DICTIONARY OF CANADIAN BIOGRAPHY

DICTIONARY OF CANADIAN BIOGRAPHY

DICTIONNAIRE BIOGRAPHIQUE DU CANADA

FRANCESS G. HALPENNY GENERAL EDITOR

JEAN HAMELIN DIRECTEUR GÉNÉRAL ADJOINT

VOLUME V

TORONTO

MARY P. BENTLEY supervisory editor JANE E. GRAHAM associate editor
HENRI PILON executive officer

ROBERT LOCHIEL FRASER III, STUART R. J. SUTHERLAND
senior manuscript editors
CURTIS FAHEY, JAMES A. OGILVY manuscript editors

PHYLLIS CREIGHTON translations editor
SUSAN E. BÉLANGER bibliographies editor
DEBORAH MARSHALL editorial assistant

QUEBEC

HUGUETTE FILTEAU, MICHEL PAQUIN codirecteurs de la rédaction
THÉRÈSE P. LEMAY rédactrice-historienne principale

CÉLINE CYR, CHRISTIANE DEMERS, JAMES H. LAMBERT
JACQUELINE ROY, ROBERT TREMBLAY rédacteurs-historiens

JEAN-PIERRE ASSELIN réviseur-historien
SUZANNE ALLAIRE-POIRIER éditrice

TRANSLATOR J. F. FLINN

UNIVERSITY OF TORONTO PRESS

LES PRESSES DE L'UNIVERSITÉ LAVAL

DICTIONARY
OF CANADIAN
BIOGRAPHY

VOLUME V

1801 TO 1820

UNIVERSITY OF TORONTO PRESS

Toronto Buffalo London

© University of Toronto Press and
Les Presses de l'université Laval, 1983
Printed in Canada

ISBN 0-8020-3398-9 (regular edition)

Canadian Cataloguing in Publication Data
Main entry under title:

Dictionary of Canadian biography.

Added t.p. in English and French.
Issued also in French.
Contents: v.1. 1000–1700. – v.2. 1701–1740. – v.3. 1741–1770. –
v.4. 1771–1800. – v.5. 1801–1820. – v.9. 1861–1870. – v.10. 1871–1880. –
v.11. 1881–1890.
Includes bibliographies and indexes.
ISBN 0-8020-3142-0 (v.1)   ISBN 0-8020-3240-0 (v.2)
ISBN 0-8020-3314-8 (v.3)   ISBN 0-8020-3351-2 (v.4)
ISBN 0-8020-3398-9 (v.5)   ISBN 0-8020-3319-9 (v.9)
ISBN 0-8020-3287-7 (v.10) ISBN 0-8020-3367-9 (v.11)
1. Canada – Biography
FC25.D52 1966   920′.071   C66-3974-5
F1005.D49 1966

Contents

INTRODUCTION   vii

ACKNOWLEDGEMENTS   xv

SUBJECTS OF BIOGRAPHIES   xvii

EDITORIAL NOTES   xxiii

LIST OF ABBREVIATIONS   2

BIOGRAPHIES   3

APPENDIX   887

GENERAL BIBLIOGRAPHY   907

CONTRIBUTORS   941

INDEX OF IDENTIFICATIONS   951

GEOGRAPHICAL INDEX   969

NOMINAL INDEX   985

Introduction

VOLUME V is the eighth volume of the *Dictionary of Canadian biography/Dictionnaire biographique du Canada* to be published. Volume I, presenting persons who died or flourished between the years 1000 and 1700, appeared in 1966; volume II (1701–40) in 1969; volume III (1741–70) in 1974; volume IV (1771–1800) in 1979. A separate *Index, volumes I to IV* was issued in 1981. The publication of volumes for the 19th century began in 1972 with volume X (1871–80) and has continued with volume IX (1861–70) in 1976 and volume XI (1881–90) in 1982. At present the DCB/DBC is concentrating its efforts on completing its program for the 19th century and is at work on volumes VI, VII, VIII, and XII; volume VIII (1851–60) will be the next volume to appear.

The Introduction to volume I contains an account of the founding of the DCB by means of the generous bequest of James Nicholson (1861–1952), and of the establishment of the DBC with the support of the Université Laval. The DCB/DBC, while continuing to develop the collaboration on which its immense bicultural and bilingual project depends, has maintained the principles and standards of operation and selection set out in the preliminary pages of its first volumes. Acknowledgements of volume V record the gratitude of the DCB/DBC for the assistance of the Social Sciences and Humanities Research Council of Canada, which has supported our work generously and sympathetically. This support has enabled us to carry the project forward in the spirit and manner of its founders.

The 269 contributors to volume V, writing in either English or French, have provided 502 biographies ranging in length from fewer than 600 words to some 10,000 words. They were invited to contribute because of their special knowledge of the period and of the persons who figured in it, and have been asked to write in accordance with the DCB/DBC's *Directives to contributors*. It sets out a general aim for authors of articles:

> Biographers should endeavour to provide a readable and stimulating treatment of their subject. Factual information should come from primary sources if possible. Biographies should not be mere catalogues of events nor should they be compilations of previous studies of the subject. The achievements of the subjects should be seen against the background of the period in which they lived and the events in which they participated. Relevant anecdote and/or quotation of the subject's own words should be used discreetly to illuminate character or personality.

Volume V has been a particular challenge to contributors for a high proportion of its figures, as well as a number of important issues of the period, have received little study to date and research in original sources has had to be especially diligent.

In this volume we continue the practice, begun with volumes IV and XI, of offering finding aids for the biographies. The subjects of the biographies in volume V are listed in the preliminary pages for quick reference. Accompanying the Nominal Index are certain special indexes. An Index of Identifications directs readers to biographies largely by the occupation of their subjects. A Geographical Index in two parts arranges subjects of biographies by their birthplaces and by their places of activity; readers are thus aided in following the history of particular national groups and of particular areas of the country. We hope that these finding aids, as well as the cross-references included in the biographies (for an explanation of how to use them, see the Editorial Notes), will enable readers to pursue their interests by a variety of routes through the volume. The response by readers to the addition of such indexes to our volumes has been favourable and similar indexes will be added to published volumes when they are reprinted (see, for example, the reprinting of the English edition of volume II in 1982).

Volume V is, like its companions, a large and lively store of many tales and debates, and it has a variety of themes. Only some of these can be mentioned here. What follows therefore is a partial account of the issues and events which absorbed the people of the volume. Through all its themes, however, runs a story of change, change which was mainly the result of contemporary events elsewhere in which the people of the volume became involved. Great Britain, after it had lost the Thirteen Colonies, became preoccupied not only with the effects of the French revolution of 1789 and war against France, but with the emergence of the United States as a new power disputing its imperial role in America. Armed conflict was thus a powerful agent of change. By such conflict the political geography of North America was upset and the development of the colonies of British North America profoundly affected. The American War of Independence instigated the massive immigration and settlement of the loyalists, who had their own ideas about the future of their new homes. The War of 1812 was to test the capacity of British North America against the growing power of the United States. But change was not centred only on questions of allegiance or politics. The organization of British North America favoured the emergence of a commercial middle class determined to have a role in economic development and government administration, and developing new patterns of social activity. Throughout the period of the volume the colonists continued to expand their domain, to the detriment of the native peoples who surrounded them; they created new centres of settlement and trade, explored new territories, adjusted the social circumstances under which they lived. This pressure of people on the move in British North America, strongly felt in volume V, will continue throughout the 19th century. The Canada of today is beginning to take form.

Among the most active in tracing the contours of the new British colony of Quebec were the merchants who arrived from Britain or the American colonies during and after the conquest. At Quebec they soon dominated the import-export trade, exchanging raw materials and semi-processed goods for British manufactures. By the turn of the century the construction of breweries and distilleries, such as that owned by Robert Lester, and of shipyards owned by men like Alexander Munn timidly announced the beginnings of local industry. Stratification had appeared gradually over the 18th century as George Allsopp, Thomas Dunn, John Young, and the wily and flamboyant William Grant (1744–1805), among others, pushed their way to the fore. If in 1760 prospects of quick prosperity for all had seemed to glow brightly, the reality was otherwise, and, like James Tod, the great majority, including many leaders, became entangled in a web of credit that had grown ever more elaborate and fragile so that the slightest blow sent shock waves through it from end to end.

At Montreal British merchants launched themselves into the fiercely competitive fur trade. As the fur-bearing animals disappeared under the onslaught, operations were gradually extended as far north and west as the Athabasca country. Costs rose accordingly, and the resulting need for increased capitalization gradually forced Canadian and British traders like Pierre Foretier and John Gregory either out of the trade or into ever more complex associations and co-partnerships from which the authoritarian Simon McTavish, architect of the North West Company, emerged supreme. Ultimately, however, Montreal's future lay not in the fur trade but in the more diversified enterprises of men such as the daring and far-seeing James Dunlop, Scottish nabob *par excellence* in the city.

If the British merchants had to adapt to unfamiliar terrain in the new colony they could at least count on being financed and represented in Britain by their own countrymen, merchants such as Brook Watson. On the other hand, Canadian businessmen such as François Baby, although familiar with conditions in the colony, had been weakened by the effects of the war and, being cut off by the conquest from their French suppliers and markets, were obliged to adjust to a new metropolis; many, perhaps most, failed. Meanwhile some country merchants such as Jacques Cartier quietly amassed small fortunes, mainly through the wheat trade. Almost without exception the merchants sought to obtain land for agricultural exploitation, speculation, stabilization of their unsteady financial situation, and improvement of their social status in a society based on property. Men such as James Caldwell counted the exploitation of landed property among the most important of their business activities. As well, the better connected sought stability in government positions, some, like Thomas Scott, even abandoning business once safely ensconced.

The British merchants in the province of Quebec blamed their early reverses on having to operate in a foreign language and under unfamiliar and outdated mercantile laws and arbitrary political institutions. Led by Allsopp and Grant among others, they became more and more strident in their demands for an elected house of assembly and English mercantile law. They were opposed by Canadian seigneurs and some British office holders, who formed the French party. The questions of the constitution and laws were ultimately, if temporarily, resolved mainly by Governor Sir Guy Carleton, through the Quebec Act. But it immediately became the focus for the merchants' ire and intensified the sympathy many of them felt for at least some of the political aspirations of the American colonists.

When the Americans invaded the colony in 1775 (Benedict Arnold), the merchants were divided; some, generally of American origin (such as Moses Hazen), supported the rebels; others (John Lees), whose commercial ties were to Britain, joined American loyalists (John Coffin), British office holders (Thomas Ainslie), and seigneurs (Malcolm Fraser) in resisting the Americans. The Canadians too were divided. The great majority were generally neutral or provided often unreliable support; an exception was the carpenter Clément Gosselin, who had to retreat with the Americans. The seigneurs and office holders, such as Gabriel-Elzéar Taschereau, came to the defence of the Quebec Act, and Britain; some merchants, Jean-Baptiste Bouchette among others, actively defended Quebec while a few, such as François Cazeau, supported the invaders. With the Americans repulsed but the revolution continuing, Frederick Haldimand, who succeeded Carleton in 1778, concentrated on defending the colony and demonstrating that he would brook no dissent.

With the war over in 1783, the British merchants again raised the cry for constitutional and legal reform. By dropping the limitations they had formerly placed on Canadian participation in the political process, they obtained the collaboration of Canadians, such as Pierre Guy, who intended to use the assembly to protect French laws and Canadian customs rather than to abolish them. Despite an opposition organized mainly by seigneurs such as René-Amable Boucher de Boucherville, the reformers got their long-sought assembly through the Constitutional Act of 1791.

About the time the act came into force Britain went to war with revolutionary France. Tension mounted in Lower Canada particularly during the administration of Governor Robert Prescott, as the British envisioned Canadian mobs being whipped into revolutionary fervour by numerous French and American secret agents (John Black). This context only intensified suspicions and hostility between the Canadian and the British members in the new assembly. There Ralph Gray and other British merchants, despite the support of some Canadian and most British office holders, such as Pierre-Louis Panet and David Lynd, saw their dream of dominating the assembly vanish. The house fell to a comfortable Canadian majority, and became the political instrument of a rising professional bourgeoisie that included the leader of the group and speaker of the assembly, Jean-Antoine Panet. As the sides became more clearly drawn, the occasional divided deputy, such as Pierre-Amable De Bonne, found less and less middle ground and eventually opted for one side or the other. Gradually the British retreated to the Legislative and Executive councils, where they joined their former enemies, the Canadian seigneurs, such as Joseph-Dominique-Emmanuel Le Moyne de Longueuil, as well as Jenkin Williams and other British office holders, in opposing the assembly's pretensions to greater power. Alarmed at the rising tide of Canadian nationalism manifested in the assembly, succeeding British governors and lieutenant governors attempted to administer either over the opposition of the assembly, as did Sir James Henry Craig, or by conciliating it in the manner of Sir George Prevost.

Elsewhere in British North America the pressures of loyalist immigration led to the erection of two new colonies: New Brunswick in 1784 and Upper Canada in 1791. During the successive administrations of John Graves Simcoe, Peter Russell, Peter Hunter, and Alexander Grant, the institutional structure of Upper Canada was established and modified. The impact of the loyalists – prominent examples of this group in volume V are Richard Cartwright and Samuel Ryerse – was muted by large-scale American immigration in the 1790s, and in subsequent years the colony's powerful merchants and office holders, Robert Hamilton and Henry Allcock among them, were challenged by a parliamentary and extra-parliamentary opposition centred on individuals such as William Weekes and Joseph Willcocks. Nor was political conflict absent from New Brunswick, whose formative years were presided over by Governor (later Lieutenant Governor) Thomas Carleton. His identification with the aims and ambitions of the loyalist élite who dominated the administration and whose activities, as described in the biographies of Edward Winslow and Gabriel George and George Duncan Ludlow, had been largely responsible for the creation of the colony prompted a political challenge from James Glenie. Although some of the old inhabitants of the region, such as William Hazen, were able to maintain their position in the face of the loyalist influx, many Acadians, such as Pierre Cormier, found their lives once again disrupted as a result of it. Developments in Nova Scotia reflected similar effects of rebellion, war, and social change as the biographies of diverse figures such as Jonathan Eddy and Sir John Wentworth show. It too received new inhabitants, Irish (Alexander McNutt), Europeans (Bruin Romkes Comingo), and loyalists (Thomas Millidge) who mingled with long-time settlers (Jonathan Binney). Governors and administrators of the colony of Cape Breton such as William Macarmick found themselves in a thicket of political quarrels over power and place. In Prince Edward Island similar power cliques filled the air with clashes (Peter Stewart, Thomas Desbrisay) and the land question pitted tenants (Joseph Robinson) against owners with agents such as James Douglas playing a large role. Controversy of a different sort prevailed in Newfoundland, which during the period covered by volume V was in the throes of transition to a colony in its own right. The institutions and rights of a settled colonial society were being introduced by governors such as Mark Milbanke and Sir Erasmus Gower, although not without opposition from the merchant community, of whom Peter Ougier was a prominent leader. In the west, at Red River, yet another theme of controversy emerged with the contested appearance of the settlers of Lord Selkirk [Thomas Douglas], who began the process of adjustment from the ways of the fur trade that eventually led to a new province.

In Quebec and Lower Canada, as the life of Michel Leclerc demonstrates, the Roman Catholic Church was as dedicated as ever in tending to the spiritual welfare of its flock and its missions among the Indians. But it conducted its work in hard times: the female religious communities experienced financial problems and difficulties in recruitment (Marie-Louise Compain, named Saint-Augustin); the Recollets died out with Louis Demers; the Sulpicians were divided by an internal struggle for control of the community between Canadian and French members (Joseph Borneuf); the Séminaire de Québec was hampered in the education of clergy by a lack of members and conflicts with the bishops (Henri-François Gravé de La Rive); and the parish clergy, of which there was also a shortage, often had to serve several parishes (Pierre-Joseph Compain). Meanwhile Bishop Pierre Denaut was engaged in a menacing phase of the church's continuing struggle to preserve its rights and privileges. At the same time the Jews of Montreal under Jacob Raphael Cohen and some Protestant denominations were establishing congregations: the Presbyterians at Montreal and Quebec (Duncan Fisher, Alexander Spark) and the Baptists near the American frontier (Jedediah Hibbard). The Anglicans remained fragmented and divided under French-speaking clergy such as David-François de Montmollin until the appointment of Jacob Mountain* as bishop in 1793.

In the other colonies, although the problems were different, the sacred and the secular were also closely intertwined. The issues of church-state relations differed from colony to colony and from denomination to denomination. In Nova Scotia, for example, Charles Inglis tried to work closely with the state in his attempts to place the Church of England on a sounder footing. By contrast, James Louis O'Donel, the Roman Catholic vicar apostolic in Newfoundland, had to struggle early in his tenure to protect his church from the hostility of civil authorities. Many of the settlers who carved new homes out of the bush felt strongly the lack of the solace of religion, and the churches stepped in to fill this need. They were faced with a formidable challenge but, thanks to the leadership of priests such as Edmund Burke (1753–1820) and James Jones as well as to the labours of clergymen such as Samuel Andrews, John Bethune, Jabez Collver, James Man, and John Stuart, their faiths did take root. The denominational diversity that prevailed in the pre-1820 period is demonstrated in the religious figures listed in the Index of Identifications of volume V.

The society of volume V had many threads to its life. New settlements were attempted in all the colonies by men such as Michael Grass and John MacDonald of Glenaladale yet in the province of Quebec the old landed properties of the seigneurs continued (Antoine Juchereau Duchesnay). Administrative patterns took shape: Hugh Finlay created a postal service with links to the outside world, and Henry Duncan established the Halifax dockyard as a prime service. Concerns about social institutions were constant. Economic developments stimulated the appearance of some of these. The Agriculture Society in the district of Quebec was founded in 1789 by devotees of the agricultural revolution in Britain such as gentleman farmer Kenelm Chandler, commercially minded seigneurs such as John Nairne, and merchants, including Joseph Drapeau, who needed grains to process or export. The Quebec Fire Society grew largely out of the fear of merchants such as John Purss that their establishments could be devastated in a major conflagration. The development of education at all levels was seen to be a necessity. In the province of Quebec education was dispensed under difficult conditions by the Ursulines (Marguerite Davanne, named de Saint-Louis de Gonzague), the Sulpicians (Jean-Baptiste-Jacques Chicoisneau), the Petit Séminaire de Québec (Pierre-Jacques Bossu, *dit* Lyonnais, named Brother Félix), an occasional zealous parish priest (François Cherrier), as well as by secular teachers such as James Tanswell. In 1801 the first public school system was created under the aegis of the Royal Institution for the Advancement of Learning to which body James McGill, in a generous bequest ten years later, confided the responsibility for establishing a university. In the Maritimes as well there was a continuing concern with higher education and the establishment of social institutions (Edward Mortimer, Jonathan Odell). Other developments across the colonies testify to a concern for the quality of life. A board of medical examiners appeared in Montreal and Quebec in 1788 (Charles Blake); George Longmore, John Caleff, and John Clinch practised vaccination; and Francis Green promoted new treatment for the deaf and dumb. In settled regions the arts advanced: in silversmithing and in woodcarving François Ranvoyzé and Jean Baillairgé set high standards; artists such as William Berczy and Robert Field recorded their contemporaries, and Thomas Davies used his training as a military artist to record the landscape; theatre was attempted at Montreal by the efforts of Joseph Quesnel, and at Halifax by Charles Stuart Powell; Jacob Bailey wrote poetry in the manner of the 18th century. Printing was introduced to Prince Edward Island (James Robertson), and in Upper Canada the first non-government newspapers appeared (Silvester Tiffany). Building continued apace with architects and contractors, John Plaw and Isaac Hildrith among them, at work on public edifices.

The volume V period saw increasingly larger numbers of Europeans, such as John Lambert, travelling throughout the colonies and into the west. Naturally, the work of exploration continued: Peter Pond ventured into the little-known Athabasca country, and Alexander Mackenzie travelled down the great river that bears his name and completed the first overland crossing of North America. On the Pacific coast the Spanish kept up their investigations, with Dionisio Alcalá-Galiano and Alejandro Malaspina assuming prominent roles. A number of travellers and traders, among them Manuel José Antonio Cardero and William Richards, left a pictorial record of people and places. Also important in gathering information were the surveyors, a group assuming increasing significance as European settlement spread in the east. Whether Samuel Johannes Holland in various parts of eastern North America, Dugald Campbell in the Maritime provinces, Patrick McNiff in Upper Canada, or William Vondenvelden in Lower Canada, all point to the rising tide of settlement and changing conditions. As the influence of the Enlightenment gained hold, the men of science found British North America a treasure trove of information. The sojourns of these inquirers were either short, as in the case of Joseph Banks, Tadeo Haenke, and André Michaux, or long, as in the case of Andrew Graham and Francis Masson, but all contributed to the growing body of data about the northern half of the continent.

Volume V introduces the last major conflict fought on Canadian soil, the War of 1812. In the Maritimes this war affected the population but little, and it was the central colonies that were chiefly involved. Although the strategy was planned in Lower Canada by Governor Prevost, fighting took place largely in Upper Canada where Administrator Isaac Brock could rely for trained support upon only a handful of British soldiers. Brock and his aide-de-camp John Macdonell (Greenfield) died early in the war at Queenston Heights, their examples becoming part of the myth that would grow up around the conflict. The attempt to maintain naval superiority on the Great Lakes fell to Sir James Lucas Yeo. Almost as important as the threat of American armies was the dubious allegiance of the non-loyalist Americans such as Ebenezer Allan who by this time constituted the majority of the Upper Canadian population. Disaffection proved an enduring theme of the war when, after the American occupation of York (Toronto) in 1813, men such as Elijah Bentley revealed the democratic sympathies of segments of the population.

The decline and fall of Indian power east of the prairies is a melancholy theme of volume V. Despite the efforts of Joseph Brant [Thayendanegea] to forge a strong enough alliance with Britain to preserve the lands of the Six Nations Confederacy, the British had other concerns and the Iroquois homeland was ceded to the Americans in the post-revolutionary settlement. A decade later, when the western neighbours of the Iroquois, under the leadership of Little Turtle [Michikinakoua] and then Blue Jacket [Weyapiersenwah], fought the Americans, the British stood by. A third wave of Indian resistance, organized by Tecumseh, was dissipated when the British withdrew from the southwestern peninsula of Upper Canada, and the possibility of an Indian buffer state south of the Great Lakes that Lieutenant Governor Simcoe had dreamed of disappeared. Even on the west coast, where contact with whites was less frequent, Muquinna was confronted with the difficulties their presence created. In Newfoundland, Demasduwit, one of the last Beothuks, was captured and died.

As with other volumes, many biographies have a particular interest because of special characteristics or activities of the persons they portray. A murder committed by Xavier Gallant, known as Pinquin, became the subject of an Acadian folk ballad that survives to the present day. Isabel Gunn disguised herself as a man and worked as a labourer for the Hudson's Bay Company until her secret could no longer be hidden. Joseph Boucher de Niverville, recalling the officers of New France, participated in every campaign from 1744 to 1775–76, serving in the west, on the Plains of Abraham, and in the east. John Beardsley's efforts on behalf of the Church of England were marred by his apparently unwitting bigamy. Boston King and David George, once slaves and loyalists, became Protestant preachers who helped organize a mass exodus of Nova Scotia blacks to Sierra Leone. George Cartwright, "Old Labrador," brought five Inuit to London where they met such notable figures as James Boswell. William Burn was brought out from Scotland by Lord Selkirk to breed sheep. Andrew Graham at his posts on Hudson Bay recorded important observations of the Crees and Inuit. Alexander Grant spoke no French and his wife no English when they married but their warm relationship was a legend to all who knew the home they established at Grosse Point. The governor-in-chief of British North America, 1818–19, was Charles Lennox, Duke of Richmond and Lennox, who had given the famous ball before Waterloo and who died in office from the bite of a rabid fox. Edward Augustus, future Duke of Kent and Strathearn, paraded the Halifax garrison every morning at five, in person, and established the faithful Mme de Saint-Laurent at Prince's Lodge. Helen MacDonald of Glenaladale had to take over the management of the large family farm on Prince Edward Island when her brother went off to increase their resources elsewhere and at his bidding gave up marriage to a young officer. The spirited Friederike Charlotte Louise von Massow accompanied her officer husband on John Burgoyne*'s invasion of the American colonies in 1777, experiencing the horrors of war and subsequently sharing his life as soldier and prisoner of war, and giving to two daughters the names America and Canada. The procession is long and colourful.

Volume V joins the published volumes IX, X, XI as a contribution to the large and complex program of the DCB/DBC for the 19th century. As we leave volume V and proceed with volumes VIII and VI, we should like to pay tribute to all the members of our staff who are working with diligence and skill to ensure that our project proceeds on its appointed course.

FRANCESS G. HALPENNY

JEAN HAMELIN

Acknowledgements

THE *Dictionary of Canadian biography/Dictionnaire biographique du Canada* receives assistance, advice, and encouragement from many institutions and individuals. They cannot all be named nor can their kindness and support be adequately acknowledged.

The DCB/DBC, which owes its founding to the generosity of the late James Nicholson, has been sustained over the years by its parent institutions, the University of Toronto and the University of Toronto Press and the Université Laval and Les Presses de l'université Laval. Beginning in 1973 the Canada Council provided grants to the two university presses which made possible the continuation and acceleration of the DCB/DBC's publication program, and this assistance has been maintained and amplified by the Social Sciences and Humanities Research Council of Canada, created in 1978. We should like to give special thanks to the SSHRCC not only for its financial support but also for the encouragement it has given us as we strive to complete our volumes for the 19th century. We are grateful also for the financial assistance accorded us by the Université Laval in 1982–83.

Of the numerous individuals who assisted in the preparation of volume V, we owe particular thanks to our contributors. In addition, we have had the benefit of special consultation with a number of persons, some of them also contributors. We should like to thank: Phyllis R. Blakeley, Denise Bousquet, André Cochrane, Brian Driscoll, Raymond Dumais, Micheline Fortin, Armand Gagné, Gilles Héon, Patricia Kennedy, Raymond J. Lahey, Louis-Joseph Lépine, Allan J. MacDonald, André Martineau, Michel Roberge, Catherine Shepard, Shirlee Anne Smith, and Bruce G. Wilson.

Throughout the preparation of volume V we have enjoyed willing cooperation from libraries and archives in Canada and elsewhere. We are particularly grateful to the administrators and staffs of those institutions to which we have most frequently appealed. In addition to the Public Archives of Canada in Ottawa and the provincial archives in all the provinces, they are: in Ontario, the University of Toronto Library and the Metropolitan Toronto Library; in Quebec, the *archives civiles* and *judiciaires*, the Archives de l'archidiocèse de Québec, the Bibliothèque de l'Assemblée nationale, the Bibliothèque and Archives du Séminaire de Québec, and the Bibliothèque générale de l'université Laval. Essential help was also given by the Hudson's Bay Company Archives at the Provincial Archives of Manitoba in Winnipeg. We should like to thank as well the staffs of the *archives départementales* and *municipales* in France and of the various record offices in the United Kingdom and Republic of Ireland who answered our numerous requests for information so kindly.

The editors of volume V were helped in the preparation of the volume by colleagues in both offices. In Toronto, editorial and research assistance has been given by Wendy Cameron, Charles Dougall, Jean C. Hoff, Catherine A. Waite, and Robert G. Wuetherick.

ACKNOWLEDGEMENTS

We should like to make a special mention of the devoted services of a former bibliographies editor, Joan E. Mitchell. Deborah Marshall was in charge of the secretariat in Toronto, where secretarial and administrative services were provided by Joanne D'Abreau, Eileen McAuley, Glynis Harbour, and Adrianna Davis, assisted on occasion by Heddi Keil and Reni Grinfelds. In Quebec, Michèle Brassard, Paulette M. Chiasson, Marcelle Duquet, France Galarneau, John Keyes, and Marie-Hélène Lévesque aided the editors at one stage or another of volume V. Pierrette Desrosiers was in charge of secretarial services, assisted by Hélène Lizotte and Suzanne East and, on occasion, by Monique Fournier and Louise Barabé. We have benefited from the advice of Jacques Chouinard and Roch-André Rompré of the Service des éditions des Presses de l'université Laval and also of the staff of the Office de la langue française as well as that of the Translation Bureau of the Department of the Secretary of State.

We should like to recognize the guidance and encouragement we have received from the two presses with which the DCB/DBC is associated, and in particular from Harald Bohne, H. C. Van Ierssel, Pauline Johnston, Thomas H. Brind, and Stephen Phillips at the University of Toronto Press and Claude Frémont, Marc Boucher, and Jacques Beaulieu at Les Presses de l'université Laval.

DICTIONNAIRE BIOGRAPHIQUE DU CANADA   DICTIONARY OF CANADIAN BIOGRAPHY

Subjects of Biographies

ADHÉMAR, *dit* Saint-Martin, Toussaint-Antoine (1740–1804)
Ainslie, Thomas (1729–1806)
Ainsse, Joseph-Louis (1744–1802)
Aird, James (d. 1819)
Alberni, Pedro de (1747–1802)
Alcalá-Galiano, Dionisio (1762–1805)
Allain, Jean-Baptiste (1739–1812)
Allan, Ebenezer (1752–1813)
Allan, John (1747–1805)
Allcock, Henry (d. 1808)
Allsopp, George (d. 1805)
Almon, William James (1755–1817)
Andrews, Samuel (1737–1818)
Antrobus, John (d. 1820)
Aplin, Joseph (d. 1804)
Arnold, Benedict (1741/42–1801)
Arnoldi, Michael (1763–1807)
Askin, John (1739–1815)
Atiatoharongwen (d. 1814)

BABY, François (1733–1820)
Bad Bird. *See* Madjeckewiss
Badelard, Philippe-Louis-François (1728–1802)
Bailey, Jacob (1731–1808)
Baillairgé, Jean (1726–1805)
Baillairgé, Pierre-Florent (1761–1812)
Balfour, James (1731–1809)
Ball, Ingram (1752–1807)
Banks, Sir Joseph (1742/43–1820)
Barnes, John (d. 1810)
Bastarache, *dit* Basque, Michel (1730–1820)
Beardsley, John (1732–1809)
Bédard, Jean-Baptiste (1761–1818)
Bedout, Jacques (1751–1818)
Belcher, Benjamin (1743–1802)
Bell, James (d. 1814)
Bentley, Elijah (fl. 1799–1814)
Bentley, John (d. 1813)
Bentom, Clark (d. *c.* 1820)
Berczy, William (d. 1813)
Berkeley, Sir George Cranfield (1753–1818)
Bernard, Noël (fl. 1781–1801)
Berthelot Dartigny, Michel-Amable (1738–1815)
Bertrand, Joseph-Laurent (1741–1813)
Bethune, John (1751–1815)
Billings, Joseph (d. 1806)

Binney, Jonathan (1723/24–1807)
Bisshopp, Cecil (1783–1813)
Black, John (fl. 1786–1819)
Blackwood, John (d. 1819)
Blake, Charles (1746–1810)
Blondeau, Maurice-Régis (1734–1809)
Blue Jacket. *See* Weyapiersenwah
Boisseau, Nicolas-Gaspard (1726–1804)
Booth, Joshua (d. 1813)
Borneuf, Joseph (1762–1819)
Bossu, *dit* Lyonnais, Pierre-Jacques, named Brother Félix (1770–1803)
Botsford, Amos (1744/45–1812)
Boucher, François (1730–1816)
Boucher de Boucherville, René-Amable (1735–1812)
Boucher de Niverville, Joseph (1715–1804)
Bouchette, Jean-Baptiste (1736–1804)
Boudreau, Cécile (Pitre; Pellerin) (d. 1811)
Bougainville, Louis-Antoine de, Comte de Bougainville (1729–1811)
Bradford, Richard (1752–1817)
Brant, Joseph. *See* Thayendanegea
Brehaut, Pierre (1764–1817)
Brenton, James (1736–1806)
Brock, Sir Isaac (1769–1812)
Bruff, Charles Oliver (1735–1817)
Bruneau, Pierre (1761–1820)
Brunet, *dit* L'Estang, Véronique, named Sainte-Rose (1726–1810)
Bruyeres, Ralph Henry (d. 1814)
Bulley, Samuel (d. between 1806 and 1809)
Bunbury, Joseph (fl. 1773–1802)
Burbidge, John (d. 1812)
Burke, Edmund (fl. 1785–1801)
Burke, Edmund (1753–1820)
Burn, William (1758–1804)
Byers, Peter, known as Black Peter (d. 1815)
Byles, Mather (1734/35–1814)

CADOT, Jean-Baptiste (fl. 1723–1803)
Caldwell, Henry (d. 1810)
Caldwell, James (d. 1815)
Caleff, John (1726–1812)
Campbell, Dugald (d. 1810)
Campbell, James (fl. 1806–17)
Cannon, Edward (d. 1814)

Cardero, Manuel José Antonio (b. 1766, d. in or after 1810)
Carleton, Guy, lst Baron Dorchester (1724–1808)
Carleton, Thomas (d. 1817)
Carrefour de La Pelouze, Pierre-Joseph (1738–1808)
Cartier, Jacques (1750–1814)
Cartwright, George (1739/40–1819)
Cartwright, Richard (1759–1815)
Cassiet, Pierre (1727–1809)
Cazeau, François (d. 1815)
Céloron, Marie-Catherine-Françoise (1744–1809)
Cerré, Jean-Gabriel (1734–1805)
Chabert de Cogolin, Joseph-Bernard de, Marquis de Chabert (1724–1805)
Chaboillez, Charles (1772–1812)
Chaboillez, Charles-Jean-Baptiste (1736–1808)
Chaboillez, Louis (1766–1813)
Champion, Gabriel (1748–1808)
Chandler, Kenelm (d. 1803)
Charland, Louis (1772–1813)
Chejauk (fl. 1761–1804)
Cherrier, François (1745–1809)
Chicoisneau, Jean-Baptiste-Jacques (1737–1818)
Clark, Duncan (d. 1808)
Clark, James (fl. 1790–1807)
Clinch, John (1748/49–1819)
Coffin, John (1729–1808)
Coffin, Thomas Aston (1754–1810)
Cohen, Jacob Raphael (d. 1811)
Colen, Joseph (d. 1818)
Collet, Charles-Ange (b. 1721, d. after 1800)
Collver, Jabez (1731–1818)
Colnett, James (d. 1806)
Comingo, Bruin Romkes (1723–1820)
Compain, Marie-Louise, named Saint-Augustin (1747–1819)
Compain, Pierre-Joseph (1740–1806)
Conefroy, Pierre (1752–1816)
Cook, Louis. See Atiatoharongwen
Cormier, Pierre (1734–1818)
Cossit, Ranna (1744–1815)
Craig, Sir James Henry (1748–1812)
Craigie, John (d. 1813)
Crane. See Chejauk
Creighton, John (1721–1807)
Cressé, Pierre-Michel (1758–1819)
Cruickshank, Robert (d. 1809)
Curtis, James (d. 1819)
Curtis, Sir Roger (1746–1816)
Cuyler, Abraham Cornelius (1742–1810)

Davanne, Marguerite, named de Saint-Louis de Gonzague (1719–1802)
Davidson, Arthur (1743–1807)
Davies, Thomas (d. 1812)
Dease, John (d. 1801)
De Bonne, Pierre-Amable (1758–1816)

Decoigne, François (fl. 1798–1818)
Dejean, Philippe (b. 1736, d. in or after 1809)
DeLancey, James (1746–1804)
Delesdernier, Moses (d. 1811)
De Lisle, Jean (d. 1814)
De Lisle, Jean-Guillaume (d. 1819)
Demasduwit (d. 1820)
Demers, Louis (1732–1813)
Denaut, Pierre (1743–1806)
Dénéchaud, Jacques (1728–1810)
Desbrisay, Thomas (d. 1819)
Deschamps, Isaac (d. 1801)
Deschenaux, Pierre-Louis (1759–1802)
Deserontyon, John (d. 1811)
Digé, Jean (d. 1813)
Dixon, Charles (1730/31–1817)
Dobie, Richard (d. 1805)
Doucet, Amable (1737–1806)
Douglas, James (d. 1803)
Douglas, Thomas, Baron Daer and Shortcleuch, 5th Earl of Selkirk (1771–1820)
Drapeau, Joseph (1752–1810)
Ducharme, Jean-Marie (1723–1807)
Duckworth, Sir John Thomas (1747/48–1817)
Dumas, Alexandre (d. 1802)
Dun, John (1763–1803)
Duncan, Henry (d. 1814)
Duncan, Richard (d. 1819)
Dunière, Louis (1723–1806)
Dunlop, James (1757–1815)
Dunn, Thomas (1729–1818)
Dussaus, Marie-Angélique (1737–1809)

Ecuier, Charles (d. 1820)
Eddy, Jonathan (1726/27–1804)
Edward Augustus, Duke of Kent and Strathearn (1767–1820)
Edwards, Edward (d. 1816)
Ellice, Alexander (d. 1805)
Elliott, Matthew (d. 1814)
Elmsley, John (1762–1805)
Émond, Pierre (1738–1808)
England, Richard G. (d. 1812)

Fairfield, William (d. 1816)
Fanning, Edmund (1739–1818)
Faribault, Barthélemy (1728–1801)
Field, Robert (d. 1819)
Finlay, Hugh (d. 1801)
Fisher, Duncan (d. 1820)
Fisher, Finlay (d. 1819)
Foretier, Pierre (1738–1815)
Forsyth, Joseph (d. 1813)
Forsyth, William (d. 1814)
Forton, Michel (1754–1817)
Fraser, John (d. 1803)
Fraser, Malcolm (1733–1815)

Frobisher, Joseph (1740–1810)
Frost, James (d. 1803)

GALLANT, Xavier, known as Pinquin (d. 1813)
Gallop, William (d. 1804)
Garland, Charles (1730–1810)
Gautier, Nicolas (1731–1810)
George, David (d. 1810)
Gibault, Pierre (d. 1802)
Gillmore, George (d. 1811)
Girty, Simon (1741–1818)
Glasgow, George (d. 1820)
Glenie, James (1750–1817)
Gosselin, Clément (1747–1816)
Gower, Sir Erasmus (1742–1814)
Graham, Aaron (d. 1818)
Graham, Andrew (d. 1815)
Grant, Alexander (1734–1813)
Grant, William (1744–1805)
Grant, William (1743–1810)
Grass, Michael (d. 1813)
Gravé de La Rive, Henri-François (1730–1802)
Graves, Thomas, 1st Baron Graves (1725–1802)
Gray, Edward William (1742–1810)
Gray, Ralph (d. 1813)
Gray, Robert (1755–1806)
Gray, Robert Isaac Dey (d. 1804)
Green, Francis (1742–1809)
Gregory, John (d. 1817)
Guernon, *dit* Belleville, François (d. 1817)
Guitet, Claude (d. 1802)
Gunn, Isabel (fl. 1806–9)
Guy, Étienne (1774–1820)
Guy, Pierre (1738–1812)

HAENKE, Tadeo (1761–1817)
Haldimand, Sir Frederick (1718–91) (Appendix)
Hall, Sir Robert (d. 1818)
Hamilton, Robert (1753–1809)
Hanna, James G. (d. 1807)
Hardy, George (d. in or after 1803)
Harries, John (1763–1810)
Harris, John (1739–1802)
Hart, Samuel (d. 1810)
Haswell, Robert (1768–1801)
Hatt, Richard (1769–1819)
Hazen, Moses (1733–1803)
Hazen, William (1738–1814)
Heer, Louis-Chrétien de (b. 1760, d. before 1808)
Henry, Alexander (d. 1814)
Heron, Samuel (b. 1770, d. 1817 or 1818)
Hertel de Rouville, Jean-Baptiste-Melchior
  (1748–1817)
Hibbard, Jedediah (1740–1809)
Hildrith, Isaac (1741–1807)
Hodgson, Robert (d. 1811)
Holland, Samuel Johannes (1728–1801)

How, Deborah (Cottnam) (d. 1806)
Howe, Alexander (1749–1813)
Huet de La Valinière, Pierre (d. 1806)
Hughes, Sir Richard (d. 1812)
Huguet, *dit* Latour, Pierre (1749–1817)
Humphreys, James (1748/49–1810)
Hunter, Peter (d. 1805)
Hutchings, Richard (d. 1808)

INGLIS, Charles (1734–1816)
Iredell, Abraham (1751–1806)
Irumberry de Salaberry, Édouard-Alphonse d'
  (1792–1812)
Isham, Charles Thomas (d. 1814)

JACSON, Antoine (d. 1803)
Jarvis, William (1756–1817)
Jessen, Dettlieb Christopher (1730–1814)
Jessup, Edward (1735–1816)
John, Captain. *See* Deserontyon, John
Jones, Caleb (d. 1816)
Jones, Ephraim (1750–1812)
Jones, James (1742–1805)
Jones, John (d. 1818)
Juchereau Duchesnay, Antoine (1740–1806)
Julien, John (fl. 1779–1805)

KEVENY, Owen (d. 1816)
Kineubenae (fl. 1797–1812)
King, Boston (d. 1802)

LA FEUILLE. *See* Wahpasha
Laforce, René-Hippolyte (1728–1802)
Lahaille, Jean-Baptiste (1750–1809)
Lambert, John (fl. 1806–16)
Lambert, Patrick (d. 1816)
Langhorn, John (d. 1817)
Lawson, David (d. after 1803)
Lebrun de Duplessis, Jean-Baptiste (d. 1807)
Leclerc, Michel (1762–1813)
Le Comte Dupré, Jean-Baptiste (1731–1820)
Lee, Samuel (1756–1805)
Lees, John (d. 1807)
Le Maistre, Francis (d. 1805)
Le Moyne de Longueuil, Joseph-Dominique-
  Emmanuel (1738–1807)
Lennox, Charles, 4th Duke of Richmond and Lennox
  (1764–1819)
Lester, Benjamin (1724–1802)
Lester, Robert (d. 1807)
Liébert, Philippe (1733–1804)
Liénard de Beaujeu de Villemonde, Louis
  (1716–1802)
Little Turtle. *See* Michikinakoua
Longmoor, Robert (fl. 1771–1812)
Longmore, George (d. 1811)
Louis, Colonel. *See* Atiatoharongwen

Ludlow, Gabriel George (1736–1808)
Ludlow, George Duncan (1734–1808)
Lynd, David (d. 1802)

MACARMICK, William (d. 1815)
McBeath, George (d. 1812)
MacDonald of Glenaladale, Helen (MacDonald) (d. c. 1803)
MacDonald of Glenaladale, John (1742–1810)
McDonell (Aberchalder), John (d. 1809)
Macdonell (Collachie), Angus (d. 1804)
Macdonell (Greenfield), John (1785–1812)
MacDonell of Scothouse, Alexander (d. 1803)
McDougall, Duncan (d. 1818)
McGill, James (1744–1813)
McGillivray, Duncan (d. 1808)
MacKay, Alexander (d. 1811)
McKay, John (d. 1810)
McKee, Thomas (d. 1814)
Mackenzie, Sir Alexander (1764–1820)
MacKenzie, Kenneth (d. 1816)
McKinnon, Ranald (1737–1805)
McKinnon, William (d. 1811)
MacMhannain, Calum Bàn (fl. 1803)
McNabb, Colin (d. 1810)
McNabb, James (d. 1820)
McNiff, Patrick (d. 1803)
McNutt, Alexander (b. 1725, d. c. 1811)
McSwiney, Edward (fl. 1812–15)
McTavish, Donald (d. 1814)
McTavish, Simon (d. 1804)
Madjeckewiss (fl. 1735–1805)
Magowan, Peter (d. 1810)
Maillou, Benjamin-Nicolas (1753–1810)
Malaspina, Alejandro (1754–1810)
Malhiot, François (1733–1808)
Man, James (d. 1820)
March, Mary. See Demasduwit
Marchinton, Philip (d. 1808)
Marcoux, Pierre (1757–1809)
Margane de Lavaltrie, Pierre-Paul (1743–1810)
Martineau, Jérôme (1750–1809)
Masson, Francis (1741–1805)
Massow, Friederike Charlotte Louise von (Riedesel, Freifrau zu Eisenbach) (1746–1808)
Mathews, Robert (d. 1814)
Meares, John (d. 1809)
Melançon, Marie-Vénérande, named de Sainte-Claire (1754–1817)
Menut, Alexandre (d. c. 1805)
Mercure, Louis (1753–1816)
Mézière, Henry-Antoine (d. after 1819)
Michaux, André (1746–1803)
Michikinakoua (d. 1812)
Milbanke, Mark (d. 1805)
Miles, Abner (d. 1806)
Millidge, Thomas (d. 1816)

Mondelet, Dominique (d. 1802)
Montmollin, David-François de (d. 1803)
Montour, Nicholas (1756–1808)
Moody, James (d. 1809)
Morgann, Maurice (1726–1802)
Morris, Charles (1731–1802)
Morris, James Rainstorpe (d. 1809)
Morse, Robert (1743/44–1818)
Mortimer, Edward (d. 1819)
Mott, Jacob S. (d. 1814)
Mountain, Jehosaphat (1745–1817)
Moziño Losada Suárez de Figueroa, José Mariano (d. 1820)
Munn, Alexander (1766–1812)
Muquinna (fl. 1786–1817)
Myeerah (fl. 1805–16)

NAIRNE, John (1731–1802)
Natte, dit Marseille, Jean-Sébastien (1734–1803)
Nevins, Archibald (1782–1812)
Newman, Robert (d. 1803)
Noble, Seth (1743–1807)

ODELL, Jonathan (1737–1818)
O'Donel, James Louis (d. 1811)
Ogilvie, James (d. 1813)
Ogilvy, John (d. 1819)
O'Hara, Felix (d. 1805)
Olabaratz, Jean d' (1727–1808)
Osborn, Mary (London) (d. 1801)
Ougier, Peter (d. 1803)
Overholser, Jacob (d. 1815)

PAGAN, William (1744–1819)
Painter, John (d. 1815)
Panet, Jean-Antoine (1751–1815)
Panet, Pierre (1731–1804)
Panet, Pierre-Louis (1761–1812)
Pangman, Peter (1744–1819)
Panton, George (d. 1810)
Parent, Marie-Geneviève, named de Saint-François d'Assise (1740–1804)
Patterson, Robert (1732–1808)
Pawling, Benjamin (d. 1818)
Payen de Noyan, Marie-Catherine, named de Saint-Alexis (d. 1818)
Périnault, Joseph (1732–1814)
Perkins, Simeon (1734/35–1812)
Perley, Israel (1738–1813)
Perrault, Jacques-Nicolas (1750–1812)
Pettit, Nathaniel (1724–1803)
Philipps, John (d. 1801)
Pichard, Amable (d. 1819)
Pickmore, Francis (d. 1818)
Pilotte, Angelique (fl. 1815–18)
Pinson, Andrew (d. 1810)
Piuze, Liveright (1754–1813)

Plantavit de Lapause de Margon, Jean-Guillaume (1721–1804)
Plaw, John (d. 1820)
Poncin, Claude (1725–1811)
Pond, Peter (1739/40–1807)
Portlock, Nathaniel (d. 1817)
Pouget, Jean-Baptiste-Noël (1745–1818)
Powell, Charles Stuart (d. 1811)
Prescott, Robert (d. 1815)
Prevost, Sir George (1767–1816)
Purss, John (1732–1803)

QUESNEL, Joseph (1746–1809)

RAIZENNE, Marie, named Saint-Ignace (1735–1811)
Ramage, John (d. 1802)
Ramsay, David (fl. 1758–1810)
Ranvoyzé, François (1739–1819)
Réaume, Charles (1743–1813)
Renaud d'Avène Des Méloizes, Nicolas (1729–1803)
Richards, William (d. 1811)
Rieutord, Jean-Baptiste (d. 1818)
Roberts, Charles (d. 1816)
Robertson, Daniel (d. 1810)
Robertson, James (1747–1816)
Robertson, William (d. 1806)
Robichaux, Jean-Baptiste (d. 1808)
Robinson, Joseph (d. 1807)
Roe, Walter (d. 1801)
Rollo, James (d. 1820)
Roundhead. See Stayeghtha
Rousseaux St John, John Baptist (1758–1812)
Routh, Richard (d. 1801)
Roy, Narsise (1765–1814)
Ruckle, Barbara (Heck) (1734–1804)
Russell, Peter (1733–1808)
Ryerse, Samuel (1752–1812)

SALES LATERRIÈRE, Pierre de (d. 1815)
Sarrebource de Pontleroy, Nicolas (1717–1802)
Sawtelle, Jemima (Phipps; Howe; Tute) (d. 1805)
Sayer, John (d. 1818)
Schurman, William (d. 1819)
Scott, Jonathan (1744–1819)
Scott, Thomas (d. 1810)
Scott, Thomas Charles Heslop (d. 1813)
Seely, Joseph (b. 1786, d. in or after 1814)
Selby, Prideaux (d. 1813)
Semple, Robert (1777–1816)
Serres, Alexandre (d. 1812)
Shaw, Æneas (d. 1814)
Simcoe, John Graves (1752–1806)
Sinclair, Patrick (1736–1820)
Skerrett, John (d. 1813)
Skinner, Robert Pringle (1786–1816)
Skinner, Thomas (1759–1818)

Slade, Thomas (d. 1816)
Smith, Michael (b. 1776, d. in or after 1816)
Smith, William (fl. 1784–1803)
Smythe, Sir Hervey (1734–1811)
Spark, Alexander (1762–1819)
Spencer, Hazelton (1757–1813)
Sproule, George (d. 1817)
Stayeghtha (d. 1813)
Stewart, Charles (d. 1813)
Stewart, Peter (1725–1805)
Stout, Richard (d. 1820)
Street, Samuel (1753–1815)
Street, Thomas (d. 1805)
Stuart, John (1740/41–1811)
Suzor, François-Michel (1756–1810)

TANSWELL, James (d. 1819)
Tarieu de Lanaudière, Charles-Louis (1743–1811)
Tarieu de Lanaudière, Xavier-Roch (1771–1813)
Taschereau, Gabriel-Elzéar (1745–1809)
Taylor, Alexander (d. 1811)
Tecumseh (d. 1813)
Testard Louvigny de Montigny, Jean-Baptiste-Pierre (1750–1813)
Thayendanegea (d. 1807)
Thibodeau, Simon (d. 1819)
Thorn, Jonathan (1779–1811)
Tiffany, Silvester (1759–1811)
Tod, James (d. 1816)
Todd, Isaac (d. 1819)
Townshend, George, 4th Viscount and 1st Marquess Townshend (1723/24–1807)
Townshend, William (d. 1816)
Trahan, Grégoire, known as Gregory Strahan (d. 1811)
Trestler, Jean-Joseph (d. 1813)
Trottier Desrivières Beaubien, Eustache-Ignace (1761–1816)
Turner, William (1743–1804)

UPHAM, Joshua (1741–1808)

VIETS, Roger (1738–1811)
Viger, Denis (1741–1805)
Vondenvelden, William (d. 1809)

WAHPASHA (probably d. before 1805)
Waldron, John (b. 1744, d. in or after 1818)
Walker, Thomas (d. 1812)
Walk-in-the-Water. See Myeerah
Warren, John (d. 1813)
Watson, Sir Brook (1735/36–1807)
Weekes, William (d. 1806)
Welch, Thomas (1742–1816)
Wentworth, John (d. c. 1820)
Wentworth, Sir John (1737–1820)
Weyapiersenwah (d. c. 1810)

SUBJECTS OF BIOGRAPHIES

Wilkie, William (fl. 1820)
Willcocks, Joseph (1773–1814)
Willcocks, William (1735/36–1813)
Williams, James (fl. 1803–15)
Williams, Jenkin (d. 1819)
Winslow, Edward (1746/47–1815)
Winslow, Joshua (1726/27–1801)
Wiswall, John (1731–1812)

Wright, George (1752–1819)
Wright, Thomas (d. 1812)

YEO, Sir James Lucas (1782–1818)
Young, John (d. 1819)

ZEISBERGER, David (1721–1808)
Zheewegonab (fl. 1780–1805)

Editorial Notes

PROPER NAMES

Persons have been entered under family name rather than title, pseudonym, popular name, nickname, or name in religion, an arrangement which has the advantage of bringing together members of the same family: BOUCHER; COMPAIN. Where possible the form of the surname is based on the signature, although contemporary usage is taken into account. Common variant spellings are included in parenthesis.

In the case of French names, "La," "Le," "Du," "Des," and sometimes "De" are considered part of the name and are capitalized; when both parts of the name are capitalized in the signature, French style treats the family name as two words. Compound names often appear: Charles-Louis TARIEU de Lanaudière; Eustache-Ignace TROTTIER Desrivières Beaubien; cross-references are made in the text from the compounds to the main entry under the family name: from Lanaudière to Tarieu and from Desrivières and Beaubien to Trottier.

Where a signature was not available for a subject whose name began with Mc or Mac, the form Mac, followed by a capital letter, has been used. Scottish-born immigrants who were entitled under Scottish law to a territorial designation as part of their names appear with that designation included: John MACDONALD of Glenaladale. Scots for whom the designation was used merely as a convenient way of distinguishing one individual from another have the designation in parenthesis: John MCDONELL (Aberchalder); John MACDONELL (Greenfield). Subjects are entered under their Gaelic names only when it is clear that they spoke Gaelic and moved in a Gaelic environment: Calum Bàn MACMHANNAIN (Malcolm Bàn Buchanan). In all cases, appropriate cross-references are provided.

Married women and *religieuses* have been entered under their maiden names, with cross-references to the entries from their husbands' names or their names in religion: Deborah How (Cottnam); Marguerite DAVANNE, named de Saint-Louis de Gonzague.

Indian names have presented a particular problem, since an Indian might be known by his own name (written in a variety of ways by people unfamiliar with Indian languages) and by a nickname or baptismal name. Moreover, by the late 18th century some Indian families, such as the Brants, were beginning to use family surnames in the European style. Indian names have been used when they could be found, and, because it is impossible to establish an original spelling for an Indian name, the form generally chosen is the one found in standard sources or the one linguists now regard as correct; variants are included in parenthesis: ATIATOHARONGWEN (Thiathoharongouan, Louis Atayataghronghta, Louis Cook, Colonel Louis). Where signatures of Indians are available, as

in the case of John DESERONTYON, their form has been respected. When Indians signed both an Indian name and a Europeanized one, as did THAYENDANEGEA (Joseph Brant), they appear under the Indian name. Appropriate cross-references are included.

For reference works useful in establishing the names of persons not receiving biographies in the DCB/DBC, the reader is referred to section III of the General Bibliography.

CROSS-REFERENCES WITHIN VOLUME V

The first time the name of a person who has a biography in volume V appears in another biography his or her family name is printed in capitals and level small capitals: Pierre DENAUT; John Graves SIMCOE.

CROSS-REFERENCES TO OTHER VOLUMES

An asterisk following a name indicates either that the person has a biography in a volume already published – James Wolfe*; Louis-Joseph Papineau* – or that he or she will receive a biography in a volume to be published – Joseph-Octave Plessis*; Sir John Harvey*. Birth and death (or floruit) dates for such persons are given in the index as an indication of the volume in which the biography will be found.

PLACE-NAMES

Place-names are generally given in the form used at the time of reference; where necessary, the modern name and/or the present name of the country in which the place is located have been included in parenthesis: York (Toronto); Kesseldorf (German Democratic Republic). The English edition cites well-known place-names in their present-day English form: St Lawrence River, Montreal, Quebec, Marseilles, Rome. The *Encyclopædia Britannica* has been followed in determining whether place-names outside Canada have accepted English forms.

Many sources have been used as guides to establish 18th- and early 19th-century place-names: Bouchette, *Topographical description of L.C.*; *Cumberland House journals and inland journal, 1775–82*, ed. E. E. Rich and A. M. Johnson (HBRS pubs., 14–15, 2v., London, 1951–52); *Encyclopædia Britannica*; *Encyclopedia Canadiana*; HBRS, 27 (Williams); "Historic forts and trading posts of the French regime and of the English fur trading companies," comp. Ernest Voorhis (mimeograph, Ottawa, 1930); Mackenzie, *Journals and letters* (Lamb); Hormisdas Magnan, *Dictionnaire historique et géographique des paroisses, missions et municipalités de la province de Québec* (Arthabaska, Qué., 1925); Mika, *Places in Ont.*; *Place-names of N.S.*; Rayburn,

Geographical names of N.B. and *Geographical names of P.E.I.*; P.-G. Roy, *Inv. concessions*; W. H. Smith, *Canada: past, present and future* . . . (2v., Toronto, [1852]; repr. Belleville, Ont., 1973–74); Walbran, *B.C. coast names.* For complete information about titles given in shortened form the reader is referred to the General Bibliography.

Modern Canadian names are based whenever possible on the Gazetteer of Canada series issued by the Canadian Permanent Committee on Geographical Names, Ottawa, on the *Canada gazetteer atlas* (n.p., 1980), and on the *Répertoire toponymique du Québec* (Québec, 1979) published by the Commission de toponymie. For places outside Canada the following have been major sources of reference: *Bartholomew gazetteer of Britain*, comp. Oliver Mason ([Edinburgh, 1977]); Albert Dauzat et Charles Rostaing, *Dictionnaire étymologique des noms de lieux en France* (Paris, [1963]); *Dictionnaire universel des noms propres . . . le Petit Robert 2*, Paul Robert *et al.*, édit. (3ᵉ éd., Paris, 1977); *Grand Larousse encyclopédique*; *National Geographic atlas of the world*, ed. W. E. Garrett *et al.* (5th ed., Washington, 1981).

CONTEMPORARY USAGE

To avoid the anachronism of applying the terms "French Canadian" and "English Canadian" to the 18th and early 19th centuries, volume V follows the contemporary practice of referring to the French-speaking inhabitants of the province of Quebec simply as "Canadians." Readers should be aware, however, that in the context of the fur trade the term "Canadian" is used, as it was at the time, to refer to Montreal-based traders, whether French- or English-speaking.

Useful reference works for contemporary usage are *A dictionary of Canadianisms on historical principles*, ed. W. S. Avis *et al.* (Toronto, 1967) and *Dictionary of Newfoundland English*, ed. G. M. Story *et al.* (Toronto, [1982]).

QUOTATIONS

Quotations have been translated when the language of the original passage is different from that of the text of the biography. Readers of the DCB may consult the DBC for the original French of quotations that have been translated into English. When a passage in French is quoted from a work that has appeared in both languages, the published English version is generally used. The wording, spelling, punctuation, and capitalization of original quotations are not altered unless it is necessary to do so for meaning, in which case the changes are made within square brackets. A name appearing within square brackets has been substituted for the original in order to identify the person more precisely or to indicate that he/she has a biography within the volume or in another volume.

DATES

The discrepancy between Old Style and New Style dates affects some biographies in volume V. The Julian calendar was 11 days behind the Gregorian one in the 18th century, and its new year began on 25 March. France and Spain had adopted the Gregorian calendar in 1582. Scotland had moved the date of its new year in 1600. England and its American colonies used the Julian calendar until 1752. In volume V a subject who was, for example, born in England or the Thirteen Colonies on 16 Feb. 1739, Old Style, has his or her birth date presented as 16 Feb. 1739/40. Except for such indications of the difference in year for the period between 1 January and 25 March, no attempt has been made to adjust Old Style dates.

In spite of assiduous inquiry it is occasionally impossible to uncover a subject's birth and death dates; only the dates of his/her active career are documented. In the introductory paragraphs and in the various indexes the outside dates of activity are presented as floruit (fl.) dates.

BIBLIOGRAPHIES

Each biography is followed by a bibliography. Sources frequently used by authors and editors are cited in shortened form in individual bibliographies; the General Bibliography (pp.907–38) gives these sources in full. Many abbreviations are used in the individual bibliographies, especially for archival sources; a list of these can be found on p.2 and p.906.

The individual bibliographies are generally arranged alphabetically according to the five sections of the General Bibliography: manuscript sources, printed primary sources (including a section on contemporary newspapers), reference works, studies and theses, and journals. Wherever possible, manuscript material is cited under the location of the original documents; the location of copies used by contributors is included in the citation. In general, the items in individual bibliographies are the sources listed by the contributors, but these items have often been supplemented by bibliographic investigation in the DCB/DBC offices. Any special bibliographical comments by contributors appear within square brackets.

TRANSLATION INTO ENGLISH (a note by the translator of French biographies)

As one would expect, in contrast to the continuity with previous volumes evident in volume IV, translation of French biographies in volume V revealed a much greater and steadily increasing change in the nature of the language and vocabulary, corresponding certainly to the increasing British presence in Quebec after the early years following the conquest. This trend brought problems of a new order. The changeover to a British military establishment undoubtedly simplified the task of presenting military terms and institutions in the English text; on the other hand the development of British administration and of a parliamentary system based upon that in London, the growing role of the British merchants and entrepreneurs, and the gradual transfer of trade and commerce from France to Britain all resulted in increasing use of English terms, which often had to be recognized under the French equivalents adopted in the province. The use of cognate terms or names in the two languages, particularly in the administrative and business worlds, became fairly standard practice and normally caused little difficulty, as with the Union Company of Quebec/la Compagnie de l'Union de Québec, but required constant vigilance to discover the equivalent in the other language. The House of Assembly was officially bilingual and its statutes were a helpful source, as was the *Quebec Gazette/La Gazette de Québec*. A microfilm copy of the index to the commissions register (PAC, RG 68, General index, 1651–1841) was used frequently in establishing the English form for official appointments. The maintenance of the seigneurial system and French civil law assured the continuing use of many of the French terms found regularly in previous volumes. For some of the more unfamiliar terminology in property transactions, translation was attempted, as in "secured annuity" for *la rente constituée*, in order to give readers at least an idea of the nature of the obligation involved. *A dictionary of Canadianisms on historical principles*, ed. W. S. Avis *et al.* (Toronto, 1967), was again useful in decisions relating to translation. As in volume IV the English originals of quotations in French biographies were used when available. At the same time it had to be recognized that some of the personages of the period, such as Sir Frederick Haldimand, wrote in French as well as in English, while the fact that some of the French-speaking "new subjects" of His Britannic Majesty on occasion expressed themselves in English when dealing with English-speaking correspondents necessitated additional vigilance to determine the nature of the original quotation.

BIOGRAPHIES

List of Abbreviations

AAQ	Archives de l'archidiocèse de Québec	MAC-CD	Ministère des Affaires culturelles, Centre de documentation
AC	Archives civiles		
AD	Archives départementales	MTL	Metropolitan Toronto Library
ADB	*Australian dictionary of biography*	NWC	North West Company
AN	Archives nationales	*NYCD*	*Documents relative to the colonial history of the state of New-York*
ANQ	Archives nationales du Québec		
ANQ-M	Archives nationales du Québec, Centre régional de Montréal	NYPL	New York Public Library
		OH	*Ontario History*
ANQ-MBF	Archives nationales du Québec, Centre régional de la Mauricie–Bois-Francs	PAC	Public Archives of Canada
		PAM	Provincial Archives of Manitoba
		PANB	Provincial Archives of New Brunswick
ANQ-Q	Archives nationales du Québec, Centre d'archives de la Capitale	PANL	Provincial Archives of Newfoundland and Labrador
AO	Archives of Ontario	PANS	Public Archives of Nova Scotia
AP	Archives paroissiales	PAPEI	Public Archives of Prince Edward Island
ASQ	Archives du séminaire de Québec		
ASSM	Archives du séminaire de Saint-Sulpice, Montréal	PCA	Presbyterian Church in Canada Archives
AUM	Archives de l'université de Montréal	PRO	Public Record Office
BL	British Library	QDA	Quebec Diocesan Archives
BRH	*Le Bulletin des recherches historiques*	QUA	Queen's University Archives
CCHA	Canadian Catholic Historical Association	*RHAF*	*Revue d'histoire de l'Amérique française*
CÉA	Centre d'études acadiennes	RSC	Royal Society of Canada
CHA	Canadian Historical Association	SCHÉC	Société canadienne d'histoire de l'Église catholique
CHR	*Canadian Historical Review*		
CND	Congregation of Notre-Dame	SGCF	Société généalogique canadienne-française
DAB	*Dictionary of American biography*		
DBF	*Dictionnaire de biographie française*	*SH*	*Social History, a Canadian Review*
DCB	*Dictionary of Canadian biography*	SPG	Society for the Propagation of the Gospel
DNB	*Dictionary of national biography*		
DOLQ	*Dictionnaire des œuvres littéraires du Québec*	SRO	Scottish Record Office
		UNBL	University of New Brunswick Library
DPL	Detroit Public Library	USPG	United Society for the Propagation of the Gospel
DSB	*Dictionary of scientific biography*		
GRO	General Register Office for Scotland	UTL-TF	University of Toronto Library, Thomas Fisher Rare Book Library
HBC	Hudson's Bay Company		
HBCA	Hudson's Bay Company Archives	UWO	University of Western Ontario
HBRS	Hudson's Bay Record Society		

Biographies

A

ABERCHALDER. *See* MᶜDONELL

ADHÉMAR, *dit* **Saint-Martin, TOUSSAINT-ANTOINE** (often referred to as Anthony or Martin Adhémar but he usually signed **Adhemar St Martin**), fur trader and office holder; b. 9 Sept. 1740 in Montreal (Que.), youngest of three children of Jean-Baptiste Adhémar* and Catherine Moreau; brother of Jean-Baptiste-Amable*; d. 22 Nov. 1804 in Michilimackinac (Mackinac Island, Mich.).

Toussaint-Antoine Adhémar, *dit* Saint-Martin, was the son and grandson of royal notaries, and may himself have trained as a physician. He married Geneviève Blondeau at Montreal on 17 Oct. 1768, and shortly after their marriage he and his wife moved to Detroit (Mich.), where he entered the fur trade. For some 30 years he traded and travelled extensively throughout the hinterland south and west of the Upper Lakes, but his trading ventures were generally unrewarding and he fell deeply into debt. In 1775 he was the "principal sufferer" when British forces destroyed a cargo of trade goods from the *Chippewa*, wrecked on Presque Isle, Pa, to keep it from falling into American hands. Adhémar petitioned for compensation, noting that his loss of £400 was "of great consequence" as he was "burdened with a numerous family" and had large debts. In supporting his claim Henry Hamilton*, lieutenant governor at Detroit, wrote to Governor HALDIMAND that "while the Traders on every side [were] enriching themselves" at the expense of the government, Adhémar had often supplied military stores at prices below prevailing market value.

Such practices did not relieve Adhémar's mounting debts, but they did enhance his reputation among British officials. In 1778 he was appointed commissary for the contingent of Indians and militia accompanying Hamilton's march on Vincennes (Ind.). On 5 March 1779, unaware that Hamilton had surrendered to Colonel George Rogers Clark, Adhémar was captured while ferrying supplies and reinforcements to Vincennes. A few days later Adhémar and the other members of the Detroit militia were released once they had taken an oath of neutrality. Adhémar nevertheless retained his allegiance to the crown: in 1780 Augustin Mottin de La Balme, during his abortive raid on Detroit, referred to Adhémar as a "dangerous man," deeply committed to the British cause.

After the war Adhémar joined the newly organized Miamis Company, a small union of Detroit merchants, and in 1786 he was sent as its agent to the Miamis Towns (Fort Wayne, Ind.), several Indian villages on the portage between the Miamis (Maumee) and Wabash rivers. Adhémar's fortunes continued to decline, however. In September 1787 he relinquished his house in Detroit to William Macomb in payment of debts, and he signed over personal property and outstanding debts to John ASKIN. Adhémar's obligation to Askin was not finally resolved until 1802.

Some of Adhémar's problems were not unique to him. During the 1780s British control of the fur trade south of the Upper Lakes was threatened by the expansion of the American frontier. Although Britain had agreed in the peace treaty of 1783 to withdraw its forces from the region, British troops remained in possession of the western forts and encouraged the Indians' political and diplomatic efforts against American encroachment on their lands [*see* THAYENDANEGEA]. The resultant warfare focused on the strategic Miamis–Wabash portage as the Americans attempted to drive out the British traders and break the Indians' confederacy. Although attacks by Brigadier-General Josiah Harmar in the fall of 1790 and Major-General Arthur St Clair a year later were repulsed by the confederacy's forces under Little Turtle [MICHIKINAKOUA], considerable damage was inflicted on the traders' warehouses and the Indians' villages. These attacks, coupled with the demise of the Miamis Company by 1789, took Adhémar back to Detroit.

Adhémar's lack of success in business contrasted sharply with his career as a public official. Continuing in the militia as a lieutenant, he was nominated justice of the peace at Detroit in 1788, but later resigned since the local merchants protested the appointment of a merchant to such a post. In 1789 he was placed on the land board of the District of Hesse. Adhémar attended meetings of the board only through March 1791, although he was listed as a member for several years afterwards.

By 1792 at the latest Adhémar had moved to

Ah je juk

Michilimackinac, where he served as justice of the peace and notary (the former notary, Jean-Louis Besnard*, *dit* Carignant, having died unexpectedly in 1791). Of his eight children at least three became active in local affairs at Michilimackinac. Adhémar remained there after the British evacuation in 1796, and in that year he was named justice of the peace and notary by acting American governor Winthrop Sargent. He retained those positions until his death in 1804.

DAVID R. FARRELL

ANQ-M, CE1-51, 10 sept. 1740, 17 oct. 1768. "Board of land office, District of Hesse," AO *Report*, 1905: 1–268. [Henry Hay], "A narrative of life on the old frontier: Henry Hay's journal from Detroit to the [Miamis] River," ed. M. M. Quaife, Wis., State Hist. Soc., *Proc.* (Madison), 1914: 208–61. *Henry Hamilton and George Rogers Clark in the American revolution, with the unpublished journal of Lieut. Gov. Henry Hamilton*, ed. J. D. Barnhart (Crawfordsville, Ind., 1951). *John Askin papers* (Quaife). *Mich. Pioneer Coll.*, 9 (1886): 467, 494, 505; 19 (1891): 319, 586. Wis., State Hist. Soc., *Coll.*, 14 (1898): 20; 19 (1910): 98, 159. H. P. Beers, *The French & British in the old northwest: a bibliographical guide to archive and manuscript sources* (Detroit, 1964). *The city of Detroit, Michigan, 1701–1922*, ed. C. M. Burton *et al.* (5v., Detroit and Chicago, 1922). Christian Denissen, *Genealogy of the French families of the Detroit River region, 1701–1911*, ed. H. F. Powell (2v., Detroit, 1976). Neatby, *Quebec*. W. W. Potter, "The Michigan judiciary," *Mich. Hist. Magazine* (Lansing), 27 (1943): 418–33.

AH JE JUK. *See* CHEJAUK

AINSLIE, THOMAS, businessman, office holder, and militia officer; b. 8 Feb. 1729 in Jedburgh parish, Scotland, son of Gilbert Ainslie and Christian Rutherford; m. first 26 March 1762 Mary Potts in Jedburgh, and they had two sons and two daughters; m. secondly 2 April 1772 Elizabeth Martin in Hampton, N.H., with whom he had five sons and three daughters; m. thirdly Elizabeth Williamson in Edinburgh, Scotland, and there were no children; d. 7 April 1806 at his farm, Wells (Over Wells), near Jedburgh, and was buried in Jedburgh Abbey.

Following the early death of their father, Thomas Ainslie and his two brothers were raised by their mother and an uncle, John Ainslie. In 1748 Thomas came to North America and appears to have entered the mercantile trade, possibly at Boston, Mass. By 1757 he had settled at Halifax, N.S., where he achieved some prominence. He secured in 1759 a portion of the supply trade at Louisbourg, Cape Breton Island. Anticipating further gain through the advancement of his friend Colonel James Murray*, he went to Quebec after the capture of that city. Between June 1760 and September 1762 Ainslie served, on Murray's appointment, as administrator of the king's posts, the government-controlled fur-trading posts on the lower St Lawrence, where he also had a temporary monopoly of the trade. In London in the spring of 1762, he reported for Murray to Lord Egremont, secretary of state for the Southern Department, on the general situation in Canada. While in Britain Ainslie returned to Jedburgh where he married the daughter of James Potts, later a judge in the Court of Admiralty. The same year he acquired from the Séminaire de Québec an estate in Sillery on which stood Samos, the former residence of Bishop Pierre-Herman Dosquet*, which had been partially destroyed during the war; Ainslie rebuilt it, renamed it Woodfield, and lived there until 1767 when he moved into Quebec. In 1764 he had been appointed a justice of the peace.

Quebec had had customs services since 1760, but in April 1762 the Treasury formally established a custom-house there with Montreal as an outport; on Murray's recommendation, Thomas Knox was made collector and Ainslie controller, responsible for the audit of the collector's accounts. Within months Ainslie became collector for the province of Quebec under the authority of Charles Stewart, surveyor general of a customs district that included New York and Pennsylvania. For this imperial function Ainslie received a salary of £300, and on Murray's instructions he retained fees for collecting provincial duties continued from the French régime. The provincial-imperial duality of Ainslie's office ended in 1768, when local merchants refused to continue paying the provincial duties.

As collector, Ainslie figured prominently in the administration of customs and trade regulations in the province. Acting through poorly paid and often negligent inspection and clerical officers, he was responsible for registration of vessels, inspection of merchants' bonds, examination of incoming cargoes for dutiable goods, collection of duties, clearance of export cargoes, and enforcement of imperial trade laws. One of his most troublesome administrative problems arose from poor customs facilities at Quebec. He pressed unsuccessfully for adequate facilities for docking, inspection, and the storage of dutiable items. From 1763 his attempts to secure the King's Wharf in Lower Town Quebec for private as well as customs use generated opposition from merchants, and from a grand jury in 1764. As well, Ainslie faced the problem of the unmanageably lengthy customs frontier of Quebec which facilitated smuggling from France, frequently via the French islands of Saint-Pierre and Miquelon and the Baie des Chaleurs. At both locations contraband goods were trans-shipped and daringly run up the St Lawrence. Ainslie's capacity to control this traffic was improved in 1763 and 1764 by Murray's assignment of additional naval patrols and establishment of a vice-admiralty court necessary for prosecuting illicit trade.

Following the arrival of Lieutenant Governor Guy CARLETON in 1766, Ainslie became increasingly embroiled in the complex disputes over fees and imperial-provincial jurisdictions that encumbered customs operations throughout North America. In 1767 the Quebec custom-house was placed under the American Board of Customs, formed that year at Boston. Ainslie claimed exemption as an imperial officer from audit by authorities of the province of Quebec. This claim along with his collection since 1765 of imperially authorized fees, which he based four years later on the comparatively high fee schedule used at Halifax, were challenged in 1769 and 1770 by Carleton, who was seeking to tighten public finances and to curb excessive extraction of fees by such "men of low birth and no education." In the bitter exchange that ensued, Carleton questioned Ainslie's integrity and condemned the worst local features of an incredibly unwieldy customs system and its grossly abused fee privileges. Although supported by law and the Boston board, Ainslie, under Carleton's threat of suspension, grudgingly but prudently decided not to continue with fees until the matter of fee collection had been regulated. In 1774 the Court of Common Pleas at Quebec, to which Ainslie had appealed, restored his use of the Halifax schedule.

The institution of new duties under the Quebec Revenue Act, in force from April 1775, saddled Ainslie with other onerous responsibilities. The act imposed a discriminatory tariff aimed at fostering triangular trade between Britain, the West Indies, and Quebec. The high duty placed on imported rum, however, stimulated smuggling from the American colonies via Lake Champlain, thus putting pressure on a custom-house recently established by Ainslie at St Johns (Saint-Jean-sur-Richelieu), Que. At the Quebec docks, where Ainslie was personally involved, incidents of seizure, forceful evasion, and pursuit may also have been related to the new tariff structure. The act authorized Ainslie's retention of the cost of collecting the duties; lacking specific instruction, he deducted almost nine per cent of his receipts. The net proceeds were paid quarterly to the province's receiver general, but Ainslie repeatedly resisted provincial control and refused the controller his legitimate right of access to the accounts before they were forwarded to the Treasury.

The resulting debate was overshadowed in 1775 by the outbreak of the American revolution. Through loyalist friends, and possibly relations, residing in Boston, Ainslie fearfully monitored developments there. As a customs officer he was exempt from military service, but by October, following the American invasion of the colony, he had voluntarily become a captain in the British militia at Quebec. He

was at first pessimistic about the colony's ability to resist the invaders. "We must fall in a few days . . . ," he wrote to Sylvester Gardiner at Boston in November; "God forgive those who have so cruelly abandoned us." However, the daily record he kept between 1 Dec. 1775 and 7 May 1776, which has been regarded as the fullest and most accurate of the British narratives of the siege of the city, reveals his European imperial bias and a sense of restored confidence. He denounced the demagoguery of British "Grumbletonians" and of American "Banditti" and on 5 March 1776 described the American observance of the "bloody Boston Massacre" of 1770 as an anarchistic honouring of illegal opposition to the New England customs. Although he had never seen European troops in action during the revolution, Ainslie asserted that it was the auxiliaries of other nations who gave the Americans their strength. The defenders of Quebec had "nought to fear from the natives of America," be they Americans or Canadians; indeed from within the city walls they "wou'd laugh at an army of 10,000 habitants." The only exceptions to Ainslie's general condemnation of the ungrateful Canadians were the "nobles" and the clergy, both royalist, and the militia within the city, whose courage during the repulse of Richard Montgomery*'s desperate attack of 31 Dec. 1775 had impressed him.

Ainslie resumed regular customs collections following the American withdrawal in 1776. In addition to the custom-house at St Johns, others had been established under his authority at the gulf outports of Gaspé and Bonaventure by 1775, and later at New Carlisle. His efforts to control illicit trade, which persisted throughout and for a time after the revolutionary war, were complicated by difficulties in coordinating customs and naval operations, the laxity and inconsistency of customs in the Maritime and American colonies, and a confusing realignment of North American trade. Partially in response to these problems, more rigid registration procedures for vessels were implemented in 1786 in Quebec. Despite this measure, the incidence of counterfeit British or colonial registrations on American vessels, particularly in the Baie des Chaleurs, remained disturbingly high. On the other hand, according to Ainslie, illicit inland traffic declined noticeably when trade restrictions were relaxed.

The closure of the port of Quebec during the long winter season facilitated frequent absences by Ainslie, most often in Britain and ostensibly on customs business. In 1768 Carleton had been forced to have Ainslie ordered back after a prolonged absence, an abuse common throughout the imperial customs system. During two of his visits to London, in 1777 and 1784, Ainslie, because of his thorough familiarity with British North American trade, testified on the subject before the Privy Council. On both occasions,

Ainslie

as well as at Quebec in 1786, he sought vainly to secure appointment to Quebec's Legislative Council.

Following the return to Quebec in 1786 of Carleton, now Lord Dorchester, as governor, Ainslie's operations were subjected to repeated scrutiny. Evidently conscious of the British Customs Board's closer regulation of colonial operations, as well as its efforts to reform the fee system in Britain, Dorchester also recognized Quebec's trade deficit and the hopeless inadequacy of the colony's revenue, which was drawn largely from the British Exchequer. He pointed to the unregulated fee structures and unaudited accounts of the receiver general [see Sir Thomas Mills*; William GRANT (1744–1805)] and Ainslie himself as major factors. During a provincial revenue inquiry by the Legislative Council in 1788, the Treasury confirmed the need for stricter auditing, and damaging testimony was received from Ainslie's controller, Thomas SCOTT, who had received no share of customs fees taken since his appointment in 1769. Ainslie's loose management of the Quebec custom-house, his accounting procedures, and his augmentation to around 13.5 per cent per annum, in the year 1787, of the deduction for his fee and other costs charged against provincial revenues – in order to compensate, with some justification, for past salary reductions and an increased work load – again drew Dorchester's criticism in 1795 and 1796. Deficiencies such as those in Ainslie's administration, however, were common in the imperial bureaucracy and the Treasury tacitly supported the collector. Indeed in 1791 it had appointed him to investigate the "state of the several Ports" and customs operations in Nova Scotia, New Brunswick, St John's (Prince Edward) Island, and Cape Breton Island; his report unfortunately has not survived. Nevertheless, it is known that different commercial interests and tariff policies had dictated, instead of an integrated system, independent customs operations in Quebec, New Brunswick, and Nova Scotia, each of which suffered serious revenue liabilities and was likely understaffed. In Quebec as in Nova Scotia, the heavy incidence of smuggling and of false British registration of vessels, which enabled the evasion of several restrictive trade acts, was countered with minimal success, even though in 1794 an additional customs vessel was placed at Ainslie's disposal.

Along with his customs work, from the 1770s Ainslie had been involved in some private business activities. In November 1774 he acquired for £400 cash from the Quebec merchant Jacques Perrault*, known as Perrault l'aîné, the right to collect a debt of £500 owed by Louis LIÉNARD de Beaujeu de Ville-monde. In August 1779 he purchased for £600 three lots at the juncture of Rue Sainte-Anne and Rue du Trésor with the Place d'Armes; the purchase included two houses, one of which, on Sainte-Anne, Ainslie had been renting as his residence for a number of years. Ainslie's house faced the Place d'Armes, and in 1786 in a disagreement, apparently provoked by his negligence over snow removal, he was beaten with a musket and narrowly evaded the deadly thrust of a sentry's bayonet. The incident was an outburst of the civil-military discord that simmered beneath the surface of the "very nett [neat] New England Society," which Ainslie had once described at Quebec. In 1793 he sold to James Fisher* for £775 all the property, except his house, acquired in 1779. Also in 1793 he purchased for £6,000 a one-quarter interest in the Quebec brewery of Young and Company. Two years later Ainslie's daughter Christian (Christianna) married one of his partners, John YOUNG, and in 1796 Ainslie transferred to his son Gilbert his interest in Young and Company for £3,850 in order to start him in business. Ainslie's prosperity is not certain, however, since in 1797 he owed £3,030 to Joshua WINSLOW, a debt which was still outstanding in 1800. Ainslie had become publicly involved in the social life of the British community at Quebec only in the 1790s. In 1794 he became a member of the Association, formed that year to support the existing political system in Britain and its colonies, and lieutenant-colonel of the Quebec Battalion of British Militia. From 1794 to 1796 he was deputy grand master of the Society of Free and Accepted Masons.

Ainslie apparently never reconciled himself to life in the colony, despite his long residence, and in 1799 he put up for sale his house and a farm in Sainte-Foy, and retired to London; he was succeeded as collector of customs by Thomas Scott. Ainslie resided for a time in London but by 1804 had moved to Wells, four miles from his birthplace. In 1802 he sold for £400 a lot he had acquired in 1780 for about £200 in the *faubourg* Saint-Jean, near Quebec. In 1803 he received a grant of 700 acres in Granby Township, part or all of which he sold for £28 to Josias Wurtele* the following year. Two years later, after Gilbert Ainslie dissolved his partnership with Young, Thomas successfully sued his son for property, including the brewery. He died in his native parish in 1806.

As customs collector, Thomas Ainslie had participated in the development of trade to Quebec for almost 40 years, possibly the longest period of service for an imperial officer in that colony. His involvement in various controversies, notably the acrimonious disputes with Carleton over fees and accounts, exemplifies some of the formidable administrative problems that encumbered the entire imperial customs service during the 18th century.

DAVID ROBERTS

[Thomas Ainslie is the author of a journal on the siege of Quebec which is held by the Houghton Library, Harvard Univ., Cambridge, Mass. (MS Sparks I, Thomas Ainslie journal). At least two manuscript copies of the journal also survive; one, dated 1794, is at the Rhodes House Library, Univ. of Oxford (MSS, Can. r.2, Thomas Ainslie journal), and the other, dating from the 19th century, is at the National Maritime Museum (JOD/66, MS 58/055, Thomas Ainslie journal). The *Remembrancer; or, Impartial Repository of Public Events* (London), 6 (1778), published a text almost identical to Ainslie's journal, entitled "Journal of the most remarkable occurrences in Quebec, from the 14th of November, 1775 to the 7th of May, 1776; by an officer of the garrison," a text which was reprinted first in William Smith, *History of Canada; from its first discovery to the peace of 1763* (2v., Quebec, 1815), 2: 81–138, and then in N.Y. Hist. Soc., *Coll.*, [3rd ser.], 13 (1880). Ainslie's "Journal of the most remarkable occurences in the province of Quebec from the appearance of the rebels in September 1775 until their retreat on the sixth of May ... 1776" was published in *Blockade of Quebec in 1775–1776 by the American revolutionists (les Bastonnais)*, ed. F. C. Würtele (Quebec, 1906; repr. Port Washington, N.Y., and London, 1970), and again as *Canada preserved; the journal of Captain Thomas Ainslie*, ed. S. S. Cohen ([Toronto, 1968]). Genealogical and family information was provided by Mr C. M. Ainslie of Oxford, Eng. D.R.]

ANQ-Q, CN1-25, 18 août 1779, 11 nov. 1780, 26 févr. 1783; CN1-205, 11 déc. 1772, 16 juill. 1773, 12 févr. 1778; CN1-230, 8 févr., 22 mars 1802; 1ᵉʳ août, 1ᵉʳ sept. 1804; CN1-248, 7 nov. 1774; CN1-256, 10 Oct., 13, 16 Nov. 1793; 18 May, 15 Aug. 1798; 20 Feb. 1800; CN1-284,12 févr. 1793, 18 juill. 1795, 13 août 1800. AP, Cathedral of the Holy Trinity (Quebec), Reg. of baptisms, marriages, and burials, 21 June, 9 Aug. 1773; 21 March 1776; 7 Aug. 1777; 22 March 1782; 22 Jan. 1784; 3 June 1785; 21 July 1797. BL, Add. MSS 21735/2, 21736, 21860, 21873, 21877 (copies at PAC). GRO, Reg. of births and baptisms for the parish of Jedburgh, 12 Feb. 1729. Mass. Hist. Soc., Gardiner, etc., II: 89. PAC, MG 23, GII, 1, ser.1, 1–3; ser.3: 26; MG 55/30, no.2; RG 1, E1, 106–7, 112; RG 4, A1, 1, 12–15, 17, 19–20, 28, 30–31, 44, 50, 62; RG 68, 89; 202. PRO, CO 42/1–5, 42/10, 42/12, 42/16, 42/24–25, 42/27–28, 42/30–31, 42/34, 42/47–49, 42/51, 42/69, 42/72, 42/77, 42/100, 42/102, 42/105–9, 42/114 (mfm. at PAC). [James Jeffry], "Journal kept in Quebec in 1775 by James Jeffry," ed. William Smith, Essex Institute, *Hist. Coll.* (Salem, Mass.), 50 (1914): 135. "Official proclamations, etc.," AO *Report*, 1906: 7, 14–15. *Quebec Gazette*, 1763–1813. Robert Douglas of Glenbervie, *The baronage of Scotland; containing an historical and genealogical account of that kingdom ...* (Edinburgh, 1798), 301. *Quebec almanac*, 1780–1802. W. H. Atherton, *Historical brochure commemorating the official opening of the new customs and excise building at Montreal in nineteen hundred and thirty six* (Montreal, 1936). T. C. Barrow, *Trade and empire: the British customs service in colonial America, 1660–1775* (Cambridge, 1967). André Bernier, *Le Vieux-Sillery* ([Québec], 1977), 75. Gordon Blake, *Customs administration in Canada: an essay in tariff technology* (Toronto, 1957), 15–39, 60. Burt, *Old prov. of Quebec* (1968), 1: 46, 121, 129–32; 2: 185–86. John Ehrman, *The younger Pitt; the years of acclaim* (New York, 1969), 92, 176, 270–71, 289–92. E. E. Hoon, *The organization of the English customs system, 1696–1786*, intro. R. C. Jarvis (2nd ed., Newton Abbot, Eng., 1968). [R. L. P. Morden], *Border bairns; an Ainslie family history* (n.p., [1978]). Neatby, *Quebec*, 66, 81–82, 97. C. R. Ritcheson, *Aftermath of revolution; British policy towards the United States, 1783–1795* (Dallas, Tex., 1969), 196–97. D. M. Clark, "The American Board of Customs, 1767–1783," *American Hist. Rev.* (New York and London), 45 (1940): 777–806. W. B. Kerr, "The Stamp Act in Quebec," *English Hist. Rev.* (London and New York), 47 (1932): 648–51.

AINSSE (Ainse, Hains, Hins), JOSEPH-LOUIS (Louis-Joseph), interpreter and fur trader; b. 1 May 1744 in Michilimackinac (Mackinaw City, Mich.), son of Joseph Ainsse, a master carpenter, and Constante Chevalier, daughter of Jean-Baptiste Chevalier*; m. 6 Oct. 1775 Marie-Thérèse Bondy in Michilimackinac; d. 12 March 1802 in Varennes, Lower Canada.

During the turmoil of the Seven Years' War young Joseph-Louis Ainsse went east to stay with an uncle on Île Perrot (Que.). When the British captured Canada he was still living on the island, where he took the oath of allegiance in 1760, but in 1762 he entered the fur trade and by the spring of 1763 had returned to Michilimackinac. On 2 June local Ojibwas captured the fort [see MADJECKEWISS], and Ainsse scurried about trying to save British soldiers and traders. Captain George Etherington soon dispatched him to Detroit (Mich.) with word of the uprising. Although some later accused Ainsse of becoming rich from goods looted at Michilimackinac, he was so poor that he wore cast-off clothing. During the next year or so he was a labourer and spent one winter cutting cordwood.

Seeking his fortune, Ainsse drifted down to Fort de Chartres (near Prairie du Rocher, Ill.) and later moved to Fort St Joseph (Niles, Mich.), where his uncle Louis-Thérèse Chevallier was a prominent merchant. He also made a trip to New Orleans (La) about 1767. During his travels he became proficient in a number of Indian languages, eventually mastering nine of them.

It was probably in 1767 that Robert Rogers*, commandant at Michilimackinac, invited Ainsse to return from St Joseph and serve as interpreter. When Ainsse arrived, however, he was not formally given the position, perhaps because he did not understand English well. On 6 Dec. 1767 Rogers was suddenly arrested and accused of treason. Ainsse talked with him frequently during his imprisonment, and while Rogers's wife taught the young man English they discussed the possibility of the former commandant's escape. Late in January Ainsse reported his conversations to Captain Frederick Christopher Spiesmacher, the commanding officer. When Ainsse produced a promissory note dated 4 Feb. 1768 and alleged that Rogers had given it to him to assist his escape, Rogers was clapped in irons. Ainsse was rewarded with the coveted office of king's interpreter, his salary of a dollar a day from the Indian Department beginning on 25 January.

The position was an important responsibility at

Ainsse

Michilimackinac. Since the British commanding officer could seldom speak even one of the various Indian tongues, the interpreter served as mediator between authorities and Indians. Michilimackinac was a major centre for negotiations with the peoples of the Upper Lakes, and the summer months, when thousands came for counsel and trade, were particularly active. To be effective, an interpreter had to be trusted by both commanding officer and Indians because an inaccurate translation could create serious misunderstandings.

In the fall of 1768 Ainsse travelled to Montreal for Rogers's court martial, and he gave damning evidence. To impeach Ainsse's character, trader Henry Bostwick testified that Ainsse had plundered his goods and ordered an Indian to kill him during the uprising of 1763; as a means of bolstering this charge he had Ainsse arrested. Rogers was acquitted and Ainsse languished in jail from October 1768 to March 1769, when his case was heard. Father Pierre Du Jaunay*, Captain Spiesmacher, Benjamin Roberts*, and others testified to his good character and the jury found him not guilty. When the first canoes left for Michilimackinac in May, Ainsse returned home; nevertheless Joseph Tucker, who had replaced him as interpreter, retained the position. The next year, however, Ainsse's behaviour in a skirmish with an Indian who had attacked an unarmed trader led to his reappointment. George Turnbull, the commanding officer at Michilimackinac, was so impressed that on 8 June 1771 he restored him to office. Ainsse, he claimed, "knows every Indian Personally."

During the American revolution, the interpreter was of great importance at Michilimackinac since Britain relied on its Indian allies to hold the Upper Lakes. Moreover, Ainsse's duties were not confined to that post. On 17 June 1776 Arent Schuyler DePeyster*, the commandant, ordered him to lead a band of Ottawa warriors from Michilimackinac to aid in the recapture of Montreal. Late in October 1778 DePeyster sent him to Fort St Joseph to help Charles-Michel Mouet* de Langlade and Charles Gautier de Verville rally support among the Potawatomis, an expedition that apparently had little positive effect. In the critical year 1779, following George Rogers Clark's capture of Lieutenant Governor Henry Hamilton* at Vincennes (Ind.), Ainsse distributed thousands of pounds' worth of Indian presents, and he took part in DePeyster's large council at L'Arbre Croche (Cross Village, Mich.), aimed at ensuring the support of the Ottawas and many western tribes.

Ainsse retired from the Indian Department in 1779 and in the fall went to Montreal to winter with his family. He had become quite a prominent trader during his time in the west: he sold furs worth 12,513 *livres* that year and purchased the seigneury of Île-Sainte-Thérèse, as well as a home in Varennes. When he returned to Michilimackinac on business in the spring of 1780, the new lieutenant governor of the post, Patrick SINCLAIR, dispatched him to Fort St Joseph along with Nissowaquet* to bring Chevallier and the other residents to Michilimackinac, where they would be less vulnerable in case of American attack. Ainsse succeeded in this mission, but shortly after his return Sinclair confined him to the fort and refused to pay his expenses. Outraged, Ainsse posted a bond and went to Quebec, where on 5 October he petitioned Governor HALDIMAND for justice. When Haldimand asked the lieutenant governor to give reasons, Sinclair claimed that he had disallowed the bills because Ainsse had purchased supplies on his own instead of through the General Store, a short-lived joint trading venture the merchants of Michilimackinac had set up in 1779. Sinclair refused Ainsse permission to return to the post but eventually approved some of the bills.

In February 1785 Ainsse became a founding member of the Beaver Club, along with such notable traders as James McGILL and Joseph FROBISHER. During that year commerce in the western Great Lakes region was disrupted by inter-tribal Indian war [*see* WAHPASHA], and in the spring of 1786 the foremost traders to the area suggested that agents be sent with presents to negotiate with the tribes. Sinclair had by this time left Fort Michilimackinac (which had been moved to Mackinac Island), and they recommended Ainsse as the best person to meet with the Ottawas, Menominees, Winnebagos, Sauks and Foxes, and Sioux. He was appointed and in August the expedition set out; in the spring he led a sizeable delegation of western tribesmen back to Michilimackinac for a peace council. They requested that Ainsse winter with them once again and, though he wanted to return to his family in Varennes, he agreed.

On 10 Aug. 1787 James AIRD, Charles Paterson, and other merchants presented a petition to commandant Thomas Scott alleging that during the previous winter's expedition Ainsse had sold Indian Department goods intended as presents. Apparently he had undercut Paterson, a prominent trader, who was out for revenge. An inquiry was not begun before Ainsse left for another winter in the interior; when he returned, however, he was immediately arrested. On 24 June 1788 Scott convened a court of inquiry which collected evidence from witnesses, with Paterson serving as prosecutor. Not until 1 May 1790, at a meeting of a committee of the Legislative Council in Quebec, did Ainsse and his co-defendant John DEASE, deputy Indian agent at Michilimackinac, have an opportunity to rebut the accusations. Attorney General Alexander Gray and Solicitor General Jenkin WILLIAMS found the charges justified and their findings were upheld by the committee in a report of 28 October. Ainsse's association with the Indian Department had come to an inglorious end.

Joseph-Louis Ainsse apparently spent the remainder of his life at Varennes, where he died on 12 March 1802. His son Joseph succeeded to his seigneury, and a mixed-blood son, Ance, was known as a chief at the straits of Mackinac.

DAVID A. ARMOUR

Arch. de la Soc. hist. de Montréal, Coll. Louis-Joseph Ainsse (mfm. at PAC). Clements Library, Thomas Gage papers, American ser., 84: Roberts to Gage, 30 March 1769; 85: Carleton to Gage, 30 May 1769; 94: Turnbull to Carleton in Carleton to Gage, 31 July 1770; 103: Turnbull to Gage, 12 May 1771; supplementary accounts, Joseph Hans's account with Capt. Etherington, 2 July 1763; Nicola Bezzo's account with Etherington for the use of the king, 18 July 1763; Frederick Spiesmacher, journal, 8 Dec. 1767–18 June 1768; Indian Department pay list, 24 Sept. 1768; Benjamin Roberts, "Expenses of evidence attending Major Rogers tryal at Montreal 1769"; box 76, George Turnbull's Indian expenses, 25 May 1770–25 Nov. 1772. DPL, Burton Hist. Coll., J.-B. Barthe papers, sales book, 1775–79, 27, 30 May 1779; Thomas Williams papers, petty ledger, 1775–79, Lamoth and Ainse account, 19 July 1776. PAC, MG 18, K3, Map of Michilimackinac in 1749. Wis., State Hist. Soc., Consolidated returns of trade licences, 7 June 1777 (transcript).

[A. S. DePeyster], *Miscellanies, by an officer* (Dumfries, Scot., 1813), 274. *The Gladwin manuscripts; with an introduction and a sketch of the conspiracy of Pontiac*, ed. Charles Moore (Lansing, Mich., 1897), 666–67. *Johnson papers* (Sullivan et al.), 6, 8, 12. *Mich. Pioneer Coll.*, 8 (1885): 466–67; 9 (1886): 377–78, 545–46, 560, 569–70, 576, 581; 10 (1886): 305–7, 400, 405–6, 415, 434–40, 444, 453, 488–89, 498–99, 531–32; 11 (1887): 490–620; 12 (1887): 312–13; 13 (1888): 83–85, 107–8; 19 (1891): 299–300, 304, 425–26, 691; 20 (1892): 208; 23 (1893): 603–80; 37 (1909–10): 537, 542–45. [Robert Rogers], "Rogers's Michillimackinac journal," ed. W. L. Clements, American Antiquarian Soc., *Proc.* (Worcester, Mass.), new ser., 28 (1918): 245, 247. H. R. Schoolcraft, *Personal memoirs of a residence of thirty years with the Indian tribes on the American frontiers, with brief notices of passing events, facts and opinions, A.D. 1812 to A.D. 1842* (Philadelphia, 1851), 492–93, 610. *Treason? at Michilimackinac: the proceedings of a general court martial held at Montreal in October 1768 for the trial of Major Robert Rogers*, ed. D. A. Armour (Mackinac Island, Mich., 1967), 27–29, 37–45, 65, 67, 71–73, 78, 95. Wis., State Hist. Soc., *Coll.*, 12 (1892); 18 (1908); 19 (1910). Massicotte, "Répertoire des engagements pour l'Ouest," ANQ *Rapport*, 1932–33: 293, 304. "Colonel Arent de Peister," *"The Kingsman": the Journal of the King's Regiment* (Liverpool, Eng.), 3 (1931–33), no.2: 4–5.

AIRD, JAMES, fur trader; b. in Ayrshire, Scotland; d. 27 Feb. 1819 in Prairie du Chien (Wis.).

Little is known of James Aird's early life. He appears to have begun his career in the Indian trade west of Michilimackinac (Mackinaw City, Mich.) about 1778 or 1779. It is evident that in the latter year he was at Quebec, for on 14 June Arent Schuyler DePeyster*, commandant at Michilimackinac, wrote to Governor HALDIMAND, "The bearer of this letter young Mr. Aird has behaved as a good subject in this Country. I believe he is desirous of returning with a load." Aird was at Montreal in 1784, but by 1786 his principal location was Prairie du Chien, and he was then associated with Charles Paterson, Étienne-Charles Campion*, and others in a short-lived partnership known as the General Company of Lake Superior and the South, or the General Society [see John SAYER]. This group lodged a complaint against Indian Department representatives John DEASE and Joseph-Louis AINSSE for trading with government supplies, and Aird testified before a court of inquiry at Michilimackinac (Mackinac Island, Mich.) in June 1788. For the past year he had been trading with the Sioux on the St Peters (Minnesota) River, and he appears to have continued operating well within the Spanish territory west of the Mississippi until the early 1800s. His activities probably extended westward from the headwaters of the St Peters to the tributaries of the upper Missouri.

On 16 Aug. 1804 Aird signed a partnership agreement with Robert Dickson* and Allen C. Wilmot of Prairie du Chien and Jacob Franks of Green Bay (Wis.). This agreement foreshadowed the organization at Michilimackinac in 1805 of Robert Dickson and Company, a combination of Canadian traders who hoped through united action to protect their interests in the territory of Louisiana, which had unexpectedly become American in 1803. In its first year the company assigned Aird to the command of a trading venture up the Missouri from St Louis (Mo.). As his brigade descended the Mississippi en route to St Louis he met with a United States exploring expedition under Zebulon Montgomery Pike. The trader made such a favourable impression that Pike recommended him to James Wilkinson, governor of that portion of the Louisiana Purchase between the 33rd and 49th parallels, as "a gentleman to whose humanity and politeness I am much indebted."

Aird wintered on the Missouri from 1805 to 1808. Wilkinson attempted to prevent Canadian traders from entering the area, but Aird had been a resident of United States territory prior to 1796 when the British relinquished to the Americans those posts which they had continued to occupy since the peace treaty of 1783; never having declared himself a British citizen, Aird was legally American. Nevertheless, he met with harassment and had little success in his Missouri River ventures. On 3 Sept. 1806 the expedition of Meriwether Lewis and William Clark, returning from the Pacific, encountered him near the mouth of the Big Sioux River (S. Dak.) and noted that, "after so long an interval, the sight of anyone who could give us information of our country was peculiarly delightful, and much of the night was spent in making inquiries into what had occurred during our absence." Aird, friendly and accommodating as he had been with Pike,

Alberni

supplied the party with tobacco and flour, as well as with whatever news "he had it in his power to have collected in the Illinois. . . ."

As late as 1810 Aird was still hiring men at Michilimackinac for service on the Missouri, but about that time he himself returned to the upper Mississippi. In 1807 Robert Dickson and Company had become a part of the recently organized Michilimackinac Company, and in the winter of 1810–11 Aird was trading for the larger concern above the Falls of St Anthony (Minneapolis, Minn.) with his brother, George, and Robert Dickson. His long association with Dickson led him to give assistance to the British forces during the War of 1812, despite former protestations of American citizenship. He seems, however, to have taken no direct part in military action. In 1814–15 he again wintered on the St Peters River; he was initially expected to do well there, but in March he was reported to be starving. From 1815 until his death he continued to make his headquarters in Prairie du Chien and to conduct business in the area of present-day Minnesota and Wisconsin. Between 1816 and 1819 he traded principally for the American Fur Company.

During his four decades in the fur trade Aird, though apparently never highly successful financially, commanded great respect among those who had dealings with him. He and Mar-pi-ya-ro-to-win (Grey Cloud), a daughter of the Sioux chief WAHPASHA, had one daughter, Margaret. She had three children with Thomas Gummersall Anderson*, one of whom is said to have been present at the time of Aird's death.

RHODA R. GILMAN

[Material on James Aird is extremely fragmentary and scattered. D. S. Lavender, *The fist in the wilderness* (Garden City, N.Y., 1964), contains the most extensive information to be found in any one source. Though only partially documented, it is carefully researched and generally accurate. R.R.G.]

Baylis Public Library (Sault Ste Marie, Mich.), Mackinac notarial records (photocopies at DPL, Burton Hist. Coll.). Private arch., Mrs Joseph R. Ramee (New York), Ramsay Crooks papers, partnership agreement with James Aird, 16 Aug. 1804 (photocopy at DPL, Burton Hist. Coll.). *History of the expedition under the command of captains Lewis and Clark, to the sources of the Missouri, thence across the Rocky Mountains and down the river Columbia to the Pacific Ocean . . .*, ed. and intro. Elliott Coues (4v., New York, 1893), 3: 1203. *Mich. Pioneer Coll.*, 9 (1886): 383–86; 11 (1887): 521, 539, 552–55; 20 (1892): 518. [Z. M. Pike], *The expeditions of Zebulon Montgomery Pike, to headwaters of the Mississippi River, through Louisiana Territory, and in New Spain, during the years 1805–6–7* (new ed., ed. and intro. Elliott Coues, 3v., New York, 1895; repr. 3v. in 2, Minneapolis, Minn., 1965), 1: 24, 32, 225. Wis., State Hist. Soc., *Coll.*, 2 (1856): 226; 9 (1882): 178, 248, 294; 10 (1888): 129; 19 (1910): 316. J. H. Case, "Historical notes of Grey Cloud Island and its vicinity," Minn. Hist. Soc., *Coll.* (St Paul), 15 (1915): 371–72.

ALBERNI, PEDRO DE, army officer; b. 1747 in Tortosa, Spain; d. 11 March 1802 in Monterey (Calif.).

Pedro de Alberni joined the Volunteer Regiment of Catalonia as a cadet in 1762 and saw some active service against Portugal. In 1768 his company was detached from the regiment and transferred to New Spain as the 1st Free Company of Volunteers of Catalonia. There Alberni participated in numerous engagements against the Indians of the northern frontier (the Mexican-American border country), and, recognized as an intelligent and valuable officer, he was promoted captain and commanding officer of his company on 24 March 1783. At some time before 1789 Alberni was for seven years military commander of the province of Nayarit.

Following the temporary occupation of Nootka Sound (B.C.) in 1789 by Esteban José Martínez*, Viceroy Revilla Gigedo of New Spain decided to establish a more permanent presence there with a fortified post capable of defence against the British, Russians, or Americans [*see* James COLNETT; Joseph BILLINGS; Robert GRAY]. The viceroy assigned naval lieutenant Francisco de Eliza* y Reventa to command the expedition of three ships, and Alberni with his company was to fortify and garrison the post. Alberni received orders to prepare for northern duty in September 1789, while stationed at Guadalajara (Mexico). He was short about 15 men, and described another 23 as unfit for the rigours of northern service. Wishing to have the greatest possible number of Europeans at Nootka, the authorities of New Spain allowed him to recruit among Catalonians originally sent from Spain to serve elsewhere in the empire. Alberni requested new arms to replace worn-out equipment and demanded clothing suited to the northern climate. The consequent delays led Revilla Gigedo to charge him with insubordination and with hindering movement to San Blas (state of Nayarit), the port of embarkation. On 3 Feb. 1790 Alberni sailed with charges still pending and was held in confinement for the duration of the voyage north. These circumstances may explain his long posting to Nootka and the special efforts made by his fellow officers to commend his zeal to the viceroy.

When Eliza's expedition landed at Friendly Cove on 5 April, Alberni and his 76 soldiers began to fortify the harbour. Although their instructions called for them to mount 20 cannon, only 14 were placed. Hard labour, a poor diet, and the wet climate weakened the soldiers, who suffered from scurvy, dysentery, and colds. Alberni sent many to California missions to recuperate; by August 1790 only 31 soldiers remained.

Despite the hardships, Alberni threw himself into preparations for the coming winter. Contemporaries praised his vigour in erecting buildings with boards obtained from the Indians and in excavating wells and operating an efficient bakery. He also undertook to raise poultry and, aware of the importance of fresh vegetables, made himself one of the first gardeners on the northwest coast. In spite of Alberni's prophylactic efforts five soldiers perished during the winter, and in March 1791, 32 seamen and soldiers were dispatched to California because of illness. Throughout this period Eliza found Alberni to be a major source of strength to the garrison, maintaining military discipline and promoting harmony between officers and men by his good example.

In 1791 Alberni expanded his horticultural efforts and was able to place the settlement on a better footing for the next winter. He was instrumental in improving relations with the local Nootkas, who were distressed by a number of confrontations with the enlisted men, and by the Spaniards' occupation of the site of Yuquot, their summer village. When he learned that the Indians used flattery and songs in their own diplomacy, Alberni successfully emulated them with a simple verse for the soldiers to sing in Nootkan, praising chief Muquinna* and set to a popular Spanish melody. Alberni is credited with a large contribution to the compilation of a Nootkan-Spanish vocabulary, but he did not write any major account of the Spanish presence in Nootka Sound. Even so, he was there long enough to become an important source of information for others. Among the Spanish explorers on the northwest coast, naval officers Alejandro MALASPINA and Juan Francisco de la Bodega* y Quadra, and naturalist José Mariano MOZIÑO praised his ability and intelligence. Supported by fellow officers' reports of his conduct, Alberni was successful in having the charge of insubordination dropped.

Bodega having arrived on 29 April 1792 to assume command at Nootka Sound, Alberni left there on 1 July; after a delay in Monterey he reached San Blas late in November. On 1 July he had been promoted lieutenant-colonel, and some time after his return he served for eight months as commander of the great castle of San Juan de Ulúa at Veracruz (Mexico) and king's lieutenant of the port. When in 1796 the colonial régime once again feared foreign encroachment on the thinly settled California coast, Alberni with his company was sent to garrison San Francisco. Probably at the same time he was named military commander of the four major California presidios. Later transferred to Monterey, he died there on 11 March 1802.

CHRISTON I. ARCHER

Archivo General de Indias (Seville, Spain), Audiencia de México, legajo 1515, legajo 2424. Archivo General de la Nación (Mexico City), Sección de Historia, vol.69. Archivo General de Simancas (Simancas, Spain), Sección de Guerra y Marina, Guerra Moderna, legajo 7277. Museo Naval (Madrid), MS nos.271, 330–31. Provincial Arch. of B.C. (Victoria), "Original manuscript letters of Pedro Alberni, Commander Quadra, Gigedo and other Spanish officials concerning Spanish occupation on the northwest coast of America, 1789–93" (photocopies). J. M. Moziño [Losada] Suárez de Figueroa, Noticias de Nutka: an account of Nootka Sound in 1792, trans. and ed. I. H. Wilson [Engstrand] (Seattle, Wash., 1970). Viaje político-científico alrededor del mundo por las corbetas Descubierta y Atrevida al mando de los capitanes de navío D. Alejandro Malaspina y Don José de Bustamante y Guerra desde 1789 á 1794, ed. Pedro de Novo y Colson (Madrid, 1885). F. X. de Viana, Diario del viaje explorador de las corbetas españolas "Descubierta" y "Atrevida" en los años de 1789 á 1794 ... (Cerrito de la Victoria, Uruguay, 1849); repub. as Diario de viaje (2v., Montevideo, 1958). Cook, Flood tide of empire. C. I. Archer, "The transient presence: a re-appraisal of Spanish attitudes toward the northwest coast in the eighteenth century," BC Studies (Vancouver), no.18 (summer 1973): 3–32.

ALCALÁ-GALIANO, DIONISIO, naval officer and explorer; b. 1762 in Cabra (Córdoba province), Spain, son of Antonio Alcalá-Galiano Pareja y Valera de la Serna and Antonia Alcalá-Galiano; d. 21 Oct. 1805 in the battle of Trafalgar, off the coast of Spain.

Dionisio Alcalá-Galiano entered naval school in 1775 and began active service in 1779. An officer with scientific training, he served in various hydrographic surveys of the Spanish and South American coasts before joining the round-the-world expedition of Alejandro MALASPINA at Cadiz in July 1789. He would likely have remained obscure had not the Spanish crown decided to divert Malaspina from his intended path across the Pacific, dispatching him instead to the northwest coast of America. Malaspina's failure to discover the fabled northwest passage during his short visit in the summer of 1791, coupled with the belief of Viceroy Revilla Gigedo of New Spain that Juan de Fuca Strait might prove to be its entrance, led to a viceregal order detaching lieutenants Alcalá-Galiano and Cayetano Valdés y Flores Bazán from the expedition to lead a survey party back to the area. On Malaspina's recommendation they were both promoted frigate captain, and were placed in command of the Sutil and the Mexicana, schooners whose shallow draught made them suitable for exploration of inland waters.

The two officers took over the ships in Acapulco (Mexico) on 28 December, and under the command of Alcalá-Galiano in the Sutil they sailed on 8 March 1792. Their instructions were to complete the exploration of Juan de Fuca Strait begun in 1790 under the direction of Francisco de Eliza* y Reventa. In the event of the waterway's leading to Hudson or Baffin Bay, the schooners were to return directly to Europe, avoiding foreign ports where news of the discovery might become known. The voyage north was difficult, but both vessels arrived safely at Nootka Sound (B.C.) on 13 May. The Spanish post at Friendly Cove, now under Juan Francisco de la Bodega* y Quadra, was assuming an appearance of permanence, owing to the efforts of Eliza and Pedro de ALBERNI during the previous two years. Like other visitors of several nationalities, Alcalá-Galiano noted the good relations prevailing with the Nootka Indians and called upon chief Muquinna*.

Departing Nootka Sound on 5 June, the schooners arrived the next day at Núñez Gaona (Neah Bay, Wash.), a post newly established by Salvador Fidalgo. On 13 June, upon rounding present-day Point Roberts, they encountered the *Chatham* under William Robert Broughton, second in command of the expedition led by George Vancouver*, and on 21 June, near modern Vancouver, they met the English commander himself. Friendly relations ensued, as the spirit of scientific cooperation outweighed that of international competition: sharing information, the two sides worked together until 13 July when they resumed circumnavigation of Vancouver Island separately. Having sailed northward through Queen Charlotte Strait and demonstrated for Spain the island's insularity, Alcalá-Galiano completed his circuit on 31 August in Nootka Sound, where he found Vancouver's ships already at anchor.

Upon returning to Mexico Alcalá-Galiano began editing reports of the voyage. His was to become the best known of the Spanish expeditions to the northwest because, untypically for this era of Spanish secretiveness, his account was published, though it did not appear until 1802. Compared with many Spanish reports of the northwest coast, Alcalá-Galiano's was positive about its economic potential, and indeed his descriptions of woods and fertile lands present images of primeval beauty. His personal correspondence indicates his belief that it would be in the national interest to continue scientific experiments and exploration, and to make Spanish sovereignty permanent. He was not optimistic about the potential of the sea-otter trade as a stable economic base for settlement; the number of animals was limited and the Chinese had prohibited further importation of furs. Nevertheless, he was convinced that Spain would have to be active in the northern trade to maintain control over the region. He proposed a government-subsidized system in which the heavy copper sheets in demand among the Indians would be exchanged at cost for their furs; once their profits had been subverted British and American traders [*see* John MEARES; Robert GRAY] would lose all interest in the northwest coast. Despite Alcalá-Galiano's hopeful recommendations, his 87 days of intensive investigation of the waterways around Vancouver Island, though well received by scientists, were dismissed by Spanish officials as having done little more than satisfy scientific curiosity. Since no passage to the Atlantic had been found, they saw no motive to establish settlements.

Alcalá-Galiano returned in 1794 to Spain where he continued his geographical surveys. In 1796,

commanding the frigate *Vencedor*, he took part in the battle of Cape St Vincent, off the coast of Portugal, which Spain lost to the British navy. Later he commanded naval escort vessels convoying silver treasure fleets from Veracruz (Mexico) to Cadiz. On 21 Oct. 1805, commanding the *Bahama*, Alcalá-Galiano died in action against the British at the battle of Trafalgar. At his death he held the rank of brigadier of the naval forces.

CHRISTON I. ARCHER

Archivo General de la Nación (Mexico City), Sección de Historia, vol.71. Museo Naval (Madrid), MS nos.619, 826. *Relación del viage hecho por las goletas Sutil y Mexicana en el año de 1792, para reconocher el estrecho de Fuca . . .* (Madrid, 1802; repr. 1958). *Viaje político-científico alrededor del mundo por las corbetas Descubierta y Atrevida al mando de los capitanes de navío D. Alejandro Malaspina y Don José de Bustamante y Guerra desde 1789 á 1794*, ed. Pedro de Novo y Colson (Madrid, 1885). Cook, *Flood tide of empire*. H. R. Wagner, *Spanish explorations in the Strait of Juan de Fuca* (Santa Ana, Calif., 1933). [For another opinion on the authorship of the *Relación del viage*, see the biography of Manuel José Antonio CARDERO. DCB]

ALLAIN, JEAN-BAPTISTE, Roman Catholic priest and missionary; b. 26 Oct. 1739 in Granville, France, son of Pierre Allain, a carpenter, and Jeanne De Lille; d. 19 June 1812 at Quebec, Lower Canada.

After studying with the Spiritans, Jean-Baptiste Allain was ordained priest on 24 Sept. 1763 and then served in the bishopric of Coutances, France. In 1786 he readily accepted his assignment as a missionary to the islands of Saint-Pierre and Miquelon, going there that year. He sought letters patent as vice-prefect apostolic for the mission on 10 October of the next year and subsequently obtained them. In 1792, at the time the shock waves from the French revolution were reaching those distant islands, Allain refused to take the oath to the new Civil Constitution of the Clergy, as did his young colleague François Lejamtel*, who also came from the diocese of Coutances. In August the two priests assembled a few dozen Acadian families who had taken refuge on the little islands and fled on fishing smacks to the Îles de la Madeleine. They may consequently be considered the first French priests to seek haven in Canada from the revolution.

The two priests' first concern was to find a ship so they might go to the bishop of Quebec, Jean-François Hubert*, and secure his protection. Unable to locate one, they could not make the voyage and, it being autumn, they put themselves at the disposal of Father James JONES in Halifax, N.S. Jones was happy at the arrival of priests in the Gulf of St Lawrence region, for the Catholics there, though few in number, were nevertheless widely scattered. He entrusted to Allain the mission of Îles-de-la-Madeleine, with responsibility for ministering to the Acadians at Chéticamp, on the west coast of Cape Breton Island. Allain had himself requested this mission; he had even made arrangements with a score of families living on the islands. Lejamtel was entrusted with the missions at Arichat, on Cape Breton Island, and Tracadie, in Nova Scotia. Because the British authorities considered these French priests better suited than Irish Catholic missionaries to keep the Acadians in hand, they allowed them to settle in the country after taking the oath of allegiance.

In the summer of 1793 Allain went to Quebec for various ordinances and objects needed in the two priests' pastoral activities. Upon his return to the Îles de la Madeleine, he set to work from his residence at Havre-Aubert to organize his little mission. He saw to the election of the first parish council and the building of a chapel and presbytery. In June 1794 he was granted supplementary pastoral powers by Bishop Hubert. He went to Chéticamp and also to Magré (Margaree) on several occasions during the summer, and he took the opportunity to visit his companion Lejamtel at Arichat.

Indeed Allain was thinking of settling down permanently with his colleague. "The fatigue of the trip [to Cape Breton] and the infirmities of old age and my constitution lead me to join him as soon as I can. Besides, this place could lose a certain number of its inhabitants," he wrote. The latter observation was prompted by the difficulties being faced by the 500 or so Acadians living on the Îles de la Madeleine, about 200 of whom had come from Saint-Pierre and Miquelon. The new seigneur, Isaac Coffin*, was demanding substantial rents from his *censitaires* for lands they had occupied since their arrival. This situation of conflict seems to have played a part in Allain's decision to leave in the autumn of 1797 for Chéticamp, where he spent the winter before joining Lejamtel. The coadjutor designate of Quebec, Joseph-Octave Plessis*, noted in a letter: "However useful your residence among that small flock was, you cannot be blamed for having put some distance between it and yourself for your own safety."

In July 1799 Allain expressed a wish to settle among the 25 families at Chéticamp if no missionary was available for them. In the spring of 1800 a delegation from the locality sought him out at Arichat. The old missionary, however, turned down their request, which would have meant sharing his ministry and his upkeep with the people of Magré; he had little respect for Magré people and did not feel able to travel. Consequently the messengers went away empty-handed. In their disappointment they complained about the matter to the bishop, and this the priest did not at all appreciate.

Allain, who suffered from asthma, seems to have been a burden to Lejamtel. In the spring of 1808 Bishop Plessis of Quebec asked him to return to the Îles de la Madeleine, because the priest in charge, the Frenchman Gabriel CHAMPION, had recently died.

Allain obediently left at the beginning of the summer, stopping on his way to minister to the people at Chéticamp. Reaching the Îles de la Madeleine, he settled in with a nephew who later helped him in his mission. Allain noted that there were 68 families living on the islands when he arrived.

Subsequently he asked several times to be recalled. He was suffering from lapses of memory and was afraid of dying without receiving the last sacraments. But a successor was hard to find. In 1808 Bishop Plessis noted: "The account Mr. Allain gives us of the state of the Isles de la Magdeleine is hardly the kind to attract a missionary to them. No chapel, no adequate presbytery, a small group of people [living] in fear of being oppressed by Admiral Coffin. All that has frightened M. leFrançois [Alexis Lefrançois], who was to go there this autumn or next spring." It was not until 1812 that, some time after obtaining permission from Governor CRAIG to recall Allain, the bishop called upon the missionary, who was then 72, to give up his post. Allain left the islands in the spring and retired to Quebec, where he died on 19 June at the Hôpital Général.

MARC DESJARDINS

AAQ, 12 A, E: f.37r.; G: f.21r.; 20 A, II: 162; III: 75; IV: 12; 210 A, II: ff.25, 64, 78, 138; III: ff.33, 79, 82, 111; IV: ff.256–59; VI: f.268; VII: ff.25–26, 32, 55, 307, 337, 449; 1 CB, II: 18, 29; 301 CN, I: 2, 4, 7, 9, 11–14, 18; 312 CN, VI: 23, 25, 29, 34, 43–44, 46, 48–50, 70. AN, Col., E, 3 (dossier J.-B. Allain). Arch. municipales, Granville, France, État civil, Granville, 27 oct. 1739. *Mémoire sur les missions de la Nouvelle-Écosse, du Cap-Breton et de l'Île-du-Prince-Édouard de 1760 à 1820 . . .* (Québec, 1895). *Quebec Gazette*, 25 June 1812. Allaire, *Dictionnaire*, vol.1. Antoine Bernard, *Histoire de la survivance acadienne, 1755–1935* (Montréal, 1935). Anselme Chiasson, *Chéticamp: histoire et traditions acadiennes* (Moncton, N.-B., 1961). N.-E. Dionne, *Les ecclésiastiques et les royalistes français réfugiés au Canada à l'époque de la révolution, 1791–1802* (Québec, 1905). Noël Falaise, "Les îles de la Madeleine: étude géographique" (thèse de D. ès L., univ. de Montréal, 1954). Paul Hubert, *Les îles de la Madeleine et les Madelinots* (Rimouski, Qué., 1926). Johnston, *Hist. of Catholic Church in eastern N.S.*, vol.1. H. J. Koren, *Knaves or knights? A history of the Spiritan missionaries in Canada and North America, 1732–1839* (Pittsburgh, Pa., 1962). Frédéric Landry, *Capitaines des hauts-fonds* (Ottawa, 1978). Robert Rumilly, *Histoire des Acadiens* (2v., Montréal, 1955), 2. Albert David, "Les spiritains à Saint-Pierre et Miquelon," "Les spiritains dans l'Amérique septentrionale au XVIIIe siècle," and "Les spiritains en Acadie," in *BRH*, 35 (1929): 439, 314, and 460 respectively.

ALLAN (Allen, Allin), EBENEZER, businessman; b. 17 Sept. 1752 in Morristown Township (Morristown), N.J.; d. 13 April 1813 in Delaware Township, Upper Canada.

Allan

Ebenezer Allan may have been living in Pennsylvania during 1777 when he decided to enlist with the loyalist unit being raised by Major John Butler*. As a result of his close ties with the Six Nations, Allan was transferred in 1781 to the Indian Department. The following year he was sent as a loyalist spy to the Genesee River area in western New York. Upon his arrival there he resided for a time with Mary Jemison, the celebrated "White Woman of the Genesee" who had been adopted in girlhood by Indians. During the winter of 1782–83 he moved to the vicinity of present-day Mount Morris, where he became more a farmer and trader than an espionage agent.

When the Indian Department began reducing its staff at the close of the Revolutionary War, Allan, who by now had attained the rank of lieutenant, was one of the officers dismissed. With this blow, it seems, he began to reconsider his allegiance to the British cause. His new attitude was probably reflected in his decision during the summer of 1783 to act as an intermediary in peace negotiations between the American government and the Six Nations. In December British authorities arrested and imprisoned Allan to prevent him from attending the council that culminated in the Treaty of Fort Stanwix in October 1784. In letters to Major Robert MATHEWS, Governor HALDIMAND's military secretary, Allan complained bitterly about his arrest, claiming that since the end of the American revolution he had been treated in "a most cruel and inhuman manner, Robbed, Striped, Plundered, and now imprisoned in a Detestable prison like A common Criminal without even knowing my crime, or my prosecutors confronting of me." He remained in prison for ten months, a period that was divided among jails at Fort Niagara (near Youngstown, N.Y.), Montreal, and Cataraqui (Kingston, Ont.).

After his release in late 1784 Allan returned to the Genesee valley, where he continued to farm and trade. In 1789 he completed a sawmill and a grist-mill at the Genesee Falls, thus becoming the first white settler on the site of Rochester. But an unsuccessful series of disputes with American authorities over titles to Indian land ultimately led him to abandon the Genesee region. Early in 1794 he appears to have purchased extensive holdings on the American side of the Detroit River and Lake Erie, and a farm at Petite Côte (Windsor), Upper Canada. In May Allan and a number of associates, including his brother Aaron, petitioned the Executive Council of Upper Canada for a grant of a township on the Thames River, where they proposed to establish a settlement. Although this petition was rejected, Allan, as a reduced lieutenant, was granted 2,000 acres in newly surveyed Delaware Township, some 40 miles up the Thames River from Moraviantown. The council also promised 200 acres to each settler Allan brought into the province.

In the summer of 1794 Allan, his family, and associates became the first white settlers in Delaware Township. Allan had his cattle driven in from the Genesee valley in July, built a sawmill and a grist-mill near the mouth of the present Dingman Creek within a year, and expanded his operations soon after to include the manufacture and sale of liquor. Yet, despite this auspicious beginning, life in Upper Canada soon began to go sour for Allan. By the early 1800s, as a result of unsuccessful and dubious land speculation on both sides of Lake Erie, Allan was hard pressed for capital to satisfy such creditors as John ASKIN and Isaac TODD, and in 1801 he sold most of his holdings in Delaware Township to Moses Brigham and Gideon Tiffany*. To make matters worse, from 1798 Allan was embroiled in quarrels with some of his neighbours, including Thomas Talbot* of Port Talbot, and with various government officials. His troubles with his neighbours stemmed largely from his failure to build a church on a clergy reserve lot, something he had agreed to do upon obtaining the land in 1794. In 1803 the Executive Council gave Allan one more year to construct the church; then all orders in council in his behalf were rescinded. Moreover, Allan was twice brought to trial in the early 1800s, once for forgery and once for larceny. Although he was acquitted on each occasion, he did not escape the clutches of the law for long: in 1804 or 1805 he was convicted of an unknown offence and imprisoned in the district jail at Turkey Point, where he remained until some time in early 1806.

Allan's experiences during these years, as well as his long period of imprisonment in British jails at the end of the Revolutionary War, probably explain why he became an American sympathizer after the outbreak of the War of 1812. When in mid July 1812 an American scouting party advanced as far eastward as Delaware Township, Allan and two neighbours, Andrew Westbrook* and Simon Zelotes Watson, accompanied the invaders back to Sandwich (Windsor). Allan and Westbrook then returned home with copies of American brigadier-general William Hull's proclamation to the people of Upper Canada, and actively circulated a petition requesting Hull to detach a force for the protection of those who did not wish to take up arms against the Americans. British commander Isaac BROCK was faced with an alarming situation, for on the western frontier of the province desertions were numerous, many militiamen were refusing to march, and whole villages were asking for Hull's protection. Appalled by "the state of apathy in that part of the country," Brock instructed Daniel Springer of Delaware Township to organize a force and overawe the disaffected. Within a few days both Allan and Westbrook were made prisoners, and Allan was conveyed to Niagara (Niagara-on-the-Lake). Released early in 1813, he died in Delaware Township on 13 April.

Allan's disregard for social conventions was well

revealed in his domestic life. During his years in Delaware Township he was surrounded by "wives" and numerous children. Polygamy, however, was nothing new to him, for while residing in the Genesee valley he had been accustomed to living with several women at a time. By 1780 he had married Kyen-danent or Sally, a sister of the Seneca chief Captain Bull. About 1780, as well, he "married" a white woman, Lucy Chapman, and, still later, added another white woman, Mary (Milly) Gregory, to his household. His "wives," with the exception of Sally, and all his children accompanied him to Upper Canada.

One of Allan's critics, the author of a history of Rochester published in the 1830s, described him as a "Tory bloodhound; with a character which combines the lasciviousness of a Turk with the blood-thirstiness of a savage," and this view was shared by several other 19th-century American writers. Yet many of Allan's contemporaries spoke favourably of him: John Butler, for example, recommended him to Lieutenant Governor SIMCOE "as a Loyalist to be depended upon," and John Askin deemed him "as active & enterprizing a man as any in the province & perfectly sober." In fact, Allan was neither a saint nor a villain, but simply a product of the frontier – self-reliant, capable, and hardworking, yet short-tempered, vindictive, and cruel. Because he lived close to nature and was primarily motivated by self-interest, his allegiance to higher authority was never strong.

DANIEL J. BROCK

AO, RG 22, ser.134, 4: 178–79. BL, Add. mss 21822: 301–3, 348–49. Middlesex West Land Registry Office (Glencoe, Ont.), Abstract index to deeds, Delaware Township, instruments 6–7, 68 (mfm. at AO, GS 611). Ont., Ministry of Citizenship and Culture, Heritage Administration Branch (Toronto), Hist. sect. research files, Middlesex RF.19, Ebenezer Allan. PAC, RG 1, L1, 22: 286, 359, 371; 23: 264; 29: 463; L3, 1: A1/43; 3: A4/49, A6/13; 4: A7/6. *Corr. of Lieut. Governor Simcoe* (Cruikshank). *De-hewamis: or, a narrative of the life of Mary Jemison: otherwise called the White Woman ...* , ed. J. E. Seaver (Batavia, N.Y., 1842). "Grants of crown lands in U.C.," AO *Report*, 1929: 57. *John Askin papers* (Quaife). "Minutes of the Court of General Quarter Sessions of the Peace for the London District ...," AO *Report*, 1933: 14, 19–20, 22, 25, 27, 33, 62, 84, 86. "U.C. land book C," AO *Report*, 1931: 7. "U.C. land book D," AO *Report*, 1931: 116, 144. "Founder of Delaware to be commemorated" (press release, Ont., Dept. of Travel and Publicity, Toronto, 16 Sept. 1960; copy at AO). *History of the county of Middlesex ...* (Toronto and London, Ont., 1889; repr. with intro. D. [J.] Brock, Belleville, Ont., 1972). M. B. Turpin, "Ebenezer Allan in the Genesee country," *Centennial history of Rochester, New York*, ed. E. R. Foreman (4v., Rochester, 1931–34), 2: 313–38. E. A. Cruikshank, "A study of disaffection in Upper Canada in 1812–15," RSC *Trans* ., 3rd ser., 6 (1912), sect.II: 11–65. F. C. Hamil, "Ebenezer Allan in Canada," *OH*, 36 (1944): 83–93. H. O. Miller, "The notorious Ebenezer Allan," *Western Ontario Hist. Notes* (London), 5 (1947): 76–82.

ALLAN, JOHN, office holder, politician, and rebel leader; b. 3 Jan. 1747 at Edinburgh Castle, Scotland, eldest son of William Allan and Isabella Maxwell; m. 10 Oct. 1767 Mary Patton; d. 7 Feb. 1805 in Lubec (Maine).

John Allan's father, a Scottish officer in the British army, brought his family to Nova Scotia in 1749 or 1750. In the early 1760s William Allan received substantial grants from forfeited Acadian lands in Cumberland County. Farmer, merchant, and Indian trader, he remained loyal to the crown during the unrest which troubled Nova Scotia in the late 1760s and early 1770s. John worked with his father both on his farms and in his trading business, married, acquired a farm of his own, and in time held offices which included justice of the peace, clerk of the sessions, clerk of the Supreme Court, and sheriff; in 1775–76 he served as member of the House of Assembly for Cumberland Township.

Allan may have been educated in Massachusetts. Whether there or elsewhere he had certainly acquired revolutionary sentiments and a number of New England ties. In 1775 and 1776 he became increasingly involved with Jonathan EDDY and others in organizing and propagandizing for revolution his discontented neighbours. He was one of those disaffected Nova Scotians who, early in 1776, urged Massachusetts and the Continental Congress to send military assistance for a projected rising. When help did not come and with arrest imminent, on 3 Aug. 1776 Allan left his wife and five children at his Upper Point de Bute farm and crossed the Bay of Fundy with other refugees, reaching Machias (Maine) on 13 August. Shortly afterwards, the Nova Scotia Council offered a reward of £100 for his capture.

Allan arrived in Machias just as Eddy was about to leave on his ill-starred expedition against Fort Cumberland (near Sackville, N.B.). This project Allan considered futile, dangerously under-equipped, and, with only 28 men, undermanned. His efforts to dissuade Eddy failed. At Passamaquoddy Bay and the Saint John River (N.B.) the small force, which Allan did not join, added a few more men, attacked British or loyal installations and ships, and did some property damage; in November it made a vain attempt to take Fort Cumberland. Among those who suffered as a result of the expedition's failure were Allan's wife and children, who were driven to the woods. Mrs Allan was imprisoned, Allan's farm was burned, and his crops, horses, and cattle were destroyed or confiscated.

Meanwhile, Allan had left Machias for Boston, where he discussed with John Adams and others aid for those eastern Indians whom he had been trying to bring actively to the support of the revolutionary

Allan

cause. He went on to George Washington's headquarters on the Delaware and again presented his case. In January 1777 he was received by the Continental Congress in Baltimore, Md, and informed it at length about the possibilities of organizing the Indians and about the Nova Scotian situation. Here he had some success. He was appointed superintendent of eastern Indians and later made an infantry colonel. On his return journey he was able to interest the Massachusetts government in his plan to take western Nova Scotia and perhaps Halifax, to establish forts on the Saint John, and to conduct from there an agency which would bring the Micmacs and the Malecites over to the American cause. In March, after more prodding from Allan, the Council agreed to provide men and supplies for an expedition to the Saint John, of which Allan eventually received the command.

The expedition of June and July 1777 had little more success than Jonathan Eddy's. Military stores and recruits were slow in coming in; in the end, under a hundred men took part. The people of the Saint John, with some exceptions, were either loyal to the crown, like the merchants William HAZEN, James Simonds*, and James White, disappointingly aloof like the formerly pro-revolutionary inhabitants of Maugerville [see Israel PERLEY], or wavering as were the Acadians and Indians. Reaching the mouth of the river on 2 June, Allan proceeded upstream and made his headquarters at the main Indian camp, Aukpaque, above St Anne's Point (Fredericton). Here he had promises of support from such pro-rebel chiefs as Ambroise Saint-Aubin* but met hostility or doubt from others, among them Pierre Tomah*. The arrival of a British naval force, with troops under Major Gilfred Studholme* and later reinforcements under Michael Francklin*, made Allan's position untenable. Taking most of the Saint John Indians with him, he made a difficult retreat by an old canoe route to Machias. They arrived in August to find Eddy there with reinforcements for the Saint John expedition, and a town preparing for a British attack. When the attack finally came, from a squadron commanded by Sir George Collier*, Allan and his Indian allies played a significant role in what was, in spite of some damage, a successful defence. Allan was made commander of forces east of the Penobscot River, an office he held to the end of the war. Probably in June 1778 he was reunited with his family.

From the summer of 1777 to the end of 1783 Allan was occupied in a continuous effort to keep the eastern Indians from joining the British in the face of increasing military and naval pressure, made more effective by Brigadier-General Francis McLean*'s seizure of Penobscot (Castine, Maine) in 1779 and by Francklin's campaign for Indian support. Bombarding Massachusetts and the Congress with letters requesting badly needed supplies, often without success,

meeting with the Indians and acquiring a French priest for them, countering Francklin's lures, Allan sometimes despaired. In the end, if he did not get much aid from the tribes, he succeeded in keeping most of them from giving effective assistance to the British. As commander at Machias, Allan had other tasks, many aimed at keeping the British out of eastern Maine.

By the last years of the revolution, Allan was becoming increasingly concerned about the future of the area he now knew so well. As early as 1779 he had expressed his belief that the British planned to keep all of Maine to the Kennebec. He was apparently the first from the American side to realize fully that the country between the present St Croix River and the Magaguadavic – now part of New Brunswick – might pass, as he saw it, illegally, to the British. In 1778 he had reported the settlement of "the disaffected" at Passamaquoddy. By the fall of 1783 he was alarmed at the arrival of loyalists at what is now St Andrews, N.B., warning both the settlers there and the American authorities that this was really United States territory. In the 1790s he played a role in the boundary negotiations he had helped to initiate. The last 20 years of his life were spent, first at Dudley (later Allan's, now Treat) Island near Lubec, where in 1785–86 he ran a rather unsuccessful trading business, numbering among his customers Benedict ARNOLD, and then at North Lubec on the mainland. He petitioned, successfully but not very profitably, for land grants in Maine and Ohio, took an active interest in Indian, town, and national affairs, and remained concerned about the boundary. After a period of increasingly ill health, he died in 1805.

John Allan's contribution to the revolutionary cause was substantial. He has been called a man of integrity and intelligence, with executive ability, foresight, and sagacity. His persistence under difficulties and his loyalty to his adopted country were noteworthy. He had much to do with the retention of eastern Maine for the United States.

ALICE R. STEWART

John Allan is the author of "Some proposals for an attack on Nova Scotia, with some other observations respecting the province, laid before the honorable council of the Massachusetts State," N.S. Hist. Soc., *Coll* ., 2 (1881): 11–16.

Mass., Dept. of the State Secretary, Arch. Division (Boston), Mass. arch., 144: 169, 175–76, 198; 166: 29; 181: 163–67; 186: 82–84; 187: 427–28; 197: 104, 139–40, 164; 201: 172–74 (transcripts at PANS). Mass. Hist. Soc., John Allan, corr., 1778–1803. PANS, RG 1, 136: 163; 212, 17 Nov. 1776; 222, no.4; 362, docs.92, 94 (transcripts). *American arch.* (Clarke and Force), 4th and 5th ser. "Calendar of papers relating to Nova Scotia," PAC *Report*, 1894. *Documentary history of the state of Maine*, ed. William Willis *et al.* (24v., Portland, Maine, and Cambridge, Mass., 1869–1916), 14–21. *Military operations in eastern Maine and N.S.* (Kidder). *DAB*.

J. H. Ahlin, *Maine Rubicon: downeast settlers during the American revolution* (Calais, Maine, 1966). Brebner, *Neutral Yankees* (1969). H. A. Davis, *An international community on the St. Croix (1604–1930)* ([2nd ed.], Orono, Maine, 1974). C. A. Day, "Colonel John Allan" (unpub. paper, Univ. of Maine at Orono, [1975]). R. I. Hunt, "British-American rivalry for the support of the Indians of Maine and Nova Scotia, 1775–1783" (MA thesis, Univ. of Maine at Orono, 1973). W. B. Kerr, *The Maritime provinces of British North America and the American revolution* (Sackville, N.B., [1941?]; repr. New York, [1970]). G. A. Rawlyk, *Nova Scotia's Massachusetts: a study of Massachusetts–Nova Scotia relations, 1630 to 1784* (Montreal and London, 1973). Raymond, *River St. John* (1943). Howard Trueman, *The Chignecto isthmus and its first settlers* (Toronto, 1902; repr. Belleville, Ont., 1975). G. H. Allan, "Sketch of Col. John Allan of Maine," *New-England Hist. and Geneal. Reg.* (Boston), 30 (1876): 353–59. D. C. Harvey, "Machias and the invasion of Nova Scotia," *CHA Report*, 1932: 17–28. Anne Molloy, "Col. John Allan, a hero for Maine," *Down East* (Camden, Maine), 13 (1966–67), no. 10: 33–37, 64–66.

ALLCHECHAQUE. *See* CHEJAUK

ALLCOCK, HENRY, judge and politician; baptized 26 Jan. 1759 in Birmingham, England, son of Henry Allcock and Mary Askin; m. Hannah —, and they had a daughter; d. 22 Feb. 1808 at Quebec, Lower Canada.

The Allcock family came from Edgbaston, near Birmingham, and moved to the city in the decade before Henry was born. He began his legal studies at Lincoln's Inn, London, in January 1785, and was admitted to the bar exactly six years later. He then practised in London specializing in equity law, which deals with matters not covered by the common law. In November 1798 Allcock was appointed a puisne judge of the Upper Canada Court of King's Bench on the recommendation of his friend, Chief Justice John ELMSLEY. By early January 1799 he was at York (Toronto), where he took the oath of office to become one of the three judges of the highest court in a virtual wilderness. His duties included attendance both at the court sessions held in the capital and at the assizes held in the local administrative towns, such as Cornwall, Kingston, Niagara (Niagara-on-the-Lake), and Sandwich (Windsor). Although the question of establishing an equity court with Allcock as judge was raised, no action was taken.

Personally, Allcock was a difficult individual, like so many of the fractious misfits who came to the province, particularly in that era. He was quickly on bad terms with his two colleagues on King's Bench, his former friend Elmsley and William Dummer Powell*. Legislative councillor Richard CARTWRIGHT remarked that what Elmsley supported, Allcock was bound to oppose. Allcock's disagreements with Powell were partly over his own insistence

on the use in Upper Canada of the full pomp and procedures of English courts. The Reverend John STUART of Kingston at first felt that Allcock was "not so rough in his manners, as the world is pleased to suppose." But he changed his mind when his son, the Reverend George Okill Stuart* of York, was upbraided by Allcock during a church service for a supposed violation of church law. Allcock then began a sort of persecution of the young cleric which, Stuart Sr asserted, was "passionately illiberal & vindictive."

Allcock was barely settled in the province before he decided to run for the House of Assembly in the election of 1800, despite the fact that he was on the bench. He was duly elected for Durham, Simcoe and the East Riding of York. Soon, however, there was a petition from some local inhabitants, including Samuel HERON, to Lieutenant Governor Peter HUNTER. They asserted that Allcock's agent, William WEEKES, had used unwarranted steps to secure the election. When a hearing was held by the assembly into the legality of the election, Allcock made use of a paper drawn up by Attorney General Thomas Scott* to argue that the house was incompetent to decide the issue and refused to leave during the proceedings, declaring that he would have to be thrown out by the "*neck and heels*." On the grounds of irregularities the house unseated him on 11 June 1801; he had, in Alexander GRANT's words, "tryed every means and did not leave a Stone unturned to keep his Seat but could not."

Allcock was, naturally, a decisive judge. John ASKIN described him at a land claims hearing in 1799 as "a very Impartial good man, but so particular & sticks so close to the law, a very unfitt man to act up to the Spirit of the Act"; he added, moreover, that Allcock "did as he pleassed without asking the Sentiments of the othe[r] Commissioners in hardly any case." The most famous case over which Allcock presided was the trial of John Small* for the murder of Attorney General John White* in a duel. Allcock, who claimed to have been friendly with White, lamented that the solicitor general, Robert Isaac Dey GRAY, "failed altogether in adducing positive evidence" of Small's guilt and the "Jury would presume nothing." Thus the defendant went free, as was usual in trials arising from duels. In 1803, at the assizes in Sandwich, Allcock sentenced two murderers to be hanged till dead and afterward hanged in chains, evidence that he was not lenient on the bench.

After Hunter arrived as lieutenant governor in 1799, Allcock gradually became one of his chief advisers, supplanting Elmsley, and helped him bring some order and regulation to the land-granting system. By 1803 Hunter was recommending him for an increase in salary as a reward for his efficiency. He also supported him for new offices. When Elmsley was appointed chief justice of Lower Canada in May

Allcock

1802, Allcock, rather than the senior judge, Powell, succeeded to the Upper Canadian post. Allcock became an executive councillor and in January 1803 he was appointed to the Legislative Council on Hunter's recommendation, becoming speaker of that house.

Whatever his office, Allcock constantly pressed for the creation of a court of chancery. In 1801 he prepared a draft bill and also proposed that he be appointed to the new court while retaining his position on King's Bench, an arrangement that would have given him two salaries. The British government delayed taking action but this did not stop Allcock from bombarding it with letters during 1802. By the end of 1803 he had decided that it would be necessary to go home to obtain action and, with Hunter's blessings, he applied for a six-month leave of absence. It was approved in March 1804 but the government refused either to increase his salary or to grant his request for a court. That fall, armed with a letter of introduction from Hunter, which solicited a salary increase for him, Allcock left for England.

While he was there, opportunity presented itself. Allcock had long been eyeing the more lucrative chief justiceship of Lower Canada. As early as 1800 he had begun studying the Lower Canadian statutes and, when William Osgoode* retired from the post in 1801, he had attempted, unsuccessfully, to gain the appointment. As 1804 closed and the hopes for the chancery judgeship faded, another possibility opened up – Elmsley was dying at Quebec and Allcock could see the chance of promotion. The main obstacle to his appointment was the Lower Canadian administrative oligarchy, who were unanimous in not wanting a third chief justice brought in from Upper Canada and who had their own candidate in Attorney General Jonathan Sewell*. Unlike Allcock, Sewell was expert in French civil law and spoke French fluently. His case was strongly presented by Lieutenant Governor Sir Robert Shore Milnes* who noted that Allcock lacked the proper dignity. Sewell was also supported by Anglican bishop Jacob Mountain* and other Lower Canadian leaders. Nevertheless, when Elmsley died in April 1805, Allcock succeeded through the influence of a British patron, the lord high chancellor, Lord Eldon. As Sewell was advised, "there was no resisting such powerful Interest."

Despite the unhappiness over his appointment, Allcock deferred arriving at Quebec until August 1806, when he was sworn in as chief justice and member of the Executive Council. He became speaker of the Legislative Council the following January. Under the circumstances, he should have looked for allies, particularly since his patron, Hunter, was now dead. The task would have been relatively easy because there were factions among the province's leaders. Instead, Allcock began to assail almost everyone in power. Like judge Robert Thorpe* in Upper Canada, by the end of 1806 he was writing to the colonial under-secretary, Sir George Shee, expounding on the evils he had found. His indictment of Lower Canadian society was truly comprehensive; neither the French nor the English members of the administration escaped his censure. Among his many complaints were that Milnes's attitude to him personally was unsatisfactory; Administrator Thomas DUNN was mishandling the renewal of the lease on the Saint-Maurice ironworks; the puisne justices, Dunn and Jenkin WILLIAMS, were too old and infirm to perform their duties properly; and there was great confusion in the courts of justice. He recommended that French executive councillors who died should be replaced by English, and he expressed the hope that the new governor would not make appointments without consultation, advising Dunn that he "expected no appointment would be disposed of without his being first consulted." Soon he was also writing to the colonial secretary, Viscount Castlereagh, stating that Dunn's memory had failed, an accusation not borne out by Dunn's correspondence. Castlereagh investigated the more substantial claims; "senile" Dunn, however, acquitted himself well. Despite Allcock's efforts, the new governor, Sir James Henry CRAIG, who arrived in October 1807, quickly fell under the influence of Sewell and Herman Witsius Ryland*, the civil secretary, with whom Allcock was also quarrelling. Thus, though he remained in office, he was excluded from the influence he cherished. Early in 1808 he died of a "bilious fever."

There is little information on Allcock's personal life. His wife having died in 1802, he was, apparently, planning remarriage near the end of his life. He had a farm near York and he had applied for 1,200 acres of land in November 1798. He did not, however, petition for his full entitlement as an executive councillor until he had left the province. He was a member of the Church of England and in 1803 he presided over a meeting of subscribers to erect the first St James church.

Evaluating Allcock does not lead to pleasant conclusions. His letters reveal a consideration for his family that did not extend to most of his acquaintances; however, he could ingratiate himself with select patrons. His personality, possibly progressively, caused difficulties wherever he went. Like many office holders, he was incredibly persistent in advancing his own interests. Yet in Upper Canada he had undoubtedly helped Hunter make the administration run more smoothly. In Lower Canada he accomplished little but trouble-making. His avarice, importuning, and quarrelsomeness were still legendary when Henry James Morgan* did the research for his first collection of biographies some 50 years after Allcock's death. He was one of the more unattractive of the many eccentrics who plagued the Canadas at the opening of the 19th century.

FREDERICK H. ARMSTRONG

Anglican Church of Canada, Diocese of Ont. Arch., (Kingston), Group 11, John Stuart papers (copies at Anglican Church of Canada, General Synod Arch., Toronto). ANQ-Q, CE1-61, 25 Feb. 1808. Birmingham Reference Library (Birmingham, Eng.), St Bartholomew (Edgbaston), reg. of baptisms, marriages, and burials; St Martin (Birmingham), reg. of baptisms, marriages, and burials. MTL, D. W. Smith papers, A10, A11, B8. PAC, MG 23, GII, 10, vol.4: 1750–53; HI, 5, vol.2; MG 24, C1: 672–82; MG 30, D1, 2: 119–53. *Corr. of Hon. Peter Russell* (Cruikshank and Hunter), 3: 15, 85. *Gentleman's Magazine*, 1803: 87; January–June 1808: 557. *John Askin papers* (Quaife), 2: 260, 351. "Journals of Legislative Assembly of U.C.," AO *Report*, 1909: 154, 174, 183, 192–94, 441; 1911: 75. Armstrong, *Handbook of Upper Canadian chronology*, 11, 13, 30, 34, 35, 38, 60, 81, 165. F.-J. Audet, *Les juges en chef de la province de Québec, 1764–1924* (Québec, 1927), 39–43. H. J. Morgan, *Sketches of celebrated Canadians and persons connected with Canada, from the earliest period in the history of the province down to the present time* (Quebec and London, 1862; repr. Montreal, 1865), 135–36. P.-G. Roy, *Les juges de la prov. de Québec*, 5. Turcotte, *Le Conseil législatif*, 15, 18, 64. Wallace, *Macmillan dict.*

A. W. P. Buchanan, *The bench and bar of Lower Canada down to 1850* (Montreal, 1925), 44–45. *Life and letters of Hon. Richard Cartwright* (Cartwright), 116–18, 121, 123, 131. Millman, *Jacob Mountain*, 68, 84, 115–16. Paquet et Wallot, *Patronage et pouvoir dans le Bas-Canada*, 41–43. D. B. Read, *The lives of the judges of Upper Canada and Ontario, from 1791 to the present time* (Toronto, 1888), 53–62. W. R. Riddell, *The bar and the courts of the province of Upper Canada or Ontario* (Toronto, 1928), 51, 61, 63, 69, 99, 102, 141, 143; *Legal profession in U.C.*, 27, 137, 152, 157, 166, 180, 182, 185; *Life of William Dummer Powell*, 91, 216. F.-J. Audet, "Henry Allcock," *La Rev. nationale* (Montréal), 5 (1923): 338–42. Alison Ewart and Julia Jarvis, "The personnel of the family compact, 1791–1841," *CHR*, 7 (1926): 211, 216. W. R. Riddell, "Toronto in the parliaments of Upper Canada, 1792–1841," Women's Canadian Hist. Soc. of Toronto, *Annual report and trans.* (Toronto), no.22 (1921–22): 14.

ALLSOPP, GEORGE, businessman, office holder, politician, and seigneur; b. *c.* 1733 in England; d. 14 April 1805 in Cap-Santé, Lower Canada.

George Allsopp served in the British Quartermaster General's Department during the 1758 expedition against Louisbourg, Île Royale (Cape Breton Island), and in 1759 as secretary to Lieutenant-Colonel Guy CARLETON, quartermaster general at Quebec. Following this service Allsopp entered the trade between Britain and Quebec, one of the earliest British merchants after the conquest to realize the commercial potential of Canada. In 1761 he came from Bristol to be junior partner, first at Montreal and then at Quebec, in the mercantile supply firm of Jenkins, Trye and Company. Since specialization often meant failure in the unstable colonial economy, Allsopp formed additional partnerships and diversified business interests, participating in the wheat, fur, and timber trades, the Gulf of St Lawrence fisheries, the manufacture of potash and spirits, and the production of iron at the Saint-Maurice ironworks. "A person of the most extensive Correspondence of [any]one in this Province without exception," Allsopp began about 1767 his lengthy association with the powerful London house of Olive, Watson and Rashleigh [*see* Sir Brook WATSON]. That firm soon became his principal financial support and commercial supplier, while Allsopp became the central agent in its consolidation of significant commercial interests in Quebec.

Allsopp's trading activities were complicated after 1761 by his conflict with James Murray*, military governor of Quebec, who had a strong aversion to the exploitative activities of the British merchants. They responded to the governor's attitudes by vilifying his numerous interventions to regulate economic activity. Personally provoked by Murray's interference with his trade and misrepresentation of him to imperial authorities in a manner capable of damaging his commercial reputation, Allsopp soon became the governor's most vehement critic.

Similar antagonism to the military prevailed elsewhere in North America following the Seven Years' War, but in Quebec the merchants also deplored Murray's attempt to gain Canadian support by attenuating the anglicizing policy of the Royal Proclamation of 1763 and his instructions, both of which were designed to assimilate the province into the British empire. The merchants supported the proclamation's exclusion of Roman Catholics from public office yet still expected the colony to be endowed with the full range of political and judicial institutions characteristic of British colonies. Allsopp and other merchants were consequently angered when, after the introduction of the long-awaited civil government in August 1764, Murray refused to institute an elected assembly, preferring to govern with an appointed council only. Tension mounted in September following Murray's ordinance establishing civil and criminal courts. The merchants felt that the resulting judicial system offered too many concessions to French civil law. They were increasingly concerned as well about the continued absence of a definite statement of property law, and precise regulations to govern complex commercial dealings. The most opinionated of the British community responded to Murray's policy in October 1764 when the first grand jury of Quebec, with James Johnston* as foreman, delivered its ill-judged presentment, part of which Allsopp had drafted. The presentment criticized the judicial system and implicitly con-

Allsopp

demned Murray's entire administration by demanding temporary recognition of the grand jury as the only representative body in the colony, with a right to review public accounts. An appended clause, later attributed to Allsopp, opposed Roman Catholic participation on juries. The irascible merchant may also have inspired the presentment's recommendation that a garrison order compelling civilians and some soldiers to carry lanterns outside after dark be amended. In March and twice in October 1764, Allsopp had been arrested for violating this order. Each encounter was marked by violence, Allsopp's vociferous denunciations of the military, and, in October, his rapid prosecution of the soldiers involved.

Allsopp vigorously campaigned for Murray's recall. In 1765 and 1766 he, the London merchant Anthony Merry, Joseph Howard*, and Edward Chinn protested Murray's restrictions of trade at the government-controlled king's posts. The resulting controversy exposed the inconsistencies of official policy, which vacillated between monopoly operation and free trade. In the midst of this debate Allsopp was appointed deputy provincial secretary and assistant clerk both of the Council of Quebec and of provincial enrolments on 15 Jan. 1766. Purchased from the absentee office holder, Henry Ellis, these largely clerical positions provided Allsopp with the security needed in a fluctuating commercial career. The appointments reached Allsopp in April, but Murray refused to install him because of his factious behaviour. The governor, however, returned to England in June, a recall for which Allsopp claimed much of the credit. Following the arrival of Guy Carleton as lieutenant governor and a thorough investigation of Allsopp's behaviour, the suspension was lifted in April 1768. The British community had been divided in its support of Allsopp's grievance over his exclusion from office. Several merchants, especially in Montreal, questioned his impartiality and disliked the militancy with which he had opposed Murray's administration. Others, such as Chief Justice William Hey*, resented the close relationship between Brook Watson and Carleton and scornfully termed Allsopp a "fallen angel." Yet by 1768 Allsopp, financier, estate executor, and local property owner as well as merchant, had become a conspicuous member of the mercantile community in the Quebec district. On 22 Dec. 1768 he married Anna Marie, the only daughter of another early merchant, John Taylor Bondfield. The Allsopps were to have ten children of whom seven, six boys and a girl, would survive infancy.

Between 1768 and 1773 Allsopp attended to both his prospering business interests and his lucrative but demanding official duties, which included the annual and often controversial issuance of tavern and fur-trade licences. Although hindered by assistants either incompetent or less scrupulous than himself, Allsopp sought to exercise his functions impartially and efficiently, conscious of his own commercial reputation and Carleton's increasing scrutiny of official fee structures in the province [see Thomas AINSLIE]. The positions brought Allsopp an annual salary of £200 from the British Treasury; he paid Henry Ellis £400 and pocketed the fees. Allsopp also served from 25 Oct. 1769 until 24 Oct. 1772 as deputy commissary general, charged with allocating provisions to garrisons throughout the province, a post in which his commercial knowledge proved invaluable. His own activities as a wholesale merchant were dependent on the credit accorded him by Watson and Rashleigh, for whom he was also, as early as 1769, the agent responsible for collecting the accounts of various retailers. Foremost among these was Samuel Jacobs*, a merchant and grain dealer in Saint-Denis on the Rivière Richelieu. In 1766 Allsopp and Jacobs combined with John Welles under the name of Jacobs, Welles and Company to exploit a potash works in Lower Town Quebec at the former king's forges, which they leased from the crown. The enterprise was soon plagued by technical and managerial problems and failed in 1772, although without serious loss to Allsopp.

Like other British merchants, Allsopp was gradually specializing in the grain trade, revived following the war, and after 1766 he began to acquire increasing amounts of wheat from Jacobs. In September 1773 Allsopp and his brother-in-law John Bondfield purchased the adjoining seigneuries of Auteuil and Jacques-Cartier about 30 miles upstream from Quebec; the property included the seigneurial gristmill on the Rivière Jacques-Cartier. Two years later Bondfield relinquished to Allsopp his share in the seigneuries. Following the acquisition of the gristmill, Allsopp began making flour, and his grain purchases resulted in a steadily increasing debt to Jacobs and other suppliers.

From 1768 to 1773 Allsopp's trade and milling operations, official duties, and cordial relations with Carleton diverted him from public debate over colonial government. During this same period, however, it was becoming increasingly clear that the merchants' political views were vastly different from those of Carleton, who as commander-in-chief was preoccupied with provincial security and Canadian loyalty under veiled threats of French retaliation and growing restiveness in the American colonies. The Quebec Act of 1774, which Carleton had largely inspired, profoundly disappointed the merchants by providing for exclusive use of French civil law and by eliminating trial by jury in civil suits. The act also dashed all hope of an assembly and provided for an appointed legislative council which the merchants felt was too small to be representative, too susceptible to Roman Catholic influence, and too dependent on the governor. Allsopp's own ill-concealed disappointment over the absence of provisions for an assembly and English commercial law stirred up opposition to him among government supporters. He was nevertheless appointed to the Legislative Council and was sworn in on 17 Aug. 1775.

During the American siege of Quebec Allsopp held the important post, between 25 Jan. 1775 and 24 Aug. 1776, of commissary general for the Quebec garrison. His misgivings about the Quebec Act, however, were being misinterpreted by Carleton and others as disloyalty, particularly since a number of Allsopp's former business associates, including Joseph Howard, Thomas Walker*, Pierre Du Calvet*, John Welles, Christophe Pélissier*, and John and Acklam Bondfield, supported the American cause. Suspicions of Allsopp's loyalty may have been partially responsible for his removal in 1777 as deputy provincial secretary and assistant clerk of provincial enrolments; the provincial secretary and clerk, George Pownall*, had been in the colony since his appointment to those offices in 1775, but Allsopp had continued to act as deputy until 1777. Allsopp's quarrelsome nature, blatant commercial bias, perceived disregard for provincial security, and desire for more English law contributed to his radical reputation, and in 1778 he was publicly assaulted as a "rebel."

Embittered by his dismissal from all his official posts by 1778, Allsopp, in spite of the pressures, was until 1791 the most consistent and militant opponent of the provincial administration. The peak of his opposition came in March 1780. Influenced by the views of the absent chief justice, Peter Livius*, and his own commercial preoccupation, the contentious merchant erupted during the near-violent session of the Legislative Council that year in a bitter but sophisticated indictment of the judicial and administrative systems sanctioned by Governor HALDIMAND. He condemned the elimination of jury trials and habeas corpus, the unauthorized privy council introduced by Carleton and continued by Haldimand, the absence of a clearly defined legal code to regulate commercial transactions and suits, and the inadequacies of the court system established under the Quebec Act. To combat the "seditious spirit" displayed by Allsopp and to counter growing support within council for reform, Haldimand suspended him in January 1783.

Although heavily engaged in politics, Allsopp did not neglect his wheat and flour trades or his agency for Watson and Rashleigh. In 1781 he had contracted with the seigneur James Cuthbert* to buy all his available wheat for 14 years. Three years previously Allsopp had begun building a large, expensive, stone grist-mill near the mouth of the Rivière Jacques-Cartier. By 1783 this project had contributed substantially to his indebtedness, already worsened by wartime trade restrictions and strained financial relations with Watson and Rashleigh. Business matters involving his agency for the London company took Allsopp to New York that year. In 1784 he went to England to negotiate a financial settlement with the firm, promote trade for his mills, and contest his exclusion from council.

In London Allsopp was drawn almost instinctively to the lobby for the repeal of the Quebec Act. He laid his arguments before various politicians, including Thomas Powys, member of parliament for Northamptonshire, Evan Nepean, an under-secretary in the Shelburne ministry, and Lord Sheffield, a recognized authority on commerce and agriculture and an opponent of William Pitt's proposed relaxation of the navigation laws. The merchant's case for administrative and judicial reform, and the reconsideration of his suspension, nevertheless fell prey to the indecisive preoccupation of the Pitt ministry with constitutional change in Quebec. In business matters he was more successful, but only after much negotiation and self-assertion. Before he returned to Quebec in the fall of 1785 he had arranged, partially through a mortgage on his new mill, to repay a debt of more than £8,660 to Watson and Rashleigh and had made agreements to supply flour and biscuit to merchants involved in the Newfoundland and Gulf of St Lawrence fisheries.

During Allsopp's absence from Quebec, reform had become a popular issue through the initiative of Lieutenant Governor Henry Hamilton* and others. Allied with Deputy Postmaster General Hugh FINLAY, Chief Justice William Smith*, and William GRANT (1744–1805), Allsopp supported measures debated between 1785 and 1787 for judicial reform, notably those favourable to commercial activity. In 1787, during a formal investigation into the administration of justice, Allsopp sharply condemned the inconsistency of decisions in commercial cases rendered by the Court of Common Pleas. Since 1777 this court had been handling all civil cases, and Allsopp, because of its inconsistency, had made every effort to avoid it. He argued that the variability in its decisions resulted from the lack of a definite legal code for the judgement of commercial transactions. Instead there was the confusing use of legal elements from the outdated French mercantile code and even from the laws of New France and of the colony of New York. Between 1787 and 1791 he continued to play a leading role in the efforts by British and Canadian committees to convince Governor Carleton, now Lord Dorchester, and the British parliament of the necessity for a representative assembly and English commercial law.

Agitation within the province over constitutional change was marked by a bewildering variety of opinion. Many merchants learned with dismay of the

Allsopp

government's intention, stated in the Constitutional Act of 1791, to divide the colony, thus separating them politically from the loyalists in what became Upper Canada. Nor did the new act completely repeal the Quebec Act or provide for a commercial code. Encouraged, however, by the provisions for an assembly balanced by a legislative council, and less concerned with the political and commercial implications, Allsopp enthusiastically claimed partial responsibility for having "produced a most excellent Constitution for Canada, preferable in several respects to that enjoyed by the other Colonies." He contested the election of 1792 for Upper Town Quebec but was defeated by his former reform associate William Grant. Allsopp was further disappointed when Dorchester's recommendation for his appointment to the first legislative and executive councils under the act was rejected by William Wyndham Grenville, the Home secretary.

In business throughout the period from 1786 to 1791 Allsopp concentrated almost exclusively on wheat buying, milling, and marketing, and the shipment of flour and biscuit from Jacques-Cartier and his Lower Town Quebec warehouses and wharf. He undertook much custom grinding in addition to the production of his own flour and biscuit. His principal markets were Montreal provisioners, the Gulf of St Lawrence fisheries, the West Indies, government supply contractors, and local consumers in Quebec. By 1788 Allsopp's milling complex, capable of producing 65,000 *minots* or 22 per cent of the colony's annual production, ranked first in the province. Fully aware of the intricate mechanics of the grain trade, he repeatedly advocated the exportation of flour rather than bulky wheat. Although Quebec merchants such as Allsopp were hampered by the negative effects of the Canadian climate and current agrarian practices on the quality of wheat and flour produced, they hoped to find compensation in the severance, following the American revolution, of supplies to the empire from American sources. In 1789, after a British act of the previous year had failed to establish reciprocal trade between Quebec and the British West Indies, Allsopp led a delegation of millers, bakers, coopers, and merchants in the presentation to Dorchester of a proposed amendment to make the act operative. Supported by the Legislative Council, the proposals were referred to Britain but lost in more pressing constitutional debates.

By 1790 Allsopp's seigneurial revenues of £600 per annum made him the eighth most important individual seigneur in the colony. His commercial stability was seriously threatened in 1793, however, when fire destroyed his main grist-mill near the mouth of the Jacques-Cartier. Allsopp was forced to renegotiate his financial obligations to Brook Watson, whose rigid control of Allsopp's financial base spurred the

merchant's contempt. In 1795 a settlement was concluded. Between that year and 1798 operations were largely restored at the stone mill; from 1795 as well Allsopp leased the nearby Portneuf baronial mill. The Jacques-Cartier seigneurial mill, which in June 1796 had also burned down, was reactivated, and a third grist-mill was added to the complex.

Although Allsopp still entered into other smaller but profitable transactions, he now viewed the processing and sale of flour as the "only eligible trade." Allsopp supplied flour to his bakeries at Jacques-Cartier and in Lower Town Quebec for the local market; he also sold flour and biscuit to the exporters Lester and Morrogh [see Robert LESTER] and to Monro and Bell [see David Monro*], suppliers to the government contractor Alexander Davison*. Allsopp was able to rely increasingly on the advice and assistance at Jacques-Cartier of his eldest son, George Waters Allsopp*, but his plan to expand his trade through the placement of his other sons in foreign market centres did not materialize. By the time of his death, John, Robert, and William had participated in the family trade at Quebec; Carleton became a merchant abroad and James entered the British army. Allsopp's wife and daughter spent much of each year throughout the 1790s at Cap-Santé near the mills, while Allsopp reluctantly resided for lengthy periods at Quebec where his business was conducted.

At Quebec Allsopp pursued various other interests ranging from the Quebec Fire and Agriculture societies to large-scale land speculation in the Eastern Townships. Complications in the controversial land-granting system prevented the family from exploiting much of Allsopp's granted land until after his death, particularly in Farnham and Maddington townships. On the basis of his knowledge of commercial law and past experience as a Court of Appeals judge (a duty of legislative councillors), Allsopp petitioned for a judgeship in 1794. This position was denied, but on 12 June 1799 he was appointed a justice of the peace for Quebec.

Governed by bitter memories of his political humiliation, Allsopp had apparently avoided any involvement in provincial politics after 1792. He nevertheless retained his faith in the British constitution, the theoretical foundation of his earlier reform campaign. In response to the French revolution he praised the constitution's balance of monarchy, aristocracy, and democracy as the most effective means of controlling an elected body. According to available evidence, Allsopp refrained from any assessment of Lower Canadian politics during the 1790s and his response to the emerging political contest between Canadian and ministerial groups for legislative control is uncertain. During the 1796 election campaign of his son George Waters, however, he did express concern over the vigour of Canadian opposition.

The longevity and extent of Allsopp's business activities establish him as a principal commercial figure in Quebec between 1760 and the 1790s. Through partnerships and diverse wholesale trading interests he quickly prospered, and as the principal agent in Canada for Brook Watson he figured significantly in that powerful merchant's penetration into virtually all aspects of the Quebec trade. Secured by this association and the apparent availability of long-term credit, Allsopp specialized increasingly in the wheat trade but gradually declined in prominence as a wholesaler. Following the construction of the Jacques-Cartier grist-mill, the turning-point of his career, Allsopp emerged as a major industrialist and, by 1788, the province's largest flour producer. Intense competition from other producers and wheat exporters, the demands of full-time management, and heavy financial obligations to Watson eventually forced him to forsake plans for retirement to England. He remained active as a businessman and magistrate until at least 1804. On 26 March 1805 the death in Quebec of his wife, who was long a stabilizing influence upon him, came as a severe blow, and he died in Cap-Santé less than three weeks later following a series of crippling strokes. The business was continued by George Waters Allsopp, but in 1808 the grist-mills were offered for lease.

DAVID ROBERTS

ANQ-Q, CN1-25, 25 janv. 1781, 1er avril 1784; CN1-205, 1er août 1775; CN1-207, 4 mars, 8 juill., 8 août 1768; 25 janv. 1774; CN1-230, 23 août 1799; CN1-256, 11 Feb., 24 June 1794; 11 Feb. 1795; E4, 1, 10; E18; P-313. BL, Add. MSS 21679: 171–72, 244; 21726: 135; 21734: 72; 21735/1: 201; 21789: 87; 21844: 13–15; 21864: 109–11; 21872/2: 308–50; 21877: 191; 21885: 29–30; 35915: 339 (copies at PAC). Clements Library, Thomas Gage papers, American ser., Gage to Allsopp, 26 Nov. 1770–26 Oct. 1772. PAC, MG 19, A2, ser.3, 1–25, 71–72; MG 23, A4, 16: 114–21; GII, 3, vols.3–5; GIII, 1; I13, 2: 189–92, 197–200; RG 1, E1, 106: 162; 107: 85; 108: 81–89; 111: 47–48, 61–65, 76–90; L3L: 11–26, 65–113, 146, 219, 230, 467, 501, 1078–79, 1088–89, 1100–21, 2063, 2796–825, 2865–69, 3154–73, 3256–67, 3295–305, 3716, 3736, 4591, 4701–6, 5366–77, 5385–88, 5398–403, 5407–10, 16044–49, 16080, 16126–29, 16137–226, 26590–728, 31806–2036, 32264–85, 35572–97, 40052–83, 54802–42, 60874–90, 95242–57; RG 4, A1: 5763–64, 6146–50, 6680, 7229–30, 17304–6, 21733. PRO, AO 1, 573/479, c.29401; CO 42/1–3; 42/5; 42/12; 42/18; 42/21; 42/25–35; 42/37–41; 42/44; 42/51–52; 42/56; 42/60–63; 42/66–67; 42/69–70; 42/86; 42/90; 42/101; 42/104; 42/109; 42/117; 42/124; 42/138; 42/182–96. *Docs. relating to constitutional hist., 1759–91* (Shortt and Doughty; 1918), l: 165, 205–13, 572; 2: 595, 609, 767–73, 847–54, 870–71, 902–9. G.B., House of Commons, *Journals* ([London]), 40 (1784–85). *Johnson papers* (Sullivan et al.), 6: 8. Maseres, *Maseres letters* (Wallace), 46, 50, 60, 72, 78–81. *The parliamentary history of England from the earliest period to the year 1803*, comp. William Cobbett and John Wright (36v., London, 1806–20), 24. *Quebec Gazette*, 1763–1805. *Quebec Herald, Miscellany and Advertiser*, 1788–91. *Quebec Mercury*, 20 April 1805. P.-G. Roy, *Inv. concessions*, 1: 294; 4: 70. Burt, *Old prov. of Quebec* (1968), 1: 95–96, 99–100, 118–19; 2: 30, 38–41, 43, 45–49, 116, 123. F.[-X.] Gatien, *Histoire de la paroisse du Cap Santé* (Québec, 1884), 146–48. Neatby, *Administration of justice under Quebec Act*, 156, 175, 208, 328–29, 338; *Quebec*, 88–89, 93, 161, 165, 182–83, 222. D. J. Roberts, "George Allsopp: Quebec merchant, 1733–1805" (MA thesis, Queen's Univ., Kingston, Ont., 1974). F.-J. Audet, "Les législateurs de la province de Québec, 1764–1791," *BRH*, 31 (1925): 490–92. P.-G. Roy, "L'honorable George Allsopp," *BRH*, 45 (1939): 157.

ALMON (Allmon), WILLIAM JAMES, physician, surgeon, and apothecary; b. 14 Aug. 1755 in Providence, R.I., son of James Almon and Ruth Hollywood; m. 4 Aug. 1785 in Halifax, N.S., Rebecca Byles, eldest daughter of the Reverend Mather BYLES, and they had six children; d. 5 Feb. 1817 in Bath, England.

Little is known of William James Almon's life until 1771, when he was apprenticed to Andrew Anderson, a physician in New York City. With the outbreak of the Revolutionary War, Almon joined the British forces, where he probably received additional medical training from William Bruce, physician with the hospital staff. He is supposed to have tended the wounded at the battle of Bunker Hill in 1775. The next year he went with General Sir William Howe's forces to Halifax, later serving with them at the capture of New York City. On 18 June 1778, ten days before the battle of Monmouth, he was appointed surgeon's mate to the 4th battalion, Royal Artillery, and about 1780 he was sent to Halifax to be surgeon to the Ordnance and artillery garrison there. He retired from the latter post some time after 1800, but retained the honorary position he had received as surgeon general to the Nova Scotia militia. While serving as a military surgeon, Almon established after 1783 a private practice which was to become the largest and most popular in Halifax. In 1785 he was appointed, at £60 a year, physician to the poor-house, which also served as the civilian hospital. At one point he was reputedly the only qualified surgeon in the town, and during one year he assisted at more than 100 births. His last years were spent in a joint medical and pharmaceutical practice with his son Wiliam Bruce*.

Almon's diagnoses and treatments were practical for the age, being soundly based on the latest scientific theories. He used inoculation with smallpox extensively, one of his few failures being with his first-born son in 1787. Although his father-in-law humorously referred to him as the "System-Monger," he respected his expertise when Almon's autopsy on Byles's

Andrews

second wife revealed that she had died not from a diseased liver but from "the pernicious Practice of lacing & girding herself too tight."

Much of Almon's medical knowledge derived from his extensive private library, since he was a well-read man with keen scientific interests. During the 1790s he served as vice-president of the local society for the promotion of agriculture, and he also belonged to an exclusive literary, scientific, and social group often patronized by Prince EDWARD AUGUSTUS. Following a visit to the United States in 1815, Almon apparently contemplated publishing his impressions of America, but the project was abandoned when the manuscript was lost.

During the residence of Edward Augustus in Halifax Almon served as physician in ordinary to the royal household, along with Duncan CLARK and John Halliburton. The prince particularly cited him for prompt medical attention when he injured himself by a fall from his horse in 1798. The doctor and his wife were also reputedly members of the royal social circle in Halifax.

In 1816 ill health forced Almon to undertake a two-year visit to England; he died while in Bath and was buried there beneath St James Church. His widow, who returned to Nova Scotia, claimed that "seldom has there been domestic Happiness so uninterrupted as ours." Although the provisions of his will were adequate, she noted that "my beloved Husband was too Benevolent & too Hospitable to leave me Rich." The Halifax press commented, "His goodness of heart and kindness of disposition will cause him to be long remembered & loved." Not easily forgotten either were the many anecdotes told of the doctor's amusing absent-mindedness. His wife related how in March 1785 she could only gaze "in silent astonishment" when Almon, after using her new pen as a tooth-pick, broke it in two. Almon's most enduring contribution to the colonial scene, however, was his founding of the long line of distinguished physicians and civil servants in Nova Scotia who bore his surname.

LOIS K. KERNAGHAN

A portrait of William James Almon by Robert FIELD, done *c*. 1810, is in the collection of Mrs H. M. Carscallen (Ottawa) and Mrs C. R. T. Cunningham (Toronto). Rebecca Almon also had her portrait done by Field at the same time, but the whereabouts of the work, said to be one of Field's best female portraits, is unknown.

W. K. Kellog Health Sciences Library, Dalhousie Univ. (Halifax), W. J. Almon, commonplace book. PANS, MG 1, 14, 163; MG 100, 101, no.45. *Vital record of Rhode Island, 1636–1850; first series, births, marriages and deaths; a family register for the people*, comp. J. N. Arnold (21v., Providence, R.I., 1891–1912), 2, pt.1: 208. *Halifax Herald*, 23 Dec. 1896.

ANDREWS, SAMUEL, Church of England clergyman; b. 27 April 1737 in Wallingford Township, Conn., youngest son of Samuel Andrews and Abigail Tyler; m. 13 Sept. 1764 Hannah Ann Shelton of Stratford Township, Conn., and they had six children; d. 26 Sept. 1818 in St Andrews, N.B.

When he was a young boy Samuel Andrews's family left the Congregational Church and joined the Church of England. It was the time of the Great Awakening and young Samuel grew up in the midst of a clamorous ecclesiastical atmosphere. He graduated from Yale College in 1759, spent two years as a lay reader in Wallingford, and was chosen by his fellow churchmen as a candidate for holy orders.

In April 1761 Andrews proceeded to England with John BEARDSLEY and the two were ordained priests in August. Appointed a missionary of the Society for the Propagation of the Gospel to serve the Wallingford area, Andrews took up his charge in January 1762 and proved to be an untiring worker. His conscientious reports to the SPG show a steady growth in church membership while recounting the difficulties in ministering to widely scattered congregations, some of them far outside his own mission. At the time of the Stamp Act crisis in 1765 Andrews reported that under "the peculiar Circumstances of the Times" he had been preaching on the "Duty of Obedience to the higher Powers," a stand taken by most of his fellow Anglican clergy. Although his lack of sympathy with those opposing the Stamp Act marked him as a tory, his work was undisturbed until the actual outbreak of hostilities.

In June 1775 Andrews had occasion to exhibit his loyalist sympathies. At a town dinner in George Washington's honour, the guests suffered through a long-winded, patriotic opening prayer. When called on to give thanks after dinner, Andrews simply quoted Eccles. 5:2, "Be not rash with thy mouth, and let not thine heart be hasty to utter any thing before God: for God is in heaven, and thou upon earth: therefore let thy words be few." He then sat down, having displayed not only his political stripes but a well-honed sense of humour as well.

On 20 July 1775, a day prescribed by the Continental Congress for prayer and fasting, Andrews's most overt action against the rebellion took place. Choosing as his text Amos 5:21, "I hate, I despise your feast days . . . ," he gave a sermon in which he again spoke against resistance to authority, calling on Americans to do nothing "but what the laws of God approve" in order to serve their country. His remarks aroused much hostility, and in response Andrews published them to show that he was not in contempt of the fast day but was prompted by a concern for his countrymen. He was nevertheless placed under heavy bonds to keep the peace and severely restricted in his movements; only the high

24

Andrews

regard for him in the town saved him from physical violence. During the war years he ministered as best he could, but undoubtedly suffered indignities and distress. Upon renewing his correspondence with the SPG in 1782, after a lapse of six years, he was reluctant to describe "my own Concerns, since the Troubles," reporting instead on the work he had performed in that time.

After the war Andrews and his friend James Scovil, rector of Waterbury, travelled to Nova Scotia in 1784 as agents for parishioners wishing to settle there. A promise of land in the Chedabucto Bay area was obtained from Governor John Parr*, but the scheme fell through for lack of aid with moving costs and supplies. When the SPG was obliged to withdraw its support of missionaries in the United States it offered several positions in New Brunswick to its Connecticut clergy. In August 1785 Andrews advised the SPG that he would continue in its service, but it was not an easy decision. Despite his wish to enjoy British government his first concern was for his parishioners, which "would prevail against every Consideration, did I not conceive that the Penury to which I and my Family must soon be reduced, would prevent the Success of my Labours."

On 25 May 1786 Andrews arrived at Saint John and received his appointment from Lieutenant Governor Thomas CARLETON to serve the shiretown of St Andrews and the whole of Charlotte County. It was a rugged coastal and inland area just being settled, but at St Andrews itself the new rector found a well-ordered populace "of different National extractions." He set to work without delay organizing his mission, and then in October 1786 returned to Wallingford to settle his affairs and to fetch his family. While there he suffered a paralytic stroke and after a partial recovery arrived back in St Andrews on 14 July 1787. A second attack in November severely curtailed his ability to travel, but by the end of 1788 he had recovered sufficiently to resume his rounds.

Andrews's ministry in Charlotte County involved extensive and arduous travel by sea as well as land to reach remote settlements. His reports recount a continuous tale of service, illness, and financial hardship as he worked to counter "straggling New Lights," "fanatic teachers from the American States," and "ignorant Anabaptist Teachers" who "infested" the extremities of his mission from time to time. Despite repeated requests he did not obtain an assistant until just before his death, but his persistent efforts led to the appointment in 1811 of Richard Samuel Clarke as SPG missionary in St Stephen (St Stephen–Milltown).

During his years in New Brunswick Andrews maintained contact with old Connecticut friends, among them Abraham Jarvis, the second bishop of Connecticut. Andrews had played a full role in the struggle to establish an episcopate in the American colonies during his ministry there, and he espoused a similiar cause while in New Brunswick. Along with most of the loyalist clergy, however, he did not favour the choice of Charles INGLIS as bishop of Nova Scotia in 1787. Eventually Inglis's neglect of New Brunswick brought forth requests for a separate diocese, and Andrews and his fellow clergy urged Carleton to press for a bishop resident in the province.

Along with his religious orthodoxy Andrews possessed a liberal outlook and a fine sense of humour which were able to win and retain the affections of the large nonconformist element in St Andrews. The persistent exertions of the preacher Duncan McColl* to establish Methodism on a firm footing in St Andrews met with little success, and during his lifetime Andrews was able to maintain the town's allegiance to the Church of England. Only after his death did the various denominations set up their own churches, and for a decade after his death Methodism remained "a foreign element" in the town. Andrews's service in St Andrews can truly be said to have "represented a triumph for the Church of England in that parish."

Although he had no commercial interests, Andrews gathered regularly with the town's leading merchants in the Friendly Society which he founded in 1803. At its convivial gatherings members discussed science, philosophy, and other learned matters. These meetings and his printed sermons, which are superior in style and matter to many of those published by his contemporaries, show Andrews to have been a man of broad intellectual interests.

In 1791 Andrews purchased an island near St Andrews on which he lived the rest of his life, riding across the tidal bar to and from his duties. Now called Ministers Island, it commemorates his former presence in the area. At his death Andrews was widely mourned on both sides of the border. This "venerable and Pious and Primitive Missionary" performed a masterly job in organizing the church in his large pioneer mission despite frequent bouts of ill health. His diligent efforts, and those of the other loyalist clergy who worked long and hard to serve the needs of their parishioners, firmly settled the Church of England in New Brunswick.

JOHN L. WILLIAMSON

[Eleven of Samuel Andrews's sermons are known to have been printed. C. K. Shipton and J. E. Mooney, *National index of American imprints through 1800* ... (2v., Worcester, Mass., 1969), lists seven dating from 1769 to 1787. Dexter, *infra*, gives three others, two printed together in 1801 and one from 1809. The last known to be published, dated 1811 on the occasion of Andrews's 50th anniversary as a priest, is to be found in USPG, C/CAN/NB, 1, no.8. The sermon of 20 July 1775 that so aroused local sentiment against Andrews was published as *A discourse, shewing the*

Antrobus

necessity of joining internal repentance, with the external profession of it; delivered upon the general fast, July 20th, 1775 (New Haven, Conn., 1775). A portrait of Andrews is reproduced in *Acadiensis* (Saint John, N.B.), 3 (1903): facing p.197; the location of the original is not known. J.L.W.]

PANB, MC 58, "Bishop Inglis letters, 1787–1842," comp. W. O. Raymond (copies); RG 7, RS63, 1818, Samuel Andrews. USPG, B, 6, no.226 (transcript at PAC); 23, nos.4–22, 24–25; C/Am, 3, nos.37–38, 57–60; C/CAN/NB, 1, no.1a (mfm. at PAC); Journal of SPG, 15, 25–31 (mfm. at PAC). *The Church of England in pre-revolutionary Connecticut: new documents and letters concerning the loyalist clergy and the plight of their surviving church*, ed. K. W. Cameron (Hartford, Conn., 1976). F. B. Dexter, *Biographical sketches of the graduates of Yale College, with annals of the college history* (6v., New York and New Haven, 1885–1912). J. S. Andrews, *Samuel George Andrews and family* ([Rochester, N.Y.?], 1919). A. M. Baldwin, *The clergy of Connecticut in revolutionary days* (New Haven, 1936). E. E. Beardsley, *The history of the Episcopal Church in Connecticut, from the settlement of the colony to the death of Bishop Seabury* (2v., New York and Boston, 1866). R. M. Calhoon, *The loyalists in revolutionary America, 1760–1781* (New York, 1973). A. W. [H.] Eaton, *The Church of England in Nova Scotia and the tory clergy of the revolution* (New York, 1891). *An historic record and pictorial description of the town of Meriden, Connecticut, and men who have made it . . .* , comp. C. B. Gillespie and G. M. Curtis (Meriden, 1906). H. G. Kinloch, "Anglican clergy in Connecticut, 1701–1785" (PHD thesis, Yale Univ., New Haven, 1959). B. E. Steiner, *Samuel Seabury, 1729–1796: a study in the High Church tradition* ([Athens, Ohio], 1971). A. W. Mahon, "The Friendly Society," *Acadiensis* (Saint John), 7 (1907): 187–92. Maud O'Neil, "A struggle for religious liberty: an analysis of the work of the S.P.G. in Connecticut," *Hist. Magazine of the Protestant Episcopal Church* (New Brunswick, N.J.), 20 (1951): 173–89. Glen Weaver, "Anglican-Congregationalist tensions in pre-revolutionary Connecticut," *Hist. Magazine of the Protestant Episcopal Church*, 26 (1957): 269–85.

ANTROBUS, JOHN, merchant and office holder; b. *c.* 1756, probably in England; d. 8 May 1820 in Trois-Rivières, Lower Canada.

In 1779 John Antrobus was in business at Quebec, where he owned a general store in Lower Town. As a merchant he was in agreement with the political demands of the English-speaking bourgeois community: consequently in 1784 and 1788 he signed petitions in favour of a house of assembly and in 1785 was amongst those who supported Lieutenant Governor Henry Hamilton* in his efforts to meet the merchants' needs. Antrobus also participated in advancing certain claims in economic and social matters: in 1789 he signed a memorial asking for the settlement of problems affecting trade in flour and biscuit [*see* George ALLSOPP], and in 1791 another about the collection of *lods et ventes*; in 1790 he was among the signatories to a petition requesting the creation of a university in Lower Canada [*see* Jean-François Hubert*]. Also in that year he was a member of the Quebec Fire Society.

On 29 March 1787, at Trois-Rivières, Antrobus had married Catherine Betsey Isabella Cuthbert, daughter of James Cuthbert* and Catherine Cairns. The following year the couple, who were then living on Rue de la Montagne in Quebec, received from Cuthbert one piece of land in the seigneury of Berthier, and two others in that of Sorel. Some months later, in exchange for one of his Sorel properties, the government granted Antrobus the ruins of the king's ironworks in Lower Town Quebec on seigneurial tenure. In September 1788 he acquired a lot with a house and stable at Près-de-Ville, at the foot of Cap Diamant, for a yearly payment of 100 *livres* on the 2,000 *livres* borrowed for its purchase.

In 1792 Antrobus and his wife went to live on their property at Berthier. The following year he was appointed overseer of highways for the district of Trois-Rivières. In this capacity he attended particularly to coordinating the development of a system of roads throughout the district. As Trois-Rivières already had an adequate set of major roads, Antrobus proceeded at the inhabitants' instance to create a network of secondary roads to link the inland areas with the Chemin du Roy, adapting the layout to needs and circumstances. Work on a sizeable scale was undertaken in the region of Rivière-du-Loup (Louiseville). It is difficult to estimate Antrobus's income as overseer of highways because the emoluments from this office came not only from public funds but also from fees paid by the inhabitants for the drafting of surveyor's reports.

In 1797 Antrobus took his family to live at Trois-Rivières, on a property purchased for £1,200. That year he was appointed a justice of the peace and a member of the grand jury for the Court of King's Bench. His land holdings grew steadily. He had already obtained a grant in the seigneury of Sorel from Lord Dorchester [Guy CARLETON] in 1795. Three years later Joseph BOUCHER de Niverville granted him 46 acres bordering on the common lands of Trois-Rivières. In 1803 Antrobus rented out a farm at Berthier on the *métayage* system. According to the agreement the *métayer*, Jean-Baptiste Amiot, was to give him half of the grain harvested in the first year; for the next six years Antrobus was to receive £46 annually for the house, milk house, and bakehouse. In 1804 Antrobus bought two properties in the seigneury of Sainte-Marie adjoining that of Sainte-Anne-de-la-Pérade. To increase his holdings Antrobus sought to obtain about 30,000 acres in Brandon Township, but lacking financial resources he was unsuccessful in getting letters patent and going ahead with the survey.

After his wife's death in January 1806, Antrobus, who owed £1,000, began to divest himself of his holdings. That year for £100 he sold to the Reverend

James Sutherland Rudd, rector of Christ Church at William Henry (Sorel), properties he owned there. In 1809 he received £400 from the sale of three pieces of land at the foot of Cap Diamant. Three years later he sold a property at Trois-Rivières to the merchant Étienne Leblanc* for £150. For £1,020 in 1816 he sold by auction to George Pyke* a waterfront lot on Rue Champlain, Quebec, which his children had received by letters patent from the government on 9 Aug. 1806. During the period 1810–19 his creditors, Lewis Tucker, John Doty*, Ezekiel Hart*, John BLACKWOOD, and Christopher Carter, demanded that the properties he still owned be put up for sheriff's sale.

In January 1820 John Antrobus resigned from his post as overseer of highways and was replaced by his son, Edmund William Romer*. He died some months later; only two of his six children survived him and his daughter died just a few weeks later. His sole heir, Edmund William Romer, had an inventory made of his father's assets. Antrobus had left only a modest estate: some pieces of land at Trois-Rivières and some properties at Sainte-Anne-de-la-Pérade and Sainte-Marie; moreover, the sale at auction of his personal estate brought in only £51 12s.

NORMAND PAQUETTE

ANQ-MBF, CE1-50, 10 June 1820; CN1-4, 1er déc. 1795, 15 févr. 1797, 2 mai 1798; CN1-6, 11 sept. 1803, 7 mai 1806, 23 sept. 1809, 30 oct. 1815, 17 oct. 1818, 21 juin 1820; CN1-32, 20 mars 1812; CN1-91, 15 sept. 1804. ANQ-Q, CN1-16, 1er avril, 20 sept., 14 nov. 1809; CN1-83, 9 avril 1784; 4 juill., 24 sept. 1788; CN1-145, 28 Dec. 1804. *Quebec Gazette*, 11 Nov. 1779; 16 June, 3 Nov. 1785; 11 Dec. 1788; 17 Dec. 1789; 28 Jan., 4 Nov. 1790; 28 April 1791; 30 March, 27 April 1797; 30 Jan. 1806; 9 Aug. 1810; 21 Feb., 27 June 1811; 4 March 1813; 21 May, 2 July 1818; 8 July 1819. Lucie Beauvillier et Carmen Grondin, *Répertoire des baptêmes-mariages-sépultures, Trois-Rivières protestant, 1767–1875* (s.l., 1979). P.-G. Roy, *Inventaires des procès-verbaux des grands voyers conservés aux Archives de la province de Québec* (6v., Beauceville, Qué., 1923–32), 3: 158–92. Sulte, *Mélanges hist.* (Malchelosse), 21: 47–51. Édouard Fabre Surveyer, "James Cuthbert, père, et ses biographes," *RHAF*, 4 (1950–51): 81. P.-G. Roy, "John Antrobus," *BRH*, 10 (1904): 283–84.

APLIN, JOSEPH, lawyer, politician, and office holder; b. *c.* 1740 in Rhode Island; d. 26 April 1804, probably in Rhode Island.

The son of John Aplin, a lawyer in Connecticut and Rhode Island, Joseph Aplin was himself "educated to the Profession of the Law." At the outbreak of the American rebellion he was practising in Newport, R.I., but his outspoken support for the crown forced his retirement to South Kingston, a loyalist area, in the fall of 1775. Aplin remained in South Kingston, living off investments, until August 1780. He was four times

put under military arrest on charges of attempting to influence the militia not to assemble before he abandoned Rhode Island for the safety of British-occupied New York. He stayed there until the evacuation of the city in 1783, moving to Nova Scotia that December.

In Nova Scotia, Aplin quickly became involved in politics, mainly in relation to loyalist resettlement. Having visited the Saint John region, in 1784 he was active in the movement for the separation of New Brunswick from Nova Scotia, arguing vehemently that the loyalists in the Saint John valley were suffering from official neglect. That same year he served as agent in Halifax for the town of Shelburne, and in 1785 he was elected to the Nova Scotia House of Assembly for Barrington Township. Soon after Edmund FANNING, the former lieutenant governor of Nova Scotia, managed to secure his position as lieutenant governor of St John's (Prince Edward) Island in 1787, he invited Aplin there to be solicitor general. Aplin's immediate reaction to his new location was positive. There was, he wrote a friend in 1788, hardly a barren acre on "this delightful and much neglected island." Although the colony's legal system left much to be desired, for the judges were "not educated to the Law," he found a disposition to seek justice. Aplin strongly supported the reinstatement as chief justice of Peter STEWART, who had been suspended by the previous lieutenant governor, Walter Patterson*, and he became clearly identified with the Fanning–Stewart faction in Island politics. In 1788 he and Attorney General Phillips Callbeck* revised the colony's laws, which James ROBERTSON began to print that year. After Callbeck's death in 1790 Aplin was appointed attorney general.

Despite his initial favourable impressions of the Island, Aplin soon found himself in the midst of controversy, a victim of the continuing political feud between Patterson's adherents and the followers of Fanning. In 1790 he was dangerously wounded by a Patterson supporter, and in 1791, along with Fanning, Stewart, and William TOWNSHEND, he was charged with malfeasance in a case brought before the Privy Council in London by the remnants of the Patterson party led by merchant-proprietors John Cambridge*, John Hill*, and William Bowley. Aplin denied all the charges in a lengthy affidavit, and with his fellow officials was completely exonerated by the council the following year. He responded to this decision in 1793 by suing Cambridge and Bowley in the Island's Supreme Court for malicious prosecution, and had the satisfaction of winning the case.

Although branded a Fanning–Stewart man, Aplin attempted to maintain an independent position on the Island, regarding most local political squabbles as not "worth quarrelling about" and "Sore Enemies" to his "Peace of Mind." By 1797, however, he had become

Arnold

associated with a new group of critics of Fanning and Stewart (led by the controller of customs, James DOUGLAS, and Captain John MACDONALD of Glenaladale), which suspected the lieutenant governor and chief justice of privately instigating the efforts of Joseph ROBINSON and Robert HODGSON to stir up popular sentiment for an escheat of proprietorial lands in the province. This little band with which Aplin was connected advocated reannexation to Nova Scotia as the only solution to the Island's problems, arguing that the colony was too small to acquire responsible officials. That same year Aplin was charged by his enemies not only with legal malpractice once again but also with sedition. He was likely excluded from his profession and in January 1798 he resigned from the Council, telling his colleagues: "If the want of bread does not overrule my inclination, I shall never see the Island again. . . . My wish is to get rid of the Island and all its quarrels." In the wake of his resignation from the Council the Duke of Portland, the Home secretary, ordered him dismissed as attorney general.

Pursued by his creditors, Aplin, with MacDonald's assistance, managed to escape the Island in 1798 and make his way to Britain to press for reannexation and to refute the charges against him. He was unable to clear his name, however, partly because his stated reasons for resigning from the Council were regarded as frivolous and partly because the accusations that he had used "rash" expressions in criticizing Fanning – whom he had accused of being either a "tame dupe" or a wielder of "misapplied power" – were all too true. Forced to return to Nova Scotia before his money ran out, Aplin went to Annapolis Royal and resumed the practice of law. Nothing is known of his last years, but he may have died in Rhode Island since his death was reported in a Providence newspaper. Though a man of strongly held convictions, Aplin clearly did not thrive on the controversy they engendered.

J. M. BUMSTED

PAC, MG 23, E5, 2. PANS, MG 1, 793, Joseph Aplin to Jonathan Stearns, 14 May 1788. PAPEI, RG 5, Minutes, 6 Feb. 1798. PRO, CO 226/13: 97–99; 226/15, 17, 348; 226/16: 156–57; 226/18: 241–42; PRO 30/55, no.8645 (transcript at PANS). SRO, GD293/2/19/10. "Calendar of papers relating to Nova Scotia," PAC *Report*, 1894: 414–15. G.B., Privy Council, *Report of the right honourable the lords of the committee of his majesty's most honourable Privy Council, of certain complaints against Lieutenant Governor Fanning, and other officers of his majesty's government in the Island of St John* ([London, 1792]). *Vital record of Rhode Island, 1636–1850; first series, births, marriages and deaths; a family register for the people*, comp. J. N. Arnold (21v., Providence, 1891–1912), 15 [reference courtesy of Ian Aplin. J.M.B.].

Royal Gazette and Miscellany of the Island of Saint John (Charlottetown), 12, 29 April 1793. Tremaine, *Biblio. of*

Canadian imprints, 287–88. Bumsted, "Sir James Montgomery and P.E.I.," *Acadiensis* (Fredericton), 7 (1977–78), no.2: 76–102. MacNutt, "Fanning's regime on P.E.I.," *Acadiensis*, 1 (1971–72), no.1: 37–53.

ARNOLD, BENEDICT, army officer and merchant; b. 14 Jan. 1741/42 in Norwich, Conn., son of Benedict Arnold, a merchant, and Hannah King, *née* Waterman; m. first 22 Feb. 1767 Margaret Mansfield of New Haven, Conn., and they had three sons; m. secondly 8 April 1779 Margaret (Peggy) Shippen of Philadelphia, Pa, and they had four sons and one daughter; d. 14 June 1801 in London, England.

The infamy that clings to Benedict Arnold in the American popular mind has obscured the remarkable life of a man who after George Washington was the ablest general in the Continental Army. Born into an old and distinguished New England family – an ancestor of the same name had been governor of Rhode Island in the previous century – Arnold watched his once prosperous father console himself for business failures with increasingly heavy drinking. A spirited and restless boy, he began an apprenticeship as an apothecary under two of his mother's cousins, but in 1758 he ran away from home to enlist with a New York company serving in the Seven Years' War. Although soon brought back at his mother's request, he enlisted again in early 1760 and served in upper New York. With the conclusion of hostilities he returned to Norwich, only to find his family on the verge of ruin as a result of his father's alcoholism. Resuming his training as an apothecary, he remained in Norwich until his father's death in 1761. He then moved to New Haven, where, in addition to running an apothecary shop, he established a trading business. In the years before the revolution he travelled along the American coast and in the West Indies, trading lumber and horses for European manufactured goods, molasses, sugar, and rum. He also made several trips to Quebec, where he became well known as a "horse-jockey."

When the revolution broke out in 1775 Arnold was eager to defend colonial liberties against what he regarded as the oppressive policies of the British government. He reacted to news of the battle of Lexington in April by calling up his company of local militia – he had been elected captain a few months previously – and marching to Cambridge, Mass., to offer his services to his fellow patriots. There he proposed to the Massachusetts committee of safety that an attack be launched against Fort Ticonderoga (N.Y.) on Lake Champlain, arguing that "the place could not hold out an hour against a vigorous onset." Convinced by Arnold that a successful assault on the fort would serve the twin purposes of capturing badly needed gunpowder and artillery and preventing a British advance along the lake and the Hudson River route, the committee accepted his proposal, gave him a commission as a colonel, and authorized him to raise 400 men for the expedition. Arnold then set out immediately for upper New York, leaving the job of recruiting to his subordinates.

Although successful in its objectives, the campaign against the British positions on Lake Champlain was a comic-opera affair. When Arnold arrived at Castleton (Vt) on 9 May, he met Ethan Allen and a group of his Green Mountain Boys. Shocked to learn that these "wild people" were also headed for Ticonderoga, engaged in an operation that had been sanctioned by Connecticut, Arnold insisted that Allen and his men place themselves under his command. After much squabbling, a compromise was worked out whereby Allen and Arnold agreed to become joint commanders of the expedition, with the understanding that Arnold would gradually assume sole authority as his recruits began arriving. The two rivals, leading a small band of roughly 100 men, then set out for Ticonderoga. Reaching their destination on the early morning of 10 May when the garrison was still sound asleep, Allen and Arnold simply walked into the fort and, without a shot being fired, received its surrender.

Immediately after the capture of Ticonderoga, small parties of men sent out by Arnold and Allen forced the surrender, again without resistance, of Crown Point (N.Y.) and Fort George (Lake George, N.Y.). By now, however, the two leaders were once more at each other's throats, partly because of Arnold's renewed attempts to acquire overall command and partly because of his efforts to halt plundering by Allen's men. The turning-point in the dispute came on 18 May, when Arnold and some of his Massachusetts recruits raided Fort St Johns (Saint-Jean-sur-Richelieu, Que.). On his way back to Ticonderoga Arnold met Allen, who was going to the fort to conduct a raid of his own. Unlike Arnold, however, Allen was forced to retreat when British troops arrived from Montreal. Following this inglorious episode, Allen, his force dwindling rapidly, relinquished the command to Arnold. Soon afterwards a Connecticut force of 1,000 men under Colonel Benjamin Hinman arrived to reinforce Ticonderoga, and there then followed a predictable quarrel between Hinman and Arnold over who was in charge. Exasperated with the whole business, the Massachusetts authorities sent a committee to the region with instructions to transfer the command to Hinman and to investigate Arnold's "spirit, capacity, and conduct." Arnold's response was prompt. Declaring that "he would not be second to any man" and that the committee's instructions were "a most disgraceful reflection on him and the body of troops he commands," on 24 June he resigned his commission and a couple of weeks later returned to Massachusetts.

Another opportunity to serve the colonial cause was not long in coming. In June 1775, while he was still on Lake Champlain, Arnold had crossed into Quebec to determine the strength of British defences. Upon his return he informed Congress that an army of 2,000 men could mount a successful invasion of the colony, and that according to a friend in Montreal "great numbers of Canadians . . . are determined to join us whenever we appear in the Country with any force to support them." This report and similar ones from sympathizers and agents inside Quebec produced results. Congress, which had earlier opposed proposals for an invasion of Quebec, now embraced the view that such an invasion would strike a severe blow at the British position in North America and at the same time block any attempt on the part of the enemy to advance down the Hudson. On 27 June, accordingly, Major-General Philip John Schuyler, commander of the troops in upper New York, was instructed to proceed into Quebec by way of Lake Champlain and the Rivière Richelieu. Later that summer, when Schuyler's army was preparing to depart, Arnold received orders from George Washington to lead another expedition along the Kennebec and Dead rivers (Maine) and then along the Rivière Chaudière to the town of Quebec, which he was to attempt to surprise.

Arnold's famous march to Quebec should more accurately be called the swim through Maine. On 19 September an army of about 1,100 men embarked in transports from Newburyport, Mass., for the mouth of the Kennebec. Reaching the river the next day, the little fleet then sailed to Fort Western (Augusta, Maine), where 200 boats had been built for the expedition by a local inhabitant. Arnold thought that these boats had been "badly, very badly built," and one of his officers described them as "little better than common rafts." Late in September the long journey up the Kennebec began. By the time the soldiers reached the Norridgewock Falls in early October, many of the boats were "nothing but wrecks" and a large part of the provisions had been damaged. By 20 October the Great Carrying Place between the Kennebec and Dead rivers had been crossed, but the men now had to contend with a violent storm and severe flood waters, and a part of the force turned back. Towards the end of the month the others, so hungry that dogs, candles, and shoes were being eaten, reached the Chaudière. A number of boats were soon lost in this turbulent, rock-strewn river, but the men persevered and on 30 October, when they reached the Rivière Famine, signs of civilization were again seen. During the following week Arnold's force, now reduced to under 700 men, plodded steadily onwards, reaching Sainte-Marie on 6 November and Pointe-Lévy (Lauzon and Lévis), just opposite Quebec, two days later. Abner Stocking, one of many individuals who had somehow found time to keep a journal on the trip, wrote that on arriving at Quebec the men's clothes "were torn in pieces by the

Arnold

bushes, and hung in strings – few of us had any shoes, but moggasons made of raw skins – many of us without hats – and beards long and visages thin and meagre. I thought we much resembled the animals which inhabit New Spain, called the Ourang-Outang." Still, thanks largely to Arnold's determination and inspiring leadership, the journey had been completed. In a letter written in late November Arnold asserted that the march was "not to be paralleled in history."

Despite the tattered condition of his force, Arnold was convinced that the fall of Quebec was inevitable. His confidence was not entirely misplaced, since Governor Guy CARLETON and most of the regular troops of the Quebec garrison had left to meet the American army advancing from the south. However, strong winds prevented Arnold from crossing the St Lawrence until the night of 13 November, and by that time a small force of Royal Highland Emigrants under Allan Maclean* had returned to Quebec to reinforce the garrison. Undeterred, Arnold quartered his troops in farm buildings belonging to Lieutenant-Colonel Henry CALDWELL, commander of the British militia at Quebec. During the next few days, Arnold reported to Washington, the American troops "marched up several times near the walls, in hopes of drawing them out but to no effect." Twice an officer bearing a flag of truce was sent to the town with a letter demanding immediate surrender, but each time this messenger was fired upon as he approached the walls – an action that Arnold denounced as "contrary to humanity and the laws of nations." On the 18th Arnold inspected his supply of arms and ammunition, and to his surprise discovered that a large number of the cartridges were unusable and that there were no more than five pounds of ammunition for each man. Learning that Maclean was planning an attack, and this at a time when many of the Americans were "invalids, and almost naked and wanting every thing to make them comfortable," Arnold decided to retire to Pointe-aux-Trembles (Neuville), about 20 miles west of Quebec. Here he planned to await reinforcements from the south before taking any further action.

Within the town itself, countering disaffection amongst the local population was as serious a problem as guarding against an enemy attack. Disappointed by the Quebec Act of 1774, the English-speaking merchants of the colony were inclined to sympathize with the American cause, and the very group that the act had been designed to benefit – the Canadians – showed only lukewarm loyalty. When Carleton, slipping unnoticed past the American forces, returned to Quebec on 19 November, he criticized "the blind Perverseness of this People, who frustrate all His Paternal Intentions for their own Protection, Interest, and Happiness, by an unprecedented Defection without even pretending the least Cause of Com-

plaint." As for the town of Quebec, Carleton feared that its fate, because of the "many Enemies within," was "extremely doubtful, to say nothing worse." To eliminate this fifth column, he issued a proclamation ordering those who refused to perform their militia duties to "quit the Town in four Days."

The situation improved somewhat in the American camp with the arrival on 3 December of Richard Montgomery*, who had replaced Schuyler as commander of the other invasion force. During the preceding two months Montgomery had achieved everything expected of him, capturing in succession Fort Chambly, Fort St Johns, Montreal, and Sorel. Yet not everything had gone well. Leading an army that had been reduced in size from 2,000 to 800 men by the expiry of terms of enlistment, Montgomery had been forced to march to Quebec with only 300 soldiers, the remainder having been left behind to garrison Montreal. The result was that Montgomery and Arnold could muster an army which, with reinforcements of some 200 Canadian volunteers, numbered only 1,200 men; in contrast, by the end of November Quebec was defended by a force of roughly 1,800. Together Arnold and Montgomery – with Montgomery in command – led their army from Pointe-aux-Trembles to Quebec on 4 December. Taking up a position near the town, Montgomery sent an address to Carleton urging him to surrender. Predictably, this overture was ignored. A confident Arnold informed Washington that the American army was "making all possible preparation to attack the city, which has a wretched motley garrison of disaffected seamen, marines and inhabitants; the walls in a ruinous situation, and cannot hold out long."

Several factors militated against a prolonged siege of Quebec: a smallpox epidemic was wreaking havoc in the American ranks; the enlistment term of Arnold's troops was due to expire on 31 December; the small size of the American force made it seem unlikely that an effective blockade of the town could be maintained; and, most important, British reinforcements would undoubtedly arrive as soon as the spring thaw permitted navigation of the St Lawrence. All these considerations convinced Montgomery that his army should storm Quebec as soon as possible, and a council of war held on 16 December settled on precisely this course of action. The original plan called for simultaneous attacks on the Upper and Lower towns, but it was soon decided, after some Americans had deserted to the enemy, to abandon this plan in favour of a two-pronged assault on Lower Town. According to the new strategy, diversionary attacks were to be made against Upper Town, while Montgomery and Arnold proceeded into Lower Town from Cap Diamant and Saint-Roch respectively. Upon joining forces, they would attempt to fight their way along Rue de la Montagne into Upper Town.

Alternatively, and preferable from the American point of view, the presence of enemy troops inside the city would lead Carleton to move out of the strong fortifications of Upper Town and give battle in the streets below.

The attack on Quebec was planned for the first stormy night, but for the next two weeks clear weather prevented the Americans from making their move. Finally, on the night of 30–31 December, a blinding snowstorm gave them their opportunity. Leading about 200 men, Montgomery advanced from Cap Diamant to Près-de-Ville, while Arnold and a force of 600 marched from Saint-Roch to the Rue du Sault-au-Matelot. What followed can only be described as a complete rout of the American army. Thanks to information supplied by deserters, the defenders of Quebec had known of American intentions for some time, and they turned out in force when the enemy was seen advancing. At Près-de-Ville a body of British seamen and Canadian militia which included John COFFIN surprised Montgomery's troops, killing several Americans, including Montgomery himself, and forcing the invaders to retreat. Arnold's division was no more successful. After passing Porte du Palais, where they were fired upon by sailors positioned on the bluffs above, the troops continued on to a battery. Here Arnold was wounded in the leg, and Daniel Morgan assumed command. While Arnold, urging his men to press on, was carried back to the Hôpital Général, Morgan fought his way past the battery and entered Lower Town. Dissension now broke out amongst the American officers over what course to follow, with Morgan in favour of an immediate advance and other officers wanting to move no farther until Montgomery arrived with reinforcements. Morgan eventually won and the attack was renewed, but by then the defenders had turned back the Americans at Près-de-Ville and were able to concentrate their force at the other end of Lower Town. After encountering a second barrier, defended by forces under Caldwell and John NAIRNE, Morgan's men decided to retreat, but a body of troops attacked them from the rear and forced them to surrender. As Carleton said, the Americans had been "compleatly ruined . . . caught as it were in a Trap." Rebel casualties numbered between 60 and 100 killed and wounded, and about 400 soldiers had been captured; the defenders of Quebec lost only about 20 men.

Luckily for the Americans, Carleton was too cautious a commander to press on and attack the American position outside Quebec. As for Arnold, he was only too aware of his army's vulnerable position. Although he boasted that "I have no thoughts of leaving this proud town, until I first enter it in triumph," he also informed Brigadier-General David Wooster, the American commander at Montreal, that the troops at Quebec were in a "miserable condition" to receive a counter-attack. This situation was to change little in the months ahead. In late January and early February 1776 about 200 troops arrived from Montreal, and by April 1,700 more reinforcements had crossed the border into Quebec. But because of desertions and expiring enlistments, the total strength of Arnold's army remained under 2,000, of whom only half were fit for duty. With such a small force, a second attack on Quebec was out of the question; Arnold himself had told Congress on 11 January that at least 3,000 more troops would be needed for a siege, or 5,000 more for an assault. Yet surprisingly, even with the pathetically small army under his command, Arnold kept up a bombardment of the city and at the same time cut off the garrison from the surrounding countryside. Admittedly, the damage caused by American cannon was minimal, but the blockade was a success by any standard. In March a worried Carleton informed the home government that fuel was "much wanted," provisions were scarce, and some people in the city were "in great Distress."

In recognition of Arnold's services during the assault on Quebec, Congress had appointed him a brigadier-general on 10 Jan. 1776. That April Wooster assumed the command at Quebec and Arnold was transferred to Montreal. Just over a month later British reinforcements under Charles Douglas* reached Quebec, and the American troops, now led by Major-General John Thomas, retreated hastily to Sorel. At Montreal, meanwhile, Arnold had more than his share of problems. On 29 April three commissioners of Congress – Charles Carroll, Samuel Chase, and Benjamin Franklin – arrived with instructions to win the support of the Canadian population. This task was hopeless from the start. After the débâcle of 31 December, the Canadians had grown noticeably less enthusiastic about the invasion, and in the next few months their attitude changed to one of open hostility as the American army began commandeering supplies and insisting on the use of paper currency. The situation was particularly bad in Montreal, for here Wooster had conducted an idiotic crusade to overawe the populace by closing "Mass Houses" and by arresting a number of prominent Canadians whom he thought to be pro-British. The fruits of this policy were noted by Colonel Moses HAZEN, who observed that the Canadian peasantry in the Montreal area were "waiting an opportunity to join our enemies," while the "better sort of people . . . would wish to see our throats cut, and perhaps would readily assist in doing it." The congressional commissioners attempted to rectify matters by cultivating the good will of the nobility and clergy and by establishing a printing press to spread the American message [see Fleury Mesplet*], but their efforts were in vain – as were those of Arnold himself. At first Arnold

Arnold

had adopted a lenient policy towards the Canadians, releasing the persons whom Wooster had imprisoned and respecting property rights whenever possible. However, he too soon gave up all hope that the local population could be won to the American side. Arguing that the Canadians should be "coerced, as I am convinced that they are in general our bitter enemies," Arnold secured from the commissioners authority to seize property and to pay for it in paper currency. In the event that his troops had to evacuate Montreal and were hindered from doing so by the populace, Arnold intended to burn the city to the ground.

Arnold had other problems as well. On 19 May the American garrison at Les Cèdres, a post located west of Montreal between Lake St Francis and Lac Saint-Louis, surrendered to a force of Indians, Canadians, and British regulars under Captain George Forster, the commander at Fort Oswegatchie (Ogdensburg, N.Y.). The following day a band of Indians and Canadians, the latter led by Jean-Baptiste-Jérémie Testard de Montigny, captured a detachment of American troops whom Arnold had sent to reinforce Les Cèdres. With his prisoners in tow, Forster began to march towards Montreal, but he was compelled to retreat when he learned that Arnold and 600 troops had entrenched themselves at Lachine. Setting off in pursuit, Arnold came within sight of the enemy just outside Vaudreuil. Here he discovered not only that the captured American officers had arranged an exchange of prisoners with the British, but also that under the terms of this "cartel" the freed Americans were prohibited from taking up arms again – a restriction that was not to apply to the British side. What was even more galling, when Arnold warned that he would punish the Indians severely if they refused to give up their prisoners, the Indians retorted that in the event of an American attack "they would immediately kill every prisoner, and give no quarter to any who should fall into their hands hereafter." Backed into a corner, Arnold agreed to sign the cartel on the condition, which Forster accepted, that the clause relating to the military service of the freed soldiers was deleted. He then left for Montreal, while Forster made his way back to Oswegatchie.

The American army was now in desperate straits. "Neglected by Congress below . . . ," Arnold wrote in a letter of 31 May, "distressed with the small-pox; want of Generals and discipline in our Army, which may rather be called a great rabble . . . our credit and reputation lost, and great part of the country; and a powerful foreign enemy advancing upon us, – are so many difficulties we cannot surmount them." By this time more than 5,000 reinforcements had arrived under Brigadier-General John Sullivan, but it was all too little too late. Soon after Sullivan reached Sorel and assumed command of the American army, some

10,000 British and German regulars under Carleton began advancing southwards. Determined to mount a counter-offensive, Sullivan sent 2,200 troops against Trois-Rivières, which it was thought was defended by only 800 regulars and Canadians; however, when the Americans reached the town they discovered that the garrison there had been reinforced by 7,000 soldiers from Carleton's army. A short battle ensued in which the Americans were badly beaten, losing more than 200 men as prisoners and about 50 dead and wounded. When Arnold heard that Sullivan wanted to remain in Sorel until the British were upon him, he urged his superior to reconsider: "I am fully of the opinion not one minute ought to be lost in securing our retreat. . . . Let us quit [Quebec], and secure our own country before it is too late." After some hesitation, Sullivan accepted Arnold's advice and withdrew from Sorel on 14 June. A day or two later Arnold evacuated Montreal upon learning that a British fleet commanded by Carleton was approaching the city. By the 17th both Sullivan and Arnold had arrived at Fort St Johns. Here, with the British hard on their heels, the two officers decided to retreat to Crown Point. Characteristically, Arnold stayed behind until the very last moment. After all the troops had set off, Arnold and an aide, Captain James Wilkinson, rode out on horseback to determine the position of the British. When they spotted John Burgoyne*'s soldiers, they hurried back to the fort, shot their horses, and boarded the last remaining boat. Arnold's insistence on pushing off this boat himself led Wilkinson to comment tersely on his general's determination to be "the last man who embarked from the shores of the enemy."

So ended the American struggle for the "fourteenth colony." In studying the invasion, American historians have generally concentrated on matters of detail: the small size of the army, the ravages of smallpox, the unwillingness of the Canadians to commit themselves to the revolutionary cause. A more crucial matter has been ignored: the fuzzy thinking that surrounded the campaign as a whole. The overall objective had been clear from the outset. The campaign had been intended to strike a blow at Britain's position in North America and to block any British attempt to use Quebec as a base from which to invade the Thirteen Colonies. Yet congressional and military leaders had never assessed the problems that would be faced by an American army in Quebec. Predictions about the reaction of the local population were always wildly optimistic. Moreover, the results of an anticipated British counter-offensive were not seriously considered. If their army had been larger, and better supplied, the Americans might have performed more effectively against Burgoyne and Carleton than they did; but in the end superior British force would have prevailed. All that the campaign accomplished – and perhaps the importance of this should not be underestimated – was to give the Thirteen Colonies some valuable breathing-space before Britain launched an attack on them from the north.

Arnold did not have time to ruminate over the mistakes of the past. Immediately after the Americans had been driven across the border, Carleton set his sights on regaining control of Lake Champlain, and to achieve this objective he instructed Charles Douglas and other naval officers to supervise the construction of a fleet at Fort St Johns. On the American side, Major-General Horatio Gates gave Arnold the task of building a navy on Lake Champlain capable of blocking the British offensive. Throughout the summer of 1776 Arnold, from a base at the southern end of the lake, worked tirelessly to create a navy from nothing. Despite his complaint that "we have a wretched motley Crew, in the Fleet; the Marines the Refuse of every Regiment, and the Seamen, few of them, ever wet with salt Water," he did succeed in building up a respectable little force consisting of two schooners, four galleys, eight gondolas, and several smaller vessels.

In early September, ignoring Gates's orders to conduct a purely defensive campaign, Arnold sailed with a number of his boats to the upper end of the lake, eventually anchoring 25 miles above Fort St Johns. Enemy batteries soon forced him to retreat south-wards, and on 23 September he took up a position off Valcour Island (N.Y.). Things then remained quiet until 11 October, when a large British fleet of more than 20 vessels, commanded by Carleton himself, rounded the southern tip of Valcour Island and detected the American force. Believing that he could never outsail the faster British fleet, Arnold resolved to give battle. In the ensuing engagement the Americans fared badly, and that night Arnold executed a daring retreat under cover of darkness. The next day, Carleton, furious to learn that the Americans were nowhere in sight, set off in chase and caught up with Arnold's flotilla at Split Rock Point (near Essex, N.Y.), about 14 miles from Valcour Island. After a short battle during which the American force continued to retreat gradually, Arnold ran his boats ashore and set them ablaze; he then led his men to Crown Point. Without question, the Americans had suffered a serious defeat, losing virtually their entire fleet. Yet the British victory was a hollow one, for the time spent in constructing a navy meant that an offensive into the northern colonies would have to be postponed until the following year. As for Arnold, his superiors were almost speechless when they heard of his exploits. Gates wrote to Schuyler: "It has pleased Providence to preserve General Arnold. Few men ever met with so many hairbreadth escapes in so short a time."

Arnold did not see further action until 1777, when he assisted in repulsing a British raid against Danbury, Conn. Here he again displayed the courage for which he was by now famous, and in appreciation of his "gallant conduct" Congress presented him with a horse, "properly caparisoned." That July he resigned his commission because of a quarrel with Congress over his rank, but on the urging of Washington he withdrew his resignation and proceeded north to help deal with Burgoyne's invasion force, then advancing through northern New York. Upon reaching Schuyler's base at Stillwater, N.Y., Arnold learned that an expedition sent to relieve Fort Stanwix (Rome, N.Y.), which was besieged by an army of British regulars, loyalists, and Indians under Barrimore Matthew St Leger*, had been turned back at Oriskany. Well aware of the importance of Fort Stanwix – its capture would lead the loyalists of the area to join forces with Burgoyne – Arnold volunteered to lead a second relief expedition. On 10 August he set out from Stillwater, and by the 21st he had arrived at Fort Dayton (Herkimer, N.Y.). Assuring Gates that "you will hear of my being victorious, or no more," he issued a proclamation denouncing St Leger's "banditti of robbers, murderers, and traitors" and promising a pardon to all loyalists who surrendered within ten days. This offer was ignored, but Arnold then employed a ruse which, in the end, made battle unnecessary. On the suggestion of one of his officers, he instructed a simpleton by the name of Hon Yost Schuyler to mingle with St Leger's Indians and spread rumours of the vast size of the American army. Hon Yost played his part to the hilt, and the panic he caused forced a general retreat by St Leger and his allies.

Fresh from this triumph, Arnold rejoined the northern army, now commanded by Gates, at Bemis Heights. As eager as ever for battle, he urged Gates to attack Burgoyne's force, which in mid September crossed the Hudson River and began marching southwards along the western bank. Gates, however, preferred to conduct a defensive campaign and ordered Arnold to remain at headquarters. Despite his cautious strategy, the two armies did clash on 19 September at Freeman's Farm. Arnold's detachment took part in this battle, but historians are divided as to whether Arnold himself was present. Whatever the case, there can be no doubt about his role in the next, decisive engagement of the campaign. On the morning of 7 October Burgoyne's troops launched another attack against the American lines. Ignoring Gates's orders – by now they were not even on speaking terms – Arnold rode out to join the battle. In a striking display of courage, he personally led an assault that resulted in the capture of an enemy redoubt. Shot in the same leg that had been wounded at Quebec, Arnold was taken back to the military hospital at Albany, where he promptly began denouncing the surgeons "as a set of ignorant preten-

Arnold

ders." Yet, though he was in a mood to complain, his spirits must have been lightened by the knowledge of what he had accomplished. With the taking of the redoubt the British had been placed in an impossible position and Burgoyne had opened negotiations for surrender. On the 17th the British laid down their arms and the Saratoga campaign – probably the most important in the Revolutionary War – came to an end. Burgoyne himself blamed his defeat on Arnold, and many military historians take the same view.

As it happened, Arnold was never again to see action in an American uniform. The story of his treason is well known, and only a brief summary of the facts can be presented here. In 1780, just after joining the British, Arnold published an address to the American public in which he put forward two arguments to justify his decision to change sides: first, that he had never supported the idea of independence but merely had wished for a redress of legitimate colonial grievances; and second, that he was simply not able to continue supporting the American cause once an alliance with France, "the enemy of the Protestant faith," had been concluded. This apologia, however, cannot be taken seriously, for prior to 1780 Arnold had not given the slightest indication that he was opposed either to colonial independence or to the French alliance. A more convincing explanation for his treason can be found if attention is paid to some of the personal problems he experienced during the war. From an early date Arnold's arrogance had made him a number of enemies, and in 1776 he had had to defend himself publicly against accusations of misconduct levelled by two lower-ranking officers, Moses Hazen and John Brown. Congress eventually cleared Arnold of these charges, but in other ways it too proved to be a thorn in his side. In February 1777 Arnold's pride was deeply wounded when Congress appointed five of his fellow brigadiers-general to the rank of major-general; soon afterwards, following the engagement at Danbury, Arnold also received the long-awaited promotion to major-general, but it was only in January 1778 that his seniority was restored above the other five officers. Later that year Arnold was made commander at Philadelphia, recently evacuated by British forces. Here he married the young Margaret Shippen, daughter of a former chief justice of Pennsylvania and a woman whose beauty was allegedly to dazzle George III. But in Philadelphia he again incurred the enmity of many important people, and in early 1779 the Pennsylvania Council charged him with using his military office for private gain. Although a committee of Congress exonerated him, Congress itself ignored the committee's report and proceeded with a court martial. This body found evidence to substantiate two of the charges and suggested to Washington that Arnold be reprimanded. Reluctantly, Washington complied.

For Arnold, the Philadelphia imbroglio was the last straw. Convinced that a man of his talents deserved better treatment, in May 1779 he began sending military intelligence to the British commander-in-chief, Sir Henry Clinton, using as intermediaries the loyalists Joseph Stansbury and Jonathan ODELL. By the following year the game had advanced one stage farther, with Arnold's request for command of the strategically important garrison at West Point, N.Y. An unsuspecting Washington granted his wish in August 1780, and shortly afterwards Clinton agreed to pay Arnold £20,000 if he were able to arrange the surrender of West Point. At a clandestine meeting on 22 September, Arnold and Major John André, Clinton's aide-de-camp, conferred over how the surrender was to be accomplished. The following day André was captured by a rebel patrol and the incriminating papers in his possession were forwarded to Washington, who was on his way to West Point to meet with Arnold! Incredibly, Arnold too had learned of André's capture and, a mere hour before Washington's arrival, he fled down the Hudson aboard his personal barge. Washington, shocked and cruelly disappointed at the treason of a man he greatly admired, sent an aide-de-camp after Arnold, but it was too late: the former American officer reached the safety of the armed sloop *Vulture* and made his way to New York City. André, however, was not so fortunate, being hanged as a spy on 2 October. Following the execution Washington wrote: "I am mistaken if Arnold is not undergoing at this time the torments of a mental hell."

For his defection, Arnold was awarded a lump sum of £6,315 and an annual pension of £360; he was made a brigadier-general in the British forces, with an annual income of several hundred pounds; and he was authorized to raise a loyalist battalion, in which his sons also received commissions. The next couple of years gave him little opportunity to display his military abilities, but he and his unit, the American Legion, did participate in marauding expeditions into Virginia and Connecticut. In December 1781, having abandoned all hope of a future for himself in the colonies, he moved with his family to England. There, although he was consulted on the course of the war, he was unable to obtain the military employment he wanted so badly. In 1785 he submitted a memorial to the loyalist claims commission, recounting why he had decided to join the British army and requesting compensation for the £30,000 he claimed he had lost as a result of this decision. He soon asked that his memorial be withdrawn, mainly because his wife had just received a pension of £360. By now Arnold was determined to make a large fortune that would guarantee his family's future, and either in late 1785 or early 1786 he immigrated to New Brunswick with the intention of resuming the occupation of a West

Indian trader. From his point of view this move had much to offer, since with the closing of the West Indies to American shipping after 1783 the trade of British North America with that market had increased significantly.

"Give you joy of the acquisition," wrote Sampson Salter Blowers* in a letter informing Ward Chipman* that Arnold had landed in Halifax and was on his way to Saint John. This comment was typical of the reception Arnold was to receive in his new home. Shortly after arriving in Saint John he established a trading partnership with his son Richard and Monson Hayt, a former loyalist officer whom he had met in New York. Using a ship constructed by Nehemiah Beckwith of Maugerville, the firm conducted a profitable trade with the West Indies, and Arnold was soon secure enough financially to send home for his wife. As before, however, he continued to be enmeshed in controversy. Widely unpopular amongst the loyalists because of the honours that had been showered upon him, Arnold did nothing to improve matters by provoking a storm of litigation in the small, tightly knit community of Saint John. His firm launched several suits against its debtors, and Arnold himself sued Edward WINSLOW in 1789. At about the same time Hayt and Arnold dissolved their partnership and became involved in a complicated series of legal actions. The most significant of these concerned Hayt's charge that a fire which destroyed the firm's store in July 1788 had been deliberately set by Arnold for the sake of the insurance money. Arnold promptly sued for slander and the case went to trial before judges Isaac Allan and Joshua UPHAM in September 1791, with Hayt being represented by Elias Hardy* and Arnold by Chipman and Jonathan Bliss*. The jury found Hayt guilty but, reflecting the prevalent animosity towards Arnold, awarded damages of only 20 shillings. Thus insulted, Arnold soon afterwards returned to England.

This was not the end of Arnold's connection with British North America. In 1794 Arnold and three of his sons petitioned the Executive Council of Upper Canada for a township grant. The council set aside this request, noting that the grant would be awarded when the petitioners took up residence in the colony. By the late 1790s Arnold's sons Richard and Henry had moved to Upper Canada and taken up lands in Wolford and Augusta townships. Arnold himself never considered venturing into "that Inhospitable Wilderness," but he continued none the less to petition for sizeable chunks of Upper Canadian land as a reward for past services. Convinced that "there is no other Man in England, who has made so great Sacrifices as I have done of Property, Rank, Prospects &c., in support of Government, and no Man who has received less in Return!," Arnold petitioned in 1797 for a grant to his family of 50,000 acres. When told

that such demands were excessive, he replied that he would be satisfied with 5,000 acres for himself and 1,200 acres for each member of his family. At this point the Home Department turned for advice to John Graves SIMCOE, the former lieutenant governor of Upper Canada. In a letter of 26 March 1798, Simcoe warned the Home secretary, the Duke of Portland, that Arnold was "a character extremely obnoxious to the *original* Loyalists of America," but he also observed that there was no legal impediment to granting his petition – provided his demands were scaled down considerably. Soon afterwards Simcoe wrote another letter to Portland in which he argued that to avoid setting a dangerous precedent – other individuals with no intention of settling in the colony might be encouraged by Arnold's example – the petition should be granted at the behest of the crown rather than by the colonial authorities alone. Portland accepted this advice and on 12 June 1798 instructed Peter RUSSELL, the administrator of Upper Canada, to award Arnold a grant of 13,400 acres "on the usual terms and conditions, that of residence alone excepted." On 29 October of the following year these lands – situated in the townships of Gwillimbury East and Gwillimbury North – were granted to Arnold by order in council.

Arnold's last years in England were miserable ones. He still was unable to obtain a military command, and in July 1792 he had to fight a duel with the Earl of Lauderdale after the latter had impugned his honour in the House of Lords. In 1793, in a bid to improve his financial position, he again established a West Indian trading company. The following year he was captured on Guadeloupe by French forces but soon escaped. He then worked for a time as a volunteer under Sir Charles Grey, the British army commander in the West Indies, acting as an agent of West Indian commercial interests and assisting in the supply service; his conduct during this period was responsible for Portland's decision to grant his request for land in Upper Canada. Returning to England in 1795, he tried his hand at privateering but suffered heavy losses. Towards the end of his life he was plagued with ill health. When he died on 14 June 1801, his wife Margaret offered a sad comment on his last years: "For his own sake the change is a most happy one, as the disappointment of all his [pecuniary] expectations, with the numerous vexations and mortifications he has endured, had so broken his spirits and destroyed his nerves, that he has been for a long time past incapable of the smallest enjoyment." Arnold was buried in the crypt of St Mary's, Battersea (London), where his wife was also buried three years later. In his will he bequeathed his estate to Margaret, though he also made provision for his sister Hannah and his sons Richard and Henry; John Sage, an illegitimate son he had fathered (apparently in New Brunswick), was left 1,200 acres of land in Upper Canada and a small annuity. The claims against the estate were so great, however, that Margaret had little left over after paying the debts.

Benedict Arnold certainly had his flaws. A vain, arrogant, and stubborn man, he was not capable of the tact that was important in both civilian and military life. He also was sensitive and proud, so proud in fact that he could not rise above his misfortunes by taking a lofty, stoical attitude; instead, as his treason demonstrated perfectly, he agonized over insults and slights to his honour, waiting for the day when revenge would be his. Yet, if Arnold was not a great man, there can be no doubt concerning his abilities as a military officer. He was an inspiring leader of men, whether he was conducting his troops through the Maine wilderness or mounting a charge against a British redoubt at Bemis Heights. In addition, he was brave to the point of recklessness. During the Quebec invasion, the naval engagement on Lake Champlain, the Saratoga campaign, the battle at Danbury – at all these times Arnold showed how remarkably courageous he really was, and his men admired him for it. Unfortunately, because of his treason, Arnold's accomplishments on the field of battle were quickly forgotten. In one sense, this was unfair, for Arnold was only one of many to change sides during the course of the war. Moreover, since the revolutionary government was too young a creature to have acquired any genuine legitimacy before 1783, Arnold, and others like him, could easily defend their treason by arguing that they were simply returning to their original allegiance. But of course, Arnold was not an ordinary traitor – he was Washington's ablest general, admired by Americans and British alike. He was also a traitor who compounded his crime with treachery, accepting money in exchange for military intelligence and the surrender of an American garrison. In these circumstances, it is hardly surprising that, in the American popular mind, Arnold's name has become a byword for treason and deceit. Every revolution needs a villain, or set of villains, who somehow personify disloyalty to the national cause, and in Benedict Arnold the American people found what they were looking for.

CURTIS FAHEY

PAC, MG 11, [CO 42] Q, 11–12; RG 1, L3, 1: A1/28–29, 45; 3: A5/24. PRO, CO 42/285: 195–205, 218–34; 42/321: 206–19, 222–26, 232. Ainslie, *Canada preserved* (Cohen). *American arch.* (Clarke and Force), 4th ser., vols.2–6; 5th ser., 1–3. [Charles Carroll], *Journal of Charles Carroll of Carrollton, during his visit to Canada in 1776, as one of the commissioners from Congress*, ed. Brantz Mayer (Baltimore, Md., 1845). *Corr. of Hon. Peter Russell* (Cruikshank and Hunter), vol.2. [Jacob Danford], "Quebec under siege, 1775–1776: the 'memorandums' of Jacob Danford," ed. J. F. Roche, *CHR*, 50 (1969): 68–85. [Hugh Finlay], "Journal of the siege and blockade of Quebec by the American rebels, in autumn 1775 and winter 1776," Literary and Hist. Soc. of Quebec, *Hist. Docs.* (Quebec), 4th ser. (1875): [3]–25. *Letters of members of the Continental Congress*, ed. E. C. Burnett (8v., Washington, 1921–36), 1–2. *March to Quebec: journals of the members of Arnold's expedition*, ed. K. L. Roberts (New York, 1938). U.S., Continental Congress, *Journals of the Continental Congress, 1774–1789*, ed. W. C. Ford *et al.* (34v., Washington, 1904–37), 4–5, 7. M. M. Boatner, *Encyclopedia of the American revolution* (rev. ed., New York, 1974). *DAB*. *DCB*, vol.4 (biogs. of Sir Charles Douglas and Richard Montgomery). *DNB*. Reid, *Loyalists in Ont.*

I. N. Arnold, *The life of Benedict Arnold; his patriotism and his treason* (Chicago, 1888). B. R. Boylan, *Benedict Arnold: the dark eagle* (New York, 1973). J. T. Flexner, *The traitor and the spy: Benedict Arnold and John André* (New York, 1953). D. S. Freeman, *George Washington: a biography* (7v., New York, 1948–[57]), 3–5. C. G. Robinson, *Pioneer profiles of New Brunswick settlers* (Belleville, Ont., 1980). J. H. Smith, *Our struggle for the fourteenth colony: Canada and the American revolution* (2v., New York, 1907). Stanley, *Canada invaded*. J. G. Taylor, *Some new light on the later life and last resting place of Benedict Arnold and of his wife Margaret Shippen* (London, 1931). Carl Van Doren, *Secret history of the American revolution . . .* (New York, 1941). W. M. Wallace, *Traitorous hero; the life and fortunes of Benedict Arnold* (New York, [1954]). A. T. Mahan, "The naval campaign of 1776 on Lake Champlain," *Scribner's Magazine* (New York and London), 23 (January–June 1898): 147–60. E. L. Teed, "Footprints of Benedict Arnold, late major-general congressional army of the American colonies, late brigadier-general British army," N.B. Hist. Soc., *Coll.*, no.20 (1971): 57–97. L. B. Walker, "Life of Margaret Shippen, wife of Benedict Arnold," *Pa. Magazine of Hist. and Biog.* (Philadelphia), 24 (1900): 257–66, 401–29; 25 (1901): 20–46, 145–90, 289–302, 457–97; 26 (1902): 71–80, 224–44, 322–34, 464–68.

ARNOLDI, MICHAEL, silversmith; b. 19 June 1763 in Montreal (Que.), son of Peter Arnoldi, a soldier who came from Hesse (Federal Republic of Germany), and Philipina Maria (Phébé) Horn; d. unmarried 27 Aug. 1807 in Trois-Rivières, Lower Canada.

Michael Arnoldi seems to have served his apprenticeship in Robert CRUICKSHANK's shop in Montreal, since he was already in business with him by the time he was 21. In fact, an announcement in the *Quebec Gazette* of 14 Oct. 1784 advised the creditors and debtors of the firm of Cruickshank and Arnoldi that it would be dissolved on 1 November and that Cruickshank was "duly authorized" to collect accounts and to settle debts. When in 1787 a legal separation was being arranged between his sister Phebe*, who lived with him, and John Justus Diehl, Arnoldi was residing at Saint-Philippe-de-Laprairie. That post seems to have been a busy one, where numerous silversmiths producing trade silver, for example Dominique Rousseau*, John Oakes*, and Christian Grothé, at some point owned properties.

In 1788 Arnoldi stamped his mark on a silver cross

he had made for the church in Varennes. Despite the announcement of 1784, he remained in partnership with Cruickshank until 17 Feb. 1789, when Cruickshank bought up the "Stocks Goods Wares and Merchandize," as well as the accounts of the firm, for £150. In September, Arnoldi drew up a handwritten will bequeathing his furnishings and clothes to his brother Peter, and all his other belongings to his mother. At that time he was residing on Rue Saint-François in Montreal.

Arnoldi was still living there when he signed a lease with his brother Peter and John Oakes on 9 May 1792; the two rented his shop and silversmith's tools, valued at £113 12s. 4d., for a period of two years. The partners were to pay rent for the house and also to provide him with lodgings, heat, food, and laundry and to supply him "annually with a suit of extra-fine cloth of his choosing." There was a clause pressing him not to move away, since the young partners would be deprived of the benefits of his knowledge. The lease indicates the reasons for Arnoldi's action: "Given his disabilities and being no longer able to attend to his aforementioned profession of silversmith, . . . [he wishes] to aid the aforementioned Sieurs Pierre Arnoldi, his brother, and John Oakes in the aforementioned profession of silversmith." A magnificent tea service resulted from this brief association: it bears Michael's mark accompanied by another with the initials AO, for Arnoldi and Oakes. But the lease was annulled prematurely on 8 Jan. 1793, and the partners then owed Michael £17 14s. 4d. for the tools not returned to him. In April he disinherited Peter and made his mother his sole heir.

In February 1794 Arnoldi, "a silversmith living in Montreal," inherited £150 from Johann Michael Mayer. He is believed to have subsequently purchased an inn at Trois-Rivières and to have given it to his mother on 11 April 1799. In return she was to undertake to keep him. In June an Arnoldi bought tools at the sale in Montreal of silversmith Louis-Alexandre Picard*'s estate, but it may have been Peter, who was in business as a silversmith on Rue Notre-Dame in 1797. In fact virtually nothing is known about Arnoldi's life from 1795 until his death in 1807 at Trois-Rivières. At that time he was still mentioned as being a silversmith.

His own mark and his brother Peter's are strikingly similar: the initials MA or PA are inscribed in a rectangle with a clipped upper right corner. A number of authors have until now attributed the mark CA to Charles Arnoldi, a brother. However, all the known primary sources say that Charles was a clockmaker. It may be supposed that the mark CA was used by the firm of Cruickshank and Arnoldi, especially since its shape and style of writing resemble unmistakably the mark used by Cruickshank, the principal partner. During the five years or so that it was in business, the

firm was in a position to turn out the numerous objects of trade silver and the other examples of the silversmith's art that bear the mark CA.

Michael Arnoldi's brief career turned out to be important because of the partnerships formed and the superiority of his work to that of many other silversmiths. The abundance, variety, and aesthetic qualities of his works bear witness to his talent and enthusiasm, which unfortunately were trammelled by the state of his health.

ROBERT DEROME

[Works by Michael Arnoldi are held in Quebec City at the Musée du Québec and at the archbishop's palace; in Montreal by the Religious Hospitallers of St Joseph; in Ottawa in the Henry Birks Collection of Silver at the National Gallery of Canada; and in two churches in the province of Quebec: Sainte-Famille (Boucherville) and Sainte-Geneviève (Berthierville).

In my view statements by Édouard Fabre Surveyer, infra, in particular that Arnoldi was still practising in Montreal in 1802 and that he was reported to have taken on as apprentice his nephew Peter Diehl (incorrectly named John Justus Diehl), should be treated cautiously. A notarial act (ANQ-M, CN1-29, 5 Feb. 1800) indicates that this nephew was placed with surgeons as an apprentice for seven years. R.D.]

ANQ-M, CN1-29, 19 Feb. 1783; 1 March, 11 Sept. 1787; 16 Jan., 17 Feb. 1789; 2 Sept. 1793; 18 Feb. 1794; CN1-121, 1er sept. 1789, 9 mai 1792, 6 nov. 1793; CN1-134, 18 févr. 1817; CN1-185, 27 Dec. 1806; 23 July, 22 Aug. 1807; CN1-269, 6 June 1799. MAC-CD, Fonds Morisset, 2, A762/J65.3.2, A762/M621.1. Quebec Gazette, 14 Oct. 1784, 30 Jan. 1806. Quebec Mercury, 24 Jan. 1817. W. H. Carter, Metallic ornaments of the North American Indians, 1400–1900 (London, Ont., 1973); North American Indian trade silver (2v., London, 1971). Robert Derome, "Delezenne, les orfèvres, l'orfèvrerie, 1740–1790" (MA thesis, univ. de Montréal, 1974). Langdon, Canadian silversmiths. Traquair, Old silver of Quebec. Édouard Fabre Surveyer, "Une famille d'orfèvres," BRH, 46 (1940): 310–15. É.-Z. Massicotte, "Dominique Rousseau, maître orfèvre et négociant en pelleteries," BRH, 49 (1943): 342–48. H. T. Schwarz, "Les orfèvres de la Nouvelle-France," Vie des arts (Montréal), no.24 (automne 1961): 39–43.

ARTIGNY, MICHEL-AMABLE BERTHELOT D'. See BERTHELOT

ASKIN (Erskine), JOHN, fur trader, merchant, office holder, and militia officer; b. 1739 in Aughnacloy (Northern Ireland), son of James Askin, a shopkeeper, and Alice Rea (Rae); d. 1815 in Sandwich (Windsor), Upper Canada.

According to family tradition, the Askins were related to John Erskine, 23rd Earl of Mar, whose unsuccessful revolt in 1715 forced some of the family to move to Ireland from Scotland. John Askin came to North America in 1758 and was a sutler with the British army at Albany, N.Y. Following the capitulation of New France he entered the western fur trade

Askin

and formed a series of partnerships, the most notable of which included Major Robert Rogers*. Bankrupted by Pontiac*'s uprising of 1763, the firm was dissolved, but Askin was not cleared of his debts until 1771. Meanwhile, some time in the mid 1760s Askin had moved to Michilimackinac (Mackinaw City, Mich.). He ran a trading store in the settlement, was commissary for the garrison, and farmed. It was at Michilimackinac that he formed the close ties with traders Isaac TODD, James McGILL, and Alexander Henry* that were to be of such significance in his business and personal life. He also established a cordial relationship with Arent Schuyler DePeyster*, commandant during the 1770s, and had likely been on good terms with his predecessors as well. Not only were such friendships valuable in themselves to Askin; they were also important to his economic interests. Commandants were in a position to regulate trade with the Indians, allocate shipping space (private vessels being prohibited on the Great Lakes during and after the American revolution), and tacitly approve illegal purchases of land from the Indians. In 1780 a conflict with Patrick SINCLAIR, who had recently arrived to take charge at Michilimackinac, may have been instrumental in Askin's decision to move to Detroit (Mich.).

In 1781 Askin signed a co-partnership agreement with merchants Robert HAMILTON and Richard CARTWRIGHT. He was to take care of the business (selling supplies to the Indian trade and the garrisons and buying furs) at Detroit and the upper posts while Hamilton and Cartwright managed affairs at Fort Niagara (near Youngstown, N.Y.). The firm of Todd and McGill was to look after the Montreal aspects of the concern. When the co-partnership was dissolved in 1784 it was indebted to Todd and McGill for £9,261. That same year Askin entered into partnership with William ROBERTSON, a Detroit merchant, and this arrangement was not terminated until 1787. Meanwhile, in 1786, Askin joined with five other Detroit firms in the Miamis Company, an attempt to bring to the trading business south of the Great Lakes the efficiency and profitability of the North West Company. Circumstances were different, however. The animal population was declining and the Indians were in a state of more or less open warfare with the Americans [see MICHIKINAKOUA]. Fur exports from Detroit continued to drop – from 5,000 packs in 1784 to 1,900 in 1796. By 1789 the Miamis Company was dead. Askin was becoming increasingly indebted to his Montreal suppliers Todd and McGill and Alexander Henry but, although the situation prompted a number of requests for payment, the friendly relationships never deteriorated and these merchants, now among the foremost in Canada, continued to shield Askin from financial ruin.

Askin was not oblivious to the precarious state of the fur trade and he made many efforts to generate income from other sources. In 1788 the British had opened the Great Lakes to private vessels, and Askin took the opportunity to go into the shipping business. In 1793, probably through the influence of Todd and McGill, he obtained a contract to supply corn and flour to the NWC. Selling provisions to the garrison was always important to a merchant and from 1791 to 1795 particularly another chance of sales to the government presented itself – the furnishing of supplies to the Indians who had gathered on the Miamis (Maumee) River to make a last stand against the Americans. Askin did not neglect these opportunities.

Much of Askin's hope for prosperity seems to have been pinned on his land speculations. As early as 1789 Todd and McGill reproved him for having £8,000 tied up in real property. "It is more than any man in business should keep from the circulation of his Trade and in the part of the Country where yours is placed the tenure of it is but uncertain . . . ," wrote McGill, advising him to sell at least half what he owned. In the 1790s, however, Askin engaged in even larger scale speculation. By 1794 the British government had agreed to evacuate the posts south of the Great Lakes that it had retained after the 1783 treaty with the United States, and many British residents of Detroit tried to accumulate land holdings from the Indians before the transfer to American authority occurred. With his son John, Patrick McNIFF, and others he was a member of a partnership that acquired from the Indians a huge tract along the south shore of Lake Erie – the Cuyahoga Purchase. He was also involved in an attempt to get title to the entire lower peninsula of Michigan. The American government opposed these schemes and both came to nothing. Over the years Askin succeeded in accumulating numerous properties in Upper Canada, which was to become his home after 1802. As a merchant he was in a favourable position to acquire land for debts, and no doubt by this means as well as through various purchases he built up his holdings. From 1791 to 1794 he sat on the district land board, which dealt with the location of claims and title to them. Either he or his son John was appointed in 1798 to the Heir and Devisee Commission, a body that was to rule on the validity of certain types of claim. Both offices would have made their holder well informed about what land might be available for purchase.

From the American revolution to 1796 Detroit was under military government, with little civil jurisdiction. In 1789 Askin became a justice of the peace there, and in this capacity took part in the enforcement of "such regulations . . . as are generally practiced in the internal polity of the towns of Quebec and Montreal and which are most conducive to prevent public nuisances, and to preserve the health and convenience of the inhabitants." Although Askin continued to reside in Detroit after it was turned over to the Americans in 1796, he chose to remain a British subject and became a JP for the Western District of Upper Canada in 1796.

In the spring of 1802 Askin moved to Sandwich, a change of location he had apparently been intending to make for some time. Although much of his land passed to Todd and McGill in payment of his debts, they gave him back the property on which he established his estate, Strabane, near Sandwich, and he acted as land agent for them. He continued to hold extensive lands of his own, acquiring the nickname the Count of Kent. As in his early years he took a great interest in farming, recording in a diary the day-to-day activities of his farm. He seems to have lived in considerable comfort. An inventory of his estate in 1787 listed among other things carriages, silver plate, mahogany furniture, and a well-stocked library.

Although Askin's first three children, John, Catherine, and Madelaine, were probably born to the Indian slave Manette (Monette) whom he freed in 1766, he made no distinction between them and the nine children of his marriage to Marie-Archange Barthe, contracted at Detroit on 21 June 1772. His connection with the Barthes, a prominent local family, soon gave him a relative in high office, since in 1774 his wife's sister married Alexander GRANT, an officer in the marine forces on the Great Lakes and later an executive councillor. John Askin Jr became collector of customs for Amherstburg in 1801 and storekeeper for the Indian Department at St Joseph Island, Upper Canada, in 1807. Askin's other children married British military officers or members of locally influential families. Catherine's second marriage was to Robert Hamilton. Thérèse married Thomas McKEE, son of the deputy superintendent general of Indian affairs in Upper Canada, Alexander McKee*.

Askin's correspondence with those of his children who lived at a distance reveals a great fondness and pride. Looking back in his old age he wrote, "All my Children . . . continue to behave as I could wish And I think Mrs Askin and I have lived so long at peace with each other that I do not dread any rupture will take place in future." His kindness extended beyond his own family. In a letter of 1778 from Michilimackinac to trader Charles Paterson he rebuked Paterson for allowing a child "that every body but yourself says is yours" to be sold to the Ottawas. Askin had retrieved the child and he informed Paterson, "He's at your service if you want him, if not I shall take good care of him untill he is able to earn his Bread without Assistance." Mixing good sense with humour he wrote to another colleague, Sampson Fleming, who had recently become the father of a baby boy, "I beg you will not kill him with d-m-d Physick. . . . If I hear any more of your tampering with him & Mrs Fleming permits me, I will go down & take him from you."

His attitude towards his role as lieutenant-colonel of militia is equally charming. "On[c]e a year," he reported in 1805 to DePeyster, "I put on my best Cloths & as Colonel Commands the Militia . . . make them Fire in Honor to the best of Kings. If we dont all Fire at once thats no matter[.] a Drink generally closes the Scene."

Distant though Askin was from the cultural centres of his time, his letters ring with the rationalist assumptions of his age. Writing to Alexander Henry in 1796 he remarked, "I think before a man's two hours dead he Knows more about . . . [religion] than all those who remain behind. at Same time surely there can be no risk, in being what all the world agrees is good; and this is in the power of all who are disposed to be so."

During the War of 1812 Askin had four sons, two sons-in-law, and ten grandchildren fighting for the British and one son-in-law for the Americans. As his health failed, his son Charles took over responsibility for the family estate and Askin died at the age of 76.

DAVID R. FARRELL

AO, MS 536. DPL, Burton Hist. Coll., John Askin papers. PAC, MG 19, A3. "Board of land office, District of Hesse," AO *Report*, 1905: 1–268. *John Askin papers* (Quaife). *Windsor border region* (Lajeunesse). H. P. Beers, *The French & British in the old northwest: a bibliographical guide to archive and manuscript sources* (Detroit, 1964). D. R. Farrell, "Detroit, 1783–1796: the last stages of the British fur trade in the old northwest" (PHD thesis, Univ. of Western Ont., London, 1968). *History of Wayne County and the city of Detroit, Michigan*, ed. C. M. Burton et al. (4v., Chicago, 1930), 1. I. A. Johnson, *The Michigan fur trade* (Lansing, Mich., 1919). N. V. Russell, *The British régime in Michigan and the old northwest, 1760–1796* (Northfield, Minn., 1939). Wilson, "Enterprises of Robert Hamilton." C. M. Burton, "Detroit biographies: John Askin," *Burton Hist. Coll. Leaflet* (Detroit), 3 (1924–25): 49–64. John Clarke, "The role of political position and family and economic linkage in land speculation in the Western District of Upper Canada, 1788–1815," *Canadian Geographer* (Toronto), 19 (1975): 18–34. M. M. Quaife, "The John Askin papers, volume II: 1796–1820," *Burton Hist. Coll. Leaflet*, 9 (1930–31): 67–82. Malcolm Wallace, "Pioneers of the Scotch settlement on the shore of Lake St. Clair," *OH*, 41 (1949): 173–200.

ATIATOHARONGWEN (**Thiathoharongouan**, meaning his body is taken down from hanging or one who pulls down the people; also known as **Louis Atayataghronghta**, **Louis Cook**, and **Colonel Louis**), Mohawk chief; b. *c.* 1740 in Saratoga (Schuylerville, N.Y.); d. October 1814 on the Niagara frontier.

Atiatoharongwen was the son of a black man and a Saint-François Abenaki woman. All three were captured in a French attack on Saratoga, probably that

Atiatoharongwen

conducted in 1745 by Paul Marin* de La Malgue. Atiatoharongwen's father became a servant in Montreal (Que.), but the boy was rescued by the Indians of Sault-Saint-Louis (Caughnawaga, Que.) from a French officer who, thinking him a black, had claimed him as a prize. Mother and son then went to live with the Caughnawagas, where Atiatoharongwen became attached to the Jesuit missionary Jean-Baptiste Tournois* and was eventually converted to Roman Catholicism. Although illiterate throughout life, Atiatoharongwen became fluent in Mohawk, French, and English. The boy evidently possessed a keen mind, and he demonstrated a precocious interest in the councils of the tribe.

Along with other Caughnawaga warriors, Atiatoharongwen served with the French in the Seven Years' War. He took part in the campaign against Major-General Edward Braddock in 1755 and was wounded during a skirmish with the British at Carillon (near Ticonderoga, N.Y.) in the spring of 1756. That August he participated in the conquest of Oswego (N.Y.) [see François-Pierre de Rigaud* de Vaudreuil] and in July 1758 fought against James Abercromby* in the defence of Carillon, where his bravery, ability, and knowledge of French had earned him the command of a party of Indians; he was also with the Indian forces of François de Lévis* in the French attack on Quebec in April 1760.

After the war Atiatoharongwen returned to Caughnawaga, where on 11 July 1763 he married Marie-Charlotte. Some time before the outbreak of the American revolution, he moved to the vicinity of the St Regis reservation. Never reconciled to British rule, in 1775 he became strongly attached to the American cause and, although most Caughnawagas preferred to remain neutral, he persuaded a small number to become partisans. He visited General George Washington in his camp at Cambridge, Mass., in August 1775, bringing news of the favourable disposition of the Indians and Canadians towards the American colonists. Later that year he returned to the province of Quebec as a messenger to assist Brigadier-General Richard Montgomery*'s expedition, and subsequently he served the Americans on numerous occasions as a scout and messenger.

When Atiatoharongwen again visited Washington in January 1776, he offered to raise 400 or 500 men. Washington hesitated, not sure that the Indians' contribution would justify the expense of engaging them; Major-General Philip John Schuyler advised him not to employ them "if we can decently get rid of their offer." By 1777 Atiatoharongwen was in command of the Indian Rangers, a company attached to the 1st New York Regiment; that year he led a party of Oneidas and Tuscaroras in the American victory over Major-General John Burgoyne* near Saratoga, where his warriors distinguished themselves by their bravery. On 15 June 1779 Atiatoharongwen was awarded a lieutenant-colonel's commission by the second Continental Congress. In October 1781, at the head of 60 warriors from the Oneida settlements, he helped Lieutenant-Colonel Marinus Willet resist Major John Ross*'s raid on the Mohawk valley.

After the war Atiatoharongwen lived with the Oneidas, probably at Kanōʔalohaleʔ (Sherrill), N.Y., and briefly at Onondaga (near Syracuse), N.Y., where he married Marguerite (Monique) Thewanihattha (Tewennihata); they would have several children. About 1789 he returned to land he held near St Regis and became a chief at the reservation. In 1792 he went to Philadelphia to confer with Secretary of War Henry Knox on the tense situation in the Ohio region, which the British had refused to evacuate following the American revolution, and he promised to use his influence to keep the Indians there peaceful.

In 1796 a deputation consisting of Atiatoharongwen, Thomas Williams [Tehoragwanegen*], and others represented the St Regis and Caughnawaga Indians and their allies in negotiations with the government of New York State to obtain compensation for the lost use of vast tracts of land. On 31 May a treaty extinguishing the Indians' claims was reluctantly signed by the Indian delegates for the sum of £1,230 and an annuity of £213. Criticized by their people for having signed the agreement, the delegates, and especially Atiatoharongwen, sought to deflect culpability to Joseph Brant [THAYENDANEGEA]. They charged that he was responsible for the 999-year land leases signed in 1787 and 1788 which the Americans had used to undercut the delegates' position; in fact Brant had only witnessed the documents, as had Atiatoharongwen himself. The latter was chosen to go yearly to collect the annuity generated by the treaty, but according to the Roman Catholic missionary at St Regis, Roderic MacDonell, writing in 1801, "he makes away with the greatest part of the money and disposes of lands on the American lines without consulting the Indians" at St Regis or Caughnawaga, so annoying them that they intended to sue him.

Attempts by British officials in the Canadas to break Atiatoharongwen's allegiance to the Americans with the enticement of a pension were unavailing, but few at St Regis shared his attachment, his personal following being, wrote MacDonell in 1801, "about four families." During the War of 1812 he was again commissioned by the Americans and was active in campaigns on the Niagara frontier. He died there, much lamented by his comrades, as a result of injuries received in a fall from his horse during a skirmish, and was buried near Buffalo, N.Y.

Atiatoharongwen had been, according to the historian Franklin Benjamin Hough, "tall and athletic, broad shouldered and strongly built, with a very dark complexion, and somewhat curly hair, which in old age became gray"; MacDonell described him as "a black man." His considerable talents both on the battlefield and in council had made his services highly valued by his French and American allies and his activities a constant source of irritation for British officials.

BARBARA GRAYMONT

[The Gallery of Fine Arts, Yale University (New Haven, Conn.), has in its collection a small pencil sketch by John Trumbull of Atiatoharongwen labelled "Col. Joseph Lewis, chief of the Oneida Indians." This and other sketches served as preliminary drawings for Trumbull's "Death of General Montgomery in the attack of Quebec," also at Yale University. However, the artist made no claim to have accurately represented Atiatoharongwen or any but three of the other figures. Atiatoharongwen did have his portrait done during a visit to Albany, N.Y., but the painting has been lost.

The most comprehensive and valuable biographical account of Atiatoharongwen is in F. B. Hough, *A history of St. Lawrence and Franklin counties, New York, from the earliest times to the present time* (Albany, 1853), 182–98, based on information obtained by Hough from one of the chief's daughters, Mary. None the less, Hough's statement that Atiatoharongwen and his parents were captured at Saratoga (Schuylerville, N.Y.) "towards the close of 1755" is to be questioned since it conflicts with other data in the account and with events of the time.

There is a reference to Atiatoharongwen under the probably erroneous name of Quitawape in *Anthony Wayne . . . the Wayne–Knox–Pickering–McHenry correspondence*, ed. R. C. Knopf (Pittsburgh, Pa., 1960; repr. Westport, Conn., 1975), 59. B.G.]

AP, Saint-François-Xavier (Caughnawaga), Reg. des baptêmes, mariages et sépultures, 11 juill. 1763; Saint-Régis, Reg. des baptêmes, mariages et sépultures, 6 juill., 3 nov. 1801. National Arch. (Washington), Military record of Lewis Atayataghronghta; Pension record of Nicholas Cusick; RG 360, M247, roll 158, item 147, 3: 391. NYPL, Philip Schuyler papers, Indian boxes, box 14. N.Y. State Library (Albany), New York State land papers, 42: 135. PAC, RG 10, A1, 486: 58–62; A6, 659: 181407–9. *The balloting book, and other documents relating to military bounty lands in the state of New York* (Albany, 1825), 140, 151. N.Y., Commissioners of Indian Affairs, *Proceedings of the commissioners of Indian affairs . . .*, intro. F. B. Hough (2v. in 1, Albany, 1861), 37–40, 73, 101, 122, 132–33, 135, 139–41, 143, 150, 153–55, 176, 196, 222, 229, 231, 233, 272–74, 311, 349, 351, 353–54, 358, 365. U.S., Congress, *American state papers* (Lowrie et al.), class 2, 1: 123, 235, 616–20. George Washington, *The writings of George Washington, from the original manuscript sources, 1745–1799*, ed. J. C. Fitzpatrick (39v., Washington, 1931–44), 3: 397–98; 4: 274–75, 280. Gallery of Fine Arts, Yale Univ., *Key to "Death of General Montgomery in the attack of Quebec"* (n.d.). *Handbook of American Indians* (Hodge), 2: 723. F. B. Hough, *A history of St. Lawrence and Franklin counties . . .*, supra, 126–46. J. R. Simms, *Frontiersmen of New York, showing customs of the Indians, vicissitudes of the pioneer white settlers, and border strife in two wars* (2v., Albany, 1882–83); *History of Schoharie County, and border wars of New York . . .* (Albany, 1845). Eleazer Williams, *Life of Te-ho-ra-gwa-ne-gen, alias Thomas Williams, a chief of the Caughnawaga tribe of Indians in Canada . . .* (Albany, 1859), 44–45.

AUCHECHAQUE. *See* CHEJAUK

AVÈNE DES MÉLOIZES, NICOLAS RENAUD D'. *See* RENAUD

B

BABY, FRANÇOIS, businessman, militia officer, office holder, politician, seigneur, and landowner; b. 4 Oct. 1733 in Montreal (Que.), tenth child of Raymond Baby and Thérèse Le Compte Dupré; d. 6 Oct. 1820 at Quebec, Lower Canada.

François Baby's father was a fur trader who had been sufficiently successful before his death, four years after François's birth, to enable the boy to be educated at the Jesuit college at Quebec. His mother's family being deeply involved in the fur trade, and his eldest brother Jacques Baby*, *dit* Dupéront, being engaged in it by 1753, François too became active in what had become a family profession; another brother, Louis, was also a fur trader. By 1757 François was in partnership with Jacques and the youngest brother, Antoine, under the name of Baby Frères. While his brothers worked the fur-trade regions, François resided at Montreal, receiving and forwarding imported trade goods, exporting furs, and handling accounts with correspondents in Paris, Bordeaux, and in La Rochelle, where they included François Havy*, partner of Jean Lefebvre*.

During the Seven Years' War François shared to some extent in his brothers' military glories. He may have been at the battle of the Monongahela (near Pittsburgh, Pa) in 1755 under Daniel-Hyacinthe-Marie Liénard* de Beaujeu, and he undoubtedly served under François de Lévis* at the siege of Quebec in the spring of 1760. He thus merited with Jacques, Louis, and Antoine the applause of Governor Vaudreuil [Pierre de Rigaud*], who certified in July "that the sieurs Baby brothers, merchants of Montreal, have on all occasions given the greatest proofs of their zeal and disinterest in the service of the king [and] that they have distinguished themselves by their bravery and their talents, in almost all the actions that they have undertaken against the English. . . ."

The war did not prevent the Babys from continuing in business or keeping an eye to their future interests. In February 1760, well before the capture of Montreal

Baby

by the British, Simon Jauge of Bordeaux advised François by way of England, no doubt in response to queries from him, that he might make contact in London with the firm of Thomas, Thomas and Son, Jauge's correspondent there. Taken prisoner to England in September, François likely did call on the London firm before obtaining a passport to go to France. He settled in La Rochelle, probably with the intention of remaining in France if Canada was not recovered, since, like Jacques, he had refused to swear allegiance to the king of Great Britain. The Babys, nevertheless, were selling their furs on the London market and importing English trade goods by 1762. From France, François endeavoured to ensure the supply of trade goods to his brothers and maintained contacts with British and French trading houses. When it became clear that the conquered colony would remain a British possession, he liquidated most of the family's French assets and oversaw the transfer of commercial relations to London in order to be of consequence in the reconstituted trade. Through his French correspondents he was put in touch with a number of London firms, including Joseph and Henry Guinaud, which soon became his principal supplier.

Baby returned to Montreal late in 1763 and once again acted as intermediary for Antoine and Jacques, who were based at Detroit (Mich.). However, he soon established his own wholesale business at Quebec, importing British spirits and manufactures; by 1765 he had taken up residence there. Although he travelled often to Montreal to conduct his brothers' business, a permanent agent was needed in the city, and the merchant Pierre GUY was chosen. Perhaps while in London, Baby had, along with Joseph and Henry Guinaud, entered into partnership with Michel Chartier* de Lotbinière, who needed financing for a scheme to buy seigneuries. But by 1766, seeing no return on his investment, Baby put an end to the association. In the same year he altered his relations with his principal London supplier – known from 1765 as Guinaud and Hankey – and established a mutual account, whereby it shared in the profits or the losses on its merchandise sold by Baby in the colony; as well, Baby received a commission on sales and another for handling all the London firm's cargoes to and from Quebec. In 1767 Baby's indebtedness to Guinaud and Hankey was £1,270 17s. 7d., a comment on his credit worthiness in London; that year he received merchandise valued at £2,825 4s. 6d. on behalf of the mutual account.

Like most merchants in the highly unstable commercial context of the 1760s, Baby sought security through diversification. He added to his items of commerce such products as planks, peas, oats, apples, silverware, cottons, helmet plumes, and maidenhair ferns, valued for their medicinal proper-

ties. He also speculated in wheat and furs. In 1769 he was the third largest investor in the fur trade, but by the early 1770s Robert Hankey was complaining that the poor quality of Baby's furs, obtained largely from Jacques in the Detroit area, resulted in serious marketing problems in London. In addition to these activities Baby operated at least one schooner and possibly other vessels on the St Lawrence and its tributaries, ensuring delivery of purchases to his warehouses and sales to his customers, and carrying on a cargo trade for other merchants when possible.

In 1773 grave problems in London and France required Baby's return to Europe. No longer satisfied with Hankey (Henry Guinaud had become bankrupt in 1769), Baby transferred his accounts with that merchant to Thomas Pecholier, also of London, while maintaining long-standing relations with Thomas, Thomas and Son. Once again he crossed to France. He had wound up most of his family's affairs there before leaving in 1763, but not until this trip was he able to close the books on his and his brothers' holdings in paper money from the French régime as well as on certain other monetary transactions. The family, including François, had lost heavily in these matters; for example, on one occasion in the late 1760s bills of exchange drawn on Bordeaux for 11,666 *livres* netted François only 6,056 *livres* after discount. But, despite his losses, and unlike many other Canadian merchants, he had survived the difficult transition to the new economic order in the colony. Indeed, he had done quite well; in 1772 he purchased better quarters, a stone house on Rue Sous-le-Fort, at a cost of about £350.

In the course of surviving economically Baby had acquired strongly conservative political views and the social and economic credentials to become a spokesman for the Canadian bourgeoisie. His social prominence as early as 1766 is indicated by the invitation he received to sign an address of welcome that was to be offered to Lieutenant Governor Guy CARLETON; his acceptance signalled his complete reconciliation to the British presence. Consequently, in 1773, with the British government labouring over a new constitution for the province, Baby was charged by the Canadian merchants and seigneurs with presenting a petition in London defining their position to the British authorities. It requested the preservation of traditional laws, privileges, and customs, the restoration of the boundaries of New France in order to include in the province Labrador and the fur trade of the west, and the distribution of patronage without distinction between British and Canadian subjects. Baby's defence of the petition was apparently of great value to Carleton, whose views corresponded closely to those of the seigneurs; the former attorney general of Quebec, Francis Maseres*, who opposed the petition in large measure, affirmed in 1774 that it "has been made the foundation of the Quebec Act." Baby arrived back at Quebec in May 1774 and was rewarded for his efforts with a public letter of thanks from the defenders of the act. Probably he expected more and was disappointed at having been passed over in the appointments to the Legislative Council, formed in 1775 by virtue of the Quebec Act, in favour of others who, he wrote bitterly to Pierre Guy, "thought and worked more for their own interests than for the public good." He added, "I am very much afraid that the time is not far off when Canadians will be unable to console themselves for having asked for the new form of government."

Baby took up the threads of his business once again and began looking to new ventures. In June 1775 he commissioned construction of a new schooner at Bécancour, paying in advance the entire cost price of about £280. He engaged in sealing and fur trading at the post of Saint-Augustin (Que.) in partnership with François-Joseph Cugnet*, Gabriel-Elzéar TASCHEREAU, and Nicolas-Joseph de Lafontaine de Belcour. They invested £1,400 in the first year's operations, choosing to market their products in London through Thomas, Thomas and Son. With this new enterprise, Baby transferred his interest from the old northwest to the Labrador coast.

Operations had only begun, however, when the American invasion of the colony [see Benedict ARNOLD; Richard Montgomery*] brought Baby's business to a temporary standstill. On 5 Aug. 1775 he was commissioned a captain in the Quebec militia, which he helped to organize, and in 1776 he was made commissary of military transport. Following the retreat of the Americans, Carleton appointed Baby, Taschereau, and Jenkin WILLIAMS to inquire into disloyalty among the Canadians east of Trois-Rivières during the invasion. Given the circumstances, the commissioners were required to display realism, restraint, diplomacy, and sensitivity. On 22 May they set out on a tour of parishes that would last seven weeks. Beginning around Quebec and the Île d'Orléans, they proceeded upriver along the north shore as far as Trois-Rivières, and then descended the south shore to Kamouraska. In each parish they collected information from the priest, mustered the militia, replaced officers who had collaborated with the Americans, publicly burned American commissions, and harangued the assembly on their duty of loyalty. They withdrew commissions from officers in 37 of some 50 parishes and fully absolved the local captain in only two. However, apart from the withdrawal of commissions, the only punishment recorded was the confiscation of weapons from those held to be lacking in sympathy to the government; it was a markedly mild and intelligent response. Apparently about this time Baby was appointed adjutant general of militia, and in 1778 he was promoted lieutenant-colonel.

Baby's conduct during the invasion also won for him the coveted appointment to the Legislative Council and he was sworn in as a member on 30 June 1778. Moreover, Governor HALDIMAND also took him into his unconstitutional privy council, composed of those councillors on whom he could depend for support. In late 1778 or early 1779 he appointed him a justice of the peace for the District of Quebec. Although an exaggeration, it became common opinion that he was, in the words of a woman from Boucherville, "all-powerful in the service of His Excellency the General Haldimand." Baby was one of a select few to establish a personal friendship with the usually reserved governor, and in 1780 and 1781, when Haldimand wished to buy land anonymously for a country estate at Montmorency Falls, he confided the task to Baby. Personally affable, courteous, and dignified, and now possessed of money, military rank, and political power, Baby indulged fully in the glittering social life of the upper class. In 1778 Georges-Hippolyte Le Comte* Dupré, known as Saint-Georges Dupré, wrote to him, "I imagine you are like a butterfly, flying from belle to belle. I would have been charmed to have taken part in all your celebrated festivities." By 1786 the attentions of the now 52-year-old social butterfly had alighted on 15-year-old Marie-Anne Tarieu de Lanaudière, daughter of the seigneur Charles-François Tarieu* de La Naudière, and they were married on 27 February. The couple would have 12 children, of whom 6 would survive Baby.

Baby's entrance into the governing class gradually reduced his commercial activities to secondary importance. In 1779 the Saint-Augustin operations suffered severe depredations at the hands of American corsairs; the same year Baby cut his connections with Thomas, Thomas and Son. However, his experience with the Labrador trade and his relations with Haldimand made him an ideal partner for the merchants George* and Alexander* Davison, who wanted to wrest from Thomas DUNN, William GRANT (1744–1805), and Peter Stuart the lease of the king's posts, and with it obtain a virtual monopoly of the fur trade and fisheries along the north shore of the lower St Lawrence. The Dunn group's lease expired in 1777 but, thanks in part to Lieutenant Governor Henry Hamilton*, they were able to retain the posts until 1786. Haldimand's influence carried, however; Hamilton was dismissed for his action, and on 21 June 1786 Baby and his partners signed a new lease to take effect on 1 October. Baby nominally held a one-third share in the enterprise, but in fact he no longer had a merchant's interest in the project. He had probably joined the Davisons mainly because of the political influence he could bring to bear; on 9 September, as the new lessees took over the posts, he sold his share for a pension of £150 per annum for the duration of the

Baby

lease and reimbursement of his expenses for obtaining it. Thenceforth, with the exception of a small investment of £750 in the fur trade in 1787 and the posting as late as 1790 of an occasional bond for outfits sent by Jacques and Jacques's son James Baby*, François was no longer engaged in commerce.

Politically, as well as socially and economically, Baby had drifted away from the Canadian merchants, the leadership of whom had fallen to his friend and former agent, Pierre Guy. In council, Baby was a loyal supporter of Haldimand, who shared few of the merchants' concerns. In early 1780, for example, in opposition to merchants on council such as Dunn, Grant, and George Allsopp, Baby voted in favour of Haldimand's proposal to fix the price of wheat. He became one of the most active and intelligent Canadian members of the French party, led by Adam Mabane*, which sought the preservation of the Quebec Act virtually in its entirety. In 1782 Mabane went so far as to promote Baby as successor to Hector Theophilus Cramahé* in the position of lieutenant governor, but Haldimand proposed Hamilton. Although Canadian and British merchants continued to have diverging opinions on some points, they gradually eliminated their more important differences and worked out a number of joint political demands requiring fundamental reform, if not a complete rejection, of the Quebec Act. Baby fought their demands, including that for an elected assembly, which the Canadian merchants adopted publicly after Haldimand's departure in November 1784.

As adjutant general of the militia Baby was responsible for the application of the first militia law, passed in 1777. The ordinance established a hierarchy of officers consisting of a commander-in-chief, and an adjutant general, colonels and subordinate officers at Quebec, Montreal, and Trois-Rivières, and captains and subordinate officers in the parishes. As well as assisting the regular army in the defence of the colony, the militia was required to provide it with transport and other services, collectively known as the corvée, not all of which were subject to remuneration. The vagueness of the ordinance left much latitude for arbitrary actions and despotism on the part of the army and the militia officers; Baby was the channel through which the resulting wave of complaints poured into Carleton's, and later Haldimand's, office. But Carleton and the seigneurs, who formed the backbone of the French party, had been extremely embarrassed by the failure of the habitants to fight the Americans. They (and Baby shared their view) systematically opposed reforms suggested mainly by Hugh Finlay, Henry Caldwell, and Allsopp to reduce arbitrariness, on the grounds that the militia had to be taught to submit to constituted authority. Not until 1787, with the French party much weakened following Haldimand's return to Britain, were changes finally introduced in a general militia law and in another more clearly defining the corvée. In 1788 Baby was lieutenant-colonel in the Canadian militia at Quebec.

By May of that year, through an inheritance from the estate of his father-in-law, Baby had become one of several co-proprietors of the seigneuries of Saint-Vallier and Saint-Pierre-les-Becquets. In January 1790 his revenues from these seigneuries were estimated at only £40, but Baby expanded his holdings in them shortly after. In June he purchased a farm in Saint-Vallier for about £300, and two years later he paid another co-seigneur Pierre-Ignace Aubert* de Gaspé about £125 for his one-eighth share in Saint-Pierre-les-Becquets. Yet, when appointed by Dorchester in 1790 to a committee of council charged with reporting on seigneurial tenure, Baby and another seigneur, Charles-Louis Tarieu de Lanaudière, were among those who urged its abolition. Thus, while Baby was no longer a merchant, neither was he, in his own mind, a full-fledged seigneur.

Baby was above all an office holder, and like many office holders he conducted some property transactions, although on a relatively small scale. Being wealthy and a devout Roman Catholic, he preferred to lend money through the purchase of life annuities, a form of lending acceptable to the church. He paid the borrower a certain sum in return for an annuity yielding six per cent per annum of that sum (the legal rate of interest at the time) for as long as the borrower kept the capital; the latter could buy the annuity back at any time. Between 1789 and 1806 Baby purchased at least 22 annuities for a total of 147,134 *livres*, or approximately £6,130. He had an excellent and wide-spread reputation for fairness among the élite of the colony; the largest annuities were purchased from seigneurs, merchants, and priests from Saint-Jean-Port-Joli to Montreal.

In 1792 Baby cut perhaps his last remaining link with the merchant community when he sold his house on Rue Sous-le-Fort and moved to Upper Town, at first on Rue du Parloir, then by 1795 on Rue Buade. In 1791 he was appointed to the Executive Council and in 1792 to the Legislative Council, both bodies having been created by the Constitutional Act of 1791. In 1794, 1802–3, and 1806–7 he was speaker of the Legislative Council. He was given the opportunity to act as administrator of Lower Canada in the governor's absence, but he declined on the grounds that he could not comply with the Test Act. He did receive two lesser appointments, however, those of commissioner to administer the Jesuit estates (1800) and commissioner for the relief of persons owing *lods et ventes* (1801).

During the 1790s and early 1800s Baby was prominent in the movement to promote loyalty in the city at a time when sympathy for revolutionary France, then at war with Britain, ran high [*see* David

McLane*; Robert PRESCOTT]. In June 1794 he was a member of the directing committee of the Association, formed that year to support British rule in the colony, and he signed its public declaration of loyalty to the constitution and government; in January he had signed an address to Prince EDWARD AUGUSTUS on his departure from Quebec. By 1795 he was colonel of a newly formed battalion of Canadian militia at Quebec. In June 1799 he and Jean-Antoine PANET were the only two Canadians among 13 leading citizens who launched a voluntary subscription campaign to support Britain's war effort.

Baby reaped a number of rewards for his public expressions of loyalty and his years of service to the British colonial administration. In 1792 he applied for land on the south shore of the St Lawrence, and it was recommended that he be granted 1,200 acres; however, an application for Templeton Township in October 1793 was dismissed. In 1802, on the recommendation of Lieutenant Governor Sir Robert Shore Milnes*, he was granted a life pension of £150 per annum. Six years later his salary as adjutant general was raised from £91 to £320 sterling. Moreover, as an executive councillor he was entitled to 12,000 acres of land: in 1809 he received 7,340 acres in Sherrington Township, and the remainder was granted in Tingwick Township in 1818. The following year he also received 1,800 acres in Chester Township for his militia service during the American invasion and occupation of 1775–76.

By 1810 age and ill-health had begun to impair Baby's abilities. With war in the air, in October 1811 he accepted the invitation of the commander-in-chief, Sir George PREVOST, to resign as adjutant general in return for the sinecure of chief road commissioner, which carried a salary of £150. He was replaced as adjutant general by François Vassal* de Montviel. In 1812 Baby also resigned as commissary of militia transport. He remained attached to the militia, however, as colonel of the Cap Santé battalion.

Baby had also ceased to play an active role in the affairs of state. Although he supported Prevost in his conflict with the English party, his support was probably passive, both because of his age and of his political ties with members of that party. He remained relatively active in business, however. By 1811 he had apparently acquired a number of life annuities sold by habitants of the *faubourg* Saint-Roch to the estate of the merchant William Grant. Between 1814 and 1820 Baby purchased life annuities costing a total of £4,643. In addition, he came to the rescue of his son François by paying a debt owed by François of £700.

Baby remained to the end a highly sociable man, and his home was renowned as a rendezvous of the Quebec élite. He and his wife conducted themselves socially in a manner that the church found exemplary given their rank; at the numerous gatherings she hosted, Marie-Anne invariably dressed with a modesty that contrasted with the stylish finery of her female guests. Bishop Plessis*, ordinarily critical of the worldliness of the colony's governing class, found that Baby's piety commanded his respect and friendship. At Baby's death, the directors of the Séminaire de Québec, wishing to express their gratitude for his active support of the institution, had him buried in their chapel, the *fabrique* of Notre-Dame Cathedral having closed its church to burials the year before.

To many Canadians of his time, Baby had been anglicized. He seems to have counted among his closest friends three of the most prominent members of the English party, Jonathan Sewell*, Herman Witsius Ryland*, and William Smith*, all of whom signed his burial record. Politically, he was much more comfortable with the authoritarianism of his British colleagues of the Executive and Legislative councils than with the democratically inclined politics of the Canadian party in the House of Assembly. But if some thought he had sold his birthright to preserve his economic well-being, others felt that he had genuinely sought to serve Canadian interests as a leading member of the governing clique for almost half a century.

JOHN CLARKE

[The prime source for studying François Baby is the voluminous Baby collection at AUM, P 58. Transcripts and microfilm copies are available in PAC, MG 24, L3. Dale Miquelon made full use of this collection in his study of Baby's business career in "Baby family." The journal kept by Baby, Gabriel-Elzéar Taschereau, and Jenkin Williams is at the Bibliothèque nationale; it has been edited by Ægidius Fauteux and appears in ANQ *Rapport*, 1927–28: 435–99; 1929–30: 138–40, under the title "Journal par Messrs Frans Baby, Gab. Taschereau et Jenkin Williams. . . ." It has also appeared separately as *Journal de MM. Baby, Taschereau et Williams, 1776* (Québec, 1929). The author is grateful to the Social Sciences and Humanities Research Council of Canada for its financial assistance and to James H. Lambert for his contribution. J.C.]

ANQ-M, CE1-51, 4 oct. 1733. ANQ-Q, CE1-1, 27 févr. 1786, 9 oct. 1820; CN1-16, 8 juin, 2, 4, 26 juill., 14, 19 sept. 1816; CN1-83, 9 sept. 1786; 6 mai 1788; 11 août 1789; 31 mai, 28, 30 juin 1790; 11 déc. 1791; 18 mai, 21 juin 1792; 6 mars 1793; 10 juin 1794; CN1-99, 29 mars 1811, 20 juin 1814; CN1-107, 1er août 1817; CN1-202, 4 oct. 1765; CN1-205, 29 avril 1779; 9 mai, 13 juin 1780; 23 janv. 1783; CN1-207, 28 mars, 30 oct. 1770; 16 juin 1772; 4 oct. 1773; CN1-212, 4 avril, 7, 25 mai, 20 juill. 1818; 6 févr., 8, 22 juin 1819; 25 mai 1820; CN1-224, 13 oct. 1790; CN1-230, 8 juin 1795; 25 févr. 1797; 26 févr., 14 mai, 15 août 1798; 15 mars 1805; 26 mars 1806; 18 mars 1816; CN1-248, 29 mars, 23 juin 1775; CN1-253, 28 Sept. 1811, 26 April 1813; CN1-262, 9 oct. 1795; 16 juill. 1796; 9 mars, 13 avril 1797; 16 févr. 1798; 11 mai 1802; 12 mars, 14 août 1805; 20 mai 1806; 8 mai, 18, 19 août 1817; CN1-284, 14 sept. 1787. PAC, MG 11, [CO 42] Q, 24: 67; 88: 193; MG 30, D1, 3: 88–115; RG 1, L3L : 45–57, 111, 168, 863–66, 1095,

Bad Bird

1140–41, 1325, 1557–58, 1587, 2136, 2170, 4061, 4420, 18095–96, 18148–51, 18156–60, 18166, 18170–83, 33206, 72228, 97930; RG 4, A1: 22954, 23798, 24145, 27580; B28, 110; RG 8, I (C ser.), 32: 208; 372: 206, 208; 1169: 98; 1714: 1, 13, 95. PRO, CO 42/46: f.262; 42/47: 259 (mfm. at PAC). "Les dénombrements de Québec" (Plessis), ANQ *Rapport*, 1948–49: 71, 120, 170. *Quebec Gazette*, 29 Sept. 1766; 19 May 1774; 22 July 1777; 14 Jan. 1779; 24 Nov. 1785; 28 Sept. 1786; 14 Aug., 11 Dec. 1788; 23 April 1789; 2 May, 28 Nov. 1793; 13 Feb., 3 July 1794; 27 June 1799; 4 Dec. 1800; 7 May 1801; 14 June 1804; 10 Oct. 1811; 27 April, 24 Dec. 1812; 30 Dec. 1813; 19 Oct. 1815; 14 May, 3 Aug., 5 Oct. 1818; 12 Oct. 1820.

[É.-A.] Baby, *Mémoire de famille: l'honorable C.-E. Casgrain . . .* (Rivière-Ouelle, Qué., 1891). P.-B. Casgrain, *Mémorial des familles Casgrain, Baby et Perrault du Canada* (Québec, 1898). Miquelon, "Baby family." Neatby, *Quebec*, 23–24, 66, 73, 149, 156–57, 165, 181, 189, 198, 200, 202–3. Tousignant, "La genèse et l'avènement de la constitution de 1791," 167–69, 227. Michel Brunet, "La Conquête anglaise et la déchéance de la bourgeoisie canadienne (1760–1793)," *Amérique française* (Montréal), 13 (1955), no.2: 19–84. P.-B. Casgrain, "L'honorable François Baby," *BRH*, 12 (1906): 41–46.

BAD BIRD. *See* MADJECKEWISS

BADELARD (Badelart), PHILIPPE-LOUIS-FRANÇOIS, army officer and surgeon; b. 25 May 1728 in Coucy-le-Château, France, son of Philippe-Martin Badelard, a cooper, and Esther Bruyer; m. 23 May 1758 Marie-Charlotte Guillimin, widow of the merchant Joseph Riverin*, in L'Ancienne-Lorette (Que.), and they had two children, one of whom, Louise-Philippe, married Jean-Antoine PANET in 1779; d. 7 Feb. 1802 at Quebec, Lower Canada, and was buried two days later in L'Ancienne-Lorette.

Little is known about Philippe-Louis-François Badelard's life in France other than that he practised medicine and surgery in a hospital at Metz and served in the French regular troops before coming to Louisbourg, Île Royale (Cape Breton Island), in 1757 as surgeon-major to the two battalions of the Régiment de Berry. That year he set out with his regiment for Quebec on the *Toison d'Or*, but the vessel was shipwrecked three leagues from its destination. Having survived this tragic accident, he reached the quarters that had been assigned his regiment on Île d'Orléans on 27 September. Badelard was present at the battle of the Plains of Abraham and was taken prisoner by John FRASER, a soldier in the 78th Foot.

Under the British régime Badelard was first appointed surgeon to the Canadian militia, and in this capacity took part in the defence of Quebec against American forces in 1775 [*see* Benedict ARNOLD; Richard Montgomery*]. On 15 May 1776 he was commissioned as surgeon to the Quebec garrison. It is, however, thanks to his study of the Baie-Saint-Paul malady that his name still figures in the annals of Canadian medicine. In 1776, three years after the appearance of the disease, the origin of which was apparently connected with the presence of Scottish soldiers at Baie-Saint-Paul, Badelard was appointed by Governor Guy CARLETON as a replacement for a Dr Menzies of Quebec to investigate the nature of the malady and to treat its victims free of charge. On various occasions between 1776 and 1784 he went to visit the parishes where the disease had shown up. During the latter year, when the epidemic was affecting five per cent of the population of the province, he wrote a brochure entitled *Direction pour la guérison du mal de la baie St-Paul*, one of the earliest medical texts published in Canada. It was printed in 1785 at government expense and distributed free in both rural areas, which were the main seat of infection, and urban districts. A condensed version had already appeared four times in the *Quebec Gazette* in 1784. In his account Badelard remarked that the symptoms were first a throat inflammation and the appearance of ulcerated pustules on the genitals, then severe pain in the joints, and in the final stages swelling of the periosteum followed by general destruction of the victim's bone tissue. On the basis of these symptoms he suggested a treatment for the malady, which he did not yet dare identify but which Charles BLAKE, a Montreal surgeon, and then François-Xavier Swediaur, a doctor in Scotland, were to term correctly a venereal disease. The measures he advised to combat the illness in fact turned out to be of a curative nature. He said almost nothing about possible prophylaxis. Indeed, recourse to prevention seems scarcely to have attracted his attention. In addition to purges and lukewarm baths, in his opinion mercury proved the most effective treatment, although the therapy caused some patients to lose teeth, to go blind, and to suffer loss of memory. It was also important for those affected to watch what they ate and to have a light diet based on vegetables, cereals, dairy products, and meat broth.

Badelard was well known as a surgeon, in particular for his skill in performing cystotomies. In addition to his army duties he had a sizeable civilian practice. From 1765 to 1779 he, along with others, was doctor to the Séminaire de Québec, and he counted Bishop Jean-Olivier Briand* among his patients. His reputation finally led to his sitting on the Quebec Medical Board in 1801 and 1802.

Badelard was fairly well-to-do, as the 6,075 *livres* (5,499 of it in payment orders) he brought to his marriage indicate, and he lived in a fashionable part of Quebec. He resided on Rue des Jardins until 1784, and then on Rue Saint-Louis, where he owned two houses, one valued at £200 in 1785. His wife also held a piece of land at L'Ancienne-Lorette. Upon the death of his parents he had inherited some properties at Coucy-le-Château; he left the usufruct of these to his sister

Louise-Suzanne, probably in 1788, on the occasion of a trip to France. On 13 July 1797 he repossessed through the courts a two-storey stone house on Rue des Ursulines whose owner, George Wilds, was unable to meet payments; it was resold some months later for £234. At his death Badelard gave 12,000 *livres* to the Hôpital Général of Quebec to set up in perpetuity a foundation to provide shelter in the winter for four poor people.

Although he was one of the most respected and heeded specialists in the French-speaking wing of the medical profession, Badelard apparently was not an easy person to get along with; at any rate Louis-Joseph de Montcalm* had complained of this characteristic several times, and Marie-Charlotte Badelard left her husband around 1770 to escape from his "bad behaviour" and the "violence" he inflicted on her. In matters of religion he was not devout, and it is said that when he died, the parish priest of Notre-Dame-de-l'Annonciation at L'Ancienne-Lorette, Charles-Joseph Brassard* Deschenaux, tried to prevent his burial in the parish cemetery.

JACQUES BERNIER

Philippe-Louis-François Badelard is the author of *Direction pour la guérison du mal de la baie St-Paul* (Québec, 1785), a shorter version of which was published earlier in the *Quebec Gazette*, 29 July, 5, 19 Aug., 28 Oct. 1784, under the title "Observations sur la maladie de la Baye . . . données au public par ordre de son excellence le gouverneur."

AD, Aisne (Laon), État civil, Saint-Sauveur de Coucy-le-Château, 25 mai 1728. ANQ-Q, CN1-83, 31 août 1786; CN1-92, 28 oct. 1784, 11 août 1785; CN1-115, 23 mai 1758; CN1-205, 17 oct. 1781, 17 juill. 1782; CN1-206, 26 juill. 1798; CN1-230, 27 mai 1803; CN1-284, 13 sept. 1797; ZQ-75. AP, Notre-Dame-de-l'Annonciation (L'Ancienne-Lorette), Reg. des baptêmes, mariages et sépultures, 23 mai 1758, 9 févr. 1802. ASQ, C 35; Évêques, no.17. PAC, MG 23, GV, 8; RG 8, I (C ser.), 1714A. "Les dénombrements de Québec" (Plessis), ANQ *Rapport*, 1948–49: 23, 73, 122. "Cahier des témoignages de liberté au mariage commencé le 15 avril 1757," ANQ *Rapport*, 1951–53: 52. *Quebec Gazette*, 1 Oct. 1789, 4 Nov. 1790, 11 Feb. 1802. *Quebec almanac*, 1788–1801. M.-J. et G. Ahern, *Notes pour l'hist. de la médecine*, 21–32. Sylvio Leblond, "Une conférence inédite du docteur Joseph Painchaud," *Trois siècles de médecine québecoise* (Québec, 1970), 59. J.-E. Roy, "La maladie de la Baie," *BRH*, 1 (1895): 138–41. Benjamin Sulte, "Le docteur Badelart," *BRH*, 21 (1915): 343–47; "Le mal de la baie Saint-Paul," *BRH*, 22 (1916): 36–39.

BAILEY, JACOB, Church of England clergyman and author; b. 16 April 1731 in Rowley, Mass., second child of David Bailey and Mary Hodgkins; m. August 1761 Sally Weeks of Hampton, N.H., and they had at least six children; d. 26 July 1808 in Annapolis Royal, N.S.

Jacob Bailey was born into a humble farming family but received a sound education through the interest of Jedediah Jewett, Congregational minister at Rowley, who prepared him for Harvard College. After receiving his AB from Harvard in 1755, he taught school in a few New England towns and then returned to Harvard in 1758 to take his AM. Subsequently, he served briefly as a Congregational preacher in New Hampshire before his growing admiration for the doctrines and episcopal government of the Church of England led him to convert to that denomination in 1759. He was ordained an Anglican clergyman in London on 16 March 1760, and upon returning to America in the summer of the following year he immediately took up his clerical duties at Pownalborough, a sprawling parish on the northeastern frontier of Massachusetts (in the vicinity of West Dresden, Maine).

Bailey's appointment to Pownalborough was supported by Dr Sylvester Gardiner, a prominent Boston Anglican and one of the leading promoters of the Plymouth Company, which was developing this new frontier. But the Congregationalists in the Plymouth Company were opposed to Church of England domination of the area, and there was a group in Pownalborough who worked vigorously to undermine its presence. As colonial America drifted towards open rebellion, this religious friction took on political overtones and rapidly intensified. Bailey, appalled by "the obstinacy, the madness, the folly, the perfidy" of the rebels, was determined to remain loyal to his church and king. As a result, from 1774 on he was at various times mobbed, assaulted, shot at, and forced to flee for his life; and on two separate occasions in 1776 he was called before the local committee of correspondence, once for not reading proclamations issued by the Continental and Provincial congresses, and once for preaching a seditious sermon, praying for the king, and refusing to read the Declaration of Independence in his parish church. Angered by this constant harassment, and complaining bitterly that he was "reduced to such Poverty and Distress as frequently and for a Considerable Time to be destitute of even the Necessaries as well as the comforts of Life," Bailey chose to leave Pownalborough for Nova Scotia in June 1779 so that he would not have to do "great Violence to . . . his Conscience."

Upon arrival in Halifax, Bailey and his family were warmly received and given material assistance [*see* John Breynton*]. The Society for the Propagation of the Gospel soon appointed him to Cornwallis in the Annapolis valley, and in October 1779 he left Halifax for his first Nova Scotia mission. At Cornwallis he found himself surrounded by "Whigs, independants, Anabaptists, new lights, and beltgurded connecticut saints," and his own congregation was so small and weak that he often preached to more non-Anglicans

Baillairgé

than Anglicans. Moreover, as loyalist refugees the Baileys encountered resentment and hostility from the established inhabitants. Declaring that "the number of King Killers are in proportion ten times greater here than in the dominions of Congress," Bailey wrote wistfully that "my warmest wishes are to return to the remainder of my poor parishioners [at Pownalborough]. . . . Could I have tarried among them without promoting both my own and their destruction no temptation would have induced me to leave them."

In the summer of 1782 Bailey left Cornwallis for a new parish, Annapolis Royal; his successor in Cornwallis, John WISWALL, arrived the following year. At Annapolis, where he remained until his death in 1808, Bailey found sharp and serious divisions within the community, and as parish clergyman he spent much of his time attempting to lessen hostility between pre-loyalist "Bluenoses" and loyalist refugees. He also proved to be a fairly energetic missionary. The parish of Annapolis, like that of Pownalborough, extended far beyond the outskirts of the town, and Bailey paid regular visits to the outlying areas of Granville, Clements, and Digby, travelling in all kinds of weather to perform baptisms, marriages, and burials at the homes of his parishioners. In addition, he performed the duties of deputy chaplain to the local garrison even though the stipend attached to this position remained in the hands of his brother-in-law, Joshua Wingate Weeks. Only in 1794 was Bailey awarded the appointment by his former friend and Harvard classmate, Lieutenant Governor John WENTWORTH.

Bailey's literary accomplishments mark him as one of the first important figures in Canadian literature. Although only a few of his works were published, many of his writings circulated fairly widely in manuscript form among friends and acquaintances, before and after his death. His most significant achievement was his poetry. As a young man he had written light lyrical poetry; but in Nova Scotia, in the wake of the persecution and injustice he had suffered at rebel hands, he discovered a talent for verse satire in the style of the English poet Samuel Butler. Between 1779 and 1784 he wrote some outstanding anti-rebel satires, including a long work entitled "America," in which he pointed out the causes of the revolution from a loyalist perspective. After the conclusion of the war Bailey dropped "America" and began work on his longest poem, "Jack Ramble, the Methodist Preacher," a religious satire which put forward the view that the growing influence of non-conformist religion in Nova Scotia threatened not only the interests of the Church of England but also the social and political stability of the province. He worked for more than ten years on this poem, leaving it incomplete in 31 books.

Bailey also produced a considerable number of prose works, including substantial pieces on theology,

morality (designed especially for children and young ladies), American history, and the geography of Maine and Nova Scotia. In addition, there are three incomplete epistolary novels and fragments of three plays among Bailey's papers. The most interesting play is "Majesty of the mob," a dramatization of a trial before a committee of correspondence. Of the novels, "Serena," the story of a loyalist girl caught up in the cruel machinations of the rebellion, is the best written and the most interesting.

Bailey died at age 77 and was survived by his wife, three daughters, and three sons. He had been a man of many parts, all of which reflected his profound commitment to his church and king.

JULIE ROSS and THOMAS VINCENT

Jacob Bailey was the author of "Behold the vaunting hero," *Royal Gazette and the Nova-Scotia Advertiser* (Halifax), 11 Dec. 1798, and "Observations and conjectures on the antiquities of America," Mass. Hist. Soc., *Coll* . (Boston), 1st ser., 4 (1795): 100–5. Three of Bailey's poems are printed and discussed in *Narrative verse satire in Maritime Canada, 1779–1814*, ed. T. B. Vincent (Ottawa, 1978).

Lincoln County Cultural and Hist. Assoc. (Wiscasset, Maine), Pownalborough courthouse coll., Jacob Bailey papers. PANS, MG 1, 91–104. *The frontier missionary: a memoir of the life of the Rev. Jacob Bailey, A.M., missionary at Pownalborough, Maine; Cornwallis and Annapolis, N.S.*, ed. W. S. Bartlet (Boston, 1853). J. M. Ross, "Jacob Bailey, loyalist: Anglican clergyman in New England and Nova Scotia" (MA thesis, Univ. of New Brunswick, Fredericton, 1975). R. P. Baker, "The poetry of Jacob Bailey, loyalist," *New England Quarterly* ([Cambridge, Mass.]), 2 (1929): 58–92. T. B. Vincent, "Alline and Bailey," *Canadian Literature* (Vancouver), no.68–69 (spring–summer 1976): 124–33; "Keeping the faith: the poetic development of Jacob Bailey," *Early American Literature* (Amherst, Mass.), 14 (1979–80): 3–14; "Some examples of narrative verse satire in the early literature of Nova Scotia and New Brunswick," *Humanities Assoc. Rev.* (Kingston, Ont.), 27 (1976): 161–75.

BAILLAIRGÉ, JEAN, carpenter, wood-carver, and architect; b. 31 Oct. 1726 in Blanzay, France, son of Jean Baillairgé, a carpenter, and Jeanne Bourdois; d. 6 Sept. 1805 at Quebec, Lower Canada.

Jean Baillairgé, who was the second of six children, came from a family of craftsmen in the building trade. His father and his brother Pierre seem to have practised as master masons or "house carpenter[s]," but not as architects, despite the contention of the family's biographer, Georges-Frédéric Baillairgé. In 1741 Jean Baillairgé emigrated to New France. He landed at Quebec on 30 August, having travelled on the same ship as Bishop Pontbriand [Dubreil*], the sixth bishop of Quebec. A legend was immediately spun from these few facts: young Baillairgé became the protégé of the bishop, who is supposed to have sent him to complete his training at the École des Arts et Métiers at Saint-Joachim, near Quebec, and then placed him as an apprentice with an architect. That the bishop was interested in his young travelling companion's lot seems plausible enough, but recent studies show that the École des Arts et Métiers was largely a fabrication of 19th-century historians in search of such an institution to serve as evidence for the emergence of a Quebec school of art. Young Baillairgé could not have completed his training at the school, since its supposed sponsor, the Séminaire de Québec, had at that time only a farm and a country retreat at Saint-Joachim. Notary Jean-Joseph Girouard*, Baillairgé's grandson, maintained that his grandfather had apprenticed with a Quebec architect. This second course seems more likely if the term architect is understood to mean a master mason or a well-known carpenter and contractor, unless Baillairgé had had the opportunity to work under the direction of the king's engineers.

In any event, it was probably during the 1740s that Baillairgé received "an education equal to his profession," enabling him to draw well, make accurate plans, and also calculate correctly. A study of his work confirms that he was one of the craftsmen who had been trained in New France and had learned the trade on the work site rather than at school. Baillairgé may have become his own master in 1746, as his biographers assert, but this seems quite unlikely. In fact, had he completed his apprenticeship at that date, he would have worked in another craftsman's shop before personally engaging himself for work on a site.

On 1 June 1750 Baillairgé, "a carpenter," married Marie-Louise Parent at Quebec; the couple were to have 11 children, of whom only three daughters and two sons survived infancy. After his marriage Baillairgé and his wife went to Sainte-Anne-de-la-Pocatière (La Pocatière), where he worked on the church in 1751. Art historian Gérard Morisset* claims that in this instance Baillairgé did the interior decoration; however, he seems rather to have done the carpentry under the direction of a contractor or a wood-carver, someone such as François-Nöel Levasseur*, with whom Baillairgé had become acquainted in 1748.

Returning to Quebec, where he lived on Rue Saint-Jean, Baillairgé went into partnership in 1753 with Armand-Joseph Chaussat, who had shared the voyage from France with him and may have been his comrade in apprenticeship; he then contracted to do the panelling for the chapel of the congregation of the Jesuit college and the carpentry for a two-storey house at the corner of Rue Buade and Rue du Trésor. That year the two partners had adjoining houses built for themselves on Rue des Casernes (Rue de l'Arsenal). During the Seven Years' War Baillairgé enlisted in the militia and fought on the Plains of Abraham in 1759. After the conquest he built several houses at Quebec for various individuals in the years 1762–68. In addition he redid or completed the carpentry on his own house, which he sold to Francis Maseres* in 1768 after building a house and shop for himself on Rue du Sault-au-Matelot. Among the houses he built during that period, the one on the Place Royale that was repaired in 1764 after the fire in Lower Town and is now called the Maison Dumont is unquestionably the most noteworthy.

Having doubtless acquired a good reputation, Baillairgé was asked by the churchwardens of the parish of Notre-Dame in Quebec in 1766 to submit a plan for rebuilding the parish church and cathedral, which had burned in 1759, 10 years after being built from the plans of the engineer Gaspard-Joseph Chaussegros* de Léry. Baillairgé's design was approved, but thereupon a controversy arose about whether the simplified building proposed was in keeping with the stature of the cathedral of Quebec among the parish churches. Bishop Briand* deferred to the views of those opposing Baillairgé's design and in the end he lost the contract for the rebuilding. No doubt disappointed, Baillairgé announced in the *Quebec Gazette* on 11 May 1769 that he intended to leave the province. He put his own house on Rue du Sault-au-Matelot up for sale, along with another one he had just had built on the market-place in Upper Town, as well as some tools, wood, and furniture. However, in 1770 he reconsidered his decision to move, presented a plan for rebuilding the cathedral belfry, and this time was successful. This may have been the determining factor in his decision to continue his career at Quebec.

The belfry project gave new impetus to Baillairgé's career; he undertook to decorate the interior of the churches of Saint-Charles at Bellechasse in 1772, Saint-François the next year, and Saint-Thomas (at Montmagny) in 1775. After serving in the third company of the Quebec militia during the American invasion in 1775–76, Baillairgé apparently lived for a while at Saint-Augustin-de-Desmaures, in order to work on the church there. In all these localities Baillairgé acted as a contractor, calling in workmen to carry out the projects. For instance, he took on apprentices and went into association with wood-carver Antoine JACSON. From 1781 he could count on the help of his son François*, who had returned from Paris after three years of study. The following year they began decorating the interior of the church at L'Islet, with François concentrating on the overall concept as well as on the execution of the fine wood carving and the statuary. In 1787 the Baillairgés took on the task of decorating the interior of the cathedral of Quebec with the help of Jean's second son, PIERRE-FLORENT, who had given up his theological studies

Baillairgé

two years earlier to work in his father's shop. But at the cathedral it was again François who conceived the overall plan and executed the decorative designs. Baillairgé continued to be the contractor for the carpentry; he prepared the panelling and attended to the structural aspects.

As François had decided to devote his time to the atelier he had opened on his own after the project at L'Islet, his father continued to collaborate with Pierre-Florent. In 1794 father and son thus began building the retable in the church of Saint-Jean-Baptiste at Saint-Jean-Port-Joli, Baillairgé's last major work and the only one in this category still in existence. Baillairgé had probably built only one type of retable (as the decorated structure housing the altar in the sanctuary was then called), drawing his inspiration from the one in the Jesuit chapel at Quebec. In plan and elevation, disposition of the carved decorative elements, and overall proportions, the Jesuit model – at least as it is shown in the engraving made after the drawings done in 1759 by Richard Short* – seems evident. In the retable the traditional character of Baillairgé's art is obvious.

Along with these interior decoration projects, for which Baillairgé would present the plans and then hire workmen for the job, a number of other pieces of liturgical furnishing are generally attributed to him. He is believed to have carved several tabernacles, including those of the church at L'Islet and the church of Saint-Joseph at Maskinongé. These two works, which were done about 1790, are based on a single design by Pierre-Florent. But François Baillairgé had already provided this type of tabernacle at Saint-Joachim in 1783. It bore the stamp of the European training that had led him to create a form breaking with the traditional model developed and defended by the Levasseurs [see François-Noël Levasseur] until about the mid 18th century. The rest of the liturgical furnishings produced by Jean Baillairgé's workshop are less well known. In general all the works that were completed during this period were replaced early in the 19th century.

In addition to his career as a contractor for church decoration, Baillairgé became an expert much sought after to settle disputes, appraise works, and judge the craftsmanship of his peers. On a few occasions he was identified as the architect supervising works executed according to his own plans.

Baillairgé lost his wife in 1798, and after that he apparently slowed down his activity considerably, leaving the field open to his two sons. He closed his shop on Rue du Sault-au-Matelot and in 1801 he went to live in a new house he had just built on Rue d'Auteuil. He died on 6 Sept. 1805, leaving no great fortune, since he had borrowed money frequently a few years before his death, particularly to build his last home. According to Girouard, Baillairgé was strict and pious but of a jovial nature, with "one of those old and original countenances that one scarcely ever sees and that bore no resemblance whatsoever to ordinary, worn, flattened, expressionless faces."

Jean Baillairgé is an important figure in the history of Quebec art. In the fields of wood-carving and architecture he filled the gap created by the death or departure of the craftsmen active before the conquest. But he was also the founder of the Baillairgé dynasty, which occupied a predominant place in the history of Quebec art and architecture from the 18th to the 20th centuries. Unfortunately the family name is too often associated with a series of works which, taken together, were used to reinforce the description of artistic production in Quebec as exclusively traditional. Certainly Jean Baillairgé's training made him one of the champions of traditional art, the models for which were works executed before the conquest. Since he was aware of deficiencies, however, he had sent his son François to study in France, thus making possible a renewal of the traditional art, which by 1780 had become rather ossified in style. The few pieces of Jean Baillairgé's work that have been preserved are less important for their formal qualities than for the witness they bear to the reassertion, through the use of tradition, of the French character of the art being created in the colony during a period of some 30 years after the conquest. Detailed study and the analysis of the formal characteristics of the works of Jean Baillairgé's descendants, François, Thomas*, and above all Charles*, reveal that they endeavoured to revive the tradition by assuring the training of competent successors, and by bringing to the practice of their craft aesthetic principles in the best of prevailing taste.

LUC NOPPEN

AD, Vienne (Poitiers), État civil, Blanzay, 31 oct. 1726. ANQ-Q, CE1-1, 1er juin 1750, 8 sept. 1805; CN1-83, 7 juill. 1788; CN1-91, 31 mai 1750; CN1-92, 13 sept. 1788, 22 mars 1796; CN1-151, 16 sept., 20 déc. 1753; CN1-202, 22 juin 1762; CN1-205, 19 juin 1777; CN1-230, 9 mai, 6 oct. 1801; 3 sept. 1802; 25 juin 1803; 23 mai 1804; CN1-248, 19 août 1753, 27 mai 1768; CN1-250, 9 mai 1762; CN1-262, 30 août 1796; CN1-284, 7 avril 1795; P-92. MAC-CD, Fonds Morisset, 2, B157/J43. Quebec Gazette, 11 May 1769. G.-F. Baillairgé, Notices biographiques et généalogiques, famille Baillairgé . . . (11 fascicules, Joliette, Qué., 1891–94), 1. F.-M. Gagnon et Nicole Cloutier, Premiers peintres de la Nouvelle-France (2v., Québec, 1976), 2. Raymonde [Landry] Gauthier, Les tabernacles anciens du Québec des XVIIe, XVIIIe et XIXe siècles ([Québec], 1974), 42–43. David Karel et al., François Baillairgé et son œuvre (1759–1830) (Québec, 1975). Luc Noppen, Notre-Dame de Québec, son architecture et son rayonnement (1647–1922) (Québec, 1974), 145–51; "Le renouveau architectural proposé par Thomas Baillairgé de 1820 à 1850 au Québec ou le néo-classicisme québécois" (thèse de PHD, univ. de

Toulouse, France, 1976). Traquair, *Old silver of Quebec*. Marius Barbeau, "Les Baillairgé, école de Québec en sculpture et en architecture," *Le Canada français* (Québec), 2e sér., 33 (1945–46): 247–55. P. N. Moogk, "Réexamen de l'école des arts et métiers de Saint-Joachim," *RHAF*, 29 (1975–76): 3–29. Gérard Morisset, "Jean Baillairgé (1726–1805)," *Technique* (Montréal), 21 (1947): 415–25; "Une dynastie d'artisans: les Baillairgé," *La Patrie* (Montréal), 3 août 1950: 18, 42, 46. A. J. H. Richardson, "Guide to the architecturally and historically most significant buildings in the old city of Quebec with a biographical dictionary of architects and builders and illustrations," Assoc. for Preservation Technology, *Bull.* (Ottawa), 2 (1970), nos.3–4: 72–73.

BAILLAIRGÉ, PIERRE-FLORENT, joiner, wood-carver, office holder, and militia officer; b. 29 June 1761 at Quebec, son of Jean BAILLAIRGÉ and Marie-Louise Parent; m. there 24 Nov. 1789 Marie-Louise Cureux, *dit* Saint-Germain, and they had seven children; d. there 9 Dec. 1812.

Pierre-Florent Baillairgé, the son and brother of wood-carvers, first turned towards the priesthood. He entered the Séminaire de Québec in 1777, and studied there until 1784. Then he was sent to the Collège Saint-Raphaël in Montreal, where he taught the fifth-year classes (Belles-Lettres) while continuing his theological studies. However, having had difficulties with the director, Jean-Baptiste Curatteau*, he gave up his studies in the spring of 1785 and returned to Quebec; he immediately made a place for himself in the workshop of his father and his brother François*. The three of them would execute several contracts for decorative wood-carving in churches of the Quebec region.

The late 18th century witnessed a revival of religious building in the colony, which was now British. The churches that had been bombarded or burned during the Seven Years' War had to be rebuilt, and burgeoning rural villages, particularly on the south shore of the St Lawrence, had to be provided with the churches they needed. Beginning in 1786 the task of decorating the chancel of the church of Notre-Dame in Quebec mobilized the resources of the Baillairgé workshop. Jean and François designed the project and Pierre-Florent saw to its execution. He probably acted as foreman, making arrangements with those responsible for doing the work and collecting payments due. Work on this site, completed by the rebuilding of the sacristy, was not finished until 1793. Meanwhile Pierre-Florent and his father fulfilled other contracts; for instance they made the tabernacle and the base of the altar, which were carved of wood, painted, and gilded, for the church of Saint-Joseph at Maskinongé in 1790, and did the woodwork on the two side altars in the Île d'Orléans church of Sainte-Famille.

In 1794 Pierre-Florent helped make the panelling for the chancel of the church of Saint-Jean-Baptiste at Saint-Jean-Port-Joli. He carved frames to works by Louis Dulongpré* for the *fabrique* of Rivière-Ouelle; he made tabernacles and side altars for other churches. With Jean Baillairgé's death in September 1805, responsibility for the shop fell to Pierre-Florent, since François was then occupied with his work as an architect. In 1806 Pierre-Florent took on two apprentices, Pierre Alary and François Lauriot, and continued with the wood-carving contract that he had already commenced for the church of Saint-Louis at Kamouraska. In a letter to the parish priest, Alexis Pinet, he asked for a payment to be made a few months in advance to enable him to complete the job before the end of the year; otherwise he would reluctantly "be obliged to take on other work to support [his] family." In 1808 he delivered the tabernacle for a chapel in the church of Saint-Charles-Borromée in Charlesbourg; it was to be his last piece of wood-carving. Like other joiners, however, he was retained in arbitration cases, particularly for the measuring of wood for carpentry.

Baillairgé seems to have been well thought of in the community of craftsmen such as Pierre ÉMOND, François RANVOYZÉ, Edward CANNON, and the like who left their stamp on the cultural life of Quebec at the outset of the 19th century. In 1805 he was a lieutenant in Quebec's 1st Militia Battalion. From 1807 to 1810 he contributed to *Le Canadien*, publishing songs and epigrams, aimed particularly at Governor CRAIG. If his writings display a certain lack of deference and a certain boldness, they reveal scant poetic gift. On the other hand he was credited with great musical talent by his niece Émilie Berthelot. He also contributed to the Quebec Fire Society. In 1812 he was appointed treasurer for roads in the town and was promoted to the rank of militia captain. In the same year, during a trip to the country to inspect a church, Baillairgé caught pleurisy and died. He left his widow and five young children an income largely from the rent of houses in nearly every part of the town.

Pierre-Florent Baillairgé was a product of the woodworking tradition, and he simply conformed to it. No great artist in his field, he was above all a craftsman faithful to the French tradition introduced by his father, with whom he collaborated but whom he never replaced. His style is uninspired and lacks vigour, the decoration consisting of floral elements that scarcely conceal the construction of the article. The joiner, far more than the wood-carver, is manifest in his style. The early creations of François Baillairgé and his son Thomas* – for example, the imposing baldachin in the church of Saint-Joachim – make one quickly forget the former seminarist, who always takes second place.

RAYMONDE GAUTHIER

Balfour

ANQ-Q, CE1-1, 29 juin 1761, 24 nov. 1789, 11 déc. 1812; CN1-83, 22 nov. 1789; CN1-147, 11 juill. 1806; CN1-212, 24 févr. 1832; CN1-230, 20 juill. 1810. AP, Notre-Dame de Québec, Cahiers des délibérations de la fabrique, 1777–1825: 103, 163, 175; Saint-Louis (Kamouraska), Livres de comptes, I. ASQ, Fichier des anciens. MAC-CD, Fonds Morisset, 2, B157/P622.7. [Émilie Berthelot-Girouard], "Les journaux d'Émilie Berthelot-Girouard," Béatrice Chassé, édit., ANQ *Rapport*, 1975: 26–27. "Les dénombrements de Québec" (Plessis), ANQ *Rapport*, 1948–49. *Le Canadien*, 1807–10. *Quebec Gazette*, 14 Sept. 1809, 25 June 1812, 24 May 1824. *L'art du Québec au lendemain de la Conquête (1760–1790)* (Québec, 1977). Tanguay, *Dictionnaire*, 2: 100. F.-X. Chouinard et Antonio Drolet, *La ville de Québec, histoire municipale* (3v., Québec, 1963–67), 2: 70. Raymonde [Landry] Gauthier, *Les tabernacles anciens du Québec des XVIIe, XVIIIe et XIXe siècles* ([Québec], 1974). David Karel *et al.*, *François Baillairgé et son œuvre (1759–1830)* (Québec, 1975), 78. Luc Noppen, *Les églises du Québec (1600–1850)* (Québec, 1977), 134, 218, 242; *Notre-Dame de Québec, son architecture et son rayonnement (1647–1922)* (Québec, 1974), 167, 170. Luc Noppen et J. R. Porter, *Les églises de Charlesbourg et l'architecture religieuse du Québec* ([Québec], 1972), 27. "*Le Canadien* en 1810," *BRH*, 1 (1895): 77. Gérard Morisset, "Pierre-Florent Baillairgé (1761–1812)," *Technique* (Montréal), 21 (1947): 603–10. "Pierre-Florent Baillairgé," *BRH*, 8 (1902): 25–28.

BALFOUR, JAMES, Church of England clergyman; b. 15 Aug. 1731 in the parish of Banchory-Ternan, Scotland; m. 13 Oct. 1766 Ann Emray in Trinity, Nfld, and they had four children; d. 1809 in Newfoundland.

James Balfour was baptized in the Presbyterian Church and left Scotland in 1757 to seek employment in England. There he became a schoolmaster at Wadley (London) and joined the Church of England. Early in 1764 he applied to the Society for the Propagation of the Gospel to be appointed a missionary, and the SPG decided to send him to Trinity Bay in Newfoundland. He was ordained by the bishop of London and by the end of the year had settled in his mission at Trinity.

Balfour's first impressions were unfavourable. He was shocked to find that a frequent form of sexual union was common-law marriage with several temporary changes of partner. No one would offer him lodging lest his presence "should check some favourite Vice." His congregation at Trinity itself consisted of only ten families, but they built him a house and by 1766 he was asserting that there was "the most agreeable Harmony & Contentment Subsisting between my People and Me." Such euphoric comments soon ceased, and in the 11 years of his ministry in Trinity Bay he made frequent complaints to the SPG. The population of Trinity feuded, probably intercepted his letters, and, if Irish, were prone to "mob and housebreak." The sabbath was broken by music, dancing, and work. At Scilly Cove (Winterton) on the east side of Trinity Bay, a "barbarous lawless place," the inhabitants paraded behind a piper every Sunday, while down the coast at New Perlican a state of civil war existed between Irish and English. Nor was Balfour himself immune from personal danger: in March 1769 he was attacked by a German surgeon and a merchant's clerk for no apparent reason. "I received several blows," he reported, "this I did not in the least resent, but bore patiently, as our Order must not be Strikers." When Governor John Byron* visited Trinity that July Balfour recounted the incident and offered his forgiveness on a promise of future good behaviour. However, the governor insisted that his assailants apologize "very Submissively" and pay a small fine.

Balfour had problems beyond the unruliness of the population. His congregation melted away in winter and, since it consisted of planters and servants, was too impoverished to afford the cost of repairs to the church. The rich of Trinity were Quakers, Presbyterians, or Roman Catholics and refused to help; as a result, the church was in "a ruinous condition." Nevertheless, by 1771 Balfour was able to report steady progress, greater concern for divine worship, and a subscription to repair the church, and the following year he stated that he had nearly 40 communicants. Even so, lawlessness persisted, and he had to be careful at burials. On one occasion the marks on a corpse aroused his suspicions, a murder was discovered, and a criminal hanged. By October 1774 Balfour was complaining, "Believe me! these are Uncouth Regions here indeed, for a Man to spend his short Life in." That year the SPG acceded to his request to be transferred to Harbour Grace, where he expected to find peace and more money.

Balfour arrived in Harbour Grace on 6 Oct. 1775, but although he was well received by the people of the town his hopes were soon disappointed. The inhabitants of Carbonear had been influenced by the Methodist teachings of his predecessor Laurence Coughlan* and consequently wanted either a Methodist or a Presbyterian minister; moreover, they claimed the church was their property and refused him entrance. An order from Governor Richard Edwards* in 1780 enabled Balfour to use the Carbonear church, but in January 1784 he was bothered when a Methodist preacher intruded into the pulpit in the middle of a service. These difficulties foreshadowed the sectarian troubles of the 19th century.

During the 1780s Balfour became increasingly dispirited and ill, claiming that he could get no money from the people in the dislocation of trade following the American revolution, complaining about the poor weather, and noting apprehensively that the congregation had expressed a wish for a younger man. The nadir came in 1791 when he quarrelled with the schoolmaster of Harbour Grace, William Lampen,

52

who had a low opinion of him. Lampen appealed to the SPG, enclosing a petition from some of the inhabitants which complained that Balfour was frequently drunk and that he performed divine service only five or six times a year, and adding his own allegation that Communion had not been administered for a year and a half. After receiving some counter-petitions and after consulting with Judge John Reeves* and others, in March 1792 the SPG dismissed Lampen and discontinued Balfour as a missionary. An unhappy and harassed man, Balfour suffered a fate not uncommon to old and tired missionaries. In view of his age, infirmities, and length of service, he was allowed his salary of £70 as a pension, and he continued to hold it until his death in 1809.

FREDERICK JONES

Lambeth Palace Library (London), Fulham papers. USPG, B, 6; C/CAN/Nfl., 1; C/CAN/PRE; Journal of SPG, 16–26. [C. F. Pascoe], *Classified digest of the records of the Society for the Propagation of the Gospel in Foreign Parts, 1701–1892* (5th ed., London, 1895). Prowse, *Hist. of Nfld.* (1896).

BALL, INGRAM, politician and judge; b. 1752 at Stonehouse Manor in Stonehouse, Gloucestershire, England, eldest of six children of Robert Ball and Mary Dickerson; m. first Anna Coutts; m. secondly Margaret Childs; there were 12 children from the two marriages; d. 18 March 1807 near Sydney (N.S.).

Ingram Ball was the elder brother of Alexander John Ball, who became a rear-admiral in the Royal Navy and the first British governor of Malta. He entered the 33rd Foot as an ensign on 12 Feb. 1772, and in June of the following year exchanged to the 7th Dragoons as a cornet. Promoted lieutenant on 29 May 1776, he was advanced to captain-lieutenant in January 1780, but resigned from the army that November. It has been claimed that during the War of American Independence he served on the staff of Lieutenant-General Lord Cornwallis. Ball came to Cape Breton in 1788 with his wife and six children and settled west of Sydney on the site of the present-day village of Ball's Creek. He soon became involved in the political life of the colony, being appointed to the Executive Council on 22 June 1789 by Lieutenant Governor William MACARMICK. Ball aligned himself with a faction in the council headed by Ranna COSSIT, the Church of England clergyman in Sydney, which was opposed to one led by David Mathews*, the attorney general. Both groups sought to control the colony through manipulation of the lieutenant governor and council, an essential step since a house of assembly was never convened.

When Macarmick left Cape Breton in 1795, Mathews became administrator and used his new power to harass and dismiss members of the rival clique. In his capacity as first (and, at this point, only) assistant judge of the Supreme Court, a position to which he had been appointed by Macarmick, Ball functioned as chief justice. Unfortunately, however, some of his judgements were in opposition to those of Archibald Charles Dodd*, a magistrate and an ally of Mathews. Dissatisfied with Ball's decisions, Mathews appointed Dodd first assistant judge in June 1797, an action that appears to have suspended Ball from the Supreme Court. At some time during Mathews's term of office he also dismissed Ball from the council. As tension between Mathews and his adversaries grew during 1797, a group of sailors led by his son roamed about terrorizing those inhabitants who opposed the administrator. During Ball's absence they broke into his home, "a Strumpet in their Company," and "teized & tossed about" Mrs Ball for some time. The following year Mathews used a debt charge as an excuse to jail Ball.

In June 1798 James OGILVIE arrived to assume control of the government. He soon released Ball and reappointed him to his seat on the council, dismissed Dodd from the Supreme Court, and replaced him with two joint chief justices, Ball and William SMITH. By early 1799 Ball and Smith were at loggerheads; unable to agree on judgements, they split decisions and nullified the power of the Supreme Court. The cause of this rivalry appears to have been Ball's change of allegiance to Mathews's group, Smith tending to favour Cossit and his allies. The reasons for Ball's volte-face are not clear. In May 1799 John Murray* replaced Ogilvie as administrator. He favoured the Cossit faction and soon fell out with Ball, calling him an "old Military Debauchée" and accusing him of being drunk "from Morning to night." Ball was finally removed from his positions as joint chief justice and councillor on 22 Dec. 1799, and in the spring of 1800 he was convicted of perjury and sentenced to jail for 12 months. Murray's successor, John Despard*, took an interest in his case and in May 1801 obtained the British government's consent to the remission of the remainder of Ball's sentence.

After his release Ball took no active part in Cape Breton politics and retired to his farm. His career reveals the acrimonious state of political life during the early years of the colony's existence, due largely to factionalism and favouritism arising from the absence of a house of assembly and the scramble for the small number of offices available.

R. J. MORGAN

PAC, MG 11, [CO 217] Cape Breton A, 10: 86; [CO 220] Cape Breton B, 5: 44–45. PRO, CO 217/113: ff.200–1, 534; 217/114; 217/115: f.87; 217/116; 217/117: ff.21, 29, 125, 143–45; 217/118: f.13. [William Smith], *A caveat against emigration to America; with the state of the island of Cape*

Banks

Breton, from the year 1784 to the present year; and suggestions for the benefit of the British settlements in North America (London, 1803).

BANKS, Sir JOSEPH, naturalist; b. 2 Feb. 1742/43 in London, England, only son of William Banks and Sarah Bate; m. there 23 March 1779 Dorothea Weston-Hugessen; d. 19 June 1820 in Heston (London).

Born into a family with considerable wealth and powerful connections, Joseph Banks also inherited acute intelligence from both sides. From the beginning, influences were at work to determine his future career. His relations' estate at Burghley House in Northamptonshire had gardens splendidly laid out by the Elizabethan statesman William Cecil, who had a special flair for acclimatizing exotic trees and shrubs. Family connections linked Banks to Lord Temple, whose gardens at Stowe were among the most famous in England, and Banks's family home at Revesby Abbey in Lincolnshire adjoined vast undrained fens with astonishing populations of waterfowl. It is not therefore surprising that when a schoolboy at Eton College Banks became attracted to natural history and applied himself to its study. About 1761 or so, while attending Oxford, he began to build up a herbarium, and among its early sheets is a plant of *Geum macrophyllum* from Labrador dated 1763. A little later, plants from this region were given to him by Moravian missionaries, whose London headquarters were close to his home; it was probably through their accounts that he became interested in Greenland and Labrador. In 1766 he obtained permission for himself and Constantine John Phipps, a naval officer and former school-friend, to travel as passengers to Newfoundland in the *Niger*, part of the squadron of Governor Hugh Palliser*. In addition to her normal patrol duties, the *Niger* was taking a party of marines to Chateau Bay in Labrador to erect a blockhouse for a permanent garrison [*see* Francis Lucas*]. She anchored in St John's on 11 May 1766, a stimulating time for a naturalist. Among the birds in full breeding plumage, Banks recorded the resident black-capped chickadee; robins were plentiful and conspicuous, and there were numerous warblers. Banks was soon busy collecting many different types of plants and birds, and when intermittent snowstorms prevented this activity he went trawling in the harbour for marine life or made geological observations on rock faces then being exposed by men levelling an area for fortifications. His interest attracted attention and the locals brought him specimens. On 6 June he commented in his journal on plant distribution, which was to be a lifelong interest: "Wlkd out to day gatherd some of the Northern English Plants which grow here Every where not Coveting high Land," among them "the Little dwarf Honeysuckle, *Cornus herbacea*," and "a beautiful Kind of . . . Medlar [an *Amelanchier*, now widely treasured in English gardens]."

On 11 June the *Niger* sailed for Croque, an isolated fishing settlement on the east coast of the Northern Peninsula, where Banks made further observations and collecting trips. Illness prevented his working through much of July, but he was able to collect again when the *Niger* arrived on the Labrador coast on 9 August. He had ceased keeping a day-to-day journal in June, and his comparison of the British and French fisheries at Croque was written after his arrival in Labrador. Banks commented that "they Differ much in their methods of Fishing and have Each their Different merits," although he considered that "the Englishman indeed has the advantage as he catches considerably a larger quantity of Fish & his Fish fetch more money at Foreign markets being better cured." He then went on to describe the gutting and drying of fish, the various types of bait, and the kind of boats used, adding that British methods were in essentials much in advance of the French "but in the neatness of their Stages & manner of working they are much our superiors."

One of the most interesting aspects of Banks's records from an ornithological point of view is his arrival in Newfoundland when the spring migrants were abundant and his reaching Labrador three months later when the fall migrants were coming south in their thousands. In a letter to a former school-friend on 10 August he wrote, "This Morn went out shooting upon Labrador . . . a bird of Passage Call'd here Curlew who came 4 or 5 days ago in amazine multitudes they are very like the Curlew Jack [whimbrel] in Enland & every body here agrees most excellent eating I am Just going to set down to Dinner on some of them Broil'd. . . ." Banks took specimens back to England, and an engraving of one of these now almost extinct Eskimo curlews appeared in Thomas Pennant's *Arctic zoology* (2v., London, 1784–85). Banks's interest in archaeology was aroused by the discovery the previous year of a large quantity of whalebone on Esquimaux Island, north of the entrance to Chateau Bay, "Carefully & regularly buried upon tiles" and "supposed to be Left here by the Danes who in their Return from Groenland South about touchd upon this Coast & Left several Whaling Crews." This observation was paralleled by one made by the Moravian missionaries Christian Larsen Drachart* and Jens Haven* on nearby Henley Island, and both have a special significance in view of the archaeological work now being carried out on the ancient Basque fisheries at Red Bay just down the coast.

When the *Niger* had fulfilled her commitments she sailed for St John's, arriving on 10 Oct. 1766. Banks commented, "We all Felt great Pleasure in Returning to Society which we had so long been deprivd of St Johns tho the Most Disagreeable Town I Ever met with was For some time Perfectly agreable to us . . . it is Built upon the side of a hill facing the Harbour Containing two or three hundred houses & as near as many fish flakes interspersed which in summer time must Cause a stench scarce to be supported." "As Every thing here smells of fish so," he recorded, "You cannot get any thing that does not taste of it. . . ." On 25 October Governor Palliser gave a formal party in honour of the anniversary of the coronation of George III; ladies were so few on the island, Banks noted, that even his washerwoman was amongst the guests. An extraordinary group of gifted men was gathered in St John's at the time, among them John Cartwright, Palliser's first lieutenant and later a friend of Banks, and his brother GEORGE, who became one of Banks's collectors of plants and animals on the Labrador coast. The crew of Palliser's flagship the *Guernsey* included several men who were to play important roles in James Cook*'s Pacific explorations; James King*, for example, an able seaman with a flair for mathematics and astronomy, was to bring the *Discovery* home from the third voyage. Cook himself arrived in St John's harbour on 27 October.

Once the *Niger* had returned to England Banks set to work classifying and recording his collections with the help of the Swedish naturalist Daniel Carl Solander, who became one of his closest friends. After travels in Britain during the autumn of 1767 to examine various technological installations he returned to London in January 1768 and there heard of Cook's projected voyage to make observations at Tahiti on the transit of Venus. Banks, realizing that the *Endeavour* would visit countries unknown to any European naturalist, obtained permission to join the expedition. With him went Solander and a small, well-trained staff of scientists, draughtsmen, and collectors usually but incorrectly referred to as Banks's servants. The observations and collections made on this voyage were to provide biologists and ethnologists with a rich variety of material which is still being worked on. Furthermore, the value of sending scientists on all voyages of exploration was securely established, and the foundations of marine biology were laid. Banks's interest in languages and his personal flair for dealing with the inhabitants of lands scarcely if at all visited by Europeans were of fundamental importance in establishing peaceful relationships so that Cook could devote himself to navigation and surveying. The strong friendship that grew up between the two men is apparent from many details in their respective journals.

On their return to England in 1771 Banks and Solander, his chief companion of the voyage, were lionized. A second Pacific voyage was planned, and Banks assumed he would be in charge, but he withdrew in anger after accommodation for his party had to be considerably reduced. Instead he took his

staff to the Inner Hebrides, Iceland, and the Orkney Islands to make archaeological and geological observations. At Christmas time of 1772 George Cartwright arrived in England with a family of Inuit; Banks paid them many visits, had them painted, and questioned them carefully about their customs and beliefs. When Phipps, his companion on the *Niger*, was commissioned the same year to search for a passage northeast to India by way of the Arctic, Banks gave him a long list of desiderata: he needed information on bird and fish migrations, sea water, and ocean currents, and he asked for biological specimens. His persistent interest in the Arctic is shown in much of his correspondence, particularly in the letters received from William Scoresby, a pioneer explorer of Arctic seas.

While Phipps was away on his voyage in 1773 Banks took an active part in the running of the Royal Botanic Gardens at Kew (London), work that was to result in the development of the gardens as a great storehouse of living plants from all over the world. Early intensive work on the florae of southern Africa, Australia, and the Pacific coast of Canada was largely due to his efforts, and in addition to being in effect the director of the gardens until his death, Banks also became George III's unofficial scientific adviser. In 1776 he moved to a new house in London which had adequate room for his growing library and herbarium, and after his marriage he purchased still another house, Spring Grove at Heston, which had an extensive garden. A fellow of the Royal Society from 1766, he became president in 1778. He held this position until his death, and displayed an active interest in the administration of the society. In 1781 he was created a baronet.

Banks was one of the most influential persons connected with science in the 18th century, and his range of professional interests extended over the whole kingdom of living creatures. At the same time a geographer in the fullest meaning of the word, he assisted William Roy in the founding of the Ordnance survey and William Smith in the production of the first geological map of the United Kingdom. Deeply interested in the development of Australia, he has been called the father of the country. He was closely connected with the voyages in Australian waters of Matthew Flinders, who was accompanied by Banks's own librarian, Robert Brown. Moreover, he was successful in obtaining Spanish merino sheep for breeding in England and then in Australia, although these efforts are less well known than his sponsorship of Captain William Bligh in the famous attempts to transfer bread-fruit from Tahiti to the West Indies. For many years Banks was associated with Matthew Boulton in his attempts to reform the currency, and he was also one of the founders of the African Association, and a supporter of Mungo Park in his travels to find the source of the Niger River. Thanks in part to Banks's efforts the Royal Institution, an organization for the promotion of science, was founded in 1800, and it rapidly became one of the most important independent research institutions in Europe.

Although crippled with gout for the last 30 years of his life, Banks retained his wide-ranging curiosity until his death. One characteristic suggests how this curiosity led to his many activities: he had the gift of finding interests in common with people of all ages and classes, which made his life one of perpetual, rich discovery in the widest sense. Equally at home with kings, gardeners, and scientists, he was a pallbearer for Samuel Johnson as well as for William Aiton, the great Kew gardener. Typically, he asked that his own funeral be as simple as possible. Banks is commemorated in Canadian waters by Banks Island off the British Columbia coast, named in 1788 by Archibald Menzies*, who had been a collector for Banks, and by Banks Island in the Arctic archipelago, named shortly after Banks's death by William Edward Parry*. Parry had paid a visit to Banks in 1817 and his account tells how they discussed Greenland ice: surely an event typical of Banks's whole life as a man of science.

AVERIL M. LYSAGHT

[Banks's meticulously ordered papers met a dismal fate after his death when many of the documents were put up for sale by a relative in defiance of Banks's provision that the manuscripts were ultimately to be deposited in the British Museum. As a result of various auctions the material was scattered all over the world; what is available in Canada includes his manuscript of Newfoundland plants and birds and some paintings of Newfoundland birds, all at the McGill Univ. Libraries (Montreal). Because authoritative material was not readily accessible Banks fell into relative obscurity after his death, and no definitive biography has been published. Such a work was written by Edward Smith early this century, but after repeated rejections by publishers he shortened it into a popular work entitled *The life of Sir Joseph Banks* . . . (London and New York, 1911; repr. New York, 1975). It was the only biography available until the appearance of Hector Charles Cameron's short but carefully documented study, *Sir Joseph Banks, K.B., P.R.S., the autocrat of the philosophers* (London, 1952). Charles Lyte has since published a popular life entitled *Sir Joseph Banks* (Newton Abbot, Eng., 1980). A.M.L.]

Joseph Banks, *The Endeavour journal of Joseph Banks, 1768–1771*, ed. J. C. Beaglehole (2v., Sydney, Australia, 1962); *The journal of Joseph Banks in the Endeavour* (Guildford, Eng., 1980); "Some early letters from Joseph Banks (1743–1820) to William Phelp Perrin (1742–1820)," ed. A. M. Lysaght, Royal Soc. of London, *Notes and Records* (London), 29 (1974–75): 91–99. *The Banks letters: a calendar of the manuscript correspondence of Sir Joseph Banks* . . . , ed. W. R. Dawson (London, 1958). *The journals of Captain James Cook on his voyages of discovery*, ed. J. C. Beaglehole (4v. in 5 and portfolio, Cambridge and London, Eng., 1955–74), 1. A. M. Lysaght, "A note on the Admiralty copy of Cook's journal in the Endeavour,"

"Joseph Banks in the Niger and the Endeavour," and "Banks's artists in the Endeavour," in James Cook, *The journal of H.M.S. Endeavour, 1768–1771* (Guildford, 1977), 10–12, 25–36, and 37–47 respectively. *ADB. DNB. DSB.* A. M. Lysaght, *Joseph Banks in Newfoundland and Labrador, 1766: his diary, manuscripts and collections* (London and Berkeley, Calif., 1971). Yolande O'Donoghue, *William Roy, 1726–1790: pioneer of the Ordnance Survey* (London, 1977). A. M. Lysaght, "Joseph Banks at Skara Brae and Stennis, Orkney, 1772," Royal Soc. of London, *Notes and Records*, 28 (1973–74): 221–34; "Some eighteenth century bird paintings in the library of Sir Joseph Banks (1743–1820)," British Museum, Natural Hist., *Bull., Hist. Ser.* (London), 1 (1953–59): 254–371.

BARNES, JOHN, army officer and politician; b. *c.* 1746, probably in Great Britain; d. 30 April 1810 in Bath, England.

John Barnes entered the Royal Military Academy in Woolwich (London) as a cadet on 16 Aug. 1760. It was at this institution that future engineer and artillery officers of the British army received their technical training. The following year he received a commission in the Royal Artillery with the lowest rank, that of lieutenant fireworker. He was promoted second lieutenant in 1771 and first lieutenant in 1774.

Barnes came to the province of Quebec in the summer of 1776 with the military reinforcements sent to counter the American invasion [*see* Benedict ARNOLD; Richard Montgomery*]. He was probably an officer in one of the four artillery companies that, having left Woolwich in March 1776, were dispatched to Chambly and Montreal. Because of the state of war the British army in the province was increasing its headquarters staff. As a result, on 8 September Barnes was appointed assistant to the quartermaster general, Thomas CARLETON. The quartermaster general's department contained a deputy quartermaster general and three other assistants also chosen from among the officers. Barnes, who was responsible for the Montreal sector, had to organize the transport of troops, arms, and supplies and to develop plans for billeting the soldiers.

From the autumn of 1778 Barnes carried out the same duties at Sorel. With the arrival of the loyalists, however, his tasks were broadened to include quartering those who were in the armed forces and putting up those who were simply refugees. He also had to intervene to try to settle the problems caused by the insubordination of the self-proclaimed minister of the Church of England in Sorel, Thomas Charles Heslop SCOTT. He was promoted second captain in 1779 and captain in December 1782, and was put in command of an artillery company stationed in Sorel. Even though his company returned to England in October 1783, Barnes remained its captain until 1794, since his work at headquarters relieved him from the obligation of accompanying his unit.

In 1783, after the War of American Independence, Barnes became the person responsible for distributing supplies to the loyalists in that part of the province east of Cataraqui (Kingston, Ont.). He also had to assemble loyalists for resettlement in such areas as Baie des Chaleurs [see Nicholas Cox*] and Cataraqui [see Michael GRASS]. Furthermore Governor HALDIMAND entrusted Barnes with the responsibility for making land grants to a group of loyalists under Alexander White which he had authorized to settle in the seigneury of Sorel, on the south shore of the St Lawrence. In September 1784, in accordance with the governor's instructions, Barnes set off on a tour to inspect the loyalist settlements in the eastern part of Quebec. His mission was to prepare a list of those who were receiving supplies, to uncover abuses, and to pick out those making no effort to establish themselves. This tour took a year. On its conclusion Barnes reported the loyalists' satisfaction but recommended that their allowances not be cut off on 1 June 1786 but instead be continued until 1 September to enable them to subsist until the harvest.

In October 1785 Henry Hope*, who held the post of quartermaster general, became commander-in-chief of the British troops, replacing Barrimore Matthew St Leger*. He decided to entrust management of the quartermaster general's department to Barnes, who was given the title of deputy quartermaster general. This post carried with it the task of supervising the Provincial Marine and the office of the barrack master general. After his promotion Barnes moved to Quebec, where military headquarters were located.

In the first elections to the House of Assembly of Lower Canada in 1792 Barnes was elected for William Henry. This riding corresponded to the town of Sorel, which since 1787 had been called William Henry. He represented it until the end of the first parliament in 1796. His legislative career amounted to supporting the English party. During this period he was promoted major in 1794 and lieutenant-colonel the following year. On 21 Dec. 1795, at Quebec, he married 21-year-old Isabella Johnson from nearby Belmont; Anglican minister Philip Toosey* officiated and Henry CALDWELL, a friend of Barnes, served as witness.

In 1799 the post of deputy quartermaster general was transferred to Halifax, N.S.; Barnes resigned from office but obtained the post of deputy barrack master general, which allowed him to remain at Quebec. In 1801, as the senior officer there, he commanded the garrison. That year he obtained leave to go to England and on 15 August, after 25 years in the colony without a break, he departed. Officially he remained on the rolls as deputy barrack master general in North America until September 1802, but he never returned to the Canadas. He was promoted colonel in the army in 1802, colonel of the Invalid Battalion of

the Royal Artillery in 1803, and finally major-general in 1809. He died the following year in Bath.

John Barnes was one of many staff officers. Trained in the professional corps of the British artillery, he spent the greatest part of his career in administration and logistics. Since promotions in the Royal Artillery were made according to seniority, Barnes received them periodically, even though he was not serving with his regiment. His rise was swifter in wartime, and he took advantage of the expansion of the British empire in North America to carve out a place for himself in the military hierarchy.

CHRISTIAN RIOUX

ANQ-Q, CE1-61, 21 Dec. 1795; CN1-256, 19 Dec. 1795. BL, Add. mss 21697; 21699; 21700; 21714: 331–428; 21723: 14, 298–300; 21724: 251–56, 387, 399; 21744: 82; 21796–98; 21848: 219–20 (mfm. at PAC). PAC, RG 1, L3^L: 43397; RG 8, I (C ser.), 29: 56–57; 209: 62; 512: 129; 744: 57, 63–64, 72, 74. PRO, CO 42/46: f.89; 42/48: ff.201–3, 215; 42/49, 6 April 1786; WO 17/1507: ff.7–12; 17/1508: ff.1–9; WO 28/6: f.183; 28/7: ff.71, 73, 90, 94 (mfm. at PAC). "Les dénombrements de Québec" (Plessis), ANQ Rapport, 1948–49: 16, 66, 119. Kingston before War of 1812 (Preston), l, 71. Quebec Gazette, index. F.-J. Audet et Fabre Surveyer, Les députés au premier parl. du Bas-Canada, 17–24. Battery records of the Royal Artillery, 1716–1859, comp. M. E. S. Laws (Woolwich, Eng., 1952), 47–83. "Collection Haldimand," PAC Rapport, 1887: 411, 413, 433, 440–41, 469, 471–75. Desjardins, Guide parl., 143. Kelley, "Church and state papers," ANQ Rapport, 1948–49: 332, 339. List of officers of the Royal Regiment of Artillery . . . , comp. W. H. Askwith (4th ed., London, 1900), 12. "Papiers d'État," PAC Rapport, 1890: 173–74, 278. Quebec almanac, 1792–1801. Quebec directory, 1790, 1791. Azarie Couillard-Després, Histoire de Sorel de ses origines à nos jours (Montréal, 1926), 127, 133, 158–61. Earle Thomas, "The loyalists in the Montreal area, 1775–1784" (paper presented to the annual meeting of the CHA, Halifax, 1981), 18–21. Hare, "L'Assemblée législative du Bas-Canada," RHAF, 27: 371–73.

BASTARACHE, dit Basque, MICHEL, settler; b. 7 Feb. 1730 in Annapolis Royal, N.S., son of Pierre Bastarache, dit Le Basque, and Marguerite Forest; m. there 12 June 1753 Marguerite Gaudet, and they had at least seven children; d. 15 Jan. 1820 in Tracadie, N.B.

When the deportation of the Acadians began [see Charles Lawrence*], Michel Bastarache, dit Basque, and his brothers Pierre and Jean-Baptiste settled in the area around Fort Beauséjour (near Sackville, N.B.), where they became renowned for their bravery. In August 1755 Michel and Pierre were taken captive; Pierre was imprisoned in Fort Cumberland (the former Fort Beauséjour), and Michel at Fort Lawrence (near Amherst, N.S.). Michel escaped, with 85 other Acadians, during the night of 1–2 October through a tunnel they had dug under the walls of the fort, but he

Beardsley

was soon recaptured and taken to Fort Cumberland. On 18 October he and Pierre were among the 960 Acadians who, on Robert Monckton*'s orders, were embarked on ships bound for South Carolina.

Forcibly uprooted from his native land and separated from his family, Bastarache could not endure exile. Thus in the spring of 1756 he fled through the woods, accompanied by a dozen of his compatriots, including Pierre. Together they made their way on foot across the colonies of North Carolina, Virginia, Pennsylvania, and New York. When they reached the shores of Lake Ontario, they fell into the hands of the Iroquois. But a fur trader who had considerable influence with the Indians secured the captives' release by paying the ransom demanded; he took them to Quebec, where they arrived in September 1756. That similar exploits occurred is attested in a letter dated 19 April 1757 from Governor Vaudreuil [Rigaud*] to the minister of Marine: "8 Acadians who fled Carolina have reached the Saint John River. 4 of these Acadians have come to Quebec. I have questioned them."

From Quebec Bastarache and his brother went to Panaccadie (Moncton, N.B.), where a few Acadian families were in hiding since the search for Acadians was still going on in the region. There Bastarache learned that his wife had sought refuge on Île Saint-Jean (Prince Edward Island). Despite the risks of the trip, he went to the island, found his wife, and returned with her to go into hiding at Miramichi (N.B.), where Pierre Du Calvet* found them living in 1761. Within two years, however, they and four children were prisoners at Fort Cumberland. There, on 24 Aug. 1763, the family joined with some 70 others in indicating their desire to go to France, but because they were considered British subjects they were refused permission to leave.

Bastarache's whereabouts over the next few years are not certain. By 1769, however, he was at Cape Maringouin, where a number of former prisoners from Fort Cumberland had settled; on 9 April he had three children baptized there by Abbé Charles-François Bailly* de Messein. Later he went to live on the west bank of the Memramcook River, at a place now called Cormier Cove, on lands belonging to Joseph Goreham*. Probably in 1787, Bastarache and his son-in-law Joseph Saulnier moved to Tracadie, north of Miramichi Bay, and settled on adjoining lots. The two men may be regarded as the founders of Tracadie, for although the Robert, dit Lebreton, family had been in the region a few years before, they did not settle there permanently until later. Bastarache built his house on the shore, near a spring, and shortly began farming. After a few years he quit his land, on which the parish church would be built around 1800; he then went to live farther inland.

In 1815, when Dr Andrew Brown* was gathering material for his history of Nova Scotia, and in particular of the Acadian people, James Fraser*, a Miramichi merchant, recounted the exploits of the Bastaraches: "Michael OBask and his Brother Peter OBask with 12 others travelled through the Woods from Carolina some say from New Orleans to the head of the river St Lawrence and from there came in a Canoe to Cumberland to vizit their wives familys and native land. Both the Basks are alive in the neighbourhood of Miramichi." According to Placide Gaudet*, however, Pierre had died on 25 March 1796. Michel passed away at Tracadie on 15 Jan. 1820, at the age of 89; he left a great many descendants, among them the Basques of Gloucester County.

CORINNE LaPLANTE

Arch. paroissiales, Saint-Joseph et Saint-Jean-Baptiste (Tracadie, N.-B.), Reg. des baptêmes et sépultures. CÉA, Fonds Placide Gaudet, 1.15-16, 1.38-4. PANB, RG 10, RS108, Petition of Pierre Bastarache, 3 Sept. 1795; Petition of Charlemagne Bastarache, 6 Oct. 1803. "Liste des Acadiens prisonniers au fort Beauséjour, en 1763," Soc. hist. acadienne, Cahiers (Moncton, N.-B.), no.7 (mars 1965): 21–25. "Notes from tradition and memory of the Acadian removal," Collection de documents inédits sur le Canada et l'Amérique, [H.-R. Casgrain, édit.] (3v., Québec, 1888–90), 2: 94. "Papiers Amherst (1760–1763) concernant les Acadiens," R. S. Brun, édit., Soc. hist. acadienne, Cahiers, 3 (1968–71): 301. "Quelques documents du musée du fort Beauséjour," R. [S.] Brun, édit., Soc. hist. acadienne, Cahiers, 2 (1966–68): 275–78. Registre de l'abbé Charles-François Bailly, 1768 à 1773 (Caraquet), [C.-F. Bailly de Messein, compil.], S. A. White, édit. (Moncton, 1978), 30. Arsenault, Hist. et généal. des Acadiens (1965). Émile Lauvrière, La tragédie d'un peuple: histoire du peuple acadien de ses origines à nos jours (nouv. éd., 2v., Paris, [1924]). Paul Surette, Memramkouke, Petcoudiac et la reconstruction de l'Acadie, 1763–1806 ... (Moncton, 1981), 27. R. S. Brun, "Histoire socio-démographique du sud-est du Nouveau-Brunswick: migrations acadiennes et seigneuries anglaises (1760–1810)," Soc. hist. acadienne, Cahiers, 3 (1968–71): [58]–88. Placide Gaudet, "Arbre généalogique de la famille Bastarache," La Voix d'Évangéline (Moncton), 29 janv. 1942: 11; "Michel et Pierre Bastarache," Le Moniteur acadien (Shédiac, N.-B.), 16 avril 1889; "Tracadie, N.-B.," Courrier des Provinces maritimes (Bathurst, N.-B.), 17 janv. 1895; "Tracadie, N.-B.," L'Évangéline (Weymouth Bridge, N.-É.), 17 nov., 1er déc. 1892. "L'odyssée de Pierre et Michel Bastarache, 1755–56," Soc. hist. acadienne, Cahiers, 4 (1971–73): 163–64.

BEARDSLEY (Beardslee), JOHN, Church of England clergyman; b. 23 April 1732 in Ripton (Shelton), Conn., son of John Beardsley, a farmer and land surveyor, and Keziah Wheeler; d. 23 Aug. 1809 in Kingston, N.B.

John Beardsley was baptized by the Reverend Samuel Johnson, afterwards president of King's

College (Columbia University), but nothing further is known of his early life until 1758, when he entered Yale College. He left Yale after two years, because of anti-Anglican sentiment there, and then continued his studies at King's under Johnson. He would have graduated with his classmates in 1761 had he not departed before commencement to seek ordination in England. Sharing both the spring voyage and its purpose was Samuel ANDREWS, later missionary at St Andrews, N.B. Among those who recommended Beardsley for holy orders was his future father-in-law, the Reverend Ebenezer Punderson, who described him as "a Person of an Unspotted Character & of an Excellent Temper & Disposition, Sound in his Principles of Religion, Firmly Attach'd to our most excellent Ch[urc]h." Beardsley was ordained deacon on 6 Aug. 1761, and raised to the priesthood by the archbishop of Canterbury 17 days later. The degree of AB *honoris causa* was conferred by King's College in 1761 and the degree of AM in 1768.

Beardsley began his ministry as missionary of the Society for the Propagation of the Gospel at Groton and Norwich, Conn., where he arrived early in 1762. The inhabitants of Groton were apparently lax in fulfilling their obligations towards him, however, and he eventually asked to be transferred. Late in 1766 he removed to Poughkeepsie in Dutchess County, N.Y., an area he had earlier served from Groton. "I shall . . . take Care that they pay the poor Man his Salary," Dr Samuel Auchmuty of New York informed the SPG. "He is not very bright, but is honest and industrious in his calling. . . ." Beardsley's parish was a scattered one, in which he claimed to ride 3,000 miles a year in the performance of his duties. His devotion and physical exertions resulted in the building of Trinity Church at Fishkill and Christ Church in Poughkeepsie.

Beardsley opposed the revolutionary movement and as a result suffered "repeated insults" and many misadventures before finally taking refuge in New York City late in 1777. He and his family were allowed to take away with them only "their wearing apparel and necessary bedding and provisions for their passage, and no other goods or effects whatsoever." The following year Colonel Beverley Robinson, one of his former parishioners and a prominent freemason, asked him to act as chaplain of the Loyal American Regiment, and his name appears on the muster-rolls of this unit, which saw service in New York, New Jersey, Pennsylvania, and the south. Some time during 1779 or early 1780 Beardsley himself became a member of the masonic fraternity, and by 1781, when a provincial grand lodge was organized provisionally in New York, he was the unanimous choice for the office of junior grand warden. He remained active until 1783, when he resigned his office on deciding to leave New York. On 8 March of that year, before his departure, Beardsley joined 17 other clergymen in preparing "A Plan of Religious and Literary Institution for the province of Nova Scotia," which was the origin of King's College, opened as a grammar school at Windsor, N.S., in 1788 and now situated in Halifax.

In the summer of 1783 Beardsley followed many of his former parishioners to Parrtown (Saint John, N.B.). At his own suggestion he became an itinerant minister, visiting settlers on both sides of the Saint John River as far as St Anne's Point (Fredericton). He also assisted James Sayre in the new communities at the river's mouth. When the rector of Maugerville, John Sayre, died in 1784, Beardsley received a unanimous call to remove there. Christ Church in Maugerville stands as a monument to his labours in the settlement. His letters to the SPG reveal that he was active as well in ministering to nearby communities, particularly Burton. While in Parrtown Beardsley had been invited to become master of Hiram Lodge No. 17, the first masonic body in New Brunswick, and in Maugerville he was an active member of St George's Lodge No. 19, of which Samuel RYERSE was the first master. In 1793 Beardsley was appointed chaplain of the King's New Brunswick Regiment.

By the time Beardsley was established in Maugerville he had already been married several times. His first marriage, to Sylvia Punderson, likely took place in 1763 or earlier, since on 26 Sept. 1764 he informed the SPG of the existence of a wife and child. Sylvia died some time after February 1771, when twins were born to them, and Beardsley seems then to have married Catharine Brooks, who died in Poughkeepsie on 5 Feb. 1774. Shortly thereafter he took as his wife Gertrude Crannell. Whether Gertrude accompanied him to New Brunswick is not known: by a deed registered on 10 June 1786 Beardsley and "Anna, my wife" transferred a town lot in Saint John, but no other evidence of "Anna" has been found. Around 1792 Beardsley and his then wife separated, and Mrs Beardsley departed for New York. On 28 Oct. 1798 he was married again, to Mrs Mary Quain of Saint John, apparently believing that his former wife had died in the United States. When it became clear that she was in fact still living, "people in general were much scandalized, and . . . his congregation were so much offended as to declare they would no longer adhere to or attend him." An "astonished and distressed" Bishop Charles INGLIS instituted an investigation into the matter, and the inquiring clergymen concluded that Beardsley had not been justified in remarrying. Inglis himself found "no proof of prudence or consideration" in Beardsley's having trusted to unsubstantiated rumours about his wife's death or in his having continued to "cohabit" with Mrs Quain once it had become clear that his former wife was still alive: "What must the world think of a man who has two

Beaubien

wives alive at the same time, and no divorce from either of them? And what must be thought of a clergyman who is in this predicament?" Though Beardsley seems initially to have complied with the bishop's instruction to separate from Mrs Quain, this situation apparently did not endure. His resignation was accepted in 1801 on the grounds that "his late, & present conduct utterly disqualifies him for a Missionary." The incident had caused some anguish to Beardsley's fellow missionaries and to Inglis, who held him in high regard. "His conduct," the bishop had concluded, "was rather marked by weakness and dotage than depravity."

How many children Beardsley and his wives had is not known. Though the twins appear to be the only children of his marriage to Sylvia Punderson found in church registers, he was said in 1768 to have had a large family. Ten years later, after his arrival in New York, he noted that his family was 12 in number, five of whom were under the age of seven. One son, John Davis, served for a time as schoolmaster at Maugerville. It was apparently he who in 1798 refused an invitation to take holy orders because no government allowance was attached to his proposed mission at Prince William, a decision which, it was reported, "very much disgusted his worthy Father." Another son, Bartholomew Crannell*, became a prominent lawyer and judge. The distinguished historian William Odber Raymond* was a great-great-grandson.

In 1807 Lieutenant Governor Thomas CARLETON was able to arrange half pay as a military chaplain for "poor Beardsley," who at some point after his resignation went to live with his daughter Hannah Dibblee in Kingston; there he died on 23 Aug. 1809, the 48th anniversary of his ordination, and was buried under the chancel of Trinity Church. Though he is sometimes referred to as the Reverend Dr Beardsley, no evidence of a doctoral degree has been found. In 1916 the Grand Lodge of Free and Accepted Masons of New Brunswick erected a brass tablet to his memory in Trinity Church, and in 1967 the same institution, to mark its centennial, established the John Beardsley medal as the highest honour for distinguished service to freemasonry in New Brunswick. By this means the loyalist clergyman and father of freemasonry in New Brunswick is remembered today.

C. ALEXANDER PINCOMBE

Saint John Registry Office (Saint John, N.B.), Libro A2: 47 (John Beardsley, deed to Thomas [?] Thitlock, registered 10 June 1786). PAC, MG 23, C6, ser.1, 3: 27–38. USPG, B, 2, nos.22, 30; 3, nos.24, 28, 39; 23, nos.54, 152, 292; Journal of SPG, 16: 267; 17: 51–52, 86–87; 21: 297; 23: 350–51, 376–77; 24: 90; 25; 26: 372; 27: 358; 28: 173. *Minutes of the committee and of the first commission for detecting and defeating conspiracies in the state of New York, December 11, 1776–September 23, 1778 . . .* (2v., New York,

1924–25). *The records of Christ Church, Poughkeepsie, New York*, ed. H. W. Reynolds (2v., Poughkeepsie, 1911–[?]). *New-York Gazette, and Weekly Mercury* (New York), 14 Feb. 1774. E. E. Beardsley, *A sketch of William Beardsley: one of the original settlers of Stratford, Conn.; and a record of his descendants to the third generation . . .* (New Haven, Conn., 1867). I. H. Beardsley, *Genealogical history of the Beardsley-lee family in America, 1635–1902* (Denver, Colo., 1902). F. B. Dexter, *Biographical sketches of the graduates of Yale College, with annals of the college history* (6v., New York and New Haven, 1885–1912). W. F. Bunting, *History of St. John's Lodge, F. & A.M. of Saint John, New Brunswick, together with sketches of all masonic bodies in New Brunswick from A.D. 1784 to A.D. 1894* (Saint John, 1895). R. V. Harris, "Rev. John Beardsley (1732–1809), founder of freemasonry in New Brunswick," Canadian Masonic Research Assoc., [*Papers*] (n.p.), nos.32–33 ([1956]): 1–11.

BEAUBIEN, EUSTACHE-IGNACE TROTTIER DESRIVIÈRES. *See* TROTTIER

BEAUJEU DE VILLEMONDE, LOUIS LIÉNARD DE. *See* LIÉNARD

BÉDARD, JEAN-BAPTISTE, carpenter and surveyor; b. 18 May 1761 in Charlesbourg (Que.), son of Thomas Bédard and Marie-Angélique Fiset; m. first 17 April 1792 Marie-Anne Toupin at Quebec, Lower Canada; m. secondly 13 June 1815 Madeleine Daigle in Saint-Ambroise (Loretteville), Lower Canada; d. 7 Jan. 1818 at Quebec.

Jean-Baptiste Bédard's career as a carpenter began in 1782, when he was hired by the Séminaire de Québec through the influence of his brother Thomas-Laurent*, who was its superior. He was sent that year as a "contractor" to Bellevue, the summer residence for its students at Saint-Joachim; later, and until 1787, he was given responsibility for various pieces of construction and maintenance work on the seminary's buildings in Quebec. Even after being appointed a surveyor in 1790 he continued to make his services available to its ecclesiastics. He carried out survey work for them in the seigneury of Beaupré, the sub-fief of La Trinité, and at Baie-Saint-Paul. In 1796 he also received payment for building the framework for the seminary's chapel.

Bédard was admitted to the surveying profession apparently without any previous training. A study of his reports shows that most of his activity took place between 1790 and 1795. He lived at Quebec and worked mainly in the neighbouring seigneuries, such as Rigaud-Vaudreuil in the Beauce, where in the autumn of 1791 he drew up no fewer than 116 reports for its owner, Gaspard-Joseph Chaussegros* de Léry the younger.

From 1796, surveying began to take second place in Bédard's career, since he gradually returned to his initial interests, those of the master carpenter. The list of important building projects in which he was involved is long. At an early stage he acquired a certain reputation, following the difficulties encountered by Martin Cannon; the stone bridge that Cannon had put up over the Rivière Jacques-Cartier collapsed in the spring of 1802. Bédard appeared before commissioners Gabriel-Elzéar TASCHEREAU, Jonathan Sewell*, and John CRAIGIE with a new model to replace it, a bridge equipped with a complex system of trusses and arches. In the summer of 1804 the bridge was finally rebuilt by Bédard for £50 to the great satisfaction of the commissioners, who had been somewhat afraid that their good name would be sullied by the collapse of the first structure.

Probably encouraged by this success, in 1806 Bédard asked for the exclusive right to put up wooden bridges based on two models that he had devised. By an act of 16 April 1807 the House of Assembly did, in fact, grant him that privilege for a period of 14 years, but it is impossible to determine how many bridges were built according to Bédard's plans. In any event, he was approached in 1810 about building one over the Montmorency, but the cost of the work was considered too high by the overseer of highways for the Quebec region, Jean-Baptiste-Philippe d'Estimauville*. Bédard is also thought to have prepared the plans for a bridge over the Saint-Maurice in 1816.

In 1807 Bédard had been associated with the construction of the famous market in the Upper Town that Major William Robe designed. This circular market, considered a daring architectural design, was not built according to the initial plans and was not at all appreciated by the townspeople, to the point that in 1815 Joseph Bouchette* wrote that it must not "continue to be public proof of bad taste." Bédard, who had constructed the roof of the market, must have been aware of the bill passed by the assembly in 1815 which ordered the building demolished to prevent the risk of fire.

When construction of the Quebec prison (from 1862 the home of Morrin College) was undertaken in 1808 under François Baillairgé*'s direction, all the carpentry work was entrusted to Bédard. Similarly, in 1817 he was given a contract for £2,390 to extend Quebec's Rue Saint-Paul.

Bédard's knowledge was also put to use in the construction of religious buildings. For example, between 1799 and 1804 he put up the framework, roof, and bell-tower of the Anglican church in Quebec, which later became the Cathedral of the Holy Trinity. The bell-tower in particular was called a skilful piece of work by the architect in charge, Major Robe, with whom Bédard worked on occasion. In 1809 Bédard erected the framework of St Andrew's, the Presbyterian church in Quebec, and then in 1813 he built the roof, vault, and steeple of the church at nearby Saint-Augustin. The parish syndics there had undertaken to supply him with nine men liable for the corvée to help him in his work. To get all these large-scale projects started, Bédard resorted to obtaining loans, generally for less than £100, from important persons or members of his family. These liquid assets served particularly for buying the lumber, which came mainly from a merchant in Sainte-Anne-de-la-Pérade (La Pérade).

A master carpenter's work is difficult to evaluate, the architectural qualities of a building usually being attributed to the person who conceives the project, and not to the one who carries it out. Also, recent studies in architectural history show no awareness of Bédard's contribution to important works such as the Quebec prison, Holy Trinity, or St Andrew's. It is certainly not presumptuous to affirm that he was one of the few local craftsmen who succeeded in adapting quickly to the new styles in architecture that the British were trying to introduce to Lower Canada. His ingenuity in bridge-building was, moreover, recognized by his contemporaries.

When he died in 1818, Jean-Baptiste Bédard was living on Rue Saint-Joachim at Quebec, in a luxurious two-storey stone house that he had had built eight years earlier by Pierre-Florent BAILLAIRGÉ, at a cost of £347. He also owned some pieces of property in the *faubourg* Saint-Roch.

GILLES LANGELIER

Jean-Baptiste Bédard's surveyor's reports for 1790 to 1817 are at ANQ-Q, CA1-3.

ANQ-Q, CE1-1, 17 avril 1792, 7 janv. 1818; CE1-7, 18 mai 1761; CE1-28, 13 janv. 1815; CN1-16, 7 avril 1809; CN1-26, 1er juin 1808; CN1-230, 3 mai 1804; 6 mai, 19 juin 1809; 3 avril, 6 juill. 1813; 4 juin, 12 déc. 1814; 17 avril, 8 juill., 5 déc. 1817. ASQ, C 37: 5, 8, 20, 22, 45, 53, 93, 104, 152–53, 155, 169; S, S-168; S-169. PAC, RG 1, E15, A, 288–89; E17; RG 4, A1: 27670–71; B33, 18. Bas-Canada, *Statuts*, 1807, c.15; 1815, c.7. *Quebec Gazette*, 24 June 1790; 10 April 1806; 26 Feb., 26 March, 2, 9, 16 April, 7, 21 May 1807; 10 Jan. 1818. Omer Bédard, *Généalogie des familles Bédard du district de Québec* (Québec, 1946), 42–43, 52–53, 98–99. Bouchette, *Description topographique du Bas-Canada*, 468–69. Luc Noppen *et al.*, *Québec: trois siècles d'architecture* ([Montréal], 1979), 54–55, 320. A. J. H. Richardson, "Guide to the architecturally and historically most significant buildings in the old city of Quebec with a biographical dictionary of architects and builders and illustrations," Assoc. for Preservation Technology, *Bull.* (Ottawa), 2 (1970), nos.3–4. F. C. Würtele, "The English cathedral of Quebec," Literary and Hist. Soc. of Quebec, *Trans.* (Quebec), new ser., 20 (1891): 80.

BEDOUT, JACQUES, naval officer; b. 13 Jan. 1751 at Quebec, son of Jean-Antoine Bedout, a merchant and member of the Conseil Supérieur of Quebec, and Françoise Barolet; m. first Marie-Jeanne Daigre,

Bedout

probably in Saint-Domingue (Haiti); m. secondly 31 May 1804 Jeanne Pécholier, *née* Lafont, in Bordeaux, France; no children were born of these marriages; d. 17 April 1818 in Pauillac, France.

Jacques Bedout began sailing as a cabin-boy on board merchant ships in 1763; by 1776 he had completed 16 voyages to America, England, the West Indies, and France, and along the Guinea coast. In this way he got to know the seas and rose in the merchant marine, becoming second mate in 1768, first mate in 1770, and captain in 1772.

Having arrived in France at the beginning of 1777, Bedout on 25 January received a temporary commission as sub-lieutenant in the royal navy and sailed for the West Indies on the *Coursier*. In America he joined the rebels; on 30 July 1777 he took command of the privateer *Défense*, which had been equipped at Boston, Mass., for operation under the American flag, and on 10 August engaged in combat with a British privateer. On 13 December he fitted out at Bordeaux the privateer *Congrès*, with which he fought two British ships off the entrance to Chesapeake Bay on 14 Feb. 1778. After three hours of combat he had to strike his flag; taken prisoner to New York City, he escaped to embark as second in command on board the American frigate *Vengeance*, in which he returned to France. Then, at the request of Rear-Admiral the Comte Du Chaffault de Besné, who valued his abilities, Bedout took up service again in the royal navy. He was a supernumerary officer on the *Diadème* in June 1778, and on the *Neptune* in the squadron under the Comte d'Orvilliers in October. In March 1779 he helped fit out the *Protée*, and in April transferred to the *Couronne* to take part in the Channel campaign. In February 1780 he sailed for the West Indies on the frigate *Railleuse* and participated in the capture of Tobago. He then took ship at Saint-Domingue, sailed through the Bahamas, and in October 1781 reached Chesapeake Bay; there he fought in the battle in which the Comte de Grasse's squadron repulsed the British forces under Rear-Admiral Thomas GRAVES and brought on the capitulation at Yorktown, Va, thus assuring the victory of the rebels and the independence of the American colonies.

In July 1782 Bedout received command of the corvette *Saint-Louis*, which was to escort convoys bound for the West Indies. After returning to France in December 1782 on the *Railleuse*, he was transferred the following January to the *Andromaque*, which was being dispatched to take the peace treaty signed at Versailles to the United States. Promoted lieutenant on 1 May 1786, and thus permanently attached to the navy, Bedout used the leave given at that time to officers of his rank to command the *Pourvoyeuse* on a trading voyage along the Guinea coast from January 1786 to May 1787.

Bedout was promoted lieutenant-commander on 1 May 1792 and captain on 27 Aug. 1793. He then received command of the *Terrible*, a 110-gun ship in the squadron at Brest, France, under the Comte de Villaret de Joyeuse. In June 1794 he transferred to the *Tigre* and took part in the battles off the Île de Groix in which Villaret de Joyeuse tried without success to loosen the blockade of the coasts of Brittany. Wounded four times, with nearly half his crew lost and his ship unable to manœuvre or fight, Bedout had to surrender and was taken prisoner. He was quickly freed; on 22 June 1796 he was acquitted by a court martial and received the *armes d'honneur* – sabre, sword, pair of pistols, sextant, and telescope – to which the Directory added a gratuity of 18,000 *livres*. He was immediately given command of the *Indomptable* in the squadron assigned to escort the expeditionary corps being sent to make a landing in Ireland.

On 12 April 1798 Bedout was promoted rear-admiral, and the following year he commanded the second squadron, with the *Républicain* as flagship, under Admiral Eustache Bruix. This force sailed from Brest in April 1799, reached Toulon, went on to supply the army of Italy at Genoa, and returned to Brest in July without encountering the enemy. In November Bedout took command of a squadron of five ships of the line and three frigates that sailed from Lorient to Rochefort to protect the region against British attack. When he was relieved of his post by Admiral Denis Decrès, Bedout tendered his resignation, but it was refused.

In October 1802 Napoleon entrusted him with command of a new squadron of five ships of the line, with the *Argonaute* as flagship, which sailed from Brest in January 1803 for Genoa; there it took on 5,000 Polish soldiers for transport to Saint-Domingue. Bedout carried out this mission and then set sail for Europe. During the return crossing his squadron captured one British privateer and destroyed another. Worn out by illness, Bedout had to land in Spain at El Ferrol (El Ferrol del Caudillo) in November and give up his command. His active career was finished. His name, however, continued to appear on the rolls, and he was not placed on the retired list until 1 Jan. 1816. At his death in 1818 he left an estate consisting solely of two-thirds of a rather small wine-producing property.

Jacques Bedout was always rated highly by his superiors, who constantly praised his talents, ardour, activity, nautical knowledge, and skill in handling ships. He was obviously an excellent officer.

ÉTIENNE TAILLEMITE

AN, Marine, C¹, 159: f.301v.; C⁷, 147 (dossier Bedout). ANQ-Q, CE1-1, 14 janv. 1751. Louis Nicolas, *La puissance navale dans l'histoire* (3v., Paris, 1958–60), 1. Georges Six,

Dictionnaire biographique des généraux et amiraux français de la Révolution et de l'Empire . . . (2v., Paris, 1934), 1: 72. P.-G. Roy, "Le contre-amiral Jacques Bedout," *BRH*, 34 (1928): 641–55.

BEHZER, TRAUGOTT LEBERECHT. *See* PIUZE, LIVERIGHT

BELCHER, BENJAMIN, merchant, militia officer, and politician; b. 17 July 1743 in Gibraltar; m. 5 June 1764 Sarah Post in Cornwallis, N.S., and they had five sons (including twins) and one daughter; d. there 14 May 1802. By his son Benjamin, Belcher was the grandfather of Clement Horton Belcher*, the Halifax publisher and bookseller.

Little is known of Benjamin Belcher's early life other than that he was born at Gibraltar, probably of English parentage; he likely came to Halifax, N.S., some time around 1760. There was apparently no family connection between Belcher and Chief Justice Jonathan Belcher*, who was originally from Boston, Mass., and who had come to Nova Scotia in 1754 after residence in England and Ireland. With the encouragement of two friends, John BURBIDGE and William Best, Belcher took up residence at Cornwallis about 1764. A man of enterprise and ability, he appears to have had no difficulty establishing himself in the community, though it was not until 1797 that he received a grant of 606½ acres, formerly the property of Joseph Goreham*, at Terry's Creek (Port Williams). The grant lay along the road connecting Terry's Creek with Horton Corner (Kentville), known today as Belcher Street. Adjacent to his home Belcher maintained a general store, which served a wide area of the surrounding countryside. He also traded with the West Indies, his brigs carrying horses, foodstuffs, and lumber there and returning with molasses and rum.

During the American revolution the population of Kings County was at best neutral, but Belcher took an active role in defence of the established order. As lieutenant of the volunteer militia of Cornwallis, he executed a courageous and daring exploit against a rebel force in the Bay of Fundy. On 21 April 1781 he and 28 volunteers aboard the armed sloop *Success* were responsible for the capture of 30 rebels in two gunboats who had been harassing navigation in the bay, and subsequently brought them to Cornwallis Township for trial.

In the provincial election of 1785 Belcher was returned as a member for Cornwallis Township, taking his seat on 8 December. Though defeated by Jonathan Crane in 1793, he petitioned the legislature on the grounds that his opponent had exercised undue influence on election day. A select committee investigated and declared him elected member for Kings County on 30 March. He held the seat until 1799, when Crane was victorious. While a member Belcher was a moving spirit in the affairs of the house. He actively participated in sessional business, frequently serving as deputy speaker, and he manifested a particular interest in provincial finance and trade and the condition of the poor. Belcher also sat on several select committees, including the one which drew up articles of impeachment against the Supreme Court judges James BRENTON and Isaac DESCHAMPS, the one which dealt with the Jamaican maroons [*see* Sir John WENTWORTH], and the one which recommended the establishment of what later became King's College [*see* Charles INGLIS]. His involvement in assembly affairs must have made a political career attractive to him, for in 1801 he offered himself as a candidate for Queens County in the forthcoming by-election. He was turned down, on the grounds that, as Simeon PERKINS noted, it would "be rather a disgrace to the County to chuse another abroad." Little more than a year later he passed away at the age of 58, leaving a substantial estate which included seven black slaves, with whose care he charged his family in his copious will.

From all accounts Belcher was a man endowed with breeding and education, which he combined with business acumen and a genuine regard for the less privileged. He was a devout adherent of the Church of England, and served as warden for the Church of St John in Cornwallis from 1784 until his death. His will specified that £300 be put towards the construction of a new church and that tablets inscribed in gilt letters with the Lord's Prayer, the Ten Commandments, and the Creed be erected in the chancel; they stand there to this day.

SHIRLEY B. ELLIOTT

Kings County Court of Probate (Kentville, N.S.), Estate inventory and will of Benjamin Belcher, probated 16 May 1802 (mfm. at PANS). N.S., Dept. of Lands and Forests (Halifax), Crown land grants, old book no.20: 43 (mfm. at PANS). PANS, MG 4, 18. N.S., House of Assembly, *Journal and proc.*, 1785–99. Perkins, *Diary, 1797–1803* (Fergusson). *Nova-Scotia Gazette and the Weekly Chronicle*, 8 May 1781. A. W. H. Eaton, *The history of Kings County, Nova Scotia* . . . (Salem, Mass., 1910; repr. Belleville, Ont., 1972). J. E. M. Rand, *Historical sketch of Church of St. John, 1810–1960, and the parish of Cornwallis, Nova Scotia, 1760–1960* (n.p., [1960]).

BELL, JAMES, merchant, carpenter, and landowner; b. *c.* 1739 in Great Britain, likely in England; m. Margaret Christie, daughter of William Christie of Stirling, Scotland; d. probably 5 July 1814 in Chambly, Lower Canada.

By his marriage James Bell became the nephew of Gabriel Christie*, who had come to Canada during the Seven Years' War and whose purchase of numerous

Bellefleur

seigneuries during the period 1764–66 made him the uncontested master of the upper Richelieu region in the second half of the 18th century. James Bell arrived at Chambly with his wife and probably a son, Alexander, some time between 1765 and 1772, and he settled on the banks of a stream, the Rivière Montréal (Rivière L'Acadie). He traded in wheat, meat, spirits, building materials, carriages, and horses. Like many British merchants who had come to Canada at that time, he tried to take advantage of circumstances and established links with the Canadians on whom his success in business directly depended. He did not let language or religion stand in the way but mastered French and occasionally allowed people to call him Jacques; he even had a son and a daughter baptized in the Roman Catholic church of the parish of Saint-Louis (Saint-Joseph) at Chambly: William in January 1773 and Margaret the next year. In business he used French-speaking notaries and for his construction work he hired several Canadians.

Bell was an opportunist, particularly during the American invasion of 1775–76. The assertion that he embraced the American cause probably requires qualification: rather, Bell saw the arrival of the revolutionary troops on the Richelieu as a chance to make money. Therefore, like a number of British merchants in Montreal such as Thomas Walker*, he did not hesitate to offer the enemy his help. His knowledge of the terrain, his great skill as a carpenter, and his resources as a merchant made him valuable to the invaders. Working in turn under Major John Brown and brigadiers-general Richard Montgomery*, David Wooster, and Benedict ARNOLD, he helped to supply them and was particularly involved in overseeing the repair work on Fort Chambly and the building of numerous bateaux, "gundeloes," and carriages, for which he also supplied much of the material. But the American army had limited means and Bell suffered the fate of many other suppliers: nine invoices, totalling £2,100 15s. 9d., remained unpaid.

In the summer of 1776 the retreating enemy troops left Quebec soil. After that Bell offered his services to the king. With men he had hired, he cut considerable quantities of wood for the crown, built a barracks and two blockhouses at the mouth of the Richelieu, and constructed many bateaux as well as a score of artillery tumbrels. In June and July 1777 he went to Fort Ticonderoga (near Ticonderoga) and then to Fort George (Lake George) with the British expedition sent into New York under Major-General John Burgoyne* to confront the American army.

Back at Chambly again, Bell encountered difficulties in his commercial pursuits. In 1781, with his business in stone and other materials at a standstill, he asked Governor HALDIMAND for a job, as well as a licence to cut wood and quarry limestone for construction. He could not obtain reimbursement of

the considerable sum the American government owed him, which he estimated in 1792 at £4,021 10s. 11d., despite numerous attempts and even a brief change of residence to "Little Charzy" (Chazy, N.Y.). Unable to repay his own debts, he was sued by Simon Fraser Sr, Moses Hart*, and David Alexander Grant in the period 1795–1802; as a result, on a number of occasions he suffered distraint or sale by auction, which stripped him of some 20 pieces of land in the seigneury of Chambly, the barony of Longueuil, and Hemmingford and Shefford townships. Shortly before 1800, at the time he moved to Quebec, Bell was close to ruin. In 1802 he presented a petition to the British government seeking lands for himself and his family in recognition of his "unquestionably uniform" loyalty and the services he had rendered the king during the American revolution.

James Bell nevertheless returned to spend his final years on the banks of the Rivière Montréal; he may have made a living there from some acres of land that he apparently still owned at Chambly. Sick and bed-ridden, he made his will on 27 April 1814; leaving his children William and Margaret £6 each, he made his wife his residual legatee. He died early in July probably on the 5th, at the age of 75, and was borne to his grave with ceremony by fellow masons from Dorchester Lodge No.3, of Dorchester (Saint-Jean-sur-Richelieu), which he had helped found in 1792. His wife endeavoured to obtain payment from the United States of the debt owed her husband, but she died on 10 Sept. 1831 without having succeeded.

JACQUES CASTONGUAY

ANQ-M, CE1-39, 14 janv. 1773, 9 juin 1774; CE1-79, 12 Sept. 1831; CN1-43, 27 avril 1814. ANQ-Q, CN1-284, 10 nov. 1800. AP, Saint-Athanase (Iberville), Notes du notaire Didace Tassé, 19 sept. 1874. Arch. du séminaire de Trois-Rivières (Trois-Rivières, Qué.), Fonds Hart, G, no.1, F-B, 57. BL, Add. MSS 21734: ff.276–77. PAC, RG 1, L3L: 1333, 1353, 1453, 20179–94, 30977, 41941, 84753, 95242–44. *Montreal Gazette*, 21 July 1814. *Quebec Gazette*, 26 Feb. 1795; 26 Sept. 1799; 14 May 1801; 5 Aug., 25 Nov. 1802. [R. F. Gould and W. J. Hughan], *A library of freemasonry* . . . (4v., London and Montreal, 1911), 4: 478. J.-O. Dion, "James Bell," *BRH*, 7 (1901): 248–49.

BELLEFLEUR, DOMINIQUE MONDELAIT, *dit. See* MONDELET

BELLEVILLE, FRANÇOIS GUERNON, *dit. See* GUERNON

BENAR, NUEL. *See* BERNARD, NOËL

BENTLEY, ELIJAH, farmer, Baptist minister, and office holder; son of Samuel Bently, "a steady Loyalist during the american war"; m. with three children; fl. 1799–1814.

Elijah Bentley's life in Upper Canada is little more than a series of fragments highlighted by his trial for sedition during the War of 1812. In 1799 Samuel Bently, a blacksmith and scythe-maker, probably from Rhode Island or Massachusetts, led his sons Reuben, Elijah, and Ira and two sons-in-law into Upper Canada. Reuben and Elijah brought their families; the others planned to return for theirs upon obtaining land. Elijah farmed briefly on a rented lot in Clinton Township and in 1801 received a grant, which he patented, in Markham Township, also the choice of the rest of his family. When Elijah sold his lot in 1805, he had cleared more than eight acres, fenced seven, and built a house. Whether he subsequently purchased or rented another lot is not known, but, by his own account, he continued to reside and farm in the area until 1814.

The Bentleys had probably been Baptists in the United States, and following their arrival in Upper Canada Elijah became increasingly involved in the province's rapidly expanding Baptist community. The church advanced steadily before the War of 1812: in 1802 missionaries of American Baptist associations commenced regular tours in the colony, and Michael SMITH, the Baptist preacher and author, reported in 1813 that there were 15 churches and 11 resident preachers. Bentley himself had established a church at Markham in 1803. Two years later he was ordained by elders Reuben Crandall*, Joseph Winn, and Abel Stevens*. He hoped to take advantage of the wording of the Marriage Act of 1798, which extended the authority to perform legal marriages, hitherto the privilege of the Church of England, to "members of the Church of Scotland, or Lutherans, or Calvinists." The act was intended to defuse opposition to the Church of England's favoured position, but it was clearly limited to Lutherans and Presbyterians. Although one Baptist minister, Crandall, had gained the right to solemnize marriages, Bentley's own hopes were quickly dashed. After setting aside his initial application because it lacked "sufficient proof" of his ordination, on 8 April 1806 the Court of Quarter Sessions for the Home District, which included William JARVIS and William WILLCOCKS, rejected it as "being under the signature of one, who states himself a Baptist." Bentley next appears in records in 1809, when at a church conference in Townsend (Nanticoke) he urged the Baptists there to break with the Vermont-based Shaftsbury Association and join the Thurlow Association, which had been formed in 1802 in Thurlow Township. The next year, as an agent of the Thurlow Association, he visited Baptist churches throughout the province.

Bentley's activities were not limited to the church. On 10 April 1805 he was appointed one of three constables for Markham. More important was the notice taken of the Bentley family's espousal of Robert Thorpe*'s candidacy in the election of 1807. Lieutenant Governor Francis Gore* believed the political inclinations of the opposition associated with Thorpe to be democratic. Moreover, he considered American emigrants, such as the Bentleys, to have "brought the very worst principles of their own constitution with them." The papers of the Executive Council contain an alphabetical list of 346 signatories, including the Bentleys, to an 1807 petition supporting Thorpe. It is worth noting that 12, and possibly 13, of the 32 men charged in 1813 with treason in the Home District had signed the 1807 petition.

Just a month before the outbreak of war in June 1812, Bentley was assisting Surveyor General Thomas Ridout* with a project of some sort in Markham. The war upset the equipoise of his life. The dubious allegiance of non-loyalist American settlers, whom Smith estimated at 60 per cent of the population, now became one of the foremost concerns of military and civil officials. Even after the victories at Detroit and Queenston Heights in 1812, disaffection and treason plagued the colony's military administrators. The occupations of York (Toronto) in 1813 revealed to élites throughout the province a sub-political seam of discontent and republican sentiment within the Home District. Public declarations of sympathy for the enemy, incautiously uttered tavern oaths denouncing monarchy, crude egalitarian declamations, and fraternization with the enemy spurred civil authorities such as William Allan* and William Dummer Powell* to urge coercive measures "to suppress the disloyal and confirm the wavering." The administrator of the province, Francis Rottenburg*, was duly alarmed and on 13 Aug. 1813 he ordered the acting attorney general, John Beverley Robinson*, to report on "dangerous and treasonable inclinations." The next day Robinson met with Allan, Ridout, Alexander Wood*, Duncan Cameron*, and John Strachan*. On the 16th they submitted a cursory analysis which caught the prevailing spirit of official anxiety by pressing the need for "the influence of some present example." Robinson suggested the formation of a committee to prepare an official report. Rottenburg agreed; the aforementioned group, with Robinson replaced by his brother Peter*, began work immediately.

The committee reported on 29 September; 64 depositions had been taken and 32 men were subsequently charged. Although anxious to make examples, the members of the committee were not the dupes of their own prejudices. Of the depositions, they astutely commented: "Some are mixed with prejudice, some with malice, others are clear and pointed." The greatest number for one person, 11 in all, concerned Bentley. One deponent, Samuel HERON, had heard Bentley deliver a sermon in which he "thanked God there was never such freedom for

Bentley

poor people in York as there was since General [Henry] Dearborn set foot in it." Others claimed that Bentley had publicly described himself as a "great friend to the United States And no friend to the King" and that he had directed American troops to government stores, "endeavoured to alienate the minds of His Majesty's Subjects from the Government," and sought a parole for his son Benjamin. One even commented, perhaps justly, that Bentley was "more dangerous from his great opportunities as a Preacher."

Bentley was charged with seditious utterance, spreading false intelligence, and inviting the militia to accept Dearborn's offer of parole. He appeared before the Home District Assizes on 26 Oct. 1813 but on Robinson's motion was released on bail for trial on 31 March 1814. On this occasion the trial judges were the chief justice, Thomas Scott*, and the associate justice, Ridout. Bentley pleaded not guilty, but after hearing the testimony of four witnesses the petit jury found him guilty. The following day Scott sentenced him to serve six months in jail and to give bonds to keep the peace for five years. On 18 July a chastened Bentley petitioned George Gordon Drummond*, Rottenburg's successor, to commute the remainder of his sentence on the grounds that "a larger confinement threatens the ruin of his health & property." Whether he was released is not known. Presumably he survived his incarceration and immediately returned to the United States with his family. Members of the extended family continued to reside in Markham, but Samuel and Ira, who were indicted at the great treason trial held at Ancaster in 1814 [see Jacob OVERHOL-SER], also left. Although the war proved only a temporary set-back to the Baptists in Upper Canada, without Bentley the church in Markham took 25 years to recover.

Bentley's arrest and imprisonment highlight a basic feature of Upper Canadian politics in the years prior to the war – the association, by many government officials, of American settlers with democratic politics. This perception was undoubtedly true. The most notorious traitors, the men of Joseph WILLCOCKS's Company of Canadian Volunteers, were (with the exception of Willcocks himself) American-born. At a less active level of involvement, a man such as Bentley illustrates perfectly the meaning of "dubious allegiance." Although his political impulses were always suspect, he was willing to avow openly his sympathy for a more democratic and egalitarian society only when it seemed that the province had been lost to the Americans. In the end the British prevailed, but the actions of men like Bentley undermined the traditional civilian opposition to military demands for martial law or the suspension of habeas corpus. Sedition and treason during the war hardened the anti-American, anti-democratic strain in the colony's political culture and resulted in attitudes that shaped political battles years later, such as the alien issue of the 1820s [see Barnabas Bidwell*].

ROBERT LOCHIEL FRASER III

[I am grateful to Dr Marget Meikleham, who kindly shared the results of her own research in American Baptist sources. These records did not provide any further clues to Bentley's career after 1814. R.L.F.]

AO, MS 4, J. B. Robinson letterbook, 1812–15: 13–14; Thomas Scott to Robinson, 30 March 1814; MU 1368, Elijah, Ira, and Samuel Bentley; RG 1, A-I-6: 4458–60; C-IV, Markham Township, concession 8, lot 4; RG 22, ser.134, 4: 138, 151–52. MTL, York, U.C., papers relating to the capitulation. PAC, MG 9, D7, 2, 25 Feb. 1809 (copies at Canadian Baptist Arch., McMaster Divinity College, Hamilton, Ont.); RG 1, E3, 100: 186; L3, 32: B5/31–32, 54, 85, 92; RG 5, A1: 6514–15, 6523–24, 6528–30, 6569, 6613, 6615, 6617, 6622, 6628, 6630, 6632, 6634, 6644, 6654, 6676, 6829, 8674–75, 10757–59. PRO, CO 42/342: f.63. Toronto Boroughs and York South Registry Office (Toronto), Abstract index to deeds, Markham Township: 219, 227, 410, 421 (mfm. at AO, GS 5867). *Doc. hist. of campaign upon Niagara frontier* (Cruikshank), 6: 81. *Documents relating to the invasion of Canada and the surrender of Detroit, 1812*, ed. E. A. Cruikshank (Ottawa, 1912), 106–7. "Minutes of Court of General Quarter Sessions, Home District," AO *Report*, 1932: 54, 69, 77, 81–82, 84, 116–17, 129, 198. "Political state of U.C.," PAC *Report*, 1892: 94–96. Michael Smith, *A geographical view, of the province of Upper Canada, and promiscuous remarks upon the government . . .* (Hartford, Conn., 1813). *History of Toronto and county of York, Ontario . . .* (2v., Toronto, 1885), 1: 118. Stuart Ivison and Fred Rosser, *The Baptists in Upper and Lower Canada before 1820* (Toronto, 1956).

BENTLEY, JOHN, musician and office holder; b. *c.* 1756 in England; d. 10 Nov. 1813 at Quebec, Lower Canada.

John Bentley, a young English harpsichordist, was living in Philadelphia, Pa, at the end of the American revolution. In 1783 he founded the City Concerts in Philadelphia, the first city in the new republic to have regular musical entertainment. This fortnightly series of vocal and instrumental music drew capacity audiences during runs lasting from October 1783 to April 1784 and from November 1784 to April 1785. In August 1785 Bentley and his wife, Catherine, left for New York with the Lewis Hallam troupe of comedians. Bentley played the harpsichord, led the orchestra when one was required, and composed incidental music as well as the music for three pantomimes, *The cave of enchantment*, *The genii of the rock*, and *Touchstone, or harlequin traveller*. At the end of the New York season in November 1785, two members of the Hallam troupe, William Moore* and Edward Allen, formed their own company; Bentley joined it as musical director, and with his wife played minor roles.

In the first week of March 1786, after having performed for two months at Albany, N.Y., the troupe arrived at Montreal, where they were welcomed with pleasure by the military and the new commercial class. One of their productions was a new pantomime, *The enchanters, or the triumph of genius*, with music by Bentley. After some months the company moved to Quebec, starting its summer season on 21 July. Catherine died there in October, shortly after giving birth to a son. In January 1787 Bentley returned with part of the company to Montreal, where, late in the year as the group was breaking up, he advertised as a teacher of geography, Latin, and English, "known to be the most Sublime, Beautiful, Copious, Energetic and comprehensive Language now us'd on the Habitable Globe."

In January 1788 Bentley was again at Quebec, and there on 11 Jan. 1789 he married Mary Colley Gill, 32-year-old widow of a Quebec businessman, William Gill. They rented a house on Rue des Remparts, where in February 1790 she died in childbirth. Bentley moved to a house along the Rivière Saint-Charles, but it was destroyed by fire in May 1791. He had entered fully into the musical life of the city, being active in subscription concerts of vocal and instrumental music, and was associated with local and touring theatrical groups. At a meeting held on 26 Dec. 1791 to celebrate the passing of the Constitutional Act, he sang an ode which he had set to music; the text was printed in the *Quebec Gazette* of 5 Jan. 1792.

In 1797 Bentley was appointed overseer of highways and bridges for Saint-Charles Ward. In August 1798 he was sworn in as high constable, and on 21 Dec. 1799 he married Deborah, daughter of Hugh McKay, his predecessor in the office. In December 1798 Bentley had been appointed surveyor of the city and suburbs of Quebec, and in May 1801 he replaced William VONDENVELDEN as inspector of roads for the city and parish at a salary of £100 per annum. One of his responsibilities was to enforce the law requiring citizens to maintain the streets in front of their property, and he regularly warned them through the newspapers of this duty; in early March 1811 he successfully prosecuted John Neilson* "for having neglected to cut the Cahots" before his house. Bentley also supervised road construction and paving, and during his tenure the Upper Town market and Rue de la Montagne were paved and streets constructed in the growing suburb of Saint-Jean. When in 1810 a contractor complained in the *Quebec Mercury* that Bentley had sent him a French advertisement for submission of tenders, Bentley apologized in the *Quebec Gazette*, adding that he was "likewise sorry that your education has been so much neglected as not to understand the French language, especially, being now in a part of the world where it is so universally spoken that I should suppose you must pass some of your hours unpleasantly without the knowledge of it."

Bentley was responsible as well for maintaining the integrity of public roads, which were being continually encroached upon, particularly by merchants desperate to expand their quarters in cramped Lower Town. His task was rendered difficult by the failure of the justices of the peace, who administered the city and of whom the most influential were merchants, to confirm a city plan proposed by Vondenvelden in 1801 which would have delineated clearly public and private property. Bentley seems to have been the first road inspector to make a serious attempt to defend public property when in 1802 he sued the shipbuilder John Goudie* for blocking a public road over a beach lot owned by William GRANT (1744–1805).

Bentley appears to have encountered serious financial difficulties in the early 1800s. In March 1803 he and his wife sold for £45 to the auctioneer John JONES 1,400 acres of land that they had been granted in Tring Township in 1801. In July 1804 Bentley's debts to a number of creditors, including Jones and Louis DUNIÈRE, totalled £211, excluding a sum, not then determined, that he owed to the firm of Lester and Morrogh [*see* Robert LESTER]. He was obliged to turn over to his creditors two horses and harnesses, two carrioles, one train, one cart, and a large amount of furniture, dishes, and sundry items from his home at the Bateau Yard in Lower Town.

Bentley continued to be active in the theatre, acting as ticket agent for touring American troupes and managing a theatre until December 1806. The touring companies visited Quebec at least once a year between 1804 and 1811, although absent in 1805 and 1807. Local troupes, except that formed by officers of the garrison, were few and short-lived, competition from the officers and the visitors being so strong. Individual local actors might, however, join the officers or the touring companies. Productions were given in theatres which were actually rooms arranged temporarily in barracks or over taverns, such as the Military Theatre, the Garrick Theatre, or one situated over the New Tavern and described by an American actor as "a paltry little room of a very paltry public-house, that neither in shape nor capacity merited the name of theatre." Two theatres for the performing arts, constructed in succession in 1804, the Brobdignac and the Patagonian, died within a year.

Bentley's primary interest, however, remained music; indeed, in 1805 some citizens, writing in the *Quebec Mercury*, had complained that "it would serve the public materially if the High Constable would attend a little more to his duty in having the streets properly levelled . . . and not bestow his entire

Bentom

attention on his Crochets and Quavers." He had been engaged by the Church of England congregation in 1801 as an organist and in 1802 as choirmaster. When the Cathedral of the Holy Trinity was consecrated by Bishop Jacob Mountain* on 28 Aug. 1804, the surpliced choir consisted of thirteen boys and four men. The Reverend James Sutherland Rudd of William Henry (Sorel) wrote to the Reverend John Strachan* that the service "was chanted and had a fine effect. The organ is a fine ton'd instrument." In 1813 Bentley was receiving £40 per annum for teaching singing to the choir and a dollar for each time he played the organ. From 1810 to 1813 he was also organist at Notre-Dame Cathedral, at a salary of £40 per annum with the responsibility of training a successor.

Bentley's third wife had died in 1809, and on 2 Nov. 1811, at age 55, he married Margaret Hutton, 28, widow of Captain James Hutton. In April 1812 they rented for £80 a year a house and garden on the Chemin du Roy at Saint-Sauveur, just outside the city. Bentley died on 10 Nov. 1813. According to Oscar George Theodore Sonneck, he "deserves to be considered one of the most important figures in the musical history of Philadelphia"; in the 25 years he lived at Quebec his main interest had been music, and he deserves to be considered an important figure in that city's musical history as well.

Dorothy E. Ryder

Two chants attributed to John Bentley are published in *A collection of original sacred music, arranged in full score, with organ or piano forte accompaniment*, comp. F. H. Andrews (Montreal, 1848), 81–82.

ANQ-Q, CE1-61, 11 janv. 1789, 21 déc. 1799, 2 nov. 1811, 11 nov. 1813. AP, Notre-Dame de Québec, Cahiers des délibérations de la fabrique, 1777–1825: 345. PAC, MG 24, B1, 79; 84. *Montreal Gazette*, 16 March 1786; 1 March, 4, 11, 25 Oct., 11 Nov. 1787. *Quebec Gazette*, 1790–1813. *Quebec Mercury*, 1805–13. *Encyclopedia of music in Canada* (Kallmann et al.), 79. Baudouin Burger, *L'activité théâtrale au Québec (1765–1825)* (Montréal, 1974), 109, 111, 113–14, 118, 144–49, 192, 321. J. T. Howard, *Our American music; three hundred years of it* (rev. ed., New York, 1939), 70, 105–6. J. N. Ireland, *Records of the New York stage from 1750 to 1860* (2v., New York, 1866–67; repr., 1966). Millman, *Jacob Mountain*, 89. T. C. Pollock, *The Philadelphia theatre in the eighteenth century, together with the day book of the same period* (Philadelphia, 1933; repr., New York, 1968). Ruddel, "Quebec City, 1765–1831," 518–19, 543, 562. G. O. Seilhammer, *History of the American theatre* (3v., Philadelphia, 1888–91; repr., New York, 1968), 2: 165, 170–75, 194–200. O. G. [T.] Sonneck, *Early concert-life in America (1731–1800)* (Leipzig, [German Democratic Republic], 1907), 78–79, 125–26. F. C. Würtele, "The English cathedral of Quebec," Literary and Hist. Soc. of Quebec, *Trans.* (Quebec), new. ser., 20 (1891): 86. Nazaire LeVasseur, "Musique et musiciens à Québec: souvenirs d'un amateur," *La Musique* (Québec), 1 (1919): 26–27.

BENTOM, CLARK, missionary and surgeon; b. *c.* 1774 in England, likely near London; d. in Jamaica, probably early in 1820.

The little that is known of Clark Bentom's life comes mainly from his own pen. Possibly orphaned as a child, since he never mentions his parents, he became at about age 19 a footman to William Wilberforce, the British abolitionist, and was apparently much influenced by him. When Bentom was about 24 he was accepted into the Missionary Society, formed in 1795 and later known as the London Missionary Society. He was ordained on 13 Nov. 1798, and on 20 December, in company with some 27 other missionaries, he set sail for "Otaheiti" (Tahiti). However, the group's ship, the *Duff*, was captured by a French privateer off Montevideo (Uruguay), and only in October 1799 were the missionaries able to return to England, by way of Lisbon, Portugal. Reporting to the society in 1800 on the conduct of the missionaries, the British philanthropist Zachary Macaulay stated that Bentom "had a good deal of information, but was conceited uppish and overbearing," and that he had abused one of the group "for a Coward in Religion because he declined Singing when on board the Privateer." During his captivity Bentom had apparently been impressed by a fellow prisoner, Dr Samuel Turner, and after his return to London he studied surgery at the Lock Hospital, undoubtedly seeing medicine as another means to climb the social ladder.

A request for a minister having come to the society from a congregation at Quebec, Bentom was asked to go. On 24 March 1800 he and another missionary, John Mitchell, sailed from Liverpool on board the *Ephron*, which, although it encountered no French privateers during the crossing, on two occasions experienced anxious moments at the appearance in the distance of unidentified ships. Bentom and Mitchell arrived at Quebec on 1 June to find the colony agitated by rumours of Napoleon Bonaparte's designs to reconquer it for France. "Our coming here has occasioned much conversation among all descriptions of persons," Bentom noted in his journal. "Some report us as Aliens and perhaps Conspirators. Others ask us if we are of respectability if we have brought letters of recommendation to any of the 'gentry' ie visitants of the Chateau the residence of the governor. It is esteemed great presumption . . . to invite preachers from England without the concurrence of the 'Superior Orders.'" Bentom was asked by the little congregation to remain at Quebec; Mitchell proceeded to Montreal. Bentom's congregation consisted mostly of evangelical former members of the Presbyterian

Scotch Church. A request to share that congregation's room (used during the week as a court-house) in the Jesuit college was rejected by the Presbyterian minister, Alexander SPARK. By July a room capable of holding 200 people had been rented from one of Spark's elders, who also attended Bentom's services, and in the first few months it was filled to capacity by the curious. They soon ceased to return, however, and the congregation had dropped to 37 members by January 1801, when, at its request, Bentom "formed a church as nearly Presbyterian as circumstances would admit." By October 1801 he reported having 50 to 60 communicants. To supplement his meagre income he occasionally practised surgery.

Bentom, like most clergymen of this period, was fairly critical of his fellow ministers. He confided to his journal that Spark appeared to be "in a way as old as Satan's rebellion." Of the Anglican bishop of Quebec, Jacob Mountain*, he wrote in his journal: "I am sadly afeard his Lordship is at present nothing but an unprofitable servant and unless mercy prevent will be cast into outer darkness for ever. I really never saw so much pride ascend a pulpit before it is so evident that few perceive it not. This makes him little beloved and little thought of." The bishop did not extend the hand of friendship either and must have let his feelings be known in Quebec society. In 1801 he described Bentom to the archbishop of Canterbury, John Moore, as "a very young man, but remarkably confident; and possessing that sort of noisy and random eloquence which captivates weak and enthusiastic people." He added that Bentom had "not scrupled to perform the ceremony of mock Marriage for some of his deluded followers." To Mountain, it was inconceivable that registers of civil status could be given to clergymen other than those of the Church of England, the Roman Catholic Church, or (and he was grudging here) the Church of Scotland.

Bentom, who claimed the right to carry out normal ministerial functions, baptized, married, and buried in spite of increasing pressure from Mountain and Attorney General Jonathan Sewell*, the bishop's close friend. In 1801 and 1802 he succeeded in having his registers authorized by Thomas DUNN, a judge of the Court of King's Bench. In January 1803, however, authorization was refused. As a matter of conscience, Bentom continued to perform ceremonies without a register, and in March he was charged by Sewell with illegally exercising the office of a clergyman. The trial was delayed, and in 1804, while on a missionary tour of New York, Bentom had an inflammatory pamphlet printed which explained his position. After his return to Quebec the same year, he lost the case to hold registers and was consequently forbidden to act as a minister in the colony. Moreover, he was later found guilty of having libelled ministers of the crown in his pamphlet. He was sentenced to six months in jail from 1 Nov. 1804 to 30 April 1805, fined £50, and ordered to deposit a bond of £300 as security that he would keep the peace. The fine was paid by "Christian friends" at Glasgow, Scotland, principally the great philanthropist David Dale. During his imprisonment his congregation and other friends stood by him, and after his release an unrepentant Bentom performed two marriages and two baptisms in the three-month period before he set sail for England early in August 1805.

In England Bentom was disappointed by the reaction of the Missionary Society to his plea for assistance. It had not helped him during his troubles, and it did not intend to help him afterwards. Consequently Bentom left the society, no doubt to its relief, and enlisted in the Royal Navy as a ship's surgeon. He very likely joined the squadron, under the command of Rear-Admiral Sir John Borlase Warren, that sailed for Madeira and the West Indies in late January 1806. Bentom served as a ship's surgeon for several years, possibly until Napoleon I was defeated at Waterloo in 1815. He then retired to Jamaica, where he died, probably early in 1820.

Bentom lived at the end of an age. It fell to him to oppose his common sense to a too rigid ecclesiastical and legal structure. It would have been easy for him, after having climbed the social ladder from footman to missionary and surgeon, to have complied with the wishes of Mountain and the "Superior Orders" of Quebec society. He might then perhaps have been accepted by them, or at least have avoided their harassment. But this independent Englishman had a robust, outspoken courage and a conscience that would not let him compromise on matters of principle. In a letter to the Missionary Society on 28 Nov. 1804 he stated, "As a man and a citizen I have acted uprightly whether altogether becoming the character of a meek and humble christian is a point that must be left to my conscience when I have peace free from the hands of my enemies – But when a man becomes a christian among us must he cease to be an Englishman?" He suffered for what he believed, and in so doing struck a blow against the presumption of the Church of England that it should be regarded legally as the established church in the colony. Clark Bentom played his part in advancing the rights of nonconformists to worship as they chose and be recognized and protected by law.

CYRIL STEWART COOK

Clark Bentom is the author of "Journal and observations on my passage to Quebec arrival &c" in the Council for World Mission Arch., Methodist Missionary Soc., at the School of Oriental and African Studies, Univ. of London (London). A microfilm copy of this manuscript is available at ANQ-Q.

Berczy

Bentom published *Talebearing a great sin, a sermon preached Lord's Day February 22, 1801; to which is added thoughts on the glorious gospel of Christ* (Quebec, 1801) and *A statement of facts and law relative to the prosecution of the Rev. Clark Bentom, Protestant missionary from the London Missionary Society, for the assumption of the office of a dissenting minister of the gospel in Quebec, by the king's attorney general of Lower Canada* (Troy, N.Y., 1804).

C. S. Cook (Ottawa) has in his possession a copy of George Spratt, "A history of the church and congregation meeting for worship in St. John's Chapel, St. Francis St., Quebec." AP, Chalmers-Wesley United Church (Quebec), Reg. of baptisms, marriages, and burials, 1801–5. School of Oriental and African Studies, Univ. of London, Council for World Mission Arch., Methodist Missionary Soc., Corr., folder 7, nos.1, 3–8, 15, 18, 21–22, 24–28 (mfm. at ANQ-Q); Candidates papers, 15 Aug. 1798; London Missionary Soc., Board minutes, 11 Nov. 1799; North American corr., 28 Nov. 1804. [James Kerr], *Letter to Mr. Clark Bentom* ([Quebec, 1804]). "Religious intelligence," *Missionary Magazine* (Edinburgh), 10 (1805): 440–42. *London Missionary Society; a register of missionaries, deputations etc., from 1796 to 1923*, ed. James Sibree (London, 1923). Richard Lovett, *The history of the London Missionary Society, 1795–1895* (2v., London, 1899), 1: 64. Rev. Dr. Burns, "A visit to Quebec and Lower Canada . . . , Nov. and Dec. 1852," *Ecclesiastical and Missionary Record for the Presbyterian Church of Canada* (Toronto), 9 (1852–53): 57. W. R. Riddell, "When a few claimed monopoly of spiritual functions: Canadian state trials – the king against Clark Bentom," *OH*, 22 (1925): 202–9.

BERCZY, WILLIAM (born **Johann Albrecht Ulrich Moll** but before his arrival in North America he used **Wilhelm Albert Ulrich von Moll** and **Albert-Guillaume Berczy**; later he occasionally signed **William von Moll Berczy**), painter, architect, author, and colonizer; baptized 10 Dec. 1744 in Wallerstein (Federal Republic of Germany), son of Albrecht Theodor Moll and Johanna Josepha Walpurga Hefele; m. 1 Nov. 1785 Jeanne-Charlotte Allamand* of Lausanne, Switzerland, and they had two sons, William Bent* and Charles Albert*; d. 5 Feb. 1813 in New York City.

Much of the early life of William Berczy, one of the more colourful characters in the history of Upper Canada, is rather obscure. The son of a prominent diplomat, he attended the Academy of Fine Arts in Vienna (Austria) in 1762 and the University of Jena (Friedrich Schiller University) in 1766. In his later life Berczy wrote accounts of his education and youthful travels, but it is difficult to determine to what degree the stories of his adventures are factual since he had a tendency to add fictional touches. If one of his writings is taken at face value, while on a diplomatic mission to Poland in the 1760s he had to hide in a Turkish harem and was captured by a Hungarian bandit. It may have been at this time that his nickname, Bertie, became Bertzie (in Hungarian, Berczy). This was to be the name by which he was known in Upper and Lower Canada.

In the 1770s Berczy, now earning his living as a merchant and perhaps as a painter as well, moved back and forth between cities in northern Germany, Poland, Hungary, and Croatia. Towards the end of the decade he broke all ties with his family and moved to Florence (Italy) where he assumed a new identity, that of Albert-Guillaume Berczy, painter of miniatures. One can only presume that financial difficulties or some problem with his quick temper required this break with the past. Although still travelling frequently, he remained based in Florence until about 1790, when he and his wife took up residence in London, England. There he continued his career as a painter, displaying some of his works in the Royal Academy of Arts, and at the same time he made the connections that eventually resulted in his move to Upper Canada. In 1791 the Genesee Association, a group of British speculators who were trying to develop a large tract of land in western New York, hired Berczy to advertise this land in Europe and recruit peasants who, as assisted immigrants, would make the area prosperous and therefore attractive to investors. Using Hamburg (Federal Republic of Germany) as his headquarters, Berczy enlisted over 200 immigrants, principally from northern Germany, despite the hostility of local officials. He himself agreed to act in an advisory capacity to the new settlement, and in May 1792 the first contingent of colonists, with Berczy and his family among them, sailed for America.

The group soon discovered that the reality of the scheme was far removed from the proposals made to them in Europe. After reaching Philadelphia, Pa, in July, the settlers spent the next few months cutting a road from Northumberland County, Pa, to the Genesee country, a distance of about 100 miles. When they arrived at the site of the settlement, near present-day Canaseraga, N.Y., Charles Williamson, the local agent of the Genesee Association, refused to provide the land and supplies promised. Berczy, who was borrowing money to help the colonists, became embroiled in a lengthy struggle with Williamson for control of the settlement. He saw himself as protector and mentor of all those whom he had brought out. Although he never lost sight of his own interests, he sacrificed much over the next few years in defence of this group. In 1794 Berczy travelled to New York City to seek aid from the German Society of New York. While there he assisted in the formation of a new association, known as the German Company, devoted to obtaining and developing land in Upper Canada.

This group of men, which included Samuel STREET, New York–Bremen merchants, and some prominent Republican politicians, purchased three townships in Upper Canada, two of which adjoined the Iroquois reserve on the Grand River. Hoping to obtain more land by grant, Berczy and others journeyed to Newark (Niagara-on-the-Lake), where in April 1794 they petitioned for one million acres on the north shore of Lake Erie. The settlers for this vast tract of land would consist of Berczy's colonists in the Genesee country and others brought from Germany. The company intended to spend $60,000 and to settle at least 800 people in its first five years.

The Executive Council, anxious to attract settlers to Upper Canada, did not grant the one million acres requested but made a generous offer none the less: on 17 May it awarded Berczy and his partners 64,000 acres west of the Grand River and a promise of more when this land was settled. Berczy returned to the American side and supervised the exodus of his settlers to Upper Canada. With the help of men hired by Street and some Indians from the Grand River reserve, the majority of settlers were spirited past the guards Williamson had put everywhere to stop such an event. After a long journey, they reached the colony in late June. In discussions between Berczy and Lieutenant Governor SIMCOE, who was anxious to develop the site of his temporary capital, York (Toronto), Berczy was offered a larger grant if he would move his settlement eastwards. Berczy agreed to this proposal and by the end of the year the colonists had established themselves on their new lands in Markham Township.

Berczy's settlers were of considerable use to Simcoe. In keeping with his desire to develop the province as quickly as possible, the lieutenant governor offered Berczy a contract to finish building Yonge Street north from the York area to Lake Simcoe within one year. Work on this project commenced in late September 1794, just after the Queen's Rangers, the men responsible for beginning construction of the road, had withdrawn to garrison duty. In the next few months the settlers cleared Yonge Street as far as the Holland River while at the same time working on a road into their Markham settlement and on mills, stores, and storehouses. In the end, however, Berczy was unable to complete Yonge Street within the year, partly because of the excessive number of projects on which his men were engaged but also because of a shortage of supplies and mounting expenses. During 1795 Berczy was hard pressed to meet the needs of his settlers, and by February 1796 he was complaining that "many of his associates are almost starving. . . ." The situation became so desperate in the winter of 1795–96 that one-third of the Markham settlement moved to Newark.

Berczy's grand scheme now began to crumble. His American associates were reluctant to increase their investment in Markham Township without some prospect of an early return, and so he continued to borrow money and supplies, as he had done in New York. To compound his problems, in May 1796 Simcoe issued a proclamation declaring forfeit the lands of all township proprietors who had failed to meet their settlement obligations. Peter RUSSELL, the administrator of the colony after Simcoe's departure, suggested a compromise which gave the proprietors 1,200 acres each and confirmed the 200-acre grants of the settlers they had brought into the province. Although this plan was rejected by Berczy and several other proprietors, it was adopted by the Executive Council in July 1797. At this point Berczy, convinced he had lived up to the terms of the original agreement, began the process of appeal to the British government that was to occupy the remainder of his life.

Prominent men supported Berczy's cause. Governor Robert PRESCOTT put his case before the Home Department as one deserving sympathetic attention because of Berczy's efforts at colonization. When Berczy visited London in 1799 to plead his case personally, Sir Joseph BANKS and Alexander Davison*, former legislative councillor in the province of Quebec, used their influence in his favour. Regrettably for Berczy, however, the decison of the British government was to compensate him only if the Executive Council in Upper Canada agreed. The Executive Council, and in particular Chief Justice William Osgoode*, had opposed any compensation from the beginning, believing Berczy to be one of a legion of land speculators who had appeared from the United States. Its opinion was not changed by the ruling of the home authorities, and as a result no compensation was forthcoming.

While devoting as much of his effort as possible to seeking justice, Berczy also had to deal with his creditors. Besides his own debts, there were those he had contracted in order to provide for his settlers. Considering these obligations a debt of honour, he worked the rest of his life to discharge them and did pay off a significant amount, but not without spending a term in debtors' prison after his arrival in London in 1799. As far as the Markham settlement was concerned, Berczy's financial problems had serious consequences. Since he considered himself almost as the settlers' father, he was reluctant to press them for repayment of the money they owed him. After 1802, however, he had no choice but to begin court actions against some of the more prosperous. The ill feeling generated by this move marked the end of Berczy's career as a colonizer. To satisfy his creditors, who included Samuel HERON, John Gray*, and William WILLCOCKS, Berczy was ultimately forced to dispose of all his lands, mills, and other assets in the York area. From 1805 he lived in Montreal, where his landlord was the painter Louis Dulongpré*, and in Quebec.

In order to pursue his cause in London once again, Berczy went to New York City just before the outbreak of the War of 1812 with the object of appealing for financial help from the surviving

Berkeley

members of the German Company. Two of his old supporters, Timothy Green and former vice-president Aaron Burr, provided a $10,000 credit, but because of the war he was unable to go on to England. In poor health even before he left Canada, Berczy died in New York on 5 Feb. 1813, and was buried in an unmarked grave, a sad end to the years of struggle. In 1818 his son William Bent submitted a petition to the Executive Council of Upper Canada requesting compensation for his father's losses in the province and was granted 2,400 acres as a final settlement.

Despite the great difficulties Berczy experienced after 1796, these last years of his life had many compensations. Men of importance in York, Montreal, and Quebec befriended him, and artistically this was probably his greatest period. Indeed it could be argued that Berczy's work in art, literature, and architecture rivals his accomplishments as a colonizer.

Berczy left behind numerous unpublished manuscripts on historical and literary subjects. Contemporary opinion was highly favourable about his topographical study of the Canadas, the final draft of which disappeared at his death. Some authorities, then and now, have claimed that Joseph Bouchette* plagiarized this manuscript in his *A topographical description of the province of Lower Canada . . .* (London, 1815) – a claim, however, that seems to be without foundation. In architecture, Berczy's crowning achievement was the winning of a competition in 1803 for the design of Christ Church, Montreal; a sketch of this building shows a derivative architectural style, but one that was well executed. As a painter, Berczy mixed styles in his secular and religious works, but generally he showed the influence of the neo-classicism popular at the time. On the whole, his works are uneven, ranging from paintings of excellence to many second-rate miniatures, which he did in order to earn a living and to pay his debts. Two of his best-known paintings are portraits, one of Joseph Brant [THAYENDANEGEA], *circa* 1800, and one of Isaac BROCK; but his undoubted masterpiece is the Woolsey family portrait, a magnificent piece described by the art historian Dennis Reid as "one of the few exceptional Canadian paintings of the first half of the century." In his own time Berczy was recognized as one of the finest painters in the Canadas, and his work still stands up well beside that of many Canadian painters who came after him, including Joseph Légaré*, Antoine Plamondon*, and Théophile Hamel*.

Berczy's colonization efforts were not nearly as successful as he had hoped, and his assistance to Simcoe in the development of Upper Canada was of a modest nature. Nevertheless, his career was not without achievement. His Markham Township colony compares favourably with the expensive settlements established in Upper Canada by the British government three decades later [*see* Sir Francis Cockburn*; Peter Robinson*], and his paintings are a significant accomplishment in 19th-century Canadian art. If Berczy had set himself less ambitious personal goals, perhaps he would not have appeared so unsuccessful. Yet had he done so, he would not have achieved as much as he did.

RONALD J. STAGG

[The major sources of information on the life of William Berczy are the two volumes by John Andre: *William Berczy* and *Infant Toronto as Simcoe's folly* (Toronto, 1971). Both books are well documented and demonstrate a mastery of the material, but are hampered by poor organization and a peculiar writing style. John Andre retains copies of many European documents used in his works. A manuscript biography of Berczy by Helen I. Cowan at the MTL complements Andre's studies. Cowan's notes on references, though a bit difficult to follow, are an excellent source of additional material. Copies of some of the documents used are included with the manuscript.

Berczy papers are to be found in PAC, MG 23, HII, 6; AO, MS 526; and the Coll. Baby (AUM, P 58, S), which also includes numerous letters by him among its Corr. générale (P 58, U). A series of letters to his wife from the last-named collection was published under the title "William von Moll Berczy" in ANQ *Rapport*, 1940–41: 1–93. Considerable material regarding Berczy can also be found in the Simcoe papers in PAC, MG 23, HI, 1, and AO, MU 2782–808; the Peter Russell papers in PAC, MG 23, HI, 2, and at MTL; the Russell family papers in AO, MS 75; the Jarvis family papers in PAC, MG 23, HI, 3; and the William Jarvis papers at MTL. Berczy appears in the Samuel Street papers, AO, MS 500, and in the correspondence of William Osgoode in PRO, CO 42/22 (mfm. at PAC). Information on his land dealings can be found in PAC, RG 1, L3, 28: B2/45; 30: B3/212; 31: B4/50, 68, 158; 34: B7/27; 40: B11/172, 185. Also of use are "William Berczy's Williamsburg documents," ed. A. J. H. Richardson and H. I. Cowan, Rochester Hist. Soc., *Pub. Fund Ser.* (Rochester, N.Y.), 20 (1942): 139–265, which prints a journal and other documents from the Berczy papers at AUM, and the Pulteney estate minute-book in the Johnstone papers at the Ontario County Hist. Soc., Canandaigua, N.Y. Among the secondary sources the following are relevant: F. R. Berchem, *The Yonge Street story, 1793–1860: an account from letters, diaries and newspapers* (Toronto, 1977); Gates, *Land policies of U.C.*; and L.-R. Betcherman, "Genesis of an early Canadian painter: William von Moll Berczy," *OH*, 57 (1965): 57–68. R.J.S.]

BERKELEY, Sir GEORGE CRANFIELD, naval officer; b. 10 Aug. 1753, third son of Augustus Berkeley, 4th Earl of Berkeley, and Elizabeth Drax; m. 23 Aug. 1784 Emilia Charlotte Lennox, sister of Charles LENNOX, and they had two sons and three daughters; d. 25 Feb. 1818 in London, England.

After his education at Eton College, George Cranfield Berkeley entered the Royal Navy in 1766. From 1767 to 1769 he served on the *Guernsey* under

Hugh Palliser* at Newfoundland, and in 1774 he was promoted lieutenant. In 1780 he became a captain, and the same year commanded the sloop *Fairy* off Newfoundland, capturing nine American privateers. Promoted rear-admiral in 1799 and vice-admiral in 1805, in 1806 he was named commander of the North American squadron, his first independent command.

When Berkeley reached his headquarters at Halifax, N.S., in July 1806, Britain's relations with the United States were strained owing to smuggling and the refitting of French warships in American ports. One of his first letters to the Admiralty spoke of the Îles de la Madeleine as "a receptacle for the smuggled produce of the States of America, and of course a most essential injury to our Newfoundland and Nova Scotia fishery." His attention, however, focused on Chesapeake Bay, where in September a French squadron, much battered by a hurricane, took refuge and underwent repairs. In order to watch the enemy force he moved his headquarters to Bermuda, where he remained until May 1807.

With his ships blockading the French and thus having to put into American ports for wood, water, and other necessary provisions, some desertion inevitably occurred. Berkeley demanded the return of the deserters, several of whom had enlisted in the United States Navy. No article of any treaty between the United States and Great Britain required the surrender of such deserters, but the American government had permitted French naval officers to reclaim their deserters on land. Berkeley resolved that, if necessary, force would be used to assert this right at sea. Thus, when in June 1807 the United States frigate *Chesapeake* sailed from Norfolk, Va, with a crew that included some English deserters, she was challenged by one of Berkeley's squadron, the *Leopard*. In Berkeley's words, the *Leopard* "proceeded to search her, and was by the pertinacity of the American Captain compelled to use force." Three American seamen were killed, with one officer and 12 seamen wounded. The fury unleashed in the United States by this action caused Berkeley, now back in Halifax, to fear the immediate outbreak of general hostilities; and he at once applied to the Admiralty for reinforcements. "The Province of Nova Scotia," he remarked, "which contains our only Arsenal, can only be attacked from the Bay of Fundy, where it will be necessary to have a constant naval force." This unhappy altercation, of little consequence, added perhaps a dram to the growing cupful of American grievances that characterized the years leading to war in 1812. In British North America, however, the provincial administrations considered the situation serious enough for active military preparations to be undertaken, and in 1808 the British government sent troop reinforcements to the provinces.

Berkeley was transferred from his North American post and promoted to command the squadron on the coast of Portugal from 1808 to 1812. Upon his retirement from active life at sea he was named lord high admiral of Portugal by a grateful ally. He was appointed a knight of the Bath on 1 Feb. 1813.

Berkeley had a long career in parliament, though there is no record that he ever spoke in the House of Commons. In 1774 he had been a candidate at Cricklade, but withdrew the day before the poll. In 1776 he lost a very expensive contest for Gloucester. He was finally elected unopposed there in 1783, and held the seat until 1810.

He died on 25 Feb. 1818. The details of his will indicate a considerable fortune, much of which was left to his son George Henry Frederick.

JULIAN GWYN

[A considerable amount of material relating to Berkeley's naval career survives outside the PRO. In the MTL, the Sir George Cranfield Berkeley papers, 1806–12, cover four inches of shelf space. Five letter-books and order-books are in the National Library of Scotland (Edinburgh), Dept. of MSS, MSS 9932–36, while the Warwickshire County Record Office (Warwick, Eng.) has letters catalogued as CR 114A/165–67, 348, 574, 616–17, and 632(6) in the Seymour of Ragley papers. The National Maritime Museum holds a number of items, including AGC/1 (G. C. Berkeley, corr., 1804); AGC/B/3 (G. C. Berkeley, corr. and account of the Peninsular War, December 1808–May 1812); KEA/9 (G. C. Berkeley, letters to Keats, 1800); LBK/36 (G. C. Berkeley, order-book, 15 Jan. 1809–8 Aug. 1810); YOR/2 (G. C. Berkeley, letters to Yorke). A calendar of his North American papers is published in American Hist. Assoc., *Annual report* (Washington), 1900, 1: 608–23. J.G.]

PRO, ADM 1/496: ff.453, 614; 1/497: ff.271–72, 425–28; ADM 6/21–25; PROB 11/1604/216. *DNB*. L. [B.] Namier and John Brooke, *The House of Commons, 1754–1790* (3v., London, 1964), 2: 85.

BERNARD, NOËL (Bernard Noel, Nuel Benar, Neville Bernard), Malecite leader; fl. 1781–1801 in the Saint John valley of New Brunswick.

Possibly the earliest reference to Noël Bernard is dated 21 Oct. 1781, when he received a gun at the "Indian House" of William Hazen and Company at Indiantown (Saint John). Although he was associated at various points in his life with Meductic (four miles upriver from present-day Meductic) and Tobique (Tobique Indian Reserve), his base of operations appears to have been in the Madawaska region. His son Louis claimed that both Noël and his father had been born and buried there.

Meductic was for many years the site of a Malecite summer village, but its residents had fled to the Madawaska region prior to 1784 in face of loyalist immigration up the Saint John. Sponsored by the New England Company, Anglican missionary Frederick Dibblee* in 1788 established a school for Indians at

Berthelot

Meductic. He gave out supplies generously in the hope of encouraging the Malecites to allow their children to attend. Attracted equally by the fact that Meductic was unoccupied – the soldiers to whom it had been granted having failed to take up their claims – numbers of Malecites arrived. Bernard, with his wife Antoinette and five children, Marie-Madeleine, Jean-Baptiste, Louis, Zacharie, and Marie, came in 1788 or 1789. Sunum Benar, literally his son Bernard, who follows on Dibblee's list of those who received supplies, was likely an adult, unmarried son. The quantity of goods the two obtained was well below the average given to the hundred or more parties who visited Meductic during those years. How long Bernard remained is not known.

The establishment in 1792 of a Catholic chapel, that of Saint-Basile-le-Grand, no doubt helped attract Malecites and other Indians to the Madawaska area. Bernard's daughter Marie-Madeleine was buried in the cemetery on 20 May 1795. Louis Bernard, interviewed in 1841, claimed that he and his family were the sole survivors of a band of five or six hundred, whose village was arranged in regular streets when he was a child.

Following the failure of Dibblee's Meductic school in the early 1790s, the New Brunswick government evolved a plan to settle the "Indian problem." A reserve of 16,000 acres was established on 4 Sept. 1801 at the confluence of the Tobique and Saint John rivers and given to Bernard and his tribe. The House of Assembly expressed the hope that, since the reserve contained fertile soil for agriculture, adequate woodlands for hunting, and several good salmon pools, the Malecites from the entire Saint John valley would have sufficient resources there to follow a traditional way of life until such time as they might become farmers. Many, however, preferred to remain in the vicinity of present-day Kingsclear, Saint John, Woodstock, and Madawaska. A migratory people with traditional hunting-grounds, they were not attracted to the settled existence of the farmer.

VINCENT O. ERICKSON

Arch. paroissiales, Saint-Basile (Saint-Basile-le-Grand, N.-B.), Reg. des baptêmes, mariages et sépultures, 1792–1823 (mfm. at PANB). N.B. Museum, Simonds, Hazen, and White papers, F20: 96, no.98 (memorandum, W. White, 21 Oct. 1781). *Military operations in eastern Maine and N.S.* (Kidder), 306. N.B., House of Assembly, *Journal*, 1838: app.12; 1842: xcii–cxxviii. *Source materials relating to the New Brunswick Indian*, ed. W. D. Hamilton and W. A. Spray (Fredericton, 1976). H. R. Schoolcraft, *Historical and statistical information respecting the history, condition and prospects of the Indian tribes of the United States . . .* (6v., Philadelphia, 1851–57; repr. New York, 1969), 5. W. F. Ganong, "A monograph of historic sites in the province of New Brunswick," RSC *Trans.*, 2nd ser., 5 (1899), sect.II: 213–357. W. O. Raymond, "The first English proprietors of the parish of Woodstock," *Dispatch* (Woodstock, N.B.), 31 July 1895; "The founding of Woodstock," *Dispatch*, 10 July 1895; "The Meductic fort and its surroundings," *Dispatch*, 29 Jan. 1896; "The old Meductic fort," N.B. Hist. Soc., *Coll.*, 1 (1894–96), no.1: 221–72.

BERTHELOT DARTIGNY (d'Artigny), MICHEL-AMABLE, lawyer, notary, judge, and politician; b. 10 Aug. 1738 at Quebec, eighth child of Charles Berthelot, a merchant, and Thérèse Roussel, daughter of surgeon Timothée Roussel*; d. there 10 May 1815.

Michel-Amable Berthelot Dartigny studied at the Séminaire de Québec from 1749 to April 1751 and again from January 1754 to July 1757. On 24 Jan. 1771 he became a lawyer after passing the prescribed examination for obtaining a commission. On 7 February he gave notice in the *Quebec Gazette* that he had entered into a partnership to practise with Jean-Antoine Saillant*, his cousin by marriage. This partnership was dissolved three years later. In the mean time Berthelot Dartigny received a commission as notary on 28 Jan. 1773, and from then on he practised law as both a lawyer and a notary. On 20 July of that year he married Marie-Angélique Bazin, the 22-year-old daughter of the late Pierre Bazin, merchant at Quebec.

In 1779 Berthelot Dartigny and his colleagues in the town of Quebec founded the Communauté des Avocats, a lawyers' society which counted about ten members. The aims of this body included making the profession respected, providing mutual assistance, discussing matters of interest to the bar, safeguarding its prerogatives, and taking disciplinary measures against members who acted in a dishonourable manner. In 1780 it set the lawyers' dress for court hearings, and the following year it got the court to agree that the table for the bar and the benches around it would be reserved exclusively for the use of the lawyers and the sheriff; previously anyone could sit at the table and rummage among the lawyers' papers while they were pleading.

On 6 Dec. 1784 the society, of which Berthelot Dartigny was treasurer, entered into a battle of major importance. In a representation to Lieutenant Governor Henry Hamilton* it deplored the fact that "a great number of people [who have] no legal knowledge and [who have] gone into bankruptcy after having followed various crafts and trades to an advanced age, seek a lawyer's commission as a last resort"; it asked that only candidates who had worked for five years in a lawyer's office be admitted to the profession. On 11 December the lawyers belonging to the association protested the granting of a lawyer's commission to a bankrupt merchant, Alexandre DUMAS. They were obliged to admit him on 30 March 1785, but reforms were not long in coming. On 30 April an ordinance by the Legislative Council decreed that in future to obtain a lawyer's commission candidates would have to study regularly in a lawyer's office, a registry office, or a civil court, and undergo an entrance examination in the practice of law. Furthermore, the ordinance separated the professions of notary and lawyer. This last provision put an end to the Communauté des Avocats as an effective force, since more than half of its approximately 15 members chose to be notaries. For his part Berthelot Dartigny decided in May 1786 to continue as a lawyer. In December 1791 he received a provisional commission as a judge of the Court of Common Pleas for the District of Quebec, which was conditionally renewed in September 1793.

Berthelot Dartigny had in the mean while acquired numerous pieces of property in the town. From 1778 to 1791 he bought seven vacant lots for small sums, and in 1778 he purchased a piece of land and a house that he sold again the following year with a profit of 1,200 *livres*. In 1779 he obtained by tender a dwelling on Rue Saint-Joseph (Rue Garneau), and then bought a property and a house on Rue Sainte-Famille for 2,300 *livres* in cash and an annual payment of 50 *livres*. At an auction sale in 1788 he purchased a lot and residence on Rue des Carrières, where three years later he bought another piece of property with a two-storey stone house for 6,000 *livres*, 3,500 in cash. During this period Berthelot Dartigny also made loans for modest amounts to people of small means. As well, in January 1786 he lent £300 to Pierre Du Calvet*, perhaps with the inheritance he had received from his father, who died in Paris, France, in 1780.

In addition to his legal activity and his business transactions Berthelot Dartigny was interested in political life. He was in favour of the creation of a house of assembly, and in 1788 he signed a petition asking for one. Then in 1792, in the first elections held in Lower Canada, he ran as a candidate in the riding of Quebec. When he was defeated by Ignace-Michel-Louis-Antoine d'Irumberry* de Salaberry and David LYND, he contested the result. In the *Quebec Gazette* of 12 July 1792 he denounced the unexpected closing of a polling station; the measure had prevented 62 electors who were prepared to vote for him from doing so, with the result that Lynd obtained a majority of 26 votes. He also published a pamphlet entitled *Conversation au sujet de l'élection de Charlesbourg*. Salaberry, however, had been elected in two ridings, and he chose Dorchester, which left a seat vacant at Quebec. Berthelot Dartigny was then proclaimed elected by acclamation on 18 Feb. 1793; he marked the occasion by having 1,200 *livres* distributed among the poor. The first bill that he brought forward, in 1793, provided for the abolition of Article 128 of the Coutume de Paris, which deprived inn- and tavern-keepers of the right to take legal action for the recovery of money owing for food, drink, and other

items sold or consumed on their premises. This bill received the support of only three members and was overwhelmingly rejected by the assembly.

In 1796 Berthelot Dartigny was again a candidate for Quebec, but was defeated. He also lost against Pascal-Jacques Taché* in the riding of Cornwallis in 1798. He was finally elected for Kent on the death of its member, Jacques Viger, and he represented that constituency in the assembly from March 1798 until 4 June 1800. In the elections of 1800 he returned to the attack successfully at Quebec, which he represented until 27 April 1808. Berthelot Dartigny regularly voted with the Canadian party. In February 1805 he was on a committee to draft a bill for the construction of one prison in the district of Quebec and another in the district of Montreal. The proposal to finance the works through duties on imports roused strong opposition among the merchants, who tried in vain to have the tax levied on land. On the other hand, during the 1808 session Berthelot Dartigny supported the English party on the bill concerning the ineligibility of judges to sit in the assembly [*see* Sir James Henry CRAIG; Pierre-Amable DE BONNE]. In addition to being a member of the assembly, he sat on several commissions: in June 1799 he was appointed a commissioner for the construction of a court-house at Quebec, in July 1800 for the management of the Jesuit estates, in June 1801 for the upkeep and care of the insane and foundlings, and finally, in March 1808, for the building of a prison at Quebec.

During these years Berthelot Dartigny had at different times taken into his service five apprentice lawyers, among them his own son Amable*, Alexandre MENUT's son, and Charles-Étienne*, the son of Gaspard-Joseph Chaussegros* de Léry. He had not, however, done much investing in real estate, buying only a lot on Rue Saint-Louis in 1797 and two small stone houses on Rue des Carrières in 1800 and 1801. In 1802 he received a farm as a reward for his services in the defence of Quebec at the time of the American invasion in 1775–76 [*see* Benedict ARNOLD; Richard Montgomery*]. In fact, on 5 June 1788 he had asked for land grants for three militia companies that served during the siege of the town, but it was not until 1802 that the government acceded to this request. After 1809 Berthelot Dartigny leased out several of the houses he owned, including the second storey of his residence on Rue Sainte-Anne, for rents that varied from £40 to £120 each a year.

Berthelot Dartigny died in 1815 at 76 years of age, the doyen of the Quebec bar. He had been a widower since November 1792, and in his will, made in 1813, he left all his belongings to his three living children, along with a life annuity of 365 shillings to his maidservant. His personal estate included a library, valued at about £60, which comprised some 56 titles in 94 volumes in addition to the issues of the *Quebec*

Bertrand

Gazette since 1774. He held debts amounting to £750 and, except for the £416 owing to his older son Michel and the £21 to his daughter Geneviève, wife of the notary Joseph Badeaux*, he owed only £87 to various creditors. On 12 May 1815 his body was buried in the Sainte-Famille chapel in Notre-Dame church, since his heirs had not been able to obtain permission to have him interred as he had wished in the little cemetery attached to the chapel.

Both through his legal activities and through his participation in political life and in business, Michel-Amable Berthelot Dartigny had acquired a certain standing in the Quebec region. Thus the Rue D'Artigny, which was opened up in 1829 on a piece of land that had belonged to him, was named in his honour. It was after his father had returned to France in the autumn of 1758 that he had come into possession of this property, held in roture, which had been bought by his father from Louis Rouer* d'Artigny's heirs ten years earlier. Michel-Amable had then added Dartigny to his name, but he was the only one to use this double patronymic, and his children bore only the name of Berthelot.

CLAUDE VACHON

Michel-Amable Berthelot Dartigny is the author of a pamphlet entitled *Conversation au sujet de l'élection de Charlesbourg* (Québec, s.d.). His minute-book (1773–86) is at ANQ-Q, CN1-25.

ANQ-Q, CE1-1, 10 août 1738, 20 juill. 1773, 16 nov. 1792, 12 mai 1815; CN1-16, 18 avril 1805, 21 févr. 1809; CN1-26, 23 avril 1798; 25 avril, 11 mai 1812; CN1-83, 30 juill. 1781; 21 févr., 30 mars 1782; 23 sept. 1782; 2 sept. 1783; 2 mai 1787; 27 mars, 18 oct. 1794; CN1-92, 12 sept. 1797, 28 avril 1802; CN1-178, 11 sept. 1800; 30 sept. 1803; 10 août, 24 sept. 1805; 12 mai 1809; 19 avril, 18, 28 août 1810; 25, 28 févr., 8 avril, 10 mai 1811; 24 mars 1812; 26 janv., 12 mars, 12 mai, 21 juin 1813; 20 avril, 17 juin 1814; CN1-205, 2 sept. 1772; 3 avril, 22 mai, 22 sept. 1778; 9 janv., 15 mars, 31 déc. 1779; 7 janv., 16 août 1780, 30 juill. 1782; 4 nov. 1783; 12 juin, 17 août, 23 nov. 1784; 13, 26 août, 31 oct. 1785; 21 janv., 27 mars, 10 avril 1786; CN1-207, 7 mai, 9 juin 1774; CN1-224, 20 juill., 17, 29 août 1785; 13 févr., 5 juin, 15 sept. 1787; 28 juin, 28 août 1788; 19 févr., 29 avril 1789; 28 déc. 1790; 20 avril, 5, 10 mai, 17, 22 juin, 18 juill. 1791; 28 mars, 21 août 1792; CN1-230, 14 avril, 21 sept., 27 nov. 1792; 27 sept., 3 déc. 1793; 17 févr., 22 juill., 1er août, 17 déc. 1794; 10, 24 juill., 3 août, 5 oct. 1795; 11 août, 4 nov. 1796; 21 sept., 14 nov. 1797; 7 févr. 1798; 30 juill. 1800; 1er juin 1808; CN1-248, 24 juin 1774; CN1-262, 31 mai 1815; P1000-11-185. ASQ, mss, 13, 10 juin 1792. PAC, RG 68, 1: 281–82. "Acte de prise de possession de la cure de Québec par messire Joseph-Octave Plessis (2 juin 1792)," ANQ *Rapport*, 1921–22: 94–95. [André] Doreil, "Lettres de Doreil," Antoine Roy, édit., ANQ *Rapport*, 1944–45: hors-texte 2. "Ordonnances édictées pour la province de Québec par le gouverneur et le conseil de celle-ci, de 1768 à 1791 . . . ," PAC *Rapport*, 1914–15: 168–72. *Quebec Gazette*, 7 Feb. 1771; 24 Feb. 1774; 15 Jan. 1789; 12 Jan., 12 July, 22 Nov. 1792; 10 July

1794; 29 March, 5 April 1798; 20 June 1799; 27 Dec. 1804; 17 Sept. 1807; 24 March 1808; 18 May 1815.

F.-J. Audet, "Les législateurs du Bas-Canada." F.-J. Audet et Fabre Surveyer, *Les députés au premier Parl. du Bas-Canada*, 38–44. Caron, "Inv. de la corr. de Mgr Briand," ANQ *Rapport*, 1929–30: 132. Charland, "Notre-Dame de Québec: le nécrologe de la crypte," *BRH*, 20: 277. Desjardins, *Guide parl.*, 131, 136. Lucien Lemieux, "Juges de la province du Bas-Canada de 1791 à 1840," *BRH*, 23 (1917): 87. "Papiers d'État – Bas-Canada," PAC *Rapport*, 1891: 14, 203; 1892: 162. *Quebec almanac*, 1782: 22; 1791: 42, 82; 1792: 152, 158; 1794: 67, 122, 125; 1799: 71; 1800: 81; 1801: 75; 1805: 20–22; 1810: 21–23; 1815: 48. P.-G. Roy, *Les juges de la prov. de Québec*, 51. Tanguay, *Dictionnaire*, 1: 530; 2: 159–60, 250; 7: 61. Chapais, *Cours d'hist. du Canada*, 1: 203; 2: 117. R. C. Dalton, *The Jesuits' estates question, 1760–1888: a study of the background for the agitation of 1889* (Toronto, 1968). J.-E. Roy, *Hist. du notariat*, 2: 28, 60, 181. P.-G. Roy, *Les rues de Québec* (Lévis, Qué., 1932), 10–11. Monique Duval, "L'histoire de Québec par ses rues; l'esprit de famille régnait chez les Berthelot," *Le Soleil* (Québec), 16 janv. 1980: G3. "La famille Berthelot d'Artigny," *BRH*, 41 (1935): 9–10. Hare, "L'Assemblée législative du Bas-Canada," *RHAF*, 27: 372–73, 376–77, 379–80. Maréchal Nantel, "La Communauté des avocats," *Cahiers des Dix*, 10 (1945): 263–91; "Querelles du palais," 9 (1944): 271–72. J.-P. Wallot, "La querelle des prisons (Bas-Canada, 1805–1807)," *RHAF*, 14 (1960–61): 69–70, 262, 265, 268.

BERTRAND, JOSEPH-LAURENT, Roman Catholic priest; b. 6 Nov. 1741 in Montreal (Que.), son of Jacques Bertrand, a mason, and Marie-Louise Dumouchel; d. 29 Oct. 1813 in Rivière-du-Loup (Louiseville), Lower Canada.

On 31 Aug. 1762, in Montreal, Joseph-Laurent Bertrand married Marie-Thérèse Dulignon, who died shortly afterwards. Finding himself widowed and with no children, Bertrand was attracted to the religious life; he entered the Petit Séminaire de Québec in 1768. Five years later he began theological studies, and in the course of these, like many of his colleagues, he taught at the Petit Séminaire [see Henri-François GRAVÉ de La Rive]. On 18 Aug. 1776, at the age of 34, Bertrand was ordained priest by Bishop Briand*.

After serving as curate for two years in the parish of Saint-Joachim, near Quebec, Bertrand was appointed parish priest of Sainte-Anne, at Yamachiche, in 1778. Two years later lightning destroyed the parish church and its rebuilding led to heated disputes. The parishioners were divided over the choice of a site. The parish priest also joined in the debate, apparently with no great skill or tact; he was in favour of the old site but did not win. As a result of this setback his position became intolerable and he asked to be transferred.

In 1786 Bishop Louis-Philippe Mariauchau* d'Esgly put him in charge of the neighbouring parish, Saint-Antoine-de-Padoue, at Rivière-du-Loup, which until then had been served by the Recollets from Trois-Rivières. When he took up his new post Bertrand's first concern was to make an inventory, with the help of churchwarden Joseph Lesage, of the *fabrique*'s possessions. In 1790 Bishop Hubert* of Quebec appointed him archpriest and the following year, lauding his prudence, made him confessor extraordinary to the Ursulines of Trois-Rivières.

In 1792 Bertrand wanted to provide his parish, which had more than 300 families, with a new church. Once again the same troubles he had encountered at Yamachiche began to develop. The parishioners split over the choice of a site and both sides sent numerous letters and petitions to the bishop. Hubert hesitated a long time before settling the question. "We have found the parish about equally divided," he wrote to Bertrand in March 1796. Finally he gave Solomon's judgement, ordering that the existing church "be repaired or added to on the site where it stands at the present time." In this decision the opposing parties perceived the discreet but persuasive influence of Bertrand and they would not yield. The bishop delegated the task of reaching an agreement to the vicar general of Trois-Rivières, François-Xavier Noiseux*, who succeeded in reconciling the parties. Finally, between 1803 and 1805 the church was demolished and another was erected on a new site. In 1806 Bertrand had a school, which accommodated two classes, built across from the presbytery.

In the mean time various curates had agreed to go to assist Bertrand, whose authoritarian reputation had spread beyond the bounds of his humble parish. In 1797 Bishop DENAUT sent François Plessis-Bélair, who stayed four years. He was replaced by Michel-Charles Bezeau, who stayed only a few months, then by Louis Delaunay, and subsequently by François-Xavier Marcoux. Although Marcoux was young, he administered the parish after Bertrand's death pending the appointment of the new incumbent, Jacques Lebourdais, *dit* Lapierre, a nephew of Bishop Bernard-Claude Panet*.

In 1804 Bertrand sued Pierre Lavergne, who the preceding year had refused to provide the host for the new church in the parish of Saint-Léon-le-Grand. This parish, which had been set up in 1800 by detaching a region from the parish of Saint-Antoine-de-Padoue, was served by Father Bertrand. Lavergne justified his refusal by claiming that he had remained a member of the parish of Saint-Antoine-de-Padoue, because Saint-Léon-le-Grand had no legal existence: the bishop of Quebec had not had the right to create parishes since the conquest, he maintained. Lavergne lost in the Court of King's Bench but went to the provincial Court of Appeal. Before the case was heard, Lavergne petitioned Attorney General Jonathan Sewell* to intervene; Sewell, who agreed with Lavergne's claims, accepted. Finally, as a result of the

decision handed down in 1806 by the chief justice of the District of Montreal, James Monk*, Lavergne won. Although the lawsuit had raised the important and complex question of the legal status of the Roman Catholic church after the conquest, Monk in rendering his decision explicitly stated that "the court . . . was deciding nothing concerning the important questions that have been debated in the case."

Bertrand's worries gradually undermined his health and he developed ulcers and rheumatism. He died on 29 Oct. 1813, a week before his 72nd birthday. According to Louiseville's historian, oblate Germain Lesage, Bertrand "had for twenty-seven years been in charge of a large and restless population," among whom he left "a highly respected memory."

RAYMOND DOUVILLE

ANQ-M, CE1-51, 8 nov. 1741, 31 août 1762. ANQ-MBF, CE1-15, 30 oct. 1813. ASQ, C 35: 258, 269, 273, 293; MSS, 11. PAC, MG 11, [CO 42] Q, 115: 96–111. *Le Canadien*, 13, 20 déc. 1806. Allaire, *Dictionnaire*, vol.1. Caron, "Inv. de la corr. de Mgr Briand," ANQ *Rapport*, 1929–30: 113; "Inv. de la corr. de Mgr Hubert et de Mgr Bailly de Messein," 1930–31: 227, 248, 267; "Inv. de la corr. de Mgr Mariaucheau d'Esgly," 1930–31: 192; "Inv. de la corr. de Mgr Plessis," 1927–28: 232, 239. Napoléon Caron, *Histoire de la paroisse d'Yamachiche (précis historique)* (Trois-Rivières, Qué., 1892). Chapais, *Cours d'hist. du Canada*, 2: 139–40. Germain Lesage, *Histoire de Louiseville, 1665–1960* (Louiseville, Qué., 1961).

BETHUNE, JOHN, Church of Scotland clergyman; b. 1751 in Brebost (probably near Orbost), Scotland, son of Angus Bethune and Christian Campbell; m. 30 Sept. 1782 Véronique Waddens, daughter of Jean-Étienne Waddens*, in Montreal, Que., and they had nine children; d. 23 Sept. 1815 in Williamstown, Upper Canada.

John Bethune was born into a respected family on the Isle of Skye, his father being descended from one of the lairds of Balfour. Nevertheless, his youth was apparently marked by poverty: he held a college bursary in his third year at King's College (University of Aberdeen), and in 1770 the Synod of Glenelg, at the request of the Presbytery of Skye, granted his family £5 to help meet the expenses of his education. After graduating from King's College with a BA in 1769 and an MA in 1772, Bethune returned to the Isle of Skye and was licensed as a Church of Scotland minister. In July 1774 the Presbytery of Skye came under criticism from the synod for having licensed Bethune before he could be presented to its meeting. From the standpoint of the presbytery, however, time had been of the essence. Soon after returning from Aberdeen, Bethune had decided to emigrate with some members of his family to North Carolina, a colony that had become a place of refuge for thousands of Highlanders in the

Bethune

years after the 1745 rebellion. It thus seems highly probable that in hastily licensing Bethune the presbytery had been inspired by a desire to prepare him for the ministry in America.

The Bethunes arrived in North Carolina in 1773, and on 14 June 1775 John was recruited as chaplain to the 1st battalion of the Royal Highland Emigrants (later known as the 84th), a loyalist unit raised by Allan Maclean*. Before assuming this post, he saw action at the battle of Moores Creek Bridge in February 1776, probably while serving as chaplain to the North Carolina royal militia. Along with hundreds of other Highlanders, he was captured at this battle by the victorious rebels and imprisoned. For a time he was held in Philadelphia, Pa, and it was from here on 31 Oct. 1776 that he and a group of fellow prisoners requested permission to rejoin their families. Although the evidence is unclear, he possibly was released at this time and made his way to New York City. Be this as it may, he is not heard of again until his arrival in late 1778 in Halifax, N.S., where the 2nd battalion of the Royal Highland Emigrants was stationed.

After reaching Nova Scotia, Bethune acted as chaplain to the 2nd battalion, assisted recruitment amongst Scottish Highlanders, and ministered to the loyalist settlers. His stay in the colony, however, was brief. By August 1779 he had moved to Montreal to take up his appointment as chaplain to the 1st battalion of his regiment. There he performed his regular duties as chaplain, administering the ordinances of marriage and baptism for military personnel of the 84th and other regiments. Since the Presbyterians of the city lacked a church of their own, Bethune attended the services conducted by the Anglican rector of Montreal, David Chabrand* Delisle. It was Delisle who married Bethune and Véronique Waddens in September 1782.

From 1783 until the disbanding of the 84th in the following year, Bethune was stationed at the garrison on Carleton Island (N.Y.). On demobilization, he spent a year at Fort Oswegatchie (Ogdensburg, N.Y.) before returning to Montreal in 1786. In Montreal he lived on his half pay but continued to perform marriages and baptisms for army personnel. Around him other Montrealers rallied – Presbyterian Scots, Dutch and German loyalists, and Anglican friends. Being sufficiently numerous to form a congregation, Bethune's followers rented a large room on Rue Notre-Dame where, on 12 March 1786, Bethune conducted a Presbyterian service. He continued to minister to his "small but interesting" congregation until May 1787, when on the invitation of a group of Highland settlers he moved to the western area of the province, soon to become Upper Canada. Although his Montreal congregation was short-lived, it is noteworthy as the first Presbyterian congregation west of the town of Quebec and as a precursor of the St

Gabriel Street Church, the mother church of Presbyterianism in Canada.

Bethune devoted the remainder of his life to his ministry among the Highland settlers in Glengarry County, Upper Canada, and to his family of six sons and three daughters. His ability to preach in Gaelic placed him in good stead with his new flock, and the welcome he received was repaid with years of dedicated service. In Williamstown, his place of residence, he formed a Presbyterian congregation and soon had the satisfaction of seeing a log church built, to be replaced by a stone structure before his death. In neighbouring Lancaster, Martintown, and Cornwall, he preached, organized congregations, and encouraged the building of frame churches. Besides the financial support he received from his congregation, he was awarded 2,000 acres as a retired chaplain, and his land holdings were increased in 1811 with the grant of a town lot in Cornwall. In 1789 he began drawing an annual salary of £50 from the local government. This salary was discontinued shortly after the formation of the new province of Upper Canada, but it was soon restored when 150 Presbyterians in the counties of Glengarry and Stormont signed a petition protesting that Bethune was "not a recent adventurer, but a gentleman of approved Loyalty" and that his government salary was necessary to keep him "above Want, and Consequently above contempt."

Bethune's relations with Lieutenant Governor SIMCOE were complicated by the controversy surrounding the Marriage Act of 1793, a measure which confined the solemnization of marriages to clergy of the Church of England and justices of the peace. In March 1796 Presbyterians in Grenville County drew up a petition complaining that the act made them "aliens in their own country." In his reply to the petitioners, Simcoe stated that their appeal was "the Product of a Wicked Head and a most disloyal Heart." Later he informed the Home secretary that criticisms of the marriage act would be followed by demands for the partition of those lands set apart for the "National Clergy." He also noted that Bethune, whom he had admitted had "the character of a most loyal man," "signed the Petition, and is said to be the Author."

Bethune was one of only a few Church of Scotland ministers who served in Upper Canada before the War of 1812. Still, he was not totally isolated from other clergymen, both of his own and of other denominations. He and his family frequently returned to Montreal for extended visits when a christening or church business was pending, and on these occasions he came into contact with fellow clergymen, including John Young*, his successor as Presbyterian minister in Montreal. With the Roman Catholic priest in Glengarry County, the Reverend Alexander McDonell*, he lived in peace, but he was careful to warn his flock that, although they should remain friendly with their Catholic neighbours, they should "flee from their principles, as from the face of a serpent." He was also on intimate terms with John Strachan*, the Anglican clergyman. When Strachan taught school at Cornwall during the years 1803 to 1812, Bethune entrusted him with the care of his sons, and later he even allowed two of them, John* and Alexander Neil*, to take Church of England orders since he could not afford to send them to Scotland for their education.

Little else is known about Bethune. He seems to have taught school in Cornwall from 1812 to 1814; he may have been present as a chaplain at the attack, led by George Richard John Macdonell*, on Ogdensburg, N.Y., in February 1813; and in June 1815 he was appointed road commissioner for the Eastern District. A few days before his death in 1815, he delivered an address to his Williamstown congregation in which he drew attention to his "precarious health" and stressed the need for an assistant minister. Noting that "there is as great an apathy respecting this essential measure, as if it were certain that I should outlive the whole Congregation," he warned his parishioners that if he died before an assistant could be provided, they would soon fall victim to the "snares" of the Roman Catholic Church, an "arrogant communion" whose members believed themselves to be "the exclusive favorites of heaven." He also stated that there were "private gentlemen" in Lower Canada who would "gladly give you every assistance in their power" in the search for a Highland minister, but that "without timely and vigorous exertion on your own part, the matter will languish away in useless talk; a fault very common in all your public transactions."

Bethune is the most honoured and respected of Canada's pioneer Church of Scotland ministers, and his children were a credit to him. John and Alexander Neil rose high in the Church of England's hierarchy, the former becoming dean of Montreal, the latter bishop of Toronto. Of his other sons, James Gray* became a banker, Angus* was made a chief factor of the Hudson's Bay Company, and Donald* founded a prominent shipping firm. A daughter, Cecilia, married John Kirby*, the Kingston merchant and legislative councillor. The best known of his descendants is Norman Bethune*, one of the heroes of the Chinese revolution.

E. A. McDougall

John Bethune's address, *To the members of the Presbyterian congregation at Williamstown, and of the other Presbyterian congregations connected with them in Glengary*, was printed in Montreal in 1815. A copy is available at the AO in Church records coll., MU 545, no.34 (Martintown, St Andrew's Presbyterian).

PAC, RG 1, L1, 26: 132; 27: 74, 273; 28: 300; L3, 28: B2/43; 37: B10/34; 67: B misc., 1788–95/96; RG 5, A1: 2196–97, 8236, 9974–75, 10568–69. PCA, St Gabriel Street Church (Montreal), Reg. of baptisms, marriages, and burials. PRO, WO 17/1496: ff.112, 115, 118, 121, 123, 125, 127, 130, 132, 136, 140 (mfm. at PAC). SRO, CH2/568 (Synod of Glenelg, Minutes, 1725–1929). *Corr. of Lieut. Governor Simcoe* (Cruikshank), vols.3–4. [James Croil], *A historical and statistical report of the Presbyterian Church of Canada, in connection with the Church of Scotland, for the year 1866* (Montreal, 1867). Douglas, *Lord Selkirk's diary* (White). "Grants of crown lands in U.C.," *AO Report*, 1928: 36. *Kingston before War of 1812* (Preston). "The mission of Cornwall, 1784–1812," ed. A. H. Young, *OH*, 25 (1929): 481–97. *The state records of North Carolina*, ed. W. L. Saunders and Walter Clark (26v., Raleigh, N.C., 1886–1907; repr. New York, 1968), 10–12, 25. "U.C. land book B," *AO Report*, 1930: 24. *Kingston Gazette*, 3 Oct. 1815. *Montreal Gazette*, 25 Sept. 1815. *A dictionary of Scottish emigrants to the U.S.A.*, comp. Donald Whyte (Baltimore, Md., 1972). Hew Scott *et al.*, *Fasti ecclesiæ scoticanæ: the succession of ministers in the Church of Scotland from the Reformation* (new ed., 9v. to date, Edinburgh, 1915–), 5. [Thomas Whyte], *An historical and genealogical account of the Bethunes of the Island of Sky*, ed. A. A. Bethune-Baker (London, 1893).

R. Campbell, *Hist. of Scotch Presbyterian Church*. William Gregg, *History of the Presbyterian Church in the dominion of Canada . . .* (Toronto, 1885). J. G. Harkness, *Stormont, Dundas and Glengarry: a history, 1784–1945* (Oshawa, Ont., 1946). J. A. Macdonell, *Sketches illustrating the early settlement and history of Glengarry in Canada, relating principally to the revolutionary war of 1775–83, the war of 1812–14 and the rebellion of 1837–8 . . .* (Montreal, 1893). [Alexander McDonald], "Letter-book of Captain Alexander McDonald, of the Royal Highland Emigrants, 1775–1779," N.Y. Hist. Soc., *Coll.*, Pub. Fund Ser. (New York), 15 (1882): 464. E. A. [K.] McDougall, "The American element in the early Presbyterian Church in Montreal (1786–1824)" (MA thesis, McGill Univ., Montreal, 1965). James MacKenzie, "John Bethune: the founder of Presbyterianism in Upper Canada," *Called to witness: profiles of Canadian Presbyterians . . .*, ed. W. S. Reid (2v., [Toronto] and Hamilton, Ont., 1975–80), 1: 95–110. J. S. Moir, *Enduring witness: a history of the Presbyterian Church in Canada* ([Hamilton, 1974?]). S. D. Self, "A history of the Presbyterian Church in the townships of Charlottenburgh and Lancaster, within the county of Glengarry, Upper Canada (Ontario)" (essay, Presbyterian College, Montreal, 1958). P. H. Bryce, "The Quinte loyalists of 1784," *OH*, 27 (1931): 5–14. E. A. Cruikshank, "A memoir of Lieutenant-Colonel John Macdonell, of Glengarry House, the first speaker of the Legislative Assembly of Upper Canada," *OH*, 22 (1925): 20–59. "John Bethune, 1751–1815," *Presbyterian News* (Raleigh), 30 (1965), no.12: 8–9. Harry Piers, "The fortieth regiment, raised at Annapolis Royal in 1717; and five regiments subsequently raised in Nova Scotia," N.S. Hist. Soc., *Coll.*, 21 (1927): 115–83. A H. Young, "The Bethunes," *OH*, 27 (1931): 553–74.

BIÈVRE, FRANÇOIS-MICHEL SUZOR DE. *See* Suzor

BILLINGS, JOSEPH, sailor and explorer; m. Ekaterina von Pestel; d. 1806, probably in Russia.

Although British documents indicate that Joseph Billings was born in 1758 at Turnham Green

Billings

(London), England, other sources place his birth at Yarmouth, and his Russian service record states that he was 37 in 1798. He enlisted in the Royal Navy on 8 April 1776 as an able seaman and joined the *Discovery* which, with the *Resolution*, was sailing under James Cook*'s command for the north Pacific. In the course of the voyage, during which Billings became an astronomer's assistant, the expedition was at Nootka Sound (B.C.) from 29 March to 26 April 1778, and subsequently visited Alaska, the Bering Sea, the Kamchatka peninsula (U.S.S.R.), and the Portuguese port and depot of Macao (near Canton, People's Republic of China). Billings was still an able seaman when he was transferred to the *Resolution* in September 1779, but he was promoted warrant officer upon the expedition's return to England in October 1780.

Nothing is known of Billings's activities immediately following his arrival home, but in 1783 he made application to enter the Imperial Russian Navy at the same rank he held in Britain. His Russian service record shows him as a lieutenant from 1 Jan. 1783, but he was probably not in Russia until October at the earliest. At that time the Empress Catherine and her advisers were planning explorations of the extreme northeastern parts of her dominion, and Billings, as Cook's former "companion," appeared a suitable choice as a leader. In August 1785, spurred by news that the Comte de Lapérouse [Galaup*] had commenced his exploratory voyage, Catherine formally commissioned Billings to command "an expedition . . . for bringing to perfection the knowledge acquired under her glorious reign, of the seas lying between the continent of Siberia and the opposite coast of America." Billings was also to report on the fur trade in Alaska and to claim for Russia territory not previously discovered by any European power.

Billings set out from St Petersburg (Leningrad) on 25 October. In his travels eastwards through Russia he met his former shipmate, the New Englander John Ledyard; he would have enlisted him, but Ledyard was arrested as a French spy. Captain James Burney, who knew them both from the voyage with Cook, recorded later in a book on Russian northeastern exploration that Catherine should have jailed Billings and given his commission to Ledyard. Travel overland to the east coast and preparations there took a great deal of time, and it was not until the summer of 1789 that Billings made his first attempt to set out to sea; when one of his two ships succumbed to a storm he went only as far as Petropavlovsk (Petropavlovsk-Kamchatskii) to winter over. On 9 May 1790, the lost ship replaced, the expedition finally set sail and, moving up the Aleutian chain, landed on Unalaska Island on 3 June. The ships went as far as Prince William Sound before turning back toward the Kamchatka peninsula to seek winter quarters. During the stormy return voyage Billings's deficiencies as a navigator, combined with his arrogance and stubbornness, became increasingly apparent. In June 1791 Billings's ship was again in the Aleutians, but Billings decided to abandon further exploration of America for his other commissioned task: to map the northeastern Russian coastline. Disappointment was general, but, as his secretary Martin Sauer wrote, "the representations of every officer who had hitherto presumed to have an opinion, were always treated by the Commander with petulant and illiberal retorts." At St Lawrence Bay (Guba Sv. Lavrentiya) on the Chukotsk peninsula Billings put his plans into effect. He led a survey party overland to the northwestward, but it suffered starvation and ambush and produced little of value; meanwhile the vessel, commanded by the expedition's surveyor, Gavriil Andreevich Sarychev, went back to explore the Aleutians.

The expedition was largely reunited at last on 2 Jan. 1794 at Yakutsk, and it returned to St Petersburg in March, having added little in its nine years to geographical knowledge of the north Pacific littoral. Nevertheless, reports of the expedition brought to light the Alaskan natives' "abject slavery" to Russian traders, and possibly led to improvements in their circumstances, which George Vancouver* was to observe when he visited an Alaskan trading post. In 1790 Billings had been in communication with the Spaniard Salvador Fidalgo near Kodiak, but this encounter of rival imperial interests had no immediate political consequences owing to Spanish preoccupation with the Nootka Sound controversy [*see* James COLNETT; Esteban José Martínez*], which was to undermine Spain's claims to all the northwest coast of America. Valuable charts of the north Pacific were compiled by Sarychev; a later explorer, Admiral Ivan Fedorovich Kruzenshtern, in describing these hydrographic accomplishments tended to praise Sarychev at the expense of Billings.

In 1796 Billings was transferred to the fleet in the Black Sea, where he conducted coastal surveys. In 1799 he published his findings in an atlas which surpassed in accuracy and completeness anything previously available. In November of that year he was retired on full pension with the rank of captain-commodore. He died in 1806, leaving an uncertain record of achievement in Arctic and north Pacific discovery, but clearly having aided the process whereby Russian interests in Alaska were expanded, consolidated, and eventually regulated.

BARRY M. GOUGH

James Burney, *A chronological history of north-eastern voyages of discovery; and of the early eastern navigations of the Russians* (London, 1819; repr. Amsterdam and New York, 1969). *The journals of Captain James Cook on his voyages of discovery*, ed. J. C. Beaglehole (4v. in 5 and portfolio, Cambridge and London, Eng., 1955–74), 3, pt.II: 1474. G. A. Sarychev, *Puteshestvie flota kapitana Sarycheva po severovostochnoĭ chasti Sibiri* . . . (2v. in 1, St Petersburg [Leningrad], 1802); *Puteshestvie kapitana Billingna* . . . (St Petersburg, 1811). Martin Sauer, *An account of a geographical and astronomical expedition to the northern parts of Russia . . . by Commodore Joseph Billings* . . . (London, 1802; repr. Richmond, Eng., 1972). *Bol'shaia Sovetskaia entsiklopediia*, ed. A. M. Prokhorov *et al.* (3rd ed., 30v., Moscow, 1970–78), 3: 949. *DNB*. Cook, *Flood tide of empire*. B. M. Gough, *Distant dominion: Britain and the northwest coast of North America, 1579–1809* (Vancouver, 1980). R. V. Makarova, *Russians on the Pacific, 1743–1799*, ed. and trans. R. A. Pierce and A. S. Donnelly (Kingston, Ont., 1975). L. H. Neatby, *Discovery in Russian and Siberian waters* (Athens, Ohio, 1973).

BINNEY, JONATHAN, merchant, politician, judge, and office holder; b. 7 Jan. 1723/24 in Hull, Mass., son of Thomas Binney and Margaret Miller; d. 8 Oct. 1807 in Halifax, N.S.

As a young man, Jonathan Binney went into commerce in Boston, Mass. On 8 Jan. 1746/47 he married Martha Hall of Charlestown (Boston), daughter of the merchant Stephen Hall, and the couple immigrated to Halifax in 1753 in search of better economic prospects. Binney's early years in Nova Scotia were a mixture of success and personal tragedy. His business affairs prospered, becoming increasingly linked with those of Michael Francklin* and with Joshua Mauger*'s commercial empire, which dominated the province's trade. In 1757 he became a leader in the local movement for representative government; late that same year he buried his wife in St Paul's churchyard "with babe in her arms." When the first house of assembly was called in Nova Scotia in 1758, Binney represented Halifax Township, as he continued to do until his elevation to the Council in 1764. On 26 July 1759 he married Hannah Adams, sister of Henry and John Newton, thus further cementing his alliance to the "Halifax party" of Francklin and Mauger. A year later he buried the remaining child of his first marriage.

By the 1760s Binney was making a name for himself as an opponent of executive authority, as an assiduous collector of appointive offices, and as a figure of controversy. He was an active participant in the strike of the assembly in 1761, which attempted to thwart Lieutenant Governor Jonathan Belcher* in his efforts both to implement Board of Trade policy opening the Indian trade and to end legal protection for debtors, especially those owing debts outside the province. In 1762 Belcher, acting on the advice of the Board of Trade, dismissed Binney and other ringleaders of the strike from those public offices held by gubernatorial fiat. Binney, characteristically, responded by collecting "Subscriptions thro' the Town"

supporting the innocent victims of executive tyranny. It was a posture he would later improve upon in the course of his conflicts with Governor Francis Legge*. The ban on office holding did not last long. In 1764 Binney acquired the posts which brought him into conflict with authority, first with the assembly and later with the governor, when he became collector of provincial duties and magistrate at Canso, a major fishing and trading port. Binney constructed a house there, and claimed to spend most of the summer months at his job. His duties were many in that distant corner of the province: in 1766, for example, "with the assistance of some gentlemen of the Navy, who happened to be near Canso," he dispersed a group of warlike Indians.

The problem with the Canso appointments was getting payment for his efforts. The legislature in 1764 voted Binney £75 for one year only, and the Council continued the allowance in 1765 in defiance of the assembly's wishes. Thereafter, Binney's salary was a major bone of contention in the struggle between Council and assembly for control of the provincial purse. The assembly regularly refused or failed to vote him a further allowance, though the Council provided one until 1769; Binney got into the habit of paying himself by deducting the first £75 of his customs receipts and fines from his remittances to Halifax. In 1768 Binney added the short-lived posts of collector of customs and excise and judge on St John's (Prince Edward) Island to his collection of offices, in January 1772 he became a judge of the Inferior Court of Common Pleas for Halifax County, and in 1774 he began collecting Cape Breton duties in return for a flat payment of £50 a year.

Binney's posts at Canso were a long-standing grievance of the assembly when Francis Legge took up his duties as governor of the province, and soon after Legge's arrival in Halifax on 6 Oct. 1773 the assembly resolved "that the charge of £75 per Annum to Jonathan Binney Esquire for being first Magistrate at Canso, is and has been repeatedly disallow'd by this House." At this point Legge supported Binney as a "serviceable and necessary" office holder, an opinion that would gradually change as the governor came to oppose the old Francklin faction of which Binney was such an obvious member. When, in the wake of an audit of the province's ill-kept books begun in late 1774, Legge and his chief legal officers such as James Monk* decided to take action against those with accounts outstanding to the treasury, Binney and his brother-in-law John Newton were their first major targets. In fairness to Binney, it should be emphasized that his case was not a simple example of rampant corruption, though Legge saw it as merely the visible tip of a great iceberg of fiscal abuse. Binney was doing a job for which he was entitled to remuneration, and his chief offence was the political one of paying

Bisshopp

himself "without warrant from the governor and against the sense of the legislature." Nevertheless, he, and Newton, were arrested and treated as criminals, being carried to Halifax jail in March 1775.

A jury specially selected by Legge – it even included a member of the committee which had done the audit – in the presence of the governor found Binney liable for £445 16s. 3d. and costs. Refusing to pay, Binney was confined to jail from 4 May to 14 July with his wife and family. It is not clear whether the recalcitrance that sent the Binneys to jail was part of a deliberate attempt to become martyrs to Legge's tyranny, but it seems likely. In any event, incarcerating the family was a serious blunder on Legge's part. Binney, wrote John Butler*, was "carres'd by the whole Gentlemen in Town & the Commanding Officer of the Troops visited him with his officers in a Body." He was finally released by special request of the legislature, which was in the process of closing ranks against the governor. According to Legge, "Mr. Binney's affair was compared to Mr. [John Wilkes's] and in Order to keep up the spirit of Malevolence, the Members of the Assembly were every Day carried to visit him, till by Public Votes they had compleated all their Addresses." The affair, despite its comic-opera overtones, had serious implications for the governor.

Whether Binney's imprisonment was the cause or the excuse for the astounding turn-about of the 1775 assembly, which ceased to support Legge and instead backed his critics, will probably never be known. But Binney's "sufferings" were a prominent part of the case against Legge which the victim carried personally and successfully before the Board of Trade in London. In his absence, the assembly obligingly struck off Binney's debt. Always a centre of controversy, Binney found himself involved on his return from England in a lengthy court battle over some fencing he had caused to be torn down at Canso, was accused in 1777 of illicit trading with the Americans, and in 1784 was charged with certifying New England fishermen as native Nova Scotians in order to sell them fishing licences at Canso for two dollars each. He seems to have retired from public business in the mid 1780s, although he did not die until 1807, leaving his estate to his two sons, Stephen Hall and Hibbert Newton.

Jonathan Binney was a typical example of the first generation of New England merchants and politicians in Nova Scotia. If his affairs always seemed to teeter on the brink of the unsavoury and illicit, it was because in those early times one could not be successful in the harsh climate of the Maritimes by being genteel.

J. M. BUMSTED

Halifax County Court of Probate (Halifax), B76 (estate papers of Jonathan Binney). PAC, MG 11, [CO 217] Nova Scotia A, 69: 41–42; 94: 58; 97: 353; 101; 105: 248; MG 23, A1, 1: 252–61, 693–97. PANS, MG 100, 111, no.13; RG 1, 44, docs.1, 39; 222, docs.4, 49–52, 69–70; 284, doc.8. [Nova Scotia archives, 1:] Selections from the public documents of the province of Nova Scotia, ed. T. B. Akins and trans. Benjamin Curren (Halifax, 1869), 729. Genealogy of the Binney family in the United States, comp. C. J. F. Binney (Albany, N.Y., 1886). Brebner, Neutral Yankees (1969), 65–67, 243–54.

BISSHOPP (Bishop, Bishoppe, Bisshop), CECIL, army officer; b. 25 June 1783 at Parham House (West Sussex), England, eldest son of Sir Cecil Bisshopp and Harriet Anne Southwell; m. 6 April 1805 Lady Charlotte Barbara Townshend, granddaughter of George, Viscount TOWNSHEND; d. about 16 July 1813 and was buried on 17 July in Stamford (Niagara Falls), Upper Canada.

Cecil Bisshopp devoted his life to service in the British military. As a young man he joined the prestigious 1st Foot Guards and was commissioned ensign on 20 Sept. 1799. A promotion to lieutenant on 16 Oct. 1800 carried with it the rank of captain in the army. He went on half pay in 1802 but on 3 Sept. 1803 exchanged back into the 1st Guards. Promoted brevet major on 1 Jan. 1812, he briefly served as major in the 98th Foot in the spring of the same year. In 1802 he had served as private secretary to Rear-Admiral Sir John Borlase Warren at St Petersburg (Leningrad, U.S.S.R.) and participated in the expeditions to La Coruña, Spain, and Walcheren, Netherlands, in January and July 1809. He was a member of parliament for Newport from 1811 to 1812. Appointed inspecting field officer of militia in Upper Canada on 6 Feb. 1812 with the local rank of lieutenant-colonel, Bisshopp sailed for the Canadas, "to fight the Yankies," three months after the outbreak of the War of 1812 in June.

Bisshopp remained in Montreal briefly before proceeding, with some foreboding, to his posting in Upper Canada "amongst the Indians." In addition to inspecting the Canadian militia, Bisshopp also was given the responsibility for commanding the regular troops and militia stationed between Chippawa and Fort Erie. Considered by Major-General Roger Hale Sheaffe* "an active intelligent Officer," on 28 Nov. 1812 Bisshopp moved "with great celerity" to repulse a large American force at Frenchman Creek. The next several months were quiet, but the Americans commenced an offensive along the Niagara frontier in the spring of 1813 with the capture of Fort George (Niagara-on-the-Lake). In accordance with Brigadier-General John Vincent*'s pre-arranged plan, Bisshopp withdrew his troops from Fort Erie to join the main force at Burlington Heights (Hamilton). From this location on 6 June Lieutenant-Colonel John Harvey* mounted a successful attack upon the Americans at Stoney Creek, and two days later Sir

James Lucas YEO's fleet bombarded and dispersed the enemy encamped at Forty Mile Creek. During these engagements Bisshopp commanded the reserve. Later in the month he played a nominal role in the Indian victory at Beaver Dams (Thorold) [*see* William Johnson Kerr*], an episode usually associated with the heroine Laura Secord [Ingersoll*].

By mid summer of 1813 the British had pushed the invaders back to Fort George. Here the Americans assumed a defensive posture, thus allowing the British to make occasional forays across the Niagara River. Bisshopp was chosen to lead one such raid against Black Rock (Buffalo), N.Y. In the early morning of 11 July his force of regulars and militia [*see* Thomas Clark*] stormed the fort, overran the batteries, and burned the blockhouses, barracks, and naval yard, as well as a large schooner. A considerable quantity of public stores and ordnance, including eight pieces of artillery, was taken. To this point, according to surgeon William Hackett, the raid had "succeeded to the very letter." But Bisshopp decided to remove 123 barrels of salt, "a most scarce and valuable article," causing a critical delay which allowed the Americans time to regroup. Bolstered by a party of Tuscarora Indians, they attacked the British on the beach. A surprised Bisshopp commented of the Indian presence that "he would as soon have expected to see a body of Cossacks." Under a galling fire, the raiders retreated precipitately. Bisshopp suffered wounds to the left thigh, left wrist, and upper right arm. Hackett hoped for a full recovery, noting that the officer was "a very young man with an unbroken constitution tho' apparently delicate." But his "constitution was not equal to the shock" and after lingering for three to five days, during which time he talked almost incessantly of England and his family, Bisshopp died.

On 21 March 1813 Bisshopp had written that he wanted to be of "real service" to his country. In the event, he made an important contribution to the success of the British army, symbolizing the best qualities of a regular officer serving in the Canadas. He was generous, donating £100 for the "aid and relief" of distressed families, and was popular with the militia and civilian population. His letters to his sister suggest a man of affable and affectionate nature. Indeed, at Black Rock a captured American civilian described him as "a mild humane-looking man . . . rather tall and well made and . . . of exceeding few words." The rector of York (Toronto), John Strachan*, thought useful lessons might be derived from Bisshopp's heroic example, and in December 1813 composed a "Life of Col. Bishoppe." He saw in the officer "the most successful" emulation of Sir Isaac BROCK's "invaluable qualities," particularly a willingness to "carry the war" into the United States. Further, pointing out that there was more to the defence of the Canadas than the British regulars, Strachan noted that

Bisshopp "attached to himself in a very remarkable degree the Militia of the Country . . . this neglected body of men." Commenting on the crucial contribution of the Indians, Strachan claimed Bisshopp "knew well how to turn these sons of nature to the best advantage." Bisshopp's life, like those of Brock and John MACDONELL (Greenfield) before him, seems the stuff of the 19th-century myth of the militia's role in the War of 1812. Strachan sought to use it to political advantage, sure that the young officer "will be remembered . . . with the most endearing regret."

ROBERT S. ALLEN

PAC, MG 11, [CO 42] Q, 317: 14–22; MG 19, A3, 13; MG 24, F4. *Doc. hist. of campaign upon Niagara frontier* (Cruikshank), 3: 319–22; 4: 20, 225–33; 6: 230; 9: 359. "Early records of Niagara" (Carnochan), *OH*, 3: 70. [J. F. Richardson], *Richardson's War of 1812; with notes and a life of the author*, ed. A. C. Casselman (Toronto, 1902; repr. 1974), 300. *Select British docs. of War of 1812* (Wood), 1: 650–51, 654–58; 2: 163–64. [John Strachan], *The John Strachan letter book, 1812–1834*, ed. G. W. Spragge (Toronto, 1946), 4–9, 52. *Burke's peerage* (1970), 2663, 2908. G. E. Cokayne, *The complete peerage of England, Scotland, Ireland, Great Britain and the United Kingdom, extant, extinct, or dormant* (new. ed., ed. Vicary Gibbs et al., 13v. in 14, London, 1910–59), 12, pt.II: 953–55. G.B., WO, *Army list*, 1800–13. M. A. FitzGibbon, *A veteran of 1812: the life of James FitzGibbon* (Toronto, 1894; repr. 1972), 10–11, 107–11. Ernest Green, "Some graves on Lundy's Lane," Niagara Hist. Soc., [*Pub.*], 22 (1911): 4–6.

BLACK, JOHN, shipbuilder and politician; b. *c.* 1764 in Scotland, son of William Black and Jane McMun; fl. 1786–1819.

John Black emigrated from Scotland to Quebec about 1786 and in 1787, along with William King, hired out as a ship's carpenter on the Baie des Chaleurs for £40 per annum. In 1789 he and King established a shipbuilding firm at Quebec, but King withdrew two years later. In February 1792 Black, now "in easy circumstances," bought from the merchant Ralph GRAY a lot in Lower Town on Rue Saint-Nicolas where he established a shipyard and built a house. By September, having conducted affairs "to a great extent" with the firm of Fraser and Young, in which the merchant-politician John YOUNG was a partner, Black owed it £800; most of this sum had probably been advanced to him as working capital, Fraser and Young reserving the option to purchase some of Black's ships. Later that year Black relinquished his business to take up a government appointment as master shipbuilder on Lake Ontario. He quickly found his salary insufficient, however, and returned to Quebec late in 1793 to recommence his own enterprise. The following year he employed about 60 carpenters and sawyers, as well as labourers.

Because Black had extensive contact with the

Black

labouring class and had acquired a knowledge of colloquial French, he was employed as an *agent provocateur* by Attorney General James Monk* in the wake of militia riots at Quebec in May 1794. Operating among Canadian artisans and habitants of Quebec and the surrounding area, Black posed as a French sympathizer and attempted to elicit revolutionary statements from those with whom he spoke. In playing this role, Young later observed, Black "allowed his Zeal to carry him to unguarded lengths." The highlight of his intelligence activity came on 17 July 1794 when he claimed to have arrested two of the leading rioters of the Charlesbourg area, where for three days in late May hundreds of armed men had defied the government and bloodthirsty Jacobin slogans had been heard. A month later, much to his surprise, Black was himself arrested as a voluble "Democrat" on the deposition, before a Canadian magistrate, of a follower of the two leaders he had taken. Monk failed to intervene, and Black was denied bail. He was successful on a second application and his case was discharged by *nolle prosequi* on 24 March 1795. After this incident Black's merchant clients, who had never previously suspected his loyalty, turned from him, and his business failed. As Black later complained to John Neilson*, proprietor of the *Quebec Gazette*, "I passed for a disturber of publick peace a villen an Enemy to my King and Country the Scoff & reproach of the Times."

In the general election for the House of Assembly in 1796, Black was a candidate in the county of Quebec, composed largely of Canadians, and he successfully exploited the resentments of the habitant voters, then suffering through hard times, by advertising himself as a reliable fellow who had never "reposed on the downy couch of luxurious opulence." According to Young and Chief Justice William Osgoode*, the voters saw Black as a determined opponent of the government. Once elected, however, Black sought to rehabilitate himself in the eyes of the powerful, and generally supported the colonial administration in the second legislature from 1797 to 1800. In early May 1797 he was given an excellent opportunity to restore the government's confidence in him when David McLane*, an undercover agent for France, thinking Black was disaffected, sought his help in recruiting a fifth column of Canadians to seize Quebec with the assistance of Vermont adventurers. Black denounced McLane to Young, who was an executive councillor, and arranged for the spy's arrest. At McLane's trial for treason in July 1797, Black was a leading witness for the crown.

In 1798 Black joined Young and Henry Caldwell in a venture to refit the ship *Lively*, sell her in England, and share equally the profit or loss; Young and Caldwell provided the capital, Black the expertise. In June Black sailed in the *Lively* for London. Nearing the English Channel, the ship was captured on 3 July by a French privateer; she was soon after retaken by the British, but Black had already been carried as a prisoner to Bayonne, France. Within a fortnight he escaped and, posing as a Dane, crossed the Pyrenees and made his way via Madrid and Lisbon to London, where he informed the government of French plans against Ireland and the British colonies. He returned to Quebec in June 1799.

Through the good offices of the lieutenant governor, Robert Prescott, and the civil secretary and clerk of the Executive Council, Herman Witsius Ryland*, as well as Young's friend and patron Prince Edward Augustus, Black had begun seeking some tangible reward for his loyalty and suffering since 1794. He requested an appointment anywhere in the British empire, but suggested more specifically the posts of king's shipbuilder and port captain at Quebec; he also asked for a grant of two islands near William Henry (Sorel). None of these requests was approved, but on 30 Dec. 1799 he, as leader, and 43 associates were granted five-sevenths of Dorset Township, comprising 71,030 acres on the west bank of the Rivière Chaudière. Black had previously arranged to acquire from his associates for a nominal sum all but 8,000 acres of the grant. In July 1800 he transferred his entire interest in Dorset to Young as payment of a debt which had reached £3,144.

Black again ran for the assembly in 1800 but soon withdrew his candidacy in favour of Attorney General Jonathan Sewell*. On 14 May 1801 Black, now 37, married Jane, the 18-year-old daughter of a Quebec merchant, Sentlow Rawson; they were to have at least two children. In July Black went £1,000 into debt to buy from the notary Pierre-Louis Deschenaux three lots with buildings at La Canoterie in Lower Town. Black was apparently already indebted to his father-in-law, who in March 1802 had all Black's property on Rue Saint-Nicolas sold at auction. In October Black acquired three more lots contiguous to his own at La Canoterie, and their development over the next three years added greatly to his debt. In February 1806 most of his holdings were sold at auction at the suit of the merchant Martin Chinic* and acquired by Pierre Brehaut; in April Black ceded the rest to Rawson. Advertising his "twenty-six years professional experience," he attempted, but apparently without success, to continue in shipbuilding from a house and lot at 19 Rue Champlain rented for £40 from John Mure*.

In an effort to recoup his losses, Black went to England in the summer of 1806 to renew his request for patronage. He took with him an address, signed, he claimed, by more than 1,500 residents of Quebec including many leading merchants and officials, which expressed appreciation for his many services to the community; however, the notary Thomas Lee* certified only 613 signatures. To gain official favour he submitted to Prince Edward Augustus a memorial on the political state of Lower Canada, in which were reflected the assumptions of the English party during the period from 1791 to 1810. For Black the Canadian majority in the assembly was to be trusted neither to advance the commercial development of the province nor to pass legislation needed in the interests of security; as well, the political vulnerability of the British minority was increased by the absence of property qualifications for members of the assembly. Every general election, according to Black, brought forth Canadian candidates of little status, education, loyalty, or talent save demagoguery, and from one end to the other the country rang with the slogans: " 'Dont vote for an English-Man, dont vote for a Seignior, a Merchant, a Judge or a Lawyer.' " Black's solution was a union of the two Canadas or, failing that, the creation of eight two-member ridings in the Eastern Townships. He also advocated an income qualification for members of the assembly of at least £150 per annum from land or in permanent salary. Union and a property qualification would remain staple demands of British merchants and government officials until both were finally achieved in the Act of Union of 1840.

Black's hopes for virtually any preferment – he added to his earlier requests the lease of the Saint-Maurice ironworks and appointment as agent for the government-owned seigneury of Sorel – were not realized. He took up residence in England and became partner in a firm trading to Canada, Shepperd and Black; by 1809, however, it was bankrupt. That summer he returned to Quebec on board the *Bonne Citoyenne*, and was wounded in the leg during a naval engagement in which the British ship captured a French frigate. At Quebec, Black pressed his claims on Governor CRAIG, who, finding him to be a man of no capital or credit, warned Lord Castlereagh, the Colonial secretary, against leasing him the Saint-Maurice ironworks. Craig also informed his superior that Black had been adequately compensated and should not be provided with a government salary. A disappointed Black returned to England later in 1809. Over the next seven years he crossed the Atlantic several times in his dogged efforts, now concentrated on obtaining a land grant in Upper Canada, to be rewarded for his earlier services. He probably eked out an existence with temporary positions, such as that in 1815 of agent for the Quebec merchant Henry Black. John Black appears to have returned permanently to Britain in 1817 and to have died in Scotland some time after 1819.

Black was a man of ordinary talents who readily enough, it seems, accepted his lot as a sycophantic client of the governing clique, on whose favour his economic well-being evidently depended. Despite the intelligence and political services he rendered his masters, Black experienced recurrent rebuff and, when he no longer appeared useful, abandonment.

F. MURRAY GREENWOOD

ANQ-Q, CE1-66, 14 May 1801; CN1-83, 25, 27 sept. 1792; CN1-145, 6 Jan. 1802, 14 Aug. 1804; CN1-171, 29 Oct. 1806; CN1-178, 21 août 1813, 13 nov. 1815; CN1-230, 14 déc. 1801; 19 déc. 1803; 5 janv., 3 avril 1805; CN1-256, 21 June 1787, 27 Sept. 1792, 20 Aug. 1794, 6 March 1798; CN1-262, 4 mars, 14 mai, 29 juill. 1801; 18 janv., 29 avril, 1er, 18, 29 oct. 1802; 2, 5 nov., 14 déc. 1803; 9 févr., 7, 13 juin, 9, 10 juill., 11 août 1804; 4 févr. 1805; 17 avril 1806; CN1-284, 1er févr. 1792; CN1-285, 3 déc. 1799; 24, 26, 29, 30 juill., 18 sept. 1800; 13 févr., 23 juill. 1804; 13 sept. 1809. PAC, MG 11, [CO 42] Q, 81: 566–68, 615–20, 675–79; 106: 41–42, 45, 60–63, 68, 72, 76a, 559–70, 683; 108: 110, 127, 182, 194, 208–10; 110: 24–27; 113: 99–102; MG 24, B1, 1: 112–18; 2: 68–70; MG 30, D1, 4. Bas-Canada, chambre d'Assemblée, *Journaux*, 1797–1800. *Docs. relating to constitutional hist., 1791–1818* (Doughty and McArthur; 1914), 323–25. "French republican designs on Canada," PAC *Report*, 1891: 67–69. Osgoode, "Letters" (Colgate), *OH*, 46 (1954): 151. *R. v. David Maclane* (1797), 26 St.Tr., 721. *Quebec Gazette*, 12 May, 4 Aug. 1791; 3 April 1794; 26 March 1795; 16 June 1796; 10 Aug. 1797; 10 April, 5, 19 June 1800; 22 Oct. 1801; 4 March 1802; 10 March 1803; 8 Aug., 14 Nov. 1805; 24 April, 5 June, 31 July, 23 Oct. 1806; 24 Aug. 1809; 23 May 1823. F. M. Greenwood, "The development of a garrison mentality among the English in Lower Canada, 1793–1811" (PHD thesis, Univ. of B.C., Vancouver, 1970). Ivanhoë Caron, "John Black," *BRH*, 27 (1921): 3–19. W. R. Riddell, "Canadian state trials; the king *v*. David McLane," RSC *Trans.*, 3rd ser., 10 (1916), sect.II: 321–37.

BLACK PETER, PETER BYERS, known as. *See* BYERS

BLACKWOOD, JOHN, merchant, land speculator, seigneur, militia officer, office holder, and politician; b. probably in England; m. secondly 23 April 1793 Jane Holmes, widow of the merchant Charles Grant, at Quebec, Lower Canada; d. 24 June 1819 in Bath, England.

John Blackwood, whose career as a merchant spanned more than 40 years, was an excellent example of the colonial businessman who became rich by extending his activities to the economic, social, and political spheres, and who retired to the metropolitan centre at the end of his life, leaving to his family a heritage of experience and wealth. He combined skilfully the abilities of a businessman, a politician who knew how to secure favoured treatment and important alliances for himself, and a member of the bourgeois oligarchy who exerted his influence on the machinery of state by which control was ensured and the social order perpetuated. His capabilities found in the imperial system a favourable setting in which to unfold. In his case, as in that of so many merchants, to

Blackwood

speak solely of personal initiative would be insufficient. The man and the system fitted together and backed each other up perfectly.

Blackwood is first mentioned as being in the colony at the time of the American invasion in 1775–76 [see Benedict ARNOLD; Richard Montgomery*], when he took part in the defence of Quebec. Subsequently, in 1783, he was in business at Quebec with Charles Grant under the company name of Grant and Blackwood. Upon his partner's death the following year, Blackwood bought part of his buildings and fixtures for the sum of £2,000. In 1793 he succeeded in getting hold of Grant's other assets by marrying Jane Holmes, his widow; through this marriage Blackwood became the manager of his former partner's wharfs, warehouses, and store, located near Rue Saint-Pierre at Quebec.

Independently of the fortune of £6,237 net that Jane Holmes brought to the marriage and that he continued to administer even after her death in 1805, Blackwood became rich, largely from the import-export trade he carried on through different companies – among them John Blackwood and Company (1792–1816), Blackwood J. Sr and Jr, and Blackwood and Patterson (circa 1803–5) – in the areas of Quebec, Trois-Rivières, and Montreal, where his son John, who must have been born of his first marriage, settled early in the 19th century. As an importer of products such as rum, sugar, coffee, wine, and woollens, and also as an exporter of various kinds of produce, especially wheat, Blackwood was naturally very concerned about the accessibility of foreign markets. For this reason he formed a common front with other exporters in 1789, was interested in a plan to establish trade between the West Indian colonies and Lower Canada via Bermuda in 1807, and wanted the export of non-strategic products to the United States to continue after war broke out in 1812. His business led him, moreover, to travel frequently to England, where he made contact with large trading firms. Thus in 1809 he was the Quebec agent for the firm headed by John Inglis, Edward Ellice*, and John Bellingham Inglis of England, and even for Joseph-Geneviève Puisaye*, Comte de Puisaye.

Blackwood maintained excellent relations with the well-established trading houses in the colony such as E. Gray, and McTavish, Frobisher and Company. He also acted as trustee for the estates of several merchants. His business led him to lend money to various individuals, particularly merchants, sometimes in cash, sometimes in merchandise, for amounts from £434 to £1,643. During this period he had little compunction in having the sheriff seize and sell the assets of at least 14 debtors who had failed to honour their obligations. In 1806 he offered the government of Lower Canada £5,000, which he claimed to have collected from "my own small business," in return for bills of exchange. When he died in 1819 he still had £7,361 of debts owing to him in Lower Canada.

Even though his career as a merchant was many-sided, Blackwood was also a large landowner involved in speculating. From 1793 to 1817 he made nearly a score of property deals, either in his own name or, on two occasions, as an administrator of the Union Company of Quebec, which he and other businessmen had founded in 1805. Being well regarded by the Executive Council in Lower Canada, he was granted favours that enabled him to increase his real estate holdings. For example, in 1796 the council authorized him to extend the pieces of land that he owned in the port of Quebec, convert them to free and common socage, and improve the quays to accommodate vessels of 300 tons burden. In 1801 he profited from a big reduction on his dues in lods et ventes to the crown, which went from £151 to £12, and two years later he received from the government a grant of 400 acres in Milton Township in recognition of his devoted services during the defence of Quebec against the American troops. In 1802 he paid the government £47 for lods et ventes, an indication of the large number of his transactions.

From the early 19th century Blackwood multiplied his purchases and sales of property, as well as his renting of farms, building sites, and waterfront lots all over the colony, in both town and country. In 1805 and 1807 he bought several lots on the Anse au Foulon at Quebec which he sold a few years later for £3,000. In addition he took advantage of sheriff's sales to buy 12 of the 48 shares in the Dorchester Bridge in 1808 [see David LYND], part of the seigneuries of Mille-Vaches and Mingan with trading posts that same year, and then the fief of Rivière-Magdeleine in the Gaspé in 1810. The last purchase, incidentally, caused a comical incident: as the new seigneur, Blackwood made bold to write to Governor Sir James Henry CRAIG in French with a view to rendering fealty and homage, and this action angered Craig, who could not accept a subject of British origin addressing him in a language other than English. Blackwood nevertheless rendered fealty and homage on 6 July 1810.

Blackwood had a manifest influence also in the numerous societies (civic, community, religious, and patriotic) with which he was associated. From 1789 until 1793, for example, he was a member of the Agriculture Society in the District of Quebec, and from 1790 until 1815 he belonged to the Quebec Fire Society, of which he was treasurer in 1791 and secretary in 1798. From 1793 to 1798 he sat on the governing council of the Quebec Assembly, which brought together people who had defended the province against American invasion, and from 1794 he took a militant role within patriotic societies; in 1813 he was president and treasurer of an association formed in 1794 to support British rule. In 1809 and

1810 he served as secretary of a society responsible for building a Presbyterian church at Quebec, for which the government had granted a lot. His most important contribution, however, was made in 1809 as a founding member of the Committee of Trade, the ancestor of the Quebec Board of Trade [see John Jones]; this body, which brought together merchants in particular, was organized to present to the government the views of businessmen on such matters as the creation of a banking establishment, the administration of the custom-house, and navigation on the St Lawrence. Blackwood also played his part in the social life of the community through public subscriptions: he contributed to funds to help the victims of the Rue du Sault-au-Matelot fire at Quebec in 1793, to aid Great Britain during the war from 1799 on (£10 a year), and to help the destitute passengers of the *Neptune* in 1802.

Blackwood belonged to the close circle of people who held prestigious offices connected with the direction of society and of those who benefited from government favours. Thus he was commissioned militia lieutenant in 1787, and then promoted captain in 1800. He held the office of justice of the peace in the District of Quebec several times between 1794 and 1815; in particular he was a magistrate at the time of the special sessions of the peace dealing with the malignant fevers that were raging at Quebec in January 1800. In 1797 he was a member of the jury of the Court of King's Bench that delivered a guilty verdict against David McLane*, who had been charged with plotting revolution, and in 1812 he presided at the sittings of the Quebec grand jury. In addition Blackwood was often asked to act as a commissioner, whether to set up regulations for pilotage on the St Lawrence (1802–3), build a new market and prison at Quebec (1807–8), receive the oath of allegiance (1812), or administer the Jesuit estates (1814).

All these offices required not only social relationships, but also Blackwood's participation in political life. Like other important people, when the occasion arose he signed petitions to governors and protectors such as Lord Dorchester [Guy Carleton], Prescott, and Prevost, and to eminent figures such as Prince Edward Augustus. As early as 1788 he had joined with other merchants to denounce the position of the Canadian seigneurs, who were opposed to the creation of an elective assembly in the colony; he and his colleagues demanded such an institution in 1789 and 1790, and he also came out in favour of a non-sectarian university. In 1805, through a by-election occasioned by the death of William Grant (1744–1805), he was elected to the Lower Canadian House of Assembly for the Upper Town of Quebec. It is not known whether his decision to enter the political arena was triggered by the debate on the Gaols Bill

[see Jonathan Sewell*]. It is certain, however, that Blackwood, along with some British merchants, had signed a petition asking the Legislative Council to block this bill. Re-elected in 1808 and 1809, Blackwood also ran in 1810 but seems to have withdrawn before polling was completed.

Except for the 1806 session, when he was frequently absent, Blackwood sat, often as chairman, on committees of the assembly which dealt with matters as varied as the preparation of addresses in reply to the speeches opening the session, regulations to curb the desertions of apprentices (1807 and 1809), port regulations (1807), security of the state (1807, 1808, 1809, and 1810), the by-laws of the Quebec Benevolent Society (1807), construction of a prison at Quebec (1807 and 1809), parliamentary precedents (1807), justice (1807), public accounts (1807 and 1808), the taking of a census and road-building in the Eastern Townships (1807, 1808, 1809, and 1810), trade with the West Indies (1808), the founding of a bank (1808), exchanges between the United States and Canada (1809), weights and measures (1809 and 1810), and speculation on the Quebec markets (1810).

On controversial questions such as the salary of assembly members in 1807, the Eastern Townships in the same year, the right of members of the Jewish faith to sit in the assembly in 1808 and 1809, and the expulsion of judge Pierre-Amable De Bonne in 1809 and 1810, Blackwood sided with the administration's party, which included the British group and a few Canadian allies. He did, however, diverge from its stand on some issues, for example on the principle that judges should not be eligible to sit in the assembly, in 1808; the election as speaker of Jean-Antoine Panet, with whom he had business relations, in 1809; and the contesting of the election of Jean-Thomas Taschereau* and Pierre Langlois in 1810. But Governor Craig considered him a "respectable" man and approved publicly of his conduct in the 1809 session. As for the Canadian party, it classed him among the "anti-Canadians" and opponents of having the civil list paid by the assembly. In 1810 Blackwood (or his son John) was involved, together with some Montreal justices of the peace, in a plot to have the leaders of the Canadian party in Montreal accused publicly of disloyalty and then arrested [see Sir James Henry Craig]; but James Brown*, the proprietor of the *Montreal Gazette*, refused to play along, and the plan fell through.

From London Sir William Grant* (1752–1832), the former attorney general of the province, recommended in 1812 that Blackwood be appointed to the Legislative Council; having received a favourable opinion from Governor Prevost, the British government named him to that office on 9 April 1813. The appointment was not without irony in view of the fact that Blackwood did not approve of the "particular experiment" that the governor was pursuing in naming to important offices the people whom his predecessor, Craig, had dismissed.

In 1815 John Blackwood decided to liquidate his affairs and return to England. He gave to the four children born of his wife's first marriage part of their inheritance, of which he had had the usufruct, and appointed an agent with power of attorney. His furniture, library, and house were later put up for sale at public auction. He came back to Lower Canada only in 1816, three years before his death, for a trip. Blackwood ended his days in England with a fortune and a prestige that had been acquired through decades of intelligent labour and carefully selected alliances in the colony.

JEAN-PIERRE WALLOT

John Blackwood is the author of *Election circular* published at Quebec in 1792 but a copy has not been located.

ANQ-Q, CN1-16, 7 avril, 12 mai, 14 nov. 1809; CN1-26, 26 janv. 1806, 26 mars 1808; CN1-83, 22 avril 1793; CN1-92, 22 mars 1793; CN1-197, 15 nov. 1819; CN1-205, 20 nov. 1782, 17 sept. 1783, 7 mai 1784; CN1-230, 21 oct., 29 nov. 1806; 8 avril 1807; 14 juill. 1810; 29 janv. 1813; 8 mars 1814; 12, 17 avril 1815; 24 mars, 15 avril 1817; CN1-262, 13 août 1805; CN1-285, 14 nov. 1800; 16 févr., 26 juill. 1804; 2 juin 1806; P-240, 3: ff.5–7; P1000-18-334. PAC, MG 11, [CO 42] Q, 79-1: 228; 84: 158–59; 97: 101–3; 112: 51–55; 117-1: 147; 118: 87; 119: 151; 120: 182–83; MG 23, GII, 6; MG 24, B1, 81; MG 30, D1, 4: 745–47; RG 1, L3^L: 58–64, 344, 420, 649–51, 1265, 1495, 1988, 2069, 2645, 4108, 4477–80, 4701–6, 4923–26, 21791–833, 25830–46, 26590, 26629–31, 26650–51, 26664, 26671–72, 26697–728, 62500–1, 88985–9016, 97803–33; RG 4, A1: 22197, 22737–38; RG 7, G14, 33; G15C, 15: 251; RG 8, I (C ser.), 111: 321–25; 372: 176A; RG 68, General index, 1651–1841: ff.59, 271, 278, 280, 329, 335, 338, 343, 345. Bas-Canada, chambre d'Assemblée, *Journaux*, 1803–10. *Doc. relatifs à l'hist. constitutionnelle, 1791–1818* (Doughty et McArthur; 1915), 375. *Le Canadien*, 1806–10. *Le Courrier de Québec*, 1806–8. *Montreal Gazette*, 1805–10. *Quebec Gazette*, 1782–1819. *Quebec Mercury*, 1805–10. Turcotte, *Le Conseil législatif*, 76. Paquet et Wallot, *Patronage et pouvoir dans le Bas-Canada*, 129. J.-P. Wallot, "Le Bas-Canada sous l'administration de sir James Craig (1807–1811)" (thèse de PHD, univ. de Montréal, 1965); *Un Québec qui bougeait*, 55, 58, 154.

BLAKE, CHARLES, army officer, surgeon, apothecary, landowner, office holder, and businessman; b. 13 Aug. 1746 in Bath, England, son of John Blake; m. first 12 April 1783 Mary Sunderland in Montreal, Que.; m. there secondly 31 March 1804 Harriet Antill, and they had two daughters; d. there 22 April 1810.

Nothing is known about Charles Blake's early years. On 3 June 1770 he was appointed surgeon to the 54th Foot, a British regiment stationed in Ireland. On 15 May 1772, retaining the same duties, he was transferred to the 34th Foot, which was also posted in

Ireland. He arrived in the province of Quebec in the spring of 1776 with the troops under Major-General John Burgoyne* sent to fight the Americans. His first experience in North America was disappointing. While serving as chief surgeon during the 1777 expedition against Fort Stanwix (Rome, N.Y.) under Lieutenant-Colonel Barrimore Matthew St Leger*, he lost his kit and surgical instruments in the course of the force's retreat. On his return to the province, he was temporarily assigned to the post of royal surgeon at the Hôpital Général in Montreal. He received a commission on 12 Oct. 1779 as surgeon to the Montreal garrison, where he carried on his profession until December 1783, after the end of the American Revolutionary War.

In January of the following year, immediately after he was placed on half pay, Blake went into partnership with Dr Henry Nicholas Christopher Loedel* to practise medicine and to trade in pharmaceutical products. The partnership, in which Blake put up two-thirds of the capital, turned out to be profitable; moreover, the firm soon enlarged the scope of its activities and ventured into the real estate field. At the outset the two partners owned a pharmacy well situated on Rue de la Grande-Parade. They not only imported drugs and medicaments from an apothecary in Bristol, England, but also prepared their own with the help of assistants. Their customers came from among doctors in Montreal and in regions as far away as Niagara, and the patients in their medical practice were mainly prominent people. The partners sometimes taught the rudiments of medicine to beginners. Thus in 1800 Peter Diehl began a seven-year period of training with them; Blake considered him almost a son and sent him to medical schools in England for further study. John Horatio Ferris, who prepared medicaments under Blake and Loedel, accompanied them for three months on their visits to the sick, having each case explained to him; he also had full access to the books on pharmacy and surgery in their library.

Blake played an important role in the development of a statute that from 1788 would establish some supervision of the medical profession in Quebec. The last initiative in this area dated back to an ordinance of 1750 promulgated by Intendant François Bigot*. Blake had been commissioned in September 1782 to investigate the Baie-Saint-Paul malady [see Philippe-Louis-François BADELARD; James Bowman*]. In 1787 he and some colleagues presented a report to the committee of the Legislative Council on population, agriculture, and settlement of crown lands which had been established the preceding year by Lord Dorchester [Guy CARLETON]. In his discussion he suggested a treatment to arrest the Baie-Saint-Paul malady and used the occasion to criticize harshly the practice of medicine in the province; he even asserted that certain doctors had killed more of His Majesty's subjects than had the late war against the Americans. To remedy the situation he proposed that examining boards be set up in Montreal and Quebec with authority to license candidates for professional practice. The ordinance of 1788 gave effect to Blake's recommendations, and he was appointed to the first Montreal board of medical examiners, an office he retained until his death.

Blake's business affairs prospered at the same time; about 1800 he purchased a two-storey stone house on Rue Notre-Dame which later became his residence. He also owned two other houses, on Rue de la Capitale, and a farm with an orchard in the *faubourg* Saint-Laurent. In 1803 he obtained a grant of 1,797 acres of crown land in Clifton Township, Lower Canada, and subsequently he bought lots in several Upper Canadian townships. He shared certain of these properties with Dr Loedel. Socially his situation was enviable; his relations with the most eminent medical practitioners, army officers, lawyers, and merchants give proof of his importance. Moreover, he lent large sums to members of the bourgeoisie in Montreal and the surrounding region at six per cent, the usual rate; in 1794, when he renewed his contract with Loedel, the debts owing to the partnership amounted to £2,681. A number of his fellow citizens chose him as guardian, proxy, or administrator of their property, probably because of the reputation that he had acquired while a justice of the peace for the District of Montreal from 1796 until 1810.

An outstanding figure of the professional petite bourgeoisie at the opening of the 19th century, Blake had succeeded in winning recognition from colonial officialdom, as well as certain favours. Having launched into new fields of activity, such as retail trade, investing in property, lending money, and even buying slaves, at the end of his life he was moving upwards in society.

GILLES JANSON

ANQ-M, CE1-63, 12 April 1783, 31 March 1804, 1 March 1806, 8 Aug. 1809, 24 April 1810; CN1-16, 13 févr. 1804; CN1-29, 22 Feb. 1786; 22 Feb., 30 April, 9 July 1787; 14 Nov. 1788; 3 June 1790; 26 July 1792; 23 Sept. 1793; 16 May 1794; 1 Oct., 2 Dec. 1795; 31 March 1796; 18 Jan., 13 March 1797; 27 Feb. 1798; 29 Nov. 1799; 5 Feb., 17 Nov. 1800; 29 May, 6 Sept. 1802; 28 Jan., 20 Oct., 12 Dec. 1803; 7 Jan., 5 Oct. 1804; CN1-74, 3 mai 1803; CN1-185, 31 Jan. 1797; 29 June 1799; 15, 22 Oct. 1802; 11 May 1803; 8, 21 March, 30 April, 28 May 1804; 16 Aug. 1805; 20 March, 1 Aug. 1806; 19 Feb., 12 Oct. 1807; 19 Feb., 2 July, 20 Aug. 1808; 23 Feb. 1809; 15 March, 15 May 1810; CN1-254, 19 janv. 1785. AUM, P 58, G2, 1801–9. BL, Add. MSS 21721: 61, 158; 21722: 312; 21735/1: 60; 21740: 120, 186, 201, 213; 21742: 104; 21744: 45; 21772: 81; 21790: 107; 21796: 43; 21799: 4, 6, 26; 21821: 50, 81; 21873: 8, 256 (copies at PAC). PAC, MG 11, [CO 42] Q, 27-2: 497–554. *Doc. relatifs à l'hist. constitutionnelle, 1759–1791* (Shortt et Doughty; 1921), 2: 569, 917–18. "Une correspondance médicale: Blake à Davidson," P.-A. Fiset, édit., *Laval médical* (Québec), 23 (1957): 419–48. *Quebec Gazette*, 3 Nov. 1785; 15 May 1788; 16 July 1789; 19 July 1792; 25 July 1799; 22 March 1804; 16 July 1809; 26 April, 22 Nov. 1810; 26 March 1818. *Quebec almanac*, 1788–1819. Langelier, *Liste des terrains concédés*, 1175. Abbott, *Hist. of medicine*. M.-J. et G. Ahern, *Notes pour l'hist. de la médecine*, 52–55. William Canniff, *The medical profession in Upper Canada, 1783–1850* . . . (Toronto, 1894; repr. 1980). J. J. Heagerty, *Four centuries of medical history in Canada and a sketch of the medical history of Newfoundland* (2v., Toronto, 1928), 1. Louis Richard, "La famille Loedel," *BRH*, 56 (1950): 78–89.

BLONDEAU, MAURICE-RÉGIS, fur trader, militia officer, and office holder; b. 23 June 1734 in Montreal (Que.), son of Jean-Baptiste Blondeau, a merchant, and Geneviève Angers; d. there 13 July 1809 and was buried two days later.

Maurice-Régis Blondeau's family came from Saumur, France. François arrived in New France some time before 1650. One of his three sons, Maurice, went into the fur trade and rose to prominence in the Montreal bourgeoisie. Maurice's nephews at Quebec, Thomas, Joseph, and Jean-Baptiste, who were orphaned as children, entered the fur trade in the 1720s. Jean-Baptiste settled in Montreal and specialized in trading among the Indians of the Illinois country.

On 10 May 1757 Maurice-Régis was hired by Joseph-Michel Cadet*, purveyor general to the French forces in Canada, to work for a year, with a salary of 900 *livres*, mainly at Fort Saint-Frédéric (near Crown Point, N.Y.). Subsequently he probably lived in the west; after Pontiac*'s uprising subsided he is believed to have gone to Michilimackinac (Mackinaw City, Mich.) from Fort Dauphin (Winnipegosis, Man.) and Fort La Reine (Portage la Prairie, Man.). In the spring of 1767, on his behalf, his father looked after the hiring of voyageurs to go to Michilimackinac and Grand Portage (near Grand Portage, Minn.).

Blondeau returned to Montreal and on 26 Oct. 1767 married Marie-Josephe Le Pellé Lahaye, the 31-year-old widow of Pierre-Louis Deslandes. At their marriage, Blondeau agreed to community of property; he retained 10,000 *livres* for himself and gave his wife a dower of 3,000 *livres* and a preference legacy of 1,500 *livres* in addition to jewellery, linen, and "a bedroom suite."

Early in May 1768, "his departure for the posts in the *pays d'en haut* being imminent," Blondeau gave his wife power of attorney to manage all his affairs during his absence. In 1769 he sent 3 canoes and 19 men, with a cargo worth £1,350, to Michilimackinac and on to La Mer de l'Ouest (a term still used at this time to mean Manitoba and the territory beyond). The following year he sent 4 canoes, 20 men, and £1,506

Blue Jacket

in goods to La Mer de l'Ouest. Blondeau carried on trade particularly south of Lake Winnipeg and in the Fort La Reine vicinity. Later he moved farther west. He sent 3 canoes, 28 men, and a cargo worth £1,642 up the Red Deer River in 1772, and 3 canoes and 22 men up the Saskatchewan River the next year.

The expansion of the fur trade increased costs and forced the merchants to form partnerships. In 1774 Blondeau, with Jean-Baptiste-Amable Adhémar* as partner, sent 4 canoes, 29 men, and goods valued at £1,300 to Lake Superior. The following year he joined with James McGill, Isaac Todd, and Benjamin* and Joseph Frobisher to fit out 12 canoes and send 103 men to Grand Portage, where a coalition was formed to exploit the resources of the northwest. The year 1779 marked the beginning of a major shift to concentration that would give rise to the North West Company. From 1779 to 1785 Blondeau traded in the Lake Superior region in partnership with Gabriel Cotté*, who became his brother-in-law in 1783, and John Grant. In the 1780s Blondeau stood surety for the trading voyages of Jean-Baptiste Cadot and Cotté to Sault Ste Marie (Mich.) and Michilimackinac. In 1785 he was one of the founding members of the Beaver Club in Montreal.

Blondeau had acquired various properties in Montreal. He had paid 8,000 *livres* in 1770 for a two-storey stone house with an adjoining storage vault on Rue Saint-Paul. In 1775 he purchased another house on the street for 1,800 shillings. The following year he bought two more houses, one on Rue de l'Hôpital for 3,000 shillings and the other on Rue Saint-François for 4,000 shillings. In 1778 he hired a man-servant and a maid, thus displaying his quite ample means. That same year he sold for 18,000 *livres* the house on Rue Saint-Paul bought in 1770, in addition to a property 720 feet square on the same street. In 1783 Blondeau hired another man-servant.

Blondeau was active in 1785 on the Canadian committee of the reform movement in Montreal, which was championing a new constitution. Two years later he testified before the commission that Chief Justice William Smith* had empowered to investigate accusations concerning the courts of justice. In 1791 he was a captain in Montreal's 1st Militia Battalion and from 1794 to 1802 a major. He became a militant member of the association founded to support the British government in 1794, of which McGill was president. In addition, from 1795 to 1799 Blondeau served as justice of the peace in Montreal.

For a score of years Blondeau was involved in the administration of the Jesuit estates. On 26 May 1792 Jean-Joseph Casot* appointed him procurator of the community to oversee the management of the seigneury of Prairie-de-la-Madeleine. His primary concern was the sale of lots. Then on 22 June 1801 George Pyke*, the secretary of the commission for the Jesuit estates, appointed him the agent for the property in the District of Montreal. He put up a bond of £750 as security, and two guarantors committed themselves for the same amount. His remuneration was equal to ten per cent of the moneys received.

Maurice-Régis Blondeau died on 13 July 1809 in Montreal, "after two years of unbelievable sufferings." His wife survived him only briefly, dying on 31 August of the same year.

François Béland

ANQ-M, CE1-51, 23 juin 1734, 26 oct. 1767, 15 juill. 1809; CN1-120, 4 mars, 27 juin 1778; 2 août 1783; CN1-200, 22 May 1802; CN1-290, 9, 13 nov. 1776; 3 juill. 1778; 9 avril 1784; CN1-308, 10 mai 1757; 19, 27 avril, 21 mai, 24 oct. 1767; 4 mai 1768; 1er déc. 1769; 3, 21 mars 1770; 15 mai 1775; CN1-313, 26 mai 1792. "L'Association loyale de Montréal," ANQ *Rapport*, 1948–49: 257–73. *Docs. relating to NWC* (Wallace), 451. *Quebec Gazette*, 20 July 1809. Archange Godbout, "Nos ancêtres au XVIIe siècle," ANQ *Rapport*, 1957–59: 401–5. "Papiers d'État," PAC *Rapport*, 1890: 207–8. "Papiers d'État – Bas-Canada," PAC *Rapport*, 1892: 162. Innis, *Fur trade in Canada* (1956), 191–94. Rumilly, *La Compagnie du Nord-Ouest*, 1: 60–61.

BLUE JACKET. *See* Weyapiersenwah

BOISSEAU, NICOLAS-GASPARD, office holder and militia officer; b. 16 June 1726 at Quebec, son of Nicolas Boisseau*, court clerk, and Marie-Anne Pagé, *dit* Carcy; d. 27 May 1804 in the parish of Saint-Thomas (at Montmagny), Lower Canada.

Nicolas-Gaspard Boisseau followed in the footsteps of his father, who early instructed him in legal practice and procedure so that he might one day replace him as chief clerk of the provost court of Quebec. In 1743 Nicolas Boisseau wrote to Intendant Gilles Hocquart*, bringing this training to his attention and requesting a commission for the boy as assistant clerk of the provost court, to encourage him to continue. Having made a report to the king, Hocquart on 5 Dec. 1743 appointed the young Boisseau "to carry out, in the absence of Sieur Boisseau Sr the duties of assistant clerk of the aforementioned provost court, to record the proceedings, draw up the decisions, and even sign the documents [issuing] from it."

Some months later, on 25 March 1744, the very day that the elder Boisseau was named chief clerk of the Conseil Supérieur of Quebec, Nicolas-Gaspard at the age of 17 was appointed by the king to succeed his father as clerk of the provost court. At the same time the king granted him letters waiving the age limit, since he had not yet reached the prescribed age of 25. The Conseil Supérieur recognized him officially on 12 Oct. 1744. As clerk he registered all the deeds of that court and all the documents brought to him for custody in his registry; he was also the depositary of the minute-books of deceased notaries who had practised in the Government of Quebec. These duties he performed to the general satisfaction of the colonial authorities. On 6 Oct. 1754, at Saint-Thomas, Boisseau married Thérèse, daughter of Louis Couillard, seigneur of Rivière-du-Sud. Unlike some of the king's servants in Canada [see François Bigot*; Joseph-Michel Cadet*], Boisseau does not seem to have taken advantage of the Seven Years' War to enrich himself; when he bought a two-storey stone house on Quebec's Rue Saint-Pierre in 1758, he had to assume a debt of 14,500 *livres*.

In 1759 Boisseau's house was partly demolished by bombardment. He then moved with his family to his parents-in-law's property at Saint-Thomas, where his wife died on 15 Jan. 1760. Without employment and saddled with a further debt of 2,483 *livres* for repairs to his house, Boisseau was in dire straits; to support his family he found himself obliged to sell "his deceased wife's few sticks of furniture and old garments," as well as his own clothes and some furniture saved at the time of the siege of Quebec, where, he declared, "he lost the rest of his household belongings . . . being left penniless and burdened with many debts." A widower with three young children to look after, Boisseau married again: on 30 Jan. 1764 at Saint-Pierre, Île d'Orléans, he wed Claire Jolliette, widow of François Volant de Chamblain, a ship's captain.

At 37 Boisseau had no intention of withdrawing from public life. Having returned to Quebec in 1764, he joined 6 compatriots and 14 British merchants in signing a presentment in English from the grand jury [see James Johnston*]. Subsequently, after they had asked for a translation and realized they had misunderstood the text, which had simply been read to them in English and not explained, the seven French-speaking jurors signed a protest to disclaim their signatures. On 30 Sept. 1766 Governor Murray* appointed Boisseau French clerk of the Court of Common Pleas of the District of Quebec, succeeding Jean-Claude Panet*. That year he was also made keeper of the minutes of notaries who had gone out of practice.

At the time of the American invasion in 1775 [see Benedict ARNOLD; Richard Montgomery*], the British authorities asked Boisseau to take command of one of the three militia companies which were to be raised on Île d'Orléans; Adam Mabane* and William GRANT (1744–1805) commanded the others. To persuade the islanders to enlist, Mabane used tactics that annoyed the habitants. Armed with sticks, they were preparing to give him a rough time when Boisseau intervened to calm them down. On 1 May 1776, probably as a reward for his loyalty to the British crown, the authorities confirmed him in his job as clerk of the Court of Common Pleas. He held this post jointly with David LYND, retaining it, and also the office of clerk

of the peace accorded him on 31 March 1777, until 22 Sept. 1783. He then retired to Île d'Orléans.

On 2 Aug. 1784, to compensate him for having undertaken the census of Île d'Orléans without pay in July, Governor HALDIMAND made Boisseau justice of the peace for the entire province of Quebec. He kept this post, which was considered a sinecure and which exempted him from all corvées and seigneurial duties, until his death on 27 May 1804 at Saint-Thomas. He had probably gone there to join his son Nicolas-Gaspard*. A notary since 1799, this son of Boisseau's second marriage practised at Saint-Vallier and Saint-Thomas and also represented the county of Orléans in the House of Assembly from 1792 to 1796.

The Boisseaus illustrate how a tradition of serving the state is established in a family from one generation to the next; in this service they showed themselves faithful and devoted.

ANDRÉ LACHANCE

AN, Col., B, 78: f.39; C[11A], 120: f.351; E, 37 (dossier Nicolas Boisseau). ANQ-Q, CE1-1, 16 juin 1726; CE1-12, 30 janv. 1764; CE2-7, 16 janv. 1760; 5, 29 mai 1804; CN1-76, 29 janv. 1764; CN1-190, 15 mars 1765; E1, 31: f.115. PAC, MG 23, GV, 1. *Doc. relatifs à l'hist. constitutionnelle, 1759–1791* (Shortt et Doughty; 1921), 1: 192–95. F.-J. Audet et Fabre Surveyer, *Les députés au premier parl. du Bas-Canada*, 65. J.-B. Gareau, "La Prévôté de Québec, ses officiers, ses registres," ANQ *Rapport*, 1943–44: 124–25. Le Jeune, *Dictionnaire*, 2: 199. P.-G. Roy, *Inventaire des jugements et délibérations du Conseil supérieur de la Nouvelle-France, de 1717 à 1760* (7v., Beauceville, Qué., 1932–35), 4: 206, 210. Tanguay, *Dictionnaire*, 2: 330. P.-G. Roy, *La famille Boisseau* (Lévis, Qué., 1907), 1–2, 19–20, 33.

BOOTH, JOSHUA, miller, office holder, politician, and militia officer; b. 1758 or 1759 in Orange County, N.Y., son of Benjamin Booth; m. Margaret Fraser, daughter of a loyalist and former army officer, and they had six daughters and five sons; d. 27 Oct. 1813 in Ernestown Township, Upper Canada.

Little is known of Joshua Booth's early life. He served with the British loyalist forces during the American revolution but details of his service are obscure. He was probably the Joshua Booth listed in 1780 as a private in De Lancey's Brigade. Booth appears on the United Empire Loyalist list as a sergeant. After the revolution he immigrated to Upper Canada and was granted land in Ernestown Township. He acquired at least another 1,500 acres of land in Ernestown and Thurlow townships as a result of successful petitions on his own and his wife's behalf. About 1793 he began to exploit the useful sites for grist-mills and sawmills within his Ernestown grants and what was then called "the Gore between Kingston and Ernestown." In 1802 he was also granted a lease

Borneuf

of the "King's Mill" at Ernestown, a sawmill on lot 18, concession 5. On the basis of these activities a local historian concluded that by the time of his death, Booth was the most successful mill proprietor and landowner in the area.

Booth held several local offices which indicate a measure of regional prominence. In 1792, when the land board of the Mecklenburg District was abolished, Booth was named to the land board of Lennox and Addington, Hastings and Prince Edward along with Peter Van Alstine, Alexander Fisher*, and Archibald McDonell*. In the same year he was elected to the House of Assembly for the riding of Ontario and Addington, serving until the first parliament was dissolved in 1796. It is not known whether Booth played a role of any importance in this early assembly. On 15 July 1796 he was appointed a justice of the peace for the Midland District and he received his last commission on 16 March 1808. As a justice, Booth was a member of the Court of Quarter Sessions of the Midland District which met four times yearly, in both a judicial and an administrative capacity, alternating between Adolphustown and Kingston. At best Booth was an infrequent attender: 3 of 15 sessions between 8 July 1800 and 24 Jan. 1804, and 5 of 25 sessions from 27 Jan. 1807 to 26 Jan. 1813. On 2 Sept. 1797 and again on 21 July 1800 he had been named with Richard CARTWRIGHT, Hazelton SPENCER, and Joseph FORSYTH to the first Heir and Devisee Commission for the Midland District. Of four sessions between 16 Sept. 1802 and 3 Sept. 1803 Booth attended three.

During the War of 1812 Booth was a captain commanding a company of the 1st Addington Militia. His death occurred suddenly while he was leading a detachment of militia in search of militiamen absent from duty without leave and to retrieve a number of missing boats washed ashore along the front of Ernestown. His widow received from the province an annual pension of £20.

J. K. JOHNSON

AO, RG 1, A-I-6: 328; A-II-1, 1: 218; A-II-5, 2; RG 22, ser.54, 2. Lennox and Addington County Museum (Napanee, Ont.), Lennox and Addington Hist. Soc. coll., T. W. Casey papers: 11849 (mfm. at PAC). PAC, RG 1, L3, 27: B1/9, 98, 135–36; 30: B3/183; 67: B misc., 1788–95/138; 184: E, Ernestown Mills/2; L7, 52A; RG 5, A1: 7781–87; RG 8, I (C ser.), 1881; RG 9, I, B4, 2: 2; 6: 216; RG 68, General index, 1651–1841: ff.248–50, 405–6, 411, 419–20. PRO, CO 42/147: 150. "Board of land office, District of Hesse," AO Report, 1905: 211. Corr. of Lieut. Governor Simcoe (Cruikshank), 5: 222. "Petitions for grants of land" (Cruikshank), OH, 24: 27. "Surveyors' letters, etc.," AO Report, 1905: 467. "U.C. land book C," AO Report, 1931: 75. Armstrong, Handbook of Upper Canadian chronology, 58. Reid, Loyalists in Ont., 25. William Canniff, History of the settlement of Upper Canada (Ontario) with special reference to the Bay Quinte (Toronto, 1869; repr. Belleville, Ont., 1971), 442–43, 534, 642. W. S. Herrington, History of the county of Lennox and Addington (Toronto, 1913; repr. Belleville, 1972), 358–59. J. F. Pringle, Lunenburgh or the old Eastern District: its settlement and early progress . . . (Cornwall, Ont., 1890; repr. Belleville, 1972), 375. T. W. Casey, "Our first representatives in parliament," Lennox and Addington Hist. Soc., Papers and Records (Napanee), 4 (1912): 28–29. C. C. James, "The first legislators of Upper Canada," RSC Trans., 2nd ser., 8 (1902), sect.II: 93–119.

BORNEUF, JOSEPH, Roman Catholic priest, Sulpician, and bursar; b. 26 Sept. 1762 at Quebec, son of Pierre Borneuf, a merchant, and Marie-Madeleine Degrès; d. 15 Nov. 1819 at the Séminaire de Saint-Sulpice in Montreal, Lower Canada.

After studying at the Petit Séminaire de Québec, Joseph Borneuf entered the Grand Séminaire at the age of 22. There he received a spiritual and theological education similar to that being offered at the non-Jansenist seminaries in France, which typically was old-fashioned, superficial, and lacking in originality. At the end of his theological studies, during which he had also taught in the rigorous milieu of the Petit Séminaire, Borneuf was ordained priest by Jean-Olivier Briand* on 8 Oct. 1786. The following year, along with Michel LECLERC, Jean-Baptiste Marchand*, and three other Canadians, he joined the Séminaire de Saint-Sulpice in Montreal, where he became a member of the community on 21 Oct. 1788.

This influx of new recruits provided the seminary with a Canadian majority – almost despite itself: the superior, Étienne Montgolfier*, and Gabriel-Jean Brassier* had tried in vain to bring Sulpicians from France to maintain French predominance. Moreover, given the advanced age of the last French Sulpicians who had arrived before the conquest, the young Canadians were in a good position to accede to high responsibilities, as the bishops of Quebec expressly wished them to do. In 1793, for example, Bishop Hubert* proposed that Borneuf be appointed parish priest of Montreal. However, the seminary, which was responsible for the appointment to this post, chose the Frenchman Candide-Michel Le Saulnier*, who had arrived that year, rather than Borneuf. In addition, the French revolution, which had softened the British authorities' opposition to the recruiting of French ecclesiastics [see Gabriel-Jean Brassier], led to the immigration of 11 new French Sulpicians in 1794. Their arrival restored numerical superiority to the French and at the same time relegated the Canadians to posts that, although important, were devoid of prestige and authority. Borneuf's subsequent career as a priest was entirely devoted to administering the Sulpicians' seigneurial properties, under the firm direction of French superiors: first Brassier, who appears to have allowed him considerable initiative, and then Jean-Henri-Auguste Roux*, who would not delegate authority.

It seems, in fact, that Borneuf had begun to assume the duties of bursar as early as 1789, through his direct involvement in the legal dispute over the Sulpicians' seigneurial rights, a dispute that the British authorities would allow to continue for some four decades more. The lawyers engaged to fight the claims of the *censitaires* who were contesting these rights consulted him, kept him informed of the progress of the cases, and submitted their bills to him. Borneuf was also concerned with the collection and administration of the funds deriving from the *cens et rentes* and *lods et ventes*, as well as with the operation of the mills on Montreal Island, which were under the seminary's exclusive control. Although it is still impossible to draw up a complete table of the economic activity supervised by Borneuf, it has been discovered that 93 per cent of the Sulpicians' revenues in 1799 came from various seigneurial rights, and that the tithe accounted for less than 2 per cent. The breakdown of expenses for this year was: 60 per cent for the upkeep of the seminary and the members' living expenses, 26 per cent for social services and education, 5 per cent for legal expenses, and the remainder for a variety of other uses. In 1815, towards the end of Borneuf's term of office, the seminary doubled the sums for education and good works in order both to meet the needs of the population and to justify its enormous revenues in the eyes of the British government.

For unknown reasons Borneuf resigned as bursar in 1796 but three years later was reinstated. By the beginning of the 19th century, however, the French priests at the seminary were sufficiently acquainted with the situation in Montreal to take complete control. As a result there are few further traces of Borneuf's activity. On the pastoral level he was restricted to the modest function of confessor at the church of Notre-Dame, to the nuns of the Hôtel-Dieu, and to the nuns of the Congregation of Notre-Dame, for whom he also served as chaplain from 1796 to 1798. In addition Borneuf was appointed in 1794 to attend the meetings of an association founded in that year to support the British government.

A discreet and reliable subordinate, Borneuf died on 15 Nov. 1819, before a prolonged crisis was precipitated by the accession to the bishopric and by the activity in Montreal of Jean-Jacques Lartigue*, a Canadian colleague at the seminary.

LOUIS ROUSSEAU

ANQ-Q, CE1-1, 26 sept. 1762. ASSM, 21, papiers Borneuf; 33, 17 nov. 1819. "L'Association loyale de Montréal," ANQ *Rapport*, 1948–49: 261. Caron, "Inv. de la corr. de Mgr Hubert et de Mgr Bailly de Messein," ANQ *Rapport*, 1930–31: 211, 296; "Inv. de la corr. de Mgr Mariaucheau d'Esgly," ANQ *Rapport*, 1930–31: 192. Desrosiers, "Corr. de cinq vicaires généraux," ANQ *Rapport*, 1947–48: 113–14, 121, 123. Gauthier, *Sulpitiana*. Tanguay, *Dictionnaire*, 2: 360. Lemire-Marsolais et Lambert, *Hist. de la CND de Montréal*, 6: 312. Louis Rousseau, *La prédication à Montréal de 1800 à 1830; approche religiologique* (Montréal, 1976).

BOSSU, *dit* **Lyonnais**, **PIERRE-JACQUES**, named **Brother Félix**, Recollet, Roman Catholic priest, and professor; b. 8 Nov. 1770 at Quebec, son of Jean-Michel-Jacques Bossu, a blacksmith, and Catherine Jean; d. there 19 Aug. 1803.

In 1782 Pierre-Jacques Bossu, *dit* Lyonnais, entered the Petit Séminaire de Québec, where he "applied himself to studying earnestly and steadfastly, a model of docility and good behaviour." In 1790, thanks to an allowance given to impoverished pupils, he finished the Philosophy program. He then entered the Recollet noviciate and took the name Brother Félix. When this early period of training was completed, Bossu returned to the seminary to follow the courses in mathematics and science given by Antoine-Bernardin Robert* in the 1791–92 school year. On 30 April 1792 he and four other students publicly defended theses in mathematics, ballistics, astronomy, and physics. Prince EDWARD AUGUSTUS, Lieutenant Governor John Graves SIMCOE of Upper Canada, and officers from the garrison were present at this defence.

After completing his studies Bossu began to prepare himself for holy orders at Quebec and Montreal. But in 1796 the Recollet order was dissolved and all the professed who had been admitted after 1784 were secularized [*see* Louis DEMERS]. Bossu, who reverted to his baptismal name, asked to be admitted to the Grand Séminaire de Québec. He was still only a subdeacon when, without any difficulty, he obtained admission as a member of the community of the seminary on 4 Aug. 1797; on 20 August he was ordained priest by Bishop DENAUT. At the seminary, Bossu taught philosophy to begin with in 1797–98, and theology for the next two years; in 1801–2 he gave the courses in rhetoric.

Because of the limited number of priests who were members of the community of the seminary, Bossu had to fulfil several administrative functions in addition to teaching. From 1798 to 1800 he ran the Grand Séminaire, and he sat on the council of the seminary from 7 July 1799. After becoming director of the Petit Séminaire and prefect of studies in 1800, on 2 March 1802 he was elected second assistant to the superior, Antoine-Bernardin Robert. That summer Bossu went to Île aux Coudres for a rest. On 8 Aug. 1803 he became first assistant to the superior, and he would probably have climbed the final step if a serious illness had not intervened. Bossu did not recover and on 19 August, at only 32 years of age, he

Botsford

died at the Hôpital Général of Quebec. He was buried in the cemetery of that institution.

HONORIUS PROVOST

AAQ, 22 A, V: f.697r. Arch. de l'Hôpital Général de Québec, Hôpital, reg. des décès, 20 août 1803. ASQ, MSS, 12; 437: 47–50; MSS-M, 134, 208, 978; Séminaire, 103, no.21a. Allaire, *Dictionnaire*, 1: 65.

BOTSFORD, AMOS, lawyer, office holder, judge, politician, landowner and improver, and merchant; b. 31 Jan. 1744/45 in Newtown, Conn., son of Gideon Botsford, "a respectable farmer," and Bertha Bennett; m. 1770 Sarah Chandler, and they had three children; d. 14 Sept. 1812 in Saint John, N.B.

After graduating from Yale College in 1763, Amos Botsford studied law under the prominent New Haven attorney Jared Ingersoll, was admitted to the bar, and, in 1768–69, lectured in law at Yale. At the outbreak of revolutionary hostilities he refused to take the oath of allegiance to the new state constitution and was excluded from his professional practice, thereby losing an income estimated to be £600 annually. He remained in New Haven until 6 July 1779 when, with the withdrawal of Major-General William Tryon's forces, he sought shelter at New York City. His properties, valued at more than £1,200, were confiscated by the Connecticut authorities.

In the fall of 1782 Botsford was appointed agent for the Lloyd Neck Associated Loyalists; under commission from Sir Guy CARLETON he was sent to Nova Scotia with Frederick Hauser and Samuel Cummings to arrange with Lieutenant Governor Andrew Snape Hamond for the settlement of the refugees scheduled to arrive during the ensuing year. Botsford reached Annapolis Royal on 20 Oct. 1782 with the advance group of New York loyalists. The following months were spent with Cummings and Hauser in making an extensive survey of the Bay of Fundy and the environs of the Saint John River (N.B.). Their report, sent to Dr Samuel Seabury and Sampson Salter Blowers*, president and secretary of the Board of Agents, and published in the New York *Royal Gazette* on 29 March 1783, was enthusiastically received.

That spring Botsford was appointed soliciting agent for the loyalists settled at Conway (Digby, N.S.). In his exertions to obtain provisions and land grants for this group, Botsford ran into disagreement with the provincial authorities, and especially with Governor John Parr* and Charles MORRIS, the surveyor general. In Conway, as well, a group of dissatisfied loyalists accused him of mismanagement and of giving preferential treatment to the élite.

Upon the formation of the province of New Brunswick in 1784, Botsford moved to Dorchester.

He received the appointments of clerk of the peace, judge of the Inferior Court of Common Pleas, and registrar of deeds for the newly created county of Westmorland. In the first provincial election, held in November 1785, he was returned as a representative to the House of Assembly; and, during the first session of the house, held at Saint John on 3 Jan. 1786, he was chosen speaker. He subsequently gained re-election in 1792, 1795, 1802, and 1809, and retained his position as speaker of the house until his death.

Amos Botsford took an active interest in politics at both the provincial and the county level. He strenuously opposed the choice of St Anne's Point (Fredericton) as the site of the capital, and joined with the Saint John interests who fought for its retention in that city. During the turbulent debates over the appropriation of finances that saw the assembly and the executive at loggerheads, the usually moderate Botsford threw his support behind James GLENIE, and in the 1795 elections he favoured the anti-government candidates Stair Agnew* and Samuel Jarvis in York County. In Westmorland County, he acted in his capacity as magistrate to oversee the escheat of lands held by delinquent grantees, and fully supported the centralizing activities of the provincial government in its attempt to eradicate the persistent mood of "township" autonomy. But Botsford failed to attain his greatest political aspiration. Despite his solicitations to Edward Goldstone Lutwyche, the colony's agent in London, and Viscount Castlereagh, the Colonial secretary, he was never awarded the chief justiceship and a seat on the Council.

Botsford's private career comprised his legal, agricultural, and commercial activities. His extensive law practice extended throughout Westmorland and Cumberland counties, while his interest in agriculture was especially evident following his move from Dorchester to Westcock in 1790. There he acquired a large acreage of marsh and upland and, like his neighbour Charles DIXON, he actively pursued farming, both personally and with hired labour and tenants. He also established a retail business, and in association with Saint John interests, especially with William PAGAN, William HAZEN, and Jonathan Bliss*, his commercial activities expanded considerably. By 1798 he was advising his son, who had settled in Saint John following his graduation from Yale, that "Law and farming together will answer here – or trade, so that you need have no gloomy prospects."

Amos Botsford died on 14 Sept. 1812 while on a visit to Saint John. His two daughters, both of whom had married sons of Thomas MILLIDGE, had predeceased him. His only son, William*, had moved from Saint John to Westcock in 1808 to become a partner in his father's legal and business interests, and succeeded him as member of the House of Assembly for

Westmorland County, later being appointed solicitor general, member of the Council, and judge of the Supreme Court.

JAMES SNOWDON

Mount Allison Univ. Arch. (Sackville, N.B.), Webster Chignecto coll., Botsford family papers. N.B. Museum, Botsford family papers; Milner coll., nos.2, 12–13. PAC, MG 23, D1, ser.1, 15: 96; D4; F1, ser.5, 19: 3710, 3717. PANB, RG 2, RS7, 2/1; RS8, Unarranged Executive Council docs., 1784; RG 10, RS107/1/1: 333; RS108, Petition of Amos Botsford, 1788; Petition of Charity French, 1791. PRO, PRO 30/55, no.270 (mfm. at PAC). UNBL, MG H2, 5: 1. [Ezra Stiles], *The literary diary of Ezra Stiles, D.D., LL.D., president of Yale College*, ed. F. B. Dexter (3v., New York, 1901), 2: 355. "United Empire Loyalists: enquiry into losses and services," AO *Report*, 1904: 785. *Royal Gazette* (New York), 29 March 1783. F. B. Dexter, *Biographical sketches of the graduates of Yale College, with annals of the college history* (6v., New York and New Haven, Conn., 1885–1912). L. H. Gipson, *Jared Ingersoll: a study in American loyalism in relation to British colonial government* (New Haven and London, 1920; repr. under title *American loyalist: Jared Ingersoll*, 1971), 349. F. E. Murray, *Memoir of LeBaron Botsford, M.D.* (Saint John, N.B., 1892), 1–15. I. W. Wilson, *A geography and history of the county of Digby, Nova Scotia* (Halifax, 1900; repr. Belleville, Ont., 1975), 46, 48, 52.

BOUCHER, FRANÇOIS, mariner, merchant, and office holder; b. 10 Dec. 1730 at Quebec, eldest son of François Boucher, a mariner, and Marie-Anne Martel, an innkeeper; m. 12 Feb. 1759 Marie-Joseph Tremblay in the parish of Saint-Louis (at Saint-Louis-de-l'Isle-aux-Coudres, Que.), and they had seven sons and four daughters; d. 3 May 1816 at Quebec.

From childhood François Boucher was in contact with the seafaring world through his mother, who kept an inn near the port of Quebec. His father, a captain on fishing vessels, probably passed on to him a taste for the mariner's life and the rudiments of that profession, since by 1758 François Boucher was engaged by a shipowner as a sea captain at 200 *livres* a month.

During the 1760s Boucher also became a river pilot on the St Lawrence, a sideline to his work as a ship's captain. It is impossible to determine exactly when he started serving as a pilot, but the fact that he lived on Île aux Coudres, the point of departure for pilots guiding ocean-going ships to Quebec, may suggest that he was among a score of candidates who received licences for the first time in 1769 and who were the only ones authorized to pilot such vessels. Moreover, he taught navigation to Joseph Bonnet, an apprentice pilot from the island who was licensed in 1777, and his own name appears on the first known list of pilots, dated 13 June 1780. In 1781 Boucher's experience in inland navigation was turned to account when he was chosen by Governor HALDIMAND to serve with Peter Napier, Augustin Raby*, and Martin Dechinique* on the committee to examine those seeking qualification as pilots on the St Lawrence. Four years later he was even one of the group of examiners licensing his son Pierre.

In 1784 Boucher sold his property on Île aux Coudres for 800 *livres* and went to live at Quebec. In the years that followed he seems to have concentrated on shipping and commerce. Thus from 1792 to 1797 he bought or hired schooners to trade in flour and various products. His transactions took him to both shores of the St Lawrence and sometimes to more distant places such as Baie des Chaleurs and Halifax, N.S. To ensure the growth of his business he went into partnership with his son Louis-Michel, and together they set up three stores, at Quebec, Saint-Thomas-de-la-Pointe-à-la-Caille (Montmagny), and Kamouraska, and then a distillery at Saint-Roch-des-Aulnaies. On 17 Oct. 1799 the firm closed down because of financial difficulties arising particularly from the shipwreck of one of its vessels; at that time it owed £5,318, including £3,700 to George Davison and Company of London, England. Unable to pay their debts, the two Bouchers had to surrender some of their real and personal estate to John BLACKWOOD, the creditors' agent. This bankruptcy apparently took Boucher's properties at Quebec, since in 1800 he rented a two-storey stone house for £25 a year, and six years later leased another, much larger one from Jean-Baptiste LE COMTE Dupré for £90 a year.

On 12 Aug. 1803 Sir Robert Shore Milnes*, the lieutenant governor of Lower Canada, awarded Boucher the important post of captain of the port of Quebec, to succeed James FROST who had died on 18 June. In view of the complexities involved in ensuring the efficiency and improvement of navigation on the St Lawrence, the parliament of Lower Canada in 1805 set up Trinity House of Quebec, on the English model of Trinity Houses. Founded in 1514, these establishments were highly respected in marine matters by the early 19th century. Boucher was reappointed to his duties within this organization with the new title of harbour-master. Trinity House also had a master, a deputy master, and a superintendent of pilots, as well as five wardens chosen from among the merchants of Quebec and Montreal. In particular these officers were to look after anchorage, the building of quays and lighthouses, and the removal of obstructions from sea lanes; in addition they could make regulations concerning ships' security and recommend the licensing of pilots.

A sudden increase in traffic at the port of Quebec in 1810, evident in the docking of 600 ships that year, prompted Boucher to ask for an assistant to carry out his tasks more efficiently. On 18 May 1811 Lieutenant

Boucher de Boucherville

Governor Francis Nathaniel Burton* agreed to his request and authorized Trinity House to take on an assistant to the harbour-master. However, on 30 May Boucher resigned his office. Because of his long years of service he received an annual pension of £150 and remained an honorary member of Trinity House. John Lambly, who was also an experienced mariner, immediately succeeded him as harbour-master.

ROCH LAUZIER

ANQ-Q, CN1-178, 29 janv. 1806; CN1-207, 6 oct. 1758, 2 mars 1759; CN1-256, 11 Sept., 29 Oct. 1792; 9 June 1795; CN1-262, 17 oct. 1799. BL, Add. MSS 21805: 14; 21879: 248; 21882: 44 (copies at PAC). Port of Quebec Arch. (Quebec), Corr., Paul Boucher à Louis Beaudry, 8 févr. 1943; Trinity House, letters patent, 6 May 1805; minute-books, I: 541; II: 42, 47–48. Bas-Canada, *Statuts*, 1805, c.12. "Les dénombrements de Québec" (Plessis), ANQ *Rapport*, 1948–49: 32, 82, 131, 185. "Ordonnances édictées pour la province de Québec par le gouverneur et le conseil de celle-ci, de 1768 à 1791 . . . ," PAC *Rapport*, 1914–15: 11–14. "Le recensement de Québec, en 1744," ANQ *Rapport*, 1939–40: 122. "Le recensement du gouvernement de Québec en 1762," ANQ *Rapport*, 1925–26: 141. *Quebec Gazette*, 31 Oct. 1799; 23 June, 25 Aug. 1803; 16 May 1805; 6 June 1811; 20 June 1816. P.-G. Roy, *Inventaire des jugements et délibérations du Conseil supérieur de la Nouvelle-France, de 1717 à 1760* (7v., Beauceville, Qué., 1932–35), 3: 197. Tanguay, *Dictionnaire*, 2: 379, 387. "Le pilotage sur le Saint-Laurent," *BRH*, 19 (1913): 117.

BOUCHER DE BOUCHERVILLE, RENÉ-AMABLE, army and militia officer, seigneur, office holder, and politician; b. 12 Feb. 1735 at Fort Frontenac (Kingston, Ont.), son of Pierre Boucher* de Boucherville, an officer in the colonial regular troops, and Marguerite Raimbault; d. 31 Aug. 1812 in Boucherville, Lower Canada.

Following his father's example René-Amable Boucher de Boucherville chose a military career. As a cadet in the colonial regular troops, during May 1754 he participated in a reconnaissance mission led by Joseph Coulon* de Villiers de Jumonville near Fort Duquesne (Pittsburgh, Pa). Jumonville's force was attacked and scattered by a detachment of the Virginia militia under George Washington. Boucher de Boucherville was taken prisoner and sent to Virginia. He regained his freedom after Louis Coulon* de Villiers's victory at Fort Necessity (near Farmington, Pa) in July 1754. Promoted second ensign in 1755, he acquired the rank of ensign on the active list two years later. François de Lévis* entrusted him in July 1757 with a reconnaissance mission on the north shore of Lac Saint-Sacrement (Lake George, N.Y.). In September 1759 he took part in the battle on the Plains of Abraham and was seriously wounded. He was captured by the British forces and sent to England; an exchange of prisoners enabled him to go to France, where he remained until his return to the province of Quebec after the Treaty of Paris was signed in 1763.

Upon his father's death in 1767 René-Amable inherited a quarter of the seigneury of Boucherville. Having obtained a dispensation for consanguinity, on 6 June 1770 he married 17-year-old Madeleine Raimbault de Saint-Blaint in Montreal. The marriage contract acknowledged community of property and accorded the bride a jointure of 3,000s. The couple went to live at Boucherville, where their eleven children were born; only Madeleine-Charlotte, Pierre-Amable, Charles-Marie, and Thomas-René-Verchères* reached adulthood.

At the time of the American invasion of the province [*see* Benedict ARNOLD; Richard Montgomery*], Boucher de Boucherville made an open display of his loyalty to the crown. In July 1776 he commanded a reconnaissance patrol that pushed as far as Crown Point, N.Y., and the following year he served as a captain under the command of John Burgoyne*. Boucher de Boucherville later claimed that he had been a faithful royalist throughout the invasion and had risked his life, leaving his family and abandoning his own interests to serve the king. He hoped to be rewarded for his support.

The colonial administration was slow in meeting Boucher de Boucherville's expectations. In 1784 Governor HALDIMAND recommended him for the seat in the Legislative Council that had been left vacant by the death of Luc de La Corne*. The following year he was appointed overseer of highways for the district of Montreal by Lieutenant Governor Henry Hope*, and in 1786 he finally received a place on the Legislative Council, which he retained until his death. Boucher de Boucherville made it a point of honour to attend all meetings of the council and proved a tenacious defender of the régime instituted under the Quebec Act.

Like the majority of Canadian seigneurs Boucher de Boucherville was opposed to the constitutional reform desired by the Canadian petite bourgeoisie and the British merchants. To counteract the burgeoning reform movement, the seigneurs set up a committee whose principal members were René-Ovide Hertel* de Rouville, Joseph-Dominique-Emmanuel LE MOYNE de Longueuil, François-Marie Picoté* de Belestre, and Pierre-Amable DE BONNE and his brother-in-law, Michel-Eustache-Gaspard-Alain Chartier* de Lotbinière. In a petition of December 1784, which bore the signatures of most of the seigneurs and co-seigneurs from the south shore of Montreal, among them Boucher de Boucherville, this committee expressed its disagreement with the proposals for reform. Because he derived a large income from seigneurial dues, he shared the fears of the Canadian seigneurs at the rise of the British merchant class, one of whose aims was to call in question the seigneurial system.

After the Americans had withdrawn, Boucher de Boucherville had in fact devoted himself to managing his seigneury. In 1782 he bought his brothers' and sisters' rights of succession to it, paying each of them 2,700 *livres*. Eager to improve the roads on his property, Boucher de Boucherville took advantage of his position as overseer of highways to have various roadworks done in the period 1786–98. In 1810 the seigneury had more than 2,250 inhabitants. The village of Boucherville had a church built from Pierre CONEFROY's plans, a presbytery, a chapel, a boys' school, and a convent run by the nuns of the Congregation of Notre-Dame. This village in the Montreal region enjoyed a reputation as a centre of Canadian social life. Indeed, the small community of Boucherville included several families descended from the nobility or from the élite of the colony who, because of their style of life and degree of wealth, lived apart from the local population.

In 1806, pleading advanced age, René-Amable Boucher de Boucherville had resigned as overseer of highways in favour of his son-in-law, Louis-René Chaussegros* de Léry. He continued, however, to serve as colonel in the militia, a rank he had acquired in 1790. He died on 31 Aug. 1812 and his funeral was held in the parish church, where he was buried on 2 September.

CÉLINE CYR

ANQ-M, CE1-22, 2 sept. 1812; CE1-51, 6 juin 1770; CN1-158, 24 avril 1782; CN1-308, 5 juin 1770. Arch. du séminaire de Trois-Rivières (Trois-Rivières, Qué.), Fonds Boucher, K1, nos.63–69. AUM, P 58, U, Boucher de Boucherville à Baby, 23 mai 1777, 31 oct. 1781, 4 févr. 1782, 10 nov. 1796, 13 mai 1797, 9 mai 1800, 9 oct. 1804, 20 sept. 1810; Boucher de Boucherville à Perrault l'aîné, 29 juill. 1771. G.-J. Chaussegros de Léry, "Journal de Joseph-Gaspard Chaussegros de Léry, lieutenant des troupes, 1754–1755," A.[-E.] Gosselin, édit., ANQ *Rapport*, 1926–27: 366. "Papiers d'État," PAC *Rapport*, 1890: 151. "Tableau général des différentes grades des officiers de la Marine servants en Canada . . . ," PAC *Rapport*, 1886: clxxviii. *Montreal Gazette*, 7 Sept. 1812. *Quebec Gazette*, 29 June 1786, 22 Jan. 1789, 17 Sept. 1812. *Quebec almanac*, 1791–1810. Bouchette, *Topographical description of L.C.*, 196–98. Le Jeune, *Dictionnaire*, 1: 214. P.-G. Roy, *Inv. concessions*, 2: 280; 3: 36. Lanctot, *Le Canada et la Révolution américaine*, 188. Stanley, *L'invasion du Canada* (MacDonald), 160. Tousignant, "La genèse et l'avènement de la constitution de 1791." Montarville Boucher de La Bruère, "Les Boucherville à l'étranger," *Cahiers des Dix*, 1 (1936): 233–57. P.-G. Roy, "Les grands voyers de la Nouvelle-France et leurs successeurs," *Cahiers des Dix*, 8 (1943): 181–233.

BOUCHER DE NIVERVILLE, JOSEPH (sometimes called **Joseph-Claude**; he signed **Chevalier Niverville**), army and militia officer, seigneur, Indian Department official, and office holder; b. 22 Sept. 1715 in Chambly (Que.), son of Jean-Baptiste Boucher* de Niverville and Marguerite-Thérèse Hertel de La Fresnière; m. 5 Oct. 1757 Marie-Josephte Châtelin in Trois-Rivières (Que.), and they had 11 children; d. there 30 Aug. 1804.

Joseph Boucher de Niverville began his military career as a cadet in the colonial regular troops in 1734 when he took part in the expedition that Nicolas-Joseph de Noyelles* de Fleurimont led against the Foxes. During the next two years he took advantage of his sojourn in the Detroit area to engage in the fur trade with goods supplied by Montreal merchant Pierre Guy*. In 1737 Niverville was assigned to serve under Gaspard Adhémar* de Lantagnac, the commandant at Fort Chambly. Two years later he went to Louisiana with Charles Le Moyne* de Longueuil's detachment, which was sent to subdue the Chickasaws. He obtained an expectancy of an ensigncy in 1742, and on 1 May 1743 the king granted him his commission as second ensign.

The War of the Austrian Succession, which spread to North America in 1744, gave Niverville an opportunity to distinguish himself. The following year he campaigned in Acadia, where he took seven prisoners and managed to capture an eight-gun British ship, boarding it with the help of four Indians. Between mid March and mid May 1746 he led a party of Abenaki warriors to within about 30 leagues of Boston, Mass., returning to Quebec with two English prisoners, one of whom he himself had captured. In early June he left Quebec for Acadia with the detachment under Jean-Baptiste-Nicolas-Roch de Ramezay* which was to meet the French squadron commanded by the Duc d'Anville [La Rochefoucauld*]; his younger brother, François Boucher de Niverville (Nebourvele) Grandpré, with whom he has often been confused, was also with the expedition. During this campaign, which lasted some six months, Niverville took part in the raid led by Joseph-Michel Legardeur* de Croisille et de Montesson against the British detachment at Port-La-Joie (Fort Amherst, P.E.I.).

Niverville carried out half a dozen missions during 1747, from New England to the government of Montreal. In the spring, he took a raiding party of some 10 Canadians and 60 Abenakis through the country south of Lake Champlain into Massachusetts. Although unable to bring back prisoners, the party destroyed five forts and about a hundred houses, killing six or seven hundred horned cattle, sheep, and pigs as well. This expedition also brought back to the authorities in Quebec the news that the enemy seemed

Boucher de Niverville

to be preparing to attack Fort Saint-Frédéric (near Crown Point, N.Y.). During another mission not long after, Niverville captured two Mohawks, and at the end of June he was one of the detachment under Louis de La Corne* that intercepted a group of Indian, English, and Dutch raiders at the Cascades (near Île des Cascades, Que.). Appointed ensign on 15 Feb. 1748, Niverville took command of various militia units in the government of Montreal during that year. He also led two war parties into New England, one of which attacked Fort Massachusetts (North Adams, Mass.) in August but did not succeed in taking it.

The year 1749 was a transitional one in Niverville's career. Along with his two young brothers, Niverville Grandpré and Pierre-Louis Boucher de Niverville Montizambert, he ranged through the Ohio valley with the detachment commanded by Pierre-Joseph Céloron* de Blainville. He barely escaped death during this campaign when he was captured by some Shawnees at Sonioto (Portsmouth, Ohio) along with fellow soldier Philippe-Thomas Chabert* de Joncaire. Shortly after his return to Montreal, he was ordered by Governor Jacques-Pierre de Taffanel* de La Jonquière to join an expedition set up under Jacques Legardeur* de Saint-Pierre to search for the western sea. The party left Montreal early in June 1750 and reached Fort La Reine (Portage la Prairie, Man.) that autumn. Niverville was to establish a new post west of Fort Paskoya (Le Pas, Man.) to serve as a base for an expedition west towards the Rockies, and he set out again almost immediately. On 29 May 1751 he dispatched two canoes with ten men from Fort Paskoya; he became seriously ill, however, and was unable to join them as he had intended. His men built Fort La Jonquière (probably in the vicinity of Nipawin, Sask.), but when they returned to Paskoya, Niverville was still in critical condition. It was not until spring 1753 that he was able to leave the fort. He succeeded in overtaking Legardeur's party just before it arrived at Lake Superior, and the expedition reached Montreal near the end of the summer without having found the western sea.

On 25 Jan. 1754 Niverville acquired half the seigneury of Chambly, buying out his brothers and sisters with whom he had inherited it jointly two years earlier; the other half had gone to the eldest brother, Jean-Baptiste. Forced to rest as a result of the illness he had contracted in the west, Niverville did not resume active service until May 1755, when he took command of the region of Michilimackinac (Mackinaw City, Mich.). He was recalled by August, however, to lead the Abenaki contingent in the army under Jean-Armand Dieskau*. Promoted lieutenant on 17 March 1756, he again headed up the Abenakis the following year at the capture of Fort William Henry (also called Fort George, now Lake George, N.Y.). In 1758 Niverville spent most of his time

recruiting Indian warriors but saw action in July at the battle of Carillon (near Ticonderoga, N.Y.). Late in May 1759 he was sent to Baie-Saint-Paul (Que.) at the head of a detachment of Abenakis and Canadian militia to prevent an enemy landing. When the British proceeded upriver, Niverville returned to Quebec and fought in its defence; he was with the French army when it withdrew to Montreal. A month or so earlier, on 20 August, his young wife and his mother-in-law had been slightly wounded by their Indian slave Marie*, an incident which resulted in what seems to have been the last sentence of capital punishment under the French régime.

On 28 April 1760, Niverville took part in the battle of Sainte-Foy. In the fall of 1761 he embarked for France along with his brother Niverville Grandpré, who had been the last Canadian officer to surrender to the British in Acadia, several months after the capitulation of Montreal.

Although he received the cross of Saint-Louis on 17 July 1763, Niverville was disappointed at the treatment given the Canadian officers in France and that November he was back in Trois-Rivières. On 21 Feb. 1766 he attended the assembly of seigneurs of the Montreal district convened by Governor Murray*. Early the following year, he became owner of almost all the lands that had belonged to his deceased father-in-law: the "marquisat Du Sablé," the seigneury of Sainte-Marguerite, the fief of La Poterie, and an unnamed fief. These new holdings, all at or near Trois-Rivières, greatly increased his income, which since his return had essentially depended on the dues from half the seigneury of Chambly. In 1767 as well, Niverville was a member of the grand jury that heard the bill of indictment brought by Thomas Walker* against Captain Daniel Disney. On this occasion he swore the oath of allegiance to the British crown, as did three other knights of Saint-Louis who were also members of the jury: François-Marie Picoté* de Belestre, Pierre-Roch de Saint-Ours Deschaillons, and Claude-Pierre Pécaudy* de Contrecœur. This action gained him a place among the 12 Canadian seigneurs proposed by Governor Guy CARLETON in 1769 for a possible legislative council, but his name was not retained.

Despite his 60 years Niverville took an active part in the defence of the province during the American invasion of 1775–76. It was probably at this time that he was granted the post of superintendent of Indians for the Trois-Rivières district, which he was to retain until 1796. In September 1775, on Carleton's orders, he left Montreal at the head of a small group of Indians and Canadians to relieve the garrison of Fort St Johns on the Richelieu, then being besieged by Richard Montgomery*. He encountered an American detachment at La Prairie, however, and turned back to Montreal without engaging it in combat. On 11

Boucher de Niverville

November, after the capitulation of Fort St Johns, Carleton abandoned Montreal to head for Quebec with the British regulars. Delayed at Lavaltrie for several days by contrary winds, Carleton learned that the Americans had already established batteries at Sorel. By means of a stratagem devised by Jean-Baptiste BOUCHETTE, during the night of the 16th the governor, his aide-de-camp, Charles-Louis TARIEU de Lanaudière, and Niverville passed by Sorel and reached Trois-Rivières, where Niverville left the group. During the winter the invaders, who occupied Trois-Rivières, did not molest royalists like Niverville but merely confiscated their weapons. After the British fleet arrived at Quebec in the spring of 1776, the Americans fell back on Sorel, and then began a counter-offensive, sending Brigadier-General William Thompson to launch a surprise attack on Trois-Rivières. On the morning of 8 June Thompson's advance guard was surprised and taken prisoner by a patrol under Niverville, without being able to give the alarm. When the American army arrived, it faced the steady fire of defenders who were ready for it [see François Guillot*, dit Larose]. Niverville's part in the defence of the province brought him a lieutenant's half-pay.

Appointed a justice of the peace in 1780 or a little before, Niverville discharged this responsibility at least until April 1798 when he was retired because of his advanced age. While in office Niverville was involved in several notable events in the life of Trois-Rivières, such as the 1787 inquiry into the suicide of Dolly Manuel, one of the Hart family's servants, the drawing up of regulations for the town market in 1791, and the reorganization of the Fire Society in 1796.

On 4 March 1790 Niverville was appointed colonel of the militia battalion for Trois-Rivières and the area to the north. On 12 August he had Jonathan and Joseph Sills and Malcolm Fraser Jr imprisoned for refusing to report for a militia exercise. This action resulted in his being disparaged in an anonymous pamphlet, probably written by Jonathan Sills, entitled La Bastille septentrionale ou les trois sujets britanniques opprimés . . . and published in Montreal and Trois-Rivières in 1791. He was even sued by his "victims." Defended by lawyer Arthur DAVIDSON, he had the complete support of the general staff in this affair and does not seem to have been seriously disturbed by it. In 1800 an ensign was assigned to act as his adjutant, and he was granted 1,200 acres of land. He did not retire until June 1803 and at the time of his death the following year he was the last knight of Saint-Louis in Canada.

Niverville's military career was without doubt one of the longest of any Canadian officer in the 18th century. He participated in many important expeditions which took him to the eastern, southern, and western limits of New France's vast territory. After the conquest he soon gained the new authorities' confidence and won several favours; however, the importance of these was exaggerated by Michel-Eustache-Gaspard-Alain Chartier* de Lotbinière when he wrote to a friend in September 1802 that the Chevalier Niverville lived on "the blessings of the government which is very generous and under which Canadians are in general quite happy." Niverville's decision to settle in a secondary town like Trois-Rivières along with his lack of interest in politics – he confined himself to signing the petition of Canadian seigneurs opposing the creation of a house of assembly in 1788 and to acting as president of the local committee of the association founded in 1794 to support British rule in the province – partially explain why he did not play as prominent a role after the conquest as did other members of the Canadian nobility.

PIERRE DUFOUR

AN, Marine, C⁷, 226 (dossier Boucher de Niverville). ANQ-M, CN1-259, 2, 9 sept. 1735. AUM, P 58, C3/83; U, Niverville à Baby, 10 janv., 26 févr. 1772; 29 mai 1773; 11 févr. 1779; 21 nov. 1800; Dame de Niverville à Baby, 26 févr. 1772. McGill Univ. Libraries (Montreal), Dept. of Rare Books and Special Coll., ms coll., CH350.S310. *Coll. des manuscrits de Lévis* (Casgrain). *Collection de documents inédits sur le Canada et l'Amérique*, [H.-R. Casgrain, édit.] (3v., Québec, 1888–90). [Anthony Henday], "York Factory to the Blackfeet country, the journal of Anthony Hendry, 1754–55," ed. L. J. Burpee, RSC *Trans.*, 3rd ser., 1 (1907), sect.II: 307–59. *Journals and letters of Pierre Gaultier de Varennes de La Vérendrye and his sons . . .*, ed. L. J. Burpee (Toronto, 1927). Jacques Legardeur de Saint-Pierre, "Mémoire ou journal sommaire du voyage de Jacques Repentigny Legardeur de Saint-Pierre . . . ," PAC *Rapport*, 1886: clvii–clxiii. *NYCD* (O'Callaghan and Fernow), vol.10. "Papiers Amherst (1760–1763) concernant les Acadiens," R. S. Brun, édit., Soc. hist. acadienne, *Cahiers* (Moncton, N.-B.), 3 (1968–71): 257–320. *Papiers Contrecœur et autres documents concernant le conflit anglo-français sur l'Ohio de 1745 à 1756*, Fernand Grenier, édit. (Québec, 1952). "Protêt des marchands de Montréal contre une assemblée des seigneurs, tenue en cette ville le 21 février 1766," É.-Z. Massicotte, édit., *BRH*, 38 (1932): 68–79. *Quebec Gazette*, 11 Dec. 1788; 8 July 1790; 13 Jan., 17 Nov. 1791; 10, 17 July 1794. Ægidius Fauteux, *Les chevaliers de Saint-Louis en Canada* (Montréal, 1940). *Historic forts and trading posts of the French regime and of the English fur trading companies*, comp. Ernest Voorhis (copy, Ottawa, 1930). J.-J. Lefebvre, "La descendance de Pierre Boucher (1617–1722), fondateur de Boucherville," SGCF *Mémoires*, 5 (1952–53): 67–96. Le Jeune, *Dictionnaire*. A.-G. Morice, *Dictionnaire historique des Canadiens et des Métis français de l'Ouest* (Québec et Montréal, 1908). *Quebec almanac*, 1780, 1782, 1788. P.-G. Roy, *Inv. concessions*. Tanguay, *Dictionnaire*, vol.1. Wallace, *Macmillan dict.*

J.-C. Bracq, *L'évolution du Canada français* (Montréal et Paris, 1927). J.-D. Brosseau, *Saint-Jean-de-Québec; ori-*

Bouchette

gine et développements (Saint-Jean[-sur-Richelieu], Qué., 1937). André Chagny, *Un défenseur de la "Nouvelle-France," François Picquet, "le Canadien" (1708–1781)* (Montréal et Paris, 1913). Antoine Champagne, *Les La Vérendrye et le poste de l'Ouest* (Québec, 1968). Raymond Douville, *Aaron Hart; récit historique* (Trois-Rivières, Qué., 1938). Jean-Paul de Lagrave, *Les origines de la presse au Québec (1760–1791)* (Montréal, 1975). Paquet et Wallot, *Patronage et pouvoir dans le Bas-Canada.* P.-G. Roy, *La famille Godefroy de Tonnancour* (Lévis, Qué., 1904); *La famille Tarieu de Lanaudière* (Lévis, 1922); *Hommes et choses du fort Saint-Frédéric* (Montréal, 1946). Stanley, *L'invasion du Canada* (MacDonald); *New France: the last phase, 1744–1760* (Toronto, 1968). Sulte, *Mélanges hist.* (Malchelosse), 10. J.-P. Tremblay, *La Baie-Saint-Paul et ses pionniers* ([Chicoutimi, Qué.], 1948). Trudel, *L'esclavage au Canada français,* 142, 297, 362; *Le Régime militaire dans le gouvernement des Trois-Rivières, 1760–1764* (Trois-Rivières, 1952). R. S. Allen, "The British Indian Department and the frontier in North America, 1755–1830," *National Hist. Sites,* no.14 (1975): 5–125. T.[-M.] Charland, "Les neveux de madame de Beaubassin," *RHAF,* 23 (1969–70): 68–91. Raymond Douville, "Charles Boucher de Niverville, son ascendance et sa carrière politique," *Cahiers des Dix,* 37 (1972): 87–122; "La dette des États-Unis envers les ursulines de Trois-Rivières," *Cahiers des Dix,* 22 (1957): 137–62. Roland Lamontagne, "La construction du fort Saint-Jean, 1748–1749," *RHAF,* 15 (1961–62): 35–40. Gérard Malchelosse, "La famille Pommereau et ses alliances," *Cahiers des Dix,* 29 (1964): 193–222; "Un procès criminel aux Trois-Rivières en 1759," 18 (1953): 206–26. Jacques Mathieu, "Un négociant de Québec à l'époque de la Conquête: Jacques Perrault l'aîné," *ANQ Rapport,* 1970: 27–82. A.-G. Morice, "L'abbé Émile Petitot et les découvertes géographiques au Canada," *Le Canada français* (Québec), 2ᵉ sér., 7 (1921–22): 225–35, 319–39. Gérard Parizeau, "Joseph Bouchette: l'homme et le haut fonctionnaire," *RSC Trans.,* 4th ser., 9 (1971), sect.ɪ: 95–126. L.-A. Prud'homme, "Les successeurs de La Vérendrye sous la domination française . . . , 1743–1755," *RSC Trans.,* 2nd ser., 12 (1906), sect.ɪ: 65–81. Benjamin Sulte, "Le chevalier de Niverville," *RSC Trans.,* 3rd ser., 3 (1909), sect.ɪ: 43–72; "Les miettes de l'histoire," *Rev. canadienne,* 5 (1868): 585–92. Albert Tessier, "Deux enrichis: Aaron Hart et Nicolas Montour," *Cahiers des Dix,* 3 (1938): 217–42. Henri Têtu, "M. Jean-Félix Richer, curé de Québec, et son journal, 1757–1760," *BRH,* 9 (1903): 97–122, 129–47, 161–74, 289–307, 321–46, 353–73.

BOUCHETTE, JEAN-BAPTISTE, businessman, mariner, and militia and naval officer; b. 5 July 1736 at Quebec, son of Marc Bouchette (Bouchet) and Marie-Thérèse Grenet; d. there 28 April 1804.

The youngest of five children of a seaman from Saint-Malo, France, Jean-Baptiste Bouchette was bred to the sea even though his father had died shortly after he was born. About 1760 he went into the fishing business in the Gulf of St Lawrence, and by 1765 he was an established merchant residing on Rue Champlain, Quebec. That year he became an equal partner with the firm of Johnston and Purss [*see* James Johnston*; John PURSS] for the development of a fur-trade and fishing post, probably in the Gulf region, during the following nine years. Bouchette was to deliver food and trade merchandise to the station, attend to the society's interests there, and bring back the fish and furs.

At Quebec on 27 Sept. 1773 Bouchette, whom Pierre de SALES Laterrière called "not a handsome lad," married Marie-Angélique Duhamel; Laterrière described her as "beautiful, buxom and well-built," and claimed to have been "tied [to her] by a love more than Platonic for quite some time" before her marriage to Bouchette. The marriage was said to have been arranged by Marie-Angélique's father, Julien, another seaman from Saint-Malo.

By 1775 Bouchette owned and commanded his own schooner and had earned the name *la tourte*, the wild pigeon, "for the celerity of his voyages." On 11 November the schooner, armed and fitted for government service during the American invasion of Quebec, was one of the escort vessels for the convoy evacuating troops from Montreal with Guy CARLETON. Contrary winds forced the convoy to anchor near Sorel, and by the 16th it appeared to be trapped by American batteries. Carleton and his aide-de-camp, Charles-Louis TARIEU de Lanaudière, escaped in a small boat skilfully piloted by Bouchette and after some adventures arrived safely at Quebec on the 19th. For this service Bouchette won a commission in an artillery company of militia during the siege of Quebec, and on 28 April 1776 Carleton appointed him lieutenant and commander of the armed sloop *Hope,* in which he provided a number of essential services to the British squadron under Captain Charles Douglas*. On 11 Sept. 1777 Carleton commissioned Bouchette a master and commander, as well as captain of the armed vessel *Seneca* on Lake Ontario, and he served on the Great Lakes until his discharge in 1784.

Bouchette returned to Quebec, and in October 1785 was among those who signed an address of departure to Lieutenant Governor Henry Hamilton*, praising his administration. Two years later his old patron Carleton, now Governor Lord Dorchester, granted him a commission as captain of militia at Quebec. By 1788 Bouchette, once again a civil mariner, was living on Rue Saint-Pierre and apparently enjoying a social position of some respectability. However, his social status concealed a grave financial situation; he was indebted to the firm of Fraser and Young, of which the politician John YOUNG was a partner, for £1,359. Young was prepared to accept £906 to be paid without interest over two years, with Bouchette's schooner the *Angélique,* built the previous year, serving as guarantee. In June 1789 Bouchette borrowed £278 from Thomas DUNN to discharge some of the debt, but in April 1790 the *Angélique* had to be sold to pay part of the remainder.

The previous summer Bouchette had given power of attorney to his wife to try to wind up his affairs at Quebec and had returned to naval service on Lake Ontario. In 1791, when the Provincial Marine was again expanding, Dorchester made Bouchette a master and commander, a commission confirmed for Upper Canada by Lieutenant Governor SIMCOE on 16 August. After the death of Commodore David Beaton in December 1794, Bouchette became the senior officer and succeeded to Beaton's post on the lake. Although there were complaints that Bouchette took gratuities for the carriage of passengers and cargo on naval vessels, the distinguished French traveller La Rochefoucauld-Liancourt* reported him by all accounts entirely incorruptible.

Bouchette's years in command would leave him disappointed and embittered. He must have been upset that his eldest son, Joseph*, was unable to follow in his footsteps because of a severe retrenchment in the Provincial Marine after 1794, when Jay's Treaty reduced tensions with the United States. In 1795 Bouchette complained to La Rochefoucauld-Liancourt of disharmony among various departments of the military and naval establishment at Kingston, Upper Canada; none the less, because Bouchette had his family and lands at Kingston, he was among the strongest critics of a project to make York (Toronto) the centre of Provincial Marine activities, even though between 1791 and 1797 he received important grants of land at York for himself and his children.

By 1799 Bouchette's grievances had led him to act the tyrant with his officers and to cooperate less and less with the military authorities. In 1801 he ceased altogether to communicate with his superiors, so that the fort major in Upper Canada, Lieutenant Donald Campbell, had to take over his administrative responsibilities. Crippled with rheumatism, ill and unable to sail with his vessel in November of that year, Bouchette was nevertheless refused permission by Lieutenant Governor Peter HUNTER to go to Quebec for the winter and seemed to withdraw into himself still further. A plan was formulated by a protégé of the Duke of Kent [EDWARD AUGUSTUS], and accepted by Bouchette himself, to retire him on full pay. It was all very sad, and Bouchette must have wished Dorchester, who had retired to England in 1796, had never left Canada. The negotiations dragged on until 1803 when the infirm and weary, but no doubt defiant, old man went too far. Faced with an accusation of disobedience by the commanding officer of the port of Kingston, Captain Holt Mackenzie, reportedly "Capt Bouchette snapped his fingers quite close to Capt Mackenzie's Face, & throwing his hat violently on the Floor said he did not care one damn for either him or

the General [Lieutenant Governor Hunter]." At the subsequent inquiry three charges against him were substantiated, and in September Captain John Steel* took over the Provincial Marine. Bouchette returned to Quebec where he died on 28 April 1804 and was buried in the Cimetière des Picotés. One week before his death he had been granted 400 acres of land in Nelson Township and 99 acres in Somerset, both in Lower Canada; however, his estate was so hopelessly indebted to the merchants John Forsyth* and John Young that his family was obliged to renounce it.

Perhaps the tedium of a remote garrison town, combined with cultural isolation, lay behind Bouchette's tragic decline in Upper Canada; certainly *la tourte* had suffered, with Dorchester's departure, from the changing of the old order. Nevertheless Bouchette, who had stemmed from long-established seafaring families, managed, in spite of everything, to perpetuate some of their maritime tradition in Upper Canada. And, by virtue of the marriages and careers of most of his nine children, he founded several prominent families of both Upper and Lower Canada: Joseph had entered into the employ of an uncle by marriage, the surveyor Samuel Johannes HOLLAND, and became surveyor general of Lower Canada; Luce, Bouchette's youngest daughter, married in 1811 the Quebec seaman and hero of the War of 1812, Charles-Frédéric Rolette*; four other daughters married merchants in the Detroit River region; and prominent descendants of this widespread family were still being noticed for their contributions to life and letters in English and French Canada more than 130 years after the death of their progenitor.

W. A. B. DOUGLAS

ANQ-Q, CE1-1, 5 juill. 1736, 27 sept. 1773, 30 avril 1804; CN1-92, 30 oct. 1788, 15 sept. 1789; CN1-148, 20 sept. 1765; CN1-178, 31 août 1804; CN1-224, 29 juin, 7 sept. 1789; CN1-253, 31 janv. 1820; CN1-256, 26 Sept. 1788, 28 Sept. 1789, 29 April 1790. BL, Add. mss 21744: 28; 21804. PAC, MG 23, HI, 1, ser.1, 6: 325–27; RG 8, I (C ser.), 723–26. PRO, CO 42/34: f.259 (mfm. at PAC). *Corr. of Lieut. Governor Simcoe* (Cruikshank). [Pierre de Sales Laterrière], *Mémoires de Pierre de Sales Laterrière et ses traverses*, [Alfred Garneau, édit.] (Québec, 1873; reimpr., Ottawa, 1980), 71. *Invasion du Canada* (Verreau), 176, 233–34. *Kingston before War of 1812* (Preston), 16, 210, 242, 350, 362. [F.-A.-F. de La Rochefoucauld-Liancourt], "La Rochefoucault-Liancourt's travels in Canada, 1795, [translated by Henry Neuman] with annotations and strictures by Sir David William Smith . . . ," ed. W. R. Riddell, AO *Report*, 1916: 79–80, 92. *Town of York, 1793–1815* (Firth), xxxii, 12, 39, 44, 232. *Quebec Gazette*, 29 Sept. 1766, 13 Nov. 1770, 15 June 1775, 3 Nov 1785, 13 Nov. 1788, 3 May 1804. Langelier, *Liste des terrains concédés*, 600, 607. Stanley, *Canada invaded*, 68–69, 147, 152. Édouard Fabre Surveyer, "The Bouchette family," RSC

Boudreau

Trans., 3rd ser., 30 (1941), sect.II: 135–40. Benjamin Sulte, "Jean-Baptiste Bouchette," RSC *Trans.*, 3rd ser., 2 (1908), sect.I: 67–83.

BOUDREAU (Boudreault, Boudreaux, Boudrot), CÉCILE (Pitre; Pellerin), b. *c.* 1714 in Annapolis Royal, N.S., probably the daughter of Charles Boudrot and Marie-Josephe Landry; m. there *c.* 1731 Jean-Baptiste Pitre, and they had 11 children; m. secondly October 1762 Pierre Pellerin in Nicolet (Que.); d. there 13 Jan. 1811.

Having escaped the massive and cruel deportation of 1755 [*see* Charles Lawrence*], Cécile Boudreau, her husband, and her children joined about 200 Acadian families who scattered into the woods bordering the Memramcook, Shepody, and Petitcodiac rivers (N.B.). Fortunately these families were able to count on the aid of missionary François Le Guerne* and of Charles Deschamps* de Boishébert, a captain in the colonial regular troops. The two men worked together to ensure the survival of the Acadians, provide for their sustenance, and organize their resistance to the British.

Foreseeing the second phase of the expulsion, which would be carried out in 1758 [*see* Robert Monckton*], many of the families, including Cécile Boudreau's, moved up the coast to Miramichi in 1757. They were exhausted, and suffered from starvation as a result of poor crops and from epidemics. Several of them then resigned themselves to following Boishébert's troops, which had been recalled to Québec for the winter of 1757–58.

The situation at Quebec seemed little brighter. There was a dearth of supplies and a severe famine. The Acadians had to make do with cod and rotten meat. According to the testimony of several persons, these poor living conditions brought about the death of a number of Acadians. On 9 June 1758, amid the general gloom and inactivity, Cécile Boudreau had to bury her husband, who had fallen victim to the smallpox epidemic raging at the time. A month earlier she had done the same for her son Jean, barely eight years of age, and four days after her husband's interment she buried one of her daughters.

It was for such reasons that the Acadian refugees then sought to flee Quebec. Some joined Le Guerne, who had become parish priest of Saint-François, on Île d'Orléans. Others settled in the Beauce or in the regions of Saint-Joachim and Bellechasse. In 1758 a large number went to Saint-Grégoire (Bécancour); others, including Cécile Boudreau's family, chose Nicolet. This locality, which their missionaries and the Abenakis had drawn to their attention, turned out to be a good place for a settlement. It was situated near the St Lawrence, which gave access to the gulf and to Acadia, where everyone hoped to live once again. The region offered an abundance of woods and lakes that enabled them to ensure their subsistence; moreover it was remote and tranquillity was easily found.

When along with other Pitres and Boudreaus, Orillon-Champagnes, Gaudets, Laurts, Melançons, Bastaraches, Commeaus, and Rouisse-Languedocs, Cécile Boudreau arrived in this new setting to find fresh hope and take root, she still had five children with her; one of them, François, would receive a commission later as captain in the militia. She married Pierre Pellerin in 1762 and was widowed 30 years later. She apparently reached the age of 97, still strong, lucid, and courageous. An unfortunate fall then forced her to take to her bed. After 18 days during which she was willing to drink "only a little water and two shots of rum," she died.

A long way from Nicolet the *Quebec Gazette*, a major paper of the province, printed a paragraph about this strong and incomparable woman which formed a longer and better tribute than any cold tombstone could offer. It told of the circumstances of her death and concluded: "This venerable Acadian constantly retained all her mental faculties with remarkable freshness and good health until the accident which brought her to the grave."

ADRIEN BERGERON

ANQ-MBF, CE1-13, 14 janv. 1811. Arch. du séminaire de Trois-Rivières (Trois-Rivières, Qué.), Louis Richard, "Notes sur l'arrivée des Acadiens dans le district de Trois-Rivières après 1755." *Quebec Gazette*, 31 Jan. 1811. Arsenault, *Hist. et généal. des Acadiens* (1965). J.-E. Bellemare, *Histoire de Nicolet, 1669–1924* (Arthabaska, Qué., 1924). Adrien Bergeron, *Le grand arrangement des Acadiens au Québec* . . . (8v., Montréal, 1981), 2: 35, 43; 5: 163, 165. P.-G. Roy, *La ville de Québec sous le Régime français* (2v., Québec, 1930), 2: 295–96.

BOUGAINVILLE, LOUIS-ANTOINE DE, Comte de BOUGAINVILLE, army officer; b. 12 Nov. 1729 in Paris, France, son of Pierre-Yves de Bougainville, member of the king's council and notary at the Châtelet, and Marie-Françoise d'Arboulin; m. 27 Jan. 1781 Marie-Joséphine de Longchamps-Montendre in Brest, France, and they had four children; d. 20 Aug. 1811 in Paris and was buried in the Pantheon with full military honours on 3 September.

Like all young men of good family in his time, Louis-Antoine de Bougainville received a sound classical education; he showed a particular aptitude for mathematics, which he first studied under Alexis Clairaut and Jean Le Rond d'Alembert. In 1754 and 1756 he published a *Traité de calcul intégral* in two volumes which won for him the patronage of the Comte d'Argenson, minister of War and member of the Académie des Sciences.

In 1750 Bougainville enlisted in the Mousquetaires Noirs; he was then 21 and rather old to enter the military profession. Three years later he became adjutant in the Régiment de Picardie. He was recommended to General François de Chevert and served as his aide-de-camp in 1754 before going to England in October as secretary to the Maréchal de Lévis-Mirepoix, who had been named ambassador extraordinary to the court in London following incidents in the Ohio valley [*see* Ange Duquesne* de Menneville]. After returning to France in February 1755 Bougainville was promoted lieutenant in the Régiment d'Apchon and resumed his service with Chevert. On 12 Jan. 1756 he was elected to the Royal Society of London. He received a commission as captain on 27 February, and when Louis-Joseph de Montcalm* was promoted to command the French regulars in Canada, Bougainville was attached to his service as aide-de-camp. They sailed from Brest aboard the *Licorne* on 3 April.

The French and the British were again at war in North America, and Bougainville, who had no combat experience, took an active part in the military campaign. In July and August 1756 he participated in the attack on Oswego (Chouaguen, N.Y.) and its capture, which secured control of Lake Ontario for the French. His conduct earned warm praise from Montcalm, who recommended him to the minister: "You would not believe the resources I find in him. He is capable of giving a good description of what he sees. He exposes himself readily to gunfire, a matter on which he needs to be restrained rather than encouraged. I shall be much mistaken if he does not have a good head for soldiering when experience has taught him to foresee the potential for difficulties. In the mean time there is hardly a young man who, having received only the theory, knows as much about it as he." Montcalm hoped to see his aide-de-camp enter the Académie des Sciences.

In September 1756 Bougainville scouted the British positions in the key Lake Champlain sector, which Governor Vaudreuil [Rigaud*] was considering attacking to neutralize the threat from this direction. In August 1757 he took part in operations in the region and was chosen by Montcalm to carry to Vaudreuil the news of the surrender of Fort George (also called Fort William Henry; now Lake George, N.Y.), a clear victory that Montcalm did not know how to exploit fully.

Naturally Bougainville was involved in the incessant quarrels between Vaudreuil and Montcalm. It seems, however, that unlike Montcalm he quickly understood the kind of warfare to wage in Canada: adopt the Indians' methods, expose oneself as little as possible, avoid pitched battles, and harass the enemy unceasingly by ambushes. On the other hand he seems to have shared Montcalm's prejudices against the

Canadians. He told Berryer, the minister of Marine, in a memoir that "the troops of the regular army and of the colonial regulars are in an admirable frame of mind. They will shed their blood for every step that has to be conceded to the enemy," he said, but the militia and the Indians "[are] vain in victory, are incapable of any other sort of warfare, little suited for the defensive, are easily and profoundly discouraged in adversity, [and] have no courage or constancy."

Bougainville's participation in the Lake Champlain operations did not keep him from preparing plans for an attack against the British establishments on Hudson Bay which was to be conducted with four ships of the line, a frigate, and troops from New France. In contrast to the objectives that Jean-François de Galaup*, Comte de Lapérouse, would achieve in 1782, Bougainville's plan called for permanent occupation, not a destructive raid. To ensure the success of the undertaking he wanted to obtain the assistance of Gabriel Pellegrin*, deputy port captain, who was a great expert on Canadian waters; however, circumstances prevented the plan from being carried out.

In July 1758 Bougainville, fighting at Montcalm's side, was wounded in the battle of Carillon (near Ticonderoga, N.Y.), which ended in "overwhelming defeat" for the British. None the less, the French victories scarcely touched the enemy's military strength; the gravest menaces still loomed over the colony, and Vaudreuil and Montcalm continued to differ on the measures to be taken to meet them.

In September 1758 Vaudreuil and Montcalm decided that they would send an officer to France to announce Montcalm's victory, report on the lamentable state of the colony, and ask for aid. Their choice fixed on Bougainville. But knowing that he was wholly devoted to Montcalm, Vaudreuil also sent Major Michel-Jean-Hugues Péan*. Bougainville sailed from Quebec aboard the *Victoire* on 15 Nov. 1758 and landed at Morlaix, France, early in 1759. It was probably during the crossing that he wrote the four reports he gave to Berryer in which Montcalm's pessimistic views, sometimes made even gloomier, are conveyed. One of them set out the colony's needs in men and material. It mentioned the absence of guns and munitions, stating that in Canada there were only two engineers, eight artillery officers, eighty-six gunners or bombardiers, and no sappers or artillery or engineering workers. Appreciably overestimating enemy forces, Bougainville noted that "10,000 men lacking ammunition and supplies, have to defend three virtually unprotected frontiers against at least 60,000 [who are] in a position to attack all three simultaneously because of their heavy numerical superiority and abundant means of every sort. . . . It seems to me therefore that the court should treat Canada today like a sick person whom one sustains

Bougainville

with stimulants, that is, should send only what is absolutely necessary for a prolonged defence." Among the absolute essentials Bougainville included four ships that could make the defence of Quebec easier. He also advocated that batteries be built at Gaspé, Pointe aux Bouleaux on the north shore of the St Lawrence, Île aux Coudres, Cap Tourmente, Île d'Orléans, and Pointe-Lévy (Lauzon and Lévis); as well, he seemed to have a high regard for the "mobile redoubts," boats armed with a cannon, which were the brain-child of Louis-Thomas Jacau* de Fiedmont. He also took advantage of his audience with Berryer to denounce Bigot*'s administration.

Having been promoted colonel and knight of Saint-Louis, Bougainville on 28 March 1759 sailed from Bordeaux on the *Chézine* and landed at Quebec on 10 May. He had not, in the end, obtained much for the colony. His arrival, heralding the advent of reinforcements, "put fresh heart into an entire people who during one of the harshest winters had been reduced to a quarter-pound of bread and a half-pound of horse meat" a day, and occasioned general rejoicing, which turned out to be short-lived. Although more than 20 supply ships had reached Quebec at the same time as the *Chézine*, France had not considered it expedient to send more than 300 men to prop up the imperilled colony, or to defend it further, following Bougainville's advice in this regard.

Soon after his return Bougainville left with Anne-Joseph-Hippolyte Maurès* de Malartic to reconnoitre defensive positions around the town, and in June 1759 he took command of the camp at nearby Beauport. On 27 June the British landed on Île d'Orléans, on 29 and 30 June at Pointe-Lévy, and then on 9 July at Montmorency. After the fighting on 31 July when the British unsuccessfully attacked the camp at Montmorency, Bougainville, with the 500 men under his command, was given the mission of guarding the communications between Quebec and Montreal and ensuring that the supply routes to Quebec were not cut off. Thus he followed the movements of the British fleet up to Pointe-aux-Trembles (Neuville); here on 8 August he twice repelled attempted landings. On 17 August he drove back a force disembarking at Deschambault, and later he prevented the British from landing at Saint-Augustin. But on 13 September the British succeeded in getting a foothold at Anse au Foulon, which was ill defended by Louis Du Pont* Duchambon de Vergor. Surprised to see the enemy troops so close to Quebec, Montcalm then committed serious errors, among which were failing to give Bougainville orders to trap James Wolfe* between two fires and neglecting the basic principle of concentration of force. Because of poor communications Bougainville, whose troops, brought up to 1,200 men, were widely strung out

along the St Lawrence, found it impossible to assemble his men and take part in the battle of the Plains of Abraham. After the surrender on 18 September he went to take up a position in the direction of Saint-Augustin and came back to Quebec to negotiate an exchange of prisoners and settle the fate of the sick and wounded who had been left behind in the hospital.

During the winter of 1759–60 he directed operations to harass the British garrison of Quebec until Vaudreuil sent him at the beginning of March 1760 to command the Île aux Noix sector on the Richelieu; here the situation quickly took a tragic turn because of desertions and the defection of the Indians, who went over *en masse* to the British. On 22 Aug. 1760 an attack by William Haviland* was repulsed, but on 27 August Bougainville had to evacuate the area, with the troops retreating through a wooded area, leaving only an officer and 30 men to protect the wounded. He was reprimanded by Bigot for this action. On 7 September he acted as a messenger between Vaudreuil and Amherst* in the negotiations for the surrender of Montreal. The town was defenceless and full of refugees who begged Vaudreuil to save their lives and belongings. Bougainville was taken prisoner along with the rest of the army and returned to France.

Bougainville's career in New France has been diversely judged. François de Lévis* had a low opinion of him and considered him a poor soldier. Some historians have held that he was partly responsible for New France being abandoned by France, and also for the defeat on the Plains of Abraham, because at that point it was he who was in charge of the defence of the shoreline beginning at Anse au Foulon. However, since Bougainville in this period had not assumed a post with great responsibility and was only carrying out orders, these judgements are too severe.

Not long after Bougainville's return to France an expedition against Brazil was being mounted, and there was some thought of entrusting command of the troops to him, but the signing of peace put an end to this project. Then he contemplated creating, with the help of Canadian refugees, a new colony that would make up for the loss of New France. The Duc de Choiseul, who had become minister of Marine, encouraged this endeavour. On 15 June 1763 Bougainville was appointed a naval captain and on 22 September he set out from Saint-Malo, France, with the *Aigle* and *Sphinx* to found a colony on the Îles Malouines (Falkland Islands), where he landed on 3 Feb. 1764 [*see* Antoine-Charles Denis* de Saint-Simon]. The court of Madrid naturally took umbrage at this incursion into what it considered its own preserve, and the islands had to be ceded back to Spain.

In the mean time Bougainville had conceived the

project of a voyage of exploration and discovery around the world, which immediately received Choiseul's approval. On 5 Dec. 1766 he sailed from Brest on the frigate *Boudeuse* for an expedition that was to last 28 months and that would take him to Montevideo (Uruguay), to the Îles Malouines, which he ceremonially handed back to Spain, and then to Rio de Janeiro, Brazil, where he was joined by the flute *Étoile*, under François Chenard de La Giraudais. After calling in again at Montevideo the two ships sailed through the Strait of Magellan, where they made contact with the so-called Patagonian giants, and then crossed the Pacific, making a stop at Tahiti that created a great literary and philosophical stir; over the following years, the Tahitian visit inspired a good many works claiming to demonstrate the superiority of "savage" over "civilized" society. After exploring the New Hebrides (Vanuatu), the Solomon Islands, New Ireland, and the north coast of New Guinea, Bougainville returned to France via the Molucca Islands, Batavia (Djakarta, Indonesia), Île de France (Mauritius), and the Cape of Good Hope. He landed at Saint-Malo on 16 March 1769, having carried out, with the loss of only seven lives, the first voyage around the world by an officer of the French navy. The account of this voyage, published in 1771, met with great success and was immediately translated into English.

In March 1770 Bougainville was admitted permanently into the navy as a captain, and in December 1771 he was elected an associate member of the Académie de Marine; he then examined the possibility of making a scientific voyage to the polar regions, but this project came to nothing. In 1775 he served as second in command on the frigate *Terpsichore*, in 1776 on the *Solitaire*, and in 1777 as commander of the *Bien-Aimé* in a squadron on manœuvres. In April 1778 he received command of the *Guerrier* in the squadron that Vice-Admiral the Comte d'Estaing was to sail to American shores and then to the West Indies. Consequently he took part in the capture of Grenada on 6 July 1779 and in the unsuccessful attack on Savannah, Ga, in October 1779. Promoted rear-admiral on 8 December, he commanded the *Auguste* in the Comte de Grasse's squadron in 1781–82 and distinguished himself in September 1781 in the battle of Chesapeake Bay, which led to the surrender of Yorktown, Va, and the independence of the United States. In January and February 1782 Bougainville took part in the fighting at St Christopher (Saint Kitts–Nevis) in the Leeward Islands, and in its capture, and he participated in the battle of the Saintes on 12 April. His conduct on the last occasion brought him a reprimand from a court martial held at Lorient, France, in 1784.

Bougainville, who had been received into the Académie de Marine as a regular member on 2 Dec.

1784 and had been admitted into the Order of Cincinnatus from the time of its foundation, became the minister's adviser on scientific questions and in this capacity assisted in preparations for the Comte de Lapérouse's voyage. In February 1789 he was made a member of the Académie des Sciences, and in October 1790 he received command of the Brest squadron, which he quickly relinquished because of the confusion and general disorganization associated with the French revolution. Promoted vice-admiral on 1 Jan. 1792, he resigned on 22 February and assisted the king at the time of the riot on 20 June. During the Terror he was arrested and imprisoned in Coutances; after the fall of Robespierre he was released, and on 19 Dec. 1795 he became a member of the new Institut de France.

Appointed successively member of the commission to prepare the expedition to Egypt in July 1798, senator in December 1799, member of the Bureau des Longitudes, associate in the organization of Nicolas Baudin's expedition to Australia in 1799, count of the Empire in 1808, and president of the court martial held in connection with the battle of Trafalgar, Louis-Antoine de Bougainville was laden with honours at the end of an exceptionally full career which had enabled him to develop his many talents. A brilliant mathematician, clear-headed warrior, successful navigator, and skilful diplomat, Bougainville had a mind open to all the sciences and a clear, precise style of writing. He showed himself an excellent observer of the diversity of people he encountered during his various missions and can with reason be considered a founder of modern ethnography. Shaped by an advanced culture, he was one of those who, giving at times an appearance of superficiality, combined elegance with depth.

ÉTIENNE TAILLEMITE

Louis-Antoine de Bougainville is the author of *Traité de calcul intégral, pour servir de suite à l'"Analyse des infiniments-petits" de M. le marquis de l'Hôpital* (2v., Paris, 1754–56) and of *Voyage autour du monde, par la frégate du roi la "Boudeuse," et la flûte l'"Étoile"; en 1766, 1767, 1768 & 1769* (Paris, 1771; réimpr., 1772, 1781; nouv. éd., Neuchâtel, Suisse, 1772; réimpr., 1773; nouv. éd., Lille, France, 1889; nouv. éd., introd. de P. Deslandres, Paris, 1924; nouv. éd., Étienne Taillemite, édit., Paris, 1977). The latter work was translated into English by J. R. Forster (Dublin, 1772) and into Spanish by Josefina Gallego de Dantin (Madrid, 1921). The manuscript "Journal de la *Boudeuse* (1766–1769)" can be found at AN, Marine, 4JJ, 142. His "Mémoire sur l'état de la Nouvelle-France à l'époque de la guerre de Sept Ans" has been published in *Relations et mémoires inédits pour servir à l'histoire de la France dans les pays d'outre-mer*, Pierre Margry, édit. (Paris, 1867), 37–84, as well as in ANQ *Rapport*, 1923–24: 1–70, as "La mission de M. de Bougainville en France en 1758–1759," an article which brings together the various reports presented by Bougainville at the time of his voyage. In 1964 Edward Pierce Hamilton translated and edited some writings by Bougainville in *Adventure in the wilderness: the American journals of Louis Antoine de Bougainville, 1756–1760* (Norman, Okla.). Étienne Taillemite has published all the navigation journals of Bougainville and his companions in *Bougainville et ses compagnons autour du monde* (2v., Paris, 1977). The journal that Bougainville kept while in Canada was published by Amédée-Edmond Gosselin in ANQ *Rapport*, 1923–24: 202–393.

AN, Col., C^{11A}, 104: ff.184, 188–92, 200–3, 267; 105: ff.17–18; C^{11E}, 10: ff.213–24; Marine, B^4, 141–48; 152; 161–70; 192–93; 195; 205–6; 236; C^7 (dossier Bougainville). Guy Frégault, *François Bigot, administrateur français* (2v., [Montréal], 1948). René de Kérallain, *Bougainville à l'escadre du comte de Grasse* (Paris, 1929); *Bougainville à l'escadre du comte d'Estaing* (Paris, 1927); *Les Français au Canada, la jeunesse de Bougainville et la guerre de Sept Ans* (Paris, 1896); *La prise de Québec et la perte du Canada d'après des publications récentes* (Paris, 1906). J.-É. Martin-Allanic, *Bougainville navigateur et les découvertes de son temps* (2v., Paris, 1964). Michèle Duchet, "Bougainville, Raynal, Diderot et les Sauvages du Canada: une source ignorée de l'histoire des deux Indes," *Rev. d'hist. littéraire de France* (Paris), avril–juin 1963.

BOURK (Bourke). *See* BURKE

BRADFORD, RICHARD, Church of England clergyman; b. 2 April 1752 in Rotherhithe (London), England, son of Richard Bradford, a farmer, and Susanna Cole; d. 12 May 1817 in Montreal, Lower Canada.

Richard Bradford's parents died when he was young, and little is known about his early life and education. In 1783 he married Sarah, the daughter of the Reverend John Jefferey, vicar of Ludham and of Potter Heigham in Norfolk, and it is probable that he studied for the ministry under Jefferey, a Cambridge graduate. Bradford was ordained deacon at Norwich in 1785 and priest in 1788. After serving from the latter date as curate for various churches in the Ludham area, he emigrated to New York State in 1793 with his wife and eight children. A gap occurs in his history until 1800, when the Bradfords are found living in Ulster County, N.Y.; Richard was then principal of an academy at nearby Catskill. In 1802 the Protestant Episcopal Church appointed him to the recently formed congregation at Catskill. During his incumbency of about two and a half years he was instrumental in the building of St Luke's Church. In 1804 he and Charles Caleb Cotton* were highly recommended to Bishop Jacob Mountain* of Quebec by the British consul general at New York City, Thomas Barclay*, and, with the approval of the bishop and of the Society for the Propagation of the Gospel, Bradford opened in October 1805 a mission in Chatham Township, Lower Canada.

Circumstances surrounding the beginnings of the mission are obscure. An application was made for a clergyman as early as 1798, but it was not encouraged since the local subscription was not absolutely secured to the incumbent. Six years later the bishop assured Lieutenant Governor Sir Robert Shore Milnes* that a missionary would receive £100 from government, £50 from the SPG, and a possible £30 from local subscriptions. It was apparently because of this assured income that Bradford was offered and accepted the post, and thus became the founder of the Church of England in the Ottawa valley. For almost three years he laboured not only in Chatham Township but also in the adjacent seigneury of Argenteuil and beyond. The largely non-Anglican population was composed of Scottish immigrants, loyalists, and late loyalist settlers from New England, lumbermen, disbanded soldiers, and retired fur traders. Bradford himself established a farm on 96 acres given him in 1806 by a local proprietor, Colonel Daniel ROBERTSON, and in 1808 purchased 1,000 acres for £125 from Pierre-Louis PANET, seigneur of Argenteuil.

In the latter year Bradford was asked by Jehosaphat MOUNTAIN, bishop's official (commissary) for Lower Canada, to replace the Reverend James Sutherland Rudd at William Henry (Sorel). Having arrived there on 1 June 1808, he remained until September 1811; his parish registers attest to his faithful services to both the civil population, apparently composed of disbanded and retired soldiers, loyalists, and merchants, and to the 49th Foot, of which he was appointed chaplain in 1810. He presented a class of 32 for confirmation by the bishop in 1809. In applying to the SPG that year for an addition to Bradford's stipend, the bishop called him "a man of very respectable exemplary conduct."

Bradford strengthened his bonds with Chatham Township in August 1810 by purchasing for £2,500 a 5,000-acre property from the merchant Daniel Sutherland* and the estate of Colonel Robertson. He now owned more than 6,000 acres, receiving rental income on the small proportion that was settled. The rest was held partly as a heritage for his sons and partly, no doubt, for speculation, since Chatham and Vaudreuil were becoming increasingly settled. It was possibly his interest in the region's economic prospects that motivated him in 1810 to accompany Captain John By* on a trip to investigate the water-power possibilities of the Lachute falls. In the autumn of 1811, arrangements having been made for a replacement at William Henry, Bradford returned with great relief to Chatham where some of his family had remained, moved into the large and elegant Robertson house, which he had acquired, and resumed work in his former mission. In October 1813, when Bishop Mountain paid the mission his one and only visit, Bradford was absent and was severely reprimanded. As a result of this absence no confirmations were made during his incumbency. By 1816 ill health had slowed down his efforts, and he died in Montreal on 12 May 1817.

Bradford's middle-class, rural background in England, modest education, and experience with colonial society in New York State between 1793 and 1804 had all prepared him well for the frontier society in which he worked at William Henry and Chatham, but particularly in the latter place. The only settled clergyman in his widespread Ottawa pastorate, aided by a broadminded attitude toward non-Anglicans and undoubtedly by the Church of England's exclusive right to hold civil registers, Bradford served his flock without denominational distinction. A landowner and farmer, burdened with family cares (he had 11 children), he lived as many of his people lived and understood their problems. If he was unable to get a church built, it was no doubt largely because of the interlude at William Henry, the unsettlement of the war years, and the denominational diversity of those to whom he ministered. His successor, the Reverend Joseph Abbott*, who arrived in 1818 to take up a post at St Andrews (Saint-André-Est, Que.) and two years later married Bradford's daughter Harriet, was disappointed by the settlers' resistance to church discipline, but wrote of the glorious harvest he reaped from the good seed sown by his predecessor.

THOMAS R. MILLMAN

[In [C. F. Pascoe], *Classified digest of the records of the Society for the Propagation of the Gospel in Foreign Parts, 1701–1892* (5th ed., London, 1895), 868, it is said that, according to tradition, Richard Bradford served as a midshipman under Captain James Cook*; recent investigations have turned up nothing to confirm this. T.R.M.]

ANQ-M, CM1, 1er mai 1817. QDA, 332, H. C. Stuart, "The episcopate of Jacob Mountain." St Luke's Church (Catskill, N.Y.), Vestry minutes, 24 Aug. 1801–23 April 1805. USPG, Journal of SPG, 29: 68–74; 30: 16–17. *Montreal Herald*, 17 May 1817. Christie, *Hist. of L.C.*, 6: 69. G. D. McGibbon, *Glimpses of the life and work of the Reverend Richard Bradford as scholar, school principal, chaplain, priest of the Church of England and S.P.G. missionary* (Calgary, 1970), 8, 31, 74, 88, 118. Millman, *Jacob Mountain*, 106, 138, 140, 195, 212–13. E. C. Royle, *An historical study of the Anglican parish of Vaudreuil* (Hudson Heights, Que.), 1952), I-8–9. Cyrus Thomas, *History of the counties of Argenteuil, Que., and Prescott, Ont., from the earliest settlement to the present* (Montreal, 1896), 294. M. E. S. Abbott, "Social history of the parish of Christ Church, St Andrews, Que., from 1818 to 1875," *Montreal Churchman* (Montreal), 22 (1934), no.6: 8; no.7: 12; no.12: 8–9. J.-J. Lefebvre, "Louise Réaume-Fournerie-Robertson (1742–1773) et son petit-fils le colonel Daniel de Hertel (1797–1866)," *RHAF*, 12 (1958–59): 329.

BRANT, JOSEPH. *See* THAYENDANEGEA

BRASSARD DESCHENAUX. *See* DESCHENAUX

BREHAUT, PIERRE (Peter), cooper, businessman, and politician; b. 7 June 1764 in Guernsey, son of Pierre Brehaut and Marie Todevin; m. 30 Jan. 1792 Thérèse Bellenoy at Quebec in the Anglican church (later the Cathedral of the Holy Trinity), and they had four children; d. 2 May 1817 at Quebec.

Pierre Brehaut came of a family which had settled in the Channel Islands in the 14th century and which had developed ties with sea-borne commerce and the colonies. Seeking a career abroad, the young Brehaut sailed for Quebec around 1788. Soon after his arrival he was hired as a cooper by businessman Louis DUNIÈRE. From 1792 on, he practised his trade independently. He operated a shop close to Quebec's port facilities, where the import-export trade was centred, and engaged now and then in sales of wines and spirits imported from Guernsey and the West Indies.

Brehaut's business seems to have prospered, since on 19 Nov. 1800 he acquired for £3,250 Dunière's properties at the foot of Cap Diamant: a 200-foot river-front lot with wharf, warehouse, two sheds, and a stable. He was then able to set on foot a wholesale-trading enterprise that opened the way to capital accumulation. In 1802 Peter Lemesurier joined the firm and aided in its financing for a four-year period. Under the name of Peter Brehaut and Company the partners specialized in the grain trade and the import of wine and spirits. Concerned to defend his economic interests, Brehaut identified himself with the merchants' cause in the notorious "prisons debate" of 1805 in the Lower Canadian House of Assembly [*see* Jonathan Sewell*]; his name appears on a petition demanding a tax on land to finance them rather than on the revenues of commerce. In 1806 he reconstructed the firm with new partners, including Thomas Higginbottom, and then enlarged its storage space with the building of additional warehouses. The quantity and variety of the goods offered to customers in March 1811 are evidence of the scale of the firm's transactions: 4,000 bushels of wheat, 1,200 of peas, 1,000 of salt, as well as such other items as flour, biscuit, cordage, American leather, and millstones. In May 1811 Brehaut joined forces with merchant William Grant Sheppard and the latter's brother Peter in the firm of Brehaut and Sheppard. Through commercial connections with Samuel Dobree and Company of London and Janvrin and Company in Jersey, the firm reached new overseas markets in Ireland, Portugal, and the West Indies. The 55 accounts receivable from clients in the Quebec region in May 1814 give an indication of the scale of its operations in the local market.

As a recognized spokesman of the trading interest, Brehaut won election to the assembly on 13 May 1814 as member for the riding of Quebec. When Sir George Gordon Drummond* dissolved the house in February

Brenton

1816, he cited in justification, and as evidence of the stubborn ill-will of the members, the declarations made to their constituents by Brehaut and Pierre BRUNEAU. This action did not prevent the re-election of both men on 25 April. In his second term Brehaut sat on committees dealing with economic matters such as several on public accounts, one on a bill to regulate trade with the United States, and another regarding the establishment of a banking institution in Lower Canada.

On 4 Sept. 1815 a fire had damaged the buildings of Brehaut and Sheppard. This misfortune was compounded by dissolution of the partnership on 1 May 1816. Far from ceasing his activity, however, Brehaut embarked in June 1816 on the rebuilding and enlargement of his facilities. Some 150 men worked on the site at erecting sheds designed to store from 150,000 to 200,000 bushels of grain. In the same year Brehaut purchased from Thomas DUNN the Cape Diamond Brewery, which adjoined his wharf and store. The acquisition, made for £12,600, enabled him to enter the production sector and to establish closer ties with producers of barley and hops, while securing the services of an expert London master-brewer, Thomas Purcell.

Some years earlier Brehaut had purchased the Manoir Saint-Roch, located in the suburb of that name and formerly the seigneurial property of William GRANT (1744–1805). The original house had been built in the 17th century for the wealthy fur trader Charles Aubert* de La Chesnaye. In 1815 and 1816 Brehaut acquired, on Rue Saint-Louis, two dwellings of note which are still standing: the Maison Maillou and the Maison Kent, the latter house having been the site where Jean-Baptiste-Nicolas-Roch de Ramezay* signed the capitulation of Quebec in 1759, and the residence of Prince EDWARD AUGUSTUS, in 1792–94. Thus, to his interests in trade and brewing, Brehaut added important holdings in real estate.

In the wake of the Irish immigration movement which began in 1816, 45 families were landed that summer at Brehaut's wharf. Destitute, they sought his aid and he immediately agreed to house them in his buildings while they waited for land grants in the area of Nicolet.

It is not known to what extent Brehaut was successful in restarting his commercial operations after the difficulties of 1815. Early in 1817, not long before his death, he painted a rather gloomy picture of the state of the economy: "Poverty is worse in Quebec than I have seen it these twenty years; not a ship on the stocks, no employment for workers." It would not be surprising if his affairs had suffered a blow from the recession that followed the Napoleonic Wars.

As a separation of dwelling and the sale of furnishings from the Manoir Saint-Roch reveal, Brehaut's marriage had collapsed some time before he drowned in the St Lawrence on the night of 2 May 1817. He was said to have lost his footing while inspecting his piers and warehouses as was his custom, but there were no witnesses. A year later his widow married his former partner, William Grant Sheppard, and Brehaut's friends marked the occasion by staging a derisive charivari.

If Brehaut's wharf was long a Quebec landmark, this was in large part due to its owner's role in the commercial life of the city and in the building up of its overseas trade, particularly with the West Indies.

STANLEY BRÉHAUT RYERSON

ANQ-Q, CE1-61, 30 janv. 1792; CN1-26, 8 mai 1806; CN1-83, 22 sept. 1792; CN1-171, 3 nov. 1809; CN1-178, 2–3, 5, 7, 9–13, 16–18, 26 mai 1814; CN1-262, 19 nov. 1800, 25 févr. 1805, 28 avril 1806, 2 mai 1816; CN1-285, 3 mai 1806. PAC, MG 24, D15. Bas-Canada, chambre d'Assemblée, *Journaux*, 6–7 févr. 1816. "Les dénombrements de Québec" (Plessis), ANQ *Rapport*, 1948–49: 28, 83, 132, 181. *Montreal Herald*, 9 Sept. 1815. *Quebec Gazette*, 16 Aug. 1792; 21 July 1803; 8 May 1806; 16 May 1811; 23 May 1815; 4 Jan., 14 March 1816; 8 May 1817. Desjardins, *Guide parl.*, 136. Wallot, *Un Québec qui bougeait*, 55–58. P.-G. Roy, "La famille Brehaut," *BRH*, 45 (1939): 146–50.

BRENTON, JAMES, lawyer, militia officer, politician, office holder, and judge; b. 2 Nov. 1736 in Newport, R.I., 13th child of Jahleel Brenton and his first wife Frances Cranston, eldest daughter of Governor Samuel Cranston; m. first 30 May 1762 Rebecca Scott in Newport, and they had one son, Edward Barbizon*, who became a judge of the Supreme Court of Newfoundland; m. secondly 28 April 1766 Elizabeth Russell in Halifax, N.S., and they had nine children; d. there 3 Dec. 1806.

James Brenton, a junior member of the Rhode Island bar, came to Nova Scotia as a young man and on 9 Dec. 1760 was admitted to the provincial bar. He subsequently joined a volunteer militia company, and by 1764 had risen to the rank of captain-lieutenant. Between 1765 and 1770 he represented Onslow Township in the House of Assembly, and between 1776 and 1785 he sat for Halifax County. On 31 Oct. 1778 he succeeded Richard Gibbons* as solicitor general, and on 12 Oct. 1779 William Nesbitt* as attorney general. With the death of Charles Morris* he was elevated to the bench as an assistant judge of the Supreme Court on 8 Dec. 1781. On 10 Dec. 1799 he was appointed to the Council. He deputized for Richard Bulkeley* in the Vice-Admiralty Court from 17 Nov. 1798, and after Bulkeley's death in December 1800 he became judge of the court, an office from which he was removed the following year in favour of Alexander Croke*.

Brenton's career in law seems to have been one of

continuous conflict. As a young lawyer he was forced to apologize for questioning the impartiality of the bench in April 1762. In the assembly his legal talents were constantly in use in the redrafting and revising of new and existing laws as assembly and Council struggled for domination during the 1760s and 1770s. And while serving on the Supreme Court, Brenton and his colleague Isaac DESCHAMPS became involved in the so-called "judges' affair."

The death of Chief Justice Bryan Finucane in August 1785 had left Brenton and Deschamps as the only two members of the Supreme Court, and dissatisfaction with their performance caused a secret session of the assembly in 1787 to request of Lieutenant Governor John Parr* and the Council an investigation into the judges' behaviour. Parr's reply indicated that he and the Council were not in favour of an inquiry. The issue became the chief one in the 1788 assembly by-election for Halifax County and, after the victory of the Council-supported candidate Charles Morris*, feelings ran so high that the Halifax garrison was called out to quell three days of post-election riots. Shortly after the election the Council published an acerbic vindication of Brenton and Deschamps. This account prompted equally intemperate letters condemning the judges and Council from two loyalist lawyers, Jonathan Sterns and William Taylor, who were struck from the roll of attorneys by Deschamps for contempt of court. In March 1789 the assembly received a reply from Parr to its request for an investigation, and although the response was couched in diplomatic terms it again upheld the judges. Nevertheless, the following year the assembly voted to impeach Brenton and Deschamps. Parr referred the case to Britain, but it was two years before the Privy Council ruled in favour of Brenton and Deschamps. Although the initial charges were damaging to Brenton, the faint vindication of the Privy Council, which recognized that the judges might have erred but found that the fault lay in "the frailty of human nature," may have been more so. In the final analysis Brenton was a victim of the loyalist determination not to be excluded from positions of power and influence in the Nova Scotia hierarchy. Brenton had seen the collision between loyalists and pre-loyalists coming and had tried to avoid it; he abandoned any thought of seeking re-election in 1785 when he realized that the contest would be carried on with the "Violence and heat of party opposition." But he could not escape the consequences of the controversy. The unpopularity of his decisions on the Vice-Admiralty Court and the desire for harmonious relations between Britain and the United States dictated his removal from the court in favour of Croke, "a gentleman least connected with the United States."

Ironically, although Brenton was at the centre of an emerging "family compact," and despite John Bartlet

Brebner*'s characterization of him as "ambitious," he died a far from wealthy man, leaving a personal estate of only £200. His salary as a Supreme Court judge had been discounted as much as 35 per cent since its warrants had to be negotiated on the Treasury. Indeed, without the lucrative period he spent on the Vice-Admiralty Court in 1800–1, when the French revolutionary wars caused a great increase in business and revenue, many of his debts might have gone unsettled. In fact, his widow was forced to petition the assembly for assistance, noting that the family home would have to be sold to satisfy the remaining debts, which amounted to £600. A minor figure on the Nova Scotia scene, Brenton may deserve recognition for his family ties to such persons as Joseph Gerrish*, John and Sir Brenton* Halliburton, and Charles INGLIS.

ALLAN C. DUNLOP

PANS, MG 9, no.109: 49–50; RG 1, 302. PRO, CO 217/60 (mfm. at PANS). *Extracts from the proceedings of his majesty's council [Feb. 21 and 28, 1788, in reference to complaints of improper and irregular administration of justice in the Supreme Court of Nova Scotia . . .]* ([Halifax, 1788?]). W. E. Boggs, *The genealogical record of the Boggs family, the descendants of Ezekiel Boggs* (Halifax, 1916), 73–74. B. [C. U.] Cuthbertson, *The old attorney general: a biography of Richard John Uniacke* (Halifax, [1980]), 19–21. John Doull, *Sketches of attorney generals of Nova Scotia* (Halifax, 1964). Margaret Ells, "Nova Scotian 'Sparks of liberty,'" *Dalhousie Rev.,* 16 (1936–37): 475–92. L. H. Laing, "Nova Scotia's Admiralty Court as a problem of colonial administration," *CHR,* 16 (1935): 151–61.

BROCK, Sir ISAAC, army officer and colonial administrator; b. 6 Oct. 1769 in St Peter Port, Guernsey, eighth son of John Brock and Elizabeth De Lisle; d. 13 Oct. 1812 at Queenston Heights, Upper Canada. He never married, and there seems to be no real evidence to support the stories that have been told of a romantic attachment in Canada.

The Brock family were moderately wealthy. Isaac Brock evidently received his earliest education in Guernsey, where we are told he was remembered by his schoolfellows as an excellent swimmer and boxer, and by his family "chiefly for extreme gentleness." When ten years old he was sent to school in Southampton, England, and subsequently studied for a year "under a French Protestant clergyman at Rotterdam, for the purpose of learning the French language." As of 2 March 1785, at the age of 15, he obtained by purchase an ensigncy in the 8th Foot, the vacancy being caused by the promotion of his eldest brother, John, from lieutenant to captain in the same regiment. His early years in the service were spent in England. He became a lieutenant in 1790. Later that year he took advantage of the government's authoriz-

Brock

ing a number of new independent companies to obtain the rank of captain by raising the men for one of them; he then exchanged into the 49th Foot, in which his captaincy was dated 15 June 1791. Thereafter his career was linked with the 49th. He joined it in Barbados, and did duty there and in Jamaica until 1793, when he was sent to England on sick leave. His nephew and biographer tells the story of how, soon after he joined the 49th, a professional duellist in the regiment forced a quarrel upon him. On being challenged Brock insisted that the exchange of shots should take place, not at the usual range, but across a handkerchief. The duellist refused, and in consequence left the regiment.

On returning to England Brock was employed in recruiting, and subsequently was in charge of recruits on the island of Jersey. He purchased a majority in the 49th as of 24 June 1795, and rejoined the regiment after it came back to England from the West Indies in July 1796. He became a lieutenant-colonel in the 49th by purchase on 25 Oct. 1797, and before the end of the year was the regiment's senior lieutenant-colonel and in command of it. In August 1799 the 49th sailed with an expedition under Sir Ralph Abercromby directed against north Holland. In this campaign Isaac Brock had his first experience of battle. The 49th was part of a brigade commanded by Major-General (later Lieutenant-General Sir) John Moore. The advanced brigades, including Moore's, landed at Den Helder on 27 August with slight opposition, and Abercromby's force took up a strong position in which it beat off a French attack on 10 September. In these operations the 49th was not actively involved; the regiment was inexperienced and had been in poor condition when Brock took it over, and Moore was probably sparing it. It is interesting to speculate about the possible influence of this celebrated leader and trainer of troops on Brock; but no comment by Brock on Moore (or vice versa) seems to have survived. After the arrival of the Duke of York with additional British troops and a body of Russians, the allied force took the offensive. On 2 October, in the action called on the colours of British regiments Egmont-op-Zee (more properly Egmond aan Zee), the 49th was heavily engaged and did well. It was a disjointed battle fought among sand-dunes, ending in the enemy's withdrawal. The 49th had 33 fatal casualties. Brock himself was slightly wounded, evidently by a spent ball. He wrote to his brother John, "I got knocked down shortly after the enemy began to retreat, but never quitted the field, and returned to my duty in less than half an hour." The allies were now able to occupy Egmond and Alkmaar, but in another battle on 6 October in which the 49th were not present they were badly mauled. The Duke of York proposed a convention, allowing his army to embark freely for England; the French agreed, and thus ingloriously the campaign ended.

Early in 1801 Brock's regiment was selected to be the main component of the military force carried in the fleet under Admiral Sir Hyde Parker which was dispatched to the Baltic to overawe Denmark. Brock, however, was not the senior army officer present; this was Lieutenant-Colonel William Stewart of the Rifle Corps (subsequently the Rifle Brigade), though only one company of that regiment was present. The troops' intended role in the attack on Copenhagen was to assault, along with a body of bluejackets, the batteries built on piles in the harbour, notably the formidable Trekroner battery. This was likely to be an extremely costly operation. Fortunately, it was not attempted, chiefly because some of the leading vessels ran aground during the approach on 2 April so that the ships never silenced the batteries sufficiently to make it remotely practicable. The 49th were distributed among the ships of Vice-Admiral Lord Nelson's squadron which attacked the Danish craft moored off Copenhagen. Brock himself was in the *Ganges*, though at the end of the action he visited Nelson's flagship, the *Elephant*. The regiment shared the casualties of this bloody engagement, suffering 13 killed and 41 wounded.

When the 49th were ordered to Canada in 1802, Brock had still had comparatively little battle experience, having been present in two general actions, one of which was primarily a naval battle. The regiment embarked in June, and at Quebec on or about 25 August Lieutenant-Colonel Brock landed in the country with which his name was to be connected in history. The intention had apparently been to send the 49th to the far western posts, but they were kept in Montreal for the winter, and proceeded to Upper Canada in the spring of 1803, the headquarters going to York (Toronto), with a wing of the regiment under the junior lieutenant-colonel, Roger Hale Sheaffe*, at Fort George (Niagara-on-the-Lake, Ont.).

Brock at once encountered the problem of desertion, which was particularly serious at posts close to the American border. In the summer of 1803 seven soldiers deserted from York in a stolen boat. Brock set off across Lake Ontario in pursuit with a party of the 49th in a bateau. At Fort George he sent an officer's party by boat along the American shore of the lake to search for the deserters, while he himself turned back along the Canadian shore in case they were coasting it. The other party in fact apprehended the men on American soil, with the assistance of one or more Indians, and they were brought back to Canada – a violation of American law, which however seems to have led to no protest. Later the same season the officers at Fort George got wind of a conspiracy, said to have been brought on by the severity of Sheaffe, to imprison the officers and desert to the United States. Before taking any action, the officers thought it well to send particulars to Brock at York. He at once crossed the lake in a schooner, and arrived at the fort gate alone. Finding that the guard turned out to receive him was commanded by the sergeant and corporal reported to him as the ringleaders, he ordered them into confinement on the spot, ending the conspiracy at a stroke. The conspirators and the deserters lately apprehended were shipped off to Quebec, where after court martial seven of them were shot the following March.

Brock was promoted colonel as of 30 Oct. 1805, and about the same time went home on leave. While in England he made detailed recommendations for dealing with desertion in Canada, arguing that a veteran battalion formed of reliable old soldiers should be organized to occupy the border posts. His advice was acted on shortly; and this expedient was resorted to again a generation later, when the Royal Canadian Rifle Regiment was formed in 1840–41 on Brock's principles for the same purpose, and did duty until the withdrawal of the British troops from central Canada in 1870. While Brock was still on leave there was apprehension of war with the United States, and he decided of his own volition to cut his leave short and return to his post. He left London for the last time on 26 June 1806. In September he found himself in temporary command of all the troops in Canada, with headquarters at Quebec, and this situation lasted until Sir James Henry CRAIG arrived to take up the appointments of governor-in-chief and commander of the forces in October 1807.

During this period of authority Brock worked with characteristic energy to improve the defences of the country. His chief care was to strengthen the fortifications of Quebec, the position on which communication with Britain ultimately depended. He reconstructed the walls facing the Plains of Abraham, and built an elevated battery mounting eight heavy guns in the temporary citadel made during the American Revolutionary War, with the object of commanding "the opposite heights," that is, those south of the river. This came to be known as "Brock's Battery," a name which Craig changed on his arrival to the King's Battery. Brock's activity brought him into difficulty with the civil government of Lower Canada (then administered by Thomas DUNN) on several issues: civilian encroachments on military lands; the use of waste land near the Jesuit college in Quebec for drill; responsibility for the cost of the Indian Department; Brock's request for civil labour to work on the fortifications; and his desire that part of the militia should be called out for training, and volunteer corps authorized and armed. The colonel got little satisfaction on any of these questions. One useful reform which lay entirely within his military competence Brock was able to carry out. Late in 1806 he gave orders that the "marine department" on the lakes and rivers of the Canadas should be under the

superintendence of the deputy quartermaster general. The Provincial Marine's chief function was providing transport service for the army, but from this time on it was increasingly developed as a force capable of naval action in case of war. Under one assistant quartermaster general at Kingston and another at Amherstburg it was more effectively administered than ever before, and it seems fair to say that Brock's action in 1806 was largely responsible for the existence of the force that six years later gave him naval command of the Great Lakes and thereby made possible his successful defence of Upper Canada.

Craig after his arrival made Brock a brigadier-general (an appointment rather than a rank, shortly confirmed from England) and placed him in command at Montreal. A few months later he returned to Quebec, where he remained until July 1810, when Craig sent him to take charge in Upper Canada. This command he retained until his death. He frequently complains in his letters of being left idle in Canada ("buried in this inactive, remote corner") while the main body of the British army is winning laurels in Europe. But the danger of war with the United States (and, he himself said, the possibility of a French-Canadian rising in the event of a French invasion) kept him where he was. Finally, early in 1812, letters from London indicated readiness to give him employment in Europe, but by then the aspect of affairs in North America was very threatening; and on 12 February Brock wrote, "I beg leave to be allowed to remain in my present command." On 4 June 1811 he had been promoted major-general; the same extensive block promotion brought this rank to Sheaffe as well. In October 1811 Francis Gore*, the lieutenant governor of Upper Canada, left for England on leave (he did not return until the war with the United States was over); Brock now became "president" and administrator of the government of the province. For the final year of his life he headed both the military command and the civil government.

Financial disaster had struck the Brocks in 1811. The general's brother William was senior partner in a London firm of bankers and general merchants which failed. William had advanced Isaac some £3,000 to purchase his commissions in the 49th, with no intention of ever requiring payment; but the loans had been entered, without Isaac's knowledge, in the firm's books. He now unexpectedly found himself faced with a demand for payment which he could not meet, but he made the whole of his new civil salary over to his brother Irving, to begin discharging the debt or to relieve distress in the family, as he thought best.

In February 1812, under the shadow of impending war with the United States, Brock met the provincial legislature. He found it less than fully cooperative; it refused to suspend habeas corpus, and the new militia act it provided was made effective only until the end of

Brock

the next session. It did, however, permit the organization on a voluntary basis within each paper militia battalion of two "flank companies" which might train for up to six days a month (though no provision was made for pay). Volunteers came forward willingly, and these companies, already organized and to a slight extent trained, were Brock's first resource for strengthening his small force of regulars when war broke out.

In December 1811 Brock had explained his war plans in a letter to Lieutenant-General Sir George Prevost, who had become governor-in-chief and commander of the forces in September. Emphasizing the importance of the cooperation of the Indians, he said that to obtain this it would be vital to seize Michilimackinac (Mackinac Island, Mich.) and Detroit (Mich.) at the outset of hostilities; he advocated in effect a bold policy of limited local offensives. The United States declared war on 18 June 1812. There were then about 1,600 British regular troops in Upper Canada, including the 10th Royal Veteran Battalion (not well fitted for field operations) and the Royal Newfoundland Regiment, chiefly employed with the Provincial Marine; the effective force consisted mainly of the 41st Foot and a company of the Royal Artillery. As soon as news of the outbreak reached him, Brock reinforced the Niagara frontier from York and went there himself. The weakness of his force, combined with letters from Prevost advising restraint lest hostile action should unite the divided American people, caused him for the moment to curb his natural impatience to take the offensive. In a succession of letters to Captain Charles Roberts, commanding at Fort St Joseph (St Joseph Island, Ont.) at the head of Lake Huron, he showed an untypical vacillation; but the last of them authorized Roberts to use his own judgement as to whether or not to attempt an attack on Michilimackinac. Roberts made the attack and it succeeded, and, as Brock had anticipated, this small early victory brought the Indians of the Upper Lakes region to the British standard.

On 12 July Canada was invaded on the Detroit frontier by Brigadier-General William Hull. There was now no doubt of American aggressive intentions, and Brock plunged into energetic counter-measures. The omens, however, were unfavourable. Hull's invasion, and the proclamation he issued, demoralized the Canadian militia along the Detroit, and they deserted in numbers, some going over to the enemy. Brock's counter-proclamation of 22 July was confident in tone, but it revealed his inner doubts: even if the province should be overrun, he declared, there was no question of its being "eventually abandoned" by the British government. He again met the Upper Canada legislature on 27 July, and again found it lukewarm; it was still unwilling to suspend habeas corpus. On the 29th he wrote to the adjutant general at headquarters in Montreal:

"My situation is most critical, not from anything the enemy can do, but from the disposition of the people – The population, believe me is essentially bad – A full belief possesses them all that this Province must inevitably succumb – This prepossession is fatal to every exertion – Legislators, Magistrates, Militia Officers, all have imbibed the idea, and are so sluggish and indifferent in their respective offices that the artful and active scoundrel is allowed to parade the Country without interruption, and commit all imaginable mischief. . . .

"What a change an additional regiment would make in this part of the province! Most of the people have lost all confidence – I however speak loud and look big. . . ."

Patriotic Canadian historians have sometimes been reluctant to recognize this aspect of the situation. It is, however, essential to an adequate assessment of Brock. Many commanders would have allowed the current despondency to discourage them into adopting a supine defensive attitude. Brock took the offensive.

The British troops on the Detroit still held the fort at Amherstburg. Brock informed Prevost that he proposed to collect a force at Long Point on Lake Erie to relieve Amherstburg. He sent thither 100 militia volunteers from York, and followed them himself. Colonel Thomas Talbot* had much difficulty with the militia in and around his settlement north of Lake Erie, but finally obtained a fair number of volunteers. On 8 August Brock embarked his small striking force of about 300 men (only about 50 of whom were regulars) at Long Point, and after a stormy voyage they reached Amherstburg on the 13th. Hull, discouraged by the threat to his communications along the Lake Erie shore posed by the Provincial Marine, Indians, and British detachments, had already withdrawn from Canada to Detroit. Brock's total force was about 1,300 men, of whom 400 were militia and 600 were Indians. Hull had something over 2,000, including a detachment of about 500 he had sent out to protect an approaching supply column; and Fort Detroit was well armed with artillery. Brock's decision to attack across the Detroit River on 16 August was bold. His first intention was to take up a defensive position on the American side and offer battle in the open, but apprehension of trouble from the detachment in his rear led him to advance at once upon the fort, which was being fired on by a battery on the Canadian shore. The mere threat of attack was enough; Hull surrendered Detroit and his army, with 35 guns and other stores which were very useful for the defenders of Upper Canada.

In a private letter Brock described the appreciation that led to his audacious action: "Some say that nothing could be more desperate than the measure, but I answer that the state of the Province admitted of nothing but desperate remedies. I got possession [through the capture of an American vessel by the

Provincial Marine] of the letters my antagonist addressed to the Secretary at War, and also of the sentiments which hundreds of his army uttered to their friends. Confidence in the General was gone, and evident despondency prevailed throughout." He added that he crossed the river against the advice of his colonels; "it is therefore no wonder that envy should attribute to good fortune what in justice to my own discernment, I must say, proceeded from a cool calculation of the *pours* and *contres*."

There seems no doubt that the presence with Brock of a large number of Indians contributed materially to the moral deterioration of Hull and his force. Brock had assisted the process by remarking in a letter in which he demanded Hull's surrender that, while he did not propose to "join in a war of extermination," the Indians would be "beyond controul the moment the contest commences." (In fact, at both Michilimackinac and Detroit the Indians' conduct was beyond reproach.) A relationship of mutual confidence and regard had been established between Brock and the Shawnee chief TECUMSEH, who was the effective leader of the Indians at Detroit; it was reflected in the fact that Brock is said to have presented to Tecumseh his sash (which Tecumseh modestly passed on to a senior chief), while Tecumseh gave Brock his sash in exchange. This story has been questioned, but the presence of an "arrow" sash among the general's uniforms as received by his family seems to provide rather strong presumptive evidence for it.

In Upper Canada the effect of the dramatic and almost bloodless victory at Detroit was electric. Brock wrote to his brothers on 3 September, "The militia have been inspired by the recent success with confidence – the disaffected are silenced." No one now doubted that the country could be defended. From Detroit Brock hastened back to the Niagara front. Prevost, he heard, had negotiated with Major-General Henry Dearborn, commanding the American forces in the eastern sector, a temporary agreement by which both sides in that region would refrain from offensive action. This resulted from a suggestion by the former British minister in Washington, D.C., Augustus John Foster, now at Halifax, N.S., who on receiving news of Britain's withdrawal of the orders in council interfering with American trade – orders in council which had been one cause of the war – had set about trying to restore peace. President James Madison refused these overtures, and Brock complained that the abortive "armistice" had merely allowed the enemy to bring up more troops to the frontier.

The chief menace was now on the Niagara. Here, as along the whole frontier, Brock's problem was defending a long line with inadequate forces, always uncertain where the Americans might strike. On 12 October his brigade-major, Thomas Evans*, crossed the river at Queenston under a flag of truce and saw on the American side boats in readiness for crossing. Returning to Brock at Fort George he argued that an attack at Queenston was imminent. It seems likely that Brock was not fully convinced, for he remained at Fort George. Before daylight on the 13th, however, gunfire from the direction of Queenston announced that an attack was in progress. Brock, who probably had slept in his clothes, at once mounted and rode hard towards the scene of action, followed at a short interval by his two aides-de-camp, one of whom was Lieutenant-Colonel John MACDONELL (Greenfield), attorney general of the province. The general's idea was presumably to make a personal assessment of the situation, for he does not seem to have left orders for the Fort George garrison to move. The flank companies of the 3rd York militia battalion (the "York Volunteers") were stationed at a battery at Brown's Point, about two miles below Queenston. After brief hesitation their commander, Captain Duncan Cameron*, marched them towards the sound of the guns. John Beverley Robinson*, a subaltern in the Volunteers, in a letter written the next day, describes how Brock, overtaking them, "waved his hand to us, and desired us to follow with expedition, and galloped on with full speed to the mountain."

Brock's own 49th Foot had arrived from the lower province to reinforce Upper Canada in August, and its grenadier and light companies, along with militia companies from Lincoln and York, were opposing the enemy landing in Queenston, supported by a three-pounder field-piece and another gun on the river bank below. The Americans had suffered considerably and when Brock galloped into the village the situation must have seemed fairly well in hand. The early stages of the battle were not well documented, but it appears that the 49th light company had been posted on the heights above Queenston, and was called down before Brock's arrival (or, less probably, by the general himself) to join in the fight below. Brock rode up to the "redan" battery (one gun) part way up the hill, and there was surprised by the appearance of enemy troops above him. This was a force under Captain (later Major-General) John Ellis Wool, which had found a way up by a "fisherman's path." Brock and the gunners abandoned the battery and hastily retreated down the hill. Realizing the importance of evicting Wool from his commanding position before he could be reinforced, the general collected the troops near by and led them up the slope on foot. Wool's account, which is not very clear, indicates that the Americans were driven back some distance, but at this moment Brock – six feet two and a splendid target – fell a victim to an enemy sharpshooter. As the bullet-hole in his extant coatee proves, he was struck full in the heart and must have died without a word. This, indeed, is the evidence of George Stephen Benjamin Jarvis*, a Canadian volunteer with the 49th, who was beside him. The attack ebbed back down the hill.

Brock

At some point the general had uttered words which at once became famous. The *York Gazette* four days later gave "Push on brave York Volunteers" as "the last words of the dying hero," the Volunteers "being then near him." But as Robinson's letter amply proves, the York Volunteers were not yet on the field when Brock fell; they entered Queenston as his body was being carried back. A more plausible account is given in a letter written at Brown's Point on 15 October, and published in the *Quebec Mercury* of 27 October: "The York volunteers to whom he was particularly partial, have the honor of claiming his last words[;] immediately before he received his death wound he cried out, to some person near him to push on the York volunteers, which were the last words he uttered." Another possibility is that the words were said when he passed the Volunteers on the road, as described by Robinson; but the fact that the *Mercury* letter was itself pretty clearly written by one of the Volunteers makes this rather unlikely.

Brock's death left Macdonell the senior officer on the ground. He proceeded to lead the Volunteers and the other troops at hand in another attack against the heights. But Macdonell's horse was shot under him, he himself was mortally wounded, and this attack too failed. Brock's body was left in a house in Queenston, and the survivors of the defending force retired to the north end of the village. The battle seemed lost. Early in the afternoon, however, General Sheaffe came up from Fort George with fresh troops including several companies of the 41st and some field-guns. The Americans in possession of the heights were left without support from across the river. Following in the footsteps of a force of Indians under John Norton*, which had arrived earlier and was harassing the enemy, Sheaffe's men climbed the escarpment some distance inland, advanced along the summit, and destroyed the invading force completely, taking nearly 1,000 prisoners. Brock was amply avenged.

Brock never knew that four days before his death the Prince Regent had recognized his victory at Detroit by appointing him an extra knight of the Order of the Bath. He and Macdonell were buried with ceremony on 16 October in a bastion of Fort George, an American salute across the river echoing the British minute-guns. In 1824 they were reburied under an imposing monument on the summit of Queenston Heights. This was blown up in 1840, supposedly by a "border ruffian" named Benjamin Lett*. The memory of Brock was still extraordinarily strong in Upper Canada, and on 30 July in the same year 8,000 people from all parts of the province met at Queenston to plan an even more striking memorial. This ultimately took the form of the lofty column, "the stateliest monument that has been raised to an individual anywhere in Canada," which still dominates the romantic battle-field where Brock fell. In London he is commemo-rated by a modest memorial voted by parliament in St Paul's Cathedral.

Isaac Brock was one of the people to whom it is given to change the course of history. But for the presence in Upper Canada in the summer of 1812 of this able and magnetic general officer (and a single battalion of British regular infantry) the province would certainly have fallen to the United States; whether or not it was recovered would have depended on the determination of the British government. As it was, the morale of the community never fell again to the point it had reached before it was revived by Brock's daring stroke against Detroit. The *York Gazette*, reporting his death, said, "Inhabitants of Upper Canada, in the Day of Battle *remember* BROCK." And indeed it seems hardly too much to say that Brock's spirit continued to animate the people of the province for the rest of the war. His action at Detroit, we have seen, was criticized as being unduly rash; and the same has been said of his last charge at Queenston Heights. Boldness was his way; but boldness almost always succeeds when the enemy is ill prepared and irresolute, and it saved Upper Canada in 1812. As Robinson said long afterwards, but for the misfortune of a well-placed bullet his attack at Queenston might have succeeded too. His personality was both attractive and compelling, and the memory of it combined with the dramatic success achieved during the brief four months of his war leadership and the manner of his death to make him warmly remembered as a Canadian hero.

C. P. STACEY

[What appears to be the only authentic portrait of Brock is a pastel profile now in the possession of Captain M. H. T. Mellish of St Peter Port, Guernsey, who inherited it from Miss Edith Tupper. It has been attributed to James Sharples, but seems almost certain to be the work of William BERCZY. It has often been reproduced and copied in various forms; it indicates that he was a remarkably handsome man. (A picture which has been published as representing Brock, "from a miniature in possession of Miss Sara Mickle," seems to the present writer likely to be a portrait of Sir George Gordon Drummond*.) The uniform in which Brock was killed, formerly owned by his heirs in Guernsey, is in the Canadian War Museum, Ottawa. It includes the arrow sash which may be Tecumseh's. Another uniform of Brock's, with a sword and a military sash, is in the McCord Museum at McGill University. Both coatees carry the lace of a brigadier-general; it seems possible that Brock never obtained a major-general's uniform after his promotion in 1811.

The power of the Brock legend in Canada is reflected in the fact that no important known documents concerning his Canadian activities seem to have escaped publication. It is reflected also in the number of biographies of Brock that have been written in Canada. Nevertheless, there is no extended modern biography. Virtually everything that has been written about him, including the present article, is heavily indebted to the book edited by his nephew, Ferdinand Brock Tupper, *The life and correspondence of Major-General Sir*

Isaac Brock ... (London, 1845), which appeared in an enlarged 2nd edition in 1847. Apart from incorporating family information, this book has the special importance of publishing a large number of letters from and to Brock, of which the originals in many cases appear to have perished. Of the Canadian books, the longest are D. B. Read, *Life and times of Major-General Sir Isaac Brock, K.B.* (Toronto, 1894), and [Matilda] Edgar, *General Brock* (Toronto, 1904). Neither is completely satisfactory. Of the shorter biographies, four are meant for school use: W. R. Nursey, *The story of Isaac Brock, hero, defender and saviour of Upper Canada, 1812* (Toronto), first published in 1908, which contains a large admixture of imagination; H. S. Eayrs, *Sir Isaac Brock* (Toronto, 1918); T. G. Marquis, *Sir Isaac Brock* (Toronto, n.d.), which is very slight; and D. J. Goodspeed, *The good soldier; the story of Isaac Brock* (Toronto, 1964). W. K. Lamb, *The hero of Upper Canada* (Toronto, 1962), is brief but perceptive.

Among collections of documents, *Doc. hist. of campaign upon Niagara frontier* (E. A. Cruikshank), vols.3–5, is essential though often badly transcribed. Valuable also is the same editor's *Documents relating to the invasion of Canada and the surrender of Detroit, 1812* (Ottawa, 1912). [Isaac Brock], "Some unpublished letters from General Brock," ed. E. A. Cruikshank, *OH*, 13 (1915): 8–23, contains little of importance. *Select British docs. of War of 1812* (Wood) is important, though internal evidence indicates that in some cases the documents were transcribed not from the originals but from other printed collections. Of more incidental importance are [Horatio Nelson], *The dispatches and letters of Vice Admiral Lord Viscount Nelson*, ed. N. H. Nicolas (7v., London, 1845–46), 4; Norton, *Journal* (Klinck and Talman); and *Ten years of Upper Canada in peace and war, 1805–1815; being the Ridout letters*, ed. Matilda Edgar (Toronto, 1890).

Of many general secondary books and articles the following may be mentioned: Andre, *William Berczy*; Pierre Berton, *The invasion of Canada, 1812–1813* (Toronto, 1980), and *Flames across the border, 1813–1814* (Toronto, 1981); J. W. Fortescue, *A history of the British army* (13v. in 14, London, 1899–1930), 4, pt.II; 8; Hitsman, *Incredible War of 1812*; A. T. Mahan, *Sea power in its relations to the War of 1812* (2v., London, 1905), still the best strategic study; F. L. Petre, *The Royal Berkshire Regiment (Princess Charlotte of Wales's)*, this being the former 49th Foot (2v., Reading, Eng., 1925); Dudley Pope, *The great gamble* (London, 1972), concerning the battle of Copenhagen; [C. P. Stacey], "The defence of Upper Canada, 1812," *Introduction to the study of military history for Canadian students*, ed. C. P. Stacey (4th ed., Ottawa, 1955), 65–74; L. E. Buckell, "British uniforms in the American War of 1812," Soc. for Army Hist. Research, *Journal* (London), 28 (1950): 29–30, corrected in details in N. P. Dawnay, "The staff uniform of the British army, 1767 to 1855," Soc. for Army Hist. Research, *Journal*, 31 (1953): 64–84; Ludwig Kosche, "Relics of Brock: an investigation," *Archivaria* (Ottawa), no.9 (winter 1979–80); 33–103.

Other sources include: *Kingston Gazette*, 19 May, 29 Aug., 24, 31 Oct. 1812; *Quebec Mercury*, 27 Oct. 1812; *Times* (London), 23 Nov. 1812; *York Gazette*, 17 Oct. 1812; G.B., WO, *Army list*, 1786, 1791, 1795–96, 1812.   c.p.s.]

BROWN, Mr. *See* COMINGO, BRUIN ROMKES

BRUFF, CHARLES OLIVER, silversmith and goldsmith; b. 1735 in Talbot County, Md, son of James Earle Bruff; m. October 1763 Mary Letellier in New York City; d. 27 Jan. 1817 in Liverpool, N.S.

Charles Oliver Bruff was descended from a long line of Maryland silversmiths and goldsmiths. He evidently served his apprenticeship with his father in Talbot County, and between 1760 and 1763 he worked in partnership with his brother James Earle in Elizabeth Town (Elizabeth), N.J. Early in 1763 he began working independently in New York City, and within a few years his shop was described in a local newspaper as a "fashionable resort" which was "sure to attract attention." Here Bruff produced some of his finest silver tankards, covered bowls, mugs, and table silver, all stamped with his mark, COB. He also offered engraving, seal cutting, and a wide variety of precious jewellery, including buckles, rings, brooches, lockets, necklaces, and assorted "trinkets for Ladies."

The outbreak of the revolution gave Bruff an ideal opportunity to expand his business: although he later stated that he was by inclination a supporter of the British crown, he was also shrewd enough to attract the patronage of rebels by making swords with such rousing inscriptions as "Magna Charta and Freedom." His true political sympathies did not become apparent until the summer of 1776, when he decided to join the British army under Sir William Howe that had recently landed on Long Island. For the next few years his life remains something of a mystery; indeed, he is not heard of again until late 1782, when he joined a group of loyalists who were planning to found a new town, untainted by republicanism, at Port Roseway, N.S., soon to be renamed Shelburne. Arriving in Shelburne, probably in May 1783, with a household that included his wife, five children, and eight servants, Bruff was granted a town lot and additional land in the adjacent countryside. By January 1785 he was once again operating a shop where, according to one newspaper advertisement, he made and repaired "all sorts of goldsmith and jewellery work."

After the summer of 1785 Shelburne's population dwindled rapidly as most of the settlers either returned to the United States or dispersed to Halifax, England, and Upper Canada. Bruff, however, remained in Shelburne despite the waning demand for his skills. In April 1786 he made himself highly unpopular by refusing to serve as town constable, an act that prompted the grand jury to sentence him to jail for contempt of court. Later in the same year he again revealed the cantankerous side of his character when appearing before the loyalist claims commission. Presenting a testimonial from no less a personage than the mayor of New York City, Bruff claimed almost £4,000 in compensation for the loss of more than 3,000 acres in Maryland and 25 acres of silver and

Bruneau

lead mines in Pennsylvania. The commission, finding these claims wildly extravagant, repeatedly warned Bruff of possible charges of perjury, and one of the judges wrote on his account of the proceedings that "the man is insane." Eventually Bruff was awarded an additional land grant in Lunenburg County but he failed to obtain compensation in cash – a failure that became all the more difficult to bear when he learned shortly afterwards that he and his brother Peter Schuyler had been disinherited by their father.

Little is known about Bruff's life from the 1790s until the time of his death in 1817. There is reason to believe that by the early 1790s he was no longer practising his craft, for in the Shelburne assessment rolls of 1792 and 1793 he is described as a "tinker." He may have moved to Liverpool in 1794: on 30 Dec. 1793 Simeon PERKINS noted in his diary that "one Mr. Bruf, of Shelburne . . . has agreed to set up his Business here . . . is about to take Capt. Zebulon Perkins House for £6 a year." The next mention of his name in documentary sources occurs in 1817, when his death in Liverpool at the age of 82 was commented upon in the *Acadian Recorder* of Halifax. Only one example of his craftsmanship has been found in Nova Scotia. Now in the possession of the Nova Scotia Museum, it is a two-handled wafer-iron for the communion host with cross-hatched discs five and three-quarter inches in diameter. The inscription around the border reads "Charles Oliver Bruff – Maker."

DONALD C. MACKAY

PAC, MG 9, B9, 14 (incomplete photocopy at PANS). PANS, MG 4, 140 (photocopy); 141 (typescript); RG 1, 444–44½; RG 34-321, P, 1. PRO, AO 13, bundle 11 (copies at PAC). *The arts and crafts in New York: advertisements and news items from New York City newspapers*, comp. R. S. Gottesman (3v., New York, 1938–54), 1–2. Perkins, *Diary, 1790–96* (Fergusson); *Diary, 1797–1803* (Fergusson). "United Empire Loyalists: enquiry into losses and services," AO *Report*, 1904: 139–41. *Acadian Recorder*, 8 Feb. 1817. *Royal American Gazette* (Shelburne, N.S.), 24, 31 Jan. 1785. Marion Gilroy, *Loyalists and land settlement in Nova Scotia* (Halifax, 1937). J. E. Langdon, *American silversmiths in British North America, 1776–1800* (Toronto, 1970); *Canadian silversmiths & their marks, 1667–1867* (Lunenburg, Vt., 1960). D. C. Mackay, *Silversmiths and related craftsmen of the Atlantic provinces* (Halifax, 1973). Sabine, *Biog. sketches of loyalists*, 2: 487. H. B. Dawson, *New York City during the American revolution . . .* (New York, 1861). J. M. Phillips, *American silver* (London, 1949). Harry Piers, *Master goldsmiths and silversmiths of Nova Scotia and their marks . . .*, ed. U. B. Thompson *et al.* (Halifax, 1948). J. H. Pleasants and Howard Sill, *Maryland silversmiths, 1715–1830 . . .* (Baltimore, Md., 1930).

BRUNEAU, PIERRE, merchant, politician, and militia officer; b. 22 July 1761 at Quebec, son of Pierre-Guillaume Bruneau, a merchant-furrier, and Marie-Élizabeth Morin, *dit* Chêneverd; m. there 30 Aug. 1785 Marie-Anne Robitaille, and they had seven children; d. 13 April 1820 in his native town.

Pierre Bruneau spent his childhood at Quebec and at an early age became involved with the trade in fur goods through his father, who had had a shop in Lower Town since at least 1758. Wanting to follow in his father's footsteps in the business field, he first studied at the Petit Séminaire de Québec from 1771 to 1780. Presumably he learned bookkeeping while subsequently working in his father's shop, since the management of the latter's "business in pelts" was entrusted to him in 1786. That year Pierre-Guillaume Bruneau had decided to return to his native town of Poitiers, which he had left in 1754 to come to New France. Pierre quickly expanded the company's scope, in particular by going into trade in grain, cloth, and spirits. He seems to have been quite prosperous in his business affairs, sufficiently so that in 1791 he could pay 9,000 *livres* for a big stone house on the Place du Marché (Place Notre-Dame), near the harbour at Quebec, to serve as his residence and as premises for a store of his own.

In 1794 Bruneau was one of those signing the loyalist manifesto, a sort of act of faith in the British authorities in the face of a supposed threat that revolutionary France would stir up popular unrest in the colony. Two years earlier Bruneau had joined the Quebec militia as an ensign. Probably because of his loyalty to the crown the government granted him 400 acres in Nelson Township in 1804. At the same period he opened a second store at Chambly and increased his purchases of grain.

Around 1802, in search of new opportunities for investment, Bruneau had bought two houses on Rue Sainte-Famille and one on Rue Saint-François, which he then rented at £40 to £50. In 1806 one of the houses on Rue Sainte-Famille was converted by the tenant into a hospital for British soldiers. In order to finance his commercial enterprise Bruneau had to resort fairly regularly to loans from British shipowners and rich merchants. In 1807, as a result of overestimating his ability to repay, he found himself in debt to Quebec merchant James TOD for £6,351. To get out of this impasse he promised to sell the three properties on Rue Sainte-Famille and Rue Saint-François and turn over the proceeds to his creditor, and to pay him £250 a year until 1812, failing which all his assets were to be seized. This precarious situation forced Bruneau to consider new solutions for making his firm more profitable. Consequently in April 1807 he hired Charles Labbé, a journeyman muff-maker, who worked at making fur articles under the direction of Mme Bruneau. But seven months later Labbé was imprisoned for defaulting on his contracts; released on bail, he nevertheless went back to work for Bruneau. In any case, the 148 fur hats that Bruneau shipped to Rivière-Ouelle in August 1812 seem to indicate a new burst of activity in his enterprise. Even more revealing is the fact that in 1814 he succeeded in repaying his debt to James Tod. However, he still owed £1,246 to the firm of Brehaut and Sheppard [see Pierre BREHAUT], which had supplied him with spirits and other goods.

From 1810 to 1816 Bruneau represented Quebec's Lower Town in the House of Assembly of Lower Canada. As a member, he sided with the Canadian party, particularly when it was necessary to stand up for the assembly's privileges. During the War of 1812 he served in the forces defending the colony as major of Quebec's 2nd Militia Battalion. This detachment assured the defence of Quebec and carried out reconnaissance missions in the surrounding regions. Early in 1816, hostilities with the United States having ended, Bruneau sent his electors a manifesto in which he rejected the principle of judges being eligible to sit on the Legislative Council. This question, which also roused the ire of the Canadian party, brought about the dissolution of the house by Sir George Gordon Drummond*. In the ensuing elections Bruneau was beaten in his riding by François Languedoc*. He tried without success to contest his opponent's election on grounds of fraud and intimidation. In April 1816 he succeeded, however, in getting elected by acclamation in Kent, which he represented until his death.

Engrossed in his political activity, Bruneau increasingly delegated the management of his business affairs to people competent in the field. Thus on 23 May 1815 he hired William Morin as a clerk at a salary of £60 a year; for his part Morin was to see to the smooth operation of the stores at Quebec and Chambly, concentrating mainly on buying and shipping grain. Three years later Bruneau gave his wife power of attorney to administer his affairs. On 9 April 1820, four days before his death, he bequeathed to her the usufruct of all his property. In 1810 he had already made over to his son René-Olivier the sum of 3,000 livres in the form of an annuity to help him enter holy orders. Of his other children, Julie married Louis-Joseph Papineau* in 1818, and Théophile became a lawyer and Patriote.

Pierre Bruneau was active in the community as a member of the Quebec Fire Society from 1790 to 1820 and as churchwarden of the parish of Notre-Dame from 1807 to 1814. When he died the *Quebec Gazette* commented appreciatively, "This excellent man brought to trade [and] to private life a courteousness and gentleness of character such that he deservedly never earned any enemies and rightly had many friends."

IN COLLABORATION

ANQ-Q, CE1-1, 30 janv. 1758, 22 juill. 1761, 30 août 1785, 15 avril 1820; CN1-224, 15 juill. 1786; CN1-230, 3 mars 1791, 1er avril 1816, 9 avril 1820; CN1-262, 12 mai 1806; 6 févr., 23 avril 1807; 23 août 1810; 2 août 1812; 19 oct. 1814; 23 avril 1815; 7 juill. 1818. ASQ, Fichier des anciens. *Doc. relatifs à l'hist. constitutionnelle, 1791–1818* (Doughty et McArthur; 1915), 492n. "Cahier des témoignages de liberté au mariage commencé le 15 avril 1757," ANQ *Rapport*, 1951–53: 39. *Quebec Gazette*, 10 July 1794; 30 Dec. 1813; 14 March, 4 April 1816; 17 April 1820. Ægidius Fauteux, *Patriotes de 1837–1838* (Montréal, 1950), 148. Langelier, *Liste de terrains concédés*, 600, 1199. *Officers of British forces in Canada* (Irving), 143. *Quebec almanac*, 1792–1820. P.-G. Roy, *Fils de Québec* (4 sér., Lévis, Qué., 1933), 2: 127. Chapais, *Cours d'hist. du Canada*, 3: 23–24. Henri Têtu, "L'abbé André Doucet, curé de Québec, 1807–1814," *BRH*, 13 (1907): 18.

BRUNET, *dit* L'Estang (L'Étang), VÉRONIQUE, named **Sainte-Rose** (she signed **Verronique Létant**), sister of the Congregation of Notre-Dame and superior (superior general); b. 13 Jan. 1726 in Pointe-Claire (Que.), daughter of Jean Brunet, *dit* L'Estang, and Marguerite Dubois; d. 12 June 1810 in Montreal, Lower Canada.

Véronique Brunet, *dit* L'Estang, came from one of the eight families named Brunet that immigrated to Canada during the second half of the 17th century; three of these added the names L'Estang, Bourbonnais, and Bellehumeur. Véronique entered the noviciate of the Congregation of Notre-Dame in Montreal in 1744 and made her profession two years later under the name of Sister Sainte-Rose. She then went as a missionary in turn to the Lower Town in Quebec, Pointe-aux-Trembles (Neuville), and Sainte-Famille on Île d'Orléans. She was back in Quebec when the town was captured by the British in 1759; at that time, it is reported, she was advised "to remain hidden as far as possible because of her great beauty and . . . other visible charms," lest in walking about town as usual she attract the attention of the strangers, in whose presence people did not always feel safe.

In 1771 Sister Sainte-Rose was called back to the house in Montreal to assume the office of assistant to the superior, Sister de l'Assomption [Marie-Josèphe Maugue-Garreau*]. The following year she became superior. The community was then facing numerous financial difficulties, largely because of the political events of the previous two decades and a fire in 1768. The new superior strove to increase the community's resources by assigning more sisters to such money-making projects as church repairs, laundering, and embroidery. In 1773 the sisters were able to take advantage of the housing of the Collège Saint-Raphaël in the Château de Vaudreuil [see Jean-Baptiste Curatteau*] to acquire supplementary income: they puttied most of the casement windows and made the bulk of the aiguillettes worn by the schoolboys.

The missions also were feeling the effects of the difficult times. The Lac-des-Deux-Montagnes (Oka) mission, where the sisters' work had been supported until the conquest through a royal gratuity of 3,000

Bruyeres

livres annually, was maintained after 1760 solely through private grants, particularly those from the generous missionary François-Auguste Magon* de Terlaye. Sister Sainte-Rose solved the financial problem by signing an agreement with the Sulpician seminary on 14 July 1772. In return for performing specific tasks, the foremost being teaching in the mission's schools for girls, the sisters were to receive from the seminary 200 *piastres* a year and certain goods in kind: the pure wheaten flour and the bran from 45 bushels of wheat, 12 cords of sound wood, hay for feeding 2 cows over the winter, and free pasture during the summer. However, the community's poverty prevented the mother house from offering direct financial assistance to the missions, even in the most difficult situations. Thus, when in 1776 the sisters at the Pointe-aux-Trembles mission had to rebuild their convent, which had been destroyed by the American troops under Benedict ARNOLD after the attack on Quebec, they admitted to Bishop Briand* of Quebec that they were undergoing many privations in order not to ask for anything from the community, "which was itself very hard up."

In 1778, when her term as superior came to an end and Marie RAIZENNE, named Saint-Ignace, took office, Sister Sainte-Rose was elected mistress of novices; she held this post until 1784, when she again became superior. By then the colony as a whole was benefiting from the state of peace. Boarding pupils were returning to Montreal in numbers and, following a decision of the council on 20 Sept. 1786, the superior sent away the day-boarders whom the community had resigned itself to taking in 1771. Relieved of the heavy financial worries that had marked her first term as superior, Sister Sainte-Rose gave her attention to clarifying certain points in the rule that concerned, among other things, the vow of permanence and the status of the sisters who did the rough work. Few changes were instituted in the missions. The one in Lachine, where the convent was falling into ruin and had few pupils, moved to Pointe-Claire in 1784. The Champlain mission near Trois-Rivières, which had been forced to suspend work three times since its founding in 1676 and which was experiencing problems similar to those in Lachine, closed down permanently in 1788.

After leaving the superiorship in 1790 Sister Sainte-Rose became assistant mistress of novices and for two years served as first counsellor. As well, she turned to giving religious instruction to Montreal girls who lacked the time and means to attend regular classes; in this way she took part in the congregation's efforts to offer "adult education," a service for which modern democratized education would like to claim the credit. Towards the end of her life she devoted her energies to washing and mending the clothes of the servant girls whom the community employed for

meagre wages and supplied with their keep. Sister Sainte-Rose, who had twice been superior general of the community, attended to these tasks until her long life came to an end in 1810, after 66 years in the Congregation of Notre-Dame.

ANDRÉE DÉSILETS

ANQ-M, CE1-37, 14 janv. 1726. Arch. de la Congrégation de Notre-Dame (Montréal), Fichier général; Personnel, V; Reg. général. Archange Godbout, "Nos ancêtres au XVIIᵉ siècle," ANQ *Rapport*, 1957–59: 393. Tanguay, *Dictionnaire*, 1: 94–95; 2: 496, 500; 5: 373–74. Lemire-Marsolais et Lambert, *Hist. de la CND de Montréal*, 5; 6: 205–6. Trudel, *L'Église canadienne*, 2: 338, 340, 347.

BRUYERES, RALPH HENRY, military engineer; b. *c.* 1765 in Montreal, Que., son of John Bruyères* and Catherine-Élisabeth Pommereau; m. there 16 April 1790 Janet Dunbar, daughter of Captain William Dunbar; d. 15 May 1814 at Quebec, Lower Canada, survived by his wife and four children.

Ralph Henry Bruyeres was the son of a Huguenot who had come to Canada during the Seven Years' War as an officer in the British army and who had settled there afterwards, and of the co-heiress of the seigneury of Bécancour. He was commissioned a second lieutenant in the engineers on 22 Dec. 1781. The date of his first assignment is unknown, but it is recorded that he was serving as a supernumerary engineer at Quebec in 1784. Promoted first lieutenant on 24 May 1790 and captain-lieutenant on 31 Dec. 1795, he achieved the rank of captain on 1 July 1799. Bruyeres saw active service in Flanders in 1793 and in the Netherlands in 1799, and after a brief sojourn at Dover, England, returned to Lower Canada. He reported for duty at Montreal in July 1800, but was soon transferred to Quebec.

In the spring of 1802 Bruyeres was dispatched on a tour of inspection in Upper Canada, an exercise which gave him invaluable insights into the problem of defending the immense reach of frontier between Montreal and the Niagara River. His formal reactions were embodied in a "Report of the state of the public works and buildings at the several military posts in Upper Canada" addressed to Colonel Gother Mann*, commanding engineer in the Canadas. This document presented a dismal picture of neglect and decay but, although its author made many recommendations for remedial action based on current or future estimates, they apparently had only minimal effect since official policy necessitated that the meagre funds available for defensive works should be expended at Quebec.

Bruyeres became commanding engineer in the Canadas on his promotion to lieutenant-colonel on 1 July 1806, Mann having left in 1804. Like Mann, he was frustrated by a lack of funds, but by 1807 the deterioration in Anglo-American relations [*see* Sir George Cranfield BERKELEY] convinced him that at least the first phase of Mann's plan for Quebec – an advance work of four interdependent towers ranged across the Plains of Abraham – should be implemented immediately. He planned to use adaptations of the formidable towers erected in Halifax, N.S., under the direction of the Duke of Kent [EDWARD AUGUSTUS], but Sir James Henry CRAIG, who became governor in chief of British North America in 1807, preferred the Martello type then favoured in Britain for coastal defence. With this change in plan Bruyeres was authorized to proceed. His great work was completed early in 1812, by which time Craig had been succeeded by Sir George PREVOST.

The outbreak of war with the United States on 18 June 1812 forced Bruyeres to concentrate on the frontier posts, in particular Kingston, Upper Canada, which, although it was the headquarters of the marine establishment on the lakes, remained undefended. On 19 Jan. 1813 he reported to Prevost on the state of Kingston, affirming that he had ordered the immediate strengthening of its defences, and for its protection urged an early attack on the rival American base at Sackets Harbor, N.Y. His report of 13 February on York (Toronto) and the Niagara frontier commented adversely on York as a naval base since he considered its site not properly defensible. On 1 March he was granted the acting rank of colonel in Upper Canada, and on 1 September Prevost ordered that he be detained in that province indefinitely. In the mean time Bruyeres had received urgently needed reinforcements: several engineers and a substantial detachment of the Royal Sappers and Miners. A severe illness forced him to return to Quebec during the autumn, but while he was still convalescent news of the British capture of Fort Niagara (near Youngstown, N.Y.) in December persuaded him to return to Upper Canada. He supervised repairs to the fort and then, in severe winter weather, returned to Quebec fatally ill. His obituary in the *Quebec Mercury* described him as a meritorious officer "fallen victim to professional zeal" who was a "good citizen of Quebec." In his will he left his immediate family the sum of £14,500, a not inconsiderable fortune in 1814.

JOHN W. SPURR

PAC, RG 8, I (C ser.), 387, 512, 692, 1170, 1220–1, 1227. PRO, PROB 11/1580/505. *Select British docs. of War of 1812* (Wood), vol.2. *Quebec Mercury*, 17 May 1814. *Roll of officers of the Corps of Royal Engineers from 1660 to 1898 . . .*, ed. R. F. Edwards (Chatham, Eng., 1898). Hitsman, *Incredible War of 1812*. Whitworth Porter *et al.*, *History of the Corps of Royal Engineers* (9v. to date, London and Chatham, 1889– ; vols.1–3 repr. Chatham, 1951–54), 1. Gérard Malchelosse, "La famille Pommereau et ses alliances," *Cahiers des Dix*, 29 (1964): 193–222. I. J.

Saunders, "A history of Martello towers in the defence of British North America, 1796–1871," *Canadian Hist. Sites*, no.15 (1976): 5–170.

BUCHANAN, MALCOLM BÀN. *See* MACMHANNAIN, CALUM BÀN

BULLEY, SAMUEL, ship's captain and merchant; b. probably 1737, son of John Bulley of Abbotskerswell, England; m. 1766 Joanna Wood, and they had four sons and four daughters; d. between 1806 and 1809 in Teignmouth, England.

The firm of Bulley and Job was one of a dozen which arose in and around the town of Teignmouth between 1770 and 1820, all owing their existence to the Newfoundland fishery, and especially the deep-sea fishery on the Grand Banks. The Bulleys, together with almost every other family in the region, had been connected with the Newfoundland fishery for generations, but few had ever derived wealth or status from the trade, particularly when compared with the merchants of Poole, Topsham, or Dartmouth. Their opportunity came with the end of the Seven Years' War, which signalled an expansion in the Newfoundland fishery lasting for nearly 30 years and allowed many servants, ship's captains, bye-boat keepers, and planters to rise in the world. The men from the villages around Teignmouth chose as their vehicle the bank fishery, which expanded rapidly after 1763. Entry was easy because the vessels were small and cheap, whilst the profit from fishing was enlarged by that which came from transporting the horde of servants and bye-boat keepers who migrated annually between the British Isles and Newfoundland.

The early career of Samuel Bulley is uncertain, mainly because there were three persons of this name operating from Devon to Newfoundland between 1750 and 1780. He probably began as an apprentice to one of the Devon bye-boat keepers or shipowners, but in 1770 he obtained a vessel of his own, which he commanded for five years in the bank fishery. He was probably in partnership with the Wilking family, owners of a plantation in St John's. The War of American Independence must have caused great problems for Bulley since between 1775 and 1783 his name disappears both as a shipowner and as a visitor to Newfoundland. He probably became a junior partner in the firm of Samuel Cocking and Company. However, with the end of the war Bulley formed a new partnership with Daniel Codner of Kingskerswell and Elias Rendell of Combeinteignhead. In 1788 John Job, who seems to have been brought up by Bulley after he was orphaned in 1766 and had served his apprenticeship as a cooper, was sent to St John's to manage the Newfoundland end of the trade. Soon afterwards Job married one of Bulley's daughters and became a partner in the company. By 1796 Codner

Bunbury

and Rendell had dropped out and the firm took on the title of Bulley and Job. Bulley's two eldest sons, Samuel and Thomas, were now in their teens and in 1797 Samuel Jr was sent to Newfoundland as agent under the tutelage of John Job. A year later Thomas, at the age of 18, became commander of the firm's brig *Flora*. In 1799 the *Flora*, with Job and the two boys on board, was taken by a French privateer on the voyage out to Newfoundland. They returned to England only after an uncomfortable captivity of six months. This set-back must have sorely tried Samuel Bulley, who was left with no one to organize the trade in St John's. Despite it, and despite other wartime losses, the firm seems to have flourished, for whilst the Dartmouth and Poole merchants were reducing their trade under the impact of the war, Bulley and Job steadily increased in size. Their shipping fleet, for example, averaged but one vessel a year between 1786 and 1793; between 1798 and 1806 they averaged four.

When the Treaty of Amiens was signed in 1802, Samuel Bulley could look back with relief, if not pleasure, upon the survival of his business during the long war years. However, times were changing: the bank fishery, seriously hit by enemy attacks and by the depredations of naval press-gangs, which pressed many of the most experienced seamen, was declining rapidly. At the same time the whole of the west-of-England–Newfoundland connection was weakening as the resident population in Newfoundland increased and the Industrial Revolution was expanding the manufactories of northern and central England at the expense of those established in the West Country. As a result the trade to Newfoundland was increasingly being organized from Liverpool and London rather than from Dartmouth, Exeter, or Poole. In 1805 the firm made a decision which was to prove its salvation: John Job and Bulley's youngest son, William Wilking, opened a branch in Liverpool. Samuel Sr probably had little to do with the decision for by now he was seriously ill. He died soon after, leaving Job and his sons with a modest fortune and a secure base for the future.

K. MATTHEWS

Devon Record Office, 53/6, box 34, will of Daniel Codner of Kingskerswell, 1798; 2954A; 3119A; 3289S/1–2; 3419A; 3420A; Exeter City Arch., town customs accounts, 1750–1806. Maritime Hist. Group Arch., Keith Matthews, "Profiles of Water Street merchants" (typescript, 1980). PANL, GN 2/1; P5/11. PRO, ADM 7/154–55; 7/363–400; BT 98/3–17; CO 194. St James Anglican Church (Teignmouth, Eng.), West Teignmouth, parish records. *Lloyd's List. London Evening-Post. Public Advertiser* (London). *Trewman's Exeter Flying Post, or Plymouth and Cornish Advertiser* (Exeter). *Whitehall Evening-Post or London Intelligencer* (London). Keith Matthews, *A "who was who" of families engaged in the fisheries and settlement of Newfoundland, 1660–1840* ([St John's], 1971). *Reg. of shipping*. C. G. Head, *Eighteenth century Newfoundland: a geographer's perspective* (Toronto, 1976). Keith Matthews, "A history of the west of England–Newfoundland fishery" (PHD thesis, Univ. of Oxford, 1968); *Lectures on the history of Newfoundland: 1500–1830* (St John's, 1973).

BUNBURY, JOSEPH, army officer and Indian Department official; fl. 1773–1802.

Joseph Bunbury became an ensign in the 49th Foot on 20 Feb. 1773 and a lieutenant on 14 Jan. 1775, during which year he presumably accompanied the regiment to North America. On 13 April 1782 he was promoted captain in the same regiment in Ireland. One anecdote relates that during a dinner at Dublin Castle he and the Duke of Rutland, lord lieutenant of Ireland, "happened to get drunk together," and in the course of the evening Rutland offered him a vacant captaincy in the 5th Foot, although it had already been promised to David William Smith*. Certainly on 24 Dec. 1785 Bunbury transferred to a captaincy in the 5th, with which he probably arrived at Quebec on 26 July 1787. On 14 May 1789 he became "Officer Commanding Kingston and its Dependencies," a post which included responsibility for Carleton Island (N.Y.) and Oswegatchie (Ogdensburg, N.Y.). He held this important command when the Kingston dockyard came into existence and in fact he may have helped bring about a decision on its exact location by seeking approval for the building of a new wharf.

Bunbury probably accompanied his regiment to Detroit (Mich.) when he left Kingston at the end of July 1790. While stationed in Detroit he undertook a variety of duties, such as presiding over a board of survey into the condition of Fort Lernoult. In June 1792 the 5th Foot was posted to Fort Niagara (near Youngstown, N.Y.), where it remained until the fort was handed over to the United States four years later. Also in the summer of 1792, Bunbury seems to have travelled between Detroit, Fort Erie (Ont.), Niagara, and the rapids of the Miamis River (Maumee, Ohio) on behalf of the army, the Indian Department, and Lieutenant Governor SIMCOE. The area was a critical one in these years, for the conflict between the Americans and the Delawares, Shawnees, Miamis, and other western tribes over the Ohio country was coming to a head [see MICHIKINAKOUA; WEYAPIERSENWAH] and the British were deeply concerned about the outcome. In the summer of 1793 Simcoe ordered that Bunbury, because of his acquaintance with the western Indians, join lieutenants Prideaux SELBY and James Givins* in accompanying the United States commissioners who were on their way to the rapids of the Miamis to discuss boundaries with the Indians. In February 1794 Bunbury attended a council at Buffalo Creek (N.Y.) where representatives of the Six Nations and the western Indians discussed land cessions with the Americans. On 15 June 1794 Simcoe praised him in a letter to Lord Dorchester [Guy CARLETON] for helping to resolve a dispute between Joseph Brant [THAYENDANEGEA] and another Six Nations chief. "I am much indebted on this and many other occasions to the assistance of Captain Bunbury," wrote Simcoe. Meanwhile, on 1 March 1794 Bunbury had been promoted major and on 22 July 1794 he signed a document at Niagara in his capacity as president of a committee of five officers detailed to examine the stores landed at that place by the *Mississauga*.

In August 1794 reports that an American army under Major-General Anthony Wayne had advanced as far as the Glaize (Defiance, Ohio) prompted Simcoe to order Bunbury to Turtle Island, at the mouth of the Miamis (Maumee) River, with a detachment from the 5th Foot and the Queen's Rangers. This site was considered by many the best point at which to meet any American threat to Canada's southwestern frontier. Wayne defeated the Indians at the battle of Fallen Timbers (near Waterville, Ohio) on 20 August but then withdrew most of his army, and British troops in the area did not take any part in the fighting. Before the end of the month Bunbury had led part of his force to Fort Miamis (Maumee), the post nearest the battlefield, at the request of Major William Campbell, whose garrison was depleted by sickness. Campbell himself became ill and Bunbury had to assume command of that post as well as Turtle Island. By the time Simcoe arrived a month later Bunbury, along with six other officers, was also unwell. Early in October he sailed for Fort Erie.

In 1795 Bunbury continued his interest in Indian matters; in March he was present along with John Butler*, deputy superintendent of the Six Nations, at Newark (Niagara-on-the-Lake), Upper Canada, when Red Jacket [Sagoyewatha*] and two other Seneca chiefs from Buffalo Creek reported on a meeting with the Americans. Shortly thereafter he was made an aide-de-camp to Simcoe and expressed a wish for a permanent position in the Indian Department. On 21 July 1796 he was appointed agent of Indian affairs in Lower Canada.

After this appointment there is little information to be found on Bunbury. On 1 Jan. 1798 he was promoted lieutenant-colonel and shortly afterwards returned to Britain – on a leave of absence, as he reportedly claimed later. This move was apparently at an inopportune time, and he seems to have become involved in the internal politics of the Indian Department. On 24 Oct. 1800 John Chew wrote to Prideaux Selby from Montreal: "What will be done next I do not know, but I think our friend Bunbury Stands some Chance of being Superceded without he plays his Cards well in England. . . ." Evidently he did not, for on 6 June 1801 the Home secretary, the Duke of Portland, approved Lieutenant Governor Sir Robert Shore Milnes*'s February recommendation that Bunbury be replaced. The last mention of him is in a letter dated 24 April 1802.

Little is known of Bunbury's private life, save a reference in March 1801 to his marriage to the 16-year-old daughter of an unnamed attorney. Although there is no assessment of his performance as an Indian agent, he was not infrequently praised as an army officer, particularly by Simcoe, who on one occasion in 1794 ranked him and four other captains in Canada as "probably second to no men in their respective ranks and situations."

CARL CHRISTIE

PAC, MG 11, [CO 42] Q, 86-1: 132; MG 19, F1, 5: 41–42, 157–60, 165–70, 175–85, 191–93, 255, 263, 275–77, 295, 297–300; 6: 205–8; 8: 56–57, 131–32; RG 8, I (C ser.), 249: 348; 511: 1v, 1½, 6, 79–80; RG 10, A1, 1–4; 486: 3856–57; A2, 8–12; B8, 768: 10; 10019: 135; 10020: 16. *Corr. of Lieut. Governor Simcoe* (Cruikshank). *John Askin papers* (Quaife). *Kingston before War of 1812* (Preston). G.B., WO, *Army list*, 1774, 1777, 1783, 1787, 1795, 1799. *The service of British regiments in Canada and North America . . .*, comp. C. H. Stewart ([2nd ed.], Ottawa, 1964). Horsman, *Matthew Elliott*. H. M. Walker, *A history of the Northumberland Fusiliers, 1674–1902* (London, 1919), 198.

BURBIDGE, JOHN, soldier, landowner, office holder, militia officer, judge, and politician; b. *c.* 1718 in Cowes, England; m. first Elizabeth —; m. secondly 14 Oct. 1775 Rebecca Dudley, widow of Benjamin Gerrish*; there were no children of either marriage; d. 11 March 1812 in Cornwallis, N.S.

Little is known of John Burbidge prior to his arrival in North America. He was at Louisbourg, Cape Breton Island, in 1747, where he was one of the "Serjeants [acting] as Foremen" of artisans, and he came to Halifax at its founding in 1749, reputedly erecting the first frame-house in the settlement. He removed from Halifax to Cornwallis about 1764 and through his active acquisition of land came to possess a 300-acre farm called Bilkington Park. On it he is reputed to have introduced the Nonpareil and Golden Russet apples and to have developed a pear which received his name.

During his lengthy life Burbidge held many positions. He was clerk to Richard Bulkeley*, the paymaster of public works at Halifax, in 1753 and overseer of public works in 1759, was elected a churchwarden at St Paul's in 1760, and the same year was appointed clerk of the market house. The following year he was named a justice of the peace for Halifax County, and in 1762 a captain in the Halifax militia. Upon his removal to Cornwallis he became major of the Kings County militia, justice of the peace, collector of customs, and the county's first

Burke

registrar of deeds. On 18 Oct. 1776 he was named a judge of the Inferior Court of Common Pleas, and in 1792 colonel commandant of the county militia. Burbidge also served as a member of the House of Assembly on two occasions: between 1759 and 1765 for Halifax Township and between 1765 and 1770 for Cornwallis Township.

Burbidge was an active and devout member of the Church of England, and through the nomination of the archbishop of Canterbury was named a member of the Society for the Propagation of the Gospel on 16 July 1784. He was a founder of the Church of St John in Cornwallis, and donated the land and substantial sums of money for it. In 1802, when the congregation decided to build a new church, their effort was aided by a generous donation from Burbidge as well as a bequest from Benjamin BELCHER. The old Fox Hill cemetery was also situated on land Burbidge had presented. His letters to the society were a constant call for greater effort and diligence on the part of the Anglican clergy, who he felt were being outdone by the dissenting ministers.

During the American revolution Burbidge warned that the "violent and audacious Robery" carried on by American privateers off the coast could seriously reduce the amount of fresh provisions which the area provided to Halifax, and in 1778 he was successful in persuading the authorities to erect a barracks and station troops at Cornwallis. At the close of the conflict he led the complaints when New England beef was permitted to flood the Halifax market and drive prices down. In 1784 he unsuccessfully appealed for the reservation of lands for prominent loyalists.

The same year Burbidge suffered a severe knee injury, which for a time restricted his activities and probably contributed to his request in 1785 that additional judges be appointed to the bench. The calendar of the Inferior Court of Common Pleas for that year included 67 civil cases plus regular business, which forced the judges to sit seven hours a day for five days a week.

Burbidge's final years appear to have been tranquil. In 1790 he drew up a memorandum freeing his slaves, provided them each with two sets of clothes (including one for Sunday), and ordered that they be taught to read. He is reputed to have entertained Prince EDWARD AUGUSTUS when the latter was en route from Halifax to Annapolis Royal in 1794. Although his hearing was apparently poor, he remained active. As late as 1807 he was corresponding with the SPG and the following year he travelled to Wilmot with the elderly John WISWALL and returned under a "Scorching Sun." Burbidge died in his 95th year and was buried in the Fox Hill cemetery. The net value of his estate exceeded £1,500, which he left to various nephews and nieces and their children.

ALLAN C. DUNLOP

Acadia Univ. Arch. (Wolfville, N.S.), "The Burbidge family, Kings County, Nova Scotia," comp. B. R. Bishop (typescript, n.d.). Kings County Court of Probate (Kentville, N.S.), Book 2: 38–41 (will of John Burbidge, 1 Dec. 1810) (mfm. at PANS). PANS, MG 1, 161; E. L. Eaton, "The Sheffield farm and other properties in Cornwallis Township" (typescript, 1961). A. W. H. Eaton, *The history of Kings County, Nova Scotia . . .* (Salem, Mass., 1910; repr. Belleville, Ont., 1972). Fingard, *Anglican design in loyalist N.S.*

BURKE (Bourk, Bourke, DeBurgo), EDMUND, Roman Catholic priest, Dominican, and vicar general; b. in Ireland, apparently in County Tipperary; fl. 1785–1801.

Edmund Burke arrived in Newfoundland on 15 June 1785 as a young priest recommended to the Newfoundland mission's first superior, James Louis O'DONEL, by the bishop of Waterford. O'Donel himself had come to St John's just a year earlier, as had the island's only other authorized priest, Patrick Phelan at Harbour Grace. Burke became parish priest of Placentia, a district with a substantial Roman Catholic majority.

The circumstances of Burke's appointment disclosed O'Donel's difficulties in asserting authority over the vagrant clerics in his jurisdiction. Also at Placentia in 1785 was Father Patrick Lonergan (Landergan), another Dominican, who had come to Newfoundland from France that same year. Lonergan, a man "of very violent and turbulent spirit," not only exercised his spiritual functions in competition with Burke, but also endangered the church's standing by assaulting a Protestant and by "tumultuously" assembling a party of Catholics. O'Donel excommunicated Lonergan, and complaints about him went from Placentia to Governor John Campbell, who ordered his removal from Newfoundland the same year. Although Lonergan remained, he died wretchedly on Fogo Island shortly thereafter.

Burke, however, had considerable initial success at Placentia. With the cooperation of Saunders and Company, which collected money from its Roman Catholic servants, he obtained both a house and land for a chapel in 1785 and, with the governor's permission, construction of the chapel began almost immediately. In the mean time, Burke was allowed to hold services in the court-house. Even in his first year he made a number of converts from the Church of England.

Burke's status brought him to the attention of the new surrogate, Prince William Henry, who arrived in Placentia in 1786 as captain of the *Pegasus*. The prince soon noted that "more Respect and Regard tis shewn him . . . than either the Surrogate himself or any of the Justices of the Peace." Confronted by this indication of priestly power, William Henry took immediate steps to counteract it. He decreed that Roman Catholics were to be especially attentive to the magistrates and that no Protestants were to be married or have their children christened by the priest. He forbad use of the court-house for Catholic services and, indeed, called into question Burke's authorization to build a chapel. Apparently at O'Donel's request, Governor John Elliot intervened to ask that William Henry be more moderate in his dealings with Catholics, but this resulted only in the prince's wrath being redirected towards Burke's superior. Arriving in St John's, he threatened to burn the chapel there and went so far as to throw an iron file at O'Donel, slightly wounding him. With the prince's departure the affair subsided, but it showed how tenuous was the footing of the Catholic clergy in Newfoundland.

Nevertheless, Burke's mission flourished. By 1788 he had three chapels in his district, including a "very neat" one at Placentia itself. His parishioners numbered more than 3,000 and Burke, who was engaged in the fishing business, had an estimated annual income of £300. That same year Placentia's newly arrived Anglican clergyman, John HARRIES, noted with alarm that so strong was Roman Catholicism that it was effectively "the establish'd religion, and our own Church within the limits of Toleration." Conversions from the Church of England continued; in 1791 Burke was reported to have made many converts as far away as Fortune Bay.

Late in 1791 Burke became ill, and he was obliged to spend several months in England before he recovered. From 1795 he appears to have had an interest in an appointment in the United States; he even visited there in that connection. Finally he left Placentia for Boston, probably in 1798, but then declined a good appointment. The next year he went instead to Halifax, N.S., which he had visited several times before. So extensive was the migration of Newfoundland Irish from Placentia to Halifax in this period that they now constituted the majority of Halifax Catholics. James JONES, the superior of missions in the Maritime colonies, asked Burke to replace him, convinced that the Dominican was the fittest person to manage his unruly congregation. Burke assumed this responsibility upon Jones's departure in August 1800. Although it was not then clear that Jones would not return, Bishop Pierre DENAUT officially appointed Burke parish priest of Halifax and vicar general of Nova Scotia on 25 September.

Immediately after Jones's leaving, Burke faced a major crisis. The committee of seven elders elected to administer parish temporalities became dominated by John Stealing, who thought the parish had been "priest-ridden" under Jones. Burke had given the committee a free hand with finances, but Stealing went farther in asserting his authority. He had the committee accept his own set of rules for parish government, which included the removal of the priest at pleasure and the denial of Christian burial to non-contributors. The latter regulation provoked a confrontation with the congregation, who believed the committee to have exceeded its authority and who in May 1801 protested to Bishop Denaut. Denaut's coadjutor, Joseph-Octave Plessis*, felt that Burke had blundered in his dealings with the committee, although Burke claimed that he had first seen the new rules only several months after their adoption and that in the mean time he had had to contend with a serious smallpox epidemic and with an attack of rheumatism which had left him bedridden for some months. The dispute was settled only by a pastoral letter of Denaut in September, which censured several of the committee's rules. By May 1801, when Jones's intention not to return to Nova Scotia had become apparent, Burke felt himself relieved of any commitment to Halifax. He asked Plessis to replace him so that he could return to Europe and left Halifax that autumn, apparently for England. Nothing is known of his subsequent career. He was succeeded at Halifax by a secular priest, also named Edmund BURKE.

Burke could be innovative. At Halifax he read the Epistle, Gospel, and Collect of the day in English before the sermon, so as better to instruct the people; he used English hymns and anthems before and after mass. He introduced a catechetical program for children, as he had probably done also in Newfoundland. His achievements at Placentia were impressive; so was his increase of parish income at Halifax by £150. Despite a drinking problem, which he apparently overcame, Burke was well regarded. The events of his career reflect the difficulties of others of the first generation of English-speaking Catholic priests in Canada.

RAYMOND J. LAHEY

AAQ, 12 A, G: f.2; 210 A, III; 30 CN, I. Arch. of the Archdiocese of Halifax, Edmund Burke papers (mfm. at PANS). Archivio della Propaganda Fide (Rome), Scritturi riferite nei Congressi, America Antille, 2 (1761–89); 3 (1790–1819). Nfld. Public Library Services, Provincial Reference Dept. (St John's), Nfld., Court of Sessions and Surrogate Court, "Records of Placentia," 2 (8 Aug. 1786–29 Dec. 1803); 3 (5 July 1805–5 July 1806). PANL, GN 2/1, 10. USPG, C/CAN/Nfl., 1. M. F. Howley, *Ecclesiastical history of Newfoundland* (Boston, 1888; repr. Belleville, Ont., 1979). Johnston, *Hist. of Catholic Church in eastern N.S.*

BURKE (Bourke), EDMUND, Roman Catholic priest, vicar apostolic, educator, and author; b. 1753 in Maryborough (Portlaoighise, Republic of Ireland); d. 29 Nov. 1820 in Halifax, N.S.

Educated at the Université de Paris, Edmund Burke was ordained in 1775 or 1776 and for more than a decade did pastoral work in County Kildare (Republic of Ireland). On the advice of the archbishop of Dublin, he left for Quebec in 1786 after having aroused the ill will of influential people through his support for a

Burke

particular episcopal aspirant. Upon his arrival he was immediately appointed professor of philosophy and mathematics at the Séminaire de Québec. According to a newspaper article published after his death, his lectures at the seminary were thronged by students eager to hear "a man celebrated in the University of Paris, as excelling most men of his day in mathematical science, and also the classics, particularly in the Greek and Hebrew languages."

Despite his popularity at the seminary, Burke was anxious to become more involved in teaching religion to a larger number of people. Believing that preaching the gospel "is a more rational employment for a priest than giving lectures in astronomy," he sought and received a pastoral charge: in 1791 he was appointed to the parishes of Saint-Pierre and Saint-Laurent on the Île d'Orléans, and he remained there until 1794. In that year Lieutenant Governor SIMCOE of Upper Canada, concerned about the presence of republican agitators in the vicinity of the western posts, appealed to Lord Dorchester [Guy CARLETON] for the appointment of a Roman Catholic clergyman to the River Raisin area near Detroit (Mich.). This appeal was relayed to Bishop Hubert*, and as a result Burke was appointed not only missionary to the River Raisin region but also vicar general and superior of the missions of Upper Canada.

Burke, possibly the first English-speaking Roman Catholic priest to work west of Glengarry County, Upper Canada, arrived at Fort Miamis (Maumee City, Ohio) in February 1795, determined "to counteract the Machinations of Jacobin Emissaries . . . amongst the Settlers and numerous Tribes of surrounding Indians." On the whole, he proved fairly effective in maintaining order. His presence seems to have undercut the attempts of the local inhabitants to have Jean-Antoine Ledru*, a man suspected of republican sympathies, appointed their parish priest. In addition, he tried to assist Simcoe in suppressing the sale of liquor to the Indians, and, "by persevering diligence and at the risque of his life," he persuaded the settlers to honour their obligation to serve in the militia. Yet, perhaps because of his very success, Burke constantly felt threatened in his new mission. Claiming that in the River Raisin area "you never meet a man, either Indian or Canadian, without his gun in his hand and his knife at his breast," Burke complained that "brigands" kept him in "continual danger" of his life. To protect himself, he wrote shortly after his arrival, "I have been obliged to keep two Christian Indians well armed, who slept in my room together with a hardy Canadian. I never walked out but in company and always armed." A couple of years later he asserted that the members of his flock, although baptized in the Roman Catholic Church, were "wicked men given to every vice, but especially to drunkenness and sins against nature. Scarcely can you find a girl of ten years that has not suffered violence."

When Fort Miamis and Detroit passed under American control in 1796, Burke moved across the border into Upper Canada, becoming chaplain to the military garrison at Fort George (Niagara-on-the-Lake). During the next few years, as vicar general and superior of missions, he helped to lay the foundations of the Roman Catholic faith in Upper Canada by conducting frequent and extensive missionary tours. At the same time he constantly sought assistance from Rome and Quebec in his efforts to increase the number of priests in the colony; unfortunately, he never received the clergy he needed. The low point in his career came in 1801, when an officer at Fort George accused him of attempting to "violate his wife by force." Burke angrily denied the charge, which indeed seems to have had no basis in fact, and denounced his accuser for spending all his time in the "Grog shop" and consorting with prostitutes.

Burke left Upper Canada in May 1801, when he succeeded his namesake, Edmund BURKE, as vicar general of Nova Scotia, still under the jurisdiction of Quebec. He arrived at Halifax in October. As vicar general he attempted to establish a seminary but encountered considerable opposition from Lieutenant Governor Sir John WENTWORTH and Charles INGLIS, the Anglican bishop; eventually the seminary was granted the necessary licence by the provincial government, but it never opened because Burke found it impossible to obtain qualified teachers. Inglis's hostility to the scheme, as well as his attacks on Roman Catholics and dissenters in his charge of 1803, led Burke to denounce his Anglican opponent in a postscript to his 1804 *Letter of instruction to the Catholic missionaries of Nova-Scotia, and its dependencies*. Wentworth, in turn, reprimanded Burke for attacking Inglis in an "unreasonable and reprehensible" manner, a criticism that was echoed by Attorney General Richard John Uniacke*. Burke, however, remained unrepentant and as determined as ever to defend the interests of his church. After his assault on Inglis in 1804 he wrote that the Anglican bishop "was completely upset by the dose he received. It is good for him, perhaps it will cure him of his itch for calumniating Catholics, all of whom this bad man would annihilate, if he could." The following year he replied to criticisms of his *Letter of instruction* levelled by two prominent Anglican clergymen, William Cochran* and Robert Stanser*, and in 1809 he again revealed his talent for polemics in a debate over the merits of the Roman Catholic faith with the Reverend Thomas McCulloch*, an anti-burgher Presbyterian minister and teacher in Pictou.

In the summer of 1815 Burke crossed the Atlantic, partly for medical reasons and partly to lobby for changes in the ecclesiastical status of Nova Scotia. After a brief visit to Ireland, a country he regarded as the most beautiful and "charming" in the world, he travelled first to London and then to Rome. As a result of reports he submitted to the Vatican, Nova Scotia became a vicariate apostolic – a step which removed it from the jurisdiction of Quebec and placed it directly under the control of Rome. This first division of the diocese of Quebec, perhaps Burke's greatest contribution to the religious life of Nova Scotia, formally went into effect in July 1817, one year after his return to Halifax. Honoured with the title of bishop of Sion and vicar apostolic of Nova Scotia, Burke was consecrated at Quebec by Bishop Plessis* on 5 July 1818, at the age of 65.

With his new authority Burke had the independence he needed to carry out his work in Nova Scotia. In 1819 he and the Reverend Angus Bernard Mac-Eachern* of Prince Edward Island held discussions on the establishment of a seminary at Arisaig, N.S. This institution did not materialize, but Burke assisted in founding a Trappist monastery near Tracadie [see Jacques Merle*]. Prior to his death in 1820 he had also started a boys' and girls' school at Halifax and had ordained five young men to the priesthood. Further, he had recommended the building of a new cathedral, and he laid the cornerstone of this building – St Mary's Cathedral – on 24 May 1820.

Estimates of Burke's character vary. In 1794 Bishop Hubert called Burke fickle, but he also described him as "a sociable character, a man of edifying conversation, and above all recommendable for his profound science." Lord Selkirk [DOUGLAS] was more critical, claiming in late 1804 during a visit to Halifax that "Burke appears to me a man of real genius, acuteness & ability . . . but he seems to be sanguine & far from cool headed, & perhaps in possible combinations of circumstances might be a dangerous enemy." He also noted that Burke was "reputed bigotted" and was not as popular with his congregation as the Reverend James JONES had been. On the whole, however, it would be a mistake to place too much credence in Selkirk's statements. Burke seems to have been highly respected in Halifax society and, despite his clashes with a number of churchmen, remained on generally good terms with the members of other denominations. One 19th-century historian wrote that Burke never permitted "differences of opinions to interfere with that kindly and gentlemanly intercourse with his friends for which he was so remarkable." As a result of his tolerant spirit, the Roman Catholics of Halifax, who numbered approximately 2,000 in 1820, were more easily accepted in the wider community than they had been prior to his arrival.

R. A. MacLean

Edmund Burke is the author of *Letter of instruction to the Catholic missionaries of Nova-Scotia, and its dependencies* (Halifax, 1804); *Remarks on a pamphlet entitled Popery condemned by Scripture and the Fathers* (Halifax, 1809); *Remarks on the Rev. Mr. Stanser's examination of the Rev.*

Mr. Burke's Letter of instruction to the C.M. of Nova Scotia; together with a reply to the Rev. Mr. Cochran's fifth and last letter to Mr. B. published in the Nova-Scotia Gazette . . . (Halifax, 1805); *A treatise on the first principles of Christianity . . .* (2v., Halifax, 1808–10); and *A treatise on the ministry of the church . . .* (2v. in 1, Dublin, 1817).

PAC, RG 5, A1: 582–97 (mfm. at AO). PANS, Biog., Edmund Burke, docs. (mfm). [John Carroll], *The John Carroll papers*, ed. T. O'B. Hanley (3v., Notre Dame, Ind., 1976). *Corr. of Lieut. Governor Simcoe* (Cruikshank), vols.3–5. Douglas, *Lord Selkirk's diary* (White). Landmann, *Adventures and recollections*, 2: 25–27. [Thomas McCulloch], *Popery condemned by Scripture and the Fathers: being a refutation of the principal popish doctrines and assertions maintained in the remarks on the Rev. Mr. Stanser's examination of the Rev. Mr. Burke's Letter of instruction to the Catholic missionaries of Nova Scotia, and in the reply to the Rev. Mr. Cochran's fifth and last letter to Mr. Burke . . .* (Edinburgh, 1808). *Acadian Recorder*, 2 Dec. 1820. Caron, "Inv. de la corr. de Mgr Denaut," ANQ *Rapport*, 1931–32; "Inv. de la corr. de Mgr Hubert et de Mgr Bailly de Messein," ANQ *Rapport*, 1930–31; "Inv. de la corr. de Mgr Mariaucheau d'Esgly," ANQ *Rapport*, 1930–31; "Inv. de la corr. de Mgr Plessis," ANQ *Rapport*, 1927–28; 1928–29; 1932–33. Akins, *Hist. of Halifax City*, 132, 136, 145, 185–86, 192. [H.-R. Casgrain], *Mémoire sur les missions de la Nouvelle-Écosse, du cap Breton et de l'île du Prince-Édouard de 1760 à 1820 . . . réponse aux "Memoirs of Bishop Burke" par Mgr O'Brien . . .* (Québec, 1895). Dooner, *Catholic pioneers in U.C.* Johnston, *Hist. of Catholic Church in eastern N.S.*, vol.1. L. A. Merrigan, "The life and times of Edmund Burke in Nova Scotia, 1801–1820" (MA thesis, St Mary's Univ., Halifax, 1971). Cornelius O'Brien, *Memoirs of Rt. Rev. Edmund Burke, bishop of Zion, first vicar apostolic of Nova Scotia* (Ottawa, 1894). L. K. Shook, *Catholic post-secondary education in English-speaking Canada: a history* (Toronto, 1971). Brother Alfred [A. J. Dooner], "The Right Rev. Edmund Burke, D.D., 'Apostle of Upper Canada,' bishop of Zion, first vicar apostolic of Nova Scotia: 1753–1820," CCHA *Report*, 8 (1940–41): 35–49. P. W. Browne, "Father Edmund Burke," *Mid-America* (Chicago), 13 (1930–31): 314–23.

BURN, WILLIAM, land agent; b. August 1758 in Beanley, England; d. 15 Sept. 1804 in Baldoon, Upper Canada.

Son of a Northumberland farmer, William Burn went to his mother's native Scotland to become a sheep farmer at Kirkland, near Kirkcudbright, apparently as a tenant on property acquired by the Earl of Selkirk [DOUGLAS]. Burn had a local reputation for reliability and good management of his flock and, when in 1802 Selkirk began to project a settlement in Upper Canada, Burn was hired in June at £80 per annum as one of the earl's first assistants. Although Selkirk had by this time been discouraged by government from his original plan to transport and settle Irish emigrants in British North America, he sent Burn to Ireland in the summer of 1802 to recruit 100 labourers for a proposed sheep farm in Upper Canada to be connected with a settlement of Highland

Burn

Scots. For reasons which are not clear only about a dozen Irishmen were signed on, to embark at Tobermory with some breeding sheep in a ship chartered by Selkirk.

As so often happened, Selkirk's carefully coordinated plans were soon in ruins. The *Bess* proved unseaworthy, and Burn himself had second thoughts about leaving for America (he was obviously under considerable pressure to remain from a Miss Bacon to whom he was "pledged"). He finally agreed to go for one winter to "set things agoing." The delay forced the earl to revise his original plans and Burn was sent directly from Liverpool to New York City without Irishmen or sheep in order to take over the flock already collected at White Creek, near Cambridge, in upstate New York. Burn departed on 2 October, arrived in New York City on 10 December, and left a week later with Alexander Brown, an experienced Scots shepherd sent out with his dogs by Selkirk. They reached White Creek on 24 Dec. 1802 and wintered in the area.

In the spring of 1803 Burn learned that Miss Bacon, whom he had expected to join him, found family circumstances "make it necessary she should remain near them." This news changed his plans, and he plunged energetically into his new assignment without further thought of his engagement or of an immediate return to Scotland. By this time Selkirk had been forced to alter the destination of his emigrants, now overwhelmingly Scottish, from Upper Canada to Prince Edward Island, and Burn was instructed to keep the flock in New York for the summer. Not until June was Selkirk able to send an impatient and increasingly uncomfortable Burn further instructions. The earl now had the crown's promise of a land grant of his choice in southwestern Upper Canada. Burn was to scout the country between the Niagara and Detroit rivers for a proper location for both a settlement and a sheep farm, on which Selkirk intended to build up a flock of 1,000 first-class breeding ewes. In a subsequent letter from Prince Edward Island, he instructed Burn to tour the northern United States with an eye for attractive sheep breeds and local sheep-rearing practices, but Burn was never able to make this trip.

Burn left White Creek for Queenston, Upper Canada, in early September 1803 and spent the autumn with a surveyor exploring lands on Lake Erie and the Thames River. After consulting with the earl about land and sheep in December 1803 at York (Toronto), he set off for the Thames; Selkirk joined him there briefly in late January 1804. Burn carefully surveyed the Chenal Écarté area on the northeast corner of Lake St Clair, where Selkirk had decided to locate the settlement he would call Baldoon after the ancestral lands his family had been forced to sell in 1793. Burn returned to Queenston in February only to

be ordered by Selkirk from Albany to proceed immediately to Baldoon to clear land and sow Indian corn, potatoes, and timothy in anticipation of the earl's arrival there around 1 May. With ten oxen Burn departed on 4 April, reaching Baldoon on 9 May. He hired local labour and began to clear and to plant, noting in his journal little of importance until Selkirk's arrival on 8 June with "2 Gentelmen or sumthing like Gentelmen" – Sheriff Alexander McDonell* (Collachie) and a Dr Shaw. It is difficult to determine whether Burn was more upset by the fact that the large number of menservants in the party put a strain on the settlement's limited sleeping accommodation, or by the earl's failure to order a day's drinking to celebrate his arrival. Moreover, it became clear that Burn would no longer be in charge, but would probably have to work under McDonell's supervision, for Selkirk had offered the sheriff the appointment as his agent in Upper Canada.

During the summer of 1804 increasing quantities of local grain whisky were shipped to Baldoon, and Burn and his men fell victim to what Selkirk in a different context described as the "malignant effect of the American climate"; adjustment to the new environment produced terrible emotional difficulties and men turned to the readily available alcohol for relief. By the end of August the small party was ravaged by fever, probably malarial in origin – Baldoon was located on marshland ideal for sheep pasturage but also for breeding mosquitoes. The major party of 101 Highlanders finally arrived on 5 September in the midst of an epidemic. Their high rate of mortality was probably a result of diseases contracted on their long journey to Baldoon, but Burn died on 15 September after two weeks of a fever acquired locally. McDonell later blamed Burn's demise as much on "the effects of excessive intemperance" as on "the prevailing fever," and the two factors undoubtedly worked together. Certainly eight barrels containing 39 gallons each of whisky had been consumed at Baldoon since July. The settlement lacked winter provisions and the housing Selkirk had ordered constructed; and Burn's books and papers were in complete disarray. Selkirk was never able to put Burn's affairs sufficiently in order to determine whether his aged mother in Scotland was entitled to any back pay.

William Burn was not a success in North America. His failure illustrates the problems of immigrants in coming to terms with new conditions, and the difficulties of outside entrepreneurs such as Lord Selkirk in obtaining dependable assistants to execute their plans.

J. M. BUMSTED

PAC, MG 19, E1, ser.1, 37: 14190–92, 14207, 14230, 14233–34, 14253–57, 14262–63, 14266–68, 14272–75,

14278–81, 14301, 14308–23; 39: 14908–13 (transcripts); MG 24, I8, I, 1: 18–19; 9: 2–4. Douglas, *Lord Selkirk's diary* (White), 326. J. M. Bumsted, "Settlement by chance: Lord Selkirk and Prince Edward Island," *CHR*, 59 (1978): 170–88. F. C. Hamil and T. [S. E.] Jones, "Lord Selkirk's work in Upper Canada: the story of Baldoon," *OH*, 57 (1965): 1–12. B. A. Parker, "Thomas Clark: his business relationship with Lord Selkirk," *Beaver*, outfit 310 (autumn 1979): 50–58.

BYERS, PETER, known as **Black Peter**, labourer; b. probably after 1796 on St John's (Prince Edward) Island; d. March 1815 in Charlottetown, P.E.I.

By the middle of the second decade of the 19th century slavery had probably come to an end on Prince Edward Island. There were, however, many former slaves among the small black population in the colony. One family of this community was that of John Byers, known as Black Jack, who was identified in 1796 as "a Negro of Colonel Robinson"; the master was undoubtedly Joseph ROBINSON, at that time an assistant judge of the Supreme Court. Byers and his wife, Amelia, had probably come to the Island with Robinson after the American revolution. They had a number of children but just where Peter stood in the family is not certain. We know nothing of Peter except for the events leading up to his death. He apparently had no difficulties with the law until 1815, although his father had been charged with theft the previous year. The elder Byers had been defended by Charlottetown lawyer James Bardin Palmer* and found not guilty of the charge.

Early in 1815 the shop of James Gibson, a tobacconist, was broken into during the night and a sum of about £5 taken. A number of the coins were identifiable, among them "an English half crown of the coin of King William having a hole on the arms side near the centre thereof." On 24 February Peter Byers gave this piece and several others to millwright John Spittal in payment of an outstanding debt. Spittal, who had been warned to look out for the stolen coins, went directly to the authorities. A warrant was issued for Byers's arrest and he was questioned at length.

Over the next three days the financial dealings of the entire Byers family came under investigation; it appears that several of them had been found to have unexplained funds. Under repeated examination a welter of conflicting testimony emerged. Peter himself at first claimed that the half-crown which had led to his arrest was among money he had received as wages and given to his mother, who later returned the coin to him. John and Amelia, however, stated that none of their funds had come from Peter and that money they had recently dispensed had been found by John on the road. When Peter was re-examined on 4 March, he finally admitted his involvement in the theft, stating that he and William Billinger, another black, had planned to rob the store but that Billinger had been the one who had broken down the door and removed the money from its hiding place. He explained his new story by saying that he had "told so many Lyes on this subject that he could not rest." Billinger, however, had an alibi, having been so drunk on the evening in question that he had been unable to leave the house where the drinking had taken place; this story was supported by Billinger's employer, William Gardner.

The matter came up for trial on 8 March before Chief Justice Thomas Tremlett* and Peter pleaded guilty. Three days later he was sentenced. Although pleading benefit of clergy had previously resulted in lighter sentences for those convicted of capital crimes, an act of 1792 had removed theft and burglary from the list of clergiable offences. For Peter, then, there was no relief: he was condemned to be hanged. Twelve days earlier in the same courtroom his brother Sancho had received the same sentence for stealing a loaf of bread and a pound of butter.

The sentences were carried out by the end of the month. Their harshness was not disproportionate to that of others handed down in the period and reflected the values of colonial society. Security of property was protected by the law, and breaking and entering, especially at night, was considered a heinous crime; even when criminal law was reformed in 1836, burglary remained a felony punishable by death. Peter and Sancho Byers were sentenced to hang, not because they were black, but because they were judged to be guilty and there was no other penalty for such guilt.

H. T. HOLMAN

PAC, MG 24, D99: 8–10. PAPEI, RG 6, Supreme Court, case papers, 1814, King. v. John Byers; 1815, King. v. Peter Byers, King v. Sancho Byers; minutes, 1814–15. St Paul's Anglican Church (Charlottetown), Reg. of baptisms (mfm. at PAPEI). J. A. Mathieson, "Bench and bar," *Past and present of Prince Edward Island . . .* , ed. D. A. MacKinnon and A. B. Warburton (Charlottetown, [1906]), 121–42.

BYLES, MATHER, Church of England clergyman and versifier; b. 12 Jan. 1734/35 in Boston, Mass., eldest son of the Reverend Mather Byles and Anna Gale, *née* Noyes; d. 12 March 1814 in Saint John, N.B.

Mather Byles came from a distinguished Puritan background. He was the great-grandson of the clergyman Increase Mather and a grandnephew of colonial governor Jonathan Belcher; his father was a well-known tory Congregational minister, poet, and wit. A precocious boy, Byles entered Harvard College at the age of 12 and graduated in 1751. He was later to

Cadot

receive the degree of MA from Harvard in 1754 and from Yale College in 1757, and he obtained a DD from Oxford in 1770. Byles was happily married three times: to Rebecca Walter on 12 May 1761 in Roxbury (Boston); to Sarah Lyde on 10 Feb. 1777 in Halifax, N.S.; and on 2 Oct. 1788, also in Halifax, to Susanna Reid, *née* Lawlor, who proved a good mother to his 13 children by his first two unions. His descendants include a number of outstanding Nova Scotia families, one of his daughters having married William James ALMON and two others a son and grandson of Thomas DESBRISAY.

In 1757, after two years as librarian of Harvard College, Byles became a liberal Congregational minister in New London, Conn. In 1768 he was converted to the Church of England, went to England where he received a licence from the bishop of London, and then took up duties as minister of Christ Church, Boston, and missionary of the Society for the Propagation of the Gospel. After a stormy tenure with a Whiggish congregation, he resigned and would have taken up a position in Portsmouth, N.H., had the outbreak of hostilities not prevented him. In 1776 he fled with the British troops to Halifax, where he lived precariously as chaplain to the garrison and assistant to the rectors of St Paul's Church. In May 1784 he went to England to press his claims for compensation as a loyalist. Awarded £120 and an annual pension of £100 in the form of "a perfect Sinecure," the lifetime chaplaincy of the Halifax garrison, he returned to Halifax in May 1785.

In August 1788 Byles visited Saint John, N.B., and received a "Unanimous" call to become rector of Trinity Church. He moved there with his family in May 1789. At first the congregation met in temporary quarters, but on Christmas morning 1791 Byles conducted the first service in the newly built church that became the centre of loyalist, Anglican worship in Saint John. It was also supported by the Presbyterians, who had no minister, and thus was frequently overcrowded. Byles served with distinction until early 1814 when he went blind. He died on 12 March 1814 in the very chair in which his father and grandfather had died.

Byles was paternalistic and somewhat puritanical and cynical. He was not impressed by England, the Anglican episcopacy, or the whole "dissipated Age." Unlike many loyalists he was not awed by aristocracy or royalty, refusing, for example, to act "like a Fool" by attending a dinner in Halifax for Prince William Henry. But like many loyalists he was not bitter towards the United States: "I wish my Country-Men Joy on the Attainment of their wishes." He was erudite and a competent satirist. In Halifax he gave vent to his frustrations by ridiculing in verse many of the city's leading citizens in a way, Governor John Parr* complained, "unbefitting a man of God."

Byles was a cantankerous individual, quarrelling in Halifax with his fellow clerics, John Breynton*, Henry Caner, and Joshua Wingate Weeks, but remaining friendly with Bishop Charles INGLIS. He did not like Nova Scotia, leaving "without the least Regret . . . the most contemptible [area] my Eyes ever beheld": "I desire never to forget that the most irreligious People I ever knew were at the same Time the most ignorant, the most stupid, & the most unhappy." In contrast, he was happy in New Brunswick partly because he liked his job. He reported to his famous loyalist sisters, Katherine and Mary, who continued to reside in Boston, that "it has pleased a good God to gild your Brother's Evening Sky": "I am connected with as worthy a People as I ever knew."

WALLACE BROWN

A portrait of Mather Byles by his nephew Mather Brown, now in the possession of the American Antiquarian Society, Worcester, Mass., is reproduced in Shipton, *infra*.

PAC, MG 23, D6, 1: 21, 35, 41, 56, 58–59, 63, 66–67 (transcripts). *A catalogue of all graduates in divinity, law, medicine, arts and music who have regularly proceeded or been created in the University of Oxford, between October 10, 1659, and December 31, 1850 . . .* (Oxford, 1851). Shipton, *Sibley's Harvard graduates*, 13: 6–26. A. C. Potter and C. K. Bolton, *The librarians of Harvard College, 1667–1877* (Cambridge, Mass., 1897). A. W. H. Eaton, *The famous Mather Byles: the noted Boston tory preacher, poet, and wit, 1707–1788* (Boston, 1914). [This book is about Byles's father but contains much on the son. W.B.]

C

CADOT (Cadotte), JEAN-BAPTISTE, fur trader and interpreter; baptized 5 Dec. 1723 in Batiscan (Que.), son of Jean-François Cadot and Marie-Josephe Proteau; d. in or after 1803.

Jean-Baptiste Cadot first went to the Upper Lakes in 1742, engaging himself at age 18 to Jean-Baptiste-

Nicolas-Roch de Ramezay* for a journey to the Nipigon country. Perhaps he was encouraged by his father, who had made a voyage to Michilimackinac (Mackinaw City, Mich.) in 1717. In 1750 Cadot was again in the west, this time in the employ of Louis Legardeur* de Repentigny and Louis de Bonne* de

Missègle, who together had been granted a seigneury at Sault Ste Marie (Mich.). The rushing rapids in the St Marys River were a key point in the water route to the interior, since all canoes going between Lake Huron and Lake Superior had to be portaged or pulled through the swift water. Repentigny erected a small fort, and when he left the area Cadot stayed on as his agent.

Cadot adjusted to his wilderness home by taking a Nipissing woman named Athanasie (or possibly Anastasie) to live with him. When a daughter was born in August 1756 they regularized their relationship by marriage at Michilimackinac on 28 October. Three years later another daughter was born and in 1761 a son, Jean-Baptiste. Cadot's wife was a great asset to him since she was related to the Ojibwa chief MADJECKEWISS and was highly respected. The family spoke only Ojibwa at home, and Cadot's skill with language and oratory won him the position of chief with the local band of about 50 warriors.

By 1762 the British controlled the Sault. Cadot, having a small farm there and being responsible for a family, quickly accommodated himself to the trader Alexander Henry* and the small garrison of Royal Americans (60th Foot) commanded by John Jamet*. In late December fire destroyed three of the four buildings in the fort, sparing only Cadot's house. Most of the soldiers returned to Michilimackinac, but Jamet was too severely burned to be moved. Late in February, however, Cadot and Henry undertook a very difficult winter trip to return him to his unit, after which Cadot returned home.

It would have been better for Jamet and Henry if they had stayed at the Sault. The Ojibwas under Madjeckewiss and Minweweh*, inspired by Pontiac*'s siege of Detroit (Mich.), took Michilimackinac on 2 June 1763, killing Jamet and capturing Henry. The Indians at the Sault, however, were kept out of the affair by the efforts of Cadot. In May 1764 Henry was permitted by Wawatam*, his Ojibwa guardian, to go to the Sault. Madjeckewiss also arrived there with his band and would have harmed Henry but for Cadot's intervention. On 22 July Athanasie gave birth to another son, Michel. When the Cadots took the child to Michilimackinac to be baptized on 13 August by Pierre Du Jaunay* the British had not as yet reoccupied the post.

Upon the return of the British on 22 September their commander, Captain William Howard, kept the soldiers at Michilimackinac and planned to rely on Cadot to represent him at the Sault. In May 1765 Cadot was sent there with a wampum belt to acquaint the Indians with the negotiations for peace undertaken by Sir William Johnson*, superintendent of northern Indians. One month later Cadot vividly demonstrated his influence over the Indians by leading 80 canoes to Michilimackinac for a treaty. When the Indians

requested that traders be allowed to go to Lake Superior, Howard, heeding Cadot's advice, gave him permission to trade at La Pointe (Wis.). Establishing a partnership with his former associate Alexander Henry, Cadot stayed at the Sault while Henry traded successfully in the vicinity of Chequamegon Bay (Wis.).

In August 1766 Cadot was appointed as Indian interpreter, a position he held for at least a year; he earned 8s. per day and was provided with presents to dispense. Regarded as "that vigilant Friend of the English," in March 1767 he showed that his reputation was deserved when he persuaded the Indians at the Sault to exchange their French flag for a British one. Working for Robert Rogers*, commandant at Michilimackinac, and also for Johnson, Cadot had become one of the most influential people in the Upper Lakes.

During the summer of 1767 Cadot aided Henry Bostwick, John Chinn, and Alexander Henry in the search for copper deposits along Lake Superior, and he was named as one of Bostwick's associates when a group of British investors received approval in London to establish mines in the area. During the next few years Cadot served the concern by maintaining good relations with the Indians and keeping them from interfering with the mines. Though the operation proved unprofitable, Cadot's reputation soared. In 1771 Johnson considered him to be one of the "Two Most faithfull Men amongst the French," and in the same year George Turnbull, the commandant at Michilimackinac, said Cadot "has an universall good character amongst both Canadians and Indians."

In 1775 Cadot was part of a large group of traders, including JOSEPH and Thomas Frobisher, Alexander Henry, and Peter POND, who travelled west to trade. At Cumberland House (Sask.), after being entertained by Hudson's Bay Company officer Matthew Cocking*, they set out in various directions. Cadot, with four canoes, went to pass the winter at Fort des Prairies (Fort-à-la-Corne). The western trade prospered, and Sault Ste Marie grew in importance as a provisioning post. Cadot maintained an association with Henry until at least 1778, when he established joint ventures with Jean-Baptiste Barthe, an agent for John ASKIN.

It was not until 1780 that the American revolution directly affected Cadot. Patrick SINCLAIR, lieutenant governor of Michilimackinac, decided to attack the Spaniards at St Louis (Mo.) and, feeling that "the Indians are under the absolute authority of Mr. Cadot, who is a very honest man," he dispatched Cadot with a war party along the southern shore of Lake Superior to try to gain Indian support. A number of Indians enlisted by Cadot did help in the attack on St Louis, but it was repulsed. In October 1781 Cadot was again put on the payroll as an interpreter. In September 1783 Daniel ROBERTSON, now commandant at Michili-

Caldwell

mackinac, sent Cadot and Madjeckewiss to the Chequamegon region in an unsuccessful effort to stop a war between the Ojibwas and the Foxes and Sioux.

About 1767, following the death of Athanasie, Cadot had married Marie Mouet, a Canadian. In October of that year they had a son, Joseph-Marie, who apparently died young. During 1772–73 Cadot sent young Jean-Baptiste to Montreal, where he studied at the Collège Saint-Raphaël from 1773 to 1780. By 1786 Cadot's sons were working with him under the name of Messrs Cadot and Company and from 1787 evidently conducted most of the firm's activities. On 24 May 1796 the venerable trader, pleading the infirmity of old age and apparently too feeble even to sign his name, formally turned over the business to Jean-Baptiste and Michel. During his career Cadot had been the major trader at Sault Ste Marie, and although he never became rich he appears to have had a comfortable income. His son Jean-Baptiste was admitted in 1801 to partnership in the North West Company, but he was expelled two years later for drunkenness. The date of the elder Cadot's death is unknown: one account suggests 1803, but he may have been alive as late as 1812. Louis-Honoré Fréchette* made Cadot the central figure of "Le drapeau fantôme," a poem published in his collection *La légende d'un peuple* (Paris, [1887]).

DAVID A. ARMOUR

Clements Library, Thomas Gage papers, American ser., 103: Turnbull to Gage, 12 May 1771; 104: Turnbull to Gage, 6 July 1771; supplementary accounts, "Account of Sir William Johnson's Indian Department expenses to Sept. 25, 1767"; "Speismacher Indian transactions, Dec. 8, 1767–July 18, 1768." DPL, Burton Hist. Coll., J.-B. Barthe papers, invoice book, 1778–80; sales book, 1775–79; ledger, 1775–79. McCord Museum, J.-B. Blondeau, account book, 1777–87. PAC, MG 19, A2, ser.1, 3. PRO, CO 700, Canada no.38E. Univ. of Notre Dame Arch. (Notre Dame, Ind.), Wisconsin diocesan coll., Cadotte ledger. Wis., State Hist. Soc., Consolidated returns of trade licences, 1777, 1779, 1781–83, 1785–86 (transcripts). *Les bourgeois de la Compagnie du Nord-Ouest* (Masson). Jonathan Carver, *Travels through the interior parts of North America, in the years 1766, 1767, and 1768* (3rd ed., London, 1781; repr. Minneapolis, Minn., 1956), 131–32, 141–43. Henry, *Travels and adventures. John Askin papers* (Quaife), vol.1. *Johnson papers* (Sullivan et al.). *Mich. Pioneer Coll.*, 9 (1886), 10 (1886), 11 (1887), 20 (1892), 37 (1909–10). [Robert Rogers], "Rogers's Michillimackinac journal," ed. W. L. Clements, American Antiquarian Soc., *Proc.* (Worcester, Mass.), new ser., 28 (1918): 224–73. *U.S. v. Repentigny* (1866), 72 U.S. 211, 223–26, 241–43, 247, 251–52. Wis., State Hist. Soc., *Coll.*, 11 (1888), 12 (1892), 18 (1908), 19 (1910). *Dictionnaire national des Canadiens français (1608–1760)* (3v., Montréal, 1958). Massicotte, "Répertoire des engagements pour l'Ouest," ANQ *Rapport*, 1929–30: 221, 424. Tanguay, *Dictionnaire.* Joseph Tassé, *Les Canadiens de l'Ouest* (2v., Montréal, 1878), 1. Wallace,

Macmillan dict. Cadotte family stories, comp. T. H. Tobola (Cadotte, Wis., 1974). Maurault, *Le collège de Montréal* (Dansereau; 1967), 186. Walter O'Meara, *Daughters of the country: the women of the fur traders and mountain men* (New York, 1968). [This work confuses Cadot's first and second wives. D.A.A.]

CALDWELL, HENRY, army and militia officer, politician, seigneur, landowner, businessman, and office holder; b. *c.* 1735 in Ireland, fourth son of Sir John Caldwell and Anne French; m. 16 May 1774 Ann Hamilton of Hampton Hall (Republic of Ireland), sister of Hugh Hamilton, bishop of Ossory; d. 28 May 1810 at Quebec, Lower Canada.

Henry Caldwell was appointed ensign in the second battalion of the 24th Foot on 5 Sept. 1756. On 7 Oct. 1757 he was promoted lieutenant in the same battalion, which was converted into a new regiment, the 69th Foot, on 23 April 1758. That year, during the capture of Louisbourg, Île Royale (Cape Breton Island), he attracted the attention of Brigadier-General James Wolfe*, who recommended him to William Pitt. On 30 Dec. 1758 Caldwell was promoted to the rank of captain in the army and on 16 May 1759 he became assistant to quartermaster general Guy CARLETON; in this capacity he was attached to Wolfe's general staff during the siege of Quebec. (Wolfe bequeathed him 100 guineas in his will, drawn up in June 1759.) Caldwell was commissioned captain in the 93rd Foot on 22 Jan. 1760 but on 14 March 1764 he transferred to the 36th when the 93rd was disbanded. According to tradition, in the late 1760s Caldwell, a "handsome soldier," was the inspiration for Colonel Ed Rivers, one of the protagonists in *The history of Emily Montague*, a novel by Frances Brooke [Moore*]. Caldwell obtained the rank of major in America on 2 Sept. 1772 and retired from the army in March 1774, perhaps in order to remain in Quebec.

In April 1774 Caldwell took a 99-year lease on the property in the province that belonged to former governor Murray*. This comprised the seigneuries of Lauson, Rivière-du-Loup, Madawaska, and Foucault (later Caldwell's Manor), the last located along the Rivière Richelieu and the present Vermont border. In addition the property included the house and lands of Sans Bruit, situated about three miles from Quebec on the Chemin Sainte-Foy, a house on Rue Saint-Jean in Upper Town, and what was called Gorgendieres Farm in the seigneury of Sillery. The new leaseholder immediately began to improve the seigneury of Lauson, building a grist-mill there. But Benedict ARNOLD's campaign during the American invasion of 1775–76 severely affected Caldwell's property near Quebec: his house at Sainte-Foy was used as the rebels' headquarters and was burned along with all its contents, and the mills on the seigneury of Lauson were pillaged. Caldwell took part in the defence of the town as lieutenant-colonel commanding the British militia, and his military experience proved a great asset, particularly during Richard Montgomery*'s unsuccessful attack in the night of 30–31 Dec. 1775. When the siege of the town ended, Caldwell was chosen to carry the dispatches reporting the victory to London. His military service earned him the king's praise (Lieutenant-Colonel Allan Maclean* was also so honoured) and £500 sterling; in addition he was promoted to the honorary rank of lieutenant-colonel in America on 10 Jan. 1776 and appointed to Quebec's Legislative Council on 21 May.

After his return, Caldwell set about rebuilding, and he bought a number of lots around Quebec, for which he paid about £500 cash. From May 1778 he rented out the Sans Bruit property including about 400 acres of cleared land, a large garden, and buildings, as well as a farm on the Rivière Saint-Charles that had once belonged to Joseph-Michel Cadet*, and, from November, a large house and outbuildings on Rue Saint-Jean. In 1782 he signed over the lease on the seigneuries of Rivière-du-Loup and Madawaska to Malcolm FRASER. When the American revolution ended in 1783, Caldwell was able to attract a number of loyalists to Caldwell's Manor, where he repaired the mill, helped build a church, and erected a manor-house. But his plans were thwarted by the rigorous application of an order from the imperial government forbidding the colonization of border areas. He was able to breathe new life into the seigneury of Lauson, however, through active promotion; although only about 20 land grants had been made before 1783, more than 100 were made between 1786 and 1794, 151 between 1795 and 1798, and 69 between 1798 and 1800. Probably partly to finance this expansion, he also leased out numerous other pieces of property during the 1780s and 1790s, sold many of his lands after 1791, and borrowed nearly £2,000 between 1786 and 1794.

A founder of the Agriculture Society, which was established at Quebec in the spring of 1789, Caldwell became one of its 16 first directors and in 1791 its chairman. He also supported it financially and would have liked to see this type of organization spread throughout the province to promote agriculture, particularly the improved breeding of livestock and the growing of hemp, for which he took a prize in 1791.

Early in the 19th century Caldwell became an important landowner; on 28 Feb. 1801 he reached an agreement to buy for £10,180 sterling all the property Murray had owned at the time of his death, property he had leased for almost 30 years. The following year he purchased the seigneury of Gaspé for £500 and that of Saint-Étienne, which adjoined Lauson, as well as 1,798 acres in Farnham Township. In 1804 he bought 12,262 acres in Westbury Township, and the next year

26,153 in Melbourne Township. To acquire these large blocks, Caldwell was ready to dispose of other properties. Thus he sold the house on Rue Saint-Jean, numerous lots in Sans Bruit and around Quebec, as well as 6,000 acres behind the seigneury of Rivière-du-Loup and pieces of land in Melbourne Township, for a total of about £5,000. Nevertheless, in 1803 and 1804, he was obliged to borrow £3,000. In 1807 he exchanged Cadet's former property in a suburb of Quebec for 14,800 acres in the Eastern Townships plus £300, and three years later he sold land at Anse au Foulon for £1,500.

At about this time Caldwell was able to make substantial profits from increases in the price of wheat because he had bought or built numerous mills. He exported large quantities; between 1797 and 1804 he bought four boats and he hired a skipper in 1803 to deliver flour to St John's, Nfld. In 1809 he constructed a 4,000-square-foot wharf in the basin of the Rivière Chaudière that could accommodate 20 boats, and he was planning to build a large warehouse capable of holding 100,000 bushels of wheat. Caldwell was also involved in supplying the troops stationed in North America. In 1810 he sold more than 1,775,000 pounds of flour to the government for £21,822.

In 1804, because of the European blockade imposed by Napoleon, Caldwell had persuaded Henry Dundas, first lord of the Admiralty, to develop Canadian timber resources for the Royal Navy. He was able to organize effectively the cutting and selling of timber by setting up sawmills beside his grist-mills and exercising his feudal privilege of taking back from his *censitaires*, for compensation, any small plots that had been granted them. After 1806 he began driving settlers away from the seigneury of Lauson by his practice of retaining rights to all oak suitable for royal ships when the *censitaires'* land titles were renewed. His sawmills were the best known in Quebec and the Etchemin mills at the mouth of the Rivière Etchemin were among the largest. Important visitors who went to see the falls of the Chaudière were sometimes invited to tour Caldwell's installations.

Caldwell was involved in colonial politics because of ambition as much as interest. He took up his seat on the Legislative Council when he returned from England in the summer of 1777 and asked to receive remuneration from the date of his appointment. A man of rather tempestuous nature and strong personality, he naturally found himself in conflict with the governors of the time. In 1778 he opposed the governor over certain details of the militia law in particular; he wanted a clearer definition and distribution of the obligations of militia captains and habitants. The following year, however, he supported HALDIMAND, albeit unsuccessfully, in his attempts to speed up the administration of justice. In 1781 Caldwell requested the post of lieutenant governor in

Caldwell

succession to Hector Theophilus Cramahé*. Although Haldimand, who thought him "a very Honorable Worthy Man, and very Zealous for the King's Service," recommended him more warmly than he did Henry Hamilton*, it was the latter who obtained the position. On 8 July 1784, however, Haldimand appointed Caldwell acting deputy receiver general to replace temporarily William GRANT (1744–1805), who had been summoned back to London to account for his administration. Like his predecessor, Caldwell tried to collect amounts owed for the seigneurial fees of *quint* and *lods et ventes*, but without success. He held this position until George Davison* was appointed to it on 1 Sept. 1787.

When Governor Guy Carleton, now Lord Dorchester, set up Legislative Council committees in November 1786, Caldwell was put on the one studying problems of the militia, highways, and communications. The following year he was a member of the committee on education in the province, chaired by Chief Justice William Smith*. Caldwell was one of the allies on council of this controversial figure and according to Alexander Fraser, writing in 1789, he seemed eager to cultivate Smith's friendship. Fraser went on to describe him as "a man of honourable sentiments . . . [who] errs from caprice (tinctured perhaps a little with interested views) rather than any love of disorder, or want of warm attachment to the mother country." After the constitutional reform of 1791 Caldwell was named to the new Legislative Council; he was sworn in on 7 Feb. 1793 and sat on it for the rest of his life.

Caldwell remained active in the militia although he frequently complained about younger officers winning advancement. In July 1787 he was promoted colonel of the Quebec Battalion of British Militia, a rank he held until June 1794, when, "induced by special circumstances," he resigned and was replaced by Francis LE MAISTRE. Not long after, Caldwell joined an association established in 1794 to support the British government in Lower Canada. On 25 July 1794 he was sworn in as receiver general of Lower Canada with an annual salary of £400, to succeed Joshua WINSLOW. He discharged the responsibilities of this office until 1808, when his son John* took over; the latter was officially appointed to the post two years later. In 1823 it was discovered that Henry Caldwell had embezzled nearly £40,000 during the exercise of his duties, including almost £8,000 from the Jesuit estates, which he had managed as treasurer of the commission set up to administer them.

Henry Caldwell died on 28 May 1810 at Belmont, his residence near Quebec, at the age of about 75. His funeral took place on 31 May at the Anglican Cathedral of the Holy Trinity in Quebec. His wife had died six years earlier, and he left all his personal goods and property to his only son except for the seigneury of Lauson, which he bequeathed to his grandson Henry John, and what was left of Sans Bruit, which went to his granddaughter Ann; he also left various gifts to relatives and friends.

MARCEL CAYA

Henry Caldwell is the author of an account of the siege of Quebec by the American army. Written in the form of a letter addressed to General Murray in 1776, it was published in Quebec in 1866 by the Literary and Hist. Soc. of Quebec as *The invasion of Canada in 1775; letter attributed to Major Henry Caldwell*, and reprinted in 1868, 1887, and 1927. The manuscript itself has not been located.

AC, Québec, Testament olographe de Henry Caldwell, 5 juin 1810 (*see* P.-G. Roy, *Inv. testaments*, 2: 299). ANQ-Q, CE1-61, 21 Feb. 1804, 31 May 1810; CN1-16, 27 janv. 1806; CN1-26, 29 sept. 1797; CN1-83, 12 juill. 1784; 9 juin, 21 oct., 6 nov. 1786; 8 août 1788; 5 janv., 22 juin 1789; 7 avril 1790; 9 févr., 12 oct. 1792; 26 mars, 28 sept. 1793; 22 oct. 1794; CN1-91, 25, 26 août, 9 nov. 1791; 26 mars 1792; CN1-171, 12 May 1808; 27 March, 24 May 1809; 5, 8 May 1810; CN1-178, 6, 17 mars, 30 avril, 1er juin, 4 déc. 1795; 20 sept. 1797; 14 mars 1798; 25 juill. 1807; 17 août 1808; CN1-205, 6 févr. 1778; 9, 15 janv. 1779; 10 nov. 1781; 8 avril 1782; 8 avril 1792; CN1-224, 20 janv. 1792; CN1-230, 9 déc. 1794; 22 sept., 5 déc. 1798; 4, 15, 21 sept. 1801; 1er déc. 1804; 8 août 1807; CN1-245, 5 août, 4 sept. 1782; CN1-256, 10 Feb., 6 March, 28 May 1798; CN1-262, 15 févr., 30 avril 1796; 8 mars, 14 août, 5 sept. 1797; 8, 16 févr., 3 mai 1798; 27 févr., 8, 15, 28 mars, 20 juin, 12 août, 1er, 17 oct. 1799; 10 janv., 4, 30 avril, 7 mai, 4, 5, 10 juin 1800; 28 janv., 11, 28 févr., 21 avril 1801; 23 mars, 21 juin, 7 juill., 2, 9, 17, 19 août, 26 sept., 19, 29 oct. 1802; 3 mars, 2, 23 juin, 14 juill., 30 août, 1er, 12 sept., 2, 23 nov., 1er déc. 1803; 7 févr., 29 mars, 5, 11, 20 avril, 6 mai, 30 juin, 28 août, 20 sept., 24 oct., 28 nov. 1804; 12, 26 mars, 31 mai, 3, 16, 17 juill., 3 août, 27 sept., 12 oct., 22 déc. 1805; 25 janv., 20 oct. 1806; 4, 14 mars, 6 nov. 1807; 4 févr., 25 avril, 1er août, 4, 5, 26 oct., 15 nov., 2 déc. 1808; 6 juin, 26, 30 juill., 10, 31 août, 9, 14 sept., 19 oct., 11 nov., 11 déc. 1809; 30 janv., 2 mars, 4, 28 avril, 1er mai 1810; CN1-284, 5 déc. 1791, 22 mars 1792; CN1-285, 20 mai 1803, 8 mars 1805; P-20. BL, Add. mss 21736: 63; 21859: 314; 24322: 24 (copies at PAC). PAC, MG 11, [CO 42] Q, 12: 4, 6; 13: 297; 17-1: 61; 43: 801–2; 65: 158; 69-1: 88; 112: 154; MG 18, L4 (copies); MG 24, B118; MG 30, D1, 6: 747–48, 750, 755; RG 4, A1; RG 68, 90: f.284.

A defence prepared and intended to be delivered at the bar of the Court of King's Bench, held in the city of Quebec; in the month of November, 1790; on a prosecution for a libel; at the instance of Henry Caldwell, esquire . . . (Quebec, [1790]). Bas-Canada, Conseil législatif, *Journaux. Doc. relatifs à l'hist. constitutionnelle, 1759–1791* (Shortt et Doughty; 1921). Knox, *Hist. journal* (Doughty), 1: 179, 332; 2: 91. Smith, *Diary and selected papers* (Upton). *Montreal Gazette*, 7 May 1789. *Quebec Gazette*, 15 Sept. 1774; 23 Feb. 1775; 12 Dec. 1776; 29 Jan., 26 Feb., 22 Oct. 1778; 24 Aug. 1780; 22 March 1781; 25 April 1782; 6 Feb. 1783; 1 Jan., 4 March, 12 Aug., 30 Dec. 1784; 27 Jan., 28 July 1785; 4 Jan., 5, 26 July 1787; 14 Aug., 11 Dec. 1788; 23 April, 14 May 1789; 25 March, 15 April 1790; 24 March, 7 April, 5, 19 May 1791; 22 March 1792; 21 Feb., 11 April, 2,

16, 23 May, 11 July 1793; 1, 4, 16 Jan., 13 Feb., 3 April, 26 June, 3, 10 July 1794; 2 April, 4 June 1795; 29 June, 10 Aug., 5 Oct., 14 Dec. 1797; 5 April 1798; 21 March, 2 May, 15 Aug. 1799; 3, 10 April, 29 May, 25 Sept., 25 Dec. 1800; 1 Jan., 5 March, 2 April, 14 May, 11 June, 12, 26 Nov. 1801; 23, 30 Sept. 1802; 13, 27 Jan., 24 March, 26 May 1803; 23 Feb., 15 March, 14 June 1804; 24 Jan., 2 May, 27 June 1805; 12 June 1806; 19 March, 9 July 1807; 3 March, 12 May, 16, 30 June, 21 July 1808; 13 April, 14 Sept., 23 Nov. 1809; 17, 31 May 1810. F.-J. Audet, "Les législateurs du Bas-Canada." "Collection Haldimand," PAC *Rapport*, 1888: 1079–82. Desjardins, *Guide parl.*, 24, 47, 56. Kelley, "Jacob Mountain," ANQ R*apport*, 1942–43: 228, 247; "The Quebec Diocesan Archives: a description of the collection of historical records of the Church of England in the Diocese of Quebec," ANQ *Rapport*, 1946–47: 195, 214. Langelier, *Liste des terrains concédés*, 10. "Papiers d'État," PAC *Rapport*, 1890: 74, 76, 78, 100, 130, 250. "Papiers d'État – Bas-Canada," PAC *Rapport*, 1891: 11, 80, 100, 121; 1892: 175, 177, 182, 186, 216, 229–31; 1893: 21. *Quebec almanac*, 1788: 47; 1792: 118; 1794: 71, 88; 1805: 21; 1810: 22. Turcotte, *Le Conseil législatif*, 4, 17, 51–52.

Burt, *Old prov. of Quebec* (1968). Caron, *La colonisation de la prov. de Québec*, 2: 253, 256. R. C. Dalton, *The Jesuits' estates question, 1760–1888: a study of the background for the agitation of 1889* (Toronto, 1968), 48–49, 79, 81, 85. Macmillan, "New men in action," *Canadian business hist.* (Macmillan), 61. Neatby, *Quebec*, 165–66. J.-E. Roy, *Hist. de Lauzon*, vol.3. Ruddel, "Quebec City, 1765–1831," 31, 261, 263–64, 414. Trudel, *L'esclavage au Canada français*, 141. F.-J. Audet, "Les législateurs de la province de Québec, 1764–1791," *BRH*, 31 (1925): 535; "Zachary Macaulay," *BRH*, 3 (1897): 7. Ivanhoë Caron, "Les censitaires du coteau Sainte-Geneviève (banlieue de Québec) de 1636 à 1800," *BRH*, 27 (1921): 166, 170–72. P.-B. Casgrain, "Le moulin de Dumont," *BRH*, 11 (1905): 71. "La famille Caldwell," *BRH*, 42 (1936): 3–6. J. M. LeMoine, "The Hon. Henry Caldwell, L.C., at Quebec, 1759–1810," RSC *Trans.*, 2nd ser., 9 (1903), sect.II: 29–37. Frère Marcel-Joseph, "Les Canadiens veulent conserver le régime seigneurial," *RHAF*, 7 (1953–54): 57, 62, 227–29. Maurice O'Bready, "The Eastern Townships contemplated as a British stronghold," *RHAF*, 15 (1961–62): 234–35. Eugène Rouillard, "Les chefs de canton," *BRH*, 2 (1896): 185. P.-G. Roy, "Le testament de l'honorable Henry Caldwell," *BRH*, 29 (1923): 202–4.

CALDWELL, JAMES, merchant, militia officer, and office holder; d. 18 April 1815 in Montreal, Lower Canada.

Nothing is known of James Caldwell's origins, date of arrival in the province of Quebec, or beginnings in business, but by 1784 he was established in Montreal, where he signed the petition seeking an assembly for the province. Three years later he was listed as a lieutenant in the British Militia of the Town and Banlieu of Montreal. In October 1790 he joined other Montreal merchants in requesting Governor Lord Dorchester [Guy CARLETON] to create a custom-house in Montreal to reduce the costs, losses, and delays caused by the fact that there was only one office,

located in Quebec. Caldwell was dealing in wine, beer, various foodstuffs, hardware, and other goods. In 1793 and 1794 he exported wines to Upper Canada and the Great Lakes region.

Being a shrewd businessman, Caldwell no doubt had his mind set on picking up a share of the lands being granted by the government in the new Lower Canadian townships. From 1792 to 1812 he, along with partners such as Alexander Auldjo*, submitted a constant stream of petitions. In accordance with the system of township leaders and associates in effect until about 1809, an applicant, having first secured the support of the Executive Council, senior officials, and governor, would recruit some associates to sign his application for a land grant; as soon as the letters patent were issued, the associates, who ordinarily received 1,200 acres each, would transfer all but 200 acres to the leader for a nominal sum. In 1802 Caldwell took part in the allocation of half of Aston Township, and in 1806 he received letters patent for 1,853 acres for himself, his wife Louisa Melvin, and their three children, Alexander, Louisa, and Amelia (Mary).

Caldwell seems to have maintained excellent relations with the powerful class of businessmen and ubiquitous officials, and this practice probably helps account for the numerous government appointments he received. Along with Auldjo and François Desrivières, in 1805 he became a warden in Montreal of Trinity House of Quebec, which at the urging of John YOUNG had been founded that year by the assembly. In addition to holding that honourable and lucrative post, he was made a commissioner for the improvement of inland navigation between Lachine and Montreal in the same year, and then in 1806 a justice of the peace. Early in 1810, when Stephen Sewell*'s election to the assembly for Huntingdon was contested, Caldwell served as one of the commissioners to hear the witnesses for both sides. His duties as a magistrate were increased in 1812 by a commission authorizing him to receive the oath of allegiance. The following year, when the Act for the Relief of Insane Persons and for the Support of Foundlings came into effect, he was again made a commissioner, in company with Desrivières. In 1814, having declined appointment as a returning officer, Caldwell accepted a commission to oversee the removal of the old walls and fortifications of Montreal, and also became a commissioner for the building and repair of churches.

While attending to his commercial activities, which he had not given up, and to his administrative duties, Caldwell had steadily risen in the ranks of the local militia, becoming captain in 1797, major in 1811, and lieutenant-colonel of the 1st Battalion in 1813. He was also interested in the arts and letters and accumulated a collection of books, maps, and engravings. In this respect he seems to have been fairly typical of certain

Caleff

businessmen of the time, such as his friends James McGILL, Joseph FROBISHER, and William McGillivray* who, ready to take any opportunity to increase their wealth, also extended their influence to charitable, educational, or cultural works, thus assuring their social advancement.

Worn out by a long and painful illness, James Caldwell died on 18 April 1815. His funeral was conducted by the Reverend Jehosaphat MOUNTAIN, minister of Christ Church, where he had owned a pew.

MARIE-PAULE LaBRÈQUE

ANQ-M, CE1-63, 20 avril 1815. PAC, RG 1, L3^L: 17745, 17747, 26831. Bas-Canada, chambre d'Assemblée, *Journaux*, 1795: 140. *Doc. relatifs à l'hist. constitutionnelle, 1759–1791* (Shortt et Doughty; 1921), 2: 733–43. *Montreal Gazette*, 20 April 1815. *Montreal Herald*, 22 April 1815. *Quebec Gazette*, 28 Oct. 1790; 31 July 1794; 14 May 1795; 30 May 1799; 16 May 1805; 20 March, 17 July 1806; 3 Nov. 1808; 6 July 1809; 15 Feb., 12 July 1810; 2 Sept. 1813; 22 Sept. 1814; 27 April 1815. *Quebec almanac*, 1788: 52; 1798: 106; 1810: 39; 1815: 47–48, 58, 65, 90. Desjardins, *Guide parl.*, 130, 134. Langelier, *Liste des terrains concédés*, 10, 17, 675, 1286. F. D. Adams, *A history of Christ Church Cathedral, Montreal* (Montreal, 1941), 57. P.-G. Roy, *La ville de Québec sous le Régime français* (2v., Québec, 1930), 2: 318. G. F. McGuigan, "La concession des terres dans les Cantons de l'Est du Bas-Canada (1763–1809)," *Recherches sociographiques* (Québec), 4 (1963), no.1: 86–87. P.-G. Roy, "La Trinity-House ou Maison de la Trinité à Québec," *BRH*, 24 (1918): 105–10.

CALEFF, JOHN (he also signed **Calef**), surgeon; b. 30 Aug. 1726 in Ipswich, Mass., son of Robert Calef, a clothier, and Margaret Staniford; m. first 10 Dec. 1747 Margaret Rogers of Ipswich, and they had two children; m. secondly 18 Jan. 1753 Dorothy Jewett of Rowley, Mass., and they had 15 children, 4 of whom were stillborn; d. 23 Oct. 1812 in St Andrews, N.B.

The fourth generation of his family to live in Massachusetts, John Caleff was educated at the Boston Latin School and was later "bred to Physic," as medical training was then termed. In 1745 he was the surgeon of a provincial ship-of-war at the capture of Louisbourg, Île Royale (Cape Breton Island), by forces under William Pepperrell* and Peter Warren*. When war was renewed in 1756, Caleff served again as a surgeon, first at the provincial hospital at Albany, N.Y., and then for five years with a provincial regiment under generals Lord Loudoun and Jeffery Amherst*. At the end of the war he returned to Ipswich, where for several years he acted as a civil magistrate and militia officer. Elected to the General Court of Massachusetts in 1764, he was one of the "17 rescinders" in the assembly who in 1768 opposed the distribution of a circular letter criticizing British taxation policy. His position made Caleff "obnoxious" to many Ipswich residents and he was the subject

of such harassment that in 1774 he was forced to apologize publicly for his action.

During the 1770s Caleff became increasingly interested in the townships developing east of the Penobscot River (Maine). Late in 1772 the inhabitants of the region chose him as their agent to attempt in London to obtain royal confirmation of the land grants made them by the Massachusetts government or, alternatively, to have a separate government established in the area. Nothing came of his mission, but in 1779, when rebel threats finally forced him to abandon Ipswich and flee to the Penobscot region, he found that both the British government and the local inhabitants were actively planning a separate administration. In February Caleff went to Nova Scotia to urge the establishment of a military post at Penobscot, and four months later troops under Brigadier Francis McLean* began the construction of Fort George (Castine, Maine). Caleff was present during the famous 21-day siege of the fort by rebel forces in July–August; for his leadership McLean appointed him inspector, commissary, chief justice of the peace, and superintendent of Indians at Penobscot.

In May 1780 the Penobscot residents again chose Caleff to press their interests in London. That August the British government approved the establishment of a separate provincial government in the region, to be called New Ireland, and appointed its chief officials. The new province died aborning, however, with the news in 1781 of the surrender of Lieutenant-General Charles Cornwallis's army at Yorktown, Va, and the abrupt cessation of all British military operations in America. Caleff continued to urge implementation of the plan, emphasizing the loyalty of the inhabitants and the possibility of Penobscot's becoming a base of operations for the recapture of the New England colonies, but the New Ireland project was, as Lord North informed him, impossible.

While in England Caleff published his account of *The siege of Penobscot* and received an appointment as assistant physician to the royal hospital in Nova Scotia. When he arrived back in North America in 1782, he found to his dismay that his commission had been lost en route and, furthermore, that during his absence his appointments as inspector and commissary at Penobscot had been given to Robert Pagan*. Feeling frustrated and abused, Caleff returned to England in 1784 to get a new commission and to present his petition for compensation before the loyalist claims commission. The commissioners were unusually impressed by Caleff's wartime services and losses. "We found so much poverty mixed with so much Loyalty," they reported, and they recommended that he be given £50 immediately to clear his debts in London and pay his passage home. On his claim of almost £10,000 the commission awarded him a lump sum of £2,400 and an annual income of £100.

Caleff was intercepted on his return voyage by a family friend and warned to stay away from the Penobscot area. Accordingly, he joined his wife and nine surviving children, who had fled to the new loyalist community of Saint John, N.B. On 25 Aug. 1784 he was appointed surgeon to the British garrison at Fort Howe and lived an apparently quiet life in Saint John except for one amusing contretemps with Bishop Charles INGLIS. Throughout his life Caleff was a fervently religious man. He had served in 1770 as a pallbearer at the funeral of the famous Great Awakening preacher, George Whitefield; he acted as a part-time chaplain at both Fort George and Fort Howe; and he was a vestryman of Trinity Church in Saint John. During one of his many trips to England he met the patroness of Methodism, the Countess of Huntingdon, who was keenly interested in spreading Methodist principles among the people of North America and who in the 1780s sent him a large collection of Bibles, various hymn-books, and two Methodist ministers to further the work. Enraged when Bishop Inglis refused to ordain one of these ministers or to allow either to preach in Trinity Church, Caleff vented his anger by spreading a particularly degrading rumour connecting Inglis with a local prostitute. The bishop was scandalized and hastened to assure the archbishop of Canterbury that Caleff was "a weak enthusiastical man" who alternated between fits of religious fervour and bouts of drunkenness and blasphemous behaviour. He threatened Caleff with a slander suit, whereupon Caleff publicly repudiated his "ludicrous" tale. This incident is the only recorded scandal in Caleff's long career.

In 1791 Caleff moved his family to St Andrews, where most of his Penobscot associates resided [see William GALLOP]; however, he returned sufficiently often to Saint John to retain his post as garrison surgeon. He was an early member of the Friendly Society, founded in 1803 by the Reverend Samuel ANDREWS, and over the years he acquired considerable property in the town. His will suggests that he continued to practise medicine until his death in 1812. His most trying professional moment was doubtless the smallpox epidemic which struck St Andrews in 1800. With some assistance he inoculated and tended more than 500 persons, all but 3 of whom, he proudly reported, survived the dread disease. Caleff's wife predeceased him some time after 1800, and only 5 of his 17 children were alive at his death.

In recorded history, Caleff's significance undoubtedly derives from his advocacy of the interests of the Penobscot loyalists. Yet one suspects that he made an equal or even greater contribution in an area that remains largely unrecorded: his constant attendance upon the sick and wounded, during both peace and war, for more than six decades. Particularly in Charlotte County, N.B., where Caleff was for many years the only available doctor, his professional services must have been an invaluable source of comfort and security to the residents of that young colonial community.

ANN GORMAN CONDON

John Caleff is the author of *The siege of Penobscot by the rebels; containing a journal of His Majesty's forces . . .* (London, 1781); it was later edited by Nathan Goold and republished in the *Magazine of Hist. with Notes and Queries, Extra Numbers* (New York), 3 (1910), no.11.

Clements Library, Shelburne papers, 66: 169–73, 183–85 (transcripts at PAC). N.B. Museum, H. T. Hazen coll.: Ward Chipman papers, John Caleff to Thomas Carleton, 22 Nov. 1786. PAC, MG 23, C6, ser.1, 1: 131–32, 135–37, 139–40 (transcripts; copies at UNBL). PANB, RG 7, RS63, 1811, John Caleff; RG 10, RS108, Petitions of John Caleff, February 1785, 12 Aug. 1802. PRO, AO 12/109: 45, 101–2; AO 13, bundle 73 (mfm. at UNBL). G.B., Hist. MSS Commission, *Report on American manuscripts in the Royal Institution of Great Britain*, [comp. B. F. Stevens, ed. H. J. Brown] (4v., London, 1904–9), 3: 229–30. *Royal commission on American loyalists* (Coke and Egerton). *Winslow papers* (Raymond). Jones, *Loyalists of Mass. Robert Calef of Boston and some of his descendants*, comp. A. C. Boardman (Salem, Mass., 1940). *Vital records of Ipswich, Massachusetts, to the end of the year 1849 . . .* (3v., Salem, 1910–19). Condon, "Envy of American states." R. W. Sloan, "New Ireland: loyalists in eastern Maine during the American revolution" (PHD thesis, Mich. State Univ., East Lansing, 1971). D. R. Jack, "The Caleff family," *Acadiensis* (Saint John, N.B.), 7 (1907): 261–73. R. L. Jackson, "Physicians of Essex County," Essex Institute, *Hist. Coll.* (Salem), 83 (1947): 255–56. Henry Wilmot, "Life and times of Dr. John Caleff, a prominent loyalist," N.B. Hist. Soc., *Coll.*, 4 (1919–28), no.11: 277–81.

CAMPBELL, DUGALD (Dougald), army officer, surveyor, judge, and office holder; b. 1758 or 1759 in Scotland; d. 12 April 1810 in Fredericton, N.B.

Little is known of Dugald Campbell's background, except that he was a nephew of Patrick Campbell*, a farmer, merchant, and soldier of Fort William, Scotland, who wrote an interesting account of an expedition in 1791 and 1792 to New Brunswick, the Canadas, and the northeastern American states. They belonged to a branch of the Campbell family which appears to have long held the hereditary office of keeper of the royal forest of Mamlorn, near Achallader. Dugald married Jacobina, daughter of Donald Drummond, a member of the MacGregor family of Balhaldie, near Stirling, Scotland, who had settled at Poughkeepsie, N.Y.; her sister Susan married Captain Archibald McLean, an officer in the New York Volunteers who was later, for many years, a member of the New Brunswick legislature. Dugald and Jacobina were to have three sons and two daughters; the eldest son, Alexander, served as a lieutenant in the

Campbell

104th Foot in the War of 1812 and later settled on a farm in Etobicoke Township, Upper Canada.

Commissioned as an ensign in the 42nd Foot (Royal Highland Regiment) in April 1777, and promoted lieutenant in 1781, Campbell served with the first battalion of the regiment in New York and was in command of a detachment disbanded at Parrtown (Saint John, N.B.) in 1783. In 1784, under Campbell's leadership, the Highlanders moved to the Nashwaak River, about 15 miles from St Anne's Point, the main centre for the loyalist regiments then being settled on the Saint John River. In April 1784 Campbell was designated by Governor John Parr* to assist in laying out a town at St Anne's. Two months later the province of New Brunswick was created, and early in 1785 Parr's plan for a town was set aside when Thomas CARLETON, the first governor of the new province, decided that the capital, to be called Fredericstown, should be built on the site. Campbell was then made responsible for surveying and subdividing a new town with streets 66 feet wide intersecting at right angles; houses were to be centred laterally on the street line of quarter-acre lots, each 66 feet by 165 feet. He was also one of the trustees appointed for effecting the speedy settlement of the capital and prepared the first plan of the town plat. Later he declared that the surveying was out of his line of duty and that he had received no compensation for his work. It did, however, bring him close to the governor, whom he later served as aide-de-camp and with whom he was to be associated until Carleton's departure from the province in 1803.

It seems likely that the patronage of Major-General John Campbell, commanding officer of the forces in Nova Scotia, was a factor in Dugald Campbell's being specifically named by Parr in the document ordering the survey of St Anne's; yet he was an experienced and capable surveyor who was to be employed from time to time as an assistant engineer with the army for the rest of his life. In the winters of 1784 and 1785 he surveyed the Saint John River from its mouth to Grand Falls, and produced a map of which the historian William Francis Ganong* says: "It is remarkable for the fidelity with which it records the Indian names of the river, to which the translation is often added." In 1791, when he accompanied his uncle Patrick on an expedition up the Saint John River, he was responsible for erecting barracks and for provisioning new posts at Presque Isle and Grand Falls designed for the defence of the frontier. Six years later he made a survey of the Magaguadavic River in connection with the settlement of the boundary dispute with the United States, completing work which had been begun by Isaac Hedden (Heddon) in 1796. The most dramatic episode in his career as a surveyor came late in 1799; seeking full-time employment as a military engineer, he succeeded in interesting the Duke of Kent [EDWARD

AUGUSTUS], then commander-in-chief at Halifax, in the possibility of developing more effective military communications by linking Halifax with Quebec through New Brunswick. The project was abandoned after a few months "as the breach formed by the projection of a part of the American territory in the best and perhaps the only practicable route for that purpose, appears to be an insuperable bar." A map of the road from Fort Cumberland (near Sackville) to Fredericton, dated 1799, is related to Campbell's proposal and may have been prepared by him. In 1807 he joined Lieutenant Colonel George Johnstone on a tour of the western part of New Brunswick during which he prepared a plan of the frontier to accompany a project for its defence. Campbell's extensive acquaintance with the topography of southern and western New Brunswick also led to his being employed to prepare a report on the province's roads, with recommendations for improvements, which was published by order of the House of Assembly in 1803.

When his uncle visited him in 1791 and 1792, Campbell was living near Fredericton, in a neighbourhood preferred by officials and loyalist officers. He continued to live in or near Fredericton but also built a country residence, Taymouth Farm, on a 580-acre grant on the Nashwaak River at its junction with a little river which he renamed the Tay. His farm home was a substantial one-storey building made of timber hewn square, dovetailed on the corners with each log laid in mortar, nicely shingled on the outside, and well finished within. Local people called it the Campbell Castle, an allusion, no doubt, to Taymouth Castle in Scotland, the stronghold of the Breadalbane branch of the clan. Many of the settlers in the little Gaelic-speaking community on the Nashwaak resented Campbell's taking for himself the only large block of good land and assigning them unusually small lots which were "all length and no breadth."

In 1802 Campbell was at the centre of the last and most bitter of the political episodes in the struggle between the official group around Carleton and the radical forces in the assembly led by James GLENIE, who, like Campbell, had earlier been employed by the military as an assistant engineer. When Hedden, the clerk of the House of Assembly, died, Carleton, following the practice in Britain, where the right to name the clerk of the House of Commons was part of the royal prerogative, appointed Campbell to the post. His right to do so was challenged by a majority of members of the assembly who, citing Nova Scotian precedent based on the earlier practice of the New England colonies, defied Carleton and elected one of his most outspoken opponents, Samuel Denny Street*. The two sides then played out the classical roles of a confrontation between crown and parliament, with the majority in the house attempting to use the assembly's right to frame money-bills to have the salary of the office paid to their nominee. When the Council objected and requested a conference, opponents of the lieutenant governor refused to attend sessions and escaped the serjeant-at-arms by getting out of town, leaving the assembly without its quorum of 13. The lieutenant governor's supporters then defied the rules. The rump of the assembly under the leadership of John Coffin* deleted Street's name from the annual revenue bill and passed it in a session with only eight members present. The Council and the lieutenant governor accepted their action as valid and Campbell received the salary for the labour that Street had performed. He continued to hold the office even when he returned to full-time soldiering, having a deputy carry out the duties when necessary. The election that followed the 1802 session of the legislature was contested with a rancour and hostility unparalleled in the early history of the province. In October Campbell, who had been a justice of the Inferior Court of Common Pleas since 1791, joined six of his fellow magistrates for York County in a petition praying that Caleb JONES be removed from the bench for conducting himself in a disloyal manner in his canvass as a candidate for the assembly. Supporters of the lieutenant governor formed a majority in the new assembly, but the campaign left a legacy of bitterness in the New Brunswick community.

In the early days of the province Campbell served as a major in the militia of York County. He always regarded himself as a soldier and, when the regular troops were withdrawn from New Brunswick at the beginning of the war with France, he obtained a commission as a captain in the King's New Brunswick Regiment, a unit recruited for local defence in the years from 1793 to 1802. During part of this time he served in Saint John: in 1797 he was in command of the light company of the regiment on garrison duty in a newly erected blockhouse at the Lower Cove, and for a time, in 1800, he was commanding officer in the city. Finally, in 1803, he had an opportunity to resume his career as a regular officer on active service; he became an acting captain in a newly approved regiment, the New Brunswick Fencibles, which was to become a line regiment, the 104th Foot, in 1810 shortly after Campbell's death. The regiment sought recruits throughout British North America, and, pursuing this endeavour, Campbell early in 1804 made a winter journey from Fredericton to Quebec that was a prelude to the famous winter march of the regiment nine years later; in February he arrived in Quebec "very much fatigued from the uncommon badness of the way which I was under a necessity of paving with Dollars to render it in any degree passable. I took off my snow shoes at the Riviere des Caps without any regret, after having wore them about three hundred miles." He remained in Quebec for several weeks in command of a large body of recruits.

He received a company in the regiment in September 1804. Most of the rest of his life was spent on regimental duty at Fredericton and Saint John.

Born into a family of forest-keepers accustomed to a robust outdoor life on the Scottish moors, trained as a soldier and surveyor, Dugald Campbell adapted readily to physical conditions in loyalist New Brunswick. He accepted the values of a society based on clientage and official patronage but rewards for loyal service were small in a poor colony. The office of clerk of the assembly was the only significant office that the government of New Brunswick was able to offer to a man who had no high-placed support in Britain. Campbell had neither the time nor the resources to develop a gentleman's estate or to give leadership to the tiny Highland community that he established on the Nashwaak, but he made a significant and long-lasting contribution to the province in helping to plan and subdivide the town of Fredericton, in surveying and mapping rivers, in laying out roads, and in organizing military communications. Ganong thought highly of Campbell's work, commenting on the excellence of his recording of Indian place names and suggesting, on the basis of his skill as a draughtsman, that he may have drawn the originals of the three excellent illustrations in Patrick Campbell's book on his North American travels.

D. M. YOUNG

N.B., Dept. of Natural Resources, Lands Branch (Fredericton), Map of Fredericton, comp. Dugald Campbell, 1785; Plan of the Nashwaak grant; Town plat of Fredericton. PAC, MG 23, D1, ser.1, 59; RG 8, I (C ser.), 227; 718: 145, 155; 1218: 107–8. PANB, H1-203.172-1800, "Survey of the proposed road between Fredericton and the Miramichi, copied from an actual survey made by Dougald Campbell . . ."; RG 2, RS6; RS8, Unarranged Executive Council docs., Petition of the magistrates of the county of York, 14 Oct. 1802; RG 7, RS75, Dugald Campbell, 1827; RG 10, RS108, Petition of Dugald Campbell, 1808. Private arch., Mrs Ralph Miles (Fredericton), Letters between W. O. Raymond and J. A. Young, Young to Raymond, 21 Feb. 1921; Papers relating to transfer of portions of Campbell farm at Taymouth, N.B. PRO, CO 700, New Brunswick, no.12 (copy at PANB). UNBL, MG H2, Dugald Campbell to Edward Winslow, 14, 21 July 1800 (mfm. at PAC).

Campbell, *Travels in North America* (Langton and Ganong). N.B., House of Assembly, *Journal*, 1802–3. *Winslow papers* (Raymond). I. L. Hill, *Fredericton, New Brunswick, British North America* ([Fredericton, 1968?]). MacNutt, *New Brunswick*. L. M. B. Maxwell, *An outline of the history of central New Brunswick to the time of confederation* (Sackville, N.B., 1937). George Patterson, *Memoir of the Rev. James MacGregor, D.D.* . . . (Philadelphia, 1859). W. A. Squires, *The 104th Regiment of Foot (the New Brunswick Regiment), 1803–1817* (Fredericton, 1962). Wright, *Loyalists of N.B.* W. F. Ganong, "Additions and corrections to monographs on the place-nomenclature, cartography, historic sites, boundaries and settlement-

Campbell

origins of the province of New Brunswick," RSC *Trans.*, 2nd ser., 12 (1906), sect.II: 3–157; "A monograph of the cartography of the province of New Brunswick," RSC *Trans.*, 2nd ser., 3 (1897), sect.II: 313–427. Jonas Howe, "Dugald Campbell's map," *New Brunswick Magazine* (Saint John), 2 (January–June 1899): 233–39.

CAMPBELL, JAMES, specialist in hemp production; fl. 1806–17.

There were quite a number of James Campbells in Quebec during the period 1783–1824: three of them, a loyalist, a half-pay officer of the 84th Foot, and a half-pay soldier of the 78th Foot, requested land in various townships; a fourth was convicted of assault. The James Campbell who was a specialist in the production of hemp emigrated from Scotland in 1806, shortly after Charles Frederick Grece*, who was also a specialist in this domain. According to official documents (but not the later claims of the two entrepreneurs), the British government had promised them advances of £400 each to introduce hemp culture into Lower Canada; the arrangement included a right of withdrawal by the government, should the need arise. This initiative was one of a series of measures that had been adopted in London and the colony beginning in the 1790s.

Full of big ideas, Campbell landed at Quebec in the autumn of 1806 with 18 skilled workers – farmers, millwrights, carpenters, and blacksmiths – and the members of his family. Shortly after his arrival Thomas DUNN, the civil administrator of Lower Canada, promised him all possible assistance from the government. London's real or imagined promises did not materialize: there was no cleared land to be given Campbell immediately, nor any seed. The Executive Council did, however, agree to reimburse him for part of his expenses, up to £300, on presentation of "satisfactory" receipts. At the beginning of 1807 the government bought some land at Bécancour; Campbell was to be allowed to occupy it without charge for five years and would receive fair reimbursement for improvements he made to it. Isaac Winslow Clarke*, the government agent, promised to obtain 300 bushels of seed so that he might begin growing hemp as soon as possible. Dunn reported on these efforts to the British government. Campbell's nephew John LAMBERT, well known for his account of his travels in Lower Canada, claimed that the Executive Council had refused to provide Campbell with additional financial aid until he put up buildings and manufactured some hemp, and also that the seed obtained for him was sterile. Campbell made a fresh attempt with the council. That body was aware of the risk of losing the advance payments already granted to Campbell, and anxious to realize a profit on the £2,400 invested in hemp-growing; thus it reluctantly made him another loan and considered obtaining reimbursement by using him to process, at a reasonable price, all the hemp produced in the Trois-Rivières region, which the government had promised to buy. There had been some question of whether it would be possible to get this crop started without a government promise to purchase all the raw hemp at a fixed price.

In 1807 Campbell had little success in raising a crop because of the poor quality of the seed. The following year Governor CRAIG praised Grece's efforts but called Campbell a slacker and a speculator who did not carry out his promises despite frequent requests for funds. However, in September Campbell announced the opening of a hemp-mill on his land. As the government turned a deaf ear to his grievances, in 1811 Campbell presented a long petition to the Executive Council giving his version of things. He claimed that in London he had first been appointed agent for inspecting hemp in the districts of Trois-Rivières and Quebec – although the British government strictly forbad anyone to be a producer and inspector at the same time – and that he had been promised a grant of 150 acres of cleared land in Lower Canada, with certain implements being put at his disposal free of charge; as for remuneration, he was to receive a sum of money to pay for his voyage, an advance of £400, a salary of £200 a year for life if he carried out his obligations, and £43 for every ton of marketable hemp harvested. In fact he had received land of mediocre quality that could not produce a crop without three or four years of hard work; he had also lost his 18 experts, in addition to several months of salary advances to them, because of the impossibility of setting to work immediately and also because of the strong demand for skilled manpower in the colony. Having been forced to mortgage his property, he had been faced with an attachment on the order of £2,000 just when he was reaching his goal. All in all, he said, he had lost more than £2,168.

The council was unmoved and agreed only to continue Campbell's salary until 1 Nov. 1811, a decision that was confirmed by the Privy Council committee for trade in London. Then Campbell's trail becomes blurred: it may have been he who signed an address to Governor PREVOST in 1813. In any event, along with Grece he submitted a new plan to the government in 1814; the last reference to him was made when some land was put up for sheriff's sale at Trois-Rivières in 1817.

Craig attributed the lack of success of Grece's and Campbell's efforts to the strong demand for manpower in the timber trade and the consequent general rise in salaries that made hemp growing unprofitable. For his part Campbell blamed the colonial government's inaction and the poor seed. Lambert, a shrewd observer, noted that for 20 years Canadians had experienced nothing but failure in that field: why, he asked, would they give up growing wheat, which had proved more profitable, for a doubtful gamble that demanded expertise, capital, and a market artificially stimulated by high subsidies? He even mentioned the existence of a supposed plot implicating members and agents of the Executive Council who were said to have provided spoiled seed. These, he said, were the real reasons for the failure in hemp culture, and it would be wrong to attribute it as did William VONDENVELDEN to the prejudices of the Canadians or opposition from the merchants, seigneurs, and clergy. At bottom, "the French Canadians are like the rest of the world, fond of getting money with as little trouble as possible."

JEAN-PIERRE WALLOT

PAC, MG 11, [CO 42] Q, 99: 249; 101-1: 2; 101-2: 372; 102: 44; 103: 20, 35–36; 107: 159, 373; 117-1: 104–38, 141–43, 146; 117-2: 185; 120: 7; 128-1: 196; RG 1, E1; L3^L: 27–42, 283, 538, 563, 575, 577, 641–46, 686–704, 2084, 2971–74, 3075–82, 3797, 3906, 5320–26, 5341–48, 15218–33, 22162, 30960–1018, 31095–112, 65819–22, 72579–83, 78473–76, 81241–360, 83434–39, 85235–44, 882484–303, 90996–1013, 96388; RG 4, A1. John Lambert, *Travels through Lower Canada, and the United States of North America in the years 1806, 1807, and 1808 . . .* (3v., London, 1810), 1: xiv–xviii, 183, 198, 232, 468–95; 2: 57. *Quebec Gazette*, 1 Sept. 1808, 30 Dec. 1813, 24 April 1817, 18 Jan. 1821, 1 April 1824.

CANNON, EDWARD, master mason and businessman; b. probably in 1739 in Ireland; m. Helena (Eleanor) Murphy, probably in 1764, and they had 11 children; d. 28 July 1814 at Quebec, Lower Canada, and was buried two days later in the Cimetière des Picotés.

Little is known of Edward Cannon's youth. He seems to have received a good education, which is reflected in his correspondence by a firm hand, legible characters, and a precise style. By 1774 he had left his native land and was living at St John's, Nfld, where he followed his trade as a mason. During the 20 years or so that he spent in Newfoundland he worked on the fortifications and other government buildings. At the time of the American revolution he was in a corps of independent volunteers [*see* Robert Pringle*]. In 1792 he made a request for land, but received no response, and this may have been the reason for his leaving Newfoundland and going to Quebec.

The Cannon family took up residence at Quebec in 1795. Edward entrusted his daughters to the Ursulines' care and then began to practise his trade with his older sons, Ambrose and Laurence, who were joined by John* in 1800. It was at this period that his career branched out. On 30 April 1800 William VONDEN-VELDEN, surveyor of the highways, streets, and lanes for the town, ordered 700 to 800 square *toises* of paving stones for Rue Saint-Pierre. Cannon was to receive "the sum of five shillings and ten pence in legal

currency" per *toise* for his work, and agreed to complete the paving job by August if the materials were supplied and the rubbish littering the ground cleaned up. The work was finished on 19 June, although some appraisers thought that it did not fully conform to the order. Subsequently Cannon undertook to do the masonry for the Anglican church at Quebec; the foundation stone having been blessed on 11 Aug. 1800, this major piece of work was finished in 1804.

In the period when the church was being built, Cannon began investing in real estate. He bought pieces of land from Thomas Reddy, Augustin Paradis, Richard W. Jones, and Hugh Hogan's widow in 1801, and from Robert Dees in 1802. In addition he petitioned the crown for land and received several hundred acres. All these properties were in Aston, Milton, and Clifton townships. Cannon did not live on his lands and as a result suffered one particular set-back. In 1809 he lost the 200 acres bought from Paradis for 23 shillings; it went to John Doty*, who also claimed to have bought this land from Paradis. Cannon was interested in acquiring properties in town as well, and on 21 June 1803 bought from Pierre-Édouard Desbarats* a two-storey stone house with stable and shed on Rue Sainte-Geneviève.

When the assignment for the Anglican church was finished, Cannon made an agreement with the *fabrique* of Baie-Saint-Paul to add an extension including two chapels and a sacristy in stone to the parish church. This kind of contract was divided into sections: Cannon undertook to provide and pay the masons and to put up the scaffolding; the churchwardens were to supply the materials and labourers and also to look after feeding, lodging, and transporting the masons. Payment for the work was made daily according to its progress measured in *toises*; the churchwardens were to make supplementary payments if they required cut stone for the openings.

Cannon and his sons took on other big projects. The Union Company of Quebec, which had been incorporated on 25 March 1805 and which wanted to provide the town with a fine hotel, awarded the building contract to Cannon. The cornerstone was laid on 14 August and the work must have been carried out rapidly, since the hotel opened on 1 November. Located on Rue Sainte-Anne, it had three storeys, and Cannon received £1,427 14s. 6d. for the work. The following year Trinity House at Quebec commissioned him to build a round lighthouse on Île Verte. In 1808, still working with his sons, he undertook construction of the Quebec prison, using plans by François Baillairgé*. In October he hired three masons for the job, paying a monthly wage of ten Spanish *piastres* for the duration of their contract. Moreover, the growth in population that the town experienced at the turn of the century stimulated a

Captain John

great deal of other construction. Cannon was consequently entrusted with building shops and residences for the leading citizens. Like all the masons of the period he also did a certain number of expert appraisals. Until his death, Cannon kept up his regular activity, signing a final contract in August 1813.

As a result, although he had been late setting up in business, Cannon was able to take advantage of the unprecedented and swift expansion of the town of Quebec to demonstrate his competence in undertaking building jobs and thus to acquire an excellent reputation and a good clientele. He was not, however, a creator; since there were architects such as François Baillairgé on the Quebec scene, he was restricted to carrying out other people's ideas.

Living in Upper Town, Cannon shared the life of those prominent in Quebec. In 1799 and 1813 he signed addresses to governors PRESCOTT and PREVOST; from 1803 he subscribed to the Quebec Fire Society. He mingled with people who were in his own or related professions, such as Charles Jourdain*, *dit* Labrosse, and François Baillairgé.

Edward Cannon was active, energetic, and enterprising. A shrewd businessman, he was able to fit his sons quickly into his operations and to prepare a successor. His third son, John, inherited his clientele and also won the confidence of both English- and French-speaking clients.

RAYMONDE GAUTHIER

ANQ-Q, CN1-16, 29 mars 1809, 10 déc. 1820; CN1-26, 9 sept. 1802, 15 août 1805, 25 févr. 1806, 11 juin 1808, 8 juill. 1809, 3 mai 1810, 10 juin 1812, 10 janv. 1814; CN1-27, 6 déc. 1813; CN1-145, 21 juin, 18 sept. 1801; 21 juin 1806; CN1-171, 27 juin 1808; CN1-178, 1er juin 1804; 25, 26 oct. 1808; 3 oct. 1810; 8, 9 févr. 1814; CN1-230, 30 avril, 19 juin 1800; 28 déc. 1804; 7 juin 1814; CN1-253, 21 avril 1813, 21 juill. 1814; CN1-256, 13 mars 1800; CN1-262, 6 mai 1801, 9 août 1813; CN1-284, 21 juin 1803, 3 juill. 1813; CN1-285, 1er déc. 1800; 15, 17 févr. 1801; 11 mai 1802; 24 mai 1804; 3 août 1809. MAC-CD, Fonds Morisset, 2, C226/E25.5/1. "Les dénombrements de Québec" (Plessis), ANQ *Rapport*, 1948–49: 174. Geneviève G. Bastien et al., *Inventaire des marchés de construction des archives civiles de Québec, 1800–1870* (3v., Ottawa, 1975). E. H. Dahl et al., *La ville de Québec, 1800–1850: un inventaire de cartes et plans* (Ottawa, 1975). Jacques Bernier, "La construction domiciliaire à Québec, 1810–1820," *RHAF*, 31 (1977–78): 547–61. Robert Cannon, "Edward Cannon, 1739–1814," *CCHA Report*, 1935–36: 11–22. P.-G. Roy, "L'Hôtel Union ou Saint-George, à Québec," *BRH*, 43 (1937): 3–17. F. C. Würtele, "The English cathedral of Quebec," Literary and Hist. Soc. of Quebec, *Trans.* (Quebec), new ser., 20 (1891): 63–132.

CAPTAIN JOHN. *See* DESERONTYON, JOHN

CARDERO, MANUEL JOSÉ (Josef, Joseph) ANTONIO, artist and sailor; b. 31 Oct. 1766 in Écija, Spain, son of Salvador Dieguez Cardero and Antonia Romero; m. Gregoria Rosalia de la Vega, probably in 1798; d. in or after 1810 in Spain.

Little is known of the early life of Manuel José Antonio Cardero. In July 1789 he sailed from Cadiz as a cabin boy to Dionisio ALCALÁ-GALIANO, on Alejandro MALASPINA's scientific and exploratory expedition, which was intended to circle the globe. The absence or disability of original members of the artistic corps provided Cardero with the opportunity to emerge from obscurity by demonstrating his talent. He made his first drawings at Guayaquil (Ecuador), more than a year after the departure of the expedition from Spain. With enthusiasm and increasing skill he drew many zoological illustrations and landscapes under the tutelage first of José Guío and then of Tomás de Suria*, two of the official artists. On 2 May 1791 Malaspina left Acapulco (Mexico) bound for the north. By the time the expedition had reached its first anchorage at Port Mulgrave (Yakutat Bay, Alaska) in late July, Cardero's merit was evident. Malaspina described him as "a simple amateur, not devoid of taste or artistic feeling," but his drawings from Port Mulgrave and from the expedition's August visit to Nootka Sound (B.C.) are a historian's delight in their fidelity of detail and their completeness. Incapable of the artistic licence of the trained specialist, Cardero produced highly realistic work in pencil, pen and ink, ink wash, and colour. As an unofficial artist, however, he received little recognition for his labours during this portion of the expedition.

In early 1792 Alcalá-Galiano and Cayetano Valdés y Flores Bazán were detached from the main expedition to explore Juan de Fuca Strait, which it was thought might be the entrance to the legendary northwest passage. For their small expedition, undertaken in the schooners *Sutil* and *Mexicana*, the officers requested Cardero's services and insisted he receive double his previous salary. Though described by contemporaries as a small man of but little strength, he served the expedition well as artist, pilot, and scribe. There is strong evidence that he was the true author of the narrative of the voyage, *Relación del viage hecho por las goletas Sutil y Mexicana en el año de 1792 . . .* , which has traditionally been attributed to Alcalá-Galiano or José Espinosa y Tello. Cardero's artistic work included Indian portraits, a view of the new Spanish settlement at Núñez Gaona (Neah Bay, Wash.), and scenes along the inside passage as the schooners travelled from southeast to northwest. Some 25 drawings survive from this period, and they demonstrate increasing proficiency. Cardero was also responsible for producing a series of coastal profiles as aids to future navigation.

The *Sutil* and the *Mexicana* returned to Acapulco in the fall of 1792, and Cardero continued on to the Royal Academy of San Carlos (National Autonomous University of Mexico) in Mexico City, where he finished his artwork. In February 1794 he arrived back in Spain, and as a reward for his significant services he was promoted in May 1795 to a lieutenant in the naval supply corps. He is not known to have turned his hand to art ever again and, if he did not, he was the first European artist to dedicate himself exclusively to drawings of the Pacific coast. Cardero served as a lieutenant in Cadiz until about 1810 when his name disappears from the register of Spanish naval officers, a circumstance suggesting either death or retirement during the Napoleonic occupation of Spain.

DONALD C. CUTTER

[Cardero's baptism is recorded in the registers of the parish church of Nuestra Señora de Santa María (Écija, Spain). Details about his family and career can be found in the Archivo Museo Don Alvaro de Bazán (Viso del Marqués), José Cardero, expediente personal, and in the Archivo General Militar (Segovia), Joseph Cardero, expediente matrimonial. Artistic works signed by him or attributed to him are held by the Museo de América and the Museo Naval, both in Madrid. The Museo Naval's MS no.1060, "Relación del viage hecho por las goletas Sutil y Mexicana . . . ," is in Cardero's hand and has been published as *Relación del viage hecho por las goletas Sutil y Mexicana en el año de 1792, para reconocher el estrecho de Fuca . . .* (Madrid, 1802; repr. 1958). D.C.C.]

Voyages of enlightenment: Malaspina on the northwest coast, 1791–1792, ed. Thomas Vaughan et al. ([Portland, Oreg.], 1977). D. C. Cutter, "Early Spanish artists on the northwest coast," *Pacific Northwest Quarterly* (Seattle, Wash.), 54 (1963): 150–57; *Malaspina in California* ([San Francisco], 1960); "The return of Malaspina," *American West* (Cupertino, Calif.), 15 (1978), no.1: 4–19. D. C. Cutter and Mercedes Palau de Iglesias, "Malaspina's artists," *El Palacio* (Santa Fe, N.Mex.), 84 (1976), no.4: 19–27. [For another opinion on the authorship of the *Relación del viage*, see the biography of Dionisio Alcalá-Galiano. DCB]

CARLETON, GUY, 1st Baron DORCHESTER, army officer and colonial administrator; b. 3 Sept. 1724 in Strabane, Ireland, third son of Christopher Carleton and Catherine Ball; m. 21 or 22 May 1772 Lady Maria Howard, third daughter of the 2nd Earl of Effingham, in Fulham (London), England, and they had 11 children; d. 10 Nov. 1808 at Stubbings House, near Maidenhead, and was buried in St Swithun's Church, Nately Scures, England.

The Carletons, originally from Cumberland County, England, but resident in Ireland since the beginning of the 17th century, belonged to that Protestant Ascendancy which has so well supplied the British army and colonial service. When Guy Carleton was about 14 his father, a modest landowner by Irish standards, died, and the following year his mother married the Reverend Thomas Skelton, who supervised the boy's education. On 21 May 1742 the 17-year-old Carleton was commissioned an ensign in the 25th Foot (Rothes's) in which he became a lieutenant three years later. On 22 July 1751 he joined the 1st Foot Guards as a lieutenant (with the army rank of captain); on 18 June 1757, having become aide-de-camp to the Duke of Cumberland, he was made captain-lieutenant in his regiment (and a lieutenant-colonel in the army); and on 24 Aug. 1758 he was appointed lieutenant-colonel of the newly formed 72nd Foot. Meanwhile, he had acquired a champion in James Wolfe*, who in 1752 recommended him as military tutor to the young Duke of Richmond and six years later requested his services for the siege of Louisbourg, Île Royale (Cape Breton Island). Reportedly annoyed by Carleton's disparagement of the German mercenaries, however, George II demurred, and it required the intervention of William Pitt the elder and Lord Ligonier, the commander-in-chief, before Wolfe could obtain the quartermaster general and engineer he wanted for the assault on Quebec.

During that campaign Carleton, who had received his appointment together with a colonelcy in North America on 30 Dec. 1758, was responsible for setting up an advance base on Île aux Coudres and a fortified supply depot on Île d'Orléans. He also conducted an amphibious operation at Pointe-aux-Trembles (Neuville), returning with intelligence, some provisions, and more than 100 Canadian civilians who had been evacuated from Quebec. On the Plains of Abraham he commanded the 2nd battalion of the Royal Americans (60th Foot), which was one of three battalions deployed under Brigadier-General George TOWNSHEND at the left of the British battle-line. The head wound he received while pursuing the enemy may explain his leaving the colony in October 1759. If he had not performed spectacularly, he had done well enough, retaining the esteem of Wolfe and acquiring another patron in Vice-Admiral Charles Saunders*.

Between 1759 and 1763 Carleton participated in two more campaigns. On 8 April 1761 he was seriously wounded in an attack on Port-Andro, on Belle-Île-en-Mer, off the northwest coast of France; and on 22 July 1762, while acting in Cuba as quartermaster general to the army under the Earl of Albemarle, he suffered another wound in the siege of Havana. Having been made a colonel on 19 Feb. 1762, he transferred two years later from the 72nd Foot to the 93rd, and on 3 Oct. 1766 became a brigadier in North America. On 7 April 1766 he was named "Lieutenant Governor and Administrator" of Quebec, but since Governor James Murray*, who had been recalled to London, remained officially in charge, Carleton was not commissioned "Captain General and Governor in Chief" until 12 April 1768.

His appointment is hard to explain: he had no experience in civil government and only a limited acquaintance with the situation in Quebec. On the other hand, he did have powerful connections: George

Carleton

III, who welcomed the nomination of such a "galant & Sensible Man," favoured him throughout his career; Henry Seymour Conway, who as secretary of state for the Southern Department had chosen him, exercised considerable influence in the Rockingham administration; and the Duke of Richmond, his former pupil, would shortly take over the Southern Department. Several members of the succeeding Grafton and North governments would also lend him their support – particularly Lord Shelburne, who followed Richmond as secretary of state; Sir Charles Saunders, who served briefly as first lord of the Admiralty; and lords Hillsborough and Dartmouth, who consecutively held the secretaryship for the American Colonies after its creation in 1768. Thus although he became involved in an acrimonious and eventually disabling feud with the next Colonial secretary, Lord George Germain, Carleton enjoyed the inestimable advantage, which Murray had lacked, of a solid political base at home.

Conditions were also opportune inside Quebec. With indisputable command of all the troops in the colony, the new governor was spared the dissension that had characterized his predecessor's dealings with Ralph Burton*. He could rely on Hector Theophilus Cramahé*, who continued as civil secretary and, thanks to Carleton, was to become the acting receiver general, a judge of the Court of Common Pleas, president of the Council of Quebec, administrator of the colony, and finally lieutenant governor. Both the first chief justice, William Hey*, and the attorney general, Francis Maseres*, were able lawyers who, although dissenting from Carleton's subsequent recommendations, supported his initial policies; and while the second chief justice, Peter Livius*, was to prove troublesome, another attorney general, William Grant*, would provide effective assistance. Most propitious of all, the merchants, many of whom had become disaffected to the colonial administration under Murray, were showing good will.

Whether or not Carleton genuinely sympathized with the commercial interests, he did make a few gestures in their direction. Shortly after his arrival at Quebec, on 23 Sept. 1766, he agreed to study the representations of those who, like John McCord, wanted to see fewer restrictions on the fur trade and fisheries, and he was soon recommending the removal of restraints in the western territory; he suspended the introduction of English bankruptcy laws, to which several merchants had objected; he endorsed the leasing of the Saint-Maurice ironworks to a group of businessmen that included such notorious malcontents as James Johnston* and George ALLSOPP; and he not only suggested, to no avail, that the former be made a councillor, but insisted on the reinstatement of the latter as deputy provincial secretary and assistant clerk of provincial enrolments and of the council, positions from which Allsopp had been suspended by Murray.

At the same time, whether from motives of policy or in reaction to their resentment over his succession, Carleton apparently wanted to distance himself from some of Murray's closest advisers. In any case, he was determined to establish control over the council, which had in effect been substituted for the assembly promised in the Royal Proclamation of 7 Oct. 1763.

An opportunity arose in a dispute over the fur-trading lands known as the king's posts, which had been leased exclusively to Thomas DUNN, William GRANT (1744–1805), and John Gray. On 8 Aug. 1766, before Carleton's arrival, the council had ordered the destruction of unauthorized posts built on these lands by Allsopp and his partners, Edward Chinn and Joseph Howard*. Carleton, however, considered the restrictions on trade at the king's posts "such a Mockery" that with the connivance of five councillors – Hey, Cramahé, James Goldfrap, Thomas Mills*, and Paulus Æmilius Irving* – he suspended the "unjust" order. And when four of the councillors who had not been consulted – Adam Mabane*, François Mounier*, James Cuthbert*, and Walter Murray* – protested, along with Irving, against "the method lately adopted of calling together a part of the Council," he told them that he intended to confer with whomever he chose, provided only they were "Men of good Sense, Truth, Candor, and Impartial Justice."

A second incident enabled Carleton to tighten his control. In November Thomas Walker*, whose protests over the acquittal of his assailants in the episode that had precipitated Murray's recall led to his case being reopened, prevailed on the authorities to arrest six new suspects, including judge John Fraser, and refused to give the necessary consent to their being allowed bail. When certain councillors not only signed a petition requesting the governor to intervene but also took part in a public demonstration, Carleton used the occasion to bring them to heel. Whether he really judged it necessary, as he explained to Shelburne, "to make some Example, thereby to deter all from such Disorders; and particularly to convince the Canadians, such Practices are not agreeable to our Laws and Customs," he dismissed Mabane and Irving. The result was all he could have wished for, and probably what he had been trying to achieve: a cowed and submissive council, and a chance to chart a new course for Quebec.

Although prejudiced against Murray's henchmen, however, Carleton soon came to appreciate his reasoning. As early as 25 Nov. 1767 he informed Shelburne that most of the "old Subjects," whom he characterized as "disbanded Officers, Soldiers, or Followers of the Army . . . Adventurers in Trade, or such as could not remain at Home," would probably leave the province within "a few Years." In contrast, the "new Subjects," who "multiply daily," would become relatively even more numerous, so that "barring a Catastrophe shocking to think of, this Country must, to the end of Time, be peopled by the Canadian Race. . . ."

But it was not numerical proportions, cultural differences, or even social merits that preoccupied Carleton: his principal concern at this time seems to have been, rather, security. Fearing that the French might yet return, apprehensive of a revolt by the habitants, and nervous about the growing dissension in the Thirteen Colonies, he had, according to his own calculations, only 1,627 troops and 500 British immigrants with whom to face 76,675 conquered people (including some 7,400 Indians). It was not merely just but politic, then, to rule the colony in a manner acceptable to the overwhelming majority – so that "the Canadians are inspired with a cordial Attachment, and zeal for the King's Government." And the surest way of doing that, as Murray had seen, was to rule them indirectly, through their "natural" leaders, the seigneurs and clergy.

Accordingly, Carleton went out of his way to conciliate the former, proposing that they be made eligible for seats in the council, given administrative positions, offered commissions in "a few Companies of Canadian Foot," and even compensated (through an increase in the price of liquor licences) for the cessation of their French stipends. In particular, he supported those who, like Joseph Deguire*, *dit* Desrosiers, felt they were being victimized; recommended pensions for others, such as Jean-Baptiste-Marie Blaise Des Bergères de Rigauville, who had been given appointments by Murray; and secured positions for the ones, including Blaise, Gaspard-Joseph Chaussegros* de Léry, Joseph Fleury* Deschambault, Louis-Joseph Godefroy* de Tonnancour, Luc de La Corne*, Claude-Pierre Pécaudy* de Contrecœur, François-Marie Picoté* de Belestre, Charles-François Tarieu* de La Naudière, and Thomas-Ignace Trottier* Dufy Desauniers, who were willing to serve the British crown.

Carleton also extended the concordat arranged between Murray and Bishop Jean-Olivier Briand*, thereby not only gaining the cooperation of the Roman Catholic hierarchy but exercising some influence in ecclesiastical affairs. Having "made a Point of attending to the Motions of all the Clergy, both Secular and Regular, to Study the Character of the Men," he encouraged Jean-Baptiste Curatteau*, who in 1767 had begun the secondary school that was to become the Petit Séminaire de Montréal; he helped Sister de l'Assomption [Marie-Josèphe Maugue-Garreau*] to purchase the fief of Saint-Paul for the Congregation of Notre-Dame in Montreal; and he defended the Jesuits against charges by the renegade priest Pierre-Joseph-Antoine Roubaud* that they were remitting "considerable Sums" to France. Most

important, he effectively ensured the continuance of the episcopacy by approving the appointment of a coadjutor, despite Hillsborough's refusal to authorize one and at the cost of Dartmouth's subsequent disapproval. Indeed, it was his candidate, Louis-Philippe Mariauchau* d'Esgly, who, in accordance with the governor's wish to see Canadians preferred, became the first native-born bishop, on 12 July 1772.

If the British régime were to be made acceptable, however, ordinary Canadians would have to be looked after as well. To help the economy Carleton promoted the production of grain, hemp, flax, potash, and iron; opposed the prohibition of Canadian manufacturing, which some merchants thought would reduce the sale of British goods; obtained permission for fur traders, such as Daniel-Marie Chabert* de Joncaire de Clausonne, to travel among the Indians; recommended that Canadians be employed as guides and interpreters on exploring expeditions; sustained their claims to the winter seal fishery off the north shore of the St Lawrence; and insisted that they had as much right as the British to indemnification for the paper money issued by the French government before the conquest. He was also interested in social reform: under his guidance the council passed ordinances to repair the highways, to prevent and control fires, to regulate bakers and river pilots, to license public houses, and to check the offering of credit by innkeepers; following his recommendation to Shelburne in December 1767, preparation of a draft ordinance, and repetition of his recommendation in March 1768, the British authorities agreed, in July 1771, that all new land grants should be conferred in seigneurial tenure only; and both the collection of fees by officials and exercise of power by the justices of the peace were limited.

Carleton strongly objected to the British fee system, under which salaries were supplemented by emoluments for particular services. Declaring that "as there is a certain Appearance of Dirt, a Sort of Meanness in exacting Fees on every Occasion, which seems still stronger from the Novelty, and by comparison with the former Government, I think it necessary for the King's Service, that his Representative, at least, should be thought unsullied," he publicly renounced all the perquisites attached to his own office. Then in December 1767 he advised Shelburne "that none of the Principal Officers of Government and Justice, neither Governor, Judge, Secretary, Provost Martial, or Clerk of the Council should receive Fee, Reward or Present from the People." Apart from the question of whether fees could be legally altered by executive action, their abolition would have required much higher salaries, which the British government was simply unable to pay. But although Carleton could not eradicate the practice, he did manage to restrict it, obtaining permission from Hillsborough "to restrain

Carleton

the Fees of Office within some settled and certain Bounds," getting the council to determine them, dismissing officials who overcharged, and even persuading the home authorities to increase salaries.

In response to complaints about the justices of the peace, Carleton appointed a committee of inquiry, which confirmed that they often exceeded their authority, and were particularly prone to taking lands in execution, or even committing to prison, "for the payment of ever so small a debt." An ordinance was therefore passed on 1 Feb. 1770 to transfer jurisdiction over all cases involving private property, as well as disputes entailing sums of less than £12, from the justices of the peace to the Court of Common Pleas. This law also provided Montreal with its own Court of Common Pleas, replaced the English practice of legal terms with the French tradition of continuous sittings, regulated executions against property in cases of debt, and limited the fees for bailiffs. However, the offence taken by the justices (including Pierre Du Calvet*, who had originally criticized his colleagues), together with the remonstrance drawn up by Charles Grant on 21 April 1770, signified the need for a general review of the administration of justice.

Carleton seems to have already concluded that the anglicizing policy implicit in the proclamation of 1763 ought to be mitigated, if not discarded. As early as December 1767 he told Shelburne that Murray's ordinance of 17 Sept. 1764 had gone too far in implementing the English legal system, and that it would be advisable to "leave the Canadian Laws almost entire." Two years later, in September 1769, on the basis of reports by Maurice MORGANN, who had been sent out from England to investigate the situation, and Chief Justice Hey, who took issue with some of Morgann's findings, he rejected Maseres's opinion that anglicization should be hastened. Instead, he advocated precisely the opposite: while some English laws and practices – the criminal law, habeas corpus, jury trials for personal actions, the "custom of the merchants" in commercial cases, and the laws of trade and navigation – might continue, in all other respects the French system ought to be restored. Furthermore, the bailiffs should be dismissed, the militia officers given back their civil authority, police magistrates appointed in every town, weekly courts held in each district, and the legislative authority of the governor and council affirmed and enlarged. To support these views, Carleton sent home an abridgement of the French laws prepared by his French-language secretary, François-Joseph Cugnet*, who had made a preliminary summary in late 1767 or early 1768 and who, at the governor's request, would later collaborate with Joseph-André-Mathurin Jacrau* and Colomban-Sébastien Pressart* on the compilation known in the colony as the "Extrait des Messieurs," published in London in 1772–73.

Legal reform, or perhaps reaction, was Carleton's main response to Quebec's institutional problems: as he explained to Shelburne in November 1767, the "Body of Laws" would be "the Foundation of all, without which, other Schemes can be little better than meer Castles in the Air." The other proposed remedy – the introduction of representative government – not only failed to interest but positively alarmed him: as he added to Shelburne in January 1768, whatever the merchants might claim, "the better Sort of Canadians fear nothing more than popular Assemblies, which, they conceive, tend only to render the People refractory and insolent." Convinced that "the British Form of Government, transplanted into this Continent, never will produce the same Fruits as at Home," he warned that "a popular Assembly, which preserves it's full Vigor, and in a Country where all Men appear nearly upon a Level, must give a strong Bias to Republican Principles." In any event, "such was the peculiar Situation of Canada, tho' I had turned that Matter often in my Thoughts, I could hit off no Plan that was not liable to many Inconveniencies, and some Danger."

At this stage, the home authorities do not appear to have entirely agreed with Carleton. Although the Norton–de Grey opinion of 10 June 1765, the Yorke–de Grey recommendation of 14 April 1766, and the instructions to the governor that were drafted though not sent in June 1766, all reveal that they had likewise been contemplating a fuller use of French laws and customs, they seem to have developed opposing views on the question of representative government. In May 1767 Shelburne advised the calling of an assembly; Carleton's instructions of 1768 ordered the summoning of one "as soon as the more pressing Affairs of Government will allow"; and in July 1769 the Board of Trade decided it was "necessary in the present State of Quebec, that a complete Legislature should be established." Carleton thereupon resolved to press his arguments personally. On 1 Aug. 1770, leaving Cramahé as administrator, he embarked for London, where he spent the next four years lobbying for a constitution that would "preserve good Humour and a perfect Harmony" in the colony.

The British government's response was the Quebec Act of 1774 (14 Geo. III, c.83), together with the Quebec Revenue Act (14 Geo. III, c.88) and three sets of instructions issued in 1775. The outstanding difference between the statutes and the proclamation of 1763 is that Quebec was now denied an assembly. Instead, the colony was given a "legislative Council," whose members would be appointed and might be dismissed by the governor; whose bills he might overrule or reserve for consideration by the home authorities; and whose powers of taxation were limited to the indirect financing of public roads and buildings. Moreover, the policy of anglicization was to be not just retarded, but reversed. Canadians were assured of "their Property and Possessions, together with all Customs and Usages relative thereto, and all other their Civil Rights"; cases relating to "Property and Civil Rights" would be settled according to "the Laws of *Canada*" only; Roman Catholics would be permitted to hold public office; and the "accustomed Dues and Rights" of the Church of Rome (as well as, by inference, those of the seigneurs) would be enforceable. Finally, much of the commercial empire that had been cut away in 1763 was restored: Quebec would once again comprise the fisheries off the Labrador coast as well as the western fur-trading hinterland down to the junction of the Ohio and Mississippi rivers.

It is impossible to estimate the extent to which Carleton was responsible for these arrangements. They are in conformity with both the general views he had been expounding for some time and the particular opinions he expressed in his testimony before the House of Commons on 2 and 3 June 1774; and in one negative respect – the decision to omit a provision in the third draft specifically authorizing conversions from seigneurial to freehold tenure – his influence can definitely be traced. But other authorities also played a part, and the contribution of lords Dartmouth, Hillsborough, and Mansfield, and especially of the law officers, James Marriott, Edward Thurlow, and Alexander Wedderburn, should not be depreciated. Besides, in several crucial respects the Quebec Act ran counter to Carleton's policies. The testimony of Hey and Maseres had raised concerns that were shared by many leading statesmen, including Lord Chatham, Lord John Cavendish, Edmund Burke, Charles James Fox, Thomas Townshend, Isaac Barré, John Dunning, and John Glynn, as well as Lord Effingham and Sir Charles Saunders. Consequently, the use of English criminal law, which Carleton had begun to question and would later regret, was to be mandatory; English property law might be invoked and land granted in free and common socage; the "Laws and Customs of *Canada*" might be altered through ordinances passed by the governor and council; and provision might be made "for the Encouragement of the Protestant Religion, and for the Maintenance and Support of a Protestant Clergy." As will be seen, the anglicizing tenor of these arrangements is still more apparent in the governor's instructions, which would have produced a much less "Canadian" dispensation than Carleton favoured, or than the Quebec Act is often presumed to have instituted.

Carleton was not given to explaining his objectives, and one can do little more than speculate on the reasons behind his policies. He could have been trying to furnish Quebec with the laws and institutions he considered appropriate for a society that would always be predominantly Canadian. He could have been hoping to avoid the type of quarrel that had arisen with the Thirteen Colonies. He could have been apprehensive about letting the British immigrants acquire a legislative power they might use against the Canadians. He could have been intent on enforcing order in the west, or cultivating the Indians, or checking American settlement. And his overall strategy could have been to ensure Canadian passivity, at least, in the event of either an attempt by France to retake Quebec or a revolution south of the border.

Whatever the reasons behind Carleton's policies, some of the results were as unwelcome as they had been unforeseen, or at any rate underestimated. Although the seigneurs and clergy were gratified, the habitants, liable once more for both seigneurial dues and ecclesiastical tithes, were actually disquieted, while the merchants, denied both English law and representative government, regarded the Quebec Act "with horror," and denounced Carleton as "the first contriver & great promoter of this Evil." On the other hand, although some Canadian habitants and British merchants did join the American insurgents, the majority remained passive, and their behaviour might have been partly due to the indisputable benefits that both communities had received. Most of the Canadians probably realized that their "Property and Civil Rights," as well as their religion, would be much less secure under the Americans than under the British; and most of the merchants must have known that their natural interests, which had been furthered by the boundary extensions, placed them on the loyal side too. It might well be that the Quebec Act helped to keep Canada British, after all.

Following his return to Quebec on 18 Sept. 1774, Carleton ran into difficulties with both the Council of Quebec, in which the merchants had gained strength, and the British government, which sought to clarify, or possibly amend, its policy on anglicization. One of his first actions was to appoint as councillors seven Roman Catholic seigneurs and several members of the French party – including Adam Mabane, whom he had dismissed in 1766. But while the home authorities confirmed all these appointments in the instructions of 3 Jan. 1775, they also enjoined a number of concessions to the British colonists: the new Legislative Council should introduce the writ of habeas corpus and consider making English law "if not altogether, at least in part the rule" for cases in contract and tort; the courts should be thoroughly reorganized, with British predominance being ensured even in the Court of Common Pleas; and an earnest attempt should be made to encourage "the Protestant Church of England," which was the only body entitled to the powers and privileges of "an established Church."

Carleton's reaction to these instructions was typically high-handed. Ignoring Dartmouth's injunction

Carleton

"to persuade the natural born subjects of the justice & propriety of the present form of Government and of the attention that has been shewn to their Interests," he made up his mind not merely to keep his orders secret, but to resist any movement towards anglicization. Accordingly, when the council, which first met on 17 Aug. 1775, took up Hey's proposals for reforming the legal system, Carleton sided with the seigneurs and French party against the introduction of habeas corpus, trial by jury in civil cases, and a limited use of English commercial law. He then prorogued the council, and from 1776 administered Quebec with the advice of a "Board of Council," which had been authorized in his instructions for transacting business, "Acts of Legislation only excepted." To this board, known as the governor's "privy council," he appointed five councillors whom he thought he could trust: Cramahé, Mabane, Thomas Dunn, John Collins*, and Hugh FINLAY.

Evidently concerned about the concessions planned for the British colonists, Carleton also modified the legal system envisaged by the home authorities. Following their instructions, he established new courts of Common Pleas for the districts of Quebec and Montreal, and ensured that each of them had two British and one Canadian judge. However, his nominees for judicial office revealed his own leanings: Mabane and Dunn, who had been in the old court, were joined on the Quebec bench by Jean-Claude Panet*, while Gabriel-Elzéar TASCHEREAU was appointed to the court at Montreal, along with Peter Livius and William Owen, who had received their commissions in England. Then, as a means of enforcing civil processes, Carleton created six "conservators of the peace," again choosing men who might be counted on to sympathize with the Canadians: in addition to Mabane, Dunn, Panet, and John (Jean) Marteilhe, he named two other judges of the old Court of Common Pleas – John Fraser and René-Ovide Hertel* de Rouville. And for the first time under the British régime, Roman Catholics were made justices of the peace.

Carleton exercised even more discretion in carrying out his ecclesiastical instructions. To reassure Briand, who was upset by a reference in the Quebec Act to the "King's Supremacy," he interpreted this term as not implying a denial of the pope's status as head of the church. While not acceding to a request by Étienne Montgolfier*, the superior of the Sulpicians in Montreal, that the seminaries be allowed to recruit in France, he did allow two Frenchmen, Arnauld-Germain Dudevant* and Jean-Baptiste LAHAILLE, to immigrate in 1775, join the Séminaire de Québec, and remain in the province after ordination. He made light of his duty to confine the powers of the bishops, to oversee the appointments to benefices, and to inspect the religious communities. Rather than suppressing

the Jesuits, he established good relations with the superior general, Augustin-Louis de Glapion*, and effectively connived at the continuance of the order in Canada despite its dissolution by the pope. And he was slack to the point of being remiss in "encouraging" the Church of England. Indeed, although he failed to prevent the collation of two Anglican clergymen – the former Recollet Leger-Jean-Baptiste-Noël Veyssière* and a Swiss Protestant, David-François de MONTMOLLIN – to Trois-Rivières and Quebec, he did stop the latter from collecting tithes, and so setting a precedent. As a result of all this forbearance, the Roman Catholic hierarchy, which could have hindered Carleton's policies, became not merely a neutral but an ally.

With the outbreak of the American rebellion and consequent threat of an invasion, Carleton needed all the help he could find. The dispatch of two of his five regiments to Boston during September of 1774, in compliance with a request from Major-General Thomas Gage*, the commander-in-chief, had seriously weakened the colony's defences. A regiment of British colonists, the Royal Highland Emigrants, was raised, and Carleton revived his plans for a Canadian corps, which again failed to materialize. His main hope, however, was the militia, to which, as he assured both Gage and the home authorities, the people were bound to rally. When they failed to do so, he vainly tried to meet Dartmouth's quota of 6,000 men by proclaiming martial law in June 1775, and two years later, following an investigation of disloyalty in the militia [see François BABY; Edward William GRAY], the council passed an ordinance designed to strengthen the government's authority in imposing military service. But while the militia was enlarged and ultimately proved more than useful, the support expected from the Canadians was never forthcoming. Indeed, many new subjects, such as Maurice Desdevens* de Glandons, Clément GOSSELIN, and Philippe Liébert, as well as some British and American colonists, including Moses HAZEN, James Livingston*, Zachary MacAulay*, and Thomas Walker, actively backed the rebels, in certain cases even to the point of joining their army.

Profoundly disenchanted, Carleton developed a distrust bordering on contempt for the Canadians: as he bitterly observed to Germain in September 1776, "I think there is nothing to fear from them, while we are in a state of prosperity, and nothing to hope for when in distress; I speak of the People at large; there are among them who are guided by Sentiments of honour, but the multitude is influenced only by hopes of gain, or fear of punishment." He also disclaimed responsibility for their poor showing, and in so doing presaged his later policy: writing to Major-General John Burgoyne* on 29 May 1777, he protested that "if Government laid any great Stress upon Assistance from the Canadians, for carrying on the present war, it surely was not upon Information proceeding from me, Experience might have taught them, and it did not require that to convince me, these People had been governed with too loose a Rein for many years, and had imbibed too much of the American Spirit of Licentiousness and Independence administered by a numerous and turbulent Faction here, to be suddenly restored to a proper and desirable Subordination."

As for the other potential ally, the Indians, Carleton was accused by Major-General Charles Lee of inciting them "to take up the Hatchet against the Colonies." In fact, while agreeing that they could play a supportive role and should be kept well disposed, he adamantly refused to turn them loose on American settlers. Gage had favoured their employment since September of 1774; Germain had come round to the idea by March of 1777; a number of officials in the colony – notably Edward Abbott, the lieutenant governor of Vincennes (Ind.) – argued that they could save British lives; and the Johnson faction in the Indian Department – particularly Guy Johnson*, Christian Daniel Claus*, and Joseph Chew* – were all for an Indian war. Carleton, however, stipulated that they be used only "in concert with Troops," where they would be "under proper management." Meeting the Six Nations at Oswego (N.Y.) in July 1775, he forbad them to take the war-path; in July 1776 he sent back a group of Ottawas who had gone to Montreal to offer their services; in August of the same year he ordered Burgoyne to dismiss the Indians under his command; and in February 1777 he begged Major John Butler* and Captain Richard Berrenger Lernoult to prevent their warriors from engaging in independent excursions. His official justification was that the Indians were undependable, but his principal reason might be discerned in his explanation to Lernoult: "However proper and justifiable it may be, to make use of the Indians in a defensive War, or to chastize the real criminals – yet true policy, as well as humanity, forbids an indiscriminate attack, such as is intended by the Savages, wherein women and Children, aged and infirm, the innocent as well as the guilty will be equally opposed to their fury."

On 27 June 1775 the second Continental Congress decided to invade Quebec. In accordance with Gage's orders to defend the Richelieu valley, the historic invasion route, Carleton rushed most of the troops he had at Quebec to Montreal, where he set up headquarters, and at Fort St Johns (Saint-Jean-sur-Richelieu) and Fort Chambly held off Brigadier-General Richard Montgomery* till early November. He was then forced back to the capital, now threatened by another invading army led by Benedict ARNOLD across Maine. In the ensuing siege, which was to drag on for six months, the only assault on Quebec, during the early morning of 31 December, was repulsed at the

cost of no more than 20 British casualties, some 60–100 Americans having been killed or wounded and about 400 captured. Carleton has been both criticized for not having launched an immediate counter-attack and commended for having waited until the arrival of a flotilla bringing reinforcements on 6 May 1776 [see Sir Charles Douglas*].

His pursuit of the decamping invaders has provided more argument, and some perplexity. On three occasions – near Trois-Rivières, when he had Brigadier-General William Thompson trapped between forces to the east and west; at Fort St Johns, when he had Brigadier-General John Sullivan within his grasp; and on Lake Champlain, when he declined to attack Fort Ticonderoga (N.Y.) even after having destroyed Arnold's fleet – Carleton failed to press home an apparent advantage. This "extraordinary" conduct, as Alfred Leroy Burt* calls it, has raised questions about his motives, and a suspicion, supported by references to the uncommon solicitude shown towards his prisoners, that he was trying to demonstrate the clemency insurgents might expect if they would only come to their senses. Whether he was charitable and politic or merely dilatory and overcautious, however, the upshot, according to Burt, was that "Carleton's inaction when the Americans were scrambling to get out of the country ruined the campaign of 1776 and possibly altered the outcome of the war."

The home authorities apparently felt much the same: while nominating Carleton for the knighthood he was awarded on 6 July 1776, seven members of the cabinet could not refrain from observing that "some parts of his conduct were doubtful"; and the king, although later granting him the "Government of Charlemount" in Ireland as a sinecure for "his meritorious defence of Quebec," conceded that "he may be too cold and not so active as might be wished which may make it advisable to have the part of the Canadian Army which must attempt to join Gen. [Sir William] Howe led by a more enterprizing Commander." This reaction shocked Carleton, who had been promoted general in North America on 1 Jan. 1776, but who now learned that the strategy he had devised, of separating New England from the other colonies, was to be put into effect by Burgoyne, his second in command. On 27 June 1777, offended and disgruntled, he tendered his resignation, which was immediately accepted. Since his successor, Frederick HAL-DIMAND, was unable to arrive for another year, however, Carleton remained in command at Quebec till 27 June 1778.

Meanwhile, he had been contending with Lord George Germain, who had replaced Dartmouth as secretary of state for the American Colonies on 10 Nov. 1775, and was now criticizing the conduct of the war. Hoping to influence strategy and bent on

Carleton

exercising his patronage, Germain endeavoured to get Carleton recalled, helped to put Burgoyne in charge of the projected invasion, and insisted on certain appointments, including that of Livius, on 21 Aug. 1776, as chief justice. Carleton's retorts to these manifestations of "private enmity and resentment" were so intemperate that even the king, writing in March 1778, felt he was "highly wrong in permitting his pen to convey such asperity to a Secretary of State and therefore has been removed from the Government of Canada."

Trouble also occurred in the Legislative Council, which Carleton had finally re-convened in January 1777. Although approved by the attorney general, William Grant, three ordinances dealing with the administration of justice greatly disturbed the British colonists. Not only were English commercial law, jury trials in civil cases, and the writ of habeas corpus still withheld, but the system had been made even more "French": through the restriction of the Court of King's Bench to criminal cases, the Court of Common Pleas was left with sole jurisdiction in civil suits (though appeals might be made to the council); and procedure in all the civil courts was to follow French forms (though the English rules of evidence would apply in commercial cases). Chief Justice Livius, who also objected to Carleton's protracted reliance on the "privy council" and refusal to disclose both their proceedings and such instructions as the councillors had a right to know, was particularly upset. But the airing of his grievances only led to his own dismissal and another proroguing of the Legislative Council. Despite his disenchantment with the Canadians, the governor continued to resist the anglicization of Quebec's legal system.

Carleton left Canada on 30 July 1778. In May 1780 North appointed him to the Commission of Public Accounts, which investigated the government's financial administration, and two years later, on 2 March 1782, following his recommendation by the king as "the Man who would in general by the Army be looked on as the best officer," he succeeded Sir Henry Clinton as commander-in-chief in North America. Nemesis now overtook Germain: since he would not agree to this succession without either a retraction or an investigation of Carleton's charges against him, he was virtually forced to resign. Carleton subsequently asked to be relieved of his command, informing Conway, the commander-in-chief in both the Rockingham and the Shelburne governments, that he was not prepared "only to be employ'd as a mere Inspector of Embarkations" and "will serve no more out of Europe." However, he was persuaded to stay on by Thomas Townshend, who as Shelburne's Home secretary had become responsible for colonial affairs.

The fretfulness Carleton displayed was probably due to his lack of success as a negotiator. On 21 March he and Rear-Admiral Robert Digby had been named

joint commissioners "for restoring peace and granting pardon to the revolted provinces in America," with instructions "to reconcile and reunite the Affections and Interests of Great Britain and the Colonies." The French minister in Philadelphia, Pa, was alarmed, reporting that "Sir Guy Carleton was the best choice that England could have made to win back the Americans: he is much respected here on account of his humane and generous conduct when he was Governor of Canada." But he need not have worried: the Americans were too suspicious of Shelburne's plans for a "Federal Union," and Congress rebuffed Carleton's overtures, in which it discerned "insidious steps" to damage the alliance with France. Whether Carleton and Maurice Morgann, who had been sent out to help, could have behaved more effectively is debatable, but it seems likely that the project was bound to fail from the start.

Carleton's other major concern while at New York, from May 1782 till November 1783, was to evacuate some 30,000 troops and up to 27,000 refugees. The latter included several thousand former slaves who, over George Washington's protests, were helped to emigrate to the Caribbean and to Nova Scotia, where about 1,200 settled near Halifax [see Boston KING]. Carleton also urged the lieutenant governor of Nova Scotia, Sir Andrew Snape Hamond, and then the new governor, John Parr*, to grant loyalists free land and a year's provisions, and prompted Haldimand to do the same for those who entered Canada.

Early in December 1783 Carleton sailed for England, where he passed the next three years. During this interval Haldimand resigned and Quebec was administered by Lieutenant Governor Henry Hamilton* and then by Lieutenant Governor Henry Hope*. By April of 1786 Townshend, now Lord Sydney and Home secretary in William Pitt's first government, had accepted the notion of a governor general for the whole of British North America – as suggested by Carleton and William Smith*, formerly chief justice of New York and soon to become chief justice of Quebec, in order to provide the basis for a union of the remaining British colonies. Eventually, however, the government decided to create only a "multiple" governor-in-chief, who would hold separate commissions as governor of Quebec, Nova Scotia, and New Brunswick (each of which was to have its own lieutenant governor as well) and who would be able to exercise his authority over any one of these colonies only when he was in it. Carleton regretted this reduction, and in 1790 and 1793 repeated his call for a proper governor general. Nevertheless, he agreed to return to North America with separate commissions, dated 22 and 27 April 1786; the position of commander-in-chief over all three provinces, as well as Newfoundland; and the title of Baron Dorchester, which was created on 21 Aug. 1786.

His reputation as both a soldier and a statesman had

been damaged, but he could still count on some political support: the king, if a bit disappointed, remained a patron; Rockingham, Shelburne, Conway, and Richmond continued to back him; and although on rather cool terms with William Wyndham Grenville, and coming close to a rupture with Henry Dundas, Dorchester got on fairly well with the other Home secretaries – Sydney, who was his first chief, and the Duke of Portland, his last. On the other hand, his position in Quebec was inherently unstable. Several of his old partisans – Mabane, Fraser, Paul-Roch Saint-Ours, Panet, Baby – were as opposed as always to anything that smacked of anglicization, and the lieutenant governor, Hope, agreed. Others, however – notably Grant, Collins, and Samuel Johannes HOLLAND – had come to accept the need for a more English legal system and often sided with such anglicizers as Smith, Henry CALDWELL, Sir John Johnson*, and the attorney general, James Monk*. Although strongly influenced by Smith, Dorchester was not completely won over, and his attempts to balance between these two groups were to prove debilitating.

Both Dorchester and Quebec had changed during the eight years he was away. For his part, he had become much less sympathetic to, or perhaps nervous about, the Canadians; and much more understanding, and respectful, of the British colonists. As for the province, the emergence of three interests had created different requirements and alliances. Anticipating a lucrative trade with the British West Indies, from which the Americans would presumably be excluded by the laws of trade and navigation, those merchants who hoped to develop a commerce based on staples other than fur were particularly eager to obtain both English law and an assembly, which they considered prerequisite for the roads, canals, harbours, banks, credit, and taxes they would need. Meanwhile, a rising Canadian bourgeoisie, although intent on retaining their property and civil rights, had come to support the demands for representative government – if for very different reasons. And the loyalists, while apparently not so concerned about an assembly as the merchants, were anxious to secure their lands under free and common socage.

Dorchester had elucidated his views concerning Canada's economic prospects when testifying on 16 March 1784 before the Committee for Trade, to which Pitt had referred the question of whether American shipping and produce should be admitted to the British West Indies. He agreed with the neo-mercantilists, such as Lord Sheffield, William Knox, and George Chalmers, that national security required the confinement of the colonial carrying trade to the British merchant marine, which served as both a training ground and a reserve for the Royal Navy. But, he added, there was also no reason why the islands should import products from the United States: Quebec and Nova Scotia would be capable of supplying them "to the whole extent both of lumber and provisions before the end of the year 1785." Impressed by this expert opinion, the Committee for Trade recommended that not only all American ships but also all American products – providing similar products were obtainable "in sufficient plenty, and at reasonable prices" from within the British empire – be barred from the British West Indies. The Pitt government accordingly decided not to continue Shelburne's liberalizing policy, but to revert to the exclusive principles of the old colonial system.

As events showed, however, direct trade between the United States and the British West Indies could not be prevented. Had Dorchester overrated the resources of British North America – or did his testimony involve an ulterior calculation? In the long run, the agricultural development of western Quebec did produce a quantity of staples. But whether or not Dorchester foresaw this outcome, his contention that adequate supplies would be forthcoming within two years' time implies something else: that he was banking, in the short run, on the trans-shipment of American products via the St Lawrence. In other words, he might have been endorsing a restrictive policy on the eastern seaboard because he was prescribing a liberal one in the western hinterland – and so was attempting not only to uphold the mercantilist practices on which British seapower depended, but also to preserve the economic integrity of the Ohio and Mississippi basin.

To achieve these ends, Dorchester effectively limited the British government's order in council of 24 March 1786, which prohibited the importation of American products into "any of the ports of the Province of Quebec," by defining "ports" as "seaports." Then, on 18 April 1787, he issued an order allowing the free exportation of all Canadian products (except furs) to the United States, and the free importation of certain American products (lumber, naval stores, and some foodstuffs) into Quebec by way of Lake Champlain and William Henry (Sorel). On 27 April 1787 the council passed an ordinance freely admitting pot and pearl ash, as well as tobacco, along the same route; on 14 April 1788, after the home authorities had decided to leave the regulation of inland trade to the colonial government, Dorchester's order of the previous year was confirmed by another ordinance; and on 12 April 1790 a third ordinance added pig-iron to the list of imports exempted from duties. Finally, following a request by the governor and council that all products freely imported from the United States into Quebec be freely allowed into imperial markets, Westminster enacted a statute (30 Geo. III, c.29, 1790) that treated American products sent by way of the St Lawrence to Britain as if they were of Canadian origin. But this is as far as Dorchester got: the crucial concession of free access

Carleton

for those products to the British West Indies was not granted; and partly for that reason – though mainly, no doubt, because the Quebec merchants were just too distant and isolated, as well as inexperienced and inefficient – his grand scheme of a Caribbean monopoly remained a pipe-dream.

On a more modest scale, however, much was done to improve both economic and social conditions. Some of the restrictions on transportation through the Great Lakes were removed; arrangements were made to settle debts incurred in wartime; during the "Hungry Year" of 1788–89, when a poor harvest led to food shortages, an embargo was placed on the export of grain and other foodstuffs; the Agriculture Society was founded to inculcate better farming methods; the postal service to London, deprived of its New York link during the American revolution, was reoriented through New Brunswick and Halifax; a bridge was built across the Rivière Saint-Charles; and following the reports of three committees established by the governor in the autumn of 1786, ordinances were passed to regulate the militia, the police, medical practitioners, river pilots, suppliers of horses and carriages, and retailers of wines and spirits. Although Dorchester may not have been directly responsible for all these achievements, some of which were clearly inspired by others [see Hugh Finlay; David LYND], he at least sanctioned them. And he continued his patronage of the loyalists, setting up administrative districts in the area southwest of Montreal, providing each district with salaried judges as well as a land board to supervise settlement, and – most surprisingly, in view of his former policy – urging the home authorities to permit grants of land in freehold, thus paving the way for the reintroduction of English tenure in 1791.

Dorchester's ecclesiastical policy, which continued along the lines he had laid down during his previous administration, also contributed to the well-being, or at least the stability, of the colony. Admittedly, his designation of Charles-François Bailly* de Messein as coadjutor in 1788, after Jean-François Hubert* had succeeded d'Esgly as bishop, led to some discord within the Roman Catholic hierarchy; and Dorchester seems to have been particularly disappointed by the failure of the plans, proposed by Smith and favoured by Bailly, for a non-sectarian university. On the other hand, by permitting a number of *émigré* priests from France to enter the colony after 1791, the governor gained influential support for the British régime, while at the same time helping the sorely depleted clergy to perform their social as well as religious role.

In contrast to his involvement in economic and social affairs, Dorchester was singularly detached, if not inert, in the matter of legal reform. Disillusioned, uncertain, and irresolute, he apparently decided to let the committee on justice, which he had also estab-

lished in the autumn of 1786, wrestle with the problem. On one side were Smith and Finlay; on the other, Mabane, Saint-Ours, and Thomas Dunn; in between, John Fraser. The furore over Smith's judgement in *Grant* v. *Gray*, delivered on 29 Dec. 1786, epitomized the difference of views. In general, Smith reasoned that the Quebec Act "was not meant to exclude English laws," which should accordingly govern causes between the "natural born subjects of Great Britain"; moreover, now that the writ of habeas corpus and trial by jury in civil suits had been instituted – respectively under Haldimand in 1784 and Hamilton in 1785 – it was time to anglicize the legal system further, starting with commercial cases. The proponents of the "charter theory" of the Quebec Act disagreed: with the possible exception of the loyalist districts in the west, Canada should be kept as Canadian as possible; indeed, not only should the essential principles of French jurisprudence be re-affirmed, but both the use of English rules of evidence in commercial cases and the right to jury trials in civil suits ought to be discontinued.

These differences – which induced Smith and Saint-Ours to propose conflicting bills in March 1787, when the ordinance that permitted jury trials was due to expire – were carried to an extreme in April 1787 by Attorney General Monk. His open advocacy of both legal and governmental anglicization, accompanied by his public censure of certain judges, prompted an indignant appeal to the governor from Mabane, Fraser, and Panet, and Dorchester was forced to intervene – though not before renewing the ordinance permitting jury trials, as amended by Smith. But although the inquiry he ordered furnished ample evidence of the complexity and uncertainty of the law, as well as establishing the arbitrary conduct of certain judges, nothing came of it. Dorchester merely passed on the records to Sydney who, despite the protestations of Adam Lymburner* on behalf of the merchants, did no more than replace Monk with Alexander Gray as attorney general.

By now it had become apparent that a fundamental revision of Quebec's governmental system was unavoidable. Not only were the demands for an assembly more clamorous than ever, but the home authorities were predisposed to listen. Their attitude, while doubtless entailing some political principles, was most likely precipitated by practical economics: the administration of Canada was costing Britain more than £100,000 a year; the proceeds obtained under the Quebec Revenue Act were insufficient; because of the renunciation implied in the Colonial Tax Repeal Act of 1778 (18 Geo. III, c.12), it was unacceptable to tax a colony directly; and therefore an assembly was indispensable. But it must somehow be made acceptable to those Canadians who were afraid that the British colonists might be inadequately restrained, to those

British colonists (including Monk) who conversely feared that the Canadians might get out of hand, and to everybody who objected to increased taxes. And looming over all these considerations was the shadow of the American revolution, which had seemed to demonstrate that a colony with representative government became increasingly refractory and eventually independent.

The British government tried to resolve the predicament with the Constitutional Act of 1791 (31 Geo. III, c.31). This statute was based on an expedient that became standard practice for colonies with irreconcilable social differences – partition. Quebec would be divided into two provinces: "Lower Canada" for the Canadians; "Upper Canada" for the British colonists. With each group thus assured of its not being dominated by the other, both could be granted assemblies, which would be able to impose taxes. At the same time, to prevent these assemblies from evolving into the too powerful legislatures that had fomented the revolt of the Thirteen Colonies, they would be subject to the sort of checks and balances that applied at Westminster: upper houses, with the power to refuse bills, would be imposed; the governors, provided with secure sources of income and ample powers of patronage, would also have a power of disallowance; and the British government would have a third veto. In addition, both Canadas would be socially assimilated to Great Britain: while French laws and customs would be continued in Lower Canada, freehold tenure would be available there as well; only English common law would be allowed in Upper Canada; the "Protestant" religion would be encouraged in both provinces by the setting aside of clergy reserves and endowment of Church of England parsonages; and provision would be made for a hereditary membership in the upper houses, and so for the foundation of a British North American aristocracy.

In devising these solutions, the home authorities received little help from Dorchester. Whether because of his distrust of the Canadians, wariness of the British colonists, dislike of representative government, or preference for conciliar rule, he advised no more than a modification of the existing structure. Confessing to Sydney in June 1787 that he was "as yet at a loss for any plan likely to give satisfaction, to a people so circumstanced as we are at present," he added in November 1788 that partition was "by no means adviseable at present." If it must be done, he could "see no reason, why the inhabitants of those western districts should not have an Assembly, as soon as it may be organized without detriment to their private affairs, nor against their having so much of the English system of laws, as may suit their local situation, and condition." But he did not think either of these innovations suitable for the rest of Canada, and

warned that even in the west, "particular care should be taken to secure the property and civil rights of the Canadian settlers of Detroit." Encountering such an indeterminate and chary attitude, William Grenville, who succeeded Sydney as Home secretary in June 1789, decided to go ahead on his own and so, possibly under the influence of Lymburner and Maseres, contrived the Constitutional Bill.

Dorchester did not remain entirely outside the discussions, however, and it may be that his contribution to constitutional developments in 1791 has been as underestimated as his impact in 1774 is exaggerated. On 8 Feb. 1790 he abandoned his initial reticence and tendered advice on a number of subjects, including the distribution of seats in the assemblies, the qualifications for members and electors, the implementation of freehold tenure, the conversion from tenure in fief, the reservation of crown lands, the disposition of the District of Gaspé, and the union of British North America under a governor general. Moreover, he seems to have been at least partly responsible for two decisions of some consequence: in November 1788 he had suggested to Sydney that if partition could not be avoided, the line of separation should be drawn along the Ottawa River, so as to place not only the western seigneuries but also Montreal within the lower province; and in February 1790 he told Grenville that since "the fluctuating state of Property in these Provinces" made a hereditary upper house inappropriate at that time, "it would seem more advisable to appoint the members during life, good behaviour, and residence in the province." The British government's acceptance of both these ideas meant that Upper Canadians were deprived of a seaport (and so of the ability to raise their own duties on goods imported by sea), and that Lower Canadian society included an economically, socially, and politically dominant British minority. But at least British North America, if saddled with a natural oligarchy, was spared an artificial aristocracy.

On 18 Aug. 1791, before the Constitutional Act came into force (on 26 December), Dorchester sailed for England on leave, entrusting the administration of Lower Canada to Lieutenant Governor Sir Alured Clarke* until his return two years later, on 24 Sept. 1793. In the mean time, John Graves SIMCOE had become lieutenant governor of Upper Canada, an office that made him subordinate to Dorchester in the latter's capacity both as commander-in-chief and (though in a less clearly defined way) as governor-in-chief. Temperamentally incompatible, the two men were soon at loggerheads over matters ranging from supervision of the Indians and operation of the commissariat through the choice of a capital for the western province to the lieutenant governor's independent ways and habit of appealing directly to the home authorities. The principal subject of discord,

Carleton

however, was defensive policy, which Simcoe linked to settlement in his plans for a string of fortified towns. Arguing variously that the costs were too high, that the Americans might be alarmed, and that the defences of the city of Quebec would be dangerously weakened, Dorchester frustrated these plans by refusing to provide the requisite troops.

His own defensive measures were intensified after France declared war on Britain in February of 1793 and her envoy to the United States, Edmond-Charles Genêt, started to intrigue with Canadians as well as Americans. Dorchester instructed everyone "to discover and secure" seditionists; tightened military regulations and enforced discipline; persuaded the legislature to pass both a militia act and an alien act (which suspended the writ of habeas corpus); requested more regulars from Britain; renewed his pleas for the construction of a "proper citadel" at Quebec; ordered Simcoe to build and garrison a new Fort Miamis (Maumee, Ohio); and fostered relations with the Indians, who he hoped would serve as a barrier against American expansion into the Ohio country. But there he went too far: on 10 Feb. 1794, in what he assumed was a private address to a deputation from the western tribes, he denounced the incursions of Americans into their territory, adding that "I shall not be surprised if we are at War with them in the Course of the present Year, and if we are a Line must then be drawn by the Kings Warriors." Leaked to the American press, which blew them up in disregard of everything that Dorchester had stood for concerning the Indians, these reflections were considered sufficiently inflammatory by the government of the United States to warrant a protest to London, and Henry Dundas, who had succeeded Grenville as Home secretary in 1791, advised a little more restraint. This was too much for Dorchester who, simmering over the government's apparent condonation of Simcoe's intractability, declared himself fed up with the "present political Influenza" at home. On 4 Sept. 1794 he asked to be relieved of his governorship, advising later that it be "entrusted to an officer of superior judgment and abilities to mine, who I hope will at the same time have authority sufficient to carry on the King's Service both civil and military."

Despite several appeals from a bemused Portland, who had replaced Dundas in July, Dorchester declined to reconsider his resignation. However, two years passed before the arrival of his successor, Lieutenant-General Robert Prescott, and notwithstanding his declared intention to "contract my interference within as narrow limits as possible," his influence continued to be felt. Although not directly involved in the negotiations leading to Jay's Treaty – which reflected his policy of free trade in the interior and mercantilism on the seaboard – he was responsible for executing its terms, and so oversaw both the evacuation of the western forts and the resettlement of those Indians who wished to live in British territory. In September 1795 he again tried to alleviate the distress resulting from a crop failure by proclaiming an embargo on the export of food; the following year he established a precedent by laying a statement of the crown's provincial revenue and annual expenditure before the legislature; he finally started to plan for the maintenance of a Protestant clergy; and he made a number of appointments, including those of William Osgoode*, as the new chief justice, and James Monk, to the Court of King's Bench at Montreal (both having agreed to relinquish the customary fees). Then on 9 July 1796 Dorchester left Canada for good.

During the last years of his life, he kept up his military connections. Having been promoted major-general on 25 May 1772 and lieutenant-general on 29 Aug. 1777, he had become a general of the army on 12 Oct. 1793; he had also been made colonel of the 47th Foot on 2 April 1772, transferring to the 15th Dragoons on 16 July 1790. Back in England, he moved to the 27th Dragoons on 18 March 1801, and then to the 4th Dragoons on 14 Aug. 1802. Most of his time, however, was spent in the countryside, where he had acquired three houses: Greywell Hill, Basingstoke, the present family seat; Kempshot House, close by; and Stubbings House, near Maidenhead, where he died in his 85th year. The barony of Dorchester became extinct with the death of the 4th baron on 18 Nov. 1897, and although another barony was granted to Henrietta Anne Carleton, a cousin of the 4th baron, on 2 Aug. 1899, it too became extinct with the death of the 2nd baron on 20 Jan. 1963.

Commentators have left us with a confusing impression of Carleton's personality. Contemporary epithets include cold, severe, sour, and morose, but also cool, intrepid, incorruptible, and disinterested. Biographers have added arbitrary, reactionary, ruthless, and vindictive, as well as benevolent, honourable, humane, and just. Lieutenant William Digby of the 53rd Foot, finding him "one of the most distant, reserved men in the world," complained of the "rigid strictness in his manner, very unpleasing, and which he observes even to his most particular friends and acquaintance." When recommending him as commander-in-chief in 1779, however, North maintained that he was "so much of a soldier, and so little of a politician, such a resolute, honest man, and such a faithful and dutiful subject, that he owns he wishes to see him intrusted with a part of our defence in this critical moment." To his early biographers, Arthur Granville Bradley and William Charles Henry Wood, he was a heroic figure: not merely the "Father of British Canada," but "the great justifier of British rule beyond the seas." Later writers turned iconoclastic: according to Burt, "Though he has been known as one of the greatest proconsuls in the history of the British

Empire, his judgment and his character were not always as sound as has been assumed." His severest judge, Donald Grant Creighton*, juxtaposes the "cocksure" Carleton, "so confident, so voluble, so emphatic," with the "baffled" Dorchester, "old and irritable and emptied of ideas," and sums him up as "a political Tory and a social conservative, with a complacent belief in his own importance and an ingrained relish for authority."

As a statesman, he will probably always be something of an enigma. Almost morbidly secretive (he had his wife destroy all his personal papers), he so coloured his accounts that his calculations, let alone motives, are peculiarly difficult to discover. Yet perhaps a general pattern can be discerned. It seems to have been Carleton's preoccupation with security during his first administration, between 1766 and 1778, that made him pander to the Canadians, and particularly to the seigneurs and clergy. But his favourable attitude towards them does not necessarily imply, as is commonly assumed, that he found the British colonists, as Murray had, innately antipathetic; on the contrary, there are indications that Carleton felt some sympathy for the latter from the start. At any rate, by the time of his second governorship, between 1786 and 1796, he had decided both that the Canadians could not be relied on to support the British régime and that Quebec was not destined to remain predominantly Canadian "to the end of Time." And it might have been these calculations, rather than any sort of conversion, as is also commonly assumed, that made him willing not only to assist the loyalists and merchants, but to accept some anglicization of the legal system. The introduction of an assembly, however, was another matter, and in his consistent opposition to that, Carleton may well have revealed the essence of his character as well as his politics: he was an autocrat, instinctively against representative government – and not just for the Canadians but probably, despite his disclaimers, for the British colonists as well. If it was really unavoidable, it should take a much more conservative, and stable, form than that under which the Thirteen Colonies had been, as Smith deplored, "abandoned to Democracy." But everyone would be much better off under his own system of conciliar administration.

It is even more difficult to assess Carleton's policies than it is to explain them. Attempts to do so have usually been made with reference to the relations between Canada's "two founding peoples" or in terms of a putative struggle between "insurgent commercial capitalism and a decadent and desperately resisting feudal and absolutist state"; and to an unusual degree the resulting judgements have tended to reveal subsequent, more than contemporary, concerns. Yet again, some general conclusions might be ventured.

Certain of Carleton's calculations were clearly based on faulty premises: Quebec was not a feudal society, and the habitants could not be conciliated by catering to the seigneurs and clergy; the merchants could not function efficiently without laws and institutions that were familiar, certain, practical, and auxiliary; and neither the British colonists nor the Canadians could be indefinitely denied some form of representative government. Carleton's limitations and errors in such cases, however, do not detract from his insights and accomplishments in others. His protection and sponsoring of the loyalists, his grasp of Canada's economic potential, and his vision of a united British North America all testify to his statesmanship. And whatever critics might think of the way he attempted to conciliate the Canadians, it could well be, as the citizens of Montreal alleged on his departure, that his "prudence and moderation" did assure "internal peace and tranquillity," on the whole.

Certainly his principal, and most controversial, legacy was the Quebec Act – or rather, the administrative system he created on the basis of this act. Amidst the amazing variety of interpretations concocted by historians, there is agreement in one respect: between 1770 and 1786 a turning-point occurred in the history of both Canada and the British empire, and Guy Carleton, for better or worse, was to a large extent responsible for it. Although Murray had made allowance for the distinctive needs and wants of the Canadians, it was still possible, and in 1770 seemed probable, that the British government would promote the anglicization of Quebec, as it had invariably done in the case of conquered colonies. Whether such a course was preferable to the one Carleton charted – whether a more balanced mixture of anglicization and conservation would have been possible, and better – is open to question. What cannot be denied is that by bolstering French laws and Canadian customs and institutions, Carleton enabled them not just to survive, but to flourish. And although it might be argued that the "charter view" of the Quebec Act has been overstated, it does seem that a groundwork was laid for the special status that many French Canadians have claimed up to the present day. In so far as he can be held accountable for this groundwork, Carleton may be praised, or blamed, accordingly.

From an imperial perspective, the consequences of the Quebec Act have also been both far reaching and controversial. By encouraging the use of French principles and practices, Carleton developed the precedent established by Murray into a model for other colonies in which foreign populations had to be conciliated. Moreover, his administrative system served as a prototype for a new form of colonial government: starting with St Domingo (Haiti) in 1794, "crown colony" government, as it was later

Carleton

called, became a standard form for not only conquered but settled colonies. And with this alternative available for dependencies that were considered unready or unsuitable for representative institutions, the way was cleared for others to develop "responsible government." The evolutionary process by which members of the second British empire attained their independence thus owes something, however paradoxically, to Guy Carleton's administration of Quebec.

G. P. BROWNE

BL, Add. MSS 21697–700, 21743, 21806, 21808, 21864 (copies at PAC). Hampshire Record Office (Winchester, Eng.), Reg. of baptisms, marriages, and burials for the parish of Nately Scures, 16 Nov. 1808. Library of Congress (Washington), Continental Congress papers, nos. 35, 41–43, 58, 78, 154, 166 (copies at PAC). PAC, MG 23, A1; A4, 14, 16, 18, 20, 29–30; A6; A8; GI, 5; GII, 6; 9; 14, vols. 2, 7; 15; 19, vol. 3; HI, 1; MG 40, B1, 3, 6–10, 13, 15, 17; RG 1, E1, 19, 28–31, 43, 46–47, 105–15; RG 4, B3, 1; B6, 2–6; B9, 9; RG 7, G5, 1; RG 14, A1, 1, 3, 7; A3, 3–7; RG 68, 90, 93, 95. PRO, CO 42/26–107; PRO 30/55; WO 1/11; 1/14 (mfm. at PAC). [Ainslie], *Canada preserved* (Cohen). *American arch.* (Clarke and Force), 4th ser., vols. 3, 4. *Annual reg.* (London), 1758–91. *Blockade of Quebec in 1775–1776 by the American revolutionists (les Bastonnais)*, ed. F. C. Würtele (Quebec, 1906; repr. Port Washington, N.Y., and London, 1970). *British colonial developments, 1774–1834: select documents*, ed. V. T. Harlow and A. F. Madden (Oxford, 1953). "Collection Haldimand," PAC *Rapport*, 1885–88. *A collection of several commissions, and other public instruments, proceeding from his majesty's royal authority, and other papers, relating to the state of the province in Quebec in North America, since the conquest of it by the British arms in 1760*, comp. Francis Maseres (London, 1772; repr. [East Ardsley, Eng., and New York], 1966). *The correspondence of King George the Third from 1760 to December 1783 . . .*, ed. J.[W.] Fortescue (6v., London, 1927–28; repr. 1967). *Corr. of Lieut. Governor Simcoe* (Cruikshank).

Jacob Danford, "Quebec under siege, 1775–1776: the 'memorandums' of Jacob Danford," ed. J. F. Roche, *CHR*, 50 (1969): 68–85. *Docs. relating to constitutional hist., 1759–91* (Shortt and Doughty; 1907); *1791–1818* (Doughty and McArthur; 1914). [Hugh Finlay], "Journal of the siege and blockade of Quebec by the American rebels, in autumn 1775 and winter 1776," Literary and Hist. Soc. of Quebec, *Hist. Docs.* (Quebec), 4th ser. (1875): [3]–25. G.B., Parl., *Debates of the House of Commons in the year 1774, on the bill for making more effectual provision for the government of the province of Quebec, drawn up from the notes of Sir Henry Cavendish . . .* (London, 1839; repr. [East Ardsley and New York], 1966); *The parliamentary register: or history of the proceedings and debates of the House of Commons (and House of Lords) containing the most interesting speeches . . .* (112v., London, 1775–1813). "Journal par Baby, Taschereau et Williams" (Fauteux), ANQ *Rapport*, 1927–28: 435–99; 1929–30: 138–40. Knox, *Hist. journal* (Doughty); *The justice and policy of the late act of parliament for making more effectual provision for the government of the province of Quebec . . .* (London, 1774). [Francis Maseres], *An account of the proceedings of the British, and other Protestant inhabitants, of the province of Quebeck, in North-America, in order to obtain an house of assembly in that province* (London, 1775); *Additional papers concerning the province of Quebeck: being an appendix to the book entitled, "An account of the proceedings of the British and other Protestant inhabitants of the province of Quebeck in North America [in] order to obtain a house of assembly in that province"* (London, 1776); *Maseres letters* (Wallace). *Naval documents of the American revolution*, ed. W. B. Clarke and W. J. Morgan (8v. to date, Washington, 1964–), 4–6. "Ordonnances édictées pour la province de Québec par le gouverneur et le conseil de celle-ci, de 1768 à 1791 . . . ," PAC *Rapport*, 1914–15. "Ordonnances faites pour la province de Québec par le gouverneur et le conseil de la dite province depuis le commencement du gouvernement civil," PAC *Rapport*, 1913: 90–91. *The parliamentary history of England from the earliest period to the year 1803*, comp. William Cobbett and John Wright (36v., London, 1806–20), 17–19. "Proclamations du gouverneur du Bas-Canada, 1792–1815," PAC *Rapport*, 1921. "Proclamations issued by the governor-in-chief . . . ," PAC *Report*, 1918. *Reports on the laws of Quebec, 1767–1770*, ed. W. P. M. Kennedy and Gustave Lanctot (Ottawa, 1931). *Quebec Gazette*, 1766–96.

G.B., WO, *Army list*, 1740, 1755, 1758, 1761, 1763–66, 1770–72, 1777–78, 1789–1808. "Papiers d'État – Bas-Canada," PAC *Rapport*, 1890, 1891. Pierre Benoît, *Lord Dorchester (Guy Carleton)* (Montréal, 1961). J. G. Bourinot, *Canada under British rule, 1760–1900* (Cambridge, Eng., 1900). A. G. Bradley, *Lord Dorchester* (Toronto, 1907; new ed. under the title *Sir Guy Carleton (Lord Dorchester)*, [1966]). G. S. Brown, *The American secretary; the colonial policy of Lord George Germain, 1775–1778* (Ann Arbor, Mich., 1963). Michel Brunet, *Les Canadiens après la Conquête, 1759–1775: de la Révolution canadienne à la Révolution américaine* (Montréal, 1969). A. L. Burt, *Guy Carleton, Lord Dorchester, 1724–1808* (Ottawa, 1955); *Old prov. of Que.* (1968); "The problem of government, 1760–1775," *The Cambridge history of the British empire* (8v., Cambridge, 1929–59; repr. of vols. 1–2, 1960–61), 6: 146–72; *The United States, Great Britain and British North America from the revolution to the establishment of peace after the War of 1812* (Toronto and New Haven, Conn., 1940). Chapais, *Cours d'hist. du Canada*. Christie, *Hist. of L.C.*, vol. 1. Victor Coffin, *The province of Quebec and the early American revolution; a study in English-American colonial history* (Madison, Wis., 1896). Reginald Coupland, *The Quebec Act; a study in statesmanship* (Oxford, 1925). Craig, *Upper Canada*. Creighton, *Commercial empire of St. Lawrence*. F.-X. Garneau, *Histoire du Canada depuis sa découverte jusqu'à nos jours* (4v., Québec, 1845–52). M. H. Gorn, "To preserve good humor and perfect harmony: Guy Carleton and the governing of Quebec, 1766–1774" (PHD thesis, Univ. of Southern Calif., Los Angeles, 1978). G. S. Graham, *British policy and Canada, 1774–1791; a study in 18th century trade policy* (London and New York, 1930); *Sea power and British North America, 1783–1820: a study in colonial policy* (Cambridge, Mass., 1941). Lionel Groulx, *Vers l'émancipation (première période); cours d'histoire du Canada à l'université de Montréal, 1920–1921* (Montréal,

1921). V. T. Harlow, *The founding of the second British empire, 1763–1793* (2v., London and New York, 1964). *A history of the organization, development and services of the military and naval forces of Canada* . . . (3v., n.p., n.d.). W. P. M. Kennedy, *The constitution of Canada; an introduction to its development and law* (London, 1922). William Kingsford, *The history of Canada* (10v., Toronto and London, 1887–98). P. E. Leroy, "Sir Guy Carleton as a military leader during the American invasion and repulse in Canada, 1775–1776" (PHD thesis, 2v., Ohio State Univ., Columbus, 1960). Duncan McArthur, "The new régime," *Canada and its prov.* (Shortt and Doughty), 4: 21–49. Piers Mackesy, *The war for America, 1775–1783* (Cambridge, 1964). John Mappin, "The political thought of Francis Maseres, 1766–69" (MA thesis, McGill Univ., Montreal, 1968). Neatby, *Administration of justice under Quebec Act*; *Quebec*; *The Quebec Act: protest and policy* (Scarborough, Ont., 1972). John Norris, *Shelburne and reform* (London, 1963). Ouellet, *Bas-Canada*; *Hist. économique*. P. R. Reynolds, *Guy Carleton: a biography* (Toronto, 1980). John Shy, *Toward Lexington: the role of the British army in the coming of the American revolution* (Princeton, N.J., 1965). P. H. Smith, "Sir Guy Carleton: soldier-statesman," *George Washington's opponents: British generals and admirals in the American revolution*, ed. G. A. Billias (New York, 1969), 103–41. C. P. Stacey, *Quebec, 1759: the siege and the battle* (Toronto, 1959). L. F. S. Upton, *The loyal whig: William Smith of New York & Quebec* (Toronto, 1969). A. C. Valentine, *Lord George Germain* (Oxford, 1962). Rex Whitworth, *Field Marshal Lord Ligonier: a story of the British army, 1702–1770* (Oxford, 1958). W. [C. H.] Wood, *The father of British Canada: a chronicle of Carleton* (Toronto, 1916). G. M. Wrong, *Canada and the American revolution; the disruption of the first British empire* (New York, 1935).

Elizabeth Arthur, "French Canadian participation in the government of Canada, 1775–1785," *CHR*, 32 (1951): 303–14. H. R. Balls, "Quebec, 1763–1774: the financial administration," *CHR*, 41 (1960): 203–14. R. A. Bowler, "Sir Guy Carleton and the campaign of 1776 in Canada," *CHR*, 55 (1974): 131–40. A. L. Burt, "The quarrel between Germain and Carleton: an inverted story," *CHR*, 11 (1930): 202–22; "Sir Guy Carleton and his first council," *CHR*, 4 (1923): 321–32; "The tragedy of Chief Justice Livius," *CHR*, 5 (1924): 196–212. Jane Clark, "The command of the Canadian army for the campaign of 1777," *CHR*, 10 (1929): 129–35. R. A. Humphreys and S. M. Scott, "Lord Northington and the laws of Canada," *CHR*, 14 (1933): 42–61. L. P. Kellogg, "A footnote to the Quebec Act," *CHR*, 13 (1932): 147–56. M. G. Reid, "The Quebec fur-traders and western policy, 1763–1774," *CHR*, 6 (1925): 15–32. *Rev. of Hist. Pubs. relating to Canada* (Toronto), 1 (1896): 68–80. P. H. Smith, "Sir Guy Carleton, peace negotiations, and the evacuation of New York," *CHR*, 50 (1969): 245–64. William Smith, "The struggle over the laws of Canada, 1763–1783," *CHR*, 1 (1920): 166–86. F. H. Soward, "The struggle over the laws of Canada, 1783–1791," *CHR*, 5 (1924): 314–35.

CARLETON, THOMAS, army officer and colonial administrator; b. *c.* 1735 in Ireland, youngest son of Christopher Carleton and Catherine Ball; m. 2 May 1783 Hannah Foy, *née* Van Horn, in London, England; d. 2 Feb. 1817 in Ramsgate, England.

Thomas Carleton's career and achievements have been overshadowed by the better-known exploits of his elder brother GUY, Lord Dorchester, and by the plans and actions of the New Brunswick loyalist élite with whom Thomas worked closely in founding and shaping a new colony. His cryptic style and sporadic letter-writing habits – "I'm so seldom guilty of the crime of writing long ones," he acknowledged to his patron, Lord Shelburne – have handicapped historians attempting to study the man. Even the public Carleton may not be accurately displayed since, with Jonathan ODELL functioning as his provincial secretary and Edward WINSLOW as his military secretary, he possibly appears, in William Odber Raymond*'s words, "to much greater advantage in his official correspondence than he would otherwise have done."

In 1753, after a childhood in Ireland, Thomas joined the 20th Foot as a volunteer. He quickly rose in rank, becoming a lieutenant and adjutant by early 1756, and saw considerable service in Europe during the Seven Years' War. On 27 Aug. 1759 he was promoted captain. Posted with his regiment to Gibraltar following the peace in 1763, Carleton was restless and in 1766 appealed to Shelburne, "as my only resource," that in the event of another war his patron (then secretary of state for the Southern Department) would not "suffer me to be shut up with a set of Gourmands in this horrid Prison." During a ten-month leave of absence he visited Minorca, Algiers, and different parts of France and Italy, eventually rejoining his regiment and returning to England in 1769. Appointed major on 23 July 1772, he again took leave to tour in Europe. No doubt it was because he was a well-travelled man of the world that Shelburne recommended him to accompany Lord John Pitt, eldest son of the Earl of Chatham, to Canada. But in March 1774 Thomas postponed the trip in favour of more adventurous service with the Russian army, then battling "with the Turks on ye Lower Danube." After visiting Constantinople (Istanbul) and wintering in St Petersburg (Leningrad), he returned to England in 1775.

In August 1775 Guy Carleton, governor of Quebec, recommended that his brother be made quartermaster general to the forces there, and the following year, now with a lieutenant-colonelcy in the 29th Foot, Thomas took up the appointment. As the American Revolutionary War progressed he became, like his brother, increasingly critical of the ministry's handling of the military effort. In fact, his censure was so intense that at one point he sarcastically commented, "This letter contains the worst kind of Treason against the Minister so I shant put my name to it." Towards the end of the war he watched with interest the fluctuating fortunes of Shelburne and wondered whether a return

Carleton

to England might be in order: "One risques being estranged to their Friends if not forgot by them, from long absence. . . ." By June 1782, however, a "happy change of administration" had placed Shelburne in his "proper sphere," and Thomas looked forward to joining his brother, now Sir Guy, at New York City and eventually to receiving another Canadian appointment.

Before leaving for New York he had a number of problems to iron out with his commanding officer, Frederick HALDIMAND. The two had clashed several times, with the ever prickly Carleton feeling that he was treated as "a Cypher" and his rank not respected. A final confrontation occurred when Haldimand demanded that he resign his position as quartermaster general before his departure. This Carleton refused to do until he had received another appointment, and he left Quebec without the matter having been resolved. After a brief stop at New York, where he found no position vacant, Carleton journeyed to England. There, in the shelter of Shelburne's country estate, he wrote to Haldimand arguing that his rather abrupt leave-taking had been justified by the need to explain in England the expenditures of his quartermaster's department. Evidently unconvinced, Haldimand removed Carleton's name from his staff list, appointing Colonel Henry Hope* in his place. With his military record tarnished and his career threatened, Carleton was not helped when, after February 1783, Shelburne (by then prime minister) was rendered powerless as the leadership of his party passed to William Pitt. Not surprisingly, when an appointment as governor of the newly created colony of New Brunswick was offered in the summer of 1784, Thomas accepted it.

He had not, however, been in a completely helpless position. The Carleton name was still respected and Sir Guy was under consideration for the post of governor in chief of British North America. In addition, finding a governor for New Brunswick had proved no simple task: both General Henry Edward Fox and Colonel Thomas Musgrave had already declined the office. Indeed, Thomas had had a strong enough bargaining position to get a commitment from the ministry that his New Brunswick service would be temporary, to be followed by the lieutenant governorship of Quebec. Later, however, he was to consider his appointment "one of the most fortunate events of my life," and he had accepted it none too soon as it turned out. Haldimand sailed to England in the fall of 1784, and the next year Carleton expressed his "uneasiness" over the apparent decline of his reputation with the Home secretary, Lord Sydney. As he wrote to Shelburne, "If I had persisted in refusing this Government [the government of New Brunswick], the hostility of a Minister might have been fatal, now . . . altho formidable it may be withstood."

Carleton's concern about possible attacks from Haldimand and Sydney revealed his insecurity, an insecurity no doubt heightened by the fact that others, both above and below him, had clearer ideas about the form the new colony should take. During the campaign for the partition of Nova Scotia in 1783–84 members of the aspiring loyalist élite, such as Winslow and Ward Chipman*, were active and articulate, and Sir Guy, who was "warm for the new Government," also had considerable influence. Thomas, on the other hand, seems not to have played a significant role. He apparently had no voice in the appointment of the first New Brunswick council (not surprisingly, perhaps, given the crush of office seekers waiting to be rewarded), while the occupant of at least one other post, and probably more, "was fixed upon by Col. Carleton at the recommendation of his Brother." Carleton was no doubt consoled by his colonel's rank (awarded on 20 Nov. 1782), a War Office commitment that two regular regiments would be stationed in New Brunswick, and the understanding that his appointment would be temporary. After taking the oaths of office on 28 July 1784, he sailed in early September for Halifax, N.S., accompanied by his wife as well as by Odell, Chipman, Gabriel George LUDLOW, and other newly appointed office holders.

In late November, after stopping briefly in Halifax, Carleton and his entourage reached Parrtown (Saint John), which became the governor's temporary capital. Although clearly instructed to call an assembly as soon as possible, Carleton decided "to finish every thing respecting the organization of the Province that properly belonged to the prerogative before a meeting of Representatives chosen by the people." Hence New Brunswick was to be governed in its first year by Carleton and the Council, a body composed largely of loyalists which consistently offered "unanimous advice." This close cooperation between the governor and the loyalist élite profoundly influenced the shape of the new colony. Indeed, Carleton's conception of a proper colonial society was not greatly different from theirs. Like his brother, he was the product of an Anglo-Irish milieu, where the need for a ruling class, an established church, and a controlled parliament were accepted, and his views, modified by his military interests, matched the hopes of the loyalists for "a stable, rural society governed by an able tightly knit oligarchy of Loyalist gentry."

By the time of Carleton's arrival the indifference of Governor John Parr* of Nova Scotia to the new settlements of loyalists and soldiers on the Saint John River had combined with the winter chill and insufficient provisions to slow colonial development. Moreover, Guy Carleton's thoughts concerning a march to the north to open new land on the upper Saint John and the consolidation of existing settlements seemed on the point of abandonment. Drawing upon his elder brother's suggestions, his own inclinations, and the aspirations of the élite, Thomas moved quickly and enthusiastically to revitalize the faltering colony. Prior to the calling of an assembly, there was a whirlwind of significant measures. Because of its central location, St Anne's Point, renamed Fredericton, was "fixed on" as the new capital, a chief justice, assistant judges, and an attorney general were appointed, counties and parishes were created, and a charter of incorporation was issued for Saint John. It was strongly asserted as well that of the three rivers known by the name St Croix, the one commonly called the Scoodic should form the western boundary of New Brunswick. The most pressing needs of the recently arrived loyalists were also dealt with. Applications for grants were processed and land registered or in some cases escheated. Carleton also arranged that the period during which the refugees were to receive free provisions be extended to May 1787 and that, if necessary, they be allowed to use American boats, rather than rely on "British bottoms," to transport their possessions to New Brunswick. The assignment of loyalists to land already occupied by pre-loyalist settlers, both Acadian and English, created a problem which Carleton and the Council resolved by ordering the new claimants to pay compensation to "the occupants for their Improvements." Arrangements were made in the case of the Acadians for their resettlement in other parts of the colony.

By the end of 1785 the main lines of New Brunswick's future development had been established. It was to be a well-governed outpost of the empire, with settlement patterns dictated by what Carleton considered to be the colony's military needs, and blessed with a deferential, well-ordered society; it was to be a loyalist "asylum" that would eventually be the "envy of the American States," a society quite unlike that taking shape in post-revolutionary America. The affinity, both in thought and in action, between the governor and his loyalist advisers makes it difficult to disentangle their perceptions and desires. Carleton clearly had appropriated many loyalist beliefs; yet the élite was at times equally receptive to and unquestioning about the governor's dictates. In the matter of appointments, which in the first years went almost exclusively to loyalists, Carleton's explanation of the qualifications of his nominees revealed his respect for the refugees. "These are Gentlemen," he wrote, "not only of real merit, but also distinguished by services and sufferings during the late Rebellion. . . ." No doubt Odell, Ludlow, Winslow, Chipman, and others wholeheartedly endorsed his selection of such "Enemies of Faction," such opponents of "violent party spirit," and would equally support the constitutional arrangements Carleton hoped to evolve. At the municipal level,

although the charter for Saint John granted a certain amount of democracy to the electorate, Carleton was at pains to point out that "there is a sufficient influence retained in the hands of Government," through the governor's direct appointment of mayor, sheriff, recorder, and clerk, "for the preservation of order and securing a perfect obedience." At the provincial level, Carleton bluntly stated, "It will be best that the American Spirit of innovation should not be nursed among the Loyal Refugees by the introduction of Acts of the Legislature, for purposes to which by the Common Law and the practice of the best regulated Colonies, the Crown alone is acknowledged to be competent." The vigilant exercise of the crown's rights was to be accompanied by the "strengthening [of] the executive powers of Government [to] discountenance its leaning so much on the popular part of the Constitution."

Such views and actions soon came under fire both from within New Brunswick and from London. In early November 1785 the first provincial election turned into a turbulent affair when troops had to be sent to quell a riot in Saint John. The contest, as William Stewart MacNutt* describes it, was "government men against those who had not been admitted to privilege" [see Elias Hardy*]. Fines and jail terms were eventually meted out and the six disputed seats in Saint John were awarded to the Jonathan Bliss*–Ward Chipman group, the governor's friends. To Carleton it was a lesson "to hold the Reins of Government with a strait hand, and to punish the refractory with firmness," and also demonstrated the need for more military forces to be stationed in the area. After receiving Carleton's report on the election Sydney approved the way the governor had dealt with the "intemperate behaviour of Mr. Hardy" and his followers, but on other matters he was far from happy with Carleton's performance. Questions had been raised about the governor's delay in forwarding to London the fee schedule he and the Council had established and also about his hesitation in calling an assembly. What had most disturbed Sydney were the legal problems created by the hasty incorporation of Saint John, since "no Authority is given in Your Commission for granting Charters of Incorporation." At the same time Carleton was involved in a wrangle with Major-General John Campbell, commander of the troops in eastern Canada, concerning Carleton's jurisdiction over the troops in New Brunswick, only one regiment of which had as yet arrived.

Thomas's position strengthened considerably with the appointment of his brother, soon to be Lord Dorchester, as governor-in-chief in early 1786 (at which time Thomas received a new commission as lieutenant governor). Sydney made it clear that military problems would be resolved by the elder Carleton, and no doubt Thomas would benefit over the

Carleton

aggrieved Campbell. Even before receiving word of this favourable turn of events Thomas had shown himself willing to challenge Sydney's criticisms. He defended the legitimacy of all his actions and, elaborating upon his successes, he assured the Home secretary "that faction is at an end here." In truth, Carleton and his loyalist allies were very much the masters of New Brunswick. The first assembly met in January 1786 to, as Carleton phrased it, "put the finishing hand to the arduous task of organizing the Province." Opposition disappeared, with the assembly demonstrating a total willingness to cooperate. By 1788 the shift of the seat of government to Fredericton had been completed and the assembly held its first meeting there in July. The absence of controversy moved Carleton to comment in opening the 1789 session that "by provident attention, in former Sessions, to the various exigencies of this infant colony, the business I have at present to recommend to your deliberation, is reduced to little more than a renewal of temporary laws. . . ."

Thomas's cause and career by now were closely bound up with the fortunes of his brother and of his own allies in the colony, the loyalist leaders. To some observers, Thomas was a virtual puppet of the governor general. In reality, while Thomas welcomed Dorchester's appointment and in 1788 risked a hazardous winter journey of 350 miles on foot to be at his sick brother's side, there were issues over which the two men disagreed. The New Brunswick–Quebec boundary provides one example, with Thomas successfully defending the Madawaska region as part of his colony. None the less, Carleton's fate was linked with his brother's, and in the late 1780s enemies were sniping. Haldimand in England continued his caustic comments about Thomas, "who certainly does not deserve favours," while Parr in Nova Scotia freely lampooned both brothers in his private correspondence. The latter's remarks were particularly embarrassing to Thomas because they were addressed to Shelburne. But, although aware of Parr's hostility, Thomas never successfully countered his insinuations. Parr's willingness to criticize the Carletons without any apparent fear of offending Shelburne perhaps explains why Thomas's connection with this once concerned patron withered away by the end of the 1780s.

Even more damaging to Thomas Carleton were suggestions of misrule and incompetence within New Brunswick. Although he was cautiously optimistic about the colony's potential, particularly in agriculture, which he believed must take precedence over trade, his assessment of progress in the first few years was balanced and realistic. In a report to Dorchester in 1787 he openly recognized some of the economic setbacks experienced in the colony and indirectly acknowledged the slowness of its overall develop-

ment. He stopped short, however, of attaching blame. Others were not so hesitant about who was at fault. "This Province would by this time have had thrice the Number of Inhabitants it now has, had not its Government been inimical to its Settlement," wrote James GLENIE in November 1789. Glenie was to be a perennial thorn in the side of the administration and, at times, his comments were exaggerated and unfair. In this instance he had received a power of attorney to act for Andrew Finucane in the struggle to regain title to Sugar Island, which the government had allowed disbanded soldiers to settle. Glenie perceived a conspiracy to deprive Finucane of his property and Carleton was implicated: "The Govr. is to have his share in Consequence of a joint Purchase which he and Judge [Isaac Allan] have made in the Neighbourhood of the Island." A lieutenant governor and a clique enriching and protecting themselves by means of the offices they enjoyed were allegedly thwarting the colony's development. Regardless of the validity of Glenie's charges, they were serious accusations, and many more would be heard by officials at home in the years ahead. Finucane having complained to London about his treatment, in September 1789 Carleton had been forced to offer a detailed explanation of the process by which the family had lost its rights to Sugar Island. On the surface it looked as if due process of law had been scrupulously observed, but the seeds of suspicion had been planted.

Suggestions of misrule, an apparent loss of support from Shelburne, a colony developing slowly, all these had severely complicated and possibly compromised Carleton's career. His original hope, of serving only briefly in New Brunswick, had virtually vanished by 1790. Admittedly, the manner in which his removal was postponed gave the impression that satisfaction with his performance was the cause. The lieutenant governorship of Quebec had been offered to him in 1786. "At the same time," wrote Lord Sydney with reference to New Brunswick, "I should not fulfill his Majesty's Commands, were I not to acquaint you . . . [that] His Majesty is persuaded that His Service would receive considerable benefit by your continuance in that Province." While Carleton loyally expressed a willingness to carry on, he privately confided that "if my staying in the Province is thought of consequence My Lord Sydney should have tempted me with something more solid than empty words." A year later more was offered with the news that on Campbell's departure he was to be made brigadier-general in America and given command of the troops in New Brunswick. But his 1788 visit to Quebec reminded Carleton of the way he was being passed over while others moved ahead. His complaints brought soothing reassurances from England that the king intended to reward his services "as soon as a favourable opportunity shall present itself." Nevertheless, although he

158

was consulted when the Quebec lieutenant governorship came open again in 1789, the same argument against his removal was offered. What could Carleton do but "express my perfect acquiescence in His Majesty's desire that I should remain at New Brunswick."

Carleton was above all else a military man and it would have been easy for him to concentrate on this career, neglecting his civil responsibilities, once the prospect of further colonial appointments dimmed. To his credit, he continued to speak out concerning New Brunswick's needs in other areas. Threats to change or set the northern, western, and southern boundaries to the colony's disadvantage were effectively challenged throughout his lieutenant governorship. The news that parliament had approved a grant for the creation of a college in Nova Scotia prompted Carleton to request the same funding for a "public Seminary of learning" in New Brunswick. Although the home government refused its support and the colony had to be content with a grammar school in Fredericton, the assembly cooperated in granting land and limited funding and the first steps had been taken towards the creation of the College (eventually the University) of New Brunswick. What Carleton was powerless to change, however, was the colony's economic decline. His report in 1791 that the importation of provisions from the United States was continuing and that lumber had been added to the list of permitted imports graphically revealed its predicament. British restrictions on further land grants within the colony, imposed in 1790 in the hope that crown lands could be sold, were a major set-back; at the same time land values fell, grain- and sawmills went idle, immigration ceased, and the debts of even the élite mounted. Imperial indifference was capped in 1794 when American vessels were again given access to the West Indies trade, a decision that destroyed New Brunswick's "ocean-going commerce" and reinforced agricultural underdevelopment.

Some compensation, from Carleton's point of view, was provided by the emergence of the province, at least temporarily, as the military bastion he had originally envisioned. In 1788 he had argued that more military posts were needed to protect the line of communication with Quebec and "to encourage settlements in their neighbourhood," and in 1790, with the arrival of the second of the two regiments promised the colony, the line of outposts stretching northward could be achieved. Garrisons were already being maintained at Saint John and Fort Cumberland (near Sackville); under Dugald CAMPBELL new posts were now established at Grand Falls and Presque Isle. Carleton was also able to station "a respectable Corps at Fredericton, which I conceive to be an object of great importance; The situation is centrical and peculiarly advantageous for the Troops." Questions

were raised immediately about the concentration of manpower and ordnance stores at Fredericton rather than in Saint John. Eventually Carleton was overruled by the War Office and forced to accept the greater military importance of Saint John. For a brief moment, however, he was in his element with paymasters, barrack-masters, and town majors in Fredericton, along with an entire regiment doing nothing according to Glenie but "mounting guard on the Governor's Farm." Then in late 1792 an upset and protesting Carleton received orders to transfer one regiment to Halifax, and the following February the second was dispatched to the West Indies. Replacing the regulars was "a Corps not exceeding 600 Men" to be raised by Carleton within the colony and commanded by him "but without any Pay in consequence thereof." No doubt softening the blow was the major-general's rank he received in the regular army on 12 Oct. 1793, as well as an appointment as colonel commandant of a battalion of the 60th Foot in August 1794. War with France had precipitated these decisions and, again to his credit, Carleton responded as a loyal soldier and governor. While encouraging recruitment for the new corps, the King's New Brunswick Regiment, Carleton also rushed through a new militia bill, strengthened Saint John's defences, and made a personal contribution of £500 to a fund for the defence of Britain. Loyalty must have been mixed with bitter disappointment, nevertheless, when Prince EDWARD AUGUSTUS was welcomed to the colony in 1794. The prince assumed command of all troops in New Brunswick and Nova Scotia, eclipsing Carleton and, with his base in Nova Scotia, guaranteeing that Thomas's colony would never be the heart of the British defences in eastern Canada.

At the same time the lines were being drawn within New Brunswick for a confrontation between the lieutenant governor and Council and the elected assembly, a battle that disrupted the colony for a considerable time and finally soured Carleton on New Brunswick. James Glenie would have a major role, although the sincerity of his championing of assembly rights is questionable. The lieutenant governor, Glenie claimed, had been placed by his friends "in a Situation which nature never intended him for, and for which he is by no means qualified by Education, Capacity or Experience"; he was, moreover, to blame for New Brunswick's failure to prosper, being "by Constitution an Enemy to Business and by practice an utter stranger to it." These attacks on the lieutenant governor have been assessed by the historian George Francis Gilman Stanley as of "little weight in London." Yet some of the charges were presented to Home Secretary Henry Dundas, no friend of the Carleton family. When Carleton complained in 1792 of Council positions being awarded without his "concurrence," and his authority being thus under-

Carleton

mined, Dundas was quick to lecture him on "an unbecoming doubt of the wisdom and discretion of His Majesty's Councils." In the major confrontation between executive and assembly, however, Carleton at least had some support from the Duke of Portland, who succeeded Dundas.

The election of 1793 replaced a cooperative assembly with one far more critical and assertive, and Carleton found some of his recommendations ignored. The simmering discontent reached a peak in 1795. Defence expenditures by the lieutenant governor in Saint John and St Andrews were rejected by the assembly and, in retaliation, the appropriation bill, which provided for salaries for assembly members, was rejected by the Council, as was a proposal to have the Supreme Court sit in Saint John as well as in Fredericton. This agitation was typified by Glenie's bill, "Declaratory of what Acts of Parliament are Binding in this Province," again a measure passed by the assembly and vetoed by the Council. Dissolution of the assembly in August 1795 and the election of new legislators provided no relief for Carleton and the Council; the deadlock remained and government ground to a halt from 1795 to 1799. Much of the assembly's restlessness, in Carleton's opinion, was due to the Fredericton emphasis of his government, since the "mercantile Interest" of Saint John, Charlotte, and Westmorland counties still hoped that the seat of government might be moved to Saint John. He saw in this attempt to undermine his master-plan a conspiracy of "a few Members, who evidently have a predilection for the Republican Systems formerly prevalent in the chartered Colonies of New England." Portland attempted throughout to rule on each of the thorny issues being debated, usually expressing a cautious approval of the position taken by Carleton and the Council. As the dispute dragged on, however, an increasing exasperation with "idle and groundless differences" emerged in his correspondence.

Even New Brunswick grew weary of the conflict. A more conciliatory mood was produced in the assembly when Carleton manipulated evidence of the home authorities' displeasure, on one occasion carefully selecting passages from Portland's letters for the information of Amos BOTSFORD, speaker of the house. The opposition cause was further weakened when, in the 1797 session, Glenie dared to introduce a censure motion against the lieutenant governor himself. With the exception of Stair Agnew* and three others, the assembly drew back at this direct attack on the king's representative. Still it was not until the 1799 session, when Carleton laid before the house extensive extracts from Portland's correspondence outlining "the principles and rules of legislative proceeding," that the deadlock was broken. Both sides compromised: the assemblymen separated provision for their salaries from the appropriations for other services; the Council waived its opposition "to some irregularities in the bills of this Session" and passed supply bills for the preceding four years. Though the further adjustments that marked the 1799 and 1801 sessions seemed to vindicate the executive (the assembly, for example, tolerated Council review of appropriation items before inclusion in the final bill), in fact a fundamental shift in power was under way. At the heart of the struggle, Botsford believed, had been the assembly's "inherent and indubitable privileges," whose vigilant protection and development were totally compatible with "the well tried loyalty of those, who compose the House of Assembly": "they had not acted from a spirit of opposition or obstinacy or want of parliamentary information . . . they had sacrificed no essential rights, and only altered the mode in granting, from a desire of harmony and in conformity to the sentiments and the clear light thrown on the subject by his Grace's important communications." In reality, New Brunswick was witnessing the emergence of the assembly's "political hegemony" as power passed to the elective branch of government.

This erosion of executive power ran contrary to Carleton's philosophy of government and, when linked with the almost total erosion of his military authority, convinced him of the need to remove himself from New Brunswick. By 1800 he was quite frank about the slow economic development of the colony, blaming short-sighted imperial policies for this failure. The now ten-year-old restriction on land grants was a particularly sore point. Some satisfaction had been achieved in 1798 with the temporary resolution of boundary problems with the United States, the Scoodic River being confirmed as the western boundary of New Brunswick [see Thomas WRIGHT], and in 1800 Carleton's continuing encouragement of "the Infant College" culminated in a provincial charter of incorporation. But in the military sphere, his pride and authority received a series of blows. Despite his strenuous opposition, his right to appoint the town major and barrack-master in Fredericton was lost in 1796 and the deputy paymaster's office was removed from his patronage in 1798. Halifax's position as the military centre of British defences was confirmed in September 1799 when Edward Augustus, now Duke of Kent and Strathearn, assumed command of the forces in British North America with headquarters in the Nova Scotia capital. Shortly afterwards, arguing that these changes had altered "the nature of the charge I have been honoured with" and reduced him to "a public Accountant," an embittered Carleton asked permission to resign.

While Portland expressed surprise and regret, he promised to act on the request. On the other hand, the Duke of Kent seemed honestly concerned at the possible loss. Informed by the duke that the service of the New Brunswick Regiment was to be extended and that it might be "shortly placed on the establishment of Fencibles," Carleton began to reconsider. He now believed his resignation had been premature, and rather tactless, and, employing the change in status of the New Brunswick Regiment as an excuse, he begged Portland "to bury in oblivion" his resignation. Portland complied and Carleton continued in office. There were better ways to leave New Brunswick than an abrupt resignation after a harsh censure of the ministry and Carleton would seek them. In the interval, perhaps he could enjoy the political lull and his remaining military responsibilities.

It was to be a short interval. The legislature had not met since February 1799, but when it reconvened in January 1801 Robert Pagan* introduced a motion censuring Carleton for expending funds on the legislative building at Fredericton without the approval of the legislature. It did not pass, but served as a painful reminder of the continuing close scrutiny of executive actions. The following year a squabble broke out over who should be appointed as clerk of the assembly, the house favouring Samuel Denny Street* while the Council and Carleton wanted, and appointed by letters patent, Dugald Campbell. Obsessed with what he perceived to be emulation of unacceptable American practices, Carleton saw in assembly appointment of the clerk "one of those usages of the late New England Provinces." Contention and disappointment also marred Carleton's military service. Citing weather conditions, expense, and lack of military manpower, he opposed one of the Duke of Kent's pet projects, a primitive telegraph system stretching from Saint John to Fredericton and eventually from Halifax to Quebec. Meanwhile the New Brunswick Regiment was ordered disbanded. In June 1802, capitalizing upon the peace between France and England, Carleton requested a leave of absence to attend to his private affairs and the request was granted. Early in October 1803, accompanied by his wife, son William, daughters Emma and Anne, and stepson Captain Nathaniel Foy, he sailed for England, never to return to New Brunswick. The direction of the colony was left to Gabriel George Ludlow, the first of a series of administrators who were to govern in Carleton's absence over the next 13 years.

Once home, Carleton did not immediately forget his responsibilities as lieutenant governor. Indeed, the generally accepted theory that he had little interest or involvement in civil matters, leaving these to his loyalist advisers as Edward Winslow hinted and a number of historians have asserted, is contradicted by the evidence. Though concerned about "the little prospect of being able to draw the attention of Ministers towards our part of the world," and handicapped of course by the lack of any extensive correspondence except with Winslow, he kept a watchful eye on activities in New Brunswick and did not hestitate to speak out. Among his concerns were the salary arrears of Society for the Propagation of the Gospel workers in New Brunswick, the colony's desire to issue paper currency, and changes in legislation dealing with the import and sale of goods. He continued to oppose as futile the attempt to collect quitrents, imposed when the restriction on land grants was lifted in 1802, and advocated an increase in the "slender salary" of the New Brunswick Supreme Court judges [see Joshua UPHAM]. Testaments to the loyalty and ability of some who had served under him were penned, but the interests of his friends were more directly served by his quick nomination of replacements when vacancies occurred on the Council or in the judiciary. Ironically, a controversy over one such vacancy completely alienated a once loyal supporter and convinced Carleton of his impotence within ministerial circles. In 1806 he nominated Ward Chipman for a judgeship on the Supreme Court, arguing that Edward Winslow's talents "would not atone for the want of Law knowledge." The ministry nevertheless dared to appoint Winslow, who had acquired important connections in England, and the lieutenant governor was outraged. Shortly thereafter, having learned of Carleton's opposition, Winslow was urging his patrons "to send us out some active and respectable man for a Governor" in place of Carleton, who continued to collect £750 each year while residing "for his amusement . . . at Ramsgate in England."

The affront to Carleton, as Edward Goldstone Lutwyche, one of his severest critics, observed, left him "some reason to be displeased." Chances of his returning to New Brunswick, a prospect he had several times considered, now were reduced considerably. By this time as well, residence at Ramsgate, winter visits to Bath, periods with Lord Dorchester at Stubbings House (near Maidenhead), and sojourns in London had seduced his family. One observer correctly predicted that it would be difficult for the Carletons again to endure life in New Brunswick. But when ordered to return in August 1807, Carleton actually prepared to do so, until he learned that Lieutenant-General Sir James Henry CRAIG had been appointed governor and commander-in-chief in British North America. As he then bluntly informed Viscount Castlereagh, the secretary for War and the Colonies, "Officers of a superior rank in the King's Army, cannot with propriety serve under the Command of inferiors . . . a situation of that sort must not only be very painful to such senior officers, but prove greatly injurious to the King's Service." An anonymous bureaucrat, obviously flustered by this missive, merely noted on it: "What ought to be done on this?" Carleton had washed his hands of New Brunswick and in the years ahead, despite periodic requests from the colony that a new lieutenant governor be appointed,

Carleton

the home authorities left him alone. His military and civil careers, in effect, had ended but he chose to remain lieutenant governor of New Brunswick until death, on 2 Feb. 1817, removed him. He was buried beside Lord Dorchester in St Swithun's Church at Nately Scures, near Basingstoke. Only then did the British government appoint a successor, George Stracey Smyth*.

Carleton as man and governor is difficult to assess. Often judgements of him are based on the comments of individuals who were his strongest critics after his departure from the colony. Thus Winslow's description of him as "costive and guarded," with an "inactive disposition and constitutional coldness," or Lutwyche's comment on "a drone with a sinecure," are frequently repeated. Worse yet, Glenie's many accusations have been assumed to be valid and James Hannay* can paint Carleton as "reactionary," "tyrannical," "obstinate," "unpopular," and "dull-witted," to cite only a sample of his choicer adjectives. On the other hand, there were those who praised Carleton's "zeal for the welfare of this Province," his "exact frugality in the managing that which belongs to the public," his "integrity, urbanity, and rectitude of conduct [which] have greatly endeared him to every good person in this Province." The faithful Jonathan Odell was moved to poetry at the mere rumour of Carleton's return to the colony, concluding his ode: "*Carleton returns*, rejoicing to impart/Fresh Hope and Joy to every loyal heart." Carleton was a man who kept his distance, even from those supporters who should have been closest to him. Yet his isolation is neither surprising, in view of his emphasis upon rank and position, nor to be condemned, since in dispensing the limited patronage available he could approach the chore, sometimes to the annoyance of his loyalist advisers, with impartial detachment. He was very much his own man and although, like any officer or official of his day, he recognized the need for support from patrons or relatives, he did not hesitate to oppose his superiors if his own or his colony's interests were threatened. To be sure, some of the resultant controversies were brought on by his abruptness, tactlessness, incorrect assessment, or even obstinacy on occasion. Yet perhaps among the most attractive qualities of the crusty old soldier were his bluntly straightforward approach when aroused and the honest evaluation of both his own and New Brunswick's problems. Was he a mere rubber stamp of the loyalist élite? Certainly he responded to much of the advice offered by those around him, but it is hard to accept the picture of him as a totally passive participant in the shaping of New Brunswick. Even if at times he only articulated the ideas of his advisers, he was the unquestioned supervisor who made at least some of their dreams a reality, who explained colonial measures and requested home government support on all the crucial matters. A prickly individual who consistently protested any derogation of his position, he is highly unlikely to have blindly followed the élite's suggestions or signed any dispatch he did not fully approve.

If his administration failed to make New Brunswick the "envy of the American states," it was at least partially because both Carleton and his colony were the victims of a changing empire. "The Original connexions and attachments are long since worn out," wrote Benjamin Marston* in 1790. This was Carleton's problem after the loss of Shelburne's support and the decline in influence of his elder brother. This was New Brunswick's problem when it discovered that it was far from the most valued possession in the empire and that the needs of other colonies, such as the West Indies, took priority. Carleton did not believe that "to reign is worth ambition tho' in Hell" and, when faced with growing neglect and possible insult, he retired from the fray. His brother is acclaimed as "the Father of British Canada" and Thomas Carleton deserves to be acknowledged as the key figure among the founding fathers of New Brunswick.

W. G. GODFREY

[The official correspondence of Thomas Carleton is fairly extensive, and frequently duplicated at various archival institutions in collections that bear different names but consist of essentially the same material. At the PAC the basic collection is MG 11, [CO 188] New Brunswick A, 1–26, while at the PRO the following are worthwhile: CO 188/1–23; CO 189/1–11; CO 190/1–5; CO 191/1–5; and CO 193/1–2. The Thomas Carleton letterbooks at PANB (RG 1, RS330, A1–A8) also contain transcripts from the official correspondence. Carleton's military career can be followed in collections such as PRO, WO 1/2–14, and BL, Add. MSS 21848 (Haldimand papers), both available on microfilm at PAC, and PAC, RG 8, I (C ser.), 15. At the BL the original Haldimand papers were examined and Add. MSS 21705, 21708–9, 21714–18, 21720, 21725, and 21728–36 were useful.

Private papers concerning Carleton are sparse. At the PAC the following were used: Thomas Carleton papers (MG 23, D3), Shelburne papers (MG 23, A4, 20–34 (transcripts)), and Chipman papers (MG 23, D1, ser.1, 1, 6). Available at UNBL is the basic source for this period of New Brunswick's history, the Winslow family papers (MG H2, 1–17). At the N.B. Museum the Thomas Carleton papers and the Odell family papers contain a small number of interesting items. In England the papers of leading figures who might be linked with Carleton were checked. At the PRO references to the governor are found in the Chatham papers (PRO 30/8, bundle 56); at the BL Carleton material is contained in the Windham papers (Add. MSS 37875), Liverpool papers (Add. MSS 38345, 38388, and 38393), and Dropmore papers (Add. MSS 59230).

The most important printed primary source is *Winslow papers* (Raymond). Other rewarding sources are *Annual reg.* (London), 1817; N.B., Legislative Council, *Journal* [1786–1830], vol.1; [Frederick Haldimand], "Private diary of Gen.

Haldimand," PAC *Report*, 1889: 123–299; "Royal commission to Thomas Carleton" and "Royal instructions to Thomas Carleton," N.B. Hist. Soc., *Coll.*, 2 (1899–1905), no.6: 394–403 and 404–38 respectively; and G.B., WO, *Army list*, 1758–1817. Carleton's marriage is recorded in *The register book of marriages belonging to the parish of St George, Hanover Square, in the county of Middlesex*, ed. J. H. Chapman and G. J. Armytage (4v., London, 1886–97), 1.

Among the secondary sources, books treating Carleton in New Brunswick are Hannay, *Hist. of N.B.*, vol.1; J. W. Lawrence, *Foot-prints; or, incidents in early history of New Brunswick, 1783–1883* (Saint John, 1883); W. S. MacNutt, *The founders and their times* (Fredericton, 1958) and *New Brunswick*; and Wright, *Loyalists of N.B.* The better-known Carleton, Lord Dorchester, is examined in *DNB*; A. G. Bradley, *Lord Dorchester* (Toronto, 1907; new ed., *Sir Guy Carleton (Lord Dorchester)*, [1966]); Burt, *Old prov. of Quebec* (1968); and W. [C. H.] Wood, *The father of British Canada; a chronicle of Carleton* (Toronto, 1916). An appreciation of the imperial background is provided by H. T. Manning, *British colonial government after the American revolution, 1782–1820* (New Haven, Conn., 1933) and John Norris, *Shelburne and reform* (London, 1963). Useful studies of the loyalists are Carol Berkin, *Jonathan Sewall; odyssey of an American loyalist* (New York, 1974); Wallace Brown, *The good Americans: the loyalists in the American revolution* (New York, 1969) and *The king's friends: the composition and motives of the American loyalist claimants* (Providence, R.I., 1965); W. H. Nelson, *The American tory* (Oxford, 1961); and M. B. Norton, *The British-Americans: the loyalist exiles in England, 1774–1789* (Boston and Toronto, 1972).

Worthwhile articles dealing with Carleton are W. F. Ganong, "Governor Thomas Carleton," *New Brunswick Magazine* (Saint John), 2 (January–June 1899): 72–78; Alec Martin, "The mystery of the Carleton portrait," *Atlantic Advocate* (Fredericton), 54 (1963–64), no.4: 28–33; and [W. O.] Raymond, "The first governor of New Brunswick and the Acadians of the River Saint John," RSC *Trans.*, 3rd ser., 8 (1914), sect.II: 415–52, and "A sketch of the life and administration of General Thomas Carleton, first governor of New Brunswick," N.B. Hist. Soc., *Coll.*, 2 (1899–1905), no.6: 439–81. Other helpful articles are T. W. Acheson, "A study in the historical demography of a loyalist county," *SH*, no.1 (April 1968): 53–65; A. L. Burt, "Guy Carleton, Lord Dorchester: an estimate," CHA *Report*, 1935: 76–87; Marion Gilroy, "The partition of Nova Scotia, 1784," *CHR*, 14 (1933): 375–91; W. H. Nelson, "The last hopes of the American loyalists," *CHR*, 32 (1951): 22–42; G. [A.] Rawlyk, "The federalist-loyalist alliance in New Brunswick, 1784–1815," *Humanities Assoc. Rev.* (Kingston, Ont.), 27 (1976): 142–60; W. O. Raymond, "Elias Hardy, councillor-at-law," N.B. Hist. Soc., *Coll.*, 4 (1919–28), no.10: 57–66; G. F. G. Stanley, "James Glenie, a study in early colonial radicalism," N.S. Hist. Soc., *Coll.*, 25 (1942): 145–73; and J. C. Webster, "Sir Brook Watson: friend of the loyalists, first agent of New Brunswick in London," *Argosy* (Sackville, N.B.), 3 (1924–25): 3–25.

Many valuable studies remain in dissertation form, including T. F. Buttimer, "Governor Thomas Carleton: unsung and unpopular" (BA thesis, Mount Allison Univ., Sackville, 1977); Condon, "Envy of American states"; C. L.

Duval, "Edward Winslow; portrait of a loyalist" (MA thesis, Univ. of N.B., Fredericton, 1960); D. R. Facey-Crowther, "The New Brunswick militia: 1784–1871" (MA thesis, Univ. of N.B., 1965); J. S. MacKinnon, "The development of local government in the city of Saint John, 1785–1795" (MA thesis, Univ. of N.B., 1968); P. A. Ryder, "Ward Chipman, United Empire Loyalist" (MA thesis, Univ. of N.B., 1958); and J. P. Wise, "British commercial policy, 1783–1794: the aftermath of American independence" (PHD thesis, Univ. of London, 1972). The thesis by Twila Buttimer considerably influenced the sympathetic handling of Carleton offered in this biography. w.g.g.]

CARREFOUR DE LA PELOUZE, PIERRE-JOSEPH (baptized **Joseph**), army officer and author of a journal; b. 10 March 1738 in Saumur, France, son of Abraham Carrefour de La Pelouze and Gabrielle-Marie Vernas; d. 6 July 1808 in London, England.

At the age of 18, Pierre-Joseph Carrefour de La Pelouze, "having left his father's house," entered the Régiment de Berry as a lieutenant. In September 1756 his regiment was ordered to India, a posting that pleased La Pelouze and appealed to his taste for the exotic. After the unit had made lengthy preparations, a counter-order forced the entire complement to go to Brest and then to sail for Canada. This new arrangement also delighted the young officer, who received a captain's commission at that time.

After a rather difficult crossing the squadron entered the port of Louisbourg, Île Royale (Cape Breton Island), on 22 June 1757. La Pelouze took advantage of his short stay in the fortress to visit the town; he found it badly built, small, dirty, and reeking unbearably of fish. After a brief stay in harbour, on board ship, the Régiment de Berry went on to Canada, an "infinitely better" country in the opinion of La Pelouze, and reached Quebec without incident 26 days later. During his first winter La Pelouze thought he was still too young to take part in the gambling and balls that occupied the local population; he contented himself with visiting the region, getting to know the inhabitants, and observing their ways and customs.

In the spring of 1758 La Pelouze went with his regiment to Fort Carillon (near Ticonderoga, N.Y.); on 8 July he was in the forces which under Louis-Joseph de Montcalm* gained a noted victory over James Abercromby*. Through hearsay and experience La Pelouze was initiated into the Indians' style of warfare, which he described as cruel. Indeed the details of the dress, religious beliefs, form of worship, manners, and especially the cruelty of these allies of New France made a strong impression on him.

La Pelouze's regiment took up winter quarters that year at Quebec. However, it returned to Carillon in May 1759. La Pelouze worked at strengthening the fort as much as possible, but this turned out to be a waste of effort. When Jeffery Amherst* laid siege to it

Cartier

on 23 July, most of the troops under François-Charles de Bourlamaque* had already withdrawn to Île aux Noix, on the Richelieu. There La Pelouze, who was engaged in building fortifications, heard of the battle fought on the Plains of Abraham by Montcalm, Vaudreuil [Rigaud*], and James Wolfe*. The account of it in his journal is brief and contains few details. Nothing happened at Île aux Noix in 1759 and La Pelouze went with his detachment to take up winter quarters near Montreal. In April 1760 he left for Quebec with the army of 7,000 under François de Lévis*. Wounded in the battle of Sainte-Foy, he spent two months in hospital before sailing for France in August 1760.

La Pelouze subsequently continued his military career as a captain in the Régiment d'Aquitaine in 1763, and then as major of the Régiment de Boulonnais in March 1774. In August of that year he became king's lieutenant at Bonifacio in Corsica, and on 16 Jan. 1778 he received the cross of Saint-Louis. He retired on 4 April 1781 with a pension of 1,250 *livres*. The next mention of him is in 1792, when he had returned to the army and was holding a commission as a major. Soon after, he emigrated to England where he died on 6 July 1808.

Pierre-Joseph Carrefour de La Pelouze's journal is more a report of his voyage to Canada. This account, which in tone is sometimes jocular, sometimes shocked, but always exaggerated, is interesting not for the freshness of its information (in particular about the Seven Years' War), but for its detailed description of the life led by a young and enthusiastic officer enthralled by new experiences.

JACQUELINE ROY

Pierre-Joseph Carrefour de La Pelouze's "Voyage et campagne au Canada" is held by Houghton Library, Harvard Univ. (Cambridge, Mass.), MS Can., b 8, 49 M-180.

AD, Maine-et-Loire (Angers), État civil, Saumur, 10 mars 1738. Arch. du ministère des Armées (Paris), Service hist. de l'Armée, A[1], 9598. *NYCD* (O'Callaghan and Fernow), 10: 1085.

CARTIER, JACQUES, businessman, militia officer, and politician; b. 10 April 1750 at Quebec, son of Jacques Cartier, *dit* L'Angevin, and Marguerite Mongeon; d. 22 March 1814 in Saint-Antoine-sur-Richelieu, Lower Canada.

Jacques Cartier's father, a merchant living on Rue Saint-Jean, Quebec, benefited from his friendship with Michel-Jean-Hugues Péan*, middle man between the intendant François Bigot* and government suppliers, to obtain contracts for a large part of the flour supplies until 1757. He also engaged in the export of salt and fish to France. Though he managed to accumulate only a very modest fortune by the time

of his death it was apparently sufficient to send his son Jacques to Jean-Baptiste Curatteau*'s secondary school at Longue-Pointe (Montreal) in 1767. Two years later Jacques had established himself as a merchant at Quebec, perhaps with the financial support of François BABY, for whom he appears to have acted as a fur-purchasing agent in 1771.

In 1770 Jacques and his brother Joseph had gone to the Richelieu region to sell fish. Jacques established himself as an independent merchant at Saint-Antoine-sur-Richelieu by 1772, the year after his father's death. On 27 Sept. 1772 he married Cécile Gervaise, niece of the parish priest, Michel Gervaise. They were to have a daughter Cécile and a son Jacques, father of Sir George-Étienne Cartier*. Jacques's brother Joseph became a merchant across the river in Saint-Denis.

Jacques Cartier bought grain in, and shipped it from, the Richelieu area. As a vital transportation route between the St Lawrence valley and the American colonies, and as the richest region in Quebec for the cultivation of wheat, the Richelieu valley was attracting the attention of such merchants as George ALLSOPP, Gabriel Christie*, Edward Harrison*, and Samuel Jacobs*. At the beginning of September 1775, Cartier offered to supply François Baby if the Quebec merchant speculated in wheat. Cartier's plans were abruptly interrupted, however, when the Americans invaded Canada in the fall of 1775 via the Richelieu valley. As late as 1 September Cartier had written to Baby: "Nothing new here. Things are very quiet. People no longer speak of the Bastones." Ironically, Brigadier-General Richard Montgomery* had started out from Crown Point, N.Y., with an invasion force of 1,200 men the day before. Cartier, unlike many Canadians, was active on the British side, serving as a militia officer and billeting British troops in his home.

Having failed in their objective to capture Quebec, the Americans were driven back to Crown Point, via the Richelieu valley, by July 1776. Cartier lost no time in re-establishing his business; in August he signed a contract to supply wheat to the Montreal merchant Jacob Jordan*. By 1781 Cartier was branching into milling, having agreed to pay François-Claude Boucher 36 *minots* of wheat annually for the privilege of building a grist-mill on his seigneury of Contrecœur. Cartier was probably a retail merchant as well. Just before the American invasion he had placed an order with François Baby for 15 quintals of assorted iron pieces, and in 1798 he purchased from Charles-Joseph Lefebvre-Duchouquet, parish priest of Notre-Dame-de-Saint-Hyacinthe (Notre-Dame-du-Rosaire), a lot of household goods which he was free "to dispose of for his profit."

Cartier's affairs seem to have prospered since in 1782 he built the most imposing home in the area, La

Maison aux Sept Cheminées, overlooking the river on the edge of Saint-Antoine-sur-Richelieu. The house was constructed in three sections, with fireproof rooms for merchandise at each end, and a large meeting room or salon connected with offices above. The property had its own wharf so that boats could be loaded and unloaded directly at the stores.

By the 1780s Cartier's business was providing him with capital to make loans to local inhabitants. Father Gervaise, at the time of his death in 1787, owed Cartier nearly £900. The merchant had Gervaise's effects and properties sold at auction to collect the debt, and himself bought from among the properties a farm, two vacant lots, and a grist-mill, all in the vicinity of Saint-Antoine-sur-Richelieu. By the late 1790s Cartier was extending his activity as a lender beyond the Richelieu valley. In 1798 he won a suit against Antoine Papineau of Chambly and Toussaint Truteau of Montreal for collection of £630. In 1803 he lent £1,287 to the Quebec speculator and property-holder Joseph DRAPEAU, and £1,000 to the notary Jacques Voyer*, also from Quebec. The following year he lent 5,500 *livres* to Jean-Baptiste Blais of Saint-Pierre-de-la-Rivière-du-Sud and in 1808 £1,485 to Jean-Baptiste Noël, seigneur of Tilly. He occasionally accepted payment of debts in land, for instance in February 1807 from Drapeau a lot in Quebec's Lower Town, and a few months later, in settlement of other suits, several rural lots in the Richelieu area with a total value of nearly £240.

In 1800 Cartier launched a new commercial venture, a postal service linking Saint-Antoine-sur-Richelieu, Saint-Denis, Saint-Ours, and William Henry (Sorel). Although an application for postal service in the Richelieu valley had been made to Hugh FINLAY, deputy postmaster general, as early as 1781, Cartier appears to have been the first to take action. He extended the service to Saint-Hyacinthe, but eventually discontinued this portion because, as the Saint-Hyacinthe notary Louis Bourdages* explained to him, his proposal seemed too grasping to the people of Saint-Hyacinthe and "smacks a little of mercantile aristocracy."

Cartier was deputy in the House of Assembly for Surrey from 1804 to 1809 and was one of the more regular attenders, voting consistently with the Canadian party against the ministerial group. Major in the 2nd Boucherville battalion of militia from about 1800, Cartier became lieutenant-colonel for the same region on 21 Feb. 1808. In May 1810 he wrote to François Baby, adjutant general of the militia, about a dispute between himself and his colonel, Joseph Boucher de La Bruère de Montarville. The details of the dispute are unknown, but it revolved around the proclamation issued by Governor CRAIG in late March justifying his suppression of the Quebec newspaper *Le Canadien* and imprisonment of several of its editors. Professing

to have "embraced the just cause of the government" since 1775, Cartier asked for Baby's support, adding that if Baby considered him wrong, he would resign. In the latter event, he wrote, "Be assured that with all my heart I will be as good a subject and loyal as before." Cartier remained in the militia and about 1813 was transferred to the new Verchères battalion.

Jacques Cartier died in March 1814, the year of his illustrious grandson's birth. His obituary described him as a generous and kindly man, widely liked and respected. The description would appear to be substantiated by Cartier's burial on 24 March in the parish church of Saint-Antoine "with the honours appropriate to his rank . . . , before a large congregation of respectable people" from Saint-Antoine and surrounding parishes. He left a sizeable fortune for the time, more than 150,000 *livres*. His effects included a library in which books on history and law were prominent; among the authors were Bossuet, Voltaire, Raynal, and Blackstone. Cartier's estate enabled his son Jacques, who had no interest in his father's business, to live in the agreeable manner of a wealthy country squire. Cartier's nephew Joseph took over the business, which continued to prosper under his direction.

HENRY B. M. BEST

ANQ-M, CE1-13, 27 sept. 1772, 24 mars 1814. ANQ-Q, CN1-60, 22 sept. 1804; CN1-230, 9, 19 juin 1804; 14 févr. 1807; 19 févr. 1809; CN1-248, 14 sept. 1771. AUM, P 58, U, Cartier à Baby, 19 août 1771, 1ᵉʳ sept. 1775; Cartier à Cuvillier, 15 oct. 1812. PAC, RG 4, B17, 8, 26 April 1785; 12, 26 Aug. 1786; 15, 28 Jan. 1790; 16, 7 Jan. 1799; 22, 11 May 1803; 27, 9 June 1806; 20 April, 20 June 1807; 31, 20 June 1812; 32, 5 May 1813; RG 9, I, A1, 2: 439A–39C. Private arch., Cartier estate (Montreal). Soc. d'hist. régionale de Saint-Hyacinthe (Saint-Hyacinthe, Qué.), sér.21, dossier 1, no.1.5. *Montreal Gazette*, 29 March 1814. *Officers of British forces in Canada* (Irving), 195–96. F.-J. Audet, *Contrecœur; famille, seigneurie, paroisse, village* (Montréal, 1940), 154, 159–60. [Noëlie Dion, Sœur Marie-de-la-Paix], *La petite histoire de chez nous, Saint-Antoine-sur-Richelieu* (Saint-Hyacinthe, 1938), 28, 38. Guy Frégault, *François Bigot, administrateur français* (2v., [Montréal], 1948), 1: 381. Maurault, *Le collège de Montréal* (Dansereau; 1967), 185. Alastair Sweeny, *George-Étienne Cartier: a biography* (Toronto, 1976), 19–21, 24, 39, 41, 91. B. J. Young, *George-Étienne Cartier, Montreal bourgeois* (Kingston, Ont., and Montreal, 1981), 2–5, 7, 138, 146. "Les disparus," *BRH*, 41 (1935): 293. Hare, "L'Assemblée législative du Bas-Canada," *RHAF*, 27: 379.

CARTWRIGHT, GEORGE, entrepreneur, sportsman, and diarist; b. 12 Feb. 1739/40 in Marnham, England, second of ten children of William Cartwright and Anne Cartwright; d. unmarried 19 May 1819 in nearby Mansfield.

George Cartwright was born into an old landed

Cartwright

family which had risen to prominence in the 16th century and was now in straitened circumstances. The father was a man of modest but distinct originality within his circle in Nottinghamshire; the mother was a daughter of George Cartwright of Ossington; and three of their sons achieved celebrity in different fields. John first pursued a naval career and through it was closely connected with George's early ventures in Newfoundland, and later, after his resignation in protest against participation in the American Revolutionary War, became a radical pamphleteer. Edmund, the youngest, was a scholar, poet, experimental agriculturist, and inventor of the power loom. Finally there was George himself.

Educated at Newark and at Randall's Academy, in Heath (West Yorkshire), George was entered at the age of 15 or 16 as a gentleman cadet in the Royal Military Academy at Woolwich (London), where he was instructed for a year; and on 6 March 1754 he sailed to India with a dozen other cadets to take up commissions in the army as they might become available. In 1755 he became an ensign in the 39th Foot, but to his regret missed being with the detachment commanded by Robert Clive at the retaking of Fort William (Calcutta), the capture of Chandernagore from the French, and the victory at Plassey over the nawab of Bengal. Recalled home, the regiment was stationed in Ireland at Limerick, and Cartwright was promoted lieutenant on 2 Feb. 1759. Early in 1760 he accompanied the Marquess of Granby to Germany as aide-de-camp and served as a staff officer with the British contingent under Duke Ferdinand of Brunswick. He returned to England at the end of the Seven Years' War as a captain in the army (from 21 May 1762). Burdened by debt, he went on half pay.

In the spring of 1765 he was residing in Scotland both to live economically with a mistress and entourage and "to indulge my insatiable propensity for shooting." The following winter he spent in London and in cruising with his brother John to control the smuggling trade in home waters. In the spring of 1766, on John's appointment as first lieutenant of the *Guernsey*, flagship of Commodore Hugh Palliser*, George sailed with the governor-designate to Newfoundland where he spent a season cruising along the northeast coast. Returning to England, he obtained a captaincy in the 37th Foot through the influence of Granby, now commander-in-chief, joined the regiment in Minorca, but was invalided home with malaria in 1767. A second voyage to Newfoundland with John followed in the spring of 1768, in the course of which he played a part in the expedition dispatched by Palliser under John's command into the interior of the island to establish friendly relations with the Beothuks at Red Indian Lake. An interest in the region and its native peoples coupled with disappointing

prospects for advancement in the army determined Cartwright on his next career as a trader and entrepreneur in Labrador, and in 1770 he went on half pay.

Competition between English and French fishermen, the often fierce rivalry between different English merchant houses, the endemic hostility between natives and Europeans, raids by American privateers, and the problems created by the divided jurisdiction of Quebec and Newfoundland authorities provided an unstable and troubled setting for Cartwright's activities during 16 years on the coast. The scene of his operations from 1770 to 1786 was the stretch of coastline between Cape Charles, where he occupied Nicholas Darby*'s old site, and Hamilton Inlet. From the stations he established he engaged with his servants and sharemen in the fisheries for cod, salmon, and seals, and the trade in furs. His ventures were undertaken in a number of financial arrangements and partnerships: between 1770 and 1772 with Francis Lucas*, Jeremiah Coghlan*, and Thomas Perkins, the latter two of Bristol; on his own account with money advanced by his father in 1773; with Robert and John Scott from 1773 to 1776; with Benjamin LESTER of Poole between 1783 and 1786; and others. There were years of success, but others of failure, and in 1778 his posts were plundered by American privateers with losses amounting to £14,000. The final result, not to be attributed to Cartwright himself, was bankruptcy, the causes of which are recorded in detail in the journal which he kept for most of these years and which he published in 1792 after his return to England.

The journal contains much else. It is, among other things, a detailed seasonal record of the exploitation of coastal resources by one who combined keen entrepreneurial interests with an inextinguishable zest for the chase which made him nature's nemesis; a finely observed record of natural history and meteorology; and, above all, testimony to a persistent, curious, and resourceful mind. In his relations with the native peoples of Labrador, especially the Inuit, Cartwright displayed an honesty which led to mutual trust. In 1772 he took a family of five Inuit to England, where they created considerable interest, meeting with the king, members of the Royal Society including Joseph BANKS, and James Boswell, who reported to a sceptical Samuel Johnson his ability to communicate with them by sign language. The poet Robert Southey, who had met Cartwright in 1791, recorded in his *Common-place book*: "I read his book in 1793. . . . This man had strength and perseverance charactered in every muscle. . . . The annals of his campaigns among the foxes and beavers interested me far more than ever did the exploits of Marlbro' or Frederic; besides, I saw plain truth and the heart in Cartwright's book – and in what history could I look for this?

Coleridge took up a volume one day and was delighted with its strange simplicity." What has only recently been properly recognized, however, is the interest of Cartwright not only in the Inuit language and its study, but also in making himself a glossarist of 18th-century Newfoundland English; and he was a close student of and perhaps contributor to the work of such scientific contemporaries as Banks, Thomas Pennant, and Daniel Carl Solander. Of his sole essay as a poet, "Labrador: a poetical epistle" (composed in 1784), Cartwright himself warned the reader: "Tho' I have often slept whole nights on mountains as high as that of famed Parnassus, yet, never having taken a nap on its sacred summit, it cannot be expected, that I should have awoke a Poet." Yet less interesting verses have attracted the industrious attention of Canadian literary historians, and among writings from the New World a more singular 18th-century document than the journal itself is hard to find.

After 1787 Cartwright resided in England, where he had inherited with his brother John a share of their father's estate. He was occupied from time to time in the legal consequences of his Labrador ventures and partnerships and with attempts to establish rights to certain Labrador coastal properties; and in 1793 he gave evidence before a committee of the House of Commons on affairs in Newfoundland and Labrador. His military experience led to his appointment during the Napoleonic Wars as barrack master at Nottingham where in later years, known by the sobriquet "Old Labrador," he was a distinguished and popular figure. A handsome man of strong and robust figure and unbending tory principles, he was courtly and agreeable in conversation. He died in 1819 at the age of 80, characteristically occupied on his deathbed with proposals to the Hudson's Bay Company to establish trading-posts on the coast of Labrador, where his name is borne by a settlement at the entrance to Sandwich Bay.

G. M. STORY

[There are documents relating to Cartwright's applications for land grants and fishing rights in Labrador, 1785–88, in the PAC, RG 1, L3^L: 28. Miscellaneous family papers are in the possession of Patricia and John Cartwright, Johannesburg, South Africa; *see* Ingeborg Marshall, "Inventory of the Cartwright papers" (typescript, 1979; copy at the Memorial Univ. of Nfld. Library, Centre for Nfld. Studies, St John's). G.M.S.]

Maritime Hist. Group Arch., Cartwright name file. [George Cartwright], *Captain Cartwright and his Labrador journal*, ed. C. W. Townsend (Boston, 1911); *Journal of transactions and events, during a residence of nearly sixteen years on the coast of Labrador* . . . (3v., Newark, Eng., 1792). *DCB*, vol.4 (biogs. of Jeremiah Coghlan and Sir Hugh Palliser). *DNB* (biogs. of Edmund Cartwright and John Cartwright). C. R. Fay, *Life and labour in Newfoundland* (Toronto, 1956), 78–82. W. G. Gosling, *Labrador: its*

discovery, exploration, and development (London, 1910), 222–50. J. P. Howley, *The Beothucks or Red Indians: the aboriginal inhabitants of Newfoundland* (Cambridge, Eng., 1915; repr. Toronto, 1974, and New York, 1979), 49–54. H. A. Innis, *The cod fisheries; the history of an international economy* (rev. ed., Toronto, 1954). A. M. Lysaght, *Joseph Banks in Newfoundland and Labrador, 1766: his diary, manuscripts and collections* (London and Berkeley, Calif., 1971). *The life and correspondence of Major Cartwright*, ed. F. D. Cartwright (2v., London, 1826; repr. New York, [1972]). P. [A.] O'Flaherty, *The rock observed: studies in the literature of Newfoundland* (Toronto, 1979), 34–42. Prowse, *Hist. of Nfld.* (1895), 598–601. C. W. Townsend, *Along the Labrador coast* (London, 1908), 207–28. G. M. Story, "'Old Labrador': George Cartwright, 1738–1819," *Newfoundland Quarterly* (St John's), 77 (1981–82), no.1: 23–31, 35. W. H. Whiteley, "Newfoundland, Quebec, and the administration of the coast of Labrador, 1774–83," *Acadiensis* (Fredericton), 6 (1976–77), no.2: 92–112; "Newfoundland, Quebec, and the Labrador merchants, 1783–1809," *Newfoundland Quarterly*, 73 (1977), no.4: 17–26.

CARTWRIGHT, RICHARD, businessman, office holder, judge, politician, militia officer, and author; b. 2 Feb. 1759 in Albany, N.Y., son of Richard Cartwright and Joanne Beasley; m. *c*. 1784 Magdalen Secord in Cataraqui (Kingston, Ont.), and they had eight children; d. 27 July 1815 in Kingston, Upper Canada.

Richard Cartwright's father was a native of England who had emigrated to New York in 1742 and his mother was from a "loyal Dutch family." By the early 1770s Richard Cartwright Sr had established himself as a pillar of the community in Albany: he owned a successful inn and a valuable tract of land near Cherry Valley; he was also deputy postmaster of Albany and active locally in the Church of England. His prosperity allowed his son to attend private primary and advanced schools where he studied "the classics and higher branches of education," in preparation for a career in the church. Although the outbreak of the American revolution ended young Richard's plans for the ministry, his appetite for learning remained. Despite a badly deformed left eye, he read extensively, wrote lucid and often evocative prose, and trumpeted the virtues of "Reading, Writing, Thinking or Conversing Sensibly." In later years Cartwright – widely read, intelligent, and blessed, it was said, with a photographic memory – was a man of intellectual stature who sometimes overawed his contemporaries in the pioneer community of Upper Canada.

The life of the Cartwright family in New York was totally disrupted by the American revolution. At first Richard Cartwright Sr was able to avoid confrontation with the rebels who controlled the Albany region. In 1775 he contributed supplies to the attack on Fort Ticonderoga (near Ticonderoga, N.Y.) led by Ethan Allen and Benedict ARNOLD, and he also turned over

Cartwright

at least two suspicious letters to rebel leaders. But with the Declaration of Independence the older Cartwright felt compelled to withdraw to a more neutral position. His neutrality, however, was challenged in February 1777 when the Albany committee of correspondence seized a letter written by Richard Cartwright Jr to his sister, Elizabeth Robison of Niagara (near Youngstown, N.Y.). The contents of the letter were obviously incriminating since Richard Jr was ordered to "enter into security for his future good behaviour." It seems that by October 1777 Richard Jr's good behaviour could no longer be guaranteed and his father gained permission from the committee to allow Richard Jr and his young niece, Hannah, to leave for British territory. Richard's parents, tainted by the loyalism of their son, suffered personal abuse, had their property "destroyed & plundered," and in July 1778 were "conveyed away by a Guard to Crown Point."

In an account of his journey to the province of Quebec written in 1777, and also in his later writings, Richard Cartwright Jr tried to clarify the basis of his loyalty to the British empire and constitution. Shortly after his departure from New York, he explained his reasons for leaving: "The distracted Condition of my native Country, where all Government was subverted, where Caprice was the only Rule and Measure of usurped Authority, and where all the Distress was exhibited that Power guided by Malice can produce, had long made me wish to leave it . . . notwithstanding the tender Feelings of Humanity which I suffered at Parting from the fondest of Parents, and a Number of agreeable Acquaintance it gave me a sensible Pleasure to quit a Place where Discord reigned and all the miseries of Anarchy had long prevailed." To loyalists such as Cartwright the British constitution symbolized institutions and traditions – for example, a government with an appointed upper house and executive, trial by jury, and habeas corpus – which guaranteed order, authority, and liberty under law. The other dimension of his loyalism was his belief in the "Unity of the Empire," under "the supremacy of Parliament," "considered as co-extensive with the British Dominions." In other words, it was his conviction that the many different branches of the British empire should be united under the authority of parliament, which ensured order, stability, and a uniformity of interests throughout the empire's various parts. Taken together, Cartwright's view of the empire, his commitment to the British constitution, and his strong awareness of his loyalist origins influenced both his response to public issues and the direction in which he sought to guide Upper Canada.

After journeying overland to Montreal, Cartwright eventually became secretary to John Butler*, major commandant of a loyalist regiment based at Fort Niagara. He spent 1778 and 1779 on military expeditions into northern New York and gained experience in military provisioning while making valuable commercial contacts. In May 1780 he left the military to enter a partnership with Robert HAMILTON. The following year Hamilton and Cartwright – with the help of their principal suppliers, James McGILL and Isaac TODD of Montreal – formed a partnership with John ASKIN of Detroit. All of these merchants were eager to tap not only the lucrative fur trade but also the supply of British garrisons. Cartwright's movements for the next couple of years are difficult to trace, but by 1783 he may have been looking after the firm's operations in eastern Upper Canada from a store on Carleton Island (N.Y.). In 1784 the partnership with Askin was amicably dissolved, and that same year or perhaps in 1785 Cartwright moved from Carleton Island to Cataraqui on the mainland. Shortly after moving, Cartwright married a member of a well-known loyalist family, Magdalen Secord, sister-in-law of Laura [Ingersoll*]. She would provide her husband with eight children, unflagging devotion and love, and unquestioning support.

At Carleton Island and later in Cataraqui (renamed Kingston in 1788), Cartwright found himself in an excellent position to realize his considerable entrepreneurial potential. He possessed untiring energy and a passion for detail, controlling every aspect of his growing business. Continuing in partnership with Hamilton until 1790, Cartwright was able to use the military contacts he had developed in Niagara to win supply contracts for the Kingston garrison; in the early 1790s William ROBERTSON and Isaac Todd lobbied successfully in England to win an exclusive contract for Cartwright, Hamilton, Askin, and David Robertson to supply the Upper Canadian garrisons between 1793 and 1795. Cartwright also acted as a key link in the "commercial empire of the St Lawrence," which stretched from London to Montreal and through Kingston to Niagara, Detroit, and the northwest. In Kingston, Cartwright received and forwarded, for a five per cent commission, goods that McGill and Todd were sending into the interior. He exported Upper Canadian products – lumber, wheat, flour, potash, and pearl ash – through Montreal, and imported, via his Montreal agents, English manufactures and other goods which he sold very profitably to the growing civilian population. The virtual monopoly that Cartwright and other Kingston merchants, such as Joseph FORSYTH, Peter Smith*, and John Kirby*, had over the economic life of the region translated itself into that dependent relationship between debtor and creditor which has characterized so many frontier societies. Thus, from the mid 1780s on, Cartwright was able to take full advantage of his location and his myriad of friends and associates. Even he admitted, however, that much depended on British support and British capital. He pointed to "the numerous garrisons and public departments established amongst us" and observed that "as long as the British Government shall think [it] proper to hire people to come over to eat our flour, we shall go on very well, and continue to make a figure."

Despite all of his early advantages, in 1786 Cartwright had found himself in a vulnerable economic situation and he therefore decided to pull back, as he put it, "into a narrow Compass." But by 1788 the general economic situation had improved and Cartwright involved himself in shipbuilding with the construction of the 120-ton *Lady Dorchester*. Six years later he joined a number of other merchants in building the *Governor Simcoe*.

Cartwright had learned early in his business career that diversification and flexibility were absolutely essential if a reasonable profit was to be earned. His general store in Kingston has been accurately described as "the most important business centre" in the community. He also owned a blacksmith's shop and a cooper's shop in Kingston. In 1792 he purchased the government mills Robert Clark* had built at Napanee – 25 miles west of Kingston – and immediately enlarged them to increase the production of flour. The flour produced at Napanee was of unusually fine quality and within a few years Cartwright was sending it to Niagara and to Montreal. At Napanee, moreover, he constructed a large "Shop," a sawmill, a fulling-mill, a distillery, and a "tavern and other buildings." In 1815 he estimated that, for the 1806 to 1814 period, the operations in Napanee had "produced a profit of £11,011-19-8 equal to £1376-10 per Annum." According to Cartwright, "few if any mercantile houses in Kingston have done business to equal advantage for the same time." His profit from his Kingston businesses must have been at least as large as that from Napanee.

Flour had become by the mid 1790s such an important staple for Cartwright that he stressed, "unless we can make our payments by this means our business is likely to become very languid in this province." In 1801 more than 25 per cent of all the flour shipped to Montreal from Kingston was Cartwright flour. The Kingston merchant was also very much involved in the salted pork trade. In 1794, for example, 800 barrels of pork were produced in Kingston – 75 per cent more than in 1793. The remarkable increase was traced to one man – Richard Cartwright.

Realizing the growing importance of the flour and pork trade to Montreal and beyond, and the disadvantages of being dependent upon bateaux, Cartwright in 1794 began "to think seriously of attempting to facilitate the Export of our produce to Montreal, by means of Scows and Rafts." In 1801 he was busy constructing his own scows and he proposed sending them laden with flour directly from Napanee to Quebec. Despite the loss of one of his scows on the St Lawrence River in 1802, Cartwright's enthusiasm for what he regarded as a most practical and inexpensive mode of transport never waned.

Not only was Cartwright interested and active in almost every aspect of trade; he also encouraged local manufacturing. He was involved in making canvas for the British navy during the War of 1812 and also in distributing knitted products made locally. Moreover, together with other members of the Kingston élite such as Peter Smith, Lawrence Herchmer, and Allan MacLean*, he felt obliged in 1811 to keep the *Kingston Gazette* alive by purchasing it for a time from its disenchanted owner [*see* Stephen Miles*]. Cartwright considered the *Gazette* to be an influential means whereby he and his fellow leaders could mould the attitudes and values of the inhabitants of eastern Upper Canada. It is, therefore, not surprising that, under the pseudonym "Falkland," Cartwright contributed many articles to the *Gazette* on the eve of and during the War of 1812. In these he underscored the loyalist and British traditions which he felt were at the core of Upper Canadian society.

When Cartwright died in 1815 he left to his wife and children not only all of his valuable business enterprises and his houses and personal property in Kingston and York (Toronto) but also more than 27,000 acres of land to be found throughout much of Upper Canada. He obviously was an unusually gifted and successful entrepreneur. One of the major reasons for his commercial success, without question, was his scrupulous honesty and his remarkable eye for detail. He took no unfair advantage of his clients and he expected the same treatment in return. Another reason was his flexibility and his commercial diversification. He had succeeded, as he had once expressed it in 1815, in making all his enterprises "mutually to assist to play into each other."

Cartwright's economic views coincided with his economic interests. He opposed "Interference in the Management of Private Property" – whether stringent laws regarding bankruptcy and financial disclosure or restrictions on trade – as being "inconsistent with Civil Rights." But he also advocated that government should encourage the production of certain cash crops by providing bounties and by inspecting Upper Canadian exports to ensure their high quality. He was especially opposed to restrictions on Upper Canadian trade with Lower Canada or the United States and used his influence (as one of three Upper Canadians on an interprovincial commission) to obtain in 1798 free trade with the United States. This reciprocity agreement ended only when the United States imposed restrictions in 1801. Cartwright argued that free trade would benefit Upper Canada since the northern United States would become integrated into the St Lawrence commercial system and English manufactures and

Cartwright

Canadian produce would reach American markets through Canadian ports, such as Kingston, and through the hands of Canadian merchants, such as Richard Cartwright. Early in his life Cartwright had pondered the difficulty of distinguishing between schemes "set on Foot" for the good of one's country and those advocated from "some private consideration." His conclusion, that it was impossible even for the individuals involved to distinguish between them, might aptly summarize the relationship between the interests of Upper Canada and those of Richard Cartwright.

Cartwright's stature in the community and his sense of duty to serve and promote the "good of the society" led to his appointment as a justice of the peace some time in the mid 1780s, and he served as chairman of the magistrates in his district once the Court of Quarter Sessions began meeting in 1788; in that year he was also appointed a judge of the Court of Common Pleas. He was regarded as a conscientious, astute judge who added "dignity to the court." In 1797, and again in 1800, Cartwright was named with Joshua BOOTH, Hazelton SPENCER, and Joseph Forsyth to the first Heir and Devisee Commission for the Midland District. In 1800, as well, Cartwright was appointed one of the commissioners in the Midland District for administering the oath of allegiance to settlers claiming land. His other appointments included: member of the Mecklenburg land board (established in 1788), militia officer (1793), county lieutenant (1792), and, most important, legislative councillor (1792). Moreover, he actively encouraged the improvement of Upper Canada's educational facilities. In 1799 Cartwright brought to Upper Canada a young Scottish teacher, John Strachan*, who was destined to educate many of the next generation of Upper Canadian leaders. A few years later, in 1805, Cartwright wrote a memorandum on education which resulted in a decision by the legislature to appropriate £400 for the purchase of scientific instruments for Strachan's Cornwall school.

An important event in Cartwright's political career was his quarrel with Upper Canada's first lieutenant governor, John Graves SIMCOE. At stake were two different perceptions of Upper Canada as a British colony. Simcoe wanted Upper Canada to become a miniature of England with a landed aristocracy, an established church, and institutions which would be replicas of those in England – as Cartwright said, "he [Simcoe] thinks every existing regulation in England would be proper here." In contrast, Cartwright believed that, although colonial institutions should be modelled on those of the mother country, the stress should be on "the spirit of the constitution," not "on copying all the subordinate establishments without considering the great disparity of the two countries in every respect." On these grounds, Cartwright, though an Anglican, opposed the exclusive privileges given to the Anglican clergy in the Marriage Act of 1793 since there was inadequate "provision for the marriages of Dissenters," who comprised a majority of the population. Similarly, he opposed the Judicature Act of 1794, whereby Upper Canadian courts were centralized as in England, because the scattered population along with the shortage of lawyers made such centralization impractical. Not only did Cartwright think that British institutions had to be adapted to Upper Canadian needs and conditions, but he also felt that the independent views of colonial leaders, such as himself, should be respected by British lieutenant governors. He believed that he had been appointed a legislative councillor because of his "Knowledge of the country and legislation to be most applicable to the situation of the colony; not merely to show my Complaisance to the person at the head of the Government." Besides, Cartwright felt that he, unlike Simcoe, had made a long-term commitment to the colony. "All my prospects, as well for myself as my family," he wrote, "are confined to this province: I am bound to it by the strongest ties, and with its welfare my interest is most essentially connected." It is understandable why he was convinced that it was his right and duty to oppose policies that would jeopardize the colony's future.

Moreover, Simcoe's land policy – to encourage American emigrants to settle in Canada – challenged Cartwright's vision of Upper Canada as an "asylum for the unfortunate Loyalists reduced to poverty and driven into exile by their attachment to Britain." This was the issue that upset Cartwright the most since, unlike Simcoe, he felt that Upper Canada was primarily a loyalist colony. "Loyalists heard, with astonishment and indignation, persons spoken of as proprietors of townships whom they had encountered in the field under the banners of the rebellion," Cartwright stated. Also, by opening Upper Canada to American settlers, Simcoe had "dispel[led] the opinion fondly cherished by the Loyalists, that the donation of lands to them in this country was intended as a mark of peculiar favour and a reward for their attachment to their Sovereign." Cartwright argued that it was important in Upper Canada to "lay a solid foundation" and stress the character of immigrants, not their numbers. Americans, though resourceful, intelligent, and capable farmers, held subversive "political notions," such as an "affection of equality," and lacked "habits of subordination." They thus threatened the stable, peaceful, and ordered community which was Cartwright's Upper Canada.

Another challenge to Cartwright's Upper Canada came in the first decade of the 19th century from a group of government critics, one of whom, John Mills Jackson*, wrote a pamphlet, *A view of the political situation of the province of Upper Canada ...*

(London, 1809), which was very critical of the authorities. Cartwright responded in his *Letters, from an American loyalist* (1810) by denouncing critics such as Jackson, Robert Thorpe*, Joseph WILL-COCKS, and William WEEKES, in terms reminiscent of his earlier denunciations of the American rebels, as a "Faction" of demagogues and "turbulent Spirit[s]" who were making "indecent aspersions against the Government," "throwing obloquy" on it, and "cabal-[ling] against" it. Like the rebels, argued Cartwright, these demagogues' "seditious exertions" were under-mining the authority of government and law and disrupting the peace, order, and good government of Upper Canada. Jackson and his friends had offend-ed Cartwright's loyalist sensibilities when they suggested that the loyalists had acted from mercenary motives. Aroused, Cartwright replied that "they were animated by no mercenary motives," and encouraged the 19th-century myth about the upper class origins of the loyalists by asserting "that the generality of those gallant men, so little known, and so much under-valued by their pretended Advocate, were men of Property; and some of them the greatest Landholders in America." Obviously, Cartwright's most deeply held preconceptions about himself as a loyalist had been challenged. And like other loyalist leaders, he became increasingly concerned about preserving the judicial and political *status quo*. By 1807 it was virtually impossible to distinguish Cartwright's views from those expressed by the government élite in York. In fact, Cartwright had become part of the élite. He was a particularly close associate of Lieutenant Governor Francis Gore* and one of his principal advisers.

Yet another significant threat to Cartwright's adopted colony came with the outbreak of the War of 1812. As a militia officer, he was active as early as 1807 in inspiring Upper Canadians to resist the anticipated American invasion. He viewed the war – with Britain and Canada aligned against France and the United States – as a cosmic struggle in which Britain represented order and freedom and her opponents the "Horrors of Anarchy" and the "Fetters of Despotism." Upper Canadians, according to Cartwright, should "not shrink from the trial should it occur." Inspired by the pride "that must glow in the Brest of every Man to be numbered among a Nation so renowned as Great Britain," they should show their gratitude and do everything possible to turn back the invader, mindful of the "abuse and degradation" that loyalists especially would suffer at the hands of the Americans. In his "Falkland" articles in the *Kingston Gazette*, Cartwright showed that he was proud of the achievements of the colonial militia, meagre as they may seem to the critical historian. This pride was also evident in a letter of 1813 in which he discussed the victory at Crysler's Farm: "Notwithstanding General

[James] Wilkinson's schemes of conquest . . . the reception he met with at Chryslers farm [from] our little band of Heroes is a foretaste of what he is to expect of his further progress."

The last five years of Cartwright's life were clouded by personal tragedy. He was a kind and loving father and husband, but he was also a patriarch who expected and received devotion and obedience from his wife and eight children. His ambitions for his children were lofty and he carefully planned and guided their careers. He therefore suffered a crushing blow from which he never really recovered when his two eldest sons – James and Richard – died in 1811, only to be followed to the grave by his daughter, Hannah, whom he loved dearly, and his third son, Stephen. Cartwright died himself on 27 July 1815 from what may have been throat cancer. He was only 56.

Despite his personal afflictions, Cartwright had many reasons to regard his life as a successful one. Besides achieving considerable personal wealth and exerting great influence in his community, he had witnessed and participated in the development and maturing of his adopted colony. Five years before his death, Cartwright summarized in a very personal way Upper Canada's accomplishments: "I have been a resident in this country before there was a human habitation within the limits of what is now the Province of Upper Canada. . . . I have seen this wilderness in the course of a few years, converted into fruitful fields, and covered with comfortable habita-tions. I see around me thousands, who without any other funds than their personal labour, began to denude the soil of its primaeval forests, in possession of extensive and well cultivated farms. . . . I see this property unincumbered with feudal burdens, undi-minished by quit-rents or taxes, guarded by the wisest laws, equally and impartially administered. I see the proprietor himself protected from vexatious arrest or arbitrary imprisonment. I have seen the benevolent intentions of the British Government towards the Colony, exemplified in every measure that could tend to promote its prosperity; and crowned, by imparting to it, its own unrivalled constitution, as far as it was practicable to impart it to a dependent Province. I have seen the foundations laid of institutions and establish-ments for the promoting of knowledge, and diffusing religious instruction, which however weak and humble in their present state, will 'grow with our growth, and strengthen with our strength.'"

Not only had Upper Canada grown and prospered, but the loyalists had repaid the "paternal care" of their sovereign, for their settlement "in this remote corner of his Empire, has been crowned with such complete success." Looking back over these achievements, Cartwright concluded that "this is a scene on which the benevolent mind must dwell with peculiar compla-

Cassiet

cency." Richard Cartwright in 1810 was evidently very much at peace with himself about the wisdom of his 1777 decision. And so would be his wife and the four children – Mary Magdalen, Thomas Robison, Robert David, and John Solomon* – who survived him. Mary had married Captain Alexander Thomas Dobbs of the Royal Navy in 1814; Thomas would die at the age of 27 in 1826, a year before his mother's death. Robert became an Anglican minister and the father of Sir Richard John Cartwright*, and John a distinguished Kingston lawyer and politician.

GEORGE RAWLYK and JANICE POTTER

[The authorship of *Letters, from an American loyalist in Upper Canada, to his friend in England; on a pamphlet published by John Mills Jackson, esquire: entitled, A view of the province of Upper Canada* (Halifax, [1810]) has usually been attributed to William Dummer Powell*. However, a letter from Cartwright to Powell in 1810 proves conclusively that Cartwright was the author. In this letter Cartwright wrote: "You will by this Time have seen my two last Letters on Jacksons Pamphlet which the Gov[r] took with him for your Perusal. As we are soon to have a printing Press set up here it is his Excellency's Wish that they should be published seriatim in the Kingston Gazette. On further Consideration however I am inclined to think they would be better under the Form of a Pamphlet at first, that those who incline to read may have the whole at once before them; and be afterwards more widely circulated through the Medium of the News Papers if it should be thought expedient." *See* QUA, Richard Cartwright papers, Cartwright to Powell, 29 July 1810. G.R. and J.P.]

AO, MS 43, Richard Cartwright to J. Gray, 24 Aug. 1793. PAC, MG 23, H1, 7, Richard Cartwright, "A journey to Canada" (mfm. at QUA). QUA, Richard Cartwright papers; [E. E. Horsey], "Cataraqui, Fort Frontenac, Kingstown, Kingston" (typescript, 1937), 233. *Kingston before War of 1812* (Preston). *Loyalist narratives from Upper Canada*, ed. J. J. Talman (Toronto, 1946), 44–53. *Minutes of the Albany committee of correspondence, 1775–78* . . . , ed. James Sullivan and A. C. Flick (2v., Albany, N.Y., 1923–25), 1: 672. John Strachan, *A sermon, on the death of the Honorable Richard Cartwright; with a short account of his life; preached at Kingston, on the 3d of September, 1815* (Montreal, 1816). "United Empire Loyalists: enquiry into losses and services," AO *Report*, 1904: 1001–2. *Kingston Gazette*, 4, 11 Feb., 3 March, 29 Aug. 1812; 17 Aug., 19 Oct. 1813. Reid, *Loyalists in Ont.* MacDonald, "Hon. Richard Cartwright," *Three hist. theses.* M. G. Miller, "The political ideas of the Honourable Richard Cartwright, 1759–1815" (research essay, Queen's Univ., Kingston, Ont., 1975). Wilson, "Enterprises of Robert Hamilton."

CASSIET (Cassiette), PIERRE, Roman Catholic priest and missionary; b. 29 Jan. 1727 in Montaut (dept of Landes), France, son of Pierre Cassiet and Jeanne Dangoumau (Dengomau); d. there 24 March 1809.

There never was any question that Pierre Cassiet, the son of a pious teacher in Montaut, would seek his vocation in the church. After religious and classical studies at the Petit Séminaire in Agen, Cassiet went to Paris to continue his training at the Séminaire des Missions Étrangères. Following his ordination, about 1751, he was chosen for missionary work in Cochin China (Vietnam); however, shortly before his departure he was asked to replace a priest who was prevented by illness from taking up a post in Acadia.

In March 1752 the Abbé de L'Isle-Dieu, the bishop of Quebec's vicar general in France, had written to Rouillé, the minister of Marine, stressing the need for more missionaries in French Acadia to assist Jean-Louis Le Loutre*. Two priests were sent out that summer. Late in December Le Loutre himself came to France, and he returned the following year with two companions: Henri Daudin* from the Séminaire du Saint-Esprit and Pierre Cassiet from the Séminaire des Missions Étrangères. Daudin was destined to serve the Acadians living under British rule in Nova Scotia, while Cassiet was supposed to join Abbé Pierre Maillard* on Île Royale (Cape Breton Island). But once again plans were changed. A priest intended for Île Saint-Jean (Prince Edward Island) having been unable through ill health to make the trip, Cassiet was sent to serve Malpeque, a largely Micmac mission established earlier on the island by Maillard. His time there was short: by the end of 1753 he had moved to Saint-Louis-du-Nord-Est (Scotchfort), where he served both Acadians and Indians. According to tradition, he encouraged the Indians to plant beans, peas, and flax and to raise domestic animals.

At the time of the deportation of the Acadians from Nova Scotia in 1755 [*see* Charles Lawrence*], many desperate refugees escaped to Île Saint-Jean. But the fate of the inhabitants there was to prove no better. The fall of the fortress of Louisbourg, Île Royale, to British forces under Edward Boscawen* and Jeffery Amherst* in July 1758 brought with it the capitulation of Île Saint-Jean. Colonel Lord Rollo* was sent there to accept its surrender and remove the inhabitants. The threat of deportation facing their parishioners, Cassiet and Abbé Jean Biscaret obtained Rollo's permission to go to Louisbourg and plead with its captors that the Acadians be allowed to remain on their lands. Their efforts were to no avail; the deportation began almost immediately. Cassiet was placed on a ship that three months later reached Plymouth, England. Eventually he was able to make his way to Morlaix, France, where he remained for a time recovering from an illness contracted on board.

His health restored, Cassiet spent some time at the Séminaire des Missions Étrangères in Paris while seeking a pension. In February 1759 the French government awarded him 200 *livres* for his losses at the hands of the British, and the following year he received a further 400 *livres* for his services in Acadia.

Some years later, in 1772, he refused a benefice worth 6,000 *livres* per annum but accepted one yielding 160 *livres*.

After a visit to Rome, where in recognition of his bravery in Acadia Pope Clement XIII presented him with a relic of the true cross (still in the possession of the parish of Montaut), Cassiet served as parish priest of Audignon, France, from 1763 to 1766. In 1767 he ministered at Castelnau-Tursan, and the following year he became a canon of the collegiate church of Saint-Girons at Hagetmau. In 1772 he decided to join the Prêtres du Calvaire at Bétharram. There he was instrumental in reviving the annual pilgrimage to the sanctuary chapel of Notre-Dame-de-Bétharram. Chosen superior in 1783, he encouraged the cultivation of grapes and market garden products and greatly increased the revenues of the order.

Once again, however, Cassiet was to experience exile. In 1792, during the French revolution, he fled to Spain. When permission was granted, he returned to France in 1801 but, since only two of the Bétharram fathers remained, he chose to spend his last years in Montaut, where he died in 1809.

DELLA M. M. STANLEY

AD, Landes (Mont-de-Marsan), État civil, Montaut, 30 janv. 1727, 25 mars 1809. AN, Col., C¹¹ᴮ, 38: 269 (transcript at PAC); F¹ᴬ, 45: f.57; 192: 46, 139 (copies at PAC). Arch. communales, Montaut (dép. des Landes), Reg. de délibération de la commune de Montaut de 1790 à l'an XII, Pierre Cassiet, Serment de fidélité; Reg. des baptêmes, mariages et sépultures. CÉA, Fonds Placide Gaudet, 1.51-12, 1.54-23, 1.55-3. [Pierre de La Rue], "Lettres et mémoires de l'abbé de L'Isle-Dieu," ANQ *Rapport*, 1935–36: 378, 381, 383. "Tableau sommaire des missionnaires séculiers . . . ," ANQ *Rapport*, 1937–38: 184. Allaire, *Dictionnaire*, 1: 103. L.-C. Daigle, *Les anciens missionnaires de l'Acadie* ([Saint-Louis-de-Kent, N.-B., 1956]), 16. J.-H. Blanchard, *The Acadians of Prince Edward Island, 1720–1964* (Charlottetown, 1964), 22–30. H.-R. Casgrain, *Une seconde Acadie: l'île Saint-Jean–île du Prince-Édouard sous le Régime français* (Québec, 1894), 279–84, 394–98. D. C. Harvey, *The French régime in Prince Edward Island* (New Haven, Conn., and London, 1926), 180–93. Henri Lassalle, *Notre Dame de Bétharram, un sanctuaire béarnais* (Pau, France, 1941), 240–41. Émile Lauvrière, *La tragédie d'un peuple: histoire du peuple acadien de ses origines à nos jours* (2v., Paris, 1922), 2: 62–64. Robert Rumilly, *Histoire des Acadiens* (2v., Montréal, 1955), 1: 397–407, 417, 434, 527; 2: 574–75. Abbé Sébie, *Étude biographique sur M. l'abbé Cassiet, supérieur des missionnaires de Bétharram dans le XVIIIᵉ siècle* (Auch, France, 1863).

CAZEAU, FRANÇOIS, merchant; b. *c.* 1734 in Saint-Cybard, France, son of Léonard Cazeau and Anne Aupetit; m. 14 May 1759 Marguerite Vallée in Montreal (Que.), and they had six children; d. 11 May 1815 in Paris, France.

François Cazeau came to New France a few years before the conquest and probably settled in Montreal. Subsequently he became a fur merchant and engaged in trade at Michilimackinac (Mackinaw City, Mich.). His business seems to have prospered, for in 1763 he declared that he had 19,777 *livres* in card money.

In 1774 Cazeau showed his sympathy for the American cause by circulating in the Montreal region a *Lettre adressée aux habitans de la province de Québec, ci-devant le Canada*; this pamphlet had been printed for the first Continental Congress by Fleury Mesplet*, who was then living in Philadelphia, Pa. During the invasion of the province [*see* Benedict ARNOLD; Richard Montgomery*], Cazeau supplied the American troops, on occasion provided shelter for rebel officers, and busied himself distributing Congressional messages to the Canadian population. In 1777 he bought three large bateaux and had them loaded with supplies, clothing, and food to equip the American troops stationed at Fort Ticonderoga (near Ticonderoga, N.Y.). But the British army, which had arrived in force in that region, captured and sank Cazeau's boats. He continued nevertheless to support the Americans. For example, in May 1779 he saw to the distribution throughout the province of a proclamation by French vice-admiral the Comte d'Estaing which urged the Canadians to rise against Britain. The following year Cazeau was accused of treason; Governor HALDIMAND ordered his arrest and had him imprisoned in the Recollet house at Quebec. In the autumn of 1780 the London merchants Brook WATSON and Robert Rashleigh demanded that his assets be sold by the sheriff.

In 1782 Cazeau escaped from prison and took refuge in the United States. The following year he asked the Quebec authorities to allow him to visit his family. Haldimand gave his consent and Cazeau came back to the colony, where he collected various documents attesting to his pro-American activities to back his request to Congress for compensation for the losses he had incurred during the invasion. In the autumn he returned to the United States, where he took steps to further his cause with Congress. Shunted from office to office, from one official to the next, for more than four years, he secured only vague promises. He decided to leave for France in the autumn of 1786.

Cazeau presented repeated requests to the government of France for help in obtaining settlement of the moneys owing him. But the French revolution delayed resolution of the matter. In 1792, however, the Legislative Assembly looked into the dossier and supported Cazeau in his representations to the American Congress. In 1801 Congress granted him 2,240 acres of land in New York State. At the insistence of one of his sons Cazeau returned to the United States and began petitioning Congress again, requesting reimbursement in money rather than land.

Céloron

Consequently he did not claim his 2,240 acres, and after taking other fruitless steps, he went back to France in 1802.

Old, sick, poor, and alone, François Cazeau nevertheless persisted in clamouring for his due. But it was all to no avail: on 11 May 1815 he died, without having won his case. The proceedings continued to drag on before the courts, but his heirs were no more successful than he in gaining anything from them.

JEAN-FRANCIS GERVAIS

ANQ-M, CE1-51, 14 mai 1759. PAC, MG 23, B19. *Quebec Gazette*, 27 Aug. 1776, 3 Aug. 1780. Tanguay, *Dictionnaire*, vol.2. Wallace, *Macmillan dict*. Corinne Rocheleau-Rouleau, "Une incroyable et véridique histoire: l'affaire Cazeau, 1776–1893," Soc. hist. franco-américaine, *Bull*. (Boston, Mass.), 1946–47: 3–31. Benjamin Sulte, "François Cazeau," *BRH*, 22 (1916): 115–20.

CÉLORON, MARIE-CATHERINE-FRANÇOISE, Religious Hospitaller of St Joseph, superior of the Hôtel-Dieu in Montreal (Que.); b. 15 Aug. 1744 in Montreal, elder daughter of Pierre-Joseph Céloron* de Blainville and Catherine Eury de La Pérelle; d. there 26 May 1809.

Marie-Catherine-Françoise Céloron was only 14 when her father died. Two years later, on 4 Nov. 1761, she became a boarder with the Sisters of Charity of the Hôpital Général of Montreal (Grey Nuns), paying 100 *livres* a year for her board. Her mother and her sister Marie-Madeleine also entered the community but, whereas they took the veil there, Marie-Catherine-Françoise left the Hôpital Général on 11 April 1762 to begin her noviciate at the Hôtel-Dieu the next day; she was not yet 18. The community accepted her without any financial conditions, since her dowry was to come from an endowment. On 9 Feb. 1763 she donned the white veil, and on 18 October the habit. On 23 Oct. 1764 she took her vows.

Marie-Catherine-Françoise Céloron was a tall, pretty woman, with a good education and fluent command of both French and English, valuable assets later when the authority of the community was vested in her. In addition she was lively and quick-witted, as her correspondence with her cousin Ignace-Michel-Louis-Antoine d'Irumberry* de Salaberry shows.

During her 47 years of religious life Sister Céloron was called upon to fulfil a number of responsibilities and in discharging them she always proved a model for her companions. After her noviciate, and for 33 years, she carried out the duties of domestic bursar, which consisted mainly of looking after the property of the community and the hospital, attending to the upkeep and cleanliness of the premises, supervising the work of the kitchen and the laundry, ensuring supplies of wood, water, and wine, and looking after the storing, proper use, and distribution of the fruit, vegetables, grain, and meat. From 1797 to 1800 she was a hospital nun, a post that was considered very important and that required extensive experience and recognized authority. Sister Céloron had to admit the sick, have them looked after according to the doctors' instructions, maintain quiet and order in the wards, and assign tasks to the sisters responsible for nursing care.

In 1800 Sister Céloron was elected assistant to the superior. Apparently her administrative abilities were appreciated, since she was elected superior on 9 July 1805 and re-elected on 9 July 1808. From a financial standpoint, the years during which she held that office were the worst the hospitallers had to go through. As a result of the French revolution the community was deprived of the interest on its investments in France and thus was without a vital part of the income necessary for its upkeep. To remedy this drop in income the nuns set up various money-making projects, including a bakery and works for making candles and soap; they also did various kinds of gilding and embroidery. During these difficult years Sister Céloron showed great wisdom and no less skill in the temporal and spiritual administration of the community. On 26 May 1809, at the age of 64, Marie-Catherine-Françoise Céloron died in the convent of the Hôtel-Dieu after a painful illness.

JACQUES DUCHARME

ANQ-M, CE1-51, 15 août 1744; CE1-141, 26 mai 1809. ANQ-Q, P1000-19-347. Arch. des Religieuses hospitalières de Saint-Joseph (Montréal), Affaires temporelles de la communauté, comptes rendus triennaux; Vie religieuse de la communauté, annales; Entrées, vêtures, professions et décès; Reg. des délibérations faites dans les assemblées capitulaires. Arch. des sœurs grises (Montréal), Reg. de l'entrée des pauvres de l'Hôpital Général de Montréal, 1694–1796: 47, 54, 60; Reg. de l'entrée des sœurs grises de Montréal, 1737–1889: 4–5. AUM, P 58, U, Céloron à de Salaberry, 15 août, 16 sept., 30 déc. 1805; 29 déc. 1806; 29 déc. 1807. [É.-M. Faillon], *Vie de Mlle Mance et histoire de l'Hôtel-Dieu de Villemarie dans l'île de Montréal, en Canada* (2v., Villemarie [Montréal], 1854), 2: 285–308. *L'Hôtel-Dieu de Montréal (1642–1973)* (Montréal, 1973). P.-G. Roy, *La famille Céloron de Blainville* (Lévis, Qué., 1909), 47; *La famille d'Irumberry de Salaberry* (Lévis, 1905), 130–44.

CERRÉ (Séré, Serré), JEAN-GABRIEL, merchant; b. 12 Aug. 1734 in Montreal (Que.), son of Joseph Serré and Marie-Madeleine Picard; m. 24 Jan. 1764 Catherine Giard, daughter of Antoine Giard*, in Kaskaskia (Ill.), and they had four children; d. 4 April 1805 in St Louis (Mo.).

By the mid 1750s Jean-Gabriel Cerré was in the Illinois country as a merchant. He established himself at Kaskaskia but apparently retained close personal and commercial ties with his birthplace. His eldest daughter married Montreal notary Pierre-Louis PANET, and Cerré made periodic visits to the city throughout his career. He shipped goods from there to Illinois in 1767, 1775, and 1777 and, since the regions had close economic links, probably in other years as well. He dealt in the usual trade goods, including guns and ammunition, cloth, tobacco, and metal objects. It would appear that he was not just a storeman; he spent the winter of 1776–77, for instance, among the Mascoutens and Kickapoos.

Cerré became a leading merchant and member of the Illinois community in a turbulent era of its history. His behaviour during the many régimes through which he lived suggests that he believed strongly in the importance of obeying established authority. In the years from 1764 to 1778, when the British ruled the area, he seems to have conducted himself correctly. Even in 1777 and 1778, when British control was being undermined by American agents, he upheld the authority of the administrator, Philippe-François Rastel de Rocheblave. It has been suggested that Cerré's loyalty was encouraged by the threat posed to his business by American competitors who were invading Illinois. Whatever the case, after George Rogers Clark seized the region for Virginia in the summer of 1778 Cerré recognized the *fait accompli* and vowed to be a "good and submissive subject." On the promise of future repayment he used his credit to buy supplies for Clark's men, and he rented his forge to the Americans as well.

Virginia established civil government for the conquered territory in December 1778, and the following May Cerré allowed himself to be elected justice of the peace for Kaskaskia and district. By the terms of their commission he and the other JPs could also sit as judges of a county court with jurisdiction in civil and criminal cases. The law which they were to interpret was basically French with some modifications from Virginia practice. Cerré was not a legal expert; concerning his later description to Congress of the judicial system under the French and British régimes, historian Clarence Walworth Alvord has stated that he showed "a surprising ignorance" of the subject. He appears, however, to have been an honest man whose opinions were respected in the community.

The French inhabitants of Illinois had hoped that the establishment of courts would protect them from the free-for-all that was developing under the occupation by American frontiersmen. As soon as the JPs were commissioned they submitted a petition complaining of depredations by the troops, land grabbing by speculators, and the unrestricted sale of liquor to Indians and black slaves. The government was unable to impose order, however, and the inhabitants grew less willing to make sacrifices for its support. By the autumn of 1779 the Americans were employing coercion to get supplies. The result was an emigration, particularly by the more prosperous residents, across the Mississippi to Spanish territory. Cerré had accumulated considerable property on the west bank around St Louis and Ste Geneviève by the 1770s, and in late 1779 or early 1780 he moved to St Louis.

Under Spain's rule his business flourished and he was soon the wealthiest man in the vicinity. His daughter Marie-Thérèse married Auguste Chouteau in 1786, a union that brought together the community's two leading merchant families. His son Paschal was later employed by the Americans as a secretary and interpreter to Indian treaty commissions. Cerré received several land grants from the Spanish authorities. He had a house in town, a country property, and a stock farm; in 1791 he owned 43 slaves – far more than anyone else in St Louis. A grant in 1800 referred to him as "one of the most ancient inhabitants of this country, whose known conduct and personal merit are recommendable." His acquaintance with change had not ended, however. During the next few years Spanish Louisiana was ceded to France and then purchased by the United States. Thus by the time of his death in 1805 Jean-Gabriel Cerré had experienced no fewer than six régimes; despite these upheavals he had managed to become one of the most prosperous merchants in the Mississippi valley.

DONALD CHAPUT

Mo. Hist. Soc. (St Louis), J.-G. Cerré papers; *see also* references to Cerré MSS in the Billon, Chouteau, Papin, and Soulard colls. and in the St Louis arch. Wis., State Hist. Soc., Draper MSS, ser.J, J.-G. Cerré letters. *Cahokia records, 1778–1790*, ed. C. W. Alvord (Springfield, Ill., 1907). [J.-G. Cerré], "Cerré to George Rogers Clark," *American Hist. Rev.* (New York and London), 8 (1902–3): 498–500. *George Rogers Clark papers* . . . [1771–84], ed. J. A. James (2v., Springfield, 1912–26). *John Askin papers* (Quaife), 1: 105–7. *Kaskaskia records, 1778–1790*, ed. C. W. Alvord (Springfield, 1909). *Mich. Pioneer Coll.*, 9 (1886); 10 (1886); 19 (1891): 472–73. *Old Cahokia: a narrative and documents illustrating the first century of its history*, ed. J. F. McDermott *et al.* (St Louis, 1949), 113. *The Spanish régime in Missouri* . . . , ed. Louis Houck (2v., Chicago, 1909; repr. 2v. in 1, [New York], 1971), 2: 374. Wis., State Hist. Soc., *Coll.*, 18 (1908). *DAB*. Massicotte, "Répertoire des engagements pour l'Ouest," ANQ *Rapport*, 1932–33: 289, 303–4. Tanguay, *Dictionnaire*, vol.7. Benoît Brouillette, *La pénétration du continent américain par les Canadiens français, 1763–1846* . . . (Montréal, 1939). [W. B. Douglas], "Jean Gabriel Cerré: a sketch," Mo. Hist. Soc., *Coll.* (St Louis), 2 (1900–6), no.2: 58–76; repr. in Ill. State Hist. Soc., *Trans.* (Springfield), 1903: 275–88.

CHABERT DE COGOLIN, JOSEPH-BERNARD DE, Marquis de CHABERT (he signed both Chabert and **Chabert-Cogollin**), naval officer, hydrographer,

Chabert

and author; b. 28 Feb. 1724 in Toulon, France, son of Joseph-François de Chabert and Madeleine de Bernard; m. 1 Dec. 1771 Hélène-Marguerite-Barbe Tascher; d. 1 Dec. 1805 in Paris, France.

Grandson of a rear-admiral and eldest son of a post-captain who died of wounds received in action, Joseph-Bernard de Chabert de Cogolin followed family tradition when he entered the navy as a midshipman in July 1741. After several voyages in the Mediterranean, where he displayed an interest in science and a talent for drawing charts that brought him to the attention of the minister of Marine, he was appointed sub-section leader of midshipmen and posted to Brest. In 1746 he made two voyages to reconnoitre the coasts of Acadia and correct the defectiveness of French charts. While in the frigate *Castor* he drew a chart of the roads and harbour of the Baie de Chibouctou (Halifax harbour), and later the same year he was sent in the *Sirène* to reconnoitre the harbour at Annapolis Royal and spy out the British ships anchored there. The next spring he joined Jacques-Pierre de Taffanel* de La Jonquière's squadron in the *Gloire* and was taken prisoner by the British during the battle off Cape Ortegal, Spain. After repatriation Chabert was promoted ensign in April 1748 and retained in Paris by the minister, who wanted him to learn astronomy in order to instruct naval officers. Two years later he was chosen to go to Île Royale (Cape Breton Island) and continue his survey of the shores of Acadia. His expedition was organized by Roland-Michel Barrin* de La Galissonière, then head of the Dépôt des Cartes et Plans de la Marine in Paris.

Chabert reached Louisbourg in August 1750 and immediately began to make a long series of observations about the waters of Île Royale. Although the weather was continually bad, he entered what is now the Strait of Canso, obtained a longitude from the shore, and twice observed the astronomical latitude. He also recorded tides and compass variations and charted the strait. At Canso itself he carried out similar observations and drew a second chart before returning to Louisbourg. He then surveyed the coast of Île Royale from Guyon Island, southwest of Cape Gabarus, northward beyond Scatarie Island. During the winter he had a hut constructed on the ramparts at Louisbourg and despite the rigours of the climate successfully established the longitude of the town before spring. In June 1751 he departed for Cape Sable at the southern extremity of Nova Scotia to determine its latitude and longitude and then coasted along the shore. At the conclusion of his survey he discovered the length of Nova Scotia to be about 15 to 20 leagues shorter than was shown on contemporary charts. The following month he successfully located Sable Island, and in August he charted the southern coast of Newfoundland from Cape Ray to Cape Race.

Returning to France in November, Chabert was attached to the Dépôt de la Marine under La Galissonière's direction and prepared his surveys for publication. The result appeared in 1753 as *Voyage fait par ordre du roi en 1750 et 1751, dans l'Amérique septentrionale*. The work is in two parts: the first is an abridgement of his journal accompanied by charts; the second is devoted to his astronomical observations. It contained the most accurate hydrographic survey of the east coast that had yet been made, and the ministry of Marine subsidized publication by taking 200 copies for its own use. In 1754 Chabert was made a knight of the order of Saint-Louis as a reward for his services and two years later he was promoted lieutenant.

Chabert served briefly at sea between 1756 and 1758 but then returned to the Dépôt de la Marine. Over the next quarter of a century he contributed frequently to the Académie des Sciences, of which he became a member in 1758. In 1760 he was instrumental in selecting the site in the south Pacific for the French observation of a transit of Venus. During the next decade Chabert devoted himself to charting the Mediterranean, work he had begun in the 1750s. In 1771 he was promoted post-captain and two years later became deputy head of the Dépôt de la Marine. A further promotion, as brigadier of naval forces, followed in 1776. After the signing of the Franco-American alliance Chabert obtained command of the *Vaillant* in Vice-Admiral Jean-Baptiste-Charles d'Estaing's West India squadron (1778–79), and he later served under Rear-Admiral François-Joseph-Paul de Grasse (1781–82). On 5 Sept. 1781 he was seriously wounded while engaging five ships of the line in Thomas GRAVES's fleet. He was promoted rear-admiral in January 1782.

On 1 Jan. 1792 Chabert's long years of service were rewarded with promotion to vice-admiral. The revolution forced him to flee to England but he returned to France in 1802. While engaged in his last great work, a general sea atlas of the Mediterranean, he was struck by blindness. At the time of his death he was laden with all the honours the country could bestow: senior admiral of the French navy, commander of the Order of Saint-Louis, and member of the Académie des Sciences and the Académie de Marine. He was also a member of scientific institutions in Berlin, Stockholm, and Bologna and of the Royal Society of London. His long career had been marked by scholarship in hydrographic surveying and courage in combat.

J. S. PRITCHARD

[Joseph-Bernard de Chabert de Cogolin's *Voyage fait par ordre du roi en 1750 et 1751, dans l'Amérique septentrionale, pour rectifier les cartes des côtes de l'Acadie, de l'isle Royale & de l'isle de Terre-Neuve; et pour en fixer les principaux points par des observations astronomiques*

(Paris, 1753) has been reprinted ([East Ardsley, Eng., and New York], 1966).

Most of the biographical material concerning Chabert can be found in AN, Marine, C⁷, 58 (dossier Chabert-Cogolin); this file is more extensive than most. Other manuscript sources are AN, Marine, B², 343: f.413; B³, 535: f.123; B⁴, 63: ff.261–61v; 3JJ, 272–73; and Bibliothèque nationale (Paris), MSS, Fr., 12224: ff.405–6. Three of Chabert's letters in AN, Marine, 3JJ, and the report of his expedition to Louisbourg delivered to the Académie des sciences in Paris in 1753 have been reprinted in Roland Lamontagne, *Chabert de Cogolin et l'expédition de Louisbourg* (Montréal, 1964). Biographical notices appear in *Biographie universelle* (Michaud et Desplaces); *DBF*; and *Nouvelle biographie générale . . .* , [J.-C.-F.] Hoefer, édit. (46v., Paris, 1852–66).   J.S.P.]

CHABOILLEZ, CHARLES, fur trader; b. 21 March 1772 in Montreal, Que., son of Charles-Jean-Baptiste CHABOILLEZ and Marguerite Larchevêque; m. 11 Jan. 1811 Jessy Bruce, aged 19, in the Cathedral of the Holy Trinity at Quebec, Lower Canada; d. 26 Dec. 1812 in Mascouche, Lower Canada, and was buried three days later in the cemetery of the parish of Saint-Louis at nearby Terrebonne.

Charles Chaboillez entered the Collège Saint-Raphaël in Montreal in 1783; founded in 1767 by the Sulpicians, this institution had been attended by men such as Antoine Tabeau and Jean-Baptiste Cadot Jr who later became voyageurs. It is not known whether Chaboillez was a pupil there for more than a year or whether he enrolled elsewhere to learn arithmetic and English. On 18 May 1791 he was hired for a four-year period by Joseph FROBISHER to work as a clerk in the North West Company for the sum of £25 and a new outfit of clothes. At the end of his contract he remained in the company's service. After spending the winter of 1795–96 at Île-à-la-Crosse (Sask.), he headed east for Cumberland House (Sask.), which he reached on 1 June 1796.

As the son of a fur trader with a solid reputation and the brother-in-law of Simon McTAVISH, Chaboillez was in a good position to carve a place for himself in the NWC; the experience he had acquired as a company clerk in a territory where competition was keen also worked in his favour. On 13 July 1796, at Grand Portage (near Grand Portage, Minn.), he signed the agreement drawn up on 30 October of the previous year that altered the composition of the company. This convention, which was not to come into effect until the spring of 1799, granted him one of the 46 shares in the enterprise.

Having signed the agreement, Chaboillez participated in the NWC's expansion northwest of the Great Lakes. Beginning in 1796 he was assigned to the Red and Assiniboine river region, where he had to compete with American merchants. According to the explorer

David Thompson*, he built a post on the Rat River, a tributary of the Red. When Thompson met him the following year, Chaboillez was established farther south, near the Pembina River. The journal which he kept of his activities from 4 Aug. 1797 to 21 June 1798 gives numerous details about the fur trade and its conduct. In 1799 he became proprietor of the Lower Red River department and had under his orders a young clerk, Alexander HENRY.

While he was in charge of the Fort Dauphin department, from 1804 to 1807, Chaboillez tried to open up a new area for trade in the upper reaches of the Missouri River. In 1804 he organized the first expedition, entrusting its leadership to the clerk François-Antoine Larocque*. Larocque, who was accompanied by Charles McKenzie* among others, went to the country of the Mandans with the objective of establishing trading links with them. The following year Larocque travelled close to the Rockies, to the great displeasure of the Mandans and the Gros Ventres (Hidatsa); the latter were afraid that they would lose their position as middlemen if the NWC made direct contact with the Crows in that region. On 18 Nov. 1805 Larocque was back and expressed himself somewhat disappointed with the results of the expedition. The following summer Chaboillez, accompanied by Alexander Henry, visited the Mandans and the Fall Indians. According to reports by McKenzie and James Caldwell, the Indians were not very impressed with the rather slovenly appearance of the two company partners. The limited success of these expeditions obliged the NWC to put an end to them.

At the annual meeting in 1807 the company made Chaboillez proprietor at Fort Pic, north of Lake Superior. When he went to Fort William (Thunder Bay, Ont.) in 1809, he had to answer serious charges concerning his last financial period. The meeting decided to wait until all the evidence was in hand before making its decision. However, it is impossible to find out more about the matter, since the minutes of subsequent meetings make no further mention of it.

It was probably on this occasion that Chaboillez, who was 37, decided to retire from the fur trade, although he maintained his relations with a few of the partners of the NWC such as his brother-in-law Roderick McKenzie* and David Thompson. He remained briefly in Montreal before taking up permanent residence at Terrebonne around 1810. Here on 3 Feb. 1811 he had his four natural children baptized; born in the west, they were then from 6 to 11 years of age. When he died in 1812 he left £1,050 to three of these children, £120 to relatives and friends, and sole ownership of the remainder of his property to his wife, including an annual income of £120 from a capital of £2,000.

Coming from a family that had been closely

Chaboillez

involved in the fur trade, Chaboillez had been drawn into it by the age of 19. First as a clerk and then as a partner in the NWC, he was not afraid to face competition with rival enterprises or to use means such as intimidation and rum. He regularly attended the annual meetings of the company, and from 1809 was a member of the Beaver Club. His relations with the chief partners of the NWC were sufficiently good for him to avoid officially the fate of Jean-Baptiste Cadot Jr, a partner who was expelled in 1804 for "drunkenness and riotousness."

GRATIEN ALLAIRE

The journal Charles Chaboillez wrote in 1797 and 1798 is at PAC, MG 19, C1, 1.

AC, Terrebonne (Saint-Jérôme), État civil, Catholiques, Saint-Louis (Terrebonne), 29 déc. 1812. ANQ-M, CE1-51, 21 mars 1772; CM1, Charles Chaboillez, 12 févr. 1813; CN1-29, 18 mai 1791. ANQ-Q, CE1-61, 11 janv. 1811; CN1-285, 8 janv. 1811. Les bourgeois de la Compagnie du Nord-Ouest (Masson). Docs. relating to NWC (Wallace). Five fur traders of the northwest . . . , ed. C. M. Gates ([Minneapolis, Minn.], 1933), 141, 158, 170–71. D. W. Harmon, Journal of voyages and travels in the interior of North America between the 47th and 58th degrees of N. lat., extending from Montreal nearly to the Pacific . . . , ed. W. L. Grant (2nd ed., Toronto, 1911), 98–109, 124–27. [F.-A. Larocque], Journal de Larocque de la rivière Assiniboine jusqu'à la rivière "Aux Roches Jaunes," 1805, ed. L. J. Burpee (Ottawa, 1911). Mackenzie, Journals and letters (Lamb), 459, 479–80, 483–85, 496. [David Thompson], David Thompson's narrative, 1784–1812, ed. R. [G.] Glover (new ed., Toronto, 1962). Raymond Masson, Généalogie des familles de Terrebonne (4v., Montréal, 1930–31), 1: 387–90. A.-G. Morice, Dictionnaire historique des Canadiens et des Métis français de l'Ouest (Québec et Montréal, 1908). M. W. Campbell, NWC (1957), 77, 117–18. Innis, Fur trade in Canada (1970). Morton, Hist. of Canadian west. Rumilly, La Compagnie du Nord-Ouest. Massicotte, "Les Chaboillez," BRH, 28: 184–88, 207–9, 241–42, 274–76, 311–13, 325–32, 355–59. E. A. Mitchell, "The North West Company agreement of 1795," CHR, 36 (1955): 126–45.

CHABOILLEZ, CHARLES-JEAN-BAPTISTE (he signed **Charles**), fur trader and merchant, and militia officer; b. 9 July 1736 at Michilimackinac (Mackinaw City, Mich.), eldest son of Charles Chaboillez, voyageur and fur trader, and Marie-Anne Chevalier; m. 27 Oct. 1769 Marguerite Larchevêque, the 20-year-old daughter of merchant Jacques Larchevêque, dit La Promenade, in Montreal, Que.; they had nine children, but only five survived infancy; d. there 25 Sept. 1808.

Charles-Jean-Baptiste Chaboillez concentrated his trading activity at Michilimackinac, in the area south of Lake Superior, and in the Mississippi region. At first he was very successful. After his father's death in 1757 his mother settled in Montreal, where on 1 Sept. 1763 she bought a spacious house on Rue Saint-Paul for 9,000 livres. During the next two decades Chaboillez and his brothers were active in the fur trade. According to a receipt dated 1768 Chaboillez had sent pelts to his mother and brother Pierre-Louis in Montreal in 1765. Apart from this slim indication the available documents throw little light on their commercial relations.

Chaboillez's business continued to prosper. When he married in 1769 his fortune, as declared in the marriage contract, amounted to 30,000 livres in cash. His wife brought to the joint estate 40,000 livres in the form of a lot with house, furnishings, silverware, and cash. The following year an investment of £2,550 in the fur trade put him in the forefront of Canadian investors.

Chaboillez's movements over the next 30 years cannot all be established. The documents located, however, make it possible to trace them in broad outline. Until about 1780 he wintered in the region of Grand Portage (near Grand Portage, Minn.) and the "Grande Rivière," and went to Montreal for the summers. Then it seems the order was reversed: the winters were spent in Montreal, the summers on trading trips. After May 1793, when he gave his wife a power of attorney, he was to be found in Montreal less and less. He was absent when his wife died in May 1798 and during the period when the estate was settled. In 1802 he was appointed storekeeper for the Indian Department at St Joseph Island in Upper Canada and was there when his daughter Marie-Charlotte-Domitille died in October 1805. John Askin Jr replaced him in the summer of 1807. It was at this time that he returned to Montreal, where he died the following year.

Chaboillez's activities in the three decades prior to 1802 are known only in part. He was one of the clients of Jean Orillat*, a Montreal merchant. In 1778, after wintering in the region of Grand Portage, he was supplied from Michilimackinac by John ASKIN Sr on instructions from his wife, who was his agent in Montreal. He maintained business relations with Benjamin Frobisher*, who went surety for him in 1778 and again in 1783. That year Frobisher and Chaboillez guaranteed an expedition costing £3,500 which Benjamin and his brother JOSEPH sent to Grand Portage. In 1785 Frobisher and Chaboillez financed the dispatch to Lake Superior of two canoes fitted out by the latter. In the course of that year he went into partnership with other Montreal outfitters and merchants at Michilimackinac, one being Étienne-Charles Campion*, to form the General Company of Lake Superior and the South. The objective of this company, known also as the General Society, was to engage in the fur trade in the upper Mississippi region for a period of three years. During the winter of

1792–93 Chaboillez was in partnership with George Edme Young, and they engaged 42 men to go to Michilimackinac (by then located on Mackinac Island, Mich.) and the Mississippi. It is possible that the hiring of 29 men by Young in 1791–92 marked the beginning of this partnership.

Chaboillez's other concerns were divided between Montreal and Michilimackinac. He had acquired farms in the Montreal region, including one on the Côte de Liesse on Montreal Island and another in the seigneury of Châteauguay, both purchased in 1779. In 1788 he also owned three islands near the tip of Montreal Island; on one of these, Île à l'Aigle, there was a farm with animals and valuable farming equipment. In 1786, while at Michilimackinac, he signed a petition to Bishop Hubert* of Quebec requesting a missionary for the locality. The following year he was elected a churchwarden of the parish of Sainte-Anne-de-Michillimakinac. While he was in Montreal in 1790 he signed an address supporting Hubert in the conflict between him and his coadjutor, Charles-François Bailly* de Messein. At about the same time Chaboillez was appointed captain in Montreal's 2nd Militia Battalion and in 1799 he was promoted major. His name was not on the rolls after 1802.

By the time Chaboillez died in 1808 his fortune had vanished; his business seems to have been in serious difficulties from the 1790s. In June 1798, according to the inventory made of the assets of the joint estate after his wife's death, his debts amounted to £11,435, £10,635 being owed to McTavish, Frobisher and Company and £420 to Simon McTavish himself. Moneys owing to him amounted to £4,056, and the furnishings were sold for £658. As his wife owed only £453, the heirs renounced the joint estate and contented themselves with that of their mother. McTavish, who was his son-in-law, died in 1804; his will released Chaboillez from all debt and gave him an annuity of £150. No will or inventory of Chaboillez's property has been found, probably an indication that he left very little. On the basis of documents currently available, no explanation of this decline can be given. The most that can be said is that the turning-point probably came around 1790.

Chaboillez had held an important place in the fur trade. Writing to Benjamin Frobisher in 1778, John Askin Sr remarked that Chaboillez was firmly established: "I know no person so well off in the North Trade as he is." In April 1786 Chaboillez, together with McTavish, the Frobisher brothers, JAMES and Andrew McGill, and the other merchants who were interested in the Michilimackinac trade, sent two memoirs to Sir John Johnson*, superintendent general of Indian affairs, asking him to help establish peace among the Indian tribes in the upper Mississippi region.

Charles-Jean-Baptiste Chaboillez belonged to the fur-trading bourgeoisie. His brothers, who were fur merchants, were linked by marriage with the Chapoton, Nouchet, and Baby-Cheneville families. His mother was the daughter of the merchant Jean-Baptiste Chevalier*. Chaboillez was also a founding member of the Beaver Club in Montreal. His only son, CHARLES, for whom he has often been mistaken by historians, was the second of four Canadians who became partners in the North West Company. His daughters Marie-Marguerite and Rachel married, respectively, Simon McTavish and Roderick McKenzie*, influential members of that company. A third daughter, Adélaïde, married Joseph Bouchette*, surveyor general of the Canadas.

GRATIEN ALLAIRE

A portrait of Charles-Jean-Baptiste Chaboillez held by the McCord Museum is reproduced in D. A. Armour and K. R. Widder, *At the crossroads: Michilimackinac during the American revolution* (Mackinac Island, Mich., 1978), 75.

ANQ-M, CE1-51, 27 oct. 1769; 30 avril 1775; 13 sept. 1786; 4 juill. 1797; 2 mai 1798; 15 juill., 27 sept. 1808; CN1-29, 20, 25–27 juin, 24 déc. 1798; CN1-74, 31 mars, 8 nov. 1788; 29 janv. 1790; 29 déc. 1791; 27 déc. 1792; 4 mai, 21 oct. 1793; 5 août 1794; 15 sept. 1799; CN1-121, 1er oct. 1793; CN1-290, 31 mai 1768, 13 janv. 1770; CN1-308, 1er sept. 1763, 25 oct. 1769; CN1-309, répertoire. ANQ-Q, CN1-230, 28 oct. 1805. PAC, MG 19, B3: 4 (transcripts); RG 4, B28, 115. *Docs. relating to NWC* (Wallace), 134–43, 432. *John Askin papers* (Quaife), 1: 52, 55, 91, 94–96, 98, 112, 115, 118, 123, 128–30, 133–34, 146–47, 150–51, 153–54, 156–57, 162; 2: 398, 534, 545, 553–54. J.-B. Perrault, *Jean-Baptiste Perrault, marchand voyageur parti de Montréal le 28e de mai 1783*, L.-P. Cormier, édit. ([Montréal], 1978), 55–56. "Requête des voyageurs de Michillimakinac en 1786," Henri Têtu, édit., *BRH*, 10 (1904): 66–68. John Tanner, *A narrative of the captivity and adventures of John Tanner . . .* , ed. Edwin James (Minneapolis, Minn., 1956), 19, 51. Wis., State Hist. Soc., *Coll.*, 12 (1892): 76–82, 92; 18 (1908): 254–55, 486–88, 494, 500, 511; 19 (1910): 4, 6–7, 9, 11, 13, 17, 31, 34, 38, 154, 160–61, 239–40, 243–45. *Quebec Gazette*, 16 June, 3 Nov. 1785; 11 Oct. 1787; 7 Aug. 1788; 27 May 1790. J.-J. Lefebvre, "Répertoire des engagements pour l'Ouest . . . ," ANQ *Rapport*, 1946–47: 303–69. Massicotte, "Répertoire des engagements pour l'Ouest," ANQ *Rapport*, 1932–33: 245–304; 1942–43: 261–397. A.-G. Morice, *Dictionnaire historique des Canadiens et des Métis français de l'Ouest* (2e éd., Québec, 1912), 61–62. *Quebec almanac*, 1791: 50; 1800: 111; 1801: 110; 1805: 74–75. Wallace, *Macmillan dict.* M. W. Campbell, *NWC* (1957), 20, 76–77, 143. Davidson, *NWC*, 14, 16, 23–25. Innis, *Fur trade in Canada* (1956), 195–96. Miquelon, "Baby family," 182–95, app.A. L. J. Burpee, "The Beaver Club," CHA *Report*, 1924: 73–92. J. E. Igartua, "The merchants of Montreal at the conquest: socio-economic profile," *SH*, 8 (1975): 290. É.-Z. Massicotte, "Le Beaver Club," *BRH*, 36 (1930): 323–27; "Les Chaboillez," *BRH*, 28: 184–88, 207–9, 241–42, 274–76, 311–13, 325–32, 355–59.

Chaboillez

CHABOILLEZ, LOUIS (baptized Joseph-Louis), notary, militia officer, office holder, and politician; b. 14 Oct. 1766 in Montreal, Que., son of merchant Louis-Joseph Chaboillez and Angélique Baby-Chenneville; nephew of Charles-Jean-Baptiste CHABOILLEZ; m. 10 Nov. 1789 Marguerite Conefroy in Pointe-Claire, Que., and they had seven children, five of whom died in infancy; d. 19 July 1813 in Montreal.

Louis Chaboillez belonged to the fourth generation of a family engaged in the fur trade since the early 17th century. He did not, however, continue the family tradition. Rather, on 24 July 1787 he received a commission to practise as a notary, and on 1 August Isaac TODD and James MCGILL called on him to draw up hiring contracts for the west. The preparation of such agreements seems to have been a sort of speciality for Chaboillez, who became the leading Montreal notary in the field; in 1813 hiring contracts form a third of his minute-book, which contains slightly more than 10,000 deeds. He recruited his clientele as much from among independent traders as from British firms such as McTavish, Frobisher and Company, Todd, McGill and Company, or Parker, Gerrard, and Ogilvy.

In 1797 Chaboillez held the rank of captain in Montreal's 2nd Militia Battalion. On 17 December he was elected a churchwarden of the parish of Notre-Dame, but he resigned on 22 April of the following year, when he was called upon to replace notary Jean-Guillaume DE LISLE as clerk of the *fabrique*. On 22 May 1799 he was appointed a justice of the peace, and in November he became a member of the commission for the building of churches and parsonage houses. Under the name of Mathieu he belonged to the Club des Apôtres, founded that year; the 12 members of the club, which lasted only a few months, were concerned with gastronomy and organized a monthly supper. On 11 Oct. 1802 he was appointed secretary of the commission responsible for repairing Montreal's fortifications.

In 1804 Chaboillez ran for Montreal East in the elections to the Lower Canadian House of Assembly. Elected along with McGill, he sat until 27 April 1808 and split his votes between the English party and the Canadian party. Thus he fought the bill for financing prisons through import duties [*see* Jonathan Sewell*], but supported the one on the exclusion of judges from the assembly [*see* Sir James Henry CRAIG; Pierre-Amable DE BONNE]. During his term the government granted him a commission authorizing him to receive the oath of half-pay officers.

Chaboillez subsequently withdrew from the political scene and continued to practise as a notary. From August 1809 until his death he speculated in building sites in Montreal. There is no inventory of his property, and thus it is impossible to evaluate his fortune and his standard of living.

CÉLINE CYR

ANQ-M, CE1-37, 10 nov. 1789; CE1-51, 14 oct. 1766, 22 juill. 1813; CN1-121, 28 oct. 1795, 11 juill. 1809; CN1-126, 31 août 1810; 25 mai, 13, 30 juill. 1811; 15 févr. 1812; 13 juill. 1813; CN1-194, 6 mai 1811; CN1-269, 21 Aug., 21 Oct. 1809; 21 Dec. 1810; 4 April 1811; CN1-313, 16 oct. 1795; CN1-375, 9 nov. 1789. *Montreal Gazette*, 20 July 1813. *Quebec Gazette*, 17 Nov. 1785, 27 May 1790, 19 July 1792, 6 July 1809. *Quebec almanac*, 1797–1801, 1805, 1810. F.-J. Audet, *Les députés de Montréal*, 70–71. Desjardins, *Guide parl.*, 134. Langelier, *Liste des terrains concédés*, 1253. Hare, "L'Assemblée législative du Bas-Canada," *RHAF*, 27: 379–80. Massicotte, "Les Chaboillez," *BRH*, 28: 184–88, 207–9, 241–42, 274–76, 311–13, 325–32, 355–59. Victor Morin, "Clubs et sociétés notoires d'autrefois," *Cahiers des Dix*, 13 (1948): 122–27.

CHAMPION, GABRIEL (Gabriel-Antoine), Roman Catholic priest and teacher; b. 17 Dec. 1748 in Le Ménil-Rainfray, France, son of Gilles Champion and Anne Cordon; d. 18 Jan. 1808 in Arichat, N.S.

Immediately upon ordination to the priesthood in 1778 Gabriel Champion became curate at the church of Notre-Dame in Romagny (dept of Manche); by his own statement, he was expelled on 29 May 1790 "for having refused to take the oath to the [Civil] Constitution of the Clergy enacted by the Assemblée Nationale." He then served as chaplain to the Bernardine nuns of the Abbaye-Blanche at Mortain, but on 6 Sept. 1792 he was forced to leave France. He went to England and remained there until his departure for North America in 1800.

Champion was one of the French priests whom Jean-François de La Marche, the bishop of Saint-Pol-de-Léon – himself an exile – recruited to swell the ranks of the clergy in the diocese of Quebec, where there had been a serious shortage of priests since the conquest. By the 1790s their numbers had so dwindled that the needs of the people could not be met. In a memoir prepared in 1790 for the governor, Lord Dorchester [Guy CARLETON], Bishop Hubert* attributed the shortage to numerous factors: the return of many priests to France after the conquest; the prolonged closing of the Séminaire de Québec; the dispersal of the clergy during the war; the six-year vacancy in the see of Quebec [*see* Jean-Olivier Briand*]; and the severance of ties with France, the traditional source of priests and missionaries for the colony. In the years after the conquest the British government had been reluctant to allow French priests to come to Canada, for fear of encouraging among the inhabitants too great an attachment to their former mother country. But with the coming of the French revolution and the appearance in Great Britain of thousands of refugee priests, Champion among them, this attitude had changed.

During the winter of 1800–1 Champion served the Acadians at Bay Fortune on Prince Edward Island. The following summer he was assigned to Cape Breton, with residence at Chéticamp; he was also to minister to Magré (Margaree) and Bay Fortune. He remained at Chéticamp for six years, expending himself unstintingly in frequent and exhausting visits to his scattered flock. Although Jacques-Ladislas-Joseph de Calonne* had been given the responsibility of taking the sacraments to the inhabitants of the Îles de la Madeleine, to all appearances it was Champion who went there regularly.

In 1805, at the end of Lent, Champion suddenly went blind. He sought treatment in Halifax, where Edmund Burke (1753–1820), the vicar general of the bishop of Quebec, put him up. He recovered his sight sufficiently to return to Chéticamp in the autumn and resume his ministry; but his health was shattered. He wrote Bishop Plessis* from the Îles de la Madeleine in June 1807 that he was still hampered by the same disability and also "by a shortness of breath" that "reaches down to [my] heart" and "probably portends an early death." Replying to this pathetic letter, Plessis suggested that he take his retirement in Halifax, in Arichat, or at the Hôpital Général of Quebec; the bishop also promised him an annual pension of 200 *piastres*. No longer daring to remain alone in his missions, Champion in the autumn of 1807 had someone take him to Arichat, to stay with his colleague François Lejamtel*. There he died on 18 Jan. 1808. His death, Burke informed the bishop of Quebec, "leaves a gap that Your Lordship will have difficulty filling."

Gabriel Champion was known for his kindness and his devotion. He had opened the first school at Chéticamp, where in all likelihood he was the only teacher. Unpretentious and modest, he had contented himself with a primitive chapel and wretched presbytery. He was undemanding, and probably not well versed in liturgy or canon law. At his death the church and presbytery were not "in great order," and, as Lejamtel wrote, thought had to be given to obtaining "the things necessary for divine service." But Champion had a generous nature. He bequeathed part of his meagre possessions to the church and the poor of Chéticamp. His parishioners had great affection for him: in addition to the tithe, they supplied him with wood, more meat than he needed, and "many other things, and all of it free." "They miss [him] very much," Lejamtel wrote to Bishop Plessis. After Champion's death his colleague Jean-Baptiste Allain visited Chéticamp but he did not return there; the mission fell to Lejamtel. Six years were to pass before Chéticamp could count on the presence of another priest, Antoine Manseau*.

Anselme Chiasson

AAQ, 301 CN, I: 22; 310 CN, I: 22; 312 CN, III: 94, 100; IV: 18; V: 7; VI: 18, 39, 48, 50, 53; VII: 6–7. Allaire, *Dictionnaire*, 1: 109. Tanguay, *Répertoire* (1893), 165. Anselme Chiasson, *Chéticamp: histoire et traditions acadiennes* (Moncton, N.-B., 1961), 113–17. N.-E. Dionne, *Les ecclésiastiques et les royalistes français réfugiés au Canada à l'époque de la révolution, 1791–1802* (Québec, 1905), 296–98. Johnston, *Hist. of Catholic Church in eastern N.S.*, 1: 185–94, 202, 211, 224, 273.

CHANDLER, KENELM, Ordnance officer and landowner; b. *c.* 1737 in Tewkesbury, England, son of Nathaniel Chandler; d. 8 Dec. 1803 in Quebec, Lower Canada.

Kenelm Chandler entered the British army at about 18 years of age, and was initially attached to the commissariat department and transport service. In 1764 he was sent to Quebec as clerk of the survey in the civil branch of the Board of Ordnance. Soon after his arrival he also served as acting barrack master, in which capacity he had some involvement in the disputes between Governor Murray* and Brigadier Ralph Burton*.

In November 1775, following the outbreak of the American revolution and the invasion of Canada [*see* Benedict Arnold; Richard Montgomery*], Chandler was also appointed assistant commissary of artillery. He was present throughout the siege of Quebec in late 1775 and early 1776 and for his services was further made barrack master at Île aux Noix and Fort St Johns, on the Richelieu, in December 1776. The following year, as assistant commissary in the artillery, he accompanied Lieutenant-General John Burgoyne*'s expedition as far as Fort Ticonderoga (N.Y.), where he remained until that post was evacuated at the end of the year. Subsequently, he was stationed at Fort St Johns; still clerk of the survey and assistant commissary in the artillery, he also assumed the duties of barrack master there.

In October 1779, following the death of Benjamin Rumsey, the Ordnance storekeeper, Chandler was named to that post, thus becoming the head of the Ordnance's civil branch in Canada. Since this promotion required that he be resident at Quebec, his brother Thomas was appointed his deputy at Fort St Johns. In the autumn of 1782 Chandler found himself in a serious dispute with Alexander Davison* and John Lees, partners in a military supply firm with which Chandler no doubt conducted business as Ordnance storekeeper. Chandler's relations with the two merchants deteriorated, and Adam Mabane* was

181

to note on 30 October that "in consequence of some Transaction at ye Coffee House Davison and Lees desired him to meet them on the Heights where he exchanged a shot wt each of them"; no one seems to have been injured. While continuing to hold his other appointments, Chandler had been promoted in 1781 from assistant commissary to commissary and paymaster in the Field Train, positions he continued to hold until the general reduction of the artillery staff in March 1785. In recognition of the "great merit" shown in the discharge of his duties, Governor HALDIMAND appointed Chandler barrack master at Quebec in January 1784. Shortly thereafter Chandler and the Ordnance were involved in furnishing implements to loyalist families then setting out to create new settlements in Quebec. In 1785 Chandler occupied a spacious two-storey house next to Thomas SCOTT on Rue des Pauvres (Côte du Palais).

After Haldimand's departure from Quebec in 1784, Chandler acted as agent for the Haldimand property at the Montmorency Falls, a task which he performed much to the general's satisfaction. In 1791 he witnessed the probate of Haldimand's will, and at the sale of the Montmorency property in 1799 he was attorney for Haldimand's heir-at-law. In 1786 Lord Amherst* had named Chandler his agent to promote a long-standing claim to the Jesuit estates, promised to him as a reward after the conquest of Canada [see Augustin-Louis de Glapion*]. In December of the following year Lord Dorchester [Guy CARLETON] appointed a commission to report on the location, condition, monetary value, and legal status of the Jesuit estates as well as on the nature and quality of the soils; Chandler was named first commissioner. He was obliged to prod his colleagues along in the face of obstacles placed in the way of their investigations by the Jesuits. Finally, in May 1789, despite the objections of Gabriel-Elzéar TASCHEREAU and Jean-Antoine PANET, Chandler, with the aid of Thomas Scott and John COFFIN, pushed through a report concluding that the crown had the right to grant the estates to Amherst; the commission did not, however, designate the precise properties to be granted. Later that year, fearing the political consequences of such a grant, Dorchester refused to act on Chandler's petition requesting on Amherst's behalf letters patent to the estates.

Chandler appears to have had an active interest in agriculture, and in 1789 he was among the initial subscribers to the Agriculture Society in the District of Quebec; the following year he served as a director. In 1792 he applied as leader according to the system of township leaders and associates [see James CALDWELL] for two townships north of Quebec to be called Stoneham and Tewkesbury. Philip Toosey*, one of Chandler's associates, was able to establish a farm in Stoneham well before the grant of that

township was officially made in 1800, when Chandler personally received 1,200 acres. The following year Chandler added about 8,500 acres bought from several of his associates for around £200. By 1802 he had begun developing Stoneham and had himself established a small farm there. In anticipation of the grant of Tewkesbury, he had already signed agreements in 1798 with many of his associates for the simple transfer to him of their shares once the grant was made, and in 1799 he had even tentatively sold several lots to Mathew Bell* and David Monro*. When the township was granted the following year, however, Chandler was excluded from the list of grantees, although his brother-in-law, George Wulff, received 1,200 acres. Chandler's interest in agriculture remained lively, and in May 1802 he was named to the board for the encouragement of the cultivation of hemp.

On 4 Aug. 1801 Chandler finally married, being then more than 60 years of age. His bride, Charlotte Dunière, was the sister of Louis DUNIÈRE, a prominent Quebec merchant. Chandler and his bride at first occupied a house at 66 Rue Saint-Vallier, where Chandler had been living since at least 1795. In February 1803 he bought a two-storey stone house on Rue Saint-Henri in which he and his wife lived comfortably. Their furniture was mahogany, the salon walls decorated with 36 small paintings, and the cellar stocked with port, Madeira, and other wines as well as rum, cider, and beer. Chandler's library of 168 volumes contained books on agriculture, history, geography, philosophy, and science by such authors as the Comte de Buffon, the Earl of Chesterfield, Edward Gibbon, David Hume, and Joseph Priestley. He frequently gave friends the keys to his farm in Stoneham for parties which lasted several days, and kept it provisioned for their use.

Less than two and a half years after his wedding, Chandler died at his home following "a painfull illness, which he bore to the last with exemplary fortitude and resignation." He had served the government in Quebec for almost 40 years and, in the words of the *Quebec Gazette*, had been "equally estimable in his public and private character for integrity and goodness of heart." Apart from his home at Quebec valued at £850, Chandler owned four houses in Tewkesbury, England, producing an annual revenue of £234. Although he had debts totalling £7,530, of which £7,165 was owed to the government in his capacities as Ordnance storekeeper and barrack master at Quebec, Chandler was creditor for debts totalling more than £10,600, including £573 from John BLACKWOOD, £1,803 from the firm of Blackwood and Patterson, £1,654 from James TOD, and £1,241 from Louis Dunière. His estate, of which the net estimated value was £4,730, was divided between his wife and a natural son, Kenelm Conor Chandler, who was born to Elizabeth Conor about 1773 and who would himself occupy the post of barrack master at Quebec from 1811 to 1819.

GLENN A. STEPPLER

ANQ-Q, CN1-256, 31 Oct. 1796; 29 Jan., 5, 23 Feb. 1798; 25 Feb., 2 Nov. 1799; CN1-262, 26 févr., 25 juill., 8, 25 oct., 12 déc. 1803; 13 nov. 1804; CN1-284, 27 déc. 1798, 21 mai 1800, 13 mars 1801; CN1-285, 7 avril 1802. BL, Add. MSS 21666; 21684; 21720; 21723; 21727; 21732; 21736; 21737; 21744; 21816; 21850; 21890–92. PAC, MG 23, GII, 1, ser.1, 2: 219–22, 240, 280; GII, 22; MG 24, A6; MG 30, D1, 7; RG 1, L7, 35–36; RG 8, I (C ser.), 29, 505, 511, 546–47, 744. [Adam Mabane], "Some letters of Mabane to Riedesel (1781–1783)," ed. Édouard Fabre Surveyer and Dorothy Warren, CHA *Report*, 1930: 81–82. *Quebec Gazette*, 24 Nov. 1766; 1 Sept. 1768; 14 Feb. 1782; 17 March 1785; 23 April 1789; 28 Jan., 25 March 1790; 5 May, 15 Dec. 1791; 11 April 1793; 13 Feb., 3 July 1794; 27 Dec. 1798; 18 July 1799; 20 May 1802; 15 Dec. 1803; 8 Jan. 1818; 18 Feb. 1819. Langelier, *Liste des terrains concédés*, 897. Burt, *Old prov. of Quebec* (1933), 86, 102. R. C. Dalton, "The history of the Jesuits' estates, 1760–1888" (PHD thesis, Univ. of Minn., Minneapolis, 1957), 93, 111–15, 118–28. A. St-L. Frigge, "The two Kenelm Chandlers," *BRH*, 49 (1943): 108–13.

CHARLAND, LOUIS, surveyor, office holder, architect, and militia officer; b. 6 April 1772 at Quebec, son of Alexis Charland and Marie Poulin; m. first 17 Jan. 1803 Marie-Joseph Fearson on Île Perrot, Lower Canada; m. secondly 22 Feb. 1810 Sarah Jones in Montreal, Lower Canada; d. there 3 Sept. 1813.

Louis Charland entered the Petit Séminaire de Québec in 1785 and finished his studies there in June 1792. Shortly afterwards he started to learn surveying with a man by the name of Jones. In 1793 he was appointed deputy provincial surveyor by Samuel Johannes HOLLAND, surveyor general of Lower Canada. That year also he gave the public the benefit of his scientific knowledge by providing answers in the *Quebec Gazette* to questions concerning geometry and surveying. Having received his commission as a surveyor in August 1795, he worked until 1799 in the Quebec area, where he does not seem to have been very busy, judging by the limited number of reports of surveys done for the region.

At that period the maintenance of roads and streets in Montreal was the subject of much complaint by the citizens. In 1799, therefore, the House of Assembly passed a bill amending one adopted three years earlier concerning the construction and upkeep of roads in Lower Canada. The 1799 act stipulated, among other things, that two surveyors would be appointed, one at Quebec and one at Montreal, and that each would receive an annual salary of £100 and would be put under the immediate authority of the justices of the peace, whose powers extended to municipal govern-

ment. At 27, Charland became the first surveyor of the highways, streets, and lanes in Montreal, and he took up permanent residence in that town to pursue other professional work as well. He signed many boundary surveys or measuring reports in Montreal and the surrounding area, and sometimes these documents were accompanied by plans prepared with exceptional care.

As road surveyor Charland was responsible for supervising the maintenance of roads, streets, and bridges, hiring the manpower for repair work, and levying fines. He held this office without interruption from his initial appointment in June 1799 until his death in 1813. In this capacity he drew up in 1801 the "Plan de la ville et cité de Montréal avec les projets d'accroissements"; his intent was to make the boundaries of the urban agglomeration, in which the suburbs were developing more rapidly than the central area, correspond more closely to the actual situation.

Charland's name is also linked with the demolition of the old fortifications which, in addition to being of no military use, were a serious block to the town's growth. In 1803, following the recommendation of the commissioners John Richardson*, James McGILL, and Jean-Marie Mondelet*, who were entrusted with directing the demolition, Charland prepared a plan of the fortifications to serve as a reference for future development of the town. On the work site he took charge of inspecting such projects as the extension of streets and the repair of embankments; he signed payment authorizations, and proceeded to survey numerous places where the fortification walls stood, in order to return them to their legitimate owners. He continued to do such jobs, which brought him supplementary income, until his death. The work of demolition itself was not completed until 1817. During his years in Montreal Charland had in addition prepared an undetermined number of plans for public buildings, among which were the Montreal court-house (1799), the prison (1808), for which he directed the work, and the buildings on the Place du Marché (1809).

While making his career in the public service Charland had undertaken other projects, and some of these turned out well. In collaboration with the surveyor and printer William VONDENVELDEN he prepared *A new topographical map of the province of Lower Canada*. It was published in London in 1803 and was only surpassed 12 years later by the work of Surveyor General Joseph Bouchette*. To accompany their map Charland and Vondenvelden published at Quebec in the same year a volume entitled *Extraits des titres des anciennes concessions de terre en fief et seineurie*. Charland was also capable of conceiving ambitious projects; for example, on 27 Feb. 1812 he put an advertisement in the *Quebec Gazette* announcing his intention to claim the exclu-

Chejauk

sive right to open a canal between Montreal and Lachine.

Charland was less successful in his attempts to obtain land in the Eastern Townships from the government. In 1796, with a group of associates, he asked for 64,000 acres in the Lac Mégantic region which were refused him; his request that year for a grant of 5,000 acres in the vicinity of Brompton and Orford townships was also rejected. In the latter case the land ended up in the hands of another surveyor, Samuel Gale*. From 1801 until his death Charland served as a militia officer; in April 1812 he obtained the post of adjutant and six months later became deputy quartermaster general of the Montreal mititia.

Louis Charland was more than the "good official" he has been termed. His contemporaries certainly had confidence in him, to judge by the number of offices he held concurrently. The excellence of his cartographic works and his plans is likewise recognized. Jacques Viger*, who succeeded him as road surveyor, could have testified to it: commissioned to do a plan of Montreal, he had difficulty obtaining payment because it was apparently too much like Charland's works.

GILLES LANGELIER

Louis Charland's surveyor's notebooks for 1793–1813 are deposited at the ANQ-M, CA1-16. With William Vondenvelden, Charland published *A new topographical map of the province of Lower Canada compiled from all the former as well as the latest surveys . . .* (London, 1803) and compiled *Extraits des titres des anciennes concessions de terre en fief et seineurie, faites avant et depuis la Conquête de la Nouvelle France par les armes britanniques dans la partie actuellement appellée le Bas-Canada . . .* (Québec, 1803).

ANQ-M, CN1-16, 25 juill. 1809. ASQ, Fichier des anciens; Fonds Viger-Verreau, Sér.O, 0165–71 (copies at PAC). PAC, MG 30, D1, 7; RG 1, E15, A, 280, 290, 317; E17; L3^L: 29603–10; RG 4, A1: 21716–18; B33, 18; RG 8, I (C ser.), 1203½G: 13. *Quebec Gazette*, 7, 14 Feb., 7 March, 4 April 1793; 20 Aug. 1795; 20 June 1799; 27 Feb., 23 April 1812; 16 Sept. 1813. Bouchette, *Topographical description of L.C. Quebec almanac*, 1795–1813. J.-C. Marsan, *Montréal en évolution: historique du développement de l'architecture et de l'environnement montréalais* (Montréal, 1974), 160. É.-Z. Massicotte, *Faits curieux de l'histoire de Montréal* (Montréal, 1922), 62–63. Albertine Ferland-Angers, "La citadelle de Montréal (1658–1820)," *RHAF*, 3 (1949–50): 509. P. Scribe, "Louis Charland," *BRH*, 34 (1928): 330–36.

CHEJAUK (Ah je juk, Allchechaque, Auchechaque, Crane), leader of a segment of the sucker clan of either the Ottawas or the Northern Ojibwas; fl. 1761–1804.

Chejauk's life spanned the hectic days of the middle and late 18th century when the Hudson's Bay Company was engaged in intense competition, first with the French and later with the North West Company. In his younger years the Ojibwas and the Ottawas were probably still in the process, begun in the 17th century, of expanding northwest into the northern regions of present-day Ontario and into modern Manitoba. Until the late 1750s most of the members of the two tribes traded with Canadians, but upon the withdrawal of these traders after the British conquest, the inland Indians north of Lake Superior began carrying their furs to the HBC posts on Hudson Bay and James Bay.

It is difficult to pinpoint the first mention of Chejauk, since early spellings of Indian names are highly variable and the English term Crane did not appear until the 1790s. However, he probably moved about in company with one of his brothers, Captain Tinnewabano (known as the Tinpot), who can be traced more easily. Tinnewabano is first mentioned in 1761 in the journal of the HBC's Fort Albany (Ont.), where he and his brothers traded annually from 1761 to 1771. In 1767 Usakechack (perhaps the Crane) was at Albany to examine the trade goods and likely to compare them with those which the Montreal traders had begun to bring to the interior. By 1771 the latter had become so numerous in the northwest that most of the Ottawas and Ojibwas ceased making the long, strenuous trip to James Bay. There is no unmistakable mention of the Crane until the HBC's establishment of inland posts.

In 1777 Tinnewabano sent his grand pipe as a gesture of friendship to the newly established Gloucester House (on Washi Lake, Ont.); he refused, however, to go there even though he was reported to be near by. The next year he traded there but he is reported to have gone to Fort Severn in 1779. During the early 1780s he again traded at Gloucester, but it is not known whether the Crane was with him. After the founding of Osnaburgh House in 1786 and the Cat Lake outpost in 1788, both the Crane and his brother traded at these stations fairly regularly. Nevertheless, they dealt with the traders who would give them the best prices, whether they represented the HBC or the NWC. By the 1770s at the latest the Crane and Tinnewabano each headed a separate band or family. In 1795 "Captain Allchechaque (or Auchechaque)" was reported to be "the father of 23 children, 16 of which is Sons, the eldest only arriv'd at manhood, and the youngest in the Cradle." Almost certainly he was a polygynist, as were most band leaders. The Crane's band may have comprised from 30 to 35 persons during the 1790s.

The year 1799 appears to have marked the point from which the Indians' normally pacific relations with the traders deteriorated. Tinnewabano, having murdered an Indian from Martin Falls or Severn, fled with his gang to Sandy Lake. The Crane was concerned for his own safety, knowing that the relatives of the murder victim would "make no distinctions between Tin-pot & any of his relations." During the next two decades the Crane's band (called the Cranes or the Crane Indians) and the Tinpots directed their hostilities toward the trading posts. The precise causes of the strife are unknown, but they may have been exacerbated by some combination of the lavish distribution of alcohol, severe treatment of the Indians by a few traders, and ruthless competition among the traders themselves; further, rivalry among the Indians over fur-bearing areas may have led to violence between bands and against traders who dealt with competing bands. In June 1803 William Thomas reported the arrival of four Tinpots at Osnaburgh House with few furs to trade, noting, "I understand they have murdered 3 Canadians & plundered the House." Thomas considered them to be "run about Blackguards." In September eight of the Crane's sons threatened Osnaburgh House, and in March 1804 Thomas feared an attack since "the Old Crane and 14 of his Sons" had been lingering within 30 miles of the post since January. Instead, five canoes of Cranes arrived at Martin Falls on 27 May. There Jacob Corrigal reported that they brought no furs and had evil intentions toward either the traders or the local Indians, who upon their arrival fled downstream. The Cranes at first refused to speak to Corrigal, but two days later they came armed into the fort and forced him to give them credit. Had not three other Indians lured them away to drink brandy, there might have been serious trouble. By late morning on 2 June the weary traders, who had been keeping watch day and night, aimed two swivel cannon at the Indians' tents and told them to leave. They did so "in a very confused hurry," and by November they were once again causing anxiety to the traders at Osnaburgh House.

In 1807, after James Swain had erected the Trout Lake post (on Big Trout Lake), he urged some Indians to guide him to the south where the Cranes and the Tinpots resided; they refused, afraid of falling "a sacrifice to their cruelty." The Cranes had become the most dreaded Indians in present-day northern Ontario. Nothing further is recorded of the Crane Indians until the period after 1810, when more trouble occurred. By this time, however, the Crane himself was in all likelihood dead: he is last named in 1804. He appears to have been succeeded by his eldest son, Matayawenenne (Maitwaywayninnee). It is possible that his brother Tinnewabano outlived him by a few years, for he is mentioned by Swain in 1807. Descendants of the Crane and his family now reside at Weagamow Lake, and they are still known as Crane Indians, some 175 years after their original leader's death.

CHARLES A. BISHOP

PAM, HBCA, B.3/a/50–67; B.10/e/2; B.30/a/1–6; B.78/a/1–14; B.86/a/1–18; B.123/a/8; B.155/a/1–36; B.155/e/1–3; B.198/a/1–31; B.220/a/1–3; E.2/7–9. C. A. Bishop, *The Northern Ojibwa and the fur trade: an historical and ecological study* (Toronto and Montreal, 1974). E. S. Rogers, *The Round Lake Ojibwa* ([Toronto], 1962).

CHERRIER, FRANÇOIS, Roman Catholic priest and vicar general; b. 15 Jan. 1745 in Longueuil (Que.), son of François-Pierre Cherrier*, a notary and merchant, and Marie Dubuc; d. 18 Sept. 1809 in Saint-Denis, on the Rivière Richelieu, Lower Canada.

François Cherrier was the second of 12 children; he spent his youth at Longueuil, where his father had settled in 1736. In 1765 he resumed his studies at the Petit Séminaire de Québec, which had been closed since the city had come under siege in 1759. Subsequently he chose the priesthood, pursuing his theological education at the Grand Séminaire. Ordained priest by Bishop Briand* on 20 May 1769, he served briefly as curate in the parish of Saint-Antoine at Longueuil, and then in Sainte-Famille at Boucherville. In the latter post he benefited for five months from the judicious advice of the local parish priest, vicar general Étienne Marchand*, who was eager to have him as a regular companion.

In November 1769 Bishop Briand named Cherrier curate to act for the parish priest at Saint-Denis. The parishioners had for some time been criticizing the administration of both their parish priest, Jean-Baptiste Frichet, who was now ill and in the Hôpital Général of Quebec, and the officiating priest, Michel Gervaise, who was accused of being miserly and of being seldom present in the parish. In September and October 1769 the churchwardens had consequently petitioned the bishop of Quebec for a new parish priest. From his earliest days in Saint-Denis Cherrier won the esteem of his flock, according to Marchand, who in December 1769 noted: "Monsieur Cherrier is doing very well there. The habitants are very pleased." The following year his family came to live at Saint-Denis, where his father practised his profession as a notary. Upon Frichet's death in 1774 Cherrier became parish priest.

During the American invasion in 1775 many of his parishioners at Saint-Denis openly supported the rebels. This did not stop Cherrier, who remained loyal to the British crown, from giving shelter in his presbytery on 17 September to Jean Orillat* and a certain Léveillé, the bearers of a proclamation of amnesty granted by Governor Guy CARLETON.

Cherrier displayed deep concern for the education of the young. In 1773 he had informed Bishop Briand of his plan to build a convent and asked him to exert pressure on the neighbouring parish priests, some of whom were reluctant, to get them interested and induce them to contribute to carrying out the project. Claude-Pierre Pécaudy* de Contrecœur, the seigneur of Saint-Denis, let Cherrier have a piece of land in

Chicoisneau

1774, specifying that the building of the convent could not be undertaken for six years. The house was begun in 1780 and completed in 1783, the year of the institution's founding by Marie-Louise COMPAIN, named Saint-Augustin, and Catherine d'Ailleboust de La Madeleine, named de la Visitation, nuns of the Congregation of Notre-Dame. In 1805 Cherrier also founded a boys' school with boarding facilities, in which Pierre-Marie Mignault* taught. This school was closed after some years' operation. In 1792 Cherrier had undertaken to have a new church built, and it was consecrated on 30 Oct. 1796.

The bishops of Quebec always had the highest regard for him, and Bishop Briand had not been sparing in his admiration. When Jean-François Hubert* was coadjutor, Cherrier accompanied him on a pastoral visit. After Hubert became bishop, Cherrier took up his defence when the *Quebec Gazette* of 29 April 1790 published an insulting letter by coadjutor Charles-François Bailly* de Messein. Bishop Hubert often relied on the wisdom of the parish priest of Saint-Denis. Thus in 1793, deploring young Canadians' lack of inclination for the priesthood, Hubert consulted him on the advisability of bringing in French priests. Cherrier was not in favour of the idea. On 9 Dec. 1797 Bishop DENAUT recognized Cherrier's abilities by appointing him vicar general for the parishes south of Montreal. Bishop Plessis*, who succeeded Denaut in 1806, freely expressed the same confidence by renewing his letters as vicar general and consulting him on many occasions, notably on the delicate question of the course to be taken with regard to the British authorities.

On 18 Sept. 1809, worn down by the illness that had sapped his strength for 12 years, Cherrier died at the age of 64. Jean-Baptiste Kelly* succeeded him as parish priest at Saint-Denis. In his will Cherrier bequeathed his library of more than 400 books – an imposing one for the period – to Bishop Plessis for the use of the new Séminaire de Nicolet.

François Cherrier belonged to a family that, according to historian Francis-Joseph Audet*, became one of the most influential in the Montreal region at the end of the 18th century and remained so for more than 50 years. Two of Cherrier's brothers, Benjamin-Hyacinthe-Martin and Séraphin, would attain prominence on the political stage of Lower Canada, and among his nephews were the first bishop of Montreal, Jean-Jacques Lartigue*, a noted lawyer, Côme-Séraphin Cherrier*, and two renowned politicians, Louis-Joseph Papineau* and Denis-Benjamin Viger*.

GILLES CHAUSSÉ

AAQ, 12 A, F: f.4r.; 210 A, I: f.139; II: ff.65, 118; 1 CB, VII: f.98; CD, Diocèse de Québec, II: f.63. Arch. de la chancellerie de l'archevêché de Montréal, 901.004, 769-5, -6, -9, -11. ANQ-M, CE1-12, 16 janv. 1745; CE2-12, 21 sept. 1809. Arch. de la chancellerie de l'évêché de Saint-Hyacinthe (Saint-Hyacinthe, Qué.), XVII, C-25. ASQ, C 36: 3, 43, 48. Allaire, *Dictionnaire*, 1: 119. F.-J. Audet, *Les députés de Montréal*, 411. J.-J. Lefebvre, "Articles généalogiques: la famille Cherrier, 1743–1945," SGCF *Mémoires*, 2 (1947): 148. P.-G. Roy, "Les notaires au Canada sous le Régime français," ANQ *Rapport*, 1921–22: 47. Tanguay, *Dictionnaire*, 3: 52–53; *Répertoire* (1893), 138. J.-B.-A. Allaire, *Histoire de la paroisse de Saint-Denis-sur-Richelieu (Canada)* (Saint-Hyacinthe, 1905), 133–41, 172–87, 275–302. Lemire-Marsolais et Lambert, *Hist. de la CND de Montréal*, 5: 366–68. J.-B. Richard, *Les églises de la paroisse de Saint-Denis-sur-Richelieu* ([Saint-Hyacinthe], 1939). J.-E. Roy, *Hist. du notariat*, 2: 11. Henri Morisseau, "La famille Cherrier de Saint-Denis-sur-Richelieu," *Rev. de l'univ. d'Ottawa*, 16 (1946): 310–18. Gabriel Nadeau, "Jean Orillat," *BRH*, 41 (1935): 653–56.

CHICOISNEAU, JEAN-BAPTISTE-JACQUES, Roman Catholic priest, Sulpician, teacher, and director of the Collège Saint-Raphaël in Montreal (Que.); b. 17 March 1737 in Meung, France, son of Guillaume Chicoisneau and Hélène Gaulthier; d. 28 Feb. 1818 in Montreal, Lower Canada.

Jean-Baptiste-Jacques Chicoisneau, who had already been tonsured, entered the Séminaire d'Orléans in France on 1 Nov. 1756. He was ordained priest on 16 May 1761 and taught at the seminary until 1765, when he became superior of the community of philosophy students at the Séminaire Saint-Irénée in Lyons. He returned to the Orléans seminary to take up a similar post in 1782.

At the time of the French revolution the Sulpicians, who were secular priests without responsibility for parish ministry, were expelled from the seminaries. Chicoisneau, like many others, emigrated. In 1792 he joined the second group of Sulpicians that went to Baltimore, Md, where the Séminaire de Saint-Sulpice in Paris had founded an establishment the previous year. He arrived on 29 March and was appointed bursar by the superior of the seminary in Baltimore, François-Charles Nagot. Probably because of his inability to learn English, Chicoisneau left Baltimore for Lower Canada in May 1796, bearing two letters, one from Bishop John Carroll of Baltimore recommending him warmly and the other from the Duke of Portland, the British Home secretary. Governor Lord Dorchester [Guy CARLETON] gave him permission to enter Lower Canada.

On 1 July 1796 Chicoisneau was admitted to the community of the Séminaire de Saint-Sulpice in Montreal as a member. In view of his teaching experience he was appointed that year to succeed Jean-Baptiste Marchand* as director of the Collège Saint-Raphaël (usually known as the Collège de Montréal), where at the same time he held the offices of bursar and physics teacher. At that period the college, located in the Château de Vaudreuil, was a secondary institution which went right up to the Philosophy course and which had at the primary level one English class and one French. It provided instruction to some 100 pupils, half of whom were boarders. The latter were governed by the rules enforced in the *petits séminaires* (classical colleges). They got up at 5:30 a.m., devoted four and a half hours to study, four to classes, and three and a half to recreation. They were summoned to mass or prayers four times a day and on Sundays and feast days went to the parish church in Place d'Armes. In winter pupils had half a day off each week and in summer a day off. The boarders had to pay 360 *livres* a year, the day-boarders half that amount, and the day pupils 48 *livres*.

In teaching physics, Chicoisneau repeated the classical experiments in electrostatics and did studies of air, using the terms of the time. For example he ended his short treatise on air by citing the French chemist Antoine-Laurent de Lavoisier's theory (in dispute, he noted) according to which water was an element composed of dephlogisticated air and inflammable gas. As bursar, Chicoisneau managed the college budget and was able to show surpluses thanks to generous contributions from the Séminaire de Saint-Sulpice in Montreal. On 3 June 1803 a fire in the east end of Montreal spread to the college, causing considerable damage. College classes had to be moved to the seminary until the new *petit séminaire* was opened in 1806.

In October 1806 Chicoisneau was replaced as director by Jacques-Guillaume Roque*; he then became assistant to Claude PONCIN, a fellow Sulpician, who was chaplain to the Hôpital Général of Montreal and whom he would succeed in 1811. For 12 years Chicoisneau devoted himself to serving the nuns and the underprivileged. The Grey Nuns' annals even credit him with the sudden cure in 1817 of a person possessed by the devil. In addition to this pastoral activity Chicoisneau was in charge of the Congrégation des Hommes de Ville-Marie, a brotherhood dedicated to the Virgin Mary.

Jean-Baptiste-Jacques Chicoisneau died suddenly on 28 Feb. 1818, at the age of 80, while engaged in prayer with the community. He was buried under the chancel of the church of Notre-Dame in Montreal on 2 March. Jean-Henri-Auguste Roux*, superior of the Séminaire de Saint-Sulpice, asserted in homage, "He constantly gave proof of his complete and unvarying attention to duty and of his charity towards his brothers."

J.-BRUNO HAREL

AD, Loiret (Orléans), État civil, Meung, 17 mars 1731. ANQ-M, CE1-51, 2 mars 1818. Arch. du collège de Montréal, Cahiers de l'administration; Cahiers manuscrits de préparation de cours de J.-B.-J. Chicoisneau. ASSM, 11, 47–49; 24, Dossier 6; 25, Dossier 1; 49. Olivier Maurault, "Galerie de portraits des supérieurs du collège de Montréal," *Cahiers des Dix*, 25 (1960): 191–217. N.-E. Dionne, *Les ecclésiastiques et les royalistes français réfugiés au Canada à l'époque de la révolution, 1791–1802* (Québec, 1905). [É.-M. Faillon], *Vie de Mme d'Youville, fondatrice des Sœurs de la charité de Villemarie dans l'île de Montréal, en Canada* (Villemarie [Montréal], 1852). J. W. Ruane, *The beginnings of the Society of St. Sulpice in the United States (1791–1829)* (Baltimore, Md., 1935).

CLARK (Clarke), DUNCAN, physician, surgeon, and apothecary; b. *c.* 1759 in Scotland; m. 7 Feb. 1789 Justina Sophia Bayer in Halifax, N.S., and they had at least five sons; d. there 10 Sept. 1808.

Considerable confusion surrounds the circumstances of Duncan Clark's early life. He enlisted in the 82nd Foot, probably in Scotland, and likely served with it in the American revolution; when the regiment was disbanded at Halifax in October 1783 Clark received half pay as an ensign. He may have had some medical training prior to his enlistment, but his subsequent expertise was likely gained during his regimental career. He may possibly have served as a surgeon's mate, for at this time surgeons' mates often purchased ensigncies in order to augment their pay and improve their status.

The month his regiment was disbanded Clark began his Halifax practice as a temporary replacement for the absent surgeon to the naval dockyard. He received a salary of 4*d.* per month per man in the yard, which amounted to approximately £25 per year. By September 1785 the incumbent still had not returned, and Clark therefore petitioned the dockyard commissioner, Henry DUNCAN, for the appointment, also requesting an adequate salary. Duncan's comment that he was "a very able surgeon . . . whose [emoluments] are no way adequate to his service" gained Clark the position, which he apparently retained for life. In 1804 he received the additional appointment of physician general and inspector of the Nova Scotia militia hospital. During the residence of Prince EDWARD AUGUSTUS, Clark served as physician in ordinary to the royal household, along with his friends William James ALMON and John Halliburton. He also maintained a large and popular medical practice in Halifax, and like several other doctors augmented his income by operating a pharmaceutical dispensary.

A congenial, dignified, and well-educated man, Clark is perhaps best remembered for his contributions to the Halifax social scene. He was a member of the North British Society by 1784, and after filling various committee positions and club offices he served as president in 1789, and again in 1797. Clark was also an active freemason, being master of St John's Lodge No.211 as early as 1786. He subsequently

Clark

attained the position of grand master in the provincial grand lodge in 1800. Succeeded the following year by Sir John WENTWORTH, he remained as deputy grand master until 1807. Clark was also a member of a select informal intellectual circle which met regularly at the Great Pontack Inn for the discussion of literary and scientific subjects, followed by an evening's conviviality. Prince Edward Augustus often attended these gatherings.

Clark was reputedly a wealthy man, and in the 1790s is supposed to have invested successfully in several privateering ventures. Neither of these contentions has been substantiated. His few attempts at landholding, notably in the Hammonds Plains area near Wentworth's rural retreat, were financially unsuccessful; at his death most of the acreage remained unimproved. His total estate amounted to only £705, of which £497 was owing to creditors. One might suppose that any profits had been expended in maintaining a high standard of living, but the inventory of his personal effects suggests only a mediocre middle-class household. Certainly it was by his character and medical expertise alone that Duncan Clark made his mark on the colonial scene.

LOIS K. KERNAGHAN

Halifax County Court of Probate (Halifax), C62 (estate papers of Duncan Clark) (mfm. at PANS). Halifax County Registry of Deeds (Halifax), Index to deeds, 1–2; Deeds, 23–28 (mfm. at PANS). PANS, "Masonic grand masters of the jurisdiction of Nova Scotia, 1738–1965," comp. E. T. Bliss (typescript, 1965); MG 13, 2.

CLARK (Clarke), JAMES, merchant, lawyer, and office holder; b. in Quebec, probably at Trois-Rivières, son of James Clark and Jemima Mason; m. 29 Aug. 1795 Elizabeth Hare in Newark (Niagara-on-the-Lake), Upper Canada, and they had four children, three of whom survived infancy; fl. 1790–1807 in Upper Canada.

James Clark's father, a native of Somerset, England, came to Quebec in May 1768 with the 8th Foot. He was posted to Trois-Rivières and served there until 1777, when he was appointed naval storekeeper at Carleton Island (N.Y.). Several of his children, including James, were educated "at a French and English Seminary" and were, as their younger brother John recalled many years later, "good scholars for that period." According to John's memoir, James and his elder brother Peter became merchants at Montreal, and Peter appears on the lists of Indian trade passes for 1782 and 1785. In 1785 Clark Sr was sent to Napanee (Ont.) to run the government grist-mill that Robert Clark* (no relation) was building there. When in 1788 western Quebec was divided into the four administrative districts that later became Upper Canada, James Clark Sr was appointed to the

Mecklenburg District land board and Court of Common Pleas, and made a justice of the peace. That same year he was appointed naval storekeeper at Kingston and took up residence there, becoming a leader of the new community. This relocation may have had some effect on his sons; John Clark wrote that in 1790 James and Peter moved to Kingston where they engaged in the Indian trade.

The division of Quebec and the establishment of a separate government for Upper Canada in 1791 opened up new possibilities for patronage, and the elder Clark may have influenced Lieutenant Governor SIMCOE's appointment of Peter Clark as clerk of the Legislative Council on 29 Sept. 1792. Peter died in 1793 as a result of a duel and on 27 May of that year was succeeded by his brother James, who then moved to the provincial capital at Newark. Clark's duties included administering oaths, supervising the copying of the council's minutes, transmitting messages from the speaker of the council, and sending out copies of statutes to local clerks of the peace. He was the chief administrative officer of the council and in conjunction with his counterpart in the House of Assembly, for many years Angus MACDONELL (Collachie), coordinated the work of successive parliaments. In 1796 the responsibility for superintending the printing of acts by the king's printer seems to have unexpectedly devolved upon him. The following year he petitioned the Executive Council for additional remuneration since this new burden was, he believed, "distinct" from the duties of his office. But a committee of the council, headed by Chief Justice John ELMSLEY, refused his petition on the grounds that his salary of £125 per annum was "very ample compensation" for all the activities associated with his position.

It is possible that Clark had received some legal training. As early as 1790 he acted as his father's attorney in civil suits before the Court of Common Pleas. In 1794 he was one of the original 16 men called to the bar by act of parliament. He was also one of the founding members of the Law Society of Upper Canada, which was established in 1797. Between 1799 and 1802 judgements against him in the Court of King's Bench usually identified him as "one of the attornies" but it is not known whether he was a practising member of the bar.

Like most Upper Canadians, Clark petitioned the government for land, and he received 1,200 acres which he located in Murray, Pittsburgh, and Marysburgh (North and South Marysburgh) townships. In 1797, the year he moved with the government to the province's new capital at York (Toronto), he was granted a town lot there, and also a 200-acre farm lot in the vicinity, with the stipulation that no warrant be issued for the latter parcel of land until he had actually settled on it.

Clark was a minor office holder who did his job

competently and conscientiously but, unlike Macdonell for instance, made little impact either socially or politically upon York society. By 1799 debt had become a constant feature of his life. Between that year and 1804 he had five judgements against him in civil court for varying sums. His situation thereafter became increasingly desperate and by 1805 he was issuing drafts against his salary as clerk, hoping that Receiver General Peter RUSSELL would honour them. Merchants such as George Forsyth and William and James* Crooks promptly forwarded their claims to Russell. In late 1805 Clark owed the Crooks brothers £100; they noted in applying to Russell about his draft, "We have made some sacrifice in the way of assistance to his family to obtain it." On one occasion Clark even denied, to no avail apparently, that the signature on a particular draft was his own.

The last years of Clark's life were characterized by insolvency, dissipation, and woe. In January 1806 Russell's half-sister, Elizabeth*, noted in her diary the possibility that Clark's position might become vacant because of "his ill state of health or death." Already the official families of York were scrambling to secure his office for one of their number. The clerk's salary and contingent account were a generous reward for working only six weeks a year. In the midst of the turmoil surrounding the clerkship, Clark's infant daughter died in March 1806; seven months later his wife died as well. Yet Clark held on to his position. He served during the legislative session of February–March 1806 and as late as November was still acting in his official capacity.

The combination of stresses, however, proved too much for Clark to bear and he turned to alcohol. Completely without influence, he became an even more tempting target for the York élite. According to Mrs Anne Powell [Murray*], early in 1806 government officials had agreed to remove him but Administrator Alexander GRANT had been unwilling to initiate the change. The new lieutenant governor, Francis Gore*, however, felt that Clark "should no longer hold a responsible situation to which his vices render'd him inequal." On 13 Feb. 1807 Mrs Powell wrote to her husband that, according to Legislative Councillor Richard CARTWRIGHT, Gore had decided to give the clerkship to the Powells' son, John. The only problem was that "James Clarke was upon the spot, & it was painful to dispossess him entirely." So it was agreed that John Powell should offer to share the salary with Clark. The offer was put to Clark some time on 13 or 14 February; he refused. Mrs Powell dismissed him as "long devoted to the most confirmed habits of intoxication, & for some time . . . advancing with hasty strides to that grave, which can alone cover his disgrace." The government acted quickly. Clark's brother later recalled that he had had to relinquish his position "from habits of indulgence, to the great regret of his family." A regular of the law society, Clark

attended his last meeting on 18 Feb. 1807. The following day, John Powell became clerk of the council. The disgraced Clark then disappeared from sight; there is no record of his subsequent whereabouts. His health, however, was very poor and it is likely that he died shortly thereafter.

In collaboration with RICHARD A. PRESTON

AO, MS 75, James Clark to Peter Russell, 23 Jan. 1803, 22 March 1806; James Crooks to Russell, 10, 27 March 1806; W. & J. Crooks to Russell, 27 Nov. 1805; George Forsyth & Company to Russell, 17 Jan. 1806; RG 22, ser.131, 1: ff.62–63. Law Soc. of U.C. (Toronto), Law Soc. of U.C., minutes, 17 July 1797–18 Feb. 1807. MTL, William Dummer Powell papers, A93: 75–82. PAC, RG 1, L3, 90: C2/151; 91: C3/49; 92: C4/23; RG 4, B28, 115, 1782, 1785; RG 5, A1: 2186–87; RG 68, General index, 1651–1841: f.74. "Accounts of receiver-general of U.C.," AO Report, 1914: 754–55, 763. [John Clark], "Memoirs of Colonel John Clark, of Port Dalhousie, C.W.," OH, 7 (1906): 157–93. Corr. of Lieut. Governor Simcoe (Cruikshank), 4: 192–93, 196; 5: 151–52. "District of Mecklenburg (Kingston): Court of Common Pleas," AO Report, 1917: 211–13, 236, 349. "Early records of Niagara" (Carnochan), OH, 3: 14, 16, 22, 54, 68–69. "Journals of Legislative Assembly of U.C.," AO Report, 1909: 162, 473–74. "The journals of the Legislative Council of Upper Canada . . . ," AO Report, 1910: 16, 116. Parish reg. of Kingston (Young), 161. Town of York, 1793–1815 (Firth), 259. "U.C. land book C," AO Report, 1930: 151, 153. "U.C. land book D," AO Report, 1931: 170, 174.

CLINCH, JOHN, doctor, Church of England clergyman, office holder, and judge; b. 9 Jan. 1748/49 in Cirencester, England, one of twin children of Thomas Clinch of Bere Regis, England; m. 17 June 1784 Hannah Hart of English Harbour, Nfld, and they had seven sons and one daughter; d. 22 Nov. 1819 in Trinity, Nfld.

John Clinch went to school in Cirencester with Edward Jenner, later the discoverer of vaccination, and both moved to London to study medicine under John Hunter, a noted anatomist and surgeon. Clinch then practised medicine in Dorset, where he obtained a knowledge of Newfoundland from Benjamin LESTER, merchant of Poole and of Trinity. He also began a Sunday school on the model of that of Robert Raikes, whom he had encountered in Gloucester. An evangelical by conviction, he ignored denominational differences and took the children to worship in a Congregational chapel at Poole.

In 1775 Clinch moved to Bonavista in Newfoundland, where he earned his living as a doctor and acted as a lay reader in the Anglican church. Eight years later he relocated to Trinity, where he married. Being concerned at the "decay of true Religion, and the success of Popery," in the absence of a clergyman he organized public worship, read sermons, and performed marriages, baptisms, and burials. In 1784 the

Coffin

inhabitants petitioned the Society for the Propagation of the Gospel to appoint him missionary, and Clinch asked the SPG that he be appointed without having to visit England for ordination. The SPG insisted, however, and after enquiries had been made concerning his character and a personal recommendation received from Richard ROUTH, collector of customs in Newfoundland, he was ordained in England and appointed as missionary to Trinity Bay in 1787.

During his 32 years as a missionary Clinch constantly complained of a lack of financial support. In 1789 he could collect only £24 to repair the church, and three years later he was forced to do it at his own expense. By 1815 the building was falling down, and even with a gift of £100 from the SPG not enough could be collected to erect a new one. His congregation was poor, its members at times obliged to travel to England to seek relief from their home parishes. The cost of living rose dramatically in 1805 because of the war with Spain, and again in 1809 because of the renewal of the American embargo on British products. Typhus spread, there were outbreaks of smallpox, and in 1799 and again in 1804 "inflammatory fever . . . raged with violence." The Church of England gradually lost support in the bay to the Methodists. In 1794 George Smith, a Methodist preacher, visited Trinity, and by the following year he had persuaded some people of Bonavista to petition for his appointment as SPG missionary. This attempt failed, but by 1810 William Ward, a Methodist minister from England, had settled at Trinity in competition with Clinch. The latter lamented that Trinity Bay, which a few years previously had been entirely Church of England, had "become a nursery for itinerant fanatic preachers."

Had he been just a missionary, Clinch might have enjoyed greater success as an evangelist. As it was, he performed a multiplicity of functions. By 1799 he had become a salaried judge of the surrogate court of Newfoundland, and at other times he acted as a magistrate, surveyor, and collector of customs. An active freemason, having been initiated into the Poole Lodge of Amity No.137 in 1780, he became in 1816 a founder and the first master of the Union Lodge No.6981 of Trinity. Clinch also found the time to compile a glossary of 112 Beothuk words, many of them not previously known.

But most of his energy went into caring for the sick. It is likely that he performed one of the first vaccinations in the New World, in 1798 on his wife's nephew Joseph Hart. His old friend Jenner had told him about the new procedure and had even sent threads of vaccine. With these, and others supplied through Jenner's nephew George Charles Jenner, SPG missionary at Harbour Grace, Clinch was soon busy. In January 1802 he reported to Jenner, "I began by innoculating my own children and went on with this salutary work till I had innoculated 700 persons of all ages and descriptions, many opportunities soon offered at St John's (where the smallpox was making great ravages) which offered convincing proofs of the safety of the practice to the inhabitants and servants in Trinity Bay; they saw (at first, with astonishment) that those who had gone through the Jennerian inoculation, were inoculated with the smallpox, and exposed to the infection without the least inconvenience." Encouraged by Governor Charles Morice Pole and enthusiastically adopted by Dr John McCurdy of St John's, the practice spread to Ferryland, Placentia, and Halifax, N.S.

Clinch had a large family; indeed, he joked with the SPG on the yearly arrival of another child. His first three sons were mentally retarded; the fourth, John, became a doctor after serving an apprenticeship to a surgeon and apothecary in Cirencester; the youngest, Joseph Hart, became an Anglican clergyman in Boston, Mass., renowned for his scholarship in Hebrew. Mary Elizabeth, the only daughter, was married in 1823 to William Bullock*, Clinch's successor in the Trinity mission. Clinch himself died of a stroke after a long illness.

As a missionary John Clinch had little success and his religious endeavours are, perhaps justly, completely ignored by historians. As a medical man, however, he has a good claim to the title of the first Canadian vaccinator.

FREDERICK JONES

Dorset Record Office, D365/F7–F8. USPG, C/CAN/Nfl., 1; Journal of SPG, 26–32. William Densham and Joseph Ogle, *The story of the Congregational churches of Dorset, from their foundation to the present time* ([Bournemouth, Eng., 1899]). H. P. Smith, *History of the Lodge of Amity No.137, Poole* (Poole, Eng., 1937). J. W. Davies, "A historical note on the Reverend John Clinch, first Canadian vaccinator," Canadian Medical Assoc., *Journal* (Toronto), 102 (1970): 957–61.

COFFIN, JOHN, businessman, militia officer, and office holder; b. 19 Aug. 1729 in Boston, Mass., son of William and Ann Coffin; d. 25 Sept. 1808 at Quebec, Lower Canada.

At the outbreak of the American revolution John Coffin was established in Boston as a merchant, distiller, and shipowner. Although usually discreet and reserved, he did not conceal his loyalist sentiments; nor did other members of his family, some of whom decided to emigrate. He himself reached Quebec early in August 1775 on his schooner *Neptune*, with his wife, Isabella Child, their 11 children, and a few belongings.

Upon arrival Coffin bought a lot at Près-de-Ville, on the St Lawrence at the foot of Cap Diamant, and set about building a distillery there. But with American

Coffin

troops on the verge of attacking Quebec, the site was hastily converted into a defensive post and fitted out with guns. Coffin volunteered for the militia and joined a small force which early on the morning of 31 Dec. 1775, during a violent storm, stopped the attack led by Major-General Richard Montgomery*, killing him and turning back his men. Governor Guy CARLETON, militia captain Thomas AINSLIE, and lieutenant-colonels Henry CALDWELL and Allan Maclean* attributed this success to the militia officers and to Coffin himself. In July 1776 Maclean paid him tribute: "To your resolution and watchfulness . . . in keeping the guard at the Pres-de-Ville under arms, waiting for the attack which you expected; the great coolness with which you allowed the rebels to approach; the spirit which your example kept up among the men, and the very critical instant in which you directed Capt. [Adam] Barnsfare's fire against Montgomery and his troops, – to those circumstances alone do I ascribe the repulsing the rebels from that important post, where, with their leader, they lost all heart."

In May 1778 Coffin, through William GRANT (1744–1805), the attorney acting for Sir Thomas Mills* who was away in London, bought the house on Rue Saint-Louis which had formerly belonged to Michel-Jean-Hugues Péan* and in which Louis-Joseph de Montcalm* had died; Coffin had already been living in it for "about three years." He was unable, however, to pay immediately the £1,000 that the land, house, sheds, and other outbuildings were worth. In the period 1778–81 he borrowed £465 from Thomas DUNN, and in March 1780 he signed a note to Grant for £1,058 to pay for his property, yet at the end of that year he in turn lent £2,500. In February 1783, as a result of "the misfortunes suffered in his business through the present war," Coffin could not honour his obligations to Grant and therefore ceded him his house as repayment for the debt. He went to live at Près-de-Ville, on the site of his distillery, and then after 1785 returned to Rue Saint-Louis. In 1790 he obtained a loan of £190 from Jacob Jordan*, to whom he still owed £150 in March 1801.

As a loyalist Coffin presented numerous claims to the government, for example in 1776, 1778, 1783, and 1784. He estimated the rebel damages to his establishment and his ship at £961, not counting the confiscation of his property by Massachusetts in 1779. He also asked the British government for a land grant, and in 1802 received a certificate generously promising him, his wife, and nine of their children 1,200 acres of land apiece. These grants were to be taken up in the townships reserved for loyalists, but no exact place or period of time was specified. Because the letters patent for each 200-acre lot cost £5, Coffin and his immediate family did not follow up this offer; one of his grandsons, Lieutenant-Colonel William Foster

Coffin*, did avail himself of it and obtained 1,200 acres of land in 1864.

Nevertheless John Coffin probably found compensation in the various offices he held. He was made a justice of the peace for the District of Quebec in 1785, and a lieutenant in the Quebec Battalion of British Militia in 1787. Late in December of that year Carleton, now Lord Dorchester, appointed him one of the commissioners to inquire into the whole matter of the Jesuit estates [see Augustin-Louis de Glapion*]. By 1788 at the latest, he held the posts of deputy surveyor general of woods and deputy inspector of police at Quebec. The following year his name was listed as one of the owners of the first bridge across the Saint-Charles, which was called the Dorchester Bridge; in this capacity he was authorized to levy tolls for its use [see David LYND]. In July 1794 he became commissioner of police for the town and district of Quebec, with a salary of £100 a year, and in August was made a captain in his militia battalion. In 1795 he received another promotion, this time to the post of surveyor general of woods for Lower Canada, a sinecure with an annual salary of £200 which he enjoyed for the rest of his life. In subsequent years Coffin received various commissions, including one for administering the oath to members of the Legislative Council and the House of Assembly and another for examining applications for crown lands. He was also one of the commissioners named to superintend the House of Correction at Quebec. He carried out these responsibilities until his death on 25 Sept. 1808. On three occasions his widow petitioned for a pension, but no action was taken upon her requests.

A confirmed loyalist, John Coffin helped to support the British crown in his adopted country by his own actions and by his family's influence. From the time of its founding at Quebec in June 1794 he had been a member of an association established to uphold the British government in Lower Canada. Of his family, to which two more children had been born after his arrival in Canada, two sons, Thomas* and Nathaniel*, were members of the assembly, as was his son-in-law John CRAIGIE, who was married to his daughter Susannah. His son William became a captain in the 15th Foot, James was assistant commissary general in the army at Quebec, and John, perhaps preceded in office by his father, held the post of deputy commissary general from 1794 to 1800. His daughter Margaret married Roger Hale Sheaffe*, who succeeded Sir Isaac BROCK as military commander in Upper Canada.

MARIE-PAULE LaBRÈQUE

ANQ-Q, CE1-61, 23 sept. 1808; CN1-25, 22 mai 1778, 23 mars 1780, 6 févr. 1783, 29 juill. 1784; CN1-83, 1er juill.

Coffin

1784; 13 juin 1785; 31 mai, 30 juill. 1790; 30 déc. 1793; CN1-178, 21 mai 1800; CN1-205, 23 août 1775, 19 sept. 1777, 31 juill. 1781; CN1-230, 30 mars 1801; CN1-262, 29 août 1797. PAC, RG 4, A1: 18850, 20057. Bas-Canada, chambre d'Assemblée, *Journaux*, 1795: 89–90. Ainslie, *Canada preserved* (Cohen), 36. *Blockade of Quebec in 1775–1776 by the American revolutionists (les Bastonnais)*, ed. F. C. Würtele (Quebec, 1906; repr. Port Washington, N.Y., and London, 1970), 103–4. Boston, Registry Dept., *Records relating to the early history of Boston*, ed. W. H. Whitmore et al. (39v., Boston, 1876–1909), [5]: *N.I. Bowditch, "Gleaner" articles*, 238. *Doc. relatifs à l'hist. constitutionnelle, 1759–1791* (Shortt et Doughty; 1921), 1: 721–23. "United Empire Loyalists: inquiry into losses and services," AO *Report*, 1904: 343. *Quebec Gazette*, 10 Aug. 1775; 12 May 1785; 26 July 1787; 3, 31 July, 23 Oct. 1794; 3 Sept. 1795; 29 Sept. 1808.

Quebec almanac, 1788: 18, 20, 47; 1796: 82; 1798: 82; 1800: 88–89; 1801: 75; 1805: 18–19, 21, 27, 40; 1808: 19, 21. F.-J. Audet et Fabre Surveyer, *Les députés au premier Parl. du Bas-Canada*, 70. Langelier, *Liste des terrains concédés*, 1270. "Papiers d'État," PAC *Rapport*, 1890: 305–6, 327. "Papiers d'État – Bas-Canada," PAC *Rapport*, 1891: 15, 114; 1893: 32, 34, 44, 60. "Papiers d'État – Bas-Canada, 1787–1841," PAC *Rapport*, 1930: 27. J. M. LeMoine, *St. Louis Street and its storied past . . .* (Quebec, 1891), 9. P.-G. Roy, *La ville de Québec sous le Régime français* (2v., Québec, 1930), 2: 356. Stanley, *L'invasion du Canada* (MacDonald), 98–99, 112–15. Stark, *Loyalists of Mass.* (1910), 125, 137, 234, 243–46. Ivanhoë Caron, "Les censitaires du coteau Sainte-Geneviève (banlieue de Québec) de 1636 à 1800," *BRH*, 27 (1921): 164. P.-B. Casgrain, "La maison d'Arnoux où Montcalm est mort," *BRH*, 9 (1903): 71. W. F. Coffin, "On some additional incidents in connection with the siege and blockade of Quebec, in 1775–6," Literary and Hist. Soc. of Quebec, *Trans.* (Quebec), new ser., 10 (1872–73): 5–20. Philéas Gagnon, "Le premier pont sur la rivière Saint-Charles," *BRH*, 4 (1898): 55. P.-G. Roy, "La famille Coffin," *BRH*, 40 (1934): 229–32; "Sir Jeffery Amherst et les biens des jésuites," *BRH*, 12 (1906): 153.

COFFIN, THOMAS ASTON, office holder; b. 31 March 1754 in Boston, Mass., son of William Coffin and his wife Mary; one daughter, Sarah, was born of his liaison with Sarah Johnston, and he and Louise Bertin of the *faubourg* Saint-Roch, Quebec, had two others, Marie-Louise and Louisa; d. 31 May 1810 in London, England.

Thomas Aston Coffin studied at Harvard College, Boston, where he obtained his AB in 1772. He remained loyal to the crown during the American revolution, as did other members of his family, including his uncle JOHN, who emigrated to Quebec in 1775. When the war ended, Coffin was private secretary to Sir Guy CARLETON, commander-in-chief of British forces in North America; Carleton had been sent to New York in 1782 to oversee, with others, the evacuation of the loyalists and His Majesty's troops. This mission completed, Carleton embarked for England on the *Ceres* late in 1783, accompanied by

Coffin. In London Coffin was part of Brook WATSON's circle, Watson being the chief author of Carleton's appointment as governor general in 1786.

Appointed civil secretary and controller of public accounts by Carleton, now Lord Dorchester, Coffin arrived at Quebec on 23 Oct. 1786 with the new governor general and the new chief justice, William Smith*. A recognized expert in his field, Coffin also sat on the board of examiners of the public accounts of the army for the province beginning in February 1789. In addition to these public offices, he was appointed an attorney for Brook Watson and Company in November 1793, along with David LYND and James Monk*, to look after this London firm's interests in the province. In 1796 Coffin was named to the new post of inspector general of public accounts, created because of increasing public revenues, with a salary of about £665. He also became a justice of the peace for the District of Quebec in June 1799.

Like many other office holders, Coffin was active in the life of the community. He gave financial assistance to the Agriculture Society, founded in 1789, and was one of its first members. He also supported the Quebec Fire Society to which he regularly subscribed. In November 1793 he contributed to a relief fund for victims of a fire on Rue du Sault-au-Matelot. Coffin was one of those who signed an address reaffirming their loyalty to the crown and the constitution which was presented to Prince EDWARD AUGUSTUS in January 1794 on his departure from Quebec. Five years later Coffin donated to a fund to assist Great Britain's war effort against France.

When the British authorities decided to establish the headquarters of the commander-in-chief for British North America in Halifax, N.S., in 1799, Coffin was obliged to move there and resign his civil offices in Quebec. By way of compensation he received from the War Office an appointment as controller general of army accounts in British North America and an increase in salary. But after being summoned back to England, he was able to settle permanently at Quebec while retaining his new duties.

Coffin amassed a sizeable fortune which he invested in property. In November 1802 he bought three pieces of land on Grande Allée for £324 cash. During February 1803 he purchased two houses on Rue Saint-Louis for a total of £1,050, of which he paid £650 in cash. In addition, he lent almost £4,800 to commissary general John CRAIGIE in October 1804.

In 1804 Thomas Aston Coffin was able to resume his position as inspector general of public accounts. He was recalled to England in 1807, however, and replaced by John Hale*. In December 1808 he auctioned off his library of more than 600 volumes of valuable books as well as various articles, including "a quantity of handsome china, plated [vases], . . . a capital beaver coat." The *Quebec Gazette* announced the following October the sale at auction of "HIS valuable HOUSEHOLD FURNITURE . . . Brussels Carpets . . . about 20 superb Paintings and Prints. – Views in Bohemia, Isle of Wight," and "several setts of Elegant Chintz window Curtains." Coffin died at London in 1810. The following year his estate put his "handsome well built Stone HOUSE" up for sale. The house had been constructed in 1796 on a lot on Rue Saint-Louis acquired from François Baillairgé* in August 1795; with the houses of Jonathan Sewell* and Thomas Place, it had introduced to Quebec the Palladian design then common in England and the United States.

MARCEL CAYA

ANQ-Q, CN1-83, 8 juin 1789, 26 août 1794; CN1-224, 30 déc. 1788; CN1-230, 17 août, 1er sept. 1795; 26 nov. 1799; 16 oct. 1804; CN1-256, 21 nov. 1793; 11 févr., 18 juin, 14 juill. 1795; CN1-262, 16, 18 avril 1796; 29 sept. 1797; 20 nov. 1802; 16, 22 févr. 1803; 20 avril 1804; 28 mars 1805; CN1-284, 9 déc. 1795, 16 févr. 1796. PAC, MG 23, GII, 20; MG 30, D1, 8: 545–46; RG 4, A1, 12 June, 11 Sept. 1799; 31 Dec. 1804; RG 8, I (C ser.), 223: 136; 224: 86, 91–92. Boston, Registry Dept., *Records relating to the early history of Boston*, ed. W. H. Whitmore *et al.* (39v., Boston, 1876–1909). Smith, *Diary and selected papers* (Upton). *Montreal Gazette*, 20 Aug. 1810. *Quebec Gazette*, 23 April 1789; 28 Jan., 25 March 1790; 5 May 1791; 11 April, 28 Nov. 1793; 13 Feb. 1794; 4 June 1795; 29 June 1797; 21 March, 10 Oct. 1799; 10 April 1800; 26 May 1803; 14 June 1804; 27 June 1805; 1 Dec. 1808; 12 Oct. 1809; 21, 28 March 1811. *Quebec almanac*, 1791: 38, 82; 1792: 104, 109; 1794: 71, 122; 1796: 64; 1797: 132; 1798: 86; 1799: 80; 1800: 90, 93; 1801: 77, 80; 1805: 17, 27. Bouchette, *Topographical description of L.C.*, 451. Doris Drolet Dubé et Marthe Lacombe, *Inventaire des marchés de construction des Archives nationales à Québec, XVIIe et XVIIIe siècles* (Ottawa, 1977), 208, 388. Kelley, "Jacob Mountain," ANQ *Rapport*, 1942–43: 215–16. "Papiers d'État," PAC *Rapport*, 1890: 273–74. "Papiers d'État – Bas-Canada," PAC *Rapport*, 1891: 28–29, 67–68, 126, 131, 198; 1892: 207; 1893: 4. Wallace, *Macmillan dict.* Caron, *La colonisation de la prov. de Québec*, 2: 256. Ruddel, "Quebec City, 1765–1831," 573. Stark, *Loyalists of Mass.* (1910), 234.

COGOLIN, Marquis de CHABERT, JOSEPH-BERNARD DE CHABERT DE. *See* CHABERT

COHEN, JACOB RAPHAEL, Jewish minister; b. *c.* 1738, perhaps on the Barbary Coast; m. 5 Dec. 1764 Rebecca Luria in London, England, and they had five daughters and a son; d. 9 Sept. 1811 in Philadelphia, Pa.

Jacob Raphael Cohen was educated in London where he became a *mohel* or ritual circumciser. When in 1777 or 1778 the Spanish-Portuguese congregation of London, Shaar Hashomayim, was asked by the Shearith Israel congregation in Montreal to recom-

mend a spiritual leader, they suggested Cohen. Ministers without ordination as rabbis – men of piety with dedication to the obligations of their office – have not been uncommon in Jewish history. On 13 Feb. 1778 Cohen was engaged for three years at £50 per annum to act as *shochet* (ritual slaughterer), *hazan* (precentor), teacher of Hebrew and of the religious tradition, and reader from the sacred scrolls of the Pentateuch. The engagement was made in London on behalf of the Montreal congregation by the merchant Hyam Myers, who had lived in Montreal from the early 1760s to 1774.

Cohen probably arrived at Montreal in 1779, the first minister to a Jewish community in the province of Quebec. His congregation consisted largely of the families of successful merchants who had come to the new British colony during and immediately after the conquest from England, the American colonies, Barbados, Jamaica, and Curaçao. In the early 1760s perhaps ten per cent of Montreal's merchants had been Jews but, since commercial conditions there had proved to be difficult, most had soon left for New York City or Philadelphia. Nevertheless, on 30 Dec. 1768 those who remained had formed Shearith Israel, the earliest Jewish congregation in Canada. Although the majority of its members were Ashkenazim, descendants of German and East European Jews, they had adopted the Spanish-Portuguese Sephardic rite, practised in the senior institution of British Jewry, London's Shaar Hashomayim Synagogue, with which they had maintained constant contact.

As prescribed by Sephardic custom, the social and religious life of the Montreal congregation was supervised, almost autocratically, by the *junta* or communal heads, all zealous adherents to aristocracy, conservatism, and orthodoxy. In 1768 the founders of the congregation had been accorded a double vote on all matters brought up at communal meetings, a privilege they could pass on to their eldest sons. In this manner internal unity and a strong orthodox spirit had been forged, so that by 1777, although small, the congregation was sufficiently established to build a synagogue, Shearith Israel, the first north of the Thirteen Colonies; it was constructed on a site on Rue Notre-Dame, which had been made available to the congregation by the David family [*see* David David*].

Cohen probably ministered, according to Sephardic custom, under the strict control of the powerful lay committee. One of his earliest ceremonies appears to have been a blessing for three benefactors of the synagogue, Abraham Judah, Phoebe Samuel, and Naphtali Joseph; blessings were also said for the congregations in London, New York, Curaçao, and Surinam. Cohen extended his services to Jewish communities outside Montreal: at Trois-Rivières he performed the circumcision ceremonies for two of

Colen

Aaron Hart*'s sons, Benjamin* in 1779 and Asher Alexander in 1782. The Jewish communities were small, however, numbering only 20 families in Montreal and five in Trois-Rivières and Berthier combined, and in the three years of his ministry Cohen performed only four circumcisions and two marriages. In 1781 Cohen made his own translation of an ancient and complex halachic document, the Aramaic *ketuba* or marriage contract, probably not rendered into English previously.

Cohen's incumbency appears to have been satisfactory to his congregation and peaceful, until his last year when he complained of not having been fully paid for the term of his engagement. The congregation split, a minority supporting Cohen, who in September 1782 sued Lucius Levy Solomons*, apparently the *parnas* or lay leader of the congregation, for £50. Cohen won his case in the Court of Common Pleas but the decision was reversed on a technicality in the Court of Appeals on 6 May 1784.

Cohen had departed for England in 1782 but found himself stranded in New York City, where his ship had been diverted to repatriate British troops. The Jewish community there was temporarily without a minister, their *hazan*, Gershom Mendas Seixas, a supporter of the revolution, having fled to Philadelphia. Cohen filled the position of *hazan* until Seixas's return in 1784, at which time he left to replace Seixas at the Mikveh Israel Synagogue of Philadelphia. Cohen died at Philadelphia in 1811 and was replaced as *hazan* by his son, Abraham Haim.

Following Cohen's departure from Montreal, Shearith Israel had begun to go into a long decline, in part as a result of the government's refusal to recognize it as an incorporated body; it was, in consequence, prevented from maintaining legal registers of births, marriages, and deaths, and experienced problems of administration and property ownership. In the course of the ensuing decades the congregation almost disintegrated. During this time it was served by laymen, and occasionally by the clergy of the New York congregation; in 1803 a layman from Rivière-du-Loup (Louiseville), Barnett Lyons, officiated at the marriage of Henry Joseph* and Rachel Solomons at Berthier-en-Haut (Berthierville), and in 1811 the minister of the Shearith Israel Synagogue of New York, the Reverend Jacques Judah Lyons, circumcised the sons of Ezekiel* and Benjamin Hart at Montreal, and of Henry Joseph at Berthier-en-Haut. When the Montreal congregation obtained legal recognition in 1830, its renewal commenced; however, it was not until 1840, when it appointed David Piza, that it was again able to support a permanent *hazan*.

DAVID ROME

[Jacob Raphael Cohen kept a record book of his activities as a minister which is one of the important sources for Jewish history in North America in the late 18th and early 19th centuries. In addition to the list of circumcisions, marriages, and burials, it provides a written description of liturgies, a rare find in the Jewish tradition. It has been published by A. D. Corré and M. H. Stern as "The record book of the Reverend Jacob Raphael Cohen" in *American Jewish Hist. Quarterly* (New York), 59 (1969): 23–82. D.R.]

PAC, MG 11, [CO 42] Q, 33: 17–30. *First American Jewish families*, comp. M. H. Stern (Cincinnati, Ohio, and Waltham, Mass., n.d.), 180. Solomon Frank, *Two centuries in the life of a synagogue* (n.p., n.d.), 28–60. A. M. Hyamson, *The Sephardim of England; a history of the Spanish and Portuguese Jewish community, 1492–1951* (London, 1951), 150. Louis Rosenberg, *Some aspects of the historical development of the Canadian Jewish community* (Montreal, n.d.). B. G. Sack, *History of the Jews in Canada, from the earliest beginnings to the present day*, [trans. Ralph Novek] (Montreal, 1945). Edwin Wolf and Maxwell Whiteman, *The history of the Jews of Philadelphia from colonial times to the age of Jackson* (Philadelphia, 1957), 124, 141–42, 190, 195, 203, 244–47. [B. G. Sack], "A suit at law involving the first Jewish minister in Canada," *American Jewish Hist. Soc., Pubs.* ([New York]), 31 (1928): 181–86.

COLEN, JOSEPH, HBC chief factor; b. *c.* 1751 in England; d. July 1818 in Cirencester, England.

In April 1785, having had extensive experience in both "mechanic & mercantile Affairs" and being "perfect master of his Pen in writing and figures," Joseph Colen was engaged as a writer by the Hudson's Bay Company for five years at £20 per annum. He was to assist Humphrey Marten*, chief at York Factory (Man.), and to oversee the rebuilding of the factory, destroyed in 1782 by Jean-François de Galaup*, Comte de Lapérouse – a project that was too much of a burden for the gouty Marten.

Marten retired in 1786 and William Tomison*, his successor as chief factor, was ordered to reside inland. Consequently, Colen was appointed resident chief at York at £40 per annum plus a premium on made beaver. Though in command at the factory, Colen was subject to the orders of Tomison when the latter visited York. On taking up his new appointment Colen was directed by the HBC's London committee to forward "the building of a new Factory." In 1793 the last flanker was covered and two years later the stockade enclosed three acres of ground, one-half of which was "occupied by buildings – The rest intended for Gardens."

To meet the competition from the North West Company south and west of York Factory, Colen had sent men inland to establish new posts: in 1790 Charles Thomas ISHAM settled on Swan River (Man.) and James Spence went to Split Lake, and in 1791 William Hemmings Cook* built Chatham House on

Wintering Lake. In 1794 Colen tried to organize an expedition to the Athabasca country and ordered boats for use on the inland waterways. That spring he travelled about 109 miles up the Hayes River on the first wooden boat ever to navigate inland from Hudson Bay, and there he selected a site for a provisioning depot which was to be called Gordon House. Its position considerably shortened the route travelled by the inland traders, who now needed to bring their canoes only as far as Gordon House to exchange their furs for supplies brought from York by boat.

Colen's position as resident chief was not an easy one. Tomison did not cooperate on the Athabasca expedition, did not approve of boats, and in general tried to thwart every plan that did not benefit the posts on the Saskatchewan River. In 1794 Colen returned to London to report to the governor and committee on various aspects of the trade. When he arrived back at York the following year he had been appointed chief factor at an annual salary of £130 plus £10 for a servant. The change in status was based on the premise that Tomison would be retiring in 1795. The expected retirement did not occur, however, and that year Tomison established Fort Edmonton (Edmonton, Alta). In 1796, 1797, and 1798 Colen journeyed to Gordon House to hold councils and contract with the inland men. New posts were established and much time devoted to inland transport.

Colen was recalled by the London committee in 1798; his salary was terminated in March 1799. The reasons were not stated, but one was the impatience of the committee with the jealousy and rivalry between Colen and Tomison. In conducting affairs at York Colen was hampered by his lack of knowledge of inland operations, and he was lax in overseeing the accounting of the York Factory goods and provisions. In fairness to Colen it should be said that he was a man of ideas, an innovator and a thinker, rather than a shrewd businessman. These characteristics are demonstrated by his interests in medicine, tree husbandry, the distilling operation at York, and the collecting of shrubs for London, and by his possessing at York Factory a personal library of some 1,400 volumes.

On his retirement from the company Colen apparently did not return to business life, but he was an active member of the Society for the Encouragement of Arts, Manufactures, and Commerce, in London. Sought out in 1802 by Lord Selkirk [DOUGLAS] for an opinion on his scheme to introduce Scottish emigrants to present-day Manitoba through Hudson Bay, Colen gave a favourable opinion. Colen appears to have spent the last ten years of his life in Cirencester.

SHIRLEE ANNE SMITH

PAM, HBCA, A.1/46: f.51; A.1/47: ff.58, 126; A.5/2: ff.127d, 147d, 148–49; A.5/3: ff.46, 56d, 83, 136; A.5/4: ff.51–51d; A.6/13: ff.156–56d; A.6/15: ff.23, 64, 137; A.6/16: f.54d; A.11/116: ff.87, 129, 133; A.11/117: ff.59d, 114d–15; B.239/a/85: f.44; B.239/a/91: ff.4, 6–6d, 10–10d, 31d, 33; B.239/a/95: ff.17d, 20d; B.239/a/96: ff.1, 8d, 9d, 27d, 30d, 32d, 33–34, 40d, 58d; B.239/a/99: ff.3, 6–6d, 15d–16; B.239/a/100: ff.15d–16, 23–24, 26–26d; B.239/a/102: ff.3, 6, 7d, 39d; B.239/b/58: ff.116–17, 126–27d; B.239/b/79: ff.2d–4; F.3/2: ff.63d–64. Royal Soc. Arch. (London), MC 1 (40), Joseph Colen to Joseph Banks, 29 Dec. 1811 (transcript at PAM, HBCA). *Gentleman's Magazine*, July–December 1818: 88. *Journals of Hearne and Turnor* (Tyrrell), 593. *Saskatchewan journals and correspondence: Edmonton House, 1795–1800; Chesterfield House, 1800–1802*, ed. A. M. Johnson (London, 1967). Soc. for the Encouragement of Arts, Manufactures, and Commerce, *Trans.* (London), 13 (1795)–22 (1804).

COLLACHIE. *See* MACDONELL

COLLET, CHARLES-ANGE, Roman Catholic priest and canon; b. 1 Oct. 1721 at Fort Saint-Joseph (Niles, Mich.), son of Claude Collet, a soldier in the colonial regular troops, and Marguerite Fauché; d. some time after July 1801.

In 1726 or 1727 Claude Collet came to live in Montreal (Que.), and his son, Charles-Ange, attended one of the very few classical schools established in the town at that time. In 1743 Charles-Ange went to continue his studies at the Séminaire de Québec, where he was the recipient of an allowance accorded to poor pupils. The following year Collet presumably began studying theology, and on 8 December he received the tonsure and minor orders. The bishop of Quebec, Henri-Marie Dubreil* de Pontbriand, ordained him to the priesthood on 23 Sept. 1747, and some months later Collet became priest in charge of the parish of Saint-Pierre at Sorel; he remained there at least until September 1750.

However, by 1748 at the latest, Collet, for unknown reasons, had expressed the desire to return to work at the seminary in Quebec. Bishop Pontbriand and the Séminaire des Missions Étrangères in Paris considered his request, and on 12 Aug. 1751 he was admitted as a member of the community of the Séminaire de Québec. In Collet's case the seminary disregarded one of its rules and gave him the privilege of retaining the honoraria for the masses he offered, in order to help his poor relatives. From the time he joined the seminary until he left for France, Collet acted as curate in the parish of Notre-Dame, at the same time serving the church of Notre-Dame-des-Victoires. On a couple of occasions, one of them in 1757, he preached at the clergy retreat. On 2 June 1758 the bishop of Quebec honoured him with a canonry conferring the dignity of penitentiary, as a

Collver

replacement for Canon Joseph-Thierry Hazeur* who had died the year before. Since he was thereby provided with the small fixed personal income enjoyed by the canons of the chapter of the cathedral of Quebec, Collet gave up his membership in the community of the seminary.

At the beginning of the siege of Quebec by the British in 1759, Collet and his colleague Gilles-Louis Cugnet were put in charge of a temporary hospital. Later Collet went to join Canon Pierre-Joseph Resche* at the Ursuline convent to find shelter in the long hours of bombardment. Collet, Resche, and Cugnet were present at Louis-Joseph de Montcalm*'s funeral, which was held in the Ursuline chapel on 14 September. In the autumn Collet received the approval of the vicar general, Jean-Olivier Briand*, to depart for France in search of a better climate for his health. He left Canada on one of the British vessels assigned to repatriating the French garrison. Briand later called this departure a "desertion." Wanting to act as chaplain during the crossing, Collet even borrowed a vestment from the chapter and a chalice to say mass at sea.

Charles-Ange Collet never returned to Canada. He retired to Thiais, south of Paris, where he apparently was put in charge of a small parish. The letters he sent to Canada nevertheless give evidence of his regret at having left the country, especially when the French revolution broke out. At that time, like many other non-juring priests, he had to flee to England and no trace of him has been found after July 1801. He was at that time the last surviving member of the chapter of Quebec, which had, indeed, ceased to exist after the conquest.

HONORIUS PROVOST

ASQ, Fonds Viger-Verreau, Sér.O, 019; Lettres, M: 117; P: 120–21; R: 16; S: 6, 6bis, 90, 107; MSS, 12: f.18; Polygraphie, VII: 21, 27: XVIII: 11–15; Séminaire, 7, no.72a; 11, no.25. [Catherine Burke, *dite* de Saint-Thomas], *Les ursulines de Québec, depuis leur établissement jusqu'à nos jours* (4v., Québec, 1863–66), 2: 323. A.-E. Gosselin, *L'Église du Canada après la Conquête*, 1: 153; "Le chanoine Charles-Ange Collet," *BRH*, 30 (1924): 389–96.

COLLVER (Culver), JABEZ, settler and Presbyterian minister; b. 19 June 1731 in Groton, Conn., second son of John Collver and Freelove Lamb; m. Anna —, and they had 13 children; d. 29 Dec. 1818 in Windham Township, Upper Canada.

Jabez Collver's ancestors settled in Connecticut in the 17th century. Many of them became Rogerenes, a religious sect persecuted by the Connecticut colonists; his grandfather therefore took his entire family to New Jersey shortly after Jabez Collver's birth. There his father, a shoemaker, died in 1733. The family settled near Schooley's Mountain, Morris County, where Jabez presumably received his scant education. He

experienced "spiritual manifestations" and in 1760 was ordained "according to the Cambridge Presbyterian order," which combined elements of the Congregational and Presbyterian doctrines. He moved north to Sussex County, buying land there in 1774, and was pastor of the Beemer (Congregational) Meeting-House at Wantage for many years.

Some sources state that Collver served as a chaplain in the Continental Army during the American revolution, but in 1794 he claimed that he had been imprisoned and had lost considerable property because of his loyalty, and in 1798 he petitioned, though unsuccessfully, for loyalist status. During or before 1788 he moved to Chemung Township, N.Y., where he and his family acquired 1,200 acres. He was the first resident minister in the area, but "did not preach much," spending most of his time farming and speculating in land. He conveyed all his property to his sons in 1791, and moved down the Susquehanna River to Wysox, Pa.

In 1792, encouraged by Lieutenant Governor John Graves SIMCOE's proclamation of 7 February "to such as are desirous to settle" in Upper Canada, Collver came to the province and received "such private encouragement" from Simcoe "in person" that he "ventured to remove . . . into the Province." In the spring of 1794 Collver, aged 62, immigrated with his wife, some of his family, and his livestock. Eventually seven sons, one daughter, and a number of grandchildren and cousins came to Upper Canada. Collver petitioned for land on 11 June 1794 and three days later received a grant of 1,000 acres, which he patented on 12 March 1797. Most of the land was in Windham Township, Norfolk County, where he lived; his relatives were also given land, much of it in the same county. In his petition he stressed his loyalty, the size of his family, and his meeting with Simcoe, but did not mention his ordination.

There was apparently some doubt about his status as a minister. The Marriage Act of 1798 permitted ministers "of the Church of Scotland, or Lutherans, or Calvinists" to perform marriages if they were licensed by the Court of Quarter Sessions for their district [*see* Elijah BENTLEY]. When Collver applied for his licence on 12 April 1800, his credentials were at first accepted, but at the next session, on 8 July, Chairman Samuel RYERSE protested and the application was refused. Collver brought forward seven members of his congregation, including three sons and a cousin, but was again refused. He was finally licensed on 13 March 1804. He had, however, been performing marriages illegally since at least 1795.

For almost 25 years Collver worked as a farmer and minister in Norfolk County. He was the second resident Presbyterian minister in Upper Canada and throughout his ministry the only one living west of the Niagara peninsula. He was a typical backwoods

196

preacher, visiting the isolated clearings in a home-made cart. He did not attend the first meeting of the Presbytery of the Canadas in 1818, probably because of age and distance, but possibly because his lack of "academical education" did not merit an invitation. Collver was also a typical immigrant of the Simcoe period, a so-called late loyalist. He spent his entire life along the fringe of settlement in America, moving often in search of land.

In his old age Collver wrote a lengthy manuscript account of his religious experiences; by 1906 it was no longer extant. After the death of his son Nathan in 1792 he was responsible for publishing *A very remarkable account of the vision of Nathan Culver*, which went into many editions.

EDITH G. FIRTH

AO, RG 1, A-I-6: 609–10, 2223–24. Donly Museum, Norfolk Hist. Soc. coll., Thomas Welch papers, 1013–14; Miscellaneous papers, 4806–9. MTL, D. W. Smith papers. PAC, RG 1, L3, 89: C1/12. [Nathan Culver], *A very remarkable account of the vision of Nathan Culver, late of Newtown (New-York)* . . . (Windsor, Vt., 1793; 5th ed., Boston, 1795; Portsmouth, N.H., 1796), repr. under title *The remarkable vision of Nathan Collver* . . . (Cobourg, [Ont.], 1846). H. S. McCollum, "Some old Presbyterian documents," *Canada Presbyterian* (Toronto), 7 Feb. 1879: 226–27. "Minutes of the Court of General Quarter Sessions of the Peace for the London District . . . ," AO *Report*, 1933. [Thomas Proctor], "Narrative of the journey of Col. Thomas Proctor, to the Indians of the north-west, 1791," *Pennsylvania archives* . . . , ed. Samuel Hazard *et al.* (9 ser. in 119 vols., Philadelphia and Harrisburg, Pa., 1852–1935), 2nd ser., 4: 470. U.C., *Statutes*, 1798, c.4. "U.C. land book D," AO *Report*, 1931: 174. *Sources in Collver-Culver genealogy*, ed. William Yeager (Simcoe, 1976). T. F. Chambers, *The early Germans of New Jersey: their history, churches and genealogies* ([Dover, N.J., 1895]; repr. Baltimore, Md., 1969), 297–99. W. J. Dey, "An historical sketch of St. Paul's Church, Simcoe, 1793–1906," W. J. Dey and Elsie Little, *St. Paul's Presbyterian Church, Simcoe, Ontario, 160th anniversary, 1793–1953* ([Simcoe?, 1953]): 1–21. William Gregg, *History of the Presbyterian Church in the dominion of Canada* . . . (Toronto, 1885; 2nd ed., 1905). *History of Sussex and Warren counties, New Jersey, with illustrations and biographical sketches of its prominent men and pioneers*, comp. J. P. Snell *et al.* (Philadelphia, 1881), 297. E. A. Owen, *Pioneer sketches of Long Point settlement* . . . (Toronto, 1898; repr. Belleville, Ont., 1972). H. B. Peirce and D. H. Hurd, *History of Tioga, Chemung, Tompkins and Schuyler counties, New York; with illustrations and biographical sketches of some of its prominent men and pioneers* (Philadelphia, 1879), 238. W. H. Wood, "Additions and corrections to the Colver-Culver genealogy," ed. D. L. Jacobus, *American Genealogist* (New Haven, Conn.), 31 (1955): 129–54.

COLNETT, JAMES, ship's captain and maritime fur trader; he may possibly have been the same person as the James Collnett baptized 18 Oct. 1753 in Stoke Damerel (Plymouth), England, son of James Collnett and Sarah —; d. September 1806 in London, England.

James Colnett began his naval career as an able seaman in the *Hazard* on 28 June 1770. On 4 September of the following year he became a midshipman under James Cook* in the *Scorpion*, and transferred to the *Resolution* when the great explorer was readying for his second Pacific voyage. During the expedition, Colnett sighted New Caledonia on 4 Sept. 1774, and Cook named Cape Colnett on that island after him. Having demonstrated skills in navigation, Colnett became master of the *Adventure* during the American Revolutionary War; subsequently he rose to first lieutenant of the *Bienfaisant* and then the *Pegase* before being placed on half pay on 17 Aug. 1786. About a month later he obtained Admiralty permission to command the expedition of the *Prince of Wales* and the *Princess Royal* (Charles Duncan*, master), owned by Richard Cadman Etches and Company (also known as the King George's Sound Company) and bound on a trading voyage to the northwest coast of North America and to China. Leaving England in 1786, Colnett first visited the northwest coast the following year; he traded there for two summers, wintering in the Sandwich (Hawaiian) Islands, and reached Canton (People's Republic of China) on 12 Nov. 1788. There he became involved with another British trader, John MEARES, who with the King George's Sound partners formed the Associated Merchants Trading to the Northwest Coast of America that winter. Colnett was installed as commodore of the Associated Merchants' fleet of five or six ships, and as the *Prince of Wales* was to return to England with a cargo of tea, another vessel, the *Argonaut*, was purchased.

In accordance with his new employers' instructions, when Colnett left China in the spring of 1789 he took with him in the *Argonaut* 29 Chinese artisans and everything essential for building ships and planting a permanent, well-defended settlement at Nootka Sound (B.C.). To be called Fort Pitt in honour of the prime minister, it would be the first in a series of posts designed to establish British claims to the coast. But at the same time the viceroy of New Spain, Manuel Antonio Flórez, was becoming concerned with the possibility of foreign encroachment, particularly by Russia, along the northwest coast, which was claimed as a Spanish possession. Accordingly, in the spring of 1789 Esteban José Martínez* was sent north with a small expedition to establish a temporary post at Nootka Sound. Thus the stage was set for a clash between Spain and Britain in their contest for trade and dominion in the Pacific.

Colnett reached Nootka Sound from Macao (near Canton) on 2 July 1789 to find that Martínez had established a Spanish settlement. Polite relations between the two men soon deteriorated to the point

Colnett

where a violent argument erupted aboard Martínez's ship, culminating in the arrest of Colnett and the detention of his vessel. "It is likely that the churlish nature of each one precipitated things . . . ," José Mariano Moziño later wrote, "since those who sailed with them both complained of them equally and condemned their uncultivated boorishness." The *Argonaut* and the *Princess Royal* (which had on its arrival on 12 July likewise been seized) were taken into Spanish service, and they and their crews were sent to the Spanish naval headquarters at San Blas (state of Nayarit, Mexico). The prisoners were kept at nearby Tepic, although Colnett was allowed to go to Mexico City in March 1790 for a personal interview with the Count of Revilla Gigedo, Flórez's successor. Revilla Gigedo did not acknowledge that the British position was correct, but under orders from Madrid he told Colnett that the British vessels would be released and compensation made in salaries and provisions. Although he constantly bemoaned the conditions of his confinement, Colnett was in fact courteously treated.

The *Argonaut* and the *Princess Royal* were released on 9 July 1790 and, embarking the English and Chinese who wished to return to Nootka, Colnett set sail, calling at Bodega Bay (Calif.) and Clayoquot Sound (B.C.) before arriving at Nootka in January 1791. Despite being prohibited from trading by Revilla Gigedo, Colnett secured 1,000 sea-otter skins between October 1790 and March 1791, although this involved some deception of Francisco de Eliza* y Reventa, commandant at Nootka. When Colnett arrived at Macao on 30 May he discovered that Chinese ports were closed to fur traders, and on his own initiative he sailed to Japan, becoming the first British trader to attempt to reopen trade with the Japanese since 1673. Having had only minor success in marketing his cargo there and in Macao, he sailed for England, where he sold the remainder to the East India Company for £9,760.

In the mean time the incident at Nootka had caused a serious dispute between Britain and Spain. Stirred up by Meares's somewhat biased and inaccurate account of events, the British government determined to demand Spanish acknowledgement of British rights on the northwest coast. When Spain refused to give it, pressure to declare war arose and a large fleet was outfitted. For its part, the Spanish government was equally ready for a conflict to defend its claims, but was partially dependent on aid from France. When developments during the French revolution rendered this assistance uncertain, Spain was forced to back down. In the Nootka Convention of 1790 she acknowledged the British right to trade and navigation on the northwest coast, and apparently agreed to return all land on Nootka Sound taken from British subjects in 1789. Hereafter increasing pressure from Britain, Russia, and the United States would combine to limit Spanish claims to the northwest coast.

Once back in England, Colnett was nominated by the Admiralty to command the *Rattler*, a merchant ship which was to examine Pacific ports that might be suitable for British whalers. The vessel sailed in January 1793, spent a year in harbours from Chile to Lower California, and returned to England in November 1794. During the voyage Colnett surveyed the Revillagigedo Islands, Coco Island, the Galapagos archipelago, San Ambrosio Island, and San Félix Island, charts of which were published by Aaron Arrowsmith in 1798. Colnett's narrative of this expedition, which appeared the same year, was instrumental in opening up the south Pacific sperm whale fishery and related branches of commerce.

After eight years in the merchant service, Colnett returned to the Royal Navy on 18 Dec. 1794, to be given commander's rank and command of the sloop *Merlin*. He was soon transferred to the *Hawk*, in which he surveyed part of the eastern coastline of England to determine suitable locations for gun emplacements. On 4 Oct. 1796 Colnett was appointed to command the *Hussar*, and was promoted captain the next day. While convoying the East India packet-boat through the English Channel, the ship was wrecked off Brittany, and Colnett and his crew were taken prisoner by the French. After further commands, which included convoy duty in the Baltic, Colnett left active service on 7 March 1805, having spent 35 years at sea. He died in September 1806 at the probable age of 51. Colnett seems never to have married, but his will provided for "the education, clothing, and maintenance of my natural daughter Elizabeth Caroline Colnett, daughter of Catherine Aulte," during her minority. When she reached 21, the balance of the estate of £5,000 was to pass to her.

James Colnett was a capable officer, surveyor, and servant of the crown. At Nootka he acted as a British proconsul and his contribution to the Nootka Sound controversy is well established, though the blame is not his alone. He had a high opinion of himself: his *Argonaut* journal shows he never lost the chance to glorify his position and authority, a hazardous penchant when combined with his frequent boasting of the greatness of the British nation. Martínez's insistence that Spanish claims and rights could not be encroached on led to Colnett's taking what some have regarded as intemperate actions; Meares and others believed Colnett actually became mentally unbalanced as a result of his capture. If this was so, he recovered and was subsequently employed on important tasks in the merchant and naval services. His name survives in the Pacific at Cape Colnett and Colnett Bay on the western coast of Mexico, Cape and

Comingo

Mount Colnett in New Caledonia, Colnett Strait (Tokara Kaikyō) south of Japan, and Colnett Mountain on Vancouver Island.

BARRY M. GOUGH

James Colnett is the author of *A voyage to the South Atlantic and round Cape Horn into the Pacific Ocean . . .* (London, 1798; repr. Amsterdam and New York, 1968). His *Argonaut* journal, PRO, ADM 55/142, has been published as *The journal of Captain James Colnett aboard the Argonaut from April 26, 1789, to Nov. 3, 1791*, ed. F. W. Howay (Toronto, 1940).

PRO, ADM 55/146. West Devon Record Office (Plymouth, Eng.), St Andrew, Stoke Damerel (Plymouth), Reg. of baptisms, marriages, and burials, 18 Oct. 1753. J. M. Moziño [Losada] Suárez de Figueroa, *Noticias de Nutka: an account of Nootka Sound in 1792*, trans. and ed. I. H. Wilson [Engstrand] (Seattle, Wash., 1970). J. T. Walbran, *British Columbia coast names, 1592–1906 . . .* (Ottawa, 1909; repr. Vancouver, 1979), 102–3. Cook, *Flood tide of empire*. B. M. Gough, *Distant dominion: Britain and the northwest coast of North America, 1579–1809* (Vancouver, 1980).

COLONEL LOUIS. *See* ATIATOHARONGWEN

COMINGO (Comingoe), BRUIN ROMKES (he assumed the name Comingo after his arrival in Nova Scotia; also known as **Mr Brown**), fisherman and German Reformed minister; b. 21 Oct. 1723, probably in Groningen, Netherlands; m. first Ebjen (Eljen; perhaps also known as Fruche) —; m. secondly 4 Sept. 1753 Renée Des Camps in Lunenburg, N.S.; m. there thirdly 1783 Catherine Margaret Bailly; d. there 6 Jan. 1820.

Bruin Romkes Comingo, a wool-comber, was living in the Dutch province of Groningen when he emigrated to Nova Scotia in May 1751. At that time he set sail for Halifax with his wife, Ebjen, and four children as part of a scheme whereby Britain hoped to populate the colony with "foreign Protestants" and thus offset the superior numbers of the Catholic French and their Indian allies. Unable to pay his family's passage, Comingo, like most of his fellow emigrants, travelled as a government redemptioner. Upon arrival in Halifax he was obliged to labour for a time on the public works before being sent with the body of foreign Protestants in June 1753 to establish what is now the town of Lunenburg. Here he received a grant of land and became a fisherman; at some point in the 1760s he appears to have moved to Chester. But the life of an ordinary settler was not to be his fate, for in 1770 he was ordained a minister of the German Reformed Church.

Though the British government had made no allowance for the religious needs of the new settlers in Nova Scotia, there had been a non-Anglican congregation in Halifax from its beginning in 1749, composed mainly of Congregationalists from New England and Presbyterians from the north of Ireland. In Lunenburg, however, many years passed before the foreign Protestants were able to enjoy the services of their own churches. The Reverend Jean-Baptiste Moreau*, a former Roman Catholic priest, had arrived with the settlers in 1753 and had established the Anglican parish of St John in which he ministered to a flock representing a variety of Protestant denominations. Moreau clung to this task until he died in 1770, but by then the division of his congregation according to confession had already begun. In 1769, three years before the Lutheran settlers acquired a minister of their own from Germany, 60 German Reformed families left St John to establish a separate church. After failing to find a suitable minister either in Europe or in the colonies to the south, they chose from among themselves Bruin Romkes Comingo, a man lacking the liberal education and theological training usually required but respected for his piety and integrity.

The Presbyterian and Congregational churches shared a common confession with the German Reformed Church, and the bond among them enabled the local clergy to declare themselves an *ad hoc* presbytery, the first such body in Canada, for the purpose of carrying out the ordination. A great occasion was made of the ceremony, which was held on 3 July 1770 at Mather's (St Matthew's) Church in Halifax in the presence of Governor Lord William Campbell*, members of the Council, and representatives of other denominations. In a sermon the Reverend John Seccombe*, Congregational minister at Chester, argued that grace was to be preferred in a man to educational qualifications and that God had given Comingo the "Tongue of the learned." The three other clergymen present – the Presbyterians James Murdoch (Horton) and James Lyon* (Onslow) and the Congregationalist Benajah Phelps (Cornwallis) – also took an active part in the proceedings: Murdoch, in justifying the ordination of a man who lacked formal theological training, quoted precedents from British churches in similar circumstances; Lyon presented the charge; and Phelps offered the "right hand of fellowship" with a short address.

Details of Comingo's ministry are scant, but it is known that his congregation flourished and contributed in kind to the upkeep of their pastor. When he retired from full-time duties in 1818 – he was then 95 years of age – his Lunenburg flock acquired the services of a German-speaking minister from Europe, Johann Adam Moschell*.

RONALD ROMPKEY

Lunenburg County Registry of Deeds (Chester, N.S.) (mfm. at PANS). PANS, MG 1, 742, no.vi; MG 4, 91, 13 July

199

Compain

1783; 94; 96; MG 100, 125, no.14a (photocopy); Places, Lunenburg County, Winthrop Bell, Reg. of Lunenburg families, 171 (mfm.). PRO, CO 217/11: f.114; 217/14: ff.117, 133. St Andrew's Presbyterian Church (Lunenburg, N.S.), Dutch Reformed Church records, 1770–1870 (mfm. at PANS). St John's Anglican Church (Lunenburg), Reg. of births and marriages, 1752–70, 4 Sept. [1753] (mfm. at PANS). St Paul's Anglican Church (Halifax), Reg. of baptisms, marriages, and burials, 7 Nov. 1751, 4 Sept. 1753, 17 Aug. 1754 (mfm. at PANS). John Seccombe, *A sermon preached at Halifax, July 3d, 1770, at the ordination of the Rev. Bruin Romcas Comingoe to the Dutch Calvanistic Presbyterian congregation at Lunenburg* (Halifax, 1770). *Acadian Recorder*, 22 Jan. 1820. Bell, *Foreign Protestants*. M. B. DesBrisay, *History of the county of Lunenburg* (2nd ed., Toronto, 1895). I. F. Mackinnon, *Settlements and churches in Nova Scotia, 1749–1776* ([Montreal, 1930]). W. C. Murray, "History of St. Matthew's Church, Halifax, N.S.," N.S. Hist. Soc., *Coll.*, 16 (1912): 137–70. Juw fon Wearinga, "Ds. Brún Romkes (Camminga?), 1723–1820," *It Beaken* (Assen, Netherlands), 19 (1957): 216–33; "The first Protestant ordination in Canada; the story of Brún Romkes Comingo, 1723–1820," United Church of Canada, Committee on Arch., *Bull.* (Toronto), 11 (1958): 19–32.

COMPAIN, MARIE-LOUISE, named **Saint-Augustin**, sister of the Congregation of Notre-Dame and superior of the community (superior general); b. 28 Jan. 1747 in Montreal (Que.), daughter of Pierre Compain, *dit* L'Espérance, a wig-maker and barber, and Françoise Vacher; d. there 2 May 1819.

Marie-Louise Compain belonged to a family which had five children who chose the religious life: her brother, Pierre-Joseph COMPAIN, was a priest, two of her sisters became nuns at the Hôtel-Dieu in Montreal, and another followed her into the Congregation of Notre-Dame. Marie-Louise grew up next door to this community, on Rue Saint-Jean-Baptiste in Montreal, and attended its primary school. She entered the noviciate in 1764 and took her vows two years later under the name of Sister Saint-Augustin. In 1768 she began teaching in the mission at Saint-François-de-la-Rivière-du-Sud (Saint-François-de-Montmagny), and in 1774 she was appointed mistress of boarders. The following year she went to teach at Pointe-aux-Trembles (Neuville). She was recalled in 1783 and put in charge of setting up a mission at Saint-Denis on the Richelieu, where the parish priest, François CHERRIER, had just finished building a convent. Sister Saint-Augustin became mistress of novices at the mother house in 1788, and the following year she was named assistant; she fulfilled this responsibility until she was elected superior in 1796. At the end of her six-year term of office she was re-elected, exceptionally, by a two-thirds majority; with the permission of vicar general Jean-Henri-Auguste Roux*, who was superior of both the Sulpician seminary and the Congregation of Notre-Dame, she retained her responsibilities until 1808.

During Sister Saint-Augustin's 12 years as superior, the community was faced with problems related to development and income. There had been 70 sisters in the community in 1760 and 56 at the time of the fire in 1768 [see Marie-Josèphe Maugue-Garreau*]; in 1800 the Congregation of Notre-Dame had only 58 sisters, 30 of whom were serving as teachers in the 12 boarding and other schools. Among the 28 who were living in the mother house there were three classes: aged sisters; high-ranking officers and classroom-sisters who having retired from teaching now held various posts in the pharmacy, sacristy, or infirmary and carried out light manual tasks; and lastly the sisters who had been accepted to do the heavy tasks such as farm work, shoemaking, baking, and candle making. The drop and then stagnation in the community's numbers after the conquest could be attributed to economic conditions in the colony rather than to the change of political régime: the dowry of 2,000 *livres* had become an obstacle to recruiting new members. To overcome this difficulty the coadjutor, Bishop Plessis*, advised Sister Saint-Augustin in 1805: "Do everything possible to increase the number of your members . . . be flexible about dowries . . . remember what I have told you, that the greatest wealth of a community is to have good members."

But at that time the community could not give up any of its sources of income, since it had already lost the largest and most regular one, the annuities paid from France, which had been cut off by the French revolution. Although the first thing that Sister Saint-Augustin had done upon the signing of the Treaty of Amiens between Great Britain and France in 1802 was to write to the procurator of the Congregation of Notre-Dame in Paris, lawyer Jean-Louis Maury, to obtain payment of the arrears in the annuities, the community received only those for 1790 and 1791. Furthermore, the amount of these annuities was sharply reduced, since they had been drawn in the past in assignats (promissory notes issued by the French revolutionary government) and had depreciated when this currency dropped in value. As for the other annuities and arrears, the procurator was pessimistic as long as they were going to be treated like annuities belonging to French citizens. Since war had broken out again between France and Great Britain in 1803, no more annuities were received and, lacking income, the community was forced to sell some property.

In 1808 Sister Saint-Augustin became the assistant, and the next year the mistress of novices. She again assumed responsibility for both the spiritual and temporal affairs of the community in 1814. That year, with the restoration of the Bourbon monarchy in France, the sisters of the congregation had been able to establish relations with Alexandre Maury, the son of their former French procurator. Sister Saint-Augustin learned with satisfaction that the French government would deal justly with the religious communities in Canada that produced documented claims. The Congregation of Notre-Dame was in a position to do this but the liquidation, which was entrusted to two commissions, a British one to receive the claims and a French one to examine them, was extremely slow. After working for two years the commissions declared themselves ineffectual and recommended that the two countries reach an agreement on the diplomatic level. Plenipotentiaries then estimated all the claims put forward by Great Britain, including capital and interest, at 60 million francs, a sum the French government was unable to pay. Consequently Britain assumed the obligations, on certain conditions that France accepted. Like the other Canadian communities the Congregation of Notre-Dame henceforth could apply to the British government for payment of its annuities and immediate reimbursement for arrears, with interest up to 22 March 1818.

With this hope Sister Saint-Augustin passed away on 2 May 1819. She had dominated 17 years of the history of the Congregation of Notre-Dame with her strong personality, at a period when financial problems kept apostolic ardour in check. It is clear that the sisters had held her in great esteem and that under her firm and intelligent direction they had felt sheltered from the difficulties of the time.

ANDRÉE DÉSILETS

ANQ-M, CE1-51, 9 juin 1732, 29 janv. 1747. Arch. de la Congrégation de Notre-Dame (Montréal), Fichier général; Personnel, VI; Reg. général. Tanguay, *Dictionnaire*, 5: 119. Gosselin, *L'Église du Canada après la Conquête*. Lemire-Marsolais et Lambert, *Hist. de la CND de Montréal*, 5: 129–30; 6. Trudel, *L'Église canadienne*, 2: 344–47.

COMPAIN, PIERRE-JOSEPH, Roman Catholic priest and doctor; b. 11 April 1740 in Montreal (Que.), son of Pierre Compain, *dit* L'Espérance, a barber and wig maker, and Françoise Vacher; brother of Marie-Louise COMPAIN, named Saint-Augustin; d. 21 April 1806 in Saint-Antoine-sur-Richelieu, Lower Canada.

Pierre-Joseph Compain was able to leave Montreal and begin studies at the Séminaire de Québec in the autumn of 1754, probably through the influence of the priests of the Séminaire de Saint-Sulpice in Montreal, where his father was barber. The siege of Quebec by the British in 1759 forced him to cut short his senior year (Rhetoric) and return to Montreal. For a few years he studied surgery there, under Charles-Elemy-Joseph-Alexandre-Ferdinand Feltz*, but he apparently remained undecided about his future. On 27 July 1766, at Rivière-du-Loup (Louiseville), he married Geneviève Arseneau, who died within a few months.

During this brief period Compain was engaged in commerce. In October 1768, having been a widower for two years, he resumed his studies at the Séminaire de Québec. On 3 July 1774, at the age of 34, he was ordained priest by Bishop Briand*.

Since the Canadian church was faced with a shortage of priests at this time, Compain was often obliged to minister to several parishes. He began as curate at Saint-Pierre, Île d'Orléans, with responsibility also for Saint-Laurent. Scarcely a year after his ordination he became parish priest of Île aux Coudres. From 1775 to 1788 he served as pastor on that island and over an immense territory stretching from Les Éboulements through La Malbaie to Tadoussac. A legend was born at this period which would be recounted by the local Indians more than a century after Compain's death. In the night of 11 April 1782 the Jesuit Jean-Baptiste de La Brosse* died at Tadoussac. At that moment, according to the tradition, the bells of all the churches on the north shore of the St Lawrence, including those on Île aux Coudres, spontaneously tolled the knell. Convinced that his colleague had died, Compain set out in a canoe, and despite the ice floes still adrift on the river he covered nearly 50 miles to conduct the missionary's funeral.

Eager for harmony in his flock, Compain often acted as adviser or mediator to the habitants. Along with others he bitterly attacked the militia captain of Île aux Coudres, Zacharie Hervé – who had refused his counsel – calling him a swine, a drunkard "who judges his cases only in the canteen and only when the parties have him drink his fill." In September 1788, on the orders of his bishop and against his own wishes, he had to leave his parishioners. He became parish priest of Saint-Étienne at Beaumont, where he served until November 1798. Then another appointment took him to Saint-Antoine-sur-Richelieu.

The clerical state did not prevent Compain from practising medicine. Like Louis-Nicolas Landriaux*, Compain learned from Surgeon-Major Feltz a cure for cankers, which were a common malady at that time. The secret was to make his reputation. In February 1794 he announced in the *Quebec Gazette* that "having found out the true secret of curing Cancers by causing them to fall off without cutting them," he was advising afflicted persons that they might "confidently apply to him and expect to be treated with the charitable attention which that malady requires." Compain's therapy consisted of bleeding and purging the patient, applying to the canker a poultice of ground oats passed through a sieve and moistened with a few drops of water, and then covering it with a cobweb. This remedy may not have had all the efficacy attributed to it, but some doctors believed in it. Consequently in 1796 George LONGMORE, a Quebec surgeon, contracted to share Compain's secret and to pay him £529 for the right to use it. The parties agreed

Conefroy

that in the event of Longmore's death the secret would be passed on to Dr John Mervin Nooth*, who concurred with this arrangement. On 29 Aug. 1798, however, Compain and Longmore modified their contract [see George Longmore]. In February of the following year Compain, "desirous of relinquishing of the care of curing Cancers," passed his secret on to the nuns of the Hôtel-Dieu in Quebec and in Montreal as well as to the Ursulines of Trois-Rivières. In return he asked them to make a communion every month for his health and not to divulge the prescription for the famous remedy before his death. The existence of the remedy was so widely famed, and it was so favourably regarded, that as late as 1855 Dr Joseph Painchaud* reported he had used it successfully in treating facial cancers.

Pierre-Joseph Compain evidently had some degree of culture, for he possessed a fairly large personal library. After his death 189 volumes were bequeathed to the newly founded Séminaire de Nicolet.

GILLES JANSON

AAQ, 12 A, C: f.127; 20 A, II: 95; 210 A, IV: f.214; V: f.169; 22 A, V: f.431. ANQ-M, CE1-13, 22 avril 1806; CE1-51, 11 avril 1740; CN1-255, 21 août 1795; CN2-11, 10, 21 avril, 16, 20 mai, 2 sept. 1806. ANQ-MBF, CN1-80, 26 juill. 1766. ANQ-Q, CN1-92, 27 juin 1796. Arch. de la chancellerie de l'évêché de La Pocatière (La Pocatière, Qué.), Île aux Coudres, I, 3: 10 sept. 1788. Arch. des Religieuses hospitalières de Saint-Joseph (Montréal), Vie religieuse de la communauté, délibérations capitulaires, 25 févr. 1799. ASQ, mss, 431: 274. AUM, P 58, U, Compain à Baby, 23 mars 1777, 20 sept. 1787. BL, Add. mss 21724: 31 (mfm. at PAC). PAC, MG 11, [CO 42] Q, 84: 160–67. Le Canadien, 15 janv. 1855. Quebec Gazette, 20 May 1790, 6 Feb. 1794, 28 Feb. 1799. Alexis Mailloux, Histoire de l'Île-aux-Coudres depuis son établissement jusqu'à nos jours, avec ses traditions, ses légendes, ses coutumes (Montréal, 1879). P.-G. Roy, À travers l'histoire de Beaumont (Lévis, Qué., 1943), 161–62. "Le remède de M. Compain pour le cancer," BRH, 12 (1906): 23–24. René Bélanger, "L'abbé Pierre-Joseph Compain, prêtre et médecin, 1740–1806," Saguenayensia (Chicoutimi, Qué.), 13 (1971): 106–7; "Les prêtres séculiers du diocèse de Québec, missionnaires au Domaine du roi et dans la seigneurie de Mingan, de 1769 à 1845," SCHÉC Rapport, 23 (1955–56): 15. Gabriel Nadeau, "La bufothérapie sous le Régime français; Mme d'Youville et ses crapauds," L'Union médicale du Canada (Montréal), 73 (1944): 917–28; "Un savant anglais à Québec à la fin du XVIIIe siècle: le docteur John-Mervin Nooth," L'Union médicale du Canada, 74 (1945): 49–74.

CONEFROY, PIERRE, Roman Catholic priest, vicar general, and architect; b. 28 Dec. 1752 at Quebec, son of Robert Conefroy, a merchant, and Marie-Josette Métivier; d. 20 Dec. 1816 in Boucherville, Lower Canada.

Pierre Conefroy grew up in comfortable circumstances, living on Rue Buade, in Quebec's market square. After studies at the Séminaire de Québec he was ordained priest by Bishop Briand* on 21 Dec. 1776. In May 1774 his parents had provided him with a life annuity of 150 livres, payable in two annual instalments as soon as he became a subdeacon.

Following his ordination Conefroy spent four years in the parish of Saints-Anges at Lachine. In 1781 he became parish priest of Saint-Joachim, Pointe-Claire. There he established a convent of sisters of the Congregation of Notre-Dame in 1784, supervising construction of their house, which was completed in 1787; he had had the presbytery enlarged according to his own plans the year before. From 19 to 21 May 1787 Jean-François Hubert*, coadjutor to Bishop Louis-Philippe Mariauchau* d'Esgly, held a pastoral visitation, and his report gives some picture of the administration of the parish under Conefroy: it noted how accounts were approved, the cost of the various religious services was set, and income was divided between the parish council and the priest. Following his description of parish affairs, Hubert concluded the report by noting some aspects of Conefroy's private life: his mother, his two sisters, and a young female servant lived with him, and he had in his library Abbé Guillaume Raynal's Histoire philosophique et politique . . . , the Morale des jésuites . . . , and works by Diderot. On the whole Conefroy enjoyed his bishop's confidence; he had authority to confess and give absolution for reserved sins throughout the Government of Montreal.

In September 1790 Conefroy left Pointe-Claire for the more important responsibility of Sainte-Famille, at Boucherville, where he succeeded Charles-Marie-Madeleine d'Youville*. As well as being a more remunerative posting, this parish charge carried with it the hope of promotion, since Boucherville was the usual place of residence of the vicar general. In 1801 Conefroy built its third church from plans he drew himself, and he undertook to repair the presbytery. He held to a traditional approach while keeping in mind the needs of his own day; for this church he turned to the major concepts employed in religious architecture during the preceding era and in his design used a Latin cross, ending in a semicircular apse. He was entering on a period of intense activity, since people from all over the province began to consult him about building or enlarging churches. It was then customary for a priest to direct the investigations that legally preceded the building of any church; Conefroy belonged to the group of priests who were interested in architecture and were often consulted. He prepared estimates and plans that, without being original, methodically set out various data on church construction relating to building materials, customs of the builders' craft, and adaptation to the climate. From this consolidation of an architectural tradition came the standardization of parish architecture, and hence the title of architect-priest which has been given to Conefroy. Virtually until the 1830s, Conefroy's design influenced the construction of churches, particularly those of Saint-Roch-de-l'Achigan, Saint-Antoine in Longueuil, and Saint-Antoine-de-Padoue at Rivière du Loup (Louiseville).

Conefroy accompanied Bishop DENAUT on his visitation of the Maritimes from 3 May to 11 November 1803. In 1805 the bishop again chose him as a companion for a trip to Baie des Chaleurs planned for the summer of 1806. In 1808 Conefroy was appointed vicar general by Bishop Plessis*, and he retained this office for the rest of his life. His correspondence with his bishop gives proof of broad culture as well as of his attention to his work and his sustained interest in the building of various churches, particularly the one at Longueuil.

In December 1815 he had such a bad attack of gout that he thought himself near death. Recovering with difficulty, he remained weak but continued to carry out his ministry until his death on 20 Dec. 1816. His zeal for his work had earned him the esteem of his bishop and his parishioners.

CLAUDETTE LACELLE

AAQ, 20 A, II: 101; 1 CB, II: 28–46; 303 CD, I: 2; 61 CD, Notre-Dame de Québec, I: 18; 69 CD, I: 104–6; IA: 15–16; 60 CN, VI: 70. MAC-CD, Fonds Morisset, 2, C747.3/P622. Caron, "Inv. de la corr. de Mgr Denaut," ANQ Rapport, 1931–32; "Inv. de la corr. de Mgr Hubert et de Mgr Bailly de Messein," 1930–31; "Inv. de la corr. de Mgr Plessis," 1927–28; 1932–33. Desrosiers, "Corr. de cinq vicaires généraux," ANQ Rapport, 1947–48. Le diocèse de Montréal à la fin du dix-neuvième siècle ... (Montréal, 1900). Tanguay, Répertoire (1893). Désiré Girouard, Les anciennes côtes du lac Saint-Louis, avec un tableau complet des anciens et nouveaux propriétaires (Montréal, 1892). Gosselin, L'Église du Canada après la Conquête, 1–2. [Louis Lalande], Une vieille seigneurie, Boucherville; chroniques, portraits et souvenirs (Montréal, 1890). Morisset, Coup d'œil sur les arts. Luc Noppen, Notre-Dame de Québec, son architecture et son rayonnement (1647–1922) (Québec, 1974). Gérard Morisset, "L'influence de l'abbé Conefroy sur notre architecture religieuse," Architecture, Bâtiment, Construction (Montréal), 8 (février 1953): 36–39.

COOK, LOUIS. See ATIATOHARONGWEN

CORMIER, PIERRE, settler; b. 3 Aug. 1734 in Rivière-des-Héberts (near River Hebert), N.S., son of Pierre Cormier and Cécile Thibodeau (Thibaudeau); d. 24 March 1818 in Memramcook, N.B.

Pierre Cormier's family moved about 1750 to the French-controlled side of the Chignecto Isthmus, perhaps in response to the blandishments of Jean-Louis Le Loutre*, and in 1752 they were living at Aulac (N.B.). Early in 1755 Pierre married Anne Gaudet, daughter of Augustin Gaudet and Agnès Chiasson of nearby Tintemarre (Tantramar). Anne was often called Nannette; hence Pierre came to be nicknamed Pierrot à Nannette. They were to have five sons and two daughters.

Cormier's repute derives from the colourful tradition of his escape from the British on the eve of the Acadian deportation of 1755 [see Charles Lawrence*]. There is more than one version of this tradition, but the greatest credibility may be given that recorded in 1877 by the genealogist Placide Gaudet*, who had the advantage of consulting many of Cormier's grandchildren. According to Gaudet's account, Pierrot, taken prisoner with his brothers at Jolicœur (Jolicure, N.B.), was put aboard a Carolina-bound deportation vessel but slipped overboard the night before its departure. By creeping through the tall hay on shore he attained an aboiteau guarded by British soldiers and, when their backs were turned, clambered onto the butt of a timber over the water. Swinging from one butt end to another, he succeeded in crossing the aboiteau unobserved. On the other bank he again crept through the fields until he was able to break for the woods. After narrowly evading a band of soldiers tracking him with a dog, he arrived at an extent of water separating him from an Acadian encampment. Once recognized he was soon crossed over. Learning from these families that his own had fled the night before toward Quebec, Pierrot immediately left in search of them. The Cormiers were reunited at Sainte-Anne (near Fredericton, N.B.), where they remained until Robert Monckton*'s raids persuaded them to move to Kamouraska (Que.), likely in 1758.

According to another tradition, Pierrot, Jacques, and François Cormier were serving in the militia at the fall of Quebec in 1759. Subsequently they joined a French frigate at Pointe-Lévy (Lauzon and Lévis), lured with other young Acadians by promises of passage to France. After engagement with two British war vessels near the Îlets Jacques-Cartier, the frigate ran aground. Only about 60 of 160 crew members managed to swim ashore through the icy April waters, but these included the three Cormier brothers. This tradition likely refers to the encounter off Cap-Rouge between Jean Vauquelin* and Robert Swanton* in May 1760.

Pierre Cormier and Anne Gaudet resided at L'Islet (Que.) between 1761 and 1764, but about 1765 they returned to Sainte-Anne with his mother and four brothers. By July 1783 Pierrot had cleared 20 acres of a tract he had continuously occupied for 13 years. The Acadians of Sainte-Anne had not secured title to their farms, however, and grants to disbanded soldiers and loyalists were soon encroaching on what they considered to be their land. They deemed the small acreage reserved to them insufficient to support their families. Learning of vacant land on the west side of

Cossit

the Memramcook River, about 20 families removed there between autumn 1786 and summer 1787, including those of Pierre Cormier and four of his married children. Pierrot had meantime lost his Nannette, and his aged mother died during the trip.

The vacant land at Memramcook had been granted to Joseph Goreham* and then sold to Joseph Frederick Wallet DesBarres*. On 5 June 1792 the Cormiers and others presented a memorial to the New Brunswick government complaining of the "extravagant" demands of Desbarres's assign, Mary Cannon*, and arguing that his land should be escheated and granted to them in consideration of the substantial improvements made during their occupation. Their efforts were thwarted by DesBarres and his agents, but it was not until after 1809 that they were turned out to find other places to live in the Memramcook valley.

STEPHEN A. WHITE

AD, Charente-Maritime (La Rochelle), État civil, Beaubassin, 1712–48 (mfm. at CÉA). AN, Section Outre-mer, G¹, 466, no.30. Arch. paroissiales, Saint-Thomas (Memramcook, N.-B.), Reg. des baptêmes, mariages et sépultures (mfm. at CÉA). CÉA, Fonds Placide Gaudet, 1.28-6, 1.33-7, 1.64-24; "Notes généalogiques sur les familles acadiennes, c.1600–1900," dossier Cormier-3. PANB, RG 10, RS108, Petition of William Anderson, 1785; Petition of Charles Bickle, 1785; Petition of French inhabitants of Dorchester, 1809; Petition of John Jouett, 1785; Petition of John Ruso, 1785; Petition of Joseph Sayre, 1786. PANS, RG 1, 409. Tanguay, *Dictionnaire*, 3: 129. Clément Cormier, "La famille Cormier en Amérique," *L'Évangéline* (Moncton, N.-B.), 8 août 1951: 4–5; 10 août 1951: 5. Placide Gaudet, "La famille Cormier," *Le Moniteur acadien* (Shédiac, N.-B.), 22, 29 janv. 1885.

COSSIT (Cossitt), RANNA (Rene), Church of England clergyman and politician; b. 29 Dec. 1744 in North Granby, Conn., second son of Rene Cossitt and Phoebe Hillyer; m. June 1774 Thankful Brooks in Claremont, N.H., and they had 13 children; d. 13 March 1815 in Yarmouth, N.S.

Ranna Cossit graduated from Rhode Island College with an AB in 1771 and then studied theology in England, where he was ordained by the bishop of London early in 1773. He immediately began his ministry as a missionary of the Society for the Propagation of the Gospel at Claremont. As a result of his strong loyalist stand during the period leading up to the American revolution, the local committee of safety had by April 1776 ordered him to be confined and disarmed; he nevertheless refused to sign the declaration of independence of the people of New Hampshire that July. Despite American suspicions of the loyalty of all Anglicans and his own diminished congregation, Cossit remained in Claremont during the war. In 1782 he visited Quebec to inform British officials about conditions in New England, and after

his return to Claremont he corresponded with British agents and supplied them with American newspapers.

After the revolution Cossit sought to interest Governor Frederick HALDIMAND of Quebec in a scheme for settling New Englanders in the Eastern Townships, but when the governor refused to countenance the plan Cossit sought an appointment in the Maritime provinces from the SPG. In April 1785 William Morice, secretary of the SPG, offered him a salary of £50 to act as minister in Sydney, the capital of the newly established colony of Cape Breton, and later in the year proposed a regular supplement of £50; moreover, the government was to provide him with a salary of £100 to act as garrison chaplain. Cossit accepted and arrived in Sydney on 2 June 1786. Since neither a parsonage nor a church had been provided, Cossit built a parsonage himself in 1787 and the same year began work on a church; named St George's, it was not finally completed until 1805 at the earliest. He also visited remote settlements such as Louisbourg, Main-à-Dieu, and Cow Bay (Port Morien) and hired the colony's first schoolmaster, Hiram Payne.

Cossit was appointed a member of Cape Breton's Executive Council on 29 Aug. 1786, and he became more and more deeply involved in the colony's political affairs. He cooperated with lieutenant governors Joseph Frederick Wallet DesBarres* and William MACARMICK, but fell into a sharp dispute with David Mathews*, who became administrator of the colony on Macarmick's departure in May 1795. The altercation arose ostensibly because Mathews blamed Cossit for his failure to be elected churchwarden of St George's, but its roots are to be found in Cossit's support of DesBarres and Macarmick in their disputes with Mathews and his fellow loyalist Abraham Cornelius CUYLER. After the departure of Macarmick, the opposition to Mathews centred around Cossit and James Miller, the superintendent of mines, whom Mathews alleged was dishonest and incompetent. When in the fall of 1795 Cossit, as was his right as SPG missionary, appointed a new schoolmaster to replace Payne and obtained the approval of Bishop Charles INGLIS, Mathews tried to block the appointment. Cossit allowed classes to be held in his home, so Mathews had the teacher arrested for debt. He even went so far as to appoint his own schoolmaster, a Roman Catholic.

This dispute placed Cossit in the forefront of the opposition to Mathews. During 1797 Mathews contrived to dismiss Cossit's allies Ingram BALL and William McKINNON from their government positions and, fearing their complaints to the Home Department, had a petition circulated which praised him as a "popular ruler." In June Cossit and others sent a memorial to the British government demanding the appointment of a new lieutenant governor. This action seems to have been responsible for Mathews's replacement as administrator by Major-General James

OGILVIE that December. Before Ogilvie's arrival in June 1798, however, Mathews had Cossit imprisoned for three months for a £25 debt which Cossit allegedly owed to Mathews's son.

During his tenure Ogilvie came to the conclusion that Mathews was responsible for the factional quarrels, an opinion shared by his successor, Brigadier-General John Murray*. Mathews's hostility to Murray drove the latter into an alliance with Cossit and his supporters, and Murray dismissed Mathews and his followers from various offices, replacing them with allies of Cossit. The Mathews faction immediately tried for Murray's removal, exploiting his unpopularity with the Duke of Kent [EDWARD AUGUSTUS] in Halifax. Murray was in fact replaced, but when his successor as administrator, Major-General John Despard*, arrived in June 1800 Murray refused to surrender the civil command. In this stand he had the support of Cossit, while Mathews and his followers rallied behind Despard. Despard finally established his authority in November, and then appealed to the British government to remove Cossit from Cape Breton for the sake of harmony. Cossit failed to regain political power, and after Mathews's death in July 1800 his supporter Archibald Charles Dodd* continued to persecute the minister.

By 1801 Cossit was ready to leave and asked Inglis for a post in Nova Scotia. But by the time Inglis offered him his choice of two parishes in the spring of 1803, Cossit had changed his mind and wished to stay. Continued complaints from Despard finally brought Inglis to Cape Breton in July 1805. After three days of discussion Inglis persuaded Cossit to leave, lest the scandal of his political conflicts should lead colonists into becoming "Methodists, Catholic or infidels." Cossit formally resigned from the Sydney mission on 18 July 1805, and Inglis appointed him to Yarmouth, where he was inducted as rector of the new parish on 23 Jan. 1807. He shortly began the construction of a church, which was completed by Christmas, and actively ministered to the surrounding settlements of Chebogue, Plymouth, and Tusket. After his removal from Sydney he was not involved in political affairs. He died on 13 March 1815 and was buried at Yarmouth.

Everything about Ranna Cossit breathes individuality and vitality of character: his self-devised spelling of his name, his outspoken loyalist stand, his founding of the Church of England in Cape Breton and Yarmouth, and his active role in the politics of Sydney. He began the formal education system in Sydney and was a founder of the masonic order in Cape Breton. Cossit was an activist whose mark on Cape Breton was recognized by the opening of his home, Cossit House, by the Nova Scotia Museum on 29 Aug. 1977.

R. J. MORGAN

Cossit House (Sydney, N.S.), Ranna Cossit, letterbook. PAC, MG 11 [CO 217], Cape Breton A, 8; MG 23, C6, ser.1, 6. PRO, CO 217/112–38. USPG, Journal of SPG, 27–29 (mfm. at PAC). *Genealogical and family history of the state of New Hampshire: a record of the achievements of her people in the making of a commonwealth and the founding of a nation*, comp. E. S. Stearnes et al. (4v., New York and Chicago, 1908), 1. Morgan, "Orphan outpost." O. F. R. Waite, *The early history of Claremont, New Hampshire; a paper read before the New Hampshire historical society . . . at a meeting held at Claremont on September 29, 1891* (Concord, N.H., 1894); *History of the town of Claremont, New Hampshire, for a period of one hundred and thirty years from 1764 to 1894* (Manchester, N.H., 1895). Mason Wade, "Odyssey of a loyalist rector," *Vt. Hist.* (Montpelier), 48 (1980): 96–113.

COTTNAM, DEBORAH. *See* How

CRAIG, Sir JAMES HENRY, army officer and colonial administrator; b. 1748 at Gibraltar, son of Hew Craig; d. unmarried 12 Jan. 1812 in London, England.

Why do social and economic forces come together in a particular fashion at a specific place and point in time? In this connection historians continue to debate the relative influence of men, structures, and circumstances. These three elements are inextricably intertwined in the destiny of Sir James Henry Craig. He tried to bring about a sharp shift in the evolution of Lower Canadian society at the beginning of the 19th century, at the very moment when a series of transformations was taking place: penetration by the capitalist market under the impetus of the Atlantic trading network; ideological ferment and polarization around the redefinition of power relationships between the actors in society, old and new, following amputation of the commercial empire of the St Lawrence, the arrival of the loyalists, division of the province of Quebec into Upper and Lower Canada, and introduction of a rudimentary system of parliamentary government into the colony; and economic, demographic, and military pressures from the United States.

The rise of the timber trade after 1807, the year Craig arrived in the colony, combined with sporadic commercialization of agricultural products and the decline of the fur trade to complete the restructuring and modernization of the Lower Canadian socioeconomy, through its direct impact and its repercussions. This economic expansion, which from the mid decade brought in its wake a marked movement towards urbanization, an increase in manpower, the creation of an integrated local market, a rationalization of production, a rise in prices and wages, increased consumption, and open speculation in landed property, in brief the penetrative power of the market, disrupted, even in the countryside, the

Craig

traditional way of life and the old human relationships.

New social groups emerged, including the petite bourgeoisie drawn from the liberal professions, small merchants (often in the country), and the more prosperous craftsmen. These people, for the most part Canadians, articulated in the Canadian party and its newspaper *Le Canadien* [*see* Pierre-Stanislas Bédard*; François Blanchet*] an explicit form of nationalism that was linked with democratic concepts and values and with a plan for economic development centred on Lower Canada. They ran up against the recent alliance of great landowners, higher officials, and rich merchants, nearly all British, who by contrast defended aristocratic and British values and advocated economic development on a continental scale. These conflicts, building upon each other, crystallized in the political arena on constitutional, social, ethnic, and economic planes, and were already beginning to paralyse a many-sided polity that included the military apparatus under command of the governor, the Legislative and Executive councils, which were dominated by the British party, and the House of Assembly, which was under the influence of the Canadian party. The obvious favouritism towards the British elements shown by the authorities would accelerate the ossification of political institutions. On the one hand the Canadian party demanded "supremacy of the legislature," as in Britain, and control of the Executive Council, which they called "the ministry." On the other hand the British party countered with plans to assimilate the Canadians through British immigration, an aristocratic form of government, development of the Eastern Townships, abolition of the seigneurial system, and abrogation of French civil law, which was considered a nuisance.

Caught between the immediate pressure brought to bear by the Executive Council and the more indirect but no less real pressures from a Canadian bourgeoisie that was considered too democratic, the Catholic Church sought to acquire legal status, stabilize and then increase its numbers, improve the training of its priests, strengthen its presence in education, and more effectively keep in line independent or recalcitrant members of the laity [*see* Pierre DENAUT].

In addition to these tensions, the turbulence of Lower Canadian society was becoming increasingly pronounced as a consequence of the repercussions of the wars in Europe and even more the threat of armed conflict with the United States looming as a result of the provocations to which Britain was subjecting neutral countries, the impressment of American sailors on the high seas, and the stirring-up of the Indian tribes in the interior of the continent [*see* TECUMSEH].

Craig tried to act directly on all these levels, but he met with uneven success because he so often ran up against structures which remained sturdy and a set of circumstances that often proved to be the deciding factor.

James Henry Craig, who came from a respectable Scottish family, was born at Gibraltar; his father was a judge of the civil and military courts in the British fortress. In 1763, at the age of 15, he joined the army as an ensign in the 30th Foot. In 1770 he was promoted aide-de-camp to Colonel Robert Boyd, lieutenant governor of Gibraltar. Next he took command of a company of the 47th Foot, and he was serving in this capacity in the American colonies from 1774. After the outbreak of the War of Independence the following year, he took part in the battle of Bunker Hill, in Massachusetts, where he was badly wounded. Nevertheless he accompanied his regiment to the province of Quebec in 1776, met the American invaders at Trois-Rivières, and commanded the advance guard that forced them back over the border. The next year he was twice wounded, once seriously, during engagements at Fort Ticonderoga (near Ticonderoga, N.Y.), Hubbardton (East Hubbardton, Vt), and Freeman's Farm, N.Y. Major-General John Burgoyne*, who thought highly of him, recommended him for the rank of major in the 82nd Foot in recognition of his services. From 1778 to 1781 he served with his regiment in Nova Scotia, at Penobscot (Castine, Maine), and in North Carolina. Constantly on the go during these campaigns, he mainly led light infantry troops. His successes suggest that he possessed initiative and resourcefulness to an unusual degree.

Having attained the rank of lieutenant-colonel in 1781, Craig became adjutant general of the Duke of York's army in the Netherlands in 1794, and then major-general. In 1795 he collaborated with Vice-Admiral Viscount Keith and Major-General Alured Clarke* in wresting the Cape Colony (South Africa) from the Dutch. Now at the peak of his military career, he became governor of the new possession and remained in this post until 1797. After receiving the Order of the Bath, he sailed that year for Madras and the Bengal region in India, where he again engaged in battle. Having been made a lieutenant-general in January 1801, he returned to England and for three years served as commander of the Eastern District. In 1805, despite his poor health, the British government commissioned him to serve as a local general in the Mediterranean, in command of an expeditionary corps in Italy which was to effect a junction with the Russian army. The battles of Ulm and Austerlitz made these plans futile, and Craig had to fall back on Sicily. Suffering from chronic dropsy, he returned to England in 1806. Since he was unable to remain inactive and seemed to recover, he accepted the post of governor-in-chief of British North America in 1807, succeeding Robert Shore Milnes*.

206

On 18 Oct. 1807, with great pomp and ceremony, Craig disembarked at Quebec from the ship of the line *Horatio*. A large crowd and a 15-gun salute greeted this short but stately figure. His brief, triumphant appearance was, however, only an interlude, since it was rumoured that Craig had taken to his bed and was dying. On all sides, and particularly in the English party, prayers were said for his recovery. From the time of their first contact the governor's civil secretary, Herman Witsius Ryland*, had felt the stirrings of great admiration for his new chief and a breath of hope; he was confident that the British would be backed up by an energetic governor, provided he lived. The Canadians also rejoiced; *Le Canadien* surmised that, like a second Hannibal, the new governor might well purge the Canadian Carthage of the clique of "placemen." The British anticipated a resolutely British policy, whereas the Canadians expected redress for the wrongs of which they claimed to be victims.

As noted, Craig arrived in the midst of very difficult circumstances. Seriously ill at the outset, he had to rely on his civil secretary for information about the colony and for expediting correspondence. He took the customary oaths from his bed on 24 October, and he did not write or dictate any letters until 9 November. His first concerns were quite naturally for military matters, especially since war between Great Britain and the United States seemed imminent. He was convinced that if the British did not make use of the Indians, the Americans would. Consequently he gave orders that greater efforts than ever be made to win them over, but that they should be made in a prudent manner, without any allusion to the possibility of a conflict, because certain tribes wanted to drag Britain into a new war to recover their lands from the United States. However, in the event of conflict he envisaged restraining their cruelty. From the time of his arrival Craig devoted much energy and money to rebuilding fortifications in the province, particularly at Quebec. As for the Canadian militia, it had displayed exemplary loyalty when put on a war footing in the summer of 1807. Craig, however, was sparing in his congratulations on this ardour and took the few deserters to task at length; this attitude, which was characteristic of Craig's perfectionist and punctilious side, startled the Canadian militia.

Yet on his arrival Craig had not been unfavourably inclined towards the Canadians. He gave no evidence of preconceived hostility towards them. Abbé François-Emmanuel Bourret, Bishop Joseph-Octave Plessis*'s agent in London, had conversed with the governor before the latter's departure, and in a letter to Plessis had remarked: "You will have reason to be satisfied with Sir J. Craig." Furthermore, in December 1807 the governor awarded commissions as militia officers to some Canadians, including a captaincy to

Pierre-Stanislas Bédard, the leader of the Canadian party.

Craig liked show. Consequently the opening of the parliamentary session on 29 Jan. 1808 was described by the newspapers as "the most brilliant that ever took place in this province." The two great debates dominating the session were linked to the Canadian party's attempt to secure a stable majority in the House of Assembly. In fact, despite their numerical superiority most of the Canadian members deserted the legislature early in the session because they could not afford a prolonged stay in the capital. Thus, at the end of the sessions the British and their Canadian allies – called "placemen" by *Le Canadien* – sometimes found themselves in the majority. The Canadian party had twice failed in the attempt to pass a bill providing an expense allowance for members of the assembly coming from outside Quebec. Hence it sought instead to expel some members of the opposing party who were vulnerable: those who were members of the judiciary and a Jew, Ezekiel Hart*, who had been elected for Three Rivers in 1807.

In debating the bill on the ineligibility of judges, however, the members of the Canadian party advanced only honourable grounds. They expressed the opinion that participation of judges in elections undermined their impartiality, or at least sapped the electors' confidence in justice, and observed that in England judges sat only in the House of Lords. Encouraged by most of the British members, judges Pierre-Amable DE BONNE and Louis-Charles Foucher* replied that educated men and government spokesmen were needed in the assembly, and that the bill amounted to an act of vengeance by *Le Canadien*. During an exchange Bédard extemporized brilliantly on the existence of a "ministry" in the colony because Lower Canada had been given a constitution similar to that of Britain. Finally, after many debates, adjournments, and dramatic turns of events, the assembly passed the bill on the ineligibility of judges on 4 March 1808. But the Legislative Council blocked it, in order, according to Michel-Eustache-Gaspard-Alain Chartier* de Lotbinière, "to stop the encroachments" of the assembly on royal prerogatives. It is easy to understand the indignation of *Le Canadien*, which proclaimed the "right to have representation free from all [governmental] influence," noting that otherwise one had tyranny. Such language could only rile a governor concerned about his authority and image. Other articles violently denounced the "little ministry" that was advising the governor; the policy of the paper may explain the hardening of Craig's attitudes towards the Canadians between April and June 1808.

After shorter but just as violent debate, on 14 March 1808 the assembly passed a resolution expelling Hart, the member of Jewish origins who was allied with the British party; since he had taken the oath in accordance with the custom of his religion rather than with the constitution of 1791, he could not "attend, sit, or vote in this House." The decision was the result of a mixture of political opportunism, anti-Semitism, and legalism. Some Canadian members had, however, defended Hart, whereas some of the British, including Attorney General Jonathan Sewell*, had voted for the resolution. Contrary to legend Craig showed Hart little sympathy; he curtly gave him to understand through his secretary that he could not intervene in the matter.

Friction arose in other areas too. Pierre-Stanislas Bédard and Jean-Thomas Taschereau* failed in their attempt to have a committee study the "alterations" to be made in the British system of free and common socage for landholding and the "precautions" to be taken against the introduction of "Yankees" and "dangerous aliens" from the United States. On the other hand the assembly succeeded in passing a good many useful measures concerning public works, justice, and other matters during the 1808 session. Craig took the opportunity to congratulate it on the work accomplished. His correspondence reveals his great satisfaction. He even stressed the "moderation" of the deliberations, except in the discussions on the ineligibility of judges when personal animosities had surfaced.

During the 1808 session partisan debates had continued to arouse passions, especially through the medium of the newspapers. The *Quebec Mercury*, the British party's organ at Quebec [*see* Thomas Cary*], insulted the language, customs, religion, and education of the Canadians; it considered assimilation to be necessary in itself and advantageous for the victims. *Le Canadien* – and on certain points the *Courier de Québec*, the organ of the Canadian members of the British party – spoke disparagingly of American immigrants, denounced plans for assimilation as leading inevitably to annexation to the United States, criticized the English judges who were unfamiliar with French law, and accused the clique of placemen of gobbling up lucrative posts, halting the implementation of the constitution, and blocking the avenues to promotion for Canadians. Just before the elections in June 1808 *Le Canadien* and various pamphlets even more stridently denounced privileges and the wasting of public funds. To the fury of the British, *Le Canadien* urged the people to reject the placemen, their adversaries, and to elect only Canadian representatives devoted to their interests. On the hustings more than one candidate resorted to ethnic appeals. The administration was, however, successful in bringing about the defeat of Jean-Antoine PANET, the speaker of the assembly. But the Canadian party had foreseen this and had him elected in Huntingdon riding. Although there were 50 seats to be filled, only 14 British members – as against 16 in

the previous parliament – escaped defeat in the elections, and even at that most leading officials and merchants in the colony had had to be conscripted into the campaign. The astute Pierre-Amable De Bonne held his own against the Canadian party and was re-elected along with a handful of his supporters. Among the members of the Canadian party newly elected were Louis-Joseph Papineau*, aged 21, Denis-Benjamin Viger*, and Joseph Levasseur-Borgia*.

Having kept his distance somewhat from political quarrels until April 1808, Craig had then quickly become the leader of the British party. This sudden metamorphosis can be explained by the democratic aspirations of the Canadian party, its virulent attacks on the executive authority and ultimately on the governor, who topped the pyramid of placemen, and then by its questioning of the prerogatives vested in the institutions representing imperial sovereignty and the colonial oligarchy. As a paternalistic and energetic soldier who had fought American democracy in the United States, Craig was not a person to let himself be attacked without counter-attacking strongly. Sick and somewhat reserved, he depended upon the people about him to keep informed of the changing situation in the colony. These people, who shared the same political interests, may have been able to influence him skilfully by suggestion, even though the governor emerged naturally as the supreme leader of the British party. In a long memoir composed in May 1808 Ryland painted a pessimistic picture of the political situation for him and recommended measures that were dear to the members of the British party: reinforcement of the preponderance of the British in the councils, the magistracy, and public office; creation of English Protestant schools and control of the Catholic clergy so as to assimilate the Canadians and convert them to Protestantism; settlement of the Eastern Townships by British people and an artificial increase in the number of ridings for this region. These solutions would become a *leitmotiv* within British circles in the colony.

Immediately after the elections in June 1808 Craig avenged the British party by dismissing those officials and militia officers who were associated with the newspaper *Le Canadien*. The British applauded this martial gesture. Some Canadians who held office or sought it lost no time in showering praise upon the governor's "wisdom" and incriminating their compatriots; this was the attitude adopted by Paul-Roch Saint-Ours in particular. But through his intervention Craig set off a chain reaction that led the Canadian party to harass the government even more, thus further provoking the anger of the proud and authoritarian governor and the fury of his entourage. *Le Canadien* denounced governmental "abuses" more strongly than ever, publishing in detail the expenditures on the civil list, comparing them with "useful expenditures," and then making known its objective of gaining control of revenues. In return the *Mercury* accused *Le Canadien* of heaping abuse upon the merchants and office holders solely out of ambition and jealousy.

In his correspondence for the months of July and August 1808 Craig even cast doubt on the loyalty of the Canadians in the event of war. Just as had Lieutenant Governor Milnes in 1800, he regretted the marked decline of the old seigneurial aristocracy and portrayed the new parliamentary leaders – for the most part lawyers, notaries, and shopkeepers who came from the people – as ambitious revolutionaries, "violent," "unprincipled," "dangerous," and "ingratiating." As for the rest of the Canadians, "they are French at heart." Even the clergy, he noted with great distaste, recruited its personnel from among "the lowest classes of the people." He predicted a stormy session and an early dissolution of parliament.

Craig did not think highly of the Catholic clergy. In the winter of 1808–9 Bishop Plessis had met with him before asking the assembly to incorporate parishes that had been created since 1721, a measure necessary to solve the innumerable problems stemming from their lack of civil recognition [*see* Joseph-Laurent BERTRAND]. Indeed, some Canadians had gone so far as to demand that the clergy retrocede lands that their ancestors had given to *fabriques*. Others, for no good reason, threatened the bishop with an appeal to the "royal prerogative," which in theory had been imposed by the Royal Proclamation of 1763 and the Quebec Act. If the parishes had no legal status, how could they own or transfer property, or collect tithes? The interview between Craig and Plessis occurred in a "rather heated" atmosphere, according to the bishop, who distrusted the dispositions "of the present ministry." Craig had clearly expressed his desire to subject the bishop and his church to the royal prerogative. Moreover, the church was suffering from a critical lack of priests; Plessis noted that there were no more than 166 for the more than 200,000 Catholics spread across an immense territory. Of that number, a score were teaching in colleges. It was therefore necessary to abandon some small parishes in order to meet the needs of the large ones. In the towns a large proportion of the élite from the liberal professions did not attend church, especially because of the church's teachings on lending money at interest. Thus morals were growing lax, and the habitants were becoming unruly in their conduct. In commiserating with a discouraged parish priest, Bishop Plessis observed: "People are always people, and peasants always peasants; more ready to receive than to give, making promises in order to have a parish priest and making no effort to keep him once they have him."

Early in 1809 Craig, worried by the tension between Britain and the United States, asked London for military reinforcements, but without success. He sent a spy, John Henry*, to the United States to ferret out information on public opinion, the plans and military capacity of the republic, and the rumours of a split between New England and the rest of the country over the American embargo, which was ruinous for the seaboard states. He even gave Henry authority to negotiate with separatist leaders if an opportunity occurred. In the event Henry passed on little useful information, and Craig recalled him in May after progress had been made in the negotiations between London and Washington. In 1812 Henry sold his correspondence to the American government, which published it to rally public opinion further.

Some correspondents of the *Montreal Gazette* capitalized on the international tension to urge the parties in Lower Canada to make peace. *Le Canadien* and the *Mercury* nevertheless persevered in their vendetta. The themes remained the same, but the gibes became more scathing. *Le Canadien* dwelt more on constitutional concepts and persisted in its opposition to American immigration. To those Canadians who wanted to keep Lower Canada to themselves the *Mercury* retorted that it would take them centuries to develop and settle the province. According to a journalist writing in the *Mercury* under the pseudonym of Scaevola, the Canadians were prolonging to no avail a backward, feudal, decadent, and inert society. Instead of whining about the distinction between the races, the Canadians, he said, should themselves do away with it "by becoming English." Another journalist refused to admit that Canada belonged only to "papists."

These articles illustrate the vigour of the confrontation. Furthermore, in 1809 the great problems facing Lower Canada were examined in two pamphlets and a book. In *Considérations sur les effets qu'ont produit en Canada, la conservation des établissemens du pays, les mœurs, l'éducation etc. de ses habitans*, Denis-Benjamin Viger maintained that the British party's plan to submerge the Canadians through the immigration of American "rebels" would steer the colony towards annexation to the United States. Great Britain's interest dictated that she should keep the province for the Canadians: only they could maintain the colony in the empire, as much through interest as through religious conviction. Two months later Ross Cuthbert* answered him in *An apology for Great Britain*. Canada, he said, was a young country with a potential for immense development, thanks to the British and Americans. The French Canadians, with their wretched "patois," represented only a hundredth of the empire's population; their medieval laws handicapped trade, and their assimilation would in no way be unjust. On the contrary, they ought to collaborate in it, since their survival was neither possible nor desirable: "inert in its nature," this people "exhibit[ed] its infant face, surcharged with the indications of old age and decay." Finally, in London an English merchant by the name of Hugh Gray published *Letters from Canada, written during a residence there in the years 1806, 1807 and 1808*. He went further than Cuthbert and suggested concrete means of carrying out assimilation: the union of the Canadas and subordination of the Canadian clergy.

For some obscure reason Craig had delayed the opening of the next session of the assembly until 10 April 1809. This decision prompted *Le Canadien* to make some comments on the constitution, the rights of the assembly, and the abuses of the "ministry." During the short session only five statutes were passed, for the most part simple re-enactments. Three questions took up almost all the sittings. First, the assembly corrected certain "insinuations" in the speech from the throne about the existence of unfounded "jealousies" in the province. Bédard seized this hoped-for occasion to deliver a long speech on the necessity of ministerial responsibility, without which the assembly would have to entertain the "monstrous idea" of turning against the person of the king's representative. The question of the ineligibility of judges took up the greater part of the debates. The Canadian party again sought passage of the bill disqualifying them from sitting in the house. Judge De Bonne's energetic resistance led to the creation of a committee to investigate the elections, which brought in a devastating report against the judge as candidate. Premature prorogation on 15 May 1809 put an end to the polemic, at least in the assembly.

Ezekiel Hart, who had been re-elected for Three Rivers in 1808, had taken the oath in the Christian manner and in the form prescribed by law. The assembly again expelled him by resolution in 1809, but this time the exclusion verged on illegality. Craig had already consulted the Executive Council, which recognized Hart's right to sit in the assembly and recommended that London censure this body, but that the governor not dissolve it. The hot-headed Craig disregarded the recommendation so as to provoke the confrontation that he had been predicting since 1808. He at last had the pretext for carrying out his plan to bring the assembly to heel, indeed, to impress the people and get them to elect members favourable to the government. In Craig's eyes new elections would deal with the dangerous and unruly Canadian party, which dared to brave his authority and criticize his policy. He therefore burst unannounced into the assembly chamber, and in a long speech proroguing the house he gave the majority a dressing down for having frittered time away on trivialities, "personal animosities," and "unconstitutional" measures. He did, however, distribute a few compliments to the Legislative Council and to the British group in the assembly.

Craig justified his conduct to the Colonial secretary, Viscount Castlereagh, by affirming that he had wanted to show the assembly he could not be "intimidated" by threats, and consequently to dispel any thought that he was afraid in the slightest of the Canadian party. He also said that he had wanted to avoid any violent measures on the part of the assembly, refute its claim to dispose of unlimited powers, and put a stop to agitation among the population. In his optimism the governor predicted the defeat of a great many of his opponents in the coming elections. In June 1809 he even campaigned throughout the province. At Trois-Rivières, Montreal, William Henry (Sorel), Dorchester (Saint-Jean-sur-Richelieu), and elsewhere his faithful supporters and some of the people gave him a rousing welcome and applauded his policies. In the euphoria of the moment the governor imagined that winning the election was simply a matter of subjugating a small clique of agitators who had no influence on the loyal population. He had considered it fitting to innovate by openly involving himself in politics. He anticipated approval from the electors and from London. In reality he had gone too far, too quickly: the people and the Colonial secretary were going to let him know it.

As the elections were not held until the autumn of 1809, the Canadian party had time to rally and to convince the population that the "ministers" had rejected its representatives because they had protected the rights of the people too well. In this long and merciless campaign *Le Canadien* played an important role. Feigning horror, the paper recapitulated the people's alleged reproaches with regard to the governor's conduct. It attributed the responsibility for Craig's actions to the "ministers," portraying them as profiteers who put pressure on the people because they feared supervision by its free representatives. Voters were urged to choose members who shared their interests. Finally, *Le Canadien* displayed on the front page extracts from the English bill of rights of 1689 opposing intervention in elections by the government and officials. Polling took place in an atmosphere of extreme excitement. There was no lack of threats, brawls, and false reports, or, again, of nationalist appeals. Despite unheard-of efforts by the government, the electors returned an assembly that was virtually identical to the preceding one, with the British holding only 14 seats. Bédard was even elected in two ridings. The Canadian party was satisfied and in its newspaper drew the conclusion that its constitutional theories had been confirmed by the people, the supreme judge.

From London Castlereagh rebuked the governor for his extravagant language. Craig, he said, would have to control himself in the future. In addition he agreed with the assembly concerning the ineligibility of judges and Hart's expulsion. He asked Craig to give his approval to any law disqualifying judges henceforth from being members of the assembly.

The year 1810 began in a climate of political crisis. The newspapers were still exchanging sarcasms and quibbles that revealed the contradictory aims of the two opposing blocs. Having learned a few lessons, Craig modified his tactics. At the opening of the session he delivered a moderate speech and announced that he would ratify a law decreeing "in the future" the ineligibility of judges. Full of confidence the assembly reprimanded the governor for his past conduct; then, as economic prosperity was bringing large sums into the public coffers, it offered to assume the total cost of the civil administration. Paying the piper would enable it to call the tune. Plainly this offensive fitted into the logic of the assembly's claims concerning both financial and ministerial responsibility. The governor perceived clearly the intention of the Canadian party. Nevertheless he noted the novelty of the offer and promised to transmit the assembly's proposal to London. In his correspondence with the home authorities Craig called the request most dangerous; to agree to it, he said, would establish the complete domination of the country by the assembly. Finally, irritated by a Legislative Council amendment to delay enforcing the ineligibility of judges until the next elections, the assembly unilaterally declared judge De Bonne's seat vacant. Craig jumped on this patently unconstitutional action and on 1 March 1810 again dissolved parliament.

Throughout the debates and electoral campaigns of 1808 and 1809 newspapers such as *Le Canadien* and especially the *Mercury* had persisted in fanning the fire. The former had discoursed upon the rights of the people and the assembly, ministerial responsibility, the certain link between assimilation of the Canadians and Americanization, and the wasting of public funds for the benefit of a small clique. The *Mercury* had slandered the Canadian leaders, calling them Jacobins and climbers, had extolled the virtues of trade, and had treated Canadian society with contempt, considering it backward and ill adapted to the modern world and thus destined to disappear. All this rhetoric was, of course, interlarded with insults which each side heaped on the other.

Setting new elections in motion in 1810 could only stir up further controversy, especially since the government launched full speed into the campaign. Officials and government pensioners signed addresses complimenting Craig and had to campaign actively. To defend the government's cause and harass *Le Canadien*, they even founded a French newspaper, *Le Vrai Canadien*, which was published by Pierre-Amable De Bonne, Jacques Labrie*, and others. *Le Canadien* then vented its fury against the "ministry" and its "rotten bunch" of creatures drawn from the "rich" and the "upper classes" whom the people

maintained through paying the "tallage." In an electoral manifesto the Canadian party attributed the dissolution of parliament to one main cause: the officials' fear that the assembly would gain control of the civil list and prevent increases in the expenditures it covered. The electors had therefore to choose as a bloc the candidates of the Canadian party or the others. A song printed in *Le Canadien*'s shops urged the electors to drive out the governor's "rabble" that was kept by the taxes levied on the people.

Craig was determined to strike a decisive blow. He used *Le Canadien*'s stinging language as a pretext to have its presses seized on 17 March 1810 and he had a score of those chiefly responsible for it imprisoned on a charge of "treacherous practices." A document found on the paper's presses and listing all the Canadians' grievances since the conquest was also seized. The government's plan provided as well for incarcerating the principal Canadian leaders in Montreal; a party thus decapitated would have difficulty in campaigning. But James Brown*, proprietor of the *Montreal Gazette*, refused to print an article given him by James McGill, Isaac Ogden*, Jean-Guillaume De Lisle, and possibly John Blackwood – all of them office holders – which reportedly contained an unsubstantiated accusation that the prospective prisoners had received sums of money from the French consulate in Washington. The government had therefore to be content with a smaller haul, which, however, at Quebec included Charles Lefrançois*, *Le Canadien*'s printer, and François Blanchet, Jean-Thomas Taschereau, and Pierre-Stanislas Bédard, its founders.

The Executive Council allowed rumours of treason and conspiracy to be spread, although they had no substance. The pro-governmental papers rejoiced in them and pretended to believe them. In an impassioned proclamation Craig denounced the "wicked, seditious, and traitorous writings" that had forced him to take harsh measures. He circulated his proclamation across the province through militia officers, magistrates, and judges. He asked Bishop Plessis to appear before the Executive Council, assured him that a conspiracy existed, censured "the almost criminal apathy" of the clergy, and ordered him to intervene. Plessis anticipated that the members of the Canadian party would be re-elected; this made him even more fearful of the government's vengeance. He begged the priests therefore to read the governor's proclamation in the churches and to preach loyalty, "which may very well be done with commonplaces." For his own part he set an example by denouncing notions of the liberty and sovereignty of the people.

In his correspondence Craig justified the dissolution of parliament by alleging the need to counter the spread of the spirit of democracy in a province that was in an "extremely critical" state. After the arrests the governor explained to the home authorities that a democratic party with many members had distilled the disaffection and distrust in the population and had aroused the animosity between British and Canadians. He even gave it to be understood that there had been some question of a "massacre"; to be sure, he was not afraid of this eventuality, but he emphasized how worked up the population was – proof, in his view, of the good sense of his energetic intervention to rally the shaken masses to his side.

The British party emerged from the test of the elections weakened, having won only 12 seats; it was embittered, and craved revenge. This desire was gratified through the large number of informers, eager for favours, found amongst the Canadians. The phenomenon of informing was so widespread that it contradicts somewhat the traditional theme of the "reign of terror" and the Canadians' heroic resistance to it. At an opportune moment, the government would reward its zealous servants and punish those who were "seditious." As for the political prisoners, the government intended to release them one by one, without bringing them to trial but exacting large amounts of bail after they had displayed what was considered sufficient contrition. Blanchet and Taschereau submitted to these demands; the latter even went so far as to reveal to the jubilant governor certain consultations and disputes among the editors of *Le Canadien*. Bédard was the only one to defy the governor to the end. He was unyielding and refused to admit to any offence, even an involuntary one, demanding instead a trial to clear his honour and prove the correctness of his political opinions. For a moment Craig hoped to use his brother, Abbé Jean-Charles Bédard*, to make him give in, but the abbé proved just as tough and stubborn. As a result Bédard spent more than a year in prison.

For its part the Canadian party came out of the elections stronger than ever. Having foreseen what was going to happen, Craig gave up trying to convince the people in haste and endeavoured to subjugate the assembly through fear. By 1808 he had already taken up his position firmly and definitively, thereby inaugurating a period of increasing political conflict. He was not only fighting against "ignorance," the "rabble," political liberalism, and the democratic aspirations of an assembly which was defying him and in his view threatening the imperial and aristocratic order; he was opposing a Catholic Church become too independent, and he was struggling on behalf of the class of "respectable people" – the merchants and higher officials – which seemed to him the best educated and most dynamic one in the colony. He was also fighting very strongly for British colonization and the disappearance of the "French" characteristics of the Canadians. His energetic intervention in 1810 had been aimed only at preventing an insurrection that he

apprehended might occur. For him and for many others of British origin, such as Jonathan Sewell, the democratic danger went hand in hand with the danger of nationalism. In fact, the Canadians had remained "completely French" and felt "hatred" for the British. Worse still, they considered themselves "as forming a separate nation," hence their relentless fight against British immigration.

In the long term Craig, supported by British merchants such as John YOUNG and John Richardson* and higher officials such as Sewell, Ryland, and Anglican bishop Jacob Mountain*, revived in part the suggestions of his predecessor, Sir Robert Shore Milnes, and advocated assimilation of the Canadians because otherwise they always would be French, and therefore enemies of the English, and because they blocked the development of British colonization and trade. A whole range of means would eventually lead to this end: either union of the Canadas, combined with over-representation of the Eastern Townships in the assembly so as to assure British dominance of the house, or the abolition of the assembly and establishment of a council that would be predominantly British and drawn from the oligarchy. Other means were also envisaged, such as immigration from Britain and the United States, abolition of the seigneurial system, subjection of the Catholic priests, and seizure by the government of control over education.

What was involved, then, was a proper offensive designed to correct the "error" of 1791. It crowned the efforts of Milnes and the British party. Craig sent Ryland to London to promote this ambitious plan, but the secretary cooled his heels there for more than two years. Certainly by 1810 the British government recognized the defects of the 1791 constitution, but it did not dare introduce a legislative measure to correct them for various reasons: the fragility of its political power, the illness of King George III, the European war then monopolizing the ministers' attention, the American danger which dictated prudence in dealing with the Canadians in the colony, and the divergent views held by the higher officials in Lower Canada on the means to be adopted.

Early in 1811 Craig exercised astonishing mastery over the assembly because of the absence of the leader of the Canadian party, Bédard, who was still in prison. The gap in the party's leadership caused fear and confusion among its elected members; rivalries sprang up between the regions and among the candidates for Bédard's position. The assembly even went so far as to renew the law that had enabled Bédard to be imprisoned! Consequently the steps it took to free Bédard proved timid and fruitless. In March 1811, after the session was ended, Craig had him released, not because of weakness but to show clearly to the people by the delay that it was he who governed the province, and not the assembly. During the session the assembly refused, however, to hand its general revenues over to the government and renewed the Gaols Act of 1805 only "to help meet the civil expenses of this Province, in the form and manner that will be adopted by the legislature of this Province." Meanwhile Craig vainly tried to persuade Bishop Plessis to give up his authority voluntarily before London forced him to do so. The bishop was not unaware of the purpose of Ryland's mission in England, but he refused to give in to the governor's blackmail, observing that "it would not grieve me to be put on board a warship, rather than betray my conscience."

Governor Craig was playing a losing game, at least for the immediate future. He was up against a particularly unfavourable set of circumstances outside the country and structures within that were not easy to change (the demographic situation, the civil laws, the seigneurial system, the parliamentary institutions, and so on). He was very ill and since 1810 had been asking to be replaced. Against his own wishes he remained in his post at the insistence of the British government, but late in June 1811, feeling himself failing rapidly, he sailed for England, to the great regret of the British in the colony and of his protégés. He was dying when he reached London, and he passed away there shortly afterwards, on 12 Jan. 1812. If the British government replaced him with Sir George PREVOST, it was not to appease the Canadians, as traditional historical works claim, but simply because the former lieutenant governor of Nova Scotia was the only experienced senior officer who could get to Quebec quickly and could meet all contingencies there, including a war with the United States that seemed imminent.

London, moreover, did not disapprove of the team in the colony whose aim was to render it British; indeed, the Prince Regent officially recognized Craig's services before he died, and the Colonial secretary, Lord Liverpool, recommended Ryland to Prevost in July 1811. Craig did not, then, die broken and defeated, as has been claimed; he remained convinced that he had done his duty and that he had in part been successful. Although the British government felt unable to amend the 1791 constitution in the immediate future, Craig could nevertheless hope that one day the supremacy of the British and of the upper classes would be recognized once and for all in the colony. For the time being he had contained the "spirit of insubordination" in the assembly and had alerted London to the disadvantages of the constitution, both where relations between the mother country and the colony were concerned and on the social, national, and economic levels.

Craig has been described sometimes as a man of transparent simplicity who was misled by bad advisers, and at other times as a man whose touchy disposition was responsible for the birth of French-Canadian nationalism. An examination of his military and civil correspondence reveals instead an energetic leader (it was he who ran the British party and not the reverse), skilful and stubborn, capable of manipulating people and even of machiavellianism. A member of the upper classes, he liked the display of wealth and had the reputation of being a generous host. A resolute soldier who was punctilious but also concerned about the well-being of his troops, he was quick to react to real or presumed affronts, and also to pardon the guilty parties if they were repentant. As governor he did not disdain the constant use of patronage, authority, and threats to achieve his goals. This impulsive being had ventured too roughly into Canadian politics without having really weighed all the complexities of a situation that had made his predecessor, Milnes, more devious but perhaps in the long run more effective. Unyielding on the whole, Craig also had a warm and engaging side, as witnessed by the loyal friendships he formed in Lower Canada and as evidenced by the sale of numerous prints portraying him. His contemporaries lauded his personal generosity to the poor. He had been a member of the Quebec Fire Society, but does not seem to have been much involved in other associations.

No mere plaything in the hands of the officials or narrow-minded soldier reputed to have created French-Canadian nationalism through his policy of confrontation, Sir James Henry Craig appears rather as the person who brought out into the open a whole set of conflicts that turned two heterogeneous blocs in the colony against each other. These antagonisms focused on issues related to democracy and the emancipation of the colony as well as on the struggle between the mass of people, who were above all Canadian and rural, and the "people" in the English tradition – the oligarchy of landowners, higher officials, and wealthy merchants, which was largely British; the people expressed their preferences and plans through the assembly, whereas the oligarchic "people" defended itself by maintaining its supremacy within the Legislative and Executive councils and by resort to its privileged ties with London. The war situation would prevent any immediate resolution of these structural conflicts.

JEAN-PIERRE WALLOT

[Most of the information on James Henry Craig's career as a colonial administrator (1807–11) was taken from collections of papers relating to affairs of state. The ANQ-Q has the official records (correspondence, resolutions, and reports) of Craig in its RG 2 series. The PAC also holds many of the official records such as the petitions he received (RG 4, A1), his civil correspondence (RG 7, G1, G2, G14, G15, and G18), his military correspondence (RG 8, I (C ser.)), his recommendations to the Lower Canadian Legislative Council (RG 14, A1) and Executive Council (RG 1, E1), his

Craigie

reports on the militia (RG 9, I) and Indian affairs (RG 10), and his dispatches to the Colonial Office (MG 11, [CO 42] Q).

Collections of personal papers contain numerous letters concerning Craig from 1807 to 1811. These may be found at the AAQ in the correspondence of Bishop Plessis (210 A); at the ANQ-Q in the papers of Jean-Antoine Panet (P-200), the Papineau family (P-417), Jonathan Sewell (P-319), and Jean-Thomas Taschereau (P-238); at the PAC in the papers of Jonathan Sewell (MG 23, GII, 10), John Neilson* (MG 24, B1), and Herman Witsius Ryland (MG 24, B3); at the Archives du séminaire de Trois-Rivières (Trois-Rivières, Qué.) in the Hart papers; at the ASQ in the Viger–Verreau papers (Sér.O, 095–125; 0139–52 (copies at PAC)); and at the AUM in the Baby collection (P 58).   J.-P.W.]

Bas-Canada, chambre d'Assemblée, *Journaux*, 1807–11. Robert Christie, *Memoirs of the administration of the colonial government of Lower-Canada, by Sir James Henry Craig, and Sir George Prevost; from the year 1807 until the year 1815 . . .* (Quebec, 1818). [Ross Cuthbert], *An apology for Great Britain, in allusion to a pamphlet intituled, "Considérations, &c. par un Canadien, M.P.P."* (Quebec, 1809). *Doc. relatifs à l'hist. constitutionnelle, 1791–1818* (Doughty et McArthur; 1915). Hugh Gray, *Letters from Canada, written during a residence there in the years 1806, 1807, and 1808 . . .* (London, 1809; repr. Toronto, 1971). *Mandements, lettres pastorales et circulaires des évêques de Québec*, Henri Têtu et C.-O. Gagnon, édit. (18v. parus, Québec, 1887–   ). Un Canadien, M.P.P. [D.-B. Viger], *Considérations sur les effets qu'ont produit en Canada, la conservation des établissemens du pays, les mœurs, l'éducation, etc. de ses habitans . . .* (Montréal, 1809). *Canadian Courant and Montreal Advertiser*, 1807–11. *Le Canadien*, 1807–11. *Le Courier de Québec*, 1807–8. *Montreal Gazette*, 1807–11. *Montreal Herald*, 1811. *Quebec Gazette*, 1807–12. *Quebec Mercury*, 1807–11. *Le Vrai Canadien* (Québec), 1810–11. Hare et Wallot, *Les imprimés dans le Bas-Canada*. *Quebec almanac*, 1807–11. Christie, *Hist. of L.C.*, vols.1, 6. J. E. Hare, *La pensée socio-politique au Québec, 1784–1812: analyse sémantique* (Ottawa, 1977). Lemieux, *L'établissement de la première prov. eccl.* Manning, *Revolt of French Canada*. Ouellet, *Bas-Canada*. Paquet et Wallot, *Patronage et pouvoir dans le Bas-Canada*. J.-P. Wallot, "Le Bas-Canada sous l'administration de sir James Craig (1807–1811)" (thèse de PHD, univ. de Montréal, 1965); "Les Canadiens français et les Juifs (1808–1809): l'affaire Hart," *Juifs et Canadiens*, Naïm Kattam, édit. (Montréal, 1967), 111–21; *Un Québec qui bougeait*. F. G. Morrisey, "The juridical situation of the Catholic Church in Lower and Upper Canada from 1791 to 1840," *Studia Canonica* (Ottawa), 5 (1971): 279–321. Fernand Ouellet, "Mgr Plessis et la naissance d'une bourgeoisie canadienne (1797–1810)," SCHÉC *Rapport*, 23 (1955–56): 83–99. Gilles Paquet et J.-P. Wallot, "Le Bas-Canada au début du XIXᵉ siècle: une hypothèse," *RHAF*, 25 (1971–72): 39–61; "Groupes sociaux et pouvoir: le cas canadien au tournant du XIXᵉ siècle," *RHAF*, 27 (1973–74): 509–64. J.-P. Wallot, "Le clergé québécois et la politique: le 'règne de la terreur' (1810)," *Annales de Bretagne et des pays de l'Ouest* ([Rennes], France), 88 (1981): 457–75.

CRAIGIE, JOHN, office holder, businessman, and politician; b. probably in 1757, possibly in Kilgras-ton, Scotland, third son of John Craigie; d. 26 Nov. 1813 at Quebec, Lower Canada.

John Craigie came to Quebec in 1781 to replace John Drummond as deputy commissary general for the British army in Canada. He had been recommended by Lord Adam Gordon, who described him to Governor HALDIMAND as a man with considerable experience in bookkeeping. When the commissary general, Nathaniel Day, left Canada in 1784, Craigie was appointed by Haldimand to succeed him as head of the commissariat, which was responsible for purchasing, storing, and distributing the army's provisions and building materials. The next year Craigie became private secretary to Lieutenant Governor Henry Hope*, who in April 1786 recommended him unsuccessfully for the seat on the Legislative Council left vacant by the death of Conrad Gugy*. Craigie also carried out the responsibilities of storekeeper general and deputy inspector general of public accounts in Lower Canada.

On 13 Nov. 1792 he married Susannah, daughter of John COFFIN and widow of James Grant. The following year Craigie and his brother-in-law Thomas Coffin* went into partnership with Thomas DUNN and Joseph FROBISHER to found the Batiscan Iron Work Company, which operated iron mines and ironworks on the east bank of the Rivière Batiscan, near Sainte-Geneviève-de-Batiscan. Along with these various concerns he pursued a political career: elected for Buckingham in 1796, he sat in the Lower Canadian House of Assembly until June 1804. During the 1797 session he secured the passage of an act regulating trade with the United States and he proposed the establishment of public schools, particularly in rural regions, and the creation of workhouses or other buildings to provide shelter for the needy. In 1802 he was chairman of an assembly committee which recommended that the growing of hemp be encouraged.

Nevertheless, Craigie maintained his interest in the Batiscan ironworks, which he and his brother-in-law ran from 1800. That year the company, which had sought to lease the Saint-Maurice ironworks, was thwarted by Mathew Bell*'s group; with the complicity of Lieutenant Governor Robert Shore Milnes*, Bell won out, beating Craigie's group by a tender that offered £50 more than whatever his competitor bid. In October 1800, however, Milnes recommended Craigie for appointment to the Executive Council, pointing out that he had always supported the government in the assembly. In fact Craigie from 1797 to 1800 had rather divided his support between the Canadian party and the English party, although he favoured the latter; he was appointed an honorary member of the Executive Council in 1801. From that moment on he became the most steadfast representative of the English party in the second parliament.

Craigie also had several temporary responsibilities:

in 1794 he was a director of the Quebec Library, and in 1801 he was appointed commissioner for the care of the insane, for the building of the Anglican church (Cathedral of the Holy Trinity) at Quebec, and for the construction of a bridge over the Rivière Jacques-Cartier; he acted as commissioner for the construction of a new building for the Hôpital Général of Quebec in 1803. His successes were mirrored in his social life. By 1792, at least, he was living on Rue Sainte-Anne, in the most fashionable quarter of Upper Town, and in 1804 he purchased a house on Rue Saint-Louis from Adam Mabane*'s sister Isabell for £1,300. Among the godparents of the Craigies' 12 children were Milnes, Dunn, Frobisher, George ALLSOPP, Roger Hale Sheaffe*, Henry CALDWELL, and Isabell Mabane.

But Craigie's success proved more apparent than real. He did not have the money for his new house and paid only an annual interest of £78. In 1805 he began to use funds belonging to the army for his personal undertakings; when he was found out, he was dismissed as commissary general in 1808 by Governor CRAIG, who unsuccessfully proposed replacing him on the Executive Council as well. Moreover Craigie was sentenced to pay back the money that had been misappropriated. In 1811 his stables on Rue Haldimand were destroyed by fire, and in the course of the following year the mines and ironworks at Batiscan were abandoned, after they had consumed the funds that Craigie had filched from the state. In November 1813, at about 56 years of age, Craigie died. He had still not paid for his house, he owed £24,000 to the government, and he had a host of small debts. On the other hand he was the principal owner of the Batiscan Iron Work Company's holdings and had a piece of land on the Plains of Abraham. In March 1815 his wife renounced the estate in her own and her children's name.

John Craigie represented what was probably a fairly common breed of person in Canada. Coming from a prominent Scottish family, he was to try his luck in a French colony which had been conquered by Great Britain and in which those of English tongue were well placed to assume positions of authority in the midst of a French-speaking population. With some political backing, he tried to climb the ladder of success and make his fortune with the state's money. In his case the attempt ended in failure.

CHRISTIAN RIOUX

ANQ-Q, CE1-61, 23 Aug. 1784, 13 Nov. 1792, 30 Nov. 1813; CN1-16, 31 mai 1815; CN1-230, 19 déc. 1804; 11–14 janv., 16–17 févr., 28–29 déc. 1814; 30 janv., 21 mars 1815. BL, Add. MSS 21724: f.121; 21734: f.63; 21736: f.191; 21737: ff.215–17, 225 (mfm. at PAC). PAC, RG 4, A1, 29–32; RG 8, I (C ser.), 325: 104–6. PRO, CO 42/19: f.187; 42/46: f.96; 42/49: ff.198, 200; 42/66, 8 nov. 1788; 42/87: f.433; 42/93: ff.166–67; 42/109: ff.266–79; 42/115: f.162; 42/116: ff.425–44; 42/117: ff.6–7; 42/136: f.229, 15 Aug. 1808. "Les dénombrements de Québec" (Plessis), ANQ Rapport, 1948–49: 21, 72, 121, 172. Quebec Gazette, 9 Aug. 1787, 3 July 1794, 24 Oct. 1799, 1 Jan. 1801, 14 Nov. 1805, 14 July 1808, 19 Sept. 1811, 17 Sept. 1812, 9 Dec. 1813. F.-J. Audet et Édouard Fabre Surveyer, Les députés de Saint-Maurice et de Buckinghamshire, 1792–1808 (Trois-Rivières, Qué., 1934), 6, 54–58. Desjardins, Guide parl. Quebec almanac, 1788: 19; 1791–1813. É.-Z. Massicotte, Sainte-Geneviève de Batiscan (Trois-Rivières, 1936), 77–79. Albert Tessier, Les forges Saint-Maurice, 1729–1883 (Trois-Rivières, 1952), 116–17. Hare, "L'Assemblée législative du Bas-Canada," RHAF, 27: 374–76. Le Mauricien (Trois-Rivières), 1 (1937), no.6: 8.

CRANE. See CHEJAUK

CREIGHTON, JOHN, office holder, militia officer, judge, and politician; b. 1721 in Glastonbury, England; m. first Maria —; m. secondly 8 Dec. 1760 Lucy Clapp in Lunenburg, N.S., and they had three sons and three daughters; d. there 8 Nov. 1807.

John Creighton began his career as a lieutenant in the dragoons, and was present at the battle of Fontenoy in 1745, but in 1749 he went on half pay. That year he, his wife, and two servants accompanied Edward Cornwallis* to Nova Scotia, sailing on board the *Charlton*. Although in comfortable circumstances, he apparently welcomed the opportunity to go to Mirligueche (Lunenburg) with the Germans and Swiss in 1753, both to secure challenging employment and to add to his income. Intending that he play a leading role in the founding and development of the settlement, the authorities in Halifax made him a justice of the peace and militia captain before he left there. In the latter capacity he commanded the settlers in Creighton's division, one of the six divisions of Lunenburg, and thus to this day all deeds relating to lands given to settlers within this division bear his name.

In the early years of the settlement Creighton served on the commission for laying out and assigning 300-acre lots; in 1753 he was gazetted as a judge of the Inferior Court of Common Pleas, although he did not actually serve in that capacity until the court was created seven years later; in June 1755 he reported personally to the Council about the victualling of the settlement; in 1776 he became judge of the Probate Court. These were some of the multiplicity of duties which the authorities at Halifax conferred on someone they trusted. In return, he was among the few who were permitted to send men to Grand Pré to procure cattle and horses after the expulsion of the Acadians in 1755.

Trust in Creighton may have developed more slowly among the Germans and Swiss, since in the election to the first house of assembly in 1758 he received but a single vote; between 1770 and 1775, however, he served as an assemblyman for Lunenburg County. Although Governor Lord William Campbell*

Cressé

recommended his appointment to the Council as early as 1767, it was not until 6 May 1775, after Governor Francis Legge* had described him as "a man of good character & understanding, in easy circumstances, well affected to His Majesty," that he was finally admitted. But it was folly to hope that the Council could be anything other than a Halifax body in those days, communications being what they were, and over the next 13 years Creighton attended only a handful of its meetings. He was there for the last time on 6 Oct. 1785, before being superseded on 3 Jan. 1788 for inability to attend.

Creighton is best known for his conduct during the American privateer raid of 1 July 1782 on Lunenburg. Some 90 men from several vessels landed near the town, took the small garrison of regulars prisoner, and then began to pillage. As a lieutenant-colonel in the militia, Creighton occupied the blockhouse and wounded three of the enemy before being captured with two of his men. The town itself was largely spared, but Creighton's belongings were not. His house and its effects were burned, although his black servant Silvia, who protected his son with her body, saved some valuable coins and plate by lowering them into the well. The assembly later voted to pay Creighton and his fellow captives £109 19s. in compensation.

In social standing Creighton was probably unique among Lunenburgers. His eldest son, John, was educated in England and served in the British army, as did his youngest son, Joseph, for whom Creighton bought a captaincy costing £950. His sons-in-law Hibbert Newton Binney and Lewis Morris Wilkins*, who married his daughters Lucy and Sarah, were both members of the Halifax establishment, of which Creighton was in effect the Lunenburg representative. Outside Nova Scotia his major holding was £9,000 in three per cent Consols, which were to bring his widow an annual net income of about £245. His descendants have held a wide variety of offices ranging from that of sheriff to that of councillor in every generation to the present.

J. MURRAY BECK

PANS, MG 4, 92: 1–10 (typescript). Private arch., Mrs D. Burke (Lunenburg, N.S.), H. W. Hewitt, "History of the town of Lunenburg" (typescript; photocopy at PANS). Bell, *Foreign Protestants*, 410; 415, n.11a; 488; 491; 575, n.5a. M. B. DesBrisay, *History of the county of Lunenburg* (2nd ed., Toronto, 1895), 62–68.

CRESSÉ, PIERRE-MICHEL, seigneur and militia officer; b. 19 Sept. 1758 at Quebec, son of Louis-Pierre Poulin* de Courval Cressé and Charlotte-Louise Lambert Dumont; m. 2 Jan. 1792 Marie-Victoire Fafard Laframboise in Trois-Rivières,

Lower Canada, under a contract providing for husband and wife to administer their properties separately; they had 13 children; d. there 3 Aug. 1819 and was buried the next day under the seigneurial pew in the church at Nicolet, Lower Canada.

Pierre-Michel Cressé was the first of the Poulin de Courval family to bear the name of Cressé alone. In 1764, on his father's death, he inherited two-thirds of the seigneury of Courval, which he was to reassign to his older sister Louise-Charlotte on 3 March 1796. The seigneury had originally been granted to his father and was located south of Baie-du-Febvre (Baieville) next to the seigneury of Nicolet. After his father died his mother moved to Nicolet, whose absentee seigneur was his grandfather, Claude Poulin de Courval Cressé; there she raised her family and built the seigneurial manor-house. In May 1785, upon his grandfather's death, Cressé inherited two-thirds of this property. He became the first seigneur of Nicolet to reside there since the death of his ancestor Michel Cressé in 1686.

Upon taking possession of his domain Cressé brought back into force the seigneur's honorary rights, which had fallen into abeyance. Thus he claimed precedence in church and demanded to have the seigneurial pew in the place of honour, the first on the right in the nave; he also insisted on following immediately after the parish priest in processions and on being the first to receive the host at the Eucharist, the candles at Candlemas, and the ashes and the palms during Lent. In addition, with his first deeds of land in 1785 he re-established the custom of planting the May tree, obliging each new *censitaire* to "help plant a tree in front of the main door of the seigneur's house every year on the first day of May, on pain of a fine of 3 *livres* 20 *sols* each time he is absent."

Cressé also firmly insisted upon his pecuniary rights, and this engendered a lengthy dispute with the parish priest of Nicolet, Louis-Marie Brassard*. On 21 Sept. 1770 Brassard had purchased in his own right a lot of 4 *arpents* in width by 40 in depth which had originally been granted freehold and on which stood a house. Cressé would only acknowledge a depth of 30 *arpents* to this lot; in addition he refused to exempt it from the *cens et rentes*, contrary to the attitude most seigneurs adopted towards their parish priests. On 17 Feb. 1787 he sued Brassard to force him to take title within a week and to pay the arrears of the *cens et rentes*. At the hearing on 23 Nov. 1788 in the Court of Common Pleas for the District of Montreal the judges, John Fraser, René-Ovide Hertel* de Rouville, and Edward Southouse, handed the matter over to arbitrators: Joseph BOUCHER de Niverville for the seigneur and Charles-Antoine Godefroy* de Tonnancour for the parish priest; they were authorized by the court to add a third "in case of a split judgement."

The two arbitrators could not reach agreement, and

Antoine Lefebvre de Bellefeuille, the overseer of highways for Trois-Rivières, was chosen to join them. On 22 June 1789 Boucher and Lefebvre came out in favour of the seigneur: "Monsieur Brassard will pay him rent for the aforementioned land grant at the regular rate." On 4 October Godefroy made it known that he was opposed to official approval of the minutes, which he had refused to sign because of "the glaring error into which the two arbitrators fell" in mistaking the land under dispute for another lot that Brassard owned west of the Rivière Nicolet. Finally, in 1790, the court annulled the arbitration and ordered Cressé to give a new title-deed to the priest. The seigneur refused to give in and persisted in maintaining that the lot was only 30 *arpents* in depth.

At his death on 27 Dec. 1800 Brassard bequeathed the 40-*arpent* lot to the parish council of Nicolet as a site for a free primary school. This transfer in mortmain was not recognized in law, and Pierre Brassard, the parish priest's brother, became the legal heir. Faithful to the deceased priest's intentions, he gave the house and land to Pierre DENAUT, bishop of Quebec, on 21 Nov. 1803. The school, however, had opened two years earlier and in 1803, at the request of his coadjutor, Joseph-Octave Plessis*, Bishop Denaut had instituted Latin classes. On 18 March 1806 Plessis, who was by then bishop of Quebec and was still interested in the school, bought the land for 5,000 *livres* from Marguerite-Amable Denaut, the bishop's niece, who had inherited it. Plessis was on good terms with Cressé and was accorded a new title-deed to the land on 3 Aug. 1812. He bound himself to pay the seigneur "the sum of 11 *livres* 10 *sols*, the *livre* [being] at 20 *sols*" for the *cens et rentes*. The contract stipulated that the land measured 40 *arpents* in depth. Thus ended a dispute that had lasted more than 25 years.

Meanwhile, in 1802, because the boundaries of the new township of Aston had to be laid out, Cressé had had his land surveyed by Jeremiah McCarthy*. By misinterpreting the land grant made to his forefathers, he managed, through this survey, to annex part of Aston; within the township he had two concessions of 120 lots each surveyed and he granted more than 30 lots to *censitaires* who paid him *cens et rentes*. He was left in peace to enjoy the fruits of this encroachment.

During the War of 1812 Cressé served as lieutenant in the 4th battalion of Select Embodied Militia. Early in 1817 his health was seriously impaired and he left Nicolet to go to live at Trois-Rivières. He then put his seigneury up for sale; included were the manorial farm, another farm measuring 7 *arpents* by 40, and the seigneurial buildings, comprising the manor-house, outbuildings, and banal mills. He perhaps thought it wise to take this action because of the inaccurate boundaries established through the survey in 1802; because of their age, none of his 13 children was in a

position at that time to take over the seigneury. Charles-François-Xavier Baby* purchased it on 9 Jan. 1819, "with all seigneurial rights attached to it, both pecuniary and honorary," for £12,000 payable in an invested annuity of £660 redeemable on payment of the capital. But Baby could not meet his obligations. On 6 March 1821 Cressé's heirs had the seigneury sold by the sheriff, and Captain Kenelm Conor Chandler bought it for the modest sum of £6,500. He later had problems because of Cressé's survey.

Throughout his life Pierre-Michel Cressé had been determined to keep the seigneurial traditions alive; his attachment to a seigneur's honorary and pecuniary rights became his constant preoccupation.

ALBERTUS MARTIN

ANQ-M, CN1-383, 3 mars 1796. ANQ-MBF, CN1-4, 17 janv. 1797; CN1-5, 25 juin 1780; 13 août 1782; 20, 21 oct. 1785; 2, 18 janv., 7, 9 févr. 1786; 1er janv. 1792; CN1-6, 30 janv. 1800, 2 févr. 1806, 3 août 1812; CN1-29, 21 sept. 1770; CN1-32, 16 juill. 1801; 9 janv., 24 août 1819; CN1-76, 21 mai 1716. AP, Immaculée-Conception (Trois-Rivières), Reg. des baptêmes, mariages et sépultures, 2 janv. 1792; Notre-Dame de Québec, Reg. des baptêmes, mariages et sépultures, 20 sept. 1758; Saint-Jean-Baptiste (Nicolet), Reg. des baptêmes, mariages et sépultures, 4 août 1819. Arch. de l'évêché de Nicolet (Nicolet), Cartable Nicolet, I: 7. Arch. du séminaire de Nicolet (Nicolet), AO, Polygraphie, I: 20–40. P.-G. Roy, *Inv. concessions*, 5: 86. J.-E. Bellemare, *Histoire de Nicolet, 1669–1924* (Arthabaska, Qué., 1924). J.-A.-I. Douville, *Histoire du collège-séminaire de Nicolet, 1803–1903, avec les listes complètes des directeurs, professeurs et élèves de l'institution* (2v., Montréal, 1903), 1: 1–10.

CRUICKSHANK, ROBERT, silversmith, merchant, office holder, and militia officer; b. *c.* 1748, probably in Aberdeen, Scotland; d. at sea 16 April 1809.

The paucity of sources has led to various hypotheses about Robert Cruickshank's origins; according to the most plausible one he was born in Aberdeen, where the family name was common. Cruickshank appears to have learned the silversmith's craft in the British Isles. He may have visited the United States: an Alexander Crouckeshanks, who came from London, opened a silversmith's shop in Boston in 1768; it is conceivable that he was one of Robert's relatives and that Robert worked with him. Whatever the case, by 1773 Cruickshank was settled in Montreal. A year later he signed a petition to the king asking for the restoration of habeas corpus and trial by jury in civil suits, which had been abolished that year by the Quebec Act.

By 1782 Cruickshank was solidly established in business. He owned a house on Rue Notre-Dame, next to the former prison; his resources and the volume of

Cruickshank

his affairs made it possible to undertake building and renovation on a large scale. To his property he added a shop measuring 23 feet by 12, with an impressive "forge chimney." Thus, just as Ignace-François Delezenne* had done in 1758 and Pierre HUGUET, *dit* Latour, would do in 1803, Cruickshank progressed from a craftsman's shop in his own house to an enterprise requiring premises separate from his private residence, in which to install a workshop and store. These three were the only silversmiths in the late 18th and early 19th centuries to make the transition. The change was not wholly fortuitous: they were forced into it by the phenomenal volume of orders for trade silver. In moving from the status of craftsman to that of bourgeois they had to provide a workshop and suitable tools for their numerous apprentices and journeymen. Their large clientele also had to have access to adequate premises – hence the store.

Judging by his partnerships with other craftsmen and the number of apprentices he took on, Cruickshank led a busy professional life. A soup-tureen in the museum of the church of Notre-Dame in Montreal, which bears the marks of Cruickshank and Jacques Varin*, *dit* La Pistole, suggests that the two silversmiths collaborated. In 1777–78 Cruickshank seems to have had Michael ARNOLDI as an apprentice; they later became partners. The firm of Cruickshank and Arnoldi, which may have used the mark CA, was not finally dissolved until 1789. In 1790–91 Cruickshank was in contact with the silversmith Jean-Henry Lerche, whose mark JHL imitated the style of writing in the mark RC. Cruickshank seems to have gone into partnership with Peter Arnoldi around 1793–94, for a tea service in the Henry Birks Collection bears their respective marks. Cruickshank was also connected with clockmakers, jewellers, and engravers: his "good old friend" John Lumsden until 1802; Charles Irish, who had been hired in London in 1803 for a three-year period; and perhaps Charles Arnoldi, Michael's brother, who is believed to have replaced Irish. In addition to silverware, therefore, his store carried clocks, jewellery, trinkets, and hardware, and certainly included many objects imported from England. Cruickshank took on the following apprentice silversmiths in turn: Michel Roy in 1791 for six years, Frédéric Delisle in 1795 for seven years, René Blache in 1796 for four years, Peter Bohle, son of the silversmith Charles-David Bohle, in 1800 for seven years, and Narcisse Auclair in 1805 for seven years. (Auclair's apprenticeship papers were transferred to Nathan Starns, his brother-in-law and guardian, on 16 Oct. 1807.)

Cruickshank belonged to the Montreal group of silversmiths. There was a clear division between this group and the one in Quebec: the former were businessmen, the latter primarily craftsmen. The marks of François RANVOYZÉ, Laurent Amiot*, and François Sasseville* belonged to craftsmen who did their own work; Cruickshank's and Huguet's can be called studio marks, because an associate, journeyman or apprentice, may have made the piece. With the Quebec silversmiths it is possible to follow the logical evolution of the craftsman's style, but study of the Montreal group becomes very complicated, since ten pieces of work bearing the same mark may have been executed by as many different silversmiths. Furthermore Cruickshank seems to have put his mark on imported objects. Nevertheless his work, which is characterized by refinement, shows greater homogeneity than does Huguet's. That was an inevitable consequence of their respective training: Cruickshank was a professional silversmith, but Huguet was a wig maker who became a silversmith overnight around 1780.

In addition to conducting his trade Cruickshank served as a banker, issuing promissory notes and lending money at interest. He proved a skilful, well-organized, meticulous administrator. Towards the end of his career he was, moreover, active mainly as a merchant. His full professional life was matched by an intense social one that gave him a place among the important people of Montreal. He made a contribution to the paving of the Place du Marché in 1785–86 and to the Agriculture Society in 1791. He held the office of justice of the peace (1795–1809) and served in the militia, first as a lieutenant (1788–97) and then as a captain (1800–9), in the town's 1st Militia Battalion. As a magistrate he signed a petition to Sir Robert Shore Milnes* for the reconstruction of the Montreal prison, burned in 1803. His name also appears on the list of founders of Christ Church in 1805 [*see* Jehosaphat MOUNTAIN]. Although less is known of his private life, he associated with the English-speaking élite, particularly James McGILL, EDWARD WILLIAM and Jonathan Abraham Gray, Joseph FROBISHER, and Stephen Sewell*.

In August 1789 Cruickshank married Ann Kay, a widow with eight children; she died the following year. His only daughter, Elizabeth, married the merchant Arthur Webster in 1803, at which date the couple were both of age. Webster quickly won his father-in-law's confidence. Just before leaving for Great Britain in October 1807, Cruickshank left him full power of attorney to run all his business affairs "wherever they are in Upper or Lower Canada or the United States of America." The exact reasons for his trip are not known, but both business matters and his private life were probably involved. No doubt Cruickshank had to import many articles from London suppliers. During his return voyage in 1809 he died on board the *Eweretta*.

All of Cruickshank's estate must have gone automatically to his daughter and son-in-law; thus there was no inventory after his death, which would have been of considerable value. It may be hazarded, however, that he owned a very large business, comparable to Huguet's. In addition there were certainly numerous properties, including a piece of land bought after the Château de Vaudreuil burned in 1803. But his departure in October 1807 had already marked the end of the career of one of Lower Canada's most important silversmiths who had initiated a profound change in both the product and its marketing. He had introduced a new treatment and a new aesthetics that met with great success and enabled his production to compete with contemporary English and American work. With him the silversmith's craft in the colony had moved away from French influence into the British tradition.

ROBERT DEROME

ANQ-M, CE1-63, 14 Aug. 1789, 12 Dec. 1790; CN1-16, 13 déc. 1802; CN1-29, 2 Sept. 1786, 17 Feb. 1789, 11 Sept. 1795; CN1-121, 2 nov. 1796; CN1-128, 1er juin 1801, 20 déc. 1803; CN1-184, 14 Aug. 1789; CN1-185, 31 Dec. 1800; 21 Sept. 1803; 7 Jan. 1804; 4 Nov. 1805; 15 Oct. 1806; 9, 16 Oct. 1807; CN1-313, 19 avril 1782; 21 janv., 6 sept. 1791. MAC-CD, Fonds Morisset, 2, C958.8/R639. PAC, RG 8, I (C ser.), 77: 101–6a. *Quebec Gazette*, 14 Oct. 1784, 22 June 1809. *Quebec almanac*, 1791, 1795–1809. Robert Derome, *Les orfèvres de la Nouvelle-France, inventaire descriptif des sources* (Ottawa, 1974); "Delezenne, les orfèvres, l'orfèvrerie, 1740–1790" (MA thesis, univ. de Montréal, 1974). H. N. Flynt and M. G. Fales, *The Heritage Foundation collection of silver, with biographical sketches of New England silversmiths, 1625–1825* (Old Deerfield, Mass., 1968), 193. A. R. George, *The House of Birks* (n.p., 1946). *Hochelaga depicta . . .*, ed. Newton Bosworth (Montreal, 1839; repr. Toronto, 1974), 103. Graham Hood, *American silver, a history of style, 1650–1900* (New York and London, 1971). C. J. Jackson, *English goldsmiths and their marks . . .* (2nd ed., London, 1921), 218, 530–31. Langdon, *Canadian silversmiths*. R. H. Mayne, *Old Channel Islands silver, its makers and marks* (Jersey, 1969). Benjamin Sulte et al., *A history of Quebec, its resources and people* (Montreal and Toronto, 1908), 230. Traquair, *Old silver of Quebec*. Jean Trudel, *L'orfèvrerie en Nouvelle-France* (Ottawa, 1974), 226–27. Édouard Fabre Surveyer, "Une famille d'orfèvres," *BRH*, 46 (1940): 310–15. E. A. Jones, "Old church silver in Canada," RSC *Trans.*, 3rd ser., 12 (1918), sect.II: 135–50. É.-Z. Massicotte, "L'argentier Huguet-Latour," *BRH*, 46 (1940): 284–87. Gérard Morisset, "Un perruquier orfèvre," *La Patrie* (Montréal), 2 juill. 1950: 28, 31.

CULVER. See COLLVER

CURTIS, JAMES, merchant, politician, office holder, judge, and land agent; d. 19 Nov. 1819 at his farm, Poplar Grove, Covehead, P.E.I.

Little is known of James Curtis's background before his arrival on St John's (Prince Edward) Island around 1770 as footman to Phillips Callbeck*. He did not long remain in that menial capacity, but served successively as clerk to Callbeck and to David Higgins*. Higgins, in partnership with Scotland's

lord advocate, James William Montgomery, was attempting to establish a settlement at Three Rivers (the region around Georgetown). After leaving Higgins, Curtis removed to the Montgomery settlement on Lot 34, which was under the supervision of David LAWSON, setting up in Covehead as a "petty trader" and storekeeper. In 1779 he was elected to the House of Assembly.

Curtis first came to prominence in 1781, when as deputy provost marshal he personally handled the auction of the proprietorial lots sold by order of the Council some time between 13 and 15 November of that year [*see* Walter Patterson*]. With David Lawson's assistance he managed in 1783 to obtain credit from the Glasgow merchant Patrick Colquhoun for fishing equipment and sundries to be sold at his store, although by Lawson's own account Curtis was already £6,000 in debt. At about this time Curtis married Lawson's daughter Elizabeth and became an integral part of the Covehead faction, which supported Governor Patterson in his efforts to prevent the sales of 1781 from being overturned by the proprietors and the British government. Curtis was elected to the House of Assembly in 1784 as a Patterson adherent, and he won again in 1785 after a bitter contest between the governor's followers and the supporters of Chief Justice Peter STEWART and the former lieutenant governor, Thomas DESBRISAY.

Soon after Edmund FANNING managed to secure his position as lieutenant governor of the Island in 1787, another election was called, in which "Captain Fletcher's list" of Patterson supporters, Curtis among them, was victorious. Because the sheriff refused to make the return for the election, citing violence at the Charlottetown poll, writs for a second election were immediately issued, and Curtis was again successful. He served as secretary of the Board of Resident Proprietors and Agents, which Patterson organized in 1787 to fight the Fanning régime, and was subsequently dismissed by Fanning from his post as storekeeper to the disbanded troops and loyalists on the Island for misappropriation of funds. In 1789, during the visit of Bishop Charles INGLIS, Curtis was accused of spreading the rumour that tithes for the Church of England were about to be introduced on the Island.

In 1791, when merchant-proprietors John Cambridge*, John Hill*, and William Bowley charged Fanning and his chief officers with malfeasance in a suit before the Privy Council in London, Curtis helped collect the local evidence against the administration. The following year he went to England with a petition from many inhabitants condemning the lieutenant governor, but the Privy Council ignored it and, in fact, completely exonerated Fanning and the other defendants. Like so many Patterson supporters, however, Curtis eventually made his peace with Fanning, and he became, in the words of Captain John MACDONALD of Glenaladale, a "chief understrapper" for the new

219

administration, much as he had been for the old one.

In a by-election held in 1797 Curtis was again returned to the assembly and three years later, although without legal background or training, he was appointed an assistant judge of the Supreme Court. According to Island gossip, "the night before his promotion he slept in a Stable at Charlottetown." From the time of his appointment until the arrival of Chief Justice Thomas Cochrane in 1801, Curtis tried most of the cases heard before the court, since Chief Justice Stewart was often indisposed (and finally resigned late in 1800) and fellow assistant judge Robert Gray* seldom attended. Curtis was active in the assembly as well: in 1797 he served on the legislative committee that censured MacDonald, and in the same year he chaired the committee whose investigation of the land situation led the assembly to petition the British government for escheat of proprietorial holdings. He was easily re-elected to the assembly in 1803 as a "friend of the people." From 1801 to 1805 and from 1813 to 1817 he served as speaker of the house.

In the 1800s Curtis was running a ship's-chandler shop at Rustico, but he increasingly acquired agencies from absentee proprietors. He began by representing Ann Callbeck, Phillips's widow, and in 1804 succeeded James DOUGLAS as agent for the Montgomery interests. The latter agency undoubtedly gave him particular satisfaction, for his father-in-law had been summarily dismissed by the Montgomerys as agent in 1788 and had spent his last years living with Curtis in semi-disgrace. Unlike Douglas, Curtis was not a particularly active agent.

One of Curtis's final acts of public importance was to testify against lawyer William Roubel* in 1812, his evidence forming part of the documentation used to disbar Roubel. Along with fellow judges Caesar Colclough* and Robert Gray, he had been heavily criticized for his involvement in party politics by Roubel and other members of the Loyal Electors led by James Bardin Palmer*. The following year Roubel prosecuted Curtis for perjury, but his suit before the Privy Council was unsuccessful.

James Curtis died in November 1819, survived only by his wife. His career was typical of those of many minor political figures on the Island who helped to maintain a high level of political conflict in the early days of its history.

J. M. BUMSTED

PAC, MG 11, [CO 226] Prince Edward Island A, 17: 335–37; 27: 236–39; MG 23, E5, 1. PAPEI, Acc. 2702, Smith–Alley coll., James Curtis, "Extracts of examinations upon oath before the House of Assembly regarding the sales of the lots," April 1786. PRO, CO 226/11; 226/13. SRO, GD293/2/17/9; 293/2/78/28, 43; 293/2/80/17. [John MacDonald?], *Remarks on the conduct of the governor and Council of the Island of St. John's, in passing an act of assembly in April of 1786 to confirm the sales of the lands in 1781* . . . (n.p., [1789]). *Prince Edward Island Gazette* (Charlottetown), 20 Nov. 1819. *Royal American Gazette, and Weekly Intelligencer of the Island of Saint John* (Charlottetown), 29 Sept. 1787. MacNutt, "Fanning's regime on P.E.I.," *Acadiensis* (Fredericton), 1, no.1: 45–49.

CURTIS, Sir ROGER, naval officer; b. 4 June 1746 in Downton, Wiltshire, England, only son of Roger Curtis, a prominent farmer, and Christabella Blachford; m. December 1778 Jane Sarah Brady, daughter and heiress of Matthew Brady of Gatcombe House (Gatcombe), England, and they had two sons and one daughter; d. 14 Nov. 1816 at Gatcombe House.

At the age of 16, Roger Curtis travelled to Portsmouth to join his first ship, the *Royal Sovereign*, on 22 June 1762. After voyages in this and other vessels, he spent three years on the Newfoundland station during the governorship of Hugh Palliser* as a midshipman in the frigate *Gibraltar*. He then served briefly in the *Venus* and the *Albion* under Captain Samuel Barrington, who became a lifelong friend.

On 28 Jan. 1771 Curtis was promoted lieutenant and posted to the sloop *Otter*. In her he spent the next three summers on the coast of Labrador and rapidly became familiar with the geography, fisheries, and peoples of this remote region. At the end of his second summer he compiled a lengthy account of the coast, dedicating it to the secretary of state for the American Colonies, Lord Dartmouth, who was especially interested in the welfare of the natives. He sweepingly dismissed the land of Labrador itself as "nothing more than a prodigious heap of barren rocks," but was enthusiastic about the prospects for a valuable cod fishery. He strongly believed that it should be carried on by annual ship fishers from Great Britain rather than by Canadians from fixed posts on the coast. As far as he could see, the Inuit lacked any kind of religion, laws, or government, but he noted that they did not drink, seldom quarrelled with each other, and as yet had few diseases, not even smallpox, and "consequently have the happiness to be without Physicians."

In 1773 the British government took a renewed interest in the Labrador coast and its fisheries. One result was that Curtis was directed both to visit the Moravian missionaries at their post at Nain and to see whether there were resources "capable of being rendered national advantages" on the northern coasts. On 14 July he left Chateau Bay in the armed shallop *Sandwich*, with an Inuit pilot. After travelling along the coast almost to Hudson Strait and visiting Nain, the *Sandwich* returned to Chateau Bay on 26 August. Governor Molyneux Shuldham* had by then arrived and Curtis was able to report to him directly. Shuldham described Curtis favourably as a "very sensible Officer" and forwarded home accounts the lieutenant had drawn up on the northern coast of Labrador and the Moravian mission there.

Curtis accompanied his report on northern Labrador with a chart of the coast which he considered superior to any yet produced. It outlined the sea coast fairly accurately, but he obviously had not had the time to explore the many intricate bays and inlets, although he was able to quash the notion that Davis Inlet might be a passage to Hudson Bay and beyond. He felt that valuable seal and walrus fisheries could be carried on in northern Labrador: Inuit were at a loss to describe the vast numbers of seals which came to certain places in the spring and fall, and walruses flocked ashore on islands north of Nain. He identified the chief tribes or settlements of Inuit and estimated their total population from observation and information at about 1,625, which was probably reasonably accurate.

Curtis was full of praise for the Moravian Brethren and wonder at the work already accomplished [see Christian Larsen Drachart*; Jens Haven*]. Speaking through a missionary interpreter, he had warned the assembled Inuit at Nain against killing or robbing Europeans or other Inuit, and the natives had pledged fidelity to the king of Great Britain and obedience to his representatives. The mission settlement, concluded Curtis, was "of infinite use to the Fishery upon this Coast, as by softning the manners of the Savages, the Adventurers will run but little risk of future annoyances, and I think [they are] extremely deserving of the Protection and the Encouragement of Government." Curtis's favourable report on the mission undoubtedly helped the Moravians to secure in 1774 land grants for further posts. His offer to continue his explorations in 1774 was not taken up, but he did succeed in having his impressions of Labrador presented to the Royal Society that year by Daines Barrington, a brother of Captain Barrington.

Authorities on the Labrador coast have had mixed opinions of Curtis's work. Thomas Pennant in his *Arctic zoology* (2v., London, 1784–85) stated that the Labrador coast "so admirably described by that honored name, Sir Roger Curtis, is barren past the efforts of cultivation," although since his work was based on the information of others he would have had no grounds to be critical of Curtis's statements. Captain George CARTWRIGHT, who lived on the coast in the 1770s and 1780s and who had no doubt met Curtis there, noted rather sourly in his copy of Pennant that Curtis had pirated his chart and invented most of his account of the country, since he was ignorant of the good soil and large trees to be found in many parts. William Gilbert Gosling*, the historian of Labrador, condemned Curtis's chart as "very crude and incorrect," and a modern scholar, Averil M. Lysaght, has argued that some of the Moravian charts were better. Since Curtis's explorations were largely confined to the sea coast, his impressions of the barrenness of the country are understandable.

Curtis never returned to Labrador after 1773. He was now high in the favour of Shuldham, and when the latter was appointed commander-in-chief on the North American station in 1775, he took Curtis with him to New York. Admiral Lord Howe, who succeeded Shuldham, quickly came to regard Curtis with equal esteem. In April 1777 he was promoted captain and given command of the *Eagle*, Howe's flagship. Curtis was sent to the Mediterranean in 1780 as captain of the frigate *Brilliant*. In April 1781 he brought a relief convoy into besieged Gibraltar and organized a naval brigade which was active in the defence of the fortress against the Spaniards. After Lord Howe raised the siege in 1782, Curtis was promoted commodore and knighted. At the same time he had to defend himself against a sharp personal attack launched by a disgruntled naval officer, Lieutenant Coll Campbell, who had served in the *Brilliant*. Campbell wrote a pamphlet charging him with errors of judgment and, in some cases, downright dishonourable behaviour under stress. Although some of the accusations had substance, the naval establishment remained solidly on the side of the hero of Gibraltar and nothing came of the charges.

According to a contemporary biographer, Sir Roger possessed elegant and engaging manners, a highly developed understanding, and a warm and friendly heart. He was certainly articulate and well spoken, with a talent for getting along well with people whose friendship he wished to cultivate. In 1783 he was appointed ambassador to the emperor of Morocco and the Barbary States, and was successful in restoring good trading and diplomatic relations. Another diplomatic mission, secret in nature, took him to Sweden, Denmark, and Russia in 1789. On the outbreak of war with France in 1793, Curtis took command of the *Queen Charlotte*, the flagship of his old patron Lord Howe. The famous victory of the "Glorious First of June," 1794, brought him promotion to rear-admiral and a baronetcy. In 1799 he was advanced to vice-admiral and appointed commander-in-chief at the Cape of Good Hope. There he established the beginnings of the famous naval base at Simonstown. Sir Roger retired from active sea service at the Treaty of Amiens (1802) but became a full admiral in 1804 and in January 1809 was appointed commander-in-chief at Portsmouth naval base, where he had joined his first ship almost 50 years before. Through his wife, Curtis had come into possession of Gatcombe House, and he lived there until his death in 1816. His eldest son, Roger, a captain in the navy, predeceased him, and the bulk of the estate thus descended to his second son, Lucius, also a navy captain.

Curtis's connection with Canada came at the beginning of an illustrious career when he was a young and ambitious officer anxious to make his mark. He was the first British naval officer to survey the northern coast of Labrador and no other followed him for almost 50 years. That his reports were in some

Cuyler

respects superficial and naïve is not surprising, given his youth, his lack of training, and the limited time at his disposal. If they reflected the biases natural to an 18th-century naval officer, they also contained a humanity and sense of fairness which such officers often displayed. In spite of their imperfections, they advanced knowledge of a difficult and remote region.

WILLIAM H. WHITELEY

The following reports by Sir Roger Curtis on Labrador are located in the PRO: "A short account of the territory of Labradore" (CO 194/30: ff.156–91), dated 1772; "An account of the Moravian mission upon the coast of Labrador" (CO 194/31: ff.58–65), dated 1773; and "Remarks upon the northern parts of the coast of Labrador" (CO 194/31: ff.38–53), dated 1773. All are available on microfilm at the PAC, which also possesses the original of Curtis's "Proposal for a further exploration of the northern coast of Labrador" (MG 23, A1, 2: 2417–29), dated 1773. His observations on the region were published in "Particulars of the country of Labrador, extracted from the papers of Lieutenant Roger Curtis, of his majesty's sloop the 'Otter,' with a plane-chart of the coast," Royal Soc. of London, *Philosophical Trans.*, 64 (1774): 372–88. His 1784 "Memorandum relative to my embassy to the emperor of Morocco" is preserved in the National Maritime Museum, JOD/157/1–2.

PRO, ADM 1/470, 1/2118; ADM 36/6801, 36/7456, 36/7530; ADM 51/663; ADM 52/1387; PROB 11/1586/610. *Annual biog. and obituary* (London), 1 (1817): 380–91. "Biographical memoir of Sir Roger Curtis, Bart. . . . ," *Naval Chronicle*, 6 (July–December 1801): 261–76. [Coll Campbell], *A new edition of the appeal of a neglected naval officer: to which are now added, the reply of Sir Roger Curtis, intersected with remarks of Lieut. Campbell . . .* (London, [1785]). *Naval Chronicle*, 36 (July–December 1816): 440. James Ralfe, *The naval biography of Great Britain . . .* (4v., London, 1828), 2: 32–44. *DNB*. W. G. Gosling, *Labrador: its discovery, exploration, and development* (London, 1910). A. M. Lysaght, *Joseph Banks in Newfoundland and Labrador, 1766: his diary, manuscripts and collections* (London and Berkeley, Calif., 1971).

CUYLER, ABRAHAM CORNELIUS, office holder and politician; b. 11 April 1742 in Albany, N.Y., son of Cornelius Cuyler and Catalyntje Schuyler; m. 10 April 1764 Jane Elizabeth (Jannetie) Glen in Schenectady, N.Y., and they had three sons and two daughters; d. 5 Feb. 1810 in Montreal, Lower Canada.

Abraham Cornelius Cuyler was born into a prominent New York family of Dutch descent which exercised much influence in the Albany region. After serving as president of the general sessions of the peace, in 1770 he became mayor of Albany; at various times he also served as coroner of the city and county and as an officer in the militia. With the outbreak of the American revolution Cuyler took an active loyalist stand, and on 4 June 1776 he and some others were arrested as they celebrated George III's birthday. Imprisoned in Albany and then in Hartford, Conn., he

escaped in December to New York City, where he was joined by his wife and family. The next year Cuyler and a party of volunteers accompanied Sir Henry Clinton's unsuccessful expedition up the Hudson River to relieve rebel pressure on John Burgoyne*'s force. In October 1779 he was appointed lieutenant-colonel commandant of a proposed force of loyalists, but the unit never materialized. The following August he was made colonel of a group of loyalist militia on Long Island. By the fall of 1782 Cuyler and his family had moved to Montreal, and the same year he was appointed inspector of refugee loyalists in the Quebec City area. During the war the rebel government had expropriated his property, which he valued at £6,000.

While residing in Quebec Cuyler probably met Samuel Johannes HOLLAND, who had surveyed Cape Breton Island in 1766 and was optimistic about the island's potential. Perhaps influenced by Holland, Cuyler decided to form a settlement there for some 3,000 loyalists then in Quebec. With typical enthusiasm, he sent Captain Jonathan Jones to inspect the island in the fall of 1783 and then in November sailed for England to pressure the Home Department into approving his project. In England, he discovered that plans were under way for the division of Nova Scotia into a number of colonies. With the backing of Sir William Howe, an acquaintance from America and a member of the Privy Council committee for trade, he asked for the separation of Cape Breton from Nova Scotia and, when that was granted, successfully solicited the appointments of secretary and registrar of the new colony. Cuyler was also allowed to bring his loyalists to Cape Breton, but by the time permission was given it was already October 1784, and most of the prospective settlers decided to remain in Quebec. Hence only 140 persons arrived at Louisbourg and St Peters that year, and when Cuyler himself came to Louisbourg the same year he discovered that Governor John Parr* of Nova Scotia had not been informed of the loyalists' coming and consequently could not provide supplies. In the mean time Joseph Frederick Wallet DesBarres* had been appointed lieutenant governor of Cape Breton, and he and a group of English settlers founded the town of Sydney in the spring of 1785. Cuyler went to Sydney by July, took office, and was sworn into the Executive Council. He was also granted 500 acres across the harbour from Sydney, a property he named Yorkfields.

It soon became apparent that Cuyler and DesBarres could not work together. The lieutenant governor had dreams of a bright future for Cape Breton, and his military background made him accustomed to implicit obedience and determined that his position would not be undermined or challenged; Cuyler was influential and ambitious, anxious to offset his financial losses, and unwilling to play a minor role in the colony's development. Together with David Mathews*, a former mayor of New York City and attorney general of Cape Breton, he soon came into conflict with DesBarres.

The main contention centred around the recurring shortage of supplies during the colony's first years. Officially, only troops and loyalists were eligible to receive the supplies furnished by the British government, but since no other supplies were available this policy discriminated against the English settlers who had come with DesBarres. In an attempt to solve the problem, in the autumn of 1785 DesBarres tried to assume control of the distribution of government supplies, but Lieutenant-Colonel John Yorke, the garrison commander, claimed the responsibility. Cuyler and Mathews aligned themselves with Yorke, in an attempt to retain the allegiance of their fellow loyalists and thereby to strengthen their own power and weaken DesBarres's. The dispute raged throughout the winter and into the spring of 1786; supplies were obtained by DesBarres only when he seized those found in a ship wrecked off Arichat. Meanwhile Cuyler's opposition to DesBarres continued. In the summer of 1786 he signed a petition of the lieutenant governor's opponents demanding his removal. When this aim was achieved the same year, the apparent vindication of Cuyler and Mathews increased their determination to control the colony's affairs.

The new lieutenant governor, William MACARMICK, attempted to heal the rift that had developed between Cuyler, Mathews, and their followers and the supporters of DesBarres, but both sides soon incurred his wrath. The break between Cuyler and Macarmick occurred in February 1789, when a number of shipwrecked Irish convicts had to be accommodated in Sydney. This emergency drained the town's food supply, and Cuyler criticized Macarmick's decision to feed the convicts, claiming that council minutes had been doctored to show that he himself had earlier supported the measure. Macarmick therefore suspended Cuyler from the council in June and in an attempt to effect his destruction launched an investigation into his behaviour, accusing him of mismanagement of land grants, intemperate language, and general obstructiveness. The investigation was poorly handled and did not result in any definite proof of misconduct, but Macarmick, determined to restore concord in council, forced every councillor except Mathews to agree that Cuyler was guilty, and obtained his

suspension from office in August. Cuyler was so infuriated at this decision that for two weeks he refused to surrender the council minutes. He then left for England to appeal his case to the Home Department. Though he received only a mild rebuke and was reinstated in office, he did not remain long in Sydney after his return in October 1790. Prior to his arrival he had had circulated a pamphlet attacking Macarmick, and after resigning his offices he left Cape Breton early in 1791.

Cuyler then returned to Albany a number of times in unsuccessful attempts to regain some of his property. In 1795 he and his family were granted 4,000 acres in Farnham Township, east of Montreal. Cuyler then joined a group of ten other persons in an attempt to gain the entire township, but when this grant was secured in 1799 he was again in Albany and so failed to obtain his share. In 1802 he moved from Farnham to Montreal, where he spent his final years.

Abraham Cuyler is a pathetic figure. Obviously a man of ambition and ability, he lost a good deal in the American revolution, was frustrated by the lack of opportunity for advancement in Cape Breton, and because of his settling late in Lower Canada failed to obtain an important position in that colony's ruling structure. Though he was responsible for bringing the first sizeable number of settlers to Cape Breton after the fall of Louisbourg in 1758, his influence on the colony's development was largely disruptive. The faction that he and Mathews created to oppose DesBarres developed into one which was at odds with administrators throughout the life of the colony.

R. J. MORGAN

PAC, MG 11, [CO 217] Cape Breton A, 1: 9, 13–15, 16–18, 37–38, 136–37, 151; 2: 370–71; 3: 112–15; 7: 25–26; Nova Scotia A, 108: 240–42; [CO 220] Cape Breton B, 4: 126; 5: 4–13, 84–90, 134–37, 179–80, 249–50; 6: 15–16, 92–93, 115–296; RG 1, L3^L: 34628, 34665–67, 34827–28. A. H. Cuyler, *Cuylers of Canada and other places* (n.p., 1961). A. C. Flick, *Loyalism in New York during the American revolution* (New York, 1901). Jonathan Pearson, *Contributions for the genealogies of the first settlers of the ancient county of Albany, from 1630 to 1800* (Albany, N.Y., 1872). R. [J.] Morgan, "Joseph Frederick Wallet DesBarres and the founding of Cape Breton colony," *Rev. de l'univ. d'Ottawa*, 39 (1969): 212–27; "The loyalists of Cape Breton," *Dalhousie Rev.*, 55 (1975–76): 5–22.

D

DAER and SHORTCLEUCH, 5th Earl of SELKIRK, THOMAS DOUGLAS, Baron. *See* DOUGLAS

DARTIGNY, MICHEL-AMABLE BERTHELOT. *See* BERTHELOT

DAVANNE, MARGUERITE, named de Saint-Louis de Gonzague, Ursuline and superior; b. 3 Oct. 1719 in Paris, France, daughter of Louis Davanne, a merchant, and Marguerite Germain; d. 23 March 1802 at Quebec, Lower Canada.

Marguerite Davanne, who had come to New France

Davidson

with her parents, went to the boarding-school operated by the Ursulines of Quebec before entering their noviciate in 1737. A sum of about 1,900 *livres* was drawn from a foundation for the dowry that her mother was unable to provide. Her father had come to the colony because of financial difficulties, but when his situation failed to improve he had been obliged to exile himself again, this time to India, in the hope of rebuilding his fortune. He had disappeared without a trace. Her mother had returned to France and, believing her husband dead, had remarried after a few years. The situation turned to tragedy when he reappeared; in his rage he had his wife confined to a convent for life. According to the Ursuline annalist, when Marguerite learned of these events, she fainted. "The ebony-black hair of the young novice turned as white as snow overnight."

Marguerite assumed the name Saint-Louis de Gonzague upon taking the habit on 21 Jan. 1738. She made her profession two years later, on 4 Feb. 1740, and then became mistress of boarders. During the siege of Quebec in 1759 she was one of the ten nuns who remained in the convent from 13 July to 13 September; the other members of the community sought refuge in the Hôpital Général, away from the shelling. On 21 September the nuns returned to their convent to find it uninhabitable. Governor Murray*, who wanted to entrust some of his wounded soldiers to the care of the nuns, provided the superior of the community, Marie-Anne de la Nativité [Migeon* de Branssat], with the financial aid necessary for the soldiers' keep and for the indispensable repairs.

In 1766 Marguerite de Saint-Louis de Gonzague, who had "a happy disposition, a sound mind and good judgement, [and] a gentle and kindly personality," replaced Marie-Joseph de l'Enfant-Jésus [Esther Wheelwright*] as superior of the community. After her three-year term ended, she held the office of zelatrice (councillor) from 1769 to 1772 and then served again as superior from 1772 to 1778. She was elected depositary (bursar) of the community in 1778, and in 1781 began her third term as superior. In all this time the community, which had been impoverished by the Seven Years' War, received no aid from France. The Ursulines went ahead with the urgent repairs, towards which Bishop Briand* of Quebec contributed personally. To the financial problems of the community were added those of recruiting novices and of insufficient personnel. In 1776, for example, the community complained that "the girls have no great inclination for religion," and the Ursulines had to refuse day-pupils for lack of nuns to teach them. In 1787 the wife of Governor Lord Dorchester [Guy CARLETON] asked for French instruction for her eldest daughter and received permission from Briand to attend the lessons herself. They were given by Marguerite de Saint-Louis de Gonzague, who was completing her final term as superior.

On 4 Feb. 1790 Marguerite de Saint-Louis de Gonzague, who at the time held the offices of mistress of novices and assistant to the superior, celebrated her 50th anniversary as a nun. Despite her age and poor health, she continued to be active. She again served as zelatrice in 1796 and 1797, and then as assistant until 1799. In that year, on 16 December, she was relieved of all official duties. The discreets (councillors) nevertheless valued the advice of this experienced nun. Consequently the new superior, Marguerite Marchand, named de Sainte-Ursule, obtained an episcopal ordinance from Bishop DENAUT which departed from the convent's rules. In consideration of her long and important services Marguerite de Saint-Louis de Gonzague was allowed to attend every meeting of the community's council as an eighth councillor. Said to be "very conscientious in all her duties, insistent about regularity, [and] active and untiring in her work, even in her final years," she kept up her attendance at the meetings until her death on 23 March 1802.

GABRIELLE LAPOINTE

AAQ, 12 A, D: f.22v. Arch. du monastère des ursulines (Québec), Actes d'élection des supérieures; Actes de professions et de sépultures, 1; Actes des assemblées capitulaires, 1; Annales, 1; Conclusions des assemblées des discrètes, 1; Reg. des entrées, vêtures, professions et décès des religieuses, 1. [Catherine Burke, *dite* de Saint-Thomas], *Les ursulines de Québec, depuis leur établissement jusqu'à nos jours* (4v., Québec, 1863–66). [Joséphine Holmes, *dite* de Sainte-Croix], *Glimpses of the monastery, scenes from the history of the Ursulines of Quebec during two hundred years, 1639–1839* . . . (2nd ed., Quebec, 1897).

DAVIDSON, ARTHUR, advocate and judge; b. 12 Nov. 1743 in the parish of Kennethmont, Scotland, elder son of Walter Davidson; m. first 3 March 1785 Jane Fraser, daughter of Alexander Fraser* and Jane McCord, and they had three children, Jane, Elizabeth, and Walter*; m. secondly 9 March 1799 Eleanor Birnie; d. 4 May 1807 in Montreal, Lower Canada.

On 10 July 1766 Arthur Davidson, Master of Arts of King's College, Aberdeen, landed at Quebec. Following his indenture to Henry Kneller*, an attorney and later the attorney general, he was admitted to the bar of the province of Quebec on 2 Oct. 1771. His legal talents were appreciated from the start: even before qualifying as an advocate he had been employed by William Brown* of the *Quebec Gazette* to prepare a suit for debt against Brown's partner, Thomas Gilmore*. In 1778, along with Thomas DUNN and Jenkin WILLIAMS, he helped Francis Maseres* execute Kneller's will.

Davidson also took an interest in public affairs. He assisted George Pownall*, clerk of the Legislative Council, and in 1779 became secretary of the Quebec Library, founded that year by Governor HALDIMAND.

Hoping to succeed Pownall, who had indicated a wish to retire, he visited London during the winter of 1779–80 in order to lobby various officials, including his chief patron Lord George Germain, secretary of state for the American Colonies and president of the Board of Trade. When Pownall decided not to resign, however, Davidson resolved to try his luck in Montreal, where he settled in October 1780.

Despite his achievements, he had not been content in Quebec. In late 1779 he counselled his relations not to emigrate, advising them that "the times are exceeding gloomy and discouraging at present," and confessing that "if it was not that I am in some measure settled in this country, and can do better in it than perhaps anywhere else, I should not live here myself." In particular, he seems to have become disenchanted with governmental activity: as he rather cryptically complained towards the end of 1778, his position with Pownall "prevented my being able to use my Interest last winter (an opportunity which I shall never have again) to procure some other place." At any rate, Davidson apparently made up his mind after leaving Quebec to concentrate on a legal career.

He did undertake to represent Pownall, who was now the provincial secretary, in Montreal, but it is not clear what this representation entailed or how long it continued. He also accepted a number of minor appointments: by 1789 he had become a superintendent of inland navigation, by 1792 he was a member of the Land Granting Department, and in 1799 he was appointed to commissions that supervised the repairing of churches and the erection of a court-house for the District of Montreal. Such positions, however, imply not so much political ambition, let alone influence, as a sense of public responsibility.

Meanwhile, Davidson was building up a lucrative practice. In 1784 he was able to pay 7,000 *livres* cash down for a house on Rue Saint-Jacques costing 10,000 *livres* and by 1800, when appointed a judge, he was reputed to be "independent as to Fortune." Later on he appears to have run into financial difficulties, perhaps as a result of expenses incurred over the seigneury of Saint-Gilles, which his father-in-law Alexander Fraser had transferred to Walter Davidson in 1791, and which Davidson was managing in trust for his son. In any event, the total value of his estate in 1807 was £960 3s. 2d., which had to be divided equally among his three children and second wife. The latter was consequently obliged to apply for relief to Governor CRAIG, who in 1808 granted her a concession of land as a means of support.

Davidson's most notable action as a lawyer was his testimony in 1787 before a commission appointed by Governor Lord Dorchester [Guy CARLETON] to inquire into the administration of justice in the province of Quebec. Bitterly criticizing the Court of Common Pleas, which had been devised by Governor Murray* to enable Canadians to invoke their former laws, employ their own lawyers, and argue cases in French, Arthur Davidson deplored the confusion and acrimony caused by references to both the English and the French legal systems and emphasized the dissatisfaction of "the first Characters in the community; and particularly *Mercantile* Characters." Specifically, he protested that the judges issued irregular summonses, misapplied the rules of evidence, thwarted counsel in the questioning of witnesses, delayed and seldom explained the legal grounds for their judgements, assessed costs arbitrarily, failed to keep clear and full records, and sometimes saw parties and reached a decision before hearing a case. Furthermore, John Fraser behaved towards him "with evident marks of private Spite, prejudice or resentment"; Fraser's colleagues on the Court of Common Pleas, Edward Southouse and René-Ovide Hertel* de Rouville, "countenanced, in their usual complaisant manner, this most indecent treatment"; and all three judges plainly lacked "a professional Education and Practice, and for want therefore are not possessed of legal Ideas." Finally, the Canadians were far too indulged: not only were the English-speaking advocates frequently required to plead in French – "an unfair and unreasonable exaction as being without equality or reciprocation whatsoever" – but unlicensed Canadian lawyers were allowed to represent clients before the court despite the act passed in 1785 to regulate admission to the bar.

Some years later, in 1795, the solicitor general, Jonathan Sewell*, sought Davidson's advice concerning the enforcement of this act. Petitions requesting exemption from its regulations had been presented to the House of Assembly by Joseph-François Perrault*, Thomas Cary*, and Louis Fromenteau, and Sewell was sufficiently alarmed to propose a counterpetition from the Montreal bar. In his reply Davidson applied his earlier testimony diplomatically. Assuming that the assembly would sympathize with the petitioners, he concluded that "nothing we could say would have any weight with them." Accordingly, he suggested that a petition should be sent to the Legislative Council instead, and if this proved inadequate, that a joint petition from the Montreal and Quebec bars be presented to the governor. It is not known whether his advice was followed, but the bills passed by the assembly on behalf of Perrault, Cary, and Fromenteau never became law.

By this time Davidson's legal reputation had led to his employment by the government as both a defence attorney and a prosecutor. In the list of civil expenditures for 1794 he is recorded as having defended Joseph BOUCHER de Niverville, colonel of militia at Trois-Rivières, against charges brought by three militiamen, and also as having prosecuted 28 actions for the recovery of debts owed to the Lake Freights Company. The latter proceedings alone netted him more than the annual salary of a puisne judge, and he had obviously become one of the most successful advocates in the district.

On 1 Feb. 1800 Arthur Davidson was appointed by the new lieutenant governor, Robert Shore Milnes*, to the Court of King's Bench for the District of Montreal. This court had been created by the Judicature Act of 1794, which also divided the province into the judicial districts of Quebec, Montreal, and Trois-Rivières. Consisting of the chief justice for the district and three puisne judges, it replaced the contentious Court of Common Pleas and so heard both civil and criminal cases.

In 1802 Milnes commended Davidson and his fellow judge Isaac Ogden* for their "Vigilant attention" in bringing to his notice the alleged misbehaviour of a lawyer, Pierre Vézina, at Trois-Rivières. The lieutenant governor stressed the "public Importance" of the conduct of attorneys in court, and declared his "fixed Determination to assist the Judges by every means in his power in restraining and punishing every species of MalPractice." During the same year Davidson joined the other Montreal judges in recommending that lawlessness in the interior, or Indian, territory be checked by authorizing the courts of Lower and Upper Canada to try felonies committed outside their provinces, and in 1803 this recommendation was given effect by the passage of a statute. However, order could not be effectively imposed until after the merger of the rival North West and Hudson's Bay companies in 1821.

Throughout his judicial career Davidson continued to distance himself from politics. Despite the common practice of judges to belong to one or both of the councils, he did not participate actively in either the executive or the legislative side of government, and he does not appear to have made any close political ties. Nevertheless, he apparently harboured social, if not ethnic, predilections, which were clearly revealed in an opinion he submitted during June of 1803. The eight judges of Lower Canada were then asked whether lands granted in free and common socage should be governed in respect of descent and dower according to the laws of England or those of Canada (primarily, the customary law of Paris). Five of them – John ELMSLEY, Thomas Dunn, Jenkin Williams, Isaac Ogden, and Davidson – argued in favour of English law, while the other three – James Monk*, Pierre-Amable DE BONNE, and Jean-Antoine PANET – maintained that French law should regulate land transfers. The majority opinion was eventually adopted in the Canada Tenures Act of 1825.

In developing his argument Davidson disclosed not only the policy that probably lay behind that opinion but also his own concerns. Generally, he approved of the trend towards greater reliance on English law, and he especially welcomed, as favouring the merchants, the use of English rules of evidence and trials by jury in commercial actions. But he was also anxious to support the new settlers, and so urged that the system of free and common socage should be both confirmed and extended. This consolidation, he asserted, would not only bolster the position of the present freeholders but induce others to join them – in short, further British settlement of the province.

Such views, added to his testimony in 1787 and advice in 1795, provide a context for estimating the significance of Arthur Davidson. A well-trained, able, and conscientious lawyer, unlike so many legal practitioners during the early years of British rule, he was clearly intent on improving both the standards of his profession and the quality, or at least the consistency, of the law. At the same time, on the fundamental issue of relations between the British and the Canadians – or possibly between the merchants and new settlers on the one hand and the adherents of a quasi-feudalistic ideal on the other – he evidently sided with those who sought to resolve the growing tensions by promoting a more intensive anglicization of Lower Canada.

G. P. BROWNE

McCord Museum, Arthur Davidson papers. PAC, MG 11, [CO 42] Q, 30: 548–88, 638–68, 765–801; 71: 396–98; 84: 165, 173–74; 89: 144, 153–55; 92: 196–202, 283; 93: 58, 194–95; 97: 95, 130–34, 155; 102: 298; 107: 77–85; 293: 230–45; RG 4, A3, 3, no.41; 5, no.25; RG 7, G15C, 7: 64, 341, 411, 431, 444–45, 459–61. Bas-Canada, chambre d'Assemblée, *Journaux*, 1795: 83, 87–88, 101, 183–86, 201–2, 217–20, 235–36, 239–40, 247–48, 261–62, 267–68, 273, 315–16; 1805: 170–77. "Courts of justice for the Indian country," PAC *Report*, 1892: 136–46. "Lower Canada in 1800," PAC *Report*, 1892: 9–15. *Quebec Gazette*, 23 March 1775, 13 Nov. 1777, 21 Jan. 1779, 6 Sept. 1781, 9 Sept. 1784, 20 Jan. 1785, 20 June 1799, 14 May 1807. *Quebec almanac*, 1782–1808. P.-G. Roy, *Inv. concessions*, 1: 25; 5: 535; *Les juges de la prov. de Québec*, 147. Édouard Fabre Surveyer and D. A. Heneker, *The bench and bar of Quebec* (Montreal, 1931), 2–21, 26, 28. Douglas Brymner, "Report on Canadian archives," PAC *Report*, 1892: i–lix. Ægidius Fauteux, "Les bibliothèques canadiennes et leur histoire," *Rev. canadienne*, nouv. sér., 17 (janvier–juin 1916): 195. É.-Z. Massicotte, "Quelques rues et faubourgs du vieux Montréal," *Cahiers des Dix*, 1 (1936): 135–36.

DAVIES, THOMAS, army officer and painter in water-colours; b. *c.* 1737, probably in Shooter's Hill (London), England, son of David Davies; m. Mary —, and they had two children; d. 16 March 1812 in Blackheath (London), England.

On 1 March 1755 Thomas Davies was appointed a gentleman cadet at the Royal Military Academy, Woolwich (London). Like other artillery officers of his period he studied drawing, presumably under the obscure Gamaliel Massiot, drawing-master at Woolwich from 1744 to 1768. Topographical drawing was the only means at the time of making a rapid and accurate visual record of military value and, as such, required the utmost attention to detail and fidelity to nature, usually to the detriment of idealism. Consequently most soldier-artists never rose above the level of craftsmen. Topography, however, had also become fashionable as an art in the 18th century, for the nobility had begun seeking portraits of their estates and representations of the developing New World. The water-colour sketch or drawing, inexpensive and easily handled, most aptly filled this demand. An early English artist in this field was Paul Sandby, who soon established himself as one of the best and most influential water-colourists of his time.

In 1756 Davies was appointed lieutenant fireworker in the Royal Artillery and the following year he was promoted second lieutenant. He was sent on an abortive expedition against Louisbourg, Île Royale (Cape Breton Island), in 1757, and a water-colour drawing of Halifax that year is Davies's earliest dated picture. It exhibits the dryness of line and lack of colour of the military artist, but it combines diagrammatic accuracy with a picturesqueness of conception that would become characteristic of Davies. Several flights of birds indicate the sportsman and a burgeoning ornithologist. From 1758 come a diagrammatic record of Amherst*'s siege of Louisbourg and two views made during a stint with Colonel Robert Monckton*'s force, which laid waste the Acadian settlements in the Saint John valley (N.B.).

In 1759 Davies was promoted first lieutenant and joined Amherst's expedition to Lake Champlain. He recorded both Fort Ticonderoga (near Ticonderoga, N.Y.) and the new British fort at Crown Point and served as "Batteaux-Master" for the artillery. After wintering in New York he was with Amherst's campaign of 1760 against Montreal. On the St Lawrence he painted a colourful view of Fort La Galette (near Ogdensburg, N.Y.); he himself was in charge of one of the row-galleys shown in the picture attacking a French sailing vessel. He also recorded the rough passage of the rapids, the last obstacle before Montreal, where he was the first to hoist the British flag over the city. Over the next few years he was employed in surveying the St Lawrence and also the south shore of, and rivers flowing into, Lake Ontario as far as the Niagara River. A map of the channels of the Genesee River, dated 1760, and a view of its falls at present-day Rochester, N.Y., done the following year, survive, as does a schematic drawing of Niagara Falls dated 1762. The same year Davies painted a water-colour of Montreal from Île Sainte-Hélène. Representing the picturesque style to perfection, it shows the town behind an elegant couple languidly reclining under a screen of trees laced over with fretted vines in the approved 18th-century manner. In these

pictures the attention to flora and fauna indicates a growing interest in natural history. Two views of Martinique and a plan of Havana, Cuba, all from 1762 as well, were probably copied from another artist's work since Davies seems to have been in North America in 1761 and 1762.

In 1763, at the end of the Seven Years' War, Davies returned to England, but he was back in New York the following year. It is possible that he had met Paul Sandby in England since a view of Flushing on Long Island, dated 1765, and one of Greenbush on the Hudson River from 1766 show the influence of Sandby's broad horizontal planes of composition and transparent washes of colour. A series of American waterfalls sketched in 1766, in particular those of the Genesee and of Niagara, mark the beginnings of a personal style characterized by strong compositions and glowing colours. In 1767 Davies's company again sailed for England. During a six-year stay he exhibited American views and flower-pieces at the Royal Academy, London, and in 1768 published six engravings, dedicated to Amherst, of his waterfalls. In 1771 he was promoted captain and placed in command of a newly formed company of artillery at Woolwich, where Sandby had been drawing-master since 1768.

In 1773, on the eve of the American revolution, Davies again sailed for America, arriving at Halifax. His company moved to Boston the following year and doubtless saw action at Bunker Hill in June 1775. After William Howe's evacuation of Boston in March 1776, it withdrew to Halifax, but soon reappeared on Long Island to join in the descent on New York. Davies made records of the actions at White Plains in October 1776 and at Fort Washington (New York) in November, as well as of Lieutenant-General Charles Cornwallis's pursuit of General George Washington into New Jersey. In 1777 Davies took command of the artillery of Fort Knyphausen (formerly Fort Washington) and from its heights later painted two fine landscapes of the Hudson.

By mid 1779 Davies was back at Woolwich and in 1780, as Amherst's aide-de-camp, he made charming drawings of ladies and gentlemen strolling among the troops stationed in the London parks during the Gordon riots. Over the years he had been cultivating an interest in birds, and he now began to win recognition for his work as a naturalist. Several of his drawings of exotic birds were engraved in Dr John Latham's *General synopsis of birds*, published in London in three volumes from 1781 to 1785. In 1781 Davies was elected a fellow of the Royal Society of London. Promoted brevet major the following year, he became a lieutenant-colonel in 1783, when he apparently took command of the artillery at Gibraltar, of which he painted a number of views.

In 1786 he returned to America by way of Madeira

and the West Indies, where he painted views enriched with natural and human detail, and in the autumn assumed command of the artillery at Quebec. It was during this peace-time posting that he executed his handsomest water-colours, mostly of Quebec and region, and developed his style to its highest point of excellence. From the competent yet narrowly topographical manner of the 1750s and the broader, picturesque technique of the 1770s, he now arrived at a style which, though still detailed, was monumental in composition, as well as delicate in its lines, simple and stylized in its rendering of forms, and rich in colour. To 20th-century eyes it seems to blend the virtues of the English water-colourist with those of an accomplished primitive and the illuminators of oriental manuscripts.

Davies returned to England in 1790 and rose in rank to colonel in 1794, major-general in 1796, and lieutenant-general in 1803. He became a member of the Linnean Society of London, publishing two articles in its *Transactions*, and continued his painting of views based on his own sketches or those of other artists. His last, and probably finest, work was a masterly panoramic view of Montreal, dated 1812, the very year of his death.

Davies was the most talented of all the early topographical painters in Canada, surpassing his predecessor Richard Short*, his contemporaries Hervey SMYTHE and James Peachey*, and his successors George Heriot* and James Pattison Cockburn*. Breaking with the tradition of the tinted drawing, he painted directly on white paper with a full range of pure, rich colours, and the fullness of his handling of the water-colour medium was almost unrivalled. His lack of formal training as an artist gave him a personal vision, intense in its expression of the land. Full of authentic details of places and of the houses, costumes, and occupations of the people, his representations correspond remarkably with the descriptions left by such observers as Pehr Kalm*, Isaac Weld*, Frederick George Heriot*, Frances Moore*, and Joseph Bouchette*. Though Davies, because his work was hidden away in private collections, had no direct influence on later Canadian artists, his perception of nature places him in the central tradition of Canadian art. The brilliance, breadth, and clarity of his landscapes would not be found again until the advent of the Group of Seven.

R. H. HUBBARD

[Five of the six engravings of waterfalls in North America published by Davies in 1768 are also part of what is apparently the single-copy publication of *Scenographia Americana, or a collection of views of North America and the West Indies* . . . (London, 1768). The same subject-matter figured in numerous engravings and was used to illustrate Andrew Burnaby, *Travels through the middle settlements in North America, in the years 1759 and 1760; with observa-* *tions upon the state of the colonies* (3rd ed., London, 1798), and other works.

Davies published a number of articles on zoology and, in particular, ornithology. A letter, dated 12 March 1770, to John Ellis of the Royal Society on preparing dead birds for preservation appeared in slightly modified form in the *Philosophical Trans.* of the Royal Soc. of London, 60 (1770): 184–87. Davies later published in the *Trans.* of the Linnean Soc. (London) "An account of the jumping mouse of Canada, dipus canadensis . . . ," 4 (1798): 155–57, with a tinted engraving at page 85; "Account of a new species of muscicapa, from New South Wales . . . ," 4: 240–42, with a tinted engraving at page 242; and "Description of menura superba, a bird of New South Wales," 6 (1802): 207–10, also with a tinted engraving, at page 207.

In 1954 the National Gallery of Canada acquired from the Earl of Derby's library most of the water-colours Thomas Davies did of Canadian subjects. This acquisition stirred interest in Davies, and two years later K. M. Fenwick and C. P. Stacey published "Thomas Davies, soldier and painter of eighteenth-century Canada," *Canadian Art* (Ottawa), 13 (1956): 270–76, 300. Preparations for the National Gallery of Canada's major exhibition in 1972 of the collection gave rise to three publications by R. H. Hubbard: "Thomas Davies, gunner and artist," RSC *Trans.*, 4th ser., 9 (1971), sect.II: 327–49; *Thomas Davies in early Canada* (n.p., 1972); and *Thomas Davies, c.1737–1812: an exhibition organized by the National Gallery of Canada* (Ottawa, 1972), with a preface by C. P. Stacey. Some of the water-colours catalogued and reproduced in the last-named work are held by the Royal Artillery Institution, the British Library, and the Natural Hist. Museum in London; by the New York Hist. Soc. and the New York Public Library in New York City; the Winterthur Museum, at Winterthur, Del.; the Detroit Institute of Arts; the Royal Ontario Museum in Toronto; the PAC in Ottawa; and a number of private collections. The PAC's holdings have been reproduced on microfiche in "T. Davies – C. Williams – G. R. Dartnell – D. Lysons – F. H. Varley," comp. B. G. Wilson, *Arch. Canada microfiches* (Ottawa), 10 (1978). R.H.H.]

DEASE, JOHN, Indian Department official; b. probably 1744 in County Cavan (Republic of Ireland), son of Richard Dease and Anne Johnson; m. *c.* 1779 Jane French, and they had eight children, including Peter Warren Dease*; d. 12 Jan. 1801, at the age of 56, in the *faubourg* Sainte-Marie (Montreal), Lower Canada.

Educated in both Ireland and France, John Dease became a doctor, following the same profession as an uncle and brother. He sailed to New York in the summer of 1771 to take a position as personal physician to his uncle Sir William Johnson*, superintendent of northern Indians. During the next three years he lived at Johnson Hall (Johnstown, N.Y.), attended conferences with the Indians, and watched over Sir William's declining health. An executor of Johnson's will, he inherited £500 and 2,000 acres of land on Lake Champlain when the superintendent died in 1774.

On 16 April 1775, just as the American revolution was breaking out, Dease was appointed deputy agent of Indian affairs for the Middle (Cataraqui) District by Guy Johnson*, Sir William's successor. Along with Christian Daniel Claus* and Alexander McKee*, he drew an average salary of £200. The rebels soon drove the Johnson clan from the Mohawk River and Dease took up residence at Fort Niagara (near Youngstown, N.Y.) and Montreal. Little is known about his career between 1775 and 1780, probably because he did not do much. Although generally well liked and considered a "good natured honest man," Dease was apparently not given any important assignments.

Late in 1780, with Johnson's support, Dease attempted to secure from Governor HALDIMAND a captain's commission so that he would have the authority to command when the absence of other officials left him in charge of Indian affairs at Niagara. Haldimand during the next two years repeatedly denied Dease's requests for a commission, saying that the appointment might create jealousies. He felt that the Johnson family had too much power in the Indian Department, and he thought well of Lieutenant-Colonel John Butler*, who was also a deputy agent at Niagara. Butler and Dease apparently had a satisfactory working relationship until August 1782, when Dease let it be known that his appointment was senior to Butler's; Butler resigned in a huff, but his resignation was not accepted. Not even Guy Johnson backed Dease in the dispute. He explained to Haldimand that, although Dease's commission predated Butler's, he had "always considered Mʳ Butlers Experience, and the approbation he found to the Northward as Inducements Sufficient for my giving him the Compliment of Seniority." Butler and Dease patched up the quarrel.

In April 1783 Sir John Johnson*, who was by that date in charge of the Indian Department, recommended Dease for the post of deputy agent at Michilimackinac (Mackinac Island, Mich.), perhaps to protect his job while government expenditures were being reduced after the end of the American revolution. The appointment, however, was not made for several years. Late in the summer of 1783 Dease accompanied Joseph Brant [THAYENDANEGEA] and other Six Nations deputies when they left for Detroit to talk about unity with the western Indians, Creeks, and Cherokees. In September Dease made his first trip to Michilimackinac, bearing the official word of the cessation of hostilities between the British and the Americans. Following his return to Niagara he was involved in sensitive conferences with the Six Nations, whose lands had in effect been turned over to the Americans by the British in the Treaty of Paris (1783). Meanwhile, beyond the upper Great Lakes, intertribal Indian wars were seriously disrupting the western fur trade. In April 1786 the affected merchants petitioned Sir John Johnson for special envoys to end the hostilities. Captain Michael Byrne, the Indian Department commissary at Michilimackinac, dispatched Joseph-Louis AINSSE to the Sioux country in the summer of 1786, and on 1 October Sir John appointed Dease to go to Michilimackinac as deputy agent and settle the troubles.

Dease arrived at the post in June 1787 to replace Byrne in the direction of Indian affairs. Almost immediately he raised the ire of the local merchants, who, organized into the General Company of Lake Superior and the South, were used to having things their own way. They believed that on his expedition the previous year Ainsse had damaged their business by trading privately in goods intended as presents for the Indians. Dease strengthened their conviction that their trade was being undercut by the Indian Department when he gave some department employees part of their pay in articles from the stores and when he loaned supplies to a former employee whose goods had not yet arrived from Detroit. The ban on such practices, which appear to have been common, had been repeated in the instructions issued by Sir John Johnson on 10 May 1787, following receipt of orders from Governor Lord Dorchester [Guy CARLETON]. Dease further angered the merchants by refusing to let one of them, Charles Paterson, speak at an Indian council on 11 July. Three weeks later, at L'Arbre Croche (Cross Village, Mich.), Nissowaquet* and his band of Ottawas bitterly complained that there was only one trading house at Michilimackinac. Dease expressed his sympathy for their situation.

Dease also offended the commandant at Michilimackinac, Thomas Scott, who requested lists of the presents distributed to the Indians. Dease did not respond and later remarked that he "found nothing in his instructions that induced him to think himself accountable to Captain Scott for his management of the Indian Department." Moreover, despite Scott's opposition he sent Ainsse west again in August on the Indians' insistence.

On 10 Aug. 1787 the merchants protested to Scott about the behaviour of Dease and Ainsse, and four days later they sent formal accusations to Lord Dorchester. He ordered a court of inquiry, which convened at Michilimackinac on 24 June 1788 with Scott presiding. For two weeks the charges and cross-examination dragged on. Dease was subsequently ordered down country to answer the charges against him. Either he did not receive the directive or he ignored it; he spent the summer of 1789 negotiating with the Indians at Michilimackinac. Finally, on 22 Aug. 1789, Sir John Johnson demanded that he come immediately to Montreal, and on 16 October the dejected agent departed.

It was not until 20 April 1790 that a committee of the Legislative Council began hearings on the case.

De Bonne

Late in May, while it was pondering, Dease received permission to return west to get his family. On 5 June the committee decided that in his administration at Michilimackinac he had acted contrary to Dorchester's orders, and it asked Sir John Johnson for his opinion as to whether Dease's departure from instructions was unavoidable. Johnson replied in October that "no deviation . . . was necessary to effect the purpose of his mission. . . ." The committee immediately concluded that Dease's conduct was indefensible and referred the matter to Dorchester. No punishment was apparently imposed, though Dease's service in the department ended. He was, in fact, a victim of the Indian Department's problems. In wartime the authorities had been somewhat tolerant of its casual accounting practices and unforeseen expenditures. Dease apparently approached the management of Indian affairs at Michilimackinac with the methods and attitudes he had learned at Niagara during the revolution, and the results ended his career. The problems, however, remained. Within months of Dease's departure from Michilimackinac, Charles Gautier de Verville, who had been left in charge of Indian affairs, was writing that he had been obliged to ignore the commandant and take coal from the king's stores for the department's blacksmith.

Dease spent the last decade of his life on half pay. In his will, made at his home "in the suburbs of saint Mary near the . . . City of Montreal" on 4 Jan. 1801, he named Sir John Johnson an executor. Thus, even in death he remained linked closely with the Johnson clan. He left a relatively modest estate, and his body was interred in the cemetery of Saint-Antoine, in the parish of Notre-Dame, on 19 January.

DAVID A. ARMOUR

[The author wishes to thank J. P. Birkett of the PAC for making available information collected there on John Dease. D.A.A.]

ANQ-M, CE1-51, 19 janv. 1801, 21 déc. 1802; CM1, John Dease, 4 Jan. 1801. AO, MU 1750. Arch. de la Soc. hist. de Montréal, Coll. Louis-Joseph Ainsse, 98, 100 (mfm. at PAC). BL, Add. MSS 21761: 112, 205; 21762: 45, 98, 138, 146, 151, 225, 227, 230, 235; 21763: 18, 48, 54, 56–59, 110, 114, 152, 224, 348, 355; 21764: 204; 21766: 24; 21767: 151, 157, 201; 21768: 33, 51–53, 91–92; 21769: 138; 21775: 10, 26, 29, 35–39, 102, 152, 213, 218, 281, 305, 311; 21779: 60–61, 74–76, 83–86, 91, 96–97, 109, 123–27, 143; 21876: 18, 22. PAC, MG 11, [CO 42] Q, 24-2: 435; 25: 136–44; 26-2: 364–67, 527–33. *Johnson papers* (Sullivan et al.), 8: 263, 313, 438, 497, 845–46, 914–15, 964, 984, 1048, 1063, 1109, 1163; 12: 962, 1010–11, 1013, 1030–31, 1043–44, 1071–72, 1075–76, 1122; 13: 634–35. *Mich. Pioneer Coll.*, 11 (1887): 322, 388, 483–620; 12 (1887): 12–13, 20; 13 (1888): 81–89, 106–8; 20 (1892): 163–64, 171, 174, 304, 362; 23 (1893): 603–80; 25 (1896): 108; 32 (1902): 339. Wis., State Hist. Soc., *Coll.*, 9 (1882): 467; 12 (1892): 83–84, 89–96.

Calendar of the Sir William Johnson manuscripts in the New York State Library, comp. R. E. Day (Albany, N.Y., 1909), 493, 527. B. L. Dunnigan, *King's men at Mackinac: the British garrisons, 1780–1796* (Lansing, Mich., 1973). Barbara Graymont, *The Iroquois in the American revolution* (Syracuse, N.Y., 1972), 282–84. M. W. Hamilton, *Sir William Johnson, colonial American, 1715–1763* (Port Washington, N.Y., and London, 1976), 79, 334. R. S. Allen, "The British Indian Department and the frontier in North America, 1755–1830," *Canadian Hist. Sites*, no.14 (1975): 5–125.

DE BONNE, PIERRE-AMABLE, militia officer, lawyer, seigneur, office holder, politician, judge, and author; b. 25 Nov. 1758 in Montreal (Que.), son of Louis de Bonne* de Missègle, an infantry captain who was killed at Quebec in 1760, and Louise Prud'-homme; d. 6 Sept. 1816 in Beauport, Lower Canada.

Pierre-Amable De Bonne is an intriguing figure because of the complexity of his character, thought, and actions, indeed, because of the very contradictions he embodied. A man deeply rooted in the past, he also prefigured the future. As a seigneur he defended his own privileges and those of his class; yet at the same time he knew how to exploit fully the parliamentary institutions he had fiercely opposed. A member of the liberal professions and a politician, he had virtually no equal as an election organizer and political strategist. At the height of his career he was the most important – and most hated – of the "chouayens," another Canadian party name for the "traitors" and "placemen"; in fact his ambition and initiative did quickly bring him lucrative offices in the public service. He emerged as the leader of the French-speaking section (which dwindled in time) of the administration's party in the Lower Canadian parliament. He served the government, however, and not the British faction itself. Hence he never qualified the nationalist positions that he had adopted at the outset of his career. Taking inspiration from the most famous *philosophes* and writers of the Age of Enlightenment, this "cultivated gentleman" found his place in the cultural life of his community through the theatre and journalism. Even though he posed as a practising Catholic after his second marriage, for a long time he had openly led a licentious life which went absolutely counter to the morality of his time, and he did not hesitate to undermine the Catholic clergy's influence with the government. His uncontested leadership and his remarkable skill made him the most feared adversary of the Canadian party, since with a handful of allies he held the balance of power in a house of assembly in which few members were regularly present until 1808. It was for this reason that the Canadian party was so hostile towards him.

Birth dictates duty. De Bonne purported to descend from the family of the constable François De Bonne, Duc de Lesdiguières, a claim that earned him the gibes of many of his compatriots, particularly in *Le Canadien*. His father, moreover, had called himself "Sieur de Missègle" and with Louis Legardeur* de Repentigny had acquired the seigneury of Sault-Sainte-Marie in 1750. In 1770, after his death, De Bonne's mother had married Joseph-Dominique-Emmanuel LE MOYNE de Longueuil; Le Moyne would be left two large seigneuries, Nouvelle-Longueuil and Soulanges, by his father, Paul-Joseph Le Moyne* de Longueuil, known as the Chevalier de Longueuil.

De Bonne began his classical studies at the school founded by the Sulpicians in Longue-Pointe (Montreal) and continued them from 1773 at the new Collège Saint-Raphaël in Montreal. In the summer of 1775, having completed his sixth year (Rhetoric), which concluded the course of study then offered at that institution, he entered the Petit Séminaire de Québec for Philosophy, the final two years of the classical program.

During the siege of Quebec by the Americans in the winter of 1775–76 [*see* Benedict ARNOLD; Richard Montgomery*], De Bonne took part in the defence of the town as an ordinary soldier in Captain Pierre Marcoux's company. He became an ensign and in 1776 went on the Lake Champlain campaign; promoted lieutenant, he was taken prisoner by the Americans in 1777, following the surrender of Major-General John Burgoyne*'s army. Upon his release he returned to the province of Quebec, but being unable to obtain adequate compensation from the government was forced out of active service. As a result he realized that a military career offered limited prospects to a French Canadian serving in the militia under the British régime. This perception did not prevent him from accepting the post of lieutenant-colonel of the Quebec militia battalion in 1796, and that of colonel of the Beauport, Charlesbourg, and Côte de Beaupré militia in the autumn of 1809, or from other involvement occasionally, for example delivering a patriotic speech to Colonel Jean-Baptiste LE COMTE Dupré's battalion in the summer of 1807. Soon after returning to the province De Bonne took up the study of law in Montreal, and in January 1780 he asked Governor HALDIMAND for a commission as a lawyer. He obtained it on 14 March, apparently along with one as a notary.

In 1781 De Bonne rendered fealty and homage for half of the fief and seigneury of Sault-Sainte-Marie, of which he declared himself sole heir. He added to his holdings with the passing years: in December 1784 he signed a petition to the king as "seigneur of Sault-Sainte-Marie and Choisy"; in 1794 he bought for 28,800 *livres* the sub-fief of Grandpré, on the Route de la Canardière near Quebec, and the following year built a château on it; in 1802 he purchased a property in the seigneury of Notre-Dame-

des-Anges, at Beauport, for 3,000 *livres*, and a lot in the *faubourg* Saint-Roch at Quebec which he resold in 1806; in addition he rented or sold lots at Montreal and Quebec and had the promise of a property on the south shore of the Rivière Saint-François. These transactions went hand in hand with borrowing (12,000 *livres* in 1800, for instance) and lending (to the extent of 60,000 *livres* in 1812 alone), as well as with a standard of living which suggests an unquestionable financial independence that could not have come solely from his emoluments (20,400 *livres* annually around 1810) as a member of the Executive Council and judge of the Court of King's Bench.

On 9 Jan. 1781, at Vaudreuil, De Bonne married Louise Chartier de Lotbinière, daughter of the seigneur (and later marquis) Michel Chartier* de Lotbinière and Louise-Madeleine Chaussegros de Léry. The marriage was soon a spectacular failure, with tradition attributing loose conduct to one spouse or other, or to both of them. In 1782, a few months after the death of their only son at five months of age, the couple separated by mutual consent. In 1790 Louise went off to the United States with Charles-Roch Quinson de Saint-Ours, who turned back near the border, and Samuel McKay, by whom she had a son of the same name in Williamstown, Mass.; she died there in 1802. Historians stress that good relationships were maintained between De Bonne and the Chartier de Lotbinière family: witness the agreement in 1804 by which De Bonne relinquished enjoyment of the usufruct of his wife's property that had been provided for in their marriage contract. However, in 1798 Michel-Eustache-Gaspard-Alain Chartier* de Lotbinière had complained of his brother-in-law's loose behaviour, claiming, "[He] is running around, [while] his wife is in a deplorable state." Soon after, De Bonne seduced Catherine Le Comte Dupré, the wife of Antoine JUCHEREAU Duchesnay; this affair ended with a gentleman's agreement before notary Félix Têtu and Attorney General Jonathan Sewell*. On 16 Jan. 1805 De Bonne took as his second wife 23-year-old Louise-Élizabeth Marcoux, the daughter of André Marcoux, a farmer, and Louise Bélanger, of Beauport; they were married under a contract providing for husband and wife to administer their properties separately, with the guarantee of an annual allowance of 3,000 *livres* for her in the event of his death. This marriage was regarded by the Canadian party as a self-interested one designed to dispel rumours that De Bonne had joined the ruling British oligarchy.

On the professional level the return of peace in 1783 offered young De Bonne a new field, which he was able to exploit to draw attention to himself and prepare for a long political career. However, his activism cannot be explained by personal ambition alone. His first political contest brought him into a struggle in

De Bonne

which the basic stakes went well beyond the aims of a mere careerist. The decision he took to defend the system of government established under the Quebec Act was as much due to a desire to promote the privileges and class interests of the seigneurial gentry to which he belonged as to the sense of nationalism that was developing within this social group in face of the demands of the anglophone bourgeoisie.

To offset the requests for constitutional reform put forward by the British minority, the seigneurial élite of Montreal took the initiative of petitioning the king for a more equitable redistribution of the seats in the Legislative Council; the seigneurs called in question the composition of this political body, claiming that since two-thirds of its members were subjects of Great Britain, the British were assured of "preponderance always," enabling them to "make changes and alterations [to the] laws . . . in relation to their interests." But this clearly expressed desire to seize legislative power was to create a deep split among the French Canadian majority between those favouring the creation of an assembly and those defending the established régime. De Bonne rushed into the fray with such determination that he took the lead in a veritable campaign against reform. Indeed, he never stopped fighting until the plan for a new constitution was submitted to the British parliament for approval.

With "the very humble address of the Roman Catholic citizens and inhabitants of different conditions in the province of Quebec" in December 1784, the opening round was fired in the campaign of opposition to the reform movement; De Bonne's name appeared at the head of the list of signatories. The committee responsible for drawing up this address to the king was composed of the leading members of Montreal's seigneurial élite: De Bonne, his brother-in-law Michel-Eustache-Gaspard-Alain Chartier de Lotbinière, judge René-Ovide Hertel* de Rouville, and legislative councillors Joseph-Dominique-Emmanuel Le Moyne de Longueuil (De Bonne's stepfather) and François-Marie Picoté* de Belestre. The importance of this manifesto has not escaped historians, who have taken it as a faithful reflection of the conquered people's views. Duncan McArthur even called it the "first definite declaration of French-Canadian nationalism" and discerned in it a revealing indication of the "essentially conservative character" of that nationalism. Rather it ought to be seen as the ideological expression of the seigneurial class, which had to fight a rearguard action in the hope of retaining privileges from the *ancien régime*. Linked through his status as a seigneur and his claims of nobility to the fate of a social group in decline, De Bonne in the end fell back on conservative positions, compromising his reputation in the eyes of the rising new professional élite to which he might have belonged had he been of another generation.

The alliance that his reformist compatriots had established with the English-speaking bourgeoisie impelled De Bonne to a vigorous and sustained fight. His opposition was more forceful and energetic because he was conscious of the dangers that the alliance of bourgeois forces in the colony represented for the future of his social group. The choice of Adam Lymburner*, a Scottish merchant from Quebec, as the reformers' delegate to London was not one to allay the seigneurs' misgivings. How could they be indifferent in the face of the French-language report in the *Quebec Gazette/La Gazette de Québec* that Lymburner, by his assertions during his first appearance before a committee of the House of Commons in the spring of 1788, had led the members of parliament to believe that the various classes of the province's population "unanimously desired the abrogation of the laws of Canada"? The English version of this report was, however, somewhat qualified, stating that the Canadians were "almost unanimous." In the face of this affront De Bonne and his peers organized a second address to the king in which they boldly declared, "Not once were the great landowners of our nation and the various estates that in general comprise it consulted about making innovations of such importance to their welfare and their common interests." The same authors also drew up a memorial to the governor, Lord Dorchester [Guy CARLETON], in which they denounced the actions of Lymburner in "using their name inappropriately and recklessly."

The administration of justice constituted a privileged realm in which it was easy for the opponents of reform to show their defensiveness since professional solidarity bound them more effectively than class solidarity. Chief Justice William Smith* was to learn to his cost in 1787 that it was very rash to undertake a reorganization of the judicial system in the face of the opposition of the French party in the Legislative Council and of the judges themselves. The judges' position was so strongly protected by the established system that Smith was unsuccessful in his attempt to prove their misbehaviour and partiality in the courts of common pleas. The three judges for the District of Montreal, John Fraser, René-Ovide Hertel de Rouville, and Edward Southouse, simply refused to take part in Smith's inquiry and had themselves represented by none other than De Bonne, their attorney. Thus began the latter's initiation into his future responsibilities as a judge.

However much he was a gentleman of the *ancien régime* through his links with the seigneurial gentry, De Bonne belonged none the less to the contemporary world. His rich collection of books reveals a man open to the spirit of the Enlightenment. Although legal tomes occupied an important place, there were also many medical treatises, as well as a great variety of works of history and diverse literary genres. Voltaire and Jean-Jacques Rousseau were represented by more than 50 volumes, Jean-François Marmontel by 17. Abbé Guillaume Raynal's noted *Histoire philosophique et politique* . . . , published clandestinely in 1770, was side by side with Louis-Sébastien Mercier's *Tableau de Paris*, a 12-volume work published in Paris from 1781 to 1790. Surprisingly, at the time of his death De Bonne owned the 57 volumes of the *Annual register*, which had begun appearing in London in 1758, the year of his birth.

De Bonne had a marked theatrical bent. With such other Canadians as Joseph QUESNEL, Jean-Guillaume DE LISLE, and Joseph-François Perrault*, he was a director of the Théâtre de Société which was founded in the autumn of 1789 and successfully completed its initial theatrical season from December 1789 to February 1790 – a first for Montreal. The four shows put on included Molière's *Le médecin malgré lui*, Quesnel's *Colas et Colinette, ou le Bailli dupé*, and three plays by Jean-François Regnard. Against ecclesiastical censure and the threats of the parish priest of Notre-Dame in Montreal, François-Xavier Latour-Dézery, the directors held their ground. A public debate ensued in the *Montreal Gazette* and went on until the end of the theatre season. The clergy succeeded, however, in having productions by the Théâtre de Société suspended for a few years. A troupe of the same name gave some performances in the years 1795 to 1797, and presented Beaumarchais's *Le barbier de Séville* for the first time in the city. This brief reappearance of theatrical activity in Montreal was followed by a new eclipse which lasted until the turn of the 19th century. The town of Quebec resisted clerical censure better, thanks to the presence of the governor and of royal visitors who liked to amuse themselves with stage entertainment; De Bonne was able to take advantage of their inclinations when he was appointed to the Court of King's Bench of the District of Quebec.

If De Bonne did not put his acting talents on stage, he used them to advantage in the political arena. Each of his election campaigns gave him the opportunity to display his predilection for public show and for theatrical devices: trenchant speeches, a cultivated oratorical style, publicity material, and addresses in the House of Assembly and elsewhere. The period from 1790 to 1794 was the most fruitful for De Bonne's professional and political future, although through a curious irony of history these years marked the introduction of the new constitutional régime that he had so violently opposed. He had been a justice of the peace since 1788, but it was his office as clerk of the register of landed property, which he held from 1790 to 1794, that involved him in the workings of the colonial administration. In 1791 he also served as assistant to the French secretary to the governor and Council.

In 1792 De Bonne launched into his first election campaign by running as a candidate with Michel-Eustache-Gaspard-Alain Chartier de Lotbinière, his brother-in-law, in the riding of York just west of Montreal. Being assured of support from the two principal lay seigneurs of the constituency, his brother-in-law Chartier de Lotbinière and his step-father Le Moyne de Longueuil, and from the polling officer, his friend Hubert Lacroix, at a time when voting took place openly in front of the assembled crowd, De Bonne ventured to campaign for the candidates of his choice in the three ridings of Quebec County, Upper Town, and Lower Town. In his *Avis aux Canadiens*, of which 350 copies were printed, he warned his compatriots against electing members of the English-speaking bourgeoisie. He urged them to choose only "people of property, importance, and character" who had the same interests as they did. The British response, of which 700 copies were distributed, was a lengthy denunciation of "the insidious insinuations" of the future member from York.

At the opening of the session late in 1792, a third of the assembly's members were English-speaking. De Bonne immediately attracted attention by trying to force the election of a speaker. He supported Louis DUNIÈRE, who had nominated lawyer Jean-Antoine PANET. Despite counter-proposals from the British, who put forward the names of James McGILL and William GRANT (1744–1805), Panet won by 28 votes to 18. This debate lasted two days. No such short span of time resolved the fundamental question of the status of the French language as against the English in a colonial legislature under the tutelage of the British crown. In January 1793 De Bonne moved a resolution laying down as a basic principle the existence of a threefold duality resulting from the dual origin of the laws (French civil and English criminal laws), and the bi-ethnic composition both of the population and of its representatives in the legislature. It followed that the records of the assembly should be kept in both languages. Since this resolution left undecided the crucial matter of the language of legislation, John Richardson* introduced an amendment that only the English texts of acts and parliamentary debates would be recognized in law. The lengthy debate that ensued gave rise to vehement speeches by the supporters of one or the other proposition: unilingual laws or the legality of both languages. The speeches on the French-speaking side that most impressed people at the time, those by De Bonne, Joseph Papineau*, and Pierre-Stanislas Bédard*, have not been preserved. Their loss is the more regrettable since they might have made it possible to establish important parallels in the realm of nationalist ideology between De Bonne, Bédard, and Papineau at that period. Perhaps they would have revealed why the colonial government had an interest in enlisting De Bonne – the most

De Bonne

vindictive of the three – on its side with tempting offers the following year: judge of the Court of Common Pleas on 8 Feb. 1794, judge of the Court of King's Bench for the District of Quebec on 16 December, and as the crowning gesture member of the Executive Council on New Year's Eve. This meteoric rise was due less to his career as a lawyer and his professions of loyalty during the popular disorders in 1794 than to his talents as an ambitious, energetic, and popular politician.

As a judge and holder of high office De Bonne had a successful but unremarkable career. In 1797 he showed greater harshness than did his English-speaking colleagues towards 12 Canadians charged with violent resistance to the application of the road law of 1796. In May 1800 Chief Justice William Osgoode* asked Lieutenant Governor Robert Shore Milnes* to dismiss De Bonne from his offices because of his immoral conduct – he accused him of double adultery, then of scandalous talk – and his repeated absences from sittings of the court. At Milnes's request De Bonne defended himself against the second accusation by affirming that in three years he had been absent only 65 days (25 more, in fact, than the elderly judge Thomas DUNN!). The lieutenant governor took his side with the home authorities: De Bonne's absences, Milnes said, had not interrupted the court's sittings and his presence in the assembly was important for the government. In short, the judge's influence on the electors and the members of the assembly was more important than his personal conduct and his absenteeism.

In 1802 and 1803 De Bonne was empowered to hear some cases involving crimes committed at sea. In 1803 he again showed his attachment to Canadian laws; like his colleague in Montreal, Pierre-Louis PANET, and in opposition to most of the English-speaking judges in the colony, he maintained that French law applied in questions of inheritance and dower, even for lands held in free and common socage. London decided in favour of English law in 1804. The following year De Bonne and his colleagues participated in revising police rules and regulations for Quebec. In 1809, along with judges Sewell, Jenkin WILLIAMS, and James Kerr*, he prepared the *Orders and rules of practice in the Court of King's Bench, for the District of Quebec, Lower Canada*, the publication of which prompted the assembly to initiate impeachment proceedings against Sewell in 1814. In 1810 he again helped revise the police rules and regulations for Quebec. He retired in 1812 and gave up his seat to judge Jean-Olivier Perrault*.

De Bonne made his career primarily in politics. His talents as an organizer and a skilful orator, indeed as a demagogue, won him election to the assembly from 1792 until 1810 without interruption. If Bédard was unquestionably the first French Canadian to make a profession of politics, De Bonne may be considered the first professional political schemer in Lower Canada. His rapid advancement in public office, his ostentatious loyalism, his steady support for government measures in the house, his unquestionable influence on voters and on some Canadian "placemen" in the assembly, the apparent abandonment of his nationalism of the 1780s and 90s, earned him the resentment and then the ferocious hostility of those in the Canadian party. He returned their feelings. Nothing, however, lends support to the theory that he gave up his nationalist position, witness his stand on civil laws concerning lands in free and common socage (1803) and his attitude in the assembly whenever Canadian laws seemed threatened. De Bonne was the system's man: he got along well in it and defended it; he shared its aristocratic and conservative values; he feared the social threat that the rise of the new professional bourgeoisie and its values represented for society. Unless it is seen in this light, the bitterness of the struggles of the years 1800–10 is incomprehensible. Behind the opposition between men and parties, diverse conceptions of society, government, and power were embodied in the combatants; different ideas of the nation also emerged, as De Bonne's adhesion to the seigneurs' nationalism in the period 1780–90 demonstrated.

De Bonne's political career was long and varied. Besides participating in the early debates of 1792–94 he sat on numerous committees, one of which urged that the Jesuit estates be used for educating the Canadians. In 1794 he introduced a bill for the arrest and detention without trial of people accused or suspected of treason; through an irony of history, this law would serve to imprison the chief editors and the printer of *Le Canadien* in March 1810 [*see* Sir James Henry CRAIG; Pierre-Stanislas Bédard]. A member for York from 1792 to 1796, he was elected in 1796 for Three Rivers after being defeated in the riding of Hampshire. When the session opened in 1797, the judge and assemblyman proposed John YOUNG as speaker of the house, but Panet was re-elected by 29 votes to 12.

De Bonne was re-elected in the same riding in 1800, after being defeated in Northumberland; at the opening of parliament he was nominated for speaker, but he too lost to Panet. During the 1801 session he presented two petitions in the name of his constituents: the first asked that a second judge be appointed for Three Rivers and that four sessions of the Court of King's Bench be held annually; the second requested that a public school be set up. He also played a leading role in the expulsion of Charles-Jean-Baptiste Bouc* in 1801, 1802, and 1803, despite the efforts of a segment of the Canadian party led by Bédard and Michel-Amable BERTHELOT Dartigny. The coalition of the British and Canadian placemen led by De Bonne got the better of the Canadian party, which was weakened by the absence of its members on very close votes, for example 12 to 10 and 8 to 7. During the long debates on the creation of the Royal Institution for the Advancement of Learning, De Bonne sided regularly with the government, except in the case of the amendments to protect the existing Canadian schools and institutions.

In 1802 the real weakness of the Canadian party, despite its theoretical majority, led it to propose, as in 1799, a bill to grant an "allowance" to the speaker and members of the assembly. De Bonne proved the fiercest opponent of the measure, making skilful use of procedure and demagoguery, so that the house had to postpone discussion of the bill indefinitely. The bitter opposition by the administration's party was explained by the fact that it held the balance of power in several critical debates.

In 1804 De Bonne ran against Jean-Antoine Panet in Upper Town. Faced with certain defeat, he withdrew and ran in the riding of Quebec County, where he was elected. His address to the voters is a good example of his theatrical sense and effective demagogic techniques: he mentioned that he had sacrificed his desire to retire to the "honourable preference" of his constituents, who, despite the "scandalous poison" spread about by his enemies, had shown that the people supported the participation of judges in politics. He intended, consequently, to uphold the government's rights against abuses, corruption, and attacks upon liberty.

De Bonne did not take part in the great debates in 1805 and 1806 on the building of new prisons. But at the end of 1806 he became involved in the founding of *Le Courier de Québec*, a newspaper combining passionate denunciations of the Canadian party and its organ, *Le Canadien*, with literary and philosophical texts from the Enlightenment. *Le Courier de Québec* none the less defended "the Canadian nation," "Canadian education," and the French language, among other things, and even denounced the monopolizing of positions and trade by some of the British. Was this approach so far removed from the seigneurs' recriminations in 1784?

In 1807 De Bonne succeeded through obstructive methods in blocking the bill proposed by the Canadian party for "payment of members" of the assembly. According to the judge this measure might attract scoundrels, as well as people unfit for seats because of lack of education, character, and property. By contrast he praised voluntary service. It was not surprising that in the following session the Canadian party secured the adoption of a bill making judges ineligible to sit in the house, which was rejected by the Legislative Council. Despite what was said about the necessity of keeping justice and judges above all suspicion, the objectives of the Canadian party were more clearly evident when it expelled the Jewish assemblyman Ezekiel Hart*, who belonged to the British party, because he had taken the oath in accordance with the forms prescribed by his religion rather than by the 1791 constitution. In the ensuing elections in June 1808 the Canadian party called upon voters to elect only members "independent of the government and the Legislative Council." It attacked De Bonne through articles and manifestos in *Le Canadien*: the basest motives were imputed to him, his dissolute conduct was raked up, and his objectivity as a judge was called in question. De Bonne and his allies brought about the defeat of Jean-Thomas Taschereau* and Jean-Antoine Panet, but Panet was rescued in Huntingdon riding. As for De Bonne, he was one of the few members of the administration's party who did not go under: beaten in Northumberland, he was re-elected in Quebec County.

In the 1809 session De Bonne vainly tried to have Denis-Benjamin Viger* elected speaker. The Canadian party again brought forward the bill on the ineligibility of judges. De Bonne fought back, using all the resources of his vast parliamentary experience. At the moment when a house committee was tabling a report that was damning for him, the judge was saved by the sudden prorogation of parliament by an enraged Governor Craig. The 1809 elections took place in a highly charged atmosphere. The Canadian party and its newspaper bore down even more on placemen and in particular De Bonne, for their corruption, cynicism, demagoguery, and "undue influence" on voters. De Bonne was even accused by one of his alleged mistresses of having boasted that he had "duped" the Canadians, "their wives, their priests, their religion, and their pope." All the same, De Bonne weathered the storm and was re-elected by acclamation in Quebec County. In the 1810 session, however, tired of this fencing and confident of receiving London's support, the assembly declared De Bonne's seat vacant on a simple resolution. Craig again dissolved parliament. In the ensuing elections De Bonne tried to obtain nomination, but a voters' meeting chose other candidates. The seizure of *Le Canadien* and the arrest of its chief editors and its printer gave De Bonne and his friends the opportunity to denounce the Canadian party's "sedition" in their newspaper, *Le Vrai Canadien*, and to seek votes, though with little success, for the government's candidates.

In 1812 De Bonne retired to his estate of La Canardière, whose château and gardens Joseph Bouchette* praised. The Centre Hospitalier Robert-Giffard is now on the site of the château. De Bonne did not retire fully, since he was appointed a commissioner to receive the oath of allegiance in 1812 and 1814 and a member of the commission to administer the Jesuit estates in the summer of 1815. He also acted as agent for four other commissioners.

De Bonne had several differences with the clergy. In 1797 his attempt to create a new parish between Nicolet and Bécancour by legislative enactment

DeBurgo

earned him the ill will of the Catholic hierarchy and the hostility of Governor PRESCOTT, who considered him "a great enemy" of the church and "a very bad subject." In 1809 De Bonne wrote to Craig objecting to the excessive liberty enjoyed by the Catholic Church and accusing Bishop Plessis* of having taken advantage of the governor's absence on a trip to go ahead with the creation of a new parish. Strangely enough, he was appointed a commissioner with authority to build and repair churches in 1799 and 1805. Given his behaviour and the material in his library, it is ironic that De Bonne is reported to have become "devout" after his second marriage.

De Bonne was a member of the high society of his time; he signed numerous addresses of good wishes to various governors and important people, and in 1794 he assisted at the anniversary dinner of the veterans of the siege of Quebec. He was a member of the Quebec Fire Society from 1795 until 1808, and subscribed to the fund set up to support Britain's war effort in 1794 and to the Waterloo fund in 1815.

De Bonne died at his estate on 6 Sept. 1816. Burial took place on 10 September in the church of La Nativité-de-Notre-Dame at Beauport, with a host of persons of consequence in the colony, both Canadian and British, in attendance. A deed dated 9 Dec. 1816 mentions a distant relative, Marie-Anne Hervieux, wife of Jean-Baptiste-Melchior HERTEL de Rouville, as his sole heir. As for the judge's widow, in 1816 she asked the government, in vain, for a pension. She hanged herself in a hospital for the insane in 1848, when suffering from a severe anxiety attack.

PIERRE TOUSIGNANT and JEAN-PIERRE WALLOT

Pierre-Amable De Bonne is the author of *Précis ou abrégé d'un acte qui pourvoit à la plus grande sûreté du Bas-Canada ...* (Québec, 1794). Tremaine, *Biblio. of Canadian imprints*, describes broadsheets he published during election campaigns for the Lower Canadian assembly.

ANQ-Q, CN1-16, 11 juin 1806, 2 août 1816; CN1-26, 8 mai 1800, 30 avril 1807; CN1-92, 23 juin 1794; CN1-99, 16 janv. 1805; CN1-178, 12 mai 1802; CN1-224, 26 août 1789; CN1-230, 14 juill., 5 sept. 1792; 15 févr., 30 avril, 15 mai 1799; 14 févr., 12 juin, 10 oct. 1800; 28 janv., 20 oct. 1801; 25 juin 1803; 16 mars 1804; 6 juill. 1812; 9 déc. 1816; 13 juill. 1818; P-239. Arch. de la chancellerie de l'archevêché de Montréal, 901.012. McGill Univ. Libraries (Montreal), Dept. of Rare Books and Special Coll., MS coll., CH304.S264. PAC, MG 11, [CO 42] Q, 83: 23, 193; 85: 165, 172, 180–88; 86-1: 142; 89: 2; 92: 159–60; 93: 194–95; 98: 270; MG 23, GI, 6; MG 24, B2: 78–81; MG 30, D1, 10: 97–260; RG 1, L3ᴸ: 40180–316; RG 4, A1: 17667, 24529; RG 8, I (C ser.), 15: 2–5; 199: 4–5; 688E: 474; 689: 188; 1714: 101; RG 68, General index, 1651–1841: ff.2, 8, 83–88, 223, 229, 259, 280–345, 532, 535. Bas-Canada, chambre d'Assemblée, *Journaux*, 1793, 1800–12. *Doc. relatifs à l'hist. constitutionnelle, 1759–1791* (Shortt et Doughty; 1921). *Doc. relatifs à l'hist. constitutionnelle, 1791–1818* (Doughty et McArthur; 1915). *Le Canadien*, 1806–10. *Le Courier de Québec*, 1806–8.

Quebec Gazette, 1786–1818. *Le Vrai Canadien* (Québec), 1810–11. F.-J. Audet et Fabre Surveyer, *Les députés au premier Parl. du Bas-Canada*, 95–153. Hare et Wallot, *Les imprimés dans le Bas-Canada.* "Papiers d'État," PAC *Rapport*, 1890–93. P.-G. Roy, *Inv. concessions*, 5: 73. A. W. P. Buchanan, *The bench and bar of Lower Canada down to 1850* (Montreal, 1925), 57–58. Baudouin Burger, *L'activité théâtrale au Québec (1765–1825)* (Montréal, 1974). Chapais, *Cours d'hist. du Canada*, 2: 63–67, 187–95. Christie, *Hist. of L.C.*, 1: 126, 177, 200–1, 230. Duncan McArthur, "Canada under the Quebec Act," *Canada and its prov.* (Shortt and Doughty), 3: 122–23. Maurault, *Le collège de Montréal* (Dansereau; 1967). Ouellet, *Bas-Canada.* Tousignant, "La genèse et l'avènement de la constitution de 1791." J.-P. Wallot, "Le Bas-Canada sous l'administration de sir James Craig (1807–1811)" (thèse de PHD, univ. de Montréal, 1965); *Un Québec qui bougeait.* "La bibliothèque du juge De Bonne," *BRH*, 42 (1936): 136–43. Bernard Dufebvre [Émile Castonguay], "Une journée de M. De Bonne," *Rev. de l'univ. Laval* (Québec), 10 (1955–56): 304–18, 405–25, 524–50. Ignotus [Thomas Chapais], "Notes et souvenirs," *La Presse* (Montréal), 1ᵉʳ oct. 1904: 8; 26 nov. 1904: 8; 24 déc. 1904: 9; 14 janv. 1905: 16; 21 févr. 1905: 7; 19 avril 1905: 8. É.-Z. Massicotte, "Un théâtre à Montréal en 1789," *BRH*, 23 (1917): 191–92. P.-G. Roy, "L'indemnité de nos députés," *BRH*, 10 (1904): 118–22. Benjamin Sulte, "Jean-Baptiste Cadot," *BRH*, 6 (1900): 83–86. Pierre Tousignant, "La première campagne électorale des Canadiens en 1792," *SH*, 8 (1975): 120–48.

DEBURGO. *See* BURKE

DECOIGNE, FRANÇOIS, fur trader; b. in Berthierville (Que.); fl. 1798–1818 (in the latter year he retired to Montreal, Lower Canada).

Although in 1818 François Decoigne could be described as "the celebrated Mons De Quoine," little is now known of his life or career. It is likely that he was in the west by 1795, for Gabriel Franchère*, who travelled with him in 1814, implies that Decoigne had been in the vicinity of Fort George (near Lindbergh, Alta) 19 years earlier. In September 1798 David Thompson* saw him working there as a clerk for the North West Company under John McDonald* of Garth. In May 1799 Thompson directed Decoigne to build a post at the mouth of the Lesser Slave River (near Slave Lake, Alta), where Peter Fidler* met him the following January. For the trading season of 1800–1 Decoigne returned to the North Saskatchewan, wintering this time some 20 miles upstream from Fort George, where he built Fort de l'Isle. By 1804 he had become the senior clerk in the NWC's Athabasca department, and he apparently remained in that position for several years.

On 20 June 1806 Alexander HENRY recorded Decoigne's arrival with McDonald at Fort Bas-de-la-Rivière (Fort Alexander, Man.), and by August 1808 Decoigne was apparently under Henry's command. That winter Decoigne reopened the NWC's old South Branch House to trade in opposition to the Hudson's Bay Company's nearby Carlton House (near Batoche,

Sask.); he was still on the South Saskatchewan in the spring of 1810 when Henry heard the report that Decoigne's men had lost 120 tauraux (hide bags filled with pemmican) through carelessness.

By 1813 Decoigne had moved farther west, and that year he built Rocky Mountain House (Jasper House, Alta). In May of the following year Franchère arrived from the Columbia River, and on the 24th they set out together for Fort William (Thunder Bay, Ont.), where the NWC partners held their annual rendezvous. The company minutes of July 1814 record that "Mr Decoigne broke in upon a Depot taking therefrom two Pieces – and being in other respects reported to be extravagant has been ordered out & goes to Montreal – nothing otherwise against his Character."

Decoigne was not to remain in the east for long. On 3 October Colin Robertson*, outfitting the first HBC expedition supplied from Montreal, engaged him to return to the Athabasca country. Described by Robertson as "one of the best traders the North West Co. ever had," Decoigne was highly successful in his first two seasons at the HBC post on Lesser Slave Lake, but in December 1816 the NWC seized his post and his supplies. Though he wanted to retire to Montreal, he was induced by the HBC's offer of a salary of £300 to remain in the west for one more winter. Establishing himself on Lake Athabasca, Decoigne "was blocked up in his house all winter and did not see an Indian." Nevertheless, his earlier efforts had evidently had an effect, for in August 1818 Robertson was able to report to Lord Selkirk [DOUGLAS] that "the exertions or as some say the extravagence of Decoigne has established the Lesser Slave Lake on a permanent footing." That spring Decoigne, dissatisfied with the HBC's reckoning of his account, left the west to settle in Montreal.

The relative obscurity of François Decoigne's career typifies our fragmentary knowledge of the Nor'Westers. Although hundreds of men, many of comparable rank, were employed by the NWC, references to them and to their work are scarce. Information is lacking not because the company failed to make formal agreements with its men or to keep records of their transactions, but because many NWC documents were lost or destroyed in the years following union with the HBC in 1821. A few Nor'Westers kept personal diaries and their associates sometimes receive mention in them. HBC journals carry references to traders of the rival company, and those men who were still employed after the union appear then as HBC employees. Nevertheless, the histories of many men of the NWC, like that of Decoigne, may never be known in great detail.

In collaboration with MARJORIE WILKINS CAMPBELL

UTL-TF, MS coll. 30. *Docs. relating to NWC* (Wallace), 290. Gabriel Franchère, *Journal of a voyage on the north west coast of North America during the years 1811, 1812, 1813, and 1814,* trans. W. T. Lamb, ed. and intro. W. K. Lamb (Toronto, 1969). *New light on early hist. of greater north-west* (Coues). [Colin Robertson], *Colin Robertson's correspondence book, September 1817 to September 1822,* ed. E. E. Rich with R. H. Fleming (London, 1939; repr. Nendeln, Liechtenstein, 1968), 210. A.-G. Morice, *Dictionnaire historique des Canadiens et des Métis français de l'Ouest* (2e éd., Québec, 1912). J. G. MacGregor, *Peter Fidler: Canada's forgotten surveyor, 1769–1822* (Toronto and Montreal, 1966). Morton, *Hist. of Canadian west.*

DEJEAN (Dijean, Dysan, Deian), PHILIPPE (Philip), merchant, notary, office holder, and judge; b. 5 April 1736 in the parish of Saint-Étienne, Toulouse, France, son of Philippe Dejean, a legal officer, and Jeanne de Rocques de Carbouere; m. first 12 Jan. 1761 Josette (Marie-Joseph) Larchevêque in Montreal, Que.; m. secondly Marie-Louise Augé, and they had three children; m. thirdly 25 Nov. 1776 Théotiste Saint-Cosme in Detroit (Mich.), and they had two sons; d. in or after 1809.

The first document attesting to Philippe Dejean's presence in the New World is the certificate of his marriage in 1761. The Detroit historian Clarence Monroe Burton speculated that he had emigrated from France in 1760 to escape his creditors, but nothing is recorded of his early life. By October 1766 he had established himself as a merchant at Detroit. The Royal Proclamation of 1763, which had initiated civil government for Quebec, had drawn the province's boundary just west of the Ottawa River, and "the Indian country" beyond it remained under martial law, with justice being dispensed by the post commandants. Detroit had hundreds of settlers and an active commercial life, and it fitted awkwardly into this structure. Its commandants attempted to cope with the volume of legal work by delegating their duties. Thus in April 1767 Philippe Dejean was appointed justice of the peace, notary, tabellion, and vendue master by Captain George Turnbull. His powers as JP were narrowly defined; he could take evidence under oath and could appoint one member to any board set up for settling a dispute by arbitration, but he was to "give no judgment or final award." Justice by arbitration was inadequate to the needs of Detroit's merchants, and in July a temporary court was established "to be held Twice in every month . . . to decide all actions of debts, Bonds, Bills, Contracts and Trespasses above the sum of Five Pounds New York Currency." Dejean was named judge.

The Quebec Act of 1774 brought Detroit within the boundaries of the province's civil administration, and Governor Guy CARLETON was instructed to establish a court of king's bench for the settlement and its vicinity. The American revolution intervened, however, and there was a long delay. In the mean time, the lieutenant governor appointed for Detroit and region,

DeLancey

Henry Hamilton*, seems to have continued some of the judicial arrangements evolved when the area was under martial law. He recognized Dejean as JP and even condoned the extension of his jurisdiction beyond the limits recognized in English law. Instead of always sending accused persons to Montreal, Dejean empanelled juries, conducted trials, and apparently sentenced several individuals to be hanged. He is said even to have reversed verdicts of juries with which he disagreed. In 1775 and 1776 Governor Carleton's attention was absorbed by the American invasion of the province, but in February 1777 he sent a warning letter to Hamilton: the lieutenant governor had been given a commission of the peace and warrants had to be signed by him, not by Dejean, "whose authority is not known here." In the autumn of 1778 a presentment by a Montreal grand jury stated that Dejean had "acted & transacted divers, unjust & illegal, Terranical & felonious acts" and Hamilton had "tolerated suffered & Permitted the same." The matter was referred to Lord George Germain, secretary of state for the American Colonies. He declared himself willing to excuse their actions if no substantial injustice had been done; like the new governor, Frederick HALDIMAND, he believed that the wartime crisis justified technical illegality.

Meanwhile the arrival of rebel forces under George Rogers Clark in the Illinois country had prompted Hamilton to lead a counter-expedition there in the autumn of 1778. Anxious to obtain a statement from the lieutenant governor that he had been acting on orders, Dejean travelled with the reinforcements that left Detroit in February 1779 for Fort Sackville (Vincennes, Ind.), where Hamilton was wintering. A surprise attack by Clark resulted in the capture of the fort and the interception of the reinforcements. Dejean, along with Hamilton and a number of others, was sent prisoner to Virginia. He arrived in Williamsburg in June; after four months' imprisonment he was paroled and he returned to Vincennes. On 28 July 1780 he wrote to the commandant of Detroit and to Governor Haldimand asking that his family be allowed to join him in Vincennes and, still worried about his legal status, he took the opportunity to assert that in his judicial activities he had only been obeying orders. Haldimand refused his request and wrote nothing that would ease his mind about his status.

Entries in the ledgers of the Detroit firm of Macomb, Edgar, and Macomb suggest that by November 1780 Dejean had returned to the community and was active as a merchant until January 1782. It is difficult to follow his movements after that date. A letter written from Normandy in 1786 to Governor James Bowdoin of Massachusetts states that Dejean had returned to France, where he had for some time been "much esteemed" by the Marquis de La Fayette, and that he was proposing to relocate in Boston. On the other hand, in July 1790 court proceedings concerned with the appointment of a curator for his estate refer to his having left the Detroit region in 1789 and lived outside British dominions thereafter without informing anyone of his whereabouts. By August 1790 he had returned to Vincennes and may have married for a fourth time, Théotiste Saint-Cosme having died in 1788. Documents relating mainly to the ownership of property connect his name with that settlement until 1809. No record of his death has been discovered.

Detroit tradition is hostile to Dejean. William W. Potter is typical in portraying him as "a pompous, pious bungler who was willing to send any suspect to the gallows on short notice for the fee there was in it." His reputation in the United States has no doubt suffered because of his association with Henry Hamilton, whom American historians in the past have castigated for employing Britain's Indian allies against frontier settlements during the revolution. Although the evidence does suggest Dejean had a concern with status and a readiness to overstep the bounds of his jurisdiction, consideration of the unusual political and legal environment in which he undertook his responsibilities must mitigate any condemnation.

BURTON HISTORICAL COLLECTION STAFF

Archdiocese of Detroit, Chancery Office, Reg. des baptêmes, mariages et sépultures de Sainte-Anne (Detroit), 2 Feb. 1704–30 Dec. 1848 (transcripts at DPL, Burton Hist. Coll.). Arch. municipales, Toulouse (France), État civil, Saint-Étienne (Toulouse), 5 avril 1736. DPL, Burton Hist. Coll., Detroit notarial papers, 1737–95, A-D-2; Macomb, Edgar, and Macomb, ledgers, 1778–82. *Knox County, Indiana: early land records and court indexes, 1783–1815*, comp. J. B. Barekman (3v. in 1, Chicago, 1973). *Mich. Pioneer Coll.*, 3 (1880): 17, 22–23; 9 (1886): 346, 437, 463, 469, 505, 508–9, 513, 647, 649; 10 (1886): 293–94, 336, 410; 19 (1891): 548–51. *The territorial papers of the United States*, comp. C. E. Carter and J. P. Bloom (28v. to date, Washington, 1934–   ; repr. vols.1–26 in 25v., New York, 1973), 7: 336–37. *Windsor border region* (Lajeunesse). Wis., State Hist. Soc., *Coll.*, 10 (1888): 433. *The city of Detroit, Michigan, 1701–1922*, ed. C. M. Burton et al. (5v., Detroit and Chicago, 1922). Christian Denissen, *Genealogy of the French families of the Detroit River region, 1701–1911*, ed. H. F. Powell (2v., Detroit, 1976). Silas Farmer, *The history of Detroit and Michigan . . .* (2nd ed., 2v., Detroit, 1889). W. R. Riddell, *Michigan under British rule: law and law courts, 1760–1796* (Lansing, Mich., 1926). Peter Marshall, "Imperial policy and the government of Detroit: projects and problems, 1760–1774," *Journal of Imperial and Commonwealth Hist.* (London), 2 (1973–74): 153–89. W. W. Potter, "Michigan's first justice of the peace," *Mich. Hist. Magazine* (Lansing), 6 (1922): 630–41.

DELANCEY (de Lancey, De Lancey, Delancey), JAMES, army officer and politician; b. 6 Sept. 1746 in Westchester County (New York City), fourth son and seventh child of Peter De Lancey and Elizabeth

Colden; m. *c*. 1780 Martha Tippett (Tippetts), and they had six sons and four daughters; d. 2 May 1804 in Round Hill, N.S.

James DeLancey was a member of one of the most prominent families in the colony of New York. Although several DeLanceys were active politically, James served quietly as sheriff of Westchester County (1769–76) and as an officer of the county militia. Most of his time was devoted to looking after the family estates. In the years immediately prior to the American revolution, James was openly and emphatically tory in his sentiments. After the outbreak of fighting, he was forced by local patriot leaders to give his parole, which he promptly broke, having decided that it was neither morally nor legally binding.

DeLancey then made his way to New York City, where in 1777 he raised a picked force of horsemen drawn from his own county. The company was to harass the enemy near New York City and to procure supplies for the use of the British army from the so-called "Neutral Ground" between the British and American positions. Governor William Tryon of New York commented, "This Troop is truly [the] 'Elite' of the Country . . . I have much confidence in them, for their spirited behaviour." Over the next five years DeLancey's "Cowboys," as they were called, became one of the best known and most feared of the loyalist units. The many exciting adventures of the "Outlaw of the Bronx" (DeLancey had his headquarters near the Bronx River) gave him a glamorous image among both loyalists and patriots in New York. Although taken once, he was exchanged, and he continued to harass the enemy throughout the war; even George Washington was well aware of his activities and much desired his capture.

The cessation of fighting in the New York region in 1782 ended DeLancey's military career. Having suffered proscription and the confiscation of his property by the New York Act of Attainder of 1779, he decided to leave and in late 1782 or early 1783 arrived in Nova Scotia along with thousands of other loyalists. With his young wife, infant child, and six slaves, DeLancey settled on his 640-acre land grant at Round Hill in Annapolis County, where his other nine children were born. It is probable that he had been able to bring at least part of his wealth with him, since by the 1790s he was certainly a well-to-do man.

DeLancey took an active part in the development both of his own farm and of Annapolis County in general. In 1790 he was elected to the House of Assembly, in succession to his brother Stephen, to represent Annapolis Township, an office he held until his elevation to the Council in June 1794. He resigned from this position in June 1801 because of ill health.

Near the end of his life DeLancey became involved in a famous debate over the legality of slavery in Nova Scotia. One of his slaves, Jack, ran away to Halifax, where he was employed by one William Woodin. In 1801 DeLancey sued in the Supreme Court for the payment of the wages Jack had earned. Woodin's lawyer, Attorney General Richard John Uniacke*, argued that Jack was a free man since Nova Scotia had no law to make him otherwise. When the court awarded DeLancey £70 in damages, Uniacke appealed, giving the subject of slavery a full airing. At DeLancey's request, Joseph APLIN, former attorney general of Prince Edward Island, prepared an extensive legal defence of slavery. Aplin's brief had no effect upon the case, however, and the charge of trespass which DeLancey subsequently brought against Woodin was dismissed. DeLancey offered documentary proof of his ownership of Jack, but the court did not order that he be returned, and DeLancey died before he could regain possession of his slave.

After several years of declining health, DeLancey died at Round Hill on 2 May 1804. A family tradition maintains that he was poisoned by a disgruntled female slave to whom he had promised freedom on his death, but there is nothing to point to the validity of this story. His widow survived until 22 Dec. 1836.

BARRY M. MOODY

DeLancey family burying ground (Round Hill, N.S.), James DeLancey, gravestone. PANS, MG 100, 133, no.36. [George Washington], *The writings of George Washington, from the original manuscript sources, 1745–1799*, ed. J. C. Fitzpatrick (39v., Washington, 1931–44), 18: 343; 22: 303. *DAB. Directory of N.S. MLAs*, 87. Calnek, *Hist. of Annapolis* (Savary), 341. R. S. Longley, "The DeLancey brothers, loyalists of Annapolis County," N.S. Hist. Soc., *Coll.*, 32 (1959): 55–77. T. W. Smith, "The slave in Canada," N.S. Hist. Soc., *Coll.*, 10 (1899): 105–11.

DELESDERNIER (Le Derniers, Les Derniers), MOSES, landowner and "improver," office holder, land agent, and author; b. *c*. 1713 in Russin (canton of Geneva, Switzerland); d. 8 Sept. 1811 in Halifax, N.S.

Moses Delesdernier and his first wife, Judith Martin (Martine), emigrated to London, England, in 1740, and ten years later came to Halifax with Gideon Delesdernier, either Moses's brother or his uncle. In Nova Scotia Moses became involved in Abram Dupasquier's scheme to recruit settlers from the Palatinate (Federal Republic of Germany) and returned to Europe in the fall of 1750. The venture proved most unsuccessful and he was back in Halifax in August 1751.

By early 1754 Delesdernier was at Pisiquid (Windsor), where, he claimed, Governor Edward Cornwallis* had given him a grant of land. The Acadians in the area apparently gave "their consent to Le Derniers residence among them," and there he became probably the first non-Acadian marshland farmer in the province. During the deportation of the

Delesdernier

Acadians in 1755 [*see* John Winslow*] he acted as commissary agent for the New England troops. He later asserted that he and his servants had joined the troops and that their activities had resulted in the surrender of many Acadians and the procurement of their cattle for Halifax. He must initially have gained the Acadians' trust and was sympathetic to their predicament, but he also understood and seems to have accepted the motives of the government in carrying out the "banishment."

Delesdernier prospered at Pisiquid, where Governor Charles Lawrence* made him a present of 30 acres. At the same time, however, he borrowed heavily from Michael Francklin* and Joseph Gerrish* in order to improve and settle his lands. In 1760 he was appointed truckmaster for trade with the Indians. His first wife had died childless in 1759 and two years later he married Eleanor Bonner, *née* Pritchard, with whom he was to have ten children.

By 1765 Delesdernier was in trouble with his creditors Francklin and Gerrish, having been "too sanguine" in his attempts to promote settlement of his lands. They forced him to sell most of his property to them to clear his debts, but being "sensible of his great misfortune" they appointed him their agent for the settlement of the new township of Hillsborough on the Petitcodiac River (N.B.). Delesdernier moved there and in 1768 became a justice of the peace for the region; by 1770 his establishment included nine persons and 800 acres. Three years later he settled his final debts with Gerrish, but only through the loss of all his Windsor properties. In the summer of 1774 Delesdernier went to the southern colonies to recruit settlers for Hopewell Township, south of Hillsborough, and in Philadelphia met Richard John Uniacke*, his future son-in-law. That same year he returned to Hillsborough with Uniacke, and the following spring both moved to Hopewell; by this time Delesdernier had become the official agent of the Hopewell proprietors, who included Major-General Frederick HALDIMAND, like himself a French Swiss. Delesdernier rashly bound himself to a £500 penalty in undertaking to settle a dispute between the proprietors and the executors of the former agent and when he failed to do so lost all his cattle.

The rebellion fomented by Jonathan EDDY in Cumberland County (N.S.) during 1776 was to leave Delesdernier impoverished and discredited by government. According to him, a number of "disaffected" settlers went to New England in the spring of 1776. He himself, after drawing up a petition of loyalty, moved his family and stock to the protection of nearby Fort Cumberland (near Sackville, N.B.) before the rebels in the county took reprisals. Upon Lieutenant-Colonel Joseph Goreham*'s proclamation of 7 November ordering the population to support the king's troops, Delesdernier offered oxen and salt to the garrison.

Threats against his property and family forced him, however, to sign an "Association" against the king. After the defeat of Eddy's force Delesdernier swore a protest against this signing, and although he "stood tryall" he was acquitted of disloyalty. The truth would seem to be that he was indeed innocent of collusion with the rebels, as Goreham explained to Haldimand in a letter of October 1778. However, a son of Gideon's, Lewis Frederick Delesdernier, had sided with the rebels, and Uniacke had been sent a prisoner to Halifax to stand trial for treason. Delesdernier's losses during the rebellion had left him destitute and "prejudice and Malice" prevailed against him because of his family connections with suspected rebels. Early in 1777 he was dismissed from all official employment for "disaffection to government."

Delesdernier nevertheless continued to live in Cumberland County. In July 1779 he was elected to the House of Assembly of St John's (Prince Edward) Island in unknown circumstances, but he did not attend a session and his seat was declared vacant in October. In the same year, at the age of 66, he went on a trading voyage to Quebec, where he applied to Haldimand for permission to ship provisions to the Bay of Fundy. He was able to restore himself sufficiently in government favour to be reappointed a justice of the peace in 1781 and to obtain grants of land in the upper Petitcodiac and River Philip areas. He gradually sold off these lands, as he did his other properties. His financial situation must have deteriorated somewhat in later years, since in 1798, with the support of Uniacke and Lieutenant Governor Sir John WENTWORTH, he petitioned the British government for 20,000 acres in Nova Scotia, claiming that "after the trial of Adversity . . . he is drove by last extremity to solicit . . . Protection and Assistance." His petition was refused and he and his wife moved to Halifax to be cared for in their old age by Uniacke.

Delesdernier was the author of two manuscripts on aspects of the early history of the Maritimes which were consulted by Andrew Brown* in 1791 for his draft history of Nova Scotia. At some time between 1785 and 1790 he wrote "Observations on the progress of agriculture in Nova Scotia and New Brunswick for consideration of proprietors in both provinces." After making some remarks on the techniques of marshland farming, he went on to propose a regularized scheme for bringing in German and Swiss redemptioners to dike and drain the marshlands of Westmorland and Cumberland counties. About 1790 he wrote "Observations on the situation, customs and manner of the ancient Acadians." He believed that the Acadians, who were quite illiterate, had lived in a state of nature and in great harmony, and had been largely self-sufficient. Those who had returned following the deportation had maintained an "inviolate separation" from all others and had retained their "superstitious bigotry," but were "very peaceable useful members of civil society."

B. C. CUTHBERTSON

Information on Delesdernier's land holdings may be found at the Cumberland, Halifax, and Hants county registries of deeds, whose records are available on microfilm at PANS. His two manuscripts are in the Andrew Brown papers at BL, Add. MSS 19071: ff.259–64; 19073: ff.126–35.

PANS, MG 100, 134, no.6; RG 1, 134: 126; 163: 112; 212: 334; 367, docs.13, 14; 367½, doc.17; RG 20; RG 39, C, 1–35. PRO, CO 217/170: 266. Bell, *Foreign Protestants*. E. C. Royle, "Pioneer, patriot and rebel, Lewis Delesdernier of Nova Scotia and Maine, 1752–1838" (typescript, n.p., 1972) (copy at Univ. of N.B. Library, Fredericton). B. C. U. Cuthbertson, "The old attorney general: Richard John Uniacke, 1753–1830" (MA thesis, Univ. of N.B., 1970); *The old attorney general: a biography of Richard John Uniacke* (Halifax, [1980]). E. C. Wright, *The Petitcodiac: a study of the New Brunswick river and of the people who settled along it* (Sackville, N.B., 1945).

DE LISLE, JEAN (he sometimes signed **De Lisle de La Cailleterie**), notary and merchant; b. *c.* 1724 in Nantes, France, son of Jean-Guillaume De Lisle, a merchant, and Angélique Chevalier; d. 11 March 1814 in Montreal, Lower Canada.

In the 1750s, for unknown reasons, Jean De Lisle emigrated to New York. There, in 1756, he married Ann Denton, and the next year they had a son, JEAN-GUILLAUME. In April 1764 De Lisle was with his son at Quebec, where he declared possession of 280 *livres* 15 *sols* in card money. Three years later he enrolled Jean-Guillaume in the secondary school that Sulpician Jean-Baptiste Curatteau* was opening in his presbytery at Longue-Pointe (Montreal). Curatteau, who also came from Nantes, and his superior, Étienne Montgolfier*, assumed responsibility for the expenses of the boy's education and board. On 15 July 1768 De Lisle received from Governor Guy CARLETON a commission to practise as notary in the District of Montreal. In the same year he was authorized to draw up survey reports, a line of work he carried on for three years. In 1771 he is supposed to have witnessed a miraculous event: on the evening of the death of Mme d'Youville [Dufrost*] he saw a "perfectly formed" cross shining above the Hôpital Général.

In 1783 De Lisle and Jean-Baptiste-Amable Adhémar* were chosen as Canadian delegates to London, England, where they were to present to George III a petition for the reform of the government and the judicial system. With the tacit consent of Bishop Briand*, and despite Governor HALDIMAND's opposition, they were also to ask on behalf of the Catholic population for a bishopric in Montreal, as well as for permission to bring priests from France, since clerics were badly needed in Canada. The delegates reached London late in November. They delivered a memoir on the religious aspect of their mission to Lord North, the Home secretary, the following month. While waiting for his reply, De Lisle and Adhémar went to Paris early in 1784 with the intention of recruiting priests there. They were back in London in March, and with Carleton's support they met North's successor, Lord Sydney; Sydney refused to allow any French priests to enter Canada, even those already living in London. Nevertheless, because of Haldimand's impending recall and the anticipated reappointment of Carleton, De Lisle's report to Bishop Briand on the religious issue, made after his return to Montreal in the summer of 1784, was quite optimistic. Although Adhémar and De Lisle had failed to accomplish the political objectives of their mission, the latter continued to work actively for constitutional reform. He joined the Canadian reform committee established in Montreal in November 1784, which brought together notary Joseph Papineau* and merchants Maurice-Régis BLONDEAU, Pierre GUY, Joseph PÉRINAULT, Pierre FORETIER, Joseph-François Perrault*, and Jean Dumas* Saint-Martin.

In 1787 De Lisle gave up his notarial practice, which was taken over by his son. It was then, apparently, that he became a merchant. He imported various wares from England, such as hardware, building materials, tools for sundry trades, kitchen utensils, dishes, and cutlery, which he stored in a shed built on to his house on Rue Saint-François-Xavier.

De Lisle was elected a churchwarden of the parish of Notre-Dame in Montreal on 27 Dec. 1787 [*see* Jean-Guillaume De Lisle]. On 15 Oct. 1790 he joined other leading Montreal citizens in signing a petition that requested from Carleton, now Lord Dorchester, a charter for the creation of a university. Two months earlier, on 3 August in Montreal, he had been married again, to Suzanne Lacroix-Mézière, sister of Henry-Antoine MÉZIÈRE. The couple were to have a daughter and three sons, only one of whom, Augustin*, would reach adulthood. In 1795 De Lisle had an 18-year-old black slave baptized in the church of Notre-Dame, giving him the name Guillaume.

De Lisle's erudition and knowledge of mathematics and physics astonished his contemporaries. He wrote a manuscript entitled "Hydrostatique, 1798," which contains numerous calculations, problems with their solutions, a method (illustrated by a drawing) for determining the specific weight of bodies lighter than water, and tables of the specific weights of various metals and alloys. His library was well stocked with literary works and monographs on history, philosophy, theology, mathematics, physics, electricity, magnetism, geography, astronomy, and chemistry. In addition he owned many laboratory instruments, which his son Augustin inherited. De Lisle seems to have followed the political evolution of his native land with interest. Among his papers were found copies of

De Lisle

the French republican calendar, as well as of newspaper articles favourable to the future emperor Napoleon I, letters exchanged between the latter and Pius VI in 1797, and a speech delivered by the emperor on 2 Jan. 1805.

Although not a figure of major importance, Jean De Lisle served his adopted country with intelligence and devotion. The journalist who announced his death rightly called him a "respectable man who combined deep and wide knowledge with all the social virtues, who in short delighted in the study of philosophy [the sciences] and always promoted it with success."

LÉON LORTIE

Jean De Lisle's "Hydrostatique, 1798," is held by the Bibliothèque de la ville de Montréal, Salle Gagnon. His minute-book for 1768–87 can be found at ANQ-M, CN1-120.

ANQ-M, CE1-51, 3 août 1790, 13 mars 1814; CN1-313, 1er juill. 1790, 28 déc. 1809. ASQ, Fonds Viger-Verreau, Carton 48, nᵒˢ 3–10. "Le gouverneur Haldimand et les prêtres français," *BRH*, 12 (1906): 248–52. "MM. Adhémar et Delisle," *BRH*, 12 (1906): 325–41, 353–71. Georges Bellerive, *Délégués canadiens-français en Angleterre, de 1763 à 1867 . . .* (Québec, [1913]). [François Daniel], *Nos gloires nationales; ou histoire des principales familles du Canada . . .* (2v., Montréal, 1867), 2: 250, 424. [É.-M. Faillon], *Vie de Mme d'Youville, fondatrice des Sœurs de la charité de Villemarie dans l'île de Montréal, en Canada* (Villemarie [Montréal], 1852), 318–21. Galarneau, *La France devant l'opinion canadienne*, 290–91. Lemieux, *L'établissement de la première prov. eccl.*, 16, 22. Maurault, *Le collège de Montréal* (Dansereau; 1967). J.-E. Roy, *Hist. du notariat*, 2: 44–45. Tousignant, "La genèse et l'avènement de la constitution de 1791," 309. Léon Lortie, "Deux notaires amateurs de science: Jean De Lisle et son fils Augustin-Stanislas De Lisle," *RSC Trans.*, 3rd ser., 55 (1961), sect.I: 39–47. É.-Z. Massicotte, "Les arpenteurs de Montréal au xviiie siècle," *BRH*, 24 (1918): 340; "La famille de Jean De Lisle de la Cailleterie," *BRH*, 25 (1919): 175–86; "Jean De Lisle et Jean-Guillaume De Lisle," *BRH*, 150–52; "Une page de l'histoire du collège de Montréal," *BRH*, 23 (1917): 207–11. Benjamin Sulte, "La délégation envoyée en Angleterre en 1783," *BRH*, 7 (1901): 213–16.

DE LISLE, JEAN-GUILLAUME, merchant, notary, and militia officer; b. *c.* 1757 in New York, son of Jean DE LISLE, a notary, and Ann Denton; m. 26 July 1779 Radegonde Berthelet, daughter of Joachim Berthelet, a lawyer and justice of the peace, in Montreal (Que.), and they had four sons and three daughters; d. there 4 July 1819.

Jean-Guillaume De Lisle, who arrived in the province of Quebec around 1764, was one of the first 16 pupils enrolled in the secondary school founded in June 1767 by the Sulpician Jean-Baptiste Curatteau* at Longue-Pointe (Montreal). This institution later became the Collège Saint-Raphaël. He finished his studies in 1771, but left with an unfavourable

impression of the school; his father, on the other hand, held the director in high esteem. Jean-Guillaume completed his education under the guidance of his father, to whom he was clerk and apprentice notary for five years.

In 1785 De Lisle formed a partnership with the Montreal merchant Maurice-Régis BLONDEAU to underwrite one of Jean-Baptiste CADOT's fur-trade expeditions to Sault Ste Marie (Ont.). Also in 1785 he signed a petition addressed by merchants and traders to Lieutenant Governor Henry Hamilton*, asking him to facilitate their commerce. After this year there is no record of further commercial activity on his part. He received a commission as a notary for the District of Montreal on 15 Nov. 1787, and then took over the practice which his father was giving up. In December 1792 he obtained another commission entitling him to practise anywhere in the province.

On 27 Dec. 1788 De Lisle had replaced Simon Sanguinet* as clerk of the *fabrique* of Notre-Dame in Montreal, and he retained the office until 1798. In this capacity he drafted the proposals that the church-warden in charge, Louis Cavilhe, put to a meeting held on 6 Sept. 1789 to choose a new director for the Collège Saint-Raphaël following Curatteau's resignation. Since the *fabrique* owned the Château de Vaudreuil, the building in which the college was housed, the churchwardens took the liberty of intervening in its internal administration and suggested that Charles Chauveaux be appointed director. In addition they proposed that a broader and more liberal curriculum be adopted, because in their opinion the college gave good preparation for the priesthood to those seeking it but left the rest ill equipped to succeed in the world [*see* Gabriel-Jean Brassier*]. The church-wardens also wanted the college to offer the final part of the classical program, Philosophy; at that time it was taught only at the Séminaire de Québec, to which Montrealers sent their sons at considerable expense.

The Sulpicians did not give in to all the requests of the *fabrique* since Jean-Baptiste Marchand* was chosen as director of the college in preference to Chauveaux. The *fabrique* did, however, obtain a philosophy teacher, Ignace Leclerc, who took up his post in 1790. The following year the college diversified its teaching, offering courses in English and mathematics. In 1790 De Lisle and other prominent citizens of Montreal signed a petition in support of the Sulpicians' request to Lord Dorchester [Guy CARLETON] for a charter to create a university college in the city; the Sulpicians' plan was developed as an alternative to the proposal to create a non-denominational university that had been put forward by a commission chaired by Chief Justice William Smith* [*see* Jean-François Hubert*].

De Lisle also participated in the social, cultural, and military life of the Montreal community. Thus, in

November 1789, he joined with Louis Dulongpré*, Joseph QUESNEL, Pierre-Amable DE BONNE, Jacques-Clément Herse, Joseph-François Perrault*, and François Rolland in founding the Théâtre de Société in Montreal. In December this company, with De Lisle as a player, put on a comedy which the parish priest of Montreal, François-Xavier Latour-Dézery, condemned, with a warning that the church would refuse absolution to anyone attending the performances [see Joseph Quesnel]. On 10 Dec. 1790 De Lisle was made master of the Frères du Canada, of whose Montreal lodge he had been master two years earlier. This society, founded in 1766 and probably masonic, had six or seven members, among them Herse, Jean-Philippe Leprohon*, and Philippe-François Rastel de Rocheblave. In 1797 De Lisle was president of the Fire Society of Montreal. He lived in the *faubourg* Saint-Antoine and owned at Côte-des-Neiges (Outremont) an orchard and vegetable garden which Michel Bibaud*'s father agreed to take care of on 22 Feb. 1798. In 1799 he was a member, under the name Apôtre Jean, of the Club des Apôtres founded that year; interested in gastronomy, its 12 members organized a monthly supper, but the club lasted only a few months.

In 1805 De Lisle was a captain-lieutenant in Montreal's 2nd Militia Battalion. Promoted captain in 1812, he served as such in the War of 1812, during which he reached the rank of major. By 1815 he had become a lieutenant-colonel. At that period he dedicated to his superior in the militia, Pierre GUY, a work on the administration of *fabriques* that he said he had begun writing when he was clerk; but the work remained in manuscript form.

On 21 July 1817 Jean-Guillaume De Lisle made a handwritten will, naming his wife as sole legatee of his property and executor of his last wishes; she had obtained a separation of property in 1803 by a decision of the Court of King's Bench. De Lisle died two years later, on 4 July 1819, in Montreal.

LÉON LORTIE

Jean-Guillaume De Lisle's minute-book for 1787–1819 is held by the ANQ-M, CE1-121.

ANQ-M, CE1-51, 26 juill. 1779, 6 juill. 1819. *Quebec Gazette*, 16 June 1785, 15 June 1815. *Quebec almanac*, 1805, 1810, 1815. [François Daniel], *Nos gloires nationales; ou histoire des principales familles du Canada . . .* (2v., Montréal, 1867), 2: 253–55. Maurault, *Le collège de Montréal* (Dansereau; 1967). Morisset, *Coup d'œil sur les arts*, 55–56. Ægidius Fauteux, "Jacques-Clément Herse," *BRH*, 35 (1929): 219–21. J. E. Hare, "Le Théâtre de société à Montréal, 1789–1791," Centre de recherche en civilisation canadienne-française, *Bull.* (Ottawa), 16 (1977–78), no.2: 22–26. "Le livre de M. Delisle," *BRH*, 12 (1906): 255. É.-Z. Massicotte, "La famille de Jean De Lisle de la Cailleterie," *BRH*, 25 (1919): 175–86; "Les Frères du Canada," *BRH*, 23 (1917): 219–21; "Jean De Lisle et Jean-Guillaume De Lisle," *BRH*, 25 (1919): 150–52; "Notre-Dame-des-Neiges," *Cahiers des Dix*, 4 (1939): 141–66; "Une page de l'histoire du collège de Montréal," *BRH*, 23 (1917): 207–11. Victor Morin, "Clubs et sociétés notoires d'autrefois," *Cahiers des Dix*, 13 (1948): 117–27.

DEMASDUWIT (**Shendoreth, Waunathoake, Mary March**), one of the last of the Beothuks; b. *c.* 1796; m. Nonosbawsut, and they had one child, who died as an infant in 1819; d. 8 Jan. 1820 at Bay of Exploits, Nfld.

In September 1818 a small band of Beothuk Indians, not for the first time, pilfered the salmon boat and the equipment and gear of John Peyton Jr at the mouth of the Exploits River on the northeast coast of Newfoundland. The governor, Vice-Admiral Sir Charles Hamilton*, in response to a request from the injured settlers and others, authorized the dispatch of a party to recover the stolen property. The expedition was also intended to act, with unperceived incongruity, on behalf of the British and Newfoundland authorities in still another of the efforts made over a long period to establish friendly relations with the dwindling survivors of the Beothuk people. Its goal was Red Indian Lake, the principal winter quarters of the Beothuks, which had already been the scene of officially sponsored searches by the naval officers John Cartwright in 1768 and David Buchan* in the winter of 1810–11. This expedition, like its predecessors, was unsuccessful; indeed it was to prove a tragic and perhaps decisive failure.

Led by John Peyton and his father John*, a small band of heavily armed furriers set out on 1 March 1819 up the frozen Exploits into the interior, arriving unobserved at the shores of Red Indian Lake on the 5th. As they closed in on a group of three wigwams, a dozen or more Indians fled into the woods or across the expanse of ice. One of the latter group, labouring in the snow and pursued by John Peyton Jr, threw herself down, exposing her breasts in a gesture of supplication, and was captured; this was Demasduwit. As she was dragged back to the main party of settlers, one of the Indians, later identified as her husband Nonosbawsut, followed at a distance by another, approached the group brandishing a club. An elaborate but mutually incomprehensible exchange of words followed, though the intent of the Indian, release of the woman, must have been obvious. A desperate scuffle followed between Nonosbawsut and the furriers; in the mêlée one of the furriers stabbed Nonosbawsut with a bayonet, shots were fired, and he fell mortally wounded. It is a plausible conjecture that his death removed the most experienced and decisive leader of the surviving Beothuks, sealed the enmity between the two competing peoples, and hastened the disintegration of the remnants of the tribe. Peyton's party examined the encampment, identified the stolen

Demers

property (including kettles, knives, axes, fish-hooks, fishing-lines, and nets), and returned to the coast, their captive several times attempting to escape.

Taken to Twillingate, Demasduwit was placed in the care of the Anglican missionary John Leigh*; and when spring navigation opened on the coast Leigh and Peyton Jr brought her to St John's by schooner. There she remained for several months, a familiar figure in the capital (where she was known as Mary March) and a visitor to the governor's residence, where Lady Hamilton executed a well-known portrait. Gentle, intelligent, and tractable, Demasduwit is said to have evinced particular attachment to her captor, Peyton Jr. He and other members of the party were absolved of the killing of her husband by a grand jury at St John's on 25 May, which found that there was "no malice on the part of Peyton's Party to get possession of any of [the Indians] by such violence as would occasion Bloodshed."

Anxious to return the captive to her people, and in accordance with a proposal to this effect from a group of influential inhabitants of both St John's and Notre Dame Bay, who raised a subscription towards the cost, the governor had her placed aboard a vessel and sent northward on 3 June 1819, Leigh boarding at Trinity. There followed, between 18 June and 14 July, a number of attempts to place her in the hands of Beothuk tribesmen known to be at their summer stations on the coast and river estuaries. All proved unsuccessful, however, and Demasduwit was again given into the care of Leigh at Fogo and Twillingate, the occasion permitting him to continue the compilation of a vocabulary of the Beothuk language from information derived from her. In September 1819, Buchan arrived in Notre Dame Bay aboard the *Grasshopper* with instructions to take the captive inland during the winter freeze-up when travel would be easier; and in late November Demasduwit was brought aboard the vessel to be in readiness for the execution of the new plan. But, her health now greatly deteriorated, she succumbed to tuberculosis at Ship Cove, near Botwood, on 8 Jan. 1820.

On his own authority, Buchan decided to salvage what he could of the situation and on 21 January, accompanied by John Peyton Jr, he led a party of 50 marines and some furriers up the Exploits to return Demasduwit's body to Red Indian Lake. Covertly watched by the Beothuks (including Demasduwit's niece Shawnandithit*), the party arrived at the empty winter encampment on 9 February. There the body, carefully arrayed, was left with gifts in one of the wigwams, and the expedition returned by a longer route to the coast. Shawnandithit later described to William Eppes Cormack* how the body of Demasduwit was placed with that of Nonosbawsut in a sepulchre by her people. In its final resting-place it was seen by Cormack in November 1828 when, on the

last melancholy expedition in search of the Beothuks, he reached the unfrozen expanse of Red Indian Lake, the shores of which had once been the inland home of the unfortunate tribe, and found them abandoned and silent.

G. M. STORY

[The principal contemporary sources, the originals of many of which are preserved in the PANL, are printed in J. P. Howley, *The Beothucks or Red Indians: the aboriginal inhabitants of Newfoundland* (Cambridge, Eng., 1915; repr. Toronto, 1974, and New York, 1979); no significant additional sources concerning Demasduwit have since been found. Howley was also able to draw upon a number of eye-witnesses: John Peyton Jr (pp.91–94), John Leigh (127–29), and a Mr Curtis (179–80). Shawnandithit's information recorded by Cormack is given at pp.227–28.

Near-contemporary accounts and information are given by the following: L. A. Anspach, *A history of the island of Newfoundland . . .* (London, 1819); R. H. Bonnycastle, *Newfoundland in 1842: a sequel to "The Canadas in 1841"* (2v., London, 1842); Charles Pedley, *The history of Newfoundland from the earliest times to the year 1860* (London, 1863); and Philip Tocque, *Wandering thoughts; or, solitary hours* (London, 1846).

In secondary sources, recent studies include: John Hewson, *Beothuk vocabularies* (St John's, 1978), 33–55; F. W. Rowe, *Extinction: the Beothucks of Newfoundland* (Toronto, 1977), 61–70; Peter Such, *Vanished peoples: the archaic Dorset & Beothuk people of Newfoundland* (Toronto, 1978); the same author's novel, *Riverrun* (Toronto, 1973); and J. A. Tuck, *Newfoundland and Labrador prehistory* (Ottawa, 1976), 62–76. For discussions on the problems regarding portraits *see* Ingeborg Marshall, "The miniature portrait of Mary March," *Newfoundland Quarterly*, 73 (1977), no.3: 4–7; and Christian Hardy and Ingeborg Marshall, "A new portrait of Mary March," 76 (1980), no.1: 25–28. G.M.S.]

DEMERS, LOUIS (baptized **Jean**), Roman Catholic priest, Recollet, superior, and architect; b. 30 Dec. 1732 in Saint-Nicolas (Quebec), son of Louis Demers and Thérèse Gagnon; d. 2 Sept. 1813 in Montreal, Lower Canada.

Jean Demers, who took the name Louis when he made his profession as a Recollet, was ordained priest on 24 Sept. 1757, only a few years before the British government forbad the Recollets in Canada to recruit new members. Following the conquest Father Louis, like others of his order, turned to the parish ministry. He was prompted by his need for a livelihood and also by goodwill towards the secular clergy, whose numbers diminished after 1760. He served at Saint-Michel, near Quebec, from 1760 to 1761, Saint-Charles (at Saint-Charles-des-Grondines) from 1762 to 1764, and La Nativité-de-Notre-Dame (at Bécancour) from 1764 to 1767.

In 1767 Father Louis was appointed parish priest of Saint-Pierre-les-Becquets, where he remained until 1789; at the same time he ministered to the seigneuries of Deschaillons, until 1789, and Gentilly, from 1767 to 1774 and from 1779 to 1789. At Saint-Pierre-les-Becquets, he had a presbytery and a mill built, but on occasion he seems to have overstepped his pastoral mandate. Some people complained to Bishop Briand* that he took the liberty of drawing up contracts. Briand was annoyed and called on him in 1774 to refrain from such activity, stating explicitly, "That is forbidden." With the help of master mason Antoine Maillou, Father Louis also became a builder of churches. Although he was probably less famous as an architect than his nephew, Abbé Jérôme Demers*, would be, he was responsible for the second church at Sainte-Anne-de-la-Pérade (La Pérade), which was completed in 1771, and the first church for the parish of Saint-Édouard (at Gentilly), which was built in 1781–87. The construction of the latter led to a dispute in 1773 between Briand and the parishioners who disapproved of the site that the bishop had chosen for the future church. Briand suspected Father Louis of being in league with the "rebels" and forbad him to give them the sacraments.

In 1789 Father Louis, who according to Bishop Hubert* was "an excellent religious, full of love and zeal for the faith," was named superior of his order's monastery in Montreal. Suggestions that he pursued architectural activities there and that he showed some talent as a painter have not yet been substantiated. In Montreal he shared the preoccupations and labours of the secular clergy. From 1792 he was attached as chaplain to the militia headquarters in the city of Montreal, but he appears to have devoted himself primarily to ministering to the sick. Indeed, 50 years after his death people still spoke of his charity and of the miraculous power of his ointments and plasters.

By 1791 the Recollet order in Canada had only five members left. With the passing of the years its extinction became inevitable. Hubert's decree of secularization on 14 Sept. 1796, which affected all those who had made their profession since 1784, destroyed the community's hope of surviving. Father Louis, who was anxious about the fate of the few remaining Recollets, received assurances from the government in August 1798 that they would not be disturbed in their ministry. He had, however, to resign himself to liquidating the community's chattels. In 1811 he sold the retable (housing the altar) and tabernacle from the Recollet church to the parish of Saint-Grégoire-le-Grand, near Nicolet, which has preserved them. In 1813 he gave the remaining goods to the churchwardens of Notre-Dame in Montreal, the Sulpicians, and the nuns of the Congregation of Notre-Dame.

Father Louis spent his last years with his brother, who had joined the order under the name of Brother Alexis, in the house next to the Recollet church in Montreal, where one of their nieces looked after them.

With his death on 2 Sept. 1813 at the Hôpital Général, the last Recollet priest in Canada was gone; he was buried two days later in Notre-Dame church, among the priests from the Séminaire de Saint-Sulpice. Almost immediately the British government seized the Recollets' property in Montreal.

MAURICE FLEURENT

AP, Notre-Dame de Montréal, Reg. des baptêmes, mariages et sépultures, 4 sept. 1813; Saint-Édouard (Gentilly), Cahier des délibérations de la fabrique, 1784–1930: 7–10, 14; Saint-Nicolas, Reg. des baptêmes, mariages et sépultures, 1er janv. 1733. Arch. de l'évêché de Nicolet (Nicolet, Qué.), Carton Saint-Édouard de Gentilly, 1752–1939, no.2, 13, 21 juill. 1773; no.5, 21 août 1773; Carton Saint-Pierre-les-Becquets, 1766–1886, no.1, 11 juill. 1766; no.3, 10 janv. 1774. Arch. des franciscains (Montréal), Notes de O.-M. Jouve. Le séminaire de Québec (Provost), 459. Allaire, Dictionnaire, 1: 153. Tanguay, Dictionnaire, 3: 527. Jean Belisle, "Le mythe récollet: l'ensemble de Montréal" (thèse de MA, univ. de Montréal, 1974). Marcel Deshaies, Ma paroisse: Bécancour (s.l., 1977). Lucien Dubois, Histoire de la paroisse de Gentilly (s.l., 1935), 93. Mariette Fréchette-Pineau, "L'église de Saint-Grégoire de Nicolet (1802)" (thèse de MA, univ. de Montréal, 1970), 55–56. O.-M. Jouve, Les franciscains et le Canada: aux Trois-Rivières (Paris, 1934), 302–5. Hormidas Magnan, La paroisse de Saint-Nicolas: la famille Pâquet et les familles alliées (Québec, 1918), 25–26. Morisset, Coup d'œil sur les arts, 52. Luc Noppen, Les églises du Québec (1600–1850) (Québec, 1977), 232. É.-T. Paquet, Fragments de l'histoire religieuse et civile de la paroisse Saint-Nicolas (Lévis, Qué., 1894). Marcelle Rivard, Gentilly, 1676–1976 (s.l., 1976), 41. J.-E. Roy, Hist. de Lauzon, 1: viii. Trudel, L'Église canadienne, 1: 98, 123–25, 219, 351, 353, 360; 2: 184–85, 192, 199, 213–14, 426; Le Régime militaire dans le gouvernement des Trois-Rivières 1760–1764 (Trois-Rivières, Qué., 1952), 153. Charles Trudelle, Le frère Louis (Lévis, 1898), 22. S. Lesage, "Les récollets en Canada," Rev. canadienne, 4 (1867): 303–18.

DENAUT, PIERRE, Roman Catholic priest and bishop; b. 20 July 1743 in Montreal (Que.), son of André Denaut and Françoise Boyer; d. 17 Jan. 1806 in Longueuil, Lower Canada.

Pierre Denaut, the seventh son of a Montreal mason, went to the Latin school run by the Sulpicians in Montreal and then in 1758 entered the Petit Séminaire de Québec. In the summer of 1759, before the British bombardment of Quebec began, he took refuge at the Séminaire de Saint-Sulpice in Montreal along with some fellow students and a few teachers; there he continued his studies and began his theology, having received a scholarship of 100 livres from the foundation created by Bishop Saint-Vallier [La Croix*]. He was still studying when he held the position of secretary to Étienne Montgolfier*, vicar general of Montreal, and then to Étienne Marchand*, also vicar general of Montreal and the parish priest of

Denaut

Sainte-Famille at Boucherville. On 25 Jan. 1767 Bishop Briand* ordained him priest in the Île d'Orléans church of Saint-Pierre. Then he appointed him parish priest of Saint-Joseph, at Les Cèdres, with responsibility for the mission chapel of Saint-Michel, at Vaudreuil, and Denaut served in this position from 5 Sept. 1773 to 30 Oct. 1775; he was subsequently named to Île Perrot, where he remained from 16 Jan. 1786 to 14 Oct. 1787. In 1788 he was made an archpriest, and on 25 October of the following year he became parish priest of Saint-Antoine at Longueuil, a charge he held until his death. This parish was prosperous and its people were, according to Denaut, "good, docile, religious." Except for one occasion, when some "stubborn people" reproached him for living too luxuriously, Denaut maintained excellent relations with his parishioners. He had two nephews and a niece staying with him, he associated with the neighbouring seigneur of Longueuil, David Alexander Grant, and once a week he visited a colleague or had a meal at the Sulpician seminary in Montreal. He led a regular life given over to pastoral duties, prayer, and study. He opened a primary school which some 15 pupils were attending in the 1790s.

Bishop Hubert* held Denaut in high esteem. In 1790 he raised him to the rank of vicar general. Then on 26 May 1794 he informed Lord Dorchester [Guy CARLETON] that from among the candidates whom Dorchester had suggested to him he was choosing Denaut as coadjutor to replace Charles-François Bailly* de Messein, who had died a few days earlier. Hubert reported this selection to Rome, stating that the future bishop's personal qualities, "his love of ecclesiastical discipline, his respect for the Holy See . . . [created] the most auspicious prejudice in his favour." Pius VI gave his approval in a bull dated 30 Sept. 1794, and Hubert proceeded to consecrate the new bishop in the church of Notre-Dame in Montreal on 29 June 1795. With his assent Denaut remained in Longueuil, and from there attended to matters in Montreal. On 1 Sept. 1797 Hubert, "worn out by fevers and fatigue," resigned in favour of his coadjutor.

The tenth bishop of Quebec was a modest, humble, reflective man, touchy at times, yet filled with the desire to serve "the glory of God and the public good." He became head of the Roman Catholic Church in Canada amid difficult circumstances: the diocese was immense, and the church was in a precarious state. Although he bore the title of bishop of Quebec, the British government recognized him as the superintendent of the Catholic Church in Canada. He had neither a salary nor official prerogatives. Certain ecclesiastical appointments were made in concert with Lieutenant Governor Robert Shore Milnes*, whom he had to inform of all other appointments. The government was disputing the ownership of the bishop's palace

with him. He lacked priests; discipline and training among the clergy left something to be desired. The women's communities were poor and short of people; the men's, not having civil recognition, were quietly dying out. To the evils that had become commonplace – drunkenness, bad books, mixed marriages – had been added in 1793 the presence at Quebec of Jacob Mountain*, the first Anglican bishop and a member of the Legislative Council. This man, who was full of a sense of his prerogatives and who wanted to subject the Catholic Church to the royal supremacy, had solid connections in the civil government, such as the clerk of the Executive Council and civil secretary to the governor, Herman Witsius Ryland*, and the attorney general, Jonathan Sewell*.

Denaut administered his diocese from Longueuil, not from Quebec. This was an unusual gesture. A humble spirit, more pastor than politician, more anxious to administer his church than to enhance its civil status, Denaut may have preferred the calm of Longueuil to the busier life at Quebec. Perhaps it was a strategy that had been devised in Hubert's time to achieve gradual British acceptance of the idea of a bishop in Montreal: "Once this step has been taken," Hubert may have thought, "we can try something more." If this was the case, the strategy had many disadvantages, one being that the slowness of communications was a possible source of misunderstanding between the bishop and his coadjutor at Quebec, especially when the latter had to deal quickly with the civil authorities.

However that may be, Denaut's first gesture, following the example of his predecessors, was to ensure the survival of his church. On 2 Sept. 1797 he took the oath of allegiance along with Joseph-Octave Plessis*, whom Hubert had chosen as coadjutor and had had accepted by Governor PRESCOTT. On 10 September Denaut asked the prefect of the Congregation of Propaganda to approve the choice of Plessis for the coadjutorship so that the episcopal succession would be assured. Denaut and Plessis, two complementary personalities, esteemed each other highly without, however, always understanding each other: the former watched over principles, the latter, who maintained "social relations" with the chief justice and the Anglican bishop, carried on the negotiations with the government. These were all the more numerous since Mountain went to work to defend his prerogatives, and some Protestant politicians to limit the powers of the Catholic bishop.

Late in the winter of 1798, when a bill to create the parish of Saint-Grégoire, at Bécancour, was introduced in the House of Assembly, some members disputed the bishop's authority to set up parishes canonically. Denaut entrusted to his coadjutor the lobbying of the government needed to obtain passage of a general bill, "reforming and amending the ordinance of 1791," that would clearly give to the bishop and the governor the authority to create parishes. This question, like the one concerning the Royal Institution for the Advancement of Learning in 1801, was only the visible tip of an anglicizing movement whose aim, set out by Sewell that same year in his report on the religious situation in Lower Canada, was to subject the Catholic Church to royal authority. The means envisaged by the attorney general included the exercise by government of the right to appoint parish priests, the attachment of the Catholic hierarchy to the political order through government stipends, the exclusion of foreign priests, and the official recognition of the episcopal function in order to bring its holder under tighter control. On the advice of Jean-Henri-Auguste Roux*, vicar general and superior of the Sulpician seminary in Montreal, Denaut adopted an intransigent attitude but a defensive strategy that was centred on cordial relations with the lieutenant governor and the presentation of memoirs setting out the rights of the Catholic Church. The general line was to demand nothing, but to take all possible advantage of a régime that was tolerant.

In 1805, when Milnes took it upon himself to ask London for a "commission" which would give the Catholic bishop a status similar to that of his Anglican counterpart, Denaut, who under the circumstances wanted "only the continuation of tolerance, support, protection," became concerned. Sewell's demands prompted him to prefer "a precarious state" to a "solid establishment" that would strip the bishop of his basic rights. He was ready to resign rather than agree to what was being proposed to him. Denaut considered the request to London inopportune: the British government, which was deeply involved in European affairs, would not have time to amuse itself "with bagatelles." He was afraid of the clique leading the Lower Canadian government, not Milnes himself, who "is too wise and too much a politician to let himself be swept away" in the direction that Mountain wanted.

After long negotiating sessions between Plessis and Sewell, and for no other reason than to avoid displeasing the lieutenant governor, in July 1805 Denaut agreed to sign two petitions, one to the lieutenant governor and the other to the king. In them he asked that his title of bishop be recognized officially, that he be accorded free exercise of all the temporal rights devolving upon a Catholic bishop, and that he receive the emoluments which it would please the king to attribute to this dignity. The petitions did not mention the disagreement between the parties over the irremovability of parish priests and the procedure for establishing parishes, but they were quite explicit about the political reasons for this understanding. The rights and dignities were requested in order that the Catholic Church might "guide and restrain the clergy

and the people," and "impress more strongly on people's minds the principles of attachment and loyalty to their sovereign."

Denaut's pastoral and administrative work is of some interest. He managed his diocese with the help of a coadjutor at Quebec and of vicars general in each of the districts of Lower Canada, a vicar general in the Maritimes, and another in Upper Canada. He made a tour, visiting Kingston and Detroit in 1801, some parishes in Upper Canada the following year, and the Maritimes in 1803. These exhausting journeys could have been enough to convince him of the necessity of subdividing his diocese. Such a plan was favoured by the Congregation of Propaganda, which, in accordance with the desire that Hubert had formerly expressed, twice suggested to Denaut the creation of suffragan dioceses. But the bishop considered this suggestion premature: the government would put obstacles in the way, and the resources needed for establishing new diocesan churches were lacking. He preferred to postpone settlement of the problem, and concentrated his efforts on strengthening discipline in the clergy and among the faithful, providing for the spiritual needs of the parishes and missions, and improving the situation of the religious communities. In these matters he was inflexible. The seniority and the merit of the candidates were the two criteria that he took into account in appointing parish priests. He did not allow dispute over the choice of sites for churches once he had had consultations and had made a decision in all justice and equity, and he insisted that parish priests be assured of a decent living. Thus he did not hesitate to threaten recalcitrant parishioners with being deprived of the sacraments from a resident priest if they did not provide for his upkeep or even with not having a church at all if the site for it were disputed. "The cross is raised; the church will be built there, or nowhere," he told the dissatisfied members of the parish of Notre-Dame-de-la-Visitation at Champlain. He began to levy charges for certain dispensations that he granted, both "to strengthen the sinews of discipline" and to provide the bishop with the income to administer his church. He put an end to the celebration of patronal feasts in parishes where they gave rise to disorders. He followed the situation of the communities closely, advising the Jesuit Jean-Joseph Casot* in his relations with the government and helping the nuns of the Hôtel-Dieu in Montreal to reorganize their finances and the Sulpicians to finance the building of their seminary.

Denaut died at Longueuil on 17 Jan. 1806, after being ill only a few hours; he was buried three days later in the parish church. In keeping with the instructions in his will, dated 3 May 1803, the executor, Pierre CONEFROY, had an inventory made on 27 Jan. 1806 of the deceased's property, which he then put up for auction on 24 and 25 February. Denaut

Dénéchaud

left personal effects that were sold for 12,000 *livres* and that included a library of 418 volumes, consisting of 106 titles among which were works of Rousseau, Voltaire, Raynal, Molière, and Racine. In addition he left two sums of money, one of £489 11*s*. 8*d*., the other, which came from tithes and debts owed him by the *fabrique*, of 1,190 *livres*; accounts receivable, which were set at some 24,000 *livres*, including a piece of land at Nicolet that had been sold to Plessis for 5,000 *livres*; settled annuities with a capital of 51,986 *livres*, 31,200 of which had been lent to René Boucher de La Bruère; and title-deeds to 200 acres in York Township and two properties of 120 acres each that had been granted in the Madawaska region (Que./ N.B.). From these assets were deducted the debts he owed, estimated at 15,054 *livres*. The difference constituted the legacy bequeathed to his great-niece Marguerite-Amable Denaut, who was to pay Denaut's sister an annuity of 600 *livres* a year.

If Pierre Denaut's portrait shows us a man with a round, chubby face marked by good nature, his correspondence reveals a thoughtful and energetic will, a mind full of humour, a man respectful of his associates, magnanimous to those close to him and to his flock, and appreciative of the attentions that each and every one lavished upon him. Having lived at a period when passive resistance was the best guarantee of survival for the Catholic Church in Canada, he left few traces in the collective memory.

JEAN HAMELIN and MICHEL PAQUIN

[Although Henri Têtu includes a short account of Pierre Denaut in *Notices biographiques; les évêques de Québec* (Québec, 1889; réimpr. en 4v., Québec et Tours, France, 1930), 76–111, there is as yet no full biographical study and historians have examined his career only in relation to particular issues.

Bishop Denaut's papers, or rather those remaining after Pierre Conefroy "burned everything that was not related to Denaut's private affairs or to parish ministry," are scattered: his correspondence for the years he was priest of Saint-Joseph, at Les Cèdres, Que., and of Saint-Antoine, at Longueuil, is held, respectively, by the Archives de la chancellerie de l'évêché de Valleyfield (Valleyfield) and the Archives du diocèse de Saint-Jean-de-Québec (Longueuil). The correspondence during his episcopacy as well as the records of his administration are at AAQ, 210 A, II; IV. There are also a few documents concerning Denaut at the ASQ, but its holdings consist mainly of copies of items at the AAQ. Complete indexes are available to the materials at the AAQ and ASQ, and an inventory is published in Caron, "Inv. de la corr. de Mgr Denaut," ANQ *Rapport*, 1931–32: 129–242. In addition, most of Bishop Denaut's episcopal pronouncements have been published in *Mandements, lettres pastorales et circulaires des évêques de Québec*, Henri Têtu et C.-O. Gagnon, édit. (18v. parus, Québec, 1887–), 2: 509–50. Finally, Têtu published extracts from Denaut's diary and from his correspondence with Plessis in "Visite pastorale de Mgr Denaut en Acadie en 1803," *BRH*, 10

(1904): 257–68 and 289–300, as well as an account of Denaut's trip to Detroit in 1801 in "Requête des voyageurs de Michillimakinac en 1786," also in *BRH*, 10: 97–106.

The authors are grateful to Professor Jean-Pierre Wallot for allowing them to consult his notes on Bishop Denaut. J.H. and M.P.]

ANQ-M, CE1-12, 17 janv. 1806; CE1-51, 21 juill. 1743; CN1-74, 3 mai 1803; 27 janv., 24, 25 févr. 1806. PAC, MG 11, [CO 42] Q, 68: 191; 92: 2; 98: 5; 100: 8; 101-1: 401; 112: 158; RG 8, I (C ser.), 63: 105–8; 206: 46; 512: 131. *Quebec Gazette*, 23 Jan. 1806. Lambert, "Joseph-Octave Plessis." Lemieux, *L'établissement de la première prov. eccl.*, 41–58, 65, 73. Robert Rumilly, *Histoire de Longueuil* (Longueuil, 1974), 76–111. Wallot, *Un Québec qui bougeait*, 169–224.

DÉNÉCHAUD, JACQUES, surgeon, apothecary, and landowner; b. 11 July 1728 in Saint-Savin, France, son of Pierre Dénéchaud, a surgeon, and Antoinette Lubet; m. 17 Nov. 1756 Angélique Gastonguay at Quebec, and they had seven children; d. there 25 Sept. 1810.

Jacques Dénéchaud studied medicine in France with a doctor by the name of Cavelier who practised at Saint-Savin. On 5 May 1751 he obtained from the Bureau des Commissaires Royaux du Grand Amiral de France at Brouage a certificate authorizing him to serve as a surgeon on seagoing vessels. With this document in hand, Dénéchaud, having taken the customary oath of allegiance to the king of France, sailed for New France and reached Quebec in 1752. He immediately settled there and engaged in private practice in addition to his duties as a naval doctor. Enjoying, no doubt, a sizeable income, on 12 Dec. 1758 he bought a three-storey stone house on Rue Saint-Jean for 5,300 *livres*, a sum he paid off in three years. This house, which had belonged to his father-in-law, Jean-Baptiste Gastonguay, was to be his residence until 1791.

From 1769 to 1810 Dénéchaud practised medicine at the Hôtel-Dieu where in all probability he set up an apothecary's shop. His professional competence cannot be doubted, for in 1788 he was one of the first doctors to obtain a licence to practise from the Quebec Medical Board. This body, which had been set up at the request of the Legislative Council to prevent quacks from practising, in 1788 also awarded certificates as surgeons and pharmacists for the District of Quebec to Pierre Chicou, *dit* Duvert, Ignace Friedel, Élie Laparre, Pierre-Henri Lebreton, *dit* Lalancette, and George Weis.

In addition to his medical practice Dénéchaud launched into a series of real-estate deals. From 1772 to 1796 he purchased at least seven lots and houses in Upper Town worth about £800 in all. Some of the properties were later sold for a gross profit of 150 per cent; others were rented to individuals for £25 to £50 a year. During the active period of Dr Dénéchaud's career, he was consulted by many people who wanted him to act as their proxy in business dealings or as their executor. It is impossible, however, to determine whether he demanded a fee for his services. Nevertheless, the management of large sums of money certainly enabled him to become a big money-lender at Quebec. In the period from 1782 to 1809 he advanced more than £5,258 in the form of multiple loans with interest at the legal rate of six per cent; over the years he was owed sums ranging from £25 to £500 by a clientele principally composed of merchants, craftsmen, and office holders in Quebec.

Dénéchaud managed closely both his own business affairs and those entrusted to him. Consequently he was not above seeking repayment of outstanding debts through the courts. In 1788, as executor for Barthélemy Cotton*, he obtained the attachment of a house on Rue Mont-Carmel in Quebec belonging to Jacques Chevalier and Joseph Dussau and their wives. Dénéchaud displayed more flexibility in his dealings with his children. In 1791 he gave an advance share in his estate, amounting to £527, to two of his sons, Pierre and Claude*, who were in partnership as merchants. He also rented them a house on Rue de la Fabrique for £16 a year, which they were to pay to their brother Charles-Denis, "to help him attain the ecclesiastical state he has chosen."

Jacques Dénéchaud died on 25 Sept. 1810 in his home on Rue Couillard, where he had been living since 1792. At the time of his death he was the last of the French doctors who had settled at Quebec before the conquest. He bequeathed to the nuns of the Hôtel-Dieu all his surgical instruments and medicaments, as well as £100 to help defray the costs of restoring their chapel. Having lost his wife 28 years earlier, he left his children entire possession of his house and the usufruct of all his other property, in both real and personal estate.

Little is known of Dénéchaud's social life other than that he was a churchwarden of the parish of Notre-Dame in the 1780s. Years later, in 1848, Joseph Morrin* observed: "He was a man of genius who charmed [others] with his pleasant conversation; he attended his patients with kindness and possessed qualities which will ever make his memory cherished."

ÉDOUARD DESJARDINS

ANQ-Q, CN1-25, 2 févr. 1775; 26 nov. 1776; 23 mars 1782; 6, 22 mars 1786; CN1-26, 13 sept. 1802, 7 juin 1806; CN1-79, 29 janv. 1759; CN1-83, 31 mai 1782; 25 janv. 1783; 26 févr., 18 juin 1784; 9, 18 oct. 1786; 6 juill. 1787; 28 mars 1788; 20, 24 déc. 1792; 22 févr., 16 avril, 1er août 1794; CN1-148, 20 févr. 1766; CN1-178, 15 juin 1795; 19 avril 1796; 4 févr., 19 juill. 1797; 13 avril 1798; 7, 18 sept., 3 nov. 1801; 22 août 1804; 19 mars 1805; 2 sept. 1807; 16 août 1808; 21 janv. 1810; CN1-193, 8 janv. 1805; CN1-200, 23 mai 1788; CN1-205, 30 avril 1777, 18 sept. 1782; CN1-207, 1er sept., 1er oct. 1770; CN1-224, 19 janv. 1780; 10 mars 1785; 13 avril 1786; 11 mai 1787; 12 janv., 3 oct. 1789; 7, 20 avril 1790; 18, 24 mai, 17 juin, 6 sept., 10 déc. 1791; 27 août 1792; CN1-230, 2, 3 déc. 1789; 19 août 1794; 1er sept. 1802; 19 juin 1809; CN1-248, 18 juill. 1772; 23 août, 2 déc. 1773; CN1-250, 11 déc. 1756, 26 mars 1761, 23 mars 1769; CN1-262, 26 sept., 26 oct. 1795; 23 mai, 12 juin, 16 août 1796; 9 juin, 14 août, 9 oct. 1798; 24 janv., 20 sept. 1803; 16 oct. 1804; 19 sept. 1808; CN1-284, 23 avril 1792; 30 déc. 1794; 6, 14 juin, 2 nov. 1796; 10 mars 1797; 16 sept. 1798; 19 juill. 1799. "Les dénombrements de Québec" (Plessis), ANQ Rapport, 1948–49: 17, 64, 114, 163. Quebec Gazette, 3 Nov. 1785, 18 Sept. 1788, 4 Nov. 1790, 13 Jan. 1803, 27 Sept. 1810. Tanguay, Dictionnaire, 3: 338. Abbott, Hist. of medicine, 33–34, 47. M.-J. et G. Ahern, Notes pour l'hist. de la médecine, 144–53, 348, 460.

DESBRISAY, THOMAS, colonial administrator, office holder, and politician; b. 1732 or 1733, likely in Dublin (Republic of Ireland), son of Theophilus DesBrisay (baptized Samuel-Théophile de La Cour de Brisay) and Magdalen de Vergese d'Aubussargues; m. c. 1753 Ellen Landers (Landen), and they had 16 children; d. 25 Sept. 1819, aged 86, on Prince Edward Island.

Of Huguenot ancestry, Thomas Desbrisay was a member of "one of the oldest branches of a highly respectable family." Appointed an ensign in the 35th Foot (Donegall's) at the age of 10, he attained the rank of captain in the Royal Irish Artillery on 8 Feb. 1760. This career was terminated when, on 31 July 1769, he was commissioned lieutenant governor, secretary, and registrar of St John's (Prince Edward) Island. Ten years were to elapse before he took up the appointment. Having acquired land on the Island, he busied himself for a few years with attempts to recruit settlers in Ireland. In 1773, however, the British government, unwilling to encourage emigration, expressly forbad him to continue his efforts.

On 8 July 1771, apparently believing that Desbrisay was soon to arrive, Governor Walter Patterson* had appointed him a justice of the peace for Queens County. Three years later Patterson was to describe the absentee lieutenant governor as "very unfit to hold any Offices under His Majesty." He charged that Desbrisay had attempted to interfere in the proper allocation of colonial funds; moreover, he had mortgaged his properties and, without discharging the mortgages, sold parcels of land to prospective settlers who were subsequently ruined by the expense of a voyage from the British Isles and the loss of their purchase money, the deeds they had received from Desbrisay being of no effect. Desbrisay was nevertheless retained as lieutenant governor, and in the summer of 1779 was ordered by the secretary of state for the American Colonies to take up his appointment.

Because Patterson was absent from the colony

Deschamps

when Desbrisay arrived on 10 October, the latter, as senior officer, assumed command. During a nine-month period he granted some 400 crown lots in Charlottetown Royalty, apportioning 58 town lots and 58 pasture lots to himself and members of his family. The British government considered his behaviour sufficient grounds for dismissal but acquiesced in Patterson's proposal that instead Desbrisay and the others who had acquired lots should be made to surrender the bulk of them to the crown in open court. Desbrisay's role in this affair no doubt explains why the remarkable number of requests for preferment that he addressed to London went unanswered. His hatred for Patterson, who had exposed him, must have intensified in 1781 when the governor claimed for himself a large portion of the land sold that November because of the proprietors' failure to pay quitrents.

With the reorganization of the colonial administration in 1784 the office of governor of St John's Island was eliminated. Patterson, as a consequence, became lieutenant governor, and Desbrisay lost both his post and his seat on the Council. He was, however, appointed clerk of the Council on 22 Jan. 1785. Unwilling to "sit, as clerk, at the foot of a Board where I was appointed by His Majesty President," he was permitted to exercise his duties by deputy, and Charles STEWART was chosen for the position. The presence of a non-member clerk at the Council meetings, a custom which was continued after Desbrisay's death, represented a departure from British tradition, and the upper house of Prince Edward Island became unique in this respect. In 1789 Desbrisay was reappointed to the Council by Lieutenant Governor Edmund FANNING.

Injured pride also figured in Desbrisay's resentment at Phillips Callbeck*'s being recommended in 1781 to command a company for the defence of the colony in preference to him, at former chief justice Peter STEWART's claim to precedence over him at Council meetings in 1801, and at William TOWNSHEND's being appointed temporary commander-in-chief of the colony in 1813 to the exclusion of his own claim as senior councillor. As late as 1818, when Desbrisay was described as being "infirm and aged even to superannuation," Lieutenant Governor Charles Douglass Smith* remarked that "it would hurt the old man's feelings much ever to be removed from the council."

Because of failing eyesight, Desbrisay had his grandson, Theophilus, assist him in the performance of the duties of secretary and registrar for some 15 years before his death. He came to believe that Theophilus was entitled to these offices and sought to negotiate a succession, over the strong objections of Lieutenant Governor Smith, who felt that, with so many offices being filled by patronage, his own recommendations stood for nothing. Desbrisay's attempt failed when the Colonial Office, citing the

"inconvenience of making a particular office hereditary in any family," declared itself ready to consider Theophilus for some other position.

On 29 Sept. 1819 Smith recorded that Desbrisay's son, Theophilus DesBrisay*, Protestant rector of Charlotte parish, "was yesterday under the necessity of officiating at the funeral of his own father." Both Theophilus and a sister had married into the family of Peter Stewart; another of Thomas's sons and a grandson had married daughters of the Reverend Mather BYLES. The family was influential in colonial and provincial affairs for many years. Thomas's great-grandson, also named Theophilus, was mayor of Charlottetown from 1867 to 1872 and again from 1875 to 1877.

F. L. PIGOT

Huguenot Soc. of London, Henry Wagner coll. of Huguenot pedigrees (MS). P.E.I. Heritage Foundation (Charlottetown), Compiled family files, Desbrisay, nos.8, 18 (photocopies). PRO, CO 226/1: 33, 127–28; 226/2: 41–45; 226/5: 65–66; 226/6: 30–31; 226/7: 44–46, 54, 136–39; 226/8: 35–37; 226/9: 98–100; 226/17: 103–4; 226/18: 239–40; 226/22: 203; 226/29: 149–50; 226/31: 62–64; 226/34: 100–1; 226/35: 21–22, 250–52, 255–56, 394–97. R. J. Dickson, *Ulster emigration to colonial America, 1718–1775* (London, 1966). *Historic highlights of Prince Edward Island* (Charlottetown, 1955). Frank MacKinnon, "Some peculiarities of cabinet government in Prince Edward Island," *Canadian Journal of Economics and Political Science* (Toronto), 15 (1949): 310–21.

DESCHAMPS, ISAAC, merchant, office holder, judge, and politician; b. *c*. 1722; by his first marriage he had one son; m. secondly 17 Oct. 1758 Sarah Ellis in Halifax, N.S.; d. 11 Aug. 1801 in Windsor, N.S.

Isaac Deschamps is usually described as a Swiss, although he may have been born in England and almost certainly lived there at least briefly. He came to Nova Scotia in 1749, but he was not among the contingent of settlers with Edward Cornwallis*. At the time of his arrival Deschamps seems to have been a man of some substance, and may have had previous business experience, possibly in association with Joshua Mauger*. He acquired land and evidently opened a general store in Halifax; two additional grants of land the next year suggest a measure of industry and success. By 1751, however, he was employed by Mauger, then victualler to the navy. Late in 1753 Deschamps seems to have been sent to Lunenburg on undisclosed official business, either to aid in the settlement there or to investigate the recent riots [*see* Jean Pettrequin*; Sebastian Zouberbuhler*].

The following year Deschamps was placed in charge of Mauger's truckhouse at Pisiquid (Windsor), where he traded with Indians, Acadians, and the garrison of Fort Edward. Fluent in French and English, he was given permission "to do any little business the French Inhabitants want without any particular appointment." He was also called upon to interpret, and to translate such documents as petitions from the Acadians, an oath of allegiance, and the deportation order of 1755 [see John Winslow*]. In 1759 he received one-sixth of a large tract of land near the fort, and on the hill below the fort he erected a house and barns. During the next few years he was given additional land, including that on which his buildings stood, and he also received grants in the new settlements at Falmouth, Newport, and Horton.

In June 1760 Deschamps began his career as a provincial official when he received the dual appointments of truckmaster for the Indian trade at Fort Edward and justice of the peace for Kings County. The following year he was named judge of the Inferior Court of Common Pleas and judge of probate for the county, and in 1764 he took office as custos rotulorum as well. He had also become involved in colonial politics: with the creation of counties in 1759 he became the first member of the House of Assembly for Annapolis County, and between 1761 and 1770 he served for Falmouth Township.

During these years Deschamps was busy with a multitude of official and semi-official tasks, which included providing horses for the military, assisting at Indian treaty ceremonies, welcoming back those Acadians who elected to return to the Minas Basin region, and arranging land grants and interim provisioning for new settlers. In addition to holding numerous minor offices in the administrations of several townships, Deschamps was often employed by the Council as their liaison in the Windsor area. His connections with the Halifax élite secured his inclusion in several land grants throughout the province, as well as appointments in May 1768 as judge of the Inferior Court of Common Pleas, judge of probate, and superintendent of settlement in the short-lived administration established by Lieutenant Governor Michael Francklin* on St John's (Prince Edward) Island. He took his duties on the Island seriously and apparently carried them out well, but he was required to return to Nova Scotia in 1769 when the Island became a separate colony.

The 1770s saw Deschamps plunge into a new round of official tasks. Named second assistant judge of the Supreme Court on 24 May 1770, four years later he became one of the three judges of the newly created Court of Exchequer. Between 1770 and 1783 he represented Newport Township in the assembly, and also acted as clerk of the house. On the local scene, Deschamps served as a trustee for school lands at Horton, Falmouth, and Newport, and a prime mover in the establishment of a chapel at Windsor in 1771. The onset of the American revolution brought new duties: in 1776 he was made barrack master at Fort Edward, and on 27 August of the same year he became

first assistant judge of the Supreme Court. In 1781 he was appointed a justice of the peace and judge of probate in Hants County.

Deschamps was elevated to the Council in 1783, but his many duties, some involving the settlement of loyalists, prevented him from attending more than a quarter of its meetings. His connections with the Council allowed him to acquire two large grants in 1784, one at Windsor and the other in Cumberland County, but there is no evidence that he made illicit profits from such patronage.

On the death of Chief Justice Bryan Finucane in August 1785, Deschamps, as senior judge, became acting chief justice. Although he had not received any legal training, he had had years of experience in various courts and had entered in his diary extensive notes on previous decisions. Nevertheless, Deschamps and his colleague James BRENTON had an all but impossible task in trying to provide biannual circuit courts in six townships throughout the province. Accusations of partiality against the judges, and the assembly's own dissatisfaction with their performance, led the house in 1787 to request of Lieutenant Governor John Parr* and the Council an investigation into the judges' behaviour. Thus started the so-called "judges' affair" [see James Brenton]. During the dispute lawyers Jonathan Sterns and William Taylor published letters early in 1788 attacking both the Supreme Court and the Council, and Deschamps struck their names from the roll of attorneys for contempt of court. Despite the appointment of Jeremy Pemberton as chief justice the same year, the "judges' affair" flared up again in 1790 when the assembly impeached Brenton and Deschamps. The Privy Council heard the case early in 1792 and, although it cleared the judges of all but having "mistaken the Law" in a few instances, it recommended that the position of chief justice be held by a person fully trained in the law.

During the latter part of his life Deschamps was plagued by personal difficulties. Not only did three grandchildren die between 1776 and 1778, and his daughter-in-law in 1779, but he was also saddened by the deaths of his wife's orphaned nephews. During the late 1780s a Halifax newspaper published an excerpt from a French book which made what Deschamps considered to be accusations about his role in the expulsion of the Acadians. With Richard Bulkeley* he wrote a refutation of the offending piece, but he had to face the problem again in 1790 when the Nova-Scotia Magazine republished the excerpt. Two years later only Deschamps's last-minute appeal to the Council saved his son George from being branded a public debtor and imprisoned, but his undertaking to pay his son's debts proved too ambitious and he was forced to ask that they be liquidated in yearly instalments of £50. By this time Deschamps's

Deschenaux

activities had become more limited, although as late as 1799 he accepted an appointment as road commissioner for Kings County. His wife had died in April 1798 after a long illness, and three years later Deschamps himself died at the age of 79.

Isaac Deschamps had a long and busy life in Nova Scotia, and few spoke ill of him. In the middle of the "judges' affair" a correspondent to the *Nova-Scotia Gazette and the Weekly Chronicle* commented, "A Gentleman of a more tender and benevolent Heart than Justice Deschamps, does not at this Day exist in Nova-Scotia." Deschamps's honesty can hardly be questioned: in a day when many profited from patronage open to them, he left only a tiny estate. Kindly and compassionate to all persons, he was an untiring public servant, and it is noteworthy that there were so few complaints about his work in so many commissions and duties. One of his wife's nieces remembered Isaac and Sarah Deschamps as "of hospitable dispositions, polite and agreeable manners, of easy fortunes . . . surrounded by numerous . . . friends and acquaintances, who loved and honored them; while the humble classes . . . many of whom largely shared their bounty as well as their sympathy in the welfare or afflictions to which . . . they were subject – loved, respected and prayed for them." The description is a suitable tribute to a man who, at the same time, played a significant public role as an official in the early days of British settlement in Nova Scotia.

GRACE M. TRATT

BL, Add. mss 19069, 19071–73 (transcripts at PANS). Dalhousie Univ. Arch. (Halifax), MS 2-164, Isaac Deschamps, diaries. Halifax County Court of Probate (Halifax), D52 (will of Isaac Deschamps) (mfm. at PANS). Hants County Registry of Deeds (Windsor, N.S.), book 2: 48, 66, 74, 76; 3: 73, 76, 83, 94, 98, 103, 141, 217, 242, 267; 4: 22, 48, 127, 138, 178–79, 203, 302–3A, 304–5; 5: 145; 6: 189, 212 (mfm. at PANS). N.S., Dept. of Lands and Forests (Halifax), Crown land grants, book 2: 53; 3: 191; 4: 100, 243; 7: 194; 15: 63 (mfm. at PANS); Halifax allotment book, index: 40, 56, 126, 176, 372 (mfm. at PANS). PANS, MG 1, 258; 281: 5; 731A-B; 828; MG 9, no.109; MG 100, 134: 97–100 (Isaac Deschamps, "Description of agricultural systems of the Acadian French in their system of dyking"); RG 1, 35, doc.1; 51: 296–97; 135; 163–69; 204: 14–15; 209–14; RG 39; C, 1.

Acadiensia Nova (1598–1779): new and unpublished documents relating to Acadia . . ., ed. W. I. Morse (2v., London, 1935), 1: 45–47. "The case of the Acadians stated," *Nova-Scotia Magazine* (Halifax), 2 (January–June 1790): 287–89. [*Nova Scotia archives, I:*] *Selections from the public documents of the province of Nova Scotia*, ed. T. B. Akins and trans. Benjamin Curren (Halifax, 1869). [G.-T.-R.] Raynal, "Historical account of Nova-Scotia," *Nova-Scotia Magazine*, 2 (January–June 1790): 82–87. [Stephen Skinner], "Diary of Stephen Skinner, 1783–1787," PANS, Board of Trustees, *Report* (Halifax), 1974: 23. [John Winslow], "Journal of Colonel John Winslow of the

provincial troops, while engaged in removing the Acadian French inhabitants from Grand Pre . . . ," N.S. Hist. Soc., *Coll.*, 3 (1883): 165. *Nova-Scotia Gazette and the Weekly Chronicle*, 25 March 1788. *Nova Scotia Royal Gazette*, 3 April 1798, 4 July 1809. *Directory of N.S. MLAs*. S. E. Titcomb, *Early New England people; some account of the Ellis, Pemberton, Willard, Prescott, Titcomb, Sewall and Longfellow, and allied families* (Boston, 1882). Akins, *Hist. of Halifax City*. Arsenault, *Hist. et généal. des Acadiens* (1965), 1: 167. Brebner, *Neutral Yankees* (1937). Duncan Campbell, *Nova Scotia, in its historical, mercantile and industrial relations* (Montreal, 1873). "Family of Deschamps," [William Courthope], *Memoir of Daniel Chamier, minister of the reformed church, with notices of his descendants* (London, 1852), 56–91. G. V. Shand, *Historic Hants County* (n.p., 1979). L. F. S. Upton, *Micmacs and colonists: Indian-white relations in the Maritimes, 1713– 1867* (Vancouver, 1979). F.-J. Audet, "Isaac Deschamps (1772–1801)," *BRH*, 41 (1935): 175–78. Margaret Ells, "Nova Scotian 'Sparks of liberty,'" *Dalhousie Rev.*, 16 (1936–37): 475–92. *Hants Journal* (Windsor), 23 Dec. 1974: 3. R. E. Kroll, "Confines, wards, and dungeons," N.S. Hist. Soc., *Coll.*, 40 (1980): 93–107. G. V. Shand, "Windsor, a centre of shipbuilding," N.S. Hist. Soc., *Coll.*, 37 (1970): 39–65.

DESCHENAUX (Brassard Deschenaux), PIERRE-LOUIS, notary, lawyer, office holder, and judge; b. 13 Feb. 1759 at Quebec, son of Joseph Brassard* Deschenaux and Madeleine Vallée; m. there first 14 June 1784 Geneviève Dumon, who died two years later; m. secondly 11 April 1787 Marie-Joseph Perrault; d. 31 Dec. 1802 in Trois-Rivières, Lower Canada.

Pierre-Louis Deschenaux spent his childhood at Quebec during the turbulent period that followed the Seven Years' War. He studied at the Petit Séminaire de Québec from 1768 to 1779. When he left it his father urged him to take up a legal career; with this in mind he placed him for two years as a clerk in the office of notary Charles Stewart at Quebec. Such training was quite unusual at that time, since most notaries learned their profession on their own. On 18 June 1781 Deschenaux received a commission from Governor HALDIMAND authorizing him to practise as a notary anywhere in the province, and on 17 November he was made a lawyer.

After receiving his two commissions Deschenaux immediately set up office at Quebec. From the beginning he received assistance from Stewart, who sent him some of his clients. He was soon engaged in complex cases, including one concerning the Cugnet family's inheritance. This matter, which was already a controversial one, quickly involved him in a conflict of interests. On 2 Sept. 1783 he and another notary proceeded to inventory the estate of Louise-Madeleine Dusautoy (Dusaultoir), widow of François-Étienne Cugnet*. From September 1783 to July 1784 he also acted as attorney for François-Joseph Cugnet* in the lawsuit that Cugnet brought against the executor for his mother, Mme Dusautoy. To prevent the concurrent exercise of two closely related legal functions by one person, Lieutenant Governor Henry Hamilton* on 30 April 1785 approved an ordinance which forbad the simultaneous practice of the professions of notary and lawyer. Deschenaux therefore gave up law to devote himself solely to being a notary in the Quebec region.

From 1786 to 1794 his office seems to have been quite popular, since three candidates for the notarial profession came to train as clerks there, one being Félix Têtu Jr. Deschenaux's reputation brought him various posts, such as justice of the peace for the District of Quebec in 1788 and commissioner of crown lands in 1794. In 1793, upon his father's death, Deschenaux had inherited several pieces of property. This legacy, and the shares he purchased from the other three heirs for £870, secured him full possession of three houses and six lots on Rue des Pauvres (Côte du Palais) at Quebec. Through this inheritance he also became part-owner of the seigneury of Neuville, near Quebec, which he had already been managing for some years.

Having given up his practice as a notary and having been reinstated as a lawyer on 27 Nov. 1794, Deschenaux on 18 December was appointed a judge of the Provincial Court of Three Rivers. This newly created court had authority to hear civil cases involving sums not exceeding £10. A court of king's bench, composed of the judge of the Provincial Court of Three Rivers and two judges from the courts of king's bench of Montreal and Quebec, exercised jurisdiction in criminal matters. This promotion to a prestigious office did not prevent Deschenaux from showing his displeasure at receiving less remuneration than the judges of other courts of king's bench. On 29 Oct. 1796 he sent Lieutenant Governor Robert PRESCOTT a request that his annual salary be raised from £300 to £500, like that of his opposite numbers in Montreal and Quebec. Moreover he always made a point of signing official documents as a judge of the Court of King's Bench.

Deschenaux's judicial career at Trois-Rivières was undistinguished; nevertheless the few judgements he delivered reveal a deep knowledge of the law and a spirit of humanity. As a prominent individual he took an interest in social life and the well-being of the local citizens. He was, for example, president of the Fire Society and with Abbé François-Xavier Noiseux* he organized a public subscription, to which he contributed generously himself, to equip the town with adequate fire protection. Towards the end of the 1790s he gave financial assistance to his cousin Louis-Marie Brassard*, the former parish priest of Saint-Jean-Baptiste at Nicolet, to set up the elementary school from which the Séminaire de Nicolet would develop. On Brassard's death in 1800 he promised to contribute

£50 a year to support the little school, which opened on 10 March 1801.

Pierre-Louis Deschenaux was buried at Trois-Rivières on 3 Jan. 1803 "in the nave of the church, in the presence of a great crowd of people," as the parish register records. The huge Tonnancour house, which he had owned since 11 April 1795, became the property of the military authorities and was converted into a residence and barracks. The *fabrique* of the parish of Immaculée-Conception at Trois-Rivières purchased it in 1822, to turn it into the new presbytery, and later into the first bishop's palace.

RAYMOND DOUVILLE

Pierre-Louis Deschenaux's minute-book for 1781–94 is held at ANQ-Q, CN1-83.

ANQ-Q, CE1-1, 13 févr. 1759, 14 juin 1784, 11 avril 1787; CN1-157, 1er juin 1790, 4 déc. 1801; CN1-224, 31 juill. 1786; CN1-230, 5 juin, 30 oct. 1793; 14 janv. 1794. ASQ, Fichier des anciens. BL, Add. MSS 21735/1: 144 (copy at PAC). PAC, MG 11, [CO 42] Q, 78: 124–25. Qué., Conseil législatif, *Ordonnances*, 1785, c.4. *Montreal Gazette*, 7 Aug. 1788. *Quebec Gazette*, 16 Oct. 1794. *Quebec almanac*, 1788–1801. P.-G. Roy, *Les juges de la prov. de Québec*, xii–xiii, 163. J.-E. Bellemare, *Histoire de Nicolet, 1669–1924* (Arthabaska, Qué., 1924), 185, 369. J.-A.-I. Douville, *Histoire du collège-séminaire de Nicolet, 1803–1903, avec les listes complètes des directeurs, professeurs et élèves de l'institution* (2v., Montréal, 1903), 1: 5–9. J.-E. Roy, *Hist. du notariat*. F.-J. Audet, "Les juges de Trois-Rivières," *BRH*, 6 (1900): 244–47.

DESERONTYON (Odeserundiye), JOHN (Captain John), Mohawk chief; b. in the 1740s, probably in the Mohawk valley of New York; d. 7 Jan. 1811 at the Mohawk settlement on the Bay of Quinte, Upper Canada.

As a young boy John Deserontyon accompanied Sir William Johnson* to Niagara (near Youngstown, N.Y.) when the British laid siege to that fort in 1759, and he was with the forces under Major-General Jeffery Amherst* that descended the St Lawrence to attack Montreal (Que.) the following year. In the spring and early summer of 1764, during the disturbances associated with Pontiac*'s uprising, he was one of a party guarding whites from Seneca attacks, probably in the Niagara region [see Kayahsota?*]. In mid summer he joined the forces led by Colonel John Bradstreet* which were sent to Detroit (Mich.) to help impose peace on the Delawares and Shawnees. Like other Mohawks, Deserontyon was bitter about Bradstreet's conduct of the expedition, recalling that "he only made a great loss to the King. There was a vessel wrecked, and a great number of his people died with hunger, & we the Mohawks scarcely returned to Niagara."

At some time prior to the American revolution

Deserontyon

Deserontyon became a chief in the village at Fort Hunter (N.Y.). When the war erupted, the native people were courted by both the British and the Americans. Deserontyon openly sided with Britain and the interests of the Johnson family, as the majority of Mohawks ultimately did. Early in the summer of 1775 he was with a party that escorted Guy Johnson* and Christian Daniel Claus* to Montreal. The decision to leave their families at this dangerous time in order to aid Johnson and Claus was not easy for the Mohawks but, Deserontyon later wrote, "we thought that it would be very hard if we should lose them for it was only them helped us." He subsequently returned to the Mohawk valley and that fall Sir John Johnson*, who was still resident there, sent him to Montreal with a letter. Deserontyon arrived at Fort St Johns (Saint-Jean-sur-Richelieu) while it was under siege by the Americans and barely escaped when the British decided to surrender to Richard Montgomery*'s forces. Reaching Montreal early in November he "found the people that were on the King's side all troubled – did not know what to do" and that Governor Guy CARLETON "did neither know what would be done for the people, for the Americans were already at La Prairie." In May 1776 Sir John, having learned that an expedition was about to be dispatched from Albany to seize him and his property, sent Deserontyon to ascertain the date of the troop's departure. This object the chief accomplished, slipping past the American guards in the darkness and thus helping Johnson make his escape to Montreal. In the autumn Deserontyon and many Fort Hunter Mohawks also fled north.

Throughout the conflict Deserontyon was actively engaged in raids into northern New York by way of Oswego (N.Y.) or the Richelieu valley, raids which were an indispensable source of intelligence to the British. Following a council with Major John Butler*, apparently in the spring of 1777, he went to Quebec, where he met Major-General John Burgoyne*, just arrived from England with orders to invade New York. The main thrust of Burgoyne's attack was to be the Richelieu valley, but a secondary advance under Barrimore Matthew St Leger* was to be made down the Mohawk valley; it was in the latter aspect of the campaign that Deserontyon participated. Early in July he was a leader of a party that spied out the defences of Fort Stanwix (Rome, N.Y.), which St Leger was planning to attack. The party discovered that the fort was much stronger than had been thought, but the over-confident commander proceeded without the necessary artillery or reinforcements. While the siege was going on, a force composed largely of Indians defeated a body of American militia approaching to relieve the fort. Deserontyon fought in this battle of Oriskany, as did Joseph Brant [THAYENDANEGEA] and Kaieñ?kwaahtoñ*, and he likely returned to Oswego with Brant after the siege was abandoned in

August [see Benedict ARNOLD]. In September he was with some Indians who set out from there to join Burgoyne's forces south of Lake George, N.Y. As the group passed Fort Stanwix it encountered scouts from the fort and Deserontyon was seriously wounded. He had recovered sufficiently by 1779, however, to lead at least two scouting parties up the Richelieu valley, and each time he brought back several prisoners to be interrogated by the British. In the autumn he left Lachine, Que., where most of the Fort Hunter Mohawks had settled, to take part in Sir John Johnson's expedition, which was heading west to retaliate for the recent American devastation of Six Nations country. A year later he was reported to have led a raid from Montreal to the area south of Saratoga (Schuylerville, N.Y.) and on 13 May 1781 he wrote to Daniel Claus, then deputy agent for the Six Nations in Canada, informing him that he and his party had returned safely to Carleton Island (N.Y.) from Canajoharie (near Little Falls). "I propose going to Niagara about some public Business and shall be back in a few days," he added. Claus entrusted him with the responsibility of going to the Iroquois settlement at Caughnawaga, Que., in January 1782 to investigate the reported presence of a spy, a report Deserontyon's acquaintances there denied. The spring and summer saw Deserontyon leading more forays into the Mohawk valley, destroying mills and cattle and taking prisoners.

In spite of pledges offered at the outset of hostilities and reiterated as late as 1780 by Guy Johnson, then superintendent of the Six Nations, many of the Iroquois feared that their property and rights in New York would be lost once peace returned, and indeed the preliminary articles signed on 30 Nov. 1782 made no provision for Indian interests. In the spring, following the institution of a cease-fire, Deserontyon accompanied Brant and other embittered Six Nations spokesmen to a meeting in Montreal with Governor HALDIMAND. Understandably Haldimand tried to reassure the deputation that his government would not abandon them. In the event of their not being permitted to reoccupy ancestral lands in New York the governor, though he had no official authority for so doing, eagerly discussed with Brant and Deserontyon the expediency of settling the Indians "on the north side of Lake Ontario." Although this arrangement was far from being a satisfactory alternative, the deputies returned to Fort Niagara and tried to convince their comrades of Britain's good intentions. The Six Nations' concern about the future was reflected, however, in the arrangements they made in August and September with tribes to the west – Delawares, Shawnees, Cherokees, Creeks, Ojibwas, Ottawas, and Mingos – to oppose American expansion.

When in September the definitive treaty of peace was concluded between Britain and the United States, again no provision was made to restore the Six Nations' lands in New York. By that time Brant and Deserontyon had seemingly resigned themselves to the situation and had already toured a site on the Bay of Quinte surveyed for the Six Nations by Samuel Johannes HOLLAND (although Deserontyon claimed years later that Nova Scotia had first been selected and then discarded as an asylum). Brant had initially seemed satisfied with the choice of Quinte, but by March 1784 he had decided instead in favour of a region he had visited some years before – the valley of the Grand River. Political and strategic considerations appeared to govern Brant's change of mind: the site offered greater proximity to his allies the western Indians and to his kinsmen the Senecas and Onondagas, who were still clinging to a vulnerable position on the flanks of American settlement in New York. Brant's decision, however, did not go down well with Deserontyon, who much preferred the Bay of Quinte site on the equally strategic grounds that it afforded a haven far removed from the Americans, a people he likened to "a worm that cuts off the corn as soon as it appears." Indeed even before Haldimand arranged the transfer of the Grand River lands to Brant and his people the Fort Hunter Mohawks had left Lachine for the Bay of Quinte. Though he sympathized with the arguments of both sides, the anxious Haldimand was put out by this turn of events, for he had maintained all along that "a determined Union and Attachment can alone support . . . [the Mohawks'] Strength and Consequence. . . ." Sir John Johnson was less polite; he openly ridiculed Deserontyon's decision to stick by the Quinte location. So did Brant, who resented his fellow chief's refusal to follow his lead and join his Mohawks and other Six Nations families on the banks of the Grand.

Deserontyon's reluctance may have been shaped as much by tradition as by strategic considerations. The creation of distinctive and autonomous villages within the tribal framework was not an unusual practice among the Iroquois. For example, the village at Fort Hunter had been a community deliberately set off from the one at Canajoharie, where Brant often made his headquarters, and this history of a separate existence may well have inspired the Fort Hunter Mohawks' decision to organize a settlement of their own at the Bay of Quinte. Anoghsoktea (Isaac Hill) and Kanonraron (Aaron Hill) elected to join Brant on the Grand, but their stay was short-lived. Within four years, following lengthy and bitter disputes with the strong-willed Brant, they returned crestfallen and repentant, much to Deserontyon's grim satisfaction.

Meanwhile Haldimand, though still aiming at uniting the two communities into one settlement, had none the less assisted Deserontyon. He arranged the purchase from the Mississaugas of a 12 by 13 mile tract fronting on the bay and transferred it to the Fort Hunter Mohawks. The transaction was made official on 1 April 1793, when after repeated requests from Deserontyon Lieutenant Governor SIMCOE formally authorized the grant of the tract to its residents. Contrary to Deserontyon's wishes, however, the right to dispose of the land as they saw fit was not bestowed.

Like other Six Nations leaders, Deserontyon was compensated by Britain for losses suffered during the war. Having left behind in New York 82 acres of cultivated land, a barn, house and furniture, sleigh, carriage, wagon, and various farm animals, he received a lump sum of £836, yearly presents, and an annual pension of £45, together with an assurance that his son Peter John would be properly educated at a boarding-school. In recognition of his services to the Indian Department he was also given 3,000 acres of land.

Deserontyon was active on behalf of the educational and spiritual welfare of his Mohawks. In response to his entreaties, a teacher named Vincent, who would also double as a catechist, was appointed to the settlement in 1785 on the understanding that his salary would be paid by the Indian Department. This move and the visits paid by John STUART, formerly the Anglican missionary at Fort Hunter, were received with great joy by Deserontyon and his fellow Indians. Official assistance was also offered to the little community, which in 1788 numbered about a hundred, with the construction of the necessary schoolhouse and church. The latter edifice, when finally completed late in 1791 through the exertions of the Mohawks themselves and with the aid of a small grant from the Society for the Propagation of the Gospel, was graced with some of the communion silver that Deserontyon had recovered in 1783 from the chapel at Fort Hunter.

All these developments augured well for the settlement, particularly when Vincent was recruited to assist Stuart, now the parish clergyman at Cataraqui (Kingston), in the translation into Mohawk of the Gospel of St Matthew. In 1789, however, with the work apparently unfinished, Vincent was dismissed and his place taken by an Indian teacher named Peter. Although the latter's credentials were deemed sound enough, he turned out to be an alcoholic and had to be let go in turn, a state of affairs that was said to have thrown the community into confusion. In 1791 John Norton* was appointed, but he shortly quit the post on the grounds that the work was too confining and the Indians too demanding. The problem of providing adequate instruction for Indian youth was not, it would appear, satisfactorily resolved in Deserontyon's lifetime.

Although the authorities ultimately swallowed their objections to the chief's decision to stay at the Bay of Quinte and appreciated his offer of aid in 1794 when another Anglo-American war threatened, his leader-

Des Méloizes

ship was not without controversy. He annoyed Haldimand and the Indian Department in 1784 by trying to provide for the local Mississaugas when supplies were distributed to the Mohawks as loyalists. Moreover, the factionalism endemic among the Six Nations also proved a serious problem at the Bay of Quinte settlement. Following the Hills' return from the Grand River, disputes reminiscent of those that had disrupted Brant's domain broke out. The source of the trouble is not clear. Deserontyon claimed that Isaac Hill refused to attend council meetings and had set up his own council, and that members of Hill's faction had opened public houses, the sign over one being a picture of the devil. Hill alleged that Deserontyon had inflated his expenses for the trip he made to Albany with Brant in 1797 to obtain compensation for lands the Mohawks had lost. The struggle culminated in the killing by Hill's party of two of Deserontyon's relatives and in the intervention of William Claus*, the acting deputy superintendent general of Indian affairs in Upper Canada. Claus summoned a council in September 1800 to air and, if possible, resolve the differences between the warring groups. Only after Hill publicly agreed to exclude himself from the settlement's affairs did an adamant Deserontyon agree to shake hands and permit the dangerous episode to close.

But Deserontyon's problems did not end there. The closing years of his life were troubled by the so-called timber war brought on when white lumbermen encroached on Indian lands. Although the depredations were condemned by both Deserontyon and John Ferguson*, a local Indian Department official, the chief was accused by his enemies of serving as a paid broker for white timber interests while purportedly acting for the Indians. He strongly denied the charge, but the issue was still unresolved when he died on 7 Jan. 1811.

Like Joseph Brant, Deserontyon had been educated in a school run by whites and was considerably acculturated to their customs. Nevertheless, he was described by Daniel Claus as "the clearest & best speaker of the 6 Nations according to the old way." He was also an accomplished warrior and chief. His career illustrates the role played by the Six Nations as Britain's allies during the American revolution. It also serves to illuminate the problems encountered by the Indian loyalists in the new province of Upper Canada. The town of Deseronto is named in his honour.

C. M. JOHNSTON

[More than half a century ago Deserontyon was rescued from near-oblivion by the diligent efforts of historian M. Eleanor Herrington. Traditionally, researchers and biographers, beginning with William Leete Stone in his *Life of Joseph Brant – Thayendanegea* (2v., New York, 1838), were preoccupied with the dramatic and well-publicized exploits of Brant. Herrington's study, "Captain John Deserontyou and the Mohawk settlement at Deseronto," *Queen's Quarterly* (Kingston, Ont.), 29 (1921–22): 165–80, and the more recent work of Barbara Graymont, *The Iroquois in the American revolution* (Syracuse, N.Y., 1972), have placed in their debt all subsequent scholarship on the subject of Deserontyon. c.m.j.]

AO, RG 1, A-I-1, 1–2. BL, Add. mss 21723–25; 21763: 175, 257, 443; 21774: 113; 21779: 322–24; 21784: 34–37 (mfm. at PAC). PAC, MG 19, F1, 4: 12, 17, 69; RG 10, A2, 15: 121–24; 26: 7–8. PRO, CO 42/69, 42/228. USPG, *Journal of SPG*, 25–33. *Corr. of Lieut. Governor Simcoe* (Cruikshank), 1: 182; 2: 178, 252–53; 3: 341. *Kingston before War of 1812* (Preston), 21–23. Norton, *Journal* (Klinck and Talman), xxxiii, 274, 280, 285. Thomas Rolph, *A brief account, together with observations, made during a visit in the West Indies, and a tour through the United States of America, in parts of the years 1832–3; together with a statistical account of Upper Canada* (Dundas, [Ont.], 1836), 273–74. "Surveyors' letters, etc.," AO *Report*, 1905: 489–94. *Valley of Six Nations* (Johnston), 46, 49, 51, 54, 58–59, 76. J. W. Lydekker, *The faithful Mohawks* (Cambridge, Eng., 1938), 139–89. E. A. Cruikshank, "The coming of the loyalist Mohawks to the Bay of Quinte," *OH*, 26 (1930): 390–403. G. F. G. Stanley, "The Six Nations and the American revolution," *OH*, 56 (1964): 217–32. C. H. Torok, "The Tyendinaga Mohawks . . . ," *OH*, 57 (1965): 69–77.

DES MÉLOIZES, NICOLAS RENAUD D'AVÈNE. *See* RENAUD

DESRIVIÈRES BEAUBIEN, EUSTACHE-IGNACE TROTTIER. *See* TROTTIER

DIGÉ, JEAN (baptized **Jean-Charles**), mariner, politician, and office holder; b. *c.* 1736 in the "parish of Forillon" in the diocese of Avranches, France, son of Jacques Digé and Jeanne Augé; d. 14 July 1813 in Sainte-Anne-de-la-Pocatière (La Pocatière), Lower Canada.

Jean Digé, who was the son of a sailor, did not have the opportunity of going to school or learning to read and write, but he had practical training in seafaring. When he came to Canada he settled in Sainte-Anne-de-la-Pocatière; on 16 May 1762, before setting off on a long cod-fishing voyage, he drew up a will there in the presence of a notary, leaving most of his belongings to François Lévêque, who was soon to become his father-in-law. On 30 Jan. 1763 he married Véronique Lévêque, who was 26. At that time, in addition to owning the equipment essential for his work as a sailor, including a fishing boat, Digé was the proprietor of two farms, one at Sainte-Anne-de-la-Pocatière, the other at Rivière-Ouelle; he also had a horse, carriole, plough, and 2,950 *livres* 10 *sous* in bills of exchange plus 330 *livres* in cash. At least two children were born of this marriage; Jean, a son, died in 1782 at the age of 16.

Digé, who was quite well off, acquired a measure of

credibility among his peers. He appears as sub-bailiff of Sainte-Anne-de-la-Pocatière in September 1767, and again in September 1773. In the 1792 elections to the House of Assembly he was returned, with Pierre-Louis PANET, as member for Cornwallis, a riding which then extended from the seigneury of La Pocatière to the constituency of Gaspé. Digé was one of the four members of the first parliament of Lower Canada who had been born in France. He played no major role in the assembly, largely contenting himself with voting. On three occasions he supported the English party, but he voted with the Canadian party seven times, in particular for the election of Jean-Antoine PANET as speaker and against according legal status to the English language. As he had little education, he probably felt the problems being discussed were beyond him. Besides, since members of the assembly received no remuneration, Digé was doubtless not much attracted to the work. It is conceivable, given the cost of living at Quebec, that he lived on his boat for the duration of the sessions. He represented his riding from 10 July 1792 until 31 May 1796. In the 1796 elections he withdrew his candidature before the poll was held.

In 1797 Digé was surveyor of roads for Sainte-Anne-de-la-Pocatière. That year he leased out a farm in the seigneury of Rivière-Ouelle; by the evidence he could then sign his name. From that time on he seemed content to live on the income from his farms and his career as a sailor. Since 3 March 1810 he had been a widower, and on 20 April 1812, at the age of about 76, he took as his second wife Marie-Charlotte Sajos (Sageot), widow of Pierre Darris, with whom she had had a son. On 13 July of the following year Digé died, "after being ill for twelve hours." His body was buried the next day in the church of Sainte-Anne-de-la-Pocatière. His wife lived to the age of 99 and died on 28 Sept. 1845.

Jean was the only Digé to emigrate to Canada from France. Having no male descendants, he was unable to perpetuate his name in Canada. He was, however, the founder of a line of Pelletiers through the marriage of his daughter Geneviève with Joseph Pelletier on 6 Nov. 1786.

PIERRE MATTEAU

ANQ-Q, CE3-1, 20 avril 1812; CE3-3, 30 sept. 1845; CE3-12, 20 févr. 1782, 6 nov. 1786, 5 mars 1810, 15 juill. 1813, 4 déc. 1831; CN3-18, 16 mai 1762, 26 janv. 1763. AP, Sainte-Anne-de-la-Pocatière (La Pocatière), Reg. des baptêmes, mariages et sépultures, 30 janv. 1763. Quebec Gazette, 17 Sept. 1767, 9 Sept. 1773, 29 July 1813. F.-J. Audet, "Les législateurs du Bas-Canada." F.-J. Audet et Fabre Surveyer, Les députés au premier Parl. du Bas-Canada, 154–59. Desjardins, Guide parl., 126. Quebec almanac, 1794: 66; 1796: 59. Répertoire des mariages de Rivière-Ouelle, 1672–1972; troisième centenaire, Armand Proulx, compil. (La Pocatière, 1972), 120. Répertoire des mariages de Sainte-Anne-de-la-Pocatière (comté de Kamouraska) (1715–1965), J.-E. Ouellet, compil. (Québec, 1968), 11. Hare, "L'Assemblée législative du Bas-Canada," RHAF, 27: 366, 368, 371–73. "Jean Digé, premier député de Cornwallis," BRH, 40 (1934): 55–62.

DIJEAN. See DEJEAN

DIXON, CHARLES, gentleman farmer, merchant, office holder, judge, and politician; b. 8 March 1730/31 in Kirklevington, England, son of Charles Dixon and Mary Corps; m. 24 June 1763 Susanna Coates, and they had eight children; d. 21 Aug. 1817 in Sackville, N.B.

Charles Dixon apprenticed as a bricklayer under his father and followed the trade at nearby Yarm until the age of 29, when he purchased a paper factory at Hutton Rudby. He engaged in this business with considerable success until 1771, but, growing discouraged by "the troubles that were befalling my native country" and attracted by the accounts of Nova Scotia circulated by agents of Lieutenant Governor Michael Francklin*, "I came to a resolution to leave all my friends and interests I was invested with, and go to Nova Scotia." Dixon, his wife, and four children were among the first contingent of Yorkshire emigrants to Nova Scotia, a group of 62 who sailed from Liverpool on 16 March 1772 aboard the Duke of York.

Following a short stay in Halifax, the Dixons arrived at Fort Cumberland (near Sackville, N.B.) on 21 May 1772. Dixon was aware of the poverty and distress pervading the region but, believing they were "largely due to indolence and lack of knowledge," he purchased a farm of 2,500 acres at Sackville. Some of this land he worked with his sons, selling his surplus produce in Halifax; part was let out to tenants. Appreciative of the region's agricultural potential, he encouraged both the Yorkshire and the New England residents to improve the productivity of the Tantramar area by constructing more dikes and reclaiming salt-marsh. With supplies purchased in Halifax he also established a small retail business.

Dixon took a moderate stand against the revolutionary enthusiasm sweeping Nova Scotia in 1775–76. Though in December 1775 he signed the memorial from the inhabitants of Cumberland County expressing their determination not to fight against the rebels, he later claimed he had done so "for Quietness Sake." Because raising local militia to defend the province might increase political tensions and aggravate the labour shortage in Cumberland, he proposed in a letter to John Butler* on 14 Jan. 1776 that the rebel activities of John ALLAN and Jonathan EDDY be checked by a force of British regulars. In June of that year the Royal Fencible Americans, a provincial unit, manned Fort Cumberland. Also in June the Nova Scotia Council replaced rebel sympathizers with loyal supporters in

Dobie

county government, appointing Dixon a justice of the peace and a judge of the Inferior Court of Common Pleas. Although his home was sacked and his family harassed during Eddy's siege of Fort Cumberland in November, he strenuously opposed retaliation against rebel participants following Eddy's defeat, claiming such a policy would "soon terminate in the destruction and ruin of the whole country." Thereafter Dixon complemented Joseph Goreham*'s military endeavours with his judicial office and his agricultural leadership in securing peace and prosperity among the inhabitants of Cumberland County.

Following the separation of New Brunswick from Nova Scotia in 1784, the colony's newly appointed Council made Dixon collector of customs for Sackville. He was defeated in his bid for a House of Assembly seat in the 1785 elections, but when a committee of the house rejected the election of Thomas Dickson because of voting irregularities, it awarded one of the four Westmorland County seats to Dixon; he held it until his retirement from provincial politics in 1792. Little is known of his record in the house, but along with Amos BOTSFORD, a fellow member for Westmorland, he was a supporter of James GLENIE. Throughout his political career Dixon was also active in county government, acting variously as justice of the peace, commissioner of highways, surveyor of highways, assessor, and overseer of the poor.

Like the majority of the Yorkshire settlers in Nova Scotia and New Brunswick, Charles Dixon was a Methodist and a man of deep religious conviction. Educated in the Church of England tradition, he had been converted to Methodism in 1765, one year after hearing Thomas Seccombe, a follower of John Wesley: "His preaching was such as I never before heard, for his word was with power, it made me cry out in the bitterness of my soul, what must I do to be saved?" At Sackville, Dixon worked industriously to establish his adopted religion. To this end, he strove to set a Christian example by freeing his black slave Cleveland, whom he had purchased at Halifax for £60, offered financial assistance to the needy, helped build the first Sackville meeting-house, and donated land for a parsonage, providing in his will for its maintenance. He died at his home on 21 Aug. 1817, survived by his wife, three sons, and four daughters.

JAMES SNOWDON

Dixon family papers are in the possession of Jean Dixon (Sackville, N.B.); many of the documents have been published in *History of Charles Dixon, one of the earliest English settlers of Sackville, N.B.*, comp. J. D. Dixon (Sackville, 1891). Mary Phillips (Hitchin, Eng.) has compiled genealogical records of the Dixon family.

PAC, MG 9, A12, 11, vol.3. PRO, CO 217/52: 110. "Calendar of papers relating to Nova Scotia," PAC *Report*, 1894: 363. N.B., House of Assembly, *Journal*, 1786–92. Brebner, *Neutral Yankees* (1969).

DOBIE, RICHARD, fur trader, businessman, and militia officer; b. *c.* 1731 in Liberton, Scotland; d. 23 March 1805 in Montreal, Lower Canada.

Richard Dobie, who apparently was of quite humble origins, is believed to have been a merchant in Scotland before he came to the province of Quebec shortly after the conquest. In 1761 he rented a stone house on Rue Saint-Paul in Montreal, and before long he was engaged in the fur trade. In July 1764 he bought a canoe in partnership with Lawrence Ermatinger*. That September he chose a Canadian partner, Pierre Montbrun, who was to proceed to the trading posts. Dobie fitted out two canoes, assumed all the expenses, and was to attend to selling the furs. They may have been dealing with Indians in the vicinity of Fort Timiskaming (near Ville-Marie, Que.), since Dobie later recalled having sent 30 bales of goods to that post for the 1764–65 season, or they may have been trading in the region southwest of the Great Lakes. Profits were divided equally between the two men; their agreement lasted two years.

In 1767 Dobie went into partnership with Benjamin Frobisher*, who travelled to the trading posts and wintered there, while Dobie remained in Montreal. In the beginning the partners operated southwest of the Great Lakes; in 1767 they organized an expedition to La Baye (Green Bay, Wis.) and the following year they hired a number of men to go to Michilimackinac (Mackinaw City, Mich.). They endeavoured to make their first forays into the northwest in 1769 and 1770. In 1769 they received licences for five canoes bound for Michilimackinac. Benjamin and JOSEPH Frobisher tried to get into the northwest, but their expedition was stopped by Indians at Rainy Lake (Ont.). The following year the partners sent three canoes to Michilimackinac and Grand Portage (near Grand Portage, Minn.). In November 1770 the partnership was dissolved for reasons and under conditions unknown.

Dobie's business seems to have slowed down until 1777, when another phase in his career began, marked by the expansion of his role as an outfitter and financial partner. Thus, in the years following, Dobie stood out as one of the principal fur traders and outfitters southwest of the Great Lakes and in the region around Lake Superior and Lake Nipigon (Ont.). From 1777 until 1790 he stood surety, on his own or with others, for a number of expeditions carrying merchandise worth close to £100,000. The value of the expeditions varied from £2,500 in 1777 to £22,000 in 1783, and most of them went off to Michilimackinac, Niagara (near Youngstown, N.Y.), and Detroit (Mich.). Only two, with merchandise worth £3,224, proceeded to the northwest. These were led by Jean-Étienne

Waddens* and his partner, Venance Lemaire, *dit* Saint-Germain, in 1778 and 1781 and consisted respectively of three and four canoes, which headed towards Grand Portage and beyond. After Waddens was murdered in 1782, Dobie seems to have abandoned his interest in the fur trade of that region.

Dobie apparently was most deeply engaged in the trade southwest of Michilimackinac and the Great Lakes. He maintained relations in this area with some of the leading merchants and fur traders, including Étienne-Charles Campion* and William GRANT (1743–1810), as well as with other, smaller traders. Dobie agreed to stand surety for Campion when he was buying furs in 1780, serve as his attorney in Montreal in 1782, and be his guarantor when he received trading licences in 1781, 1782, 1783, and 1787. He continued to support him when Campion went into partnership with Jean-Baptiste Tabeau to send seven canoes and £3,000 of merchandise to Michilimackinac (by then located on Mackinac Island, Mich.) in 1789, and eight canoes with a cargo valued at £5,000 the following year. Dobie seems to have played the role of surety and outfitter for the short-lived General Company of Lake Superior and the South, which specialized in the fur trade as far south as the Illinois country and westward to the head of the Missouri; Campion joined it in 1785, and it was dissolved about 1787. Just like Campion, William Grant, a fur trader and Montreal merchant, held an important place in the business affairs of Dobie, who supplied him with surety on his expeditions in 1781, 1782, 1783, 1786, 1787, and 1788.

Dobie generally carried on his business as outfitter and financial backer alone, but occasionally he joined other merchants to put up surety for a fur trader. Among those merchants were John Grant and his partner Robert Griffin, William Grant and Campion, who became partners in Grant, Campion and Company in 1791, and Thomas Forsyth, one of the partners in Robert Ellice and Company. In 1788 Dobie decided to take in Francis Badgley* as a partner, to reduce the burden of running his business and to permit him to devote more time and energy to the fur trade in the Timiskaming region. The company was to look after outfitting fur traders and to buy and sell furs, and Badgley was to receive a third of the profits. The association ended in 1792.

In 1787 Dobie had formed a partnership with James Grant* to go into the fur trade at Fort Timiskaming for a period of seven years. Dobie was to supply everything that was needed, and he was authorized to collect a commission on all transactions. Grant was to winter at the post and take care of trading during the first two years at least. Dobie took two-thirds of the profits in the first three years, and one-half of them after that. In order to be able to trade at Timiskaming, Dobie paid £2,900 to acquire the accounts receivable of the firm of Sutherland and Grant, which previously owned the trading rights there. He obtained trading licences for the years 1787–90, and he invested large sums: £4,600 in merchandise and 12 canoes in 1787; £3,500 and 12 canoes the following year; £6,100 and 14 canoes in 1789; and £3,000 and 12 canoes in 1790. About a hundred voyageurs went to Timiskaming every year. Dobie ended his participation in the fur trade of the region in 1791 when he sold all his interests to the firm of Grant, Campion and Company in Montreal.

Although by far the most important, furs were not the only staple in which Dobie was interested. For several years he bought wheat from various rural merchants and exported it through the port of Quebec. In 1773 he received a few bushels from a merchant in Varennes as payment for dry goods. Five years later he bought 2,600 bushels, and in 1786 he went into partnership with William Maitland and Alexander Auldjo* to buy 10,000 bushels, which were shipped overseas.

Dobie was also interested in production. In 1769, for example, the company of Dobie and Frobisher bought ginseng from Pierre FORETIER. Five years later Dobie tried to organize production of that root. He hired someone named Laforge and a team of men to go to La Galette (near Ogdensburg, N.Y.) and stay there, and he instructed Laforge to work "primarily at having ginseng of the best possible quality produced." Similarly in 1784 he advanced money to Alexander Milmine, a potash manufacturer at Île-Jésus, Que., so he could buy ashes, convert them, and supply Dobie with at least 18 tons of potash in the eight months following the signing of the contract. Dobie was also interested in wood; in 1779 he owned a small sawmill near Sorel, probably on Île Ronde, which turned out 30 to 40 boards a day.

Dobie imported from Great Britain a great variety of products which he sold not only to the fur traders but also to merchants in the countryside around Montreal, particularly at Chambly, Varennes, and Terrebonne. He even supplied goods to a merchant in Cornwall (Ont.).

There are numerous indications that Dobie played a role as financial go-between for the government of the colony during Governor HALDIMAND's term of office. In the summer of 1779, for example, Dobie was working for Haldimand and seems to have travelled as far as Niagara. His main function was to pay accounts and advance money to various governmental services. Thus, between June 1782 and June 1784 Dobie advanced £8,403 to the engineers and £2,386 to the Indian Department. In July 1784 he paid an account for £2,418 owed by that department at Detroit, and he received sums that were owing to it. That year Dobie was also responsible for distributing various amounts to recruiting agents. In the winter of 1782 the

Dobie

lieutenant governor of Michilimackinac, Patrick SINCLAIR, had drawn four promissory notes on Dobie and William Grant for £34,586 in all. Unfortunately the government refused to reimburse £3,563 of that amount, and Dobie had to face the holders of the notes by himself. At the same period, 1783–85, Dobie was the Canadian agent for William Cullen of London for remitting money to half-pay officers from several regiments.

Around 1790 Dobie retired from business and invested his capital in order to draw a comfortable income. He lent both modest sums, such as £125 to a barber to repair his house, and much larger amounts, such as £1,650 to Simon McTAVISH in 1795 and £6,750 to the firm of Parker, Gerrard, and Ogilvy in 1804.

Dobie's participation in political life reflected his interests as a merchant engaged in the fur trade. For example, he added his voice to those calling for the trade to be reorganized after the conquest, and he intervened several times to defend the interests of the merchant-traders. He was one of the spokesmen for the Montreal merchants when they asked for a house of assembly. In a letter to Christian Daniel Claus* he said of Governor Guy CARLETON, "Tho his head is weak and soft, I consider his heart and intentions are good." He also informed Claus of his dissatisfaction with the manner in which the old subjects of Great Britain were being treated. "French fawning and flattery enough will answer your purpose superior to your long and faithful service to your King and Country." His antagonistic relations with the governor had consequences for others, since Chief Justice Peter Livius* was dismissed in 1778 as a result of a trial involving Dobie [see Jean-Louis Besnard*, dit Carignant].

Dobie held a place in the public life of Montreal that witnessed his success in business, his wealth, and his prestige. He was a member of the grand jury of the District of Montreal on a number of occasions, and he was also active in the British Militia of the Town and Banlieu of Montreal, with the rank of captain from 1788 until 1797, and major from 1798 till 1803. He was a member of the Presbyterian congregation of Montreal, and in 1791 he was elected chairman of its prestigious and powerful committee to manage temporalities [see Duncan FISHER], an office that he seems to have retained until 1800. He became a member of the masonic lodge known as St Peter's, No.4, Quebec, at Montreal, in 1772 and was master several times.

Dobie accumulated an impressive fortune in business and the fur trade that enabled him to enjoy a comfortable, even luxurious, standard of living. This fortune also gave him the means to see to the material well-being of the numerous members of his family. His illegitimate daughter, Anne Freeman, who had

probably been born before he arrived in Montreal, married John Grant. At least four children were born of this marriage, three daughters and one son: Ann, who married Samuel Gerrard*; Catherine, the wife of Jacob Jordan*; Elizabeth, who was married to James Finlay; and Richard. Dobie made a substantial gift to his son-in-law soon after his marriage to enable him to buy a house and establish a trust fund to protect his family from need. Subsequently he provided the three Grant daughters with generous dowries, and bequeathed a substantial part of his estate to them and their offspring. He also demonstrated that he attached great importance to his family by his attention to the provision of financial backing for his son-in-law and his granddaughters' husbands in their business careers. Thus he helped John Grant and his partner Robert Griffin from 1784 to 1786, Jordan in 1801, and Gerrard on different occasions.

Richard Dobie was a man of considerable importance but he has seldom attracted the attention of scholars. This omission seems to be closely linked to the fact that he was not one of the promoters of the fur trade in the Canadian northwest and that he was not in the North West Company. He was interested in the fur trade in a region that was highly profitable and important in its time, but which after 1794 was handed over to the Americans and disappeared, as it were, from the field of interest of Canadian historians. As a merchant and outfitter Dobie contributed to the emergence of a greater concentration of both fur traders and merchants. Associated informally with William Grant and Campion, and in partnership with Badgley, he collaborated in setting up a relatively stable network of fur traders whom he outfitted virtually exclusively. This network, as well as Dobie's interest in Timiskaming, seems to have been taken over completely by Grant, Campion and Company in 1791. That firm, along with Forsyth, Richardson and Company, Todd, McGill and Company [see Isaac TODD; James McGILL], and Alexander Henry*, subsequently negotiated the division of the trading zones with the NWC in 1792 and confronted it in the Canadian northwest after Jay's Treaty in 1794.

JOANNE BURGESS

[The author wishes to thank Alan Stewart of the Groupe de recherche sur les bâtiments en pierre grise de Montréal for letting her consult some of his research materials. J.B.]

ANQ-M, CN1-29, 13 June, 12–14, 18 Oct. 1786; 30 March 1787; 12 Jan., 31 Oct. 1792; 26 Feb. 1795; CN1-128, 15 oct. 1793; CN1-184, 25 Feb. 1784, 27 May 1788; CN1-185, 1 March 1798, 21 Nov. 1800, 3 April 1801, 3 May 1803; CN1-269, 9 Aug. 1793; CN1-290, 2 juin 1761; 19 avril 1765; 23 janv. 1767; 17 mai 1768; 25 févr., 20 mai 1769; 20 avril 1770; 8 févr. 1774; 5 févr., 13 août 1777; 12 juin, 18 oct. 1780; 11 mai 1782; 14 oct. 1784; 19 avril, 23 mai 1785; 13 févr. 1786; CN1-308, 5 sept. 1764. BL, Add. MSS 21724–25; 21734–35; 21770; 21772; 21814; 21822;

21859; 21864; 21877 (copies at PAC); 35915: 228–32. PAC, MG 8, G65; MG 19, F1, 4: 87; F2, 3, 22 July 1784; MG 22, A9, 4: 42; MG 24, L3: 2535–36, 2540–44, 6170–71, 7506–8, 7510–11, 18278–313, 20242–48; RG 4, B16, 2, 3 Aug. 1778; RG 4, B17, 7, 19 Feb. 1784; 17, 24 July 1799; B28, 110–15; RG 8, I (C ser.), 280: 155. *Docs. relating to NWC* (Wallace), 436. *Quebec Gazette*, 27 April 1769; 11 Nov. 1770; 31 March 1774; 18 May 1782; 13 Nov. 1783; 2 June 1785; 22 June 1786; 10 May 1787; 11 Dec. 1788; 12 Nov., 24 Dec. 1789; 26 April, 13 Sept. 1792. *Quebec almanac*, 1788–1803. Massicotte, "Répertoire des engagements pour l'Ouest," ANQ *Rapport*, 1942–43; 1946–47. Burt, *Old prov. of Quebec* (1968), 1: 248–49. R. Campbell, *Hist. of Scotch Presbyterian Church*, 69–70, 117. Creighton, *Commercial empire of St. Lawrence*, 24. Davidson, *NWC*, 14. Innis, *Fur trade in Canada* (1956), 184, 193–99, 215. Robert Rumilly, *Histoire de Montréal* (5v., Montréal, 1970–74), 2: 36, 83. W. S. Wallace, *The pedlars from Quebec and other papers on the Nor'Westers* (Toronto, 1954), 22–24, 62. W. E. Stevens, "The organization of the British fur trade," *Mississippi Valley Hist. Rev.* ([Cedar Rapids, Ind.]), 3 (1916–17): 172–202.

DORCHESTER, GUY CARLETON, 1st Baron.
See CARLETON

DOUCET, AMABLE,
office holder; b. 23 April 1737 in Annapolis Royal, N.S., second son and third child of Pierre Doucet and Marie-Josèphe Robichaud; d. 21 June 1806 in Grosses Coques, N.S.

Eighteen-year-old Amable Doucet was deported to Massachusetts with his parents and siblings in 1755 [*see* Charles Lawrence*]. The family was allocated to the town of Newbury and is listed there in 1756, 1758, and 1760. Amable, his father, and eldest brother were among the five Acadian men at Newbury in 1758 capable of work.

Apparently during his exile in New England, Amable was betrothed to a relative, Marie Doucet, daughter of François Doucet and Marguerite Petitot, *dit* Saint-Sceine (Sincennes), and sister of Pierre*. Subsequently, while Amable's own family removed to Quebec, Amable and Marie decided, as did her family, to go back to Nova Scotia. In 1764 the British authorities had informed Governor Montagu Wilmot* that Acadians who took the oath of allegiance should be allowed to return to their native land, and in 1767 the Nova Scotia government specifically set aside lands for an Acadian settlement on St Mary's Bay. According to traditional accounts, though they vary as to the exact date, it was about 1770 that François Doucet's family went from Salem, Mass., to what was later called Pointe-de-l'Église (Church Point); church records show, however, that Amable Doucet, at least, was back in Nova Scotia by 21 Sept. 1769.

In early 1774 Marie Doucet died, leaving Amable with two children. Her burial place at Pointe à Major was later chosen as the site for the first Acadian cemetery in the area. Amable married secondly, on 18 Oct. 1774, Marie-Gertrude Gaudet, daughter of Joseph Gaudet and Gertrude Le Blanc; they were to have ten children, the youngest of whom would marry François-Lambert Bourneuf*.

On 14 May 1772 Amable Doucet had been granted 350 acres at what is now Comeauville, and in 1801 he received part of 21,300 acres allotted to a group of Acadians of the St Mary's Bay region. Over the years he was involved in numerous other land transactions. At some point he settled at Grosses Coques.

Doucet played a significant role in local Acadian religious life. Extant parish records show that he conditionally baptized children and officiated at marriages during the sometimes long periods when no missionary was available [*see* Joseph-Mathurin Bourg*]. Doucet also enjoyed the confidence of his compatriots in other community matters. Several petitions, addressed to both religious and civic authorities, show that he was foremost among his fellow citizens. His name and signature come first in these documents, which regard such diverse matters as grants of land, parish boundaries, the securing of a French royalist priest, and the site of the parish church. A petition of 1 March 1790 by Doucet and several others requesting that Pierre Le Blanc* receive land omitted from his allotment displays a fairness that merits much respect.

On 6 April 1792 Doucet was appointed town clerk for Clare Township by the Annapolis County Court of Sessions, and on 3 Sept. 1793 he became a justice of the peace. He was the first Acadian to be appointed magistrate in Nova Scotia after the expulsion; however, his maternal grandfather, Prudent Robichaux, had served in a similar capacity at Annapolis Royal from 1727. As the only Acadian magistrate in the county, Doucet affixed his signature to many legal transactions, but he was involved in few extraordinary matters. On 28 Feb. 1803 he presided over a special general sessions at his home in Grosses Coques, where a person was found guilty of petty larceny and sentenced to be flogged. Doucet's participation in this proceeding and the fact that by his will, dated 17 June 1806, he bequeathed to his wife a black slave named Jérôme may be taken to signify that his ideas were generally no more progressive than those of his time.

STEPHEN A. WHITE

ANQ-Q, ZQ-60 (photocopies at CÉA). Arch. of the Diocese of Bathurst (Bathurst, N.B.), Caraquet, Reg. des baptêmes, mariages et sépultures, 1768–73. Arch. of the Diocese of Yarmouth (Yarmouth, N.S.), Saint-Jean-Baptiste de Port-Royal (Annapolis Royal), Reg. des baptêmes, mariages et sépultures, II (1727–55) (mfm. at CÉA). CÉA, Fonds Placide Gaudet, 1.23-15, 1.24-6, 1.24-32, 1.24-34, 1.88-9, 1.88-10, 1.88-12; Extraits des reg. de la Pointe-de-l'Église, N.-É. (transcripts); "Généalogies acadiennes," 1435-1,

Douglas

1435-2; "Notes généalogiques sur les familles acadiennes, c.1600–1900," dossier Doucet-2: f.41; Fonds H.-J. Hébert, dossier Mass. Mass., Dept. of the State Secretary, Arch. Division (Boston), Mass. arch., 23: 350; 24: 368. PANS, RG 20A, 2 (photocopies at CÉA).

Nova Scotia archives, II: a calendar of two letter-books and one commission-book in the possession of the government of Nova Scotia, 1713–1741, ed. A. McK. MacMechan (Halifax, 1900), 172. Donat Robichaud, *Les Robichaud: histoire et généalogie* (Bathurst, [1967]), 151–52. Tanguay, *Dictionnaire*, 3: 438. P.-M. Dagnaud, *Les Français du sud-ouest de la Nouvelle-Écosse . . .* (Besançon, France, 1905), 24–25. [J.-]A. Deveau, *La ville française* (Québec, 1968), 123, 186, 189. [Élie LeBlanc], *Église Saint-Bernard: commencée en 1910, complétée en 1942, diocèse de Yarmouth* ([Yarmouth, 1942]), 31. I. W. Wilson, *A geography and history of the county of Digby, Nova Scotia* (Halifax, 1900; repr. Belleville, Ont., 1975), 40, 58, 97–98, 109, 136, 227, 243, 430. C.-J. d'Entremont, "Amable Doucet, écuyer du roi," *Le Courrier de la Nouvelle-Écosse* (Yarmouth), 16 mars 1978: 10; "Les 'terres françaises' de East Ferry: Amable Doucet avait un testament," *Le Courrier de la Nouvelle-Écosse*, 9 mars 1978: 1. [Placide Gaudet], "La construction d'une église à la baie Sainte-Marie," *Le Moniteur acadien* (Shédiac, N.-B.), 26 juill. 1889: [2]; "Grande démonstration religieuse dans le premier cimetière acadien de la baie Ste-Marie," *L'Évangéline* (Weymouth Bridge, N.-É.), 8 sept. 1892: [2]; "Imposante démonstration religieuse," *L'Évangéline*, 16 juill. 1891: [2]; "Premiers habitants de la baie Ste-Marie," *L'Évangéline*, 2 juill. 1891: [2]; "Les premiers missionnaires de la baie Ste-Marie . . . ," *L'Évangéline*, 6 août 1891: [3].

DOUGLAS, JAMES, office holder and land agent; b. *c.* 1757 in Edinburgh, Scotland, son of John Douglas, a writer there, and younger brother of John Jr, who became a well-known Edinburgh advocate; d. 26 Sept. 1803 on Prince Edward Island.

After obtaining a commercial education, James Douglas spent some time in the counting-house of Sibbald and Company, merchants of Leith, Scotland, trading to the West Indies. In 1779 he immigrated to America, where he took up a clerkship with a firm of traders operating in the frontier region between the Niagara and Detroit rivers. Able, honest, and righteously Calvinistic in outlook, in 1781 he complained to Governor Frederick HALDIMAND that William Taylor and George Forsyth, his employers at Fort Niagara (near Youngstown, N.Y.), had been engaged with Colonel Guy Johnson*, superintendent of the Six Nations, in a large-scale fraud involving official presents to friendly Indian tribes. This embezzlement of several years' duration had netted the perpetrators upwards of £15,000. Douglas went to Montreal in 1781 and assisted the governor in a successful prosecution of the merchants. On his return to Niagara he apparently set up in business on his own account, but he found himself ostracized and harassed by all the traders of the region, who resented his part in the termination of an exceedingly profitable racket in which they saw no harm.

Having suffered heavy losses in his trade and finding himself in an intolerable situation, Douglas, with Haldimand's backing, petitioned the British government for some form of compensation on account of his services. Instead of receiving financial assistance, however, he was appointed controller of customs on St John's (Prince Edward) Island at the meagre salary of £40 per annum. Married by this time to the daughter of a Detroit merchant, and with several children to support, he moved to the Island in 1787. (His first wife apparently died there, for about 1789 he married Waitsill Haszard (Hassard); the couple were to have at least eight children.) Taking up his appointment on arrival as second in command to William TOWNSHEND, the collector of customs, Douglas entered a society in which cliques of poorly paid officials fought as in a jungle for perquisites and preferment. Amid all these tensions, he maintained a high reputation for probity, and did his utmost to keep out of the squabbles over land, fees, and salaries. He found, however, that his fees as controller were negligible since the colony's trade was negligible.

In 1788 Douglas was appointed an assessor in the adjudication pending between James William Montgomery, the Island's largest proprietor, and his agent, David LAWSON. Montgomery, a regular supporter of the Henry Dundas group that dominated Scottish politics, had long been prominent in public life there and in 1788 was serving as lord chief baron of the exchequer. He was also a leading agricultural improver. Having acquired lands on St John's Island, first in the notorious lottery of 1767 and later by purchase, he had determined to create there an estate similar to those he owned in Scotland, which were based on a capable tenantry enjoying long leases, and on experienced supervision, sound agricultural practices, and strict accounting procedures. Although, given the difficulties, Lawson's attempt to establish a flax farm on Montgomery's Lot 34 was reasonably successful, he fell foul of the lord chief baron's exacting standards in bookkeeping and was dismissed as agent in 1788. Douglas's part in the appraisal of Montgomery's estates so impressed the proprietor's son William*, an army officer on leave from Halifax to attend to the family's Island affairs, that he recommended to his father the appointment of Douglas as agent for most of the extensive Montgomery interests. Douglas was put in charge of lots 30, 34, 12, and 7, under the superintendency of Lieutenant Governor Edmund FANNING. Seven years later he visited Scotland and met Montgomery Sr, who, already impressed by his agent's performance and integrity, committed himself fully to Douglas as the trusted servant of his interests. Montgomery certainly needed such a servant, for his past experience, both with Lawson and with David Higgins*, had been dismal. In Douglas he found, as historian J. M. Bumsted has observed, "that *rara avis* in colonial North America, a scrupulously honest man."

With the cooperation of Fanning, Douglas was eventually able to straighten out the complicated issue between Montgomery and Lawson. A final arbitration in 1793 established Lawson's total debt to the lord chief baron at £9,219 12s. 2½d., but Montgomery, realizing that Lawson was, in fact, impoverished, was not vindictive. On the contrary, he arranged for Douglas to give his former agent an annual payment of £12. Meantime Douglas had been active in the general administration of Montgomery's estate. A system of regular accounting had been instituted, and rentals and back rentals collected. As early as 1789 Montgomery was receiving a small income from his lands. The tenantry on his properties increased slowly, but steadily; tenants were generally not turned out if they failed to pay full rentals, for Montgomery wisely preferred occupancy to eviction. Arrears and back rentals were, however, assiduously recorded by Douglas, the arrears alone amounting to £3,400 by 1802. More land was brought into cultivation, and the extensive Montgomery holdings made genuine, if uneven, progress under Douglas's able stewardship. His efforts did much to justify the initial expenses of his remarkable employer.

Douglas's devotion to the interests of this employer eventually involved him in Island politics. Among Montgomery's tenants who had never paid any, or at most only a slight proportion, of their rents were several members of the "inner ring" of the governing clique, including the Reverend Theophilus DesBrisay* (son of Thomas DESBRISAY, the secretary and registrar), Councillor Joseph ROBINSON, and Chief Justice Peter STEWART. When Douglas moved against them, they set out to break him. In 1797 Douglas took the chief justice to court in an effort to collect arrears of rent but found himself blocked by the Stewart family's tight control of the judicial apparatus. Within a few months Stewart's son-in-law, William Townshend, who as collector of customs was Douglas's superior, complained to London that Douglas had illegally entered a ship with smuggled goods from the United States at Three Rivers (Georgetown). Luckily for Douglas, he had the support of Montgomery at home, and John MACDONALD of Glenaladale and Joseph APLIN took his part in the colony. The Montgomery–Stewart dispute dragged on for some years, with the chief justice managing to evade the attempt to bring him to account. The crisis was eased only after his resignation from the bench in 1800.

Although provoked himself by Stewart's evasion, Montgomery reproached his agent for becoming a "violent party man" in the contest with the chief justice. Douglas replied frankly that his disputes with the Stewart clique were indeed "very high political concerns." In this his judgement was excellent, and his statement no more than the bare truth. The partiality of the judicial system was not the only political issue in which he had become involved in his attempt to administer his employer's estate. Of Montgomery's tenants, Joseph Robinson, in particular, had since 1796 actively campaigned for the escheat of the holdings of absentee proprietors, most of whom, unlike the lord chief baron, had made no attempt to develop their lands. In time Douglas had come to believe that Lieutenant Governor Fanning and Chief Justice Stewart were behind this agitation (which he saw as a conspiracy to defraud the proprietors of their holdings), as well as the attempt to ruin him personally.

The core of opposition to the Fanning administration, Douglas, MacDonald, and Aplin maintained that annexation to Nova Scotia was the best solution for the colony's political and economic ills. Montgomery, however, did not favour annexation. He believed that the proprietors' interests would suffer if the colony were ruled from Halifax and that their discomfiture would harm the Island. Although he admitted that most of the absentees had failed to meet their commitments, he held that the colony would progress only if proprietors such as himself were prepared to finance emigration and provide the capital needed for the stimulation of commerce. When in 1797 the House of Assembly passed resolutions calling upon the British government either to oblige the proprietors to develop their lands or to establish a court of escheat, Montgomery was specifically mentioned as an outstanding example of a landholder who had done much to fulfil his obligations. Early in the new century it seemed that the home authorities might act on these resolutions [see John Stewart*], but in the end the matter was shelved.

An old man by 1802, Montgomery turned over his affairs to his heir, but he retained a keen interest in his Prince Edward Island holdings right up to his death in April 1803, his estate there "being the last subject on which he spoke." Douglas himself died five months later, of "rapid asthmatic consumption." He had been a strong and principled advocate of the Montgomery interests, which after his death were entrusted to James CURTIS, and of more impartial government. In the integrity of his principles, in the maintenance of his employer's concerns amid the miasma of petty jobbery in which he found himself on the Island, and in the brave defence which he more than once had to mount against the groundless allegations of his enemies among the controlling clique, James Douglas truly stands out as an admirable personality.

DAVID S. MACMILLAN

Douglas

National Library of Scotland (Edinburgh), Dept. of MSS, MS 1399: ff.70–71. Private arch., Sir David Montgomery (Kinross, Scot.), Montgomery–Spottiswood corr. (copies at SRO; researchers wishing to consult the originals should contact the National Register of Archives, Scotland). St Paul's Anglican Church (Charlottetown), Reg. of baptisms, 1790–1804 (mfm. at PAPEI). SRO, GD293/2, 293/3. D. S. Macmillan, "New men in action," *Canadian business hist.* (Macmillan), 44–103. Bumsted, "Sir James Montgomery and P.E.I.," *Acadiensis* (Fredericton), 7, no.2: 76–102. Bruce Wilson, "The struggle for wealth and power at Fort Niagara, 1775–1783," *OH*, 68 (1976): 146.

DOUGLAS, THOMAS, Baron DAER and SHORTCLEUCH, 5th Earl of SELKIRK, colonizer and author; b. 20 June 1771 on St Mary's Isle (near Kirkcudbright), Scotland, son of Dunbar Hamilton Douglas and Helen Hamilton; m. 24 Nov. 1807 Jean Wedderburn in Inveresk, Scotland, and they had three children; d. 8 April 1820 in Pau, France.

Thomas Douglas was the seventh son of the 4th Earl of Selkirk, and though two of his brothers had died in infancy he had no prospect of inheriting the title until his mid twenties. Then, between 1794 and 1797, all four of his remaining brothers died, two of yellow fever in the Caribbean and the others of tuberculosis. In 1799, on the death of his father, Thomas Douglas became earl at 28 years of age.

As a boy Douglas had been quiet and not strong, but he was apparently well liked at the University of Edinburgh which he entered at the age of 14. There he followed a general course in the humanities with some studies in law. He belonged to a lively group which included Walter Scott, who in later years remembered him as "one of the most generous and disinterested of men"; and there were many to testify to his charm of manner and winning smile though he remained reserved and laconic. His education was filled out in 1792 with some months of travel in the Highlands of Scotland, an experience which was to influence the course of his life decisively. This journey was followed by a period of travel in Europe until 1794. Two other matters seem to have been of particular importance in his growing-up years. The first was a raid on St Mary's Isle by the American privateer John Paul Jones in 1778, when young Tommy was only seven. Though there was no bloodshed or brutality the boy found it a frightening experience, and in later years he believed it had left him with a dislike of Americans that he never wholly overcame. Secondly, though he inclined toward intellectual pursuits, in 1796 he took up the working of one of his father's farms to learn what a landowner must know.

Douglas never lost interest in the Highlands after his travels there, and he studied Highland affairs and learned some Gaelic. He had been shocked by the effect of the clearances with their callous, if inevitable, uprooting of helpless people who obviously were capable and deserving of a better life. Though he had not been in a position to help he had begun to develop a theory of emigration that might both restore hope to dispossessed people and strengthen Britain overseas. An opportunity to apply his theories arose even as he came into his title and fortune. In 1798 a rebellion in Ireland brought on by starvation and rack-rents had been put down harshly. The young earl spent some months in 1801 travelling there to study conditions at first hand. Everything he saw tended to confirm his views, and in the winter of 1801–2 he put forward to the Colonial Office a "radical cure" for Ireland's troubles. He believed the same qualities that had made men leaders in rebellion could be of value in a different setting. To provide real opportunities and new challenges would change the whole thrust of an oppressed society.

Selkirk advanced these arguments repeatedly and with enthusiasm to the Colonial Office, but they met with little favour. The Irish were regarded as intractable, and hopeless prospects as colonists; moreover the government was opposed to large-scale emigration. In this long and wearing correspondence all Selkirk's qualities appeared: his capacity for imaginative planning, his energy, and a stubborn determination so intense as to become self-defeating. Finally recognizing that the government would not countenance the resettlement of Irish rebels, Selkirk proposed the emigration of Highlanders instead. By the summer of 1802 he was thinking of "the Falls of St. Mary" (Sault Ste Marie, Ont.) as a site and, since the government was hinting at cooperation if he selected a "maritime situation," he offered to combine his efforts in Upper Canada with colonization on Prince Edward Island as well. As his plans for the Upper Canadian venture went forward it became clear that costs would be higher than he had anticipated. The government, influenced by the strength of anti-emigration sentiment in Britain, informed him in February 1803 that it was unwilling to grant him special assistance. He was therefore obliged to turn to Prince Edward Island, since he had already recruited a number of Highland emigrants and contracted for ships and supplies. By July 1803, when the expedition set out, it had been delayed too long for much clearing of land or planting in the first year. Selkirk's ship, the *Dykes*, reached the Island on 9 August, two days after the *Polly*; the *Oughton* would arrive on the 27th [*see* James WILLIAMS]. Despite the lateness of the season, hindrances from local government, and disputes over land claims and preferences among the settlers, the colony was from the first a success to match Selkirk's dreams and support his arguments. By the time he left in late September 1803 his people were well on the way to being happily established, mainly on lots 57, 58, 60, and 62.

Selkirk gave his next year to travel in the United States and the Canadas, tirelessly observing, questioning, and taking notes. He informed himself about the terrain, crop expectations and prices, conditions of trade, and local government. Above all he was interested in the degree and speed of adaptation by immigrants, especially those from the Highlands. Though he found great variations in progress as a result of differing effort and ability, he concluded that all were better off than they would have been at home. He had prepared himself as well as was possible through study for his Prince Edward Island venture, but now he had the added benefit of on-the-spot reconnaissance and of discussion in depth. It all went down in a diary written in the evenings by candle-light or when bad weather prevented travel by day. He was determined to be an expert on the problem he had made his own.

Having started his travels in Halifax, N.S., he went to Boston, Mass., then across New York State to Newark (Niagara-on-the-Lake), and on to York (Toronto), capital of Upper Canada. He stayed there from 20 Nov. 1803 to 4 Jan. 1804, becoming well known and well liked. Part of his time was spent in studying maps of the western part of the province in search of a site for another colony. His efforts were encouraged by Lieutenant Governor Peter HUNTER, who had received instructions from the Colonial Office telling him to grant Selkirk 1,200 acres plus land for his settlers in any township of the earl's choice that had not already been claimed. Selkirk chose his site – to be called Baldoon after an ancestral estate – near the junction of Lake St Clair and the Detroit River. Then in January he left York by sleigh for Montreal. The trip down Lake Ontario and the St Lawrence tended to confirm his view that unless the border area was filled up rapidly by British immigrants it would inevitably be absorbed by the United States.

In Upper Canada he had seen and heard much about the fur trade. In Montreal he learned more of its importance, its glamour, and its power. Here were the great houses of the Montreal agents and partners – led by William McGillivray* – who lived in considerable comfort and state as became the "Lords of the North." They were nearly all fellow Scots, glad to welcome an eminent compatriot and to make his stay among them pleasant. Characteristically he was full of questions about the country and about the fur trade, which they were happy to answer at the time but later considered to have been an indication of sinister designs by Selkirk on their business.

By late spring 1804 he was back in York, where he engaged Alexander McDonell* (Collachie), sheriff of the Home District, as manager of the Baldoon project. Travelling toward the site, the two men agreed on elaborate and ambitious building plans, and construction started on their arrival in early June. The first small group of settlers was already on the way. On 9 July Selkirk turned for home, stopping some weeks in Prince Edward Island where his settlement was already well rooted and prospering in little more than a year.

In Scotland he prepared *Observations on the present state of the Highlands of Scotland, with a view of the causes and probable consequences of emigration* (London, 1805), advancing his theories in the face of opposition from the Royal Highland and Agricultural Society of Scotland and the Colonial Office and using the success in Prince Edward Island to support his claims. The fact that there had already been warnings of disaster at Baldoon was largely ignored. Located on swampy ground and suffering from mismanagement, that colony was becoming a tragic and costly failure [*see* William BURN], although despite sickness, death, and bad crops settlers would remain in the area.

His rank and wealth had made Selkirk prominent; the book, clearly and persuasively written, made him a celebrity. Other books, both to challenge and to support his arguments, were rushed out. In February 1806 he was invited to go as British minister to Washington. Although he accepted, in the end the appointment was not made. In the spring of 1806 he applied for an immense grant of 300,000 acres in New Brunswick but attached conditions that could not be accepted. Turning his back on his North American interests he flung himself into domestic affairs with characteristic energy. On 4 Dec. 1806 he was elected to the House of Lords as one of 16 representative peers for Scotland. He became involved in the abolition of the slave trade, the problem of national defence, and parliamentary reform. On national defence he made himself something of an expert, and when in 1808 he published a proposal for national service his ideas were respectfully received. On parliamentary reform he was cautious and conservative, having been horrified by the excesses of the French revolution and disappointed in the working of democracy in the United States.

His efforts as parliamentarian, colonizer, and author were bringing Selkirk some of the pleasant rewards of prominence and service. In 1807 he was made lord lieutenant of the Stewartry of Kirkcudbright; he was shortly to be elected a fellow of the Royal Society of London and to become a member of the prestigious Alfred Club in that city. And in 1807 came the greatest reward of all. The shy, rich, and distinguished bachelor of 36 was married to Jean Wedderburn, aged 21. His attractive, intelligent, and

Douglas

courageous wife was to be the source of most of his future happiness and an unfailing and invaluable support in the troubles that lay ahead. The marriage also brought him two strong future allies, Andrew Wedderburn, Jean's brother, and John Halkett*, her cousin, who was later to marry Selkirk's favourite sister, Katherine. Though with his marriage and involvement in government Selkirk appeared to have put aside any interest in the emigration question, he probably never entirely lost sight of it. But the most obvious area, Upper Canada, seemed closed to him; the failure of Baldoon and the attitude of the ruling clique made it hopeless to try further in that province. There remained Red River, which he had proposed back in April 1802 for an Irish settlement. He had been told then that it could not be discussed as a site since it was in the territory of the Hudson's Bay Company. By 1808, however, the loss of free markets in Europe due to the Napoleonic Wars had seriously reduced the value of HBC shares, and this devaluation seems to have revived his hope of colonizing Red River, since it provided a favourable opportunity for him to secure an interest that would get him a hearing. In July he began to buy HBC stock on his own, and also jointly with Sir Alexander MACKENZIE, whose objective – though Selkirk could not have known it at the time – was to gain influence for the rival North West Company. In the next year Wedderburn and Halkett also began to buy the stock at its attractive price, and at about this time Wedderburn became a member of the HBC's governing committee. Thus Selkirk and his allies, although they never came close to a controlling interest in the company, gained a strong voice.

The idea of the company's developing an agricultural settlement at Red River as a refuge for retired fur traders and a source of food that had otherwise to be brought from England had already been discussed by the committee and had some support. It was against this background that Selkirk early in 1811 put forward his plan, which called for a large grant of land anchored to a substantial settlement. When news of the proposal reached the NWC the partners did not take the settlement idea very seriously but considered that if it should succeed it might destroy their trade, for the site was astride their route to Athabasca and they were already in financial difficulty through loss of markets and rising costs. (And indeed the HBC had recently considered a proposal by former NWC partner Colin Robertson* that it should initiate serious competition via Montreal for the rich Athabasca trade.) Too late the NWC attempted to block the grant. In June 1811 agreements were signed by Selkirk and the HBC under which, in return for founding an agricultural settlement and some other considerations, he was to have some 116,000 square miles – an area five times the size of Scotland and much of it

magnificent land – for 10 shillings. Lady Selkirk would later call it, with playful bitterness, his Kingdom of Red River.

The Red River colony, if not absolutely ill-conceived, as the Nor'Westers asserted, was born under an unlucky star. For ten years it was to be the focus of the mounting struggle between the two great fur-trading companies, a struggle that cost many lives, ruined the NWC, destroyed Selkirk's great fortune, and contributed to his early death.

During his earlier tour of Upper Canada Selkirk had met Miles Macdonell*, brother-in-law of Alexander McDonell, and now the earl chose him to superintend operations in the Red River colony. The HBC officially named him the first governor of Assiniboia in June 1811, and he arrived with the first colonists late in the summer of 1812. Both Selkirk and Macdonell had been warned that the Nor'Westers would not tolerate the settlement, but its initial crises came from natural causes: lack of adequate shelter and of a stable food supply. When Macdonell, to meet the food crisis, forbad the taking out of provisions from the grant, which had traditionally provided most of the pemmican for the fur brigades, the Nor'Westers regarded the measure as the declaration of war they had been expecting. Though in 1814, the first year of the ban, a mutually creditable compromise was reached with John McDonald* of Garth, a leading winterer, senior NWC partners such as William McGillivray considered compromise beneath their dignity, and there were to be no more reasonable dealings at Red River.

Selkirk had from the first planned to visit the colony once it was established, and he had even led Macdonell to believe that he would appear in 1813 at the head of a force of soldiers – to protect the settlement against the Americans, with whom Britain was at war. Although in the first three years there seemed to have been little to show for his enormous expense, by the autumn of 1814 the earl felt the worst was over. But in a letter written from Montreal at that time Colin Robertson, whose plan for competition in the Athabasca country had now been approved, advised him that the senior NWC partners were openly rousing natives against the settlement. Selkirk asked the Colonial Office to provide protection for the settlers and made arrangements to go out himself in September 1815. The government refused its support, and when he reached New York in late October he heard that the colony had been destroyed. The Nor'Westers had frightened or seduced 140 of the settlers from their loyalty to Selkirk and carried them down to Upper Canada. The remainder were driven away, their crops and houses destroyed. Macdonell, who had given himself up on a promise of amnesty for the settlement, was arrested on a dubious warrant and taken as a prisoner to Lower Canada. With his wife Selkirk went directly to Montreal to challenge the Nor'Westers on their own ground. Through the autumn and winter of 1815 he gathered information on the events and prepared to go to Red River himself, strongly supported and with the powers of a justice of the peace for the Indian Territory, in the spring of 1816. He also found time to complete a book entitled *A sketch of the British fur trade in North America; with observations relative to the North-West Company of Montreal* (London, 1816). The work was an indictment of Nor'Wester methods that was never answered. In the end it may have harmed Selkirk more than the NWC since it revealed little that had not been well known, and officially overlooked, for a long time; but it did suggest a more active concern with the fur trade than was consistent with Selkirk's professed aims as a disinterested colonizer.

In fact Selkirk, whom the Nor'Westers took to calling the Trading Lord, did have an official capacity in the trade, being authorized by the HBC to open negotiations for amalgamation with the NWC. The talks were to be confidential and conducted through a third party, but since each company argued from a fixed position unacceptable to the other, the negotiations served only to sharpen existing tensions; and they were soon common knowledge in Montreal, bearing an interpretation injurious to both Selkirk and the HBC.

In March 1816 came astounding news. A messenger from Colin Robertson at Red River – Jean-Baptiste Lagimonière* – had come 1,800 miles on foot in the depth of winter to report that the colony had been restored. Robertson had met the fleeing settlers and led them back to Red River; and Robert SEMPLE, the new governor, had arrived with another group of settlers. The colony was as strong as before and more determined than ever to survive. The news presumably sharpened North West resolve even as it raised Selkirk's spirits. Both parties seem to have concluded that this summer would be decisive for the settlement. Because of Colonial Office direction and threats against Selkirk's life the acting governor, Sir George Gordon Drummond*, provided him with a small force of regular soldiers, and Selkirk recruited an additional 90 men from the disbanded De Meuron's Regiment.

The departure of the NWC spring brigade from Montreal for Fort William (Thunder Bay, Ont.) was an annual event. In 1816 a larger party than usual left, and advance elements had gone ahead with clear instructions to finish off the settlement, preferably with a front of Indians, but by storming the fort if necessary. Close behind the main body of Nor'Westers came Selkirk's flotilla of soldiers with 12 boatloads of supplies and arms for the colony. But they were already too late.

At Sault Ste Marie on 25 July Selkirk learned that the colony had been broken up by the Métis [*see* Cuthbert Grant*]. Governor Semple and about 20 colonists had been killed at Seven Oaks (Winnipeg) and the rest driven away, except for a few who were prisoners at Fort William. Selkirk, roused to passionate anger, led his force straight to Fort William, risking a pitched battle, and in mid August arrested nine of the NWC partners after a preliminary hearing. He then decided to occupy their fort for the winter, impounded their furs, and sent the partners off as prisoners to Montreal, including William McGillivray himself. A search of the fort under warrant disclosed the NWC's complicity in the crimes at Red River. Until this point Selkirk's steps had been at least correct in form; the law had formed the basis of all his arguments and of his instructions to Miles Macdonell. Reckless of opinion he now entered into a dubious transaction with the one remaining partner at the fort, Daniel McKenzie*, a notorious drunkard. Under it he bought the company's furs and all the supplies at the fort in return for a distant and non-liquid asset, one of his estates in Scotland. He was later to refer to his "ill-judged conduct" at Fort William, and certainly it lost him sympathy and further impugned the purity of his motives as a colonizer.

More serious, though more understandable, he twice refused obedience to warrants for his arrest which reached Fort William from Upper Canada in the late autumn. The one he believed to be spurious and the other no longer valid; he compounded the offence by locking up a constable who sought to use force. He undoubtedly was also influenced in his refusals by hearing that Owen KEVENY, one of his agents, had been murdered after submitting to an NWC warrant. However justified his refusals may have been, they were to be given more weight in Quebec and in London than all the tragic acts in the mounting dispute.

Meanwhile, the course of events had caused the new governor-in-chief at Quebec, Sir John Coape Sherbrooke*, to appoint commissioners of inquiry in October. Their task was to represent the crown in the Indian Territory and "to quiet the existing disturbances." Selkirk had been asking for such a commission repeatedly but he was to find the Nor'Westers claiming the credit for it. In the spring of 1817 the NWC came west in force, including the partners released on bail. They found Fort William intact, and the supplies purchased from McKenzie left behind under caretakers, whom they promptly arrested and sent to Montreal under guard. Lord Selkirk had left for Red River on 1 May. Behind the Nor'Westers came the commissioners with a small detachment of troops, and behind them a further detachment of De Meuron's along with more supplies for the colony.

Douglas

Mail which reached Selkirk on his way chilled his optimism. The tone of Sherbrooke's letters and even more that of a proclamation in the name of the Prince Regent made him apprehensive. The latter called for a cessation of hostilities and a restitution of property. It assumed throughout that the struggle was purely a trade war in which the parties were equally guilty; it took no notice of Selkirk or the settlement as special factors.

At first Selkirk believed that the senior commissioner, William Bacheler Coltman*, would prove wise and just, but Coltman's conduct fulfilled the letter and followed the spirit of the Prince Regent's proclamation. Moreover, he expressed the gravest doubts of the validity of the HBC charter though prominent lawyers re-examined and confirmed its soundness in 1811. If the charter was not valid neither was the grant to Selkirk, and the acts of Miles Macdonell as governor were of doubtful legality. To this assessment Coltman added doubts about the feasibility of the settlement, since like many he had accepted NWC propaganda about the unsuitability of the soil for crops. And if the settlement was not feasible its creation could only have been a tactical move in a fur-trade war.

Though there was much satisfaction for Selkirk in the weeks at Red River, and though his settlers returned to fine crops and felt at last secure in his presence among them, the future was full of uncertainty. A purchase of land from the Indians had been arranged, but Selkirk could not give clear title to the settlers. Too much depended on Coltman's report.

In his hope for justice from the commission Selkirk was frustrated and bitterly disappointed. He himself was charged for his actions at Fort William, but the obvious instigators of the killing at Seven Oaks, Archibald Norman McLeod* and Alexander Greenfield Macdonell*, were allowed time to get out of reach before Coltman saw fit to charge them. When Selkirk announced his intention of returning to Montreal through the United States, for a variety of reasons including fear of assassination, Coltman angrily imposed £6,000 bail for his appearance in court in Lower Canada. The Nor'Westers spread the word that the Trading Lord had escaped justice and would not again be seen in the Canadas.

Selkirk made an immense circuit through the United States; he arrived at York on 10 Jan. 1818 and then went on to the assizes at Sandwich (Windsor), Upper Canada, to answer the warrants he had originally resisted. In these proceedings and in all that followed he felt himself hopelessly entangled in a web of perjury, postponements, and manipulation of justice that was both maddeningly frustrating and deeply shocking. The trip to Sandwich saw no trials completed but he was bailed for £250 on the same offences for which Coltman had imposed bail of £6,000. During the winter and spring, preliminary hearings at Quebec on offences by the Nor'Westers found true bills in nearly all cases to do with the murders of settlers and destruction of Selkirk's settlement. But a dozen prisoners and key witnesses escaped or jumped bail and slipped away to the Indian Territory, among them Cuthbert Grant*, leader of the Métis at Seven Oaks.

Selkirk, whose health had been robust under the rigours of a year and a half of hard living and travel, now sickened under months of the law's delays. In February 1818 it was decided that all the cases from Quebec would be moved to York for trial at the request of the NWC partners, on the plea that Lower Canadian juries would be hostile. In York, still a small village, there was some doubt that a competent jury could be empanelled. In August Selkirk went the 700 miles to Sandwich from Montreal for his own trials. There, after a bitter wrangle, just as he and his lawyer, Samuel Gale*, believed he was about to be acquitted, Chief Justice William Dummer Powell* adjourned the court *sine die*. At that moment a local newspaper carried word that for the first time since 1806 he had not been elected as a representative Scottish peer; this news would certainly be interpreted in the Canadas as a loss of favour with the British government. He was sick of justice in the Canadas, and having seen by accident Colonial Secretary Lord Bathurst's letter of 11 Feb. 1817 that had resulted in his official persecution, he determined to return to England to confront the Colonial Office.

Leaving his clever and courageous wife to watch his interests from Montreal, he returned to London. Though now seriously ill he continued the fight from his sick-bed, informing and arousing his friends. The whole miserable controversy was set out in what was to be his last book, *A letter to the Earl of Liverpool* . . . ([London], 1819). In addition he kept a watch over the affairs of his settlements at Prince Edward Island and Red River, adjudicating disputes and forwarding supplies, though his own finances were approaching ruin. His health at first improved but the stress was too great and at last produced a dangerous haemorrhage. By mid May 1819 it was reported that he was "far advanced in a deep consumption"; by August this news was known at Red River and beyond, to the grief and dismay of his supporters and the undisguised glee of the Nor'Westers.

Nevertheless, his efforts were at last having some success. His brother-in-law, Sir James Montgomery, had won in February 1819 a motion in parliament asking for papers on the Red River controversy. When presented they contained Coltman's report along with Colonial Office correspondence and amounted to a massive exposure of NWC methods. It was a vindication of sorts, but only a few friends and enemies were much interested, and Selkirk was no longer able to follow up effectively.

In June his family returned from Montreal and plans were made for a journey to a warmer climate in search of health. By mid September preparations were complete, and what Selkirk referred to as their "caravan" wound its way toward the south of France. Early in October they reached Pau, found it charming, and settled in for the winter. Though it was not the right climate for a chest complaint Lord Selkirk's health appeared to improve. There was a constant stream of news from England, and word of a probable amalgamation of the fur companies, both of which were now in serious financial trouble. There was a tempting NWC offer for Selkirk's HBC stock, a sale that would have helped his desperate financial affairs. But he would countenance no arrangement that would not provide for the well-being of his settlers. Selkirk's health was now steadily declining. He still wrote on Red River affairs, and spoke sadly of the colony as the place "where we had the prospect of doing so much good." On 8 April 1820 he died, and he was buried in the Protestant cemetery at nearby Orthez.

Selkirk did not live to see the amalgamation of the HBC and the NWC, only a year away; nor would such a controversial figure have a place in the memory of the new company, though to his supporters he remained a hero, and to his settlers a noble legend. Lady Selkirk, in a letter to his sister Katherine, wrote, "I feel confident if we have patience he will have ample justice, and when the North West Company are forgotten his name and character will be revered as they ought." The *Montreal Gazette* of 8 June reported his death and commented: "It may be said of this nobleman that the endowments of his mind as well as his other qualifications made him be as much respected as the exalted rank he inherited from his ancestors. . . . Perhaps some people would deduct something from his worth on account of his rage for colonization."

JOHN MORGAN GRAY

[Selkirk's personal papers are available at the PAC in MG 19, E1, and the journal he kept on his North American visit of 1803–4 has been published as *Lord Selkirk's diary* (White). A fuller note on sources may be found in J. M. Gray, *Lord Selkirk of Red River* (Toronto, 1963). J.M.G.]

MTL, William Dummer Powell papers. PAC, MG 11, [CO 42] Q; MG 19, E4; RG 5. *Docs. relating to NWC* (Wallace). G. W. Lefevre, *The life of a travelling physician, from his first introduction to practice; including twenty years' wanderings through the greater part of Europe* (3v., London, 1843), 1: 21–75. [Colin Robertson], *Colin Robertson's correspondence book, September 1817 to September 1822*, ed. E. E. Rich with R. H. Fleming (London, 1939; repr. Nendeln, Liechtenstein, 1968). C. [B.]

Martin, *Lord Selkirk's work in Canada* (Oxford, 1916). J. P. Pritchett, *The Red River valley, 1811–1849: a regional study* (New Haven, Conn., 1942). J. M. Bumsted, "Settlement by chance: Lord Selkirk and Prince Edward Island," *CHR*, 59 (1978): 170–88; "Lord Selkirk of Prince Edward Island," *Island Magazine*, no.5 (fall–winter 1978): 3–8. F. C. Hamil, "Lord Selkirk in Upper Canada," *OH*, 37 (1945): 35–48. W. S. Wallace, "The literature relating to the Selkirk controversy," *CHR*, 13 (1932): 45–50.

DRAPEAU, JOSEPH, merchant, seigneur, and politician; b. 13 April 1752 in Pointe-Lévy (Lauzon and Lévis, Que.), son of Pierre Drapeau, a farmer, and Marie-Joseph Huard, *dit* Désilets; m. 14 Oct. 1782 Marie-Geneviève Noël* in Saint-Antoine-de-Tilly, Que., and they had six daughters; d. 3 Nov. 1810 at Quebec, Lower Canada.

Although he was not destitute, Joseph Drapeau probably possessed little when he left Pointe-Lévy, where his father farmed 90 acres of land to keep his large family. He went to live at Quebec, probably early in the 1770s. He served in the militia during the American invasion of 1775–76 [*see* Benedict ARNOLD; Richard Montgomery*]. In April 1779 he obtained a permit to sell alcoholic beverages, and then two years later a hotel-keeper's licence. At the time of his marriage he owned a house and a general store on the Place du Marché (Place Notre-Dame) in Lower Town, with an inventory evaluated at £1,066. His 16-year-old wife, the daughter of the seigneur of Tilly, Jean-Baptiste Noël, brought 4,000 *livres* to the joint estate. Because of the dearth of information on the early years of his career, however, it is impossible to know how he came to be a merchant or what conditions and means enabled him to set up his business.

Drapeau's commercial operations rapidly spread beyond the limits of Lower Town. In 1788 he went into partnership with Louis Bourdages*, a merchant in Upper Town, who in return for capital undertook to sell at his store goods that Drapeau would furnish. Drapeau entered into a similar partnership in 1793 with Louis Bélair, a merchant in Baie-Saint-Paul, to whom he supplied imported and manufactured products in exchange for the surplus grain produced in the region. Their flourishing business even made necessary the purchase of a schooner, the *Marie*, which would ply between Quebec and Baie-Saint-Paul until 1804, when the commercial agreement came to an end.

In 1794 Drapeau negotiated the building of a ship in Louis Garennes's shipyard on Île aux Grues. In March 1795 the sloop *Saint-Pierre*, commanded by Louis Bodoin, whom Drapeau had urged "to be active and as vigilant as he can . . . in order to make the aforesaid sailing as profitable as possible," was carrying goods and passengers between the ports of Montreal, Quebec, Baie-Saint-Paul, and Rimouski.

In 1799 Drapeau owned his own shipbuilding yard in Baie-Saint-Paul. He personally hired the carpenters and caulkers, and he paid them four shillings a day for work "from sunrise to sunset, except for the time needed to take meals," deducting from their wages "two days' salary for each day lost." In July the brig *General Prescott* left the shipyard. Drapeau, who was obtaining his supplies from British firms in business at Quebec, particularly those of John BLACKWOOD and Adam Lymburner*, decided to trade directly with Europe. He fitted out the *General Prescott* to sail to Halifax, N.S., then to Liverpool, Bristol, and London, and from there to Lisbon. In November 1801 the 235-ton *Denault* left Baie-Saint-Paul for London where it was sold. The following year three schooners, the *Marguerite*, the *Amelia*, and the *Marie*, came off the stocks in his shipyard. The first was sold in 1802; the other two were used by Drapeau for his commerce until they were sold in 1808 and 1809. In 1803, at his quay on Rue du Sault-au-Matelot at Quebec, Drapeau had a schooner built which François Vassal* de Montviel and Jacques Voyer* bought that same year for £600. In 1805 Martin Chinic* purchased for £450 the schooner *Clairet*, which had been built at Quebec the previous year.

Like the other merchants and traders of the time Drapeau was induced to give credit to some of his clientele. Between 1780 and 1806 he held debts amounting to more than £5,000. The amounts due by note, ranging from £3 to £1,500 and payable at set dates, bore legal interest at 6 per cent. The debtors were mainly from the Quebec and Baie-Saint-Paul regions, but also from as far away as Rivière-Ouelle, Rimouski, Saint-Ours, Carleton, and Caraquet, N.B. Drapeau demanded solid guarantees. He did not hesitate to employ any legal recourse and thus to seize the property of debtors who were too slow in making repayment: an owner's land, a skipper's ship, and even rights of inheritance or widows' claims to dower. He made use of all legal means, procurations or juridical proceedings, to obtain what was due him.

In 1784 Drapeau had begun to invest his profits in landed property. He paid £450 for a three-storey stone house on Rue de la Montagne that year. The following year he bought by tender before the Court of Common Pleas a lot fronting on the St Lawrence with a two-storey stone house and a quay. In 1797 he bought from James TOD three lots on Rue du Sault-au-Matelot. In 1803 the nuns of the Hôtel-Dieu of Quebec let him have a piece of land on the St Lawrence and another on the Rivière Saint-Charles.

Drapeau was a conscientious manager and applied himself to making his landed property turn a profit. In May 1795 he rented out for £17 a year the ground floor of the house in which he was living on the Place du Marché. He increased this rent to £42 the following year, then to £100 in 1805. He converted his house on Rue du Sault-au-Matelot into a bakery in 1797 and received five Spanish *piastres* a month for it, and £30 a year from 1798. He leased out the house he owned on Rue Saint-Pierre and received an annual rent of £45. His house on Rue de la Montagne, which was rented for £27 a year, was leased in 1804 to hat-makers, who converted it into a shop and warehouse, paying £50 annually for it. The detailed leases stated precisely the condition of the buildings and the area allocated to the lessees in the sheds or stables. They described meticulously their obligations and set down exactly the terms of payment. Most often the lessees had to agree to specific demands upon them such as redoing the roof, repairing a wall that had been damaged, clearing the snow off the porches, digging a culvert, or even piling the cordwood in a precise spot in the yard. If they were behind in their payments, Drapeau cancelled the lease and found a new tenant.

Like many merchants Drapeau had his eye on the properties belonging to seigneurs. Within ten years he had accumulated large land holdings. In February 1789 he bought the seigneury of Champlain. In August of the following year he paid Simon Fraser and John YOUNG £300 for the seigneury of Lessard, also called La Mollaie or Pointe-au-Père. That year as well he purchased the seigneury of Nicolas-Riou, known as Baie-du-Ha!Ha! At the same time he engaged in clever land transactions with René Lepage's numerous heirs which made him the owner of four other seigneuries: Rimouski and Saint-Barnabé, Grand-Métis (Lepage, Thivierge, Anse-aux-Coques, Pointe-aux-Bouleaux, or Mitisses), Pachot or Rivière-Mitis, and Sainte-Claire. In 1791 and 1792 he made an arrangement with the owners of Rivière-du-Gouffre and became its titular seigneur. In August 1793, ill and fearful that he might leave his wife and daughters in "difficulties or misfortune through not being able, or not knowing how to develop and administer the aforesaid properties," he sold almost all his landed property to Louis Bélair for £6,950. The next month, probably having recovered his health, he cancelled the sale. In December 1797 Drapeau parted with the seigneury of Champlain, selling it to Alexander ELLICE for £525. The following year he reinvested his capital, buying half of the seigneury of Île d'Orléans. In 1805 Drapeau succeeded in acquiring a twelfth of the seigneuries of Rigaud-Vaudreuil, Gentilly, Perthuis, Beauvais, Rivière-Duchesne, and Sainte-Barbe-de-la-Famine, properties that belonged to Alexandre-André-Victor Chaussegros de Léry. He had, however, to let these lands go four years later when the seller's brother, Louis-René Chaussegros* de Léry, exercised his right of lineal repurchase. He succeeded nevertheless in making £118 17s. on this transaction.

Drapeau rarely paid cash for his purchases. He preferred to arrange a bond or to make payment in the form of a life annuity or merchandise. He always managed to take advantage of seizures, sheriff's sales, and auctions, thus obtaining cheaply properties that he resold at a profit.

Drapeau lost no time in rendering fealty and homage for the seigneury of Champlain in May 1789 and he began erecting a mill in June. Three years later he had a similar building put up at Rivière-du-Gouffre. He was much concerned with profits in these construction contracts, requiring guarantees of reliability, setting delivery dates, and even providing for penalties in the event he was not satisfied. When he leased out his mills at Baie-Saint-Paul, Rimouski, Rivière-du-Gouffre, or Île d'Orléans, he took care to describe their condition in detail and to have the millers' obligations put in writing.

As soon as he had bought his properties, Drapeau the seigneur lost no time in taking inventory of them. In January and February 1791 the notary Alexandre DUMAS issued in his name 54 new title deeds for land grants to tenants on the seigneury of Champlain. In the spring Dumas visited all the farms at Rimouski to give deeds for land grants, collect the *cens et rentes*, and draw up the register of landed property. The notaries Jean Néron and Barthélemy FARIBAULT surveyed the seigneury of Rivière-du-Gouffre, drawing up new title deeds or leases *à cens*.

Drapeau did not hesitate to seize the farm of a tenant who was in debt and unable to pay the seigneurial dues, or to cancel a land sale if the seller had cheated him by lying about the size or condition of the buildings; he even interfered in the *censitaires'* affairs, for example stipulating in a sale that the new purchaser could not "lease the above-mentioned piece of land to any persons practising the trade of tavern-keeper without express consent and permission in writing." He advised his steward at Champlain, Joseph-Alexandre Raux, "to bring action through the competent court, both by personal judgement and condemnation and by seizure and distraint of their property" against tenants who were late in paying their dues. He entrusted the administration of his seigneuries to his brothers-in-law, Louis Bélair at Baie-Saint-Paul and Augustin Trudel at Rimouski.

Drapeau's public life was uneventful and unmarked by scandal. In 1785, as a member of the merchant community, he supported Lieutenant Governor Henry Hamilton* when he was recalled to England. He was very concerned about the problems of education, and in 1787 joined in petitioning Lord Dorchester [Guy CARLETON] to do everything in his power to ensure the reopening of the Jesuit college. In 1790 he became a member of the Fire Society and the Agriculture Society. The following year he joined the Canadian Militia of the Town and Banlieu of Quebec as an ensign, and in April signed a petition to the king favouring the remission of the *lods et ventes*. He indicated his loyalty to the British crown by joining an association formed in 1794 to support the constitution and government. Three years later he was a member of the jury of the Quebec Court of King's Bench.

During the 1804 electoral campaign Drapeau attacked the candidate in the riding of Orléans, Jérôme MARTINEAU, accusing him publicly of having extorted 40,000 *livres* from the Séminaire de Québec. When threatened with legal action he withdrew his charge and cleared Martineau's reputation. In 1809 Drapeau ran in Northumberland riding. Elected on 23 November, he supported the Canadian party, voting in particular for the exclusion of judges from the assembly [*see* Sir James Henry CRAIG; Pierre-Amable DE BONNE]. His political career, however, was brief, for he died on 3 November of the following year.

Since there are no records, little is known of Drapeau's family life. He lived on the Place du Marché at first, and then from 1798 on Rue du Sault-au-Matelot. His household consisted of a servant or two and probably some slaves. His wife assisted in running his affairs, frequently accompanying him to the notary's office to initial transactions. At times Drapeau behaved generously towards members of his family. He took in his invalid sister, paid for his brother Charles's studies to become a notary, granted lands to his brothers and sisters, and had his daughters educated in the Ursuline convent. He was, however, parsimonious when it came to subscribing to causes. For example, he refused to contribute to the building of the church at Rimouski, and the habitants complained to Bishop Plessis*, who nevertheless took up his defence.

Drapeau was an intelligent businessman who invested in sectors of the economy that could earn him profits. He derived income from his business, interest on his loans, rents from his houses, dues from his seigneuries, and profits from his shipbuilding. He paid close attention to the management of his property, and it was probably through ability as much as parsimony that he succeeded in building the considerable fortune that his widow and daughters continued to manage after his death.

CÉLINE CYR and PIERRE DUFOUR

ANQ-Q, CE1-19, 13 avril 1752; CN1-26, 10 juin 1800; 23 févr., 6, 23 sept. 1803; 23 janv., 27 juill., 3 nov. 1804; CN1-63, 24 sept. 1810; CN1-83, 22 juill. 1786, 28 janv. 1789; CN1-92, 8, 16 mai 1788; 22 juin 1789; 17 août 1790; 6, 15 févr., 15–16 mai, 14 sept., 14 oct. 1791; 4 oct. 1792; 15 juin, 12 août 1793; 28 avril, 24 oct. 1794; 20 mars, 29 mai, 5 sept. 1795; 30 janv., 28 août 1797; 8 janv. 1798; 11 févr. 1799; 16 août 1800; CN1-99, 13–17 mai, 8 sept. 1797; 1er févr., 21 mars 1798; 28 août 1805; CN1-147, 6 juin 1804, 21 déc. 1805, 9 sept. 1806; CN1-178, 27 mai 1809, 8 juin

Ducharme

1810; CN1-224, 30 oct. 1782; CN1-230, 30 déc. 1797, 24 mai 1800, 22 mai 1805, 5 avril 1809; CN1-245, 4 juill. 1784; CN1-262, 23 sept. 1803; CN1-284, 12 déc. 1796; CN1-285, 1er oct. 1799; 5 févr., 27 oct. 1800; 17 nov. 1801; 24 juin 1802; CN4-16, 10–15 sept. 1792; P1000-32-592. PAC, MG 30, D56; RG 1, L3L: 37980–8083; RG 42, ser.1, 183: 11, 15, 34, 48, 57, 63, 68, 79, 91–92. *Quebec Gazette*, 29 April 1779; 17 May 1781; 20 June 1782; 28 Jan., 22 April 1790; 28 April 1791; 3 July 1794; 6 April 1797; 24 Jan. 1799; 7 June 1802; 8 Nov. 1810. *Quebec almanac*, 1791. F.-J. Audet, "Les législateurs du Bas-Canada." Bouchette, *Topographical description of L.C.* Desjardins, *Guide parl.*, 135. P.-G. Roy, *Inv. concessions.* J.-A. Lavoie, *La famille Lavoie au Canada, de 1650 à 1921* (Québec, 1922). P.-G. Roy, *L'île d'Orléans* (Québec, 1928); *Toutes petites choses du Régime anglais* (2 sér., Québec, 1946). J. W. M., "Notes sur les seigneuries du district de Rimouski," *BRH*, 17 (1911): 237–46, 257–67, 312–20, 331–38, 353–68. "Les seigneuries du négociant Drapeau," *BRH*, 43 (1937): 81–82.

DUCHARME, JEAN-MARIE, fur trader and politician; b. 19 July 1723 in Lachine (Que.), son of Joseph Ducharme and Thérèse Trottier; m. there first 3 Aug. 1761 Marie-Angélique Roy, *dit* Portelance; m. there secondly 3 Feb. 1789 Françoise Demers, *dit* Dumé; d. there 20 July 1807.

Jean-Marie Ducharme's birthplace was the embarkation point of canoes bound for the west, and his father was a farmer who engaged in the fur trade. It is not certain when Jean-Marie entered the trade himself but by the 1750s he was described as a "skilful voyageur." The first official record of his business activities dates from 1752, when he sent a canoe of merchandise to the Illinois country; however, as his subsequent career reveals, he had little regard for formalities such as permits, and he may already have been involved for some time. When traders from Pennsylvania moved into the Ohio valley, Governor Ange Duquesne* de Menneville of New France launched a military expedition to occupy the upper reaches of the river. Ducharme assisted Claude-Pierre Pécaudy* de Contrecœur's forces as a courier in 1754 and helped construct Fort Duquesne (Pittsburgh, Pa) in 1755. During the fall of 1755 he supervised a group of men bringing supplies to the fort from the Illinois country. Later Ducharme resumed his trade, sending a canoe to the Illinois in 1757.

By the winter of 1762–63, Ducharme had shifted his operations to the vicinity of La Baye (Green Bay, Wis.) and accommodated himself to the British merchants who had moved into the region following the conquest of New France. When an Indian uprising erupted in the Great Lakes area in 1763 [*see* MADJECKEWISS], the British military immediately prohibited the transporting of gunpowder and ammunition into the interior. Ducharme, willing to defy the law for profit, took several canoes of ammunition up the Ottawa River route to Michili-

mackinac (Mackinaw City, Mich.) and La Baye in August. Stories were being circulated among the Indians of the region that France had sent its forces to reconquer Canada, and Ducharme tried to counter such rumours. British merchants in Montreal were enraged, however, by his profitable journey. In October 1764, on his return to Lachine, they petitioned Lieutenant Governor Ralph Burton* to have him arrested. Slipping by a detachment of soldiers sent to apprehend him, Ducharme fled. The soldiers seized his furs, hidden in a neighbour's cellar, and found his four canoes in an orchard. Some time later he was apprehended, convicted, and imprisoned in Montreal, but through the intervention of Governor Murray* he was given a relatively mild punishment. Years later, Ducharme's exploit still rankled with Indian Department official Christian Daniel Claus*.

When peace came back to the Great Lakes, Ducharme once again turned to the Illinois country, as trade licences of 1769 and 1772 indicate. He centred his trade in Cahokia (Ill.), but westward across the Mississippi were rich lands controlled by the Spaniards, who excluded traders of other nations. Tempted by the potential of commerce with the Little Osages along the Missouri River, Ducharme took two canoe-loads of merchandise into the territory under cover of darkness in October or November 1772. When Spanish authorities at St Louis (Mo.) learned of his presence, they were appalled. The Little Osages had given them particular trouble and all trade had been prohibited. A Spanish detachment under the command of Pierre de Laclède Liguest was sent out in February 1773 to apprehend the intruders. It encountered them on 11 March and tried to get them to surrender peacefully. Refusing, Ducharme provoked an exchange of gunfire in which he was wounded in the thigh. He returned the fire and then fled with his Iroquois servant. His crew surrendered, and his canoes, furs, and merchandise were confiscated and taken to St Louis. Word of the affair sped eastward where it was much talked about.

Ducharme himself returned to Montreal and, undaunted by his adventure, obtained a licence on 13 May 1773 to trade at La Baye or the Mississippi. For the next two years he continued in business, purchasing most of his supplies from Jean-Louis Besnard*, *dit* Carignant, in Montreal.

The outbreak of the American revolution did not at first hinder trade. However, while Ducharme was spending the winter of 1775–76 with his family at Lachine, Richard Montgomery*'s army captured Montreal. Ducharme remained neutral, but he did sell the Americans supplies. Though he later helped expel the invaders, British authorities put him in jail for having furnished them with food.

By 1777 Ducharme was once again active in the Indian trade and the following year took two canoes to

Prairie du Chien (Wis.). At this time he probably had another clash with the Spanish authorities. His son Paul recalled that Jean-Marie was imprisoned by the Spaniards during 1778 or 1779 and threatened with execution. Only by proving he had ransomed Spanish captives from the Indians did he obtain his release. In 1779 the American success against Henry Hamilton*'s forces at Vincennes (Ind.) caused grave uncertainty among the traders at Michilimackinac. Consequently 32 of them, including Ducharme's cousin Laurent*, pooled their resources on 1 July 1779 in a general store to be managed for the common good. Jean-Marie Ducharme was one of the largest partners, contributing two canoe-loads valued at 30,000 *livres* in all. He was also appointed one of the enterprise's managers. At that time his place of residence was listed as "the Mississippi."

During the winter of 1779–80 Lieutenant Governor Patrick SINCLAIR of Michilimackinac received a circular letter from the secretary of state for the American Colonies encouraging him to take offensive action against the Spaniards. Spain had recently declared war against Britain, and by promising a monopoly to traders who helped capture Spanish territory along the Mississippi Sinclair raised an expedition of traders and Indians to attack St Louis. Ducharme became one of the leaders. While Joseph Calvé led a force against St Louis, Ducharme's group crossed the river and attacked Cahokia, which had surrendered to the Americans in 1778. Though he knew the village intimately, Ducharme's attack was repulsed, as was the assault on St Louis. Sinclair was infuriated by the expedition's failure and accused Calvé and Ducharme of treachery. Ducharme was particularly castigated for letting two French prisoners escape. Governor HALDIMAND gave Sinclair permission to arrest him and send him to Montreal, but the quick-tempered Scot must have calmed down and realized that his charges could not be proved. A couple of years later Ducharme had another encounter with Sinclair, who accused him of trading without a licence and assessed a fine of 22,500 pounds of hay.

Some time after this incident the old trader apparently retired to his farm at Lachine. White-haired and nearly blind, he still walked erect and was active enough to serve Montreal in the House of Assembly from 1796 to 1800. He died at Lachine the day after his 84th birthday. Several sons survived him, including Dominique*, who gained distinction during the War of 1812.

DAVID A. ARMOUR

Clements Library, Thomas Gage papers, American ser., 25: "Summary of Jean Marie DuCharme affairs," 12 Aug. 1764, in Burton to Gage, 11 Oct. 1764. DPL, Burton Hist. Coll., Thomas Williams papers, petty ledger, 1775–79, Pond and Williams account, 19 July 1774. Soc. d'archéologie et de numismatique de Montréal, 31: "Invoice of two canoes sent to Mr. Jn. Mie. Ducharme for Michilimackinac" (mfm. at PAC). Wis., State Hist. Soc., Abstracts of Indian trade licences in Canadian arch., Ottawa, 1767–76, and consolidated returns of trade licences, 1777, 1779 (transcripts). [L. C. Draper], "Interview of L. C. Draper with Pascal Leon Cerré, St Louis, Oct. 1846," Mo. Hist. Soc., *Coll.* (St Louis), 2 (1900–6), no.6: 51–54. "Ducharme's invasion of Missouri, an incident in the Anglo-Spanish rivalry for the Indian trade of upper Louisiana," ed. A. P. Nasatir, *Mo. Hist. Rev.* (Columbia), 24 (1929–30): 3–25, 238–60, 420–39. *Mich. Pioneer Coll.*, 9 (1886): 559–60, 568, 586, 650, 658; 10 (1886): 254, 305–7, 442–43, 585; 19 (1891): 303, 305, 529–30; 27 (1896): 668–69. *NYCD* (O'Callaghan and Fernow), 10: 407. *Johnson papers* (Sullivan *et al.*), 4: 511, 516, 540; 5: 377–80; 8: 841; 12: 1027–28; 13: 622. *Papiers Contrecœur et autres documents concernant le conflit anglo-français sur l'Ohio de 1745 à 1756*, Fernand Grenier, édit. (Québec, 1952), 209, 215, 303, 370, 372–73. [Wilson] Primm, "History of St. Louis," *The early histories of St. Louis*, ed. J. F. McDermott (St Louis, 1952), 119–20. "Spain in the Mississippi valley, 1765–1794: I, the revolutionary period, 1765–1781," ed. Lawrence Kinnaird, American Hist. Assoc., *Annual report* (Washington), 1945, 2: xxiv, 214–18. Wis., State Hist. Soc., *Coll.*, 3 (1857): 231–34; 11 (1888): 99; 18 (1908): 161–62, 358–59; 19 (1910): 293. *Catalogue de la collection François-Louis-Georges Baby*, Camille Bertrand, compil. (2v., Montréal, 1971), 1: 420, 543. *Dictionnaire national des Canadiens français (1608–1760)* (3v., Montréal, 1958), 1: 437. Massicotte, "Répertoire des engagements pour l'Ouest," *ANQ Rapport*, 1930–31: 439; 1931–32: 348. Joseph Tassé, *Les Canadiens de l'Ouest* (2v., Montréal, 1878), 1: 341–50. *The Spanish in the Mississippi valley, 1762–1804*, ed. J. F. McDermott (Urbana, Ill., 1974). F.-J. Audet, "Jean-Marie Ducharme (1723–1807)," *RSC Trans.*, 3rd ser., 33 (1939), sect.I: 19–29. A. P. Nasatir, "The Anglo-Spanish frontier in the Illinois country during the American revolution, 1779–1783," Ill. State Hist. Soc., *Journal* (Springfield), 21 (1928–29): 291–358. Don Rickey, "The British-Indian attack on St. Louis, May 26, 1780," *Mo. Hist. Rev.*, 55 (1960–61): 35–45.

DUCHESNAY, ANTOINE JUCHEREAU. *See* JUCHEREAU

DUCKWORTH, Sir JOHN THOMAS, naval officer and governor of Newfoundland; b. 9 Feb. 1747/48 in Leatherhead, England, son of the Reverend Henry Duckworth and Sarah Johnson; m. July 1776 Anne Wallis, only child and heiress of John Wallis of Camelford, England, and they had one son and one daughter; m. secondly 14 May 1808 Susannah Catherine Buller, daughter of William Buller, bishop of Exeter, and they had two sons; d. 31 Aug. 1817 in Plymouth, England.

Descended from an old landed family, John Thomas Duckworth went to Eton College as a young boy but at the age of 11, on the invitation of Edward Boscawen*, decided to join the Royal Navy. He

Duckworth

entered Boscawen's ship of the line *Namur* on 24 July 1759 at Portsmouth. After serving in it and in the *Prince of Orange*, he joined on 5 April 1764 the 50-gun *Guernsey* at Chatham. The *Guernsey* was the flagship of Commodore Hugh Palliser*, the newly appointed governor of Newfoundland, so it was as a young midshipman that Duckworth first saw the island to which he was to return to govern half a century later. He spent two happy and instructive years in the *Guernsey*: Palliser was one of the ablest of the 18th-century governors of Newfoundland, Joseph Gilbert, an accomplished chart-maker, was master of the *Guernsey*, and Michael Lane, who was to follow James Cook* as surveyor of Newfoundland, was the schoolmaster in the ship.

Duckworth passed his lieutenant's examinations on 13 May 1766 and was confirmed in that rank on 14 Nov. 1771. With the outbreak of the American revolution, he saw action in North America and the West Indies as first lieutenant in the frigate *Diamond*. On 16 June 1780 he was promoted captain and soon afterwards became flag-captain to the admiral of the West Indies squadron, Sir George Brydges Rodney, in the *Princess Royal*. After a period "on the beach" between wars, he was appointed in 1793 commander of the 74-gun *Orion* in the Channel fleet of Admiral Lord Howe, and took part in the victory over the French fleet off Ushant on the "Glorious First of June," 1794. In the following years of the long war, Duckworth commanded ships and squadrons in home waters, the West Indies, and the Mediterranean. In April 1800 he intercepted a large and rich Spanish convoy off Cadiz, and his share of the prize money was said to have been £75,000. The following year he was knighted. He was commander-in-chief on the Jamaica station from 1803 to 1805 and was appointed vice-admiral on 23 April 1804. Early in 1806 Duckworth was engaged in a blockade of Cadiz, which he broke off to pursue a French squadron across the Atlantic to the Leeward Islands and destroy it off San Domingo (Hispaniola) on 6 February. He received the thanks of both houses of parliament, a yearly pension of £1,000 from the House of Commons, and the freedom of the City of London. The following year he took a squadron into the Dardanelles with peace terms for the Sublime Porte, but through no fault of his own had to return without reaching Constantinople (Istanbul) or contacting the Turkish potentate.

On 26 March 1810 Duckworth was appointed governor of Newfoundland and commander-in-chief of the squadron there. Nearing the end of a long career, wealthy, and but recently remarried, he seems to have hesitated about taking the command of a relatively minor squadron on a rather remote station. The appointment was sweetened by promotion to full admiral, and in his flagship, the 50-gun *Antelope*, he reached St John's harbour on 9 July after a "very tedious passage" of 27 days. At this time the Newfoundland command included, besides the great island itself, the coast of Labrador, Anticosti Island, and the captured French islands of Saint-Pierre and Miquelon. Duckworth's frigates, sloops, and schooners were dispersed widely throughout this domain, patrolling the seas from Davis Strait to the Gulf of St Lawrence. The governor himself remained in St John's, except for a tour of the northern outports of Newfoundland and the southern coast of Labrador in August 1810, the first such visitation in 30 years.

Newfoundland was in the throes of transition from a summer fishing settlement to a permanently settled colony and Duckworth had to preside over this process as best he could. The island had a population of some 30,000, largely concentrated on the shores of the eastern bays and the Avalon peninsula, with about 7,000 of them in the ancient capital of St John's. Although the once mighty migratory fishery was rapidly dwindling, the antiquated anti-settlement laws remained formally in effect, and Newfoundland lacked many of the institutions of a settled country. The governor, for example, still stayed only for the summer, and ruled without the mixed benefits of advisory council and elected house of assembly. The home government was, however, beginning to face the realities of change, and in 1811 parliament passed legislation allowing fishing ships' rooms in St John's harbour to be converted into private property. Duckworth had the designated lands surveyed and let at public auction in renewable leases of 30 years, on condition that the buildings erected be in stone or brick, that streets be of an ample width, and that adequate sewers be built [*see* Thomas George William Eaststaff*]. He proposed that the annual rentals be devoted to the "most essential wants" of Newfoundland, which to his mind were better magistrates and more missionaries.

By 1812 Duckworth recognized that the old laws favouring the migratory fishery were now obsolete – "it is no longer a question of preference between two systems, that which was justly the favourite is now no more." However, he did not believe that a full colonial government with a legislature was either necessary or desired by the inhabitants, and he strongly opposed handing over powers to the increasingly vocal St John's élite of merchants and professional men. Dr William Carson* became particularly obnoxious to Duckworth, with his pamphlets attacking the governor's arbitrary powers and calling for an elected local legislature. Sir John denounced the pamphlets as indecent and libellous and enforced his "peremptory determination" not to reappoint Carson as surgeon to the Loyal Volunteers of St John's, the local militia unit.

On the other hand Duckworth helped to plant and

274

Duckworth

nurture some of the institutions essential to a civilized society. He took a great interest in the building and repair of churches, from Twillingate on the northeast coast round to the Burin peninsula and Fortune Bay on the south coast. The Anglican church in St John's especially engaged his attention. Since the pews were all rented out, his soldiers and seamen had to stand in the aisles and poor people were completely excluded. A government grant of £250 was paid in 1812 after the church had been repaired and enlarged according to his wishes. He pressed the archbishop of Canterbury to send out more missionaries, for whom government allowances and pensions were available, and recruited some from Devon, where he made his home. Duckworth worked with the Reverend Lewis Amadeus Anspach* to improve the rudimentary school system. In 1811 he readily accepted the proposal that a public hospital be built in St John's, financed by subscriptions from the merchants and "very moderate" assessments imposed on the fishermen and seamen of the port.

Of all the Newfoundland governors, Duckworth made the most persistent attempts to rescue the Beothuk Indians from oblivion. As soon as he arrived in 1810, he issued proclamations ordering the Micmacs, the Inuit, and the white population to treat the Beothuks with kindness. A reward of £100 was offered to anyone who established friendly contact on a continuing basis. In October he ordered Lieutenant David Buchan* to sail north to the Exploits River, anchor his schooner the *Adonis* there for the winter, and "proceed to discover the haunt of the Native Indians." Buchan did reach the interior wigwams of the elusive natives but had to withdraw after the unfortunate murder of two marines. The governor reported home that although the enterprise had ended in tragedy, the zeal and manly endurance shown was worthy of better success. He readily gave his lieutenant permission to winter in Newfoundland, the better to resume the search the following spring.

In 1812, however, the outbreak of war with the United States cut short the well-intentioned enterprise. Duckworth arrived in St John's on 16 July to find the townspeople in a state of alarm, anticipating an American descent. He immediately cancelled his projected trip to the south coast, ordered all his warships to sea to patrol the coasts, and tried to put the capital itself in defensible condition. With the aid of a citizens' committee of defence, he revived and enlarged the militia force, which was renamed the St John's Volunteer Rangers, and which came to comprise over 500 well-trained officers and men. He strengthened the seaward defences of the town and established a signal station on a nearby promontory to warn of the approach of enemy ships. In outports up and down the coast the residents formed themselves into companies and laboured, under the guidance of

officers sent with warships bearing ordnance supplies from St John's, to erect gun batteries able to beat off privateers. Although American privateers swarmed in Newfoundland waters, only a few communities were attacked, and the royal ships themselves captured a goodly number of the marauders. When Duckworth left Newfoundland for the last time at the end of October, the leading merchants and inhabitants of St John's, with the notable exception of Dr Carson, presented a farewell address thanking him for the measures taken to protect the trade and fisheries in general and St John's in particular.

However successful his tenure as governor had been, Duckworth had no wish to prolong it, and on 2 Dec. 1812, barely a week after arriving home, he tendered his resignation, after being offered a parliamentary seat for New Romney, on the Kent coast. He was created a baronet on 2 Nov. 1813 and in January 1815 was appointed commander-in-chief at Plymouth naval base, where he died in August 1817. The body was brought back to Wear House, his country seat on the Devon coast, and the funeral took place on the afternoon of 9 September in Topsham church. He was laid to rest in the family vault, in a coffin covered with crimson velvet studded with 2,500 silvered nails.

Duckworth's career was distinguished but at times controversial. To some contemporaries he was a generous and brave man and a skilful naval officer, although others accused him of being selfish and of lacking decisiveness. As governor of Newfoundland he seems to have been capable. He sought the best and most impartial advice on problems of the day, reported to the home government promptly and thoroughly, and displayed real energy and resolve in the crisis of 1812. He saw clearly that the migratory fishery was finished and that the future lay with the settlers for whom the island had become home, but he did not so clearly see that they must inevitably desire to govern themselves. It is not unfitting that a major thoroughfare in St John's bears the name of the governor who helped lay some of the foundations of the modern city.

WILLIAM H. WHITELEY

[Sir John Thomas Duckworth's career, especially as governor of Newfoundland, is well documented by a mass of papers in several repositories. His Newfoundland station papers were preserved in private hands and in 1970, through the efforts of the then premier of Newfoundland, Joseph Roberts Smallwood, they were purchased for the PANL, where they became P1/5, Duckworth papers, files 1–24. Correspondence of Duckworth as governor of Newfoundland is also found in the letterbooks of the Department of the Colonial Secretary (PANL, GN 2/1, 21–24). Dispatches from Newfoundland to the Colonial Office and Admiralty are in the PRO in CO 194/49–53 and ADM 1/477. Duckworth's admiral's journal from 1810 to 1812 is in ADM 50/73 and

275

Dumas

should be studied in conjunction with the log of his flagship *Antelope* between 1809 and 1813, which is in ADM 51/2123. His will is in PRO, PROB 11/1598/570.

The National Maritime Museum (London) has an important collection of Duckworth papers (DUC/1–46); DUC/16–18 contains Newfoundland squadron papers, 1810–12, and DUC/30 is Duckworth's official letterbook for 1812. Yale Univ. Library, Beinecke Rare Book and MS Library (New Haven, Conn.), Osborn coll., has account books, letterbooks, order-books, and correspondence for the period 1790–1817, and another series of Duckworth items beginning in 1785. The Univ. of Chicago Library has Newfoundland papers of Duckworth, especially those dealing with American fishing rights and issues raised by the War of 1812. There is a small but interesting collection of Duckworth manuscripts, largely of a family nature, in QUA. In 1977 the PAC produced a microfilm collection of Duckworth papers, integrating the small collection of PAC originals with the papers in the PANL and QUA, and adding selections from the National Maritime Museum material (PAC, MG 24, A45). Since then the Univ. of Chicago papers have been added.

Printed material on Duckworth, especially for the Newfoundland years, is relatively scanty, and there is no full-scale biography. Biographical accounts in dictionaries are reasonably full, except for the Newfoundland period. The *DNB* has the best balanced account. The life in James Ralfe, *The naval biography of Great Britain* . . . (4v., London, 1828), 2: 283–301, is unreliable and incomplete on several points. It is based largely on an obituary in *Gentleman's Magazine*, July–December 1817: 275, 372–74. Another obituary appeared in *Naval Chronicle*, 38 (July–December 1817): 262–64, which had earlier printed a "Biographical memoir of Sir John T. Duckworth, K.B. . . ." in vol.18 (July–December 1807): 1–27.

For Duckworth in Newfoundland the following general histories are of use: L. A. Anspach, *A history of the island of Newfoundland* . . . (London, 1819); *The Cambridge history of the British empire* (8v., Cambridge, Eng., 1929–59), vol.6; Joseph Hatton and Moses Harvey, *Newfoundland: its history, its present condition, and its prospects in the future* (Boston, 1883); Paul O'Neill, *The story of St. John's, Newfoundland* (2v., Erin, Ont., 1975–76); Charles Pedley, *The history of Newfoundland from the earliest times to the year 1860* (London, 1863); Prowse, *Hist. of Nfld.* (1895). The PANL published [L. A. Anspach], *Duckworth's Newfoundland: notes from a report to Governor Duckworth by Rev. Louis Amadeus Anspach* ([St John's, 1971]). See also the *Royal Gazette and Newfoundland Advertiser* (St John's), 1810–12, for notices of official ceremonies, addresses, and proclamations.   w.h.w.]

DUMAS, ALEXANDRE, businessman, militia officer, notary, lawyer, and politician; b. *c.* 1726 in Nègrepelisse, France, son of Jean Dumas and Marie Favar; d. 11 July 1802 at Quebec, Lower Canada.

By means of mercantile partnerships and marriages, the large Dumas family of the Montauban region in southern France was associated with virtually all the drapers from that region involved in the Quebec trade through such ports as La Rochelle and Bordeaux during the last two decades of the French régime in Canada. Alexandre Dumas came to Quebec in 1751 with a cousin, Jean Dumas* Saint-Martin, probably as the agent of the La Rochelle merchant Jean Chaudrue. The following year Alexandre's young brother Antoine-Libéral joined him as a clerk. They had all been preceded to the colony by Alexandre's cousin Jean-Daniel Dumas*, who had arrived in 1750 as an officer in the colonial regular troops. A Huguenot, Alexandre represented one of the 14 or 15 French Protestant firms in the colony by 1754, a group that included Joseph Rouffio*, François Havy*, Jean Lefebvre*, and François* and Jean-Mathieu* Mounier. Between about 1755 and 1757 Dumas became directly associated at Quebec with at least two other Protestant merchants, both from Montauban: Antoine Fraisses de Long and Joseph Senilh. Although Huguenot merchants were collectively treated with suspicion by Bishop Henri-Marie Dubreil* de Pontbriand – the result of ancient religious conflict in Europe – Governor Ange Duquesne* de Menneville and Intendant François Bigot* repeatedly defended them, reporting in 1755 that they carried on three-quarters of the trade to the colony. This domination continued down to the conquest.

One of Dumas's commercial interests during the French régime was the Gulf of St Lawrence fisheries, and it would remain a field of activity after 1759. On 1 April 1756 Pierre Révol*, a former salt smuggler of some notoriety, leased the post of Gros Mécatina, and later that month Dumas and Servant Durand, a Quebec navigator, joined him in purchasing buildings there. Révol went bankrupt that year, however, and Dumas and Jean Dumas Saint-Martin reached a settlement with his creditors, leading Révol in 1757 to accept a government appointment in Gaspé. During his absence, Dumas's acquaintance with his wife, Marie-Charlotte, blossomed into open adultery, a much talked-about affair that ended in January 1758 in a private settlement, after Révol had returned to Quebec for the winter season. Dumas was compelled to leave Quebec until Révol returned to Gaspé, and then to go to France in the fall at the latest; he had also to provide the unfortunate Mme Révol with an annuity. The scandal overshadowed Dumas's own financial difficulties: in May 1758 Senilh had instituted legal action to seize houses belonging to Dumas at Quebec.

Dumas was back in the colony by July 1760. At L'Islet on 6 October he renounced his faith in order to marry a Roman Catholic, Marie-Joseph Requiem, *née* La Roche; they would have four children, one of whom survived infancy. Dumas's was one of only a few marriages involving formerly Protestant merchants (Antoine-Libéral abjured the following year to marry Marguerite Cureux). Alexandre's change of faith was short-lived; two children were baptized in the Protestant church, and on 16 Oct. 1764 Dumas signed the controversial presentment of the Quebec grand jury, which in one clause objected to Roman Catholic jurors in cases involving British litigants [*see* George ALLSOPP].

Dumas had operated as a retailer before the conquest, and he continued to do so thereafter within French and Canadian trading circles. About 1762 he was joined by Jean Taché* in exploiting Gros Mécatina, and in 1764 Dumas participated with one Louis Nadeau in grist-milling on the Rivière Saint-Charles. By 1766 Dumas had entered into partnership with Henri-Marie-Paschal Fabre, *dit* Laperrière, known as Pascal Rustan. But as a result of the influx of British merchants and the colony's new mercantile alignment with London, he also transacted at Quebec with such merchants as Alexander Mackenzie and William Bayne, and with the firm of Moore and Finlay [*see* Hugh FINLAY]. At least twice in the 1760s Dumas visited London for business reasons; notarial records for that period provide revealing but incomplete evidence of his dealings with French merchants in London, Paris, and Bordeaux, usually in connection with his pre-conquest accounts and often on behalf of other correspondents in the colony. In 1766 he headed a delegation at Quebec which petitioned Governor Murray*, without success, for an ordinance to regulate unrecoverable debts incurred before 1760.

On 9 June 1767 Dumas, Christophe Pélissier*, Dumas Saint-Martin, Brook WATSON of London, and five others secured a 16-year lease from the crown to a large tract of land that included the seigneury of Saint-Maurice and the Saint-Maurice ironworks near Trois-Rivières. In 1771 Dumas hired Pierre de SALES Laterrière as the company's agent at Quebec, responsible for the sale of iron products from Dumas's store. Despite his enterprising involvement in the ironworks, which he probably wished to develop as a secure industrial base, Dumas encountered mounting financial problems in his own business. In 1764 he had held Canadian notes and bills of exchange worth over £39,000 but in 1769, during the collapse of the paper money market, he failed, according to Laterrière, with a debt of £33,000. A year later the Bordeaux firm of Rigal and Peeholier obtained a judgement in France against Dumas on an account stretching back to 1755, and in 1771, by which time the partnership with Rustan had been dissolved, much of Dumas's property was sold at the suit of Jean Orillat*, a Montreal merchant.

During the American invasion of Quebec in 1775–76, Dumas served as a captain in the Canadian militia and participated in repelling the assault led by Benedict ARNOLD on Rue du Sault-au-Matelot. As well, Dumas reportedly built a "machine" for grinding wheat in the blockaded city. On 15 Sept. 1776 he married another Catholic, the popular Marie-

Françoise Meignot, daughter of Louis Fornel* and Marie-Anne Barbel*; they had no children. Within months of their marriage Alexandre and his wife, who had assumed the business interests in France of her former husband, had authorized the London firm of Watson and Rashleigh to collect a debt in Dunkerque, France.

Early in 1778 Dumas acquired the lease to the Saint-Maurice forges and later that year moved there to take over their management from Laterrière. This and other commercial activity appear to have resulted in renewed personal indebtedness, mainly to Alexander Davison* and John LEES, and in 1779 Dumas was charged with forestalling the wheat market, which in the shadow of the American Revolutionary War was a forum for vigorous speculation. In September 1782 he petitioned Governor HALDIMAND for a renewal of the Saint-Maurice lease, due to expire the following year. However, on 3 Feb. 1783 it was granted to Conrad Gugy*, in part, perhaps, because the ironworks had fallen into disrepair. The decision led to pressure upon Dumas by his creditors and to a suit against him by the province's deputy receiver general, William GRANT (1744–1805), for the sale of equipment and ironware still in Dumas's possession at Quebec.

Dumas's failure to secure the lease forced him to withdraw from business and to consider a new occupation. He had apparently had an interest in law for some time; in 1776 he possessed nearly 90 books on law, and at an auction that September of property owned in common with his first wife, who had died probably shortly before, he bought back two-thirds of them. On 12 May 1783 he was examined as a candidate for the position of notary by Adam Mabane*, Thomas DUNN, and Pierre PANET, and three days later he was commissioned. About this time he moved back to Quebec from the forges. The next year, on 8 December, Haldimand commissioned him a lawyer as well, in response to a petition by Dumas but contrary to an earlier ruling by the governor forbidding the simultaneous holding of commissions as notary and lawyer. The move thrust Dumas into the midst of controversy over the regulation of the bar at Quebec. On 6 December the lawyers' society, the Communauté des Avocats, had opposed Dumas's likely admission on the grounds that the bar was adequately supplied and that, in view of his age and failures in business, he was an unfit candidate. When he received his commission despite these objections, the lawyers complained on the 11th to the Court of Common Pleas, which informed them in January that nothing could be done about Dumas but that such an abuse would not happen again. Dumas was admitted to the Communauté des Avocats on 30 March 1785; although it entered a final protest on the court register, and a regulatory ordinance was passed in April during the stormy legislative session of that year [*see*

Dumas

Henry Hamilton*], Dumas did not relinquish his commission until 9 Aug. 1787. He appears to have achieved some success as a notary; he served in the execution of Hugh Finlay's estate, and among his most frequent clients were Joseph DRAPEAU and James TOD.

Dumas did not figure prominently in the political debates of the 1780s that aligned many of the British merchants desiring English laws and a British constitution against the French party, led by Mabane, which sought to protect French laws and Canadian customs through retention of the Quebec Act. An investigation in 1787 into the administration of justice in the province reveals, however, that Dumas had challenged in court the validity of the partnership of Davison and Lees on the ground that it had not been registered according to the French mercantile code, with which he was undoubtedly conversant, but which the British merchants strenuously sought to have replaced by British law and custom. Ever adaptable, Dumas probably saw, like such Canadian political leaders as Pierre GUY, that the House of Assembly, accorded by the Constitutional Act of 1791, would provide a new forum for the defence of French law and Canadian customs. In 1792, during the province's first general election, he proudly proclaimed in the *Quebec Gazette* and before the Constitutional Club at Quebec his support for British constitutional principles. Despite recurring rheumatism, he represented, along with Charles Bégin, the county of Dorchester in the assembly between 1797 and 1800. On 14 of 19 occasions he voted with the Canadian party, successors to the French party in defending French laws and Canadian customs, against the English party led by John YOUNG. He was instrumental in 1799 in securing an amendment to the Highways Act of 1796 to create more efficient administrative districts under the act.

Between about 1793 and his death Dumas was active in purchasing and selling property in the Quebec area on his own behalf, and he frequently acted as legal agent on land matters for Jeremiah McCarthy* and others. Recommended in 1800 for a land grant on account of his early service in the militia, Dumas patented lots two years later in Windsor and Simpson townships, where land was allotted only to veterans of the Canadian militia companies that had served at Quebec during the American siege. Dumas had remained active in the militia, and by 1802 he had risen to lieutenant-colonel in Quebec's 2nd Militia Battalion.

Dumas died unexpectedly within weeks of his marriage on 15 May 1802 to Catherine Lee, daughter of Thomas Lee, a Quebec merchant, and was buried from the Anglican church at Quebec. He had demonstrated little constraint in matters of decorum and religion, a propensity not uncommon within Quebec society but which, compounded by mercantile failures, had evidently besmirched his public image. Forced out of business by the loss of the Saint-Maurice lease and his final decline within the credit structure of 18th-century commerce, Dumas transferred his mercantile contacts and legal abilities to notarial practice.

DAVID ROBERTS

[Alexandre Dumas is the author of a speech which appeared first in a draft version in the *Quebec Gazette*, 24 May 1792, and which was apparently later published separately. He may also have written the series of articles published under the pseudonym of Solon in the *Quebec Gazette* from 23 February to 15 March 1792 under the heading of "Pour accompagner la nouvelle constitution." D.R.]

AN, Col., B, 99: f.5; 101: ff.15, 18; D²ᴰ, 1 (mfm. at PAC). ANQ-Q, CE1-61, 15 Sept. 1776; 15 May, 13 July 1802; CN1-25, 14–16 sept., 9 nov. 1776; 9 déc. 1779; 8 nov. 1780; CN1-79, 30 avril 1756; 7, 30 déc. 1757; 19 juin 1758; CN1-83, 6 mars 1787, 16 avril 1794; CN1-99, 26 janv. 1800; CN1-103, 12 juill. 1769; CN1-122, 18 avril 1769; CN1-148, 10, 25 janv. 1763; 8 oct., 9, 16, 19 nov., 11 déc. 1764; CN1-189, 24 oct. 1763; 15 mars 1764; 23 avril, 3, 19 juin, 2 août 1766; 17 nov. 1767; CN1-205, 31 mai 1777; 31 mai, 1ᵉʳ, 20 sept. 1783; CN1-207, 19 oct. 1753; 12 nov. 1755; 29 juill., 30 déc. 1756; 27 juin, 23 nov. 1757; 11 janv. 1758; 24 oct. 1761; 8 mai, 29 oct. 1762; 8 avril 1764; 21 nov. 1766; 22 août, 14 nov. 1770; CN1-230, 23 févr. 1796; 7 mars, 3 avril 1801; 12 juill. 1802; CN1-248, 31 oct. 1754; 20 avril, 30 mai, 18 sept. 1756; 10 déc. 1764; 8 août 1766; 27 juill. 1768; 27 oct. 1770; 31 mai 1775; CN1-250, 3 août 1769, 9 juin 1770; CN1-284, 19 déc. 1793; 23, 25 juin 1794; 2 avril 1796; 30 mars 1797; 15 août 1799; 14 mars 1801; 15 mai 1802. BL, Add. MSS 21735: 108; 21879: 91–92, 215 (copies at PAC). PAC, MG 23, GII, 10, vol.3: 935–42; MG 24, L3: 6787, 6800–1, 6936–39, 6941–44, 6958; MG 30, D1, 11: 711–13; RG 1, L3ᴸ: 38708–17; RG 4, A1: 3652–59, 5865–67, 7790–92, 7796–99; B8, 1: 130–32, 165–73; B17, 7: [1784]; RG 8, I (C ser.), 1714: 1, 37–40; RG 68, General index, 1651–1841: ff.8, 542, 574.

A collection of several commissions, and other public instruments, proceeding from his majesty's royal authority, and other papers, relating to the state of the province in Quebec in North America, since the conquest of it by the British arms in 1760, comp. Francis Maseres (London, 1772; repr. [East Ardsley, Eng., and New York], 1966). Bas-Canada, chambre d'Assemblée, *Journaux*, 1796–1802. "Les dénombrements de Québec" (Plessis), ANQ *Rapport*, 1948–49: 32, 83, 120. "Inventaire des biens de feu Sʳ Pierre du Calvet," J.-J. Lefebvre, édit., ANQ *Rapport*, 1945–46: 365, 379. "Journal du siège de Québec du 10 mai au 18 septembre 1759," Ægidius Fauteux, édit., ANQ *Rapport*, 1920–21: 218. "Rôle général de la milice canadienne de Québec . . . ," Literary and Hist. Soc. of Quebec, *Hist. Docs.*, 8th ser. (1906): 269–307. Pierre de Sales Laterrière, *Mémoires de Pierre de Sales Laterrière et de ses traverses*, [Alfred Garneau, édit.] (Québec, 1873; réimpr., Ottawa, 1980). *Quebec Gazette*, 1764–1802. "Archives Gradis," ANQ *Rapport*, 1957–59: 35, 41, 52. Bouchette, *Topographical description of L.C.* "Cahier des témoignages de liberté au mariage commancé le 15 avril 1757," ANQ *Rapport*, 1951–53: 95, 122, 148. *Dictionnaire national des Canadiens français (1608–1760)* (2ᵉ éd., 3v., Montréal, 1965), 1.

Hubert Létourneau et Lucille Labrèque, "Inventaire de pièces détachées de la Prévôté de Québec," ANQ *Rapport*, 1971: 403. P.-G. Roy, *Inv. concessions*, 3: 234; 4: 134; *Inventaire des jugements et délibérations du Conseil supérieur de la Nouvelle-France, de 1717 à 1760* (7v., Beauceville, Qué., 1932–35), 5: 200. Tanguay, *Dictionnaire*, 3. Tremaine, *Biblio. of Canadian imprints*, 360, 378. J. E. Hare, *La pensée socio-politique au Québec, 1784–1812: analyse sémantique* (Ottawa, 1977). Neatby, *Administration of justice under Quebec Act*; *Quebec*. J.-E. Roy, *Hist. de Lauzon*, vol.3; *Hist. du notariat*. P.-G. Roy, *Toutes petites choses du Régime anglais* (2 sér., Québec, 1946), 1. Sulte, *Mélanges hist.* (Malchelosse), vol.6. Albert Tessier, *Les forges Saint-Maurice, 1729–1883* (Trois-Rivières, Qué., 1952). Louise Trottier, *Les forges: historiographie des forges du Saint-Maurice* (Montréal, 1980). Marcel Trudel, *L'Église canadienne*, vol.1. André Vachon, *Histoire du notariat canadien, 1621–1960* (Québec, 1962). J. F. Bosher, "French Protestant families in Canadian trade, 1740–1760," *SH*, 7 (1974): 179–201. M. Dumas de Rauly, "Extraits d'un livre de raison de la famille Dumas, de Nègrepelisse, dite de Lacaze . . . ," Soc. archéologique de Tarn-et-Garonne, *Bull. archéologique et hist.* (Montauban, France), 11 (1883): 111. Édouard Fabre Surveyer, "Notre Alexandre Dumas (1727–1802), député de Dorchester," *RSC Trans.*, 3rd ser., 41 (1947), sect.I: 1–14. Hare, "L'Assemblée législative du Bas-Canada," *RHAF*, 27: 375. Jacques Mathieu, "Un négociant de Québec à l'époque de la Conquête: Jacques Perrault, l'aîné," ANQ *Rapport*, 1970: 31, 36. "La 'représentation' des grands jurés de Québec en 1764," *BRH*, 11 (1905): 369–75. A. G. Reid, "General trade between Quebec and France during the French regime," *CHR*, 34 (1953): 18–32. P.-G. Roy, "La famille Dumas," *BRH*, 45 (1939): 161–64; "Le faux-saunier Pierre Revol," *BRH*, 50 (1944): 225–35.

DUN (Dunn), JOHN, Church of Scotland minister, merchant, and office holder; b. 11 Dec. 1763 in Fintry, Scotland, second son of James Dun, a farmer; d. on or about 6 Nov. 1803.

Little is known of John Dun's early life, except that he had been "regularly educated." When he graduated in 1788 from the University of Glasgow with an MA, he was living in Largs, a coastal village west of Glasgow. On 5 July 1791 he was licensed to preach by the Presbytery of Irvine. Within two years he emigrated to the state of New York where he was accepted as a licentiate by the Presbytery of Albany and received the vacant charge of Cherry Valley. His name appears in American Presbyterian records for 1794, but by the fall of that year he was resident at Newark (Niagara-on-the-Lake), Upper Canada.

It seems probable that while he was at Cherry Valley Dun had visited John Young*, minister of the Scotch Presbyterian Church in Montreal, who had advised him to apply for an appointment at Newark, where the Presbyterian congregation was numerous and prosperous and in 1792 had built a meeting-house. The two men may already have been acquainted for

Young had been born in Beith, Scotland, not far from Largs; he too had been licensed by the Presbytery of Irvine and had emigrated to New York where he had ministered before moving to Montreal. In late 1793 or early 1794 Dun reached an agreement with the Newark Presbyterians which provided him with a room and a salary of £300 New York currency for a three-year period; it also called for a ten-week trial "to Judge, if his Loyalty, piety, prudence & other ministerial qualifications" were acceptable.

Although his ministry was to commence on 13 June 1794, Dun arrived some three months later, bearing a recommendation from Richard DUNCAN, a merchant and legislative councillor who alternated his residence between New York and Upper Canada, to Surveyor General David William Smith*. On 30 Sept. 1794 a committee of the Newark congregation, composed of Ralfe Clench*, Robert Kerr*, and Andrew Heron, resolved to build a new church and to raise adequate funds for the support of a clergyman. The following day Dun called together the elders of the congregation; they formed a session and at once held their first meeting with Dun as moderator. The financial terms of a new contract with Dun differed slightly from those of the original. He agreed to itinerate between Newark and Stamford Township where a church had been built in 1791. His salary was £100 New York currency annually.

On 1 Nov. 1794 after the successful completion of his trial period Dun petitioned Lieutenant Governor John Graves SIMCOE for 1,200 acres of land, promising that "if your Petr reside here it shall constitute his glory and ambition, to sow the Seeds of Loyalty, Morality and religion among his congregation." On 8 Nov. 1795 Simcoe wrote to the Duke of Portland that local support in the Newark area for the construction of a church for the Church of England minister Robert Addison* had diminished because "unfortunately the last year a Presbyterian Clergyman having arrived from Scotland the Inhabitants of all denominations built a place of Worship, so that I apprehend very little assistance will be expected from them in the Erection of the Episcopal Church." Simcoe's obvious displeasure notwithstanding, Dun's petition was successful and on 31 Dec. 1798, 800 acres were finally patented in Ancaster Township and 400 in Pelham Township.

Two and a half years after his arrival in Newark, Dun abruptly left the ministry. His reasons are uncertain, but in a land petition of 28 Dec. 1796 he mentions his resignation because of "certain discouraging circumstances," stating that he "professes the Christian religion, & obedience to the Laws and has lived inoffensively in the Country." He was succeeded briefly in 1802 by his friend John Young who had had to resign his Montreal pulpit because of alcoholism. It was only with John Burns*'s arrival in Newark, now

Duncan

Niagara, in 1805 that the congregation finally secured a regular minister. Dun might have been successful in Scotland ministering to an established congregation. In Newark he was isolated, the nearest Church of Scotland minister being John BETHUNE at Williamstown in Glengarry County. He was therefore unable to secure ordination and could not perform marriages and christenings, rites essential to a pioneer community. Moreover, had ministers of his denomination been at hand to offer counsel and companionship it is possible the scepticism that beset him might have been allayed. But although he left the pulpit Dun continued his association with the church and rented a pew.

Dun now began a career as a merchant. In his 1796 petition he had asked for a town lot in Newark and a patent was issued on 3 Aug. 1799. On 26 December he sold one of his Pelham lots for £25, possibly to finance the building of his store. He established himself in the town as a general merchant offering a variety of wares for sale ranging from books to rum, coffee, sugar, and dry goods. Whether or not he was a successful merchant is not known, but in January 1801 he advertised that circumstances had obliged him "to deny credit even to his most punctual customers." In 1800 he was one of the signatories in the petitioning campaign of small merchants, office holders, and loyalist officers against the improvements proposed for the Niagara portage by the leading merchant in the province, Robert HAMILTON, and his associates. By 1802 Dun had acquired a measure of local prominence. That year he was elected town assessor and the following year pound-keeper. In 1803 he drowned when the sloop *Lady Washington* went down in Lake Ontario.

Dun had not married and died intestate, leaving his creditors to petition for administration of his estate. Robert Hamilton and Dun's principal creditors, Patrick Robertson and Company of Montreal, to whom he owed at least £1,400, sought control from Lieutenant Governor Peter HUNTER. The decision was made in favour of the Robertson company's authorized local agents, the Niagara merchant John MacKay and Samuel Hatt*, brother of RICHARD.

E. A. McDOUGALL

Ancaster Land Registry Office (Ancaster, Ont.), Abstract index to deeds, I: ff.33, 99 (mfm. at AO). AO, RG 1, A-I-6: 347–48; C-IV, Ancaster Township, concession 1, lot 31; concession 2, lot 31; concession 12, lots 14–17; Pelham Township, concession 12, lots 14–17; RG 22, ser.155, will of John Dun; RG 53, ser.2-2, 2: ff.3–4. GRO, Reg. of baptisms, burials, and marriages for the parish of Fintry, Stirlingshire; Reg. of baptisms, burials, and marriages for the parish of St Ninian's, Stirlingshire. Niagara Hist. Soc. Museum (Niagara-on-the-Lake, Ont.), Newark/Niagara Township, minute-book, 1 March 1802, 7 March 1803 (mfm. at AO). PAC, RG 1, L3, 149: D1/41, 150; D2/31, 70.

Pelham Land Registry Office (Welland, Ont.), Abstract index to deeds, 236–38 (mfm. at AO, GS 2870). SRO, CH2/197/6 (Presbytery of Irvine, minute-books, 1759–84). Strathclyde Regional Arch. (Glasgow), TD 59/21, Presbytery of Glasgow, minute-books, March 1749–11 Aug. 1762. "Accounts of receiver-general of U.C.," AO *Report*, 1914: 736, 739, 746, 750, 774. *Corr. of Lieut. Governor Simcoe* (Cruikshank), 4: 134–35. "Journals of Legislative Assembly of U.C.," AO *Report*, 1909: 135-36. Presbyterian Church in the United States of America, General Assembly, *Acts and proc.* (Philadelphia), 1794: 23. *Niagara Herald* (Niagara [Niagara-on-the-Lake]), 24, 31 Jan. 1801. *Upper Canada Gazette*, 3 Nov. 1804. Hew Scott et al., *Fasti ecclesiæ scoticanæ: the succession of ministers in the Church of Scotland from the Reformation* (new ed., 9v. to date, Edinburgh, 1915–), 7: 632. *The matriculation albums of the University of Glasgow from 1728 to 1858*, comp. W. I. Addison (Glasgow, 1913), 133. *A roll of the graduates of the University of Glasgow from 31st December, 1727 to 31st December, 1897 with short biographical notes*, comp. W. I. Addison (Glasgow, 1898), 168. E. R. Arthur, *St. Andrew's Church, Niagara-on-the-Lake* (Toronto, 1938), 3, 27. *An historical narrative of some important events in the life of First Church, St. Catharines, 1831–1931*, ed. J. A. Tuer (Toronto, 1931), 1–3. *History of St. Andrew's Presbyterian Church, 1791–1975* ([Niagara-on-the-Lake, 1975]). A. L. Lonsdale and H. R. Kaplan, *A guide to sunken ships in American waters* (Arlington, Va., 1964). Wilson, "Enterprises of Robert Hamilton."

DUNCAN, HENRY, naval officer, office holder, and politician; b. *c.* 1735; m. 27 Nov. 1761 Mary French in Dartmouth, England, and they had two sons and one daughter; d. there 7 Oct. 1814.

Little can be ascertained about Henry Duncan's early years. It is likely that he was born in Dundee, Scotland, and it is possible that he was related to Adam Duncan, victor of the battle of Camperdown. He entered the Royal Navy on 10 May 1755 as an able seaman on the *Nassau*, perhaps after early service with the East India Company. Following a period in the Mediterranean, the ship went to Halifax, N.S., in 1757 under Vice-Admiral Francis Holburne, as part of the planned expedition against Louisbourg, Île Royale (Cape Breton Island). Duncan passed his lieutenant's examination on 3 Jan. 1759 and was appointed to the *America*. After service on several other ships he was paid off at the peace in 1763. Duncan remained on half pay for six years, during which time he was promoted commander (26 May 1768). From 1769 to 1772 he commanded the *Wasp* sloop on the home station. On 7 Feb. 1776 he was promoted captain and appointed flag-captain to Lord Howe in the *Eagle*, on board which he was present at the actions off New York City. After again serving as Howe's flag-captain in the *Victory* at the third relief of Gibraltar in 1782, on 17 Jan. 1783 he was once more placed on half pay.

Duncan's enforced leisure lasted only until 2 April, when he was appointed resident commissioner of the

Halifax dockyard by Howe, now first lord of the Admiralty. As commissioner, Duncan was the representative of the Navy Board, the administrative arm of the Admiralty, and orders from London to the dockyard officers and reports from them were transmitted through him. He was in charge of the clerical and shipwright officers, organized local contracts, and negotiated with the commanders of naval vessels over the problems of refitting and storing ships. Immediately after his arrival in October he faced several difficulties. Among them were the need for shipping to England large quantities of stores evacuated from New York and Florida, a local shortage of food which required his supplying transports to take it where needed, and the influx of the loyalists, who had been arriving in Halifax since May. Duncan was instrumental in shipping the refugees elsewhere in Nova Scotia, as in April 1784 when Governor John Parr* requested him to move some persons from Port Mouton to Passamaquoddy Bay (N.B.). Later problems included the supervision of pilots for the Bay of Fundy, a scarcity of specie, a shortage of stores from England to build up the yard establishment, and, most important, the friction generated between Duncan and active commanders who wished to have a dominant role in the allotment of supplies to their ships. One quarrel stemming from this friction resulted in the dismissal of the storekeeper of the yard, George Thomas, by Sir Charles Douglas*, commander-in-chief in North America. Thomas went to London to clear his name and was reinstated.

During Duncan's long tenure the dockyard was continuously developed since Halifax had achieved a new importance with the independence of the southern colonies. A hospital was completed in 1783, the careening wharf was improved throughout the 1780s, and the dockyard property was enlarged in 1790. In the late 1780s Duncan travelled to the Miramichi River, N.B., in search of mast timber. Although this trade developed, his early reports on the availability of large masts proved to be overenthusiastic, since the trees selected were found to be decayed in the centre.

In Halifax, Duncan was a member of the North British Society, and was elected its president in 1796. He was appointed by Parr a member of the Council in 1788 but rarely attended, resigning in 1801. Duncan was also associated in a business way with a fellow Scot, Alexander Brymer, deputy paymaster of the forces. Brymer is reputed to have made £250,000 from his position. There is very little evidence about Duncan's ability to profit similarly from his post, but he can hardly have amassed such a large amount. At the same time, however, he more than likely made some profit: he had a good deal of freedom in the awarding of local contracts and in such matters as the disposal of ships not worth repairing; moreover, his access to government hard cash must have been an advantage in a society which was often short of specie. In 1796 Lieutenant Governor Sir John WENTWORTH described him as "very rich," and his occupation as "the best employment in this county or these provinces." Duncan's will gives evidence of comfortable if not great wealth, including a house and land at Dartmouth, N.S., and a "plantation" in St John's, Nfld.

In the spring of 1797 Duncan returned to London for treatment of "a complaint in his head, which breaks through the upper part of his eye." He was replaced as commissioner in 1799 by Isaac Coffin*. During his time in England Duncan, still paid as commissioner, was appointed to Coffin's position at Sheerness, Kent. Duncan returned to Halifax on 19 Aug. 1800, sold his land, and left again for London on 11 November. On 21 Jan. 1801 he was appointed deputy controller of the Navy Board, and resigned on 20 June 1806.

The evidence for Duncan's tenure as commissioner suggests that he was a tough and experienced officer, efficient by the standards of the age and not devoid of imagination. He enjoyed good relations with Parr and probably with Wentworth as well; moreover, he took the part of his men in the dockyard and was not cantankerous or hot-headed, as he demonstrated by maintaining his calm during the Douglas–Thomas quarrel of 1783–84. Relations between naval officers and the commissioner were, however, likely to be troublesome whatever the personalities involved because sea-going officers looked down on the administration, even in the person of formerly active officers such as Duncan. In this difficulty Duncan's position was strengthened by his being on good terms with Charles Middleton, controller of the Navy Board during the 1780s.

Duncan's elder son, Henry, entered the navy in 1781 but was lost at sea off Newfoundland in 1801. His daughter, Isabella, married Lieutenant Thomas Twisden in Halifax on 14 Dec. 1790. Nothing is known of his son Arthur.

R. J. B. KNIGHT

National Maritime Museum, HAL/F/1–2 (Halifax Yard, Commissioners' letterbooks, 1783–89). PRO, ADM 106/1330; 106/2027–28; 106/3174; CO 217/37: f.74; PROB 11/1562/604. *The naval miscellany*, ed. J. K. Laughton *et al*. (4v. to date, London, 1902–), 1.

DUNCAN, RICHARD, army officer, merchant, judge, and office holder; b. in Berwick-upon-Tweed, England, son of John Duncan and Maria March; m. October 1784 Mary Wright in Montreal, Que., and they had one son and one daughter; d. February 1819 near Schenectady, N.Y.

Richard Duncan came to America in 1755 with his

Duncan

father, a lieutenant in Thomas Gage*'s 44th Foot, and in 1758 he himself was commissioned ensign and quartermaster in the regiment. At the conclusion of the Seven Years' War he left the army and joined his father, now an Indian trader, at Schenectady. Between 1761 and 1766 on his own and in various partnerships with merchants such as James Sterling*, John Porteous, James Phyn, and Alexander ELLICE, John Duncan had established posts at Niagara (near Youngstown, N.Y.), Detroit (Mich.), and Michilimackinac (Mackinaw City, Mich.). He also founded the firm which on his retirement in 1767 became Phyn, Ellice and Company. Richard rejoined the army in 1765 as an ensign in the 55th Foot but, after brief service in Ireland, he returned in 1768 to aid his father, who had experienced financial difficulties. By the time of the American revolution the Duncans had acquired extensive landholdings but had also accumulated a joint debt of £3,000.

Though his family remained in Schenectady throughout the revolution Duncan was an active loyalist. In June 1776 he assisted Adjutant General Allan Maclean*'s escape to Canada and the following year he joined John Burgoyne*'s army at Saratoga (Schuylerville, N.Y.). After the surrender on 17 October, Duncan travelled to the province of Quebec where he was commissioned captain in the first battalion of Sir John Johnson*'s King's Royal Regiment of New York. At the conclusion of the war he went on half pay and settled at Rapid du Plat (Mariatown, Ont.). For his services he and his family received large quantities of land, to which he added more by purchase.

Duncan enjoyed the continuing support of Johnson, the most influential man in the new western settlements, and was rewarded in other ways as well. On 24 July 1788 Lord Dorchester [Guy CARLETON] organized four new administrative districts in what was to become Upper Canada and Duncan, along with such other local notables as John McDONELL (Aberchalder) and John Munro*, reaped the benefits. He was appointed to the magistracy, the Court of Common Pleas, and the land board of the Luneburg District, and he attended the meetings of all three institutions regularly until the autumn of 1791. That year his father died and he returned to Schenectady to handle "the wreck of an estate left under the greatest embarrassment." In 1792 his local and provincial prominence was recognized when he was made lieutenant of the county of Dundas [see Hazelton SPENCER] and one of the nine original legislative councillors. Five years later he became a member of the district Heir and Devisee Commission.

From 1791 until 1805 Duncan spent most of his time in New York though he carried out the duties of his Upper Canadian offices intermittently for a number of years. He made his first appearance in the council on 17 June 1793. Of the ten sessions before his removal for non-attendance in 1805, he attended only four. His participation was negligible and his effectiveness limited to a minor piece of legislation in 1798 establishing the boundaries of Eastern District townships. Speculating in land was Duncan's major concern in Upper Canada during the 1790s. Like many of the loyalist officers in the district he took advantage of the township grants proclaimed by Lieutenant Governor SIMCOE in 1792. With associates such as Peter Drummond, Munro, and particularly Thomas Fraser*, in 1793 he received seven townships. When in 1796 the government considered taking action against Duncan and his associates for non-fulfilment of their settlement obligations, he attempted to fend off the threat. The spokesman of the group, Duncan tried on 2 July to enlist Surveyor General David William Smith* as a silent partner but failed. Eight days later he wrote to Smith again, concerned that he had given "some offence to the Governor." Indeed, he had thought that Simcoe's favourable response to "some hints" he had offered on the subject of the townships would have resulted in the Executive Council complying "with our wishes." Having been unsuccessful in deterring the administration, Duncan sought compensation of 10,000 acres per proprietor, but when the township grants were rescinded in 1797 he and his partners received only 1,200 acres apiece.

Duncan does not seem to have lived in Upper Canada at all after 1809 or 1810, though he had intended to return permanently and wished to resume his seat on the council. He remained at his father's former home, the Hermitage, near Schenectady until his death.

J. K. JOHNSON

AO, RG 1, A-I-6: 347–48, 792–95, 1937–39. PAC, MG 9, D8, 8 (transcript; mfm. at AO); RG 1, L3, 149: D1/62; 150: D3/7, 84; RG 5, A1: 2202, 2272, 3405, 3477, 4195; RG 68, General index, 1651–1841. PRO, AO 12/32; AO 13, bundle 12. *Corr. of Lieut. Governor Simcoe* (Cruikshank), 1: 10–11, 88–90, 147–48. "District of Luneburg: Court of Common Pleas," AO *Report*, 1917: 353–451. "Grants of crown lands in U.C.," AO *Report*, 1928: 44, 117, 160. *Johnson papers* (Sullivan et al.), 4: 237, 266; 5: 11, 47, 163; 7: 457; 10: 569–70. "The journals of the Legislative Council of Upper Canada . . . ," AO *Report*, 1910: 21, 28–29, 58–59, 133–37, 205. *NYCD* (O'Callaghan and Fernow), 7: 502, 508. Osgoode, "Letters" (Colgate), *OH*, 46: 88. "U.C. land book B," AO *Report*, 1930: 2–4. "U.C. land book C," AO *Report*, 1930: 174; 1931: 44. "U.C. land book D," AO *Report*, 1931: 168, 172. Armstrong, *Handbook of Upper Canadian chronology*, 33. G.B., WO, *Army list*, 1759, 1766. J. S. Carter, *The story of Dundas . . .* (Iroquois, Ont., 1905; repr. Belleville, Ont., 1973), 449–63. Duncan Fraser, *William Fraser, senior, U.E., and his descendants in Fulton County, New York, and Grenville County, Ontario* (Johnstown, N.Y., 1964), 12. Gates, *Land policies of U.C.,*

40–41. R. H. Fleming, "Phyn, Ellice and Company of Schenectady," *Contributions to Canadian Economics* (Toronto), 4 (1932): 8–11.

DUNIÈRE, LOUIS, merchant, landowner, militia officer, and politician; b. 7 May 1723 at Quebec, son of Louis Dunière and Marguerite Durand; m. there 1 July 1748 Élisabeth Trefflé, *dit* Rottot, and they had 17 children; d. 31 May 1806 at Berthier (Berthier-sur-Mer), Lower Canada.

Louis Dunière's father, a native of Saint-Saturnin (Saint-Cernin), France, arrived in the colony shortly before 1714; at Quebec he was active as a merchant, in association with François Perrault* after 1719. Working with his father, young Dunière doubtless acquired from him the rudiments of bookkeeping and other elements of commerce. In 1744, at the age of 21, he was still living at his parents' house on Rue Saint-Pierre. When he married four years later, he was a man of business, with property valued at 14,020 *livres*.

Dunière embarked on operations in real estate with the purchase of lands at Saint-Thomas-de-la-Pointe-à-la-Caille (Montmagny) in 1754 and 1757; in 1762 he became manager of the seigneury of Bellechasse. When the census was taken that year, he owned 43 head of livestock and a large quantity of seed, and he employed six servants. With a growing surplus of produce, he entered into a three-year business partnership in the grain trade with Henry Boone, a Quebec merchant, on 20 Sept. 1769.

On 4 Aug. 1775, just before the American invasion [*see* Benedict ARNOLD; Richard Montgomery*], Dunière was appointed a captain in the Canadian militia at Quebec, his company being assigned to the defence of the *faubourg* Saint-Louis. The part he played in the siege of Quebec is unrecorded; but he still held the captaincy at his death.

In the early 1780s Dunière continued to manage his commercial enterprise, as the transactions recorded in his account-books of the period show. He also made a business trip to London, returning in 1782 in company with Henry Hamilton*, just named lieutenant governor of Quebec, and several merchants, including Thomas Aylwin*, Adam Lymburner*, John LEES, and Meredith Wills, his future son-in-law. The years following witness a diversification of Dunière's interests: in association with three other Quebec merchants, his son-in-law Pierre MARCOUX, John ANTROBUS, and Jacques-Nicolas PERRAULT, he obtained from Lieutenant Governor Henry Hope* in 1786 a permit to establish a sedentary fishery on the Labrador coast, near a Moravian mission [*see* Jens Haven*], to take cod, salmon, and seals. At Quebec, Dunière bought properties that would serve his grain-trading ventures: on 21 Oct. 1788, for £1,000,

he acquired from the London businessman John Fraser a house, sheds, and wharf along the river at the foot of Cap Diamant. Around this time he went into ship building but, being unable to devote himself fully to it, in 1793 rented his yard to Patrick Beatson*.

Politically, Dunière had, in addresses and petitions, frequently assured the British authorities of his loyalty. He was not backward, however, in voicing complaints about the administration of justice or proposing the introduction of hemp growing in the colony. On three separate occasions, in 1784, 1785, and 1790, he joined with others (both British and Canadians) in calling for the establishment of representative institutions in the province. Their aspirations on this score were to be fulfilled in 1791, and in June 1792 Dunière was elected for Hertford to the House of Assembly of Lower Canada. At the opening of the first session, in December, Dunière as the oldest member of the chamber proposed Jean-Antoine PANET as speaker. Over the vehement opposition of the British mercantile élite, Panet was chosen by 28 votes to 18. During his term in the assembly, Dunière took a stand opposing the exclusive legal recognition of the English text of laws and parliamentary debates; he also supported a bill to allocate the proceeds of the Jesuit estates to the education of young people. At the time of the 1796 election Dunière withdrew from active politics, but his son Louis-François* was chosen for Hertford. Still following in his father's footsteps, Louis-François in his turn nominated Panet to the post of speaker of the assembly the next year.

Despite his advancing years, Dunière remained deeply involved in business dealings. In 1796 the army purchased £428 worth of supplies from him. That same year he applied for a permit to export to England supplies in his warehouses – 2,000 quarters of flour, 1,500 quintals of biscuit, 1,200 bushels of peas, and 600 of Indian corn. He was associated at this time with the Montreal merchant Francis Badgley* in the firm of Dunière, Badgley and Company. In 1800 Dunière appears finally to have abandoned commerce, selling to his former employee Pierre BREHAUT the lot, wharf, and buildings at the foot of Cap Diamant.

Thenceforth Dunière concentrated his investments in landed property, in which he had already demonstrated an interest. In 1801 he acquired by an emphyteutic deed all the titles to the seigneury of Bellechasse in return for an annual rent of 1,500 *livres* and 450 bushels of wheat payable to the nuns of the Hôpital Général at Quebec. He thereby became owner of a domain at Berthier comprising a stone house, four frame-houses, three mills, a barn, and other buildings. In 1789 he had been among the founders of the Agriculture Society of the District of Quebec, and two years later he had signed a petition opposing any proposal to commute seigneurial tenure to freehold.

Dunlop

Overburdened with debt – he owed £1,241 to the heirs of his brother-in-law Kenelm CHANDLER, the keeper of Ordnance, and £1,556 to John PAINTER, a Quebec merchant – Louis Dunière sold the domain of Berthier in 1805. He was still residing in the area at his death on 31 May 1806.

STANLEY BRÉHAUT RYERSON

ANQ-Q, CE1-1, 7 mai 1723, 1er juill. 1748; CN1-83, 21 oct. 1788; CN1-178, 6 mars 1798; CN1-205, 20 déc. 1782; CN1-250, 20 sept. 1769; CN1-256, 31 May 1791; CN1-262, 19 nov. 1800, 8 oct. 1803, 25 févr. 1805. PAC, RG 1, L3L: 39017. "La milice canadienne-française à Québec en 1775," *BRH*, 11 (1905): 227. "Le recensement de Québec en 1744," ANQ *Rapport*, 1939–40: 130. "Le recensement du gouvernement de Québec en 1762," ANQ *Rapport*, 1925–26: 38. *Quebec Gazette*, 24 Jan. 1765; 20 Sept. 1766; 27 June 1782; 30 June 1785; 18 Dec. 1788; 17 Dec. 1789; 24 March, 19 Aug. 1791; 24 May, 20 Dec. 1792; 13 Feb. 1794; 26 Jan. 1797; 17 June 1799; 29 Dec. 1803. *Quebec almanac*, 1788–1805. F.-J. Audet et Fabre Surveyer, *Les députés au premier Parl. du Bas-Canada*, 176–85. Ouellet, *Hist. économique*, 153. Paquet et Wallot, *Patronage et pouvoir dans le Bas-Canada*, 129. Tousignant, "La genèse et l'avènement de la constitution de 1791," 447. Édouard Fabre Surveyer, "Les deux premiers députés du comté de Hertford (Bellechasse-Montmagny): Pierre Marcoux et Louis Dunière," *Le Canada français* (Québec), 32 (1944–45): 404–17. Hare, "L'Assemblée législative du Bas-Canada," *RHAF*, 27: 371–73. "La mission de MM. Adhémar et Delisle en Angleterre en 1783–84," *BRH*, 32 (1926): 623–25.

DUNLOP, JAMES, businessman and militia officer; b. November 1757 in Glasgow, Scotland, third and youngest son of David Dunlop, merchant and textile manufacturer, and his wife, a daughter of James McGregor of Clober; d. unmarried 28 Aug. 1815 in Montreal, Lower Canada.

James Dunlop received a "sound commercial education," which included instruction in "bookkeeping, mathematics and navigation," probably at the High School of Glasgow. Like many other young men of the city's mercantile class, he was sent out to Virginia, the focus of the tobacco trade and the main centre of Scottish overseas enterprise; he arrived, it seems, early in 1773 and settled on the James River opposite Jamestown as an employee of William and John Hay, correspondents of his brothers Robert and Alexander Dunlop, partners in Glasgow. At the outbreak of the American revolution, according to James's nephew, Alexander Dunlop of Clober, he served as a loyalist in several campaigns in Virginia and the southern colonies.

Early in 1779 Dunlop came to Quebec and, in the upper part of a house on Rue Saint-Pierre, established a small store in which he sold dry goods, hardware, groceries, and "fancy goods," imported on credit from Glasgow. Having lost his slender working capital

during the revolution, he formed a partnership with Andrew Porteous and worked closely with John Porteous and Daniel Sutherland*, all of Montreal. The Porteouses were members of a family connection which included a number of Patersons equally active in the trade of the colony, was already well established in the province, and was also of Ayrshire origin. Like many other Scottish merchants in the colony, Dunlop was involved in the scandal surrounding John Cochrane, agent at Quebec between 1779 and 1782 of a British firm responsible for providing Governor HALDIMAND with the specie needed by the colonial administration. Cochrane, without authorization, had advanced on credit to colonial merchants large sums in bills of exchange, and Haldimand's suits at law against some of the tardy debtors, through judge Adam Mabane*, provoked a financial crisis in the colony. The amount given to Dunlop had been small in comparison with the advances to many of these merchants, but in 1787 he still owed £3,000.

Dunlop's energy, resourcefulness, and desire to open new fields of endeavour had meanwhile driven him in 1781 to dissolve his partnership with Porteous, and, apparently the following year, to set himself up in Montreal, which was burgeoning as the centre of Canadian commerce. He continued, nevertheless, to import and export to some extent through Quebec where he maintained an agent, John Pagan. By 1785 Dunlop was established in a warehouse, with its own wharf, on Montreal's main business thoroughfare, Rue Saint-Paul. It was probably from there that he sold the large assortments of dry goods, cutlery, alcoholic beverages, sugar, and other products that he continued to import. Foreseeing the possibilities in the flour and lumber trades, he began in the early 1780s to travel extensively throughout the colony, negotiating purchases of grain and timber. His activities in this business, and the wide range of contacts he established, had placed him in a strong position by 1788 when an act of the British parliament permitted vessels from Canada to carry lumber and provisions to the West Indies and to bring back, free of duty, sugars and rum to the value of the outward cargo. By 1789 he was also exporting shiploads of choice Canadian oak to Leith, Scotland.

Wines and spirits were another specialty. Dunlop imported high-grade rums and whiskies from Greenock and found a ready market among habitants and fur traders. His rum, identified by the initials J. D. and a thistle burnt into the barrel, was highly regarded. Before the war with Spain began in 1796, he imported from Cadiz shiploads of Spanish, Madeira, and Portuguese wines, supplying the domestic cellars of most of the fur-trade magnates, including Simon McTAVISH. Dunlop also imported from Cadiz on a large scale rum, sugar, and tobacco. He maintained a useful network of agents, mostly Scottish firms, in

Dunlop

Tuscany (Italy) at Leghorn, in Spain at Cadiz and Barcelona, in Portugal at Lisbon, and on Madeira. Spirits also formed a large part of his trade with York (Toronto), where he supplied Alexander Wood* and William Allan* beginning in 1798. Dunlop was linked to Upper Canada as well through his association with Richard DUNCAN and his group of "insatiate" (according to Chief Justice William Osgoode*) land speculators, among them Coll McGregor and James Caldwell of New York State. In 1794 their petition for hundreds of thousands of acres in the Beauharnois region of Lower Canada was rejected, as was another in 1796 by less important men, in an association of which Dunlop was leader, for the entire 64,000 acres of Derry Township on the north shore of the Ottawa River.

In Montreal Dunlop rented a house on Rue Saint-Paul until March 1788. By 1795 he was ensconced, on the outskirts of the city, in a handsome mansion that became a social centre; visitors to Montreal testified to Dunlop's warm-hearted hospitality, which was characteristic of Montreal's Scottish nabobs. His liveried servants were invariably brought from Scotland. Like most of the city's Scottish merchants, he had been a member of the Protestant Congregation of Montreal (Christ Church), an Anglican body, but he had joined the Scotch Presbyterian Church, later known as the St Gabriel Street Church, when it was formed in the early 1790s.

Dunlop also participated in the public life of the city. In 1792 he offered himself as candidate for the House of Assembly in the riding of Montreal West, but the electors preferred James McGILL and Jean-Baptiste-Amable Durocher. As fear rose among the British population of the activities of French revolutionary agents operating in Lower Canada from the United States [see David McLane*; John BLACK], Dunlop became active in the British Militia of the Town and Banlieu of Montreal; he joined it as an ensign in 1790 and was promoted lieutenant in 1794.

Dunlop exploited fully the favourable economic conditions in the period of potential and open conflict with France and then the United States that lasted from 1793 to 1814. In 1797 he wrote that his business activities had become so numerous and so varied that he required additional staff from Scotland. By 1802 his headquarters on Rue Saint-Paul were among the largest mercantile premises in the colony. Dunlop's exports for 1803 were estimated to be worth a total of £60,000, surpassed among Montreal firms only by the North West Company and Parker, Gerrard, Ogilvy and Company [see John OGILVY]. His original import business had by then been overshadowed by new lines of activity; in 1800 he stated that his imports from Scotland made him no profit, but that he was rapidly accumulating a large fortune through bill brokering, shipowning, and the export of bulk products.

Dunlop had engaged in bill brokering since the Cochrane scandal, and in the interim he had learned to deal in government bills of all kinds, routing them via New York where good gains could be made in specie. It was the war with France, however, that launched him into the field of high finance. In the early 1800s he was purchasing bills drawn on the paymaster general – £21,000 worth in June 1800 alone – at a discount of almost two per cent and selling them in New York for specie at a premium of almost two per cent. Bill brokering was his major activity as a financier, and he conducted it with skill and foresight. By 1812 he was the most important operator in British North America and the recognized channel through which the mercantile fraternity of Montreal and Quebec disposed of army bills, as is evidenced by the records of his transactions with Frederick William Ermatinger* among others. The magnitude of Dunlop's dealings entitle him to be considered Canada's first large-scale bill broker.

The war with France had also spurred Dunlop to move into shipbuilding. In 1793 he took a long-term lease on a lot at Pointe-à-Callière, Montreal, where he constructed a shipyard, staffing it with skilled craftsmen brought from the Clyde and New York and local men and apprentices who were acquiring shipbuilding skills. From this yard came the vessels for his trade with Europe and the West Indies, as well as for privateering. In order to augment his fleet more rapidly he bought vessels, such as the schooner *Marie* in 1794 from the Quebec merchant John Munro, the sloop *Peggy* three years later, and, in 1805, the *Industrie*, constructed by the Quebec shipbuilders François and Romain Robitaille. In 1806 Dunlop's fleet numbered three large ocean-going vessels, and seven smaller craft for the river and coastal trades. By the end of 1811 he had six vessels named after members of the Dunlop family, and that May the launching of the last of these, the *James Dunlop*, built at a cost of £10,000, attracted a crowd of 5,000. The following year Dunlop laid the keels of three more large vessels, one of them, the *George Canning*, of 482 tons. In 1814 he purchased the *Earl St Vincent*, an East Indiaman of over 900 tons, and was planning to buy several others. Shipbuilding costs in Lower Canada were approximately 35 per cent higher than on the Clyde, but Dunlop had faith in the future of the industry in British North America if first-class materials were used by competent craftsmen.

War had sharpened demand in Britain for bulk products such as potash, lumber, grain, and flour; in the autumn of 1797 Dunlop remitted bills to Glasgow for more than £17,000, derived from grain exports in the preceding eight months. By 1800 he was considering the ambitious project of cornering Canadian flour and potash supplies, and in 1805 he nearly succeeded in monopolizing the latter, which he

Dunlop

exported on a large scale at a handsome profit for use in the cotton, linen, and woollen mills on the Clyde. Similarly, in the years 1812 and 1813, when Scotland suffered a crisis in provisioning that led to the formation of "meal-mobs," Dunlop dispatched several thousand tons of flour from his stocks, the most extensive in the province, and was able to secure considerable returns. With the Scottish market, supply contracts for the British army on the Iberian peninsula, and provisioning of the forces in North America during the War of 1812, he bid fair to being the key operator in the Canadian grain trade.

The interlocking of Dunlop's shipbuilding and privateering activities with his commodity operations is shown by the special permission accorded him on 22 July 1812 by the Legislative Council of Lower Canada: he was authorized to dispatch his large and heavily armed vessel, the *James Dunlop*, to Lisbon with army provisions despite Napoleon's embargo, since "her force [of armament] . . . will in all probability be equal to her protection." He was so confident in the strength of his ships, all of which were accorded letters of marque as privateers, that he refused to insure them throughout the war, apparently considering insurance rates excessive; his risk was justified, since he lost only the *James Dunlop*, wrecked in 1812 during a storm off the coast of Anticosti Island but well compensated for by the capture of an enemy ship. In 1814 he boasted in a letter to his sister in Glasgow that he had done "more good business since the War began than ever I did in the same space of time" and that he was the wealthiest man in the province. Even making allowance for his natural ebullience, there seems little reason to doubt the assertion: in November 1813 one of his cargoes of imported goods was valued at £50,000 including duty; six months later he remitted what was apparently the largest bill of exchange – £32,500 – yet sent from the colony; in August 1815 he had a stock of goods in hand estimated at £100,000; and that year the *Montreal Herald* noted that his fortune was "supposed to be greater than ever was acquired by any individual in this country."

Dunlop's ability to exploit the favourable economic climate in the 1790s and early 1800s was due in part to the wide range of business contacts that he had established in Canada and Britain. He had earned the confidence of the Montreal merchants from the time he settled in the city, and in the 1780s and 1790s was frequently called upon to act as trustee for the estates of deceased businessmen. He never engaged in the fur trade as did many of the Montreal merchants, but out of solidarity with them he had signed in 1782 and 1785 several petitions in which the fur magnates requested from the government protection and freedom in the prosecution of that trade. Although he separated from Andrew Porteous, Dunlop maintained his connection

with the Paterson–Porteous group; its members, and especially the younger ones (the Robertsons, John Ogilvy, and their close allies), were active in opposition to the NWC in the 1790s and, as part of the Parker, Gerrard, and Ogilvy empire, the group became one of the most important elements in the trade between Quebec and Britain. Like John Porteous, Dunlop was on close terms with James and Andrew McGill, with whom he shared a Glasgow background, and in 1806 he was executor of the latter's estate.

Unlike the merchants of the fur trade, whose business was transacted through London, Dunlop conducted his affairs in Britain largely with Scottish correspondents. He had contacts with James Dunlop of Garnkirk, the Dunlops of Lockerbie, and his brothers Alexander, a bookseller, and Robert, a linen manufacturer, who still acted in Glasgow as purchasing agents and exporters for the wide range of dry goods and other commodities Dunlop imported. However, his most important Scottish agent was Allan, Kerr and Company of Greenock, a leading firm in the trade to the Canadas.

Throughout the early 1800s Dunlop continued to participate enthusiastically in the Montreal militia. A captain in 1803, he became a major, commanding four companies of the 1st Battalion, including the artillery. In June 1811 he and Étienne Nivard Saint-Dizier were chosen to take an address from the citizens of Montreal to Governor CRAIG, who was about to depart for London. In November 1812 part of the militia, including Dunlop's artillery company, was placed on alert. The following year he expressed the hope that the American invaders would penetrate to Montreal so that "my Great-Guns will make Thousands of them Sleep with their Fathers." His military service, however, involved him in a dispute that led to his court martial in December 1813. He was accused of insulting a subordinate officer at Lachine named Hart Logan when an enemy attack was expected, and of being drunk at the time. Dunlop told Logan that he "esteemed him less than the driver of a milk cart," an insult typical of Ayrshire parlance but perhaps also derived from the little dogcarts used to transport milk in the colony at this period. Ordered to apologize to Logan by a military court presided over by his friend James McGill, Dunlop refused and lost his commission. The incident did Dunlop no damage in the community; he was commended by many for his pride and sang-froid before the tribunal. Dunlop was distressed when the war with the United States ended in 1814, and he wrote to George Canning, ambassador extraordinary to Portugal, as well as to the member of parliament for Glasgow, that "we will never again have the same good opportunity of bringing the United States to our own terms."

In August 1815, perhaps as the result of an

excursion late in July to the Chaudière Falls near Quebec, Dunlop developed inflammation of the bowels, for which he seems to have put off medical attention. He died on 28 August in Montreal. At the time of his death he was full of new projects: planning more and larger vessels for his fleet, embarking on a massive scheme to import and speculate in thousands of tons of Irish flour, and pondering the possibility of instituting a regular passenger service across the Atlantic. In a letter in 1814 to his brother-in-law he had claimed to "have been more bold in my Speculations than any other person or Company in this Province," and the *Quebec Gazette* acknowledged that he had been "one of the most eminent, respectable and enterprising" merchants in Montreal. In Dunlop the colony lost a lively businessman who might have made a great contribution in the ensuing period of commercial growth and formation of banks. Within two years of his death, the Bank of Montreal was founded, and his vision of regular transatlantic passenger service was being pursued by other men.

A colourful and imaginative figure, Dunlop was a worthy contemporary of Simon McTavish, also known as "the Marquis," and other characters who composed the Montreal trading circle. Throughout his life, though very much a progressive businessman of the enterprising 18th-century type, he had been keenly conscious of his heritage, coming as he did from a cadet branch of the ancient Ayrshire house of Dunlop, and being linked as well to the Scottish national hero William Wallace. Dunlop's pride in his lineage made him irascible if crossed and quick to take affront, although most who encountered him noted his good-natured hospitality, tolerance, and aplomb. To his relatives in Scotland he was extremely generous, but tended to be "steering." They regarded him with some trepidation. During his visits home they experienced his impulsive rages, particularly over the education and upbringing of his nephews and nieces, matters that profoundly concerned him; as his nephew Alexander Dunlop of Clober recalled, "The Canadian was kind, but overbearing." Dunlop's characteristic sang-froid was manifested on the occasion of a fire that razed his Montreal warehouse; as he watched the blaze, seated on a sofa rescued from the building, he remarked, "Why should not a man enjoy his own fireside?" In Clober's words, he was "a prompt, active and dashing fellow, with indomitable intrepidity, both in maintaining sword and pen. He took fortune by storm, and dared his all to secure it."

The executors of Dunlop's will, dated 12 July 1811, included James McGill (who died two years before Dunlop), John Forsyth*, Isaac Todd, William Lindsay* Jr, John Harkness, and Adam Lymburner Macnider* in Canada; Andrew McNair, his brother-in-law, at Glasgow; and Allan, Kerr and Company and John Denniston, Scottish mercantile and financial

magnates at Greenock. Between £150,000 and £200,000, representing the bulk of Dunlop's fortune, went to his nephews and nieces in Scotland; his sister received an annuity of £1,000. Dunlop also left an endowment of £5,000 to an illegitimate son, James, born in 1810 to Mrs Elizabeth Whitlaw, apparently of Glasgow. Dunlop and Company was wound up following the owner's death, and it appears that the amounts received by Dunlop's heirs fell far short of the real value of the estate.

James Dunlop was a mercantile man of outstanding talent and originality, far beyond his contemporaries, even the fur-trade magnates, in techniques and vision. He was directly responsible for opening up several important lines of Canadian commercial activity, and, certainly, he was one of the founding fathers of Canadian finance.

DAVID S. MACMILLAN and A. J. H. RICHARDSON

James Dunlop seems to be the only British merchant of prime importance in Canada in the 18th century whose personal business correspondence at the height of his career has survived. It may be consulted at the SRO, GD1/151, and at the PAC which holds a microfilm copy (MG 24, D42).

ANQ-Q, CN1-145, 26 July 1805; CN1-256, 12 Nov. 1794, 8 Nov. 1797; CN1-262, 18 juin 1805. PAC, MG 19, A2, ser.3, 33; E1, ser.1, 52: 19771 (copies); RG 1, L3^L: 38841–44; RG 8, I (C ser.), 688E. Private arch., W. H. Dunlop of Doonside (Ayr, Scot.), Dunlop papers. PCA, St Gabriel Street Church (Montreal), Reg. of baptisms, marriages, and burials, 31 Aug. 1815 (mfm. at ANQ-M). PRO, CO 42/48: ff.40–41 (mfm. at PAC). Alexander Dunlop of Clober, *Reminiscences of Alexander Dunlop of Clober, 1792–1880* (Ayr, 1967). *Town of York, 1793–1815* (Firth), 116–17, 126. *Quebec Gazette*, 1779–1815. *Quebec almanac*, 1791–1816. J. F. Bayne, *Dunlop parish; a history of church, parish, and nobility* (Edinburgh, 1935). R. Campbell, *Hist. of Scotch Presbyterian Church*, 96. Archibald Dunlop, *Dunlop of that ilk; memorabilia of the families of Dunlop, with special reference to John Dunlop of Rosebank ... with the whole of the songs, and a large selection from the poems, of John Dunlop* (Glasgow, 1898). Macmillan, "New men in action," *Canadian business hist.* (Macmillan), 44–103; "The Scot as businessman," *The Scottish tradition in Canada*, ed. W. S. Reid (Toronto, 1976; repr. 1979), 179–202; "Demon of the bill brokers," *Canadian Banker and ICB Rev.* (Toronto), 84 (1977), no.1: 14–18.

DUNN. *See also* DUN

DUNN, THOMAS, businessman, seigneur, office holder, politician, judge, and colonial administrator; b. 1729 in Durham, England; m. 27 Nov. 1783 Henriette Guichaud, widow of Pierre Fargues, at Quebec, and they had three children; d. there 15 April 1818.

Unfortunately nothing is known about Thomas

Dunn

Dunn's life before he arrived in Canada. His purpose in coming to set up in the town of Quebec soon after the general capitulation in September 1760 was undoubtedly to take advantage of the various possibilities for economic development afforded by this huge, newly conquered territory. His earliest ventures were those of an enterprising man whose objectives were already firmly fixed. In his early thirties, he gives the impression of being a true member of the rising bourgeoisie, in full possession of the means to achieve his ends. Having in hand some of the assets essential for carving out a place at the top in this future British colony, he would turn them to account on every level – political, judicial, legislative, economic, family, even military – and would have an exemplary career within the framework of an imperial system controlled directly by the mercantilist policy of the metropolitan authorities. Perhaps to a greater degree than in any of his contemporaries, in him personal interests, family interests, and the interests of the state would be joined together in a productive and mutually supportive union.

Dunn's success was even more remarkable because he acted skilfully, prudently, and circumspectly in the management both of his own business and of public affairs. He never let himself be drawn into intrigues and factions, unlike many of his British compatriots, and he always stayed out of party quarrels and rivalries. Reflective and level-headed by disposition, he was too far-sighted to let himself be manœuvred and too discerning not to exploit fully any situation potentially advantageous to him. In this way, throughout half a century of political life he succeeded in retaining his influence with the colonial authority and in profiting fully from the patronage system. He did it with such consummate art that historian Donald Grant Creighton* thought him merely "an undistinguished octogenarian resident of the colony"; unlike so many other more "distinguished" members of the bourgeoisie, however, Dunn left a sizeable fortune at his death. Following Creighton's example, historian Fernand Ouellet mentions Thomas Dunn only once, in his capacity as administrator of Lower Canada. In fact, like so many entrepreneurs under the French régime and the new one, Dunn personified the colonist who took advantage of the imperial system – patronage, networks of friendship and information, lucrative posts, and political power – to attain not only wealth but also the highest office to which a resident of Lower Canada could aspire, that of administrator of the colony.

Before Canada had been handed over definitively to Great Britain by the Treaty of Paris in February 1763, Dunn had already thought of creating a small commercial empire for himself by obtaining the trading lease to the king's posts with his partner John Gray, also of Quebec; William GRANT (1744–

1805) soon became a co-lessee. This acquisition would guarantee a monopoly of the fur trade and the fisheries throughout the crown's domain, an immense area stretching from the eastern limits of the seigneury of La Malbaie to Sept-Îles and including the kingdom of the Saguenay with the posts of Tadoussac and Chicoutimi. James Murray* himself, as "governor of Quebec and its dependencies," authorized this leasing in the king's name. The agreement, signed on 20 Sept. 1762, provided for renewal of the lease for a 14-year period from 1 Oct. 1763 at an annual rent of £400, a relatively trivial sum for a net return estimated at more than five times that figure – £2,500.

Once this first step had been taken, Dunn sought to consolidate his monopolistic control with the purchase of the seigneury of Mille-Vaches, an enclave of 12 square leagues inside the crown's domain below Tadoussac. Originally granted to Robert Giffard* de Moncel, this seigneury had passed into the hands of François Aubert* de La Chesnaye, and Dunn purchased it from his son, Ignace-François, on 23 Feb. 1764. With a foothold of this sort Dunn, as an ambitious bourgeois, was in a good position to extend his commercial empire to the entire lower north shore of the St Lawrence. That same year he paid £2,550 to buy a property with a stone house on Rue Saint-Louis at Quebec for his permanent residence, and in 1769 he acquired an adjacent piece of land. He obtained from the government the grant of a lot in Lower Town on which to build a wharf for commercial purposes. From 1767 to 1783 he also rented the seigneury of Saint-Étienne with some associates.

An opportunity to broaden his already wide field of activity came when on 11 Sept. 1770 his friend and partner William Grant married in a public ceremony Marie-Anne-Catherine Fleury Deschambault, the dowager baroness of Longueuil and great-granddaughter of Louis Jolliet*. By this matrimonial alliance, Grant entered the great family of the descendants and heirs of the renowned explorer, the first seigneur of the Île d'Anticosti, who had engaged in the exploitation of the fisheries around the islands of Mingan, to which he had received a grant. Such matrimonial ties facilitated a link with the descendants and heirs of François Byssot* de la Rivière, who had received the initial grant of the mainland property of Mingan and whose children had been associated with the Jolliets in developing the north shore fisheries. As an astute businessman, Dunn lost no time in using Grant's advantageous marriage to extend his monopoly. Thus, on 18 Oct. 1771 some ten representatives and agents of the great family to which Grant's wife belonged met in the presence of notaries Pierre PANET and Jean-Antoine Saillant*; they gave Dunn and Grant, his partner, a trading lease to the Mingan and Anticosti posts for a 15-year period from 1 Aug. 1772. A trading lease provides a useful basis for estimating the profitability of an operation, which in this case derived its income principally from cod, salmon, porpoise oil, and the hides of seals. The trade seemed sufficiently lucrative for a third partner, Peter Stuart, to be taken in.

Before the trading lease expired the trio of Dunn, Grant, and Stuart succeeded in buying almost all of the seigneuries of Mingan (the mainland and the islands) and Île d'Anticosti, as the "agreement and covenant" signed on 12 Dec. 1789 before notaries Pierre-Louis DESCHENAUX and Charles Stewart recognized. This document describes the complex series of transactions that each of them had engaged in, separately or jointly, to purchase the heirs' property rights. It shows that, through his connections by marriage, William Grant had been able to acquire "the fair and true half" of everything that had been bought by the three partners, for the sum of £2,241.

This stranglehold on the posts along the lower north shore of the St Lawrence made up for the loss of the monopoly on the crown's domain, which Dunn and his partners had suffered early in the autumn of 1786. In 1785 they had been able to get their trading lease on the king's posts renewed for only one year, and this new agreement had been approved in the nick of time by Lieutenant Governor Henry Hamilton* when the authorities in London were on the verge of favouring François BABY and the Davison brothers, Alexander* and George*.

Dunn could take this blow without too much complaint, because from the outset of his career in the province of Quebec he had always enjoyed the régime's patronage. When civil government was instituted in August 1764 he obtained a commission as justice of the peace for the districts of Quebec and Montreal; he retained this office until 1815, and eventually saw his mandate extended to all the districts of Lower Canada, including Gaspé. He had become a member of the Quebec Council which had been created by Murray in 1764, and also a master in the Court of Chancery. His connections with Thomas Mills*, the first receiver general for the colony, and Hector Theophilus Cramahé*, the civil secretary, fostered a sort of triumvirate, which Murray's successor, Guy CARLETON, turned into a committee of the Council to examine public accounts (honoraria, expenditures, and claims) from the beginning of the British régime. In 1763 and 1769 Dunn acted as king's attorney in succession matters.

Mills's departure in August 1767 strengthened Dunn's position through the process by which responsibilities were devolved upon those benefiting from patronage. Thus when the duties of receiver general were handed down to Cramahé, Dunn became next in line. He acceded to the acting receiver generalship on 31 July 1770, the day Cramahé was called on to be administrator of the province in Carleton's absence. The redistribution of offices on the eve of Carleton's departure indeed proved doubly profitable for Dunn. Not only did he inherit the acting receiver generalship, which he retained until the spring of 1777 when his partner Grant in turn inherited it; he also became judge of the Court of Common Pleas for the districts of Quebec and Three Rivers, a post he held until the judicial system was reorganized in 1794. In addition he sat on the Circuit Court in 1771 and 1772, the Prerogative Court in 1779, and the Court of Appeal in 1788. The Thomas Dunn who was paymaster for the navy on the Great Lakes during the American invasion was apparently a namesake.

Eager to take advantage of the various fruits of the conquest, Dunn had of course taken an interest in the Saint-Maurice ironworks, which were initially taken over by the military authorities and then leased out after civil government was established. In June 1767 Carleton granted the first contract, for a 16-year period, to eight partners – one of them being Dunn – who had joined forces around a dynamic citizen of Trois-Rivières, Christophe Pélissier*. Of the eight, Alexandre DUMAS and Jean Dumas* Saint-Martin were of French descent and had recently immigrated to the province. Of the six English-speaking partners, who were all merchants, Benjamin Price* and Dunn were members of the Council; three others, George ALLSOPP, Colin Drummond, and James Johnston*, resided at Quebec, while Brook WATSON lived in London. Each partner's share had been set at one-ninth of the costs of running the ironworks. Restarting operations at the works, which had been abandoned for two years, required sums so far beyond the expectations of the interested parties that the anticipated returns failed to materialize. The entire group of English-speaking merchants from Quebec liquidated their shares within a few years. Johnston was the first to take this step, and in April 1771 Dunn, Drummond, and Allsopp, who was acting for himself and for Watson, followed his example. Their agreement of sale, signed before notaries Jean-Antoine Saillant and Simon Sanguinet*, showed capital outlays totalling £615 apiece. In exchange for their shares in the ironworks Pélissier promised to deliver to the four shareholders 90 tons of pig-iron each, within a period of a year and a half. The deal proved profitable; the promise was kept, and the transaction was completed in 1772.

Finding themselves with 360 tons of pig-iron on their hands when they were connected to the world of maritime trade presented no difficulties. After all, the business class to which Dunn belonged possessed the irreplaceable asset of being able to trade in all kinds of merchandise. In the era of sailing ships, when ballast was in great demand, the weight of the pig-iron met the needs of shipowners and shippers; moreover, the simple presence of a Brook Watson in this deal sufficed to guarantee disposal of the product. Far from losing his investment in the Saint-Maurice ironworks, Dunn recovered it at the point when he was extending his commercial grip on the lower north shore.

The Quebec Act consolidated Dunn's well-established position within the administration of the colony. His name headed the list of members of the new Legislative Council, and he was called to serve on the privy council instituted by Carleton. The creation of such a body favoured concentration of the legislative, executive, and judicial powers in the hands of a group of privileged councillors, which included only one Catholic French-Canadian, François Baby. Although the home authorities severely disapproved of it, this system of government was maintained by Carleton's successor, General HALDI-MAND, until the end of the War of American Independence. Dunn adapted to the system as well as he did to the change of generals at the head of the province.

Exemplary in his attendance both at the privy council meetings in the Château Saint-Louis and at the Legislative Council sessions in the bishop's palace, Dunn acquired a reputation as a moderate by avoiding involvement in partisan fights, unlike his impetuous compatriots George Allsopp and William Grant. Although he made common cause with his colleagues in the English party to obtain certain rights held dear by every good British subject – particularly with respect to personal liberty and security in accordance with the common law – he attached himself to the French party to uphold the system of government instituted under the Quebec Act. Dunn remained aloof from the battle for constitutional reform that broke out after Governor Haldimand's departure. He had too much business sense to let himself be caught in the interplay of party divisions and fights and thus risk compromising his privileged situation as a member of the anglophone bourgeoisie who was also in the colonial government.

Late in the spring of 1785, Dunn received permission to absent himself from the province, and he stayed in England until the spring of 1787. The editor of the *Quebec Gazette* reported that on the day he sailed, 19 June, Dunn was accompanied to the pier by Lieutenant Governor Hamilton and the "most respectable inhabitants," who expressed to him "their sincere regret for his departure and their earnest wishes for his speedy return." In addition to the good wishes of the French-speaking lawyers, Dunn had already received a few days earlier warm tributes from the leading members of the English-speaking bourgeoisie at Quebec, who praised "the justice and moderation, with which you have fill'd the most respectable offices," as well as the "conduct in all occasions" which showed a "man of sound wisdom, rectitude and benevolence."

Dunn did not go alone; he sailed "with his family."

His wife, Henriette Guichaud, was the daughter of the late Jacques Guichaud and widow of Pierre Fargues, both of whom had been merchants at Quebec. The marriage had occurred at least two years earlier, since the contract was signed on 27 Nov. 1783 before notaries Pierre-Louis PANET and Pierre-Louis Deschenaux. In a departure from the Coutume de Paris the couple reserved "the freedom to make their wills as they please, as is permitted them by the [Quebec] Act." Although Dunn agreed to community of property and recognized his spouse's right to "a fair half of all his property" in the event of his death, he provided that in the reverse case neither "the children of the first marriage . . . with the Sieur Fargues, nor those who may be born [of their marriage] or other collateral heirs could lay claim to any part of the said joint estate." As for the "goods and chattels pertaining to the joint property régime with [the late] Pierre Fargues," the contract stipulated that Henriette Guichaud had the "right to half of the said goods, and in respect of her under-age children to the other half." Finally, Dunn bestowed a fixed jointure of £400 upon his future wife. This marriage agreement plainly bore the stamp of the bourgeois individualism that characterized Dunn. Evidently he was no more interested in linking himself with a family clan than he was in integrating himself into the French Canadian milieu. In 1801, however, the couple agreed to help the children of the first marriage get established by granting £3,000 to Henriette Fargues and £2,000 to each of the sons, Thomas* and Jean Fargues, to be taken out of the joint estate after the deaths of husband and wife. They were to have three sons of their own, Thomas and William, who would both pursue military careers, and Robert.

From the 1790s Dunn's career was directed primarily towards the judicial, administrative, and political spheres. He remained none the less active in business, particularly until 1807 or 1808. As in the past he continued to speculate in landed property. In the period from 1764 till his death he bought at least ten lots, four houses, and several farms; he sold about the same number of lots, seven houses, a shed, and half of the shares in a schooner; in addition he rented out various pieces of land and exchanged building sites. He also concluded several land deals as assignee, executor, attorney, and commissioner in various capacities. An inventory of the notarized deeds reveals that on nearly 50 occasions Dunn lent sums of cash or goods varying in value on average from £500 to £1,000 and up to £3,000, at a regular rate of 6 per cent and on one occasion 10 per cent. Only once did he borrow. By an irony of fate, Bishop Plessis*, who denounced lending at interest, borrowed £600 from Dunn in 1807 and £400 in 1818, both times at 6 per cent interest.

In addition to the important transactions already mentioned, Dunn bought the seigneury of Saint-

Armand, on the shores of Lake Champlain, in December 1788. By 1792 he requested a grant of land to round out his seigneury, which had been truncated when the border between Lower Canada and the United States had been laid out. In 1802 he demanded, but to no avail, that the British authorities intervene to obtain compensation from the American government. On the other hand his membership on the Executive Council of Lower Canada had certainly not been unconnected with his receiving Dunham Township, together with 34 other associates, in 1796. This was the first time that an entire township was the object of an official grant in Lower Canada. In addition to reserves, the township comprised 40,895 acres and was divided into 200 lots; it soon became Dunn's sole property. Later he obtained 58 lots in Stukely Township through Lieutenant Governor Robert Shore Milnes*'s recommendation to the home authorities; they decided that as well as being entitled to request lands in the regular manner Dunn could ask for them as a member of the Executive Council. In a notarized deed of 1803 Dunn is mentioned as a co-seigneur of the seigneury of Champlain, together with John CRAIGIE and Joseph FROBISHER. Two years later, as co-owner of the Batiscan Iron Work Company along with Craigie, Joseph Frobisher, Benjamin Joseph Frobisher*, and Thomas Coffin*, he bought a series of building sites in the Batiscan region. But by 1808 he had withdrawn from this company, in which he seems to have lost a substantial sum. At a sheriff's sale that year he bought the Cape Diamond Brewery of Quebec, with the adjoining wharfs and sheds. Unable to resell this property at a profit, he struck a bargain with John Racy for its use. In 1811 the agreement became a simple lease to Racy for £1,200 a year. The brewery and warehouses burned in 1815.

In 1825, seven years after Dunn's death, a partial inventory of the joint estate revealed a residual amount of £15,758 still owing to him, a capital sum of unknown size invested in England, on which two of his sons had already received the interest, and numerous properties: seven building sites, four houses, a third of the seigneury of Mille-Vaches, a third of the seigneury of Mingan, a quarter of the seigneury of Île-d'Anticosti, all of the seigneury of Saint-Armand, Dunham Township (minus the government and clergy reserves), a quarter of Stukely Township, and various other unidentified lots. Unlike Grant, who had died burdened with debts despite his reputation as a great entrepreneur, Dunn had left a large estate and its assets were still flourishing seven years after his death.

At the time the constitution of 1791 went into effect, Dunn had been a member of the Legislative and the Executive councils of Lower Canada. As the senior member of the executive he took part in crucial sessions on land distribution, the audit of public accounts, and affairs of state. In 1794, at the time the

judicial system was being reorganized, he became a judge of the Quebec Court of King's Bench. In 1801, shortly before he left for London, where he spent a year, he was appointed presiding judge of the Court of Appeal. In 1803 he sided with the majority of the British judges in upholding the application of English civil law in matters of succession and jointure for lands held in free and common socage. He took part in the revising of municipal police regulations for Quebec in 1805, and then for Quebec, Montreal, and Trois-Rivières in 1809. During the period of disturbances in 1794 he was president of the Quebec branch of an association founded to support British rule in Lower Canada. He was frequently a member of commissions with various tasks: construction of churches at Trois-Rivières and Quebec in the period 1791–1805, building of a court-house at Quebec between 1799 and 1801, administration of the Jesuit estates from 1801, and application of the 1801 law concerning the collection of *lods et ventes* on crown lands held in simple roture.

The flourishing state of Dunn's fortune, which can be attributed to his business dealings, did not keep him from taking full advantage of his public offices. In addition to having obtained immense stretches of land, around 1802 he received emoluments amounting to £850 sterling from the various offices he held, and £2,350 in the years 1805–7 as administrator of Lower Canada. In the latter capacity he took advantage of the situation to appoint his stepson, Thomas Fargues, storekeeper general of the Indian Department, despite Sir John Johnson*'s attempts to get the post for his son. In 1802 Dunn, citing his long and undeniable services, laid claim to a respectable pension, similar to the one that Chief Justice William Osgoode* had received. Lieutenant Governor Milnes supported his request, and London agreed in principle to a pension of £500 sterling annually, drawn on the revenues of Lower Canada. Dunn postponed his retirement for a few years, however, because of the substantial emoluments provided by his office as administrator of Lower Canada, and also because of the financial losses he had incurred in the exploitation of the Batiscan ironworks. He did not draw his pension until 1809, after he had resigned from his judgeship.

As president of the Executive Council Dunn was civil administrator of Lower Canada from the departure of Lieutenant Governor Milnes in August 1805 until the arrival of Governor CRAIG in October 1807. Once more he managed to stay above the fray at a time of fierce conflict between the Canadian and British parties in the House of Assembly. The furious outbursts of the *Quebec Mercury* against the Canadians provoked several confrontations in the 1806 session: warrants for arrest and summonses were issued by the assembly against the editors of the *Montreal Gazette* and the *Quebec Mercury*; some Canadians drew up a memorial supporting the Gaols

Dunn

Act of 1805 which Dunn agreed to send to London, but not without stressing the irregularity of the procedures of the house; a quarrel erupted between the two parties over the translation of John Hatsell's work *Precedents of proceedings in the House of Commons* . . . (London, 1781). Facing a divided assembly, Jean-Antoine PANET as speaker decided in favour of the translation but Dunn prudently deferred the decision until an officially appointed governor arrived. The year ended with the founding of the newspaper *Le Canadien* to defend the Canadians' interests and give expression to their loyalty. Each side showered insults and innuendoes on the other; the *Quebec Mercury* in particular urged that after more than 40 years of British rule the Canadians should be assimilated, and *Le Canadien* accused a small clique of privileged people of wanting to "anglify" the Canadians and hand them over to the Americans.

During 1806 also, the crown missed a unique opportunity to bring the Catholic Church under royal jurisdiction, a step advocated in the period from 1793 to 1805 by Anglican bishop Jacob Mountain*, Lieutenant Governor Milnes, Attorney General Jonathan Sewell*, and Provincial Secretary Herman Witsius Ryland*. On 18 Jan. 1806 Bishop DENAUT died. To Ryland's fury, and in the absence of Milnes, Mountain, and Sewell, who were all in England, Dunn rendered an immense service to the church when he swore in Plessis as bishop of Quebec on 25 January, and Bernard-Claude Panet* as coadjutor a few days later, without referring the matter to the British government. He claimed to have based his actions on precedent in this matter. The good relations existing between Dunn and Plessis may have played an important role. Or again, perhaps there was weight to Ryland's caustic query: what man of 77 could pass up the opportunity of making a bishop? Plessis and Panet would live to see the crown give up any serious design to bring the Catholic Church under its authority by taking advantage of a vacancy in the episcopate.

During the 1807 session fierce debates again brought the Canadian and British parties into conflict, particularly over the issue of payment of assemblymen who represented ridings distant from Quebec, over petitions from the Eastern Townships requesting that roads be built and various improvements be carried out, and over a bill for recovering small debts. Even with all this disagreement 16 bills received royal assent, and Dunn was able to avoid the drastic measures resorted to by his successor Craig, in spite of newspaper quarrels and *Le Canadien*'s long dissertations on ministerial responsibility.

Dunn even took advantage of the threat of war occasioned by the bloody skirmish between the British vessel *Leopard* and the American ship *Chesapeake* off the New England coast in June 1807 [*see* Sir George Cranfield BERKELEY] to carry out successfully the first general call-up of the militia since the conquest. In the colony as a whole, the population behaved with zeal and loyalty. Large numbers of volunteers came forward. Dunn was so astonished, and perhaps so relieved, that he wrote an order of the day to congratulate the militiamen and praise them warmly. This attitude of the good paterfamilias seems to have been the image of him retained in the public mind.

Dunn had been less successful in his attempt on behalf of the government to settle the question of the lease on the Saint-Maurice ironworks in 1806. It had been awarded at auction to the former lessee, the firm of Monro and Bell, for £60 annually, which was £790 less per year than the sum agreed to in the preceding lease. Despite the suspicions of Chief Justice Henry ALLCOCK and Colonial Secretary Lord Castlereagh, there does not seem to have been any bribery involved in the deal, although the Executive Council had neglected to take certain elementary precautions, such as setting a minimum price. Dunn defended himself, maintaining that the only other offer came from a company of Canadians without much money. After his arrival Craig cancelled the lease and exonerated Dunn, explaining that at the age of 77 Dunn was not at his best for presenting a situation in its true colours.

The confidence and universal esteem that Dunn enjoyed, and his status as senior member of the Executive Council, explain why he again presided over the destiny of Lower Canada from June to September 1811, between Craig's departure and the arrival of his successor, Sir George PREVOST. This time circumstances spared him unpleasant surprises.

Despite his various occupations, Dunn had served as treasurer of the relief committee for poor Protestants in 1768 and of the committee to help the poor of Quebec in 1769; he also subscribed to the relief fund for the poor in 1784 and 1818. He was a member of the Agriculture Society in the District of Quebec from 1789 to 1793, and of the Quebec Fire Society from 1790 to 1815; as well, he was one of the charter members of the fund to support the war that Great Britain was waging against France from 1797 to 1801. He contributed to the Waterloo Fund in 1815 and to the building of a road linking the Plains of Abraham with Cap-Rouge in 1817.

Thomas Dunn passed away at Quebec on 15 April 1818. During his lengthy career he had stood out in nearly all areas of life in the colony, from business to the judiciary and affairs of state. His family life had apparently been happy and filled with satisfaction.

PIERRE TOUSIGNANT and JEAN-PIERRE WALLOT

ANQ-Q, CN1-26, 17 juill. 1798, 28 juill. 1801, 16 janv. 1802, 15 juin 1803; CN1-83, 2 oct. 1783; 13 juin 1785; 30 mai, 13 déc. 1788; 27 mars, 24 août, 12, 22 déc. 1789; 21, 22 juin, 27 août, 11 sept. 1790; 12 oct. 1792; CN1-92, 13 août 1801; CN1-205, 10 avril, 26 juin 1775; 18 juill. 1776; 23

juill., 23 oct. 1777; 11 avril, 23 mai, 6 oct. 1778; 19, 21 oct. 1780; 15 oct. 1781; 27 nov. 1783; CN1-230, 16 févr., 5 juill., 11 août 1796; 3 mars 1798; 1er avril 1801; 17 août 1809; 9 mars, 12 août 1811; 24 avril 1815; 16 mars, 4, 6 avril, 31 mai, 5 nov., 18 déc. 1816; 26 févr. 1817; 27 mai 1822; 9 sept. 1825; CN1-248, 9 août 1764; 2, 27 août 1769; 7 mai 1770; 4 avril 1771; 13 oct. 1772; 27 avril 1773; 4 oct. 1775; CN1-262, 11 oct. 1797; 31 déc. 1798; 28 nov. 1799, 17 janv. 1800; 23 oct. 1804; 18 janv., 28 mars, 5 sept. 1805; 15 sept., 3 nov. 1807; 2 avril 1818. ASQ, C 36: 73, 96, 102, 104, 106; Polygraphie, IX: 63; XIX: 49; XXV: 34, 40. PAC, MG 11, [CO 42] Q, 13: 211–13; 24-1: 67, 69, 335, 338–52; 26-2: 394–405, 409, 466; 87-1: 176; 90: 265–66; 92: 13, 161; 93: 137–71; 97-A: 40–41, 139; 100: 298–304; 101-1: 73; 101-2: 425; 102: 256; 104: 7–38, 66–72; 106-2: 327–29; 109: 24–43; 112: 255; MG 23, GIII, 3; MG 24, B10; RG 1, E1, 7: 198, 212; RG 1, L3L: 143, 186, 788–862, 1362, 1580, 2162, 4365–66, 4574–87, 35572–97, 39169–81; RG 7, G1, 2: 174–75; 3: 48–49, 167, 250; RG 8, I (C ser.), 722A: 38, 79, 82, 87, 92; 772A: 82; 1908: 41; RG 68, General index, 1651–1841: ff.222–23, 229, 259, 266, 272, 275–77, 322–45, 521, 531–38, 543–46, 569, 625, 628, 650, 653. Bas-Canada, chambre d'Assemblée, *Journaux*, 1793–1818. *Doc. relatifs à l'hist. constitutionnelle, 1759–1791* (Shortt et Doughty; 1921), 1: 252; 2: 579, 647. *Le Canadien*, 17, 24, 31 janv., 28 févr., 21, 28 mars 1807. *Le Courier de Quebec*, 28 févr. 1807. *Montreal Gazette*, 1805–11. *Quebec Gazette*, 24 Nov. 1768; 26 Jan. 1769; 25 March 1784; 23, 30 June 1785; 12 Oct. 1786; 24 May 1787; 4 Aug. 1788; 23 April 1789; 28 Jan., 25 March, 8 July 1790; 5 May 1791; 11 April 1793; 3, 10 July 1794; 4 June 1795; 29 June, 1 Aug. 1797; 2 July 1799; 15 Jan., 26 Feb. 1801; 27 June 1805; 14 July 1808; 22 June 1809; 20 June 1811; 7 Feb., 19 Oct., 9 Nov. 1815; 13 March 1817; 12 March, 16 April 1818. *Quebec Mercury*, January–March 1807. F.-J. Audet, "Les législateurs du Bas-Canada." Hare et Wallot, *Les imprimés dans le Bas-Canada*, 315–27. P.-G. Roy, *Inv. concessions.* Christie, *Hist. of L.C.*, 1: 127, 200–1, 233–34, 255, 257, 260; 6: 25–27, 84–86. Creighton, *Commercial empire of St. Lawrence*, 161. Ouellet, *Bas-Canada*, 122. Paquet et Wallot, *Patronage et pouvoir dans le Bas-Canada*, 43n. Wallot, *Un Québec qui bougeait*, 63–74, 186–87.

DUPLESSIS, JEAN-BAPTISTE LEBRUN DE. *See* LEBRUN

DUPRÉ, JEAN-BAPTISTE LE COMTE. *See* LE COMTE

DUSSAUS, MARIE-ANGÉLIQUE (she also signed **Dussaust** and **Dussaut**), hospital nun and assistant to the superior of the Sisters of Charity of the Hôpital Général of Montreal (Grey Nuns); b. 20 June 1737 in the parish of Saint-Joseph (Lauzon, Que.), daughter of Jean Dussaus and Marie-Angélique Huard; d. 7 June 1809 in Montreal, Lower Canada.

On 14 Aug. 1756 Marie-Angélique Dussaus joined the community of Grey Nuns, founded in 1737 by Mme d'Youville [Dufrost*]. In choosing to enter the Hôpital Général of Montreal, rather than a community in the region of Quebec, she may have been influenced by Charles-Marie-Madeleine d'Youville*, the son of the founder, who had been parish priest of Saint-Joseph since 1754. On 12 Dec. 1759 Marie-Angélique took vows as a domestic nun, a subordinate class devised by Mme d'Youville, who was anxious to enlarge the community but was unable to do so because a clause in the letters patent of 1753 limited the number of directors to 12.

In 1754 Mme d'Youville had begun to take in a few foundlings, and by 1760 she was able to accept them all. At that point she called on Sister Dussaus to take charge of them. According to Mother Élisabeth McMullen, superior of the community from 1843 to 1848, Sister Dussaus had great personal gifts, and from the beginning of her life in religion her enthusiasm for work and her exemplary devotion had attracted attention. During the 36 years she consecrated to foundlings, the Hôpital Général admitted 954 of them. Some were placed with families; the others stayed at the hospital, where they remained until the age of 18 and rendered some services. In addition to giving the children a great deal of care, Sister Dussaus had to exercise great ingenuity to find means of meeting their needs, since the hospital received no financial assistance from the government for this work.

Marie-Angélique Dussaus carried out her task well, and the community considered her worthy to replace Marie-Josephe Benard as assistant to the superior, Thérèse-Geneviève Coutlée*. The directors – Sister Dussaus had been one since 1778 – elected her to this office with a majority of votes on 28 Jan. 1796. Catherine Papin, *dit* Barolette, took charge of the foundlings in her place. Flexible, pious, capable of self-denial, blessed with great discretion and good sense, according to Mother McMullen, Sister Dussaus showed much skill in performing the sensitive tasks her community had entrusted to her.

Marie-Angélique Dussaus died suddenly on 7 June 1809, having devoted most of her career to caring for unfortunate children. Her funeral took place on 8 June at the Hôpital Général, and she was buried in the institution's church.

GEORGETTE SÉGUIN

Arch. des sœurs grises (Montréal), Dossier de sœur Marie-Angélique Dussaus; Mémoire de sœur Julie Casgrain-Baby, 57–60; Notices biographiques (1741–1848); Reg. des baptêmes et sépultures de l'Hôpital Général de Montréal, IV; Reg. des minutes du Conseil général; Reg. des professes perpétuelles, 3; Reg. pour les enfants trouvés; C.-M.-M. d'Youville, "La vie de madame Youville, fondatrice des Sœurs de la charité à Montréal." Allaire, *Dictionnaire*, 1: 543. [É.-M. Faillon], *Vie de Mme d'Youville, fondatrice des Sœurs de la charité de Villemarie dans l'île de Montréal, en Canada* (Villemarie [Montréal], 1852), 185–92.

DYSAN. *See* DEJEAN

Ecuier

E

ECUIER, CHARLES, Roman Catholic priest, Sulpician, and musician; baptized 20 Nov. 1758 in Montreal (Que.), son of Jean Ecuier and Marie-Josephte Cimère; d. 29 May 1820 in Yamachiche, Lower Canada.

Charles Ecuier's parents – his father was a soldier in the Régiment de Béarn – came to Canada during the Seven Years' War. They settled in Montreal, where they had at least five children. Charles probably went to the primary school run by the Séminaire de Saint-Sulpice in Montreal. From 1771 to 1778 he pursued secondary studies at the college founded at Longue-Pointe (Montreal) by the Sulpician Jean-Baptiste Curatteau*, which was moved in 1773 to Montreal and named Collège Saint-Raphaël. He took the final two years of the classical program (Philosophy) at the Petit Séminaire de Québec from 1778 to 1780, and on 15 August of the latter year he began theological studies at the Grand Séminaire. To enable him to enter the priesthood, on 7 Aug. 1781 his parents bestowed a life annuity of 150 shillings on him by mortgaging the family patrimony, which consisted of a seven-acre property with an orchard, located at Côte-Saint-Antoine (Westmount) and valued at 20,000 *livres*. On 5 April 1783 Ecuier was ordained priest in Montreal by Bishop Briand* of Quebec.

Ecuier, on whom his earliest teachers, the Sulpicians, had left a strong mark, joined that society and in the month of May 1783 began to minister in the parish of Notre-Dame in Montreal. He was given specific responsibility for the Confrérie de la Sainte-Famille, a religious association for women, and he succeeded Étienne Montgolfier* as chaplain to the nuns of the Congregation of Notre-Dame, an office he held from 1788 to 1790. On 21 Oct. 1788 he was admitted as a member of the Séminaire de Saint-Sulpice in Montreal, and on 2 September of the following year was appointed to the assembly of the seminary's assistants. According to Gabriel-Jean Brassier*, the assistant to the superior, Ecuier did not spare himself, and his health suffered as a result. In the summer of 1790 his doctor, François-Xavier Bender, recommended appointment to a country charge as the sole cure for the illnesses he had suffered in the preceding six months. Ecuier left the Sulpician seminary on 18 September, and on 11 October took charge of Saint-Joachim parish (at Pointe-Claire).

There were roughly 150 families in this rural parish, about 50 of whom lived in the village. Ecuier hoped to change the immoral ways of certain of his parishioners, but some were not ready to meet his wishes. Furthermore, there were disagreements within the *fabrique* over the distribution of responsibilities,

duties, and salaries between the sacristan and the nuns of the Congregation of Notre-Dame. In September 1793, on the occasion of the feast of the parish's patron saint, there was a violent confrontation between the priest and some of his parishioners, with threats of physical violence being uttered; Ecuier consequently refused to celebrate the feast that had been planned. Vicar general Brassier severely condemned the parishioners but nevertheless suggested to Bishop Hubert* that Ecuier be moved. Early in October 1793 Ecuier took charge of the parish of Purification-de-la-Bienheureuse-Vierge-Marie (at Repentigny). On arrival he did not know where to live because the presbytery was in ruins, but he was not discouraged. He had the buildings belonging to the *fabrique* repaired and the interior of the church repainted. In 1799, to ensure a better source of income, the *fabrique* decided to have a rood-loft built. Despite these extensive alterations, income always exceeded expenditures while Ecuier was at this parish.

Ecuier twice came before the Court of King's Bench. In October 1797 the merchant James Woolrich demanded payment of an account, which Ecuier repaid with interest and charges in March 1799. The priest's lawsuit against Joseph Poitevin d'Anglebert and his wife Marie-Anne Garnom caused more of a sensation. Ecuier had lent money and rendered all sorts of services to these two, who were distant relatives from France. He suspected them of wanting to leave Canada in a hurry and demanded that their property be seized. The process-server estimated the sequestered property at £94; however, the couple retaliated, seeking £100 in damages. The dispute caused a great stir in the little village. There was no judgement, but Ecuier and vicar general Jean-Henri-Auguste Roux* informed Bishop DENAUT of Quebec that the difference had been resolved in the priest's favour in February 1799.

Late in October 1802 Ecuier was appointed to the larger church in Yamachiche, and in this parish, which had been deeply divided by quarrels under his predecessors, he was able to restore peace. He made improvements to the church, and added a new presbytery in 1804 and a sacristy, rood-loft, and dwelling for the schoolmaster in 1807. Although he was a big, strong man of somewhat dour appearance, with a weather-beaten and rather forbidding countenance, and although he evidently lacked eloquence, Ecuier was able to win the trust of his parishioners, thanks to the liveliness of the music and of the way in which he conducted the liturgy. He was an accomplished musician and is supposed to have left a *Sanctus*, a *Magnificat*, and a number of motets and

Eddy

psalms of remarkable musical quality. He also had a beneficent influence in clerical circles: he took under his protection John Holmes*, a Protestant who was converted to Catholicism in 1817 and who became an eminent priest and member of the Séminaire de Québec.

Charles Ecuier gave up his ministry in February 1820 because of illness, and he died on 29 May. Vicar general François-Xavier Noiseux* and a great many priests and ecclesiastics showed their esteem for him by attending his funeral. He was buried under the sanctuary of the church then standing at Yamachiche, but his remains are now in the parish cemetery.

J.-BRUNO HAREL

AAQ, 1 CB, VII: 4; IX: 161; 71-31 CD, I: 81; 303 CD, I: 20. ANQ-M, P-10, 30 oct. 1797, cause no.64; février 1798, cause no.32; CN1-158, 7 août 1781. AP, Purification-de-la-Bienheureuse-Vierge-Marie (Repentigny), Cahier des délibérations de la fabrique; Sainte-Anne (Yamachiche), Cahiers des délibérations de la fabrique, 1789–1843; Reg. des baptêmes, mariages et sépultures, 1812–20. Arch. de la chancellerie de l'archevêché de Montréal, 355.104, 793-3, 794-1, 799-1; 355.110, 793-2, -3, -4. ASSM, 21; 24, Dossier 5; Dossier 6. Le séminaire de Québec (Provost), 465. Allaire, Dictionnaire. Gauthier, Sulpitiana, 202. Napoléon Caron, Histoire de la paroisse d'Yamachiche (précis historique) (Trois-Rivières, Qué., 1892). Helmut Kallmann, A history of music in Canada, 1534–1914 (Toronto, 1960), 40.

EDDY, JONATHAN, army officer and office holder; b. 1726/27 in Norton, Mass., son of Eleazar Eddy and Elizabeth Cobb; m. 4 May 1749 Mary Ware, and they had four sons; d. August 1804 in Eddy Township (Maine).

Jonathan Eddy's military career began in 1755, when he enlisted in the New England force under John Winslow* which was to participate in an expedition against the French Fort Beauséjour on the Chignecto Isthmus of Nova Scotia [see Robert Monckton*; Louis Du Pont* Duchambon de Vergor]. Three years later he received a Massachusetts captain's commission to raise a company for "the Reduction of Canada," but the expedition was aborted after James Abercromby*'s bloody failure before Fort Carillon (near Ticonderoga, N.Y.). Then in the early spring of 1759 Eddy received another captain's commission to recruit men from the Norton region to serve at Fort Beauséjour, now renamed Fort Cumberland. Eddy remained there from 5 May 1759 until 30 Sept. 1760.

After his discharge in 1760, Eddy returned to Norton. Three years later he and his family moved to the Chignecto region. Like thousands of other New Englanders, he had been attracted to Nova Scotia by the offer of cheap and fertile land and by the promise of an abundant future. He emigrated to a land he knew

well. Soon after his arrival he became deputy provost marshal of Cumberland County, and from 1770 to 1775 he served as a member of the House of Assembly. Apparently Eddy did not take his Halifax responsibilities too seriously, for on 20 July 1775 his seat was declared vacant for non-attendance. At approximately the same time, Eddy and his friend John ALLAN were taking the lead in the development of a revolutionary movement in the Chignecto region while they grew increasingly enthusiastic about the patriot cause in New England. Many New Englanders who had settled in Nova Scotia became opposed to provincial authority as events developed in their native country, and Eddy and Allan were greatly encouraged by what they perceived to be a growing anti-British feeling throughout the province. During late 1775 and early 1776 Eddy in particular seemed to be obsessed with precipitating a major insurrection in the colony as quickly as possible, an end he hoped to achieve by encouraging George Washington and the Continental Congress to send an "army of liberation" to Nova Scotia as had been done in Canada [see Richard Montgomery*]. Consequently, in February 1776 Eddy and 14 associates left the Chignecto region to discuss the situation with Washington. On 27 March the American general listened patiently to Eddy's arguments for invading Nova Scotia but because of "the present uncertain State of things" could not offer any military assistance. A rather disillusioned Eddy next made his way to the Congress at Philadelphia, Pa; there his urgent request also fell upon insensitive ears. In May he returned to Cumberland County, and decided to make a final appeal to the General Court of Massachusetts for an offensive to liberate Nova Scotia.

In August the Massachusetts government rejected Eddy's proposal, but promised to provide supplies and ammunition for any force he was able to raise. Eddy immediately set off for Machias (Maine) where, he knew, there was some support for his scheme. Once at Machias, however, he was able to recruit only about 20 men. On 13 August, just when this liberating "army" was about to set sail for Nova Scotia, John Allan arrived. Allan did everything in his power to dissuade Eddy from carrying out what he considered to be a foolish enterprise. But instead of listening to the wise advice of his associate, Eddy ordered his men to Passamaquoddy Bay (N.B.), where seven new recruits were found, and then to Maugerville (N.B.), where 27 Yankee settlers and 16 Indians including Ambroise Saint-Aubin* enlisted. The small force then slowly made its way towards the Chignecto Isthmus with the aim of taking Fort Cumberland, capturing on the way a detachment posted by the fort's commander, Lieutenant-Colonel Joseph Goreham*. On 5 November Eddy's force, strengthened by a few Acadians from Memramcook (N.B.), arrived near the British

295

Edward Augustus

fort. By this time Eddy had learned that the Halifax authorities had issued a proclamation offering rewards of £200 for his capture and £100 for Allan's.

The pro-American Cumberland settlers were profoundly disappointed with the small size of Eddy's force and its lack of artillery, and in order to counteract this feeling Eddy made wild promises about the imminent arrival of hundreds of American reinforcements. When these assurances failed to lift the prevailing mood of gloom, he began to threaten his former friends with the destruction of their homes and property, hoping thereby to intimidate them into supporting his proposed attack on the fort. About 100 eventually joined, to give Eddy 180 men as against roughly the same number in the fort.

On 12 November Eddy sent in a summons to surrender, which was rejected by Goreham. Accordingly, on the night of the 14th the rebels (who numbered only 80, the rest of their force being on outpost duty and guarding prisoners) attempted an assault, but they were easily driven off; a further attack on the 22nd had no greater success. Eddy thereupon established a blockade in the hope that American reinforcements would soon arrive. But on the 27th British troops under Thomas Batt and Gilfred Studholme* arrived from Windsor, N.S., and on the morning of the 29th they cooperated with the garrison in an attack which drove the invaders towards Memramcook. Once the area was cleared, Goreham published an amnesty which pardoned nearly all of the Cumberland settlers but which specifically excluded Eddy, who made his way to Maugerville and then to Machias. Although he was later to entertain ideas about another attack on Fort Cumberland, no further invasions of Nova Scotia took place during the revolution, and American efforts shifted to attempts to draw the Indians of the region to their side [see John Allan].

In many respects, the so-called Eddy rebellion was a comic-opera affair. It showed, however, not only how weak the revolutionary movement was in Nova Scotia but also how little real interest there was in New England in the liberation of what has been termed "New England's outpost." In the final analysis, especially when it is realized that the Royal Navy's presence in Nova Scotia waters exerted a profound influence on the strategic realities of the area, it appears obvious that Eddy's task was a hopeless one.

On returning to Machias, Eddy was placed in charge of the settlement's protection, and in August 1777 he participated in the defence of Machias against an attack by the squadron of Sir George Collier*. After the incident, probably because of the spirited criticism of John Allan and other former Cumberland friends over his handling of the defence, Eddy returned temporarily to his birthplace, and then in 1781 moved to nearby Stoughtonham (Sharon).

During 1782 and 1783 he was Stoughtonham's representative to the General Court. In 1784 he decided to settle on the east side of the Penobscot River (Maine) in what would become Eddy Township. Here he became the factotum of the community which developed on the site. He was chairman of the committee which called his old Maugerville friend Seth NOBLE to the church at Kenduskeag Plantation (Bangor), and on 19 June 1790 he was appointed a special judge of the Court of Common Pleas, a registrar of probate and wills, and a justice of the peace for Penobscot County. In 1800 he was also named the local postmaster. Eddy became involved in trade with Grand Manan Island, N.B., in 1785 after he purchased the schooner *Blackbird*. In 1801 Congress acknowledged Eddy's service to the revolutionary cause by granting him 1,280 acres in the Chillicothe district (Ohio). Eddy did not live on this land, however, and died in Eddy Township in August 1804; his wife survived him by a decade.

G. A. RAWLYK

Mass., Dept. of the State Secretary, Arch. Division (Boston), Mass. arch., 144: 161–68; 164: 176, 366–67; 192: 205–11; 195: 335–37; 197: 372; 198: 13, 54–56, 62, 97, 239–41; 239: 371. PAC, MG 11, [CO 217] Nova Scotia A, 94: 330–38; 95: 108–10, 113–15; 96: 93, 354–57, 383–85. *American arch.* (Clarke and Force), 5th ser., 2: 734; 3: 881, 909. "Calendar of state papers relating to Nova Scotia," PAC *Report*, 1894: 345, 355–57, 359–65. *Military operations in eastern Maine and N.S.* (Kidder). [George Washington], *The writings of George Washington, from the original manuscript sources, 1745–1799*, ed. J. C. Fitzpatrick (39v., Washington, 1931–44), 4: 437–38. *Directory of N.S. MLAs*, 110, 389. Charles Eddy, *Genealogy of the Eddy family* (Brooklyn, N.Y., 1881), 19. J. H. Ahlin, *Maine Rubicon: downeast settlers during the American revolution* (Calais, Maine, 1966), 11–157. Brebner, *Neutral Yankees* (1969), 271–87. S. D. Clark, *Movements of political protest in Canada, 1640–1840* (Toronto, 1959), 53–74. W. B. Kerr, *The Maritime provinces of British North America and the American revolution* (Sackville, N.B., [1941?]; repr. New York, [1970]), 62–82. J. W. Porter, *Memoir of Col. Jonathan Eddy of Eddington, Me.: with some account of the Eddy family, and of the early settlers on Penobscot River* (Augusta, Maine, 1877). G. A. Rawlyk, *Nova Scotia's Massachusetts: a study of Massachusetts–Nova Scotia relations, 1630 to 1784* (Montreal and London, 1973), 219–40. J. D. Snowdon, "Footprints in the marsh mud: politics and land settlement in the township of Sackville, 1760–1800" (MA thesis, Univ. of N.B., Fredericton, 1975). G. [T.] Stewart and G. [A.] Rawlyk, *A people highly favoured of God: the Nova Scotia Yankees and the American revolution* (Toronto, 1972), 45–76. D. C. Harvey, "Machias and the invasion of Nova Scotia," CHA *Report*, 1932: 17–28.

EDWARD AUGUSTUS, Duke of KENT and STRATHEARN, army officer; b. 2 Nov. 1767 at

Edward Augustus

Buckingham Palace, London, England, fourth son of George III, King of Great Britain and Ireland, and Charlotte Sophia of Mecklenburg-Strelitz; d. 23 Jan. 1820 in Sidmouth, England.

At a very early stage Edward Augustus lost the favour of his father, and he never regained it. The king, disliking him strongly, was for many years determined to keep him out of England. Destined for the army like several of his brothers, he received his secondary and military education in Hanover and Lüneburg (Federal Republic of Germany) and at Geneva (Switzerland), where he was desperately unhappy and began to contract the debts which were to plague him all his life. He also had bad luck, best exemplified by the loss at sea on seven occasions of expensive sets of military dress and equipage. On 30 May 1786 he was gazetted colonel, and then in April 1789 received the colonelcy of the 7th Foot. When he returned to London from Geneva the following year without leave, his father immediately sent him to take command of his regiment at Gibraltar. It soon became evident that the prince was a strict disciplinarian even by the standards of the age and that he was passionately concerned with the minute points of military dress and decorum. In 1791 the 7th, which was chafing under Edward's command, was ordered to Quebec. As a prince of the blood Edward naturally entered the highest social circles there, and he was especially friendly with leading Canadian families. With Ignace-Michel-Louis-Antoine d'Irumberry* de Salaberry he maintained a correspondence for the rest of his life and he took a lively interest in the military careers of Salaberry's three sons, including ÉDOUARD-ALPHONSE and Charles-Michel*. In 1792 he paid a brief visit to Lieutenant Governor SIMCOE at Newark (Niagara-on-the-Lake), Upper Canada.

On the outbreak of war with France in 1793 Edward (who was promoted major-general on 2 October) eagerly volunteered for service, and he served as a brigade commander at the reduction of Martinique and St Lucia in 1794. He then went to Halifax, N.S., where he was appointed commander of the forces in Nova Scotia and New Brunswick. The prince took a stern view of drunkenness and gambling and even, according to contemporaries, made an inexorable stand against what he considered the loose morals of society at large. It was his custom to parade the Halifax garrison every morning at five and to attend in person. The continuing severity of his punishments for breaches of military conduct made him unpopular. At the same time, however, his actions were punctuated by conspicuous acts of humanity to the troops.

In view of the war with France, Edward embarked on an ambitious program of reconstruction of the Halifax fortifications, which had fallen into considerable disrepair after the American revolution. A new citadel was built to replace the old one, and Citadel Hill itself was cut down to accommodate the new works. Other batteries and fortifications including several towers were also erected, and a boom was placed across the Northwest Arm to prevent an enemy fleet from entering and bombarding the town from the rear. One innovation was the creation of a signalling system to facilitate communications between Halifax and the outposts. Although these works were built at a cost much higher than the original estimates, only a decade later many were in virtual ruins.

The prince injured his leg by a fall from his horse in 1798, and when his doctors (including William James ALMON and John Halliburton) suggested convalescence in England he eagerly took up the idea and left Halifax in October. In March 1799 parliament granted him an annual income of £12,000, and the next month he was created Duke of Kent and Strathearn; promotions to general and as commander-in-chief of the forces in British North America followed in May. Edward returned to Halifax in September 1799, but ill health cut short his stay and he left again in August 1800. This sojourn completed his North American experience: his ambition to become governor-in-chief of British North America was never realized. Except for a brief and unfortunate second term at Gibraltar from May 1802 to the spring of 1803, when he was recalled because of rumours of harsh discipline, his active military career was finished. He was promoted field-marshal by seniority in September 1805. Though somewhat protected by his older brothers from his father's strong adverse prejudices, he was unable to obtain important office, and most of the remainder of his life was spent in retirement on his estate at Ealing (London). He became president or benefactor of a great many charitable societies, and was much interested in the socialist doctrines of Robert Owen. For pecuniary reasons he resided at Brussels (Belgium) from 1815 to 1818.

Prince Edward is remembered in Halifax for initiating plans for the construction of the clock tower at the foot of Citadel Hill (although it was not begun until after his departure), for his contribution to the building of St George's Round Church, for his active interest in helping Nova Scotians he had known while there, and for his residence on Bedford Basin at Prince's Lodge which he leased from Lieutenant Governor John WENTWORTH, with whom he maintained close and friendly relations. There he lived with Thérèse-Bernardine Mongenet*, known as Mme de Saint-Laurent. She had come to Gibraltar in 1790 at his request and followed him faithfully on his travels to Quebec, Halifax, Ealing, and finally to Brussels where they parted. There can be no doubt that he was remarkably devoted to this companion who shared fully in his life. In 1818, after 27 years with Julie, as she was better known, the danger of failure in the royal

Edwards

succession obliged him to respond to public and family pressure for his marriage. He made a generous financial settlement upon Mme de Saint-Laurent, and on 29 May 1818 at Coburg (Federal Republic of Germany) married Victoria Mary Louisa, widow of the prince of Leiningen. The birth of Princess Victoria, the future queen, one year later was the result wished for by public opinion. The duke was proud of her, and he and the duchess paraded the baby at every opportunity. In December 1819 he took his family to a country house in Devon, where he died of pneumonia a month later.

Much about Edward Augustus's life is still unknown. Rumour spoke of children by Mme de Saint-Laurent and others, stories which Queen Victoria much disliked and endeavoured to suppress, and Sir William Fenwick Williams* took pleasure in not denying that he was the duke's son.

In collaboration with W. S. MacNutt

The later correspondence of George III, ed. Arthur Aspinall (5v., Cambridge, Eng., 1962–70). *The life of F.M., H.R.H. Edward, Duke of Kent, illustrated by his correspondence with the De Salaberry family, never before published, extending from 1791 to 1814*, ed. W. J. Anderson (Ottawa and Toronto, 1870). *Royal Gazette and the Nova-Scotia Advertiser*, 1794–1800. *DNB*. G.B., WO, *Army list*, 1786–1820. David Duff, *Edward of Kent: the life story of Queen Victoria's father* (London, 1938; repr. 1973). Mollie Gillen, *The prince and his lady: the love story of the Duke of Kent and Madame de St. Laurent* (Toronto, 1971). Erskine Neale, *The life of Field-Marshall His Royal Highness, Edward, Duke of Kent, with extracts from his correspondence, and original letters never before published* (London, 1850). Harry Piers, *The evolution of the Halifax fortress, 1749–1928*, ed. G. M. Self et al. (Halifax, 1947).

EDWARDS, EDWARD, bookseller, printer, publisher, journalist, office holder, and militia officer; b. *c*. 1756; d. 1 Sept. 1816 in Montreal, Lower Canada.

In 1781 Edward Edwards became the Montreal bookseller and agent for William Brown*, a printer at Quebec. He joined in the political protests of the day by signing in November 1784 the petition of old and new subjects for an assembly. The following year he signed two petitions supporting Lieutenant Governor Henry Hamilton*. In July 1785 Edwards, who was identified as "a bookseller and director of the press," was one of the creditors of printer Fleury Mesplet*, who owed him £300. Again in that year, Governor HALDIMAND reputedly asked him to keep an eye on the material in the new paper that Mesplet was getting ready to launch, the *Montreal Gazette/Gazette de Montréal*.

In February 1794, when the printing equipment that Edward William GRAY had been renting to Mesplet (who had died the previous month) was sold at auction, Edwards made a successful bid for a roller press, a binding press, and a small press, as well as paper and type, paying 1,802 *livres* 5 *sous* for the lot.

On 16 July 1795 Edwards, who had opened an office on Rue Saint-Vincent, announced that he intended to continue publishing the *Montreal Gazette*. The previous week Louis Roy*, a printer at Quebec, had made known his desire to take it over. Edwards's paper appeared on 3 August, followed by Roy's 15 days later. For more than a year the two weeklies bearing the same name competed with each other. At the outset Roy stole the limelight by emphasizing local affairs, whereas Edwards devoted more space to foreign news. Edwards, who had been postmaster since 1786, had easy access to newspapers from abroad and did not hesitate to reprint them. Sometimes he prevented them from being distributed to his rival, who openly denounced these unfair tactics. In 1797, for lack of financial means, Roy had to hand his paper over to his brother Joseph-Marie, who was not successful in keeping it alive. The paper ceased publication in November, leaving the field open to Edwards.

Under the management of Edwards the *Montreal Gazette* was simply a news-sheet. Its columns were filled with official proclamations, public notices, announcements of sheriff's sales, advertisements, and information on the intellectual and business worlds. Edwards reprinted extracts from British and American newspapers several months after their publication. Anxious to avoid any controversial subject, he rarely published letters from readers.

Besides forms, a few calendars, a song, and an exercise book, Edwards printed Jay's Treaty in 1795, a sermon by James Marmaduke Tunstall* three years later, and a collection of fables by the English writer Robert Dodsley around 1800. The poor quality of printing in these works, which is in strange contrast with the care Mesplet lavished on production or with that displayed by John Neilson* of Quebec, may explain the fact that Edwards's printing shop issued no works from 1801.

In 1805 Edwards began having difficulties. In March he published in his newspaper the somewhat sarcastic toasts proposed by Montreal merchants at a banquet where Isaac TODD presided. The House of Assembly, which met in February 1806, called the article untruthful, scandalous, and seditious, and voted to arrest Todd and Edwards. To escape imprisonment the two men took flight and nothing further came of the matter.

The arrival of three professional printers in Montreal in 1807 put an end to the monopoly Edwards had enjoyed. Nahum Mower* launched the *Canadian Courant and Montreal Advertiser* in May; the brothers James* and Charles Brown began publishing the *Canadian Gazette/Gazette canadienne* in July.

298

Edwards could not meet the competition. In fact, his health had begun to fail and he was even forced to give up his position as postmaster in October. Thus, in early 1808, sick and in debt, he sold the *Montreal Gazette* to the Browns, who the following month announced their intention to rejuvenate it. Edward Edwards apparently then retired from business. In 1813 he was still a captain in the militia, a post he had held since 1800. He died in Montreal on 1 Sept. 1816.

JOHN E. HARE

ANQ-M, CE1-63, 3 Sept. 1813. *Quebec Gazette*, 20 July 1786, 16 July 1795, 8 Oct. 1807, 16 Sept. 1813. Beaulieu et Hamelin, *La presse québécoise*, 1: 5–6, 12, 22. Hare et Wallot, *Les imprimés dans le Bas-Canada*, 293–94, 352. Tremaine, *Biblio. of Canadian imprints*, 162, 164, 424, 449, 498–99, 524, 540, 575, 584, 623–29. R. W. McLachlan, "Fleury Mesplet, the first printer at Montreal," RSC *Trans.*, 2nd ser., 12 (1906), sect.II: 268, 300, 302. Pierre Tousignant, " 'La Gazette de Montréal' de 1791 à 1796" (thèse de MA, univ. de Montréal, 1960). Wallot, *Un Québec qui bougeait*, 63–65.

EISENBACH, FRIEDERIKE CHARLOTTE LOUISE VON RIEDESEL, Freifrau zu. *See* MASSOW

ELLICE, ALEXANDER, merchant, shipowner, landowner, and seigneur; baptized 28 May 1743 in the parish of Auchterless (Kirktown of Auchterless), Scotland, eldest son of William Ellice of Knockleith and Mary Simpson of Gartly; m. *c.* 1780 Ann (Anne) Russell; d. 28 Sept. 1805 in Bath, England, and was buried 5 October in Bath Abbey.

The son of a prosperous miller, Alexander Ellice attended Marischal College (University of Aberdeen), and was admitted to the Scottish bar. Apparently foreseeing little opportunity for success in the legal profession or in his homeland, in 1765 he led his four brothers to Schenectady, N.Y. Early in 1766, with an investment of £714 11*s.* 10*d.*, he entered into partnership with James Phyn, brother of his brother-in-law and possibly a cousin, and with John Duncan, to engage in the fur trade and general merchandising in upstate New York and the lower Great Lakes area. The firm, known as Phyn, Ellice and Company following Duncan's retirement in 1767, prospered and expanded; in 1768 Ellice's brother Robert*, and in 1769 the Detroit fur trader John Porteous, were taken into the partnership. To broaden its financial base, the company took on contracts to supply provisions for military posts and presents used by the Indian Department, and it moved into the grain trade. Ellice invested his profits shrewdly in mortgages and land in prosperous northern New York, including a valuable mill-site, acquired from Sir William Johnson*, at Little Falls. Thanks to his solid connections, in January 1770 Ellice was granted a royal patent for 40,000 acres near Cooperstown.

Until 1768 Phyn, Ellice and Company disposed of its furs at New York, but in that year, finding the New York market glutted, it sold in London. At the same time, dissatisfied with its New York suppliers, it began ordering goods directly from Britain, at first from WILLIAM and Alexander Forsyth, Glasgow friends of the Phyn and Ellice families, and then, having discovered that it was cheaper to deal with London, from Neale and Pigou, who were located there. However, in 1769 the embargo placed the previous year by American merchants on British imports prevented Phyn, Ellice from delivering its goods to the interior. To circumvent the embargo in 1770, the company had its imports shipped to Quebec, where it obtained a licence to send trade goods valued at £6,000 to Porteous at Detroit. In 1771 and 1772 Phyn, Ellice, and Porteous evolved a scheme to beat their Montreal competitors by obtaining from the British government a virtual monopoly of the supply trade to the Indian agents in the North American interior. Ellice conducted negotiations in London in the spring of 1772, but the scheme fell through.

The partnership with Porteous was terminated in the summer of 1773, and one year later a new one was established with Alexander and William Macomb of Detroit. When in October 1774 the American colonies severed commercial relations with Britain, Phyn, Ellice and Company, which now did all its business direct with London, was placed in a difficult situation. It again circumvented the embargo by importing through Montreal, where it had engaged Isaac TODD as its agent, but the ruse was detected and Ellice was severely reprimanded by the committee of correspondence at Schenectady. Phyn and Ellice had already decided that their future in the fur trade lay with Britain. At the end of 1774 Phyn left to establish a London office; the following summer Ellice went to Niagara (near Youngstown, N.Y.), ostensibly on business, but instead of returning to Schenectady, in October 1775 he continued on to England. Most of the Schenectady assets were liquidated and the remainder transferred to Ellice's brother James, who had been brought into the company some years before.

In 1776 Ellice came to Montreal, where he established Alexander Ellice and Company and began restoring Phyn, Ellice's business with the fur-trade outfitters it had formerly supplied from Schenectady. The Canadian trade being as yet relatively unstructured, he was able as well to furnish simultaneously several of the major Montreal traders, including James McGILL, Simon McTAVISH, and George McBEATH. In 1777 Ellice's investment in the fur trade of about £42,300 was by far the largest of any merchant based in the colony. That year he also stood security for

Ellice

other traders to the value of £84,500 and in 1778 to the value of £71,000. In 1778 Robert arrived at Montreal, and the following year he and John Forsyth* took over operations there under the name Robert Ellice and Company, freeing Alexander to assure communications between the London and Montreal offices.

During the American Revolutionary War Robert Ellice and Company and Phyn, Ellice's Schenectady branch furnished military supplies to, and acted as messengers and paymasters for, their respective sides. Between 1778 and 1783 the Montreal company received £28,233 for its services to the British forces. After the war Phyn, Ellice appears to have moved into the triangular trade involving America, the West Indies, and Europe. Thirty-two departures of its vessels were recorded at Quebec between 1786 and 1804; although in most cases the ships were bound for London, some went to Newfoundland, to Cadiz, or to the West Indies. Like other firms of the time, Phyn, Ellice probably held shares in at least some of the vessels it used in order to ensure a certain control of transport to market. As well, in time of war, unless captured by privateers, sunk, or confiscated by the British navy, ships were good speculative investments. Formal agreements among a number of merchants for the use of a ship during a voyage or a series of voyages enabled them to spread the costs in case of loss. Ellice's commerce in the Caribbean region and with the American Atlantic colonies led to his acquisition, for non-payment of debts, of sugar plantations in the former and landed estates in the latter.

It was as a financier, supplier, and middleman in the Canadian fur trade, however, that Ellice made most of his fortune. From 1781 to 1783 he stood security for traders to the value of £227,000 and in 1789 and 1790 to a total value of £77,200. He was heavily involved in the trade south and west of the Great Lakes through Robert Ellice and Company but the best profits were increasingly to be made in the northwest, where the trade was becoming concentrated in the hands of fewer and larger co-partnerships. Beginning in 1784 Phyn, Ellice and Company furnished trade goods to McBeath and Peter POND, each of whom owned a one-sixteenth share in the North West Company; yet it also supplied Gregory, MacLeod and Company [see John GREGORY], the NWC's major competitor until 1787. Following the formation of McTavish, Frobisher and Company [see Simon McTavish] in November 1787, Phyn, Ellice – known since a reorganization in January 1787 as Phyn, Ellices, and Inglis – obtained a contract to supply half of the new company's goods.

Since 1779 Ellice had been travelling frequently between Montreal and London, apparently maintaining residences in both cities. He seems to have acquired the confidence of, and probably some influence among, merchants on both sides of the Atlantic. In 1778 he had been made a member of a committee of Montreal importers to determine a method, acceptable to both London and Montreal merchants, for the disposal of imported goods damaged in transit by salt water. The following year he was among eight surveyors elected to oversee the newly established procedure. In 1786 Ellice presided over a gala dinner held by London merchants trading to Quebec in honour of Lord Dorchester [Guy CARLETON], recently appointed its governor-in-chief, and William Smith*, the new chief justice. He was in the colony again in October 1790 and signed a petition for the establishment of a non-sectarian university [see Jean-François Hubert*]. When, however, a few days later, he took ship for London in the company of McTavish, James McGill, and John Richardson*, it was apparently to establish a permanent residence in the imperial capital. None the less, he returned occasionally to the province, where his business activities continued undiminished. Upon Robert Ellice's death in 1790 the Montreal office was reorganized as Forsyth, Richardson and Company, Ellice being related by marriage to the two principals, John Forsyth and John Richardson. In 1798 Forsyth, Richardson became a partner in the New North West Company (sometimes called the XY Company), formed that year to compete with the NWC, and Phyn, Ellices, and Inglis found itself in the position of major supplier for both sides; indeed it became the London agent for the New North West Company. In 1804 Ellice and his son Edward*, ostensibly on behalf of the New North West Company, attempted to purchase a controlling interest in the HBC. Although unsuccessful, their bid of £103,000 provided a dramatic demonstration of Alexander's financial power. When the rival Montreal firms united in the reorganized NWC that year, Phyn, Ellices, and Inglis was able to maintain its position as a principal supplier to the new co-partnership. In 1857 Edward would assert proudly, "My father supplied the great part of the capital by which the whole north-west trade was conducted." Between 1802 and 1807 Ellice's London office registered an annual gross balance in excess of £1,000,000.

As was his custom, Ellice invested part of his profits in land holdings. Although these investments were essentially a means of achieving financial security, Ellice evinced a certain interest in agriculture, for in 1794 he became a member of the Montreal branch of the Agriculture Society. In 1795 he bought for £9,000 from Michel Chartier* de Lotbinière the seigneury of Villechauve, commonly known as Beauharnois, which measured 324 square miles. Ellice evidently intended to retire there eventually, but in the mean time, through a manager, he built a large manor-house, renamed the sub-fiefs of the seigneury for members of his family, and laid out areas for new development. To complement the seigneury he acquired most of the adjacent townships of Godmanchester and Hinchinbrook. Other lands were acquired in settlement of debts, such as 16,000 acres in Upper Canada from the fur-trading firm of Leith, Jameson and Company. In 1803 Ellice was granted 6,690 acres in Clifton Township, Lower Canada. The same year he sold the seigneury of Champlain, purchased from Joseph DRAPEAU in 1797, to Joseph FROBISHER and his partners in the Batiscan Iron Works Company.

In 1803 Ellice, having been in poor health for some time, retired from Phyn, Ellices, and Inglis. He died two years later, leaving an estate worth in excess of £450,000. It included nearly 350,000 acres of land in New York and the Canadas, as well as property in Prince Edward Island, Britain, and elsewhere, shares in the London and Montreal companies, ships, stock holdings, and mortgages. The estate was divided fairly equally among his widow and ten surviving children, some of whom had been born in Canada since Ann had often accompanied her husband on business trips. The diverse and generally successful careers pursued by the brood, including the army, the navy, the church, business, and landowning, were typical routes to prosperity followed by the sons of the rising upper middle class; none of Ellice's inheritors, however, benefited more from his father's work, or managed his heritage with greater astuteness, than Edward, who became the true successor to the Ellice empire.

In his remarkable 40-year business association with the Canadas, Alexander Ellice had contributed much to their economic life, which depended so heavily on the fur trade. The place he had opened for the Ellices in colonial affairs would endure, with modifications, until the seigneury of Beauharnois passed out of the family in 1866.

JAMES M. COLTHART

GRO, Reg. of births and baptisms for the parish of Auchterless, 28 May 1743. National Library of Scotland (Edinburgh), Dept. of MSS, MSS 15113–15, 15126, 15139. *Docs. relating to NWC* (Wallace). Smith, *Diary and selected papers* (Upton), 2: 94. *Bath Chronicle* (Bath, Eng.), 28 Sept. 1805. *Quebec Gazette*, 9 Sept. 1779; 7 Sept. 1780; 23 Aug. 1781; 28 Oct. 1784; 28 Oct., 4 Nov. 1790; 11 July 1793. Langelier, *Liste des terrains concédés*, 4, 13–14. P.-G. Roy, *Inv. concessions*, 4: 229–30. C. R. Canedy, "An entrepreneurial history of the New York frontier, 1739–1776" (PHD thesis, Case Western Reserve Univ., Cleveland, Ohio, 1967). J. C. Clarke, "From business to politics: the Ellice family, 1760–1860" (D.PHIL. thesis, Univ. of Oxford, Eng., 1974). J. M. Colthart, "Edward Ellice and North America" (PHD thesis, Princeton Univ., N.J., 1971), 12–24. Merrill Denison, *Canada's first bank: a history of the Bank of Montreal* (2v., Toronto and Montreal, 1966–67). Innis, *Fur trade in Canada* (1956), 195. D. E. T. Long, "Edward Ellice" (PHD thesis, Univ. of Toronto, 1942), 4–12.

Miquelon, "Baby family," 184, 188–89. Rich, *Hist. of HBC*. Rumilly, *La Compagnie du Nord-Ouest*, 1: 50, 62, 76, 88–91, 259. R. H. Fleming, "McTavish, Frobisher and Company of Montreal," *CHR*, 10 (1929): 140; "Phyn, Ellice and Company of Schenectady," *Contributions to Canadian Economics* (Toronto), 4 (1932): 7–41. H. A. Innis, "The North West Company," *CHR*, 8 (1927): 314–15. Ouellet, "Dualité économique et changement technologique," *SH*, 9: 256–96. W. S. Wallace, "Forsyth, Richardson and Company in the fur trade," RSC *Trans.*, 3rd ser., 34 (1940), sect.II: 187–94.

ELLIOTT, MATTHEW, farmer, Indian Department official, politician, and militia officer; b. *c.* 1739 in County Donegal (Republic of Ireland); d. 7 May 1814 at what is now Burlington, Ont.

Matthew Elliott came to North America in 1761 and settled in Pennsylvania. During Pontiac*'s uprising he served as a volunteer in Colonel Henry Bouquet's forces, going with him to the relief of Fort Pitt (Pittsburgh, Pa) in 1763 and against the Indians of the Ohio country the following year. In the decade before the American revolution Elliott traded among the Shawnees on the Scioto River, in what is now Ohio. In 1774 he was the emissary for the Shawnees who met Lord Dunmore, the governor of Virginia, when he advanced into the Ohio country. On the eve of the revolution Elliott was the partner of Alexander Blaine of Carlisle, Pa. He continued to trade in the Ohio region during the winter of 1775–76, and in the summer of 1776 acted as an American emissary to invite the Shawnees and Delawares to a treaty at Fort Pitt. He kept this episode secret later in his life when he became a loyalist.

During the winter of 1776–77 Elliott again journeyed to the Shawnee towns, and in the spring he visited British-held Detroit in an attempt to regain goods stolen from him by Senecas. Arrested as a suspected American spy, he was sent to Quebec but was soon allowed to return to Pittsburgh on parole. He arrived there in early 1778. Apparently feeling he had little to gain by staying, in March he fled to Detroit along with Alexander McKee* and Simon GIRTY. He served as a scout on Henry Hamilton*'s expedition to Vincennes (Ind.) in the autumn of 1778 but left before Hamilton was captured by the Americans in February 1779. For the remainder of the revolution Elliott served as a British Indian agent. He saw action at the defeat of American captain David Rodgers on the Ohio in the summer of 1779 and during Captain Henry Bird's expedition against Kentucky in 1780. The next spring he accompanied a band of warriors into Kentucky once again. Later in the year he headed the party that forcibly removed from their homes a colony of Indians converted by the Moravians and settled along the Muskingum (Tuscarawas) River (Ohio) [see Glikhikan*]. These Indians had on an earlier occasion saved Elliott's life, but he brought along some trade

Elliott

goods, intending to buy up their cattle for a few dollars each and sell them at high prices in Detroit; the possibility of a quick profit was never far from his thoughts. In 1782 he fought near present-day Upper Sandusky, Ohio, in the defeat of American colonel William Crawford and again at Blue Licks (near Cowan, Ky).

After the revolution Elliott established himself on a farm at what later became Amherstburg, Upper Canada. His home developed into a show-place in the region; he eventually owned over 4,000 acres and many slaves, a number of whom he had acquired in the course of raids during the revolution and refused to relinquish despite government pressure. In partnership with William Caldwell* he renewed his trading activities, dealing with the Indians south of Lake Erie and bringing flour, cattle, bacon, and other provisions from Pittsburgh to sell at Detroit as well. But it was becoming increasingly difficult to do business in that disputed area and the firm went bankrupt in 1787. In spite of this misfortune and the handicap of illiteracy, Elliott became a justice of the peace for the new District of Hesse in 1788.

Elliott continued to encourage the Shawnees to oppose the American advance across the Ohio River, and in 1790 he became assistant to McKee, who was Indian superintendent at Detroit. Along with McKee, in the early 1790s Elliott helped organize the various tribes to resist American military expeditions and refuse American requests for land cessions. His main area of operations was along the Miamis (Maumee) River. Much of his time was spent in distributing British supplies to the Indians, a necessity if the warriors were to stay assembled, and it is likely that he went beyond official British policy in his efforts to strengthen their resistance. Elliott was present at the battle of Fallen Timbers in August 1794, but as an observer not as a participant; the British chose not to support the Indians militarily and the Indian forces were crushed.

Meanwhile, earlier in the decade Elliott had made amends for his harsh treatment of the Moravians and their converts, first by allowing them to take refuge on his farm and then, because they wished to be at a distance from the corrupting influences of the white community, by arranging for them to settle near what is now Thamesville, Ont. [see David ZEISBERGER]. He even attended the service at their meeting-house on Christmas Day 1791.

In the summer of 1796 Elliott became "superintendent of Indians and of Indian Affairs for the District of Detroit," but he was suspected of peculation and was involved in clashes with the military authorities. In December 1797 he was dismissed. The Indian Department was traditionally careless in its accounting and secretive about its business, and Elliott appears to have been about as honest as the average

officer. He had been accustomed to working in an atmosphere of crisis, and after that atmosphere evaporated following the signing of Jay's Treaty in 1794, he failed to adapt to the more orderly practices of peace-time administration. During the next ten years he made considerable efforts to secure reinstatement. He even travelled to England in 1804, but his efforts failed despite recommendations by Sir John Johnson*, superintendent general of Indian affairs, and David William Smith*, former speaker of the Upper Canadian House of Assembly. His farm, however, was prospering. In 1796 one traveller, Isaac Weld*, described it as "cultivated in a style that would not be thought meanly of even in England." From 1800 to 1804 he was a member of the House of Assembly, attending regularly and participating actively in the proceedings. He was re-elected in 1804 and 1808 but attended less frequently because of other business. On several occasions he appeared before authorities at York (Toronto) on behalf of groups of his constituents who were seeking land grants.

When after 1807 another crisis erupted in British-American relations, the great importance of Elliott's influence among the Indians was recognized. In the spring of 1808 he was reappointed superintendent in place of Thomas McKee, Alexander's son. During the years preceding the War of 1812 he helped persuade the Indians within American territory to join the British in the event of war, supplied them with provisions, and encouraged the confederacy being organized by the Shawnee TECUMSEH and his brother the Prophet [Tenskwatawa*] for the purpose of resisting American encroachments on Indian lands. In the war itself he was actively in the field, leading the Indian allies of the British and bearing the rank of lieutenant-colonel in the Essex County militia. He was present in August 1812 at the taking of Detroit from the Americans and the next month accompanied the Indians on Major Adam C. Muir's abortive expedition against Fort Wayne (Ind.). In order to ease the pressure on provisions at Detroit, Elliott led a large number of Indians to winter at the rapids of the Miamis River (Maumee, Ohio), where the Americans had abandoned supplies of corn and cattle. In 1813 he was at the battle of Frenchtown and the sieges of Fort Meigs (near Perrysburg, Ohio) and Fort Stephenson (Fremont, Ohio). The British commander, Henry Procter*, blamed him for failing to prevent the Indians from killing American prisoners, and it is possible that Elliott, being over 70 and having lost his son Alexander in the war, did not make every effort; however, the warriors in their growing bitterness were more and more inclined to take revenge on the Americans who were driving them from their lands. In the autumn he was with the Indians who covered Procter's retreat and who fought with desperation in the battle of Moraviantown. During the last months of

302

his life his base of operations was the Burlington area and in the winter of 1813–14 he led the Indians in raids on the Niagara frontier. He became ill and died on 7 May, after almost half a century's experience of border warfare.

Elliott for many years had lived with a Shawnee woman, and she was the mother of Alexander and of Matthew, who was active among the Shawnees in the Amherstburg region for many years. In 1810 Elliott married young Sarah Donovan, and they had two sons, Francis Gore and Robert Herriot Barclay. Perhaps influenced by some "ungentlemanly remarks" of Elliott's, an American prisoner whom he had ransomed from the Indians about 1793 left the following description of his rescuer: "Elliott's hair was black, his complexion dark, his features small; his nose was short . . . turning up at the end, his look was haughty, and his countenance repulsive." Throughout his career Elliott was always willing, and often able, to turn any situation to his own advantage, but he was also effective in maintaining British influence among the Indians along the borders of Upper Canada.

REGINALD HORSMAN

An extensive bibliography on Elliott is contained in Reginald Horsman, *Matthew Elliott, British Indian agent* (Detroit, 1964). Particularly useful sources include the following: BL, Add. MSS 21661–892 (transcripts at PAC). Carnegie Library (Pittsburgh, Pa.), George Morgan, letter books, 1775–79. DPL, Burton Hist. Coll., John Askin papers; Solomon Sibley papers. Pa., Hist. Soc. (Philadelphia), Yeates family papers, corr., 1762–80. PAC, MG 11, [CO 42] Q; MG 19, F1; RG 1, E3, 12–13; RG 4, B17, 13–14; RG 8, I (C ser.); RG 10, A1, 1–4; A2, 8–12. PRO, AO 12/40, 12/66, 12/109. *Corr. of Hon. Peter Russell* (Cruikshank and Hunter). *Corr. of Lieut. Governor Simcoe* (Cruikshank). *Frontier defense on the upper Ohio, 1777–1778* . . . , ed. R. G. Thwaites and L. P. Kellogg (Madison, Wis., 1912; repr. Millwood, N.Y., 1973). J. [E. G.] Heckewelder, *Narrative of the mission of the United Brethren among the Delaware and Mohegan Indians, from its commencement, in the year 1740, to the close of the year 1808* . . . (Philadelphia, 1820; repr. [New York], 1971), 232–36, 244–45, 276–77. *Mich. Pioneer Coll.*, 9 (1886), 10 (1886), 12 (1887), 15 (1889), 20 (1892), 23 (1893), 24 (1894), 25 (1894). Isaac Weld, *Travels through the states of North America, and the provinces of Upper and Lower Canada, during the years 1795, 1796, and 1797* (London, 1799), 343–59. *Windsor border region* (Lajeunesse). [David Zeisberger,] *Diary of David Zeisberger, a Moravian missionary among the Indians of Ohio*, ed. and trans. E. F. Bliss (2v., Cincinnati, Ohio, 1885), 1: 3–17; 2: 153–54, 173–75, 179–81, 203–6, 210–11.

ELMSLEY (Elmsly), JOHN, judge and politician; b. 1762 in the parish of Marylebone, London, England, eldest son of Alexander Elmsly (Elmslie) and Anne Elligood; m. 23 July 1796 Mary Hallowell in London, and they had five children including John Elmsley*; d. 29 April 1805 in Montreal, Lower Canada.

The Elmslie family came from the parish of Touch, Kincraigie, in Aberdeenshire, Scotland, where they were small farmers and Quakers. In the mid 18th century Alexander and his brother Peter moved to London, changed the spelling of their name to Elmsly, and joined the Church of England. John Elmsley entered Oriel College, University of Oxford, on 3 Dec. 1782, graduating with a BA in 1786 and an MA in 1789. He was called to the bar at the Inner Temple on 7 May 1790. Through connections with the Home secretary, the Duke of Portland, Elmsley secured the chief justiceship of Upper Canada in April 1796, when he was resident at Lincoln's Inn. On 20 Nov. 1796 he arrived at Newark (Niagara-on-the-Lake) with his friend, the Reverend Thomas Raddish (Reddish); his bride and her loyalist father, Benjamin Hallowell, followed later after a lengthy visit in Boston, Mass., their home until March 1776.

Lieutenant Governor John Graves SIMCOE had left the province in July, choosing Peter RUSSELL to act as administrator in his absence. The government officials were rather unwillingly preparing to follow Simcoe's orders and move the seat of government from Newark to York (Toronto). Elmsley objected strongly to the move because he thought that there would be great difficulty in finding lodgings and jurors for the Court of King's Bench and the Home District court, both of which automatically held their sessions in the capital. He and Russell quarrelled acrimoniously on this issue thoughout most of 1797. In July 1797 a resolute Elmsley paid £1,105 for a house in Newark. Russell insisted that the capital be moved, and in June 1797 met his first parliament in York. A compromise was reached by passing a bill permitting the courts to remain at Newark for a further two years. Elmsley finally moved to York in the spring of 1798, building a large house that later became the lieutenant governor's residence.

Russell and Elmsley continued to disagree about almost everything. In November 1797 Russell had renewed his own temporary appointment as a puisne judge, first made by Simcoe in 1795. Elmsley immediately objected, and his objection was upheld by the Duke of Portland on the principle of separation of judicial and executive authority. Other issues continued to divide the administrator and the chief justice.

In April 1799 Peter HUNTER was appointed lieutenant governor of Upper Canada and commander of the forces in the Canadas, and on 16 August he arrived in York. Because his military responsibilities necessitated long absences from the province Hunter left its administration mainly to a committee of the Executive Council consisting of Russell, Æneas SHAW, and Elmsley, who was chairman. During the early years of the Hunter administration Elmsley was the most powerful man in the province, but he later

Émond

lost much of his influence to his own nominee as judge, Henry ALLCOCK, and to the attorney general, Thomas Scott*.

While he was in Upper Canada Elmsley was particularly concerned with land granting problems, the provisional agreement with Lower Canada on tariffs, and the administration of the courts and law. In land and tariff matters he was greatly influenced by his friend Richard CARTWRIGHT and generally supported the loyalist and merchant point of view. In legal matters he tried to adapt English law to Canadian circumstances. He objected, for example, to the complicated English machinery by which married women alienated property, and introduced a bill to make such transactions easier. In this attitude he was consistently opposed by Allcock, who believed that there should be absolutely no tampering with English law, procedures, and precedents.

Elmsley wrote reports on many subjects in Upper Canada, especially in the early years of Hunter's administration. They are usually clear and sensible, but as in his private correspondence he revealed a tendency to dramatize events, his own actions, and his deteriorating relations with others. He was one of the few university graduates in the province, and was much given to elegant phrases and Latin quotations, a habit that may not have endeared him to all his colleagues.

At the time of his appointment to Upper Canada, Elmsley was promised promotion to the chief justiceship of Lower Canada, should it become vacant. In 1800, however, he withdrew his claim because he feared that he would lose money with another move. Despite his reluctance he was appointed to the Lower Canadian post in May 1802, following the resignation of William Osgoode*. The salary was increased from £1,000 to £1,500 a year, and he was to be called to the Executive and Legislative councils with a "seat next in Rank to the Lieutenant Governor."

Elmsley was urged to hurry to Quebec, but he waited for Hunter's return to York and did not take the oaths of office in the lower province until 29 Oct. 1802. Although he was "perfectly master of the French language" and had studied "the old norman law" in France, he was at a disadvantage in Lower Canada because he constantly had to depend on others for specialized knowledge and advice on French jurisprudence. It probably did not help that he regarded the French judicial system as inferior to the English. In any event his career in Quebec was brief. From June to November 1803 he was on leave in England, and in November 1804 he became seriously ill. In February 1805 he went to Montreal intending to travel in the United States to recover his health, but he died there on 29 April 1805. His widow and children returned to England; his large houses in York and

Quebec were both eventually bought by the government.

In this period the position of chief justice was extremely important in the administration of the province. In both Upper and Lower Canada Elmsley was president of the Executive Council and speaker of the Legislative Council. He was particularly powerful in Upper Canada because there was no resident lieutenant governor throughout his entire career there. His difficulty in working with others, however, combined with occasional impetuousness to prevent his accomplishing all that he wished. Like so many of the early government officials he was obsessed with his own importance and with his precarious personal finances. Although his contemporaries all agreed that he had great ability, his quarrelsomeness, especially with Russell and Allcock, greatly reduced his influence.

EDITH G. FIRTH

AO, MS 75; MS 78. MTL, John Elmsley letterbook; William Dummer Powell papers; Peter Russell papers; D. W. Smith papers. PAC, MG 23, GII, 10, vol.4: 1596–99; HI, 3; 5; RG 1, E1, 46–48; E14, 10–11. PRO, CO 42/120–31, 42/320–42. QUA, Richard Cartwright papers. *Corr. of Hon. Peter Russell* (Cruikshank and Hunter). *Corr of Lieut. Governor Simcoe* (Cruikshank). *Gentleman's Magazine*, 1805: 677. *Alumni Oxonienses; the members of the University of Oxford, 1715–1866 . . .*, comp. Joseph Foster (4v., Oxford and London, 1888), 2: 423. Armstrong, *Handbook of Upper Canadian chronology*. F.-J. Audet, *Les juges en chef de la province de Québec, 1764–1924* (Québec, 1927), 37–38. D. B. Read, *The lives of the judges of Upper Canada and Ontario, from 1791 to the present time* (Toronto, 1888), 43–52. *The register book of marriages belonging to the parish of St George, Hanover Square, in the county of Middlesex*, ed. J. H. Chapman and G. J. Armytage (4v., London, 1886–97), 2: 151. Dooner, *Catholic pioneers in U.C.*, 193–201. *Life and letters of Hon. Richard Cartwright* (Cartwright). MacDonald, "Hon. Richard Cartwright," *Three hist. theses*. W. R. Riddell, *The bar and the courts of the province of Upper Canada, or Ontario* (Toronto, 1928); *Legal profession in U.C.*; *Life of William Dummer Powell*. E. A. Cruikshank, "A memoir of Lieutenant-General Peter Hunter," *OH*, 30 (1934): 5–32. E. G. Firth, "The administration of Peter Russell, 1796–1799," *OH*, 48 (1956): 163–81.

ÉMOND, PIERRE, master carpenter and woodcarver; b. 24 April 1738 at Quebec, to a "father and mother not married to one another"; m. there 6 Sept. 1762 Françoise Navarre; d. there 3 Oct. 1808.

The circumstances of Pierre's birth remain obscure but he was taken in charge, probably as an infant, and given his name by Pierre Émond, a native of Rivière-Ouelle (Que.). He was trained as a carpenter in either the workshop of François-Noël* and Jean-Baptiste-Antoine* Levasseur, already well

Émond

established at Quebec, or that of Jean BAILLAIRGÉ. The second possibility is more plausible, because in various aspects of style Émond's work has much in common with that of Baillairgé's son PIERRE-FLORENT.

Émond's career was mainly spent working for the religious communities in the town of Quebec. He was employed in particular by the Séminaire de Québec, the Hôtel-Dieu, and the Hôpital Général, which after the Seven Years' War had to repair their damaged buildings. He began his career as a carpenter quite early, at the age of 21, and he was at no loss for orders. The Séminaire de Québec made extensive use of the talents of the young man, who lived a stone's throw from its walls. In 1761 Émond, who at that time was referred to simply as a carpenter, rented "part of a two-storey stone house situated near the ramparts and near the close of Messrs the priests of the seminary of the said town of Quebec." In 1768, the year in which Jean Baillairgé produced the plans for reconstructing the church of Notre-Dame in Quebec, Émond took on the job of repairing the Hôpital Général, where he carried out large-scale works in 1769 and 1770, particularly in the chapel; the plan for the latter, which indicates that the building had been occupied by the Recollets, was completely changed. Émond drew attention to himself at that time by his technical skill and his patience in awaiting payment for his services. He was to remain "the usual workman" for the nuns of the hospital until his death.

The seminary's property at Petit Cap (Cap Tourmente) was developed after 1778; Émond supervised the building of the house, known as Château Bellevue; he drew up the plans and, with the help of mason Michel-Augustin Jourdain, executed the portal and tower of the chapel. Some time after 1799 he supervised the construction of the chapel of the Hôtel-Dieu and added a porch to it [see Marie-Geneviève PARENT, named de Saint-François d'Assise]. At the same period Émond did various smaller pieces of work for the Ursulines, including repairs to their chapel tower, a task that seems to have been his speciality. He also produced plans for churches. For example, his name is mentioned in the contract for building the church of Saint-Ambroise (Loretteville, Que.).

Although Émond excelled in carpentry, much of his time after 1785 was taken up with ornamental wood-carving and statuary. In that period Bishop Briand* commissioned him to embellish his private chapel within the precincts of the seminary. The decoration, a very delicate piece of work, consists solely of a wall-retable with a slightly projecting central portion on which rest the branches of an olive tree which in turn frame a canvas depicting the marriage of the Blessed Virgin. The churchwardens of the *fabrique* of Notre-Dame entrusted Émond with the task of carving two retables (the structures housing the altars), one in 1789 for the Sainte-Anne chapel, and the second in 1803 for the Sainte-Famille chapel. This agreement may have been made in order to have him share in the work being done by the Baillairgés, who were responsible for the masterly ornamentation of the cathedral's chancel. Émond continued his decorative work until his death, producing for the parishes around Quebec tabernacles, crosses, candlesticks, and other furnishings designed to enhance the splendour of liturgical ceremonies or to provide storage in the sacristy for the numerous vestments required.

At the same time, in conjunction with his professional activity Émond on a few occasions acted as agent for his fellow citizens and as referee in disputes concerning buildings in progress. At the time of the American invasion in 1775, he was a corporal in the Quebec militia. In 1790 he became a member of the Fire Society. In addition, when occasion arose he joined with the local notables in signing petitions to the governor, particularly on educational matters. On 27 Dec. 1797 he was elected a churchwarden of the *fabrique* of Notre-Dame.

Stylistically Émond belonged to the French régime, doing wood-carvings for customers who were not greatly concerned about change. Although his production shows a high degree of workmanship – Bishop Briand's chapel is an eloquent witness – Émond displayed no desire for new directions beyond what was required by his situation as a craftsman employed on a regular basis by the religious communities. Moreover, the presence at Quebec of François Baillairgé*, who had been trained in France and who was acutely aware of the new trends, discouraged any attempts at competition.

Pierre Émond kept working until his death in 1808. He left no children and does not seem to have trained apprentices. The inventory of his assets lists among his personal effects a few books, including one treatise on architecture and two on astronomy. The architectural tradition of New France died with him; François and, later, Thomas Baillairgé* were of another school.

RAYMONDE GAUTHIER

ANQ-Q, CE1-1, 24 avril 1738, 6 sept. 1762, 5 oct. 1808; CN1-16, 22 juill. 1806; 31 juill. 1807; 28 mai, 16 juin, 30 août, 26 déc. 1810; CN1-25, 23 avril 1778; CN1-26, 31 déc. 1805, 31 déc. 1806; CN1-83, 2 mai 1785; 26 janv., 11 févr., 19 nov. 1792; CN1-92, 31 mars, 8 avril 1785; 2 mai 1786; 29 oct., 6 nov. 1795; 19 avril 1802; CN1-99, 10 mars 1808; CN1-178, 23 janv. 1797, 28 janv. 1798, 23 mai 1808, 13 mars 1809; CN1-205, 20 janv. 1780; 5 sept. 1781; 8 avril, 14 nov. 1783; 18 févr. 1784; 27 avril 1785; 16 juill. 1798; CN1-224, 21 janv. 1783; CN1-230, 21 avril 1795; 27 nov. 1798; 14 nov. 1799; 14 mars, 6, 21 mai 1803; 7, 9 mai 1805;

England

CN1-248, 5 sept 1762, 31 mai 1764; CN1-250, 18 juill., 12 oct. 1761; CN1-284, 13 mai 1789; 26, 31 mars, 13 mai 1791; 19 nov. 1792; 17 oct. 1795; 2 mars 1797; 11 mars, 30 oct. 1800; 30 janv. 1801; 24 mars, 1er oct. 1804; 11 août 1807; 17 févr. 1808. Arch. de l'Hôpital Général de Québec, Communauté, Journal, I: ff.113, 132, 161. Arch. du monastère de l'Hôtel-Dieu de Québec, Lettres, carton 5, nos.1–5. ASQ, Évêques, nos.29–38. MAC-CD, Fonds Morisset, 2, E54.5/P622. Raymonde [Landry] Gauthier, *Les tabernacles anciens du Québec des XVIIe , XVIIIe et XIXe siècles* ([Québec], 1974). Morisset, *Coup d'œil sur les arts.* Luc Noppen, *Les églises du Québec (1600–1850)* (Québec, 1977), 29, 35, 164, 176, 188, 190, 246; *Notre-Dame de Québec, son architecture et son rayonnement (1647–1922)* (Québec, 1974), 145–55. Luc Noppen et al., *La maison Maizerets, le château Bellevue: deux exemples de la diffusion de l'architecture du séminaire de Québec aux XVIIIe et XIXe siècles* (Québec, 1978). Jean Palardy, *The early furniture of French Canada* (Toronto, 1963). J. R. Porter, *L'art de la dorure au Québec du XVIIe siècle à nos jours* (Québec, 1975). Ramsay Traquair, *The old architecture of Quebec . . .* (Toronto, 1947). Gérard Morisset, "La chapelle de monseigneur Briand," *La Patrie* (Montréal), 18 févr. 1951: 26–27; and "Le sculpteur Pierre Émond (1738–1808)" in RSC *Trans.*, 3rd ser., 39 (1946), sect.I: 91–98, and in *La Patrie*, 30 août 1953: 28–29.

ENGLAND, RICHARD G., army officer and office holder; b. *c.* 1750 in Lifford, County Clare (Republic of Ireland); m. Anne O'Brien, daughter of James O'Brien of Ennistymon, County Clare, and they had at least one son and one daughter; d. 7 Nov. 1812 in London, England.

Richard G. England first entered the British army on 20 Nov. 1765, when he was commissioned ensign in the 47th Foot; in 1770 he became a captain. The regiment was sent in 1773 to North America, where England served with distinction during the American revolution. He was wounded at Bunker Hill, Mass., in 1775, took part in the relief of Quebec in 1776 [*see* Richard Montgomery*], and accompanied John Burgoyne*'s expedition in 1777, being taken prisoner in October with the rest of Burgoyne's force at Saratoga (Schuylerville, N.Y.). Following his release he was promoted lieutenant-colonel of the 24th Foot on 20 Feb. 1783.

The 24th was sent to Canada in 1789, and after three years at Montreal and Quebec it was ordered to garrison Detroit and the western posts, which the British had continued to occupy since the treaty of 1783. England arrived at Detroit in June 1792 and became commandant there. By virtue of his position he assumed the presidency of the land board of the District of Hesse (renamed the Western District in October), chairing all meetings from 29 June 1792 to 12 Dec. 1794, when the board was dissolved. Although the main work of the board, whose members included John ASKIN and Jean-Baptiste-Pierre TESTARD Louvigny de Montigny, was simply to adjudi-cate claims and grant certificates for land, England himself did much to encourage immigration into the area. He had difficult relations with "that infamous fellow," deputy surveyor Patrick McNIFF, whom he believed unsuited for his job and whom on one occasion he criticized for plotting only half the lots the commandant thought should be made available to settlers. England did not neglect his own interest in land; in 1795 he successfully petitioned for 2,000 acres on the Thames River (Ont.).

As commandant of Detroit in the 1790s, England was naturally much involved with the dispute then occurring between the Indians and the Americans over the Ohio valley. He cooperated with Indian Department officials such as Alexander McKee* and Matthew ELLIOTT in their efforts to support the Indians, and took the initiative himself in reassuring the native peoples of British aid. On orders from Lieutenant Governor SIMCOE, he built and garrisoned Fort Miamis (Maumee, Ohio) in the spring of 1794 as a further reminder of British presence in the region. Despite the worsening situation, England retained his reputation as a humane and gallant officer. At his own expense he procured the release of more than 50 Americans held prisoner by the Indians, clothed them, and sent them home, earning one grateful captive's praise as a "gentleman and a man of great humanity." In the changed situation following the American victory over the Indians at Fallen Timbers (near Waterville, Ohio) in August 1794, England had to deal with disaffection among the inhabitants of the Detroit region. That same year he detained Jean-Antoine Ledru* on suspicion of republican agitation, and both he and Edmund BURKE (1753–1820) later accused leading citizens of Detroit of clandestine correspondence with the Americans. When he received word that Detroit was to be relinquished to the Americans, England determined to maintain a British presence in the region. At a site on the Canadian side of the Detroit River he constructed several buildings which later formed the basis for the town of Amherstburg. He sternly suppressed the attempt by some spiteful and resentful soldiers to destroy public and private property before the evacuation of Detroit, which took place without incident on 11 July 1796.

England then proceeded with his family (whom he had brought to Detroit with him) to Quebec where that year they took ship for home. Britain was now at war with France, and a French privateer captured the Englands and took them to France. His wife and family were released but it was some time before he was permitted to join them in London. He saw no more active service, but was appointed colonel of the 5th Foot on 21 Aug. 1801 and lieutenant governor of Plymouth on 9 Aug. 1803, and received promotion to lieutenant-general on 25 Sept. 1803.

Six feet six inches tall and of "large dimensions," England was described as "a cheerful, open countenanced, masculine soldier." He was noted for his fondness for good living and his wry sense of humour, and was the subject of jocular anecdotes while at Detroit and elsewhere. Among his other characteristics was his strong attachment to his family. His brother Poole served with him in the 47th, and after being placed on half pay in 1783 settled in Kingston, where in 1797 he was clerk of the peace. England's son Richard, born at Detroit in 1793, established a reputation in the Crimean War and died a lieutenant-general.

FRANKLIN B. WICKWIRE

Gentleman's Magazine, July–December 1812: 500. *John Askin papers* (Quaife). *The later correspondence of George III*, ed. Arthur Aspinall (5v., Cambridge, Eng., 1962–70), 3: 199–200. J. A. McClung, *Sketches of western adventure* . . . (Maysville, Ky., 1832; repr. New York, 1969), 300. *Windsor border region* (Lajeunesse). G. B. Catlin, *The story of Detroit* (Detroit, 1923). H. M. Chichester and George Burges-Short, *The records and badges of every regiment and corps in the British army* (London, 1895). *DNB* (biog. of Sir Richard England). J. B. M. Frederick, *Lineage book of the British army, mounted corps and infantry, 1660–1968* (Cornwallville, N.Y., 1969). Silas Farmer, *History of Detroit and Wayne County and early Michigan: a chronological cyclopedia of the past and present* (3rd ed., 2v., Detroit, 1890).

ERSKINE. *See* ASKIN

F

FAIRFIELD, WILLIAM, businessman, office holder, and politician; b. 1769 or 1770 in Pawlet Township (Vt), third child and second son of William Fairfield and Abigail Baker; m. first Elizabeth Billings, and they had four children; m. secondly Clarissa Fulton, and they had three children; d. 6 Feb. 1816 at Ernestown (Bath), Upper Canada.

In 1777 William Fairfield's father, a farmer in southwestern Vermont who had managed to clear only a small portion of his 300 acres, lost much of his property to the American army that was advancing to meet the force led by John Burgoyne*. The following year, after Burgoyne's defeat in the Saratoga campaign, Fairfield Sr joined the loyalist corps later commanded by Edward JESSUP, and he served with this unit for the duration of the war. In 1779 his wife and children, including young William, moved to Machiche (Yamachiche), Que., and with the conclusion of hostilities in 1783 the entire family made its way to the lands west of the Ottawa River set aside for loyalist units. The men of Jessup's Rangers were allotted townships No.6 (Edwardsburg), No.7 (Augusta), and part of No.8 (Elizabethtown), all along the St Lawrence, as well as No.2 (Ernestown), west of Cataraqui (Kingston). By July 1784 Fairfield and his family had settled in Township No.2, where they received a grant of 550 acres of land. Within a short time William Sr had become a prosperous merchant, and in 1793 he finished building a large two-storey house, near present-day Amherstview, for his family of 12 children.

William Fairfield Jr, evidently in charge of a mill by the early 1790s, built a home in the village of Ernestown in 1796. During the years before the War of 1812 Ernestown grew rapidly, partly because of its location at the mouth of the Bay of Quinte and partly because of its role as the supplier of foodstuffs to Kingston. Several decades later the historian William Canniff* went so far as to claim that in the pre-war period Ernestown "rivalled even Kingston itself, in respect to rapid increase of inhabitants, the establishment of trade, building of ships, and from the presence of gentlemen of refinement and education." William was a prominent figure in this flourishing community. A partner with his brothers Benjamin and Stephen in Benjamin Fairfield and Company, William was involved in milling, shipbuilding, and merchandising. After the death of their father in December 1812, the brothers carried on his mercantile business, contracting with the commissariat to supply the garrison at Kingston. William, although still maintaining a residence in Ernestown, managed the Kingston operations; Stephen was responsible for Cornwall; and Benjamin tended affairs in Ernestown. The brothers dealt in hay, pork, flour, tea, shoes, oil, tobacco, and snuff, but their main commodity was beef. In 1814, for instance, they contracted to supply 7,000 to 15,000 pounds of beef per week and had some difficulty fulfilling the contract until the commissariat gave them a permit to import cattle from New York State.

William was active in other ways as well. Besides serving as a justice of the peace and as a commissioner of the roads, he entered the House of Assembly in 1799 for the riding of Ontario and Addington, to sit in the place of Christopher Robinson*, who had died the previous year. The administrator of the province, Peter RUSSELL, claimed that, in choosing Fairfield over Attorney General John White*, the voters of Ontario and Addington had revealed their "low

Fanning

Ignorance" and their preference for "an illiterate young Man of their own level & neighbourhood." Along with his brothers Benjamin and Stephen and Robert McDowall*, Fairfield was on a local committee responsible for the establishment in March 1811 of Ernestown Academy. Founded with the object of instructing "Youth in English reading, speaking, grammar and composition, the learned languages, penmanship, arithmetic, geography and other branches of Liberal Education," this institution was a symbol of popular opposition to the Kingston grammar school, which was widely disliked in the Midland District because of its classical curriculum and its monopoly of government funds. The academy also symbolized the wide gulf between the radicals of Ernestown, a group of which the Fairfields were apparently leading members, and the conservatives of Kingston, for its first "preceptor" was the American democrat Barnabas Bidwell*. Although Bidwell's appointment provoked a vitriolic debate in the *Kingston Gazette*, the school continued in operation until the War of 1812, when it was converted into a barracks. After the war it served briefly as a church before reverting to its role as a school in 1818.

William Fairfield died on 6 Feb. 1816 at his home in Ernestown "after a confinement of 9 days, with a bilious fever, accompanied by an inflammation of the liver." In the absence of a clergyman, Bidwell conducted the funeral. An obituary in the *Kingston Gazette* noted that "this is the first link that has been broken in a family chain of twelve brothers and sisters, all arrived at years of maturity. In his death not only his family, but also the Township and the District have lost a valuable member. . . . As a magistrate and a man, he was characterized by intelligence, impartiality, independence of mind and liberality of sentiments."

MARGARET SHARP ANGUS

Anglican Church of Canada, Diocese of Ont. Arch. (Kingston), St John's Church, Ernestown, reg. of baptisms, marriages, and burials. BL, Add. MSS 21786, 21822, 21828–29. PAC, RG 1, L1, 22: 516, 584; 25: 161; 27: 19; L3, 186: F3/77; 188: F10/7; 195A: F misc./35; RG 68, General index, 1651–1841: ff.424, 428. QUA, Fairfield family papers. [E. P. Gwillim (Simcoe)], *Mrs. Simcoe's diary*, ed. M. Q. Innis (Toronto and New York, 1965). *Kingston before War of 1812* (Preston). *The loyalist trail*, comp. R. M. Bruce ([Kingston, 1965]). *Parish reg. of Kingston* (Young). "United Empire Loyalists: enquiry into losses and services," AO *Report*, 1904: 224–27, 283–85, 350, 654, 799, 867, 877–78, 909–10, 1019, 1021. "U.C. land book C," AO *Report*, 1931: 88. *Kingston Gazette*, 26 March 1811; 10 Feb., 6 April 1816. Armstrong, *Handbook of Upper Canadian chronology*. C. C. J. Bond, *City on the Ottawa: a detailed historical guide to Ottawa, the capital of Canada* (Ottawa, 1967). William Canniff, *History of the settlement of Upper Canada (Ontario) with special reference to the Bay Quinte* (Toronto, 1869; repr. Belleville, Ont., 1971). W. S. Herrington, *History of the county of Lennox and Addington* (Toronto, 1913; repr. Belleville, 1972). G. H. Patterson, "Studies in elections and public opinion in Upper Canada" (PHD thesis, Univ. of Toronto, 1969). Reid, *Loyalists in Ont.* E. R. Stuart, "Jessup's Rangers as a factor in loyalist settlement," *Three hist. theses*.

FANNING, EDMUND, army officer, colonial administrator, and land agent; b. 24 April 1739 in that part of Southold Township, N.Y., which is now Riverhead, son of Captain James Fanning and Hannah Smith; d. 28 Feb. 1818 in London, England.

Edmund Fanning graduated from Yale College in 1757 and moved to Childsburgh (Hillsborough) in Orange County, N.C., where five years later he was admitted to the bar. Rapidly acquiring offices and reputation, in the 1760s he served variously as a militia colonel, registrar of deeds, assemblyman for Orange County, and a Superior Court judge. Reputed "the best educated man in the province," Fanning became a particular favourite of Governor William Tryon, but he was also the object of great public outcry as an interloping pluralist and exploiter of the common people. According to one set of contemporary satirical verses:

> When Fanning first to Orange came
> He looked both pale and wan,
> An old patched coat upon his back
> An old mare he rode on.
>
> Both man and mare wa'nt worth five pounds
> As I've been often told
> But by his civil robberies
> He's laced his coat with gold.

By 1768 Fanning had become the chief symbol of corruption for the Regulation – an outburst of popular back-country opposition to seaboard domination – and the main target as well for the mob violence associated with it. His house was on several occasions set aflame, and in 1770 he was dragged through the streets of Hillsborough, a humiliation that contributed to Tryon's forcible suppression of the Regulation in a pitched battle at Great Alamance Creek the following year.

When Tryon was transferred to the governorship of New York in 1771, Fanning was more than pleased to abandon North Carolina and accompany his patron as private secretary. He subsequently served as surrogate of New York City from 1771 and provincial surveyor general from 1774. On 6 July 1774 the University of Oxford awarded him a doctorate of civil laws. At the outbreak of the American rebellion Fanning received permission to raise and command a force of loyalists known as the King's American Regiment or the

Associated Refugees, which soon became notorious in the colonies for the ferocity of its fighting and cruel treatment of the enemy.

Fanning has been portrayed in American historical mythology as an evil tyrant (an interpretation given much circulation by the publication in Boston in 1771 of a work attributed to Hermon Husbands, *A fan for Fanning, and a touch-stone to Tryon, containing an impartial account of the rise and progress of the so much talked of Regulation in North-Carolina*). There is thus a disparity between his earlier notoriety and assessments of his subsequent career in St John's (Prince Edward) Island, where, it has often been claimed, he was an ineffectual governor. To some extent, of course, the American reputation was undeserved; most modern scholars agree that Fanning in North Carolina was made the scapegoat of popular opinion. But his experiences there made a strong impression upon him, and on the Island he became almost compulsive about courting popular favour and working behind the scenes, thus disguising his real position on potentially controversial matters. Although some contemporary Island critics saw him as an impotent dupe of others – and some later scholars as a drifter with the tide – during most of his lengthy administration he was in command of the situation, his survival for 17 years a tribute to the cunning of his policies. When the Earl of Selkirk [DOUGLAS] in 1803 described Fanning as having "no superabundant head," the remark was merely that of an impetuous and energetic young man about an older and wiser one on the eve of retirement, and it should not be taken as a fair estimate of Fanning throughout his career.

After the war Fanning settled in Nova Scotia, where on 23 Sept. 1783 he was sworn in as lieutenant governor. Two years later, on 30 Nov. 1785, he married Phoebe Maria Burns (who had been, whispered his enemies, his cook and housekeeper); the couple subsequently had a son and three daughters. Fanning gave up his Nova Scotia sinecure in 1786 to replace Walter Patterson* as lieutenant governor of St John's Island, surrendering his comfortable existence in Halifax for a "small, unfinished, comfortless, rented cottage" in Charlottetown. He regarded the appointment as an interim one until he would replace John Parr* at the head of the Nova Scotia administration; however, the first months after his arrival on 4 November were hardly designed to confirm his wisdom in accepting the position.

Taking advantage of the ambiguities of the formal wording of Fanning's appointment – "during Lieutenant-Governor Patterson's absence" – the incumbent refused to surrender the seals and the administration of the Island until he was ready to depart it. Because he had defied orders to restore the proprietorial lots he had had sold in 1781, Patterson was being recalled to Britain to face an inquiry and was desperately buying time to cover his tracks and justify his behaviour. When the Home secretary, Lord Sydney, officially dismissed him in the spring of 1787, Fanning and Patterson's brother John came to an arrangement which confirmed most of Patterson's supporters in their offices, especially on the Council. The former lieutenant governor remained on the Island until 1788, at the head of the Board of Resident Proprietors and Agents, an organization of his leading followers that claimed to speak for proprietors of 302,000 acres and agents for 427,000 more, over half the land on St John's.

Under the circumstances, Fanning was forced to find support wherever he could. He turned in two directions. A few loyalist refugee friends from Nova Scotia and New Brunswick – Robert Gray*, Joseph ROBINSON, and Joseph APLIN – were invited to the Island and given minor appointments until Fanning could make room for them on the already over-crowded civil list. But while the new arrivals offered moral support and convivial company for the new lieutenant governor, Fanning needed local assistance as well, and he inevitably turned to the faction on the Island that had opposed Patterson and his policies. This group – led by Peter STEWART, whom Patterson had suspended as chief justice and whom Fanning was soon to reinstate, and consisting mainly of Stewart's sons CHARLES and John* and other relations – was a powerful one with a good deal of popular backing in outlying districts. In the first election to the House of Assembly, called by Fanning in July 1787, two opposing lists of candidates ("the Richmond Bay list," organized by John Stewart, and the pro-Patterson "Captain Fletcher's list," organized by Alexander Fletcher) contended for the voters' support in polling which was for the first time conducted in places outside Charlottetown. Although the Richmond Bay group did well at Princetown (Malpeque) and St Peters, the Patterson faction captured the majority of seats. However, "confusion and disorder" at the Charlottetown poll enabled the sheriff to refuse to declare their victory, and another election was immediately called. The resulting legislature was no more satisfactory to Fanning and he convoked it infrequently; it was not until 1790 that he obtained an amenable assembly.

Despite Walter Patterson's departure for Britain in 1788 and the dismissal the following year of Attorney General Phillips Callbeck* (considered by many the brains of the former administration), old hostilities died hard. In 1789 John Patterson claimed that Fanning had not honoured their earlier compromise, and he made the agreement public to prove his case. Fanning had, in fact, reshuffled some offices to make room for his loyalist friends. More significant in keeping animosities alive were the activities of the Stewart faction, which had suffered heavily during the

Fanning

Patterson years and which now sought revenge. The principal targets were merchant-proprietors John Cambridge*, John Hill*, and William Bowley – all Patterson supporters – who were attempting to build up an Island commerce with both the United States and Britain; John Patterson was somehow connected with the New York part of the trade. In 1789 William TOWNSHEND, who was both collector of customs and Chief Justice Stewart's son-in-law, confiscated a schooner owned by Cambridge and Bowley, insisting that its trading with the Island was part of a large-scale scheme to evade customs duties. Further custom-house proceedings against the merchants followed. The partners denied any conspiracy to trade illegally, maintaining that their major sins were continued political support for the Pattersons and a refusal to cut the Stewart faction in on the profits. The charges and countercharges, which persisted for years, are now impossible to sort out, for as Townshend himself lamented, "in this Island . . . affadavits are frequently but too easily obtained." Fanning had attempted at the outset to cool his subordinate's zeal for preventing smuggling, but ultimately he found himself, along with Townshend, Peter Stewart, and Joseph Aplin, a defendant against charges of malfeasance and persecution brought by the merchants before the Privy Council in 1791.

At first Cambridge and his friends had the support in London of many of the Island's absentee proprietors; however, the merchants insisted on denouncing the political partisanship of their opponents, when their complaints of official corruption and judicial partiality were both more serious and more legitimate, and they weakened their case. Fanning, moreover, had gained the approbation of several key landowners (particularly the lord chief baron of the Scottish Exchequer, James William Montgomery, and George, Marquess TOWNSHEND) by becoming their Island agent, and he managed through his personal emissary, Robert Gray, to marshal most proprietorial opinion on his side. The complaints were dismissed as without foundation by the Privy Council in 1792. One result of the proceedings, however, was that Fanning was put under a cloud at the very moment a successor was being sought for Lieutenant Governor Parr of Nova Scotia, and John WENTWORTH got the appointment instead. But in the longer run the vindication of Fanning and his officers in 1792 effactually destroyed the Patterson faction on the Island.

The merchants themselves turned to years of legal wrangling with one another over financial responsibility for the fiasco. For his part, Fanning accepted the unlikelihood of transfer to a more prestigious appointment and began to consolidate his personal and public position on the Island. He bought at auction for bargain prices most of the landed property of the now bankrupt Walter Patterson, expanded his agencies for absentee proprietors, and occasionally had the satisfaction (as in the arbitration of a long dispute between Lord Chief Baron Montgomery and his Island agent, David LAWSON) of bringing former Patterson supporters to ruin. He apparently reconciled himself to his home in Charlottetown, and by 1794 he could write that he had many fruit-bearing trees in "one of the best Gardens I ever saw," nearly two acres in extent.

Although he had emerged relatively unscathed from the Privy Council affair, Fanning was not free of controversy. The failure of absentee proprietors to pay quitrents on their lands and the question of escheat of their holdings for non-fulfilment of the terms of the grants were matters of high public interest on the Island. Fanning's own supporters, led by the Stewart clan, were anxious either to force payment of quitrents (which would help fund the civil list and thereby enhance their salaries as government officials) or to reclaim for the crown the holdings of absentee owners so that local proprietors (mainly themselves) could take them over. Since most inhabitants and officials were united in their hostility to the absentee proprietors, the land question was the principal Island issue upon which a broadly based administration could be created. Although, as a proprietor himself, Fanning, like the Stewarts, had only a narrow interest in escheat, he carefully promoted the issue. His experiences in North Carolina had taught him the dangers of open hostility to popular opinion, and he was not uninfluenced by a desire for personal aggrandizement.

It was rumoured in the late 1790s that Fanning and the Stewarts had planned a major offensive against the absentees for 1791 but had been stymied by the need to gain proprietorial support in the Privy Council proceedings. By 1795, however, Fanning felt secure enough to act, although he did so circumspectly. In that year he approved legislation passed by the assembly that moved in the direction of putting land into the hands of residents by enacting that all those who had been or would thereafter be in possession of land for a period of seven years should be confirmed in their freehold or leasehold tenure of it. In giving his approval, moreover, Fanning did not insist on the suspending clause, normal in Island legislation, which provided that the act would not take effect until confirmed by the crown. Opponents of the legislation, including Attorney General Aplin, claimed that its intention was to defraud the proprietors, since anyone could build a hut on land under a fraudulent deed and subsequently claim ownership. Whatever the other effects of the act, it would serve to legitimize Fanning's title to Patterson's lands.

The offensive continued in 1796 with the publication of a brief pamphlet by Fanning's friend Joseph Robinson calling for more active proprietorial investment or the creation of a crown-appointed court of escheat for the Island. The following year the

310

assembly maintained the pressure, appointing a committee which made a detailed examination of the failure of most proprietors to live up to the terms of their grants. Before transmitting its report with his approval to Whitehall, Fanning saw to it that those proprietors for whom he was agent were specifically omitted from the criticisms. In the case of Montgomery, who had attempted to develop his property, such exemption was legitimate. Townshend's lands on Lot 56, on the other hand, were almost totally unimproved; nevertheless, Fanning would later boast to him of his "Endeavours in getting them reported by the House of Assembly, as fully settled agreeable to the Conditions of the Grant, & therefore exempted from being escheated for nonsettlement, which must greatly enhance the Value of Your Lordships Lot."

In his careful encouragement of the movement for escheat Fanning hoped for both popular favour and personal gain. But he failed to allow for two other factors which affected his position. One was the extent to which the entire judicial system of the Island had got out of hand. Characteristically, Fanning had earlier evaded his obligation to review Supreme Court decisions, preferring instead to devolve his Chancery duties upon the Council and to participate only in tied cases. Since Chief Justice Stewart and his assistant judges, Gray and Robinson, were also members of the Council, appeals went – said Fanning's critics – "from the Chief Justice and Assistant Judges to the Chief Justice and Assistant Judges." Moreover, increasing amounts of litigation in the Supreme Court were directed against the Stewarts, mainly over private business dealings; given Peter Stewart's position and the fact that his son Charles served as clerk of the court, complaints about the judicial system voiced by Attorney General Aplin, his successor John WENTWORTH, and several proprietors proved more and more credible. The corruption and inefficiency of the judicial process became the major weapon that Fanning's critics and those defending the proprietors wielded against the lieutenant governor's administration.

The second problem was Captain John MACDONALD of Glenaladale, a fiery Scots Highlander who was one of the principal resident proprietors. MacDonald was not afraid to take on the entire Island, if necessary, and he was a genius at converting bits of Island gossip and scandal into incisive, epigrammatic condemnations of its leaders. As early as 1790 MacDonald had decided that there was little to choose between the Patterson and Fanning governments, the change representing only the institution of "deep far fetched despicable Yankey cunning instead of audacious open tyranny." Fear-a-Ghlinne – as he was known in Gaelic – emerged in the mid 1790s as the leader of opposition to the Fanning–Stewart administration; later he recruited James DOUGLAS and Joseph

Aplin to the small party of critics. None of these men accepted Fanning's protestations of non-involvement in the escheat business; they were absolutely certain that the lieutenant governor not only knew what was going on, but was actively manipulating events behind the scenes. "No one is safe from his malice, and the power he has to gratify it," wrote Douglas to Montgomery, "[he] having all the different departments of Justice and the Government at his discretion." This new opposition to Fanning was doubly dangerous: not only did it assume a public role in defending the absentee proprietors, but in its advocacy of annexation to Nova Scotia it had a simple and practical solution to the Island's political and economic problems.

Fanning worked hard to blunt the attacks upon himself and his government. MacDonald was censured by the assembly in 1797 on the basis of a letter he had directed to the lieutenant governor accusing him of countenancing "a Levelling Party" in the colony. The following year Aplin was dismissed as attorney general upon Fanning's complaints to the British government about his seditious speech and behaviour. Douglas was a bit harder to reach, since he kept out of politics and was the trusted agent of Montgomery, the Island's largest absentee proprietor. Douglas did find himself defending his integrity as controller of customs in the face of complaints brought to London by William Townshend, but Fanning more effectively neutralized Douglas's criticisms by pointing out to his employer the dangers of annexation, which would turn land-hungry Nova Scotians loose on the Island's proprietors. Thus Fanning succeeded in damping the movement against him, particularly on the Island, and the extent to which the land question united local warring factions was a tribute to his political perspicacity and management. He was unable to prevent British proprietors from becoming extremely suspicious of the escheat movement, but he managed to persuade them that only he could control the ground swell of popular hostility to leasehold, rents, and absenteeism that threatened to overwhelm the proprietorial system. More than any other early Island governor, he succeeded in maintaining a credibility with all the conflicting interest groups involved with the Island.

Although the land question was in the forefront during the latter part of Fanning's régime on the Island, in many ways it obscured the larger problem of economic underdevelopment. Critics claimed that the lieutenant governor had not done enough to help the Island prosper, but the years of warfare between 1793 and 1801 were probably more responsible for its slow rate of growth. Fanning had been hoping to retire for some years and, when in 1804 he was finally given permission to step down effective in 1805, the Island was well out of its economic doldrums and entering a

Faribault

period of almost unprecedented prosperity. The British government allowed him an annual pension of £500 from the revenues of the Island. Although he spent some months in London in 1805, his satisfaction with the Island was such that he continued to reside in Charlottetown until 1813, when old age forced him to move permanently to London; he was living in Upper Seymour Street at the time of his death. Fanning had always stood in good favour at the War Office, and he received regular promotions in the army list, eventually becoming a full general in April 1808. His last years were marred by the death in 1812 of his only son, who had joined the British army at the age of 14. His three daughters, all unmarried at the time of his death, inherited extensive property in Vermont and on Prince Edward Island.

Edmund Fanning has not received the same attention as some other loyalist governors of British North America, but he was perhaps the most successful of the breed. Alone among the early administrators of Prince Edward Island he emerged from the colony with his reputation intact. That he escaped untarnished was to a large extent the result of his careful, and ambiguous, stand on the land question.

J. M. BUMSTED

PAC, MG 9, C3; MG 11, [CO 226] Prince Edward Island A, 17: 212, 224, 246–71; MG 23, E5; E7. PAPEI, Acc. 2702, Smith–Alley coll., Edmund Fanning to James Cary, 12 June 1794; Fanning to Marquis Townshend, 10 Jan. 1803, 2 March 1804; RG 3, House of Assembly, Journals, 1795; RG 6, RS2, Chancery Court, box 1: "Report of committee of Council for hearing appeals from plantations on petition of William Bowley to Privy Council, heard 6 March 1799." Private arch., Jean and Colin MacDonald (St Peters, P.E.I.), MacDonald family papers, John MacDonald to Helen MacDonald, 7 July 1790 (copy at PAPEI). PRO, CO 226/10: 39–40; 226/10: 129–35 (mfm. at PAC); PROB 11/1603/170 (copy at PAPEI). SRO, GD 293/2/19/6, 9; 293/2/78/22, 24; 293/2/79/23–24; 293/2/80/22. *Gentleman's Magazine*, January–June 1818: 469. G.B., Privy Council, *Report of the right honourable the lords of the committee of his majesty's most honourable Privy Council, of certain complaints against Lieutenant Governor Fanning, and other officers of his majesty's government in the Island of St. John* ([London, 1792]). *The Regulators in North Carolina: a documentary history, 1759–1776*, comp. W. S. Powell et al. (Raleigh, N.C., 1971). *The state records of North Carolina*, ed. W. L. Saunders and Walter Clark (26v., Raleigh, 1886–1907; repr. New York, 1968), 7–8. Stewart, *Account of P.E.I.*, 220–25. *Royal American Gazette, and Weekly Intelligencer of the Island of Saint John* (Charlottetown), 29 Sept. 1787. *DAB*. G.B., WO, *Army list*, 1792–1808. Sabine, *Biog. sketches of loyalists*, 1: 415–19. Carl Bridenbaugh, *Myths and realities: societies of the colonial south* (Baton Rouge, La., 1952), 160–67. *Canada's smallest prov.* (Bolger), 64–75. A. T. Dill, *Governor Tryon and his palace* (Chapel Hill, N.C., [1955]). M. D. Haywood, *Governor William Tryon and his administration in the province of North Carolina, 1765–1771 . . .* (Raleigh, 1903). H. T. Lefler and A. R. Newsome, *North Carolina, the history of a southern state* (3rd ed., Chapel Hill, 1973), 180–90. A. B. Warburton, *A history of Prince Edward Island, from its discovery in 1534 until the departure of Lieutenant-Governor Ready in A.D. 1831* (Saint John, N.B., 1923), 239–41. Bumsted, "Sir James Montgomery and P.E.I.," *Acadiensis* (Fredericton), 7, no.2: 94–99. A. P. Hudson, "Songs of the North Carolina Regulators," *William and Mary Quarterly* (Williamsburg, Va.), 3rd ser., 4 (1947): 477. MacNutt, "Fanning's regime on P.E.I.," *Acadiensis*, 1, no.1: 37–53.

FARIBAULT, BARTHÉLEMY, notary and office holder; b. 26 April 1728 in Montbizot, France, son of Bernard Faribault and Madelaine Hamon; m. 3 Sept. 1761 Catherine-Antoine Véronneau in Saint-François-du-Lac (Que.), and they had ten children; d. 21 June 1801 in Berthier-en-Haut (Berthierville), Lower Canada.

Barthélemy Faribault belonged to a family trained in the law: his father and three of his brothers were notaries. Seeking to follow the same path, Faribault became a notary in Paris. How long he practised in his native land is not known. He came to New France as military secretary to Governor Ange Duquesne* de Menneville about 1752. From 1755 to 1760 he held the post of scrivener in the Bureau de l'Intendance (Bureau de la Marine) at Quebec and in the last year received a salary of 1,200 *livres*.

Faribault decided to remain in the country after the conquest; in 1760 he settled in Bécancour and tried to set up a business there. Probably because of the economic instability of the colony at that time, he gave this project up in favour of returning to the notarial profession. On 22 July 1763 he received a commission from Major-General Thomas Gage* authorizing him to practise at Berthier-en-Haut, Île Dupas, Lanoraie (Lanoraie-d'Autray), Lavaltrie, and Saint-Sulpice, provided that he establish residence in Berthier-en-Haut. He was probably the first notary to receive such a commission under the British régime. He remained at Berthier-en-Haut as a notary until 1790.

Soon after his arrival Faribault had acquired as clients Pierre-Noël Courthiau, seigneur of Berthier, and several of his *censitaires*, who consulted him on land sales or for confirmation of title deeds. On 16 April 1765 he obtained the grant of a site on which he built his residence. Ownership of the seigneury passed that year to James Cuthbert*, who, like his predecessor, continued to transact his affairs with Faribault. For example, the notary was asked to draw up the notarial contracts for the building of St Andrew's, a Protestant church, in 1786 and 1787.

Relations between Faribault and Cuthbert gradually deteriorated, however, particularly after the notary refused the hand of one of his daughters to Alexander Cuthbert, the seigneur's son, in 1789. The situation grew worse the following year after Faribault attempted to settle an ongoing quarrel between James Cuthbert and Jean-Baptiste-Noël POUGET, parish priest of Sainte-Geneviève-de-Berthier (at Berthierville). Offended and infuriated by Faribault's attitude, Cuthbert made life unbearable for him; he prevented his *censitaires* from having recourse to his services and even threatened him with death. Faribault recounted this episode in a four-page poem composed in alexandrine verse.

Since he had a commission issued in 1784 that authorized him to practise as a notary anywhere in the province, Faribault decided in 1790 to take up residence at L'Assomption in order to escape Cuthbert's reprisals. He did not return to Berthier-en-Haut until 30 Sept. 1798, a few days after the seigneur had died.

Little else is known about Faribault's life. On 1 Aug. 1780 he had complained to Governor HALDIMAND about the exactions he had suffered from Captain Olivier in connection with the billeting of soldiers. Because of his status as a notary it was acknowledged that he might henceforth be exempted from the obligation. Other than this incident and his differences with Cuthbert, Faribault probably led a quiet life centred largely on his profession and family. The records mention his participation in higher office in the region only in 1792, when he was appointed commissioner of the Court of Requests at L'Assomption and returning officer for the riding of Leinster.

When he died in 1801, Barthélemy Faribault owned a piece of land one *arpent* square with a house and small stable, as well as a lot next to his place of residence. His personal estate was sold for £918. Judging by the law-books in his library, Faribault was undoubtedly a learned man. He probably passed on to his sons a liking for the notarial profession, since three of them followed in his footsteps, including Joseph-Édouard*, who did his training with him.

MARTHE FARIBAULT BEAUREGARD
and CLAUDE LESSARD

Barthélemy Faribault's minute-book is deposited at AC, Richelieu (Sorel), and contains 7,876 acts for the years 1763 to 1801.

AD, Sarthe (Le Mans), État civil, Montbizot, 26 avril 1728. AN, Col., D²ᶜ, 47; 48 (copies at PAC). ANQ-M, CN1-308, 16 avril 1765; CN3-31, M.-L. de Glandon-Desdevens, 4 juill. 1801; CS1-1-11, Doc. de la famille Faribault. AP, Sainte-Geneviève-de-Berthier (Berthierville), Reg. des baptêmes, mariages et sépultures, 23 juin 1801; Saint-François-du-Lac, Reg. des baptêmes, mariages et sépultures, 3 sept. 1761. Bibliothèque de la ville de Montréal, Salle Gagnon, MSS, Barthélemy Faribault, 25 oct. 1760. BL, Add. MSS 21879: 263 (copies at PAC). PAC, RG 4, B8, 1: 18–20, 220. "Journal du siège de Québec du 10 mai au 18 septembre 1759," Ægidius Fauteux, édit., ANQ *Rapport*, 1920–21: 149, 215. [Pierre de La Rue], "Lettres et mémoires de l'abbé de L'Isle-Dieu," ANQ *Rapport*,

1935–36: 396. André Vachon, "Inventaire critique des notaires royaux des gouvernements de Québec, Montréal et Trois-Rivières," *RHAF*, 11 (1957–58): 270–76. H.-R. Casgrain, *Faribault et la famille de Sales Laterrière* (Montréal, 1925). S.-A. Moreau, *Précis de l'histoire de la seigneurie, de la paroisse et du comté de Berthier, P.Q. (Canada)* (Berthierville, 1889). J.-E. Roy, *Hist. du notariat*, 2: 13, 133, 194. P.-G. Roy, *La famille Faribault* (Lévis, Qué., 1913).

FÉLIX, PIERRE-JACQUES BOSSU, *dit* **LYONNAIS,** named **Brother.** *See* BOSSU

FFRASER. *See* FRASER

FIELD, ROBERT, painter; b. *c.* 1769, probably in London, England; d. 9 Aug. 1819 in Kingston, Jamaica.

Although the details of Robert Field's early career in England are obscure, it is known that he received his early training at the Royal Academy schools, London, in 1790. In 1794 he moved to the United States as part of the influx of British artists and craftsmen enticed by the prosperity of the new republic. After settling briefly in Baltimore, Md, he took up residence in the nation's capital, Philadelphia, Pa. There he immediately joined a group of artists led by Charles Willson Peale, the noted painter and naturalist, in establishing the Columbianum, or American Academy of the Fine Arts, an organization whose plan, according to Field, was "the most enlarged, liberal and grand of any in the world." When American-born artists objected to the academy's authoritarian, quasi-monarchical structure – George Washington was to play a role analogous to that of George III as the first patron of the organization, and "visitors" were to travel from city to city judging which individuals were to be admitted to membership – Field and seven other English expatriates founded the rival Columbianum, or National College of Painting, Sculpture, Architecture and Engraving. This body collapsed within a few months, but the American Academy continued in operation until it was superseded by the Pennsylvania Academy of the Fine Arts in 1805.

Field spent 14 years in the United States, working as a miniature painter in Baltimore, Philadelphia, Washington, and Boston; during this period he produced miniatures of George and Martha Washington, Thomas Jefferson, and a wide range of people prominent in the social, economic, and political life of American society. In May 1808 he left the United States for Halifax, N.S., a city that was enjoying unprecedented prosperity because of its position as a base for British naval operations. Shortly after his arrival in Halifax, he set up his studio in Alexander Morrison's bookshop, and in a newspaper advertisement he announced his intention "to exercise his

Figueroa

profession, as portrait painter, in oil and water-colours, and in miniature." In the years that followed he continued to produce miniatures, but he also painted more than 50 oil portraits of government officials, military officers, merchants, and assorted members of the Halifax "gentility"; among his subjects were Bishop Charles INGLIS, former lieutenant governor Sir John WENTWORTH, Sir George PREVOST, Sir John Coape Sherbrooke*, and Sir Alexander Forrester Inglis Cochrane, vice-admiral in the Royal Navy (whose portrait was shown at the Royal Academy exhibition in London in 1810). In addition, Field was an important figure in Halifax social circles: he was an honorary member of the Charitable Irish Society, and in 1812 and 1813 he served as an officer of St John's Masonic Lodge No.211.

In a few years Field depleted the potential market for oil portraits in Halifax, and early in 1816 he moved to Jamaica, settling first in Montego Bay and then in Kingston. He died on 9 Aug. 1819, apparently of yellow fever, and was buried in an unmarked grave in the old "West Ground" cemetery, now called the Strangers' Burial Ground, near the Kingston parish church.

Generally recognized as one of America's leading miniaturists, Field was probably the most professionally trained painter to settle in Canada at the beginning of the 19th century. Working in the conventional neo-classic portrait style of Henry Raeburn and Gilbert Stuart, he showed little stylistic variation in his works. None the less, the oil portraits painted during the Halifax stage of his career stand as a striking illustration of patronage of the arts in colonial Canada.

SANDRA PAIKOWSKY

Pa., Hist. Soc. (Philadelphia), Academy of Fine Arts, minutes and papers, 1794–1830; F. J. Dreer coll., painters and engravers. PANS, MG 20, 66; MG 100, 141, no.10. *Notes on American artists, 1754–1820, copied from advertisements appearing in the newspapers of the day; to which is added a list of portraits and sculpture in the possession of the New-York Historical Society,* comp. William Kelby (New York, 1922; repr. 1970). *Acadian Recorder,* 2 Jan., 25 Nov. 1815; 31 Aug. 1816; 11 Sept. 1819. *British Colonist* (Halifax), 3 Oct. 1848. *Kingston Chronicle and City Advertiser* (Kingston, Jamaica), 18 March, 11 Aug. 1819. *Nova Scotia Royal Gazette,* 7 June 1808, 14 Sept. 1814. Art Gallery of N.S., *[Robert Field, 1769–1819]; an exhibition organized by the Art Gallery of Nova Scotia, Halifax, October 5 to November 27, 1978* (Halifax, 1978). Mantle Fielding, *Dictionary of American painters, sculptors, and engravers; with an addendum containing additional material on the original entries,* comp. J. F. Carr (New York, 1965). J. R. Harper, *Early painters and engravers in Canada* ([Toronto], 1970). *The New-York Historical Society's dictionary of artists in America, 1564–1860,* comp. G. C. Groce and D. H. Wallace (New Haven, Conn., and London, 1957). J. C. Smith, *British mezzotinto portraits; being a descriptive catalogue of these engravings from the introduction of the art to the early part of the present century* . . . (4 pts. in 5v., London, [1878–84]). D. M. Stauffer and Mantle Fielding, *American engravers upon copper and steel* . . . (3v., New York and Philadelphia, 1907–17; repr. New York, 1964). H. B. Wehle and Theodore Bolton, *American miniatures, 1730–1850* . . . *& a biographical dictionary of the artists* (Garden City, N.Y., 1927; repr. New York, 1970). Theodore Bolton, *Early American portrait painters in miniature* (New York, 1921). William Dunlap, *A history of the rise and progress of the arts of design in the United States* (2v., New York, 1834; repub., ed. Rita Weiss and intro. J. T. Flexner, 2v. in 3, 1969). Harry Piers, *Robert Field, portrait painter in oils, miniature and water-colours and engraver* (New York, 1927). C. C. Sellers, *Charles Willson Peale* (New York, 1969). Frank Cundall, "More about Robert Field," *Connoisseur* (London), 77 (January–April 1927): 187. C. R. Grundy, "Robert Field, an Anglo-American artist," *Connoisseur,* 76 (September–December 1926): 195–98. Barry Lord, "Portraits of a young hero: two versions of Robert Field's 'Portrait of Lieutenant Provo William Parry Wallis,'" National Gallery of Canada, *Bull.* (Ottawa), 20 (1972): 13–21. Harry Piers, "Artists in Nova Scotia," N.S. Hist Soc., *Coll.,* 18 (1914): 112–19. G. C. Williamson, "Robert Field, American miniature painter," *Connoisseur,* 79 (September–December 1927): 50–51.

FIGUEROA, JOSÉ MARIANO MOZIÑO LOSADA SUÁREZ DE. *See* MOZIÑO

FINLAY, HUGH, merchant, office holder, seigneur, politician, and landowner; b. *c.* 1730, possibly in Glasgow, Scotland, third son of Robert Finlay, tanner and cordwainer, and Susanna Parkins; m. *c.* 1769 Mary Phillips at Quebec, and they had ten children; d. there 26 Dec. 1801.

Hugh Finlay sailed from Glasgow for Quebec early in 1763, bringing several assets that promised him success. He had family connections in the business communities of both Glasgow and London and sufficient capital to join a wholesale merchant partnership at Quebec. His fluency in French would prove helpful, not only in business but also in launching an administrative career, for bilingual British immigrants were rare in the colony. Indeed, the beginnings of a career in government were evident before he left, since Finlay had the assurance that he would be appointed postmaster of the colony upon his arrival.

At Quebec, Finlay formed a partnership with Stephen Moore, a merchant who had established himself in the town by August 1761, less than two years after its capture by British forces. Their partnership illustrates the methods and risks of commercial venture in this transitional period. They acquired premises on Rue Saint-Pierre in Lower Town and in March 1764 a lot and house at Baie-Saint-Paul from the surgeon Jean-Baptiste RIEUTORD, perhaps to serve as commercial outlets. The following month they purchased a bakery on Rue Saint-Charles from François Foucault*, formerly a member of the Conseil Supérieur of New France, for 21,000 *livres*. Foucault exacted payment in coin, shunning the rapidly devaluating paper currency, so that the acquisition was immediately burdensome for the new partnership. Moore and Finlay opened a retail business at their Rue Saint-Charles location and sold a wide range of goods, advertised almost poetically in the *Quebec Gazette*; among their wares were bindings, buckles, buttons, and boots, muslins, moltons, and "mazamets," pickles in boxes and pork in barrels, silks, satins, sailcloth, and swan-skin, as well as "Tycks, Tweelings, Tickenburghs, Taffeties, Tumblers," and tar. The mid 1760s, however, were difficult for many North American merchants, regardless of their business or cultural connections. Moore and Finlay soon found themselves deeply in debt at the same time as debts to them mounted; in December 1764 the Quebec merchant Alexandre DUMAS owed them £4,000, and the Richelieu valley merchant Charles Curtius was indebted to the amount of £2,200 by November 1766. Despite Finlay's advantages, to which should be added the diligence that marked his entire career, Moore and Finlay had operated little more than a year before having to turn the business over to their creditors in August 1765. Three months later they sold for £3,000 their Rue Saint-Pierre premises and a beach lot granted to them in June.

While he was operating in partnership with Moore, Finlay had also begun investing in land on his own. In 1764 he purchased from Foucault the latter's seigneury, on the upper Richelieu at the entrance to Lake Champlain, for 15,000 *livres* in gold and silver coin spread over five years. Three years later, along with Francis Mackay, surveyor general of the king's woods, and the Montreal merchant Samuel McKay, Finlay was granted Lot 55 on St John's (Prince Edward) Island.

Finlay's appointment as postmaster at Quebec had been arranged in the last months of the administration of the Earl of Bute, probably by the Earl of Egmont, and confirmed on 10 June 1763 by Benjamin Franklin and John Foxcroft, joint deputy postmasters general of North America, acting on instructions from London. Local merchants, with the support of Governor Murray*, had petitioned as early as 1762 for a regular postal service. Finlay soon built a weekly postal service between Quebec and Montreal via Trois-Rivières and a monthly post south through Skenesborough (N.Y.) and Albany to meet the mail packet service between New York City and Falmouth, England. He obtained from the government directions to the keepers of post houses to provide horses for mail couriers at one-half the rate to the public and to

ferrymen to pass couriers over their rivers promptly and without charge. In view of the shortage of currency, Finlay met expenses with "tickets," payable upon his announcement that cash had arrived at the Quebec post office. The posts were unexpectedly successful, returning a profit to the British Post Office Department and giving Finlay a good income of one-fifth of the receipts. In less than a decade the system was profitable enough to support a twice-weekly service on the colony's post roads, and two posts a month to New York.

Finlay's abilities were soon recognized as useful to the government in other ways. In October 1764 he was appointed a justice of the peace for the District of Quebec in Murray's unconventional civil government. On 25 Sept. 1765 he was named to the Council of Quebec, the governing body of the colony, and he held a comparable position during the remaining 36 years of his life. With British patronage independent of Murray, Finlay quickly became an advocate for the British merchant community, which was often in opposition to the governor, and his support was most vehement in its demand that the English legal rights promised in the Royal Proclamation of 1763 be applied to the colony. Since his postal service was dependent on the post-house system, and no one had been commissioned to exercise authority over the keepers of post houses, Finlay unofficially assumed responsibility in council for them and consequently for the conveyance and accommodation of travellers on the post roads. In 1767 he issued a notice applying to the colony regulations governing the post-house system in Britain; the keepers were confirmed in their monopoly of the post roads and protected from abuse by users. About 1770 he had instructions printed codifying the duties of keepers and post-riders. In council he defended keepers against the billeting of troops and the exactions of militia ordinances in such a manner that his moderate, but persistent, objections to arbitrariness constituted a defence of the Canadians in general.

Late in 1772 Finlay left for London with a recommendation from Foxcroft that he be appointed surveyor of the post roads in North America. He apparently was befriended by the joint postmasters general, Baron Le Despencer and Henry Frederick Thynne (known from 1776 as Carteret). He agreed with the latter that he would investigate troubles in the extensive landholdings of the Carteret family in North Carolina. On 5 Jan. 1773 Finlay was appointed "Surveyor of the Post roads in the Continent of North America." Back at Quebec that summer, he advised Le Despencer on choice properties for sale in the colony. These services for his patrons further strengthened the position Finlay had gained from his trip to London.

Possibly in part as a response to complaints by

Finlay

merchants at Quebec that mail service to New England via Montreal was slow and unreliable, Finlay set out in September 1773 with Indian guides and an interpreter to scout a direct route by canoe and on foot up the Chaudière and down the Kennebec to Falmouth (Maine). From there he travelled southward to survey the post roads, all the while investigating the postal employees and noting the weaknesses of, and suggesting improvements in, the postal system. His industry, common sense, and extraordinary perception are evident in a journal he kept during the tour. Unrivalled as a detailed account of the postal system, it is also a sensitive record of colonial attitudes towards this most visible and vulnerable department of royal government immediately prior to the American revolution. In New Hampshire, Finlay joined Governor John WENTWORTH in recommending a new road through the White Mountains and down the Rivière Saint-François to the St Lawrence. After careful study of facilities as far as New York, Finlay hurried south to spend several months in North Carolina, where he looked into Carteret's land problems. In Virginia by May 1774, he abruptly ended his tour upon learning that he had been named on 31 January to replace Franklin as one of the joint deputy postmasters general of North America.

Finlay arrived back at Quebec on 26 June 1774. That year the British government, after long urging by Guy CARLETON, abandoned the anglicizing policy of the Royal Proclamation of 1763 by passing the Quebec Act. Although appointed in 1775 to the Legislative Council created by the act, Finlay disagreed with many policies embodied in the measure, which denied the demands of the British merchant community. Moreover, Carleton chose to ignore instructions that would have softened the blow to the merchants. However, in the context of the American invasion of the colony in the autumn of 1775 [see Benedict ARNOLD; Richard Montgomery*], Finlay muffled his opposition. A member of the garrison defending the besieged town of Quebec that winter, he was probably the author of a detailed journal that illustrates clearly the bitterness and distrust engendered by the Canadians' reluctance to fight the Americans.

The revolution dealt Finlay several blows. It eliminated his option of becoming an agent for the Carteret family in North Carolina. It also ruined the prospect of a career in North Carolina politics – he had been nominated for a seat in that colony's Council by the governor, who described him as "a gentleman of education and good fortune, of an excellent character and great understanding." As well, the American invasion destroyed the postal link to the south and prompted complete censorship of internal as well as ship mail. In consequence, the postal service was all but destroyed, Finlay's income as postmaster evapor-

ated, and his recent appointment as joint deputy postmaster general of North America became insignificant.

Finlay still had the confidence of Carleton, who feared he could not dominate a legislative council deprived by war of some of his most faithful councillors. In 1776 he chose Finlay as one of five members of a board with which he briefly administered the province unconstitutionally. The following year Finlay argued for the introduction of trial by jury in certain types of cases, but he was opposed by the majority in the restored regular council; when he learned that Carleton, too, was opposed to the measure, he dropped it for the duration of the war. However, at the same time he was in serious conflict with Carleton, publicly and privately, over the broad and arbitrary powers given to the military under a new militia law [see François BABY]. Finlay insisted on the need for more public and specific rules governing militia duty. His concern about widespread discontent with the measure, of which he was well aware by virtue of his position as postmaster, was doubled by his need to defend the keepers of post houses, who risked becoming particular victims of the corvée clauses in the law. The failure of the Canadians to oppose the Americans in 1775–76, however, had angered Carleton and the dominant party of loyal seigneurs in the council, rendering them strongly opposed to any lightening of the burden on the habitants. Finlay's insistence resulted in his being dropped as an inner council adviser, although he remained a member of the regular council.

The arrival of HALDIMAND to replace Carleton in 1778 brought Finlay no immediate comfort, since he was soon busy fighting Carleton's characterization of him to the new governor. It was apparent, moreover, that Haldimand was no more willing than his predecessor to free the mails from complete censorship. Neither would the new governor, who feared that the capture of the mails by Americans might compromise Britain's military situation, acquiesce in Finlay's urgings for restoration of normal postal service. Finlay's continued representations in defence of the keepers of post houses, and the flood of their minor problems that he passed on to Haldimand for solution, were intended to support his drive for a formal appointment, with pay, as superintendent of the colony's post houses. Faced with procrastination on Haldimand's part and the combination of a growing family and a shrinking income, Finlay resorted to the bolder tactics that had won the day on an earlier occasion: in the fall of 1778 he sailed for England. There he organized a petition from merchants trading to the colony and gained the aid of his friends at the Post Office, who encouraged the secretary of state to support Finlay both in his struggle to restore normal postal service and in his desire to become superintendent of post houses. Despite this prompt and powerful backing, both decisions were left to Haldimand. The war continued to defeat Finlay.

Back at Quebec by August 1779, Finlay did not allow his need of the governor's support to soften his stand in the Legislative Council on reform of the judicature, but neither was Haldimand's military perspective on the subject altered by Finlay's efforts in London or at Quebec. In the summer of 1780 Finlay at last obtained Haldimand's authorization to supervise the post houses, but without salary; immediately after, Finlay showed characteristic zeal in a tour he conducted of post houses and in his report, which called for road and bridge improvements. Although Finlay remained a political adversary, Haldimand came to trust him; in January 1781 Finlay ostensibly undertook another tour of post houses, but in fact, on Haldimand's orders, he was secretly gathering information on discontent with, and clandestine opposition to, the government. His report was perceptive and cautious, advising that most people would obey orders when required.

Finlay's status as an office holder was confirmed in September 1780, when he acquired from the former attorney general, Francis Maseres*, a single-storey stone house on Rue des Casernes (Rue de l'Arsenal) in Upper Town, paying immediately the entire purchase price of £300 sterling; until then he had lived on Rue du Sault-au-Matelot, a commercial street in Lower Town. Like many office holders he engaged in property transactions; in May 1781 he bought one-half of a house on Rue Saint-Jean, again paying the full cost of £300 in cash, and by April 1783 he was renting out part of a house on Rue Saint-Paul, another Lower Town business street. Finlay apparently retained his contact with the merchant community; in May, for example, he was given power of attorney by the merchant John YOUNG to represent the interests of three English firms during Young's absence in Halifax, N.S.

In the fall of 1781 Finlay had returned to London at the urging of a worried Carteret, whose fears for his family's North Carolina properties were fully justified since they were ultimately lost. While in London, Finlay took the opportunity to seek a salary for his duties as superintendent of post houses, and he eventually succeeded. He returned to Quebec in June 1782 in the company of the new lieutenant governor, Henry Hamilton*, who became a valuable ally in council during the last two years of Haldimand's administration. Finlay's political influence probably reached its height in the years following the peace with the United States. In the session of 1784 he was one of Hamilton's most prominent supporters. They obtained the re-introduction of habeas corpus, suspended since 1774, into the provincial judicial system; it was a measure for which he and the merchant William

GRANT (1744–1805) had long fought. The following year he was president of the council and secretary and principal adviser to Hamilton, with whom he had established close personal relations. The lieutenant governor would be namesake and godfather to Finlay's ninth child.

Although habeas corpus had been won in 1784, several other judicial proposals had been lost, but Haldimand's departure revived hopes for reform. In 1785 Finlay introduced into council a major ordinance calling for the institution of trial by jury for some cases, the introduction of English commercial law and of English law of evidence in damage suits, and the inscription in the court records of the judge's charge to the jury; all but a limited use of trial by jury, however, were defeated by the French party led by Adam Mabane*. Finlay also lost a bid to reform the Court of Appeals, composed of the lieutenant governor or chief justice and any five legislative councillors. One of only a few council members sufficiently conscientious to read law, Finlay roundly condemned as anarchical the practice adopted by most councillors of rendering judgements on the basis of equity. He wanted to limit membership in the court to those councillors who were bilingual and prepared to sit regularly.

If Finlay was the backbone of the merchants' campaign for judicial reform, his doubts about the wisdom of their demands for a house of assembly probably contributed significantly to Britain's hesitation to grant the request. He had acquired a well-earned reputation for being moderate and informed about the Canadians' opinions; he had also gained the ear of the under-secretary of state for the Home Department, Evan Nepean. Finlay repeatedly argued that the habitants did not care for an assembly, especially if it meant the introduction of taxation, and that before the political future of the colony were confided to them it would be advisable to educate and anglicize them through the establishment of free parochial schools with English-speaking masters. He feared that, if given the vote without proper preparation, the Canadians would elect Canadian deputies who would constitute an assembly ill fitted to govern a commercial country and would legislate to preserve French laws and Canadian customs; his prediction would prove far more accurate than that of assembly promoters, such as Grant and George ALLSOPP, who felt confident that the British would easily dominate Canadian legislators.

The return of Carleton, now Lord Dorchester, as governor-in-chief in 1786 reduced Finlay's direct influence. In matters of legal reform he bowed to the leadership of the new chief justice, William Smith*. His one personal initiative, a drive in 1790 for the establishment of prerogative courts to probate wills and administer the laws of guardianship, was defeated by the French party. Politically, Alexander Fraser

Finlay

noted in 1789, Finlay was much attached to Grant but was "less violent and less formidable." By that time he had been converted to the idea of an assembly, possibly by the limited prospects for further judicial reform under the existing constitution; he continued to insist, however, on the need to educate and anglicize the Canadians in order for an assembly to function satisfactorily. If less prominent, Finlay continued to be influential in council; in 1787 he finally saw the militia ordinance reformed, and the same year he translated into an important bill, passed in 1788, recommendations made by doctors Charles BLAKE and James Fisher* to regulate the medical profession. He was also active socially, as an officer in the Quebec Battalion of British Militia, as secretary of the Agriculture Society from its foundation in 1789 until at least 1794, and as a trustee of the Quebec Library in 1790, 1792, and 1793.

Less occupied by politics after 1786, Finlay was able to devote more time to the postal service. He had received the position of deputy postmaster general of the province of Quebec in 1784. Although he was still anxious to restore the mail services via New York that had previously been so successful, he was forced to develop an alternative overland route to Halifax. In 1787 he undertook yet another postal odyssey, again keeping a journal, and he ultimately prepared a full report on the roads and post houses between Quebec and Halifax. Characteristically, he recommended unified authority over the whole route, and thus obtained his own appointment in 1788 as deputy postmaster general of British North America with authority over Joseph Peters* of Nova Scotia and Christopher Sower* of New Brunswick. He also obtained a stopover at Halifax of the monthly Falmouth–New York packets in each direction of their transatlantic voyages, although it was only practicable eight months of the year. Finlay was able to extend the postal service through Upper Canada to Detroit (Mich.), and in 1792 he negotiated a landmark postal convention with the United States, re-establishing postal service with it and providing for passage of mails between Britain and Lower Canada across American territory in the four months of each year when the Halifax route could not be used.

Although successful in rebuilding the postal service that furnished part of his income, by 1789 Finlay was, according to Alexander Fraser, "in very indigent circumstances, having only his office as Postmaster & Salary as Counselor to support himself, his wife, & near a dozen children." In April he sold his house on Rue des Casernes and a vacant lot elsewhere to pay a debt of nearly £500 that his father-in-law had contracted and he himself had guaranteed. Two months later he bought a modest farm, called Woodside, along the Rivière Saint-Charles, promising to pay the purchase price of £300 by 1793; in

March 1792, however, he offered the farm for sale. He must have been renting Woodside for some time, since it was there that the traveller Joseph Hadfield had visited his family in 1785; Hadfield found Finlay "a very sensible and agreeable man" and his wife, Mary, "a very agreeable, polite woman." Four years later Bishop Charles INGLIS stayed with Finlay during his pastoral visit and found the family "numerous and amiable." The happy household was plunged into grief in November 1791 by the death of Mary; the élite of Quebec society, including Prince EDWARD AUGUS-TUS, attended her funeral.

Finlay sought by various means to supplement his inadequate income. Most involved exploitation of his political influence, and the efforts of a number of his political superiors to aid him testify to their recognition of his worth as an administrator and adviser. In April 1788 he sought the lease of the Saint-Maurice ironworks, then exploited by Davison and Lees [see John LEES]. Although his petition was recommended by the Legislative Council, he did not obtain the concession. However, in August 1791, when George Pownall*, provincial secretary, left for England, he deputed Finlay to act in his stead. The following month Finlay was appointed to the Executive Council created by the Constitutional Act, and in December 1792 he was named to the new Legislative Council. In May Lieutenant Governor Alured Clarke* had appointed him clerk of the crown in chancery. In 1792 as well, Home Secretary Henry Dundas intervened on Finlay's behalf with the postmaster general when a large deficit surfaced in Finlay's Post Office accounts. His situation had not improved by 1794 when he went to London to request compensation for unpaid services to the government; among other duties he had served as chairman of various council committees because he was bilingual and had acted as interpreter for the Court of Appeals as well as translated into French and transcribed that court's decisions. As compensation, he again requested the lease of the Saint-Maurice ironworks, but added to it the posts of commissioner to determine the boundary with the United States, auditor of Lower Canada, and chairman of the Executive Council's land committee. With the support of Dorchester and Dundas he obtained the latter two positions, but their combined salary remained inadequate to his needs.

Perhaps it was desperation that prompted Finlay to become involved in a land speculation scheme in the fall of 1795. The plan, involving John Jacob Astor*, called on Finlay to use his position as chairman of the land committee to gain approval of grants for as many as 24 townships. The scheme collapsed because of a temporary halt put on new free concessions of township land that fall. Finlay himself, along with about 40 associates, had expected to be granted Stanbridge Township. Desperate for money, he sold

318

36,000 acres of Stanbridge in advance for £1,000 sterling, but he was obliged in October 1796 to mortgage Woodside and pledge his salary to repay the sum when he found himself under suspicion of speculation by Governor Robert PRESCOTT and was unable to obtain letters patent to the land. The same month he was forced to sell the house on Rue du Sault-au-Matelot to pay off another debt. These difficulties were in addition to his Post Office debt, aggravated by the bankruptcy of the postmaster of Trois-Rivières. No longer willing to tolerate the ever-increasing arrears, the British government dismissed Finlay from the Post Office in October 1799; he was replaced in April 1800 by George Heriot*.

Finlay's long and able service to the government of the colony helped postpone, but could not deflect, the rigours of the English civil law that he had so ardently advocated; in 1801 the Court of King's Bench ordered Finlay to pay £1,408 to the Post Office. That September Finlay finally received the patent on the Stanbridge grant from Lieutenant Governor Robert Shore Milnes*, and the following month he sold 32,400 acres to Isaac TODD and James McGILL, two Montreal merchants to whom he was heavily in debt, for £3,750. The sale was too little too late. At the time of Finlay's death on 26 Dec. 1801, Todd and McGill were only among the larger of Finlay's probably numerous creditors. One month later Milnes brought to the notice of the colonial secretary, Lord Hobart, the pecuniary distress into which Finlay's family had fallen. His children were forced to renounce their inheritance, and the creditors would take years to recover debts from the estate, which they confided to the trusteeship of John Mure*. Despite his financial ruin, however, at his death Finlay remained the respected senior member of the Legislative Council and loyal whig office holder, who had earned his subsequent designation of "father of the Canadian post office."

I. K. STEELE

A copy of the "Journal kept by Hugh Finlay, surveyor of the post roads on the continent of North America, during his survey of the post offices between Falmouth and Casco Bay in the province of Massachusetts and Savannah in Georgia, begun the 13th Sept. 1773 & ended 26th June 1774" is held at the National Arch. (Washington), RG 28. It was edited by F. H. Norton and published under this title at Brooklyn, N.Y., in 1867, and reprinted in 1975 as *The Hugh Finlay journal; colonial postal history, 1773–1774* with an introduction by C. M. Hahn. A journal of the siege of Quebec in 1775–76 which is attributed to Finlay has been published as "Journal of the siege and blockade of Quebec by the American rebels, in autumn 1775 and winter 1776" in Literary and Hist. Soc. of Quebec, *Hist. Docs.* (Quebec), 4th ser. (1875): [3]–25.

ANQ-Q, CE1-61, 30 Dec. 1801; CN1-16, 27 janv., 17 févr. 1809; CN1-26, 18 déc. 1801; CN1-83, 24 avril 1783,

18 févr. 1788, 21 avril 1789; CN1-92, 23 janv., 16 févr. 1802; CN1-148, 22 mars, 11 déc. 1764; CN1-205, 26 juin 1775; 26 janv., 30 sept. 1780; 25 févr., 31 mai 1783; CN1-207, 21 nov. 1766; CN1-224, 26 mai 1781; CN1-248, 23 avril 1764; CN1-256, 18 June 1789, 11 Oct. 1796; CN1-262, 3 oct. 1796, 19 mars 1798, 2 oct. 1801. BL, Add. mss 21860; 21877: 407. PAC, MG 23, GII, 9; MG 30, D1, 12: 730–91; MG 40, L, 1; 3A; 60 (copies). PRO, CO 42/25–135, especially 42/46, 42/61, 42/87, and 42/104. *Doc. relatifs à l'hist. constitutionnelle, 1759–1791* (Shortt et Doughty; 1921), 2: 697–98, 729–33, 830–33, 841–45, 941–43. Joseph Hadfield, *An Englishman in America, 1785, being the diary of Joseph Hadfield*, ed. D. S. Robertson (Toronto, 1933), 130. *The papers of Benjamin Franklin*, ed. L. W. Labaree *et al.* (21v. to date, New Haven, Conn., [1960–]), 10: 221–23, 252–53, 279–80, 284–85; 19: 273, 359, 374–75, 415. *Quebec Gazette*, 4 Oct., 20 Dec. 1764; 28 May, 13 June, 25 July, 18 Aug., 19 Sept., 3 Oct. 1766; 20 Aug. 1767; 22 March 1770; 15 June 1772; 30 June 1774; 25 Aug. 1775; 15 May, 12 June 1777; 3 Sept., 29 Oct. 1778; 19 Aug. 1779; 25 Oct. 1781; 27 June, 7 Nov. 1782; 6 Nov. 1783; 3 March, 18 Aug. 1785; 5, 26 July 1787; 14, 21 Aug. 1788; 2 April, 31 Dec. 1789; 28 Jan., 25 March 1790; 18 Aug., 17 Nov. 1791; 23 Feb., 8, 29 March, 10 May 1792; 3 Jan., 11 April 1793; 2 July 1795; 6 Feb. 1798; 27 June 1799; 8 May 1800; 31 Dec. 1801; 28 Jan., 28 April, 25 Nov. 1802; 7 April, 12 May, 3 Nov., 1 Dec. 1803. Kelley, "Church and state papers," ANQ *Rapport*, 1953–55: 108. *Quebec almanac*, 1788: 47; 1801: 102. Tremaine, *Biblio. of Canadian imprints*, no.153. Abbott, *Hist. of medicine*, 47. A. H. Clark, *Three centuries and the Island: a historical geography of settlement and agriculture in Prince Edward Island, Canada* (Toronto, 1959). Neatby, *Administration of justice under Quebec Act*, 28, 47–50, 76, 97, 100–1, 115–17, 135, 137, 140, 168, 196–255, 322; *Quebec*, 79–80, 161, 165–67, 190–91, 203, 206–25. William Smith, *The history of the Post Office in British North America, 1639–1870* (Cambridge, Eng., 1920), 1, 37–58, 76, 79, 84–86, 89–90.

FISHER, DUNCAN, shoemaker; b. *c.* 1753 in the parish of Little Dunkeld, Scotland, probably the son of Duncan Fisher, a farmer, and Christian (Christen) Creighten; d. 5 July 1820 in Montreal, Lower Canada.

Duncan Fisher settled as a farmer near Argyle, N.Y., in 1773. In July 1777 he was recruited to transmit verbal dispatches to Major-General John Burgoyne* at Skenesborough (Whitehall) and continued as a volunteer without pay until the convention signed near Saratoga (Schuylerville) on 17 October after the campaign. He then came to Montreal, probably joining his brother James, a fur trader. Their brothers John, a merchant, and Alexander, a hosteller, as well as their cousins Finlay FISHER, a schoolmaster, and Alexander Fisher, apparently established themselves in the city about the same time. By 1783 Duncan was in business as a shoemaker. The following year he and Finlay were among the signatories to a petition asking that Quebec be granted an assembly. Duncan and his brothers Alexander and

Fisher

John were described in the early 1790s as "Gentlemen of the Northwest." No other evidence has been found to indicate that Duncan participated directly in the fur trade; in 1799, however, he was a supplier of goods to the fur-trade firm of McTavish, Frobisher and Company [see Simon McTavish; Joseph Frobisher]. Fisher's business evidently prospered, since in June 1793 he paid the impressive sum of 18,000 *livres* (about £900, Halifax currency) for a house on Rue Saint-Paul belonging to the estate of Marie-Anne Hervieux, widow of the merchant Jean-Baptiste Le Comte* Dupré. From 1792 to 1803 Fisher made many applications as a loyalist for land in different parts of the province, and was supported by such prominent figures as Alexander Auldjo*, James McGill, John Richardson*, and Sir John Johnson*; in 1802 he received 1,200 acres in Roxton Township, Lower Canada.

After his arrival in Montreal Fisher supported the English "Protestant Congregation," in which many Scots worshipped [see David Chabrand* Delisle]. As early as 1785, however, he was subscribing funds for a Presbyterian congregation, which was to hold its first service on 12 March 1786 following the arrival of the Reverend John Bethune. In 1787 Bethune left Montreal, and the Presbyterians appear to have attended services at the English Church (Christ Church) until 1791, when Presbyterianism was put on a permanent footing after the arrival from New York State of the Reverend John Young*. A congregation called the Society of Presbyterians was formed, and on 8 May 1791 Fisher was elected, along with Richard Dobie and 16 others, to the first temporal committee. Fisher that year began conducting correspondence with the Presbytery of Albany to secure Young's services as "stated supply," that is to have Young fill the position of pastor without, however, his being officially called and inducted into the post. In 1791 as well the temporal committee charged Fisher with the task of locating and negotiating the purchase of a lot on which a church could be built. In April 1792 ground was finally acquired on Rue Saint-Philippe (Rue Saint-Gabriel) and the construction of a church begun, Fisher being a member of the building committee. In the mean time the congregation worshipped, following the service of the Church of Scotland, in a church on Rue Notre-Dame placed at its disposal by the Recollets. On 7 Oct. 1792 Young was able to conduct divine service for the first time in the new Scotch Presbyterian Church, later known as St Gabriel Street Church, which had cost £850 and could seat 650 people; however, construction would not be completed until 25 years later, at a total cost of £2,268. Fisher was appointed one of ten trustees, to hold property on behalf of the congregation, and he helped to administer its mortgage discharge fund. He was elected among the congregation's first elders, a post he held until his death, and was for a time clerk of the session, the most important lay office in the congregation.

In 1802 Young, who was an alcoholic, was obliged to resign his position, and Fisher, along with most of the leading Scottish merchants, supported a call to James Somerville*. Since Somerville was still a licentiate, the Presbytery of Montreal was re-established in September 1803 to ordain him; it consisted of Bethune, Alexander Spark, minister at Quebec, and Fisher, who represented the Scotch Presbyterian Church. Somerville then became the congregation's first regularly inducted minister. However the "American party" in the church, which had preferred another candidate, Robert Forrest, formed a new congregation, keeping the keys to the church. Fisher was one of those appointed by the "Scotch party" to secure its rights, and the delegates were able to recover the keys.

On 27 Feb. 1783, in a Presbyterian ceremony at Montreal, Duncan had married Catherine Embury, daughter of Philip, the founder of Methodism in the United States. Catherine appears to have been as strongly Methodist as her husband was Presbyterian, and she brought up their children with Methodist leanings. She helped establish her denomination in Montreal and was a member of the Wesleyan Methodist congregation (St James Street Methodist Church) after its foundation in 1809. The Fishers had five daughters, one of whom died in infancy, and four sons. Their daughters were noted for their beauty, and since Duncan had apparently acquired a reasonable fortune, and he and Catherine had become socially prominent in their respective denominations, the girls were able to make excellent marriages. The eldest, Jannet, married the Reverend John Hick, who helped organize Methodism in the city; another, Margaret, married successively the merchants William Hutchison and William Lunn*; the third, Elizabeth, married another merchant, John Torrance*; and Nancy, the youngest, married John Mackenzie, also a businessman. Nancy's daughters married the Reverend Alexander Mathieson* and the merchant Robert Esdaile. The Fishers' son Duncan became a prominent lawyer in Montreal, and married the widow Budden, mother of Edwin Henry King*, president of the Bank of Montreal. Duncan's descendants moved into some of the most important places in Montreal, and Fisher stands as a founder of some of the city's leading 19th-century families.

Frederick H. Armstrong

ANQ-Q, CN1-83, 5 oct. 1793. PAC, MG 23, GIII, 32; RG 1, L3ᴸ: 417, 5243, 21086, 41917–18. PCA, St Gabriel Street Church (Montreal), Reg. of baptisms, marriages, and burials, 5 July 1820 (mfm. at ANQ-M). St Andrew's Presbyterian Church (Williamstown, Ont.), Reg. of baptisms and marriages, 27 Feb. 1783, 13 March 1785 (mfm. at PAC). "United Empire Loyalists: enquiry into losses and services," AO *Report*, 1904: 1106–7. *Montreal Gazette*, 12 July 1820. *Montreal Herald*, 8 July 1820. *DAB* (entry for Philip Embury). W. H. Atherton, *Montreal, 1535–1914* (3v., Montreal and Vancouver, 1914), 2: 93–94. R. Campbell, *Hist. of Scotch Presbyterian Church*, 69–70, 72–75, 77, 81, 126. J. S. Moir, *Enduring witness; a history of the Presbyterian Church in Canada* ([Hamilton, Ont., 1974?]), 49–50, 64–65.

FISHER, FINLAY, schoolmaster; b. *c.* 1756 in Dunkeld, Scotland; d. 14 Jan. 1819 in Montreal, Lower Canada.

In June 1775 Finlay Fisher and his brother Alexander emigrated from Scotland to the colony of New York, where Finlay began farming in Charlotte (Washington) County. In June 1777 both joined Major-General John Burgoyne*'s forces and in October were taken prisoner at the battle of Bemis Heights. Released in accordance with the convention signed after the British surrender, they came to Montreal about the same time as their cousins DUNCAN, James, John, and Alexander Fisher. Finlay and his brother claimed to have lost £150 2*s.* 6*d.* as a result of having had to abandon their farm.

In 1778 Fisher founded what was apparently the second English-language school in the city, the first having been opened five years earlier by John Pullman. In 1780 Fisher joined with a certain B. Macho to open a school where they would teach reading, writing, orthography, arithmetic, and book-keeping, as well as English, French, Latin, Italian, Spanish, German, and Dutch grammar and where they would tutor privately. Fisher apparently prospered from his fees, since in 1783 he rented a house on Rue Saint-Paul for the high rate of £60 per annum. That year he shared in the salary of £100 reserved for a schoolmaster at Montreal; the Reverend John STUART received £50 and Fisher and another Scot named Christie £25 each. Christie left the same year, but it was not until May 1786 that his share was transferred to Fisher. By 1789 Fisher was sufficiently prosperous to make a loan of £137. That December he held an open house at which his students' works were displayed; according to the *Montreal Gazette*, the visitors "went away highly pleased with this interesting and useful entertainment."

In 1790 Fisher taught 42 pupils, aged 6 to 15, who, with the exception of 7 free scholars, paid either 6*s.* 6*d.* or 7*s.* 6*d.* per month. He taught most of the subjects offered ten years earlier with Macho, but had added to them geometry, geography, navigation, and surveying. His school was kept "after the old Scottish model, . . . the Presbyterian children learning the catechism, and all pupils repeating a psalm or a paraphrase, every Monday morning." In 1791 Fisher's was one of 17 English-language or bilingual

schools taught by Protestant teachers and serving a Protestant population in the colony of about 10,000. According to David Chabrand* Delisle, Church of England rector at Montreal, the Canadians, who had only 40 schools for a population of 160,000, "prefer the English schools to their own," but only a few were able to afford them. Some time after the adoption in 1801 of a law creating the colony's first public schools, administered by the Royal Institution for the Advancement of Learning, Fisher's school was incorporated into its system.

Fisher appears to have continued to prosper, and in January 1818 he acquired a single-storey stone house on Rue Saint-Joseph (Rue Saint-Sulpice) for the imposing sum of £1,140, although he did not pay cash for it. He rented out this house, and himself lived in a "commodious" two-storey stone house on the same street.

Until at least 1792 Fisher was a member of the Protestant Congregation, an Anglican body, but when in 1791, after the arrival of the Reverend John Young*, a Presbyterian congregation was formed, Fisher also joined it. He died, apparently unmarried, in January 1819. According to the *Quebec Gazette* he was "much and justly regretted" as "one of those meritorious characters who discharged the various and important duties of a Teacher of Youth, with a fidelity that cannot fail to call forth the applause of every good member of society."

J. KEITH JOBLING

ANQ-M, CN1-187, 31 janv. 1818. ANQ-Q, CN1-284, 8 juin 1789. BL, Add. MSS 21877: 265–66v. PAC, MG 23, HII, 1, vol.1: 403–5; RG 1, L3ᴸ: 66353; RG 4, B17, 25, 25 July 1805. PCA, St Gabriel Street Church (Montreal), Reg. of baptisms, marriages, and burials, 18 Jan. 1819 (mfm. at ANQ-M). PRO, AO 12/27: 227, 237 (mfm. at PAC); AO 13, bundle 12: 414–17; CO 42/71: ff.289v–91v, 471, 482. P. Campbell, *Travels in North America* (Langton and Ganong), 119. "United Empire Loyalists: enquiry into losses and services," AO *Report*, 1904: 362–63. *Montreal Gazette*, 31 Dec. 1789; 19 Dec. 1793; 20, 29 Jan., 3, 10 Feb. 1819. *Quebec Gazette*, 15 June 1780; 16 July 1789; 19 July 1792; 25 July 1799; 1 Aug. 1805; 19 Nov. 1818; 18 Jan., 18 Feb. 1819. Kelley, "Church and state papers," ANQ *Rapport*, 1948–49: 329, 337. "Les maîtres d'écoles de l'Institution royale de 1801 à 1834," Ivanhoë Caron, compil., *BRH*, 47 (1941): 22. L.-P. Audet, *Histoire de l'enseignement au Québec* (2v., Montréal et Toronto, 1971), 1: 269, 325, 343; *Le système scolaire*, 2: 137, 139, 345. R. Campbell, *Hist. of Scotch Presbyterian Church*, 238. Douglas Brymner, "Rapport sur les archives canadiennes," PAC *Rapport*, 1889: xxi–xxiii. Massicotte, "Les Chaboillez," *BRH*, 28: 274.

FORETIER, PIERRE, businessman, landowner, seigneur, office holder, and militia officer; b. 12 Jan. 1738 in Montreal (Que.), son of Jacques Foretier and Marie-Anne Caron; d. there 3 Dec. 1815.

Foretier

Pierre Foretier came from a family of tradesmen. His grandfather Étienne Foretier was a baker in Montreal; his father, a shoemaker, had obtained master's papers in 1721 in Paris, where he apparently worked at his trade for some years before returning to New France. After 1735 Jacques Foretier lived in Montreal, where he extended his activity to the operation of a small tannery in the *faubourg* Saint-Laurent. In 1743 he went into partnership with a merchant-tanner, Jean-François Barsalou, for the joint use of their tanning mills. Jacques Foretier died in 1747, and his wife kept the tannery going for some years; she died in 1754.

Orphaned at 16, Pierre Foretier was placed in the care of the children of his mother's first and second marriages, with whom he lived until he himself married. He seems to have resided at first with his half-brother, Jacques Paré, probably in the seigneury of Châteauguay, and then with his half-sister, who was married to Bazile Desfonds, a shoemaker in the *faubourg* Saint-Laurent who had once been apprenticed to his father. On 16 Jan. 1764, in Montreal, Foretier married Thérèse, daughter of the merchant Jean-Baptiste Legrand. Their five daughters were to marry men prominent in Lower Canada, among them Denis-Benjamin Viger*, Louis-Charles Foucher*, and notary Thomas Barron. Four years after his wife died in 1784, Foretier married Catherine Hubert, widow of the merchant Thomas Baron; she too predeceased him, and there were no children from this marriage.

Pierre Foretier's business career began in 1761, the date of the earliest references to his trading and land transactions. From 1762 he appears as a trader or merchant, probably dealing in dry goods and various articles for the fur trade. Around the same time he set up one or several stores. In 1775–76 he was running his father-in-law's store on Rue Saint-Paul, and he owned another on Rue Notre-Dame. Ten years later he was selling fine cloth, crockery, cutlery, clothing, shoes, combs, books, and a variety of small articles in a store connected to his house on Rue Notre-Dame, which apparently was the only one then belonging to him; his business was worth 14,324 *livres*. Subsequently he abandoned this sort of trade, which he had carried on by himself, but there is no indication as to when he closed his store.

His partnerships with other merchants had a very different purpose. Late in 1764 or early in 1765 Foretier had joined with Joseph PÉRINAULT to enter the fur trade. The two formed a partnership in April 1765 with Henry Boone, a Montreal merchant, and a Mr Price, Boone's partner at Quebec, to engage in the fur trade and to run a canoe loaded with merchandise to Michilimackinac (Mackinaw City, Mich.). The total capital invested amounted to at least 11,657 *livres*, 5,285 being put up by Foretier and Périnault; they were to receive a third of the profits. Price and

Boone attended to selling the furs, Périnault stayed at Michilimackinac, and Foretier served as supplier for the expedition. This agreement was not renewed. Foretier and Périnault probably maintained an interest in the fur trade in 1766 and 1767, but there is no record of their activity. Their partnership seems to have come to an end around 1767. In 1769 Foretier on his own sent a canoe with merchandise worth £150 to Lake Ontario, and four years later he invested more than £800 to send two canoes and seventeen *engagés* to Michilimackinac. He accompanied this final expedition and stayed in the *pays d'en haut* in 1773.

The following year Foretier took a new partner, Jean Orillat*. The company was active in the fur business, particularly in 1777 and 1778, when it invested £9,930, and then an additional £2,625, in the trade. Foretier and Orillat fitted out their own canoes, but they also advanced merchandise and funds to other traders. In addition the company sought to diversify its activities; from 1776 and apparently until 1782, it furnished the government of the colony with powder. In 1776 Foretier and Orillat obtained a contract for supplying the British government with articles for presents to the Indians. The contract amounted to £14,000, and they received a five per cent commission. Because Orillat had been taken prisoner by the Americans during the invasion of 1775–76, the authorities made James Stanley Goddard responsible for looking after Indian presents. Although the partnership between Foretier and Orillat was disrupted by the war, it continued until Orillat's death in 1779; the company's accounts were not officially settled until 1783. Foretier, who had been the largest Canadian investor in the fur trade in 1774 and 1777 and had placed substantial sums in it in 1778, got out of it after Orillat's death, although in 1782 he went security for Joseph Sanguinet's expedition to Michilimackinac (Mackinac Island, Mich.). Foretier's career took a different direction, and the transformation is probably attributable in part to changes occurring in the fur trade and to the increasing difficulties faced by Canadian merchants [*see* Étienne-Charles Campion*]. But another factor influenced the thrust of Foretier's commercial activity: from 1780 his real estate holdings were becoming more and more profitable.

Foretier's earliest property investments dated from 1761, when he began to purchase land in the *faubourg* Saint-Laurent, at the level of what is now Sherbrooke Street. He first bought two small parcels in the sub-fief of La Gauchetière, and then in 1762 acquired 30 acres at Côte du Baron, to which he added 6 more in 1764. Foretier embarked on his first development project in the *faubourg* Saint-Pierre, subdividing his land and selling the lots. But this initial venture failed; the *faubourg* Saint-Pierre was too isolated and too far from the town to attract many buyers.

Foretier made his principal purchases in 1765. With

his partner at that time, Joseph Périnault, he bought two parcels of land from Marie-Anne-Noële Denys de Vitré – her three-quarters of the sub-fief of Closse (a property located partly in the *faubourg* Saint-Laurent) and her three-quarters of the seigneury of Île-Bizard – as well as 54 secured annuities (23 on Closse). Périnault made his share over to Foretier in 1767, and two years later Foretier purchased the remaining quarters of the two properties, which belonged to Mathieu-Théodore Denys de Vitré. In 1769, then, Foretier owned all the sub-fief of Closse, an immense area 2 *arpents* wide and over 45 *arpents* in depth. Later, particularly after 1780, he purchased a number of adjacent lots, either in the sub-fief of La Gauchetière or at the northern tip of Closse.

Foretier's purchase of the Closse sub-fief was part of a long-term strategy, since it offered little prospect of quick subdivision; its development would extend over nearly half a century. Foretier's main concern at the time of purchase seems to have been to reduce the cost of his investment to the bare minimum. Thus he reached an agreement with the Sulpicians, who were the seigneurs of Montreal Island, that his sub-fief would be added to their domain and then granted back to him in simple roture (for an annual rent); in this way he avoided paying the heavy cost of the *quint*, a tax amounting to a fifth of the price. A first deed of merger concerning three-quarters of the sub-fief was concluded in 1765, and a second one concerning the last quarter in 1778. Around 1790, however, the Closse sub-fief was being developed. Foretier realized how much income he had forgone in making over the *cens et rentes* and *lods et ventes* to the Sulpicians. Pleading that the Sulpicians had "taken" his sub-fief from him, he launched a suit to regain possession of his seigneurial rights, which he won in 1796. He was able consequently to add revenues as seigneur to the profits from subdividing and the secured annuities.

Particularly in the years 1797–1806, Foretier also developed a large number of lots he had acquired between 1781 and 1784 in the southwest of the *faubourg* Saint-Laurent. Once again, as with his other properties, he bought, subdivided, and sold lots, usually by means of secured annuities. This last block of land, which was close to the old town, may have been his most lucrative property investment.

Foretier owned about a quarter of the *faubourg* Saint-Laurent, the equivalent of the area within the town's fortifications. To make these purchases he had invested 83,000 *livres* over a period of 50 years; the land that he subdivided brought him 186,000 *livres*, which made his total profit 103,000 *livres*. To this sum was added the income from the secured annuities and his seigneurial rights, as well as from the sale of produce and the rental of meadows and wood and pasture lands.

Foretier's real estate operations were not limited to the urban setting; his strategy for developing Île-Bizard was, however, very different from the one he used in the *faubourg* Saint-Laurent. He sought first to consolidate his hold on the seigneury by buying back the five sub-fiefs already granted on it; he could not control the pace of development unless he had sole authority to grant land. The process took several years, for the last sub-fief was not rejoined to the domain until 1788. It is interesting to note that the grants he made reflected the timing of his acquisition of urban properties, the periods of greatest activity being 1765–74, 1785–89, and 1795–1805. The number of land grants rose from 83 in 1781–82 to 107 in 1813; the population of Île-Bizard grew to 508 in the same period and included not only farmers but a number of tradesmen. Foretier took a close interest in the running of his seigneury. He erected a communal mill in 1772–73 and rebuilt it after a fire in 1790. He paid close attention to the situation of his *censitaires* and kept meticulous accounts. At the end of his life his grandson, Hugues Heney*, was running the seigneury and accounted to him for the smallest details of his management. The seigneury of Île-Bizard certainly contributed heavily to Foretier's fortune. In 1781–82, for example, the communal mill brought him 1,800 *livres*, the *cens et rentes* 1,087 *livres*.

From his youth Foretier had been interested in commerce, the fur trade, and landed property, all activities requiring considerable initial capital. Astonishingly enough, he apparently lacked both the capital and the contacts that would explain his rise in the business world. No signs of a large family fortune can be found: his parents' estates were modest indeed. Some attribute his success to money from his first wife, but Thérèse Legrand brought him no dowry. Jean-Baptiste Legrand, a fairly well-to-do merchant, probably gave Foretier the benefit of his experience and his financial help, but there is no record of a substantial loan or gift to his son-in-law to enable him to launch his career. Certain elements of Foretier's success consequently remain obscure. On the other hand, his real estate ventures demonstrate his ability to make good deals and to purchase sites on terms that did not necessitate the initial outlay of large sums. Thus Foretier's earliest acquisitions were all made through secured annuities, with the capital not being paid off until much later. Even his biggest purchases, Closse and Île-Bizard, were not acquired with cash but rather by a life annuity of 3,000 *livres*, which Foretier had to carry with Périnault from 1765 to 1767 and then by himself until 1789. The other large disbursements at the start of his career were in 1769 (1,100 *livres*) and 1770 (3,000 *livres*). It was not until the period 1780–92 that Foretier made other purchases with cash or repaid secured annuities. He also frequently transferred both bonds and secured annuities to minimize the transactions that had to be settled in ready money. It is highly probable that in commerce and the fur trade Foretier had had recourse to similar

Foretier

methods to turn a profit on his initial capital, which may have been relatively modest.

Foretier also played an important role in the public life of Lower Canada. Along with other Canadian and British merchants he took part in the reform movement before 1791, and he was one of the members of a committee of Canadians from the Montreal district working for this cause [*see* Jean DE LISLE]. He was also among those asked to stand as candidates in the first elections for the House of Assembly of Lower Canada in 1792. He ran for Montreal West, where he was defeated. In 1796 he was again a candidate but decided to withdraw before the elections. Appointed a justice of the peace in 1779, he retained that office until his death; as one of the most prestigious JPs of the District of Montreal he was responsible for swearing in provincial officials. He sat on many committees and commissions: he was a member of the commission appointed to investigate aliens arriving in the province (1776), of a committee appointed by the Montreal merchants to study the problem of damaged goods (1779) [*see* Alexander ELLICE], and of the commission to superintend the House of Correction at Montreal (1803–7); he was also "commissioner with authority to carry out church repairs" (1794–1814).

During the occupation of Montreal by American troops in 1775–76 Foretier showed himself an active loyalist. He had letters delivered to Guy CARLETON in Quebec and lent support to a small force of Canadians and Indians being formed at Vaudreuil, providing them with munitions and supplies. He made this contribution to the British cause despite the presence in his home of an American colonel with his aides-de-camp and servants, and despite the close watch kept on him. When hostilities ceased, Foretier continued to show support for the government. He was an active member of the Canadian militia of Montreal, serving in succession as major of the 2nd Battalion (1789–1800) and then as its lieutenant-colonel (1801–3), and as colonel of the 3rd Battalion (1804–15).

Foretier also took a close interest in matters of religion. In 1783 he went to London to seek permission from the government to recruit Catholic priests as teachers for the Collège Saint-Raphaël in Montreal. Two years later he was elected church-warden in the parish of Notre-Dame, an office he held until at least 1787. He may also have been interested in various charities, since he bequeathed large sums to the parish of Notre-Dame, the Hôtel-Dieu, and the Hôpital Général. These legacies amounted to 36,000 *livres*, about a quarter of a fortune estimated at 140,000 *livres* in addition to the value of his lots and buildings.

Foretier's way of life and the considerable fortune he had accumulated bear witness to his success in the business world and public life. He occupied an imposing residence on Rue Notre-Dame that had belonged to his father-in-law, Jean-Baptiste Legrand. In addition to the furniture and numerous and sometimes luxurious fixtures, he had a huge library and a collection of silverware. He also owned a seigneurial manor at Île-Bizard. The inventories made after his first wife's death in 1785 and his own death in 1816 make it possible to examine the evolution of his fortune. In 1785 Foretier was still engaged in both commercial and real estate activities; his links with the fur trade had just been broken. The situation is clearly revealed by the assets of the joint estate, which were estimated at 344,493 *livres*: these included, among other items, the inventory of the store (14,394 *livres*), secured annuities (116,548 *livres*), debts in connection with the landed and seigneurial property (20,901 *livres*), debts of a commercial type due in the form of notes, bonds, and accounts receivable (126,970 *livres*), and even debts owing to the firm of Foretier and Orillat (34,179 *livres*). The last two categories, however, included a large number of doubtful debts that swelled the assets. The liabilities of the joint estate amounted to only 109,915 *livres*, making its net worth 234,578 *livres*, plus 31 lots and buildings. Thirty years later Foretier's wealth was based essentially on his real estate. Of assets valued at 140,142 *livres*, the secured annuities (119,327 *livres*) represented the most important element, followed by the property and seigneurial debts (11,139 *livres*). His liabilities were only a fraction of what they were in 1785 and arose primarily from small current expenses; his properties were free of debt. Foretier had therefore accumulated a fortune estimated at 140,011 *livres*, as well as 34 lots and buildings of unknown value.

When Foretier died, he left a will and numerous codicils designed to prevent his huge fortune and numerous properties from being split up. He stipulated that his estate not be subdivided and tried to exclude certain members of his family, in particular his son-in-law Denis-Benjamin Viger, from any part in managing it and from the income it brought in. Foretier's heirs refused to accept the restrictions imposed on them by the will; they contested the deceased's right to dispose of the assets which their mother, Thérèse Legrand (who had died in 1784), had bequeathed to them and of which he had enjoyed only the usufruct. They agreed, therefore, to disregard the terms of the will and to share the estate equally. Foretier, however, had named his neighbour and friend, Jean-Baptiste-Toussaint Pothier*, as his executor, and Pothier saw to it that Foretier's wishes were respected. Pothier launched a suit which, after extensive legal proceedings, gave rise on 20 Feb. 1827 to a decision by the Court of King's Bench for the District of Montreal in his favour. On appeal, the provincial Court of Appeals at Quebec on 30 April 1830 set aside the judgement, ruling that the terms of

Foretier's will were invalid in the case of Thérèse Legrand's estate and applied solely to the assets in Foretier's estate. The decision made it necessary to evaluate and divide the assets of the two estates and led to another series of lawsuits which dragged on until 29 March 1841, when Foretier's own assets and those bequeathed by Thérèse Legrand were finally separated. It was not until 23 July 1842, however, that the assets from the Legrand estate were divided among the various heirs. Thus for more than 25 years the improvement of the sub-fief of Closse and the other properties in the *faubourg* Saint-Laurent was halted, and in his own way Foretier continued to influence property development in Montreal.

Pierre Foretier was a notable figure in the early years of the British régime. His career spanned more than half a century and encompassed a crucial period in the economic and social development of Lower Canada. His participation in business was not confined to one sector: he was both a retailer and a wholesale merchant, a supplier and financial backer in the fur trade, a lender and speculator, a seigneur and the largest Montreal property owner of his generation. Through the breadth and diversity of his activities he defies simplistic definition. His role in the political and social life of his era also illustrates the complexity of the Lower Canadian merchants' reactions to the transformation their society experienced in the decades after the conquest.

JOANNE BURGESS

[I wish to thank Alan Stewart of the Groupe de recherche sur les bâtiments en pierre grise de Montréal who shared with me his research notes and knowledge of Pierre Foretier. J.B.]

Pierre Foretier is the author of "Notes et souvenirs d'un habitant de Montréal durant l'occupation de cette ville par les Bostonois de 1775 à 1776," PAC *Rapport*, 1945: xxv–xxviii.

ANQ-M, CC1, 12 juin 1747, 18 juin 1754; CE1-51, 1er janv. 1695, 13 janv. 1738, 10 juin 1747, 16 janv. 1764, 22 juin 1784, 25 févr. 1788, 18 févr. 1813, 5 déc. 1815; CN1-108, 13 juin 1747, 22 juill. 1754; CN1-134, 22 janv. 1816; CN1-290, 28 févr. 1769, 23 avril 1773, 19 juill. 1779; CN1-308, 18 oct. 1761; 3 août, 23 sept., 5 oct. 1762; 8 déc. 1763; 8, 15 janv., 20 mai, 23 juin, 11 août 1764; 8 mars, 25 avril, 9, 28 oct. 1765; 13 juill. 1769; CN1-313, 21 déc. 1785, 25 févr. 1788; CN1-339, 3 nov. 1736; CN1-363, 11 févr. 1769, 29 déc. 1778, 15 juin 1779; CN1-372, 22 oct. 1740, 21 déc. 1743, 25 sept. 1744, 12 août 1746, 30 sept. 1748, 23 janv. 1766; CN1-375, 30 déc. 1767. ANQ-Q, E21, 3: ff.534–39 (copies at PAC). BL, Add. mss 21699: 187, 405, 481, 598–601, 693; 21735: 232, 611; 21879: 65–70 ; 21884: 1–2 (mfm. at PAC). PAC, MG 8, F57; F138; MG 11, [CO 42] Q, 15: 236–40; 26-1: 42; 30-1: 107–14; 67: 142; 100: 222; 101-1: 173; MG 17, A7-2, ser.I, sect.8 (mfm.); MG 19, F2, 3, 25 Sept. 1776; MG 24, I179; L3: 5255, 7502–3, 8104, 17380, 17393, 17399, 17406, 17408, 17488, 17501–2, 17567, 17576, 18153–56, 18247–49, 18254–56, 19457–58, 22872–77, 22992–93, 26208–10, 26861–76, 27643–58, 27662–94, 31074–81, 33245–46 (transcripts); RG 1, L3ᴸ: 38, 36043–44, 42267–70; RG 4, B28, 110–15.

Mémoire de Denis-Benjamin Viger, écuyer, et de Marie-Amable Foretier, son épouse, appelans; contre Toussaint Pothier, écuyer et autres intimés, à la Cour provinciale d'appel, d'un jugement de la Cour du banc du roi de Montréal, pour les causes civiles du 20 février 1827 (Montréal, 1827). *Montréal en 1781 . . .* , Claude Perrault, édit. (Montréal, 1969). *Montreal Gazette*, 7 June 1792. *Quebec Gazette*, 5 Sept. 1776, 9 Sept. 1779, 30 Oct. 1783, 17 June 1784. F.-J. Audet, *Les députés de Montréal*, 168–70. *Quebec almanac*, 1780–1815. *Histoire de l'Île-Bizard*, (s.l., 1976). J. E. Igartua, "The merchants and *négociants* of Montreal, 1750–1775: a study in socio-economic history" (PHD thesis, Mich. State Univ., East Lansing, 1974), 115–16. Miquelon, "Baby family." Fernand Ouellet, *Éléments d'histoire sociale du Bas-Canada* (Montréal, 1972), 281–94. Tousignant, "La genèse et l'avènement de la constitution de 1791." Hélène Charlebois-Dumais et Alan Stewart, "Un aperçu du développement de la propriété foncière à Montréal: la carrière de Pierre Foretier, 1760–1815," *Communication to the Society for Study of Architecture in Canada* (Montreal, 1980). J.-J. Lefebvre, "Études généalogiques: la famille Viger, le maire Jacques Viger (1858): ses parents, ses descendants, ses ascendants, ses alliés," SGCF *Mémoires*, 17 (1966): 203–38. É.-Z. Massicotte, "Le bourgeois Pierre Fortier," *BRH*, 47 (1941): 176–79; "Les tribunaux de police de Montréal," *BRH*, 26 (1920): 182. Gabriel Nadeau, "Jean Orillat," *BRH*, 41 (1935): 644–84.

FORSYTH, JOSEPH, merchant and office holder; b. *c.* 1760 in Huntly, Scotland, son of William Forsyth and Jean Phyn; m. first *c.* 1797 Ann Bell in Kingston, Upper Canada, and they had one son; m. there secondly *c.* 1803 Alice Robins, and they had six children, including James Bell Forsyth*; d. there 20 Sept. 1813.

Exactly when Joseph Forsyth came to British North America is not known. On 24 Nov. 1784, with his brothers John* and Thomas, he signed a petition urging repeal of the Quebec Act [*see* George ALLSOPP], and most accounts place his arrival in that year; in a memorial of 31 Jan. 1795, however, he claimed residence in Upper Canada of "Fifteen years and upwards." Nor are his whereabouts in the early years entirely clear. In 1786 he was described in a lawsuit at Montreal, Que., as a resident of Detroit (Mich.), and the following year his name was among those supporting the Church of England clergyman there. But by 31 May 1789 he had settled in Kingston, and his prominence dates from his association with that town. Tied by kinship to a powerful mercantile network, Forsyth was now advantageously situated to avail himself of the opportunities afforded by local retailing, the supply of garrisons, and the forwarding trade between Montreal, Kingston, the Niagara area, and Detroit.

Forsyth

Although in July 1789 Forsyth described his activities as being "partly with a view to supplying Loyalists who have authorised our Friends Messrs Phyn Ellice & Inglis of London to receive Compensation allowed them by the British Governm't," it appears his major concern until 1793 was supplying the garrisons. He acquired exclusive rights to the government wharf where he erected a large storehouse. Such were the improvements made to the property that when the commissariat repossessed it after his death, they paid £2,836 in compensation. Since 1786 the policy of the army had been to provision the upper posts with the produce of farmers in the surrounding areas. But problems such as distance of farms from the garrisons, the inability of local areas to produce surpluses, the want of a circulating medium of exchange, and the peculiarities of payment combined to enable a handful of merchants to control the lucrative trade. Forsyth's share of this market seems to have been substantial. Until 1795 Kingston merchants supplied Detroit because of that area's lack of wheat surpluses. Moreover, a crop failure at Niagara in 1789 gave the Kingstonians a monopoly there for a two-year period. Anticipating that this windfall would be repeated in 1792 Forsyth and several others, including Richard CARTWRIGHT, Robert Macaulay*, and Thomas Markland*, bought almost 4,000 barrels of flour. But a bumper crop at Niagara reduced their market to 500 barrels at Kingston; export to Lower Canada could be undertaken only at a substantial loss. Dependent "chiefly" upon flour for their remittances, the merchants petitioned Lieutenant Governor SIMCOE to purchase their surplus for government stores. However, Commissary General John CRAIGIE saw no reason to indemnify them.

The collapse of the Niagara market in 1792, combined with the award to rival merchants the following year of a two-year contract to supply the garrisons, seems to have pushed Forsyth's enterprises in new directions. In late 1793 he approached the Schenectady, N.Y., merchant John Porteous about the possibility of a market there for the "pretty abundant" wheat at Kingston but without any success. The next year he invested in John Denison's brewery at Kingston and leased him the lands and necessary buildings for £125 for one year. Later, Forsyth called in his share of the investment; Denison was unable to pay and Forsyth assumed control. By 1802 the brewery was in an "advanced state of decay." His new partner in the business, Alexander Wood* of York (Toronto), wanted to retain the property but Forsyth was anxious to sell it to James Robins, his future father-in-law, for £1,000 plus interest.

Forsyth had petitioned successfully in 1793 for a town lot in York, but he does not appear to have been concerned with land as a speculation until 1795. Early that year he enquired on behalf of three relatives – his uncle Alexander ELLICE, his cousin John Richardson*, and his brother John – about the conditions attached to township grants in Upper Canada [see Richard DUNCAN]. Later that year Forsyth and his brothers each petitioned for grants of 1,200 acres and by late November 1799 he had received patents for lots in Clarke, Cramahe, Haldimand, Percy, Scarborough, and Thurlow townships. He also acquired land by purchase and in lieu of cash payments for goods, and further increased his holdings as a result of lawsuits against debtors. On such occasions, it was not unusual for him to seek advice from the surveyor general about the quality and value of the lots in question. It is probable that Forsyth regarded land as a long-term investment and retained most of his holdings at his death.

About 1795 Forsyth began to act as a Kingston agent, first for Receiver General Peter RUSSELL and by 1797 for Surveyor General David William Smith*, issuing supplies and notes. He seems to have continued to operate in this capacity until 1800, and again in 1803–4. These contacts brought additional benefits and he became a personal forwarder, receiver, and supplier for other York officials, such as John McGill* and Robert Isaac Dey GRAY.

In 1797 Forsyth's name reappears on the victualling accounts of the commissariat. That year he supplied the garrison at Kingston with 67,200 pounds of flour and 550 barrels of peas. The volume of this business declined to 23,744 pounds of flour and 41 bushels of peas the following year, remained steady in 1799, and dropped to a mere 200 bushels of peas in 1800. It was three years before he again supplied the garrison – a modest 220 bushels of peas. In 1804 he delivered 80 barrels of pork and 19,000 pounds of flour. After that date pork became the major article of supply: 16,640 pounds in 1805, 4,000 pounds in 1807, and 25,000 pounds in 1808 and 1809. Once again trade with the garrison declined and the last record of business is an account for 500 bushels of peas in 1811.

The garrison was an unstable albeit profitable market. In 1800 Upper Canadian merchants began for the first time to export wheat and flour to Lower Canada; Forsyth shipped 400 barrels of flour, 5 of potash, and 80 bushels of wheat. The following year the increase in his trade was dramatic. From the Kingston area he shipped 803 barrels of flour to Montreal in partnership with Robins, and 250 barrels for another merchant; with Robins he shipped from Niagara 298 barrels of flour and from Detroit 1,103, as well as 6 barrels of potash. An annual account *circa* 1802, presumably for the Kingston area alone, indicates how quickly he had adjusted to the demands of the new market. That year he shipped 1,739 barrels of flour, 25 barrels of potash, 20 barrels of pork, and 563 pounds of butter to Montreal.

Forsyth's was one of a handful of shops maintained by the leading Kingston merchants and local retailing continued to be a major part of his enterprises. He sold a wide variety of goods, and his imports at Coteau-du-Lac in 1801 included large amounts of many luxury items. Extension of credit was necessary for any merchant in a province lacking a circulating currency, and served to build and secure a fixed clientele. One notable development of this practice occurred during the War of 1812, when Forsyth banded together with other large merchants such as John Kirby* to form a rudimentary bank. The sole purpose of the short-lived Kingston Association, established on 28 Aug. 1813, was to issue bills in exchange for specie.

Forsyth's interest was limited to business; he had apparently no political ambitions. An early supporter of the Church of England in Kingston, he served as vestryman in 1794, and churchwarden of St George's Church in 1797 and 1803. As justice of the peace he attended 7 of 9 meetings between 1802 and 1804, and 8 of 25 between 1808 and 1813. He also served on the first Heir and Devisee Commission for the Midland District. In 1807 he was a road commissioner. On 14 June 1813 he became collector of customs. Forsyth appointed Richardson and William Mitchell, "my Partner in Business," executors of his estate, dividing it equally among his children. The documents that survive portray a man single-minded in his devotion to business. But an obituary eulogized him as "a fond husband, an affectionate father, and . . . the constant patron of all who had the honor of his confidence; in hospitality he could not be exceeded, and as a magistrate he was irreproachable; none ever filled that honorable station with more credit."

DAVID S. MACMILLAN

AO, MS 88, Elizabeth Russell to Joseph Forsyth, 8 Aug. 1809; MS 392, 20-164 (Court of Common Pleas, Montreal District, court docs.), no.3 (Hoyles & Small *v*. Joseph Forsyth, 13 June 1786); MS 522, William Jarvis to John Peters, 23 Nov. 1793; Joseph Forsyth & Co. to Peters, 6 Feb. 1796; MS 525, John Denison to Joseph Forsyth & Co., accounts, 10 April 1794, 2 Oct. 1795, 15 April 1796; Kingston Brewery to Forsyth & Co., account, 12 April 1794; indenture between Forsyth and Denison, 1 Oct. 1795; RG 1, A-I-6: 481–82, 1503–4, 1582–83, 1795, 1853, 1857, 1893, 1984–85, 2055, 2139, 2173, 2460, 2466–67, 3147–48, 3163, 3418, 3461, 3532, 3580, 3609; A-II-1, 1: 222, 386, 402; C-I-4, 40: 84; RG 22, ser.54, 1–2; ser.155, will of Joseph Forsyth. Buffalo and Erie County Hist. Soc. (Buffalo, N.Y.), C64-4 (Porteous papers), nos.41–43, 1272–78, 1280, 1282 (mfm. at PAC). Durham Land Registry Office (Whitby, Ont.), Abstract index to deeds, Clarke Township, 2: 7–10 (mfm. at AO, GS 3852). MTL, Peter Russell papers, Joseph Forsyth to Russell, 14 Oct. 1795; 2 Nov. 1796; 2 Nov., 8 Dec. 1797; 15 April, 24 May, 2, 12 June, 13, 20 July, 3–4 Aug., 1 Sept., 12 Dec. 1798; 30 May 1800; 21 Aug. 1803; John Gray to Russell, 23 Dec. 1803; 18 Feb.

1804; Alexander Wood papers, business letterbooks, I–III. Northumberland East Land Registry Office (Colborne, Ont.), Abstract indexes to deeds, Cramahe Township, 1: 213–14; Percy Township, 1: 111 (mfm. at AO, GS 4727, 4792). PAC, RG 1, E3, 100: 206–11; L3, 185: F1/6, 28; 186: F4/11; 186a: F5/19; RG 8, I (C ser.), 77: 34; 111: 156; 112: 34; 115A: 49, 62; 115B: 70, 92, 348; 115C: 3, 179, 244; 115D: 1; 115E: 53–54, 66, 187, 246, 271–72, 302; 115F: 101, 203–4, 220–21, 256; 272: 191; 505: 156; 688E: 89, 136, 138; 724: 113; 913: 53, 57; 930: 63; RG 16, A1, 133, unsigned draft memo, 14 June 1813; RG 68, General index, 1651–1841: f.419. PRO, CO 42/317: ff.186–89, 191, 193–94, 197–205. QUA, Richard Cartwright papers, letterbook (transcript at AO).

"Accounts of receiver-general of U.C.," AO *Report*, 1914: 739–40, 742–45, 752, 774. *Corr. of Lieut. Governor Simcoe* (Cruikshank), 2: 217. "District of Luneburg: Court of Common Pleas," AO *Report*, 1917: 438, 445. "District of Mecklenburg (Kingston): Court of Common Pleas," AO *Report*, 1917: 202, 213, 241, 250–51, 275, 346. *Docs. relating to constitutional hist., 1759–91* (Shortt and Doughty; 1907), 502–9. *Docs. relating to NWC* (Wallace), 442–43. "Grants of crown lands in U.C.," AO *Report*, 1929: 53, 129. *John Askin papers* (Quaife), 1: 303, 367. *Kingston before War of 1812* (Preston), 109–10, 145–46, 189–90, 202, 280a–b, 296. *Parish reg. of Kingston* (Young), 25, 32, 57, 65–67, 69, 72, 91, 94, 110, 112, 129, 137, 151, 158. [John Richardson], "The John Richardson letters," ed. E. [A.] Cruikshank, *OH*, 6 (1905): 24. "U.C. land book D," AO *Report*, 1931: 123. *Kingston Gazette*, 31 Aug., 23 Sept. 1813. *Montreal Herald*, 2 Oct. 1813. *Heritage Kingston*, ed. J. D. Stewart and I. E. Wilson (Kingston, Ont., 1973), 37. MacDonald, "Hon. Richard Cartwright," *Three hist. theses*, 127. Wilson, "Enterprises of Robert Hamilton," 62, 64, 111. W. S. Wallace, "Forsyth, Richardson and Company in the fur trade," RSC *Trans.*, 3rd ser., 34 (1940), sect.II: 187–94.

FORSYTH, WILLIAM, merchant, office holder, and politician; b. *c.* 1749 in Scotland; d. 14 Oct. 1814 in Tealing, Scotland.

Prior to the American revolution London merchant houses virtually monopolized trade between Nova Scotia and Britain [*see* Sir Brook WATSON]. By the 1780s, however, this English hegemony was disintegrating as a result of Scotland's rise as a commercial power. One reflection of this development was the large number of Scottish entrepreneurs who emigrated to post-revolutionary Nova Scotia. The most notable of these was William Forsyth.

Little is known of Forsyth's background. He was a Presbyterian, apparently of Lowland stock. Having gained business experience in and around Glasgow, he moved to Halifax where he began advertising as a general merchant in July 1784. The British and European goods handled by Forsyth were mostly shipped to him by his two Greenock-based partners, George Robertson and James Hunter. In common with other Halifax merchants of the post-revolutionary era, Forsyth avoided exclusive dependence on the local garrison market. He established commercial contacts

Forsyth

across the Maritime regional hinterland, and by the late 1780s Forsyth and Company was trading along the coast from Saint John, N.B., to the Gaspé and Newfoundland. Indicative of the scale of his operations was the fact that between June 1787 and December 1788 Forsyth received goods valued at £48,786 6s. 4d. from his Scottish partners. Additional quantities were brought in during this same period for sale on a commission basis for various British manufacturers. These imports were then exchanged with a host of Halifax and outport merchants mostly for timber and fish, which Forsyth and Company shipped to markets in Britain, the Caribbean, and the United States.

A company letterbook which survives for the period 1796–98 provides insight into the difficulties experienced by Halifax merchants in carrying out their complex, multilateral trade relations. The lack of reliable information on the all-important but rapidly fluctuating commodity prices in the Caribbean remained a source of constant anxiety. Additional problems came in the form of squabbles over the quality of cargo, disputes over late payments, incompetent and often drunken captains, mutinous and deserting crewmen, thievery, losses from storm and disease, and harassment from customs officers. Further complications arose from the fact that war then raged between Britain and revolutionary France. Forsyth and Company repeatedly complained of being deprived of continental markets, of suffering losses to enemy privateers, of having crews depleted by press-gangs, and of seeing the Royal Navy raid American shipping to the point where war with the United States threatened. As compensation, the firm found that war allowed it to sell to an expanded garrison market while simultaneously speculating in the prize-goods market.

The single greatest advantage derived from war by Forsyth and Company related to a surge in the Royal Navy's demand for ship timber. In 1788 the firm won a seven-year contract to provide the navy with masts, yards, and spars; on one occasion, in 1789, Forsyth secured these materials by entering into an arrangement with William Davidson*, the New Brunswick lumber merchant. As a timber contractor, Forsyth became intimately associated with John WENTWORTH, surveyor general of the king's woods. When Wentworth became Nova Scotia's lieutenant governor in 1792 he used his authority to promote the interests of Forsyth, whom he termed "my most respected valuable Friend." As a result, government contracts continued to flow to Forsyth; he was appointed a magistrate and overseer of the poor; and in 1801 he formally joined Wentworth's inner circle as a member of the Council. Wentworth and Forsyth were also associated in two abortive development schemes, one to build a canal from Halifax to the Bay of Fundy, and

the other to establish a chartered bank in Halifax. Further, in 1802 Wentworth granted Forsyth and two other Halifax merchants a 21-year monopoly on coal-mining in the province. This patronage *coup* was foiled, however, when the imperial government refused to ratify the lease.

Forsyth's entrepreneurial success was reflected in the various partnership changes that took place within his firm. In 1797 William Smith, a new son-in-law, joined Forsyth and Company. Smith subsequently moved to Liverpool, England, where he conducted a branch operation in conjunction with Forsyth's son Thomas. In 1806 John Black*, manager of the firm's Saint John branch and an important merchant in his own right, moved to Halifax as a partner. Three years later Forsyth left Nova Scotia to live permanently in Greenock. Although he remained involved in the business of the transatlantic firm, Black now assumed control of the Halifax operations.

Forsyth's departure from Halifax aroused no comment, largely because he had never played a major role in community affairs. On his arrival he had joined the North British Society, and in 1788 he served as its president. During the mid 1790s he was on the executive of the short-lived Halifax Marine Society, a philanthropic organization established in 1786 by a group of shipmasters and merchants. But, in essence, Forsyth maintained a low social profile and after 1802 displayed a decreasing interest in Nova Scotia; frequent absences in Scotland gave him a poor attendance record in Council. Wentworth's ouster as lieutenant governor in 1808 probably contributed to Forsyth's decision to return to Scotland. Under the direction of John Black, however, Forsyth and Company remained an active force on the Halifax waterfront for more than a decade. Furthermore, the link between Nova Scotia and Glasgow that William Forsyth had helped to forge persisted throughout the 19th century.

D. A. SUTHERLAND

Halifax County Registry of Deeds (Halifax), Deeds, 37: ff.273–75; 39: ff.29–31, 35–36; 61: ff.66–67 (mfm. at PANS). PANS, MG 3, 150–51; MG 13, 2: ff.626–35; 3, Alexander Anderson to Forsyth, Smith and Co., 12, 22 Sept. 1802; 4: 37–38; RG 1, 49, John Wentworth to S. W. Prentice and John Henderson, 28 July 1792; Wentworth to George Pyke, 25 Nov. 1805; 51: ff.45–47; 52: 259–61; 53: 222–23, 458–61; 458, doc.1. PRO, CO 217/78: f.248. N.S., House of Assembly, *Journal and proc.*, 21 June 1798. Perkins, *Diary, 1766–80* (Innis); *Diary, 1780–89* (Harvey and Fergusson); *Diary, 1790–96* (Fergusson); *Diary, 1797–1803* (Fergusson). *Acadian Recorder*, 26 Nov. 1814, 30 Dec. 1815, 14 Sept. 1822. *Nova Scotia Royal Gazette*, 12 Oct. 1784; 11 Jan. 1785; 16 Dec. 1794; 20 Sept. 1796; 12 Sept. 1797; 20 Sept. 1798; 21 March, 25 July 1805; 28 April, 7 July 1807; 20 Feb., 21 Nov. 1810. *An almanack . . . calculated for the meridian of Halifax in Nova-Scotia . . .* , comp. Theophrastus (Halifax), 1799. North British Soc., *Annals of the North British Society, Halifax, Nova Scotia, with portraits and biographical notes, 1768–1903*, comp. J. S. Macdonald ([3rd ed.], Halifax, 1905). Murdoch, *Hist. of N.S.*, vol.3. J. R. Armstrong, "The Exchange Coffee House and St. John's first club," N.B. Hist. Soc., *Coll.*, 3 (1907–14), no.7: 60–78.

FORTON, MICHEL, gold- and silversmith, maker and seller of jewellery, and engraver; b. 25 Nov. 1754 at Quebec, son of Jean Forton, a pulley maker, and Louise Chamard; d. there 12 Feb. 1817.

Michel Forton's career cannot be traced further back than 1775, when he signed a document concerning an expedition for Michilimackinac (Mackinaw City, Mich.) that had been fitted out by Joseph Schindler*, a specialist in trade silver. As an apprentice to Schindler he gave evidence in a lawsuit brought against the silversmith at Detroit in 1776. Forton may have known him through his brother Jean Forton, a first cousin by marriage of Joseph Lucas, who had also been Schindler's apprentice.

In 1790 Forton was in Quebec, where he had a shop at 19 Rue de la Montagne. In March 1795 he hired 14-year-old James Sullivan as an apprentice for a period of six years. In accordance with an unusual and interesting condition that Sullivan's father had put in the apprenticeship agreement, Forton immediately had the boy attend drawing classes given by François Baillairgé*. Moreover, Forton undertook to send him to the school for a year. Baillairgé's diary reveals that he produced for Forton many little wood carvings which the latter probably used as models in making silver pieces or jewellery: a squirrel, heads of a griffin, a stag, and a unicorn, a half-length figure of a griffin, a bull, a dog, a rooster, and numerous other models including a crown and a star. In his diary Baillairgé also calls Forton an engraver.

The Court of General Sessions of the Peace in 1795 ordered that from 21 October anyone using a forge or an oven would have to do so in premises entirely finished in stone or brick. Quebec silversmiths Michel Forton, François RANVOYZÉ, James G. HANNA, Laurent Amiot*, James Orkney*, Jean-Nicolas Amiot, and Louis-Alexandre Picard* signed a petition demanding exemption from this regulation because of their particular working conditions: no accident could be caused by their forges, since they used very little fire at a time and never for a sustained period; moreover, according to the testimony of Picard, who had engaged in his craft at Quebec for 40 years, there had never been an accident in any workshop and it would be detrimental to silversmiths to have to work on pavements, because they would inevitably lose their gold and silver clippings in them; finally, since they had to remain seated most of the time while working, their health might be damaged irreparably

by the insalubrious dampness of the paved premises. It is not known if anything came of the petition.

The 1798 census was the first document to list Forton as a jeweller. Sullivan was still with him. In 1805 Forton bought for £400 a property on Rues "St. George and de Laval," which he rented to Charlotte Duchouquet. After adding a storey and an attic to this house, he rented it to lawyer Andrew Stuart* in 1811, and then to merchant James TOD in 1813. He also rented a property, with houses and outbuildings, on Rue Saint-Vallier in the *faubourg* Saint-Roch, to merchant Joseph Fournier in 1811. Furthermore Forton lent at interest sums ranging from £50 to £150. Clearly he was a rich man by the time of his death on 12 Feb. 1817.

Michel Forton's social life was as ordered and quiet as his professional activity. He was a member of the Quebec Fire Society, which counted the local élite in its ranks, and he did not hesitate to show his loyalty to the British crown upon occasion. The mark identified with his initials is found on numerous household articles and a few snuff boxes. But his shop also carried gems and jewellery, as well as arrowroot, a "very useful and very scarce article." Limited in quantity, his work is sober, unpretentious, and free of major defects; in short, an average production of reasonable quality.

ROBERT DEROME

Works by Michel Forton are to be found in Quebec City at the Musée du Québec, the Séminaire de Québec, and the Hôtel-Dieu, in Montreal at the Hôpital Général, and in Ottawa at the Henry Birks Collection of Silver at the National Gallery of Canada.

ANQ-Q, CE1-1, 25 nov. 1754, 13 févr. 1817; CN1-26, 27 sept. 1804; 23 oct., 25 nov. 1805; 21 mai 1806; 23 mars, 3 déc. 1807; 5 mai 1809; 30 janv., 6 févr. 1811; CN1-27, 18 févr. 1813; CN1-92, 27 mars 1795; CN1-189, 20 déc. 1766; CN1-205, 21, 23, 25 mars 1775; CN1-230, 3 juill. 1806, 14 oct. 1818; P-398, journal, 1784–1800: 158–59, 166, 171–73, 175–77, 180–81, 185. MAC-CD, Fonds Morisset, 2, F74/M623; R213.5/F825; S336/J83. "Les dénombrements de Québec" (Plessis), ANQ *Rapport*, 1948–49: 126. *Quebec Mercury*, 18 Feb. 1817. Langdon, *Canadian silversmiths*. F. W. Robinson, "Silversmiths of early Detroit," Detroit Hist. Soc., *Bull.* (Detroit), 9 (1952–53), no.2: 5–8.

FRASER, JOHN, soldier and schoolmaster; b. *c.* 1734, probably in Scotland; d. 13 Feb. 1803 at Quebec, Lower Canada.

John Fraser served in the 78th Foot during the Seven Years' War and fought in the battle of the Plains of Abraham on 13 Sept. 1759. During the British pursuit after the action, Fraser gave chase to a fleeing French doctor, Philippe-Louis-François BADELARD. Badelard aimed his pistol at him, but the strong and

Fraser

agile Fraser, a giant of a man, overcame him before he could fire. In later years the former adversaries became neighbours, and Fraser would regularly greet Badelard with a friendly "Good-day, my prisoner."

After his discharge Fraser settled at Quebec. There, as elsewhere in the colony, a shortage of schools existed in the aftermath of the conquest. In the 1760s Roman Catholic religious communities, such as the Jesuits, the Ursulines, and the Congregation of Notre-Dame, re-established their primary schools in the city, but the small and mainly Protestant British community was not so well served. Fearing the linguistic and religious consequences of sending their children to French-language Catholic institutions, its members made efforts to establish English-language schools in the city. Fraser probably became the first English-language schoolmaster at Quebec, and had been teaching for some time when on 1 Sept. 1765 Patrick McClement, the first schoolmaster authorized and subsidized by government, opened a school in the Jesuit college. Between 1766 and 1769 three more schools were opened at Quebec, one of them by James Jackson, who succeeded McClement in June 1768 as the official schoolmaster. Fraser had petitioned in 1768 for government certification but had been refused. On 25 Sept. 1769, however, he succeeded Jackson as "Official Schoolmaster at Quebec," and, combining the government subsidy of £30 per annum with fees charged for each student, he apparently experienced modest success thereafter. Competition was evidently minimal, since in 1773 some of the city's Protestant inhabitants complained to the British government about a shortage of schools. Prior to 1778 Fraser lived on Rue Sainte-Anne, but in that year he bought for £200 cash a single-storey stone house at 3 Rue des Jardins and moved there with his wife, Agnes Maxwell, and their daughter. Agnes may have been an alcoholic; the previous year Fraser had printed a notice in the *Quebec Gazette* warning liquor retailers that, since "she had for some time past behaved in a very disorderly Manner drinking to the great Disquiet of my Family," he would no longer be responsible for her bills.

By 1790 there were six English Protestant schools at Quebec educating nearly 200 scholars; among the schoolmasters, however, only James TANSWELL, with £100 per annum, and Fraser, with £30, were receiving government subsidies. That year Fraser taught reading, writing, spelling, and arithmetic at his home to 14 boys and 4 girls between the ages of 4 and 16 years for a fee of 15 shillings per quarter, and from 1791 to 1798 he taught between 10 and 18 scholars per annum. Not all were Protestants: Georges-Barthélemi Faribault*, for example, attended Fraser's school for a few years. In 1801 the efforts begun as early as 1784 to create a system of publicly supported schools, designed not only to educate English Protestants but also to anglicize Canadians, finally issued, as a result of pressure by Anglican bishop Jacob Mountain*, in the formation of the Royal Institution for the Advancement of Learning. Fraser's school immediately became part of its system.

Fraser died two years later and was buried on 16 February by the Presbyterian minister Alexander SPARK. Surviving him were his second wife, Ann Hudson, two daughters (one by each marriage), and a stepson; to them Fraser left a modest succession, including a library of approximately 180 volumes and a grant of 400 acres in Granby Township, patented one month earlier. The *Quebec Gazette* stated that "a large number of respectable citizens of Quebec" were indebted to the "old and respected" schoolmaster for their education. The school at 3 Rue des Jardins continued to exist after Fraser's death, with Daniel Wilkie* as master.

MARIANNA O'GALLAGHER

ANQ-Q, CN1-284, 9 mars, 17 mai, 28 déc. 1803; CN1-285, 23 mai 1800. AP, St Andrew's (Quebec), Reg. of baptisms, marriages, and burials, 16 Feb. 1803. PAC, MG 11, [CO 42] Q, 48-2: 651–54. "Les dénombrements de Québec" (Plessis), ANQ *Rapport*, 1948–49: 71, 121, 172. *Quebec Gazette*, 5 Sept. 1765; 19 June 1777; 3 March, 9 June 1803. "A list of Protestant house keepers in the District of Quebec (Octr. 26th, 1764)," *BRH*, 38 (1932): 753–54. L.-P. Audet, *Le système scolaire*, 2: 136, 139, 231, 344, 347. P.-G. Roy, "Le chirurgien Badelard," *BRH*, 2 (1896): 45; "Le premier professeur d'anglais au Canada," *BRH*, 31 (1952): 416–17.

FRASER (ffraser), MALCOLM, army and militia officer, seigneur, and office holder; b. 26 May 1733 in Abernethy, Scotland, son of Donald Fraser and Janet McIntosh; d. 14 June 1815 at Quebec, Lower Canada, and was buried five days later in St Matthew's cemetery.

In July 1757 Malcolm Fraser purchased an ensigncy in the 78th Foot. The following month his regiment landed at Halifax, N.S., and Fraser subsequently took part in the sieges of Louisbourg, Île Royale (Cape Breton Island), and Quebec. When the regiment was disbanded in 1763 he retired on a lieutenant's half pay. His loyal services as a soldier entitled him to petition for land. On 27 April 1762 Governor Murray* granted him the seigneury of Mount-Murray, which was situated within the boundaries of the former seigneury of La Malbaie. Only two such grants in fief and seigneury were made by the British government, the other one being given to Fraser's companion in arms John NAIRNE. That same year Fraser rented from Murray part of the seigneury of Île-d'Orléans including the parishes of Sainte-Famille and Saint-Jean, and in 1766 Murray granted him 3,000 acres at the back of his seigneury of Rivière-du-Loup. During the American Revolutionary War Fraser became a captain and paymaster in the 1st battalion of the Royal Highland Emigrants [see Allan Maclean*]. He gave the alarm when the Americans who were besieging Quebec launched their attack on 31 Dec. 1775 under Richard Montgomery*. Later his company was stationed mainly in the Montreal and Richelieu valley regions. When his battalion was disbanded in June 1784, Fraser again went on half pay, but it was withdrawn five years later because of the discovery of irregularities in his regimental books. He had to wait until 1795 to clear his reputation and again collect his half pay, along with arrears.

After the American invasion Fraser continued to acquire landed property. He bought the seigneury of L'Islet-du-Portage from Gabriel Christie* in 1777. Two years later he purchased for £1,000 the portion of Île-d'Orléans that he rented from Murray. In 1782 he took over part of a long-term lease that Murray had given Henry CALDWELL. The territory, which was rented for £90 per annum for the first 11 years and £100 after that, comprised the seigneuries of Rivière-du-Loup and Madawaska and the fief of Île-Rouge. In 1786 he received 3,000 acres in Chatham Township. Fraser also turned out to be one of the major landowners in the Upper Town of Quebec. In the period 1777–91 he bought five houses and lots on Rue des Grisons, between Rue Sainte-Geneviève and Rue Mont-Carmel. His common-law wife, Marie Allaire, herself purchased some land on Rue des Grisons, of which Fraser took over the mortgage. Around 1790 he also acquired the house belonging to merchant John McCord on Rue de la Fabrique. In addition, in 1782 Fraser had set up the Madawaska Company in partnership with Caldwell. He had become a money-lender as well. He lent out the sum of £300 in 1773 and £1,000 in 1784. Three years later he made a loan of £200 to Hugh Blackburn, a miller at Mount-Murray.

Thus, beneath the exterior of a landed gentleman, Fraser showed himself to be an astute businessman, whether he was investing in property or putting out money. He did not hesitate to invest even when he had to mortgage his seigneuries. The seigneury of L'Islet-du-Portage had a mortgage of £400 on it in 1790, and again in 1810. In 1791 there was a mortgage on Mount-Murray made out to surgeon James Fisher*. On occasion Fraser leased his seigneuries, contenting himself with collecting the rent from them. They brought him income from fishing, wheat, saw logs, and seigneurial dues.

Fraser was an absentee seigneur. At Quebec he held for many years the office of justice of the peace, to which he was first appointed in 1764. He was a founding member of the Agriculture Society, which was created in 1789, and he became a subscriber to the Fire Society in 1790. Three years earlier he had been appointed a major in the Quebec Battalion of British Militia, a posting he retained until 1794. In May of that year Governor Lord Dorchester [Guy CARLETON] promoted him colonel in the Kamouraska battalion of militia, and in 1805 he was colonel of the Baie-Saint-Paul battalion of militia. During the War of 1812, despite his advanced years Fraser led the militiamen from Baie-Saint-Paul to Quebec.

By 1803 Fraser had begun divesting himself of his real estate, giving his son Simon his 3,000 acres in Chatham Township on condition that Simon secure letters patent. Two years later he sold his share in the seigneury of Île-d'Orléans to Louis Poulin, a miller at Sainte-Famille. Finally, in 1810, he gave his son Joseph his seigneury of L'Islet-du-Portage.

One of Fraser's biographers, William Stewart Wallace*, asserts that he had numerous illegitimate children, five of them with Marie Allaire, who came from the seigneury of Beaumont. Three other children, Ann, William, and John Malcolm*, were born later of his liaison with Marguerite Ducros, dit Laterreur, who was from the seigneury of Mount-Murray. In his will, dated 4 Nov. 1811, Fraser bequeathed an annual pension to her and divided his Canadian estate among all his children.

YVON DESLOGES

ANQ-Q, CN1-103, 3 sept. 1765; CN1-205, 19 déc. 1777, 10 août 1784; CN1-224, 6 mai 1786; CN1-245, 11 mai 1780, 3 août 1784; CN1-256, 17 March, 25 May 1791; 5 July, 1 Sept. 1794; 6 Oct. 1795; CN1-262, 11 déc. 1795; CN1-284, 22 juill. 1791; P-81; P-297. ASQ, Polygraphie, XXXVI: 22g. PAC, MG 23, B7; GIII, 23, vol.1: 2–9, 191, 575; vol.5; K1; RG 1, L3^L: 29, 37, 43, 408, 2368, 2643, 2649, 43277, 43282, 43329, 43332, 43355, 43361–62, 43369, 54137–41, 72886; RG 8, I (C ser.), 15: 18; 187: 3–4; 931: 28, 109. L.-P. Lizotte, La vieille Rivière-du-Loup, ses vieilles gens, ses vieilles choses (1673–1916); le pays des beaux couchers de soleil (s.l., 1973). G. M. Wrong, A Canadian manor and its seigneurs; the story of a hundred years, 1761–1861 (Toronto, 1908). W. S. Wallace, "Notes on the family of Malcolm Fraser of Murray Bay," BRH, 39 (1933): 267–71.

FROBISHER, JOSEPH, fur trader and dealer in furs, politician, landowner, office holder, and militia officer; b. 15 April 1740 in Halifax, England, son of Joseph Frobisher and Rachel Hargrave; d. 12 Sept. 1810 in Montreal, Lower Canada.

Joseph Frobisher was the eldest of a family of seven. Three of the five boys, Joseph, Benjamin*, and Thomas, came to try their luck in the province of Quebec after the conquest, the first two around 1763 and their brother about six years later. They were not rich when they arrived, but they were filled with a desire to put the small capital that they did possess to profitable use. It was only by gradual steps that they became determined to dominate the fur trade in the northwest, and in fact the entire economy based on pelts [see Benjamin Frobisher].

Frobisher

The Frobishers' enterprise was initially a family one, and to some degree it retained that character until 1787. The three brothers got along together and complemented one another rather well. As Benjamin had the strongest personality and a distinct talent for organization and administration, he gave up the long journeys in the west fairly early and took over the management of the company in Montreal. Joseph, who had enormous respect for his younger brother, seemed to accept this division of duties without difficulty. On 14 April 1787 he wrote to their suppliers in London: "My worthy brother, yes, I may say father died this morning after an illness of seven days only." By contrast Thomas made his career almost entirely in the west, travelling from Grand Portage (near Grand Portage, Minn.) to the most distant trading posts. For nearly 20 years he spent only brief periods in Montreal, where on 12 Sept. 1788, having just returned from the west, he died at the age of 44. Joseph, who divided his time between Grand Portage, other posts, and Montreal, had more varied experience; yet it was limited, having been within the management of a big enterprise which had become complex and largely impersonal though it had retained certain traits of a family organization. When Benjamin died, Joseph wrote to reassure the London suppliers, "The business here and in the Upper Countries will not suffer by the unforseen accident for I can venture to say without flattery, that I am thoroughly acquainted with every branch of it." He was, however, not unaware that he was exaggerating somewhat, since a week later he wrote to Simon McTavish that he had "never as you know taken any part in the management of the general concern of our House here."

There is no doubt that Joseph had played an essential role in the struggles of the late 1770s and the next decade that accompanied the emergence of the North West Company [see Simon McTavish], in which the firm of Benjamin and Joseph Frobisher held an important place. He had shared his brothers' dreams, and he had proved exceptionally effective against all competitors in the field. There had been particularly fierce rivalry with Gregory, MacLeod and Company [see John GREGORY], which in 1787 still constituted a threat. As a result of all this Joseph had earned the respect of the business world. It is none the less true that questions of financing, transactions concerning the supplying of trade goods, and strategies leading to multiple partnerships with other enterprises had in part escaped his attention. For this reason Benjamin's death was a tragic event for him.

In reality the firm of Benjamin and Joseph Frobisher was not in a sound state at that period. For ten years the company not only had been making heavy investments in the west – especially for outfitting – but had made a poor recovery from the difficult problems encountered since the end of the American revolution.

Joseph pointed out in 1783, for example, that they had had to sell off at 1s. 9d. a gallon a huge stock of spirits bought for 5s. a gallon. To complicate matters, Governor HALDIMAND that year had secured court orders for the repayment of a debt of £14,999 in connection with the Cochrane affair [see James DUNLOP]. On this matter Joseph admitted, "The public exposure of our situation soon reached our friends in England and would have put a total stop to our credit and the means of carrying on the trade to the North West (which we had established at great expence) had not friends stood forth and assured our correspondents." The poor conditions on the international fur market had continued, so that when Benjamin died the firm of Benjamin and Joseph Frobisher was still in a critical state. In fact, the settlement of Benjamin's estate led to a declaration of bankruptcy.

It was the old debt to the government, which had never been repaid, that lay at the heart of the company's difficulties. Since it was no longer possible to obtain further extensions, and Joseph did not have the funds needed for full repayment, he made the government an offer to pay the debt off at the rate of 9 shillings on the pound, which was then worth 20 shillings. Thanks to the dowry that Charlotte Jobert had brought to their marriage and the support of his friends Thomas DUNN, Robert LESTER, Robert Morrogh, Thomas SCOTT, Isaac TODD, and James McGILL, who put up security for him, Joseph finally succeeded in settling this thorny question. On 22 Dec. 1787 he wrote to Dunn, "It hurts my feelings very much to find after laboring very hard for 20 years to be worse than when I began business, however there is no help for it, I am content and flatter myself that in future I will be more lucky."

Sorely tried, humiliated, but not downhearted, Frobisher had already begun to reorganize his business. When McTavish had proposed in April 1787 that they unite their interests and suggested that he himself succeed Benjamin as administrator of the enterprise, Joseph replied, "I agree with you in opinion that throwing our interests together seems to be the most certain means of giving stability to our concern and defeating the hopes which our opponents may form from the distressing event of my poor brother's death." The founding of McTavish, Frobisher and Company in November 1787 entailed a reorganization of the North West Company, which made it possible for Gregory's firm to be included as a member. In addition, the partnership with McTavish, for which Frobisher had his friends' approval, was designed to reassure the London suppliers; the latter, added Frobisher, "will with greater confidence give us their support in a joint capacity than apart."

The reorganization, which in theory ensured the pre-eminence of McTavish, the principal director in Montreal, and of Frobisher, the dominant figure at

Grand Portage, in practice ended in reducing the influence and authority of the one who had been only a first-rate deputy. Within a few years McTavish was in firm command of the partnership, and of the NWC as a whole. Under him management became more complex and offices multiplied. Even if Frobisher still considered himself "the principal of the House," he was now only one of a number of highly competent deputies, among them Gregory, James Hallowell Sr, William McGillivray*, and John Fraser. He complained of this to McTavish and in 1791 pointed out that his role was now limited "to outdoor business, hiring of men and public duty." His feelings of frustration and the tensions that abounded, especially when McTavish stayed in England as he did with increasing frequency, can be readily understood. On 6 Aug. 1794 McTavish wrote to Frobisher, "Really, Sir, I am quite confounded at such inconsiderate conduct on your part. . . . I should go out in the spring and take a part in the future deliberations on the management of the business in Canada." These calls to order did not put an end to the conflict, and in November Hallowell wrote concerning Frobisher, "I am sorry that any expression of me should seem intended to amend his feeling, we are convinced of his abilities, and have the fullest confidence in his honor, altho we have in some instances differed in opinion."

Despite the infringements upon his status within the firm, Frobisher profited from the NWC's successes. In the period from 1787 to 1798, the year in which he retired from the company, he succeeded in rebuilding his fortune. Not only did he occupy a place of honour in the Beaver Club of Montreal, of which he was for a long time the secretary, but he took an interest in other economic activities. In 1793, for example, he purchased a fifth of the shares in the Batiscan Iron Work Company [see John CRAIGIE]. On 28 May 1803, with his partners in the ironworks, he bought from Alexander ELLICE the seigneury of Champlain, near Trois-Rivières, which was rich in forest resources. In addition he became one of the first five shareholders in the Company of Proprietors of the Montreal Water Works, which had been set up in 1801 to supply the town and surrounding area with drinking water. He had owned riverside lots at Sorel since 1786. Like many dealers in furs Frobisher was interested in landed property on a large scale. He was less attracted by seigneurial properties than by township lands. In 1801 he sold to Edward Cartwright the islands that he owned in the St Lawrence. The following year he obtained from the government 11,500 acres in Inverness Township under the system of township leaders and associates [see James CALDWELL]. Then he bought from Samuel Phillips, Jean-Baptiste Jobert, McGillivray, and Todd a fifth of Chester, Halifax, Ireland, and Inverness townships.

Frobisher was indisputably a man of substance in the society of Montreal and the province. On 30 Jan. 1779, before Anglican minister David Chabrand* Delisle, he married Charlotte Jobert, a girl of about 18 who was the daughter of the surgeon Jean-Baptiste Jobert and Charlotte Larchevêque. The latter was the daughter of a dealer in pelts and the sister-in-law of the fur trader and dealer Charles-Jean-Baptiste CHABOILLEZ. Twelve children were born of Frobisher's marriage, one of whom was Benjamin Joseph*. If John Fraser is to be credited, Frobisher was "a very unfortunate man in his children and connections." He was nevertheless well placed in the merchant community and linked by marriage to influential Canadian families; he was also active in political life. He joined in the movement to obtain parliamentary institutions [see George ALLSOPP; William GRANT (1744–1805)], and once they were in place he won election in Montreal East. However, he evidently did not attend the House of Assembly very often, since in the first four sessions he took part in only four votes. Indeed, like other fur merchants elected in 1792 – such as John Richardson*, James McGill, and George MCBEATH – who found it difficult to give up their businesses to take part in the assembly's work, Frobisher refused to seek a second term in 1796. Two years before, when an association to support the British government in Lower Canada had been founded, he had signed the declaration of loyalty to the crown and had been appointed to the committee in Montreal that was responsible for recruiting other members.

An important and prestigious figure, Frobisher was the beneficiary of government patronage. He was appointed a justice of the peace in 1788 and his commission was renewed repeatedly, the last time being in 1810. He was made one of the commissioners responsible for removing the old walls surrounding Montreal in 1802. On four occasions in the period 1805–10 the government granted him commissions. In addition he helped administer a pension fund for aged voyageurs. In 1800 he held the rank of captain in the British Militia of the Town and Banlieu of Montreal, and by 1806 he had been promoted major in the 1st Militia Battalion of the town. Frobisher was also active in religious affairs. Even though he was a churchwarden of Christ Church, an Anglican congregation, he subscribed in 1792 to a fund for the construction of the Scotch Presbyterian Church (later called St Gabriel Street Church) in which the firm of McTavish, Frobisher and Company had a pew until 1805. After Christ Church burned down in 1803, Frobisher was a member of the committee for building a new one [see Jehosaphat MOUNTAIN].

During his last 20 years Frobisher had a busy social life. Around 1792 he began to put together an estate called Beaver Hall; it eventually consisted of about 40 acres outside the town, on which he had a huge secondary residence built. There, and in his house on Rue Saint-Gabriel in Montreal, he displayed hospital-

Frost

ity on a scale that revealed both the extent and the importance of his social relationships. In 1794 he entertained Bishop Jacob Mountain* at a dinner for about 40 people, and showed him around the town and its outskirts, putting his driver and a chaise at the disposal of the bishop and his suite. Mountain appreciated this welcome and noted, "This Mr. Frobisher is an immensely rich merchant, a most worthy, honest and beneficent man. He is at the head of a house which has the first fur-trade in the country." Towards the end of his life Frobisher was still very active socially. In January 1806, for example, he noted in his diary 16 occasions on which he dined out and 5 dinners at home at which guests were present; in February he noted only 10 dinners at home without guests.

Frobisher died in Montreal on 12 Sept. 1810. His estate was not settled finally until June 1819, three years after his wife's death on 23 June 1816. The one sale of his personal property brought in £8,765.

FERNAND OUELLET

ANQ-M, CE1-51, 25 juin 1816; CE1-63, 30 Jan. 1779, 15 Sept. 1810. ANQ-Q, CN1-230, 15 août 1797, 2 oct. 1807, 7 juill. 1808; CN1-256, 30 July 1790; CN1-284, 11 oct. 1791; CN1-285, 24 juin, 30 août, 23 oct. 1802. PAC, MG 19, A5, 3; RG 4, B28, 115. "L'Association loyale de Montréal," ANQ *Rapport*, 1948–49: 253–73. *Les bourgeois de la Compagnie du Nord-Ouest* (Masson). "Le commerce du Nord-Ouest," PAC *Rapport*, 1888: 46. *Docs. relating to NWC* (Wallace). Jacob Mountain, "From Quebec to Niagara in 1794; diary of Bishop Jacob Mountain," ed. A. R. Kelley, ANQ *Rapport*, 1959–60: 140–42. *Montreal Gazette*, 21 July 1808, 17 Sept. 1810. *Quebec Gazette*, 16 June, 3 Nov. 1785; 29 Nov. 1787; 28 Feb., 14 Aug. 1788; 19 Nov. 1789; 21 June, 20 Dec. 1792; 17 July 1794; 25 July, 12 Dec. 1799; 20 Sept. 1810; 4 July 1816; 24 Jan. 1820; index.
F.-J. Audet, "Les législateurs du Bas-Canada." F.-J. Audet et Fabre Surveyer, *Les députés au premier Parl. du Bas-Canada*, 205–30. Desjardins, *Guide parl.*, 134. Massicotte, "Répertoire des engagements pour l'Ouest," ANQ *Rapport*, 1943–44: 386; 1944–45: 309–401; 1946–47: 319, 324–37. "Papiers d'État," PAC *Rapport*, 1890: 46–65, 209. *Quebec almanac*, 1800: 104; 1801: 103; 1805: 46; 1810: 58. Wallace, *Macmillan dict.* M. W. Campbell, *NWC* (1957). R. Campbell, *Hist. of Scotch Presbyterian Church*, 81, 95–96. Innis, *Fur trade in Canada* (1956). É.-Z. Massicotte, *Sainte-Geneviève de Batiscan* (Trois-Rivières, Qué., 1936), 78–79. G. R. Swan, "The economy and politics in Quebec, 1774–1791" (PHD thesis, Univ. of Oxford, 1975), 94. W. S. Wallace, *The pedlars from Quebec and other papers on the Nor'Westers* (Toronto, 1954). R. H. Fleming, "McTavish, Frobisher and Company of Montreal," *CHR*, 10 (1929): 136–52. Hare, "L'Assemblée législative du Bas-Canada," *RHAF*, 27: 371–73. Ouellet, "Dualité économique et changement technologique," *SH*, 9: 256–96. W. S. Wallace, "Northwesters' quarrel," *Beaver*, outfit 278 (December 1947): 9–11.

FROST, JAMES, ship's captain, naval officer, and office holder; b. *c.* 1745, probably in England; m.

Phoebe (Phebe) Wallen, and they had three children; d. 18 June 1803 at Quebec, Lower Canada.

James Frost's career in Canada can be traced back only to 1775. At that time he was the owner and captain of the merchant ship *Charlotte* and probably lived at Quebec. Upon the American invasion of the province in 1775 [*see* Benedict ARNOLD; Richard Montgomery*], he enlisted in the British forces and turned his ship over to Governor Guy CARLETON, who armed it. In return Frost was appointed a first lieutenant in the marine forces and commander of the *Charlotte*. When his ship was laid up in the winter, Carleton named him first lieutenant to a detachment of seamen in the garrison of Quebec and he served in that capacity during the siege. In the spring of 1776, after reinforcements had arrived, the British forces struck out, pursuing the Americans to the frontier. Frost took part in the offensive as captain of the *Charlotte* but lost his ship in the rapids on the Richelieu.

Immediately after this unfortunate event Carleton entrusted Frost with the post of assistant to the master attendant, the officer responsible for building and fitting out ships for the British navy, at St Johns (Saint-Jean-sur-Richelieu); because of its location this village would serve as port for the fleet that was to engage the American warships on Lake Champlain. In 1777 Frost was promoted master attendant and storekeeper at St Johns, thus becoming a naval staff officer.

Having discharged these duties for almost five years, Frost applied for the post of captain of the port of Quebec, which had become vacant with Peter Napier's death but was also coveted by Lieutenant Richard Peter Tonge. On 21 Feb. 1782, because of his faithful service to the British armed forces since 1775 and the glowing recommendations of his superiors, Frost received the appointment from Governor HALDIMAND. Before taking office, however, he had to withdraw from all commercial affairs that might be incompatible with his new responsibilities. At that time the captain of the port of Quebec, together with the superintendent of pilots, had to enforce the regulations concerning pilotage on the St Lawrence and the laws regarding quarantine of ships calling at Quebec. In addition he was required to make and sign a collection of all the statutes and regulations concerning pilots and navigation and to have it printed and sold to every ship's captain for a sum not to exceed five shillings. He also had sole authority to make decisions about the anchoring and mooring of ships in the port of Quebec. In 1787, at the request of Lord Dorchester [Carleton], Frost, whose competence was recognized, was consulted about the state of navigation on the St Lawrence and asked what improvements might be desirable. Frost's successor to the office of port captain of Quebec, after his death on 18 June 1803, was François BOUCHER.

Since 1795 Frost had lived in a house on Rue

Saint-Pierre in Quebec; this house, on a site fronting on the St Lawrence, had been purchased for £200. He left an estate of £2,050, including his residence, which was valued at £1,250.

ROCH LAUZIER

ANQ-Q, CE1-61, 20 June 1803; CN1-16, 19 mars 1808; CN1-230, 20 oct. 1795, 9 nov. 1798; CN1-256, 20 Oct. 1786. BL, Add. MSS 21803: 165–67; 21876: 126, 130. Bas-Canada, *Statuts*, 1795, c.5. "Les dénombrements de Québec" (Plessis), ANQ *Rapport*, 1948–49: 86, 136. *Doc. relatifs à l'hist. constitutionnelle, 1759–1791* (Shortt et Doughty; 1921), 2: 886. Qué., Conseil législatif, *Ordonnances*, 1788, c.5; 1790, c.1. *Quebec Gazette*, 23 June 1803.

FUBBISTER, JOHN (Mary). *See* GUNN, ISABEL

G

GALIANO. *See* ALCALÁ-GALIANO

GALLANT, XAVIER (Francis-Xavier), known as **Pinquin (Pinquaing)**, settler and convicted murderer; b. *c.* 1760, probably in Ristigouche (Que.), son of Louis Gallant and Anne Chiasson; m. Madeleine Doucet; d. 6 Nov. 1813 in jail in Charlottetown, P.E.I.

When the Acadians living on Île Saint-Jean (Prince Edward Island) were deported in 1758, Louis Gallant and his family took refuge at Baie des Chaleurs, settling first at Ristigouche, and later at Shippegan (Shippagan, N.B.). At some point Xavier Gallant, known as Pinquin, and two of his brothers crossed to Île Saint-Jean and settled there. Gallant and his wife had eight children, seven of whom were still alive in 1812. The family were living as tenants on Lot 16, on the shores of Malpeque Bay.

Gallant was, it seems, an affable man, a good worker, and a practising Catholic. Nevertheless, on Thursday, 11 June 1812, in a state of insanity he killed his wife, slitting her throat in a woodlot on his farm. After the murder he went home, asked about her, and claimed he did not know where she was. For two days he tramped through the woods with his children, looking for her, but she was not found. The following Saturday he fled; the children called in the neighbours, who organized search parties. The next morning Gallant was seen at the edge of the woods, and his cousin Jean-Baptiste Gallant managed to approach him. Xavier admitted that he had murdered his wife and told him the location of her corpse. At the neighbours' urging he led them to the spot where he had concealed it under a pile of leaves. The body was taken to Gallant's home and he was questioned in the presence of 12 witnesses. He confessed to having deliberately killed her and was taken to the Charlottetown jail.

On 3 July Gallant was tried before Chief Justice Caesar Colclough*, his associate judges Robert Gray* and James CURTIS, and a jury of 12 men of British origin. The crown assigned Solicitor General James Bardin Palmer* to defend the accused, and Attorney General Charles STEWART prosecuted. John Frederick Holland*, a member of the grand jury, was sworn in as interpreter, since a number of the witnesses did not speak English.

In the course of the trial, which lasted just a day, 11 witnesses appeared, 6 for the crown and 5 for the defence. Among them were three of the defendant's sons: Victor and Fidèle for the crown and L'Ange for the defence. According to the evidence, people had become aware of Gallant's mental problems some years earlier, soon after he had concluded a deal, apparently netting him several hundred dollars, with a man named Marsh (probably the merchant Thomas Marsh). His son Fidèle stated in court that "this was the cause of his father's derangement"; he who had previously been hard-working, amiable, and kind to his family stopped working. The money, which Gallant kept hidden in various places, including the attic, gave rise to numerous quarrels; he often accused his wife and children of stealing it. Obviously deranged, he sometimes imagined, according to Fidèle, that his wife was his daughter-in-law, believed that his dog had bewitched him, thought that his house was going to be seized, and would no longer go to church since he was afraid of being attacked and arrested. Fidèle further testified that Gallant said he had killed his wife because she "was not mindful enough of Household affairs and did not take care of him – that he was obliged to cook his own Victuals."

Found guilty, Gallant was sentenced to be hanged, but his lawyer sought a stay of execution. On 16 July Lieutenant Governor Joseph Frederick Wallet DesBarres* consulted the Council and its members agreed unanimously to a reprieve. In the mean time Gallant remained locked up in the Charlottetown jail under the guard of the jailer Caleb Sentner, who was supposed to receive 15 shillings weekly for the prisoner's keep, the money to come from the liquidation of Gallant's property that the coroner was to arrange.

On 9 April 1813 Gallant's case had still not been

Gallop

settled. Certain questions about the legality of the proceedings under which he had been convicted were yet unresolved. The prisoner's execution was therefore again respited and the matter referred to the Prince Regent. In September Gallant was still in prison. The jailer informed Lieutenant Governor Charles Douglass Smith* that he had received no money from the coroner for Gallant's keep since February. He complained that he did not have the means to take care of him, deplored the unhealthy and uninhabitable state of the prison, and stressed the prisoner's horrible condition. Gallant's health was already seriously affected; he died in his cell a few weeks later, on 6 November. A judicial inquiry conducted by coroner Fade Goff* at the prison concluded that he had died "of the Visitation of God, and in a natural way." On the day of Gallant's death the problem of the prison and of the prisoners' keep was a major subject of discussion at a meeting of the Council. At the end of the deliberations it was decided that any prisoner unable to meet his own needs would thenceforth receive public assistance without undue delay.

The story of the sad fate of Gallant and his wife has been handed on in the Acadian oral tradition through a ballad and legends. The ballad, composed by an unknown author, is still in the repertory of many traditional Acadian singers. Folklorists have collected it in Prince Edward Island, New Brunswick, and Quebec, where it has been found on the Îles de la Madeleine, in the Gaspé, and on the north shore of the St Lawrence. It appears in Conrad Laforte's *Catalogue de la chanson folklorique française* under the title "Le meurtrier de sa femme." This tragic narrative song relates in detail the events surrounding the murder and the murderer's death. There are diverse renditions of the lament which do not agree on every point. For example, in certain versions, such as that of Eva Richard, the wife of Thomas Savoie, of Sheila, N.B., Gallant dies in prison of hunger and thirst. In others he dies infested with worms and lice, as Benoni Benoît, also from Sheila, sings. According to certain legends found on Prince Edward Island, Gallant was a pirate and had supernatural powers. A treasure he was supposed to have buried near the village of Miscouche was the object of searches towards the end of the 19th century. During the trial reference had been made several times to the accused man's bizarre beliefs in the supernatural and in witchcraft as well as to a relatively large sum of money in his possession.

The story of Xavier Gallant has survived orally down to the present because of the very nature of his mournful and moving tale and also because it may well recount the first murder committed by an Acadian on the Island. The tragic ballad has certainly contributed greatly to keeping Gallant's memory alive, both among his numerous descendants on the Island and among the Acadians in many corners of the Maritimes and Quebec.

GEORGES ARSENAULT

Centre d'études sur la langue, les arts et les traditions populaires (Québec), Coll. R. Bouthillier–V. Labrie, enregistrement 1238; Coll. Roger Matton, enregistrement 186. PAPEI, Acc. 2702, Smith–Alley coll., "The King vs Francis Xavier Galant . . . , 1812," report by Charles Serani; "The petition of Caleb Sentner, keeper of his majesty's gaol at Charlotte Town . . . ," 1813; RG 5, Minutes, 1812–16 (mfm. at PAC); RG 6, Supreme Court, inquests, "Inquest taken on the body of Francis Xavier Gallant . . . ," 1813; minutes, crown side, 1811–13; Trinity term, R. v. Xavier Gallant, indictment, 1812. PRO, CO 226/26: 189–92. *Le catalogue de la chanson folklorique française*, Conrad Laforte, compil. (Québec, 1958). Patrice Gallant, *Michel Haché-Gallant et ses descendants* (2v., s.l., 1958–70), 2. *Illustrated historical atlas of the province of Prince Edward Island . . .* , comp. J. H. Meacham (Philadelphia and Charlottetown, 1880; repr. Belleville, Ont., 1972). Georges Arsenault, *Complaintes acadiennes de l'Île-du-Prince-Édouard* (Montréal, 1980). J.-H. Blanchard, *Rustico: une paroisse acadienne de l'île du Prince-Édouard* ([s.l., 1938]).

GALLOP, WILLIAM, merchant and office holder; date and place of birth unknown; d. unmarried 1804 in St Andrews, N.B.

Little is known of William Gallop's activities before his arrival in 1780 at Fort George (Castine, Maine) on the Penobscot River. He was one of many loyalist refugees who descended on the region following the establishment of a British military post under Brigadier-General Francis McLean* in 1779. Excited by the proposed creation between the Penobscot and St Croix rivers of a loyalist haven to be known as New Ireland, a project in which Dr John CALEFF particularly interested himself, Gallop acquired two lots of land at Penobscot and constructed a house there.

Previously, Gallop had served for six months as a pilot on HMS *Greyhound* and he had periodically turned privateer in the British interest. His experience as a mariner and his joint ownership of certain vessels operating out of Boston, Mass., during the revolutionary years may have been deciding factors in his selecting the Penobscot River as his future home. Other commercially oriented businessmen such as Robert Pagan* and Thomas Wyer* were already established there, and they had likely conducted business transactions with Gallop at one time or another.

When news arrived in 1783 that the St Croix and not the Penobscot would be the northern boundary of the American colonies, Gallop's experience as a pilot undoubtedly influenced his being chosen one of the agents to represent the Penobscot Associated Loyalists. Along with his fellow agents, Pagan, Wyer, William PAGAN, Colin Campbell, and Jeremiah Pote, he coordinated and executed the evacuation of Penobscot and selected Passamaquoddy Bay (N.B.) for the loyalists' new home. The very fact that Gallop did not receive a town lot in the new community of St Andrews during the initial draw for lands points to his activity as a principal figure in evacuating the nearly 500 residents who left Penobscot over a four-month period. Not until April 1784 did he settle in the town. The respect he had earned among the settlers and their agents is reflected in the extensive litigation that followed to secure for him a suitable town lot and water frontage, the latter a necessity for his livelihood.

As an original promoter of the St Andrews settlement, Gallop was appointed in 1784 one of the first magistrates for the township, a position he held for the next 20 years. On 28 March 1786, two years after the establishment of New Brunswick as a separate province, he was made registrar of deeds, conveyances, and wills for Charlotte County, continuing in that capacity until 1789. During the initial months of settlement Gallop shared in the exercise of a mill privilege at Oak Point Bay (Oak Bay), near St Andrews. As vendue master, in 1785 he gained the exclusive right to sell lucrative water lots in the town. His participation in various land dealings and commercial exploits with other leading members of the community contributed in no small way to the rapid rise of St Andrews as an entrepôt. Despite its early promise, however, the St Andrews economy faltered as a result of internal and uncontrollable external factors during the first two decades of settlement. As for Gallop, his involvement in county and provincial affairs did not extend beyond the positions he received in the 1780s. Limited opportunities and encumbering mortgages had placed him in an insolvent state by the time of his death in 1804.

ROGER NASON

PANB, RG 2, RS7, 22: 2646; RG 7, RS63, 1805, William Gallop; RG 10, RS108, petition of William Swain, 1784; petitions of William Gallop, 1785; petitions of Nathanial Palmer, 1785. N.B., Dept. of Natural Resources, Lands Branch (Fredericton), land grants, book A: 165–75. Joseph Williamson, "The proposed province of New Ireland," Maine Hist. Soc., Coll. (Portland), 3rd ser., 1 (1904): 147–57. Winslow papers (Raymond). Jones, Loyalists of Mass. H. A. Davis, An international community on the St. Croix, 1604–1930 (Orono, Maine, 1950). MacNutt, New Brunswick. R. W. Sloan, "New Ireland: loyalists in eastern Maine during the American revolution" (PHD thesis, Mich. State Univ., East Lansing, 1971). W. H. Siebert, "The exodus of the loyalists from Penobscot and the loyalist settlements at Passamaquoddy," N.B. Hist. Soc., Coll., 3 (1907–14), no.9: 485–529. Joseph Williamson, "The British occupation of Penobscot during the revolution" and "The proposed province of New Ireland" in Maine Hist. Soc., Coll., 2nd ser., 1 (1890): 389–400, and 7 (1876): 199–206 respectively.

GARLAND, CHARLES, office holder, planter, merchant, and judge; b. 1730 in Mosquito (Bristol's Hope), Nfld, son of George Garland; married, with one son; d. 8 March 1810 in Harbour Grace, Nfld.

Charles Garland was born into one of the oldest established families in Conception Bay. In the 1670s his grandfather John Garland resided at Mosquito, a small cove between Carbonear and Harbour Grace, and was a typical 17th-century fisherman-planter. Charles's father, George, was evidently the only son of John, and he became prominent enough to be appointed, in 1732, one of the first justices of the peace for Conception Bay. Charles himself was made a justice in 1755, a position he held until 1792, when he also acquired the offices of deputy customs collector and naval officer. In 1799 he became a judge of the surrogate court of Newfoundland with an annual stipend of £60, and retained this appointment until his death. Throughout most of his public career Garland also tried to gain a livelihood from trade and the fishery.

As one of Newfoundland's pioneer peace officers, Garland performed a varied role in a controversial office during a period of extreme uncertainty, instability, and change. He served under many different naval governors, whose views and interpretations of the acts governing the island varied. His authority was frequently challenged by British merchants and sea captains and his conduct and integrity were occasionally questioned. While his principal duties were the settlement of criminal cases (involving personal assaults and drunkenness) and the arbitration of civil cases (particularly those arising from property disputes or involving charges of debt between merchants and fishermen or between fishermen and their servants), he was also frequently required to enforce decrees of the governors and to provide them with information. Perhaps one of the more notable episodes of his magistracy happened in 1755, when he was ordered by Governor Richard Dorrill* to investigate a complaint that, contrary to law, a Roman Catholic priest had celebrated a public mass in Conception Bay. Garland's preliminary inquiry determined that a priest had held mass at Caplin Cove, north of Carbonear, but that he had left and gone to Harbour Main. Together with the other justice of the peace for Conception Bay, Garland went to Harbour Main and elicited a confession from one Michael Katem, a planter, that a priest had celebrated a public mass in one of his storehouses. Katem was fined £50, the building was demolished, and he was ordered to sell all his possessions in Newfoundland before 25 November. The same expedition also uncovered another Catholic sympathizer in Harbour Main named

Gautier

Michael Landrican, who suffered much the same punishment.

More praiseworthy were Garland's efforts in organizing resistance to the French invasion of Newfoundland in 1762 [see Charles-Henri-Louis d'Arsac* de Ternay]. He recruited 50 volunteers in Conception Bay to serve with Lieutenant-Colonel William Amherst's expedition to recapture St John's, and provided boats and small vessels to assist in the landing of troops. These activities, in addition to his supplying the British garrison in St John's with provisions after the French were routed, earned him an official commendation and were reported in the *London Chronicle, or Universal Evening Post.*

Although Garland apparently took an active part in the cod fishery and in the passenger and provisions trade, he seems to have supported his family mainly by renting out fishing rooms and other properties to migratory fishermen and planters. He owned and leased properties in Mosquito, Harbour Grace, Carbonear, and Devil's (Job's) Cove, and asserted hay-cutting and grazing rights to land on Little Bell Island, the Harbour Grace islands, and Carbonear Island. Much of the conflict between migratory fishermen and settlers during the 18th century, and more particularly between English ship's captains and local magistrates, focused on the possession of fishing rooms. In 1763, for example, Garland's rights to two rooms in Harbour Grace were challenged by ship's captains, but he was able to prove to the governor's satisfaction that both properties had been inherited from his father. There seems little doubt that the Garlands, like other settlers in Newfoundland and English merchants who established fixed premises on the island, could have acquired their holdings only by encroaching on and converting to private property fishing rooms formerly used as ship's rooms by migratory fishermen, aided in this practice by the indifference of the governors or their inability to enforce the acts respecting property possession. Ironically, as a magistrate Garland on at least one occasion acted to prevent encroachment on a ship's room when in 1755 he ordered the structures built on one by a Jersey merchant in Harbour Grace to be burned while the merchant was in Jersey for the winter.

Garland's close association with the governors appears to have been a major factor in his having property disputes settled in his favour, but he did fall from grace, at least temporarily, with Governor Hugh Palliser*, who suspended him from office in 1765 for failing to settle a trade account with a Devon merchant. The latter had consigned some goods for Garland to retail late in 1762, and three years later he claimed that no account had been rendered. The following year, however, Garland was reappointed a justice of the peace.

Few details are available on Garland's role in the fishery and trade, but he apparently was closely connected with several merchant traders and during the 1780s owned shares in a number of ships. In addition, documents related to the bankruptcy of John Thomey and Company of Bristol and Harbour Grace in 1792 suggest that Garland had been involved in the Irish passenger traffic to Newfoundland on Thomey's account. In his later years, especially from 1792 until his death, Garland was able to live comfortably off his pay as a customs and naval officer and as a surrogate judge. He had additional income from his rented properties, but withdrew from commerce and trade.

Such individuals as Charles Garland and his father were not only the first pillars of civil government in Newfoundland but were also the intermediaries between the British governors and the Newfoundland settlers in the transition of the island from a base for an English fishery to a settled colony. When Charles Garland was born, Conception Bay had only a few hundred permanent settlers, was dominated by the migratory fishermen, and was ruled by the fishing admirals. When he died, it was the most populous district in Newfoundland, with over 5,000 inhabitants. Chaotic and contentious conditions still prevailed in the courts and in the general administration of justice, but the offices and institutions that were needed for future improvements had at least been founded.

W. GORDON HANDCOCK

Dorset Record Office, D365. Hunt, Roope & Co. (London), Robert Newman & Co., Newfoundland letterbook, 1844–50 (mfm. at PANL). Maritime Hist. Group Arch., Garland, Charles; Garland, George, name files. PANL, GN 2/1, 2/2; P7/A/53. Supreme Court of Nfld. (St John's), Registry, administration of Charles Garland estate, granted to Elizabeth Garland, 3 May 1834. PRO, CO 1/35, 1/38, 1/41, 1/47, 1/55; CO 41/7; CO 194/4, 194/24, 194/41; CO 199/18; CO 324/7. St Paul's Anglican Church (Harbour Grace, Nfld.), Reg. of burials (mfm. at PANL). G.B., PRO, *Calendar of state papers, colonial series, America and West Indies* (44v. to date, London, 1860–), 36: 283, 375–79. W. G. Handcock, "An historical geography of the origins of English settlement in Newfoundland: a study of the migration process" (PHD thesis, Univ. of Birmingham, Eng., 1979), 16–18, 40–41. McLintock, *Establishment of constitutional government in Nfld.*, 59. Prowse, *Hist. of Nfld.* (1895), 222, 293–94.

GAUTIER, NICOLAS (sometimes **Joseph-Nicolas**), mariner, port official, and militia officer; b. 31 Aug. 1731 in Annapolis Royal, N.S., son of Joseph-Nicolas Gautier*, *dit* Bellair, and Marie Allain; d. 6 Nov. 1810 in Saint-Malo, France.

Nicolas Gautier was the third son of an Acadian family famous for its fight against British rule, and his

338

life was repeatedly interrupted in one way or another by the great imperial struggle between France and Britain during the 18th century. When the War of the Austrian Succession spread to North America in 1744, Nicolas's father declared for the French cause and, with his two eldest sons, Joseph and Pierre, actively aided the French forces. He was consequently outlawed, and his possessions destroyed; in 1748 he moved with his family to Île Saint-Jean (Prince Edward Island), where he died in 1752.

Joseph-Nicolas had been an adept pilot, and this knowledge, as well as his anti-British feelings, he passed on to Nicolas and Pierre. As early as 1751 Nicolas was employed by Claude-Élisabeth Denys* de Bonnaventure, commander at Île Saint-Jean, in reconnaissance missions and in transporting Acadian refugees to the island. From 1752 to 1756 he acted as assistant port captain at Port-La-Joie (Fort Amherst, P.E.I.). Afterwards he commanded a corvette and, when the British besieged Louisbourg, Île Royale (Cape Breton Island), in 1758, he used it to try to help keep open the lines of supply and communication between the fortress, its outpost at Port-Toulouse (near St Peters), and Île Saint-Jean.

The capitulation of Louisbourg to Jeffery Amherst* and Edward Boscawen* on 26 July brought the cession of Île Saint-Jean in its train [see Andrew Rollo*]; Nicolas and his family fled to the mainland. At Restigouche (Que.) he joined his elder brother Pierre in the militia, as adjutant; the small number of colonial regular troops were commanded by their brother-in-law Jean-François Bourdon* de Dombourg. After the general capitulation at Montreal on 8 Sept. 1760, the colonial regulars returned to France. Nicolas remained at Restigouche until October 1761 when, in a sudden raid, Captain Roderick MacKenzie, commandant of Fort Cumberland (near Sackville, N.B.), seized some 300 Acadians and transported them to Halifax. Nicolas and his younger brother Jean-Baptiste were among those seized.

At Halifax Nicolas married Anne, daughter of Joseph Leblanc*, dit Le Maigre; they were to have at least six children. They returned to French territory only in 1766, when they joined Nicolas's brother Pierre and numerous other displaced Acadians on the islands of Saint-Pierre and Miquelon, which had been restored to France in 1763 to serve as ports for her fishing fleets [see François-Gabriel d'Angeac*]. Pierre's career had been somewhat more active than Nicolas's: he was a partisan with his father during the 1740s; on several occasions he reconnoitred military activities at Halifax, occasionally taking British scalps and prisoners; in 1755–56 he even undertook an arduous overland winter journey from Shediac to Quebec and back to deliver official despatches. He also worked for the French government as a private entrepreneur: between 1763 and 1766 he made three voyages between France and Saint-Pierre, transporting supplies to build up the new colony. In the latter year he was rewarded with an appointment as port captain of the islands, a position he had previously held at Île Saint-Jean. He did not, however, remain at Saint-Pierre. By 1769 it was evident that there were far too many Acadians dependent on the colony's scarce resources and the French government removed many of them to France. Pierre Gautier went – perhaps as an inducement for others to leave – but did not stay in France. That year he was appointed port captain at Gorée (off the coast of Senegal), where he died in 1773 or early 1774.

Nicolas settled with his family on Miquelon where he fished and, according to references found in census records, acted as a coastal pilot. He appears to have passed a fairly uncomplicated life devoted to increasing his family and winning his daily bread until 13 Sept. 1778 when, France having declared war on Britain during the American revolution, the British descended on the islands, quickly extracted a capitulation from Governor Charles-Gabriel-Sébastien de L'Espérance*, and transported the inhabitants to France. There they remained until the islands were returned to France in 1783. At this time Gautier was made port lieutenant at Miquelon, with annual pay of 800 livres. Although he seems to have acted as port captain of Saint-Pierre for several years, he did not officially receive the appointment until 1792. Soon afterwards, on 14 May 1793, several British men-of-war with troops under James OGILVIE conquered Saint-Pierre, and again the population was deported. Gautier settled in Saint-Malo, where he seems to have been a pilot and where he passed the rest of his life.

Although the family's extreme devotion to the French cause was exceptional among Acadians, the trials, tribulations, and transportations that Franco-British imperial rivalries visited on the Gautiers were suffered by the Acadians in general. Nicolas Gautier became a refugee a half dozen times during his life as the direct result of four separate wars. His eldest brother, Joseph, settled near Bonaventure (Que.), on the Gaspé coast; Pierre died in Africa; their youngest brother, Jean-Baptiste, ultimately settled in Rustico (P.E.I.); and one of their sisters, Marguerite, died in France.

ANDREW RODGER

AN, Col., B, 120: f.361v; 123: f.4; 125: ff.57, 63v, 100; C^{11B}, 30: 21, 31 (transcripts at PAC); C^{12}, 22: ff.44v, 60v; E, 200 (dossiers Pierre Gautier, Nicolas Gautier); F^3, 54: f.469v; Section Outre-mer, G^1, 413; 458–59; 463: ff.5, 118. *Les derniers jours de l'Acadie (1748–1758), correspondances et mémoires: extraits du portefeuille de M. Le Courtois de Surlaville, lieutenant-général des armées du roi, ancien major des troupes de l'île Royale*, Gaston Du Boscq de Beaumont, édit. (Paris, 1899). "Documents: recense-

George

ments de 1760," R.-S. Brun, édit., *Rev. d'hist. de la Gaspésie* (Gaspé, Qué.), 8 (1970): 30–36. Placide Gaudet, "Acadian genealogy and notes," PAC *Report*, 1905, II, pt.III: 174. [Joseph de La Roque], "Tour of inspection made by the Sieur de La Roque; census, 1752," PAC *Report*, 1905, II, pt.I: 88. Arsenault, *Hist. et généal. des Acadiens* (1978). J.-H. Blanchard, *Rustico: une paroisse acadienne de l'île du Prince-Édouard* ([s.l.], 1938]). J.-Y. Ribault, *Les îles Saint-Pierre et Miquelon des origines à 1814* (Saint-Pierre, 1962); "La population des îles Saint-Pierre et Miquelon de 1763 à 1793," *Rev. française d'hist. d'outre-mer* (Paris), 53 (1966): 5–66.

GEORGE, DAVID, Baptist preacher; b. *c.* 1743 in Essex County, Va, son of African slaves John and Judith; d. 1810 in Freetown, Sierra Leone.

As a young slave to a man named Chapel, David George was employed fetching water and carding cotton, and when he grew older he took his place among the adult slaves in the corn and tobacco fields. His master was "a very bad man to the Negroes": George witnessed with horror his mother being stripped and whipped, and he himself was scourged "till the blood has run down over my waistband." In 1762, when he was about 19 years old, his independent spirit asserted itself, and he ran away. Pursued by his master's son, he fled farther and farther south, eventually finding refuge, in 1764 or 1765, among the Natchez Indian nation. There a white man by the name of George Galphin (Gaulfin, Gaulphin) purchased him from the Indians and set him to work on his estate at Silver Bluff, near the Savannah River and about 12 miles from Augusta, Ga.

At Silver Bluff George married Phillis, another slave, and began a family. Soon afterwards, upon being introduced to the Christian religion by a fellow black, he started attending religious services held on the estate by George Liele, a free black Baptist preacher, and "brother Palmer," whom one scholar has identified as Wait Palmer, a white Baptist preacher from Connecticut. At some point between 1773 and 1775 Palmer organized the Silver Bluff Baptist Church, the first black Baptist church, and possibly the first black church of any denomination, in North America. George became the leading elder and preached between the visits of Palmer and Liele.

With the outbreak of the revolution in 1775 Lord Dunmore, the governor of Virginia, issued a proclamation offering freedom to any rebel-owned slave who joined the loyalist forces. Thousands of slaves, attracted by Dunmore's offer, deserted their masters and flocked to the British. At Silver Bluff, George later stated, preachers were not allowed to visit the slaves "lest they should furnish us with too much knowledge." In these circumstances the black congregation elevated George to the position of pastor. In 1778, when the British took Savannah and were pressing close to Silver Bluff, Galphin fled his estate and left the slaves to fend for themselves. George and a group of 50 others then went out to greet the British and to claim protection as black loyalists.

A list of black loyalists dated 1791 shows that George became a soldier in the loyalist cause. In his own memoir, however, he makes no such claim. According to this source, he worked on the fortifications of Savannah during the siege by American forces, but for most of the war he joined his colleague Liele in preaching amongst the black loyalists, supporting himself by keeping a small butcher's stall. When Savannah fell to the Americans he moved to Charleston, S.C., and when a similar fate befell that city he accompanied the British and thousands of white loyalists to Halifax, N.S. He arrived there in December 1782.

Determined to carry the Gospel to his fellow blacks, George moved in June 1783 to Shelburne, N.S., where 1,500 black loyalists had settled two months previously. At first the local magistrates forbad him to hold his services in town, and so he set up camp "in the woods" where his preaching drew blacks from "far and near." However, when a sympathetic white gave him a town lot, George began conducting his meetings in Shelburne itself. By mid 1784 a chapel had been built and George had attracted a congregation of 50 blacks and several whites.

George's problems were not at an end, of course, for as a black and as a dissenter he continued to encounter opposition not only from the white settlers but also from the blacks of other denominations. In the summer of 1784 a near-riot occurred when a mob attempted to prevent the baptism of a white couple at one of George's services. Following this episode, according to George, "the persecution increased, and became so great, that it did not seem possible to preach, and I thought I must leave Shelburn." The climax came in late July and early August, when unemployed soldiers, resentful of cheap black labour, attacked the black district of Shelburne and forcibly drove George from his chapel. Along with many Shelburne blacks George sought refuge in nearby Birchtown. He remained there a few months, preaching and baptizing another 20 black loyalists. Even here, however, he encountered hostility, this time from black Anglicans and Methodists. He therefore returned to Shelburne in December 1784 and regained possession of his chapel.

From Shelburne, George's fame as a preacher began to spread: in the 1780s he was invited to preach in communities throughout Nova Scotia and New Brunswick. At Saint John, N.B., he held a mass baptism in the river, with both blacks and whites present, but some other whites complained and he was forced to obtain a licence permitting him "to instruct the Black people in the knowledge, and exhort them to the practice of, the Christian religion." The clear implication was that he was not to preach or baptize among the white citizens. After organizing black Baptist congregations in both Fredericton and Saint John, he returned to Nova Scotia, visiting Preston, where he founded a chapel, Horton Township, and Liverpool.

George's missionary tours won him the largest following of any contemporary Baptist preacher, white or black, in Nova Scotia and New Brunswick. His success partly derived from his impassioned preaching style; a Shelburne white who visited George's chapel described a scene where the congregation was so overcome that they could not refrain from crying out hosannas, and George himself was obliged to interrupt his sermon because of the tears streaming down his face. Another reason for his success was the fact that his brand of religion satisfied some of the most deeply felt needs of the black loyalists. From the time of their arrival in Nova Scotia, they had been treated in a discriminatory fashion: unlike their white counterparts, who received three years' provisions upon settling in the colony, black loyalists received enough to last only 80 days, and as a result were forced to support themselves by working on the roads. Further, only one-third of the black loyalists who moved to Nova Scotia obtained land grants, and even these fortunate few were given plots only large enough for kitchen gardens. Under such conditions, it was hardly surprising that George enjoyed great success as a preacher, for his chapels offered blacks freedom and equality, the very things they did not enjoy in a society dominated by whites. At the same time, since the black loyalists were mostly former slaves, they naturally felt drawn to a preacher who provided them with an opportunity to manage the affairs of their church in complete independence from any outside white authority.

Besides spreading the Baptist message through Nova Scotia and New Brunswick, George joined other black preachers, notably Boston KING and Thomas Peters*, in implementing plans for a mass emigration of black loyalists to Sierra Leone. In 1790 several hundred blacks, upset by their failure to obtain the grants of land to which they were entitled, appointed Peters to bring their grievances to the attention of the British government. In response to these complaints of ill-treatment, the Sierra Leone Company, a philanthropic organization dedicated to the creation of a colony of freed slaves, offered to transport the black loyalists to Africa, to provide them with free land, and to guarantee them full rights as British subjects. David George became an enthusiastic supporter of this scheme, and he assisted Lieutenant John Clarkson of the Royal Navy, whom the Sierra Leone Company sent to Nova Scotia to recruit emigrants, in carrying his invitation to the blacks of Shelburne County.

"The White people in Nova Scotia were very

unwilling that we should go," George later recalled, "though they had been very cruel to us, and treated many of us as bad as though we had been slaves." The fact was that the landless black loyalists provided the bulk of labour available in Nova Scotia, and as customers they created a market for the produce of white-owned farms. George was personally threatened with violence; false debts and charges were concocted to keep the blacks in place; bribes were offered; and a vigorous propaganda campaign claimed that the Sierra Leone Company intended to sell the free blacks into slavery. Despite this opposition 1,196 black loyalists, about one-third the total black loyalist population of Nova Scotia and New Brunswick, embarked with Clarkson in January 1792. Included among them were almost all the Baptists from George's chapels in Saint John, Fredericton, Preston, and Shelburne. Clarkson organized his black emigrants into companies, each under a captain who was to maintain discipline and relay information, and over the entire body he placed three superintendents, Thomas Peters, the Methodist preacher John Ball, and David George.

Unfortunately, the great promise of Clarkson's mission was not to be fulfilled. Physical discomfort, the failure of the company to provide free land, and above all the fact that the independence-seeking black loyalists found themselves subordinate to a white government appointed in London, led to a confrontation on 8 April 1792 between Clarkson and Thomas Peters. Since George had great admiration and friendship for Clarkson and little sympathy for Peters, he rallied his Baptists, then the largest religious group in the colony, to Clarkson's support. He was therefore responsible at that early point for the maintenance of company authority in Freetown.

In December 1792 George accompanied Clarkson to London, where he stayed until August 1793, visiting English Baptists and collecting financial support for his African mission. He also dictated his memoirs to the editor of the *Baptist annual register*, thus leaving for posterity one of the few existing black loyalist documents. While he was in London his compatriots in Sierra Leone came into conflict with their new governor, William Dawes, the workers struck against their company employers, and a public meeting sent delegates to England in an unsuccessful bid to acquire a new form of government. George missed all this activity and its emotional impact, and consequently he was prepared on his return to the colony to continue to believe in the good faith of men who had treated him with kindness and justice.

In Sierra Leone, George devoted himself to the "Lord's vineyard" both figuratively and literally: he kept an alehouse and engaged in mission work among the neighbouring Africans and his Freetown congregation. Until his death in 1810 he continued to shun

Gibault

revolts against the company's authority. Those Baptists who sympathized with the demands of the more radical "Nova Scotians" split with their pastor, initiating a decline in George's influence and in the position of the Baptist denomination. After 1808 the Baptists slipped from the primacy of place they had enjoyed in 1792 and became the smallest denomination in the colony, a denomination increasingly associated with poverty and low status.

But if there is no monument to him in Sierra Leone, David George is still regarded as a key figure in the early history of the Baptist church in Nova Scotia and New Brunswick. Through his efforts and those of later preachers such as Richard Preston*, the Baptist church was gradually built into the largest denomination among Maritime blacks. To these people, George remains a heroic and beloved pioneer.

JAMES W. ST G. WALKER

David George's autobiography, "An account of the life of Mr. David George, from Sierra Leone in Africa; given by himself in a conversation with Brother Rippon of London, and Brother Pearce of Birmingham," was published in the *Baptist annual reg.* (London), 1 (1790–93): 473–84. Some of George's letters from Sierra Leone appeared in *Baptist annual reg.*, 2 (1794–97): 94–96, 215–16, 255–56, 409–10.

BL, Add. MSS 41262A–41264. Huntington Library (San Marino, Calif.), Zachary Macaulay papers. PANS, MG 1, 219; MG 4, 140–41, 143 (copies); MG 100, 220, no.4 (photocopy). PRO, CO 217/63; CO 270/2–5. USPG, Dr. Bray's Associates, minute-books, 3. [John Clarkson], "Diary of Lieutenant J. Clarkson, R.N. (governor, 1792)," *Sierra Leone Studies* ([Freetown, Sierra Leone]), no.8 (March 1927). [Boston King], "Memoirs of the life of Boston King, a black preacher, written by himself, during his residence at Kingswood School," *Methodist Magazine* (London), 21 (1798): 105–10, 157–61, 209–13, 261–65. C. [H]. Fyfe, *A history of Sierra Leone* (London, 1962). E. G. Ingham, *Sierra Leone after a hundred years* (London, 1894). P. E. McKerrow, *A brief history of the coloured Baptists of Nova Scotia . . .* (Halifax, 1895; repr. Dartmouth, N.S., 1975). A. P. Oliver, *A brief history of the colored Baptists of Nova Scotia, 1782–1953; in commemoration of centennial celebrations of the African United Baptist Association of Nova Scotia, Inc.* ([Halifax, 1953]). J. W. St G. Walker, *The black loyalists: the search for a promised land in Nova Scotia and Sierra Leone, 1783–1870* (London, 1976); "The establishment of a free black community in Nova Scotia, 1783–1840," *The African Diaspora: interpretive essays*, ed. M. L. Kilson and R. I. Rotberg (Cambridge, Mass., and London, 1976), 205–36. E. G. Wilson, *The loyal blacks* (New York, 1976). R. W. Winks, *The blacks in Canada: a history* (Montreal, 1971). W. H. Brooks, "The evolution of the Negro Baptist Church" and "The priority of the Silver Bluff Church and its promoters" in *Journal of Negro Hist.* (Washington), 7 (1922): 11–22 and 172–96 respectively. C. [H]. Fyfe, "The Baptist churches in Sierra Leone," *Sierra Leone Bull. of Religion* (Freetown), 5 (1963): 55–60. Anthony Kirk-Greene, "David George: the Nova Scotian experience," *Sierra Leone Studies*, new ser., 14 (1960): 93–120. J. W. St G. Walker, "Blacks as American loyalists: the slaves' war for independence," *Hist. Reflections* (Waterloo, Ont.), 2 (1975): 51–67. A. F. Walls, "The Nova Scotian settlers and their religion," *Sierra Leone Bull. of Religion*, 1 (1959): 19–31.

GIBAULT (Gibaut), PIERRE, Roman Catholic priest and missionary; baptized 7 April 1737 in Montreal (Que.), eldest child of Pierre Gibault and Marie-Joseph Saint-Jean; d. 16 Aug. 1802 in New Madrid (Mo.).

Information on the early years of Pierre Gibault is sketchy. He probably attended the Jesuit college at Quebec, and in 1759 he made a journey to Detroit (Mich.) and Michilimackinac (Mackinaw City, Mich.), perhaps as a helper in a trading company. On 19 March 1768, following two years of theological studies at the Séminaire de Québec, he was ordained by Bishop Briand*, and early in June he left for the Illinois country as vicar general. There he was to join Sébastien-Louis Meurin, already advanced in age and the only priest between Michilimackinac and New Orleans (La) since the hasty departure of Jacques-François Forget* Duverger and the expulsion of the Jesuits in 1764. Much to Briand's annoyance, Gibault was accompanied by his mother and sister.

Making his official residence at Kaskaskia (Ill.), the major village, he regularly visited all the French settlements from Vincennes (Ind.) to Ste Genevieve (Mo.). During the first few years Gibault's Kaskaskia parishioners were devoted to him, but they came to resent his frequent absences in other settlements. Under the French régime the state had subsidized the church, but once the region came under British authority the people had to support their priest by tithing. They grew restless and critical. Unjust accusations against him were forwarded to Quebec and, though unwarranted, plagued him till his death.

Gibault's claim to historical fame rests on his role in George Rogers Clark's capture of the Illinois country. In 1778 Clark received a commission from the governor of Virginia to invade the west, and on 4 July he marched into Kaskaskia. Spokesmen for the village, Gibault included, agreed to cooperate with the invaders and Clark promised to leave them in peace. He seized the other villages in the vicinity and then, intending to proceed against Vincennes, consulted Gibault. The missionary, he reported, declared "he would take this business on himself and had no doubt of his being able to bring that place over to the American Interest without my being at the Trouble of Marching Troops against it. . . ." Gibault and Jean-Baptiste Laffont, a doctor, spent a day or two discussing the situation with the inhabitants of Vincennes, who then swore loyalty to the Americans. Gibault also conveyed Clark's regards to Tobacco's

Son, chief of the Piankeshaws, and that Miami tribe remained neutral or friendly thereafter. The missionary's activities earned him the wrath of British authorities: Lieutenant Governor Henry Hamilton* of Detroit thought he should be hanged. Bishop Briand, who had condemned collaboration with the rebels, suspended him from his ecclesiastical functions on 29 June 1780. Perhaps Gibault did not receive the bishop's letter. At any rate he continued ministering to the Illinois settlements and later denied any complicity with the rebels. To Americans, however, he is sometimes known as the patriot priest.

With the arrival of other missionaries, Gibault moved across the river to Ste Geneviève in 1780. There he came under the civil jurisdiction of the Spanish crown and the ecclesiastical authority of the bishop of Santiago de Cuba. Possibly none too comfortable in that situation, after five years he removed to Vincennes. In 1788 he requested recall to Quebec but Bishop Hubert* refused. "After the disadvantageous opinion that the government has formed of him, I can not prudently consent to his return," he noted. The next year Gibault returned to Kaskaskia because all the priests who had come to the Mississippi valley had departed for one reason or another.

In 1787 the Northwest Ordinance had brought American civil government to the valley. Residents were required to justify the legality of their claim to land they occupied. Gibault sent in a petition asking recognition of his private claim to the land on which the church and the pastor's residence at Cahokia (Ill.) stood. Though the request was granted by President George Washington, the newly appointed American bishop, John Carroll, objected, considering the land ecclesiastical property. For Pierre Gibault, this was the last straw. He moved to the recently founded village of New Madrid, becoming a Spanish citizen in 1793. From 1792 until his death he was pastor of the parish of Saint-Isidore (the Immaculate Conception).

JOSEPH P. DONNELLY

[Larger-than-life bronze statues of Gibault have been erected in Ste Geneviève and Vincennes. An extensive bibliography of material relating to his life appears in J. P. Donnelly, *Pierre Gibault, missionary, 1737–1802* (Chicago, 1971). Material particularly useful in the preparation of this article includes: AAQ, 7 CM, VI; Archdiocese of St Louis, Chancery Office (St Louis, Mo.), Reg. de la paroisse de Conception de Notre Dame des Cascaskiae; *George Rogers Clark papers* . . . [1771–84], ed. J. A. James (2v., Springfield, Ill., 1912–26), 1; J. F. McDermott, "The library of Father Gibault," *Mid-America* (Chicago), 17 (1935): 273–75. J.P.D.]

GILLMORE, GEORGE, Church of Scotland clergyman; b. probably 1720 in County Antrim (Northern Ireland); m. Ann Allen, and they had at least seven children, six of whom survived infancy; d. 20 Sept. 1811 in Horton Township, N.S.

In 1762 George Gillmore was a student in logic, metaphysics, and natural philosophy at the University of Edinburgh, and he appears to have studied there the following year as well; no record has been found of his graduation. In 1769 he decided to emigrate to the American colonies, and after a voyage of 11 weeks – a voyage marked, he said, by the blasphemous behaviour of crew and passengers – he landed at Philadelphia (Pa) on 9 September. He preached and taught school for a time in Massachusetts and Connecticut before moving in October 1770 to Voluntown, Conn., to take up a post as a supply preacher. There is some doubt about the date of his ordination: Gillmore once claimed it took place in 1769, but the records of the Presbytery of Boston, the body responsible for the ordination, indicate that the ceremony took place on 2 July 1773. Whatever the case, Gillmore remained in Voluntown, serving his congregation and at the same time paying ministerial visits to several communities in New Hampshire, until the outbreak of the revolution. Because he refused to "pipe the popular Tune of Tumult Faction Sedition and Rebellion," his fortunes took a turn for the worse. Denounced as a tory by the governor of the colony and deserted by his own flock, Gillmore was forced to stop preaching in 1775, and for the next year or so he devoted himself entirely to farming. Still harassed by local rebels, he and his family moved to Nobletown (near Albany, N.Y.) in the winter of 1776–77. There he farmed, preached, and taught school until the surrender at Saratoga (Schuylerville, N.Y.) in October 1777 of the force led by John Burgoyne*. Ejected again from his parish because of his loyalist views, Gillmore then taught school in Spencertown, N.Y., until late 1782, when the triumph of the rebel cause compelled him to leave his family and flee to the province of Quebec.

After a winter spent at St Johns (Saint-Jean-sur-Richelieu), Gillmore went to the town of Quebec in an unsuccessful attempt to obtain financial assistance. Within a few months he had moved on to Sorel, where he was later joined by his family. Financially, Gillmore was now extremely hard-pressed, for the only employment he was able to find in Sorel was as deputy chaplain to the garrison and the salary for performing this duty was in the form of rations. By November 1784 he was back in Quebec, where he was soon complaining that "hearers are few, circumstances low, minds shut up and purses closed. . . ." However, he did obtain from Governor HALDIMAND "a certificate and recommendation as a minister and Loyalist for the Province of Nova Scotia," and the following spring Henry Hope*, the commandant at Quebec, secured a passage to Halifax for the entire Gillmore family.

Gillmore

The Gillmores reached Halifax in July 1785 and spent the summer there. Desperate for assistance of some kind, Gillmore submitted a petition to Governor John Parr* in which he stressed that he and his family had been reduced to "cold, hunger, and nakedness" as a result of their decision to remain loyal to the crown. This appeal evidently had an effect, for soon afterwards Gillmore moved to Windsor to begin serving Presbyterian congregations that had been organized at that place and at Newport by the Reverend James Murdoch. In February 1786, moreover, he obtained a grant of land at Ardoise Hill, which became the family's home for the next five years.

Gillmore's problems, however, were not yet at an end. Shortly after his arrival in the Windsor area he noted that "there be some members of our church here by profession but few in reality. Persons are loath to appear in the profession of our holy religion, lest they should bring on themselves the odious names of oddity and singularity." To compound his anxieties about the state of religion in his mission, Gillmore received no support from his impoverished flock and consequently he and his family still lived on the bare edge of subsistence. In a 1786 petition to the loyalist claims commission – an earlier one had been drawn up at Sorel – he emphasized the seriousness of his plight and pleaded for assistance to compensate him for the £700 he had lost because of the "wasting and Consuming Fire" of the American revolution. For some reason, consideration of this petition was deferred. Eventually, with the help of concerned friends, he was able to buy a passage overseas, where he intended to press his claims upon the government. Arriving at Greenock, Scotland, in January 1788, he spent a month in Glasgow before travelling to London. In the capital he presented two petitions to the Treasury, supported by recommendations from the Reverend Samuel Andrew Peters, a prominent Anglican loyalist, and Henry Hamilton*, formerly lieutenant governor of Quebec. In the second petition, dated 5 May, Gillmore stated: "I have been in peril oft by sea, by land, and false Brethren . . . I have wandered about without cloathing as good as sheep; or Goatskins – I have lodged in caves and Dens – I have suffered hunger – and am now destitute." The government responded to this appeal by awarding him an annual pension of £20, an amount Gillmore considered inadequate. By the fall he was back in Nova Scotia and had resumed his ministry at Windsor and Newport.

Evidently a conscientious clergyman, Gillmore took an interest in the state of Presbyterianism outside his own mission: in 1786 he assisted three other Presbyterian clergymen, Hugh Graham* of Cornwallis, Daniel Cock of Truro, and David Smith of Londonderry, in organizing the Associate Presbytery of Truro, the first such body in the colony. As for his relations with other denominations, Gillmore, being of "Covenanter" stock, had no use for episcopacy, and in the 1780s he was a strong defender of the interests of his church and dissenting sects in their contest with the established Church of England. After the appointment in 1787 of Charles INGLIS as the Anglican bishop of Nova Scotia, Gillmore referred contemptuously to "the pomps and vanities of a Bishop, whose greatest strength of argument consists in £1,000 per annum and a coach with two white horses." His anger mounted later that year when Inglis cast aspersions on dissenting denominations in a sermon preached before the legislature. Responding to this sermon in a series of letters to an unnamed correspondent, Gillmore defended his dissenting brethren and violently attacked the Church of England. He announced his determination to guard against "all usurpations of episcopacy, tithes, and spiritual courts, taking place in this colony under the sanction of the civil magistrate." He also emphasized that Protestant dissenters should join forces in this "time of common danger."

In 1791 Gillmore moved to Horton and assumed responsibility for the church at Grand Pré, where he continued to preach "till prevented by the infirmities of age," probably some time in the early 1800s. He was instrumental in having the church (known today as the Presbyterian-Covenanter Church) rebuilt on a different site, a task begun in 1804 and completed, except for the tower and spire, by 1811. Although Presbyterianism was "at a low ebb" in Horton, Gillmore was a "sound evangelical preacher of gospel truth" who strengthened the Presbyterian tradition in the area to the point where it was able to survive the 22-year ministerial vacancy that followed his death. It was during Gillmore's ministry that the Presbyterians of Horton severed their formal association with the American Congregational Church, although some aspects of Congregational doctrine did remain.

Gillmore was a pious man who retained to the end a fervent belief in the eternal happiness that awaited the righteous. Writing to a daughter a few years before his death, he noted: "Were we not to meet with discouragements in our pilgrimage journey through life, we should not vehemently long to arrive at the land of rest and light to the wearied traveller. 'But there remaineth a rest for the people of God' – a rest of perpetual activity, singing and praising evermore. . . ." He died on 20 Sept. 1811, at the age of 91, and was buried in the Grand Pré churchyard. His gravestone, which was later removed and placed inside the church, bears a Latin inscription which notes, in part, that "unholy contact with the irreligious crowd did not turn him from the right path." Many of Gillmore's descendants entered the ministry, and Charles D. Hunter, his grandson, established the

Hunter Building Fund that assists church building in Nova Scotia.

In collaboration with ELIZABETH A. CHARD

George Gillmore is the author of *A sermon preached before a lodge of free and accepted masons, at Sorrel in Canada, on the day of St. John the Evangelist, 1783* (London, 1788), a copy of which is preserved in the library of the Mass. Hist. Soc.

PANS, MG 1, 328 (typescript); 742, no.ix. PRO, AO 12/23: 56; 12/102: 226; 12/109: 158; AO 13, bundles 13; 41; 70, pt.I; 83; 96, pt.I; 137. United Church of Canada, Maritime Conference Arch. (Halifax), George Gillmore, diary, 1769 (mfm. at PANS). A. W. H. Eaton, *The history of Kings County, Nova Scotia . . .* (Salem, Mass., 1910; repr. Belleville, Ont., 1972). William Gregg, *History of the Presbyterian Church in the dominion of Canada . . .* (Toronto, 1885). "Historical statement, 1754–1968," *Grand Pre Presbyterian-Covenanter Church, 1804–1970: 166th anniversary service . . .* ([Grand Pre, N.S.], 1970; copy in PANS, MG 100, no.28). I. F. Mackinnon, *Settlements and churches in Nova Scotia, 1749–1776* ([Montreal, 1930]). Alexander Maclean, *The story of the kirk in Nova Scotia* (Pictou, N.S., 1911). J. S. Moir, *The church in the British era: from the British conquest to confederation* (Toronto, 1972); *Enduring witness; a history of the Presbyterian Church in Canada* ([Hamilton, Ont., 1974?]). "The late Rev. George Gilmore," *Christian Instructor* (Pictou), 5 (1860): 161–65, 225–29, 257–63, 289–94, 321–23. S. F. Tucker, "The vicissitudes of a loyalist clergyman," RSC *Trans.*, 3rd ser., 7 (1913), sect.II: 107–16.

GIRTY, SIMON (the name may originally have been Geraghty), Indian Department interpreter; b. 1741 at Chambers' Mill (near Harrisburg, Pa), son of Simon Girty and Mary Newton; m. August 1784 Catharine Malott, a captive of the Delawares, and they had at least two sons and a daughter; d. 18 Feb. 1818 in Amherstburg, Upper Canada.

Simon Girty was born at the beginning of the last great period of Indian-white warfare east of the Mississippi, and his entire life was spent in the vortex of the struggle. His father was evidently killed by an Indian during a drunken fight some time in the 1740s and his mother remarried. The entire family was captured by a war party about 1756 and Girty's stepfather was burnt at the stake. With his mother and brothers George and James, Simon spent the next three years amongst the Indians. Simon lived with Senecas – apparently Mingos, as the Iroquois residents of the upper Ohio were known to the British. This experience later provided his enemies with the basis for many distortions of fact, including the labelling of Girty as "the white savage."

Girty probably spent most of the time between his release and the American revolution as a trader in the Ohio valley. His command of the Seneca language must have been a valuable asset, and he no doubt picked up some Delaware and Shawnee, the two other major languages of the region. He served as an interpreter at Fort Pitt (Pittsburgh, Pa) on a number of occasions and was a second lieutenant in the Pennsylvania militia. Perhaps because of his association with Alexander McKee*, an Indian agent and known loyalist, Girty was confined to Pittsburgh after the American revolution reached the "back country." Together with McKee and Matthew ELLIOTT, he fled the town in the spring of 1778, and this escape set the stage for the central episodes of his career.

Having made their way to Detroit (Mich.), the three were given posts in the British Indian Department, Girty as interpreter to the Six Nations. He must have been an impressive figure. Someone later recalled: "He was a splendid-looking man, was fully six feet high, and had a large head and large black eyes." Familiar with Indian ways, Girty, Elliott, and McKee were able to harness native resentment of American expansion to overall British military strategy. In the summer of 1779 a mixed party of Indians accompanied by Girty and Elliott ambushed Captain David Rodgers's American detachment which was attempting to bring munitions up the Ohio River to Fort Pitt. Girty then wintered in Shawnee country, returning to Detroit in March 1780. From 25 May to 4 August he was away again, this time with both Elliott and McKee on Captain Henry Bird's expedition, which was headed for the falls of the Ohio. On the insistence of Indian leaders, the party changed its course and followed the Licking River into Kentucky. Evidently the Indians, facing their old enemies the Kentucky settlers, were restrained from killing prisoners only with difficulty, but the raid was a success: two posts were captured and more than 300 captives taken.

The Americans responded to these and other skirmishes by sending punitive missions against Indian villages. In March 1782 Lieutenant-Colonel David Williamson's forces wantonly murdered some 90 Christian Delawares at the Moravian settlement of Gnadenhutten (Ohio) [*see* Glikhikan*]. When an expedition under Colonel William Crawford was defeated in June near what is now Upper Sandusky, Ohio, some Delawares under their chief Konieschguanokee (Captain Pipe) took revenge by torturing the unfortunate commander to death. Elliott and Girty were both present; Girty apparently indulged in some mirthless jesting with Crawford as he was dying. American propaganda fed on such scenes, and the growth of Girty's "savage" reputation dated from this occasion.

In his official capacity as interpreter Girty was present at most Indian conferences in the Detroit region during and after the revolution. With McKee and Elliott he observed the defeat of the Indian confederacy at the battle of Fallen Timbers (near

Glasgow

Waterville, Ohio) on 20 Aug. 1794 [see WEYAPIER-SENWAH]. Following the British withdrawal from the posts south of the Great Lakes in 1796 Girty remained on the Indian Department payroll, earning 4s. 8d. a day, but the heyday of his activity had ended.

After the revolution Girty and some other Indian Department officers had obtained a tract of land at what is now Amherstburg. Large numbers of Indians settled near by and worked as hired help on the farms. During the War of 1812 the Indian Department requisitioned some of Girty's corn to feed its clients, and his claim to the government was one of the last official contacts he had with his former employer. When Major-General Henry Procter* retreated from the Detroit frontier in the fall of 1813, Girty undoubtedly went along; there had been a price on his head since Crawford's death. After the invaders withdrew he returned, and his final years were spent quietly: he was old, nearly blind, and liked nothing better than recounting tales of his past career in his favourite public house.

Girty was a man of great ability in working with native leaders, but his manners were rough, his disposition temperamental, and his capacity for drink legendary. His superiors did not always appreciate such a combination of talents. "James Girty is sulky," wrote Henry Bird in 1780, "and Simon Girty is useless." Girty plied his Indian farm-workers with rum and even succeeded in getting Moravian Indians drunk, much to the disgust of David ZEISBERGER and other missionaries. Behind such incidents lurked a type of grim humour, born of the harsh conditions in which he had spent his life. His behaviour gave just enough substance to the old propaganda for some to take seriously the stories of his viciousness. These tales were spread by people who could not see that hostilities between the western tribes and the new republic were caused, not by the behaviour of men like Girty, but by the white settlers' insatiable hunger for land and their government's failure to honour its agreements with Indians.

DOUGLAS LEIGHTON

PAC, MG 19, F1, 2; MG 23, HI, 4; RG 8, I (C ser.), 88: 1; 258; RG 10, A1, 2; A2, 13. *Mich. Pioneer Coll.* Wallace, *Macmillan dict.* (1963). Thomas Boyd, *Simon Girty, the white savage* (New York, 1928). C. W. Butterfield, *History of the Girtys . . .* (Cincinnati, Ohio, 1890). F. X. Chauvin, *Simon Girty (1741–1818); an address before the descendants of Simon Girty at Lakeside Park, Kingsville, Ont., September 5th, 1932* (n.p., n.d.; copy at UWO). D. R. Farrell, "Detroit, 1783–1796: the last stages of the British fur trade in the old northwest" (PHD thesis, Univ. of Western Ont., 1968). Horsman, *Matthew Elliott*. U. J. Jones, *Simon Girty, the outlaw*, ed. A. M. Aurand (Harrisburg, Pa., 1931). R. S. Allen, "The British Indian Department and the frontier in North America, 1755–1830," *Canadian Hist. Sites*, no.14 (1975): 5–125. N. V. Russell, "The Indian policy of Henry Hamilton: a re-valuation," *CHR*, 11 (1930): 20–37.

GLASGOW, GEORGE, army officer; d. 28 Oct. 1820 in London, England.

George Glasgow was appointed a cadet in the Royal Artillery on 2 April 1771, gazetted a second lieutenant on 8 Sept. 1774, a first lieutenant on 7 July 1779, and a captain-lieutenant on 29 Sept. 1784. He remained in this intermediate rank until 25 Sept. 1793, when he was promoted captain and appointed second in command of a company of the 1st Battalion, Royal Artillery, which shortly thereafter mustered in Flanders as part of an expeditionary force commanded by the Duke of York. It is not certain that Captain Glasgow participated in Britain's ill-starred campaign in the Low Countries in 1793 and 1794, but it is known that on 20 Oct. 1794 he was transferred to the 4th Battalion and posted to command a company stationed at Quebec, Lower Canada. His company remained at Quebec until May 1799, when it was dispatched to Montreal. By February 1800, however, it had returned to the capital.

On 3 Dec. 1800 Glasgow was promoted major, and then on 25 Dec. 1801 lieutenant-colonel. The first promotion removed him from the roster of company commanders and signalled his eligibility for a superior command; the second made him the senior artillery officer in the Canadas. Two further promotions, to colonel on 24 July 1806 and to major-general on 4 July 1811, established him securely within the senior echelon of the British command structure on this continent. No other member of this establishment could equal his long service in Lower Canada.

On receipt of the news of the American declaration of war against Great Britain on 18 June 1812, Lieutenant-General PREVOST, captain-general and governor of British North America, acted swiftly to ensure that the most vulnerable sectors of his extended frontier were assigned to subordinates who had had extensive experience in field operations. The defence of Quebec, his capital and vital port of entry for supplies and reinforcements, he entrusted to Glasgow who, although never involved in operations, possessed much command and staff experience as well as a thorough knowledge of the terrain and military problems of Lower Canada. In this, his first major command, Glasgow seems to have given general satisfaction since he retained it until July 1815, save for brief periods of special duty in Upper Canada in January 1814 and February 1815 and in Montreal in December 1814 and January 1815. From 14 June to 25 Sept. 1813, while Prevost was preoccupied in Upper Canada, Glasgow served as president administering the government of Lower Canada.

Meanwhile, Glasgow had not neglected the artillery, which was critically under strength. In June 1812 he was able to deploy only four companies comprising 18 officers and 420 gunners, and few horses or drivers were available to constitute a field train. With Britain fully committed in Europe, only minimal strength could be spared for the struggle in North America and, despite Glasgow's complaints, by the end of 1813 his corps of gunners had increased by a scant 116 although by this time he had 149 drivers of all ranks. None the less, by skilful improvisation – principally, according to its commander, by "calling in the assistance of additionals from the Line and Militia and leaving the Field Guns with scarcely half their complement of artillery men" – his small force made an honourable and important contribution to every battle in 1812 and 1813. Napoleon's defeat in the spring of 1814 permitted Britain to post large reinforcements to Canada, and Lieutenant-Colonel Edward W. Pritchard, who succeeded Glasgow in command of the artillery in July, inherited a force which by autumn had grown to eight companies.

Glasgow's staff appointment became redundant with the end of the war and the beginning of demobilization, and in August 1815 he was granted leave to return to England. He had served continuously in Canada for 21 years and had played a most important role in the War of 1812, demonstrating a high degree of competence, if not brilliance. Retired on 23 Sept. 1815 with a pension of £700 per annum, he received one last promotion, being gazetted a lieutenant-general on 12 Aug. 1819.

Glasgow had married Margaret Green, who predeceased him; they were survived by nine children, eight of whom had been born in Canada.

JOHN W. SPURR

PAC, RG 8, I (C ser.), 679, 686, 690, 693, 730, 1221, 1224, 1232. PRO, PROB 11/1637/673; WO 17/1513–19 (mfm. at PAC). *Doc. hist. of campaign upon Niagara frontier* (Cruikshank), vol.1. *Battery records of the Royal Artillery, 1716–1859*, comp. M. E. S. Laws (Woolwich, Eng., 1952). G.B., WO, *Army list*, 1771–1820. *List of officers of the Royal Regiment of Artillery . . .*, comp. W. H. Askwith (4th ed., London, 1900). *Officers of British forces in Canada* (Irving), 2, 9, 21, 261. Hitsman, *Incredible War of 1812*, 29, 45, 138, 177.

GLENALADALE, HELEN MacDONALD OF. *See* MacDONALD

GLENALADALE, JOHN MacDONALD OF. *See* MacDONALD

GLENIE, JAMES, army officer, military engineer, businessman, office holder, and politician; b. 1750 in Fife, Scotland; m. in the early 1780s Mary Anne

Locke, and they had at least two sons; d. 23 Nov. 1817 at Ebury House, Pimlico (London), England.

No stranger to controversy on whatever side of the Atlantic he found himself, James Glenie was a colourful and opinionated figure in New Brunswick's early history. His intellectual ability and talent won him the support of prominent English patrons, whereas his unceasing attacks on Thomas CARLETON and the loyalist élite helped forge an opposition coalition which has been acclaimed as a popular reform movement. He moved easily from the highest circles in London to the struggling communities of Sunbury County, at times a principled opponent of any scheme harmful to the best concerns of the public, and, on other occasions, a defendant given to special pleading on behalf of his own or a patron's particular interests.

The son of an army officer, Glenie embarked upon divinity studies at St Andrews University in 1766 but instead blossomed into an excellent mathematician, winning two prizes in that discipline in 1769. Equipped with an MA, and having gained the support of the chancellor of St Andrews, the Earl of Kinnoull, he decided upon a military career and received a cadet's place at the Royal Military Academy, Woolwich (London). Commissioned a second lieutenant on 3 Nov. 1776 in the Royal Artillery, Glenie had as his colonel George, Viscount TOWNSHEND, who was also master general of the Board of Ordnance and who would prove a supportive, as well as somewhat demanding, patron in the future. Dispatched to Quebec in late 1776 or 1777, Glenie served during the American Revolutionary War in the unrewarding counter-offensives of John Burgoyne* and Barrimore Matthew St Leger*, but he came into his own under Governor Frederick HALDIMAND. In the summer of 1778 Glenie accompanied Lieutenant William Twiss* to Oswegatchie (Ogdensburg, N.Y.) and Cataraqui (Kingston, Ont.) in search of a suitable site for a supply depot which Haldimand hoped to establish at the eastern end of Lake Ontario. Once Twiss had decided upon Buck Island (N.Y.), which he proposed to rename Carleton Island, he sent Glenie to report to Haldimand, expressing his confidence in him. Haldimand agreed with Twiss's proposal for a post on Carleton Island, but as soon as the proposed works were well launched Twiss was to leave for Montreal and Glenie would "oversee and carry on that Business in your absence."

By late September Glenie was able to report the completion of a five-foot parapet and the imminent completion of a barracks which would house the garrison in the approaching winter. Already there were problems, however. Glenie complained that the soldiers labouring on the post lacked "the knowledge of working well," and he soon found himself embroiled in a series of disputes with Captain Thomas

347

Glenie

Aubrey, who was in command at Carleton Island. Others, including Lieutenant Thomas Bunbury, complained of "hard treatment and ill usage" at Aubrey's hands, but it was Glenie who was singled out for a warning from Haldimand. Reports of "Complaints and disagreements" between Glenie and Aubrey brought a Christmas Day reminder from Haldimand for Glenie to bear in mind that "he who commands must command in every thing, and be obeyed without hesitation, by every person under him as he is alone answerable."

When squabbling continued none the less, Haldimand suggested the possibility of Glenie's recall. Twiss agreed that a recall might be wise but still thought him "the most capable Officer I know in the Province" to undertake a necessary survey of the north shore of Lake Ontario. By May 1779 it was too late to rescue Glenie since a petition he circulated against Aubrey and a charge that he had "*Signed a false Return*" left him under arrest and facing a court martial. To the double embarrassment of Haldimand, Glenie's services were still badly needed and in the fall word arrived that Glenie had been transferred to the corps of engineers (his commission as a second lieutenant was dated 23 Feb. 1779) and Lord Townshend wanted him sent home to England. Because of a variety of problems, there was a long delay before Glenie was brought to trial, and Haldimand felt that until this judicial question was resolved it would be "highly improper" to allow him to return home.

For his part, Glenie initially described Aubrey's accusations as "vague & indeterminable," offered a spirited defence of his conduct, outlined the insufferable insults he had patiently endured, and asked permission to move to the eastern part of the colony, "where I can find more conveniency of amusing myself in the mean time with Study, as nothing can be more insupportable than idleness." By November, now in Quebec, he diplomatically accepted Haldimand's decision not to allow him to proceed to England and expressed his willingness to be "employed as Captain Twiss shall direct, till such time as the affair between Capt. Aubrey & me can be settled without Inconveniency to the Service." As a result, although charges were laid against Glenie in the spring of 1779, his court martial did not take place until the summer of 1780 and in the interval he continued on active and valued service, largely at Sorel. While under this cloud, he was the recipient of a significant honour at home. Two mathematical papers were presented to the Royal Society by Francis Maseres* on his behalf and earned him election as a fellow in March 1779.

Would such a brilliant young officer be cashiered? Not likely, at least to Lord Townshend's way of thinking, since several months prior to the trial he

virtually assumed acquittal: "Mr. Glenie as his affair is likely to turn out favorably is ordered to remain on the Canada Staff." Finishing the trial in late August, the court-martial board, which included Lieutenant-Colonel Thomas Carleton, on 24 October presented what must have been a rather surprising verdict to some of Glenie's supporters. He was found innocent of signing a false return but "Guilty of having behaved unbecoming the Character of an Officer and a Gentleman on many occasions." He returned to England disgraced, his military career apparently ended, but bearing a letter from Haldimand to Townshend describing him as "a very promising Engineer." "He possesses great knowledge and great application, and from a belief that his faults have arisen from his want of knowing the rules of the Army, I would thro' your Lordship recommend him for any Employment where great abilities and great application are necessary, But where Subordination is not the first and most necessary Qualification." Haldimand made identical remarks in a letter to Lord Amherst*, and a variation on the same theme was offered to Colonel William Roy of the engineers, who was urged to intervene to prevent Glenie from being ruined. Within a matter of months the decision was overturned. In late January 1781, on the grounds of irregularities in the court-martial proceedings and Glenie's good service both before and after arrest, the king, while disapproving of his conduct towards Captain Aubrey, remitted the sentence and restored Glenie to his rank and duty in the engineers.

With his career rescued, Glenie should perhaps have trod carefully, but he now had substantial obligations to his protectors and, in truth, seemed to relish controversy. In 1782 Townshend was replaced as master general of the ordnance by the Duke of Richmond, who soon was proposing an elaborate coastal fortification plan, the estimated cost of which was substantial to begin with but would soon escalate. Glenie scoffed at the plan and was enlisted by Townshend's secretary to write a condemnatory pamphlet which appeared in 1785 as "by an officer." Its assertions that the duke's fortifications would eventually cost forty to fifty million pounds, enough to construct a completely new navy, made it a damaging indictment. Richmond attempted a reply, but, when his legislative proposals came to a vote in parliament in February 1786, they were defeated. Not surprisingly, Richmond would not be "satiated until he had hounded Glenie from the Corps [of engineers]."

Meanwhile Glenie had returned to active service in North America and was realistically looking for new sources of income to supplement, or replace, his military pay. In the late summer and early fall of 1785 he supervised work parties of the 54th Foot in the Saint John River area of New Brunswick and, as a result of a tour up the Oromocto River, he submitted a proposal

348

for the proper development of this part of the province. Thinking that the Oromocto region was "admirably calculated for grazing & the rearing of Cattle; of which the beneficial Effects are almost instantaneous when compared with those arising from Agriculture," on 4 August he proposed to import cattle, clear 60 to 100 acres of land before winter, and begin to raise livestock if Carleton, now governor of the province, and the New Brunswick Council would immediately grant him 200 acres. In addition, Glenie asked for an assurance that, when the restrictions concerning the size of land grants expired, his grant of 200 acres would be augmented with another grant, adjoining the first, of at least 1,000 acres, "which is the smallest Quantity for any Person to embark in a Scheme of this Nature." A cool governor and Council responded with a qualified offer of 200 acres, but a disappointed Glenie never took it up. Instead he resubmitted his proposal in October 1785 in a joint petition with William Gordon of St Anne's Point (Fredericton), William Donaldson and James Gordon of Saint John, and Alexander Fraser of Grenada. Again the advantages of cattle-raising on the Oromocto were emphasized and the memorialists promised that, if they were awarded a tract of 5,000 acres, they would each put "not less than twenty Milch Cows upon their Lands early next summer, together with the necessary houses and Servants." An unimpressed governor and Council granted only what was "agreeable to the General Regulations" and only to "Such of the Memorialists as are in the Province & not already provided for"; again the offer was refused. Hence, even before Glenie took up permanent residence in New Brunswick his schemes had been twice frustrated by Carleton and the loyalist-dominated Council, the same Carleton who had participated in his Quebec court martial.

Glenie returned to England some time after receiving the response to his second petition for land. His stay there, however, was short. Realizing that Richmond's opposition would damage his military career, in September 1787 he resigned his commission, granted on 15 November of the previous year, as a lieutenant in the engineers. The next month Glenie and his family arrived in New Brunswick aboard the brig *Providence*, for Glenie a return to familiar country but for his wife, Mary Anne Locke, probably her first visit. Glenie settled on land at Gooldsborough (near Oromocto) in Sunbury County, but the only land claims recorded in his name were two later grants, one of 235 acres in Queens County in 1790 and one of 880 acres in York County in 1794. While he was in London the firm of Blair and Glenie had been formed to participate in the mast trade, and it was through this enterprise that Glenie hoped to make his fortune. Andrew Blair would secure from the Admiralty contracts for masts and Glenie would get the masts to

Saint John. By 1790 he had a "Mast Pond with the appurtenances, situate near Portland Point [Saint John]," as well as mast ponds at French Lake on the Oromocto and just below Gagetown on the Saint John River. But once again, he ran afoul of Carleton and the loyalist élite, whose plans for agrarian development would be disrupted by over-aggressive masting operations. Offsetting this opposition was the friendship and support of John WENTWORTH, surveyor general of the king's woods in North America, and soon to be, in 1792, lieutenant governor of Nova Scotia. Always ready to help Blair and Glenie in fulfilling their contracts, when Glenie requested a timber licence in 1790 Wentworth was quick to issue one "for so many Trees as were necessary." Not only was Wentworth very cooperative with Glenie, but Glenie in turn was willing to report "illegally cut" timber and "trespassers." The latter were promptly prosecuted by Wentworth, sometimes with money conveniently advanced by Glenie. In business dealings and management of the forest resources the Glenie–Wentworth connection was extremely strong, no doubt reinforced by the rapport and respect each had with and for the other.

Given the treatment of his land petitions, the hostility towards his masting activities, and his own confidence in his connections and abilities, it was predictable that Glenie would quickly move to an all-out attack on Carleton and his loyalist advisers. In a by-election held in November 1789 he was elated when "the People unsollicited & contrary to my Wishes chose me Member of Assembly for the County of Sunbury." This victory was achieved allegedly despite "every Strategem every low Artifice & Lie [which] was practised and made use of by the Govr's pitiful Junto for months before to prevent it." According to Glenie, the rulers of New Brunswick "are cursedly alarmed. For they suppose that a Majority of the House will follow me & that their villainous Practices will not only be examined into but brought to Light & exposed." But it would be well over a year before the House of Assembly met and Glenie could launch his attack there. In the interval, examples of "villainous Practices" were enthusiastically unearthed and used to underline the shortcomings and abuse of power by Carleton and his advisers. When Glenie's accusations and name-calling are digested – "illiterate Moon-Struck Judge" (Isaac Allan), "ignorant uncouth Dutch Boor" (councillor Christopher Billopp*), "ignorant stuttering Chief Justice" (George Duncan LUDLOW), and "a man on whom nature has fixed the stamp of Stupidity" (prominent loyalist Beverley Robinson) were some of the thumbnail sketches of New Brunswick's leading citizens – they seem designed not to change the system but merely to replace one ruling clique by another. Instead of the "unprincipled Harpies" current-

Glenie

ly being appointed, Glenie proposed Jonathan Bliss* or "My neighbour Daniel Bliss" as excellent candidates for judicial appointments. For Council vacancies, he suggested Phineas Shaw, William Gordon, and "several other European Gentlemen very well qualified who will not be Tools like those recommended."

Glenie was far from a tribune of the common people at this moment, and his electoral success in Sunbury County probably owed more to his taking as a pattern the approach and appeal of a William Davidson* than to later issues such as assembly power. Davidson had been elected to represent Sunbury County in the Nova Scotia House of Assembly and then in 1785 represented Northumberland in the New Brunswick assembly. In both instances, the fact that he was at the time of election the most prominent employer of individuals in each of the counties was a major help. This deferential attitude on the part of the electorate was likely still present when Glenie moved into Sunbury with his masting contracts and, coupled with his outspoken anti-loyalist proclamations in an area with a large pre-loyalist population, contributed substantially to his acceptance. Admittedly, when the assembly opened on 5 Feb. 1791 he became an active participant and soon demonstrated an alert sensitivity to the needs of his Sunbury constituents. Within a few days he presented a petition from a number of Maugerville inhabitants asking that the boundaries of land grants in their township and throughout the province be clearly defined. Quickly pressed into service on a variety of committees, Glenie opposed Carleton's plan for "fitting up" part of Christ Church in Fredericton to accommodate the Supreme Court and the assembly, and a marriage and divorce bill that was decidedly pro-Anglican and neglectful of other denominations. He also contributed to a committee report that found "very great irregularities and important deviations from the Impost Law" in the treasurer's department.

Again in the 1792 session he remained quite active. Spurred on by a petition from his Sunbury constituents calling for a more liberal marriage act, he moved for leave to bring in such a measure. Apparently the session ended before this was done. At the same time, he condemned those in power in New Brunswick, particularly Carleton, in private correspondence with at least one prominent British government official. As a result of Glenie's promise "to send you occasionally some Observations respecting this Province," Evan Nepean, under-secretary of the Home Department, was presented with a devastating criticism of Carleton's policies. Fredericton "has been very injudiciously fixed on as the Seat of Government." It was "altogether incapable of Defence" yet £4,000 had already been expended on a barracks, money that "might as well be thrown into the River." Carleton's

decision to establish military posts farther up the Saint John River was scorned because of the transportation expenses involved, the fact that "two small Blockhouses" could have done the job just as well, and, if it was argued that they were needed to facilitate settlement, why were they erected on American territory? Surely, Glenie argued, it was Carleton's "Duty to make himself acquainted with the Boundary Line between the United States & the Province, he was sent out to govern, before he adopted Measures not only tending manifestly to bring the Mother Country into immediate Expence but peculiarly calculated for involving her in Troubles & Disputes eventually."

Even Glenie's old adversary, the Duke of Richmond, no doubt without realizing it, agreed with the basic thrust of Glenie's military analysis, that Fredericton should not be the military centre of New Brunswick, and Carleton was forced to abandon some of his Fredericton pretensions. Other of Glenie's complaints are more suspect. Carleton sincerely believed in the need to strengthen the New Brunswick claim to areas in dispute with the Americans, to build strong lines of communication with Quebec, and above all to facilitate settlement by military protection if necessary. Hence, it is difficult to accept Glenie's accusations of what amounted to wasteful ignorance and self-aggrandizement on Carleton's part.

Quite possibly some of Glenie's complaints were related to the fact that in late 1791 Wentworth had made him the deputy surveyor of the king's woods in New Brunswick. Shortly thereafter Carleton upset Wentworth by charging that he discouraged the settlement of New Brunswick. The Carleton case was best explained by loyalist Daniel Lyman, who argued that "the reserves made by the Surveyor General of Woods . . . should be taken off, – and a stop put to any more being made. . . . Most of the reserves I have seen are made in places calculated for agriculture . . . large tracts of miles in extent are precluded from being given to settlers." The policy of controlling white pine timber for the benefit of the crown, or for the enrichment of certain mast contractors, such as Glenie and William FORSYTH, was apparently conflicting with the idea of a settled agrarian society cherished by Carleton and the loyalists. If Carleton's and Lyman's views prevailed, Glenie stood to lose both as a mast contractor and as an office holder. By the summer of 1792 he was busy prosecuting trespassers, confiscating illegally cut timber, and trying to harvest as much as possible for himself. Thus the discrediting of Carleton would be a considerable impetus to Glenie's economic concerns, and possibly the defeat of Carleton's military expansion and settlement plans for northern New Brunswick would preserve another area for the exploitation of its timber resources.

Whether because of difficulties in his masting

business or because of his determination to undermine Carleton, in 1793 Glenie returned to England; although re-elected to the assembly after its dissolution in December 1792, he was unable to attend the 1793 or 1794 sessions. In London both Nepean and Henry Dundas, the Home secretary, were presented with thoughtful commentaries on the defence policies of Carleton which soon moved beyond military matters to chastise both Carleton and his brother Lord Dorchester [Guy CARLETON] for much that was wrong in New Brunswick and British North America generally. Glenie had earlier argued that the two regular regiments stationed in New Brunswick were unnecessary but he also took issue with the decision to allow Carleton to raise a New Brunswick regiment to replace these regular units, now withdrawn. To Glenie this decision would result in a substantial drain on the colony's limited manpower resources, which were already in decline due to the short-sighted policies of Carleton and his followers. A combination of the existing provincial militia, a few howitzers at the mouth of the Saint John River, and a couple of sloops in the Bay of Fundy was all that was required. Of course the line of posts up the Saint John valley should be downgraded since the "natural line of Defense . . . is from St. Andrews or Passamaquoddy along the Bay of Fundy to Fort Cumberland [near Sackville, N.B.]." These were, for the most part, comments that deserved consideration, but Glenie soon launched into the usual accusations of ignorance and maladministration which probably hurt rather than helped his argument. The Council must be changed because it was "composed Entirely of Americans (there not being one European in it, though there ought always to be at least a Majority)." Moreover, it was Glenie's rather ludicrous suggestion that the new regiment Carleton was raising would be American as well: "It is obvious – the Lieut Governor & his American Field Officers will be under the necessity of introducing men from the States & putting Arms into the hands of Enemies & thereby contribute to the Dissemination of Principles perhaps still more hostile to the Constitution of this Country than even those of the French themselves." Thus were the loyalists accused of disloyalty; but the Carleton family was accused of even greater sins. Just as his brother, Lord Dorchester, "through the most unpardonable negligence lost the whole of [Canada], Quebec excepted" – a somewhat puzzling reference to the American invasion of 1775–76 – so Thomas was about to lose New Brunswick. Glenie was "unavoidably led to the Conclusion that the Carleton Family is fated to be the Ruin of British America & think if it be continued & for only a few years longer, these Provinces will be lost to the Crown of Great Britain for ever."

The Carletons might have been in disfavour, particularly with Dundas, but to displace a lieutenant governor on the basis of Glenie's shrill accusations, at a time when the defence of Britain and the empire required continuity rather than disruption, was an unlikely action. Consequently, Glenie's direct lobbying in England produced no change in New Brunswick. And if his attacks on Carleton were proving fruitless, even more discouraging was the fate of Glenie's masting operations. By late 1794 and early 1795 unnecessary waste and cut-throat competition in the masting trade forced Wentworth to urge the several contractors to accept an agreement that left Forsyth and Company in control rather than Blair and Glenie. Relieved of his commercial responsibilities, Glenie still had his appointment as deputy surveyor and plunged into "prosecution on behalf of the Crown" with his usual vigour. Meanwhile, despite his absence, the assembly had not been idle. In 1793 and 1794 it had challenged Carleton and the Council on a number of issues – including the proposed quarters of the legislature and Supreme Court, times and places of Supreme Court sessions, and aid to Carleton's cherished college – and appeared headed for a confrontation. The moment was right and Glenie was ready.

The assembly session of February and March 1795 brought consistent disagreement between the lower house and the Council, which was allied with the lieutenant governor, and time and again Glenie emerged at the centre of the skirmishes. When a committee was struck to prepare an address to Carleton requesting that he "order such of His Majesty's instructions to be laid before this House as may tend to the information of the same," Glenie was appointed. When word was sent to the Council drawing its attention to the bill for setting the times and places of convening the Supreme Court, Glenie was dispatched with Robert Pagan* to carry the message. Again, when the Council failed to accept the above bill, Glenie was appointed to a committee to search for precedents for holding a conference with the upper house. He served on committees to bring in bills "For establishing the Due and Equal Administration of Justice," "To regulate the Practice of the Courts of Law," and "For regulating and establishing a Table of Fees" for the courts. The introduction of Glenie's own Declaratory Bill and the assembly's refusal to accept Carleton's defence expenditures in St Andrews and Saint John made the Council increasingly assertive of its and the governor's rights and privileges. The assembly's anticipation of the need to take its grievances to the home government prompted the addition of Glenie and others to a committee appointed at the previous session to correspond with the province's agent in London, William Knox. When the Council rejected a money bill, which included an appropriation for the payment of assembly members, Glenie was among those appointed to respond to the

Council's objections. In the last case a well-argued response was made to the Council's position, which historian Ann Gorman Condon, describing it as a "sophisticated, terse reply" asserting the assembly's "exclusive right to originate money bills," feels was the work of Elias Hardy*. None the less, Glenie had made a substantial contribution to the impasse which existed between assembly and Council by the time the house was prorogued on 5 March.

Once Carleton decided to attempt to secure a more amenable assembly through an election in September and October 1795, Glenie was quite willing to take to the hustings to outline his active and vigilant defence of the assembly's, and thus the people's, rights. The proposed act concerning Supreme Court sessions, Glenie explained, was pushed "in order to carry the administration of Justice by that Court into every County and to every Man's door as much as possible; The very purpose, I conceive, for which the Judges receive their salaries." He pointed out that this bill had been passed by the assembly five times only to be rejected by the Council, and even when "I delivered a message myself putting them in mind of it as a Bill tending greatly to promote the happiness and convenience of His Majesty's subjects in this Province," no satisfactory explanation of the Council's setting it aside was offered. The assembly's refusal to grant money for the erection of a legislative and court building at Fredericton was explained as the result of its judgement that "the Province [was] not in a situation to bear without great inconvenience to the people, the raising of such sums as would have been necessary. . . ." Moreover, Glenie expressed his opinion, growing out of his own considerable experience, that the buildings would be far more expensive than estimated.

A concern about unwarranted or premature expenditures was also behind the assembly's unwillingness to approve funds for a college. This "barely-existing Colony" could ill afford the proposed grant, which was in any case "not half sufficient." Emphasis should be placed on a parish school system meeting local and broader needs first, for "however much some persons may dislike the general dissemination of knowledge among the people and reckon it dangerous, it ought in my opinion to be the first object of attention in every well regulated state." The assembly's refusal to accept Carleton's defence expenditures in St Andrews and Saint John was due to the fact that responsibility for such expenses rested with the home government. As for the most important issue of assembly power over the public purse, Glenie told his constituents that to have accepted the Council's claims "would have been tantamount to an absolute surrender of your purses, property, rights and liberties, into the hands of the Council at once. . . . It is a proposition, to which I hope in God no House of Assembly will ever give its assent. For it is a parliamentary maxim as old as parliament itself, that those who have the sole right of granting have an unquestionable right to dispose of what they grant."

Glenie had made a powerful case for a vigilant and active assembly sensitive to the needs of the overwhelming majority of New Brunswickers. Controlling needless and wasteful spending, making education and the courts accessible to the people, and enhancing the elected assembly's position and power within the governmental system were all issues that would have a definite appeal to many who were not among the privileged loyalist élite. Glenie went even further, however, in apparent anticipation of a possible counter-argument that the parliamentary system he envisioned was quite different from that in operation in the mother country. Essentially, he argued that there was a need for adaptation of the English system to suit colonial realities. "True it is," he agreed, "that our Legislature consists of three distinct Branches, like that of Great Britain," but the House of Lords was quite different from the New Brunswick Council and Supreme Court, which occasionally were one and the same in that the judges "sometimes form a majority of the Legislative Council." Whereas the House of Lords was "a dignified, opulent and independent body," and its members could only be removed by "an Act of the British Legislature," New Brunswick councillors and judges "hold their seats not hereditarily, not even during good behaviour, but during the pleasure of His Majesty's servants and ministers, and are removable at their pleasure, without any reasons assigned." Since the colony lacked the finer balance and independence of the mother country, the opportunities for arbitrary rule were apparently increased. "If therefore an attentive, watchful and vigilant opposition has ever been found necessary in the House of Commons to preserve the rights and liberties of the people in Great Britain, it must certainly be doubly requisite here, where two Branches of the Legislature are in a great measure thrown into one scale." Glenie on the hustings in 1795 was Glenie the reformer and people's tribune at his best. Rising above character assassination and unsubstantiated accusations, and even to a considerable extent above the personal bitterness and selfishness that lay behind earlier attacks on Carleton and the élite, he had persuasively argued the case for many of the assembly's actions during the 1795 session and pinpointed some of the needs of New Brunswick as well as some of the nuances of the constitutional debate.

Against this background, the Declaratory Bill which Glenie had introduced during the 1795 session, and which had been passed by the assembly but rejected by the Council, was to him the key to enhancement of assembly power and to the emasculation of the other branches of government. To Glenie this measure was "unquestionably the most important and salutary one in its tendency which was ever introduced into that House." Shorn of the various clauses removed during debate, the bill maintained that New Brunswickers "are extremely desirous of having the Constitution & Government of said Province brought as near, as their local Circumstances will permit, to that of the mother Country, and of enjoying the Benefit of all the Laws of England and Acts of the British Parliament applicable to their colonial Situation down to as late a Period, as the fundamental Principles of constitutional Law will admit of their being construed as extended thereto." The reception date for English statute law proposed in the bill was 1750, erroneously assumed to be the British settlement date for Nova Scotia, rather than the restoration year of 1660, the date decided upon by Carleton and his advisers in the early days of New Brunswick's existence. Thus, under the bill all acts passed by the British parliament before 1750 were to apply to New Brunswick, in so far as colonial circumstances permitted. By the same token, "no Act of Parliament made or passed since the Beginning of the Year of our Lord 1750 shall be held taken or construed as extending to this Province without express Words in the Act itself shewing the Intention of the British Legislature."

Glenie himself, his enemies, and scholars such as James Hannay*, George Francis Gilman Stanley, and Samuel Delbert Clark have greatly exaggerated the significance of this proposed bill, as David G. Bell has pointed out in a carefully argued article. Bell makes clear that the bill stopped well short of any challenge to British parliamentary authority over New Brunswick; it was "far from radical," and, contrary to Glenie's hopes, it would not have "reduce[d] judicial discretion." It probably would have indirectly encouraged the movement towards a more responsive, representative system, and a more active assembly, in that the period from 1660 to 1750 was marked by considerable improvement in English jurisprudence, the passage of statutes "that defined and established the principles of the Constitution and the liberties of the subject," and the enactment of "such fundamental libertarian safeguards as the *Bill of Rights*." But Daniel Lyman certainly erred when he described the bill as going "further than the first address or declaration of the American Congress assembled at Philadelphia, when they were about to separate themselves from Great Britain."

Be that as it may, the Declaratory Bill was portrayed as a radical measure and its proponent, seen as equally radical, was the lightning-rod that absorbed the loyalist thunderbolts. As Lyman put it, "This Mr. Glenie is known to be in the correspondence with some of the most violent members of the opposition in the British Parliament – at least, he avows himself so – and his sentiments or declarations are such as tend to the subversion of all government of Church and State." The outraged response, in view of the limited nature of the bill, prompts a question about Glenie's contribution to the cause of assembly rights. Although he symbolized this particular cause, his radical rhetoric precluded acceptance of much of what he proposed. At the same time, other more cautious exponents of assembly privileges could portray themselves as loyal moderates and work towards the same goals in a less flamboyant fashion. Thus both Elias Hardy, spokesman for assembly control of the purse, and Amos BOTSFORD, shortly to be a voice for moderate reform, opposed Glenie's Declaratory Bill while certainly not abandoning many of his other goals. In short, Glenie's attacks accelerated a broadening of the rather closed loyalist political culture into a more accommodative structure where opposition could no longer immediately be silenced or dismissed as disloyal republicanism. Ironically, at the very moment when Glenie was at his political peak, his radical political image was clearing the way for a more respectable reform movement, guided by others and contributing to his own decline.

This development was not readily apparent in the election of 1795 since the electorate appeared to approve of Glenie and the assembly party's conduct by returning a majority of members even more hostile to the governor's supporters. Glenie himself won easily in Sunbury County, topping the poll with 79 votes, although one of the defeated candidates who had received 22 votes challenged the outcome. William Hubbard charged that Glenie and his running-mate, Samuel Denny Street*, had provided "Meat Drink and Entertainment *in order to induce* the said Voters to give their voice" for them. Not surprisingly, the assembly rejected Hubbard's accusations and, by a vote of 13 to 8, declared Glenie and Street legitimately elected. None the less, in the new assembly Glenie was much less active than in the previous session. To be sure, he did reintroduce the bill regulating the times and places of Supreme Court sittings, and he also served on committees for other bills. As well, he was among those appointed to correspond with William Knox concerning the Supreme Court issue. But when a very strong motion was passed requesting that Carleton direct at least one of the Supreme Court judges to reside at Saint John, Glenie, despite his expertise on the question, was not among the three-man delegation appointed to present this resolution to the lieutenant governor. Likewise, although Glenie was a member of the assembly committee that met with a committee of the Council concerning a revenue bill, he did not occupy the limelight when this committee reported back to the assembly. A lengthy indictment of the Council's

Glenie

actions, ending with a ringing declaration that the elected members were "resolved to continue to assert the Privileges of the House of Assembly and the Honor of their Constituents," was instead presented by Daniel Murray, a Massachusetts loyalist who had voted against the Declaratory Bill. When the Council offered a blistering reply, it was again Murray, on behalf of the committee, who spelled out the assembly's detailed and determined position.

In December 1796 Glenie was honoured by the mayor and corporation of Saint John with the freedom of the city. Still, when the assembly met the following January he received an open rebuff from this body. If the words of one of Glenie's opponents are accurate, however, perhaps he had done his work all too well and further bold assertions of the assembly's rights were unnecessary. Edward WINSLOW assessed the house that gathered in 1797 as follows: "We have fellows here who three years agoe did not know that Magna Charta was not a Great Pudding – will analyse all the principles of Government – Trace 'Jurisprudence to its Source' – fix political Longitudes & Latitudes & establish the boundary line between prerogative and privilege." Consequently, when Carleton dared to lecture the assemblymen on deviations "from the line of conduct at all times pursued by the British House of Commons, by which you have so often professed the laudable intention to be solely guided," a committee was struck to reply. Apparently the response, urging the lieutenant governor not to press for measures that "will involve the province in perplexities and difficulties which might prove pernicious to public credit," was not strong enough for Glenie. He introduced two motions suggesting that Carleton's statements were "contrary to the fundamental principles of our colonial constitution" and that his assertion "manifestly tends to destroy the independence of this branch of the Legislature." Both resolutions were rejected. Even when he softened his position in a third motion, the assembly rejected it by a vote of 17 to 5. The impasse continued but other assembly leaders were fighting the battle in their own way and thus disassociating themselves from Glenie's more abrasive approach. Still, Glenie continued to vote with the majority on important issues such as refusing to accept the Council's demand that expenses of assemblymen be removed from the revenue and appropriations bill. By now, however, even some of Glenie's friends and patrons outside the house appeared to be wavering. After the session ended Glenie and John Coffin* decided that their differences of opinion could be resolved only by a duel, in which Glenie came off the loser with a flesh wound in his thigh. Such activities produced the comment from John Wentworth that "in a late conversation with H.R.H. [EDWARD AUGUSTUS] we lamented the late accident which the public papers informed us you had sustained, we both concurred in wishing that you would forever Substitute the pursuits of Philosophy; or rather science, to politics – from whence you would derive the greatest good to the world at large, and gratify all your friends."

During the short session of 1798, also a stalemate, Glenie was involved in one of the major manœuvres by the assembly. Although apparently bypassed in dealings between the lower house and the Council or the lieutenant governor, Glenie was recruited to serve on the committee to prepare a letter to the Duke of Portland, the Home secretary, outlining the assembly's position. Speaker Amos Botsford, after the assembly approved the letter, sent it to Portland as a summary of "the present deplorable situation of this Colony." Emphasizing the loyalty of the assembly to the sovereign and the British constitution, the letter briefly outlined the deadlock, the appropriation and revenue problems, and the shortcomings of the judiciary – all matters Portland had already heard far too much about – and stressed the need for instructions to the lieutenant governor to rectify the problems. By now Portland was not the only one who found the continuing controversy increasingly tiresome. In New Brunswick the electorate was becoming restive, and with good reason: supplies had not been voted for the past five years because of the legislative deadlock, and without revenue the province was unable to undertake public works. At the same time, as the decade closed, a measure of prosperity and an awareness of the French menace to the mother country were diverting attention to other matters. In Kings and York counties petitions were circulated, and eventually presented at the 1799 session, urging the assembly to restore "harmony between the two Branches of the Legislature" by removing the pay measure from other appropriations. In the press it was even suggested that the assembly was the tool of a profiteering merchant community since, though duties could not be collected without a revenue bill, there had been no fall in prices. Carleton was also active, shrewdly placing extracts of Portland's correspondence into Botsford's hands to underline the growing impatience of the British government. The mounting pressure paid off in the 1799 session. Parts of Portland's correspondence were now submitted to the house and, as Botsford described it, "the principles of Legislation were therein so clearly pointed out, and the anxious desire of the House such, that Bills were prepared and passed, and concurred by the Council: in these Bills no point was given up by the House, they only varied the Mode, and every item they had put into their former Bills which had been negatived, now passed." All disputes had been "amicably adjusted" in what Botsford perceived as a vindication of the assembly. To Carleton also, it was a satisfactory outcome in that the pay item had been set apart by the assembly and the Council waived "their objections to some irregularities," hoping "that, by the present recovery of harmony and mutual confidence, they should contribute most effectually to the adoption of a more regular system of proceeding in future."

What did James Glenie think of all this? Initially there was a strange silence but before 1800 expired he had written and published a satire, based on the Apostles' Creed, in which he lampooned, among others, Provincial Secretary Jonathan ODELL, "maker of Militia officers and Just Asses of the Peace, and plotter of all head quarter intrigues visible and invisible, the only beloved of Simple Tom." Obviously, the compromise arrangements did not go far enough for Glenie. Nothing short of a purge of the upper house and a recall of the lieutenant governor would satisfy him. The old Glenie, an abusive and bitter name-caller, re-emerged and the reasoned arguments for legal and constitutional reforms were forgotten. His bitterness no doubt was heightened by the realization that even in the assembly, the cause of which he had briefly championed, he could no longer count on anything like majority support.

There was no assembly session in 1800 and Glenie busied himself with his duties as deputy surveyor of woods, duties that took on a new urgency as a result of the European situation. "Masts and other Spars and naval timber must of course be preserved, and an immediate supply be provided," reminded Wentworth, who continued to rely on and confide in Glenie as an old friend. Whether because of these activities, or perhaps because of disillusionment with his assembly colleagues, when the legislature met again in January 1801 Glenie was not present. He managed to appear for eight days at the tag-end of the thirty-two day session, the worst attendance record of any member except for two who did not appear at all. When he did attend on 10 Feb. 1801 it was for a specific reason: this was the day a censure of Carleton was to be attempted. Between sessions, the lieutenant governor had expended funds on the construction of a building in Fredericton to house the assembly and the Supreme Court, and to some members this arbitrary executive act had to be challenged. Glenie supported a motion by Pagan that Carleton's action was "unconstitutional, and infringes the unalienable right of the House of Assembly to originate all Appropriations of Public Money." Not only did the assembly overwhelmingly reject this censure by 14 votes to 5, but it then passed a motion affirming the need for a new building in Fredericton, thus vindicating the lieutenant governor. Glenie retreated to his surveying duties, ever vigilant and with plenty of legal advice for Wentworth, and turned to loftier schemes, such as trying to get financial support for a survey of a possible canal between the Bay of Fundy and the Gulf of St Lawrence.

During the session of 1802, however, Glenie returned for his last campaign in the assembly, a campaign that culminated in a boycott of its proceedings. At issue was who should become clerk of the house during the illness and following the death of Isaac Hedden (Heddon). Glenie successfully moved that Samuel Denny Street be acting clerk and then served on a committee "to search for precedents, as to the powers authorities and privileges, in the appointment to the Clerkship." Clearly, Glenie and a majority of assemblymen felt that the assembly had the power to recommend appointment to the clerkship and, once Hedden died, Glenie moved, again successfully, that Street should be recommended to the lieutenant governor for the post. Carleton's response revealed equally clearly his feeling that the crown controlled this appointment and he therefore chose Dugald CAMPBELL. Glenie retaliated by moving that the house appoint Street and by 11 votes to 9 his motion passed, but the Council was quick to block the clerk's salary which the assembly tried to provide for Street and, of course, stood with Carleton in upholding the legitimacy of Campbell's appointment. To force an adjournment Glenie and like-minded assemblymen stopped attending the sessions, thus depriving the assembly of a quorum; but even when there were only eight members present the sessions continued, despite the opposition of two of this number, Street and Thomas Dixon. The serjeant-at-arms was dispatched to inform Glenie that the house required his attendance, but Glenie replied "that he did not consider them as a House, and that he would not go near them." As a result, only a handful of members finished the session, Dugald Campbell received the clerk's appointment and salary while Street performed the duties, and the issue was taken to the electorate since Carleton called an election for October 1802. There followed an extraordinary debate in the press of New Brunswick as both sides presented in elaborate detail the legitimacy of their case. The election itself resulted in a rout of Carleton's opponents. Even in Sunbury County, Glenie and Street barely scraped back in, with 101 and 93 votes respectively compared to their opponents' 87 and 82, and the results were to be disputed.

First to be challenged was Street, who was denied victory when the sheriff of the county scrutinized his votes and those cast for his opponent, Elijah Miles*, and then declared Miles elected, a decision eventually supported by the assembly. Another petition sought to have Glenie unseated because of the impact his accusations against the government had had "upon the minds and the fears of the Electors." It was alleged that Glenie had spoken of "Such Gigantic strides of Despotism . . . that the like has not been known since the days of Henry the Eighth the most despotic Prince that ever ruled on the English throne." Glenie was not unseated, but a clear indication of his political demise was provided when he dared to reopen the clerkship question. His motion in the 1803 session that the

Glenie

house choose a clerk was defeated by 15 votes to 8, and instead a motion was passed to make clear that this office "is a Patent Office, and the appointment thereof vested in the Crown." If it was any consolation, Glenie's attacks had taken their toll on the crown's representative and Carleton was preparing to leave New Brunswick. Prior to the lieutenant governor's departure in October 1803, his faithful and equally abused Council attempted a final defence against the charges so frequently levelled. In praising Carleton the Council testified that "we have had the honor, for many years, to be witnesses intimately acquainted with the inflexible integrity and disinterested purity of your Administration; and we consider our faithful testimony, on this occasion, not only as a debt due to personal merit, but as a document of public importance." The need for the document reflected the severity of the attacks launched over the years. Moreover, the Council emphasized that "an equal regard to the Prerogatives of the Crown and the Rights of the People has been the constant Rule of your Government, which hereafter will afford a bright example to your Successors." This was more than face-saving rhetoric for it revealed how deeply Glenie had stung the conscience and pretensions of Carleton and the loyalist élite.

To all intents and purposes, Glenie's political career was ended. He now concentrated on his duties as deputy surveyor of the king's woods which, it was expected, would be more demanding as a result of a renewal of land granting in New Brunswick and new naval contracts. Without Wentworth's continued support even this appointment might have been lost to Glenie; before Carleton returned to England he suggested to Wentworth that George SPROULE should be appointed deputy surveyor in New Brunswick, but this advice was not acted upon. Nevertheless, Glenie had never realized his financial ambitions in New Brunswick and in May 1804 he was busy planning a visit to England which Wentworth hoped "may be prosperous and happy, in every respect, and your return to your friends here be speedy and in perfect safety." In the winter of 1804–5, after arranging the appointment of Street as acting deputy surveyor of woods, James Glenie left loyalist New Brunswick, never to return. According to one report, published in 1817, his departure came as a surprise to his own wife. Lieutenant-Colonel Joseph Gubbins claimed that the "notorious Glenny" had "fled from this Province without making the least provision for his wife, or acquainting her with his intentions." Left impoverished, she was able to make ends meet only with the help of her husband's creditors, who were sympathetic to her plight, and the "neighbouring peasantry."

In January 1805 a no doubt apprehensive Carleton, now in England, questioned Edward Winslow: "What's become of that worthy son of Beliol, Mr.

Glenie? I understood he was to come home this winter." What became of Glenie remains somewhat of a mystery since little is known of the remainder of his life. Through the intervention of the Earl of Chatham, in 1806 Glenie was appointed "Professor of East India Cadets" and in 1807 "Inspecting Engineer in some of the West India islands." However, his penchant for controversy remained and in 1809 his critical comments concerning the Duke of York, connected with a parliamentary inquiry into the alleged sale of military commissions by York's mistress, gave such offence to the duke that Glenie was stripped of both positions. His mathematical talents remained – he presented a paper to the Royal Society in 1811 – but his efforts to attract students were largely unsuccessful. Consequently, he died in poverty on 23 Nov. 1817, the same year that Carleton passed on, and was buried in the churchyard of St Martin-in-the-Fields, London. His wife had remained in New Brunswick and continued to live in Sunbury County, known to her neighbours as Lady Glenie, until her death on 26 Feb. 1847. They had at least two sons, one (Melville) a military officer and the other an Anglican minister; the at times rather undisciplined and anti-establishment Glenie no doubt appreciated the irony.

The obituary notice of James Glenie that appeared in the Halifax *Free Press* and then was reprinted in the *New Brunswick Courier* was full of praise. The Duke of Kent, it reported, respected Glenie's "personal merit" and "superior mental endowments." It also claimed of Glenie that "in the discharge of his public duties he was particularly eminent," with "a sound judgment, united to great political sagacity and foresight" and that "many individuals in the sister Province" acknowledged "the value of his counsel, and the prudence of his admonitions." One wonders whether his officer-son, then stationed in Halifax, was the source of this eulogy! Whig historians in search of the first glimmerings of responsible government have continued this eulogistic approach, hailing Glenie as "a reformer of the most advanced type" who was "a full half century in advance of his time." More recently, William Stewart MacNutt* attempted a balanced assessment, observing that Glenie's reform reputation was "subject to damaging qualifications" since "many of his motives were vindictive and mischievous." None the less, MacNutt concludes, "it was perhaps he who first led a movement that by any stretch of the imagination could be called popular against the upholders of the royal prerogative, who first employed a popular assembly as a forum for the seizure of power from privileged hands."

Concerning his motivation, it should now be clear that his economic interests and personal bitterness were frequently behind his attacks on Carleton and the loyalist élite. Yet, to his credit, there was a real desire to serve his Sunbury constituents and, however briefly, a real commitment to constitutional change in New Brunswick. Unfortunately, his proposals and principles were never spelled out in sufficient depth, at least in the evidence available at present, and often were clothed in an aggressive rhetoric which further obscured rather than clarified. One can be more decisive on the question of whether Glenie ever "led a movement" to seize power from the privileged. The assembly party of the mid 1790s was very much a loose coalition of those who felt disillusioned or deprived in Carleton's loyalist New Brunswick. Religious issues (dissenters versus Anglicans), economic issues (mast contractors and merchants versus an aspiring landed gentry), geographic divisions (coastal versus inland counties), nationality differences (pre-loyalists versus loyalists, Scots versus Englishmen, Europeans versus Americans), metropolitan rivalries (Saint John versus Fredericton), and quite simply loyalists out of power versus loyalists in power were some of the ingredients that went into the cauldron of the colony's politics and produced the alignment of an assembly party versus a governor's party. But to describe the assembly party as led by Glenie or as a Glenie faction greatly overestimates his role. Such a coalition of varied interest groups was bound to be plagued by constant shifts in loyalty as the issues under discussion changed and would have been virtually impossible to lead. Assembly rights appeared to be the one constant, shared at some point by all the anti-Carleton groups, but even on this issue Glenie sometimes parted company with the majority, or some quickly parted company with Glenie, over how far, how fast, and even how, changes should be achieved. Indeed, Glenie seemed committed to change from the bottom up – that is, a greatly enhanced role for the lower house – only in the 1795 to 1796 period; once Council and assembly had agreed on a compromise he retreated to his earlier position of change from the top down, a new governor and Council. Thus, despite his radical image and his assertions concerning the assembly's privileges and the people's rights, James Glenie falls far short of being the consistent, committed, and influential leader of a reform movement. He was an erratically brilliant individual, however, and his very presence contributed to the legitimization of dissent and opposition. It also was a forceful reminder to Carleton and the loyalist élite that what they assumed in 1784 to be a coherent and united New Brunswick had, by the time of Carleton's departure for England and Glenie's withdrawal from politics in 1803, proved itself a much more pluralistic and diverse society.

W. G. GODFREY

[James Glenie is the author of a number of mathematical works, including *The history of gunnery, with a new method of deriving the theory of projectiles in vacuo, from the properties of the square and rhombus* (Edinburgh and London, 1776); *The doctrine of universal comparison, or general proportion* (London, 1789); and *The antecedental calculus; or, a geometrical method of reasoning . . .* (London, 1793). The two essays that Francis Maseres submitted to the Royal Soc. of London appear as "Propositions selected from a paper on the division of right lines, surfaces, and solids" and "The general mathematical laws which regulate and extend proportion universally . . . ," *Philosophical Trans.*, 66 (1776): 73–91 and 67 (1777): 450–57, respectively. Another two papers, "A problem concerning the construction of a triangle, by means of a circle only . . ." and "A letter from James Glenie, esq., to Francis Maseres, esq., containing a demonstration of Sir Isaac Newton's binomial theorem," were subsequently published in a collection edited by Maseres, *Scriptores logarithmici; or a collection of several curious tracts on the nature and construction of logarithms . . .* (6v., London, 1791–1807), 4: 333–42 and 5: 205–16. His contributions to the Royal Soc. of Edinburgh include "A short paper on the principles of the antecedental calculus" and "A geometrical investigation of some curious and interesting properties of the circle" published in its *Trans.* (Edinburgh), 4 (1798), pt.II, sect.I: 65–82, and 6 (1812): 21–69, respectively. He is not, however, the author of a report in volume 7 (1813) concerning "a boy born blind and deaf" as reported in the *DNB*; he has evidently been confused with a "Mr Professor Glennie of Marischal College, Aberdeen," whose "Answers to some queries . . ." on that matter appear on pp.16–20.

Glenie's opposition to Richmond's defence policy was conducted in print, beginning with *A short essay on the modes of defence best adapted to the situation and circumstances of this island; with an examination of the schemes that have been formed for the purpose of fortifying its principal dockyards on very extensive plans, which are ready to be carried into execution by his grace the Duke of Richmond, now master-general of the ordnance*, published anonymously as "by an officer." This essay, Richmond's *An answer to "A short essay . . . ,"* and Glenie's *A reply to the "Answer . . ."* were all published in London in 1785. Glenie later published *Observations on the Duke of Richmond's extensive plans of fortification, and the new works he has been carrying on since these were set aside by the House of Commons in 1786; by the author of the "Short essay"* (London, 1794).

At the PAC, the basic collection for the early period of New Brunswick history is MG 11, [CO 188] New Brunswick A, 1–26. Glenie's military career can be traced in the Haldimand papers, BL, Add. MSS 21709: 95–96, 129–31; 21712: 67–68; 21714: 255–58; 21715: 6–9; 21720: 147–49; 21722: 361–62; 21726: 209–10; 21734: 10–11; 21741: 40; 21743: 146–47; 21764: 19–20; 21787: 6, 14–15, 36, 43–45; 21788: 5, 12; 21801: 9–10; 21814: 29–30, 40–43, 46–47, 143–50, 200, 210–12, 257–58, 265, 273; 21874: 180–81; 21877: 412 (mfm. at PAC). The PANS contains the valuable Wentworth letterbooks, RG 1, 49–54, which allow a reconstruction of the Wentworth–Glenie relationship. Also useful are the Wentworth papers, MG 1, 939–41, and the Saint John River papers, RG 1, 409 (mfm. at N.B. Museum). A variety of documentation concerning Glenie's political career is found at PANB in RG 4, RS24, S6-B25, P14; S8-B17; S9-B5, B8, B9, B17, P4; S10-B17, P2, P6; S11-P3; S13-B14, Z9; S14-Z1; S15-B6, B19; S16-B3, B16,

Gosselin

P16, P17, Z7. Other valuable items here are RG 7, RS72A, Mary Ann Glenie, 1847; and RG 10, RS108, Petition of James Glenie, 3 Aug. 1785; Memorial of Glenie *et al.*, 8 Oct. 1785. His land grants are catalogued in N.B., Dept. of Natural Resources, Lands Branch (Fredericton), Index to grants, 1765–1848. The basic collection at the PRO is of course CO 188/1–23. At the N.B. Museum are some interesting items, a number of which are very valuable. These include SB 39: 118; Colwell coll.; Glenie family CB; H. T. Hazen coll.: Ward Chipman papers; and Jarvis papers.

Among printed primary sources, the following are extremely useful: *Annual reg.* (London), 1809; "'Creon': a satire on New Brunswick politics in 1802," an anonymous poem originally issued the same year, edited by T. B. Vincent and republished in *Acadiensis* (Fredericton), 3 (1973–74), no.2: 80–98; *Gentleman's Magazine*, July–December 1817; [Joseph Gubbins], *Lieutenant Colonel Joseph Gubbins, inspecting field officer of militia: New Brunswick journals of 1811 & 1813*, ed. Howard Temperley (Fredericton, [1980]), 32–33; *Kingston before War of 1812* (Preston); N.B., House of Assembly, *Journal*, 1788–89, 1791–99, 1801–3, 1805; and *Winslow papers* (Raymond). Useful contemporary newspapers include the *New Brunswick Courier* (Saint John), 1818; the *Royal Gazette* (Saint John), 1785–1804; and the *Saint John Gazette*, 1787–1805. The following reference sources are valuable: William Anderson, *The Scottish nation; or the surnames, families, literature, honours, and biographical history of the people of Scotland* (3v., Edinburgh and London, 1869), 2; *DCB*, vol.4 (biogs. of William Davidson and Elias Hardy); *DNB*; and G.B., WO, *Army list*, 1777–87, 1817.

Secondary sources providing helpful background information or mention of Glenie include S. D. Clark, *Movements of political protest in Canada, 1640–1840* (Toronto, 1959); John Ehrman, *The younger Pitt: the years of acclaim* (London, 1969); Hannay, *Hist. of N.B.*, 1; Macmillan, "New men in action," *Canadian business hist.* (Macmillan), 44–103; MacNutt, *New Brunswick*; L. M. B. Maxwell, *An outline of the history of central New Brunswick to the time of confederation* (Sackville, N.B., 1937); Whitworth Porter *et al.*, *History of the Corps of Royal Engineers* (9v. to date, London and Chatham, Eng., 1889–   ; vols.1–3 repr. Chatham, 1951–54), 2; Wright, *Loyalists of N.B.*; and Graeme Wynn, *Timber colony: an historical geography of early nineteenth century New Brunswick* (Toronto, 1981). Worthwhile dissertation material includes R. C. Campbell, "Simonds, Hazen and White: a study of a New Brunswick firm in the commercial world of the eighteenth century" (MA thesis, Univ. of N.B., Saint John, 1970); Condon, "Envy of American states"; W. D. Moore, "Sunbury County, 1760–1830" (MA thesis, Univ. of N.B., 1977); G. C. W. Troxler, "The migration of Carolina and Georgia loyalists to Nova Scotia and New Brunswick" (PHD thesis, Univ. of N.C., Chapel Hill, 1974); and Graeme Wynn, "The assault on the New Brunswick forest, 1780–1850" (PHD thesis, Univ. of Toronto, 1974). Useful articles are D. G. Bell, "A note on the reception of English statutes in New Brunswick" and "The reception question and the constitutional crisis of the 1790's in New Brunswick," *Univ. of New Brunswick Law Journal* (Saint John), 28 (1979): 195–201 and 29 (1980): 157–72; "Population patterns in pre-confederation New Brunswick," ed. Graeme Wynn, *Acadiensis* (Fredericton), 10 (1980–81), no.2: 124–38; G. F. G. Stanley, "James Glenie, a study in early colonial radicalism," N.S. Hist. Soc., *Coll.*, 25 (1942): 145–73; and Graeme Wynn, "Administration in adversity: the deputy surveyors and control of the New Brunswick crown forest before 1844," *Acadiensis*, 7 (1977–78), no.1: 49–65. W.G.G.]

GOSSELIN, CLÉMENT, carpenter and army officer; b. 12 June 1747 in Sainte-Famille, Île d'Orléans (Que.), son of Gabriel Gosselin and Geneviève Crépeaux; m. first 22 Jan. 1770 Marie Dionne in Sainte-Anne-de-la-Pocatière (La Pocatière), Que.; m. secondly 15 Jan. 1787 Charlotte Ouimet in Longueuil, Que.; m. thirdly 8 Nov. 1790 Catherine Monty, probably in Champlain, N.Y.; d. 9 March 1816 in Beekmantown, N.Y.

Clément Gosselin, the youngest of a large family, left Île d'Orléans probably at the age of about 20, and settled at Sainte-Anne-de-la-Pocatière, where he owned some land at the time of his first marriage in January 1770. When American troops invaded Quebec five years later, Gosselin supported the revolutionary cause. It is likely that he was one of about 200 Canadians who took part in the attack – disastrous for the Americans – that was launched against the town of Quebec by Richard Montgomery* on the night of 30–31 Dec. 1775. The defeat made the invaders' military situation precarious and also effectively checked the current of sympathy towards them that had developed amongst some part of the Canadian population. But Gosselin was not shaken in his convictions.

From January to May 1776 he travelled throughout the various parishes on the south shore of the St Lawrence from Pointe-Lévy (Lauzon and Lévis) to Sainte-Anne-de-la-Pocatière, recruiting volunteers for the Congressional troops. In this task he was aided by his father-in-law, Germain Dionne, who furnished clothing and supplies to the new recruits. Gosselin also called and presided over parish meetings for the election of militia officers, to whom he delivered Congressional commissions. Moreover, from the steps of the churches he read the orders and proclamations issued by the Americans, and he sometimes even forced the king's officers themselves to read them. Together with Pierre Ayotte, a habitant from Kamouraska who was equally devoted to the revolutionary cause, Gosselin organized a system of bonfires, under close guard, to warn the Americans of any approaching British ships.

On 4 March 1776 Gosselin became a captain in the regiment commanded by Moses HAZEN, and on 25 March he took part in the attack on the advance guard of the force that had been mustered by Louis LIÉNARD de Beaujeu de Villemonde at Saint-Pierre-de-la-Rivière-du-Sud. On 3 May, three days before the Congressional troops lifted the siege of Quebec, Gosselin presided at a meeting in the parish of

Gower

Saint-Vallier. No trace has been found of his activity during the next 15 months. Instead of following his regiment in the American retreat to New England, he seems to have chosen to go underground and probably hid in the region of Sainte-Anne-de-la-Pocatière. In August 1777 he managed to sell his land to Jean-Marie Chouinard, but some months later he was arrested and imprisoned at Quebec.

In the spring of 1778 Gosselin was freed, and along with his father-in-law and his brother Louis he rejoined his regiment at White Plains, near New York. In the mean time the idea of invading the province of Quebec was regaining favour in the American colonies, particularly after the treaty of alliance with France was concluded on 6 Feb. 1778. With this possibility in mind the men in Hazen's regiment opened a road from Newbury (Vt) to the Quebec border. Some Canadians were also entrusted with spying missions. Thus from the summer of 1778 until the summer of 1780 Gosselin returned secretly to the colony a number of times, spreading the rumour that an invasion by the Congressional armies was imminent and that this time they would be accompanied by French regiments. Naturally this talk created serious anxieties for Governor HALDIMAND, who feared that the Canadians would defect if French troops returned. But in the autumn of 1780 Congress finally abandoned all plans for invasion.

Gosselin was wounded on 4 Oct. 1781 in Virginia at the battle of Yorktown, which was to bring the American Revolutionary War to an end. In June 1783, after the conclusion of the Treaty of Versailles, he was promoted major and discharged. The next year New York State gave lands on the shores of Lake Champlain to the Canadian veterans who had served in the Congressional troops. Gosselin received 1,000 acres but parted with them soon after, probably preferring to return to his carpenter's trade, the occupation he had followed before the American invasion of the province. He lived at Champlain until early in 1791 and then moved to the Saint-Hyacinthe region in Lower Canada. Around 1800 he stayed briefly at Sainte-Marguerite-de-Blairfindie (L'Acadie), and then in 1803 settled at Saint-Luc, where he lived until early in 1815.

Historian Gustave Lanctot* passes severe judgement upon Canadians like Clément Gosselin who took up the cause of the American revolution. He calls them "restless and ambitious individuals" who "saw in the invasion an opportunity . . . for profit and adventure." They were "only a fraction of the population, although a hostile, aggressive, and often unscrupulous one." Such an interpretation scarcely stands up to an analysis of the facts. Rather it seems to be an offshoot of a current of Canadian nationalist thought that was born with the conquest and that has constantly sought to highlight the loyalty of the French-Canadians to the British crown, probably through a desire to see resolved the tensions and frictions which have arisen between two sociocultural groups inhabiting the same territory for more than two centuries.

PIERRE DUFOUR and GÉRARD GOYER

Arch. du collège de Sainte-Anne-de-la-Pocatière (La Pocatière, Qué.), CAC 1038, nos.726.3, 726.5. BL, Add. MSS 21844: 387–91. "Journal par Baby, Taschereau et Williams" (Fauteux), ANQ *Rapport*, 1927–28: 435–99; 1929–30: 138–40. Caron, "Inv. de la corr. de Mgr Plessis," ANQ *Rapport*, 1927–28: 215–316. *DAB*. J. E. Hare, "Le comportement de la paysannerie rurale et urbaine de la région de Québec pendant l'occupation américaine 1775–1776; note de recherche," *Mélanges d'histoire du Canada français offerts au professeur Marcel Trudel* (Ottawa, 1978), 145–50. Lanctot, *Le Canada et la Révolution américaine*. Robert Rumilly, *Histoire des Franco-Américains* (Montréal, 1958). N.-E. Dionne, "L'invasion de 1775–76," *BRH*, 6 (1900): 132–33. Edmond Mallet, "Les Canadiens-français et la guerre de l'Indépendance américaine," *BRH*, 3 (1897): 156–57; "Le commandant Gosselin," *BRH*, 4 (1898): 6–10. E.-L. Monty, "Études généalogiques: le major Clément Gosselin," SGCF *Mémoires*, 3 (1948): 18–38. T. Saint-Pierre, "Les Canadiens et la guerre de l'Indépendance," *BRH*, 6 (1900): 209–13.

GOWER, Sir ERASMUS, naval officer and governor of Newfoundland; b. 3 Dec. 1742 near Cilgerran, Wales, eldest of 19 children of Abel Gower of Glanafon and Letitia Lewes; d. unmarried 21 June 1814 in Hambledon, Hampshire, England.

Erasmus Gower entered the Royal Navy in 1755 under the care of his uncle, Captain John Donkley. His service was extensive and varied. Between 1764 and 1766 he was on the *Dolphin* during the round-the-world voyage of Commodore John Byron*, and in the latter year was promoted lieutenant. In March 1770 he was shipwrecked on the coast of Patagonia (Argentina), and reached the Falkland Islands only to be expelled by a Spanish force. During the American revolution he saw service in both the West and the East Indies and in January 1783, while in command of the frigate *Medea*, captured the Dutch East Indiaman *Vrijheid* at Cuddalore (India). Between 1786 and 1789 he was flag-captain to Commodore John Elliot on the Newfoundland station, and in 1792 he was knighted prior to his taking out to China, in the *Lion*, a British embassy under Lord Macartney. He also served under Sir William Cornwallis in an action off the French coast in 1795 and was present at the mutiny at the Nore in 1797. Although his British biographies note that he held no "active employment" after his promotion to rear-admiral of the white in February 1799, his greatest service to Canada began with his promotion to vice-admiral of the white and his appointment as governor of Newfoundland in the spring of 1804.

Gower

Gower arrived at St John's on 20 July 1804 and for the next three years followed the usual pattern of Newfoundland governors by remaining on the island over the summer and then returning to England in the autumn with the fishing fleet. The obvious care which he applied to the day-to-day administration of the island is exemplified in his meticulous annual returns of shipping and fishery statistics, to which he appended lengthy explanatory observations. Although he was greatly concerned with the defence of St John's, much of his attention was concentrated on administration, in the long term, of all Newfoundland, which by the time of his tenure was clearly a year-round settlement, a "colonized" place. His earlier service there gave him a perspective on the changes which had occurred as the fishery altered from one with a large proportion of its vessels migrating seasonally from Britain into a sedentary one. Governor James Gambier*, Gower's predecessor, who had also recognized these realities, had suggested the appointment of a permanent government secretary, the establishment of Protestant schools, the construction and rebuilding of jails, and the leasing of disused properties still reserved for the migratory fishing ships in acknowledgement of the changed conditions.

Gower agreed with Gambier's measures, strengthened them, and extended them – no small feat in the tangle of approvals and entrenched policies then part of Newfoundland government. He retained Gambier's secretary and pointed out persistently the importance of a permanent secretary to provide continuity. He worked diligently for a fair judicial system and adequate remuneration for its officials, reorganized their offices, and, to replace a system in which magistrates and clerks were paid directly from what they could collect, allocated fines and fees to a general fund from which commensurate salaries could be paid. He also took the charitable fund that had been started by Governor William Waldegrave and supported by his two successors, Sir Charles Morice Pole and Gambier, and built it into a society for improving the condition of the poor. The society provided for both the relief of the indigent and the instruction of children of both sexes in morality, reading, and practical skills. This latter development quickly resulted in the establishment of a large school building and an enrolment of 150 pupils. The institution had political and governmental importance as well, for the Roman Catholics had been more active than the Protestants in providing schooling. Gower did not hesitate to recommend that the government continue funding this educational effort. He emphasized government support for the Church of England in a number of ways, and he also strongly supported the attempt to obtain a salary and pension for the Roman Catholic bishop in Newfoundland, James Louis O'DONEL, in recogni-

tion of his work with the "labouring class," which had through his efforts remained loyal and peaceful in the nervous times of the Napoleonic Wars.

In a settlement that was growing, and in new directions, Gower recognized the importance of property and land for the support of the fishery and trade, for agriculture, and for housing. The ships' rooms in St John's, places on the harbour traditionally reserved for seasonal fishing vessels which arrived early from Britain, were no longer so used. Gambier had begun a quiet general survey of them; Gower extended the survey to much of the island and developed a policy to allow their being leased from the crown. To meet a pressing demand for agricultural land at St John's, Gower, again following Gambier's lead, made available on 21-year leases land back from the 200-yard strip traditionally reserved for fishery use, and by the end of 1805 this amounted to more than 300 acres. On the line of the 200-yard limit he laid out a street with house lots on its inland side. Rents from all these lands went for the support of the programs of the civil establishment and the Church of England.

Nevertheless, the official British attitude was still that Newfoundland should not become a colony. One of the main reasons was that the migratory ship fishery was seen as necessary to the continuance of the Newfoundland trade and as a training ground for the Royal Navy. Gower, however, compared the statistics of 1787–89, years of a peak in the Grand Banks fishery, with those for 1805 and showed that, although the migratory fishery had fallen away to little, shipping to and from the island in the latter year came close to employing the same number of men as had been engaged in the earlier period. A further official policy was that Newfoundland should rely on Britain for its supplies. Gower pointed out that the Newfoundland fishery had to remain competitive; otherwise it could not continue as a British exchange earner or as a "Nursery of Seamen." If it were to be able to compete with the New England fishery it had to have a much freer hand in importing supplies from the cheapest market, and its people had to have the clear right to possess land and to grow more of their own food. Gower's attitude to his instruction regarding the islanders' clouded property rights illustrates the tenor of much of his three years of Newfoundland administration: "Conceiving it therefore to be impracticable, I should recommend it to be rescinded, or so altered as to recognize the existing customs, and thereby relieve the Governor from the embarrassment of holding an Instruction contrary to the nature and interest of the object which it is his duty to promote, and give confidence and encouragement to those who adventure in it."

Gower left Newfoundland for the last time on 25 Oct. 1806, and his successor John Holloway* was appointed the following spring. He saw no further service, but was promoted admiral of the white on 31 July 1810.

C. GRANT HEAD

A lithograph of a portrait of Gower is reproduced in W. L. Clowes, *The Royal Navy: a history from the earliest times to the present* (7v., London, 1897–1903), 4: 261.

PRO, CO 194/44: ff.3–3v, 5–8, 16, 17–47, 59, 62vff., 75v, 81, 113–16, 155–63v, 170, 201–5, 256v, 258v, 259–59v; 194/45: ff.14–16v, 26–27, 28v–32v, 34–39, 59–60, 78–81, 82–82v, 84–84v, 96–97, 107–8, 119–22, 129–34, 201–2, 233–35, 263–65v, 332–34. *Gentleman's Magazine*, January–June 1814: 702; July–December 1814: 289–90. "Biographical memoir of Sir Erasmus Gower, knight," *Naval Chronicle*, 4 (July–December 1800): 257–89; "Additional biographical memoir of Admiral Sir Erasmus Gower," *Naval Chronicle*, 30 (July–December 1813): 265–301. *DNB*.

GRAHAM, AARON, office holder and judge; b. *c.* 1753, probably in England; m. a cousin of Sir Henry Tempest, and they had two sons; d. 24 Dec. 1818 in London, England.

Described as incomparably the greatest civil servant in the history of Newfoundland, Aaron Graham was secretary to four governors during the period from 1779 to 1791. Contemporary witnesses attributed the success of these governors in large measure to Graham's skill, zeal, and industry; some of them characterized him as a spirited and admirable aide and even as the virtual governor of the island.

Almost nothing is known about Graham prior to his appointment in 1779 as secretary to Governor Richard Edwards*, although it is possible he may have acted as a barrister in London. He doubtless served an effective apprenticeship with Edwards, a "very careful and attentive administrator." Graham seems to have had some mercantile connections at this time since in 1782 he owned the *Maria*, which transported navy victuals to Newfoundland. Another vessel consigned to him and carrying a cargo of salt was apparently lost or captured on its voyage out. About his service to Governor John Campbell between 1782 and 1786 there is little information. John Elliot, a prudent, intelligent, and firm governor, took office in 1786 and the following year informed the home authorities that Graham had been extremely helpful to him in matters of civil government and that he had been acting as *custos rotulorum* since 1783 without pay. Elliot commended Graham for his complete knowledge of Newfoundland and recommended that he continue to be "personally attached" to the governor.

By the time Mark MILBANKE was appointed governor in 1789 the administration of civil justice in Newfoundland had broken down. In an attempt to find a solution Graham met the governor-designate in London and initiated a search of Milbanke's commission. From his reading, he advised Milbanke that he could appoint a court of common pleas with regular judges to replace the inefficient and vulnerable system which had been in use. Graham's interpretation of the commission was untechnical but very clever, since it was to spur a careful investigation of the whole judicial system by the British government. Meanwhile, the civil court was duly constituted in the summer of 1789 with Graham as one of its judges, and although deemed illegal by the home authorities it functioned that year and the next. Despite major complaints from West Country merchants, the British government decided that a civil court was necessary, and in 1791 the House of Commons passed an act to create a court designated grandly as "The Court of Civil Jurisdiction of Our Lord the King at St. John's, in the Island of Newfoundland." It was to be presided over by John Reeves*. Graham served as one of the two assessors to Reeves, who acknowledged that Graham's competence was crucial in establishing the new court on a firm footing. With some changes the court was continued on an annual basis until 1809, when it became permanent.

Late in 1791 Graham returned to England, where he became a police magistrate in London. In 1793 he was called to testify before a committee of the House of Commons appointed to inquire into the state of the trade to Newfoundland. Insofar as Graham was concerned, the inquiry became in effect a careful examination of his role as adviser to Milbanke in instituting the Court of Common Pleas. Graham acquitted himself admirably, claiming that the court was an attempt to legalize what had been done from necessity for so long in the administration of justice. His testimony and that of Reeves underline the exaggeration in the complaints against the court and the tyranny and greed of the West Country merchants.

In his capacity as a police magistrate, Graham was appointed by the Home Department to launch an inquiry into the naval mutinies at Spithead and the Nore in 1796 and 1797. It is clear from his final reports that he believed most of the suspicions entertained about the presence of Jacobin agitators were without serious foundation. By 1805 he had become involved in the Drury Lane Theatre, and he has been variously described as one of the principal shareholders, manager, superintendent, and supervisor of affairs. He may very well have been involved in the theatre before he retired from the bench because of ill health. His indisposition developed into a serious illness which afflicted him for the last five years of his life. At the time of his death in 1818 he had one living son, who had attained the rank of captain in the Royal Navy.

CALVIN D. EVANS

Graham

PRO, ADM 1/472: f.22; CO 194/21: f.352; 194/38: f.290; 194/41: f.23. L. A. Anspach, *A history of the island of Newfoundland* . . . (London, 1819), 209. *Gentleman's Magazine*, 1798: 84, 646–47. G.B., House of Commons, *Reports from committees of the House of Commons which have been printed by order of the house and are not inserted in the Journals*, [1715–1801] (16v., London, [1803–20]), 10: 409–32, "Second report from the committee appointed to enquire into the state of the trade to Newfoundland, 24 April 1793"; 433–503, "Third report . . . , 17 June 1793." J. R. Smallwood, "A dictionary of Newfoundland biography," *The book of Newfoundland*, ed. J. R. Smallwood (6v., St John's, 1937–67), 5: 571. R. H. Bonnycastle, *Newfoundland in 1842: a sequel to "The Canadas in 1841"* (2v., London, 1842), 1: 132–35. James Dugan, *The great mutiny* (London, 1966), 155–65, 175, 193, 242, 323–32, 396, 440, 455, 460. John MacGregor, *Historical and descriptive sketches of the Maritime colonies of British America* (London, 1828; repr. East Ardsley, Eng., and New York, 1968), 230–31. McLintock, *Establishment of constitutional government in Nfld.*, 9n., 59–77. W. J. Macqueen Pope, *Theatre Royal, Drury Lane* (London, 1945), 224. Paul O'Neill, *The story of St. John's, Newfoundland* (2v., Erin, Ont., 1975–76), 2: 554–55. Charles Pedley, *The history of Newfoundland from the earliest times to the year 1860* (London, 1863), 158–63. Prowse, *Hist. of Nfld.* (1895), 345–60, 599, 662. John Reeves, *History of the government of the island of Newfoundland* . . . (London, 1793; repr. New York and East Ardsley, 1967), 162–67.

GRAHAM, ANDREW, HBC chief factor and naturalist; b. in Scotland, probably in the mid 1730s; d. 8 Sept. 1815 in Prestonpans, Scotland.

Andrew Graham joined the Hudson's Bay Company as a youth in 1749 and went first to the most northerly of its trading stations, Prince of Wales's Fort, also known as Churchill (Man.). Among the more interesting of his duties was service on three of the summer slooping expeditions which traded with the Inuit living in the northern parts of Hudson Bay. In 1753 he was appointed assistant writer at York Factory (Man.), where under chief factor James Isham* he held positions of increasing responsibility. From 1761 to 1774 Graham was master at Fort Severn (Ont.) save for two seasons, 1765–66 and 1771–72, which he spent as acting chief at York, and a year's leave in 1769–70. From March 1774 until August of the following year he was at Prince of Wales's Fort once again, this time as chief factor. Graham retired from the company's service in 1775 and lived in or near Edinburgh until his death.

Since the opening of the HBC archives Graham has emerged both as a key figure in the company's inland expansion of the late 18th century and as an important early naturalist. His main claim to recognition rests on the remarkable series of manuscript "Observations" he wrote from 1767 onwards. Begun perhaps as an elaboration and a continuation of the notes kept by Isham in the 1740s, they contain narratives of life at posts on the bay, detailed trade lists, meteorological and astronomical observations, transcripts of journals by company explorers, and the first known vocabularies of the Fall (Gros Ventre) and Sarcee Indians. In actual fact, these short vocabularies, together with much else of Graham's rather sketchy information about the interior Indians, were obtained from other company men, for Graham himself never travelled inland. On the other hand, his much fuller sections on the Crees derived from his own experience at York and Severn, and they are among the most detailed accounts we possess of the bayside Indians. Even more interesting to anthropologists are Graham's comments on the Inuit he had seen along the west coast of Hudson Bay, for written material on their culture in this early period of European contact is otherwise almost non-existent. Above all, Graham's manuscripts contain long sections on the natural history of the bay region, the fullest on birds. Together with his written observations, Graham from 1770 onwards made extensive collections of natural history specimens (again, birds predominated) and sent them to London.

The first shipments of Graham's specimens, together with some of his notes, were described by naturalist Johann Reinhold Forster in three papers published in the Royal Society's *Philosophical Transactions* in 1772 and 1773. Graham had no scientific training and made elementary mistakes in his classifications; nevertheless, his invaluable first-hand observations and the specimens he continued to send home formed the basis for much of the second volume of Thomas Pennant's celebrated *Arctic zoology* (2v., London, 1784–85) and his *Supplement* (London, 1787), as well as of the North American material in the third volume of John Latham's *A general synopsis of birds* (3v. in 6, London, 1781–85). But after the appearance of Forster's articles, acknowledgments to Graham by the world of learning had almost ceased. His material was circulated among naturalists in England by his old colleague and fellow collector in the bay, surgeon and naturalist Thomas Hutchins*, who was corresponding secretary of the HBC in London from 1783 until his death in 1790; and Hutchins seems to have appropriated the credit for observations that were wholly or mainly Graham's. Graham suffered more plagiarism as well: several of the more reliable sections of Edward Umfreville*'s *The present state of Hudson's Bay* . . . (London, 1790) were taken straight from Graham's manuscript journals.

In addition to their importance to natural science, the "Observations" provide an unrivalled picture of the company's trading methods in the mid 18th century. Here Graham was more than a mere collector of information, important though his remarks are for the insight they give about private trade and other matters on which the official records are usually reticent. His two seasons as acting chief at York coincided with an increase in pressure on the HBC's trade by rival pedlars from Canada. To counter this threat Graham in 1766 sent six men on separate inland expeditions to investigate and block Canadian penetration along the river routes leading down to the bay; but by the time he returned to York five years later it was clear this strategy had failed. In 1772 on the advice of John Cole*, a deserter from the Canadians, not only did he order Matthew Cocking* inland on the most ambitious journey by a company servant since Anthony Henday*'s explorations, but in August he also sent a crucial memorandum together with a map to the London committee arguing that a permanent inland post should be established at Basquia (The Pas, Man.), possibly with Samuel Hearne* in command. It was this plan that the committee, long since worried about the company's deteriorating position in the bay, accepted the next year; and in 1774 Hearne, after discussing the project with Graham at Churchill, left for the Saskatchewan River to set up a post. This action marked a radical departure from the company's traditional practice of drawing the Indians down to the bay to trade.

Graham's family life was a complicated one. He had married Patricia Sherer in Edinburgh on 6 May 1770; he had at least two mixed-blood children in Hudson Bay, both of whom seem to have joined him in Scotland after his retirement; and at some stage he married Barbara Bowie. During his retirement Graham kept in touch with the London committee and with former colleagues in Hudson Bay, who even long after he formally retired sent him information concerning, for example, the raids on Prince of Wales's Fort and York conducted by the French under Jean-François de Galaup*, Comte de Lapérouse, in 1782. He continued revising and recopying his "Observations" until the last known version of 1791; and the next year he sent his remaining journals, together with some maps, to the company in London. Despite an appeal in 1801 for financial help, which the London committee answered with the award of an annual gratuity, Graham died, as his will indicates, a man of some substance – though one whose contribution to Europe's knowledge of the Canadian north seems to have been totally forgotten long before his death.

GLYNDWR WILLIAMS

[Ten volumes of Andrew Graham's manuscript "Observations on Hudson's Bay: twenty-five years in the company's service, fifteen years chief factor at Severn, York and Churchill settlements," dated between 1767 and 1791, are in PAM, HBCA, E.2/4–13; a slimmer manuscript, "Remarks on Hudson's Bay trade . . . 1769," is in the Huntington Library (San Marino, Calif.), HM 1720. Annotated selec-

tions from these documents, including the important memorandum of 26 Aug. 1772 from Graham to the London committee, together with a biographical sketch of Graham and a full analysis by Richard Glover of Graham as a naturalist, are contained in HBRS, vol.27 (Williams). A profusion of other documentary material on Graham also exists in PAM, HBCA: notably his York Factory journals for 1765–66 and 1771–72 (B.239/a/56, 66), the York Factory correspondence book for this period (A.11/115), his Severn House journals (B.198/a), and his journal at Churchill for 1774–75 (B.42/a/42). G.W.]

GRANT, ALEXANDER, army officer, businessman, office holder, and politician; b. 20 May 1734 in Glenmoriston, Scotland, son of Patrick Grant and Isobel Grant; m. 30 Sept. 1774 Thérèse Barthe, and they had 11 daughters and 1 son; d. 8 May 1813 in Castle Grant, his residence at Grosse Point (Grosse Point Farms), Mich.

Alexander Grant claimed to have been "in the very early part of his Life bread to the sea." Before accepting an ensigncy in the newly raised 77th Foot (Montgomery's Highlanders) on 4 Jan. 1757 he seems to have entered the Royal Navy in 1755 and served as a midshipman. His regiment was in North America in 1758 and the following year saw service on Lake Champlain with Major-General Jeffery Amherst*'s army. Captain Joshua Loring*, Amherst's naval assistant, had been charged with the construction of a flotilla to wrest naval control of the lake from the French, and when on 11 Oct. 1759 the *Boscawen*, a 16-gun sloop, was ready for action, Grant was given command. In the only engagement of any consequence, Loring forced Jean d'OLABARATZ to abandon his ships. Grant remained on the lake for the duration of the Seven Years' War. In 1760 he assumed command of the vessels and naval station at Fort Ticonderoga (N.Y.), where he performed his duties to Amherst's satisfaction. He went on half pay in 1763 but remained connected with the naval establishment. When Loring retired (possibly the same year), Grant, according to his own account, succeeded him; exactly what position the two men held is not clear.

Initially Grant's headquarters were located at the dockyard on Navy Island in the Niagara River. At some point no later than 1771, the naval department was moved to Detroit (Mich.), where Grant had had some connection as early as September 1764. He spent winters in New York City until 1774, when he took up permanent residence in Detroit, probably as a result of his marriage that year to Thérèse Barthe. His duties as naval superintendent included management of the dockyards, construction and repair of vessels, deployment of ships, purchase of materials, and transportation of stores, including private merchandise. Because private shipping was almost nonexistent, commercial goods were allowed as cargo in the crown's ships.

Grant

The power to allocate this cargo space put Grant at the hub of the commercial network between Detroit and New York. Recognizing a golden opportunity, he began to build his own vessels, first at Navy Island, then at Detroit, for use on the lakes. In 1767 John Blackburn, the English merchant who had won the Treasury contract to man, victual, and repair the crown's vessels on the lakes, and his New York factor, Henry White, signed an agreement with Grant making him their local agent. After 1768 he consolidated his position by monopolizing all shipping on the lakes.

Naturally enough, favouritism shown by Grant in apportioning limited space met with antagonism. In 1769 James Sterling* and the Schenectady firm of Phyn, Ellice and Company built the sloop *Enterprise* at Detroit to transport their goods over Lake Erie; several months later they sold the ship to Grant. The following year they mounted a more effective challenge to Grant's empire by building the 45-ton sloop *Angelica*. Then in 1772 they erected a trans-shipment depot at Fort Erie (Ont.). The timing was propitious. During the summer of 1771 Grant suffered a financial setback, losing his new sloop *Beaver* and a second ship. One merchant reported that the losses "will Discourage the traders from Imploying his Vessell." The *Angelica* reaped the benefits of Grant's misfortune but he was determined to regain his hegemony. In return for an attractive package of rebates and preferential rates on Grant's ships, Detroit merchants agreed not to patronize his rivals. While the main battle raged for control of the lakes, a skirmish of a different sort broke out between Grant and Phyn, Ellice. This fight was occasioned by the breakdown of negotiations over freight charges on dry goods. Grant immediately ordered 100 hogsheads of rum to sell in competition with the Schenectady merchants in their northwest markets. So determined was he to undercut their retail business that he was willing to absorb a significant loss. Moreover, he took further steps to interrupt the firm's cash flow by stalling movement of their goods over the Niagara portage until the close of the navigation season for winter. Rifts soon appeared among his competitors; Sterling, the first to capitulate, sold his shares in the *Angelica* to Grant. By December 1773 Phyn, Ellice also gave in and sold him the remaining shares. Once again he was master of the lakes.

Changes resulting from the outbreak of the American revolution solidified Grant's official position and initially strengthened his commercial empire. The restrictions on private shipping inaugurated in 1776 were followed by a complete ban the next year. Sir Guy CARLETON instructed the naval department to continue the practice of assisting the merchants when cargo space was available. But the war put a further burden on the already strained capacity of the naval establishment to handle the needs both of the military and the merchants. Out of necessity the crown turned to Grant. As a result, by 25 Aug. 1775 three of Grant's own vessels, the schooner *Hope*, the sloop *Angelica*, and the schooner *Faith*, were employed in the king's service on Lake Erie at a rent of £8 per month. By 1777 the *Caldwell* was being used on Lake Ontario at £12 monthly. That same year Grant received the naval command of lakes Ontario, Erie, Huron, and Michigan. In 1778 the naval department was divided into three separate commands, with Grant appointed to lakes Erie, Huron, and Michigan.

The complete dependence of merchants on Grant for shipping was a major source of frustration. In 1778 John ASKIN had to beg Grant's favour to make provision for his goods. On 5 Jan. 1780 the Detroit merchants petitioned Governor HALDIMAND regarding the losses and delays suffered from the prohibition of private shipping. Several months later Charles Grant, a Quebec merchant, noted in a report to the governor on the fur trade that, in connection with trade carried over lakes Ontario and Erie, "improper preferences have been given in transporting goods to Niagara and Detroit, by which means it is represented that the Trade of these countries has fallen into a few hands, to the great detriment of many honest men. . . ." The same year Grant sold "his Vessels on the Lakes" to the government; however, as late as 1784 there was still an amount of £893 sterling outstanding on the transaction. The military monopoly of shipping was broken in that year when the North West Company was allowed to build a vessel at Detroit; in 1787 private vessels were allowed on Lake Ontario and the following year the Upper Lakes were opened.

Expenditures by the Provincial Marine at Detroit were considerable. By the end of the revolutionary war Grant commanded an establishment of 77 naval personnel and 11 civilians. Substantial sums were expended on naval stores and victuals. In August 1778 Haldimand issued rules for drawing bills of expenses and furnishing vouchers. The following year, complaining that Grant's vouchers seemed "so irregular," he ordered an inquiry into his accounts because the "enormous expenses . . . oblige me to establish order there." That May he wrote John Schank*, the naval commander on Lake Ontario, that Grant could retain his command only if he behaved. For his part, on two occasions Grant called for an investigation into his general accounts, but Haldimand refused.

Grant's income both from his official positions and from commerce was altered significantly during the war. He had lost his half pay in 1776 and suffered a reduction in salary after the war. He had, of course, profited by the rental and subsequent sale of his ships, but the sale also seems to have brought his participation in private shipping to an end. Moreover, he had lost 12,000 acres of land in New York which he valued at £6,000, New York currency. Thus he petitioned in 1784 for a "permanent subsistence . . . adequate to his long service" and sought confirmation of a land grant given him by the Indians.

Grant soon rose to a position of civil pre-eminence. His first appointment was justice of the peace on 3 Jan. 1786 and he was reappointed continuously until his death. When in 1788 western Quebec was divided into administrative districts, he was named to the land board of the Hesse District. In 1790 Sir John Johnson* recommended him for the executive council of the proposed province of Upper Canada. Two years later, at Lieutenant Governor SIMCOE's request, Grant, "at once to be stamped with eminence and respectability of his professional situation," was one of the five councillors appointed that year. Along with the other two executive councillors from Detroit, James Baby* and William ROBERTSON, he was also named to the Legislative Council. Although, as Administrator Peter RUSSELL later reported, distance and official duties often kept Grant from attending meetings of the councils, the very fact of the appointments testified to his stature in the province.

Grant also collected a host of regional offices. He was named to the first Heir and Devisee Commission for the Western District on 30 June 1798 and received his last appointment on 9 March 1812. In January 1799 Grant, Baby, and Thomas MCKEE were collectively entrusted with the office of deputy superintendent general of Indian affairs upon the death of Alexander McKee*. Two months later the temporary commission was withdrawn when William Claus* acceded to the post. Alexander McKee's demise brought Grant another reward, the appointment as lieutenant of the county of Essex on 23 Aug. 1799.

The greater part of Grant's time and energy was devoted to the marine, an important concern for it gave the British control of the lakes and secured the supply of the western posts. Although aware of this fact, historians have stressed the marine's inadequacies, particularly the incompetence of some personnel and the decrepitude of the ships. In testimony given before the Legislative Council of Quebec in 1788, Robertson complained that with one exception "the king's Vessels . . . are mostly unfit for Service without a thorough repair." Simcoe recognized the problem and how necessary it would be to increase and upgrade the marine forces in the event of hostilities with the United States, but nothing was done. He claimed that Grant was "fully conpetent to his technical trust and worthy of confidence." Yet it is clear that the commodore was not without his faults. He lacked, for example, initiative in professional matters. When in 1794 Simcoe was concerned about a chronic shortage of men in the marine, Grant replied with blithe reassurances which simply ignored the seriousness of the situation. The matter was finally resolved only by

the intervention of the commandant of Detroit, Richard G. ENGLAND. Grant's difficulties with the marine accounts recurred again and again. On 14 Oct. 1797 he was reprimanded for making expenditures without proper authority; in June 1801 Lieutenant Governor Peter HUNTER expressed his concern that considerable sums had been expended on ship repairs without prior submission of estimates.

The unexpected death of Hunter in August 1805 thrust the administration of the province on Grant. A meeting of the Executive Council was convened by Russell on 7 September; it was decided by the members present – Russell, Æneas SHAW, and John McGill*, one of Hunter's principal advisers – that Grant, as the senior councillor, should be asked to come to York (Toronto) immediately. He arrived in the capital on the 10th and assumed the office of administrator the following day. Russell, a previous administrator, who had gone along with the council's decision on the 7th, began the next day to assert his claim to precedence. He even made a case for his own seniority (although in 1799 when he had tried to assert his entitlement to the presidency of the council, he had allowed that others were senior to him). Grant suggested to his friend John Askin that Russell's machinations resulted from the "advice of a new Comer, and a Country Gentleman of yours high in the law Department here" – an allusion to judge Robert Thorpe*. Grant's appointment elicited harsh criticism from Thorpe who regarded him as old and inefficient, the servile tool of Hunter's "Scotch instruments," such as McGill. As Thorpe put it, "the system of the last Government was extortion and oppression . . . the desire of the present was to continue it. . . ."

Whatever may be said about Thorpe's analysis, it was true that Grant continued in the Hunter line. Grant had been uneasy after assuming office but, "with the assistance of two very honourable men perfectly know'n the intention and secrets of our worthy late Lieut Governor, regarding the business of this province," he quickly acquired a measure of equanimity. McGill and Thomas Scott*, among Hunter's main lieutenants, became the chief courtiers of Grant's administration. On Grant's behalf, however, it may be said that there was a certain amount of reasonableness to his chosen course. Privately he explained to Lord Castlereagh that he did not "feel myself at Liberty, in my Temporary situation to discontinue what he [Hunter] had authorized." As to the role of Scott and McGill, their influence derived from their abilities and familiarity with executive government under Hunter. Grant was his own man and on occasion deviated from his predecessor. But his immediate concern was continuity and he had few office holders to pick from as advisers. Shaw left his farm for meetings of council only. Russell felt aggrieved and besides he had not been in Hunter's circle. Judge William Dummer

Grant

Powell* might have been a possibility, but he too had been an outsider under Hunter.

At York, Grant lived with William Allan*, a local merchant, rather than stay at the official residence. The initial anxiety to do well soon passed and he became "perfectly easy in my mind, which I was not at first. . . ." It seemed that his personal contentment reflected the state of provincial society: "All seems to be satisfied, with matters gone on queitly." This apparent quietude in the body politic was not long lasting. On 4 Feb. 1806 Grant opened the legislature. Several weeks later he reported that the "house of Commons do's nothing but vomiting grievance and Complaints Against the Administration of General Hunter and plaguing me, and his favoureds." He pointed to Thorpe and William WEEKES as the "fomenters of all the disorder amongest the Commons." In private correspondence Thorpe complained that the "expence of the useless Marine . . . is enormous . . . the President [Grant] is now building a Ship for his son in law that will cost three thousand pounds." Grant had, in fact, ordered the construction of a new provincial yacht at Amherstburg but whether for the purpose suggested by his critic is not known.

Grant's only major departure from Hunter's administration was one of style, not policy. As he put it, "Tho my late good worthy predesessor was Sensible & Clever, he latterly dealt very harse with most of the people that had any business with him." Grant's manner was conciliatory. In October 1805 he had written the Colonial secretary, the Earl of Camden, that the bill for granting land to aliens stood little chance of passing "from almost the universal prejudice . . . against Aliens of every description becoming settlers." When the bill was overwhelmingly defeated in the house, Grant sensibly let it lie. Led by Weekes, the assembly urged executive action against some of Hunter's more contentious reforms, such as the restrictions on loyalist and military land claimants and the revised table of fees for land grants. On the latter issue, Grant held firm, but with the former he promised to investigate and, in the end, issued proclamations restoring the lost privileges.

One particular item stands out in the business of the legislative session. Weekes's committee on public accounts asserted that £617 13s. 7d. had been spent by Hunter without prior authorization by the assembly. He had, in fact, carried on this practice since 1803 without arousing complaint. Citing Hunter's action as a violation of its "first and most constitutional privilege," the house urged that the money be restored to the provincial treasury. When it brought the matter to his attention, Grant reported that he could find no authority for such an appropriation by the governor and had the funds restored.

Grant did nothing to exacerbate political ill feeling and he did, in a brief period, a good deal to remove some of its sources. After the legislature was prorogued, he missed the excitement of the political arena. He urged one correspondent to send "Something to Enliven us it's cursed dull since the sessions is over." Indeed, it was so dull that he decided to take a trip to Niagara (Niagara-on-the-Lake) and Queenston for a few days. The remaining months of his administration proved relatively quiet; he was succeeded on 25 Aug. 1806 by the new lieutenant governor, Francis Gore*.

Although he was still one of the targets of Weekes's railing at the fall assizes at Niagara in 1806, old age was taking its toll and his participation in public affairs was rapidly declining. In 1807 Gore, apparently acting on the assumption that Grant wished to be relieved, appointed François Baby* to succeed him as county lieutenant. The old man was gracious and thanked the lieutenant governor for his consideration "in easing me from the great Fatigues and trouble attendant on the situation." When he found out that he had acted in error, Gore issued a new commission for Grant on 17 December. Grant remained good-natured about the affair and wrote that, "Mrs Grant was so glad at my being Superseded . . . I suppose she will be displeased now." He rarely attended council, pleading by way of explanation "my advanced age – and infirmities." In January 1812 a report on the state of the marine by Captain Andrew Gray bluntly recommended that Grant be superannuated on the grounds that "he cannot be of any service; but may possibly do harm, by standing in the way of others." He retired on 30 March of that year and was replaced by George Benson Hall*.

The most vivid depictions of Grant emanated from the pen of George Thomas Landmann*, a British military engineer. He commented on Grant's "round, plump, pocked-marked face as red as a pomegranate" and described him as "an old Scotchman, a large stout man, not very polished, but very good-tempered, [who] had a great many daughters, all very good-looking, all very lively, all very fond of dancing, and all very willing to get married as soon as possible." Certainly, Grant lacked polish. He was only semi-literate and totally without pretence. According to an anecdote often related by his contemporaries, on being introduced to Prince EDWARD AUGUSTUS, Grant unabashedly exclaimed, "How do you do, Mester Prince? How does yer Papaw do?"

While Grant was administrator Askin wrote him: "I think you would rather be with them [his family] than siting in state. Your not one of those men who prefers honors to Family comforts." At the centre of Grant's world were his wife and children, and their farm at Grosse Point. It was, in his words, "a very fine farm of excellent land with a good Mansion House & all other buildings – fine garden & a large orchard." Except when required elsewhere on official business, he spent all his time there. Indeed, even after Detroit was transferred to the Americans in 1796 and naval headquarters moved to Amherstburg, he continued to reside on the farm. Its operation was superintended by his beloved wife, twenty-four years his junior. When they married she spoke no English and he no French. The predicament caused him to send to New York City for a dictionary but did not prove an obstacle to their relationship. They had 12 children and he clearly was in love with her all their life together. She was at "the helme" of the family and would never quit her post, causing Grant to comment that even his adopted son, John, "who is much interested and alert, cannot do any thing without consulting Mr^s Grant except kissing his Wife." Grant, when he was away, urged close friends such as Askin to try to get her away from the farm for a few days but apparently their efforts were rarely successful. Late in 1805 Grant was so relieved by Askin's account of an improvement in her health "that I feel myself growing quite hearty and well danced fifteen couple down the other night." He was equally glad to hear that Askin planned to invite her to his house for a visit "as you and her talks now and then la la la, which makes the old lady shake her sides." After her death on 11 Nov. 1810, Grant wrote his brother that she was "as good a mother and as kind a wife [as] perhaps ever was." Grant himself died at his residence in 1813 and was buried at Sandwich (Windsor), Upper Canada.

In collaboration with CAROL WHITFIELD

AO, MS 75; MS 497, Alexander Grant, draft of memorial, 17 June 1786; copy of letter, Grant to Alpine Grant, 15 July 1811. BL, Add. MSS 21735/2: f.555; 21783: f.405; 21876: ff.135–37. Clements Library, Thomas Gage papers, American ser., 44: Alexander Grant to Gage, 11 Oct. 1765; 59: Grant, report of vessels at Niagara, 16 Nov. 1766; 79: Grant to John Brown, 2 Aug. 1768; 84: bill of Henry White to Grant, 8 April 1769; 93: Grant to Gage, 21 July 1770; 119: Grant to White, with bill, 27 April 1774. PAC, MG 23, HI, 3, vol.10: 20; RG 5, A1: 2668, 5183; RG 8, I (C ser.), 722A: 36–37, 70, 94–95; 723: 8, 40, 42–43, 111, 115, 164; 725: 3, 13, 32, 36–37, 39–43, 62, 191; 726: 9, 24, 38, 41, 48, 73, 81, 116, 139, 215, 217; 727: 15, 22–23, 40; 728: 23, 36, 84–85; RG 68, General index, 1651–1841: ff.249–52, 287, 310, 325, 403, 406, 409, 412, 419, 422–23, 542, 630. PRO, CO 42/339: ff.163, 167–68; 42/340: ff.3, 5–6, 9, 17, 340; 42/342: ff.35, 43, 88, 108, 110, 146–48; WO 17/1489: ff.12, 15–16, 18–19, 23–32; WO 34/50: ff.35, 37, 50, 54, 61, 63, 83, 86–88, 140–41, 144–46, 196, 201, 207, 209, 216, 259; 34/64: 168, 220, 224; 34/65: 15, 40–41, 109, 111, 137, 166. QUA, Richard Cartwright papers, letterbook (transcript at AO).

"Board of land office, District of Hesse," AO *Report*, 1905: 1–268. *Corr. of Hon. Peter Russell* (Cruikshank and Hunter). *Corr. of Lieut. Governor Simcoe* (Cruikshank). *John Askin papers* (Quaife). *Johnson papers* (Sullivan et al.), 4: 540; 8: 105–6, 223–24; 10: 130–31. "Journals of Legislative Assembly of U.C.," AO *Report*, 1911: 57–116. Knox, *Hist. journal* (Doughty), 2: 195–96; 3: 56–57, 61–64, 72, 74. Landmann, *Adventures and recollections*, 1: 10–12. *Mich. Pioneer Coll.*, 11 (1887): 640–41, 647; 17 (1890): 604; 19 (1891): 32, 304–5, 312–13, 336, 343, 346, 366, 368, 431, 433, 436, 450, 492–93, 495, 502, 507, 520, 555–56, 559, 592–93, 601–2, 626, 644, 649, 653, 659, 664, 667; 20 (1892): 1–2, 5–6, 8, 88–89, 158, 237, 256–57, 307–8, 669–70; 23 (1893): 186, 264, 268–69, 342, 347, 353–54; 24 (1894): 6; 25 (1894): 25, 148, 151, 153, 191, 194–95, 201, 221–22, 229. "The north west trade," PAC *Report*, 1888: 59–62. "Ordinances made for the province of Quebec by the governor and Council of the said province, from 1768 until 1791 . . . ," PAC *Report*, 1914–15, app.C: 205–11. "Petitions for grants of land" (Cruikshank), *OH*, 24: 71–72; 26: 195–96. "Political state of U.C.," PAC *Report*, 1892: 32–37, 40–41, 46–47. "The probated wills of persons prominent in the public affairs of early Upper Canada: second collection," ed. A. F. Hunter, *OH*, 24 (1927): 383–85. *Select British docs. of War of 1812* (Wood), 1: 248–58, 288–89. *Town of York, 1793–1815* (Firth), 184, 259, 261, 263. *Windsor border region* (Lajeunesse), 65, 106, 158, 172, 176, 193, 210–12, 225. Wis., State Hist. Soc., *Coll.*, 11 (1888): 185–200.

Upper Canada Gazette, 21 Sept. 1805, 17 May 1806. Armstrong, *Handbook of Upper Canadian chronology*, 13, 33, 141. G.B., WO, *Army list*, 1759: 131; 1763: 138; 1784: 282. *Officers of British forces in Canada* (Irving). C. R. Canedy, "An entrepreneurial history of the New York frontier, 1739–1776" (PHD thesis, Case Western Reserve Univ., Cleveland, Ohio, 1967), 226, 231, 239–40, 243–44, 250, 337–47, 355. Craig, *Upper Canada*, 43, 58, 61. Creighton, *Commercial empire of St. Lawrence*, 71. E. A. Cruikshank, "The contest for the command of Lake Erie in 1812–13," *The defended border: Upper Canada and the War of 1812 . . .*, ed. Morris Zaslow and W. B. Turner (Toronto, 1964), 84–85. G. A. Cuthbertson, *Freshwater: a history and a narrative of the Great Lakes* (Toronto, 1931), 120, 283. D. R. Farrell, "Detroit, 1783–1796: the last stages of the British fur trade in the old northwest" (PHD thesis, Univ. of Western Ont., London, 1968), 94–95, 99, 110, 174, 244–46. Gates, *Land policies of U.C.*, 59, 74–77, 324. J. M. Hitsman, *Safeguarding Canada, 1763–1871* (Toronto, 1968), 57, 60–61. C. P. Stacey, "Another look at the battle of Lake Erie," *The defended border: Upper Canada and the War of 1812 . . .*, 105–7. W. S. Wallace, *The family compact: a chronicle of the rebellion in Upper Canada* (Toronto, 1915), 4–5, 10–11. Wilson, "Enterprises of Robert Hamilton," 60, 111–13, 141. W. A. B. Douglas, "The anatomy of naval incompetence: the Provincial Marine in defence of Upper Canada before 1813," *OH*, 71 (1979): 3–25. R. H. Fleming, "Phyn, Ellice and Company of Schenectady," *Contributions to Canadian Economics* (Toronto), 4 (1932): 13–16. "The king's shipyard," *Burton Hist. Coll. Leaflet* (Detroit), 2 (1923–24): 18–32. G. F. Macdonald, "Commodore Alexander Grant (1734–1813)," *OH*, 22 (1925): 167–81. M. M. Quaife, "Detroit biographies: Commodore Alexander Grant," *Burton Hist. Coll. Leaflet*, 6 (1927–28): 65–80.

GRANT, WILLIAM, merchant, seigneur, office holder, and politician; b. 15 June 1744 in Blairfindy, Scotland, son of William Grant and Jean Tyrie; d. 5 Oct. 1805 at Quebec, Lower Canada.

Grant

William Grant, the son of the laird of Blairfindy, a Jacobite in the Scottish uprising of 1745, was one of at least three brothers to enter the British overseas trade. A bright lad, possessed of a liberal education, he was engaged about 1756 by Robert Grant, a kinsman from the valley of the River Spey, Scotland, and the agent in Halifax, N.S., of naval supply contractors based in London, England; Robert soon formed his own firm in London. In the fall of 1759, having secured a contract to supply the navy at Quebec, he sent William, who was only 15 but fluent in French, to the province of Quebec as agent for his company, Alexander, Robert, and William Grant. Indeed, Scottish firms were prominently represented among the merchants drawn to the colony, which, as a result of the conquest, entered a period of significant change in entrepreneurial control and metropolitan alignment.

Grant quickly established agencies at Quebec and Montreal for his kinsman's firm. In 1763 he entered into partnership at Quebec with two other agents of the company, Peter Stuart and John Gray, and, in a context of economic instability, aggressively pursued various speculative opportunities. Among them were the supply of merchandise and the lending of capital to French and Canadian merchants obliged to rebuild their businesses. In September and October 1764, for example, he lent £750 to two Quebec merchants, most of which was drawn from the Grant firm. Like many other merchants, he also engaged in the fur trade. In September 1761 he associated with James Stanley Goddard and Forrest Oakes* to conduct the trade at Michilimackinac (Mackinaw City, Mich.). Four years later he acquired exclusive trading rights at that place and Baie-des-Puants (Green Bay, Wis.) from Pierre de Rigaud* de Vaudreuil de Cavagnial. The nominal sale price was 160,000 livres, but Grant never paid it all; as a result of pressure from officials in the British Indian Department and rival traders, the purchase was voided in 1767. Another rival group of merchants, including the turbulent George ALLSOPP, was unsuccessful, however, in attempting to have declared void a lease granted in 1762 by James Murray* to Thomas DUNN and John Gray (in which Grant soon became a co-lessee) to conduct the fur trade at the government-controlled king's posts on the lower St Lawrence River. It was possibly through this involvement that Grant became interested from about 1764 in the lucrative seal and salmon fisheries in the same region, where he exploited two posts in the Île Saint-Augustin with Jacques Perrault*, known as Perrault l'aîné. In 1766 he purchased from Dunn one-third of the seigneury of Mille-Vaches, also on the lower St Lawrence.

Considerable risk was involved in Grant's exploits related to his speculation in the colony's French paper currency between 1761 and 1770 [see James Murray]. Among the agents he used in France for conducting this and other business were Thomas-Marie Cugnet, former Quebec agent for the Compagnie des Indes, and Louis Charly* Saint-Ange, a Montreal merchant, both of whom returned to France in 1764 when Grant submitted a claim for 279,350 livres. Grant himself left for Britain and France in November to sell a vessel for John Gray, order goods from the proceeds, and probably to promote redemption by the French government of paper money. While at Bordeaux, perhaps motivated by spiralling debt, Grant let himself be persuaded by Irish merchants to use the ship instead to smuggle wine into the colony through his establishments in Labrador, that coast being a well-used contraband route. The ship was wrecked off the Strait of Belle Isle, however, with heavy loss to Grant. Following his return to Quebec he became involved in the wheat and flour trade; Samuel Jacobs*, a merchant from Saint-Denis, on the Rivière Richelieu, was one of his major suppliers of grain from about 1766.

Grant's principal business activity in the 1760s was probably the acquisition of landed property, including some of the largest houses in Quebec and Montreal. Owners who had left the colony for France following the conquest had been given 18 months from the signing of the Treaty of Paris to dispose of their property and, operating in such a buyer's market, Grant invested heavily. On 22 Oct. 1763 he purchased from Étienne Charest* for 30,000 livres a lot and stone house on Rue Saint-Pierre at Quebec, to which he soon added the neighbouring property; on them he constructed an important wharf, which eventually became known as the Queen's Wharf. In 1765 he and John Grant (possibly his brother) obtained the concession of a beach lot also on Rue Saint-Pierre. About the same time Grant purchased for 22,500 livres from Joseph-Michel Cadet* another lot on the same street; in June 1769 he sold a house and one-third of the lot for 30,000 livres. As well as concentrating on the commercial thoroughfare of Rue Saint-Pierre, with its frontage on the St Lawrence River, Grant looked to the faubourg Saint-Roch as a long-term investment, since it seemed destined to receive the overflow of population from the old city. On 29 Sept. 1764 he purchased from Marie-Josephte-Madeleine Hiché, for 250,000 livres, all of her property at Quebec, consisting principally of the faubourg Saint-Roch, formerly belonging to her father, Henry Hiché*. Probably aware that development of the land would be slow, Grant, undoubtedly with the complicity of some local notaries and government officials, elevated what had been a simple roture to the rank of fief, and took the title of seigneur of Saint-Roch. He thus demonstrated a practical knowledge of the seigneurial system: the concession of lots with cens et rentes, and especially lods et ventes, would ultimately be more profitable to him through the rents and taxes they would bring than the sale of parcels of land in free and common soccage. At the same time the arrangement would give him a stronger hold over the inhabitants of the *faubourg* and a freer hand in its development. In 1766 he added to his holdings in Saint-Roch a large lot bought from François Mounier* and Jean (John) Marteilhe. In June 1769 he acquired the former residence of Lieutenant-General Louis-Joseph de Montcalm* in Upper Town on Rue des Remparts. In the Montreal area he had bought on 16 Aug. 1764 for 100,000 *livres* all the Canadian possessions of Charly Saint-Ange; two days later he purchased the Château Ramezay for 275,000 *livres*. At least some of Grant's major purchases were to have been made in payment orders, with payment deferred over a specified period of time, during which the orders diminished in value.

Seigneuries also being available at low cost, Grant showed an early and constant interest in them. In September 1764 he purchased from François-Joseph de Vienne* for 30,000 *livres* the sub-fief of La Mistanguienne or Montplaisir, and in July 1768 he acquired the seigneury of Aubert-Gallion near Quebec for £100. Grant capped his early drive for the acquisition of seigneuries by marrying Marie-Anne-Catherine Fleury Deschambault, widow of the seigneur Charles-Jacques Le Moyne de Longueuil; having declared himself to be a Catholic, Grant was married secretly at Montreal by the Jesuit Pierre-René Floquet*, with special dispensation from Governor CARLETON, and publicly on 11 Sept. 1770 by the Church of England minister David Chabrand* Delisle. The union placed at Grant's disposal at least some of the Longueuil seigneurial resources, notably Mingan, and a farm on Île Sainte-Hélène, near Montreal.

By 1766, sustained by London credit, Grant was probably one of the leading British merchants at Quebec. His expenditures had brought him heavily into debt, but he received liberal extensions from the firm of Alexander, Robert, and William Grant toward an account evaluated at over £80,000 in 1768, a year after the London firm's dissolution. With "great dexterity and cleverness," he held out on any debt settlement and gained a notorious reputation in the mercantile community for his skilful manipulation of finances and commodity supply. In November 1767 Robert Grant had complained to an acquaintance that his firm's Quebec debtors, and "particularly William Grant," paid "less attention to their words characters and credit than the worst thief you ever knew in the Highlands of Scotland." By 1772 Samuel Jacobs was also frustrated by Grant's methods. "You promise and then think no more of it," he charged. After the breakup of the Grant firm, William retained or reorganized his associations with clansmen at Quebec, Montreal, and London, and he eventually became a senior member of his "Family" in the colony.

Grant regarded politics as a legitimate forum for promoting commercial improvements, and had no more doubt of his political than of his commercial abilities. In 1764, having declared himself a Protestant in order not to be excluded from political office, he asked his London associates to lobby for his appointment to the governing Council of Quebec, but Murray, who had a low opinion of merchants in the colony generally, warned the home government against this "conceited boy." In 1767 Grant earned the animosity of a large part of the merchant community by having printed in the *Quebec Gazette* an opinion of Attorney General Francis Maseres* on bankruptcy laws that gave concern to many creditors [*see* George Suckling*]. Grant was initially wary of such irascible critics of military rule as Allsopp. But by 1768 Grant's "friends" were reportedly among the "wrong-headed small party," composed mainly of merchants, "who are resolved to oppose the Govt," and he supported demands for the repeal of the Quebec Act as an imperfect constitution, for representative government, and for the introduction of English commercial law (a difficult area since English mercantile law had not been codified). His youth and personal reputation hindered him, however, from aspiring to leadership until his marriage, by allying him with some of the oldest and most respectable families in the colony, gave him a proper social base. In 1773 he was elected by the merchants of Quebec to a committee to spearhead constitutional reform.

In business in the 1770s Grant consolidated his position in the Gulf region by purchasing the claims of some of the numerous co-seigneurs of Mingan and by leasing fishing and sealing rights from those who would not sell. Yet Grant and his partners, Dunn and Peter Stuart, had difficulty exploiting their holdings until 1774 when Labrador was returned to the jurisdiction of Quebec from that of Newfoundland. Like their predecessor Hugh Palliser*, governors John Byron* and Molyneux Shuldham* of Newfoundland wished to promote the ship fishery on the Labrador coast as a nursery for British seamen. Consequently, they ignored the title claims of the colonial proprietors, who annually saw their sealing grounds invaded by British ship fishers and colonial interlopers profiting from the lack of enforcement of property rights. At Quebec, Grant reclaimed lots in Saint-Roch from indebted holders, and in September 1772 he announced the completion in the *faubourg* of a new wind-operated grist-mill. He also speculated in land at La Canardière, and on 25 Aug. 1774 he sold to Ralph GRAY for £1,500 the sub-fief of La Mistanguienne, by then known as Grandpré. Shortly before he had sold the Montcalm house to Allsopp.

In 1775, during the American revolution, Grant's

Grant

economic aspirations were confronted by the threat of invasion and the spectre of ruin. "Determined to stand or fall with the King's Govrnmt," Grant joined the militia of "undisciplin'd citizens" raised to defend Quebec and openly denounced the rebels: "the best & shortest way" of trying American prisoners, he proclaimed in September, "would be to shute them at once." Britain should either give in to the rebellion or "pursue it with all her vigour." "Government from its Supremacy is become despicable," he candidly admitted. Beneath his bravado, however, lay anxiety, commercial apprehension, and frustration with the neutrality of the Canadians. Having moved from his "manor" at Saint-Roch to lodgings in Upper Town, both for security and in order to join in the defence of the city, on 15 November Grant dictated his will, leaving one-third of his estate to his wife and the remaining two-thirds to his relatives. His properties suffered heavily from American depredations in the winter of 1775–76. Many of his buildings were destroyed at Quebec and at Saint-Roch, where his house, after having been a "hornet's nest" of skirmishing and shelling, was burned by the British for defensive purposes. He also lost a vessel destined for Boston with relief supplies, as well as several fishing posts, destroyed in retaliation for his razing of American stations and for his widely known anti-American sentiments.

Grant's financial base, however, remained intact, and after the departure of the Americans, and perhaps a period of reconstruction, he renewed his property speculation and development. In October 1778 he bought a lot with a grist-mill and a sawmill at Cap-Santé near Quebec for 5,000 *livres*, selling it two years later for 7,200 *livres*. At Quebec in 1781 he acquired land around the Coteau Sainte-Geneviève in the *faubourg* Saint-Jean and two lots on Rue du Sault-au-Matelot, and sold a lot and stone house on Rue Saint-Pierre to Jean-Baptiste-Amable Durocher for 22,700 *livres*. At Montreal, after having rented the Château Ramezay to the government since 1773, in August 1778 Grant sold it for 2,000 guineas to Governor HALDIMAND for its continued use by the government. In 1779 he bought the seigneury of Beaulac and part of that of Chambly. Two years later he sold a share in the seigneury of Jolliet, probably acquired by marriage, to his wife's relative Gabriel-Elzéar TASCHEREAU, with whom he had conducted business on several occasions.

Between 1779 and 1786 Grant strengthened his position in the lower St Lawrence by buying out several more of the co-seigneurs of Mingan and acquiring a share in the seigneury of Île-d'Anticosti. By 1783 he, Dunn, and Adam* and Mathew Lymburner also dominated sealing along the Labrador coast from Petit Mécatina to beyond Blanc-Sablon. Nevertheless, Grant's fishing operations failed at least

twice in the 1780s. At the same time he was expanding his milling facilities. In 1778 and 1779 he had begun constructing grist-mills at various locations, including Saint-Roch, the seigneury of Belœil, and Île Sainte-Hélène, from where David Alexander Grant, a son of his elder brother David, supervised his uncle's milling, shipbuilding, and seigneurial interests in the Montreal region. The substantial amounts of capital required for these activities were secured in part through loans; although in March 1780 Grant was able to lend £1,058 to John COFFIN, one year later he was obliged to borrow £4,076 from David Alexander Grant and in July 1784 £1,000 sterling from Attorney General James Monk*.

Grant's ostentatious loyalism in 1775–76 had borne fruit in 1777 when he was appointed to the Legislative Council. As well, through a business association with the absentee receiver general of Quebec, Sir Thomas Mills*, and the acting appointee at Quebec, Dunn, in April 1777 Grant was appointed by Mills deputy receiver general in Dunn's place. These appointments brought some financial stability to a fluctuating commercial career, but plunged Grant into political controversy. Responsible as deputy for the collection and custody of provincial funds, Grant inherited an inadequate system of revenue collection and soon encountered problems with provincial officials over accountability and fees. His efforts to improve the system were ineffective; his proposal in the council to enforce collection of property transfer taxes – the *quint* from the seigneurs and the *lods et ventes* from holders of urban lots – was rejected for fear of the reaction it would cause. These problems were in any case overshadowed by political agitation in council, where, by October 1780, Grant had established himself before Haldimand as a self-seeking opponent of such wartime measures as the regulation of wheat pricing and of the governor's postponement of war-loss claims (including Grant's) and administrative reform.

Following Allsopp's suspension from council in 1783, Grant became leader of the opposition to Haldimand's policies. In the tumultuous session of 1784, he pressed for the introduction into the province of the "Common and Statute Law of England," including habeas corpus, which had been suspended in 1774. Under the Quebec Act Canadians would remain subject to arbitrary government by council, he reasoned, and only the full extension of British rights would "secure and attach them to their King and Country – And render them beneficially and commercially useful to the present state." He also pressed for an elective assembly, declaring that he looked on "Representation and Freedom in Government as absolutely necessary Springs to give Vigour and Motion to the new Commercial Machine." On 22 April, however, at the height of his campaign, his proposal for an address by council requesting an "elective Grand Council," British commercial law, and optional trial by jury – "that bulwark of English security" – was defeated.

Behind Grant's presentments of 1784 seethed a confrontation with council and Haldimand over unauthorized fee claims Grant had made as deputy receiver general, irregularities in his accounts, and his resolve to claim war compensation from provincial funds. The receiver general's accounts being traditionally uncontrolled by regular audit, Grant refused to submit to provincial inspection or to demands for some £8,000 in revenue that he had reputedly retained. In August 1784 he was obliged to sail for London to settle his accounts before the Treasury. Haldimand, who had regarded his conduct toward Grant as "indulgent and moderate," nevertheless took the opportunity to name Henry CALDWELL as acting deputy receiver general rather than David Alexander Grant, William's nominee.

In London, operating from a circle of clansmen, Canadians, and sympathetic British merchants and politicians, Grant sought private contracts and lobbied, with others, for assembly government and for imperial trade regulations favouring merchants in the colony. In February 1785 he met William Smith*, a close associate of Sir Guy Carleton, and Smith listened sympathetically to Grant's presentation of the merchants' political position. He lent Smith, who hoped to be named chief justice of Quebec, several volumes on the laws of the colony. Along with Isaac TODD, Grant organized the London merchants trading to Canada in an effort to hasten the replacement of Haldimand by Carleton, who was more sympathetic to the merchants' political aspirations.

Haldimand's rapid replacement was important to Grant for personal reasons as well. He and Dunn, who was also in London, were anxious to renew their lease of the king's posts. Their hopes lay with the London merchant Brook WATSON, a friend of Carleton, while their rivals for the lease, George Davison* and his associates, counted on Haldimand, then also in England. "I find Mr. Grant has been using his influence among his Scotch friends to counteract your intentions as well as mine in favour of Davison," the permanent under-secretary, Evan Nepean, informed Haldimand. Carleton became governor, but Haldimand's influence ultimately prevailed in the matter of the king's posts, even though, thanks to Lieutenant Governor Henry Hamilton* at Quebec, Grant and his partners retained the posts until October 1786. They subsequently sued Davison and his associates for more than £10,000 in claimed improvements and equipment at the posts, but in 1791 they settled out of court for £1,800. As a result of Carleton's influence, however, no revenue charge was brought against Grant while he was in England.

Grant arrived back at Quebec in October 1786. He failed to oust Caldwell as deputy receiver general, and in the council yielded political leadership to Smith, now chief justice. However, encouraged by progress made during his absence, and occasionally advised by Allsopp, Grant resumed his strident demands for judicial and political reforms, venting his hatred of Adam Mabane* and the French party, which defended the Quebec Act, the existing judicial system, and the outmoded French mercantile code. Expert in both English and French laws, and experienced as a Court of Appeals judge (a function of legislative councillors), Grant was acutely aware of the merchants' principal complaints about the judicial system: the lack of a definite commercial code in the colony and inconsistency on the part of provincial judges in receiving evidence and rendering judgements. Grant himself had figured in two relevant judicial rulings – those of the British Privy Council in 1785 on St Ange v. Grant, and Smith on Alexander Gray v. Grant a year later – from which the chief justice prescribed the use of English law where both litigants were British. As a member of the council committee organized by Carleton (now Lord Dorchester) in 1786 to inquire into commerce and police regulations, Grant further politicized mercantile interests by eliciting from the merchants at Quebec, the most radical reform element in the province, a petition for English law. In April 1787, in part as a result of his incendiary rhetoric, "party rage" broke out over judicial reform. Dorchester was obliged to order a full-scale inquiry into the administration of justice. Grant testified that the courts frequently resorted to equity, especially in commercial cases, confirming the practical difficulties of applying English or French law. The inquiry nevertheless ended in confusion and impasse.

Grant continued to be preoccupied in council with the political articulation of the merchants' commercial aspirations. In 1789 he was appointed superintendent at Quebec of inland navigation, responsible, among other tasks, for the registry by owners residing there of vessels plying the Great Lakes. In 1790 and 1791 Grant's committee on commerce and police regulations inquired into inland navigation and produced a bill recommending that the fur trade be freed of many of the government restrictions that encumbered it. "Left to itself it will flourish and expand – Touch it, it decays or dies," he asserted. Among the restrictions that the bill recommended for abolition was that on the sale of rum to Indians; at the time Grant was proprietor of two of the colony's five distilleries, which, "owing to the difficulty of procuring molasses, shipping and other local and temporary inconveniences," according to the merchant community, were producing at only half capacity. The bill, which became law in 1791, swept away the system of regulatory fur-trade passes in operation since 1764. Grant also took a lively

Grant

interest in regulations bearing on fishing and the wheat and flour trade (in both of which he was still engaged) as well as those concerning piloting.

The late 1780s were difficult years for Grant. Not only did he lose the king's posts, but like others he was affected by a general depression and instability that had settled on the colony following the American revolution. Moreover, the collapse of the system of provincial financing, which began in 1782 and involved mercantile purchase of Treasury bills [see James DUNLOP], drew Grant, among others, perilously close to ruin. In February 1787 he contracted a major debt of £2,250 to Peter Stuart. By 1788, however, his seigneurial possessions were bringing in rents of £300 per annum. At Quebec he continued to accumulate land around the Coteau Sainte-Geneviève. In June 1791 he rented 23 Rue Saint-Pierre, with wharf and dependencies, to Fraser and Young [see John YOUNG]. In the Montreal area his interests were still administered by David Alexander Grant, and in February 1791 he sold a major portion of them to his nephew for £6,000. By August, when Grant was in a position to lend nearly £550 sterling, he seemed to have emerged from his most trying period of difficulty. In October he was paid £1,000 by the Montreal merchant William Maitland not to press claims to the estate of Maitland's deceased wife (and Grant's sister), Jane Elizabeth.

Having always been active in the merchants' political struggles, Grant was in the forefront when, in the late 1780s and early 1790s, new social institutions began to emerge at Quebec, often dominated by the merchants. In April 1789 he was among the 21 charter members of the Quebec Benevolent Society, founded to support members in need as a result of illness, old age, or other causes. Between 1789 and 1795 he was four times a trustee of the Quebec Library; he was a charter subscriber to the Agriculture Society in 1789 and a director in 1791 and 1793. In January and February 1792 he was the principal organizer and president of the Constitutional Club, reputedly composed of those 165 citizens of Quebec who had gathered at Franks' Tavern on 16 Dec. 1791 to celebrate the Constitutional Act. A debating society that met fortnightly, the club sought to promote knowledge of the British constitution and "diffuse . . . a spirit of Commercial and Agricultural industry." Recognizing the improving grasp by Canadians of British parliamentary authority, Grant carefully scheduled a discussion on "the rights of Canadian citizens" under the Quebec and Constitutional acts. On 26 Jan. 1792, in ostentatious display of his standing in the colony, Grant received to dinner at Bijoux, his country home near Quebec, Prince EDWARD AUGUSTUS, his suite, and Lieutenant Governor Alured Clarke*. In 1794 Grant was deputy grand master of the Moderns order of freemasons in Lower Canada.

Although Grant had taken an active interest in obtaining the new constitution, he was not reappointed to the Legislative Council. Determined to remain a political leader, however, in June 1792 he sought election in Upper Town Quebec to the first House of Assembly. With the energetic support of Charles-Louis TARIEU de Lanaudière, a long-time friend and vice-president of the Constitutional Club, and the merchants Mathew and John* Macnider, he was elected with Jean-Antoine PANET, largely on the support of artisans, eligible labourers, and Canadian and British businessmen. Thanking his English-speaking electors in the *Quebec Gazette*, Grant, never one to underestimate his own capacity, implored heaven to "enable me to do that which may be for the good of the EMPIRE and agreeable to your wishes"; the French text of his letter made no mention of the empire. Viewed as a potentially influential member of the assembly, he confidently lent other representatives his many volumes by John Locke, Sir William Blackstone, Baron Montesquieu, Voltaire, and others on political theory and constitutional law. In December 1792 Grant was proposed as speaker by James McGILL, one of his former clerks, on the strength of his bilingualism, his knowledge of constitutional law, and his experience in government. Objections were raised to Grant's nomination, ostensibly because his election had been contested by a defeated candidate, Allsopp, on the grounds of Grant's "having opened houses of entertainment. giving cockades etc. To the prejudice of a Free Choice." Grant then nominated McGill. The Canadian majority, however, unified by an emerging national awareness, preferred Panet. Allsopp's petition, signed by only 15 of the more than 600 voters, was rejected by the assembly in March 1793, but the defeat of Grant and McGill for the speakership was the first indication that the British merchants had been over sanguine in their expectation of dominating the assembly and using the power of taxation and control of tariffs to forge a new commercial environment in the colony.

In the first parliament, which lasted until 1796, Grant was very prominent, acting frequently in 1792–93 as spokesman for Chief Justice Smith, obtaining for fellow members the privileges accorded members of the British House of Commons, and proposing legislation. Most of his bills, however, including two to establish a system of welfare for the poor and another to promote parish schools, were defeated. He generally voted with the minority English party, favouring, among other measures, freehold tenure, public rather than church-controlled education, and the primacy of English as the legal record of assembly proceedings. But, as one of the most independent ministerial supporters he also voted against a proposal by John Richardson* to prevent the use of French in the legislative process, and effectively killed another by Thomas Coffin* that would have

372

taken from the Roman Catholic bishop of Quebec the exclusive right to divide Catholic parishes. In 1794, still distrustful of the colonial judges, Grant opposed a judicial reform bill "in the most artful way he could," according to a long-time antagonist, Attorney General Monk. Supported by Joseph Papineau* and others in the Canadian party, Grant sought vainly to have inserted in the bill a radical clause, initially Smith's invention, by which the proceedings of the proposed court of king's bench would conform completely to those of the English court in all cases in which the crown was a party. Re-elected in 1796, Grant supported the English party more consistently in the second parliament, siding with it in 17 of 21 votes. He did, however, vote for Panet as speaker in preference to John Young. In 1800 he was defeated in the elections for Upper Town by Augustin-Jérôme Raby*.

Commercially, in the prosperous 1790s Grant rebounded from his difficulties of the previous decade. His mills, bakeries, wharfs, timber-yards, and warehouses bustled; according to John Grant, a supply contractor at Halifax, N.S., his flour "was very well liked by the bakers." Grant continued to function as a wholesale importer, supplying merchants like Edward William GRAY of Montreal with goods ranging from Jamaican rum, sugar, and coffee to the varied cloths of John Hounsom, a linen-draper in London. With Adam Lymburner he operated a fleet of schooners to service their Labrador fisheries. The partners strengthened their position in that region even further by acquiring in 1792 from John Young a debt of £545 owed to him by rival traders Nathaniel and Philip Lloyd, along with Young's mortgage on the Lloyds' seigneury of Saint-Paul in Labrador; in 1796 they bought out more of the co-seigneurs of Mingan and Île-d'Anticosti. The following year Grant added to his seigneurial holdings that of Pierreville, acquired jointly with David Alexander Grant and Nicholas MONTOUR, and in March 1799 another share in the seigneury of Chambly. That year he divided the first two ranges of Aubert-Gallion into 118 lots for concession. In 1792 and 1793 he had acquired at Quebec, for £286, 17 of the 48 shares in the Dorchester Bridge over the Rivière Saint-Charles [see David LYND]. He also added to his holdings in and near the *faubourg* Saint-Jean, notably in 1796 and 1798 around the Coteau Sainte-Geneviève. On Chemin Sainte-Foy he acquired several lots and a house, called Upper Bijou House, which in 1797 he rented to the schoolmaster James TANSWELL, for seven years at £40 per annum. The following year he purchased from Pierre-Louis PANET a three-storey stone house on Rue Saint-Pierre, which was rented by Allsopp in 1799.

Grant's investment in Saint-Roch began to pay handsomely as the settlement of the *faubourg* expanded rapidly after 1795. Unfettered by city ordinances, since local justices of the peace had decided that they did not apply to Saint-Roch, Grant had a free hand in conceding lots and in laying out streets that he made only half the width of those in the city. In January 1797 he leased to his miller, George Miller, a large meadow lot with house, bake-house, barns, and two windmills for five years at an annual rate of £245. Just as the rhythm of Grant's concessions in Saint-Roch was accelerating, however, his subterfuge in having elevated his roture holding to a seigneury was brought to the attention of Attorney General Jonathan Sewell*, and in 1798 Grant was sued by the crown in a case that was to last for several years. The same year the Court of King's Bench ruled in a suit that Monk had launched on behalf of the Treasury in 1793 over irregularities in Grant's accounts as deputy receiver general; the court established crown priority in all cases against Grant. As well as legal vexations, Grant experienced continuing financial worries in the 1790s despite the recovery of many of his enterprises. In 1797 and 1798 he borrowed at least £1,365 from three creditors.

In 1801 the ever-enterprising merchant undertook the experimental cultivation of hemp, the British government having been persuaded that Lower Canada might become a secure supplier of the material, which was vital to the navy. In May 1802 Grant was appointed to the newly formed Board for the Encouragement of the Cultivation of Hemp. Yet it is doubtful that he was any more successful in this ill-fated enterprise than James CAMPBELL or Charles Frederick Grece* would be. In May 1801 he made his last seigneurial acquisition, that of Rivière-David, from Montour for £1,271. In 1800 he had been granted, according to the leader and associates system [see James CALDWELL], the patent on Grantham Township, comprising 27,000 acres; this acquisition was a blatant example of the rampant acquisitiveness of British merchants for lands in the Eastern Townships. Three years later he purchased several hundred acres in Barford, Granby, Milton, and Clifton townships. In 1803 Grant, Stuart, and Dunn leased to McTavish, Frobisher and Company for 19 years at £500 per annum their share of the fishing and sealing grounds in the seigneuries of Mingan and Île-d'Anticosti; Grant received half the rent. About this time his association with the firm of Lymburner and Crawford for fishing and sealing in the lower St Lawrence was running into difficulty. Lymburner and Crawford was forced into bankruptcy by mid May 1804, at which time Grant owed it nearly £11,000. That month their operations on the Labrador coast from Itamamiou (Étamaniou) to Bras d'Or (Brador) were advertised for auction by John JONES. Grant, however, bought Lymburner and Crawford's half of the enterprise for £4,750 on 19 Sept. 1804, and then, three days later, sold one-third of the operations to Charles William Grant*, eldest son of David Alexan-

Grant

der, for £3,166. In April, William paid £1,125 for Lymburner and Crawford's share in the seigneuries of Mingan and Saint-Paul. Meanwhile, having stood security for £11,700 of Lymburner and Crawford's debts, he had been obliged in December 1804 to pay £2,700 of them.

Grant's operations in the lower St Lawrence region, however expensive, seem not to have affected his property transactions at Quebec between 1800 and 1805. He acquired land along and north of the Grande Allée, just outside the city in Charlesbourg, and again around the Coteau Sainte-Geneviève and in Saint-Roch. In the last place he also reclaimed concessions for debt, and, the population continuing to grow rapidly, made new concessions and even sold land outright. In February 1803 he leased the Queen's Wharf to the merchant George Symes for seven years at £600 per annum, and two years later he rented a three-storey stone house on Rue Saint-Pierre to the auctioneering firm of Jones and White. Grant's overall transactions in this period nevertheless buried him deeper in debt. Between 1801 and 1803 he borrowed at least £955; in 1803 he owed Stuart and Dunn £1,315 for merchandise furnished on credit and was ordered by the Court of King's Bench to pay £777 to Charles Ward Apthorp of New York.

Since his electoral defeat in 1800 Grant had remained marginally active in politics. In 1802 he supported a petition for land on which to build a Presbyterian church at Quebec. From May to July 1805 he acted as adviser to the coadjutor bishop, Joseph-Octave Plessis*, in negotiations with Sewell and Lieutenant Governor Sir Robert Shore Milnes* to have recognized in law the title and position of the Roman Catholic bishop of Quebec. Grant had established good relations with the Roman Catholic hierarchy as a commissioner, since 1792, for the construction and repair of churches in the District of Quebec. In 1798 he had been an adviser to Plessis when the coadjutor had sought, unsuccessfully, to have legislation passed that would recognize in law the boundaries of existing and future Catholic parishes. In 1804 the irrepressible merchant was returned as representative for Upper Town in the assembly. In the first session, the following year, he voted seven times with, and four times against, the English party. His most notable breaking of the ranks occurred during a vote on a controversial bill to finance the construction of prisons at Quebec and Montreal through a tax on imports rather than on land. Merchant though he was, it was the landowner in Grant that dominated, and he was the only British member to vote for the bill. In 1805 the veteran office holder received his last appointment, that of deputy master at Trinity House of Quebec, organized that year for the supervisiond of navigation.

Since 1790 Grant had been gradually withdrawing from direct involvement in some business interests. He remained, none the less, an active man until his death on 5 Oct. 1805, of an "inflamation in his bowels, after a short illness," at his home on Rue des Pauvres (Côte du Palais). "None of those close to him dared call a priest, or speak in any way of religion to the sick man . . . ," Plessis wrote to Bishop Pierre DENAUT. "After his death, a Catholic burial was discussed, but Col. [Louis-Joseph de Fleury*] Deschambault refused to come and make the proposal to me, foreseeing that I would reject it." Grant was buried on 8 October from the Anglican Cathedral of the Holy Trinity.

William Grant had been an enigmatic man. Intelligent, shrewd, and visibly ambitious, he was known closely by only a few friends and relatives; to others he appeared an impetuous and often presumptuous character. In 1789 another British resident, Alexander Fraser, had given what would seem to be a just assessment of him: "Mr. Wm. Grant is a man of first rate Abilities thoroughly vers'd in the French Laws, and well informd in those of England, particularly such as relate to commercial business. . . . He has a readiness in discovering Men's Characters, & the talent of profiting by their foibles when he has any purpose to serve and his own thoughts are unfathomable, being a complete Master of every art of simulation or dissimulation, & possesses a shameless composure of temper and countenance that cannot be removed by reproach or abuse. – He is besides this a plausible and good Orator; quick with his Pen, and when requisite of indefatigable application." One of the most aggressive members of the British bourgeoisie at Quebec, Grant had married into the seigneurial nobility but never divested himself of his strong attachment to the mercantile group. He left for his executors, John Richardson, the powerful Montreal merchant who had married his niece, and Dunn, who soon renounced the responsibility, an enormous and tangled estate. Among Grant's possessions was an imposing and varied library of nearly 600 volumes, many of them on law and history. Debts owed Grant totalled at least £9,300, of which his associates in the Labrador fisheries owed nearly £9,000. His own debts totalled at least £23,700; more than £13,500 were directly related to the Labrador operations. Among the numerous large creditors was the London firm of Brickwood, Daniel and Company, possibly Grant's principal supplier. His estate was ordered in 1807 to pay £8,756 to the government, Grant having during his lifetime evaded reimbursement of the shortfall in his receiver general's accounts. In 1809 his estate was condemned to compensate the crown £9,729 for *lods et ventes* collected by Grant as "seigneur" of Saint-Roch. Richardson contested the latter judgement, but the ultimate resolution of the matter is unknown.

Grant's property holdings at the time of his death

were vast. He owned all of the seigneuries of Aubert-Gallion, Beaulac, and Rivière-David, one-half of those of Mingan and Île-d'Anticosti, one-third of Mille-Vaches, small fractions of Saint-Paul, Saint-Joseph-de-la-Nouvelle-Beauce, and Deschambault, and a total of 45,000 acres of land in Grantham, Granby, Milton, Clifton, and Barford townships. At Quebec he owned most of the *faubourg* Saint-Roch, as well as properties (many with stone houses on them) in the *faubourg* Saint-Jean and on Rue Saint-Pierre, Rue du Sault-au-Matelot, and Rue des Pauvres; he still held, too, his 17 shares in the Dorchester Bridge. All his possessions, however, were insufficient to cover his debts, and in 1807 his universal legatee, Charles William Grant, renounced his rights to the succession. Grant had left a lifetime annuity of £200 to his wife, who died in 1818. By 1811, in order to settle claims, Richardson had disposed of virtually the entire estate.

DAVID ROBERTS

A pencil sketch of William Grant was published in Gilbert Parker and C. G. Bryan, *Old Quebec: the fortress of New France* (Toronto, 1903), 221, in Gwillim, *Diary of Mrs. Simcoe* (Robertson), 98, and finally in F.[-J.] Audet and Édouard Fabre Surveyer, "William Grant," *La Presse* (Montréal), 7 mai 1927: 21, 24. According to John Ross Robertson*, an engraving at the PAC was the basis for the sketch but neither the sketch nor the engraving appears among its present holdings.

AAQ, 20 A, III: 149; 210 A, IV: f.196. ANQ-M, CE1-63, 11 Sept. 1770. ANQ-Q, CE1-61, 8 Oct. 1805; CN1-16, 2 févr., 19 mars, 2 avril, 15–17 juin 1805; 4 mars, 25 mai, 11, 18, 25 juin, 23, 25, 31 juill., 8 août, 2, 7 sept., 14, 31 oct. 1807; 27 avril 1808; 24 janv., août–décembre 1809; janvier, février, avril, mai 1810; 28 juill. 1813; CN1-25, 23 août 1775; 22 mai, 24 juill., 5 oct. 1778; 23 mars, 31 août 1780; 1er, 13, 28 févr., 22 mars, 3 avril, 5 mai, 6, 16 juill. 1781; 6 févr., 26 juin 1783; 16 févr., 1er, 17 avril, 26 mai, 29 juill., 2, 17 août, 14, 21 oct. 1784; CN1-83, 19, 20 déc. 1783; 6 oct., 30 déc. 1786; 16 févr., 24 avril, 19 mai, 14 juin, 5 juill., 28 déc. 1787; 12, 31 janv., 8, 14, 28 mai, 30 sept., 15, 16, 20 déc. 1788; 28–30 avril, 22, 28, 31 mai, 5 oct., 12 déc. 1789; 30 mars, 31 mai, 25 août, 14 oct., 20 déc. 1790; 26 janv., 10 févr., 13 mai, 20 août, 7 déc. 1791; 14 févr., 24, 31 mars, 7, 11 avril, 16 oct. 1792; 16 févr., 26 oct., 17 nov., 23 déc. 1793; 20 févr., 6, 15 sept., 28 oct. 1794; CN1-92, 1er, 27 oct., 5 nov. 1798; CN1-145, 29 avril, 4 mai 1802; 4 févr., 15 mai 1803; CN1-178, 12 mai 1795, 12 avril 1797; CN1-193, 22, 28 déc. 1804; CN1-205, 5 juill., 23 sept 1773; 16 juill. 1774; 10 avril, 15, 17 nov. 1775; 3 juin 1778; 29 mars 1780; 22 juin 1784; CN1-207, 22 oct. 1763; 18, 29 août, 4, 7, 8, 12, 29 sept., 15, 30 oct. 1764; 2 oct. 1765; 27 août, 15, 16 sept. 1766; 27 nov. 1767; 7 janv. 1769; 21 août, 12, 18 oct. 1771; 25 août 1774; CN1-230, 2 avril 1792; 3 juin, 5 déc. 1795; 13 févr., 2 juill., 15 août 1796; 3 mai, 10 oct. 1798; 23 août 1799; 5 avril 1800; 1er août 1801; 21 avril 1802; 19 nov. 1803; 14 mai, 19 sept., 13 déc. 1804; 4 janv., 5 avril 1805; 31 oct. 1806; 22 juin 1807; 22, 30 avril 1808; 17 janv. 1809; CN1-248, 11 juill. 1768; 14 nov. 1769; 14 nov. 1770; 2, 3 août 1773; 6 juin, 1er, 20 juill., 5, 23 août 1774; 18 févr., 12

avril, 17 mai, 13, 17 juin, 6 juill. 1775; CN1-256, 3 Feb. 1787; 30 Oct. 1790; 25 June, 24, 29 Oct. 1791; 30 Oct. 1792; 20 May, 30 Sept. 1793; 13 June, 25 Sept. 1794; 22 Oct. 1795; 23 Oct. 1796; 20 Jan., 27 April, 27 May, 2 Nov. 1797; 2 Nov. 1799; CN1-262, 16 oct., 12 déc. 1795; 18 févr., 4 juin, 21, 25, 26 juill., 27 sept., 27 oct., 8 nov. 1796; 27 juill., 14 août 1797; 10, 15, 20, 26, 28 juill. 1798; 29 janv., 23 févr., 29 avril, 13 mai, 29 juin, 23 sept., 8, 10 oct. 1799; 5, 23 mars, 10, 12 mai, 6, 16, 17 juin, 29 juill., 30 août, 18 sept., 14, 20 oct., 1er, 10, 13, 14 déc. 1800; 17, 28, 29 avril, 5, 22 mai, 15, 25 juin, 15 juill., 2, 5, 25 oct., 13, 22 nov., 5, 13, 18, 22–26 déc. 1801; 12 janv., 23 mars, 5 avril, 9 mai, 7 juin, 7, 12 juill., 5, 6, 9 août, 15 sept., 9, 14, 20 oct., 18 nov., 1er, 2, 22, 31 déc. 1802; 3, 14 janv., 4, 5, 21 févr., 9 juin, 19 juill., 2 août, 24, 27, 29 sept., 27 oct., 20, 22 déc. 1803; 9, 10 juill., 24 août, 21, 22 sept., 30 oct., 7, 28 nov., 20 déc. 1804; 13 févr., 26 juill., 9 sept., 5, 7 nov. 1805; CN1-284, 8 mai, 1er juill., 21–23, 28 sept. 1795; 21 janv., 7 juill. 1796; 11 janv., 1er juill. 1797; 13 nov. 1798; 19 juill., 5, 15 oct., 3 déc. 1799; 5, 18, 19 sept., 3 déc. 1800; 14 avril, 16 juill., 3, 7, 12 sept. 1801; 21 mars, 15 avril, 28, 30 juin 1802; CN1-285, 29 sept. 1798; 10 oct. 1801; 21 mai 1802; 29 janv., 8, 17 août, 8 oct. 1803; 7, 27 févr. 1805; P-240.

BL, Add. mss 21702: 50; 21716: 65, 93–96; 21719: 141, 190, 193; 21724: 33; 21735: 505–7, 630–31; 21858: 1–9, 47–48, 86–90, 92, 96–101; 21859: 47–48, 60–62, 177–80, 193–99, 206–7, 259–60, 271 (copies at PAC). McCord Museum, William Grant papers. PAC, MG 19, A2, ser.3, 2: 14; 3: 52–53, 59–61, 161–63; 4: 45–46, 51–52, 68, 75–76, 82; 8: 22; 15: 1873–94; 18: 2528–35; 20: 2755, 2764, 2842; 21: 2859, 2870–71; 22: 3027, 3031, 3049; MG 23, A6; GII, 3, vols.2–5; vol.15: 54–69; MG 24, L3: 7435, 18059–68, 23808–11, 26286–88, 26908–16, 47680–81, 47717–21; MG 30, D1, 14; RG 1, E1, 105–15; L3L: 47657, 47660–66, 47668–72, 47686–709, 47722–83; RG 4, A1: 110, 114–15, 177, 4368, 4538, 4715; RG 42, ser.1, 183; RG 68, General index, 1651–1841: ff.1, 222, 308, 326, 531, 543, 677. Private arch., David Roberts (Toronto), A. J. H. Richardson, "The Grant group" (copy). PRO, CO 5/115: ff.208–14; CO 42/12: ff.285–86; 42/19: ff.206–29; 42/25: ff.37–38, 167–68; 42/26: ff.270–73; 42/28: f.327; 42/36: f.290; 42/47: ff.259–61; 42/48: ff.223–51, 257–61; 42/49: ff.281–337; 42/52: ff.142–47; 42/63: ff.17–18; 42/66: ff.195–99, 398–99; 42/67: ff.128, 130; 42/86: ff.37, 88–206; 42/97: ff.202–3, 252, 254, 259; 42/100: f.350; 42/117: f.359; 42/120: ff.157–59; 42/121: ff.121–22; 42/134: ff.93–105 (mfm. at PAC). UTL-TF, ms coll. 31, box 24. Bas-Canada, chambre d'Assemblée, *Journaux*, 1792–1810. Gwillim, *Diary of Mrs. Simcoe* (Robertson; 1911), 98. [Frederick Haldimand], "Private diary of General Haldimand," PAC *Report*, 1889: 151, 177, 219–21, 227, 229–33, 263, 295. James Jeffry, "Journal kept in Quebec in 1775 by James Jeffry," ed. William Smith, Essex Institute, *Hist. Coll.* (Salem, Mass.), 50 (1914): 121, 123, 135, 137, 139–40. Smith, *Diary and selected papers* (Upton), 1: 202, 216, 246–47, 250, 292; 2: 3, 46–47, 60, 173, 177–82. *Quebec Gazette*, 2 Aug., 8 Nov. 1764; 21 March 1771; 10 Sept. 1772; 22 June, 25 Sept. 1775; 12 Dec. 1776; 19 Oct., 28 Dec. 1786; 17 April, 14 Aug., 30 Oct., 11 Dec. 1788; 22 Jan., 9 April, 17, 31 Dec. 1789; 7, 21 April 1791; 19, 26 Jan., 2, 23 Feb., 17, 24 May, 21 June, 5 July 1792; 3, 24 Jan., 7, 21 March, 11 April 1793; 9 Jan., 29 May, 10 July, 7 Aug. 1794; 12 Feb., 7 May 1795; 16 Feb. 1797; 27 June, 14

Grant

Nov. 1799; 29 May, 3 July 1800; 30 May 1802; 17 Feb. 1803; 26 April, 17 May, 21 June, 27 Dec. 1804; 16 May, 10 Oct., 14 Nov. 1805; 2 Jan. 1806; 23 July, 12, 19 Nov. 1807; 3, 17 March, 28 April, 6 Oct. 1808; 7 Dec. 1809; 8 March, 8 Nov. 1810; 16 May, 26 Sept. 1811; 12 Jan. 1815.

F.-J. Audet et Fabre Surveyer, *Les députés au premier Parl. du Bas-Canada*, 231–57. "Précis des actes de foy et hommage," PAC *Rapport*, 1884: 1, 3, 11, 18, 26. P.-G. Roy, *Inv. concessions*, 1: 17, 24; 2: 20, 63, 203; 3: 196–98, 201, 213–15, 248; 4: 82, 143, 189; 5: 3, 10–11, 20, 79–80, 208. Tremaine, *Biblio. of Canadian imprints*, nos.770, 772A. Mary Allodi, *Printmaking in Canada: the earliest views and portraits* (Toronto, 1980). Burt, *Old prov. of Quebec* (1968), 1: 128, 245, 249; 2: 34, 121–23, 129, 169, 182–83, 186–91. D. S. Macmillan, "The Scot as business-man," *The Scottish tradition in Canada*, ed. W. S. Reid (Toronto, 1976; repr. 1979): 183–87. Mildred Morgan, "The office of receiver general and its tenure by deputy in the province of Quebec, 1763–1791" ([MA thesis, McGill Univ., Montréal], 1937), 26–27, 45–54, 91–103, 109–15, 124–35, 140–58, 161–65. Neatby, *Quebec*, 184–86, 191–92. Ruddel, "Quebec City, 1765–1831," 38–40, 291, 512–13, 520–21, 543, 558, 580. W. S. Wallace, "Strathspey in the Canadian fur-trade," *Essays in Canadian history presented to George MacKinnon Wrong for his eightieth birthday*, ed. Ralph Flenley (Toronto, 1939), 278–95. F.[-J.] Audet et Édouard Fabre Surveyer, "William Grant," *La Presse* (Montréal), 7 mai 1927: 21, 24. Louise Dechêne, "La rente du faubourg Saint-Roch à Québec, 1750–1850," *RHAF*, 34 (1980–81): 569–87. Hare, "L'Assemblée législative du Bas-Canada," *RHAF*, 27: 372–75, 379–80. Robert La Roque de Roquebrune, "M. William Grant: homme d'affaires," *Nova Francia* (Paris), 2 (1926–27): 123–32. J.-J. Lefebvre, "William Grant (1744–1805): conseiller législatif (1778–1784)," *BRH*, 58 (1952): 25–27. W. H. Whiteley, "Newfoundland, Quebec, and the Labrador merchants, 1783–1809," *Newfoundland Quarterly* (St John's), 73 (1977), no.4: 18.

GRANT, WILLIAM, fur trader, merchant, and office holder; b. 1743 in Kirkmichael, Scotland, son of John Grant and Genevieve Forbes; m. 27 Feb. 1787 Marguerite Fafard, *dit* Laframboise, in Trois-Rivières, Que., and they had five children; d. 20 Nov. 1810 near William Henry (Sorel), Lower Canada.

William Grant, usually known as William Grant "of Three Rivers" to distinguish him from William GRANT of Saint-Roch and from at least two other contemporaries of the same name, came from a large family which had many members active in the fur trade during the early decades of British rule. He arrived in the province of Quebec soon after the conquest. In 1767 he was a resident of Montreal and was already involved in the fur trade as a merchant. He pursued this career for almost 20 years, on his own as well as with associates, in the region southwest of Michilimackinac (Mackinaw City, Mich.) and in the vicinity of lakes Superior and Nipigon. His public life does not seem to have had the same importance; his

only appointment appears to have been as justice of the peace for the District of Three Rivers in 1792.

In 1767 Grant and Richard DOBIE were sent the proposals of the merchants of Michilimackinac concerning the reorganization of the fur trade in order that they might be examined and then forwarded to London, England. For the next ten years nothing is known of Grant's activities. In 1777 he stood surety for Ezekiel Solomons when the latter dispatched a canoe with £250 worth of merchandise to Michilimackinac. The next year he and Solomons were issued two permits allowing them to send five canoes bearing goods valued at £1,650 to Lake Nipigon; Grant himself wintered at Michilimackinac. Prior to 1777 he was also in business with John Grant, Dobie's son-in-law; the arrangements governing the partnership, which was dissolved in 1780, are unknown.

During the 1780s Grant continued to be active in the fur trade. He regularly obtained permits and often wintered in the *pays d'en haut*. He was particularly interested in the region around Lake Superior, to which he sent a canoe loaded with £50 of goods in 1780, and in the hinterland of Michilimackinac, to which he forwarded four canoes and a cargo worth £2,000 in 1781, four canoes bearing £3,500 of goods the next year, and five canoes valued at £5,000 in 1783. In 1782 he had formed an association with Gabriel Cotté* to trade at the posts on Lake Nipigon and on the Pic River (Ont.). The partners agreed to supply trade goods and share profits on an equal basis. In 1785 Alexander Shaw, who had been in the employ of Grant and Cotté, entered the partnership and the three men agreed to divide profits and losses equally. The arrangement seems to have lasted only one year.

From 1780 to 1786 William Grant rarely stood surety for other traders; he posted a single bond in 1782. He was then working with Dobie who played an important role in Grant's career during these years. Dobie was usually one of the financial backers for Grant's expeditions and he acted as outfitter for the partnerships Grant formed with Cotté and with Shaw. In the late 1780s Grant obtained numerous trade permits for Michilimackinac (by then located on Mackinac Island, Mich.). He forwarded four canoes with £2,800 of trade goods in 1786, two canoes valued at £450 the following year, and a single canoe worth £200 in 1788; he is known to have wintered there in 1786 and 1790. During the same period, he seems to have taken a more active interest in the commercial aspect of the trade; he collaborated with Dobie in outfitting a whole network of fur traders and he acted as a bondsman with him. Their informal association ended in 1788 when Dobie entered into partnership with Francis Badgley*.

This experience, and his professional and social ties with Dobie, were to prove extremely useful to Grant during the final phase of his career in the fur trade. In 1791 he joined with Étienne-Charles Campion*, a Michilimackinac trader, and Samuel Gerrard*, a Montreal merchant and Dobie's relative by marriage, in establishing the firm of Grant, Campion and Company, which was destined to play an important role in the trade southwest of the Great Lakes and in the Timiskaming region. Grant was responsible for overseeing the firm's general operations while Campion handled the trade "with the Indians in the *pays d'en haut*" and Gerrard kept the books. Grant and Campion each received three-eighths of the profits while Gerrard took the remaining quarter.

The company seems to have taken over the fur-trading network previously supplied by Dobie. It provided trade goods to various Michilimackinac merchants as well as to traders throughout the region extending from Lake Superior to the Mississippi. It hired voyageurs, paid their wages, and sold the furs consigned to it, in either Montreal or England. The firm was also directly involved in the fur trade at Michilimackinac, where Campion was very active, and in the Timiskaming region where it seems to have held exclusive trading privileges and was represented by Charles Phillips.

Grant, Campion and Company was one of the most important firms engaged in the fur trade to the southwest of Grand Portage (near Grand Portage, Minn.), Michilimackinac, and Detroit (Mich.) in the early 1790s. With Todd, McGill and Company, Forsyth, Richardson and Company, and Alexander Henry*, the firm entered into negotiations with the North West Company concerning the allocation of trading zones, and in September 1792 the parties agreed not to prejudice one another's interests. The distribution of shares in the NWC was then modified, with Grant, Campion and Company receiving one of them. However, in November 1794 Grant decided to wind up the affairs of the firm in November of the following year. In a long letter to Simon McTavish, he explained that the precarious state of the fur trade in the area southwest of the Great Lakes, along with violent stomach pains and problems with his eyesight which made writing extremely difficult, had rendered him less and less able to conduct any kind of business. His decision seems also to have been influenced by the knowledge that Britain might soon be compelled to surrender the southwest posts. The partnership was thus dissolved in November 1795. Campion died soon after and Grant's involvement in the fur trade ended.

William Grant had also engaged in wholesale and retail trading of products imported from Great Britain. He carried on this business first in Trois-Rivières, where he had married in 1787, acquired property in 1788, and brought up his family. While he was active in Grant, Campion and Company, he had a partner based at Trois-Rivières, James Mackenzie, whom he supplied with imported merchandise for the local market; the firm of James Mackenzie and Company was dissolved on 1 Oct. 1796. Grant soon chose a new associate, Claude Laframboise, with whom he remained in partnership until 1800, doing business under the name of William Grant and Company in Trois-Rivières and Grant and Laframboise in Montreal. Grant left Trois-Rivières and in 1801 settled with his family in Nicolet, which was the home of his wife's brother-in-law, Pierre-Michel CRESSÉ, the local seigneur. He apparently continued to be interested in commerce and spent some years in William Henry before his death. It is possible that his many moves reflected financial difficulties. He seems to have left a very modest estate; following his death, the sale of his effects raised only 2,657 *livres*.

William Grant was a prominent figure in the history of the fur trade in the 18th century. As both trader and merchant, he contributed to the prosperity and growth of the region southwest of the Great Lakes; he withdrew from the trade on the eve of the surrender of that region's posts to the Americans following the signing of Jay's Treaty in 1794. He played an important role in the growing concentration of the fur trade in this area and in the emergence of an opposition to the NWC.

JOANNE BURGESS

ANQ-M, CN1-29, 10 nov. 1791; CN1-185, 14 janv., 6 févr. 1800; CN1-290, 13 août 1777, 19 avril 1785, 12 avril 1786. PAC, MG 24, L3: 2540–41, 6615, 6643–44, 6651–52, 6765–66, 26285; RG 4, B28, 115: 2248, 2269, 2269A, 2283, 2303, 2312, 2321, 2321A, 2332, 2340, 2343. *Docs. relating to NWC* (Wallace). *Quebec Gazette*, 10 Aug. 1780, 31 May 1787, 4 Dec. 1788, 10 Dec. 1795, 13 March 1800. *Quebec almanac*, 1792–1803. M. W. Campbell, *NWC* (1973), 92–96. Davidson, *NWC*, 14. E. E. Rich, *The fur trade and the northwest to 1857* (Toronto, 1967), 189–90. W. S. Wallace, "Strathspey in the Canadian fur-trade," *Essays in Canadian history presented to George MacKinnon Wrong for his eightieth birthday*, ed. Ralph Flenley (Toronto, 1939), 278–95. Raymond Douville, "Un William Grant trifluvien," *BRH*, 47 (1941): 362–65. W. E. Stevens, "The organization of the British fur trade," *Mississippi Valley Hist. Rev.* ([Cedar Rapids, Ind.]), 3 (1916–17): 172–202.

GRASS, MICHAEL, office holder; b. *c.* 1735 in Strasbourg, France; m. first Mary Ann —; m. secondly Margaret Swartz, and they had at least six children; d. 25 April 1813 in Kingston, Upper Canada.

Michael Grass was part of the considerable emigration of Palatinate Germans to North America in the 18th century. He arrived on 22 Sept. 1752 at Philadelphia, Pa, where he remained for a while,

Grass

earning his living as a saddler. He subsequently moved to Tryon County, N.Y., where he operated a saddlery in addition to farming and thereby achieved a modest prosperity. A captain in the local militia, he refused to join the rebels after the outbreak of the American revolution. In 1777 he fled to New York City where he served as a lieutenant in the volunteer militia.

Grass's historical reputation derives from his connection with the settlement of loyalists at Cataraqui (Kingston, Ont.) after the revolution. Family tradition and popular lore accord him the position of founder. These accounts maintain that he had been a prisoner at the old French Fort Frontenac (Cataraqui) during the Seven Years' War, and thus, towards the end of the revolution, when the British commandant at New York City, Sir Guy CARLETON, asked him about the area he was in a position to recommend it. Grass may have had some familiarity with Cataraqui; there is, however, no evidence to corroborate this version of the settlement's founding.

A more plausible account is as follows. On 26 May 1783 Governor HALDIMAND ordered Surveyor General Samuel Johannes HOLLAND to Cataraqui to consider "the facility of establishing a settlement" there. Two months later, Major John Ross* was ordered to prepare the site for a military post. In the mean time, numbers of loyalist refugees, including Grass, were awaiting evacuation from New York City to Nova Scotia; on 12 June Grass had written on behalf of a group of them that "we cannot think of going to another place in the Universe for the many Benefits that will flow from that Settlement [Cataraqui] to the Settler." On 2 July he was given a temporary commission of captain for the second of the eight companies organized for transportation to Quebec. This group, many of whom were Associated Loyalists, probably numbered fewer than 500. Grass's transport Camel was the first of nine to reach Quebec, arriving there on 12 August. Three days later, Haldimand's military secretary, Robert MATHEWS, indicated to Ross the governor's intention to settle many of the New York exiles in the neighbourhood of Cataraqui. The actual decision, however, was not made until Haldimand had received reports indicating the suitability of the area for farming. In early September, while most of the New York loyalists prepared to winter at Sorel, Grass and 37 men ascended the St Lawrence River with a survey party to mark out the settlements at Cataraqui. When he returned to Sorel in late fall he found there another company from New York led by Major Peter Van Alstine. The presence of a new group led to jealousy and factionalism; Grass and several other captains complained of persons who "Presume to Place themselves at our head without our consent or Approbation."

In January 1784 Grass and others petitioned Haldimand for large-scale assistance in setting up their farms. They also indicated their preference for a "Form of Government . . . similar to that which they Enjoyed in the Province of New York in the year of 1763." Haldimand informed them that their requests were impossible to meet and reminded them that if they were not happy with his plans he could provide them passage to Nova Scotia. Several months later the governor was angered by Grass's seeming claim on behalf of himself and his "party" that they had "first found out and planned the settlement." Grass demurred, however, reportedly claiming "he only ment that he was the first of the *Loyalists* who before they left New York pointed out that [Cataraqui] as the most desirable place to go to. . . ." After a winter of discontent, the loyalists began the trek to their new home on 24 May 1784. The settlement from the Bay of Quinte to Cataraqui was divided into numbered townships; Grass's party of some 220 was granted Township No.1 (Cataraqui).

Grass's leadership in the new community was short-lived. He was appointed a justice of the peace for the Montreal District (which then included the new loyalist townships) on 18 April 1785. In this capacity, he signed a petition for English land tenure, local courts, and municipal government, as well as for more schools and clergymen. However, when in 1788 Carleton (now Lord Dorchester) established four new administrative districts in western Quebec to meet loyalist needs, Grass was not appointed to any of the new civil offices. After this period his contribution to local society was limited; he was, for instance, a benefactor of the local Church of England congregation and served as vestryman in 1789.

The legend of Michael Grass, founder of Cataraqui, cannot be sustained by the evidence. But there remains, to his credit, an image of a determined, possibly even imaginative, leader who resisted the normal direction of refugee emigration from New York City and helped not only to influence, but to push to conclusion, the decision to settle the wilderness later known as Ontario. Perhaps he is best remembered for a letter that he wrote to the *Kingston Gazette* in 1811, harking back to the days when, "strong in my attachment to my sovereign, and high in the confidence of my fellow subjects, I led the loyal band, I pointed out to them the scite of their future metropolis, and gained for persecuted principles a sanctuary[,] for myself and followers a home."

LARRY TURNER

BL, Add. MSS 21716: 132; 21723: 212–13; 21784: 9–14; 21786: 42–44, 92–95; 21798: 322, 326, 343–45, 360–63; 21806: 65; 21808: 151–55, 158, 168, 174; 21825: 110, 117, 124, 133, 143, 145, 152; 21827: 1–4, 300, 351; 21828: 68, 80; 21875: 133–34 (transcripts at PAC). Frontenac Land

Registry Office (Kingston, Ont.), E270 (will of Michael Grass). PAC, RG 1, L3, 203A: G3/63; 204: G6/3; 205: G10/38; 206: G12/30; 206A: G12/81; 222: G misc., 1789–95/104–5; G misc., 1794–1830/67. PRO, ADM 9/9; AO 13, bundle 13: 118–20 (mfm. at PAC); CO 5/111: 118; PRO 30/55/11; 30/55/21; 30/55/38; 30/55/50–51; 30/55/73 (copies at PAC); T 1/1597; WO 36/3; WO 60/22–23; 60/27; 60/32–33. "Early records of Ontario," ed. Adam Shortt, *Queen's Quarterly* (Kingston, Ont.), 7 (1899–1900): 51–59. "Grants of crown lands in U.C.," AO *Report*, 1928: 148, 167, 169. *Kingston before War of 1812* (Preston), xlii, 25, 36–37, 49–51, 72–73, 91–95, 138. *Loyalist narratives from Upper Canada*, ed. J. J. Talman (Toronto, 1946), 75–76. *Minutes of the Albany committee of correspondence, 1775–78 . . .* , ed. James Sullivan and A. C. Flick (2v., Albany, N.Y., 1923–25), 2: 1142–43. *The settlement of the United Empire Loyalists on the upper St Lawrence and Bay of Quinte in 1784; a documentary record*, ed. E. A. Cruikshank (Toronto, 1934; repr. 1966), 37–38, 40–42, 67, 78–79, 111–12. "Settlements and surveys," PAC *Report*, 1891: 11–12. "United Empire Loyalists: enquiry into losses and services," AO *Report*, 1904: 1257–58. *Kingston Gazette*, 10 Dec. 1811. *DCB*, vol.4 (biog. of John Ross). *Pennsylvania German pioneers: a publication of the original lists of arrivals in the port of Philadelphia from 1727 to 1808*, comp. R. B. Strassburger, ed. W. J. Hinke (3v., Norristown, Pa., 1934; repr., 2v., Baltimore, Md., 1966), 1: 572–73. Reid, *Loyalists in Ont.*, 131. Sabine, *Biog. sketches of loyalists*, 2: 522. H. C. Burleigh, "Captain Michael Grass," H. C. Burleigh, *Forgotten leaves of local history: Kingston* (Kingston, 1973), 81–86. William Canniff, *History of the settlement of Upper Canada (Ontario) with special reference to the Bay Quinte* (Toronto, 1869; repr. Belleville, Ont., 1971), 650–51. Dennis Duffy, *Gardens, covenants, exiles: loyalism in the literature of Upper Canada/Ontario* (Toronto, 1982). E. R. Stuart, "Jessup's Rangers as a factor in loyalist settlement," *Three hist. theses*, 76–78, 137. D. E. Grass, "Michael Grass and the Grass family of Kingston," *Hist. Kingston* (Kingston), no.12 (1964): 6–10.

GRAVÉ DE LA RIVE, HENRI-FRANÇOIS, Roman Catholic priest, superior of the Séminaire de Québec, and vicar general; b. 25 April 1730 in Vannes, France, son of Charles-Yves Gravé de La Rive, at one time a judge in commercial court, and Louise-Jeanne-Marguerite Mercier; d. 4 Feb. 1802 at Quebec.

Having completed classical studies in his home town, Henri-François Gravé de La Rive went to finish his education in Paris, first at the Académie de Paris, and then at the Sorbonne, where he obtained the degrees of master of arts in 1753 and bachelor in theology the following year. He received the subdiaconate on 16 June 1753 and the diaconate on 31 March 1754. On 15 March 1755 he was ordained priest at Rouen, from which he was preparing to sail for Canada with Urbain Boiret*. They arrived at Quebec on 26 July and settled in at the seminary.

On 16 Feb. 1759 Gravé was appointed a director of the institution. In the summer, when the British siege of the city began, the seminary was evacuated. The superior, Colomban-Sébastien Pressart*, and Gravé went to Montreal at the same time as Bishop Henri-Marie Dubreil* de Pontbriand, with a few students from the senior classes, and took refuge at the Séminaire de Saint-Sulpice. There Gravé taught philosophy, at the same time acting as chaplain to the Sisters of Charity of the Hôpital Général of Montreal (Grey Nuns).

Gravé returned to Quebec in September 1761, when the restoration of the seminary was sufficiently advanced for the priests to live in it. The following year, at the end of Pressart's term of office as superior, the Séminaire des Missions Étrangères in Paris appointed his successor, according to the pre-conquest practice; it named Pierre Maillard*, a missionary in Acadia, or failing him, Gravé. But Governor Murray* objected to these appointments, denying that Paris had any right to interfere in Canadian matters. Henceforth the priests of the Séminaire de Québec had to elect their superior themselves, and Murray remained opposed to the election of the two designated candidates. In July 1762 Boiret was elected, and Gravé served as assistant to the superior. When the Petit Séminaire reopened in 1765, it had to assume the responsibilities formerly discharged by the Jesuit college, which had closed its doors permanently. It now had to offer classical studies, which had previously been provided solely by the Jesuit institution; it was also obliged to accept day pupils as well as students seeking to enter the liberal professions. Since the priests were unable to undertake the increased burden of work, theological students were pressed into service as masters or professors.

On 13 April 1768, after the death of Jean-Félix Récher*, parish priest of Notre-Dame in Quebec, the seminary decided to give up its union with this parish charge and, as a result, the right to designate the priest. Gravé objected to this renunciation, claiming that the union was a legal act, obligatory and inalienable. He even registered his dissent in the presence of a notary and never reconsidered his position. In 1768 also, Gravé took over a cause that Father Récher had upheld before him; with the backing of a colleague, Joseph-André-Mathurin Jacrau*, he supported the churchwardens of Notre-Dame in their refusal to make their newly restored church the diocesan cathedral. When Bishop Briand* finally took possession of the church as his cathedral six years later, all those who had been opposed had given in, except Gravé. In 1768 Gravé had replaced Boiret as superior of the seminary and he held that office until 1774.

In 1777–78 Gravé assumed the responsibilities of bursar and in the latter year was again elected

Graves

superior. In 1779 he was a member of the first board of the Quebec Library, and from 1780 he was chaplain to the Ursulines. At the end of his term as superior in 1781 he again became bursar and retained that post until 1787. The Hôpital Général was able to take advantage of Gravé's administrative experience: he held the office of temporal director of that institution from 1784 to 1789. In 1784, although he was personally in favour of the steps that Jean-Baptiste-Amable Adhémar* and Jean DE LISLE took in London to request constitutional reform, Gravé maintained that the clergy must remain neutral, without however disapproving of those supporting the reform.

In December of that year the new bishop of Quebec, Louis-Philippe Mariauchau* d'Esgly, renewed Gravé's letters as vicar general, which had originally been granted by Briand in 1781. But in 1788, D'Esgly reproached Gravé for insubordination and took away his powers. The coadjutor, Jean-François Hubert*, upheld Gravé, and when Hubert replaced D'Esgly in June 1788, he hastened to reinstate Gravé as vicar general. The preceding year Gravé had once more been elected superior of the seminary and he remained in office until 1793.

The clergy did not greatly appreciate the introduction of parliamentary government in 1791. "Those who, in my opinion, reflect a little are very angry at this change," Gravé observed, "for there are several of our vain Canadians and many English, admirers of the [French] National Assembly, who are already talking of establishing the rights of man as principles in the laws." In March 1791, as superior of the seminary, proprietor of several seigneuries, Gravé signed a petition along with 59 other Canadian seigneurs against the proposal to replace seigneurial tenure by free and common socage; this proposal had already been put forward by loyalists in 1788 and had been supported by Charles-Louis TARIEU de Lanaudière [see Thomas-Laurent Bédard*].

In 1793 Gravé became the director of the Grand Séminaire, a post he retained until 1795, when he took charge of the Petit Séminaire for the next three years. In 1797 Bishop DENAUT renewed his letters as vicar general. The following year he was elected superior for a final term of four years. Over and above all these duties Gravé taught theology and took an interest in philosophy. In addition he wrote a small catechism, consisting of 72 lessons for pupils in the Petit Séminaire.

In 1800 Bishop Denaut asked Gravé's opinion when the British authorities introduced the practice of making Catholics swear on the Protestant Bible in law courts. Gravé encouraged the bishop to fight this action, whereas coadjutor designate Joseph-Octave Plessis* and vicar general Philippe-Jean-Louis Desjardins* did not see anything objectionable about it. Denaut favoured Gravé's view.

Although he had some reactionary views and a Breton's stubbornness, Gravé certainly possessed superior talents and human qualities, as is borne out by the important responsibilities repeatedly entrusted to him by the bishops of Quebec and by his colleagues at the seminary. Even after his dissent on the issue of the parish charge of Quebec in April 1768, people evidently did not bear a grudge against him, since on 20 August he was elected superior. François Sorbier* de Villars, superior of the Missions Étrangères in Paris, held him in high esteem. The religious communities in Quebec regarded him with deep respect and affection. After his death the *Quebec Gazette*, which published eulogies of him on 11 and 18 Feb. 1802, claimed: "Lastly, and it was one of the most prominent traits of his character, his Majesty had not a more faithful a more devoted or a more affectionate subject than Mr. Grave." If this affirmation contains no flattery, it is proof of splendid loyalty in the last upholder of the *ancien régime*.

HONORIUS PROVOST

AAQ, 1 CB, VI: 124. AD, Morbihan (Vannes), État civil, Vannes, 25 avril 1730. ASQ, Fonds Viger-Verreau, Carton 17, no.46A; Lettres, P, 124; mss, 12; 13; 342; mss-m, 427; Paroisse de Québec, 103, 112; Polygraphie, IX: 106–7; Séminaire, 13, no.24. *Le séminaire de Québec* (Provost). *Quebec Gazette*, 11, 18 Feb. 1802. Caron, "Inv. de la corr. de Mgr Briand," ANQ *Rapport*, 1929–30: 74, 106; "Inv. de la corr. de Mgr Denaut," 1931–32: 135; "Inv. de la corr. de Mgr Hubert et de Mgr Bailly de Messein," 1930–31: 203; "Inv. de la corr. de Mgr Mariaucheau d'Esgly," ANQ *Rapport*, 1930–31: 187, 198. [Catherine Burke, named de Saint-Thomas], *Les ursulines de Québec, depuis leur établissement jusqu'à nos jours* (4v., Québec, 1863–66), 3. Antonio Drolet, *Les bibliothèques canadiennes, 1607–1960* (Ottawa, 1965), 91. Gosselin, *L'Église du Canada après la Conquête*. J.-E. Roy, *Souvenirs d'une classe au séminaire de Québec, 1867–1877* (Lévis, Qué., 1905). Trudel, *L'Église canadienne*, 2. "La mission de MM. Adhémar et Delisle en Angleterre en 1783–84," *BRH*, 32 (1926): 621.

GRAVES, THOMAS, lst Baron GRAVES, naval officer and governor of Newfoundland; b. 23 Oct. 1725 in Thanckes, England, second of three sons of Captain Thomas Graves and his second wife, Elizabeth Budgell; m. 22 June 1771 in Ottery St Mary, England, Elizabeth Williams, daughter and co-heiress of William Peere Williams of Cadhay House, and they had two sons and three daughters; d. 9 Feb. 1802 at Cadhay House.

Thomas Graves grew up in a seafaring family and first saw Newfoundland in the summer of 1739 or 1740 as a youthful volunteer in the squadron of Commodore Henry Medley, then governor of the island. Soon afterwards he transferred to the *Norfolk*, commanded by his father, and in 1741 took part in the

Graves

unsuccessful expedition against Cartagena (Colombia). On 25 June 1743 he was promoted lieutenant and posted to the 50-gun *Romney*. When peace came in 1748, he took up the systematic study of principles of gunnery and fortification and mastered the French language. Promoted captain in 1755, he commanded a number of warships in the early years of the Seven Years' War.

On 14 May 1761 the governor of Newfoundland, James Webb*, died unexpectedly just prior to setting out for his government. Graves received his commission as governor and commander-in-chief the following day, and sailed for Newfoundland on the 26th. He convoyed the annual fleet of West Country fishing ships safely across the Atlantic, arriving in St John's on 1 July. After supervising the summer fishery and settling the usual disputes, he sailed for Europe in November with 66 merchant ships. Since he first escorted ships to the Portuguese market and then had to wait to convoy the trade from Portugal to England, Graves did not arrive back in Plymouth until 18 March 1762. He followed the same pattern throughout his three years as governor, but the following summers were not to be so uneventful.

On his outward voyage in 1762 Graves received news from Captain Charles Douglas* of the *Siren* that four French warships had been seen approaching St John's. When the governor made the Newfoundland coast near Cape Race early in July, he learned that St John's had already fallen. He promptly reinforced the garrison on Bois Island in Ferryland harbour and then made his way through an iceberg-strewn sea to Placentia, the only other garrisoned centre remaining in British hands. There he made use of his engineering skills to repair the forts.

In the mean time, Lord Alexander Colvill*, commander-in-chief of the North American squadron, had sailed for the island from his headquarters at Halifax, N.S.; on 14 August he arrived at Placentia and eight days later Graves sailed with him to blockade St John's, taking about 50 fishermen of Conception Bay as volunteers. Colvill was joined off St John's by troop transports under Lieutenant-Colonel William Amherst and the soldiers were landed on 13 September at Torbay, some ten miles north of the capital. The enemy squadron under Charles-Henri-Louis d'Arsac* de Ternay fled St John's harbour three nights later and the French surrender followed on 18 September. With the departure of Colvill in early October, Graves was left to deal with the debris of war and to sort out property claims. Not only St John's and Bay Bulls, but several flourishing outports to the north, chief among them Harbour Grace, Carbonear, and Trinity, had been ravaged and their populations scattered. As Graves put it, the fishery had "almost stood still in the eastern and northern parts of the island."

Under the peace terms of 1763, Labrador, as part of New France, became British territory, and was placed under the jurisdiction of the naval governor at Newfoundland. Graves was instructed to encourage the development of an English ship fishery on the Labrador coast and to supervise the mixed fishery on the French Shore of northern Newfoundland in accordance with the treaty provisions, which allowed the French to continue to catch and dry fish there. He decided to bring out a surveyor to begin charting the largely unknown coasts of his station. Although Hugh Palliser* is usually thought of as the great patron of James Cook*, it was Graves who got Cook appointed surveyor of Newfoundland in 1763, badgered the Admiralty for the necessary stores and instruments, and purchased the small schooner *Grenville* for him at Newfoundland. When Graves left the governorship, Cook assured him that the survey would probably go ahead until finished, adding "this useful and necessary thing the World must be obliged to you for."

In the summer of 1763, Captain John Ruthven reported from the treaty coast that the French were cutting down trees to build boats and erect warehouses, and were leaving boats behind after the end of the season. He was burning any he could lay his hands on, but asked for guidance. Graves in St John's strove to provide a reasonable interpretation of the treaty terms, one which he hoped would be approved by the home authorities. He pointed out to Ruthven that the treaty limited the French to erecting only stages made of boards and huts necessary for fishing and drying fish, and he ordered him to destroy all other buildings with their contents after giving due notice. Boats built of Newfoundland timber should also be destroyed, but boats brought from France, even if left during the winter, should not. Ships continuing to fish after the season was over should be driven off the coast, again after proper notice was given. Above all, both British and French fishers must recognize British sovereignty over the coast and the authority of the governor and his surrogates to settle all disputes.

By the time that Graves returned to England in March 1764 the French ambassador had lodged "heavy complaints" about the actions of his captains on the treaty coast, especially in compelling French fishers to leave by 10 September. Graves in reply defended the September date as "the custom of the country" and taxed the French with simply making excuses in order to remain over the winter to trap furs, fell timber, and build boats, and with living in what were almost "little French towns." The Admiralty in May 1764 reprimanded Ruthven for the "violence and temerity" of his actions, and Graves's successor, Hugh Palliser, was instructed to prevent British fishermen and his own officers from interrupting the French fishery in future. At the same time the Admiralty assured Graves that it was "perfectly well

381

satisfied with his conduct at Newfoundland." Indeed it was due in large part to Graves's resolute policies that the British government was able to reject completely a French claim for an exclusive fishery on the treaty coast.

Looking back on his three years as governor, Graves frankly pointed out that many of the ancient laws, especially those supporting the English ship fishery, were outmoded and disregarded. He also commented that the naval officer was handicapped as governor by his unfamiliarity with civil government, by the absence of disinterested advisers, and by his short term of office: "The first summer the Governour cannot be supposed to know anything of ye matter – the second he has treasured up an heap of inconsistant & opposite accounts of the Customs & Interest of the Country deliverd to him just as the views of the party's lead them – the third summer he begins to know People somewhat & to Distinguish between truth & falshood, then he is turned out and heard of no more, so that were he ever so well inclined, & to take ye utmost pains, no great matter cou'd be expected from him."

In December 1764 Graves was appointed to command a squadron dispatched to investigate merchants' complaints against the governors of British forts on the west coast of Africa. On his return he commanded a succession of warships, mostly in home waters. He sat briefly in parliament in 1775 as member for East Looe in Cornwall, but neither spoke nor voted. The American revolution brought Graves to active service once more. In 1779 he served in Vice-Admiral John Byron*'s fleet in the West Indies, in 1780 he was in the Channel fleet commanded by Sir Charles Hardy*, and in July 1781 he succeeded Mariot Arbuthnot* as commander-in-chief of the North American squadron. In September he failed to break the French naval blockade of the British army at Yorktown, Va, and its surrender followed in October. Inevitably, Graves was criticized, but the French fleet was superior and probably only a commander of Nelsonian talents could have dislodged it. Upon leaving the North American command in November, Graves went to the West Indies. After the battle of the Saintes he sailed for England in July 1782 in charge of a motley squadron composed mainly of prizes. Many sank in a storm, and his flagship the *Ramillies* had to be destroyed after sustaining heavy damage.

Graves was promoted vice-admiral of the blue in September 1787 and soon after became commander-in-chief at Plymouth. On the outbreak of war with France in 1793 he was appointed second in command of the Channel fleet under Lord Howe and the next year advanced to full admiral. In the *Royal Sovereign* he defeated three enemy ships of the line in the battle of the "Glorious First of June," 1794, and was rewarded with an Irish peerage. However, the battle

marked the end of his long sea career; badly wounded in the right arm, he was forced to retire to his estate in Devon. James Northcote painted his portrait and Francesco Bartolozzi engraved his likeness against a background depicting the great naval victory.

Thomas Graves is one of the most interesting of the early governors of Newfoundland and held the office at a critical time in the island's development. His personality comes through in his correspondence since he did not hesitate to express himself candidly, even on personal matters. The Newfoundland command, with its absence of prize money and the endless involvement in fishing disputes, cannot have been attractive to him. Nevertheless, the Newfoundland historian, Daniel Woodley Prowse*, praises "the cool, methodical way in which he sets to work to defend the Colony, his admirable arrangements, his lucid judgments, his entire freedom from the bigotry of the age." Whether or not he liked Newfoundland, he brought to his task a professionalism and sound judgement that made him a successful governor.

WILLIAM H. WHITELEY

National Maritime Museum, GRV/101–20. PANL, GN 2/1, 3. PRO, ADM 1/482, 1/1835–36, 1/4126; ADM 2/88, 2/90, 2/535–37; ADM 51/50; CO 194/15, 194/26; CO 195/9 (mfm. at PAC); PROB 11/1378/546. "Biographical memoir of the right hon. Thomas Lord Graves . . . ," *Naval Chronicle*, 5 (January–June 1801): 377–408. "Some account of Admiral Lord Graves," *European Magazine, and London Rev.* (London), 28 (July–December 1795): 147–56. John Charnock, *Biographia navalis; or, impartial memoirs of the lives and characters of officers of the navy of Great Britain, from the year 1660 to the present time . . .* (6v., London, 1794–98), 6: 126–43. *DNB. Prowse, Hist. of Nfld.*

GRAY, EDWARD WILLIAM, merchant, notary, lawyer, office holder, and militia officer; b. 4 Dec. 1742 in London, England, son of John Gray; d. 22 Dec. 1810 in Montreal, Lower Canada.

Edward William Gray came to Montreal in May of 1760 aboard the British warship *Vanguard*. Settling there, he engaged for a few years in the general trade of the colony. In 1764 he served as deputy registrar, acting provost marshal, and deputy commissary for the District of Montreal; that December, as provost marshal, he arrested the soldiers suspected of assaulting the merchant Thomas Walker* and transported them to Quebec. On 12 June 1765 he was formally appointed deputy for the Montreal District of the absentee provost marshal, Nicholas Turner. He was commissioned a notary public on 7 Oct. 1765 and a lawyer three years later. On 13 Jan. 1767 Gray married Margaret Oakes and through his marriage became related to the fur traders Forrest Oakes* and Lawrence Ermatinger*. About this time as well he opened a vendue and commission business, importing goods from London merchants, advertising their arrival in the local press, and then auctioning them; he also sold on commission.

In 1775, at the beginning of the American revolution, Gray was appointed major of a corps of volunteers he had raised among the Montreal merchants. During the rebel occupation of the city that winter, he was regarded with suspicion by American brigadier-general David Wooster, the civil and military administrator of Montreal and district. When Major-General Richard Montgomery*'s defeat at Quebec on the night of 30–31 December became known, Wooster ordered the arrest of Gray, Ermatinger, and ten other prominent citizens, but he was obliged to release them under public pressure. On 16 Jan. 1776 he demanded the disarming of three Montreal suburbs considered loyal to the British, and to ensure the cooperation of the citizens he had Gray and René-Ovide Hertel* de Rouville taken hostage; however, once again public opinion forced Wooster to release his prisoners. Ultimately he decided to rid the city of its most prominent loyalists and on 6 February, when Gray and three Canadians, including Georges-Hippolyte Le Comte* Dupré and Thomas-Ignace Trottier* Dufy Desauniers, refused to surrender their British commissions as militia officers, they were arrested and imprisoned at Fort Chambly.

On 1 May 1776, perhaps even before Gray's release, Governor Guy CARLETON appointed him postmaster at Montreal, a position he held until replaced by Edward EDWARDS in 1786. Gray was also named on 1 May 1776 to succeed Turner as provost marshal, but with the title of sheriff. As sheriff Gray served summonses to witnesses and defendants in court cases, executed writs of distraint against accused debtors, and enforced punishments imposed by the courts, including arrests and the maintenance of prisoners in jail, and the selling of property at auction for payment of debt. Another of his duties was the collection of rents due to the government from leased crown and clergy reserve lots. Under an ordinance of 1787 the sheriff became responsible also for summoning grand jurors to hear criminal cases in the Court of King's Bench. The task of compiling jury lists was not always easy, and Gray kept a list "of Persons who . . . treated me with Contemptuous language." His average annual income as sheriff between 1777 and 1786 was £471, of which approximately £100 was salary and the rest fees.

Gray received a number of other commissions after the American withdrawal from Canada in 1776. On 25 June he was appointed by Carleton to a three-man commission to investigate in the District of Montreal the nature and extent of Canadian collaboration with the enemy during the American invasion; that August he was named a justice of the peace. He received a

commission as notary for the province at large on 23 Aug. 1781, but because of his many official duties, he practised little. In April 1783 he was appointed a manager, responsible for ticket sales, of a lottery for the building of a new jail at Montreal; the lottery apparently failed for the old prison, dating back to the French régime, continued in use.

Even though a full-time sheriff, Gray maintained his commercial interests. In November 1785 he acquired at auction the printing equipment of Fleury Mesplet*, but was then obliged to rent it back to Mesplet, who was the only person in Montreal capable of using it; Gray finally sold the press to Edward Edwards about 1794. In August 1787, the same month that his brother Jonathan Abraham advertised the opening of a vendue and commission business in Montreal, Gray announced that he was continuing his auction business, located on Rue Saint-Vincent, despite rumours to the contrary; these had been generated perhaps by his neglect of the concern as a result of illness and the demands of the sheriff's office. Indeed, he felt that he could expand, even though conditions were far from favourable for such a venture; the North West Company was absorbing many of the smaller merchants, and others found it more economical and practical to order through large importing houses in the city. On 1 May 1792, in order to ensure continuation of the business, Gray took into partnership his nephew by marriage Frederick William Ermatinger*, giving him a one-third share in the firm, now called Gray and Ermatinger. Gray withdrew in October 1795 because his position as sheriff was occupying most of his time. He had already relinquished his post of justice of the peace in 1791, and in 1798 he ceased entirely to practise as a notary. Jonathan Abraham, who had received a commission as notary for the District of Montreal on 31 March 1796, and had it extended to Lower Canada at large in 1798, eventually became one of the most prominent notaries in Montreal. As a member of the commercial community Gray had been active in the merchants' attempts to influence the political and economic direction of the colony [see George ALLSOPP]. In 1784, for example, when Lawrence Ermatinger experienced financial difficulties, Gray complained that there was no law in the colony to enable a creditor to recover his money from a bankrupt or sue the bankrupt's debtors. In 1790 and 1791 he was a director of the Montreal branch of the Agriculture Society, which sought to stimulate commercial agriculture in the colony.

Gray continued to be active in the militia and on 16 July 1787 was appointed by Lord Dorchester [Guy Carleton] colonel commandant of the British Militia of the Town and Banlieu of Montreal; thereafter he was commonly known in the city as "the Colonel." Jonathan Abraham became an ensign in the regiment

Gray

the same year, was promoted lieutenant by 1790, and became captain in 1803. By the early 1790s the British inhabitants of Lower Canada had begun to fear that the French revolution, through its influence on the Canadians, might overthrow British rule in the colony. When in July 1794, following the example of Quebec, some citizens of Montreal under the chairmanship of James McGILL formed an organization to support British rule – called simply the Association – Gray became a member of its managing committee. In October 1796 he was "roughly seized" by a number of Canadians influenced by revolutionary thinking and news of an imminent French invasion of Canada and was prevented from arresting a Canadian charged with disobeying a controversial road law. Three years later he was a member of a committee, which included McGill, Simon McTAVISH, and John Richardson*, to receive and remit voluntary subscriptions raised to aid Britain in the prosecution of the war in Europe.

Throughout the 1790s and early 1800s Gray continued to accumulate government appointments. He was a returning officer in Montreal for the House of Assembly elections in 1792, 1796, and 1801. On 29 May 1805 he was appointed a commissioner for the building of churches and parsonages and on 22 July a commissioner for repairing them. As sheriff he was responsible for the Montreal prison, and in March 1804, at the request of Lieutenant Governor Sir Robert Shore Milnes*, he reported on the reasons for its distressing inability to contain its occupants. The debate over the financing of a new prison became one of the more heated in Lower Canadian politics.

In addition to all his public and business activities Gray was active socially. He had joined the freemasons on 16 Oct. 1760 aboard the *Vanguard*, and on 12 March 1762 was secretary of a meeting in Montreal to organize the first lodge in the city, later called St Peter's No.4, Quebec. In 1779 he was an instigator of the movement to establish a branch in Montreal of the Quebec Library, founded that year by Governor HALDIMAND. Although they were from a Quaker background, Edward William and Jonathan Abraham were members of the Protestant Congregation of Montreal, an Anglican body; in 1789 Edward William was one of its trustees and Jonathan Abraham its treasurer, and in 1805 both were members of the committee for building Christ Church [*see* Jehosaphat MOUNTAIN].

Edward William Gray died in 1810 after an illness of eight days, having been sheriff, his obituary noted, "with honor to himself and satisfaction to the public." According to his request, he was buried without pomp in the Protestant cemetery (Dufferin Square), but the funeral was attended by a large number of his friends and fellow citizens. He was survived by his wife (they had no children) and succeeded as sheriff by Frederick

William Ermatinger. Gray's brother, Jonathan Abraham, died on 31 July 1812; another brother, John*, became first president of the Bank of Montreal.

MYRON MOMRYK

ANQ-M, CE1-63, 13 Jan. 1767, 24 Dec. 1811. PAC, MG 11, [CO 42] Q, 85: 321; MG 19, A2, ser.3; MG 23, GII, 3, vols.3, 5–6; MG 24, I20; RG 68, General index, 1651–1841: ff.7, 223, 305, 323–24, 531, 572–73, 654, 666. "First masonic initiation in Quebec," PAC *Report*, 1944: xxxii. "The Walker outrage, 1764," PAC *Report*, 1888: 5. *Montreal Gazette*, 19 Nov. 1789, 19 Oct. 1790, 23 June 1808, 21 Jan. 1811. *Quebec Gazette*, 8 Aug. 1765; 23 July 1772; 11 March 1779; 8, 15 May 1783; 9 Sept. 1784; 16 July 1785; 29 June 1786; 6 Sept. 1787; 16 July 1789; 28 Oct. 1790; 24 May 1794; 10 Jan. 1811. Caron, "Inv. de la corr. de Mgr Denaut," ANQ *Rapport*, 1931–32: 133. "List of members and first meeting of the Montreal Grand Lodge," PAC *Report*, 1944: xxxii–xxxiii. *Quebec almanac*, 1780: 33; 1782: 24; 1791: 84; 1800: 88. W. H. Atherton, *Montreal, 1535–1914* (3v., Montreal and Vancouver, 1914), 2: 55. *Hochelaga depicta: the early history and present state of the city and island of Montreal . . .*, ed. Newton Bosworth (Montreal, 1839; repr. Toronto, 1974), 103. Neatby, *Administration of justice under Quebec Act*, 41, 52–53, 100, 334–36, 342–43. S. M. Scott, "Chapters in the history of the law of Quebec, 1764–1775" (PHD thesis, Univ. of Michigan, Ann Arbor, 1933), 149. Stanley, *Canada invaded*, 110–11. "Edward William Gray," *BRH*, 20 (1914): 220. Ægidius Fauteux, "Les bibliothèques canadiennes et leur histoire," *Rev. canadienne*, nouv. sér., 17 (janvier–juin 1916): 195. "Les maîtres de poste de Montréal depuis la cession," *BRH*, 8 (1902): 16–17. É.-Z. Massicotte, "Les shériffs de Montréal," *BRH*, 29 (1923): 107–9. J.-P. Wallot, "La querelle des prisons (Bas-Canada, 1805–1807)," *RHAF*, 14 (1960–61): 67.

GRAY, RALPH, soldier, tailor, businessman, politician, and seigneur; b. *c.* 1736–40, probably in Scotland; d. 27 Dec. 1813 in Beauport, Lower Canada.

Ralph Gray came to Canada during the Seven Years' War as a regimental tailor with the rank of private in the forces of Major-General Jeffery Amherst*. He fought at Louisbourg, Île Royale (Cape Breton Island), and at Quebec, where he served as an orderly sergeant; he was wounded in the attack at Montmorency Falls on 31 July 1759 and during the battle of the Plains of Abraham on 13 September. He later purchased his discharge, concluding ten years of military service, and by May 1761 he was established as a tailor on Rue des Pauvres (Côte du Palais), Quebec. In March 1764 he and his wife, Mary Ann Scott, purchased a stone house on Rue de la Fabrique, Gray paying in cash the cost price of nearly £600. On 23 Jan. 1765 he was appointed by Governor Murray* one of four sub-bailiffs at Quebec for a one-year term; he had been filling this minor constabulary position unofficially since late 1764, when civil courts were established. During his first years as a tailor, Gray provided a largely British and urban clientele with clothing fashioned from a variety of imported but commonplace woollen and cotton fabrics. His business prospered, and by 1769 he was advertising in the *Quebec Gazette* a larger and more sophisticated stock of materials, including Irish linens, silks, elegant European velvets, and a greater variety of woollens and cottons; accessory items such as handkerchiefs, hats, and table-cloths were also imported.

In the early 1770s Gray sought to expand and diversify his business interests. In February 1773 he petitioned, apparently unsuccessfully, for land to the rear of the seigneuries of Lachenaie and L'Assomption in the Montreal area. On 25 Aug. 1774 he bought from the Quebec merchant William GRANT (1744–1805) the sub-fief of Grandpré, formerly known as La Mistanguienne or Montplaisir, at La Canardière, east of Quebec; he paid the full purchase price of £1,500 within four years. Gray thus joined the small group of British merchant-seigneurs in the province. Meanwhile, he was acquiring property at Quebec, in the form of a house on Rue Saint-Jean by adjudication in April 1774 and another in August on Rue des Pauvres by purchase for £200 from the merchant Samuel Jacobs*. Probably in 1774 as well, Gray entered into partnership with the Quebec merchant Duncan Munro, and in April 1775 they acquired from another Quebec merchant, John Bondfield, property and unpaid debts in the Chambly region. The partnership of Gray and Munro was terminated by 1 June 1775. Gray, now an experienced importer, expanded his business, announcing in June 1777 that he had opened a new store for the wholesale merchandising of a "full range of goods," including drapery, hosiery, haberdashery, stationery, cutlery, and groceries.

By February 1778 Gray was sufficiently wealthy to be able to retire from business at Quebec to a home called New Garden at La Canardière; from there he managed the rentals of his houses in the city and intensified his property transactions. That month he sold the house on Rue Saint-Jean for about £550. In January he had rented most of Grandpré to the Quebec notary Charles Stewart for £132; in February 1779 Stewart purchased it for £2,000 sterling. The following month Gray sold for £600 another house acquired by adjudication, on Rue de la Montagne, and in April he paid more than £400 for a farm at La Canardière and a lot with two stone houses on Rue Saint-Louis. In May 1781 he exchanged a farm in the parish of L'Immaculée-Conception at Saint-Ours, acquired at a sheriff's sale, for a lot and house on Rue Saint-Vallier.

As well as deriving income from his property transactions and the rental of his houses, Gray, like other merchants, functioned as an estate executor, property sales agent, and financier. In 1781 the local tailoring partnership of Ritchie and Ferguson was indebted to him for £1,058 and the estate of George Hipps owed him £703. In August 1784 he lent £500 to the postmaster at Berthier-en-Haut (Berthierville), Alexander McKay. In April 1789 Gray and eight others, including David LYND, obtained letters patent for a toll-bridge, called Dorchester Bridge, over the Rivière Saint-Charles.

During the early 1790s Gray disposed of several of his properties at Quebec, but in October 1792 he was obliged to take back from Stewart much of Grandpré in partial payment of a debt of £1,650. Gray conceded several lots according to seigneurial tenure in an effort to exploit his sub-fief; in February 1800 he sold a large farm, part of which was in Grandpré, to judge Pierre-Amable DE BONNE for £3,150 sterling. The following April Gray bought a house and three lots at Beauport, but from that time he appears to have lived off revenues generated from property sales, putting out part of his influx of capital in the form of loans.

By March 1807, when Gray drew up his will, it was obviously a man of substantial means who contemplated the bequests he would bestow. To his young nephew Benjamin Ritchie, son of the deceased tailor Hugh, whose estate was heavily indebted to him, he left £600 and a number of effects. To relatives, most of whom were in Scotland, he left £1,600 and two shares in the Union Hotel at Quebec. His largest beneficiary, however, was Ann Ritchie, Benjamin's sister, who had for some time nursed Gray's invalid wife and who was to receive £2,000, two shares in the Dorchester Bridge, Grandpré (now known as Montplaisir), and a farm in the parish of Beauport. The bequest was made on condition that she continue to live with, and nurse, Gray's wife in addition to taking over from Gray the care of the indigent wife of a former tenant, and of an old slave, Néron Bartholomy, should he decide to remain in slavery after Gray's death; should he opt for freedom but remain with Ann, she was to pay him £12 a year for his services as a freeman.

Until 1808 Gray had participated little in politics, although he had occasionally manifested sympathy with some of the political aspirations of the local merchant community. In May 1808, however, he invoked his 48 years' residence at Quebec and his age, situation, and fortune to seek election to the House of Assembly. He had, perhaps, been caught up in the increasingly charged political atmosphere of the colony; in the assembly most of the Canadians, who formed the majority, were seriously disaffected and the colonial government was supported only by a small group of representatives, composed mainly of British merchants. On 16 May Gray and De Bonne, a known ministerial adherent and influential politician, were elected for Quebec County on the strength of their support in Beauport and Charlesbourg.

A major point of conflict in the assembly was the assertion by the Canadian majority that De Bonne, as a judge, was ineligible to sit in the house; Gray consistently supported the ministerial defence of De Bonne's right to sit. Challenges to De Bonne's eligibility were met by Governor CRAIG with dissolution of the assembly in 1808 and 1809. During the fiercely contested elections of 1809, Gray and 16 others were identified as composing a group favourable to the government by the newspaper *Le Canadien*, established in 1806 as the outspoken voice of Canadian political interests. Although the group's number was significantly reduced in the elections of November 1809, Gray and De Bonne were re-elected for Quebec County. In the assembly Gray reaffirmed his support for Craig in votes on the control of civil expenditure and the eligibility of judges to be elected.

Faced with the assembly's independent dismissal of De Bonne at the height of political crisis, Craig again dissolved it in February 1810. Gray, who was one of only a few members who commanded the governor's respect, sought re-election despite ill health and the death of his wife on 27 February. In a strained electoral climate intensified by Craig's seizure of *Le Canadien* in March, Gray articulated the British fear of Canadian social and political domination. Failing to comprehend the complex Canadian position and suspecting revolutionary motivation, he denounced the Canadian leaders as "Demagogues of faction" and condemned their nationalist aspirations as the seditious and "wicked machinations of a few evil disposed persons." In a public address on 27 March the former merchant testified to the "rapid advances" made by Canadians since the conquest "under the powerful protection of the British Government." He further defied the Canadian group by equating continued prosperity and political stability with assimilation and electoral support for candidates favouring the government. In the election, which lasted from 29 March to 3 April, Gray and Joseph-François Perrault*, a government official and pioneer Canadian educational reformer, were defeated. On 5 April the *Quebec Gazette* printed a letter, signed by Gray and Perrault, protesting electoral irregularity and recklessly identifying "the Congreganistes Sacristains and Beadles of the ROMAN CHURCHES" and specific influential Canadian families as the agents of their defeat. Gray denied association with this rash letter, declaring that he had authorized only a statement of gratitude to his electoral supporters.

Following his defeat Gray returned to Millbank, a residence he occupied at Beauport. On 22 Aug. 1810 he married Phoebe (Phebe) Wallen, widow of James FROST, former captain of the port of Quebec. They separated, however, in February 1813; by the articles of separation, Gray, in order to satisfy his "natural obligation" as a husband "to find and provide the said Phoebe Wallen Gray with the means of living in a befitting manner," promised to pay her £100 per annum for the duration of their separation. Gray apparently had no children from either of his marriages, but by 21 Feb. 1810 he had adopted an orphan, whom he had baptized Frost Ralph Gray and to whom he was, according to Craig, a "good father."

Gray died unexpectedly at Beauport on 27 Dec. 1813 and was buried three days later from St Andrew's (Presbyterian) Church at Quebec. He had been, according to the *Quebec Mercury*, a man "much esteemed for the goodness of his disposition and charitable acts." In 1811 he had had to cut his Scottish relatives out of his will and reduce bequests to other heirs in order to take into account a smaller fortune and his second wife. Only his devoted niece, Ann, who had married Colonel John Thomas Zouch the previous year, suffered no diminution of bequests, and she inherited what was probably a sizeable estate. Phoebe Wallen, after receiving her first and only separation allowance of £100, was subsequently paid a life annuity of £126 per annum as specified in her marriage contract, even though by the articles of separation she had agreed to renounce its benefits.

DAVID ROBERTS

ANQ-Q, CE1-61, 22 Aug. 1810; CE1-66, 30 Dec. 1813; CN1-25, 4 oct. 1781; CN1-26, 21 nov. 1807, 14 mai 1808, 23 mars 1810; CN1-83, 25, 29, 30 janv., 15 févr., 31 juill. 1782; 23 mars 1785; 3 févr., 3 mars 1787; 15 oct. 1788; 29 avril, 5 sept. 1789; 19 avril, 2 juill. 1790; 22 mars, 4 nov. 1791; 26 janv., 22 févr. 1793; CN1-178, 20 juill. 1796; 9 nov. 1797; 6 déc. 1802; 8, 26 mars 1803; 3 mars 1804; CN1-205, 17 nov. 1775; 3 janv., 12 févr. 1778; 6 févr., 13, 16 mars, 13 avril 1779; 18 janv. 1780; 26 mars, 30 mai, 2 oct. 1781; 1er mai 1783; 10 mars 1784; CN1-207, 21 juin 1773; 2 mai, 25 août, 5 nov. 1774; 13 avril 1775; CN1-224, 14 juin 1779, 12 août 1784; CN1-230, 28 juill. 1798; 15 févr., 30 avril, 21 nov. 1799; 14 févr., 7 mai 1800; CN1-248, 31 mars 1764; CN1-250, 5 avril 1761; 5 mars, 14 juill. 1762; CN1-253, 28 Jan., 11, 12, 15 Feb., 6 July 1814; CN1-256, 17 Jan. 1782; CN1-262, 16 janv. 1796; 20 févr., 15 avril 1797; 5, 17 avril 1800; 7 mars 1801; 24 sept. 1804; 1er sept. 1806; 6, 18 mars, 21 juin, 7 juill. 1807; 29 juin, 6, 14 août 1810; 9 mars, 21 sept., 14 oct. 1811; 14 mai 1812; 25 févr. 1813; CN1-284, 22 mars 1791; 1er févr., 18 sept., 20 oct., 23 nov. 1792; 16 avril 1793; 6, 23 mai 1795; 19 févr. 1797; 7 oct. 1801; 17 avril 1802; 28 juin 1803; 20 mai 1804; 14 août, 30 oct. 1810. PAC, RG 1, L3ᴸ: 2951, 47653–54; RG 4, A1, 149: 37. PRO, CO 42/66: 176–81; 42/141: 32.

Bas-Canada, chambre d'Assemblée, *Journaux*, 1806–13. *Gentleman's Magazine*, January–June 1818: 645. *Le Canadien*, 9 oct., 29 nov. 1809; 6 janv. 1810. *Quebec Gazette*, 24 Jan., 28 Feb. 1765; 21 May 1767; 17 Aug. 1769; 15 June 1775; 19 June, 10 July 1777; 4 Feb., 1 April 1779; 20 Dec. 1781; 24 July 1794; 15 Jan. 1801; 5, 19 May 1808; 5

Gray

Oct., 30 Nov. 1809; 1, 15 March, 5, 12 April 1810; 22 April, 30 Dec. 1813; 25 May 1818. *Quebec Mercury*, 28 Dec. 1813. Christie, *Hist. of L.C.*, vol.1. F. M. Greenwood, "The development of a garrison mentality among the English in Lower Canada, 1793–1811" (PHD thesis, Univ. of B.C., Vancouver, 1970). Manning, *Revolt of French Canada*, 41–62. Neatby, *Quebec*, 229–30. Philéas Gagnon, "Le premier pont sur la rivière Saint-Charles," *BRH*, 4 (1898): 55. Hare, "L'Assemblée législative du Bas-Canada," *RHAF*, 27: 381–86. L. A. H. Smith, "'Le Canadien' and the British constitution, 1806–1810," *CHR*, 38 (1957): 93–108.

GRAY, ROBERT, merchant captain, fur trader, and explorer; b. 10 May 1755 in Tiverton, R.I., son of William and Elizabeth Gray; d. in the summer of 1806, probably at sea.

Robert Gray's widow was to state in a memorial submitted to the United States Congress in 1846 that her husband had served in the naval forces during the Revolutionary War, but no documentary proof has been found. He first comes to notice in 1787. Shortly before this, businessmen in New England had learned that the fur of the sea otter, plentiful on the northwest coast, had fetched high prices in China when sold there by members of James Cook*'s last expedition. Eager for Chinese goods, a group of Boston merchants headed by Joseph Barrell sent to the northwest an expedition led by John Kendrick*. It consisted of the ship *Columbia Rediviva*, under Kendrick, and the small sloop *Lady Washington*, commanded by Gray.

The ships sailed from Boston on 30 Sept. 1787, but Kendrick was a dilatory commander and they were a full year on the way to Nootka Sound (B.C.). Gray arrived on 17 Sept. 1788, in time to meet John MEARES, who was about to sail for the Sandwich (Hawaiian) Islands, and he witnessed the launching of Meares's schooner *North West America*. Kendrick arrived on 22 September and decided it was too late to trade for furs; both ships lay idle in the sound until March 1789. Gray in the *Washington* then sailed on a trading cruise, ranging the coast from Juan de Fuca Strait to Bucareli Bay (Alaska), and proving the insularity of the Queen Charlotte Islands. When he returned to Nootka on 17 June he found the *Columbia* still at anchor, and discovered that the Spaniards under Esteban José Martínez* had taken possession of the sound. During the following month James COLNETT, commanding British merchant ships owned in part by Meares, arrived with the intention of establishing a trading post. Although this objective led to a clash with Martínez, and thus to the Nootka Sound controversy, the Spanish commander did not molest Gray or Kendrick, who remained on good terms with him. On 16 July the Americans left Nootka and sailed south to Clayoquot Sound (B.C.). There Kendrick transferred the furs the *Washington* had collected to the *Columbia*, and sent the latter to China and thence

back to Boston under Gray's command. She arrived at Boston on 9 Aug. 1790, the first vessel to carry the Stars and Stripes around the world.

The venture was not a financial success, but it was clear there was a good prospect that subsequent voyages would prove profitable. American merchants, unlike their British competitors, were not hampered by the necessity of securing licences from chartered companies holding monopolies, and were unaffected by the long wars that were to plague Europe. The *Columbia*'s voyage initiated for New England a trading contact with the northwest coast that was to continue for 40 years, and American ships soon completely dominated the maritime fur trade.

Barrell reorganized his enterprise, in which Gray became a partner, and on 28 Sept. 1790, after a respite of only six weeks, the *Columbia* sailed again. Gray was a fine seaman, and under his driving command the ship reached Clayoquot Sound in little more than eight months, on 5 June 1791. The next few months were spent trading on the coast. Late in September Gray found winter quarters in the sound where he built Fort Defiance, apparently at present-day Lemmens Inlet in Meares Island. The small sloop *Adventure* was completed there and launched in February 1792 [*see* Robert HASWELL]; she was sold to the Spaniards at the end of the trading season.

Relations with the Indians had been reasonably good, but Gray's ship had been threatened several times, and in January a plot by Wikinanish* to seize the *Columbia* and kill her crew was discovered. Gray was not a man to be trifled with. On 27 March, just before the ship left Clayoquot Sound, he retaliated by ordering the burning of Opitsat, a large Nootka village of some 200 houses. The order was carried out by one of the mates, John Boit, who confesses in his journal that he was "greived to think Capt. Gray shou'd let his passions go so far. . . . This fine Village, the Work of Ages, was in a short time totally destroy'd."

Sailing southward, Gray met George Vancouver*'s ships on 29 April, and on 7 May discovered and named Grays Harbor (Wash.). On the 11th came the climax of his career, the discovery of the Columbia River, which he named after his ship. Others had suspected the existence of the river, but Gray was the first who dared to take his ship through the forbidding breakers and shoals that stretched across its mouth. By so doing he gave the United States one of its strongest claims to the Oregon country.

By 24 July Gray was back in Nootka Sound, where Juan Francisco de la Bodega* y Quadra, the new Spanish commandant, was awaiting Vancouver's arrival to negotiate a settlement of the rival claims to the sound. From Gray and Joseph Ingraham (second mate of the *Columbia* in 1789) Bodega secured a joint statement supporting his contention that Meares's claims against the Spaniards were unfounded. After a

Gray

brief trading cruise Gray returned to Nootka Sound in September, when he reported to Vancouver his discovery of the Columbia and gave him a rough sketch of its estuary. The *Columbia* left the coast on 3 Oct. 1792 and returned to Boston by way of China on 26 July 1793.

On 3 February the following year Gray married Martha Atkins; they had four daughters and a son, Robert Don Quadra, who died in childhood. Except in 1799–1800, when trouble developed with France and he was briefly in command of the privateer *Lucy*, Gray spent his late years in coasting ships sailing out of Boston. The exact date of his death is not known, but he is believed to have died of yellow fever in 1806 while on a voyage to Charleston, S.C.

W. KAYE LAMB

[The Mass. Hist. Soc. (Boston) holds the logs of Robert Haswell, an officer on both voyages: "A voyage round the world onboard the ship Columbia-Rediviva and sloop Washington," [1787–89], and "A voyage on discoveries in the ship Columbia Rediviva," [1791–93]. It also holds John Boit's log of the second voyage, "Remarks on the ship *Columbia*'s voyage from Boston (on a voyage round the Globe), 1790–1793," and an account of it by John Box Hoskins, supercargo, "The narrative of a voyage to the north west coast of America and China on trade and discoveries performed in the ship *Columbia Rediviva*, 1790, 1791, 1792 and 1793." The ship's official logs are lost, but Robert Greenhow secured an extract recording the discovery of Grays Harbor and the Columbia River and printed it in *The history of Oregon and California, and the other territories on the northwest coast of North America* . . . (Boston, 1844; repr. Los Angeles, 1970), 434–36. These logs and journals, together with miscellaneous letters and other papers, are included in *Voyages of the "Columbia" to the northwest coast, 1787–1790 and 1790–1793*, ed. F. W. Howay ([Boston], 1941; repr. Amsterdam and New York, [1969]), although Haswell's log of the second voyage comes from the incomplete transcript held by the Bancroft Library, Univ. of California (Berkeley), the only text available at the time.

Additional details appear in the following: "Captains Gray and Kendrick; the Barrell letters," ed. F. W. Howay, *Wash. Hist. Quarterly* (Seattle), 12 (1921): 243–71. "Letters relating to the second voyage of the 'Columbia,'" ed. F. W. Howay, Oreg. Hist. Soc., *Quarterly* (Eugene), 24 (1923): 132–52. Jack Fry, "Fort Defiance: relics discovered last summer may establish the wintering place in 1791–2 of Captain Robert Gray," *Beaver*, outfit 298 (summer 1967): 18–21. F. W. Howay, "Voyages of Kendrick and Gray in 1787–90," *Oreg. Hist. Quarterly*, 30 (1929): 89–94. F. W. Howay and Albert Matthews, "Some notes upon Captain Robert Gray," *Wash. Hist. Quarterly*, 21 (1930): 8–12. E. S. Meany, "The widow of Captain Robert Gray," *Wash. Hist. Quarterly*, 20 (1929): 192–95. D. H. Mitchell, "The investigation of Fort Defiance: verifications of the site," *BC Studies* (Vancouver), no.4 (spring 1970): 3–20. S. E. Morison, "The Columbia's winter quarters of 1791–92 located," *Oreg. Hist. Quarterly* (Salem), 39 (1938): 3–7. W.K.L.]

GRAY (Grey), ROBERT ISAAC DEY, office holder, lawyer, judge, and politician; b. *c.* 1772, probably in New York, son of James Gray and Elizabeth Low; d. unmarried 7 or 8 Oct. 1804 in the wreck of the *Speedy* on Lake Ontario.

At the outbreak of the American revolution the Gray family fled to the province of Quebec where James Gray was appointed major in the 1st battalion of Sir John Johnson*'s King's Royal Regiment of New York. At the end of the war Gray received land and took up residence just east of the loyalist settlement of New Johnstown (Cornwall, Ont.). Robert Isaac Dey Gray received his early education and acquired an interest in law at Quebec, probably under the tutelage of his godfather Isaac Ogden*.

Young Gray benefited from the prominence of his father, who had been appointed lieutenant of the county of Stormont by Lieutenant Governor SIMCOE. On 5 Sept. 1793 Gray became surrogate court registrar for the Eastern District, serving until his appointment as district court judge for the Home District on 7 June 1796. Along with 15 others he was called to the bar in October 1794 by an act of the legislature. The following month Simcoe recommended him for the vacant office of solicitor general "not only on his Father's merits" but to enable him to further his education in England "and by these means acquire the habits and character of the English Bar." The Duke of Portland, the Home secretary, approved Simcoe's choice in May 1795 but wondered whether "the present state of the Province required both an Attorney and Solicitor General." Gray became a barrister in Trinity term 1797 and served as treasurer of the Law Society of Upper Canada from 1798 to 1801.

It was usual in Upper Canada for both the solicitor and the attorney general to hold seats in the House of Assembly and act as administration spokesmen. Gray was no exception. He was elected for the riding of Stormont in the election of 1796 and to the new riding of Stormont and Russell in 1800 and 1804. No scholarly study has yet been made of the alignments in Upper Canada's parliaments; none the less it is possible to pick out significant events in Gray's participation in the assembly. He was one of the more active members but did not dominate proceedings as did oppositionists such as Angus MACDONELL (Collachie) or David McGregor Rogers*. Although a slave-holder himself, in 1798 he was among the minority that opposed Christopher Robinson*'s bill extending slavery within the province. The following year he voted with the majority defeating a bill to allow Methodists the right to solemnize marriage. In 1800 he was among the eastern members who opposed Samuel STREET's election as speaker and the next year cast his vote against Surveyor General David William Smith*'s election to the speakership. Gray led the resistance to Macdonell's contempt proceedings in 1803 against the clerk of the crown and pleas, David Burns, yet during the same session he supported Macdonell's Assessment Bill. In 1804 he favoured the passage of the notorious Sedition Bill [*see* Robert Fleming Gourlay*]. He regularly served as the assembly's liaison with the Legislative Council and consistently resisted the assembly's attempts to curtail or limit the prerogatives of the lieutenant governor. He initiated several pieces of legislation usually concerning the reform of law and its administration and took a particular interest in the regulation of inland trade and designation of ports of entry [*see* Colin McNabb].

When Attorney General John White* was killed in 1800, Gray temporarily assumed the duties of that office until the arrival of Thomas Scott* in 1801. As solicitor general Gray often represented the crown in criminal cases across the province. On 7 Oct. 1804 he embarked from York (Toronto) on the schooner *Speedy* to prosecute a murder case. The ship went down with all hands off Presqu'ile Point, Brighton Township, that or the following day. Other victims included Macdonell and the recently appointed judge of the Court of King's Bench, Thomas Cochrane.

At his death Gray owned 12,000 acres of land and had debts of £1,200. By his will he freed the old family slave Dorinda (Dorine) Baker and left a trust of £1,200 to provide for her welfare. Earlier in the year on a trip to Albany, N.Y., he had purchased her mother Lavine for $50 and "promised her that she may work as much or as little as she pleases, while she lives." He gave £50 and 200 acres each to Dorinda's sons, John and Simon Baker. The remainder of his estate he divided among his relatives and friends including £20 to former Chief Justice John Elmsley "in token of my regard and esteem."

ROBERT J. BURNS

PAC, MG 23, HII, 11; RG 5, B2. *Corr. of Lieut. Governor Simcoe* (Cruikshank), 1: 10–11; 3: 178; 4: 6, 35. "Journals of Legislative Assembly of U.C.," AO *Report*, 1909. "Petitions for grants of land" (Cruikshank), *OH*, 26: 197. "The probated wills of men prominent in the public affairs of early Upper Canada," ed. A. F. Hunter, *OH*, 23 (1926): 332–33, 337–38. Henry Scadding, *Toronto of old*, ed. F. H. Armstrong (Toronto, 1966), 210–11, 334–35. *Town of York, 1793–1815* (Firth), lvii. "U.C. land book B," AO *Report*, 1930: 15, 58, 82. "U.C. land book C," AO *Report*, 1931: 24. Armstrong, *Handbook of Upper Canadian chronology*, 23, 160, 164. Wallace, *Macmillan dict.* Burns, "First elite of Toronto," 85. J. F. Pringle, *Lunenburgh or the old Eastern District; its settlement and early progress . . .* (Cornwall, Ont., 1890; repr. Belleville, Ont., 1972), 406. Riddell, *Legal profession in U.C.* G. C. Patterson, "Land settlement in Upper Canada, 1783–1840," AO *Report*, 1920: 89. W. R. Riddell, "Robert Isaac Dey Gray, the first solicitor-general of Upper Canada, 1797–1804," *Canadian Law Times* (Toronto), 41 (1921): 424–32, 508–18.

GREEN, FRANCIS, army officer, office holder, author, and judge; b. 21 Aug. 1742 in Boston, Mass., second son of Benjamin Green* and Margaret Pierce; m. there first 18 Oct. 1769 Susanna Green, his double cousin, and they had five children; m. secondly 19 May 1785 Harriet Mathews, daughter of David Mathews*, in Halifax, N.S., and they had six children; d. 21 April 1809 in Medford, Mass.

Francis Green was educated in Halifax and Boston schools and in 1756 was admitted to Harvard College. He did not finish his degree, however, since in 1757 he was called to join the 40th Foot, in which his father had obtained him an ensign's commission. Francis took part in the siege of Louisbourg, Île Royale (Cape Breton Island), in 1758 [*see* Jeffery Amherst*] and remained there until June 1760, when his regiment was ordered to Quebec to reinforce James Murray*. He was promoted lieutenant in 1761 and saw service in the West Indies the following year. After the war Green spent several years as one of Major-General Thomas Gage*'s secretaries, but in 1766, seeing little chance of advancement, he sold his commission.

Green then went into the importing business with his father, who was in Halifax, and as the Boston partner of the firm he established a reputation as a rising young merchant. During the political controversies of the 1760s and 1770s Green initially supported the colonial party, but when he was dropped from its ranks in 1769 for violating the non-importation agreement he joined the government supporters. In June 1774 at several town meetings he counselled abolition of the committees of correspondence then forming, and his loyalist sentiments resulted in his being attacked by mobs at Norwich and Windham, Conn., while on a business trip in July. On the outbreak of hostilities in 1775 Green sided with the British and on 1 November was appointed captain in the Loyal American Associates. He served throughout the siege of Boston, and when the British evacuated Boston for Halifax in March 1776 Green, with his three children (his wife having died of fever in November 1775), three servants, and some of his goods and furniture, accompanied them.

The next spring Green followed the British army to New York City. There, sometimes in partnership with other loyalists such as George Leonard*, he outfitted vessels for privateering. Although he had hopes of aiding the British cause and retrieving his fortune, they were dashed in December 1779 when five of his vessels were lost to enemy action or shipwreck. In the autumn of 1780 he therefore went to England in an attempt to obtain compensation, and in July 1781 he was granted an annual pension of £100. His subsequent claim for £36,209 lost in goods, money, and extensive land holdings in Massachusetts, Connecticut, and New Hampshire was less fortunate: most of

Greenfield

the component claims were disallowed for lack of proof, and he received only £295.

Green returned to Nova Scotia in June 1784 and in November was appointed sheriff of Halifax County, succeeding William Shaw*. His finances had, despite his difficulties, evidently remained healthy, since in April 1785 Penelope, sister of Edward WINSLOW, wrote to Ward Chipman* that Green "enjoys all the pomp of this pompous Town . . . gives dinners two or three times a week & tomorrow evening all the Noblesse are to be entertained at his house, a Ball and supper superb." In his official duties Green encountered problems. Several prisoners escaped in 1786 from the jail, which was falling into disrepair and was consequently not secure. The following year Green was sued by John Stairs for allowing a man Stairs had had confined for debt to escape. Green blamed the poor state of the jail, claiming that he had repeatedly advised the Council of its condition, but to no avail. Green lost the suit, and to meet the costs he had to sell 100 acres of land near Dartmouth which he had inherited from his father.

Green's son Charles had been discovered to be deaf when six months old, and while in Britain during the revolution Green had placed the boy in Thomas Braidwood's academy for the deaf and dumb in Edinburgh, where Charles had learned to speak, read, and write. Encouraged by this improvement, Green published anonymously a pamphlet entitled *"Vox oculis subjecta"; a dissertation on the most curious and important art of imparting speech* in the hopes that other establishments of the kind would be stimulated. His son accidentally drowned in 1787 but Green persisted and, although he was disappointed initially, his visits to England and France before 1784 and his publication of other pamphlets between 1788 and 1793 were partially responsible for the establishment of a charitable school for the deaf and dumb at Bermondsey (London).

In 1793, after the death of his elder brother Benjamin, Green acted as temporary treasurer of the province in association with George Thesiger. In 1794 he was appointed a judge of the Inferior Court of Common Pleas. Financial difficulties plagued him, however. Assured that strong feelings against loyalists had died down in the United States, in 1796 he sold his property at Preston, which included a fine house, to the commissioners of the maroons [*see* Sir John WENTWORTH] and the next year returned with his family to his native state, where he settled at Medford. For some years he worked as a marine insurance underwriter at Boston but in 1798 and 1799 suffered losses of $25,000. Thereafter he once more devoted himself to the education of the deaf and dumb, publishing various essays in an attempt to have a school for them established in America. He became an authority on the subject and is regarded as a pioneer in the education of the deaf.

Francis Green is the author of *"Vox oculis subjecta"; a dissertation on the most curious and important art of imparting speech, and the knowledge of language, to the naturally deaf, and (consequently) dumb* (London, 1783); this was republished in part under the title *A new edition of "Vox oculis subjecta," part I* . . . (Boston, 1897).

PAC, MG 23, D1, ser.1, 2: 591–616. PANS, MG 1, 332D (copy); MG 100, 131, no.15; RG 20A, 19, no.53; RG 39, J, 8: 29. PRO, AO 12/105: 19; 12/109: 60; AO 13, bundle 45: 464–529; bundle 73: 714–25. Boston, Registry Dept., *Records relating to the early history of Boston*, ed. W. H. Whitmore *et al.* (39v., Boston, 1876–1909), [24]: *Boston births, 1700–1800*, 246. "United Empire Loyalists: enquiry into losses and services," AO *Report*, 1904: 1208–10. *Winslow papers* (Raymond), 58, 59, 288. *DAB*. Jones, *Loyalists of Mass.*, x, xviii, 12, 83, 153–54, 194. R. H. R. Smythies, *Historical records of the 40th (2nd Somersetshire) regiment* . . . (Devonport, Eng., 1894), 18–38. Stark, *Loyalists of Mass.* (1907), 123–25, 132–37. P. R. Blakeley, "Francis Green – 'A suffering loyalist and friend to the British government,'" *Nova Scotia Hist. Quarterly* (Halifax), 9 (1979): 1–14.

GREENFIELD. *See* MACDONELL

GREGORY, JOHN, fur trader and merchant; b. *c.* 1751 in England; d. 21 Feb. 1817 in Montreal, Lower Canada.

John Gregory may have been connected in Britain with Mark and Thomas Gregory, a London firm that had entered the fur trade shortly after the conquest. He came to North America in 1773 and that year formed a partnership with the fur trader James Finlay, who had considerable experience in the field, having been one of the first British traders to reach the lower Saskatchewan River by 1766. Little is known of Gregory's life as a trader, but he did spend some time on the Sturgeon River (Sask.). By the end of the 1770s he was displacing Finlay as the dominant partner; in 1777 Gregory invested £2,500 to Finlay's £11,770, but the following year Gregory's investment was £6,790 to Finlay's £4,750, and in 1782 £15,805 to Finlay's £750. Their efforts were concentrated primarily on Detroit (Mich.) and secondarily on Michilimackinac (until 1781 Mackinaw City, then Mackinac Island, Mich.). In 1783 Gregory made what appears to have been his largest investment, £18,460, of which £17,500 was in the Detroit trade.

After the retirement of Finlay in 1783 or 1784, Gregory formed a new partnership with Normand MacLeod*, who had connections at Michilimackinac; in 1784 they traded principally to that post, with a secondary interest in the Mississippi valley. That year two traders excluded from the North West Company during its reorganization in the winter of 1783–84, Peter PANGMAN and Peter POND, persuaded Gregory, MacLeod and Company to move into the northwest trade. Pond opted finally to join the NWC, but Pangman and his associate, John ROSS, were made wintering partners in Gregory, MacLeod, as was Alexander MACKENZIE, a clerk in Gregory's Montreal counting-house since 1779. Although Joseph FROBISHER affirmed that Gregory, MacLeod furnished the backbone of the opposition to the NWC, the competition was unequal, the latter being larger, more experienced in the northwest trade, and better financed; in 1785 it sent 25 canoes to Grand Portage (near Grand Portage, Minn.) while Gregory, MacLeod could send only eight. By 1786 the challengers were in grave financial difficulty. That December their creditors chose from among themselves three trustees, Robert Ellice and Company, Richard DOBIE, and Edward William GRAY, to receive and distribute among them all returns of the next season's trade. Moreover, rivalry with the NWC, always fierce, had become violent: in the summer of 1787 Gregory, who was attending his company's annual general meeting at Grand Portage, was shaken when one of his clerks, Roderick McKenzie*, arrived unexpectedly with news of the murder of Ross by Pond's men in the Athabasca country. When Simon McTAVISH of the NWC arrived at Grand Portage for its annual meeting, he proposed that Gregory, MacLeod join the NWC in order to avoid further bloodshed, an invitation that Gregory wisely realized could hardly be declined. By the agreement of entry later that year each partner in Gregory, MacLeod received a one-twentieth share in an expanded NWC. The competition had cost Gregory dearly, however; by 1792 he had still not discharged all the debts he had brought with him into the NWC and MacLeod was disclaiming all responsibility for them.

None the less Gregory soon achieved a certain prominence within the NWC. In 1790 he was named one of its representatives at the annual meetings at Grand Portage, where the wintering partners exchanged their furs for trade goods, and later that year he purchased MacLeod's share in the company. He appears to have acquired the respect of McTavish, who on leaving for London in 1791 arranged secretly to entrust Gregory with control of the Montreal business during his absence, much to the chagrin of Frobisher; he complained that Gregory did not manifest sufficient regard for his experience and position as a senior partner. That year Gregory's election to the Beaver Club, membership in which was limited to men who had wintered in the Indian country, signalled his acceptance within the NWC, for its members dominated the club and controlled entry into it.

In 1793 Gregory was apparently in charge of the hiring of traders, and, with William McGillivray*, was director of operations at Grand Portage. Two years later he was made a partner in McTavish, Frobisher and Company, the principal outfitting firm in the NWC; he was again to act as representative, with McGillivray and Mackenzie, at the annual meetings at Grand Portage. As well, he made numerous trips to New York to conduct negotiations for the shipping of furs to the Far East, an alternative to European markets disrupted by the Napoleonic Wars. In 1799 Gregory held two of the ten shares in McTavish, Frobisher, which had been reorganized following Frobisher's retirement, and he was assigned the superintendence of the "Outfits Packing and Shipping Concerns." When McTavish died in 1804, he bequeathed £100 to Gregory, his "friend and partner." Later that year Gregory signed the agreement which brought to an end the competition in the northwest between the NWC and the New North West Company (sometimes called the XY Company) [see John OGILVY]. On 31 May 1806 Gregory retired from McTavish, Frobisher and from the fur trade.

On 22 Feb. 1778 Gregory had married at Montreal Isabella Ferguson, and they had several children. Their three daughters were described as "very fine, lovely girls" by George Thomas Landmann*, a British officer, in 1799; the youngest, Maria, married the fur trader David Mitchell in 1806. A son, George, married Jane Prescott Forsyth, daughter of the Montreal merchant John Forsyth*.

It would appear that during the 1780s Gregory had begun spending most of his time in Montreal. He owned a stone house on Rue Saint-François, which he sold before June 1789, probably to McTavish, Frobisher; about 1799 he was living on Mount Royal next to McGillivray and Mackenzie. In 1787 he had been a member of a grand jury that complained of the inadequacy of Montreal's jail and court-house. He was a staunch member of the Scotch Presbyterian Church, later known as St Gabriel Street Church.

In 1802 Gregory received, according to the system of township leaders and associates [see James CALDWELL], 1,200 acres in Arthabaska Township; he soon added the grants of his associates to make a total of 11,550 acres. The same year, and in 1804, he bought several contiguous lots along the Chemin des Tanneries (Rue Carrière) at Montreal; there, in the woods on the bank of the Rivière Saint-Pierre, he built a manor-house called Woodland, from which a long poplar-lined drive was cut out to the road. Gregory died at Woodland at about age 66 on 21 Feb. 1817. He had been, according to the *Montreal Herald*, "one of our most respectable citizens."

MARJORIE WILKINS CAMPBELL

Grey

ANQ-M, CE1-63, 22 Feb. 1778, 21 Feb. 1817. PAC, RG 4, B28, 115. *Docs. relating to NWC* (Wallace). "Fur-trade on the upper lakes, 1778–1815," ed. R. G. Thwaites, Wis., State Hist. Soc., *Coll.*, 19 (1910): 266. Landmann, *Adventures and recollections*, 2: 65. Mackenzie, *Journals and letters* (Lamb), 10, 78; *Voyages from Montreal through the continent of North America to the frozen and Pacific oceans in 1789 and 1793 with an account of the rise and state of the fur trade* (2v., New York, 1922), xliii. J.-B. Perrault, *Jean-Baptiste Perrault, marchand voyageur parti de Montréal le 28e de mai 1783*, L.-P. Cormier, édit. ([Montréal], 1978), 93. *Montreal Herald*, 1 March 1817. *Quebec Gazette*, 9 Sept. 1779; 16 June, 3 Nov. 1785; 17 May 1787; 25 June 1789; 28 Oct. 1790; 23 Jan. 1800; 11 March, 3 June 1802; 5 May 1803; 18 Dec. 1806; 15 Dec. 1808; 22 March 1810; 5 Aug. 1813; 6 March 1817; 13 Sept. 1819; 21 Dec. 1820. Langelier, *Liste des terrains concédés*, 57, 1413. Lefebvre, "Engagements pour l'Ouest," ANQ *Rapport*, 1946–47: 326–41. Massicotte, "Répertoire des engagements pour l'Ouest," ANQ *Rapport*, 1944–45: 353, 355–57. M. W. Campbell, *NWC* (1957), 48, 53–54, 68–70, 91, 93, 121–22, 127, 152. R. Campbell, *Hist. of Scotch Presbyterian Church*, 97. Davidson, *NWC*, 14, 17, 24–26, 47, 62, 73, 83, 200. Innis, *Fur trade in Canada* (1970), 199–200, 249–55; *Peter Pond, fur trader and adventurer* (Toronto, 1930), 106–7. Miquelon, "Baby family," 188–91. Morton, *Hist. of Canadian west* (1973), 336–47. Rumilly, *La Compagnie du Nord-Ouest*, 1: 92–93, 102, 104, 124, 138, 141, 143–44, 179, 239. L. J. Burpee, "The Beaver Club," CHA *Report*, 1924: 73–74. É.-Z. Massicotte, "Coins historiques de Montréal d'autrefois," *Cahiers des Dix*, 2 (1937): 121. E. A. Mitchell, "The North West Company agreement of 1795," *CHR*, 36 (1955): 126–45. Ouellet, "Dualité économique et changement technologique," *SH*, 9: 286. W. S. Wallace, "Northwesters' quarrel," *Beaver*, outfit 278 (December 1947): 8.

GREY. *See* GRAY

GUERNON, *dit* **Belleville, FRANÇOIS**, soldier and wood-carver; b. *c.* 1740 in Paris, France, son of François Guernon, an innkeeper, and Marie Coulon; m. first 10 Aug. 1761 Marie Dalpech, *dit* Bélair, in the parish of Saint-Sulpice (Que.), and they had eight children; m. secondly 28 Jan. 1793 Marie Martin, a widow, at Saint-Jacques-de-la-Nouvelle-Acadie (Saint-Jacques), Lower Canada; d. there 17 Aug. 1817.

François Guernon, *dit* Belleville, a grenadier in the Régiment de Berry, sailed for New France in the spring of 1757. Discharged after the defeat of the French troops, he settled at Saint-Pierre-du-Portage (L'Assomption, Que.). It is likely that Guernon did his apprenticeship as a wood-carver after his release from the army, possibly with Philippe LIÉBERT or Antoine Cirier*.

In 1762 he was paid for a piece of carving done in the chancel of the church at Saint-Pierre-du-Portage, where Liébert worked on the interior decoration from 1760 to 1774. Guernon could have met Liébert when the latter was beginning his work and may have decided to learn the wood-carver's craft with him, for in this period and until about 1770 Guernon lived at Saint-Sulpice, the parish next to Saint-Pierre-du-Portage. On the other hand, in 1772 Guernon, who was then residing in Montreal, was first mentioned as a wood-carver in the account-book of the parish of Saint-Enfant-Jésus, at Pointe-aux-Trembles (Montreal); the record indicates other sums were paid to him in 1773 and 1774. Between 1743 and 1781 Cirier received payment for various pieces of work from the *fabrique* of Pointe-aux-Trembles, and in 1773 Liébert's name also appeared in the parish account-book. The three wood-carvers may have worked in close collaboration in this period. Whether he had learned his craft with Liébert or with Cirier, it is certain that around 1772 Guernon had established relations with the best wood-carvers in the Montreal region.

In 1775 or 1776 Guernon and his family went to live at the mission of Lac-des-Deux-Montagnes (Oka). It was probably during these years that he did seven reliefs to decorate the shrines and chapels of a Way of the Cross that the Sulpicians had built for the Indians. From 1742 and until about 1776 seven paintings brought from France had decorated the Way of the Cross at the Lac-des-Deux-Montagnes mission and had been a means of teaching religion to the Indians. The Sulpician François-Auguste Magon* de Terlaye was anxious to preserve these works and he put them in the church to protect them. But since he wanted to retain their value for teaching, he ordered exact reproductions, this time in wooden sculptures in relief that would be more suited to the climate and would weather it better. Although remaining faithful to the originals, Guernon simplified the composition in several instances.

In 1777 Guernon may have worked on the decoration of a chapel in the mission church. At this period he settled in Saint-Jacques-de-la-Nouvelle-Acadie, on one of the two properties that the Sulpicians had granted him on 8 June 1774, on the upper reaches of a stream called the Vacher. Later, on 12 March 1782, he sold the other piece of land to his son Jean-Baptiste.

From 1777 to 1784 he practised his craft in the church at Saint-Pierre-du-Portage, where in 1783 he collaborated with Jean-Louis Foureur*, *dit* Champagne, and perhaps with Cirier. The following year he carved some tabernacles for the church of Sainte-Anne at Varennes, and in 1790 he worked at the church in Saint-Sulpice. His last known works date from 1791–92 and were done for the church at Saint-Pierre-du-Portage. Two other works have been attributed to Guernon: the tabernacle in the sacristy at Caughnawaga and a large relief in wood entitled

"Saint Martin partageant son manteau avec un pauvre," which was formerly part of the decoration of the church of Saint-Martin on Île Jésus.

François Guernon, *dit* Belleville, was illiterate and he had no known apprentices. Nevertheless he seems to deserve as important a place in the history of early art in Quebec as his contemporaries Liébert and Cirier. Many of his works have survived and through their characteristics they bear eloquent witness to the production of the wood-carvers of the second half of the 18th century.

JOHN R. PORTER

Six of the seven reliefs carved for the stations of the cross at Oka are extant, although two have suffered some damage. The relief "Saint Martin partageant son manteau avec un pauvre" is now held by the Musée du Québec at Quebec.

AC, Joliette, État civil, Catholiques, Saint-Jacques, 28 janv. 1793, 19 août 1817; Saint-Sulpice, 10 août 1761, 2 mai 1762, 26 févr. 1766, 23 avril 1768; Minutiers, Joseph Daguilhe, 9 août 1761, 29 juin 1770; Terrebonne (Saint-Jérôme), État civil, Catholiques, L'Annonciation-de-la-Bienheureuse-Vierge-Marie (Oka), 7 mars 1775; 23 avril, 20 sept. 1776 (copies at PAC). ANQ-M, CN1-120, 8 juin 1774; CN1-364, 12 mars 1782. AP, Saint-Enfant-Jésus (Pointe-aux-Trembles), Livres de comptes, 1726–1865. ASSM, 8, A; 36, André Cuoq, "Notes inédites pour servir à l'histoire de la mission du Lac-des-Deux-Montagnes" (typescript) (copy at PAC). MAC-CD, Fonds Morisset, 2, G933.5/F825. *Sculpture traditionnelle du Québec* (Québec, 1967), 76. Marius Barbeau, *Trésor des anciens jésuites* (Ottawa, 1957), 19, 150, 152. Morisset, *Coup d'œil sur les arts*, 18, 34; *Les églises et le trésor de Varennes* (Québec, 1943), 18, 31. J. R. Porter et Jean Trudel, *Le calvaire d'Oka* (Ottawa, 1974), 24–25, 93–101. Christian Roy, *Histoire de L'Assomption* (L'Assomption, Qué., 1967), 96–131. Ramsay Traquair, *The old architecture of Quebec . . .* (Toronto, 1947), 249, 289, 292. Olivier Maurault, "Les vicissitudes d'une mission sauvage," *Rev. trimestrielle canadienne*, 16 (1930): 16. Gérard Morisset, "Le trésor de la mission d'Oka," *La Patrie* (Montréal), 13 nov. 1949: 18. L.-B. Richer, "Les chapelles d'Oka," *Québec-Histoire* (Québec), 1 (1971–72), nos.5–6: 46–48.

GUITET (Guité), CLAUDE, settler; b. *c.* 1738 in Carcassonne, France, son of René Guitet and Élisabeth Peyrot; d. 20 Nov. 1802 in Maria, Lower Canada.

According to family tradition, Claude Guitet was a member of the expeditionary force of six infantry battalions that was sent to North America in the spring of 1755 under Jean-Armand Dieskau* to consolidate France's position in the New World. Vice-Admiral Edward Boscawen* lay in wait for the convoy in the Gulf of St Lawrence, and on 10 June, at a point southeast of Newfoundland, he captured two vessels, the *Alcide* and the *Lys*. The latter had on board 330 soldiers of the Régiment de Guyenne and the Régiment de la Reine. Guitet was one of them, and he was probably taken to the British colonies.

Guitet is known to have been in Boston, Mass., in 1772; he had been assimilated into the Acadian community that had formed from those landed on the coast of Massachusetts at the time of the expulsion [*see* Charles Lawrence*]. He married Modeste Landry in Boston on 8 January; the couple had to have a civil marriage, because a local law prohibited Roman Catholic priests from living there. The ceremony was conducted by an uncle of the bride, Louis Robichaux*, who had been authorized to officiate on such occasions by the bishop of Quebec's vicar general in Halifax, N.S., Pierre Maillard*, in 1761. In 1775 the Guitets went to join the Landry family, which had settled in the region of Quebec. Guitet then hastened to show the parish priest of Notre-Dame at Quebec the deed certifying the validity of his civil marriage and finally had his marriage celebrated in rites of the Roman Catholic Church on 28 July 1775. Two sons who had been born in Boston attended the ceremony and were baptized. During the time he lived in the Quebec region, Guitet made his living as a house painter.

When he was about 50, Guitet went to settle in the Gaspé; two of his brothers-in-law, Claude and Jean Landry, had been living there at Carleton since at least 1770. Guitet met again with Pierre Loubert, who had also been on the *Lys* and who was married to a sister of Modeste Landry. Having served in the British army during the American revolution, around 1784 Loubert had received 750 acres of land near Carleton on the Rivière Cascapedia. Apparently he then offered part of his property to Guitet. At the time of the 1784 census the locality, which was soon named Maria after Sir Guy CARLETON's wife, had only two families, Guitet's not being listed; he must therefore have arrived some time between then and the spring of 1790, when one of his sons was godfather at a baptism in Carleton.

Claude Guitet died at the age of about 64, leaving only one of his sons, Joseph, to continue the family line. In the mid 19th century his descendants owned the greater part of Loubert's land.

MARIO MIMEAULT

ANQ-Q, CE1-1, 28 juill. 1775. AP, Saint-Joseph (Carleton), Reg. des baptêmes, mariages et sépultures, 29 nov. 1802. BL, Add. MSS 21862, 7, 9 août 1784. *Familles de Maria et leur généalogie*, [D. Paradis, compil.] ([Maria, Qué., 1967]). Patrice Gallant, *Les registres de la Gaspésie (1752–1850)* (6v., [Sayabec, Qué., 1968]). Tanguay, *Dictionnaire. Centenaire de Caplan, 1875–1975* (Caplan, Qué., 1975), 72. *Le centenaire de la paroisse de Maria, 1860–1960* ([Montréal, 1960]). Guy Frégault, *La guerre de la Conquête* (Montréal et Paris, [1955]; réimpr.,

Gunn

[1966]), 129–32. Émile Lauvrière, *La tragédie d'un peuple: histoire du peuple acadien, de ses origines à nos jours* (3ᵉ éd., 2v., Paris, 1922), 2. Antoine Bernard, "Les origines du pays de Carleton, 1760–1810," *Rev. d'hist. de la Gaspésie* (Gaspé, Qué.), 4 (1966): 101–2. "Le combat de l'*Alcide*," *BRH*, 50 (1944): 152–54.

GUNN, ISABEL (known variously as **Isabella Gun, John Fubbister**, and **Mary Fubbister**), HBC servant; b. probably in St Andrew's Parish, near Kirkwall, Scotland; fl. 1806–9.

Isabel Gunn's foray into the history of the northwest was as short as it was dramatic. In the summer of 1806 this Orkney girl, apparently intent on following a faithless lover, disguised herself as a boy and signed on with the Hudson's Bay Company as a labourer under the name of John Fubbister. Her contract was for three years at £8 per annum. Arriving at Moose Factory (Ont.), Fubbister was transported with the other hands to Fort Albany, only to find that her lover was serving at the outpost of Eastmain (Que.). The Albany journal for 1806–7 reports that Fubbister actively performed the servants' tasks, especially helping to freight goods inland. Apparently her true identity was a well-kept secret, although it was known at least to one John Scarth, a long-time HBC employee who had sailed with Fubbister from Stromness.

In the fall of 1807 Fubbister was part of a brigade sent to winter at Pembina (N. Dak.) on the Red River. Here again she "worked at anything & well like the rest of the men" until the morning of 29 December when to everyone's astonishment Fubbister gave birth to a son. Her confinement actually took place at the North West Company's post at Pembina, it being customary for the men at rival posts to share holiday festivities. As the HBC men were leaving, Fubbister, feeling poorly, asked Alexander HENRY who was in charge of the post if she might stay behind at his house. A short time later Henry found her "extended out upon the hearth, uttering most dreadful lamentations, he stretched out his hand towards me and in a piteful tone of voice begg'd my assistance, and requested I would take pity upon a poor helpless abandoned wretch, who was not of the sex I had every reason to suppose. But was an unfortunate Orkney Girl pregnant and actually in childbirth, in saying this she opened her jacket and display'd to my view a pair of beautiful round white Breasts." Within an hour the baby was born, and mother and child were soon bundled into a carriole and sent back to the HBC post. The father was reputed to be Scarth.

How the true sex of John Fubbister could have been concealed for so long remains a mystery, but once the truth was out, she was known by the name of Mary and sent back to Albany in the spring of 1808. For the next year she was employed as a washerwoman, a traditionally female role in which she did not excel. She may also have acted as nurse to the pupils of the school established by the company at Albany that year. Her son was baptized by the schoolmaster William Harper in October. The chief factor at Albany, John Hodgson*, appears to have been sympathetic to the young woman's plight; she did not want to return to the Orkneys but it was against company policy to allow white women at any of its posts. Thus in September 1809 Isabel Gunn was "discharged from your Honours Service" and sent home with her son by the annual ship. According to popular account, she was to suffer further misfortune and ended her life a vagrant.

SYLVIA VAN KIRK

PAM, HBCA, B.3/a/109, 111; E.3/3. *New light on early hist. of greater northwest* (Coues). Malvina Bolus, "The son of I. Gunn," *Beaver*, outfit 302 (winter 1971): 23–26.

GUY, ÉTIENNE, politician, surveyor, and militia officer; b. 16 Feb. 1774 in Montreal, Que., son of Pierre GUY and Marie-Josephte Hervieux; m. 16 Nov. 1801 Catherine Vallée in Lachine, Lower Canada, and they had six children, three of whom reached adulthood; d. 29 Dec. 1820 in Montreal.

Étienne Guy came from one of the leading bourgeois families of Montreal at the end of the 18th century. When he was six he inherited a 30-acre farm belonging to Étienne Augé*, a family friend. This property, located in the *faubourg* Saint-Antoine, formed part of the lands farmed by his father, at least until 1799, first because Étienne was very young when he inherited it, and then because his father steered him in another direction for his career.

Guy studied initially at the Collège Saint-Raphaël in Montreal, from 1785 till 1792; then his father sent him to Princeton to finish his education at the College of New Jersey, with the avowed aim of having him learn English. He arrived in the United States in October 1794, got to know New York and Philadelphia, and tried, with limited success, to master the English language. Disappointed with his progress, he confided to his father that everyone was paying him compliments on the way he spoke English, but that no one understood him. After being questioned by his father, who found this stay in the United States extremely costly and who regularly had to borrow money from relatives to meet his needs, Guy was summoned back to Montreal at the end of January 1796.

A few months after his return Guy stood as a candidate in the riding of Montreal in the 1796 elections for the Lower Canadian House of Assembly and was elected, together with Jean-Marie DU-CHARME. He was then only 22 and he still had to rely

Guy

on financial support from his family, since members of the assembly received no salary and none of their expenses were paid.

Guy could hardly be called one of the leading members of the second parliament. But neither was he the silent member who, according to historian Francis-Joseph Audet*, was content "to vote with the majority when the occasion arose." If he did not intervene regularly in debates during the first two sessions, he nevertheless took part in the assembly's work, particularly when it dealt with trade. Thus on 8 March 1797 he was appointed to a committee responsible for preparing a law on commerce between Lower Canada and the United States. Some weeks later he was on a committee to study a bill on the inspection and export of flour. During the endless debates on a bill concerning roads and bridges in March 1798 he spoke out occasionally in support of certain amendments. By contrast, in the 1799 and 1800 sessions he took no part in committee work, and his name does not appear in recorded votes. On 15 April 1799, at the time of proceedings to expel Charles-Jean-Baptiste Bouc*, he was "excused because of illness at home." The fact that he had obtained his commission as a surveyor in the spring of 1798 might explain his absenteeism. Faced with a choice between an unpaid political career and a stable profession, Guy quite obviously decided on the latter. He probably did not stand in the 1800 elections. His surveying work shows one interest in particular: he signed numerous reports and plans concerning transactions carried out by his father.

Like most of the prominent citizens of his time, Guy served in the militia. From adjutant of Montreal's 2nd Militia Battalion in 1797, he rose to major in the Longue-Pointe battalion of militia in 1812. This unit took part in the operations against Plattsburgh, N.Y., in September 1814, but Guy himself did not necessarily participate in the fighting. Having sought promotion to lieutenant-colonel, Guy subsequently obtained that rank and held it until his death in 1820.

Unlike the other members of his family, Étienne Guy did not have a career in business. He took up politics for a few years, but he chose the peaceful profession of surveyor over the uncertainties of public life.

GILLES LANGELIER

AUM, P 58, A4/60, 68; L/33. Bibliothèque nationale du Québec (Montréal), Dép. des mss, mss-101, Coll. La Fontaine, Extraits des reg. de Montréal, 1793–1812: 65, 75, 84, 96, 108, 115. PAC, MG 24, L3: 6624–32, 6636–38, 6645–46, 6653–55, 6658–62, 6681–85, 6689–90, 6703–7, 6761–62, 6773–79, 6793–95 (copies); MG 53, 55; RG 4, B33, 18; RG 8, I (C ser.), 1708: 10–14; 1717: 30; RG 9, I, A1, 13; A7, 20. Bas-Canada, chambre d'Assemblée, *Journaux*, 1797–1800. *Montreal Gazette*, 30 May, 27 June 1796; 21 July 1800. *Quebec Gazette*, 10 May 1798; 25 July 1799; 2 July 1812; 7 June 1819; 12 Sept., 26 Dec. 1822; 4 Sept., 6 Nov., 18 Dec. 1823. *Quebec almanac*, 1799–1820. F.-J. Audet, *Les députés de Montréal*, 352–55. *Officers of British forces in Canada* (Irving), 172. T.-P. Bédard, *Histoire de cinquante ans (1791–1841), annales parlementaires et politiques du Bas-Canada, depuis la Constitution jusqu'à l'Union* (Québec, 1869), 27–45. André Bernard et Denis Laforte, *La législation électorale au Québec, 1790–1967* (Montréal, 1969). É.-Z. Massicotte, *Faits curieux de l'histoire à Montréal* (Montréal, 1922), 63–64.

GUY, PIERRE, militia officer, merchant, and landowner; b. 11 Dec. 1738 in Montreal (Que.), son of Pierre Guy* and Jeanne Truillier, *dit* Lacombe; m. 1 May 1764 his cousin Marie-Josephte Hervieux, under-age daughter of the late Louis-François Hervieux* and Louise Quesnel Fonblanche; d. 7 Jan. 1812 in Montreal, Lower Canada.

Pierre Guy, who lost his father when he was nine, was educated at the Petit Séminaire de Québec, and at La Rochelle, in France. He then came back to New France; having been made an ensign in the militia in May 1755, he took part in the Seven Years' War. Following the conquest Mme Guy, who had managed the family business since her husband's death, sent young Pierre to France with instructions to attend, among other things, to settling her affairs with merchants in La Rochelle. Between 1761 and 1763 she terminated her dealings with the merchants Jean Pascaud, Paillet, and Meynardie, entrusting her funds and any of her merchandise that remained in storage to the firm of Denis Goguet*, "the best and safest house in La Rochelle," according to her son. In his letters to Mme Guy, Goguet, like Paillet and Meynardie, never tired of praising the exemplary conduct of Pierre, who was steadily pursuing his studies with teachers he had chosen.

Guy, who had hopes that Quebec would be restored to France, was soon faced with sad reality. As he was obliged in consequence to entrust his mother's interests to an English firm, he sought information from Goguet about Daniel Vialars, a Huguenot merchant established in London. Before leaving for England, Guy, who no longer thought it would be possible to ship his mother's merchandise to the colony, had written to her that he had had to resign himself to selling it at a 25 per cent loss. When he reached England in May 1763, he congratulated himself on this deal, since the merchants who were then letting their merchandise go were suffering losses running to 40 per cent.

During his stay in London Guy bought nothing because he considered prices too high. In addition he felt that the glut of English products on the Canadian market would force merchants there to offer discounts. In 1763 he returned to Montreal and set himself up as a merchant. Three years later he

395

Guy

received from his mother 15,315 *livres* in merchandise coming to him from his father's estate. He had already obtained from his father-in-law's estate 42,628 *livres* in bills of exchange and payment orders and 500 *livres* in a single bill of exchange. On 26 Sept. 1768 he received from that estate a further sum of 6,292 *livres*, this time in cash. On 16 June 1770 he noted in a day-book that on the orders of his wife's aunt he had been credited by Goguet with 35,365 *livres* for the rest of his father-in-law's estate. That year Guy also inherited about 23,000 *livres* on his mother's death.

The make-up of Guy's initial capital influenced his activities as a merchant. For want of a large supply of cash in the period 1764–69, and possibly because of a greater interest in landed property, he had to content himself with handling relatively small business affairs, and he bought little in London, preferring to obtain goods through merchants in Montreal and Quebec. Vialars, who at Guy's request in 1765 was not to send him his order until negotiations on Canada paper were completed, delivered merchandise to him but neglected to provide a detailed account of the state of his affairs. Guy was greatly displeased to learn that this firm had traded only part of his paper. On 14 Nov. 1768 Guy gave Vialars to understand that he might sue him if his orders were not respected and that if Vialars wanted to be paid, he had to send him full statements of his account. At that point, however, his bills of exchange and payment orders were liquidated. Indeed, on 1 Sept. 1767, 13,165 *livres* of an initial sum of 42,628 *livres* had been paid into Guy's account.

From 1770 to 1774 Guy's business prospects brightened. He was now able to buy more dry goods from London, especially textiles and clothing. Through the agency of Jean Vienne, a Montreal merchant, he entered into relations with the firm of Thomas Linch in 1772. Having built himself a house with spacious vaulted cellars the previous year, he offered to sell trade goods on commission for Daniel Vialars and his son Antoine. They accepted and continued their association with him until 1774, when Antoine Vialars came to Montreal. As the Vialars had been slow to send the statement of Guy's current account, he had not been able to pay what he owed them promptly and was charged five per cent interest on the balance due. Feeling himself wronged, Guy refused to pay the interest. In the end he obtained satisfaction in October 1774, through a compromise deemed fair by both parties.

Guy was one of the twelve prominent citizens who on 12 Nov. 1775 signed the act of capitulation of Montreal, which was occupied by American troops under Richard Montgomery*. The following year his store was pillaged by some of the invaders. He estimated that he had lost £129 in merchandise. After the Americans had retreated, he turned his mind to replenishing his stocks. He bought goods worth more than £1,855 from the firm of Brook Watson and Robert Rashleigh in London. Subsequently the precarious state of international trade, the increased cost of merchandise and insurance, and perhaps an excess of prudence led him year after year to cancel his purchases from that company. From then on he obtained his supplies from merchants in Montreal and Quebec.

Between 1766 and 1777 Guy had made purchases amounting to more than £4,880 from London firms; this figure represented but half of the market value of his imports, which largely consisted of textiles and clothing. During that period he had had occasion to complain many a time: the products received did not necessarily match what he had asked for; he was charged higher prices than other merchants; orders were shipped to third parties, who forwarded them after long delays; his invoices and statements of account contained errors detrimental to his interests. Guy therefore kept a watchful eye on his affairs, and hence was extremely demanding of his suppliers.

Guy's commercial activities extended far beyond the usual run of business. Although he had not engaged much in the fur trade on his own account, he had collaborated with Jacques Baby*, *dit* Dupéront, and François Baby, who were in business at Detroit and Quebec respectively. Guy served as middleman for the two brothers. François forwarded the merchandise needed for the fur trade to Montreal. From there Guy saw that it was sent to Detroit. Jacques sent the furs to Guy, who followed the instructions given him to verify the contents of the packages, pay the men working for the Babys, and arrange for the furs to be stored.

As a landowner Guy had houses and land in the town of Montreal and in the suburbs. Between 1766 and 1768, for example, he bought the Ranger and La Bourgogne lands in the *faubourg* Saint-Antoine and the *faubourg* Saint-Joseph for 12,805 *livres*. The La Bourgogne property, which was encumbered with payments owing to the Séminaire de Saint-Sulpice, brought Guy into conflict with the seminary's superior, Étienne Montgolfier*, over extinguishing these payments. Unable to reach a compromise with Montgolfier, Guy had to make them for 12 years. As a result of this misadventure he became extremely distrustful in business matters and was prompted to act with caution when dealing with the seminary.

Guy nevertheless devoted much of the money earmarked for extinguishing the payments on La Bourgogne to putting his two farms back into shape. He purchased agricultural implements, repaired the farm buildings, and had the land fenced, cleared of trees and stones, and manured. Then he increased his development capital and invested large sums to make the farms profitable. In the period from 1774 to 1781 there was a real scarcity of hay, an essential commodity for the army. Guy took the opportunity to put most of his farmland into hay. When the price dropped, he again diversified production. Since, given his storage for crops, he could speculate on prices, he found that slumps in farming and crop failures were advantageous and enabled him to make substantial profits in some years. The greater part of the income his farms produced came from his hayfields and orchards, which he managed himself as owner. He received supplementary income from market-gardening, growing grain, and raising livestock – cattle, sheep, horses, and poultry. For this work he sometimes used hired hands or tenant farmers, and often both together.

Beginning in the 1790s Guy bought other lands in the *faubourg* Saint-Joseph and the *faubourg* Saint-Antoine, and on the Coteau Saint-Louis; he also bought a few lots on Rue Saint-Éloy, Rue Saint-Laurent, and Rue Saint-François. From his wife he had acquired a site on the Place du Marché which he exchanged for half of a house belonging to his sister on Rue Saint-Paul.

Guy's case illustrates well the economic choices open to the Canadian petite bourgeoisie under the British régime. If his real estate purchases would serve to build up the family estate that he was bent on bequeathing to his children, they also fitted in with investment and development goals. The attention that he gave to improving the Ranger and La Bourgogne lands and the exemplary way in which he managed to run them leave no doubt about his capitalistic and enterprising spirit. Consequently, only after he assured himself that the money he had put into real estate was earning a profit did he turn from the general store inherited from his parents, and even then he did not give it up completely. This evolution became more evident during the War of American Independence, a period which gave him the opportunity to benefit from his production, so that when peace returned his preoccupations as a farming entrepreneur clearly took precedence over his other activities.

The rationality of this choice cannot be analysed solely in terms of a personal option without obscuring the impact that the conquest had had upon the import trade from Europe organized by his father under the French régime and continued by his mother until the end of the Seven Years' War. Personal inclination and interest in real estate investments were assuredly not the only factors leading to the transformation of his parents' trading house into an ordinary retail business that was up against the competition of the rising bourgeoisie. The constraints imposed by the British merchants' stranglehold on commercial exchanges between the colony and the mother country were too keenly felt by Guy for them not to enter into his decision.

Guy had become aware of the consequences of the separation from France while still a young man. As he was living there when the Treaty of Paris was concluded in 1763, he experienced the effects of the complete breaking off of trade. He was obliged to liquidate the goods held by his mother on consignment in the port of La Rochelle and thenceforth had to turn to new suppliers in London. Belonging to a social milieu directly affected by the change of mother country and experiencing the difficulties in resuming commercial operations within a new imperial framework, he was prompted, once back in the colony, to strengthen his ties with his compatriots of the Canadian petite bourgeoisie. Through his marriage with his cousin he was related to a family of merchants involved in the same business network as his father and father-in-law had been.

Guy's concerns were not confined to the realities of the new economic situation; he soon was made aware of the social and political problems engendered by the establishment of a civil government for the province under the British régime. In the autumn of 1764, after the Quebec grand jury affair had prompted the first serious confrontation with representatives of the English-speaking minority over the fundamental issue of the conquered people's rights [*see* James Johnston*], Guy made common cause with his compatriots in Quebec town; in an address initiated by the Canadian members of the grand jury they appealed to the "kindness and sense of justice" of the new king, George III. Guy's support on this occasion seems especially noteworthy since few French-speaking Montrealers followed his example, except for the members of his wife's family. Yet the cause was crucial for the future of the new British subjects, as their first political manifesto declared. "What would become of the general prosperity of the Colony, if those who form the principal section thereof, become incapable members of it through difference of Religion?" they demanded. From this principled position, Guy would support and then promote his compatriots' rights until recognition by the imperial government was attained. If at a period prior to 1774 he limited his solidarity to supporting their petitions, after the American revolution he engaged in militant activity to obtain constitutional reforms.

Until the Quebec Act the intransigent attitude of the Protestant minority prevented any political alliance between the members of the Canadian petite bourgeoisie and the British merchants. Since, according to Guy, the demands of the latter were "entirely opposed to ours," any attempt at reconciliation was futile and the new subjects were obliged to make "separate representations." These took the form of a petition and memorial to the king which the leading citizens of Montreal signed early in the autumn of 1773. In addition to requesting that their former laws and

Guy

customs be retained, they begged their "generous sovereign" to preserve "the glorious title of sovereign of a free people" by granting them "in common with your other subjects, the rights and privileges of citizens of England." François Baby, Guy's friend, was given the mission of going to London to plead with the ministry "the common cause" of all the Canadians.

The leading representatives of Montreal society, drawn from both the merchant and professional petite bourgeoisie and the seigneurial class, rallied to the "common cause," but the behaviour of some of the seigneurs after assent had been given to the Quebec Act made Guy indignant. Seeing them act like perfect courtiers of the colonial administration, he confided to Baby: "I believe that they seek rather to secure protection of people in high places for themselves than to show themselves patriots and to inform the government of what might be conducive to the people's happiness and the encouragement of trade." To which his Quebec confidant replied: "It is probable, as you have pointed out to me, that your [Montreal] politicians and ours have given more thought to their own interest and worked more for it than for the good of the public. . . . I very much fear the time is not far off when Canadians will not be able to console themselves for having asked for the new form of government." But unlike Baby, who, once in the Legislative Council, adapted to the system of government set up under the Quebec Act, Guy remained true to his principles and to the interests of the Canadian petite bourgeoisie. Not only did he disapprove of the régime of favours and privileges granted to the seigneurial élite; he was also indignant at the abuses of power by the colonial government, which, when it was under the tutelage of governors Guy CARLETON and Frederick HALDIMAND, was labelled the "system of the generals" by people at the time.

Nothing was more instrumental in demonstrating the need for constitutional reform than experience of that system, which was kept in place until the end of the War of American Independence by the critical revolutionary situation. The British merchants hastened to assert themselves as soon as peace had returned, but the Canadian petite bourgeoisie waited until Governor Haldimand left before following their example by endorsing openly the plan for reforms put forward by Pierre Du Calvet* in his noted indictment, *Appel à la justice de l'État; ou recueil de lettres au roi, au prince de Galles, et aux ministres; avec une lettre à messieurs les Canadiens, . . . une lettre au général Haldimand lui-même; enfin une lettre à milord Sidney* (London, 1784). Guy was one of the most active and fervent members of this reform movement which rallied the English- and French-speaking bourgeois forces about its main objective, the setting up of an assembly "made up, without distinction, of old and new subjects." Judging by the militancy that he displayed until the advent of the 1791 constitution, Guy may be considered to have had the interest of the public at heart and to have devoted himself to this cause as a "true patriot and friend of humanity," as notary Jean DE LISLE, a compatriot and fellow Montrealer, put it.

Guy also devoted much of his energy to the militia. On 3 May 1787 Lord Dorchester [Guy Carleton] commissioned him lieutenant-colonel of the Canadian militia raised in the town of Montreal. Fifteen years later, on 21 April 1802, Sir Robert Shore Milnes*, lieutenant governor of Lower Canada, granted him a commission as colonel of Montreal's 2nd Militia Battalion.

Guy and his wife had 14 children, of whom five reached adulthood. They seem to have had little contact with the children in infancy, entrusting them rather to nurses. This practice probably explains the apparently detached and laconic notes Guy wrote in his ledger on their deaths and the cost of burying them, and also the itemized account he kept for each home where they were nursed. Yet he was not always so unfeeling in the presence of death, and he was far from devoid of paternal affection. When his eldest son died at the age of six, he confided his pain and sorrow to François Baby, observing that Baby "did not yet know how sad it is to lose children of that age. And nothing teaches us better not to spoil them and love them too much, regrets are [then] less intense."

As a new British subject Guy thought his children's education and future could not be assured unless they knew English. He therefore sent his sons Louis* and ÉTIENNE to study at the College of New Jersey, in Princeton. The youngest son, Joseph, who was a poor student, did not go there for further education. He signed on to work as a clerk at Michilimackinac (Mackinac Island, Mich.) in 1798. Guy was somewhat anxious about letting him go. He penned innumerable letters reiterating a great many edifying recommendations. He explained that a man should "be more pleased with what he earns than with what he inherits." In 1802 Joseph returned to Montreal, rented a store from his father on the Place du Marché, and set up for himself. Two years later he opened a second store at Michilimackinac, but his ventures were far from flourishing. Soon he was short of cash and could not pay his creditors. Being very attached to his family and aware that his life was drawing to a close, Guy longed to leave the surviving members happy. Yet he was to be an impotent observer of the blighted hopes of his youngest son. Joseph concentrated his business at Michilimackinac, but he went bankrupt and left for a self-imposed exile in Baltimore, Md. There he vegetated in a clerical job. He no longer dared even to write to his father, knowing the hurt he had inflicted on him. His hope was that the legacy coming to him at his father's death would put an end to his exile by enabling him to pay his creditors.

However, when Pierre Guy drew up his will some days before his death in 1812, he decided otherwise. His assets were divided into five equal shares. Those going to Louis and Étienne were encumbered with two life annuities of 600 *livres* each, to be paid annually to their sisters until they were provided for by marriage or in some other way. Anxious to prevent Joseph from being deprived of his heritage by his creditors, he took all possible steps to ensure that his share would be immune from seizure, and in so doing he condemned his son to a lifetime of exile. For it was Joseph's children who would inherit; their father would receive only the usufruct from the legacy.

GINETTE JOANNETTE and CLAIRE JORON

ANQ-M, CE1-51, 11 déc. 1738, 30 avril 1764, 23 déc. 1765, 30 oct. 1770, 9 janv. 1812; CN1-290, 4 avril, 8 oct. 1766; 6 déc. 1770; CN1-363, 4 juin 1785. AUM, P 58, A1/22, 58, 158; A2/19, 23; A3/62; A4/60; A5/252, 271; C2/157, 165; G2/113, 124, 128, 133, 154, 192; H3/21; P1/19, 28, 43; P2/55–56, 82; U, Goguet à Mme Guy, 8 févr. 1762; Pierre Guy, reg. 37; Paillet et Meynardie à Mme Guy, 28 févr. 1762, 15 mars 1763; Pascaud à Mme Guy, 1er mai 1761. PAC, MG 23, GV, 7: 49. *Docs. relating to constitutional hist., 1759–91* (Shortt and Doughty; 1918), 1: 223–26, 504–6, 508–10. *Montréal en 1781 . . .* , Claude Perrault, édit. (Montréal, 1969). F.-J. Audet, *Les députés de Montréal*, 226, 228–29, 354. Louise Dechêne, *Habitants et marchands de Montréal au XVIIe siècle* (Paris et Montréal, 1974). J. E. Igartua, "The merchants and *négociants* of Montreal, 1750–1775: a study in socio-economic history" (PHD thesis, Mich. State Univ., East Lansing, 1974). Miquelon, "Baby family." Neatby, *Quebec*, 23–24, 73, 132–33, 145, 239, 247. Benjamin Sulte, *Histoire de la milice canadienne-française, 1760–1897* (Montréal, 1897). F.-J. Audet, "1842," *Cahiers des Dix*, 7 (1942): 215–54. J. E. Igartua, "The merchants of Montreal at the conquest: socio-economic profile," *SH*, 8 (1975): 275–93. Jacques Mathieu, "Un négociant de Québec à l'époque de la Conquête: Jacques Perrault l'aîné," ANQ *Rapport*, 1970: 27–82.

H

HAENKE, TADEO (Tadeáš, Thaddeus), scientist and explorer; b. 1761, probably on 5 October, in Kreibitz (Chřibská, Czechoslovakia), son of Elias Georg Thomas Hänke and his wife Rosalia; d. unmarried in 1817 near Cochabamba (Bolivia).

Tadeo Haenke took university courses in mathematics and astronomy in Prague, and at age 25 went to Vienna University to study medicine and botany. Knowledgeable and enthusiastic, he was recommended by Professor Nikolaus Josef Jacquin to Alejandro MALASPINA, the commander of a Spanish scientific and exploratory expedition which was expected to circle the globe. The *Descubierta* and the *Atrevida* left Cadiz on 30 July 1789 but Haenke, after a dash for that city, arrived there a few hours too late to embark. Obtaining passage for Montevideo (Uruguay), Haenke went in pursuit, only to suffer shipwreck off the South American coast on 23 November, shortly before the expected time of arrival; he was forced to swim ashore with some of his equipment under his arm. Again he missed the expedition. He consequently undertook a historic crossing of the pampas and the southern Andes, finally joining the expedition at Valparaíso (Chile) in mid April 1790. On the way Haenke had practised his specialties, taking notes on zoology, mineralogy, and particularly botany.

Once he became an active member of the expedition Haenke worked closely with its chief of natural science, Antonio Pineda, and the botanist Luis Neé, but his superior knowledge permitted him consider-able latitude and independence. Stops were made at various ports on the way northward until the expedition reached Acapulco (Mexico) in February 1791 and prepared for a voyage to the northwest coast. Leaving Acapulco on 2 May, the vessels sailed far to the north before touching land. The first stop, late in June, was at Port Mulgrave (Yakutat Bay, Alaska), and there Haenke resumed his study of natural history. In boats he and others visited a small bay to the north where an island not far from Malaspina Glacier was named for him. Possessed of wide-ranging interests and skills, Haenke turned his hand to recording the music of the Tlingit Indians, and also demonstrated his own musicianship by playing the harpsichord on board the *Descubierta* for the entertainment of his colleagues.

On 12 August the expedition, having sailed south along the coast, arrived in Nootka Sound (B.C.) where Pedro de ALBERNI was in charge of the Spanish settlement of Santa Cruz de Nutka. Here Haenke enlarged his collections, classifying specimens according to the Linnaean system. His results form the oldest systematic ordering and cataloguing of the botanical species of present-day western Canada. Haenke was disappointed in his relatively small collection of plants; he could not find many species distinct from those of Europe, but he did discover a great number of conifers which differed from European varieties, and also found that the natives used spruce beer as an effective antiscorbutic. While he was in Nootka Sound Haenke continued his observation of the music of the coastal Indians and recorded some of the music of the local Nootkas.

The expedition left Nootka Sound on 28 August and reached Acapulco in mid October. After a voyage across the Pacific to the Orient and Australia, Malaspina's ships returned to the Americas. In October 1793 Haenke went ashore with a companion at Callao (Peru) to begin an overland journey to Buenos Aires (Argentina), where he was to rejoin the expedition in October or November of the following year. The proposed schedule would have proved impossible even if Haenke had tried to follow it, but he became so engrossed in his studies in the heart of South America that he spent the remainder of his life there. He continued to draw the salary he had received as a member of the expedition until his death some 24 years later near Cochabamba after significant exploration in present-day Peru, Bolivia, and Brazil.

Haenke's skill and hard work were greatly appreciated by associates, government officials, and the European scientific community. More than any other member of the Malaspina party Haenke has received recognition, being considered by some a worthy precursor to the more famous German naturalist Friedrich Wilhelm Karl Heinrich Alexander von Humboldt. Haenke's incessant, tireless, and efficient labour embraced a variety of scientific fields including chemistry, botany, geology, astronomy, geography, and mineralogy. His writings, both published and unpublished, have won for him the attention of a number of biographers and the occasional reprinting of some of his works.

DONALD C. CUTTER

Archivo General de la Nación (Buenos Aires), Fondo Biblioteca Nacional, legajo 48, doc.38; legajo 130, doc.115; legajo 138, doc.123; legajo 286, doc.4319; legajo 314, doc.5127; Sala IX, Fondo período colonial-gobierno, 4-6-1, Reales órdenes y cédulas, Consulado antecedentes T.I.: f.280; 24-4-14, Reales órdenes, libro 68: ff.71–72; 25-2-2, Reales órdenes, libro 24: ff.157, 170; 25-4-13, Reales órdenes, libro 67: f.49; 30/6/5, Interior leg. 47, exp.24; Communicaciones y resoluciones reales, libro 9: f.68. Biblioteca y Archivo Nacional de Bolivia (Sucre), MSS concerning Tadeo Haenke. Museo Naval (Madrid), MSS relating to the Malaspina expedition. C. W. Arnade and Josef Kühnel, *El problema del humanista Tadeo Haenke; nuevas perspectivas en la investigación haenkeana* (Sucre, 1960). L. H. Destefani and D. [C.] Cutter, *Tadeo Haenke y el final de una vieja polémica* (Buenos Aires, 1966). Josef Kühnel, *Thaddaeus Haenke, Leben und Wirken eines Forschers* (Prague, 1960).

HAINS. *See* AINSSE

HALDIMAND, Sir FREDERICK. *See* APPENDIX

HALL, Sir ROBERT, naval officer; baptized 2 Jan. 1778 in County Tipperary (Republic of Ireland); his father remains unidentified, while his mother is known only through the probate of his will, where she appears as "Mary Roche, heretofore Hall"; d. unmarried 7 Feb. 1818 in Kingston, Upper Canada.

Robert Hall's early years have not attracted the attention of naval biographers. It is known, however, that he was gazetted a lieutenant in the Royal Navy on 14 June 1800, a commander on 27 June 1808, and a captain on 4 March 1811. He attracted attention for sterling service in the defence of a fort on the Gulf of Rosas, Spain, in November 1808 while in command of the bomb-ketch *Lucifer*. On 28 Sept. 1810 he enhanced his reputation when, as commander of the 14-gun *Rambler*, he captured a large French privateer lying in the Barbate River, Spain.

In September 1811 Hall was appointed to command a flotilla entrusted with the defence of Sicily against naval forces operating from French-occupied Naples. He achieved a major success at Pietrenere (Italy) on 15 Feb. 1813 in a raid on a convoy of about 50 armed vessels, French supply ships escorted by many Neapolitan gunboats. With only two divisions of gunboats carrying four companies of the 75th Foot he neutralized the enemy's shore batteries and captured or destroyed all 50 ships. In recognition of this feat he was made a knight commander in the Sicilian order of St Ferdinand and of Merit. Permission to accept this honour was granted by the Prince Regent on 11 March, at which time Hall was described as a post-captain and a brigadier-general in the service of Ferdinand IV of Naples.

On 27 May 1814 Hall was designated acting commissioner on the lakes of Canada, to reside at Quebec; his actual headquarters would be the naval dockyard at Kingston. He was not immediately available and did not report for duty in Kingston until mid October. His new assignment involved a dual responsibility: to the commander-in-chief on the lakes, Sir James Lucas YEO, for the building, outfitting, supply, and maintenance of naval vessels, and to the Navy Board in London for the administration of the navy yard at Kingston and its dependencies on the Upper Lakes and Lake Champlain, and all naval victualling and stores depots in the two provinces.

The new commissioner's immediate concern was the implementation of Yeo's plans for a decisive campaign against the Americans in 1815. These involved the completion of a 56-gun frigate, the construction of two 74-gun ships of the line (their proposed armament was later increased to 110 guns) and a number of gunboats in the Kingston yard, the building of a 36-gun frigate on Lake Huron, and the completion of two brigs, three 36-gun frigates, and eleven gunboats on Lake Champlain. To this ambitious program Hall made an important addition: a scheme to rid the naval units of transport duties, which had impaired their fighting efficiency, by building two 500-ton armed transports, 20 gunboats and 4 mortar boats, and 50 bateaux for the army. He dispatched this proposal to the Navy Board late in December 1814, but all plans for a campaign in 1815 became redundant when on 1 March of that year Governor PREVOST was notified of the ratification of an Anglo-American peace signed at Ghent (Belgium) on Christmas Eve 1814.

The peace posed immediate and serious problems for Hall and his staff. The yard and its dependencies had incurred expenses of some £40,000 in wages alone in 1814, the building of the Lake Ontario squadron's flagship, the *St Lawrence* (launched on 10 Sept. 1814), had been immensely costly, and a huge outlay was required to pay for the ships under construction. Immediate retrenchment seemed an obvious necessity to Hall and Yeo, but, in the absence of orders from England and without any official assessment of even the short-term future of Anglo-American relations, prudence dictated the maintenance of a strong fleet in being. Their reaction was therefore to halt construction, save on one of the 74-gun ships, to cancel contracts, and to pay off labour hired against the requirements of the 1815 program. During the spring the largest ships were placed in reserve, and late in July Commodore Sir Edward Campbell Rich Owen, who had succeeded Yeo on 20 March, dispatched Hall to England for consultations with the Admiralty about the future naval establishment in the Canadas.

Hall remained in England for more than a year, during which time the British government was engaged in negotiations with the United States which eventually led to the Rush–Bagot agreement of April 1817 to demilitarize the lakes. On 29 Sept. 1815 Hall was named commander on the lakes and resident commissioner at Quebec, thus combining the two senior naval appointments in the Canadas. The first authorized him to style himself commodore; the second confirmed him in the post of commissioner. He was knighted on 15 July 1816 and, distinguished with the additional honour of a companionship in the Order of the Bath, returned to Kingston on 9 September.

Apart from useful discussions concerning a peace establishment for his command, the one important result of Hall's mission was a general agreement that the dilapidated wooden buildings of the Kingston yard would gradually be replaced by permanent stone structures. This project was one which Hall had long advocated, and he made a start towards its implementation on 4 Dec. 1816 when he invited tenders for the construction of a huge stone warehouse. No tenders were submitted, however, since the size of the building placed it completely beyond the resources of any local contractor, and there the matter rested. But in the late spring of 1817 Hall was confronted with a vastly more serious problem. On 29 May he acknowledged orders dated 26 February which stated that the whole of the fleet on the lakes should be placed in reserve and its crews paid off. It is assumed that at the same time he also received a letter of 21 February which ordered him to strike his broad pennant. It is not known whether Hall was privy to his government's intentions, but these communications clearly foreshadowed the imminent proclamation of the Rush–Bagot agreement. He promptly assured the board that its orders would be put into effect on 30 June, and he proved as good as his word. Henceforth he was to preside over naval affairs in the Canadas solely as commissioner.

The last seven months of Hall's life were devoted to the administration of the peace establishment devised for his command, to the unending task of keeping the fleet in repair, to plans for improvements to the yard, and to arrangements for strengthening subsidiary bases on the Upper Lakes. He was seriously ill with a lung infection in October, recovered sufficiently to return to duty for a few weeks at the end of the year, but died of this disease at his quarters at Point Frederick on 7 Feb. 1818. An affable, gallant, and cultivated officer, Hall in his Canadian posting had proved himself a conspicuously fair-minded, innovative, and efficient administrator. His heirs were a natural son, Robert Hall, born in 1817 to a Miss Mary Ann Edwards, and his mother Mary Roche, who was his residuary legatee. The son, baptized on 2 Nov. 1818 by George Okill Stuart*, rector of St George's Church in Kingston, became a vice-admiral in the Royal Navy and died in London on 11 June 1882 after having served for ten years as naval secretary to the Admiralty.

JOHN W. SPURR

Anglican Church of Canada, Diocese of Ont. Arch. (Kingston), St George's Cathedral (Kingston), Reg. of baptisms, 1818. PAC, RG 8, I (C ser.), 1–3, 8, 18. PRO, ADM 1/1953; ADM 42/2167–70, 42/2174–75, 42/2177; ADM 106/1997–98 (mfm. at PAC); ADM 107, passing certificates, index; PROB 11/160/7/371. *Annual reg.* (London), 1814: 436. *Gentleman's Magazine*, January–June 1818: 260. William James, *The naval history of Great Britain, from the declaration of war by France in 1793 to the accession of George IV* (new ed., 6v., London, 1860), 5–6. *Naval Chronicle*, 24 (July–December 1810); 25 (January–June 1811); 29 (January–June 1813); 34 (July–December 1815); 36 (July–December 1816). *Kingston Gazette*, 1814–18. *Montreal Gazette*, 1814. Frederic Boase, *Modern English biography . . .* (6v., Truro, Eng., 1892–1921; repr. London, 1965), 1: 1289. G.B., Adm., *The commissioned sea officers of the Royal Navy, 1660–1815*, [ed. D. B. Smith et al.] (3v., n.p., [1954?]), 2: 334. W. L. Clowes, *The Royal Navy; a history from the earliest times to the present* (7v., London, 1897–1903), 5: 522. J. M. Hitsman, *Safeguarding Canada, 1763–1871* (Toronto, 1968), 115.

Hamilton

HAMILTON, ROBERT, businessman, politician, judge, and office holder; b. 14 Sept. 1753 in Bolton, Scotland, son of John Hamilton and Jean Wight; m. first 1785 Catherine Askin, widow of Samuel Robertson, and they had five sons; m. secondly c. 1797 Mary Herkimer, widow of Neil McLean*, and they had three sons and a daughter; d. 8 March 1809 in Queenston, Upper Canada.

The power and influence of Robert Hamilton derived largely from his association with the fur trade and the supply of the British army. Like many middle class Scots of the late 18th century he came to British North America through connections in the fur trade. In March 1778 he signed a three-year contract with the Ellice brothers in London, England. They were Lowland Scots long prominent in the southwest fur trade (below and to the west of lakes Huron and Superior) and were major provisioners of the British forces during the American Revolutionary War. By July 1779 Hamilton was in the province of Quebec where he served an apprenticeship as a clerk at Montreal and at Carleton Island (N.Y.) while building up a small trade at the upper posts on his own account. In May 1780 he left the Ellices to form a partnership with the New York loyalist Richard CARTWRIGHT at Fort Niagara (near Youngstown, N.Y.). There they built a solid trade with the British army and its quasi-military adjunct, the Indian Department. British officers were impressed by the respectability, the patriotism, and the dependability of the firm.

Hamilton and Cartwright were supplied and, in part, financed probably by the Montreal firm of Todd and McGill, one of the oldest and most prosperous houses in the southwest fur trade. Isaac TODD and James McGILL arranged a copartnership between their Niagara associates and John ASKIN, their most successful client at Detroit (Mich.). Hamilton's contacts with the military and new associations within the southwest fur trade laid the basis for the remarkable enterprises he built in early Upper Canada. Indeed, the Laurentian mercantile networks provisioning and supplying the military and the fur trade were the most highly developed organizations in the geographically fragmented and institutionally weak province before the War of 1812. Association with them brought a few privileged merchants the only substantial affluence and power the young colony had to offer.

In 1782 Hamilton and Cartwright opened a branch of their firm at Oswego (N.Y.) but, with the winding down of the war, they moved it to Carleton Island in 1783. The decade after the war was not a propitious time for Niagara merchants: of the 18 firms receiving goods there in 1783, only four were still functioning in 1789. The rest had been driven under by the post-war depression, the drying up of military demand, and the unpromising market offered by the pioneer loyalist community. Hamilton, however, operating in continuing partnership with Cartwright until 1790, not only survived this period but prospered by concentrating his efforts on forwarding and receiving for the fur trade rather than on local merchandising. The advantages of this decision were solid: the fur trade required little investment and yielded a steady profit not directly dependent on the price of goods or the state of the local market.

Some time in 1784 or 1785 Hamilton established himself at Niagara, and shortly thereafter began building a residence and shop at what was to become Queenston (Ont.). Cartwright established himself at Cataraqui (Kingston, Ont.). By the late 1780s, according to one observer, they became agents for the shipping of all private goods on Lake Ontario. This thriving trade required extensive transportation facilities beyond the means of small up-country merchants such as Hamilton. Fortunately, capital was provided and construction undertaken both by leading Montreal merchants and by the British military. It was the good luck of Hamilton that his suppliers, Todd and McGill, were the first to build a major private vessel on the lake after the war. He then became the Niagara agent for the 120-ton *Lady Dorchester*, built in 1788, as well as for Todd and McGill's second ship, the 137-ton *Governor Simcoe*, built in 1794. Their monopoly of private shipping ended that same year but the enterprise continued to be profitable thereafter. The transportation infrastructure – storehouses, wharfs, and portages – was built by the military, and initially Hamilton was able to use army facilities for his own carrying business. The profits he realized from the carrying trade while the local economy remained depressed and primitive provided a solid base for expansion of his enterprises and his subsequent rise to prominence.

The Niagara area was the major trans-shipment point on the route to the west. The main portage was located on the east (American) side of the Niagara River until the end of the revolution. Then the Montreal fur traders successfully lobbied for the right to portage their goods on the west bank and subsequently awarded their business to Hamilton and another local merchant, George Forsyth (brother of JOSEPH), who was also closely connected to the fur trade. In 1791, with the major Montreal trading companies providing support and financial sureties, Hamilton, Forsyth, John Burch*, and Archibald Cunningham won the lucrative contract for the portaging of all military goods. Since the army had already built transportation facilities, Hamilton's overhead was low and, more important, his profits were high.

In addition to his partnership with Cartwright, his contacts with the army, and his associations within the fur trade, Hamilton developed a network of family alliances to secure his interests. In 1785 he married the daughter of his partner, John Askin, thus cementing an alliance that would serve both families for more than a generation. The marriage brought him other contacts at Detroit, most notably the powerful William ROBERTSON. That same year Hamilton began to establish his own Scots relations in the Niagara peninsula. Over the next seven years, he sent home for four of his cousins: Thomas Clark* and the Dicksons, Robert*, Thomas*, and William*. Each served an apprenticeship in his enterprises before being placed in businesses that were, in fact, adjuncts of Hamilton's own and were, as well, closely linked to the fur trade and military supply. Hamilton and his cousins remained closely allied during his lifetime. Their circle expanded to include even Old World acquaintances, such as Robert Nichol*, and the second generation of the Dickson–Clark families in a complex net of business agreements, partnerships, coordinated land speculations, and mutual lobbying for office and patronage.

The supply of the army and fur trade was the mainstay of Hamilton's businesses. The victualling part of it was almost exclusively for the army because the fur trade tended to purchase its provisions closer to its western centres of operation. With the aid of Todd and McGill and the assent of the military, Hamilton became in 1786 the agent for the supply of flour to the Niagara garrison, which was the only significant market for local produce until shipment began down Lake Ontario to Lower Canada in 1800. Distance and fluctuating supply kept local prices high and the market proved capacious: until 1798, the military purchased all the produce the Niagara peninsula could offer. Because of the comparatively large garrison and Niagara's strategic location as the major supply centre for western posts, by 1800 the army was buying 61 per cent of its total victualling requirements for the colony at Niagara. Hamilton claimed the lion's share of the Niagara market, providing annually between 35 and 100 per cent of local military purchases by value. His virtual monopoly was a consequence of the military's desire to buy in bulk, of the momentum generated by his early establishment in business, and, in no small part, of the preference and special privileges the military awarded him because of his reputation.

Portaging also retained its importance in the regional economy. By the late 1780s, the only period for which statistics are available, an average of 30 per cent of all trade goods by value were moving west by the lakes route over the Niagara portage; 40 per cent of all furs returned east by the same route. The southwest remained the major destination of these goods: 80 per cent of private supplies passing over the portage in 1790 were for Detroit or Michilimackinac (Mackinac Island, Mich.) rather than the far west. The volume of this traffic was substantially augmented by military

items, in the main, provisions for the upper posts. Hamilton was fortunate; he continued until his death to receive an unbroken string of lucrative portaging contracts from the military. Total profits on the portage in 1798, for instance, were in the range of £2,500 New York currency, a substantial sum for the three up-country merchants then involved.

Hamilton's provisioning and carrying operations were notable in providing him with a sizeable amount of disposable capital; at this early period all his customers paid him in specie, an important advantage for a merchant in a society where currency was always scarce. All indications point to the likelihood that he invested this money in local enterprises, particularly retailing and land speculation. Whereas the shops of most merchants were small, localized concerns, Hamilton's Queenston store, where he sold large quantities of common goods and a wide selection of luxury items, was the equivalent of a modern regional retailing centre. It drew customers from the length and breadth of the peninsula, and by 1803 he had for some time employed an agent annually to collect his 500 to 600 accounts over as many as 22 townships. He also owned and operated a horse-powered grist-mill, a tannery yard, and a distillery. At his death in 1809, 1,200 individuals owed him the astounding sum of £68,721 New York currency.

Hamilton undoubtedly was the chief land speculator in early Upper Canada. The total known amount of land in which he held an interest by purchase, grant, or mortgage was 130,170 acres. If contiguous, his lands would have stretched one township deep from the Niagara River almost to Burlington Bay (Hamilton Harbour). About 50 per cent of them were located in his own county of Lincoln, with a second major concentration in the counties of Oxford and Norfolk. He had acquired his land rapidly, purchasing close to 43 per cent of his holdings in the peninsula (other than those obtained by grant or mortgage) between 1791 and 1799. Although he invested heavily in land, much of it undoubtedly came to him as payment for outstanding debts. Only 11 per cent of his total holdings came as direct grants from the crown.

Hamilton considered land a commercial speculation. He did not believe in the social desirability or economic potential of establishing great landed estates for himself or his heirs. Rather he saw economic development depending upon yeoman farmers, preferably of American origin, who would clear and work one or two lots; to such individuals he planned to sell his lands. In the main, Hamilton showed little concern for either the quality or the saleability of his acquisitions. A large portion was interior and isolated, with poorly drained soils, land that would not come under cultivation rapidly. With the financial resources at his disposal, he was confident that his family could hold large parcels of land, even poor land, long

Hamilton

enough for it to become marketable. This was long-term speculation; during his lifetime, he disposed of only 13 per cent of his total holdings.

From an early period, the political power of Hamilton's economic patrons assured him office. When the government in distant Quebec made its initial appointments for the upper country, it sought recommendations from those who knew the region best – officers of the British military and Indian Department and prominent members of the Montreal fur-trading community. Hamilton's patrons in these circles, particularly Sir John Johnson*, assured his appointment in 1786 as one of the original justices of the peace at Niagara, in 1788 as a member of the land board of the Nassau District and as a judge of the district Court of Common Pleas, and finally, in 1792, as a member of the Legislative Council of Upper Canada. Hamilton proved assiduous in attending to his official duties. Although he seldom exploited his offices directly for personal gain, he was able to use them to affect general matters related to his commercial activities.

The political and social goals of Robert Hamilton were pragmatic and limited; he showed little interest in institutional or social development. In the council, he was rarely concerned with any issue not directly touching himself or his mercantile connections. Despite the restricted nature of his politics, he was nevertheless embroiled in political controversy throughout much of his career. He was at the centre of a commercial élite extending to Kingston and Detroit that dominated affairs along the Great Lakes. His economic power gave him an unparalleled influence over regional society and that power and influence were, not unnaturally, resented; indeed, they became a major issue of the early politics of the peninsula.

The sharpest challenge to Hamilton's ascendancy came during the administration of Lieutenant Governor SIMCOE. The most immediate concerns of contemporaries were economic: the transfer of land, the satisfaction of claims for debt, and the control of the market of greatest significance to the province, army provisioning. It is a measure of Hamilton's prominence that he, with Cartwright, was the focus of debate on these issues and for a time the Simcoe administration was marked by a clash between the regionally based major merchants attempting to defend their privileges and the newly established provincial executive trying to centralize power in its own hands. Simcoe's initial disdain for merchants, shared by many of his 18th-century military colleagues, contributed to the animosity between the two groups. The political élite, often unaware of or naïve about local conditions, was spurred to action by regional grievances against mercantile domination.

The first significant dispute between the two groups emerged from province-wide agitation over the control of army provisioning. Todd, in conjunction with Robertson, had lobbied successfully for a contract giving preference to their foremost Upper Canadian clients, Cartwright, Hamilton, Askin, and David Robertson, William's brother. The resulting monopoly generated much controversy and Simcoe manœuvred to secure cancellation of the contract in 1794. Although successful, his action had little impact on the pattern of supply because the government took no additional measures to loosen the economic grip of the major merchants. A second bone of contention was the supposed influence of merchants such as Hamilton in the local courts and land boards. Simcoe attempted to address this complaint by altering the structure of the courts and by abolishing the boards. Because of the merchants' entrenched social power, however, these moves were only partially successful.

Transfer of land was the third, and potentially most contentious, issue. Before 1796 land holding was based on certificates that gave possession, but not necessarily ownership and the right to alienate. Land speculators, Hamilton chief among them, who had acquired a good deal of land by purchasing certificates, feared the government might not uphold their legality. In this matter, Simcoe proved sympathetic; however, a final solution was not reached until 1797 with the establishment of the first Heir and Devisee Commission, whose commissioners, including Hamilton, were allowed great latitude in recognizing the legality of land transfers.

Towards the end of his administration Simcoe increasingly acknowledged the legitimate and, indeed, the necessary influence of merchants on the economy and even on the politics of the colony. One signal of this change was his appointment in 1796 of Hamilton as lieutenant of the county of Lincoln, the most important office in the region [see Hazelton SPENCER]. After Simcoe's administration Hamilton's interest in legislative politics declined sharply. The major conflict had been between officials and entrepreneurs over their respective powers and prerogatives. Now that those battles had been fought and the relationship between the political and economic élites had been defined to his satisfaction, Hamilton, from being a frequent opponent of government, became a staunch, if generally quiescent, supporter of it.

Hamilton exercised immediate personal control over patronage within his own area from the establishment of the Nassau District in 1788 until his death. When he became lieutenant of the county of Lincoln he had the right to appoint or recommend justices of the peace and to nominate militia officers. Moreover, he had great power over the selection for offices in the whole area west of York (Toronto). By his use of a potent combination of political and economic influence, he was able to place his sons, his cousins, and the whole second generation of the Askin family in official as well as commercial posts. Hamilton was not part of any local compact of office holders nor did he stand in a client-patron relationship to a provincial "family compact." His power over patronage rested largely on his own local influence. So far as it did depend upon the provincial political structure, it rested squarely upon his personal connection with the lieutenant governors. His most profitable association in this regard was with Peter HUNTER. Of the 13 appointments outside his own district that Hamilton influenced, 8 were made during Hunter's administration. Indeed, the reformer Robert Thorpe* complained of the "scotch pedlars" who "had insinuated themselves into favour with General Hunter . . . there is a chain of them linked from Halifax to Quebec, Montreal, Kingston, York, Niagara & so on to Detroit. . . ." Thorpe labelled these Scots a "Shopkeeper Aristocracy." As he implied, Hunter was connected to many of the merchants by their Scottish origins. He had served as an officer in British North America in the immediate post-revolutionary period when links between the military and the Laurentian traders were especially strong. He had been commandant at Fort Niagara in 1788 and, from 1789 to 1791, he had served at Montreal. During this period he became acquainted with a number of merchants and maintained these relationships up to his return to the province in 1799 as lieutenant governor.

In his later years Hamilton's immediate concerns were to protect and nurture the patronage and influence obtained from the provincial government, for himself and his connections, and to defend his interests in the regional politics of the peninsula. He was, however, less successful in the politics of his own area than in provincial politics and patronage. Indeed, the privileges Hamilton and the merchants associated with him derived from outside contacts fuelled popular resentment. Hostility to monopoly which had first broken out in 1791 reached its peak in 1799 and 1800. A proposal by Hamilton, Clark, and George Forsyth to make extensive improvements to the Niagara portage, to be financed by higher charges, caused a local furore and resulted in a massive petitioning campaign. This hostility to the merchants carried over into the election of 1800, when loyalist officers such as Ralfe Clench* and office holders such as Isaac Swayze* campaigned successfully against the merchants' candidates and excluded them from seats in the peninsula. Hamilton, however, in conjunction with his cousins and other connections such as John WARREN and Thomas WELCH, was able to secure the election of Surveyor General David William Smith* in the riding of Norfolk, Oxford and Middlesex. The division between the major merchants and the coalition of officers, office holders, and petty merchants diminished after 1806 with the rise of a parliamentary opposition, usually associated with

Thorpe, William WEEKES, and Joseph WILLCOCKS. The perceived radicalism of this group drove the merchants and their former opponents together in common cause against their radical foes.

In his private affairs, Hamilton adopted to the full the lifestyle of a gentleman. In 1791, when others in the peninsula might be considering the construction of their first permanent homes, Hamilton began to build an impressive Georgian mansion. Perched on the escarpment, high above the Niagara River at Queenston, the house with its two-storey greystone façade, side wings, and covered galleries, rose incongruously above its modest wooden neighbours and the pioneer clearings. Hamilton entertained lavishly at his home and his guests included Prince EDWARD AUGUSTUS, who, in 1792, stopped there for refreshment during his visit to the falls at Niagara. Elizabeth Posthuma Simcoe [Gwillim*], wife of the lieutenant governor, was a constant companion of Mrs Hamilton. Surrounding his home, Hamilton kept a fairly extensive farm, a practice that reinforced his public image as a man of the landed gentry. He and his children showed a marked respect for books and learning. To indicate his own status and to prepare his offspring for their future social roles, Hamilton was assiduous in their education; all received their higher education in Scotland.

His respectability was based upon more than possession of the trappings of gentility. Hamilton closely associated himself with those institutions that provided concrete opportunities for benefitting the community, such as the Niagara Agricultural Society. He was a founding member and its second president, succeeding Simcoe. The society kept a small library that it eventually donated to the Niagara Library, another institution of which he was a founding member. He was also a provincial deputy grandmaster in the Masonic Lodge of Upper Canada.

Robert Hamilton died on 8 March 1809 after a prolonged illness. His passing was accorded the respect owed by his community to its most prominent citizen. "His funeral, as you may imagine, was attended by a vast concourse," wrote a former tutor of the Hamilton children, "and since the first settlement of the country nothing of this kind has occurred to occasion so much real sorrow." Hamilton's enterprises survived him only for the remarkably brief span of three years. The pillars of his commercial edifice, provisioning and portaging, had been cracking in the last decade of his life. After 1800 army provisioning had become progressively less significant in the local economy with the opening of an export market in Lower Canada. This development stimulated major competition to Hamilton's firm from men such as James Crooks* and Richard HATT and slowly lowered its effectiveness. Again, after 1800, portaging became less profitable with the decline of fur-trading activity, most notably in the southwest. Military shipping also

Hanna

declined as agricultural output in the vicinity of the army posts became sufficient to supply garrisons' needs. Finally, the establishment of a powerful and well-financed portaging rival on the American side of the Niagara River exacerbated Hamilton's situation.

His heavy investment in land and extensive use of credit in his retail operation made it difficult for Hamilton to offset his declining profits in portaging and provisioning. This situation was complicated after his death by the ineptitude of his heirs, the coming of the War of 1812, and a complex will that virtually froze the assets of his estate until 1823. Although some of his sons such as Alexander*, George*, and John* rose in time to be successful entrepreneurs, office holders, and public figures in the higher echelons of Upper Canadian society, none succeeded to the social and political predominance that his enterprises had made Robert Hamilton's prerogative.

BRUCE G. WILSON

AO, MS 75; MU 492, "The Goring family," Hamilton to Goring, 4 Oct. 1779 (transcript); MU 500, Richard Cartwright, letterbook, 1793–96; RG 22, ser.155, will and inventory of Robert Hamilton. BL, Add. MSS 21785: 25; 21786: 73; 21787: 127. Buffalo and Erie County Hist. Soc. (Buffalo, N.Y.), AOO-261 (Robert Hamilton papers), "Hamilton family genealogical chart." Donly Museum, Norfolk Hist. Soc. coll., Thomas Welch papers, 1641–42 (mfm. at PAC). DPL, Burton Hist. Coll., John Askin papers. GRO, Reg. of births and baptisms for the parish of Bolton, 16 Sept. 1753; Reg. of marriages for the parish of Bolton, 17 Oct. 1748. Middlesex East Land Registry Office (London, Ont.), Abstract indexes to deeds (mfm. at AO). Middlesex West Land Registry Office (Glencoe, Ont.), Abstract indexes to deeds (mfm. at AO). Niagara North Land Registry Office (St Catharines, Ont.), Abstract indexes to deeds (mfm. at AO). Niagara South Land Registry Office (Welland, Ont.), Abstract indexes to deeds (mfm. at AO). Norfolk Land Registry Office (Simcoe), Abstract indexes to deeds (mfm. at AO). Oxford Land Registry Office (Woodstock, Ont.), Abstract indexes to deeds (mfm. at AO). PAC, MG 11, [CO 42] Q, 71-1: 234–37; 305: 189; MG 19, A1, 3 (transcripts); A3, 20: 6532; F6, 1: 144; MG 23, HI, 1, ser.3, 2: 329; 8: 471, 475; 10: 16; ser.4, 1–8 (transcripts); MG 24, B130, Thomas Clarke to Helen Clarke, 11 Oct. 1803 (copy); D4; I26; RG 1, E1, 9: 195–96; 28: 284–85, 289; RG 4, B28, 5: 43–44, 46–49; 9: 206; 115; RG 5, A1: 490–91, 1574–75, 1588–91, 1774–81, 1785–86, 1932–37, 3107–28, 3509–10; RG 8, I (C ser.), 108: 132; 115D: 1, 50, 129, 131. QUA, Richard Cartwright papers, letterbooks (transcripts and mfm. of transcripts at AO). UWO, William Robertson papers, Robert Hamilton to Robertson, 20 Oct. 1791; Robertson to Hamilton, 14 Jan. 1805, 17 Jan. 1806. *Corr. of Hon. Peter Russell* (Cruikshank and Hunter). *Corr. of Lieut. Governor Simcoe* (Cruikshank). "District of Nassau: register of the lots in the townships of that district; book no.3," AO *Report*, 1905: 337–47. Douglas, *Lord Selkirk's diary* (White). [E. P. Gwillim (Simcoe)], *Mrs. Simcoe's diary*, ed. M. Q. Innis (Toronto and New York, 1965), 14–15. *John Askin papers* (Quaife). "Names only,

but much more," comp. Janet Carnochan, Niagara Hist. Soc., [*Pub.*], 27 (n.d.). Armstrong, *Handbook of Upper Canadian chronology*. Chadwick, *Ontarian families*. J. R. Robertson, *The history of freemasonry in Canada from its introduction in 1749* . . . (2v., Toronto, 1899), 1: 181, 367. Wilson, "Enterprises of Robert Hamilton."

HANNA, JAMES G., clock and watch maker, gold- and silversmith, and merchant; b. *c.* 1737 in Ireland; d. 26 Jan. 1807 at Quebec, Lower Canada.

It is likely that James G. Hanna was trained and worked as a clock and watch maker in Dublin until about 1763. He then emigrated to Quebec and established himself in the house of merchant John McCord on Rue Buade. On 5 July 1764 he placed an advertisement in the *Quebec Gazette* announcing that he "Makes and mends all Sorts of Watches and Clocks, Jewels, &c. with the greatest Care and Expedition." The following year he sold various articles including jewellery, clocks, finery for trade with the Indians, and materials for clock and watch makers. Located at 15 Rue de la Fabrique, his shop, the Eagle & Watch, quickly became a store for imported goods. Every year he brought in from England a great many fashionable items which enabled the Quebec bourgeoisie to enjoy a style of life like that in London. Jewellery, silverware, arms, scientific instruments, and a variety of other articles were meticulously listed in his advertisements. The popularity of grandfather clocks among the middle class is attributed to him. Hanna imported the movements, which he assembled and fitted into cases made by Quebec cabinet-makers. He also brought in supplies for artists and silversmiths. His business prospered.

Little is known of Hanna's first marriage other than that the couple had two daughters: Jane, who married James Orkney*, a clock and watch maker, and Mary, who married John Macnider*, a tradesman. On 9 Dec. 1787 in the Presbyterian church at Quebec, Hanna took a second wife, Elizabeth Saul, and they had nine children.

In 1788 Hanna paid the Jesuits £360 for a property on Rue de la Fabrique on which stood a frame house that he had bought earlier; eventually, in 1805, he would take up permanent residence there. In January 1794 he set up his store, which had previously been in his home, in the corner house across from the post office. In 1799 he bought the dwelling next door to his from Joseph Kimber for £450; he rented it, to merchants George King and George Chapman among others, before selling it for £400 in 1802. Hanna also owned a house with a bakery on Rue Sainte-Hélène (Rue McMahon), which he rented to master bakers.

Hanna's social life befitted a member of the town's élite. He subscribed to the Quebec Fire Society and the

Quebec Benevolent Society. In 1790 he supported the endeavours to set up a university there [see Jean-François Hubert*], and in 1791, along with other Quebec merchants, he signed the petition in favour of the payment of *lods et ventes*. When governors, administrators, and distinguished visitors arrived or departed, he joined the prominent citizens and merchants of the town in signing the addresses of welcome or appreciation that were presented to them. In 1795, along with six other silversmiths, he petitioned for exemption from a law regulating the use of forges [see Michel FORTON].

In 1803 Hanna went into partnership with his son James Godfrey* and hired a workman who could repair watches and clocks. He then gradually withdrew from the business. He died at Quebec on 26 Jan. 1807, leaving a modest estate to his family. His home was well furnished, with assorted valuable articles and a library of more than 50 volumes. Only a few serving dishes and articles of trade silver, bearing the mark IH in a rectangle, remain as a witness to James Hanna's accomplishments.

SYLVIO NORMAND

ANQ-Q, CE1-66, 9 Dec. 1787; 9 Nov. 1788; 3 July, 5 Sept. 1790; 2 Sept. 1792; 23 April 1794; 26 April 1795; 6 March 1797; 30 June 1799; 16 April 1801; 1 Jan. 1804; 29 Jan., 9 Aug. 1807; CN1-16, 2 déc. 1811; CN1-26, 21 mars 1799, 26 févr. 1800; CN1-171, 26 Jan. 1807, 15 Jan. 1808; CN1-224, 12 août 1788; CN1-230, 24 juill. 1795; CN1-284, 20 mars 1805; CN1-285, 26 févr. 1801. MAC-CD, Fonds Morisset, 2, H243/J27.5/2. "Les dénombrements de Québec" (Plessis), ANQ *Rapport*, 1948–49: 15, 120, 164. *Quebec Gazette*, 5 July 1764; 8 Aug. 1765; 3 Nov. 1785; 4 Nov. 1790; 2 June, 11 Aug. 1791; 16 Jan., 13 Feb., 10 July 1794; 29 June 1797; 21 March, 18 July 1799; 11 Dec. 1800; 3 Nov. 1803; 19 Feb. 1807. *Quebec directory*, 1790. Langdon, *Canadian silversmiths*, 80.

HARDY, GEORGE, overseer of roads, businessman, and master mariner; b. *c.* 1740, probably in East or West Knighton, England; d. in or after 1803.

George Hardy first enters the historical record in a letter dated 12 Jan. 1769, now in the county archives at Warwick, England, from the Nova Scotia surveyor Charles MORRIS to one John Butler, agent for John Pownall, at that time proprietor of Lot 13 on St John's (Prince Edward) Island. The previous summer Morris had visited the eastern part of Pownall's lot, on the west side of Malpeque Bay in the neighbourhood now known as Port Hill. There he had found evidence of settlement by about 20 Acadian families but reported, "There is now no Houses on it worth repairing except the one Mr Hart lives in this Man came there last summer from New York with a large Family and Stock and proposes if the land is to be let upon reasonable Terms to bring ten Families from thence who understand both Farming and Fishing."

Until the discovery of this letter the earliest evidence of George Hardy's pioneer existence on St John's Island lay in Thomas Curtis's detailed account of the shipwreck of the brig *Elizabeth* off the northern shore in November 1775; however, Morris's "Hart" can be identified beyond reasonable doubt as Hardy. According to Curtis's account, Hardy lived 14 miles across the ice from the wreck, itself situated in the vicinity of Cavendish Inlet on the long sand-hills off the shore. A map prepared by Morris and accompanying his letter shows "Hart's house" at the centre of the area previously occupied by French-speaking settlers, not far from the modern Port Hill wharf and roughly ten miles in a straight line from Cavendish Inlet. The site of the house is still clearly visible as a crop mark in air photographs. Clearly traceable also is a track from the site westwards in the direction of Ramsay Creek, the nearest safe harbour for boats and small vessels.

Here Hardy lived in isolation, the sole European known to have been settled in the western part of the Island in 1769. By 1775 only one other settler, Donald Ramsay, had come to join him, and theirs were the only two houses within reach of the *Elizabeth*. The vessel had been conveying settlers and stores for Robert Clark*'s settlement at New London, and Hardy was of great help to the passengers in their attempts to recover the cargo some months after the disaster. He emerges from Curtis's account as a resourceful and skilled woodsman and pioneer, and also, in Curtis's own words, as "a remarkabl honest good natured man."

There are shadowy indications of Hardy's subsequent career in public records. He was an overseer of roads in the 1780s. In August 1787 he and George Penman, who had been paymaster of the Island's first British garrison and had recently settled on the site now known as Old Port Hill Farm, purchased the schooner *Mary*, built two years before. The partners sold her in 1788. The following year Hardy was arrested on a murder charge but acquitted on a plea of self-defence. He remained a settler on Lot 13 until it changed ownership in the early 1790s. When the old Acadian clearings then began to fill up and the question of rent arose, he moved with his family out into the wilderness again, to the neighbourhood of the present Alberton, farther north and west on the Island. He appears in the census report of 1798 as the only settler on Lot 6, with a family, presumably his second, of five boys and four girls under 16 years of age. In the same year he was registered at the Charlottetown custom-house as the sole owner of the new schooner *Lark*, and she remained his property and command until she was lost in the Baie des Chaleurs in 1803. Hardy may have lost his life in this accident, but there appears to be no record of his death.

George Hardy's known career, and indications in Curtis's account, suggest that one of his occupations

Harries

may have been the support and supply of merchant vessels engaged in illegal trade. Be that as it may, he emerges from the fragmentary records as a successful man of the wilderness, kind and generous, with the skills needed for survival in extreme conditions, living beyond the limits of settlement and moving on when these overtook him.

BASIL GREENHILL

PAC, RG 42, ser.1, 459. Warwickshire County Record Office (Warwick, Eng.), CR 114A/562 (Seymour of Ragley papers). *Journeys to the Island of St. John or Prince Edward Island, 1775–1832*, ed. D. C. Harvey (Toronto, 1955). Duncan Campbell, *History of Prince Edward Island* (Charlottetown, 1875; repr. Belleville, Ont., 1972). Basil Greenhill and Ann Giffard, *Westcountrymen in Prince Edward's Isle: a fragment of the great migration* (Newton Abbot, Eng., and [Toronto], 1967; repr. Toronto and Buffalo, 1975).

HARRIES, JOHN, Church of England clergyman and office holder; b. 1763 in Wales; m. Phoebe —, and they had nine daughters and one son; d. 22 Jan. 1810 in St John's, Nfld.

Ordained in Wales by the bishop of St David's in 1787, John Harries served a short period as curate at Camrose and at St Martin's Church, Haverfordwest. On 16 April 1788 he was assigned, by the Society for the Propagation of the Gospel, to Placentia in Newfoundland, in response to a request by the principal inhabitants for a clergyman, whom they promised to support. Prince William Henry, who had visited the area in 1786 while on naval duty, had added his petition and also given 50 guineas and a handsome set of communion plate towards a church.

Upon his arrival in Placentia in 1788 Harries found only 120 Anglicans in a summer population of 3,500 in the town and nearby outports. The district was dominated by the Roman Catholics, and thanks to the efforts of Father Edmund BURKE (fl.1785–1801) many Anglicans had been converted. Harries lamented that "the Protestants of Placentia are nearly all proselyted" and noted that "no controversial pamphlet on Roman Catholicism can be distributed with safety." Anglican worship had been kept up in the court-house prior to Harries's arrival, and the building of a church begun, but the settlers had not even a surplice available for the missionary. Moreover, collections from the congregation for his support raised only £23 in 1788, as compared to £300 from Burke's parishioners. Governor Mark MILBANKE obtained Harries free board and lodging by appointing him chaplain to the garrison in 1789, but Harries was evidently disappointed with the smallness of his emoluments. Thus when in 1790 the financially more appealing St John's mission became available, Harries made a successful application to be transferred

there. By the time of his departure from Placentia in 1791 he had visited Fortune Bay and had started a school at Burin. In addition, the church at Placentia, complete with bell and spire, had been finished.

Harries arrived at St John's on 10 May 1791 to find the church "in a very ruinous situation." So cold was the building in winter that his congregation preferred to worship with the Methodists or Catholics, whose churches were warmer. However, the Congregational preacher John Jones*, described by Harries as a "very exemplary, pious, old man," allowed the Anglicans the use of his chapel while Governor William Waldegrave settled disputes about the site of a new church. A grant of £400 from the SPG and 200 guineas from King George III secured its completion in 1800.

Harries constantly worried about money, even though he was well paid by the standards of the time. In 1794, for instance, he received £74 as deputy chaplain to the garrison, £70 from the SPG, £50 from the government, and £30 16s. 3d. in collections, and five years later the total increased by £30. The money was, however, insufficient to meet the demands of his large family. He lived in a dilapidated two-room house, attempts to obtain funds by public subscription failed because of the opposition of enemies whom he described as wild fanatics and "still more dangerous infidels," and his family often went hungry. Of his ten children, three predeceased him.

Despite these handicaps, Harries was an active missionary. He visited Harbour Grace several times in the absence of other clergymen, went down the coast to Bay Bulls and Ferryland, and even ventured as far as Harbour Breton. At St John's he competed successfully with the Methodists but not with the Roman Catholics, and lamented that the latter had a bishop, James Louis O'DONEL, able to perform confirmations. Harries also undertook some official duties as a magistrate, and as *custos rotulorum* from 1803. He died of consumption, a scourge which carried away his two eldest children in Newfoundland and others later. After his death his widow and family were assisted by the SPG and went to England.

FREDERICK JONES

USPG, C/CAN/Nfl., 1–3; Journal of SPG, 25–30. [C. F. Pascoe], *Classified digest of the records of the Society for the Propagation of the Gospel in Foreign Parts, 1701–1892* (5th ed., London, 1895). Prowse, *Hist. of Nfld.* (1896).

HARRIS, JOHN, land agent, judge, merchant, office holder, and politician; b. 16 July 1739 in Elizabethtown, Pa, third son of Thomas Harris and Mary McKinney; m. 1766 Elizabeth Scott, and they had at least two sons and one daughter; d. 9 April 1802 in Truro, N.S.

The opening up of Nova Scotia to British settlement

in 1759 [*see* Charles Lawrence*] resulted in the formation of many land companies to obtain grants in the province. One such organization was the Philadelphia Company, which in October 1765 obtained from Governor Montagu Wilmot* a grant of 200,000 acres on the northern shore of Nova Scotia. Thomas Harris and his three sons, Matthew, Robert, and John, were all involved in the company and consequently in its attempts to settle the grant. John, the youngest, was a graduate of the College of New Jersey (Princeton University), where he had obtained his AB in 1763; having studied medicine after his graduation, he had become a doctor. It was he who was generally in charge of the company's affairs in Nova Scotia and who led the first of the settlers there in 1767 aboard the brigantine *Betsey*. The party, which numbered ten adults, including Robert PATTERSON, and 15 to 19 children, arrived in Pictou harbour on 10 June. During the first night, while the ship was anchored in the harbour, a son was born to Harris and his wife.

The region appeared rather forbidding to this first group of English-speaking settlers. The land was almost completely wooded, and the harbour frontage given them was swampy, for the best land surrounding the port had been granted to Alexander McNUTT. Moreover, Truro, the nearest settlement, was 40 miles inland. Nevertheless, the settlers began clearing the land and during the next two years were joined by others from Pennsylvania and Maryland. By January 1770 there were 176 people in Pictou, as the community was called, and the town had acquired an air of permanency. Harris was one of the more prosperous inhabitants: he had six servants or labourers living with him, he owned 11 head of livestock, and his land had produced 50 bushels of wheat and oats the previous year. The arrival of the first large contingent of Scottish settlers on the *Hector* in 1773, and that of another group of Scots, who had initially established themselves on St John's (Prince Edward) Island, in 1774, added to the stability of the community.

During the first few years of the community Harris was heavily involved in attending to the needs of those who had settled the company's land. In addition to being the company agent, responsible for selling lots to applicants, he had been made a justice of the peace in October 1767 and a magistrate in 1771. His medical training undoubtedly proved useful, but no records of his practice have survived. He and his brother Matthew were also involved in coastal trading; John owned the shallop *Dolphin*, which was wrecked in a storm off Cape George in November 1771.

At the time of the American revolution the Scots, who formed the majority of the settlers in Pictou, were passively loyal, but there was also an American faction in the settlement. Harris, who had friends and relatives on the rebel side, belonged to this faction in spite of his crown appointments. He contrived to carry on trading with the American colonies, and Lieutenant Governor Michael Francklin* once seized a cargo belonging to him and his brother Matthew in the belief that they were trading with the rebels. Although no charges were laid against Harris, because of his known sympathy with the American cause considerable resentment developed against him in Pictou. Perhaps as a result of this antagonism, but possibly also for business reasons, Harris moved to Truro in 1777.

During his residence in Truro Harris was much involved in community and provincial affairs. He became clerk of the township in 1779, a registrar of deeds, and a justice of the peace, and he represented Truro in the House of Assembly between 1781 and 1785. In 1793 he became a judge of the Inferior Court of Common Pleas. He continued to enjoy positions of influence despite his views on the American revolution. It is probable that his political beliefs had changed somewhat, given that he had remained in Nova Scotia. Harris's career, which is notable for his promotion of settlement at Pictou, illustrates the dilemma faced by American settlers who arrived in Nova Scotia before the revolution.

R. A. MacLean

PANS, MG 9, no.170; MG 100, 161, no.53; 207, no.6 (typescript); 228, no.13; RG 1, 212; RG 46, folder 3. "A direct road between Annapolis Royal and Halifax," PANS, Board of Trustees, *Report* (Halifax), 1937: 37–44. *Acadian Recorder*, 26 Oct. 1816. *Directory of N.S. MLAs*. Robert Stewart, *Colonel George Steuart and his wife Margaret Harris: their ancestors and descendants . . .* (Lahore, India, 1907). J. M. Cameron, *Political Pictonians: the men of the Legislative Council, Senate, House of Commons, House of Assembly, 1767–1967* (Ottawa, [1967]). George MacLaren, *The Pictou book: stories of our past* (New Glasgow, N.S., [1954]). G. G. Patterson, *Studies in Nova Scotian history* (Halifax, 1940). George Patterson, *A history of the county of Pictou, Nova Scotia* (Montreal, 1877). R. F. Harris, "A pioneer Harris family and the pre-loyalist settlement of Pictou," N.S. Hist. Soc., *Coll.*, 33 (1961): 103–35. Alexander Mackenzie, "First Highland emigration to Nova Scotia: arrival of the ship 'Hector,'" *Celtic Magazine* (Inverness, Scot.), 8 (1883): 140–44. *Pictou Advocate* (Pictou, N.S.), 2 Oct., 18 Dec. 1947.

HART, SAMUEL, merchant and politician; b. *c.* 1747, probably in England; m. *c.* 1780 Rebecca Byrne of Philadelphia, Pa, and they had four children; d. 3 Oct. 1810 in Preston, N.S.

Samuel Hart's origins are obscure. Apparently born in England of Jewish stock, he moved to Philadelphia some time prior to the outbreak of the American revolution. During the war he evidently became identified with the tory cause since he arrived at Halifax from New York City about 1785 as part of the general loyalist exodus to Nova Scotia. Operating from premises at the corner of Hollis and George streets purchased for £900, Hart conducted a general import-export business. His newspaper advertisements emphasized the sale of dry goods brought in from London, but entries in the diary of Simeon PERKINS, a Liverpool merchant, indicate that Hart engaged in the West Indies trade and handled a virtually unlimited range of commodities. Certain contemporaries, including Perkins and William FORSYTH, disapproved of Hart's allegedly "sharp practices," but he nevertheless prospered, particularly after war broke out between Britain and revolutionary France in 1793. The bankruptcy of his brother Moses Hart, a London merchant, caused Samuel some distress in the late 1790s because he had guaranteed Moses's debts. By 1801, however, Samuel had recovered to the extent of being able to pay off all mortgages on his Nova Scotia property. At this point Hart owned urban and rural real estate valued at more than £4,000.

Not content with material success, Samuel Hart aspired to social recognition, even if that required suppression of his Jewish identity. In March 1793 he had himself baptized an Anglican and by 1801 he owned a pew in St George's Anglican Church in Halifax. He also invested £655 in the purchase of a large country estate, complete with mansion, at Preston, to the northeast of Halifax. There he "spent his summers . . . and entertained elaborately." By playing host to officers of the British army and navy, Hart and his wife acquired a reputation for being "gay and fashionable people." To cultivate further his image as a respectable man of property, Hart had his portrait painted during a visit to London in 1795. Moreover, through the use of "ledger influence" directed against his outport debtors, Hart gained entry to the provincial assembly. As the member for Liverpool Township between 1793 and 1799 he predictably allied himself with other Halifax merchants against those rural and allegedly democratic interests led by William Cottnam Tonge*. On one occasion Hart broke with the merchants to support an increase in import duties. It is probable that he did so only because the tax increase was being urged by Lieutenant Governor Sir John WENTWORTH. All of these efforts secured Hart no more than a precarious degree of acceptance from Halifax's social élite, however. Significantly, he failed to be named a magistrate or be elected to the executive of the Halifax Commercial Society.

In 1797 Samuel Hart declared in a codicil to his will that "the Blessing of God" appeared to be with him in business. That optimism vanished between 1803 and 1805. A severe slump in Halifax trade deprived Hart of income just at the time when his social ambitions made material abundance essential. He mortgaged his property and desperately began coercing his debtors for immediate payment. Hart should have been able to survive this crisis since Halifax trade had begun to revive by 1807. Unfortunately, however, the pressure of events proved too much for Hart's mind. In 1809 he was declared legally insane. A year later he died, a pathetic figure who spent the last days of his life chained to the floor of a room in his Preston mansion. His wife, Rebecca, and their three children, two girls and a boy, inherited virtually nothing. Debts overwhelmed the estate's assets, and ultimately Hart's creditors were obliged to accept payment of 4s. 10d. on the pound. Samuel Hart's tragic fate underscored the difficulties facing Jews who aspired to social acceptance in early British North America.

D. A. SUTHERLAND

Anglican Church of Canada, Diocese of Nova Scotia Arch. (Halifax), St George's Anglican Church, Halifax, pew rentals, 17 July 1801 (mfm. at PANS). Halifax County Court of Probate (Halifax), H45 (estate papers of Samuel Hart) (mfm. at PANS). Halifax County Registry of Deeds (Halifax), Deeds, 24: ff.10–14; 32: ff.443–45, 484; 34: ff.405–7; 38: ff.185–86; 39: ff.270–73 (mfm. at PANS). PANS, MG 3, 150, William Forsyth & Co. to George Andrew, and to David Colter, 12 Nov. 1796. PRO, AO 13, bundles 80; 96, pt.II. Royal Bank of Canada (Liverpool, N.S.), Simeon Perkins, diary, 1804; corr., Perkins to Messrs. Cochran, 9 Feb. 1793 (transcripts at PANS). St Paul's Anglican Church (Halifax), Reg. of baptisms, 17 March 1793 (mfm. at PANS). N.S., House of Assembly, *Journal and proc.*, 1793–99. Perkins, *Diary, 1790–96* (Fergusson). *Halifax Journal*, 3 Oct. 1810. *Nova Scotia Royal Gazette*, 21 Feb. 1786; 6 Nov. 1787; 16 June 1789; 21 June 1796; 7 Oct. 1802; 24–31 Jan., 7 March, 26 Sept. 1805; 20 Feb. 1810. *Directory of N.S. MLAs*. M. J. [Lawson] Katzmann, *History of the townships of Dartmouth, Preston and Lawrencetown, Halifax County, N.S.*, ed. Harry Piers (Halifax, 1893; repr. Belleville, Ont., 1972). J. P. Martin, *The story of Dartmouth* (Dartmouth, N.S., 1957). N.S., Provincial Museum and Science Library, *Report* (Halifax), 1932–33, 1934–35.

HASWELL, ROBERT, fur trader; b. 24 Nov. 1768, probably in Hull, Mass.; m. 10 Oct. 1801 Mary Cordis in Reading, Mass., and they had two daughters; d. 1801 at sea.

The eldest son of William Haswell, a lieutenant in the Royal Navy, Robert Haswell had had experience at sea before joining the *Columbia Rediviva* as third mate at Boston on 30 Sept. 1787. This ship, commanded by John Kendrick*, and the sloop *Lady Washington*, under Robert GRAY, had been fitted out by Joseph Barrell and five business associates to participate in the fur trade on the northwest coast. The log kept by Haswell during the voyage is extremely valuable, since it is the only surviving contemporary account of Boston's pioneering adventure in the sea otter trade.

In the course of the voyage southwards through the Atlantic, Haswell rose to the position of second officer. At the Falkland Islands, after a dispute with Kendrick, he was transferred to the *Lady Washington* as second officer, a position he still held when the expedition reached Nootka Sound (B.C.) in September 1788. The following spring, while the *Columbia* remained at anchor in the sound, the sloop sailed along the coast seeking out Indians to trade with. On this trip Haswell met the Indian leaders Callicum and Muquinna* and gained a sufficiently intimate knowledge of the Nootkas to compile a vocabulary of their language. In July Kendrick sent the *Columbia*, with Gray in command and Haswell resuming his position as second officer, back to Boston via the Sandwich (Hawaiian) Islands and Canton (People's Republic of China). She arrived at her home port in August 1790, having circumnavigated the globe.

Just six weeks later Haswell sailed in her again for the northwest coast, this time as Gray's first officer. The ship reached Clayoquot Sound (B.C.) on 5 June 1791 and traded on the coast for the summer season, Gray following the owners' instructions to avoid Nootka Sound, which was held by a Spanish garrison under Francisco de Eliza* y Reventa and Pedro de ALBERNI. The expedition wintered at Adventure Cove (Lemmens Inlet, Meares Island), where the 45-ton sloop *Adventure* was constructed. In March 1792 Haswell was placed in command of this tiny vessel, which proved to be "a very good seaboat," and in April he sailed in search of trade to the Queen Charlotte Islands and the adjacent coast. On 17 June he made contact with Gray, who was sailing north after having discovered the Columbia River, and the next day, in Nasparti Inlet (B.C.), he delivered to the *Columbia* the sea otter skins and other pelts he had acquired. Shortly afterwards the *Columbia* struck a rock, and Gray was forced to call upon the Spaniards in Nootka Sound for assistance. The Americans established friendly relations with the men they had hitherto avoided, and on 28 September they sold the *Adventure* to the new Spanish commandant, Juan Francisco de la Bodega* y Quadra, for 75 prime sea otter skins. Haswell returned to the *Columbia* as first mate and sailed in her for Boston, arriving there by way of China late in July 1793.

In the next five years Haswell made two voyages to the East Indies. On 4 March 1799 he entered the United States Navy as a lieutenant, and he remained in the service until April 1801. During this time he served in the *Boston*, gaining a share of the prize money when she captured the French corvette *Berceau*. On 5 April Haswell, aged 32 and now residing with his family in Charlestown (Boston), left Massachusetts for the last time in command of the trading vessel *Louisa*. His proposed itinerary was familiar: around Cape Horn to the northwest coast, to

China, and back to Boston; but the ship was lost at sea before reaching her initial destination.

Haswell's success in his career indicates that he was a trusted officer and a competent trader, although John Box Hoskins, supercargo on the *Columbia*'s second voyage to the northwest coast, was ambivalent in his assessment. Hoskins admitted in his journal, "it is to him we are indebted for what knowledge we have yet attained" of the coastline. Nevertheless he wrote to Barrell, "Mr. Haswell . . . has said to his officers, that he would make 10,000 *Dollars*, he would then go to England that the Owners might go to hell and his wages and per Centage with them." In his writing Haswell often underlined his own independence and good judgement, sometimes at the expense of his superiors; but he appears to have been an intelligent leader and a good navigator.

BARRY M. GOUGH

Robert Haswell's "A voyage round the world onboard the ship Columbia-Rediviva and sloop Washington," [1787–89], and "A voyage on discoveries in the ship Columbia Rediviva," [1791–93], are at the Mass. Hist. Soc. The first of these logs, including the Nootka vocabulary he compiled, was published in *Voyages of the "Columbia" to the northwest coast, 1787–1790 and 1790–1793*, ed. F. W. Howay ([Boston], 1941; repr. Amsterdam and New York, [1969]), pp.3–107, and a portion of the second at pp.293–359. F. W. Howay, "Some notes on Robert Haswell," Mass. Hist. Soc., *Proc.* (Boston), 65 (1932–36): 592–600.

HATT, RICHARD, businessman, judge, office holder, politician, and militia officer; b. 10 Sept. 1769 in London, England, son of Richard and Mary Hatt; m. December 1799 Mary Cooley in Ancaster, Upper Canada, and they had nine children; d. 26 Sept. 1819 in Dundas, Upper Canada.

Richard Hatt immigrated to Upper Canada in 1792. Two years later he was working in the "Mercantile business," probably with John MacKay at Niagara (Niagara-on-the-Lake). Hatt's family joined him in 1796. By this time he was MacKay's partner but, with the financial backing of his father, he decided to strike out on his own. He moved to Ancaster village in the region known as the Head of the Lake (the vicinity of present-day Hamilton Harbour) where he opened a store, probably that same year. His intention was to become a miller and by 1798, in partnership with his brother Samuel*, he had completed construction of a grist-mill in the village. Prospects were not as encouraging as he had hoped, and he began to look for a new site with better potential for development.

In 1800 he purchased land for a flour-mill on the nearby Spencer Creek, three miles above its inlet to Coote's Paradise. Here he established a milling complex, known as the Dundas Mills, that soon

Hazen

became the dominant enterprise at the Head of the Lake. By his death it included a distillery, a potashery, a general store, two sawmills, a coopery, a blacksmith shop, several farms, and numerous houses, store-houses, and other buildings. Most of his profits seem to have been reinvested in either the expansion or the upgrading of his enterprises, but he did engage in some land speculation. In 1808 he and his brother were involved with John Norton* in an attempt to purchase from the Six Nations a tract on the Grand River. Three years later he entered an agreement to rent a mill there from David Phelps for 12 years at $300 per annum. The brothers' partnership continued until 1816, when Samuel moved to Lower Canada.

Hatt's mills spurred the settlement of the valley in which they were located. In 1801 the area was surveyed and a town plot laid out for Coote's Paradise, after 1814 Dundas. Hatt had great hopes for the fledgling community; in 1810 his name headed a petition urging the government to make it the administrative centre of the proposed new district at the Head of the Lake. The War of 1812 intervened and, when the Gore District was established in 1816, Barton Township (Hamilton) became the district capital.

During the war Hatt had served as a major in the 5th Lincoln Militia. He saw action throughout the conflict and was severely wounded at the battle of Lundy's Lane on 25 July 1814. From the spring of 1813 until late 1814 the Head of the Lake was often occupied by British troops and their Indian allies. Although Hatt had lost some goods to invading American armies, he sustained his heaviest losses at the hands of the British and especially the Indians; his total claim for damages after the war amounted to £2,898 (provincial currency).

Hatt was primarily a businessman but he had other interests as well. He was appointed justice of the peace in 1800 and served in that capacity until his death. Before the war he was a road commissioner and after it he was appointed judge of the new district court and also of the surrogate court. In 1812 he had purchased Joseph WILLCOCKS's printing-press; six years later he took up his interest in newspapers again, as proprietor of the *Upper Canada Phoenix*. Hatt's political involvement came late; he first entered the House of Assembly after successfully contesting a by-election in the riding of Halton in 1817. During the spring session in 1818 he chaired the important committee on public accounts. His death in 1819 ended a successful and varied career in Upper Canada.

In collaboration with BRUCE A. PARKER

AO, RG 22, ser.155, will of Richard Hatt. PAC, RG 1, L3, 222a: H1/66; 224: H3/161; RG 8, I (C ser.), 1219: 266; RG 19, 3747, claim 503; RG 68, General index, 1651–1814: ff.407–8, 412–16, 418, 422, 425–26, 431, 537. "Journals of Legislative Assembly of U.C.," AO *Report*, 1912: 66–67, 432; 1913: 10, 208. "Petitions for grants of land" (Cruik-shank), *OH*, 24: 77–79. *The history of the town of Dundas*, comp. T. R. Woodhouse (3v., [Dundas, Ont.], 1965–68), 1: 14–27.

HAZEN, MOSES, army officer, office holder, landowner, seigneur, and merchant; b. 1 June 1733 in Haverhill, Mass., third child of Moses Hazzen, merchant, and Abigail White; m. 5 Dec. 1770 Charlotte de La Saussaye in Montreal, Que.; they had no children; d. 5 Feb. 1803 in Troy, N.Y., and was buried 8 February in Albany, N.Y.

Moses Hazen enlisted in an American colonial unit in 1755 and, according to the historian Francis Parkman, served that year under Lieutenant-Colonel Robert Monckton* at Fort Beauséjour (near Sackville, N.B.). In 1756 he was at Lac Saint-Sacrement (Lake George, N.Y.). Out of the army the following year, he shipped to Halifax provisions and supplies for the projected British attack on Louisbourg, Île Royale (Cape Breton Island). On 7 April 1758 he was commissioned first lieutenant in John McCurdy's company of Major Robert Rogers*'s rangers, and he served under Brigadier-General James Wolfe* at the capture of Louisbourg. Wintering at Fort Frederick (Saint John, N.B.), and having succeeded in January 1759 to command of McCurdy's company, Hazen led it the following month on a raid to Sainte-Anne-du-Pays-Bas (Fredericton, N.B.), burning the settlement and taking prisoners, among them Joseph Godin*, *dit* Bellefontaine, *dit* Beauséjour, who had been a thorn in the British side; the raid earned Hazen a captaincy.

In 1759 Hazen's company was included in the expedition to Quebec, and he transferred to that front Rogers's form of brutal partisan warfare, boldly volunteering himself and his men for numerous expeditions into the countryside around Quebec. He was on one such operation when the battle of the Plains of Abraham was fought on 13 September. As the British waited out the winter of 1759–60 within the walls of Quebec, Hazen's daring sorties impressed Brigadier-General James Murray*. Badly wounded in the thigh at the battle of Sainte-Foy in April 1760, Hazen was eventually obliged to give up his ranger company. On 21 Feb. 1761, with the recommendation of Murray, who attributed to him "so much still Bravery and good Conduct as would Justly Entitle him to Every military Reward he Could ask or Demand," Hazen was allowed to purchase, for 800 guineas, a lieutenant's commission in the 44th Foot. From 1761 to 1763 his regiment performed garrison duty at Montreal, and when it was reduced to nine companies in 1763 he retired on half pay.

Hazen settled at Montreal, and in 1765 he was appointed by Murray a justice of the peace. Two years later he was a member of the grand jury in the Thomas

Walker* assault case. Meanwhile he had begun acquiring land for settlement and speculation. In the early 1760s he obtained proprietary shares in two towns in New Hampshire and the grant of another town, later known as Moortown (Bradford, Vt). In 1764 he was among the British officers and associates who formed a company, later known as the Saint John River Society, to acquire vast tracts of land in the Saint John valley (N.B.) [*see* Beamsley Perkins Glasier*]. The same year Hazen and Lieutenant-Colonel Gabriel Christie* jointly purchased the seigneuries of Sabrevois and Bleury on the east bank of the Rivière Richelieu and five farms on the site of Saint-Jean (Saint-Jean-sur-Richelieu). The two men thus became masters of the rich upper Richelieu valley. With Christie furnishing most of the capital, but absent for long periods, Hazen strenuously developed their holdings, clearing lands, settling tenants, building two sawmills, and erecting a manor-house at present-day Iberville.

An appointment by Murray in 1765 as deputy surveyor of the king's woods facilitated Hazen's entry into the timber business. The following year he signed a personal agreement with Samuel McKay, deputy surveyor for the navy in Canada, and a London naval supplier, John Henniker, to provide a large number of masts. Standards for masts were sufficiently high that it was probably necessary to cut on property to which Hazen and McKay did not have title, and when in 1767 they floated 200 logs from the Lake Champlain area to Montreal, the timber was seized by Benjamin Price* and Daniel ROBERTSON as having been cut on their land. From 1766 Hazen was in and out of court on a number of commercial matters. That October a Saint-Jean merchant, Joseph Kelly, published in the *Quebec Gazette* a letter accusing Hazen of having "villainously seduced" his wife while he was absent on business in July, and then of having had him imprisoned at Quebec for a non-existent debt when he had come there to obtain redress.

By 1766 Hazen's expensive development schemes had provoked Christie to impose stringent restrictions on the activities of his fast-moving, ambitious partner, who, however, tended to interpret them after his own fashion. He incurred large debts on the seigneuries, and in 1766 he mortgaged his half of them to Christie for £800. He continued to borrow heavily and obtained £2,000 from his brother WILLIAM and William's partner, Leonard Jarvis. In 1770 Christie insisted on a division of their property. Hazen got land in and around Fort St Johns (Saint-Jean-sur-Richelieu), a farm near by, and the southern half of Bleury, including the manor; he thus became seigneur of Bleury-Sud. That fall some of his goods and livestock were advertised for sale at a sheriff's auction, and the following spring another sheriff's auction of land was advertised in order to pay a debt owed to Joseph

Fleury* Deschambault. These set-backs did not prevent Hazen from pushing ahead the development of his seigneury, on which he built a forge, an ashery, and a second sawmill to replace one lost to Christie in the division of properties. In 1773 he petitioned Governor Guy CARLETON for a large tract of land adjoining Bleury-Sud to the east as well as for a seigneury for his brother William and another for Jarvis; none of these requests was granted before the outbreak of the American revolution in 1775.

Alarmed at the first news of open rebellion in the colonies to the south, in February 1775 Hazen visited Carleton at Quebec; the governor, describing him as a brave and experienced officer, recommended him for a commission and in March sent him with dispatches to Lieutenant-General Thomas Gage* at Boston. Two months later Hazen brought Carleton word of Benedict ARNOLD's incursion to Fort St Johns. He then returned to his seigneury and, since his lands lay along a probable American invasion route, he spent the summer pondering his situation. Temperamentally Hazen was incapable of remaining neutral, but his decision as to which side to join would be based in good part on the prospects of success of each of the contending parties, and hence on the ultimate disposition of his properties.

In the fall of 1775 the Americans began a two-pronged invasion of Canada, one force entering the colony via the Richelieu valley [*see* Richard Montgomery*]. It had first, however, to retake Fort St Johns, where the defences had been stiffened under Major Charles Preston. Hazen was sent an authorization from Carleton to raise troops and to join Preston, but, as yet unsure of which side to adopt, he equivocated. Perhaps hoping to stave off the invasion, which could only wreak havoc on his lands, instead of reporting to Preston he visited the American commander, Philip John Schuyler, and told of bleak prospects for American success. As a result, a council of war decided to abort the invasion, but it reversed its decision when James Livingston*, an American established at Chambly, described the situation in a far more optimistic light. Because of his equivocal behaviour, Hazen was arrested by an American detachment. It was obliged to abandon him, however, by an approaching British force, which arrested him in turn. Preston sent Hazen to Carleton at Montreal, where he was placed in close confinement after, he later claimed, having refused Carleton's offers of the command of a British regiment or retirement to Britain for the duration of the war. Following the capture of Fort St Johns on 3 November, Carleton was obliged to depart Montreal precipitously for Quebec; he took Hazen with him, but, when nearly captured en route, had to leave him to the Americans.

Hazen, now obviously committed to the American side, joined in the siege of Quebec. After the failure on

413

Hazen

31 Dec. 1775 of Montgomery's desperate attack on the city, Hazen and Edward Antill, an American resident of Quebec who had been expelled by Carleton, were sent to the second Continental Congress at Philadelphia with the news of Montgomery's death and a request for reinforcements. Congress decided to raise two Canadian regiments of 1,000 men each. Command of the first was given to Livingston, and that of the second, with the rank of colonel, was offered to Hazen. His reticence to accept was overcome by a guarantee of compensation for loss of his British half pay and assurances that his Canadian property would not be confiscated by the British since the American invasion could not fail.

Hazen returned to Montreal and began recruitment in competition with Livingston, offering the equivalent of 40 *livres* for enlistment, plus monthly pay. One of his recruiters in the Richelieu valley was the merchant James BELL. At first Hazen enjoyed success with the disaffected Canadians, but recruitment fell off as a result, Hazen asserted, of bad behaviour on the part of American troops and civilians in Canada, the paucity of troops in the colony, and payment in paper money and certificates that the quartermasters subsequently refused to redeem. By the end of February Hazen had 150 soldiers; a month later he still had only 250. Even the hiring as chaplain of the Jesuit Pierre-René Floquet*, in an attempt to overcome the church's discouragement of recruitment, failed to have much effect.

In late March 1776 Hazen took command of Montreal, when Brigadier-General David Wooster was ordered to replace Arnold before Quebec. Soon after his arrival at Montreal, Arnold sent Hazen to take command at forts St Johns and Chambly; Hazen was also to prepare the American line of retreat along the Richelieu valley. His experience with the Canadians prompted him in May to write Brigadier-General John Sullivan, who was preparing a last stand at Sorel: "Do not rely on any real assistance from the Canadians whom you are collecting together – I know them well; be assured that, in our present situation, they will leave us in the hour of difficulty. . . . What are we to expect from a handful of such men, against the well-known best troops in the world?" When Hazen joined the retreat from Canada in June, of the maximum of 477 men that he claimed to have recruited, only about 175 followed him.

Hazen's regiment remained intact throughout the revolution, supplemented by recruitment from the American states. It saw action at Staten Island, N.Y., Brandywine and Germantown (Philadelphia), Pa, and Yorktown, Va, earning an excellent reputation. Hazen's was among the most insistent voices for a second invasion of Canada, and in January 1778 he was appointed deputy quartermaster general for an invasion force to be led by the Marquis de La Fayette;

the project was abandoned, however, on 13 March. In September 1778 Hazen launched yet another campaign for an invasion of Canada [*see* Sir Frederick HALDIMAND] and the following year Hazen's unit built a prospective route, called the Hazen Road, across northeastern Vermont toward Missisquoi Bay, but the second invasion never took place. Hazen fought for the promotion and the prerogatives of his men by repeated petitions to General George Washington and to Congress, but succeeded only in obtaining a brevet promotion for himself to brigadier-general in 1781.

Hazen's men were furloughed in June 1783 and the regiment disbanded in November. His Canadians joined their families in refugee camps at Albany and Fishkill, N.Y., where they received rations from Congress; some drifted back to Canada [*see* Clément GOSSELIN]. Before the end of the war Hazen had tried to get land grants for them, and, although Congress had failed to take action, the state of New York created the Canadian and Nova Scotia Refugee Tract along Lake Champlain. In 1786 the refugees moved to their new lands.

After the war Hazen fought a running battle with Congress for compensation for his losses in Canada, for his disbursements to recruit and maintain his regiment, and for loss of his British half pay. His estate had been pillaged by both armies, and during the retreat of 1776 his manor had been razed to deny it to the British. In 1783 the Saint John River Society's lands, including Hazen's share, were escheated. The following year Gabriel Christie won a suit against him in the Court of Common Pleas at Montreal, obtaining judgement for £1,900 sterling. He had Hazen arrested twice at New York for debt and in August 1785 had his Richelieu valley holdings seized for sale at sheriff's auction. Hazen won on appeal but saw the decision reversed by the British Privy Council. In 1790, at a sheriff's auction, Christie acquired Bleury-Sud and some of Hazen's other lots around Fort St Johns.

In spite of his debts and set-backs Hazen had extensive plans for land speculation and colonization in the United States; all came to naught, particularly after a stroke in 1786 disabled him for life. In 1787 he settled at New York, but then moved to Troy. In the years following the war he enjoyed cordial business relations with James Bell in Canada. By 1790, however, after unsuccessfully petitioning Congress for years to reimburse $6,000 of personal funds advanced for the American cause, Bell sued Hazen for $826 of advances that Hazen had guaranteed. Having won his suit, in 1794 Bell had attached part of Hazen's lands in Clinton County, N.Y., including 1,000 acres in the Refugee Tract and a model farm, which Hazen had been developing on the shores of Lake Champlain. In the last 20 years of his life Hazen was arrested 14 times for debt, and he instituted as many suits against others. A court adjudged him of unsound mind in 1802; nevertheless, he was arrested twice for debt only weeks before his death on 5 Feb. 1803. On paper he died a wealthy man, but his widow was unable to collect claims totalling $42,000 against Congress and individuals before her death in 1827; the executor of Hazen's estate ultimately obtained payment from Congress of some of the claims.

As a soldier Moses Hazen displayed extraordinary leadership qualities. A combative man, he was happiest in action. Courageous and impetuous, he was also throughout his life restless, frustrated by obstacles, stubborn, and hypersensitive about his honour; in 1790 Secretary of War Henry Knox referred to him as "the unfortunate Hazen . . . , nature has marked him with as obstinate a temper as ever afflicted humanity." A driving man, Hazen was even more a man driven by the need to be in motion, but he never established a sense of direction.

ALLAN S. EVEREST

For a detailed bibliography on Moses Hazen see A. S. Everest, *Moses Hazen and the Canadian refugees in the American revolution* (Syracuse, N.Y., 1976). The following sources are also useful: "Inventaire des biens de Luc Lacorne de Saint-Luc," J.-J. Lefebvre, édit., ANQ *Rapport*, 1947–48: 62; "L'outrage Walker, 1764," PAC *Rapport*, 1888: 14; "Pierre du Calvet," J.-J. Lefebvre, édit., ANQ *Rapport*, 1945–46: 367; *Vital records of Haverhill, Massachusetts, to the end of the year 1849* . . . (2v., Topsfield, Mass., 1910–11), 1: 167.

HAZEN, WILLIAM, businessman, politician, and office holder; b. 17 July 1738 in Haverhill, Mass., youngest son of Moses Hazzen and Abigail White and brother of MOSES; m. 14 July 1764 Sarah Le Baron of Plymouth, Mass., and they had at least 16 children; d. 23 March 1814 in Saint John, N.B.

William Hazen's father died in 1750, leaving a small inheritance to each of his five children. Nine years later, when soldiers were needed for Jeffery Amherst*'s campaign into Canada, William enlisted. After the war he set up as a merchant in what became Newburyport, Mass., and with the remainder of his small inheritance as capital he participated in the traditional staple trade of the New England "sedentary" or wholesale merchant.

Hazen's interest in Nova Scotia was sparked by the activities of his two cousins James* and Richard Simonds, who had begun in the early 1760s to investigate business prospects around the mouth of the Saint John River (N.B.), and also by the closing to New England of the back-country trade after the Royal Proclamation of 1763. For established merchants the end of the Seven Years' War meant dull trading, but for younger merchants such as Hazen the close of the

war and the cancellation of wartime contracts often led to bankruptcy. With his business flagging, Hazen looked to Nova Scotia for opportunities to expand. In 1763 he was associated in a commercial venture with James Simonds, and the following year a partnership was formed to pursue the fishery, the fur trade, and other activities at Portland Point (Saint John, N.B.), where the Simonds brothers had obtained a licence to occupy lands from Lieutenant Governor Montagu Wilmot*.

The firm created on 1 March 1764 had three senior partners: Samuel Blodget, an established merchant in Boston, James Simonds, and Hazen. The three junior partners were Richard Simonds, James White, another of Hazen's cousins, and Robert Peaslie, Hazen's brother-in-law. The firm extended to Nova Scotia a pattern of trade already established in the Thirteen Colonies: Hazen and Blodget resided in New England where they operated as sedentary merchants; James Simonds and the junior partners set up a trading-post at Portland Point that was typical of back-country merchants. A perusal of the firm's account-books reveals how trade was carried on in fish, fur, and feathers. These staples were sent from Nova Scotia to Hazen and Blodget, who sold the furs to British merchants, the fish to West Indian planters, and the feathers to coastal traders. Hazen and Blodget acquired the manufactured goods and provisions that Simonds and the junior partners used in domestic trade with the settlers who moved into Nova Scotia prior to the American Revolutionary War [see Israel PERLEY]. The firm also exploited the limestone quarries at Portland Point and supplied the garrison at nearby Fort Frederick. A sawmill was soon established, schooners were built, and both lumber (some of it acquired from settlers in payment of debts) and lime were exported. To further the company's trade Simonds established branch operations 60 miles inland from Portland Point on the Saint John River and 70 miles south at Passamaquoddy Bay.

Early in 1765 Richard Simonds died and a few months later Peaslie retired from the company. In May 1766 Blodget also withdrew, and his share in the firm was bought by Hazen and Leonard Jarvis, whom Hazen had brought into the company in 1765. Consequently, on 16 April 1767, a new partnership was formed between Hazen, Jarvis, Simonds, and White. As associates of the Saint John River Society [see Beamsley Perkins Glasier*], members of the original company had acquired large grants of land in the Saint John River valley in 1765. Seven years later Hazen decided to settle on part of his property, but the move was delayed until 1775. By that time conflict between the Thirteen Colonies and Great Britain had caused trade between Nova Scotia and New England virtually to cease, although Hazen managed to carry it on for a short time by using circuitous routes and

Hazen

questionable business practices. The company pursued the West Indian trade until the end of 1775, when it became both too hazardous and too expensive.

Like many New Englanders, Hazen had mixed feelings about the revolutionary war. His elder brother Moses was a general in the revolutionary army and family contacts were maintained; however, incursions into Nova Scotia by soldiers from New England persuaded Hazen that his future lay within the British empire. Although in 1776 the company was undisturbed by Jonathan EDDY's ragtag army that attacked but failed to capture Fort Cumberland (near Sackville, N.B.), in the summer of 1777 Hazen and White were held prisoner for a time by forces under John ALLAN and that autumn the company's stores were robbed by marauding privateers from the Thirteen Colonies. The firm complained bitterly to government officials in Halifax and later that year troops under Gilfred Studholme* began construction of Fort Howe, which overlooked the company's warehouses at Portland Point. In 1778 the firm played a role in British attempts to secure the neutrality of the Micmac and Malecite Indians, who were being encouraged by Allan to support the American cause. As deputy to Michael Francklin*, superintendent of Indian affairs, James White was particularly influential; as commissary at Fort Howe, Hazen was responsible for distributing supplies to the Indians.

In 1773, Jarvis having left the company, Simonds, Hazen, and White had contracted a verbal agreement to carry on their trade. Five years later, with the business at Portland Point at a standstill, Simonds broke from the firm and moved inland. By 1781, however, Hazen had established a new partnership with White and Francklin. Francklin's contacts with the government at Halifax helped secure a masting contract for the company and, despite the rivalry of William Davidson*, the business prospered. The new firm also dealt in furs, which were sent to the London firm of Brook WATSON and Robert Rashleigh. Francklin, in effect, took the place of the sedentary merchant in the partnership and Halifax became the firm's entrepôt for overseas trade.

Although the loyalists who arrived on the Saint John River in 1783 had little sympathy with pre-loyalists, Hazen was quickly recognized as a community leader, for his position at Portland Point was pre-eminent. He served as a loyalist agent, and he was the only pre-loyalist to be chosen in 1784 to sit on the Council of the newly created province of New Brunswick. He continued to be active in provincial politics and also served on municipal committees in Saint John, acting as commissioner of highways and overseer of the poor from 1791 to 1797. The influx of loyalists gave considerable impetus to his business. He was able to rent out the company's wharfs and buildings and he supplied the new settlers with manufactured goods and lumber. Although many of his early land grants had been escheated, he had received other large holdings in compensation and was able to turn his property to profit by collecting rents from newly arrived tenants. In the late 1780s he was managing a grist-mill at Saint John which he owned jointly with Ward Chipman* and Jonathan Bliss*, both loyalists. When commercial relations were resumed with the United States after the war Hazen re-established his coastal trade, and with the end of privateering he was able to pick up the West Indian trade. He again engaged in shipbuilding, frequently selling a ship and its cargo to overseas merchants, and he continued his masting business, though demand declined after the war. Although prosperous, Hazen's latter years were troubled by an extensive litigation with Simonds and White over the lands their company had acquired. The issue was not finally resolved until 1810.

Hazen's career illustrates the dexterity of the 18th-century businessman, and his ventures into fishing, lumbering, shipbuilding, and trading were portents of New Brunswick's future. His entrepreneurial skills both gave direction to the new colonial economy and guaranteed a future for the Hazen family. His progeny, which included at least 11 sons and 5 daughters, became stalwarts of the community. One daughter married Ward Chipman and another Amos BOTSFORD's son William*; a grandson, Robert Leonard Hazen*, became a prominent lawyer and politician in New Brunswick.

ROD CAMPBELL

N.B. Museum, H. T. Hazen coll.; Leavitt family papers; Simonds, Hazen, and White papers; James White papers. "Letters written at Saint John by James Simonds, A.D. 1764–1785," ed. W. O. Raymond, N.B. Hist. Soc., Coll., 1 (1894–97), no.2: 160–86. "Selections from the papers and correspondence of James White, esquire, A.D. 1762–1783," ed. W. O. Raymond, N.B. Hist. Soc., Coll., 1 (1894–97), no.3: 306–40. "The James White papers, continued, A.D. 1781–88," ed. W. O. Raymond, N.B. Hist. Soc., Coll., 2 (1899–1905), no.4: 30–72. Winslow papers (Raymond). W. T. Baxter, The house of Hancock; business in Boston, 1724–1775 (Cambridge, Mass., 1945; repr. New York, 1965). J. B. Brebner, Neutral Yankees (1969); New England's outpost: Acadia before the conquest of Canada (New York and London, 1927; repr. Hamden, Conn., 1965, and New York, [1973]). R. C. Campbell, "Simonds, Hazen and White: a study of a New Brunswick firm in the commercial world of the eighteenth century" (MA thesis, Univ. of N.B., Saint John, 1970). Hannay, Hist. of N.B., vol.1. W. S. MacNutt, The Atlantic provinces: the emergence of colonial society, 1712–1857 (Toronto, 1965). Raymond, River St. John (1910). A. M. Schlesinger, The colonial merchants and the American revolution, 1763–1776 (New York, 1957). W. O. Raymond, "At Portland Point," New Brunswick Magazine (Saint John), 1 (July–December 1898): 6–20, 65–79, 132–45, 186–201, 263–79, 316–32; 2

(January–June 1899): 21–33, 78–91, 140–51, 205–22, 249–63, 311–25.

HEBBARD. *See* HIBBARD

HECK, BARBARA. *See* RUCKLE

HEER, LOUIS-CHRÉTIEN DE, painter and gilder; b. 3 Nov. 1760 in Bouxwiller, France, son of Jean-Tobie Heer, commissary at the court of Bouxwiller, and Frédérique-Louise Ouvrier; d. some time before 1808.

Louis-Chrétien de Heer was baptized in the Lutheran faith and had three godfathers and two godmothers, all of whom were in the service of the gentry of Bouxwiller and the surrounding region. De Heer arrived in North America in 1776 as colour-bearer in the Regiment Specht in the troops from Brunswick which had come as mercenaries to support the British forces engaged in the American Revolutionary War.

After the war de Heer settled in Montreal, and there, on 25 July 1784, in Christ Church (Anglican), he married Marie-Angélique Badel, daughter of Antoine Badel, a tailor. In the period between 1785 and 1790 the couple had four daughters, who were baptized in either Montreal or Quebec, the two towns in which he practised his trade as painter and gilder.

In 1787 de Heer, who was living on Rue des Pauvres (Côte du Palais) at Quebec, put an advertisement in the *Quebec Gazette* announcing: "He will draw Pictures either in Oil or in Pastel, Landskips, Tapistries of all sorts . . . and he also engages to teach in a very short time such persons as may be inclined to learn Painting." But as this activity did not provide enough to live on, two years later he signed an important contract with the parish priest of Saint-Charles, near Quebec – despite the fact that he was a Protestant – by which he undertook to do the gilding on the baldachin of the church and to execute seven paintings for the chancel portraying Christ and six of the apostles, as well as one of the Holy Ghost for the sanctuary and another of St John the Baptist for the baptismal font.

In September 1789, however, de Heer was back in Montreal, on Rue Saint-Paul, still looking for more lucrative contracts. His advertisement, which appeared this time in the *Gazette de Montréal*, promised "good work at a moderate price." De Heer, it stated, "flatters himself on being able to gild with oil, sizing and copal varnish, and in addition offers to give all possible instruction . . . in painting." He was anxious to attract clients, and it is apparent from his peregrinations that he could not find sufficient patronage in either town. He returned to Quebec, where in July 1790 he advertised his usual services, painting and teaching, and also informed the public

"that he has received by the last ships from Europe, an Assortment of superfine Paints, books of various Flowers, Land capes, &c." To survive, however, he had to appeal to his clientele by substantially reducing his prices for "the Pictures of half length." That year he worked at gilding the retable (as the decorated structure housing the altar in the sanctuary was then known) in the church of Notre-Dame-de-Bon-Secours at L'Islet.

De Heer's Catholic clients and also his wife's family probably had an influence on him, for in September 1792, in the sick ward of the Hôtel-Dieu at Quebec, he abjured his Protestant faith and became a Catholic. In 1800 he and some former comrades in arms signed a petition for a tract of land, which was refused them. There is no subsequent information about the artist until 25 Jan. 1808, when his daughter Marie-Louise married Pierre-Guillaume De Lisle. In their marriage contract de Heer was reported to be absent from the country; the marriage certificate said that he was dead.

A great many religious paintings and portraits of citizens, military personnel, and ecclesiastics are attributed to Louis-Chrétien de Heer. None of these works is signed, however, and there is no documentary confirmation of these attributions, with the exception of a painting of St Louis in the church of Saint-Michel, at Vaudreuil, which bears de Heer's name in block letters. De Heer probably had great difficulty in living on the income from his painting. Compared with the works of such contemporaries as François Malepart* de Beaucourt, Louis Dulongpré*, and William BERCZY, the portraits attributed to de Heer are stiff and naïve in technique. His subjects, whether soldiers or ecclesiastics, are shown full face, with little depth. His use of colour and his emphasis on surface pattern make him, however, one of the best primitive portrait artists in Lower Canada. Like other little-known painters, he was an itinerant. Through force of circumstance de Heer was versatile; through misfortune he was in competition with several more accomplished artists.

SUZANNE LACASSE GALES and PETER MOOGK

AD, Bas-Rhin (Strasbourg), État civil, Bouxwiller, 3 nov. 1760. ANQ-M, CE1-51, 13 mai 1785, 30 nov. 1790, 25 janv. 1808, 6 janv. 1825; CN1-158, 25 juill. 1784; CN1-269, 23 janv. 1808. AP, Notre-Dame-de-Bon-Secours (L'Islet), Livres de comptes, 2: 81; Notre-Dame de Québec, Abjurations, 8 sept. 1792. ASSM, 19, tiroir 66A. MAC-CD, Fonds Morisset, 2, H459/L888.4. PAC, RG 1, L3^L: 94214. *Montreal Gazette*, 17, 24 Sept. 1789. *Quebec Gazette*, 16 Aug. 1787, 29 July 1790. J. R. Harper, *Early painters and engravers in Canada* ([Toronto], 1970), 153–54; *Painting in Canada, a history* (Toronto and Quebec, 1966), 73, 75, 78, 424. Gérard Morisset, *La peinture traditionnelle au Canada français* (Ottawa, 1960), 63–66.

Henry

HENRY, ALEXANDER, fur trader, explorer, and writer; drowned 22 May 1814 in the Columbia River off Fort George (Astoria, Oreg.).

Nothing is recorded of the birth or early life of Alexander Henry the younger. He was a nephew of Alexander Henry* the elder, and had other relatives in the fur trade, including a cousin of the same name (the elder Alexander's second son) and cousins William and Robert*; his brother, Robert, was also a fur trader. Alexander Henry the younger is known for his copious journal, begun in 1799, which is one of the best records from the early 19th century of the fur trade in the vast area from Lake Superior to the mouth of the Columbia River.

Henry began trading among the Ojibwas in the Lower Red River department of the North West Company in 1791, after which nothing is known of his career until the first journal entry, made in the autumn of 1799 on the Whitemud River (Man.). He spent the winter of 1799–1800 at a post near Fort Dauphin Mountain (Riding Mountain, Man.), leaving there in the spring for Grand Portage (near Grand Portage, Minn.), until 1803 the location of the company's annual rendezvous. In July 1800 he returned to the interior, moving south from Lake Winnipeg up the Red River. Passing Sault à la Biche (St Andrews Rapids, Man.), where formerly Crees and Assiniboins had assembled in large camps at the edge of meadow country, on 18 August Henry met waiting Ojibwas at the mouth of the Assiniboine River and traded rum for their dried buffalo meat. Though there had once been a missionary and a church in that location, Henry observed that little progress had been made in "civilizing the natives," and that their numbers had been greatly reduced by smallpox. Those with whom he traded were very much in fear of attack by the Sioux from the south. They had excavated shelter trenches for the security of their people, a measure later to be adopted by the Métis during the North-West rebellion of 1885.

Henry, with a party of 28, proceeded up the Red River, crossing the 49th parallel to the mouth of the Pembina River, where the first NWC settlement on the Red stood, and continuing to the Park River mouth, near which he erected a fort. The post was well defended in case of attack by the Sioux, but that winter was uneventful. In the spring of 1801 Henry built a new post near present-day Pembina, N.Dak., leaving Michel Langlois in charge. The returns of the previous winter had been healthy in the Lower Red River department, and continued to be good despite competition from both the Hudson's Bay and the New North West (XY) companies. On 30 June 1801 he received a partnership in the NWC, to commence with the outfit of 1802. For several years Henry traded successfully at Pembina, annually leading a summer brigade first to Grand Portage, and after 1803 to Kaministiquia (Thunder Bay, Ont.), the company's new point of rendezvous on Lake Superior. One of his journal entries for this period provides a picture of the men and their master who made these long voyages: "Canoes heavy loaded has nearly knocked the men up nothing but a certain pride and ambition, natural to the North Men keeps them pushing forward with every exertion in their power; but is a very disagreeable task for the Master to undergo when he joins his own Brigade in a difficult and tedious part of the route. Little or nothing is said in the course of the day . . . but no sooner is your tent put up in the evening then you are attacked by every one in his turn. some complain of having a bad Canoe, others a heavy one. . . . Some want Bark, Others Gum. . . . Having listened to all their numerous complaints and redressed them as far as lays in your power, you must attend to the sick and administer accordingly."

In 1806 Henry led a trading and exploring party into the Missouri River basin. While visiting among the Mandans he met trader Jean-Baptiste Lafrance from Brandon House (Man.). Henry was shown American flags that had been presented to a Mandan chief by captains Meriwether Lewis and William Clark on their way to the Pacific. In his journal Henry records many Mandan customs and notes the physical features which have led to apocryphal accounts that this tribe was descended from the Welsh. He also met with Cheyenne, Crow, and other Indians. In August 1806 Henry arrived back at his Pembina post.

Two years later he left Pembina for the last time, following company orders to move to the Saskatchewan River. On his way he met David Thompson*, making his second expedition to the Columbia River, on 18 August near Cumberland House (Sask.). Henry wintered at Fort Vermilion (at the mouth of the Vermilion River, Alta), travelling down to Fort William (the new name of Kaministiquia) the following summer. At this point in his journal Henry gives a lengthy ethnographic report on the Crees and appends a quinquelingual vocabulary of English, Ojibwa, Cree, Slavey, and Assiniboin. In 1809 he went to Fort Augustus (Edmonton) and then back to Fort Vermilion. He traded at what he called New White Earth House (near the mouth of Wabamun Creek) during 1810 and wintered that year even farther west, at Rocky Mountain House. In 1811 he crossed the Great Divide by "the Rocky Mountain portage" (Howse Pass) to visit the watershed of the river now named the Kootenay. He traded among the Peigans, Salish, and Sarcees that year and the next.

In 1813 the NWC dispatched Henry and Alexander Stewart (Stuart), both partners, to establish trade at the mouth of the Columbia River, where John Jacob Astor* had set up a depot [see Duncan McDougall]. They were to work in conjunction with the *Isaac Todd*, sent from London via Cape Horn under Royal

Navy escort to oust the Americans, with whom the British were now at war. Henry records the Nor'Westers' purchase of Astoria (which they renamed Fort George), HMS *Racoon*'s arrival, Indian raids, and finally the *Isaac Todd*'s arrival. Reports of these episodes by Gabriel Franchère*, Ross Cox*, and Alexander Ross* corroborate Henry's narrative. He provides useful data on chief Comcomly and the Chinook Indians, and also records his visit to Lewis and Clark's westernmost post, Fort Clatsop (near Astoria), and his trips into the Cowlitz and Willamette River valleys. On 22 May 1814 Henry, with Donald McTAVISH and five sailors, was going in an open boat from Fort George to the *Isaac Todd*. The boat capsized, and Henry and McTavish drowned.

During his years in the greater northwest, Alexander Henry travelled from Lake Superior to the Columbia River mouth, living for long periods of time at various outposts and crossing the Rocky Mountains several times. His journal is an important source for anthropological and ethnological study. The journal entry for 25 Feb. 1803 observes: "Now the Indians are totally neglecting all their ancient customs and manners and to what else can this degenracy be ascribed but to their intercource with us. . . . If there is a murder committed among the Soulteux it is always in a drinking match, so that we may in truth say that Liquor is the mother of all evil even in the North West." Yet Henry was principally a businessman and he had little sympathy for his customers. He judged them by European standards. A good illustration is found in his journal entry for 4 March 1814, which describes certain Chinook women whom he found taking their daily bath by the sea: "They were perfectly naked, and my presence did not affect their operations in the least. The disgusting creatures were perfectly composed, and seemed not to notice me. Although they stood naked in different postures, yet so close did they keep their thighs together that nothing could be seen."

Early in 1801 (quite against his will, according to his journal) Henry had taken an Indian wife, daughter of the Ojibwa chief Liard. Returning to his room after New Year's celebrations, he found that she had occupied it and, he reported, "the devil could not have got her out." It is not certain how many children they had, but his Fort Vermilion roster indicates one man, one woman, and three children in his quarters. His will, executed at Fort William on 15 July 1813, indicates that he had three "reputed sons" born in the west during the 1790s. It also mentions his three daughters and one son, children of an Indian woman "who has been in the habit of living with me since the year 1802" and who was the daughter of the Buffalo, an Ojibwa chief.

BARRY M. GOUGH

A transcript of Henry's journal, made from the original by George Coventry* about 1824, is in PAC, MG 19, A13. Included as well is an outline of the contents, probably also by Coventry. Sections of the journal have been published in an adulterated version in *New light on early hist. of greater northwest* (Coues). Excerpts also appear in "Henry's Astoria journal," *The Oregon country under the Union Jack: a reference book of historical documents for scholars and historians*, comp. B. C. Payette (Montreal, 1961; 2nd ed., 1962), 1–170, and C N. Bell, "Henry's journal . . . ," *Man., Hist. and Scientific Soc., Trans.* (Winnipeg), 31 (May 1888); 35 (1889); 37 (1889). Henry's will is in ANQ-M, CM 1, 7 Oct. 1815. *See also* L. J. Burpee, *The search for the western sea: the story of the exploration of north-western America* (London, 1908; new ed., 2v., Toronto, 1935).

HERON, SAMUEL, businessman, office holder, and militia officer; b. 1770 in Kirkcudbright, Scotland; d. 1817 or 1818 in York Township, Upper Canada.

Samuel Heron emigrated from Scotland at an early age, and after a short stay in New York City he moved to the Niagara peninsula in Upper Canada, where by 1793 his brother Andrew was a merchant in the town of Newark (Niagara-on-the-Lake). In the spring of that year Samuel settled on a 200-acre tract of land near Ashbridges Bay on Lake Ontario; there Mrs Sarah Ashbridge and her family had just settled, and on 14 Dec. 1794 he married Mrs Ashbridge's daughter Sarah.

On 3 Sept. 1793 Heron petitioned the Executive Council for a town lot in York (Toronto) and 200 acres of land, but was granted only a back town lot. It is not clear when Heron settled at York, but by January 1795 he had opened a general store in the town and was selling goods to William BERCZY's settlers in Markham Township. That June he was reported among the 14 heads of households at York.

Heron must have developed close contacts with Berczy, for in 1795 or 1796 he was the latter's partner in the construction of a grist-mill on the Don River, the mortgagee of Berczy's land, and, after Berczy's departure from the province, his agent in several business matters. In 1796 he began a shipping service between York, Newark, and the Genesee River (N.Y.) in partnership with Abner MILES. Heron's business in York apparently prospered: by 1799 it included a tavern and by 1800 a shop for two tailors. His success seems to have enabled him to become a local financier as well as agent or trustee for the disposition of the land and property of many settlers in and near York.

Heron was an avid land speculator, though on a small scale. On 30 Aug. 1794 he had petitioned the Executive Council for 200 acres of land and was granted a lot on Yonge St in Vaughan Township, which he leased to John Lyons. In 1796 his petition for another 200 acres was turned down, but in 1797 and

Heron

1799 he was successful in obtaining two 200-acre grants. He hoped to sell these lots quickly for profit rather than settle on them as the government intended. Heron also purchased considerable land, notably a mill site on lot 9, Yonge Street, on the west bank of the Don River (later to be known as Hogg's Hollow or York Mills). By 1801 he was advertising for sale a total of 3,000 acres in Scarborough, Vaughan, and Norwich (Whitby and East Whitby) townships.

By the late 1790s Heron seems to have become a respected figure in York society: he was collector of municipal assessments in 1797 and 1798, a town warden in 1797 and 1799, and an assessor in 1802. In 1797 he also became a master freemason and the following year he was made lieutenant in the York militia. Heron was anxious for recognition of his status. Although he already had two town lots, he petitioned twice in 1797 for a prestigious waterfront lot; his requests were refused. In 1799, however, after two more petitions, his grant in York was increased to an acre.

In 1800 Heron's widespread contacts with farmers and townsfolk in the York area probably prompted him to seek a seat in the House of Assembly at the first election for the new constituency of Durham, Simcoe, and the East Riding of York. His name was proposed on 22 March in the *Upper Canada Gazette* by "A Farmer," who was concerned that the man elected should "neither directly, or indirectly receive any emoluments from, or in office under government." Admitting that Heron lacked "a refined education," the writer argued that with "a large share of mother wit and good sense" he was "an honest, upright and just man." The campaign shaped up as a contest between gentleman office holders and a humbler man in closer contact with the settlers. Curiously, on 12 July Heron announced that he would not be a candidate. But when polling began on 24 July he was definitely in the race. As the candidates, judge Henry ALLCOCK, Provincial Secretary William JARVIS, John Small*, and Heron, brought forward their adherents, Heron appeared to be gathering support from the countryside, and Jarvis gave his backing to Allcock. When a disturbance developed over the arrest of a drunken supporter of Heron, the poll was adjourned. But at the insistence of Allcock's scrutineer, William WEEKES, two more votes for his candidate were subsequently recorded, giving the judge a majority of two. Then he successfully demanded that the poll be closed. Heron immediately protested, but the riot act was read and the crowd dispersed. Later that day Heron and 97 others petitioned Lieutenant Governor Peter HUNTER for a new election; however, Hunter referred them to the assembly. In June 1801 the assembly unseated Allcock and ordered a new election; Heron did not stand and the petitioners' advocate, Angus MACDONELL (Collachie), was elected.

Heron's election defeat was followed in February 1801 by the death of his wife. His marriage on 10 Dec. 1802 to Sarah Conott (Connott) may have lifted his spirits, but he faced serious financial trouble. Like merchants such as Miles, Heron was pressed by the colony's shortage of cash and by problems arising from his own land speculation. Each year between 1799 and 1801 he ran notices demanding payment of outstanding debts and advertising for sale some of his "excellent wood land"; in fact, in 1800 he announced prematurely that he was "about to decline business." Later that year he mortgaged all his property to the Montreal merchant John Gray* for £1,875, one-half of which sum was due early in 1802. On 12 Feb. 1803 Gray foreclosed – as he had another York merchant, William WILLCOCKS – and put up for sale Heron's property in York and in Scarborough, Vaughan, York, Crowland, and Norwich townships, totalling more than 2,500 acres valued at £1,338.

Heron, now simply a "Yeoman" and perhaps hoping to make a new start, was granted in the summer of 1804 a lot in the town of Niagara. Simultaneously arrangements were under way to pay off Berczy's longstanding debts, his principal creditors being Heron, Willcocks, and Gray. For the £1,937 owed him Heron was awarded 600 acres of land worth £550, Berczy's 400-acre farm worth £300, and £459 cash. This infusion of funds probably allowed him to remain on his mill site on Yonge Street, where he constructed a grist-mill and sawmill. In 1805 he was elected an overseer of highways and fence viewer. His attempt to obtain a tavern licence was unsuccessful, but by 1810 he was running a distillery "capable of making 18 gallons of Whiskey per day," and a potashery. Financial problems still troubled him, and every year between 1809 and 1812 he attempted to sell off some or all of his property. After his death he was still indebted to Gray. On 5 Jan. 1817 Heron was granted a tavern licence in York Township. In the spring of 1819 the annual census listed Heron's third wife, Lucy, as a widow.

Samuel Heron had risen from humble origins in Scotland to local prominence as a pioneer merchant on the Upper Canadian frontier. Yet his eagerness for social recognition had been checked by the self-styled gentry who occupied the chief offices of the provincial government. Heron's final downfall, however, was his own doing. After a few years of mercantile success his plunge into land speculation was fatal to his business in York. He finished his life in quiet obscurity in the backwoods of York Township, without ever abandoning his enterprising schemes.

CRAIG HERON

AO, MS 526; RG 1, A-I-1, 55: 205; RG 53, ser.2-2, 1. MTL, William Allan papers, William Berczy papers;

William Jarvis papers, B38: 10; B53: 153; Alexander Wood papers, William Berczy to Joseph Forsyth, 10 Nov. 1802; York, U.C., minutes of town meetings and lists of inhabitants, 1797–1819. PAC, MG 23, HII, 6, vol.1: 14–15, 271–72, 429; vol.2: 453–54; MG 24, I9, 14: 4173–74, 4177, 4179, 4185–86, 4189; RG 1, L3, 3: A4/4; 223: H2/10, 107; 224a: H4/47, 59, 67; 225a: H7/7; 251: H misc., 1788–95/4, 90. "Grants of crown lands in U.C.," AO *Report*, 1929: 52, 104, 159, 161. "Minutes of Court of General Quarter Sessions, Home District," AO *Report*, 1932: 5, 29, 59, 68, 82, 93, 114, 123–24, 126–27, 176. *Town of York, 1793–1815* (Firth), 13, 68, 70, 88, 193. "U.C. land book B," AO *Report*, 1930: 26, 122. "U.C. land book C," AO *Report*, 1930: 150. "U.C. land book D," AO *Report*, 1931: 102, 147, 184. *Upper Canada Gazette*, 5 July 1797; 1 Dec. 1798; 16 March, 3 Aug. 1799; 8 Feb., 17, 31 May, 7 June, 30 Aug., 13 Sept. 1800; 21 Feb., 15 Aug. 1801; 24 July, 11 Dec. 1802; 12, 19 Feb. 1803; 6 July 1809; 7 Feb. 1810; 15 July 1811; 26 Feb. 1812; 10 July, 27 Nov. 1817.

John Andre, *Infant Toronto as Simcoe's folly* (Toronto, 1971), 49, 54–55, 68–69; *William Berczy*. W. T. Ashbridge, *The Ashbridge book; relating to past and present Ashbridge families in America* (Toronto, 1912), 102–3. Janet Carnochan, *History of Niagara . . .* (Toronto, 1914; repr. Belleville, Ont., 1973), 250. E. C. Guillet, *Pioneer life in the county of York* (Toronto, 1946), 43–44, 46; *Toronto from trading post to great city* (Toronto, 1934). P. W. Hart, *Pioneering in North York: a history of the borough* (Toronto, 1968), 63, 84, 145–46, 156. *A history of Scarborough*, ed. R. R. Bonis ([2nd ed.], Scarborough, Ont., 1968), 66–67. *History of Toronto and county of York, Ontario . . .* (2v., Toronto, 1885), 2: 64–65. G. E. Reaman, *A history of Vaughan Township: two centuries of the township* (Toronto, 1971), 33, 117. J. R. Robertson, *The history of freemasonry in Canada from its introduction in 1749 . . .* (2v., Toronto, 1899), 1: 608. *Robertson's landmarks of Toronto*, 3: 396. Henry Scadding, *Toronto of old: collections and recollections illustrative of the early settlement and social life of the capital of Ontario* (Toronto, 1873). R. J. Burns, "God's chosen people: the origins of Toronto society, 1793–1818," CHA, *Hist. papers*, 1973: 213–28. E. G. Firth, "Alexander Wood, merchant of York," *York Pioneer* (Toronto, 1958): 5–29.

HERTEL DE ROUVILLE, JEAN-BAPTISTE-MELCHIOR, army and militia officer, office holder, seigneur, and politician; b. 21 Oct. 1748 in Trois-Rivières (Que.), son of René-Ovide Hertel* de Rouville and Louise-Catherine André* de Leigne; d. 30 Nov. 1817 in Chambly, Lower Canada.

Jean-Baptiste-Melchior Hertel de Rouville joined the Régiment du Languedoc as an ensign in 1760. Shortly after the conquest he went to France with his regiment. In December 1764 he sailed for Corsica, where he took part in the war against Pascal Paoli, the patriot. He returned to France in December 1770 and two years later came back to the province of Quebec. Like his father, Rouville was a supporter of the new régime and did not hesitate to defend the crown when American troops invaded [*see* Benedict ARNOLD;

Richard Montgomery*]. In the autumn of 1775 he helped defend Fort St Johns, on the Richelieu. He was taken prisoner and spent 20 months in captivity in the American colonies. After his return he secured a captain's commission; he retired on half pay in 1783.

That year Rouville obtained a commission as justice of the peace for the District of Montreal. On 8 May of the following year, in Chambly, he married Marie-Anne, daughter of Jean-Baptiste Hervieux, a Montreal merchant. The marriage contract recognized the community of property of husband and wife, while according the bride a jointure of 6,000 shillings and separate property of 31,000 shillings. Rouville, who already owned half a league of land in the seigneury of Chambly, obtained from his father as part of his future inheritance half a league of land at Chambly, including the flour mill; through an exchange he acquired a further half league at the same place.

In 1787 Rouville was appointed to the commission on the Jesuit estates [*see* Kenelm CHANDLER], and like his Canadian colleagues [*see* Gabriel-Elzéar TASCHEREAU] he rejected the claims of the crown. Being a conservative, Rouville opposed the constitutional reform desired by the merchant bourgeoisie of the colony, who requested it in a petition to the king in 1788. The following year Rouville went to live at Chambly, where he obtained a commission as militia colonel in 1790.

On his father's death in 1792 Rouville received by primogeniture half of the seigneury of Rouville and part of the seigneury of Chambly. That year he ran successfully in the first elections for the House of Assembly of Lower Canada; he represented the riding of Bedford from 10 July 1792 till 31 May 1796. In the house he supported the Canadian party, particularly in the choice of Jean-Antoine PANET as speaker. Rouville's loyalty to the crown was probably responsible for his appointment to the Legislative Council in 1812. That year he also received command of the 2nd Battalion of the Chambly militia. In 1813 he was appointed justice of the peace for the districts of Quebec, Montreal, and Three Rivers.

Jean-Baptiste-Melchior Hertel de Rouville died in Chambly on 30 Nov. 1817 and was buried on 3 December in the parish church. At that time he was described as "one of those men [who are] consistently honourable, fair, and upright." He had bequeathed the seigneury of Rouville (the other half of which he had purchased in 1797) and his share in the seigneury of Chambly to his son Jean-Baptiste-René*. His daughter, Marie-Anne-Julie, wife of Charles-Michel d'Irumberry* de Salaberry, received 48,000 *livres* and a sub-fief of 4,704 acres in the seigneury of Chambly. The children took possession of their inheritance upon their mother's death on 25 Jan. 1819.

CÉLINE CYR

Hibbard

ANQ-M, CE1-39, 3 déc. 1817; CN1-43, 24 sept. 1814; CN1-290, 8 mai 1784. ANQ-MBF, CE1-48, 21 oct. 1748. AUM, P 58, U, Hertel de Rouville à Baby, 30 mars 1780; 7, 26 janv., 7 févr. 1798; 26 janv. 1802; Hertel de Rouville à Guay, 29 sept. 1817; Hertel de Rouville à Perrault l'aîné, 2 août 1771; 8 janv., 13 juin 1782; 7 juill., 11 août 1788; Hertel de Rouville à Sullivan, 8 sept. 1814. "Papiers d'État," PAC Rapport, 1890: 305–6. La Gazette de Québec, 1er avril 1813, 11 déc. 1817. F.-J. Audet, "Les législateurs du Bas-Canada." Desjardins, Guide parl., 124. P.-G. Roy, Inv. concessions, 2: 199; 4: 64, 77–78. Wallace, Macmillan dict. Armand Cardinal, Histoire de Saint-Hilaire; les seigneurs de Rouville (Montréal, 1980). F.-J. Audet et Édouard Fabre Surveyer, "Jean-Baptiste-Melchior Hertel de Rouville," La Presse (Montréal), 1er oct. 1927: 53. Hare, "L'Assemblée législative du Bas-Canada," RHAF, 27: 361–95.

HIBBARD, JEDEDIAH (baptized **Jedadiah Hebbard**), surveyor and Baptist elder; b. 14 Oct. 1740 in Canterbury, Conn., son of John Hebbard, farmer, and Martha Durkee; d. 4 Oct. 1809 in St Armand East (Frelighsburg), Lower Canada.

One of 13 children born into a Congregational family, Jedediah Hibbard received only a good common-school education, but being of a studious nature, he read much, especially on religious subjects, and in March 1760 he was admitted to Hampton First Congregational Church at Hampton, Conn. At Mansfield on 15 Jan. 1764 he married Martha, daughter of Nathaniel Porter, a prosperous Congregationalist from Canterbury; they were to have nine children.

Soon after his marriage Hibbard joined the New Lights, a sect which vigorously preached the separation of church and state, and many of whose members suffered arrest for their refusal to pay taxes in support of Congregational churches, Congregationalism being the established domination in Connecticut; his wife, however, remained a staunch Congregationalist. In 1765 Hibbard moved to Lebanon, N.H., where he took up farming and over the next decade established a certain social prominence. He also began preaching and, like many moderate New Lights, joined the Free Will Baptist Church, in which he was ordained an elder in 1773. He often made long missionary trips through what is now central and northern Vermont and into Quebec. An ardent revolutionist, in 1777 he fought against Major-General John Burgoyne* at Fort Ticonderoga (near Ticonderoga), N.Y., and near Saratoga (Schuylerville). He returned to the Lebanon area, probably the following year, and about 1780 he founded a church. He occasionally preached at Cornish (Cornish Flat), N.H., a short distance to the south, where he settled about 1784, founded a church in 1789, and served as pastor for the next seven years.

Hibbard continued to travel as a missionary preacher, and in the summer of 1796 he visited the seigneury of Saint-Armand in Lower Canada. He decided to settle there, probably with the intention of extending the Baptist religion in Lower Canada, where the first congregation had been organized in 1794 at Caldwell's Manor near the Vermont border. In August 1796 he and two sons purchased 800 acres of land among the rolling foothills of Pinnacle Mountain from the seigneur Thomas DUNN for £186. Hibbard supported his family by farming and surveying as other settlers moved into the area. A community soon grew which was named Abbott's Corner after Dr Jonas Abbot, one of the first settlers. In December 1797 Hibbard joined the first masonic lodge in the Eastern Townships, Select Surveyors No.9, at Missisquoi Bay. As well he continued to preach, evangelizing the surrounding region, including northern Vermont, and exercising considerable moral and social influence over the settlers in the seigneury of Saint-Armand. In 1799 Hibbard and elder William Marsh, who had founded a congregation in Sutton Township in 1797, established the Baptist Church in the future townships of Hatley and Stanstead. On 6 August they organized a congregation at Abbott's Corner, and the same year, apparently with Martha's money, the Hibbards erected a large frame-house there in which a Baptist conference may have been held in 1801. A small frame building, one of the first Baptist churches in Lower Canada, was built on a hill north of the settlement in 1802; Hibbard became its pastor and remained so until his death on 4 Oct. 1809. He was buried in the only cemetery properly maintained in the area, that of the established Church of England, by the Anglican missionary Charles James Stewart*.

Traces of Hibbard's life and influence in the Missisquoi Bay area are evident today in the large frame-house that still stands in Abbott's Corner, in the survey lines that mark property boundaries in the region, and in the flourishing Baptist churches in the villages of the border townships. Unfortunately, the church he founded in Abbott's Corner is now closed; the little frame structure was abandoned in 1830 and replaced 11 years later by a brick building, which is no longer in use as a church.

IN COLLABORATION

ANQ-M, CN1-74, 30 août 1796. Canterbury, Conn., Vital statistics, IA: 158. Conn. State Library (Hartford), Indexes, Barbour coll.; Conn. church records; Family bible records. Genealogy of the Hibbard family . . . , ed. A. G. Hibbard (Woodstock, Conn., 1901), 48–49. Illustrated atlas of the dominion of Canada . . . (Toronto, 1881), 11. W. H. Child, History of the town of Cornish, New Hampshire, with genealogical record, 1763–1910 (2v., Concord, N.H., [1911?]), 1: 73, 118–19. C. A. Downs, History of Lebanon, N.H., 1761–1887 (Concord, 1908), 20–23, 30–31, 40–43, 62, 66. G. H. Montgomery, Missisquoi Bay (Philipsburg, Que.) (Granby, Que., 1950), 132. Cyrus Thomas, Contributions to the history of the Eastern Townships . . . (Montreal, 1866), 96–98.

HILDRITH, ISAAC, builder and surveyor; b. 1741 in Ellerton-upon-Swale (Ellerton, North Yorkshire), England; m. Ann Wood, also of Ellerton-upon-Swale; d. 16 Sept. 1807 in Shelburne, N.S.

After emigrating to Norfolk, Va, in 1770 Isaac Hildrith pursued various occupations. Established as a small storekeeper and house carpenter, he was also employed as a surveyor, preparing reports on a survey of the James River Falls and, in 1774, on canal proposals for the North and Elizabeth river systems. When the revolution broke out in 1775 he rejected solicitations from the rebels and joined the forces of Lord Dunmore, the governor of Virginia, serving first as a surveyor and builder of military fortifications, and later as lieutenant commanding a company engaged in the defence of the Great Bridge Fort near Norfolk.

Hildrith lost all his property when Norfolk fell to the rebels in January 1776. Resigning his commission on 5 August, he returned to England the following month to reside in his birthplace of Ellerton-upon-Swale. From here he submitted to the Treasury in 1778 the first of several petitions requesting financial recompense for losses suffered in service to the crown. Although the government decided to defer its consideration of this petition, Hildrith tried again in July 1781 and was awarded £100 and passage for himself and family back to America, where he hoped to retrieve his Virginia property. Soon afterwards the Hildrith family moved to Charleston, S.C., and they remained there until the city was evacuated by British troops in December 1782. They then travelled to Kingston, Jamaica, and later, in June and July 1783, to Shelburne, N.S., via New York. In Shelburne, Hildrith obtained a land grant of 360 acres and established himself in reasonable comfort; he was variously described as merchant, farmer, and associate with Aaron White in the firm of Hildrith and White, carpenters.

Hildrith's importance in Nova Scotia's history is based on his activities as the so-called architect of two public buildings, the first being Christ Church, Shelburne. However, in this, as in the later case of Government House, Halifax, it would be more accurate to describe Hildrith as the master builder since there is no evidence of original design work on his part. In May 1788 the vestries of the Anglican parishes of St Patrick and St George, Shelburne, purchased a lot for the building of a church [see George PANTON]. Although the estimate of £620 submitted by Hildrith and White was the higher, the firm's design for the building was accepted as "superior in Strength, Convenience and Beauty." A plain rectangular clapboard building, 65 by 42 feet, containing 82 pews, with galleries around three sides

and a small cupola for a bell over the front end, the church mirrored the New England design of the period. Divine service was held for the first time in the new building on 25 Dec. 1789.

The picture of Hildrith's activities is sketchy, but it is none the less a fairly typical reflection of the Nova Scotian loyalist who, by juggling a variety of occupations and by taking advantage of every opportunity to exercise a talent, re-established his position and acquired a modest competence. After 1797 Hildrith travelled frequently to Halifax, a city that offered greater scope for his surveying and building skills, and some time around 1802 he took up permanent residence there. His first assignment in Halifax was the preparation, in partnership with Theophilus Chamberlain*, of a report on a projected Shubenacadie canal. In July 1797 the Council agreed to a House of Assembly resolution that a committee be appointed "to procure a fit person to make a survey of the water and ground between Shubenacadie River and Halifax Harbour" and to report on the cost of a canal between Minas Basin and Halifax. The Hildrith–Chamberlain report recommended such an inland navigation system and presented an estimate of approximately £24,000 for the project. The commissioners recommended the construction of a canal; the assembly studied a resolution in June 1798 that a committee be established to petition for the incorporation of a canal construction company; and Lieutenant Governor Sir John WENTWORTH promised his support for such a petition, naming a company chaired by Andrew Belcher*. However, the 1798 legislative session ended with no further action on the proposal. The Shubenacadie canal question was not taken up again until 1814, with construction finally begun in 1826.

Meanwhile, on 23 June 1797 the assembly resolved upon the construction both of a "public building for the Accommodation of the General Assembly, Supreme Court, and Court of the Admiralty and public Offices," and of a new residence for the lieutenant governor. A lot was purchased to meet the first objective, but the pressure of executive complaint over the condition of the current Government House effected a change of plans: in July 1799 the assembly announced that "whereas the present Government House is in so ruinous a condition as to be unfit for the residence of the Governor or Commander in Chief of the Province, it becomes more immediately necessary to proceed to the Erection of a House suitable for his reception and Accommodation." The assembly voted £6,900 to cover the costs. The allocation was later increased to £10,500, in return for increased grants to the provincial road system, but as costs continued to mount Government House became a bone of contention between the assembly and the lieutenant governor, contributing to the acrimony of legislative

Hins

proceedings during the last years of the Wentworth administration.

Hildrith worked for seven years on Government House, assisted by John Henderson as chief mason. In a contemporary newspaper account of the laying of the cornerstone Hildrith is identified as "architect," a designation reappearing in other sources; but it is likely that this title was applied loosely, meaning the official charged with the interpretation of plans. There has been a tradition that the Scottish architects Robert and James Adam designed the building; however, certain significant characteristics of the Adam style are lacking, and the claim is countered by the likelier supposition that use was made of one of the various books of English architectural designs then circulating in the United States and British North America. Government House is built on simple lines, a three-storey central section with two-storey wings, reflecting some classical influence, constructed solidly of Nova Scotian free-stone and other local materials. Lieutenant Governor Wentworth's successor, Sir George PREVOST, thought it a far grander building than the state of the province warranted.

On 31 Dec. 1806 Hildrith resigned his position, with Government House still not completed in all details. In 1803 he and John Henderson had been granted house lots in the north suburbs of Halifax. Further appreciation of his efforts was shown on 23 Jan. 1807, when the assembly voted £50 "as a testimonial of the favourable opinion entertained by the legislature of his ability, integrity, diligence, and zeal." On 16 September of the same year Hildrith died in Shelburne and was buried in Christ Church cemetery. The inscription on his tombstone summed up his life and character with a simplicity characteristic of the works he left behind – "a loyal subject, an able architect, and an honest man."

M. SUSAN WHITESIDE

Christ Church (Shelburne, N.S.), cemetery, gravestone of Isaac Hildrith. PANS, MG 4, 140 (photocopy); MG 24, 43; 72, no.10; RG 1, 303; RG 5, A, 6–14; GP, 1; S, 8: c.1, c.9, c.12; RG 20A, 12A, 1785, no.81. PRO, AO 13, bundle 24: 262–64; bundle 31: 50–52 (copies at PAC). Shelburne County Court of Probate (Shelburne), no.279, will and estate of Isaac Hildrith, proved 5 Feb. 1808. Shelburne County Museum (Shelburne), Christ Church, Shelburne, vestry book, 1788–1908; burial reg., 1783–1813 (mfm. at PANS). J. S. Martell, "Government House," PANS *Bull.* (Halifax), 1 (1937–39), no.4. N.S., House of Assembly, *Journal and proc.*, 1792–98. *Colonial Churchman* (Liverpool, N.S.), 1 Dec. 1836. *Royal Gazette and the Nova-Scotia Advertiser*, 16 Sept. 1800. Sabine, *Biog. sketches of loyalists*, vol.2: 530. Akins, *Hist. of Halifax City.* J. S. Martell, *The romance of Government House* (Halifax, 1939). C. B. Fergusson, "Isaac Hildrith (c.1741–1807), architect of Government House, Halifax," *Dalhousie Rev.*, 50 (1970–71): 510–16. Marion Robertson, "Isaac Hildrith: a Shelburne loyalist," *Nova Scotia Museums Quarterly* (Halifax), 1 (1970), no.2: 18–21.

HINS. *See* AINSSE

HODGSON, ROBERT, carpenter, merchant, politician, army officer, office holder, and lawyer; b. *c.* 1765 in England; m. 8 June 1797 Rebecca Robinson in Charlottetown, St John's (Prince Edward) Island, and they had at least one son; d. there 5 Jan. 1811.

Robert Hodgson went to Port Roseway (Shelburne), N.S., in 1782 from Sandwich, England. Some time later he migrated to St John's Island where, although not a loyalist, he received from Lieutenant Governor Edmund FANNING a large grant of land from the donation made by the Island's proprietors for the settlement of American refugees [*see* Walter Patterson*]. Until 1790 he worked as a journeyman house-carpenter, and after briefly operating his own shop he went into business with John Brecken at a large store in Charlottetown. This partnership was dissolved in 1795, and thereafter Hodgson appears to have supported himself and his family by that common Island practice, pluralism. His enemies always saw his meteoric rise from carpenter to "landed gentleman" both as evidence of the misuse of patronage by Fanning and his supporters, who were largely the family and relations of Chief Justice Peter STEWART, and as an illustration of the way such patronage enabled men to raise themselves above their social stations.

Hodgson had entered politics in 1790, when he was elected to the House of Assembly, and he became a justice of the peace for Charlottetown in 1795. The following year he assisted his future father-in-law, Colonel Joseph ROBINSON, in distributing among the population the colonel's controversial pamphlet, *To the farmers in the Island of St. John, in the Gulf of St. Lawrence*, which called for the introduction of a court of escheat to take back unimproved lots from inactive proprietors. Hodgson also travelled the Island collecting signatures on a petition for escheat. The lieutenant governor's critics – particularly Captain John MacDONALD of Glenaladale and James DOUGLAS – believed that the land question had been raised at the instigation of the Fanning–Stewart faction, whose nefarious political purposes it was intended to serve, and found partial confirmation of this interpretation in the fact that shortly after the pamphlet's appearance in 1796 Fanning granted Hodgson a commission in one of the Island's fencible corps.

The escheat movement gained momentum the following year when an assembly committee, of which Hodgson was a member, drew up a series of resolutions asserting the failure of most of the Island's proprietors to fulfil the terms of their grants and requesting that the British government either compel the proprietors to act or move to confiscate their lands. These resolutions were passed by the assembly and forwarded by Fanning to Whitehall. In the same year another committee, chaired by Hodgson, passed a number of resolutions critical of Captain MacDonald, labelling as "a torrent of falsehoods" his accusations that Fanning had encouraged the promulgation of "levelling" principles on the Island. When MacDonald sent through Fanning a memorial to Prince EDWARD AUGUSTUS, then in Halifax, N.S., protesting Hodgson's chairmanship, the lieutenant governor turned it over to Hodgson, recommending a prosecution for defamation of character. Hodgson was, however, dissuaded from court action by Attorney General Joseph APLIN, who by this time had become associated with Fanning's critics. Aplin was soon thereafter dismissed from office for his hostile attitude to the government. As for Hodgson, he and Robinson recirculated *To the farmers* in 1798, thus helping to keep the escheat issue before the public.

In 1800 Hodgson was appointed deputy clerk of the Supreme Court, replacing Charles STEWART, and that same year he added the post of coroner to his collection of offices. He served as sheriff in 1801, and often acted as collector of customs during William TOWNSHEND's frequent and prolonged absences from the Island. Despite a serious paralytic stroke in 1802, Hodgson remained active in Island affairs. His popularity among the voters was demonstrated in 1803, when he was simultaneously elected to the assembly from three constituencies – Georgetown, Prince County, and Queens County – winning every vote in the first, though he chose to sit for the second. His unpopularity with some, however, was illustrated in 1805 by a series of incidents in which the windows of his house were mysteriously broken; the culprit was never found. In 1806 Hodgson served as speaker of the assembly, and two years later he was admitted to the Island's list of practising attorneys-at-law. He never fully recovered his health after 1802, however, and he died in 1811, mourned by most of the people as an early supporter of their rights. His son Robert* had a distinguished career on the Island, ultimately serving as its first native lieutenant governor.

J. M. BUMSTED

PAPEI, Benjamin Chappell, diary, 19 Nov. 1805; RG 3, House of Assembly, Journals, 15, 17, 19, 22 July 1797; RG 6, Supreme Court records; RG 9, Customs, shipping reg., 1 (1787–1824). PRO, CO 226/17: 438–39; 226/18. SRO, GD293/2/19/6, 10. [Joseph Robinson], *To the farmers in the Island of St. John, in the Gulf of St. Lawrence* (n.p., n.d.). Stewart, *Account of P.E.I.*, 220–25. MacNutt, "Fanning's regime on P.E.I.," *Acadiensis* (Fredericton), 1, no.1: 50.

HOLLAND, SAMUEL JOHANNES, army officer, military engineer, surveyor, office holder, politician, and landowner; b. 1728 in Nijmegen, Netherlands; d. 28 Dec. 1801 at Quebec, Lower Canada.

Samuel Johannes Holland entered the Dutch artillery in 1745 and served during the War of the Austrian Succession. He was promoted lieutenant in 1747, following the siege of Bergen op Zoom, Netherlands. On 31 Aug. 1749 he married Gertrude Hasse at Nijmegen, and the following year they had a daughter, who may have died in infancy. However, possibly having made contact with the Duke of Richmond, Holland in 1754 emigrated to England to seek advancement under the British flag, leaving Gertrude in the Netherlands. By March 1756, with the duke's aid, he had received a commission, backdated to 29 Dec. 1755, as lieutenant in the Royal Americans (62nd, later 60th, Foot) in which the Earl of Loudoun was colonel-in-chief and Frederick HALDIMAND a lieutenant-colonel. Holland came to North America with Loudoun in early 1756. With the help of others, he prepared a map of New York province that would be widely used for 20 years. Promoted captain-lieutenant in 1757, he was assigned to reconnoitre Fort Carillon (near Ticonderoga, N.Y.), but early in 1758 he was transferred as assistant engineer to the expedition against Louisbourg, Île Royale (Cape Breton Island). Under the command of Brigadier-General James Wolfe*, he surveyed the ground adjacent to the fortress, took soundings, prepared plans, and gave engineering advice during Wolfe's operations against the town before its capitulation on 27 July. Having been constantly under fire, he was highly commended by Wolfe to Richmond for his bravery and technical competence. Afterwards, Holland surveyed the fortifications, the town, and the surrounding territory. That winter he and his new survey pupil, James Cook*, drew a chart of the St Lawrence gulf and river in preparation for the attack on Quebec. Holland also plotted surveys and made plans in Halifax, N.S., and supervised the construction of Fort Frederick (Saint John, N.B.). Promoted captain on 24 Aug. 1759, he participated actively that summer in the siege of Quebec. He narrowly escaped death on one occasion when his boats were run down by a schooner. During the battle of the Plains of Abraham on 13 September, he returned wounded to Wolfe's side from dangerous engineering operations only to find him dying. At the battle of Sainte-Foy the following spring Holland temporarily replaced the wounded chief engineer, Patrick Mackellar*. After the French siege was lifted, he was employed in surveying the settled parts of the St Lawrence valley [*see* John Montresor*] and in drawing up plans for a new citadel at Quebec.

In 1762 Holland took his maps to London, where he submitted a proposal to the Board of Trade for a survey of all British possessions in North America in order to facilitate settlement. It was finally accepted in February 1764 and, along with his surveys and an excellent recommendation from Governor Murray*, earned him the appointment on 6 March of surveyor general of the province of Quebec, with a salary of £365 per annum. When he offered to fill the post of

Holland

surveyor general of the Northern District of North America at no increase in salary, the authorities were quick to accept. On 23 March he received instructions to survey all British possessions north of the Potomac River, beginning with St John's (Prince Edward) Island, the Îles de la Madeleine, and Cape Breton Island because of their importance for the fisheries.

Before proceeding to St John's Island, Holland delivered to Murray at Quebec the British government's instructions for organizing the civil government of the colony. Murray appointed him to the newly established Council of Quebec on 13 Aug. 1764; the following month he was named a justice of the peace. After appointing John Collins* to direct surveying in the province during his absence, Holland left for St John's Island, where he arrived early in October. Armed with a wide range of scientific instruments and assisted by the deputy surveyor, Thomas WRIGHT, and a number of engineer officers, volunteer apprentices, non-commissioned officers, and privates, Holland conducted his survey of St John's Island under harsh climatic conditions. He divided it into counties of approximately 500,000 acres, parishes of around 100,000 acres, and townships of about 20,000 acres, surveying them with precision by fixing latitudes and longitudes from astronomical observation; he also took careful soundings in coastal waters. On maps and in accompanying reports he recorded the principal rivers and harbours, and established the sites of projected towns, including the capital, which he named Charlottetown. He analysed possible land uses around these sites, providing a detailed account of forest resources, plant life, and the quality and extent of the soils, as well as an assessment of the climate, particularly for agriculture. By October 1765 he was able to send the first of his maps and reports to England, where they renewed an interest in land speculation that had manifested itself the previous year [see Walter Patterson*]. When the Island was apportioned by lottery in 1767, Holland received Lot 28. That year he sent a few farmers and disbanded soldiers to settle it, and by 1798 there were 136 people living there. As an absentee landlord, Holland collected little rent from the tenant farmers during his lifetime.

In 1765 Holland had surveyed the Îles de la Madeleine with Lieutenant Peter Frederick Haldimand*; they then moved on to Cape Breton Island, where work had been begun by Charles Morris* in 1764. It was divided in the same manner as St John's Island. The completed maps and reports, which Holland had sent to London by July 1767, indicated that in addition to its fisheries Cape Breton was valuable chiefly for its coal, building stone, and gypsum, although it was also suited in a few areas to agriculture. As on St John's Island, Holland's survey was intended to be the basis for land grants, but long

after his report was approved settlers continued to receive mere licences of occupation rather than full title-deeds. In 1768 Holland expressed the view that Cape Breton Island could not develop its resources energetically as long as it remained administratively dependent on Nova Scotia; it was separated from that colony in 1784. While the survey on Cape Breton Island was being finished, in 1767 Holland's survey parties were working in the Gaspé around Baie des Chaleurs and on Anticosti Island. Work was also carried out in the late 1760s on both shores of the lower St Lawrence River. In 1767 Holland had proposed that British explorers look for a northwest passage from the Atlantic Ocean to the Pacific, but he received little encouragement for the project.

Holland made his home at Louisbourg for much of the period 1765–67. Possibly as early as 1762 at Quebec he had begun living with Marie-Joseph Rollet, then 21 years old, and their first child, John Frederick*, was born on St John's Island. In January 1768 Holland wrote to Haldimand, "You must know my Dear General that I have Carryed the jock too far with my Little Bedfellow as I have got now, besides little St. Johns Jack and Louisburgh Henry . . . what has most Spoiled Sport . . . a little Girl last for a Christmas Box." By September 1769 another girl had been born, and the couple wished it were in Holland's power to make Marie-Joseph his wife "for the children's sake." His separation from Gertrude Hasse had been amicable and, except in 1763 and 1770, Holland recognized an obligation by paying her an annual allowance from 1756 to 1780. (Her petition in 1784 to the British government to have him renew payments was unsuccessful.) During 1772, however, he secured the opinion of judges and the attorney general in New Hampshire that a marriage with Marie-Joseph would be legal, and it is likely that it was contracted soon after. By May 1773, when the brood counted three boys and four girls, Holland was referring to their mother as his "little wife." They would eventually have ten children.

By the autumn of 1767 Holland was residing at Quebec, where in October 1766 he had been granted a small lot adjacent to the Château Saint-Louis. The following year he purchased six lots and a residence on the Côte Saint-Jean for about £400 from the heirs of Jacques de Lafontaine* de Belcour; by May 1769, when he made four small loans totalling about £120, he was residing in the house. He bought land near the Saint-Jean gate in March 1770, and about this time he was renting his home, called Holland House, to Advocate General George Suckling*. While at Quebec Holland participated in the proceedings of the council, and he was appointed to committees dealing with land, roads, and public works. He also served on the public accounts committee and in 1768 on a board set up to determine whether George ALLSOPP, suspended from several offices he had purchased, should be allowed to take them up.

Holland apparently did not reside long at Quebec; by 1770 he was directing survey parties in the enormous task of mapping Atlantic coastal lands from the Saint John River (N.B.) to New York City in the context of a project to supply the British government with the best possible maps of the Atlantic seaboard at a time when her American colonies were drifting toward revolution. Simultaneously, and theoretically in collaboration with Holland, Joseph Frederick Wallet DesBarres* was employed by the Admiralty in conducting excellent, but more laborious, hydrographic surveys around Nova Scotia. Early in 1775 the Board of Trade regretted that Holland was depending on DesBarres's surveys in order to complete "the General Map we have been so impatient for." As a result, before the outbreak of the American Revolutionary War, the board had received from Holland many excellent detailed maps but no general survey. In the course of their work in the Atlantic colonies, Holland and his colleagues put to use instruments, newly developed in Britain, such as the astronomical clock and the refracting telescope. Holland produced the first accurate map of New Hampshire and advocated the separation of Maine from Massachusetts, recommending the Saint John River as the boundary with Nova Scotia. In 1769–70 he served on the New York–New Jersey boundary commission, and in 1774 he was a representative for New York on a commission to settle its boundary with Pennsylvania. He was preparing to run the boundary line between New York and Massachusetts when the revolution broke out.

During this period Holland lived at Portsmouth, N.H., until 1773, when he moved to Perth Amboy, N.J. As a measure of security for his family, he sold his army commission in 1772, realizing £1,500, which he banked at New York City. By the time the revolution began, he had obtained 3,000 acres of land in New Hampshire and 24,000 acres in Vermont. He thus had ties to the American colonies and offers were made to him to join the revolutionaries, who valued his skills. But his entire career had been linked to Britain and, leaving his family in hiding at Perth Amboy, he fled to England in 1775. During his stay in London he cooperated with DesBarres, then working on a compilation of charts and sailing directions for North American coastal waters that were published in various forms from 1777 as *The Atlantic Neptune*. . . . On 4 Jan. 1776 he was commissioned a major in the army, and later that year, as a British aide-de-camp, he accompanied the commander of the Hessian troops, Leopold Philipp von Heister, to America. Holland appears to have seen action near New York City, and in March 1777 he organized a colonial unit called the Guides and Pioneers.

In October 1778 Governor Haldimand called Holland to Quebec to resume the duties of provincial surveyor general. After wintering at Halifax, Holland and his family, who had joined him in New York City, arrived at Quebec in the spring of 1779. He was appointed, temporarily, muster-master for the Hessians in the province. In 1779 as well he was named to the Legislative Council, established four years earlier under the Quebec Act. Except in 1788–89, when he was on leave in Britain, and in 1789–90, when he was seriously ill, he attended council meetings regularly. He supported Haldimand's administration on most issues against an opposition comprising Lieutenant Governor Henry Hamilton*, Allsopp, Hugh Finlay, William Grant (1744–1805), and others. However, during Hamilton's own administration, from 1784 to 1786, Holland voted for optional jury trials in civil suits and other measures introduced by the Hamilton faction. Under Lord Dorchester [Guy Carleton] he was a cautious supporter of the policies of Chief Justice William Smith*, including judicial reform; in 1787 and 1791 he supported Smith in 27 of 38 votes, a record at variance with the opinion of his contemporary Alexander Fraser that he voted with Smith "sometimes," but "only from blunder and mear want of sense and no other Cause." In tending to support the administration of the moment Holland was probably acting in his own best interests as an office holder, as would seem to be confirmed by Fraser's remark that "no Man wishes to do whatever is agreeable to Govt. more than he."

Having again taken up residence at Holland House along the road to Sainte-Foy, Holland added extensively to his holdings in the Côte Saint-Jean area in 1780, 1782, and 1790. He established a large farm of about 200 acres, and his mansion was renowned for its grandeur. By 1788 he had acquired the fief of Saint-Jean, probably from Murray. In addition to his expenditures for land purchases, between 1784 and 1791 Holland was able to lend a total of more than £1,700. By 1790, thanks to his influence with Evan Nepean, a commissioner of the Privy Seal, he had apparently received some compensation from the British government for losses sustained during the American revolution; on the other hand, his salary as surveyor general was mysteriously reduced by £65 per annum, and in New York, New Jersey, and Vermont, where he attempted to recover his properties, he was embroiled in suits at law with what he termed "a Lawless crew."

The British government's decision to make extensive land grants to loyalists after the American revolution made it necessary to reduce routine work in the settled areas in order to accelerate the surveying of vast tracts never before considered for settlement in the region that was to become Upper Canada. In order to report on suitability for habitation, in May and June

Holland

1783 Holland inspected lands around Cataraqui (Kingston, Ont.) and sent a small party, including James Peachey*, to the Niagara region. Holland's relatively favourable reports led to large-scale surveying on the upper St Lawrence, on the north shore of Lake Ontario westward from Cataraqui, in the Niagara peninsula, and along the Detroit River opposite Detroit (Mich.). There being a need for the quick production of farm lots, Holland ordered the laying out of townships divided into concessions, in turn divided into lots, which were to be awarded by ballot without regard to land quality.

Most of the work in the new areas fell to Collins. After visits to them in late 1783 and the spring and summer of 1784, Holland was increasingly confined by failing health and paper work to the Quebec office, where he supervised at a distance survey teams from the Gaspé to Detroit; however, he was able to make trips to Britain in 1784 and 1787. In 1792 responsibility for surveys in the western regions passed to the Surveyor General's Office for Upper Canada, and Holland's deputies turned their attention to the new, or eastern, townships of Lower Canada, for which claims to grants were soon flooding into the Executive Council [see Robert PRESCOTT]; 22 townships were surveyed during the succeeding decade.

Holland's health continued to alarm him. An attack of palsy, probably in 1790, prevented him from carrying out his duties fully until March 1792; in April John Graves SIMCOE noted, "Poor Holland, that good and faithful servant of the Crown, is worn out in body, tho' in full possession of his intellect." Holland was, moreover, omitted from the new Legislative Council, formed in 1792, and he thus lost the councillor's salary of £100 per annum. From 1796 he began leasing his farm to others. In April 1801 he transferred the entire duties of the Surveyor General's Office to William VONDENVELDEN, who had been performing them for several years past, and promised him one-half of the surveyor general's fees and more than 5,500 acres of land in Kingsey Township as compensation. The previous month Holland had gathered 39 associates, according to the system of township leaders and associates [see James CALDWELL], to petition for Kingsey, which comprised 64,000 acres on the Rivière Saint-François. For his part, Vondenvelden promised to use his influence to obtain another grant for Holland. The latter's lingering illness, however, had reached its final stages; he died at Holland House on 28 Dec. 1801. Three days later, after the funeral service at the Anglican church, his body was escorted to the farm by a band, a detachment of 200 soldiers, and numerous dignitaries. He was buried beside a son, Samuel Lester, killed at age 19 in a duel in which he had used a pair of pistols given to Holland by Wolfe.

If Holland's debts at his death amounted to only a little over £100, his movable property was assessed at less than £300. It included nearly 150 maps and 17 atlases as well as a varied library of well over 100 titles, embracing geography and modern history, military and naval subjects, classics, philosophy, political thought, language, and literature. Holland also left 32 original engravings and more than 60 oil paintings, one-half of them portraits; some of the paintings were probably by his own hand. In 1792 Mrs Simcoe [Elizabeth Posthuma Gwillim*] had admired his "fine prints of Italy and Mount Vesuvius," and he appears to have befriended the artist William BERCZY, who described him in 1799 as "this respectable old man" and "good old Holland," always so sensitive to the desires of others. Most of Holland's atlases, books, and paintings were purchased by his Sainte-Foy neighbour, Henry CALDWELL, or by Joseph Bouchette*, step-nephew of Marie-Joseph and Holland's eventual successor as surveyor general. Holland also left extensive property holdings; in 1805, moreover, his family was granted some 11,000 acres in Kingsey Township.

Samuel Johannes Holland holds an important place in the history of Canadian science and technology for his role in setting high standards of accuracy in land measurement and mapping, for his contributions to astronomy and geography, and for the training in surveying and cartography which he provided directly or indirectly to so many. In the northeastern United States he won fame for his mapping and contributions to boundary settlements. In Prince Edward Island he is remembered as a founder of the colony and revered by some as an ancestor, his son John Frederick (and from about 1802 his widow, Marie-Joseph) having taken up residence there; his maps and reports remain important sources for the historical geography of the Island and of Cape Breton. At Quebec, as a politician he was a reliable, well-read defender of conservative values, but it is the many maps and the layout of townships in Upper and Lower Canada under his competent administration that constitute the chief legacy of the Canadian career of this great surveyor and cartographer. The topographical name "Holland" in several provinces is a reminder of the prominent role he played in the shaping of this country.

F. J. THORPE

[Samuel Johannes Holland was the author of: "Observations made on the islands of Saint John and Cape Briton; to ascertain the longitude and latitude of those places, agreeable to the orders and instructions of the Rt Honourable the Lords Commissioners for Trade and Plantations"; "Astronomical observations . . ."; "A letter to the astronomer royal . . . containing some eclipses of Jupiter's satellites, observed near Quebec"; and "Astronomical observations . . . ," published in the Royal Soc. of London, *Philosophical Trans.* (London), 58 (1768): 46–53; 59 (1769): 247–52; 64 (1774):

171–76; and 64 (1774): 182–83 respectively. He was apparently also the author of *Miscellaneous remarks and observations on Nova Scotia, New Brunswick, and Cape Breton; supposed to be written by the surveyor general of Nova Scotia* (Boston, 1794). His report of 1768 on Cape Breton Island, along with his correspondence relating to the survey and other documents, were edited by Daniel Cobb Harvey* and published at Halifax in 1935 under the title *Holland's description of Cape Breton Island and other documents*.

The National Map Coll. at the PAC holds originals of Holland's maps as well as photocopies of many others located in the ANQ-Q; G.B., Ministry of Defence, Hydrographic Dept., Admiralty Arch. (Taunton); PRO; BL; British Museum (London); Clements Library; and Library of Congress (Washington).

Aspects of Holland's career have received attention from various writers, but only one, Willis Chipman, attempted to deal with his whole life. A land surveyor in the Holland tradition, Chipman published "The life and times of Major Samuel Holland, surveyor-general, 1764-1801," *OH*, 21 (1924): 11–90, a scissors-and-paste biography containing most, but not all, of the pertinent data. Other writers, including Don W. Thomson in *Men and meridians; the history of surveying and mapping in Canada* (3v., Ottawa, 1966–69), have tended to accept Chipman's word as law, even his speculations regarding Holland's second marriage and ancestry. Chipman, however, overlooked or ignored some sources available to him, and this despite the help of the archivist Francis-Joseph Audet*, whose files in PAC, MG 30, D1, 15, reveal extensive collation of data on Holland and some research. Nothing has been found in archives in the Netherlands regarding Holland's ancestry, social class, or education, and no record has been found of his second marriage, but letters from Holland to Haldimand in BL, Add. MSS 21679, 21728, and 21730, provide a few tantalizingly candid glimpses of a man whose private life is otherwise largely enshrouded in documents about property, arrears of salary, or the baptism of the younger children. Nevertheless, the sources on Holland's land surveys and colonial parliamentary career can answer most of the essential questions that might be asked in a full-length treatment of his public life. F.J.T.]

The *DCB* should like to acknowledge assistance generously provided it by Mr Wim Van Veen of Toronto.

Algemeen Rijksarchief (The Hague), Raad van State, no.1538: f.220. ANQ-Q, CE1-61, 28 Dec. 1801; CN1-25, 27 sept. 1784; CN1-83, 8 sept., 11, 21 oct. 1784; 19 sept. 1785; 19 oct. 1787; 31 janv., 11 mai, 23 sept. 1789; 15 janv., 30 juin, 12, 16, 28 août, 16 sept. 1790; 15 janv. 1791; CN1-92, 3 mars 1791; CN1-157, 5 mars 1801, 20 sept. 1805; CN1-209, 9 sept. 1762; 22 oct. 1767; 7, 30 mai 1770; 25 sept. 1772; CN1-250, 2 mai 1769; CN1-253, 18 Feb. 1826, 13 March 1827; CN1-256, 8 June 1792; 13 June 1795; 7 Jan. 1796; 2 Feb., 5, 27 April 1797; 25 April 1801; CN1-262, 20 juin 1801; CN1-284, 14 oct. 1800; 27 oct. 1801; 19, 29 janv., 8 févr. 1802. Dalhousie Univ. Arch. (Halifax), MS 2-33. Municipal Arch., Nijmegen (Netherlands), vital statistics, 31 Aug. 1749, 24 June 1750. PAC, MG 11, [CO 42] Q, 17: 324–27, 742; 56: 852; MG 23, A4, 64: 60 (copy at PAC); B14; MG 24, K2, 6: 1–2, 17–23, 241–46, 267–71, 278–80; RG 1, E1, 1–7; RG 1, L3ᴸ: 52575–640; RG 8, I (C ser.), 600: 92; 604: 164; RG 14, A1, 2; 4. PRO,

AO 3/140: 63, 104; CO 5/51: 126; 5/70: 19–26; 5/71: 133–36; 5/74: 263–66; 5/75: 201–4; CO 42/16: 230, 259; 42/55: f.399v. (copies and mfm. at PAC).

Docs. relating to constitutional hist., 1759–91 (Shortt and Doughty; 1907), 48, 50, 277, 279, 854–57. *Documents relating to the colonial, revolutionary and post-revolutionary history of the state of New Jersey*, ed. W. A. Whitehead *et al.* (42v., Newark, N.J., 1880–1949), 9, 10. Gwillim, *Diary of Mrs. Simcoe* (Robertson; 1911), 57. Knox, *Hist. journal* (Doughty), 2: 391n. *Military affairs in North America, 1748–1765: selected documents from the Cumberland papers in Windsor Castle*, ed. S. [McC.] Pargellis (New York and London, [1936]; repr. [Hamden, Conn.], 1969), 364, 439n., 446. [William Berczy], "William von Moll Berczy," ANQ *Rapport*, 1940–41: 16–17. [James] Murray, *Governor Murray's journal of Quebec, from 18th September, 1759, to 25th May, 1760* ([Quebec and Montreal, 1871]), 27. *NYCD* (O'Callaghan and Fernow), 7: 845. Smith, *Diary and selected papers* (Upton), 2: 145–46, 167, 169, 181. *Quebec Gazette*, 4 Oct. 1764; 12 Nov., 3 Dec. 1767; 22 March 1770; 12 Sept. 1771; 19 March 1772; 5 Aug. 1786; 11 Dec. 1788; 10 Sept. 1789; 19 Dec. 1793; 3 July 1794; 6 April 1797; 5 Feb. 1800; 7 Jan., 4 Feb. 1802. *Biblio. of Canadiana* (Staton and Tremaine), no.671. G.B., WO, *Army list*, 1756–1800. Richard Brown, *A history of the island of Cape Breton, with some account of the discovery and settlement of Canada, Nova Scotia, and Newfoundland* (London, 1869), 352. Duncan Campbell, *History of Prince Edward Island* (Charlottetown, 1875; repr. Belleville, Ont., 1972), 3–17. A. H. Clark, *Three centuries and the Island, a historical geography of settlement and agriculture in Prince Edward Island, Canada* (Toronto, 1959), 44–47. G. N. D. Evans, *Uncommon obdurate: the several public careers of J. F. W. DesBarres* (Toronto and Salem, Mass., 1969), 11–13, 23, 62. [C.-N.] Gabriel, *Le maréchal de camp Desandrouins, 1729–1792; guerre du Canada, 1756–1760; guerre de l'Indépendance américaine, 1780–1782* (Verdun, France, 1887), 323–28. Andrew McPhail, "The history of Prince Edward Island," *Canada and its prov.* (Shortt and Doughty), 13: 332–36. L. S. Mayo, *John Wentworth, governor of New Hampshire, 1767–1775* (Cambridge, Mass., 1921), 43–44. W. A. Russ, *How Pennsylvania acquired its present boundaries* (University Park, Pa., 1966). Henry Scadding, *Surveyor-General Holland; a notice of Samuel Holland, first surveyor-general of lands for the northern district of North America . . .* (Toronto, 1896). Abraham Wolf, *A history of science, technology, and philosophy in the eighteenth century* (London, 1938), 122–23, 144–45. F.-J. Audet, "Samuel Holland," *Cahiers des Dix*, 23 (1958): 187–94. N.-E. Dionne, "L'arpentage en Canada: le major Samuel Holland, 1764–1801," *Le Journal* (Montréal), 6 oct. 1900: 3. N. N. Shipton, "General James Murray's map of the St Lawrence," *Cartographer* (Toronto), 4 (1967): 93–101. W. A. Whitehead, "Northern boundary line: the circumstances leading to the establishment, in 1769, of the northern boundary line between New Jersey and York," N.J. Hist. Soc., *Proc.* (Newark), 8 (1856–59): 157–86.

HOW, DEBORAH (Cottnam), schoolmistress; b. *c.* 1725 in Canso, N.S., daughter of Edward How* and his first wife; m. *c.* 1742 Ensign (later Captain)

Howe

Samuel Cottnam of the 40th Foot, and they had at least two children; d. 31 Dec. 1806 in Windsor, N.S.

Deborah How was raised in Canso, where her father was the leading merchant and civilian official. The family's strong New England ties and her father's fluency in languages assured her a sound education, likely at home. She was married at an early age, and her first child, Martha Grace, was 11 days old when Canso fell to the French in May 1744 [see Patrick Heron*]. The community's buildings were burnt and the garrison families were removed as prisoners to Louisbourg, Île Royale (Cape Breton Island), from where they were sent to Boston in July.

Mrs Cottnam's activities for the next 30 years remain obscure. Her husband was at the fall of Louisbourg in 1758 [see Jeffery Amherst*] and continued there until, in declining health, he resigned his commission in 1760. By 1764 he was a merchant in Salem, Mass., where he had been living in 1762 and where he remained until 1773, when he brought his family to Nova Scotia. Although he held "avow'd [loyalist] principles & fix'd attachment to Government," it is likely that financial difficulties precipitated the move.

By July 1774 Mrs Cottnam had returned to Salem with her unmarried daughter Grizelda Elizabeth (Grissey) to open a school for young ladies. After the outbreak of war she moved to Halifax, where by 1777 she was again operating a "Female Academy" with her daughter. The boarding- and day-school catered to the colonial establishment and loyalist gentry, numbering among its pupils the daughters of Joseph Frederick Wallet DesBarres* and Mather BYLES. Reading, writing, arithmetic, and French were the principal subjects; dancing and sewing were also taught, the latter being Grissey's speciality. Pupils worked samplers, muslin cuffs, and tuckers, while their minds were treated to such matters as "Locke upon inate ideas." The duration of schooling varied, but most girls were considered adequately educated at about age 14.

Although her pupils came from cultured families, it is evident that Mrs Cottnam offered them additional intellectual stimulation and a superior education for the time. After graduating, Rebecca Byles was "imploy'd in translating a very long Sermon for Doctor [John Breynton*], from French into English; & in reading Pamela and Terences Plays in French; [also] in hearing Popes Homer." It was said that Mrs Cottnam possessed "everything that [was] excellent in Woman," and she had both the respect and the admiration of her students. Rebecca Byles paid her a high compliment in noting that boys were poorly educated in the colonies, but that "Girls . . . have the best Education the place affords, and the accomplishment of their Minds is attended to as well as the adorning of their Persons; in a few years I expect to see

Women fill the most important Offices in Church and State."

The Halifax establishment did not appreciate Mrs Cottnam's importance to their community until the loyalist families of Saint John, N.B., persuaded her to open a school there in 1786. Having found Halifax "very expensive & not . . . very pleasing," she and Grissey were not sorry to leave. Although they were happier in Saint John, the financial difficulties continued, with Grissey noting that it was hard indeed for her mother "to be reduced at her year to the dreadful necessity of earning a scanty subsistence . . . in keeping a school, & with difficulty gaining a sufficiency to live with decency." Matters were alleviated somewhat in 1793 with the death of Edward How's widow, Marie-Madeleine Winniett; the £100 yearly pension which she had enjoyed was continued to Mrs Cottnam, who had received nothing from her father's estate. By 1793 she had returned to Halifax, but her final years were spent in Windsor at the home of her daughter Martha Grace, the widow of Winckworth Tonge*.

LOIS K. KERNAGHAN

Mass. Hist. Soc., J. M. Robbins papers, 1774–77. PANS, MG 1, 163; MG 12, miscellaneous, 6, nos.13–14; RG 20A, 11. *Weekly Chronicle* (Halifax), 9 Jan 1807. G. A. Rawlyk, *Yankees at Louisbourg* (Orono, Maine, 1967).

HOWE, ALEXANDER, army officer, politician, judge, and office holder; b. 19 Dec. 1749 in Annapolis Royal, N.S., son of Edward How* and Marie-Madeleine Winniett; m. first 14 May 1778 his cousin Helen McKellar Bontein in Gravesend, England, and they had ten children; m. secondly 6 Sept. 1803, in Annapolis Royal, Margaret Ann Green, granddaughter of Benjamin Green*; d. 9 Jan. 1813 in Dartmouth, N.S.

Finances and patronage were predominant themes in Alexander Howe's life. His mother, widowed when he was less than a year old, used a small pension and influential family connections to provide military careers for her four sons. Howe claimed that he began his military career as a volunteer under Lieutenant-Colonel William Amherst during the Newfoundland expedition of 1762 [see Charles-Henri-Louis d'Arsac* de Ternay]. On 24 July 1767 he was gazetted an ensign in the 36th Foot by purchase; a lieutenancy followed on 31 Jan. 1771. After service in Jamaica, England, and Ireland, Howe was commissioned captain of his own independent company on 13 April 1781. This risky financial venture proved unsuccessful (it was expensive to establish, and the winding down of hostilities caused problems), and in 1782 the company was incorporated into the 104th Foot.

The state of Howe's finances and the lack of

military prospects in 1783 induced him to sell his commission and return the following year to Nova Scotia, where, again at considerable expense, he began farming at Granville. He was quickly drawn into the social and administrative problems created in Annapolis County by the arrival of the loyalists. The immigrants had all but submerged the established families, who nevertheless were determined to share in the government. In the November 1785 elections for the House of Assembly, Howe was the only pre-loyalist to contest any of the four Annapolis seats. When his opponent David Seabury was elected, Howe protested to Halifax, charging polling irregularities and vote solicitation by the loyalist sheriff, Robert Tucker. A second election, held amid "quarrels, broken heads and bloody noses," again returned Seabury, but Howe's repeated complaints led to the vote's being declared invalid. By a decision of the assembly, Howe took his seat, jubilant at overthrowing "the machinations of as complicated a Sett of Rascals as ever Existed" in their "inordinant thirst for power." The loyalists viewed Howe similarly, complaining of his friendliness with the Halifax establishment. According to Jacob BAILEY, the "late election was wholly put aside upon the evidence of one party only."

Although Howe consistently supported the stand of the pre-loyalist assembly reactionaries in such matters as the impeachment of Supreme Court judges James BRENTON and Isaac DESCHAMPS, he evidently enjoyed the ultimate support of his electors, for he retained an Annapolis County seat until 1799. On 20 Nov. 1785 he was appointed a justice of the peace and a judge of the Inferior Court of Common Pleas for Annapolis County, and on 11 March 1788 he was also named collector of impost and excise duties for the county. In 1791 Lieutenant Governor John Parr*, intending to provide Howe with "a little employment, and . . . a little Cash," appointed him to recruit the Annapolis County blacks wishing to emigrate to Sierra Leone [see Thomas Peters*]. Although Parr did not encourage the scheme, Howe tackled the job zealously, noting that "(however much I stand in need of Cash) I had much rather have . . . approbation than any pecuniary reward." He later claimed to have sent to Halifax one-third of the blacks who emigrated and to have undertaken several perilous journeys in his work.

In 1793 Lieutenant Governor John WENTWORTH commissioned Howe captain of a company in the newly raised Royal Nova Scotia Regiment. In July 1797 Howe was appointed superintendent of the fractious Jamaican maroons quartered at Preston, near Dartmouth. Although he was a capable administrator as a result of his previous experience in Jamaica and Nova Scotia, Howe viewed these blacks as a source of cheap local labour, and failed to comprehend their

confusion over the climate and their isolated situation. He was also, inevitably, drawn into the intrigue surrounding Wentworth's handling of the situation; his efforts to supervise the maroons were continually undermined by persons attempting to discredit the lieutenant governor. On 9 July 1798 he was replaced by the more forceful Theophilus Chamberlain*.

Howe's friendly relations with EDWARD AUGUSTUS, Duke of Kent, secured him an appointment in 1802 as assistant commissary and storekeeper in Prince Edward Island; his regiment disbanded the same year. He was also named to the Council that year by Lieutenant Governor Edmund FANNING and on 13 Dec. 1806 became a justice of the peace, but family tragedy (two of his sons died in 1804 after eating poisonous berries), financial difficulties, and isolation plagued Howe on the "forlorn Isle." The final blow came on 25 Aug. 1811 when he was relieved of his position as commissary and placed on half pay.

Howe left Charlottetown with the esteem of Islanders, but he had to sell his furniture to finance the return to Nova Scotia. He petitioned the Duke of Kent for assistance, noting that he had "no anchor of Hope to rely on save only the Protection of H.R.H. the Benevolent Duke," but he died before an answer arrived, with little to show for his career except "a long life spent in the Service . . . supported by an upright Conscience and satisfied that I have done my duty, to the best of my abilities, in whatever station I have been placed."

LOIS K. KERNAGHAN

PANS, MG 1, 472–74A; RG 5, E, 1. PRO, CO 217/68, Wentworth to Portland, 12 Aug. 1797; 217/69, Wentworth to Portland, 23 June 1798. *Nova Scotia Royal Gazette* (Halifax), 13 Jan. 1813. Calnek, *Hist. of Annapolis* (Savary). J. [M.] Ross, "Jacob Bailey: portrait of an Anglican clergyman in eighteenth century Nova Scotia" (essay, Dalhousie Univ., Halifax, 1972). J. W. St G. Walker, *The black loyalists: the search for a promised land in Nova Scotia and Sierra Leone, 1783–1870* (London, 1976). Margaret Ells, "Nova Scotian 'Sparks of liberty,'" *Dalhousie Rev.*, 16 (1936–37): 475–92.

HOWE, JEMIMA. *See* SAWTELLE

HUET DE LA VALINIÈRE, PIERRE, Roman Catholic priest and Sulpician; baptized 10 Jan. 1732 in Varades, France, son of Charles Huet de La Valinière and Olive Arnaud; d. 29 June 1806 in L'Assomption, Lower Canada.

Pierre Huet de La Valinière entered the Grand Séminaire de Nantes in November 1752. Once he had become a subdeacon and therefore attached to his diocese, he received permission from his bishop to join the Sulpicians, a step he took after staying for a time at the Séminaire de Saint-Sulpice in Paris. At the request of his superior general, Jean Couturier, La Valinière sailed for New France, where he arrived on 9 Sept. 1754. He completed his training for the priesthood with the Sulpicians in Montreal. Upon his ordination by Bishop Henri-Marie Dubreil* de Pontbriand on 15 June 1755, he was initiated into ministry in Notre-Dame parish in Montreal, among the Iroquois at the Sulpician mission of Lac-des-Deux-Montagnes (Oka), and at the Hôpital Général of Montreal, working in all three places with other Sulpicians. He was named parish priest of Saint-Joseph, at Rivières-des-Prairies (Montreal), in 1759, and of Saint-Henri-de-Mascouche (Mascouche) in 1766. Three years later he was transferred to the parish of Saint-Sulpice, near Montreal, where he had responsibility also for Saint-Antoine at Lavaltrie. La Valinière next served as parish priest of Saint-Enfant-Jésus, at Pointe-aux-Trembles (Montreal), in 1773; the following year he replaced his colleague Jacques Degeay* at L'Assomption.

Meanwhile New France had been conquered by the British. The gradual extinction of the religious communities had been the subject of a royal instruction, and the Jesuits, Recollets, and even the Sulpicians found this policy hard to accept. It is therefore scarcely surprising that some priests among them were strongly opposed to the new political régime: the Jesuits Joseph Huguet*, Bernard Well, and Pierre-René Floquet*, the Recollet Claude Carpentier, and the ex-Recollet Eustache Chartier* de Lotbinière. La Valinière is believed to have had similar leanings, for in 1771, not long after his arrival in the parish of Saint-Sulpice, he was accused of disloyalty to the British authorities. Although Étienne Montgolfier*, who was both his superior and vicar general of the District of Montreal, had in 1768 already lamented his colleague's "immoderate conduct" and "fierce frame of mind" even towards Bishop Briand*, he had said that La Valinière had convinced him of the falsity of such allegations and he was pleased that the priest "said the prayers . . . usual for the king." Montgolfier succeeded in stopping the legal action launched against La Valinière by justice of the peace Gordon of Saint-Sulpice, who had the support of the seigneur of Berthier, James Cuthbert*.

The American invasion of 1775 and the occupation of Montreal that November caused a variety of reactions with respect to the British government [see Benedict ARNOLD; Richard Montgomery*]. A large part of the Canadian nobility and bourgeoisie, as well as most of the Catholic clergy, came down in favour of defending Canada; however, on the whole the people remained neutral, and a majority of the English-speaking merchants of Montreal and Quebec heartily welcomed the revolutionaries. As for La Valinière, those who doubted his loyalty had reason to be suspicious. Writing from L'Assomption to his super-

ior, Montgolfier, he wanted to know why, since God had declared for the invaders, "at least for a while," the clergy should not themselves follow suit. For one thing, many of his parishioners were joining the rebels, having been persuaded to do so by Thomas Walker*, a Montreal merchant and justice of the peace who owned a local farm and who ardently supported the Americans. Worse still, when La Valinière learned that Jean-de-Dieu-François Robert and Charles-François Lemaire de Saint-Germain, the parish priests of Saint-Sulpice and Saint-Antoine at Lavaltrie, had been arrested by the invaders, taken to Sorel, and threatened with deportation for having declared too openly their loyalty to King George III, he went to see the prisoners and in some obscure way obtained Robert's release. To his detractors this action was proof that he maintained good relations with the revolutionaries and their supporters.

In September 1776, when the Americans had gone home and Governor Sir Guy CARLETON was restoring order in the province, La Valinière was severely reprimanded by Montgolfier. The superior reproached him with having compromised the Sulpicians' honour, insisting that he deserved to be laid under an interdict and indeed sent back to France. La Valinière was not impressed: to be called a *Bostonnais* did not distress him in the least. First he declared to Bishop Briand that he had "done as much for the king's service as any priest in the province." He had often preached obedience to the king, although each time there had been disapproving murmurs from his congregation; he had warned the governor of the movements of Walker and his supporters; he had urged his own servant to enlist in the royal garrison; he had refused the sacraments to those supporting the rebels. On the other hand he had restrained royalist passions when hostilities had ended, in order to avert pillage and acts of vengeance. Hence his nickname *Bostonnais*. To his colleague Gabriel-Jean Brassier*, the bursar of the Sulpician seminary in Montreal, he specifically stated that his contact with pro-American parishioners had come in the course of his pastoral duties. It was part of a priest's calling, he added, "to love the sheep of his flock, no matter how errant they may be, as long as he sees a prospect of retrieving them." Montgolfier, Briand, and Carleton did not believe in his innocence, however. La Valinière went to Quebec to see Briand and tried in vain to refute the slanders that were being spread about him. The bishop offered him the choice of returning to France, retiring to the Sulpician seminary in Montreal, or becoming a parish priest in the Quebec district. La Valinière chose the last option. When he delayed going to his new charge of Saint-Roch-des-Aulnaies, Briand warned him that he would lose all his powers as a priest if he were not there by the end of January 1777 and told him "not to seek to justify himself or cause any scandal."

However, a petition was already being circulated at L'Assomption. It soon reached Bishop Briand, bearing the signatures of 575 men who claimed they were joined by their wives, their children, and people from the neighbouring parishes. They had constantly witnessed La Valinière's devotion to the king and to his ministry, and they considered it harmful that the bishop and the governor had been deceived "by two or three black sheep who never listened to their pastor's voice." They recalled his patience in instructing all his parishioners, although in so doing he acquired as many enemies as he won over people led astray by the rebels. La Valinière had merely preached charity to all and so had led some people to heap countless insults upon him. They were sorry to see these people succeed in their plan to oust the parish priest. Bishop Briand admitted that the content of the petition had greatly reduced the impact of the false statements about the priest's loyalty to the king that had been circulating. Addressing the parishioners of L'Assomption, the bishop declared: "What causes me to remove him from your parish is not what you allege; M. de La Valinière knows that. The reason informing my action is simply his own good, his interest, and the affection I have for him." The bishop had, moreover, conveyed the tenor of the petition to the governor in order to clear the patriotic priest in his eyes, and the two men were happy to have the proof of his innocence. Nevertheless, La Valinière changed parishes in January 1777, although in the mean time he had considered joining his Sulpician colleagues at the seminary in Montreal instead; Bishop Briand adhered to his priest's first choice and proceeded with the appointment already made. The real reason for his departure remained unstated, but it may have been simply to separate him from pro-American Canadians. Three months after arriving in the parish of Saint-Roch-des-Aulnaies the priest apologized to his bishop for still not having preached in favour of obeying the king. He thought the parishioners had already adopted that disposition towards the sovereign. Bishop Briand assured him that he should not be distressed at not having insisted on that point since his arrival. "I do not think anyone is malicious enough to blame you for that."

But the Franco-American alliance of February 1778 kindled patriotic sentiments in many Canadians of French birth, and this reaction heightened the distrust of the French felt by the new governor, Frederick HALDIMAND. La Valinière became parish priest of Sainte-Anne (at La Pocatière) in September 1778. His recent past, possibly new verbal outbursts on his part, and the need for a scapegoat seem to have prompted the governor's decision to deport him to England in 1779. He had ten days to get ready. Haldimand urged the bishop to advise La Valinière "not to indulge in his usual petulance, to be careful about the manner in

which he conducts himself and speaks until he leaves." He described the priest to the secretary of state for the American Colonies, Lord George Germain, as "a rebel in his heart, . . . fiery, factious and turbulent"; this punishment, he said, would serve as a lesson to his fellow religious, who would consequently become "more careful and circumspect." In 1780 La Valinière left England for France where, the following year, he presented the Comte de Vergennes, minister of Foreign Affairs, with a plan for insurrection in the province of Quebec, or at least for its recapture by France. The signing of the Treaty of Versailles in 1783 destroyed all this inveterate patriot's hopes.

Although he had left the Society of Saint-Sulpice in 1779 upon being expelled from the British colonies and had been refused hospitality by the Sulpicians in Paris when he came from England in 1780, La Valinière managed to stay for five years with the Sulpicians in Nantes, part of the diocese from which he had come. The contacts thus renewed with his deepest roots were not, however, enough to hold him. At the age of 53 he again left for the province of Quebec. But Lieutenant Governor Henry Hamilton*, with the assent of Bishop Louis-Philippe Mariauchau* d'Esgly of Quebec, forbad him to reside there, and the great traveller went to the United States. He first carried on his ministry among the Canadians, French, and Acadians in New York City. In June 1786 he became a missionary at Kaskaskia (Ill.), in the Mississippi valley. During his three years' apostolate in that region La Valinière quarrelled with his parishioners and with the priests in the neighbouring parishes, Paul de Saint-Pierre and Pierre GIBAULT. In 1790 he was named parish priest at Split Rock, N.Y.

That year La Valinière published in New York a controversial catechism, *Curious and interesting dialogue between Mr. Goodwish and Dr. Breviloq* . . . , in both French and English. Two years later he brought out at Albany a 50-page fascicle entitled *Vraie histoire, ou simple précis des infortunes, pour ne pas dire, des persécutions qu'a souffert & souffre encore le révérend Pierre Huet de La Valinière. . . .* In this publication, as indeed in the first one, the author portrays himself as a martyr to the American cause at the time of the invasion of Canada in 1775–76.

On the pastoral side there was again dissension between La Valinière and his parishioners; his church and presbytery were even burned down. He had to leave New York in 1792. He was able, however, to return to Lower Canada; Lieutenant Governor Alured Clarke* did not object to his return, the international situation having changed greatly in view of the French revolution. La Valinière's rights as a British subject were finally restored in 1798. But on the ecclesiastical side he was denied any clerical office. He lived in poverty first at Saint-Sulpice, then at Repentigny.

Hughes

Having succeeded in borrowing money from a member of the parish of Saint-Sulpice, he bought a piece of land at L'Assomption. In 1802 he even took steps through solicitor general Louis-Charles Foucher* to have his innocence at the time of the American invasion publicly acknowledged. Having finally retired to Saint-Sulpice, the wandering priest was buried there; he had died after falling from a carriage on a return journey from L'Assomption. He was 74.

Pierre Huet de La Valinière no doubt gives the impression of having been "a restless spirit . . . capable of causing his colleagues a great deal of trouble," as Bishop Hubert* of Quebec had described him in 1788 to Bishop John Carroll, the official responsible for missions in the United States. Bishop d'Esgly called him the "wandering Jew of Canada" and thought him discontented and turbulent. Perhaps less a man of ideas and principles than an unstable and difficult person, he seems to have been incapable of hiding his political preferences, even in public. As a result, during the war between the British and the Americans, when Governor Haldimand was bent on exercising his authority to the full, La Valinière suffered the painful consequences of his patriotic leanings and rash temperament. For this reason, his pastoral work has been left in obscurity, even though it may have been as valuable as that of many other priests. By failing to develop to a larger extent close ties with his parishioners or with fellow Sulpicians – indeed by provoking conflicts without truly realizing what he was doing – Huet de La Valinière isolated himself and lived as an outsider all his life.

LUCIEN LEMIEUX

Pierre Huet de La Valinière is the author of *Curious and interesting dialogue between Mr. Goodwish and Dr. Breviloq, French and English, where every body may find easily the arms for defending his religion and may clear it of all false assertions made against it* (New York, 1790), which was also published in French, and of *Vraie histoire, ou simple précis des infortunes, pour ne pas dire, des persécutions qu'a souffert & souffre encore le révérend Pierre Huet de La Valinière . . .* (Albany, N.Y., 1792). The archives of the Mass. Hist. Soc. holds La Valinière's "Simple et vrai récit de la conduite du rév.^{d} P. de La Valinière depuis son arrivée aux Illinois le 20 juin 1786," a copy of which is at the PAC.

AAQ, 60 CN, I: 26. AD, Loire-Atlantique (Nantes), État civil, Varades, 10 janv. 1732. Arch. de la chancellerie de l'archevêché de Montréal, 355.114, 776-1, -2, 777-1, -3, -4; 901.005, 777-1; 901.115, 776-1. Arch. de la chancellerie de l'évêché de La Pocatière (La Pocatière, Qué.), Saint-Roch-des-Aulnaies, I, 12: 9, 18 mai 1777. Arch. du ministère des Affaires étrangères (Paris), Mémoires et doc., Angleterre, 47: 203–86 (copies at PAC). ASQ, Fonds Viger-Verreau, Sér.O, 0144: 31–38. ASSM, 14, Dossier 18. AUM, P 58, U, La Valinière à Foucher, 2 mai, 17, 27 juin, 7 nov. 1802. Bibliothèque nationale (Paris), 2008 (copies at PAC). PAC, MG 11, [CO 42] Q, 16-2: 689–91. PRO, CO 42/24.

Allaire, *Dictionnaire*, 1: 316. Caron, "Inv. de la corr. de Mgr Briand," ANQ *Rapport*, 1929–30: 121; "Inv. de la corr. de Mgr Hubert et de Mgr Bailly de Messein," 1930–31: 205, 265–66, 279, 314; "Inv. de la corr. de Mgr Mariaucheau d'Esgly," 1930–31: 189. Desrosiers, "Corr. de cinq vicaires généraux," ANQ *Rapport*, 1947–48: 85–86, 91, 97–98, 119. Gauthier, *Sulpitiana*, 218. Louis Bertrand, *Bibliothèque sulpicienne, ou histoire littéraire de la Compagnie de Saint-Sulpice* (3v., Paris, 1900), 2. Lanctot, *Le Canada et la Révolution américaine*, 138. Laval Laurent, *Québec et l'Église aux États-Unis sous Mgr Briand et Mgr Plessis* (Montréal, 1945), 51–53. Christian Roy, *Histoire de L'Assomption* (L'Assomption, Qué., 1967). T. F. Cleary, "Huet de La Valinière," *Mid-America* (Chicago), 15 (1932–33): 213–28. Gustave Lanctot, "Un sulpicien récalcitrant: l'abbé Huet de La Valinière," SCHÉC *Rapport*, no.3 (1935–36): 25–39. Henri Têtu, "L'abbé Pierre Huet de La Valinière, 1732–1794," *BRH*, 10 (1904): 129–44, 161–75.

HUGHES, Sir RICHARD, naval officer, office holder, and colonial administrator; b. *c.* 1729, probably in Deptford (London), England, eldest son of Richard Hughes of the Royal Navy and Joanne Collyer; m. Jane Sloane, and they had three sons (all of whom predeceased him) and two daughters; d. 5 Jan. 1812 in East Bergholt, England.

Richard Hughes entered the Portsmouth Naval Academy in 1739 and three years later joined the *Feversham*, commanded by his father. On 2 April 1745 he was promoted lieutenant of the *Stirling Castle*. In 1752 he went to the West Indies on the *Advice*. While there he lost the sight in his left eye when he accidentally pierced it with a table fork in trying to kill a cockroach. During the next 25 years he served in various places, including the East Indies and the Mediterranean.

In 1778 Hughes was appointed resident commissioner of the Halifax dockyard; on 12 March of the same year he became lieutenant governor of Nova Scotia, succeeding Mariot Arbuthnot*, but he was not sworn into office until 17 August. When he was replaced as lieutenant governor on 31 July 1781 by Sir Andrew Snape Hamond he returned to Europe. On 23 Sept. 1780 he had succeeded his father as second baronet; the honour had been conferred upon the senior Hughes in 1773 on the occasion of George III's visit to Portsmouth, where he was commissioner of the dockyard.

During his period as lieutenant governor, Hughes's chief concern, as Arbuthnot's had been, was the protection of the province. Halifax was an important port and supply depot for the British forces in North America, and constant rumours of a French attack kept Hughes and the military commanders, among them Francis McLean*, on the alert. The strengthening of the defences was naturally of considerable importance, and as a result of pressure from the home government Hughes persuaded the House of Assembly in 1779 to raise £5,000 for provincial defence by a series of new taxes. The depredations of American privateers [see Simeon PERKINS] forced him to maintain a small armed vessel to prevent their attacks on settlements and trading vessels. He also had blockhouses constructed at various points along the coast, and in 1779 he unsuccessfully applied for permission to equip two small vessels to protect the Canso fishery. Hughes supported the efforts of Michael Francklin*, superintendent of Indian affairs, to obtain supplies for the Micmacs and Malecites, and he ratified the treaty with the Indians concluded on 24 Sept. 1778 at Menagouèche (Saint John, N.B.) [see Nicholas Akomápis*]. Peace with the Indians enabled Hughes to carry out his favourite project of obtaining cargoes of masts from the Saint John River for the use of the Royal Navy [see William Davidson*].

Wartime brought other problems. In the winter of 1780–81 the Halifax grand jury and Court of Quarter Sessions protested against the navy's impressment of seamen from Lunenburg, Liverpool, and Chester who had brought provisions and fuel to Halifax, and requested the lieutenant governor's intervention. Hughes issued a proclamation on 22 Jan. 1781 reminding all that "impressing Men for the Kings Service, without permission of the Civil Authorities, is contrary to, and an Outrageous breach of Law." This requirement caused trouble for Hughes some years later when he returned to Halifax as naval commander-in-chief. In July 1790 he applied to Lieutenant Governor John Parr* and the Council for permission to impress 70 men to replace deserters and discharged sailors. Their refusal forced him to undertake a recruiting campaign, whose expenses Henry DUNCAN, the naval commissioner, refused to pay and for which he was criticized by the Admiralty.

After his return to Europe in 1781, Hughes commanded a division in Lord Howe's fleet at the relief of Gibraltar the following year, and at the conclusion of peace in 1783 he became commander-in-chief in the West Indies. One of his captains was Horatio Nelson, who drew his admiral's attention to the fact that he did not have the legal power to suspend the navigation acts to allow trade with the United States, as Hughes had been persuaded to do by some merchants, and who also refused on legal grounds to obey the naval commissioner at Antigua whom Hughes had appointed. Nelson criticized Hughes for not living in "the style of a British admiral . . . he does not give himself that weight that I think an English admiral ought to do."

On 10 April 1789 Hughes was appointed naval commander-in-chief for eastern British North America, but his flagship, Adamant, did not arrive in Halifax until August. At the time the navy had a particular responsibility for the enforcement of the navigation acts and the prevention of smuggling, and

it was also expected to stop American ships from encroaching on the fishing grounds. Hughes's squadron consisted of four to six ships, and in summer he cruised with some of them to St John's (Prince Edward) Island, the St Lawrence, and Quebec, while the rest patrolled the fishing grounds. Because large warships ran the risk of being wrecked if they chased smugglers close to shore, Hughes obtained permission to buy three or four small vessels of shallow draught for this purpose. He was also allowed to send these schooners to Boston or New York to collect the mail from the royal packets in the winter, when they did not call at Halifax. He hoped thus to establish a winter mail service, since while he had been lieutenant governor he had become fully aware of "the great Interruption given to the Public Correspondence with this Station during the Winter Months." However, his hope was disappointed when one schooner was driven by storms to the West Indies and another was caught in ice off Nantucket Island, Mass., for eight weeks.

While in Nova Scotia, Hughes was promoted vice-admiral of the blue on 21 Sept. 1790. On 13 April 1792 he was ordered by the Admiralty "to Strike [his] Flag," and his squadron reached Spithead on 18 May. Though he saw no more active service, he continued to be promoted, reaching his highest rank, admiral of the red, on 9 Nov. 1805.

PHYLLIS R. BLAKELEY

PANS, RG 1, 45, docs.58–101; 346, doc.83. PRO, ADM 1/492; CO 217/54: ff.89–243; 217/55: ff.1–190. Gentleman's Magazine, January–June 1812: 91. F.-J. Audet, "Governors, lieutenant-governors, and administrators of Nova Scotia, 1604–1932" (typescript, n.d., copy at PANS), 179–81. Burke's peerage (1921), 1190. DNB. Brebner, Neutral Yankees (1969). W. L. Clowes, The Royal Navy; a history from the earliest times to the present (7v., London, 1897–1903). Murdoch, Hist. of N.S., vol.2: 591–619.

HUGUET, dit LATOUR, PIERRE, wig maker, silversmith, and merchant; b. 24 Jan. 1749 at Quebec, son of Claude Huguet, merchant, and Charlotte La Motte; d. 17 June 1817 in Montreal, Lower Canada.

Nothing is known of the early life at Quebec of Pierre Huguet, dit Latour. Nor is it known when he moved to Montreal. There on 26 Feb. 1770 he married Charlotte Desève, widow of Jean Leheup, dit Latulippe. Huguet was identified as a wig maker one month later in the inventory of property owned jointly by Desève and her first husband. Pierre and Charlotte soon had two sons, Pierre, baptized in September 1771, and Louis, baptized in May 1773; Huguet's younger brother, Louis-Alexandre, a silversmith, was godfather to the second. Pierre was a witness at his brother's marriage in January 1776, as was Louis-

Huguet

Alexandre's friend Dominique Rousseau*, another silversmith. "Latour wig maker" and "Latour silversmith" were among those who purchased objects at a sale of the estate of François Simonnet* in December 1778. Two years later a relative, Marie-Anne Chaboillez, widow of Pierre Parent, transferred her stone house on Rue Notre-Dame to Huguet in return for board, lodging, and a lifetime annuity. He lived and had his shop and store on these premises until a few months before his death.

In 1781 Huguet entered the silver trade; on 17 September, still describing himself as a wig maker, he signed a one-year contract with Simon Beaugrand, a 21-year-old silversmith, who was to make as many ear-rings as possible for Huguet. Huguet agreed to supply the silver, and Beaugrand was to pay 600 *livres* per annum for his board and lodging. For each 100 pairs of ear-rings, Beaugrand was to be paid "four *piastres* worth five shillings each." Two days earlier another contract had been prepared for the master silversmith François Larsonneur, but it was not signed until October; Larsonneur had learned his craft between 1775 and 1780 at Quebec with Joseph Lucas, himself a former apprentice, like Louis-Alexandre Huguet, of Joseph Schindler*. Larsonneur agreed to make 800 pairs of ear-rings per month for one year; he was to be paid £48, "of which he will receive two Portuguese [gold coins]" at the end of each month. Huguet was to supply board, lodging, and the silver.

On 21 Aug. 1785 Huguet, now described as a silversmith, engaged as an apprentice for four years Michel Létourneau, who promised to learn the craft from Huguet "or his deputies"; henceforth Huguet would always be identified as a silversmith. After the death of his first wife in June 1787, he married Josette Valois on 16 Nov. 1788. The inventory of his workshop, compiled in January 1788 by the silversmiths Narsise ROY and Pierre Foureur, *dit* Champagne, included tools valued at 918 *livres*; domestic silver, such as bowls, jugs, goblets, sugar-tongs, various spoons, forks, and ladles, valued at 422 *livres*; trade silver, mainly ear ornaments, pins, bracelets, crosses, and brooches, valued at 857 *livres*; Indian silverware estimated at 448 *livres*; and bulk silver to a value of 113 *livres*. The inventory also included elaborate personal belongings, indicative of a sophisticated style of life. It is likely, judging from Huguet's will of 1812, that in 1788 his son Pierre at the age of 17 began to work as a silversmith in the shop. Huguet was also busy with other matters at around this time; in December 1786 he had bought land in the *faubourg* Saint-Antoine, and in 1790–91 he was occupied with an inheritance from Josette's mother and with a bequest left to his step-daughter, Marguerite Leheup, *dit* Latulippe.

On 10 Oct. 1791 Huguet engaged Augustin Lagrave as apprentice for seven years, and in March 1795 he hired Faustin Gigon for a similar term. The first records of repairs by Huguet to religious silver of the church of Notre-Dame date from this period. In 1795 he was involved in having a second storey added to his house on Rue Notre-Dame. Not pleased by the progress of the work, he protested against his contractors, stating that his family and business would suffer from the delays; moreover, taking care of the shop behind his house had become difficult because he had had to rent lodgings at a distance.

As well as repairing silver, Huguet had been making trinkets for the fur trade. Between 1797 and 1801 the North West Company spent £4,184 3*s*. 5*d*. on silver ornaments, and of this amount £3,068 8*s*. 9*d*. was paid to Huguet. The McGill brothers, JAMES and Andrew, were also among his clients. In March 1797 Huguet cancelled the apprenticeship of Augustin Lagrave, and replaced him in September with François Blache, about 16 years old, whom he engaged to age 21. Huguet also engaged Salomon Marion* as apprentice in July 1798 for a term of five years. On 6 June 1799 Huguet was among several silversmiths, including Charles Duval*, John Oakes*, Jean-Henry Lerche, and Christian Grothé, at the sale of the estate of the silversmith Louis-Alexandre Picard*, held at the home of another silversmith, Michel Roy; Huguet bought several tools for £68 8*s*. The following year he sold Indian silver to his neighbour, the merchant Joseph Borrel, for 1,219 *livres*. In April 1802 he engaged 18-year-old Paul Morand* as apprentice until he reached age 21. The previous year Huguet had been a witness to the marriage of his niece, Magdeleine Huguet, to the silversmith Jean-Baptiste Dupéré.

That Huguet's business was increasing is confirmed by an inventory, made in 1802 after the death of his second wife, of the property that they owned jointly. Total assets were valued at 56,674 *livres*, including 30,525 *livres* in cash. Tools, valued by the silversmiths Narsise Roy and Nathan Starns, were now worth 2,272 *livres*. Huguet's shop included linens appraised at 862 *livres*, domestic silver worth 738 *livres*, and trade silver valued at 1,284 *livres*. Three surviving children from this marriage were placed under Huguet's care: Louis-Maximilien-Théodore, 12, Agathe-Henriette, 6, and Scholastique, 5. In the same year, Huguet's son Louis, who had renounced his plans to become a priest to go into business, married Claire Trudeau, one of whose friends was the silversmith Joseph Normandeau.

In 1803 Huguet decided to move his store into a new building to be constructed behind his house. Of stone, two storeys high, and equipped with a forge, it was to cost 3,180 *livres*. That Huguet began at this time to make, rather than repair, religious silver is confirmed by payments received from various churches; they date from 1803 and continue until his death.

From this period on, Huguet also bought, rented, and sold several properties, administered estates, and made loans. He was identified as a "bourgeois" for the first time in 1805. On 24 Oct. 1809 he married Marie-Louise Dalciat, widow of Claude-Joseph Petit-Claire, a watchmaker. This third marriage provided for the separation of property, a rare arrangement in Canadian society at that time. Most of Huguet's business contracts were handled by his son Louis, commissioned notary in 1804, and by Huguet's friend the notary Jean-Baptiste Desève.

In 1810 Huguet took his last known apprentice, Alexander Fraser, aged 15 years; his term was to last until he reached 21. In the same year a much more important contract was settled with Salomon Marion, whose apprenticeship ended in 1803 and who now had his own shop. Marion agreed to work one year "exclusively" for Huguet, making several religious items. Huguet controlled the market in Montreal; as a matter of fact, neither Marion nor Morand, another ex-apprentice, was able to develop a clientele until after Huguet's death. The contract with Marion shows that the identification PH was less the mark of a craftsman than a commercial label put on objects sold by Huguet but manufactured by apprentices or contract workers. This fact is important to remember in any study of Huguet's styles, especially of religious silver, in which Marion and Morand specialized.

In his will, Huguet bequeathed to his son Pierre all the tools and movables in his store as well as the use of the house and property on Rue Notre-Dame, "wanting to repay and recognize the good services rendered to him by his son for 24 years." In 1813 Huguet named Pierre his executor in place of the painter Louis Dulongpré*. Huguet was also generous to his daughter Agathe-Henriette when in 1816 she married Duncan Cameron McDonell. By this date the silversmith seems to have retired; he was then living in the *faubourg* Saint-Antoine. At his death in 1817 Huguet's affairs were in order and his bequests clear. He had always been a keen businessman and a good judge of people, qualities that made him one of the leading silversmiths at the turn of the century. The younger Pierre, identified in contracts as "bourgeois," managed his father's properties until his own death on 11 Sept. 1828.

Huguet's career as a silversmith is fascinating in many respects. It followed a simple but logical development, reflecting the evolution of the market. His production was originally oriented exclusively towards trade silver, but by 1788 he was also producing domestic silver. He entered the religious silver market by repairing religious vessels as early as 1794, and it was only in 1803 that he produced silver articles for the church. That he attained a certain predominance in his field is indicated by the agreement of 1810 with Marion and confirmed by his acquaintance with almost every silversmith in Montreal, as well as by the inability of his apprentices Marion and Morand to enter the market until after his death. He certainly was among the richest in his craft, but it is difficult to consider him as a craftsman; his activity was more that of a bourgeois, who hired apprentices and masters to work for him while he looked after marketing and administration. His closest competitor in the city, Robert CRUICKSHANK, employed fewer silversmiths. Thus, one should not be surprised that objects bearing Huguet's mark have less aesthetic unity than those of François RANVOYZÉ, Laurent Amiot*, Cruickshank, or Marion; Huguet's aim for his work was not that it be decorative but rather lucrative.

ROBERT DEROME and NORMA MORGAN

[It would be interesting to study the division of work in Huguet's shop in terms of the social classes to which silversmiths belonged and to determine Huguet's own position in the Montreal market. Further research might also reveal the specific roles played by his brother Louis-Alexandre and his son Pierre. We disagree, however, with Ross Fox that Louis-Alexandre "directed Pierre's workshop until his dismissal sometime before 1792"; no document supports such a hypothesis and all the information on relationships which has been located in original sources has been given in this article. R.D. and N.M.]

ANQ-M, CE1-51, 26 févr. 1770; 1er sept. 1771; 26 mai 1773; 22, 30 janv. 1776; 30 juin 1783; 7 janv. 1784; 5 juin 1787; 6 sept. 1795; 12 oct. 1801; 5 nov. 1804; 24 oct. 1809; 19 juin, 20 oct. 1817; CN1-16, 4 juill. 1802, 11 oct. 1809, 20 mars 1810, 2 mars 1813; CN1-74, 16 janv. 1788; 24 juill. 1792; 27, 28 sept. 1802; 14 juill. 1812; CN1-121, 21 janv. 1776; 16 déc. 1778; 2 nov. 1796; 12 déc. 1816; 15 mars, 21 mai, 17 juin, 5, 15 juill. 1817; CN1-126, 21 avril 1813; CN1-128, 21 août 1785; 11 déc. 1786; 30 août, 7 sept., 13 nov. 1790; 1er avril 1791; 21 janv., 30 mars, 23, 24 sept. 1795; 23 mars 1796; 6 mars, 1er mai, 25 sept. 1797; 23 juill. 1798; 20 sept. 1800; 28 avril 1802; 20 déc. 1803; 20 nov. 1804; CN1-158, 15 sept. 1780; 15, 17 sept. 1781; CN1-185, 3 Feb., 23 March 1808; 10 July 1811; CN1-194, 16 févr. 1805; CN1-243, 13 oct. 1804; 4, 6 avril 1807; 31 janv., 26 déc. 1809; 13 févr., 14 juin 1810; 13 avril 1811; 29 janv. 1812; 7 juill. 1813; 8, 26 janv., 19 juill., 17 oct., 29 nov., 20 déc. 1814; 3 oct. 1815; 20 févr. 1816; 7 févr. 1817; 7 juin 1819; 4, 8 févr. 1820; 15 févr. 1821; 18 mars, 10 avril 1822; 8 févr., 12 mars 1823; 8 févr. 1825; 4 mars 1826; CN1-269, 6 juin 1799; CN1-372, 27 mars 1770; CN1-375, 16 nov. 1788. ANQ-Q, CE1-1, 24 janv. 1749, 10 août 1754; CN1-25, 20 avril 1775; CN1-189, 20, 22 déc. 1766. MAC-CD, Fonds Morisset, 2, H894.5/L888.9; H294.5/P622/1.

Quebec almanac, 1806: 53. Robert Derome, "Delezenne, les orfèvres, l'orfèvrerie, 1740–1790" (thèse de MA, univ. de Montréal, 1974). Langdon, *Canadian silversmiths*, 19. Gérard Morisset, *Coup d'œil sur les arts; Évolution d'une*

Humphreys

pièce d'argenterie (Québec, 1943), 20–21. R.A.C. Fox, *Quebec and related silver at the Detroit Institute of Arts* (Detroit, 1978), 82–83. Traquair, *Old silver of Quebec*. É.-Z. Massicotte, "L'argentier Huguet-Latour," *BRH*, 46 (1940): 287. Gérard Morisset, "Un perruquier-orfèvre," *La Patrie*, 2 juill. 1950: 28–29, 31.

HUMPHREYS, JAMES, printer, publisher, merchant, and politician; b. 15 Jan. 1748/49 in Philadelphia, Pa, son of James Humphreys and Susanna Assheton; m. Mary Yorke, probably of Philadelphia; d. there 2 Feb. 1810.

In 1763 James Humphreys entered the College of Philadelphia (University of Pennsylvania) to begin the study of medicine. Soon disenchanted, he left the college before receiving his degree and was apprenticed by his father to William Bradford, a well-known Philadelphia printer who remained a strong supporter of the British crown until the passage of the Stamp Act of 1765. Under Bradford, Humphreys learned the printing trade and possibly some of his loyalist political philosophy. By 1770 his apprenticeship was completed, and two years later he established his own business.

Humphreys's first recorded imprint, a pamphlet for the Society of the Sons of St George, appeared in 1772. The following year he produced a Greek grammar for the College of Philadelphia, probably the first book of its kind printed in the Thirteen Colonies. In the 1770s his establishment issued at least 80 separate items. Among those printed before the revolution were a few novels, a five-volume edition of the collected works of Laurence Sterne, an occasional almanac, and a number of pamphlets on politics, religion, and agriculture. He also began publication in 1775 of a newspaper, the *Pennsylvania Ledger: or the Virginia, Maryland, Pennsylvania, & New Jersey Weekly Advertiser*. Although the *Ledger* claimed to be "Free and Impartial," Humphreys stated several years later that he had become unpopular amongst Philadelphia rebels because of his paper's commitment to the British cause.

Refusing to renounce his allegiance to Britain after the outbreak of revolution in 1775, Humphreys was frequently denounced as a traitor by the local committee of correspondence. His loyalism also made him a convenient target for Benjamin Towne, a rival newspaper publisher who proved extremely adroit at using anti-tory sentiment to drive his competitors out of business. In mid November 1776 Towne published a letter, purportedly from Humphreys but probably written by Towne himself, in which "all friends of arbitrary government" were urged to come to the assistance of the British forces. Shortly afterwards Humphreys, fearing reprisals for his loyalist sympathies, abandoned the *Ledger* and fled from Philadelphia into the countryside. It was not until the fall of 1777, when Philadelphia was occupied by British troops, that he returned to the city and resumed publication of his newspaper.

During the British military occupation of Philadelphia, Humphreys received the major share of government printing: about 50 broadsides, mainly proclamations on army and naval matters or notices of benefit concerts for war widows, appeared under his imprint. When the British troops evacuated Philadelphia in June 1778, Humphreys accompanied them to New York, where he established himself as a merchant and, in partnership with Valentine Nutter, printed Richard Brinsley Butler Sheridan's *The duenna*. At the end of the war he went to England to present a petition to the loyalist claims commission, a petition that was supported by testimonials from Joseph Galloway, one of Pennsylvania's most prominent loyalists, and William Franklin, the last royal governor of New Jersey. Eventually, after he had moved to the new loyalist settlement of Shelburne, N.S., Humphreys was awarded the substantial sum of £800, two-thirds of the amount he had claimed, in compensation for his losses.

Humphreys arrived in Shelburne some time in late 1784 or early 1785 and immediately resumed his career as printer and merchant. In May 1785 he launched his four-page weekly, the *Nova-Scotia Packet: and General Advertiser*, the third newspaper in the town. Unlike its competitors, James ROBERTSON's *Royal American Gazette* and the *Port-Roseway Gazetteer; and, the Shelburne Advertiser*, Humphreys's paper concentrated almost entirely on news, notices, and advertisements of local interest. As Shelburne's population dwindled, the *Nova-Scotia Packet* was issued in a smaller format and less frequently; by 1790 it seems to have suspended publication. In the years that followed Humphreys continued his mercantile activities, selling such miscellaneous items as farm and household goods, books, and spirits. He also served as a justice of the peace, and from 1793 to 1796 he was a member of the House of Assembly.

Discouraged by prospects in Nova Scotia in general and by French privateering attacks in particular, Humphreys returned to Philadelphia some time between June 1796 and April 1797. After a brief attempt in 1798 to publish another newspaper, the *Weekly Price Current*, he concentrated on book-printing, assisted by several of his sons and daughters, who continued the business for two years after his death in 1810. Described by a contemporary as "a good and accurate printer, and a worthy citizen," he was buried in the cemetery of Christ Church, Philadelphia.

GERTRUDE TRATT

Christ Church in Philadelphia (Philadelphia), Reg. of burials, 4 Feb. 1810. PRO, AO 12/38: 101; 12/95; 12/100: 149; 12/109 (mfm. at PAC). *Royal commission on American loyalists* (Coke and Egerton). *DAB*. *Directory of N.S. MLAs*. Charles Evans *et al.*, *American bibliography* . . . (14v., Chicago and Worcester, Mass., 1903–59; repr. New York and Worcester, 1941–59; repr. New York, 1941–67), 4–5. C. K. Shipton and J. E. Mooney, *National index of American imprints through 1800* . . . (2v., Worcester, 1969), 1. G. E. N. Tratt, *A survey and listing of Nova Scotia newspapers, 1752–1957, with particular reference to the period before 1867* (Halifax, 1979). Tremaine, *Biblio. of Canadian imprints*. D. C. McMurtrie, *The royalist printers at Shelburne, Nova Scotia* (Chicago, 1933). J. P. Edwards, "The Shelburne that was and is not," *Dalhousie Rev.*, 2 (1922–23): 179–97. W. O. Raymond, "The founding of Shelburne; Benjamin Marston at Halifax, Shelburne and Miramichi," N.B. Hist. Soc., *Coll.*, 3 (1907–14), no.8: 212, map facing 228. J. J. Stewart, "Early journalism in Nova Scotia," N.S. Hist. Soc., *Coll.*, 6 (1888): 91–122. D. L. Teeter, "Benjamin Towne: the precarious career of a persistent printer," *Pa. Magazine of Hist. and Biog.* (Philadelphia), 89 (1965): 316–30.

HUNTER, PETER (baptized **Patrick**), army officer and colonial administrator; baptized 11 July 1746 in Longforgan, Scotland, son of John Hunter of Knap and Euphemia Jack; d. 21 Aug. 1805 at Quebec, Lower Canada.

Peter Hunter belonged to a family of landed gentry in Perthshire. In January 1767 he purchased an ensign's commission in the 2nd battalion of the 1st Foot. He was promoted lieutenant in 1770, served in Minorca from 1771 to 1775, and had become a captain when the regiment returned to England. Commissioned major in 1779 in the 92nd Foot, he went with it to the West Indies the following year. By the end of 1781 he had transferred to the 1st battalion of the 60th. In November 1782 he was promoted to the army rank of lieutenant-colonel (he received the regimental rank in 1787).

Hunter's unit was posted to Halifax, N.S., in 1786 and the next year he assumed command of the 4th battalion. Early in 1788 he became commander of the western posts of Quebec, with his headquarters at Fort Niagara (near Youngstown, N.Y.). Responding to the still prevalent effects of a partial famine in 1787, he authorized immediate distribution of provisions from the commissary without waiting for orders from Quebec. Within a few years rumours were circulating that the men in charge of the distribution, Robert HAMILTON and John Butler*, had profited by his charity. The military efficiency Hunter displayed at this time, as well as the local suspicion aroused, were to be characteristic of his future administration in Upper Canada.

In 1789 Hunter went to England on leave. Despite the request of Lord Dorchester [Guy CARLETON] for

his return to Quebec, that October he was appointed temporary superintendent of the settlement which became known as British Honduras (Belize). This post, which he would hold until March 1791, was to give him his only experience of civil government before he went to Upper Canada. He handled problems in an authoritarian manner, which the complex situation in Honduras perhaps required and with which its elected magistrates complied; Upper Canada was to provide a different context for governing. After his return to England, Hunter obtained the army rank of colonel in 1793; he then served as a general officer on the Continent in 1794–95 and in the Caribbean in 1795–96. Following the Irish rebellion of 1798, he became military governor of County Wexford, where he pursued a moderate policy.

On 10 April 1799 Hunter was appointed lieutenant governor of Upper Canada, succeeding SIMCOE, and commander of the forces in the two Canadas with the local rank of lieutenant-general. He arrived at Quebec on 13 June. His civil responsibilities – and those of his counterpart in Lower Canada, Robert Shore Milnes* – were almost immediately increased. The governor-in-chief, Robert PRESCOTT, sailed for home on 29 July and thereafter took no part in government, although he retained his office until 1807. In August 1800 Hunter's military superior, the Duke of Kent [EDWARD AUGUSTUS], also returned to England, leaving Hunter with sole responsibility for the troops in the Canadas. He was promoted full lieutenant-general in April 1802 and, in June 1804, was made colonel of the 9th Foot.

The military situation was, in fact, Hunter's first concern. In August–September he had made a brief visit to Upper Canada, but had then returned to Quebec to devote his attention to military affairs. His assessment of his command was to remain unaltered over the next six years. He argued that the regular troops at his disposal – 1,528 in Lower Canada and only 696 in Upper Canada – were insufficient in number even for peace-time needs. Moreover, the provincial unit, the Royal Canadian Volunteer Regiment, was under strength and Hunter saw little hope of rectifying the situation. The quality of the troops was also a matter of concern, with poor discipline and desertions plaguing both British and local units. Hunter's protests against the state of his command were, however, partly formal in nature: he himself recognized that the main theatre of operations during the Napoleonic Wars was elsewhere. Although his civil administration was occasionally troubled by rumours of revolutionary conspiracies, he was to report no serious threats to the Canadas.

Hunter's early dispatches from Upper Canada reflected his superiors' expectation that he could

Hunter

manage his unwieldy appointments. The express purpose of his visit in 1799 had been to set up a means of carrying on government during his necessary absences. The visit confirmed assumptions that his presence would be required only while the legislature was in session and that a standing committee of the Executive Council could handle the administration while he was elsewhere. Hunter's proposal for a committee had the approval of the Home secretary, the Duke of Portland. The former administrator, Peter RUSSELL, and judge William Dummer Powell* would have preferred the more usual procedure of appointing an administrator; Hunter, however, informed the Executive Council in 1799 that he must have sole authority to govern the province "upon the principles which his own judgement suggests and for which alone he can consent to be responsible." He instructed the committee to correspond with him and empowered it to conduct routine business during his absence.

The committee consisted of Russell, Æneas SHAW, and John ELMSLEY, who was replaced in 1802 by Henry ALLCOCK. The three original members had the authority to call in a fourth (they usually turned to John McGill*) if one of them were going to be absent. McGill became a regular member in 1802 and Attorney General Thomas Scott* joined later. Although he had no formal place in the government, Hunter's secretary, James Green*, was involved in much of its operation and acted as a liaison with the council when the lieutenant governor was in York (Toronto) and with the committee when he was away. Hunter's favoured advisers, and the ones whose careers he tried hardest to promote, were those willing to devote long hours to administrative problems: Allcock, who became more influential than Elmsley even before the latter left for Lower Canada; McGill, whose competence increasingly won Hunter's respect; and Scott.

From 1800 until 1802 Hunter's practice was to attend the spring meeting of parliament in York and then to return to Quebec, where, occasional visits to the upper province aside, he spent the rest of the year. In the winter of 1802–3 he began to spend more time in Upper Canada. Thereafter he met the legislature between January and March, and remained in the province for the greater part of the year. The reasons for Hunter's new schedule lay in York rather than in Quebec and went beyond his publicly stated desire to accommodate members of the legislature who preferred a winter to a spring meeting. His private correspondence of February 1802 mentions two problems which likely led to this change. In the first place, he learned from Scott that internal conflicts had developed within the executive. Secondly, a public agitation over certain aspects of land policy had been initiated by discontented individuals, in particular Joseph-Geneviève Puisaye*, Comte de Puisaye, and

Joseph Brant [THAYENDANEGEA]. The latter concern was especially pressing; opposition of this sort was new to the province and the change in Hunter's schedule was a tacit acknowledgement that administration could no longer be left, for the most part, to others.

Hunter's subsequent career in Upper Canada has received harsh treatment from historians. Often the lieutenant governor has been judged by the criticisms his administration engendered. He arrived in Upper Canada, however, with little experience of colonies that prized British institutions and had elected assemblies. He was something of a martinet, impatient, and used to resolving problems in a military manner. As Isaac TODD observed, "Genl Hunter is verry exact and wishes all under him to be so." But if his difficulties were in part due to temper and tactlessness – his "brutality of manners was proverbial throughout the whole army" – they were also the result of his attempt to bring order and dispatch into the machinery of government and, particularly, into the land-granting system.

Land granting was a primary function of the Executive Council. More important, the acquisition of land touched the immediate interests of all orders of society. Hunter identified two basic problems: first, the lack of systematic government policy designed to encourage the orderly settlement of the province and, secondly, the inability of government officials to carry out the work of the council in an efficient manner. Any attempt to implement reforms in an area of vital concern to society as a whole was bound to meet resistance and generate discontent. Yet Hunter pushed ahead, undeterred by the potential for discord.

His efforts to limit large speculation in land ran into immediate difficulties, partly because so many speculators had influential connections in England. Developers such as the Comte de Puisaye, the Earl of Selkirk [DOUGLAS], Richard Beasley*, and William BERCZY were a constant source of trouble. On the other hand, the successful settlements associated with Thomas Talbot* and Alexander McDonell* had their origins during Hunter's administration. At another level, Hunter tried to avoid opening new townships until those already established were filled. The policy was not unreasonable but it was frustrated by a general reluctance to settle the surveyed eastern sections of the province, which had much poorer land than the western regions. To bring a measure of efficiency to the administration of land granting he made laudable efforts to increase clerical staff and to regularize office hours and procedures. Similarly he brought to imperial attention the physical difficulties of operating the legislature out of a two-room building that doubled as a church, and the inconvenience of forcing officials to keep their papers in, and run their offices from, private homes.

In two key areas Hunter pressed his reforms forward with a determination that caused him much unpopularity and left a legacy of bitterness that came to the fore in the administrations of his successors, Alexander GRANT and Francis Gore*. Hunter loathed incompetence and laziness. Just as men such as Allcock and McGill were marked by favour for their ability and industry, officials such as William JARVIS, the provincial secretary, and John Small*, the clerk of the Executive Council, were singled out for their lack-lustre performance of their duties. Jarvis, for instance, had a backlog of land patents waiting to clear his office. The consequent delays were vexatious for settlers and led to frequent reprimands of the provincial secretary. Hunter pushed him to issue more patents. Jarvis, however, had every reason to drag his feet, since the fees he was authorized to charge did not cover his expenses and he lost money on every transaction. As part of his investigation of the land-granting system Hunter initiated a review of the existing fee structure. In 1804 a new schedule implemented a scale of higher fees for government officials to charge for their services. Yet such was Hunter's antagonism toward the provincial secretary that during discussions of the revised schedule he overrode his council's advice to compensate Jarvis for his losses, in spite of the apparent justice of his claim. Thus a reform that was intended to improve the efficiency of officials by adequately rewarding their efforts produced only antagonism in one instance.

Not only Jarvis was irritated by the new schedule. The higher fees had the unpopular effect of increasing the costs for all who applied for land. Similarly, Hunter's initiatives to control free grants (grants on which no fees were payable) touched all who had not yet taken up the land they were entitled to claim as loyalists or as military settlers. McGill, in his capacity as inspector general of public accounts (a new post established by Hunter in 1801 to parallel the inspector generalship of Lower Canada), conducted a thorough investigation into individual claims to loyalist status. As a result of his findings, between 1802 and 1804 Hunter struck more than 900 names off the list of those eligible for free grants. At the same time, he tried to impose a time-limit on the validity of all claims on the government by male loyalists (females were exempted). His proclamation of December 1802 bluntly stated that there would be no recourse for claimants who failed to appear before the commissions sitting at eight different centres across the province. For having "so grossly neglected their own Interest," they would lose legal title forever. No other issue generated such outraged protests. The parliamentary opposition associated with William WEEKES and Robert Thorpe* seized upon it after Hunter's death, and in 1806 the time-limits were removed.

There was more to Hunter's concern for efficient administration than a desire for regularity in process. According to Thorpe, who gave no source for his claim, Hunter sent almost £30,000 to England during his period as lieutenant governor. Thorpe characterized Hunter's attitude toward fees as one of "rapaciousness, to accumulate money by grants of land was all he thought of." At issue was not the number of grants issued but rather the number of patents completed. The fees of government officers, including the governor, were calculated upon the latter only. Gore, who initially defended Hunter against the charges, later considered his predecessor's actions in pushing through so many patents a "very unusual" method of collecting for himself revenue that was more properly due his successor. Gore compared Hunter's fees between 1 July 1802 and 30 June 1805 with his own fees for a three-year period. The results were interesting: Hunter had collected £4,393 whereas Gore only managed £1,870. Hunter's private agents, Lester and Morrogh [see Robert LESTER], recorded remittances totalling more than £3,400 that were made to Hunter's personal account for a 17-month period in 1804 and 1805. If this sum was typical, Hunter turned a tidy profit, though far less than Thorpe claimed for him.

Hunter's dissatisfaction with the administrative practices in Upper Canada was paralleled by a bleak assessment of colonial society as a whole. He had little hope for the colonies as a school for the professions. Just as he regretted the inexperience of provincial army officers, which in his view accounted for the ill discipline of the Canadian volunteers, so he deplored the standards of the legal profession. Although he failed in the end to carry the case with the law officers of the crown, Hunter strongly supported Allcock's arguments for establishing a court of chancery in Upper Canada. His assumption was, however, that such a court would be staffed from England: local lawyers had no experience of equity courts and some had no formal training of any sort. Again, although he worked hard in 1803 to secure money for building Anglican churches in the province, he looked only to an English clergy to minister to the colonial outpost.

Hunter's rather severe outlook was lightened by his appreciation of the colony's commercial potential. In the area of trade Hunter even used his military authority to forward the commercial policies of his civil administration. Major public works were the responsibility of the Royal Engineers and the lieutenant governor worked closely with Gother Mann*, the commanding engineer at Quebec, to improve the internal transportation network of the Canadas. Hunter gave first priority to the St Lawrence River system, which had received little attention since the first locks were built between 1779 and 1783. Although Hunter and Mann had only occasional success in gaining approval for purely military construction, they fared better when they could point to the additional benefit of possible commercial use. On his own authority Hunter approved an immediate start on essential repairs to the locks in 1801. The following year Mann began work on a new canal to be cut at Mille Roches and the Cascades (near Île des Cascades), Lower Canada, at an estimated cost of £2,583. Mann judged the various improvements made under Hunter sufficient to accommodate the larger barges operating on the St Lawrence since 1783. Ambitious Upper Canadian merchants such as Richard CARTWRIGHT hoped for more, but they were perhaps partly mollified when Hunter revived the regulations concerning river traffic that Lord Dorchester had introduced in 1795. Instead of returning empty from Upper Canada to Montreal, crown vessels were allowed to accept goods owned by private merchants at a modest cost to the shippers.

When no military justification existed to use the engineers, Hunter, particularly in 1804, urged the legislature of Upper Canada to undertake road building. He presided over the completion of the Danforth Road and the opening of the first section of road in the Talbot settlement. Although he recognized that the province could not afford substantial improvements on its own, he believed that revenues could be increased. With his support, legislation was passed establishing ports of entry and providing for collection of duty on goods entering the province from the United States [see Colin McNABB].

Hunter was particularly interested in mercantile policy. As commander-in-chief he concerned himself directly with the large purchases of provisions made by the commissariat. Provisioning the British army was already a mainstay of merchants in both Upper and Lower Canada. Hunter encouraged the commissariat to buy as much as possible from them, and under his direction the quantity of flour and peas purchased in the two provinces increased substantially. He also used the commissariat to expand and diversify the economy of Upper Canada. In 1800 merchants there began for the first time to ship wheat and flour to wholesalers in the lower province [see Joseph FORSYTH]. In a directive of 1803 Hunter tried to open a new line of trade by ordering Commissary General John CRAIGIE to buy in the upper province as much flour as possible for use in Lower Canada. The army had bought flour in Upper Canada since the 1780s, but during Hunter's administration the commissariat also purchased salt pork and fresh beef, usually through McGill in his capacity as agent for purchases.

By 1803 Hunter's superiors in Great Britain had advanced well beyond his comparatively cautious support of the provisioning trade in the Canadas. They looked to the saving in transportation costs if the Canadas could supply food for the troops throughout British North America and possibly even for those in the West Indies. Local opinion supplied Hunter with the corrective to any undue optimism. Lieutenant-General Henry Bowyer, commander of the forces in Nova Scotia, requested provisions from Hunter in Quebec rather than from his usual suppliers in the United States with poor grace and only because he was ordered to do so. He doubted that Hunter could spare anything but flour, pointed out the problems of delivery in the absence of regular shipping from Quebec to Halifax, and questioned whether, even if flour were sent, it would match the American product in quality or price. Cartwright and Hamilton, Hunter's chief advisers on questions of commerce, counselled him to hold back, citing in particular the immaturity of Upper Canada's agriculture. They welcomed the prospect of a certain market for the surplus produce of farmers but cautioned that, in the absence of such a market in the past, the province could not immediately assure supply. In fact, with respect to beef and pork, Cartwright stated bluntly that the Canadas were "at present far from being equal" to the supplying of its own demands. He concluded therefore that too much should not be attempted for fear of jeopardizing future orders by failure. Under Hunter, the commissariat gave steady support of merchants selling Canadian produce, but always with reference to supply and always with a sufficient surplus in hand to guard against disappointment.

Although Cartwright and Hamilton approved Hunter's exertions, he received little credit outside the small circle they represented. Moreover his efforts contributed to the jealousy and resentment felt by those whose careers he did not promote. Hunter championed the merchant community because he felt comfortable with the methods of businessmen and because he supported their aspirations for the province. He made no secret of whom he favoured and, after his death, McGill described him as "my much lamented Patron." Those outside this charmed circle saw with Thorpe a "Shopkeeper Aristocracy" of "scotch Pedlars" who had long "irritated & oppressed the people." The benefits to individual farmers and to small traders were in the future and could not be appreciated immediately. Hunter received no more praise in the province for his interest in fostering economic growth than he did for trying to introduce the best business methods to the administration of government offices.

Contemporary criticism of Hunter was inspired as much by his style of governing as by his policies, and the tone of the criticism has largely been taken over by historians. Certainly Hunter's autocratic manner was more suited to a regiment or even a large family business. His brusqueness was probably temperamental; however, it was no doubt exacerbated by poor health. By 1799 he was suffering from stomach ailments characterized by dysentery and biliousness.

Hutchings

In addition he was plagued by gout. He had none of the arts or graces that enable power to be used, and decisions to be made, without giving offence. With the exception of Scott and his aide-de-camp, Major William Samuel Curry, few people penetrated Hunter's stiff and unapproachable manner, let alone established an informal relationship with him. On a personal level, Hunter's black-and-white view of humanity led naturally to favouritism. Most of the men he promoted were able, but many government officials believed their own advancement had been blocked by his obvious dislike of them.

When Hunter died unexpectedly in August 1805 he left a province beset with problems. After his death the House of Assembly broke out in an uproar. According to his successor, Alexander Grant, the session of 1806 was spent "vomiting grievance and Complaints Against the Administration of General Hunter and plaguing me, and his favoureds." The loudest complaints concerned his disregard of the assembly's claim to initiate money bills. From 1803 on, Hunter had had certain expenses paid from revenues raised by the house, without its prior approval. It is probably a mark of his formidable presence that when he subsequently submitted the accounts, they were approved without protest.

How far can Hunter be held responsible for the outbreak of parliamentary opposition, usually associated with Weekes, Thorpe, and Joseph WILLCOCKS, after his death? The discontent that Thorpe uncovered on the western circuit and in the Niagara peninsula in 1806 was caused more by regional resentments and inequalities than by the governor's personality or policies. Yet, there was substance to Thorpe's claim that Hunter had treated the people of the province like soldiers, by which he meant without consideration. Loyalists, American settlers, assemblymen: many groups emerged from his term of office more conscious of themselves as distinct interest groups, and more willing to pursue and protect their interests in the realm of politics. Hunter's attempted administrative reforms were necessary. "The wonder . . . is," as Cartwright put it, "that such culpable negligence should be tolerated so long." But these initiatives went against the grain of Upper Canadian society: too many groups and too many people were affected. As a result, the province became more polarized and the potential for opposition to government increased.

IN COLLABORATION

ANQ-Q, CE1-61, 24 Aug. 1805. AO, MS 75; MU 1730. BL, Add. MSS 8075, 104: 85–87 (transcript at PAC). PAC, MG 23, GII, 10, vol.4: 1750–53; MG 24, A6, civil letterbook, 40, 98, 110, 117–19; military letterbook, 1, 38, 78, 81, 137, 291, 324 (transcripts); RG 1, E14, 13; RG 8, I (C ser.), 107: 102; 108: 26, 52, 83, 92–93, 105, 121, 127; 109: 18, 126; 223: 290; 225: 12, 16, 19, 21, 35, 40, 51–52. PRO, CO 42/324: f.311; 42/327: ff.18, 75, 77; 42/328: f.237; 42/330: f.83; 42/331: ff.8, 51, 53; 42/333: f.108; 42/334: f.21; 42/335: ff.5, 14v.; 42/336: ff.49, 106; 42/342: f.167; 42/343: ff.160, 166; 42/348: f.107; 42/350: f.301; PROB 11/1433/775.

Archives of British Honduras, ed. J. A. Burdon (London, 1931–35), 1: 23–24, 35–37, 45–46. *Gentleman's Magazine*, 1805: 971. *John Askin papers* (Quaife), 2: 231, 399, 486, 493, 506. "The journals of the Legislative Council of Upper Canada . . . ," AO *Report*, 1910: 175–78, 205. "Political state of U.C.," PAC *Report*, 1897: 57, 69. "Proclamations by governors and lieutenant-governors of Quebec and Upper Canada," AO *Report*, 1906: 199–230. "Proclamations of the governor of Lower Canada, 1792–1815," PAC *Report*, 1921: 79–80. C. A. H. Franklyn, *A genealogical history of the families of Montgomerie of Garboldisham, Hunter of Knap and Montgomerie of Fittlesworth* (Ditching, Eng., 1967). G.B., WO, *Army list*, 1767–1805. D. B. Read, *The lieutenant-governors of Upper Canada and Ontario, 1792–1899* (Toronto, 1900), 41–51. S. L. Caiger, *British Honduras, past and present* (London, 1951), 94–95. Craig, *Upper Canada*, 42–65. Narda Dobson, *A history of Belize* (London, 1973), 74, 91–92. Gates, *Land policies of U.C.*, 62–74. A. R. Gibbs, *British Honduras: an historical and descriptive account of the colony from its settlement, 1670* (London, 1883), 47. *Life and letters of Hon. Richard Cartwright* (Cartwright), 89–90, 115–16. Riddell, *Life of William Dummer Powell*, 91–93, 217. E. A. Cruikshank, "A memoir of Lieutenant-General Peter Hunter," *OH*, 30 (1934): 5–32. E. G. Firth, "The administration of Peter Russell, 1796–1799," *OH*, 48 (1956): 163–81.

HUTCHINGS, RICHARD, ship's captain and merchant; b. *c.* 1740, probably in Newfoundland, son of Robert Hutchings, a Devon planter in St John's; m. 1769 Hannah Sparke, daughter of merchant Henry Sparke, in Dartmouth, England, and they had at least two sons; d. there 1808.

Although Richard Hutchings began life with nothing but the advantage of a father who was known to the merchants of St John's, he reached maturity in England at a time when the fishery was expanding and any lad of ambition could hope to find useful employment. He eschewed direct involvement in the fishery by going to sea in trading ships, and in 1760 was appointed commander of the *Mary and Ann*, a sack ship of Dartmouth. His vessel was taken by a French privateer on the way to Newfoundland in 1761, but he ransomed her for £750 and for the next ten years led an uneventful life as a ship's master. In 1766 he became commander of the *Prince of Brunswick* sack ship owned by the firm of Henry and Robert Sparke of Dartmouth. What little time he had ashore he spent in Dartmouth, where he attracted the approbation of Henry Sparke and, more to the point, the affection of Sparke's daughter.

Henry Sparke's trade was growing rapidly and in 1771 Hutchings was appointed his agent in St John's. He lived there every summer and for several winters

443

until 1782, and as one of the few resident merchants took an important place in the primitive society. He dutifully signed petitions complaining about the custom-house [see Richard ROUTH], competition from New England merchants, and the pernicious effects of Palliser's Act (which enforced the payment of wages to fishermen and their return to Britain each year), but he was appointed to no office. He was a prominent supporter of the Church of England in St John's – one of a desperately small band in those irreligious times. He was also the first surveyor of roads (unpaid and unofficial) in Newfoundland.

Hutchings's retirement to Dartmouth in 1782 was occasioned by the death of his father-in-law two years earlier. Sparke had sons of his own but they betrayed neither aptitude nor interest in the business, and Hutchings probably returned to Dartmouth in order to manage the main concern. Under his hands it flourished: by 1785 the firm of Sparke, Hutchings, and Sparke owned six vessels and was one of six firms that more or less monopolized the importation of bread and flour into Newfoundland.

In 1786 circumstances changed abruptly when the Sparke heirs decided to terminate the partnership. This event resulted in a heavy withdrawal of capital, and forced Hutchings to look for new premises with which to carry on his trade in Newfoundland. He chose the harbour of Cape Broyle, south of St John's on the so-called Southern Shore, lightly inhabited at this time but an excellent place for operating bank ships. It was not a good decision. The Southern Shore was already heavily populated with merchants and the economic possibilities of the area were not great. Even in Cape Broyle another firm, that of Henry Sweetland and Company, was already established. Hutchings and the other merchants fought tooth and nail for the trade of the resident planters of the region, and in 1787 he embroiled himself in a legal dispute concerning the debts owed him by a planter. The local magistrate, who was also a merchant, found against him. Hutchings then appealed to Captain Edward Pellew, the naval surrogate, who also found against him. In 1788 Hutchings appealed Pellew's decision to the Court of Quarter Sessions in Devon and won on the grounds that the surrogate had no authority to hear the case. This judgement, which exposed the fact that practically none of the courts of law in Newfoundland were legally constituted, brought about the collapse of the system of civil justice in 1789 and led to the establishment of regular courts under the aegis of John Reeves* [see also Aaron GRAHAM; Mark MILBANKE].

With the termination of this case, Hutchings returned to the shadows as just another merchant. His trade, although not large, was sufficient to provide a decent living and in 1789 he decided to give up the annual voyages to Newfoundland, appointing one of his ship's captains to act as agent for him. By now his two sons were approaching manhood and Hutchings made what, from his point of view, may have been an unfortunate decision concerning their education. He sent both of them to Portugal, where they learned much about the commission trade and the importation of fish, training which hardly fitted them for the rude life of an outport merchant. The elder son Charles reluctantly went to Newfoundland in 1799 only to be taken prisoner when returning to England in January 1800. He soon returned from captivity and settled in Cape Broyle, but his brother, Henry, never took any part in the business. By 1805 the firm was trapped in a small outport with no possibility for expansion. Richard Hutchings now owned only two vessels, and when he died in 1808 the great promise of the 1780s was gone. Charles continued the business, but in 1810 he too retired to Dartmouth to live off the residue of his fortune and the business was left to a succession of agents. In 1829 the premises at Cape Broyle were sold.

K. MATTHEWS

Devon Record Office (Exeter, Eng.), 2992A; 2993A. Dorset Record Office, D365/F2–F10. Hunt, Roope & Co. (London), Robert Newman & Co., journals and letterbooks (mfm. at PANL). PANL, GN 1/13/4; GN 2/1; GN 5/1/B, Harbour Grace records; GN 5/1/C/1, Ferryland records; GN 5/2/A/1; GN 5/4/A. PRO, ADM 1/471–76; 7/154–55; 7/363–400; 68/89–219; BT 1; BT 5; BT 6/187; 6/189–91; BT 98/3–17; CO 194; 324/7; IR 26/140/121; T 64/82. *Lloyd's List. St. James's Chronicle or the British Evening Post* (London). *Trewman's Exeter Flying Post, or Plymouth and Cornish Advertiser* (Exeter). *Reg. of shipping.*

I

INGLIS, CHARLES, Church of England clergyman, bishop, and author; b. 1734 in Glencolumbkille (Republic of Ireland), third son of the Reverend Archibald Inglis; m. first February 1764 Mary Vining of Salem County, N.J.; m. secondly 31 May 1773 Margaret Crooke of Ulster County, N.Y., and they had four children; d. 24 Feb. 1816 in Aylesford, N.S.

Raised in a clerical family of Scottish descent, Charles Inglis was educated privately, his father's early death depriving him of the opportunity to attend university. He emigrated to the American colonies before his 21st birthday, reputedly as a redemptioner, the means by which the poorer sort of emigrant in the 18th century commonly secured the expensive trans-atlantic passage. After he had taught for three years at a Church of England school in Lancaster, Pa, Inglis obtained the required testimonials to enable him to be admitted to holy orders in England. Ordained deacon and priest by the bishop of Rochester on 24 Dec. 1758, the young cleric returned to America as missionary to Dover, Del., where he served for six years. Early in 1766 he left the employment of the Society for the Propagation of the Gospel to accept appointment as one of the curates at Trinity Church, New York, though, fortunately for his later career, he remained in close touch with the Anglican missionary society. In New York the aspiring curate became involved in the unsuccessful campaign for the creation of colonial bishoprics and promoted the cause of missionary work amongst the Iroquois, a cause that received a considerable boost when John STUART was appointed SPG missionary at Fort Hunter. He also furthered his deficient classical education by taking advantage of the cultural opportunities which an urban centre provided.

During the years of deteriorating relations between Britain and the Thirteen Colonies, Inglis, like many of his loyalist contemporaries, came to the conclusion that excessive colonial liberty was the root cause of Anglo-American problems. He also began to feel that the weakness of the colonial church, which was surrounded on all sides by disloyal dissenters, was the direct result of the imperial government's failure to model American society on its English counterpart. His tory views, articulated in such discourses as the *Letters of Papinian* and *The true interest of America impartially stated*, exposed him to patriot hostility until the British occupation of New York in September 1776. That turn of events, combined with his succession to the rectorship of Trinity Church after the death of Samuel Auchmuty in 1777, won for him influence, safety, and a number of lucrative military chaplaincies behind military lines.

For Inglis, the end of the war coincided with tragic personal events: the death of his elder son and of his second wife. At the same time, the evacuation of New York in November 1783 forced him to resign his rectorship and return to England, where he spent the next three years jockeying with fellow refugees for pensions and preferments. Although he was unable to find the comfortable living in the United Kingdom for which he yearned, he did secure, with the patronage of Lord Dorchester [Guy CARLETON], appointment in 1787 as first bishop of Nova Scotia, a position he held until his death. His diocese included not only the colony of Nova Scotia but also Newfoundland, St John's (Prince Edward) Island, the old province of

Quebec, and Bermuda. In 1793 this vast sphere of jurisdiction was narrowed with the appointment of Jacob Mountain* as bishop of the new see of Quebec, a diocese that embraced both Upper and Lower Canada.

Inglis entered upon his new duties amidst considerable opposition from the local clergy. Not only were they unused to hierarchical interference, but they were also angry that they had been denied a voice in the selection of their bishop. Furthermore, they were antagonistic towards Inglis because of his lack of formal education and his wartime career in New York, a career that in their view smacked of personal opportunism. Inglis also found Lieutenant Governor John Parr*, who was jealous of his gubernatorial authority, reluctant to share the local leadership of the established church. Even the SPG, long accustomed to exercising a remote but decisive influence over church administration at the mission level, initially became involved in jurisdictional clashes with Inglis. Eventually Inglis's patience, tact, and appeals to the archbishop of Canterbury resolved his differences with the SPG; Parr's death in 1791 removed another source of friction, and the appointment of an amenable fellow loyalist, John WENTWORTH, heralded a more harmonious era which Inglis's erastian outlook helped to maintain.

In the case of the clergy, Inglis knew that the loyalists among them (comprising with their clerical sons one-half of the clergy in the Maritime portion of his diocese during the course of his episcopate) would prove difficult to manage. Many of them had been raised as dissenters in New England, their attitudes shaped as much by colonial traditions as by loyalist politics. For this reason they could rejoice in the creation of a colonial episcopate at the same time as they applauded its strictly circumscribed nature. It suited them well that the bishop had no patronage with respect to livings, no financial control over stipends, no cathedral, dean, and chapter to support his dignity, and no temporal powers or jurisdiction over the laity. Inglis, for his part, had neither the desire nor the authority to treat his clergy as subordinates. He was, however, determined to command at least token respect. One of the methods he employed was an essential component of English diocesan supervision: the triennial visitation. Conducted as plenary sessions, these visitations were initially resented by some of the missionaries, but Inglis countered their opposition by making attendance at the meetings compulsory. He was relatively successful in the results and continued to hold regular but separate visitations for the clergy of Nova Scotia and New Brunswick until his health deteriorated in 1812.

Yet, if Inglis was determined to uphold his episcopal authority, he also attempted to maintain harmonious relations with his clergy. To this end, he used the triennial visitations to consult with the clergy, not to dictate to them; his approach at these meetings mirrored a desire to follow a course of brotherly love and to appear as no more pre-eminent than a first among equals. He also pursued a policy of minimal interference in the day-to-day affairs of individual churches. On only one occasion did he take severe disciplinary action against a member of his clergy. In 1790 he was forced to dismiss the Reverend John Eagleson* of Cumberland County for drunkenness and incompetence. Astutely, he conducted the inquiry with the assistance of two of his clergy, Thomas Shreve and William Twining, a procedure that produced the appearance of a concerted decision by the church's spiritual leaders. Inglis subsequently claimed that this episcopal act was his "most painful undertaking," and he never again resorted to such an extreme course despite the misconduct and ineffectiveness of several of his clergy.

Inglis's unwillingness to exert close personal supervision over the affairs of his diocese had the advantage of winning the support of independent-minded clergymen. Yet one aspect of his policy of non-interference – the infrequency of his confirmation tours – proved extremely damaging to the Anglican cause. It is debatable whether this failure to visit the diocese's churches was a deliberate strategy designed to further amicable relations, or rather a convenient shunning of a responsibility that was made doubly tiresome by primitive conditions of travel. Whatever the case, Inglis managed only one trip to St John's Island, in 1789 on his way to the Canadian portion of his diocese. Disputes in Sydney between the Reverend Ranna Cossit and the civil authorities forced Inglis to travel to Cape Breton in 1805, but he never troubled to visit Guysborough or Yarmouth at the opposite ends of the Nova Scotia peninsula, let alone tour distant Newfoundland. His other official tours were few, hardly an effective approach for one who saw himself essentially as a pioneer in church affairs. Nor did his sedentary habits provide much of an inspiration to a numerically weak denomination.

Although Inglis showed little interest in the concerns of individual churches, he did have a plan for the development of the church as a whole. One of his chief aims was to persuade the British and local governments to increase their financial assistance to the established church. As it turned out, he was forced to rely on the British government for most of the church's funds, since local congregations and the colonial legislatures were reluctant to assume a greater share of financial responsibility. Nevertheless, he obtained enough financial aid from parliament, the SPG, and the colonial government to raise clerical stipends and to build or complete the modest wooden churches of the diocese.

Another part of Inglis's plan was to provide the church with a larger corps of clergymen, and he therefore devoted himself to nurturing an educational institution for the benefit of the Anglican élite. Aware that the church's future welfare depended on a stronger framework at the parish level, Inglis believed the primary aim of his college should be to produce well-trained native clergy. But the composition of the statutes of King's College, opened at Windsor as a grammar school in 1788 and chartered as a university in 1802, was entrusted in 1803 not just to the bishop but to two of the church's secular leaders, Alexander Croke* and Sampson Salter Blowers*, mere pettifogging lawyers, Inglis thought, who were out to vitiate his plans for a clerical seminary. Inglis strongly supported a statute requiring all applicants to the new institution to subscribe to the Anglican articles of religion, but he feared that other statutes did not go far enough towards consigning the care of the college to the bishop and ensuring the predominance of clergymen on the staff. A few years later, in 1806, he eagerly embraced the change made by the archbishop of Canterbury whereby non-Anglican matriculants would be allowed to study at King's but would be denied their degrees until they subscribed to the Thirty-Nine Articles. Thus from the first he promoted a college that was as contemptuous of dissenters as the Oxbridge model he naturally admired. There was no reason to expect any other policy from a tory churchman, politicized by the American revolution, confirmed in his predilections by the French revolution, and dedicated to the concept of an established church.

Inglis had withdrawn into semi-retirement in 1795, moving from the provincial capital of Halifax to Windsor, and the following year he settled on his country estate near Aylesford. One critic of this move suggested that Inglis feared a French attack; Inglis himself claimed that the sea air adversely affected his health and that the valley was a more central location for his diocesan residence. As a gentleman farmer he pursued an enthusiasm for agriculture, his lands being admired for their fine orchards and progressive tenantry. During his Aylesford years effective control of the bishopric passed from the reticent, unambitious father to the precocious, aggressive son, John*, whom Inglis groomed as his successor and appointed his secretary and ecclesiastical commissary for Nova Scotia in 1802. It was largely out of concern for the future career of his son that Inglis was attracted back to Halifax in 1808 by an increase in salary and appointment to the Council. Subsequently, he participated only sporadically in the affairs of state until he suffered a stroke in 1812 which left him largely incapacitated for the last few years of his life. Although he failed to secure the immediate episcopal succession for his son, he left him a wealthy man. His bequests to John and two daughters included the Aylesford estate and over 12,000 acres of land in the Annapolis valley.

A bewigged prelate, slender of build and dapper in attire, Inglis enjoyed books and rural pastimes, particularly when surrounded by his small but closely knit family. This leisurely style of life reflected his reluctance to become involved in local political squabbles which paled into insignificance when compared either with the heady ferment of the American revolution or with the momentous events on the continent of Europe. The years of his episcopacy formed an anti-climax to a controversial career. His failure to become more active in the concerns of both church and community may have been extremely judicious in the circumstances, but it also reflected his satisfaction at drawing a handsome salary in return for minimal exertion and as a reward for past rather than present services to the British empire.

Inglis's character and career have been distorted by hagiography. Much of the historical praise is based on his distinction as the first colonial bishop of the Church of England, a landmark, admittedly, but hardly an adequate ground on which to assess his reputation. The other enthusiasms of Inglis's post-humous partisans have been more fundamentally misleading. Most damaging to historical inquiry has been their refusal to recognize that the bishop's views on education were as illiberal as those of the staunchest churchmen in his diocese. Another of their failings has been their uncritical interpretation of Inglis's record as bishop. In picturing him as an energetic, hard-working administrator, Inglis's champions have missed the underlying personal objective of his episcopate: a tranquil, comfortable retirement to compensate for his steadfast loyalty. By the same token they have misinterpreted his approach to official duties. Far from displaying the energy and zeal with which he has been credited, he studied to be quiet, to maintain a discreet presence, and to confine himself as much as possible to the less controversial concerns of his denomination. True, it was as a result of his moderate churchmanship and guarded approach that the Church of England emerged from these years without deep divisions. But Inglis's additional success in maintaining relatively good relations between the Church of England and rival denominations should not be attributed to any astute appreciation on his part of the inescapable realities of religious pluralism. It should rather be seen as a reflection of the fact that at this early stage in the social development of Nova Scotia, the leaders of non-Anglican churches were not as sophisticated, articulate, and sensitive to the inequities of church establishment as they were shortly to become.

JUDITH FINGARD

[Charles Inglis's publications include *The true interest of America impartially stated, in certain stictures on a pamphlet intitled "Common sense"; by an American* (Philadelphia, 1776); *The letters of Papinian: in which the conduct, present state and prospects, of the American Congress are examined* (New York, 1779); *Remarks on a late pamphlet entitled "A vindication of Governor Parr and his Council" . . . by a consistent loyalist* (London, 1784); *Dr. Inglis's defence of his character, against certain false and malicious charges contained in a pamphlet, intitled, "A reply to remarks on a vindication of Gov. Parr and his Council" . . .* (London, 1784); *A sermon preached before his excellency the lieutenant governor, his majesty's Council, and the House of Assembly, of the province of Nova-Scotia, in St. Paul's Church at Halifax, on Sunday, November 25, 1787* (Halifax, 1787); *A charge delivered to the clergy of the diocese of Nova Scotia, at the primary visitation holden in the town of Halifax, in the month of June 1788* (Halifax, 1789); *A charge delivered to the clergy of the province of Quebec, at the primary visitation holden in the city of Quebec, in the month of August 1789* (Halifax, [1789]); *A charge delivered to the clergy of Nova Scotia, at the triennial visitation holden in the town of Halifax, in the month of June 1791* (Halifax, [1792]); *Steadfastness in religion and loyalty; recommended, in a sermon preached before the legislature of his majesty's province of Nova-Scotia; in the parish church of St. Paul, at Halifax, on Sunday, April 7, 1793* (Halifax, 1793); *A sermon preached in the parish church of St. Paul at Halifax, on Friday, April 25, 1794: being the day appointed by proclamation for a general fast and humiliation in his majesty's province of Nova-Scotia* (Halifax, 1794); *The claim and answer with the subsequent proceedings, in the case of the Right Reverend Charles Inglis, against the United States; under the sixth article of the treaty of amity, commerce and navigation, between his Britannic majesty and the United States of America* (Philadelphia, 1799); *A sermon on confirmation: preached in St. John's Church, Cornwallis, on Sunday, September 13, 1801* (Halifax, 1801); and *A charge delivered to the clergy of the diocese of Nova-Scotia, at the triennial visitation holden in the months of June and August, 1803* (Halifax, 1804).

Several of his letters were published in "The first bishop of Nova Scotia: chap.IV, the first colonial episcopate," ed. W. S. Perry, *Church Rev.* (New Haven, Conn.), 50 (July–December 1887): 343–60. His papers, and those of his son John, remain in the hands of his descendants. Microfilm and transcript copies are available in PANS, MG 1, 479–82 (transcripts); Biog., Charles Inglis, letters, journals, and letterbooks (mfm.); and John Inglis, letters (mfm.). J.F.]

Halifax County Court of Probate (Halifax), I1 (will and estate papers of Charles Inglis) (mfm. at PANS). Lambeth Palace Library (London), Manners-Sutton papers; Moore papers; SPG papers, X: 189–92, 232; XI: 37–41, 45–48, 53–55, 57–58, 68–70, 77–111. PRO, CO 217/56–98. Protestant Episcopal Church in the U.S.A., Arch. and Hist. Coll. – Episcopal Church (Austin, Tex.), Samuel Peters papers, in the custody of the Hist. Soc. of the Episcopal Church (Austin). QDA, 72 (C-1), docs.9, 16, 21, 77; 75 (C-4), docs.76, 91. Univ. of King's College Library (Halifax), Univ. of King's College, Board of Governors, letterbook of the secretary, 1803–18; minutes and proc., 1 (1787–1814), 2 (1815–35); corr. relating to King's College, 1789–1889; statutes, rules, and ordinances of the University of King's College at Windsor in the province of Nova Scotia, 1803, 1807. USPG, Journal of SPG, 23–31; B, 2; X, 142–48.

T. B. Akins, *A brief account of the origin, endowment and*

Iredell

progress of the University of King's College, Windsor, Nova Scotia (Halifax, 1865). [John Inglis], Memoranda respecting King's College, at Windsor, in Nova Scotia; by one of the alumni (Halifax, 1836). DAB. Carl Bridenbaugh, Mitre and sceptre: transatlantic faith, ideas, personalities, and politics, 1689–1775 (New York, 1962). Susan Buggey, "Churchmen and dissenters: religious toleration in Nova Scotia, 1758–1835" (MA thesis, Dalhousie Univ., Halifax, 1981). R. M. Calhoon, The loyalists in revolutionary America, 1760–1781 (New York, 1973). Philip Carrington, The Anglican Church in Canada; a history (Toronto, 1963). S. D. Clark, Church and sect in Canada (Toronto, 1948). Hans Cnattingius, Bishops and societies: a study of Anglican colonial and missionary expansion, 1698–1850 (London, 1952). A. L. Cross, The Anglican episcopate and the American colonies (New York, 1902). A. W. [H.] Eaton, The Church of England in Nova Scotia and the tory clergy of the revolution (New York, 1891). Judith Fingard, Anglican design in loyalist N.S.; "The Church of England in British North America, 1787–1825" (PHD thesis, Univ. of London, 1970). V. T. Harlow, The founding of the second British empire, 1763–1793 (2v., London and New York, 1964), 2: 735–42. R. V. Harris, Charles Inglis: missionary, loyalist, bishop (1734–1816) (Toronto, 1937). H. Y. Hind, The University of King's College, Windsor, Nova Scotia, 1790–1890 (New York, 1890). G. H. Lee, An historical sketch of the first fifty years of the Church of England in the province of New Brunswick (1783–1833) (Saint John, N.B., 1880). J. W. Lydekker, The life and letters of Charles Inglis: his ministry in America and consecration as first colonial bishop, from 1759 to 1787 (London and New York, 1936). W. H. Nelson, The American tory (Oxford, 1961). M. B. Norton, The British-Americans: the loyalist exiles in England, 1774–1789 (Boston and Toronto, 1972). W. S. Perry, A missionary apostle; a sermon preached in Westminster Abbey, Friday, August 12, 1887, on the occasion of the centenary of the consecration of Charles Inglis, first bishop of Nova Scotia . . . (London, 1887). H. C. Stuart, The Church of England in Canada, 1759–1793, from the conquest to the establishment of the see of Quebec (Montreal, 1893). J. [E.] Tulloch, "Conservative opinion in Nova Scotia during an age of revolution, 1789–1815" (MA thesis, Dalhousie Univ., 1972). C. W. Vernon, Bicentenary sketches and early days of the church of Nova Scotia (Halifax, 1910); The old church in the new dominion; the story of the Anglican church in Canada (London, [1929]). [F. W.] Vroom, "Charles Inglis," Leaders of the Canadian church, ed. W. B. Heeney (3 ser., Toronto, 1918–43), ser.1: 1–33; King's College: a chronicle, 1789–1939; collections and recollections ([Halifax, 1941]).

J. M. Bumsted, "Church and state in maritime Canada, 1749–1807," CHA Hist. papers, 1967: 41–58. Judith Fingard, "Charles Inglis and his 'Primitive Bishoprick' in Nova Scotia," CHR, 49 (1968): 247–66. R. S. Rayson, "Charles Inglis, a chapter in beginnings," Queen's Quarterly (Kingston, Ont.), 33 (1925–26): 163–77. C. M. Serson, "Charles Inglis, first bishop of Nova Scotia," American Church Monthly (New York), 42 (1937–38): 215–28, 264–78. F. W. Vroom, "Charles Inglis: an appreciation," N.S. Hist. Soc., Coll., 22 (1933): 25–42. S. F. Wise, "Sermon literature and Canadian intellectual history," United Church of Canada, Committee on Arch., Bull. (Toronto), 18 (1965): 3–18.

IREDELL, ABRAHAM, surveyor and office holder; b. 29 June 1751 in Philadelphia County, Pa, third child of Robert Iredell and Hannah Luckens; m. Hester (Hetty) Marsh; d. without issue April or May 1806 in Chatham, Upper Canada.

Prior to the American revolution Abraham Iredell lived near Philadelphia. He owned more than 1,000 acres of land in Northumberland and Westmoreland counties, and was employed as a deputy surveyor in Northampton and Northumberland counties under the authority of Surveyor General John Lukens, who was probably a relative. Although of Quaker parentage, Abraham and at least one brother took an active part against the rebels after the outbreak of the war. Abraham joined the army in 1777, and both brothers eventually became lieutenants: Abraham in the Guides and Pioneers, and his brother in the Company of Armed Boatmen. The brother was killed in the taking of the Toms River blockhouse in New Jersey. Abraham, one of three members of the Iredell family who were subsequently attainted of high treason by the state of Pennsylvania, was taken prisoner at the time of the British evacuation of Philadelphia in June 1778 but was exchanged a few months later. Nothing is known of his activities during the remaining years of the conflict.

Iredell seems to have taken leave of his wife, Hetty, in late 1783, possibly to go to Britain, but he planned to return to the United States the following spring. Some time later, apparently in 1784, he and his wife immigrated to New Brunswick, settling in Saint John. Here he was commissioned a deputy surveyor under George SPROULE, surveyor general of the province, and received a grant of land along the Kennebecasis River.

By the spring of 1793 Iredell had removed to Newark (Niagara-on-the-Lake), Upper Canada, and that June he was sworn in as a deputy to Surveyor General David William Smith*. Iredell's first duty as a surveyor in Upper Canada was the completion in 1793 of the survey of Hope Township in Durham County. In June 1795, after surveying William BERCZY's grant just north of York (Toronto), he moved to Detroit to succeed Patrick McNIFF as deputy surveyor of the Western District. Within the next few years he conducted surveys throughout Kent County; the more notable were those of the town plots of Sandwich (Windsor) and Chatham, the latter being the projected site of an important naval arsenal, and a tract of land at the forks of the Thames River which Lieutenant Governor SIMCOE had chosen as the location for the capital of Upper Canada. Side by side with his accomplishments, however, were the difficulties he created by adjusting the boundaries of lots which he believed had been illegally enlarged. Confronted by an avalanche of protests from settlers in the region, Smith ordered all boundaries left as they were. Nevertheless, the confusion produced by Iredell's actions lasted until the l830s, when commissioners were appointed to arbitrate boundary disputes.

With the relinquishment of control over Detroit by the British in the summer of 1796, the Iredells temporarily settled along the left bank of the Detroit River, but in December 1797 they removed to the town plot of Chatham. Nothing ever came of plans to build a naval arsenal in Chatham, and for many years Iredell and his wife were the town's only legal residents. In 1798 they built a log house near the Thames River, on the southeast corner of Water and William streets, and soon afterwards they planted one of the first apple orchards in Kent County.

In 1800 Iredell, William Harffy, and François Baby* were appointed commissioners for administering the oath of allegiance to persons claiming land in the Western District. That same year Iredell and Walter ROE actively supported William JARVIS, Prideaux SELBY, and Matthew ELLIOTT as possible representatives for the riding of Essex in the House of Assembly. Iredell was also the returning officer for the riding of Kent in the elections of 1800 and 1804, his house in Chatham serving as the polling station. Commissioned a justice of the peace for the Western District in 1796, he continued in this office until his death.

There is a possibility that Iredell's life, like that of his one-time contemporary in the Western District, William ROBERTSON, was shortened by an excessive consumption of alcohol. He died in possession of more than 2,000 acres of land scattered about the province, goods and chattels valued at roughly £390, and a legacy left by his late father.

DANIEL J. BROCK

AO, RG 1, A-I-1, 31, 42; A-I-2; CB-1, Malden Township; RG 22, ser.6-2, Essex County, will of Abraham Iredell. "Abraham Iredell," comp. L. V. Rorke, Assoc. of Ont. Land Surveyors, *Annual report* (Toronto), 1935: 96–103. *John Askin papers* (Quaife). "Petitions for grants of land" (Cruikshank), *OH*, 24: 81–82. "United Empire Loyalists: enquiry into losses and services," AO *Report*, 1904: 200–1, 221–22. F. C. Hamil, *The valley of the lower Thames, 1640 to 1850* (Toronto, 1951; repr. Toronto and Buffalo, N.Y., 1973).

IRUMBERRY DE SALABERRY, ÉDOUARD-ALPHONSE D', military engineer; b. 20 June 1792 in Beauport, Lower Canada, son of Ignace-Michel-Louis-Antoine d'Irumberry* de Salaberry and Françoise-Catherine Hertel de Saint-François; d. unmarried 6 April 1812 at Badajoz, Spain.

Édouard-Alphonse d'Irumberry de Salaberry came from a prominent military and seigneurial family. His father, a seigneur, soldier, and man of letters who was favoured with colonial and imperial patronage, had established good connections with the élite of both linguistic groups in the colony, as well as with certain great English and French families. He would be criticized for his conspicuous desire to place his children in good jobs or good marriages; but their way of life necessarily depended on seigneurial revenues and above all on patronage and careers in the British empire.

Even at birth Salaberry was fortunate: he was baptized by Bishop Charles-François Bailly* de Messein on 2 July 1792 in the presence of his godfather, Prince EDWARD AUGUSTUS, and his godmother, Thérèse-Bernardine Mongenet*, known as Mme de Saint-Laurent, the prince's mistress, an event that did not fail to create a small scandal. On 16 July 1806 the young Salaberry, then 14 years of age, embarked for England on the *Champion*.

Salaberry did not find himself without companions when he arrived. He met with his three brothers, Maurice-Roch, François-Louis, and Charles-Michel*, who often stayed at the prince's London residence, sat in his personal box at concerts, benefited from his sponsorship, and gave ear to his counsel, all of which led them to venerate their benefactor. The prince and Mme de Saint-Laurent treated Édouard-Alphonse as if he were their own son. They underwrote his fees for a private tutor and then paid £100 a year for him to attend the Royal Military Academy at Woolwich (London). They provided him with new clothing, took him in for holidays, and gave him pocket money and presents such as money, a watch, and a gold chain, thus incurring a total expenditure of several hundreds of pounds sterling each year. In addition, at their table and at receptions and the theatre, Salaberry was in the company of many of the leading figures of the day, including the Duc d'Orléans and his brothers, the former lieutenant governor of Lower Canada, Sir Robert Shore Milnes*, and his family, Major-General Frederick Augustus Wetherall*, the Prince of Wales, and various Spanish and English generals and admirals.

Salaberry repaid his benefactors by applying himself to his studies, in which he did well, and by demonstrating to them his unfailing thanks. He gave evidence of a keen sense of duty as well as artlessness, humour, and warm-heartedness, in short an appealing blend of qualities complementing his physical transformation into a young man described as tall, strong, and charming. Towards the end of 1809 he took five or six months training in surveying before he began his service as a military engineer. His education in a Protestant institution does not seem to have caused insurmountable problems.

The Napoleonic Wars took Salaberry to Spain, and during the night of 6 April 1812 he was struck down by a musket ball while participating in the assault on

Isham

Badajoz with a division of light troops of the British army. The previous day he had had a premonition that great danger lay ahead for him. Lieutenant-Colonel Richard Fletcher, Salaberry's commander, expressed the feelings of those who knew him: "He was universally esteemed by his brothers in arms, and all mourn his death." It was a tragic end for the most gifted, in intellect and character, of the Salaberry sons. Only Charles-Michel survived to perpetuate the name of this great family. Maurice-Roch had died in India in 1809; his inconsolable parents had considered having François-Louis return home but he too died in India in 1811.

JEAN-PIERRE WALLOT

AAQ, 210 A, VI: ff.20–37. ANQ-Q, CE1-5, 2 juill. 1792; P-289, 1; P1000-55-1053; P1000-93-1905. *Quebec Gazette*, 1809–12. Le Jeune, *Dictionnaire*, 2: 608–10. Jean Langevin, *Notes sur les archives de Notre-Dame de Beauport* (Québec, 1860). P.-G. Roy, *La famille d'Irumberry de Salaberry* (Lévis, Qué., 1905). Sulte, *Hist. des Canadiens-français*, 8: 16–17. Henri Têtu, "Le duc de Kent parrain," *BRH*, 9 (1903): 347–50.

ISHAM, CHARLES THOMAS (known in youth as **Charles Price** or **Charles Price Isham**), fur trader; b. 1754 or 1755 probably at York Factory (Man.), son of HBC chief factor James Isham* and an Indian woman; d. 1814 in England.

As heir to the estate of his father, who had apparently given him the name of Price to honour a friend at York, Charles Isham was allowed to travel to England for his education, a privilege rarely granted in the 18th century to the Hudson Bay children of traders. In May 1763 the London committee of the Hudson's Bay Company asked its officers at York to "send Home Charles Price alias Isham an Indian Lad said to be the Natural Son of Mr. Jas. Isham Deceased," and in September Ferdinand Jacobs* noted, "We have sent home . . . Charles price Isham with his apparrell." That November the committee, still hesitant over the boy's surname, directed that "Charles Price . . . Servant to Mr James Isham deced, be delivered to the said Mr. Isham's Brother and Administrator Mr. Thomas Isham." On 7 May 1766 the company "Entertained Charles Price Isham, as an Apprentice . . . at York Fort, for 7 years." He first served under Andrew GRAHAM at Severn House (Fort Severn, Ont.), along with William Tomison*. In 1772 his superiors at York wrote to London, "Charles Price Isham submits himself to Your Determination a Strong Good working sober Lad." By August 1773 he had "Contracted for five years at 10£ a Year" as a labourer.

Isham's inland career began in 1774 when he "offered his service in settling Basqueawe [The Pas, Man.]" to Samuel Hearne*. That July he and Isaac Batt* left York with supplies for Hearne, who had found a site for an inland post on Pine Island Lake (Cumberland Lake, Sask.). When Matthew Cocking* and his men, also voyaging inland, came upon them, they discovered that Isham and Batt had been robbed and stranded by their Indian guides. All joined forces, but through lack of Indian aid they failed to reach Hearne, not seeing him until they reached York in mid 1775 after a "winter of futile wandering."

In 1775–76 Isham served under Cocking at Cumberland House. Plagued by a shortage of boats for inland transport, Cocking sent Isham and Robert LONGMOOR off with some Indians to build canoes. Six were constructed for the HBC, "but as Natives were the builders, and had not been fully paid for them," independent traders from Canada persuaded the Indians to sell them all but two. Isham's account of these events to Humphrey Marten* at York the next summer led Marten to instruct Tomison, the new master at Cumberland House, to have canoes built at the post itself and avoid losses by taking "great care not to pay before hand."

In 1776–77 Isham, at Cumberland and beyond with Tomison and others, was said to be the only inlander besides Longmoor with "any degree of Proficiency in Bowing or Steering canoes." Isham's efforts against Montreal-based traders earned him a murder threat from them that year: the pedlars blamed the disappearances of two of their number, who were said to have been killed by Indians, on Isham's "instilling bad Notions into the minds of the Natives to their prejudice." His responsibilities grew in this period; in September 1776 Tomison sent him "away to the Buffeloe Country to encourage the Indians to come down to Trade, Also to get what Canoes he possible can." But his success was mixed; "having wastefully Expended all his Goods" by early winter, he was obliged to join Longmoor at his post in the Eagle Hills (Sask.). The following winter he tented with Indians from November to April but lost most of their spring trade to the "French House in the Beaver [Amisk] Lake where they was trading all that they had." Subsequent journals of Cumberland House and Hudson House (near Brightholme, Sask.) note his continued active service in difficult circumstances. In November 1781 he fell ill with the smallpox then ravaging the Indian population. Unlike most Indians, but like those mixed-blood sufferers observed by Edward Umfreville*, he survived. Philip Turnor* gave him high praise in this period: "Well beloved by the Indians and taulks the Language exceeding well, the Canadians have an exceeding peak against Charles Isham but had better hurt any other Englishman as his death would be revenged both by the English and

Indians." The Canadians' "peak" was exemplified in 1782 by William Holmes*'s complaints to William Walker* that Isham had threatened his men and abducted their women. Walker defended Isham, noting that the charges were unproved; as for the women being taken, they "must agree to it, before any such thing as that could be done."

Isham continued as inland labourer, canoeman, and interpreter at £15 to £20 a year through the 1780s. A request in 1786 for personal items from England – "a Bed Tick, 4 Shirts white Good, 2 Muslin Neckcloths. A Good laced hat and 1 p^s Nankeen" – suggests persisting British tastes, and in 1788–89 he apparently revisited England, perhaps the parish of St George, Bloomsbury (London), the home address he listed in 1787–88.

In May 1789 Isham contracted as "Inland Trader & Supervisor of Canoes in Swan River" at £30 annually plus "premium on all the made Beaver I can procure." Known thereafter as "Mr. Isham," between 1790 and 1795 he was master at Swan River (Man.), Marlborough House (near Pelly, Sask.), Somerset House (near Swan River), and Carlton House (near Kamsack, Sask.) in succession, and from 1797 to 1799 at Jack River House (near Norway House, Man.). Continuing a mobile inland life, he served until his retirement in 1814 at various posts as far west as Edmonton House (near Fort Saskatchewan, Alta), and in 1812 was an interpreter for Miles Macdonell* at the new Red River colony [see Thomas DOUGLAS]. His salary varied: £80 in 1812; £40 in 1814. The 1790s in particular were not easy; like Malchom Ross* and others, Isham found himself competing with his own inland colleagues as well as Canadians. In 1791, according to Joseph COLEN, Isham built at Swan River "3 Canoes . . . of a much larger size than we have seen before, but not having proper hands to man them . . . was obliged to set off with the usual cargo." For this shortage of men Colen blamed inland officer Tomison who was constantly making "efforts to distress Swan

River." Isham wrote to London that summer, "without your honours interfere this Infant Settlement will be lost."

Although London clearly valued his service, Isham became no more than a minor officer in obscure and often difficult posts. He was probably the first Hudson Bay native, however, to rise that high (the origins of Moses Norton* being uncertain) and his colleagues ranked him as English, without making a racial distinction. At his death Isham's estate, which amounted to £1,800 in three per cent annuities, benefited four Hudson Bay children, Thomas, Mary, Jane, and James, designated as natural; like older colleagues such as Malchom Ross and George Atkinson*, and unlike some later traders, he did not seek to affirm their legitimacy. Thomas and one Price Isham were company labourers in the Winnipeg district at the time of his death, and Ishams appear in later Red River mission records.

JENNIFER S. H. BROWN

PAM, HBCA, A.1/42: ff.92, 172; A.11/115: ff.74, 137, 153, 171–72; A.11/116: ff.6–7, 14, 23, 27, 184; A.11/117: ff.98, 120–21, 128, 139, 159, 172; A.30/1: f.9; A.30/3: f.89; A.30/4: f.20; A.30/11: f.37; A.30/12: ff.31, 35; A.30/13: f.35; A.32/3: f.234; A.36/1A: f.13; B.198/a/8: f.11; B.203/a/1–2; B.239/f/3: f.11; B.239/f/6: ff.23, 40, 64. PRO, PROB 11/1564/27. St John's Anglican Cathedral (Winnipeg), Red River and St Peter's (Indian settlement), Reg. of burials and marriages. *Cumberland House journals and inland journal, 1775–82*, ed. E. E. Rich and A. M. Johnson (2v., London, 1951–52). HBRS, vol.27 (Williams). *James Isham's observations on Hudson's Bay, 1743 . . .*, ed. E. E. Rich and A. M. Johnson (London, 1949; repr. Nendeln, Liechtenstein, 1968). *Journals of Hearne and Turnor* (Tyrrell). *Saskatchewan journals and correspondence: Edmonton House, 1795–1800; Chesterfield House, 1800–1802*, ed. A. M. Johnson (London, 1967). Edward Umfreville, *The present state of Hudson's Bay . . .* (London, 1790; new ed., ed. W. S. Wallace, Toronto, 1954). Morton, *Hist. of Canadian west*.

J

JACSON, ANTOINE, soldier and wood-carver; b. some time between 1720 and 1730 in the parish of Sainte-Marguerite in Paris, France, son of Louis Jacson and Madeleine Fleury; d. 6 Dec. 1803 at Quebec, Lower Canada.

At the time of his arrival in the town of Quebec, probably in 1750, Antoine Jacson was serving in the colonial regular troops. As a soldier in Saint-Pierre's company he gave witness in a murder case on 18

March 1752. On 14 Feb. 1757 he married Marie-Marguerite Chamberland at Quebec; they were to have eight children. He is described on his marriage certificate as "a soldier in the colony" in Charles Deschamps* de Boishébert's company; the marriage contract signed a few days earlier mentioned that he was "a wood-carver born in Old France."

Jacson probably lived at Trois-Rivières soon after his marriage, since he had a son, Antoine-Joseph,

Jarvis

baptized there on 28 Dec. 1760; the certificate of baptism issued then termed him a "master wood-carver." In 1770 Jacson did some of the carving for the decoration of the church of Saint-Charles at Lachenaie, executing his first known contract. He lived in that locality for some months and had a child baptized there on 20 Sept. 1771. A month later, having returned to Quebec and settled on Rue du Cap, he signed a one-year contract with master carpenter Jean BAILLAIRGÉ. Jacson undertook to do all the carving and other pieces of work that Baillairgé requested; in addition he was to teach Baillairgé's son François* "what he [knew] about wood-carving." For this he was paid 600 *livres*. From then on François Baillairgé considered Jacson his father's associate.

Between 1781 and 1784 Jacson worked on the decoration of the church of Saint-Pierre on Île d'Orléans. There, as at Lachenaie, it is impossible to judge what he accomplished since his work is lost in a jumble of decorative elements done by a number of wood-carvers. Shortly after this contract ended, Jacson went to practise his craft in the workshop newly opened at Quebec by his former pupil, François Baillairgé, who had returned from France in 1781.

In the period 1784–87 Baillairgé, well aware of Jacson's skill, entrusted to him jobs demanding great precision. In particular he did some of the framework and the door of the tabernacle in the church of Saint-Louis in Kamouraska in October 1784, the carving on the altar ledges in the church at Saint-Henri-de-Lauzon (Saint-Henri), the tabernacle, supporting pedestal, and ornamental consoles in the church of Notre-Dame-de-Bonsecours at L'Islet in February and March 1785, the bases of the candlesticks for the church at Saint-Joachim in July 1786, the churchwardens' pew in the church of Notre-Dame-de-l'Assomption at Berthier (Berthier-sur-Mer), and the frieze in the stairway of the Château Saint-Louis at Quebec in March 1787. In addition during this period he collaborated with Pierre ÉMOND on the decoration of Bishop Briand*'s chapel. From 1787 to 1793 François Baillairgé's account-book makes no mention of Jacson. The two men apparently remained on good terms, however, since one of Jacson's sons did various small jobs for Baillairgé.

On 25 Jan. 1793, François Baillairgé recorded that "Mr Antoine Jacson began to work for me on a trial basis." Perhaps this note is to be explained by the precarious state of Jacson's health or by other difficulties. At all events, Baillairgé, who was engaged in the decoration of the church of Notre-Dame at Quebec, needed help at that moment; he entrusted to his old master the carving of the "friezes, rosettes, and framework of the high altar of the retable," retable being the contemporary term for the decorated structure that housed the altar in the sanctuary. In April, again work-ing for Baillairgé, Jacson did the carving on the framework of the painting above the tabernacle for the parish of Saint-Pierre-du-Sud.

Antoine Jacson's name appears for the last time in Baillairgé's account-book on 2 April 1796 and he probably retired at that date. He died at Quebec in 1803, leaving all his belongings to one of his sons, Louis. Jacson's work, at least as glimpsed through the fragments that have been identified, seems to have been that of a wood-carver who specialized in decorating. He executed candelabras, consoles, friezes, and rosettes, but there is no mention made of statuary.

MICHEL CAUCHON

ANQ-Q, CE1-1, 7 déc. 1803; CN1-11, 27 janv. 1757; CN1-26, 19 sept., 4 oct. 1800; CN1-83, 12 juin 1783; CN1-248, 16 oct. 1771. AP, Saint-Charles (Lachenaie), Livre de comptes, II: 47; Saint-Pierre (île d'Orléans), Livre de comptes, I. Tanguay, *Dictionnaire*, 4: 570. "Un conseil de guerre à Québec en 1752," *BRH*, 45 (1939): 355.

JARVIS, WILLIAM, office holder and militia officer; b. 11 Sept. 1756 in Stamford, Conn., fifth son of Samuel Jarvis and Martha Seymour; m. 12 Dec. 1785 Hannah Owen Peters in London, England, and they had three sons and four daughters; d. 13 Aug. 1817 in York (Toronto), Upper Canada.

William Jarvis joined John Graves SIMCOE's Queen's Rangers in 1777. He was wounded at the battle of Spencer's Tavern in Virginia on 26 June 1781 and was commissioned cornet on 25 Dec. 1782. At the cessation of the American Revolutionary War he went on half pay and returned to Connecticut. There the hostility to the loyalists often resulted in violence, and on one occasion Jarvis was injured. In 1784 or 1785 he travelled to England where he secured Simcoe as a patron. Simcoe recommended him in 1791 to the Home secretary, Henry Dundas, for the positions of provincial secretary and clerk of the Executive Council of the newly established province of Upper Canada. Although Jarvis did not receive the clerkship, he was, however, rewarded with the more important, prestigious, and lucrative post of provincial secretary and registrar. In the summer of 1792 he arrived in Upper Canada as part of Lieutenant Governor Simcoe's entourage. Soon after he settled in the capital of Newark (Niagara-on-the-Lake).

Shortly before leaving England, Jarvis had been chosen provincial grand master of the newly organized Masonic Lodge of Upper Canada. His prominence in local society was reflected by his appointment as deputy lieutenant of the county of York in 1794. Simcoe envisaged the county lieutenants as the core of an indigenous aristocracy and the basis of the local militia [see Hazelton SPENCER]. Jarvis maintained his connection with the militia and at his death was a colonel. He was appointed a magistrate in 1800 and from 1801 to 1806 served as chairman of the Court of Quarter Sessions.

From its beginning Jarvis belonged to the province's tiny governing circle, first at Newark and after 1798 at York. His career was marked by the internecine bickering which characterized this group as its members struggled to consolidate their positions and to secure places for their children. Although Jarvis's salary was £300, it was supplemented by fees. In 1794 he came into conflict with Attorney General John White* over the division of the lucrative fees on land patents. Jarvis drew up and registered all legal instruments and was responsible for the cost of parchment and wax. White, ever in search of additional income, claimed half of Jarvis's fees on the grounds that the attorney general was responsible for the crown's legal matters. He was successful, yet Jarvis still maintained the full burden of expense. Indeed he lost money on each grant processed thereafter and he petitioned in vain for relief until 1815 when he was granted £1,000. His financial problems were not, however, entirely the fault of White or an uncaring Executive Council. At times, changes in land regulations invalidated his work and often he himself was inefficient and careless. In 1800 Lieutenant Governor Peter HUNTER discovered that many of the deeds issued by Jarvis contained irregularities such as erasures and corrections, or were drawn up on paper rather than parchment. Hunter censured him and provided strict instructions for the preparation of documents – instructions which by Jarvis's estimate rendered useless £475 worth of deeds.

Jarvis's temperament occasioned frequent clashes with his peers. At Newark in 1795 he became involved in a minor *cause célèbre* over the authorship of a lampoon, purportedly in his hand, maligning several prominent families. Affronted at being suspected, Jarvis challenged four individuals to duels, and even met with one, before Receiver General Peter RUSSELL forced him to swear to keep the peace. Jarvis once confessed to his father-in-law that though he wished to be an executive councillor he "was too proud to ask them [members of the council] to recommend me." The social tension Jarvis endured within the civil administration can perhaps be understood from Mrs Jarvis's comment that White and Chief Justice John ELMSLEY "think an American knows not how to speak." Jarvis's sometimes erratic behaviour may have been in part a response to the influence of his vituperative spouse, who once explained her husband's stalled career by observing that Simcoe was surrounded by "a lot of *Pimps*, Sycophants and Lyars."

William Jarvis lived well, if not within his means, on his 100-acre park lot on the outskirts of York. Like so many of the early official families, he sought to ensconce his offspring in the developing society of York and Upper Canada. His eldest son, Samuel Peters Jarvis*, became deputy provincial secretary to Duncan Cameron* in 1827, and later chief superintendent of Indian affairs. Two of his daughters married George* and Alexander* Hamilton, sons of the wealthy Queenston merchant Robert HAMILTON, and a third married William Benjamin Robinson*.

William Jarvis was not a central figure in the York élite. Though he contested the riding of Durham, Simcoe, and the East Riding of York against Samuel HERON, Henry ALLCOCK, and John Small* in 1800 and briefly supported Judge Robert Thorpe* in 1806, he was not particularly interested or involved in politics. He was a ranking member of the province's small administration and his career illustrates some of the problems which plagued the province in its early years.

ROBERT J. BURNS

MTL, William Jarvis papers. PAC, MG 23, HI, 3, vols.1–2. *Corr. of Lieut. Governor Simcoe* (Cruikshank), 1: 45–47; 2: 288, n.1; 3: 29; 4: 10–11. "Minutes of Court of General Quarter Sessions, Home District," AO *Report*, 1932. *Town of York, 1793–1815* (Firth), lxxxi. Wallace, *Macmillan dict.* Burns, "First elite of Toronto," 289–93. *The Jarvis family; or, the descendants of the first settlers of that name in Massachusetts and Long Island, and those who have more recently settled in other parts of the United States and British America*, comp. G. A. Jarvis *et al.* (Hartford, Conn., 1879). W. R. Riddell, *The life of John Graves Simcoe, first lieutenant-governor of the province of Upper Canada, 1792–96* (Toronto, [1926]), 453–54. G. C. Patterson, "Land settlement in Upper Canada, 1783–1840," AO *Report*, 1920: 52–53, 82–83, 90–91, 117–18.

JESSEN, DETTLIEB (Detleff) CHRISTOPHER, office holder, militia officer, judge, and politician; b. 25 Feb. 1730 in Holstein (Federal Republic of Germany); m. 2 Jan. 1755 Francisca Barbara Rudolf in Lunenburg, N.S.; d. there 12 Aug. 1814.

Dettlieb Christopher Jessen came to Halifax from Hamburg (Federal Republic of Germany) in the *Speedwell* in 1751, and was among the first settlers of the town of Lunenburg in 1753. A wine-cooper by occupation, he had some education, a tolerable understanding of English, and something in the way of means. Turning these assets to advantage, he was listed as "gentleman" rather than as "artificer" in the *Speedwell*'s registers, and over the years at Lunenburg he occupied many of "the little official positions . . . which the government distributed among the better educated and more reliable of the settlers." A lieutenant in the militia in 1753, he rose to the rank of lieutenant-colonel of the county militia. For at least 11 years he was foreman of working parties, and in the

Jessup

first years of the settlement he acted as muster-master in charge of the victualling lists. A justice of the peace from the early 1760s, Jessen also served at various times as naval officer for the town, judge of the Inferior Court of Common Pleas, registrar of deeds, and collector of customs and excise. While a member of the House of Assembly for Lunenburg County between 1785 and 1793, he concentrated largely on his constituents' needs.

As lieutenant-colonel of militia, he was to the fore in defending Lunenburg against the American privateer attack of July 1782, and for his efforts had his house robbed, during the occupation of the town by the Americans, of most of his clothes, the furniture, plate, and a good deal of money, the value of which he estimated at £700. What distinguished Jessen most in his public activities, however, was his humaneness and generosity. As justice of the peace, he would not use his office to enrich himself. When anyone "through accident comes into A Scrap, I have always endeavoured to mitigate between neighbour & neighbour without taking any Feese." After outlining the procedure to be followed, he arranged for the disputants to meet, usually by themselves, and often the matter was "Ajusted without any Judge or Jury or expense either to [plaintiff] or [defendant] and those people remain Good neighbours." To avoid having to give up the justiceship, he declined an appointment as sheriff in 1783, the more so because "the Fees accruing from said office proceeds on distresses of others."

Jessen was a principal benefactor of both St John's Anglican Church and Zion Lutheran Church in Lunenburg. To the latter he donated a silver paten and two chalices; to the former £140, and, on his deathbed, a bell for its steeple and a complete set of plate for its altar.

J. MURRAY BECK

PANS, MG 4, 92 (typescript). Bell, *Foreign Protestants*, 210; 362–63, n.16a; 415, n.13a. M. B. DesBrisay, *History of the county of Lunenburg* (2nd ed., Toronto, 1895), 63–64, 109–10.

JESSUP, EDWARD, army officer, land speculator, judge, office holder, and militia officer; b. either 4 or 24 Dec. 1735 in the parish of Stamford, Conn., son of Joseph Jessup and Abigail James; m. 1760 Abigail Dibble, and they had two children; d. 3 Feb. 1816 in Prescott, Upper Canada.

Although the Jessups had lived in Connecticut for several generations, Joseph Jessup moved his family to the "Upper Nine Partners Patent" in Dutchess County, N.Y., in 1744. Edward Jessup raised a company and served as a captain in Jeffery Amherst*'s campaign of 1759 in the Lake Champlain region, and probably became aware at that time of the opportunities available in northern New York. About 1764 Edward and his brother Ebenezer moved to Albany. There they formed a partnership, and over the next decade the two engaged in land speculation on a grand scale in the upper Hudson and Lake George areas. In their speculations they were no doubt aided by their close relationship with Sir William Johnson* and John Butler*. The brothers eventually established a community, with mills and a ferry, about ten miles above Glen Falls on the Hudson. This settlement, which became known as Jessup's Landing, was a focus of loyalism in the years just before the revolution, and when Sir Guy CARLETON succeeded in driving the American forces out of the province of Quebec in the summer of 1776 the Jessups led a party of some 80 loyalists to join him at Crown Point (N.Y.).

The Jessup party was first attached to Sir John Johnson*'s King's Royal Regiment of New York, but on 7 June 1777 the King's Loyal Americans corps was tentatively established with Ebenezer as lieutenant-colonel and Edward as captain. Although the corps was not fully formed, the Jessup brothers took part in John Burgoyne*'s campaign, with Edward as commander of the bateaux service on the Hudson. Both Edward and Ebenezer were taken prisoner in the Saratoga campaign but were paroled and allowed to make their way to Quebec.

Since many members of the King's Loyal Americans were dispersed during the Burgoyne fiasco, the unit never attained its established strength and remained for the next four years a semi-independent appendage of Johnson's regiment, engaged mainly in building, repairing, and garrisoning fortifications around Montreal, Sorel, and lower Lake Champlain, although it also took part in several raids into New York. Edward went on such raids in October 1780 and again the following fall. It was probably these services, as well as his administrative capacities, that led Governor HALDIMAND to choose Edward over Ebenezer as major commandant of the new corps of Loyal Rangers, created 12 Nov. 1781 from a number of smaller military formations including the Loyal Americans. The new corps soon became known as Jessup's Rangers. Until their disbandment on 24 Dec. 1783 the Rangers were employed in the same kind of duties that had previously engaged the Loyal Americans. They were usually stationed at Sorel or Verchères and provided garrisons for posts at Yamaska, Rivière-aux-Chiens, Île aux Noix, and Dutchman's Point (near Alburg, Vt).

With the war lost, Jessup began in the summer of 1783 to plan the resettlement of his corps and was one of those who proposed the Ottawa River and the upper St Lawrence for that purpose. Although his proposal for structured settlements based on military rank was rejected, Haldimand incorporated a number of his other ideas into the plan finally adopted. In that plan Jessup's Rangers were allotted townships No.6 (Edwardsburg), No.7 (Augusta), and part of No.8 (Elizabethtown), all on the St Lawrence, as well as No.2 (Ernestown), west of Cataraqui (Kingston). Jessup spent the summer of 1784 supervising the settlement of his men on their new lands and in the fall of that year journeyed to London, England, to submit a claim for his losses during the revolution. He returned to Quebec by 1788 and took up his own land grant of 1,200 acres in Augusta Township, immediately opposite Fort Oswegatchie (Ogdensburg, N.Y.) on the St Lawrence and beside the lots granted to his son, Lieutenant Edward Jessup.

In the post-war years Jessup resumed his career as a land speculator. As a loyalist and a major he was entitled to considerable land beyond his 1,200 acres, and he shortly applied for and was granted 3,800 acres in a single block on the South Nation River (Ont.); he apparently intended to settle and develop it but there is no evidence that he was able to do so. He also had considerable land in the seigneury of Sorel, where his family lived until at least the late 1780s and possibly longer. It seems he had some standing with both Haldimand and Carleton (now Lord Dorchester), although not enough either to persuade the government to invest £6,000 in a plan to provide loyalist settlers with cattle in return for oak barrel staves, or to gain approval for a township settlement scheme he drew up with three American entrepreneurs who, he assured Dorchester, were "Loyalist in heart." Haldimand, however, made him a justice of the peace; and Dorchester, besides recommending him for the Executive Council of Upper Canada, appointed him a judge of the Court of Common Pleas and lieutenant-colonel of the Edwardsburg, Augusta, and Elizabethtown militia.

Jessup was not able to maintain his influence after the establishment of the new colony of Upper Canada in 1791. In the struggle for place at York (Toronto) it was Ephraim Jones and Solomon Jones* who won out, not Jessup; Lieutenant Governor Simcoe did not take up Dorchester's recommendation of Jessup for the Executive Council. Yet by this point age may well have begun to make Jessup less competitive since his son did achieve some standing. Edward Jr sat for Grenville in the second session of the legislature of Upper Canada, succeeded his father as lieutenant-colonel of the local militia in 1795, and was appointed a clerk of the peace for the Johnstown District in 1800 and a clerk of the Court of Common Pleas in 1802.

In 1810 Jessup and his son laid out the town of Prescott, named after Governor Robert Prescott, along the front of their St Lawrence River lands, but only two years later their own home sites were expropriated by the army for the construction of Fort Wellington. Jessup's active career, however, was now over. By 1812 he was no longer able to conduct business for himself, and when he died in February 1816 he had been bedridden and "afflicted with the palsy" for several years and could not even sign his name.

R. Arthur Bowler

AO, MS 521; MU 1107, package 4; MU 2828–31. BL, Add. mss 21670, 21678, 21717, 21766, 21822–23, 21828–29, 21874–75 (transcripts at PAC). Conn. State Library (Hartford), Indexes, Barbour coll., Stamford vital records, 1: 39. PAC, MG 23, A3; C9; K12 (originals and transcripts); MG 25, 59; RG 1, E14; L3, 254: I–J1/26–28, 40; 254A: I–J4/50; I–J5/10–11; I–J6/5; 255: J9/1; 266: I–J misc., 1788–95/24–29; I–J misc., 1795–1837/2–3; 522: W2/16; RG 8, I (C ser.), 279; RG 19, 3757; RG 68, General index, 1651–1841: ff.81, 260, 276, 292, 324, 330, 334, 403, 405, 411, 413, 415, 417, 419, 427, 534, 629, 631–32, 646, 679. PRO, PRO 30/55 (copies at PAC); WO 28/4, 28/6, 28/10 (mfm. at PAC). "Book of official instructions to the land surveyors of Upper Canada," AO *Report*, 1905: 369–70, 390–93. *Corr. of Lieut. Governor Simcoe* (Cruikshank). "Grants of crown lands in U.C.," AO *Report*, 1928: 22–24, 128–29, 138–39, 210–11; 1929: 139, 171. [J. M. Hadden], *Hadden's journal and orderly books: a journal kept in Canada and upon Burgoyne's campaign in 1776 and 1777, by Lieut. James M. Hadden . . .* , ed. Horatio Rogers (Albany, N.Y., 1884; repr. Freeport, N.Y., [1970]). *Johnson papers* (Sullivan et al.). *Loyalist narratives from Upper Canada*, ed. J. J. Talman (Toronto, 1946). *NYCD* (O'Callaghan and Fernow), vols.4–5, 8. *The settlement of the United Empire Loyalists on the upper St Lawrence and Bay of Quinte in 1784; a documentary record*, ed. E. A. Cruikshank (Toronto, 1934; repr. 1966). "Settlements and surveys," PAC *Report*, 1891: 17. *Stamford registration of births, marriages and deaths, including every name, relationship, and date now found in the Stamford registers from the first record down to the year 1825*, comp. E. B. Huntington (Stamford, Conn., 1874), 57. "Surveyors' letters, etc.," AO *Report*, 1905: 437–38, 440–41, 458–59, 482–83. "U.C. land book B," AO *Report*, 1930: 49. "U.C. land book D," AO *Report*, 1931: 171–72, 175. Alexander Fraser, "Report of the Ontario Bureau of Archives: prefatory," AO *Report*, 1909: x. H. G. Jesup, *Edward Jessup of West Farms, Westchester Co., New York, and his descendants . . .* (Cambridge, Mass., 1887). "List of documents, furnished by his honour, judge Pringle, Cornwall, Ontario," PAC *Report*, 1884: xxvi. A. C. Flick, *Loyalism in New York during the American revolution* (New York, 1901). T. W. H. Leavitt, *History of Leeds and Grenville, Ontario, from 1749 to 1879 . . .* (Brockville, Ont., 1879; repr. Belleville, Ont., 1972). E. R. Stuart, "Jessup's Rangers as a factor in loyalist settlement," *Three hist. theses*. H. B. Yoshpe, *The disposition of loyalist estates in the southern district of the state of New York* (New York, 1939). P. H. Bryce, "The Quinte loyalists of 1784," *OH*, 27 (1931): 5–14. E. A. Cruikshank, "The King's Royal Regiment of New York," *OH*, 27 (1931): 193–323.

JOHN, CAPTAIN. *See* Deserontyon, John

Jones

JONES, CALEB, slave owner and office holder; b. *c*. 1743, probably in Maryland; m. Elizabeth —; d. 21 Dec. 1816 in Saint Marys parish, N.B.

At the outbreak of the American Revolutionary War Caleb Jones was a planter and slave owner and the sheriff of Somerset County, Md. It was likely he who was called before the Maryland council of safety in 1776 and required to post bond with the Somerset County committee of observation for his good behaviour and his "paying due obedience to the orders of the honourable Continental Congress and Convention." He fled to New York City, where he joined the Maryland Loyalists, and he served throughout the war as a captain. Before the evacuation of New York City in 1783, Jones was given six months' leave of absence to explore lands in what was to become New Brunswick, and after the arrival of the loyalists there he obtained a grant on the Nashwaaksis Stream near St Anne's Point (Fredericton). In 1785 he chartered a ship and sailed from New Brunswick to Maryland, leaving behind on his land two slaves he had purchased in New York City; returning shortly after with seven slaves, he found that those working his land had run away, the first of many to escape from him. Jones's wife had remained in Maryland to collect his property, and in 1786 he returned for his family and movables. He was disappointed to find, however, that his agents there had been unable to recover any of the debts owed to him. Once back in New Brunswick he took up farming.

By the beginning of the 19th century there were a number of people in New Brunswick interested in the abolition of slavery and in February 1800 Jones became involved in an attempt to test its legality in the province. When a woman named Nancy (Ann), whom Jones was detaining as a slave, claimed her freedom, a writ of habeas corpus was issued and the case was presented to the full bench of the Supreme Court. The best legal counsel in the province was employed by both sides. Nancy was defended by Ward Chipman*, who was later chief justice, and Samuel Denny Street*. Chipman and Street were not paid for their services, but defended the slave as "volunteer[s] for the rights of human nature." Jones was represented by Jonathan Bliss*, John Murray Bliss*, Thomas Wetmore*, Charles Jeffery Peters*, and William Botsford*. The judges who heard the case were Chief Justice George Duncan LUDLOW, Joshua UPHAM, Isaac Allan, and John Saunders*. The first three were slave owners; Judge Saunders was the only opponent of slavery on the bench. To strengthen his case Chipman searched out every trial and legal decision on slavery in the British empire available to him, and his opponents undoubtedly did the same. On the conclusion of the trial Ludlow and Upham declared that slavery was legal in New Brunswick, while Allan changed his views and joined Saunders in declaring it

illegal. Since the bench was equally divided, no judgement was recorded and the slave was returned to her master; however, as a result of his decision Judge Allan released his slaves and a number of slave owners followed his example. Though the writ of habeas corpus was issued to Jones, some writers have concluded that Stair Agnew* was Nancy's real master. The confusion appears to have arisen from the fact that a female slave of Agnew's also claimed her freedom about the time of the trial.

Jones was not happy in New Brunswick and felt that he had not been compensated adequately for his losses during the war. He became involved in disputes with the government and portions of his land were escheated for non-fulfilment of the conditions of the grant. In 1802 he made an unsuccessful attempt to win a seat in the House of Assembly. At that time he was accused of making seditious remarks by seven York County magistrates, among them Dugald CAMPBELL and Stair Agnew. They requested that he be removed from his position as magistrate, to which he had been appointed in 1799, so that they would be spared "the mortification" of having to sit with him again at the Court of General Sessions. There is, however, no record of the cancellation of his commission. He continued to criticize the government and was involved in disputes over land and the ownership of slaves until his death in 1816.

W. A. SPRAY

PAC, MG 23, D1, ser.11, S. S. Blowers to Chipman, 7 Jan. 1800, [April 1800]. PANB, RG 2, RS6, 1: 38; RS8, Appointments and commissions, 2/1: 26; Magistrates, 1802: Petition to have Caleb Jones removed as magistrate; RG 10, RS108, Petition of Caleb Jones, 1802. UNBL, MG H2, 4: 104, 106 (transcript at N.B. Museum). *American arch.* (Clarke and Force), 5th ser., 1: 1344, 1356. I. A. Jack, "The loyalists and slavery in New Brunswick," RSC *Trans.*, 2nd ser., 4 (1898), sect.II: 137–85. *New Brunswick Royal Gazette* (Fredericton), 18 Feb. 1800, 14 Jan. 1817. Sabine, *Biog. sketches of loyalists*. I. C. Greaves, *The negro in Canada* (Montreal, [1930]), 19. J. W. Lawrence, *The judges of New Brunswick and their times*, ed. A. A. Stockton [and W. O. Raymond] ([Saint John, N.B., 1907]), 70–76. L. M. B. Maxwell, *An outline of the history of central New Brunswick to the time of confederation* (Sackville, N.B., 1937). W. A. Spray, *The blacks in New Brunswick* ([Fredericton], 1972), 21–25. T. W. Smith, "The slave in Canada," N.S. Hist. Soc., *Coll.*, 10 (1899): 103–4.

JONES, EPHRAIM, soldier, office holder, landowner, businessman, judge, and politician; b. 27 April 1750, in an "elegant mansion house," at Weston, Mass., ninth son of Elisha Jones and Mary Allen; m. first 24 March 1779 Charlotte Coursolles (Coursol) of Verchères, Que., and they had 12 children, eight of whom survived infancy; m.

secondly 7 May 1806 Margaret S. Beke (Beck, Beek); d. 24 Jan. 1812 in Augusta Township, Upper Canada.

Ephraim Jones is a noteworthy character in the history of early Upper Canada both because of his influence in the local life of Leeds and Grenville counties, and because his career and its extension in the work of his sons exemplify a link in that network of friends and ideological allies which, christened the "family compact" by its enemies, dominated the political affairs of the province until the 1837 rebellion.

Service to the crown during the American revolution demonstrated the loyalty of both Ephraim and his family. His father, a prosperous landowner and a colonel in the militia of Middlesex County, Mass., was an early and strenuous opponent of the revolution, and after moving to Boston in 1774 was reputedly consulted on numerous occasions by Thomas Gage*, commander-in-chief of British forces in North America, who "placed the greatest confidence in him." Six of his sons joined the loyalist standard, and five of them moved to British North America in the 1780s: Simeon settled in New Brunswick, Elisha, Josiah, and Stephen in Nova Scotia, and Ephraim in the western section of the province of Quebec, soon to become Upper Canada.

Like his father, Ephraim enjoyed the "confidence" of the British authorities. Living at East Hoosack (Hoosac), Mass., at the beginning of the war, he joined the British at Point au Fer (Rouses Point), N.Y., and served for a time with the troops commanded by Major-General Friedrich Adolph Riedesel. Shortly after, Sir Guy CARLETON appointed him commissary of forage in the army of John Burgoyne*, and in that position he was with Burgoyne and taken prisoner in the Saratoga campaign in 1777. His whereabouts for the next few years are unknown, but in 1781 he enlisted in the Loyal Rangers, under the command of Edward JESSUP, and served until that regiment was disbanded in December 1783.

Along with other men of the loyalist corps, Jones settled in the virgin territory west of the Ottawa River. Although he does not seem to have received a land grant, he apparently resided in what was shortly to be Augusta Township. He served briefly as a commissary for the loyalist settlers, thereby gaining the sobriquet "Commissary Jones," and in late 1784 Surveyor General Samuel Johannes HOLLAND, who was acquainted with Jones and "several of his Brothers" and spoke highly of his father's reputation as "a great forestander in Loyalty," recommended him as a suitable person to be entrusted with a licence for the sale of liquor. Some time later Jones moved to the Montreal area, where he was appointed a justice of the peace in 1786. Within a couple of years, however, he had returned to the loyalist settlements on the St Lawrence. In 1788 he was made a JP in the Luneburg

District, and in 1790 he obtained a grant of 1,300 acres of land in Augusta Township for the services he had rendered the crown. Far from remaining content with his initial grant, Jones quickly became a large landowner: by 1811 he had accumulated approximately 11,260 acres of land scattered over 12 townships. He also established himself as an important figure in the business life of the area, for besides being a shopkeeper he apparently operated a mill and owned an iron foundry on the Gananoque River.

The number of elective and appointive offices Jones held is an indication of his local prominence. During the first decade after the formation of the new colony of Upper Canada in 1791, Jones served as a member of the land board of Leeds and Grenville counties, and as a judge on the New Johnstown (Cornwall) Court of Requests as well as on the surrogate courts of the Eastern and Johnstown districts. He was also elected in 1792 as Grenville County's first member in the new House of Assembly. In the first session he introduced a bill, which was later passed, establishing trials by jury; and although the owner of a number of slaves, he supported the 1793 act providing for the gradual abolition of slavery in the colony.

Business success, together with a record of loyalty and administrative competence, made Jones a person who held the trust of both the government and his local community, and who could act as intermediary between the two. His function as a link between settlers and administrators was revealed in a letter of 1799 in which Stephen Burritt of Marlborough Township, who hoped to receive government aid, asked that Jones "be so well convinced of the reality of my sufferings as . . . to give me a certificate of the same and I shall acknowledge the particular favour with Gratitude." As it happened, Burritt did not have to wait long for a mark of government favour: whether Jones's influence played any role is uncertain, but in 1800 Burritt became a JP.

Jones's children also entered the Upper Canadian élite, their claims to prominence solidified by his friendships as well as by his achievements. Jones sent his son Jonas* to the school run in Cornwall by John Strachan*, who appears to have been on easy terms with the family well before his own political success was ensured. In the 1820s Jones's sons captured remunerative appointments because of their ties with Strachan and his associates such as John Beverley Robinson*, who rose to power during and after the War of 1812.

A letter written by Strachan in 1806 provides early evidence of Jones's frail health. His death in January 1812 proved a temporary setback to his children's ambitions. They were, however, to build well on the foundations he had provided. Of his daughters, Charlotte married Levius Peters Sherwood*, a leading politician and judge, and Eliza married Henry John

Jones

Boulton*, whose legal career in Upper Canada was capped with his appointment in 1833 as chief justice of Newfoundland. His sons climbed rapidly up the ladder of preference: Alpheus became collector of customs, postmaster, and agent of the Bank of Upper Canada at Prescott; William, a miller, merchant, and lumberman, was made collector of customs in Brockville; Jonas, a member of the House of Assembly, was appointed puisne judge of the Court of Queen's Bench in 1837 and became speaker of the Legislative Council in 1839; Charles*, also an assembly member and one of Brockville's most prominent early merchants, was appointed to the Legislative Council in 1828. Ephraim's family had succeeded him in the provincial patronage network.

ELVA RICHARDS MCGAUGHEY

AO, MS 520. PAC, MG 24, B7; RG 1, L1, 24: 206; 26: 157, 164, 328–29; L3, 254: I–J1/6, 21–22; I–J3/6; 254A: I–J4/1; 255: J9/14–16; RG 68, General index, 1651–1841: ff.248–49, 251, 288, 292, 325, 408, 411, 413, 415, 417, 419, 538. QUA, Solomon Jones papers. "Gleanings from the Blue Church burying ground, Augusta Township," comp. F. J. French, *OH*, 19 (1922): 91–102. "Grants of crown lands in U.C.," AO *Report*, 1928: 111, 164, 195, 197; 1929: 17, 81, 148. "Journals of Legislative Assembly of U.C.," AO *Report*, 1909: xv–43. *Parish reg. of Kingston* (Young). "The probated wills of men prominent in the public affairs of early Upper Canada," ed. A. F. Hunter, *OH*, 23 (1926): 328–59. *The settlement of the United Empire Loyalists on the upper St Lawrence and Bay of Quinte in 1784; a documentary record*, ed. E. A. Cruikshank (Toronto, 1934; repr. 1966). "United Empire Loyalists: enquiry into losses and services," AO *Report*, 1904: 751, 911–12, 917. "U.C. land book C," AO *Report*, 1931: 71. "U.C. land book D," AO *Report*, 1931: 173. Chadwick, *Ontarian families*. D. B. Read, *The lives of the judges of Upper Canada and Ontario, from 1791 to the present time* (Toronto, 1888). Reid, *Loyalists in Ont.* T. W. H. Leavitt, *History of Leeds and Grenville, Ontario, from 1749 to 1879 . . .* (Brockville, Ont., 1879; repr. Belleville, Ont., 1972). E. R. Stuart, "Jessup's Rangers as a factor in loyalist settlement," *Three hist. theses*. S. F. Wise, "Upper Canada and the conservative tradition," *Profiles of a province: studies in the history of Ontario . . .* (Toronto, 1967), 20–33. C. C. James, "The first legislators of Upper Canada," RSC *Trans.*, 2nd ser., 8 (1902), sect.II: 93–119. H. S. MacDonald, "The U.E. Loyalists of the old Johnstown District," *OH*, 12 (1914): 13–32. E. M. Richards [McGaughey], "The Joneses of Brockville and the family compact," *OH*, 60 (1968): 169–84.

JONES, JAMES, Roman Catholic priest, Capuchin, and superior of missions; b. 1742 in Dunshaughlin (Republic of Ireland); d. on or about 18 June 1805, probably in Ireland.

James Jones was the first Roman Catholic priest in Nova Scotia whose mother tongue was English. Little is known of his early life, although one of his critics,

the Reverend William Phelan of Arichat, N.S., claimed that he had been apprenticed "to a Skinner & Glover & followed his Trade & Tenets of Presbyterianism till the age of 28." He spent some time in the Capuchin monastery at Bar-sur-Aube, France, and later did pastoral work in the diocese of Cork (Republic of Ireland) for eight years. During this time he was one of the first to take the oath of allegiance prescribed for priests who wished to gain relief from the penal code.

In 1785 Bishop Louis-Philippe Mariauchau* d'Esgly of Quebec, responding to the pleas of Halifax Catholics, arranged for the transfer of Jones from Cork to Nova Scotia, where the growing population of Catholic loyalists and Irish demanded the presence of English-speaking priests. Arriving in Halifax in August of that year, Jones immediately won the respect of Vicar General Joseph-Mathurin Bourg*, who wrote that Jones was "a very good priest, a learned man full of piety and zeal, and an excellent preacher in the English language; in short, a man for whom I have greater esteem the more I know him." On his recommendation, Jones secured appointment in October 1787 as superior of the missions of Nova Scotia, Cape Breton, Îles de la Madeleine, St John's (Prince Edward) Island, and part of New Brunswick.

Jones encountered many problems in his new post: besides having to write to his superiors in French, a difficult task for him, he had to cope with a low income, poor communications, recalcitrant or weak priests, and a congregation in Halifax that stubbornly demanded a large role in the regulation of parish affairs. In his view, however, the most serious of his problems was the fact that the Roman Catholic Church in his region, lacking an adequate supply of clergy, was hard pressed to prevent its members from being led astray by "fanatical Methodists," "Scotch Calvinists,"and the clergy of the established Church of England. In April 1792 Jones reported that the Acadians, Scots, and Irish under his charge were served by only a handful of priests, including Thomas-François Le Roux*, Angus Bernard MacEachern*, and Thomas Grace*, known as Father James. Fortunately, the arrival of clerical refugees from the French revolution, which Jones denounced for its "mob rule" and its "slaughter of priests and royalty," strengthened the church's position in the Maritime colonies. In the late summer of 1792 Jean-Baptiste ALLAIN and François Lejamtel*, two priests from Saint-Pierre and Miquelon who had refused to swear allegiance to the Civil Constitution of the Clergy, fled to the Îles de la Madeleine and offered their services to Jones. Other refugee priests came to the region in subsequent years, among them Amable PICHARD, Gabriel CHAMPION, and Jean-Mandé Sigogne*.

Jones's life was not made easier by the behaviour of

one of his priests, William Phelan. A graduate of the Irish College in Rome (Italy), Phelan served in Ireland for 17 years before emigrating to Nova Scotia in 1786. Appointed to Arichat, a mission which embraced all of Cape Breton Island, Phelan was soon complaining that his flock, composed mostly of Micmacs and Acadians, was "rude and ignorant" and "totally unacquainted with any sort of restraint or subordination" – an assessment which contrasted sharply with Jones's view that the Roman Catholics of the region were "regular and disciplined" in religious practice. Apparently jealous of Jones's appointment as superior, Phelan fought him at every turn, principally by ignoring his authority and reporting directly to the bishop of Quebec, but also by conducting unauthorized missionary tours and refusing to cooperate with plans to establish an endowment fund for the Halifax mission. At length Jones, angered that Phelan spoke "so much of money," lost all patience. In April 1792 he dismissed Phelan from office and informed the Roman Catholics of the Arichat mission that they were to "act as if there were no priest, except in danger of death." Phelan, for his part, held on to his post until early 1793, when he was told to submit by the vicar general of Quebec, Henri-François GRAVÉ de La Rive.

Jones's health was poor after 1790, partly because of a fall from his horse. Afflicted with dropsy, he sought to return to Ireland, pleading that "they need here a young man, used to their ways." In August 1800 he finally secured passage home, with the understanding that he would return to Nova Scotia as soon as he was well enough; he was replaced in Halifax by an Irish Dominican, Edmund BURKE (fl. 1785–1801), who in turn was succeeded one year later by another priest of the same name. In October 1800 Jones was in London, England, where he attempted to recruit clergy for the Nova Scotia missions. He then spent a few months in Bath taking the waters, and during the course of his stay there he met several Nova Scotians. He continued to give every indication that he planned to return to the colony, but, probably because of his deteriorating health, he never did. Writing from Bath in March 1801, Jones informed Joseph-Octave Plessis*, the coadjutor bishop of Quebec, that he was about to go to Dublin to visit his relations. Thereafter he disappears from view until 30 July 1805, when his death was commented upon by the archbishop of Dublin.

Apparently a man of strong character, Jones was a hard-working priest and an eloquent preacher, although his effectiveness may have been reduced by his stern, unbending attitude and by his dismay at the "levelling, democratic" spirit of the colonial population. He seems to have been a competent administrator, but his record in managing church finances leaves some unanswered questions. Throughout his stay in Nova Scotia Jones complained to his superiors that his living conditions were poor and his income inadequate. However, after 1796 he obtained an annual stipend of £50 from the local government, and before leaving the colony he was able to deposit at least £2,000 in a Philadelphia bank for the support of the eastern missions – money that was drawn from his personal funds in Ireland, the donations of the Roman Catholic community of Halifax, and a bequest from Bishop Charles-François Bailly* de Messein of Quebec to the church in the Maritime colonies. Curiously, at Jones's death in 1805 the eastern missions received none of the funds he had accumulated. In his will he bequeathed £1,300 to the Royal College of St Patrick, Maynooth (County Kildare, Republic of Ireland), £500 to a number of charitable institutions in Dublin, and the remainder of his estate to his relations.

A. A. MacKenzie

AAQ, 12 A, H: ff.199v–200v; 20 A, II: 17; III: 181, 186; 210 A, I: f.214; II: ff.25, 125, 136, 141, 150, 166, 179, 209; III: ff.171, 191; IV: ff.42, 52, 83, 159, 208; VIII: ff.184, 543; 22 A, V: f.219; 1 CB, II: 10;10 CM, III: 130; 90 CM, I: 18–20; 30 CN, I: 20, 23; 312 CN, I–III (copies at Arch. of the Archdiocese of Halifax). Arch. of the Archdiocese of Halifax, Edmund Burke papers. Johnston, *Hist. of Catholic Church in eastern N.S.* K. E. Stokes, "The character and administration of Governor John Wentworth" (MA thesis, Dalhousie Univ., Halifax, 1934). Terrence Murphy, "James Jones and the establishment of Roman Catholic Church government in the Maritime provinces," CCHA *Study sessions*, 48 (1981): 26–42. Père Pacifique [de Valigny] [H.-J.-L. Buisson], "Le premier missionnaire de langue anglaise en Nouvelle-Écosse," Soc. de géographie de Québec, *Bull.* (Québec), 26 (1932): 46–62.

JONES, JOHN, businessman, landowner, militia officer, and politician; b. *c.* 1752; d. 3 Aug. 1818 at Quebec, Lower Canada.

John Jones arrived at Quebec in 1777. By February 1780 he was announcing imported spirits for sale in Lower Town, and he subsequently engaged at least in part in wholesale trade from a "large commodious house" with cellars and a storehouse on Rue Saint-Pierre. Having bought and sold liberally on credit, however, he became one of many victims of the depression that settled on Quebec at the end of the American revolution. On 2 June 1786 he assigned all his property to James Tod as trustee for his creditors; debts owed to him totalled £5,363, but he himself owed £12,420, of which £11,000 was due to London merchants. In February 1788 Jones's house was advertised for sale.

At the same time as his business was failing, Jones became embroiled in a dispute resulting from the formation of the Quebec Battalion of British Militia. Officer rank in the militia being a mark of social

Jones

status, Jones and two other merchants were upset when they were refused commissions and subsequently avoided their duties as ordinary militiamen. When the battalion commander, Henry CALDWELL, attempted to enforce regulations through the courts, he was ridiculed in a series of letters in the *Quebec Herald, Miscellany and Advertiser* during July and August 1790. He sued the merchants and the printer, William Moore*, for libel, but the case never came to trial, the jury having refused to return a true bill. Adding insult to injury, the accused published the defence they had prepared, appropriating a long-standing complaint of the merchant community by attacking the military for abuse of authority over civilians [*see* George ALLSOPP].

In May 1789 Jones had resurfaced in business, this time as an auctioneer and broker. He had apparently decided to profit from his experience with bankruptcy, since a major activity of the auctioneer and broker was the management and sale of bankrupt estates of individuals and companies. In 1804, for example, he advertised for auction the Labrador seal and salmon fishery that the failed partnership of Lymburner and Crawford had exploited with the Quebec merchant William GRANT (1744–1805). A significant proportion of Jones's business probably came from the auction of the effects of deceased persons. It was a common practice in the province of Quebec and Lower Canada to have a notarized inventory made of possessions at death, and then for the executor of the estate to have the effects sold at auction, the family being allowed first choice to reclaim what it wished to keep. Jones also acted as the curator of numerous estates, including, from 1795, that of the merchant Edward Harrison*. Harrison may have been his father-in-law, since he had been a witness at Jones's marriage to Margaret Harrison on 14 May 1794 at Quebec; Jones was a widower at the time. Jones also auctioned the possessions of people returning to Britain, among them Thomas Grant, whose books he sold in 1801 after having printed 200 copies of a catalogue listing them. Jones auctioned ships and ships' cargoes as well. New vessels were sold at the request of the builders, stranded or damaged ones at that of the owners or masters. Jones apparently imported some of the cargoes himself, while others, damaged in transit, were sold for the benefit of the underwriters.

In many cases auctions were held at the location of the goods – on the premises for the sale of estates, at various docks for ships' cargoes – or at places frequented by merchants, such as the Merchants' Coffee House and the Union Hotel. Jones also used his rented stores, on the King's Wharf in 1789 and on Rue Saint-Pierre, which ran along the waterfront, by 1792. In July 1802 he bought from Robert LESTER a lot, a two-storey stone house, and stores at 7 Rue Saint-

Pierre, where he had been established since at least 1799. The purchase cost £1,000, of which he paid £250 cash and the rest within three years. His stores were in addition a regular retail, and perhaps wholesale, outlet for "private" sales, often for "ready money only." There he offered dry goods and hams, cheese, and roll tobacco; he tended to specialize, however, in the sale of imported spirits, including rum, wines, gin, brandy, porter, and ale, as well as of molasses, essence of spruce, flour, sugar, salt, and teas.

Jones's business activities were not limited to retail and wholesale selling. By 1794 he was co-proprietor with William VONDENVELDEN of the New Printing Office at 21 Rue de la Montagne, Jones having imported the press and equipment from Alexander Young of London and engaged a journeyman printer from Britain. In August 1794 Jones and Vondenvelden published the first regular number of the bilingual newpaper the *Times/Le Cours du tems*. Jones's role appears to have been largely financial and managerial, and it was perhaps because he foresaw imminent failure that in May 1795 he sold his share in the enterprise to Vondenvelden for £342; the last number of the *Times* appeared at the end of July.

In the first decade of the new century Jones engaged in much property speculation, especially in the undeveloped lands of the Lower Canadian townships. With 19 associates, he, as leader, obtained in April 1800 a grant of 21,600 acres in Hunterstown Township, and in June he acquired the holdings of his adjuncts for a nominal sum according to the system of township leaders and associates [*see* James CALDWELL]; he sold 10,000 acres to James McGILL for £185 in September 1801. In 1803 he and John Munro, a Quebec merchant, acquired from Joseph Bouchette* 2,200 acres in Tring Township, and Jones alone acquired another 1,800 acres. Three years earlier he had purchased for £550 from Thomas DUNN a house in Quebec's Lower Town. Possibly by 1806 he was a shareholder in the Union Company of Quebec, owner of the Union Hotel and Coffee Room; that year he was elected administrative president of the Coffee Room, where members could read newspapers and periodicals.

As an increasingly prosperous member of Quebec's merchant community after 1789, Jones participated in its social and professional institutions. In 1797 he was finally commissioned an ensign in the Quebec Battalion of British Militia, and he rose to the rank of captain by 1812. He was more active, however, in the Quebec Fire Society [*see* John PURSS]. A member since 1790, Jones was elected secretary in 1791 and 1797 and president in 1803. That year the executive faced charges of negligence, which Jones apparently refuted satisfactorily since he was again elected president in 1806. In December 1808 he was one of the principal organizers of a lobby by the merchants of Lower Town to oblige the Phoenix Assurance Company to renew its fire-insurance policies there, the company's agent, Alexander Auldjo*, having pronounced the area an uninsurable fire-trap. Two months later he was appointed by the merchant community to a committee, chaired by James Irvine*, to study a proposal from the Committee of Trade at Halifax, N.S., to establish a similar organization at Quebec. The two committees would then join in efforts to pressure Britain into according its North American colonies more advantageous conditions of trade and greater protection against American competition in the West Indies. The proposal was accepted and the Committee of Trade of Quebec was founded that year.

Until about 1808 Jones had manifested little interest in politics, limiting his activity to signing petitions that, with one exception, concerned his business. The exception was support he gave in 1787 to a petition by Canadians asking that the Jesuit college, in use as a barracks, be once again consecrated to the education of Canadians. Perhaps concerned about the increasing polarization of Canadians and British in colonial politics [see Sir James Henry CRAIG], in May 1808 he stood as a candidate for the House of Assembly in the riding of Lower Town and, along with Pierre-Stanislas Bédard*, a leader of the Canadian party, was elected by acclamation. In the short fifth parliament of 1809 Jones sought an independent position between the majority Canadian group and the small British party, voting three times with the former and twice with the latter. The recalcitrant assembly was dissolved by an angry Governor Craig in October 1809. In the subsequent election, Jones posed at once as the candidate of conciliation and the last hope of the British electors of Lower Town, who were, he claimed, threatened by an unnamed group with exclusion from representation in the assembly. The campaign, according to the *Quebec Gazette*, was "briskly contested" but "without any animosity between the individuals of either party, a circumstance highly creditable to the Lower Town." Bédard and Jones were re-elected with 340 and 270 votes respectively to James Irvine's 220 and Ignace-Michel-Louis-Antoine d'Irumberry* de Salaberry's 118. In his address of thanks Jones castigated the government party for having introduced Salaberry from outside Lower Town in order to draw off his moderate Canadian support, and for having cast aspersions on his loyalty. In the assembly of 1810, however, perhaps having concluded that there was no middle ground on which he could stand, he was drawn or forced to the government side, voting seven times with the small British group and once with the Canadian majority. Craig again dissolved the legislature, and in the elections of 1810 for Lower Town

Jones withdrew in favour of the merchant John Mure*.

In the mean time Jones had continued his auctioneering business, and in December 1810 he announced the introduction of auctions every Thursday and Friday at his rooms on Rue Saint-Pierre in addition to the advertised auctions held irregularly. But competition had stiffened; by 1809 Quebec counted 19 licensed auctioneers grouped into seven or eight firms. In July 1811 Jones announced a co-partnership with "his old acquaintance and good friend" John Munro. The two apparently parted ways before December 1812; in September and November Jones advertised alone that he had for sale stoves, ploughshares, iron bars, and other products of the Batiscan Iron Work Company. By June 1815 he had reduced the number of auctions in his rooms to one a week, and in May 1816 he announced his partial retirement and intention to conduct outdoor sales at the premises of any friends who would employ him. "Those that have not paid their old Accounts need not appear at his Auctions," he added bluntly.

After 1810 Jones had also continued his property transactions and land speculation. In January 1813 he offered for sale or rent three prime properties at Quebec: 9 Rue de la Montagne, 7 Rue Saint-Pierre, and 51 Rue du Sault-au-Matelot, which he was then occupying, and early in 1814 the first two were rented, the second to a mercantile firm for £250 per annum. Jones himself took a house on Cap Diamant in April for £90 per annum. In March 1817 Jones and Munro divided evenly the land they held jointly in Tring Township, and Jones bought another 400 acres there from Munro in December; meanwhile, in June he had sold about 3,000 acres in Tring for £337 to James Godfrey Hanna*.

Jones died at Quebec on 3 Aug. 1818, and was buried two days later from the Cathedral of the Holy Trinity. Although he had not been in the first rank of merchants at Quebec, his career is of more than passing interest. The documentation he left not only provides a particularly clear picture of the auctioneer's role in Lower Canadian society, but also illustrates the business strategy of most contemporary merchants. Though they tended to specialize, they were obliged by the fragility of the colonial economy to diversify their activities, often by general retailing, urban property transactions, and land speculation in the Eastern Townships. Like most of his colleagues, Jones went bankrupt; unlike many others, however, he apparently succeeded a second time around. At his death debts owed to him totalled nearly £5,800, and he had over £750 in hand. He still possessed two houses on Rue Saint-Pierre and land in Hunterstown Township. In 1810 he had left his entire estate to his daughter Elizabeth Vaughan Jones, wife of the merchant James Ross. Jones and his wife, Margaret,

Juchereau

appear to have been separated for some time, since he made no provision for her in 1810, and she was absent from the colony at the time of his death.

In collaboration with MARIANNA O'GALLAGHER

There were several John Joneses active at Quebec and elsewhere in Lower Canada between 1780 and 1820, and some of them might readily be confused with the auctioneer at Quebec. In 1805 a John Jones, notary public by profession but apparently not practising, bought a house on Rue de la Montagne, and it may have been he who was arrested three times in 1810 for drunkenness and being a nuisance. He was dead by March 1817. Another John Jones, nephew of the auctioneer, became a notary in 1801, practising this profession until 1811; it might also have been he who was arrested in 1810. He lived in Lower Town, for a time on Rue de la Montagne, and speculated in property at Quebec and in several townships, including Tring, where his uncle also speculated. After 1811 he became a merchant at Quebec, eventually conducting business under the name of John Jones Jr and Company. He was a member of the Quebec Fire Society and a director of the Quebec Bank. By 1816 he had become an auctioneer, still conducting business under the name of John Jones Jr and Company, with stores on the Queen's Wharf. No apparent relation to any of the above, another John Jones arrived at Quebec in 1783 and opened a school on Rue Saint-Pierre. By 1788 he was living on Rue du Sault-au-Matelot, in 1791 on Rue de la Montagne, by 1792 on Rue du Parloir, and ten years later in a house called Bandon Lodge, in the *faubourg* Saint-Louis. He too conducted numerous property transactions at Quebec, where he owned houses and lots on Rue de la Montagne, Rue Champlain, and Rue Saint-Louis, speculated on lands in the townships, and was a member of the Quebec Fire Society. He appears to have left for Wales in 1805, giving power of attorney to his brother Joseph, a licensed auctioneer at Quebec and partner in the auctioneering firm of Jones and White (Jones, White and Melvin from 1811). In 1810 John Jones, the auctioneer and deputy for Lower Town Quebec, was joined in the assembly by John Jones, representative for Bedford County. It was probably he who possessed the fief of Yamaska in 1788; in any case he also speculated in township lands, notably in Compton. Finally, a John Jones of Quebec was a member in July 1797 of the grand jury inquiring into charges of treason against David McLane*.

ANQ-Q, CE1-61, 14 May 1794; 7, 14 May 1813; 5 Aug. 1818; CN1-16, 9 mars 1811, 19 nov. 1812; CN1-25, 16 sept. 1785, 12 janv. 1786; CN1-26, 29 janv. 1807, 15 févr. 1808, 27 janv. 1817; CN1-49, 31 March, 21 June, 23 Dec. 1817; 26 May, 8 June, 24 Aug. 1818; CN1-83, 20 mars 1784, 30 oct. 1792; CN1-99, 2 févr. 1808; CN1-145, 15 Sept. 1801; 17 July 1802; 25 Feb., 1, 2 March, 15 April 1803; 1, 4 Feb., 7 March, 5 July, 5 Aug. 1805; CN1-157, 29 avril 1796; 20 févr., 2 juin 1800; CN1-171, 16 March, 27 Sept. 1809; 28 Jan. 1814; CN1-178, 21 janv. 1805; CN1-197, 29 May, 25 June 1818; CN1-205, 9 août 1781; CN1-230, 15 juin 1796; CN1-256, 1 April 1782; 5 Sept. 1783; 24 May, 19 Sept. 1785; 2 June, 7 Aug. 1786; 23 Oct. 1789; February 1793; 13 May, 16 Sept., 23, 26 Nov., 19 Dec. 1795; 13 Jan., 18 March, 6 Sept. 1796; 2 June 1797; 15 April 1799; CN1-262, 15 avril 1814; CN1-284; 19 févr., 27 avril 1797; CN1-285, 26 août 1799, 10 juin 1800, 22 juill. 1809, 30 nov. 1811. "Requête des citoyens de la ville de Québec, 1787," ANQ

Rapport, 1944–45: hors-texte II. *Quebec Gazette*, 1780–1818. Desjardins, *Guide parl.*, 137. Hare et Wallot, *Les imprimés dans le Bas-Canada*, 28. Langelier, *Liste des terrains concédés*, 560–61. *Quebec almanac*, 1798: 105; 1805: 41. Tremaine, *Biblio. of Canadian imprints*, 643–44. F.-X. Chouinard et Antonio Drolet, *La ville de Québec, histoire municipale* (3v., Québec, 1963–67), 2: 55–59. O.-A. Côté, "La Chambre de commerce de Québec," *BRH*, 27 (1921): 26–28. Hare, "L'Assemblée législative du Bas-Canada," *RHAF*, 27: 382. J.-P. Wallot, "La querelle des prisons (Bas-Canada, 1805–1807)," *RHAF*, 14 (1960–61): 79.

JUCHEREAU DUCHESNAY, ANTOINE, army and militia officer, seigneur, and politician; b. 7 Feb. 1740 in Beauport, near Quebec, son of Antoine Juchereau Duchesnay, seigneur, and Marie-Françoise Chartier de Lotbinière; d. there 15 Dec. 1806.

In 1760 Antoine Juchereau Duchesnay, who was an ensign in the colonial regular troops, was given a difficult reconnaissance mission on the Lake Champlain frontier by Louis-Antoine de BOUGAINVILLE. After the conquest Duchesnay went over to the service of the British crown. In 1764 Governor Murray* appointed him captain of a corps of Canadians raised to take supplies to the beleaguered garrison of Detroit at the time of Pontiac*'s uprising [*see* John Bradstreet*].

On 12 Aug. 1765, at Beauport, Duchesnay married Julie-Louise, daughter of Louis LIÉNARD de Beaujeu de Villemonde and Louise-Charlotte Cugnet. In 1767 he entered the business world. The seigneur Michel Chartier* de Lotbinière gave him full responsibility for administering his possessions and properties. That year Duchesnay set up a company with René-Hippolyte LAFORCE, a ship's captain, to trade with the West Indies. But it was to the administration of the huge estate left by his father that he would principally direct his efforts. At the latter's death on 12 June 1772, he inherited the seigneuries of Beauport, Fossembault, Gaudarville, and Saint-Roch-des-Aulnaies. He had the advantage of being sole beneficiary. His older sister, Marie-Catherine, had retired to the convent of the Hôpital Général in Quebec, and for 26,200 *livres* his brother, Marie-Eustache, made over all his rights of succession to him in order to pursue a military career in France.

From then on Duchesnay worked for himself. He found buyers for the wheat harvested on his estates at Saint-Roch-des-Aulnaies and Beauport. At Gaudarville he farmed out the banal mill and had a new boat built to transport people and goods, for a fee, on the Rivière du Cap-Rouge. He proved a meticulous and thrifty administrator. His estimates for building and repairing mills, houses, and other buildings were very detailed; he did not hesitate to recommend that second-hand materials or tools be used. Accompanied by a notary he travelled over his estates making agreements, principally leases and land grants.

Almost all his livestock – dairy cattle and teams of oxen – were leased to habitants at Beauport. By 1774 there were unmistakable signs that the young land-owner was living in great comfort. He had several servants working for him. The silverware, linen, jewellery, and various articles of furniture and clothing mentioned in an inventory of his belongings made that year are striking in their quality and value. Jean Garneau, owner of the sub-fief of Duchesnay, rendered him the prestigious homage of his vasselage, which in keeping with custom was performed "bare-headed and kneeling on the ground" before the main doorway of the manor-house. The favourable situation was, however, upset by the partial pillaging of the manor-house and the almost complete loss of the assets of his estate when American soldiers were billeted at Beauport during the invasion in 1775 [*see* Benedict ARNOLD; Richard Montgomery*]. In the course of the hostilities Duchesnay volunteered with other Canadian officers for the defence of Fort St Johns (Saint-Jean-sur-Richelieu). He was taken prisoner on 1 Nov. 1775 and spent 18 months as a captive in New England.

Released from American military prison in 1777, Duchesnay immediately went back to work. It was a period of reconstruction. He claimed compensation for the property looted during his imprisonment. He had his mill at Gaudarville rebuilt. At Beauport and Saint-Roch-des-Aulnaies the flour-mills resumed production. Two sawmills were added at Saint-Roch-des-Aulnaies. New storage buildings were erected on his estates. The manor-house was repaired. Large sums had to be invested for transporting wood and materials, importing machinery for grinding and for other purposes in the mills, and hiring skilled labour. Within ten years the seigneur of Beauport became the fourth-largest producer of wheat in the entire province. The unoccupied back sections of his seigneuries of Saint-Roch-des-Aulnaies and Fossembault were divided into lots, which were granted to new settlers or sold when they had reached "some degree of clearing" and had been provided with buildings. Duchesnay did not hesitate, on occasion, to take part of his grantees' crops in the event of arrears in yearly payments or of other debts; he also resorted to the form of sale called *à réméré*, which obliged the habitant to repay his debt within a set period on pain of losing his property. A seasoned administrator, in 1782 Duchesnay forced the lessees of the flour-mills on his estates to turn over to him from one-half to two-thirds of the profits from their milling dues; by contrast only one-quarter had been taken 15 years earlier. This revenue, added to the income from the *cens et rentes* and from maritime trade, enabled Duchesnay the businessman to build up a large fortune.

As a result, he was called upon to supply capital to a large number of habitants, craftsmen, sailors engaged in trading, and prominent citizens. The manor-house served as a credit establishment, and people came from all parts – particularly from the Beauport and Charlesbourg regions, but also from Quebec and Montreal – seeking financial help. In the case of a farm loan the seigneur received the habitant in his manor-house and let him have from 200 to 600 *livres* in cash, at the legal interest rate of six per cent. Between 10 March 1788 and 6 March 1789 the notary Louis Miray registered no fewer than 18 loans, involving more than 10,500 *livres*. Duchesnay nevertheless acted with caution. Where borrowers were minors or did not come from his seigneuries, he required a guarantor. If a business loan was involved, he demanded that an account-book be kept, and in the case of a more doubtful debt, he insisted that an object of value be deposited as security.

Duchesnay's financial situation enabled him to enlarge an already impressive patrimony. Between 1779 and 1809 he purchased five properties, including building sites at Quebec and Montreal and new fiefs. He was concerned to establish his seigneurial privileges by exercising all his rights to the limit. For example, he even required habitants with property on the St Lawrence to take out fishing leases, extending his right of ownership over the water, as it were.

Duchesnay had become a powerful man. He no longer travelled on business. A clerk or steward acting in his name made the rounds of his estates, saw that contracts and leases were put into effect, and collected the various monies due – yearly payments, rents, or even debts. He had innumerable possessions: black servants, a second residence, a fountain and basin of faience in the main room at the manor-house, henceforth termed the "Château de Beauport," all designed for a spectacular effect. When on 7 May 1778 he married his second wife, Catherine, daughter of Jean-Baptiste LE COMTE Dupré, at Saint-Pierre on Île d'Orléans, Duchesnay brought many riches to the joint estate, whereas his 18-year-old wife had as dowry only promises of prospective family inheritances. When he penned his signature he never included a given name: there was only one Juchereau Duchesnay. He had sought verification and confirmation of the titles and letters of nobility devolving upon him from the ennoblement of his ancestor Nicolas Juchereau* de Saint-Denis in 1692. At the age of 52 he was at the height of his renown.

When the House of Assembly was constituted in the summer of 1792 Duchesnay, like many seigneurs from old families and many property owners, cast his eye on political power. He was elected for the riding of Buckingham. In the house he supported the Canadian party on crucial votes, particularly on the choice of a speaker [*see* Jean-Antoine PANET] and on the question of the assembly's official language. Duchesnay did not have to be re-elected, for in 1794 he was invited to become a member of the Executive Council.

In the final years of his life this office of executive

councillor, which brought no remuneration, seemed to be more and more just a crowning of his career, for he was now an old man and rarely attended the meetings. He neglected his own affairs somewhat: mills and buildings on his seigneuries, including those on his own estate, were in ruins. The many unused and aged sets of harness, sleighs, and calèches that were piled up in his courtyard conjured up an eventful and sumptuous past. He lived in retirement in his manor-house at Beauport, surrounded by his servants. His second wife had left the house in 1794, having been accused of adultery and sued by her husband. Since judge Pierre-Amable DE BONNE, a member of the assembly and a colleague of Duchesnay on the Executive Council, was directly implicated, the whole Lower Canadian political world was shaken by this painful affair. Duchesnay's wife launched an appeal to the highest courts in the colony for a separation as to bed, board, and property and for custody of her children. Her suit was dismissed. Eventually, however, the Duchesnays came to an agreement before a notary: Mme Duchesnay was awarded an annual pension for life and the right to visit her children, who were placed in boarding-schools "for their education."

Duchesnay's death in the winter of 1806 did not go unnoticed. The seigneur of Beauport had left a handwritten will specifying the rights, shares, and gifts to go to his heirs, as well as the bonds, promissory notes, and other payments due of which they would be beneficiaries. The registration of the will in a private minute-book in accordance with former French customary law gave rise to a dispute in court when the estate sued John YOUNG for repayment of a debt. The will had not been registered at the office of the clerk of the Court of King's Bench and the court consequently refused to recognize it as authentic. Nothing further was needed for the traditional struggle between the English party and the Canadian party to move from the House of Assembly to the courtroom. The newspapers of the time, particularly *Le Canadien*, were full of the matter.

Duchesnay left his family a huge fortune. The 42,000 *livres* in cash – 30,000 of it in gold coins – listed in the inventory of his property is only one indication of his wealth. The estate to be divided up was substantial. More than 165,000 *livres* in chattels, as well as the monies due and annual payments in arrears, had to be distributed among the widow and the five children inheriting – two born of his first marriage, Antoine-Louis* and Louise-Françoise, and three of his second, Jean-Baptiste*, Catherine-Henriette, and Michel-Louis*. Only Julie-Marguerite de Saint-Antoine, who was a nun in the Hôpital Général of Quebec, was left nothing under the will. The real estate went partly to his widow, but primarily to his sons; it consisted of the five seigneuries, two fiefs, and a number of pieces of land and building sites, which represented more than 100,000 acres

altogether, not to mention the manor-house, houses, and other buildings on the domains. Of the seigneurial properties belonging to Canadians, it brought in the largest revenues, being among the five most lucrative in all of Lower Canada at that period. The few books in Duchesnay's library, mainly on seigneurial rights and the Coutume de Paris, were just so many tools to serve this resourceful and active administrator. It would, however, take but one generation of heirs to impoverish and break up his immense estate.

RÉAL BRISSON

ANQ-Q, CE1-5; CN1-16, 8 avril, 2 oct. 1805; 23 mars 1807; CN1-25, 20, 27 oct. 1773; 4 mars 1774; 30 mars 1775; 15 mai, 5 oct. 1778; CN1-26, 24 juin, 5 nov. 1800; CN1-83, 22 oct. 1783; 6 mars, 5 oct. 1787; 27 mars, 3 oct., 11 nov., 19 déc. 1788; 16 janv., 13 févr., 30 juin, 26 août 1789; 2 juin 1794; CN1-148, 1er févr., 6 mars 1765; CN1-178, 6 oct., 1er déc. 1802; 21, 23 mars 1803; CN1-189, 18 oct. 1766; 20 févr., 16 nov. 1767; CN1-200, 9, 11, 24, 25 févr., 2, 3, 4, 13 mars, 25, 31 mai, 5 juill., 22, 25, 27, 29 sept., 25 nov. 1779; 25 juin, 13 nov. 1782; 1er, 7 mai 1787; 10, 12, 19, 22, 31 mars, 19 mai, 24 juin, 20 oct., 30 déc. 1788; 9 janv., 11, 21 févr., 6, 18 mars, 14, 25 avril, 12 mai, 22, 23 juill., 10, 22 août 1789; CN1-205, 3 juin 1773, 21 avril 1785; CN1-207, 18 juill. 1765, 18 avril 1769, 9 févr. 1774; CN1-230, 14, 31 juill., 13 sept., 8 oct. 1792; 6 mars 1794; 3 juill. 1797; 10 janv., 20 mars 1798; 15 nov. 1800; 4 avril 1801; 12 déc. 1804; 21 mars, 22 déc. 1806; 13 janv. 1808; 3 mai, 25 nov. 1809; CN1-248, 6 août, 12 oct. 1772; 2 mars, 3 juin 1773; 21 avril 1785; CN1-262, 30 juill. 1796; 18 mai 1797; 30 avril, 13, 23 mai 1801; 6 août 1803; 1er mai, 26 juill. 1805; P1000-54-1047. "Lettres de noblesse de la famille Juchereau Duchesnay," *BRH*, 28 (1922): 137–41. *Quebec Gazette*, 18 Dec. 1806. F.-J. Audet et Fabre Surveyer, *Les députés au premier Parl. du Bas-Canada*. "Papiers d'État – Bas-Canada," PAC *Rapport*, 1891: 63, 100–1, 197; 1892: 266–67. [François Daniel], *Histoire des grandes familles françaises du Canada, ou aperçu sur le chevalier Benoist, et quelques familles contemporaines* (Montréal, 1867), 317–46. Ouellet, *Bas-Canada*. J.-E. Roy, *Hist. du notariat*, vol.2. P.-G. Roy, *La famille Juchereau Duchesnay* (Lévis, Qué., 1903). "Les Américains à Beauport en 1775," *BRH*, 9 (1903): 175–81. "Les Juchereau Duchesnay," *BRH*, 38 (1932): 407–16. "La reddition du fort Saint-Jean en 1775," *BRH*, 12 (1906): 315–16. P.-G. Roy, "Le premier parlement canadien," *BRH*, 1 (1895): 122–23.

JULIEN (Julian), JOHN, Micmac chief; fl. 1779–1805 in the Miramichi region of New Brunswick.

In July 1779 HMS *Viper* sailed up the Miramichi River to protect British traders who had been robbed by the local Micmacs. It was wartime, and the Indians' fidelity to the crown was in doubt. Flying an American flag, the *Viper* put out a boat under French colours; after a brief fight, 16 Indians were captured and taken prisoner to Quebec. The ship's commander, Captain Augustus Harvey, concluded peace with John Julien, whom he recognized as chief of the Miramichi Indians, on 28 July 1779.

A few weeks later ten "Consequential Indians"

headed by John Julien and his brother Francis visited Michael Francklin*, superintendent of Indian affairs for Nova Scotia. They wanted to know what had happened to the prisoners and asked for supplies to carry their families through the winter. Francklin made a treaty with the ten at Windsor, N.S., on 22 Sept. 1779. For their part, the Indians acknowledged that they should have tried to stop the attacks on the traders, whom they agreed to protect in the future; they promised to hand over any of their number who were hostile and to have nothing to do with John ALLAN, the American superintendent of eastern Indians, who had been trying to win the support of the Micmacs and Malecites. In return, Francklin gave them supplies, promised not to molest them, and agreed to send traders to furnish necessities in exchange for furs. John Julien signed on behalf of the Indians of the Miramichi, Pokemouche, and Resti- gouche regions. On 30 Aug. 1783, Governor John Parr* of Nova Scotia gave John Julien and his tribe a licence to occupy, during pleasure, 20,000 acres along the shores of the Northwest Miramichi River.

The remembered version of these events can be seen in a Micmac-language document that came to light in 1931. According to this account a treaty was signed on 17 June 1794 between "King John Julian," together with his brother Francis, and King George III, represented by Governor William Milan, aboard an unnamed warship on the Miramichi. The English king said to the Indian king: "Henceforth you will teach your children to maintain peace and I give you this paper upon which are written many promises which will never be effaced." Then Julien requested land and was granted six miles on the Northwest Miramichi River. "Henceforth," said King George, "I will provide for you and for the future generation so long as the sun rises and river flows."

After the province of New Brunswick came into existence in 1784 Parr's licence was called into question since part of these Indian lands were included in a grant made to John Cort and William Davidson*. Julien requested confirmation of his lands on 8 July 1785 and Deputy Surveyor Benjamin Marston* reported on their extent on 29 Aug. 1785. Under the authority of Parr's licence the Indians claimed a strip of land one mile deep along each shore of the Northwest Miramichi for 20 miles from its confluence with the Southwest Miramichi: six and a half miles of this tract overlapped the new grant. Nothing was done

to resolve the contradiction. On 10 Jan. 1789 New Brunswick issued a licence of occupation to John Julien for 3,033 acres within present-day Newcastle parish, and warned that "all persons are hereby strictly forbidden to interrupt or molest the said John Julian and his tribe in the peaceable possession and occupancy hereby given." This acreage extended part of Governor Parr's grant farther inland from the Northwest Miramichi and formed the basis for the Eel Ground Indian Reserve. Further lands were added by licences of occupation dated 5 March 1805 for 8,700 acres (the Big Hole Tract) and 750 acres (the Indian Point Indian Reserve), both on the Northwest Miramichi River.

In 1808 Deputy Surveyor William Franklin Odell* was ordered to survey the Indian lands on the Miramichi, with the result that the 20,000 acres licensed by Parr were cut down by half. In his report of 16 Sept. 1808, Odell noted that he had "pointed out to the Indians on the plans the boundaries of the several tracts allotted to them, and *informed them that they must not expect or claim anything more* with which they expressed themselves satisfied." Since their licences of occupation ran only during pleasure, the Indians had no legal protection. A further threat to the reserves came from whites who either squatted on the land or made arrangements with the local chief. In 1805 James Oxford obtained quitclaims from Chief John Julien and the government made no effort to stop the practice, holding that it could not interfere in private purchases of Indian lands.

John Julien was chief at a critical period, for it was in his lifetime that whites established themselves throughout New Brunswick. He owed his position to his willingness to cooperate with the British during the American Revolutionary War, and he retained suffi- cient faith in them to be the only chief who made a sustained effort to have his tribal lands protected by the forms of the white man.

L. F. S. UPTON

PANB, RG 2, RS8, Indians 1/1, Benjamin Marston, Report, 29 Aug. 1785; RG 10, RS107/1/4: 13; 107/1/11: 26–27; RS108, Petition of John Julien, 1786; Petition of Matthew Oxford, 1805. PRO, CO 188/106: ff.206–23; CO 217/54: ff.206–7, 219–22 (mfm. at PAC). Indian-Eskimo Assoc. of Canada, *Native rights in Canada* (Toronto, [1970]), app.3: 16–17. L. F. S. Upton, *Micmacs and colonists: Indian-white relations in the Maritimes, 1713–1867* (Vancouver, 1979).

K

KAIGWIAIDOSA. *See* MADJECKEWISS

KENT and STRATHEARN, EDWARD AUGUSTUS, Duke of. *See* EDWARD AUGUSTUS

KEVENY, OWEN, HBC employee; murdered 11 Sept. 1816 on the Winnipeg River (Ont./Man.).

Owen Keveny, from Sligo (Republic of Ireland), was employed by Lord Selkirk [DOUGLAS] to recruit

Kineubenae

colonists in the west of Ireland and was chosen to lead a second party to the Red River settlement (Winnipeg) in 1812. Selkirk described him as a man "of a good family" and with four years' experience in a counting-house where he had given ample proof of "steadiness, activity and integrity." He was to stay in the settlement as Governor Miles Macdonell*'s second in command as long as Macdonell felt he was required.

On the 61-day trip to York Factory (Man.), Keveny gained a reputation as a harsh disciplinarian. Some of the settlers charged that they were "treated unlike men and with Tyranny." Keveny defended his harsh actions as necessary in the handling of agitators on board, whose actions he considered "more heinous than insubordination." The party of approximately 70 reached York in August 1812 and proceeded inland, reaching the settlement in late October. The winter was spent at Fort Daer (Pembina, N.Dak.), where some provisions were available. Food was scarce, nevertheless, and Keveny travelled to Brandon House (Man.) in the spring of 1813 to procure pemmican. Macdonell found him "distant & reserved" and reported to Selkirk that he was "extremely unpopular among the people on account of his discipline."

Though he showed zeal and interest in the affairs of the settlement, Keveny was determined to return home. He felt that Selkirk did not approve of his disciplinary methods and he had met at Macdonell's hands, he said, "treatment which has given him disgust." Macdonell indicated there was no further need for his services. Selkirk, however, reprimanded the governor, expressing dismay that a man of such ability had been "so completely thrown aside & employed to no useful purpose."

Keveny left Red River on 2 June 1813 and after a three-week journey arrived at York. There he spent the summer overseeing the dispatch of supplies to Red River and making arrangements for the third party of settlers. In September he travelled to Churchill (Man.) where the group, led by Archibald McDonald*, had been landed; he then returned to Britain on the HBC ship *Prince of Wales*. Early in 1815 he requested Selkirk to obtain an appointment for him in the company's service. The same year he was sent to Moose Factory (Ont.) as an accountant. When he heard that the Red River settlement had been dispersed and Macdonell taken prisoner by Nor'Westers in June 1815, he volunteered to take a party of men to restore order and "to make a stand there," believing that if Selkirk provided the means he could "bid defiance to the united efforts of the incendiaries who had so lately humbled" the settlement.

With his party, some of whom intended to settle at Red River, Keveny set out from Fort Albany (Ont.) in the summer of 1816. According to one witness, his harsh treatment led to desertions throughout the

journey and some of the group on hearing of the killing of Governor Robert SEMPLE at Seven Oaks (Winnipeg) in June did not want to continue. On 16 August at Bas-de-la-Rivière (Fort Alexander, Man.), Keveny was arrested under a warrant issued by Nor'Wester Archibald Norman McLeod*, a magistrate in the Indian Territory. The next day he was sent under guard towards Fort William (Thunder Bay, Ont.), but on the upper Winnipeg River the party turned back after hearing that Lord Selkirk had seized the fort. Quarrels among them and Keveny's own illness led them to abandon him on an island in the river. He was recaptured above The Dalles (Ont.) by another party of Nor'Westers under Archibald McLellan and shortly after, on 11 September, was murdered by a Métis named Mainville and Charles de Reinhard, formerly sergeant of De Meuron's Regiment but then an employee of the North West Company. The action seems to have been instigated by McLellan in some way. Reinhard confessed to the crime, was tried and found guilty in Lower Canada, and was sentenced to be hanged. Of the 150 charges laid against the Nor'Westers in connection with the Red River affair, his case was the only one that resulted in a guilty verdict but, because of disputes over the exact location of the crime and the jurisdiction of the Canadian courts, the sentence was never executed.

The murder of Keveny, and of Robert Semple and about 20 men in 1816, was a tragic climax to the struggle for control of the western fur trade in which the Métis people had been used by Nor'Westers against the Red River settlement and the Hudson's Bay Company. The violence of that struggle was a factor contributing to the amalgamation of the two companies in 1821.

HARTWELL BOWSFIELD

PAC, MG 19, E1, ser.1, 1: 460–67, 477–501; 2: 698–702, 712–34, 764–94, 812–24, 836–42; 3: 1006–52, 1456; 5: 1985–92; 6: 2189–94; 7: 2678–84, 2886; 8: 3199–202; 36: 13816; 41: 15879–85; 52: 20126–27 (transcripts). [Colin Robertson], *Colin Robertson's correspondence book, September 1817 to September 1822*, ed. E. E. Rich with R. H. Fleming (London, 1939; repr. Nendeln, Liechtenstein, 1968), 8, 225–28. [George Simpson], *Journal of occurrences in the Athabasca Department by George Simpson, 1820 and 1821, and report*, ed. E. E. Rich, intro. C. [B.] Martin (London, 1938; repr. Nendeln, 1968), 213n., 444. M. A. MacLeod and W. L. Morton, *Cuthbert Grant of Grantown, warden of the plains of Red River* (Toronto, 1963), 54–55, 68. C. [B.] Martin, *Lord Selkirk's work in Canada* (Toronto, 1916), 51, 56, 59–61, 128–29, 155. J. P. Pritchett, *The Red River valley, 1811–1849: a regional study* (New Haven, Conn., 1942), 93–99, 107, 123–24, 126, 192, 194, 212.

KINEUBENAE (Quinipeno, Quenebenaw), Mississauga Ojibwa chief; his name means the golden eagle; fl. 1797–1812 on the north shore of Lake Ontario.

During the War of 1812 a group of Mississaugas gathered by a river mouth at the western end of Lake Ontario. As the warriors squatted around him the old chief, Kineubenae, slowly began to tell of the fast in which, through the grace of unseen spirit powers, he had obtained protection against arrows, tomahawks, and even bullets. And he would demonstrate this gift. He took a tin kettle and, with some difficulty on account of his age, walked a short distance away from the circle. As soon as he raised the kettle up before his face a warrior was to fire, and Kineubenae would collect the bullet in the kettle. The marksman, like the others, believed in Kineubenae's "medicine" and he fired. The chief instantly fell. The band, to their horror, found that "the lead went into his head and [had] killed him on the spot." That one bullet did more than kill a respected leader; it shook the faith of many Mississaugas in their traditional way of life.

The life and death of Kineubenae symbolizes the decline of the Ojibwas known to the whites as Mississaugas. Born in the mid 18th century, Kineubenae grew up in the last decades of Ojibwa domination of present-day southern Ontario. Two generations earlier his ancestors had swept southward from the Upper Lakes and by 1700 had expelled the Iroquois. For the next 75 years Mississaugas alone would occupy the north shore of Lake Ontario [see Wabbicommicot*; Wabakinine*]. But all changed with the outbreak of the American revolution.

Kineubenae soon witnessed the arrival in his homeland of thousands of white and Iroquois refugees. Suddenly the Mississaugas were obliged to cede their territory at the western end of the lake in order to provide land for the newcomers. Retaining for themselves the "Mississauga Tract," an area lying between Burlington Bay (Hamilton Harbour) and the Credit River, they agreed in 1784 to the surrenders on the understanding, in Kineubenae's later words, that "the Farmers would help us," and that the Indians could "encamp and fish where we pleased."

In fact – as the chief himself complained in 1805 – the promises were not kept. Instead of assisting the Indians, the farmers "when we encamp on the Land . . . drove us off and shoot our dogs and never give us any assistance as was promised to our old Chiefs." Meanwhile the Mississaugas were fast disappearing. Close contact with Europeans had brought to the villages diseases such as smallpox and tuberculosis, against which they had no natural immunity. Over the period from 1787 to 1798 the Mississaugas at the western end of Lake Ontario declined from more than 500 to approximately 350.

As the principal chief of the Mississaugas on Twelve Mile (Bronte) Creek, Kineubenae frequently spoke for the Mississaugas in the early 19th century.

In 1805, for example, he negotiated with the British over the proposed sale of the "Mississauga Tract." The surviving minutes of the conference reveal that Kineubenae was a shrewd bargainer. On the first day he firmly opposed the surrender of more land, for, as he told William Claus*, deputy superintendent general of Indian affairs in Upper Canada, "the young Men & Women have found fault with so much having been sold before,: it is true we are poor, & the Women say we will be worse, if we part with any more." Only after the British applied pressure on the second day did he comply. Then, in return for ceding the entire lakefront of the tract (the Indians retained the interior section until 1818), Kineubenae extracted a promise from the British that the Mississaugas would keep the river mouths and their rights to the fisheries there.

Within a year, however, Kineubenae was protesting against the settlers' encroachments on the fisheries. In 1806 he complained about the white man who had taken over his cornfield at Bronte Creek and then destroyed it, as well as that of a poor Indian widow who had four children to support. The same white settler, Kineubenae reported, was building a weir to catch salmon on their way upstream to spawn. In addition, a white squatter at the Credit River had so disturbed the waters "by washing with sope and other dirt, that the fish refuse coming into the River as usual, by which our families are in great distress for want of food."

By 1812 Kineubenae was becoming extremely weak and on his own admission "getting too old to walk." For nearly two decades he had led his people and during this time most of their lands had been taken, the fish and game populations had declined drastically, and their own numbers had been severely reduced. Then the war between the British and the Americans had extended to the north shore of Lake Ontario. It was at this point that Kineubenae, in order to inspire his band with an example of the strength of their traditions, fasted and obtained "warrior's medicine." The fact that it could not resist the white man's bullet would, a decade later, facilitate the work of Peter Jones [Kahkewaquonaby*] in converting the demoralized Mississaugas to Christianity.

DONALD B. SMITH

PAC, RG 10, A2, 27: 420; 438; "Proceedings of a meeting with the Missisawque Indians," 3 Oct. 1810; A6, 1834: 197. PRO, CO 42/340: ff.49–53. Victoria Univ. Library (Toronto), Peter Jones coll., anecdote book, no.53 ("Powwowiska Quenebenaw's death"). *Canada, Indian treaties and surrenders . . .* [1680–1906] (3v., Ottawa, 1891–1912; repr. Toronto, 1971), 1: 23. *Corr. of Hon. Peter Russell* (Cruikshank and Hunter), 2: 304, 306. Peter Jones (Kahkewaquonaby), *History of the Ojebway Indians; with especial reference to their conversion to Christianity . . .* (London, 1861), 108–9, 155.

King

KING, BOSTON, Methodist preacher and author; b. c. 1760 near Charleston, S.C.; d. 1802 in Sierra Leone.

Boston King was born a slave on Richard Waring's plantation near Charleston. His father, who had been "stolen away from Africa when he was young," was on good terms with Waring, and his mother also was well treated because of her skills as a nurse and seamstress. King was trained as a house servant but at the age of 16, still under Waring's control, he was sent to a nearby town to be apprenticed as a carpenter. The time he spent learning his new trade was far from pleasant, for his employer often beat him "without mercy." Fortunately, when the American revolution broke out Waring adhered to the rebels, which meant that if King could flee to the British he would gain freedom. His opportunity came when the British took Charleston in May 1780. Joining a mass movement of runaway slaves to the royal standard, King now "began to feel the happiness of liberty."

The treatment provided by the British did not match the generosity of their offer of freedom. Squalid and overcrowded accommodation promoted disease, and King was one of the many to contract smallpox. After his recovery he became useful to his benefactors. As a carpenter he might have been one of that sizeable minority of black loyalists with specialized skills, many of whom plied their trades in the British service, but the absence of tools forced him to seek alternative employment as a servant. Like countless black loyalists, however, he soon was engaged in military action. By carrying dispatches through enemy lines he was responsible for the relief of 250 besieged British soldiers at Nelson's Ferry (near Eutawville), S.C., and as a crew member on a British man-of-war he helped capture a rebel ship in Chesapeake Bay. Later he was taken and re-enslaved by the American navy but escaped for a second time to British safety. Yet threats to his freedom came not only from the rebels, for innumerable runaways were betrayed and sold as slaves by loyalist militia officers. Once King himself was taken by a militia captain, but his talent for escape saved him again.

As the war drew to a close, thousands of loyalists converged on New York City, King among them. While there he supported himself as a servant and casual labourer, and married Violet, a fellow runaway who had escaped from a master in Wilmington, N.C. The publication of the preliminary peace agreement in late 1782 destroyed King's comfort, for article 7 required the British to return all American property, including slaves. As King wrote later, the prospect of being returned to bondage filled the black loyalists with "inexpressible anguish and terror," and their fears were certainly not diminished when former masters entered New York City and began seizing blacks in the streets and in their homes. At this critical point Sir Guy CARLETON, commander-in-chief of British forces, announced that his interpretation of article 7 was that black loyalists were not in fact American property at the time of the agreement and so must be allowed to evacuate with other loyalists. Issued with certificates guaranteeing their freedom by Brigadier-General Samuel Birch, the city commandant, New York's black refugees boarded the transport ships and had their names, descriptions, and personal histories recorded in the "Book of Negroes." Between 26 April and 30 Nov. 1783, 3,000 black loyalists were shipped to Nova Scotia. King, described as a "Stout fellow" aged 23, embarked with his wife on L'Abondance and sailed for Port Roseway, recently renamed Shelburne, on 31 July.

The first loyalists had reached Port Roseway in May 1783, including a party of blacks who set to work clearing the town-site and preparing roads. At a discreet six miles from Shelburne, surveyor Benjamin Marston* laid out a separate town-site for the blacks. King arrived there on 27 August in time to witness the survey and participate in the establishment of Birchtown, named for their New York protector. A muster held in January 1784 showed that Birchtown, with a population of 1,521 blacks, was the largest free black settlement in North America. Each of them received a town lot large enough for a garden, but the delay in granting farms forced them to continue to labour in Shelburne where construction assured plentiful employment.

A great religious revival occurred in Birchtown during the winter of 1783–84, part of a phenomenon seen all over Nova Scotia as the former slaves flocked to the churches for baptism. William Black*, the Methodist evangelist, paid special attention to Birchtown, which contained the largest Methodist society in Nova Scotia. Even John Wesley remarked upon the religious enthusiasm of the Birchtown blacks, and in 1785 American Methodist Freeborn Garrettson was sent from Baltimore, Md, to assist in the harvest of souls. The first person in the settlement to be converted was King's wife, Violet, who owed her deliverance from "evil tempers" to the preaching of Moses Wilkinson, a black loyalist and Birchtown's leading Methodist. In early 1785 King, too, was converted. Describing his feelings at this time, King wrote: "All my doubts and fears vanished away: I saw, by faith, heaven opened to my view; and Christ and his angels rejoicing over me." For the next few years King preached in black settlements from Shelburne to Halifax. Owing to his and other preachers' efforts, by 1790 black loyalists constituted one-quarter of Nova Scotia Methodists.

With most of his Birchtown neighbours King worked in Shelburne, as a carpenter, and supplemented his income with his garden. Because they accepted lower wages, the blacks attracted the hostility of white workers, who launched a riot in July 1784 and attempted to drive them out of Shelburne. That issue disappeared as the whites were given farms, but by 1789 Shelburne's economic difficulties created unemployment and abject distress for the blacks. King, appalled by the "poverty and distress" around him, left Birchtown and found work on a fishing boat operating out of Chedabucto Bay, where he continued to preach at every opportunity. In 1791 William Black, by then presiding elder of Nova Scotia's Methodists, appointed King preacher to the black settlement at Preston near Halifax. The Preston black community was closely knit, and the preachers in the Anglican, Baptist, and Methodist chapels were its natural leaders. King knew comfort at last, earning a decent living from his work in Preston and nearby Dartmouth, and enjoying the respect of his flock. His stay in Preston, however, was brief. Although satisfied with his life in Nova Scotia, he had a strong desire to spread "the knowledge of Christianity" amongst his African brothers, and in 1791 he joined other prominent Nova Scotia blacks, such as David GEORGE and Thomas Peters*, in assisting John Clarkson of the Sierra Leone Company to recruit emigrants for a colony of free blacks in West Africa. The support he gave Clarkson in this endeavour yielded results: almost the entire black community of Preston, many of whom were motivated by the promise of free land and self-determination in Sierra Leone, joined in the exodus.

A fleet of 15 ships – King and the Preston blacks sailed on the *Eleanor* – left Nova Scotia for Sierra Leone in January 1792. After arriving in Freetown, Violet King succumbed to a fever epidemic, but King survived to establish a Methodist chapel. His ambition was fulfilled when in August 1793 the Sierra Leone Company appointed him teacher and missionary to the Africans on the Bullom shore, opposite Freetown, making him the first Methodist missionary in Africa. To improve his qualifications for this work, the company in March 1794 sent him to England, where he attended the Kingswood School near Bristol for two years. While there he wrote a memoir of his life to 1796. On his return to Africa in late September 1796 the company employed him as a teacher in Freetown and its vicinity, but he seems to have been dissatisfied with this work since his personal goal was to minister to the indigenous Africans. He soon left the colony for a company post located amongst the Sherbro people, some hundred miles south, where he probably resumed his missionary activity. He and his second wife both died there in 1802.

King was one of three black loyalists to leave a personal account of his experiences. John Marrant*'s influential *Narrative of the Lord's wonderful dealings* is his most important legacy, and David George, still remembered as the founder of the black Baptist church in the Maritimes, published a revealing account of his life in the *Baptist annual register*. Boston King's "Memoirs" was not a major literary or historical work, but through his reminiscences it is possible to gain an impression of the life of the ordinary black loyalist during the American revolution and in early Nova Scotia.

JAMES W. ST G. WALKER

The original "Book of Negroes" is in PRO, PRO 30/55/100. A photocopy is available in the NYPL, British Headquarters papers, doc.10427, while transcript versions with slight variations can be seen in PAC, MG 23, B1, 55, and PANS, RG 1, 423. Boston King was the author of "Memoirs of the life of Boston King, a black preacher, written by himself during his residence at Kingswood School," *Methodist Magazine* (London), 21 (1798): 105–10, 157–61, 209–13, 261–65.

BL, Add. MSS 41262A–64. Huntington Library (San Marino, Calif.), Zachary Macaulay papers. N.B. Museum, F50, "Muster roll of the Black Pioneers, 1779–80"; F53, "State of the Guides & Pioneers, 27 Nov. 1780" (transcript). NYPL, Emmet coll. PAC, MG 23, D1, ser.1, 24 (transcripts at PANS). PANS, MG 1, 219; 948, docs.196, 340; MG 4, 140–41, 143 (copies); MG 100, 169, no.27a (photocopy); RG 1, 47, doc.13; 137; 213, 5 Aug. 1784; 302, doc.11; 346, doc.89; 371; 419–22. PRO, AO 12/54, 12/99, 12/102; AO 13, bundle 79; CO 217/63, 217/68; CO 267/91; PRO 30/8, bundle 344 (transcript at PAC); PRO 30/55, nos.1215, 4331, 6480, 7419, 7448, 8668, 8800, 8886, 9130, 9304, 9955 (photocopies at NYPL); WO 1/352. USPG, Dr. Bray's Associates, minute-books, 3; unbound papers, box 7; Journal of SPG, 23: 379; 25: 18–19, 24, 97.

[David George], "An account of the life of Mr. David George, from Sierra Leone in Africa; given by himself in a conversation with Brother Rippon of London, and Brother Pearce of Birmingham," *Baptist annual reg.* (London), 1 (1790–93): 473–84. [John Marrant], *A narrative of the Lord's wonderful dealings with John Marrant, a black . . .*, ed. Rev. Mr Aldridge (2nd ed., London, 1785). SPG, [*Annual report*] (London), 1784. Benjamin Quarles, *The negro in the American revolution* (Chapel Hill, N.C., 1961). J. W. St G. Walker, *The black loyalists: the search for a promised land in Nova Scotia and Sierra Leone, 1783–1870* (London, 1976). E. G. Wilson, *The loyal blacks* (New York, 1976). R. W. Winks, *The blacks in Canada: a history* (Montreal, 1971). P. R. Blakeley, "Boston King: a negro loyalist who sought refuge in Nova Scotia," *Dalhousie Rev.*, 48 (1968–69): 347–56. W. O. Raymond, "The founding of Shelburne: Benjamin Marston at Halifax, Shelburne and Miramichi," N.B. Hist. Soc., *Coll.*, 3 (1907–14), no.8: 204–77. J. W. St G. Walker, "Blacks as American loyalists: the slaves' war for independence," *Hist. Reflections* (Waterloo, Ont.), 2 (1975): 51–67. A. F. Walls, "The Nova Scotian settlers and their religion," *Sierra Leone Bull. of Religion* (Freetown, Sierra Leone), 1 (1959): 19–31.

La Cailleterie

L

LA CAILLETERIE, JEAN DE LISLE DE. *See* DE LISLE

LA FEUILLE. *See* WAHPASHA

LAFORCE, RENÉ-HIPPOLYTE, ship's captain, naval and militia officer, merchant, and diarist; b. 4 Dec. 1728 in La Prairie (Que.), son of Pierre Pépin, *dit* Laforce, and Michelle Lebert; m. 10 Jan. 1757 Madeleine Corbin at Quebec, and they had ten children; d. there 3 Feb. 1802 and was buried two days later in the crypt of Notre-Dame.

René-Hippolyte Laforce spent the first 11 years of his life at Fort Niagara (near Youngstown, N.Y.), where his father held the post of king's storekeeper. No further trace of him has been found until 1751, when he was engaged in coastal trading between Quebec and Louisbourg, Île Royale (Cape Breton Island). Three years later Laforce joined an expedition under Joseph Coulon* de Villiers de Jumonville in the Ohio valley. Although his role in this venture remains unclear, he was taken prisoner and sent to Virginia. Robert Stobo*, who was captured by the French at about this time, did not see him as a hero but thought he was at the least an important cog in the French war machine in the Ohio country.

In 1756, after his release, Laforce was appointed commander of a frigate on Lake Ontario by Governor Vaudreuil [Pierre de Rigaud*]. He took part that year in a skirmish against the British near Oswego (Chouaguen) (N.Y.). In 1758 he arrived at Niagara, and he remained there until the beginning of the siege operations the following year, which he recorded in his diary [*see* Sir William Johnson*].

Laforce apparently stayed in Kamouraska, Que., from 1762 to 1766 while retaining possession of a small piece of land on Rue Saint-Jean at Quebec. Upon his return to Quebec in 1767 he went into partnership with Antoine JUCHEREAU Duchesnay to trade with the West Indies; the two were to share equally in the profits. He was getting ready to take ship when merchant Alexandre DUMAS authorized him to recover the sums that two Martinique traders owed him. Laforce continued to travel to the islands until 1775, bringing back sugar and coffee in particular, but it seems that at some point the contract was modified and that Laforce then acted only as captain. The American revolution put an end to his commercial endeavours for a while.

When the Quebec militia was temporarily re-established in 1775, Governor Guy CARLETON appointed Laforce captain of the town's artillery company. Some days later Laforce received orders, as commanding officer of the *Providence*, to patrol the St Lawrence. He plied the river between Quebec and Sorel in 1775 and 1776 and even took part in the various operations connected with the American blockade.

Late in 1776 Carleton entrusted Laforce with the command of the schooner *Seneca*; he also supervised its construction and saw to its fitting-out. At the same time he became commanding officer of the fleet on Lake Ontario. He was in charge of the shipyard at Pointe-au-Baril (Maitland, Ont.) the following year. In 1778 Governor HALDIMAND appointed him "master and commander of His Majesty's Naval Armament upon the Rivers and Lakes within this Province." Two years later Laforce was supervising the shipyard on Carleton Island (N.Y.) and received a commission as commodore of the fleet. In 1784 he retired from service on half pay.

Laforce then resumed sailing between Quebec and the West Indies. Age and the state of his health, however, got the better of his intrepidity. In October 1788 he sold his share in a 120-ton schooner, the *Marie*, to Quebec merchant Louis DUNIÈRE. Six years later Lord Dorchester (as Carleton was now known) appointed Laforce lieutenant-colonel of the militia of Quebec and vicinity. His long and loyal services led him to ask for land in 1800; he applied at that time to the lieutenant governor of Upper Canada, Peter HUNTER, on the grounds that he had served largely in that region. His request was turned down because he was not living in the province. A few weeks before his death Laforce petitioned the lieutenant governor of Lower Canada, Sir Robert Shore Milnes*, for 5,000 acres of land.

Except for his ships Laforce does not seem to have acquired much property. Besides his lot on Rue Saint-Jean he owned a house in the Palais quarter which he rented to a shoemaker. He sold some land on Rue Saint-Nicholas; it belonged, however, to his father-in-law, who had mortgaged it in his favour.

YVON DESLOGES

René-Hippolyte Laforce's "Journal fait par le Sr Laforce, commandant les bâtiments sur le lac Ontario, du siège de Niagara, à commencer du 6 juillet 1759 jusqu'au 14 dud." is held at PAC, MG 18, N20.

ANQ-M, CE1-3, 5 déc. 1728. ANQ-Q, CE1-1, 10 janv. 1757, 5 févr. 1802; CN1-83, 20 oct. 1788; CN1-189, 16, 17 nov. 1767; CN1-205, 30 janv., 31 mars 1783; P-128;

P1000-95-1936. AUM, P 58, H2/55, 8 août 1766. PAC, RG 1, E15, A; L3^L: 57355–64. *Quebec Gazette*, 11 Feb. 1802. Charland, "Notre-Dame de Québec: le nécrologe de la crypte," *BRH*, 20: 273. Tanguay, *Dictionnaire*, 6: 295, 300. *Royal Fort Frontenac*, trans. and comp. R. A. Preston, ed. Léopold Lamontagne (Toronto, 1958). P.-G. Roy, *Les petites choses de notre histoire* (7 sér., Lévis, Qué., 1919–44), 3: 238–39. G. F. G. Stanley, *New France: the last phase, 1744–1760* (Toronto, 1968), 141. "Jumonville et ses compagnons," *BRH*, 10 (1904): 250–52. Marcel Trudel, "L'affaire Jumonville," *RHAF*, 6 (1952–53): 331–73.

LAHAILLE, JEAN-BAPTISTE (baptized **Jean**), Roman Catholic priest, superior of the Séminaire de Québec, and vicar general; b. 22 Oct. 1750 in Tarbes, France, son of Joseph Lahaille, a merchant and gold- and silversmith, and Barthelemie Grabot; d. 24 May 1809 in the Hôpital Général of Quebec.

Under the *ancien régime* colleges in France drew their pupils from bourgeois families, those of the gold- and silversmiths being among the most influential. It is not surprising, therefore, that Jean-Baptiste Lahaille attended the Collège de La Madeleine in Bordeaux; he completed his studies successfully, obtaining his baccalaureate and then, at the age of 21, his master's degree. In the period 1771–74 he studied theology and received the tonsure and minor orders. In 1775 Abbé de L'Isle-Dieu, the bishop of Quebec's vicar general in Paris, informed the Séminaire de Québec that Lahaille, who wanted to serve in the missions, had agreed to go to the province of Quebec. Having obtained Governor Guy CARLETON's permission, Lahaille landed at Quebec that year, along with another young cleric from Bordeaux, Arnauld-Germain Dudevant*. Their admission to the province constituted an exception, since after the conquest the British government had forbidden the Canadian clergy to recruit priests in France. His compatriot went back to France in 1783, but Lahaille spent the rest of his life in Quebec, although he tried on several occasions to return home or go to the missions in India. In 1799 he asked for letters of naturalization so that he could remain in Lower Canada free of harassment by British officials, who in that troubled period of the French revolutionary wars kept a close watch on foreigners and especially on Frenchmen living in the province.

On 20 Aug. 1777 Lahaille was ordained priest by Bishop Briand*; that year he was also admitted to the Séminaire de Québec as a member of the community. He taught philosophy at the Petit Séminaire from 1775 to 1778 and then became a professor at the Grand Séminaire. Although the lack of documentary evidence makes it impossible to evaluate Lahaille's teaching, it is clear that he took a great interest in the sciences. He possessed physics instruments and a graphometer, and during the summer holidays at the "cotteau Fortin" or Petit Cap (Cap Tourmente, Que.) he used his microscope to introduce the pupils to the experimental method. Lahaille extended his scientific knowledge with the help of John Mervin Nooth*, a doctor and the former superintendent of hospitals in British North America, who after his return to England in 1799 sent him information on the latest experiments conducted at the Royal Society of London.

Since few priests were admitted to the seminary as members, Lahaille devoted himself more to administration than to teaching. He held the offices of director of the Petit and the Grand Séminaire as well as that of bursar, before serving as superior from 1805 to 1809. In the early years of the 19th century, the seminary faced a serious recruiting problem that was hard to resolve because Bishop DENAUT was short of priests for the parishes and refused to allow them to be admitted as members of the seminary. Lahaille's difficulties were compounded by the fact that he disputed the diocesan authority, refusing to accept its interference in the seminary's affairs. This attitude did not please Denaut. The situation improved after Joseph-Octave Plessis* became bishop in 1806, although he shared Denaut's views. Plessis brought Lahaille around to a better frame of mind by allowing a few priests to be admitted into the community of the seminary, appointing Lahaille vicar general on 12 June 1806, and taking up residence in the seminary himself.

Jean-Baptiste Lahaille was recognized as much for his moderation, good judgement, and prudence as for his intellectual endeavours. The exemplary modesty and thoughtfulness he displayed prevented the Canadian priests from taking umbrage at this Frenchman, who was indeed the last one to head the seminary. From September 1789 Lahaille had been a confessor to the Ursulines of Quebec and the nuns of the Hôtel-Dieu and the Hôpital Général. At the latter institution, in complete serenity, he ended his days. He was buried in the seminary chapel.

CLAUDE GALARNEAU

AAQ, 210 A, II: f.193; IV: f.11; 516 CD, 1, 25 mai 1809. AD, Hautes-Pyrénées (Tarbes), État civil, Tarbes, 22 oct. 1750. ASQ, Lettres, M, 57, 58, 61, 157, 205, 209, 256, 723, 724; T, 80, 85; mss, 12: f.45; 433; Polygraphie, VIII: 63; XII: 6; XVII: 22–29. *Le séminaire de Québec* (Provost), 455. *L'Abeille* (Québec), 8 mars 1861. *Le Canadien*, 27 mai 1809. *Quebec Gazette*, 25 May 1809. Caron, "Inv. de la corr. de Mgr Briand," ANQ *Rapport*, 1929–30: 116; "Inv. de la corr. de Mgr Denaut," 1931–32: 238–39; "Inv. de la corr. de Mgr Hubert et de Mgr Bailly de Messein," 1930–31: 215; "Inv. de la corr. de Mgr Panet," 1933–34: 235; "Inv. de la corr. de Mgr Plessis," 1927–28: 267; 1932–33: 23, 26, 37, 64. Claude Galarneau, "L'enseignement des sciences au Québec et Jérôme Demers (1765–1835)," *Mélanges d'histoire du Canada français offerts au professeur Marcel Trudel* (Ottawa, 1978), 86, 89. Lemieux, *L'établissement de la première prov. eccl.*, 144. J.-E. Roy, *Souvenirs d'une classe*

Lambert

au séminaire de Québec, 1867–1877 (Lévis, Qué., 1905), 137.

LAMBERT, JOHN, traveller, author, and painter in water-colours; b. *c.* 1775 in England; fl. 1806–16.

John Lambert came to Lower Canada in 1806. He was accompanying his uncle, James CAMPBELL, who had been sent by the Privy Council committee for trade in London to promote the growing of hemp in the colony. It does not seem, however, that Lambert was in any way engaged in this project, which failed around 1810. In 1806, well before that outcome, he set off on travels about the colony and in various American states. He may already have been been thinking of writing an account of his voyage. One thing is certain: it was as a perspicacious observer with a critical and extremely sharp eye that he carried out his tour, accumulating facts and anecdotes of all kinds.

Lambert remained in Lower Canada in 1806 and 1807, visiting Quebec, Montreal, and the towns and villages in between. In each place he seems to have associated with the influential people and to have been welcomed warmly and unreservedly in British and Canadian, Catholic and Protestant homes. Later he toured the United States, from the state of New York to South Carolina, in the same fashion.

Lambert returned to Quebec in 1809 and left again for London almost immediately. The following year he brought out in three volumes his *Travels through Lower Canada, and the United States of North America, in the years 1806, 1807, and 1808*; its great success led him to prepare a second edition in two volumes in 1813, a third one the following year, and a fourth in 1816. He illustrated the work himself with rather restrained and naïve water-colours depicting some of the places visited, objects of everyday use, and the clothing worn by women, priests, soldiers, seminary students, and Indians. In 1811 Lambert also brought out, with a long and laudatory introduction on American life, a British edition of a work he considered a model of American literature, Washington Irving's essays *Salmagundi; or, the whim-whams and opinions of Launcelot Langstaff, esq., and others. . . .*

Lambert claimed that he published his *Travels*, which professed to offer a description of the social and economic situation of Lower Canada, because the colony's rapid progress had made earlier travel accounts obsolete; the last one, Isaac Weld*'s *Travels through the states of North America, and the provinces of Upper and Lower Canada, during the years 1795, 1796 and 1797*, had come out in London in 1799. In his book Lambert displayed no class or party interest. As far as possible he tried to paint a fair and realistic picture of Lower Canada, although on occasion he was unable to conceal his aversion for still-visible signs of the influence of the French régime

and for the Roman Catholic clergy; he considered the clergy useful, to be sure, because of their social vocation, but also thought they fostered ossification and backwardness amongst the Catholics.

Far from presenting a chronological account of his voyage, Lambert arranged his notes to depict in each of his chapters a different aspect of Lower Canada: geography, climate, geology, botany, and zoology. He studied both towns and countryside, estimated the size of the population, and compiled a mass of data, backed with tables, on such facets of the economy as agriculture, industry, retail trade, the fur trade, exports, imports, money, and many other elements. Lambert also paid attention to social circumstances. He described the Indians' way of life and their decline, divided the population of the towns and countryside into social classes, and with numerous anecdotes recounted the ways and customs of the habitants and the town-dwellers. He depicted, sometimes ironically but never dishonestly or antagonistically, various groups such as priests, nuns, and women; he considered the latter to be better educated than their husbands and to have great influence on them. He also tried to fathom the judicial system and French law, explain seigneurial tenure, and assess the church's hold on the Canadians.

Lambert proved just as meticulous in his description of American society; he compared it favourably with Lower Canadian society in virtually all areas: roads, farms, towns, trade, education, art, wealth – and scandals. His analysis also showed the glaring difference that already existed between the anglophones in Lower Canada and the Americans, a generation after the states had gained independence.

Biographical information on John Lambert is extremely fragmentary. And yet his short stay in Canada turned out to be of real importance, for the writings that resulted from it have been widely read and used by historians, story-tellers, and novelists. The author's desire to be objective is so evident throughout the work that many have been convinced of the merit of the account and the soundness of its arguments. There is, however, no doubt that Lambert was above all faithful to his period and his origins.

JACQUELINE ROY

[John Lambert's *Travels through Lower Canada, and the United States of North America, in the years 1806, 1807, and 1808, to which are added, biographical notices and anecdotes of some of the leading characters in the United States; and of those who have, at various periods, borne a conspicuous part in the politics of that country* was published in three volumes in London in 1810; it reappeared under slightly different titles in two volumes in 1813, 1814, and 1816. Despite its success and the wide use made of it by francophone historians, Lambert's *Travels* has never been translated. However, extracts in French have appeared in several articles, notably "Du voyage de J. Lambert en Canada (1810)," *La Bibliothèque canadienne* (Montréal), 3 (1826): 130–32; "État de la littérature canadienne en 1809," 7 (1828): 57–60; Ægidius Fauteux, "La romanesque mais peu véridique histoire de Mlle d'Artigny," *BRH*, 41 (1935): 167–71. J.R.]

C. P. De Volpi, *Québec, a pictorial record . . . 1608–1875*, trans. Jules Bazin (n.p., 1971). *DNB*. Hare et Wallot, *Les imprimés dans le Bas-Canada*, 259–62. J. R. Harper, *Early painters and engravers in Canada* ([Toronto], 1970). Norah Story, *The Oxford companion to Canadian history and literature* (Toronto and London, 1967). Tremaine, *Biblio. of Canadian imprints. Histoire littéraire du Canada, littérature canadienne de langue anglaise*, ed. C. F. Klinck *et al.*, trans. Maurice Lebel (Québec, 1970), 122, 163, 222. Sulte, *Mélanges hist.* (Malchelosse), 7: 116–18.

LAMBERT, PATRICK, Roman Catholic priest, Franciscan, and vicar apostolic of Newfoundland; b. *c.* 1755 in the parish of Kildavin, County Wexford (Republic of Ireland); d. 23 Sept. 1816 in Wexford.

Patrick Lambert first appears in 1780 at the Irish Franciscan college at Louvain (Belgium), where he became lector in philosophy. In 1783 he transferred to Rome as president of St Isidore's, also an Irish Franciscan college, but resigned this appointment the following year. He returned to Ireland in 1785, serving as guardian of the monastery in Kilkenny until 1793. Thereafter he was associated with the Wexford friary and taught at the Franciscan academy attached to it. For some years he was president of the academy, and was guardian of the friary from 1801 to 1803. While at Wexford, Lambert held several important offices in the administration of the Franciscan province of Ireland. He was the Leinster definitor from 1794 to 1801 and was elected custos in 1803. From the death of the provincial in September 1803 to July 1804, Lambert headed the order as vicar provincial.

In 1804 the ailing vicar apostolic of Newfoundland, James Louis O'DONEL, requested a coadjutor bishop with the right of succession. Early the following year, from candidates proposed by Archbishop John Thomas Troy of Dublin, Rome selected Father Bonaventure Stewart, the new Irish Franciscan provincial, but he resigned before being consecrated, and on 30 July Lambert was appointed instead. Elevated to the episcopacy with the title of bishop of Chytra on 4 May 1806 at Wexford, Lambert arrived in St John's that August. He served as O'Donel's coadjutor until the latter's resignation on 1 Jan. 1807, whereupon he succeeded as vicar apostolic.

From the beginning Lambert was unhappy in his appointment. Even before his consecration he had suggested to the Holy See that he would prefer a more temperate climate. He indeed found the weather in Newfoundland inclement, and the people "passably instructed, but not even *passably* obedient . . . with

many immersed in the Depths of lust, prone to Drunkeness, and even infected with the Rash of the new philosophy." By November 1807 he had asked the pope (in vain) to transfer him to a less arduous see or to give him a pension sufficient for retirement to Ireland.

None the less, Lambert attended faithfully to his episcopal duties. He visited Conception Bay in 1807, covering 21 leagues of coastline and confirming more than 400 persons. On a similar visitation of Ferryland district in 1810 he broke several ribs while travelling through the woods. In fact, Lambert had few priests to serve so large a territory – only five throughout most of his episcopate. The bishop therefore made it a practice to accept students for the Newfoundland mission, both Irish-born and native Newfoundlanders, who would be trained in Quebec. The first priest ordained specifically for Newfoundland, James Sinnott, a young man who had come with Lambert from Wexford, was sent to the Séminaire de Québec in 1808 and was ordained there in 1810. Although over the years Lambert sent several other seminarians to Lower Canada, only one other, William Herron*, ever attained the priesthood.

With the bishop of Quebec, Joseph-Octave Plessis*, Lambert had a cordial relationship. In 1807 and 1808 the two exchanged faculties giving one another the powers of vicars-general, and thereafter they maintained a steady correspondence. Anxious to be relieved of responsibility for part of his vast territory, in 1807 Plessis offered to transfer to Lambert responsibility for Nova Scotia, New Brunswick, and the neighbouring islands. Lambert saw nothing attractive about this offer, remarking that "I have too much sailing round the coasts of Newfoundland without going across to the Continent." He proposed instead subdivision of the Quebec diocese, with the assurance that he would gladly be a suffragan should Quebec become a metropolitan see. Plessis did not pursue the matter, but on another occasion he did raise tentatively the possibility of attaching Labrador and Anticosti Island to Newfoundland. In 1812 he also brought to Lambert's attention the situation of the Micmac Indians who had migrated from Nova Scotia to the St George's Bay area; Lambert was able subsequently to send them a priest in the summer season.

Lambert's episcopate was marked by a large number of conversions to Roman Catholicism. From 1809 to 1813 especially, the letters of Protestant clergymen evidenced the success of Lambert's priests. "Thousands along the coast" were said to have espoused Catholicism, and one Anglican missionary, John HARRIES, went so far as to warn that the island "will very soon become a Roman Catholic colony." Even Governor Sir Richard Goodwin Keats* recognized the priests as being "too successful in making

Lanaudière

proselytes" and their "Zeal and Activity" as worthy of imitation. Although numerical data are lacking, this movement seems to have been especially significant in areas where Anglicans were unattended by clergy of their own. In general, the Catholic priests were much more mobile, and more regular in their visits to out-lying areas, than their Protestant counterparts.

An even larger factor in the growth of Newfound-land's Roman Catholic population was the vast Irish immigration that occurred between 1811 and 1816, an influx which eventually caused the bishop major problems. The boom years of the Napoleonic Wars saw Newfoundland prosper. By the spring of 1815, however, the fishing economy had collapsed, and yet large numbers of Irish still poured into St John's, perhaps 6,000 in that year alone. Not only was there massive unemployment and great poverty, but these conditions soon led to divisions among the Newfound-land Irish; competitive county gangs were formed and secret oaths sworn. There were important social differences between Leinster and Munster, the two Irish provinces from which immigrants came to Newfoundland, Munster being the less anglicized and heavily Irish-speaking. The long-standing rivalry which had existed between the two spilled over into Newfoundland and in 1815 led to violence between gangs of the two factions.

Lambert had previously recorded his opinion of Irish newcomers as an "unprincipled and ignorant set of lawless wretches." Now he and his clergy denounced the disorders and secret oaths in their sermons, but to no avail. Lambert spoke no Irish, and as Leinster men he and his clergy were held suspect by the other party. Furthermore, the bishop had earlier suspended Father John Power*, a priest from Mun-ster, and this action had cost him considerable support. Indeed, the dispute between Lambert and Power appears to have greatly exacerbated interprovincial rivalry in Newfoundland. The troubles of 1815 probably contributed significantly to Lambert's deci-sion to leave the island that year.

Lambert maintained a generally good relationship with the governors of his day. A major concession had been accorded Newfoundland Roman Catholics in 1811 when the British government permitted them cemeteries of their own, thereby ending the disputes that had sometimes accompanied Roman Catholic burials in Anglican churchyards. At the recommenda-tion of Governor Keats, the government also author-ized in 1814 the payment of an annual stipend of £75 to Lambert in his official capacity as "Head of the Catholic Church." In fact, when Lambert had trouble with Power, Keats went so far as to recommend that the imperial government prohibit the immigration to Newfoundland of any priest not authorized by the bishop.

By 1813 Lambert's health was failing. He was subject to dizziness and violent headaches, apparently the result of an epileptic condition. He contemplated leaving Newfoundland even then, but he did not make a final decision until 1815, following an application to Rome to have Thomas Scallan* named as his coadjutor. On 14 November he departed for Ireland, where he took up residence at the Wexford friary. Lambert still spoke of returning to his mission even after Scallan's nomination in January 1816, but with little conviction. He was concerned that his pension was payable only during his residence in Newfound-land, and sought to have this condition modified. By June he was said to be "exceedingly ill, deranged and childish, with no hope of recovery." He succumbed to his illness on 23 September and was buried in the friary church at Wexford.

Lambert was described by Chief Justice Caesar Colclough* as "Honest, Loyal and well-intentioned," although "an irritable man of no abilities." Not robust, the bishop was perhaps ill-suited to the demands of his office, and it is clear that his appointment was one he did not relish. Nevertheless, his episcopate saw the Roman Catholic church in Newfoundland acquire new strength and stability, progress which undoubtedly owed much to Lambert's careful efforts and his moderating influence.

RAYMOND J. LAHEY

AAQ, 12 A, G, H; 210 A, V, VII–VIII; 30 CN, I. Arch. of the Archdiocese of St John's, Howley papers, transcripts of docs. in the Archivio della Propaganda Fide. Archivio della Propaganda Fide (Rome), Acta, 1805, 172; Scritturi riferite nei Congressi, America Antille, 3 (1790–1819). Basilica of St John the Baptist parish (St John's), Reg. of baptisms, 1 Jan. 1807. Collegio St Isidoro (Rome), Discretorium book, 17 July 1780, 27 Feb. 1783, 27 Nov. 1784, 25 Jan. 1785. PRO, ADM 80/151; CO 194/46, 194/49, 194/51, 194/54–56, 194/81. USPG, C/CAN/Nfl., 1–2. "Documents relating to Wexford friary and parish," comp. Pádraig Ó Súilleab-háin, *Collectanea Hibernica* (Dublin and London), 8 (1965): 126–27. *Evangelical Magazine and Missionary Chronicle* (London), 22 (1814): 75. George Conroy, *Occasional sermons, addresses, and essays* (Dublin, 1884), 315–27. M. F. Howley, *Ecclesiastical history of Newfoundland* (Boston, 1888; repr. Belleville, Ont., 1979). *Liber Dub-liniensis: chapter documents of the Irish Franciscans, 1719–1875*, ed. Anselm Faulkner (Killiney, Republic of Ire., 1978). Father Paul, *Wexford friary: a short account of the history and traditions of the Franciscan friary of Wexford* ([Wexford, Republic of Ire.?, 1949]).

LANAUDIÈRE, CHARLES-LOUIS TARIEU DE. *See* TARIEU

LANAUDIÈRE, XAVIER-ROCH TARIEU DE. *See* TARIEU

LANGHORN, JOHN, Church of England clergy-man; b. *c.* 1744 in Wales, the son of a clergyman; d.

unmarried 15 May 1817 in Natland, near Kendal, England.

Educated at St Bees School in Cumberland, John Langhorn served a curacy of 19 years, latterly at Harthill, Cheshire. In 1787, with strong support from two well-known churchmen, he was accepted by the Society for the Propagation of the Gospel as a missionary to the loyalist settlements in western Quebec. His parish comprised townships No.2 (Ernestown) and No.3 (North and South Fredericksburgh), which had been settled three years before by disbanded soldiers from the King's Royal Regiment of New York. After a journey of four months, Langhorn arrived on 5 Oct. 1787.

Aside from a few visits by John STUART of Cataraqui (Kingston), the approximately 1,500 people of the parish had had the attention of no clergy whatever. The work awaiting Langhorn was immense and he took it up immediately. Quickly he established a routine to which he adhered with little deviation for the following quarter of a century. On alternate Sundays he conducted services for two home congregations, St John's, at the front of Ernestown Township, and St Paul's, at the front of Fredericksburgh (North and South Fredericksburgh) Township. Then, during the week, winter and summer, packing his surplice and books on his back, he traversed his territory on foot, systematically visiting a network of preaching stations. The names he chose for these small congregations were either appropriately apostolic or commemorative of his Cheshire diocese. Occasionally he also moved outside his parish to visit adjacent communities. Wherever he went, in addition to the regular services of the church, Langhorn performed baptisms, marriages, and burials.

The work was hard, the conditions severe, and the rewards few, especially since the area was not promising for a Church of England missionary. The people were loyalist and, reflecting their American origins, not many of them, perhaps one in ten, were Anglican. Langhorn quickly discovered that the two townships contained a large majority of Presbyterians, Congregationalists, Lutherans, and Methodists. In 1787, he and Stuart were the only clergy at the eastern end of Lake Ontario. But within a few years, dissenting teachers and preachers were moving aggressively into the area, so that by the mid 1790s denominational pluralism was made permanent. It was accompanied by competitive pressure on the Church of England at the level of the individual congregation and of the government as well.

Langhorn's response to that pressure was unequivocal. He had a deep reverence for the distinctive doctrines and forms of the church. An obstinate man with a tender conscience, he was driven by a highly developed sense of duty. Consequently, whatever the circumstances, he refused to make concessions to dissent. Whether it was a question of deviation from Anglican forms in marriage or baptism, of approving a sectarian preacher by sharing the pulpit with him, of recognition for dissenting ordination, or of wearing the surplice while conducting the rites of the church, in all cases Langhorn demanded, in Ernest Hawkins*'s words, "strict observance of the rules of the Church." Ernestown (Bath) village, Langhorn told the SPG, was a "sore refractory town against the Church of England" and its people wanted him to behave as though all denominations and all clergy – no matter what "nonsensical gabble" they uttered – were equal and equally beyond criticism. But that was unthinkable for Langhorn. To him, dissenting clergy were schismatics and he was sure God would arrange harsh treatment for them in another world.

When no church principle was at issue, Langhorn was not uncharitable. Quite the contrary, he was well known for frequent acts of kindness that transcended denominational lines. But about the encroachments of dissent he was inflexible and as a result was in almost constant conflict and under frequent criticism. It was alleged that his attitude alienated possible converts and, in particular, drove crowds of people into the chapels of enthusiastic Methodist preachers. That criticism was made most vehemently and insistently by Stuart, a product of the apologetic Anglicanism of the Thirteen Colonies, who was willing to make some of the concessions that Langhorn refused.

Stuart was the bishop's commissary and therefore was responsible for dealing with problems that arose out of Langhorn's ministry. The difference in churchmanship between the two men made that task difficult. It was made harder still by Langhorn's other attributes. He was, in the first place, not a university man. That was a grave disability in the eyes of, for example, Bishop Charles INGLIS, who saw religion, science, and literature as interdependent and equally important. Similarly, Langhorn did not display that patina of speech and deportment characteristic of those who were accustomed to associating with the upper levels of Anglo-American society. By Inglis's account, Langhorn was "uncouth, and little acquainted with the world" (that is, of course, the *polite* world). And finally, there seems no question that in manners and appearance he was one of the most curious clergy ever to cross the ocean. Stuart remarked that Langhorn had "so many Singularities in Manner and Dress, that the Real Friends to the Interest of our Church have often wished him in England again."

For Stuart, in other words, Langhorn was an easy, indeed a tempting, target and more than once, baffled and frustrated in dealing with this strange, intractable man, Stuart succumbed to temptation and treated Langhorn unfairly. The most important instance occurred in 1804. Langhorn was engaged in public debate with Robert McDowall*, the local Presbyterian minister, on episcopal ordination. At the same time, he was being "railed at and abused" by the Methodists of Ernestown village. He finally responded to the Methodist pressure by composing one or two ribald verses or songs through which he informed the startled community "what an empty insignificant clamour these Gentry make." In reporting the incident to Bishop Jacob Mountain* and to the learned doctors of the SPG, Stuart described Langhorn as a man who was "untaught, unteachable and incorrigible" and who, if allowed to continue "to meddle with matters above his capacity" (a reference to the debate with McDowall), would do grave harm to the prospects of the church.

Stuart's was an unfair and exaggerated reaction. If Langhorn's mode of reply to his Methodist attackers was not one to be generally recommended, neither was it so shockingly improper. As to the debate with McDowall, Langhorn argued publicly because he was not prepared to let the church's position on a matter of central importance go by default. A defence of the church's status in the Canadas could never rely solely on legal arguments. The best case possible had to be made for the distinctive theological and historical position of the Church of England, and much of that case would rest upon establishing and maintaining the difference between bishop and priest and, consequently, the necessity for episcopal ordination. If the case were not made – if the church were not differentiated clearly from Protestantism on the one hand and Roman Catholicism on the other – its status would be seriously undermined.

Although he was almost recalled, Langhorn survived the crisis. He survived it, as he had others, for one fundamental reason. No matter how much they might differ from him (or, for that matter, be astounded by him), all observers agreed upon one central point: Langhorn was an honest and simple man, with a cheerful disposition and a humane and benevolent outlook. Even Stuart, at least in his calmer moments, shared this perception, as did Inglis and Mountain. And the point was affirmed later in Hawkins's history of the diocese of Toronto.

Ironically, however, it was the honesty and simplicity of the man that lay at the roots of the conflicts that swirled around him. Those were the characteristics that forced Langhorn to identify and face problems which others either ignored or dealt with inadequately. In that respect, he was anachronistic. He was what a later generation would know familiarly as a high churchman and he would have been more comfortable with the spirited and aggressive journalism of the *Church* of the mid 19th century than he was with the bland temper of his own time.

On the eve of the War of 1812 Langhorn was approaching 70 years of age. His health was beginning to fail. Through prudent management he had saved enough money to provide for himself, and he was therefore inclined to retirement. In the summer of 1813, overcoming his fear of being taken prisoner and spending his last days in France, Langhorn sailed for home. He died there four years later.

H. E. TURNER

[The most important source for John Langhorn is his correspondence with William Morice, the secretary of the SPG. Langhorn usually wrote twice annually to report on the progress of his mission. Morice prepared abstracts of these letters which were presented to the general meetings of the society and then incorporated into its journals. The letters and abstracts are to be found in USPG, C/CAN/folder 439 and Journal of SPG, 24–30. Both sources are available on microfilm at Anglican Church of Canada, General Synod Arch. (Toronto), the former under the old reference, Box IVa/38.

All of this material has been published. In 1926 A. H. Young reproduced the references to Langhorn, including Morice's abstracts, which he found in the society's journals, in "Entries in the journals of the Society for the Propagation of the Gospel in Foreign Parts relating to the Revd. John Langhorn," *OH*, 23 (1926): 534–60. It seemed at the time that the original Langhorn letters had been destroyed, but shortly thereafter some of them were discovered in the society's archives. These letters were then published by Young in "More Langhorn letters," *OH*, 29 (1933): 47–71. H.E.T.]

Anglican Church of Canada, Diocese of Ont. Arch. (Kingston), Group 11, John Stuart papers. AO, MS 35 (mfm. at McMaster Univ. Library, Hamilton, Ont.); MU 2923, ser.A (photocopies at Anglican Church of Canada, General Synod Arch.). PRO, CO 42/19 (mfm. at McMaster Univ. Library). QDA, 72 (C-1)–80 (C-9) (mfm. at Anglican Church of Canada, General Synod Arch.). *Corr. of Lieut. Governor Simcoe* (Cruikshank). *Early church records of Rev. John Langhorn and Rev. Robert McDowell*, comp. C. Loral et al. (n.p., n.d.). Ernest Hawkins, *Annals of the diocese of Toronto* (London, 1848). *Kingston before War of 1812* (Preston). Jacob Mountain, "From Quebec to Niagara in 1794; diary of Bishop Jacob Mountain," ed. A. R. Kelley, ANQ *Rapport*, 1959–60: 119–65. "Rev. John Langhorn," [comp. John Langhorn et al.], ed. T. W. Casey, *OH*, 1 (1899): 13–70. *Kingston Gazette*, 13 March, 1 June 1813.

"The correspondence and journals of Bishop Inglis of Halifax, Nova Scotia, 1775–1814," PAC *Report*, 1912: 215–88. "Completion of the correspondence and journals of the Right Reverend Charles and John Inglis, first and third bishops of Nova Scotia," PAC *Report*, 1913: 227–83. D. H. Farmer, *Oxford dictionary of saints* (Oxford, 1978). "Jacob Mountain, first lord bishop of Quebec: a summary of his correspondence and of papers related thereto, compiled from various sources," ANQ *Rapport*, 1942–43: 175–260. A. N. Bethune, *Memoir of the Right Reverend John Strachan, D.D., LL.D., first bishop of Toronto* (Toronto and London, 1870). J. W. Lydekker, *The life and letters of Charles Inglis: his ministry in America and consecration as first colonial bishop, from 1759 to 1787* (London and New York, 1936). Millman, *Jacob Mountain*. G. H. Patterson, "Studies in elections and public opinion in Upper Canada" (PHD thesis, Univ. of Toronto, 1969). *Guardian* (London), 14 March 1918: 203. [Arthur] Jarvis, "Some notes of early ecclesiastical history, Bay of Quinte District," Lennox and Addington Hist. Soc., *Papers and Records* (Napanee, Ont.), 1 (1909): 49–60. W. R. Riddell, "The law of marriage in Upper Canada," *CHR*, 2 (1921): 226–48. G. F. G. Stanley, "John Stuart, father of the Anglican Church in Upper Canada," Canadian Church Hist. Soc., *Journal* (Toronto), 3 (1956–59), no.6. A. H. Young, "The Revd. John Langhorn, Church of England missionary, at Fredericksburgh and Ernesttown, 1787–1813," *OH*, 23 (1926): 523–33.

LA OJA. *See* WAHPASHA

LAPAUSE DE MARGON, JEAN-GUILLAUME PLANTAVIT DE. *See* PLANTAVIT

LA PELOUZE, PIERRE-JOSEPH CARREFOUR DE. *See* CARREFOUR

LA RIVE, HENRI-FRANÇOIS GRAVÉ DE. *See* GRAVÉ

LATERRIÈRE, PIERRE DE SALES. *See* SALES

LATOUR, PIERRE HUGUET, *dit.* *See* HUGUET

LAUBARAS. *See* OLABARATZ

LA VALINIÈRE, PIERRE HUET DE. *See* HUET

LAVALTRIE, PIERRE-PAUL MARGANE DE. *See* MARGANE

LAWSON, DAVID, farmer, land agent, and politician; b. *c.* 1720, probably near Muthill, Scotland; m. Ellen —, and they had five children; d. after 1803 on Prince Edward Island.

A Perthshire flax farmer, David Lawson was recommended in 1769 to Scotland's lord advocate, James William Montgomery, to found and manage an agricultural settlement on St John's (Prince Edward) Island. An agreement was reached whereby Lawson, financed by the lord advocate, would develop and oversee a flax farm on Montgomery's Lot 34 in return for half the profits after seven years. Having recruited about 50 indentured servants in Perthshire, Lawson embarked with his family on the *Falmouth* and set sail from Greenock on 8 April 1770. After a long and difficult voyage – during which he was very sick – the *Falmouth* reached the Island early in June, anchoring first in Richmond (Malpeque) Bay and on the 8th in Stanhope Cove (Covehead Bay), where Lawson's party was put ashore. There, having almost no food and no fresh water, they confronted a total wilderness. Expecting "better provisions than oatmeal and salt

water" and shocked by the primeval conditions, the servants became restive and mutinous. Lawson spent most of the summer dealing with the discontent and attempting to clear land, obtain livestock, and manufacture farming equipment.

The process of clearing the forest went slowly. Not until 1772 did Lawson have sufficient land even to feed his people, let alone plant flax (they had, in the mean time, been supplied by Montgomery's agent, David Higgins*). Misfortunes dogged the tiny settlement: during the first summer one servant was killed by a log he had felled, and two others drowned bringing in a cargo of rum; a dam and mill were twice destroyed by fire before 1777. At the very point, moreover, when the farm (called Stanhope after Montgomery's Scottish estate) was becoming self-sufficient, the servants' four-year indentures ran out. Most left the Island, but some took up farms on Lot 34 and weakened Lawson's breeding herds by claiming the livestock they had been promised when signing their agreements in Scotland.

Nevertheless, within five years of his arrival Lawson had, by Island standards, a substantial farm in operation. He had become familiar with local agricultural conditions, grown some flax successfully, and sent soil samples home to Montgomery. He could not, however, demonstrate that his improvements were equal to the capital invested by Montgomery, much less that he was turning a profit. By the time his agreement with Montgomery expired, the disruption of communications caused by the American rebellion meant that he was not required to render an accounting; during the war his associate's only attempt at contact was to send him in 1777 a power of attorney to manage all the Montgomery property and interests on the Island. In 1783 Lawson added an agency for General Henry Wood and George, Marquess TOWNSHEND, proprietors of Lot 56; that same year he became administrator of the bankrupt estate of David Higgins. During the 1770s Lawson had become active in Island politics. He was four times elected a member of the House of Assembly between 1773 and 1785, he and his sons-in-law, Cornelius Higgins and James CURTIS, constituting a small Covehead group which loyally supported Governor Walter Patterson* in his struggles with the proprietors and the British government.

At the end of the war Montgomery attempted for several years, without success, to settle his accounts with Lawson and was finally forced in 1788 to send his son William* to the Island to obtain a detailed statement of affairs. Lawson procrastinated, and William eventually appeared without warning at the farm heading a party of assessors. Lawson was summarily evicted from Stanhope and replaced as agent. His problems stemmed from his initial unrealistic agreement with Montgomery: it had been fool-

Lebrun

hardy to expect a farm carved out of the wilderness to show a profit within seven years. Montgomery nevertheless insisted on a strict accounting, with a complete evaluation of assets and a full record of expenditures. Years of pioneer hardship on the Island had convinced Lawson that his labour and that of his family had made far more of a contribution to Stanhope than the proprietor's monetary investment, and he believed that an accounting such as Montgomery demanded would not reflect the value of their efforts. Moreover, he had kept no books or records, and during long periods of isolation from the outside world had been forced to support himself by whatever means were available; the evidence suggests he had become unable to distinguish what was rightfully Montgomery's. For his part, Montgomery concluded that Lawson was merely attempting to maintain a newly acquired status as a country gentleman by overlooking his obligations to his employer.

Having appointed new agents in the persons of Lieutenant Governor Edmund FANNING and James DOUGLAS, Montgomery continued to press Lawson for an accounting. Turning to the courts, in 1789 he sued Lawson as administrator of the estate of David Higgins, who had died heavily in debt to Montgomery and whose account-books Lawson had refused to give up. He was awarded £3,813 plus costs when Lawson failed to contest the action, and as a result of the decision he acquired Rustico Island, which Lawson had earlier obtained by grant from the government and which Montgomery now had sold at auction. In 1793 Lawson and Douglas agreed on mutually acceptable arbitrators – Fanning, Charles Lyons, and Joseph ROBINSON – and the business of Lawson's accounts was finally settled. In making their decision the arbitrators not only examined Lawson's management of Stanhope but undertook a new accounting of Higgins's obligations to Montgomery. They awarded Montgomery £9,219 12s. 2½d., more than half of which was really Higgins's debt assumed by Lawson as administrator of the estate.

Once having established the principle that even Islanders had to live up to contracts, Montgomery forgot the debt and ordered a regular allowance to be paid to the aged Lawson, who continued to live at Covehead with his children. His name disappears from the record after 1803.

J. M. BUMSTED

PAPEI, Acc. 2702, Smith–Alley coll., Marquess of Townshend to —, 1783. SRO, GD293/2/78/9; 293/2/79/5, 27, 33, 38, 46; 293/2/80/21; 293/2/81/2. Univ. of B.C. Library (Vancouver), Special Coll. Division, Macmillan coll., James Montgomery to Edmund Fanning, 30 April 1798. [William Drummond], "Diary of William Drummond," ed. David Weale, *Island Magazine*, no.2 (spring-summer 1977): 29. *Royal Gazette and Miscellany of the Island of Saint John* (Charlottetown), 29 July 1791. G. H. Kielly, *History of Montgomery settlers and others at Stanhope–Covehead–Brackley Pt., 1770–1970* (Stanhope, P.E.I., 1970), 90–91. Bumsted, "Sir James Montgomery and P.E.I.," *Acadiensis* (Fredericton), 7, no.2: 76–102.

LEBRUN (Le Brun) DE DUPLESSIS, JEAN-BAPTISTE, lawyer, notary, merchant, office holder, and pamphleteer; b. *c.* 1739 in Corbie, France, son of Jean-Baptiste Lebrun de Duplessis and Marie de Champigny; m. 12 Oct. 1762 Marie-Catherine Mettot at Quebec; d. 26 June 1807 in Montreal, Lower Canada.

Jean-Baptiste Lebrun de Duplessis arrived in New France in 1755 as an artillery scrivener in the Régiment de Béarn. From May 1759 to May 1760 he was a notary at Michilimackinac (Mackinaw City, Mich.). Some time between 31 August and 6 Sept. 1760 he joined up with Jeffery Amherst*, the British commander-in-chief, and assisted him as he descended the St Lawrence to attack Montreal. According to Guy CARLETON, Lebrun had deserted to the British side after escaping from prison, where he had been sent by the French authorities on a charge of stealing from the army's stores. At the end of 1760 he was taken into Amherst's secretariat, and a little later into that of Thomas Gage*, who was military governor of Montreal.

In 1762 Lebrun acted as an attorney before the military council of Quebec, and on 29 Jan. 1765 he was admitted to the Court of Common Pleas as a lawyer. He became at that time one of the six lawyers given entry to the Common Pleas, the only court in which Canadians could then practise law. On 14 March he received from Governor Murray* a commission authorizing him to plead there, as did François Lemaître Lamorille, Jean-Antoine Saillant*, and Guillaume Guillimin*. On 1 July 1766, after the test oath was lifted, Canadians obtained the right to practise as lawyers before all civil courts. Six days later Lebrun was granted a full commission as lawyer. Along with Joseph-Antoine Olry, Jean-Antoine Saillant, and Guillaume Guillimin, he was one of the first Canadians to be so accredited. In addition, on 12 December he was licensed as a notary for the District of Quebec.

Lebrun's practice, however, ran into heavy weather. On 2 Feb. 1769 he complained in the *Quebec Gazette* that he had been subjected to "calumnies" arising from an out-of-court payment which he was supposed to have demanded from two servants who had robbed him of articles worth about £40. After an investigation, on 12 April Carleton, by then governor, annulled Lebrun's commissions as lawyer and notary. As grounds for his action he cited "the various incidents of roguery and extortion" in which Lebrun was said to have indulged, among them the illegal detention of several persons. It is impossible to know whether, as the ex-lawyer claimed, the good relations he maintained with Francis Maseres* and the British merchants in the colony had had an influence on Carleton's decision. Eight days after being dismissed Lebrun announced in the *Quebec Gazette* that he hoped to leave the province. He did not, however, carry out this intention. On 23 June 1769 he sold a two-storey stone house in the Lower Town of Quebec for 3,600 *livres* and retired to a farm at L'Ancienne-Lorette that he had owned for a least a year. The proceeds of this sale, together with the 1,400 *livres* he had received the previous year from the sale of a piece of land at Rivière-du-Loup (Louiseville), guaranteed him some degree of material comfort. According to Carleton, in the ensuing years Lebrun was found guilty of sexual offences against young girls nine or ten years of age; the most serious of these, apparently, was the attempted rape of a young girl by the name of Marie Valin on 27 May 1770. Lebrun is believed to have been sentenced to a term in prison and a fine of £20 for this offence.

On 8 Jan. 1774 Lebrun wrote to Maseres from Quebec expressing approval of his memoir proposing that the exercise of French civil law in the province should be limited through the introduction of a new legal system. Lebrun added, without providing evidence to support his assertion, that three-quarters of the inhabitants of the province shared his opinion. He also used the occasion to ask that he be reinstated as a lawyer and notary or be appointed to equivalent functions, alleging that he had lost his earlier commissions because of a "whim" of Carleton's, solely on the accusation of having been "envious." Maseres forwarded this correspondence to Lord Apsley, lord chancellor of Great Britain, in an attempt to win the British government's support for his plan.

Around the same time, in a letter to the British authorities, Lebrun supported the proposal to create a house of assembly in the province, claiming that the inhabitants of the colony were in general of the same opinion. When the passage of the Quebec Act was under discussion Lord North, the leader of the British government, questioned Carleton about Lebrun's opinions. The governor replied that Lebrun was not a man to be trusted. He stated that he had initially patronized him because of the aid he had given Amherst but had subsequently disavowed him because of his bad behaviour. He even alluded to Lebrun's sexual misdeeds, noting that at the time he had pardoned him.

In 1776, during the American invasion [*see* Benedict ARNOLD; Richard Montgomery*], Lebrun supported the occupation forces. To secure supplies for them, he stole, with the help of his brother-in-law and another man, about 110 bushels of wheat from the seigneury of Saint-Roch-des-Aulnaies and took them to a property he owned at Cap-Saint-Ignace.

When the invasion was over Lebrun returned to Quebec, where he was active as a general merchant until at least 1782. In 1790, however, he was living in the parish of Saint-Sulpice, near Montreal. At that time he published a pamphlet entitled *Mémoire abrégé ou exposition justificative du cas de Jean-Baptiste Lebrun . . .* ; in it he claimed that he had lost his offices of lawyer and notary unjustly and defended himself against a charge of pecuniary theft laid by the surgeon Jean Ducondu in 1789. On 14 Jan. 1791 Lebrun petitioned Alured Clarke*, lieutenant governor of the province, to be reinstated into the practice of law. He declared that he, his wife, and nine children had been reduced to abject poverty, and recalled the services he had rendered Amherst, Gage, and Murray; he had lost his offices, he alleged, as a result of accusations made by some "jealous fanatics and despots." He included a copy of his pamphlet and also a petition from his wife and children, dated the same day and addressed to Lord Dorchester [Carleton]. In it Mme Lebrun declared that she was impoverished and asked pardon for "some trifling, perhaps involuntary offence" committed by her husband.

On 11 Feb. 1791 eight lawyers presented to William Smith*, chief justice of Lower Canada, a petition pleading the seriousness of the grounds that had led to Lebrun's dismissal; according to them the contents of his pamphlet and the charge of theft laid in 1789 cast considerable doubt on his conduct after he was dismissed. On 16 Feb. 1791 a ninth lawyer reached the same conclusion. In the end, Lebrun's petition was not granted. At the time of his death in Montreal on 26 June 1807, however, he was holding the office of bailiff.

JACQUES L'HEUREUX

Jean-Baptiste Lebrun de Duplessis is the author of *Mémoire abrégé ou exposition justificative du cas de Jean-Baptiste Lebrun, de la paroisse de St. Sulpice, dans le district de Montréal* (Montréal, 1790). His minute-book containing 65 deeds drawn up between 1766 and 1769 is at ANQ-Q, CN1-168.

ANQ-Q, CE1-1, 12 oct. 1762; CN1-250, 4 août 1768, 23 juin 1769. PAC, MG 23, A1, ser.2, 2: 240; RG 4, A1: 16153–66, 16169–74; B8, 28: 92. PRO, CO 42/5: 237; 42/6: 156. *Doc. relatifs à l'hist. constitutionnelle, 1759–1791* (Shortt et Doughty; 1921), 1: 180–85, 219–20, 516. G.B., Parl., *Debates of the House of Commons in the year 1774, on the bill for making more effectual provision for the government of the province of Quebec, drawn up from the notes of Sir Henry Cavendish . . .* (London, 1839; repr. [East Ardsley, Eng., and New York], 1966), 115–16. "Journal par Baby, Taschereau et Williams" (Fauteux), ANQ *Rapport*, 1927–28: 490, 494. [Francis] Maseres, *Réponse aux observations faites par Mr. François Joseph Cugnet, secrétaire du gouverneur & Conseil de la province de Québec pour la langue françoise, sur le plan d'acte de parlement pour l'établissement des lois de la ditte province . . .* ([London], 1773). *Quebec Gazette*, 7 Feb., 21 March, 15 Aug. 1765; 22 Dec. 1766; 12 Nov. 1767; 2 Feb., 13, 20 April 1769; 30 Nov. 1780; 29 Nov., 6 Dec. 1781; 18 July 1782.

Leclerc

P.-G. Roy, *Les avocats de la région de Québec* (Lévis, Qué., 1936), 261–62; *Inventaire des contrats de mariage du Régime français conservés aux Archives judiciaires de Québec* (6v., Québec, 1937–38), 4: 75; *Inventaire des insinuations de la Prévôté de Québec* (3v., Beauceville, Qué., 1936–39). Tanguay, *Dictionnaire*, 5: 233. W. R. Riddell, *The bar and the courts of the province of Upper Canada, or Ontario* (Toronto, 1928), 7, 14, 17–19. J.-E. Roy, *L'ancien barreau au Canada* (Montréal, 1897), 28, 30–35, 38–41, 73; *Hist. du notariat*, 2: 22–26. Philéas Gagnon, "Le premier roman canadien de sujet par un auteur canadien et imprimé au Canada," RSC *Trans.*, 2nd ser., 6 (1900), sect.i: 129–30. Marine Leland, "François-Joseph Cugnet, 1720–1789," *Rev. de l'univ. Laval* (Québec), 17 (1962–63): 833–36.

LECLERC, MICHEL, Roman Catholic priest, Sulpician, and superior of the Lac-des-Deux-Montagnes mission (Oka, Qué.); b. 10 Feb. 1762 in La Prairie (Que.), son of Michel Leclerc, master blacksmith, and Marguerite Bétourné; d. 9 May 1813 in Montreal, Lower Canada.

Michel Leclerc grew up near the Indian mission at Caughnawaga, and thus learned the Mohawk language at an early age. From 1775 to 1782 he studied at the Collège Saint-Raphaël in Montreal, where every year he won one or more prizes or honourable mentions for memory work and Latin. As the college did not yet offer the final two years of the classical program (Philosophy), Leclerc continued his studies at the Séminaire de Québec from 1782 to 1784. He was given the tonsure before the holidays of 1783, possibly so he could become study master, living during the summer at the seminary's holiday house at the "Cotteau Fortin" or Petit Cap (Cap Tourmente). Having entered the Grand Séminaire on 1 Oct. 1784, he received minor orders and the sub-diaconate from the bishop of Quebec, Louis-Philippe Mariauchau* d'Esgly, in March 1786. He then became assistant master of the pupils at the Petit Séminaire, while continuing his theological studies. The coadjutor, Jean-François Hubert*, conferred the diaconate and the priesthood on 24 and 25 March 1787.

Upon his ordination as priest Leclerc returned to Montreal, and from there Étienne Montgolfier*, superior of the Séminaire de Saint-Sulpice, sent him to join Vincent-Fleuri Guichart* at the Indian mission on the Sulpician seigneury of Lac-des-Deux-Montagnes. On 25 Oct. 1787 Leclerc replaced Antoine-Théodore Braun, a missionary there, and began his ministry among the Iroquois. On 21 Oct. 1788 he was admitted to the community of the Sulpician seminary as a member.

In addition to his missionary work Leclerc served as bursar at Lac-des-Deux-Montagnes. It was in this capacity that in 1790 he gave an account to Gabriel-Jean Brassier* of the mission's difficulties with Eustache Trottier Desrivières Beaubien, who wanted to settle in the Iroquois village, build a house, and carry on business, despite the Sulpicians' opposition. The case was brought before the Court of Common Pleas in November 1790, and in 1793 the provincial Court of Appeal settled the dispute in favour of the seigneurs, the Sulpicians.

Following the death of Guichart on 16 Oct. 1793, Leclerc took his place as superior of the mission, and for a year he ran it alone, since the shortage of priests throughout the Canadas prevented him from having an assistant. But with the arrival in Lower Canada in 1794 of French Sulpicians driven out of their country by the revolution, Leclerc was able to obtain the aid of two of them, Anthelme Malard and Jean-Louis-Melchior Sauvage de Chatillonnet.

As superior of the mission Leclerc had the double responsibility of being the keeper of souls and the representative of the seigneurs. His first duty was to administer the sacraments, preach, and teach his flock. His sermons, which were all in Mohawk, drew much of their inspiration from the works of his predecessors, according to Sulpician Jean-André Cuoq*. In 1797 Leclerc was the driving force behind the founding of a mission which would become the parish of Saint-Benoît. He also was in charge of the temporal administration of the mission of Lac-des-Deux-Montagnes and, like his predecessors [see François-Auguste Magon* de Terlaye; Vincent-Fleuri Guichart], he had to deal with the Indians' demands, which had become more insistent as the seigneury developed and as the Indians became aware of the rights enjoyed by its white settlers. The mission Indians, who unlike the settlers did not own their land, wanted to choose the sites of their farms and to have a monopoly on the exploitation of the forests. They also wanted to keep for themselves the sap drawn from the maple trees on the seigneurial domain. On 6 Nov. 1805 Leclerc reached an understanding with the Indians. Henceforth the settlers would not be allowed to cut wood on the Sulpicians' domain, make maple syrup, or harvest the hay; the Indians would not be allowed to rent their meadows or lend or rent their houses. However, the Indian claims concerning their territorial rights were to persist throughout the 19th century [see Joseph Onasakenrat*; Nicolas Dufresne*]. While the seigneury was being rapidly developed, Leclerc looked after practical matters, with the help of the bursar Joseph BORNEUF. He also organized the corvées for road-building and chose the sites for mills. In 1812, when war broke out with the United States, the civil authorities, who were interested in having the Indians take part in the conflict, asked him to pass on details pertaining to military organization.

Despite apparently delicate health Michel Leclerc carried on his ministry until March 1813. He died at the Sulpician seminary in Montreal on 9 May and was buried in Notre-Dame church two days later. Jean-Baptiste Roupe* succeeded him as head of the mission. According to his colleague François-Joseph-Michel Humbert, Leclerc was "a witty, warm-hearted man, much beloved by the Indians, whose confidence he enjoyed."

J.-Bruno Harel

ANQ-M, CE1-3, 10 févr. 1762; CE1-51, 11 mai 1813; CN1-158, 2 août 1785. Arch. du collège de Montréal (Montréal), Palmarès, 1775–81. AP, L'Annonciation (Oka), Reg. des baptêmes, mariages et sépultures (copy at PAC). ASSM, 8, A; 24, Dossier 6. J.-A. Cuoq, "Anotc kekon," RSC Trans., 1st ser., 11 (1893), sect.I: 137–79.

LE COMTE DUPRÉ, JEAN-BAPTISTE, merchant, militia officer, seigneur, office holder, and politician; b. 25 Feb. 1731 in Montreal (Que.), son of Jean-Baptiste Le Comte* Dupré and Marie-Anne Hervieux; d. 5 May 1820 at Quebec, Lower Canada.

Jean-Baptiste Le Comte Dupré belonged to the third generation of a family of merchants which had been in the fur trade since the end of the 17th century. His grandfather, Louis Le Conte* Dupré, had built up the enterprise that his father inherited in 1715. The interplay of marriages had helped create a broader network of relationships for the family, which could therefore rely on support from important mercantile families in Montreal: the Hervieuxs, Magnans, Courreaud de La Costes, Babys, Charly Saint-Anges, Pothiers, La Cornes, Gamelins, and Quesnel Fonblanches. Consequently Le Comte Dupré grew up in a commercial milieu, and it seems certain that he acquired a knowledge of business at his father's side.

In 1755 Le Comte Dupré received a commission as captain in the Montreal militia. By 1758 he had established himself at Quebec, where his mercantile activities were probably conducted as his father's business representative. There, on 13 July 1758, he married Catherine Martel de Brouague, the 15-year-old daughter of François Martel* de Brouague, commandant of the Labrador coast, and Louise Mariauchau d'Esgly. Through this marriage Le Comte Dupré extended his connections with commercial and governmental circles. Gaspard-Joseph Chaussegros* de Léry, the bride's brother-in-law, Louis-Philippe Mariauchau* d'Esgly, her uncle, as well as her cousins Eustache Lambert Dumont and Joseph and Étienne* Charest, were present, along with other guests, at the signing of the marriage contract on 8 July. Le Comte Dupré put half his fortune into the joint estate, contributing 30,000 livres, derived from his inventory of merchandise, accounts receivable, and cash. The bride brought a dowry of 26,000 livres consisting of 6,000 livres that her father was to pay her in four years and an annuity of 1,000 livres a year.

The couple took up residence in Montreal, where their first four children were born. In 1764, the year after the signing of the Treaty of Paris, Le Comte Dupré had a pessimistic view of the consequences of the change in régime, which, he said, "is going to cause a terrible upset in the colony and will complete our ruin." His fears were based in good part on the uncertainty surrounding the redemption by France of playing-card money, since he himself had put no less than 91,609 livres into it. He was also worried about the possibilities of pursuing his commercial ties with the West Indies, as well as with French merchants in Bordeaux, La Rochelle, and Paris. And he was concerned about the conduct of the Indians at Detroit (Mich.) [see Pontiac*], who "are in no better humour than last year," and about the effects of this situation on the fur trade.

Le Comte Dupré envisaged settling permanently at Quebec. In 1764 he contracted to have a house built for himself at the corner of Rue Saint-Pierre and Rue du Sault-au-Matelot; he entrusted supervision of the work to Jacques Perrault*, known as Perrault l'aîné. Two years later he moved into his new home. From Quebec he carried on his trade in wood, spirits, wheat, and furs. As an experienced businessman he kept himself well informed on commodity prices, inquired about the competence and honesty of his employees, and made sure he secured a satisfactory return on his goods, which he sold in Quebec and Montreal. In 1769 he began to invest in real estate with the purchase of the sub-fief of La Maringouinière, in the seigneury of Lauson, and a property near the Rivière Saint-Charles, where he bought a further 60 acres in 1770. He also acquired a lot on the Côte Saint-Jean, near Quebec, that year.

In 1774 Le Comte Dupré's fellow Catholics recognized his social position by appointing him the first churchwarden of the parish of Notre-Dame in Quebec. This office put him in a position during the winter to bring the bishop of Quebec, Jean-Olivier Briand*, and the churchwardens together again. Since 1764 the latter had been opposed to the fact that their parish church also served as the cathedral.

During the American invasion of 1775–76 [see Benedict Arnold; Richard Montgomery*], Le Comte Dupré, like his brother Georges-Hippolyte*, openly displayed loyalty and devotion to the British crown. In September 1775 he became a major in the Quebec militia. In the course of a routine patrol in November, when Arnold's army was camped outside the gates of the town, Le Comte Dupré is said to have discovered a plot devised by three militia sergeants. He is supposed to have immediately warned Lieutenant Governor Hector Theophilus Cramahé*, who had the traitors imprisoned. This action would explain the reprisals by the Americans, who pillaged Le Comte Dupré's properties and seized the wheat, flour, and various effects on the sub-fief of Argentenay, on Île d'Orléans, which belonged to his wife. However, in recognition of his services Governor Sir Guy CARLETON appointed him colonel in the militia of the town and district of Quebec on 4 March 1778.

In October of that year Le Comte Dupré sailed for England with his 17-year-old son Jean-Baptiste. There he talked with Lord George Germain, the secretary of state for the American colonies, informing him of the losses he had suffered during the American invasion. He returned to Quebec in July 1779. He must have made a good impression, since Germain suggested to Governor HALDIMAND that he be given a seat on the Legislative Council and be indemnified for the pillaging of his properties.

In July 1783 Le Comte Dupré purchased his brother-in-law William Johnstone's share in the sub-fief of Argentenay for £500 in cash. Two years later he became a justice of the peace, and his commission was renewed in 1786. He was appointed a member of the Legislative Council that year, and held this office until 1792. He gives the impression of having been rather conservative. In 1788, for example, he opposed the setting up of a house of assembly. He signed the numerous addresses of welcome or farewell to colonial administrators. In 1794 he joined the Association, which had been founded to support the government, and signed the declaration of loyalty to the British crown.

During the 1790s Le Comte Dupré reoriented his business career. He apparently forsook trade to become a money-lender. Between 1790 and 1799 he lent more than 57,320 *livres* to people living in the Quebec region. The debtors, who were mostly in rural areas, borrowed from him, either as individuals or in groups of two or three, amounts ranging from 200 to 3,000 *livres*, which were used to consolidate a debt, buy a farm, or purchase rights of succession. Le Comte Dupré made these loans for periods of three to five years at the legal rate of interest of six per cent.

In 1797 Le Comte Dupré was named police inspector in Montreal, replacing his brother Georges-Hippolyte, who had died that year. This post seems to have been a sinecure since he stayed at Quebec, where he continued to engage in business. His wife, who was said to be "blessed with all the social virtues, and with the equanimity that characterizes a charitable and liberal heart," died on 12 Dec. 1801. Five of the ten children born to them had not survived infancy. Three daughters had married: Catherine the seigneur of Beauport, Antoine JUCHEREAU Duchesnay, Françoise an officer in the British army, John Francis Le Moine, and Marie-Angélique a lawyer, Jacques-François Cugnet. Jean-Baptiste never married, nor did his sister Louise-Charlotte.

In 1806 Le Comte Dupré rented his house on Rue du Sault-au-Matelot to François BOUCHER, port captain of Quebec, for £90 a year, and moved to Rue

Saint-Louis in Upper Town. Despite his 75 years he continued to manage his affairs. In 1816–17 he lent £1,190 to people living in the region. He also was busy collecting arrears of *cens et rentes* from his *censitaires* on Île d'Orléans and attending to the renting of the seigneurial mill.

Jean-Baptiste Le Comte Dupré died at Quebec on 5 May 1820. His funeral service was sung in the chapel of the Séminaire de Québec; his body was then taken to Saint-François, on Île d'Orléans, where it was buried on 9 May under the seigneur's pew, in keeping with the family's wishes. The following year his personal and real estate were put up for sale by his daughters, who had inherited them; his only son had died in 1817.

CÉLINE CYR

ANQ-M, CE1-51, 25 févr. 1731, 1er août 1759, 7 août 1761, 5 déc. 1762, 19 mars 1764. ANQ-Q, CE1-1, 13 juill. 1758; CN1-25, 13 oct. 1777; 28 déc. 1780; 5 avril 1781; 10 janv., 19 oct. 1782; 9 juill., 21 août 1783; CN1-79, 8 juill. 1758; CN1-83, 15, 16, 22–24 juin, 2, 3, 5, 6, 9, 10, 14, 17, 19, 21, 22 juill., 7, 14, 31 août, 10 sept. 1790; 31 janv. 1793; 1er, 8 juill. 1794; CN1-178, 23, 24, 27 juin, 11 juill. 1796; 29 janv. 1806, 23 déc. 1809; CN1-205, 10 oct. 1782; CN1-207, 8 janv., 1er mai 1770; 4 oct., 13 nov. 1773; CN1-212, 11, 12 nov. 1817; 10, 23 juin 1818; CN1-230, 5 déc. 1794, 31 mars, 8 avril, 8, 15, 23, 30 juin, 12 août, 5, 14, 23 sept. 1795; 23–25, 29 févr., 1er, 9 mars, 6, 8, 12, 13, 23 avril, 24 mai, 13, 14 juin 1796; 21 juin, 17 août, 11 oct. 1797; 11, 23 janv., 22 mai, 21, 22 juin, 11, 24 juill., 27 août, 4 oct. 1798; 18 févr. 1799; 16, 17, 25 sept. 1806; 9, 13, 15–19, 22, 29 avril, 7 mai 1816; CN1-248, 23 août, 1er sept. 1769. AUM, P 58, U, Le Comte Dupré à Baby, 7 avril 1766; 14 mai, 10 sept. 1767; 16 avril 1768; 12, 19 avril, 3 mai 1770; 10 févr. 1774; 26 oct. 1775; 4 mai 1800; Le Comte Dupré à Perrault l'aîné, 24 mai, 15 oct. 1764.

"État général des billets d'ordonnances" (Panet), ANQ *Rapport*, 1924–25: 337. *Quebec Gazette*, 29 Sept. 1766; 7 Sept. 1775; 12 Dec. 1776; 10 July 1777; 29 Oct. 1778; 12 May, 24 Nov. 1785; 29 June 1786; 13 Nov. 1788; 15 Jan. 1789; 3 July 1794; 21 Dec. 1797; 17 Dec. 1801; 1 March 1821. Claude de Bonnault, "Le Canada militaire: état provisoire des officiers de milice de 1641 à 1760," ANQ *Rapport*, 1949–51: 447. "Papiers d'État," PAC *Rapport*, 1890: 116, 118, 230. *Quebec almanac*, 1788–1820. P.-G. Roy, *La famille Le Compte Dupré* (Lévis, Qué., 1941)."Le Compte Dupré," *BRH*, 6 (1900): 249–50. P.-G. Roy, "La famille Martel de Brouage," *BRH*, 40 (1934): 513–49; "Jean-Baptiste Le Compte Dupré, seigneur d'Argentenay," *BRH*, 33 (1927): 705–7. Henri Têtu, "Le chapitre de la cathédrale de Québec . . . ," *BRH*, 16 (1910): 65–75.

LE DERNIERS (Les Derniers). *See* DELESDERNIER

LEE, SAMUEL, office holder, judge, businessman, and politician; b. 28 March 1756 in Concord, Mass., son of Dr Joseph and Lucy Lee; m. Sarah —; d. 3 March 1805 in Shediac, N.B.

Samuel Lee was born to one of the most influential families in the Concord area. After graduating from

Lees

Harvard College in 1776, he established himself as a successful merchant at Penobscot (Castine, Maine). A supporter of the loyalist cause, in 1784 he went to Restigouche in northern New Brunswick. There he was to acquire large grants of land, some in rather questionable ways.

While on a trip to England in 1785 Lee leased a block of land on the Restigouche River which formed part of a grant previously ceded by the Nova Scotia government to John Shoolbred. When, to provide land for the loyalists, the New Brunswick government moved to escheat many of the grants issued earlier by the Nova Scotian authorities, Lee petitioned for some of Shoolbred's property on the grounds that it had not been improved. Shoolbred considered this action "unprincipled & perfidious, the Trait of a base Heart." By 1789 Lee had acquired 1,800 acres, including part of Shoolbred's grant and a further 200 acres to which others laid claim. Since he was a staunch supporter of the loyalist government, all disputes over land were settled in his favour. At his death settlers in the Restigouche area claimed that he had obtained "more land than he was entitled to hold" and that much of it "now lays waste and uncultivated to the Great Injury of the Settlement." He was also accused of having acquired land "under borrowed names." His honesty was further impugned after his death when a group of 15 men, mostly Acadians, petitioned the government for grants of the lands they occupied. Lee had supposedly agreed to apply for the grants and to pay the grant fees in exchange for goods the men had supplied him; however, the grants had not been issued, Lee had not paid the fees, and the men were in danger of losing their lands.

On 17 Nov. 1787 Lee was appointed the first justice of the peace for Restigouche, which formed part of Northumberland County, and on 10 July 1789 he was made a judge of the Inferior Court of Common Pleas. He supported government candidates in the province's first election in 1785 and in the by-election of 1791; in 1795 he was himself elected to the House of Assembly as one of the two members for Northumberland. He ran again in 1802 but was defeated by Alexander TAYLOR, who had the support of the Scottish pre-loyalists.

In 1789 Lee mortgaged his land for £7,950 to the firm of Maitland and Company of London, England, and using these funds he bought supplies and built a storehouse. By 1790 he was shipping fish to Europe; a year later he built a sawmill and began exporting timber. He also attempted to develop his land, bringing out settlers from Scotland and England. His various business activities were not successful, however: at the time of his death he owed the London company £19,000, and his property was sold in an attempt to pay his debts.

Although he was a failure in business, Lee was a leader in promoting English-speaking settlement in the Restigouche area (by 1798 he had 25 families on his lands), and he helped establish government control in this remote region. His death occurred as he was returning to Restigouche from Halifax, N.S.

W. A. SPRAY

N.B. Museum, F71, nos.101 (lease to Samuel Lee, 1785), 102 (petition of John Shoolbred, 12 Jan. 1788); Petitions, Northumberland County, no.18 (abstracts). PANB, "New Brunswick political biography," comp. J.C. and H.B. Graves (11v., typescript), XI: 51; RG 2, RS6, 2: 34; RS8, Appointments and commissions, 2/1: 8, 10; Unarranged Executive Council docs., 1787, 1802–3, 1807; RG 10, RS108, Petition of Adam Gerrard, 1800; Petition of Benjamin Marsden, 1785; Petition of Ebenezer Whitney, 1802. PRO, CO 188/3: f.94 (photocopies at UNBL). *Winslow papers* (Raymond). *Concord, Massachusetts, births, marriages, and deaths, 1635–1850* ([Boston, 1895]). W. O. Raymond, "The north shore; incidents in the early history of eastern and northern New Brunswick," N.B. Hist. Soc., *Coll.*, 2 (1899–1905), no.4: 112, 124. Lemuel Shattuck, *A history of the town of Concord; Middlesex County, Massachusetts, from its earliest settlement to 1832* ... (Boston, 1835).

LEES, JOHN (until about 1780 he added "junior" to his signature; he sometimes signed **Jean Lees**), militia officer, merchant, landowner, politician, judge, and office holder; b. *c.* 1740 in Scotland, son of John Lees, a merchant; d. 4 March 1807 in Lachine, Lower Canada.

John Lees came to Quebec with his parents immediately after the conquest. By October 1761 his father was established in Lower Town, where he remained in business until he left for Scotland around 1777. Both father and son became involved in the political struggles disturbing the colony [*see* George ALLSOPP]. In 1766 the younger Lees went to England to complain about the laws governing the administration of justice [*see* Maurice MORGANN]; he returned there for the same purpose on two other occasions. In January 1774 he was one of the 148 people who signed a petition to the king requesting a house of assembly, and in November he was amongst those who expressed a fervent desire to have the Quebec Act repealed. On 2 Dec. 1775, when the American army was at the gates of Quebec [*see* Benedict ARNOLD; Richard Montgomery*], Lees enlisted as an ensign in the militia company of which William GRANT (1744–1805) was captain; soon after he himself became a militia captain. During the siege of the town his property on Rue Saint-Pierre was severely damaged.

In 1773 Lees had entered into partnership with merchant Alexander Davison*. From the beginning the firm of Davison and Lees specialized in the import trade and in supplying the British troops in North America, two highly lucrative activities. For example, a contract to provide the army with flour brought

483

Lees

the two partners £300 a year, as well as a 25½ per cent commission on their purchases. They also became suppliers for a number of merchants in the Quebec and Trois-Rivières regions, among them Pierre Du Calvet*, who owed them £3,600 at his death in 1786, and Aaron Hart*, for whom they also acted as agent in England. As creditors for small merchants such as Alexandre DUMAS and John Justus Diehl, to whom they advanced goods on credit, they occasioned more than one bankruptcy.

Like many businessmen of the period, Lees and his partner engaged in land speculation. *Habitués* of the sheriffs' offices in Quebec and Montreal, they concentrated their activity at Quebec and in the parishes west of Trois-Rivières. In this way on 14 Oct. 1784 they bought the seigneury of Gastineau, which they sold three years later to George Davison*, Alexander's younger brother.

In 1786 Lees and the two Davison brothers obtained the lucrative lease of the king's posts for 16 years at £400 a year [*see* Henry Hamilton*]. The acquisition was made through the political contacts of the Davisons, supporters of the French party, with Lees acting as agent. François BABY was also a partner, but the others soon bought up his share and divided the profits, one-half going to George Davison, the other to Davison and Lees.

Because of their numerous activities in the Trois-Rivières region, Lees and Alexander Davison became interested in the Saint-Maurice ironworks, to which they were suppliers. As the lessee, Conrad Gugy*, had died, in March 1787 they obtained the lease and the contents of the inventory for £2,300. The next year the two partners asked the Executive Council for a ten-year extension of their lease, which was to expire in 1799; they argued that they had had many expenses and would have to invest more in the ironworks "to render them of greater and more general utility." Their request was turned down because Hugh FINLAY had applied for the lease before them and the council judged that the reasons they invoked appeared "neither favourable to the common interest, nor their own interest." Finlay, however, did not obtain the lease; in 1793 Davison and Lees sold it to George Davison, David Monro*, and Mathew Bell*.

Lees and Davison originally entered into a partnership for only a few years, but it was renewed and lasted 18, coming to an end for unknown reasons on 15 Aug. 1791. According to the terms of the final settlement, which did not occur until October of the following year, Lees made over his share, amounting to half of their business, to his ex-partner for £1,000. Davison for his part promised to repay £812 5s. 7d. which had been paid out by Lees on the company's behalf, plus "further sums not exceeding two hundred pounds currency which the said John Lees may justify." In addition, if the lease to the king's posts

was renewed, Lees was to receive £200 a year for six years. He undertook, naturally, to hand over to Davison any sums he might receive in the name of their company, which would be wound up in 1794. Lees continued until at least 1800 to serve as an official supplier to the army. During his partnership with Davison, Lees had acted on his own on a few occasions, particularly as agent for friends or merchants in difficulty with the law.

In 1792 Lees embarked on a new career. On 10 July he was elected to the first house of assembly of Lower Canada, for the constituency of Three Rivers, a seat he retained for the rest of his life. He also sat on the Executive Committee as an honorary member from late 1794 until December 1804, and then as an active member until 1807. In addition, during the last two years of his life he was a judge of the provincial Court of Appeals. He appears to have virtually abandoned the business world, although the post of storekeeper general to the Indian Department at Lachine, which he held from 20 April 1795, may have enabled him to carry out certain transactions. In any case it brought him nearly £500 a year. In his first report Lees drew attention to himself by accusing the Queen's Rangers of stealing goods and presents intended for the Indians. Later he often complained to his superiors of the expenditures he had to make personally to rent and heat his office; moreover, as his landlord was demanding such a high rent, he had to build a house in the vicinity of the storehouse.

In the House of Assembly Lees took part in the debates from the outset, opposing Jean-Antoine PANET'S election as speaker and unsuccessfully nominating James McGILL. At the second session he did the same thing, proposing, again unsuccessfully, that John YOUNG preside over the members' deliberations. He was also fiercely opposed to French being an official language of the house and, along with other members of the English party, advocated that members should be able to introduce bills in the language of their choice but that only the English version should be authoritative. In those early days of Canadian parliamentary government Lees also worked hard at drawing up the procedural rules for the assembly, of which he was one of the most regular members, being absent only three or four times from 1792 to 1804. Although he was involved in all the debates, two problems in particular engaged his attention: economic questions and the colony's security. Since he was well acquainted with the business world, he was often chosen as a member or chairman of committees on imports, duties, weights and measures, hemp growing, fishing, and the division of customs revenue between Upper and Lower Canada. As an ardent royalist who feared France's intrigues in her former colony, he proposed or supported various bills for reorganizing and

484

increasing the militia, as well as for punishing "traitors" and deserters.

In addition to these principal occupations, in 1787 Lees had received a new commission as captain in the Quebec Battalion of British Militia; he had been a member of the Agriculture Society of the district since 1789 and one of its directors from 1791 to 1793, the year in which he was on the board of directors of the Quebec Library. In June 1794 he joined the association that had been founded that year to support the British government. The next year he was one of the commissioners of the Lachine toll-roads. He also served as justice of the peace for the District of Quebec from 1795 to about 1799. Like a good many officials of the time, Lees asked for land grants; a request in 1796 came to nothing, but in 1803 he received 541 acres in Granby Township.

From 1805 he was plagued with illness and was unable to attend assembly sessions. He died at Lachine in March 1807. Since he had not married, he bequeathed his estate to his sisters Jane, Sarah, and Nancy, of Stirling, Scotland. His accounts, however, were in such disorder that James McGill, John CRAIGIE, and John Richardson* refused to serve as his executors, and the attorney general seized his books and papers. It would take five years to straighten them out.

YVES FRENETTE

ANQ-M, CE1-63, 6 March 1807; CL, 1767–99, 1er, 31 mars 1781. ANQ-MBF, CN1-6, 1er avril 1807. ANQ-Q, CN1-25, 9 déc. 1779; 9 juill., 20 sept., 25 oct. 1785; CN1-83, 29 janv. 1794; CN1-205, 6 févr. 1782; CN1-230, 21 sept. 1816; CN1-256, 25, 31 Oct. 1792; CN1-284, 29 nov. 1787, 13 juin 1796; P1000-27-502. Arch. du séminaire de Trois-Rivières (Trois-Rivières, Qué.), Fonds Hart, OC-4, Agents des Hart. AUM, P 58, J2/150. BL, Add. MSS 21738: 75–77 (copy at PAC). PAC, MG 11, [CO 42] Q, 29: 942–46; 38: 108, 119–20; 114; MG 23, I13, 1; RG 1, L3^L: 20198–201, 35318–20; RG 4, A1, 27; 92; B17, 4, 25 janv. 1784; 11; 14; RG 8, I (C ser.), 546: 138–39; RG 68, 238: 814–17. PRO, T 64/115 (mfm. at PAC). Bas-Canada, chambre d'Assemblée, *Journaux*, 1792–1807. *Doc. relatifs à l'hist. constitutionnelle, 1759–1791* (Shortt et Doughty; 1921), 1: 479. [Frederick Haldimand], "Private diary of Gen. Haldimand," *PAC Report*, 1889: 175–77. *John Askin papers* (Quaife), 2: 544. [Francis Maseres], *An account of the proceedings of the British, and other Protestant inhabitants, of the province of Quebeck, in North-America, in order to obtain an house of assembly in that province* (London, 1775), 241. *Quebec Gazette*, 3 Jan. 1793; 10 April, 3 July 1794; 12 March 1807. F.-J. Audet, "Les législateurs du Bas-Canada." F.-J. Audet et Édouard Fabre Surveyer, *Les députés de Saint-Maurice et de Buckinghamshire, 1792–1808* (Trois-Rivières, 1934), 8. "Papiers d'État – Bas-Canada," *PAC Rapport*, 1891: 63; 1892: 234, 243; 1893: 63. *Quebec almanac*, 1788: 47; 1791: 38, 43, 82; 1792: 104, 119, 158; 1794: 122; 1796: 61; 1799: 77; 1801: 80, 102. M.-F. Fortier, *La structure sociale du village industriel des forges du Saint-Maurice: étude qualitative et quantitative* (Can., National Hist. Parks and Sites Branch, *Manuscript report*, no. 259, Ottawa, 1977), 95. F.[-J.] Audet et Édouard Fabre Surveyer, "John Lees," *La Presse* (Montréal), 18 juin 1927: 53, 63. "La famille Bell," *BRH*, 42 (1936): 129. Albert Tessier, "Les Anglais prennent les forges au sérieux," *Cahiers des Dix*, 14 (1949): 176.

LE MAISTRE, FRANCIS, army and militia officer and colonial administrator; b. *c.* 1743 on Jersey, son of François-Guillaume Le Maistre and Élisabeth Théodore; d. 13 Feb. 1805 at Quebec, Lower Canada.

Francis Le Maistre purchased a lieutenancy in the 98th Foot for 300 guineas in 1760 and fought during 1762 in the West Indies. Placed on half pay in 1763, he purchased into the 7th Foot for 300 guineas three years later and then paid £400 for the position of adjutant, which he occupied for nine years from October 1767. In 1775 and 1776 he served with distinction as brigade-major at Quebec while the province was under attack by the American rebels [*see* Benedict ARNOLD; Richard Montgomery*]. Governor Guy CARLETON rewarded him in 1776 with an appointment as his aide-de-camp and that summer entrusted him with dispatches to London; in November he received a captain's commission in the 8th Foot. Le Maistre returned from London in May 1777, and in July Carleton named him deputy adjutant general to the British forces in Canada.

In November 1783 Le Maistre sailed again for England and may have remained there until 1786 when he was appointed military secretary by Carleton, now Lord Dorchester; he would hold the post until 1794. In April 1786, in London, Le Maistre purchased for £650 a nine-room, two-storey, stone "mansion" at 12 Rue Sainte-Famille, Quebec, where he arrived in July. The following year he bought a farm, perhaps for a summer home, in the village of Fargy (Beauport), and between 1787 and 1790 he acquired several lots in and around the village. His income was no match for his social aspirations, however, and in 1787 he was obliged to borrow £200 from the deputy paymaster, Joshua WINSLOW. He left the army in August 1788.

In 1792 Le Maistre began petitioning for a township in the colony; he never received a land grant, but in 1794, following the death of Nicholas Cox*, Dorchester rewarded him with Cox's positions of lieutenant governor of the District of Gaspé and inspector of trade and fisheries on the Labrador coast, for which he would receive a combined annual salary of £300. Le Maistre visited the Gaspé coast in 1795; the following year he complained that the expense of travel and of the reception at Quebec of delegations from his district necessitated an increase in his salary to £400. Perhaps because his petition was refused or because he was suffering from ill health, Le Maistre never returned to

Le Moyne

the Gaspé; nor did he ever visit Labrador. He exercised virtually no influence at Quebec in favour of his district, but the Jersey families that dominated the Gaspé economy, the Janvrins and the Robins [see Charles Robin*], were pleased with the appointment of their countryman; his very neglect of the Gaspé left them free to maintain their profitable monopoly of its trade and fishing.

Le Maistre's social status at Quebec continued to improve in the 1790s. In 1794, at a time of considerable political ferment resulting from French revolutionary influence, Carleton commissioned him colonel of the Quebec Battalion of British Militia in succession to Henry CALDWELL. Three years later he was chosen foreman of the grand jury that indicted David McLane* for treason.

Le Maistre enjoyed the social life at Quebec; in early 1798 George Thomas Landmann*, a British officer, spent many agreeable hours visiting him, his wife Margaret Stuart, their son, and two daughters. "Le Maistre was especially fond of good living, and had grown to an extra size," Landmann observed, "and whilst engaged in the pleasures of the table, he frequently entertained his friends with many anecdotes of days, long since gone by." His cultural tastes befitted a man of his social rank; his library of more than 350 volumes on history, military theory, law, finance, philosophy, and Greek, English, and French literature included such British authors as David Hume and Thomas Hobbes, Sir William Blackstone and Viscount Bolingbroke, the Duke of Marlborough and the Earl of Chesterfield, Tobias George Smollett and Jonathan Swift, and such French writers as Nicolas Boileau, dit Boileau-Despréaux, Jacques Necker, Charles Rollin, Guillaume Raynal, and Voltaire. His library also contained scientific works, and he possessed a telescope and a microscope.

When Le Maistre died in 1805 he was given a lavish military funeral attended by companies from the British garrison and militia and a "numerous assemblage of the most respectable citizens, and gentlemen of the Legislature, and a great concourse of persons of every description." Within months of this impressive burial, his widow was inundated by the demands of more than 60 creditors for payment of £2,250 in debts. Among the largest creditors were Thomas Aston COFFIN, inspector general of public accounts, to whom Le Maistre owed £368, and Anna Green, Winslow's widow, who in 1806 had Le Maistre's landed property sold at auction by the sheriff. Margaret Le Maistre was left destitute.

Shortly after the death of Le Maistre, Lieutenant Governor Sir Robert Shore Milnes* remarked of the Gaspé: "Public Concerns in that distant District have suffered very essentially through the want of an acknowledged Agent on the part of Government residing there." Le Maistre's inattention created a precedent for his successor, Alexander Forbes, who seems to have toured the Gaspé only once during a tenure lasting until about 1830. The position of lieutenant governor of the District of Gaspé was discontinued after that date.

DAVID LEE

ANQ-Q, CN1-26, 25 oct. 1798; 2 avril, 24 juin 1805; CN1-83, 28 août 1786; 4, 5 juin, 24 sept. 1787; 23 juill., 29 oct. 1790; 26 août 1794; CN1-256, 25 May 1795. BL, Add. MSS 21743: 88 (copy at PAC). PAC, MG 8, F25, 3: 11; MG 11, [CO 42] Q, 67: 55–56; 69: 194; 78: 166–67; 94: 73–76; 96: 32–33; 97: 43–46; MG 23, GII, 17, 1, vol.15: 52–54; MG 30, D1, 9: 200–90. PRO, PRO 30/55, no.5643 (transcript at PAC). Ainslie, Canada preserved (Cohen), 94. Landmann, Adventures and recollections, 1: 284. Quebec Gazette, 13 Nov. 1783; 30 July 1786; 14 Feb., 4 July, 28 Nov. 1805; 20 May 1806. Quebec Mercury, 16 Feb. 1805. P.-V. Charland, "Le tableau de 'l'Immaculée conception' à la basilique de Québec," BRH, 22 (1916): 3–13. David Lee, "La Gaspésie, 1760–1867,"Canadian Hist. Sites, no.23 (1980): 126.

LE MOYNE DE LONGUEUIL, JOSEPH-DOMINIQUE-EMMANUEL, army and militia officer, seigneur, and politician; b. 2 April 1738 in the seigneury of Soulanges (Que.), son of Paul-Joseph Le Moyne* de Longueuil, known as the Chevalier de Longueuil, and Marie-Geneviève Joybert de Soulanges; d. 19 Jan. 1807 in Montreal, Lower Canada.

Joseph-Dominique-Emmanuel Le Moyne de Longueuil's noble descent and his membership in one of the most prestigious families in the military history of New France quite naturally marked him out for a military career. He soon passed through the lower ranks; he entered the colonial regular troops at the age of 12, and after a mere 6 months, on 1 April 1751, he was promoted second ensign. In this capacity he led a group of Hurons from Notre-Dame-de-Lorette (Loretteville, Que.) to Fort Duquesne (Pittsburgh, Pa) in 1754 as part of an expedition sent under Louis Coulon* de Villiers to consolidate the French position in the Ohio country. The long-standing links between the Le Moyne de Longueuil family and the Indian nations explain in large part the role that Longueuil played with the Hurons throughout his military career under the French régime. On 3 July 1754 he led them at the capture of Fort Necessity (near Farmington, Pa), an operation directed by Villiers to avenge the death of his brother Joseph Coulon* de Villiers de Jumonville. Longueuil took command of a detachment of Hurons from Notre-Dame-de-Lorette on 27 April 1755 and led it from Quebec to the Ohio River. He was promoted ensign in May, and on 9 July took part with his detachment in the battle of the Monongahela near Fort Duquesne. In 1757 he participated in both phases of the campaign that ended with the surrender of Fort George (also called Fort William Henry; now Lake

George, N.Y.): he was detailed to second his father in commanding France's Indian allies during the raid by François-Pierre de Rigaud* de Vaudreuil in March, and was given the same responsibility during the August offensive of Louis-Joseph de Montcalm*. As a result of having scoured the region between Fort Carillon (near Ticonderoga, N.Y.) and Fort Orange (Albany, N.Y.) during the summer of 1756 – a type of military action in which he seems to have excelled – Longueuil was well acquainted with the territory south of Lake Champlain and all its forts. After apparently having taken part in the defence of Carillon in 1758 [see Montcalm], he spent the rest of that summer in reconnaissance or skirmishing operations; then in the autumn Montcalm gave him command of a company of volunteers ordered "to keep a daily watch on the shores of Lac Saint-Sacrement," as Lake George was then called by the French.

On 1 Jan. 1759 Longueuil was appointed adjutant to the troops at Trois-Rivières and also promoted to the rank of infantry lieutenant. He participated in the Beauport campaign, experienced the bitter defeat on the Plains of Abraham on 13 September, and then withdrew to the vicinity of the Rivière Jacques-Cartier to spend the winter under the orders of Jean-Daniel Dumas*. During the battle of Sainte-Foy, on 28 April 1760, he was wounded in the thigh. He left the colony, probably in the six months following the capitulation, and went to Paris, France, where he stayed at the home of his great-uncle, the aged Jean-Baptiste Le Moyne* de Bienville. After repeated requests, both from himself and from influential persons, he was granted a captain's commission on 1 July 1766 and accorded a pension of 400 *livres* from 25 July, an unusual award in view of his youth.

Longueuil's decision to come back to Canada was probably influenced by two factors: his unfitness for service and the death on 7 March 1767 of Bienville, whose will named him heir to a quarter of his estate. He returned home, and on 10 March 1770 in Montreal he married Louise Prud'homme, the widow of Louis de Bonne* de Missègle and mother of Pierre-Amable DE BONNE. Although he continued to pay attention to the great questions of the day, Longueuil led a rather secluded life until the American invasion [see Benedict ARNOLD; Richard Montgomery*] gave him the opportunity to put his military experience at the service of the crown. On 7 Sept. 1775 he took command of about a hundred Canadian volunteers and led them from Montreal to Fort St Johns (Saint-Jean-sur-Richelieu). Under the orders of François-Marie Picoté* de Belestre his detachment put up a steady resistance for 45 days against the invader's assaults. Following the surrender of the fort early in November 1775, Longueuil was sent to Albany and New Jersey, and by all indications was kept prisoner until May 1777.

On 25 Nov. 1777 Governor Sir Guy CARLETON appointed Longueuil inspector of militia, an office with which he was already familiar since he had carried out its duties on various occasions during the summer of 1775 and particularly since his return from captivity. This responsibility was not the only reward for his loyalty. On 20 Aug. 1777 the king assented to Longueuil's appointment as a legislative councillor. His swearing-in on 7 July 1778 marked the beginning of nearly 30 years of political life. The direction taken by his career demonstrates the concerns of this nobleman who, reassured by the Quebec Act of 1774 and well served by the turn of military events, from then on endeavoured to preserve his gains by taking refuge in a deeply conservative political attitude. His open hostility to the establishment of parliamentary institutions did not, however, prevent him from pursuing his career under the new régime created by the constitution of 1791, when he found himself called to the executive and legislative councils of Lower Canada.

Longueuil's political activity reflects quite faithfully the assumptions and values of the seigneurial nobility of the period. For Longueuil was also a landowner. The seigneuries of Soulanges, Nouvelle-Longueuil, and Pointe-à-l'Orignal, which his father had left him, brought him an annual income of £300 during the ten-year period from 1780 to 1790. Longueuil managed his properties from Montreal, where he lived, and concentrated his efforts particularly on Soulanges, which provided him with almost all his income from landed property. Pointe-à-l'Orignal was, on the other hand, put up for sale in 1784.

Although the name of Longueuil is deeply engraved in the political annals of the period, various factors often forced him to remain somewhat removed from the political foreground. His place of residence and his participation in Montreal affairs often kept him from council meetings, for example. But there was more to it than that: the politician had never really shed his military uniform. Having performed his duties as inspector of militia until 24 Dec. 1783, Longueuil was promoted to the rank of major on 12 July 1790 in recognition of his services during the American invasion. On 10 May 1794 he became colonel of the Vaudreuil militia. Finally, his appointment on 22 Jan. 1796 as lieutenant-colonel in the Royal Canadian Volunteer Regiment came as a consummation of his military career. The raising of this colonial regiment, which was required by the military situation in Europe and Great Britain's need of all her forces, made it possible to replace the troops recalled by incorporating English- and French-speaking recruits from the Canadas into the regular army. On 25 June 1796 Longueuil was put in command of the first of the regiment's two battalions – the one that was formed

Lennox

for recruits speaking French and was permanently stationed in Lower Canada; he continued to demonstrate his loyalty and retained his post until the regiment was disbanded in September 1802.

Longueuil died on 19 Jan. 1807 at his home in the *faubourg* Saint-Antoine in Montreal. Having no immediate heirs, since his only son had died in infancy, he had on 21 Nov. 1806 bequeathed his seigneuries of Soulanges and Nouvelle-Longueuil to his nephew, Jacques-Philippe Saveuse* de Beaujeu.

GÉRALD PELLETIER

AN, Col., D²ᶜ, 48: ff.309v., 349, 403v.; 49: ff.353, 379, 382, 386–88, 390, 392, 399, 401, 403, 405, 408v., 425–26, 428, 430, 432; 58: ff.23v., 26v., 27; 59: f.8; 61: ff.126v., 134, 161; E, 290 (dossier Le Moyne de Longueuil). ANQ-M, CE1-23, 18 janv. 1773; CE1-51, 10 mars 1770, 21 janv. 1807; CN1-308, 9 mars 1770 (copies at PAC). BL, Add. MSS 21687: 30, 655–56; 21708: 56; 21721: 169; 21738: 5; 21739: 1; 21749-1: 73; 21777: 72–76; 21796: 58–59; 21831: 1; 21879: 27–29; 21884: 12 (copies at PAC). PAC, MG 11, [CO 42] Q, 11: 284; 12: 170; 13: 164–65; 25: 241–42; 27-1: 64; 38: 241, 365–66; 39: 11–12; 40: 142; 57-1: 227–30; 67: 50–51; 81-2: 501; 82: 282; 83: 6, 216–17; 85: 2l3; 87-1: 98–100; 98: 198; 101-2: 440; MG 24, L3: 6819–21, 24931–32, 29469, 29473–75, 29477–78 (copies); RG 1, E1, 108: 44; 111: 52.

[L.-A.] de Bougainville, "Le journal de M. de Bougainville," A.[-E.] Gosselin, édit., ANQ *Rapport*, 1923–24: 256–57. G.-J. Chaussegros de Léry, "Journal de Joseph-Gaspard Chaussegros de Léry, lieutenant des troupes, 1754–1755," A.[-E.] Gosselin, édit., ANQ *Rapport*, 1927–28: 358–59. *Coll. des manuscrits de Lévis* (Casgrain), 1: 89–91; 2: 256–58; 7: 197–98. *Doc. relatifs à l'hist. constitutionnelle, 1759–1791* (Shortt et Doughty; 1921), 1: 490–94; 2: 684–85, 857–59, 917–18; *1791–1818* (Doughty et McArthur; 1915), 13–32, 172. *Documents inédits sur le colonel de Longueuil*, Monongahéla de Beaujeu, édit. (Montréal, 1891). [Antoine] Foucher, "Journal tenu pendant le siège du fort Saint-Jean, en 1775, par feu M. Foucher, ancien notaire de Montréal," *BRH*, 40 (1934): 135–59, 197–222. *Invasion du Canada* (Verreau), 31, 34, 42–44, 66–67, 166, 229, 313–14, 320–21, 324–25. *NYCD* (O'Callaghan and Fernow), 10: 620–21. *Papiers Contrecœur et autres documents concernant le conflit anglo-français sur l'Ohio de 1745 à 1756*, Fernand Grenier, édit. (Québec, 1952), 187. [J.-G. Plantavit de] Lapause [de Margon], "Les 'mémoires' du chevalier de La Pause," ANQ *Rapport*, 1932–33: 308. "Remplacement d'officiers de guerre," ANQ *Rapport*, 1923–24: 37. Nicolas Renaud d'Avène Des Méloizes, "Journal militaire tenu par Nicolas Renaud d'Avène Des Méloizes, chᵉʳ, seigneur de Neuville, au Canada du 19 juillet 1756 au 30 octobre de la même année," ANQ *Rapport*, 1928–29: 12. *Montreal Gazette*, 26 Jan. 1807. *Quebec Gazette*, 29 May 1777; 29 Aug. 1782; 24 June 1784; 19 May 1785; 15 July 1790; 3 May 1792; 20 March 1800; 7 May, 18 June, 13 Oct., 19 Nov. 1801; 11 Feb. 1802; 22 Sept., 8 Dec. 1803; 21 June 1804; 29 Jan., 23 April 1807.

F.-J. Audet, *Les députés de Montréal*, 36. Caron, "Inv. de la corr. de Mgr Briand," ANQ *Rapport*, 1929–30: 104.

Louise Dechêne, "Les dossiers canadiens du notaire Pointard," ANQ *Rapport*, 1966: 115–18, 127–31. Le Jeune, *Dictionnaire*. P.-G. Roy, *Inv. concessions*, 1: 220–21; 3: 144–45; 4: 176, 274–75. É.-J.[-A.] Auclair, *Histoire de la paroisse de Saint-Joseph-de-Soulanges ou Les Cèdres (1702–1927)* (Montréal, 1927), 20–21, 50–52, 61, 65. Caron, *La colonisation de la prov. de Québec*, 1: 131, 257, 282. E. J. Chambers, *The Canada militia, a history of the origin and development of the force* (Montreal, 1907), 27. Grace King, *J. B. LeMoyne, sieur de Bienville* (New York, 1892), 325–27. Lanctot, *Le Canada et la Révolution américaine*, 79, 194, 202–3. Tousignant, "La genèse et l'avènement de la constitution de 1791," 166–68, 216, 316–17, 320–24, 329, 380–81, 400–5. Monongahéla de Beaujeu, "Le colonel de Longueuil," *BRH*, 7 (1901): 255. "La famille Bailly de Messein," *BRH*, 23 (1917): 201. A.[-E.] Gosselin, "Notes sur la famille Coulon de Villiers," *BRH*, 12 (1906): 230–31, 291. J.-J. Lefebvre, "Michel-Eustache-Gaspard-Alain Chartier de Lotbinière (1748–1822)," ANQ *Rapport*, 1951–53: 374, 378–80. "La loyauté des Canadiens en 1775," *BRH*, 31 (1925): 370–75. Frère Marcel-Joseph, "Les Canadiens veulent conserver le régime seigneurial," *RHAF*, 7 (1953–54): 46–63. É.-Z. Massicotte, "Une inscription énigmatique," *BRH*, 30 (1924): 403–5. Fernand Ouellet, "Officiers de milice et structure sociale au Québec (1660–1815)," *SH*, 12 (1979): 55, 64–65. "La reddition du fort Saint-Jean en 1775," *BRH*, 12 (1906): 315–18. "Le 'Royal Canadien' ou 'Royal Canadian Volunteers,'" *BRH*, 7 (1901): 372. C.-A. Santoire, "Le colonel de Longueuil," *BRH*, 7 (1901): 292.

LENNOX, CHARLES, 4th Duke of RICHMOND and LENNOX, colonial administrator; b. 9 Sept. 1764 in England, eldest son of Lord George Henry Lennox and Lady Louisa Kerr, daughter of William Henry Kerr, 4th Marquess of Lothian; m. 9 Sept. 1789 Charlotte Gordon, daughter of Alexander Gordon, 4th Duke of Gordon, and they had seven sons and seven daughters; d. 28 Aug. 1819 near Richmond, Upper Canada.

Charles Lennox was apparently born in a barn, his mother having taken ill suddenly during a fishing trip. As a boy he joined the Sussex militia, in which he was promoted to a lieutenancy in 1778. Some six years later he became secretary to his uncle, Charles Lennox, 3rd Duke of Richmond and Lennox, as well as to the Board of Ordnance. On 29 Aug. 1787 he was commissioned a captain in the 35th Foot, and on 26 March 1789, thanks to the influence of Richmond with Prime Minister William Pitt, Lennox obtained a captaincy in the Coldstream Foot Guards, which carried with it a lieutenant-colonelcy in the army at large. The commander of the Coldstreams, Frederick Augustus, Duke of York and second son of King George III, was indignant to learn of the promotion, particularly since Richmond was a political enemy. When York made disparaging remarks about the courage of the Lennox family, Charles challenged him to a duel, and the encounter took place on 26 May. Lennox grazed the duke's curl with a ball, after which

488

York fired into the air, declaring that he bore his opponent no animosity. Lennox's brother officers esteemed that he had "behaved with courage, but from peculiarity of circumstances, not with judgement"; their ambiguous verdict probably encouraged him to transfer back to the 35th Foot as lieutenant-colonel on 15 June. Fond of sports – his father was the founder of the Goodwood horse-races – Lennox was popular with officers and men alike. After serving with his regiment in the West Indies in 1794, he was appointed aide-de-camp to the king in January 1795. Promoted major-general three years later, on 17 March 1803 he became colonel of the 35th Foot. He was made lieutenant-general in 1805 and general on 1 June 1814.

In 1790 Lennox had been elected to his father's seat of Sussex in the House of Commons, and he was re-elected in 1796, 1802, and 1806. He succeeded to the dukedom of Richmond and Lennox on the death of his uncle on 29 Dec. 1806. The following April he was appointed lord lieutenant of Ireland. His administration was comparatively quiet, despite his opposition to the removal of any political disabilities imposed by British law on Roman Catholics. In June 1812 he wrote to the Colonial secretary, Lord Bathurst, that he would remain in Ireland only so long as "nothing is done for the Catholics." Despite his rigid political and religious views, Richmond's interest in horse-racing, hunting, and other sporting activities, and his lavish hospitality, ensured him a certain popularity among the Irish. His appointment ended in 1813, and the following year he temporarily closed the family estate of Goodwood for reasons of economy and moved his family to Brussels (Belgium). There, on 15 June 1815, the Duchess of Richmond gave the famous ball at which Wellington learned of Napoleon's advance into the Netherlands. Richmond was present at Waterloo, but simply as a civilian. The Richmonds continued to live in Brussels until 1818; on 8 May of that year the duke was appointed governor-in-chief of British North America. He does not appear to have sought the appointment, but he willingly accepted it.

Richmond arrived at Quebec on 29 July 1818, accompanied by his family and his son-in-law, Sir Peregrine Maitland*, who had been appointed lieutenant governor of Upper Canada. The duke had instructions from London to improve the defences of British North America, to expand inland navigation, and to encourage the settlement of disbanded soldiers and other British immigrants in the various colonies. After a preliminary survey, Richmond recommended the strengthening of the forts at Quebec, Île aux Noix, and Île Sainte-Hélène in Lower Canada and at Kingston in Upper Canada, the opening of navigation on the Ottawa and Rideau rivers, and the construction of canals at Lachine, Lower Canada, and between lakes Ontario and Erie; canalization of the Ottawa

began during his régime. Among other suggestions were the improvement of the militia and the building of a military road between Lower Canada and New Brunswick.

Richmond had also received instructions to continue the policy of his predecessors, Sir George PREVOST and Sir John Coape Sherbrooke*, by conciliating Canadian political and religious leaders. He gave assurances to Bathurst that he had overcome the initial suspicions of Bishop Plessis*, the result of his anti-Catholic record in Ireland, but Plessis nevertheless found Richmond less well disposed than Prevost or Sherbrooke had been. Accustomed to having direct access to the governor, the bishop found Richmond "in general . . . buttoned up tight about affairs and scarcely communicative." "Everything is done by interim secretaries," he added, "we have enemies among the most notable people." Moreover, Richmond breathed new life into the Royal Institution for the Advancement of Learning, which was responsible for the colony's public schools and was much contested by Plessis [see Joseph Langley Mills*]. Later Richmond asked Anglican bishop Jacob Mountain* to draft plans for a university to be founded under the auspices of the Royal Institution with the aid of a bequest from the merchant James McGILL.

In politics, rather than conciliating the Canadian party, Richmond took counsel from the rival English party, and most notably from John YOUNG in the crucial matter of provincial finances. The revenues of the executive alone being insufficient to meet the expenses of the civil administration, in 1818 Sherbrooke, with the approval of the Colonial Office, had arrived at a compromise with the House of Assembly, dominated by the Canadian party under Louis-Joseph Papineau*, whereby the assembly would meet the current expenses of government and wipe out a large accumulated deficit in return for an annual consideration of the estimates. However, Sherbrooke's poor health and subsequent departure had prevented the passage of a regular supply bill sanctioning the arrangement in legislation. In March 1819 Richmond, who feared for the independence of the crown if Sherbrooke's compromise was adopted, presented the assembly with the estimates of expenses for the year, prepared by Young, reintroducing items, such as sinecure salaries, that Sherbrooke had agreed to drop as part of the compromise. When the assembly once again eliminated these items, Richmond seized the opportunity to contest its claim to control the estimates and prorogued the legislature, lecturing the lower house on its responsibilities in a manner reminiscent of the unpopular Governor CRAIG. Richmond had been angered as well by the assembly's refusal to follow the British practice of providing for a civil list, guaranteeing at least some of the salaries of office

L'Estang

holders during the life of the king. To strengthen the hand of the administration, he sought to enforce the collection of *lods et ventes*, a crown revenue, and urged London to replace provincial acts regulating trade and imposing import duties by imperial ones, in order to ensure for the executive funds sufficient to make it independent of moneys voted by the assembly. Also concerned by the assembly's disposition to ignore the Legislative Council, which was dominated by the English party, Richmond adopted as his own that party's recommendation for the union of Upper and Lower Canada as a means of neutralizing the Canadian party in a combined elective assembly.

As in Ireland, Richmond considered the encouragement of leisure an important means of popularizing his administration, at least among the élite. According to Frederic Tolfrey, an officer of the garrison, Richmond, who had been "one of the finest tennis-players in England" and an excellent racket-baller, "joined the officers around him in all manly games with an unaffected urbanity and good nature that endeared the Duke to all." He was patron of the Garrison Racing Club, and he encouraged the Tandem Club, formed to make winter excursions into the countryside, by taking his turn in a rotation among the principal families of the town to supply the excursionists' luncheons. He also did much to promote the theatre; his sons and entire staff joined the garrison theatre group, and he himself attended all presentations, inviting the players afterwards to supper at the governor's residence, the Château Saint-Louis. Tolfrey noted as well that "balls and parties were more numerous than ever; the hospitality at the Chateau was conducted on a scale of princely liberality, and the magnificent gold plate and racing cups of the Noble Duke astonished the Canadians not a little whenever any large State parties were given, and to which the natives on these occasions were invited."

During the summer of 1819 Richmond undertook an extensive tour of Upper and Lower Canada. At William Henry (Sorel, Que.) he was bitten on the hand by a fox. The injury apparently healed, and he continued to York (Toronto) and Niagara (Niagara-on-the-Lake, Ont.), even examining military sites as far distant as Drummond Island. Returning to Kingston, he planned a leisurely visit to the settlements on the Rideau. During this part of the journey the first symptoms of hydrophobia appeared. The disease developed rapidly and on 28 August he died in extreme agony in a barn a few miles from a settlement that had been named in his honour. Some accounts suggest that the duke had been bitten by a dog; stronger contemporary evidence, however, supports the view that he had received the rabies infection from a fox. Richmond's body was brought back to Quebec, where on 4 September it was buried in the Cathedral of the Holy Trinity.

Personally popular among the British élite in the Canadas, the Duke of Richmond was out of sympathy with the popular party in Lower Canada, whose claims outraged his ideas of the inviolability of the crown's prerogative. His most enduring legacy in Lower Canadian politics was the conversion of his brother-in-law and close friend, the Colonial secretary, Lord Bathurst, to the English party's view that compromise with the assembly over provincial finances was impossible. Relations between the British government and the assembly were thenceforth to deteriorate almost unrelentingly. Owing to Richmond's early death, however, the political storm burst not over his own head, but over the heads of his successors.

GEORGE F. G. STANLEY

ANQ-Q, CE1-61, 4 Sept. 1819. PAC, MG 24, A14. Bas-Canada, Conseil législatif, *Journaux*, 1819. *Docs. relating to constitutional hist., 1791–1818* (Doughty and McArthur; 1914); *1819–28* (Doughty and Story; 1935). *Gentleman's Magazine*, January–June 1819: 466–67. W. P. Lennox, *My recollections from 1806 to 1873* (2v., London, 1874). *The life and letters of Lady Sarah Lennox, 1745–1826* . . . , ed. [Mary Dawson], Countess of Ilchester and [G. S. H. Fox-Strangeways], Lord Stavordale (2v., London, 1901), 1: 300; 2: 69–70. "La mort du duc de Richmond," *BRH*, 8 (1902): 30–31. "Particularités de la maladie et de la mort du duc de Richmond, par un officier de son état-major," *BRH*, 10 (1904): 43–50. *Spencer and Waterloo: the letters of Spencer Madan, 1814–1816*, ed. Beatrice Madan (London, 1970). *Montreal Herald*, 4 Sept. 1819. *Quebec Gazette*, 21 May, 22 June, 27, 30 July, 20, 31 Aug., 14, 28 Sept., 5, 19 Oct., 2 Nov., 7 Dec. 1818; 28 Jan., 11 Feb., 8 March, 13, 27 May, 14, 17 June, 1, 5 July, 5, 30 Aug., 2, 6, 20, 23, 27 Sept. 1819; 20 Jan. 1820.

Burke's peerage (1890), 1159–60. Caron, "Inv. de la corr. de Mgr Plessis," ANQ *Rapport*, 1928–29: 125, 129. *DNB*. "State papers, Lower Canada," PAC *Report*, 1897: 253–56, 275–82. Lambert, "Joseph-Octave Plessis." L. M. Lande, *The 3rd Duke of Richmond, a study in early Canadian history* (Montreal, 1956). Duncan McArthur, "History of public finance, 1763–1840," *Canada and its prov.* (Shortt and Doughty), 4: 496–506, 509–11; "Papineau and French-Canadian nationalism," 3: 289–93. [Daniel] MacKinnon, *Origin and services of the Coldstream Guards* (2v., London, 1833), 2: 30–32, 496–97. Manning, *Revolt of French Canada*, 43, 122–23, 133–34, 152, 200, 235. Millman, *Jacob Mountain*, 76, 175, 178, 181, 212, 274. Frederic Tolfrey, *The sportsman in Canada* (2v., London, 1845), 2: 198–221, 236–52. Douglas Brymner, "La mort du duc de Richmond," *BRH*, 5 (1899): 112–14. E. A. Cruikshank, "Charles Lennox, the fourth Duke of Richmond," *OH*, 24 (1927): 323–51. "Le duc de Richmond," *BRH*, 10 (1904): 41–42. "Les funérailles du duc de Richmond," *BRH*, 42 (1936): 511–12.

L'ESTANG (L'Étang), named Sainte-Rose, VÉRONIQUE BRUNET, *dit. See* BRUNET

LESTER, BENJAMIN, office holder, agent, and businessman; b. 13 July 1724 in Poole, England, fourth son of Francis Lester, merchant and cooper of

Poole, and Rachel Taverner, daughter of William Taverner*; m. *c.* 1750 in Trinity, Nfld, his cousin Susannah Taverner, daughter of Jacob Taverner of Trinity; d. 25 Jan. 1802 in Poole, survived by one son and three daughters.

Benjamin Lester's father, mayor of Poole in 1716, owned at least one ship in the Newfoundland trade in the 1730s and apparently concentrated on dealing in oil. Benjamin himself went to Newfoundland about 1737, evidently in the employ of John Masters, an eminent Poole-Newfoundland merchant who had married another daughter of William Taverner, and his Irish partner, Michael Ballard. The death of Benjamin's father in 1737 presumably had made it necessary for him to pursue his own career, and his youth and probable lack of capital meant that he was unable to set up on his own in the fishery. In 1749 he was appointed a magistrate at Trinity, and in 1750 was acting as Ballard's agent as victualler to the Trinity garrison.

Masters and Ballard died in 1755 and 1756 respectively, and Lester subsequently emerged as a merchant on his own account, eventually acquiring a substantial share of the Newfoundland fishery in partnership with his elder brother Isaac. Isaac, who had apparently inherited his father's coopering business, remained in Poole, where he was well placed to supervise the British end, recruiting men and handling ships and supplies for the fishery. Benjamin's interests centred on Trinity, where he normally spent the fishing seasons until he left Newfoundland in 1776 and where he built a large brick house, but they extended over Trinity and Bonavista bays and up to Fogo, as well as to the banks fisheries. His outstations included Scilly Cove (Winterton), Tickle Harbour (Bellevue), and Bonavista. Lester exploited the coast of Labrador as well from 1767, and in 1778 he pioneered the use of shallops there for seal fishing by water so that full advantage could be taken of the spring fishing season. By the 1770s he owned at least 12 ships, and by 1793 his fleet had grown to nearly 30, probably the largest then owned by a Poole merchant. He built many of his vessels in Trinity and had two sixth rates for the Royal Navy constructed there in 1790.

Lester was responsible for surrendering Trinity to the French during the attack on Newfoundland in 1762 commanded by Charles-Henri-Louis d'Arsac* de Ternay. Criticized by some of the inhabitants, who had at least talked of resistance, he was made to give up his magistrate's commission by Governor Thomas GRAVES, but was shortly afterwards exonerated from charges of collaboration. In his defence it must be said that his conduct during the occupation undoubtedly minimized not only his own losses but those of the community in general.

Lester's trade does not appear to have suffered greatly during the War of American Independence, in spite of difficulties in supplying provisions to Newfoundland and the depredations of American privateers off the coast. During the boom years of the 1780s he prospered greatly. In 1787 his eight bankers, manned by 87 men, caught 9,000 quintals of cod, and in the 1789 season he shipped to Europe 50,087 quintals of new fish and 2,469 of old fish, nearly seven per cent of the total taken in Newfoundland that year, together with 1,183 tierces of salmon. In addition, nearly 4,000 quintals of old fish were sold to the West Indies. The French revolutionary wars were a more serious threat to his interests. He lost seven of his ships between 1795 and 1798 and was affected by the closing of the Italian market and the depression in the Spanish and Portuguese markets, but his business was able to survive these difficulties. In 1800 he was assessed in Poole at £3,000 value in export and import rates, by far the greatest amount for a Poole merchant, and in 1801 his stations on Venison Island and elsewhere caught 2,900 of the total of 8,084 seals taken in Labrador that year.

Lester's relations with other Poole merchants established in the Trinity area and trading in the same regions varied. Those with Samuel and Joseph White and Peter Jolliffe appear to have been initially friendly, but he quarrelled over business with Richard Waterman of Trinity and Jeremiah Coghlan* of Fogo during the late 1760s. About a decade later he became an opponent of John Jeffrey of Poole, who inherited the Whites' business, but his relations with Jeffrey's sometime partner Thomas STREET were generally good. In 1776 he quarrelled with John Slade* of Twillingate when Slade engaged some men who had already taken service with Lester.

Lester had emerged as a spokesman of the Newfoundland merchants in Poole in their dealings with government by 1773, when he represented their opposition to the establishment of the custom-house in St John's. In 1775, despite opposition in Poole, he secured the dispatch of a petition supporting the barring of the Americans from the Newfoundland trade, and gave evidence before the House of Lords in support of a bill to exclude them. After his final return to England in 1776 he used the political influence his brother had built up in Poole to have himself elected mayor of the town in 1779 and from 1781 to 1783, and he also served as member of parliament for the borough between 1790 and 1796. In the attempt to obtain better terms in the peace settlement of 1783 he attacked the concessions made over the French Shore and the French retention of Saint-Pierre and Miquelon. Lester supported Lord Sheffield, a leading authority on commerce, in opposing American trading rights with British colonies, and as one of the Poole representatives at the Privy Council committee for trade's inquiry into this issue in 1785 he urged limitations on American trade with Newfoundland. But Lester and the other Poole merchants were

Lester

persuaded by the government to accept the need for imports of foodstuffs from the United States into Newfoundland, and by 1788 they had come to realize that American supplies were essential, to the extent that they protested when the government sought to stop American supplies in favour of those from Quebec. Lester entered a further protest in 1791 when the government again attempted to restrict imports of American supplies. In 1793 Lester was a member of the House of Commons inquiry into the Newfoundland trade. Active too in securing posts in the Newfoundland government for his acquaintances, he assisted Richard ROUTH to become the customs collector in 1782, and D'Ewes Coke to obtain the customs controllership in 1783.

Since Lester's only son, John, did not take much interest in the family firm, on Lester's death his Newfoundland business passed effectively to his son-in-law George Garland, who had formerly assisted him in managing his trade, and then to the latter's sons George* and John Bingley. Starting his career with apparently few advantages, Benjamin Lester had demonstrated great energy and enterprise in exploiting the Newfoundland fisheries and trade. Although he came to change his mind on such matters as the custom-house and American trade with Newfoundland, his attitude to the commerce and government of the island was fundamentally conservative, and typical of the view of the West Country merchants, who felt that they knew better than government or missionaries how to manage the island's affairs, and who wished to be as free as possible from interference with the conduct of their business in Newfoundland. Characteristically, in 1764 Lester promised that the newly appointed Anglican clergyman in Trinity, James BALFOUR, would not "want for my assistance while he behaves as a Gentleman of his Cloth." In his last years he opposed the extension of civil government in Newfoundland, telling Prime Minister William Pitt in 1792 that the establishment of a supreme court at St John's [see John Reeves*] would make Newfoundland "a colony filled with lawyers; all harmony will subside, and the ruin of that valuable branch of trade of fishery will be fatal to this country."

D. F. BEAMISH

BL, King's Maps CXIX, 107b. Dorset Record Office, 2694 (Life history of John Masters); D365; P227/RE3–RE10, reg. of christenings, marriages, and burials, 1722–1812. Poole Borough Arch. (Poole, Eng.), no.226 PBA, Town dues, 1731–32. PRO, BT 1/2: f.165; CO 194/12: f.184; 194/21: ff.35, 84; PRO 30/8, bundle 151. USPG, B, 6, no.157. *The parliamentary history of England from the earliest period to the year 1803*, comp. William Cobbett and John Wright (36v., London, 1806–20), 18: 426–27. Derek Beamish *et al.*, *Mansions and merchants of Poole and Dorset* (Poole, 1976). McLintock, *Establishment of constitutional government in Nfld.*, 67–74. E. F. J. Mathews, "The economic policy of Poole, 1756–1815," (PHD thesis, Univ. of London, 1958). A. C. Wardle, "The Newfoundland trade," *The trade winds: a study of British overseas trade during the French wars, 1793–1815*, ed. C. N. Parkinson (London, 1948), 227–50.

LESTER, ROBERT, businessman, militia officer, politician, and landowner; b. *c*. 1746 in Galway (Republic of Ireland); d., probably unmarried, 12 July 1807 at Quebec, Lower Canada.

Robert Lester arrived at Quebec around 1770, and by 1772 he had established himself there as a merchant. In the winter of 1775–76, during the siege of the city by brigadiers-general Benedict ARNOLD and Richard Montgomery*, he was a captain of militia. Along with Captain Anthony Vialar, he kept the orderly book in which were recorded the duties of the militia garrison. In 1779, when Governor HALDIMAND founded the Quebec Library, Lester was appointed treasurer in an executive that included Henri-François GRAVÉ de La Rive, François BABY, James Monk*, Arthur DAVIDSON, and the merchant Pierre Fargues. That February Lester purchased from Nicolas-Gaspard BOISSEAU for 15,200 *livres* a lot and two-storey stone house at 7 Rue Saint-Pierre, where he established his residence and business.

In the 1770s and 1780s Lester gradually built up a trade based principally on the import, for wholesale marketing, of cloth and spirits and on the export of wheat. For some years he conducted business as an individual, and he continued to do so after he formed Robert Lester and Company, which was in existence by 1786. By March 1787 he had taken in as a junior partner his nephew Robert Morrogh, and as early as April 1790 the firm was known as Lester and Morrogh. Like many other merchants, he acted as a business attorney and an estate trustee. He was probably aided in this work by a certain fluency in French, a definite asset for a British merchant in Quebec at this time. In 1780 he was given power of attorney by Henriette Guichaud, Pierre Fargues's widow, to regulate her husband's succession. This assignment may have brought Lester into frequent contact with the influential merchant Thomas DUNN, who married Mme Fargues in 1783. In June 1785 Dunn gave Lester power of attorney to manage some of his affairs. A procuration the same year from the powerful Montreal firm of Todd and McGill may have been the start of Lester's long and fruitful relationship with Isaac TODD, and helped extend beyond Quebec the reputation for probity that he had acquired. In 1789 he acted as attorney for Robert Ellice and Company of Montreal and for the merchants Robert HAMILTON of Queenston (Ont.) and Richard CARTWRIGHT, Robert Macaulay*, and Thomas Markland* of Kingston (Ont.), for whom Todd and McGill were agents at Montreal.

Another aspect of Lester's business was the making of numerous small loans to ordinary people. During

Lester

the period of economic stress following the American revolution the number of Lester's debtors, mainly tailors and tavern-keepers unable to pay for supplies, increased, and he was obliged several times to have property seized for sale at public auction. Lester himself apparently had to struggle to survive. By January 1782 he owed £12,000 in the Cochrane affair [*see* James DUNLOP]. In November of the following year he borrowed £1,200 from the surgeon James Fisher*, promising to pay it back in three years; by December 1787, however, he had paid no more than £200, and could pay the remainder only with a loan from Dunn.

In the 1780s Lester began to participate in the public life of the colony. A devout Catholic, he earned the confidence of the clergy, and in February 1784 he was one of six men authorized to receive and remit to the parish priest of Quebec money and goods destined for the poor and sick of the town. The previous year, when a draft petition for political reform was sent by the merchants of Montreal for the concurrence of their Quebec colleagues, Lester and William GRANT (1744–1805) led a successful drive to revise a clause on qualifications for members of a proposed elective house of assembly in order to admit Roman Catholics. He signed petitions requesting an assembly in 1784, 1788, and 1789, and in 1789 and 1790 he was a member of a 15-man committee formed to protest delay of constitutional and judicial reform. In 1786 he had been among those who signed a petition opposing the collection by government of *lods et ventes* on past property sales. The following year he was a member of a committee of merchants that submitted a report to the Legislative Council recommending the introduction of English law for the regulation of business, the incorporation of Quebec and Montreal, and the use of the Jesuit estates to establish an English-language college. That July he became a captain in the British militia at Quebec. He was among the founding subscribers to the Agriculture Society in April 1789, and the following month he was a member of the grand jury at Quebec. In December Robert Lester and Company was among those firms that protested recently introduced restrictions on the import of rum, arguing that they adversely affected the export of flour and biscuit. The following year Lester signed a petition in support of the founding of a non-sectarian university, even though it was opposed by Bishop Jean-François Hubert*.

Constitutional reform, including provision for a house of assembly, was finally achieved through the Constitutional Act of 1791. Lester ran for election to the assembly in Lower Town, a riding which, although in large part commercial, was inhabited principally by artisans and workers. The resident population, mainly Canadian with a significant Irish minority, was overwhelmingly Roman Catholic, and Lester may have benefited substantially from the

support, no doubt discreet, of the Séminaire de Québec. Thus, as an Irish-Catholic merchant, well known in the community, Lester tapped a fairly broad base of sympathy, including both Canadians and British merchants, among the latter, John PURSS, James TOD, and John BLACKWOOD. He and John YOUNG took 66 per cent of the vote to defeat Adam Lymburner* and Jean-Antoine PANET in the two-seat riding. In the first parliament, from 1792 to 1796, Lester was a faithful adherent of the minority English party, voting with it on 15 of 16 occasions. This adherence was also manifested by his election in 1794 to the standing committee of the Association, formed that year to support British rule in Canada in the context of war with revolutionary France, persistent rumours of a French invasion, and revolt among Canadian militiamen. In October, Lord Dorchester [Guy CARLETON] promoted Lester major in the Quebec Battalion of British Militia; he became lieutenant-colonel about May 1799.

Defeated by Young and Augustin-Jérôme Raby* in the elections of 1796, Lester none the less remained active in public affairs. In February 1797 he and Morrogh were among the petitioners against a prohibition on the export of unsaleable flour as causing a great loss to merchants. In June 1799 he joined 12 leading citizens of Quebec who opened a general subscription in support of Britain's war effort; Lester subscribed £30 per annum for the duration of the war, a contribution exceeded only by those of Dunn and Jenkin WILLIAMS. Lester had continued to be active in the burgeoning social life of Quebec. He was elected a director of the Agriculture Society in 1792 and 1793 and treasurer from 1792 to 1795; he was also repeatedly elected treasurer of the Quebec Library. In November 1793 he made one of the largest individual contributions to a fund for the relief of sufferers in a fire on Rue du Sault-au-Matelot.

Lester's relations with the Catholic hierarchy intensified during the 1790s. When the French revolution cut communications between Quebec and Rome by way of Paris, it may have been Lester's firm that provided a new route; after 1792 exchanges were made through Francis Morrogh at Lisbon, Portugal, a regular port of call for Lester and Morrogh's ships. Lester's relations with Bishop Hubert had undoubtedly introduced him to the latter's secretary, Joseph-Octave Plessis*; when Plessis took possession of Notre-Dame Cathedral as the new parish priest of Quebec in June 1792, Lester was among the official witnesses. In 1794 Lester and Morrogh made cash advances to four exiled French priests, including Jean-Baptiste-Marie Castanet*, who had immigrated to Lower Canada. The following year Lester was the most active among four people designated to collect gifts of clothes and food from the citizens of Quebec for the subsistence of four French royalist families who had fled Guadeloupe.

Lester

The 1790s, a decade of economic prosperity in Lower Canada, were for Lester and Morrogh years of diversification and rapid expansion. Their business had led them to build up their own fleet of ships, and they undoubtedly chartered others. They became among the leading Lower Canadian exporters of wheat and flour. Lester's close relations with Plessis may have given him access to an important source of grain, the tithe collected by parish priests; in 1798 Plessis, now coadjutor designate to Bishop Pierre DENAUT, authorized the sale to Lester of the grain tithe from the parish of Saint-Laurent on Île d'Orléans. By 1790 Lester and Morrogh had moved into the trade in timber and staves. That year, with Todd and the Quebec merchant Peter Stuart, they took a 30-year lease from the Ursulines on three lots in the *faubourg* Saint-Jean. In February 1794 Lester gave power of attorney to Richard Cartwright to manage lands that he had acquired in Upper Canada. Lester himself continued to be an active business agent and attorney: among new clients were the priest Edmund BURKE (1753–1820), who in 1794 left Quebec for the Upper Canadian missions; the London merchant Alexander ELLICE, for whom Lester negotiated the purchase of the seigneury of Villechauve in 1795; and the Halifax merchants Thomas, James, and William Cochran. Since 1789 Lester and Morrogh had been partners in the Montreal Distillery Company, but in 1794 it was dissolved and the property sold to Nicholas MONTOUR; Lester and Morrogh continued, nevertheless, to import spirits and supply local inns and taverns.

The firm's increased activities necessitated an expansion of its facilities. In 1792 it was still being operated from the waterfront property on Rue Saint-Pierre. From 1795 to 1798 at least, the company also rented a wharf from John Blackwood for £175 per annum. In July 1795 it purchased for £850 from the London merchants Brook WATSON and Robert Rashleigh a lot on Rue du Cap-Diamant (Boulevard Champlain) with house, wharf, bakehouse, potash works, stores, and outhouses. The following month the partners bought for £1,750 from Catherine Trottier Desauniers Beaubien, widow of the merchant François Lévesque*, a lot at 2 Rue Saint-Pierre with a two-storey stone house, vaults, storehouses, and wharf; by 1798 Lester had made this his residence, leaving 7 Rue Saint-Pierre to Morrogh. They also undertook major construction projects on their properties.

This expansion was paid for in large part by borrowing. The partners obtained £2,000 from Dunn in August 1795 and another £1,000 two years later. In September 1797 they borrowed £350 from Fisher and in August 1799 the Sulpician superior at Montreal, Jean-Henri-Auguste Roux*, lent them £500 from his personal fortune. In 1801 Lester and Morrogh were among the largest debtors to the estate of the Trois-Rivières merchant Aaron Hart*. That September they borrowed another £2,500 from Fisher. Perhaps sensing themselves over-extended, they sold their property at 7 Rue Saint-Pierre in July 1802 to the auctioneer John JONES for £1,000, paid over three years.

In June 1800 Lester again sought election to the assembly. He easily topped the poll in Lower Town, receiving votes from 357 of the 408 electors; Young was the other successful candidate. Between 1801 and 1804 Lester voted 15 times, always with the English party. In 1801 he was appointed one of five commissioners to execute a law for the relief of persons who had purchased lands on which heavy arrears of *lods et ventes* were due to the crown, and in 1804 he was appointed treasurer of a commission for the erection of a court-house at Quebec.

In the early 1800s Lester's ties with the Catholic clergy broadened. He established excellent relations with Bishop James Louis O'DONEL, vicar apostolic of Newfoundland. In 1802 he acted as financial adviser to the Hôpital Général of Quebec, and that August Bishop Plessis wrote to Denaut that Lester was "more than ever the friend of the priests." In June 1803 Lester was at Halifax, a guest, along with Denaut, of Edmund Burke. His prominence in colonial politics and his unimpeachable credentials as a supporter of the administration may have been exploited by Denaut and Plessis in their relations with the colonial and imperial governments. By the early 1800s they had become aware that Lieutenant Governor Sir Robert Shore Milnes*, influenced by Anglican bishop Jacob Mountain* and Attorney General Jonathan Sewell*, was abandoning the quiet pragmatism that had characterized the state's relations with the church under governors Murray* and Carleton. In its place appeared a certain aggressiveness on the part of the government, which now sought to control the church in the hopes of using its social power to strengthen the political position of executive government in the colony. Lester offered advice to Plessis and used what influence he had on behalf of the hierarchy. About 1803 he was delegated to mollify the angered lieutenant governor when it became clear that the *emigré* French priest Philippe-Jean-Louis Desjardins*, whom Milnes had permitted to visit France, intended to stay there even though that country was at war with Britain. In November 1804, when Lester was in London on one of his business trips, Plessis asked him to obtain from the British government the letters patent for a grant of land at Quebec, made some time before by Milnes to the Congregation of Notre-Dame. Lester also tried, but with limited success in an inhospitable political climate, to obtain foreign priests for seminaries at Quebec and Halifax. In June 1806, when Plessis, who had succeeded Denaut as bishop of

Quebec, sought an English vicar general to fill a crucial position as his agent to the British government, Lester persuaded him to nominate an exiled French Sulpician, François-Emmanuel Bourret, whom he had met during earlier visits to London.

To his ever-widening range of activities Lester was adding those of land speculation in the Eastern Townships and the production of beer. In April 1801 he, as leader according to the system of township leaders and associates [see James CALDWELL], received a grant of 23,100 acres in Barnston Township. Two years later he was granted 500 acres in Granby and 200 acres in Milton for his role in the defence of Quebec in 1775–76. In June 1800 Lester and Morrogh hired the master mason Charles Jourdain*, *dit* Labrosse, to construct a brewery on their property on Rue du Cap-Diamant at Près-de-Ville. The brewer James Mason Godard (Goddard) left his partnership with Young at the St Roc Brewery in February 1801 to join Lester and Morrogh, whose Cape Diamond Brewery was to begin about April producing porter and Burton and mild ale, as well as table and small beer. At the same time Lester and Morrogh continued to import spirits; they also sold Upper Canadian flour.

Perhaps the most important enterprise conducted by Lester and Morrogh after 1800, however, was the provisioning of the army, in association with Todd. The associates filled the role of middlemen, negotiating purchases, mainly of flour and peas, from local merchants when possible, but importing when necessary, to fill orders principally for the commissariat. In December 1801 they received orders for 3,000 barrels of flour and 5,000 bushels of wheat. The same year Lester and Morrogh themselves made the lowest bid to supply 500 gallons of rum. Responding to directions from the lieutenant governor of Upper Canada, Peter HUNTER, to obtain as many of their provisions as possible from that colony rather than from the United States, in 1803 Todd and Lester and Morrogh entered the Upper Canadian market through Todd's relations with the principal partners of James and Andrew McGill and Company. Similarly, a decision by the British government to supply its troops in the Maritimes from the Canadas resulted in an increase in business for the partners; in 1804 and 1805 they were invited to supply Nova Scotia and neighbouring colonies as well as Lower Canada. Todd and Lester and Morrogh continued to act as purchasing agents until at least 1806, when they supplied provisions later valued by the government at £31,694. However, in November 1807 Commissary General John CRAIGIE stated that the merchants owed the government more than £2,800 for credit advanced.

On the surface, by the year 1805 Lester and Morrogh had finally achieved prosperity and security: provisioning orders were large; they were Peter Hunter's personal financial agents for the transfer of money to London; and in May Lester obtained the grant of a beach lot at Quebec, allowing room for further expansion. Although their partnership with Godard in the Cape Diamond Brewery terminated acrimoniously at the end of 1805, in April 1806 they signed a new contract with William Hullett to buy his entire crop of hops up to 6,000 pounds at 1*s*. 6*d*. per pound. The following January they renewed for five years the contract of the brewery's maltster, George Oakley. They also continued to import liquors.

In fact, however, neither Lester nor his company was well. "Our friend Mr Lester leaves for London in a state that makes me fear we will not see him again," Plessis wrote to Bourret in November 1806. "At least the good man will have before God the consolation of having honoured and practised his religion in a manner very edifying for the church and its friends." His will, handwritten before his departure, indicates that Lester was not optimistic of success on his trip. By May 1807, when he returned to Quebec, word of financial disaster was abroad. Lester and Morrogh had had to borrow £2,500 in August 1805 from the collector of customs, Thomas SCOTT. Two years later the Montreal merchant Alexander Henry* informed John ASKIN at Sandwich (Windsor), Upper Canada, that the firm was bankrupt. In June 1807 Plessis remarked that he had offered Lester condolences on a reversal "that has just ruined him completely." One month later he was dead. The Catholic hierarchy had lost one of the few laymen it trusted. For Plessis the loss was a personal one; for Bourret it was also a "public calamity." Lester was buried on 15 July in the crypt of Notre-Dame at a service attended by prominent merchants and officials of the colony.

At the time of Lester's death, 79 debtors owed him or his firm more than £7,400. Major ones were located in St John's, Nfld, Halifax, and London; Joseph FROBISHER of Montreal owed £423 and Plessis £326. Lester's and Lester and Morrogh's properties, equipment, and merchandise were valued at more than £29,000. The house and business at 2 Rue Saint-Pierre were worth more than £5,300, the wharf and one-half of the store at Près-de-Ville £6,000, and Lester's one-half share in the Cape Diamond Brewery £6,900. Yet the beneficiaries of his will – Fisher, Morrogh, and relatives in Spain and Portugal – were obliged to renounce the succession in order not to be engulfed in debts totalling more than £42,700.

Lester's collapse was only one of many [see John Jones; James Tod] that severely hampered the establishment of a stable economy in Lower Canada. The British traveller Hugh Gray remarked in 1809 that "it is very well known, that many of the goods imported are never paid for, the importers becoming insolvent." He felt that the enforced idleness of trade from November to May each year and lack of

Lester

acquaintance by British merchants with the customs of the people were major problems, but that the principal cause of bankruptcy was an habitual over-extension of credit. Importers easily obtained credit in Britain to purchase their merchandise on the expectation of paying for the order, with interest, from sales to retailers in the colony. Most retailers, however, were themselves obliged to buy on credit, and the importers watched the interest on their debts in Britain mount, even during the idle winter season. Moreover, most merchants, like Lester and Morrogh, depended on credit to expand their facilities or diversify their activities. The numerous bankruptcies of debtors deprived the creditors of part of the capital, interest, and, in the case of sales, profits, on which they relied to pay their own debts; each bankruptcy echoed through the entire credit system, and when the failure was as important as Lester's – Alexander Henry had predicted it would "fall heavily on Individuals" – the reverberations were heard as far away as London, where Lester and his company owed nearly £4,000 to Inglis, Ellice and Company and £1,367 to Isaac and Henry Thompson. In all, Lester had 87 creditors; in Lower Canada, the majority of these – and the largest – were at Quebec and Montreal. At Quebec he and his firm were indebted, for example, to Dunn for more than £5,000, to Fisher for more than £2,500, and to Craigie for £942, while at Montreal they owed £1,041 to James and Andrew McGill and Company and £728 to Forsyth, Richardson and Company, as well as substantial sums to Todd and James McGill among others.

Between 1807 and 1809 all of Lester's possessions were sold to pay part of his debts. They included a surprisingly small library of 13 titles. The artist William Berczy was astonished to learn that at a sale of Lester's effects in 1808 "one of the most beautiful masterpieces of Vandick [Sir Anthony Van Dyke]," which the merchant had acquired for 25 guineas at Lisbon and which "in London or Paris would sell easily for 300 *louis*," was bought for a mere five *louis* by the Anglican clergyman and schoolmaster John Jackson*.

Robert Lester was among the most prominent merchants of his time at Quebec and possessed the respect of business colleagues all over British North America and in London. He was considered fully dependable by both the government and the Roman Catholic hierarchy, a reputation he alone enjoyed; his standing enabled him to work discreetly – a manner of proceeding favoured by both parties – to maintain good relations between them under increasingly difficult conditions. Finally his personal rapport with the Canadian hierarchy may have constituted an excellent beginning to relations between the clergy of the town of Quebec and an Irish Catholic population that, as the 19th century progressed, grew rapidly and made its presence felt increasingly in the city's religious and social life.

In collaboration with Marianna O'Gallagher

AAQ, 20 A, III: 87; 210 A, V: f.207. AC, Québec, Testament olographe de Robert Lester, 23 juill. 1807 (see P.-G. Roy, *Inv. testaments*, 3: 82). ANQ-Q, CE1-1, 15 juill. 1807; CN1-16, 21, 24 juill., 4 août 1807; CN1-25, 25 mai 1782; 30 janv., 26 nov. 1783; 22 mars, 15 août 1785; CN1-26, 29 déc. 1798, 3 août 1801; CN1-83, 20 oct., 2 nov. 1786; 16 mars, 29 oct. 1787; 22 mars 1788; 31 mars, 2 juill., 24 déc. 1789; 8 juin, 27 août 1790; 8 avril, 15 sept. 1794; CN1-92, 12 avril 1790; 28 déc. 1792; 22 févr., 22 mars 1796; CN1-145, 15 Sept. 1801, 17 July 1802, 7 March 1805, 27 Jan. 1807; CN1-205, 3 févr. 1779; 28 févr., 25 sept. 1780; 27 déc. 1783; CN1-224, 26 juill. 1781, 15 juin 1785, 16 juill. 1787, 14 juill. 1788, 9 mars 1789; CN1-230, 3 déc. 1794, 26 août 1795, 4 sept. 1797, 11 déc. 1798, 23 août 1799, 27 juin 1800, 12 sept. 1801, 24 août 1805, 23 avril 1806, 26 oct. 1808, 27 sept. 1809; CN1-256, 7 Aug. 1786; 2 Feb. 1788; 30 July, 22 Nov. 1790; 14 Sept. 1791; 29 May 1792; 1 March, 26 June 1793; 14 Feb., 21 Nov. 1794; 25 March, 14 July 1795; 16 Feb., 5 Aug. 1796; 4 Sept. 1797; 26 April 1800; CN1-262, 23 août, 4 nov. 1802; 8 nov. 1806; CN1-284, 3 juill. 1788. ASQ, MSS, 13, 10 juin 1792. PAC, MG 11, [CO 42] Q, 29: 530–34, 873–79; MG 55/23, no.110; RG 1, L3L: 60761; RG 8, I (C ser.), 107: 4–5, 27, 176, 188, 209; 108: 26, 52, 83, 92–93, 121, 164; 109: 18, 86, 89, 121; 110: 73, 76, 136; 111: 205; 112: 10; 113: 95; 225: 12, 16, 19, 21, 35, 40, 51–52.

[William Berczy], "William von Moll Berczy," ANQ *Rapport*, 1940–41: 50–51. "Les dénombrements de Québec" (Plessis), ANQ *Rapport*, 1948–49: 36, 86, 135, 185. Hugh Gray, *Letters from Canada, written during a residence there in the years 1806, 1807, and 1808 . . .* (London, 1809; repr. Toronto, 1971), 175, 228–30. John *Askin papers* (Quaife), 2: 543. "Manifestes électoraux de 1792," *BRH*, 46 (1940): 100. "Orderly book begun by Captain Anthony Vialar of the British militia . . . ," ed. F. C. Würtele, Literary and Hist. Soc. of Quebec, *Hist. Docs.* (Quebec), 7th ser. (1905): 155–265. "Les prises de possession de bénéfices ecclésiastiques sous le Régime français," ANQ *Rapport*, 1921–22: 95. *Quebec Gazette*, 1772–1809. F.-J. Audet, "Les législateurs du Bas-Canada." Caron, "Inv. de la corr. de Mgr Denaut," ANQ *Rapport*, 1931–32: 174, 197, 206, 212–13; "Inv. de la corr. de Mgr Hubert et de Mgr Bailly de Messein," 1930–31: 303, 319; "Inv. de la corr. de Mgr Plessis," 1927–28: 229, 236, 249, 254, 257; 1932–33: 8, 11, 18, 22, 28, 30–31, 35–39, 41–42, 46. Charland, "Notre-Dame de Québec: le nécrologe de la crypte," *BRH*, 20: 275. Desjardins, *Guide parl.*, 137. Langelier, *Liste des terrains concédés*, 9, 971, 977. *Quebec almanac*, 1788: 47; 1796: 82; 1801: 102; 1805: 22. Creighton, *Commercial empire of St. Lawrence*, 28, 120. Lemieux, *L'établissement de la première prov. eccl.*, 31. J. M. LeMoine, *Picturesque Quebec: a sequel to Quebec past and present* (Montreal, 1882), 81–82. Ouellet, *Bas-Canada*, 295. G. R. Swan, "The economy and politics in Quebec, 1774–1791" (PHD thesis, Oxford Univ., 1975), 173, 190. F.[-J.] Audet et Édouard Fabre Surveyer, "Robert Lester," *La Presse* (Montréal), 2 juill. 1927: 38. Édouard Fabre Surveyer, "Robert Lester (1746–1807), député de la basse-ville de Québec," *Rev. de l'univ. Laval* (Québec), 7 (1952–53): 622–27. Hare, "L'Assemblée législative du Bas-Canada," *RHAF*, 27: 371–73, 376. Albert Tessier, "Deux enrichis: Aaron Hart et Nicolas Montour," *Cahiers des Dix*, 3 (1938): 225. "Un bon ami de Mgr Plessis," *BRH*, 42 (1936): 678–80.

LIÉBERT, PHILIPPE (baptized **Philippe-Pierre**), painter and wood-carver; b. 9 Aug. 1733 in Nemours, France, son of Philippe Liébert and Anne Des Porques; m. 31 March 1761 Françoise Lenoir, daughter of Vincent Lenoir, a joiner, in Pointe-aux-Trembles (Montreal, Que.), and they had ten children; d. 27 Sept. 1804 in Montreal, Lower Canada.

It is not known when Philippe Liébert arrived in New France, or under what circumstances, but in 1760 his name was recorded in the ledgers of the parishes of Saint-Pierre-du-Portage (Assomption-de-la-Sainte-Vierge), at L'Assomption, and Purification-de-la-Bienheureuse-Vierge-Marie, at Repentigny. In 1760 and 1761 he made a retable (the structure that housed the altar) for the church at Repentigny, probably in collaboration with Antoine Cirier*. The tabernacle, which has predellas decorated with foliated scrolls and scallops, is surmounted by classical columns with pedestals and entablature, a projecting monstrance, and a recess above two reliquaries. To execute this early piece of work Liébert had drawn inspiration from both Gilles Bolvin*'s exuberant style and Cirier's more delicate approach. The work as a whole gives an impression of timidity and lack of experience. Subsequently Liébert used this type of composition only in side altars.

The retable in the church at L'Assomption, which was begun at the same time but completed later, in 1764, gave Liébert an opportunity for refinement. After drawing the plans for the tabernacle, the balustrade, and the base of the altar, he carried them out in a style that has been described as "rather ornate Louis XIV, crossed with Regency motifs and accented with certain Louis XV details." He also furnished for the parish six candlesticks, the side altars, and the pulpit.

But it was from 1764 that Liébert undertook his first major piece of work: the decoration of the sanctuary in the church at Sault-au-Récollet (Montreal North), which was completed only in 1793. For it he carved a retable "in the Recollet style" that falls within the tradition introduced by Claude François*, named Brother Luc, notably in his work for the chapel of the Hôpital Général of Quebec in 1671. The retable is characterized by four columns (two of which bear the baldachin), sacristy doors with painted reliefs, and vaulting with carved trusses. Liébert had freed himself from the influence of Bolvin and Cirier, and this retable gives proof of an important evolution in his style.

These early contracts made Liébert known, and he became the fashionable wood-carver in the Montreal region. He supplanted Paul-Raymond Jourdain*, *dit* Labrosse, who died in 1769, and Cirier, who became mired in debt and sank into oblivion. In 1765 he received the contract for making a pulpit, a church-wardens' pew, and stalls for the church of Notre-Dame in Montreal. Five years later he carved the hands of the big clock at the Séminaire de Saint-Sulpice in Montreal, and the following year he executed the three retables for the church of Saint-Louis at Terrebonne. In 1777 he carved and decorated with bas-reliefs a tabernacle consecrated to St Joseph for the Religious Hospitallers of St Joseph of the Hôtel-Dieu in Montreal. Between 1783 and 1791 he executed for the church at Varennes an altar, a tabernacle, and frames for four recent paintings by François Malepart* de Beaucourt.

From this point on Liébert had complete mastery of his art. With his apprentices, among them Joseph Pépin* and Urbain Desrochers*, he now turned out his principal works. At Saint-Martin on Île Jésus, for example, he was commissioned between 1787 and 1798 to make the side altars, two bas-reliefs, the pulpit, the churchwardens' pew, three sets of candlesticks, the paschal candlestick in Louis XV style, and the high altar. In 1790 the Grey Nuns of the Hôpital Général in Montreal ordered from him a high altar, and a side altar consecrated to the Sacred Heart; the latter attracts attention because of its exceptionally pleasing contours and the harmonious distribution of the decorative reliefs carved on the flat surfaces. Between 1791 and 1798 he made an "altar of Roman inspiration," a pulpit, and a churchwardens' pew for the church at Saint-Cuthbert.

From 1792 to 1799 Liébert worked on a high altar for the church at Vaudreuil; its arrangement is dense but not overloaded and reveals the artist's very considerable facility. Behind the base of the crucifix dominating the tabernacle door is an Ecce Homo, familiarly referred to as the "beautiful Lord" of Vaudreuil, which is one of the wood-carver's masterpieces.

On 18 May 1795 Liébert joined forces with his son-in-law Jean Gaston, a confectioner. The two rented from Basile Proulx a house on Rue Saint-Jacques in Montreal in which they both lived and carried on their respective professions. They shared the profits and losses, the purchasing of materials, and other expenses such as the wages of the shop boys and servants, housekeeping costs, and food. The agreement provided for a 10-year association, but on 1 October the partnership was dissolved. Gaston then owed his father-in-law 900 *livres* to cover the investment in furnishing his café. The following year Liébert moved to the precinct of the convent of the Grey Nuns, with whom he signed a lease for life. The

Liénard

rent was moderate but the nuns also profited by doing the gilding for Liébert's carvings. Between 1799 and 1803, under a contract with the *fabrique* of Sainte-Rose on Île Jésus, Liébert made the candlesticks, the crucifix, and a high altar with baldachin, decorated with two remarkable statuettes representing St Rose and the Madonna and Child.

Many other less important contracts had come Liébert's way in the course of his long career. Although his religious wood-carving may be quite easily traced through parish ledgers, it is more difficult to know whether he pursued his art in other spheres. Given the customs of the period and the inventory that was made of his estate after his death, it may be assumed that he did some work in wood-carving for civil institutions, some fine cabinet-making, and even religious and civil architecture.

In the spring of 1804 Philippe Liébert cancelled his lease with the Grey Nuns and went to live in the *faubourg* Saint-Laurent, where he died on 27 September, leaving an estate in excess of 9,000 *livres*. An accomplished and prolific craftsman to whom some paintings – such as the portraits of Louis Normant* Du Faradon, Mme d'Youville [Marie-Marguerite Dufrost* de Lajemmerais], and Étienne Montgolfier* – are also attributed, Liébert represents a high point in late 18th-century art.

MICHEL CAUCHON

AC, Joliette, Minutiers, Eugène Archambault, 2 déc. 1834. AD, Seine-et-Marne (Melun), État civil, Nemours, 9 août 1733. MAC-CD, Fonds Morisset, 2, L716.4/P551.

LIÉNARD DE BEAUJEU DE VILLEMONDE, LOUIS (baptized **Louis-Joseph**), army and militia officer and seigneur; b. 16 Sept. 1716 in Montreal (Que.), third son of Louis Liénard* de Beaujeu and Thérèse-Denise Juchereau de Saint-Denys, *née* Migeon de Branssat; d. 5 June 1802 in Cap-Saint-Ignace, Lower Canada.

Born into a noble family with a long military tradition, Louis Liénard de Beaujeu de Villemonde was granted a second ensign's commission in the colonial regular troops in 1732 and promoted first ensign six years later. In 1741 he was serving at Fort Saint-Frédéric (near Crown Point, N.Y.) and in 1743 at Fort Niagara (near Youngstown, N.Y.); the following year he received his lieutenant's commission. He and his brother Daniel-Hyacinthe-Marie Liénard* de Beaujeu sailed in June 1746 with Jean-Baptiste-Nicolas-Roch de Ramezay*'s expedition for Baie-Verte (N.B.). On 22 September he was sent by Ramezay to receive orders for his troops from the Duc d'Anville [La Rochefoucauld*], who had come from France with a large force to clear the British out of Acadia. Beaujeu fought in the battle of

Grand Pré on 11 Feb. 1747 against Lieutenant-Colonel Arthur Noble*. During the Acadian campaign Beaujeu, who was a pious Roman Catholic, killed a British soldier who was also Catholic and, according to the author Philippe-Joseph Aubert* de Gaspé, this incident still affected Beaujeu at the end of his life.

On 18 July 1747 at Quebec Beaujeu married Louise-Charlotte, daughter of François-Étienne Cugnet*, member of the Conseil Supérieur. One year later he was reporting on the fortifications at Fort Saint-Jean, on the Richelieu, when he was called back to Quebec for Louise-Charlotte's burial; she had died giving birth to their daughter, Julie-Louise. Beaujeu was promoted captain in 1751, replacing Pierre Gaultier* de Varennes et de La Vérendrye, and made commander of the posts of Kaministiquia (Thunder Bay, Ont.) and Michipicoton (Michipicoten River, Ont.). On 22 Feb. 1753 at Quebec he married 17-year-old Geneviève Le Moyne de Longueuil, daughter of Paul-Joseph*, and they would have seven children. That July he was at Michilimackinac (Mackinaw City, Mich.), where he had been placed in command, but by 15 October he was commander at Fort de la Presqu'île (Erie, Pa). He was again in command at Michilimackinac in May 1754, but does not seem to have remained there long.

On 20 July 1755 Beaujeu was granted the seigneury of Beaujeu on the west shore of Lake Champlain, but the concession apparently did not receive royal confirmation. He was at Fort Carillon (near Ticonderoga, N.Y.) in July 1756, and on the 30th he was sent by François de Lévis* at the head of 100 Canadians and 120 Indians on a mission to take prisoners on the route between Fort Lydius (also called Fort Edward, now Fort Edward, N.Y.) and Fort William Henry (also called Fort George, now Lake George, N.Y.). He captured six soldiers in an ambush of an advance guard, but was prevented by the Indians in his force from attacking the main party. For his action he earned the strong praise of Lévis in a letter to Governor Vaudreuil [Pierre de Rigaud*].

Beaujeu was back in command at Michilimackinac by 1757, and in February 1759 he was awarded the cross of Saint-Louis. He reportedly became wealthy through trade at Michilimackinac, although such activity by commandants was contrary to regulations; in May and June 1758 he hired five men at Montreal to bring trade goods up for his use. His wife was criticized in October 1759 for abusing the protective services for personal property sent to Montreal from the captured city of Quebec by having loaded aboard ship coffers more than half of which "certainly contain merchandise on which can be made three or four hundred per cent." In July 1760 Beaujeu hired two men in Montreal to bring trade goods to Michilimackinac. Just before the fall of Montreal in September

Liénard

Governor Vaudreuil sent him orders through Charles-Michel Mouet* de Langlade, who had been given command of Michilimackinac, to withdraw to the Illinois country. Beaujeu departed in October with 4 officers and 128 soldiers and wintered at Rivière à la Roche (Great Miami River, Ohio); there the Sauks and Foxes obliged him to trade all his merchandise, the value of which he later estimated at more than 65,000 *livres*, for provisions for his men. In 1761 he arrived at Fort de Chartres (near Prairie du Rocher, Ill.) where his men were placed in garrison, and by the end of the year he had taken ship from New Orleans (La) to France. The following year he was at Kaskaskia (Ill.), and, the Seven Years' War having ended, he spent the winter of 1763–64 at Fort de Chartres, bringing the influence of the French army to bear on the Indians to end their hostilities with the British. In 1767 he was described as resident in "Missisipi."

In October 1769 Beaujeu's wife, by an agreement with her brother Joseph-Dominique-Emmanuel Le Moyne de Longueuil, acquired the seigneury of Île aux Grues, Île aux Oies, and adjacent islands where the Beaujeus then went to live; Beaujeu had a manor constructed on Île aux Grues and busied himself with the settlement of the seigneury. He was there in the autumn of 1775 when the American revolutionary army invaded the colony [*see* Benedict ARNOLD; Richard Montgomery*]. In March 1776, with the Americans besieging Quebec, Governor Guy CARLETON requested Beaujeu, whom one of the defending garrison called "that partisan of tried fidelity," to raise a relief force among the Canadians along the south shore of the St Lawrence below Quebec. Beaujeu gathered a force of about 150 men, but when his advance guard was captured at the house of Michel Blais* in the village of Saint-Pierre-de-la-Rivière-du-Sud, he dispersed the remainder and went into hiding. Beaujeu's son Charles-François, who was in the French navy, fought on the American side during the revolution.

Beaujeu apparently lived the last 25 years of his life in financial difficulties. By the early 1770s he owed £500 to Jacques Perrault*, known as Perrault *l'aîné*. In February 1779 he sold his "fine large House two Stories high," situated on the Place d'Armes at Quebec. In August 1782 the seigneury was offered for sale, but not sold. Two years later Beaujeu borrowed £144 from Samuel Johannes HOLLAND, and in August 1789 he sold the two small islands of Île Patience and Île au Canot, forming part of his seigneury as the fief of Grandville, to the merchant Alexander Wilson for £20. Nevertheless Beaujeu continued to live the life of a seigneur: in November and December 1788 he signed petitions opposing the political reform movement led by the colony's merchants [*see* Jean-Baptiste-Amable Adhémar*; George ALLSOPP]; in July 1790 he was promoted to the provincial rank of

captain and given half pay for his part in the American revolution; and when, in October of that year, the brigantine *Atlas* was lost in a gale off the Île aux Grues, the surviving crew and passengers were generously received by Beaujeu and given shelter among the families inhabiting the island. In June 1800 he again offered the seigneury for sale, but he had not sold it by the time of his death on 5 June 1802. His estate was so indebted that his inheritors renounced it. In August 1802 the seigneury, by then fully settled, was sold at public auction to the merchant Daniel Macpherson for £2,100.

DAVID DANIEL RUDDY

AN, Col., D^{2C}, 57: f.153v.; 58: f.25; 61: ff.10v., 48v., 128v.; Marine, C^2, 55 (copies at PAC). ANQ-Q, CE1-1, 18 juill. 1747, 22 févr. 1753; CN1-11, 19 févr. 1753; CN1-92, 4 août 1789; CN1-230, 27 août, 9 sept. 1802. PAC, MG 18, N13 (photocopy). "Acte de mariage de Louis Liénard de Beaujeu et Geneviève Lemoine de Longueuil," *BRH*, 54 (1948): 239–40. "Acte de mariage de Louis Liénard de Beaujeu et Louise Charlotte Cugnet," *BRH*, 52 (1946): 59–60. *Coll. des manuscrits de Lévis* (Casgrain), 2: 33–34, 40, 43, 60; 8: 21–22; 10: 32–33. "État général de la noblesse canadienne, résidant actuellement dans la province de Québec, ou au service de l'armée française, ainsi que le lieu de leur résidence en novembre 1767," PAC *Rapport*, 1888: 35. "État général des billets d'ordonnances" (Panet), ANQ *Rapport*, 1924–25: 260. *Invasion du Canada* (Verreau), 195–97. Wis., State Hist. Soc., *Coll.*, 3 (1857): 216; 7 (1876): 139, 180, 182, 186–87; 8 (1879): 213; 16 (1902): 386; 17 (1906): 71, 432; 18 (1908): xvi, 84–85, 131, 221–22, 479, 484; 19 (1910): 33–35, 37, 51–56, 59–61. *Quebec Gazette*, 30 April 1778; 18 Feb. 1779; 29 Aug. 1782; 13 Nov., 11 Dec. 1788; 22 Jan. 1789; 15 July, 4 Nov. 1790; 19 June 1800.

Ægidius Fauteux, *Les chevaliers de Saint-Louis en Canada* (Montréal, 1940), 172. Massicotte, "Répertoire des engagements pour l'Ouest," ANQ *Rapport*, 1932–33: 250–51, 259. P.-G. Roy, *Inv. concessions*, 1: 222–23; 5: 88. [François Daniel], *Histoire des grandes familles françaises du Canada, ou aperçu sur le chevalier Benoist, et quelques familles contemporaines* (Montréal, 1867), 262–66; *Le vicomte C. de Lévy, lieutenant-général de l'empire français, ingénieur en chef de la grande armée, et sa famille* (Montréal, 1867), 202, 225, 227. Lanctot, *Le Canada et la Révolution américaine*, 148–50. J.-M. Lemieux, *L'île aux Grues de l'île aux Oies: les îles, les seigneurs, les habitants, les sites et monuments historiques* (Ottawa, 1978), 89–92. Alexandre Mazas, *Histoire de l'ordre royal et militaire de Saint-Louis depuis son institution en 1695 jusqu'en 1830 . . .* (2e éd., 3v., Paris, 1860–61), 2: 174. J.-E. Roy, *Hist. de Lauzon*, 2: 60–61. P.-G. Roy, *Hommes et choses du fort Saint-Frédéric* (Montréal, 1946), 350. Joseph Tassé, *Les Canadiens de l'Ouest* (2v., Montréal, 1878), 1: 23–24, 93, 95, 103. Marc de Villiers Du Terrage, *Les dernières années de la Louisiane française . . .* (Paris, 1905), 146, 178, 191. Alphonse Gauthier, "La famille de Georges-René Saveuse de Beaujeu (1810–1865)," SGCF *Mémoires*, 6 (1954–55): 198. Hugolin Lemay, "Le registre du fort de la Presqu'île pour 1753," *BRH*, 44 (1938): 204, 208. N.-E. Dionne, "L'invasion de 1775–76," *BRH*, 6 (1900): 132–40.

Little Turtle

LITTLE TURTLE. *See* MICHIKINAKOUA

LONDON, MARY. *See* OSBORN

LONGMOOR, ROBERT, fur trader; b. probably in the parish of West Church, Edinburgh, Scotland, son of William Longmoor; fl. 1771–1812.

Robert Longmoor joined the Hudson's Bay Company in 1771 as a sailor, and in 1774 he accompanied Samuel Hearne* up the Saskatchewan River and helped him to establish Cumberland House (Sask.). The next year he was sent with Charles Thomas ISHAM to winter among Indians on the south branch of the Saskatchewan. Regarded by Humphrey Marten*, chief at York Factory (Man.), as the best canoeman in the company's service, he was assigned to employment "in the outdoor Pedling way." Going north from Cumberland in June 1776 to the Grass River (Man.) in search of Athapaskan Indians, he was obstructed by Alexander Henry* and JOSEPH and Thomas Frobisher, independent traders from Canada, but he managed to drive a fair trade and returned to Cumberland before the end of the month.

That year Longmoor was ordered back to England but Marten, impressed by his skills and his animosity towards the Canadian traders, sent him to Cumberland again. During the next two years Longmoor made several trading excursions from Cumberland, staying with Indians as far west as the Eagle Hills (Sask.); in the summers of 1777 and 1778 he went down to York. Encouraged by the HBC to set up a house in the buffalo country, on 27 Sept. 1778 he set out westwards from Cumberland in charge of a party which included Malchom Ross*, Isaac Batt*, and Charles Isham. Poor conditions forced them to stop at a pedlar settlement near present-day Silver Grove, Sask., where Longmoor accepted the offer of a Canadian house for the winter. His post was known at the time as the HBC's upper settlement. The following March he was joined there by Philip Turnor*, and starting out in late April they travelled down to York together, Longmoor impressing Turnor as "little or none inferior to a good Indian."

At York, Longmoor volunteered to establish the company's trade in the Athabasca country; but the emphasis was still on the Saskatchewan and in 1779, with William Tomison*, chief at Cumberland, he set up the first Hudson House (sometimes referred to later as Lower Hudson House) and remained in command there. This post was about 14 miles downstream from the place where he had spent the previous winter, which was later called Upper Hudson House. Although he was short of trade goods Longmoor managed to purchase eight Indian canoes and built two himself. In 1780 he commanded the summer brigade to York, and in September he was again sent to Hudson House with 21 men under his command. It

was a hard winter for Longmoor. The Indians had burned the prairie to drive off the buffalo and make the traders totally dependent on them for meat; trade goods were short and discipline was difficult. Fifteen of his men swore in a letter to Tomison never to serve under Longmoor again, while Longmoor himself registered a protest against the indifference and ignorance of his superiors by the bayside. Despite the hardships of the winter of 1780–81 Longmoor got his men safely down to York the following summer.

That fall Longmoor was sent to oppose the pedlars in the area of Lake Athabasca, in preparation for a strong HBC advance in 1782. But this was a winter of great distress, the Indians being ravaged by a catastrophic smallpox epidemic, and Longmoor was ordered to winter in the plains. In the summer of 1782 the inland brigades had already started back for the interior when the French under Jean-François de Galaup*, Comte de Lapérouse, captured and destroyed York on 24 August. The following spring Tomison, now in charge of inland affairs, left Longmoor in command at Hudson House when he went down to York. Finding it "a Ruinous Heap," Tomison waited as long as he dared for the ship from England and then made his way disconsolately inland without supplies. The posts on the Saskatchewan survived, however, and Longmoor continued to trade from Hudson House. In 1785 the London committee ordered him to explore the Churchill River as a possible approach route to the Athabasca country, but Samuel Hearne, now chief at Churchill (Man.), gave priority to the Saskatchewan and the following year sent Longmoor, with the young David Thompson*, to build Manchester House (near Standard Hill, Sask.) for the purpose of competing with strong Canadian opposition.

From the fall of 1787 until he returned to England in 1792 Longmoor was second in command at Churchill. In 1791 he had been ordered to accompany Captain Charles Duncan* in his attempt to find an overland route to the Pacific; but his opposition to the venture and his difficulties with Duncan prevented the expedition from starting. Nevertheless, he was re-engaged in 1793 as superintendent (an undefined office) at York, becoming shipping officer there the following year. In 1796 he asked to go inland once more and was sent to Red Deer River House (near Red Deer Lake, Man.). But his supplies were inadequate, and he spent the winter at Carlton House (near Kamsack, Sask.), trading in rivalry with HBC men from Fort Albany (Ont.) as well as with the Canadians. Although his returns were disappointing, he remained there till 1800, acting as master of the Swan River district (a jurisdiction which included Red Deer River) and building a new post on the Swan River. The obsession of Tomison with the Saskatchewan, however, led to the diversion of goods which

500

were meant to provide for the expansion of Red Deer River.

During this period York was relinquishing to Albany its claims to trade in the area of Lake Winnipeg, and in 1800 Longmoor, who had refused to go inland again before the HBC ship arrived from England, abandoned Swan River House and handed over Carlton House to men from Albany. He then went down to York, only to be sent to the Saskatchewan once more; from 1804 onwards he was assistant master at Island House (near Lake Eliza, Alta). Always more remarkable for his skill with canoes than for his literary or managerial abilities, he remained in comparative obscurity on the upper Saskatchewan until 1807, when he was once more employed for a year at York. He was again at Island House from 1808 to 1810, when he made his last journey down to York with his family. On 18 May Alexander HENRY reported him "determined to leave the River and Country instantly, and retire to enjoy the fruits of his labours, he is now worth about £1800 H.Cy the produce of near Forty Years services in this Country for the HBC°."

Longmoor seems to have taken his family responsibilities seriously. He sent six guineas a year to his father, who was living in Edinburgh as late as 1787. A son (he is known to have had one named Robert) was staying in Britain in 1808 and 1809, perhaps for an education, and Longmoor was paying for his room and board. Longmoor himself went back to Britain in 1810 but soon returned. By February 1812 he had bought a farm near Montreal and stocked it with horses, oxen, and cows. On 5 July 1814 an HBC trader noted in his journal, "Entered the lake of two mountains and passed the House where the late Mr. Longmore's family dwells. . . ."

E. E. RICH

PAC, MG 19, A13, 2: 935 (transcript). PAM, HBCA, A.5/2: ff.132, 170; A.16/33: f.130; A.16/34: f.159d; B.3/a/117b: f.17d; B.135/a/102: f.17d; C.1/423; D.13/8: f.122. *Cumberland House journals and inland journal, 1775–82*, ed. E. E. Rich and A. M. Johnson (2v., London, 1951–52). *Docs. relating to NWC* (Wallace). *Journals of Hearne and Turnor* (Tyrrell). *Saskatchewan journals and correspondence: Edmonton House, 1795–1800; Chesterfield House, 1800–1802*, ed. A. M. Johnson (London, 1967). Rich, *Hist. of HBC*.

LONGMORE (Longmoor), GEORGE, physician, army officer, office holder, and landowner; b. *c.* 1758 in Banffshire, Scotland; d. 9 Aug. 1811 at Quebec, Lower Canada.

George Longmore seems to have come from a family of some means. Probably Scottish Episcopalians – George's brother Alexander would serve as vicar of Great Baddow, England, from 1779 to 1812 –

they appear to have placed a premium on literary values. Longmore attended King's College, Aberdeen, from which he graduated AM in 1778. After studying anatomy, surgery, and the practice of medicine at the University of Edinburgh in 1780 and 1781, he came to North America in the latter year as hospital mate in the medical department of the British army. He served on the general medical staff at New York under John Mervin Nooth*, whom he came to respect as a physician and later as a friend. In November 1783 he was transferred to the province of Quebec and attached to the general medical staff of the army in Trois-Rivières. His first assignment was to attend the growing number of loyalists in Yamachiche and, when they were moved to the Baie des Chaleurs in 1784, Longmore accompanied them. In addition to performing his medical duties, from the summer of 1785 he served as justice of the peace and as secretary to Nicholas Cox*, lieutenant governor of the Gaspé. During Cox's absence in 1786–87, Longmore acted in his stead. His marriage to Cox's daughter, Christiana (Christina) Lætitia, probably about this time, confirmed his entry into the lower ranks of the colony's official society; the couple was to have five sons and five daughters.

In June 1788 the Longmores arrived at Quebec and, as a hospital mate on the general medical staff (which had been transferred there from Trois-Rivières), Longmore renewed contact with Nooth. Quebec provided avenues for private practice and professional advancement. In 1789, now an assistant surgeon, Longmore was appointed to the medical staff of the Hôtel-Dieu. Two years later, with doctors Nooth, John Gould, James Fisher*, and Philippe-Louis-François BADELARD, he was questioned by a committee of the Legislative Council on the extent and nature of the Baie-Saint-Paul disease. In March 1795 Longmore, along with Nooth, Fisher, and Frédéric-Guillaume Oliva*, answered questions in the House of Assembly concerning a quarantine bill, then pending. Longmore's professional status was acknowledged that year by his appointment to the Quebec Medical Board. In 1801 he was named a commissioner for the care of the insane and foundlings.

Longmore considered himself "of an inquisitive . . . not . . . inattentive mind." It may have been intellectual curiosity or hope of financial gain that led him in June 1796 into a strange agreement with the Roman Catholic priest Pierre-Joseph COMPAIN. Longmore paid £129 immediately and agreed to pay another £400 in two years for a secret cure for cankers, while promising to keep the secret for 10 years. It was agreed as well that, in the event of Longmore's death during a projected trip to Britain, Nooth would be informed of the cure and allowed to practise it for the profit of Longmore's family. In the year or two following this agreement Longmore

Longmore

possibly became disenchanted with the effectiveness of the remedy or the profitability of the arrangement. In 1798, following "difficulties" between him and Compain, the second payment of £400 was reduced to £75; Longmore promised not to divulge the cure before Compain's death and was restricted to practising it on himself and his family.

Longmore was not only intellectually active, he was ambitious. His trip to Britain occurred six months after he had been promoted surgeon in January 1796, and was made in order to obtain the degree of MD at King's College; he achieved his goal on 10 November. While in England he made a modest contribution to the philological collection of Sir Joseph BANKS, president of the Royal Society, of letters, in translation, by Saguenay Indians.

Returning to Quebec in 1797 as apothecary to the forces, Longmore was charged with supervising hospital supplies and medicines for all military hospitals and posts in Upper and Lower Canada and with providing basic medical necessities to regimental surgeons. As well, he sat with other senior surgeons as a member of the hospital board. In 1799, together with William Holmes*, surgeon to the forces, and Fisher, he was requested by Lieutenant-General Peter HUNTER, commander of the forces in the two Canadas, to report on an outbreak of typhus fever introduced into the port by shipping. Although he shared the prevailing view of his contemporaries that the disease had originated in the foul air below deck, Longmore later distinguished himself by introducing in its treatment a special glass apparatus, designed by Nooth, that dispersed a solution of camphor at regular intervals. Longmore would also have used "oxygen gas" – in what way is not known – but none was available. In May 1800 Longmore and Robert Jones of Montreal were recommended by the Legislative Council to receive £105 each in recognition of the care they had given to those poor families who had fallen victim to the fever.

Longmore's readiness to accept new ideas was again shown in his promotion of smallpox vaccination, introduced into Quebec in November 1801 by a young engineer officer, George Thomas Landmann*. Using "cowpox matter" sent to him from England, Longmore began "vaccine inoculation" on 16 April 1802 and personally inoculated nearly 50 patients that year while distributing the vaccine to other doctors. In 1803 he vaccinated free of charge at the Hôtel-Dieu, and published letters and informative articles on the procedure in the *Quebec Gazette*. Both medical and lay persons began to practise vaccination; in the Gaspé, Theophilus Fox, a justice of the peace, undertook to vaccinate following Longmore's instructions. Longmore, however, was the only member of the established profession to promote the new method publicly. The *Quebec Gazette* thanked him "for

having . . . come forward" to sanction vaccination despite opposition resulting from fear, ignorance, and quackery, and considered the people "under a strong obligation to that Gentleman, for the liberal manner in which he has met this business." Attendance at Longmore's clinic was disappointing, however, and not until 1815 was a public vaccination program attempted.

Longmore had anticipated becoming senior hospital officer and surgeon to the forces, but in 1803 his hopes were dashed by the appointment to that post of James Macaulay*. Furthermore, the position of apothecary was eliminated in a reduction of staff that year. The prospect of half pay, with a "wife and six children to support and educate," was bleak, but by means of a cleverly worded proposal to the commander-in-chief, Hunter, Longmore secured his reinstatement at full pay. Moreover, in 1805 he was appointed health officer to the port of Quebec, a civil post carrying a stipend of £100 per annum. Its responsibilities in regard to shipping were similar to those he had earlier carried out as apothecary, Longmore also derived an income from private practice and, between 1804 and 1807, by acting as surgeon to the civil branch of the Board of Ordnance at Quebec.

Longmore lived comfortably in the inner circle of Upper Town Quebec society. From his arrival at Quebec he successively occupied houses in excellent neighbourhoods on Rue Saint-Louis, Rue Buade, and Rue Sainte-Anne, and by 1795 he was apparently employing two domestics. As a member of the garrison he shared in the social life centred on the governor's residence, the Château Saint-Louis. He also participated to some extent in the life of the community apart from his concern for public health; he was a member of the Agriculture Society, founded in 1789, joined in a petition in 1790 for the establishment of a university, and four years later signed a declaration of loyalty to Britain in a context of political tension fomented by agents favourable to the French revolution [see David McLane*]. Although he no doubt benefited from his medical, literary, and administrative abilities, part of his social success was undoubtedly owing to influential contacts, including Nooth, Cox, Hunter, and Henry CALDWELL.

Like many of his British contemporaries, Longmore invested much time and money in the acquisition of land for speculative purposes. In the Gaspé he had acquired by 1785 nine town lots (more even than Cox) and at least one park lot, and in 1791 he purchased a 200-acre farm on Bonaventure harbour. He was also caught up in the scramble to obtain land grants in the Eastern Townships. In the early 1790s he petitioned unsuccessfully as leader, according to the system of township leaders and associates [see James CALDWELL], for land in Aberdeen and Horton townships.

Along with Nooth and several other doctors, he was an associate of Hugh FINLAY, president of the land committee of the Executive Council, in a petition for 20,000 acres along the west bank of the Rivière Saint-François. In 1803, for his services to Cox in the Gaspé, he was granted more than 11,000 acres in Kingsey Township. He also purchased 5,500 acres in Thetford Township from Nooth and 1,200 acres in Tewkesbury Township. By 1810 he was probably a man of some wealth. That August he left for England on leave of absence, possibly for reasons of health; he returned in early July 1811 and died suddenly, at about age 53, the following month.

Although easily ensconced within the colonial establishment, Longmore had constantly shown genuine concern for the health of the people in general; he had received no remuneration for 22 years' service at the Hôtel-Dieu, for example, and in 1802 he had cared for sick immigrants without charge. What set him apart from some of his contemporaries, however, was a willingness to innovate. Although formed by the medical tradition of the 18th century, he was ready to adapt to the emerging scientific medicine of the 19th century, and his understanding of the importance of preventive medicine is clear from his campaign in favour of vaccination, which, as he foresaw, would become a universal practice.

BARBARA TUNIS

Aberdeen Univ. Library (Aberdeen, Scotland), MS K.48. AC, Québec, Testament olographe de George Longmore, 20 Aug. 1811 (*see* P.-G. Roy, *Inv. testaments*, 3: 84). ANQ-Q, CE1-61, 11 Aug. 1811; CN1-92, 27 juin 1796, 29 août 1798. BL, Add. MSS 11038: ff.6, 11–12 (copies at PAC); 21857: ff.317, 321, 333, 337, 339, 351, 353, 404 (mfm. at PAC). PAC, MG 11, [CO 42] Q, 85: 55–56; RG 1, L3^L: 41633–34, 61616–82, 73334–37, 73359; RG 4, A1: 10084–99; B43; RG 8, I (C ser.), 30: 57; 200: 65–67; 287: 16–17, 46–49, 72–132, 194, 199–204, 212, 218, 218a, 218b, 219; 372: 36–142; 505: 20–21; 872: 31; 1218: 7, 10; RG 68, General index, 1651–1841. Private arch., K. H. Annett (Sainte-Foy, Qué.), William Vondenvelden, Plan des lots de la ville de New-Carlisle, 1785 (copy). PRO, PRO 30/55, no.8059 (mfm. at PAC). [William Berczy], "William von Moll Berczy," ANQ *Rapport*, 1940–41: 39, 42. Gwillim, *Diary of Mrs. Simcoe* (Robertson; 1911), 265. *Quebec Gazette*, 29 June 1786; 19 June 1788; 4 Nov. 1790; 18, 19 Aug. 1791; 13 Feb., 10 July 1794; 26 March, 4 May 1795; 30 Sept. 1802; 13 Jan., 11, 18 Aug., 27 Oct., 17 Nov. 1803; 5 April 1804; 4 July, 15 Aug. 1811. William Johnston, *Roll of commissioned officers in the medical service of the British army . . .* (Aberdeen, 1917). *Quebec almanac*, 1789; 1804–7.

Abbott, *Hist. of medicine*, 43. M.-J. et G. Ahern, *Notes pour l'hist. de la médecine*, 377. Andre, *William Berczy*, 64. Burt, *Old prov. of Quebec* (1968), 2: 82–85. William Canniff, *The medical profession in Upper Canada, 1783–1850 . . .* (Toronto, 1894; repr. 1980), 482–84. P.-G. Roy, *À travers l'histoire de l'Hôtel-Dieu de Québec* (Lévis, Qué., 1939), 191. René Bélanger, "L'abbé Pierre-Joseph Compain, prêtre et médecin, 1740–1806," *Saguenayensia* (Chicoutimi, Qué.), 13 (1971): 106–7. M. L. MacDonald, "George Longmore: a new literary ancestor," *Dalhousie Rev.*, 59 (1979–80): 267. Gabriel Nadeau, "Un savant anglais à Québec à la fin du XVIIIᵉ siècle: le docteur John-Mervin Nooth," *L'Union médicale du Canada* (Montréal), 74 (1945): 49–74. Christian Rioux, "L'hôpital militaire à Québec: 1759–1871," Canadian Soc. for the Hist. of Medicine, *Newsletter* (s.l.), April 1981: 16–19. P.-G. Roy, "Le curé Compain et la guérison des chancres," *BRH*, 29 (1923): 85–86. W. H. Siebert, "The loyalist settlements on the Gaspé peninsula," RSC *Trans.*, 3rd ser., 8 (1914), sect.II: 399–405.

LONGUEUIL, JOSEPH-DOMINIQUE-EMMANUEL LE MOYNE DE. See LE MOYNE

LOSADA SUÁREZ DE FIGUEROA, JOSÉ MARIANO MOZIÑO. See MOZIÑO

LOUIS, COLONEL. See ATIATOHARONGWEN

LOUVIGNY DE MONTIGNY, JEAN-BAPTISTE-PIERRE TESTARD. See TESTARD

LUDLOW, GABRIEL GEORGE, politician, office holder, judge, and colonial administrator; b. 16 April 1736 in Queens County, Long Island, N.Y., son of Gabriel Ludlow and Frances Duncan; m. 3 Sept. 1760 Ann Ver Planck; d. 12 Feb. 1808 in Saint John, N.B.

Gabriel George Ludlow was a member of a long-established and wealthy New York family. While his brother GEORGE DUNCAN took up the study of law, Gabriel, like his father and grandfather, turned to the world of business and property. By the end of the Seven Years' War in 1763 both brothers were moving up in the New York aristocracy. Gabriel owned an estate of more than 100 acres near Hempstead, Long Island, which he subsequently enlarged and improved; in the 1780s he estimated its value at £2,000 sterling. Although he did not attain the prestigious official position held by his brother, his prominence was marked by an appointment as justice of the peace.

As the turbulence mounted in the period before the revolution, the Ludlows stood firmly and conspicuously on the side of the king. Gabriel spent the war years as a fighting loyalist. In 1775 he was commander of the Queens County militia, and the following year he raised and was commissioned colonel of the third battalion of De Lancey's Brigade. His Long Island home became a favourite retreat for "British officers and Loyalist gentlemen." As a result of their support for the crown both Ludlows were named in an act of attainder by the state of New York in 1779 and had their property declared confiscated.

At the end of the revolution Gabriel followed his brother to England, where they joined other loyalists

Ludlow

in seeking preferment and compensation for their losses. Throughout 1783 and 1784 the group mounted a strong lobby, the major result of which was the creation of a new colony, New Brunswick, on the north shore of the Bay of Fundy to accommodate loyal refugees and their families. Already in Parrtown, the future Saint John, Edward WINSLOW had taken "three town lots on the West side of the river, in the most delightful situations I ever saw, for myself, Major [John Coffin*] and Col. Ludlow." If the colonel suffered, declared Winslow, "there is no Providence." Ludlow in fact got three lots, not one, in what had been the garden of the old French fort at the mouth of the Saint John River. Other advantages went to the élite among the loyalists. Like his brother, who became chief justice, Gabriel was appointed in 1784 to the first council of the new colony. As a military man, he was named first in order of seniority, and thus acquired a rank second only to that of the governor.

In September 1784 the Ludlows embarked for New Brunswick in company with Governor Thomas CARLETON. Gabriel's wife, Ann, had remained in her Long Island home, even though "obliged to pay rent to the Committee of Forfeitures." That fall she took ship for Saint John with her family and belongings, only to lose practically everything but lives in a cruel Bay of Fundy wreck. Still, her prospects were far superior to those of the majority of loyalists struggling in the wilderness. In 1785 her husband was appointed mayor of Saint John, and two years later he became judge of the Vice-Admiralty Court, a post he would hold until 1803; he had his half pay as well and established a mercantile business. In all, he commanded the means to construct in Ludlow House one of the landmarks of Carleton, as west Saint John was called. There, in 1794, the family was able to entertain Prince EDWARD AUGUSTUS, commander of the forces in Nova Scotia and New Brunswick.

Briefly the capital of New Brunswick, until Governor Carleton moved the administration to Fredericton, Saint John was the first city in British North America to be incorporated. Its municipal institutions, modelled on those of pre-revolutionary New York, were subject to several non-democratic restrictions, including appointment by governor and Council of the mayor, sheriff, clerk, and recorder. As mayor, Ludlow was the city's senior administrative official, and he carried out his duties conscientiously, missing only a handful of Common Council meetings during the decade he held the position. The early years were particularly busy, because Saint John had come into existence virtually overnight and a host of regulations was required to maintain order and to organize its economic and social life. Ludlow was also the city's leading judicial officer. By the charter of incorporation the mayor, recorder, and aldermen

became justices of the peace for the city and county of Saint John; Ludlow presided as well over the Inferior Court of Common Pleas, or Mayor's Court.

In 1790, when the office of common clerk became available, the mayor pressed for the appointment of his son Gabriel Ver Planck Ludlow. Carleton deliberately passed over him in favour of a whiggish English lawyer who had had a brief New York career, Elias Hardy*. Though Hardy was both deserving and talented, the Ludlows were furious. Such incidents did not improve their strained relations with the governor, who disliked them both. It was apparently Hardy who caused Ludlow's retirement as mayor. In 1794 he accused Ludlow of negligence in prosecuting the city's case against William HAZEN in a fisheries dispute; as a result, Ludlow stopped attending meetings of the Common Council in mid year. Although a subsequent inquiry by a committee of council into Hardy's performance as clerk concluded, among other things, that his accusations against Ludlow were groundless and that he was himself responsible for the failure of the city's lawsuit, a new mayor, William Campbell*, was appointed in 1795.

Ludlow held his seat on the provincial council until his death, but he increasingly refused to leave Saint John and appeared to regard the benefits of his position as a right derived from his revolutionary service rather than as a reward for any contribution he might make to New Brunswick. Nevertheless, when Carleton left the colony in 1803, Ludlow, as senior councillor, became administrator, commander-in-chief, and president of the Council. His five-year tenure has been praised by some for its tranquillity and damned by others for stagnation. The colony was a loyal member of the British empire, and the residents were described by Winslow as a "self-governed quiet people." The lack of controversy may have been an indication of growing maturity as much as a response to a quiescent administration. Ludlow, it seems, was content to leave management of affairs to his brother, who had always participated more actively in colonial administration. "Our Government goes very smoothly on," Solicitor General Ward Chipman* wrote in 1805, "the President more retired than ever at Carleton and everything done by a Committee of Council of which the Chief Justice is at the head."

The threat of war with the United States in 1807 inspired Lord Castlereagh, the secretary of state for War and the Colonies, to look to the defence of New Brunswick. In January 1808 Ludlow, as commander-in-chief, called out the colonial militia. Regarding military action as unlikely, he planned to disband them in March to save the provincial treasury. He did not get the opportunity. On Friday morning, 12 Feb. 1808, he died unexpectedly at his Saint John residence, to be succeeded as administrator by

Edward Winslow. He left his wife, two sons, and two daughters; his brother survived him by only nine months.

C. M. WALLACE

N.B. Museum, Hazen family papers. PANB, "New Brunswick political biography," comp. J. C. and H. B. Graves (11v., typescript). PRO, AO 12/25: 274; 12/90; 12/100: 134; 12/109; AO 13, bundles 19, 65. UNBL, MG H2. *Canada's first city: Saint John; the charter of 1785 and Common Council proceedings under Mayor G. G. Ludlow, 1785–1795* (Saint John, N.B., 1962). "United Empire Loyalists: enquiry into losses and services," AO *Report*, 1904: 267–70. *Winslow papers* (Raymond). *DAB*. Sabine, *Biog. sketches of loyalists*. Hannay, *Hist. of N.B.*, vol.1. J. W. Lawrence, *Foot-prints; or, incidents in early history of New Brunswick, 1783–1883* (Saint John, 1883). J. S. MacKinnon, "The development of local government in the city of Saint John, 1788–1795" (MA thesis, Univ. of N.B., Fredericton, 1968). MacNutt, *New Brunswick*. W. O. Raymond, *The London lawyer; a biographical sketch of Elias Hardy, counsellor-at-law at Saint John, N.B., A.D. 1784–1798, with some account of the incidents in which he figured* (n.p., 1894); "New Brunswick: general history, 1758–1867," *Canada and its prov.* (Shortt and Doughty), 13: 125–210; *River St. John* (1910). Wright, *Loyalists of N.B.* W. O. Raymond, "Elias Hardy, councillor-at-law," N.B. Hist. Soc., *Coll.*, 4 (1919–28), no.10: 57–66.

LUDLOW, GEORGE DUNCAN, judge and politician; b. 1734 in Queens County, Long Island, N.Y., son of Gabriel Ludlow and Frances Duncan; m. 22 April 1758 a cousin who was also named Frances Duncan, and they had one son and two daughters; d. 13 Nov. 1808 in Fredericton, N.B.

The Ludlow family arrived in America from Somerset, England, in 1694. Gabriel Ludlow, founder of the colonial branch, became a successful merchant, shipowner, and landholder. His son Gabriel married Frances Duncan and moved to Queens County, where George Duncan was born in 1734 and GABRIEL GEORGE in 1736. A second marriage produced Daniel in 1750. The wealth and status of the family gave the boys several advantages, including education in a private school. George Duncan apparently spent a short period as an apprentice apothecary before turning to the law. By the age of 30 he had been admitted to the bar and had begun a successful practice, largely in commercial cases. Official preferment soon followed: in 1769 he was appointed a judge of the colonial supreme court. His brother Gabriel was meanwhile making a mark for himself in business.

Both brothers were staunch supporters of the crown during the troubles of the pre-revolutionary years. In the mid 1770s George Duncan was forced out of New York City "to cherish the remains of loyalty in Queens County," where he and Gabriel owned substantial adjoining properties near Hempstead. With the arrival of General Sir William Howe and the British army in 1776, he returned to the city, and until the final surrender in 1783 he remained a leading royalist. In August 1779 the houses of both brothers on Long Island were plundered by rebels during their absence; the plan had been to abduct the owners in order to exchange them for rebel prisoners "of equal rank." Two months later the properties were confiscated by the state of New York. George Duncan later estimated the price of his loyalty at £6,500 in real and personal estate. Disappointed when passed over in favour of William Smith* for the chief justiceship of New York in 1780, he had resigned from the bench. Governor James Robertson consoled him in 1780 with an appointment as superintendent of police for Long Island. It had become necessary to find some means of administering justice there, and he was given "powers on principles of equity to hear and determine controversies till civil government can take place." The "little tyrant of the Island" was not popular, however, and was said to have exerted excessive influence on behalf of his friends.

Regarded as arch-tory to the core, the Ludlows apparently had no choice but to leave New York when the revolution was over, though their half-brother Daniel, also a loyalist, remained there to become a successful businessman. George Duncan sailed for England on 19 June 1783, shortly before his brother; both left their families behind until arrangements could be completed for their settlement elsewhere. In London the Ludlows joined a large and vociferous lobby of loyalist place-seekers. With the successful conclusion of the campaign to create from Nova Scotia a new province as a home for American refugees, George Duncan was selected as its chief justice. The choice was made in March or April 1784, some months before the royal proclamation establishing the province of New Brunswick was signed and before the governor was appointed. Ludlow may therefore have been the first person named to any position in New Brunswick. As chief justice he was a member of the original council that was to administer the province. Gabriel was also appointed to this body and, by virtue of his military rank, became its senior member. The Ludlow brothers held these positions, two of the most prestigious in New Brunswick, for the next 25 years. Younger members of the Council such as Edward WINSLOW, Ward Chipman*, and John Coffin* had more to offer, but their activities always took place under the cautious eyes of their seniors.

After touring Britain, especially the new manufacturing towns, the Ludlows embarked for New Brunswick in September 1784 with Governor Thomas CARLETON. Following a brief stay at Halifax, N.S., the governor's entourage made its way to Parrtown

Ludlow

(Saint John), which became the temporary capital of the new province and where Gabriel was soon to be appointed mayor. George Duncan was sworn in on 25 November. When the first session of the Supreme Court was held on 1 Feb. 1785, Benjamin Marston* recorded that "the Chief Justice gave a very judicious, sensible charge to the Grand Jury."

Saint John's early years were turbulent ones, raising the spectre of incidents similar to those in pre-revolutionary American cities. The distressed condition of the mass of the people was in sharp contrast to the circumstances of the élite, a point emphasized in the local press and taverns [see Elias Hardy*]. The first provincial election, in 1785, brought the issue to a climax. When the six hand-chosen government candidates for Saint John were defeated by the "rabble," Carleton, supported by his council and the judges, overturned the results and had his candidates declared elected. Selected members of the "rabble," including newspapermen William Lewis* and John Ryan*, were arrested, charged with "criminal" activity before the Supreme Court, and punished. The executive, of which the Ludlows were members, thus established from the beginning the tenor of New Brunswick's politics.

Governor Carleton decided that Saint John was unsuitable for the provincial capital and in 1786 moved inland to Fredericton. The chief justice naturally accompanied the administration while his brother stayed in the commercial capital of Saint John. George Duncan acquired about 1,500 acres five miles north of Fredericton for his estate, which he called Spring Hill after the residence of Lieutenant Governor Cadwallader Colden, his New York patron of the 1760s. The house, made from the "most beautiful specimens" of local woods such as bird's-eye maple and birch, was much admired. There he and his lady, who was described by Patrick Campbell* as "among the mildest and most amiable of her sex," lived out their years in New Brunswick.

As chief justice, Ludlow was more inconsistent, or more flexible, than might have been expected. In his first case Nancy Mozely (Mosley), a black, was convicted of manslaughter for killing her husband with a pitchfork. After praying benefit of clergy under an ancient tradition, she was sentenced to be branded with the letter M in the brawn of her left thumb and then dismissed. In a more celebrated case of February 1800 that considered the legality of slavery in New Brunswick, Ludlow, a slave holder, supported the owners. "Our Chief Justice," declared Ward Chipman, "is very strenuous in support of the master's rights as being founded on immemorial usuages and customs in all parts of America ever since its discovery. He contends that customs in all countries are the foundation of law, and from them the law acquires its force." Ludlow was supported on the bench by Joshua UPHAM while the other two judges were opposed. The split permitted the slave owner, Caleb JONES, to hold his property, despite British practice at the time. By 1820, however, slavery was at an end in New Brunswick, partly because of the controversy this outcome had sparked.

Ludlow's use in this case of North American as opposed to British practices was a characteristic trait. When, for example, the question of legal fees arose in 1787 he reduced the proposed scale by almost one-half to meet the needs of a struggling colony. "At the commencements of Circuit Courts, especially in this province," he explained, "peculiar difficulties must attend the practitioner, but they will gradually lessen as the population increases, and the wealth, as well as the litigation, of the inhabitants, multiply." Despite the outrage of the lawyers, Ludlow held firm "[or] the present generation would not find wherewith to purchase justice."

Wealthy landholders also found themselves at odds with Ludlow. In 1805 the ownership of fishing rights in waters adjoining property became an issue in Saint John. William HAZEN, an original grantee from the 1760s, had his claim challenged and a fishing weir removed. He charged trespass before a jury, but Ludlow "without hesitation, directed the Jury that it was an arm of the sea and common to all; that even if all the fisheries there had been expressly granted to him [Hazen], the grant would not have been worth a farthing." That attack on property rights shocked the establishment, and Ludlow's "tergiversation" was a scandal. In 1808, however, the British were to uphold his position.

The chief justice in this as in other matters was unmoved by criticism, which he received from all sides during the course of his career. James GLENIE, an early New Brunswick radical, at one point called him an "illiterate, strutting chief-justice" who must be removed to save the province, and Governor Carleton liked neither of the brothers, especially the chief justice with whom he was frequently at odds. It is not clear what prompted the difficult relationship between Carleton and the Ludlows. Perhaps he was too English and they too American, or they lacked the proper deference or were too demanding. Until 1803, however, Carleton dominated affairs. The Ludlows might quibble with him, but they supported the conservative thrust he gave to the colony. George Duncan participated in all decisions regarding legislation and justice throughout Carleton's governorship, and of the two brothers was far the more substantial and influential. Even when Gabriel became administrator of the province on Carleton's departure, it was George Duncan who, in reality, headed the government. He had the greater experience of administration and Gabriel always deferred to him.

In February 1808 Gabriel Ludlow died. Left to

carry on alone, George Duncan was grief stricken and faced the certainty of loss of power in the Council. He suffered a paralytic stroke on 6 March and remained largely incapacitated until his death at Spring Hill on 13 November. He was survived by his widow and three children.

The Ludlow brothers occupy a unique position in New Brunswick history. For 25 years they held two of the senior positions in the colony, and for five years after Carleton's return to Britain they were in control, apparently without being seriously challenged. Innately conservative, a predilection reinforced by the American revolution, they were partly responsible for the ascendency of that disposition in New Brunswick. Past their prime when they arrived in New Brunswick, the Ludlows claimed their rights as members of the loyalist élite and died respected.

C. M. WALLACE

N.B. Museum, Hazen family papers. PANB, "New Brunswick political biography," comp. J. C. and H. B. Graves (11v., typescript). PRO, AO 12/19: 310; 12/90; 12/99: 179; 12/109; AO 13, bundle 65. UNBL, MG H2. P. Campbell, *Travels in North America* (Langton and Ganong). *Documents and letters intended to illustrate the revolutionary incidents of Queen's County . . .* , comp. Henry Onderdonk (New York, 1846; repr. Port Washington, N.Y., [1970]). *NYCD* (O'Callaghan and Fernow), vol.8. *Winslow papers* (Raymond). *DAB*. Sabine, *Biog. sketches of loyalists*. Hannay, *Hist. of N.B.*, vol.1. Thomas Jones, *History of New York during the Revolutionary War, and of the leading events in the other colonies at that period*, ed. E. F. de Lancey (2v., New York, 1879). J. W. Lawrence, *Foot-prints; or, incidents in early history of New Brunswick, 1783–1883* (Saint John, 1883); *The judges of New Brunswick and their times*, ed. A. A. Stockton [and W. O. Raymond] ([Saint John, 1907]). MacNutt, *New Brunswick*. Raymond, *River St. John* (1910). Wright, *Loyalists of N.B.*

Kenneth Donovan, "The origin and establishment of the New Brunswick courts," N.B. Museum, *Journal* (Saint John), 1980: 57–64. A. G. W. Gilbert, "New Brunswick's first chief justice," *Univ. of New Brunswick Law Journal* (Saint John), 11 (1958): 29–32. J. W. Lawrence, "The first courts and early judges of New Brunswick," N.B. Hist. Soc., *Coll.*, no.20 (1971): 8–34. W. O. Raymond, "A sketch of the life and administration of General Thomas Carleton, first governor of New Brunswick," N.B. Hist. Soc., *Coll.*, 2 (1899–1905), no.6: 439–81.

LYND, DAVID, office holder, landowner, seigneur, politician, and militia officer; b. *c.* 1745, probably in Scotland; d. 29 June 1802 at Quebec, Lower Canada.

It is not known when David Lynd took up residence in Quebec. He was appointed to his first post, as English clerk to the Court of Common Pleas of Quebec, in the spring of 1767, succeeding William Kluck. Whether prior to his arrival in the colony he had acquired the legal knowledge necessary for carrying out his duties remains unclear. Whatever the case he was never admitted as a lawyer or notary in the province. Like so many other legal officers appointed in the early years after the conquest, he may have had no specific professional training when he obtained his first position. The appointment as clerk settled his career. For the rest of his life he was to hold various similar offices in the courts of the District of Quebec.

The Quebec Act, which came into force on 1 May 1775, was supposed to put an end to the existing courts. However, since Governor Guy CARLETON had determined, by a proclamation dated 26 April 1775, to maintain the former judges of the Court of Common Pleas in office as "commissioners" for civil suits, Lynd continued acting as clerk with the civil court thus created, pending the establishment of a new judicial system. But in November William Gordon arrived from London with a mandamus appointing him clerk of the crown (King's Bench) and of the Common Pleas. Annoyed at this interference by the imperial government and considering it unfair to remove from office people whose past services had given him satisfaction, Carleton limited Gordon to the post of clerk of the crown [*see* Alexander Johnston*]. Since all the parties involved in this imbroglio agreed to the compromise, Lynd was able to continue in the exercise of his duties; he also remained register of the Vice-Admiralty Court, a post to which he had been appointed on 13 May 1767.

When regular civil and criminal courts were finally set up, in February and March 1777, Lynd was confirmed as clerk of the Common Pleas, and on 31 March was appointed clerk of the peace. In these two offices he had Nicolas-Gaspard BOISSEAU as his French-speaking colleague. That same year he was chosen to serve as clerk of the crown, as deputy first to Gordon, who continued to hold the office until his death in 1781, and then to Gordon's successor, William Pollock. From 22 May 1779 Lynd acted as coroner for the District of Quebec, an office he retained until April 1792. He was also successful in obtaining an appointment in 1784 as register "for English matters" in the Prerogative Court. This court, which had been created by Governor Murray* in 1764, was mainly responsible for the probate of wills, issuing letters of administration in estate matters, and dealing with questions of tutorship and curatorship. Lynd was then in the peculiar and unique situation of monopolizing the office of English-language clerk for all the civil and criminal courts of the District of Quebec, so that in April 1786 he could call himself "clerk of the courts of judicature of this district."

The Judicature Act, which came into force in December 1794, completely reshaped the judicial system of Lower Canada, but it scarcely affected Lynd's career. Although the Vice-Admiralty Court was retained, all others were abolished. New courts of

Lynd

King's Bench were created at Quebec and Montreal as courts of first instance for both civil and criminal matters. On 11 Dec. 1794 Lynd became protonotary and register of the court for the District of Quebec, conjointly with Pierre-Louis PANET. The following year, on 12 May, he was also appointed clerk to the Court of General Sessions of the Peace, along with Joseph-François Perrault*. Lynd retained these offices until his death, but none the less continued to act as clerk of the Vice-Admiralty Court and deputy to the clerk of the crown, an office whose holder did not bother to live in the colony.

In the years preceding the Quebec Act of 1774 Lynd had made common cause with those British residents of the province who were demanding a house of assembly, even if Catholics had to be excluded from it. In the autumn of 1773 he had joined the group of old subjects who met in Miles Prenties's inn under the chairmanship of John McCord to voice their demand; along with several dozen of his compatriots, he had also signed the petitions for an assembly that were presented to Lieutenant Governor Hector Theophilus Cramahé* and to the king. During the 1780s he had continued to associate himself with the demands for constitutional change. It was not surprising, therefore, that he became a candidate in the elections of June 1792, the first to be held after the Constitutional Act of 1791 had created a house of assembly in Lower Canada. Lynd chose to stand in the riding of Quebec, his opponents being Ignace-Michel-Louis-Antoine d'Irumberry* de Salaberry and Michel-Amable BER-THELOT Dartigny. At Charlesbourg, where voting took place, a riot almost broke out after it was decided to close the poll and take down the hustings. Berthelot Dartigny, who of the three candidates had at that moment received the fewest votes, claimed his supporters had been prevented from casting theirs. The tumultuous gathering was calmed by the intervention of Prince EDWARD AUGUSTUS, who, being on familiar terms with Salaberry, addressed the crowd and urged people to disperse. Berthelot Dartigny denounced the alleged irregularities at the poll both in the *Quebec Gazette* and in a pamphlet that he published; then with a score of electors he filed a petition in the House of Assembly to contest Lynd's election.

In the end nothing further came of the matter; Salaberry having chosen to represent Dorchester riding which had also elected him, Berthelot Dartigny was admitted to sit along with Lynd, and on 2 March 1793 his supporters withdrew their petition, thus preventing the assembly from examining the merits of the dispute. Lynd sat as a member until the house was dissolved on 7 May 1796; he attended fairly regularly despite his court duties, which must have taken up much of his time. Except on one occasion he supported the English party in voting. In another debate Lynd, who owned at least two slaves, sided with those who sought to maintain slavery in Lower Canada by voting against the bill that would have decreed its abolition in 1793.

Of all Lynd's offices, that of coroner was unique in paying a salary. For the others he received only fees, which were mainly payable by the litigants and were set according to a rate that at first was fixed by ordinance and later, under a law of 1801, was determined by the judges of each court. In addition there were modest allowances for the annual trips to Montreal that he had to make as deputy to the clerk of the crown. Since he was holding too many offices at the same time, Lynd found it impossible to carry out all his obligations and regularly had to pay someone to replace him, which reduced his income correspondingly. Because of this situation he succeeded in obtaining a special allowance of £325 in 1782 and another of £200 the following year.

As if so many occupations were not enough to keep him busy – or with an eye to the main chance – Lynd managed in November 1793 to secure an appointment, along with James Monk* and Thomas Aston COFFIN, as attorney for Brook Watson and Company of London [see Sir Brook WATSON]. He thus looked after numerous legal transactions to protect the financial interests of this firm, which engaged in business in the province.

Since the greater part of Lynd's earnings came from the fees he received for the legal instruments and procedures he handled as clerk, it is almost impossible to estimate his annual income. It cannot have been inconsiderable, however, judging by the size of his investments in real estate, which were particularly numerous from 1785 to 1790. Lynd often bought, but almost never sold. At his death he owned more than 20 properties; they were located mostly in the town and suburbs of Quebec, and included five houses in the town proper and some pieces of land in the *faubourg* Saint-Roch. He held several properties *en censive* in the fiefs of Tilly and Saint-François, and he had received a grant of two lots in Granby and Milton townships for his services as a lieutenant in the British militia during the siege of Quebec by the Americans in 1775 [see Benedict ARNOLD; Richard Montgomery*]. In February 1779 he and his brother John had bought the fief of Sasseville, with the attached seigneurial rights, in Quebec's Upper Town; unable to pay his share, John gave it up in David's favour in October 1785. That year Lynd began subdividing his land in the *faubourg* Saint-Vallier with a view to selling it under terms entailing a perpetual ground-rent, a practice then common in the neighbouring *faubourg* Saint-Roch; he had four lots surveyed, for which he found takers only with difficulty.

The property to which Lynd was most attached was the farm of La Vacherie; leased to him by the Jesuits in

1771, it included a house, barn, and stable. Lynd first made it his summer home but soon moved there permanently. In 1772 he also leased the farm's water-mill, situated at the crossing over the Rivière Saint-Charles, but it is not known whether the one-year lease was subsequently renewed, or whether the mill remained in operation. To take further advantage of La Vacherie, Lynd conceived a plan to build a bridge spanning the Saint-Charles; it was to run from the land behind his farm and connect with the junction of the Beauport and Charlesbourg roads. He gathered about him eight other English-speaking citizens: Charles Stewart, Ralph GRAY, James Johnston*, John PURSS, John COFFIN, William Lindsay* (d. 1834), Nathaniel Taylor, and Peter Stuart, the last four of whom were justices of the peace for the District of Quebec. They put together the capital needed for construction, and on 22 April 1789 obtained letters patent authorizing them to collect tolls for a period of 50 years. The bridge, made entirely of wood and 701 feet long, was built in seven months under the supervision of Colonel Asa Porter; on 19 Sept. 1789 it was inaugurated by Bishop Hubert* of Quebec, and named after Governor Lord Dorchester [Carleton]. It was, wrote the *Quebec Gazette*, "without doubt the greatest work of the kind ever executed in this Province."

By an ordinance of the following year the owners also obtained a local monopoly of river crossing, by either bridge or ferry. In 1794 William GRANT (1744–1805), who was acting for the proprietors, leased out the crossing rights and the house located near the bridge for £250 a year. The Dorchester Bridge had cost £1,627. It frequently required expensive repairs, and the return on it disappointed the owners, several of whom sold their shares at a loss. Lynd himself kept until his death 4 of the 48 jointly owned shares in the bridge, which he had promoted and which remained in use until 1820.

Lynd had been a member of the Agriculture Society for the District of Quebec since its foundation in 1789, and in 1793 held office as a director. He was also a member of the Quebec Fire Society in the 1790s. From at least 1794, and probably until his death, he was a lieutenant in the Quebec Battalion of British Militia. In 1798 he gave up residence on his estate of La Vacherie and moved to Rue Saint-Stanislas in Quebec. This decision may have been taken for reasons of health, because shortly after he seems to have reduced the pace of his professional activities, particularly as protonotary of the Court of King's Bench and clerk of the peace. He died on 29 June 1802. His wife, Jane Henry, daughter of the Presbyterian minister George Henry, was appointed guardian of their under-age son, Hutchinson, a few days later. The couple had had two other children: Ann, who had married Thomas Grant, a Quebec

merchant, and died in 1799 "after a long and lingering illness," and Jane, wife of Thomas Dodd, a captain in the Royal Artillery. Lynd had also in effect brought up Marie-Magdelaine Schleiger, whose mother had committed her to his care legally in 1777, "being unable to do better than to indenture her in order to teach her how to earn her living and to provide her with food and keep." The child was only 12 at that time and was to remain seven years in Lynd's service.

David Lynd and Jane Henry had been married at Quebec without a marriage contract. The inventory of the joint estate was drawn up between 7 January and 31 May 1805. Besides the furniture and other effects in his two residences on the Rivière Saint-Charles and at Quebec, which were valued at £467, and his library, which was worth £223, Lynd left large debts totalling £2,378, an amount only slightly in excess, however, of the sum owed to him; the main part of his estate consisted of a rather impressive accumulation of landed property. The heirs – his children Jane and Hutchinson and his granddaughter Marguerite Grant – accepted the inheritance. In 1804 his widow had asked for a renewal of the lease to La Vacherie. In subsequent years, however, she and the heirs parted with some of the properties her husband had left them.

ANDRÉ MOREL

ANQ-Q, CE1-66, 1 July 1802; CN1-16, 8 juin 1813, 9 mars 1814; CN1-25, 21 avril 1786; CN1-26, 10 juin 1800, 21 mars 1801; CN1-83, 14 juin 1788; 21 avril, 13 nov. 1789; CN1-145, 30 April 1807; CN1-178, 1er avril 1797; CN1-205, 22 mai 1777, 26 mars 1784; CN1-207, 22 juin 1771, 1er oct. 1772; CN1-230, 13 oct. 1797, 26 nov. 1799, 7 janv. 1805; CN1-256, 21 Nov. 1793; 11 Feb., 14 July 1795; 25 Nov. 1799; CN1-262, 19 oct. 1796, 28 mars 1799, 1er févr. 1802. Bas-Canada, chambre d'Assemblée, *Journaux*, 1792–93: 19, 31, 81, 127, 272, 276, 291–93; 1798: 110, 117; 1799–1800: 77, 86, 191, 203; 1801: 257, 259, 270; 1802: 171, 186; 1803: 99; 1808: 137, 215; *Statuts*, 1793–94, c.6; 1795–96, c.9, art.73; 1808, c.10; 1819, c.28. M.-A. Berthelot Dartigny, *Conversation au sujet de l'élection de Charlesbourg* (Québec, s.d.). "Les dénombrements de Québec" (Plessis), ANQ *Rapport*, 1948–49: 52, 54, 95, 117, 155, 172. *Docs. relating to constitutional hist., 1759–91* (Shortt and Doughty; 1918), 1: 487–502; 2: 682, 690, 837–38. Kelley, "Jacob Mountain," ANQ *Rapport*, 1942–43: 226. "Manifestes électoraux de 1792," *BRH*, 46 (1940): 102. "Ordonnances édictées pour la province de Québec par le gouverneur et le conseil de celle-ci, de 1768 à 1791 . . . ," PAC *Rapport*, 1914–15: 114–26, 242–43. "Proclamations issued by the governor-in-chief . . . ," PAC *Report*, 1918: 17–18.
Quebec Gazette, 14 May 1767; 8 Aug. 1771; 13, 27 Oct. 1774; 16 Feb., 26 Oct. 1775; 12 Dec. 1776; 8 May, 12 June, 7 Aug., 11 Sept. 1777; 22 April 1779; 22 Aug. 1782; 19 June 1783; 29 April 1784; 23 June 1785; 5 July 1787; 31 July, 11 Dec. 1788; 23 April, 24 Sept. 1789; 28 Jan., 25 March, 5 May, 18, 19 Aug. 1791; 17 May, 28 June, 5, 12 July, 20

Lyonnais

Dec. 1792; 24 Jan., 7 March, 11 April, 4 July 1793; 13 Feb., 3 April, 29 May, 10 July, 23 Oct. 1794; 14 May 1795; 29 June 1797; 21, 28 Feb., 18 July 1799; 10 April 1800; 8 July 1802. *Quebec Herald, Miscellany and Advertiser*, 15 Dec. 1788. F.-J. Audet, "Coroners de Québec (liste revisée)," *BRH*, 8 (1902): 147; "Greffiers de la Cour des plaidoyers communs du district de Québec," *BRH*, 10 (1904): 211. F.-J. Audet et P.-G. Roy, "Greffiers de la paix à Québec," *BRH*, 11 (1905): 247. Joseph Bouchette, *The British dominions in North America; or a topographical and statistical description of the provinces of Lower and Upper Canada . . .* (2v., London, 1832), 1: 263, 268. Desjardins, *Guide parl.*, 136. J.-J. Lefebvre, "Tableau alphabétique des avocats de la province de Québec, 1765–1849," *La rev. du Barreau de la prov. de Québec* (Montréal), 17 (1957): 285–92. "Papiers d'État," PAC *Rapport*, 1890: 208–9. "Papiers d'État – Bas-Canada," PAC *Rapport*, 1893: 38, 41, 46, 65, 80, 121, 123. "Protonotaires du district de Québec," *BRH*, 10 (1904): 117. P.-G. Roy, "Coroners de Québec," *BRH*, 8 (1902): 78; *Inv. concessions*, 1: 8–9, 81–82. Tremaine, *Biblio. of Canadian imprints*, 358.

Caron, *La colonisation de la prov. de Québec*, 1: 304–12. Chapais, *Cours d'hist. du Canada*, 1: 130–31. F.-X. Chouinard et Antonio Drolet, *La ville de Québec, histoire municipale* (3v., Québec, 1963–67), 2: 92–95. Albert Jobin, *Histoire de Québec* (Québec, 1947), 94. Neatby, *Administration of justice under Quebec Act*, 22–23, 60–62, 131–33, 146–47, 300, 323–24, 333–39, 351–54. Trudel, *L'esclavage au Canada français*, 142, 297, 362. F.-J. Audet, "David Lynd, 1745–1802," *BRH*, 47 (1941): 86–89. Ivanhoë Caron, "Les censitaires du coteau Sainte-Geneviève (banlieue de Québec) de 1636 à 1800," *BRH*, 27 (1921): 162. Louise Dechêne, "La rente du faubourg Saint-Roch à Québec, 1750–1850," *RHAF*, 34 (1980–81): 569. Philéas Gagnon, "Le premier pont sur la rivière Saint-Charles," *BRH*, 4 (1898): 54–57. Hare, "L'Assemblée législative du Bas-Canada," *RHAF*, 27: 371–73. Pierre Tousignant, "La première campagne électorale des Canadiens en 1792," *SH* (1975): 120–48.

LYONNAIS, named **Brother Félix, PIERRE-JACQUES BOSSU**, *dit*. *See* Bossu

M

MACARMICK (MacCormick, Macormick), WILLIAM, colonial administrator; baptized 15 Sept. 1742 in Truro, England, son of James Macarmick, mayor of Truro in 1757 and 1766, and Philippa—; m. Catherine Buller, and they had two daughters; d. 20 Aug. 1815 in West Looe, England.

William Macarmick succeeded his father as a Truro wine merchant, and like him he was elected mayor, in 1770. He began a military career on 16 May 1759 as a lieutenant in the 75th Foot, and by 23 March 1764 he had become a captain in the 45th Foot; four years later, however, he exchanged onto half pay. During the American revolution he raised a regiment, the 93rd Foot, at his own expense, and was appointed its colonel on 2 Feb. 1780. He entered political life in 1784, allying himself with Lord Falmouth (son of Edward Boscawen*) and the tories to represent the borough of Truro in the House of Commons until February 1787. At that time he resigned to become lieutenant governor of Cape Breton Island, replacing Joseph Frederick Wallet DesBarres*. Macarmick was interested in the position because of its salary of £500 per annum and £300 in perquisites yearly out of the growing sales of coal from the Sydney mines. The appointment was due to the patronage of Falmouth, who replaced him in the Truro seat, and to Macarmick's military services during the revolution.

Before his departure for Cape Breton, Macarmick was instructed by the British government to end the factionalism in the colony, and he arrived in Sydney on 10 Oct. 1787 determined to assert his authority and end the quarrels that had plagued DesBarres. The latter had succeeded in alienating some of the most powerful officials in Sydney, particularly the loyalists David Mathews* and Abraham Cornelius CUYLER. DesBarres's alliance with their opponents on the council, led by Chief Justice Richard Gibbons*, had caused a rift which had eventually led to the lieutenant governor's recall. Macarmick attempted to reconcile the two groups. But Gibbons, in an attempt to increase his power, soon organized the Friendly Society, a group formed from volunteer militia, which Macarmick outlawed when he came to fear that it might dominate him. After other incidents, he dismissed Gibbons from his posts in 1788. This action only emboldened Cuyler, who openly disagreed with Macarmick's policies, and in 1789 he too was dismissed from the council. Five years later Mathews formed an ostensibly counter-revolutionary society, but Macarmick claimed it would "include all the principle people, [so] that I might be obliged to fill vacancies out of [it]," and managed to ban it, thus alienating Mathews. The Duke of Portland, the Home secretary, complained to Macarmick that the squabbling was hurting the colony and threatened wholesale dismissals unless it ended. This rebuke brought peace during the last six months of Macarmick's tenure.

Macarmick took the greatest interest in the military aspects of his office. Though relations between Britain and France worsened during his period on Cape Breton, and he was ordered to maintain a state of military preparedness, he was unable to obtain arms

McBeath

and ammunition until 1790. Moreover, when the French revolution broke out in 1789, the garrison of the 42nd Foot was withdrawn to Halifax, leaving only a subaltern and 20 men of the 21st Foot in Sydney. Even these were withdrawn in 1793. Macarmick thus decided on his own measures. Fearing that the Acadians living around Isle Madame might assist in a French attempt to regain Cape Breton, in 1794 he strengthened a small fort near St Peters and manned it with Jerseymen and loyalists. His most ambitious plan, however, was for the formation of a colonial militia the same year. The council, led by Mathews, opposed this measure, claiming that a militia at the call of the lieutenant governor would increase his power in the absence of a house of assembly. They insisted that the militia be summoned only in extreme emergencies and with the council's consent. Macarmick refused these terms and did not organize the militia.

The most serious encumbrance to the colony's growth during Macarmick's administration was the British government's decision in 1789 to ban land grants in the Maritime provinces in order to raise money from the sale of land, a state of affairs which lasted until 1817 in Cape Breton. Macarmick tried to lessen the effects of the ban by recognizing squatters' rights and by extending the deadline for filing land claims until 1 June 1792 for those living distant from Sydney, in which measures the British government acquiesced. Though expressly forbidden to grant land to former French citizens, Macarmick allowed a group of refugee Acadians from Saint-Pierre and Miquelon, where they had mainly worked in the fishery, to settle in the early 1790s at Isle Madame and Chéticamp. There they contributed to the island's fishery and shipbuilding. In order to foster further settlement, Macarmick also authorized the first surveys of the area from Chéticamp to Justaucorps (Port Hood), and of the Judique and Ship Harbour (Port Hawkesbury) regions. Despite his efforts, however, the increase in population during his period of office was probably slight.

At the time of Macarmick's arrival in Cape Breton, Britain showed only slight interest in the Sydney coal mines. By 1790, however, the stripping of timber from the coast of Nova Scotia had increased its cost, and coal consequently became more important for heating garrison barracks and for domestic use. The mines had been privately operated under a lease from the British government by Thomas Moxley, who died in 1792, and that year Macarmick transferred the lease to Jonathan Tremaine* and Richard STOUT. Their inefficient mining methods caused production to slump but Macarmick allowed them to continue their operation in the hope that they would pursue increased sales.

In 1794 Macarmick's perquisites from the coal sales were discontinued. When he found out, he was bitter and immediately requested leave. He set sail from Cape Breton on 27 May 1795 but retained his position of lieutenant governor until his death. Although still on half pay, he continued to be promoted in the army, being appointed lieutenant-general on 25 Sept. 1803 and finally general on 4 June 1813.

Despite factional aggravations and an impossible political and military situation, William Macarmick revealed a patient and reasonable disposition while in Cape Breton. Though the colony failed to grow during his tenure, his liberal land policies and tolerant attitude towards the Acadians contributed to Cape Breton's later development.

R. J. MORGAN

PAC, MG 11, [CO 217] Nova Scotia A, 4: 109–10, 163–65, 187; 5: 84; 6: 32–33; 7: 2–3, 7–11, 123, 125–26; 10: 80–84, 125–33, 177–79; 11: 89–90; 12: 52–53, 73–75, 276–77; [CO 220] Nova Scotia B, 3: 116–19, 125–26; 5: 44–45; 7: 97–98, 127–34; 8: 16–19, 52–57, 84–103. PRO, CO 217/119: f.190; 217/125: f.163. L. [B.] Namier and John Brooke, *The House of Commons, 1754–1790* (3v., London, 1964), 3: 78. *The royal military calendar, containing the service of every general officer in the British army, from the date of their first commission . . .* (3v., London, 1815–[16]), 1: 101. Morgan, "Orphan outpost."

McBEATH, GEORGE, fur trader, politician, office holder, and militia officer; b. *c.* 1740 in Scotland; d. 3 Dec. 1812 in Montreal, Lower Canada.

George McBeath arrived in Canada immediately after the conquest. His activity in the fur trade seems to date from 1765, the year in which Governor Murray* once more authorized the issuance of trading licences, which had been suspended two years earlier at the time of Pontiac*'s uprising. He went on his first trading expedition in 1765 and in the following years continued to fit out canoes which he took to the Lake Superior region. At this period he was concentrating his attention on the northwest. In 1772 at Michilimackinac (Mackinaw City, Mich.), McBeath was a member along with Maurice-Régis BLONDEAU, Isaac TODD, and some others of a company that sent canoes to Grand Portage (near Grand Portage, Minn.) and from there to Lake Winnipeg. In 1774 he was in Montreal, and for a time he seemed to hesitate between the northwest and the more southerly regions: Niagara, Detroit, and even the Illinois country. Having returned to Michilimackinac in 1776, McBeath went into partnership with Simon McTAVISH, who at that time maintained a close association with a number of powerful traders in Detroit: William Macomb, William Edgar, and Thomas Williams. In 1777 McBeath himself, with McTavish and Alexander ELLICE standing surety, fitted out 5 canoes with a

511

McBeath

crew of 32 which transported £2,000 of goods up to Sault Ste Marie (Mich.) and Grand Portage; in partnership with a man named Wright, he also financed the dispatch to Detroit of 20 boats with 80 men and goods worth £3,000. The following year, the last in their brief partnership, their investments amounted to £6,000 and included 6 canoes, 15 boats, and 105 men. Then for two years McBeath apparently worked by himself; he invested £7,100 in 1779–80, hiring 4 canoes, 7 boats, and 70 men for Grand Portage.

The independence of his operations was, however, more apparent than real, since in 1779 he had participated in an amalgamation of fur dealers through the purchase with Peter POND of 2 of the 16 shares of the North West Company [see Simon McTavish]. In 1781 McBeath formed a partnership with Pond and a man named Graves (probably Booty Graves) to fit out four canoes, standing surety along with Robert Ellice*. The next year, acting on his own, he sent two expeditions valued at £4,000 in all to Michilimackinac (Mackinac Island, Mich.) and in partnership, perhaps with James Grant*, under the name of McBeath and Company he made a shipment worth £3,000 to Grand Portage. But he ran into difficulties in his endeavours to supply Michilimackinac, and from then on his fortunes seem to have rested on shakier foundations. In 1783 McBeath still held his two shares in the North West Company but he fitted out only three canoes for £2,000 with Pond's aid. In April Daniel ROBERTSON, commandant at Michilimackinac, commissioned him to inform the Indians around Prairie du Chien (Wis.) of the prospect of peace between Great Britain and the American colonies and to encourage them to cease all warlike activity among themselves. The following year, in June 1784, McBeath accompanied Captain Robertson in search of a site for a British post to replace Michilimackinac.

In 1785 McBeath went to live in the parish of L'Assomption, but he nevertheless stayed frequently in Montreal. That year he was listed as one of the 19 founders of the Beaver Club. In 1787, after four years of inactivity in the fur business, he organized a final expedition with 6 canoes and £2,000 of merchandise. During that year McBeath had serious financial difficulties which obliged him to have McBeath, Grant and Company run by trustees; in addition he underwrote a debt which the firm of Sutherland and Grant contracted with Phyn, Ellices, and Inglis of London, an action which merchant John Richardson* predicted would assuredly lead to his ruin. In the course of 1787 also, Simon McTavish advised Joseph FROBISHER to buy from Thomas Forsyth the shares that McBeath still held in the North West Company. McBeath let one of them go, and in 1792 Alexander MACKENZIE purchased the second one under the terms of an engagement he had made two years earlier when

the NWC agreement was renewed; he had promised to pay £350 to McBeath, plus the value of the merchandise McBeath still had on hand in the spring. With this sale McBeath's business career finally ended.

From then on McBeath held administrative and political offices. In 1790 he was appointed commissioner for the Court of Requests of L'Assomption. In the same year he made an application to buy 3,000 acres of land in Rawdon Township, Leinster County, but he obtained only 500 acres of it nine years later. On the death of François-Antoine Larocque, the first MHA from Leinster, McBeath was elected for the county at the beginning of 1793 and sat in the House of Assembly until 1796. In 1795 he became a justice of the peace for the District of Montreal and in November 1799 he was appointed customs collector for the port of St Johns (Saint-Jean-sur-Richelieu). Later, in June 1807, he was commissioned to swear in the half-pay officers in the District of Montreal, and in June 1812 to administer the oath of allegiance. At the time of his death that year he was also lieutenant-colonel commanding the 1st Townships Militia Battalion.

Although McBeath owned a pew in the Scotch Presbyterian Church (later known as St Gabriel Street Church) in Montreal, his funeral was conducted according to Anglican rites. By his first marriage, with Jane Graham, who died on 26 May 1787, he had at least two children. In an Anglican service on 9 Sept. 1801, he had married Erie Smyth, widow of David McCrae, a fur trader and a founder of the Beaver Club. McBeath was a freemason and had been master of St Peter's Lodge No.4, Quebec, which was active in Montreal in the period between 1762 and 1793.

George McBeath was quite an important figure in the fur trade, but he never had the stature of those who at one time or another in their careers were in a position to aspire to sole control of it. Thus in 1777 the investments of the brothers John and William Kay amounted to £17,020; William and Alexander Macomb's in 1780 to £30,600; John GREGORY's in 1783 to £18,460; and Robert Ellice's in 1790 to £25,000. But in this struggle for pre-eminence the brothers Benjamin* and Joseph Frobisher and Simon McTavish were to be the winners.

FERNAND OUELLET

PAC, MG 19, B3: 4 (transcripts); RG 4, B28, 110–15. *Docs. relating to NWC* (Wallace), 4, 7–8, 40, 51, 56, 76, 89, 450, 453, 461–62. *John Askin papers* (Quaife), 1: 80, 83, 90, 92, 99, 124. "Le commerce du Nord-Ouest," PAC *Rapport*, 1888: 53. *Quebec Gazette*, 8 April 1790. F.-J. Audet, "Les législateurs du Bas-Canada." *Quebec almanac*, 1796: 63; 1810: 21, 55. M. W. Campbell, *NWC* (1973), 19, 34, 37, 52–53, 56. R. Campbell, *Hist. of Scotch Presbyterian Church*, 81, 96. Creighton, *Commercial empire of St. Lawrence*, 24, 29, 73. Innis, *Fur trade in Canada* (1956),

195–98, 200, 220. P. C. Phillips, *The fur trade* (2v., Norman, Okla., 1961), 1: 632–34. E. E. Rich, *The fur trade and the northwest to 1857* (Toronto, 1967), 141, 154, 172. F.[-J.] Audet et Édouard Fabre Surveyer, "George Mc-Beath," *La Presse* (Montréal), 6 août 1927: 53, 62. H. A. Innis, "The North West Company," *CHR*, 8 (1927): 308–21. Victor Morin, "Clubs et sociétés notoires d'autrefois," *Cahiers des Dix*, 13 (1948): 131–37.

MACDHÒMHNUILL, ALASDAIR. *See* MACDONELL OF SCOTHOUSE, ALEXANDER

MACDONALD OF GLENALADALE, HELEN (MacDonald) (Eilidh MacDhòmhnaill), estate manager; b. *c.* 1750 in Scotland, daughter of Alexander M'Donald of Glenaladale and Margaret MacDonell of Scothouse (Scotus); d. *c.* 1803 on Prince Edward Island.

Little is known of the early life of Helen MacDonald (or Nelly, as she was always called). She obviously received some sort of formal education, for she wrote fluent English as well as Gaelic. In 1772 Nelly and her younger sister Margaret (Peggy) accompanied their brother Donald on board the *Alexander* to St John's (Prince Edward) Island. The family, led by eldest brother JOHN, who arrived the following year, was attempting to create a Highland Catholic colony on the Island, partly to recoup its fortune and partly to help relieve religious persecution and economic oppression in the Highlands. Nelly and her sister shared in all the difficulties and privations of pioneering in unfamiliar wilderness. By the opening of the American rebellion in 1775, the little settlement on Lot 36 – centred at Scotchfort – had taken hold. The MacDonald brothers were desperately short of money, however, and, although Catholics, they were commissioned in the Royal Highland Emigrants (84th Foot), a regiment recruited for American service during the war. Both had left the Island before the end of 1775, Donald never to return (he was killed in battle in 1781) and John to remain away until 1792, occupied first by the war and then in Britain by political struggles related to the Island. Nelly and her sister had planned to leave the Island during the war for a more congenial location, but they never did.

With her brothers absent, supervision and management of the settlement and of the MacDonald interests on the Island devolved upon Nelly. Such responsibilities, when men were away at war or on business, were not at all unusual for women of the time, their magnitude depending on the extent of the family holdings involved. John MacDonald's continuous 16-year absence was excessive, however, while both the nature of his property and the political aspect of landownership on the Island made Nelly's task onerous and crucial. For MacDonald was not merely a landholder with a large farm; he was a self-conscious Highland laird (known in Gaelic as Fear-a-Ghlinne,

the lord of the glen) with a considerable number of dependent tenants for whom he felt responsible. As a proprietor, moreover, he was threatened by the machinations of the official clique that controlled the Island. Nelly operated at a considerable disadvantage in her attempts to manage the estate and protect her brother's interests. As a woman she could not become involved in the political and social activities necessary to establish a base of local support, although she did have enough influence to acquire some Charlottetown town lots in her own name, and because Catholics on the Island could neither vote nor hold office, she was unable to work behind the scenes in the capital through any of her numerous relations or tenants.

The demands made upon Nelly during her lengthy stewardship were considerable. She had to operate the family farm, which included more than 90 head of cattle, since without its produce survival was impossible on the isolated Island. Her success in this endeavour, such that her brother subsequently asked her advice in management matters, was due to help from the tenants and the work of soldiers she hired in Charlottetown. In the mid 1780s she even had a house built for her brother, to his specifications. Collecting rentals from tenants was more difficult, for the Island had little cash and no market for its produce; but – especially in 1781 when John feared the loss of his property unless he raised money for the quitrent payments – Nelly tried to collect, and stored the money in a strong-box in her cellar. Reporting on the progress of the estate was undoubtedly easier than garnering the political intelligence her brother demanded. He was especially interested in the Island government's sale of forfeited proprietorial lots late in 1781, a little matter that Governor Walter Patterson* neglected to mention to the government in Britain until – acting on Nelly's information – MacDonald and other proprietors forced the ministry to insist on details from Charlottetown.

In return for Nelly's efforts, John provided periodic remittances of money and luxuries (on one occasion, eight pairs of shoes, two to three yards of lasting, patterns, and two pairs of galoshes), and a constant flow of paternal advice. "You & the People should have dances & Merriment Among Yourselves," he wrote in 1780, "it is very reasonable that You Should be innocently Merry, & make the Time pass Smoothly." But only innocently merry. When Nelly met a young officer at one of the dances held in her house and contemplated an engagement, John became most concerned. The young man had "no dependence but on his commission," and his sister would not add to her "consequence by the connection," for provincial corps were little better than militia. Promising to return to look after his sister, MacDonald insisted "untill then you had better not throw yourself away" and "make yourself & me look silly in the Eyes of the

MacDonald

world." Nelly acquiesced in her brother's wishes on this occasion; as her mother wrote in 1785, "One comfort I have marrage is not nesesary to salvation – so my Dear Nelly you may . . . be happie els wher if not in marrage here." After his intervention, however, MacDonald found it necessary to complain constantly of his sister's gloomy and discontented letters and to advise her to "keep your mind as easy as possible." Finally, shortly before John was expected back on the Island in 1792, the *Royal Gazette* announced Nelly's marriage to Ronald MacDonald of Grand Tracadie. As one of her last acts of management Nelly inventoried the population – human and animal – on her brother's lots 35 and 36. Despite her efforts, many of the tenants had moved away during John's absence.

Fear-a-Ghlinne returned to the Island with a new bride. Nelly did not get on well with her sister-in-law Margaret (whose imperiousness led to her being known as "the Queen of Tracadie"), but when MacDonald went again to Britain in 1802 she found herself saddled with Margaret and advice from her brother to let his wife have her own way as to the management of the house. By this time Nelly was constantly ill, and she died shortly thereafter. Her life was a tribute to the resourcefulness of pioneer women despite the limitations and demands imposed upon them by their society.

J. M. BUMSTED

PAPEI, RG 16, Land registry records. Private arch., Jean and Colin MacDonald (St Peters, P.E.I.), MacDonald family papers, Helen MacDonald corr., 1779–1802 (copies at PAPEI). Scottish Catholic Arch. (Edinburgh), Blairs letters, 11 Dec. 1775, John MacDonald to George Hay; 4 Nov. 1776, James MacDonald to Hay. *Royal Gazette and Miscellany of the Island of Saint John* (Charlottetown), 28 Jan. 1792. J. M. Bumsted, "Captain John MacDonald and the Island," *Island Magazine*, no.6 (spring–summer 1979): 15–20; "Highland emigration to the Island of St. John and the Scottish Catholic Church, 1769–1774," *Dalhousie Rev.*, 58 (1978–79): 511–27. A. F. MacDonald, "Captain John MacDonald, 'Glenalladale,'" CCHA *Report*, 30 (1964): 21–22.

MacDONALD OF GLENALADALE, JOHN (Iain MacDhòmhnaill), army officer and colonizer; b. 29 Sept. 1742 in Scotland, eldest son of Alexander M'Donald of Glenaladale and Margaret MacDonell of Scothouse (Scotus); d. 28 Dec. 1810 on his estate, Tracadie (lots 35 and 36), P.E.I.

John MacDonald was three years old when his father, Alexander, head of the Glenaladale branch of the Clan MacDonald of Clanranald, joined the standard of Prince Charles, the Young Pretender, at its raising in 1745 on the Glenaladale property at Glenfinnan, Scotland. After the prince's hopes for a Stuart restoration perished at Culloden, his allies, including the MacDonalds, suffered serious economic

reprisals at the hands of the British government. It was nevertheless possible to send young MacDonald in 1756 to the famous Catholic seminary at Regensburg (Federal Republic of Germany), where, as a lay student, he received the thorough grounding in languages and the classics to which his later correspondence so strongly attests. Historians have noted that he could "speak, read and write seven languages" and was accounted "one of the most finished and accomplished young gentlemen of his generation."

Some time after his return to Scotland in 1761 he became the 8th laird of Glenaladale and second in command among the chieftains of the Clanranald family; however, a combination of factors eventually turned his mind to thoughts of emigration. There is evidence that MacDonald had little sympathy with the economic policies of the post-Culloden chieftains, which had led to the oppression of the tacksmen, among whom he had many relatives and friends. At a more personal level, moreover, his dependence on the Clanranalds had become so repugnant to him that he "was determined to take the first Opportunity of throwing off the Same." He began, therefore, to hope that he and his people might find "a feasible Method of leaving the inhospitable Part of the World, which has fallen to our share," and in 1770 he became involved in an emigration scheme. That year Colin MacDonald of Boisdale undertook to compel his tenants on South Uist, in the Outer Hebrides, to renounce their Roman Catholic faith in favour of the Church of Scotland, under penalty of expulsion from his estate. The Roman Catholic bishops of Scotland concluded that emigration was the only solution for these destitute people, and MacDonald became chief organizer of the plan. He purchased from the lord advocate of Scotland, James William Montgomery, Lot 36 on St John's (Prince Edward) Island, and, with the assistance of the Roman Catholic Church, undertook to settle there not only tenants from South Uist but "a Number of other people & our own friends" from the mainland. In May 1772, under the leadership of MacDonald's brother, Donald, and accompanied by Father James MacDonald*, 210 settlers departed on the *Alexander* for St John's Island. The following month the party disembarked on Lot 36 at a place subsequently called Scotchfort.

In 1773, dismayed by reports of distress from the newly established settlement, where the harvest of the previous year had been poor, MacDonald himself embarked for America, landing at Philadelphia, Pa. His progress northward, though rapid, enabled him to acquire some estimate of the capabilities of the various colonies, which served as a basis for comparison with those of St John's Island; on arrival there he concluded that his settlement could be brought to prosperity. The task of removing the settlers from the point of disembarkation to their permanent locations and

514

thereby placing the estate on a sound organizational basis was, however, interrupted by the outbreak of the American revolution. In June 1775 MacDonald received an invitation from Lieutenant Colonel Allan Maclean* and Major John Small to join them in measures to retain the allegiance of the great number of Scots Highlanders settled in the revolting colonies. It was also proposed to raise a regiment among "some hundreds of discharged soldiers from the several Highland regiments then dispersed in the different provinces on the continent of North America." Although he hesitated because, as a Roman Catholic, he would occasionally have to conform to the established church, MacDonald acquiesced. Despite the fact that he had never before belonged to the service, he was appointed captain and made company commander in the second battalion of the Royal Highland Emigrants (84th Foot). His sister HELEN (Nelly) would manage the family estate, not only while he and Donald, who was to die during the course of the war, were on active service, but for some years afterwards. MacDonald later asserted that he "did not meet the enemy," but there are accounts of his seizure of an American man-of-war, apprehended on a plundering expedition along the coast of Nova Scotia. Small referred to Captain MacDonald's "activity and unabating zeal, in bringing an excellent company into the field" and to his being "one of the most accomplished men, and best Officers of his rank, in His Majesty's Service." He was placed on half pay in 1783.

In 1781, during MacDonald's absence, Governor Walter Patterson* had initiated proceedings against certain lots which were in arrears for non-payment of quitrents. The lots were auctioned off in November of the same year, and Patterson and a few of his friends were the principal purchasers. Upon learning of the sales, MacDonald went to London in 1782 and assumed leadership of a movement to secure a remission of the quitrent arrears and the return of the lots to their former owners. Unaware at first that Lot 36 had not been sold, he argued that the quitrents on this property had run unavoidably in arrears through the expense of settlement and his absence in the service. He was, moreover, incensed over the sale to Attorney General Phillips Callbeck* of Lot 35, for which he himself had been making offers to the previous owner, General Alexander Maitland. Patterson later contended that MacDonald and many of his tenants had been pasturing their cattle and making the principal part of their hay on Maitland's lot for over a decade without compensation to the proprietor and that it was "this loss of the use of another's property which has occasioned his great activity in the business." It was, however, the determination of king in council that instructions be sent to the governor to repeal the Quit Rent Act of 1774, in virtue of which

the lots had been sold, to annul the sales, and to restore the sold lots to the former proprietors. Patterson refused to comply with these instructions and, for this and further disobedience to Home Department instructions, he was dismissed in 1787 and replaced by Edmund FANNING. MacDonald remained in London to assist in bringing criminal charges against the former governor and to serve as solicitor at the subsequent hearings before the president of the Privy Council in 1789. The purchase of Lot 35 from General Maitland was effected in 1792 after a spirited controversy with Mrs Phillips Callbeck. In the same year MacDonald married Margaret MacDonald of Ghernish (Guernish), his first wife, Isabella Gordon of Wardhouse, having died many years previously.

When MacDonald at last returned to Tracadie in 1792, he found that, despite the exertions of his sister Nelly, his affairs were in a sorry state. Despairing of his return and not having received their permanent locations of land, many of his tenants had provided for their own security by moving to the estates of other proprietors. MacDonald had not only to reinstate his lands in their former condition, but he was also faced with the necessity of retiring the accumulated arrears of quitrents. He proceeded to attempt to develop his property, concentrating on the raising of livestock and the production of hay.

He also strove to bring a measure of tranquillity to his domestic relationships. During the war years he had complained of the "foolish storms of high passion and feeling" which Nelly's letters conveyed. He once declared to her that "it makes my flesh shrink to read a paragraph of your letter." Assessing the situation in 1803, he admitted that he himself had "naturally a warm temper" and that he had been "betrayed . . . into occasional Gusts of passion"; "Mrs Macdonald is the same," he noted, while "in respect to yourself, my dear Nelly, you must not, more than others, cock up your nose, and say you are as white as snow: you too have plenty of spice." Nelly was, nevertheless, held in high regard. Writing in 1792 to prepare her for his impending marriage, MacDonald had promised, "You need not fear that I shall ever neglect you. . . . If my income were but a shilling a year, you shall have a sixpence thereof."

In 1797, following upon the publication in the previous year of Joseph ROBINSON's *To the farmers in the Island of St. John, in the Gulf of St. Lawrence*, MacDonald complained to Lieutenant Governor Fanning of the existence of a "Levelling Party" on the Island which was working for the establishment of a court of escheat and the subdivision of proprietorial lands. The party, he claimed, "has been for a year past employed in disseminating principles among our tenants and the people at large which may vie with the like which have laid France in ruins." Fanning could scarcely have been unaware that such a movement

MacDonald

existed, particularly in view of the fact that it derived its leadership from members of his own government, chiefly the family of Chief Justice Peter STEWART; but the lieutenant governor, MacDonald charged, pretended to understand that the complaint was of "a levelling party aiming immediately against Government itself by treason and bloodshed than to the sort of levelling party . . . aimed against the proprietors." When, therefore, fearing prosecution for libel, MacDonald twice refused to appear before the Council to furnish proof of the party's existence and the names of its members, that body determined that such a levelling party did not exist and that MacDonald "most pointedly declares himself to be the greatest malcontent on the face of the earth." Fanning passed the matter on to the House of Assembly, and the legislature dispatched the serjeant-at-arms to Tracadie, summoning MacDonald to defend his allegations before the house. Glenaladale disdainfully declined to appear before a group of which John Stewart*, with whom he had scuffled with weapons drawn in the streets of Charlottetown, was speaker, and in a letter to Fanning he delivered a scathing commentary on the origins and integrity of the membership of the house. Considering the matter, an assembly committee chaired by Robert HODGSON drew up a set of resolutions condemning MacDonald for his "false and groundless" assertions but decided that, in view of his "turbulent, restless and factious character" and the possibility that proceedings against him might "raise him into a degree of consequence," it should dispense with his attendance as had been required. In the late 1790s MacDonald, along with Joseph APLIN and James DOUGLAS, stood virtually alone in opposing the tightly knit Fanning administration.

Despite MacDonald's spirited resistance, the assembly of 1797 declared in favour of escheat and petitioned the British government accordingly. In the resolutions forwarded to London, however, Glenaladale's lots 35 and 36 were specifically stated to be "settled agreeable to the terms of the grants." It was not until 1802–3 that, diverted temporarily from its preoccupation with the Napoleonic Wars, the Colonial Office took action on the land question, deciding that the lands of those proprietors who did not pay reduced arrears of quitrents would be escheated. MacDonald, in London at the time in an effort to acquaint the authorities with the true state of the Island, was dismayed to learn that the receiver general of quitrents, John Stewart, "full of destroying enmity to one class, and of favor to his own," was to commence prosecutions. Judgements were obtained against a number of proprietors; however, fear on the part of both Fanning and the Colonial Office of offending the powerful landlords, coupled with the resumption of war and a change of administration in London, brought proceedings to a halt in 1804.

Although the proponents of escheat had been silenced for a time, there remained the problem of MacDonald's existing debts, greater, John Hill* once asserted, "than he will be able to liquidate during his life, independent of the quit rents." He cautioned his family to economy, averring that the alternative was "to go to pieces, scatter, and be beggars, in a place where beggars are not known and every one only thinks of himself." In 1805, still in England, he attempted to sell his Island properties, but no buyers were forthcoming. He returned home the following year with the help of a loan from the Earl of Selkirk [DOUGLAS]. Although the escheat issue was raised again during the administration of Lieutenant Governor Joseph Frederick Wallet DesBarres*, MacDonald seems to have kept aloof from Island politics until his death in 1810.

Stolidly aristocratic in his convictions, MacDonald was nevertheless mindful of the afflictions of the less privileged. He had at one time busied himself with the preparation of petitions on behalf of Highland settlers being prosecuted for back rents by William TOWNSHEND, the collector of customs. He had also laboured for the removal of the disabilities which at that time denied Roman Catholics the right to vote. One of the last controversies in which he became involved stemmed from his objection to an edict of Bishop Pierre DENAUT whereby the Catholics of St Andrew's, Naufrage, Tracadie, Three Rivers (the region around Georgetown), Bay Fortune, and East Point were to contribute to the erection of a large chapel at St Andrew's. In a letter to Father Angus Bernard MacEachern* he declared such "a magnificent Pile of unnecessary Ostentation" to be beyond the exigency and means of the people, particularly when those not within reach of St Andrew's, including the people of Tracadie, would have to build churches of their own. For a time he forbad his tenants to support the project and had his brother, Augustine, say mass at Tracadie.

Although the child of his first marriage had lived for only a few months, five children were born of MacDonald's union with Margaret MacDonald, the "Queen of Tracadie." These were Donald*, William, John*, Roderick C., and Flora Anna Maria. To them and his wife he passed on the Tracadie estate intact, although his will indicates that it was encumbered with unspecified debts. Donald, his successor as head of the estate, was the father of Sir William Christopher MacDonald*, the millionaire manufacturer and philanthropist.

F. L. PIGOT

PAPEI, Acc. 2702, Smith–Alley coll., petition of John MacDonald. Private arch., Jean and Colin MacDonald (St Peters, P.E.I.), MacDonald family papers, docs.7, 10, 19–20, 22, 26, 67 (copies at PAPEI). PRO, CO 226/3: 50–51, 107–10; 226/10: 94–125; 226/15: 182–83, 208–27,

McDonell

230–50; 226/18: 31–32, 114–17, 160–62, 166–234. Supreme Court of P.E.I. (Charlottetown), Estates Division, liber 1: f.31 (will of John MacDonald). *The lyon in mourning, or a collection of speeches, letters, journals, etc. relative to the affairs of Prince Charles Edward Stuart,* comp. Robert Forbes, ed. Henry Paton (3v., Edinburgh, 1895–96), 3. [John MacDonald], "Glenalladale's settlement, Prince Edward Island," ed. I. R. Mackay, *Scottish Gaelic Studies* (Aberdeen, Scot.), 10 (1965): 16–24. P.E.I., House of Assembly, *Journal,* 17 July 1797. *Weekly Recorder of Prince Edward Island* (Charlottetown), 1 Jan. 1811. Alexander Mackenzie, *History of the Macdonalds and lords of the isles; with genealogies of the principal families of the name* (Inverness, Scot., 1881).

Canada's smallest prov. (Bolger). J. F. S. Gordon, *The Catholic Church in Scotland, from the suppression of the hierarchy till the present time; being memorabilia of the bishops, missioners, and Scotch Jesuits* (Glasgow, 1869). F. L. Pigot, *A history of Mount Stewart, Prince Edward Island* (Charlottetown, 1975). J. M. Bumsted, "Captain John MacDonald and the Island," *Island Magazine,* no.6 (spring–summer 1979): 15–20. A. F. MacDonald, "Captain John MacDonald, 'Glenalladale,'" *CCHA Report,* 30 (1964): 21–37. MacNutt, "Fanning's regime on P.E.I.," *Acadiensis* (Fredericton), 1, no.1: 37–53.

McDONELL (Aberchalder), JOHN, army and militia officer, judge, office holder, and politician; b. *c.* 1758 at Aberchalder House, Scotland, eldest son of Alexander McDonell of Aberchalder; m. Helen Yates, probably at Fort George (Niagara-on-the-Lake), Upper Canada, and they had one son and two daughters; d. 21 Nov. 1809 at Quebec, Lower Canada.

In 1773 Alexander McDonell and his two brothers, John of Leek and Allan of Collachie, led one of the first major migrations of Highlanders to North America, settling on Sir William Johnson*'s estate in the Mohawk valley of New York. At the outbreak of the American revolution young John McDonell returned from Montreal, Que., where he was working in an accountant's office and on 14 June 1775 became an ensign in Allan Maclean*'s Royal Highland Emigrants. That October he was sent from Montreal, where he was stationed, to arrest the notorious American sympathizer Thomas Walker* at L'Assomption and during the affray he was "wounded in the arm." By April 1778 McDonell had been promoted lieutenant. While in Montreal he became acquainted with Walter Butler* and, weary of garrison duty, transferred to John Butler*'s rangers, becoming a captain on 29 August.

McDonell and Walter Butler set out to join the campaign led by William Caldwell* and Joseph Brant [THAYENDANEGEA] in September 1778 against German Flats (near the mouth of West Canada Creek), N.Y., but arrived too late. On 11 November he participated in Butler's infamous attack at Cherry Valley. Having failed to take the fort there, the expedition turned on the settlement. The next morning

Butler sent McDonell "accompanied by Mr. Brant . . . to compleat the destruction of the place," and he praised McDonell "in particular, whose activity and spirit on every occasion does him much honor." On 28 July 1779 McDonell and a small force captured the American fort at Freeland, Pa, and the following month he was with the combined party of Butler's Rangers and Indians defeated at Newtown (near Elmira, N.Y.). The rangers then retired to their headquarters at Fort Niagara (near Youngstown) where McDonell assumed the duties of paymaster. In February 1780 he accompanied Walter Butler to Montreal where they did "very little else but feasting and Dancing" and for diversion intended to tour the mountain "every other day on Snow Shoes." In June McDonell led a force of rangers and Indians in an unsuccessful attempt to bring the Oneidas to Niagara. Suffering from fever, ague, and "Rheumatism in my neck," McDonell was so ill that he had to have himself tied on his horse. Walter Butler wrote that "they killed their Horses and Dogs for food."

By this time McDonell was the only senior ranger officer available for active service. In September he commanded a large ranger contingent supporting Sir John Johnson*'s attack on the Mohawk valley. Having burned their way through the Schoharie valley, McDonell and Brant were mentioned by Johnson as having "contributed greatly to our success" in defeating on 19 October an American force which had sallied forth from Fort Stanwix (Rome). This affair was his last in the field. For the remainder of the war his primary service was as paymaster at Fort Niagara. On 1 June 1782 John Butler wrote to HALDIMAND, "Capt. McDonell is the most capable officer in the Corps . . . he is also the best liked by the Indians." The regiment disbanded in June 1784 and McDonell retired on half pay. He appeared on a list drawn up on 20 July 1784 of persons intending to settle at Niagara, but on 25 September he was on a return of disbanded troops residing in Township No.3 (Osnabruck, Ont.), and on 16 October he was on a similar list for Township No.1 (Charlottenburg). Although most of Butler's officers settled in the Niagara peninsula, McDonell apparently preferred to live along the St Lawrence River among the Highlanders.

Among the isolated post-war loyalist settlements of western Quebec, McDonell's social stature, his military service, and his acquaintance with Johnson assured him regional and later provincial prominence. On 15 April 1787 he was a signatory to the petition of "Western Loyalists" requesting, among other things, the blessing of the British constitution, English land tenure, aid to the Church of Scotland and the Church of England, and the establishment of schools. This pressure resulted on 24 July 1788 in the organization of four new administrative districts and McDonell was a reaper in the harvest of new local offices. He was

Macdonell

appointed to the land board of the Luneburg District along with John Munro* and Richard DUNCAN among others, and was reappointed to its successor, the land board of Glengarry and Stormont, on 16 July 1792. In 1790 McDonell had succeeded his father on the Court of Common Pleas attending all 13 sessions between 1790 and 1794. He was also one of the original magistrates appointed to the district Court of Quarter Sessions but attended only two of nine sessions between 1789 and 1791. In 1791 McDonell was recommended by Governor Guy CARLETON, now Lord Dorchester, in consultation with Johnson, for the Executive Council of the new province of Upper Canada. He was not chosen but his local pre-eminence was recognized by his appointment to the lieutenancy of the county of Glengarry on 2 Nov. 1792 [*see* Hazelton SPENCER].

The almost continuous hegemony of the leading McDonell families in Glengarry extended to politics and ensured the election of McDonell and his brother Hugh* in 1792 to the House of Assembly. On 17 September McDonell was chosen first speaker of the house of Upper Canada's first parliament. He was re-elected to the second parliament in 1796, but ill health prevented his attendance until 9 June 1798. He had been replaced as speaker by Surveyor General David William Smith*, who on 11 June moved with unanimous consent that "in order to mark the sense I entertain of his former situation" McDonell be given a special seat immediately to the right of the speaker. Although now regular in his attendance McDonell was rarely prominent. On 20 June he voted with the majority in favour of Christopher Robinson*'s bill extending slavery within the province; on 5 June 1800 he opposed the successful candidacy of Samuel STREET to replace Smith as speaker; and on 25 June he supported Solicitor General Robert Isaac Dey GRAY's bill to extend English criminal law in the province.

McDonell continued to be slightly involved in military affairs after the revolution as an officer in the local militia. One of the chief concerns of Lieutenant Governor SIMCOE was the military security of the province and he saw in the quasi-military society of the Highlanders an untapped resource. Thus in 1792 and 1793 he supported as "both politick & just" McDonell's longstanding request for "Highland Broadswords" – the traditional weapon of the Highlander – to arm the Glengarry militia. On 1 July 1794 Simcoe recommended him for the majority of a proposed Canadian regiment as "the most proper person . . . within this Province." Simcoe's reasoning was simple. McDonell apparently had influence with the Indians at St Regis (near Cornwall), and his position as a surrogate chieftain in his community meant that "the Highlanders will follow him in numbers." On 1 June 1796 the regiment, the Royal Canadian Volunteer Regiment, was divided into two battalions: McDonell received command of the Upper Canadian battalion and a promotion to lieutenant-colonel. In June of the following year most of the battalion under McDonell's command left Kingston for new headquarters at Fort George where they remained until disbandment in 1802. McDonell retired on half pay to the impressive residence he had built near Cornwall. In 1803 the Earl of Selkirk [DOUGLAS] observed, "His vanity in calling it 'Glengarry House' has given umbrage, as he is far from being the nearest to the chieftainship of those of the clan that are in Canada." But until the arrival of Father Alexander McDonell* in 1804, his leadership among the Gaelic-speaking Highlanders was unchallenged.

Financial insecurity, the result of too generous loans to relatives, forced his return to military life after a few years. On 9 July 1806 he proposed to raise a battalion of volunteers from among the Highlanders. Although supported by Isaac BROCK the proposal was not revived until 1811 [*see* George Richard John Macdonell*]. In 1807 McDonell received the relatively lowly appointment of paymaster to the 10th Royal Veteran Battalion stationed at Quebec. The harsh Quebec climate perhaps was too much for McDonell's poor health. In early November 1809 he caught a severe cold and died several weeks later. A contemporary biographer has given a portrait: "He was rather below the middle size, of a fair complexion, and in his Youth, uncommonly strong and active. For some time past his appearance was totally altered . . . those, who had not seen him for many years, could not recognize the swift and intrepid Captain of the Rangers."

ALLAN J. MACDONALD

AO, MS 517. BL, Add. MSS 21661–892 (transcripts at PAC). PAC, MG 9, D8, 21 (transcript; mfm. at AO); RG 1, L4, 9–16; RG 5, A1: 2188–89; RG 8, I (C ser.), 251, 272, 283, 789, 791–94. *Corr. of Lieut. Governor Simcoe* (Cruikshank). Douglas, *Lord Selkirk's diary* (White). Gwillim, *Diary of Mrs. Simcoe* (Robertson; 1911). "Journals of Legislative Assembly of U.C.," AO *Report*, 1909. "Records of the early courts of justice of Upper Canada," AO *Report*, 1917. *Canadian Courant and Montreal Advertiser* (Montreal), 28 Jan. 1811. Dooner, *Catholic pioneers in U.C.* J. G. Harkness, *Stormont, Dundas and Glengarry: a history, 1784–1945* (Oshawa, Ont., 1946). E. A. Cruikshank, "A memoir of Lieutenant-Colonel John Macdonell, of Glengarry House, the first speaker of the Legislative Assembly of Upper Canada," *OH*, 22 (1925): 20–59. W. L. Scott, "Glengarry's representatives in the Legislative Assembly of Upper Canada," CCHA *Report*, 6 (1938–39): 22–26; "The Macdonells of Leek, Collachie and Aberchalder," CCHA *Report*, 2 (1934–35): 22–32.

MACDONELL (Collachie), ANGUS, office holder, lawyer, and politician; b. in Inverness-shire, Scotland, son of Allan McDonell of Collachie and Helen

MacNab; d. unmarried 7 or 8 Oct. 1804 in the wreck of the *Speedy* on Lake Ontario.

In 1773 the Collachie family was part of an emigration of about 600 Highlanders from the lands of the Clan MacDonell of Glengarry to Sir William Johnson*'s estate in the Mohawk valley of New York. After the outbreak of the American revolution the Highlanders remained loyal to the crown and in January 1776 Major-General Philip John Schuyler took Allan McDonell and five other leaders hostage to ensure the neutrality of Sir John Johnson* and his Highland tenants. Fearing arrest by the rebels, Johnson struck out for Montreal, Que., early in the summer with about 130 Highlanders and 120 others. Old Collachie escaped in May 1779 and by August he had reached the province of Quebec where he resided, first at Yamachiche and then at Quebec, until his death in 1792.

Unlike his brother Alexander*, Angus Macdonell does not seem to have served in a loyalist corps during the revolution. Nor was he living with his father at Quebec at the end of the war. He did, however, spend a few years about this time in Montreal and Quebec where he gained a seminary education and acquired a sound grasp of the French language. In June 1785 he was at Quebec where he had been jailed for debt. After his release Macdonell began experimenting with a new method of manufacturing pot and pearl ash and in November 1788 he applied for a patent. In April 1791 the province of Quebec passed an act which granted exclusive patent privileges to him, his brothers James and Alexander, and Christopher Carter, as well as to Samuel Hopkins, a rival inventor who also had devised an improved process. That same year Macdonell and Hopkins became partners and attempted, it appears, to market their product.

The Collachie family's proven loyalty and young Macdonell's ability as a chemist apparently came to the attention of the lieutenant governor of Upper Canada, John Graves Simcoe. Informed by the Lower Canadian deputy surveyor general, John Collins*, of salt springs in Upper Canada, in 1792 Simcoe commissioned Macdonell and William Chewett* to explore the area around the Bay of Quinte and the Niagara peninsula for sites and to analyse their quality. Macdonell reported a major location on the Fifteen Mile Creek in the Niagara region and Simcoe immediately set him to work establishing a project to produce salt there for general consumption. Delays occurred in securing supplies and provisioning labourers but Macdonell, now superintendent of the works, plunged ahead, spending large sums. After three years in operation the project had produced a disappointing 450 barrels. Having declared that he was "determined to stand or fall" by the works, Macdonell was removed in 1796 and replaced by the local Church of England clergyman, Robert Addison*. Macdonell's other

government duties, it seems, had prevented him from providing effective management.

As first clerk of the House of Assembly – he had been appointed on 12 Dec. 1792 – Macdonell administered the oaths to members, recorded the business of the house, and provided for the printing of its journals and statutes. In spite of frequent tardiness in performing his duties, which exasperated Simcoe's secretary, Edward Baker Littlehales, on 29 Oct. 1794 the lieutenant governor named Macdonell secretary to the Upper Canadian commissioners – Richard Cartwright, John McDonell (Aberchalder), and John Munro* – who had been appointed to negotiate a revenue-sharing agreement about customs duties with their Lower Canadian counterparts.

Late 1798 saw the arrival at York (Toronto) of French royalist *émigrés*, led by Joseph-Geneviève Puisaye*, Comte de Puisaye, who were on their way to establish a military settlement at Windham, a few miles north of York. In 1799 Administrator Peter Russell made Macdonell his French secretary, instructing him to act as the settlement's agent. It appears that Macdonell exceeded his authority, and charges were laid against him by Puisaye. The Executive Council examined the matter in September 1800 and determined that Macdonell had engaged in unauthorized transactions in Indian land. It concluded that "he is unworthy of any favour from the Executive Government and unfit to hold any situation under it," and Macdonell was dismissed as clerk on 30 May 1801. He petitioned the assembly, which passed a resolution stating that he had not been dismissed for any irregularity in his conduct as clerk and which awarded him £300, this being the salary unpaid for two years.

Excluded from government preferment, Macdonell embarked almost immediately upon a political career. He served as Samuel Heron's scrutineer during the election of 1800 in Durham, Simcoe, and the East Riding of York. A newspaper account noted that his "interrogatories were general, but in that mild way which characterises the man." Thereafter he appeared in the House of Assembly as counsel for a group of York petitioners complaining that judge Henry Allcock's agent, William Weekes, had used improper measures to secure Allcock's election. Allcock was consequently unseated by the house and, in a by-election called in June 1801, Macdonell defeated John Small*, clerk of the Executive Council, by 112 to 32 votes. In the election of June 1804 Macdonell campaigned successfully against Weekes and former surveyor general David William Smith*. In his election address he was particularly concerned to discredit a rumour that his assessment legislation of 1803 had increased the general rates within the Home District. He claimed that he had always favoured a shifting of the public burden "from the shoulders of

Macdonell

the Industrious Farmers and Mechanics, upon those of the more opulent Classes of the Community."

During his brief years in the assembly, Macdonell was among its most energetic, productive, able, and independent members. He initiated legislation, not always successfully, to encourage the cultivation and export of hemp, to better secure land title, to establish a Court of Chancery, and to reform the fee schedules of attorneys. He was responsible for the Assessment Act of 1803 which attempted to provide more equal rates. He championed the rights and prerogatives of the assembly and in 1803 he attained a degree of notoriety for his effort to have David Burns, clerk of the crown and pleas, held in contempt of parliament for his attempt to avoid questioning on the matter of fee schedules, a favourite target of Macdonell's. His most frequent associates in the assembly were David McGregor Rogers*, Ralfe Clench*, and Robert Nelles*.

In spite of family ties Macdonell rarely worked with, or supported, the parliamentary efforts of his brother Alexander, but on one occasion, 16 Feb. 1804, the brothers joined ranks in an unsuccessful move to provide for public schools in certain parts of the province. Their initiatives were a direct response to a petition of the magistrates and leading Presbyterians of Glengarry County, including John McDonell (Aberchalder) and John BETHUNE, urging the erection of public schools in central places. The petitioners were concerned that the Highlanders were "accustomed to hear the beauties of Christianity inculcated in their mother tongue [and] . . . supposed that an English education was unnecessary." The "few schools found among them here . . . are fluctuating and of little value," the petitioners claimed, forecasting that the establishment of public schools would be a measure of "great utility, both in a political and moral view, to the rising generation . . . [to] speedily counteract the effect of an improper bias."

One of the most important facets of Macdonell's career – his legal practice – is the least known. A prominent York lawyer, he was admitted as an attorney on 7 July 1794 and became a barrister in Trinity term 1797. He was a founding member of the Law Society of Upper Canada and succeeded Robert Isaac Dey GRAY as treasurer in Easter Term 1801. In October 1804, on his way to defend an Indian charged with murder, Macdonell perished with Gray when the schooner *Speedy* sank in a gale off Brighton.

Angus Macdonell died a freemason without a strong attachment to the Catholic Church of his forefathers. An unaccomplished poet, he had distinct ability in law and politics, which was undermined by his procrastination, irascibility, and occasional indolence.

ALLAN J. MACDONALD

AO, MS 517; MU 1776–78; RG 22, ser.155, will of Angus Macdonell. BL, Add. mss 8075, 104: 1–120 (transcript at PAC). PAC, MG 24, I8; RG 1, E3; RG 5, A1: 330–32, 707–9, 1202–4. "Accounts of receiver-general of U.C.," AO *Report*, 1914: 754. *Corr. of Lieut. Governor Simcoe* (Cruikshank). "Journals of Legislative Assembly of U.C.," AO *Report*, 1909. [Alexander Macdonell], "A journal by Sheriff Alexander Macdonell," J. E. Middleton and Fred Landon, *The province of Ontario: a history, 1615–1927* (5v., Toronto, [1927–28]), 2: 1246–50. "Ordinances made for the province of Quebec by the governor and Council of the said province, from 1768 until 1791 . . . ," PAC *Report*, 1914–15, app.C: 254–55. "State papers," PAC *Report*, 1890: 281. "State papers – Upper Canada," PAC *Report*, 1891: 100, 128, 137, 158, 162. *Town of York, 1793–1815* (Firth), 163–64, 170–77, 226–29, 234, 239, 250. [Joseph Willcocks], "The diary of Joseph Willcocks from Dec. 1, 1799, to Feb. 1, 1803," J. E. Middleton and Fred Landon, *The province of Ontario: a history, 1615–1927*, 2: 1250–322. *Quebec Gazette*, May–July 1791. *York Gazette*, 2 May 1804; 4, 11 July 1807.

Dooner, *Catholic pioneers in U.C.*, 1–34. Riddell, *Legal profession in U.C.* J. R. Robertson, *The history of freemasonry in Canada from its introduction in 1749 . . .* (2v., Toronto, 1899). Henry Scadding, *Toronto of old*, ed. F. H. Armstrong (Toronto, 1966). Ernest Green, "The search for salt in Upper Canada," *OH*, 26 (1930): 406–31. H. H. Guest, "Upper Canada's first political party," *OH*, 54 (1962): 275–96. W. R. Riddell, "The legislature of Upper Canada and contempt: drastic measures of early provincial parliaments with critics," *OH*, 22 (1925): 187–91. W. L. Scott, "The Macdonells of Leek, Collachie and Aberchalder," CCHA *Report*, 2 (1934–35): 22–32; "A U.E. Loyalist family," *OH*, 32 (1937): 140–70.

MACDONELL (Greenfield), JOHN, lawyer, office holder, militia officer, and politician; b. 19 April 1785 in Greenfield, Scotland, the fourth son of Alexander Macdonell of Greenfield and Janet Macdonell (Aberchalder), sister of John McDONELL (Aberchalder); d. 14 Oct. 1812 in Queenston, Upper Canada.

Little is known of John Macdonell's early life. In 1792 his family immigrated to Glengarry County, Upper Canada, and under his father's leadership it enjoyed a measure of prominence in the military and political affairs of the county. Some sources suggest that John, like his younger brother Alexander Greenfield*, attended John Strachan*'s grammar school at Cornwall. This seems improbable. Strachan's school was established in the summer of 1803 and on 6 April of that year Macdonell became a law student. In 1862 Chief Justice John Beverley Robinson* recalled that Macdonell served in the law office of William Dickson* at Niagara (Niagara-on-the-Lake). Several historians have speculated that he was persuaded to take up law by his uncle Alexander McDonell* (Collachie), sheriff of the Home District and member of the House of Assembly for the riding of Glengarry and Prescott. In 1808, having articled for the requisite five years, Macdonell was called to the bar in Trinity term. Thereafter, according to Robinson, he "established himself very successfully in business" at York (Toronto).

Macdonell's legal career was brief but meteoric. Through Collachie he became acquainted with judge William Dummer Powell*, gaining both his friendship and his patronage. At the height of his political power during the administration of Lieutenant Governor Francis Gore*, Powell on 19 Aug. 1808 solicited an appointment for the young barrister as clerk to several court commissions for the Newcastle, Midland, Johnstown, and Eastern districts. By 1811 Macdonell was firmly established in his profession. A combination of personal ability and Powell's patronage brought recognition of his legal prominence when on 16 July he was appointed to conduct the criminal prosecutions on the western circuit in the absence of Solicitor General D'Arcy Boulton*. Powell's wife, Anne Murray*, wrote enthusiastically that "our young Friend J McDonnel goes as king's counsel." He had also begun to attract law students and that year Robinson and Archibald McLean* joined his practice. The following year the astute Ebenezer Washburn*, ever alert for suitable prospects for his family, arranged for his son Simon Ebenezer* to article with Macdonell but the War of 1812 disrupted these plans. Macdonell's professional stature had been complemented by an increasing social prominence. In December 1811 he was secretary to the subscribers to the library in York and in 1812 esquire was added to his name on the town census.

Early in his career Macdonell established a reputation for a quick temper. In 1808 he reacted strongly to a statement about his practice made in court by Attorney General William Firth* and on 16 September sent his close friend Duncan Cameron* to demand a retraction. Firth refused and Cameron challenged him to a duel on Macdonell's behalf. Firth seems to have had little use for the code so dear to the gentlemen of Upper Canada and faint-heartedly dismissed the challenge as contrary to law. Macdonell could give offence as easily as he took it. In April 1812 William Warren Baldwin* objected in court to his "wanton & ungentlemanly" expressions. Chief Justice Thomas Scott* reprimanded Macdonell but Baldwin remained dissatisfied. He demanded an apology and when Macdonell refused challenged him to a duel. They met on 3 April but Macdonell would not raise his pistol, having decided to admit his fault by receiving Baldwin's fire. Baldwin "took this as an acknowledgement of his error – we joined hands and thus this affair ended." Baldwin's initial objection seems to have been prompted by Macdonell's arrogance and success. Several weeks after the incident he wrote to his friend Firth describing Macdonell as "such a paragon of excellence that he leaves no virtue no commendable qualification for others to found pretensions on . . . the field, the cabinet and the Forum are all to be the scenes of his Renown – his honors rain not upon him, they come in tempests."

The mark of Macdonell's rapid ascent was his assumption of the duties of attorney general on 28 Sept. 1811. Firth had returned to England to defend his accounts and Boulton had been imprisoned by the French in Verdun. Gore was less than enthusiastic about the appointment and two days later urged Lord Liverpool, the Colonial secretary, "to lose no time in procuring a fit subject for that high and confidential situation" because "there is no Person at the Bar in this Province, whom I consider qualified for the office." Gore returned to England in October and Macdonell made a more favourable impression on the administrator of the province, Isaac BROCK. Macdonell's appointment was confirmed on 14 April 1812 and a warrant issued on 18 June. His nomination was a testament to Powell's influence: Brock, "who appeared to repose as much on my Judgement & Counsel as his predecessor . . . afforded Strong proof of this in naming . . . the youngest Practioner at the Bar merely on my recommendation." Powell, an able judge of men, saw in young Macdonell "a fair proportion of legal acquirement . . . Sound Discretion and highly honorable spirit." The appointment was the first for a native-trained barrister, thus suiting Powell's "object to retain the Honors of the profession amongst ourselves without risque of receiving from Europe Subjects often less suitable & no credit to the good wishes of the Minister, and to the good Service to the Colony."

The fourth and fifth parliaments of Upper Canada had witnessed the rise of opposition in the House of Assembly [see Joseph WILLCOCKS; Robert Thorpe*]; war with the United States seemed imminent. In this atmosphere of early 1812 Macdonell decided to contest the riding of Glengarry for the sixth parliament. His decision was probably influenced by his political friends, mindful of the need for a loyal assembly, and by the decision of his uncle Collachie, who had held one of the Glengarry seats since 1800, not to stand for a fourth term. Macdonells from various branches of the family had virtually monopolized the Glengarry seats since 1792 and in his election broadside John Macdonell reiterated the traditional social bonds of extended family and clan loyalty which characterized the Highland settlements of Glengarry, describing himself as "connected with many of you by the ties of blood, and possessing one common interest with you all." In May, on a leave of absence from official duties, he travelled to the Eastern District with John Beikie, the first clerk of the Executive Council, who had been encouraged by Father Alexander McDonell* to contest the riding of Stormont and Russell. Archibald McLean, one of the priest's political contacts in York and a friend of John

521

Macdonell

Macdonell, wrote of their candidacy, "At this time it is particularly to be desired that the House of Assembly should be composed of well informed Men who are *well affected* to the Government." Both were elected, Macdonell in conjunction with Alexander McMartin*. Whether Macdonell attended the first session of the sixth parliament called by Brock to pass emergency legislation occasioned by the war is unknown. After his death he was succeeded in the assembly by his uncle Collachie.

Macdonell's abilities were not apparently restricted to politics and law. Brock found him "so useful" as a soldier that on 15 April 1812 he appointed him provincial aide-de-camp with the rank of lieutenant-colonel in the militia. In his memoir of the war William Hamilton Merritt* was to comment on Brock's staff appointments as "most judicious." On 18 June the Americans declared war. Macdonell accompanied Brock to Sandwich (Windsor) in August and was at the council of war called on the 15th. Only Macdonell and Robert Nichol* approved Brock's plan to attack the American army commanded by William Hull at Detroit. That same day Macdonell and Major John Bachevoye Glegg, Brock's military aide-de-camp, were deputed by Brock "to conclude any arrangement that may lead to prevent the unnecessary effusion of blood." Within an hour they returned with the conditions of the American capitulation. On 30 August Brock wrote to Lord Liverpool that Macdonell had "afforded me the most important assistance" at Detroit, and he asked Liverpool to confirm his appointment as attorney general because of "the very important Services which I have derived . . . both in his Civil and Military Capacity."

After the victory at Detroit Brock and Macdonell returned to the Niagara frontier, alternating between their political duties at York and preparations for the next military crisis. When word reached Brock on 13 October that the Americans had attacked at Queenston he hastened there, followed by Macdonell and Glegg. After Brock met his death on the heights in an effort to retake a battery, a detachment of York militia, including Macdonell's closest friends, Cameron and McLean, and his student Robinson, joined with the 49th Foot in a new attack led by Macdonell. In Robinson's words, "McDonell was there mounted, and animating the men to charge." He was wounded in three or four places as well as trampled by his horse, and was aided to safety by McLean and Cameron. He died the next day after 20 hours of "excruciating suffering, his words and thoughts appeared ever occupied with lamentations for his lost friend [Brock]." Brock and Macdonell were buried on 16 October in what George Ridout* described as "the grandest & most solemn [burial] ever I witnessed." In 1824 and again in 1853 they were re-interred in the successive monuments to Brock.

Macdonell's gallant death, like that of Brock, became part of the lore of the War of 1812 which flourished in the 19th century. The monuments at Queenston enshrined their heroic moment. Yet the ultimate victory at Queenston belonged to Brock's successor Roger Hale Sheaffe*, and the charge led by Macdonell, although valiant, was perhaps foolhardy. Robinson observed the following day that "the attempt was unsuccessful and must have been dictated rather by a fond hope of regaining what had been lost by a desperate effort than by a conviction of it's practicability. . . ." Less than two weeks after the battle Glegg wrote that Macdonell had "appeared determined to accompany him [Brock] to the regions of eternal bliss." Possessed of a poetic sensibility and keen intelligence yet headstrong and violent, Macdonell was a man whose abilities marked him off from the generality of society. He was the epitome of a Highland gentleman. The bravery and impetuosity of his last act were entirely characteristic of such a man. His brief life was the stuff of legend. To Robinson's mind he was "as noble a youth as ever inherited his name, which is saying much."

Two stories have persisted about Macdonell: that at the time of his death he was engaged to Mary Boyles Powell, daughter of William Dummer; and that he had been converted to the Church of England from Roman Catholicism. There is no doubt that Macdonell was Mary Boyles's ardent suitor. Books of poetry he gave her, dated 1805, are still in the possession of the Macdonell family. It has often been assumed that the 500 guineas Macdonell left Mary in his will proved their relationship, if not their engagement, but this is not the case. On 22 Feb. 1812 Anne Powell wrote that her daughter Mary "assiduously avoids every mark of [Macdonell's] attention, as any other would court it. . . . Except herself no young Woman in the Province would reject a Man of 25; of Talents integrity & exemplary goodness & who at this early period is at the head of his profession." In 1815 Anne described the tragic effect of Macdonell's death: "Mary is changed beyond description . . . more to unceasing regret for her unkindness to one who merited and . . . possessed her best affection . . . the generous bequest of our ever lamented Friend was a proof of his regard, which she could not but feel a reproach for her capricious conduct." For Macdonell's religion the evidence is less conclusive. According to a still persistent family tradition Macdonell made the change at York, but the only supporting evidence is the payment of pew rent in St James' Church by Macdonell on at least one occasion for his uncle Collachie's family, with whom he had lived as a student; this does not seem significant since St James' was then the only church in York and Collachie's wife belonged to the Church of England. Collachie himself was a Catholic, as was Macdonell's brother Donald*,

MacDonell

and the first conversion within the family seems to have been that of one of Donald's sons to Presbyterianism.

In his will Macdonell left his two lots in York to his cousin James Macdonell (Collachie), another lot in Whitby Township to William Powell, grandson of William Dummer Powell, several pieces of property in Scarborough and Saltfleet townships to his niece Ann, the daughter of Miles Macdonell*, various personal bequests, and the remainder to his father.

CAROL WHITFIELD and ROBERT LOCHIEL FRASER III

AO, MS 4, Memoranda, 14 Oct. 1812; J. B. Robinson to Lord Seaton, 30 March 1854; address to the Law Society of Upper Canada, 1862; MS 88, W. W. Baldwin to William Firth, 22 April 1812; MS 496, J. B. Glegg to William Brock, 25 Oct. 1812; letter from "Archy" McLean, 15 Oct. 1812; J. B. Robinson to F. B. Tupper, 15 April 1846; MS 537, George Ridout to Samuel Ridout, 21 Oct. 1812; MU 1537, "Notice of the progress of William Dummer Powell, chief justice of the province of Upper Canada"; MU 2143, 1797, no.2, John Macdonell, "To the free and independent electors of the county of Glengary," 12 March 1812; RG 22, ser.155, will of John Macdonell; RG 53, ser.2-2, 1. Arch. of the Archdiocese of Toronto, Macdonell papers, ser.1 (added material), Archibald McLean to Alexander Macdonell, 20 May 1812. MTL, William Dummer Powell papers, A93: 287–90, 299–302, 347–60; B32: 84–85; York, U.C., minutes of town meetings and lists of inhabitants, 1797–1822. PAC, RG 5, A1: 3314–16, 5006–97, 5575–76, 5737–38, 5743–44, 5747–48, 6231–32, 6295–97; RG 8, I (C ser.), 683: 133; 688A: 183; 12031/2A: 47. PRO, CO 42/351: ff.113–15; 42/352: ff.66, 140–41, 144–45; 42/353: ff.117–19. St James' Cathedral (Toronto), Minute and record book, 1807–30, 5 Feb., 3 April 1810; 14 March, 30 Dec. 1811. Select British docs. of War of 1812 (Wood), 1: 461, 468, 471, 584–88, 614; 3, pt.II: 47, 554. York Gazette, 26 Dec. 1811, 25 March 1812.

Chadwick, Ontarian families. J. G. Harkness, Stormont, Dundas and Glengarry: a history, 1784–1945 (Oshawa, Ont., 1946). J. A. Macdonell, Sketches illustrating the early settlement and history of Glengarry in Canada, relating principally to the revolutionary war of 1775–83, the war of 1812–14 and the rebellion of 1837–8 . . . (Montreal, 1893). Riddell, Life of William Dummer Powell. W. M. Weekes, "The War of 1812: civil authority and martial law in Upper Canada," The defended border: Upper Canada and the War of 1812 . . . , ed. Morris Zaslow and W. B. Turner (Toronto, 1964), 191–204. Alexander Fraser, "Stirring career of heroic soldier: sketch of life of Lieutenant-Colonel John Macdonell," Daily Mail and Empire (Toronto), 12 Oct. 1912: 15, 25. W. L. Scott, "Glengarry's representatives in the Legislative Assembly of Upper Canada," CCHA Report, 6 (1938–39): 19–37; 7 (1939–40): 27–42.

MacDONELL OF SCOTHOUSE (Scotus), ALEXANDER (Alasdair MacDhòmhnuill), Roman Catholic priest and missionary; b. c. 1740 in the West Highlands, Scotland, probably in the traditional clan lands of the MacDonells of Glengarry, son of Angus

(Æneas) MacDonell of Scothouse and Catherine MacLeod of Bernera; d. 19 May 1803 in Lachine, Lower Canada.

Born of a Catholic father and a "heretic" mother, Alexander MacDonell entered the Jesuits' Scots College at Rome (Italy) on 23 Nov. 1759. He took his vows on 25 May 1760 and was ordained priest on 19 May 1767, having completed studies in philosophy and nearly finished theology and dogmatics. The school's register contains the notation that he was "of good disposition, with a fine mind and aptitude." He returned to the Highlands in 1767 and served in the Knoydart area of Glengarry. One source states that he was "fairly certainly domestic chaplain at Scotos." He aspired to the mitre in 1779 but the election resulted in a tie. Bishop George Hay sent the results to Rome with the recommendation that MacDonell's opponent be accepted, and Rome concurred.

The disintegration of the ancient clans which had already begun before the Jacobite defeat at the battle of Culloden in 1746 proceeded more rapidly thereafter. Few clans suffered more than the Glengarry Macdonells. In 1773 approximately 600 emigrated to New York and settled on the Mohawk valley estate of Sir William Johnson*. In the early 1780s MacDonell's Knoydart parishioners were evicted from their lands and in 1786 they prepared to emigrate, accompanied by their priest. MacDonell's letters on the eve of departure refer to mysterious failures of the past and to his own "public bankruptcy," but the Highland bishop, Alexander Macdonald, wrote that he was "of a respectable family . . . whose abilities both natural & acquired are equal to his Birth." The party, some 540 strong, sailed from Greenock and arrived in Quebec on 7 Sept. 1786. Although they had intended to settle at Cataraqui (Kingston, Ont.), the emigrants were persuaded instead to join their clansmen of the 1773 emigration now settled in the townships of Charlottenburg and Lancaster.

MacDonell was less than enthusiastic about continuous residence in a remote area and the Quebec hierarchy commenced a long-standing battle to force him to live with his kinsmen in the loyalist settlement of New Johnstown (Cornwall, Ont.). Finding life at the Séminaire de Saint-Sulpice in Montreal more attractive, he was reluctant to join his flock. On 1 Sept. 1787 the superior, Henri-François GRAVÉ de La Rive, declared to the coadjutor, Bishop Hubert*, his intention that MacDonell should set out for his mission because "he is rendering no service to the diocese" at the seminary. However the cantankerous MacDonell was not easily cowed and demanded a parish with a curate as promised by the government. Lieutenant Governor Henry Hope* intervened to deny the priest's claim that such a commitment had been made, and pressed the church to accommodate MacDonell until his own people could support him.

MacDonell

Later that month the church promised him £25 a year for four years once he had settled at New Johnstown. MacDonell was not pleased and complained to Bishop Louis-Philippe Mariauchau* d'Esgly, who agreed only to the allowance and a small pension for MacDonell's mother at the general hospital.

Meanwhile the Catholics of New Johnstown were without a resident priest and on 11 Dec. 1787 they petitioned Hubert. They wished "above all things to have a Priest settled amongst them" but, being fewer than a thousand and unable to provide adequate financial support, they suggested that the revenues of a vacant parish be appropriated for this purpose. Their choice of priest was MacDonell, "he being the only man that understandes our Country Language [Gaelic]." That same month Hubert granted their request, appointing MacDonell with a stipend of £25 a year for four years. Shortly after, MacDonell was in Quebec, infuriating the hierarchy with his "uncivil reproaches" and complaints to patrons in London about lack of proper support. Gravé de La Rive upbraided him for desiring "to be treated like a milord and abound in wealth." In turn MacDonell charged that "english priests [are treated] otherwise and more harshly than Canadian priests." When the church refused to advance him the first year's salary MacDonell brashly borrowed the sum, directing the lender to seek repayment from Gravé de La Rive, who did not refuse. In May 1788 MacDonell was in the New Johnstown settlement. That September he and the missionary to the Indians at St Regis (near Cornwall), Roderic MacDonell, wrote to their superior denying rumours of quarrelling between them over tithes.

In October 1789 James JONES, missionary at Halifax, N.S., and superior of missions, urged that MacDonell was the logical choice for the Highland and Acadian settlements on St John's (Prince Edward) Island, which had been without a priest since the death of James MacDonald* in 1785. Hubert raised the matter with his vicar general at Montreal, Gabriel-Jean Brassier*, who broached it with MacDonell. Shortly after MacDonell wrote to Hubert declaring that he had "not the least inclination . . . [because] Mr. MacDonald, my old comrade, died there in wretchedness . . . I could never . . . accept any place where it would be impossible for me to enjoy feasible access to my colleagues."

Hubert also brought up the subject of MacDonell's stipend. The priest admitted his failure "in the pastoral attention owed to my office" but added that "it has thus far always been impossible for me to settle amongst my Scots parishioners . . . [unless] I am given more abundant resources." He was also reluctant to take up permanent residence in the wilderness of New Johnstown because of the "advantages and amenities" of seminary life. Hubert replied on 18 Dec. 1789 that his allowance would be withheld unless MacDonell joined his flock. The letter had its desired effect and in 1790 MacDonell finally began to reside permanently in his parish.

In 1791 the old province of Quebec was divided into Upper and Lower Canada. For a brief period MacDonell's ministry, in what became in 1792 the county of Glengarry, seems to have been unmarked by conflict. He attended to his mission and on occasion sought dispensations from the bishop to legitimize the often complicated matrimonial entanglements of his parishioners, whose customs did not always accord with those of the church. But in 1794 Hubert was once again taking MacDonell to task for presuming to hold extraordinary powers which, in fact, had not been granted. Special minor powers were often accorded to missionaries to give them some authority to settle cases such as mixed marriages normally falling within the bishop's exclusive jurisdiction, and on 7 Nov. 1794 Hubert accorded such powers to MacDonell; they were renewed on 7 Sept. 1797. A more important issue was the reprimand by Edmund BURKE (1753–1820), superior of Upper Canadian missions, ordering MacDonell "to wear his ecclesiastical habit, to stay in Montreal only in the case of necessity, and to begin to have a church and presbytery built, and to reside there." Hubert considered MacDonell's conduct in these matters sufficiently negligent to abrogate the condition for supporting his mission set down on 18 Dec. 1789. In a note dated 7 Nov. 1794 MacDonell discharged the bishop "from every obligation in money matters towards me," adding acidly, "supposed to be my right."

In 1801 MacDonell was once again embroiled in conflict. Problems had arisen over his various attempts to ensure adequate support in the Glengarry settlement. Specifically, he had demanded increased supplies of wood, the assumption by the parish of incidental expenses incurred in clothing himself properly and administering the sacraments, and the provision of "a steady and educated servant." A servant was needed to assist him in serving mass, for "I often had to make the responses in the mass to my own self"; he could also help in attending the old, sick, and isolated. These tasks were particularly difficult because the mission was "vast in extent and split up by great barriers of forests and by Protestants," he wrote to Hubert's successor, Bishop DENAUT, in a letter of 20 April 1801. MacDonell complained that "there were no disagreements . . . while they [his parishioners] were so poor . . . now they have been a little better off, and . . . I am having more and more difficulties every year." He saw in their opposition not only "the intrigues of one demagogue or two" but the results of Upper Canada's religious heterogeneity. In 1793 he had incurred the wrath of John STUART, the Church of England clergyman at Kingston, for "assiduously . . .

endeavouring to gain Proselytes" and distributing a pamphlet, no longer extant, apparently called "A Catholic's reasons why he cannot become Protestant." MacDonell took umbrage at "the plainness of the Calvinist worship . . . the irreligion or even the paganism of the Americans . . . who have no minister of any religion called Christian . . . and the sordid greed so natural to vile hearts, [which] led them to refuse me everything." Burdened with debt and prey "to a mistaken hospitality," MacDonell had been forced to give a lien on his chalice, vestments, silverware, and books. Thoroughly plunged in all sorts of afflictions, MacDonell wrote, "I have spoiled my people and I have undermined myself." He urged Denaut to combine the Catholic usages of Scotland with the customs of Lower Canada and the Indian missions to provide a "solid and permanent footing" for religion. In May 1801 Denaut visited Glengarry in an attempt to deal with the long-simmering disputes, and he noted then that MacDonell had been sick for a month.

These quarrels within the mission came to a climax in 1802 after seven families labouring "under a load of oppression for some time past, and Debared from the Eclesiastical dues . . . like Hereticks," petitioned the bishop to provide another confessor. They resented MacDonell's extravagant demands for wood and opposed supporting a chapel which was both remote and privately owned. They claimed that most of the 170 families had resisted the priest but then acquiesced in the face of "the most Opprobious words and Slurs" and threats to withhold the sacraments. Only these seven families, castigated by MacDonell as "Cecedars," held out. Some had been without the sacraments for almost three years. On 27 Feb. 1802 MacDonell proposed to Denaut that all previous arrangements about finances be continued and in addition urged the bishop to set fixed tithes on produce. In return he was willing to turn over his chapel to the parish. On 25 April Denaut answered both priest and petitioners in a pastoral letter which two days later he ordered MacDonell to translate into Gaelic. Denaut made a bow to the legitimacy of the complaints by characterizing them as imprudent rather than ill-intentioned as MacDonell had done. However he urged piety and respect for the priest and was concerned to establish a church discipline conducive to good order. MacDonell would continue as priest and a parish would be formed under the invocation of the archangel Raphael – the name attached to the parish ever since. To support MacDonell, Denaut ordered the adoption of Lower Canadian customs with regard to tithes and casual dues. The organization of the church would be regulated by three churchwardens elected by 12 electors nominated by the parish; the priest would preside over the deliberations of the wardens. In addition the parish would begin immedi-

ately to keep proper records, to observe all ceremonies of the church practicable in a new parish, and to erect a proper church.

MacDonell did not live long under the new order. During the winter of 1803 he fell ill and was taken to Lachine where he died on 19 May. His estate, including 1,200 acres for which he had petitioned on 7 Aug. 1800, was administered by his relative Miles Macdonell*. Finding a successor seemed a problem but not for long. In October 1804 an illustrious and capable namesake, Alexander McDonell*, took over the parish. A man of much promise in his early years, Alexander MacDonell of Scothouse seems to have had his ambition frustrated in Scotland. Determined to enjoy a support equal to his status and reluctant to give up seminary life in Montreal for his wilderness mission, he proved a constant Highland thorn in the side of his French Canadian superiors throughout his ministry.

IN COLLABORATION

AAQ, 20 A, II: 161; III: 147; 210 A, I: ff.72, 78, 95, 111, 187; II: ff.46, 145, 166; IV: ff.78, 149, 198; V: f.221; VII: ff.3v, 4r; 1 CB, I: 42–43, 57, 71, 73; VI: 50; 9 CM, VI: 2, 156b; 90 CM, I: 11b; 312 CN, III: 3; 320 CN, I: 1; III: 3–8. AO, MS 444, C-1-2 (Histories of Glengarry); RG 22, ser.6-2, United Counties of Stormont, Dundas and Glengarry, administration of Alexander MacDonell. PAC, RG 1, L3, 331: M5/33. PRO, CO 42/18: ff.11–12; 42/82: ff.15–21. Scottish Catholic Arch. (Edinburgh), Blairs letters, 19 June 1786, Alexander MacDonell to George Hay; 3 Feb. 1788, MacDonell to John Geddes. "Clergy lists of the Highland District, 1732–1828," comp. F. Forbes and W. J. Anderson, *Innes Rev.: Scottish Catholic Hist. Studies* (Glasgow), 17 (1966): 148. *Mandements, lettres pastorales et circulaires des évêques de Québec*, Henri Têtu et C. O. Gagnon, édit. (18v. parus, Québec, 1887–), 2: 525–29. *Kingston before War of 1812* (Preston), 287–88. *Records of the Scots colleges at Douai, Rome, Madrid, Valladolid and Ratisbon* . . . (Aberdeen, Scot., 1906), 138–39. "Roman Catholic Church in Upper Canada," PAC *Report*, 1896, note C: 76–77. J. F. S. Gordon, *Ecclesiastical chronicle for Scotland* (4v., Glasgow, 1867), 4: 177, 263, 591. Alexander Mackenzie, *History of the Macdonalds and lords of the isles; with genealogies of the principal families of the name* (Inverness, Scot., 1881), 363.

McDOUGALL, DUNCAN, fur trader; b. probably in Scotland, son of Duncan McDougall, a lieutenant in the 84th Foot, and his wife, — Shaw; d. 25 Oct. 1818 at Fort Bas-de-la-Rivière (Fort Alexander, Man.).

Duncan McDougall's parents died when he was a boy, and it was presumably through his uncles Angus Shaw* and Alexander McDougall*, both partners in the North West Company, that he entered the firm as a clerk, probably in 1801. In the spring of 1803 Simon McTavish, the NWC's leading partner, decided to challenge the Hudson's Bay Company on its own

McDougall

ground, and Duncan McDougall took part in the scheme. A 150-ton schooner sailed to Hudson Bay to meet an overland party from Montreal. While John George McTavish* built Fort St Andrews on Charlton Island in James Bay that summer, McDougall set up a post on what became known as the Fort George River (Grande Rivière, Que.), helped by one John Hester, evidently a native descendant of James Hester, HBC officer at Fort Albany (Ont.) in the 1760s. McDougall's trade that winter was poor, however, owing to opposition from George Atkinson (Sneppy), a native-born HBC man with strong Indian ties.

In the summer of 1804 McDougall began building winter quarters at the mouth of Great Whale River (Grande Rivière de la Baleine, Que.), but he was apparently recalled to Charlton Island before the house was finished. He was probably in charge of the Nor'Westers on the Fort George River in 1804–5; certainly he was there in 1805–6 as a rival to HBC men Atkinson and Thomas Alder, who complained of the Nor'Westers' threats and violence. Neither company gained from the rivalry, and in mid 1806 the Nor'Westers burned their house and departed. In February 1807 HBC officer George Gladman noted that they had "entirely evacuated the Bay." McDougall left behind two children, George and Anne, whom Gladman listed in the Eastmain post register on 21 Aug. 1808 along with their mother, Nancy Hesther.

McDougall is next on record as one of the ex-Nor'Westers who founded Astoria (Oreg.) on the Columbia River. On 10 March 1810 John Jacob Astor* enlisted him, Alexander MacKay, and Donald McKenzie*, among others, as partners in the Pacific Fur Company and on 6 September McDougall sailed from New York City on the *Tonquin* (Capt. Jonathan THORN) as Astor's proxy, reaching the Columbia in late March 1811. He oversaw the building of Fort Astoria that spring, and the sending inland of several trading and exploring expeditions. On 15 July 1811 an NWC party led by David Thompson* arrived for a brief visit. Finding an American post in a region they had hoped to control, the Nor'Westers agreed not to encroach on its trade if the Astorians confined themselves to the west side of the Rocky Mountains.

The position of the Pacific Fur Company proved less secure, however, than the traders of either firm then realized. Only later did news reach McDougall of the loss of the *Tonquin* and its men, including partner Alexander MacKay, in a conflict with Indians in Clayoquot Sound (B.C.). On 18 Jan. 1812 the Astorians were cheered by the arrival of their colleagues Donald McKenzie and Robert McClellan (McLellan) after an arduous overland journey from St Louis (Mo.), and on 15 February another party of overlanders arrived. Prospects were discouraging,

nevertheless, because of supply shortages, illness, and other problems; and McClellan and Ramsay Crooks*, who had been recruited from Missouri River trading ventures, resigned their shares. Then, although Astor's ship, the *Beaver*, arrived safely at the post from New York in May 1812, her planned return visit later that year was aborted because of damage suffered during her travel to Russian posts in Alaska.

On 13 Jan. 1813 Donald McKenzie arrived at Astoria from inland, having learned from Nor'Wester John George McTavish that Great Britain and the United States were at war and that a British warship was being sent to the Columbia that spring to block the American trade. McTavish himself arrived at Astoria in September, confirming the news to his old James Bay associate and setting up a large encampment of Nor'Westers near the fort. McDougall, who expected an armed challenge to the American presence and who also, by some accounts, had improper sympathies with his former North West colleagues, commenced bargaining to sell Astoria. On 16 Oct. 1813 an agreement was signed that gave possession of the fort to the Nor'Westers; and on 30 November the *Racoon* arrived to support British claims. The post was renamed Fort George, and on Christmas Day McDougall accepted his own reinstatement in the NWC.

In the mean time, he had cemented trade ties with the local Chinook chief Comcomly by marrying his daughter on 20 July 1813. Alexander HENRY recorded that the transactions associated with the marriage were spread over a considerable period; on 26 April 1814 McDougall paid Comcomly the last of a bride-price of "15 guns and 15 blankets, besides a great deal of other property, as the total cost of this precious lady."

McDougall became a partner in the NWC in 1816. He remained at Fort George until 16 April 1817, when he left to journey east with Angus Bethune*, Ross Cox*, and others. Upon reaching Fort William (Thunder Bay, Ont.), he agreed to take charge of the Winnipeg River district and travelled there in August. He "died a miserable death," cause unrecorded, at Bas-de-la-Rivière on 25 Oct. 1818.

McDougall's will of 28 March 1817 offered a spirited defence of the most questionable phase of his career, his conduct at Fort Astoria in 1813. Leaving all his papers to Alexander McDougall, he affirmed they would show "that I did every thing in my power to do the utmost justice to the trust and confidence reposed in me by John Jacob Astor . . . agreeable to, and in conformity with, the Resolves of the Company passed and signed by my late Associates and myself," and that they would demonstrate "how much and how unjustly my character and reputation has suffered and been injured by the malicious and ungenerous conduct of some of my late Associates in the late Pacific Fur Company." Other legatees included two sisters, his maternal aunt and her daughters, and "my reputed or rather adopted son George McDougall." A codicil of 15 Oct. 1818 added, "Should there be any means of aiding my little Daughter in James Bay I should feel happy."

JENNIFER S. H. BROWN

[The author wishes to thank Elaine A. Mitchell for information leading to the use of McDougall's will. J.S.H.B.]

ANQ-M, CM1, Duncan McDougall, 26 Sept. 1820; CN1-29, 29 May 1801. AO, MU 842, George Nelson, Tête au Brochet diary, 16 Dec. 1818. PAM, HBCA, A.1/43: f.156; B.59/z/1: 92. PCA, St Gabriel Street Church (Montreal), Reg. of baptisms, marriages, and burials, 28 Oct. 1812 (mfm. at AO). *Les bourgeois de la Compagnie du Nord-Ouest* (Masson), vol.1. Gabriel Franchère, *Journal of a voyage on the north west coast of North America during the years 1811, 1812, 1813 and 1814*, trans. W. T. Lamb, ed. and intro. W. K. Lamb (Toronto, 1969). Washington Irving, *Astoria, or anecdotes of an enterprise beyond the Rocky Mountains*, ed. E. W. Todd (new ed., Norman, Okla., 1964). *New light on early hist. of greater northwest* (Coues), vol.2. *Northern Quebec and Labrador journals and correspondence, 1819–35*, ed. K. G. Davies and A. M. Johnson (London, 1963). Ross Cox, *Adventures on the Columbia River, including the narrative of a residence of six years on the western side of the Rocky Mountains, among various tribes of Indians hitherto unknown: together with a journey across the American continent* (New York, 1832). E. A. Mitchell, *Fort Timiskaming and the fur trade* (Toronto and Buffalo, N.Y., 1977). J. U. Terrell, *Furs by Astor* (New York, 1963).

McGILL, JAMES, merchant, office holder, politician, landowner, militia officer, and philanthropist; b. 6 Oct. 1744 in Glasgow, Scotland, second child and eldest son of James McGill and Margaret Gibson; d. 19 Dec. 1813 in Montreal, Lower Canada.

The McGill family, probably originating in Ayrshire, had been resident in Glasgow for two generations when James was born. They were metal workers and, from 1715, members of the hammermen's guild and burgesses of the city. Their fortune rose with Glasgow's when, following the Union of 1709, the English colonies were opened to Scottish commerce. In 1756, on James's matriculation into the University of Glasgow, his father was described as "mercator." The McGills had risen from tradesmen to traders.

When and in what circumstances James McGill emigrated is not known. In 1766 he was in Montreal en route to the *pays d'en haut* as "the deputy" of the Quebec merchant William GRANT (1744–1805). McGill probably wintered on Baie des Puants (Green Bay, Lake Michigan), for in June and July 1767 he was at Michilimackinac (Mackinaw City, Mich.) supervising the dispatch of canoes. He was at Montreal in 1770, but in 1771–72 he was in the field near Fond-du-Lac (Wis.). Like other traders working the southern hinterland of the Great Lakes, McGill

conducted simultaneously a number of enterprises with different partners. As early as 1767 he began trading on his own account, obtaining licences for two canoes and cargoes valued at £400. He also posted bonds totalling £2,400 for four traders, one of whom was Charles-Jean-Baptiste CHABOILLEZ, a veteran in the southwest trade. By 1769 McGill had begun his long association with Isaac TODD; about 1770 he also joined with his brother John McGill. John ASKIN of Michilimackinac, and later of Detroit (Mich.), was McGill's agent, or "forwarder," rather than a partner.

In "constant residence" at Montreal from 1775, McGill adapted his family's urban tradition to Canada. His suppliers were Brickwood, Pattle and Company of London, whose goods he distributed among traders operating in the Indian country. As a minor member of the Anglo-American merchant community, McGill may have felt it expedient to adopt its political views; once in 1770 and twice in 1774 he signed petitions praying for "a general assembly." Possibly the omission of his name from a memorial against the Quebec Act suggests an improving status that enabled him to act independently. The occupation of Montreal by the troops of the Continental Congress from November 1775 to May 1776 made him conspicuous; he had been one of the group that had negotiated the city's surrender [see Richard Montgomery*]. He had no truck with rebels, however, and his house became a loyalist rendezvous. His steadfastness cost him 14 puncheons of rum when his cellars were ransacked. "Unhappy people" was his characterization of the despoilers; "many of our Mont^rl Rebels," he added, "[have run] off with the others."

On 2 Dec. 1776 McGill's marriage with the widow Charlotte Trottier Desrivières, *née* Guillimin, was solemnized by the Reverend David Chabrand* Delisle, Montreal's first regularly appointed Anglican pastor. McGill acquired a family, the two surviving sons of Charlotte's first marriage. The elder, François-Amable*, would become McGill's partner and principal heir. The younger, Thomas-Hippolyte, would be provided with a commission in the Royal Americans (60th Foot) and his son, James McGill Trottier Desrivières, would be the object of much solicitude at the end of McGill's life. McGill was fond of children, and he appears to have been drawn especially to the one that bore his name. The years 1775–76 were decisive in McGill's career; marriage brought him into Mrs McGill's wide family circle and his commercial position was thus stabilized. His political position was unexceptional. Shortly after his marriage McGill secured the highly desirable Bécancour house between Rue Notre-Dame and Rue Saint-Paul near the Château Ramezay. It had been the property of Thomas Walker*, one of the chiefs of "our Mont^rl Rebels."

McGill

In 1776 McGill received his first public appointment, as justice of the peace. It was renewed periodically, and he was thus brought into the administration of Montreal, a function of the justices until 1833. In all, McGill held ten appointments, of which four were of significance: he served in 1788 and 1789 as a member of a commission of inquiry into Lord Amherst*'s claims to the Jesuit estates (educational endowments being considered by many as an alternative use for proceeds from these lands); participated in 1798 with Thomas Blackwood* in the French royalist colony at Windham, Upper Canada; supervised from 1802 the demolition of the old walls of Montreal and the elaboration of plans (entirely abortive) for urban renewal and beautification; and from 1800 oversaw the Lachine turnpike, the first modern road west of the city.

McGill's business also prospered. In 1775, in association with Todd, Benjamin* and JOSEPH Frobisher, and Maurice-Régis BLONDEAU, he sent 12 canoes to Grand Portage (near Grand Portage, Minn.), a shipment that "appears to mark the beginning of large-scale trade to the Northwest . . . and of the Northwest Company," according to the historian Harold Adams Innis*. Three years later McGill himself was at Grand Portage, probably the farthest point west he reached. With the adoption of the 16-share organization in 1779, McGill and Todd were among the largest shareholders in the NWC. Yet shortly afterwards the McGill group dropped out. Nevertheless, McGill himself continued to post bonds for traders going to the northwest. Todd and McGill retired to "the Ohio Country," the arc lying south of the Great Lakes. McGill noted about 1785 that this region supplied £100,000 of the total of £180,000 to be derived from the trade in all the territory between "the mouth of the Ohio . . . [and] Lake Arabaska [Athabasca]."

The warehouses on Rue Saint-Paul were the centre of the McGill empire. Furs from Detroit and Michilimackinac were exported to Great Britain. Some went by devious ways to New York and John Jacob Astor*. The suppliers of furs, the Indians, were carefully cultivated, silver jewellery being bought for them in Montreal. Imported from the West Indies were tobacco, sugar, molasses, and rum; from Britain, metalware, textiles, and powder and shot. Transportation presented problems; the continuation after 1783 of a ban on private shipping on the Great Lakes, begun as a war measure in 1777, provoked McGill to protest. Rudimentary banking was carried on: notes were discounted, foreign currency exchanged, and the pensions of loyalists and French émigrés safeguarded. McGill's good personal relations with Governor Lord Dorchester [Guy CARLETON] were exploited to corner "the flower" supply market of the Great Lakes military posts.

In 1783 the Treaty of Paris, which ceded the Ohio country to the United States, caused McGill and his associates great vexation. In London, Todd, along with other merchants, protested. McGill himself blew hot and cold. In 1785 he threatened to keep his goods at Montreal if "there was the slightest possibility" of a British withdrawal from the ceded territory. At the same time he boasted, "I am clearly of opinion that it must be a very long time before they [the Americans] can even venture on the smallest part of our trade."

In the threatened area, Detroit was of prime importance. Its geographical advantages were patent and, from 1780 or 1781, it was the home of John Askin, one of McGill's oldest associates. Askin's waning success in the fur trade, along with his vast speculation in land, put him heavily in debt to the McGill partners. In brief, they accepted land in lieu of their trade claims and found themselves in legal difficulties after 1796 when Detroit was transferred to the United States. In compensation McGill acquired land on the Canadian side of the Detroit River, along Lake St Clair, and elsewhere in Essex and Kent counties, Upper Canada.

The Detroit land deals, effected between 1797 and 1805, signalled McGill's entry into systematic land speculation. Earlier acquisitions had been made haphazardly: a farm at L'Assomption, Lower Canada, a water lot at William Henry (Sorel), Montreal properties, a distillery, and probably Burnside, his summer home at the foot of Mount Royal. From 1801 land was secured methodically; that year he acquired 10,000 acres in Hunterstown Township and 32,400 acres in Stanbridge Township, and it was probably in this period that land was secured in Upper Canada near Kingston and York (Toronto).

McGill's public career approached its apex in the late 1780s. In 1787 he was described as "Militia Mad," the euphoria being produced by the attainment of his majority; in 1810 he would become the colonel commandant of the 1st Battalion of Montreal's militia. He began to figure in petitions deploring "the anarchy and confusion" in the administration of civil law. In 1794 he denounced the disturbances in Montreal that attended the embodying of the militia. Two years earlier he had been returned for the riding of Montreal West to the House of Assembly established by the Constitutional Act. His candidacy for the speakership, the highest honour in the assembly, was a tribute to his competence in French and English. In 1792 as well he was appointed to the Executive Council. McGill did not stand for re-election to the assembly in 1796, but he was returned for Montreal West in 1800, and then for Montreal East in 1804.

Around the turn of the century new men entered McGill's business circle: François-Amable Trottier Desrivières probably in 1792 and Thomas Blackwood eight years later. The newcomers may have prompted new ventures. From 1792 to about 1794 Todd, McGill

McGill

and Company was a co-partner in the reorganized NWC. In 1796 McGill began to export squared timber. He and Todd were among the planners of a bank in 1807, and McGill himself was active in the Lachine turnpike project. Nor were the old trades neglected. In 1808 McGill joined in the protest against United States interference with the fur traders' shipping at Niagara (near Youngstown), N.Y.

McGill's business career epitomized much of the economic development of Lower Canada in the late 18th century. His stake in the fur trade reached its peak in 1782 when he made the largest investment in the colony, some £26,000. By 1790 his investment had fallen to £10,000, the fourth most important that year. Lord Selkirk [DOUGLAS] noted in 1803 that McGill had retired from the fur trade but remained in "the ordinary Colonial trade." The property on Rue Saint-Paul was sold five years later, and in 1810 the affairs of James and Andrew McGill and Company, which had succeeded Todd, McGill and Company in 1797, were wound up. New interests – "the ordinary Colonial trade," the manipulation of land, and other activities – had replaced the fur trade. By such means, in a changing economic environment, did James McGill and his fellow merchants assure the metropolitan supremacy of Montreal.

Perhaps warned by deaths in his family circle, of his brothers John and Andrew in 1797 and 1805 and of his sister Isobel, probably in 1808, McGill made his will in January 1811. The major assets were real estate in Lower and Upper Canada and investments in the United Kingdom, the latter not specified as to character or amount. There were also extensive mortgage holdings. The chief beneficiaries were Mrs McGill, her son François-Amable, and James McGill Trottier Desrivières. Old friends were remembered (even the tiresome Askin), the Montreal poor, the Hôtel-Dieu, the Sisters of Charity of the Hôpital Général (Grey Nuns), the Hôpital Général of Quebec, and two Glasgow charities. Alexander Henry* grumbled that McGill's fortune went "to strangers . . . [and] his wife's children, Mrs McGill is left comfortable, but young Desrivières will have £60,000."

McGill also left £10,000 and the Burnside estate of some 46 acres towards the endowment of a college or a university, specifying that the college or one of the colleges of the university should bear the name McGill. The Royal Institution for the Advancement of Learning, the agency of the provincial government responsible for schools, was required to open the college or university on the Burnside site before the bequest became operative. It was not till 1821 that a charter was obtained and not till 1829 that teaching began in what is now McGill University. McGill was not a theorist about education; his concern was with "endowments etc," in the Reverend John Strachan*'s phrase. Strachan certainly encouraged the benefaction. He had joined the McGill circle in 1808 when he

married Ann Wood, Andrew McGill's widow. The actual form of the bequest was doubtless drawn from McGill's own experience of some 25 years before as a commissioner in the inquiry into the Jesuit estates.

The last 18 months of McGill's life were clouded by the War of 1812. In February 1812 he warned Governor PREVOST of the approaching crisis, probably on the authority of Astor, and on 24 June he communicated the actual declaration. McGill saw no active service but, since he was senior militia officer in Montreal, with the rank of colonel, his staff duties were heavy. He was greatly concerned with the disturbances that attended some of the early militia levies. His civil responsibilities also increased: in 1813 he became temporary president of the Executive Council. He was recommended for membership in the Legislative Council, but death intervened before the appointment became effective.

McGill's death was sudden; "he had no Idea of going off half an Hour [before] he died" on 19 Dec. 1813. Two days later he was buried in the Protestant cemetery (Dufferin Square), but in 1875 the body was reinterred on the university campus. Contemporaries "reckoned [him] the richest man in Mont^l & . . . [one who could] command more cash than anyone"; they savoured "the elevated stations" he attained and admired "the sonorous voice" as he rendered voyageurs' songs at the convivial gatherings of the Beaver Club. Portraiture presents a less awesome figure. A miniature of about 1790 shows McGill in his prime. The painting by Louis Dulongpré* of only some 15 years later shows the onset of ill health.

James McGill was an 18th-century man. His economics were those of the pre-Adam Smith world. His partnerships, the most complex form of business organization that he knew, were with relatives or close friends. He shared the Enlightenment's tolerance of confessional divergences; born into the Church of Scotland, he died an Anglican, and half-way through life married a Roman Catholic. He contributed to the support of both the Presbyterian and the Anglican churches at Montreal. In 1805 he became a member of the building committee of Christ Church, which was still in the process of erection when McGill died in 1813. His support of Roman Catholic causes has been noted in connection with his will. McGill felt a strong attachment to place. He left Montreal only on business – there were no sentimental journeys to Scotland. To Montreal his chief benefaction was a university, for which, with characteristic practicality, he gave land and the nucleus of an endowment.

J. I. COOPER

[No complete biography of James McGill exists. The following studies, arranged chronologically, provide the fullest information in print. John William Dawson*, "James McGill and the origin of his university," *New Dominion Monthly* (Montreal), March 1870: 37–40, is an amplification

McGillivray

of "James McGill and the University of McGill College, Montreal," which Dawson published in *Barnard's American Journal of Education* (Hartford, Conn.), 13 (1863): 188–99. In the 1870 article Dawson incorporated the reminiscences of William Henderson, who, as a young man, had met McGill. The article was reprinted in Dawson's *Educational lectures, addresses, &c.* . . . ([Montreal, 1855–95]). Cyrus Macmillan, *McGill and its story, 1821–1891* (London and Toronto, 1921), contains a brief biographical sketch. Francis-Joseph Audet* and Édouard Fabre Surveyer included a biography of McGill in their "Les députés au premier Parl. du Bas-Canada," which appeared serially in *La Presse* (Montréal) in the late 1920s; the notice on McGill was published on 17 Dec. 1927: 66–67. The biographies were republished by Audet, with valuable notes by Gérard Malchelosse, as *Les députés de Montréal*. In 1930 Maysie Steel MacSporran submitted her MA thesis, "James McGill: a critical biographical study," to McGill Univ. The research is very complete, drawing on the collections of the PAC and on the DPL, Burton Hist. Coll. Full use has been made of this thesis. Undated, but probably from the 1960s, is a typescript in the McGill Univ. Arch. by J. M. McGill, "The early history of James McGill, university founder," based on Glasgow court and municipal records. For what may be called the Scots phase of McGill's career, J. M. McGill leaves little to add. Finally, Stanley Brice Frost has consecrated an interesting first chapter to McGill in volume one of his *McGill University: for the advancement of learning* . . . (1v. to date, Montreal, 1980–). J.I.C.]

ANQ-M, CE1-63, 2 Dec. 1776, 21 Dec. 1813; CN1-363, 2 déc. 1776. ANQ-Q, CN1-16, 27 janv., 17 févr. 1809; CN1-26, 18 déc. 1801; CN1-145, 15 Sept. 1801; CN1-262, 2 oct. 1801. McCord Museum, Beaver Club minute-book. McGill Univ. Arch., James and Andrew McGill journal, 1798–1813; James McGill will. McGill Univ. Libraries, Dept. of Rare Books and Special Coll., MS coll., CH141.S11. NYPL, William Edgar papers (copies at PAC). PAC, MG 11, [CO 42] Q, 30: 202–12; 71: 221; 85: 321–23; 119: 3–5; RG 1, E1, 29–35; RG 4, B28, 115. UTL-TF, MS coll. 31, box 24, notes on the Grant family. "L'Association loyale de Montréal," ANQ *Rapport*, 1948–49: 257–73. Bas-Canada, chambre d'Assemblée, *Journaux*, 1792–96; 1805–8. *Doc. relatifs à l'hist. constitutionnelle, 1759–1791* (Shortt et Doughty; 1921), 1: 488–89, 2: 904. *Docs. relating to NWC* (Wallace). Douglas, *Lord Selkirk's diary* (White). "Explorations au Nord-Ouest," *PAC Rapport*, 1890: 54–57. [Joseph Hadfield], *An Englishman in America, 1785, being the diary of Joseph Hadfield*, ed. D. S. Robertson (Toronto, 1933), 112. *Invasion du Canada* (Verreau), 81–82, 97. *John Askin papers* (Quaife). [John Strachan], *The John Strachan letter book, 1812–1834*, ed. G. W. Spragge (Toronto, 1946). *Montreal Gazette*, 1785–1813. *Quebec Gazette*, 1777–1813. É.-Z. Massicotte, "Inventaire des cartes et plans de l'île et de la ville de Montréal," *BRH*, 20 (1914): 65–66; "Répertoire des engagements pour l'Ouest," ANQ *Rapport*, 1942–46. *The matriculation albums of the University of Glasgow from 1728 to 1858*, comp. W. I. Addison (Glasgow, 1913). *Quebec almanac*, 1793–1814. *Third statistical account of Scotland: Glasgow*, ed. James Cunniston and J. B. Gilfillan (Glasgow, 1958).

L.-P. Audet, *Histoire de l'enseignement au Québec* (2v., Montréal et Toronto, 1971). R.-G. Boulianne, "The Royal Institution for the Advancement of Learning: the correspond-

ence, 1820–1829, a historical and analytical study" (PHD thesis, McGill Univ., 1970). Caron, *La colonisation de la prov. de Québec*, 2. I. C. C. Graham, *Colonists from Scotland: emigration to North America, 1707–1783* (Ithaca, N.Y., 1956; repr. Port Washington, N.Y., and London, 1972). Henry Hamilton, *An economic history of Scotland in the eighteenth century* (Oxford, Eng., 1963). L. P. Kellogg, *The British régime in Wisconsin and the northwest* (Madison, Wis., 1935). Miquelon, "Baby family," 188–89, 191–92, 194–95. Ouellet, *Hist. économique*. K. W. Porter, *John Jacob Astor, business man* (2v., Cambridge, Mass., 1931; repr., New York, 1966). Rumilly, *La Compagnie du Nord-Ouest*. J. H. Smith, *Our struggle for the fourteenth colony: Canada and the American revolution* (2v., New York, 1907). L. J. Burpee, "The Beaver Club," CHA *Report*, 1924: 73. Ivanhoë Caron, "The colonization of Canada under the British dominion, 1800–1815," Que., Bureau of Statistics, *Statistical year-book* (Quebec), 7 (1920): 461–535. Julian Gwyn, "The impact of British military spending on the colonial American money markets, 1760–1783," CHA *Hist. papers*, 1980: 91–92. M. G. Jackson, "The beginning of British trade at Michilimakinac," *Minn. Hist.* (St Paul), 11 (1930): 259–64. Charles Lart, "Fur trade returns, 1767," *CHR*, 3 (1922): 351–58. W. D. Lighthall, "The newly-discovered 'James and Andrew McGill journal, 1797,'" *RSC Trans.*, 3rd ser., 29 (1935), sect.II: 43–50. É.-Z. Massicotte, "Quelques maisons du vieux Montréal," *Cahiers des Dix*, 10 (1945): 239–41. T. R. Millman, "David Chabrand Delisle, 1730–1794," *Montreal Churchman* (Granby, Que.), 29 (1941), no.2: 14–16. Ouellet, "Dualité économique et changement technologique," *SH*, 9: 286, 291, 293. Ramsay Traquair, "Montreal and the Indian silver trade," *CHR*, 19 (1938): 1–8.

McGILLIVRAY, DUNCAN, fur trader and author; b. in Inverness-shire, Scotland, probably in the early 1770s, second son of Donald McGillivray and Anne McTavish, sister of Simon McTAVISH; d. 9 April 1808 in Montreal, Lower Canada.

Duncan McGillivray was one of several kinsmen of Simon McTavish whose education and careers benefited from the patronage of this Montreal fur-trade merchant. By the early 1790s McGillivray had followed his brother William* from Scotland to Montreal and into the North West Company. His career in the fur trade is best known for the years 1794–95, during which time he kept a journal at Fort George (near Lindbergh, Alta) on the North Saskatchewan River. This document provides vivid descriptions of life and travel in the northwest, of the plains Indians who, finding most of their essential needs met by the buffalo, would not "work beaver" except to obtain rum, and of the Canadian voyageurs, some of whom mutinied at the Rainy Lake (Ont.) post in the summer of 1794 while accompanying McGillivray inland.

McGillivray, a clerk at Fort George and one of 110 men serving under NWC partner Angus Shaw*, recorded the vigorous competition between the

Nor'Westers and Hudson's Bay Company officer William Tomison* and his 35 men at nearby Buckingham House. The rivals cooperated intermittently, as, for example, in putting out a fire at the HBC post on 22 March 1795. But in trade the Nor'Westers carried the day with their manpower and better stocks, and made a good profit from the "7 different nations" of Indians who arrived in the spring of 1795. The following season the NWC founded the original Fort Augustus (Fort Saskatchewan, Alta) farther upriver, and Tomison met their challenge by building Edmonton House close by. Although in November still other rivals came representing the Montreal partnership of David and Peter Grant, the main competition continued to be that between the two more established companies.

HBC records show shifts in personal relations between the rivals. Tomison and the Nor'Westers could not get along; but when in 1796 Tomison left Fort Edmonton for a year's furlough, his fellow officer George Sutherland* established a cordial relationship with Shaw and McGillivray. In November 1797, when Tomison returned, McGillivray wrote to him urging that since they would probably be neighbours for some years, they should reach "a proper understanding" and "cast away old prejudices & begin a new Score . . . for the good of Both parties And the Interests of the Country in general." New troubles developed, however, and the HBC trade suffered. On 14 May 1798 Tomison accused McGillivray of stealing furs from the Bungee (Ojibwa) Indians so that they could not pay their HBC debts, but his stern protests against these seizures of "the honourable Hudsons Bay Company's property" apparently were ignored.

In 1799 McGillivray visited Montreal. While there he became a partner in McTavish, Frobisher and Company, which had a controlling interest in the NWC, and was elected to membership in the Beaver Club. His subsequent inland activities are known only in part. In late October 1800 he was at Rocky Mountain House (Alta), having travelled up the Saskatchewan in the company of HBC man James Bird* who was en route to Acton House. After a short trip that November with David Thompson* to "the great Camps of Peagan [Peigan] Indians" near present-day High River, McGillivray undertook another trip deeper into the mountains in search of new beaver areas reported by Indians, but he was forced back by deep snow and rugged terrain. In a letter of 19 Feb. 1801 Bird noted: "Messrs. McGilvery & Thompson are going the ensuing summer . . . to examine the country west of the mountain as far as the borders of the South sea & ascertain if possible whether . . . an advantageous trade can be carried on with those parts or not either from hence or China." But severe attacks of rheumatism during the late winter and spring kept McGillivray from joining a springtime exploring journey led by Thompson and James Hughes. Whether McGillivray later that season "conducted in person the exploration planned," as Arthur Silver Morton* believed, is much disputed.

McGillivray left the interior in 1802 to work more closely with the Montreal headquarters of McTavish, Frobisher and Company (McTavish, McGillivrays and Company from 1806). For the next few years he travelled annually from Montreal to Kaministiquia (Thunder Bay, Ont.) to represent the firm at summer meetings with the NWC winterers, promoting the continued westward explorations of David Thompson and Simon Fraser* and playing an important role in drawing up specific arrangements for inland operations.

In 1803–4 McGillivray was also engaged in bids to negotiate an alliance between the NWC and the HBC, in order to counteract moves in the same direction by Edward Ellice*, London agent of the New North West (XY) Company. Since his Saskatchewan experiences McGillivray had been aware of the advantages of cooperation with the HBC; now the time seemed right for some formal agreement. In 1803 an NWC outpost was founded on Charlton Island in James Bay, strengthening the Nor'Westers' hand as the two Montreal firms each sought "to obtain a facility from the H.B. Co. to be used to the prejudice of the other." The death of Simon McTavish in 1804 was followed by the union of the North West and New North West companies and by a new series of negotiations that lasted from January 1805 until February 1806, as McGillivray bargained for the NWC to be allowed the use of routes by sea into Hudson Bay and by inland waterways from York Factory (Man.) to the Red River; he also sought to rent land at York Factory for a depot. Discussions were broken off when the HBC realized that the Nor'Westers also planned to ship furs from the bay to other than British markets, a privilege that its own charter seemed not to allow and that it did not wish to grant to others.

In the last few months of his life McGillivray composed "Some account of the trade carried on by the North West Company." This essay urged British governmental support for NWC enterprise beyond the Rocky Mountains. Success in ventures in the far west and on the ocean beyond would mean "a new field will be open for the consumption of British manufactured goods; and a vast country and population made dependant on the British Empire." McGillivray also reacted against campaigns by William Wilberforce, the British parliamentarian most influential in the abolition of the slave trade, and Lord Selkirk [DOUGLAS] to prohibit liquor sales to the Indians, supporting his argument against government intervention with a statement favouring a monopoly: if trade were "confined to a single company," that company

McGowan

would itself be led "by every motive which self-interest can supply" to reduce drunkenness among the natives.

McGillivray died in Montreal on 9 April 1808 and was buried in the family vault of Simon McTavish. He left no record of marriage, but he had one and probably two children with an Indian woman. Magdalene, born in 1801, was baptized in Montreal on 7 Oct. 1804 in her parents' absence with William McGillivray as witness. Duncan was also probably the father of company clerk William McGillivray, described by Governor George Simpson* in 1832 as a "half breed of the Cree Nation." William entered the NWC in 1814 and later served in the Athabasca country and the New Caledonia region (B.C.). He married a daughter of HBC chief factor Alexander Stewart (Stuart) and was drowned on 31 Jan. 1832 in the Fraser River.

SYLVIA VAN KIRK and JENNIFER S. H. BROWN

[The library of the Royal Commonwealth Soc. (London) holds the MSS of Duncan McGillivray's journal and of his essay "Some account of the trade carried on by the North West Company." Photocopies of both are in the PAC (MG 19, A10 and B4). A. S. Morton's edition of *The journal of Duncan M'Gillivray of the North West Company at Fort George on the Saskatchewan, 1794–5* (Toronto, 1929) is based on the PAC photocopy. The manuscript of the essay contains William McGillivray's annotations, including the new title "Sketch of the fur trade, 1809." The material was reworked and published anonymously under the title *On the origin and progress of the North-West Company of Canada . . .* (London, 1811), most likely by John Henry*, who is often cited as the author of the pamphlet. The essay as annotated by William McGillivray was published under its orignal title in PAC *Report*, 1928: 56–73. S.V.K. and J.S.H.B.]

ANQ-M, CE1-63, 8 Dec. 1801, 7 Dec. 1804. *Les bourgeois de la Compagnie du Nord-Ouest* (Masson), vol.2. *Rules and regulations of the Beaver Club* (Montreal, 1819). *Saskatchewan journals and correspondence: Edmonton House, 1795–1800; Chesterfield House, 1800–1802*, ed. A. M. Johnson (London, 1967). [David Thompson], "David Thompson and the Rocky Mountains," ed. J. B. Tyrrell, *CHR*, 15 (1934): 39–45; "David Thompson's account of his first attempt to cross the Rockies," ed. F. W. Howay, *Queen's Quarterly* (Kingston, Ont.), 40 (1933): 333–56; *David Thompson's narrative, 1784–1812*, ed. R. G. Glover (new ed., Toronto, 1962). M. W. Campbell, *NWC* (1957). Innis, *Fur trade in Canada* (1970). Morton, *Hist. of Canadian west* (1973). K. G. Davies, "From competition to union," *Minn. Hist.* (St Paul), 40 (1966–67): 166–77. A. S. Morton, "Did Duncan McGillivray and David Thompson cross the Rockies in 1801?" *CHR*, 18 (1937): 156–62; "The North West Company's Columbian enterprise and David Thompson," *CHR*, 17 (1936): 266–88. J. B. Tyrrell, "David Thompson and the Columbia River," *CHR*, 18 (1937): 12–27; "Duncan McGillivray's movements in 1801," *CHR*, 20 (1939): 39–40.

McGOWAN. *See* MAGOWAN

MACHIQUAWISH. *See* MADJECKEWISS

MacKAY, ALEXANDER (he also signed **McKay**), fur trader and explorer; b. *c.* 1770, probably in the Mohawk valley of New York, son of Donald McKay and Elspeth (Elspy) Kennedy; m. *à la façon du nord* Marguerite Waddens, daughter of Jean-Étienne Waddens*, and they had one son, Thomas McKay, and three daughters; another woman was likely the mother of his son Alexander Ross McKay; d. *c.* 15 June 1811 in Clayoquot Sound (B.C.).

Alexander MacKay participated in two momentous events in the history of North American exploration and westward expansion. As lieutenant in Alexander MACKENZIE's expedition to the Pacific Ocean on behalf of the North West Company in 1793, he was among the first Europeans to cross the breadth of the continent. In 1811, as a Pacific Fur Company partner, he became one of the founders of Astoria (Oreg.), the first English-speaking settlement on the Pacific coast.

MacKay's father, Donald, fought at Quebec in 1759 as a sergeant in the 78th Foot, a Highland regiment whose members contributed many sons to the NWC. Having settled in the Mohawk valley after the Seven Years' War, the elder McKay brought his family north as United Empire Loyalists. Although they eventually made their home in the Glengarry region of Upper Canada, at Martintown, they first lived near Trois-Rivières, Lower Canada. By November 1791 three sons, Donald, William*, and Alexander, were in the west as NWC clerks.

How much earlier Alexander MacKay had joined the NWC is not known; nor is the date of his first posting to Fort Chipewyan (Alta). He must have been stationed there in 1792, since on 10 Jan. 1793 Alexander Mackenzie asked that MacKay be transferred to Fort Fork (Peace River Landing, Alta) because "he would be of great Service to me should I undertake any expedition." MacKay joined Mackenzie on 12 April, and on 9 May, together with six voyageurs and two Indian hunters, they began their 74-day journey to the Pacific Ocean.

MacKay's activities were primarily land-based. His duties were those of a scout, and his tasks included determining the navigability of waterways and choosing the course ahead, selecting portage routes and "cutting a road" through dense bush along steep inclines, and leading the two Indians in the hunt for game. When dangerous waters dictated, MacKay and the hunters would be the first to walk, often an equally perilous course. No wonder that on 22 June he showed "great satisfaction" at riding down what is now known as the Fraser River in an Indian canoe which had joined the party; as Mackenzie observed, he "was thereby enabled to keep us company with diminution of labour."

Voyaging through uncharted territories peopled by

unknown tribes compelled Mackenzie to obtain local Indians as guides and interpreters and then to retain their services by alternating watches with MacKay. The disappearance of a guide twice during MacKay's vigils led Mackenzie to record, at the first instance, his displeasure with MacKay, and at the second, "painful reflections in my breast." Elsewhere in his journal, however, Mackenzie cites numerous examples of MacKay's courage and reliability. Perhaps the most telling occurred at the start of the return from the mouth of the Bella Coola on 23 July, when the men came close to mutiny in their "frantic terror" at the menacing Indians and treacherous terrain ahead. After describing the conclusion of the revolt Mackenzie, as if to reassure his readers about MacKay's performance, added this footnote in his journal: "It is but common justice to him, to mention in this place that I had every reason to be satisfied with his conduct." Probably written in 1800 during the preparation of the manuscript for publication, this note, as well as Mackenzie's recommendation to the NWC in 1799 that MacKay be "provided for indeed he ranks amongst the first," is convincing evidence of the explorer's lasting esteem for his subordinate.

MacKay likely spent the years between 1793 and 1800 as a clerk in the NWC's Upper English River department, near Lac La Loche (Sask.). He re-established the Île-à-la-Crosse post and in 1799 was reported to be earning £100 Halifax currency per annum. In 1800 he was made a partner and worked in the English River department (probably the Upper division) until 1804. He attended the rendezvous at Grand Portage (near Grand Portage, Minn.) in 1800 but was absent in 1801 and again in 1802, when he received two shares in the company by the agreement of that year.

After the 1805 rendezvous at Kaministiquia (Thunder Bay, Ont.), which he did attend, MacKay went down to Montreal on rotation, returning to Kaministiquia in 1806. In the assignment of departments that year, his was somewhat unusual: "to Watch De Lorme." MacKay did more than "watch" Delorme, a trader attempting to compete with the NWC by way of Grand Portage. He and his *engagés* forced Delorme to abandon his adventure by cutting trees across his path, an action later denounced by Lord Selkirk [DOUGLAS] in *A sketch of the British fur trade in North America; with observations relative to the North-West Company of Montreal* (London, 1816).

Following the winter of 1806–7, which he spent at Lake Winnipeg, MacKay returned to Fort William, as Kaministiquia was now called, where he declared his willingness to retire in place of John SAYER on the same terms Sayer had been offered. Sayer chose to retire, however, and MacKay wintered on the Winnipeg River as proprietor before returning to Fort William for the last time in 1808. Resigning on condition that he receive £1,000 for one share in the NWC and retain his second for seven years, he then retired to Montreal.

Perhaps it was this, or some other arrangement, that led to the "disgust" MacKay is said to have shared with other retired Nor'Westers and that led them to join the venture by American businessman John Jacob Astor* to found a post at the mouth of the Columbia River. Mackay, along with Donald McKenzie* and Duncan McDOUGALL, signed a preliminary agreement with Astor in New York on 10 March 1810, whereupon they began recruiting in Montreal for land and sea expeditions to the Columbia. Among those enlisted by MacKay were Gabriel Franchère*, David and Robert Stuart, and his own 13-year-old son, Thomas, all of whom joined him for the sea voyage. Another recruit was Jean-Baptiste Perrault*, who later withdrew from the land party at Michilimackinac (Mackinac Island, Mich.).

In the mean time, MacKay had joined the Beaver Club on 17 Dec. 1809 after first attending on the previous 1 April as guest of Alexander McKenzie*, nicknamed the Emperor. At his last recorded attendance, on 21 April 1810, he introduced three guests, "two Mr. Stewarts and Mr. McDougall," all associates in the Pacific enterprise.

Not in New York on 23 June 1810 for the formal ratification of the Pacific Fur Company agreement, which allotted him 5 of 100 shares, MacKay created a sensation by arriving on 3 August in a birchbark canoe manned by colourfully bedecked Canadians singing their voyageur songs. In contrast, during their forthcoming voyage on the *Tonquin*, similar displays of the Nor'Westers' spirit would provoke the everlasting loathing of its captain, Jonathan THORN. Before embarking, MacKay consulted British ambassador Francis James Jackson regarding his status and that of other British subjects in the company, should war with the United States break out. Whether he also divulged information that would contribute to the later surrender of Astoria to the NWC, as charged by Washington Irving, has not been proved. Nor can it be known whether some duplicity on MacKay's part contributed to Astor's mistaken impression that all company members from the Canadas had become American citizens.

Also controversial and perhaps, as Alexander Ross* would have it, "an egregious inversion of the ordinary rules of prudence," was Astor's very choice of MacKay for the sea voyage, his exploration and fur-trade experience having prepared him rather for the land expedition. Yet the party that sailed on 6 Sept. 1810 aboard the *Tonquin* came to consider him more their leader than Astor's proxy, Duncan McDougall. Confusion over leadership not only led the two partners to quarrel, but undoubtedly contributed to their catastrophic relationship with Captain Thorn, a

McKay

martinet against whose ruthlessness MacKay many times intervened, albeit in vain. The enmity between Thorn and MacKay, aggravated by Thorn's attempt to maroon his adversary and others of the party at the Falkland Islands, was indirectly responsible for the *Tonquin*'s final tragedy.

The ship reached the mouth of the Columbia in March 1811, and early in May MacKay led a trading and exploring party up the river. Then, at the beginning of June, he left as supercargo on the *Tonquin*'s trading mission up the Pacific coast. Before sailing he confided his premonition of impending disaster to Alexander Ross, in whose care he left his son Thomas. At Clayoquot Sound, Thorn's callous treatment of the Indians, contrary to MacKay's admonitions, evidently provoked an attack. In the fighting and the subsequent blowing up of the ship all but one of those on board the *Tonquin* were killed. Highly respected by the Indians, MacKay none the less was reportedly the first to fall.

MacKay's death, according to Gabriel Franchère, was "an irreparable loss" to the Pacific Fur Company. Characterized by his contemporaries as "brave and enterprising," though also as "whimsical and eccentric," MacKay became known in the Oregon country not only because of his role in the *Tonquin* Astoria saga, but also through his son Thomas's career there as a fur trader. Marguerite Waddens, whom he had apparently left behind when he retired in 1808, became the wife of Dr John McLoughlin*.

JEAN MORRISON

McCord Museum, Beaver Club minute-book, 1807–27 (transcript at PAC). Oreg. Hist. Soc. (Portland), MS 231 (Elliot coll.), Alexander MacKay folder; MS 927 (Mc-Loughlin–Fraser family papers), David McLoughlin corr. PCA, St Gabriel Street Church (Montreal), Reg. of baptisms, marriages, and burials, 19 Sept. 1805, 17 Oct. 1815 (mfm. at AO). [J. J. Astor], "John Jacob Aster relative to his settlement on Columbia River," ed. D. W. Bridge-water, *Yale Univ. Library Gazette* (New Haven, Conn.), 24 (1949–50): 47–69. *Les bourgeois de la Compagnie du Nord-Ouest* (Masson). P. Campbell, *Travels in North America* (Langton and Ganong). *Docs. relating to NWC* (Wallace). [Thomas Douglas], Earl of Selkirk, *A sketch of the British fur trade in North America; with observations relative to the North-West Company of Montreal* (London, 1816). Gabriel Franchère, *Journal of a voyage on the north west coast of North America during the years 1811, 1812, 1813 and 1814*, trans. W. T. Lamb, ed. and intro. W. K. Lamb (Toronto, 1969). [D. W. Harmon], *Sixteen years in the Indian country: the journal of Daniel Williams Harmon, 1800–1816*, ed.W. K. Lamb (Toronto, 1957). Mackenzie, *Journals and letters* (Lamb). [John McLoughlin], *The letters of John McLoughlin from Fort Vancouver to the governor and committee, first series, 1825–38*, ed. E. E. Rich, intro. W. K. Lamb (London, 1941). *New light on early hist. of greater northwest* (Coues). J.-B. Perrault, "Narrative of the travels and adventures of a merchant voyageur in the savage

territories of northern America . . . ," ed. J. S. Fox, *Mich. Pioneer Coll.*, 37 (1909–10): 508–619. Alexander Ross, *Adventures of the first settlers on the Oregon or Columbia River*, ed. M. M. Quaife (Chicago, 1923; repr. New York, [1969]); "Letters of a pioneer," ed. George Bryce (Man.), Hist. and Scientific Soc., *Trans.* (Winnipeg), 63 (1903). [David Thompson], *David Thompson's narrative of his explorations in western America, 1784–1812*, ed. J. B. Tyrrell (Toronto, 1916; repr. New York, 1968).

D. [S.] Lavender, "Thomas McKay," *The mountain men and the fur trade of the far west . . .*, ed. L. R. Hafen (10v., Glendale, Calif., 1965–72), 6: 259–76. J. S. H. Brown, *Strangers in blood: fur trade company families in Indian country* (Vancouver and London, 1980). Ross Cox, *The Columbia River; or scenes and adventures during a residence of six years on the western side of the Rocky Mountains . . .*, ed. E. I. and J. R. Stewart (Norman, Okla., 1957). Roy Daniells, *Alexander Mackenzie and the north west* (Toronto, 1971). J. R. Harper, *78th Fighting Frasers in Canada: a short history of the old 78th regiment or Fraser's Highlanders, 1757–1763* (Laval, Que., 1966). Washington Irving, *Astoria, or anecdotes of an enterprize beyond the Rocky Mountains*, ed. R. D. Rust (Boston, 1976). D. [S.] Lavender, *The fist in the wilderness* (Garden City, N.Y., 1964). K. W. Porter, *John Jacob Astor, business man* (2v., Cambridge, Mass., 1931; repr. New York, 1966). J. K. Smith, *Alexander Mackenzie, explorer: the hero who failed* (Toronto and New York, [1973]). J. U. Terrell, *Furs by Astor* (New York, 1963). Sylvia Van Kirk, *"Many tender ties": women in fur-trade society in western Canada, 1670–1870* (Winnipeg, [1980]). T. C. Elliott, "Marguerite Wadin McKay McLoughlin," *Oreg. Hist. Quarterly* (Salem), 36 (1935): 338–47. Dorothy and Jean Morrison, "John McLoughlin, reluctant fur trader," *Oreg. Hist. Quarterly* (Portland), 81 (1980): 377–89.

McKAY, JOHN, fur trader; probably the brother of Donald "Mad" MacKay; m. *c.* 1791 Mary Favell, daughter of John Favell and his Indian wife Titameg; d. 5 July 1810 at Brandon House (Man.) and was buried there beside his wife.

There is some indication that John McKay and Donald MacKay came from the valley of the Brora River, Scotland. They entered the fur trade by way of Montreal, and by 1788 John was working for Alexander Shaw and his son Angus at Lake St Ann (Lake Nipigon, Ont.). In 1790 he and Donald went to Fort Albany (Ont.) to join the Hudson's Bay Company, Donald taking with him a plan for crippling the Nor'Westers by competing with their communication posts and supply bases. The HBC adopted a modified version of this scheme and for the next two decades John played an important part in carrying it out. For the summer of 1791 and the outfit of 1792–93 he was sent back to Lake St Ann, an area poor in furs, but for the next four outfits he was assigned to the more important Rainy Lake post (near Fort Frances, Ont.). There he faced opposition led by Charles Boyer, Peter Grant*, Donald McIntosh, and others, who found that he enjoyed peaceful and friendly competition but was not to be cowed by threats of violence. Despite the superior numbers of his competitors he obtained about half the trade of the area.

In April 1797 James Sutherland*, the master at Brandon House, died and McKay was sent to replace him for the next outfit. Three seasons at Osnaburgh House and Martin Falls (Ont.) followed. Then in the autumn of 1801 he was posted back to Brandon House, where, with the exception of the outfit of 1806–7, he remained in charge until his death in 1810. From Brandon House he sometimes sent his traders on dangerous expeditions as far afield as the Mandan country (in the vicinity of Stanton, N.Dak.) [see Alexander HENRY]. At his post he was at first encircled by houses competing with one another, but after the consolidation of the North West and New North West (XY) companies in 1804 [see Sir Alexander MACKENZIE] the opposition united against him and became more effective. However, even though his men were greatly outnumbered and he was often short of goods, McKay continued to obtain more than his share of the trade. At the same time he accomplished the strategic aim of disrupting and weakening the provisioning system of the Nor'Westers, who were dependent for pemmican and other supplies on their Red River posts.

From about 1804 he began to show signs of failing health, and in January 1810 he contracted a cold which persisted till his death on 5 July. His wife died in childbirth on 19 March of that year. They were survived by three daughters and five sons, of whom John Richards* and William were the most notable.

With McKay's passing the HBC lost one of its most loyal and zealous servants. In letters to Albany the London committee had expressed appreciation of his work, and in 1794 he was nominated to the Albany council. He was liked also by his opponents, for he was always considerate of those in trouble. When in 1805 John Pritchard* was lost on the prairies and found almost dead from starvation McKay cared for him, and Pritchard wrote later, "My friend McKay of the Hudson's Bay Company . . . became both my surgeon and nurse." The following winter McKay himself became so ill he was delirious, and his opponents Pritchard, Charles CHABOILLEZ, and Pierre Falcon took turns in watching over him – surely a tribute to a troublesome rival. He also enjoyed to a remarkable degree the friendship and loyalty of many Indians who found him just, reliable, and sympathetic.

McKay's journals were written for the information of his employers and disclose little of his private life. They do show, however, that he was a family man, watching over and often employing his wife's brothers. As his older sons became useful he sometimes noted their accomplishments with pride.

He is revealed as a man of even temperament and humane disposition, with a sound understanding of the men who opposed him and the Indians with whom he traded. His journals rise above the usual recording of weather and daily happenings and are among the most interesting of the period.

T. R. McCLOY

PAC, MG 19, E1, ser.1, 40: 15501–42 (transcripts). PAM, HBCA, A.5/4; A.6/15, 17; A.11/5; A.32/4; B.3/a/108; B.3/b/28, 34, 42; B.22/a/5, 9–18a; B.86/a/45; B.105/a/1–4; B.123/a/6; B.149/a/1; B.155/a/14–16; B.166/a/1–2. PRO, PROB 11/1542/147. *Docs. relating to NWC* (Wallace). John Pritchard, "Lost on the Prairies," *Beaver*, outfit 273 (June 1942): 36–39. Morton, *Hist. of Canadian west*. Rich, *Hist. of HBC*.

McKEE, THOMAS, army and militia officer, Indian Department official, and politician; b. possibly *c.* 1770, probably in a Shawnee village on the Scioto River (Ohio), son of Alexander McKee* and a woman said to be a Shawnee; d. 20 Oct 1814 at the Cascades (near Île des Cascades), Lower Canada.

A son of one of the most influential Indian Department officials in the Great Lakes region, Thomas McKee enjoyed the benefits of his father's position, prestige, and connections. In 1785 he received a share in a tract of land at the mouth of the Detroit River given to members of the department by the Indians. In 1788 the Ojibwas and Ottawas granted him the lease of Point Pelee Island (Pelee Island, Ont.) for 999 years. With his father's support, on 29 March 1791 he became an ensign in the 60th Foot, part of which was stationed at Detroit; he was promoted lieutenant on 5 Feb. 1795 and captain on 20 Feb. 1796.

McKee was active in Indian affairs from an early date. Dressed as an Indian, he was with a handful of whites who participated in the unsuccessful Indian attack on Major-General Anthony Wayne's forces at Fort Recovery (Ohio) in June 1794 [see WEYAPIERSENWAH], and he was said to have subsequently encouraged the Wyandots to take up arms. In 1795 he attended the purchase of Indian lands at the Chenal Écarté (on the eastern boundary of the Walpole Island Indian Reserve), and in August 1796 he took part in a council with the Ojibwas and Ottawas of the Detroit region. On the recommendation of his father, who was the deputy superintendent general of Indian affairs in Upper Canada at the time, McKee was made superintendent of Indian affairs for the Northwestern District in 1796. His area of jurisdiction centred on St Joseph Island, Upper Canada, which in that year replaced Michilimackinac (Mackinac Island, Mich.) as the British headquarters in the Upper Lakes region. In 1797 Matthew ELLIOTT was obliged to forfeit the superintendency of Indian affairs in the Amherstburg

McKee

region, and Alexander McKee ordered Thomas to take on the office, which he added to his responsibility for the Northwestern District.

In January 1799, following the death of Alexander McKee, the office of deputy superintendent general was temporarily entrusted to James Baby*, Alexander GRANT, and Thomas McKee. There were objections to McKee's appointment, presumably relating to his drinking, but his command of Indian languages outweighed them. In any event, the warrant to all three men was withdrawn in March so that the way would be clear for William Claus* to succeed to the post. By May McKee again had the responsibility for Amherstburg. He gathered intelligence about events south of the Great Lakes, negotiated the surrender of Indian lands to the crown, and attended councils. He also became embroiled in the Indian Department's ongoing feud with the officious commandant at Fort Malden (Amherstburg), Hector McLean, who wanted to reduce the quantity of supplies given to the Indians and whose complaints had led to the dismissal of Elliott. McKee protested that McLean's actions would "Operate to the diminution if not the total extinction of our influence, and may infinitely prejudice His Majesty's Indian Interest in these parts," and the commandant was reprimanded by Administrator Peter RUSSELL and Governor Robert PRESCOTT.

McKee had been elected to the House of Assembly for Kent in 1797; he was re-elected in 1800 for that riding and sat for Essex as well. His increasing alcoholism and the requirements of his work with the Indian Department, however, limited his time for assembly matters. McKee, who may have been as much as three-quarters Shawnee himself, seems to have considered that his role was primarily to serve the Indians. Certainly he was willing to support them on particular occasions. When in 1804 an individual's rights were, in his opinion, infringed, he wrote to Prideaux SELBY, the department's assistant secretary: "The Government should consult the Indians. I am determined to make the Indians support their claims and rights and to repel force by force." At this time McKee was still greatly respected by the native people, but by 1807 the Wyandots were complaining that he was "too young and inexperienced, he loved to frolick too much and neglected our Affairs." William Claus thought McKee incompetent and, with the threat of war in the air following the *Chesapeake* affair, arrangements were made to replace him at Amherstburg with Matthew Elliott. In 1808 he lost the post, although he kept his superintendency of the Northwestern District.

Meanwhile, in 1805 or 1806, McKee had given up his commission in the 60th Foot, which was no longer serving in the Canadas. He joined the militia and in 1807 held the rank of major. During the War of 1812 he retained this rank, being attached to the 2nd Essex Militia, but served as a captain in the Indian Department. He was congratulated by the Prince Regent for the restrained behaviour of the Indians during the capture of Detroit from the Americans in August 1812 [*see* TECUMSEH] and was mentioned in dispatches for his service in other actions early in the war, although his qualities as a field commander were questioned. In March 1814 he was accused of "grave misconduct" among the Indians on the beach at Burlington Bay (Hamilton Harbour). He had allowed his followers alcohol so that they became "outrageous"; he himself got "shamefully drunk" and verbally abused them. Steps were taken to remove him from the theatre of war. In the autumn, while on his way to Montreal, he died.

By his knowledge of their languages and customs, Thomas McKee had helped maintain the friendship of the Indians who were so essential in securing the boundaries of modern Canada. Possessed of money and connections, he might have had a brilliant career. Instead he became, according to trader Alexander Henry*, "Continualy deranged with Liquor." McKee was the father of three children by an unknown mother, and on 17 April 1797 at Petite Côte (Windsor) he married Thérèse, daughter of John ASKIN; they had one son. "Poor M^{rs} McKee suffered much while she was here with her unfortunate Husband," wrote Henry from Montreal. On his death she was left in absolute want and was granted a pension of £40 per annum.

JOHN CLARKE

[The author would like to acknowledge the assistance of David Brown and Gregory Finnegan as well as that of the Social Sciences and Humanities Research Council of Canada. J.C.]

PAC, MG 11, [CO 42] Q, 80-1: 70–74; MG 19, F1, 8: 84–85, 117–18, 136–39, 236, 238–41, 243–44; 9: 7–9, 43–45, 47–49; F16: 24–26; RG 1, L4, 2: 116–20; RG 5, A1: 2707–8; RG 8, I (C ser.), 15: 46–48; 249: 177–86; 250: 385–87, 560–62; 252: 157–63, 165–72, 213–16, 317–18; 331–32, 368–69, 375–78; 256: 48, 52, 55; 257: 251, 253, 255; 258: 33–36, 54–55, 149, 516; 677: 157; 682: 286; 688: 107; 922: 34, 36; 932: 95; 1170: 53; 1222: 118, 170; 1224: 116–17; 1227: 119; RG 10, A2, 9: 9202–3, 9210–11; 10: 9406, 9598–99, 9601; 11: 9740–43, 9770–71, 9896; 12: 10533–34. *Corr. of Hon. Peter Russell* (Cruikshank and Hunter), vol.3. *Corr. of Lieut. Governor Simcoe* (Cruikshank), vol.4. *John Askin papers* (Quaife). *Mich. Pioneer Coll.*, 12 (1887): 283–89; 20 (1892): 692; 25 (1894): 92, 280. *Windsor border region* (Lajeunesse). Horsman, *Matthew Elliott*. N. W. Wallace, *A regimental chronicle and list of officers of the 60th, or the King's Royal Rifle Corps, formerly 62nd, or the Royal American Regiment of Foot* (London, 1879). R. S. Allen, "The British Indian Department and the frontier in North America, 1755–1830," *Canadian Hist. Sites*, no.14 (1975): 106–7. John Clarke, "The role of political position and family and economic linkage in land speculation in the Western District of Upper Canada, 1788–1815," *Canadian Geographer* (Toronto), 19 (1975): 18–34.

MACKENZIE, Sir ALEXANDER, fur trader, explorer, and author; b. 1764 at Stornoway, on the Isle of Lewis, Scotland, third of four children of Kenneth Mackenzie, of Melbost farm (two miles east of Stornoway), and Isabella Maciver, whose family was prominent in the town; m. 1812 Geddes Mackenzie, and they had three children; d. 12 March 1820 at Mulinearn, near Dunkeld, Scotland.

In the 1770s a severe depression developed on Lewis, and in 1774 Kenneth Mackenzie decided to join his brother John in New York. His wife had died while Alexander was still a child. Kenneth sailed for North America with his two sisters and Alexander, leaving both his daughters behind. (Alexander's older brother Murdoch studied medicine; a terse family record states that he then "followed the sea and was lost on the coast of Halifax.") Only months after the family's arrival the American revolution broke out, and Kenneth and John joined the King's Royal Regiment of New York, raised by Sir John Johnson*. Commissioned lieutenant in 1776, Kenneth served until 1780, when he died suddenly at Carleton Island (N.Y.). Young Alexander had been left in the care of his aunts, who first took him to Johnstown, in the Mohawk valley, where Sir John Johnson had large estates, and in 1778, when conditions in the valley became difficult for loyalists, sent him to Montreal, where he attended school.

His schooling was to be brief. The fur trade promised adventure and a profitable future to a sturdy, high-spirited youth, and in 1779 Mackenzie joined Finlay and Gregory, a partnership formed by James Finlay and John GREGORY that had been trading in the west since 1773. The firm was reconstituted as Gregory, MacLeod and Company in 1783, when Finlay, a well-known pioneer among Montreal's British fur traders, retired and was succeeded by Normand MacLeod*. By 1784, when he had been five years in the Montreal office, Mackenzie was anxious to try his hand at trading. Gregory entrusted him with "a small adventure of goods" which he took to Detroit (Mich.). It is evident that he had very favourably impressed his employers, for some months later MacLeod travelled to Detroit to offer Mackenzie a share in the business. The offer was conditional upon his willingness to go to Grand Portage (near Grand Portage, Minn.) in the spring of 1785 and serve in a post in the far west, a proviso quite acceptable to Mackenzie.

This expansion of the firm was prompted by radical changes taking place in the fur trade. Shortly after Canada was ceded to Great Britain in 1763, British traders from Montreal, like the French before them, ventured into what is now western Canada and began to extend their quest for furs farther and farther west. James Finlay built a post in the Saskatchewan valley in 1767 or 1768, and in 1778 Peter POND reached the

Athabasca River and discovered the richness of the fur resources in the surrounding area. As it happened, this greater interest and activity in the northwest developed at a time when the American revolution was threatening to deprive Montreal of its important stake in the trade in the area south of the Great Lakes. Detroit and Michilimackinac (Mackinaw City, Mich.), through which much of it had been channelled, would probably be in American territory, and it was certain that an independent United States would soon reserve the country south of the lakes for its own nationals. The Montreal traders who had been active in that area turned therefore to the northwest as an alternative source of furs.

Sharply increased competition in the northwest was the natural result, and it quickly became evident that this could be both costly and hazardous – costly because traders would often be faced with the necessity of outbidding one another, and hazardous because if furs could not be secured by fair methods there was always the temptation, in an unpoliced wilderness, to resort to foul means. Much of the trouble arose because the trade was carried on by individuals or small partnerships. Wider agreements were the obvious solution, and these soon began to come into being. Most notable of them was the pooling of nine partnerships in 1779, a step toward a longer-term agreement and the formal organization of the North West Company in the winter of 1783–84. It was in response to this strong competitor that Gregory, MacLeod expanded its own partnership from two members to five the following winter; the company was joined by Peter PANGMAN and John Ross in addition to Mackenzie. The small supporting staff included Alexander's cousin Roderick McKenzie*, a few months out from Scotland, who served as an apprentice clerk. When the partners met at Grand Portage in June 1785, Mackenzie himself was assigned to the English (Churchill) River department, with headquarters at Île-à-la-Crosse (Sask.). There he would be stationed until 1787.

The ambitions of the NWC were to play an important part in Mackenzie's later career. From the very beginning it was anxious to expand the scope of its trading right across the continent. As early as October 1784, in a memorial submitted to Governor Frederick HALDIMAND of Quebec, the company declared its intention "of exploring at their own Expence, between the latitudes of 55, and 65, all that tract of country extending west of the Hudson's Bay to the North Pacific Ocean." Ignoring the monopoly rights of the Hudson's Bay Company, it went on to suggest "the propriety of granting to the Company an exclusive right . . . of the Trade to the North-West . . . for Ten-Years" in return for opening up new country. Nothing came of this proposal, but the company seized every opportunity to increase its knowledge of

Mackenzie

western geography. Its immediate source of information was Peter Pond, who had been included in the 1783–84 partnership. By 1785, guided by his own travels and by his questioning of the Indians, Pond had drafted a map that included the country north of Lake Athabasca. Correct in essentials, it showed a river flowing north to Great Slave Lake, from which a second river ran on to the Arctic Ocean. Later, when he had had access to accounts of the third Pacific voyage of James Cook*, and had learned of the inlet in Alaska that Cook had mistaken for an estuary and had named Cook's River, Pond ignored his native informants, indulged in wishful thinking, and jumped to the conclusion that this was the mouth of the large river that flowed out of Great Slave Lake. In a map drawn in 1787, small streams still lead towards the Arctic, but the major river flows westwards, towards the Pacific. And in a second major miscalculation, which was to be important to Mackenzie, Pond grossly underestimated the distance from Athabasca to the Pacific. No accurate calculations of longitude had yet been made in the area around Lake Athabasca, and he placed the lake some 700 miles west of its true position.

There was a streak of violence and bad temper in Pond's nature, which was to cut short his career in the fur trade. He was already suspected of having been responsible for the death in 1782 of a rival trader, Jean-Étienne Waddens*, and in 1787 a scuffle resulted in the shooting death of John Ross, whom Gregory, MacLeod had sent to compete with Pond in the Athabasca country. Once again competition had erupted into violence. Some measure to reduce dangerous rivalry was clearly desirable, and the immediate result of Ross's death was the amalgamation of Gregory, MacLeod and the NWC. The enlarged partnership consisted of 20 shares, and Mackenzie received one of the four assigned to the four surviving partners of Gregory, MacLeod. Pond was not excluded, but it seems to have been agreed that the season of 1787–88 would be the last he would spend in the west. He returned to his post on the Athabasca River, arriving on 21 Oct. 1787, Mackenzie going with him in the dual capacity of second in command and understudy. Although Mackenzie was convinced that Pond was a murderer, the two men managed to agree fairly well. Pond was both an accomplished trader and a born explorer, and Mackenzie was anxious to learn all he could from him.

Pond left Athabasca for good in the spring of 1788 and Mackenzie took charge of the department. He was to succeed Pond as explorer as well as trader, and was soon preparing to descend the large river (now the Mackenzie) that flows out of Great Slave Lake. There is no reason to doubt that when he set out he expected to find the course of the river much as Pond had mapped it in 1787. Pond, for his part, had never

deviated from two of his basic but badly mistaken assumptions. In November 1789, before details of Mackenzie's first expedition had reached the east, Pond had several conversations in Quebec with Isaac Ogden*, who described them in a letter to his father. "There can be no doubt," Ogden wrote, "but the source of Cook's River is now fully discovered and known." And Pond's conviction that the journey from Great Slave Lake to the supposed mouth of Cook's River would be a short one is reflected in Ogden's note that "Another man by the name of McKenzie was left by Pond at [Great] Slave Lake with orders to go down the River, and from thence to Unalaska, and so to Kamskatsha, and then to England through Russia, &c." That Mackenzie was in fact acting on specific instructions is proven by his own account of the journey, which is entitled "Journal of a Voyage performed by Order of the N.W. Company, in a Bark Canoe in search of a Passage by Water through the N.W. Continent of America from Athabasca to the Pacific Ocean in Summer 1789." But there is no doubt that Mackenzie welcomed the assignment; in the preface to the printed account of his travels he described "the practicability of penetrating across the continent of America" as "this favourite project of my own ambition."

Mackenzie's headquarters in Athabasca had been at what became known as the "old establishment," founded by Pond in 1778 some 40 miles up the Athabasca River. In 1788 he sent his cousin Roderick, now serving with him, to build the first Fort Chipewyan, on the south shore of Lake Athabasca, where he joined him shortly before Christmas. It was from this new post that Mackenzie set out on his first voyage of discovery on 3 June 1789. His party consisted of four French Canadian voyageurs, a young German, whose presence is unexplained, a Chipewyan Indian known as English Chief*, and sundry native wives and retainers. Travel was slow and difficult in the upper part of the Slave River, where rapids were frequent, and ice delayed the party in Great Slave Lake, but once they entered the Mackenzie River their progress was rapid. The full length of the river, about 1,075 miles, was covered in only 14 days, at an average speed of more than 75 miles per day. For nearly 300 miles the Mackenzie followed the generally westward course that Pond had predicted, but at what is now known as the Camsell Bend the river swung round to the north and continued on, day after day, in that general direction. It became apparent at last that it could not constitute a route to the Pacific. "I am much at a loss here how to act," Mackenzie wrote in his journal on 10 July, when only two days distant from the sea, "being certain that my going further in this Direction will not answer the Purpose of which the Voyage was intended, as it is evident these Waters must empty themselves into the Northern

Ocean. . . ." But he decided to push on "to the discharge of those Waters, as it would satisfy Peoples Curiosity tho' not their Intentions." Misty weather made it uncertain for a time whether or not he had actually reached the Arctic Ocean or merely a large lake, but there is no doubt that he reached the sea. He spent four nights on Whale Island (Garry Island, N.W.T.), off the river's mouth, which he so named because of the number of white whales seen in its vicinity, and he observed the rise and fall of the tide. The return journey to Fort Chipewyan was begun on 16 July and the party reached the fort on 12 September. They had completed the round trip, totalling over 3,000 miles, in 102 days.

Although he had been the first to explore one of the world's great rivers, and in later years came to take pride in the fact, Mackenzie's first reaction was one of frustration. When he attended the annual rendezvous of the Nor'Westers at Grand Portage in 1790 he remarked in a letter to Roderick: "My *Expedition* is hardly spoken of but this is what I expected." The reaction of the partners is understandable; most of them were accustomed to making long and arduous overland journeys, and Mackenzie's explorations, having failed to find a route to the Pacific, were of no immediate practical use to the NWC. But it cannot be said that his worth was not appreciated; a new North West agreement, which was to come into effect in 1792, gave him two of the 20 shares in the company in place of the one he had held since 1787. He is said to have dubbed the Mackenzie the River Disappointment, but this is doubtful. The original of the letter in which he is alleged to have used the name has disappeared, and it occurs in only one of four surviving transcripts of this letter; in the other three the river is referred to as the Grand River.

Mackenzie had great physical strength, determination, and stamina; he tells us that he possessed "a constitution and frame of body equal to the most arduous undertakings." As the speed at which he travelled indicates, he was a hard driver of men. In Joseph Burr Tyrrell*'s view he was "a man of masterful temperament, and those who accompanied him, whether white men or natives, were merely so many instruments to be used in the accomplishment of any purpose which he had in hand." This judgement is unduly harsh. When there was some doubt whether he would reach the Arctic he noted in his journal: "My Men express much sorrow that they are obliged to return without seeing the Sea, in which I believe them sincere for we marched exceed*ing* hard coming down the River, and I never heard them grumble; but on the contrary in good Spirits . . . and declare themselves now and at any time ready to go with me wherever I choose to lead them." This was no exaggeration, for two of the four voyageurs who had travelled to the Arctic became members of his second expedition. He

had watched over the welfare of his men, had made great efforts to protect them from dangers along the way, and had brought all of them home safely.

Mackenzie had a second expedition in mind before the first had ended. He had encountered relatively few Indians and no Inuit, but when returning up the river he had tried to question any natives he met in the hope that they could give him information about rivers west of the mountains, which presumably would lead to the Pacific. Mackenzie had become aware of certain deficiencies in his knowledge and equipment that he was anxious to make good before he explored further. His observations of latitude, usually south of the true position by from 7 to 15 minutes, served well enough, but he had no instruments that would enable him to ascertain longitude. This shortcoming was emphasized, perhaps in a somewhat arrogant and embarrassing way, by Philip Turnor*, a qualified surveyor in the service of the HBC, whom he happened to meet at Cumberland House (Sask.) in June 1790. Turnor noted at the time: "Mr McKensie says he has been at the Sea, but thinks it the Hyperborean Sea but he does not seem acquainted with Observations which makes me think he is not well convinced where he has been." Mackenzie was in fact perfectly aware of where he had been, but the encounter with Turnor doubtless strengthened his determination to pay a private visit to London in the winter of 1791–92, where he could receive instruction and acquire equipment. He was nevertheless somewhat scantily outfitted when he set out on his second expedition in the autumn of 1792, as he seems to have had only a compass, a sextant, a chronometer, and a large telescope. In spite of the relative lack of equipment, the accuracy with which Mackenzie plotted his position from time to time was remarkable. Fortunately he was now aware of the great distance that would have to be covered to reach the Pacific, for Pond's mistake in placing Lake Athabasca had been detected: the true longitude of Fort Chipewyan, ascertained by Turnor, could now be compared with Cook's earlier readings on the coast.

On his second venture, Mackenzie had decided to ascend the Peace River to its source in the mountains, and then cross the divide in the expectation that he would find some river on the western slope that would lead him to the Pacific. On 10 Oct. 1792 he left Fort Chipewyan and started up the Peace with the intention of building an advance base where he could spend the winter. This was Fort Fork (Peace River Landing, Alta), near the junction of the Peace and Smoky rivers. In the spring he had difficulty in mustering a crew, but was able to leave at last on 9 May 1793. His account of the departure from Fort Fork illustrates the astonishing capacity of a fur trader's birchbark canoe: "Her dimensions were twenty-five feet long within, exclusive of the curves of stem and stern, twenty six inches hold, and four feet nine inches beam. At the

Mackenzie

same time she was so light, that two men could carry her on a good road three or four miles without resting. In this slender vessel, we shipped provisions, goods for presents, arms, ammunition, and baggage, to the weight of three thousand pounds, and an equipage of ten people." As second in command Mackenzie had chosen Alexander MacKay; two Indians, intended to act as interpreters and hunters, and six voyageurs completed the party. He was unfortunate in a number of the crewmen he had had to accept. Only a few days after the start some of them were so appalled by the portages encountered at the Peace River canyon that they urged Mackenzie to abandon the whole enterprise. Despite this and many later complaints he was able to keep the party moving and to maintain discipline and some semblance of morale.

By the end of May he had reached the point at which the Parsnip and Finlay rivers unite to form the Peace. He chose to ascend the Parsnip, following the advice of an old Indian who told him that a carrying place at its headwaters would lead over a height of land to a large river flowing to the west. This statement proved correct, but travel in the small streams and lakes that linked the larger rivers on either side of the mountains turned out to be laborious, notably in James Creek, to which Mackenzie gave the more appropriate name of Bad River. At last on 18 June he descended the McGregor River and reached the Fraser; being unaware of its existence, he jumped to the conclusion that he must have reached the upper waters of the Columbia. Four days later he had travelled down it as far as the future site of Fort Alexandria (Alexandria, B.C.), which was named after him. There he was able to hold discussion with the Indians, who strongly advised him to proceed no farther. They informed him that parts of the river were virtually impassable, and that its mouth was still far to the south. In their view much the best way to reach the ocean was by a considerably shorter route overland. He should go back up the Fraser to the vicinity of its large tributary, the West Road River, and follow its valley westward.

It was not in Mackenzie's nature to turn back in the face of difficulties, and he feared that such a change of plan might be construed as a retreat and damage the morale of his party. "In a voyage of this kind," he noted in his journal, "a retrograde motion could not fail to cool the ardour, slacken the zeal, and weaken the confidence of those, who have no greater inducement in the undertaking, than to follow the conductor of it." Such, he added, were the considerations by which his mind was "distressed and distracted." He decided nevertheless that the advice of the Indians should be followed, and the trip back to the West Road began on the next day, the 23rd.

By 4 July the canoe and surplus supplies had been cached near the junction of the Fraser and West Road rivers, and the heavily laden party began the trek to the

coast. Mackenzie's own load consisted of pemmican and other provisions weighing about 70 pounds, besides arms, ammunition, and his telescope. He travelled west in or near the valley of the West Road River, following well-beaten Indian trails most of the time. Later he ascended Ulgako Creek, a tributary of the West Road, and after leaving it continued on westward to the Tanya Lakes. Here Indian reports indicated that he could either go north to the Dean River or turn south to the Bella Coola. He chose the latter, and on his way south crossed Mackenzie Pass, at 6,000 feet the highest point reached in any of his travels. On 17 July he descended into the deep gorge of the Bella Coola and was greeted by Bella Coola Indians at a small settlement that he named Friendly Village. Two days later, having travelled down the turbulent river, he came upon six curious Indian houses built on stilts, about 25 feet high. "From these houses," Mackenzie wrote, "I could perceive the termination of the river, and its discharge into a narrow arm of the sea." In this singularly undramatic fashion he chronicled the conclusion of the first journey across North America north of Mexico.

Although small alarums had occurred, thus far Mackenzie had succeeded in maintaining good relations with the Indians he had met. By contrast, the Bella Bellas at the mouth of the Bella Coola were anything but friendly, and open clashes were narrowly averted. As a result, little exploring was done after he reached tide-water, but he did secure a canoe and paddle down North Bentinck Arm, into which the Bella Coola flows, and then he proceeded to Dean Channel. There Mackenzie encountered more Bella Bella Indians, who viewed him "with an air of indifference and disdain. One of them in particular made me understand, with an air of insolence, that a large canoe had lately been in this bay, with people in her like me, and that one of them, whom he called *Macubah*, had fired on him and his friends, and that *Bensins* had struck him on the back, with the flat part of his sword." Macubah would seem to refer to George Vancouver*, and it has been suggested that Bensins was Archibald Menzies*, the botanist who accompanied the expedition; but he was not with Vancouver when he explored Dean Channel on 2 June. None of the journals of the expedition mentions any difficulties with the Indians. What would have been a historic meeting between Mackenzie and Vancouver was missed by a little more than six weeks.

That night, the 21st, the party slept on a large rock in Dean Channel, and the next morning Mackenzie "mixed up some vermilion in melted grease" and wrote on its southeast face the famous inscription: "Alexander Mackenzie, from Canada, by land, the twenty-second of July, one thousand seven hundred and ninety-three." The rock has been identified and the words reinscribed upon it in permanent form.

Mackenzie began the return journey on 23 July and was back at Fort Chipewyan on 24 August. Once again his speed of travel was phenomenal. Frank C. Swannell, an experienced wilderness explorer, estimates that, when allowance is made for the various delays encountered, Mackenzie's average day's travel on the westbound trip, by land and water, was about 20 miles. "The real test of his ability to travel is the return trip over a known route and less heavily burdened, he having left caches behind to secure his return. On foot, from Friendly Village, on the Bella Coola, to the Fraser, he averaged 25 miles a day. The 860 miles by water was made in twenty-four days, including the portages, an average of 36 miles a day." The total distance covered, outward and homeward, was somewhat more than 2,300 miles. Once again Mackenzie brought his crew home safe and uninjured, and in spite of difficulties with the natives during the second journey, on neither of his great expeditions had he fired a shot in anger.

In one respect Mackenzie's expedition to the Pacific bore an unfortunate similarity to his journey to the Arctic: the route he had pioneered was of no immediate use to the NWC. He had added a huge tract of new country to the map of the world, but the routes that would be followed in later years by fur brigades would be discovered by Simon Fraser* and David Thompson*.

In semi-solitude at Fort Chipewyan during the winter of 1793–94, restless and highly strung, Mackenzie seems to have come close to a breakdown. In the previous autumn he had intended to make a fair copy of his journal, but, he later informed his cousin Roderick, "the greatest part of my time was taken up in vain Speculations. I got into such a habit of thinking that I was often lost in thoughts nor could I ever write to the purpose." By January 1794 he had determined to leave the west. "I am fully bent on going down. I am more anxious now than ever. For I think it unpardonable in any man to remain in this country who can afford to leave it."

But he had no intention of leaving the fur trade. On the contrary, his visit to the Pacific had roused a desire to see the trade organized on far wider and more efficient principles. On his way to Montreal in September 1794, he called on John Graves SIMCOE, lieutenant governor of Upper Canada, and outlined the project to him. He proposed that the NWC should participate in a cooperative effort that would involve the HBC and the East India Company. The former would be asked to make available its supply route via Hudson Bay, which could deliver goods cheaply to the heart of the continent; the latter would be expected to modify its monopoly rights in the China trade to permit the marketing of furs shipped from the Pacific coast. The idea was not entirely new; in 1789 Alexander Dalrymple, hydrographer of the East India

Company, had published his *Plan for promoting the fur-trade, and securing it to this country, by uniting the operations of the East-India and Hudson's-Bay companys*. Dalrymple shared Mackenzie's interest in both the Pacific coast and the river that flowed out of Great Slave Lake and, partly as a result of his urging, expeditions to explore both were planned by the British government to begin in 1790. Threatened war with Spain delayed the expedition by sea, which sailed eventually in 1791 under Vancouver. Command of the land expedition was to have been given to Captain John Frederick Holland*, who arrived at Quebec in the fall of 1790 only to hear that Mackenzie had anticipated him and had already explored the Mackenzie River.

As long as he was active in the fur trade Mackenzie was to continue to advocate some cooperative plan such as he had outlined to Simcoe, but he was diverted from it for a time by the offer of a partnership in McTavish, Frobisher and Company. A decade earlier, Simon McTAVISH had perceived that a managing agency in Montreal to purchase supplies and market furs would be essential to the success of the NWC, and he had so contrived matters that his firm not only performed these functions but also controlled a majority of the NWC shares. Mackenzie's partnership became effective in 1795 and each spring he travelled to Grand Portage to attend the annual rendezvous with the wintering partners. By degrees, however, his restless nature began to assert itself. On many points of internal policy he found himself more in sympathy with the wintering partners than with his fellow agents. His interest in a broader trading strategy revived, and this led to differences with McTavish; trade handled through Hudson Bay or the Pacific coast would not benefit Montreal, where McTavish's interests were centred. By 1799 Mackenzie was again in a highly nervous condition, and about the time his partnership expired on 30 Nov. 1799 he left abruptly for England.

He had long been anxious to publish an account of his travels, and this became his primary objective in London. His *Voyages from Montreal ... to the Frozen and Pacific oceans* was published in December 1801 and attracted wide attention. The journals of the voyages are preceded by a valuable general history of the fur trade; this may have been written in great part by Roderick McKenzie, who had been collecting materials on fur-trade history. The journals themselves were edited for publication by William Combe, a prolific writer who had previously revised the text of the *Voyages* of John MEARES, published in 1790. On 10 Feb. 1802 Mackenzie was knighted, possibly at the instigation of EDWARD AUGUSTUS, Duke of Kent and Strathearn. The single extant letter from the duke to Mackenzie, dated 1 Nov. 1819, indicates that they were on terms of friendship.

Mackenzie

In the last few pages of his *Voyages* Mackenzie had again outlined his proposal for cooperation between the NWC, the HBC, and the East India Company. In January 1802 he presented the plan to Lord Hobart, the Colonial secretary. It now included the Pacific coast fisheries, and Mackenzie was thinking of a central establishment at Nootka Sound (B.C.) and two outposts, one to the north and the other to the south. Meanwhile, a complication had arisen. In 1798, before Mackenzie had left Canada, the New North West Company, later known as the XY Company, had formed around the powerful trading partnership of Forsyth, Richardson and Company, and it soon offered the old concern spirited competition. Mackenzie had acquired shares in it as early as 1800, and by 1802 it was sometimes known as Sir Alexander Mackenzie and Company. Hobart suggested that the first step toward a wider trading arrangement should be a union of the two companies based on Montreal. Mackenzie returned to Montreal in 1802 to bring this about, but antagonism between Simon McTavish and himself was too great to make union possible. A coalition suddenly became practicable in 1804 when McTavish died. Mackenzie had long been a close friend of McTavish's nephew and successor, William McGillivray*; for several years in Montreal, when both were bachelors, they shared quarters, and their convivial life was the talk of the town. But although he had many friends and was socially popular, in the trade Mackenzie had evidently come to be considered a trouble-maker, and he was excluded from the new united concern.

At a loose end, Mackenzie was persuaded to enter politics. On 16 June 1804 he was elected to represent the county of Huntingdon in the House of Assembly of Lower Canada. Although he continued to be a member until 1808, he attended only the first session; by January 1805, as he confessed to his cousin Roderick, he was already "heartily tired of Legislation." He wished sincerely "that those who thought themselves my friends in being the means of getting me to so honorable a situation had been otherwise employed." He seems not to have taken his responsibilities as a member very seriously, since he went to London in the autumn of 1805 and made only brief visits to Canada thereafter, the last in 1810.

The description of the Red River country in Mackenzie's *Voyages* is said to have been the first to arouse the interest of Lord Selkirk [DOUGLAS] in the region, and this circumstance may have led to their meeting. In 1808 both men, anxious to influence the HBC but for quite different reasons, began buying the company's stock. Mackenzie was hoping to exert pressure to secure the use of the Hudson Bay supply route for the Montreal traders; Selkirk was interested in a land grant in the Red River country on which to found a colony. At first relations were cordial, for

Mackenzie, it seems, was under the impression that the grant Selkirk would be seeking would be modest and would not interfere with the fur trade. When the huge dimensions of the scheme became apparent he and representatives of the NWC did their utmost to prevent the grant's being made, but it was approved by the HBC's General Court at the end of May 1811. Three months later Mackenzie learned of the failure of another of his efforts to secure official backing for his plan to reorganize the fur trade: a memorandum he had submitted to Viscount Castlereagh, then Colonial secretary, in March 1808 was at last considered by the Privy Council committee for trade in August 1811, and the board declined to take any action.

By this time Mackenzie had decided to retire to Scotland. On 12 April 1812 in a letter to Roderick McKenzie he announced his marriage to Geddes Mackenzie, one of the twin daughters of George Mackenzie, a Scot who had prospered in London and had died in 1809. The bride was 14 years of age; Mackenzie was 48. Geddes and her sister had inherited the estate of Avoch, and about the time of his marriage Mackenzie purchased it for £20,000. He and Lady Mackenzie usually spent the season in London and lived the rest of the year at Avoch, where Mackenzie took an interest in local activities and improvements. A daughter was born in 1816, and two sons followed in 1818 and 1819. By the time the sons were born Mackenzie's health was failing; Bright's disease appears to have been the most likely cause. In January 1820 he went to Edinburgh to seek medical advice; in March, on the return journey to Avoch, he died unexpectedly in a wayside inn near Dunkeld.

Mackenzie's fame is based solidly upon his two remarkable expeditions, both of which penetrated far into huge areas hitherto unexplored. He was only 29 when he returned from the Pacific in 1793, and the relative ineffectiveness of his activities thereafter made his later career somewhat of an anticlimax. The union of the New North West Company with the NWC in 1804 excluded him from the fur trade in Canada, and Selkirk defeated his attempt to gain control of the HBC in 1811. Only after his death did the newly reconstituted HBC adopt many aspects of his scheme for a continent-wide fur trade.

W. KAYE LAMB

[Mackenzie's home at Avoch was burned in 1833 and his papers were lost in the fire. He had presented a fair copy of his original journal of the expedition to the Arctic to the Marquess of Buckingham; this is now in BL, Stowe MSS 793, ff.1–81. The journal of the second expedition exists only in the version edited by William Combe in the published accounts of Mackenzie's voyages. The most important surviving item in Mackenzie's own handwriting is a letterbook copy of 11 letters written from New York in 1798 (PAM, HBCA, F.3/1). Roderick McKenzie received a considerable number of letters from his cousin, but he appears to have destroyed the originals and they now exist only in transcripts (PAC, MG 19, C1), the accuracy of which is frequently doubtful. Copies of other letters are scattered through the collections relating to the fur trade in PAC, MG 19, and AUM, P 58, G1.

Fortunately the fine portrait of Mackenzie by Sir Thomas Lawrence was saved from the fire at Avoch; it is now in the National Gallery of Canada, Ottawa. A second portrait is known to have been painted by James Sharples in New York in 1798; presumably it was lost in the fire.

Mackenzie's *Voyages from Montreal, on the river St. Laurence, through the continent of North America, to the Frozen and Pacific oceans; in the years, 1789 and 1793; with a preliminary account of the rise, progress, and present state of the fur trade of that country,* [ed. William Combe], was published in London in 1801; a two-volume second edition was published in 1802. Editions were published in New York and Philadelphia the same year; a French translation and two editions in German also appeared in 1802. An abridged translation in Russian was published in 1808. Of the many later complete and partial editions the most useful follow. *Exploring the northwest territory: Sir Alexander Mackenzie's journal of a voyage by bark canoe from Lake Athabasca to the Pacific Ocean in the summer of 1789,* ed. T. H. McDonald (Norman, Okla., 1966). This was the first publication of Mackenzie's own text of the journal of his first voyage. *First man west: Alexander Mackenzie's journal of his voyage to the Pacific coast of Canada in 1793,* ed. Walter Sheppe (Berkeley, Calif., and Los Angeles, 1962). *The journals and letters of Sir Alexander Mackenzie,* ed. and intro. W. K. Lamb (Cambridge, Eng., 1970). This work, no.41 in the Hakluyt Society's extra series, includes Mackenzie's text of the journal of the first expedition, the journal of the second expedition as published in 1801, and all known letters and fragments of letters. It has an extensive bibliography. Volume 1 of *Les bourgeois de la Compagnie du Nord-Ouest* (Masson) contains "'Reminiscences' by the Honorable Roderic McKenzie being chiefly a synopsis of letters from Sir Alexander Mackenzie."

Biographies include the following: Roy Daniells, *Alexander Mackenzie and the north west* (London, 1969); J. K. Smith, *Alexander Mackenzie, explorer: the hero who failed* (Toronto and New York, [1973]), a highly critical appraisal; M. S. Wade, *Mackenzie of Canada: the life and adventures of Alexander Mackenzie, discoverer* (Edinburgh and London, 1927); and [H.] H. Wrong, *Sir Alexander Mackenzie, explorer and fur trader* (Toronto, 1927).

Other useful works are: Basil Stuart-Stubbs, *Maps relating to Alexander Mackenzie: a keepsake for the Bibliographical Society of Canada/Société bibliographique du Canada* ([Vancouver], 1968); R. P. Bishop, *Mackenzie's Rock: with a map showing the course followed by the explorer from Bella Coola, B.C., to the rock, and illustrated with views along the route* (Ottawa, [1924]); M. W. Campbell, *NWC* (1957); Morton, *Hist. of Canadian west*; Rich, *Hist. of HBC*; H. R. Wagner, *Peter Pond, fur trader and explorer* ([New Haven, Conn.], 1955); T. Bredin, "Mackenzie, Slave Lake and Whale Island," *Beaver,* outfit 294 (summer 1963): 54–55; R. H. Fleming, "McTavish, Frobisher and Company of Montreal," *CHR,* 10 (1929): 136–52, and "The origin of 'Sir Alexander Mackenzie and Company,'" *CHR,* 9 (1928): 137–55; R. G. Glover,

"Hudson's Bay to the Orient," *Beaver,* outfit 281 (December 1950): 47–51; E. A. Mitchell, "New evidence on the Mackenzie–McTavish break," *CHR,* 41 (1960): 41–47; Franz Montgomery, "Alexander Mackenzie's literary assistant," *CHR,* 18 (1937): 301–4; J. K. Stager, "Alexander Mackenzie's exploration of the Grand River," *Geographical Bull.* (Ottawa), 7 (1965): 213–41; and F. C. Swannell, "Alexander Mackenzie as surveyor," *Beaver,* outfit 290 (winter 1959): 20–25, and "On Mackenzie's trail," *Beaver,* outfit 289 (summer 1958): 9–14. w.k.l.]

MacKENZIE, KENNETH, fur trader; b. in Scotland, son of Colin MacKenzie and his wife, Margaret; drowned 26 Aug. 1816 near Sault Ste Marie (Ont.).

Kenneth MacKenzie entered the service of the North West Company on 1 May 1800 as an apprentice clerk for a five-year period. On 2 June of that year Daniel Williams Harmon* reported his departure with five other clerks from Maple Point (near Sault Ste Marie) across Lake Superior for Grand Portage (near Grand Portage, Minn.). That winter he was apparently left in charge of the Grand Portage depot in the absence of Dr Henry Munro, the wintering clerk and overseer. From the available evidence it can be inferred that he was stationed there until 1803, and subsequently at Kaministiquia (Thunder Bay, Ont.), the company's place of rendezvous on Lake Superior from that year.

After completing his apprenticeship in the fall of 1805, MacKenzie succeeded Munro, who had been transferred to the Pic (Ont.). He was presumably the McKenzie listed in 1806 as one of two clerks at Kaministiquia, for in 1807 "Mr. Kenneth McKenzie" was in charge at Fort William (the new name of the post). In 1807 also he was voted next in line for promotion to partnership, supported equally by wintering partners from the old NWC and by those from the New North West Company (sometimes called the XY Company), which had been absorbed into the NWC in November 1804 [see Sir Alexander MACKENZIE]. Succeeding to the share of John Finlay in 1808, he served as proprietor of the Fort William department until late 1815, apart from his rotation to Lower Canada in 1812–13.

MacKenzie played a small part in the War of 1812. After news of hostilities reached Fort William he wrote to Duncan Mackintosh at Sandwich (Windsor), Upper Canada, affirming the early success of NWC plans to mobilize its own people and the Indians. The letter, intercepted by American forces, was later introduced at the court martial of defeated American general William Hull as evidence justifying his decision not to invade Canada. While at Montreal in 1812 MacKenzie became a captain in the Corps of Canadian Voyageurs when it was formed in October. After the unit was disbanded in March 1813 he was among the Nor'Westers commissioned to serve in "the

McKinnon

Indian and conquered countries." That year he was admitted to the Beaver Club.

He returned to Fort William in the summer. During the rendezvous of 1815 the impending crisis that would lead to the NWC's eventual downfall loomed large. Shipments of supplies from the east had at times been disrupted during the war, and in the same period John Jacob Astor* had cornered all available supplies of twist tobacco, which the Indians preferred. These factors combined with unexpectedly low commissions and the high costs on the Columbia River and in the China trade to foster resentment among the wintering partners toward the controlling companies in Montreal. MacKenzie assumed the role of intermediary between the openly hostile winterers and the two agents representing Montreal interests, Simon McGillivray* of McTavish, McGillivrays and Company, and Alexander McKenzie* of Sir Alexander Mackenzie and Company (as the New North West Company was sometimes known). Although McGillivray believed "our friend K. rather torments than allays" the winterers' fears, he also recorded his refusal to join a wintering partners' "committee of investigation." In the fall of 1815 MacKenzie was back in Montreal where he succeeded Alexander McKenzie as NWC agent representing Sir Alexander Mackenzie and Company. His annual salary of £500 in addition to his share in the company's profits indicates exceptional influence and status, for his predecessor had received only £200 in salary and his successor Pierre Rastel* de Rocheblave would receive £400.

As the proprietor at Fort William, MacKenzie was drawn inevitably into the controversy surrounding the Red River settlement. In 1811 Lord Selkirk [DOUGLAS] had succeeded in obtaining an immense land grant for colonization of the area south of Lake Winnipeg (Man.). The NWC opposed the new colony, seeing it as a threat to their traditional source of winter provisions and as an instrument of the Hudson's Bay Company's newly aggressive trading policy. By 1814 the NWC had decided to take concerted action against their opponents, and sent Duncan Cameron* and Alexander Greenfield Macdonell* to deal with the problem. Writing to Cameron in 1815, MacKenzie, who seems to have adopted a moderate attitude, cautioned, "Do not for God sake commit yourself in either action or writing – prudence prevents misfortune." Nevertheless, settlers were frightened away in large numbers, and on 19 June 1816 their governor, Robert SEMPLE, and some 20 colonists were killed at Seven Oaks (Winnipeg) by a party of Métis in the NWC's employ. MacKenzie was at Fort William in August when Selkirk seized the fort in retaliation for the Seven Oaks affair and sent all the partners, including William McGillivray* and Alexander McKenzie and excepting only Daniel McKenzie*, to Upper Canada for trial. On 26 August MacKenzie and eight others bound for the east drowned in Lake Superior when their canoe capsized near Sault Ste Marie, where MacKenzie was subsequently buried. He was survived by his Indian wife, Louisa, and their daughter, Margaret.

Before leaving Fort William as a prisoner MacKenzie had had the presence of mind to make out his will. The names of his executors reveal close relations with the three main components of the NWC: Roderick McKenzie* of the old company, who may also have been a relative; John McLoughlin*, a spokesman for the wintering partners; and George Moffatt*, linked with both the New North West Company and the HBC. MacKenzie's rapid promotion can be attributed almost certainly to family ties, as well as to his evident capability and to his popularity with the various factions within the company. Given his commanding position as agent and his connections with Moffatt and McLoughlin, promoters of the 1821 union with the HBC, it seems entirely likely that, had death not intervened, MacKenzie would have emerged out of the ruins of the NWC as one of the principal figures in the united concern.

JEAN MORRISON

ANQ-M, CM1, Kenneth McKenzie, proved 16 Sept. 1816; CN1-29, 11 April 1796, 24 April 1800. AUM, P 58, G1/122, 131, 142 (transcripts at PAC). PAC, MG 19, A35, 7, notebook IV, memoranda, Fort William, 1815; B1, 1; E1, ser.1, 22: 8565–67 (transcripts); E2, 2, J. S. Cameron to James McTavish and Jasper Vandersluys, 29 Aug. 1816 (transcript). *Docs. relating to NWC* (Wallace). G.B., Colonial Office, *Papers relating to the Red River settlement* . . . (London, 1819). [John Halkett], *Statement respecting the Earl of Selkirk's settlement upon the Red River in North America* . . . (London, 1817; repr. East Ardsley, Eng., and New York, 1968, and [Toronto, 1970]); *Postscript to the statement respecting the Earl of Selkirk's settlement upon the Red River* ([Montreal, 1818]). [D. W. Harmon], *Sixteen years in the Indian country: the journal of Daniel Williams Harmon, 1800–1816*, ed. W. K. Lamb (Toronto, 1957). *Report of the trial of Brig. General William Hull* . . . , comp. [J. G.] Forbes (New York, 1814). [James Tate], "James Tate's journal, 1809–1812," *Hudson's Bay miscellany, 1809–12*, ed. Glyndwr Williams (Winnipeg, 1975), 95–150. [S. H. Wilcocke], *A narrative of occurrences in the Indian countries of North America* . . . (London, 1817; repr. East Ardsley and New York, 1968). C. P. Wilson, "The Beaver Club," *Beaver*, outfit 266 (March 1936): 19–23.

McKINNON, RANALD, army officer, office holder, and militia officer; b. 1737 on the Isle of Skye, Scotland; m. 20 Nov. 1768 Letitia Piggott, and they had nine children, including John, who became MHA for Shelburne County, N.S., in 1823; d. 28 April 1805 in Shelburne.

Ranald McKinnon began his career as a lieutenant in the 77th Foot, from 21 Sept. 1758. His regiment served in several North American campaigns during the Seven Years' War including John Forbes*'s expedition against Fort Duquesne (Pittsburgh, Pa) in 1758 and Jeffery Amherst*'s thrust up Lake Champlain in 1759. McKinnon was apparently present when some of the 77th took part in the recapture of St John's, Nfld, from the French in 1762 [see Charles-Henri-Louis d'Arsac* de Ternay]. Once the 77th was disbanded in 1763 McKinnon went on half pay, and some time afterwards he accompanied a party of surveyors to southwestern Nova Scotia, where they were to lay out land grants for New England settlers already there. McKinnon liked the area; with a good war record, he had no difficulty in obtaining on 1 April 1766 a grant of 2,000 acres in a place called Abuptic by the Indians. McKinnon renamed it Argyle, after a district in Scotland, and the name came to be applied to the surrounding region as well.

McKinnon was a successful farmer and gardener, possibly using slave labour to tend the orchards and field crops on his land. He also took an active part in community life: he was appointed a customs collector on 11 Nov. 1766, served as a road commissioner, and on 16 July 1771 became a justice of the peace and an officer in the militia. His military service, loyalty to the monarchy, and good relations with those in authority in Halifax were apparently well known. McKinnon was horrified by rumours of rebellion among the New England settlers in Argyle in 1775. American sympathizers within that group seemed ready to foment discord, and they tried to pressure the Acadians in the region to help their cause. But having experienced the distresses of the expulsion in 1755 [see Charles Lawrence*] and a number of them having only been permitted to resettle in Nova Scotia some years afterwards, the Acadians were not about to provoke the British. For their refusal to cooperate they were harassed by the pro-American settlers, who included Jeremiah Frost, a militia captain, and his brother John, a Congregational minister and justice of the peace. Bénoni d'Entremont* and others asked the Council for aid, and as a result Governor Francis Legge* dismissed the Frosts from their positions. Because of Ranald McKinnon's military experience and his friendly relations with the Acadians, he was appointed commander of the Queens County militia and of the Acadians in Clare Township, and was provided with troops and munitions.

The loyalty of the Acadians and some New England settlers, the show of force by the government, and the uncertainty of aid from the rebels across the Bay of Fundy all combined to prevent an active rebellion in southwestern Nova Scotia. McKinnon's prompt action in mobilizing the loyalist forces had increased his prestige, and he was appointed a captain in the Royal Highland Emigrants on 14 June 1775. But many of the "neutral Yankees" looked upon the old soldier as an informer, an opportunist, and a Halifax figure-head. McKinnon was alien to them in many other ways: he was an Anglican among dissenters, a customs official among inveterate smugglers, and an aristocrat among levellers. It is not surprising, under the circumstances, that he was physically attacked or that he was beset with lawsuits over land; perhaps more disturbing to him were the threats of barn-burning and cattle-maiming made by his enemies. After his death, his widow found it necessary to seek from the Council confirmation of her rights to the estate, since the ownership papers had been lost or destroyed.

As far as can be determined from the available material, Ranald McKinnon's major contribution to Nova Scotian history was his service as a figure of resistance to pro-American disaffection during a dangerous period of the province's history. He would have been less successful in his loyalist activities, however, had it not been for the backing of the Acadians.

A. A. MacKenzie

PANS, MG 4, 141 (typescript); RG 1, 212; 226, doc.6. [Jonathan Scott], The life of Jonathan Scott, ed. C. B. Fergusson (Halifax, 1960). Directory of N.S. MLAs. Brebner, Neutral Yankees. G. S. Brown, Yarmouth, Nova Scotia: a sequel to Campbell's history (Boston, 1888). J. R. Campbell, A history of the county of Yarmouth, Nova Scotia (Saint John, N.B., 1876; repr. Belleville, Ont., 1972). Edwin Crowell, A history of Barrington Township and vicinity ... 1604–1870 (Yarmouth, N.S., [1923]; repr. Belleville, 1973). Clara Dennis, Down in Nova Scotia: my own, my native land (Toronto, 1934). Jackson Ricker, Historical sketches of Glenwood and the Argyles, Yarmouth County, Nova Scotia (Truro, N.S., 1941).

McKINNON, WILLIAM, office holder and politician; b. in Scotland; m. with at least one son; d. 13 April 1811 in Sydney, Cape Breton Island. His grandson William Charles McKinnon* was a Sydney newspaperman and novelist who later became a Methodist preacher.

William McKinnon emigrated to the New World a considerable time before the American revolution, residing in the Carolinas, Georgia, and finally West Florida. During the War of American Independence he served as a captain in the provincial troops of West Florida. He claimed to have lost £7,900 in property and possessions during the revolution, but since parliament had made no provision for the indemnification of loyalists residing in West Florida, he awaited an appointment in one of the remaining colonies. McKinnon was finally named secretary and registrar of deeds as well as clerk and member of the Executive Council of Cape Breton; he arrived in Sydney in December 1792 and was sworn in on the 15th, replacing Abraham Cornelius CUYLER, who had left the previous year after disagreeing with Lieutenant

MacMhannain

Governor William MACARMICK's policies. The appointment plunged McKinnon into the political warfare of the colony. One faction, headed by the loyalist David Mathews*, attempted to increase the council's power at the expense of the lieutenant governor, but was opposed by another, headed by Ranna COSSIT, the Church of England clergyman in Sydney, and James Miller, the superintendent of mines. McKinnon at first supported Cossit's group, which had the favour of Macarmick. However, when the latter left in 1795 Mathews became administrator. In the spring of 1797 a controversy erupted when McKinnon's wife alleged that Chief Justice Archibald Charles Dodd*, a supporter of Mathews, had accused Cossit of robbery and sacrilege. Dodd refuted the story and retaliated by calling Mrs McKinnon "a most infamous liar" and McKinnon himself a "Damn'd Scotch Highland Brute." McKinnon's temper flared and in the council meeting of 18 May he had Mathews deliver to Dodd a challenge to a duel. Immediately afterwards Mathews dismissed McKinnon from office, alleging that he and others had given "every opposition to His Majesty's Government . . . in a manner calculated to stir up the Objects of his Conduct to revenge and perhaps Bloodshed." The duel was prevented by the intervention of Cossit.

The next year Mathews continued his attack on McKinnon. It was probably at his behest that a woman appeared in the spring and alleged that she had purchased in West Florida half of McKinnon's military pay for two years but that McKinnon had never given her the money. Mathews imprisoned McKinnon, who in vengeance took all the council and land records to jail with him and refused to surrender them. Fortunately for McKinnon, Mathews was replaced as administrator shortly afterwards by Lieutenant-General James OGILVIE, who began an investigation into the conduct of the various crown officers. To the affair of the duel, Mathews added a charge that McKinnon had defrauded a settler of 130 acres. Ogilvie decided that the threatened duel between McKinnon and Dodd had been merely a personal matter that had become entangled in political issues, and he dismissed the fraud allegation as a mistake in the transcription of the land patent. He also considered that although McKinnon's conduct had been "improper and reprehensible Yet it was by no means such, as to Authorize in any respect, Mr. Mathews to suspend him from his seat at the Council Board," and restored him to it.

This vindication did not free McKinnon from the charge of an unpaid debt, for which he was still in prison. Since it was a civil case, he required a lawyer to defend him, but Mathews was the colony's only lawyer who was not also a judge and, not surprisingly, he refused to act. Ogilvie could not obtain a suitable person from Halifax to serve as solicitor general, but

McKinnon was saved from further imprisonment by switching his political support to Mathews in return for Mathews's dropping the charges. McKinnon was freed on 5 July 1799 by Ogilvie's successor, Brigadier-General John Murray*, who also restored him to his official employments. McKinnon kept his allegiance to Mathews during Murray's term, refusing to support Murray's and Cossit's hiring of a Protestant schoolteacher and even refusing to recognize Murray's legal authority. Murray retaliated by dismissing McKinnon as secretary, registrar of deeds, and clerk of the council. After Major-General John Despard* replaced Murray as administrator in June 1800, McKinnon regained his former posts, which he then held until his death. Murray had also suspended McKinnon from the council, but in 1807 he was reinstated to that body. After 1800 McKinnon was a less controversial figure. Despard's arrival and Mathews's death that summer toned down factionalism and, although McKinnon became powerful locally in his later years, he remained aloof from the ensuing struggle for a house of assembly which culminated several years after his death in 1811. He is said to have died as a result of wounds received in 1776 on board the *Bristol* during an attack on Charleston, S.C.

William McKinnon, like other early political figures in Cape Breton, can be accused of being an opportunist. However, in the light of the colony's poverty and incomplete constitution, which made no provision for a house of assembly, power struggles in the council were almost guaranteed. In this context, McKinnon's political career was effective, since he steered an eventually successful course through the rocks of factionalism which were characteristic of the first years of Cape Breton's existence as a colony.

R. J. MORGAN

PRO, CO 217/112: ff.148, 199; 217/113: ff.152–53; 217/114; 217/115: ff.52–54, 148, 150–55, 216–18, 389–90; 217/116: f.110; 217/117: ff.20–22, 198–99; 217/118–25; 217/126: ff.97–98; 217/127–28; 217/129: f.22. Richard Brown, *A history of the island of Cape Breton, with some account of the discovery and settlement of Canada, Nova Scotia, and Newfoundland* (London, 1869), 428. J. G. MacKinnon, *Old Sydney; sketches of the town and its people in days gone by* (Sydney, N.S., 1918), 106. Morgan, "Orphan outpost," 175–81.

MACMHANNAIN, CALUM BÀN (Malcolm Bàn Buchanan), bard and settler; b. *c.* 1758 at Sarsdal, in Flodigarry on the Isle of Skye, Scotland; m. Flora MacLeod, and they had four sons and two daughters; fl. 1803.

Like his fellow passengers on the *Polly*, Malcolm Bàn Buchanan probably made a conscious decision to emigrate in response to the recruiting campaign conducted by Lord Selkirk [DOUGLAS] in the Hebrides during the autumn and winter of 1802–3. By that time emigration to the New World had become an attractive alternative to the despotism of fact which Scottish Gaels had encountered for over half a century. The final dissolution of the clan system after the Jacobite rising of 1745–46, the evictions and exploitation incident to a widespread increase in sheep farming and commercial enterprises in the Hebrides, and a rapid rise in population induced hundreds to heed the blandishments, benign and otherwise, of ambitious noblemen such as Selkirk and to leave their homeland for greener pastures abroad.

Selkirk's original scheme to locate Highland colonists in Upper Canada had foundered on opposition from the British government, and at the last minute the *Oughton*, the *Dykes*, and the *Polly*, with some 800 emigrants, were re-routed to Prince Edward Island. There the emigrants took up lands in the Belfast area and there they perpetuated their traditions and their rich heritage of song and story in their everyday language, Gaelic, for generations.

Malcolm Bàn was one of an innumerable company of bards who composed and transmitted Gaelic songs of emigration, which were seldom if ever committed to writing during their own lifetime. Seldom, too, did the formidable challenge of pioneer life daunt their spirits or outweigh their optimism and verve in the face of it.

The misfortunes attending Selkirk's subsequent colonizing ventures frustrated and even infuriated hundreds of Highlanders who had cast their lot with him. Not so Malcolm Bàn, it would seem, for the fragmentary data pertaining to him reflect none of the disenchantment and chagrin of his compatriots. By his own testimony, as recorded in his song *Imrich nan Eileanaich* (Emigration of the Islanders), he had become convinced that emigration was the obvious route from tyranny and poverty to peace and prosperity.

Thàining maighstir as ùr
Nis a stigh air a' ghrunnd,
Sin an naigheachd tha tùrsach, brònach.
Tha na daoine as a' falbh,
'S ann tha 'm maoin an déigh searg'; . . .

Ciod a bhuinnig dhomh fhì
Bhi a' fuireach 's an tìr,
O nach coisinn mi nì air brògan.

A new master has come
now into the land,
a sad, woeful matter.
The people are leaving;
Their possessions have dwindled. . . .

What would it profit me
to remain in this land,
where I can earn nothing by shoemaking.

Later in the song, he describes Prince Edward Island as *Eilean an àigh*, the isle of contentment, blessed with an abundance of fruit, grain, sugar, and even red rum.

Buchanan was a percipient Gaelic bard whose sense of adventure was kindled by the challenges of the voyage. His song delineates in fascinating detail the voyage of the *Polly* and the circumstances of the Skye emigrants. When an outbreak of typhus claimed the lives of at least two victims, he composed a lament to the two beautiful young girls of which only a couplet remains.

Chuir mi iad an cill na Frangach
'S cha chuir fuachd a gheamhraidh as iad

I buried them in the Frenchmen's grave
and the cold of winter will not remove them from it.

Malcolm Bàn settled at Point Prim near Belfast. It may be assumed tentatively that he was the Malcolm Buchanan whose name appears on a testimonial dated 5 Nov. 1811 to Selkirk's principal agent, the Reverend Angus McAulay*, for his clerical instruction in the Gaelic tongue. Similarly, he was probably the Malcolm Buchanan who, in 1818, obtained from Selkirk a one-year lease on 96 acres in lots 57 and 58. According to Alexander Maclean Sinclair*, who lived in Belfast and compiled several books of Gaelic verse, Buchanan died in Point Prim about 1828, but no documentary evidence has been found so far to support the assertion.

Long after Malcolm Bàn's death his song continued to be transmitted orally, possibly by his kinsmen, until on 29 March 1883 it was transcribed by Eoghan MacLaomuinn from an octogenarian who had learned it from the bard himself. Reflections of bards such as Malcolm Bàn are an illuminating supplement to the customary documentation used in reconstructing historic events. In its own right *Imrich nan Eileanaich* has an enduring quality, the quality that enabled Gaelic bards to chronicle in an intimate and colourful way the fate and fortune of fellow Gaels who have figured prominently in the foundation of this nation.

MARGARET MACDONELL

[The text of Malcolm Bàn Buchanan's *Imrich nan Eileanaich* is taken from *Mac-Talla* (Sydney, N.S.), 3 (1894–95), no.41: 9. It has been republished with an accompanying English translation by Margaret MacDonell, as *Emigration of the Islanders*, in "Bards on the 'Polly,'" *Island Magazine*, no.5 (fall–winter 1978): 34–39, and in *The emigrant experience: songs of Highland emigrants in North America*,

McNabb

ed. and trans. Margaret MacDonell (Toronto and Buffalo, N.Y., 1982), 105–13. The author wishes to acknowledge the assistance of Professor J. M. Bumsted in the preparation of this biography. M.MacD.]

PAC, MG 19, E1, ser.1, 39: 14862 (transcript). PAPEI, RG 16, Land registry records, Conveyance reg., liber 25: ff.204–5. Douglas, *Lord Selkirk's diary* (White), 4–5, 11–12, 17. *Gaelic bards from 1765 to 1825*, ed. A. M. Sinclair (Sydney, 1896), 80–81. *Mac-Talla*, 3 (1894–95), no.41: 1; 11 (1902–3): 79, 112. *Prince Edward Island Gazette* (Charlottetown), 18 March 1820. J. M. Bumsted, *The Scots in Canada* (Ottawa, 1982). M. A. Macqueen, *Hebridean pioneers* (Winnipeg, 1957), 73–74, 76; *Skye pioneers and "the Island"* ([Winnipeg, 1929]), 13, 30–32. J. M. Bumsted, "Lord Selkirk of Prince Edward Island," *Island Magazine*, no.5 (fall–winter 1978): 3–8; "Settlement by chance: Lord Selkirk and Prince Edward Island," *CHR*, 59 (1978): 170–88.

McNABB, COLIN, army and militia officer and office holder; b. *c.* 1764, possibly in Virginia, son of James McNabb; m. Elizabeth —, "the daughter of an old Servant of the Crown," and they had at least six children; d. 7 April 1810 at Four Mile Creek, Niagara Township, Upper Canada.

Few details are known of Colin McNabb's early life. At the outbreak of the American revolution his family, including his brother James, resided in Virginia. His father enlisted in a loyalist corps and served during John Burgoyne*'s campaign of 1777. By 1780 James Sr and probably his family were in Quebec. Some time after, Colin enlisted in Francis Legge*'s Loyal Nova Scotia Volunteers, a unit used primarily for garrison duty at Halifax. When the regiment was disbanded on 20 Oct. 1783, McNabb went on half pay as an ensign. He first appears in the Niagara area of western Quebec on the return of loyalists and disbanded troops compiled by Robert Hamilton in 1787. He was married with one daughter and had cleared 60 acres of land, 30 of which were sown with wheat.

McNabb's 25-year career as a minor local office holder stemmed from the 1787 decision of the Privy Council committee for trade to lift the prohibition on trade between the British North American colonies and the United States. Jurisdiction devolved on the colonies and the following year an ordinance was issued in the province of Quebec regulating inland commerce. To enforce the measure, superintendents of inland navigation were appointed between May 1788 and January 1789 for seven ports. McNabb's status as a reduced loyalist officer may have gained him the Niagara (Niagara-on-the-Lake) post, which he received on 23 June 1788. His responsibilities were to collect duties, to prevent smuggling, and to register vessels.

The administration of inland trade was altered by Jay's Treaty of 1794 which opened free trade with the United States. In 1796 Lower Canada enacted legislation bringing the treaty into effect, and the next year Upper Canada reluctantly followed suit. The period of transition which lasted until 1801 caused confusion for both government and superintendents. On 5 Sept. 1797 Administrator Peter Russell proclaimed the suspension of certain ordinances regulating the inland trade. On 16 November he annulled this decision except for the ordinances concerning the registration of ships. McNabb was baffled. In 1798 he petitioned Russell complaining that the lack of new instructions had inhibited the proper functioning of his office and had resulted in "great Quantities of Duteable & even Contraband articles" entering the province. Unsuccessful in his efforts to spark parliamentary initiative, and hesitant to devise measures of his own, Russell that year recommended to the Executive Council the temporary expedient of adopting Lower Canadian legislation "applicable to the local circumstances of this Province."

The problems were partially resolved by an act of 1801 which further regulated American trade, established customs duties, and designated 11 ports of entry. McNabb became collector of customs at Niagara on 6 Aug. 1801. To augment the emoluments of office, because Lieutenant Governor Peter Hunter thought the collectors' share of duties might "for some time be inconsiderable," McNabb received on 1 August the inspectorship of flour, potash, and pearl ash. In addition to the duties of the old superintendents, the collectors had also to submit quarterly accounts to Inspector General John McGill* and to compile lists of the stills, shops, and taverns within their areas of jurisdiction. McNabb supervised a deputy at Queenston, Samuel Street*.

Collectors were usually merchants such as John Warren or John Askin who could use their positions to complement their other interests. McNabb was singular in relying upon his office for the bulk of his income. Consequently problems which interrupted the efficient performance of his duty were a source of constant irritation. Some were personal: "a severe fit of sickness for two months" in 1801 prevented the punctual submission of his returns to McGill; a dispute with Street necessitated McGill's intervention to uphold McNabb's authority. There was also the constant problem of imposing new duties when information from government about new acts was not regularly transmitted. Finally, masters of Upper Canadian merchant vessels often refused to report to the collectors. Although in the early period a collector's share of duties was usually trifling, McNabb was well situated to benefit from a major provincial trans-shipment point, from his region's close proximity to the United States, and from the volume of trade generated by such prominent Niagara

McNabb

merchants as Hamilton, Thomas Clark*, and the Dicksons, William* and Thomas*. Between 1 July 1801 and 31 March 1802 McNabb received £63 for duties collected on liquor, molasses, sugar, coffee, tobacco, snuff, and salt; his counterpart for Kingston and Cornwall, Joseph Anderson, received less than half that amount, and William Allan* at York (Toronto) took in a mere £2 10s. 9d.

An action taken in the early months of 1802 was to prove McNabb's undoing. He had decided to apply duty on almost 13,000 pounds of manufactured tobacco belonging to McTavish, Frobisher and Company of Montreal and destined for trade at Detroit (Mich.) and Michilimackinac (Mackinac Island, Mich.). In spite of his objection to the legality of the duty, Robert Hamilton, the company's Niagara agent, posted a conditional bond which allowed 7,000 pounds to go forward. The remainder was held pending settlement of the dispute. The company and Hamilton contended that goods in transit for consumption outside the province were not subject to duty; in turn McNabb cited a precedent, the action of the New North West Company (sometimes called the XY Company) in directing their Niagara agents, George Forsyth and Company, to pay similar duties. Meanwhile the duties payable upon subsequent shipments of tobacco had raised the sum owed by the company to more than £700. Anxious for a compromise to avoid a lawsuit and to extricate himself, McNabb attempted to soothe the powerful Hamilton and pleaded with McGill to secure the intervention of Attorney General Thomas Scott* so that a decision could be made. McNabb's accounts for duties collected between 1 April and 31 Dec. 1802 showed arrears exceeding £730.

McNabb's action had offended powerful merchant interests. On 13 March 1803 he wrote McGill that he had seen a letter "wherein you hint that you are apprehensive that I am a lost man." On 28 March his deputy at Queenston was replaced by Hamilton's cousin, Thomas Dickson, and the port was separated from McNabb's control. On 6 April Hunter removed McNabb for defaulting in his payments. McNabb and Street refused to turn over their account-books "on the ground that they may possibly hereafter be necessary to their Justification." But the authorities did not take legal action. Hamilton subsequently paid duty on tobacco which had been imported solely for local consumption and the matter of duty on goods in transit seems to have been quietly dropped. In March 1810 David McGregor Rogers*'s committee of the assembly on public accounts condemned McNabb's continuing arrears of £87, the result of merchants' not paying duties.

Little is known of McNabb's life after the loss of the collectorship. It seems that his only means of support was his half pay. One piece of evidence indicates he was deputy commissary at Fort Niagara (near Youngstown, N.Y.) in 1796 but it is not known whether he continued to act in this capacity. His landholdings in the 1790s exceeded 1,200 acres in addition to town lots in Newark (as Niagara was then called) and York, hardly a substantial total. A 1796 petition for a lot in York stated that he was "desirous of building" there, but he shortly disposed of the lot. Between 1796 and 1798 his brothers, Alexander, James, and Simon, evinced a similar desire to relocate and by 1799 all but Colin had left Newark.

McNabb was a slave owner, a member of the Presbyterian congregation, the agricultural society, the Niagara Library, and an officer in the Lincoln militia. The travel accounts of Patrick Campbell*, who resided briefly in Niagara in 1791 and 1792, provide a hint of McNabb's life. The head of one of the area's "genteel families," McNabb appears as a convivial companion who enjoyed nothing better than an extended hunting trip and took the slightest pretext for social intercourse. On one occasion he and Ralfe Clench* guided Campbell to the Grand River settlement of Joseph Brant [THAYENDANEGEA]. The long evening provided a study in contrasts: sumptuous dining, learned conversation, heavy drinking, Indian dances, and Scottish reels. Campbell was astonished. "I do not remember I ever passed a night in all my life I enjoyed more . . . but the other gentlemen [McNabb and Clench], to whom none of these things were new, looked on, and only engaged now and then in the reels."

PETER N. MOOGK

[Some researchers have confused the careers of McNabb and his son Colin A. (d. 1820) who served with the Nova Scotia Fencibles. P.N.M.]

AO, MU 1777, Land papers, Grant to Colin McNabb, 15 May 1799; Agreement of bargain and sale, McNabb to A. Macdonell, 6 July 1799; RG 1, A-I-6: 2317–18, 2471–72. MTL, D. W. Smith papers, B7: 337; B11: 60, 117, 164, 178. PAC, RG 1, E3, 60: 93–93D; L3, 324: Mc misc., 1788–95/136; 328: M2/39, 116, 175; 330: M4/176; 330A: M4/275; RG 5, A1: 2184–85; RG 7, G16C, 2: 27, 72–73, 190; 3: 95–96, 105; RG 16, A1, 84: Warren to McGill, 15 Sept. 1801; 232, items used for years 1801–3; 297, items used for years 1801–3; RG 68, General index, 1651–1841: 525, 677. "Accounts of receiver-general of U.C.," AO Report, 1914: 732–33, 761. P. Campbell, Travels in North America (Langton and Ganong), 151, 155, 157–58, 168, 181–83. Corr. of Lieut. Governor Simcoe (Cruikshank), 1: 191; 4: 229–30, 269–70. Douglas, Lord Selkirk's diary (White), 154. "Early records of Niagara" (Carnochan), OH, 3: 9, 12, 15, 54, 69–76. "Grants of crown lands in U.C.," AO Report, 1929: 89, 144. "Journals of Legislative Assembly of U.C.," AO Report, 1909: 283–84, 435; 1911: 145, 372. Kingston before War of 1812 (Preston), 209. "Names only, but much more," comp. Janet Carnochan, Niagara Hist. Soc., [Pub.], 27 (n.d.): 10, 13, 15, 17, 21, 23. "Ordinances made for the province of Quebec by the

McNabb

governor and Council of the said province, from 1768 until 1791 ...," PAC *Report*, 1914–15: app.C, 203–11, 252. "Proclamations by governors and lieutenant-governors of Quebec and Upper Canada," AO *Report*, 1906: 190–92. "Proclamations of the governor of Lower Canada, 1792–1815," PAC *Report*, 1921: 56–63. "U.C. land book B," AO *Report*, 1930: 50, 67, 83. "U.C. land book C," AO *Report*, 1930: 162. "U.C. land book D," AO *Report*, 1931: 160. *Upper Canada Gazette*, 10 July 1794. *Upper Canada Guardian; or, Freeman's Journal* (Niagara [Niagara-on-the-Lake]), 14 April 1810. Chadwick, *Ontarian families*, 1: 21. Gordon Blake, *Customs administration in Canada: an essay in tariff technology* (Toronto, 1957). William Canniff, *The medical profession in Upper Canada, 1783–1850* . . . (Toronto, 1894; repr. 1980), 498. Janet Carnochan, "Inscriptions and graves in the Niagara peninsula," Niagara Hist. Soc., [*Pub.*], 19 ([2nd ed.], n.d.): 6.

McNABB, JAMES, businessman, office holder, and politician; b. possibly in Virginia, son of James McNabb; m. 24 March 1801 Mary Ann Fraser in Fredericksburg (North and South Fredericksburg) Township, Upper Canada, and they had one son; d. 5 April 1820 en route from York (Toronto) to Belleville.

At the commencement of the American Revolutionary War James McNabb Sr reputedly joined a loyalist regiment in Virginia. By 1777 he had joined McAlpin's Royal Americans as a military surgeon and he served with this unit until his death at the loyalist settlement of Yamachiche, Que., in 1780. His sons Alexander, James, COLIN, and Simon had probably come with him to Quebec, and by 1787 Colin and Alexander were residing in the Niagara area. In 1794 the young James McNabb's petition for land was approved by the Executive Council of Upper Canada. Two years later he settled at Newark (Niagara-on-the-Lake), where Colin was superintendent of inland navigation and Simon had entered business.

"Desirous of settling in York in the mercantile line," James McNabb petitioned for a town lot in April 1798. Alexander had already moved there to become assistant clerk to the Executive Council, and James relocated in that developing port later in 1798; Simon followed the next year. About 1800, apparently in partnership with Simon, James moved to Thurlow (Belleville), an early trade and milling centre on the Bay of Quinte. Although originally intent upon remaining in business at York, Simon was soon propelled by "unforeseen circumstances" to join his energetic brother in 1802.

The McNabbs quickly established links with leading Kingston trans-shipment merchants and financiers, notably Richard CARTWRIGHT and Donald McDonell. Although frequently pressed financially, the brothers shipped increasing quantities of flour, potash, and other staples to their forwarders. Their success made them the leading local competitors to John Walden Meyers*. This rivalry increased when in 1804 James McNabb purchased a mill site near Thurlow on Meyers' Creek (Moira River) where, with Cartwright's financial support, he built a sawmill and a grist-mill.

By 1808 the successful merchant had achieved a measure of local status. On 10 March he received his first commission of the peace for the Midland District; the last was dated 8 Jan. 1820. Between 26 April 1808 and 26 Jan. 1813 he was present at 9 of 20 sessions, a much better record than that of fellow magistrates such as Thomas Dorland*, Ebenezer Washburn*, and Joshua BOOTH. On 2 May 1808 McNabb was elected to the House of Assembly for the riding of Hastings and Township of Ameliasburgh. From 1809 until parliament was dissolved in 1812, he actively represented his constituents' interests in the assembly and, on land matters, at the surveyor general's office. Prone to attacks of pleurisy and pressured by commercial problems, he sold his mills in September 1810. The following November he dissolved his partnership with Simon and sold his valuable property in Fredericksburg. Despite his withdrawal from business, in May 1812 McNabb nevertheless pressed the government to make the thriving Thurlow community the centre for a proposed new administrative district on the Bay of Quinte.

The War of 1812 interrupted McNabb's plans for the locality but it brought him new responsibility. In 1813 and 1814 he voluntarily served as a commissarial agent, charged with the arrangement of military transport and the acquisition, storage, and shipment of supplies for the Kingston garrison. Warned to avoid coercion, McNabb had difficulty contending with constant, often critical, supply demands from the army and the antipathy of settlers such as Meyers to billeting, impressment, and fixed pricing. On 24 March 1814, the military administrator, George Gordon Drummond*, appointed McNabb, along with such prominent men as Cartwright and Dorland, a commissioner to enforce a recent act of the legislature which authorized the detention of persons "suspect of treasonable adherence to the enemy." In June the fatigued magistrate was awarded financial compensation for his service to the commissariat but was refused a military land grant.

After the war McNabb continued his squabbles with Meyers. In charges brought before Lieutenant Governor Francis Gore* in 1815 McNabb apparently discredited his rival with allegations of hindering the commissariat in supplying the army. At the same time he raised the issue of making Thurlow a town site. Gore ordered the appropriate land purchase and between March and April 1816 surveyor Samuel Street Wilmot laid out a plot at the mouth of the Moira River. McNabb used his influence to have the new town named Bellville (Belleville). In the election of June 1816 McNabb was elected for his old riding. That same year he acquired several district offices:

McNiff

war pensions commissioner, branch roads commissioner, and membership on the first Board of Education. Official stipends provided strong motivation. McNabb was crippled in 1815 by the amputation of his right leg following an accident, and the collapse of wartime prosperity apparently brought compelling material setbacks. "In consequence of the reverse of fortune I have met with I am in a manner out of business to attend to," he confessed in December 1816 when requesting additional appointments.

Although "not so hearty and well as formerly" and overburdened with his magistrate's duties, McNabb journeyed to York in February 1817 for the forthcoming legislative session. There he continued his earlier efforts to promote regional interests, notably by his unsuccessful attempts of 1817 and 1818 to have a new district formed with Belleville as its centre. During the sessions of 1817 and 1818, however, McNabb's essentially local interests were overshadowed by such smouldering provincial issues as recession, delayed compensation for war losses, dwindling immigration, and the exclusion of American settlers. Untouched by the tensions surrounding many of these issues, McNabb could oppose a touchy assembly's unjustified censure of criticism from some of its members.

Back in Belleville, however, his apparent detachment dissolved when his conservative opinions merged with personal antagonism. He displayed little tolerance towards the Bay of Quinte supporters of Robert Fleming Gourlay* – men such as Thomas Coleman, a war veteran and owner of the mills formerly belonging to McNabb. At a militia dinner in Belleville on 4 June 1818, Coleman and McNabb began a heated argument which was rekindled in a local tavern the following day. Coleman reputedly damned Gore and his supporters as a "set of perjured villains." McNabb promptly sued for libel. Matters were further strained by Coleman's attendance at the Gourlayite Upper Canadian Convention of Friends to Enquiry held at York in July. By 22 September the feud had spread to the columns of the *Kingston Gazette*. Coleman castigated McNabb as a "mean malignant man," part of the political "scum" whom he wished purged in "the people's interest." A week later McNabb abruptly brought his adversary to heel with aspersions on his war record – citing a "shameful retreat" led by Coleman.

In the remaining years of his life McNabb attended parliament with diminishing regularity, possibly because of declining health. He nevertheless remained active locally in the Midland District Agricultural Society, the Society for Bettering the Condition of the Poor of the Midland District, and the Belleville Auxiliary Bible Society; he also supported a petition of Church of England members for assistance in erecting a church. The image held of him by some local people as a vindictive justice of the peace was not

shared by the Belleville correspondent of the *Kingston Chronicle* who deplored the loss of an impartial public servant, an "affectionate husband, [and] an indulgent and a kind friend."

DAVID ROBERTS

AO, Map coll., Thomas Ridout, "Belleville, Ontario, on lot 4, Thurlow Twp.," 1812; MS 75; MU 490–92; 500–1; RG 1, A-I-6, 5–6; C-IV, Thurlow Township; RG 22, ser.54, 2. Belleville Public Library (Belleville, Ont.), Hastings County Hist. Soc. coll., 915 (Thomas Coleman papers); 2119: 202 (rebellion losses claim no.108, Christopher O'Brien). BL, Add. MSS 21765, 21826–27 (transcripts at PAC). Hastings Land Registry Office (Belleville), Abstract index to deeds, Belleville town, Hastings County, A1–A2 (mfm. at AO, GS 4158). Lennox and Addington County Museum (Napanee, Ont.), Lennox and Addington Hist. Soc. coll., William Bell papers, 1st Regiment Hastings Militia, letters, orders, 1798–1831. PAC, MG 23, HII, 1, vol.1: 562–63; RG 1, E14, 10; L3, 40: B11/213; 324: Mc misc., 1788–95/136; 325: M misc., 1792–1816/65; 327A: M2/23; 328: M2/66, 71; 328A: M2/241; 330: M4/90; 330A: M4/209, 275; 331: M5/153; 333: M8/5; 334: M9/44; 338: M11/286, 323, 366, 379; 339: M11/379; 341: M12/226; 342: M12/430; 379: M leases, 1798–1832/79, 128, 146 (mfm. at AO); RG 5, A1: 8145–47, 8276–77, 8488–89, 9071, 9611–15, 12305–12, 12991–93, 13956–58, 14067–68, 14895, 14899, 17903 (mfm. at AO); B11, 1: files 16, 20, 22; 4: file 259; RG 16, A1, 12; RG 68, General index, 1651–1841: ff.419–20, 424, 432–33, 490, 515. PRO, WO 57/15: no.225 (mfm. at PAC). QUA, Richard Cartwright papers, letterbooks. "Grants of crown lands in U.C.," AO *Report*, 1929–31. "Journals of Legislative Assembly of U.C.," AO *Report*, 1911–13. *Kingston before War of 1812* (Preston). [Robert] McDowall, "McDowall marriage register," *OH*, 1 (1899): 72–94. *Kingston Gazette*, 20, 27 Nov. 1810; 4 May 1814; 25 Nov. 1815; 22 June, 13 July, 24 Aug., 28 Sept. 1816; 22 March 1817; 30 June, 6 July, 22, 29 Sept. 1818; 8 Jan., 19, 26 Feb., 7 May 1819; 14 April 1820. *Upper Canada Gazette*, 12, 26 June 1816; 3 July 1817.

Armstrong, *Handbook of Upper Canadian chronology*. Chadwick, *Ontarian families*. G. E. Boyce, *Historic Hastings* (Belleville, 1967). William Canniff, *History of the settlement of Upper Canada (Ontario) with special reference to the Bay Quinte* (Toronto, 1869; repr. Belleville, 1971); *The medical profession in Upper Canada, 1783–1850 ...* (Toronto, 1894; repr. 1980). Craig, *Upper Canada*. MacDonald, "Hon. Richard Cartwright," *Three hist. theses*, 127, 180–81. W. C. Mikel, *City of Belleville history* (Picton, Ont., 1943). "Capt. Alexander McNabb," *Tyler's Quarterly Hist. and Geneal. Magazine* (Richmond, Va.), 5 (1923–24): 144. "The town of Belleville," *Globe and Canada Farmer* (Toronto), 6 July 1877: 1–2.

McNIFF, PATRICK, surveyor; b. in Ireland; m. first Elizabeth McDonnell; m. secondly 1 Nov. 1775 Catherine McDavitt, and they had one son and three daughters; d. May 1803 in Detroit (Mich.).

Patrick McNiff left Ireland in 1764 and settled as a

551

McNiff

merchant at Saratoga (Schuylerville, N.Y.). By the time of the American revolution, he "lived in ease and affluence . . . [with] property of upwards of £3,000." Although he signed "one Rebel Association," he did not serve in the militia. In July 1776 and again the following summer rebels looted his store. "Sent away from Saratoga . . . by order of a Committee," McNiff resettled at Albany until the spring of 1779 when local rebels heard of "some intelligence he had conveyed to Canada." McNiff fled to security behind the British lines at New York. The following year he built a house and store on Staten Island but in January 1782 rebels plundered him of goods worth nearly £300 and then imprisoned him. Released shortly after, he rebuilt his home only to abandon it in April 1783, claiming that he had been chased away.

On 6 Sept. 1783 McNiff was in New York City where he petitioned Sir Guy CARLETON for aid to go to the province of Quebec. "Perhaps one of the most distressed men living," he had been reduced to existing on the charity of friends. His plea apparently fell on deaf ears for on 30 October he again sought relief. In Sorel, Que., McNiff petitioned Governor HALDIMAND for assistance in bringing his family to the province. This memorial was accompanied by testimonies to McNiff's worthiness and honesty by such notable loyalists as Stephen DeLancey, Peter Van Alstine, and Abraham Cornelius CUYLER. Cuyler mentioned information which McNiff had provided during the war and also noted that he had "some knowledge of surveying." In spite of such high praise McNiff was forced to write on 8 Jan. 1784 reminding Haldimand of his petition. This action was apparently successful and by the summer McNiff was working as a surveyor for Surveyor General Samuel Johannes HOLLAND and possibly also Sir John Johnson* at New Johnstown (Cornwall, Ont.).

McNiff laid out the river lots in six townships, completing the plan on 1 Nov. 1786. The following year he was working near Cataraqui (Kingston, Ont.) and in April produced a sketch of the Gananoque River. He did some work there for the prominent local loyalist Joel Stone* and by the summer of 1787 was well established at New Johnstown with a house and farm, which he sold four years later. On 4 June 1788 Deputy Surveyor General John Collins* instructed McNiff to go to the Ottawa River where he surveyed parts of several townships and produced a large-scale plan of his work. On 24 July Lord Dorchester [Guy Carleton] established four new administrative districts in the western area of the province, and the following spring McNiff was appointed deputy surveyor for the District of Hesse and ordered to Detroit. He and his family left Lachine, where they had been living, in May 1789, arriving in Detroit three months later.

A dispute over land claims by local Indians prevented McNiff from surveying until the matter had been settled by the "McKee Treaty" of May 1790 [see Wasson*], signed by the local deputy agent of the Indian Department, Alexander McKee*. On 2 July the district land board issued its first survey order to McNiff which he complained about as "so imperfect and inexplicit that . . . he could not comprehend nor execute it." However, by the end of the month he had done sufficient work to be able to report to Collins that the general plan of survey, which laid out lots in neat, rectangular townships, could not be applied universally without jeopardizing the improvements already made by French settlers and loyalist squatters whose lots were located haphazardly. Moreover, swamps and marshes made huge areas uninhabitable. In August and September, after his instructions had been clarified, McNiff surveyed parts of the La Tranche (Thames) River and the townships of Colchester (Colchester South) and Gosfield (Gosfield South). Before he could complete his work, however, he fell ill.

On 31 Jan. 1791 McNiff complained to Collins that land speculators – he implied strongly that members of the land board, which included such prominent men as John ASKIN and Jean-Baptiste-Pierre TESTARD Louvigny de Montigny, were involved – were hindering the progress of settlement. He repeated these charges on 3 May to Hugh FINLAY, chairman of the land committee of the Legislative Council. In April, while surveying at Detroit, McNiff had been accused by French settlers of tampering with their fences and sidelines but he denied the charges. In June the land board complained that his plan for the La Tranche River did not correspond to the general plan of survey, but he explained that swamps and the irregularity of settled lots necessitated deviations. In September he suggested the need for reform of existing regulations; he was still complaining about this problem in 1792. Finally in March 1793 the land board agreed to allow him to survey lots which were not the standard 100-acre size.

The province of Quebec had been divided in 1791, and the following year McNiff applied to Lieutenant Governor SIMCOE for the post of deputy surveyor general of Upper Canada, extolling himself as having been the "oldest deputy surveyor in the Province of Quebec . . . the most experienced (without comparison) in settling a new country." However, David William Smith* received the post and on 3 Oct. 1792 enquired of Richard G. ENGLAND, president of the district land board, if he was satisfied with McNiff's work. England's response was positive, but not for long. In May 1793 he complained to Smith: "The shadow of a difficulty is sufficient to impede for years any service he [McNiff] is directed on." Simcoe concurred with such a judgement and on 13 May wrote to Alured Clarke*, the acting governor-in-chief, that McNiff "is not competent . . . being of a very impractical disposition." Simcoe must have been relieved when Francis LE MAISTRE, Dorchester's military secretary, informed him on 27 Jan. 1794 that McNiff was no longer needed in the Engineer Department. The land boards were dissolved in November of that year, and McNiff's fate was sealed. He was soon unemployed. In the spring of 1795 an exasperated England refused to employ him on further survey work or to recommend him for a farm lot. Clearly McNiff was not wanted; in June 1795 Abraham IREDELL was appointed deputy surveyor for the Western District. In July 1796 the British evacuated Detroit in accordance with the terms of Jay's Treaty; McNiff remained, keeping with him several important surveys which he sold to Major-General Anthony Wayne for $100. Colonel John Francis Hamtramck, who had arranged the deal, charged that "the privation of 15 shillings Halifax money per day has induced him to change his coat . . . this is the total amount of patriotism of that Gentleman." Although perhaps not the base turncoat Hamtramck saw him as, McNiff undoubtedly had flexible ethics. While a surveyor he had complained bitterly and frequently about land speculation but he speculated himself when the opportunity arose. He owned about 15 per cent of the shares in a partnership including John Askin, John Askin Jr, and Alexander Henry* which had obtained rights to a huge tract of Indian land on the south shore of Lake Erie. This speculation, known as the Cuyahoga Purchase, came to an abrupt end in 1795 because Alexander Hamilton, the former American secretary of the Treasury, expressed doubts about the legality in the United States of the Indian deeds. Henry wrote to his partners, "We have lost a fortune of at least one Million of Dollars."

In 1796 McNiff was named surveyor of Wayne County (Mich.) and judge of the Court of Common Pleas; soon after, he was appointed conductor of military stores and barrack master at a salary of $40 a month. However, tranquillity was an infrequent visitor in McNiff's life. On 15 Aug. 1798 Governor Arthur St Clair revoked his surveyor's commission; in November his fellow judges refused to sit on the bench with him. Never known for easy acquiescence, McNiff immediately charged his colleagues with all manner of crimes. Countercharges followed and the upshot was the indictment and trial of McNiff and a fellow judge; both were acquitted. Between 1798 and 1802 quarrels among the magistrates virtually closed the court. Only McNiff's death in May 1803 apparently ended the feud.

Simcoe's description of McNiff as incompetent and of a "very impractical disposition" was only half correct. Although he surveyed throughout Upper Canada for a decade few errors were subsequently discovered in his work. However, examples of his

"impractical disposition" abound. As historian Milo Milton Quaife put it, McNiff's "positive temperament . . . caused him to be involved in numerous disputes." McNiff was over-confident, stubborn, tactless, argumentative, and opinionated. He complained about everything from poor wages to a lack of stationery and he skirmished with virtually everyone he met. He remains, however, a demonstration that the squeaky wheel does not always get the grease.

RON EDWARDS

AO, Map coll., J. F. Holland, copied from Patrick McNiff, "Hesse District, a map of Lake Erie, Lake St Clair, showing claims to lands in that district," [1790]; Patrick McNiff, "Hawkesbury Township, Ont., survey," [1795]; "Lake Superior, a sketch map of the north shore . . . collected from the journal of a coasting survey and remarks by Lieut. Bennet of the 8th Regiment," 1794; "Plan of part of the east [north] shore of Lake Erie [and part of the east shore of the Detroit River] in the District of Hesse . . . ," 1790; "A plan of part of the new settlement on the north bank of the south west branch of the St Lawrence River . . . ," 1786; "A plan of the new settlements on the north bank of the south west branch of the St Lawrence River . . . ," 1786; RG 1, A-I-1, 1: 201; 2: 43, 71–72, 78; 55: 58, 74; A-I-6: 90–93, 19287–89, 23094–96; A-II-1, 1: 468; C-I-9, 2: 24. BL, Add. MSS 21875: 74–76; 21877: 347–49 (copies at PAC). MTL, D. W. Smith papers. PAC, MG 23, HII, 1, vol.1: 309, 366, 368, 395–98, 426, 444; MG 30, D1, 21: 245–47; National Map Coll., H2/400-1786; R/400-1786; H1/400-1790; H1/400-[1790]; H1/400-[1790] (1924); H1/400-1790 (1905); V1/400-1791 (1909); H3/409–Hesse-1790; V30/409-Hesse-1815; R/410-Erie-1789; R11/410-Erie-1791; H12/410-Gananoque-1787; H3/410-Superior-1795; M/430-Camden-1794; M/430-Charlottenburgh-1796; M/430-Colchester-1794; M/430-Cornwall-1786; M/430-Cornwall-1792; H12/430-Lancaster-1802; H12/430-Sandwich-1798; V3/1000-1791 (1909); 1210-Detroit-1796; RG 1, E14, 10: 515–18; L4, 1–4. PRO, AO 12/27: ff.295–301 (mfm. at PAC); PRO 30/55, 8: 263–65 (mfm. at PAC). *Corr. of Lieut. Governor Simcoe* (Cruikshank). "Documents relating to the proceedings of the district land boards," AO *Report*, 1905: cxxxi–546. *John Askin papers* (Quaife). *Windsor border region* (Lajeunesse). F. C. Bald, *Detroit's first American decade, 1796 to 1805* (Ann Arbor, Mich., and London, 1948). F. C. Hamil, *The valley of the lower Thames, 1640 to 1850* (Toronto, 1951; repr. Toronto and Buffalo, N.Y., 1973). Friend Palmer, *Early days in Detroit* (Detroit, 1906). A. P. Walker and R. W. Code, "Patrick McNiff," Assoc. of Ont. Land Surveyors, *Annual report* (Toronto), 1931: 100–4.

McNUTT, ALEXANDER, army officer, colonizer, and land agent; b. 1725, probably in Londonderry (Northern Ireland), and possibly the son of Alexander and Jane McNutt; d. unmarried *c.* 1811 in Lexington, Va.

Alexander McNutt emigrated to America some time before 1753, and settled in Staunton, Va. In 1756 he was an officer in the militia on Major Andrew

McNutt

Lewis's expedition against the Shawnees on the Ohio River. A quarrel between Lewis and McNutt after the campaign may have led to McNutt's leaving Virginia for Londonderry, N.H., where many Ulster Scots lived. He is known to have been one of the "freeholders and inhabitants" of the town in September 1758. Between April and November 1760 McNutt served as a Massachusetts provincial captain at Fort Cumberland (near Sackville, N.B.), and he was also engaged that year in raising troops for the reduction of Canada.

It was about this time that McNutt first became involved in the colonization of Nova Scotia. He apparently worked initially as a deputy for Thomas Hancock, the Boston agent of Governor Charles Lawrence*, recruiting settlers for the former Acadian lands advertised by Lawrence in January 1759. That August he was in Halifax, N.S., where he secured a written promise from Lawrence of seven townships for himself and some associates on condition that he introduce Protestant settlers. One month after the governor's death in October 1760, McNutt appeared before the Nova Scotia Council to claim the promised townships. Besides mentioning his agreement with Lawrence, he stated that he had obtained 850 subscribers for the promised lands, that he had agents in Ireland and America, and that he had already sent a vessel to Ireland to bring out settlers. During the spring of 1761 a group of about 50 families he had recruited from New Hampshire arrived in the region of Cobequid (near Truro), where they received grants of land.

Early that same year McNutt was in London, England, with a letter from Administrator Jonathan Belcher* recommending him as a proper agent to bring settlers from Ireland. On 24 February McNutt was called before the Board of Trade, and three days later submitted proposals for conditions of settlement of Nova Scotia lands; most were accepted. Although emigration from the British Isles was subject to official discouragement, McNutt was a persuasive speaker and memorialist, and his proposals were attractive since they involved the British government in no ultimate expense. In return for introducing settlers into Nova Scotia, McNutt asked for the right to select townships of 100,000 acres from land ungranted and unsurveyed at the time of his settlers' arrival, and he also requested that he receive 100 acres for every 500 granted to his settlers. John Bartlet Brebner* has pointed out that if McNutt's terms had been approved, then he and not the governor and Council would have controlled the colonization of Nova Scotia. But despite the board's recommendation that the governor be instructed to grant land on McNutt's terms, the proposals failed to receive the necessary Privy Council approval that year.

In the mean time McNutt, armed with the board's approval, had proceeded to Ireland, where he had appointed agents in a semicircle through the hinterland of the port of Londonderry. On 21 April 1761 he publicly launched his campaign with an advertisement in the *Belfast News-Letter and General Advertiser* inviting "industrious farmers and useful mechanics" to emigrate to Nova Scotia and offering 200 acres to the head of each family and 50 to each member. The response seems to have been encouraging: although he had originally decided to hire only one vessel, a second had to be engaged. By October McNutt and 300 colonists had arrived in Halifax. In contrast to the substantial New England farmers who had come the previous year [*see* John Hicks*], McNutt's immigrants were "indigent people, without means of subsistence," but they were welcomed by the authorities. Over the winter they worked in Halifax, supported with provisions borrowed by McNutt from the government and with other supplies donated by the government and private charity. In the spring of 1762 the Council gave the Irish provisions, seed corn, tools, and building materials, and arranged for a vessel to take them to Cobequid, where they became tenants on the lands of earlier settlers.

McNutt had discovered on his arrival in Halifax that the Board of Trade's instructions for land grants had not been sent to Belcher, but when he appeared before that body in March 1762 he evidently did not mention the problem. The board was then discussing Belcher's enthusiastic reports of McNutt's plans to charter 10,000 tons of shipping to transport 7,000 or 8,000 persons from the north of Ireland that summer. On 16 March McNutt submitted a memorial in which he asked the board's approval of new conditions of settlement, stating that he had already entered into contracts worth £26,000 for transportation. These conditions were much more detailed and ambitious, and included a request that all grants be made in his name so that he could parcel them out himself, "this being the only security He can have of the [payment] of [the immigrants'] Passage and Subsistence, till they have worked out that Sum." He also asked to be allowed to recommend proper persons for militia commissions in the townships to be formed. Lastly, he solicited the contracts for making and clearing roads from the new townships to Halifax and for other kinds of public works. Through these contracts, he claimed, settlers unable to reach their lands immediately would be afforded employment, and their labour would also permit them to repay him for the passage money they had obtained on credit. The board again found the conditions reasonable and recommended that grants be made to the settlers McNutt had already introduced. But at the same time it questioned whether as large an emigration from Ireland as was envisaged might not be harmful to the mother country. The Privy Council considered McNutt's plan on 29 April and decided that however useful the settlement of Nova Scotia might be "the Migration from Ireland of such great numbers of His Majestys Subjects must be attended with dangerous Consequences." It therefore ordered that the governor of Nova Scotia be instructed not to grant land to Irish settlers who had been resident in Nova Scotia or another American colony for less than five years. The landlords who constituted the British government did not favour emigration since they believed that a large population at home was necessary for prosperity. Moreover, and more important, the prospect of massive emigration from the Protestant districts of Ireland had alarmed the authorities.

McNutt had once again not waited for official blessing before opening his recruitment campaign, and in the *Belfast News-Letter and General Advertiser* of 11 March 1762 he published a laudatory letter from emigrants of the previous year. But by the time he reached Londonderry in June he knew of the Privy Council decision, and his efforts to attract settlers became noticeably less enthusiastic. Nevertheless, he made arrangements for about 170 persons to sail with him for Nova Scotia on the *Nancy* and *Hopewell*. Again the Irish arrived late in the season and proved unable to support themselves. Belcher (now lieutenant governor) found it increasingly difficult to accept the expenses that McNutt's plans entailed and objected to the cost of keeping the immigrants over the winter. But when McNutt threatened to take them to Philadelphia the lieutenant governor gave in: provisions were supplied and the immigrants were taken to New Dublin Township and elsewhere in the province, where they became tenants to others. Because Belcher had apparently not revealed to the Council his instructions not to grant land to recent Irish immigrants, and thanks to McNutt's work among the councillors, a dispute developed and several councillors protested to absentee governor Henry Ellis that Belcher was trying to stifle McNutt's attempts to introduce further settlers.

In the spring of 1763 McNutt was back in London, where he addressed several memorials to the Board of Trade. The first requested compensation for losses he claimed were the result of the board's not keeping its engagements of 1761, and subsequent ones charged that Belcher and other enemies in Nova Scotia were trying to limit his settlement plans. Favourably impressed by his claim for compensation despite his lack of proof, the board recommended that he receive a compensation grant in proportion to the number of persons he had settled in Nova Scotia, and asked the colonial authorities to determine its size. Although the Council criticized his figures, it eventually awarded him 13,500 acres in 1765. The Privy Council decision having effectively halted McNutt's schemes to introduce Irish settlers into Nova Scotia, his later

involvement with Irish immigrants was minimal. All the same, his partners in Ireland sent out one or two boatloads of settlers later in the 1760s on the *Hopewell*, the *Falls*, and the *Admiral Hawke*.

His Irish plans were not, however, McNutt's only interest in colonization. In 1761, by claiming that he had the approval of the Board of Trade, he had encouraged some disbanded New England provincial soldiers, including Israel PERLEY, to settle on the Saint John River (N.B.). And at the same time as he was protesting his losses in 1763 he was proposing to transport foreign Protestants to South Carolina on condition that he receive a grant on St John's (Prince Edward) Island. Moreover, in December 1763 he submitted a plan to introduce 200,000 settlers into Nova Scotia and elsewhere in North America without expense to government. Neither of these proposals received unqualified approval in London, and they appear to have been dropped soon afterwards.

McNutt's next involvement with Nova Scotia came in 1764. The Royal Proclamation of 1763, by establishing an Indian reserve west of the Appalachians, had restricted settlement in the central colonies. Thus when, in the following year, the British government issued new instructions covering grants in Nova Scotia which made the colony more attractive to land companies elsewhere in North America, a great interest developed in the acquisition of grants there. Hearing of this interest, McNutt arrived in Philadelphia, Pa, in September 1764. By emphasizing his experience with Nova Scotia he apparently persuaded several companies to associate with him in an attempt to gain lands; moreover, he convinced these companies that his conditions of settlement (which broadly followed his 1761 proposals) were the only ones on which settlement should take place. By March 1765 McNutt and agents for several land companies were in Halifax, where McNutt produced applications for 21 townships of 100,000 acres each and set out the conditions of settlement. Governor Montagu Wilmot* was impressed by the number of applications and wrote to the Board of Trade about the possibility of diverting to Nova Scotia "the annual current of Germans into America." But the governor was hesitant to grant land on McNutt's terms since they differed considerably from those in the new instructions, which he had received in June 1764. In addition, he himself considered that the new instructions would encourage speculation, and had voiced his misgivings to the British government. Moreover, after consulting the Council he had decided not to publish the instructions as he had been ordered until he received further information from the Board of Trade. While awaiting a reply Wilmot and the Council made reservations of 2,300,000 acres to McNutt and the agents, and proposed as a condition of the grant that settlement be completed in four years or the land would be forfeited. Wilmot wanted to prevent land from being held indefinitely in large blocks by speculators.

For five months over the summer of 1765 McNutt and the agents remained in Halifax in the hope of obtaining better terms from the provincial government. Disputes broke out, McNutt's supposed associates claiming that he was trying to deceive them. One of the agents, Anthony Wayne, who later became an American Revolutionary War general, reported that several Council members had told him that McNutt "had made Interest privately against us & Said that we had Nothing to do with the terms or any thing Else, & was only Employed as Surveyors under him." McNutt had succeeded in having his name inserted in the list of the grantees for each of the four townships reserved for Wayne and his associates, and Wayne wished to "try to Exclude him if possible, as he has been rather a Determent than of Service to us."

By October 1765 the British government had not replied to either McNutt's conditions or Wilmot's objections. McNutt and the agents demanded immediate action since the coming into effect of the Stamp Act on 1 November would add an extra £15 6s. 3d. to the cost of every township grant. Wilmot and the Council decided to make the grants, but insisted on the conditions proposed when the land had originally been reserved. Between 13 October and 1 November Nova Scotia experienced a wave of land granting in which 3,000,000 acres were parcelled out, mainly in the south, east, and northeast of the peninsula and along the Saint John, Petitcodiac, and Memramcook rivers (N.B.). McNutt acquired a township grant at Port Roseway (Shelburne), and with various associates he obtained grants along the Saint John, the northern shore, the South Shore, and the northeast coast totalling half of the total acreage granted. He contrived to have clauses inserted in the grants stating that representations were being made to the crown and any more favourable conditions that might be obtained as a result would apply to the lands ceded by these grants. Wayne's plans for the exclusion of McNutt evidently did not succeed, since McNutt received a one-fifth share in the two township grants Wayne's group was allotted. Moreover, the Philadelphia Company, one of the organizations with which McNutt had associated himself, was also disappointed. It had expected that its grant of 200,000 acres on the northern shore in present-day Pictou and Colchester counties would have a large water frontage, but McNutt and some associates from Ireland obtained most of the frontage on Pictou harbour, the best in the region, in another grant.

Despite the huge amounts of land granted, Wilmot's conditions about settlement in four years effectively stopped speculation, and the Nova Scotia land boom rapidly petered out. Only a few settlers actually arrived, and over an extended period of time most of the grants were escheated. McNutt returned to London, where in April 1766 he appeared before the Board of Trade to complain that the board's instructions had not been followed and that Wilmot and the Council had given the best lands and more favourable terms of settlement to their friends. When the Nova Scotia government was asked to comment on these charges, it denied any partiality and stated that any obstructions McNutt claimed to have encountered "had proceeded from his own intemperate Zeal & exhorbitant demands from Government." So far from hindering him, they claimed, they had included his name on every grant to the companies with which he had been associated. McNutt's charges seem to have gone no farther.

McNutt himself went back to Nova Scotia, where from time to time during the late 1760s he lived with his brother Benjamin on McNutt Island in the harbour of Port Roseway. He also seems to have resided in the Truro region, and appears on the census for that town in 1771. To support himself McNutt probably engaged in the timber trade, for in June 1767 Attorney General William Nesbitt* was ordered to prosecute McNutt for the unauthorized occupation of land and cutting of timber. McNutt evidently made no effort to develop his grants, and in 1770 the townships at Pictou harbour and on Minas Basin in which he owned land were escheated; three years later the one at Beaver Harbour went the same way. Moreover, the township at Port Roseway (which included McNutt Island) was sold in 1768 to pay a debt McNutt owed Henry Ferguson, a Halifax merchant. McNutt was taken to court at various times between 1767 and 1774 for other debts and ordered to pay several hundred pounds to his creditors, who included Michael Francklin* and Joshua Mauger*.

With the coming of the American revolution McNutt's career entered a new phase. Although he later claimed to have conformed to the principles underlying the resolutions of the Continental congresses from 1774, he seems to have remained in Nova Scotia during the early years of the rebellion. But when his house at Port Roseway was robbed in June 1778 by a party of "armed ruffians" from an American privateer who took "upwards of Three Hundred Pounds Sterling, Exclusive of Books [and] Papers," in property, he travelled to Boston to appeal to the Massachusetts Council for relief. On the way he suffered further humiliation when arrested at Salem as a "Doubtful Character." Unable to obtain immediate compensation, he went to Philadelphia to petition Congress to draw Nova Scotia into the revolution, and in March 1779 he joined with Phineas Nevers and Samuel Rogers of Maugerville (N.B.) to ask Congress for money to construct a road between the Penobscot River (Maine) and the Saint John. In September 1779

McNutt was given permission to return to Halifax to obtain papers which would prove his losses, but he was suspected by the British authorities and Francis McLean*, commander at Halifax, had been warned that McNutt "was supposed to be in correspondence with the rebels & should be watched." McNutt evidently left Nova Scotia in 1780 or 1781. In the latter year the Nova Scotia authorities received a letter describing him as "a subtle, designing fellow, [who] has endeavoured to circulate several letters and dangerous pamphlets throughout the Province."

Among these pamphlets may have been the one attributed to McNutt entitled *Constitution and frame of government for the free and independent state and commonwealth of New Ireland*, apparently printed in 1781 at Philadelphia. The new nation was intended to encompass that part of Massachusetts between the Saco (Maine) and St Croix rivers, and either by design or by coincidence had the same name and extent as a province proposed by the British government as a haven for displaced loyalists [*see* John CALEFF]. There any similarity between the two projects ended. In contrast to the imperial province, the independent New Ireland was to have a theocratic constitution based on puritanical principles. Lawyers were to be forbidden to hold offices of state, and no person not a regular member of a Christian society would hold public office. Moreover, such recreations as plays, horse-racing, cock-fighting, balls, and games of chance would be banned.

After the end of the revolution McNutt came back to McNutt Island, and both he and Benjamin are mentioned in the tax lists for Shelburne in 1786 and 1787. In September 1791 William Hale, a local merchant, was trying to collect a small debt from "Col. McNutt on the Island." McNutt's name was on the Shelburne tax list of 1794, but he moved to Virginia in 1796. The following year he executed a deed of property there in Rockbridge County, where he was also mentioned in a property case in 1802. He is thought to have died some time about 1811.

PHYLLIS R. BLAKELEY

PANS, MG 4, 140 (photocopy); RG 1, 31: docs.53, 55; 164: f.331; 166A: 41; 188: 5, 29 Nov. 1762; 3 June–2 July 1765; 189: 26 Aug., 1 Sept. 1766; 27 June 1767; 14 April 1770; 3 Oct. 1774; 219: docs.68–69; 220: doc.59; 221, no.3: doc.6; 374: ff.79–80, 93–94, 118, 122, 126–27, 135; 377, no.2: 6, 23, 27, 29, 32, 44, 112, 174, 179; 443: doc.13. PRO, CO 217/18: ff.143–44, 148–57, 198–215, 297–98; 217/19: ff.278–79, 300–1; 217/20: ff.21–24, 41–46, 82–85, 224; 217/21: ff.158–67 (mfm. at PANS). *Annals of Yarmouth and Barrington (Nova Scotia) in the Revolutionary War, compiled from original manuscripts, etc., contained in the office of the secretary of the Commonwealth, State House, Boston, Mass.*, comp. E. D. Poole (Yarmouth, N.S., 1899), 45–49. *DAB*.

Bell, *Foreign Protestants* (Toronto, 1961), 109n., 111– 12, 113n., 114–15, 117n., 122n., 123n., 547. Brebner, *Neutral Yankees* (1969). R. J. Dickson, *Ulster emigration to colonial America, 1718–1775* (London, 1966), 55, 101, 132, 134–52, 154, 163–67, 173, 179–80, 182, 191–93. E. C. Wright, *The Petitcodiac: a study of the New Brunswick river and of the people who settled along it* (Sackville, N.B., 1945), 16–23, 38–40. A. W. H. Eaton, "Alexander McNutt, the colonizer," *Americana* (New York), 8 (1913): 1065–106; "The settling of Colchester County, Nova Scotia, by New England Puritans and Ulster Scotsmen," RSC *Trans.*, 3rd ser., 6 (1912), sect.II: 221–65. Margaret Ells, "Clearing the decks for the loyalists," CHA *Report*, 1933: 43–58. W. O. Raymond, "Colonel Alexander McNutt and the pre-loyalist settlements of Nova Scotia," RSC *Trans.*, 3rd ser., 5 (1911), sect.II: 23–115; 6 (1912), sect.II: 201–15.

MACORMICK. *See* MACARMICK

McSWINEY, EDWARD, clerk and militiaman; m. with four children; fl. 1812–15.

One of the significant aspects of the 19th-century loyalist account of Canada's origins is the role of Upper Canadians and the militia in successfully repelling American invaders during the War of 1812. In fact, however, this loyalist myth (long since discredited) was in part generated by contemporaries such as John Strachan* who feared that the province would be lost by the actions of the disloyal. Since at times the foremost problem of civil government and military command was disaffection [*see* Jacob OVERHOLSER], it is not surprising that an outstanding demonstration of loyalty, no matter how suspect, could be its own reward in a society anxious for examples of zealous adherence to the crown. The hitherto untold tale of Sergeant Edward McSwiney is a case in point.

A "British European" by birth, McSwiney came to Upper Canada from the lower province to clerk for surveyor Reuben Sherwood. Soon after the outbreak of war in June 1812 McSwiney enlisted for service, becoming a sergeant in his employer's company of 1st Leeds Militia. On 10 October he stood guard at the arms depot of the Elizabethtown (Brockville) garrison. When a fellow militiaman, Andrew Fuller, attempted to take several items without authorization, McSwiney challenged him. After exchanging abusive language, the two men scuffled. A friend of Fuller's, Daniel Cloud, encouraged him to whip "the damned Rascal." Now threatened by two men, McSwiney discharged his musket, mortally wounding Fuller. McSwiney was arrested and turned over to the district sheriff.

After a lengthy incarceration he was indicted by the grand jury at the Johnstown District assizes on 7 Sept. 1813 and was tried three days later before William Campbell*. The petit jury, after hearing the evidence of eight witnesses for the crown and one for the prisoner, found McSwiney guilty. Campbell sentenced

McSwiney

him to be hanged on 18 October, thereby allowing sufficient time for the usual petitions for pardon to be made on the prisoner's behalf. Campbell himself reported to the administrator that there was no legal cause "to induce a Mitigation of his fate," but he mentioned McSwiney's "having declined to avail himself of the opportunity to escape afforded him by the Enemy on the 6th February last." On 17 September, "in his own hand writing," McSwiney penned the first of several eloquent petitions seeking royal mercy.

The petitions reveal a shrewd mind. Here was a man who knew how to make a case for himself. He drew on the commonplace elements of such documents: personal suffering, disgrace, and the plight of his family. But his genius was to emphasize aspects of his case which on a larger scale were provincial concerns raised by the exigencies of the war. In a district that was later called the most disaffected within the province, he was a man who sought "to retain life, only that he may devote it to his Country in defending it from the grasp of a malignant and inveterate foe." Taking for himself the cloak of loyalty, he tarred both his victim and the jury with the brush of treason. Fuller was "a man recently from the United States, a mercenary, or hired Substitute for one of the Militiamen, of base dissolute reputation, and strongly suspected as being inimical to His Majesty and Government." Seizing upon the desertions which had been rife among the colony's militia since the beginning of the war, McSwiney tied Fuller's action to the "daily occurrences of Mens deserting to the Enemy." Fuller's accomplice, Cloud, whom Mc-Swiney noted in a later petition had deserted to the enemy, was hostile to him because of his "strict enquiries" about Cloud's brother, also a deserter. As a man of only pure and patriotic impulses, McSwiney disavowed any malice on his part in the fatal shooting. It had occurred "in the heat of momentary passion [and was occasioned by] his Zeal for the service, his Loyalty and the most affectionate attachment to his ever beloved Sovereign and Country."

The heroic deeds of the war were not confined to the battlefield. The unquestionable proof of McSwiney's ardent loyalty was the incident mentioned by Campbell that occurred on the night of 6 Feb. 1813, when American troops raided Elizabethtown, taking several captives and, according to McSwiney, "liberating the Prisoners from the Gaol." All, that is, but one. Animated by an abiding patriotism, McSwiney remained in an empty jail. He wrote that he had "spurned the thought of becoming a Fugitive in the land of, and amongst the Enemies of his King and Country." But his refusal to leave the jail had been ignored by a jury "prejudiced against him. . . . Had [he] been a Yankee, or [been] possessed of Yankee principles . . . the Testimony would have been less criminating, and the Verdict less severe."

But McSwiney's sterling example of loyalty had made a deep impact upon local militia officers and the leading members of society in the Johnstown District. Each of his petitions bore the support of members of the local élite, including Archibald McLean* and Jonas Jones*. McSwiney's craft in framing his petition had its calculated effect. Upon receipt of the first petition, the provincial administrator, Francis Rottenburg*, "felt inclined to pardon him." Acting Attorney General John Beverley Robinson* apprised him that pardon fell within the royal prerogative and that the appropriate course of action was to postpone the execution and recommend McSwiney to "His Majesty's mercy." Campbell was shocked. He was unable to "report any thing favorable" of McSwiney and regarded even the mere application for clemency as "totally unmerited." None the less, the execution was respited "until His Majestys pleasure shall be known." At issue was not legal cause – neither Campbell nor Robinson thought much of McSwiney's claims in this regard – but his manifest loyalty on the night of 6 February. Not all, however, were as impressed by this act as the provincial administrators were. The jailer on that fateful evening noted tersely that McSwiney, in spite of his assertion to the contrary, was the "only one [in jail] at the time the Americans passed this place; it was impossible for him to make his escape unless rescued as he is kept in Irons and chained."

At this juncture the case became complicated by the change of administrations (Rottenburg was succeeded by George Gordon Drummond* in December 1813), by the rudimentary state of the attorney general's office, and by legal technicalities. McSwiney insisted that the reprieve constituted a pardon, but there was no copy of it at York (Toronto) and matters rested until January 1814, when Robinson, after receiving a copy from the Johnstown District sheriff, apprised Drummond that the convict was mistaken. McSwiney continued to languish in jail, "kept in Irons – hands as well as legs, and chained to the floor," while Robinson attempted to sort out matters. The sentence was continually respited until on 25 Oct. 1814 Governor Sir George PREVOST's secretary notified Drummond that the case was entirely within Upper Canadian jurisdiction.

Finally, on 2 Jan. 1815, Drummond forwarded to the Colonial Office McSwiney's plea for mercy, supported by petitions and his own recommendation. The local petitions urging clemency were of critical importance. Drummond described them as coming from "gentlemen . . . of the most respectable Standing . . . and they bear strong testimony of the Loyalty and Zeal for the Service of his King and Country which he [McSwiney] had evinced." Drummond added that the jury was "prejudiced against McSwiney, not only on account of his Loyalty and Activity in bringing the Seditious to justice but because the man who had . . .

provoked the occasion . . . was one like themselves." The appeal was forwarded immediately to the Home Department where it was passed to the Prince Regent and Privy Council for their consideration. Once again McSwiney's deft handiwork proved utterly convincing; a pardon was drawn up on 29 June. After passing back down the successive stages of authority, Attorney General D'Arcy Boulton* issued a fiat for McSwiney's release on 30 October. McSwiney thereafter disappeared from sight and likely left the province.

The case of Edward McSwiney is a marvellous illustration of individual cunning. Gaining a pardon was no mean feat. A lowly sergeant, he had to overcome the legal opinion of Campbell that there was not a shred of evidence to support his extravagant claims. Moreover, Robinson was totally unsympathetic for reasons probably similar to Campbell's. But men of a less legal bent were easily won. The ultimate success of McSwiney's petitions without judicial recommendation reflected the mentality of a harrowed administration; men such as Drummond were as anxious to reward loyalty as they were to suppress disaffection. Had allegiance been more certain it is possible that the beguiling productions of that most artful of dodgers, Edward McSwiney, would have received short shrift from all concerned.

ROBERT LOCHIEL FRASER III

AO, RG 22, ser.134, 4: 132, 135. PAC, RG 5, A1: 7741, 8859–930, 10596–97, 10678–79, 10860–61; RG 7, G1, 57: 108–10. PRO, CO 42/356: 3–5, 260–61, 266–67. *Select British docs. of War of 1812* (Wood), 2: 13–24. Hitsman, *Incredible War of 1812*, 105–20.

McTAVISH, DONALD, fur trader; b. 1771 or 1772 in Strath Errick, Scotland, son of Alexander McTavish; drowned 22 May 1814 at the mouth of the Columbia River.

Like many Nor'Westers, Donald McTavish entered the fur trade through kinship ties, his first cousin being Simon MCTAVISH, the North West Company's principal director. Having joined as an apprentice clerk about 1790, he apparently spent the following 18 years in the Upper English River department, as the NWC designated the basin of the upper Churchill River. Some time before 1795 he was on the Beaver River, in that department, most likely establishing the Lac Vert post (Green Lake, Sask.). David Thompson* met him at the Beaver River in 1797, and in the following year McTavish reported that he had sent Thompson from Lac Vert "by land to touch at Fort George," an NWC post on the North Saskatchewan about 40 miles west of the present-day Alberta border. Perhaps as early as 1797 McTavish was promoted to a partnership. Certainly he was a partner by 1799, for he was listed along with Angus Shaw* as a proprietor in the Upper English River department that year.

Following the company's annual meeting at Kaministiquia (Thunder Bay, Ont.) in 1804, he went on rotation to Montreal. In 1806 he was again assigned to the English River.

In the course of the 1808 meeting at Fort William (as Kaministiquia was by then named), McTavish was one of five wintering partners appointed to recommend solutions to various financial difficulties, including the problem of heavy inventories. As one of the proprietors named to the Athabasca department that year, he took charge at Fort Dunvegan (on the Peace River at 118°40′ W) in place of Archibald Norman McLeod*. Apart from his annual journey to Fort William, McTavish remained at Fort Dunvegan until 1811.

The NWC continued during this time to expand its trade westward. David Thompson explored the Columbia River and its tributaries, and the East India Company was approached for a licence that would allow the NWC to sell its furs in China. In the summer of 1811 the NWC resolved to "enter into adventure and a Trade from England, and China to the North West Coast of America" with Donald McTavish in command. On his rotation McTavish travelled to Britain for the winter of 1811–12. He purchased an estate in Scotland for his retirement and then joined William McGillivray* in London to make preparations for an expedition to the northwest coast. It may have been at this time that he was enrolled as an original member of the Canada Club, founded in 1810 to lobby the British government on behalf of Canadian commercial interests. Following the London fur sales of April 1812, he returned to Fort William, where Thompson reported not only his success in reaching the Pacific but also the establishment of Astoria at the Columbia's mouth by John Jacob Astor*'s Pacific Fur Company. Taking advantage of the recently declared war between the United States and Britain, the wintering partners determined to seize Astoria by "the sending a Vessel thereto," and at the same time confirmed McTavish's appointment as the venture's leader since "we hope much from his known integrity." Accompanied by his second in command, John McDonald* of Garth (who apparently was somewhat miffed at being "deprived" of first place), McTavish set sail for England where arrangements had been made to have the NWC ship *Isaac Todd* escorted by a naval frigate with orders "to destroy, and if possible totally annihilate," any American settlements on the northwest coast.

The *Isaac Todd*, under Captain Fraser Smith, set sail from Portsmouth on 25 March 1813, but not before most of the NWC voyageurs and clerks had been temporarily impressed into the Royal Navy. McTavish blamed McDonald for this episode and another incident at Tenerife, in the Canary Islands, where the voyageurs underwent a brief imprisonment as suspected citizens of France. At Rio de Janeiro,

McTavish

Brazil, McDonald transferred to the convoy ship. Left for the remainder of the 13-month voyage on the lumbering *Isaac Todd*, with a crew who reportedly came to detest him "beyond all measure," McTavish had for consolation the charms of Jane Barnes, a Portsmouth barmaid whom he had induced to accompany him.

The *Isaac Todd* reached the Columbia on 23 April 1814, only to find that Astoria had already been acquired by an overland party of Nor'Westers through purchase on 16 Oct. 1813 [*see* Duncan McDOUGALL], and had been renamed Fort George upon its formal possession by the sloop *Racoon* on 13 December. The management of the post was in disarray when McTavish assumed charge. He immediately demonstrated his well-known reputation for "securing the good will and alliance of the Indian Nations." Not only did he pay "uncommon attention" to all Indians coming to trade, regardless of status, and allow the chiefs to sleep inside the fort because of rain, but he managed to arrange a murder trial and execution by firing-squad of some Indians with the complete approbation of the chiefs, with whom he then "smoked the calumet of peace." But what created more of a stir was his "flaxen-haired, blue-eyed" companion, Miss Barnes, and the transfer of her affections to Alexander HENRY. Being of an "amorous temperament," however, McTavish was sympathetic to others' liaisons and understandingly gave up his room two nights later "for the convenience" of three colleagues and their Chinook women; he subsequently took a Chinook woman "in tow" himself.

On 22 May 1814 McTavish drowned with Henry when their boat capsized on its way to the *Isaac Todd*, a mishap some Nor'Westers later blamed on Captain Smith. McTavish's body was found a day or two later and buried near the fort. According to his gravestone he was 42. The following November, before his death became known in Montreal, McTavish, McGillivrays and Company, principal shareholders in the NWC, nominated him as an agent.

But for the Columbia adventure and the manner of his death, Donald McTavish might not have been one of the more memorable Nor'Westers. Yet it was through his rather typical activities in the English River and Athabasca country that he not only realized an "independent fortune" but won the respect of NWC agents, partners, and clerks. Eulogized in the *Quebec Gazette* for his "enterprising genius," he was remembered by Ross Cox*, a member of the expedition to Astoria, as "a man of bold and decided character" who appreciated merit "without reference to a man's family or connexions."

JEAN MORRISON

Oreg. Hist. Soc. (Portland), Scrapbooks, SB 49: 3. PAC, MG 19, E1, ser.1 (transcripts; mfm. at Old Fort William

(Thunder Bay, Ont.)). UTL-TF, MS coll. 30. *Les bourgeois de la Compagnie du Nord-Ouest* (Masson). *Docs. relating to NWC* (Wallace), 442–43. [D. W. Harmon], *Sixteen years in the Indian country: the journal of Daniel Williams Harmon, 1800–1816*, ed. W. K. Lamb (Toronto, 1957). Duncan McGillivray, *The journal of Duncan M'Gillivray of the North West Company at Fort George on the Saskatchewan, 1794–5*, ed. and intro. A. S. Morton (Toronto, 1929). Mackenzie, *Journals and letters* (Lamb), 476. *New light on early hist. of greater northwest* (Coues). [David Thompson], *David Thompson's narrative of his explorations in western America*, ed. J. B. Tyrrell (Toronto, 1916; repr. New York, 1968). *Quebec Gazette*, 14 Dec. 1814. B. B. Barker, *The McLoughlin empire and its rulers* . . . (Glendale, Calif., 1959), 161. J. G. Colmer, *The Canada Club (London)* . . . ([London, Ont.], 1934), 7. Ross Cox, *The Columbia River; or scenes and adventures during a residence of six years on the western side of the Rocky Mountains* . . . , ed. E. I. and J. R. Stewart (Norman, Okla., 1957). Grace Flandrau, *Astor and the Oregon country* ([St Paul, Minn.], n.d.). Alexander Ross, *The fur hunters of the far west*, ed. K. A. Spaulding (Norman, 1956). B. M. Gough, "The 1813 expedition to Astoria," *Beaver*, outfit 304 (autumn 1973): 44–51.

McTAVISH, SIMON, fur trader and dealer in furs, militia officer, office holder, landowner, seigneur, and businessman; b. *c.* 1750 in Strath Errick, Scotland, son of John McTavish of Garthbeg; d. 6 July 1804 in Montreal, Lower Canada.

Simon McTavish came from a poor family. His father was a lieutenant in the 78th Foot, a Highland regiment, and was at Louisbourg, Île Royale (Cape Breton Island), when New France fell; he returned to Scotland when the troops were demobilized in 1763. The following year Simon, who was still very young and penniless, landed at New York. He found work there with a merchant, who may also have been a Scot. This marked the beginning of his apprenticeship in business. In 1771 he petitioned the governor of New York for a grant of 2,000 acres in Albany County on behalf of his father. At that time McTavish seems to have been in business for himself, with an interest in the fur trade. In 1772 he was at Detroit, a place favoured by American traders, and there he joined forces with William Edgar, one of the most important local merchants. The following year he traded in the Niagara region. In December 1774, following the passage of the Quebec Act, he wrote, "I apprehend this Bill will be of infinite hurt to our Trade. . . . But in case it shou'd not be repealed at all, we must inevitably break off our Connexion with this Province & have our Supplies from Canada." It would appear that he was beginning to envisage moving his operations from New York and Albany to Montreal. At this point McTavish was in partnership with another Scot, James Bannerman, and he steered his fur-trading expeditions towards the region northwest of the Great Lakes, unlike a great many American merchants who were concentrating on the area south and west.

The reasons that led McTavish to establish himself in Montreal were primarily economic, although political circumstances precipitated his decision. In 1775 he was at Detroit. In June 1776 Bannerman noted the scarcity of trade goods and indicated that McTavish had already left Michilimackinac (Mackinaw City, Mich.) for Grand Portage (near Grand Portage, Minn.). As the season advanced, events seemed to confirm their pessimistic forecasts. From the end of July to 10 August, Bannerman continued to be all the more worried since he feared that the poor take of furs "here [Michilimackinac] & in the North" would not allow him to pay for "the large purchases of Goods, provisions, & Liquors" which he had been obliged to make in order to guard against the shortage of these items. "I am afraid I shall lose considerably," he wrote. By mid August McTavish was back at Michilimackinac and was getting ready for a new expedition, in which he took George MCBEATH as a partner. Pessimistic forecasts notwithstanding, as a result of arrangements made at Grand Portage McTavish was back in Montreal around the end of September 1776, content, and announcing that he was leaving for London with a cargo of pelts that he valued at £15,000. "Fortune has proved so kind a Mistress to me for some years past," he declared, "that perhaps I am too Sanguine; and the Jade may now Jilt me effectually by lowering the Prices of Furrs at home – at any rate I am determin'd to Venture."

It was customary among the merchants, voyageurs, and *engagés* to celebrate their return from the *pays d'en haut*. McTavish was never backward in joining the festivities. His trip to England was probably for business reasons and a chance to see Scotland again, where as a rich relative he undertook to pay for secondary schooling for his nephews, among them DUNCAN and William* McGillivray. But in addition it was a good chance to relax. In March 1778 he wrote to Edgar: "We have had a continual round of dissipation here, dancing Clubs drinking, &c ᵃ& yet I do not like the place . . . as we advance in Life we are more difficult to be pleased . . . I was always like a fish out of water when not in Love."

This period seems to have been an important one in McTavish's career. He tried out all aspects of the fur business: in financial matters he was connected with the London firm of Phyn, Ellice and Company [*see* Alexander ELLICE], and his partnership with Bannerman enabled him both to acquire wide experience in the field and to become aware of the possibilities that were offered by joint enterprises. In May 1777 Bannerman had informed him of his intention to retire to England in the autumn of 1778. Perhaps as a result of successes in the preceding years, their investments were particularly large: in 1777 they fitted out 27 bateaux, hired 108 men, and purchased goods worth £15,800; in 1778 they outfitted 8 canoes and 30 bateaux, engaged 178 men, and allocated £9,500 for trade goods. Bannerman did not retire until the end of the 1779 season.

McTavish does not seem to have gone very far into the northwest before 1779. Nevertheless he had begun to realize that the future of the trade in pelts lay in this direction. Consequently his meeting with the Frobisher brothers, Benjamin* and JOSEPH, was an event of paramount importance. The Frobishers had set out to build a great enterprise that would give them control of the trade in the northwest. In 1779 the formation of a coalition which in addition to the Frobishers and McTavish included Charles Paterson, James MCGILL, Isaac TODD, Robert Grant, and some fur traders of secondary rank, made evident the emergence of the North West Company. Perspectives much broader than those afforded by his partnership with Bannerman now opened up for McTavish. Moreover, the struggle for the upper hand in trading, as it developed from 1780, effectively served the interests of the Frobisher–McTavish group. McGill, Todd, and Paterson were primarily interested in trading in the southwest. Unlike the Frobishers, they were convinced that the peace treaty of 1783 between Great Britain and the United States would not really alter the balance of forces in the fur-trade economy. Consequently they were no longer in the NWC when it was reorganized during the winter of 1783–84. They confined themselves to helping finance the firms engaged in this northwest trade, keeping the southwest as their own field of endeavour. McTavish and the Frobishers, who had held 4 of the 16 shares in 1779, owned 6 of them in 1783. At that date, although McTavish had become an important member in the enterprise, the pre-eminent figure was undoubtedly Benjamin Frobisher, who was the brains of the company. The other partners, Grant, McBeath, Nicholas MONTOUR, Peter POND, Patrick Small, and William Holmes*, did not possess leadership qualities.

Despite its power in the field and the strength of its support in Montreal, the NWC was not immediately successful in establishing its supremacy. The support of Phyn, Ellice enabled Gregory, MacLeod and Company, under John GREGORY's management, to engage in the northwest trade from 1785; rivalry with this firm would become more and more intense and difficult to sustain financially. But it was an unequal struggle; in 1787 Gregory could outfit only 9 canoes, whereas the NWC got 25 ready and also made use of 4 bateaux.

The year 1787 was a decisive one for McTavish. Benjamin Frobisher's death in April would provide the opportunity to climb to the top of the NWC. He was not unaware of the fact that Joseph Frobisher, who had neither the experience nor the talent to manage a large enterprise, was incapable of succeeding his brother as general director of the company. He also knew that an organization of its size could not be

McTavish

run entirely from Montreal or Grand Portage. He therefore proposed to Frobisher that they amalgamate their firms, which, he said, between them owned half the shares in the NWC. Frobisher was quick to accept, on 22 April, the offer from McTavish, who was about to leave for Grand Portage. When McTavish reached his destination feelings were running high because of the murder of John Ross, one of the partners in Gregory, MacLeod and a former partner in the NWC. McTavish then proposed a reorganization of the NWC that would permit him to bring his rivals into the enterprise. Thus, when the firm of McTavish, Frobisher and Company was founded in November 1787, it effectively controlled 11 of the company's 20 shares – 7 held in its own right, and 4 others in the hands of Small and Montour – and it reserved only 4 shares in all for Gregory, Normand MacLeod*, Peter PANGMAN, and Alexander MACKENZIE. The admission of these valuable men into the company strengthened it and signified the elimination of all opposition from the hinterland.

From the beginning the NWC grouped together a certain number of firms: eight in 1779 and 1783–84, nine in 1787; theoretically they were all on an equal footing, with expenses and profits being divided in proportion to their respective interests in the enterprise. This principle of equality governed decision-making about the allocation of territory and about strategies for fighting competitors, both within the country and abroad. On the other hand, financing, importing trade goods, hiring men, and selling the pelts on the outside market were the responsibility of one firm, which enjoyed a kind of supremacy on the management level and profited from it. Before 1787 Benjamin and Joseph Frobisher's firm played that role; it had now passed to McTavish, Frobisher. This structure would enable McTavish to extend his hold over all NWC operations.

McTavish's influence on the company's destiny was soon felt. Within a few years he undertook to reorganize company relations with London business circles. In 1787 he was still satisfied with the system linking the company with its two London suppliers, the houses of Dyer, Allan and Company and Brickwood, Pattle and Company: "As we are supplied from Home by two Houses which we have reason to esteem we would continue the business, one-half with each. for we should have occasion for the credit allowed by both, to carry on the business on an extensive scale, as we do now." But the situation became more complicated the following year, because Dyer, Allan stopped sending goods. In June Brickwood, Pattle, which Joseph Frobisher invited to supply his company with all its merchandise, refused to commit itself further, having decided to reduce the scope of its commercial activities. Finally, in October 1788 Phyn, Ellices, and Inglis agreed to furnish the other half of the company's requirements. In order to minimize the uncertainties surrounding the sale of pelts, the obtaining of credit and insurance, and the purchase of goods, McTavish decided to found his own house in London: McTavish, Fraser and Company. He entrusted its management to his cousin John Fraser, a businessman who was thoroughly knowledgeable about trading conditions on both sides of the Atlantic. This enterprise seems to have enjoyed a degree of autonomy, since in 1794 Frobisher, James Hallowell Sr, and Gregory, who were grappling with a difficult economic situation, wrote to Fraser, "The only Idea that must in future be entertained is, *that the two Houses must stand or fall together*." But in 1799 Fraser himself reminded McTavish that McTavish, Fraser and McTavish, Frobisher were separate enterprises: "From all these considerations I trust you will not press such unpleasant & unprofitable business on us." Be that as it may, Fraser played an extremely important role. He kept very careful watch on the sales of furs and noted how consignments from the Hudson's Bay Company fared. He saw to the purchasing of goods, insured them, and had them shipped. He proved indispensable in the financial field above all; McTavish observed, "All that man can do Mr. Fraser is equal to, in matters of finance." On this subject Fraser multiplied his warnings and admonitions. To Frobisher he declared: "Nothing but a total ignorance of the situation of your affairs in this Country could have dictated your letter . . . by refusing to comply with our request, you have brought your affairs to the verge of destruction." In 1795 he wrote to McTavish himself, "In short my dear friend the business is become extremely important, & requires most serious attention." In 1793–94 the turnover of Fraser, McTavish, on which the two partners received a commission, amounted to £311,400.

The fluctuations of demand on the London market were a factor over which dealers in pelts had little control. The only solution to the problem, which was made more acute from 1793 by the French revolutionary wars, lay in diversification of markets. Around 1790, besides the American market only the Chinese one was open. From then on the NWC turned its efforts in that direction. As the furs had to pass through New York, McTavish, Frobisher was obliged to extend its network of associations. Shipments for China were organized in collaboration with two merchants connected with the fur business, Alexander Henry* in Montreal, and John Jacob Astor*, his New York partner. At first McTavish and Frobisher used American ships, which delivered the pelts and took on tea, silks, and porcelain for the return trip. These ventures cost £13,484 in 1792, £16,260 in 1793, and £22,824 in 1794. Expansion of this part of the business made it necessary to set up a new structure,

562

an office in New York. When Alexander Mackenzie took charge of this branch, he urged the company to use its own ships. In 1798 the enterprise bought the *Northern Liberties*, a 340-ton vessel, and had the *Nancy* built. In London Fraser was concerned and advised McTavish to be very cautious. He maintained that this trade was creating other problems related to competition with the HBC since the finest furs were being shipped to China. In 1799 he noted, "We have been much disappointed in the assortment of your fine Beaver . . . from which we infer that you have pickd out the best for the China market." It may also be assumed that the Chinese venture facilitated access to the American market.

Almost inevitably the fur economy led to territorial expansion. Not only was it necessary to meet the demand, but the best pelts had to be sought out. The volume of these extraordinary catches of animals was so great that resources were sure to be gradually exhausted. In the period 1764–86, 10,258,350 pelts were exported through the port of Quebec. Shipments of beaver accounted for 2,556,236 of them. As this process had been going on since the earliest days of New France, the need to extend the trading grounds can be readily understood. The realities which McTavish faced were not new, but they steadily became more compelling. The hunt for fur-bearing animals prompted a continual shift of the centres of exploitation to the west and north and also required explorers, a fact evident at the time of Pierre Gaultier* de Varennes et de La Vérendrye and even more evident around 1790. The voyages of Mackenzie, who went down the river that bears his name right to the Arctic Ocean in 1789 and travelled overland to the Pacific in 1793, were inspired by the needs of the fur economy. The explorations of David Thompson*, who journeyed as far as the Rocky Mountains in 1800 and finally reached the mouth of the Columbia River in 1811, were also dictated by the same concerns. Moving the centres of production towards the Athabasca region and beyond made more necessary than ever the elimination of competition, an essential condition for tight control of transportation costs and wages, especially since prices tended to rise.

Developing new grounds with the aim of increasing production and maintaining stricter controls led the company to establish new posts. Naturally, in this steady drive towards the west Grand Portage remained the most important staging post built under Benjamin Frobisher's reign. At the end of the century, however, when the cession of the posts in the Great Lakes region to the Americans had become a reality, a move from Grand Portage to Kaministiquia (Thunder Bay, Ont.) was foreseen. This expensive operation, estimated to have cost more than £10,000 and completed in 1803, shows clearly the key role that meeting place and transit point had played. But the construction of other,

more distant staging posts also required larger investments of funds than previously. These establishments were to serve as warehouses and distribution centres for pelts, provisions such as pemmican, and products needed for the fur trade. Their size also depended upon the danger that the HBC traders in the region represented. Personnel at these posts was increasingly organized on hierarchical lines, from the partners right down to the voyageurs. In 1804, for example, there were 17 posts comprising 837 men in all, divided as follows: at the top, 45 partners; then 76 clerks, 44 interpreters, 15 guides, and 657 voyageurs.

The empire over which McTavish reigned was thus inhabited: first by the Indians, and then by the "professionals" of the fur trade and the body of *engagés*, who came mainly from the seigneuries. Many took part in this adventure, since transporting goods from Montreal to Grand Portage mobilized a lot of manpower. In 1783 there were 3,069 men engaged in the trade. In 1795 Count Paolo Andriani estimated the number employed at 2,540 – 40 guides, 1,100 winterers, and 1,400 *engagés*. It is quite evident that wages represented an important variable in the NWC's costs. As long as agriculture had remained at subsistence level, it was easy to recruit the "professional" and seasonal manpower required by trading enterprises. At that time wages had been low. But since 1765 agriculture had grown into a commercial operation, with the result that rural manpower had become much less flexible and much less available. Consequently wages had risen rapidly, endangering the very existence of the firms. The pressure of wages, together with the scarcity of manpower and the expansion of agricultural production, continued unabated throughout the second half of the 18th century. On this matter William GRANT (1743–1810) commented in 1793: "We have now engaged upwards of two hundred wintering men. We are yet difficient in men to go and come. . . . The high price wheat fitches keeps the good hands backwards to engage." The scarcity of manpower had prompted the fur merchants to replace canoes with bateaux as far as possible in order to reduce the need for seasonally hired men and the total remuneration and substitute the less costly St Lawrence River route in part for the Ottawa River route. Ten crewmen were needed for handling a canoe but a bateau carried the same volume of goods with a crew of only four. The NWC also followed the trend initiated by traders at Detroit and Niagara (near Youngstown, N.Y.). In 1790 it had two ships on Lake Superior, one of 10, the other of 15 tons burden; in 1793 it owned the *Beaver* (45 tons) and the *Athabaska* (40 tons) on lakes Erie, Michigan, and Huron, and it assigned the *Otter* (75 tons) to Lake Superior.

When McTavish took over management of the company in 1787, he had applied rigorously the policy instituted by Benjamin Frobisher. But these man-

McTavish

power problems constantly preoccupied the people in charge of the NWC. In 1791 Joseph Frobisher told McTavish: "I likewise left orders with St Cir to Run about the Country from his Parish to Quebec. . . . The same Orders I gave also to Fainante." The following year he wrote again: "What you mention respecting Wintering Men shall be duly attended too. Mr. Gregory will be able to pick up a great Many . . . (as I shall be at Quebec the best part of the winter) I will endeavour to hire as many Stout Lads as I can. Attention will also be paid to what you recommend respecting the Young Men that may be Hired in future for the North West." The preoccupation with the labour market and its cost implications was dictated by the very way in which the enterprise worked. In 1793 Frobisher reverted to this subject: "I am going out to La Chine to send of six boats & one Canoe for [CHARLES-JEAN-BAPTISTE] Chaboillez [George Edme] Young & [Bazile] Irelande with Two Canoes for the Portage [Grand Portage], which is all the Men I Can muster & was under the necessity of hiring them for St. Mary's [Sault Ste Marie, Ont.] only; at extravagant wages . . . had we raised their wages for the Portage we would have been under the necessity of augmenting the Wages of all those that are gone up & we would have met with great difficulty in hiring Men next Winter." As the trading territory expanded, the proportion of winterers to men hired seasonally increased, and the salary problem became more critical. The NWC not only made use of bateaux between Montreal and Lake Ontario, but also exerted pressure for improved communications between Montreal and Lachine and invested in York (Toronto) for the same reasons.

The burden of wages and the increase in transportation costs and prices were the mainsprings of technological change. The same factors set in motion a process leading to the concentration of enterprises. Seen from the angle of wages, this movement aimed to create a monopoly on the labour market. As long as trade in pelts was the object of competition among a great many entrepreneurs who were fighting to get the best employees, it was impossible to control wages; these could only rise more rapidly in a situation where shortage prevailed. Thus Benjamin Frobisher's ambition, and subsequently McTavish's, to concentrate all the fur trade in the hands of the NWC was not just a manifestation of their personalities; it was fostered by economic conditions and partly by labour problems. And it was operative as long as the final objective had not been attained.

In 1787 McTavish may have believed that the NWC could thenceforth be satisfied with exploiting its domain in complete tranquillity. Its most dangerous adversary, Gregory, had been brought to the brink of bankruptcy and forced to join the company on terms set by McTavish. In 1791 Joseph Frobisher was not far

from thinking that his dream in this regard had been realized: "The North W. Co was never in such a formidable and respectable footing as it is at present . . . it would require an immence Capital & great exertions to get to the least footing there." In reality neither of them could cherish illusions of this sort for long, because the riches of the northwest were always fiercely coveted. They were desired by those who wanted to enter the trade, and would be even more eagerly desired by those who, believing that the American revolution would not alter the existing equilibrium, had limited their activity to the southwest. The depletion of resources, Jay's Treaty of 1794, and, within a few years, the attitude of the Americans, who were bent on controlling trade in the southwest, forced these firms to turn to the resources of the northwest. From 1791 the rumours about the development of opposition to the NWC became increasingly explicit. Todd and McGill let it be known that they wished to acquire an interest in the company. By then, however, McTavish and Frobisher were no longer financially dependent upon them. They were also independent of the Ellice–Forsyth–Richardson group, represented by Forsyth, Richardson and Company, the Montreal subsidiary of Phyn, Ellices, and Inglis, who were eager to take part in the northwest trade. All that these potential competitors were offered with a view to the reorganization of the NWC anticipated for 1795 was a meagre block of two shares. They of course refused it.

This refusal marked the beginning of the rise of another competing power, the New North West Company (sometimes called the XY Company) [see John Richardson*]. After its founding in 1798 this company brought into its ranks John OGILVY, the agent of Parker, Gerrard, and Ogilvy, as well as Daniel Sutherland* and, still more important, Alexander Mackenzie. After having fought alongside Gregory against the NWC, Mackenzie had joined that company at the time of the amalgamation in 1787. Then, following his successes as an explorer, he had a position and functions of increasing importance within it. Since he was ambitious and since he had his own views on the future of the company and the fur economy, his position became increasingly difficult vis-à-vis McTavish, who was predominantly responsible for policy, and McTavish's nephew and heir apparent, William McGillivray. As a result Mackenzie became a member of the new rival company.

To McTavish's way of thinking all competition was pernicious, not only for his company but also for the fur-trade economy as a whole. In 1799 he admitted that his adversaries presented a real danger, from the point of view of both the capital invested and the experience of the men engaged in the fight. In August 1800 Fraser wrote from London, "I am happy to have such favorable Accounts of your returns; to find that

564

you have so much the advantage over your Opponents." Two years later, in October, Fraser was just as optimistic about the outcome of the fight: "Your complete union must ultimately baffle the attempts of your adversary, & your success (which is really extraordinary under such circumstances) will enable you to combat them with advantage." In 1804, according to John ASKIN, the New North West Company had already spent £70,000 but had not succeeded in damaging its rival's position. Consequently, that year it had to accept the terms of an amalgamation put forward by McGillivray, who, however, excluded Mackenzie from the enterprise. As usual, competition had resulted in a rise in wages and in prices paid the Indians for furs.

Under McTavish's rule the NWC was perpetually being reorganized: five major transformations took place between 1790 and 1804. These changes were probably caused by the increase in production and the expansion of the company's domain; but in addition they also stemmed from circumstances closely linked with the life of the enterprise and the mind of its director. For example, the number of shares in the company and of people receiving them kept on growing. This situation was partly dictated by the existence of opposition, open or veiled, so that admission into the company of a real or potential competitor was a technique to reinforce its ascendancy. The increase in the number of participants also served as an instrument for promotion within the enterprise. The pressure in this respect came primarily from the clerks and partners. Around 1795, following suggestions from Duncan McGillivray, Mackenzie became the spokesman for these disgruntled elements: it is significant that the number of shares went from 20 in 1787 to 46 in 1795 and 100 in 1804.

Inevitably, the NWC became more and more embodied in the person of McTavish. Certainly the man himself knew how to impress people and inspire loyalty. In a letter to him in 1794 Hallowell observed: "I have lived in the habit of sacrificing my Opinions & my feelings to yours, for which however I must confess, I expected some credit with you; You, I am afraid, have placed this deference to a wrong Account – to a meanness of Spirit in my part, & to the want of having an opinion of my own, when the true Principles which governed my Conduct were, a sense of Obligation to, & personal regard for you – & more than all, a strong persuasion that, that regard was reciprocal. . . . In the Spring I hope we shall see you, which will relieve me in a Situation where subordinate to every one, you seem to hold me accountable for all." McTavish was certainly autocratic, and this tendency became more pronounced with time, but he could also delegate authority. The meetings at Grand Portage were not solely information sessions, and the agreements that came out of them did not depend

especially upon the presence of family members among the partners. It can be said, however, that it was through McTavish, Frobisher and Company that McTavish wielded his power. This firm's participation in the NWC went from 7 out of 20 shares in 1787 to 75 of 100 in 1804, and it received more than its due proportion of the profits.

The firm of McTavish, Frobisher was not a rigid, unprogressive institution dominated by a fixed personnel. The most experienced and capable merchants were promoted in it, and it was possible for them to push themselves forward. James Hallowell and his son William, Gregory, the McGillivrays, Alexander Mackenzie and his cousin Roderick McKenzie* were all people who had proven their efficiency in the field and had displayed particular talents. And even if several members of the McTavish clan – for which Simon had a remarkable attachment – belonged to it, this firm was not a family enterprise in the true sense of the term. Before becoming McTavish's successor William McGillivray would have to prove his capabilities: after his arrival in 1784 came nine whole years in the Athabasca department, then various and widespread responsibilities. The same was true for Duncan McGillivray, who despite his promotion in the firm remained almost all his life an effective man in the field and an explorer. Yet it remains the case that the presence of some of his relatives in both the NWC and McTavish, Frobisher and Company served Simon McTavish's interests well.

The organization of McTavish, Frobisher, which assumed so many responsibilities, was based upon criteria of efficiency. That Joseph Frobisher was soon more or less downgraded is not in the least surprising. After a few years his role in the firm was clear: hiring manpower and handling external relations. As for Gregory, he rapidly specialized as the person responsible for the warehouse – preparing the trading expeditions and the shipments of pelts for export. His subordinate at Quebec, James Hallowell, who was a relative of McTavish, for his part was increasingly limited to keeping the books, and in this capacity his authority was exercised over the clerks in the west and at Grand Portage. Before 1800 the only two people who really seemed in the running for the succession were Alexander Mackenzie, whose ideas seemed to worry McTavish, and William McGillivray. McTavish had certainly given some thought to providing for his replacement, but Mackenzie's defection to the New North West Company left him virtually no choice, and he prepared the way for his nephew McGillivray.

McTavish presided over the fortunes of a smooth-running organization which operated from Montreal west to the Rocky Mountains and east to Labrador, where in 1802 he and his associates acquired the lease to the king's posts for £1,025 a year. In addition the

McTavish

company was well represented in London, New York, and Quebec. Served by effective men of varied talents, it was not only destined to establish a monopoly directed against its competitors in Montreal, but also strove to eliminate competition, from both the Americans and the HBC. Around 1790 the latter company was not showing much drive and at that period the Nor'Westers clearly felt superior in the field. In 1792 William McGillivray wrote to the HBC factor William Tomison*, "I do not perfectly understand your threat respecting Pills but if by them you mean [musket] Balls you have certainly the weakest side & should matters come to such Extremities you will find that we can play off more ourselves – & can pay the natives dearer, should it be necessary – for playing off theirs, than is in your power in either Case." In 1791 McTavish had even asked Prime Minister William Pitt to rescind the HBC's charter. Having met with a refusal, and being quite aware of the advantages that the rival company had in dispatching trade goods to the west, he tried to obtain transit rights, which of course were refused him. Subsequently the struggle with the HBC was pushed into the background because that company was reorganizing its tactics by slow steps and competition was not yet keen. But there was to be an awakening, and at the turn of the century the question was back on the table. McTavish had certainly envisaged buying the HBC, but circumstances had not been favourable. He then decided to strike a heavy blow to force his adversary into conceding transit rights [see Duncan McDougall]. He organized two expeditions to James Bay: one overland from Montreal, the other by sea with a ship hired for the occasion. In September 1803 the two expeditions met at Charlton Island (NWT), of which they took possession in the name of the NWC. The rivalry did not end until 1821, when the amalgamation of the two companies marked the absorption of the NWC.

Because of his preoccupation with the fur business, McTavish took little interest in owning land on a large scale until 1802, although his subscription to the Montreal section of the Agriculture Society at the beginning of the 1790s does reveal an interest in farming. In 1802, at a period when agriculture was prosperous and land a source of profit, he obtained 11,500 acres in Chester Township, and he bought the seigneury of Terrebonne, near Montreal, for £25,000. From the beginning he proved a capitalist seigneur. He ran a store and two very modern flour-mills, built a bakery that made biscuit for the northwest, set up a sawmill, and encouraged the manufacture of barrels. He was not content just to collect the seigneurial rents but tried to channel the region's surplus production to his mills. The wheat he processed was intended for the local market and for export. He was, of course, in contact with former fur merchants such as Francis Badgley* and Pangman. But his relations in this business were primarily with grain merchants and exporters: Louis Dunière, Jacob Jordan*, the brothers John and William Porteous, and Thomas Porteous* as well, Henry Caldwell, William Burns* and his partner John William Woolsey*, Robert Lester and Robert Morrogh, Adam Lymburner*, David Monro*, and Mathew Bell*. McTavish's situation clearly illustrates the connections between the different sectors of the economy and proves that the fur dealers were not opposed to the commercialization of agriculture. The motives for his purchase of the seigneury of Terrebonne were certainly not those behind his buying back in 1799 of the small estate of Dunardary, for generations the home of the chief of the McTavish clan, in Argyllshire, Scotland.

McTavish's participation in the public life of his town and of the colony seems modest, compared with that of other important merchants such as James McGill and John Richardson. At most he held the rank of lieutenant in the British Militia of the Town and Banlieu of Montreal from 1788 until about 1794, and in 1796 he received a commission as justice of the peace for the District of Montreal which was renewed three years later. His elegance, his personality, and his cleverness, however, won him the nickname of "the Marquis" from his contemporaries. In October 1793 McTavish had married Marie-Marguerite Chaboillez, the 18-year-old daughter of Charles-Jean-Baptiste Chaboillez. The couple had four children, all of whom died in their twenties. At the time of his marriage McTavish had bought the house on Rue Saint-Jean-Baptiste in which he had been living as a tenant for ten years. Just before his death he began building a huge home which was not yet finished when he died on 6 July 1804. His estate amounted to more than £125,000. His will was significant, not just because it disclosed the close ties he had maintained with the whole McTavish clan, but because it revealed the friendly relations he had established with his former partners, Frobisher, Gregory, and James Hallowell. He bequeathed £700 to his doctor George Selby* and Selby's son. He gave £2,000 to two Montreal hospitals, the Hôtel-Dieu and the Hôpital Général.

Simon McTavish was certainly the colony's most important businessman in the second half of the 18th century. Like his friends the Frobishers, he was shrewd and far-sighted, but he possessed an even greater sense of organization and management. His career shows that the success of entrepreneurs cannot be reduced to a matter of patronage or be forecast simply from the amount of capital with which they began.

Fernand Ouellet

ANQ-Q, CN1-262, 15 nov. 1802. PAC, MG 19, A5; MG 29, A5, 26–28. *Les bourgeois de la Compagnie du Nord-Ouest* (Masson). *Docs. relating to NWC* (Wallace). *Quebec Gazette*, 5 May 1803, 12 July 1804. Caron, "Inv. de la corr. de Mgr Denaut," ANQ *Rapport*, 1931–32: 202–3, 205; "Inv. de la corr. de Mgr Plessis," 1927–28: 232. Massicotte, "Répertoire des engagements pour l'Ouest," ANQ *Rapport*, 1942–46. "Papiers d'État," PAC *Rapport*, 1890: 294, 340. "Papiers d'État – Bas-Canada," PAC *Rapport*, 1891: 117; 1892: 155, 211, 220, 223. *Quebec almanac*, 1788: 52; 1791: 44; 1792: 120; 1794: 89; 1797: 131; 1801: 78. Wallace, *Macmillan dict.* M. W. Campbell, *McGillivray; lord of the northwest* (Toronto, 1962); *NWC* (1973). W. S. Dunn, "Western commerce, 1760–1774" (PHD thesis, Univ. of Wis., Madison, 1971). Macmillan, "New men in action," *Canadian business hist.* (Macmillan), 44–103. E. E. Rich, *The fur trade and the northwest to 1857* (Toronto, 1967). W. S. Wallace, *The pedlars from Quebec and other papers on the Nor' Westers* (Toronto, 1954). E. A. Collard, "Simon McTavish's burial place still intact on mountain slope," *Gazette* (Montreal), 21 Feb. 1941: 10. R. H. Fleming, "McTavish, Frobisher and Company of Montreal," *CHR*, 10 (1929): 136–52. D. [S.] Macmillan, "'The Marquis': king of the fur trade" and "King of the fur trade, part 2; Scots in collision: the Marquis vs the Knight," *Canadian Banker & ICB Rev.*, 78 (1978), no.4: 28–32 and no.5: 62–66 respectively. Massicotte, "Les Chaboillez," *BRH*, 28: 328. Ouellet, "Dualité économique et changement technologique," *SH*, 9: 256–96. W. S. Wallace, "New light on Simon McTavish," *Beaver*, outfit 272 (December 1941): 48–49.

MACUINA. *See* MUQUINNA

MADJECKEWISS (Machiquawish, Matchekewis, Michiconiss, Michiguiss, Mitchikiweese, Mudjekewiss, Wachicouess, meaning a hereditary chief; **Kaigwiaidosa; Mash-i-pi-nash-i-wish** or **Bad Bird)**, Ojibwa chief; b. in present-day northern Michigan, probably *c*. 1735; d. *c*. 1805.

Madjeckewiss was born into a group of Ojibwas who wintered in hunting villages west of Lake Huron, in the region of Saginaw and Thunder bays, and spent their summers at Cheboygan (Mich.) or in hunting along the Lake Superior shore. Called Kaigwiaidosa as a young man, he was tall and weighed more than 200 pounds. By his mid 20s he was a respected war chief. In 1763, when Pontiac*'s forces besieged Detroit, Madjeckewiss welcomed the opportunity to help drive the British out of the west. Working closely with Minweweh*, Madjeckewiss planned the capture of Fort Michilimackinac (Mackinaw City, Mich.). Charles-Michel Mouet* de Langlade, a local trader, warned Captain George Etherington, but after interviewing Madjeckewiss the commandant paid no further heed. On the morning of 2 June 1763, Etherington stood outside the walls of the fort watching Madjeckewiss and his warriors vigorously engage a band of Sauks in a game of lacrosse.

Suddenly the chief threw the ball over the pickets of the fort. As the Ojibwas rushed in to retrieve the ball, waiting women handed them weapons concealed beneath their blankets. Within a few minutes the garrison was killed or captured and Madjeckewiss and his men controlled the post. After holding it for several days, they apparently departed to assist Wasson* and other Saginaw Ojibwas in the siege of Detroit.

Indian tradition recounts that, after British control in the west had been re-established, Madjeckewiss was taken captive to Quebec and imprisoned for a while. Upon his release he was given a medal, a flag, and other presents, and returned from prison with great honour. Documents suggest that he met with Sir William Johnson* at Fort Niagara (near Youngstown, N.Y.) in 1764; in 1768 he and four others went to Guy Park (near Amsterdam, N.Y.) and Johnson Hall (Johnstown) to see Sir William, report rumours of Spanish intrigue, and pledge their loyalty. Madjeckewiss was imprisoned at Michilimackinac in April 1771 after the body of a trader was found near his village. When it was determined that the man had died of natural causes the chief was released.

Throughout the American revolution Madjeckewiss was a close ally of the British. He later claimed, in circumstances that make the assertion plausible, to have been with John Burgoyne*, presumably in the invasion of New York that ended disastrously in October 1777. If trader John Long* is accurate in recalling that he encountered Madjeckewiss on the north shore of Lake Superior early in July 1777, the Ojibwa chief and his warriors must have joined the expedition in its late stages, since by early July Burgoyne had already taken Fort Ticonderoga (near Ticonderoga, N.Y.). Certainly the British at Michilimackinac found Madjeckewiss's friendship invaluable. Fearing attack by the forces of George Rogers Clark, which had seized the Illinois country in 1778, commandant Arent Schuyler DePeyster* dispatched Madjeckewiss to Detroit to encourage the Indians there. The chief hurried back to participate in the great council at L'Arbre Croche (Cross Village, Mich.) on 4 July 1779. He and ten of his band then accompanied a British officer to Fort St Joseph (Niles, Mich.) to secure the support of the Potawatomis. After returning to Michilimackinac by sailing vessel, he was sent to the Illinois country to harass the rebels. As compensation for his services, Madjeckewiss was given a log house, which was moved some 18 miles over the ice to Cheboygan that winter.

During the early months of 1780 the new lieutenant governor at Michilimackinac, Patrick SINCLAIR, organized a major attack on the Spanish village at St Louis (Mo.). He was particularly pleased when on 10 March the "very noted Chief" Madjeckewiss consent-

Maera

ed to participate. The chief assisted trader Jean-Marie DUCHARME in gaining the support of the Sauks, Foxes, and Sioux who lived along the Fox and Wisconsin rivers. On 26 May a British and Indian force numbering nearly a thousand attacked but was unable to capture the fortified town. It split up, and Madjeckewiss joined Langlade's group which retreated by way of the Illinois River. Despite the expedition's failure Madjeckewiss continued to assist the British in securing alliances and in September 1783 he accompanied Jean-Baptiste CADOT, whose wife was a relative of his, to the vicinity of Chequamegon Bay (Wis.) in an effort to stop a war between the Ojibwas of Lake Superior and the Foxes and Sioux.

As the American Revolutionary War drew to a close, the British spent less on supplying the Indians. When in 1784 Madjeckewiss came to receive presents at Fort Michilimackinac (located since 1781 on Mackinac Island), he berated Captain Daniel ROBERTSON, denouncing the British as liars and impostors who had encouraged the Indians to sacrifice their lives and then let them starve. The Indians ought to chase them out of the country, he exclaimed. In fact the Indians who lived south of the Great Lakes needed the help of Britain to hold back the advancing Americans. When the American invasion culminated in the battle of Fallen Timbers (near Waterville, Ohio) in 1794, however, the British gave no military assistance to the Indians [see John Graves SIMCOE]. Madjeckewiss and his warriors were part of the defeated confederacy of tribes. Using the name of Mash-i-pi-nash-i-wish or Bad Bird, he joined in signing the Treaty of Greenville, which surrendered most of the Ohio valley and strategic land around Niagara, Detroit, and Michilimackinac to the Americans. Through him the Three Fires, a confederacy of Ojibwas, Ottawas, and Potawatomis, made the "extra and voluntary gift" of Bois Blanc Island in the straits of Mackinac in order to gain the Americans' favour. Eager to return home, the old chief requested a horse to ride.

Although he had made his peace with the Americans, Madjeckewiss still obtained gifts from the British. During each summer from 1796 to 1799 he and his band of between 13 and 30 journeyed to the British headquarters on the Upper Lakes to beg for charity and presents from the commandants.

The exact year of Madjeckewiss's death is uncertain. DePeyster, writing in March 1804, was under the impression that he was already dead. Some years later the chief's son Madjeckewiss recalled that his father had died while attending a treaty conference on the Miamis (Maumee) River; this may have been the one held at Fort Industry (near Toledo, Ohio) in 1805. Another Indian remembered that he had died about 1806.

DAVID A. ARMOUR

Clements Library, Thomas Duggan journal, 17 July 1796; 25 July 1797; 23 June 1798; 9, 10 July, 8, 10 Sept. 1799; Thomas Gage papers, American ser., 103: Turnbull to Gage, 12 May 1771; supplementary accounts, box 76, Michilimackinac expenses, Indian expenses, Capt. George Turnbull, 25 May 1770–8 July 1772. Wis., State Hist. Soc., Doty papers, "Memorandum of travels in northern Michigan and Wisconsin," 10 July–2 Aug. 1822: 4–6. [A. S. DePeyster], *Miscellanies, by an officer* (Dumfries, Scot., 1813), 18, 32. Augustin Grignon, "Seventy-two years' recollections of Wisconsin," Wis., State Hist. Soc., *Coll.*, 3 (1857): 224–25, 232, 234. Henry, *Travels and adventures*. *John Askin papers* (Quaife), 1: 52; 2: 407. [John Long], *John Long's voyages and travels in the years 1768–1788*, ed. M. M. Quaife (Chicago, 1922), 59–65. *Mich. Pioneer Coll.*, 9 (1886): 379; 10 (1886): 365–66, 570; 11 (1887): 383, 389, 453; 12 (1887): 162, 262; 20 (1892): 417. *Johnson papers* (Sullivan et al.), 12: 544–45, 548–50, 558–63. H. R. Schoolcraft, *Personal memoirs of a residence of thirty years with the Indian tribes on the American frontiers, with brief notices of passing events, facts and opinions, A.D. 1812 to A.D. 1842* (Philadelphia, 1851), 103, 447. U.S., Congress, *American state papers* (Lowrie et al.), class II, [1]: 562–82. Wis., State Hist. Soc., *Coll.*, 11 (1888): 115, 142–43, 151–52; 12 (1892): 67–68; 18 (1908): 375–76, 393, 400–1. Erminie Wheeler-Voegelin, "An anthropological report on Indian use and occupancy of northern Michigan," *Chippewa Indians* (7v., New York and London, 1974), 5: 8–11. L. C. Draper, "Notice of Match-e-ke-wis, the captor of Mackinaw, 1763," Wis., State Hist. Soc., *Coll.*, 7 (1876): 188–94.

MAERA. *See* MYEERAH

MAGOWAN (McGowan), PETER, lawyer, politician, and office holder; b. *c.* 1763, probably in Ireland; d. 19 June 1810 in Charlottetown, P.E.I.

A disgraced young lawyer who had left London, England, under a cloud of scandal that involved certain "pecuniary embarrassments," Peter Magowan immigrated in 1789 to St John's (Prince Edward) Island, where he was immediately admitted an attorney by the Supreme Court. The following year he was elected to the House of Assembly from Kings County. After the death of Phillips Callbeck* in 1790, Magowan was for years the only practising lawyer on the Island besides Attorney General Joseph APLIN. Inevitably, he found himself acquiring as clients all those who were critical of the administration. In 1791, for example, when John Cambridge*, William Bowley, and John Hill* brought before the Privy Council in London complaints of malfeasance against Lieutenant Governor Edmund FANNING, Chief Justice Peter STEWART, and other officers, Magowan acted as Cambridge's agent on the Island and personally swore an affidavit charging Stewart with gross partiality on the bench. Not surprisingly, his legal talents were constantly disparaged by Fanning and Stewart, and he seldom won his cases. But clients complained as well. One member of the assembly charged that Magowan had altered the wording of a document, and in so doing had cost him the cause, and a sailor insisted vehemently before the Council that the lawyer had embellished an affidavit which he had signed without being able to read. Such accusations were a familiar part of the Island's legal and political scene, and it is impossible to determine either their veracity or their implications.

Six years after his arrival in the colony Magowan finally received official preferment. In 1795 he was made deputy to Thomas DESBRISAY in his capacity as secretary and registrar of the Island. Having accepted the post solely for the fees of office – Desbrisay retained the salary – Magowan found that the expense of employing a copyist exceeded his income, and he abandoned the job in 1800. Nevertheless, after 1795 he gradually moved closer to the administration, at the same time that Joseph Aplin was moving away from it. In 1797 it was Magowan who brought to the attention of the assembly the "libellous" letter Fanning had received from Captain John MACDONALD of Glenaladale, which accused the lieutenant governor of countenancing the activities of "a Levelling Party" determined to bring about an escheat of proprietorial holdings on the Island. That same year Magowan served as clerk of the committee which reported on the state of the proprietors' lots and petitioned the crown for the institution of a court of escheat. This popular stand was to ensure his re-election to the assembly in 1803. In the wake of MacDonald's charges of maladministration, Magowan brought on his own behalf a £3,000 libel action against the outspoken Scotsman. With Lieutenant Governor Fanning testifying personally for Magowan, the jury awarded the plaintiff costs and £7 10s. in damages. Magowan supplemented this small award by charging himself heavy legal fees for pleading his own case. About the same time he was broken as an ensign in the Island militia by a Halifax court martial investigating an illegal liquor shop set up to "intoxicate" privates, but he was restored to his rank when he persuaded the court he had not known of the operation.

By 1798 Magowan was helping to draw up complaints of malpractice against Attorney General Aplin, and one critic of the government, James DOUGLAS, labelled him "the favourite tool of Governor Fanning and the Stewart party." When Aplin was relieved of his office that year, Magowan served for a time as acting attorney general. He gained the post permanently in 1800, succeeding Aplin's replacement, John WENTWORTH, who had been slow to take up local residence. At the time his appointment was announced Magowan was in Quebec, Lower Canada, looking for employment, but his new position enabled him to remain on the Island in some security. After a decade of controversy, he now found a few years of peace as attorney general. By 1806, however, he had become an outspoken critic of Lieutenant Governor Joseph Frederick Wallet DesBarres* and his supporters, particularly James Bardin Palmer*. Palmer had helped organize a new political association known as the Loyal Electors, and his influence on DesBarres was suspected by Magowan, Charles STEWART, and other members of the official clique that had long dominated local politics. Magowan objected to the manner in which appointments were made under DesBarres, and he was particularly upset that commissions of the peace were being issued to people he considered unqualified for the position. He was also critical of the way DesBarres issued writs of election, finding it unfavourable to the interests of the "old party." As party politics again heated up, he remained loyal to the Stewart faction until his unexpected death in 1810.

Magowan's colourful and controversial career well illustrates the complex and personal nature of contemporary Island politics. The struggles in which he was involved continued after his death. It was, in fact, the vacancy in the attorney generalship that his demise created, and the dispute over who should fill it, that led ultimately to DesBarres's recall and Palmer's dismissal from public office [see Charles Stewart].

J. M. BUMSTED

PAC, MG 11, [CO 226] Prince Edward Island A, 17: 439–40. PAPEI, Acc. 2702, Smith–Alley coll., petition of Peter Magowan, 30 Sept. 1803; RG 3, House of Assembly, Journals, 1791, 1797; RG 6, Supreme Court records. PRO, CO 226/21. SRO, GD293/2/19/6, 10. G.B., Privy Council, *Report of the right honourable the lords of the committee of his majesty's most honourable Privy Council, of certain complaints against Lieutenant Governor Fanning, and other officers of his majesty's government in the Island of St. John* ([London, 1792]).

MAILLOU (Mailloux), BENJAMIN-NICOLAS, Roman Catholic priest; b. 29 Sept. 1753 at Quebec, son of Benjamin Maillou, a blacksmith, and his second wife, Angélique Marchand; d. 19 Jan. 1810 in Saint-Eustache, Lower Canada.

Benjamin-Nicolas Maillou entered the Petit Séminaire de Québec on 15 Nov. 1765. He began theological studies in 1773, serving at the same time as master of a class in the Petit Séminaire. Bishop Briand* ordained him to the priesthood on 21 Dec. 1776, and four days later appointed him parish priest of Immaculée-Conception at Trois-Rivières; this was an early appointment since Maillou was not yet 24. At Trois-Rivières he replaced a Recollet, Isidore (Charles-Antoine) Lemire Marsolet, to whom the parishioners were very much attached but who had resigned. The Recollets had been serving the parish for 84 years. Consequently the appointment of a secular priest was not well received; indeed it gave rise

Malaspina

to partisan quarrels, as Bishop Briand emphasized in a letter to the vicar general of Trois-Rivières, Pierre Garreau*, *dit* Saint-Onge, early in 1777: "People are saying that everything is ablaze at Trois-Rivières, some holding for the priests, the others for the Recollets." The appointment was, however, unavoidable, since the British government had forbidden the Recollets to recruit new members; in 1777 there were only nine Recollet priests, six running parishes and three staffing religious houses at Quebec and Montreal. The parishioners also complained of Maillou's youth but, when Louis-Joseph Godefroy* de Tonnancour expressed his opinion on the matter to Briand, the bishop replied to him rather brusquely: "It is true that the Sieur Mailloux is a very young priest, but it is no less certain that the post I have given him is far from agreeable, far from sought after, [and] moreover hardly capable of providing the necessities of life. . . . This very young priest probably accepted only because he was very young and did not dare refuse, showing himself disobedient, two days after swearing to me that he would obey me. . . . If you find some Recollets, take one." At that time the population of the parish of Immaculée-Conception was small (not more than 800), and indeed the difficulties occasioned by repairs to the steeple and the lack of a presbytery rendered the parish charge rather unattractive. Maillou was also given responsibility for the mission of Vieilles-Forges. Once he had taken up his duties, his first concern was to build a decent presbytery, a project to which Briand even offered to contribute from his own purse. Meanwhile the *fabrique* rented a house for 252 *livres* a year. The new presbytery was completed on 10 Aug. 1783.

Maillou, who had a rather phlegmatic temperament and was in ill health, seemed largely to neglect the preaching ministry, to the point that when he asked to be transferred to another parish Bishop Hubert* replied: "My dear Maillou, you yourself create an obstacle to this by not preaching at Trois-Rivières, especially after I warned you of your obligation in that respect. Acquire the habit, then, of instructing the people entrusted to you, and you may rest assured that I shall then share your views."

On 20 Sept. 1790 Hubert appointed Maillou parish priest of Saint-Eustache and the neighbouring missions. Maillou was greatly disappointed on arriving in the parish. The presbytery, which had been built by Father Félix Berey Des Essarts in 1774, was now scarcely habitable. Consequently Maillou went to live in the house of the former parish priest, Charles-François Perrault, which was already up for sale and which he had to leave on 1 Oct. 1791. Maillou compared himself to "the bird on the bough," and accepted the parishioners' suggestion that he go to live in one of their houses "while waiting for a lodging that belongs to the parish." Claiming that "part of the parish was biased" against him, Maillou, who was pessimistic and a bit neurasthenic, was casting his eye on the vacant charge of Saint-Joseph at Chambly, but this scheme did not meet with Hubert's approval. In 1792 the parishioners decided to take steps to have the former presbytery repaired, and the bishop even went so far as to advise Maillou, albeit without success, to retire to either the Séminaire de Saint-Sulpice in Montreal or the Lac-des-Deux-Montagnes mission (Oka) until "a comfortable, decent house accessible to the church" had been made ready for him. On 30 July 1793 the bishop of Quebec forbad Maillou to celebrate the feast of the parish's patron saint after "the battles [and] orgies of previous years."

The parishioners were satisfied with Benjamin-Nicolas Maillou's ministry despite his poor health – he suffered from frequent attacks of gout and had become an invalid. Having wasted away to a noticeable degree, he died at the age of 56; he was buried in the sanctuary of the church.

ALBERTUS MARTIN

[A portrait of Benjamin-Nicolas Maillou by Vital Desrochers, housed in the parish church of Saint-Eustache, appears to bear some likeness to the subject. A.M.]

AAQ, 210 A, I: ff.126, 144, 158, 199, 224, 245; II: ff.3, 73. ANQ-Q, CE1-1, 16 mai 1740, 1er sept. 1750, 29 sept. 1753. AP, Saint-Eustache, Cahiers des délibérations de la fabrique, 2 oct. 1791; Reg. des baptêmes, mariages, et sépultures, 22 janv. 1810. Arch. de l'évêché de Saint-Jérôme (Saint-Jérôme, Qué.), Cartable Saint-Eustache, corr., 22 mars, 18 sept. 1791; 29 août, 11, 23 sept., 20 oct. 1792. Allaire, *Dictionnaire*, vol.1. O.-M. Jouve, *Les franciscains et le Canada: aux Trois-Rivières* (Paris, 1934), 263–64. J.-E. Bellemare, "Desserte religieuse des Vieilles Forges," *BRH*, 24 (1918): 270.

MALASPINA, ALEJANDRO, naval officer and explorer; b. 5 Nov. 1754 in Mulazzo, in the duchy of Parma (Italy), third son of Carlo Morello, Marquis of Malaspina, and Catalina Melilupi; d. unmarried 9 April 1810 in Pontremoli (Italy).

Alejandro Malaspina, a Spanish subject, entered the Spanish navy in 1774 as a midshipman. He received knighthood in the order of Saint John of Jerusalem in January 1775 and two months later was promoted lieutenant. By the age of 30 Malaspina had already circumnavigated the globe, and, because he had proved on this journey both his naval expertise and a capacity for scientific investigation, he was able soon after his return to persuade the Spanish navy to undertake an exploratory and scientific mission round the world in imitation of James Cook*'s voyages.

Malaspina, now a captain, was given command of the expedition, which comprised two ships, the *Descubierta* and the *Atrevida*, both well staffed and equipped with the best scientific instruments. Among the participants sailing from Cadiz on 30 July 1789 were lieutenants Dionisio ALCALÁ-GALIANO and Cayetano Flores Valdés y Bazán, and Manuel José Antonio CARDERO, a crew member who was later to prove his artistic capabilities; Tadeo HAENKE, who would become the most prominent of the scientists on the voyage, joined the expedition only after it had reached the west coast of South America. Malaspina's itinerary included Montevideo (Uruguay), Patagonia (Argentina), the Falkland Islands, and numerous ports on the west coast of South and Central America. The original plan was to visit the Sandwich (Hawaiian) Islands; however, the idea of a northern passage through North America had been reawakened in scientific circles [see Philip Turnor*], and upon arriving in Acapulco (Mexico) Malaspina found his orders changed: he was to seek the Strait of Anian, as the Spaniards called it, supposedly navigated in 1588 by Lorenzo Ferrer* Maldonado. Exploration of the Sandwich Islands was made the responsibility of a junior officer and, with orders to inspect the coastline as far north as the 60th parallel in search of the imagined strait, Malaspina led the main body of the expedition northward. He was also to visit the Spanish outpost at Santa Cruz de Nutka in Friendly Cove (Nootka Island, B.C.), where a confrontation between his compatriot Esteban José Martínez* and James COLNETT, an Englishman, had led to an international dispute over regional sovereignty.

Having made preparations in Acapulco, Malaspina set sail on 2 May 1791. He took his vessels far to the north, making his first landfall in late June at Port Mulgrave (Yakutat Bay, Alaska, where a glacier still bears his name), and then coasting as far west as Prince William Sound. From there the explorers turned back along the shore, making coastal profiles and seeking the northwest passage in vain. On 12 August the ships entered Nootka Sound and anchored near the Spanish settlement, where Pedro de ALBERNI was in command. Journals kept by various members of the expedition indicate that their stay in the sound was fruitful. Malaspina solidified Spanish friendship with Muquinna*, the principal leader of the local Nootka Indians, while at the same time approving the purchase of several slave children in the belief that they would suffer starvation or even become victims of cannibalism if left with their original Nootka captors. Scientists gathered astronomical and geographical data; maps were made; and the Nootkas became subjects for both ethnographers and artists, who collected many native artefacts and produced a great number of drawings of the area and its people.

On 28 August the ships left Nootka Sound. After a brief visit to Monterey (Calif.), they reached Acapulco in mid October. On 20 December Malaspina set off across the Pacific, visiting various ports in the Orient and Port Jackson (Sydney, Australia) before returning to South America at Callao (Peru) the following July. After retracing its path round Cape Horn and across the Atlantic the expedition arrived home at Cadiz on 21 Sept. 1794. Malaspina soon set to work editing for publication the vast quantity of material gathered. He was promoted brigadier of the naval forces on 24 March 1795 but soon ran foul of court intrigue, in part as a result of his willingness to express the conviction that Spain's reactionary attitude toward economic and social development in her colonies was in need of thoroughgoing change. He was imprisoned in November and, having been found guilty of treason, was stripped of his rank and position the following April. After some six years in jail Malaspina was finally released on condition that he would not again set foot in Spain. He retired to his native Parma, where after a period of public service in minor positions he died at Pontremoli in the spring of 1810.

DONALD C. CUTTER

Almost all of the extensive material relating to Malaspina's expedition is in the Museo Naval (Madrid). A catalogue is in preparation. Other useful sources include the following: Archivo Museo Don Alvaro de Bazán (Viso del Marqués, Spain), Alejandro Malaspina, hoja de servicios, expediente personal. *Viaje político-científico alrededor del mundo por las corbetas Descubierta y Atrevida al mando de los capitanes de navío D. Alejandro Malaspina y Don José de Bustamante y Guerra desde 1789 á 1794*, ed. Pedro de Novo y Colson (Madrid, 1885). Emma Bona, *Alessandro Malaspina, sue navigazioni ed esplorazioni* (Rome, 1935). D. C. Cutter, *Malaspina in California* ([San Francisco], 1960); "Malaspina at Yakutat Bay," *Alaska Journal* (Juneau), 2 (1972), no.4: 42–49.

MALHIOT, FRANÇOIS, merchant, land speculator, politician, office holder, and militia officer; b. 20 Oct. 1733 in Montreal (Que.), son of Jean-François Malhiot*, a merchant, and Charlotte Gamelin; d. 28 Jan. 1808 in Verchères, Lower Canada.

The Malhiots came from the diocese of Limoges in France. Jean Malhiot, the first of the family to come to Canada, arrived some time before 1683. On 1 March 1688 he married Madeleine Marchand, who was his second wife; their son Jean-François made a fortune in the fur trade and the import-export business with France. On 18 Dec. 1724, in Montreal, he married Charlotte Gamelin, daughter of the merchant Ignace Gamelin* the elder, and they had several children, one of whom was François.

Nothing is known of François Malhiot's youth. The earliest mention of his career occurs in his marriage contract, where he is described as a "merchant" in Montreal. It may reasonably be assumed, then, that his father had initiated him into the business world and that upon his death on 28 Jan. 1756 Malhiot simply took over management of the family enterprise.

Malhiot

Whatever the case, on 11 Jan. 1768 Malhiot married his first cousin Élisabeth Gamelin, daughter of the Montreal merchant Ignace Gamelin* the younger. It was a brilliant occasion attended by many members of the Montreal élite. The marriage contract, dated 9 January, assured the wife a jointure of 6,000 *livres* and a preference legacy of 3,000 *livres*. The couple were to have 11 children.

Late in 1768 or early in 1769 Malhiot settled at Verchères. A notarized deed dated 26 April 1769 refers to him as a "merchant" living there. He sold dry goods, made mortgage loans, and speculated in wheat. In 1774 alone he bought at least 4,683 bushels of wheat. His business seems to have prospered, since in 1779 he owned a schooner, the *Coquette*, which was handled by a captain and two sailors. He resided in a stone house in the centre of the village; on his lot, which measured 120 feet by 180, he had also built a stable, a stone shed, and two wooden ones.

During the 1780s Malhiot's liquid assets grew and he was able to take up land speculation, in which he had previously seldom engaged. He sold a lot at Varennes in 1784, and a small piece of land at Verchères in 1788. The following year he bought four lots at Verchères and two others adjacent to the Chemin du Roy; then he sold four at Verchères and one in the seigneury of Varennes. In 1793 he bought half of Île Baladeau, a property "in grassland and standing timber," for 360 *livres*. The next year he purchased a farm of nearly 44 acres with a house and barn in the fief of Cap-Saint-Michel, as well as another in the seigneury of Verchères. His acquisitions turned out to be good investments. In 1794 he sold for 800 *livres* those lots for which he had paid 700 *livres* five years earlier.

From 1795 Malhiot seems gradually to have retired from business, probably relying more and more on his sons. In 1799 the notarized deeds no longer refer to him as a merchant, but as "esquire." In 1804 he made a gift of his assets to his three sons: Pierre-Ignace, François-Victor, and François-Xavier*. His fortune at that time amounted to 125,101 *livres*: 34,612 in dry and wet goods, 29,347 in properties, 7,187 in equipment and livestock, 33,869 in good debts, and 20,086 in doubtful ones. One of the latter consisted of an advance of 13,000 *livres* that he had made to Jean-Marie Coursolle on 20 April 1790, before Coursolle left for the "Pays d'en Haut." Pierre-Ignace and François-Xavier carried on the paternal enterprise in partnership; François-Victor became a clerk with the North West Company.

A shrewd and prosperous businessman, linked through his marriage with the Montreal élite, François Malhiot was one of the prominent citizens of Verchères. The interest he took in the village community made him respected by his fellow citizens. More than once he acted as executor and proxy. On 28 Dec. 1788 the churchwardens of the parish of Saint-François-Xavier at Verchères offered him a pew to show their gratitude for the role he had played in the construction of the new church. Quite naturally he began to have an influence outside his village. His entry into public life had, however, been due to circumstances beyond his control. During the American invasion in 1775–76 he had displayed his loyalty before Richard Montgomery*'s troops; his properties had been pillaged and he had been held prisoner. On 12 Nov. 1775 he was one of the 12 prominent citizens who signed the act of capitulation of Montreal.

The creation of a house of assembly in Lower Canada launched Malhiot on to the public scene again. He agreed to stand in the riding of Surrey and was duly elected in the summer of 1792. A level-headed man, he was always steadfast in his loyalty. In January 1793, at his colleagues' request, he helped prepare an address to the British crown expressing the fidelity and gratitude of its subjects in Lower Canada. In July 1794 he signed the declaration of loyalty to the constitution and the government that a group of Montreal citizens was circulating to counter the tide of enthusiasm in the colony for the ideas of the French revolution. His colleagues in the House of Assembly also turned his business experience to account. On 7 May 1793 they named him, along with James McGILL, John Richardson*, Joseph Papineau*, and James Walker, to a committee appointed to discuss with the commissioners from Upper Canada the division of customs receipts between the two provinces. According to historian Francis-Joseph Audet*, it was the most important mission that the house could entrust to a member.

Like most of those elected in 1792, François Malhiot served for only one term. He retired from public life by slow degrees. On 8 May 1799 he was appointed a justice of the peace. It is not known when he became a colonel in the militia, but the indications are that it was towards the end of his life. These two positions, which were largely honorary, kept him occupied during retirement. He died at Verchères on 28 Jan. 1808. The *Quebec Gazette*, which announced his death on 4 February, rendered him this homage: "François Malhiot, esquire, merchant, universally regretted in the District of Montreal, where his business relations and above all his good qualities had made him particularly well known . . . always merited the trust both of the government and of his compatriots. . . . He was well informed, very amiable and interesting in his friends' company, and gave happiness to a family whom he raised in the sentiments of honour and virtue and who will long miss him as a most considerate and loving father."

FRANÇOIS BÉLAND and HÉLÈNE PARÉ

ANQ-M, CE1-26, 30 janv. 1808; CE1-51, 20 oct. 1733, 11 janv. 1768; CN1-74, 6 juill. 1789; CN1-150, 26 avril 1769; 26 mars, 5 avril, 1er, 6, 11 juill. 1774; 14 juin 1777; 30, 31 mars 1779; 15 févr. 1782; 22 mai 1784; 7 août, 27, 28 sept. 1788; 24, 29 août, 22 sept., 30 nov. 1789; 20 avril 1790; 17 sept. 1793; 5 juill., 19 sept., 22 déc. 1794; 11 févr. 1799; CN1-295, 14 janv. 1804; CN1-313, 10 févr. 1802. *Quebec Gazette*, 4 Feb. 1808. F.-J. Audet, *Les députés de Montréal*, 131. F.-J. Audet et Édouard Fabre Surveyer, "Les députés au premier parlement du Bas-Canada: François Malhiot," *La Presse* (Montréal), 30 juill. 1927: 41, 50.

MAN (Mann), JAMES, educator and Methodist minister; b. in the early 1750s in New York City; d. unmarried 25 Dec. 1820 in Cape Negro, N.S., and was buried at Shelburne, N.S.

Although he lived and preached in Nova Scotia from 1783 until his death in 1820, James Man is a rather elusive figure. He was of Dutch ancestry and may have been a Lutheran in his youth. His brother John was caught up in the first phase of Methodist activity in New York City in the 1760s and for a time was minister of the Wesley Chapel (John Street Church) there; James acted as clerk to the Reverend Charles INGLIS, soon to be named the first Anglican bishop of Nova Scotia. Apparently James Man became a Methodist before leaving New York.

The Man brothers were identified, as were many other Methodists, with the loyalist cause in the American Revolutionary War and emigrated to Nova Scotia in 1783. James Man opened a school in Liverpool in 1785; Simeon PERKINS, who soon was on close terms with him, noted on 9 January that "Mr Mann the Schoolmaster Read one Sermon, & prayed very Acceptable to the Congregation." A year later Man was recruited as a probationer for the Methodist ministry by the Reverend Freeborn Garrettson, an American preacher who in 1784 had been persuaded by Thomas Coke and William Black* to come to Nova Scotia.

Methodism began spontaneously in Nova Scotia in much the same way as it had earlier in the Thirteen Colonies. William Black, the first itinerant, a member of a family of Yorkshire Methodists, looked for assistance first to John Wesley, who urged him to seek help from the societies in the United States. From 1784 until 1800, about 20 missionaries from the new Methodist Episcopal Church worked with Black, the Man brothers, and others, but by 1800 only two American preachers were still in Nova Scotia. Black once again turned to the Wesleyan Conference in England, which assumed responsibility for the societies in the Maritime provinces. When the General Wesleyan Methodist Missionary Society was established in 1818, the Maritimes were constituted as a regular missionary district under the society's direction.

James Man's career spanned this formative period in the development of Methodism in the eastern colonies. In 1786 he began work on the Barrington circuit, where, he later reported, 50 members were added to the society during the first year of his itineracy. Ordained with Black and John Man at the Philadelphia conference of the Methodist Episcopal Church in 1789, James served until his death on the Barrington, Cumberland, Liverpool, Halifax, and Shelburne circuits, and also on the Sheffield and Saint John circuits in New Brunswick. He was responsible for the building of the first Methodist church in Sackville, N.B., and in 1806 he presided at the opening of a new church in Shelburne. In 1791–92 he preached for several months in New York City; for part of 1802–3 he acted as superintendent of the societies in Nova Scotia and New Brunswick in the place of Black; Man considered Shelburne his headquarters, however, and before and after his retirement in 1812 he moved in and out of that town in response to the directions of his brethren.

The form of Methodism that James Man helped to establish in the eastern provinces had certain distinctive characteristics. As in Britain and the United States, the missionaries were genuinely peripatetic, and nominally each one was stationed each year on a new circuit. In practice, however, the older itinerants became a semi-settled ministry in that they became identified with particular centres: Black with Halifax, John Man with Newport, N.S., Duncan McColl* with St Stephen (St Stephen–Milltown), N.B., and James Man with Shelburne. As a result, Methodism was undoubtedly strengthened in these areas, but its organization lacked the flexibility of Methodism elsewhere. Similarly, although Man and his colleagues were fervent evangelists, they seem to have been more restrained than their counterparts in the Methodist Episcopal Church. Man's own sermons were said to have been "chaste, edifying and usually unimpassioned; sometimes upon the love of Calvary, but more frequently upon the terrors of the law." He shared with his fellow missionaries a strong antipathy to the antinomian outlook which the Methodists believed was characteristic of the New Light movement and its Baptist successors [*see* Henry Alline*]. Thus in 1796 he reported: "I have prevented Stephen Snow from exhorting. . . . He is strongly tinctur'd with enthusiasm & holds to no falling from Grace." A year earlier he had been concerned lest the society in Saint John should "be pick'd up" by "Antinomian innovaters." Moreover, the Man brothers believed that Methodists should be loyal subjects. Loyalism had brought them to Nova Scotia; in 1795 Man commented that "religion is low in this City [New York]. Republican principals & politics eat it out of many hearts. . . ." Later he would exclaim about the United States: "Ah sir, there is a rod in soak for them; depend upon it, there is a rod in soak for them."

In appearance, James Man was apparently a striking figure: according to one report, he was of "large stature and dark complexion, presuming generally the old custom of 'short clothes,' and

Maquilla

attending with scrupulous care to the details of dress." This impressive physical presence was matched by the strength of his character. Noted for his personal rectitude and puritanical zeal – like other preachers he often denounced balls and dancing – Man believed intensely that his task as a Methodist missionary was to rescue people from their wickedness by preaching Wesley's doctrines of free grace and Christian perfection. He travelled tirelessly throughout Nova Scotia and the Saint John valley to establish and nurture Methodist societies imbued with this gospel. His last sermon was delivered on the day of his death. A fellow preacher, Winthrop Sargeant, said of Man that "no frivolity or mirth could appear in his social intercourse, yet he was cheerful and happy"; another preacher claimed, "Even the ungodly would not allow an insinuation against his memory, but would fight for him." The Methodist community Man had helped to found in the Maritime provinces would be nourished by the memory of his sober, self-sacrificing zeal.

G. S. FRENCH

School of Oriental and African Studies, Univ. of London (London), Council for World Mission Arch., Methodist Missionary Soc., Wesleyan Methodist Missionary Soc., Corr., Canada, 1800–17 (mfm. at United Church Arch., Central Arch. of the United Church of Canada, Toronto). James Man, "Memoir of Mr John Man, missionary in Nova Scotia," *Methodist Magazine* (London), 41 (1818): 641–46. *Methodist Magazine*, 44 (1821): 622–23. "The papers of Daniel Fidler, Methodist missionary in Nova Scotia and New Brunswick, 1792–1798," ed. G. [S.] French, United Church of Canada, Committee on Arch., *Bull.* (Toronto), 12 (1959): 3–18; 13 (1960): 28–46. [The originals of these letters are in Drew Univ. Library (Madison, N.J.).] Perkins, *Diary, 1780–89* (Harvey and Fergusson); *Diary, 1790–96* (Fergusson); *Diary, 1797–1803* (Fergusson). Matthew Richey, *A memoir of the late Rev. William Black, Wesleyan minister, Halifax, N.S., including an account of the rise and progress of Methodism in Nova Scotia . . .* (Halifax, 1839). G. H. Cornish, *Cyclopædia of Methodism in Canada, containing historical, educational, and statistical information . . .* (2v., Toronto and Halifax, 1881–1903). E. A. Betts, *Bishop Black and his preachers* (2nd ed., Sackville, N.B., 1976). S. D. Clark, *Church and sect in Canada* (Toronto, 1948). G. G. Findlay and W. W. Holdsworth, *The history of the Wesleyan Methodist Missionary Society* (5v., London, 1921–24), 1. G. [S.] French, *Parsons & politics: the rôle of the Wesleyan Methodists in Upper Canada and the Maritimes from 1780 to 1855* (Toronto, 1962). T. W. Smith, *History of the Methodist Church within the territories embraced in the late conference of Eastern British America . . .* (2v., Halifax, 1877–90).

MAQUILLA (Maquinna). *See* MUQUINNA

MARCH, MARY. *See* DEMASDUWIT

MARCHINTON (Marchington), PHILIP, merchant, office holder, politician, and Methodist preacher; b. *c.* 1736 in England; d. 2 Nov. 1808 in Halifax, N.S.

Almost nothing is known of Philip Marchinton's early life. Circumstances suggest that he was born into a family with means sufficient only to give him a counting-house education. After serving a commercial apprenticeship in England, he moved in 1771 to Philadelphia, Pa, where he established himself as a general merchant. Marchinton prospered to the extent that by 1777 he owned Pennsylvania real estate worth more than £1,000. Business success was overshadowed, however, by the American revolution. Initially, Marchinton tried to remain neutral, agreeing to serve in the local militia but refusing to renounce his allegiance to the crown. Having declared himself a loyalist during Philadelphia's occupation by British forces, he had no choice but to leave the city when the army abandoned it in June 1778. The property he left behind him was subsequently confiscated by the revolutionaries. Marchinton spent the remainder of the war in New York City, sailing from there in November 1783 with 300 fellow loyalists and a personal fortune supposedly totalling £35,000.

After being storm-stayed for several months in Bermuda, Marchinton moved on to Halifax, a port that many loyalists believed would outrival Boston once New England had been excluded from the West Indies carrying-trade. Although those expectations proved over ambitious, Marchinton achieved success in his own business in Nova Scotia, thanks partly to the capital and entrepreneurial talent he brought with him and partly to his connections within the loyalist community. The precise nature of his business operations remains unknown, but he appears to have engaged in the general export-import trade as a wholesaler. He also contracted for sales of timber to Britain during the French revolutionary and Napoleonic wars. The profits he earned enabled him to acquire a large block of waterfront real estate in Halifax along with more than 12,000 acres of land, mostly located in the northeastern parts of Nova Scotia.

Material achievement quickly translated itself into social recognition for Philip Marchinton. By the early 1790s he had been appointed a justice of the peace for Halifax Township. Furthermore, from 1786 to 1793 he sat in the House of Assembly as member for Cumberland County. In the legislature he supported the campaign, led by Captain Thomas Barclay* and other loyalist members, to impeach puisne judges James BRENTON and Isaac DESCHAMPS, a campaign that essentially reflected the desire of Nova Scotian loyalists for a larger share of government patronage. He also opposed tariff measures which would have impeded the flow of imports from the United States. Although local farmers wanted tariff protection, Marchinton and other urban merchants feared that duties on American goods would drive up costs in the fishery and hinder the re-export trade to the Caribbean.

The most controversial aspect of Marchinton's public career derived from his religious zeal. Arriving in Halifax as a follower of John Wesley, he displayed his faith by leasing a house where Methodist prayer-meetings could be held. In the spring of 1786 he built a large chapel in Halifax which could accommodate up to 1,000 worshippers. Over the next few years "Brother" Marchinton preached numerous sermons and interceded with the authorities on behalf of a succession of itinerant Methodist missionaries. In 1791–92 he assisted William Wilberforce and other English evangelists in their project to resettle Nova Scotian blacks in Sierra Leone [see David GEORGE; Thomas Peters*].

Despite his continuing philanthropic enthusiasm, Marchinton was expelled from Halifax's Methodist community at the end of 1791. One contemporary complained that Marchinton had "attempted to raise himself above all discipline," a comment that 19th-century writers interpreted to mean that he refused to abstain from liquor. This purge proved costly to the Methodists, since Marchinton retaliated by closing the doors of his chapel to those who had judged him morally deficient. For a while he carried on as a renegade preacher, but a lack of public response caused him to abandon this role. In 1806 he sold his chapel, then known as "Sodom," to local Presbyterians for £500.

Marchinton's troubles possibly originated with the death of his wife, Elizabeth, at a young age on 24 Nov. 1788. Unwilling to accept her loss, he had her remains placed in a glass-covered coffin and allowed burial to take place only after the body had badly decomposed. At his death he left two children, Joseph, who served during the Napoleonic Wars with the Nova Scotia Fencibles, and Mary, who married John Welsford, lieutenant-colonel of the 101st Foot. Quarrelling during the early 1820s over division of their father's substantial estate resulted at one point in Joseph's being lodged in the Halifax jail. Memory of Philip Marchinton's somewhat eccentric presence was kept alive by his grandson, Major Augustus Frederick Welsford*, who suffered what Haligonians regarded as a hero's death in the Crimean War.

D. A. SUTHERLAND

Halifax County Registry of Deeds (Halifax), Deeds, 37: ff.327–28; 41: ff.42–44 (mfm. at PANS). PANS, RG 1, 227, nos.106, 131. [John Clarkson], Clarkson's mission to America, 1791–1792, ed. and intro. C. B. Fergusson (Halifax, 1971). N.S., House of Assembly, Journal and proc., 1786–93. Perkins, Diary, 1780–89 (Harvey and Fergusson); Diary, 1790–96 (Fergusson); Diary, 1797–1803 (Fergusson). "United Empire Loyalists: enquiry into losses and services," AO Report, 1904: 494. Acadian Recorder, 25 Oct. 1823. Nova Scotia Royal Gazette, 2 Dec. 1788; 16 Sept. 1800; 19 March, 17 May 1801; 2 Aug., 8 Nov. 1808. An almanack . . . calculated for the meridian of Halifax in Nova-Scotia . . . , comp. Theophrastus (Halifax), 1802. Directory of N.S. MLAs. R. V. Harris, The Church of Saint Paul in Halifax, Nova Scotia: 1749–1949 (Toronto, 1949). G. O. Huestis, A manual of Methodism: being outlines of its history, doctrines, and discipline (Toronto, 1885). Murdoch, Hist. of N.S., vol.3. T. W. Smith, History of the Methodist Church within the territories embraced in the late conference of Eastern British America . . . (2v., Halifax, 1877–90). W. M. Brown, "Recollections of old Halifax," N.S. Hist. Soc., Coll., 13 (1908): 75–101. K. B. Wainwright, "A comparative study in Nova Scotian rural economy, 1788–1872, based on recently discovered books of account of old firms in Kings County, Nova Scotia," N.S. Hist. Soc., Coll., 30 (1954): 78–119.

MARCOUX, PIERRE, army and militia officer and merchant; b. 2 Jan. 1757 at Quebec, son of Pierre Marcoux and Geneviève Lepage; d. 20 Nov. 1809 in Berthier (Berthier-sur-Mer), Lower Canada.

Pierre Marcoux's career has often been confused with that of his father, Pierre. The latter was born at Quebec on 9 July 1731 to the mason Germain Marcoux and Geneviève Marchand; he was already established as a merchant by the time of his marriage to Geneviève Lepage on 9 Sept. 1754, and by 1769 he was living on Rue Notre-Dame in Quebec's Lower Town. In 1773 a committee of British merchants at Quebec wanting to obtain a house of assembly invited to a meeting 15 Canadian seigneurs and merchants whom they felt capable of influencing the Canadians to support the proposal; eight, including Marcoux, attended, but their suspicions that the British were determined to exclude Canadians from election to an assembly overcame their sympathy for the measure, and they refused to endorse the campaign. The previous year Marcoux had bought a farm at Berthier, to which in March 1775 he added a lot acquired from Louis DUNIÈRE, a merchant at Quebec and his neighbour at Berthier. He became a captain of militia at Quebec in August 1775, and during the American siege of the city he commanded a company of volunteers in which his son Pierre served. It saw action in the repulse of Major-General Richard Montgomery*'s assault on the barricades of Rue du Sault-au-Matelot. In 1777 the younger Marcoux joined Major-General John Burgoyne*'s army as a lieutenant.

In the mean time, probably as early as 1776, the elder Marcoux had begun moving into maritime commerce in partnership with the Quebec merchant Louis (Louis-Martin) Marchand; they purchased a schooner for a cash payment of £900 in January 1777, and likely began making and shipping flour the following year. In 1779 Marcoux acquired from the Séminaire de Québec and the Hôtel-Dieu several lots, one of which was a beach lot, at La Canoterie in Lower Town. In February 1780 he leased the farm at Berthier for rent in kind, including half the grain. Perhaps the same year he opened a store at his property on Rue Notre-Dame, where he sold wines, porter, cider, and cheese. Marcoux had evidently become quite prosperous by this time; in September 1779 he had been able to give his daughter, Marie-Geneviève, and her new husband, his partner, Marchand, an advance of 12,000 *livres* on her inheritance. Marcoux's situation rapidly deteriorated, however; in 1781 he was obliged to borrow £2,000 from Joseph Brassard* Deschenaux.

At the end of the American revolution young Pierre was placed on half pay and granted 2,000 acres of land. On 7 June 1783 he married Marie-Anne, daughter of Louis Dunière, and struck out on his own in business. The post-war context was unfavourable, however, and as early as November he and his brother Jean-Baptiste, with whom he had formed a partnership, found themselves creditors to two merchants on the brink of bankruptcy, one of whom, the younger Louis Marchand, owed them £500. Moreover, because of "the great decrease in the price and value of goods since the Peace" with the United States, by September 1784 the three Marcouxs were indebted for a total of £1,800 in imported merchandise to the London firms of Watson and Rashleigh [*see* Sir Brook WATSON] and Rashleigh and Company, who demanded payment of at least two-thirds of the debt within three years. In October the family's three-storey stone house on Rue Notre-Dame, now occupied by Pierre and Marie-Anne (the elder Marcoux had moved to Berthier in 1783), and the two-storey house in La Canoterie with "the large and commodious store distributed properly for a manufacture of flour" were offered for sale; they were not sold, however. In the spring and summer of 1785 all the stock-in-trade, "consisting in a compleat and valuable Assortment of Dry-Goods, Groceries and Liquors," was put up for auction.

At the same time as the Marcouxs were struggling to pay off their British creditors, they were trying to finance a hazardous scheme to send a trading expedition to Baie des Esquimaux (Hamilton Inlet), Labrador. Trade was being conducted on different parts of the Labrador coast by such merchants as Adam Lymburner*, Thomas DUNN, and William GRANT (1744–1805) of Quebec and George CARTWRIGHT and Andrew PINSON of England, but Baie des Esquimaux seemed to offer excellent prospects. It had been explored in 1743 by Louis Fornel*, and then exploited commercially in the 1750s by his widow, Marie-Anne Barbel*, and her associates, but appears to have been rather neglected since. In July 1784 the Marcouxs obtained from Governor HALDIMAND a licence to send eight men and £800 worth of merchandise to Baie des Esquimaux on condition that they obey the laws regulating trade with the Indians,

but they did not send an expedition that year. In August 1785 the younger Marcoux formed a joint partnership with Dunière and two other Quebec merchants, Jacques-Nicolas PERRAULT and John ANTROBUS, to carry on a seal fishery on the Labrador coast and "a trade with the savages at the Baie des Esquimaux and elsewhere." That fall, however, Marcoux was turned back by heavy winds at the entrance to the bay and wintered at Seal Islands (Seal Islands Harbour), Labrador, about 100 miles to the southeast. He brought back to Quebec three sealskin-clad Inuit, with their whalebone utensils and weapons; they met Lieutenant Governor Henry Hope*, and paddled their kayaks in the harbour before a large crowd.

The partners subsequently secured a licence from Hope to establish fishing posts at Indian Island, between Seal Islands and Baie des Esquimaux. Marcoux set forth in the fall of 1786 with fishing gear, lumber, and the Inuit family. After an unfortunate wintering at Seal Islands, he finally got away in June 1787 for Baie des Esquimaux and established himself in an old French post at North West River, about 120 miles inside the bay. Two other Canadian traders, George Plante and Baptiste Dumontier, had wintered there the past two years and they protested, but ultimately the parties agreed to settle on opposite sides of the river, and let the natives choose the post with which they would trade. Marcoux had a successful winter, the natives "exerting themselves amazingly to kill seals to exchange for woollens, iron mongery, bread, etc." In the summer of 1788, however, Plante brought suit at Quebec against Marcoux, alleging that he had broken provincial ordinances by settling and trading in Indian country without a licence and by selling liquor to the natives. The case was held over until the following summer when Marcoux, in defence, argued that he had obtained licences, that Inuit were not Indians, and that since he was in Hudson's Bay Company territory provincial regulations did not apply anyway. The outcome of the case is unknown.

In spite of the court battles, in the winter of 1788–89 Marcoux and his partners had two vessels in Baie des Esquimaux and a third fitting out to go in the spring. Moreover, they joined forces with John MacKenzie and Company of London to approach the authorities in both England and Quebec for exclusive rights of fishing and trading in Baie des Esquimaux. Their petition of January 1789 to Governor Lord Dorchester [Guy CARLETON] claimed that a monopoly was essential to their lives and property, for if competition made it necessary to give liquor to the natives in the bay, "all attempts to improve it [would have to be] dropt for ever." Dorchester referred the petition to the land committee of the Legislative Council. Composed in part of Quebec merchants, it had rejected a similar petition from Cartwright two years earlier but was sympathetic to the request of Marcoux and his associates. Although the committee felt it could not grant a monopoly, it praised the petitioners for their enterprise and recommended that they have the preference for the sites in the bay they effectively occupied; however, the matter seems to have gone no further. Marcoux apparently continued to trade in the area in the 1790s but without great success.

Meanwhile, by 1788 the house and store on Rue Notre-Dame had been sold to Dunière and Joseph Duval, and the elder Marcoux had begun pursuing a public career. About 1789 he became lieutenant-colonel of militia for the region between Berthier and Matane. Though not taking a leading part, since 1784 he had been supporting the campaign of the Canadian merchants at Quebec to obtain a house of assembly and English commercial law [see Jacques-Nicolas Perrault]. From 1792 to 1796 he and Dunière represented Hertford County in the first house of assembly. Marcoux supported the Canadian group which developed in opposition to deputies backing the colonial administration. On 3 July 1797 he married Geneviève Alliés, but six days later he died; he was buried on the 11th under his pew in the first row of the parish church of Notre-Dame-de-l'Assomption at Berthier. He left a net debt of nearly 16,000 *livres*.

The Marcoux farm was divided equally among Pierre, Jean-Baptiste, and Marchand. In 1799 Pierre acquired Jean-Baptiste's share, and the following year sold the two-thirds for £640 to Dunière, who had already acquired Marchand's share. Marcoux seems to have settled for a time at Montreal, where in 1799 he was a member of the Club des Apôtres, a gastronomic group that Lieutenant-Governor Robert Shore Milnes* wrongly suspected of subversive activities in favour of France. By 1804, however, Marcoux was living at Berthier on the former family farm, which he was renting from Dunière. That April he received a grant of 400 acres of land in Mégantic Township.

In 1796, when Lord Dorchester had created the Royal Canadian Volunteer Regiment, Marcoux had been named captain in the first battalion; on its disbandment in 1802 he was placed on half pay as a lieutenant. He later became major in the militia and assistant to the adjutant general, François Baby. On 19 Sept. 1809 he succeeded Gabriel-Elzéar Taschereau as overseer of highways of the District of Quebec. Marcoux's health, however, had been adversely affected by his expeditions to Labrador, and on 20 November, before being able to take up his functions, he died of pleurisy at the age of 52. His burial took place three days later in the parish church of Notre-Dame-de-l'Assomption. He left his wife with a small and precarious income.

Pierre Marcoux and his father touched the society of their times at many points. They cooperated with the new régime after the conquest, entered into mercantile ventures with British partners, and were personally brave and enterprising, but they were perhaps not sufficiently cautious or astute to make successful businessmen. In his daring effort to exploit Baie des Esquimaux the younger Marcoux had worked in a vast and lonely region, under conditions too difficult to allow him to reap the rewards that his courage and enterprise deserved.

W. H. Whiteley

[Personal details of Pierre Marcoux's life and military service can be found in his wife's pension petition (1823) in PAC, RG 8, I (C ser.), 197: 60–65. The place of the young Marcoux in the siege of Quebec is recorded on page 101 in volume 1714 of the same collection. The list of those who served in the militia on that occasion was compiled by Gabriel-Elzéar Taschereau and later printed as "Rôle général de la milice canadienne de Québec passée en revue le 11 sept. 1775 . . . ; aussi, nouveau rôle de la milice canadienne qui a fait le service pendant le blocus de Québec . . . ," Literary and Hist. Soc. of Quebec, *Hist. Docs.*, 7th ser. (1905): 269–307.

Francis-Joseph Audet* and Édouard Fabre Surveyer published an article on Marcoux in *La Presse* (Montréal), 20 août 1927: 45, as part of a series on the members of the first parliament of Lower Canada. It contains details of Marcoux's last will and testament and a facsimile of his signature. In their article, however, Audet and Fabre Surveyer state that Pierre Marcoux Jr was deputy of Hertford, when in fact it was his father who represented the county. This error was corrected by Fabre Surveyer in "Les deux premiers députés du comté de Hertford (Bellechasse-Montmagny): Pierre Marcoux et Louis Dunière," *Le Canada français* (Québec), 2e sér., 32 (1944–45): 404–17.

The business activities of the Marcoux at Quebec are detailed in a large number of notarial acts, listed below, in the possession of the ANQ-Q. Their involvement in the trade and fisheries of Labrador is documented in petitions, licences, correspondence, legal depositions, and statements gathered together in G.B., Privy Council, Judicial committee, *In the matter of the boundary between the Dominion of Canada and the colony of Newfoundland in the Labrador peninsula, joint appendix* (12v., London, 1927), 7: 3356–90. The memorial for an exclusive grant of Baie des Esquimaux and the report of the Quebec land committee are in PAC, RG 1, L1, 1: 283–86. George Cartwright's *Journal of transactions and events, during a residence of nearly sixteen years on the coast of Labrador . . .* (3v., Newark, Eng., 1792), 3, has some interesting glimpses of Marcoux on the coast. Background information on the Labrador posts is found in James White, *Forts and trading posts in the Labrador peninsula and adjoining territory* (Ottawa, 1926) and in William Henry Whiteley, "Newfoundland, Quebec, and the Labrador merchants, 1783–1809," *Newfoundland Quarterly* (St John's), 73 (1977), no.4: 18–26. w.h.w.]

ANQ-Q, CE1-1, 9 juill. 1731, 9 sept. 1754, 2 janv. 1757; CE2-2, 7 juin 1753; 3, 11 juill. 1797; 23 nov. 1809; CN1-25, 30 avril 1779; 8, 19 avril, 25 juill. 1782; 1er sept. 1783;

Margane

CN1-26, 4 mars 1801; CN1-205, 9 août 1774; 10 avril 1775; 11 janv., 13, 29 mars, 19 sept. 1777; 12, 20 févr., 18 avril, 25 mai, 21 déc. 1778; 28 avril, 15 juin, 17 sept. 1779; 17 févr. 1780; 24 juill., 24 nov. 1783; 6, 21 sept. 1784; 16 avril, 23 août 1785; CN1-207, 8 sept. 1754, 10 févr. 1775; CN1-256, 31 May 1791; CN1-262, 29 sept., 10 nov. 1804; CN2-7, 30 juin 1797, 19 mars 1798. *Quebec Gazette*, 29 Sept. 1766; 18 June 1772; 29 June 1775; 28 Dec. 1780; 5 Feb., 14 Oct. 1784; 21 April, 30 June, 29 Dec. 1785; 29 June 1786; 19 April, 28 June, 20 Dec. 1792; 5 Jan. 1797; 5 Oct., 30 Nov., 7 Dec. 1809; 18 Jan. 1810. "Les habitants de la ville de Québec en 1769–1770," F.-J. Audet, compil., *BRH*, 27 (1921): 121. Hare, "L'Assemblée législative du Bas-Canada," *RHAF*, 27: 373.

MARGANE DE LAVALTRIE, PIERRE-PAUL, army and militia officer, seigneur, office holder, and politician; b. 13 Aug. 1743 in Montreal (Que.), son of Pierre-Paul Margane de Lavaltrie and Louise-Charlotte d'Ailleboust d'Argenteuil; d. 10 Sept. 1810 in Lavaltrie, Lower Canada.

Pierre-Paul Margane de Lavaltrie belonged to a family of soldiers. His grandfather, Séraphin Margane de Lavaltrie, had come to New France in 1665 with the Régiment de Carignan-Salières; his father made a career in the colonial regular troops, reaching the rank of captain and becoming a knight of the Order of Saint-Louis. Pierre-Paul probably studied for some time in Montreal before being admitted into the colonial regular troops as a cadet at the age of 13. On 25 July 1758 he was promoted lieutenant in the Régiment du Languedoc. The following year he took part in the battle of the Plains of Abraham and, after the surrender of Montreal on 8 Sept. 1760, he accompanied his regiment to France.

Lavaltrie was an only son, and at his father's request he came back to Canada after serving for some years in the French army. On his arrival in September 1765 he was received rather coldly by Governor Murray*, who suspected French army officers returning to Canada of being spies in the pay of the French monarchy. His father's death on 1 Jan. 1766 probably influenced Lavaltrie's decision not to return to France to pursue the military career on which he had embarked but to settle in Canada. On 21 February, as heir to the seigneury of Lavaltrie, he attended the meeting of the seigneurs from the Montreal district which had been called by Murray and his council, a meeting that aroused the anger of the British merchants in Montreal against the governor. A month later, at Terrebonne, Lavaltrie married Marie-Angélique, daughter of Louis de La Corne, known as La Corne *l'aîné*, and Élisabeth de Ramezay. Thus he became linked with some important families of the Canadian nobility. In the autumn of 1769 he built a manor-house at Lavaltrie and went to live there permanently. From then on he devoted himself to developing his seigneury, in particular building a

sawmill and obtaining the agreement of his *censitaires* for a church to be erected.

When the Americans invaded the province of Quebec in 1775 [*see* Benedict ARNOLD; Richard Montgomery*], Lavaltrie went to the defence of Fort St Johns, on the Richelieu, as did a good many other seigneurs. Guy CARLETON's government considered entrusting him with the task of raising a corps of Canadians to defend Montreal, but the surrender of Fort St Johns at the beginning of November 1775 led Carleton to fall back upon Quebec instead. To escape the Americans sent in pursuit of him the governor had to disguise himself; in this way, and with Lavaltrie's help in particular, he was able to reach Quebec. The next spring Lavaltrie contributed indirectly to the success of the British troops assembled at Oswegatchie (Ogdensburg, N.Y.) by seeing that munitions and supplies reached them. Upon learning of this the Americans tried to have him arrested, and he had to take refuge at Quebec, where he joined the army and served until the invaders withdrew. After hostilities ended, Lavaltrie returned to his seigneury. Inheritances from his own family and that of his wife brought him partial or full ownership of the seigneuries of Terrebonne, Argenteuil, and Monnoir (also called Ramezay), but he chose to relinquish them in order to concentrate entirely on the development of Lavaltrie.

Although he had signed a petition to the king in 1788 opposing constitutional change, Lavaltrie nevertheless stood as a candidate in Warwick when the first elections to the Lower Canadian House of Assembly were held in the summer of 1792. On the evening of his victory he declared to the electors, who were also his *censitaires* and whom he addressed as "my dear children," that he was relinquishing the right to a share of the purchase price when a property was sold, the right to repurchase, the right to demand days of unpaid labour, the right to have trees planted on May Day, and other seigneurial privileges. "I shall give you a deed to this effect drawn up before a notary whenever you desire," he added. The promise, an unusual gesture for a seigneur of the time, was carried out the following week.

As a member of the assembly, Lavaltrie was quite inconspicuous, however. At the beginning of the first session he backed the choice of Jean-Antoine PANET as speaker, and like most members of Canadian origin he was opposed to having only the English text of laws and parliamentary debates recognized as legal. But after that he did not attend sessions and he did not run in the next elections in 1796, stepping aside for his son-in-law, Charles-Gaspard Tarieu de Lanaudière, to be elected.

Lavaltrie's absenteeism from the assembly can probably be explained by the behaviour of the man he had defeated at the polls in June 1792, James

Cuthbert*. For several years Cuthbert tried to have the election annulled, claiming that because Lavaltrie was not a British subject he could not be elected. If the authorities had agreed to act on such a request, they could have been led into quashing not only Lavaltrie's election but also those of other Canadians. Cuthbert even insinuated that Lavaltrie was not loyal to the British crown, since he was reported to have refused to take the customary oath on his appointment as justice of the peace in 1788. Cuthbert's allegations do not seem, however, to have unduly excited the authorities in either London or the colony, since Lavaltrie obtained the rank of militia colonel on 13 May 1794. In addition his commission as JP was renewed in 1799, and in June 1803 Lieutenant Governor Sir Robert Shore Milnes* made him a grant according to the system of township leader and associates [see James CALDWELL] of 11,486 acres in Kildare Township, north of the seigneury of Lavaltrie.

Pierre-Paul Margane de Lavaltrie died at his manor-house on 10 Sept. 1810 and was buried three days later under his pew in the church of Lavaltrie. Through his only daughter, Suzanne-Antoinette, his property passed to the Lanaudière family. The efforts he had exerted to develop his domain had borne fruit. At the time he became seigneur, Lavaltrie had a population of only 327, but by about 1810 it had risen to more than 1,000, and the parish of Saint-Paul, which had been founded in the mid 1780s, had more than 2,500. The seigneury had acquired a good network of roads and was producing wheat and other cereals, as well as hay in large quantities; it also had one of the richest forests in Lower Canada for a variety of building woods. In 1794 the Anglican bishop Jacob Mountain* had noted in his journal: "La Valtrie is the most beautiful seigneurie between Quebec and Montreal."

PIERRE DUFOUR and GÉRARD GOYER

Invasion du Canada (Verreau). "Inventaire des biens de Luc Lacorne de Saint-Luc," J.-J. Lefebvre, édit., ANQ *Rapport*, 1947–48: 29–70. Jacob Mountain, "From Quebec to Niagara in 1794; diary of Bishop Jacob Mountain," ed. A. R. Kelley, ANQ *Rapport*, 1959–60: 119–65. "Protêt des marchands de Montréal contre une assemblée des seigneurs, tenue en cette ville le 21 février 1766," É.-Z. Massicotte, édit., *BRH*, 38 (1932): 68–79. *Montreal Gazette*, 17 Sept. 1810. *Quebec Gazette*, 13 Nov., 11 Dec. 1788; 5 Feb. 1789; 23 Dec. 1790; 20 Dec. 1792; 24 Jan. 1793; 7 Aug. 1794. F.-J. Audet et Fabre Surveyer, *Les députés au premier Parl. du Bas-Canada*. Camille Bertrand, *Catalogue de la collection François-Louis-Georges Baby* (2v., Montréal, 1971). Bouchette, *Topographical description of L.C.* Caron, "Inv. de la corr. de Mgr Briand," ANQ *Rapport*, 1929–30: 47–136; "Inv. de la corr. de Mgr Denaut," 1931–32: 129–42; "Inv. de la corr. de Mgr Hubert et de Mgr Bailly de Messein," 1930–31: 199–351.

Ægidius Fauteux, *Les chevaliers de Saint-Louis en Canada* (Montréal, 1940). Langelier, *Liste des terrains concédés*. Le Jeune, *Dictionnaire*. "Officiers du régiment de Languedoc," *BRH*, 51 (1945): 283–89. P.-G. Roy, *Inv. concessions*. Wallace, *Macmillan dict.* Burt, *Old prov. of Quebec* (1968). Ægidius Fauteux, *La famille d'Aillebout: étude généalogique et historique* (Montréal, 1917). Marcel Fournier, *La représentation parlementaire de la région de Joliette* (Joliette, Qué., 1977). Jean et Marcel Hamelin, *Les mœurs électorales dans le Québec de 1791 à nos jours* (Montréal, 1962). Paquet et Wallot, *Patronage et pouvoir dans le Bas-Canada*. Christian Roy, *Histoire de L'Assomption* (L'Assomption, Qué., 1967). P.-G. Roy, *La famille Tarieu de Lanaudière* (Lévis, Qué., 1922). Stanley, *L'invasion du Canada* (MacDonald). *Tricentenaire de Lavaltrie, 1672–1972*, Réal Pelletier, édit. (Lavaltrie, Qué., s.d.). Hare, "L'Assemblée législative du Bas-Canada," *RHAF*, 27: 379. Eugène Rouillard, "Les chefs de canton," *BRH*, 2 (1896): 183–85. P.-G. Roy, "La famille Margane de Lavaltrie," *BRH*, 23 (1917): 33–53, 65–80. Benjamin Sulte, "Le chevalier de Niverville," *RSC Trans.*, 3rd ser., 3 (1909), sect.I: 43–72.

MARGON, JEAN-GUILLAUME PLANTAVIT DE LAPAUSE DE. *See* PLANTAVIT

MARGUERITE DE SAINT-LOUIS DE GONZAGUE. *See* DAVANNE

MARIE-CATHERINE DE SAINT-ALEXIS. *See* PAYEN DE NOYAN

MARIE-GENEVIÈVE DE SAINT-FRANÇOIS D'ASSISE. *See* PARENT

MARIE-VÉNÉRANDE DE SAINTE-CLAIRE. *See* MELANÇON

MARSEILLE, JEAN-SÉBASTIEN NATTE, *dit.* *See* NATTE

MARTINEAU, JÉRÔME, merchant, business agent, and politician; b. 6 March 1750 in Sainte-Famille, Île d'Orléans (Que.), son of Augustin Martineau, a farmer, and Françoise Mercier; m. 13 April 1779 Marie-Angélique Legris at Quebec; d. there 19 Dec. 1809.

Jérôme Martineau, who was the third in a family of seven, spent his childhood and adolescence on the Île d'Orléans. In 1771 he was living at Quebec, where he worked as paymaster and business agent for the Séminaire de Québec. In this capacity Martineau was responsible for supplying the seminary with foodstuffs, building materials, fabrics, and other goods. He purchased these from merchants in the town or its vicinity, paying for them himself and then obtaining reimbursement from his employer. He also looked after the hiring of tradesmen who did various repair or maintenance jobs on the seminary's buildings and furnishings. In 1773 this employment brought him an

Mary March

annual salary of 216 *livres*; in addition he received the interest on a loan of 697 *livres* he had made to the seminary that year.

In 1777 Martineau began to speculate in land located in the seigneury of Île-Jésus, near Montreal, that belonged to the Séminaire de Québec. In the period from January 1777 to June 1781 he obtained the grant of six *censives* (seigneurial areas), with a total frontage of some 30 *arpents*, in different ranges on the island. Taking advantage of the great demand for land at that time, when almost all of the island had been taken up, Martineau sold the properties, which he had acquired free of charge, and thus made a substantial profit. In 1778, for example, the sale of a lot with a frontage of 3 *arpents* brought him 300 *livres*; a year later he made a similar deal. In October 1779, for 600 *livres*, he parted with another lot, this time of uncleared land, which he had acquired three months earlier. Such a practice was illegal by virtue of an edict of 1732 prohibiting seigneurs and owners of *censives* from selling any land with standing timber.

In 1783 the Séminaire de Québec gave Martineau authority to make grants in its name of the property situated between the Sainte-Rose and Saint-François concessions in the seigneury of Île-Jésus. In March Martineau granted three *censives* with a total frontage of 58 *arpents* to the surveyor Joseph Turgeon. In the course of the next two years Turgeon sold, in the form of secured annuities, more than 45 *arpents* of frontage, ensuring himself an annual income of 1,035 *livres* on a capital of 20,700 *livres*. These transactions, which were highly profitable, but illegal under the 1732 edict, were carried out without the knowledge of the seminary. In 1787, however, the bursar, Henri-François GRAVÉ de La Rive, discovered the scheme. At the same time he learned that Martineau had been paid by certain individuals to grant them land, a practice prohibited by the edicts of Marly in 1720.

This underhand dealing cost Martineau his position as business agent. Furthermore, on 10 Jan. 1788 the seminary told him to get out of the house which he rented from it on Rue Sainte-Famille in Quebec. On 28 January Martineau paid 11,500 *livres* cash for a house on Rue des Pauvres (Côte du Palais). He apparently continued to engage in the trade in dry goods, wheat, and flour that he had been carrying on since at least 1784. He also made investments in landed property. In 1802, as one of the associates of the leader of Leeds Township, Isaac TODD, Martineau obtained 1,000 acres on the first and second concessions in that township. Two years later he obtained an additional 706 acres in Somerset Township from the government.

Martineau had begun to take part in public affairs in the 1790s. In 1794 he signed the petition in favour of maintaining English laws. Two years later, succeed-ing Nicolas-Gaspard Boisseau*, he was elected to the Lower Canadian assembly for Orléans, a riding then including the whole island. In the assembly Martineau at first supported the Canadian party, but in the third parliament (1801–4) and the fourth (1804–8) split his vote. On the one hand he voted in favour of the bill put forward by the Canadian majority to finance the prison at Quebec through import duties; on the other hand he supported the English party when a bill making judges ineligible to sit in the assembly was introduced. In the fifth parliament, in 1809, he was one of the ten Canadian members who sided with the English party.

Martineau died at the end of 1809. Two of his colleagues in the assembly, Pierre-Stanislas Bédard* and François Huot*, attended his funeral on 22 December, together with Joseph-Bernard Planté* and the merchant Joseph DRAPEAU.

CÉLINE CYR

ANQ-Q, CE1-1, 22 déc. 1809; CE1-11, 6 mars 1750; CN1-25, 8 avril 1777; 20 nov. 1778; 11 avril, 29 juill. 1779; 10 juill. 1780; 26 févr., 30 juin 1781; CN1-83, 29 mai 1784; 30 juin 1785; 10 janv., 13 avril 1787; 28 janv. 1788; 30 juill., 9 sept. 1789; 24 avril 1792; 5 févr., 9, 23 juill. 1794; CN1-178, 28 janv., 11, 21 févr., 6, 19 mars, 2, 8, 18, 23 mai, 10 juin, 3 juill. 1795; 24 mars, 11 mai, 22 juin, 29 sept., 11 déc. 1797; 17 févr. 1798. ASQ, C 11; C 35; C 36; Évêques, no.14; Polygraphie, XXVII: 26; S, S-11: 10, 32; Séminaire, 120; 121; 122. *Quebec Gazette*, 3, 10 July 1794; 10 July 1800; 27 Dec. 1804; 2 June 1808; 26 Oct., 30 Nov., 21 Dec. 1809. Desjardins, *Guide parl.*, 136. Langelier, *Liste des terrains concédés*, 592, 1620–21. Tanguay, *Dictionnaire*, 5: 552–54. Sylvie Depatie, "L'administration de la seigneurie de l'Île Jésus au XVIIIᵉ siècle" (thèse de MA, univ. de Montréal, 1979). Hare, "L'Assemblée législative du Bas-Canada," *RHAF*, 27: 361–95.

MARY MARCH. *See* DEMASDUWIT

MASH-I-PI-NASH-I-WISH. *See* MADJECKEWISS

MASSON, FRANCIS, botanist; b. August 1741 in Aberdeen, Scotland; d., probably unmarried, 23 Dec. 1805 in Montreal, Lower Canada.

Francis Masson was appointed under-gardener at the Royal Botanic Gardens at Kew (London), England, in 1771. Until that time, Kew Gardens had received plants and seeds from a variety of persons, but William Aiton, the director, wished the institution to undertake its own gathering of specimens; Masson became its first official collector. In 1772 he was sent aboard the *Resolution* with Captain James Cook* to the Cape of Good Hope. Between that year and 1774 he made three long excursions into the interior of southern Africa to explore for plants. He returned to England in 1775, and the following year he published an account of his journeys in the *Philosophical

580

Transactions of the Royal Society of London. He began corresponding with Carl Linnaeus, the eminent Swedish naturalist, whom he idolized and who, at Masson's request, named a species of asphodel *massonia*. In May 1776 Masson was sent to the Azores, the Canary Islands, Madeira, and the West Indies, and in 1778 he published "An account of the Island of St Miguel" in the *Philosophical Transactions*. He went back to England in 1781. Two years later he ventured to Portugal, Spain, and Tangier, Morocco, and then travelled back to Portugal and Madeira, returning to England in 1785. Late that year he again set out for the Cape of Good Hope. He remained in southern Africa until 1795, and the following year he published a book on a species of *Stapelia nova* that he had discovered there; a gifted draughtsman, Masson himself produced most of the illustrations.

Early in 1797 Masson's friend Sir Joseph BANKS, president of the Royal Society, persuaded him to undertake a collecting trip to Upper Canada. He sailed in September but did not arrive at New York until late in December owing to inclement weather and the activities of French privateers. Towards the end of May 1798 he journeyed to Oswego, N.Y., and then travelled by boat along Lake Ontario, making several botanizing forays on shore. In early July he reached Newark (Niagara-on-the-Lake), Upper Canada, and went on to Queenston. He intended to visit Detroit (Mich.) but, because of adverse winds, could not take ship on Lake Erie. After further collecting around Niagara, he sailed to York (Toronto) and finally to Montreal, where he arrived on 16 October. The following day he dispatched to Banks a box of seeds and specimens of wild rice.

In early 1799 Masson met James McGILL as well as Alexander MACKENZIE and other members of the North West Company. That spring he travelled with company traders via the Ottawa River and Lake Superior as far as Grand Portage (near Grand Portage, Minn.). Back in Niagara by September, he returned through Kingston to Montreal, where he arrived in November. This voyage produced two cases of living plants, including aquatic plants, and seeds from 123 others, all of which were sent to Banks. In November 1800 he sent from Quebec herbs, shrubs, and 90 seeds. A covering letter stated that his plans for 1801 included a trip to Virginia and the Ohio River. In January 1801, however, he considered such a trip too expensive and intended rather to go up the Ottawa River with the traders to survey the botany of the Upper Lakes. None the less, specimens at Kew Gardens of two plants from Virginia linked to Masson indicate he may have visited that state during this period.

By May 1805 Masson's passage home had been arranged, but he decided to remain in Lower Canada because of dangerous French naval activity. He proposed to collect at British stations in the Gulf of St Lawrence, and appears to have done so that summer. In October he made definite plans to return to England the following spring and forwarded specimens of fruit, nut, and willow trees, complaining that heavy rains had kept him from further collecting around Montreal. However, on 23 December he died there at the home of John Gray* and two days later he was buried from the Scotch Presbyterian Church (later known as St Gabriel Street Church).

Although he did not have a strong education and published little, Masson established a solid reputation. Like his French contemporary André MICHAUX, he was intelligent, observant, and a born traveller. In the obituary of this "mild, gentle, and unassuming" man, the *Montreal Gazette* noted that "travellers who occasionally met him in remote countries . . . and men of science that knew his unremitting botanical labours and could estimate his talents, bear equal testimony of his merits and their writings incontestably evince his very uncommon success." None the less, even though Masson had introduced to England a number of plants indigenous to Canada, including the trillium (now the floral emblem of Ontario), and had brought Canadian plants to the attention of Kew Gardens, he was soon forgotten in Canadian botanical circles.

RICHARD A. JARRELL

Francis Masson is the author of *Stapeliæ novæ; or, a collection of several new species of that genus, discovered in the interior parts of Africa* (London, 1796), as well as two articles which appeared in the *Philosophical Trans.* of the Royal Soc. of London: "An account of three journeys from Cape Town to the southern parts of Africa . . . ," 66 (1776): 268–317, and "An account of the Island of St. Miguel . . . ," 68 (1778): 601–10. A collection of his specimens and water-colours of plants is found at the British Museum.

Royal Botanic Gardens (London), Record book, 1793–1809, J. A. Ewan to G. P. de Wolf, n.d. ("Chronology of Masson in Canada"). State Library of New South Wales, Mitchell Library (Sydney, Australia), Banks papers, Brabourne coll. Landmann, *Adventures and recollections*, 1: 315–16. "Of the three species of the natural order orchidæ represented in plate VI," *Journal of Science and the Arts* (New York and London), 4 (1818): 199–206. "Select orchidæ from the Cape of Good Hope," *Journal of Science and the Arts*, 5 (1818): 104–5; 6 (1819): 44–46; 8 (1820): 221–22; 9 (1820): 310–14. *Montreal Gazette*, 30 Dec. 1805. *Dictionary of South African biography*, ed. W. J. de Kock et al. (3v. to date, Pretoria, South Africa, 1968–), 1: 521–23. *DNB*. James Britten, "Francis Masson," *Journal of Botany* (London), 22 (1884): 114–23. V. S. Forbes, "Masson's travels," *South African Geographical Journal* (Johannesburg), 29 (1947): 16–18. M. C. Karsten, "Francis Masson, a gardener-botanist who collected at the Cape," *Journal of South African Botany* (Cape Town), 24 (1958): 203–18; 25 (1959): 167–88, 283–310; 26 (1960): 9–15; 27 (1961): 15–45.

Massow

MASSOW, FRIEDERIKE CHARLOTTE LOUISE VON (Riedesel, Freifrau zu Eisenbach), author; b. 11 July 1746 in Brandenburg (German Democratic Republic), daughter of Hans Jürgen Detloff von Massow, lieutenant-general in the Prussian army and commissary-in-chief under Frederick II, King of Prussia, and Miss von Crausee; d. 20 May 1808 in Berlin, and was buried in the Riedesel family vault at Lauterbach (Federal Republic of Germany).

Friederike Charlotte Louise von Massow was about 13 years old when she first met Friedrich Adolph Riedesel, a 21-year-old captain in the Brunswick cavalry and aide-de-camp to the Duke of Brunswick. Although their marriage on 21 Dec. 1762 at Wolfenbüttel (Federal Republic of Germany) was arranged by their families, with Brunswick playing a role in the negotiations, the match was clearly one of love. After the marriage Riedesel left on a tour of duty, while Friederike went to live in Berlin. There in 1766 she gave birth to a boy, the first of nine children they would have; three, including the first two, were to die in infancy. Riedesel was stationed at Wolfenbüttel, where he eventually bought a home and where the couple settled. Described by a Prussian chamberlain in 1766 as "very young, very good-looking," Friederike was also very forceful. "You have the best character in the world," her husband wrote in 1776, "but often are so unreasonable as not to hide the hate which you have for important men, and you speak in the presence of everybody. . . . You know that we have many enemies and people profit by your frankness and intrigue against you and me."

By January 1776 Riedesel had already, at the age of 38, reached the rank of colonel. When, that month, Great Britain concluded a treaty with the duchy of Brunswick for the hiring of troops to fight against the rebellious American colonies, he was appointed commander of the first contingent to be sent to America. He left Wolfenbüttel on 22 February and that night he wrote Friederike: "Never have I known greater suffering than upon my departure this morning. My heart was broken, and had I had the opportunity of going back, who knows what I might have done!" After announcing his promotion to major-general, he added, "And now, my own Mrs. General, take good care of yourself so that you can join me immediately after your confinement." The irrepressible Friederike had decided that she would accompany her husband. To her mother, who had formally ordered her to stay at Wolfenbüttel, Friederike replied: "To remain here when the best, the tenderest of husbands gave me permission to follow him would have been impossible for me. Duty, love, and conscience forbade me. It is the duty of a wife to foresake all and follow her husband."

On 14 May 1776 Friederike left Brunswick, accompanied by her three daughters, aged four years, two years, and ten weeks. From her departure Friederike kept a journal in which she recounted her adventures and observations. After a year of frustrating delay in England, the family sailed for Quebec, arriving early on the morning of 10 June 1777; when news of Friederike's arrival reached the city, "all the ships lying in harbour fired their cannon," and at noon a boat "with twelve sailors dressed in white with silver helmets and green sashes" was sent to fetch her. Familiar with *The history of Emily Montague . . .* (4v., London, 1769), the novel by Frances Brooke [Moore*] set in the colony, Friederike in her turn noted that "Quebec presents a fine view from the water," and at first fully agreed with "the lovely description of it" in Emily Montague's letters. Once landed, however, she found the city "as ugly as can be and very inconvenient to walk about in, for one has to climb mountains when walking in its streets."

Riedesel, who had been stationed at Trois-Rivières, had already left to join the forces of Major-General John Burgoyne* in preparation for an invasion of the American colonies. Friederike pressed on immediately from Quebec, finally rejoining him at Chambly, where they spent two days together in mid June. Since they could see little of each other while Riedesel was occupied with plans for the campaign, Friederike settled at Trois-Rivières and remained there for two months. Among her friends were vicar general Pierre Garreau*, *dit* Saint-Onge, cheerful, sociable, and "a man of intelligence," as well as Garreau's "so-called 'cousin.'" In a general reference, probably to the vicars general, Friederike wrote of later hearing that "each of these gentlemen had a similar 'cousin' as housekeeper and that almost every year these 'cousins' were obliged, for certain reasons, to leave town for a while in order to avoid causing scandal." She frequently visited, and dined with, the Ursulines, whom she found charming company. She described Canadians of the region as friendly and recorded her observations of their houses and way of life.

In August 1777 Friederike, taking the children, joined her husband on Burgoyne's expedition, reaching the force just before communications with it were cut off by the Americans. Approximately 2,000 women accompanied Burgoyne's troops at one time or another. Friederike found herself in a group of officers' wives, who followed at some distance behind the first line of advance. She was close enough to the front, however, to observe the battle of 19 September in the vicinity of Freeman's Farm, N.Y., and, she wrote, "knowing that my husband was taking part in it, I was filled with fear and anguish and shivered whenever a shot was fired, as nothing escaped my ear." At the battle of Bemis Heights on 7 October, "the firing grew heavier and heavier until the noise was frightful. It was a terrible bombardment," she noted, "and I was more dead than alive!" The arrival, at the house in which Friederike was staying, of wounded officers, some of whom were good friends, heightened her fears for her husband's life. At one point during the British retreat to Saratoga (Schuylerville), in an area under heavy bombardment, she was torn between accompanying her daughters to safety, as an officer had ordered her to do, or waiting for her husband to join her and consequently being separated from her children. "He knew the weakest spot in my armor and thus persuaded me to get into the calash," she wrote, "and we drove away." Like her husband, Friederike condemned Burgoyne's dilatoriness and nonchalance during the retreat. "In fact," she recorded, "Burgoyne liked having a jolly time and spending half the night singing and drinking and amusing himself in the company of the wife of a commissary, who was his mistress."

Following Burgoyne's surrender by the convention of Saratoga on 17 Oct. 1777, Friederike and the children accompanied Riedesel into captivity. For a year they lived in Cambridge, Mass., comfortably and "quite happily." In November 1778 they were ordered to Virginia; en route they met, and dined with, the Marquis de La Fayette. Friederike frankly reproached him with ingratitude when he admitted to having been the recipient of kind attentions from King George III during a recent visit to England. After an arduous trip, the Riedesels were installed at Charlottesville, Va, where they established a close friendship with Thomas Jefferson. Riedesel was paroled in the summer of 1779, and the family left for New York City. On 25 October another daughter was born, named America. After nearly a year Riedesel was exchanged and restored to active duty in command of Long Island.

In July 1781 the Riedesels returned to the province of Quebec, putting ashore along the St Lawrence below Quebec in order to finish the trip by land. Again Friederike found the habitants "hospitable and jovial, singing and smoking all the time." Although the women frequently had goitre, she noted, "otherwise the people are healthy and live to an old age." At Quebec Riedesel was received by Governor HALDIMAND, who assigned him to Sorel; there on 1 November yet another daughter, Louisa Augusta Elizabeth Canada, was born, but she died five months later. The Riedesels remained at Sorel for the next two years, making lengthy visits to Quebec at Haldimand's invitation. The general, Friederike wrote, "had been represented as a man with whom it was difficult to get along and whom no one satisfied. I not only had the satisfaction of being warmly received by him, but of having won his friendship, which lasted as long as he lived. . . . We were frank and sincere in our relations with him, for which he was all the more grateful to us, since he was little accustomed to such treatment there." At Quebec the Riedesels usually stayed at the home of Adam Mabane*. Friederike, who spoke

excellent French, recorded in her journal and letters other visits to Montmorency Falls and Montreal and her drives into the country around Sorel. These records include characterizations of the personalities of Indians, British, and Canadians, and she describes the Canadians' houses and customs, such as the making of maple syrup and the building of ice-houses for the storage of food in winter.

With the end of the war in 1783, Riedesel's return to Brunswick became inevitable; Haldimand presented Friederike with a sable cape and muff, and the officers of the garrison performed a play in her honour. After a tearful separation from the governor, the Riedesels left Quebec in August and reached Portsmouth, England, in mid September, anchoring, Friederike noted, "exactly between the ship that took me from England to Canada and that which carried us from New York to Quebec."

The later life of the Riedesels was one of relative quiet and contentment. In 1780, upon his father's death, Riedesel had succeeded to the title of Freiherr zu Eisenbach and had inherited the castle of Lauterbach. Three years later Friederike bore the male heir, Georg Karl, for which the couple had often prayed. From 1788 to 1793 Riedesel served with the Brunswick troops in the Netherlands; his wife did not accompany him. In 1794, one year after retiring to Lauterbach, Riedesel was recalled to Brunswick and placed in command of the city of Brunswick (Federal Republic of Germany), where he served for five years. He died there on 6 Jan. 1800.

Having been encouraged by her husband, Friederike published her journal and letters about the American expedition shortly after his death. Characterized by a clear and unpretentious style, the journal reveals its author to have been a devoted wife and mother, resourceful and courageous under fire, and a compassionate and generous friend to those who shared her trials. She was also a sociable, charming woman, esteemed not only by members of the élite, such as Jefferson and Haldimand, but also by Riedesel's forces, who reportedly nominated her "the most beloved woman in the army."

LORRAINE MCMULLEN

[Friederike Charlotte Louise von Massow is the author of *Auszüge aus den Briefen und Papieren des Generals Freyherrn von Riedesel und seiner Gemalinn, gebornen von Massow; Ihre Beyderseitige Reise nach Amerika und ihren Aufenthalt bettrefend; Zusammengetragen und geordnet von ihrem Schwiegersohne Heinrich dem XLIV, Grafen Reuss; Gedruckt als Manuscript für die Familie* ([Berlin, 1800]), which was a limited edition for circulation in the family. In 1801, another edition for public circulation, differing slightly from the private one, was published in Berlin under the title *Die Berufs-Reise nach America: briefe der Generalin von Riedesel auf dieser Reise und während ihres sechsjährigen Aftenthalts in America zur Zeit des dortigen*

Matchekewis

Krieges in den Jahren 1776 bis 1783 nach Deutschland geschriebene zweite Auflage. This work was translated into Dutch as early as 1802 and into English in New York in 1827 under the title *Letters and memoirs relating to the war of American independence, and the capture of the German troops at Saratoga.* This translation was not a very faithful rendering of the German, however, and William Leete Stone prepared a new translation of the journal which appeared under the title *Letters and journals relating to the war of the American revolution, and the capture of the German troops at Saratoga* (Albany, N.Y., 1867). Finally a revised translation, accompanied by an introduction and notes, was prepared by Marvin Luther Brown, Jr., and Marta Huth; this was published as *Baroness von Riedesel and the American revolution; journal and correspondence of a tour of duty, 1776–1783* (Chapel Hill, N.C., 1965). Friederike's journal and letters provide an almost unique source of information for an important period in the history of Canada and the United States. L.McM.]

BL, Add. MSS 21796–98 (mfm. at PAC). McCord Museum, Riedesel papers. PAC, MG 23, GII, 23; MG 30, D136, 5, causerie 21. [J. M. Hadden], *Hadden's journal and orderly books: a journal kept in Canada and upon Burgoyne's campaign in 1776 and 1777 by Lieut. James M. Hadden . . .*, ed. Horatio Rogers (Albany, 1884; repr. Freeport, N.Y., 1970). [Thomas Jefferson], *The papers of Thomas Jefferson*, ed. J. P. Boyd (17v., Princeton, N.J., 1950–65), 2–3. [Adam Mabane], "Some letters of Mabane to Riedesel (1781–1783)," ed. Édouard Fabre Surveyer and Dorothy Warren, CHA *Report*, 1930: 81–82. [F. A. von] Riedesel, *Memoirs, and letters and journals of Major General Riedesel, during his residence in America*, ed. Max von Eelking and trans. W. L. Stone, (2v., Albany, 1868). Benjamin Silliman, *A tour to Quebec in the autumn of 1819* (London, 1822). *Allgemeine deutsche Biographie* (new ed., 55v., Berlin, 1967–71). W. M. Dabney, *After Saratoga: the story of the convention army* (Albuquerque, N.Mex., 1954). Bernard Dufebvre [Émile Castonguay], *Cinq femmes et nous* (Québec, 1950), 59–110. E. J. Lowell, *The Hessians and the other German auxiliaries of Great Britain in the revolutionary war* (New York, 1884; repr. Port Washington, N.Y., 1965). J. N. McIlwraith, *Sir Frederick Haldimand* (Toronto, 1906), 219–20, 239, 296–304, 345. Georges Monarque, *Un général allemand au Canada, le baron Friedrich Adolphus von Riedesel* (Montréal, 1927). L. H. Tharp, *The baroness and the general* (Boston and Toronto, 1962). T. J. Wertenbaker, *Father Knickerbocker rebels; New York City during the revolution* (New York and London, 1948). [Blanche] Biéler, "Au temps où l'on faisait la guerre en famille," *Rev. trimestrielle canadienne* (Montréal), 22 (1936): 287–99. Anna Hess, "A voyage of duty: the Riedesels in America," *German-Canadian yearbook/ Deutschkanadisches jahrbuch* (Toronto), 1 (1973): 131–39. P.-G. Roy, "La famille Glackemeyer," *BRH*, 22 (1916): 195.

MATCHEKEWIS. *See* MADJECKEWISS

MATHEWS, ROBERT, army officer; m. 22 Nov. 1798 Mary Simpson in London, England; d. 5 July 1814 in Chelsea Hospital, London.

Robert Mathews may have come from Scotland, where his father was living in 1786. On 28 Feb. 1761 he was commissioned an ensign in the 8th Foot, then part of a British contingent in Germany under Duke Ferdinand of Brunswick, and he was undoubtedly present at the battles of Vellinghausen (1761) and Wilhelmstahl (1762). From 1768 Mathews was stationed in the province of Quebec; in March 1770 he purchased a lieutenancy, and on 10 April 1775 he obtained the adjutancy. During the early years of the American Revolutionary War Mathews was at the regimental headquarters of Fort Niagara (near Youngstown, N.Y.). On 5 July 1777 he was promoted captain.

Thus far Mathews's career had been indistinguishable from those of hundreds of his fellow officers, but during a sojourn in Quebec in the summer of 1778 he met the new governor, Frederick HALDIMAND. Whatever the circumstances, the two men evidently got along well. Mathews mentioned his qualifications in engineering to Haldimand, who in August dispatched him to Niagara with orders to carry on minor works as necessary. In April 1779 Captain Edward Foy, Haldimand's military secretary, died. The same month, with the help of Francis LE MAISTRE, deputy adjutant general in the province, parts of letters Mathews had written about the upper posts were read to Haldimand. Le Maistre reported to Mathews that the governor seemed well pleased with the observations and added that this favourable reception might "turn to Your Advantage." It did. One month later Mathews was on his way to Quebec, there to take up his new position as Haldimand's military secretary.

For the remainder of Haldimand's governorship Mathews would perform this task, mainly at Quebec but with the occasional side-trip elsewhere. He was to receive all incoming correspondence dealing with military matters inside the province, advise the governor on concerns that required his response, prepare letters for his signature (several clerks actually wrote the letters), and deal with business that did not require Haldimand's attention. Haldimand soon gave Mathews increasing responsibility, evidence of the rapport that developed between the two men. The topics covered in the correspondence were quite diverse. For instance, in the 11 days between 31 Jan. and 10 Feb. 1780 Mathews wrote to Major Christopher Carleton at Île aux Noix about trespassers near the fort; to Captain George Dame of Butler's Rangers ordering him to join his corps at Fort Niagara; to Brigadier-General Allan Maclean* at Montreal about payment for rum furnished to the troops; to Lieutenant-Colonel Barrimore Matthew St Leger* at Sorel stating Haldimand's concern about a quarrel between St Leger and the surgeon Charles BLAKE; to Nathaniel Day, chief commissary in the province, about the transportation of goods to the Upper Lakes posts through the Coteau-du-Lac canal; to Captain

Daniel McAlpin about the arrangements for loyalists in Montreal; and to Robert Rogers* recommending that he leave with his officers to join the men he had allegedly raised for the King's Rangers. The position of secretary came to be one of great importance as a result of Mathews's close daily contact with the governor, and his advice was doubtless sought unofficially by hopeful petitioners. At the same time, it is probable that Mathews had comparatively little influence with Haldimand because the two men were in agreement on most issues. An uncomplaining and intensely loyal subordinate, Mathews was among the few close friends of the normally reserved governor, and their personal relationship worked to his advantage. When in the summer of 1783 John NAIRNE wished to sell his majority in the 53rd Foot, Haldimand specified that his secretary was to be allowed to purchase the rank, an action which caused justifiable resentment among more senior captains.

As the war drew to a close, Mathews, like Haldimand, came to concern himself increasingly with the problems of provisioning and accommodating the loyalists who entered the province, and in the wake of the peace treaty, with the details of their settlement. Here too Haldimand gave him considerable leeway, and there is every reason to believe historian Alfred Leroy Burt*'s assertion that the loyalists were greatly in his debt for his handling of many of the petty problems that inevitably arose.

Once back in London with Haldimand in early January 1785, Mathews performed small errands and assisted in settling the governor's accounts and papers for a time. But by March 1786, with Sir Guy CARLETON's appointment as governor-in-chief of British North America impending, prospects for advancement had disappeared, and he gloomily contemplated selling out and returning to settle in the colony. Almost certainly with Haldimand's approval, however, he petitioned Lord Sydney, the Home secretary, to request from Carleton an appointment as one of his aides-de-camp. Sydney was "much embarrassed" by this highly unusual and even brash step, but Carleton consented, and that summer Mathews returned to Quebec to prepare the way for the governor's arrival. In May he had received a sinecure in the form of the lieutenant governorship of Antigua, another result of Haldimand's prodding of the government.

Mathews's second term in Quebec was uneventful. The post of aide-de-camp left him little to do, and just one year after his arrival he decided to join his regiment, whose headquarters were at Detroit (Mich.). He recorded with interest in his journal of the trip to Detroit the state of loyalist settlements along the route. Mathews was not impressed with the inhabitants of Detroit, describing them as "a sad set of Rascals" who were not above attempted bribery of the military authorities. There were frustrations in settling titles to lands and administering justice, yet when Mathews left in November one of his officers asserted that he departed "universally regretted . . . as he had been indefatigable in his endeavours to assist the settlement." Despite the inclination of Governor Carleton (now Lord Dorchester) to retain him as aide-de-camp, Mathews was not interested in remaining much longer in the province, and when the 53rd departed in August 1789 he accompanied it. It is certain that he had quickly discovered his diminished importance in the new régime.

Mathews returned to his purely military career. When war broke out with France in 1793 he went to Flanders as part of a British expeditionary force. That October he greatly distinguished himself as commander of the 53rd in the successful defence of Nieuport (Nieuwpoort, Belgium) against a greatly superior French force, and was promoted lieutenant-colonel of the regiment as a reward. The following year he relinquished this position, and in 1800 he was appointed an inspector of army clothing. On 6 Oct. 1801 he became major of Chelsea Hospital, the British army institution for invalided and superannuated soldiers, and in this quiet retreat he ended his days. The *Times* obituary praised his "universal and active benevolence of mind . . . [and] urbanity of manners." He was married to a noted Quebec beauty, who had the distinction of being the first love of Horatio Nelson. It is not known if there were any children.

Without the patronage of Frederick Haldimand, Robert Mathews would never have attained even the modest degree of success that he did. In settling the loyalists and arranging military matters, however, he displayed valuable talents. If he was unable to rise beyond a fairly low rank, it was principally a result of his patron's position on the fringes of the British hierarchy.

STUART R. J. SUTHERLAND

BL, Add. MSS 21661–892 (mfm. at PAC). PAC, MG 23, J9. PRO, WO 17/1493; 17/1496; 17/1572 (mfm. at PAC). *Times* (London), 11 July 1814. G.B., WO, *Army list*, 1763–1814. *The register book of marriages belonging to the parish of St George, Hanover Square, in the county of Middlesex*, ed. J. H. Chapman and G. J. Armytage (4v., London, 1896–97), 2: 191. C. G. T. Dean, *The Royal Hospital, Chelsea . . .* (London, 1950), 269, 307. J. R. B. Moulsdale, *The King's Shropshire Light Infantry (the 53rd/85th Regiment of Foot)* (London, 1972), 5–6.

MAYAR (Mea ire). *See* MYEERAH

MEARES, JOHN, maritime fur trader and author; b. c. 1756; d. 1809.

In 1771 John Meares entered the Royal Navy as "Captain's servant" in HMS *Cruizer* and, after serving

Meares

in several small vessels, passed his lieutenant's examination on 17 Sept. 1778, at which time he was said to be more than 22. He was promoted lieutenant the following day. He later hinted that he had been involved in naval action on Canadian lakes during the American revolution, and it has been stated that he "served against the French in the West Indies." In 1783 he entered the merchant service and sailed for eastern seas.

Meares undertook his first voyage to the northwest coast of North America in 1786, sailing from Calcutta (India) in charge of two trading ships, the *Nootka*, under his own command, and the *Sea Otter*, under William Tipping. Meares may have been the principal owner of the Bengal Fur Company, the firm that organized the expedition; he was certainly its guiding spirit. He traded in Alaskan waters and wintered in Prince William Sound, where 23 of his crew died of scurvy. In May 1787 captains Nathaniel PORTLOCK and George Dixon* found him there, his ships trapped in the ice. Portlock and Dixon, trading for the rival Richard Cadman Etches and Company (commonly called the King George's Sound Company), claimed that Meares was an interloper in a trade they declared was exclusively theirs by arrangement with the East India and South Sea companies. These two bodies together held a monopoly of British trade between the Cape of Good Hope and Cape Horn, and had the power to grant licences for commercial activity in their territory. Though captured, in effect, by Portlock and Dixon, Meares was released on bond with the understanding that he would sail directly for Macao (near Canton, People's Republic of China) and not return to the northwest coast. In the event, Meares resumed his trading on the coast, sailing to Macao only after he had obtained a saleable cargo. Dixon later charged that Meares was ungracious in accepting the help rendered by his rescuers.

In January 1788 Meares again sailed for the northwest coast, reaching Nootka Sound (B.C.) in May in the *Feliz Aventureira*, accompanied by the *Efigenia Nubiana* under the command of William Douglas. Not licensed by the East India Company or the South Sea Company, Meares sailed under the Portuguese flag, a device that allowed him to trade freely at Macao (a Portuguese possession) and pay lower customs duties at Canton. During this season of trade with the Indians, he later claimed, he bought land in the sound and obtained from the Nootka chief, Muquinna*, a promise of free and exclusive trade; other accounts differ, however, and Muquinna himself later denied the transactions, calling Meares a liar. In September Meares sailed for Macao in the *Feliz*, leaving the *Efigenia* and her tender, the 40-ton schooner *North West America*, the first vessel of European design built on the northwest coast, to winter at the Sandwich (Hawaiian) Islands.

At Canton during the winter of 1788–89 Meares and his associates formed a partnership with the King George's Sound Company, calling the new concern the Associated Merchants Trading to the Northwest Coast of America. To represent the new firm Meares sent James COLNETT, with the *Argonaut* and the *Princess Royal*, to join the *Efigenia* and the *North West America* in trade on the coast. Early in 1789 a force of Spaniards under Esteban José Martínez* was sent to establish a post at Nootka Sound in order to protect Spanish claims to the area. Between mid May and mid July Martínez seized all four Associated Merchants' vessels, contending that foreign ships were violating Spanish rights of trade and navigation on the coast and in adjacent seas. When news of the seizures reached Meares in China he sailed to England where, on 30 April 1790, he submitted his *Memorial* on the capture of British vessels at Nootka to the Home secretary, William Wyndham Grenville. In his statement Meares exaggerated the permanence of the British settlement in the sound and the losses sustained by the Associated Merchants. But anti-Spanish sentiment ran high, and the British cabinet at the height of the Nootka crisis announced the outfitting of a large fleet. Under this coercion Spain agreed to the terms eventually announced in the Nootka Convention of 28 Oct. 1790 (revised in 1793 and 1794), whereby British rights to the trade at Nootka and to navigation in the Pacific were acknowledged.

Widespread interest in the maritime fur trade and the northwest coast led Meares to bring forth in 1790 his pretentious *Voyages made in the years 1788 and 1789, from China to the north west coast*, which magnified the author's accomplishments in discovery and trade at the expense of others, including Dixon, who had aided Meares at Prince William Sound in 1787. Dixon retaliated the same year with *Remarks on the Voyages of John Meares, esq.*, an attack on the veracity of Meares's account of his exploits, to which the latter responded lamely in 1791 with *An answer to Mr. George Dixon*; in *Further remarks on the Voyages of John Meares, esq.*, published later that year, Charles Duncan* joined Dixon in a last, conclusive discrediting of the original claims.

Meares found it easy to make enemies. The Yankee trader John Box Hoskins thought he "behav'd himself scandalously" at Nootka in 1788, and "by no means like a gentleman. a character he dares to assume." Robert HASWELL, another Boston trader, was convinced of Meares's deception and "notorious falsity." Indeed, by disregarding the truth, advertising untruths, and falsifying documents Meares merited disfavour. He does not seem to have been employed in the navy again, perhaps because of his tarnished reputation. He was advanced on the navy list and by seniority was promoted commander on 26 Feb. 1795. His remaining years are obscure.

BARRY M. GOUGH

586

John Meares is the author of *An answer to Mr. George Dixon, late commander to the Queen Charlotte, in the service of Messrs. Etches and company: in which the remarks of Mr. Dixon on the Voyages to the north west coast of America, &c. lately published, are fully considered and refuted* (London, 1791); *Authentic copy of the memorial to the Right Honourable William Wyndham Grenville, one of His Majesty's principal secretaries of state; dated 30th April, 1790, and presented to the House of Commons, May 13, 1790; containing every particular respecting the capture of the vessels in Nootka Sound* (London, [1790]); and *Voyages made in the years 1788 and 1789, from China to the north west coast of America . . .*, [comp. William Combe] (London, 1790; repr. Amsterdam and New York, [1967]). The frontispiece of the last-mentioned work is a portrait of Meares after Sir William Beechey.

[James Colnett], *The journal of Captain James Colnett aboard the Argonaut from April 26, 1789, to Nov. 3, 1791*, ed. F. W. Howay (Toronto, 1940). George Dixon, *Remarks on the Voyages of John Meares, esq., in a letter to that gentleman* (London, 1790); *Further remarks on the Voyages of John Meares, esq. . . .* (London, 1791). *The Dixon–Meares controversy . . .*, ed. F. W. Howay (Toronto and New York, 1929; repr. Amsterdam and New York, 1969). *Voyages of the "Columbia" to the northwest coast, 1787–1790 and 1790–1793*, ed. F. W. Howay ([Boston], 1941; repr. Amsterdam and New York, [1969]). *DNB*. W. K. Lamb, "John Meares: fur trader, navigator, and controversialist," *Polar Notes* (Hanover, N.H.), no.2 (1960): 18–23.

MELANÇON (Melanson), MARIE-VÉNÉRANDE, named **de Sainte-Claire**, hospital nun of the Hôtel-Dieu in Quebec and superior; b. 11 Nov. 1754 in Annapolis Royal, N.S., daughter of Jean-Baptiste Melançon and Marie-Anne Robichaud; d. 13 Oct. 1817 at Quebec, Lower Canada.

Marie-Vénérande Melançon, who was of Acadian ancestry, came to Quebec with her family, probably towards the end of 1757. Like many other Acadian families emigrating at that period, the Melançons had to suffer the famine prevailing in Quebec, as well as the rigours of the Seven Years' War, and to live in poverty through the beginnings of the British régime. In 1760 and 1761 they were residing at Charlesbourg, where the parents had two children baptized.

Marie-Vénérande entered the convent of the Hôtel-Dieu on 10 Aug. 1774 at the age of 19 and on 25 Feb. 1776 was permitted to take her vows under the name of Sainte-Claire. However, as the American revolution had led to the invasion of the province of Quebec [*see* Benedict ARNOLD; Richard Montgomery*] and the city had been besieged since the beginning of December 1775, the ceremony of profession was delayed. It took place on 17 June 1776, after the Americans had lifted the siege. The Melançons were accorded exceptional terms for the dowry of their daughter, who was admitted for 2,400 *livres* instead of the 3,000 *livres* usually required for a choir nun. Nevertheless, only 1,200 *livres*, the gift of some benefactors, had been paid by the beginning of June

1776, and the parents were exempted from paying the remaining 1,200 *livres* in exchange for making over to the community of the Hôtel-Dieu their daughter's future share in their estate. In addition, Abbé Joseph-Mathurin Bourg*, vicar general of Acadia, who two years earlier had promised to give 600 *livres*, had paid 532 by 9 Sept. 1777. The reduction of her dowry can be explained not only by the Melançon family's modest circumstances, but also by the community's need for new members. Since 1755, as a result of the small number of recruits and of illness, the size of the community had decreased and the average age of its members had risen; in some 30 years only 12 postulants were taken in as choir nuns and hence in 1787 there were only 26 professed.

Until 1787 Marie-Vénérande de Sainte-Claire, who "was skilful in all things [and] was very successful with artificial flowers," contributed through the income from her handiwork to the community's efforts at liquidating heavy debts. In October of that year Bishop Hubert* named her depositary for the poor, a post she held until her election as assistant in 1799. In the latter office she worked with the superior, Marie-Geneviève PARENT, named de Saint-François d'Assise, to plan the rebuilding of the chapel, which had been destroyed in a fire at the Hôtel-Dieu in 1755, and to get construction under way in the spring of 1800. When she was elected superior in 1801 the work was still not far advanced, but the consecration ceremonies were held two years later, before the end of her first term.

Marie-Vénérande de Sainte-Claire was in charge of the community for two consecutive three-year terms, the maximum period allowed, and then became assistant again in 1807; she served in this capacity until she took charge once more in November 1813. Her name is associated with a project that took shape in the spring of 1816: the rebuilding of the hospital. In the period just after the fire of 1755, which had destroyed the hospital and the convent as well as the chapel, the nuns had had only the convent rebuilt, the ground floor of its east wing being used for the sick. The British troops occupied that floor in 1759, and not until they left in 1784 was the hospital, still located in the convent, able to open its doors to the civilian population. At that time it had ten beds for men and eight for women, fewer than under the French régime. The increase in population quickly made it too cramped, but lack of funds prevented any thought of a new building. In 1812 the nuns appealed for government aid to meet ordinary expenses and obtained an annual subsidy of £300 for the relief of the sick. For four years they saved part of this sum, and finally in the spring of 1816 the rebuilding project took shape. After debates within the community about the size of the future hospital, Marie-Vénérande de Sainte-Claire assured the bishop that her community would respect whatever decisions he took. Bishop

Menut

Plessis* considered it unnecessary to use an architect and suggested they rely upon the masons' advice. The work began on 8 Oct. 1816, but after some progress had been made the hospital nuns realized that their means were insufficient.

On 7 Feb. 1817 Marie-Vénérande de Sainte-Claire presented a petition to the House of Assembly requesting help from the government. However, some property owners on Rue des Pauvres (Côte du Palais) disapproved of the nuns' project. They alleged that the hospital's proximity to the street made the neighbourhood unpleasant and unsanitary, and that in well-organized towns hospitals were relegated to outlying areas. Not only was the air unhealthy, they said, but there would be a depreciation in the value of their properties. A counter-petition signed by 209 citizens supported the nuns. Finally the assembly yielded to the Hôtel-Dieu's request, but the bill was rejected by the Legislative Council. In April 1817 a public subscription was organized to meet the expenses of the work for that year and enable material already delivered to the building site to be utilized. The following year the nuns were successful in pressing their claim for government aid and with this assistance work went on until 1825.

Marie-Vénérande de Sainte-Claire, however, never knew the outcome of her endeavours for a malignant fever carried her off on 13 Oct. 1817 after a week's illness. During the 41 years she spent in religious life she was assistant for eight and superior for almost ten; she held the latter office at the time of her death. She had also been counsellor since 28 Jan. 1788.

FRANÇOIS ROUSSEAU

Arch. of the Diocese of Yarmouth (Yarmouth, N.S.), Saint-Jean-Baptiste-de-Port-Royal (Annapolis Royal), Reg. des baptêmes, mariages, et sépultures, 15 janv. 1755 (mfm. au CÉA). Arch. du monastère de l'Hôtel-Dieu de Québec, Actes capitulaires, I: ff.57–64; Corr., Clergé séculier, Arthur Melançon, 26 sept. 1899; Évêques, Pierre Denaut, J.-O. Plessis, et A.-B. Robert, nos.7–11; B.-C. Panet, A.-B. Robert, no.1; J.-O. Plessis, nos.1, 2; Dossier des vœux, no.116; Élections triennales et annuelles, I: 190–212, 214, 220; II: 3–21; Hôpital, Copies de lettres, requêtes, états de comptes, Législature, 1801–92: 6–10, 14–21, 23–24; Notes et mémoires des anciennes mères, armoire 5, cahiers 2/1–2; Notices biographiques, M.-V. Melançon. Tanguay, *Dictionnaire*, 5: 587. Arsenault, *Hist. et généal. des Acadiens* (1965), 1: 466–67. H.-R. Casgrain, *Histoire de l'Hôtel-Dieu de Québec* (Québec, 1878), 401, 430, 446, 470–72, 506–7, 591. Raymonde Landry Gauthier, "Les constructions de l'Hôtel-Dieu de Québec (1637–1960)" (travail présenté à l'univ. Laval, 1974), 28.

MENUT, ALEXANDRE, innkeeper and politician; b. in France; m. some time before 1777 Marie Deland, and they had at least five children; d. between March 1804 and March 1806.

Alexandre Menut came to Canada after the conquest to work as a cook for Governor Murray*, and Guy CARLETON subsequently hired him in the same capacity. On 4 Dec. 1766 he obtained a licence to sell alcoholic beverages. Two years later he opened an inn "at the Sign of the Crown," on Rue du Parloir in Quebec, where the customers were assured of being "served with Exactness, in the best English or French Manner and in the newest Taste . . . at a reasonable Price." Menut also went to serve "Dinners or Suppers" in private homes. He was granted a licence in 1769 to open a tavern and sell alcoholic beverages.

In 1775 Menut owned an inn near the Hôpital Général of Quebec. He was in the Canadian militia at the time of the American invasion [see Richard Montgomery*] but did not take part in the defence of the town. His inn became Benedict ARNOLD's headquarters during the siege of Quebec in the winter of 1775–76. In December 1776 Menut put in a claim for compensation from the government for the losses he had suffered during the invasion, but there is no indication that he received any.

Subsequently Menut opened an inn at the corner of Rue Saint-Jean and Rue Saint-Stanislas. "Menut's house" accommodated the House of Assembly balls and both English and French theatre companies during the period 1782–96. In the 1790s Menut took an interest in the problems of his adopted community. He was a member of the Quebec Fire Society in 1790, and that year he signed the petition in favour of a provincial university which both Catholics and Protestants could attend [see Jean-François Hubert*]. The following year he supported the recovery of the *lods et ventes*. In 1792 he subscribed to the Agriculture Society and was president of the Constitutional Club [see William GRANT (1744–1805)].

Menut ran for the House of Assembly of Lower Canada in 1796; along with Pascal Duplessis-Sirois, he was elected for Cornwallis, this rural riding being entitled to two members. Menut attended the four sessions of the assembly regularly and supported the Canadian party; in particular he voted for Jean-Antoine PANET as speaker. In 1801 he was re-elected, along with Joseph Boucher, but he turned away from the Canadian party to support the English party. Indeed, during the third legislature the Canadian group disintegrated and the executive seemed to be on the point of breaking the Canadians' resistance. Menut was only moving with the tide.

The *Journals* of the House of Assembly make no mention of Alexandre Menut's presence after February 1803. In March 1804 he was living in Simpson Township. It would seem that he died some time between this date and March 1806, when in a notarized deed Marie Deland declared herself a widow.

JOHN E. HARE

ANQ-Q, CE1-61, 3 Nov. 1777, 21 Sept. 1779, 14 March 1782, 15 Aug. 1784, 25 Oct. 1786; CN1-262, 6 mars 1804. "Les dénombrements de Québec" (Plessis), ANQ *Rapport*, 1948–49. *March to Quebec: journals of the members of Arnold's expedition*, ed. K. L. Roberts (New York, 1938), 147, 187, 272, 368, 695, 698. *Quebec Gazette*, 29 Dec. 1766, 7 July 1768, 24 Aug. 1769, 12 Dec. 1776, 28 Jan. 1790, 5 May 1791, 8 Nov. 1792, 11 April 1793, 26 Nov. 1795, 26 Jan. 1797, 13 Jan. 1825. F.-J. Audet, "Alexandre Menut," *BRH*, 33 (1927): 408–11. Hare, "L'Assemblée législative du Bas-Canada," *RHAF*, 27: 361–95. "Un cuisinier membre du parlement," *BRH*, 54 (1948): 93–94.

MERCURE, LOUIS, army officer, courier, guide, and settler; b. 11 May 1753 in Port-La-Joie (Fort Amherst, P.E.I.), son of Joseph Mercure and Ann-Marie Bergeaux, *née* Gautier, *dit* Bellair; m. *c.* 1773 Madeleine Thibodeau, and they had one son, Louis-Michel; d. June 1816 and was buried 8 Dec. 1817 in Saint-Basile, N.B.

Louis Mercure came from a family with a strong military tradition and reasons to resent the British régime. His parental grandfather, François Mercure, had been a captain in the colonial regular troops in Canada, as was his own father, and his maternal grandfather, Joseph-Nicolas Gautier*, *dit* Bellair, had lost all his possessions as a penalty for fighting the British in Nova Scotia. The family left Île Saint-Jean to escape deportation and moved to Quebec, where their presence was recorded in the 1760s at Sainte-Anne-de-la-Pérade (La Pérade), near Quebec, and in the Kamouraska area on the south shore of the St Lawrence. By 1774 Louis had married and was living at Sainte-Anne (near Fredericton, N.B.).

The military tradition proved stronger than any resentment against the English, and during the American revolution Louis joined the British army, becoming a lieutenant in Lieutenant-Colonel Robert Rogers*'s King's Rangers, a unit that was never fully embodied and saw no action. By 1780 Mercure was employed as a courier and guide travelling between Halifax, N.S., Penobscot (Castine, Maine), and Quebec with military dispatches. According to Madawaskan tradition, he was on one occasion nearly killed by Indians and owed his escape to knowledge of their language and customs. In 1782 he was sent by General Frederick HALDIMAND, governor of Quebec, to report on the progress of the new military road between Halifax and Quebec. Louis and his brother Michel, also a courier, must have been exceptionally skilled, for Haldimand's correspondence contains frequent references to the expense of their services and the difficulty of finding anyone to replace them.

The Mercures apparently profited considerably as couriers: for one trip between Halifax and Quebec in 1782, Louis claimed 100 dollars, and was paid 80. They evidently also took advantage of the army

authorities. One officer maintained that the brothers carried letters for merchants while on army business, and that Louis had an agreement with the Canadian canoemen to cheat those he was guiding and share the profits. However, complaints of overcharging eventually ceased, and by the end of the war the Mercures were in favour with both Haldimand and Governor John Parr* of Nova Scotia.

The Mercure brothers had acquired land in the area that was to become Fredericton, N.B. Louis may have originally settled in the central part of the future town, but by 1780 he was installed at the mouth of the Keswick River near his brother. By July 1783 he had a good house and 12 acres of land cleared. The commissioners who reported his situation to Brigade-Major Gilfred Studholme* recommended him for special consideration when lands were laid out along the Saint John River for loyalist settlers. He had a mill on the Keswick by 1784 and that year, in response to his requests and as a special mark of favour, Parr gave him 200 acres on nearby Bagweet (Lower Shores) Island.

Because he was in official favour and was able to write fluently, Louis became a spokesman for the small group of French settlers in the area, many of whom lacked title to their land. In 1783 he had told Haldimand that a number of Acadians wished to go to Quebec, in order to worship freely. Haldimand wanted to settle them on the Saint John, above Grand Falls, so that they could protect the military road to Quebec, but no action was taken to move them there. In 1785 Mercure wrote to Major Samuel Johannes HOLLAND, surveyor general of Quebec, asking for the land in the Madawaska region that Haldimand had suggested for him and 24 heads of families. He must have made a similar request to Thomas CARLETON, governor of the newly established province of New Brunswick, which also claimed this border region, since on 21 June 1785 Carleton and his council gave him permission to settle the petitioners on land of their choice in the Madawaska region. Each family could claim 200 acres. Both Mercure brothers left for Madawaska and took up land on the north bank of the Saint John River between the Iroquois and Madawaska rivers.

Louis retained a position of some authority during the early years of the settlement. In 1786 he wrote to Carleton asking for permission to assign land to Canadians entering the region, and to single men between 16 and 25 years of age "in like manner as to fathers of families on condition that they improve them." The following year he reported to Jonathan ODELL, provincial secretary of New Brunswick, on the cultivation of lots. However, his influence in Fredericton was waning: he was told that petitioners for land must apply directly to the government, and Odell asked Surveyor General George SPROULE to speed up the designation of lots, because he suspected

Me-She-Kin-No-Quah

Mercure and his friends of taking the best land, regardless of the claims of others.

Apparently no official position was given to Mercure in either the civil or the militia establishment of Madawaska. Carleton wanted him to be a magistrate, but as a Catholic he was not willing to take the necessary oath of allegiance. In spite of his convictions, he apparently took no part in the negotiations for a church and a resident priest. In the early 1790s disputes arose between the militia officers, jointly appointed by Quebec and New Brunswick since it was not clear which province controlled the area, and the magistrate, Thomas Costin, appointed by New Brunswick. Mercure's continuing authority was shown when Costin tried to enlist his help with a letter, supposedly from Sproule, asking Mercure to arrange the election of new militia officers. Mercure was elected himself, but his office was never officially recognized; Lieutenant Governor Carleton denied that militia elections could have taken place in New Brunswick, where, as elsewhere in British North America, militia officers were appointed by government. Although Mercure in his turn proceeded to criticize Costin, the dispute was eventually smoothed over. Costin told Edward WINS-LOW, a member of the New Brunswick Council, that those who opposed him were trying to make Madawaska part of Lower Canada. Mercure's views on this boundary dispute were never clarified, but he received no more favours from the New Brunswick government.

Mercure did try to move to Lower Canada; he made several applications after 1791 for the land grant due to a former lieutenant there. Since there are no references to his presence in Madawaska between 1800 and his burial in 1817, it may be that he took up residence in Lower Canada, returning late in life. It is also possible that he died in Lower Canada and that his brother and son had his remains reinterred at Saint-Basile.

Mercure has been seen by the American historian Charles Collins as a victim of English persecution who should have desired to join the United States, but the New Brunswick historian William Odber Raymond* has shown that Mercure had at least been far more fortunate than many other Acadians in his dealings with government. He was able to work with the British authorities, and used his position and education to gain personal advantage from the régime. His leadership in the Acadian community depended on his literacy and on government favour. When the favour was withdrawn, leadership passed to others in the community.

SHEILA ANDREW

BL, Add. MSS 21810 (mfm. at UNBL). CÉA, Fonds Placide Gaudet, 1.33-8, 1.33-9, 1.33-11, 1.33-12, 1.33-13, 1.33-20, 1.69-6. PAC, MG 30, C5, 1: 28, 33, 35, 38, 96, 124, 169; 2: 24, 35; 3: 40, 176 (transcripts; mfm. at PANB). PANB, RG1, RS330, A2, no.26; A3, no.21 (copies at UNBL). PRO, CO 188/2: 105–10 (photocopies at UNBL). "Sunbury County documents," N.B. Hist. Soc., *Coll.*, 1 (1894–97), no.1: 100–18. Thomas Albert, *Histoire du Madawaska d'après les recherches historiques de Patrick Therriault et les notes manuscrites de Prudent L. Mercure* (Québec, 1920). Antoine Bernard, *Histoire de la survivance acadienne, 1755–1935* (Montréal, 1935). C. W. Collins, *The Acadians of Madawaska, Maine* (Boston, 1902). [W. O.] Raymond, "The first governor of New Brunswick and the Acadians of the River Saint John," RSC *Trans.*, 3rd ser., 8 (1914), sect.II: 415–52.

ME-SHE-KIN-NO-QUAH (Meshecunnaqua). *See* MICHIKINAKOUA

MÉZIÈRE, HENRY-ANTOINE (he signed **Meziere**), printer, publisher, journalist, and author; baptized 6 Dec. 1771 in Montreal, Que., son of Pierre-François Mézière, a lawyer and notary, and Michel-Archange Campeau; d. some time after 1819, probably in France.

One of 15 children of whom nine reached adulthood, Henry-Antoine Mézière early demonstrated his independence and his taste for adventure. He ran away from home for the first time at the age of seven, crossing the St Lawrence River. At 15, alone and with no means of subsistence, he took ship for Quebec; his father brought him back, paying the expense and insisting on filial obedience in return. His father's authoritarianism seems indeed to have provoked a good deal of conflict and may explain why Henry-Antoine and his two brothers, Pierre and Simon-André, wanted to escape. Nevertheless, from 1782 to 1788 Mézière studied at the Collège de Montréal, where he proved a good student, his name being on the honours list each year for a few prizes and honourable mentions. He finished after his sixth year (Rhetoric), as did most of his Montreal contemporaries, since the college of the Messieurs de Saint-Sulpice did not offer the Philosophy class until 1789. For the college and the Sulpicians, Mézière had nothing but disrespect, even scorn. "A college in the hands of ignorant ecclesiastics was the tomb of my early years; there I acquired a few words of Latin and utter contempt for my teachers," he later wrote.

His studies ended, Mézière familiarized himself with the *philosophes* and joined the Enlightenment circle, a small group of intellectuals gathered around Fleury Mesplet*, his printing shop, and his weekly newspaper, the *Montreal Gazette/La Gazette de Montréal*. In January 1788 Mézière published his first poetry in the *Gazette* and for five years he contributed irregularly to the paper, writing poems and articles on

Mézière

the usefulness of science and on patriotic and filial love – texts in which contemporary realities lurked behind the tawdry finery of mythological allegory. Mesplet must have been glad to count this Young Turk as one of his coterie of initiates who were then in the forefront of the struggle against despotism and superstition, a struggle inspired and intensified by the progress of the French revolution. Mézière showed enthusiasm for the revolution although his commitment at times appeared to falter, for example in May 1791 when he publicly repudiated an anti-religious text he had published in the *Gazette*, claiming that he had "gone astray in seeking satisfaction from the philosophy of the age." The fact none the less remains that he was carried away by his interest in the revolution and, with the added impetus of resentment of his father's authority, he fled to the United States in May 1793. He went to New York and then to Philadelphia, Pa, where he approached Edmond-Charles Genêt, the French revolutionary government's minister to Congress, who had been given the assignment of rousing Canadians against Great Britain. In June Mézière presented him with his memoir "Observations sur l'état actuel du Canada et sur les dispositions politiques de ses habitants," in which he maintained that he and his compatriots, enlightened by the revolution, were conscious of the ruling government's despotism and tyranny and were ready to fight against British domination. Genêt took this information into account when he wrote his address "Les Français libres à leurs frères du Canada," a revolutionary pamphlet that Mézière was to take to the Canadian frontier. Returning to New York, Mézière, as Genêt's political agent, sailed on the *Éole*, one of the ships of the French fleet stationed at Saint-Domingue (Haiti). Disregarding its assigned mission to destroy the Newfoundland fisheries, retake Saint-Pierre and Miquelon, burn Halifax, N.S., and sail up the St Lawrence, the fleet sailed back to France and cast anchor in Brest on 2 Nov. 1793.

On 4 Jan. 1794 Mézière presented to Citizen Jean d'Albarade, the minister of Marine, his "Mémoire sur la situation du Canada et des États-Unis" in which he described the fate of his unhappy compatriots and their enthusiasm for the revolution. For unknown reasons he spent some months in prison before settling down to live in Bordeaux as an official. He wrote several letters to his sisters, Charlotte-Archange and Suzanne, describing his boredom and his desire for news of the family, but he received no reply. In 1816, at the time of the Bourbon restoration, he returned to the United States and took up residence in New York, where he gave French lessons for a living until he could return to Lower Canada. In order to get back he made contact with his sisters and his old friend Louis-Charles Foucher*, who had been a member of the Enlightenment circle and had become a judge. Foucher was so

effective that Mézière was back in Montreal on 3 Sept. 1816, when he signed a declaration of repentance and future loyalty in the presence of Jean-Marie Mondelet*, a justice of the peace.

Mézière expressed a desire to open an educational establishment to instil respect for the constitution in the young and to make up for the mistakes of his wild youth, but nothing came of his plans. In February 1817 he went into partnership with Charles-Bernard Pasteur and became co-owner of the newspaper *Le Spectateur canadien*. The partnership was short-lived because Pasteur, learning that Mézière had been paid by the North West Company to take up its side in disputes with Lord Selkirk [Douglas], broke off their association, and Mézière left the newspaper in June. However this experience did not end his involvement in journalism. On 1 Aug. 1818 Mézière launched a bi-monthly newspaper in Montreal, *L'Abeille canadienne*, which primarily published articles from French periodicals, mainly *La Ruche d'Aquitaine* from Bordeaux. During its six-month duration Mézière wrote only the prospectus and three articles; the paper closed down on 15 Jan. 1819. That year Mézière and his family returned to France permanently since Marie-Eugénie de Passy, his second wife, had inherited from an uncle in Bordeaux ownership of his personal property and the usufruct of his real estate, and their children had come into ownership of the real estate itself.

CLAUDE GALARNEAU

Henry-Antoine Mézière is the author of a memoir kept at AN, Col., C^{11E}, 11: ff.243–51, 262–64 (mfm. at PAC); it was published in its entirety under the title "Un mémoire de Henry Meziere" in *BRH*, 37 (1931): 193–201.

ANQ-M, CE1-51, 6 déc. 1771. Arch. du ministère des Affaires étrangères (Paris), Corr. politique, États-Unis, 37: ff.419–23. ASQ, Fonds Viger-Verreau, Carton 13, no.53; 17, nos.32–35, 49. AUM, P 58, U, Mézière à Foucher, 24 mars, 3 juin, 29 juill., 24 août, sept., 10 oct. 1816. "Le gouverneur Haldimand et les prêtres français," *BRH*, 12 (1906): 248–52. *L'Abeille canadienne* (Montréal), 1er août 1818–15 janv. 1819. *Montreal Gazette*, 10, 24 Jan., 20, 27 March, 18 Sept. 1788; 8 April, 1 July, 25 Nov., 30 Dec. 1790; 6 Jan., 12, 19 May, 25 Aug. 1791; 26 July 1792. *Quebec Gazette*, 2 Aug. 1792. F.-J. Audet, *Les députés de Montréal*, 181. Beaulieu et Hamelin, *La presse québécoise*, 1: 30, 37–38. H.-R. Casgrain, *Œuvres complètes* (3v., Québec, 1873–75), 2: 225. Galarneau, *La France devant l'opinion canadienne*. Maurault, *Le collège de Montréal* (Dansereau; 1967), 186, 190, 192. Wallot, *Un Québec qui bougeait*, 304–5. Michel Brunet, "La Révolution française sur les rives du Saint-Laurent," *RHAF*, 11 (1957–58): 155–62. Ægidius Fauteux, "Henri Mézière ou l'odyssée d'un mouton noir," *La Patrie* (Montréal), 18 nov. 1933: 34–35, 37. É.-Z. Massicotte, "Les tribunaux de police de Montréal," *BRH*, 26 (1920): 182. Mason Wade, "Quebec and the French revolution of 1789: the missions of Henri Mézière," *CHR*, 31 (1950): 345–68.

Michaux

MICHAUX, ANDRÉ, botanist and author; b. 8 March 1746 near Versailles, France, son of André Michaux and Marie-Charlotte Barbet (Barbée); d. probably 11 Oct. 1803, on Madagascar.

André Michaux was born and raised on a royal farm, of which his father was manager, on the plateau of Satory, south of Versailles. He had received only four years of formal education when in 1760 his father withdrew him from school in order to train him in practical horticulture. From his father's death in 1763 until 1769, Michaux shared the management of the farm with his brother. In October 1769 André married Cécile Claye, daughter of a rich farmer in the region of Beauce, France; she died in September 1770 after giving birth to a son, François-André, and her death plunged Michaux into a profound depression. The naturalist Louis-Guillaume Le Monnier, who lived at Montreuil near Satory, persuaded Michaux to occupy himself with the study of the acclimation to France of useful foreign plants, and for several years Michaux devoted himself to experiments at Satory. In 1777 he studied with the botanist Bernard de Jussieu in the park of the château of Versailles, and in 1779 he worked at the Jardin des Plantes in Paris.

From childhood Michaux had dreamed of travelling, and between 1779 and 1781 he went on botanizing expeditions to England, the region of Auvergne in France, the Pyrenees, and Spain. In 1782 he received an appointment as secretary to the French consul in Persia. Although he travelled far and wide in a country torn by civil war, was at one point robbed of all his possessions, and had occasion to care for, and cure, the shah, nothing excited him like the discovery of plants. "I cannot express . . . with what joy I went to visit the countryside," he wrote in July 1782. "Gazing upon that multitude of plants which covered the meadows, I was often dazzled and obliged to calm myself for several minutes. I could not sleep at night and awaited the day with impatience." He returned to France in June 1785 with an extensive collection of seeds and botanical specimens from various parts of Persia and Mesopotamia.

Later that year the French government sent Michaux to the United States to collect North American seeds, shrubs, and trees; he landed at New York City on 1 October, accompanied by his son and a gardener. In 1786 he established a nursery at Hackensack, N.J., and the following year another at Charleston, S.C., from both of which he shipped many boxes of seeds and thousands of trees to the park at Rambouillet, France. Between 1786 and 1792 he botanized through much of the United States from New York to Florida and as far west as West Virginia and eastern Kentucky; in the same period he also visited Spanish Florida and the Bahamas.

In 1792 Michaux decided to pursue his botanical studies in Lower Canada. On 2 June he met the retired fur trader Peter POND near New Haven, Conn.; Pond informed him that the fur-trade canoes to the west, which Michaux may have considered accompanying, had left Montreal at the end of April. Michaux eventually proceeded to Montreal, where he arrived on 30 June. He remained there into July, botanizing and meeting several members of the fur-trading merchant class, including Joseph FROBISHER and Alexander Henry*, whom he undoubtedly questioned about the flora of the west. He then went to Quebec, where he spent several days with Dr John Mervin Nooth*, discussing Nooth's scientific inventions, inspecting his garden, herborizing, and preparing a voyage to James Bay.

Late in July, Michaux, accompanied by a mixed-blood interpreter, left Quebec for the Rivière Saguenay. On 5 August he arrived at Tadoussac, where he hired three Indian guides, and on the 7th the party started up the Saguenay in two bark canoes. On the 10th they reached the fur-trade post of Chicoutimi, and six days later Lac Saint-Jean, where Michaux explored extensively the shores and the surrounding forest. Following the Rivière Mistassini and small rivers and lakes, he arrived at Lac Mistassini on 4 September. Two days later, after proceeding about 25 miles down the Rivière de Rupert, which flows into James Bay, he was forced by bad weather and the late season to turn back, about 400 miles short of his objective.

As on all his voyages, Michaux daily recorded in a journal the conditions of travel, the day's progress, and the plants he had observed or discovered; as well, when possible, he noted their most northerly limits. He observed, for example, that the great rapids on the Mistassini marked the limit of *Potentilla tridentata*, or three-toothed cinquefoil, and that *Gaultheria procumbens*, or wintergreen, disappeared ten leagues up the same river from Lac Saint-Jean. One of the last specimens he collected was *Primula mistassinica*, or bird's-eye primrose, found along the Rivière de Rupert, and named by him. Michaux also wrote of his admiration for his guides' ability to manipulate the canoes and added that, although he never feared drowning, "these voyages are frightening for those not accustomed to them, and I would advise the Little Masters of London or Paris . . . to stay home."

Michaux arrived at Montreal in October 1792. On 2 December he was back at New York City, and in January 1793 he shipped to France seeds he had collected. In May he met Edmond-Charles Genêt, minister plenipotentiary to the United States of the French revolutionary government, who hoped to promote the revolution in Lower Canada; Michaux gave him several memoranda containing his observations on former French colonies in North America, including Canada. Genêt persuaded Michaux to undertake a secret political mission to Kentucky, the

592

nature of which is still largely unclear. From 1793 to 1796 he continued to botanize in the United States, travelling as far west as the Mississippi River. He was increasingly hampered by the French government's failure since 1789 to support him financially, and in 1796 he was finally obliged to abandon his project. On 13 August he left Charleston, but one month later his ship was wrecked off the coast of Holland; his herbarium was damaged, some of his manuscripts were lost, and Michaux himself almost perished. He reached Paris in January 1797 to discover that, of the thousands of trees he had sent since his arrival in North America, few had survived the ravages of the revolution. Moreover, he was unsuccessful in efforts to recover the arrears of his salary or to obtain financial support for a return trip to North America.

In October 1800 Michaux was engaged as a naturalist in a scientific expedition bound for Australia under the direction of Captain Nicolas Baudin. Always more comfortable working alone, Michaux left ship at Île de France (Mauritius) in April 1801 and proceeded to Madagascar, where he died of fever – according to some historians, on 13 Nov. 1802 near Tamatave, but, according to a member of the expedition, on 11 Oct. 1803 at Tananarive.

A contemporary of Michaux wrote that his robust constitution and habits of self-sufficiency gave him a great confidence in his own powers. Michaux, he added, "was of a frank temperament, although of a taciturn nature. . . . His extreme simplicity and the desire for independence that he had acquired in his roving and solitary life gave him a singular appearance. . . . He was not a Frenchman, an Englishman, or a Canadian, but everywhere one found him closer to the natives than any other foreigner would have been. . . . If he passed through a city, he visited the markets and enquired about the origins of the produce; in the country he questioned the habitants about the smallest details relative to cultivation; to an activity that did not permit him to lose a moment's time, he united an unwearying patience." Judging by Michaux's writings, he was a man of unusual intelligence and powers of observation but neither of culture nor of literary ability.

The genus *Michauxia* in the family Campanulaceae was named in Michaux's honour by the French botanist Charles-Louis L'Héritier de Brutelles.

J. F. M. HOENIGER

André Michaux is the author of *Histoire des chênes de l'Amérique* . . . (Paris, 1801) and of *Flora boreali-americana, sistens caracteres plantarum* . . . (2v., Paris, 1803), both of which were edited by his son, François-André, and illustrated by Pierre-Joseph Redouté. The latter work, which was co-edited by Louis-Claude Richard, describes more than 1,700 plants, including 40 new genera, and remained for many years the most complete flora of

eastern North America. Michaux also published a "Mémoire sur les dattiers . . ." in the *Journal de physique, de chimie et d'hist. naturelle* (Paris), 52 (1801): 325–35.

Those of Michaux's manuscript journals that survived the shipwreck of 1796 were donated in 1824 by his son to the American Philosophical Soc. and published with an introduction and notes by Charles Sprague Sargent in their *Proc.* (Philadelphia), 26 (1889): 1–145, under the title "Portions of the journal of André Michaux, botanist, written during his travels in the United States and Canada, 1785 to 1796. . . ." An extract from the journal of his voyage to Canada was published by Frère Marie-Victorin [Conrad Kirouac*] in *Études floristiques sur la région du lac Saint-Jean* (Montréal, 1925), 22–38. Botanical specimens from this trip are still in the Muséum nationale d'hist. naturelle, Paris; photographs of several of them are at the Jardin botanique de Montréal and the Institut botanique de l'université de Montréal. The labels on the specimens, in Michaux's hand, provide valuable details about habitat. The journal of the trip lists 160 plants not mentioned in his *Flora boreali-americana*.

The exact route of Michaux's voyage has long been the subject of debate and has been examined in the following works: [L.-]O. Brunet, *Voyage d'André Michaux en Canada depuis le lac Champlain jusqu'à la baie d'Hudson* (Québec, 1861); *Notice sur les plantes de Michaux et sur son voyage au Canada et à la baie d'Hudson, d'après son journal manuscrit et autres documents inédits* (Québec, 1863), translated under the title "Michaux and his journey in Canada" and published in *Canadian Naturalist and Geologist* (Montreal), new ser., 1 (1864): 331–43; Arthème Dutilly and Ernest Lepage, "Retracing the route of Michaux's Hudson's Bay journey," *Rev. de l'univ. d'Ottawa*, 15 (1945): 88–102; and Jacques Rousseau, "Le voyage d'André Michaux au lac Mistassini en 1792," *RHAF*, 2 (1948–49): 390–423.

AD, Yvelines (Versailles), État civil, Saint-Louis de Versailles, 8 mars 1746. *Biographie universelle* (Michaud et Desplaces), 28: 219–21. *DAB*. Gilbert Chinard, "André et François-André Michaux and their predecessors; an essay on early botanical exchanges between America and France," American Philosophical Soc., *Proc.*, 101 (1957): 344–61; "Les Michaux et leurs précurseurs," *Les botanistes français en Amérique du Nord avant 1850* (Paris, 1957), 263–84. [J.-P.-F.] Deleuze, "Notice historique sur André Michaux," Muséum d'hist. naturelle, *Annales* (Paris), 3 (1804): 191–227. Jacques Rousseau, "De la forêt hudsonienne à Madagascar avec le citoyen Michaux," *Cahiers des Dix*, 29 (1964): 223–45.

MICHICONISS (Michiguiss). *See* MADJECKEWISS

MICHIKINAKOUA (Michikiniqua, Me-She-Kin-No-Quah, Meshecunnaqua, Little Turtle), Miami war chief; b. mid 18th century, son of Aque-Noch-Quah, a Miami war chief; rumoured to have Mahican or even French blood; m. secondly Polly Ford, a white captive; d. 14 July 1812 at Fort Wayne (Ind.).

Little Turtle first came to white attention at the time of the American revolution. Like other Miami chiefs an ally of the British, in 1780 he led his warriors in the

Michikinakoua

destruction at the Miamis Towns (Fort Wayne) of a force under Augustin Mottin de La Balme, who was attempting to re-establish French control in the Ohio valley. The tribes south of the Great Lakes received their supplies from the British, who after 1780 encouraged the formation of a confederacy to oppose American expansion [see THAYENDANEGEA]. When in spite of official promises American settlers moved north of the Ohio, war parties from the confederacy attacked them. Little Turtle led many such raids and by 1790 had become the leader of the united war parties of the confederacy.

After 1789 the stronger central government created by a new constitution in the United States made possible plans to retaliate against the confederated tribes. Little Turtle led the Indians in two of the three major battles that ensued. In October of 1790 he decimated the forces under Josiah Harmar which had come to attack the Miami, Shawnee, and Delaware villages at the Miamis Towns. Although Harmar burned 300 houses and 20,000 bushels of corn just at the onset of winter, and although smaller American attacks followed, the Indians were not demoralized. In November 1791 near the Miamis Towns Little Turtle inflicted on Arthur St Clair's expedition losses of 630 killed and 264 wounded, the most casualties ever suffered by Americans in a single offensive against Indians. He is reported to have gone to the Montreal area following this victory in an effort to recruit more Indians for the spring's campaigning.

British and Indian hopes were now high that the Americans would agree to limit their expansion and allow the formation of an Indian state south of Lake Erie, but the Americans, more determined than ever, were preparing another expedition. Bolstered by inflammatory talk from Lord Dorchester [Guy CARLETON] and John Graves SIMCOE, which seemed to promise military aid if needed, the confederacy braced itself to meet the army under Anthony Wayne which began advancing in the autumn of 1793. Many residents of the Miamis Towns and vicinity had moved to the Glaize (Defiance, Ohio), farther from the American frontier; Little Turtle himself had left his customary village on the Eel River (Ind.) to live there. After unsatisfactorily harassing Wayne's lines of supply and communication for months and sounding out the British at Detroit (Mich.) about the possibility of aid, Little Turtle advised the confederacy that more would be gained by negotiating than by fighting. His advice was rejected, and he turned over command to the Shawnee chief Blue Jacket [WEYAPIERSENWAH], retaining only the leadership of his Miami warriors. A few days later, on 20 Aug. 1794, Blue Jacket was outgeneralled in the battle of Fallen Timbers (near Waterville, Ohio). Losses on both sides were about equal, but the Indians abandoned the field. The greatest casualty was their alliance with the British,

who refused them aid and shelter at nearby Fort Miamis (Maumee).

Wayne remarked on the agricultural nature of the Glaize settlements, writing: "The very extensive and highly cultivated fields and gardens show the work of many hands. The margin of those beautiful rivers [the Maumee and the Auglaize] appear like one continued village for a number of miles both above and below this place; nor have I ever beheld such immense fields of corn in any part of America from Canada to Florida." This area was not placed within the boundaries exacted by the Americans at the Treaty of Greenville the following summer, but the Indians, their confederacy in shambles, surrendered most of present-day Ohio, a portion of Indiana, and other tracts. Little Turtle made an eloquent though unsuccessful attempt to secure better terms and signed the agreement reluctantly. Yet he never broke the promises of peace it contained. In return the Americans built him a house in his old village on the Eel River, provided for the purchase of a black slave for him, and financed extensive travel to the east. At Philadelphia, Pa, in 1797 Gilbert Stuart painted his portrait. There also in 1798 he impressed the Comte de Volney, a French *philosophe*, with his wit and wisdom. During one of a series of interviews, Volney asked him what surprised him most about Philadelphia. "The extraordinary diversity of personal appearance among the whites and their great numbers," he replied. "They spread like oil on a blanket; as for us, we melt like snow in the spring sunshine; if we do not alter course, the race of red men cannot possibly survive." At Washington, D.C., in 1802 Little Turtle stirred officials with his pleas for prohibition of alcohol as well as training in farming and metal-craft for his people.

After the disintegration of the confederacy in 1795 Little Turtle, like many of his contemporaries, surrendered hope for a pan-Indian movement and concentrated on the interests of his tribe alone. His opposition after 1806 to the new confederacy being created by the Prophet [Tenskwatawa*] and TECUMSEH was based on several considerations. By its insistence that Indian land was owned by all tribes in common, the confederacy threatened Miami land claims, and by advocating the removal of those chiefs who had already sold land to the Americans, it endangered his leadership. Moreover he was convinced that the Americans could not be successfully opposed by any combination of tribes. He was more effective than most chiefs in preventing his warriors from joining the confederacy; yet the Americans never completely trusted him. His prestige among the tribes in general was revived somewhat when Governor William Henry Harrison of Ohio devastated the headquarters of the confederacy at Tippecanoe (near Lafayette, Ind.) in 1811.

Little Turtle died at Fort Wayne on 14 July 1812 following treatment by an army doctor for gout. As was customary with Miamis, he was buried wearing his silver jewellery, which included several pieces with the mark of Robert CRUICKSHANK of Montreal. Lesser chiefs could not restrain the young Miami warriors from joining the new confederacy in increasing numbers after his death. In September the Americans burned his village on the Eel River but they spared his property as a mark of respect. He was, in his prime, a strong defender of native rights and was remembered as a hero among the Miamis.

HERBERT C. W. GOLTZ

C.-F. Chassebœuf, comte de Volney, *Œuvres complètes de Volney* (Paris, 1837), 715–17. *Corr. of Lieut. Governor Simcoe* (Cruikshank). *Fort Wayne, gateway of the west, 1802–1813: garrison orderly books, Indian agency account book*, ed. and intro. B. J. Griswold (Indianapolis, Ind., 1927; repr. New York, 1973). *Letter book of the Indian agency at Fort Wayne, 1809–1815*, ed. Gayle Thornbrough (Indianapolis, 1961). *Messages and letters of William Henry Harrison*, ed. Logan Esarey (2v., Indianapolis, 1922). U.S., Congress, *American state papers* (Lowrie *et al.*), class II, vols.[1–2]. S. G. Drake, *Biography and history of the Indians of North America, from its discovery to the present time . . .* (5th ed., Boston, 1836). *Handbook of North American Indians* (Sturtevant *et al.*), 15: 681. Bert Anson, *The Miami Indians* (Norman, Okla., 1970). C. M. Young, *Little Turtle (Me-she-kin-no-quah), the great chief of the Miami Indian nation; being a sketch of his life, together with that of William Wells and some noted descendants* ([Greenville, Ohio?], 1917). H. H. Tanner, "The Glaize in 1792: a composite Indian community," *Ethnohistory* (Tucson, Ariz.), 25 (1978): 15–39.

MIERAY. *See* MYEERAH

MILBANKE, MARK, naval officer and governor of Newfoundland; baptized 12 April 1724, third of six sons of Sir Ralph Milbanke of Halnaby Hall, England, and his second wife, Ann Delavall, daughter of Edward Delavall of Dissington Hall, South Dissington, England; m. Mary Webber, and they had one son and two daughters; d. 9 June 1805 in London, England.

Mark Milbanke entered the Portsmouth Naval Academy as a scholar in February 1736/37, and he spent his midshipman years on the *Tilbury*, *Romney*, and *Princess Mary*, the last commanded by Captain Thomas Smith, who was governor of Newfoundland in 1741 and 1743. Milbanke became a lieutenant on 20 April 1744 and assumed command of his first ship, the *Serpent*, on 13 Sept. 1746. He was placed on half pay at the end of the War of the Austrian Succession in 1748, and again following his service in the Mediterranean throughout the Seven Years' War.

During the American revolution Milbanke com-

manded several vessels and on occasion substituted for Lord Shuldham* as commander-in-chief at Plymouth. Although by September 1780 he had risen to vice-admiral of the blue, he held no command as a flag officer until the spring of 1782. At that time he was appointed to the fleet under Lord Howe, and he participated in several actions during the closing stages of the war. He was port admiral at Portsmouth from 1783 to 1786, but seems to have had no other important posts until 1789, when as a vice-admiral of the white he became governor of Newfoundland.

Immediately upon his arrival in the middle of July, Milbanke was given serious concern by the old problem of the dumping of unwanted human cargo in Newfoundland. In this instance the problem related to the fate of convicts. It was then the pernicious custom to ship them to the mainland colonies in America, but a ship which had left Ireland in June with 114 convicts put them ashore at outports south of St John's, where they created much uneasiness among the inhabitants. As the convicts – many of them in poor health – wandered to the capital, Milbanke had them rounded up and sent to England. These unfortunate people were unwelcome on an island where, after the fishing season, the resident community had a great enough problem ensuring their own survival.

Though by the time of Milbanke's governorship it was too late to forbid settlement in Newfoundland, it was still possible to hinder it. In accordance with his instructions, Milbanke forced the demolition of buildings beyond those needed for a temporary or seasonal fishery. Forest clearing was also discouraged if done for purposes of establishing permanent housing or for any other purpose likely to encourage settlement. Nevertheless, increasing numbers of poor Catholic Irish attempted to winter in Newfoundland after the fishing season, and the hasty dispatch of the Irish convicts was not unrelated to the danger of unrest. Milbanke believed, moreover, that if the comforts of religion were readily available the Irish would remain. He thus viewed the Catholic chapel built at St John's in 1786 as an encouragement to settlement, but also, what was worse in his eyes, to Catholicism. Although freedom of worship had been proclaimed by Governor John Campbell in 1784, he refused permission to James Louis O'DONEL, prefect apostolic in Newfoundland, to build another chapel at Ferryland.

Milbanke is best remembered for his part in ending the difficulties Newfoundland experienced during the late 1780s in the administration of justice. At the beginning of the century the only judicial authorities on the island had been the fishing admirals, who were responsible for settling disputes in the fishery. It soon became obvious, however, that the growth of the resident population made some form of rudimentary judicial organization necessary, and under governors

Miles

Henry Osborn* in 1729 and Francis William Drake* in 1750 measures were taken to appoint justices of the peace and commissioners of oyer and terminer to deal with most criminal cases. The majority of disputes requiring decisions, however, were those concerning debt, payment of wages, and property disputes, and the judicial authorities had not been given power to deal with these matters. Nevertheless, the need was such that civil cases had been heard. In addition, the governor and his surrogates, naval officers empowered by him to supervise the fishery, had taken it upon themselves to adjudicate in civil cases. Despite the illegality of the system, it functioned well enough as long as all concerned agreed to abide by the decisions. The inevitable happened in 1787 when Richard HUTCHINGS, a West Country merchant, refused to accept the decision of a surrogate and appealed it to a court in Devon. The court, not surprisingly, found that the surrogate had no legal authority to hear civil cases. News of this judgement created consternation in Newfoundland and effectively stopped the administering of civil justice during the 1788 fishing season: none of the persons who had previously ruled on civil matters wanted to take the risk of being sued, in England, for a decision made in Newfoundland. To compound the problem, a slump in the fishery that year resulted in many cases of debt requiring immediate attention.

Before he began his governorship Milbanke had consulted with his secretary, Aaron GRAHAM, who had served the previous three governors, about some way of solving the judicial impasse. On Graham's prompting he stretched the terms of his commission to permit the establishment of a court of common pleas which would hear civil cases. The new court came into being during the fishing season of 1789. It was readily accepted by the settled population, but not by the transient fishermen and merchants with their powerful West Country backing in parliament. The law officers in London denounced the court as illegal, but recognized that a similar institution was necessary. They recommended to the government that legislation be enacted to allow the establishment of a civil court, and appalled Milbanke by further suggesting that professional personnel be appointed to operate it. Legal wrangling and West Country parliamentary opposition delayed implementation of the legislation, however, and in 1790 Milbanke, now vice-admiral of the red, returned to Newfoundland to continue his illegal court.

The following year, by the act 31 Geo.III, c.29, a "court of civil jurisdiction" was created for one year, and John Reeves*, a trained jurist and a man of great integrity, was appointed its "chief judge." In 1792 a new act established a supreme court with full power to hear all civil and criminal cases; as a corollary, surrogate courts able to adjudicate on civil matters

were to be established in the outports. The system of supreme and surrogate courts was continued on an annual basis until 1809, when it was made permanent.

Following the end of his governorship in 1792, Milbanke returned to naval service and rose steadily in rank, becoming admiral of the white on 1 June 1795. His active career was concluded as commander-in-chief at Portsmouth from September 1799 to March 1803. Two years later, at the age of 81 or 82, he suffered a fatal accident by falling over the banisters of the staircase at his London home.

FREDERIC F. THOMPSON

North Yorkshire Record Office (Northallerton, Eng.), Reg. of baptisms for the parish of Croft, 12 April 1724. PRO, CO 194/21. *Gentleman's Magazine*, 1805: 589. *The Noels and the Milbankes: their letters for twenty-five years, 1767–1792*, ed. Malcolm Elwin (London, 1967). John Reeves, *History of the government of the island of Newfoundland . . .* (London, 1793; repr. New York and East Ardsley, Eng., 1967). John Charnock, *Biographia navalis; or, impartial memoirs of the lives and characters of officers of the navy of Great Britain, from the year 1660 to the present time . . .* (6v., London, 1794–98), 6: 81–83. *DNB*. R. H. Bonnycastle, *Newfoundland in 1842; a sequel to "The Canadas in 1841"* (2v., London, 1842), 1: 135–36. McLintock, *Establishment of constitutional government in Nfld.*, 62–77. Paul O'Neill, *The story of St. John's, Newfoundland* (2v., Erin, Ont., 1975–76), 2: 725–28. Prowse, *Hist. of Nfld.* (1895), 357–60. F. F. Thompson, "Transportation of convicts to Newfoundland, 1789–1793," *Newfoundland Quarterly* (St John's), 69 (1960), no.1: 30–31.

MILES, ABNER (before 1794 he signed **Mighells**), businessman and office holder; b. *c.* 1752 in Massachusetts; m. Mercy —, and they had at least four children; d. 26 July 1806 in Markham Township, Upper Canada.

Abner Miles's early life in Massachusetts remains unknown. By 1790 he had moved to the newly opened frontier settlement of Genesee Town in western New York's Ontario County, where his combined general store, inn, and cobbling business served the first wave of settlers in the region. In response to Lieutenant Governor John Graves SIMCOE's proclamation of 7 Feb. 1792, to "such as are desirous to settle" in Upper Canada, Miles and a few hundred other "Inhabitants and subjects of the United States of America" petitioned unsuccessfully in June 1793 for a township grant on the north shore of Lake Ontario. When in the spring of 1794 William BERCZY chose to move to Upper Canada with the more than 100 Germans who had arrived in the Genesee country that year under his supervision, Miles must have decided to follow. His account-books for the spring of that year show a final settlement with his New York customers. On 7 June 1794 the Executive Council of Upper Canada

596

Miles

considered a petition from Miles, apparently on behalf of a large number of settlers, requesting a tract of land six miles square on the La Tranche (Thames) River. This was the area that Berczy initially had expected to settle. Instead the council granted Miles and his family 600 acres of land and offered 200 acres to each of the male settlers. Miles was in Newark (Niagara-on-the-Lake) by the summer of 1794 and probably became aware that Simcoe planned to shift the centre of settlement from the western end of the province north of Lake Erie to the north shore of Lake Ontario behind the townsite of York (Toronto). On 26 August Miles contracted to build a large log house there for Provincial Secretary William JARVIS. In November he purchased for himself the dwelling of William Cooper* on lot 6 at a cost of two steers and a barrel each of salmon and flour – thus Miles became one of the town's earliest residents. In June 1795 there were still only 14 houses in York.

Miles soon opened a general store on lot 13 on King Street to provide a wide variety of foodstuffs, liquor, clothing, tools, building supplies, household goods, and sundries needed by the immigrants settling in and near York. In a society with little cash in circulation and no formal banking institutions Miles occasionally became a private banker. He also provided a cartage service, and beginning in the spring of 1796 ran the schooner York to Newark and Genesee in partnership with Samuel HERON. The following year he became a partner with Eli Granger of Handford's Landing, N.Y., in the construction of Jemima, the first ship built by the Americans on Lake Ontario.

By early 1796 Miles had expanded his premises to include a public house serving meals and alcoholic beverages and providing lodging for travellers. In the rugged conditions of the new settlement the tavern was doubtless one of the few centres where farmers and townsfolk could gather for recreation and discussion. Since York lacked public buildings of any size it became a focal point for such social activities as auctions, dances, and special celebrations including masonic dinners. All the annual town meetings between 1798 and 1803 were held under Miles's roof.

In 1797 and 1798 Miles was chosen overseer of highways for the town and in the latter year he also became quartermaster of the York militia. As an innkeeper he was automatically appointed a constable by the Court of Quarter Sessions. In 1800, at a meeting to choose municipal officers for Markham, Vaughan, Whitchurch, and King townships – where he held land – Miles was elected assessor of rates and collector of assessments.

Like many ambitious Upper Canadian merchants, Miles seems to have been a land speculator. Besides his initial homesteading grant and his two town lots he received in 1796 lot 21 on Yonge Street which he sold to Surveyor General David William Smith* two years

later. He did, however, patent land in Markham, Vaughan, and Whitchurch townships in 1803. At his death, a local historian has claimed, he left some 2,000 acres.

The lack of cash in the colony and Miles's probable expansion of his land holdings put a strain on his business. These problems were common to other early York merchants such as Heron and William WILLCOCKS. On 31 Aug. 1799 he placed an advertisement in the Upper Canada Gazette demanding payment from his debtors, and the following spring one of his creditors obtained a writ to sell Miles's share in the Jemima. By 1801 he had turned over the management of his York tavern to James Playter, his son-in-law, and Ely Playter; he eventually sold it to another former resident of the Genesee country, Dr Thomas Stoyell. Whether motivated by financial difficulties or by the advantages awaiting an enterprising merchant in the new settlements north of York, Miles moved up Yonge Street during 1800 to lots 45 and 46 on the boundary of Markham and Vaughan townships, a spot 16 miles from York which became known as Miles' Hill (Richmond Hill). In 1802 he again opened a store, carrying on the same trade as he had at Genesee and York. He also ran a potashery, and by 1805 was again operating a tavern. After his death in 1806 his son James continued the business on Yonge Steet.

CRAIG HERON

AO, MS 87; MU 2115, 1864, no.2; RG 1, A-I-6: 1964–65; RG 22, ser.155, will of Abner Miles; RG 53, ser.2-2, 1. MTL, William Allan papers, Abner and [James] Miles, account-books, 1793–1809; [William Berczy], "Narrative concerning an expedition in Upper Canada for settling a part of that province with Germans from Europe and the United States, volume I, 1794–1812"; "Documents and vouchers s[h]ewing to prove the facts related in volume the first, volume II, 1792–1812"; William Jarvis, estimates, accounts, and contracts with Abner Miles and others for building a house at York, also a plan of the house, [Niagara-on-the-Lake, Ont.], 26 Aug. 1794–7 May 1795; William Jarvis papers, B52: 72, 109; Abner Miles, day book B, 1 Sept. 1795–15 Dec. 1796; ledger A, August 1803–6 March 1809; York, U.C., minutes of town meetings and lists of inhabitants, 1797–1803. PAC, MG 23, HII, 6, vol.1: 8–9; RG 1, L3, 283: L1/1, 73; 327a: M2/18, 41.

"Grants of crown lands in U.C.," AO Report, 1929: 66, 104, 160. "Minutes of Court of General Quarter Sessions, Home District," AO Report, 1932: 10, 23, 29, 32, 49, 52, 78–79, 82. "Rev. William Jenkins of Richmond Hill," ed. A. J. Clark, OH, 27 (1931): 15. Town of York, 1793–1815 (Firth), 69, 223. U.S., Bureau of the Census, Heads of families at the first census of the United States taken in the year 1790: New York (Washington, 1908; repr. [Spartanburg, S.C., 1964] and Baltimore, 1966), 138. "U.C. land book B," AO Report, 1930: 50–51. "U.C. land book C," AO Report, 1930: 150. "U.C. land book D," AO Report, 1931: 128. Upper Canada Gazette, 8 Dec. 1798; 2 Feb., 31 Aug. 1799; 11 Jan., 8, 22 March, 26 April 1800; 29 Nov. 1806.

Millidge

John Andre, *Infant Toronto as Simcoe's folly* (Toronto, 1971), 12–13, 83–84, 87. *Centennial history of Rochester, New York*, ed. E. R. Foreman (4v., Rochester, 1931–34), 1: 276. E. C. Guillet, *Pioneer inns and taverns* (5v. in 4, Toronto, 1954–62), 1: 67–69; *Pioneer life in the county of York* (Toronto, 1946), 47–48; *Toronto from trading post to great city* (Toronto, 1934), 210, 295–97. G. E. Reaman, *A history of Vaughan Township: two centuries of life in the township* (Toronto, 1971), 33, 117–19, 273. *Robertson's landmarks of Toronto*, 1: 445. H. E. Bryan, "King's or Hanford's landing," Rochester Hist. Soc., *Pub. Fund Ser.* (Rochester), 14 (1936): 173.

MILLIDGE (Millage, Milledge), THOMAS, surveyor, office holder, politician, judge, and militia officer; b. *c.* 1735 in Hanover, N.J., son of John Millidge; d. 8 Sept. 1816 in Granville, N.S.

Unfortunately, little is known about Thomas Millidge's early years, and the first documentation available is the record of his marriage to Mercy Berker (Barker) on 3 Dec. 1758 in the Hanover Presbyterian Church; he was baptized only a half-way member of the church on 15 Jan. 1764. The couple were to have six children, and the church records also contain the baptismal dates of four born between 1769 and 1776, including John* and Thomas*. Having begun his working career as a surveyor, on 23 March 1767 Millidge was appointed by the East Jersey Proprietors to the lucrative position of deputy surveyor of the counties of Morris, Sussex, Bergen, and Essex. He was also appointed a justice of the peace for Morris County on 27 April 1775.

Information on Millidge's stance during the American revolution is scarce. By his own testimony, he initially tried to prevent "violent measures," and advocated legal channels for the presentation of grievances, but by November 1776 he had committed himself to the loyalist cause and had joined the British army. It is probable that, as a moderate, Millidge earned the enmity of those more vigorously opposed to the *status quo*, and was thus forced into a defensive position which became a loyalist one. He was commissioned major of the 5th battalion of the New Jersey Volunteers on 11 Dec. 1776 and served in the regiment with that rank throughout the war. In August 1778 the New Jersey authorities initiated legal proceedings against him, and in December his estate was advertised for public auction. Millidge was later awarded £1,131 of his claim for £2,777 6s. by the loyalist claims commissioners, plus a £50 yearly pension for the loss of his official income.

Thomas Millidge was one of the more fortunate of those forced to emigrate at the close of the revolution. Receiving grants in the fertile Annapolis valley of Nova Scotia, he settled first in Digby, and then in Granville, and became a substantial landowner, amassing 900 acres in Wilmot and Digby townships. He also became a deputy surveyor for the provincial government, and in this capacity laid out lands for black loyalists in Annapolis County in 1785 [*see* Thomas Peters*]. Millidge was held in high regard by Surveyor General Charles MORRIS, who often praised him. In 1785 Millidge began a long and active public life with his election to the House of Assembly as the first representative for Digby Township, a seat he held until 1793. He then served for Annapolis County from 1793 to 1806. In the latter year he was a candidate for Granville Township, but was defeated by Isaiah Shaw in a closely contested battle. Millidge was appointed to several other public offices, including those of justice of the peace on 9 Feb. 1784, judge of the Inferior Court of Common Pleas on 26 April 1793, colonel in the militia on 5 June 1793, and *custos rotulorum* on 3 Oct. 1803. One of the more active and articulate members of the assembly, he was noted for his oratorical powers and was frequently nominated to committees or asked to chair committees of the whole. Millidge concerned himself with most of the issues within the charge of government at that time, and initiated a considerable proportion of the assembly's legislation dealing with the judicial system. In this context, he agitated for an investigation into the conduct of the Supreme Court judges in 1787 [*see* James BRENTON; Isaac DESCHAMPS], and he was also interested in education, social problems, finances, and the freedom of the assembly. By 18th-century standards, he took a progressive stand on these issues.

Thomas Millidge returned to his native country but once, in 1800. An extract from a letter to one of his remaining American friends illustrates his unhappy reception: "I consider the ill treatment I received when at your place to have proceeded from [ill?] motives. However I forgive these wretches any [?] they intended me and I hope God will forgive them also. . . . I am no enemy to any person in this world and should like to go again into your country." This statement reveals a remarkable equanimity and reasonableness, and in doing so reflects the general tenor of Thomas Millidge's entire life.

CAROL ANNE JANZEN

Annapolis County Registry of Deeds (Bridgetown, N.S.), vols.7–8, 11. PANS, RG 1, 171–72; 213, 10 Oct. 1783–24 Dec. 1798. Private arch., Mr and Mrs Donald Kitchell (Whippany, N.J.), Kitchell papers, letters from Thomas Millidge to Uzal Kitchel. *Documents relating to the colonial, revolutionary and post-revolutionary history of the state of New Jersey*, ed. W. A. Whitehead et al. (42v. and index, Newark, N.J., 1880–1949), 18: 25. *Documents relating to the revolutionary history of the state of New Jersey*, ed. W. S. Stryker et al. (5v., Trenton, N.J., 1901–17), 2: 387, 593. N.S., House of Assembly, *Journal and proc.*, 1786–1806. "United Empire Loyalists: enquiry into losses and services," AO *Report*, 1904: 67–70. *Nova Scotia Royal Gazette*, 18 Sept. 1806. *Church members, marriages and baptisms, at Hanover, Morris Co., N.J.* . . .

1746–1796 ([Morristown, N.J., 1893]; repr. 1968). *Directory of N.S. MLAs*. E. A. Jones, *The loyalists of New Jersey: their memorials, petitions, claims, etc., from English records* (Newark, 1927; repr. Boston, 1972). *Loyalists and land settlement in Nova Scotia*, comp. Marion Gilroy (Halifax, 1937). Calnek, *Hist. of Annapolis* (Savary).

MITCHIKIWEESE. *See* MADJECKEWISS

MOCIÑO. *See* MOZIÑO

MOLL, JOHANN ALBRECHT ULRICH (Wilhelm Albert Ulrich von). *See* BERCZY, WILLIAM

MONDELET (Mondelait, *dit* Bellefleur; Mondelé; Monthelet), DOMINIQUE, soldier, notary, surgeon, and landowner; b. *c.* 1734 in the parish of Saint-Sulpice in Paris, France, son of Didier Mondelet and Anne Méneveau; m. 23 April 1759 at Quebec, Marie-Françoise Hains, daughter of Joseph Hains, a carpenter of English origin, and they had 13 children; d. 6 Jan. 1802 in Saint-Marc, Lower Canada.

Dominique Mondelet arrived in New France in 1757 after serving for three years in the French navy. The following year he made a declaration that he was a sergeant in the Régiment de la Reine and a saddler by profession. He probably took part in the battle at Carillon (near Ticonderoga, N.Y.) on 8 July 1758, as well as the siege of Quebec in 1759. During the winter of 1759–60 he accompanied his regiment to the Chambly region where it established quarters. A man of initiative, he took advantage of the troubled times to assume the titles of notary and surgeon. In 1762 he signed his first deeds as a notary at Saint-Charles-sur-Richelieu and was treating the sick in the neighbourhood, having probably acquired his medical training in the army. In any case, he practised as a surgeon until he died.

With substantial means at his disposal, as is shown by the 1,287 *livres* in payment orders that he had in his possession in 1763 and the letter of credit for 100 *livres* that he held on Pierre Pelletier's estate two years later, Mondelet did not hesitate to launch into property transactions. Between 1765 and 1769 he bought for 2,300 *livres* at least four adjoining pieces of land, with a large acreage suitable for farming, along the Rivière Richelieu in the seigneuries of Saint-François-le-Neuf and Cournoyer. Early in 1770 he encountered difficulties. Some of his assets were seized and sold at auction for outstanding debts; among them were two houses, one a wooden dwelling of considerable size, a store, a stable, and various other buildings. These troubles did not seem to disturb unduly Mondelet's plans for enlarging his estate on both banks of the Richelieu. Through purchases, grants, or exchanges, particularly in the period 1772–75, he obtained a

footing in the seigneuries of Rouville and Saint-Hyacinthe, and then acquired more properties in that of Cournoyer. On 30 March 1781 he made his biggest deal when Jean Jenison, the seigneur of Saint-François-le-Neuf, granted him 14 pieces of land situated between the Richelieu, the Rivière des Hurons, and the Rivière Salvail. Subsequently he took advantage of the Sunday auction sales on the steps of the parish church of Saint-Charles to buy lands adjoining his own.

As his time was taken up by his work as a notary and a surgeon, Mondelet was unable to develop all his properties on his own. Consequently he sometimes had recourse to farmers or *métayers*. Anxious to protect his interests, he made heavy demands, asking them to maintain ditches and fences, take out thistles and other weeds, and spread manure immediately after the harvest.

Although Mondelet's affairs seemed prosperous, an unfortunate development occurred that caused concern in his family. In August 1781 judges John Fraser and René-Ovide Hertel* de Rouville, who had been named by Governor HALIDMAND to investigate the practice of the notarial profession, recommended that Mondelet be dismissed from its ranks; among other things they accused him of having practised without an official commission and of frequently contravening the rules of procedure for notaries. Shortly before this recommendation was made, Mondelet had urged the governor in vain to accord him a notary's commission for the villages of Saint-Charles-sur-Richelieu, Belœil, Saint-Hyacinthe, and Saint-Antoine-sur-Richelieu. The petition he addressed to Haldimand on 2 March 1782, in which he begged to be continued in his position, met with no greater success. He seems to have resigned himself to his fate, since after that date his minute-book contains only two deeds, one drawn up in 1784 and the other the next year.

Early in the 1790s Mondelet left his home at Saint-Charles-sur-Richelieu and went to live on the left bank, at Saint-Marc. In connection with this move he sold a number of properties in the region of Saint-Charles-sur-Richelieu, particularly in the period from 1794 to 1798. He was probably engaged in the wheat trade, since on several of these occasions he stipulated that he be paid in that grain, either directly or as a life annuity. He also received nearly 8,000 *livres* from the various transactions.

As a surgeon, notary, and landowner Mondelet had gained the trust of the people in the Richelieu region. This explains why the inhabitants of Saint-Marc chose him on 27 Nov. 1793 to defend their interests when a piece of land was seized. He was also chosen in 1796 to sit in the tenant farmers' assembly which had to deliberate about the building of a church in the parish of Saint-Marc-de-Cournoyer (Saint-Marc). When he

Montigny

died, four parish priests conducted his funeral service before "a great crowd of people."

Through his work and intelligence Mondelet had carved out an enviable place for himself within the modest society of the Richelieu valley. His son Jean-Marie* followed in his footsteps and became a notary; he also served as a member of the House of Assembly and coroner for the district of Montreal. His grandsons, Charles-Elzéar* and Dominique*, would be appointed judges and play important roles on the political stage in the 19th century.

GILLES JANSON

Dominique Mondelet's minute-book, 1762–85, is deposited at the ANQ-M as CN1-295.

ANQ-M, CE1-46, 8 janv. 1802; CN1-100, 17 juin 1764, 12 févr. 1765; CN1-150, 5 oct. 1765, 30 avril 1767, 30 mars 1781; CN1-189, 24 juin 1772; CN1-217, 19 févr. 1789, 19 juin 1790; CN1-254, 21 avril 1775; CN1-255, 27 nov. 1793; CN1-295, 29 sept., 22 oct. 1794; 7 févr., 8 juin, 13 nov. 1795; 10 janv., 1er juill., 3 oct. 1796; 15 mars, 25 juill., 23 sept. 1797; 23 févr., 9 mars 1798; 20 août, 1er nov. 1799; 11 févr. 1800; 22 févr., 6 juill. 1802; P1000-48-1020. ANQ-Q, CE1-1, 23 avril 1759. BL, Add. MSS 21734: 154; 21879: 59 (copies at PAC). "Cahier des témoignages de liberté au mariage commancé le 15 avril 1757," ANQ *Rapport*, 1951–53: 43–44, 53–54. "État général des billets d'ordonnances" (Panet), ANQ *Rapport*, 1924–25: 286. *Quebec Gazette*, 9 March 1769, 1 Feb. 1770, 2 July 1772. Abbott, *Hist. of medicine*, 35. M.-J. et G. Ahern, *Notes pour l'hist. de la médecine*, 418–19. Gérard Malchelosse, *La famille Mondelet* (Montréal, 1946). F.-J. Audet, "Les Mondelet," *Cahiers des Dix*, 3 (1938): 191–216. É.-Z. Massicotte, "Les médecins, chirurgiens et apothicaires de Montréal, de 1701 à 1760," *BRH*, 27 (1921): 80.

MONTIGNY, JEAN-BAPTISTE-PIERRE TESTARD LOUVIGNY DE. *See* TESTARD

MONTMOLLIN, DAVID-FRANÇOIS DE, Church of England clergyman and landowner; baptized 18 March 1721 in Neuchâtel (Switzerland), son of Louis de Montmollin, office holder, and Salomé Gaudot; d. 17 Dec. 1803 at Quebec, Lower Canada.

David-François de Montmollin was the fifth of 11 children born into a family of the Neuchâtel minor rural aristocracy. His father held seats in the Grand Conseil and the Conseil Étroit, the governing bodies of Neuchâtel. David-François's interests were not political, however; at age 17, a catechumen of the reformed church, he entered university at Basel, Switzerland, to study medicine. He seems to have completed his studies after three years. In 1744 he went to Leiden, Netherlands, where he was received into the Flemish church the following year. By 1748 he was in London, studying medicine. There on 2 June 1762 he married Jane Bell, and they would have five children, of whom three sons survived infancy.

In 1761 the Protestants of Quebec had petitioned for a French-speaking assistant to John Brooke*, the unofficial Anglican missionary there. Brooke hoped this man would "engage the Attention of those of the Popish Persuasion as well as secure the Approbation of the French Protestants that are here." He still had not received an assistant by 1768, and it may have been decided that Brooke should be replaced by a French-speaking clergyman capable of ministering in English. Montmollin had become attached to the Huguenot parish of La Patente, Spitalfields (London). Like many London Huguenots, he had probably joined the Church of England; on 12 Feb. 1768 he was given a mandamus admitting him to the cure of Quebec. He may have owed the appointment to an influential connection; his mandamus pre-dated his ordination on 4 March by Bishop Richard Terrick of London, and he had been chosen for the post over Leger-Jean-Baptiste-Noël Veyssière*, even though Veyssière had the support of Francis Maseres*, attorney general of the province of Quebec. Montmollin arrived at Quebec, probably in June 1768, and soon encountered hostility from Governor Guy CARLETON, who feared that the appointment of French-language ministers in the colony – Montmollin at Quebec, Veyssière at Trois-Rivières, and David Chabrand* Delisle at Montreal – would offend the Roman Catholic hierarchy. More specifically, Montmollin clashed with the governor over the accommodation of the Protestants at Quebec, complaining of their having to share the Recollet chapel with the Roman Catholics.

Montmollin's congregation was extremely small, he wrote in August 1770. Of the 30 communicants in the city the most he had had at one service had been 15, and latterly he had been averaging only 3. The number of Protestants was diminishing rapidly, the French and many of the British leaving Quebec. Moreover, most Protestants in the city were Presbyterians who had their own minister, George Henry. The main problem, however, was a lack of zeal in the congregation, attributed by Montmollin to its ethnic diversity and to the previous nomadic existence of most of its members, which had left them without habits of church attendance.

Others, such as Henry CALDWELL in 1775, Christian Daniel Claus* in 1782, and the Reverend John Doty* the following year, felt that the problem at Quebec was symptomatic of a greater malaise; they ascribed the deplorable state of the Church of England in the colony to the policy of appointing French-speaking clergy, who, they argued, knew little of the English language and less of Anglican rites. In 1785 the Reverend Charles Mongan was sent to Canada to investigate, and he forwarded to the British government an anonymous memorandum in which Montmollin was described as very old and unable to speak a word of plain English; worse, his private conduct was scandalous. "What opinion must the Canadians form of our religion," it was asked, "when they daily see the Minister of it degrading the very name, by keeping a little dirty dram shop, and himself so scandalously indecent, as to measure out, & sell rum to the soldiers of the Garrison – And all this too in the *Capital* of the Province, the Seat of Government, and *Residence* of the french Bishop, & other dignified Clergy of that Church." As a result of such complaints the Society for the Propagation of the Gospel recommended that the Reverend Philip Toosey*, a recent arrival in the colony, assist one of the French-speaking clergymen. When Toosey opted for Quebec, however, he was prevented from officiating regularly by Montmollin, who considered him an intruder.

By 1788 the complaints against the three French-language ministers had reached the ears of Charles INGLIS, newly appointed bishop of Nova Scotia, with jurisdiction over the province of Quebec. He proposed to Carleton, now Lord Dorchester, that the French-language clergy remain titular rectors of their parishes, but be replaced effectively by English-language assistants; Dorchester recommended Toosey for such a position with respect to Montmollin. On 9 June 1789 Inglis arrived at Quebec to begin the first pastoral visit of the colony by an Anglican bishop. He found Montmollin totally unsuited to his post. There were no wardens or vestry in his parish, so that after 20 years of his ministry "the English were a number of detached individuals, wholly unorganized, and without any form of order or Government." On 24 June he informed Montmollin of his wish that the rector retire. Although at least 68, Montmollin was horrified by the proposal and complained bitterly to Dorchester that it should even be entertained after his many years of service.

Montmollin's principal fear was that his superannuation would deprive him of much-needed income, for he was heavily in debt. He had arrived at Quebec financially secure and possessed of rent-producing property in Switzerland. He also received a salary of £200 per annum and fees for his services to the regiments in garrison. On the other hand, the governor had refused to countenance his tithing the Catholics, and Montmollin had been unsuccessful in claiming Brooke's position and salary as chaplain to the garrison, even though Brooke had had no intention of returning to Quebec. Montmollin had first moved into a house on Rue du Sault-au-Matelot, but at the end of October 1774 he bought for £500 a three-storey stone house on Rue Buade; at the end of the year he was renting out the lower floor to a merchant. By 1782 he was in a position to make a number of small loans, but the following year he began sliding into debt as a result of efforts to establish his sons in careers: John Frederick and John Samuel were to be dry-goods

merchants, and Francis Godot an officer in the 60th Foot. Thus by 1789 Montmollin could not afford to retire; although Inglis had guaranteed his salary, he needed the fees received for religious services.

Dorchester, who was informed by Inglis that the general desire of the congregation was to have Montmollin replaced, refused to intercede on the latter's behalf, and on 31 July 1789, after "a disagreeable scene," Montmollin bowed to Inglis's insistence that he retire. In return he exacted from the bishop a certificate of good character and conduct, although Inglis's personal appreciation of him was mixed at best: "[Montmollin] had some zeal and his moral courage was pretty fair, but he did not understand the discipline or the usage of our Church. He could not pronounce nor did he understand English. His mind was sordid, his manners uncouth, and his address mean and disgusting."

Montmollin suspected Toosey, whom he described as "a Croesus, the more he has the more he wants to have," of having engineered his misfortune, but he failed in efforts to supplant him. In the spring of 1792, however, Toosey went to England, leaving Montmollin once again in charge. After his arrival at Quebec in late 1793, the new bishop of Quebec, Jacob Mountain*, who found Montmollin "very old and infirm," appointed his brother JEHOSAPHAT to assist him; in fact Jehosaphat performed "the whole duty" until Toosey's return except when on pastoral visit with the bishop, during which time Montmollin was able to exercise his functions. Between 1790 and 1795 Montmollin performed about 500 baptisms, marriages, and burials.

Early in his retirement Montmollin's financial situation continued to deteriorate. By February 1790 John Frederick and John Samuel had fled the province, leaving their father guarantor of a debt of £1,550 to the firm of Fraser and Young [see John YOUNG]. In 1794 Montmollin sold his house and a lot behind it for £1,224 and paid the debt. His fortunes improved thereafter. In 1796 and 1797 he received appointments as deputy regimental chaplain to the 5th Foot and the 60th Foot, and in November 1796 he began to make small loans, which by September 1803 totalled about £800. In January 1803, as leader according to the system of township leaders and associates [see James CALDWELL], he had received a grant of approximately 10,000 acres in Wentworth Township.

Montmollin's position as rector necessarily tied him more closely to the city's British than to its Canadian inhabitants; however, his closest personal ties were with the small Huguenot community, particularly François Lévesque*, Jean Renaud*, and the merchant Pierre Fargues. Their deaths between 1780 and 1794 left Montmollin increasingly isolated until his own demise on 17 Dec. 1803. He left to his

Montour

widow £650 in cash as well as debts owed to him and several properties.

It is difficult to judge of the quality of Montmollin's ministry on the basis of testimony by his contemporaries and near-contemporaries. If Henry Caldwell and Inglis did not esteem him, George ALLSOPP and Chief Justice William Osgoode* apparently did. In 1822 the *Quebec Gazette* referred to him as a "much respected" former minister, a description confirmed about 1848 by Bishop George Jehoshaphat Mountain*, who stated that Montmollin was still at that time remembered by some "as a respectable, well-informed, and clever old man, with his old-fashioned clerical dress, and a great white wig." However, during his lifetime Montmollin shared with Chabrand Delisle and Veyssière the scorn of the Canadians and many British inhabitants as well as neglect and virtual rejection by his own church, and afterwards the fate of historical oblivion.

JAMES H. LAMBERT

[The author would like to express his appreciation to the late George Carlyle Marler and the late Élyse de Montmollin, both descendants of David-François de Montmollin, for the invaluable assistance they gave him in the preparation of this biography.   J.H.L.]
ANQ-Q, CE1-61, 19 Dec. 1803; CN1-16, 3 janv. 1803; CN1-25, 30 oct., 7 déc. 1774; 12, 21 mai 1781; 24 mai 1782; 18 déc. 1788; CN1-99, 2 sept., 29 oct. 1804; CN1-178, 7 nov. 1796; 16 mai, 7 nov. 1797; 9 févr., 30 mars, 4 avril, 5, 11 mai, 8 nov. 1798; 29 mai 1801; 10 avril 1802; 2 sept. 1803; 20 juin, 24 juill., 6, 11 août, 29 oct. 1804; 22, 23 déc. 1808; 1er févr. 1809; CN1-224, 2 avril 1787, 30 déc. 1788, 17 mai 1790; CN1-230, 6, 28 nov. 1794; CN1-256, 20 Jan. 1790; CN1-262, 14 nov. 1797, 16 mai 1801. AP, Cathedral of the Holy Trinity (Québec), fonds A. R. Kelley, Montmollin à Lord Dorchester, juin 1789.
Arch. de l'État (Neuchâtel, Suisse), fonds S.-P. Andrié, actes perpétuels, 1754–91, 65–66; fonds Abraham Bourgeois, 1: 223; fonds C.-F. Bovet, 7: 79; fonds Boy de la Tour, lettre no.3752. BL, Add. MSS 21665: 184–85 (copy at PAC). Lambeth Palace Library (London), Fulham papers, 1: ff.106, 110–12, 167, 169–70; 38: 22, 58. PAC, MG 11, [CO 42] Q, 21: 64–68; MG 23, A1, 2: 1432–53; A4, 14: 26, 42; 18: 33–34; C6, ser.1, 1: 69, 93; GII, 1, ser.1, vol.2: 182; RG 1, L3ᴸ: 4093, 36207; RG 4, A1: 6211–12, 4 May 1818, 18 June 1819; RG 8, I (C ser.), 828: 104–5; 931: 3. Private arch., G. C. Marler (Montreal), G. C. Marler, "David Francis de Montmollin, 1721–1803: a short biography"; Edmond Perret (Geneva, Switzerland), Charles Biéler, "Heurs et malheurs du premier pasteur anglican de Québec, David-François de Montmollin de Neuchâtel (Suisse)"; Edmond Perret, "Rev. David-François de Montmollin (1721–1803), first rector of Quebec: essay for a revised estimate." PRO, CO 42/28: ff.388–89; 42/49: ff.46–47; 42/92: f.118; 42/96: f.186; 42/100: f.400v. QDA, 60 (B-14), doc.2; 83 (D-2), 15 Jan. 1783; 84 (D-3), 9 June, 27 Aug. 1789; 25 June 1792. USPG, C/CAN/Que, I: 1 Nov. 1764, 5 Aug. 1770, 9 Oct. 1782; Journal of SPG, 16: 280–82. *A collection of several commissions, and other public instruments, proceeding from his majesty's royal authority, and other papers, relating to the state of the province in Quebec in North America, since the conquest of it by the British arms in 1760*, comp. Francis Maseres (London, 1772; repr. [East Ardsley, Eng., and New York], 1966), 148–49. *Docs. relating to constitutional hist., 1759–91* (Shortt and Doughty; 1918), 1: 72. *Quebec Gazette*, 26 Feb., 13 Aug. 1784; 21 Feb. 1788. Kelley, "Church and state papers," ANQ *Rapport*, 1948–49: 307; 1953–55: 99–101, 103–5. *Registers of the church of La Patente, Spitalfields*, ed. William Minet and W. C. Waller (Lymington, Eng., 1898), 153. R.-P. Duclos, *Histoire du protestantisme français au Canada et aux États-Unis* (2v., Montréal, [1913]), 1: 36. Ernest Hawkins, *Annals of the diocese of Quebec* (London, 1849). "David-François de Montmollin," *BRH*, 42 (1936): 104–5. Roger de Montmollin, "Un Neuchâtelois, premier pasteur de Québec," Soc. d'hist. du canton de Neuchâtel, *Musée neuchâtelois* (Neuchâtel), nouv. sér., 37 (1950), no.1: 26–28.

MONTOUR, NICHOLAS, fur trader, seigneur, politician, and office holder; b. 1756 and baptized on 31 October in the Dutch church at Albany, N.Y., son of Andrew Montour and Sarah Ainse*; d. 6 Aug. 1808 on the seigneury of Pointe-du-Lac and was buried two days later in Trois-Rivières, Lower Canada.

Nicholas Montour was descended from the family of Pierre Couc, *dit* Lafleur, of Trois-Rivières, one branch of which had become assimilated to the Indians of the Ohio, Pennsylvania, and Virginia regions in the 18th century. Grandson of Elizabeth Couc*, Nicholas was an English-speaking Protestant of mixed blood. Shortly before his birth, his parents had separated, their children had been placed in Philadelphia, and his mother, who is thought to have been an Oneida, had gone to live with Indian relatives near the Mohawk River, N.Y. In 1780 she was to acquire lands on the banks of the La Tranche (Thames River, Ont.) and give part of them to Nicholas, the only child left to her.

In 1774 Montour was acting as clerk for the brothers JOSEPH and Benjamin* Frobisher on the Churchill River (Man.). Three years later he was staying at Sturgeon River Fort (Sask.), with other fur traders: Booty Graves, Charles McCormick, William Bruce, Peter PANGMAN, Peter POND, and Joseph-Barthélemy Blondeau. In March 1779 he was living on Pine Island Lake (Cumberland Lake, Sask.) in a house belonging to Blondeau, for whom he was serving as agent. While Montour was putting in his years of apprenticeship in the fur trade, the Frobishers and other seasoned traders were concentrating their efforts at Grand Portage (near Grand Portage, Minn.) in order to set up a trading organization which was to become known as the North West Company.

In August 1782 Montour, who was working as a clerk for the Frobishers, was boarding in Montreal, Que., in the home of the lawyer Antoine Foucher; four months later Foucher accused him of seducing and abducting his 26-year-old daughter with a promise of marriage. He asked Governor HALDIMAND to force

Montour to marry his daughter or to pay her an allowance for the rest of her life and take care "of the fruit of his fornication."

Under the NWC agreement of 1783–84, Montour, George McBEATH, Robert Grant, and Patrick Small are thought to have each received two shares in the company, Pond and William Holmes* one, the Frobishers three, and Simon McTAVISH three. At that time Montour was working primarily on the Saskatchewan River. After a period of ruinous competition [see John GREGORY; Simon McTavish], the NWC merged with Gregory, MacLeod and Company in 1787. Of the 20 shares that then made up the capital of the NWC, Montour, Grant, and Small each held two; John Gregory, Pangman, Alexander MACKENZIE, Normand MacLeod*, Pond, McBeath, and Holmes held one apiece; and McTavish, Frobisher and Company owned the remaining seven.

The NWC, which was contending with steadily rising production costs and extremely fierce competition from the Hudson's Bay Company and from independent traders, was going through a difficult period. In 1790, under a new NWC agreement, Montour was to receive 2 of 20 shares. That year he and Pangman wintered at Fort des Prairies (Fort-à-la-Corne, Sask.), representing the NWC. For unknown reasons Montour decided around 1792 to retire and settle in Montreal. There he became a member of the Beaver Club, a select group of merchants to which he had been admitted in 1790.

Unlike others who were investing their liquid assets in new commercial endeavours, Montour seems primarily to have wanted to enjoy life and to put his money away safely. He made two trips to London, England, one in 1792–93, the other in 1794–95. On 16 Oct. 1794 he bought from Isaac TODD and his partners the Montreal Distillery Company, an enterprise consisting of several disused buildings for which he paid £1,166. Then he decided to invest in landed property. He paid £550 for a house on Rue Notre-Dame in Montreal on 2 July 1795 and resold it in 1800. At an auction sale in October 1795 he paid £3,740 to the sheriff of Trois-Rivières, Antoine-Isidore Badeaux, to purchase the seigneuries of Pointe-du-Lac (or Normanville, also called Tonnancour) and Gastineau, which had until then both belonged to Thomas Coffin*. Montour paid £2,000 for a four-storey stone house on Rue Saint-Paul in Montreal on 12 Jan. 1797. On 15 May, in joint ownership with David Alexander Grant and Quebec merchant William GRANT (1744–1805), he purchased the seigneury of Pierreville, for which he rendered fealty and homage in 1798. Judging that the seigneury could not be divided easily, he sold his share to David Alexander Grant for £610 on 2 Dec. 1799. On 25 June 1798 he had paid £1,150 for the seigneury of Rivière-David (also called Deguire), which he sold

three years later to William Grant for £1,271. Finally, in August 1802 he bought 11,500 acres of land in Wolfestown Township through the system of township leader and associates [see James CALDWELL].

On 17 Feb. 1798 in Christ Church, Montreal, Montour had married a 21-year-old woman from Quebec, Geneviève Wills, the daughter of Meredith Wills, a merchant, and Geneviève Dunière. The marriage contract acknowledged the separation of property, accorded the wife a jointure of 40,000 shillings, and made provision for a life annuity of 4,000 shillings a year upon the husband's death. Through his marriage Montour became linked to some great Canadian families: the Le Moyne de Longueuils, the Panets, and the Dunières, who at that time counted in their ranks a judge, one member of the Legislative Council, and three of the House of Assembly.

Shortly after their son Henry Isaac Horatio was baptized in Montreal on 7 Feb. 1799 the Montours took up residence at Pointe-du-Lac. There Montour lived like a great seigneur on his domain of Woodlands. He built a manor-house, a flour-mill, and a sawmill, and then had a race-track laid out for horse-racing. He enjoyed this life of luxury and always received his friends hospitably. In 1806 he formed a company to exploit iron ore on his estate, but the scheme seems to have come to nothing.

Montour also took part in public life. On 20 July 1796 he was elected to the assembly as member for Saint-Maurice, a seat he held until the dissolution of the legislature on 4 June 1800. He voted for the English party's candidate for speaker, John YOUNG, who was beaten by Jean-Antoine PANET. On 9 May 1799 he was appointed a justice of the peace for the District of Three Rivers, and his commission was regularly renewed. Not much is known about his private life, but it is clear that he has a bad reputation with the historians who have studied him. Father Alexandre Dugré observed: "He was a sad fellow, anglicized, a Protestant, a drinker and high-liver."

Having resided for some time in a house on Rue du Fleuve in Trois-Rivières, Montour died in his manor-house. His will, dated 13 April 1805, left to his wife, the executrix, and then to his four children, the enjoyment and usufruct of his property; Henry Isaac Horatio was to receive a two-fifths share. Only the grandchildren would be entitled to full ownership. A codicil dated 10 June 1808 authorized his wife to sell properties belonging to him in Montreal to take care of the debts on his estate, which amounted to £2,771. To repay them she had to sell a house on Rue Saint-Paul and put most of his personal estate up for public auction on 28 and 29 Nov. 1808 and again on 3 May 1809. She then went to live at Quebec. Around 1810 she returned to Pointe-du-Lac, where she died on 2 March 1832. The seigneury became the property of her son-in-law, Charles-Christophe Malhiot*.

Moody

While Montour was in the west he had had a son, also called Nicholas, who spent his entire life in that region. In 1804 he was working for the NWC at Fort des Prairies, and he became an employee of the HBC after the fusion of the two firms in March 1821.

FRANÇOIS BÉLAND

ANQ-M, CE1-63, 17 Feb. 1798, 7 Feb. 1799; CN1-29, 2 July 1795, 12 Jan. 1797, 15 April 1800; CN1-74, 29 mai 1801; CN1-184, 16 Oct. 1794; CN1-313, 17 févr. 1798. ANQ-MBF, CE1-50, 8 Aug. 1808; CN1-6, 2 déc. 1799, 1er déc. 1801, 20 août 1802, 13 avril 1805, 10 juin 1808. ANQ-Q, CN1-16, 1er juin 1810; CN1-256, 17 April 1795; CN1-262, 25 juin 1798. BL, Add. mss 21879: ff.80–90 (copy at PAC). *Docs. relating to NWC* (Wallace), 3. John McLoughlin, *The letters of John McLoughlin from Fort Vancouver to the governor and committee, first series, 1825–38*, ed. E. E. Rich, intro. W. K. Lamb (London, 1941), 350–51. *Quebec Gazette*, 27 April 1797, 19 Feb. 1798, 22 May 1806, 25 Aug. 1808. F.-J. Audet et Édouard Fabre Surveyer, *Les députés de Saint-Maurice et de Buckinghamshire, 1792–1808* (Trois-Rivières, Qué., 1934), 19–25. Desjardins, *Guide parl.* P.-G. Roy, *Inv. concessions*, 2: 48–50; 3: 248–49; 5: 79, 254–55. Emmanuel Brissette, *Pointe-du-Lac; au pays des Tonnancour* (s.l., s.d.). F. C. Hamil, *Sally Ainse, fur trader* (Detroit, 1939). C. A. Hanna, *The wilderness trail; or, the ventures and adventures of the Pennsylvania traders on the Allegheny path . . .* (2v., New York and London, 1911; repr. Ann Arbor, Mich., 1967). Innis, *Fur trade in Canada* (1956), 196, 198, 200, 256. Rumilly, *La compagnie du Nord-Ouest*, 1: 86, 88, 101–2, 127–28, 138–39, 149, 152, 166, 181. Sœur Marie du Rédempteur, "La Pointe-du-Lac au 19e et 18e siècles," *BRH*, 38 (1932): 301–15. Albert Tessier, "Deux enrichis: Aaron Hart et Nicolas Montour," *Cahiers des Dix*, 3 (1938): 217–42.

MOODY, JAMES, army and militia officer, office holder, politician, and author; b. *c.* 1744 in New Jersey, son of John Moody; by his first marriage he had three children; m. secondly 21 March 1782 Jane Lynson, *née* Robinson; d. 6 April 1809 in Sissiboo (Weymouth), N.S.

James Moody occupies a special place among the thousands of loyalists who settled in Nova Scotia after the American revolution because he is widely held to have been one of the most effective British raiders in that conflict, and many of his exploits read like popular fiction. At the outbreak of the revolution he was living quietly on a farm belonging to his father in Sussex County, N.J. Like many loyalists, he was "a Lover of Peace & good Order, and loyal on Principle," but initially he had no thoughts of taking part in the struggle. Early in 1777, however, the local committee of safety ordered him to abjure his British allegiance and pledge loyalty to the United States, and he refused. He was then harassed, and after being shot at in his fields he gathered more than 70 neighbours and fled to the British lines in April.

Soon after his arrival Moody became an unpaid volunteer in the New Jersey Volunteers, and because of his knowledge of northern New Jersey was sent back there to observe rebel troop movements, enlist men for the British forces, and generally annoy the inhabitants. On all the missions he undertook he led small bodies of men deep into enemy territory, and on several occasions he narrowly escaped death or capture. At last, in July 1780, now an ensign, he was taken near Englishtown, N.J. Imprisoned at West Point, N.Y., he was treated with great cruelty by Benedict ARNOLD, who commanded there, and it was not until George Washington himself intervened that his conditions improved. In September Moody was transferred to Washington's main camp, where he was to be tried by court martial for causing the death of two rebel officers in a skirmish. Hearing that he would almost certainly be condemned to death, he decided to escape. But this was easier said than done. He had been manacled, and was guarded by a sentry placed in his cell; in addition, there was a second sentinel at the door, and four others near by, and he was in the middle of the rebel camp. Notwithstanding these apparently insurmountable difficulties, one stormy night he incredibly managed to free himself and evade his captors. After several days of travel, he arrived safely at New York City.

Moody was to be left little time to rest from his harrowing experience. In March 1781 Oliver De Lancey, adjutant general of the British army, requested his help in intercepting Washington's correspondence, and after one failure he succeeded. On another mission to capture rebel mail he had a narrow brush with death when 70 men fired at him from point-blank range. Moody was uninjured, however, and must have been thankful for the proverbial inaccuracy of the 18th-century musket. His last major undertaking occurred in November 1781 when he was sent to break into the state-house at Philadelphia, Pa, and steal congressional books and documents. The plan was exposed, and he was forced to spend two days in a cornstack without food or water to avoid capture. His brother, who had accompanied him, was caught and executed as a spy.

Moody's adventures seriously affected his health, and when Sir Henry Clinton, the retiring commander-in-chief, was leaving America early in 1782 Moody accepted his offer of a passage to England. There he memorialized the government for compensation for his losses, and was awarded a yearly pension of £100 from the Treasury. The officials were impressed with his claims, commenting that "this is a Case of great Merit & great Exertions in his Majesty's Service." Moody also had his wartime experiences published as a pamphlet entitled *Lieut. James Moody's narrative of his exertions and sufferings in the cause of government*. Although the *Narrative* was ignored by the London press, Moody had it reprinted, asserting that he did so to reply to the general disbelief in the facts it

Morgann

presented. This time he added testimonials from several prominent army officers and loyalists, all of whom signified their complete acceptance of his story. The *Narrative*, and the accompanying personal statements, doubtless helped Moody when he went before the loyalist claims commission in 1784: he was awarded £1,608 of his total claim of £1,709 for property confiscated during the war and received in addition £1,330 for his expenses in raising men for the British service. He also obtained half pay as a lieutenant (he had been promoted in August 1781) when the New Jersey Volunteers were disbanded after the war.

Now at least temporarily free from the financial difficulties that had afflicted him throughout the war and during his stay in London, in 1785 Moody went to Nova Scotia, where he had been recommended to Governor John Parr* for a grant of land. The following year he travelled to the loyalist community on the Sissiboo River that later became the town of Weymouth. Moody soon became a person of some stature in the infant settlement. In August 1788 Bishop Charles INGLIS noted when passing through the community that Moody had just launched a ship he had built and was constructing another, and that in the absence of a clergyman he led the inhabitants in prayers on Sunday. Moody must have continued the latter task for some time, since Weymouth did not receive a clergyman until 1798; in the mean time, in 1790, he and his wife conveyed land for a church and cemetery to the inhabitants of Weymouth. In conjunction with a Colonel Taylor, Moody launched another ship in 1793, and he was also active in building mills. He served as a captain in the Royal Nova Scotia Regiment from 1793 to 1802 and participated as well in local affairs. A magistrate and colonel of militia, he was made a road commissioner in 1801. Moody entered politics when he was elected to the House of Assembly from Annapolis Township in 1793. Like that of other rural members, his time in Halifax was limited owing to the difficulties of travel, but he apparently took an active part in the business of the house. One of his proposals, the separation of the western portion of Annapolis County and its establishment as an independent county, was not accepted until 1833, when Digby County was created. Following his retirement from the assembly in 1806 Moody lived on his farm; the 640-acre grant he had received in 1791 had been swelled by 2,258 acres allotted to him when Digby Township was regranted in 1801. His death left his widow in straitened circumstances, however, and she was forced to petition the British government for a continuation of her husband's pension. Her claim was supported by strong recommendations from Inglis and EDWARD AUGUSTUS, Duke of Kent and Strathearn, and she received an annual pension of £81.

STUART R. J. SUTHERLAND

Lieut. James Moody's narrative of his exertions and sufferings in the cause of government, since the year 1776 was published in London in 1782; a second edition – . . . *authenticated by proper certificates* – appeared the following year and was reprinted in New York in 1865, with an introduction and notes by Charles Ira Bushnell. The *Narrative*, without its supporting letters, has been printed with an introduction by William Stewart MacNutt* in *Acadiensis* (Fredericton), 1 (1971–72), no.2: 72–90.

PRO, AO 12/13: ff.36–38; 12/89: f.4; 12/109: 208–9 (copies at PAC). *DAB. Directory of N.S. MLAs*. E. A. Jones, *The loyalists of New Jersey: their memorials, petitions, claims, etc., from English records* (Newark, N.J., 1927; repr. Boston, 1972). *Loyalists and land settlement in Nova Scotia*, comp. Marion Gilroy (Halifax, 1937). Sabine, *Biog. sketches of loyalists*, 2: 90–97. Calnek, *Hist. of Annapolis* (Savary), 391–92. Fingard, *Anglican design in loyalist N.S.*, 59. W. S. Stryker, *"The New Jersey Volunteers" (loyalists) in the Revolutionary War* (Trenton, N.J., 1887), 57. I. W. Wilson, *A geography and history of the county of Digby, Nova Scotia* (Halifax, 1900; repr. Belleville, Ont., 1975), 59, 91, 110, 125, 322–23.

MORGANN, MAURICE, office holder; b. 1726 in London, England; d. 28 March 1802 in Knightsbridge (London).

Maurice Morgann arrived at Quebec on 22 Aug. 1768 charged with helping to prepare a report on the administration of justice in the province. Since the Royal Proclamation of 7 Oct. 1763, utter confusion had reigned in the courts. On the one hand Chief Justice William Gregory and Attorney General George Suckling*, who drafted the ordinance of 17 Sept. 1764 setting up the judicial organization of the province, maintained that the proclamation introduced English law, and the report of the Board of Trade on 2 Sept. 1765 indirectly followed the same line of argument. On the other hand, in Great Britain Attorney General Charles Yorke and Solicitor General William de Grey asserted in their report of 14 April 1766 that the proclamation had not abolished all French laws. Suckling's successor, Francis Maseres*, in a report he presented in 1766, claimed that the proclamation could not have changed the laws of the colony, because only the parliament of Great Britain had such power. Nor could the Canadians and the British in the province of Quebec agree on the laws they wanted to see enforced, the former demanding French laws, the latter English. The Court of King's Bench and the justices of the peace applied English laws; the Court of Common Pleas sometimes used English laws, sometimes equity (in the sense of natural justice), but most often French laws. The judicial organization was such that in civil matters, except in the case of lawsuits involving £10 or less, the plaintiff had the choice of proceeding either in a court that applied English laws or in one that usually applied French laws. With the exception of the chief justice, the judges had no legal training; justices of the peace

605

Morgann

were completely incompetent, and justice was as slow as it was costly.

On 28 Aug. 1767 the Privy Council, judging that it needed more information, ordered Lieutenant Governor Guy CARLETON, Chief Justice William Hey*, and Attorney General Maseres to prepare a report on the administration of justice and to suggest reforms if necessary. It further decided to send "a fit and Proper person" to the province to deliver instructions on this matter, bring the report back to London, and be able to explain the difficulties. For this delicate mission Lord Shelburne, then secretary of state for the Southern Department, chose Morgann. On 17 Sept. 1767 he notified him of his appointment and ordered him to proceed to Quebec immediately. Morgann got on good terms with Carleton immediately but was received with suspicion by Hey and Maseres, who had difficulty accepting this representative of London – a man untrained in the law and unfamiliar with Quebec. On 31 Aug. 1768 Maseres wrote: "Mr: Morgan the legislator, as we use to call him, is come. . . . He is a well-bred agreeable man but not a lawyer; and he has a pompous way of talking that seems borrowed from the house of commons cant about the constitution, &c, without having precise Ideas of what he would say."

In compliance with the Privy Council's order, Maseres delivered to Carleton on 27 Feb. 1769 a report in which he recommended reform of the administration of justice and suggested four ways of removing the uncertainty about the laws, without specifying an order of preference. One of them involved putting back into force all the French laws and introducing certain English ones, a solution Maseres himself opposed, judging by his comments. Dissatisfied, Carleton rejected Maseres's submission. Morgann fully approved of his reaction and wrote to Shelburne on 30 Aug. 1769 that the document was "extreamly defective and improper" and that it was "a strange Report."

Carleton and Hey then asked Morgann to draw up a new plan. Morgann's report pleased the governor, but not the chief justice, who decided to prepare one himself, arguing that it was improper for such a statement to be written by a stranger to the colony. Late in June 1769 Hey presented Carleton with his observations, which, according to Morgann, were inspired by his own but did not suggest specific reform. Finding Hey's report unsatisfactory, Carleton concluded that he should write one himself; he in turn took his inspiration partly from Hey's text but mostly from that of Morgann, whom he requested to provide further amplification. Carleton's report, dated 15 Sept. 1769 and signed also by Hey, recommended a reform of the judicial system and in particular proposed the creation of a third judicial district, limitation of the competence of the Court of King's Bench to criminal matters, and the appointment of seigneurs and militia captains as justices of the peace. It also advised that French laws be maintained except in criminal, commercial, and maritime matters. Finally it proposed that habeas corpus should be introduced and trial should be by jury not only in criminal matters but also in suits for damages. Morgann was very pleased with this report. On 30 Aug. 1769 he wrote to Shelburne that Carleton's report did "not vary in any material Point" from his own, and he praised the governor's qualities highly. Although Hey had signed the report, on 15 Sept. 1769 he appended to it a dissent on the question of French laws, in which he declared that he approved only of the re-establishment of those dealing with land tenure, alienation of chattels and real estate, mortgages, inheritances, marriage contracts, domestic economy, and family relationships. Maseres did not sign the report, and on 11 Sept. 1769 he too drew up a letter in which he expressed his dissent and declared his opposition to the re-establishment of French laws, except those concerning land tenure, alienation and incumbrance of landed property, mortgages, dower, and inheritances.

On 18 Sept. 1769 Carleton wrote to the secretary of state for the American Colonies, Lord Hillsborough, that he was handing over to Morgann both the report and the two letters of dissent. To these he attached summaries of the civil, criminal, and police laws in effect at the time of the conquest and the digest that François-Joseph Cugnet* had prepared of edicts, declarations, ordinances, provisions, and commissions. Carleton praised highly the assistance he had received from Morgann, who returned to Great Britain and handed over to Hillsborough the documents entrusted to him.

Morgann's mission to Canada was a major factor in the re-establishment through the Quebec Act in 1774 of most of the French civil laws, a re-establishment doubly beneficial in that it was fairer for the population and also indicated clearly that those were the laws in force. His mission also had an influence on the reform of the administration of justice, which was effected through an ordinance of 1 Feb. 1770. At the time the judicial system was reorganized after the Quebec Act, important recommendations in Carleton's report were implemented; this reorganization was not undertaken until 1777, because of the American invasion [see Benedict ARNOLD; Richard Montgomery*]. The reforms of 1770 and 1777 brought appreciable improvements to the administration of justice but a number of important problems were left unresolved.

During his stay at Quebec Morgann had drawn up a report on the church and another on revenues; they were not, however, sent to Great Britain by the governor. Morgann continued writing after his return to England. He published some essays, the most important of which, *An essay on the dramatic character of Sir John Falstaff*, first appeared in 1777. In it he wittily defended the bravery of Shakespeare's famous character.

In 1782 Lord Shelburne entrusted another delicate mission to Morgann. He was made private secretary to Carleton, who on 2 March 1782 had been named commander-in-chief of the British army in North America and charged with the task of effecting a reconciliation between the American colonies and the mother country. Morgann was in New York in May 1782, and remained there until July 1783, although on 17 June 1782 he had asked to be recalled. In 1783 he was appointed secretary of the delegation sent to Versailles to ratify the peace treaty with the United States. Three years later he was still Carleton's secretary. Morgann continued to take an interest in the issues of his day. His *Considerations on the present internal and external condition of France* was published anonymously in 1794, and *Remarks on the slave trade*, also anonymous, probably dates from this period as well. He died in Knightsbridge on 28 March 1802, having left instructions in his will that all his writings should be destroyed.

JACQUES L'HEUREUX

Maurice Morgann is the author of *An essay on the dramatic character of Sir John Falstaff* (London, 1777; repr. New York, 1970; new ed., London, 1820; 1825; ed. W. A. Gill, 1912). The anonymously issued *Remarks on the slave trade* and *Considerations on the present internal and external condition of France* (n.p., 1794) are also attributed to him.

PAC, MG 23, A4, 20: 24, 37 (transcripts). *A collection of several commissions, and other public instruments, proceeding from his majesty's royal authority, and other papers, relating to the state of the province in Quebec in North America, since the conquest of it by the British arms in 1760*, comp. Francis Maseres (London, 1772; repr. [East Ardsley, Eng., and New York], 1966). *Doc. relatifs à l'hist. constitutionnelle, 1759–1791* (Shortt et Doughty; 1921). Maseres, *Maseres letters* (Wallace). *Rapports sur les lois de Québec, 1767–1770*, W. P. M. Kennedy et Gustave Lanctot, édit. (Ottawa, 1931). *British authors before 1800: a biographical dictionary*, ed. S. J. Kunitz and Howard Haycraft (New York, 1952). *DNB. Documents of the American revolution, 1770–1783*, ed. K. G. Davies (20v., Shannon, Republic of Ire., 1972). Wallace, *Macmillan dict.* Burt, *Old prov. of Quebec* (1968), 1: 137, 152–56. Neatby, *Quebec*. Jacques L'Heureux, "L'organisation judiciaire au Québec de 1764 à 1774," *Rev. générale de droit* (Ottawa), 1 (1970): 266–331.

MORRIS, CHARLES, surveyor, politician, office holder, and judge; b. 31 Dec. 1731 in Hopkinton, Mass., eldest child of Charles Morris* and Mary Read; m. Elizabeth Bond Leggett, and they had 11 children; d. 26 Jan. 1802 in Halifax, N.S.

Charles Morris apparently came to Nova Scotia in 1760, some time after his marriage. From then until 1781 he assisted his father, Nova Scotia's first surveyor general; between 1776 and 1781 he performed the tasks of the office alone. In the course of the work he made "Frequent and Tedious Excursions" throughout Nova Scotia, and, in 1768, went to St John's (Prince Edward) Island. In 1772 the possibility that his father might lose his position spurred Morris, with his father's approval, to seek it for himself. He enlisted Joseph Frederick Wallet DesBarres* to promote his cause in England and in return looked after DesBarres's land interests in Nova Scotia. Morris, however, had to wait until after his father's death in 1781 to obtain the position, perhaps because DesBarres's interests, which he supported, conflicted with those of Lieutenant Governor Michael Francklin*, himself a prominent land speculator. Morris would have further antagonized Francklin and his friends such as Joshua Mauger* and John Butler* by supporting Governor Francis Legge* in 1775 when they sought his removal.

As surveyor general, Morris was overwhelmed with loyalist land claims. Attacks of gout forced him to rely increasingly on his son Charles* (his eventual successor) to perform some of his duties in the 1780s, and his deputies appear to have done most of the actual work in laying out the claims. Nevertheless, in 1784 he informed loyalist agent Amos BOTSFORD that he had "no time to attend on any other Business." Morris's feelings towards the loyalists were ambivalent. When they first arrived in 1783 he welcomed them as providing a basis for a barrier to the rebellious colonies and as a protection to the fisheries. But when he realized how much work they would make for him he seems to have changed his attitude, and he was obviously chagrined that members of his own family might lose property to them because they had not had time to develop it. Morris constantly complained that he was overworked and underpaid, and that he had to be content with incompetent staff, even though he apparently appointed his own deputies. On one occasion an assistant's error led him to declare that "there must either have been a Want of Professional Knowledge or the Surveyor must be of a hardy, nefarious tribe who delight in mischief." At times Morris claimed that the expenses of his office exceeded his allowances. He apparently received a salary, and in addition was entitled to fees for surveys. In the case of the surveys of loyalist land grants, however, he was to receive only one-half the usual fees, and then from the British government, since the loyalists themselves were exempt from payment. Morris claimed that he had received payment in only a few cases. When the Treasury rejected a request for additional funds in 1784 in the belief that Morris received fees on every grant and commissions from his deputies, Morris protested that "the Expence of my

Morris

Table only since these Affairs [loyalist land claims, for example] has come to double my salary." Three months later he decided to charge his deputies five per cent interest on their outstanding accounts with him.

Despite his duties as surveyor general, Morris managed to find time for other activities. Between 1770 and 1785 he served in the House of Assembly for Sunbury County and took an active part in committee work. He was registrar of the Vice-Admiralty Court from 1771 until his death, registrar of wills and probate from 1792 to 1798, surrogate general of the Probate Court from 1798 to 1802, and a justice of the peace. Legge thought so highly of him that in 1775 he recommended him for a seat on the Council. Morris did not achieve the office until 1785, however. He attended the meetings of that body regularly and supported its stands in the controversies of the late 1780s [see James BRENTON]. He apparently had good reason to agree with the Council: it reviewed his accounts as surveyor general several times a year and seems to have approved payment without question.

Land interested Morris personally as well as professionally. In his first few years in Nova Scotia he purchased several lots in Halifax and with other officials obtained large grants elsewhere. As a member of the Saint John River Society in the mid 1760s [see Beamsley Perkins Glasier*] he participated in its grants, and he also held land in Maugerville Township (N.B.), around Passamaquoddy Bay (N.B.), and in and around the Annapolis valley. Over the next 40 years Morris bought and sold numerous pieces of property; in 1774, for example, he sold 10,000 acres on the Saint John River (N.B.) to James Simonds* for £150. Despite his complaints of the expenses of his offices, Morris amassed a considerable estate, probably through his property transactions. When he died he left assets worth more than £17,000.

Charles Morris's tenure as surveyor general emphasizes the continuity of office and administration which characterized the terms of the three Morrises. Although his death attracted little attention, Morris had been friends with such prominent Nova Scotians as Simeon PERKINS, and had been magnanimous towards critics such as Francklin. After Francklin's death, Morris advised an assistant to be charitable to his heirs, noting that "Mr. Francklin was long in this Government's Service and left Nothing for his Children but Wilderness Lands."

DONALD F. CHARD

Halifax County Court of Probate (Halifax), Book 3: 256–58 (will of Charles Morris) (mfm. at PANS). Halifax County Registry of Deeds (Halifax), Deeds, 5–35 (mfm. at PANS). PAC, MG 23, D4; F1, ser.5, 3 (mfm. at PANS). PANS, MG 1, 313B; MG 100, 192, nos.17–19; Places, Nova Scotia, Land grants, Index to Nova Scotia land grants, 1730–1958 (mfm.); RG 1, 53, 136, 221, 223, 299, 395, 396B. PRO, CO 217/29, 217/36, 217/51. Perkins, *Diary, 1766–80* (Innis); *Diary, 1780–89* (Harvey and Fergusson); *Diary, 1797–1803* (Fergusson). *Nova Scotia Royal Gazette*, 10 Sept. 1801–14 Jan. 1802. *Directory of N.S. MLAs.* Brebner, *Neutral Yankees* (1969). Ethel Crathorne, "The Morris family – surveyors-general," *Nova Scotia Hist. Quarterly* (Halifax), 6 (1976): 207–16.

MORRIS, JAMES RAINSTORPE, public servant; baptized 20 May 1750 in Hopkinton, Mass., youngest son of Charles Morris* and Mary Read; m. Susannah —, and they had one son, the father of Maria Frances Ann Morris*, and one daughter; d. 29 Oct. 1809 on Sable Island, N.S., where he had served as first superintendent of the life-saving station.

Unlike his brother CHARLES, James Rainstorpe Morris has been largely unknown. The son of the first surveyor general of Nova Scotia, he served in the Royal Navy for 14 years. Exactly when he came to the province is not known, although his daughter was born in 1772 in Halifax, near where he and his family were living in 1801. That year Morris emerged from obscurity with the founding of the life-saving station on Sable Island. Lieutenant Governor Sir John WENTWORTH had considered establishing such a post at the notorious graveyard of ships and men 100 miles off the Nova Scotia coast after a vessel carrying Prince EDWARD AUGUSTUS's military equipment had foundered there in 1797, and in 1798 he had commissioned Andrew and William Miller keepers of the island in what proved to be an abortive attempt to establish a settlement. Nothing daunted, two years later Wentworth tried to interest the British government in supplying funds and equipment for a life-saving station, and in 1801 he sent one Seth Coleman to the island to report on the possibilities for permanent habitation. That June the House of Assembly voted to provide up to £600 for starting a settlement, and five commissioners including Morris's brother Charles, William FORSYTH, and Michael Wallace* were appointed to handle the details of the project. The commissioners initially tried to persuade family men to settle permanently on the island without government aid, but they eventually had to agree to wages and support. One of the applicants was James Morris.

In their report to Wentworth recommending Morris, the commissioners described him as active, resolute, and resourceful. His naval service had provided him with practical experience, and he was "much noted for his enterprise and uncommon mechanical genius," especially in "Nautical affairs." Morris accordingly received an appointment as superintendent of the island, and had his authority confirmed by the act of the legislature that established the station. He was also commissioned a magistrate and revenue officer for the island during his residence there.

The very full instructions Morris received from the lieutenant governor made him responsible for the behaviour of everybody on the island and also for the enforcement of all rules and regulations for the humane service. He was instructed to permit no persons other than those employed under him or with a licence from the lieutenant governor to settle on the island, and he was to take command of all persons shipwrecked there. In addition, he was given directions as to the disposal of goods saved from shipwrecks, instructed to explore the island, and ordered to keep a journal of all events. Although it was originally intended to have three families on the island, for financial reasons the first establishment consisted only of Morris, his family, and a staff of three men and a boy; another man, found on Sable with his family, also became part of Morris's group. Two houses, one of them temporary, were constructed, and livestock and provisions were put ashore. A flag-staff was erected at either end of the island for signalling ships in fine weather, and a cannon had been emplaced for giving warning in foggy or stormy weather. Rockets were to have supplemented the cannon, but were unavailable. On 13 Oct. 1801, the landing of equipment completed, the Sable residents were left to their own devices. Their duty was to aid castaways; their problem was to survive the winter. The first season provided the crucial test of the enterprise. Against all odds, the station succeeded, and Morris was able to report in March 1802 that the entire crew of a shipwrecked vessel had been saved. That spring he went to Halifax and added oral comments to the elaborate written reports he submitted to the commissioners. He also signed an agreement with the commissioners to remain on the island for another year.

Morris's superintendency continued until his death, and throughout it people and property were continually saved. A committee of the assembly stated in 1804 that in less than three years the station had been the means of rescuing 41 persons and about £2,300 worth of goods. The service suffered, however, from a chronic lack of resources. The money voted by the legislature was usually insufficient, and Wentworth tried in vain several times to interest the British government in contributing towards the costs and equipment of the station. In 1806, for example, Morris was ordered to send his son and another man away because there was not enough money for wages. The island's inhabitants experienced difficulties other than pecuniary ones. Morris thought at first that the settlers could live fairly comfortably by exploiting the resources of the island, but attempts to grow food were generally disappointing. Moreover, the shortage of funds meant that during the early years of the establishment no more than six months' provisions could be sent at one time, and visits of supply ships

were often erratic. Thus in November 1803 Morris informed Wentworth that since no goods had reached the island his family would have insufficient clothing and would suffer by spring. The same letter also mentioned large numbers of rats and mice, as many as 15 to 20 being caught nightly in one trap. Nevertheless, the establishment continued, even if it did not expand significantly. A report of 1808 noted that there were two stations, each with a house, flagstaff, and signal gun.

Another factor beyond Morris's control, poor health, limited his contribution during his last years. Always responsive to the call of duty, he returned from a convalescent stay on the mainland on 29 Oct. 1809, but died the same day. His son took the body to the Country Harbour area, where the family owned land, and Morris returned to obscurity, his burial place unknown. The Sable Island establishment remained at about the same size until the 1830s, and in 1867 it became the responsibility of the dominion government. James Morris had been its founder in the field and he supervised its critical embryo period. He began the life-saving service that was to become world-renowned, and he began it well. He died in this service.

In collaboration with LYALL CAMPBELL

[The library of the Mass. Hist. Soc. holds a manuscript attributed to James Rainstorpe Morris entitled "A journal kept on the Isle of Sable, Oct. 6, 1801, to June 1, 1804" (there is a gap for the period between 28 May and 1 Aug. 1802). A copy of the entries for October 1801–May 1802 is available in PRO, CO 217/76: ff.288–366. Both documents are contemporary manuscripts but in my opinion are not Morris's own work. The handwriting bears a close resemblance to that in letters signed by Lieutenant Governor John Wentworth, which suggests that the original journal was copied over by clerks in his employ. The Mass. Hist. Soc. holds a second manuscript attributed to Morris: "Remarks and observations on the Isle of Sable, 1801–1804." This report was sent to England along with the journal, and there is thus a copy in PRO, CO 217/76: ff.367–420. As with the journal, this document appears to me to be a copy, but there are drawings included which complicate the issue. L.C.]

PANS, MG 1, 544; 676, no.6; RG 1, 53; 172: 110–11; 424, nos.1–71; 425, no.1. PRO, CO 217/75–76. "[Papers relating to Sable Island]," PAC *Report*, 1895: 84–93. *Vital records of Hopkinton, Mass., to the year 1850* (Boston, 1911). L. G. Campbell, "History of Sable Island before confederation" (MA thesis, Dalhousie Univ., Halifax, 1962); "Sir John Wentworth and the Sable Island humane establishment," *N.S. Hist. Quarterly* (Halifax), 6 (1976): 292–309.

MORSE, ROBERT, military engineer and author; b. 29 Feb. 1743/44 in the parish of Lamyatt, England, son of Thomas Morse, the rector; m. 1785 Sophia Godin, and they had one daughter, Harriet, who married James Carmichael-Smyth*; d. 20 Jan. 1818 in London, England.

Morse

As was the case with several graduates of the Royal Military Academy at Woolwich (London) in the 1750s, Robert Morse received his first practical experience in the half-hearted raids on the French coast in 1758. After service in the West Indies and elsewhere, he was with the British contingent in Westphalia (Federal Republic of Germany) from 1761 to 1763, and then was employed on the construction of coastal defences in England. From 1773 to 1779 he served as chief engineer in the West Indies, but the loss of the British-held islands to the French in the latter year resulted in his return once again to coastal defence work at home.

His Westphalian service marked the point at which Morse's career diverged from that of many of his colleagues. Although he had much field experience, he seems to have discerned that the key to advancement was not the disdainful and lonely chauvinism of his fellow professionals. He knew the rights and privileges of engineers, but merely by examining the bald record of his life one must conclude that he also understood and had the advantage of "connection," and used it skilfully. He appears as a formally trained and experienced engineer who combined professional credentials with social graces to build an unusually successful career. In Westphalia he had served as aide-de-camp to the Marquess of Granby, and both there and at home varied his engineering duties with staff appointments as an assistant quartermaster general.

Morse's brief connection with Canada began in New York City, where in 1782 he was serving as chief engineer under Sir Guy CARLETON. Carleton appears to have favoured Morse, and supported the engineer's successful quest for promotion to lieutenant-colonel, obtained in 1783. By the summer of that year plans were well under way for the evacuation of New York, and it was apparent that the future condition of Nova Scotia and its defences was important to post-war British interests in North America. Possibly because he did not want to rely on Governor John Parr* of Nova Scotia, Carleton decided to obtain an independent assessment of the province by sending Morse "to obtain a general knowledge . . . and examine its Military defences, and its natural strengths and advantages." Morse was charged to study particularly the protection of navigation, fisheries, and communications links with Canada, with special attention to Saint John harbour (N.B.), the Strait of Canso, and the sensitive St Croix River area, where the boundary question was causing concern.

Morse left New York at the end of July 1783, arriving at Halifax, N.S., in August while the exodus from New York was gathering momentum. He embarked immediately on a seven-week exploration of the Fundy and Passamaquoddy areas in the armed brigantine *Maria*. Not surprisingly, he noted to

Carleton that his relations with Parr were "not such as I could wish." Parr had first learned of the mission when Morse arrived in Halifax, and there is little doubt that the querulous and beleaguered governor saw Morse as another intrusion by the detested Carleton. Parr believed that Morse thought him guilty of reserving land for himself at Passamaquoddy Bay, and as late as June 1785 he was begging his patron Lord Shelburne not to credit any stories Morse might spread in London to that effect.

The mission took much longer than expected, for Morse faced the additional engineering task of sorting out the chaotic stores situation for the Nova Scotia garrison in Halifax. During the winter of 1783–84 he busied himself inspecting fortifications in the province, advising the local army command on the repair of barracks, and gathering materials for his forthcoming report. He was styled "Commanding Royal Engineer in North America" at this period, and consequently was officially listed as stationed at Quebec; but the title fell to the senior ranking engineer in Canada, and there is no evidence that he actually went to Quebec.

He finished his report some time after July 1784, entitling it "A General Description of the Province of Nova Scotia, and a Report of the present State of the Defences. . . ." It is not clear whether he wrote it in Nova Scotia or completed it after he sailed for England in October 1784, or whether it was ever presented to Carleton, who had long since returned home.

Morse's subsequent career is a story of advancement. After promotion to colonel in 1788 and five years (1791–96) as commanding engineer at Gibraltar, he joined the Board of Ordnance's prestigious Tower Committee. He served as acting chief engineer of Great Britain, and apparently carried through a reorganization of the board. The result was the abolition of the chief engineer's office and the creation of the post of inspector general of fortifications, Morse being the first occupant, from 1802 to 1811. Until a good history of the Royal Engineers is written, there is no way of knowing whether Morse filled the post perfunctorily or governed the corps with an iron but remote hand. He reached the rank of general in 1808, and upon his retirement in 1811 was given a generous extra pension by royal warrant. His services do not seem to have been long remembered, however, for the obituary notice in the *Gentleman's Magazine* merely stated: "Jan. 28. In Devonshire Place, Gen. Morse." He was buried in Marylebone Church.

Morse's relevance to Canadian history arises from his "General Description" and perhaps his recognition from the fact that Douglas Brymner* published it in his *Report on Canadian archives for 1884*. Brymner noted that Morse had made "a suggestion for the Union of the Maritime Provinces with Canada, the Seat of Government to be in the Island of Cape

Breton." Certainly there is much in the report that is of interest, and Morse's clear style makes it very readable. His descriptions of places and natural features are brisk and factual, and his observations on natural history ring true. Nova Scotians might not like his descriptions of their weather, but they are very astute. He briefly analyses the geographical complexity of the St Croix dispute; sympathizes with the problems of the loyalists, which he attributes in part to "lack of foresight and wisdom" by the authorities (presumably provincial); and has a low opinion of the loyalty and character of the pre-loyalist inhabitants. He is on more familiar ground when he comments on the defences, and is predictably critical of the false economy which poured money repeatedly into temporary repairs while leaving no enduring fortifications. The 13 plans attached to the report are re-drawn versions of plans done by earlier royal engineers, with the exception of a fine plan of Halifax prepared for Morse by Charles Blaskowitz.

The report ends with the suggestion of "uniting these Provinces with Canada" alluded to by Brymner. In addition, Morse recommends "employing an able man to preside over the whole . . . a man of integrity and ability, with a comprehensive understanding" – Carleton?

MAXWELL SUTHERLAND

BL, King's MSS 208–9, Robert Morse, "A general description of the province of Nova Scotia, and a report of the present state of the defences . . ." (also published in PAC Report, 1884: xxvii–lix). PAC, MG 11, [CO 217] Nova Scotia A, 105: 25, 27; MG 23, A4, 88: Parr to Lord Shelburne, 27 June 1785 (typescripts). PRO, PRO 30/55, nos.5583, 8538, 8540, 9521, 9535 (typescripts at PAC). Annual Reg. (London), 1808 (new ed., 1820): 175. Douglas Brymner, "Report on historical archives," PAC Report, 1884: xi. Gentleman's Magazine, January–June 1818: 91, 377. Winslow papers (Raymond), 294. DNB. Roll of officers of the Corps of Royal Engineers from 1660 to 1898 . . . , ed. R. F. Edwards (Chatham, Eng., 1898), 8. Whitworth Porter et al., History of the Corps of Royal Engineers (9v. to date, London and Chatham, 1889– ; vols.1–3 repr. Chatham, 1951–54), 1: 98, 183–84, 189, 198; 2: 94, 204.

MORTIMER, EDWARD, businessman, militia officer, judge, and politician; baptized 6 June 1768 in Keith, Scotland, fourth child and second son of Alexander Mortimer, excise officer, and Mary Smith; m. c. 1790 Sarah Patterson, daughter of Robert PATTERSON; d. 10 Oct. 1819 in Pictou, N.S.

Edward Mortimer's arrival in Nova Scotia in the late 1780s coincided with that of other Scots whose mercantile ventures gradually redirected the province's British trade north to their homeland. An employee of the Liddell firm of Halifax and Glasgow, by 1789 Mortimer had purchased land in Pictou, the principal Scottish settlement in eastern Nova Scotia. Through the 1790s he apparently continued to represent the Liddell firm while building stores and wharves, accumulating land, and investing in lucrative transatlantic shipping. At the same time he exported timber from newly opened lands, and established himself in the supply and trade of the fisheries. The Clyde connection essential to his operation was maintained by his continuing participation in the Liddell firm, initially through Andrew Liddell in Halifax but by 1805 through partnership with Andrew and William Liddell in Glasgow and John Liddell in Halifax. In his local operations Mortimer entered into partnerships not only with John Liddell but also with John Clark on the timber-rich Miramichi River (N.B.). In 1813, all previous partnerships having been dissolved, Mortimer set up a new firm, with himself as principal and William Liddell of Glasgow and George Smith of Pictou as his associates. Nor was Mortimer's exploitation of the new land limited to the classic Maritime economy of shipping, fish, and timber: in 1818 he successfully outbid competitors for a 21-year monopolistic lease to operate the Pictou coal-mines.

Mortimer's business acumen established his mercantile pre-eminence amongst the large numbers of Scottish immigrants throughout eastern Nova Scotia and Prince Edward Island. The system by which he exchanged imported Scottish goods against future deliveries of timber, fish, and agricultural products was identical to the system prevailing in outport Newfoundland. The extensive indebtedness to his firm which this arrangement engendered made him the most powerful man in the region. Of the operations carried out by Liddell, Clark, and Mortimer prior to 1812, only those of the Pictou branch showed a profit. After Mortimer's death the debts of his associates and economic stagnation, especially in Scotland, rendered his company insolvent.

In the 1790s Mortimer established himself not only as an important local merchant but also as a leading community figure. From 1795 he was a senior officer in the Pictou militia. After Pictou became a separate judicial district in 1792, he was appointed to the Court of General Sessions and, later, to the Inferior Court of Common Pleas. Although a spasmodic attender at the Sessions, he was active in local offices and in local improvement. In 1810 he began a massive stone residence (now Norway House) for which he brought out skilled Scottish carpenters and masons; in 1812 he used these same artisans to construct a battery for the defence of the town.

Mortimer held the Scots conviction of the importance of education. He was a trustee of the Pictou grammar school from 1811 and an early, influential, and persistent advocate of the Presbyterian Secessionist scheme for establishing in Pictou an institution of higher learning where all denominations might be educated without reference to the religious tests

Mosiño

imposed at King's College, Windsor. Mortimer was both the political father and the most generous financial backer of Pictou Academy from its founding in 1815. In keeping with his inter-denominational commitments, he was a member of the Nova Scotia Bible Society, titular president of the Pictou branch of the British and Foreign Bible Society, and an ardent supporter of efforts to gain for dissenting clergy the right of marrying by licence. As an honorary member of the Halifax Scots charitable organization, the North British Society, he solicited subscriptions for publishing a dictionary of Celtic languages. He was also an enthusiastic patron of scientific agriculture, an area where Scots led by John Young* made a particular contribution in Nova Scotia. Besides being president of the first agricultural society founded in Pictou in 1817, he was an active practitioner of new techniques on his own lands.

By 1799 population increases in the distant rural areas of Halifax County had made town control of the county seats in the House of Assembly unpopular. In that year Mortimer and James Fulton* of Colchester joined William Cottnam Tonge*, a vociferous reformer intent on overthrowing loyalist domination of the assembly, in contesting the county seats. As representatives of the "country party," they received overwhelming support in the polls outside the capital and were elected along with pre-loyalist Charles Morris*, from the town of Halifax. The electoral defeat of Provincial Treasurer Michael Wallace* in this election laid the groundwork in Pictou for political antagonism which reached a climax 30 years later. Its early stages took the form of a personal conflict between the two Scots, Mortimer's rural, Scottish, Secessionist, and business view confronting Wallace's urban, loyalist, Kirk, and government position. The two men clashed especially over issues of government appropriations, local patronage, and religious privilege. After Wallace's appointment to the Council in 1802, the opposition became institutionalized in relations between the two legislative bodies, and subsequently focused on Pictou Academy.

Easily re-elected in 1806, 1811, and 1818, Mortimer as a legislator was attentive, practical, forceful, and witty. His legislative activity was directed to the promotion and defence of issues advantageous to non-urban Nova Scotia, particularly his Pictou constituents – road and bridge appropriations, improvement in the circulation of money, aid to settlers, advancement of the fisheries, encouragement to agriculture, and religious equality. In 1818 a satiric attack on Mortimer in the *Acadian Recorder* led the assembly to reprimand the *Recorder's* editor, Anthony Henry Holland*, for breach of the privileges of the house. Mortimer's early death, which left the issue of Pictou Academy in the hands of his inexperienced

successor in the assembly, George Smith, and the obdurate Reverend Thomas McCulloch*, contributed to the political and religious conflict of the 1820s.

Styled by some the "King of Pictou" and "our Oat Meal Emperor from the East," Mortimer was seen by his friends as one who "thought of Pictou and its inhabitants, almost as his own property and family, and exercised a corresponding regard over their prosperity and welfare."

S. BUGGEY

The Art Gallery of Nova Scotia (Halifax) possesses a portrait of Edward Mortimer by Robert FIELD; a photograph of the painting is available at PANS.

Colchester County Registry of Deeds (Truro, N.S.), Index to deeds, 1771–1870 (mfm. at PANS). GRO, Reg. of births and baptisms for the parish of Bellie, 20 Sept. 1763; Reg. of births and baptisms for the parish of Keith, 22 Nov. 1764, 7 Jan. 1766, 25 March 1767, 6 June 1768. Halifax County Court of Probate (Halifax), Book 4: 48–49 (will of Edward Mortimer) (mfm. at PANS). Halifax County Registry of Deeds (Halifax), Index to deeds, 1; Deeds, 28: ff.325–26; 42: ff.371–72 (mfm. at PANS). King's County Registry of Deeds (Kentville, N.S.), Index to deeds, 1764–1859 (mfm. at PANS). PANS, MG 1, 979, L. M. Wilkins to Peleg Wiswall, 11 March 1818; RG 1, 458, docs.7, 9, 25–26, 29–30; 463, docs.8, 17–18; RG 8, 2; RG 34-318, P, 1–4; RG 36, 18–27; RG 39, C, 75–131. Pictou County Court of Probate (Pictou, N.S.), wills, 1811–1940 (mfm. at PANS). Pictou County Registry of Deeds (Pictou), Index to deeds, 1771–1840; Deeds, Book 1: ff.95–96, 124–25, 129–32, 170–71, 221–22, 233–39, 251, 277–78 (mfm. at PANS).

Acadian Recorder, 7 Feb.–11 April 1818. *Colonial Patriot* (Pictou), 11 Jan. 1828. *Halifax Journal*, 20 Jan. 1812; 18 Oct., 29 Nov. 1819. North British Soc., *Annals of the North British Society of Halifax, Nova Scotia, for one hundred and twenty-five years . . .*, comp. J. S. Macdonald (Halifax, 1894), 88, 390. George MacLaren, *The Pictou book: stories of our past* (New Glasgow, N.S., [1954]). F. H. Patterson, *John Patterson, the founder of Pictou town* (Truro, 1955), 62–70. George Patterson, *A history of the county of Pictou, Nova Scotia* (Montreal, 1877), 250–55.

MOSIÑO. *See* MOZIÑO

MOTT, JACOB S., printer, publisher, office holder, bookseller, and stationer; b. *c.* 1772 on Long Island, N.Y., son of John Mott; d. 7 Jan. 1814 in Saint John, N.B.

Jacob S. Mott was a member of the printing fraternity both by family and by profession, and all the records that survive about him relate to that trade. His father was a printer, and in 1780 his sister Amelia married John Ryan*, who was to be Jacob's immediate predecessor as king's printer of New Brunswick. Before and during the American revolution Mott and his parents were resident on Long Island, a stronghold of loyalism. Although he has been called a loyalist, Jacob was only about 11 when his parents joined the exodus to Nova Scotia in 1783. In the event, Mrs Mott took one look at Parrtown (Saint John) and declared that she would "never live in such a god-forsaken place." The family immediately returned to New York, where Jacob learned the printing trade. He subsequently published in New York City *Mott and Hurtin's New-York Weekly Chronicle* (1 Jan.–16 April 1795), in partnership with William Hurtin Jr, and *Youth's News Paper* (30 Sept.–4 Nov. 1797). The latter publication was innovative in that it surveyed the news for younger readers. In 1795 Mott married Ann Hinton of New York.

Mott returned to Saint John in 1798, as a local commentator mysteriously notes, "consequent on the yellow fever." He registered as a freeman of the city with the trade of printer on 4 May 1799. Earlier that year he had purchased from his brother-in-law the *Saint John Gazette, and Weekly Advertiser* upon Ryan's appointment as king's printer and his acquisition from Christopher Sower* of the *Royal Gazette and the New Brunswick Advertiser*. The pattern was repeated in 1808 when Mott took over the *Royal Gazette* from Ryan and on 5 March himself became king's printer, a position he held until his death in 1814 "after a short illness." His wife attempted to continue publication of the *Royal Gazette*, at first leaving Jacob's name on the mast-head, then listing "Ann Mott & Son" as publishers, and finally using her name alone. She was denied appointment as king's printer because of her sex (George Kilman Lugrin* obtained the position) and subsequently dropped the word "Royal" from the newspaper's name. In spite of an appeal for public support – " as their smiles will in this instance tend to relieve the necessities of the Widow, and to foster the industry of the fatherless, she feels a just confidence that these considerations will not lessen her claim to the public favour" – she had to discontinue publication in 1815. She returned to New York, where she died in Brooklyn on 17 July 1861.

Jacob Mott had at least two sons. The elder, Gabriel F. Mott, also trained as a printer. After assisting his mother briefly in 1814, he joined his uncle in St John's, Nfld, where Ryan was publishing the *Royal Gazette and Newfoundland Advertiser*. Gabriel returned to the United States and established a newspaper, the *Blakeley Sun, and Alabama Advertiser*, in Alabama Territory in 1818. The younger son, William Hinton Mott, returned with his mother to New York.

In his printing shop on Prince William Street Jacob Mott established the first book and stationery store in Saint John. Although his contribution to journalism in New Brunswick was relatively modest, he initiated the career of the influential Henry Chubb*, who was apprenticed to him as a printer. For the most part Mott carried on the custom of reprinting large chunks of news from foreign newspapers along with official notices and advertisements. Before becoming king's printer, however, he had allowed occasional criticism of government to appear in the *Saint John Gazette*. He thus belongs to the independent tradition established by Ryan, and carried on by Chubb and the apprentices trained in the offices of his *New Brunswick Courier* over a number of years.

JO-ANN CARR FELLOWS

[There are no private papers extant. A few of Mott's accounts with the province for the period 1804–14 are in PANB, RG 4, RS24. A mortgage is on file at the Saint John Registry Office (Saint John, N.B.), Libro K1: 63. There is a letter from Mott to Edward WINSLOW, dated 28 Jan. 1811, in UNBL, MG H2. J.-A.C.F.]

Saint John Regional Library (Saint John), "Ward scrapbook of early printers and newspapers of New Brunswick and their times," vol.3 (mfm. at PANB). *Royal Gazette and New Brunswick Advertiser* (Saint John), 1808–14. *Saint John Gazette* (Saint John), 1799–1806. C. S. Brigham, *History and bibliography of American newspapers, 1690–1820* (2v., Worcester, Mass., 1947). J. R. Harper, *Historical directory of New Brunswick newspapers and periodicals* (Fredericton, 1961). Tremaine, *Biblio. of Canadian imprints*. D. R. Jack, "Early journalism in New Brunswick," *Acadiensis* (Saint John), 8 (1908): 250–65.

MOUNTAIN, JEHOSAPHAT, Church of England clergyman and author; b. 4 Dec. 1745 in Thwaite (Thwaite St Mary), England, son of Jacob Mountain and Ann Postle; m. 1769 Mary Leach, and they had six children; d. 10 April 1817 in Montreal, Lower Canada.

Jehosaphat Mountain was educated at grammar schools in Wymondham and Norwich, Norfolk. In 1777 he was admitted sizar to Gonville and Caius College, Cambridge, but did not take his degree. He was ordained deacon on 15 March 1778 and priest on 19 Sept. 1779, both at Norwich. After holding curacies in the parishes of Quidenham and Eccles (Norfolk) in 1778 and 1779, and Peldon, Cranworth, and Southburgh from 1779 to 1782, he served until 1793 as rector of Peldon. In that year he was recruited to serve in Lower Canada by his brother Jacob Mountain*, recently appointed bishop of Quebec. Jehosaphat responded the more readily because the prospect of a good salary in Lower Canada promised to help settle a worrisome burden of debt. Leaving England on 13 Aug. 1793 with Jacob, Jehosaphat, along with his wife, three children, and other family members, survived gales, separation from their convoy, and harassment by French ships before reaching Quebec on 1 November. Jehosaphat then assumed the duties of assistant to David-François de MONTMOLLIN, rector of Quebec, in the absence of Philip Toosey* who was in England from 1792 to 1794.

Mountain

On 24 Jan. 1794 Mountain was appointed assistant to Leger-Jean-Baptiste-Noël Veyssière*, rector of Trois-Rivières, but he accompanied the bishop on his visitation of the Canadas before taking up his post in September. In practice Mountain replaced Veyssière in the performance of the rector's duties, and the number of communicants rose from 4 to 18 in the year following his arrival. In early 1795 he was appointed missionary at Trois-Rivières of the Society for the Propagation of the Gospel. The appointment added the society's annual allowance of £50 to Mountain's salary of £150 as minister. In February 1796 he informed the SPG that the number of Protestants in the town was only 123, but that there were a few others at Rivière-du-Loup (Louiseville), Yamachiche, Maskinongé, and Sainte-Anne-de-la-Pérade (La Pérade). It was not always easy to reach them; indeed, the back settlements of Maskinongé were inaccessible to him in summer, the only way of getting there being by foot through woods oppressive with heat and venomous insects. Services in Trois-Rivières were held in the part of the town's court-house that Mountain had fitted up to make a church. His congregation was composed largely of Presbyterians conforming to Church of England practice for want of a minister of their own. Mountain also made occasional visits outside his mission to the Abenakis of Saint-François-de-Sales (Odanak), to Batiscan, and once to Bécancour.

Although the Mountains greatly appreciated the beauty of the countryside and the salubrity of the climate at Trois-Rivières, they felt socially isolated in the overwhelmingly French-speaking Roman Catholic community and longed at first to be back in England. Jehosaphat's hope for a rapid transfer to Montreal was dashed in 1795 when Bishop Mountain learned that the incumbency there had long since been promised to James Marmaduke Tunstall*. In 1797 Jehosaphat was appointed chaplain of the troops stationed at Trois-Rivières and was named bishop's official (commissary) for Lower Canada, a post which made him in effect the bishop's deputy, authorized to visit the clergy and to administer discipline and oaths, but not to ordain, confirm, or consecrate. The same year Mountain turned down an appointment as Philip Toosey's successor at Quebec in favour of his son Salter Jehosaphat. Mountain succeeded Veyssière at Trois-Rivières following the latter's death on 26 May 1800. Within a few months, however, he was appointed to Christ Church, Montreal, replacing Tunstall. The following year he was granted the Lambeth degree of DD by the archbishop of Canterbury.

Mountain had been at his new post in Montreal only two years when in June 1803 his church, the former Jesuit chapel, burned down. An architectural competition for the design of a new building was won by William BERCZY. The contract for the church, to be built on Rue Notre-Dame on a lot granted by government, was let in January 1805, and the cornerstone was laid on 21 June. The building committee consisted, at different times, of Mountain, Jonathan Abraham Gray, Edward William GRAY, James McGILL, Isaac Ogden*, Joseph FROBISHER, David Ross, Stephen Sewell*, Robert CRUICKSHANK, and John Platt, with Frederick William Ermatinger* as treasurer. By the autumn of 1805 the walls of a rather pretentious structure in the Renaissance style, designed perhaps to emphasize the strength of the established church, were raised and roofed in. Work soon stopped, however, for want of money. The congregation included wealthy and prominent members, but the unexpectedly high costs led it to appeal to friends for funds, and in 1808 to the imperial government for £4,000 to complete the building. In a time of war with France, Westminster wished to limit its expenditures, and feared alienating the Canadians by boldly supporting the Church of England. A government grant of £4,000 was finally made, but because of a bureaucratic blunder it was not received in Montreal until 1812. An unfavourable rate of exchange, which developed during the war, caused a loss of 20 per cent to the commissioners. Subscribers to the building fund had been assured by Bishop Mountain of a pew in the new church, but when some of them, in 1804 and again in 1814, sought confirmation that their heirs would also have a pew, a vigorous correspondence ensued with the bishop who firmly opposed the request. Bishop Mountain was also often at odds with the building committee, and Jehosaphat was called upon to act as a buffer between them. From 1803 until 9 Oct. 1814, when Jehosaphat preached at the first service in the new building, the congregation was given hospitality in the austere surroundings of the Scotch Presbyterian Church (later known as St Gabriel Street Church), some of whose members were pew-holders in the new Christ Church. The building was considerably altered before its ultimate completion in the 1820s.

The Protestant population of Montreal had grown considerably since Mountain's arrival, and after 1812 he had also been chaplain to the garrison. He obtained assistance in August 1814 with the arrival of the Reverend George Jenkins as senior military chaplain. In 1815 Jenkins was appointed evening lecturer at Christ Church, and in the autumn of 1816, with his health failing, Mountain engaged a curate, the Reverend John Leeds.

Mountain seems to have lived in relative comfort in Montreal, where by the time of his death he owned a house and vacant lot in the *faubourg* Québec and a house at Coteau-Saint-Louis; he also owned six uninhabited, uncultivated lots, totalling 1,218 acres, in the township of Wendover. When he died on 10 April 1817, an obituary in the *Montreal Herald* extolled his "extraordinary generosity and warmness of heart," while at the same time admitting his "little singularities." Mountain's was the first funeral to be conducted in the new Christ Church.

THOMAS R. MILLMAN

Jehosaphat Mountain is the author of *A sermon preached in the Episcopal Church at Montreal on the 13th September, 1814, on the thanksgiving in consequence of the general peace in Europe* (Montreal, 1817).

Anglican Church of Canada, Diocese of Montreal Arch. (Montreal), file C-11; General Synod Arch. (Toronto), Mountain–Roe–Jarvis coll. 1, Mountain A, geneal. docs., no.5; Mountain B, corr., nos.1, 4. Norfolk Record Office (Norfolk, Eng.), T169A (copies at Anglican Church of Canada, General Synod Arch., Toronto). QDA, 58 (B-12), doc.1, 2, 3; 75 (C-4): 74–76, 94; 77 (C-6): 4–5, 26, 30, 51, 54. USPG, Journal of SPG, 26: 398; 27: 76–79, 271; 28: 41–42, 130. "An account of Christ's Church in the city of Montreal, province of Lower Canada," *Canadian Magazine and Literary Repository* (Montreal), 4 (1825): 217–24. Jacob Mountain, "From Quebec to Niagara in 1794; diary of Bishop Jacob Mountain," ed. A. R. Kelley, ANQ *Rapport*, 1959–60: 129, 131, 137, 140, 151. *Montreal Herald*, 18 Dec. 1813; 22 Jan. 1814; 15 March, 12, 19 April, 17 May 1817. *Quebec Gazette*, 15 Jan., 24 Sept. 1801. Kelley, "Jacob Mountain," ANQ *Rapport*, 1942–43: 196, 206–7, 210, 220–21, 235, 256, 258. F. D. Adams, *A history of Christ Church Cathedral, Montreal* (Montreal, 1941), 40–41, 55, 60 (contains a likeness, facing p.41, of Jehosaphat Mountain by William Berczy). Andre, *William Berczy*, 60. R. Campbell, *Hist. of Scotch Presbyterian Church*, 207–14. A. E. E. Legge, *The Anglican Church in Three Rivers, Quebec, 1768–1956* ([Russell, Ont.], 1956), 37–40. Millman, *Jacob Mountain*, 2, 20, 35, 53, 55, 81, 110–11, 117, 212–13, 237 (contains a drawing of Jehosaphat Mountain by John Downman). A. W. Mountain, *A memoir of George Jehoshaphat Mountain, D.D., D.C.L., late bishop of Quebec . . .* (London and Montreal, 1866), 25–26. T. R. Millman, "Rev. George Jenkins, B.D., 1779–1821," *Montreal Churchman* (Montreal), 28 (1940), no.1: 20, 23. "Les Mountain au Canada," *BRH*, 20 (1914): 355–57.

MOZIÑO LOSADA SUÁREZ DE FIGUEROA, JOSÉ MARIANO (also **Mociño** and **Mosiño**, but he most frequently signed Moziño), natural scientist and author; baptized 24 Sept. 1757 in Temascaltepec (Mexico), son of Juan Antonio Mosiño and Manuela Losada; buried 19 May 1820 in Barcelona, Spain.

José Mariano Moziño, a Mexican of pure Spanish ancestry, was first educated in his native town and in 1774 entered the Seminario Tridentino in Mexico City as a scholarship student. He received his bachelor's degree in philosophy after just two years and on 17 July 1778 completed the course in scholastic theology and ethics. Later that year Moziño married María Rita Rivera y Melo Montaño and moved to Oaxaca, where he became a professor of ecclesiastical history, theology, and ethics at the local seminary.

His teaching career was brief. Discord arose between Moziño and his wife, and in 1784 he returned to Mexico City to enrol in medicine at the Royal and Pontifical University (National Autonomous University of Mexico). He received his bachelor's degree in medicine on 30 April 1787. While he was working toward this degree he also completed a course in mathematics at the Royal Academy of San Carlos (National Autonomous University of Mexico) and substituted in the chair of astrology and mathematics at the university.

Attracted by research, particularly in the field of medicinal plants, Moziño then entered the course in botany at the Royal Botanical Garden in Mexico City. Recognized as the year's outstanding student upon graduation in 1789, he delivered an address defending the controversial Linnaean system of biological nomenclature. Shortly afterwards, he was chosen to participate in botanical investigations north and west of Mexico City as a member of the Royal Botanical Expedition to New Spain.

Upon the recommendation of Martín de Sessé y Lacasta, director of the expedition, Viceroy Revilla Gigedo appointed Moziño to a scientific post with another expedition, led by Juan Francisco de la Bodega* y Quadra. It was to proceed to Nootka Sound (B.C.), where the commander hoped to come to some arrangement with British commissioner George Vancouver*, their nations having disputed territorial rights on the northwest coast. After departing San Blas on 3 March 1792, the group arrived at Nootka Island on 29 April and remained there until 21 September. During this period Moziño met the previous commandant, Pedro de ALBERNI, the explorer Francisco de Eliza* y Reventa, and the Nootka chief Muquinna*. The duration of Bodega's stay allowed Moziño sufficient time to compile *Noticias de Nutka* (published first in 1913), a geographical description of the area with an account of the customs, government, economy, rites, chronology, and music of the Nootka Indians. In this work he included a history of European voyages to the sound, added a dictionary of the Nootkan language, and classified more than 200 species of plants and animals. Though fascinated by Nootka Sound's attractions for the naturalist and ethnographer, Moziño was realistic in assessing Spain's official presence there. He believed that retention of the presidio offered no military or commercial advantage. Unlike Dionisio ALCALÁ-GALIANO he did not assume that Spanish control of the maritime fur trade would cause other countries to lose interest in the area, and he knew that on a coastline as complex as this a garrison of 6,000 to 8,000 men would scarcely be sufficient to guard against incursions by other Europeans. Further, even a monopoly

Mudjekewiss

of furs would not offset the enormous cost of such a force. He therefore recommended withdrawal, hoping nevertheless that individual Spaniards would be encouraged to enter the fur trade. Moziño's recommendations appear to have made little impact politically, but his manuscript was immediately recognized as valuable by the few scientists who had access to it.

Returning to San Blas and then to Mexico City in February 1793, Moziño rejoined the Royal Botanical Expedition. He subsequently undertook investigations in the present-day states of Veracruz, Tabasco, and Oaxaca, ultimately collecting as far south as Nicaragua. Early 1799 saw his return to Mexico City, where he devoted himself to cataloguing specimens. Four years later he accompanied Sessé to Spain; there he taught at the Royal Academy of Medicine in Madrid and served four terms as its president. In 1808 Joseph Bonaparte, then king of Spain, appointed him director of the Royal Museum of Natural History, but Moziño fell from favour when the Spaniards returned to power in 1812. His consequent exile to Montpellier, France, prevented him from publishing the results of his field-work, and so he entrusted some 1,400 drawings of plants of the New World, including many of the Nootka area, to Swiss botanist Augustin-Pyramus de Candolle. When in 1817 Moziño learned that he was to be allowed again into Spain he asked for the return of his drawings; before giving back the originals Candolle had copies of most of them made by hand and preserved in the Conservatoire Botanique in Geneva, where they are still housed. The Mexican scientist died on his way to Madrid and was buried in Barcelona on 19 May 1820.

IRIS H. WILSON ENGSTRAND

José Mariano Moziño collaborated with Martín de Sessé on two major botanical works, *Flora Mexicana* and *Plantae Novae Hispaniae*, published in 1888 and 1889 in Mexico City, and wrote articles on medical, botanical, and philosophical subjects. His *Noticias de Nutka, diccionario de la lengua de los Nutkeses, y descripción del volcan de Tuxtla*, edited by Alberto M. Carreño, was published in Mexico City in 1913. Translated into English and further edited by Iris Higbie Wilson [Engstrand], it was published in Seattle, Wash., in 1970 as *Noticias de Nutka: an account of Nootka Sound in 1792*.

Archivo del Ministerio de Asuntos Exteriores (Madrid), MS no.145, J. M. Moziño, "Breve diccionario de los terminos que se pudieran aprender del idioma de los naturales de Nutka"; J. M. Moziño and José Maldonado, "Catálogo de los animales y plantas que han reconocido y determinado segun el sistema de Linneo los facultativos de mi expedición." Museo Naval (Madrid), MS nos.143, 468, J. M. Moziño, "Descripción de la isla de Mazarredo, junto a la Quadra o Vancouver y noticias de aquellos países." *Diccionario Porrúa de historia, biografía y geografía de México* (1v. and *Supplemento*, Mexico City, 1964–66), 1: 1027–28. J. C. Arias Divito, *Las expediciones científicas Españolas durante el siglo XVIII: Expedición Botánica de Nueva España* (Madrid, 1968). Rogers McVaugh, *Botanical results of the Sessé & Mociño expedition (1787–1803)* (Ann Arbor, Mich., 1977). H. W. Rickett, "The Royal Botanical Expedition to New Spain, 1788–1820, as described in documents in the Archivo General de la Nación [Mexico]," *Chronica Botanica* (Waltham, Mass.), 11 (1947–48): 1–86. I. [H.] Wilson Engstrand, *Spanish scientists in the New World: the eighteenth century expeditions* (Seattle, 1981).

MUDJEKEWISS. *See* MADJECKEWISS

MUNN, ALEXANDER, shipbuilder and shipowner; b. 26 Sept. 1766 in Irvine, Scotland, son of John Munn, shipbuilder, and Catherine Edward; m. 6 Dec. 1797 Agnes Galloway at Quebec, Lower Canada, and they had 11 children, of whom six died in infancy; d. there 19 May 1812.

Alexander Munn is a shadowy figure. Since his personal and business records have apparently not survived, the only direct evidence about him consists of disparate references found in routinely generated sources such as notarial records, newspaper notices, and ship and church registers. Difficult to work, these sources do not yield a rounded portrait. But the broad picture that emerges clearly indicates he was a leading Quebec shipbuilder in the beginning stages of that highly productive sector of the city's economy. It is Munn's entrepreneurial function that provides the focus in the following sketch.

Munn undoubtedly learned the "mysteries" of shipbuilding from his father before immigrating to Quebec in or before May 1793. In the 1790s the establishment of big-ship construction in the city implied a transfer of skills and capital in person from Britain. Certainly the cumulative evidence about British American shipbuilding in general shows a heavy reliance on Britain for technology (in the wide sense of the term), capital, and markets; the emergence of a native-born shipbuilder before about 1830 is rare.

Munn first appears in Quebec records in February 1794 when he described himself as a "ship carpenter" in a notarial act; by 1803, however, he was calling himself a "shipbuilder." These descriptions superficially suggest that he rose from journeyman to master craftsman within the craft hierarchy, but in shipbuilding at Quebec at the turn of the 19th century the craft system seems to have been a vestigial formality which bore little weight in the actual economy of shipyards. Apprenticeships, which were common, were clearly used by employing shipbuilders primarily as a legal device to circumvent labour shortages, and the status of master shipbuilder did not entail any special political privilege as it did at Saint John, N.B., where it carried with it admission to the freedom of the city. The change in Munn's title is more likely explained by what appears to have been a well-observed unwritten rule reserving the use of the appellation of shipbuilder to those who operated substantial yards, as Munn did by the later date.

Beginning in the mid 1790s, at premises leased from the firm of Johnston and Purss [see James Johnston*] on the King's Wharf in Lower Town, and after 1806 as proprietor of an extensive shipyard at Anse des Mères, Munn frequently launched two large vessels a year, one in the spring and the other in the fall. In addition, a certain amount of repair work seems to have been turned out from his yards. A conservative estimate of his new production, based mainly on the certificates of ship registry, would be 17 vessels having an aggregate of 4,470 tons, built between 1798 and 1812 inclusive. The actual launchings may have exceeded these figures considerably since certificates do not always fully identify builders and no other satisfactory source exists. As with the bulk of the tonnage built in British America in the century after the American revolution, Munn's ships and brigs were constructed for the British market. His known production indicates that he built primarily on his own account, or under contract with a British agent, an example of the latter arrangement being an 1807 agreement with John Drysdale for construction of a 435-ton ship. Since contract building appears to have involved a flow of capital from the future owner to the builder at specified periods during construction, Munn's registration of ten vessels in his own name testifies to his strong financial position; he possessed, or had access to, sufficient capital to avoid the dependence usually imposed by contract construction. The source of the capital with which he established operations is unknown; presumably he drew from his family network, but it seems a safe assumption that much of the subsequent finance was generated from sales.

Alexander was one of at least five contemporary shipbuilding Munns, four of whom established themselves in Lower Canada and were probably of the same family. The fifth, Alexander's brother, James, was a shipbuilder at Troon, Scotland, in 1800 when, following the death of their father, Alexander gave him power of attorney to look after his shipping interests in Scotland. He may have been the same James Munn, shipbuilder, located at Irvine in 1803 and mentioned in the correspondence of John Scott and Sons, a shipbuilding firm of Greenock, Scotland, and Saint John, N.B.; he was one of the first steamship builders on the Clyde. A John Munn, who may have been Alexander's brother, began building at Quebec as early as the fall of 1797, and within a few years he had brought his young son John* into partnership to run a shipyard in the *faubourg* Saint-Roch, the area of the port, bordering the Rivière Saint-Charles, which later in the century was to have the largest concentration of shipbuilding in British America. David Munn,

who may also have been Alexander's brother, operated a shipyard next to Molson's Brewery in the Montreal suburb of Sainte-Marie from 1805 to about 1820, and much of his construction may have been financed by the Greenock merchant Robert Hunter, with whom he registered 14 of 17 vessels, totalling 4,916 tons. David also had business interests at Quebec; in 1812 he guaranteed the performance of John Munn and Son in a contract to build a ship for a London merchant. The same year he was one of two shipbuilders who valued the vessels in Alexander's estate, and two years later he rented Alexander's shipyard from the latter's widow.

Given the paucity of evidence, it is difficult to trace in detail the operations of the early colonial shipyards and the social formations which developed from them, not least in the instance of Alexander Munn. Nevertheless, the general outline is sufficiently clear to allow assertion that the shipyard represented a vanguard stage in colonial productive enterprise in terms of unit size, division of labour, rhythm of employment, control of materials, labour discipline, and capital requirements. Similarly, shipbuilders may be seen as a new class of entrepreneurs in the colonial setting, a variety of manufacturer as different from the contemporary master artisan as from the industrial capitalist who followed him. If only broad generalizations can be made about the work and financial structures of Munn's shipyard operation – principally from the size of vessels constructed (of those registered, between 119 and 469 tons) – there are a few precise indications of his own economic and social status. The rents for his shipyard site at the King's Wharf amounted to nearly £400 annually by about 1800, and in 1806 he paid the bankrupt estate of the London shipbuilders William and John Beatson £3,050 for the shipyard at Anse des Mères. In 1812 an inventory of his movable property (but not of the land, buildings, or cash) indicated that effects in his "Yard & Stores" were worth £1,055; as well, a sloop afloat was valued at £300, a new brig, the *James*, at £2,700, and a new ship on the blocks, the *Diana*, at £4,000. In his marriage agreement in 1797 Alexander promised Agnes £300 on his death. His estate, for which she was administratrix, did indeed leave her well established. She lived on in a newly built, substantial stone house, employing a manservant for at least one year at a salary of £20. The shipyard was subsequently leased on an annual basis to various individuals, including David and John Munn, and finally sold in 1839 to James Bell Forsyth* for £6,250.

Munn's only evident sally into a public position took place around 1807 when he became acting surveying officer of the port. Certainly he was a privileged member of Quebec society, enjoying advantages that clearly stemmed from being a shipbuilder. In addition to trips to Britain, there are

Muquinna

signs of gracious living in the inventory of his estate: two calèches and three carrioles; a lady's side-saddle; and a piano. Also, for the education of the children, Munn had employed a tutor who lived in. These luxuries were beyond the reach of his employees; one of his apprentices, for example, was engaged in 1807 for but £8 per year plus meat, drink, and lodging. There can be little doubt that they were also beyond the resources of master craftsmen, then the typical entrepreneurs of production outside shipbuilding in the pre-industrial economy of British America.

IN COLLABORATION

ANQ-Q, CE1-66, 6 Dec. 1797, 21 May 1812; CN1-16, 23 oct., 18 nov. 1807; 25 mai, 12 oct. 1811; 20 févr. 1812; CN1-49, 13, 19 June 1812; 1 March, 24, 30 April, 3 Dec. 1813; 9 Dec. 1814; 2 Aug. 1815; 4 Nov. 1825; CN1-99, 6 déc. 1797, 3 févr. 1808; CN1-145, 17 Dec. 1806; 18 Jan., 9 Feb., 13 Sept. 1809; CN1-147, 7 juill. 1804; CN1-171, 2, 27 oct. 1809; CN1-253, 25 janv. 1814; CN1-256, 15 Feb. 1794, 23 April 1795; CN1-285, 14 déc. 1803; 18, 19 janv. 1809; 11, 27 juin, 16 juill. 1810; 4 nov., 2, 4 déc. 1811; 11 mai 1812. GRO, Reg. of births and baptisms for the parish of Irvine, 26 Sept. 1766. PAC, RG 42, ser.1, 183. "Les dénombrements de Québec" (Plessis), ANQ *Rapport*, 1948–49: 180. *Quebec Gazette*, 30 March 1797; 17 Dec. 1800; 8 April, 15 July 1802; 14 April, 5 May, 25 Aug., 20 Oct. 1803; 28 Aug. 1806; 9 April 1807; 26 Jan., 18 May 1809; 27 Sept. 1810; 2 May 1811; 8 Oct. 1812. Richard Rice, "Shipbuilding in British America, 1787–1890: an introductory study" (PHD thesis, Univ. of Liverpool, Eng., 1978). D. T. Ruddel, "Apprenticeship in early nineteenth-century Quebec, 1793–1815" (MA thesis, Univ. Laval, Quebec, 1969), 58, 68, 99, 107, 115, 118, 120, 172, 174–75.

MUQUINNA (Macuina, Maquilla, Maquinna), Nootka chief on the west coast of what is now Vancouver Island, B.C.; the name, written muk^wina in a proper native orthography, means possessor of pebbles; he apparently was active from 1786 into the second decade of the 19th century.

During the early years of European contact on the northwest coast of America there was a succession of leaders named Muquinna among the group of Indians living in Nootka Sound (B.C.) who had a summer village at Yuquot (called Friendly Cove by white visitors). There is some evidence that one Muquinna* died and another individual assumed both the name and the position of leadership in 1795. The fur trader Charles Bishop was at Nootka Sound that year and he observed that Muquinna the elder was very ill. A few weeks later when he was at Clayoquot Sound, Bishop noted in his journal that Wikinanish, chief there, had informed him of the death of Muquinna. This statement is not corroborated by any other known source. In 1786 Alexander Walker* had visited Nootka Sound with the expedition of James Charles

Stuart Strange* and he noted that Muquinna the elder was "blind with age" and that Muquinna the younger had already assumed leadership. Walker described this Muquinna as "a Stout handsome young Man, with a fine manly countenance" and added that "he was the most intelligent Person we met with" at Nootka Sound. Although his birth and death dates are unknown, there can be no doubt that an Indian named Muquinna was an important leader and trading chief at Nootka Sound during the last years of the 18th century and into the 19th. His activities are recorded by Camille de Roquefeuil who was at Nootka Sound in 1817. The name Muquinna was mentioned again in 1837, although clearly with reference to a different individual, and it has been used by leaders of the Moachat group of Nootka Indians to the present day.

By the time Roquefeuil arrived at Nootka Sound in 1817 the Indians there had declined from their former pre-eminence in the area. During the peak years in the late 1780s and early 1790s they had controlled the maritime fur trade to their advantage and had become both wealthy and powerful. The provisions of the Nootka Convention had resulted in the withdrawal of the Spanish establishment from Friendly Cove in 1795. Muquinna's people reasserted their control over the site by removing whatever remained of the Spanish buildings and rebuilding their summer houses. For a few years fur traders continued to come to the cove, but the maritime fur trade was soon to pass by Nootka Sound and the Indians of Yuquot became poorer and weaker as a consequence. There must, therefore, have been considerable tension among them as they experienced a period of declining wealth, and, since northwest coast Indian leaders were expected to provide for their people, Muquinna would have been under particular pressure.

It was this pressure perhaps, along with a desire to revenge past insults by Europeans, that lay behind the attack on the fur-trading vessel *Boston* in March 1803. The *Boston* had been in Nootka Sound for several days when a quarrel broke out between the captain, John Salter, and Muquinna over a defective gun. The Indians launched a successful attack and destroyed the vessel. The only crew members who were not killed were the armourer, John Rodgers Jewitt*, and the sailmaker, John Thompson, who was spared when Jewitt interceded on his behalf. Jewitt possessed skills that were valuable to Muquinna, particularly in a period of declining power, and so for the next two years he lived as the chief's slave, making articles such as daggers for him. His *Journal kept at Nootka Sound*, published in Boston, Mass., in 1807, is a unique document which provides significant insights into the Nootkan way of life. He described the daily round of food gathering as well as the annual moves between the summer village at Yuquot and the winter village at Tahsis. In some ways the life of the Nootka

Indians continued as it always had, but clearly new stresses were developing for them and for Muquinna.

In 1803 Muquinna was still a wealthy and powerful leader: Jewitt records that he held a potlatch at which he distributed a considerable amount of property, including 200 muskets and 7 barrels of gunpowder. But Jewitt also tells how Muquinna's life was threatened by Indians who resented the fact that fur traders no longer came to Nootka Sound. Muquinna was also concerned about the possibility of retribution by the Europeans for the attack on the *Boston*. When Wikinanish made an offer to purchase Jewitt, Muquinna refused, apparently on the ground that Jewitt would act as an intermediary when another trading vessel came to Nootka Sound. The crew of the next ship, the *Lydia*, which finally did arrive in 1805, took Muquinna hostage for Jewitt and Thompson, and this temporary capture further damaged his prestige. The Indians were in great confusion, "saying that their chief was a slave to the whites." Later visitors concluded that the Indians had taken the passing of the maritime fur trade from their territory as an insult. The affront would have reflected particularly on their chief, and so Muquinna the younger probably found his later years of leadership at Nootka Sound to be fraught with tension and difficulty.

ROBIN A. FISHER

National Library of Scotland (Edinburgh), Dept. of MSS, MS 13780 [a copy prepared for publication of Alexander Walker's account]. Edward Belcher, *Narrative of a voyage round the world, performed in her majesty's ship Sulphur, during the years 1836–42* . . . (2v., London, 1843; repr. Folkestone, Eng., 1970). [Charles Bishop], *The journal and letters of Captain Charles Bishop on the north-west coast of America, in the Pacific and in New South Wales, 1794–99*, ed. Michael Roe (Cambridge, Eng., 1967). J. R. Jewitt, *A journal, kept at Nootka Sound* . . . (Boston, 1807; repr. New York, 1976). [Samuel Patterson], *Narrative of the adventures and sufferings of Samuel Patterson* . . . (Palmer, Mass., 1817; repr. Fairfield, Wash., 1967). Camille de Roquefeuil, *A voyage round the world, between the years 1816–1819* (London, 1823). Cook, *Flood tide of empire*. Philip Drucker, *The northern and central Nootkan tribes* (Washington, 1951). R. [A.] Fisher, *Contact and conflict: Indian-European relations in British Columbia, 1774–1890* (Vancouver, 1977). Jean Braithwaite and W. J. Folan, "The taking of the ship *Boston*: an ethnohistoric study of Nootkan-European conflict," *Syesis* (Victoria), 5 (1972): 259–66.

MYEERAH (Myecruh, Mayar, Maera, Mieray, Mea ire, Walk-in-the-Water; the name refers to an insect that travels on the water's surface), Wyandot chief; fl. 1805–16; d. *c.* 1817 in the Detroit River region.

In 1805 Myeerah signed the Treaty of Fort Industry by which a number of Indian tribes, including the Wyandots, ceded part of what is now northern Ohio to the United States, and in subsequent years he was prominent in land negotiations with the Americans. By the time of the War of 1812 he had become the acknowledged leader and main spokesman of the Wyandots living by the Detroit River in the vicinity of Brownstown (near Trenton, Mich.). Myeerah tried to pursue policies favourable to the Wyandots rather than simply pro-British or pro-American. More than once he pointed out that the British had deserted the Indians on previous occasions, but he also caused consternation among the Wyandots by throwing away his American medal when visiting Washington, D.C., in the winter of 1808–9.

On the eve of the War of 1812 Myeerah cast his influence on the side of neutrality, but under considerable pressure from the British and the Wyandot chief Roundhead [STAYEGHTHA] he joined the British and went to the vicinity of Fort Malden (Amherstburg), Upper Canada, where other Indians were gathered. He fought at Maguaga (Wyandotte), near his home, in August 1812, participated in the capture of Detroit the same month, and was at the battle of Frenchtown in January 1813.

Myeerah did not, however, identify Indian interests with the British cause to the extent that Roundhead or TECUMSEH did. When in the late summer of 1813 American general William Henry Harrison prepared to advance in the Detroit River region, Myeerah secretly informed the Americans that he would break from the British. At first he suggested coming to their aid once they reached Sandwich (Windsor), Upper Canada, but he decided instead to withdraw from any action to avoid the possibility that the Indian-hating American militia would attack him and his followers in spite of their intention to desert the British. Thus he simply retired from the field as the Americans advanced, notified Harrison, and allowed the general to direct his movements. On 14 October, after the battle of Moraviantown, he signed an armistice with the Americans. When a formal treaty between the Wyandots and the Americans was made in July 1814 Myeerah did not attend because he was too ill to travel, but he was acknowledged by a Wyandot chief at the council as the "principal chief" of the Brownstown band. In September 1815 he signed the Treaty of Spring Wells, near Detroit, a document that recorded the peace between the United States and the Ojibwas, Ottawas, and Potawatomis and reaffirmed previous agreements with the Ohio valley tribes. A letter of 4 June 1816 refers to Myeerah's stand on a measure desired by the American government. It is likely that he died about 1817.

An American resident of the Detroit region who had known him in his last years later described him as having "a fine, commanding person, [being] near six feet in height and well-proportioned, and as straight as an arrow. He was mild and pleasant in his deportment."

REGINALD HORSMAN

[James Foster], *The capitulation, or a history of the expedition conducted by William Hull, brigadier-general of the North-western Army, by an Ohio volunteer* (Chillicothe, Ohio, 1812); repub. in *War on the Detroit . . .* , ed. M. M. Quaife (Chicago, 1940), 211. *Indian affairs: laws and treaties*, comp. C. J. Kappler ([2nd ed.], 2v., Washington, 1904), 2: 78, 117–19. *Letter book of the Indian agency at Fort Wayne, 1809–1815*, ed. Gayle Thornbrough (Indianapolis, Ind., 1961), 35. *Messages and letters of William Henry Harrison*, ed. Logan Esarey (2v., Indianapolis, 1922), 2:

537, 573. *Mich. Pioneer Coll.*, 13 (1888): 320–21; 40 (1929): 60–61, 75–76, 461. Norton, *Journal* (Klinck and Talman), 285. "Policy and practice of the United States and Great Britain in their treatment of Indians," *North American Rev.* (Boston), 24 (January–April 1827): 422–24. [John Richardson], *Richardson's War of 1812; with notes and a life of the author*, ed. A. C. Casselman (Toronto, 1902; repr. 1974), 39, 70. L. U. Hill, *John Johnston and the Indians in the land of the Three Miamis . . .* (Piqua, Ohio, 1957), 81–82. B. J. Lossing, *The pictorial field-book of the War of 1812 . . .* (New York, 1868), 279. H. R. Schoolcraft, *Historical and statistical information respecting the history, condition and prospects of the Indian tribes of the United States . . .* (6v., Philadelphia, 1851–57; repr. New York, 1969), 2: 226.

N

NAIRNE, JOHN, army and militia officer and seigneur; b. 1 March 1731 in Scotland; d. 14 July 1802 at Quebec, Lower Canada.

John Nairne came from a Scottish family with Jacobite sympathies. After studying in Edinburgh he enlisted at the age of 14 with the Scots Brigade in the Dutch service, joining the first battalion of Stewart's Regiment. In 1757 Nairne returned to Scotland and obtained a lieutenant's commission in the 78th Foot. He arrived with his regiment on Île Royale (Cape Breton Island) in June of that year and took part in the capture of Louisbourg in 1758 and of Quebec in 1759. Like all the men in the regiment Nairne suffered rather badly from the rigours of his first winter at Quebec and gratefully accepted the warm woollen stockings that the nuns knitted for the men in kilts. The severity of the winter did not seem to demoralize Captain Nairne, who had borrowed £400 from James Murray* to buy his new commission.

In September 1761 Nairne went to La Malbaie with his friend and companion in arms, Malcolm FRASER. Satisfied with what he saw, he asked Murray for a grant of land. In his desire to secure as much acreage as possible he stressed the large number of mountains and marshes in the region that he had visited. His inclination to settle in the province probably stemmed from the poor state of his finances, which left him little hope of making a career in Scotland. In addition he thought that in the new British colony he could lead the pleasant life of the French seigneurs. On 27 April 1762 Murray divided the seigneury of La Malbaie in two and granted it to Nairne and Fraser. Fraser took Mount Murray and Nairne took Murray Bay, which included the village of La Malbaie. To buy the equipment and existing buildings Nairne had to pay out £85 6*s.* 8*d.*

Upon taking possession of his land Nairne retired from the army on half pay. He brought some soldiers of the 78th Foot with him, because he wanted above all to found a small Scottish and Protestant settlement on his lands. But the Warrens, Harveys, MacLeans, and Blackburns who came with him married Canadians, and within a generation the new settlers had created families that were Scottish in name but Canadian in religion, language, and customs – a painful miscarriage of plans for the seigneur.

Nairne applied himself to farming and to developing his domain and the seigneury, which he had surveyed in 1764. The following year he asked for a road to be built between Quebec and La Malbaie; this request and several subsequent ones went unanswered for a long time. Nairne also worked at implanting Protestantism; he corresponded with the Protestant minister at Quebec, John Brooke*, and with ministers in England, asking them to send him clergymen. Once again he suffered a setback, for there were then only five Protestant families at Murray Bay. Nairne, who proved a good farmer, constantly lamented that the Roman Catholic faith and its round of feast days prevented his *censitaires* from maintaining sufficient production. He was not rich, the seigneury brought in little revenue, and this determined Scot wanted to change his circumstances.

In 1766 Nairne entered into a relationship with Christiana Emery, a Scot whom he married on 20 July 1789 at Quebec. It would never have entered his head to share his life with someone not a compatriot. He had chosen Christiana because she was distinguished and had the qualities of austerity and industry that he was looking for. Immediately after they united their lives, the couple left on a long trip to Scotland. In 1773 Nairne went back to Scotland alone; by then he was the father of four children, of whom all but one died at Murray Bay during his absence. He and Christiana

Nairne

were subsequently to have five more children. Apart from trips to Scotland Nairne attended to his seigneury until 1775: he made land grants, built a sumptuous manor-house, undertook to market the products of the seigneury, and, being fond of hunting and fishing, at last led the seigneur's life he had dreamed of.

On 13 July 1775, in the face of an imminent American invasion of Canada [see Benedict ARNOLD; Richard Montgomery*], Governor Guy CARLETON gave Nairne the task of organizing a regiment of Canadians from La Malbaie, Les Éboulements, and Baie-Saint-Paul. On 12 August Nairne wrote to Carleton, offering to serve in any vacant captaincy. On 9 September he was summoned to Quebec and given the rank of captain in a battalion of the Royal Highland Emigrants, a regiment of Scots from the former 78th Foot. Under Henry CALDWELL's orders Nairne played a leading role in the stubborn resistance put up by soldiers and militiamen during the siege of Quebec; he killed an American soldier who was threatening Captain George Lawe, then captured the group detaining him. Nairne said he deeply regretted this campaign and the fact that he had to fight men who spoke his own language and had been brought up as he had. He fought dispassionately and considered the war a painful necessity. None the less, in loyalty to the land of his birth, he continued his military career for eight years, being promoted major in the army on 29 Aug. 1777. He served at Montreal in 1776, Île aux Noix in 1777, and Carleton Island (N.Y.) in 1779; at the last-named location he supervised the rebuilding of the fort and kept watch over the prisoners. Back in Montreal that year, on HALDIMAND's orders he arrested Valentin Jautard* and Fleury Mesplet*. Later he returned to Murray Bay, where he oversaw the building of the jail. In 1781 he was on duty at Verchères, where he was in charge of loyalists. He was made lieutenant-colonel in the army on 19 Feb. 1783; having received this commission, he waited a while, then in the autumn sold for £3,000 his commission as major in the Royal Highland Emigrants, which he had obtained three years earlier. He lost no time returning to Murray Bay to pursue the country life which made him happy.

Nairne settled permanently at Murray Bay but maintained his friendly links with Quebec, where he subscribed to the Agriculture Society, as well as to an association founded in 1794 to support the British government, and to the Fire Society. He was also in the Quebec Battalion of British Militia in 1794 as lieutenant-colonel. Everything was going well at Murray Bay. In 1798 the parish that had been created on Nairne's seigneury had more than 500 habitants, including 100 men able to bear arms; there were also mills, fishing rooms, good houses and barns, fertile fields, and a priest with whom Nairne was on excellent terms despite his reservations. Nairne owned three farms, each with 100 acres of arable land, and numerous buildings. The seigneury produced and exported wood, furs, and products from the white whale. The manor-house had become a warm and comfortable dwelling, well finished and handsomely appointed.

Nairne was possessed of indomitable pride and will-power. This man, whose refined face was full of goodness and kindness, displayed great strength of character, but he was sad, always sad. His repeated lack of success in imparting a Scottish and Protestant spirit to the settlement at Murray Bay was intensified by the fact that his children quickly disappointed him. When young they spoke only French, and Nairne had to send each of them to Scotland for several years. He himself saw to the education of those remaining at the manor-house. His efforts were to no avail. His daughter Magdalen married a Catholic, Peter Mc-Nicol; Mary secretly married a habitant, Augustin Blackburn, and never returned to the manor-house; and Christine, who remained single, turned out to be a socialite and much preferred life at Quebec to the more monotonous one at home. Nairne made a great effort to welcome visitors and in this way attract his daughter back to Murray Bay; guests spent the summer there, passing their time in hunting and fishing. Nairne's greatest sorrow, however, was occasioned by the death of his son John in India in 1799.

In 1802, when he was ill, Nairne asked to be taken to Quebec. There, on Rue des Grisons, he died on 14 July. Thomas, the only son to survive him, was unsuited for the life of a country gentlemen, and chose the army. He died on service at Carleton Island in 1813. Nairne's wife took care of the seigneury until her death in 1828.

JACQUELINE ROY

ANQ-Q, CN1-83, 11, 12 juin 1787; CN1-99, 9 juill. 1805; CN1-245, 3 août 1784, 6 juill. 1785; CN1-284, 5 oct. 1789. PAC, MG 23, GIII, 23. "By the honble James Murray, Esq, governor of Quebec etc., etc.," BRH, 40 (1934): 116. P. Campbell, Travels in North America (Langton and Ganong). Quebec Gazette, 26 July 1787; 22 April 1790; 5, 19 May 1791; 11 April 1793; 23 Oct. 1794; 17 Oct. 1799; 15 July 1802. Caron, "Inv. de la corr. de Mgr Hubert et de Mgr Bailly de Messein," ANQ Rapport, 1930–31: 245. Kelley, "Church and State papers," ANQ Rapport, 1948–49: 321. Papers illustrating the history of the Scots Brigade in the service of Holland, ed. James Ferguson (3v., Edinburgh, 1899–1901), 2: 410. "Papiers d'État," PAC Rapport, 1890: 119. P.-G. Roy, Inv. concessions, 5: 102–3. George Gale, Quebec twixt old and new (Quebec, 1915), 229. Roger Le Moine, La Malbaie, esquisse historique (La Malbaie, Qué., 1972). G. M. Wrong, A Canadian manor and its seigneurs, the story of a hundred years, 1761–1861 (Toronto, 1908). Marius Barbeau, "Pile ou face pour une seigneurie," Le Canada français (Québec), 2e sér., 27 (1939–40): 294–308. Ivanhoë Caron, "Le Chemin des caps," BRH, 32 (1926): 23–41. R. W. McLachlan, "Fleury Mesplet, the first printer

Natte

at Montreal," RSC *Trans.*, 2nd ser., 12 (1906), sect.II: 197–309. P.-G. Roy, "Les concessions en fief et seigneurie sous le Régime anglais," *BRH*, 34 (1928): 321–25; "Saint-Étienne de la Malbaie," *BRH*, 1 (1895): 123–24. W. S. Wallace, "Some notes on Fraser's Highlanders," *CHR*, 18 (1937): 131–40.

NATTE, *dit* **Marseille**, **JEAN-SÉBASTIEN**, soldier, painter, and puppeteer; b. 20 Jan. 1734 in Marseilles, France, son of Jean-Noël Natte and Françoise Gassin; m. first 6 Feb. 1758 Marguerite Ducheneau, *dit* Sanregret, at Quebec, and they had three daughters; m. secondly 5 May 1781 Marie-Louise Fluette, the widow of Joseph Barbeau; d. 12 July 1803 at Quebec, Lower Canada.

Jean-Sébastien Natte, *dit* Marseille, came to Quebec in 1757 as a soldier in the Régiment de la Reine. After the conquest he chose to remain in Canada. It is not known when he left the army, but in 1766 he called himself a painter, and in 1770 a master painter. As a house painter he worked on the church at Saint-Michel-de-Bellechasse in 1773. The account-book of the *fabrique* shows payments to Natte for two pictures: a Guardian Angel and a Blessed Virgin. But there is nothing to confirm that Natte had painted them; it is more likely that he had only restored, mounted, or framed them. In 1784 Natte painted the churchwardens' pew and the sides of the altar in the church of Notre-Dame-de-Liesse at Rivière-Ouelle and part of the interior and exterior of the church of Saint-Joseph (at Lauzon) in 1787 and 1788.

Before 1781 Natte showed himself to be a poor and unlucky businessman, experiencing numerous disappointments in his invariably frustrated attempts to acquire a house. Having been forced in 1766 to give up a lot belonging to his wife, in August 1770 he bought from François Lemonier a house at Pointe-aux-Trembles (Neuville), near Quebec, which he kept for only three months. Three years later he purchased a house on Rue Saint-Jean at Quebec, outside the walls, but it was burned during the siege of the town in 1775 [*see* Benedict ARNOLD; Richard Montgomery*]. The lot, on which the yearly mortgage payments had not been made since before the fire, became unsaleable. Natte was thus burdened with an ever-increasing debt. In 1780 a lawsuit went against him and he had to give up the lot, but he still had to pay his creditors the full amount of the arrears, which could not otherwise be recovered. Ten months after this incident Natte remarried, and from then on he seems to have had no further financial worries.

After the fire Natte had moved into a house on Rue d'Aiguillon where he later set up a puppet theatre. In 1792 he called himself a "puppet player"; it is not known how far back this theatrical activity went, but it seems to have coincided with his second marriage. Running a puppet theatre proved very profitable. The Nattes opened their theatre every year between Christmas and Lent, a period of about 10 weeks. In his *Mémoires* Philippe-Joseph Aubert* de Gaspé provides an account of it as it was remembered by his parents. The burlesque productions, which he describes as "brilliant theatre," were lively and highly amusing. In addition to speaking, the puppets did little dances accompanied by a violin, a drum, and occasionally a fife. Natte, who was distinguished by an "enormous mouth," endeavoured to "provoke to laughter the numerous spectators eager to hear the banter that he put in the mouths of his puppets." The performances, which lasted two hours, were normally for children, but Natte and his wife, Marie-Louise, regularly transported their equipment to private homes, including those of "heads of families in the forefront of Canadian society." The show, which amused adults as much as children, was often followed by a supper and sometimes even by a ball.

Natte used his talents as a painter to mount the shows; his equipment included not only "a set of puppets," but "everything that goes with it, such as a painted cardboard town, also little figures painted on cardboard and the theatre with its fittings." Among the "fittings" there may have been backdrops for the various productions included in the repertoire. For the sign on the door of the house there was a full-length picture of a grenadier, painted in "bright and striking colours." If credit for the farcical humour and the skill in painting required for the craft of puppetry belonged to Natte, it was "Mother Natte" who was responsible for putting those talents to work. Marie-Louise added sparkle to the shows, performing songs – such as "Malbrouk s'en va-t'en guerre" – and taking her seat of honour "below the stage" at every performance.

The Nattes had their greatest success when they played for Prince EDWARD AUGUSTUS, some time between 1791 and 1793. To enliven the show they presented for the first time a model of the town of Quebec, a miniature scene on which was staged "the siege of Quebec by the Americans in 1775, and . . . the sound thrashing the British and Canadians gave them," followed by a march-past of effigies of the royal family, which, it was said, caused the prince to weep.

It must be concluded, however, that even before they were outdoing themselves in this way the Nattes had made plans to retire; for in December 1790 they had arranged with a notary the sale of their house and its contents to François Barbeau, Natte's stepson. The Nattes continued to live in the house, and they were active in the puppet theatre until the death of Marie-Louise in 1795 put an end to their collaboration.

Some months later Natte listed "dauber" as his profession. By the time of the 1798 census he had left the house on Rue d'Aiguillon and had definitely given up the puppets. He was living in Lower Town in "a shabby house" near the "king's highway," where he died in 1803, long forgotten.

Barbeau's theatre did not stand up well to comparison with the Nattes'; the owner did, however, possess the virtue of perseverance, since he was able to carry on for nearly half a century. A third owner witnessed the destruction of the venerable establishment when the police came "to demolish" and "plunder" it at the time of the rebellion in 1837–38. The police are said to have stuck the names of rebels on the puppets and then carried them around the marketplace.

DAVID KAREL

ANQ-Q, CE1-1, 13 juill. 1803; CN1-122, 5 nov. 1770; CN1-189, 5 janv. 1759; CN1-205, 19 juill. 1780; CN1-284, 17 déc. 1790. Arch. municipales, Marseille, France, État civil, Saint-Martin, 20 janv. 1734. MAC-CD, Fonds Morisset, 2, N282/J43. "Les dénombrements de Québec" (Plessis), ANQ Rapport, 1948–49: 100. P.[-J.] Aubert de Gaspé, Mémoires (Ottawa, 1866), 517, 544–52. É.-Z. Massicotte, "Les marionnettes au Canada, le théâtre du père Marseille," BRH, 28 (1922): 8–13.

NEVINS, ARCHIBALD, merchant and shipowner; b. 1782 in County Kildare (Republic of Ireland), the second surviving son of Archibald Nevins and his second wife, Grace Penrose; m. Jane —, and they had four children; d. 21 Oct. 1812 in St John's, Nfld.

Archibald Nevins was the fifth of 11 children, four of whom died while infants. He was the son of a substantial Quaker farmer, and his roots in his native county extended back to the early 18th century, when his great-grandfather moved from County Antrim in northern Ireland to Edenderry on the borders of west Kildare. In 1800 Archibald's father died and his mother took her family to Waterford, where a number of her relatives resided. Before his death Archibald's father had sublet part of his lands in King's (Offaly) County and Kildare, and his widow now used this capital and income derived from other Nevins lands, amounting to several thousand pounds, to help establish Archibald's elder brother, Thomas, in Waterford's extensive overseas export trade, in which her brother Richard and Thomas's uncle William Penrose had been prominent, the latter at least since the 1770s. The money allowed Thomas to rent right away one of the most desirable mercantile premises in Waterford, strategically located on the quay. This property had been held by his uncle Richard, and Thomas launched his career beside his cousins, the sons of William Penrose, who had succeeded their father as proprietors of the leading house in Waterford's Newfoundland trade. In 1803 Archibald himself formed a mercantile partnership with another Waterford-based Quaker, George Newsom. This

partnership was clearly unsuccessful and was dissolved in November of the same year. The following year Nevins moved to his mother's home area near Arklow in County Wicklow and joined his uncle Thomas Penrose in the flour-milling trade. In 1805, with the assistance of family funds received from his brother Thomas, he moved to the south of County Carlow, where he invested in a tan-yard. These ventures also proved short-lived and he mortgaged or disposed of his interests in both places the next year.

Some time between 1806 and August 1808 Nevins moved to St John's. There he began to ship cod, cod oil, timber, and other commodities to Thomas in Waterford, who by 1807 had been joined in business by their younger brothers Pim and Penrose. The available evidence does not make clear the nature of the relationship between Archibald and this family firm. Archibald may have been acting as an agent for the firm on a salary or commission, or he may have been acting independently, paying the partners a commission. It is most likely, however, that he shared in the profits with his brothers but was not legally part of the Nevins firm. The company employed at least one vessel, the *Peggy*, exclusively in the lucrative passenger and provisions trade between Waterford and St John's. The *Peggy* had been plying this route since at least 1802, and under the Nevinses' management made as many as four transatlantic trips a year, bringing out primarily salted pork and butter, bread, flour, porter, soap, candles, and other items, including salt from Thomas's refinery for the curing of fish. These goods were consigned to Archibald, but the Nevinses also transported provisions for other St John's merchants. Nevins not only acted as a wholesaler and retailer of provisions imported through his brothers, but he also sold on commission goods exported to Newfoundland by other Irish merchants. Although by no means a large-scale supplier, he offered a wide range of supplies at his premises, which were located at the west end of St John's on the edge of the port's central business district. Apart from the traditional Irish supplies, these included American beef and butter, rum and molasses from the West Indies, tea, coffee, sugar, and tobacco from British suppliers, wine, brandy, and gin from continental Europe, and a general assortment of shop merchandise.

From the outset the Nevinses were also involved in the passenger trade, transporting young men and sometimes families from Waterford to St John's, where most of them were hired for a summer or more by planters in the rapidly expanding resident fishery. In April 1807, for example, the *Peggy* brought out 70 adults at £6 per person. Like all resident merchants or agents in the passenger trade, Archibald's task was usually to direct these migrants or immigrants to their places of employment, to collect their fares in the fall

Nevins

after their wages had been paid, and to remit the resulting bills to his brothers in Waterford.

Apart from retailing goods, Nevins supplied merchants and fishermen outside St John's, which was then emerging as the emporium for the island's trade. In 1808 he bought a 30-year-old Newfoundland brig, the *Success*, which he registered in St John's under his name, using it as a coaster and as a supplement to the *Peggy* in the transatlantic trade. In November 1809 the *Success*, just back from Waterford with provisions, sailed back again from Ferryland, south of St John's, with cod, cod oil, and timber products for Archibald's brothers, proceeded from Waterford to Liverpool for salt, and was back in St John's by late May 1810. The vessel completed another round trip to Waterford before going to Burin on the south coast that fall for another cargo of cod and oil. Nevins was also engaged in the northern fisheries, selling goods to George Garland, a Poole merchant in Trinity, and supplying five boats to Irish fishermen operating out of Pitts Harbour at Chateau Bay in Labrador. Much of his trade was, however, confined to St John's, and was particularly with the Scottish merchant community there and with Irish shopkeepers, publicans, artisans, and fishermen.

With little experience in the Newfoundland trade, Nevins probably attempted to expand his trade too rapidly. Between 1 Nov. 1810 and 27 March 1811 a number of St John's merchants and dealers used bills of exchange amounting to £1,760 drawn by Nevins on his brothers in Waterford in order to reimburse a Waterford merchant for provisions. No doubt because Archibald was drawing bills too liberally, payment was refused by Thomas Nevins and the bills were returned. Extensive litigation ensued between the trustees of Archibald's insolvent estate, the Nevins brothers in Waterford, and the various creditors and debtors in St John's. Archibald's insolvency was, however, due to more than a prodigal drawing of bills; like most merchants he had problems collecting debts from his customers. Writs issued by him, and later by the trustees, amounted to over £2,700, compared to £2,900 worth of debts against Nevins and later the insolvent estate. The court proceedings on the insolvency had not been concluded when Archibald died tragically on 21 Oct. 1812. While attempting to aid another man in trouble on board a ship in St John's harbour, he fell from the main deck to the lower hold and fractured his skull. The *Royal Gazette and Newfoundland Advertiser* reported that he had been a kind and affectionate husband and parent and that he left a disconsolate wife and four helpless children. The family home was assigned to the trustees of the estate and Archibald's widow and children left Newfoundland. His younger brother Robert moved to St John's and re-established the trade with Thomas in Waterford until one of the fires of 1817 destroyed their stores on Water Street. Thomas Nevins then withdrew from the Newfoundland passenger and provisions trade and focused instead on the growing emigrant traffic from Waterford's hinterland to the North American mainland, especially to the port of Quebec, and the concomitant timber-exporting business. He was one of the few Waterford merchants to adapt successfully his Newfoundland operations to the circumstances of trade with the mainland.

Archibald Nevins was of no importance politically, and his commercial career can hardly be considered a success. His activities are, however, important in the context of the period. Since at least the mid 18th century the Quaker merchants in Waterford had been important suppliers of provisions, on a commission basis, to West Country merchants engaged in the Newfoundland cod fishery. As in most other parts of the British Isles the Quaker merchant community in Waterford was a closely knit group which confined their mercantile associations as much as possible to immediate members of the family, close relatives, or fellow members of the Society of Friends. The typical trading arrangement involved a father and one or two sons or a combination of two or more brothers. Marriage was an important mechanism in the creation of such partnerships, the property and capital from marriage settlements frequently forming the basis for the establishment of mercantile trade. The Nevins family epitomized these patterns, but departed from Waterford Quaker trading tradition with Archibald's departure for St John's. Apart from one other family, there is no evidence of other Irish Quaker merchants taking up residence in Newfoundland despite their substantial trade with the island. The Nevinses were also unusual in operating their own ships; the other Waterford Quakers preferred to sell directly to English houses, whose ships called each spring to collect the goods at Waterford's quay. This attempt by the Nevinses towards vertical integration of the trade came in a period of transition when the old migratory fishery was being supplanted by a resident one. The intensive shipping of supplies and passengers (the vast majority of the latter now emigrants and not migratory fishermen) on the outbound voyages between Waterford and St John's was an adaptation to the rapidly changing conditions of the Newfoundland cod fishery during the Napoleonic Wars. A number of other Waterford merchants, almost all Catholic and mainly small-scale, attempted to develop similar operations, as did some of the St John's–based merchants. Most were, however, obliterated by the uncertain nature of the fish trade during and after the Napoleonic Wars.

JOHN MANNION

Maritime Hist. Group Arch., Richard Fogarty, Waterford, ledger, 1 Nov. 1810–1 Nov. 1813. PANL, GN 2/1, 19; GN 5/1/A/1-1816, minute-books, 29 July, 16 Sept.; GN

624

5/2/A/1-1812, minute-books: 66–67. Phoenix Assurance Company Ltd. (London), Jenkin Jones, report to Matthew Wilson on St John's, 6 June 1809 (photocopy at PANL). Registry of Deeds (Dublin), items 345911, 363453, 371338, 376379, 377468, 386821, 389420, 393844. Religious Soc. of Friends Hist. Library (Dublin), Nevins pedigree, comp. T. H. Webb; Waterford Meeting, reg. *Reg. of shipping*, 1802–10. *Ramsey's Waterford Chronicle* (Waterford, Republic of Ire.), 21 Aug., 9 Dec. 1817. *Royal Gazette* (St John's), 16 Aug. 1810; 13 June 1811; 2, 16 Jan., 22 Oct., 19 Nov. 1812; 15 April, 15 July 1813. *Waterford Mirror* (Waterford), 27 Nov. 1803; 23 March 1804; 26 March, 21 Dec. 1806; 28 April, 13 July, 15 Aug., 31 Dec. 1807; 24 April, 11 July, 23 Aug. 1808; 18 Jan. 1810.

NEWMAN, ROBERT, ship's captain, agent, and merchant; baptized 9 Dec. 1735 in Dartmouth, England, eldest son of Robert Newman and Mary Holdsworth; m. 1760 Ann Holdsworth; they had no children; d. 30 July 1803 in Dartmouth.

To be a merchant in the Newfoundland cod fishery during the years between 1600 and 1800, when it was carried on as a migratory trade from the southwestern counties of England, was to engage in a highly speculative undertaking where profits at times could be enormous. Unfortunately, for much of the period profits were marginal and hard to come by, and a fortune made in a few years could be, and often was, dissipated before the death of the first generation of entrepreneurs. Thus the fishery was characterized by a continuous turnover in the dominant merchant families. Few managed to establish dynasties lasting more than two or at most three generations, but there were a handful of families who traded to Newfoundland for more than one hundred years. The Newman family, however, were unique in that they appear to have become involved in the fishery almost from its commencement and did not withdraw from Newfoundland until 1907. The family were domiciled at Dartmouth and Totnes in south Devon by 1395, when they were shipping English cloth and salt fish to Bordeaux (France) and Portugal in exchange for wine. In 1589 John Newman had two vessels in the Newfoundland fishery, and for the next 300 years every generation of Newmans had its representative in the trade. One of the first families to become West Country–Newfoundland merchants, they were the last to withdraw. It is not surprising, then, that the family played a vital role not only in sustaining the fishery in Newfoundland, but even at times in maintaining the fluctuating fortunes of their home town of Dartmouth.

However, one generation stands out from the others, that which engaged in the fishery between 1775 and 1811. This era was one of constant boom and slump, of war and economic changes both within the Newfoundland trade and the English economy in general. It was an era in which most Dartmouth merchants rose quickly to fortune and crashed again, unable to adjust to new methods of trade which called for supplying settlers with goods in exchange for fish rather than fishing on one's own account. By 1810 only three Dartmouth merchants survived out of more than 15 who had been active before 1793, and only the house of Robert Newman and Company had succeeded to the extent that it was far larger than it had been in 1793. The company had commenced in 1779 with a capital of £9,000. By 1800 it had cleared a net profit of more than £90,000, much of it assiduously ploughed back into the business. In 1780 the company owned three vessels; by 1805 it owned 12, despite heavy losses during the French revolutionary wars. Its exports of fish grew from an average of 14,000 quintals per annum in the period 1780–85 to 27,000 quintals in the period 1800–5, when it accounted for some five per cent of the entire export trade of Newfoundland.

Until Robert and his brothers formed their company, the family had survived for generations but had managed to accumulate surprisingly little wealth. By the time his generation passed away, however, the Newmans had risen to enormous affluence and social position in the west of England, and had laid the groundwork for the lives of the inhabitants of the south coast of Newfoundland during the 19th century, when they operated no fewer than ten establishments there and earned their reputation as purveyors of "rum and religion."

The beginnings of the company were traditional enough. Robert Sr and his brother Richard had conducted their fishery in St John's and its outports ever since the death of their father in 1754. Robert had no fewer than six sons, of whom Robert, the subject of this biography, was the eldest. The third son, Thomas, was apprenticed to the house of Holdsworth, Land and Olive, wine merchants and commission agents in Oporto, Portugal, whilst the fifth son, Holdsworth, seems to have always operated on his own – possibly he made a marriage which alienated his father. This left four sons who followed their father into the Newfoundland trade, Robert, John, Lydston, and Richard. Robert first went to Newfoundland in the mid 1750s. In 1757 he was appointed commander of his father's vessel *Syren* and for the next three years he seems to have acted as the family agent in St John's. In 1760 he married and was elected a freeman of the borough of Dartmouth. It would appear that he and his brother John alternated as agents in St John's until the death of their father in 1774. Neither Lydston nor Richard had as yet visited Newfoundland; one assumes that they worked with their father in the Dartmouth counting-house.

The death of Robert Sr saw a reorganization of the business under, surprisingly enough, the leadership of Robert's younger brother John. However, in 1779

Newman

John died at the early age of 36 and the firm emerged the same year as Robert Newman and Company, in which Robert, Lydston, and Richard were equal partners. Under John, the company had at least survived the problems posed by the first years of the American revolution, but he had taken no fresh initiatives and had been content to run the trade as his father had done – operating banking vessels and dealing with the by-boat keepers and resident planters in St John's, Torbay, and Petty Harbour. Robert, however, was more imaginative and enterprising. Immediately upon the end of the war in 1783 he visited Newfoundland and on his return to Dartmouth persuaded his brothers that they should open a new Newfoundland house in the recently settled and expanding region of the Burin peninsula. The store opened at Little St Lawrence under the care of an agent in 1784 and by 1800 was handling as much trade as the old established house in St John's; meanwhile additional branches were opened at Burin and Little Bay in Fortune Bay. By 1812 the main Newfoundland office was moved to Harbour Breton, from which focal point the firm controlled the entire coast to the west during the 19th century.

Almost certainly it was the decision to move to an outport in a recently settled but fast-expanding region surrounded by some of the best fishing areas in Newfoundland that enabled the Newmans to survive and flourish during the 1790s whilst the firms of their compatriots who had remained in St John's and on the Southern Shore declined. They had an assured supply of fish and, compared with the St John's merchants, little competition. They were also in an area where the fishery was always carried on by resident fishermen, whereas St John's and the Southern Shore had always been dominated by a migratory fishery sustained by the bank fishery and the annual migration of by-boat keepers out from England and Ireland. During the 1790s this migratory fishery collapsed, and with it the merchants who depended upon it; Robert Newman and Company, by shifting to the south coast, not only avoided this fate, but prospered. Their decision to move was not, however, an isolated chance. It reflected the high degree of commercial acumen and mercantile virtue which Robert and his brothers possessed. Shrewd and hard working, they paid enormous attention to detail and, as their surviving ledgers demonstrate, were assiduous bookkeepers whose accounting system was much in advance of that of most of their contemporaries. They were unsentimental and harsh towards employees who failed them, but tended to support those who won their trust. Their most striking characteristics were honesty and promptitude in their business dealings and parsimony both in their personal lives – for despite their rapid accumulation of wealth they always lived simply – and towards their employees.

By 1800 the partners had prospered, as their contemporaries pointed out, "to an eminent degree," but a potential crisis, that of succession, threatened the family fortune and business. Fortunately, their brother Thomas, who had entered the Portuguese trade and was about to retire, had had two sons, Robert William and Thomas, educated in the port wine and commission trade. The partners cast their eyes around Dartmouth and decided also to allow a member of a Dartmouth family of little fortune to share the inheritance: Henry Holdsworth Hunt, son of a favoured doctor, was taken into the Newman clan and went to Oporto to replace Thomas Newman when in 1802 he retired to Bath. Robert Newman and Company opened an office in London where the partners' nephew Robert William (later joined by his brother Thomas) learned the mysteries of the Newfoundland trade under the tutelage of a trusted clerk, John Christopher, and one of their retired captains, James Lyon. The old partners continued to operate what was still the main house in Dartmouth, the succession now assured.

They had certainly not acted too hastily for on 30 July 1803 "Alderman Robert Newman, Justice of the Peace," died in Dartmouth. Richard followed in 1811 and, with Lydston declining business on account of advanced age, the Dartmouth house was more or less closed whilst the new generation took over from London. Lydston lived until the age of 89 but took no practical interest in the trade, which was developed even more by the nephews and their partners.

Before the death of Richard, however, the brothers did one more thing for the new generation. Between 1801 and 1810 Lydston and Richard purchased at least three manors and other lands worth a minimum of £30,000, and these they gave to Robert William Newman. On the strength of these holdings he was catapulted into county prominence, becoming member of parliament for Exeter in 1818, and in 1836 a baronet with a new manor-house at Mamhead and a taste for carefully chosen endowments which are extant to this day. The Newman family had had for centuries a highly respectable place in the local society of Dartmouth, but in the late 18th century Robert Newman and his brothers laid the foundations for the much higher social position of the succeeding generations.

K. MATTHEWS

Devon Record Office, 2537A; 2992A; DD60501–8053; Exeter City Arch., town customs accounts. Dorset Record Office, D203/A4–A5. Hunt, Roope & Co. (London), Robert Newman & Co., corr. from Dartmouth house and Oporto; journals and ledgers; ledger for Little Bay, Nfld. (mfm. at PANL). PANL, GN 1/13/4; GN 2/1; GN 5/2/A/1–1817, minute-books. PRO, ADM 7/154–55; BT 5/3; BT 6/87, 6/190; CO 33/13–26; CO 194; CO 325/7; CUST 65;

626

HCA 26/62; T 64/82. *Trewman's Exeter Flying Post, or Plymouth and Cornish Advertiser* (Exeter, Eng.). *Reg. of shipping.*

NIVERVILLE, JOSEPH BOUCHER DE. *See* BOUCHER

NOBLE, SETH, Congregational preacher and rebel leader; b. 15 April 1743 in Westfield, Mass., son of Thomas Noble; d. 1807, likely on 15 September, in Franklinton (Columbus, Ohio).

Like most Puritan ministers in early Nova Scotia, Seth Noble had experienced a call to preach but lacked the formal education to obtain a settled position in the established New England colonies. Having joined the church at Westfield in 1770 and expressed a desire to become a clergyman, he drifted toward New England's northern frontier, where settlers desperate for religious instruction had to be less particular.

Noble eventually ended up in Maugerville on the Saint John River (N.B.) in 1774. The community had been settled by families mainly from Essex County, Mass., in 1763 [*see* Israel PERLEY]. A covenanted church had been quickly organized, committed to the Westminster Shorter Catechism and to the Cambridge Platform of church discipline, but until Noble's arrival it had been unable to attract a permanent minister. Noble was called by the community as minister on 15 June 1774 and was initially offered £120 currency as an inducement to settle among them and an annual salary of £65 "in Cash or furs or grain at cash price." Setting a precedent which he would have to pursue throughout his career, Noble bargained hard. The "subscribers to a bond for the support of the Preached gospil among us" were forced to meet again on 29 June 1774, when they agreed to "cut and haul twenty five cords of wood" annually to Noble's house "so long as he shall continue to be our Minister." In November 1775 Noble married Hannah, daughter of Joseph Barker of Maugerville, and the couple moved into their new residence, built at the same time as the meeting-house, early in 1776. At this stage Noble's career, hitherto similar to those of hundreds of American frontier parsons, was significantly altered by the arrival of the American rebellion on the Saint John.

Nineteenth-century tradition has it that Noble wrote to George Washington advocating American conquest of the Saint John region and offering assistance in the endeavour, but no evidence to support this story now survives. What is documented is that the lay leaders of Noble's church at Maugerville, among them Israel Perley, spearheaded efforts to place the area under American control, and that Noble was one of the town's residents who left it to support the American cause. On 14 May 1776 a town meeting appointed a committee of 12 "to make immediate application to the Congress or General Assembly of the Massachusetts Bay for relief under their present distressed circumstances." The committee drafted a number of resolutions in sympathy with American resistance and claimed these were signed by 125 local residents, all but a dozen of the adult male inhabitants on the river. Later the same year the town supported Jonathan EDDY's abortive expedition against Fort Cumberland (near Sackville, N.B.). When in the spring of 1777 the government of Nova Scotia enforced an oath of allegiance to the crown upon the Saint John River settlers, Seth Noble left Maugerville. As a "proscribed person," he escaped to Machias (Maine) with Eddy and other rebel leaders, leaving his wife in Maugerville for more than two years apparently to preserve his connection with the community (and his salary), although he made it clear he had no intention of living under a British constitution. Enlisted as a private in the American forces on 17 May 1777, Parson Noble assisted John ALLAN with intelligence work on the expedition to the Saint John that year, returning to Machias in August. He was there during the British attack that month and preached a sermon "on the late event."

Noble did not soon revisit his people in Maugerville, although the Massachusetts authorities tried in 1779 to interest him again in intelligence work on the river. He spent the remainder of the war preaching with "full employ and good wages" at Woburn, Mass. When in 1784 Noble attempted through correspondence to restore his relations with Maugerville and collect his back salary, the church's leaders wrote him an angry letter, particularly incensed that their pastor should insist that they had left him by remaining in "immoral" Nova Scotia.

Returning northwards in the mid 1780s, when he received land in what became Eddy Township (Maine) through the efforts of his old associates Eddy and Allan, Noble ministered occasionally on the Penobscot River and ultimately became settled preacher at Kenduskeag Plantation (Bangor, Maine) on 7 June 1786. He visited the Saint John valley in 1791, shortly after the death of his first wife. In Bangor, where on 11 April 1793 he married widow Ruhama Emery, Noble found he was unable to collect his salary; despite supplements to his income from teaching singing and selling land, he was forced to leave in 1797, gradually finding new pulpits by migrating west – first to Montgomery, Mass., in 1801 and then to Franklinton, in the Ohio country, in 1806. Not long before his death he was married, for a third time, to Mary (Margaret) Riddle, a widow. At least one son of his first marriage took up residence in New Brunswick.

Seth Noble was a typical late-18th-century frontier Puritan parson, constantly following the expansion of settlement in hopes of a success which never

Noel

materialized. His career was distinguished only through his finding himself on the wrong side of the frontier line when rebellion came.

J. M. BUMSTED

"Documents of the Congregational Church at Maugerville," N.B. Hist. Soc., *Coll.*, 1 (1894–97), no.1: 119–52, esp. 119–20. *Military operations in eastern Maine and N.S.* (Kidder), 92, 99, 110, 129. "Papers relating to the townships of the River St. John in the province of Nova Scotia," ed. W. O. Raymond, N.B. Hist. Soc., *Coll.*, 2 (1899–1905), no.6: 287–301. G. A. Rawlyk, *Nova Scotia's Massachusetts: a study of Massachusetts–Nova Scotia relations, 1630 to 1784* (Montreal and London, 1973). G. O. Bent, "Parson Noble," *Acadiensis* (Saint John, N.B.), 7 (1907): 46–57. James Hannay, "The Maugerville settlement, 1763–1824," N.B. Hist. Soc., *Coll.*, 1 (1894–97), no.1: 63–88, esp. 74. G. B. MacBeath, "New England settlements in pre-loyalist New Brunswick," N.B. Hist. Soc., *Coll.*, no.18 (1963): 27–33. "Rev. Seth Noble, the first minister of Bangor," *Bangor Hist. Magazine* (Bangor, Maine), 3 (1887–88): 66–69. "Some of the early pioneer business men," *"Old Northwest" Geneal. Quarterly* (Columbus, Ohio), 15 (1912): 96–97.

NOEL, BERNARD. *See* BERNARD, NOËL

NOYAN, named **de Saint-Alexis, MARIE-CATHERINE PAYEN DE.** *See* PAYEN

O

OBERHOLSER. *See* OVERHOLSER

ODELL, JONATHAN, Church of England clergyman, office holder, and poet; b. 25 Sept. 1737 in Newark, N.J., son of John Odell, a joiner, and Temperance Dickinson; m. 6 May 1772 Anne De Cou in Burlington, N.J., and they had four children; d. 25 Nov. 1818 in Fredericton, N.B.

Jonathan Odell was descended in the fourth generation from William Odell, who had come to Concord in the Massachusetts Bay Colony, probably in 1635 with the Reverend Peter Bulkeley, founder of the town and former rector of the parish of Odell in Bedfordshire, England. After graduating in 1754 from the College of New Jersey (Princeton University), where he would three years later receive his AM, he taught in 1755–56 at the grammar school attached to the college. Soon, however, he became a student of medicine, and he served for a time in a medical capacity with the British forces in the West Indies. He then went to England, where he was employed for more than two years as an assistant at James Elphinston's academy in Kensington (London). While there he decided to enter holy orders; he was ordained deacon in London on 21 Dec. 1766 and priest on 9 Jan. 1767.

Licensed by the bishop of London as a missionary of the Society for the Propagation of the Gospel, Odell returned to New Jersey where Governor William Franklin inducted him into his charge at St Ann's (later St Mary's) Church, Burlington, in July 1767. He was also made responsible for the church at Mount Holly. He apparently continued the "practice of Physick": in 1768 he was elected to the American Philosophical Society for "his medical Character" and on 8 Nov. 1774 he became a member of the New Jersey Medical Society. In the early 1770s he found the religious state of his charges "not unpromising" in spite of "some inconveniences arising, from time to time, among us, from the frequent visits that are made us by a Number of Methodistic Emissaries, who are taking uncommon pains to get footing in this country. I have hitherto been in hopes," he stated, "that their diligence may be defeated by letting the novelty pass without any open warmth of opposition. . . ." Such success as he had arose from his own zeal and enterprise. Among his manifold duties was that of secretary, from 1769 to 1774, of the Corporation for the Relief of Widows and Children of Clergymen in the Communion of the Church of England in America. In the latter year events occurred that were destined to reshape his life.

From the outset of the agitation over imperial taxation Odell regretted the action of the British government and maintained that the rights of the colonies should be clearly defined. He was confident that justice could be obtained by peaceful means and set his face steadfastly against sedition and rebellion. Abstaining from political affairs, and regarding it as his duty as a clergyman to promote "a Spirit of peace and good Order" by "prudence & integrity of Conduct," he sought to secure "the future permanency of that harmony and peace, upon just and practicable grounds, which is essential to the happiness & glory of the whole Empire." Like his fellow clergyman Jonathan Boucher, who however showed something of the influence of the 17th-century absolutist Sir Robert Filmer, he believed that there were such things as justifiable rebellions, but that the American rebellion was not one of them. Not long after the outbreak of hostilities his true sentiments became known throughout New Jersey as a result of the interception of two of his letters. The Provincial Congress of New Jersey, which considered his case on 17 and 18 Oct. 1775, declined to censure him, however, on the ground that his opinions did not appear to have been designed to influence public measures, and because the congress did not wish "to violate the right of private sentiment." He was, however, too outspoken to remain for long immune, and in consequence of his having written a birthday ode in honour of the king, which was sung on 4 June 1776 by British prisoners at Burlington, he brought about his head a storm of hostility. On 20 July he was required, as a person suspected of being inimical to American liberty, to confine himself on the east side of the Delaware River within a circle of eight miles of the Burlington court-house. On 1 August he sought to be excused from this undertaking, offering to bind himself not to hold any political correspondence with the "enemy" or to furnish them with supplies or information, but this request was denied. When in mid December 1776 a detachment of Hessians reached Burlington with orders to billet in the town, some neighbours asked Odell to meet the commandant, with whom he could converse in French, and request him to guard their inhabitants from insult or injury. While their meeting was in progress, four rebel gondolas bombarded the town, and the Hessians retired, leaving Odell and other loyalists exposed to reprisals. Rebel troops with fixed bayonets hunted him with orders to take him dead or alive, but he was much beloved by the people of Burlington who would not give him up. He narrowly escaped capture while in hiding in a secret chamber of a house occupied by Margaret Morris, a Quaker who had befriended him. On 18 December he was able to flee to the British lines in New York, but he was compelled to leave his wife and children behind and was not reunited with them until 1779.

As a result of the confiscation of his property, which soon followed, Odell found himself in financial difficulties. He continued to receive support from the SPG, however, and was able to add to it 6s. a day as chaplain of the Pennsylvania Loyalists, and later of the King's American Dragoons, as well as occasional fees for services rendered the authorities, mainly in the translation of documents. In 1777 he was appointed by Sir William Howe, the commander-in-chief of the British forces, as superintendent of the printing office and of periodical publications in Philadelphia, Pa. Almost by chance he became involved in the Arnold–André affair. When in the spring of 1779 Benedict ARNOLD, probably the ablest general in the service of the revolted colonies, determined to change sides should a settlement profitable to himself be arrived at, he got in touch with Joseph Stansbury, a poet and merchant of Philadelphia, who in turn communicated with Odell. On

hearing the news Sir Henry Clinton, the commander-in-chief, and John André, Clinton's aide-de-camp, could scarcely believe their ears, but they decided to make cautious and hesitant responses to Arnold's overtures. Odell coded and decoded the messages in his house in Wall Street, New York, which became the terminus of this correspondence. It had already lasted some months when Arnold broke it off late in the summer of 1779, partly through fear of detection but mostly because he felt the British authorities did not sufficiently value his proposed services. When negotiations were resumed in the summer of 1780 they eventuated in Arnold's defection and André's capture and execution as a spy on the orders of George Washington.

Odell considered his activities as a confidential agent more important than his propagandist writings. Winthrop Sargent, the 19th-century editor of *The loyal verses of Joseph Stansbury and Doctor Jonathan Odell*, was, however, to refer to these men as "undoubtedly the two most important loyal versifiers of the time." Of Odell, Moses Coit Tyler, the author of *The literary history of the American revolution*, writes, "As a satirist, no one on that side of the controversy approaches Odell, either in passionate energy of thought or in pungency and polish of style. . . ."

Satire in prose and verse, but particularly the latter, had become the principal weapon in the literary warfare of both sides. Odell's purpose was to arouse and encourage the loyalists, sometimes through boisterous drinking-songs, but usually through attacks on the rebellious whigs involving denigration and ridicule. In the latter he followed the models of English classical satire as perfected by John Dryden, Alexander Pope, and others, particularly Charles Churchill. The habit of expressing himself in verse stemmed from his early years. "A welcome home to the Twenty-Third Regiment," written after the treaty of 1763, and a piece composed two years later, "On Pope's garden at Twickenham," indicate that the poems, satirical and otherwise, written during the Revolutionary War were not the work of a novice. Vigorous, filled with invective, hostile without reserve of any kind, they were clearly the expression of a mind inflamed by the passions of civil conflict. Many appeared in *Rivington's New-York Gazette*, a number in the *Royal Pennsylvania Gazette*, both widely read. In their virulence some of the poems went beyond the "decent, well-meant essays" promised to Sir Henry Clinton by Governor Franklin, Odell's patron. Generals, congressmen, officers of government, and "hired scribblers" are seen to be "Swarming like maggots, who the carcass scour/Of some poor ox, and as they crawl devour." The most respected leaders among the whigs – John Jay, Samuel Chase, Robert Morris – were not spared, and

Odell

only a grudging acknowledgement of merit was accorded to Gouverneur Morris. Henry Laurens of South Carolina alone escaped unscathed, though he was president of Congress. Perhaps Odell's most powerful satire was "The American times," which once was attributed to Dr Myles Cooper and which appeared over the pseudonym Camillo Querno. Here the poet calls before him those he holds responsible for the crime of the revolution, namely the fallen angels, who, able temporarily to leave Pandemonium, take on human form and wreak havoc in earthly society. For this device Odell may have been indebted to John Milton.

The period following the end of the war in 1783 was a time of great anxiety for the thousands of loyalists crowded within the British lines. It seemed to many that the terms of the Treaty of Paris had left them abandoned to their enemies at the conclusion of a conflict that had been marked on both sides by acts of savagery. Nevertheless, when it was learned that a refuge would be provided in the northern provinces, some of the leading spirits among them began to anticipate future needs, such as provision for the education of their children, and Odell was among a number who, on 8 March 1783, petitioned for the establishment of a college in Nova Scotia. But the immediate need confronting the refugees was to find some means of achieving at least a bare survival on reaching their new home. In 1784 those close to government canvassed their friends and patrons in the hope of obtaining public office in the province that was to be carved out of northwestern Nova Scotia, a measure in support of which Odell had advanced cogent arguments, as had Edward WINSLOW, the muster-master general of the loyalist corps, and his friend Ward Chipman*. When General Henry Edward Fox declined the governorship of New Brunswick, Winslow lost his chance for the provincial secretaryship, which was to go to Odell whose services had brought him into the public eye. He had acted from 1781 as assistant to Sampson Salter Blowers*, secretary to the board of directors of the Associated Loyalists, and had been appointed on 1 July 1783 as an assistant secretary to Sir Guy CARLETON, the commander of the British forces and the officer responsible for the evacuation. In December 1783 he had gone with Carleton to England, where he attended a royal levee and caught a glimpse of the monarch whose virtues and reign had so often been the inspiration of his muse. He had apparently hoped at one point to be named bishop of Nova Scotia or New York; however, when in the summer of 1784 Carleton's brother, Lieutenant-Colonel Thomas CARLETON, accepted the governorship of the new, largely loyalist province, Odell was appointed secretary, registrar, and clerk of the Council at a salary of £1,000 per annum. Odell did what he could for Winslow, a man of generous nature

who bore Odell no ill will for accepting the position which he himself had hoped to receive – although late in 1800 he gave vent to a fit of exasperation when he wrote of Odell: "His habits & manners are such as in the days of superstition might have suited a High priest of the order of Melchisedec, but are ill calculated for a civil department. His hauteur is so disgusting that he has become completely obnoxious. . . ." The fit apparently did not last long for he almost immediately added, "I really have no personal prejudices against this man."

One of Odell's first duties after arriving in New Brunswick in November 1784 was to accompany Carleton, William HAZEN, and Thomas Knox over the 90 miles of the frozen Saint John River to St Anne's Point, which they chose as the site of the future capital of the province. On 22 Feb. 1785 the governor in council ordered that immediate steps be taken to establish the new settlement, on the site of an old Acadian village; it was to be called Fredericstown in honour of one of the sons of George III. This place was to be Odell's home for the rest of his life. He lost no time in establishing himself there, and was fortunate in obtaining grants adjacent to the glebe land, on which Christ Church was soon to be built. Here he erected a new house, incorporating one already constructed, as substantial as any in the settlement. On 2 May 1796 he petitioned for additional holdings, and eventually the family came into possession of one of the largest estates in the area. Yet an observer wrote on 2 Dec. 1804 that "except merchants, no one is rich here." Social position, indeed, rested rather on the holding of office, church membership, and the possession of education and cultivated tastes. Odell attained a leading position from the beginning. When the New Brunswick academy, established as early as 1785, received its university charter in 1800, Odell was named as one of its governors together with the chief justice, George Duncan LUDLOW, the attorney general, Jonathan Bliss*, and a number of other prominent citizens. Until his retirement in 1812, when he was succeeded by his son, William Franklin Odell* (father and son together held the influential office of provincial secretary for a period of 60 years), he helped to mould the early institutions of the province, and exercised a paramount influence on political decisions, partly, it is true, because of his close personal relationship with the province's first governor.

Yet scope for the exercise of constructive talents remained limited because of the prolonged economic depression incidental to the French revolutionary wars. Even after 20 years Fredericton remained a village, though a pleasant one "scattered on a delightful common of the richest sheep pasture I ever saw," wrote Lady Hunter, wife of the senior officer on this station. There were, she observed, only 120 houses, "some very pretty, all comfortable-looking," and almost everyone had a garden. Although the diminutive capital remained largely unconnected by roads with the outside world during Odell's lifetime, the first steamboat, the *General Smythe*, was launched on the waters of the Saint John – a harbinger of change – two years before his death. Nevertheless, the frequency of balls and gregorys enlivened the social life of the place, the former marking events for which Odell wrote suitable songs and odes. On one noteworthy occasion he composed a piece sung to the tune of "Nottingham ale" in honour of Lord Nelson. It was performed in the midst of decorations so enchanting – among them a brilliant transparency of the *Victory* engaging the French and Spanish flagships, with their masts falling, and four grenadiers in full dress and arms standing at attention under arches made of evergreens – that one young lady exclaimed, "Oh, ma'am, such a place as I would wish to spend all my days in, and go to after I was dead." To the splendour of the occasion the Misses Odell contributed by their handiwork. Although Odell thus continued to write for public occasions, he also indulged in personal tributes: one to Lieutenant Governor Thomas Carleton on his departure for England in 1803; another in praise of Lady Hunter, who found him "a wonderful old man; so much life, spirit, and activity are rarely to be met with at his advanced period of life." He was not so old as to be unable to greet the War of 1812 with a "Salute to neighbour Madison," a tribute to British arms at Queenston Heights, and the like. His address to his wife "On our thirty-ninth wedding day," 6 May 1810, struck an unaccustomed note of personal emotion and tender sentiment.

Although one of his last poems was suffused with melancholy as he contemplated his own dissolution, it was in marked contrast to his generally hopeful temper and his faith in the righteousness of his conduct throughout his life. Whereas Joseph Stansbury had returned to Philadelphia after the war and had made peace with his erstwhile rebel neighbours there, Odell remained steadfast. Tyler, in an often cited passage of his *Literary history of the American revolution*, wrote: "He died, without ever taking back a word, or uttering an apology, or flinching from an opinion – a proud, gritty member of a political party that had been defeated, but never conquered or convinced."

ALFRED G. BAILEY

Jonathan Odell's poems appear in a number of 19th- and 20th-century anthologies, including *The loyalist poetry of the revolution*, ed. Winthrop Sargent (Philadelphia, 1857); the same editor's *The loyal verses of Joseph Stansbury and Doctor Jonathan Odell; relating to the American revolution* (Albany, N.Y., 1860); *The book of Canadian poetry: a critical and historical anthology*, ed. A. J. M. Smith (rev. ed., Chicago and Toronto, 1949); *Narrative verse satire in Maritime Canada, 1779–1814*, ed. T. B. Vincent (Ottawa, 1978); and *The New Brunswick poems of Jonathan Odell: a selection* (Kingston, Ont., 1982). A chronological listing of Odell's poetry is provided by *Jonathan Odell: an annotated chronology of the poems, 1759–1818*, comp. T. B. Vincent (Kingston, 1980).

N.B. Museum, Odell family papers. UNBL, MG H2; "Select loyalist memorials: the appeals for compensation for losses and sacrifices to the British parliamentary commission of 1783 to 1789 from loyalists of the American revolution who came to Canada," ed. W. S. MacNutt (photocopy of typescript, n.d.). USPG, B, 21, no.261; 24, nos.140, 146, 149. *American arch.* (Clarke and Force), 4th ser., 3: 1227; 6: 1651, 1656. *The journal of Gen. Sir Martin Hunter, G.C.M.G., C.H., and some letters of his wife, Lady Hunter . . .* , ed. and comp. Anne Hunter and Elizabeth Bell (Edinburgh, 1894). [Margaret Morris], *Margaret Morris: her journal . . .* , ed. J. W. Jackson (Philadelphia, 1949). *Winslow papers* (Raymond).

DAB. James McLachlan et al., *Princetonians, 1748–1768: a biographical dictionary* (Princeton, N.J., 1976). Sabine, *Biog. sketches of loyalists*. R. P. Baker, *A history of English-Canadian literature to the confederation; its relation to the literature of Great Britain and the United States* (Cambridge, Mass., 1920). Wallace Brown, *The good Americans: the loyalists in the American revolution* (New York, 1969). I. L. Hill, *Fredericton, New Brunswick, British North America* ([Fredericton, 1968?]). H. Y. Hind, *The University of King's College, Windsor, Nova Scotia, 1790–1890* (New York, 1890), 8. J. W. Lawrence, *Footprints; or, incidents in early history of New Brunswick, 1783–1883* (Saint John, N.B., 1883), 67–68. D. A. Loughlin, "The development of social and intellectual attitudes as revealed in the literature of New Brunswick" (MA thesis, Univ. of N.B., Fredericton, 1948), 74–111. V. L. Parrington, *Main currents in American thought* (3v., New York, 1927–30; repub. 3v. in 1, 1930; repub. 2v. to date, 1954–), 1. M. C. Tyler, *The literary history of the American revolution, 1763–1783* (2v., New York and London, 1897), 2. Carl Van Doren, *Secret history of the American revolution* (Garden City, N.Y., 1941). Wright, *Loyalists of N.B.* Jonas Howe, "The King's New Brunswick Regiment, 1793–1802," N.B. Hist. Soc., *Coll.*, 1 (1894–97), no.1: 36. Rufus King, "Memoir of Hon. William Hunter Odell," *New-England Hist. and Geneal. Reg.* (Boston), 46 (1892): 20–22.

ODESERUNDIYE. *See* DESERONTYON

O'DONEL (O'Donnell), JAMES LOUIS, Roman Catholic priest, Franciscan, and vicar apostolic; b. *c.* 1737 near Knocklofty (Republic of Ireland), son of Michael O'Donel and Ann Crosby; d. 1 April 1811 in Waterford (Republic of Ireland).

James Louis O'Donel and his brother Michael, the sons of a prosperous farmer, received their initial education from a private tutor. Both boys were then sent to Limerick to study the classics. There they expressed a wish to enter the priesthood, and were admitted into the Franciscan order. Some time about

O'Donel

the mid 1760s James Louis was sent to the Irish Franciscan college of St Isidore's at Rome (Italy), where he was ordained in 1770. After teaching philosophy and theology at Prague (Czechoslovakia) for several years, in 1777 he returned to Ireland, where he became prior of the Franciscan monastery at Waterford. On 19 July 1779 he was elected provincial of the Irish Franciscans, a position he held until 22 July 1781. While at Waterford he established a reputation as "a popular and pathetic preacher."

It was this popularity that was to be partially responsible for O'Donel's appointment to Newfoundland. For much of the 18th century the Roman Catholic population of that island had been prevented from freely exercising their religion, a series of decrees from naval governors such as Richard Dorrill* threatening fines and imprisonment for those found celebrating or attending Catholic services. Some priests arrived nevertheless, but they were forced to minister to the inhabitants secretly and under difficult conditions. By 1783, however, legal obstacles to religious liberty for Roman Catholics had been removed, and Governor John Campbell gave permission to the Roman Catholics of St John's to build a chapel. Late the same year some merchants with Waterford connections, acting on behalf of the inhabitants of St John's, applied to Bishop William Egan of Waterford for an authorized priest, who would have sufficient faculties and jurisdiction over all other priests on the island. The merchants' choice was O'Donel. Not only was he popular in the diocese of Waterford, whence came the great majority of Newfoundland's Roman Catholics, but he was also fluent in Irish, a distinct advantage for his proposed mission. Consultations followed between Egan, O'Donel, and Bishop James Talbot, vicar apostolic of the London district and the official responsible for Newfoundland, which resulted in Talbot's conditionally authorizing O'Donel as vicar general for the mission. In the mean time the matter had been referred to the Sacred Congregation of Propaganda in Rome. By decrees of 17 and 30 May 1784 Pope Pius VI constituted Newfoundland as a separate ecclesiastical territory immediately subject to the Holy See, and named O'Donel its superior (prefect apostolic).

O'Donel had meanwhile sailed for St John's, where he arrived on 4 July. Before he could effectively supervise his new mission, however, he had first to assert his jurisdiction. He attempted to send away all unauthorized clergy, but although some left quietly others were not so submissive. In 1785 O'Donel was forced to excommunicate Patrick Lonergan (Landergan), a Dominican who had come into conflict with Edmund BURKE (fl. 1785–1801), the authorized priest at Placentia. Two years later a Franciscan, Patrick Power, likewise unauthorized, arrived in Newfoundland. O'Donel apparently allowed Power to function as a priest for a time, but then Power left for an out-harbour, seemingly without O'Donel's permission, and he subsequently refused to acknowledge O'Donel's authority to deny him jurisdiction in Newfoundland. Although excommunicated, Power was active at Ferryland until the counter-influence of Thomas Anthony Ewer* caused support for him to wane, and he apparently left the area in 1790. The dispute had taken on a personal dimension when Power, reviving Irish provincial quarrels, suggested that as a Munsterman O'Donel was hostile to priests from Leinster such as himself.

Equally troubling to O'Donel were the obstructions he encountered from those in authority. Campbell's successor, Rear-Admiral John Elliot, had as one of his captains Prince William Henry, who arrived in Newfoundland in 1786. While stationed at Placentia he came into conflict with Father Burke, and O'Donel apparently asked Elliot to have the prince moderate his anti-Catholic attitude. William Henry's anger was accordingly redirected towards the superior. The prince came to St John's, and O'Donel reported that he had been slightly injured by an iron file thrown by William Henry. The affair subsided with the prince's departure. Two years later another of Elliot's captains spoke out strongly against Roman Catholics and, in particular, asked Elliot to have priests removed from the island. O'Donel claimed that Elliot was about to acquiesce when his personal appeal changed the governor's mind. O'Donel's troubles continued in 1790 under Governor Mark MILBANKE. Milbanke was hostile to Catholicism and was also determined to reduce the winter population by forcing fishermen to return home at the end of the season. Using the excuses that O'Donel encouraged residency among his parishioners – a charge which the superior admitted in letters home – and that facilities for absolution were too readily available in Newfoundland, Milbanke took action by refusing Ewer permission to erect a chapel at Ferryland. When O'Donel protested, the governor indicated that he intended to lay existing chapels "under particular restrictions" the following year. O'Donel spent an anxious winter, but with the arrival of judge John Reeves* in 1791 these plans were dropped. Although the superior had good relations with the governors thereafter, these incidents serve to show the vulnerability of the early Roman Catholic church in Newfoundland.

The mission flourished under O'Donel's care nevertheless. By 1790 he had three priests, Patrick Phelan at Harbour Grace, Burke at Placentia, and Ewer at Ferryland. All had considerable success in proselytism at the out-harbours in their districts, making many converts to Catholicism, in particular among the Anglicans. O'Donel himself seems to have had some success at conversions in St John's, where in 1786 William Henry had claimed that "many thousands" attended services in the chapel erected two years previously. Chapels were also built in Placentia, Harbour Grace, and Ferryland. The successes of O'Donel and his clergy were alarming to the Anglican ministers in St John's, Walter Price and his successor John HARRIES, and doubtless for that reason they were somewhat hostile to the superior. On the other hand, O'Donel seems to have enjoyed good relations with John Jones*, the Congregational preacher. Since Newfoundland was separated both geographically and administratively from the mainland, O'Donel had little contact with the bishops of Quebec, although he did maintain a friendly correspondence with Joseph-Octave Plessis* and sent him likely candidates for education in Lower Canadian seminaries.

By the mid 1790s the success of the Newfoundland mission had stimulated some of its priests and laymen to seek improvement in its status, and in November 1794 they addressed a petition to the pope which asked that O'Donel be elevated to the episcopacy and given the powers of a vicar apostolic. Their request was granted, and on 23 Dec. 1795 O'Donel was elected bishop of Nilopolis *in partibus*. On 5 Jan. 1796 he was transferred to the diocese of Thyatira, and then on the 22nd he was appointed vicar apostolic of Newfoundland and the captured French islands of Saint-Pierre and Miquelon. The ceremony of consecration was performed at Quebec on 21 Sept. 1796 by Bishop Jean-François Hubert*. O'Donel thus became the first English-speaking Roman Catholic bishop in what is now Canada. Immediately afterwards O'Donel left for Ireland, and did not return to Newfoundland until the following year.

One of O'Donel's main concerns during his tenure of office, and especially after the outbreak of the French revolution and the Irish rebellion, was the maintenance of peace and order among the Irish of St John's. Early in 1800 a potentially dangerous situation developed when evidence was uncovered of a mutiny planned within Thomas SKINNER's Royal Newfoundland Fencible Regiment, which was composed mainly of Irish Catholics. Rumours persisted that the plotters meant to join with the inhabitants in a general uprising, intelligence given weight by information that some soldiers and inhabitants had taken the oath of loyalty to the radical Society of United Irishmen. Thanks to O'Donel's exerting his influence in favour of loyalty and obedience among the civilian population, the juncture did not occur, and in the event the would-be mutineers were forced to abandon their plans [*see* John SKERRETT]. O'Donel's strongly loyal disposition was evident in his horror at the excesses of the French revolution. When in 1801 he set down a body of diocesan statutes, his priests were ordered to "inculcate a willing obedience to the salutary laws of England, and to the commands of the governor and magistrates of this Island." Public prayers were to be offered every Sunday for the king and the royal family, and the priests were to oppose "with all the means in their power all plotters, conspirators, and favorers of the infidel French." The bishop's efforts seem to have been generally successful, for in 1805 Governor Sir Erasmus GOWER could write that O'Donel's parishioners were notable for "industry sobriety and good order."

Notwithstanding certain periods of financial distress and the relative poverty of his parishioners, on whom he was dependent for contributions, O'Donel seems to have been adequately supported during his term in Newfoundland. Brigadier-General Skerrett made two attempts to increase his income by applying for a pension for O'Donel's services in 1800, but the documents miscarried. Then in 1804 the "Magistrates Merchants, and other principal Inhabitants" of St John's tried again, this time asking Governor Gower for his support. Gower recommended that O'Donel be paid £50 per annum while he remained in Newfoundland, and the British government approved. Although pleased to receive the pension, the bishop considered it insufficient, and he also wished to have the money payable during his retirement. His petition to improve the conditions had Gower's support, but nothing came of it.

These events took place when O'Donel was feeling himself inadequate for the toils of his mission. The combination of a slight attack of apoplexy in 1804 and other symptoms of general debility convinced him that he should retire, and he requested the Holy See to appoint a coadjutor with the right of succession. Patrick LAMBERT accordingly arrived in St John's in August 1806, and on 1 Jan. 1807 O'Donel resigned his mission. The scene of his departure from St John's that July was indicative of the respect in which he was held by Protestant and Roman Catholic alike. He was entertained at a dinner given by the most prominent merchants, and the chief personages of the town gathered to bid him farewell. As a further token of appreciation, he later received a silver urn worth 150 guineas from some merchants. These rewards recognized that O'Donel had kept the Irish population of Newfoundland peaceful in a period when rebellion and turmoil were rife elsewhere.

Upon his return to Ireland, O'Donel retired to the Franciscan monastery at Waterford. One night in late March 1811 the chair in which he was reading caught fire and, though the aged prelate was only slightly injured, the shock was too great, and he died on 1 April. He was buried in St Mary's chapel, Irishtown, near Clonmel, beneath a tombstone inscribed with an epitaph he himself is alleged to have composed.

IN COLLABORATION

AAQ, 30 CN, I. Arch. of the Archdiocese of Dublin, Troy papers, 1: 33. Arch. of the Archdiocese of St John's, Howley

Ogilvie

papers: 400–1. Archivio della Propaganda Fide (Rome), Scritturi riferite nei Congressi, America Antille, 2 (1761–89): 413 *et seq.* PANL, GN2/1, 1749–1811. PRO, CO 5/470–506; CO 194/35–44 (mfm. at PAC); WO 1/15: ff.21–22. USPG, C/CAN/Nfl., 1, nos.69, 81. "The first bishop of Newfoundland," *Irish Ecclesiastical Record* (Dublin), 2 (1866): 508–23. *Gentleman's Magazine*, January–June 1811: 497. *DNB. The Dissenting Church of Christ at St. John's, 1775–1975: a history of St. David's Presbyterian Church, St. John's, Newfoundland* (n.p., [1976]), 17–19. M. F. Howley, *Ecclesiastical history of Newfoundland* (Boston, 1888; repr. Belleville, Ont., 1979). G. W. L. Nicholson, *The fighting Newfoundlander; a history of the Royal Newfoundland Regiment* (St John's, [1964?]). Philip O'Connell, "Dr. James Louis O'Donnell (1737–1811), first bishop of Newfoundland," *Irish Ecclesiastical Record*, 103 (1965): 308–24.

OGILVIE (Ogilvy), JAMES, army officer and colonial administrator; b. *c.* 1740, possibly in Scotland; m. Penelope —; d. 14 Feb. 1813 in London, England.

James Ogilvie began his military career as an ensign in the lst Foot on 21 Sept. 1756, but in March 1757 transferred to the 4th Foot. He received his lieutenancy on 20 December of the latter year, and from 1759 to 1762 served in the West Indian campaigns of the British army. After his return to Britain, he was appointed captain on 30 March 1764. The 4th was sent to Boston, Mass., in June 1774, and Ogilvie saw a considerable amount of service during the American revolution, including participation in the battles of Long Island, Brandywine, and Germantown. In 1778 his ship was captured by the French off St Lucia, and Ogilvie was taken prisoner to France, returning to his regiment in Ireland in 1780. On 20 Nov. 1782 he was appointed colonel in the army.

The 4th was posted to Halifax, N.S., in 1787, and upon arrival Ogilvie was made brigadier commanding the Nova Scotia district. Little is known about his relations with Lieutenant Governor John Parr*, but those with Lieutenant Governor John WENTWORTH were strained, largely because their jurisdictions overlapped. After hostilities broke out between Britain and France in 1793, Ogilvie, acting on instructions from London, organized an expedition against Saint-Pierre and Miquelon consisting of members of the 4th and 65th Foot and the Royal Artillery on transports, accompanied by a frigate and several armed vessels. In concert with a force from Newfoundland, on 14 May they attacked the ill-defended French colony, which surrendered without firing a shot. Ogilvie returned to Halifax on 20 June with 570 officials, troops, and fishermen as prisoners; the remaining inhabitants of the islands were deported to Nova Scotia and the Channel Islands the next year. On 12 Oct. 1793 Ogilvie was advanced to major-general by the normal process of seniority.

In 1794 Prince EDWARD AUGUSTUS became com-

mander-in-chief of the Nova Scotia military district, and Ogilvie served under him for four years (being promoted lieutenant-general on 1 Jan. 1798) until the spring of 1798, when he received the order appointing him the administrator of Cape Breton. In order to placate Ogilvie, the Duke of Portland, the Home secretary, described the island as an "important Outpost of His Majesty's North American Possessions." Ogilvie left for Sydney, the capital, on 20 June 1798, but the wreck of his ship off Scatarie Island meant that he did not reach there until the 29th.

Upon his arrival Ogilvie replaced David Mathews* and became the second administrator of Cape Breton in the absence of Lieutenant Governor William MACARMICK. The colony, founded in 1784, had experienced much political infighting and slow economic growth. Mathews had exacerbated a difficult political situation by alienating and imprisoning members of the Executive Council such as William McKINNON, Ranna COSSIT, and Ingram BALL. Ogilvie's mandate was to investigate and put an end to these disputes. He immediately started an inquiry which lasted throughout his one-year term, and soon came to the conclusion that Mathews was the prime cause of the discontent. He was unable to prove Mathews guilty of misdeeds, and released all the imprisoned councillors except McKinnon, whose case required a lawyer for the defence. However, Mathews was the colony's only lawyer, and refused to act for him. Ogilvie was unable to hire a solicitor general in Nova Scotia, who might have acted for the defence, but McKinnon arranged to switch his political support to Mathews in return for Mathews's dropping the charges. Ogilvie was bewildered by these events and sought to leave the colony as soon as possible.

Ogilvie's chief contributions to the development of Cape Breton were his bringing 150 troops to protect the colony, undefended since 1793; his organization of the colonial militia after Macarmick's failure to do so (although this achievement appears to have been largely on paper); his improvement of the Sydney harbour defences; and his development of the coal mines. Mathews had harassed James Miller, the superintendent of mines, during his commencement of a new level at the mines, and had gone so far as to imprison him. Ogilvie released Miller, and despite a labour shortage authorized the digging of the level.

Following the appointment of his successor, Brigadier-General John Murray*, in May 1799 Ogilvie returned to Halifax, where he functioned as interim commander-in-chief until the return of the Duke of Kent [Edward Augustus] in September. He then retired from active service, but he was appointed colonel of the 89th Foot on 28 March 1801, exchanging this colonelcy for that of the 32nd Foot on 4 Sept. 1802 and receiving an automatic promotion to general three weeks later.

James Ogilvie's career in Canada reveals him to

have been an honest but unimaginative soldier. Wentworth believed him to be dilatory and unenterprising; Harry Piers considers him to have been "a cautious man and not popular, and to have lacked the great influence and constructive genius of his successor [Edward Augustus]."

R. J. MORGAN

PRO, CO 217/113-21; WO 25/747 (mfm. at PANS). Harry Piers, *The evolution of the Halifax fortress, 1749–1928*, ed. G. M. Self et al. (Halifax, 1947). Akins, *Hist. of Halifax City*, 123. T. W. Smith, "Halifax and the capture of St. Pierre in 1793," N.S. Hist. Soc., *Coll.*, 14 (1909): 80–105.

OGILVY, JOHN, merchant and farmer; b. *c.* 1769, possibly in or near Leith, Scotland, son of Jane Ogilvy, *née* Dunlop; d. unmarried 28 Sept. 1819 in Amherstburg, Upper Canada.

John Ogilvy immigrated to Canada about 1790, settling at Montreal, where he became involved in the fur trade. In 1792 he sent at least six men to Michilimackinac (Mackinac Island, Mich.) and three to the Mississippi country; the following year he sent nine to Michilimackinac. About 1796 he formed a partnership with William Parker and Samuel Gerrard*, and the new firm, called Parker, Gerrard, and Ogilvy, was soon engaged in the trade south and west from Michilimackinac. By 1800 the company, which was based in Montreal, had taken in a partner at Quebec, John Mure*, and jointly they ran a transatlantic shipping and passenger service; the arrangement lasted until 1811 at least. The partnership had continued to expand, and in 1803 it was known as Parker, Gerrard, Ogilvy and Company; that year Sir Alexander MACKENZIE entered the firm, bringing the total number of partners to nine, each of whom had one share. Its affairs in London were confided to Sir Alexander Mackenzie, Gillespie, Parker and Company, the Quebec business to Mure, and Michilimackinac affairs to George Gillespie*; Ogilvy, Gerrard, and Thomas Yeoward attended to company matters at Montreal.

Meanwhile, in the late 1790s Ogilvy, representing Parker, Gerrard, and Ogilvy, had begun trading north and west of the Great Lakes; in 1799 he sent four canoes to Grand Portage (near Grand Portage, Minn.). The following year the intense competition of the North West Company [*see* Simon MCTAVISH] drove him under the umbrella of the New North West Company, which Forsyth, Richardson and Company [*see* John Richardson*] and the Detroit firm of Leith, Jameson and Company had organized in 1798 in order to maintain themselves in the northwest trade in the face of the NWC's opposition; Parker, Gerrard and Ogilvy invested nearly £8,000 in trade goods. According to the trader John McDonald, Ogilvy was "at the head" of the reorganized New North West

Company, which was also known after 1799 as the New Company or the XY Company. By 1802 Ogilvy had joined with Mackenzie, Mure, the winterer James Leith*, and two other traders to form a partnership within the New North West Company called Sir Alexander Mackenzie and Company.

In 1803 competition between the New North West Company and the NWC was so fierce that, to maintain order in the northwest, the imperial government enacted a statute giving the courts of Upper and Lower Canada jurisdiction over the territory not included in the Hudson's Bay Company charter and providing for the appointment of five justices of the peace; two, Ogilvy and Mackenzie, were named from the New North West Company and three were appointed from the NWC. However, the statute had little effect. The competition, moreover, was proving financially ruinous to both co-partnerships, and on 5 Nov. 1804 the New North West Company was brought into the NWC and accorded 25 of the 100 shares in the restructured partnership. Ogilvy and Thomas Thain* were named agents of the New North West Company in its business with the joint firm. When, a few days later, the shares of the New North West Company, which became Sir Alexander Mackenzie and Company, were divided among its partners, Ogilvy and Mure received three shares between them and Ogilvy two shares for his role as agent; one year later Parker, Gerrard, Ogilvy and Company held the fourth largest investment of the 13 partners.

In the mean time Parker, Gerrard, Ogilvy and Company had continued in the fur trade on American territory south and west of Michilimackinac. In 1806, to meet the growing competition from American traders following the Louisiana Purchase, the firm joined with Forsyth, Richardson and Company, McTavish, McGillivrays and Company, and James and Andrew McGill and Company to establish a co-partnership called the Michilimackinac Company; Ogilvy played a major role in its formation and then, as an agent of the NWC, in negotiating a division of territory between the co-partnerships. He continued until 1810 at least his work as an agent in the NWC, one of his tasks being to establish, with less favourable conditions for the traders, new contracts with those such as Jean-Baptiste Perrault* whose terms had expired. Ogilvy took a lively interest when the affairs of the Montrealers conflicted with those of American traders; in 1810 he wrote to the London house of McTavish, Fraser and Company, which was closely connected with the NWC, warning of a projected rival trading-post to be constructed on the Pacific coast by the American John Jacob Astor*.

On 11 March 1802 Ogilvy had purchased from François Lévesque a two-storey stone house and lot on Rue Notre-Dame in Montreal; the purchase price was £1,500, of which Ogilvy paid £600 cash. He was already beginning to be active in community affairs,

Ogilvy

having in 1800 become an ensign in the British Militia of the Town and Banlieu of Montreal. Seven years later he was a member, with John Richardson and Louis CHABOILLEZ, of a committee charged with the erection of a statue to Horatio Nelson. Like many Scottish expatriates at Montreal, Ogilvy was a member of the Scotch Presbyterian Church, later known as St Gabriel Street Church, and he occupied Mackenzie's pew when the latter returned to Britain in 1805. That year Ogilvy became a trustee of the Protestant burying ground, and in 1810 he was named to the Scotch Presbyterian Church's temporal committee; he became vice-president some time thereafter. He was possibly the John Ogilvie who was lieutenant-colonel in the Rivière du Chêne battalion of sedentary militia in 1814.

In November 1814 Ogilvy – who had already disposed of his two agent's shares in the NWC – sold to Mure his half of the three shares they held jointly, for £7,050 and an annuity of £300 until 1823. Although Ogilvy ceased to be active in the fur trade after 1814 the experience he had acquired in it was highly respected. When in 1815 the Earl of Selkirk [DOUGLAS], on behalf of the Hudson's Bay Company, sought a negotiated division of the west with the NWC, he held a preliminary discussion with Ogilvy.

In 1816 the British government called upon Ogilvy's experience in the southwest fur trade by appointing him its commissioner to determine the Canadian boundary with the United States from the St Lawrence River to Lake of the Woods, in accordance with the Treaty of Ghent, which had ended the War of 1812. "There was about him, I am informed," said a surgeon who joined the commission later, "an unusual amount of public spirit and talent; but he was variable, apt to be obstinate in trifles, and immediately afterwards too pliant in matters of importance." Ogilvy conducted his business with considerable zeal, his bark canoe being a familiar sight on survey locations, but also, in the view of the British Foreign Office, with rather too much expense.

Ogilvy had continued as a partner in Parker, Gerrard, Ogilvy and Company, although probably not actively after 1816. According to the *Quebec Gazette*, "he was perhaps the only Gentleman in the district, who quitting his commerce, turned the whole of his attention and capital to agricultural pursuits"; these followed his move to one of several farms he owned near Côte-des-Neiges (Montreal), all called Airlie. In 1815 he appointed George Moffatt*, a recent partner in Parker, Gerrard, Ogilvy and Company, to administer a trust set up to provide a solid agricultural education in Scotland for a boy named John Nelson, who, it was planned, would eventually take possession of an Airlie farm. In September 1818 one of Ogilvy's cows was judged best in its category at a Montreal Agricultural Society livestock competition,

and the following January two of his hogs received honourable mention in an exhibition by the society.

That autumn Ogilvy was at work for the boundary commission in the swampy lowlands of the Detroit River when fever struck his camp; he succumbed to it on 28 September at about age 50. He had been a sociable, cultivated man, living and working in the high style of the Montreal fur-trade bourgeoisie. The traveller John Maude, who had met him while on a trip to Niagara Falls in 1800, recorded that to Ogilvy, James Cuthbert*, and Joseph FROBISHER, "I shall ever feel myself indebted; less for their civilities, than for that friendly manner with which they were accompanied." Before Maude left Montreal for the United States, Ogilvy pressed into his hands two books of poetry "as a resource against *ennui*" during the trip. In his will Ogilvy left, among other bequests, £100 to the Scotch Presbyterian Church and £200 "to the poor of Leith"; bequeathing a sum to one's native parish had become almost a custom among successful Scottish expatriates. In 1821, at the suit of George Gillespie, a number of properties belonging to Ogilvy's estate were seized from his residuary and fiduciary legatee, Moffatt, and advertised for sale at auction: there were two lots in the village of Saint-Eustache, two in the parish of Saint-Laurent on Montreal Island, one at Côte-des-Neiges, and two in the *faubourg* Saint-Antoine; all but the last two had houses on them.

MARJORIE WILKINS CAMPBELL

ANQ-M, CM1, John Ogilvy, proved 5 Oct. 1819. ANQ-Q, CN1-16, 4 nov. 1814; CN1-26, 11 mars 1802. *Les bourgeois de la Compagnie du Nord-Ouest* (Masson), 2: 23. *Docs. relating to NWC* (Wallace). Mackenzie, *Journals and letters* (Lamb), 32, 37, 40, 208, 493–94. John Maude, *Visit to the falls of Niagara in 1800* (London, 1826), 142, 160, 175–77, 181, 185, 188–89, 191, 207, 233–34, 238, 249. J.-B. Perrault, *Jean-Baptiste Perrault, marchand voyageur parti de Montréal le 28e de mai 1783*, L.-P. Cormier, édit. (Montréal, 1978), 111. *Quebec Gazette*, 11 Sept. 1800; 22 July 1802; 23 June, 27 Oct. 1808; 27 June 1811; 11 April, 28 Nov. 1816; 8 Oct. 1818; 25 Jan., 18 Oct. 1819; 6 April 1820; 4 Oct. 1821. J. R. Harper, *Everyman's Canada; paintings and drawings from the McCord Museum of McGill University* (Ottawa, 1962). Massicotte, "Répertoire des engagements pour l'Ouest," ANQ *Rapport*, 1942–43: 261–397. *Quebec almanac*, 1801: 103; 1805: 46; 1810: 58; 1815: 94. R. Campbell, *Hist. of Scotch Presbyterian Church*, 237–38. M. W. Campbell, *NWC* (1957), 124, 137, 152–55. H. G. Classen, *Thrust and counterthrust: the genesis of the Canada–United States boundary* (Don Mills, Ont., 1965), 95–101. Davidson, *NWC*, 84, 86. Innis, *Fur trade in Canada* (1970). E. A. Mitchell, *Fort Timiskaming and the fur trade* (Toronto and Buffalo, N.Y., 1977), 58, 60–61. Morton, *Hist. of Canadian west* (1973), 509, 606. R. A. Pendergast, "The XY Company, 1798–1804" (PHD thesis, Univ. of Ottawa, 1957). Rich, *Hist. of HBC*. Rumilly, *La Compagnie du Nord-Ouest*, 1: 222, 228, 251–52, 261, 264. G. J. J. Tulchinsky, *The river barons:*

O'Hara

Montreal businessmen and the growth of industry and transportation, 1837–53 (Toronto and Buffalo, 1977). R. H. Fleming, "The origin of 'Sir Alexander Mackenzie and Company,'" *CHR*, 9 (1928): 137–55.

O'HARA, FELIX, businessman, office holder, and judge; b. in Ireland; d. 9 Sept. 1805 in Gaspé, Lower Canada.

After leaving Ireland Felix O'Hara went to live in the colony of New Jersey. A naval lieutenant in the British forces, he was put on half pay shortly after the conquest of New France. In the spring of 1764 he settled at Gaspé with his wife, Martha McCormick, and two sons; theirs was one of the first English-speaking families to take up residence in that region.

Upon his arrival O'Hara became head of a fishery in Baie de Gaspé. The following year he was appointed justice of the peace. In 1767 Lieutenant Governor Guy CARLETON granted him and his partner, Quebec merchant John McCord, 1,300 acres of land located partly in the centre of the village and partly on both banks of the Rivière York. McCord seems never to have lived at Gaspé; consequently O'Hara was able to use the grant for his own benefit. Diversifying his activities, O'Hara two years later obtained a licence to sell alcoholic beverages, which he probably carried in the store he owned. In addition to fishing and trading he farmed and raised livestock; in 1777 he had 17 head of cattle. From 1780 he also owned a sawmill located at Anse aux Cousins.

After complaining to Carleton of being "abandoned, forsaken as in a desert," in 1779 O'Hara received a commission as a judge of the Court of Common Pleas established that year at Gaspé, with an annual salary of £100. But this court, of which Charles Robin* and Isaac Mann were also to be members, functioned badly because the means of communication were inadequate; both judges and litigants found it difficult to get to Percé, where the court sat. In the year following this appointment O'Hara also accepted the position of collector in the Gaspé custom-house, which at that time was a branch of the Quebec one [*see* Thomas AINSLIE]. In 1785, with the backing of the Jersey merchants trading on the coast, O'Hara asked the government to make the custom-house independent, a request that was finally granted. In addition to these functions O'Hara represented the lieutenant governor of the District of Gaspé, Nicholas Cox*, during his frequent absences. Like Cox, he complained to Governor HALDIMAND of American privateers in the district; the privateers attacked in 1782, took him prisoner, but acquitted him "of the crime of being rich."

In May 1783 O'Hara acted as guide to Justus Sherwood, who had been sent by Haldimand to the Gaspé to examine the possibility of settling loyalists there in the hope that they might engage in the fishing industry. The following year some five or six hundred loyalists began moving into the region. O'Hara immediately judged them to be malcontents, unreliable and difficult to please. He soon got into trouble with them. In 1785, because O'Hara, it seems, was showing signs of greed, the loyalists set fire to the woods on about 800 of the 1,500 acres he had received as a grant from Lieutenant Governor Henry Hamilton* that year.

In 1789, when Carleton (now Lord Dorchester) set up a land board for the District of Gaspé, O'Hara agreed to be a member of it. This board, which in addition to Cox, Robin, and O'Hara included a loyalist and two Canadians, was to examine requests for land and to issue certificates of grants. On 25 Feb. 1795 the British government at last recognized O'Hara's abilities and experience in the legal field by appointing him judge of the Provincial Court of Gaspé, which had been created in 1793, and he received an annual salary of £200.

O'Hara died at Gaspé on 9 Sept. 1805. In the will he had drawn up a month before, he bequeathed to three of his grandsons the seigneury of Grand-Pabos, which he had purchased from Haldimand's heir for 2,000 *livres* in 1796. Curiously, he left nothing to his wife, who was obliged to seek a pension from the government. In August 1806, with the support of her son Henry and Thomas DUNN, the president and administrator of Lower Canada, she obtained an annual allowance of £50.

A sensible, well-informed man according to Bishop Charles INGLIS of Nova Scotia, Felix O'Hara initiated the rapid economic development of the Gaspé area. Ambitious and interested in acquiring property, he tried to exploit its major resources – the fishery and the forests. At least three of his seven children distinguished themselves in the region. Oliver became customs agent at New Carlisle, and Edward* was the first member for Gaspé in the House of Assembly of Lower Canada. For his part, Hugh became justice of the peace at Gaspé in 1788 and his commission was renewed six years later; in 1801 he replaced his father in the custom-house at Gaspé. He also acted as business agent for a Jersey company and for Pierre BREHAUT. He died in 1818, victim of a contagious fever caught in helping some immigrants whose ship had cast anchor at Gaspé.

RÉGINALD DAY

ANQ-Q, CN1-253, 30 April 1813; CN1-262, 15 nov. 1796; CN1-284, 1er mai 1810. *Quebec Gazette*, 24 Aug. 1769, 12 May 1785, 29 June 1786, 2 April 1789, 1 March 1792, 10 July 1794, 5 March 1795, 10 Oct. 1805, 6 Jan. 1811, 10 Dec. 1818. Patrice Gallant, *Les registres de la Gaspésie (1752–1850)* (6v., [Sayabec, Qué., 1968]). "Papiers d'État – Bas-Canada," PAC *Rapport*, 1891: 25; 1892: 254–58. P.-G. Roy, *Les juges de la prov. de Québec*. C.-E. Roy et

Olabaratz

Lucien Brault, *Gaspé depuis Cartier* (Québec, 1934). Réginald Day, "Il y a deux siècles: les O'Hara à Gaspé," *Rev. d'hist. de la Gaspésie* (Gaspé, Qué.), 9 (1971): 342–97; 10 (1972): 31–35. David Lee, "La Gaspésie, 1760–1867," *Canadian Hist. Sites*, no.23 (1980).

OLABARATZ (Laubaras), JEAN D', naval officer; b. 20 Oct. 1727 in Saint-Jean-de-Luz, France, son of Joannis-Galand d'Olabaratz* and Catherine Despiaube; m. *c.* 1779 Marguerite-Angélique Collas; they had no children; d. 1 Feb. 1808 at his birthplace.

Little is known about Jean d'Olabaratz's childhood, but everything suggests that he was oriented towards a naval career from his youth. In these years his father had his own ship, and there is no doubt that he took his son with him on more than one voyage. The elder d'Olabaratz seems indeed to have had a major influence on his son, because throughout the latter's apprenticeship they were often to be found on the same bridge.

When he was 18 Jean d'Olabaratz joined the French navy. He served as a supernumerary officer in the port of Bayonne, and then as port ensign there. From 1746 to 1749 he sailed under his father in the frigate *Bristol* and the king's corvette *Catherine*; promoted lieutenant at the time of a voyage to Louisbourg, Île Royale (Cape Breton Island), in the *Intrépide*, he subsequently returned to France. In 1750 the minister of Marine, Rouillé, appointed his father port captain at Louisbourg; Jean occupied the post of port ensign, for which he obtained his brevet in 1752.

In 1755 d'Olabaratz received permission from the governor of Île Royale to embark on the *Héros*, a warship returning to France after a short mission at sea. Once more on French shores, he became port ensign at Brest. In 1756, despite his desire to serve in France, he was given command of the frigate *Aigle*, which he skilfully sailed to Louisbourg that October.

The following year, again in the *Aigle*, which was accompanied by the *Outarde*, d'Olabaratz left Rochefort, France, for Quebec. The ships captured two British merchant vessels during the crossing, and then lost sight of each other off Newfoundland. D'Olabaratz sailed into the Gulf of St Lawrence through the Strait of Belle-Isle, but as a result of wrong information he ran aground near Gros Mécatina. When he was informed of this shipwreck, Intendant François Bigot* dispatched the *Légère* to the scene; it arrived at the same time as the *Bien-Aimé*, two months after the accident. Unfortunately the following night the two ships crashed into each other in a sudden gale and were a total loss.

D'Olabaratz then requisitioned the *Roi du Nord*, a snow belonging to some French fishermen who had come to hunt seals. He loaded onto it what had been salvaged from the previous shipwrecks and set sail for Quebec. As a crowning misfortune his new ship proved unseaworthy – its hull was completely rotten and split open off Île Saint-Barnabé. The shipwrecked crew managed to reach shore. Thus it was only after months of delay that d'Olabaratz arrived at Quebec.

Early in 1758 the government of the colony gave d'Olabaratz the delicate task of ensuring the naval defence of Lake Champlain. Along with the shipbuilder Pierre Levasseur, son of René-Nicolas Levasseur*, he supervised the building of three xebecs. After they were launched, the *Muskelonge, Brochette*, and *Esturgeon* were put under the command of d'Olabaratz, who was himself under François-Charles de Bourlamaque*'s orders. His mission consisted of patrolling the waters of Lake Champlain and delaying as long as possible the advance of the British troops. On several occasions he was on the verge of engaging with enemy ships, but each time he adroitly evaded them. On 12 Oct. 1759 he was hemmed in near present-day Plattsburgh, N.Y., and after holding a council with his officers on board the *Muskelonge*, he scuttled his flotilla and returned to Montreal under cover of darkness. The incident, which has been attributed erroneously to d'Olabaratz's father, displeased the colonial authorities. After François de Lévis* had denied him command of a schooner, d'Olabaratz took passage for France. Again he had the misfortune to be shipwrecked, a little below Quebec, but he soon found another vessel on which to continue his voyage. Once at sea, it was pursued by a British ship, which speedily captured it. D'Olabaratz was taken to England, where he was detained for some time.

In the years following his tour of duty in Canada d'Olabaratz held various posts on the king's ships. In particular he served on board the flute *Salomon*, the frigate *Hareror*, and the lighter *Porteuse*. He was named lieutenant in 1775 and captain in March 1779. He then commanded the flute *Ménagère*, subsequently ending his career on board the *Fier*. In 1786 he retired with the rank of brigadier of the naval forces.

Of all the misadventures that Jean d'Olabaratz experienced in New France, the loss of the Lake Champlain flotilla remains the strangest. He never explained the motives for his action, and no court martial was held to force him to justify himself. The ships were the only ones that the government of the colony had ever built to defend its posts on the Rivière Richelieu, and at the moment when they were the most indispensable, they sank without even firing their guns.

MARC THÉORÊT

In the biography of Joannis-Galand d'Olabaratz in *DCB*, vol.4, the incidents on Lake Champlain, reported above, were attributed in error to his career rather than to his son's.

AN, Marine, B⁴, 91; C¹, 171: f.1034; C⁶, 239: ff.1–43; C⁷, 239 (dossier d'Olabaratz). *Coll. des manuscrits de Lévis* (Casgrain), 5. Harrison Bird, *Navies in the mountains: the battles on the waters of Lake Champlain and Lake George, 1609–1814* (New York, 1962), 100.

OSBORN, MARY (London), convicted murderer; b. *c*. 1773 in Bedford, Pa; m. Bartholomew London, and they may have had one child; d. 17 Aug. 1801 in Niagara (Niagara-on-the-Lake), Upper Canada.

In the early years of Upper Canadian settlement major crimes were infrequent and cases resulting in capital convictions rare. Attorney General John White* complained in 1795 to the French traveller La Rochefoucauld-Liancourt* that, although one or two people had been tried for murder in every district of the province, "they were all acquitted by the jury, though the evidence was strongly against them." Convictions were indeed difficult to obtain. But the sparing ways of the juries aside, between August 1792 and September 1800 there were six cases ending in capital convictions: four for burglary, one for forgery, and one for murder. Three of these trials were of black slaves, among them Jack York*; the first execution in the province's history was of the black slave Josiah Cuttan (Cutten) in 1792. The first execution for murder and the first execution of a woman occurred in 1801.

In the late summer of that year the attention of the Niagara peninsula was riveted on the trial of Mary London and George Nemiers (Nemire) for the murder of her husband. The trial was sensational in appeal, exposing the adultery of young lovers, the betrayal of an old husband, the role of unnamed accomplices and confidants, and clandestine trips to obtain poison. Moreover, the local appetite for scandal was whetted by the first newspaper coverage of a criminal trial held in the province. For reasons that are not entirely clear, the printer and editor of the *Niagara Herald*, Silvester TIFFANY, covered the trial and execution in detail extraordinary for a period in which local and provincial news rarely received more than short shrift. For the most part, the following account is based on his reports.

The basic outline of events leading to the trial seems clear. In 1789 Bartholomew London, a small farmer from New Jersey who claimed to have been imprisoned during the American revolution because of his loyalty to the British, entered the province with four children and four grandchildren. Drawing on the support of a fellow New Jerseyman and local office holder, Nathaniel PETTIT, he obtained a grant of 200 acres in Saltfleet Township. An older man, he appears to have been unmarried upon his arrival in the colony. At some point he married the young Mary Osborn, an emigrant from Pennsylvania whose family still resided there in 1801. How they met is unknown, but whatever the scenario it was complicated by the appearance of George Nemiers. About 28 years of age and from Carlisle, Pa, Nemiers likely worked as a

labourer on the London farm. By December 1800 Mary London and Nemiers were lovers. When Bartholomew London died on 17 Feb. 1801, Mary, then four months pregnant, and Nemiers were arrested and charged with felony and murder.

The trial began on the morning of 14 August before judge Henry ALLCOCK and his local associate justices, Robert HAMILTON and William Dickson*. The petit jury included the Niagara merchants James Crooks* and John DUN. Among the 14 witnesses were Tiffany, his brother Oliver, Dr Robert Kerr*, and Robert Nelles*. Attorney General Thomas Scott* opened the proceedings with an address to the jury which, according to Tiffany, "moistened many eyes, and captivated many hearts." Eight hours were then spent in examining the witnesses. The coroner and medical men established that London's death was a result of poisoning and not a fractured skull. The rest of the testimony was apparently circumstantial, but Tiffany, himself a witness, reported that, although there was a lack of "positive proof as to the person or persons who administered the poison," "the facts and the numerous circumstances left no room for doubt." After the jury delivered its verdict of guilty, Allcock, "who had all along 'judged with mercy,'" pronounced the "dreadful sentence." On the morning of 17 August, the lovers were to be hanged "until they be dead, dead, and afterwards their bodies to be Dissected."

The interlude of two days gave Tiffany time to interview the two convicts. Nemiers, "penitent and perfectly resigned," absolved his "honest parents . . . who discharged their duty in instructing him in the strict observance of the Sabbath and his duty to God and man . . . and blamed none but the guilty copartner in the crime . . . who lured him to unlawful intimacy and connection about 9 months ago, and from the sin of adultery to that of murder." She had first suggested "shooting the old man" and later raised the possibility of poison. Nemiers attempted to obtain poison at Ancaster, but "he there felt some remorse of conscience." Later, his moral qualms resolved, he secured two ounces of arsenic and one ounce of opium from a "medical gentleman" in Canadaigua, N.Y. (Tiffany's home after leaving the province in 1803). Insisting that "it was not the estate, but the woman he wanted," and that a third party was involved in the crime, he confessed to causing London's skull fracture with a shoe-hammer.

But it was Mary London's seeming indifference "to a sense of her true standing" that intrigued Tiffany. Possibly because she was a female, Tiffany had expected a full confession. Instead all she had offered during the trial was "a partial confession . . . framed to her own innocency and the guilt of Nemiers." When Nemiers spoke to Tiffany of a guilty third party, she "checked" him, saying "two of us to die for this is enough." But afterwards she confirmed that another had suggested murdering London to get "the old rascal out of the way." She denied administering anything more than opium to her husband, indicating that the unnamed accomplice was the culprit. But the contradictions in her story and her tendency to lie led Tiffany to disregard her statements and conceal the names of those implicated. Only once did her steely reserve falter: returning to her cell after sentencing she had cried aloud, "I am guilty, I gave the poison and knew it." To Tiffany, she later confided that she did not know who was the father of her child, Catherine, then but a few days old and baptized by Robert Addison* the day before the execution. Like Nemiers, she did not blame her parents "for any neglect." Tiffany believed that Mary first realized her fate in the preparation room on the morning of the 17th: "When she came out to her place, she said, 'May this be a warning to you all,' and prayed to God to have mercy on her soul."

The execution was attended by a "large concourse of people" and was marred when "a female (it is to be regretted it was one of that sex)" mocked the cries and gestures of Mary London. Following English practice, the bodies were turned over to medical men for dissection, the first instance in Upper Canada of a procedure that continued at least until the execution of William Kain* in 1830. As was often the case with criminal trials during this period, the convicted passed quickly from the written record and possibly from memory. Tiffany saw in the case a moral lesson: "Visible in the whole of this business, [is] the hand of Providence pursuing with vengeance offenders even in this life; for in it we see punished adultery, disregard of marriage vows, and murder: and to those who indulge themselves in the two former, it may be a lesson of instruction, that from them to the last is but a step."

ROBERT LOCHIEL FRASER III

AO, RG 1, A-II-1, 1: 143–44; C-IV, Saltfleet Township, concession 3, lots 18–19; RG 22, ser.134, 3: 22, 45, 80, 88, 94, 102, 131. Hamilton Public Library (Hamilton, Ont.), Buchanan papers, ledger of an early doctor of Barton and Ancaster, 1098. PAC, RG 1, L3, 283: L1/5, 20, 68. Wentworth Land Registry Office (Hamilton), Abstract index to deeds, Saltfleet Township: ff.124–27 (mfm. at AO, GS 1627). York North Land Registry Office (Newmarket, Ont.), Abstract index to deeds, King Township: 149 (mfm. at AO, GS 5840). "Early records of Niagara" (Carnochan), *OH*, 3: 18. [F.-A.-F. de La Rochefoucauld-Liancourt], "La Rochefoucault-Liancourt's travels in Canada, 1795, [translated by Henry Neuman] with annotations and strictures by Sir David William Smith . . . ," ed. W. R. Riddell, AO *Report*, 1916: 40. *Niagara Herald* (Niagara [Niagara-on-the-Lake, Ont.]), 15, 22 Aug. 1801. W. R. Riddell, "The first legal execution for crime in Upper Canada," *OH*, 27 (1931): 514–16.

OUABACHAS. *See* WAHPASHA

OUGIER, PETER, ship's captain and merchant; d. July 1803 in Dartmouth, England.

Some men are remembered because of their personal qualities, and others for their roles in great events. Still others are remembered merely because they happen to be mentioned in easily accessible documents and can be used as examples of the thought or groupings of their time. Peter Ougier falls into the last category. The West Country merchant is a prominent villain in the historical mythology of Newfoundland, and it fell to Ougier to appear as a witness at a well-known parliamentary inquiry into the Newfoundland trade in 1792–93. He was voluble, emphatic, and reactionary, and, in addition, the evidence of the inquiry was published in three reports. Thus whenever historians wanted a live West Country merchant, they reached for Ougier or two of the other merchants who appeared and presented them shining before the world.

It is perhaps a mistake to see Ougier as typical of the merchants of his day, although his trading methods and general outlook were much the same as those of his fellows. The merchants were fearful of change, and especially of government intervention in the affairs of Newfoundland; Ougier was, if anything, more reactionary than his colleagues. The merchants were generally pessimistic about the future of the fishery and their fortunes; Ougier was even more so. It might be said that, like a tradesman's son at a 19th-century English public school, he embraced the philosophy of his class by personal choice rather than by heredity, which would explain his fervent identification with its traditional approach to life. There are certain features of his career which lend support to this theory. To begin with, he was probably not a West Country man; his father was likely a Guernsey ship's captain who traded coastwise and to the Caribbean, Virginia, and the Carolinas, but never to Newfoundland. Ougier himself stated that he entered the Newfoundland trade from the port of Dartmouth around 1760 and that he remained constantly in it thereafter, but the available facts do not seem to bear this claim out. His first recorded appearance was in 1769, when he commanded a merchant vessel owned by Arthur French of Dartmouth which went to Newfoundland not to fish, but merely to carry fish to a Mediterranean market. In 1771 he temporarily gave up his connection with Dartmouth to command ships owned in London, and these vessels were by no means "constant traders" to Newfoundland as he claimed. Thus his early experience was in command of shipping, and not with the techniques and organization of the fishery. However, in 1775 he suddenly entered the Newfoundland fishery on his own account and in an unusually substantial way, for he purchased a plantation at Bay Bulls and began trading with no fewer than three ships. One can only surmise that he had received an inheritance, for this scale of operation was not made possible by the savings (legal or otherwise) of a merchant ship's master in the 1770s.

Ougier was probably therefore of a type which he himself was to condemn heavily in 1792, the "New Adventurer" or speculator. By entering into a trade of which he knew little, Ougier would claim, the speculator overturned the careful balance of competition between those already in the trade, and thus ruined himself and everyone else as well. Ougier's career, however, contradicted his forecasts for the "New Adventurer," since he prospered so well that by 1788 he owned eight ships, had expanded his trade into St John's, and gave employment to between 600 and 800 fishermen and seamen annually. He had also purchased an estate near Dartmouth for 5,000 guineas, and was renowned for his liberality to his friends. Even more surprisingly, he had somehow persuaded the clannish Dartmouth merchants to accept him as their leader and spokesman in a campaign to remove the "oppressions and vexations" of recent legislation such as Palliser's Act of 1775 [see Sir Hugh Palliser*] and allow them to return to the good old days in Newfoundland when laws were few (and easily broken), lawyers non-existent, and relationships between all classes of men supremely happy. Ougier's first venture into lobbying came between 1783 and 1786, when he firmly assured the British government that any restoration of trade and contact between Newfoundland and the new United States would inevitably lead to the speedy collapse of the fishery. The government was only partly impressed, intercourse was allowed, and Ougier and the rest of the merchants continued to prosper, so much so that by 1787 they were demanding that the government be more liberal in granting licences for trade with the United States.

By 1790, however, Ougier was much more alarmed at the prospects for the fishery. The postwar boom had collapsed because of overfishing and an over-extension of trade, and widespread mercantile failures had ensued. The litigation caused by these failures led to the breakdown of the legal system in Newfoundland, and thus to yet more government intervention in the shape of a bill in 1791 to create a court of civil jurisdiction [see Mark MILBANKE] and another to improve the regulation of the fishery. The merchants became hysterical; they saw the legislation as the cause of the depression, and in a carefully coordinated campaign that involved every port in Great Britain active in the Newfoundland trade, they forced the government to hold a parliamentary inquiry in 1792–93 into the state of the trade. A host of official

and mercantile witnesses including Aaron GRAHAM, George CARTWRIGHT, Sir Hugh Palliser, and John WALDRON attended, the three leading merchants being John Jeffrey of Poole (former partner of Thomas STREET) and William Newman (cousin of Robert NEWMAN) and Ougier of Dartmouth. Ougier vied with Newman in the violence (and incoherence) of his arguments against existing and proposed legislation, but the government was not impressed. Although the regulating bill was abandoned, Palliser's Act, the so-called Amending Act of 1786, which made minor changes to the previous act, and the judicial measures stood intact. Ougier and Newman repeated their prediction that the trade would collapse overnight; the government disagreed. The parliamentary committee issued a report that contained no recommendations whatsoever, and by the time it was published war with France had driven the problem out of everyone's mind.

Ougier and his fellow merchants had overstated their case, and by incoherence and repeated exaggeration had bored the government into complete antagonism. However, their predictions that the fishery was doomed did have some validity. The Newfoundland trade suffered some very serious moments during the French revolutionary wars, but soon recovered. The trade as carried on from Dartmouth did not. By 1800 severe losses had sent many of its merchants into bankruptcy, and Ougier himself could operate only two ships. Ougier also suffered a personal disappointment. His first son, Benedict, had died at the age of ten, and his surviving son, Peter, betrayed no interest in the Newfoundland trade. He in fact reverted to the ancestral instincts of his Channel Island forebears, becoming a fairly successful privateer captain. Taken prisoner himself, on his release he settled in London.

In the absence of personal correspondence or ledgers we do not know precisely why Ougier became seriously worried about his business affairs. But he was a gloomy man at heart. In the period between 1793 and 1802 he had seen other Dartmouth merchants become insolvent and drop out of the trade; moreover, like others he found himself facing a growing list of bad debts. One may imagine that in July 1803 he could also no longer bear the thought of renewed war with France and the danger to his business, which in any case would not be taken over by his son. In a moment of depression over what he supposed was his bankruptcy he committed suicide. Generous to the last, his fellow citizens gave him a Christian burial. His affairs were left in such a state that the final dividend to his creditors was not paid until 1813. But, sad irony, they were paid 19s. 1d. in the pound. Poor Ougier had probably never been bankrupt at all.

K. MATTHEWS

Overholser

BL, Add. MSS 37219. Devon Record Office, 2992A; 2993A. Hunt, Roope & Co. (London), Robert Newman & Co., ledgers and letterbooks (mfm. at PANL). PANL, GN 2/1. PRO, ADM 1/471–76; ADM 7/154–55; 7/317–19; BT 1; BT 5; BT 6/86–87; BT 98/3–17; CO 194; CO 324/7; CUST 65; E 190; HCA 26. *Lloyd's Evening Post and British Chronicle* (London). *Lloyd's List. St. James's Chronicle or the British Evening Post* (London). *Sherborne Mercury or the Weekly Magazine* (Sherborne, Eng.). *Trewman's Exeter Flying Post, or Plymouth and Cornish Advertiser* (Exeter, Eng.). *Reg. of shipping.* Keith Matthews, *Lectures on the history of Newfoundland: 1500–1830* (St John's, 1973). Prowse, *Hist. of Nfld.* Keith Matthews, "Historical fence building: a critique of the historiography of Newfoundland," *Newfoundland Quarterly* (St John's), 74 (1978–79), no.1: 21–30.

OVERHOLSER (Oberholser), JACOB, settler and convicted traitor; b. *c.* 1774 in the American colonies; m. Barbara —, and they had four children; d. 14 March 1815 in Kingston, Upper Canada.

Jacob Overholser led a life that in most respects was singularly unexceptional. A simple man, probably illiterate, he immigrated to Upper Canada with his wife and children about 1810 and settled in Bertie Township, where in 1811 he bought a farm. From all accounts he appears to have worked hard, made friends with his neighbours, and enjoyed a moderate degree of prosperity. Unlike officials at York (Toronto), the mercantile élite of the Niagara peninsula was not over concerned by the presence of American settlers, and Overholser seems to have met with the approval of John WARREN of Fort Erie, the pre-eminent man of the township, and his family.

The War of 1812 shattered Overholser's life. The peninsula was the scene of heavy fighting throughout the war and, as opposing armies moved back and forth, civilian life was altered in their wake. Without a strong and lasting military presence by either army, order often quickly broke down. A regrettable, but probably a natural enough, consequence was that some seized on this instability to settle private grudges or further personal ends. A recent American immigrant such as Overholser was a likely target for the vengeful.

Although the exact time frame is not clear, Overholser had problems with a set of louts – principally members of the Anger family – whose actions towards him were tinctured with malice. After the retreating American army burned Niagara (Niagara-on-the-Lake) on 10 Dec. 1813, these men threatened to take his land and set fire to his buildings, and on one occasion several of them stole four horses from his barn. About 20 December Overholser, together with Thomas Moore, a Quaker neighbour, approached Major-General Phineas Riall* to seek redress. The general referred the case to the Queenston merchant and magistrate Thomas Dickson*, who

ordered the animals returned. The Angers then charged that during the American occupation Overholser had accompanied the enemy when members of their family were taken prisoner. The charge was serious and Dickson had no choice but to refer the matter back to Riall and ask John Warren Jr, also a magistrate, to investigate.

Extant documents relating to Overholser's actions from about the 1st of December 1813 to 26 Jan. 1814 are so fragmentary and elliptical as to render impossible a full reconstruction of events. Before Dickson, Overholser's accusers had charged that on or about 1 Dec. 1813 he had been seen "in Company with the Americans" when Benjamin Clark and two members of the Anger family were captured. The prisoners were removed to Black Rock (Buffalo), N.Y., and the following day Overholser testified against them for having broken the conditions of a previous parole granted them by the American forces. Warren's inquiry established that the basic outline of events was true but that Overholser had been compelled by the Americans to accompany them and carry a rifle. Warren concluded that there was no substance to the charge and that the whole episode amounted to "Nothing more than an ill Disposition" by the Angers towards Overholser. Moore interjected that even if the charges were true, the Angers' crime in stealing Overholser's horses was the greater. Obviously alarmed by the possibility of charges against them, the Angers then suggested that they would return Overholser's property if the matter was dropped. Warren agreed "and there it was supposed to end." However, the Angers, a thuggish lot, took the first opportunity – the absence of Dickson and Riall – to revive their charges against Overholser, and another magistrate, apparently unfamiliar with the case, ordered him jailed. Towards the end of January 1814, through the intercession of Riall, Moore secured bail for Overholser, an extraordinary departure in circumstances involving possible charges of high treason. Later, when ordered to appear in court, Overholser voluntarily surrendered himself to the sheriff.

Overholser's situation was serious but his prospects were hopeful. The charges seemed to lack substance, his accusers were a disreputable set, and Dickson, Warren, and Riall supported him. But Overholser's fate did not turn on legal niceties; his story became intertwined with, and inseparable from, the grim determination of military and civil authorities to overawe disaffection by exemplary punishment. The genesis of this resolve deserves an explanation.

The experience of the American revolution and the examples of the French revolution and the Irish rebellion of 1798 had made the Upper Canadian élite highly suspicious of non-loyalist American settlers, anxious about political opposition, and inflexible on the meaning of loyalty. The rise of a parliamentary and extra-parliamentary opposition associated with William WEEKES, Robert Thorpe*, and Joseph WILLCOCKS exacerbated these anxieties. Although, in large part, the parliamentary opposition drew its strength from matters of local concern, it took its political language from a transatlantic whig tradition rooted in the 18th century which emphasized constitutional liberty, civil rights, and the prerogatives of elected assemblies. The heyday of the opposition, the legislative sessions of 1812, brought these ideals into conflict with the exigencies of war. Administrator Isaac BROCK had grave doubts about the effect of a largely American population upon Upper Canada's security. He feared that the war might be lost not from "any thing the enemy can do, but from the disposition of the people." In an address to the House of Assembly in which he recalled the experience of Great Britain between 1792 and 1795, a period sometimes known as the "White Terror," Brock sought sanction for emergency measures such as a suspension of habeas corpus to secure the province "from private Treachery as well as from open dissaffection." These proposals violated sacred whig principles and the assembly under the leadership of men such as Willcocks and Abraham Markle* rejected them.

Brock's suspicions about the popular mood were further confirmed by the reaction in the western areas of the province to American brigadier-general William Hull's proclamation of 12 July 1812. The problem of disaffection was kept in abeyance by the military victories at Detroit and Queenston Heights, but throughout 1813 the situation steadily deteriorated. Following the American capture of York on 27 April 1813, an event that led to an outbreak of disorder and the voicing, albeit in a coarse manner, of explicit egalitarian and democratic sentiments, the concern for constitutionalism on the part of the élite all but collapsed [see Elijah BENTLEY]. Little more than a week later prominent men of the Niagara peninsula such as James Crooks* and Robert Nichol* petitioned Major-General John Vincent* to take measures sufficiently severe to quell the traitorously inclined, and on 28 June judge William Dummer Powell* opined that in the event of a military disaster it would be difficult for the loyal to "keep down the Turbulence of the disaffected who are numerous." In July Governor PREVOST authorized the formation of general courts martial in cases requiring "an immediate example." When on 3 August the influential York merchant William Allan* charged certain people with seditious behaviour during the occupation, Administrator Francis de Rottenburg* instructed the acting attorney general, John Beverley Robinson*, to investigate the instances of "dangerous and treasonable inclinations." Several days later the Executive Council recommended increased military surveillance

and the detention of suspects, and the report of the committee appointed by Robinson to inquire into the situation at York urged the need to make examples of the disaffected. It was probably just this change in the constitutional climate of the province that prompted the treason of Willcocks and Markle in the summer of 1813.

As the military situation west of York deteriorated, the civil situation became even more acute. On 13 November 18 marauders were captured in Norfolk County. Rottenburg ordered Robinson to take prompt measures to bring the renegades to trial and advised him that a special commission – the instrument used in extraordinary circumstances to summon the full majesty of the law – would be appointed. George Gordon Drummond*, Rottenburg's successor, issued the commission on 14 December for the trial of all persons accused of treason, with special concern for the London and Home districts. Uppermost in Drummond's mind was the need "to make examples" immediately. Robinson, however, proceeded slowly. The peculiarities of the law regarding high treason required him to take great care to avoid errors. Moreover, he hoped to avoid departing from normal civil procedures because executions "by military power would have comparatively little influence – the people would consider them as arbitrary acts of punishment."

When Robinson reported to Drummond on 4 April 1814 Jacob Overholser was among the men to be charged. Drawn into a web of events beyond his own making, he was now to be lumped together with men who were avowed traitors and who had actually taken up arms. The site of the great show trial of Upper Canadian history was Ancaster. The court opened on 23 May with the three justices of the Court of King's Bench, Thomas Scott*, William Campbell*, and Powell, presiding. Three of the associate judges, RICHARD and Samuel* Hatt and Thomas Dickson, were drawn from the local magistrates, and the 17-man grand jury included some of the area's leading merchants and office holders, notably James Crooks, Robert Nelles*, and Samuel Street*. In all the jury found true bills against 21 prisoners and 50 others. Overholser was indicted on 24 May and two days later decided on John Ten Broeck and Bartholomew Crannell Beardsley* as his counsel. His trial took place on 8 June before Powell, the Hatts, and Dickson. He pleaded not guilty, a petit jury of 12 was picked, and the witnesses appeared – four for the crown (three Angers and Clark) and five for the defence, including Dickson and Warren. Unfortunately for Overholser, his Quaker friend Thomas Moore refused to take the required oath and could not be sworn.

Overholser was charged with a branch of high treason known as adherence to the enemy; his specific

Overholser

act was alleged to have been carrying arms and assisting the enemy in making prisoners of the king's subjects. According to Robinson's summary of the case and Powell's bench notes on the trial, the evidence against him was as follows. On or about 1 Dec. 1813 Overholser had accompanied an "armed party of the Enemy" to the homes of his neighbours, Clark and the Angers, who were then made prisoners. Overholser stood armed guard over them before they were taken to Black Rock. The following day he "voluntarily" appeared at Buffalo claiming that at some point before their capture Clark and the Angers had broken the terms of their parole with the American army by making him a prisoner. The ensuing day at Black Rock he attended the examination of the prisoners, who were then sent to Fort Niagara (near Youngstown), N.Y. Overholser's defence was developed along two lines. First (and this was undoubtedly the work of his counsel), he argued that since he was an American citizen the withdrawal of the protection of British forces had absolved him of the allegiance he owed the king. Thus, his action constituted only "a Trespass against the Individuals and not Treason," according to this act's definition by statute. Secondly, he repeated his testimony before Warren to the effect that he had been "impelled to join the Enemy by Apprehension of Danger to himself." But Powell noted that his defence "was not sustained by Evidence" and that the charge of treason "was fully and satisfactorily proved by the Testimony." From the bare outline of the trial in the minute-book it seems that the jury had some difficulty reaching a verdict. No doubt the testimony of John Warren Jr that the prisoner was a "quiet, inoffensive Man, always obedient to the requisitions of the Magistrates" had something to do with its discussion. The deliberations lasted for an hour and a half before Overholser was pronounced guilty.

Overholser was not alone in his misfortune: of the 21 men tried, 17 were convicted. The penalty for high treason was harsh and calculated to have a "strong and lasting" impact upon the "Public Mind." On 21 June Scott read the sentence to the convicted men: "You are to be drawn on Hurdles to the place of execution where you are to be hanged by the neck, but not until you are dead, for you must be cut down while alive and your entrails taken out and burnt before your faces, Your Heads then to be cut off, and your bodies divided into four quarters, and your Heads and quarters to be at the Kings disposal." Since Drummond and others believed that "many examples were not necessary to convince the Province that Treason will meet with its due reward," the thorny question was whom to pardon. Robinson provided him with detailed recommendations on each of the cases. As far as Overholser was concerned, Robinson termed him an "ignorant

man . . . of considerable property – a good farmer . . . not a man of influence or enterprise, and it is thought acted as he did from motives of personal enmity to the persons [the Angers and Clark] . . . who are not of themselves men of good characters." The proper objects of punishment, he noted, were not unfortunates such as Overholser, but notorious offenders. A petition for clemency signed by 95 residents of Bertie Township claimed that Overholser was "an honest peaceable Sober and Industrious Inhabitant." John Warren Jr's name headed the list of signatories and he forwarded the petition observing that Overholser was "worthy of every indulgence."

On 9 July Drummond approved Robinson's recommendations and respited the executions of nine men, one of whom was Overholser; the eight selected for execution were hanged, until dead, at Burlington Heights (Hamilton) on 20 July. Overholser was sent immediately to York and then forwarded to Kingston where he languished in a military jail awaiting confirmation of a royal pardon and transportation to Quebec and banishment. On 14 March 1815 he died of typhus fever. At the time of his death his farm was not fully paid for. A dispute over ownership ensued but his wife continued to reside there at least until January 1818. Ultimately his 196 acres were vested in the crown and sold in 1821.

The trial at Ancaster has been dubbed the "Bloody Assizes," perhaps from too great an emphasis on the executions on the heights and not enough on the trial itself and the deliberations that preceded it. From the War of 1812 until almost the present day Canadian political culture has shown little of the 18th-century whig concern with civil liberties. It is not, perhaps, unreasonable to discern in the wartime climate of opinion – the preoccupation with maintaining order and the demand by those in civil and military authority for immediate examples – an early manifestation of this tradition. Yet the wonder is that the result was not more bloody. In the end, young Robinson's insistence upon adhering "as much as possible" to the "common course of Justice" avoided the gory consequences which surely would have attended the summary treatment of traitors by the military under martial law. But, as events turned out, there were victims and Jacob Overholser was surely one. Although spared the horror of 20 July 1814, he was convicted of an overt act of treason. Correct according to statutory definition, the charge of treason against him was lacking altogether in substance. Overholser was an enemy of Clark and the Angers but he bore no treasonous intent towards Upper Canada. The magistrates knew it, his neighbours knew it, and, indeed, Robinson admitted it. This knowledge, however, was sufficient only to respite Overholser's execution, not to prevent his prosecution. The press of events – beleaguered authorities, a perilous military situation, and the perception of widespread disaffection and active treason – was his undoing.

ROBERT LOCHIEL FRASER III

AO, MS 4, especially J. B. Robinson letterbook, 1812–15; MS 74, package 27, Return of civilian prisoners confined in the Union Mill, 28 May 1814; Letter from T. Merritt, 18 July 1814; MS 500, Barbara Oberholser to Gilman Willson, bond, 9 Jan. 1818; MU 1368, Jacob Overholser; RG 4, A-I, 1; RG 22, ser.134, 4: 153–71. MTL, William Dummer Powell papers, L16, Calendar of prisoners at Ancaster, 1814: 12. Niagara South Land Registry Office (Welland, Ont.), Abstract index to deeds, Bertie Township: 210–11 (mfm. at AO, GS 2794); Deeds, Bertie Township, vol.A: 233–35 (mfm. at AO, GS 2796). Norfolk Land Registry Office (Simcoe, Ont.), Abstract index to deeds, Townsend Township, vol.A: 339. PAC, MG 11, [CO 42] Q, 318-1: 22–23, 30–31, 99–100, 124–27, 132–33, 142–43; 321: 59–68; RG 5, A1: 6514–15, 6523–24, 6528–35, 6667–73, 6704–9, 6741–43, 6761–69, 6779–81, 6787–91, 6804, 6845–52, 6859–64, 6868–75, 6880, 6902–4, 6932–33, 6937, 6939–41, 6943, 7307, 8258–61, 8511–12, 9345–46, 10200–1, 10221–23, 10340–41; RG 8, I (C ser.), 166: 84–87; 679: 148–50; 688C: 84–86a, 87–90, 97, 100–1; RG 9, I, B1, 2, Proclamation, 25 July 1814. Private arch., Christopher Robinson (Ottawa), Robinson papers (mfm. at AO). William Blackstone, *Commentaries on the laws of England* (4v., Oxford, 1765–69; repr. Chicago and London, 1979), 1: 357–61; 4: 74–93. U.C., House of Assembly, *Journal*, 1830, app., "Proceedings of the commissioners of forfeited estates," 143–60. *Kingston Gazette*, 5 Aug. 1814. *Montreal Herald*, 6 Aug. 1814. E. A. Cruikshank, "John Beverley Robinson and the trials for treason in 1814," *OH*, 25 (1929): 191–219; "A study of disaffection in Upper Canada in 1812–15," RSC *Trans.*, 3rd ser., 6 (1912), sect.II: 11–65. W. R. Riddell, "The Ancaster 'Bloody Assize' of 1814," *OH*, 20 (1923): 107–25. W. M. Weekes, "The War of 1812: civil authority and martial law in Upper Canada," *OH*, 48 (1956): 147–61.

P

PAGAN, WILLIAM, businessman and politician; b. 1744 in Glasgow, Scotland, eldest son of William Pagan and Margaret Maxwell; d. unmarried 12 March 1819 in Saint John, N.B.

The Pagan family had been active in the rising commerce of Glasgow since the 1650s. William Pagan Sr, a prominent sugar refiner there, established a strong commercial reputation through trading activities in the West Indies, in the Mediterranean, and along the Irish coast. In 1754 he and his brother John became burgesses and guild brethren of Glasgow, positions open to them because their father, David, had been admitted to the city as a merchant earlier in the century. Another brother, George, set up as a merchant in Greenock; a third, Thomas, successfully entered the London trading community as a silk-mercer. There were yet other family ties to London and the West Indies, as well as to the tobacco commerce of North America. Thus, by the 1760s, when a second generation of brothers – William, John, Robert*, and Thomas – left their home port of Glasgow for North America, they had the advantage of an existing network of commercial, financial, and political connections.

In 1766 William Pagan Jr was master of the sloop *Britannia* trading to St Eustatius. Operating in what was probably his father's vessel, he participated in the traditional trade in sugar and rum between the West Indies and the coast of North America, principally the stretch from Virginia to New York. By 1769 he had become firmly enough established in business at New York to warrant his admittance as a freeman of the city. Described as a shipping agent and shop proprietor, he likely dealt mainly in goods and supplies connected with the family businesses.

By 1777, it appears, Pagan had joined forces with his brothers Robert and Thomas under the business style of Robert Pagan and Company. Robert, at the age of 19 in 1769, had settled at Falmouth Neck, Mass. (Portland, Maine), where in partnership with the Greenock firm of Lee, Tucker and Company, he traded goods from the West Indies and Scotland in return for masts and timber. Thomas, the youngest brother, had joined him there in 1775. Later, both brothers had evacuated to Barbados and then gone on to New York, where they established Robert Pagan and Company. Meanwhile, John Pagan had been expanding his commercial horizons on another front, that of promoting the migration of settlers to America from Scotland. In 1772, as a merchant of Glasgow, he contracted with the Philadelphia Company to provide settlers for a tract of land at Pictou, N.S. [*see* John HARRIS]. The following year he financed the ship *Hector*, which carried around 200 passengers to Pictou Harbour.

The diverse operations and broad talents of the Pagan brothers brought them into contact with major businessmen and political figures on the eastern seaboard. Moreover, as a member and manager (1770–75) of the prestigious St Andrew's Society of

Pagan

New York, William enjoyed the company and respect of such worthies as the Reverend Dr John Witherspoon, president of the College of New Jersey (Princeton University) and a member of the Philadelphia Company; James Phyn, partner in the great trading business of Phyn, Ellice and Company of Schenectady, N.Y. [see Alexander ELLICE]; Colonel Beverley Robinson, a prominent New York landowner; Neil Jamieson, tobacco lord and agent for the firm of Glassford, Gordon and Company of Glasgow; William Shedden, son of Robert, head of a prominent London trading house; and Cadwallader Colden, lieutenant governor of New York. Several of these individuals were later to maintain solid ties with Nova Scotia.

By the time that Robert, William, and Thomas moved to Penobscot (Castine, Maine) in 1780, they had perfected a trading pattern which put them in touch with commercial establishments up and down the coast from Halifax to the West Indies. Spurred on by the prospect of a permanent loyalist haven at Penobscot [see John CALEFF], the Pagans cemented their links with Halifax through James McMaster and his three brothers, originally traders of Boston, Mass., but later of Nova Scotia, and through them established a close relationship with John WENTWORTH, who was to become lieutenant governor of Nova Scotia.

When it was eventually learned that the peace negotiations in early 1783 would designate the St Croix River and not the Penobscot as the boundary line between the new United States and British North America, William Pagan and his brothers made preparations to move to Nova Scotia. As an agent, along with William GALLOP, of the Penobscot Associated Loyalists, William assisted in re-settling nearly 430 families at St Andrews, in what was shortly to become the new colony of New Brunswick. His brother Robert decided to stay at St Andrews, but William moved up the coast to Saint John where, with Thomas, he established the firm of William Pagan and Company.

Reckoned by 1795 to be among the three largest of the 25 Scottish houses in Saint John, Pagan's company imported dry goods, rum, and a wide variety of Scottish manufactures. There were initial difficulties in the trade, largely due to the lack of currency with which to make remittances home in payment for goods brought in. However, as the New Brunswick timber trade developed, Pagan was able to consign an increasing number of lumber cargoes to the Clyde and also to the Mersey, where Liverpool was becoming the pre-eminent timber-importing centre in Great Britain. These exports put the firm on a sound basis for a thriving overseas commerce, and for expansion into other lines, including various forms of trade, licit and illicit, with the United States. In 1790 James GLENIE charged that Pagan and his brothers were openly looting government reserves of mast timber in the southern parts of the province. No action was taken against them, if indeed there was any truth in the allegations. The Pagans had early launched out into shipbuilding, and in the late 1780s they established a regular weekly packet service between Saint John and St Andrews. William Pagan was quick to see that the wartime scarcity of, and losses to, British shipping would put colonial-built vessels at a premium. Apart from building for his own fleet, he constructed several large ships of more than 200 tons for sale in Britain, and during the War of 1812 he was part-owner in several privateers. In 1812 his firm was acting as agent at Saint John for Lloyd's of London, and Pagan was engaged in the first marine-insurance transactions known in the colony. Unlike his brother Robert, he had early seen the advantage in diversifying his business operations. After 1800 Thomas Pagan was established on the northern shore of New Brunswick at Richibucto, where, in addition to shipbuilding, he engaged in milling and the fishery.

In his various commercial activities Pagan benefited greatly from his large network of contacts, both in North America and abroad. He expanded ties nurtured in New York by striking up a strong business relationship in New Brunswick with Colonel Robinson's son John*. Other British North American contacts included two of the largest operators in the colonies, William FORSYTH of Halifax, whose firm was a subsidiary of the Greenock house of Hunter, Robertson and Company, and James DUNLOP of Montreal. A long-standing relationship with John* and William* Black gave Pagan access to additional contacts in London and Greenock, while his association with James McMaster connected him with business circles in Boston and Portsmouth, N.H. Through Thomas at Richibucto trading connections were expanded to the Miramichi and to Pictou, N.S.; brother John guided the family's affairs at Quebec. However, the Quebec branch of the business became insolvent, and its difficulties had a reverberating effect on the whole North American operation.

It was not only through business that Pagan made his mark in New Brunswick. During the first, controversial elections to the House of Assembly in 1785 [see George Duncan LUDLOW], he was returned for Saint John County. Historian James Hannay* has described his legislative record as "honorable," for he consistently championed the cause of the assembly against what he considered to be the overweening power of the ruling hierarchy headed by Lieutenant Governor Thomas CARLETON. Pagan's interest in public affairs was also evident at the municipal level. In 1785 he became alderman for Queens Ward in Saint John and six years later he served as a fire warden. Patrick Campbell* described him in 1792 as among those "of the first character and respectability" in the city. He lived opposite St Andrew's Church in a house built of brick shipped from London. His landholdings in Saint John were extensive and included a large block at the southern end called Pagan Place.

A staunch adherent of the Church of Scotland, Pagan was one of the founders and incorporators of St Andrew's and participated directly in the building committee. In 1798 he became the first president of the St Andrew's Society of Saint John, a position he retained until 1801; he held the office again in 1806–12 and in 1815. Among the original members who met at the Exchange Coffee House were his business associates John and William Black, fellow merchants such as Hugh Johnston*, Munson Jarvis*, and Thomas Millidge*, Thomas Wetmore*, a future attorney general, and William Campbell*, the second mayor of Saint John. In 1803 Pagan was also a founding member of the Subscription Room, the first club in Saint John for which records remain.

Pagan was appointed to the New Brunswick Council in 1817, a notable event since he was the first adherent of a denomination other than the Church of England to be nominated. He thus became a member of the establishment that he had so often criticized. He was still attending council meetings when he died on 12 March 1819. The *Royal Gazette* reported that "he was ever conspicuous for his integrity, correctness and impartiality."

DAVID S. MACMILLAN and ROGER NASON

National Library of Scotland (Edinburgh), Dept. of MSS, MS 5039. PANB, "New Brunswick political biography," comp. J. C. and H. B. Graves (11v., typescript); RG 5, RS55; RG 10, RS108. PANS, MG 3, 150–51; RG 5, A, 1b, 1784. Private arch., W. H. Dunlop of Doonside (Ayr, Scot.), Dunlop papers. PRO, AO 12/11: 71; 12/61: 71; 12/109; AO 13, bundles 51, 93. SRO, Particular reg. of sasines, Renfrew. P. Campbell, *Travels in North America* (Langton and Ganong). *Royal commission on American loyalists* (Coke and Egerton). "United Empire Loyalists: enquiry into losses and services," AO *Report*, 1904. *Winslow papers* (Raymond). *The burgesses & guild brethren of Glasgow, 1751–1846*, ed. J. R. Anderson (Edinburgh, 1935). W. M. MacBean, *Biographical register of Saint Andrew's Society of the state of New York . . .* (2v., New York, 1922–25). Sabine, *Biog. sketches of loyalists*.

C. A. Armour and Thomas Lackey, *Sailing ships of the Maritimes . . . 1750–1925* (Toronto and Montreal, 1975). I. C. C. Graham, *Colonists from Scotland: emigration to North America, 1707–1783* (Ithaca, N.Y., 1956; repr. Port Washington, N.Y., and London, 1972). Hannay, *Hist. of N.B.*, 1: 340. I. A. Jack, *History of St. Andrew's Society of St. John, N.B., Canada, 1798 to 1903* (Saint John, 1903). J. S. Macdonald, *Annals, North British Society, Halifax, Nova Scotia, with portraits and biographical notes, 1768–1903* (Halifax, 1905). Macmillan, "New men in action," *Canadian business hist.* (Macmillan), 44–103. MacNutt, *New Brunswick*. R. P. Nason, "Meritorious but distressed individuals: the Penobscot Loyalist Association and the settlement of the township of St. Andrews, New Brunswick, 1783–1821" (MA thesis, Univ. of N.B., Fredericton, 1982). R. W. Sloan, "New Ireland: loyalists in eastern Maine during the American revolution" (PHD thesis, Mich. State Univ., East Lansing, 1971). J. R. Armstrong, "The Exchange Coffee House and St. John's first club," N.B. Hist. Soc., *Coll.*, 3 (1907–14), no.7: 60–78. T. M. Devine, "An eighteenth-century business élite: Glasgow–West India merchants, c. 1750–1815," *Scottish Hist. Rev.* ([Edinburgh]), 57 (1978): 40–67. Julian Gwyn, "The impact of British military spending on the colonial American money markets, 1760–1783," CHA *Hist. papers*, 1980: 77–99. D. R. Jack, "Robert and Miriam Pagan," *Acadiensis* (Saint John), 2 (1902): 279–87. W. H. Siebert, "The exodus of the loyalists from Penobscot and the loyalist settlements at Passamaquoddy," N.B. Hist. Soc., *Coll.*, 3 (1907–14), no.9: 485–529.

PAINTER, JOHN, merchant, office holder, and militia officer; b. *c.* 1745 in England; m. 1 Dec. 1786 Margaret Stuart in the Anglican church at Quebec, and they had six children; d. 11 Nov. 1815 at Quebec.

John Painter left England around 1765 and settled in the town of Quebec, probably as the representative of a British business firm. In 1771 he advertised in the *Quebec Gazette* that he had a stock of clothing from London. Subsequently he imported various goods, such as spirits, fabrics, shoes, and tools, which he sold wholesale or retail. In 1775 he purchased a schooner, the *Marie-Joseph*, for £133, probably to carry on trade along the shores of the St Lawrence. It seems reasonable to assume that for sending goods long distances he used ships belonging to the British firms he represented.

For reasons unknown Painter sold his belongings in 1776 and left the province of Quebec to return to Britain. After seven years' absence he decided to come back to the colony in order to carry on his business there. In June 1783 therefore he arrived from Bristol, England, on board the *Lively* with a variety of products that he expected to sell in the town of Quebec. His business seems to have prospered, since in 1786 he bought a lot of 28,500 square feet on the St Lawrence and a two-storey house on Rue Saint-Pierre at Quebec, where he conducted business from then on.

In an address delivered to Lieutenant Governor Henry Hamilton* in 1785 Painter declared himself in favour of trial by jury in commercial suits. Two years later he was appointed to a grand jury that reported to the Court of King's Bench in the District of Quebec. Eager for a role in politics, Painter supported the electoral campaign of Adam Lymburner* in 1792; Lymburner was, however, defeated in Lower Town Quebec.

Far from giving up business, Painter expanded his relations with merchants from abroad; in 1793 he was the representative for James Jones of Bristol and Thomas Franklin of Philadelphia, Pa. He also

Panet

established links with local producers such as the Quebec distiller James McCallum*, from whom he bought 1,666 gallons of "Esprit de Beauport" for £500 in 1801. In 1799 Painter had installed his business firm in a building on Rue du Sault-au-Matelot, which he did not buy until 1803. Two years later he was one of the chief shareholders in the Union Company of Quebec, set up to provide the town of Quebec with a fine hotel and a hall for meetings. He became a director of this company, and then chairman from 1810 to 1814. These new investments obliged Painter to step up his trading activities; in this may lie the reason for his opposition to the prison bill of 1805, which imposed a tax on commerce.

Having acquired a certain reputation in the merchant community, Painter was called upon to hold key offices in institutions dedicated to promoting commerce. For example, on 16 May 1805 Lieutenant Governor Sir Robert Shore Milnes* appointed him a member of Trinity House of Quebec, which had been founded to improve navigation on the St Lawrence [see François BOUCHER]. In addition to being treasurer in this organization from July 1805 to September 1808, Painter also served as deputy master from November 1805. In 1812 he was promoted master to replace merchant John YOUNG. During his years of service he and the other members set up a relief fund for pilots who were victims of accidents and for their families; he also had the first lighthouse on the St Lawrence built in 1809 at Île Verte and had some buoys installed. In 1809 Painter was entrusted by a gathering of Quebec merchants with another important responsibility; he was one of the seven merchants delegated to set up an association that would represent the interests of Quebec businessmen in dealing with the political authorities. This organization came into being at Quebec soon after as the Committee of Trade.

Painter also took part in Quebec community life. In 1790 he became a member of the Fire Society and served as its president in 1792 and 1799. In 1796 he received an appointment as a justice of the peace for the District of Quebec, a position he retained until his death. In addition to these prestigious offices he was commissioned an ensign in the Quebec Battalion of British Militia that year and was promoted lieutenant in 1801.

By all indications, John Painter gave up business in 1814; that year he sold the property on Rue du Sault-au-Matelot which served as his business premises and retired to a house on Rue Sainte-Ursule at Quebec, where he passed away on 11 Nov. 1815. The inventory made after his death reveals that he was worth more than £17,000, largely in debts owed him by the army, the navy, and merchants in Quebec and Great Britain. In addition to this considerable sum Painter owned nine houses in the parish of St Thomas

the Apostle in Devon, which he had inherited from his cousin Elizabeth Painter. He also had fourteen shares – six of which were worth £100 each – in the Union Company of Quebec.

ROCH LAUZIER

ANQ-Q, CE1-61, 1 Dec. 1786, 15 Nov. 1815; CN1-16, 17 janv., 23 mai 1811; CN1-26, 29 janv. 1806; 3 nov. 1807; 26 janv., 15 févr., 31 mai 1808; 3 mai 1810; 25 mars 1811; CN1-83, 16 déc. 1786; CN1-92, 17 mars 1794, 1er mars 1799; CN1-207, 11 avril 1775; CN1-230, 25 juin 1803, 8 août 1805, 6 mai 1807, 25 avril 1811, 28 nov. 1815; CN1-262, 26 janv. 1801. Port of Quebec Arch. (Quebec), Trinity House of Quebec, minute-books, I–II. Bas-Canada, *Statuts*, 1805, c.16. "Manifestes électoraux de 1792," *BRH*, 46 (1940): 99. *Quebec Gazette*, 13 June 1771; 25 May 1775; 19 Sept. 1776; 12 June 1783; 16, 23 June 1785; 8 June 1786; 17 May 1787; 11 Dec. 1788; 17 Dec. 1789; 21 Jan., 4 Feb., 25 March 1790; 14 June 1792; 16 May, 8 Aug., 12 Dec. 1805; 22 Sept. 1808; 2 May 1811; 29 Oct. 1812; 28 April 1814; 16 Nov. 1815. *Quebec almanac*, 1788–1815. Wallot, *Un Québec qui bougeait*, 57–58. O.-A. Côté, "La Chambre de commerce de Québec," *BRH*, 27 (1921): 26–28.

PANET, JEAN-ANTOINE, notary, lawyer, militia officer, seigneur, politician, and judge; b. 8 June 1751 at Quebec, the eldest son of Jean-Claude Panet* and Marie-Louise Barolet; m. 7 Oct. 1779 Louise-Philippe Badelard at Quebec; d. there 17 May 1815.

Jean-Antoine Panet probably received his education at the Séminaire de Québec. During the American invasion in 1775–76 [see Benedict ARNOLD; Richard Montgomery*] he was an ensign in the 1st company of the Quebec militia and took part in the defence of the town. He began to practise as a notary in 1772, but because of an ordinance issued in 1785 [see Pierre-Louis PANET], he had to give up this profession in 1786 to concentrate on his career as a lawyer, which he had taken up in 1773. His family's wealth and the income from his practice assured him of a fairly high standard of living. By 1777, for example, he had bought a two-storey stone house and a lot in Upper Town.

On 7 Oct. 1779 Panet made a good match when he married Louise-Philippe, daughter of Philippe-Louis-François BADELARD, surgeon to the Quebec garrison, and Marie-Charlotte Guillimin. He contributed £2,000 in cash and possessory rights to the joint estate, as well as a guarantee to his wife of a jointure of 1,500 *livres* a year and a preference legacy of £500. Fifteen children were born to the couple, five of whom reached adulthood: Bernard-Antoine (1780–1854), Marie (1788–1866), Philippe* (1791–1855), Louis (1794–1884), and Charles (1797–1877). Several, like their father, were active in the political and military spheres. By contrast, Panet's brothers and sisters left their mark mainly on the religious life of the province – in particular Abbé Jacques Panet*, Bishop

Bernard-Claude Panet*, who was appointed to the see of Quebec in 1825, and Ursulines Marie-Anne-Archange Panet, named de Saint-Bernard, and Marie-Françoise Panet, named de Saint-Jacques.

Through legacies, marriage, and his own work Jean-Antoine Panet built up a tidy fortune. In the course of his career he served as attorney in numerous cases, among others for the Séminaire de Québec, the *fabrique* of Notre-Dame in Quebec, and various persons, many of whom were British; on innumerable occasions he also acted as proxy, executor, and trustee. His comfort was assured; he and his family lived surrounded by five or six servants (chambermaids, cooks, menservants, a tutor for each child, and a nurse for each baby). In 1777 he became seigneur of Bourg-Louis. In 1795 he even refused appointment as a judge of the Court of King's Bench in Montreal and other offices; that decision would influence Lieutenant Governor Robert Shore Milnes* five years later to call for judges to be given salaries of more than £500, in view of the high incomes enjoyed by good lawyers. Panet was also involved in a great many real estate transactions and lending operations: an interest in the Union Company of Quebec from 1806 to 1808, which bought and rented buildings and lots; the purchase and resale of a large number of lots at Quebec and Trois-Rivières, not to mention obtaining grants to and selling lots on 1,400 acres in Nelson and Somerset townships; the purchase of the sub-fief of Monceaux, comprising 336 acres, in 1789; transactions arising from numerous legacies from his own family or his wife's; a score of loans ranging from £25 to £600, with interest at six per cent. In his will, which was dated 12 May 1815, Panet left half his seigneury of Bourg-Louis as well as a piece of land and a house at Quebec to his son Bernard-Antoine, made over the sub-fief of Monceaux, a house, and a building lot to his son Philippe, and assured his daughter Marie, who was married to Jean-Thomas Taschereau*, of an annual pension of £36. He also bequeathed £600 to be divided among his grandchildren upon his daughter's death. He entrusted the rest of his property to his wife, specifying that it was to be apportioned among the children not named in the will after her death.

As a lawyer Panet trained many of those seeking to enter the profession, including Amable Berthelot*, the son of Michel-Amable BERTHELOT Dartigny, in 1793, Denis-Benjamin Viger* and George Vanfelson* in 1798, his brother-in-law Bernard Badelard in 1799, and Georges-Barthélemi Faribault* in 1804.

Panet's reputation and talent earned him many offices and commissions in addition to those connected with his political activity itself. He served as a captain in the Quebec militia from 1787 to 1794 and as lieutenant-colonel in the Beauport militia battalion from 1794 to 1808. He was named a judge of the Court of Common Pleas in 1794 and judge of the Court of

King's Bench for the District of Montreal at the end of that year (a nomination he declined). He was also appointed to the commissions to examine the Jesuit estates in 1787 and to set the rate of exchange for government bills in 1812. On several occasions Panet was in the public eye, signing declarations of loyalty in 1794 and addresses to Prince EDWARD AUGUSTUS in 1794 and Governor Robert PRESCOTT in 1799. From 1790 to 1807 he was also a member of the Quebec Fire Society, and he subscribed to funds for the victims of a fire on the Rue du Sault-au-Matelot in 1793, in support of the war effort in 1799, and for the victims of a Quebec fire in May 1804.

Like a number of his compatriots, Panet waited until Governor HALDIMAND had left in November 1784 to come out openly in favour of the plan for constitutional and judicial reforms put forward by Pierre Du Calvet* in his ringing *Appel à la justice de l'État*, a work published in London that year. Less than ten days after Haldimand's departure, an event perceived by the reformers as a veritable liberation, some 15 members of the French-speaking bourgeoisie in the town of Quebec met to form a Canadian committee, and in conjunction with representatives of the British bourgeoisie prepared the text of the noted petition of 24 Nov. 1784. For the first time since the inauguration of the British régime, the forces of the English- and French-speaking middle classes were rallying to a common program of reforms; its main objective was, in the words of the original French petition, the creation of a "freely elected house of assembly . . . composed without distinction of old and new subjects," in order that they might be "confirmed in the full enjoyment of their civil and religious rights as British subjects." Since he had taken a leading role in bringing the Canadian reformers together, Panet found himself at the head of the Canadian committee for the town of Quebec, and he collaborated closely in drawing up the petition to the king and the "two houses of parliament."

When early in January 1785 Lieutenant Governor Henry Hamilton* received the English and French versions of the petition, each with an attached list of signatures, he was presented with the names of 855 "old subjects" and 1,518 "new subjects." Panet's name appeared at the head of the new subjects; nearly 400 of these were residents of the town of Quebec itself, more than a quarter of its adult male French Canadian population. In their covering letter to the lieutenant governor the members of the Canadian committees for Quebec and Montreal therefore noted rightly that a large proportion of "persons worthy of respect because of their personal qualities, their property holdings, their commercial interests, and their attachment to Great Britain" had signed the petition.

The alliance of bourgeois forces inevitably pro-

Panet

duced a quick and vigorous reaction from the seigneurial élite in the Montreal area, who mounted a veritable anti-reform campaign at the prompting of Pierre-Amable DE BONNE. This rearguard action by the defenders of the régime established under the Quebec Act was, however, doomed to failure, for far from shaking the convictions of the supporters of a new provincial constitution, it helped to galvanize the reform movement, as the numerous speeches and public stands of the Canadian committees for Quebec and Montreal show. The remarkable cohesion of the committees, whose members remained united until victory was won in 1791, was due not only to their steadfast adherence to the course they had chosen, but also to the articulate analysis of the reform leaders. The long text of the instructions that Panet drew up on behalf of the Quebec Canadian committee for the reformers' delegate, Adam Lymburner*, illustrates the point. Lymburner was to emphasize to the members of the imperial parliament that the Canadians had a legitimate right to consider themselves full British citizens and "as such" to share "without discrimination" in the constitutional prerogatives and privileges of representative government. Panet's preponderant influence within the Canadian committee for the town was to open the way for his entry on the political scene as speaker of the House of Assembly of Lower Canada.

In November 1787, probably as a result of a rumour that the Jesuit estates were to be transferred to Sir Jeffery Amherst*, 195 "respectable inhabitants" of the town of Quebec presented a petition to Governor Lord Dorchester [Guy CARLETON], pointing out that these estates really belonged to the Canadian people since the Jesuits had only held them in trust, and that they should be devoted to their original purpose, the education of Canadians. Panet, who had written this document, was appointed a member of the commission to inquire into the Jesuit estates which was set up by the government in December 1787 [see Kenelm CHANDLER]. He and his colleague, Gabriel-Elzéar TASCHEREAU, slowed down the work of the commission as much as they could, holding out for various legal conditions, including a proclamation in due form requiring the habitants to produce their title deeds, so as to establish clearly the rights of various people to the lands belonging to the Jesuit estates. In 1790 Panet and Taschereau, the two Canadians on the section of the commission drawn from the town of Quebec, refused to sign the report of the commissioners from that town and presented a separate minority report. Panet in particular was anxious that the Jesuit estates be used for educational purposes, specifically for creating a university open to Canadian and British settlers. His position fitted into the logic of a course of action common to bourgeois reformers, but it can probably also be explained by his independence of

mind in regard to the Catholic clergy; it was he who in 1808 cried out that the Séminaire de Québec was turing out young men who were "swinish, ignorant, and immoral."

The tactical alliance between the Canadian and British reformers soon fell apart. In the elections of 1792 Panet is reported to have given a speech on the steps of the church of Saint-Charles in Charlesbourg declaring that if the voters supported his candidacy and that of Berthelot Dartigny, "they would trample the English underfoot." Panet had indeed campaigned in the riding of Upper Town Quebec, where Charlesbourg was located and where he won a seat. After his victory he declared that he had "not given any cockades or liquor before or during his election," but he made a gift of £100 to the poor. When the first session of the House of Assembly was opened, Louis DUNIÈRE, seconded by Pierre-Amable De Bonne, nominated Panet for the office of speaker; he was elected by 28 to 18, despite the opposition of the British members. De Bonne's support for Panet may seem strange. The two men in reality headed conflicting movements, with De Bonne directing the reaction of the seigneurs and Panet being one of the leaders of the Canadian reform movement. The fact that De Bonne went over to his side when the speaker was being chosen can probably be explained by Panet's popularity and by De Bonne's wish to be on the winning side, and his nationalism – Panet was the only Canadian member from the town's two ridings and the only Canadian candidate for the speaker's office.

Upon his appointment as judge of the Court of Common Pleas in January 1794 Panet handed the speakership of the assembly over to Michel-Eustache-Gaspard-Alain Chartier* de Lotbinière. The reorganization of the judicial system that year led to the creation of courts of King's Bench, and Panet was offered a post as a judge in the one at Montreal. He declined and his cousin Pierre-Louis Panet was appointed in his stead. Until the end of the first parliament Jean-Antoine Panet sat as an ordinary member.

In the 1796 elections Panet was returned by acclamation in Upper Town. After his victory he offered a "hundred *piastres*" to the first woman in his riding to announce her marriage in church. At the beginning of the 1797 session De Bonne, who had joined the administration's party following his appointment as a judge of the Court of King's Bench at Quebec in 1794, nominated John YOUNG for speaker of the assembly. Panet, however, won by 17 votes. In the 1800 elections Panet was again returned, despite stronger opposition. When the new session opened, De Bonne's nomination for speaker was defeated by 16 votes, and Panet was again unanimously accorded the office, receiving congratulations from Lieutenant

Governor Milnes. Despite re-election in 1804 and a fourth term as speaker, Panet's situation was to become more difficult in the following years. The growing intensity of the conflicts between the Canadian party and the administration's party, which consisted of the British and a handful of Canadian allies, resulted in extremely virulent partisan attacks during the period 1805–10, from the time of the quarrel over prisons [see Jonathan Sewell*] until the "reign of terror" under Governor CRAIG. As speaker of the assembly Panet had to settle procedural questions and sometimes to cast his vote when the two parties in the house split evenly (particularly prior to 1808). On certain occasions he found himself in opposition to the Canadian party. But to his adversaries, his nationalism, his unquestioned support for the Canadian party on the most important matters, his share in the founding of the newspaper Le Canadien, and his altercations with De Bonne in the elections of 1808, 1809, and 1810 were just so many reasons to discredit this man who was an upright politician and a particularly honest and capable speaker.

In the 1808 elections De Bonne and Joseph-François Perrault* took advantage of the weighty influence of "placemen" in the riding of Upper Town Quebec to secure Panet's defeat by a government candidate, Claude Dénéchaud*. Panet then announced that he intended to run in Orléans, which prompted Perrault to send the parish priest, Jean-Marie Fortin, a slanderous letter casting doubt upon Panet's loyalty to the government. In any event, Panet had been re-elected in Huntingdon; this had been the very riding represented by Perrault from 1796 until 1804. Apparently the voters in the constituency had not appreciated Perrault's relations with judge De Bonne; the Canadian party had taken care to conduct its campaign with this in mind. Its brilliant victory brought Panet, as well as the other leaders of the party involved in putting out Le Canadien, a letter of reprimand from Governor Craig, who dismissed them from all their public offices, including their commissions as militia officers. Panet, who had displayed his loyalty by fighting during the siege of Quebec, made a dignified reply to the governor's secretary, Herman Witsius Ryland*, and asked him for an interview to dispel the calumnies that had been spread concerning him.

The governor's attitude could not help but strengthen the confidence that the Canadian party, which held the bulk of the seats in the assembly, had in Panet, and he was re-elected speaker despite the nomination of Denis-Benjamin Viger. After Craig had dissolved parliament in the spring of 1809, Panet won with a large majority in Huntingdon riding in the November elections. He was again speaker for the 1810 session. The imprisonment of members of the Canadian party in 1810 [see Craig] did not affect Panet, who was returned once more as member for Huntingdon and as speaker. Craig had not dared lay hands on a man who enjoyed such great prestige, although he considered him less dangerous and more easily influenced than other members of the Canadian party such as Pierre-Stanislas Bédard*.

Craig's departure and the threat from the United States cleared the political atmosphere. Panet benefited from that: Governor PREVOST gave him back his commission in the militia and recommended him for a seat on the Legislative Council, of which he became a member in February 1815. He had been returned in the 1814 elections, this time, however, in the riding of Upper Town Quebec. In January 1815 he was obliged for reasons of health to hand the speakership over to Louis-Joseph Papineau*. The assembly passed a vote of thanks "for his steady, impartial and faithful discharge of that high and important Station during Twenty two Years, by supporting on every occasion, the Honour and Dignity of the House, and the Rights and Privileges of the People." Panet's reply was full of sentiments of loyalty and faith in the ability of the constitution to ensure the peace and prosperity of the colony.

The assembly's homage was almost an epitaph. On 17 May 1815 Jean-Antoine Panet passed away at Quebec; his funeral was conducted by Bishop Plessis* in the cathedral of Notre-Dame. His wife outlived him by 15 years and died on 18 March 1830. The general esteem in which Panet was held found expression in the assembly's decision to consider paying him a pension for the rest of his life, and then to transfer it to his widow, a step which was taken in 1823.

JEAN-PIERRE WALLOT and PIERRE TOUSIGNANT

Jean-Antoine Panet's minute-book, containing the deeds which he notarized between 1772 and 1786, is deposited at the ANQ-Q, CN1-205.

ANQ-Q, CN1-16, 29–30 janv. 1816; CN1-25, 16 août, 9 sept. 1785; CN1-26, 29 janv. 1806; 3 nov. 1807; 26 janv., 26 mars 1808; CN1-83, 24 août 1786; 22 août 1787; 26 févr. 1788; 6 mars, 19 nov., 15 déc. 1789; 2, 10 juin, 11 oct. 1790; 27 avril 1792; CN1-178, 31 août 1803; 30 mai, 1er juin, 10 sept. 1804; 21 août 1809; CN1-230, 21 nov., 3, 19 déc. 1793; 13 oct. 1795; 8 janv., 24–25 févr. 1796; 9 janv. 1797; 4 avril, 7 mai, 9 juin, 4, 31 juill., 8, 10 oct. 1798; 27 janv., 18 mars, 30 avril, 27, 30 août 1799; 3 mai, 1er, 16 août, 22 sept., 16, 22 oct., 6 nov., 22 déc. 1800; 17 janv., 2 mars, 24 août, 30 sept. 1801; 13 avril, 11 mai 1802; 11 mai, 24 juin, 23 juill. 1803; 30 mai 1804; 19 juin 1805; 3, 8 mai, 24 oct., 4 nov. 1806; 11 mai 1807; 14 mai, 27, 29 déc. 1808; 7 févr., 6 mars, 10 juill. 1809; 30 janv., 30 juin 1811; 19 mars 1813; 5 oct. 1814; 12 mai 1815; CN1-262, 10 févr. 1795; 7 janv., 1er mars 1797; 5 déc. 1804; P-200. ASQ, C 35: 278, 318, 334–35; Polygraphie, XXXVI: 149, 206. PAC, MG 11, [CO 42] Q, 24: 236–38; 35: 60–116; 40: 85–105; 47: 187; 84: 172–73; MG 24, B2: 5134–41; MG 29, D72; MG 30, D1, 23: 536–680; RG 1, L3L: 1290, 2097, 75091; RG 7, G15C, 13: 158; RG 8, I (C ser.), 199: 26, 29; 703: 25; 1218:

Panet

366; RG 68, General index, 1651–1841. Bas-Canada, chambre d'Assemblée, *Journaux*, 1793–1815. *Doc. relatifs à l'hist. constitutionnelle, 1759–1791* (Shortt et Doughty; 1921), 2: 733–43; *Doc. relatifs à l'hist. constitutionnelle, 1791–1818* (Doughty et McArthur; 1915), 164, 364. *Petitions from the old and new subjects, inhabitants of the province of Quebec, to the right honourable the lords spiritual and temporal* (London, 1791). J.-T. Taschereau, "Lettre de l'honorable Jean-Thomas Taschereau, père du cardinal Taschereau, à son beau-père, l'hon. Jean-Antoine Panet," *BRH*, 9 (1903): 206–9. *Le Canadien*, 1807–10. *Le Courier de Québec*, 1807–8. *Quebec Gazette*, 1772–1815. *Le Vrai Canadien* (Québec), 1810–11.

F.-J. Audet et Fabre Surveyer, *Les députés au premier Parl. du Bas-Canada*. Caron, "Inv. de la corr. de Mgr Panet," ANQ *Rapport*, 1933–34: 235–421. Desjardins, *Guide parl*. Hare et Wallot, *Les imprimés dans le Bas-Canada*. P.-G. Roy, *Inv. concessions*, 1: 300–1; 4: 142; 5: 56–57. Christie, *Hist. of L.C.*, vols.1–2. R. C. Dalton, *The Jesuits' estates question, 1760–1888: a study of the background for the agitation of 1889* (Toronto, 1968). Paquet et Wallot, *Patronage et pouvoir dans le Bas-Canada*. P.-G. Roy, *La famille Panet* (Lévis, Qué., 1906). J.-P. Wallot, "Le Bas-Canada sous l'administration de sir James Craig (1807–1811)" (thèse de PHD, univ. de Montréal, 1965); *Un Québec qui bougeait*. Douglas Brymner, "La langue française au commencement du régime constitutionnel," *BRH*, 8 (1902): 52–55. Ignotus [Thomas Chapais], "Notes et souvenirs," *La Presse* (Montréal), 1er oct. 1904: 8; 26 nov. 1904: 8; 24 déc. 1904: 9; 14 janv. 1905: 16; 21 févr. 1905: 7; 19 avril 1905: 8. "Panet *vs* Panet," *BRH*, 12 (1906): 120–23. P.-G. Roy, "Sir Jeffery Amherst et les biens des jésuites," *BRH*, 12 (1906): 152–56. Pierre Tousignant, "La première campagne électorale des Canadiens en 1792," *SH*, 8 (1975): 120–48.

PANET, PIERRE (Pierre-Méru), notary, office holder, lawyer, judge, and politician; b. 1731 in the parish of Saint-Germain-l'Auxerrois in Paris, France, son of Jean-Nicolas Panet, a clerk in the office of the treasurers general of the Marine, and Marie-Madeleine-Françoise Foucher; m. 2 Oct. 1754 Marie-Anne Trefflé, *dit* Rottot, at Quebec, and they had 17 children, only 4 of whom survived them; d. 15 June 1804 in Montreal, Lower Canada.

Pierre Panet left France in 1746 to join his brother Jean-Claude*, who was a notary at Quebec. He immediately began to learn the notarial profession by becoming a clerk. On 15 Dec. 1754 Jean-Victor Varin* de La Marre, subdelegate of the intendant, accorded him a commission as notary for the jurisdiction of Montreal, replacing Henri Bouron. Two years later Intendant Bigot* confirmed this appointment.

With the capitulation of Montreal on 8 Sept. 1760 the court clerk, Louis-Claude Danré* de Blanzy, ceased to perform his duties and returned to France. On 19 September Panet succeeded him as clerk of the militia captains' court in the District of Montreal, a position he retained until that tribunal was abolished in 1764. During his term in office he drew up a list of the invoices for payment orders and bills of exchange in the Government of Montreal. In January 1765, a year after civil government had been restored, he and Pierre-François Mézière obtained permission to plead in the Court of Common Pleas. He did not, however, become a lawyer officially until 15 July 1768. That year he also obtained a commission to practise as a notary anywhere in the province of Quebec.

From 1760 to 1778 Panet served as clerk of the churchwardens' assembly in the Montreal parish of Notre-Dame. Despite many occupations he found time to manage the seigneury of Prairie-de-la-Madeleine, a Jesuit property, and in this capacity he made grants of some 60 farms between September 1772 and April 1778.

From the beginning of the British régime Panet had got along well with the authorities and through the years he displayed an unwavering loyalty. At the time of the negotiations preceding the adoption of the Quebec Act he recommended to the seigneur Michel Chartier* de Lotbinière, who was eager to represent his compatriots in London, that he leave this task to Governor Guy CARLETON.

On the eve of the American invasion in 1775–76 [*see* Benedict ARNOLD; Richard Montgomery*] Panet was chosen by Lieutenant-Colonel Dudley Templer as one of the eight citizens responsible for raising companies of volunteers. The measure proved unpopular, however, and Carleton had to re-establish the militia along the lines followed in the French régime. On 12 Nov. 1775 Panet was one of the 12 citizens who had to negotiate the capitulation of Montreal with Montgomery. Following Montgomery's defeat before Quebec on 31 Dec. 1775, Brigadier-General David Wooster, who was in command of the Americans in Montreal, gave orders for the loyalists, including Panet, to be arrested and disarmed. On 25 June 1776, soon after the American troops had retreated, Panet, along with Georges-Hippolyte Le Comte* Dupré and Edward William GRAY, was appointed commissioner with authority to regroup the militia of the parishes in the Montreal region, give commissions to trustworthy militiamen, confiscate arms from disloyal citizens, and draw up a report to the governor on the situation in every parish. Three months later he was entrusted with the office of commissioner to identify strangers moving about the province.

Panet aspired to the judiciary. The industry and intelligence he had displayed in his professional life made him a serious candidate. Nevertheless in 1775 he was deprived of the judicial post in Montreal by René-Ovide Hertel* de Rouville. After a few years of waiting, in April 1778 he was appointed judge in the Court of Common Pleas in the District of Quebec, replacing his brother Jean-Claude, who had died on 28 February. He then terminated his notarial and legal practice in Montreal and went to live at Quebec. He also became justice of the peace for the entire province in 1779, and on 11 November that year was made a judge of the Prerogative Court in the District of Quebec. Finally, on 24 Dec. 1788 his commission as judge of the Court of Common Pleas was extended to the District of Montreal and on 1 July 1790 to that of Trois-Rivières.

On 25 May 1791, after 13 years of intensive work as a magistrate, Panet told his children in a letter that he had just handed his resignation to Lord Dorchester [Guy Carleton]. Taken by surprise, the governor tried to dissuade him, noting that 60 was not a very advanced age and that he would much prefer him to retain office. Panet pointed out his 45 years of labour, the services he had rendered at the time of the American invasion, his own and his wife's infirmities, and his apprehensions about confronting the people who would soon be members of the House of Assembly, which he had opposed in January 1789. He also expressed the desire to spend his final years gardening and living quietly in the country.

Panet did retire to his haven at Lachenaie but he remained active. He became a commissioner for the building and repair of Catholic churches in the District of Quebec on 20 June 1791 and in that of Montreal five months later. In August of that year his commission as justice of the peace was renewed, and on 16 September he acceded to the prestigious office of member of the Executive Council of Lower Canada, which he held until his death. At the initial meeting of the assembly on 17 Dec. 1792 Panet was responsible for swearing in the members. Three members of his own family were in this first parliament: his sons Bonaventure* and Pierre-Louis and his nephew Jean-Antoine, the speaker of the house. In 1794 Panet also belonged to an association whose aim was to make the advice and recommendations of the governor known to the people.

After ten peaceful years in the country Marie-Anne Panet died suddenly on 4 June 1801 at the age of 68, and was buried in the parish of Saint-Charles at Lachenaie. She had been Panet's companion in life for nearly 47 years. A small woman, who remained pretty despite an attack of smallpox when she was 22, she was shy and ill at ease in public. Although she was considered a faithful wife, she caused her husband some anguish because of her capriciousness and jealousy. On 22 June 1801 Panet, claiming he was unable to manage his affairs, made over to his children, as their inheritance, all his property, which was valued at 111,877 *livres*. He kept only his sword, bed, and clothes and asked in return for a life annuity of £200 a year.

Having arrived at Quebec as an adolescent, Pierre Panet had taken advantage of his brother Jean-Claude's support and experience. The clarity and precision of his style are proof of a sharp and clear mind. Once he had settled down in Montreal, the city of trade, he rapidly became one of the notaries serving the bourgeoisie. His ability and good judgement were soon noticed by the authorities governing the province, and he was entrusted with various positions of responsibility. While he was engaged in a legal career he made some property deals that brought him substantial profits. His opulent homes bespeak his social status. In Montreal he lived in two-storey stone houses, one of which was on Rue Saint-François-Xavier. At Quebec he lived in a three-storey stone house on Rue Saint-Pierre that he had bought from Louis Dunière.

RAYMOND DUMAIS

Pierre Panet's minute-book for 1755 to 1778 is kept at the ANQ-M as CN1-308.

AC, Joliette, État civil, Catholiques, Saint-Charles (Lachenaie), 6 juin 1801; Minutiers, J.-É. Faribault, 8 déc. 1797; 22, 23 juin 1801. ANQ-M, CE1-51, 17 juin 1804; CL, 1767–99, 27 août 1790; CN1-74, 21 juin 1804; CN1-121, 2 mai 1802; CN1-158, 5 juin 1795; CN1-217, 7 juill. 1801; CN1-290, 13 juill. 1763; 31 août, 1er sept. 1764; 4 oct. 1777; 18 mars 1778; CN1-363, 1er déc. 1777; 11 août 1781; P1000-14-633. ANQ-Q, CE1-1, 2 oct. 1754; CN1-11, 29 sept. 1754; CN1-25, 22 sept. 1784, 28 juin 1785; E1, 41: f.3; 42: f.20; P-240, L'Assomption, Doc. de la famille Faribault. AUM, P 58, U, Panet à Baby, 3 juill. 1767, 22 mars 1779; Panet à sa fille, 2 févr. 1783; Panet à son frère, 5 nov. 1787, 2 janv. 1788; Panet à Guy, 31 janv. 1780; Panet à P.-L. Panet, 25 mai 1791, 25 déc. 1794; Panet à sa sœur, 1er juin 1791. Centre de recherche en civilisation canadienne-française (Ottawa), fonds Jacques Gouin. PAC, MG 18, K3. "État général des billets d'ordonnances" (Panet), ANQ *Rapport*, 1924–25: 231–33. "État général des états et certificats . . . ," Pierre Panet, compil., ANQ *Rapport*, 1924–25: 359. "État général des lettres de change . . . , Pierre Panet, compil., ANQ *Rapport*, 1924–25: 342–43. [Simon] Sanguinet, *L'invasion du Canada par les Bastonnois: journal de M. Sanguinet (suivi du siège de Québec)*, Richard Ouellet et J.-P. Therrien, édit. (Québec, 1975). *Quebec Gazette*, 21 April 1789; 28 Jan., 25 March, 4 Nov. 1790; 5 May 1791; 3, 10 July 1794. "Les notaires au Canada sous le Régime français," ANQ *Rapport*, 1921–22: 56–57. Michel Brunet, *Les Canadiens après la Conquête, 1759–1775: de la Révolution canadienne à la Révolution américaine* (Montréal, 1969), 240–41. Gonzalve Doutre et Edmond Lareau, *Le droit civil canadien suivant l'ordre établi par les codes, précédé d'une histoire générale du droit canadien* (Montréal, 1872), 592–95. J.-E. Roy, *Hist. du notariat*, 1: 8, 97, 183, 366–67. P.-G. Roy, *La famille Panet* (Lévis, Qué., 1906). F.-J. Audet, "Les juges de Trois-Rivières," BRH, 6 (1900): 244–47. "Lettres de noblesse de la famille Juchereau Duchesnay," BRH, 28 (1922): 137–41. Maréchal Nantel, "Les avocats de Montréal," *Cahiers des Dix*, 7 (1942): 185–213. "Les ordonnances et lettres de change du gouvernement de Montréal en 1759," ANQ *Rapport*, 1924–25: 230. "Panet vs Panet," BRH, 12 (1906): 120–23.

PANET, PIERRE-LOUIS, lawyer, notary, seigneur, office holder, politician, and judge; b. 1 Aug.

Panet

1761 in Montreal (Que.), son of Pierre PANET and Marie-Anne Trefflé, *dit* Rottot; m. there 13 Aug. 1781 Marie-Anne Cerré, daughter of Jean-Gabriel CERRÉ; d. there 2 Dec. 1812.

Pierre-Louis Panet was the seventh in a family whose first six children had died in infancy. On 26 June 1779, before he was even 18, he obtained a lawyer's commission, following the example of his father, who had chosen a career in law. On 19 Dec. 1780 he was admitted into the notarial profession. Combining the two functions had been allowed since 1765 to enable those who took advantage of the situation "to deal fully with the affairs of their clients," since they were "able to serve them in their dual capacity"; but the practice was beginning to be questioned by Governor HALDIMAND. Notaries were not, however, prohibited from acting as lawyers or clerks of law courts until an ordinance of 30 April 1785. Whether Panet practised as a lawyer cannot be confirmed; he did act as a notary in Montreal from 1781 until 1783, and then at Quebec until 1785.

On 22 Sept. 1783 Panet was appointed French-language clerk of the Court of Common Pleas in the District of Quebec, replacing Nicolas-Gaspard BOISSEAU. His wife, who was then pregnant, had left for Quebec with their first child late in the spring. Panet himself remained in Montreal to liquidate their property. On 1 June 1783 he wrote to his wife that he hoped to join her in ten days or so, but on 27 August he was still in Montreal and had not yet succeeded in selling their house. He complained that people were haggling about the price and he very much feared he would be "losing a lot of money." During the months when he was on his own he resided with Thérèse-Amable Viger, the widow of Jean Orillat*, and attended to settling the estate of the latter, for whom Pierre Panet, his father, had acted as notary for 20 years.

Panet also secured appointment as clerk "for Canadian matters" in the Prerogative Court on 25 Jan. 1785. Having had to give up practising as a notary that year, he was reduced to the sole occupation of court clerk, which provided little satisfaction. In a letter written to the seigneur Louis Couillard Des Islets around this time, he compared the splendour of a seigneur's life with the sadness and disgust that life as a court clerk brought him. He even considered giving up his position: in 1787 he wrote to Boisseau (the very person he had replaced in the Court of Common Pleas), offering to surrender the office to him for "300 *louis* at the going rate as compensation"; he was determined, he said, to retire to the seigneury of Argenteuil, which he had bought in February 1781. Late in the summer of 1790 Panet's wife decided to visit her parents in St Louis (Mo.). She went off with their son Léon, leaving her husband at Quebec with their 18-month-old daughter Louise-Amélie. The separation, which apparently was not unconnected to an already tense relationship between them, lasted a whole year.

At the time of the 1792 elections Panet first announced that he would run in the riding of Quebec, but soon changed his mind and switched to that of Cornwallis, where he was elected on 10 July along with Jean DIGÉ. Throughout the sessions of this first parliament in Lower Canada Panet attracted attention by his almost unbroken solidarity with the English party. For example, he opposed the choice of his cousin Jean-Antoine PANET as speaker of the house; according to him this office required that the person holding it be able to "express himself in the English language when he addresses the representative [of the] sovereign." Furthermore he declared it was "absolutely necessary in the long run for Canadians to adopt the English language, the only way to dissipate the repugnance and suspicions that diversity of language would always foster between two peoples united by circumstances and compelled to live together." He was also the sole Canadian, along with François Dambourgès, who voted for the bill to make the English text of parliamentary laws and debates the only official one. In the 1793 session he introduced a bill on the abolition of slavery, but his colleague Pierre-Amable DE BONNE succeeded in keeping the assembly from voting on its third reading.

The judicial reform of 1794 led to the abolition of the Court of Common Pleas and the Prerogative Court and their replacement by the Court of King's Bench, to which Panet on 11 Dec. 1794 was appointed protonotary and French-language clerk for the District of Quebec. On 8 May 1795 he became judge of this court for the District of Montreal, after Jean-Antoine Panet had refused the office. He must have greeted the new appointment with relief, for it put an end to his monotonous career as a court clerk, assured him of an annual salary of £500, and enabled him to move closer to his seigneury of Argenteuil, where he hoped some day to live. He was eager to develop this property, on which there were already several new dwellings, some gardens, and two mills in operation.

Kept busy by his duties as a judge, Panet stopped participating in the work of the assembly and did not run in the 1796 elections. Four years later he decided to return to politics, though with considerable reluctance since he thought "it did not befit him as a judge to be a candidate." Yielding to the pleas of constituents in Montreal East, he resolved that he "would do nothing to secure his election." He left Montreal to go on the assizes and was not present on any occasion when voting took place. None the less he was elected on 28 July 1800 and carried out his duties as a member assiduously, despite the annoyance that his long stays at Quebec caused him. As he had done during his first term, Panet continued to support the

English party, from whom he hoped to obtain further patronage. On 18 March 1802 he wrote to his wife that he was "surrounded . . . by envious people who are vexed to see that the governor and his wife continue to show me the same consideration." The lieutenant governor, Robert Shore Milnes*, had indeed recommended in October 1800 that Panet be made an honorary member of the Executive Council and this appointment was approved on 7 Jan. 1801 by the Duke of Portland, the Home secretary. No remuneration was attached to the office. By 1 Oct. 1800, however, Panet's salary as a judge had been raised to £750 a year as a result of a petition that the puisne judges of the Court of King's Bench had addressed to Milnes on 17 Oct. 1799. According to the lieutenant governor the salary increase was justified to ensure the recruitment of suitable people for the judiciary, since at a salary of £500 a year only second-rate lawyers would be willing to give up their profession to become judges. In August 1809 and again in October 1810 Panet joined with his colleagues on the court to ask for another increase, pleading the continual rise in the cost of living and the growing volume of judicial matters, but the request met with a refusal from Lord Liverpool, the Colonial secretary.

Panet seldom missed an opportunity to display his loyalty to the British authorities. In May 1803, for example, he passed on to Herman Witsius Ryland*, the lieutenant governor's secretary, excerpts from two incriminating letters which his father had received from a former compatriot then living in France; in substance these said that the writer had presented a memoir to Napoleon urging that Canada be given back to France. Panet feared that a "surprise attack" would be successful "if the French were favoured by the Canadian population," and he suggested that the province be equipped with a "military force sufficient to contain those who might be disaffected and to encourage the friends of the government."

Panet served as a judge and member of the Executive Council until his death, but he gave up his seat in the assembly after 1804. He is said to have declared frequently that judges should not stand for election and that "the equality of the members and the freedom of debates [in the assembly] often damaged a judge's reputation." In 1812 Panet presided at the trial of some men from Lachine who were charged with riotous assembly when the militia was called up. The accused were found guilty by a jury and were given one to two years in prison and fines of up to £100. Before pronouncing sentence Panet dwelt upon the seriousness of what each of the rioters had done and drew a parallel between the period when "under the former rule of the French . . . the country groaned in poverty and difficulty" and the years since the conquest when prosperity had prevailed. In conclusion he declared, "And you would like to destroy the

government that creates happiness for you. You would be so ungrateful as not to recognize its benefits."

Both during his years at Quebec and after his return to Montreal Panet engaged in numerous real estate transactions. In 1792 his father had given him as an advance portion of his inheritance a piece of land near the Rivière Saint-Charles, which he sold the following year. Panet often took advantage of forced sales to buy properties cheaply, in both Quebec and its suburbs. He resold them when he had to move to Montreal. On 18 Oct. 1796 he bought an immense property in the *faubourg* Québec in Montreal, on a street that now bears his name. He went to live there with his family and retained it until 1810, when he sold it to judge James Reid. In 1802 he purchased in addition an imposing house beside the Château Ramezay. He regretted having made this acquisition which was "beyond his means," and hastened to sell it to Andrew McGill the following year. In 1800 he had also sold his seigneury of Argenteuil and bought the seigneuries of Ailleboust and Ramezay; in addition he obtained a grant of 1,000 acres in Chatham Township the following year.

Pierre-Louis Panet died suddenly of a stroke on 2 Dec. 1812. At that time only 5 of his 12 children were still living. His widow tried in vain to obtain a grant of several thousand acres in Ascot and Aston townships. In 1826 she asked for a pension of £150 in recognition of the services rendered by her husband, but the assembly turned down her request.

ANDRÉ MOREL

Pierre-Louis Panet's minute-book for the years 1781 to 1783 is kept at the ANQ-M as CN1-309 and, for 1783 to 1785, at the ANQ-Q as CN1-209.

ANQ-M, CN1-363, 11 août 1781. ANQ-Q, CN1-230, 21 août 1792; 18 oct. 1793; 30 avril, 22 juill. 1794; 24 juill., 3 août 1795. AUM, P 58, U, Panet à Cerré, 1er juin, 27 août 1783; 27 sept. 1790; 27 avril, 12, 26 mai, 29 juin, 24 juill. 1791; 18 mars 1802; 10, 17 févr. 1803. PAC, MG 11, [CO 42] Q, 71-1: 98; 72-1: 16; 84: 172, 177; 85: 209; 87-1: 5. Bas-Canada, chambre d'Assemblée, *Journaux*, 1792–96; 1801–4; 1809, app.23. *Montreal Herald*, 5 Dec. 1812. *Quebec Gazette*, 20 Dec. 1792. F.-J. Audet, *Les députés de Montréal*, 47–63. Fernand Ouellet, "Inventaire de la Saberdache de Jacques Viger," ANQ *Rapport*, 1955–57: 69. P.-G. Roy, *Inv. concessions*, 3: 221–22; 5: 29, 33; *Les juges de la prov. de Québec*, 421. Caron, *La colonisation de la prov. de Québec*, 1: 189–91. Neatby, *Administration of justice under Quebec Act*, 62, 351. P.-G. Roy, *La famille Panet* (Lévis, Qué., 1906), 163–96. Trudel, *L'esclavage au Canada français*, 296. André Vachon, *Histoire du notariat canadien, 1621–1960* (Québec, 1962). Wallot, *Un Québec qui bougeait*, 107–41. Hare, "L'Assemblée législative du Bas-Canada," *RHAF*, 27: 371–73, 376. É.-Z. Massicotte, "Brève histoire du Parc Sohmer," *Cahiers des Dix*, 11 (1946): 97–117; "Quelques maisons du vieux Montréal," 10 (1945): 239.

Pangman

PANGMAN, PETER, fur trader; b. 30 Aug. 1744 in Elizabeth Town (Elizabeth), N.J.; m. 28 March 1796 Grace MacTier in Montreal, Lower Canada, and they had nine children of whom four survived infancy; d. 28 Aug. 1819 in Mascouche, Lower Canada.

Little is known of Peter Pangman's early life. By 1767 he was involved in the fur trade out of Michilimackinac (Mackinaw City, Mich.), having been licensed to trade that year in the region of the Mississippi River through La Baye (Green Bay, Lake Michigan). In 1771 he entered into a partnership in which he held one of three equal shares, another being held by Joseph Fulton and the third by the existing partnership of Forrest Oakes* and Charles Boyer. Early in the summer of 1773 Pangman paid a visit to the Hudson's Bay Company's York Factory (Man.) to look into the possibility of shipping his partnership's furs through Hudson Bay, a route which would be considerably cheaper than the one through Michilimackinac and Montreal. Chief factor Ferdinand Jacobs*, regarding Pangman as nothing more than an intruder on HBC territory, "gave him a good supply of goods to carry him back again & notice to him and another pedler to remove off the Company's Land."

In 1774 Fulton left the partnership to become an independent trader on Lake Timiskaming, and the three remaining partners now held equal shares. Pangman moved to the Saskatchewan River: Samuel Hearne*, in charge of the HBC's Cumberland House (Sask.), noted in June 1775 that Pangman was settled some 150 miles upstream from him, as were Charles Paterson, "Francis" (François Leblanc, *dit* Latour, known to the Indians as Shash or Saswee), and William Holmes*. By 1777 Pangman had moved farther westward to Sturgeon River Fort, on the North Saskatchewan at the mouth of the Sturgeon River (Sask.), where Peter POND also spent the winter of 1777–78.

As the partnership of Pangman, Oakes, and Boyer was coming to an end in 1778, Pangman sought association with other traders. That year he was involved in the establishment of Fort Montagne d'Aigle (in the Eagle Hills, Sask.), nine miles below the confluence of the Battle and North Saskatchewan rivers. During the winter of 1778–79 he was a member of a traders' alliance which included Holmes, Booty Graves, Robert Grant, and Charles McCormick. This was one of the early associations, designed to lessen competition, which eventually led to the formation of the North West Company. Maltreatment of the local Crees by John Cole* and others resulted the following spring in the Indians killing Cole and one of Pangman's men, and evicting the traders from their stronghold. By 1779 Pangman was in partnership with John Ross, and during the 1779–80 season the first NWC appears to have come into being, "Ross & Co." holding one of 16 shares. Pangman spent that

season and the ensuing winters until 1782–83 at Sturgeon River Fort, once rebuilding it after a summer in which the local Indians, probably Crees, had burned it down. William Tomison*, in charge of the HBC's Hudson House (about 30 miles farther up the North Saskatchewan), referred to him in February 1783 as "Chief Master" at Sturgeon River Fort.

Although involved in early cooperative ventures among the traders on the Saskatchewan, Pangman was not included as a shareholder in the NWC agreement of 1783–84. He and Peter Pond, who was dissatisfied with the offer of only one share in the new concern, went to Montreal with the aim of persuading John GREGORY and Normand MacLeod*, partners in Gregory, MacLeod and Company, to support them in opposition. Pond soon changed his mind and returned to the west to take up his NWC share. Pangman and his associate Ross, also excluded from the new organization, prevailed upon Gregory and MacLeod, who in 1784 admitted them, with Alexander MACKENZIE, to partnership in the firm. That year Pangman wintered on the South Saskatchewan River in competition with his former ally, Holmes. In the heat of subsequent rivalry with the NWC, Ross, who in 1786–87 was opposite Pond some 40 miles up the Athabasca River from Lake Athabasca, was killed by Pond's men during the winter. In order to avoid further bloodshed the two concerns united in 1787 to form the new, 20-share NWC, in which each of the four remaining partners of Gregory, MacLeod, including Pangman, held one share. When the agreement was renegotiated three years later he increased his holdings to two shares.

In 1790 Pangman travelled up the North Saskatchewan River to a point three miles above present-day Rocky Mountain House (Alta), farther upstream than any white trader had gone until that time. He commemorated his achievement by blazing a spruce tree which became a landmark to later travellers such as David Thompson* and Alexander HENRY.

On 1 Aug. 1793 Pangman left the west for the last time, setting out from Grand Portage (near Grand Portage, Minn.) with Robert Grant and others for Montreal. John Macdonell* recorded their departure with regret, noting at the same time that Pangman and Grant "retire from the concern with handsome competencies." On 3 Nov. 1794 Pangman bought the seigneury of Lachenaie, near Montreal, from Jacob Jordan*. In 1792 he had subscribed five guineas to the building fund for the Scotch Presbyterian Church in Montreal, and there on 28 March 1796 he married Grace MacTier. One of their sons, John, in 1837 became a member of the Legislative Council of Lower Canada. Pangman was also the father of a mixed-blood son known as Bastonnais Pangman (his given name may have been Joseph), who was prominent in Métis resistance to the attempts by Lord Selkirk

[DOUGLAS] to colonize the Red River district. Peter Pangman died in his residence at Mascouche on 28 Aug. 1819.

IN COLLABORATION

Private arch., J. B. Pangman (Toronto), A. J. Van Den Bergh, "Pedlar Pangman of the Saskatchewan" (typescript, 1963). *Les bourgeois de la Compagnie du Nord-Ouest* (Masson), 1: 10, 35, 38. *Docs. relating to NWC* (Wallace). *Five fur traders of the northwest . . .*, ed. C. M. Gates ([2nd ed.], St Paul, Minn., 1965). *Journals of Hearne and Turnor* (Tyrrell). *New light on early hist. of greater northwest* (Coues). R. Campbell, *Hist. of Scotch Presbyterian Church*. Morton, *Hist. of Canadian west*. A. S. Morton, "Forrest Oakes, Charles Boyer, Joseph Fulton, and Peter Pangman in the north-west, 1765–1793," RSC *Trans.*, 3rd ser., 31 (1937), sect.II: 87–100.

PANTON, GEORGE, Church of England clergyman; b. in Scotland, possibly at Kelso, one of eight children; d. 8 Aug. 1810 in the British Isles.

George Panton received his BA and MA from Marischal College (University of Aberdeen). In 1771, shortly after his ordination as a Church of England clergyman, he emigrated to New York where he became a "Tutor to a Young Gentleman." Two years later, in November 1773, he entered the employ of the Society for the Propagation of the Gospel as rector of St Michael's Church in Trenton, N.J., a charge he supplemented with missionary duty in the neighbouring communities of Allentown, Princeton, and Maidenhead (Lawrenceville). Just prior to the revolution he moved to Maryland to assume a post that combined the duties of schoolmaster and clergyman, but with the outbreak of hostilities in 1775 he abandoned these plans and returned to Trenton.

Panton never made a secret of his loyalist sympathies. In the early 1770s, as part of his campaign to "quiet the Minds of the People," he joined three prominent loyalists, Charles INGLIS, Myles Cooper, and Thomas Bradbury Chandler, in publishing essays supporting the British cause, and at his own expense he travelled throughout New York, Pennsylvania, and Maryland attempting to counteract "the popular system" and maintain "Civil Government." Following the skirmish at Lexington, Mass., on 19 April 1775, he drew up a petition from the freeholders of Nottingham (near Allentown) expressing their attachment to the crown and urging the New Jersey House of Assembly to use its influence to effect a speedy reconciliation with Britain. The evidence is contradictory, but it seems he left Trenton after the signing of the Declaration of Independence. In October 1776 he joined the British army in the field at White Plains, N.Y. For the next couple of months, as the army marched through New York and New Jersey, Panton played an important role in furnishing his officers, including Captain John Montresor*, with valuable

military intelligence. His services were rewarded in 1778, when he was appointed chaplain of the Prince of Wales's American Regiment. Further appreciation of his efforts in this campaign – efforts which he claimed were "known to almost every General Officer in the Middle Colonies" – was shown in the testimonials that accompanied his petition for a government pension in 1786. Among the individuals who then praised Panton's military record were Lord Charles Cornwallis, Sir William Howe, and former governors William Tryon and William Franklin of New York and New Jersey.

Panton probably spent the last years of the war in New York, performing his duties as chaplain and, in 1783, operating a military academy. With the evacuation of the city in late 1783, Panton joined those loyalist refugees who made their way to Shelburne, N.S. There he immediately became involved in a bitter struggle with a rival Anglican clergyman, a struggle that exposed a conflict between New World and Old World methods of clerical appointment. When he had been invited by some of the leaders of the settlement to be their minister, Panton, indicating his interest, had received both salary and blessing from the SPG. Because of confusion over his intentions and his health, some loyalists had assumed he was not going to take the position and therefore extended an invitation to William Walter, the former rector of Trinity Church in Boston, Mass. The ministers arrived in the community within a few days of each other, both claiming to represent the Church of England in Shelburne and each seeking support from parishioners, Governor John Parr*, and the SPG. Panton based his claim upon the invitation of the leading loyalists and the SPG's approval of him as missionary. Walter displayed petitions to show that he was the people's choice and, when neither Parr nor the SPG showed any enthusiasm for his claim, placed greater and greater emphasis upon the necessity of popular support. To Panton such appeals flouted "public authority" and encouraged principles dangerous equally to church and to government.

With fiery letters to the editors of the Shelburne papers, with petitions and meetings, accusations and counter-accusations, the dispute between Panton and Walter was acrimonious and divisive. The two parties created separate vestries – Walter's supporters were known as the "Vestry of Trinity Church," while Panton's styled themselves the "Parish of St Patrick" – and applied for SPG grants. In 1784 Parr, on Panton's recommendation, divided Shelburne into the parishes of St Patrick, St George, and St Andrew, appointing Panton to St Patrick's, Walter to St George's, and leaving St Andrew's vacant. Walter protested against this action, however, and continued arguing that he alone had the right to act as the Anglican clergyman in Shelburne. Finally, in 1785, a

Parent

worn-out and dispirited Panton gave up the fight and retired from the settlement, hoping that Walter would also resign and a new minister be appointed to heal the community's wounds. His successor at St Patrick's, John Hamilton Rowland, remained at odds with Walter until 1788, when the rival parishes of St Patrick and St George merged. Together the two congregations, under the joint care of Rowland and Walter, hired the services of local builders Isaac HILDRITH and Aaron White to begin the construction of Christ Church. In 1791, two years after the completion of the church, Walter returned to Boston, leaving Rowland as the sole rector of the United Parishes of St Patrick and St George.

With Shelburne behind him, Panton was commissioned, apparently by Parr, to solicit funds in Great Britain for "erecting Places of Worship in the several New Settlements in Nova Scotia." He arrived in England in February 1786, and the following month was successful in obtaining an annual pension of £40 from the British government. Soon afterwards the SPG appointed him to Yarmouth, N.S. By now, however, Panton seems to have given up the idea of returning to the colony, hoping instead for a suitable "provision" in Britain. On 14 March 1787 he wrote from London asking the SPG for permission to postpone his trip to Halifax because his mother was dying and wanted him to stay with her to the end. One month later he claimed that the illness of his two sisters prevented him from going to his mission.

In September 1788 Panton was at Kelso, Scotland, probably on family business. Thereafter his name disappears from view until 1811, when the British Treasury, noting his death on 8 August of the previous year, discontinued both his half pay and his pension. Although little is known of his personal life, it appears he was something of a scholar. In his petition to the loyalist claims commission in 1783, he stated that his losses during the revolution included approximately 200 books and more than 40 manuscript volumes of his own "Essays, Sermons, Belles Lettres, Criticism, Philosophical Investigations etc, the labour of many years, on which a value cannot be affixed."

NEIL MacKINNON

PANS, RG 5, A, 1a. PRO, AO 12/15: f.8; 12/63: f.2; 12/101: f.320; 12/109: f.252; AO 13, bundles 19, 62, 83, 93, 111 (mfm. at PAC); PMG 4/85: f.65; T 50/11, 50/22 (mfm. at PAC). USPG, B, 6, no.25; 25 (transcripts at PAC); C/CAN/NS 1 (transcripts at PAC). "United Empire Loyalists: enquiry into losses and services," AO *Report*, 1904: 53–54. *Nova-Scotia Packet: and General Advertiser* (Shelburne, N.S.), 1785. *Port-Roseway Gazetteer; and, the Shelburne Advertiser* (Shelburne), 1784–85. *Royal American Gazette* (Shelburne), 1784–85. *Fasti Academiæ Mariscallanæ Aberdonensis: selections from the records of the Marischal College and University, [1593–1860]*, ed. P. J.

Anderson and J. F. K. Johnstone (3v., Aberdeen, Scot., 1879–98), 2: 329, 331. Lorenzo Sabine, *The American loyalists, or biographical sketches of adherents to the British crown in the war of the revolution . . .* (Boston, 1847).

A. W. [H.] Eaton, *The Church of England in Nova Scotia and the tory clergy of the revolution* (New York, 1891). Fingard, *Anglican design in loyalist N.S.* E. A. Jones, *The loyalists of New Jersey: their memorials, petitions, claims, etc., from English records* (Newark, N.J., 1927; repr. Boston, 1972). C. F. Pascoe, *Two hundred years of the S.P.G. . . .* (2v., London, 1901). J. M. Bumsted, "Church and state in Maritime Canada, 1749–1807," CHA *Hist. papers*, 1967: 41–58. Neil MacKinnon, "Nova Scotia loyalists, 1783–1785," SH, no.4 (Nov. 1969): 17–48. W. O. Raymond, "The founding of Shelburne: Benjamin Marston at Halifax, Shelburne and Miramichi" and "The founding of the Church of England in Shelburne" in N.B. Hist. Soc., *Coll.*, 3 (1907–14), no.8, pages 204–77 and 278–93 respectively.

PARENT, MARIE-GENEVIÈVE, named **de Saint-François d'Assise**, hospital nun of the Hôtel-Dieu in Quebec and superior; b. 10 Nov. 1740 at Quebec, daughter of Joseph Parent and Marie-Anne Chatellereaux; d. there 22 Dec. 1804.

Marie-Geneviève Parent was the daughter of a master ship's carpenter who lived on Rue Saint-Vallier, in the Palais quarter. She entered the convent of the Hôtel-Dieu on 30 April 1755, when she was only 14. On 7 June the convent, chapel, and hospital burned down and the nuns were forced to take refuge with the Ursulines. Three weeks later they moved into a wing of the Jesuits' house and it was in these makeshift premises that the young novice took her vows on 15 Nov. 1756. For her dowry her father provided 2,500 *livres* in payment orders drawn on the treasurers general of the Marine; the community itself added 500 *livres* from a foundation established in 1675 by Abbé Gabriel Thubières* de Levy de Queylus to supply dowries to nuns without means.

On 1 Aug. 1757 the nuns took possession of their new convent, which had been rebuilt at the cost of a heavy debt amounting to more than 100,000 *livres*. After the surrender of Quebec in 1759 they were able to keep only part of the building for their use, since a shortage of barrack space forced the military authorities to lodge some British troops in it. Despite the rent paid for the occupancy, which was maintained until 1784, and the donations of benefactors such as Bishop Briand* and Governor Murray*, the community had to employ all possible expedients to try to discharge its large debts: the hospital nuns had to become laundresses and bakers, sell several pieces of land, and, finally, put back under development their farm at La Canardière and their seigneuries of Saint-Augustin and Île-aux-Oies. In addition to having financial difficulties the community had received few postulants since 1755 and recruitment remained slow for 30 years.

It was in this context that the chapter of the community elected Marie-Geneviève de Saint-François d'Assise novice mistress in 1772. After she had held this office for four years, her responsibilities increased: from 1776 to 1786 she was annually elected depositary of the community by the assembly of choir nuns; then she was superior from 1786 to 1792 and again from 1795 to 1801. Between her two terms of office as head of the community, she held another elective post, that of assistant.

In the autumn of 1799 the nuns of the Hôtel-Dieu, with Marie-Geneviève de Saint-François d'Assise in charge, decided to go ahead with a project they had long cherished: the rebuilding of their chapel, which had been destroyed by the fire of 1755. Their finances, however, were still precarious and insufficient for the community to undertake such an endeavour without another source of income. Thus the hospital nuns had to appeal to public charity through a subscription, launched on 15 Dec. 1799, of which Antoine-Bernardin Robert*, bursar of the Séminaire de Québec and also confessor to the nuns of the Hôtel-Dieu, took charge. Difficulties arose, however, over the size of the future chapel. Some of the nuns, notably the superior and Marie-Angélique Viger, named de Saint-Martin, favoured a more imposing building than was needed; others were readier to accept a less extravagant project. Although internally divided, the community supported the more ambitious plans which to Bishop DENAUT and coadjutor designate Bishop Plessis* seemed much too vast and which they vetoed. After an exchange of letters that reveal the fiery personalities of their writers, a compromise solution was accepted unanimously: the chapel would equal in size that of the Ursulines of Quebec. Abbé Philippe-Jean-Louis Desjardins* drew up the plans and Pierre ÉMOND supervised the work. Building itself began in the spring of 1800 and was finished in 1803; the interior decoration took several more years.

The name of Marie-Geneviève de Saint-François d'Assise is also associated with charitable work for abandoned children. In January 1801 the House of Assembly set up a committee to investigate the position of the religious communities regarding assistance to the poor. The superior first maintained that the hospital nuns' vocation was solely to care for the sick; responsibility for waifs was obviously incompatible with their duty because of the constant attention and additional expense it would entail. Nevertheless, at the assembly of the nuns held on 3 March 1801, the community reversed its stand and agreed to take care of foundlings on condition that the government assume the costs for room and board and other necessary expenses. Although the nuns advanced Christian and charitable motives to explain their change of mind, they did not conceal the anxiety that they, like the other commmunities, felt about the

fate the government would reserve for them if it did not consider them sufficiently useful to society. The hospital nuns thought it was in their interest to keep on the good side of the lieutenant governor, Sir Robert Shore Milnes*, who seemed disposed to favour them and to let them continue, "but always in proportion to the services they will render; happy [they were] to buy this favour at that price," as the minutes of their assembly noted; they undertook this work and kept it going until 1845.

At the end of 1801, in keeping with the rules of the Hôtel-Dieu a new superior, Marie-Vénérande MELANÇON, named de Sainte-Claire, succeeded Marie-Geneviève de Saint-François d'Assise, who was then elected assistant and re-elected the following year. In the annual elections of 1803 she became counsellor and in November 1804 was again elected to this office. She was to hold it little more than a month, however. Having been paralysed for more than two years, she died in December at the age of 64, after 48 years of religious life.

FRANÇOIS ROUSSEAU

ANQ-Q, CE1-1, 11 nov. 1740. Arch. du monastère de l'Hôtel-Dieu de Québec, Actes capitulaires, I: ff.59, 61; Corr., Évêques, Pierre Denaut, J.-O. Plessis et A.-B. Robert, nos.3–6; J.-F. Hubert, no.1; Dossier des vœux, no.107; Église, tiroir 1, carton 5, nos.1–13; Élections triennales et annuelles, I: 165–220; Hôpital, Copies de lettres, requêtes, états de comptes, Législature, 1801–92: 1, 3; Notes et mémoires des anciennes mères, armoire 5, cahiers 2/1–2; Notices biographiques, M.-G. Parent. "Le recensement de Québec, en 1744," ANQ Rapport, 1939–40: 52. Caron, "Inv. de la corr. de Mgr Denaut," ANQ Rapport, 1931–32: 165, 168, 183. "Habitants de la ville de Québec, 1770–1771," F.-J. Audet, compil., BRH, 27 (1921): 249. Tanguay, Dictionnaire, 6: 236. H.-R. Casgrain, Histoire de l'Hôtel-Dieu de Québec (Québec, 1878), 401, 408, 421–25, 430–31, 445–46, 449, 465–68, 488–91, 493, 495–96, 576, 591. Raymonde Landry Gauthier, "Les constructions de l'Hôtel-Dieu de Québec (1637–1960)" (travail présenté à l'univ. Laval, 1974). [On p.25, Landry Gauthier errs in identifying the author of the church's plans as Louis-Joseph Desjardins*, dit Desplantes, its future chaplain; they were in fact the work of his brother, Philippe-Jean-Louis Desjardins. F.R.]

PATTERSON, ROBERT, surveyor, merchant, office holder, and militia officer; b. 1732 in Renfrew, Scotland; d. 30 Sept. 1808 in Pictou, N.S.

Following his emigration to America, Robert Patterson worked for some time as a pedlar, and prior to 1763 apparently was also a sutler with the British army. In 1767 he was living at Cross Roads (Churchville) in Maryland. When the Philadelphia Company, an association of American land developers, organized a group of settlers to go to its newly acquired land grant on the northern coast of Nova Scotia, Patterson was selected as the expedition's

Pawling

surveyor. In May 1767 Patterson, his wife, and their five children sailed on the *Betsey* with John HARRIS's and several other families. He soon became involved in trading ventures at the new settlement of Pictou, supplying goods to both Indians and settlers in return for furs, timber, and farm produce. Professional fees from surveying and business profits soon made him relatively prosperous; his sons were educated by hired tutors, and he had the first frame-house in the settlement while the other residents lived in rude cabins. When James McGregor*, pioneer missionary to the Highland settlers in the area, preached his first sermon at Pictou in 1786, he did so in Patterson's barn, where rough benches had been improvised.

An educated man, with influential friends among the Scottish "merchantocracy" that played such a vital part in the North Atlantic trade, Patterson shortly became the leading man in the settlement. As a justice of the peace (appointed 6 April 1774) and known as Squire Patterson to distinguish him from John "Deacon" Patterson, he was the "venerable settler [who] presided over the others . . . while they, with confidence . . . yielded in most cases obedience to his counsels. . . ." He was considered "a sort of factotum for all the settlers, even celebrating their marriages."

During the American revolution Patterson, unlike most of the other settlers from America, favoured the British side. In his enthusiasm he attempted to arrest some of the disloyal inhabitants, and was warned off by threats of murder. When trying to reach Halifax for copies of the oath of allegiance which Governor Francis Legge* had ordered everyone in the province to take, he was forced to return home by an armed American settler at Truro. Possibly Patterson had not spent enough time in the American colonies to be influenced by the revolutionary movement. It is more likely, however, that as a far-sighted businessman he perceived the opportunities for profitable trade if the colony remained in Britain's good graces, and he was also well aware that the Highland Scots, the majority of Pictou's inhabitants, were strongly pro-British. In recognition of his services he was made a captain of militia in 1783.

Patterson retained his prominent position in Pictou until his death. His sons seem to have left the area – by 1900 his only descendants in Pictou County bearing the Patterson name were in Lower Barneys River, where his son George had settled after his marriage to the daughter of Nicholas Purdue Olding, a prominent loyalist magistrate sometimes called the "grandfather of the Nova Scotia Bar." Patterson strengthened his connections with Pictou when his daughter Sarah married the important local merchant Edward MORTIMER. Patterson's niece Elizabeth of Baltimore was married for a time to the brother of Napoleon, Jérôme Bonaparte, who had visited Maryland in the 1790s as an officer in the French navy. Napoleon, disliking the match, had the marriage annulled in 1805.

A. A. MacKenzie

Durham cemetery, Pictou County, N.S., tombstone of Robert Patterson. H. R. Beer, *The Pictou plantation: 1767* ([Corner Brook, Nfld., 1967]). George MacLaren, *The Pictou book: stories of our past* (New Glasgow, N.S., [1954]). J. P. MacPhie, *Pictonians at home and abroad: sketches of professional men and women of Pictou County; its history and institutions* (Boston, 1914). F. H. Patterson, *John Patterson, the founder of Pictou town* (Truro, N.S., 1955). George Patterson, *A history of the county of Pictou, Nova Scotia* (Montreal, 1877); *Memoir of the Rev. James MacGregor, D.D. . . .* (Philadelphia, 1859). *Colonial Patriot* (Pictou, N.S.), 4 Jan.–3 Dec. 1828. *Colonial Patriot and Miscellaneous Selector* (Pictou), 17–31 Dec. 1828. A. J. Crockett, "Robert Patterson: the father of Pictou," *Free Lance* (New Glasgow), 20 March 1952. *Eastern Chronicle* (New Glasgow), 1951. R. F. Harris, "A pioneer Harris family and the pre-loyalist settlement of Pictou," N.S. Hist. Soc., *Coll.*, 33 (1961): 103–35.

PAWLING, BENJAMIN, army and militia officer, farmer, office holder, judge, politician, printer, and publisher; b. *c.* 1749 in Philadelphia, Pa; m. Susan —, and they had six children; d. in Grantham Township, Upper Canada, and was buried 16 Dec. 1818.

The facts of Benjamin Pawling's early life are obscure. His parents had emigrated probably from Wales and settled at Philadelphia. After the outbreak of the American revolution their lands were confiscated and Pawling and his brother Jesse made their way to Quebec where they joined the British forces in 1777. Pawling served for seven years before being retired on half pay on 25 Jan. 1784 as a captain in John Butler*'s rangers. His brother also served with the rangers as quartermaster. Contemporary records of the unit list Pawling's occupation as "farmer" and his brother's as "private gentleman."

Although appearing on a list of loyalists who were at Detroit (Mich.) in September 1784, Pawling is known to have settled in the Niagara region as early as 1783 and indeed by that date had cleared eight acres of land. As a loyalist captain he received 3,000 acres and settled on a lot in Grantham Township on the Lake Ontario front near Twelve Mile Creek. Four years later Pawling had cleared 16 acres and sown 10 with wheat. He was as yet unmarried and the sole occupant of his land. An indication of his local prominence is the fact that he was one of several recommended on 27 Dec. 1787 by Sir John Johnson* for "civil trusts" in the proposed new administrative districts.

When the Nassau District was proclaimed in July 1788 Pawling became one of its leading local officials. Along with Butler, Robert HAMILTON, Nathaniel PETTIT, and later John WARREN, he served on the land board of the Nassau District, and subsequently on its successor, the land board of Lincoln County. He was a justice of the peace from 19 Jan. 1789 for Nassau and later for the Home and Niagara districts; his last commission as a justice was 17 May 1814. With Pettit, Pawling was named to the Court of Common Pleas on 24 Oct. 1788, joining Butler and Hamilton. The primary concerns of the land board and the court were land title and the settlement of debt, and a loyalist officer such as Pawling showed less inclination than a merchant like Hamilton to attend to these matters. Of 36 sessions of the land board between 26 Oct. 1789 and March 1792, Pawling attended 3. His attendance at the court was only marginally better: 4 of 23 sessions between 28 Oct. 1788 and 10 April 1794. Yet in 1793 he petitioned Lieutenant Governor John Graves SIMCOE to relieve him "from the weight of his public occupations," which encroached upon "the management of his own private concerns." This letter is the earliest evidence that Pawling had married and possibly had children. It is not known what effect the petition had but the abolition of the court and the county land boards in 1794 must have relieved some of his anxiety. On 19 Oct. 1797 he was appointed to the first Heir and Devisee Commission for the Home District with Hamilton, Pettit, and Warren. But again his interest was negligible. Records are available only for the seven sessions between 1 Oct. 1800 and 15 Sept. 1803, none of which Pawling attended.

In 1792 Pawling was elected to the House of Assembly for the 2nd riding of Lincoln, defeating the merchant, Samuel STREET, 148 votes to 48. Records for the early assemblies are scarce and it is not known how active a member Pawling was. In 1794 he was commissioned a major in the Lincoln militia. He resigned prior to 1806 and does not appear to have participated in the War of 1812.

On 3 Dec. 1818 the name Pawling appeared with that of Bartemas Ferguson* below the mast-head of the *Niagara Spectator* as printers and publishers. Secondary sources identify this Pawling as Benjamin, although he may have been Benjamin's nephew, the local deputy sheriff, Peter Ten Broeck Pawling. The partnership did not last long. The last issue to bear both names was 4 Feb. 1819. But the first issue to use these names was sufficient to engage Pawling the publisher in the controversy surrounding Robert Fleming Gourlay*. Throughout 1818 Gourlay had carried on an agitation in the columns of the *Spectator* and the issue of 3 December carried his letter "Gagg'd-Gagg'd, by Jingo!" which led to charges of seditious libel against Pawling and Ferguson. On 16 December, the day that Benjamin Pawling, the subject of this biography, was buried, Isaac Swayze*, a local assemblyman, reported to Major George Hillier*, the lieutenant governor's secretary, that Ferguson was "in close custidity" and Pawling was "held to bail for aperance at court, in the sum of £400 Currcy." When

the case came to trial the following August only Ferguson appeared. It would seem that Pawling the publisher was indeed the deceased Benjamin.

J. K. JOHNSON

AO, RG 1, A-II-5, 1, Niagara District reports, 1800–3; C-I-9, 1; RG 22, ser.6-2, Lincoln County, will of Benjamin Pawling; ser.134, 4–5; RG 53, ser.2-2, 1: f.230. MTL, U.C., Court of Common Pleas, Nassau District, minutes. Norfolk Land Registry Office (Simcoe, Ont.), Abstract index to deeds, Windham Township: 821, 825, 829, 831, 835, 900, 903, 910 (mfm. at AO, GS 2640). PAC, MG 23, HI, 1, ser.8, 3: 71; RG 1, L3, 400: P1/43; 418: P misc., 1775–95/54; RG 5, AI: 1909–11, 2048–49; RG 68, General index, 1651–1841: ff.149, 249–50, 289–90, 292, 402–3, 408, 410, 418, 425. "Board of land office, District of Hesse," AO *Report*, 1905: 132, 211. "District of Nassau: minutes and correspondence of the land board," AO *Report*, 1905: 304. "Early records of Niagara" (Carnochan), *OH*, 3: 13–14, 18, 67, 71. [Francis Goring], "An early diary of Francis Goring," Niagara Hist. Soc., [*Pub.*], 36 (1924): 63. *Mich. Pioneer Coll.*, 11 (1887): 435–36, 451. "Records of Niagara, 1784–7," ed. E. A. Cruikshank, Niagara Hist. Soc., [*Pub.*], 39 (n.d.): 119, 123. *Statistical account of Upper Canada, compiled with a view to a grand system of emigration*, comp. R. [F.] Gourlay (2v., London, 1822; repr. East Ardsley, Eng., and New York, 1966), 2: 439–40. *Niagara Spectator* (Niagara [Niagara-on-the-Lake, Ont.]), 3 Dec. 1818–4 Feb. 1819. Reid, *Loyalists in Ont.*, 245. Wilson, "Enterprises of Robert Hamilton."

E. [A.] Cruikshank, "Record of the services of Canadian regiments in the War of 1812; part IX: the Lincoln militia," Canadian Military Institute, *Selected Papers* (Toronto), 13 (1903): 9–41; "Ten years of the colony of Niagara, 1780–1790," Niagara Hist. Soc., [*Pub.*], 17 (1908). C. C. James, "The first legislators of Upper Canada," RSC *Trans.*, 2nd ser., 8 (1902), sect.II: 93–119. "Loyalist and pioneer families of West Lincoln, 1783–1833," comp. R. J. Powell, *Annals of the Forty* ([Grimsby, Ont.]), no.7 (1956).

PAYEN DE NOYAN, MARIE-CATHERINE, named **de Saint-Alexis**, hospital nun of the Hôpital Général of Quebec and superior; b. *c.* 1730 in Montreal (Que.), daughter of Pierre-Jacques Payen* de Noyan et de Chavoy and Louise-Catherine d'Ailleboust de Manthet (married in 1731); d. 9 Nov. 1818 at Quebec.

Marie-Catherine Payen de Noyan was placed in the care of the hospital nuns of the Hôpital Général of Quebec when she was 18 months old; this was a rather unusual step since the sisters did not normally take in such young boarders. Growing up in the shadow of the convent, she left the nuns only for brief visits with her family. When she was 14 she expressed her desire to enter the noviciate, but she had to persist in order to obtain her parents' consent. On 11 April 1745 she left the classrooms for the noviciate. Since her family had difficulty in paying the dowry, her profession was delayed by nine months; as a result it was not until 24

Pearley

Aug. 1747 that Marie-Catherine Payen de Noyan became Sister Saint-Alexis.

During her first 14 years of religious life Marie-Catherine de Saint-Alexis devoted herself to the boarders at the Hôpital Général. Subsequently she was entrusted with increasingly heavy responsibilities. In 1761 she was elected first hospitaller; in 1763 she became mistress of novices, and then, three years later, depositary (bursar). She held the latter post at a time when the Hôpital Général was in quite serious financial difficulties, since the community was recovering only slowly from the losses incurred during and after the Seven Years' War. The nuns were making every effort to satisfy their creditors: they sewed vestments, did gilding, and even had to sell some of their land.

The community was still in difficulties when Marie-Catherine de Saint-Alexis was elected superior for her first three-year term in 1772. The new superior tried to obtain help from the king of France to put the finances of the Hôpital Général on a sound footing. The nuns received no reply to inspire any hope, and once again they had to face a state of war. In 1775 some of the American troops at the gates of Quebec decided to set up their winter quarters in the Hôpital Général. Marie-Catherine de Saint-Alexis was able to keep the section of the convent reserved for the nuns untouched by the occupation, and through her conciliatory manner she won the American generals' respect. The nuns lavished on the wounded and sick soldiers the care they needed, but the occupation added to their financial problems. Thus her second term of office began on a disheartening note. She succeeded to some degree, however, in straightening out the situation in the following years by severely restricting expenditures.

Marie-Catherine de Saint-Alexis gave up the superiorship in 1779. She served as assistant until 1785, when the nuns chose her as superior, as they did again in 1788. From 1791 to 1797 she acted as discreet (counsellor) and then once more held the office of superior from 1797 to 1803. Enjoying robust health, she continued to carry out her duties as discreet until the 60th anniversary of her vows. On this occasion Bishop Plessis* attended the celebration held by the nuns. Even when she was over 80 she was always on time for services. On the 70th anniversary of her profession the community held only the simplest of gatherings, in keeping with her express desire.

Marie-Catherine Payen de Noyan died on 9 Nov. 1818, having spent 71 years in religion and more than 86 in the Hôpital Général of Quebec.

LILIANNE PLAMONDON

Arch. de l'Hôpital Général de Québec, Communauté, Journal; Reg. des entrées et des dots. [Helena O'Reilly, *dite* de Saint-Félix], *Monseigneur de Saint-Vallier et l'Hôpital Général de Québec: histoire du monastère de Notre-Dame des Anges . . .* (Québec, 1882).

PEARLEY. *See* PERLEY

PELLERIN, CÉCILE. *See* BOUDREAU

PÉRINAULT (Perrinault), JOSEPH, tailor, fur trader and dealer in furs, seigneur, office holder, and politician; b. 8 Oct. 1732 in Montreal (Que.), son of Toussaint Périnau and Marie-Joseph Cusson; d. 31 Jan. 1814 in Sault-au-Récollet (Montreal North).

Joseph Périnault belonged to a family that had probably arrived in New France around 1680. His grandfather, Jacques Périnau, was a mason by trade, and in 1688 at Boucherville had taken as his second wife the widow of a dealer in pelts. They had eight children, among them Toussaint, who in turn had 13 children, Joseph being the seventh. Joseph worked as a tailor in Montreal until 1764, but he was also interested in the fur trade and in 1752 had hired himself out to René de Couagne* to go on an expedition. By 1765 he was ready for action on a larger scale and fitted out his first canoe, with a four-man crew bound for Michilimackinac (Mackinaw City, Mich.). In April, in partnership with Montreal merchant Pierre FORETIER, he joined with two other merchants for a trading expedition; he himself acted as resident at Michilimackinac. Following the death of Marie-Élisabeth Harel (whom he had married on 14 Nov. 1757), on 8 Jan. 1766 in Montreal he took as his second wife Élisabeth Guyon Desprez, the daughter of an important dealer in pelts, who was about 26.

In 1767 Périnault tried his luck on his own again in the trade. Two years later he invested £400 to fit out a canoe with a crew of 8, and the following year put out £750 for 2 canoes and 14 hands. In the period 1772–74 his investments reached a peak, at £1,500 annually, and the expeditions consisted of 3 or 4 canoes with 25 to 32 crewmen. But in 1775 his financial engagements fell to £800, and two years later were just £150. His former partner Foretier, who was now working with Jean Orillat*, put £4,550 into the fur trade in 1774 and went ahead with his largest investment, £5,375, in 1777. This was the last year in which Périnault seems to have been directly involved in the fur trade. He may have outfitted canoes after 1777, but without taking part in any expedition himself.

Having invested directly in the fur trade for some 10 years, Périnault reduced his activity to guaranteeing other traders' expeditions. In this respect his career evolved in a manner similar to Foretier's, although on a more modest scale. From 1777 to 1786 Périnault, on his own or with Maurice-Régis BLONDEAU and

Gabriel Cotté*, stood security for £5,000 in all, a sum that served to fit out at least 8 canoes manned by 69 crewmen; Foretier guaranteed nearly £10,000 in the period 1777–82.

Like many fur merchants Périnault was interested in holding both seigneurial and other properties. On 9 Oct. 1765 together with Foretier he bought three-quarters of the seigneury of Île-Bizard, as well as three-quarters of the sub-fief of Closse, part of which was in the *faubourg* Saint-Laurent; on 28 October the new owners agreed with the Sulpicians, who were the eminent seigneurs of the Île-de-Montréal, to put the sub-fief into roture (for an annual rent). Two years later Périnault sold his share in both properties to Foretier. In late 1772 and early 1773 he and some others, including Foretier and David Chabrand* Delisle, requested a grant of crown land, apparently without success. Having bought a vast tract from the Sulpicians for about £3,500, Périnault and another fur trader, Jean-Baptiste-Amable Durocher, gave a small piece of it to the town of Montreal in December 1803 for a public market. This gesture was not, however, entirely disinterested, since the value of the whole site was likely to rise following the creation of a market.

Like most merchants, Périnault was led to cross the Atlantic several times for business or personal reasons. In August 1782, for example, he announced that he was leaving for Europe and pressed his debtors to settle with him. He returned to the province in June 1784 with Foretier. In 1790 he was in France, at Senlis, where his son Pierre-Joseph was studying theology. In November that year Bishop Hubert* of Quebec took advantage of Périnault's being overseas to ask him to take care of his temporal affairs in France, and the following October wrote to him there thanking him for the services he had rendered. Périnault came back briefly to the colony, left again for England in 1792, stayed in France once more, and then returned home in July 1793.

Périnault was a man of some consequence in the Montreal community. He was a churchwarden in the parish of Notre-Dame and late in 1781 was delegated by the *fabrique* to buy a piece of land in its name. That August he had been a witness at Pierre-Louis PANET's marriage with a daughter of the merchant Jean-Gabriel CERRÉ. In 1786 and 1787 he was listed as one of the people consulted by a committee of the Legislative Council set up by Governor Lord Dorchester [Guy CARLETON] to inquire into trade and police in the province [*see* William GRANT (1744–1805)]. From 1796 until at least 1800 Périnault was a justice of the peace for the District of Montreal. In June 1801 he was made one of the Montreal commissioners for the relief of the insane and foundlings; his appointment was renewed in 1804. Two years earlier he had been appointed to a committee established to promote the growing of hemp.

Being in favour of constitutional reform, Périnault had joined the committee of Canadians which was created in 1784 in Montreal to work for it and which counted among its members notary Jean DE LISLE and the merchants Foretier, Blondeau, and Pierre GUY. It is therefore not surprising to find him among the members of the association founded in 1794 to support the British government, to see him on the executive committee of this organization's Montreal section, which was responsible for recruitment, and even to find him twice a member of the House of Assembly established under the Constitutional Act of 1791. From 1796 to 1800 he was one of the representatives for the riding of Huntingdon; then from 1800 to 1804 he represented Montreal West with James McGILL. During his first term he voted on 11 occasions but in his second he did not participate in any vote at all; like many members who did not live in the town of Quebec and who received neither salary nor allowances at the period, he may have been finding it difficult to carry out his duties.

When he retired Périnault went to live with his son, who was parish priest of La Visitation-de-la-Bienheureuse-Vierge-Marie at Sault-au-Récollet from 1806 until 1816. He died there on 31 Jan. 1814, leaving Pierre-Joseph an income of £30 annually.

FERNAND OUELLET

ANQ-M, CE1-4, 2 févr. 1814; CE1-51, 3 oct. 1718, 8 oct. 1732. PAC, RG 1, L3^L: 36043–45; RG 4, B28, 110–15. "L'Association loyale de Montréal," ANQ *Rapport*, 1948–49: 258–59, 261, 263, 267–69. *Docs. relating to constitutional hist., 1759–91* (Shortt and Doughty; 1918), 2: 900. "État général des billets d'ordonnances" (Panet), ANQ *Rapport*, 1924–25: 248. *Quebec Gazette*, 9 Sept. 1779; 6 Dec. 1781; 29 Aug., 31 Oct. 1782; 17 June 1784; 28 April, 19 May, 23 June 1785; 11 July 1793; 17 July 1794; 5 March 1795; 25 July 1799; 20 May 1802; 9 July 1821. Allaire, *Dictionnaire*, 1: 424. F.-J. Audet, *Les députés de Montréal*, 18, 50, 124, 168–70. Caron, "Inv. de la corr. de Mgr Hubert et de Mgr Bailly de Messein," ANQ *Rapport*, 1930–31: 238–39, 256. Desjardins, *Guide parl.*, 130, 135. Massicotte, "Répertoire des engagements pour l'Ouest," ANQ *Rapport*, 1942–43: 348–53. "Papiers d'État," PAC *Rapport*, 1890: 209. *Quebec almanac*, 1797: 131; 1798: 85; 1799: 79; 1800: 91; 1801: 78; 1805: 20. P.-G. Roy, *Inv. concessions*, 3: 181; 5: 151. Tanguay, *Dictionnaire*, 6: 306. J. E. Igartua, "The merchants and *négociants* of Montreal, 1750–1775: a study in socio-economic history" (PHD thesis, Mich. State Univ., East Lansing, 1974), 84, 115–16. Miquelon, "Baby family," 182–95. Tousignant, "La genèse et l'avènement de la constitution de 1791," 309–10. Hare, "L'Assemblée législative du Bas-Canada," *RHAF*, 27: 375–76.

PERKINS, SIMEON, businessman, office holder, judge, politician, militia officer, and diarist; b. 24 Feb. 1734/35 in Norwich, Conn., fourth of 16 children of Jacob Perkins and Jemima Leonard; m.

Perkins

first 12 June 1760 Abigail Backus in Norwich, and they had one son; m. secondly 10 Sept. 1775 Elizabeth Young, widow of John Headley, in Liverpool, N.S., and they had six daughters and two sons; d. 9 May 1812 at his home in Liverpool.

Simeon Perkins was descended from John Parkyns, who arrived in Boston, Mass., from England in 1631. His parents, as the Methodist leader William Black* stated, were "respectable members of the Presbyterian or Congregational persuasion, who neglected not to instruct their son in the grand and important doctrines of the Christian faith," and Perkins remained strongly religious throughout his life. He evidently received a fair education, and was apprenticed to his first cousin Jabez Huntingdon, member of a Norwich family prominent in business and public affairs.

At about the time of his first marriage Perkins became a member of a partnership with his father-in-law and another cousin, and in May 1762 he went to Nova Scotia to establish the business of the company in the new town of Liverpool. He immediately opened a store and became directly involved in the fishery. An enterprising merchant in the broadest sense of the word, Perkins was concerned not only with catering to the needs of his fellow townsmen but also with lumbering, trading to various outside markets such as the West Indies, the Thirteen Colonies, Newfoundland, and Europe, shipbuilding, and several related operations. On 24 April 1766, moreover, he was licensed to traffic with the Indians of Nova Scotia. Perkins's commercial activities in the decade and a half preceding the American revolution involved close communication with New England, where he had relatives, friends, and trading partners. Liverpool itself was essentially a New England community in Nova Scotia, and Perkins's business undertakings epitomized the trade of the province. During these years Perkins visited his native land three times: once in November 1762 to report to his partners and plan for the future, then for a year and a half from November 1767 when Liverpool was experiencing hard times, and lastly in the spring of 1775, when increasing friction between the mother country and the colonies was causing concern.

As controversy changed to crisis, Perkins's responsibilities as lieutenant-colonel of the Queens County militia, a position he had held since 1772, took on special importance. He had, however, little success in persuading the men of Liverpool to enrol for militia duty. Although all but one took the oath of allegiance in the winter of 1775–76, they were reluctant to give active support to the British side. Nor was Perkins himself immune from the desire of many Nova Scotians to maintain connections with their relatives and friends in New England: he carried on a clandestine trade there and on at least one occasion was detected and had his goods seized. The incursions

of American privateers, however, caused a change. Rather than offer active resistance, the people of Liverpool had attempted to dissuade privateers from attacking, but raids prompted them to take a stand in their own defence. The most dramatic incident occurred on 13 Sept. 1780, when two privateers surprised and captured the fort with the garrison of troops stationed there for the protection of the town. At first the inhabitants were "Disheartned & did not Incline to make any resistance." But Perkins engineered the capture of one of the American captains, and by means of prudence and diplomacy, and with the militia now "under Arms & Determined to fight," he arranged for the recovery of the fort and the mutual release of prisoners. Within a few hours "every thing [was] restored to its former Situation without any Blood Shed." Liverpool was not bothered by privateers for the remainder of the war. Perkins was later to be concerned again with the security of the area during the French revolutionary and Napoleonic wars. Under his direction, a battery was built at Liverpool in 1793, arms and ammunition were distributed, and a guard of 36 men was mounted. Under his command, also, the Queens County milita was periodically mustered, trained, and reviewed.

During periods of warfare Perkins was actively involved in privateering. In 1779 he was one of a group of Liverpool merchants who purchased and fitted out the schooner *Lucy* as the first Liverpool privateer, and between 1798 and 1801 he was financially involved in five of the six privateers the town sent out. Fortunes in privateering fluctuated: although a venture early in 1799 resulted in five prizes estimated to be worth more than £26,000 to Perkins and his associates, other cruises that year were less remunerative and one privateer was wrecked. By 1801 prospects had so worsened that Perkins and his associates decided to sell their privateers at auction. Perkins was, however, briefly involved in further ventures in 1803 and 1805.

Fishing, trading, and privateering required ships: thus Perkins's concern with lumbering and shipbuilding. On 7 May 1765 he launched the *Nabby* and the *Polly*, two schooners he had built at Liverpool, and in June 1766 he agreed to take a quarter-share in a schooner being built at Port Medway. The American revolution hit him severely (he lost five ships to privateers), but matters improved later. Between 1789 and 1810 he was owner or part-owner of at least 20 vessels built in Liverpool and vicinity.

For many years Perkins was prominent in both local and provincial affairs. Early in 1764 he was appointed a justice of the peace and a judge of the Inferior Court of Common Pleas, and he served for 46 years in both that court and the Court of Quarter Sessions. In 1770 he was chosen as proprietors' clerk, an office which he held until 1802; he also acted as town clerk and county treasurer for a lengthy period. In 1772 he was appointed commissioner of roads. From 1777 to 1807 he was judge of probate for Queens County, from 1780 to 1790 deputy registrar of the Vice-Admiralty Court, and for many years *custos rotulorum* as well. Lieutenant-colonel of the county militia from 1772 to 1793, he served as colonel commandant from 1793 to 1807. Perkins was also for more than 30 years a member of the House of Assembly, representing Queens County from 1765 to 1799, except in 1768 and 1769. Even though he attended only 11 of 40 sessions, during his absence he was able to render service through his connections in Halifax. As an assembly-man, Perkins did effective work in a rather quiet way throughout a period affected by problems of both war and peace. Although "slow to speak," according to William Black, ". . . in deciding upon questions of importance he is said to have manifested great wisdom and integrity."

Simeon Perkins is well known for the comprehensive and voluminous diary he kept from 29 May 1766 to 13 April 1812. It is complete with the exception of the period from 22 Nov. 1767 to 15 June 1769, when he was in Connecticut, the year 1771, for which there are no entries, and the period from 5 March 1806 to 29 Nov. 1809, the record of which has been lost. When the diary was bequeathed to the town of Liverpool in 1899, it was described as "one of the most valuable and interesting records, that ever perhaps, came into the province." It is indeed a mine of information for the study of economic, political, and social institutions, shedding light not only on the life of a community but also on a region occupying a significant place in the North Atlantic triangular trade and an important position in the evolution of the second British empire. Largely devoid of flashes of wit or insight, the diary is a journal of daily events in a pioneer settlement which had little time for worldly pleasures and a constant concern for survival. Perkins kept a careful record of births, marriages, and deaths, faithfully observed the weather, and commented on all noteworthy events in Liverpool and abroad. His statement upon hearing of rumours of the end of hostilities in 1782 – "we hope for a Peace . . . that our Nation[s] may no longer Ly under the awfull Judgement of Devouring one an Other" – reflected the feelings of a great many Nova Scotians whose friends and relations were in New England. Perkins took a great interest in religious affairs, and changed from Congregationalism to Methodism late in life. He was impressed enough by Henry Alline* in 1783 to record that he had not seen "Such an Appearance of the Spirit of God moving upon the people" for some time. The following year, however, the New Light supporters were excluded from regular church meetings because Alline, in Perkins's words, "denied the Fundamental Articles of the Christian Religion." The diary also provides illuminating glimpses of the war at sea, as well as comments on losses at the hands of one's own countrymen, and shows to what extent business and military strength affected the status of Nova Scotia. It has been published in a series of five volumes by the Champlain Society. The house of Simeon Perkins in Liverpool, built in 1766–67 and extended in 1781 and 1792, has been preserved as one of the historic houses of Nova Scotia.

C. BRUCE FERGUSSON

The originals of Simeon Perkins's diary are in the possession of the town of Liverpool, and microfilm and transcript copies are in PANS as MG 1, 749–52. It was published under the title *The diary of Simeon Perkins. . .*, ed. H. A. Innis *et al.* (5v., Toronto, 1948–78).

PANS, MG 1, 748A, 851; MG 4, 77; MG 20, 215, no.10; RG 1, 40; 48; 51–54; 165; 168; 171–72; 221, doc.40; 287; 378; 499½; RG 5, A, 3, 6, 8, 10. Private arch., Seth Bartling (Liverpool, N.S.), R. J. Long, "The annals of Liverpool and Queen's County, 1760–1867" (1926) (typescript at Dalhousie Univ. Library, Halifax; mfm. at PANS). Norwich, Conn., *Vital records of Norwich, 1639–1848* (Hartford, Conn., 1913), 370. N.S., General Assembly, *Acts* (Halifax); House of Assembly, *Journal and proc.*, 1765–99. *Naval Chronicle*, 5 (January–June 1801): 174–75; repub. with comment in *Provincial: or Halifax Monthly Magazine* (Halifax), 2 (1853): 337–39. *Nova Scotia Royal Gazette* (Halifax), 3 June 1812.

Epitaphs from the old cemeteries of Liverpool, Nova Scotia, comp. Charles Warman (Boston, [1910]). G. A. Perkins, *The family of John Perkins of Ipswich, Massachusetts* (3 pts. in 1, Salem, Mass., 1889). C. B. Fergusson, *Early Liverpool and its diarist* (Halifax, 1961). *Liverpool privateering, 1756–1815*, comp. J. E. Mullins, ed. F. S. Morton ([Liverpool], 1936]). A. [McK.] MacMechan, *There go the ships* (Toronto, 1928). J. F. More, *The history of Queens County, N.S.* (Halifax, 1873; repr., Belleville, Ont., 1972). J. E. Mullins, *Some Liverpool chronicles* ([Liverpool], 1941). Murdoch, *Hist. of N.S.* R. R. McLeod, "Old times in Liverpool, N.S.," *Acadiensis* (Saint John, N.B.), 4 (1904): 96–118. *Morning Chronicle* (Halifax), 28 Nov. 1899. G. E. E. Nichols, "Notes on Nova Scotian privateers," N.S. Hist. Soc., *Coll.*, 13 (1908): 130.

PERLEY (Pearley), ISRAEL, miller, office holder, and surveyor; b. 21 July 1738 in Boxford, Mass., first son of Thomas Perley and Eunice Putnam; m. *c.* 1764 Elizabeth Mooers (Moores), and they had seven sons and seven daughters; d. 30 Aug. 1813 in Maugerville, N.B.

Son of a farmer and local office holder, Israel Perley was reared in Boxford where the New England traditions of Congregational religion and basic education left their marks. He reached his maturity during the Seven Years' War in which he served for a short time as a provincial officer, although it is not clear where. The scarcity of land in eastern Massachusetts in the 1750s and 1760s led Perley and other disbanded

Perley

soldiers to seek better prospects elsewhere, and they turned to Nova Scotia where many of them had served. Perley, who had learned surveying, was appointed in 1761 to lead a group of 12 men to explore for suitable land in the Saint John River valley (N.B.). They travelled overland from Machias (Maine) to the mouth of the Oromocto River before returning to Massachusetts. The following year Perley was among a group of 20 who ascended the Saint John River to St Anne's Point (Fredericton), where a large assembly of Indians turned them back. They settled about 12 miles below St Anne's, and as a result of advertisements placed in Boston newspapers they were joined in 1763 by about 200 others who were led from Massachusetts by Perley. When the Nova Scotia government proved slow in issuing land grants, the area the settlers had chosen having already been claimed by a group of disbanded regulars, Perley and four other memorialists petitioned the Board of Trade in London, England. Their petition was granted in 1764, with the help, the settlers believed, of Joshua Mauger*, the leading London merchant trading into Nova Scotia. The grateful settlers chose Maugerville as the name of their town.

Like other Nova Scotia communities settled at this time, Maugerville was modelled on the New England township system. Perley, as an original grantee, was therefore a "proprietor" of the town, proprietors having control over common or undivided land which, in this case, comprised acreage far back from the river behind the line of settlement as well as islands in the river. The soil proved to be the richest in the province and yields by 1767 were remarkable even from unploughed land. Perley farmed, surveyed, and joined with others in grist-mill and sawmill ventures. As a proprietor, he was called upon to play a leading role in the political as well as the economic development of the town. In 1770 he was elected representative for Sunbury County in the Nova Scotia legislature, but he probably never took his seat. At about the same time he became a justice of the peace. Within three years of the beginning of their settlement, Perley and the other settlers had formed a Congregational church and Perley became an elder. In the early 1770s they brought in their first minister, a fellow New Englander named Seth NOBLE.

The strength of their New England connections ultimately brought Perley and his community to their first crisis. Initially, when Massachusetts revolutionaries complained about British oppression and infringements on their rights, the Maugerville settlers – isolated and few in numbers – said nothing. But when protests led to open warfare and then to the brink of independence, Perley and his neighbours felt forced to act. Probably influenced by Noble, the Maugerville settlers met in mid May 1776 – on the eve of the declaration of independence – to consider the question

of their allegiance. Perley, whose father was an active revolutionary in Massachusetts and whose uncle, Israel Putnam, became an American general, favoured the revolutionary side. He served as the clerk of the meeting, articulately phrasing resolutions which rejected the British parliament's right to legislate for the colonists, asserted the justice of the Americans' resistance, called for the annexation of their settlement by Massachusetts, and pledged that the settlers would share in the "struggle for liberty" with their lives and fortunes. The meeting chose Perley one of a committee of 12 to organize the civil and military affairs of the town. Its remoteness, however, made any significant alliance impossible. Despite the activity of Yankee privateers in Nova Scotia waters, the eagerness of some Machias frontiersmen to help the Nova Scotians rebel, and the sympathy of the Massachusetts General Court, Massachusetts was unable to aid the Maugerville settlers or to act on their request for annexation. A feeble military thrust against Fort Cumberland (near Sackville, N.B.), led by Jonathan EDDY and supported by a few Maine frontiersmen, some Indians, and a handful of Nova Scotian rebels, including 27 men from Maugerville, was easily repulsed by the British. There is no evidence that Perley was among them.

By May 1777 the Maugerville settlers, with Perley again in a leading role, accepted the reassertion of British authority when Colonel Arthur Goold (Gould), of the Nova Scotia Council, came to investigate "illegal proceedure." Offering leniency and swift reconciliation for those who would take an oath of allegiance, Goold found Perley and other "rebel" leaders ready to submit. Perley wrote on behalf of the others that they had felt themselves cut off from British authority and intimidated by New England privateers into taking the action they had. He advised that there should be a general pardon and no attempt to distinguish the loyal from the disloyal. Goold agreed and by the end of May 1777 had taken oaths of allegiance from most of the settlers. Perley, however, found little protection in the general pardon. As clerk of the Maugerville meetings, he had signed the minutes and all correspondence and was thus open to the charge that he had carried on "Secret Correspondence with his Majesty['s] Rebellious Enemies." So indicted, he was brought before the Nova Scotia Supreme Court on 16 Oct. 1778, but when the crown failed to produce evidence against him the court released him on his own recognizance. Perley returned home and apparently the matter was dropped completely.

When American loyalists swelled the population of the Saint John River valley after 1783 and successfully petitioned to have a new province established, Perley's surveying skills were in great demand. Named a deputy to the surveyor general of New

Brunswick, George SPROULE, by 1786, Perley surveyed lands in various parts of the province, but especially in the Miramichi valley, and acquired a grant of 1,000 acres for himself on the Gaspereau River in what is now Queens County. Yet, though he served the crown, he resisted efforts of loyalists to acquire for the Church of England those lands held by his own church, and he remained a firm Congregationalist.

In his declining years Perley lived on his farm at Maugerville, where he died in 1813.

STEPHEN E. PATTERSON

Common Clerk's Office (Saint John, N.B.), Index of marriages and deaths, comp. C. Ward, 1972 (copy at N.B. Museum). N.B. Museum, F41; F49: nos.156, 263A, 265, 285; History of Maugerville, 1788–1928; Perley family papers; Petitions, Northumberland County, nos.72, 401; Queen's County, no.317; York County, no.521 (abstracts); Quinton family papers, John Quinton diary (typescript). PANB, RG 10, RS107/5/1, 1: 278. PANS, RG 1, 409, Arthur Gould to inhabitants of Maugerville, 9, 14, 17, 20 May 1777; Israel Perley to Gould, 12 May 1777; Perley *et al.* to Gould, 18 May 1777 (mfm. at N.B. Museum); RG 39, J, 1: 332. *American arch.* (Clarke and Force), 5th ser., 1: 703–6. "Documents of the Congregational Church at Maugerville," N.B. Hist. Soc., *Coll.*, 1 (1894–97), no.1: 119–52; no.2: 153–59. [Israel Perley], "Justice Perley's court documents," N.B. Hist. Soc., *Coll.*, 1 (1894–97), no.1: 96–99. *Directory of N.S. MLAs. A genealogical chart of the male descendants of Allen Perley*, comp. G. A. Perley (Fredericton, 1877).

Brebner, *Neutral Yankees. History and genealogy of the Perley family*, comp. M. V. B. Perley (Salem, Mass., 1906). [This work is the most comprehensive genealogy of the family, but much of the New Brunswick material is based on family tradition rather than on original research. S.E.P.] *Maugerville, 1763–1963*, comp. I. L. Hill (Fredericton, 1963). L. M. B. Maxwell, *An outline of the history of central New Brunswick to the time of confederation* (Sackville, N.B., 1937). M. H. Perley, *On the early history of New Brunswick: a portion of a lecture delivered before the Mechanics' Institute, St. John, in 1841 . . .* (Saint John, 1891). [The lecture seems to have been based on the oral tradition and is the probable source of much misinformation repeated elsewhere. S.E.P.] Raymond, *River St. John* (1910). J. C. Webster, *The forts of Chignecto: a study of the eighteenth century conflict between France and Great Britain in Acadia* ([Shediac, N.B.], 1930). James Hannay, "The Maugerville settlement, 1763–1824," N.B. Hist. Soc., *Coll.*, 1 (1894–97), no.1: 63–88. "Observer" [E. S. Carter], "Linking the past with the present," *Telegraph-Journal* (Saint John), November 1929–December 1931. S. E. Patterson, "In search of the Massachusetts–Nova Scotia dynamic," *Acadiensis* (Fredericton), 5 (1975–76), no.2: 138–43.

PERRAULT, JACQUES-NICOLAS (from at least 1785 he signed **Perrault l'aîné**), merchant, militia officer, office holder, seigneur, and politician; b. 6 Aug. 1750 at Quebec, son of Jacques Perrault*, known as Perrault *l'aîné*, and Charlotte Boucher de Boucherville; d. 7 Aug. 1812 in Rivière-Ouelle, Lower Canada.

Jacques-Nicolas Perrault, who was the son of a well-educated and prosperous merchant and grandson of the co-seigneur Pierre Boucher* de Boucherville, probably received some education before going into business with his father. After the latter's death in 1775 Perrault did not obtain a large legacy because the paternal fortune was dispersed among numerous heirs, and he continued his business activity. On 23 Nov. 1779, at the Hôpital Général in Quebec, he married Marie-Anne Amiot, daughter of a wealthy merchant, the late Jean-Baptiste Amiot*. In May of the following year the couple received 3,000 *livres* from the sale of half a property on the Place du Marché (Place Notre-Dame) in Lower Town that came from Amiot's estate. On 20 April 1782 Perrault's wife was buried in the Quebec cathedral with Bishop Briand* in attendance.

During the next ten years Perrault seems to have devoted himself to business. He shared the mercantile community's views in regard to the administration of the colony, and from 1784 he held the office of secretary of the Canadian committee of Quebec, one of two committees created at that time by the town's merchants. Like their Montreal counterparts, which were set up soon after, these bodies pursued such objectives as the repeal of the Quebec Act, the obtaining of a house of assembly, and the introduction of English commercial laws. They were dissolved in December 1791, after the Constitutional Act had been promulgated. In social matters Perrault was more conservative: in 1790 he sided with Bishop Hubert* of Quebec, who fought the proposals for a non-sectarian university and the abolition of certain religious holidays, two measures that were championed by the coadjutor, Bishop Charles-François Bailly* de Messein. In June of the same year his uncle Guillaume-Michel Perrault bequeathed to him the seigneury of La Bouteillerie, also called Rivière-Ouelle; the usufruct from it, however, was to go to his mother. In 1791 the new seigneur came out in favour of the retention of seigneurial tenure [*see* Thomas-Laurent Bédard*].

His mother's death in 1792 enabled Perrault to enter into full possession of the seigneury and marked a turning-point in his career. At the time, Perrault was still carrying on his merchandising business and was residing on Rue du Sault-au-Matelot at Quebec; a widower, he had one under-age son, Jacques, the only surviving child of his marriage. He owned some real estate and various effects valued at 4,347 *livres* 12 *sous*. His accounts receivable amounted to 1,813 *livres* 4 *sous*, nearly three-fifths of which were owed by Lester and Morrogh and James TOD; his own debts totalled 21,601 *livres* 13 *sous*. He had held the rank of

Perrault

captain in the town's militia since at least 1788, and a commission as justice of the peace in the District of Quebec for a year or more. In December 1792 the *Quebec Gazette* announced the sale by auction of the "late Madame Perrault's big, handsome house in Lower Town"; on 10 Jan. 1793, in Rivière-Ouelle, Perrault married Thérèse-Esther Hausman, *dit* Ménager, the widow of Pierre Florence, a wealthy local merchant.

Perrault then went to live at Rivière-Ouelle, becoming the first seigneur in 90 years to take up permanent residence on the seigneury. After Jean-Baptiste-François Deschamps* de La Bouteillerie's death in 1703 neither of the two heirs who had succeeded in turn to the property, Henri-Louis Deschamps* de Boishébert and his son Charles Deschamps* de Boishébert et de Raffetot, had lived there, nor had Perrault's uncle, who had bought it in 1774. Perrault was interested in developing his seigneury: he bought a lot with a sawmill, a barley mill, and a blacksmith's shop, and then built a wharf, repaired the mills, and put his sugar-bush into production. The income from the property was, however, modest; the ledgers show that the sale of wheat and products from the porpoise fishery were the sole source of the meagre living it furnished. Consequently it was really through his wife's dowry that Perrault was able to fit out a seigneurial manor-house – none other than the former Florence residence, which he had restored – and to secure the full-time services of a manservant and a maid.

A seigneur, even though in humble circumstances, Perrault enjoyed great prestige in his milieu. He acquired a reputation as a cultivated man. He was fond of good literature and owned a well-stocked library of about 300 volumes: legal treatises, history books, literary works of all kinds, even those of Voltaire, which at that time were on the Index of Forbidden Books. From at least 1796, he served in the militia, first as lieutenant-colonel, then after 1801 as colonel. He remained a justice of the peace for the District of Quebec. Perrault also acquired the goodwill of his fellow citizens by involving himself in parish activities such as furnishing the convent in 1809. From 1804 to 1808 he represented Cornwallis riding in the Lower Canadian House of Assembly. He supported the Canadian party on 11 out of 15 occasions, voting for the bill on financing the prison through import duties and one on the ineligibility of judges to sit in the assembly [see Sir James Henry CRAIG; Pierre-Amable DE BONNE]. Despite this support Perrault was not anti-British; for example, in 1807, reviewing the militia battalion of Kamouraska in his capacity as colonel, he pointed out in a spirited speech the need for solid defence in case of attack, emphasizing the Canadians' loyalty and their duties to king and country. In January 1812, in light of the policy of Governor PREVOST to attract the support of moderate Canadians for the colonial administration, he was appointed to the Legislative Council.

Perrault was able to enjoy this privilege for but a short time, however. On 7 August, after only a few days of illness, he was found dead in his bath-tub. Three days later, with Bishop Bernard-Claude Panet* officiating, he was buried in the crypt of the parish church of Rivière-Ouelle, "with the honours due his rank." The *Quebec Gazette* reported that "the large throng of people of distinction and habitants, both from this parish and the neighbouring parishes, who attended his funeral, is proof of the esteem which he enjoyed and the regrets that go with his passing." At his death his debts totalled £994, while the amount owing him was £1,206. As his son had drowned in 1797 in the rapids on the Rivière Chaudière near Quebec, the seigneury went to Perrault's brothers: Pierre, a certified lunatic, Michel, a schoolteacher, and Jean-Olivier*, a member of the Executive Council. But all three dissociated themselves from it, and in 1813 they began to sell it to Pierre Casgrain*. Perrault's wife received a life annuity of 225 *livres* in compensation.

After pursuing a commercial career for about 20 years, Jacques-Nicolas Perrault lived somewhat in the manner of those aristocratic seigneurs who preferred honours to business. After him, the seigneurs of Rivière-Ouelle belonged rather to the bourgeois kind.

PIERRE MATTEAU

ANQ-Q, CE1-1, 6 août 1750, 20 avril 1782; CE3-1, 10 janv. 1793, 10 août 1812; CN1-25, 6, 21 nov. 1779; 18 mai 1780; CN1-26, 14 oct. 1801; CN1-230, 19 nov. 1792, 5 août 1793, 3 oct. 1794, 14 mars 1795, 4 mars 1797, 2 févr. 1805, 2 déc. 1809. Soc. hist. de la Côte-du-Sud (La Pocatière, Qué.), Boîte 33, doc.34, P.-B. Casgrain, "Le manoir d'Airvault, précis historique" (typescript). "Les dénombrements de Québec" (Plessis), ANQ *Rapport*, 1948–49: 35. [Adam Lymburner], "Lettre d'Adam Lymburner à Jacques Perrault, de Québec," *BRH*, 39 (1933): 215; "Lettre d'Adam Lymburner à J. Perrault l'aîné," *BRH*, 38 (1932): 572–73. *Quebec Gazette*, 16, 30 June 1785; 20 April 1786; 18 Dec. 1788; 23 April 1789; 25 March, 13 May 1790; 24 March, 28 April, 5 May, 18 Aug., 29 Dec. 1791; 13 Dec. 1792; 11 April, 16 May 1793; 29 June 1797; 10 Sept. 1807; 25 Jan. 1810; 29 Aug. 1811; 4 June, 13 Aug. 1812. Desjardins, *Guide parl.*, 57, 126. "Papiers d'État – Bas-Canada," PAC *Rapport*, 1893: 52, 84. *Quebec almanac*, 1788–1810. *Répertoire des mariages de l'Hôpital Général de Québec (paroisse Notre-Dame-des-Anges) (1693–1961)*, Benoît Pontbriand, compil. (Québec, 1962), 7, 29. P.-G. Roy, *Inv. concessions*, 2: 251. Tanguay, *Dictionnaire*, 6: 319. Turcotte, *Le Conseil législatif*, 18, 73. P.-B. Casgrain, *Mémorial des familles Casgrain, Baby et Perrault du Canada* (Québec, 1898), 192–93. P.-H. Hudon, *Rivière-Ouelle de la Bouteillerie; 3 siècles de vie* (Ottawa, 1972),

137–39, 273–74. P.-G. Roy, *La ville de Québec sous le Régime français* (2v., Québec, 1930), 2: 300. Henri Têtu, *Histoire des familles Têtu, Bonenfant, Dionne et Perrault* (Québec, 1898), 596–99. Tousignant, "La genèse et l'avènement de la constitution de 1791," 304. Hare, "L'Assemblée législative du Bas-Canada," *RHAF*, 27: 379–80.

PERRINAULT. *See* PÉRINAULT

PETTIT (Petit), NATHANIEL, office holder and politician; b. 12 June 1724 in Sussex County, N.J., son of Nathaniel Pettit and Elizabeth Heath; m. 26 Feb. 1747 Margaret McFarland, and they had one son and six daughters; d. 9 March 1803 in Ancaster, Upper Canada.

Nathaniel Pettit's forebears emigrated in 1630 from Essex, England, to the area around Boston, Mass. The family eventually dispersed, some members settling in New Jersey where in Sussex County Nathaniel achieved financial security and legal prominence prior to the American revolution. He owned two valuable mills and in 1766 was appointed judge in the county Court of Common Pleas. In 1768 his personal standing in the community rose further with his election as one of the two members returned for the county to the provincial legislature. But his success, at a time when officials appointed by Britain came to be feared and distrusted, ultimately worked against him.

Initially Pettit was sympathetic to colonial grievances; in 1774 he was appointed at a county meeting to a ten-man committee to oppose taxation without representation and to support the suspension of imports from Britain. But on 12 Jan. 1776 he was brought before the provincial committee of safety for refusing to pay taxes levied by the revolutionary congress. He was fined and stripped of his judicial appointment, which precipitated an open declaration of his loyalty. Approaching his mid fifties, he was not physically able to join a loyalist corps, but with the aid of a former fellow member of the legislature, Joseph Barton, in late 1776 he raised a battalion of 500 men. Pettit, "lame and infirm," remained in Sussex County where his assistance to "the friends of Government . . . exposed him to the worst treatment" from the rebels. Imprisoned from 4 April 1777 to 28 May 1778, he obtained his liberty only by paying heavy fines and taking out large bonds for his future behaviour. Pettit estimated these losses "at a very moderate computation" to be in excess of £1,000. Moreover, when he left the United States he had to sell his mills and lands for less than half their value. Although he pressed his "well attested" case before the loyalist claims commission, it "was attended with no effect." With several friends he left his home and arrived in the

Niagara area of Quebec in 1787 "to solicit a settlement where he may enjoy that Liberty and comfort so amply secured by the British constitution." He received a grant of 700 acres, and in 1794 another 1,300. His lands were located in Saltfleet, Grimsby (North and South Grimsby), Burford, Ancaster, and Aldborough townships.

On 24 July 1788 Lord Dorchester [Guy CARLETON] established four new administrative districts in what was to become Upper Canada. The chief institutions in the new districts were the land board and the Court of Common Pleas; Pettit's appointment to both on 24 Oct. 1788 in the Nassau District reflected his pre-revolutionary prominence. He served on the land board with John Butler*, Robert HAMILTON, Benjamin PAWLING, and John WARREN, and also was a member of its successor, the land board of Lincoln County, established on 20 Oct. 1792. The other officials sitting on the district court were Hamilton, Pawling, and Peter Ten Broeck. The board settled matters of land title and the court handled questions of debt. Neither concern was crucial to Pettit's interests and his attendance was sporadic: he was present at only 9 of 36 sessions of the land board between 26 Oct. 1789 and March 1792 and 4 of 23 sessions of the court between 28 Oct. 1788 and 10 April 1794. The court was abolished by act of the provincial legislature in July 1794 and the land board by order in council the following November. Pettit was a justice of the peace from 19 June 1789; his last commission was dated 1 April 1803, several weeks after his death. He was named to the first Heir and Devisee Commission for the Home District on 19 Oct. 1797 and reappointed on 21 July 1800 for Lincoln County. He did not attend any of the three meetings between 1 Oct. 1800 and his death.

Pettit's stature is perhaps best reflected by Dorchester's recommendation of him on 15 March 1790, on the advice of Sir John Johnson*, as one of eight legislative councillors for the intended province of Upper Canada. Of those commissioned on 12 July 1792, five were selected from this 1790 list. For whatever reason, possibly because of advanced age, Pettit was rejected on the suggestion of Lieutenant Governor John Graves SIMCOE. However, on 27 Aug. 1792 he was elected for the riding of Durham, York, and 1st Lincoln to the first parliament of the new province. The records for this period are fragmentary and it is not known how he participated in the affairs of the assembly. He was succeeded in the second parliament by Richard Beasley*.

Pettit did not live long enough to accumulate much more than the land he had been granted. In fact, between 1800 and 1802 he sold off substantial portions of it, mostly to his sons-in-law. In his will he left the remainder to his five surviving daughters and

Philipps

£80 to his son-in-law Lawrence Lawrason, a successful London merchant. In some ways the British government had compensated Pettit for his losses; however, his advancing years did not allow him to rebuild his life to its former eminence.

In collaboration with BRUCE A. PARKER

AO, MU 2100, 1798, no.1, Robert Hamilton to Nathaniel Pettit, 31 Oct. 1797; RG 1, A-I-6: 1010–11; A-II-5, 1, Niagara District reports, 1800–3; C-I-9, 1; C-IV, Ancaster Township; Grimsby Township, concessions 1 and 2, lot 9; Saltfleet Township, concession 1, lot 9; concession 2, lots 5–6. Brant Land Registry Office (Brantford, Ont.), Abstract index to deeds, Burford Township: f.147 (mfm. at AO, GS 1822). MTL, U.C., Court of Common Pleas, Nassau District, minutes. Niagara North Land Registry Office (St Catharines, Ont.), Abstract index to deeds, Grimsby Township: ff.8, 18 (mfm. at AO, GS 1914). PAC, MG 23, HII, 18 (photocopies); RG 1, L3, 418: P misc., 1800–56/95–96; RG 68, General index, 1651–1841: ff.249–50, 402, 407, 410, 412, 535, 631. Wentworth Land Registry Office (Hamilton, Ont.), Abstract index to deeds, Ancaster Township: ff.190, 235, 270 (mfm. at AO, GS 1395). "Board of land office, District of Hesse," AO *Report*, 1905: 132, 211. "United Empire Loyalists: enquiry into losses and services," AO *Report*, 1904: 982. *Corr. of Lieut. Governor Simcoe* (Cruikshank), 1: 10–11; 4: 347–49. "Loyalist and pioneer families of West Lincoln, 1783–1833," comp. R. J. Powell, *Annals of the Forty* ([Grimsby, Ont.]), no.7 (1956). Pearl Wilson, "Nathaniel Pettit," *OH*, 32 (1937): 192–202.

PHILIPPS (Phillips, Phillipps), JOHN, surgeon, politician, apothecary, merchant, army officer, and office holder; b. *c.* 1736, the illegitimate son of John Philipps of Coedgain, Wales; m. 17 Nov. 1761 in Halifax, N.S., Judith Wood, daughter of the Reverend Thomas Wood* (she died in May 1775, survived by two daughters and four sons); d. 3 Jan. 1801 in Kensington (London), England, aged 65.

John Philipps's early career remains a mystery, although he may have arrived in Halifax about 1760 as an assistant to the naval hospital. He is not to be confused with his contemporary, John Phillipps, a surgeon and ranger officer in Lunenburg between 1753 and 1766. On 26 April 1773 Philipps received the government appointment of medical and surgical attendant to the Halifax orphan house, presided over by Richard Wenman*. This institution was denounced by Governor Francis Legge* the next year as "a decayed, inhospitable Building, Just falling into ruins." The management was equally decadent; rife with patronage and plagued by poverty, it eagerly received even such items as "2 Dozen ratt nawed Hatts" from government stores for the pitiful inmates. Legge's planned reforms for the orphan house did not include the retention of Philipps's salary, which was stopped in October 1774. He petitioned for reimbursement in 1776, noting the "considerable expence and trouble" he had been put to on behalf of the institution, in addition to his "having Inoculated [with smallpox] Twenty of the Orphan Children and many more poor persons" during the epidemic of 1775–76. Although his salary was reinstated, it was not placed on the civil list, and in June 1778 it was again discontinued. A new petition by Philipps in 1784 resulted in a grant of £130 for attendance and medicine. In retrospect, he appears to have been merely a victim of reduced government spending, since his services, given the level of medical expertise of his time, would seem to have been both adequate and competent. Indeed, Philipps was commended in 1783 for his duty as surgeon to the Royal Nova Scotia Volunteers, in which capacity he displayed "great attention and regularity in the disposal of the hospital" on George Island in Halifax harbour.

In 1773 Philipps was elected to the House of Assembly as a member for Halifax County; he held this seat until 1785, although his political career was apparently unremarkable. Indeed, Philipps's reputation in Halifax ultimately rests with an aspect of his career about which little is known. He expanded his medical practice about 1780 into a chemical and drug business located near the dockyard. In a vigorous, growing community, such a venture was a lucrative enterprise with little competition. Philipps reputedly used his business and medical practice to amass a considerable fortune and became a highly respected Halifax citizen, as is evidenced by his appointment as a magistrate in 1794. He returned to England about 1800 and died shortly thereafter; his will unfortunately gives no indication of his financial position.

LOIS K. KERNAGHAN

PANS, RG 1, 163–70; RG 5, A, 1a–b. PRO, IND 16663 (Chancery bill book, no.58, *Corbyn* v. *Pollock*, 18 March 1843). St Paul's Anglican Church (Halifax), Reg. of baptisms, marriages, and burials (mfm. at PANS). *Gentleman's Magazine*, 1801: 90. Harry Piers, "The fortieth regiment, raised at Annapolis Royal in 1717; and five regiments subsequently raised in Nova Scotia," N.S. Hist. Soc., *Coll.*, 21 (1927): 115–83.

PHIPPS, JEMIMA. *See* SAWTELLE

PICHARD (Pichart), AMABLE, Roman Catholic priest; b. *c.* 1753 in Orléans, France; d. 24 Dec. 1819 in Berthier (Berthier-sur-Mer), Lower Canada.

Ordained to the priesthood in the diocese of Orléans on 21 Dec. 1782, Amable Pichard exercised his priestly duties there for some years. It is presumed that after the outbreak of the French revolution he refused to swear allegiance to the Civil Constitution of the Clergy, for in 1799 he was in England under the jurisdiction of the exiled bishop of Saint-Pol-de-Léon,

Jean-François de La Marche. Because of a shortage of clergy in the diocese of Quebec the British government had agreed that a number of French refugee priests might be sent there [see Jean-François Hubert*], and in 1799 Pichard volunteered. At that time he was described by Bishop La Marche as "a man of mediocre talent and ability, but most unassuming and of excellent personal qualities, very virtuous as well."

Pichard arrived at Halifax, N.S., in August 1799 in company with Abbé Jacques-Ladislas-Joseph de Calonne*, brother of Louis XVI's ex-minister of finance, Charles-Alexandre de Calonne. According to Joseph-Octave Plessis*, the coadjutor designate of Quebec, Pichard was known to several priests in the diocese who had lived in Orléans and who attested to his character. After obtaining the necessary faculties from Father James JONES, superior of the eastern missions, Pichard and Calonne proceeded to Prince Edward Island, where Pichard was to divide his time among the Acadian missions of Malpeque, Rustico, and Bay Fortune. Calonne, because he spoke English, was to minister to the Irish and other Catholics at Charlottetown; the Scots on the Island were served by the Reverend Angus Bernard MacEachern*. It seems, however, that Pichard's ministry may not have kept him fully occupied: in June 1801 Plessis suggested that he might help with the New Brunswick missions. He resided in a one-room glebe-house at Rustico until the fall of 1803 when, in the wake of Bishop Pierre DENAUT's visitation of Prince Edward Island, he was transferred to Tracadie, N.S.

The first parish priest of Tracadie, Pichard also served the missions of Havre Boucher and Pomquet; in 1812 his flock was to number 310 communicants, exclusive of the Indians. Ill health, the reason for his transfer, continued to plague him, however, and in 1807 and 1809 he wrote to Bishop Plessis describing the difficulties of conducting his ministry. But the bishop was unable to offer him a new appointment in Lower Canada, since with the outbreak of the Napoleonic Wars the British government had become more reluctant to admit French emigrant priests there. In 1812 Plessis undertook a visitation of the eastern missions and it was apparently on this occasion that he decided to replace Pichard. The Micmacs complained that they did not have a priest able to understand them; moreover, there were at Tracadie a number of black Protestant families whom the bishop was anxious to proselytize. Pichard, he noted, was "no longer young enough to study a language other than his own." In 1813 he wrote Pichard promising to send him a successor the following year. "It is high time, after 14 years of mission work, that you should come and get some rest as priest of a small parish in the interior of the diocese." A year later he instructed him to remove to Quebec as soon as the opportunity arose, writing at

the time to Abbé François Lejamtel* at Arichat to urge him to supervise Pichard's departure: "You know how maladroit the good fellow is. I believe him incapable of finding a passage if you do not take a hand in it. . . ."

Pichard left Nova Scotia in 1815 to become parish priest at Berthier and was succeeded at Tracadie by Abbé Antoine Manseau*. He served his new parish until his death, while hearing confessions, on Christmas Eve 1819.

J.-ALPHONSE DEVEAU

AAQ, 1 CB, VI: 114. AP, Notre-Dame-de-l'Assomption (Berthier-en-Mer), Reg. des baptêmes, mariages et sépultures, 28 déc. 1819. Allaire, *Dictionnaire*, vol.1. Caron, "Inv. de la corr. de Mgr Denaut," ANQ *Rapport*, 1931–32; "Inv. de la corr. de Mgr Plessis," 1927–28. Tanguay, *Répertoire* (1893). J.-H. Blanchard, *Rustico: une paroisse acadienne de l'île du Prince-Édouard* ([s.l.], 1938). [H.-R. Casgrain], *Mémoire sur les missions de la Nouvelle-Écosse, du cap Breton et de l'île du Prince-Édouard de 1760 à 1820 . . . réponse aux "Memoirs of Bishop Burke" par Mgr O'Brien . . .* (Québec, 1895). Johnston, *Hist. of Catholic Church in eastern N.S.*, vol.1. J. C. MacMillan, *The early history of the Catholic Church in Prince Edward Island* (Quebec, 1905).

PICKMORE, FRANCIS, naval officer and governor of Newfoundland; b. *c.* 1756, probably in England; married, with at least one daughter; d. 24 Feb. 1818 in St John's, Nfld.

Nothing is known of Francis Pickmore before his commission as a lieutenant in the Royal Navy on 18 Dec. 1777, while he was on the Newfoundland station. On 27 June 1782 he achieved the rank of commander, and on 21 Sept. 1790 that of captain. Between 1803 and 1812 Pickmore served on various commands with Richard Goodwin Keats*, who preceded him as governor of Newfoundland. In 1806, in the *Ramillies*, Pickmore took the French raider *Marengo* in the Atlantic, and the following year he was in a force sent to capture the Danish West Indies. On 28 April 1808 he reached flag rank as rear-admiral of the blue, and he became rear-admiral of the white on 25 Oct. 1809 and of the red on 31 July 1810. He was subsequently appointed vice-admiral of the blue on 12 Aug. 1812 and reached his ultimate rank of vice-admiral of the white on 4 June 1814.

Though his commission as governor of Newfoundland was dated 18 May 1816, Pickmore did not arrive there until 5 September. He remained at St John's until November, long enough to learn that the inhabitants faced a trying winter. A fire the previous February had destroyed 120 houses, and there was a shortage of provisions throughout the island, a consequence of the economic depression that had accompanied the end of the Napoleonic Wars. One of Pickmore's officers,

Pilotte

Commander David Buchan* of the *Pike*, wintered in Newfoundland to oversee the proper distribution of supplies. Conditions for the next winter were not helped by a poor seal fishery in the spring of 1817, followed by a similarly bad summer fishery.

Pickmore returned to St John's on 30 Sept. 1817. He had been asked by the British government to remain in Newfoundland over the winter, and he was the first governor to do so. It was hoped that his presence would guarantee to the more than 70,000 settlers the continuance of law and order. One of Pickmore's personal worries was the governor's residence in Fort Townshend, intended for summer use only; he found snow had drifted into the bedrooms the previous winter. Lord Bathurst, the Colonial secretary, refused his request for money to reconstruct and advised him to rent a suitable residence. Conditions generally were worse than in the previous year: provisions were short, and lack of gainful employment had impoverished a large part of the population. The social disorders that threatened were likely to be all the more dangerous because of the continuing influx of large numbers of poor Irish, a most unwelcome group to the English population.

The expectations of a hard winter were more than fulfilled. From November 1817 to the following spring the frost, which was severe and unrelieved, iced over the harbour of St John's and made communications difficult. On 7 and 21 November fires destroyed 400 houses and left 2,000 persons homeless. The conflagrations also consumed large amounts of provisions in warehouses, so compounding the destitution. It is not surprising that all this misery was accompanied by vandalism, looting, and other social disorders of all descriptions. In Newfoundland parlance the season was known as the "Winter of the Rals" (rowdies).

Pickmore was literally worked to death by his efforts to alleviate the worst sufferings. He placed a temporary embargo on all vessels holding supplies, purchased provisions wherever possible, and sent out urgent appeals for help; subsequently, substantial aid came from Halifax, N.S., Boston, Mass., and England. For himself, the governor had been unable to find better quarters; in poor health when he arrived, he suffered great discomfort from the inadequacies of his house. The bitter cold and his ceaseless labours eventually took their toll and Pickmore died on 24 Feb. 1818, the first governor to do so in office. His duties were assumed by the senior naval officer, Captain John Bowker, until the arrival of Governor Sir Charles Hamilton* in July. Pickmore was given a "grand funeral," and his body rested in the Anglican church before being conveyed to England in the spring. During his short stay in Newfoundland he was considered to have been a ruler of "humane and amiable qualities." Contrary to statements in some secondary sources, he was never knighted.

FREDERIC F. THOMPSON

Gentleman's Magazine, July–December 1808: 156; July–December 1813: 383; July–December 1814: 496; January–June 1816: 561. *Naval Chronicle*, 40 (July–December 1818): 343–44. [James Saumarez], *The Saumarez papers: selections from the Baltic correspondence of Vice-Admiral Sir James Saumarez, 1808–1812*, ed. A. N. Ryan (London, 1968). *Royal Gazette* (St John's), 3 March 1818. G.B., Admiralty, *The commissioned sea officers of the Royal Navy, 1660–1815*, [ed. D. B. Smith *et al.*] (3v., n.p., [1954?]), 3. R. H. Bonnycastle, *Newfoundland in 1842; a sequel to "The Canadas in 1841"* (2v., London, 1842), 1: 145–49. Joseph Hatton and Moses Harvey, *Newfoundland, the oldest British colony; its history, its present condition, and its prospects in the future* (London, 1883), 97–99. McLintock, *Establishment of constitutional government in Nfld.*, 124–30. Prowse, *Hist. of Nfld.* (1895), 406–7.

PILOTTE, ANGELIQUE, servant; b. *c.* 1797 near Michilimackinac (Mackinac Island, Mich.), in her own words "the natural daughter of a Squaw, and a native of the Indian Country"; fl. 1815–18.

About 1815, because of her "good natural qualities," Angelique Pilotte was engaged as a servant to a woman on Drummond Island (Mich.). She accompanied her mistress on a trip to France but when the latter died suddenly, Pilotte returned, landing at Quebec on 4 June 1817 and making her way back to Drummond Island. With "strong recommendations in her favour," she was hired as a "waiting woman" to Elizabeth Ann Hamilton, also of Drummond Island, and they left almost immediately on a three-week voyage to the home of John Ussher (Usher) of Chippawa, Upper Canada, arriving on 29 July 1817.

Pilotte attended to her routine household duties until about 8 August when the body of a dead baby boy was discovered in a very shallow grave near the Ussher home. When questioned by her mistress the following day, Pilotte confessed to being the baby's mother, "and was for the first time apprised, that she had committed a crime in the Eye of English Law." Later that day, while "in a state of extreme convulsion," she made the same admission before justices of the peace Samuel Street* and Thomas Clark*, whereupon she was held over for trial under a bill of indictment for infanticide; the act invoked was that of 1624 (21 Jac. I, c.27), which had been passed "to prevent the destroying and murthering of Bastard Children."

The assizes began at Niagara (Niagara-on-the-Lake) on 8 Sept. 1817. A grand jury was summoned and found a true bill against Pilotte. At the outset of the trial the next day justice William Campbell*

appointed lawyer Bartholomew Crannell Beardsley*
as Pilotte's counsel; she pleaded not guilty. The
attorney for the crown, Henry John Boulton*,
prosecuted the case to a quick conclusion after the
introduction of Pilotte's confession and the examination of seven witnesses. The petit jury found her guilty
but "strongly" urged mercy. On 11 September Campbell, who later claimed that the defendant had been
convicted on "clear and sufficient evidence," sentenced
her to be hanged. His confident assertion to the contrary, however, the case was not clear-cut. Pilotte's
own petition for mercy, written on 15 September and
maintaining her innocence, was supported by the
grand jury; its members were "strongly inclined *to
give* credit to its assertions" and, like the petit jurymen, they recommended that she be pardoned. Moreover, several other petitions championed her cause.
Campbell soon decided to respite the execution and
refer the case to the administrator of the province,
Samuel Smith*, to determine whether Pilotte was a
"fit object for the exercise of the Royal Mercy." On
18 September he sent Smith copies of the pertinent
documents, along with Pilotte's petition, in which she
pleaded her innocence. A few weeks later, Smith,
noting "the very uncommon Interest the case seems to
have excited in all Ranks" and the "unusual demon-
strations" on the part of the juries in particular,
transmitted these documents to Colonial Secretary
Lord Bathurst to forward for royal consideration.

The reaction of the "respectable" to Pilotte's plight
– a reaction that was not to be duplicated at the trial of
Mary Thompson* in 1823 – was possibly the most
notable aspect of the case. On the grand jury that
supported Pilotte's petition, 11 of 20 members were
justices of the peace and included such worthies as
Robert Nelles*, William Johnson Kerr*, and William
Hamilton Merritt*. A number of the magistrates and
"principal Inhabitants" of the Niagara area, among
whom were Thomas Clark, an associate judge at the
trial and one of the JPS who originally examined
Pilotte, William Claus*, and James Crooks*, also
recommended mercy. Even the officers of the 70th
Foot stationed at Fort George (Niagara-on-the-Lake),
although admitting that "it may perhaps be out of our
line of duty," petitioned for mercy through their
spokesman, Henry William Vavasour* of the Royal
Engineers. This popular clamour is difficult to
explain, but it may be significant that many of those
who came to Pilotte's defence had connections with
the Indian community through the American revolution and War of 1812, the fur trade, the Indian
Department, and intermarriage.

By the terms of the act of 1624 Pilotte was guilty on
her own admission. The act was of unusual construction. One of the few statutes in English law that
presumed the guilt of the accused, it made the very

fact of concealment of the birth of a bastard child, later
found dead, sufficient presumption that the mother
had committed murder. Although Pilotte did not deny
that the child was a bastard, her statements about its
birth were contradictory. In her petition she maintained that the child had been stillborn en route to
Chippawa, but her confession established that the
child had been born on the Ussher property, that he
had been born alive, and that his birth had been
concealed. Claiming to have given birth in a field
adjoining the Ussher home at about 2 a.m. on the
morning of 30 July, Pilotte stated that the child
"moved its little legs, but did not move its arms."
After staying with him for an hour or so, she left him
"upon the grass then moving his legs but not crying."
She went back to the house for about two hours,
"being sick," and returned to the field to find the baby
"which was still moving its legs." After wrapping a
"cloth very tight about the child," she left him behind a
stable until about 2 a.m. on 31 July. When asked by
the magistrates why she had wrapped the infant
tightly, she replied that "it was for the purpose of
choaking it." Then, if her confession was true, she
buried the child, possibly while he was still alive.

The confession was sufficiently damning and the
statements of the witnesses supported it to the extent
that they established that the child had been born on
the Ussher property. Thomas Clark stated that the
confession "was freely made, neither threats nor
promises being used to induce or influence her." Mary
McQueen, the Usshers' servant who had shared her
bed with Pilotte, testified that Angelique had got up
two or three times during the night of 29–30 July and
appeared sickly. Mary Margaret Clark, one of three
women who had "privately examined" Pilotte, concluded that "she had lately been delivered of a Child."
Elizabeth Hamilton also reached the same conclusion.
Mary Ussher (née Street), John's wife, had gone
through Pilotte's linen and found with her clothing "an
Infant's Shift." She had not suspected her to be
pregnant but recalled that she had heard a "Strange
Noise" on the night in question, "which instantly
occurred to her was like the crying of an Infant – but
having no idea of any Infant being there, she imagined
it must have been a Cat."

As to whether the baby had been alive or dead at
birth, the evidence of the witnesses was less
conclusive. Miss Hamilton and Mrs Clark reiterated
Pilotte's assertion to them that the baby had been
stillborn; however, Pilotte's own confession made
that possibility seem highly unlikely. Moreover, a
local surgeon's testimony that the body "was perfect
in form, and had every appearance of mature birth"
was coupled with the statement that a live child so
"tightly pinned up . . . must necessarily soon be
smothered." Under cross-examination by Beardsley

Pinquin

he added that death might have been caused by "the want of proper assistance at time of delivery."

Another point that either was established by the testimony or, if not made in the first instance, emerged under cross-examination was the fact that, as Thomas Clark noted, Pilotte "appeared Simple and Stupid." No one disagreed and indeed Elizabeth Hamilton said that Pilotte "borders on Idiotism" and was "so Simple and ignorant as not to know right from Wrong, nor that she thought it a crime to Kill her own child." Later, when faced by the pressure of the combined petitions, Campbell used Hamilton's testimony on this matter as grounds for ordering a respite of execution and referring the case for further consideration.

Pilotte's petition was carefully framed, no doubt by her counsel, and emphasized the extraordinary circumstances of the case. She was a "poor girl," with "no education whatever, nor the slightest instruction in the Principles of Christian Religion." Utterly helpless, she was depicted as a victim of the judicial process. She had been unaware of her right to counsel and thus the lawyer appointed by the court to defend her had had insufficient time to prepare her case adequately. Moreover, some of the statements in her confession were flatly contradicted by her petition. Here she claimed that while in France she had had "an unhappy connection" with a friend of her employer, a British officer whom she identified as a Lieutenant Luckman of the 81st Foot, and became pregnant. During the latter days of her voyage to Chippawa she went into labour. The child was stillborn and, fearing the wrath of her mistress, she wrapped the body, brought it ashore, and on the night of 29–30 July buried the baby in a shallow grave in an open field. The petition pointed out that the presence of infant's clothing, by proving the mother's intention to care for the child, was sufficient evidence according to English legal practice to remove a case from the purview of the 1624 act. More important, it drew particular attention to the different cultural customs of Indian women in childbirth. All Pilotte knew was the "customs and maxims of her own nation"; thus, she was guilty only of "the invariable custom of Indian women to retire and bring forth their children alone, and in secret."

Pilotte had to spend many months in prison before learning of the crown's response to her plea for mercy. Transatlantic appeal was, naturally enough, a lengthy process and the delay eventually led Robert Fleming Gourlay* to claim that the government had not acted with proper dispatch, a charge that was completely unfounded. On 27 March 1818 Lord Sidmouth, acting on behalf of the Prince Regent, changed her sentence to one year's imprisonment. On 13 May Bathurst notified Smith of the royal decision.

It is extremely difficult for an historian to judge on the basis of incomplete records whether Pilotte was guilty or innocent of infanticide. Certainly, according to the act under which she was charged, the grand jury (in the first instance, the petit jury) and the judge agreed that there was sufficient evidence to proceed with a trial and ultimately to convict her. The peculiarities of that act aside, it cannot be known for certain whether the baby boy was stillborn or murdered. However, Pilotte's assertions on the former count are not very convincing. What moved the juries and local inhabitants was probably sympathy for her helplessness and simplicity before a law which, in a sense, put the Indian tradition of childbirth on trial. As for Pilotte herself, it is not known what became of her. She probably served her sentence and then returned to her birthplace and her people.

ROBERT LOCHIEL FRASER III

AO, RG 22, ser.134, 4, 9 Sept. 1817. PAC, MG 11, [CO 42] Q, 322-1: 245–76; RG 5, A1: 16102–26, 18104–5, 19067–68; RG 7, G1, 59: 13–18. William Blackstone, *Commentaries on the laws of England* (4v., Oxford, 1765–69; repr. Chicago and London, 1979), 4: 220–21. U.C., *Statutes*, 1831–32, c.1. *Niagara Spectator* (Niagara [Niagara-on-the-Lake, Ont.]), 28 Jan. 1819. W. C. Keele, *The provincial justice, or magistrate's manual, being a complete digest of the criminal law of Canada, and a compendious and general view of the provincial law of Upper Canada . . .* (2nd ed., Toronto, 1843), 86, 157. S. R. Clarke and H. P. Sheppard, *A treatise on the criminal law of Canada* (2nd ed., Toronto, 1882), 208–9. Leon Radzinowicz, *A history of English criminal law and its administration from 1750* (4v., London, 1948–68), 1: 430–36, 629.

PINQUIN (Pinquaing), XAVIER GALLANT, known as. *See* GALLANT

PINSON, ANDREW, ship's captain and merchant; b. *c.* 1728 in Abbotskerswell, England, eldest surviving son of Andrew Pinson and Ann Dodd; m. with at least one son; d. 20 April 1810 in Broadhempston, England.

Andrew Pinson was the son of a by-boat keeper who cleared a fishing room in St John's, Nfld, during the 1720s. By 1750 Andrew Sr had prospered to the degree that he owned his own trading ship, which the son then commanded. By now the father was growing old and no longer undertook the annual migration across the Atlantic, thus leaving Andrew Jr with the management of the fishery. Events went well enough until 1758, when he and his vessel were captured by a French privateer on the return voyage from Newfoundland. Pinson probably spent the next four years as a prisoner and his father, unable to continue his fishery, leased the St John's plantation to another man. The father died in 1764 and Andrew inherited little beyond the rents of the plantation. Forced to commence life anew, he chose to work for the important Bristol firm of John Noble and Company.

Noble had traded to Newfoundland since about 1740, and during the Seven Years' War had outfitted several privateers. One of them, commanded by Nicholas Darby*, found rich pickings in the Strait of Belle Isle between Newfoundland and Labrador, and also discovered the abundance of the fishing grounds in that region, which before had been almost unknown to English seamen.

Following the establishment of peace in 1763 Noble was well placed to exploit the fisheries of the northern shore, and Pinson was employed to recruit a crew in St John's, which fished at Zealot Harbour. Between 1763 and 1770 Pinson organized annual fishing expeditions from St John's to Conche and Cape Rouge on the Northern Peninsula. A rough-hewn man, Pinson had one of the worst reputations in the Newfoundland trade for ill treatment of his servants, which brought him into great disfavour with the governors, especially Hugh Palliser*, and he outraged other merchants by claiming exclusive rights to the salmon fishery in the northern harbours. John Noble, however, found him efficient and productive.

In 1770 Noble, probably at Pinson's suggestion, constructed a more or less permanent fishing station at Lance Cove in Temple Bay, Labrador, and in 1772 another at nearby Pitts Harbour. By 1775 Pinson had become a partner in the firm, and his young son William came out to Labrador as a ship's captain and summer agent. The War of American Independence proved costly for the firm since the premises they had built at L'Anse-au-Loup in Labrador and three ships were destroyed by an American privateer in 1778. However, the same privateer also destroyed George CARTWRIGHT's establishment on Sandwich Bay. This disaster forced Cartwright into one of his periods of insolvency, and Noble and Pinson acquired the premises.

During the war both Pinson and Noble outfitted privateers which enjoyed a modest success, and the end of the war encouraged them to expand their business quickly. There were as yet no planters operating independently on the Labrador coast, and indeed their only serious mercantile rival was John Slade* of Poole, at Battle Harbour. Thus the company, unlike those in Newfoundland, had to employ servants directly to catch the fish, and these men had to be transported from and to Britain every year. By 1793 Pinson and Noble had nine vessels in the carrying trade and were employing up to 250 men in catching cod and salmon, killing seals, and trading with the native peoples.

By now Pinson's son William and Noble's son John Hatt had also joined the firm as partners, and the future seemed bright. Once again, however, war intervened to interrupt expansion and in 1796 the firm was forced to destroy the premises it had rebuilt at L'Anse-au-Loup in order to prevent them from falling into the hands of the French admiral Joseph de Richery. This event, and the closure of Spanish and Italian markets as a result of the war, caused a certain amount of dislocation, but the firm seems to have ridden it out well enough. The Treaty of Amiens in 1802 allowed the partners to re-expand quickly, and by 1804 they owned seven ships and were apparently well secured. However, human relationships dislocated this flourishing trade. It would seem that Andrew Pinson and, to a lesser extent, John Noble were living too long. By 1800 Pinson's son William was 46 years old, and John Hatt Noble was well into manhood. The older men must have refused to give them enough responsibility, for William Pinson formed a new partnership with John Hine of Dartmouth, a brother-in-law and long agent and captain with the company, while John Hatt Noble formed one with Henry Hunt of Dartmouth. Noble and Hunt moved from the west of England to London, where they engaged in a complex set of business relationships with the numerous relatives of Henry Hunt; Pinson and Hine began a trade to Labrador on their own account. The breach must have been fairly amicable for both sets of partners had a fairly close relationship with the senior firm. The latter found its own salvation by sending out to Newfoundland William's son Andrew, who was now of an age to take on the responsibilities of management.

Andrew Sr's death in 1810 was rapidly followed by that of William, and both their estates fell to Andrew Jr. He severed the connection with the Noble family and traded under the name of Pinson and Hine, being an annual migrant between Dartmouth and Labrador, where he became the chief resident and a justice of the peace. John Hatt Noble inherited his father's share of the trade, and through his partner Henry Hunt re-entered the Labrador fishery under the name of Beard and Hunt. However, he was a sleeping partner and soon moved his interests to Oporto in Portugal. Andrew Pinson had a son in 1827, but died four years later at the untimely age of 43. With his death the connection of both the Noble and the Pinson families with the Newfoundland trade came to an end.

K. MATTHEWS

Bristol Reference Library (Bristol, Eng.), Bristol Presentments. East Devon Record Office, 73A/PO 46–87; 2659A; 2954A; 2992A; Exeter City Arch., town customs accounts. Hunt, Roope & Co. (London), Robert Newman & Co., ledgers and letterbooks (mfm. at PANL). PANL, GN 1/13/4; GN 2/1; GN 5/1/B/1, Trinity and Labrador records; P7/A/6. PRO, ADM 1/471–76; 7/317–19; BT 1; BT 5; BT 6/190–91; BT 98/3–17; CO 194; CUST 65.
George Cartwright, *Journal of transactions and events, during a residence of nearly sixteen years on the coast of Labrador . . .* (3v., Newark, Eng., 1792). Edward Chappell, *Voyage of his majesty's ship Rosamond to Newfoundland and the southern coast of Labrador, of which countries no account has been published by any British traveller since the*

reign of Queen Elizabeth (London, 1818). *Felix Farley's Bristol Journal* (Bristol). *Lloyd's Evening Post and British Chronicle* (London). *Lloyd's List. Newfoundland Mercantile Journal* (St John's). *Public Advertiser* (London). *Royal Gazette* (St John's). *Sherborne Mercury or the Weekly Magazine* (Sherborne, Eng.). *Trewman's Exeter Flying Post, or Plymouth and Cornish Advertiser* (Exeter). *Reg. of shipping.*

PITRE, CÉCILE. *See* BOUDREAU

PIUZE, LIVERIGHT (at birth he was named **Traugott Leberecht Behzer**), surgeon and apothecary; b. 5 Feb. 1754 in Warsaw (Poland); m. 14 Nov. 1786 Marie-Anne Aubut in Sainte-Anne-de-la-Pocatière (La Pocatière), Que., and they had 14 children; d. 22 April 1813 at Rivière-Ouelle, Lower Canada.

Liveright Piuze spent part of his childhood in Warsaw and then lived in Dresden (German Democratic Republic), where his family moved around 1763. There, from 1767 to 1772, he trained as a surgeon and apothecary under the guidance of one of his father's close relatives. Having finished his apprenticeship, he decided to seek his fortune in the British colonies, and on 18 Sept. 1773 he arrived in Philadelphia, Pa, after a long crossing in the *Britannia.* He quickly set up an apothecary's shop in that city and bought a small plantation near the Susquehanna River. In December 1776, some months after the War of American Independence had begun, he served as an assistant surgeon, first in the revolutionary militia and later at a hospital in Philadelphia. At the urging of some friends he left the American army and decided to settle in the Mississippi valley. After a number of incidents in which he almost lost his life, he was captured in February 1779 by an Indian tribe from the Delaware valley, who handed him over to Mason Bolton, lieutenant-colonel commanding the British forces at Fort Niagara (near Youngstown, N.Y.). Suspecting Piuze of being in the pay of the Continental Congress, Bolton sent him to Montreal, Que., on 9 May to be locked up. He was imprisoned at Fort Chambly until April 1780; he then went to Quebec, where he received a certificate as a surgeon from Dr Hugh Alexander Kennedy, inspector general of hospitals. After serving for some months as a surgeon on British navy vessels in the St Lawrence, he obtained his discharge on 19 Jan. 1781 and decided to settle in the province of Quebec.

Piuze almost immediately went to live in Rivière-Ouelle – a village without a doctor since 1761 – with the intention of establishing a medical practice. He was able to win the confidence of the local population in short order and had no difficulty fitting into rural society. On 1 Jan. 1786, ten months before his

marriage with Marie-Anne Aubut, he renounced Lutheranism to embrace Catholicism; the act of renunciation was signed in the presence of Bernard-Claude Panet*, parish priest of Notre-Dame-de-Liesse at Rivière-Ouelle. In 1789 his medical competence was recognized by the Quebec Medical Board, which issued him a licence to practise as a surgeon and apothecary. In addition to his doctor's fees Piuze secured income through the purchase and sale of properties at Rivière-Ouelle; in 1788 and 1793 he sold two houses, with grounds and outbuildings, the first for £140 and the second for £228.

Little is known of the rest of his career, except that in the period 1806–8 he sued a merchant and tavern-keeper by the name of Ignace Lassare in the Court of King's Bench of the District of Quebec, accusing him of having practised medicine illegally and of selling medicaments without authorization. After hearing witnesses testify that the accused had attended patients at Kamouraska, Rivière-Ouelle, and Sainte-Anne-de-la-Pocatière in 1806, the court imposed a fine of £20 upon Lassare.

In 1814, a year after the death of Piuze, Dr François Fortier came to take his place. Several of Piuze's children settled in the Rivière-Ouelle region. Rémi, the eldest, served as a notary at Sainte-Anne-de-la-Pocatière from 1808 to 1867; Édouard-Ferdinand remained in his native village where, following in his father's footsteps, he practised medicine.

JACQUES MORIN

A copy of Liveright Piuze's account in English of his adventures from the time he left Warsaw until his arrival in Quebec in 1780 is at ANQ-Q, P1000-80-1666. A translation into French by J. R. Piuze was published in *BRH*, 25 (1919): 334–66.

AAQ, 42 CD, I: 46. ANQ-Q, CE3-12, 14 nov. 1786; CN1-178, 16 sept. 1793, 2 juin 1794; CN1-256, 9 Sept. 1788; CN3-11, 13 nov. 1786; T6-1, Cour du banc du roi, 26 sept., 16 oct., 1ᵉʳ nov. 1806; 3 févr. 1808. BL, Add. MSS 21789: f.41; 21805: f.128; 21843: ff.48, 62 (copies at PAC). *Quebec Gazette*, 6 Nov. 1788, 2 May 1793. Le Jeune, *Dictionnaire*, 2: 446. *Quebec almanac*, 1792: 155. M.-J. et G. Ahern, *Notes pour l'hist. de la médecine*, 444–45. Georges Desjardins, *Antoine Roy, dit Desjardins (1635–1684) et ses descendants* ([Trois-Rivières, Qué.], 1971), 217–37. P.-H. Hudon, *Rivière-Ouelle de la Bouteillerie; 3 siècles de vie* (Ottawa, 1972), 219. Gabriel Nadeau, "L'ancêtre des Piuze," SGCF *Mémoires*, 6 (1954–55): 94.

PLANTAVIT DE LAPAUSE DE MARGON, JEAN-GUILLAUME, army officer and author; b. 14 Aug. 1721 in Pézenas, France, son of Henri Plantavit de Lapause de Margon and Grâce Maudon; d. unmarried 9 March 1804 in his home town.

Jean-Guillaume Plantavit de Lapause de Margon began his military career as an ensign in the Régiment de Guyenne on 16 May 1745. He attained the rank of lieutenant on 14 Aug. 1746, was appointed adjutant the following year, and then in 1751 was promoted captain. He arrived at Quebec on 23 June 1755 with the regular troops under the command of Jean-Armand Dieskau*.

In the summer of 1756 Lapause took part in the expedition led by Louis-Joseph de Montcalm* against the fortified base of Oswego (Chouaguen) (N.Y.). According to his own statement, he was carrying out the responsibilities of adjutant general and chief of staff, and his task was to help set up the siege of Oswego by reconnoitring the forts with François-Charles de Bourlamaque* and some engineers to determine the best tactics for the attack. He was also responsible for officering the Canadians who had come as reinforcements for the regular troops, fitting out the boats, and dispatching artillery and rations. On 14 August, after some bombardment and a short, three-day siege, the British surrendered. Following the victory Lapause was delegated to drawing up the terms and conditions of surrender and planning the evacuation. Some days later Montcalm wrote to François de Lévis*: "I cannot praise too highly my aides-de-camp, Lapause [and] Malartic [Anne-Joseph-Hippolyte de Maures* de Malartic]; I would have collapsed under the task without them, and Lapause is a sublime man who has greatly eased my burden." In addition Montcalm appointed him adjutant general, and he was also granted a pension of 300 *livres* from the royal treasury. Lapause's duties were essentially of two kinds: on the one hand he was to attend to matters of practical organization of the army, taking all decisions about rations, supply, returns of men, arms, ammunition, and equipment of every sort; on the other hand he was to carry out reconnaissance missions.

In September 1756 Lapause went with the Régiment de Guyenne to Carillon (near Ticonderoga, N.Y.), where in accordance with his duties he closely examined the situation of the post and made several suggestions for improving its security, including having extensive clearing done around the fort to prevent a surprise attack by Indians. He spent the rest of 1756 in the Quebec region, where the troops took up winter quarters. The following May the Régiment de Guyenne was ordered to do work on Fort Chambly. In July it received instructions to leave for Carillon, where Montcalm was assembling troops for the siege of Fort George (also called Fort William Henry; now Lake George, N.Y.). Lapause inspected the troops and artillery, and also gave his views on the strategic situation, some of which were adopted by Montcalm and Lévis.

At the end of June 1759 Lapause was sent to Île aux Noix, on the Richelieu, to assist in fortifying it. Then on Montcalm's orders he went to join Lévis, who was responsible for defending the frontiers of the Government of Montreal. In July Lapause took part in reconnaissance near Lake Champlain. After the fall of Fort Niagara (near Youngstown, N.Y.) in July, Governor Vaudreuil [Rigaud*] on 9 August sent him, with François-Marc-Antoine Le Mercier* and Lévis, to complete the construction of Fort Lévis (east of Prescott, Ont.), in order to meet the threat of a British invasion. In April 1760 Lapause was sent by Lévis on reconnaissance to the Rivière Jacques-Cartier, near Quebec. When Vaudreuil dispatched Lévis to recapture Quebec, Lapause was sent on ahead of the army to make preparations for its arrival and to reconnoitre the enemy's positions. Lévis instructed him to draw the army up in battle order upon arrival and to assign each battalion to its specific position, a heavy responsibility if ever there was one.

After the failure of the attempt to retake Quebec and the surrender of New France, Lapause sailed on the same ship as Lévis, reaching La Rochelle, France, on 27 Nov. 1760 and arriving in Paris on 5 December. That same year he received the cross of Saint-Louis. While in New France Lapause had written reports in which he gave his opinion on a variety of subjects, such as the causes of the food shortage in 1757. He thought Quebec's situation vulnerable and considered it desirable for France to continue to support the colony. Lapause had also kept a diary about his adventures in which he described his various missions and the course of operations during the Seven Years' War.

For Lapause there had never been any question of settling permanently in New France. He was first and foremost a career soldier. On 10 Feb. 1761 he was promoted colonel of infantry and received a gratuity of 3,000 *livres* for his services. Lévis had warmly recommended this promotion, and earlier Montcalm had asked for it with the utmost insistence. Both of them had spoken very highly of Lapause, as had André Doreil*, the financial commissary of wars in New France. Like many officers who though meritorious came from the gentry and had no fortune, he depended on the king's favour. Lévis said of him: "I think it for the good of the service to put him in the way of the most important posts and not leave him idle, since he is fit for any employment for which he may be wanted. He has the experience, abilities, and birth to merit a regiment, but not the means to buy one." In April 1761 Lapause was made an additional supernumerary colonel. In 1770 he became a brigadier and received a pension of 1,000 *livres* from the order of Saint-Louis. He seems to have ended his career in an organizing capacity, since he was posted in 1780 to Saint-Omer, France, as assistant chief of army staff to engage in work on the canal.

Plaw

Some years later Lapause would seem to have received the title of count and the rank of major-general; he then retired to his estates, dividing his time between his property at Beaune and his house at Pézenas, where he died on 9 March 1804.

JEANNINE POZZO-LAURENT

The ANQ's *Rapport* has published the manuscripts of Jean-Guillaume Plantavit de Lapause de Margon in three parts: "Les 'mémoires' du chevalier de La Pause," 1932–33: 305–97; "Mémoire et observations sur mon voyage au Canada," 1931–32: 3–46; and "Les 'papiers' La Pause," 1933–34: 65–231.

Arch. municipales, Pézenas, France, État civil, Pézenas, 14 août 1721. AD, Hérault (Montpellier), État civil, Pézenas, 9 mars 1804. [L.-A.] de Bougainville, "Le journal de M. de Bougainville," A.[-E.] Gosselin, édit., ANQ *Rapport*, 1923–24. *Coll. des manuscrits de Lévis* (Casgrain), vols.1–7, 10–12. [André] Doreil, "Lettres de Doreil," Antoine Roy, édit., ANQ *Rapport*, 1944–45. "Mémoire du Canada," ANQ *Rapport*, 1924–25. Thomas Chapais, *Le marquis de Montcalm (1712–1759)* (Québec, 1911).

PLAW, JOHN, architect and surveyor; baptized 8 Jan. 1746 in Putney (London), England, son of John Plaw and Mary —; d. 24 May 1820 in Charlottetown, P.E.I.

John Plaw, one of the first important architects to immigrate to British North America, received training for his chosen career by being apprenticed to Thomas Kaygill, a member of the Tylers' and Bricklayers' Company of London. His term began in September 1759 and lasted until January 1768 when he gained freedom by service. In 1763, while still an apprentice, Plaw had received an architectural award, or premium, given each year by the Society for the Encouragement of Arts, Manufactures, and Commerce. His submission was a detailed drawing of the Banqueting House, Whitehall, and provides evidence that he had studied the work of Inigo Jones and the Palladian movement. Plaw's architectural drawings were accepted for showing in 13 exhibitions of the Royal Academy of Arts, beginning in 1775. He was a long-time member of the Incorporated Society of Artists and in 1790 was its president.

Although Plaw became an established builder and architect in Westminster, many of his commissions were for country buildings and these became his specialty. His most famous surviving structure is the circular villa on Belle Isle in Lake Windermere built in 1774 for Thomas English, a coffee merchant of London. Several later circular houses were based on this plan, including Ickworth House in Surrey, designed by Francis Sandys, and La Gordanne, a villa in Switzerland on the north shore of Lake Geneva. Another of Plaw's more significant buildings is the Church of St Mary, Paddington (London), designed in

1788. Justly esteemed in his day, it was included in a book of selected drawings published by the contemporary German architectural historian Christian Ludwig Stieglitz.

Around 1795 Plaw moved to Southampton, attracted there, it appears, by the prospect of building military barracks, a major source of employment for architects in the second half of the 18th century. He did receive commissions to erect barracks there and on the Isle of Wight. During the 12 years he spent in Southampton he designed houses for a planned residential area called Albion Place and received some work from nearby estate owners.

While still in England Plaw published three books, and through his writings made his main contribution to architecture. *Rural architecture; or designs, from the simple cottage to the decorated villa* appeared in 1785 and was followed by *Ferme ornée; or rural improvements* (London, 1795), and *Sketches for country houses, villas, and rural dwellings* (London, 1800). The first had six reprintings and was widely read by architects, master builders, and members of the gentry in Britain and on the continent. In North America, architects such as Philip Hooker and, later, George Browne* were also familiar with Plaw's work.

In the early 1800s Plaw apparently became "discouraged and disappointed in his art" and began to seek other opportunities. Possibly drawn by the fact that Prince Edward Island urgently needed public buildings he immigrated there in 1807 with his wife Mary, her sister Betsy Ball, and nephew Joseph Ball. As architect to the Island's government he submitted plans for a new jail in 1809, several designs for a proposed court-house in 1810, and "sundry plans and designs for roads." He was also acting surveyor general during Thomas WRIGHT's absences. Although Plaw's design for the jail was accepted, the project was abandoned in January 1810 because no builders could be found to undertake it. The following April his plan for a court-house was selected and bids were received in May. Construction began in the spring of 1811. Though unfinished, the building, on Queen Square in Charlottetown, was used for the first time on 15 July 1812 when Chief Justice Caesar Colclough*, after ordering workmen to clean it, invited Bishop Joseph-Octave Plessis* to celebrate mass there. The House of Assembly began using it in August but even then it was not finished. In December 1813 Plaw listed the details yet to be completed, saying that the cost would not exceed £100. The Court House served its intended purpose until 1847 and then became in turn a flour and meal market, a city hall, and a police court before being moved off the square in the winter of 1872–73. It was demolished in 1972.

Plaw visited Halifax, N.S., in 1813 and offered to design public and private buildings. While there he prepared plans for the admiral's residence. These were accepted locally and tenders were called. His plan for a wooden building, however, was not accepted by the Admiralty in London and a design for a brick building drawn by their own architects was acted upon.

In 1814 Plaw returned to a favourite theme by designing yet another circular building, this one as a store for Waters and Birnie, a London-based firm doing business on Prince Edward Island from 1810 to 1820. It is not known whether the design was ever carried out but the theme was employed again in 1819 when Lieutenant Governor Charles Douglass Smith* obtained plans and estimates from him for a new market-house. The plan was for a 16-sided building surrounded by a colonnade of the Tuscan order and surmounted by a cupola. The market-house was not built until 1823, three years after Plaw's death, when the plan was retrieved and executed by three prominent Island builders, Isaac Smith, Henry Smith, and Thomas Hodgson.

Plaw was a competent architect who in 1810 had advertised in Charlottetown that he would give evening lessons to "carpenters and others" in the principles of geometry and architectural drawing. It seems probable that his influence spread in this way and that the precision and attention to detail found in the colony's early houses are due to his example and teaching. Unfortunately, the scarcity of records for the period he lived in America makes it difficult to assess his work. For example, until quite recently it was thought that his design for the market-house was the work of Isaac Smith, the Island's foremost builder and architect from 1830 to 1850. The hope always remains that an existing building in Charlottetown or Halifax may yet be identified as his work, and that the prints, drawings, and plates sold after his death will surface.

IRENE L. ROGERS

[John Plaw is the author of *Rural architecture; or designs, from the simple cottage to the decorated villa* . . . (London, 1785), *Ferme ornée; or rural improvements* . . . (London, 1795), and *Sketches for country houses, villas, and rural dwellings* . . . (London, 1800). They enjoyed frequent reprintings and, according to Howard Colvin, "were among the earliest of the cottage and villa books which became so popular during the first quarter of the nineteenth century."

Although recent research on Prince Edward Island has added to our knowledge of his career there, the standard study remains Colvin's *A biographical dictionary of British architects, 1600–1840* (London, 1978). The *DNB* seems to have based its mention of Plaw's Canadian activities on material published in England around 1824; the *Prince Edward Island Register* (Charlottetown) reprinted that account in its issue of 29 Dec. 1824. Speculation that Plaw might have had one or two daughters appears to be based on entries for painters with that surname in the three works by Algernon Graves cited below; Plaw's will, however, held at the Supreme Court of P.E.I. in Charlottetown (Estates Division, liber 2: f.9), makes no mention of children.

Plaw's designs of 1809 for a proposed jail in Charlottetown are not extant, but his plans for the Court House (1810) and the delightful front elevation and floor plan prepared for Waters and Birnie (1814) are at PAPEI, Acc. 2333. A plan and specifications for the Charlottetown round market done in Isaac Smith's handwriting are held at PAPEI, Acc. 2702, Smith–Alley coll., Isaac Smith papers, 555, 560, 973, and 979; Plaw's originals have not survived. The plan and specifications Plaw prepared for the admiral's house in Halifax (1813) are at the PRO in ADM 1/504 (MPI 166). A drawing and a photograph of the market-house are in M. K. Cullen, "Charlottetown market houses: 1813–1958," *Island Magazine*, no.6 (spring–summer 1979): 27–28. Unfortunately, photographs of the Court House, including those published in Cullen, *A history of the structure and use of Province House, Prince Edward Island, 1837–1977* (Can., National Hist. Parks and Sites Branch, *Manuscript report*, no.211, Ottawa, 1977), 237, 275, do not adequately represent Plaw's design because the building had been much altered by the time it was photographed. Plaw's tombstone at the Elm Avenue cemetery in Charlottetown is illustrated in C. B. Chappell, "The burial place of John Plaw," *Architectural Rev.* (London), 45 (1919): 130–31.

Marianne Morrow's contribution to this biography is gratefully acknowledged. I.L.R.]

Guildhall Library (London), Reg. of baptisms, marriages, and burials for the parish of Putney (London), 8 Jan. 1746. PAPEI, Acc. 2987; RG 3, House of Assembly, Sessional papers, 1813, "Report of survey of the state of the Court House at Charlotte-town, Dec. 6, 1813"; RG 5, Minutes, 23 June 1808; 15, 16 Jan., 7 April, 4, 10, 29 May, 25 Aug. 1810; 18 Feb. 1811; 7, 14 June, 2 Aug., 6 Dec. 1814; 7 April 1819; 11, 25 March 1823; RG 16, Land registry records, Conveyance reg., liber 15: f.337 [This document is a power of attorney issued 30 April 1807 by London merchant Samuel Yockney authorizing Plaw, who was on the eve of departing for Prince Edward Island, to collect a debt from John Cambridge*. I.L.R.]; RG 20, 1 (Council minutes), 20, 22 Aug., 21 Dec. 1855; 36 (letterbook, 1856–77), Peter MacGowan to John Currie, 28 Oct. 1873. PRO, CO 226/21, Selkirk to Auckland, 4 July 1806; CO 226/26: 5–7 (mfm. at PAPEI); CO 229/3, 18, 20 April 1809 (mfm. at PAPEI). Royal Academy of Arts Library (London), SA/43/1–56 (Soc. of Artists papers, misc.). P.E.I., House of Assembly, *Journal*, 18, 25 Aug. 1812. C. L. Stieglitz, *Plans et dessins tirés de la belle architecture* . . . (Paris, 1801). *Nova Scotia Royal Gazette*, 13, 20 Oct. 1813. *Prince Edward Island Gazette* (Charlottetown), 14 June 1820. *Weekly Recorder of Prince Edward Island* (Charlottetown), 24 Dec. 1810; 16, 25 March 1811. *A dictionary of artists who have exhibited works in the principal London exhibitions from 1760 to 1893*, comp. Algernon Graves (3rd ed., London, 1901; repr. Bath, Eng., 1970). Algernon Graves, *The Royal Academy of Arts* (8v., London, 1905–6; repub. in 4v., East Ardsley, Eng., 1970); *The Society of Artists of Great Britain, 1760–1791; the Free Society of Artists, 1761–1783; a complete dictionary of contributors and their work from the foundation of the societies to 1791* (London, 1907; repr. Bath, 1969). Erik Forssman, "Ein Pantheon am Genfer See: die Villa La Gordanne in Perroy," *Kunst als Bedeutungsträger Gedenkschrift für Günter Bandmann*, ed. Werner Busch *et al.* (Berlin, 1978), 345–66. Emil Kaufmann, *Architecture in the age of reason; baroque and post-baroque in England, Italy,*

Poncin

and France (Cambridge, Mass., 1968). John Woodforde, *Georgian houses for all* (London, 1978). Benjamin Davies, "The old church and old times," *Daily Examiner* (Charlottetown), 6 April 1896: 3. *Island Argus* (Charlottetown), 19 Nov., 10 Dec. 1872. D. R. Kent, "Hyde Hall, Otsego County, New York," *Antiques* (New York), 92 (August 1967): 188.

PONCIN, CLAUDE, Roman Catholic priest and Sulpician; b. 24 Feb. 1725 in Jarcieu, France, son of Jean Poncin, a merchant, and Marie Clameron; d. 10 May 1811 in Montreal, Lower Canada.

Claude Poncin completed the sixth year of the classical program (Rhetoric) with the Jesuits in Vienne, France, in 1744. He then did the two years of Philosophy at Bourg-Saint-Andéol, under the direction of the brilliant teacher Louis-Alexandre Crénier. From 1746 to 1749 Poncin studied theology at the Sulpician seminary in Viviers. There he obtained a solid grounding in ethics with Simon Guichard and in dogma with Jean-Baptiste Ravel. His Latin notes on the courses – more than a thousand pages in a fine, clear hand – attest to the care and application that characterized Poncin. In the course of his studies he passed through the stages leading to priesthood: tonsure, minor orders, sub-diaconate, and diaconate. Following custom, on 3 May 1748, before he was ordained sub-deacon, his father assigned him a life income of 100 *livres* a year to provide for his necessities. On 20 Dec. 1749 the bishop of Uzès, Bonaventure Baüyn, ordained him priest at Bagnols-sur-Cèze. After being admitted as a member to the community of priests of the Séminaire de Saint-Sulpice in Paris, Poncin left for Brest and Canada on 3 April 1750; he reached Montreal on 23 August.

Poncin was first assigned to teach Latin at the school maintained by the Séminaire de Saint-Sulpice in Montreal; his students included Pierre DENAUT, later bishop of Quebec. In addition Poncin was occupied with ministry in the parish of Notre-Dame, taking care of the sacristy and teaching the catechism to the children from the town and the surrounding countryside. In 1755 he became assistant to Jean-François Pélissier de Féligonde, chaplain at the Hôpital Général in Montreal, which was run by Mme d'Youville [Dufrost*]. He succeeded Pélissier as chaplain in 1777 and held this office for 34 years.

Poncin did not, however, limit himself to the encouragement of spiritual life. He was gifted with remarkable manual skill and, after studying various techniques of the period, he began to instruct the nuns of the Hôpital Général. He taught them how to make chains and chaplets, candles for everyday and church use, and also copper tubing and springs for producing altar candlesticks; in the period 1792–97 lampmaking brought the nuns a profit of 3,547 *livres*. In addition he

introduced the nuns to the art of printing; he even had printing equipment imported and consequently was able to reproduce and distribute music or repair the plain-song books. Poncin was also a lover of good music. He had brought from Bourg-Saint-Andéol a mass that he made popular in Montreal, and he learned to play the organ. An inventory of his library around 1800 reveals his chief interests. In addition to books on spirituality, preaching, and the catechism and works of literature, there were sixteen volumes on music, four on technical subjects, and one on algebra and geometry.

In 1799 the nuns and hospital residents celebrated the 50th anniversary of Poncin's ordination: poems and plays written for the occasion extolled the chaplain's qualities. The following year Poncin, who was then 75, suffered a paralytic stroke that afflicted him with deafness, making it more difficult for him to hear confessions. The seminary therefore gave him an assistant, Jean-Baptiste-Jacques CHICOISNEAU, in 1806 but Poncin was mortified. Later, blaming himself for never having preached to the parish or to the nuns, he began preparing sermons which he preached at the Hôpital Général.

In 1786 Poncin had become the first assistant to the Sulpician superior Étienne Montgolfier*, and he retained this office under Gabriel-Jean Brassier* and Jean-Henri-Auguste Roux*. In 1794 the arrival of 11 French Sulpicians who had been driven out by the revolution ensured the continuance of the Sulpicians' work in Canada. This was of the greatest comfort to Poncin in the tranquillity of his declining years.

Although he was ill, Poncin continued to edify his colleagues by his courageous acceptance of suffering; he died on 10 May 1811, at the age of 86. He was buried under the chancel in the church of Notre-Dame in Montreal two days later. In 1784 Montgolfier, who did not usually express very gentle opinions about his colleagues, had written of Poncin: "Although he does not possess any great talents, he is infinitely useful to us through his services to the house and his steadiness." Poncin's 61 years in Canada are summed up in these words. Frequently in a community the humble tasks are those that render the greatest service to the group. From this perspective all the good Poncin did can readily be appreciated.

J.-BRUNO HAREL

ANQ-M, CE1-51, 12 mai 1811. Arch. municipales, Jarcieu, France, État civil, Jarcieu, 24 févr. 1725. Arch. des sœurs grises (Montréal), Dossier Claude Poncin. ASSM, 14, Dossier 9; 15; 24, Dossiers 2, 6. Louis Bertrand, *Bibliothèque sulpicienne, ou histoire littéraire de la Compagnie de Saint-Sulpice* (3v., Paris, 1900), 2: 579–80. [É.-M. Faillon], *Vie de Mme d'Youville, fondatrice des Sœurs de la charité de Villemarie dans l'île de Montréal, en Canada*

(Villemarie [Montréal], 1852). [Albina Fauteux et Clémentine Drouin], *L'Hôpital Général des Sœurs de la charité (Sœurs grises) depuis sa fondation jusqu'à nos jours* (3v. parus, Montréal, 1916–), 1: 574–87.

POND, PETER, army officer, fur trader, explorer, map maker, and writer; b. 18 Jan. 1739/40 in Milford, Conn., eldest son of Peter Pond and Mary Hubbard; m. Susanna Newell, probably in 1762, and they had at least two children; d. 1807 in Milford.

This remarkable, eccentric, and violent man was born, according to his own account, into a family well known for five generations as "all waryers [warriors] Ither by Sea or Land." Despite objections from his parents, in April 1756 he enlisted as a private in the seventh company of the 1st Connecticut Regiment under Captain David Baldwin. In June the company sailed from Milford to New York harbour and then up the Hudson River to the Half Moon (north of Albany), where the regiment gathered for a descent on the French at Fort Carillon (near Ticonderoga, N.Y.). Winter intervened, the regiment was dispersed, and Pond returned to his parents. In 1758 an army was required for James Abercromby*'s assault on Carillon; Pond rejoined the Connecticut troops and took part in the operation. On 17 April 1759 he again enlisted, this time as a sergeant, giving his occupation as shoemaker. He joined the Suffolk County Regiment at Long Island, N.Y., for an army raised "to go a ganst Niagaray [Fort Niagara, near Youngstown, N.Y.]" under John Prideaux. At Oswego, Colonel John Johnstone of the New York Regiment singled out Pond to be with him in the journey to the Niagara region. After serving until exhaustion as orderly sergeant to Prideaux, Pond was with Sir William Johnson*, who commanded the army after Prideaux's death, at the capture of the fort. "I Got But One Slite wound Dureing the Seage," he recalled.

From Niagara, Pond returned with his regiment to Oswego and helped build a camp there in preparation for an assault on Montreal. After passing the winter of 1759–60 at Milford, where a number of French prisoners were billeted, in 1760 he received an officer's commission and for the fourth time entered the army. He went first to Albany, and then to Oswego to join Amherst*'s forces which were assembled for the taking of Montreal, the sole remaining French stronghold. He was present at the town's surrender on 8 Sept. 1760.

After the conquest Pond "thought thare was no bisnes left for me" in Canada. In 1761 he therefore turned his attention to seafaring, with the intention of making it a profession. He sailed to the West Indies, presumably from a New England port. On his return to Milford he found his father had gone to Detroit

(Mich.) on a trading voyage and his mother had died of a fever. Pond gave up seafaring, took charge of the numerous young family, and stayed in Milford for three years. It was, he later wrote, the longest time between the ages of 16 and 60 that he stayed in one place.

Having decided to enter the fur trade in the Detroit region, Pond left Milford, likely in 1765, and for six years carried on business in the west. In this period, having been abused and threatened by another trader, he killed his opponent in a duel, returned from Detroit, and proclaimed the event to authorities but was not prosecuted. Documents show that in 1771 he was in partnership with Felix Graham, a merchant trading from New York to Michilimackinac (Mackinaw City, Mich.). He made another voyage to the West Indies, apparently in 1772. On his return he accepted an invitation to renew his partnership with Graham. In 1773 Graham took a large cargo from New York to Michilimackinac by way of the Great Lakes. Pond, who "wanted Sum Small artikels in the Indan way to Cumpleat my asortment," went up to Montreal. He arranged with Isaac TODD and James McGILL to have these items shipped in their canoes and set out with them by the Ottawa River route for Michilimackinac. At that post he bought canoes and supplies, engaged men, and loaded bales. Altogether he had 12 canoes, "my small fleat," and 4,600 pounds of goods valued at more than £1,200. In September 1773 he crossed Lake Michigan to Green Bay. He visited the Menominees on the north side of the bay, the Winnebagos on "Peuans Lake" (Lake Winnebago, Wis.), and may have traded with the Foxes. He ascended the Fox River to a place where that tribe interred its dead and then portaged to the Wisconsin River, "a Gentel Glideing Stream" and part of the Mississippi drainage system. Near the end of September he arrived at the Sauk village on the north side of the Wisconsin. In his narrative he recorded cultural traits of that tribe: "Thay are . . . Les Inclined to tricks and Bad mannars then thare Nighbers . . . Sum of thare Huts are Sixtey feet Long and Contanes Saverl fammalyes . . . the women Rase Grat Crop of Corn Been Pumkens – Potatoes Millans . . . Thay are Not Verey Gellas of thare women." He then descended the river some 50 miles to a village of Foxes, "a Differant Sort of People Who was Bread at Detroit under the french Government and Clarge; till thay By Chrisanissing Grew so Bad thay [the French] ware Oblige to Go to war a Ganst them," and who now lived in "Sad Sarkamstanis." They had recently been infected by an epidemic, and Pond remained only one day, managing to do a little trading before continuing downstream to the Mississippi. There, at Prairie du Chien, he found many French traders, and Indians purchasing supplies for the winter hunt. He stayed ten days, while he dispatched nine

Pond

clerks to various tributaries of the Wisconsin and Mississippi for trade. In October 1773 he left for the St Peters River (Minnesota River, Minn.) with two other traders. On the river about 14 miles from its mouth, he found a log house which he supposed to be that of Jonathan Carver, where the explorer had wintered in 1766–67. Pond later wrote that he thought little of Carver and could have completed his whole tour in six weeks.

Pond passed the winter of 1773–74 on the high banks of the St Peters River and conducted business with the Indians in gentle competition with a French trader. When the ice broke and the water level receded, Pond's party descended the river to Prairie du Chien. He collected pelts from various tribes gathered there, against keen trade from New Orleans, the Illinois, and Michilimackinac. "All my Outfits had Dun well," he wrote, "I had a grate Share for my Part a[s] I furnish Much the Largest Cargo on the River." This statement suggests that Pond was relying heavily on bulk imports and that he had a good source of supply.

In July 1774 he was back at Michilimackinac where he found his partner Graham with a large cargo. Pond had done so well that he proposed to buy Graham out. He paid him for the 1773 cargo "and well on toward the One he had Brot me." Pond's first venture had ended. He had learned the trade, mastered the art of getting along with fellow traders and at the same time out-trading them when necessary, become familiar with wilderness travel and survival, and emerged a successful capitalist. He entered into partnership with another merchant, Thomas Williams, an arrangement that would last until 1777.

Trade from Michilimackinac to the Mississippi was severely threatened when war between the Ojibwas and Sioux broke out again. A Lake Superior trader brought news of the fighting to the fort about the first of August 1774. The commandant, Arent Schuyler DePeyster*, gathered Pond and the other traders together, had six large wampum belts made (three for each nation), and sent Pond to the Sioux and other agents to the Ojibwas. Chiefs of the opposing sides were to assemble at Michilimackinac in the spring of 1775 for a council. Pond went to Prairie du Chien and found the Sioux there not involved in the fighting. He took the occasion to go up the St Peters River to trade with a band of Yankton Sioux who had never met whites and of whose customs he left an important ethnological account. After wintering at his post on the St Peters, he assembled 11 Sioux chiefs and explained the wampum belts; he then headed for Michilimackinac with them. The group was joined at Prairie du Chien by Indians of various tribes who were waiting there. At Michilimackinac, DePeyster chaired a grand council which was followed by a decade of

peace between the warring parties [see Joseph-Louis AINSSE].

After this venture Pond never returned to the upper Mississippi, deciding instead to pursue trade in the northwest via Grand Portage (near Grand Portage, Minn.). He was at the time a partner in the firm of Pond and Graves, which seems to have been a subsidiary of Pond and Williams. Traders from Montreal and from the Hudson's Bay Company had recently begun moving into the Saskatchewan valley seeking better quality pelts. Doubtless knowing of these prospects, Pond joined Alexander Henry* on 18 Aug. 1775 near the Cree village at the mouth of the Winnipeg River. Three weeks later they were overtaken by JOSEPH and Thomas Frobisher and Charles Paterson; the whole party, consisting of 30 canoes and 130 men, reached the mouth of the Saskatchewan on 1 October. They ascended the river to the HBC's Cumberland House (Sask.), where they were greeted with civility but as unwanted guests by Matthew Cocking*. The canoes separated, and Pond went south through Little Lake Winnipeg (Lake Winnipegosis, Man.) and travelled up Mossy River to winter at his Fort Dauphin, which he locates on the northwest corner of Dauphin Lake itself. Unless an agreement to cooperate had been undertaken, Pond would have been in opposition to John Cole* at Peter PANGMAN's Fort Dauphin. (Pond was not trading with the "common concern" of Henry, Pangman, Paterson, Jean-Baptiste CADOT, and James Finlay.) At Dauphin Lake there was plenty of buffalo meat available, and he was in a position to intercept Indians bound for Cumberland House.

In 1776 Pond went to Michilimackinac and arranged to have the next season's goods brought to Grand Portage. He had realized the necessity of keeping his supply base as far forward as possible. In so doing he assisted the process whereby Grand Portage, and later Fort William (Thunder Bay, Ont.), supplanted Michilimackinac as the western supply depot of the northwest fur trade. He evidently wintered for the next two years, 1776–77 and 1777–78, at the junction of the Sturgeon River (Sask.) and the North Saskatchewan, a short distance downriver from the place where HBC employee Robert LONGMOOR would soon challenge the pedlars' hold on trade. Apparently on 17 April 1777, Pond had entered partnership with trader George McBEATH, who was also associated with Simon McTavish. It was McBeath who looked after the Montreal to Grand Portage section of the enterprise with Pond.

The success of Thomas Frobisher in 1777 at Lac Île-à-la-Crosse, on the edge of the Athabasca watershed, led others to push forward in that direction. In the spring of 1778 several traders, chiefly representing the two houses of Benjamin and Joseph Frobisher and

McTavish and Company, put into common stock their spare goods at Pine Island Lake (Cumberland Lake, Sask.). They gave management of the enterprise to Pond, who had four canoes for the expedition. He was instructed to enter the English River (the upper Churchill), follow Thomas Frobisher's route, and if possible go into the Athabasca region, a country little known to the pedlars except by Indian report. This joint concern, says Harold Adams Innis*, "was probably the direct forerunner of the North West Company."

Pond wintered on the Athabasca River, about 40 miles from the lake, in 1778–79. There he saw a "vast concourse" of Crees and Chipewyans, who went down each year to Prince of Wales's Fort (Churchill, Man.) via lengthy, difficult routes. According to Alexander MACKENZIE, who was in the Athabasca country himself a decade after, these tribes were pleased to see traders who would "relieve them from such long, toilsome, and dangerous journies; and were immediately reconciled to give an advanced price for the articles necessary to their comfort and convenience." Pond was thus able to obtain more furs than his canoes could carry. Accordingly he stockpiled the remainder in winter huts.

In the spring of 1779 Pond came heavily laden out of Athabasca at the completion of what was in effect a trading expedition of two summers' duration. On 2 July he arrived at Cumberland House "with three Canoes from the Northward very much distressed for want of food having bad Success on his Journey down his Canoes being broke upon the fall's." From the master, William Walker*, who treated him civilly for previous kindnesses, he acquired tobacco, powder, and meat. Pond told Walker that he had gone far enough north to trade with "the Northward Indians" among whom Samuel Hearne* had been with Matonabbee*. During trading, he said, he had made 140 packs of 90 pounds each but had been obliged to leave most of them behind. Since one pack contained about 60 pelts, the whole would have constituted some 8,400 made beaver. Historian Edwin Ernest Rich states that in 1779 Pond brought out more than 80,000 fine beaver skins. This would have been about 60 tons of furs – an extraordinary load for three canoes, given that the average *canot du nord* had a carrying capacity of a ton and a half. Pond told Walker freely of his discoveries and informed him of Portage La Loche. About 12 miles in length and so steep that it had taken the party eight days to complete it, this portage ran between Lac La Loche, in the Hudson Bay watershed, and the Pelican (Clearwater) River, in the Athabasca drainage.

Pond continued east to Grand Portage, and returned to Athabasca directly to bring out the furs he had left behind. The licence issued to him in Montreal in 1780 for four canoes to be sent up to Grand Portage must therefore have been given in his absence. He spent the winter of 1780–81 at Michilimackinac, arriving on 26 November with seven *engagés* in a bateau from Lake Superior and remaining at least until 10 May. He entered a partnership with McBeath and Booty Graves and returned west to winter in 1781–82 with Jean-Étienne Waddens* at Lac la Ronge (Sask.). The two men represented different and yet interrelated trading interests. Pond's was the larger and was built around the more sizeable Montreal houses, such as those of the Frobishers and Simon McTavish; Waddens was acting for an association of smaller houses, such as those of Forrest Oakes* and John Ross. The two groups were in some way affiliated, and in 1779 it had been intended that Waddens should replace Pond in trading with the Indians of Athabasca. However, rivalry between the two sets of interests was not resolved, and in a compromise arrangement the men were to trade side by side at Lac la Ronge in 1781–82. They were reported to be of distinctly different character, and ill will developed between them doubtless also because of economic competition. In February they fought, but details are not known. At the beginning of March Waddens was shot and mortally wounded, perhaps by Pond or his clerk. Waddens's widow pressed charges but historians disagree as to whether or not Pond stood trial. Relying, no doubt, on a remark by Alexander Mackenzie, Innis claims that "it may be assumed" Pond was tried and acquitted in Montreal during the winter of 1784–85. The only documentation located, however, is a deposition by Waddens's clerk, and Arthur Silver Morton* maintains that the absence of any record of a trial indicates Pond was merely examined; he suggests that the case was not taken to court because the murder had occurred in a region beyond the jurisdiction of Quebec's legal system.

Pond wintered on Lac Île-à-la-Crosse in 1782–83 and then proceeded to Athabasca, probably in the spring. The years between 1776 and 1783 had seen a growing tendency of fur-trade interests to coalesce and a series of agreements, usually annual, eventually produced the first declared North West Company, formed in 1783–84 and intended to last for five years. Pond seems to have had one of the 16 shares in the 1779 company, and in his absence he was allotted one share in the 1783–84 organization.

Pond probably explored waters downriver of Lake Athabasca, but how far is not known. He learned from Indians the approximate location of Great Slave and Great Bear lakes and perhaps of the Peace and Mackenzie rivers. Especially in 1783–84 he came into contact with many Indians from the country north of Lake Athabasca, and he secured for the Nor'Westers a trade that the HBC was unable to divert. In 1784 Pond

Pond

came out to Grand Portage and to Montreal, where in February 1785 he became a charter member of the Beaver Club.

During the winter of 1784–85 Pond drew his celebrated map, showing the rivers and lakes from the Great Lakes and Hudson Bay westward to the Rocky Mountains and northward to the Arctic. It indicates a large river flowing from Lake Athabasca to Slave (Great Slave) Lake and thence to the Arctic Ocean, called by Pond "Supposed, the Ice Sea." One copy of the map was prepared for submission to the United States Congress. In April 1785 another was given to the lieutenant governor of Quebec, Henry Hamilton*, as was a memorial signed by Pond and probably written by the Frobishers which asked Hamilton to support a scheme for discoveries of the northwestern reaches of North America under Pond's leadership. Anxious to assist Pond and prevent him from aiding the United States or another country, Hamilton urged the British government, but unsuccessfully, to help him and the Nor'Westers.

Feeling that he deserved more than the one share he had been assigned by the NWC agreement of 1783–84, Pond had at first refused it and considered joining with John Ross and Peter Pangman instead. Ultimately, however, he accepted the share, and in 1785 he returned to Athabasca via Grand Portage. John Ross also went there, to compete with him. In the summers of 1786 and 1787 Pond made excursions from his post, extending trade towards the Peace River and organizing his base and provisions. In the winter of 1786–87 competition became severe, and Ross was "shot in a scuffle with Mr. Pond's men," according to one report. The news of Ross's death resulted in a decision by the leaders of the rival interests to unite and bring an end to the murderous competition. Two of Pond's men were arrested and brought to Quebec for trial, but they were acquitted. Evidence suggests the killer was one Péché (Peshe), who afterwards traded from Slave River among the Chipewyans. HBC surveyor Peter Fidler* wrote in his journal of 1791 that "Mr. Ross was shot by one Peshe, a Canadian, by order of Pond."

In the spring of 1788 Pond left the northwest never to return. From the time of the murder of Waddens in 1782 he had been a marked man, and his time in the west limited. This situation was re-emphasized with Ross's murder five years later, despite Pond's apparent remoteness from the episode. The second death led to his withdrawal or forced retirement from the fur trade. Alexander Mackenzie profited from Pond's pioneering enterprises and geographical ideas, building a career and reputation on business activities suggested by Pond's theories and activities.

Pond continued to produce maps of the northwest. One, dated 6 Dec. 1787, he presented to Lord Dorchester [Guy CARLETON] at Quebec. Dorchester

sent it to London in November 1790, but a simplified copy had already been published in the *Gentleman's Magazine* of March 1790. Pond made yet another version, intended for the empress of Russia. These maps show that he had become aware of Captain James Cook*'s discoveries. What is now called Cook Inlet, Alaska, was thought by the captain to be a river flowing from the east, and Pond's 1787 maps strongly suggest that it drains from a gigantic Great Slave Lake. In 1789 Alexander Mackenzie explored the river leading out of that lake and found it flowed to the Arctic, as Pond's first maps had indicated. Pond's willingness to change on the basis of Cook's unsubstantiated discovery dramatically hurt his credibility as a map maker, but he was not alone in making the error.

Pond was not included in the 1790 reorganization of the NWC, having sold his share that year to William McGillivray* for £800. Dorchester had knowledge that Pond quit the province of Quebec owing to his dissatisfaction with the NWC. His intention, Dorchester said, was to seek employment in his native United States. That same year Pond visited President Ezra Stiles of Yale College, who made a copy of his map. In November 1791 he was offered an unspecified share in a projected "Company for the N.W." in opposition to the NWC by John Howard, Jacob Jordan*, and Samuel Birnie, to be supported by Jordan's backers, Brickwood, Pattle and Company of London. Pond's response to this proposal is not known. On 9 Jan. 1792 "Captain" Peter Pond and William Steedman were instructed by the American secretary of War to go to Niagara and Detroit to seek from warring Indians a request for peace [*see* MICHIKINAKOUA]. Whether Pond went has not been discovered. The latter years of his life were spent in the United States, most probably at Milford, and he passed the time reading the travels of the Baron de Lahontan [Louis-Armand de Lom* d'Arce] and Jonathan Carver. He died impoverished in 1807. Peter Pond National Historic Site, at the junction of the Sturgeon River and the North Saskatchewan, and Peter Pond Lake (Sask.) have been named after him.

Pond's contemporaries generally regarded him with a mixture of admiration and suspicion: admiration for his energetic activities; suspicion for his association with murders and for his American background. East India Company hydrographer Alexander Dalrymple doubted his loyalty to the crown. Alexander Henry, who used Pond's discoveries for his own benefit and without acknowledgement, called him a "trader of celebrity." Dr John Mervin Nooth*, who met him in Quebec, thought him "a very singular person." Judge Isaac Ogden* favoured him as "a Gentleman of Observation and Science." Trader Roderick McKenzie* said Pond "thought himself a philosopher, and was odd in his manners." Alexander Mackenzie obviously was jealous of Pond's pre-eminence and of his discoveries, actual and suggested. Explorer David Thompson* wrote of Pond: "He was a person of industrious habits, a good common education, but of a violent temper and unprincipled character." This unfavourable attitude forms a common thread in the works of later writers, including Charles Lindsey* and E. E. Rich. Even Innis, his biographer, calls his achievements "in many ways remarkable but . . . not of a sensational character."

Pond was an unusual man, more energetic, more aggressive, and more capable of organizing than most traders. Lured by profits from northern furs, he pushed farther north and west than any other trader in the 1770s and 1780s. He was the first white man to cross Portage La Loche (also known as Methye Portage) to the Athabasca River and Lake Athabasca. The discovery linked the Mackenzie watershed with the rivers flowing to Hudson Bay. In this achievement Pond succeeded where others, especially Thomas Frobisher, had failed. The first white trader to push into the Athabasca country, he induced rivals in competition to his lucrative commerce, and his activities led to the first organization named the North West Company. They also opened what Mackenzie called the "new eldorado" of the NWC, around which the company's prospects for the 1790s and afterwards revolved. Pond's use of supplies, including pemmican, and his good organization were keys to his success: they enabled him to travel farther and to trade better than his predecessors. They also set the pattern for NWC exploitation of the Athabasca country. His reputation for violence, however, invited the suspicion of other traders both inside and outside the concern and eventually forced his withdrawal from the company.

Pond was the first to outline the general features of the Mackenzie River system. His findings fired Mackenzie with the possibilities of discovery in the north and led him to follow the course of the great river to its frozen mouth in 1789. Pond's maps and suggested course of the waters of Athabasca are enduring testaments to him as a pioneer in the last great fur-bearing area of North America.

BARRY M. GOUGH

[Pond's narrative was probably written some time after he reached the age of 60. Many years later Sophia M. Mooney, the wife of Nathan Gillette Pond, discovered it in the home of former Connecticut governor Charles Hobby Pond. The account stops in 1775, and she reported that some pages had been torn off at the end. Whether or not much is missing is debatable. The manuscript is now in Yale Univ. Library, Beinecke Rare Book and MS Library (New Haven, Conn.); two photocopies are in the manuscript collection of the UTL-TF. A transcription by Mrs Pond, first published in the *Conn. Magazine* (New Haven), 10 (1906): 239–59, sub-

sequently reappeared in Wis., State Hist. Soc., *Coll.*, 18 (1908): 314–54, and in the first edition of *Five fur traders of the northwest . . .* , ed. Charles Marvin Gates ([Minneapolis, Minn.], 1933). A small part of the journal was published in the *Journal of American Hist.* (New Haven), 1 (1907): 357–65. To date the best text available is the new transcription prepared from the original manuscript at Yale by June D. Holmquist *et al.* for the second edition of *Five fur traders of the northwest* (St Paul, Minn., 1965).

Copies of Pond's maps are in BL, Add MSS 15332: c, d, e; PRO, CO 700, America North and South no.49; Ministère de la Défense (Marine), Service hist. de la Marine (Vincennes, France), Recueil 67, pièce no.30 (anciennement 208 (4044^b)); and PAC, MG 55/23, no.47. B.M.G.]

Buffalo and Erie County Hist. Soc. (Buffalo, N.Y.), C64-4 (Porteous papers), John Askin accounts, 1775. DPL, Burton Hist. Coll., Thomas Williams papers, Felix Graham and Peter Pond accounts, 1773–75. PAC, MG 11, [CO 42] Q, 24-2; 36-1: 280–310; MG 19, C1, 32A; MG 23, GIII, 8, 7 Jan. 1792; RG 4, B28, 115, 1780: 1; 1783: 1. PRO, CO 42/47: 649–51. UTL-TF, MS coll. 30. Yale Univ. Library, Beinecke Rare Book and MS Library (New Haven), Ezra Stiles papers, itinerary, 6: 406–7.

[Joseph Banks], "Peter Pond and the overland route to Cook's Inlet," ed. R. H. Dillon, *Pacific Northwest Quarterly* (Seattle, Wash.), 42 (1951): 324–29. *Les bourgeois de la Compagnie du Nord-Ouest* (Masson). *Cumberland House journals and inland journal, 1775–82*, ed. E. E. Rich and A. M. Johnson (2v., London, 1951–52). Henry, *Travels and adventures* (Bain). *Journals of Hearne and Turnor* (Tyrrell). *The journals of Jonathan Carver and related documents, 1766–1770*, ed. John Parker ([St Paul], 1976). Mackenzie, *Journals and letters* (Lamb). "North-western explorations," PAC *Report*, 1889: 29–38; 1890: 48–66. [Ezra Stiles], *The literary diary of Ezra Stiles, D.D., LL.D, president of Yale College*, ed. F. B. Dexter (3v., New York, 1901), 3: 383, 385–86, 388, 402. [David Thompson], *David Thompson's narrative of his explorations in western America*, ed. J. B. Tyrrell (Toronto, 1916; repr. New York, 1968). *DAB*.

D. A. Armour and K. R. Widder, *At the crossroads: Michilimackinac during the American revolution* (Mackinac Island, Mich., 1978). L. J. Burpee, *The search for the western sea: the story of the exploration of north-western America* (new ed., 2v., Toronto, 1935), 2: 325–53. Roy Daniells, *Alexander Mackenzie and the north west* (London, 1969). Davidson, *NWC*. H. T. Fry, *Alexander Dalrymple (1738–1808) and the expansion of British trade* (Buffalo and Toronto, 1970). B. M. Gough, *Distant dominion: Britain and the northwest coast of North America, 1597–1809* (Vancouver, 1980). Innis, *Fur trade in Canada* (1930); *Peter Pond, fur trader and adventurer* (Toronto, 1930). E. E. Rich, *Montreal and the fur trade* (Montreal, 1966). H. R. Wagner, *Peter Pond, fur trader and explorer* ([New Haven], 1955). W. S. Wallace, *The pedlars from Quebec and other papers on the Nor'Westers* (Toronto, 1954), 19–26. Glyndwr Williams, *The British search for the northwest passage in the eighteenth century* (London and Toronto, 1962).

Douglas Brymner, "Report on Canadian archives," PAC *Report*, 1889: xxxvi–xxxvii. *CHR*, 13 (1932): 205–7. H. A. Innis, "The North West Company," *CHR*, 8 (1927): 308–21; "Peter Pond and the influence of Capt. James Cook on exploration in the interior of North America," RSC *Trans.*,

Pontleroy

3rd ser., 22 (1928), sect.II: 131–41; "Peter Pond in 1780," *CHR*, 9 (1928): 333; "Some further material on Peter Pond," *CHR*, 16 (1935): 61–64. G. M. Lewis, "Changing national perspectives and the mapping of the Great Lakes between 1755 and 1795," *Cartographica* ([Toronto]), 17 (1980), no.3: 1–31. [R. W.] McLachlan, "Connecticut adventurer was a founder of famous fur trust in 1783," *Conn. Magazine* (New Haven), 10 (1906): 236–37. Mrs N. G. Pond [S. M. Mooney], "Journal of 'Sir' Peter Pond . . . : introductory," *Conn. Magazine* (New Haven), 10 (1906): 235–36. G. A. Young, "The organization of the transfer of furs at Fort William: a study in historical geography," Thunder Bay Hist. Museum Soc., *Papers and Records* (Thunder Bay, Ont.), 2 (1974): 29–36.

PONTLEROY, NICOLAS SARREBOURCE DE.
See SARREBOURCE

PORTLOCK, NATHANIEL, ship's captain, maritime fur trader, and author; b. *c.* 1748; d. 12 Sept. 1817 in Greenwich (London), England.

Nathaniel Portlock entered the Royal Navy in 1772 as an able seaman in the *St Albans*, commanded by Charles Douglas*. His rapid promotion to midshipman suggests previous experience in a merchant vessel. On 30 March 1776 he was entered as master's mate on board the *Discovery*, in which he participated in the third Pacific voyage of James Cook*; he was transferred to the *Resolution*, also on the expedition, in August 1779. Returning to England before the expedition as a messenger, he passed his lieutenant's examination on 7 Sept. 1780, at which date he was officially stated to be "more than 32." He then served in the Channel fleet on the *Firebrand*.

In May 1785, Richard Cadman Etches and other merchants entered into a partnership, usually known as the King George's Sound Company, in order to prosecute the maritime fur trade between the northwest coast and China. The owners appointed Portlock commander of the *King George* and of the expedition; George Dixon* was to command her consort the *Queen Charlotte*. As Portlock wrote, "Both of us having accompanied Captain Cook in his last voyage into the Pacific Ocean, were deemed most proper for an adventure which required no common knowledge and experience." Having sailed westwards around Cape Horn, the expedition made its first North American landfall in Cook Inlet (Alaska) on 19 July 1786, and came upon Russian traders there. Portlock soon noted a disparity in British and Russian methods of collecting furs: whereas he expected to barter for pelts and food with the local Indians, the Russians had brought native hunters with them and treated the locals harshly. The contrast was evident to the Indians as well, and at one point a native middle man requested armed assistance for his people against the Russians, but he was denied this aid.

Portlock had arrived late in the trading season, and his fur harvest was consequently poor. The two ships coasted southwards, but bad weather prevented their attempt, from 23 to 28 September, to enter Nootka Sound (B.C.), where the two captains had agreed to winter, and so the expedition refitted at the Sandwich (Hawaiian) Islands. The following spring the ships returned to the northwest coast, arriving at Montague Island (Alaska) on 24 April 1787. Some two weeks later Dixon was led by Indians to the *Nootka*, commanded by John MEARES, who with his crew had passed a desperate winter in Prince William Sound (Alaska). Portlock provided assistance to make the ship seaworthy, and it was able to sail on 18 June. Meanwhile, having learned that Meares expected one of his company's ships to arrive at Nootka Sound from China that month, Dixon in the *Queen Charlotte* had proceeded southwards to forestall it.

That winter Portlock and Dixon sailed separately to Macao (near Canton, People's Republic of China), where their combined cargo of 2,552 skins realized 54,857 dollars. Proceeding then to England, they reached Margate roads in August 1788, bringing home a consignment of tea for the East India Company. Portlock's account of the expedition, published in 1789, presents lists of the flora and fauna he observed, often with descriptions and illustrations, as well as ethnographic notes and a geographical record of the entire voyage.

Returning to service in the navy, Portlock was appointed to command the brig *Assistant*, in which he accompanied Captain William Bligh in 1791 on his second attempt to transport bread-fruit plants from Tahiti to the West Indies. The voyage was successful, and the Jamaican House of Assembly awarded 1,000 guineas to Bligh and 500 to Portlock. The ships returned to England in August 1793 and on 4 November Portlock was promoted commander. In 1799 he commanded the sloop *Arrow*, which on 9 September captured the Dutch vessel *Draak*. On 28 September he was advanced to captain, but does not appear to have had further employment at sea, perhaps owing to ill health. He died on 12 Sept. 1817 in Greenwich Hospital.

Nathaniel Portlock had done well for himself; rising from inconspicuous beginnings, he had benefited from the experience and training of Cook's third Pacific voyage. His subsequent commands in that ocean were important in demonstrating the growth of British commercial and imperial interests there. His second son, Joseph Ellison, became a major-general in the Royal Engineers and had a distinguished career in geology and natural history.

BARRY M. GOUGH

Nathaniel Portlock was the author of *A voyage round the world, but more particularly to the north-west coast of America* . . . (London, 1789; repr. Amsterdam and New

York, 1968). A portrait of him engraved by Mazel after Robert Dodd forms the frontispiece.

DNB. B. M. Gough, *Distant dominion: Britain and the northwest coast of North America, 1579–1809* (Vancouver, 1980). J. T. Walbran, *British Columbia coast names, 1592–1906* . . . (Ottawa, 1909; repr. Vancouver, 1979), 399–400.

POUGET, JEAN-BAPTISTE-NOËL, Roman Catholic priest; b. 25 Dec. 1745 in Montreal (Que.), son of Paul Pouget and Marie-Joseph Payet; d. 17 May 1818 in Berthier-en-Haut (Berthierville), Lower Canada.

Jean-Baptiste-Noël Pouget studied at the Latin school run by the Sulpicians in Montreal, where one of his classmates was Pierre DENAUT, the future bishop of Quebec. From 1769 Pouget was responsible for teaching the Latin and rhetoric classes, while continuing his studies. On 19 Sept. 1772 Bishop Briand* ordained him priest, along with Joseph-Mathurin Bourg*, in the chapel of the Hôtel-Dieu in Montreal. Pouget then became curate of Notre-Dame at Quebec; he remained there until the middle of 1773, when he was put in charge of Saint-Cuthbert, a parish in the seigneury of Berthier.

This new task was a delicate one for a young cleric. Two years earlier his predecessor, Saint-Cuthbert's first parish priest, had spent some months in prison for debt. Further, the man who had taken care of his parishioners during his incarceration had roused the wrath of the seigneur, James Cuthbert*, because he omitted "the customary prayers for the king." Lastly, the habitants of Saint-Cuthbert were certainly not the most docile in the diocese, as Pouget would soon learn. During the American invasion in 1775 his flock at first chose to remain neutral. But when on 10 October a detachment of 67 militiamen under Charles-Louis TARIEU de Lanaudière and Louis-Joseph Godefroy* de Tonnancour left Trois-Rivières for Montreal, the habitants of Saint-Cuthbert, under the direction of a man named Merlet, laid an ambush for them. They took the two commanders prisoner and only released them at Pouget's request. The parishioners of Saint-Cuthbert, like those of the neighbouring parish of Sainte-Geneviève-de-Berthier (at Berthierville), persisted in refusing to join the militia, and the vicar general of Montreal, Étienne Montgolfier*, recalled the two priests. Pouget was appointed to La Visitation-de-la-Bienheureuse-Vierge-Marie, at Sault-au-Récollet (Montreal North), late in 1775. He served there for somewhat less than two years and in 1777 was given charge of Sainte-Geneviève-de-Berthier.

Two years later the priest of Saint-Cuthbert, who was at odds with the seigneur, Cuthbert, as well as with a group of his parishioners, tried to expand his parish at the expense of Pouget's. But Bishop Briand, who was displeased with the conduct and the "out and out blunders" of Saint-Cuthbert's cleric, pronounced in favour of keeping Sainte-Geneviève-de-Berthier as it was and urged Pouget to remind his colleague in the neighbouring parish of the duties attached to his ecclesiastical state.

In 1780 the habitants of Berthier-en-Haut found a new bone of contention in the matter of a road and a bridge. To avoid giving any offence Pouget refrained from expressing an opinion in public, but on 25 June he privately intimated to Governor HALDIMAND which side he should support in the affair. Pouget was so successful in preserving general harmony that in the summer of 1781 his parishioners decided with one accord to undertake the construction of a new church. Cuthbert even promised to do all in his power to facilitate the purchase of the necessary materials. The new church was begun in 1782 and consecrated in August 1787.

In the same year some habitants of Berthier-en-Haut began to dispute Cuthbert's right to collect seigneurial dues, on the pretext that he had granted them farms which in fact were crown lands. Rightly or wrongly, Cuthbert soon convinced himself that it was Pouget who was inciting the recalcitrant *censitaires* to stand up to him. The situation worsened in the autumn of 1789, when two of Cuthbert's three sons asked Pouget to grant them permission to become Catholics; having obtained authorization from the bishop of Quebec, Jean-François Hubert*, Pouget agreed to receive their renunciation of Protestantism. This time the seigneur of Berthier lost his temper – there were complaints to the bishop of Quebec, threats of legal action (and even death threats) against Pouget, attempts to intimidate his *censitaires*, and open letters in the *Quebec Gazette* denouncing the parish priest's meddling in his seigneurial and family matters. Hubert gave Cuthbert a laconic reply, saying that Pouget's conduct seemed irreproachable to him; at the same time he exhorted Pouget to do nothing that might make matters worse. A good many *censitaires* of the seigneury of Berthier made sworn statements before a notary denouncing their seigneur's intransigence and exonerating their priest. On 2 March 1790 Alexander Cuthbert, the seigneur's son, even signed a note in which he declared that his conversion to Catholicism was in line with the freedom to choose his religion which his father had given him some years earlier. Pouget kept quiet and the quarrel finally petered out.

But Father Pouget was not yet out of range of dispute. In November 1791 Bishop Hubert entrusted him with investigating the many complaints levelled against the parish priest of Saint-Antoine, at Lavaltrie, by the habitants and the seigneur, Pierre-Paul MARGANE de Lavaltrie. The following month Hubert even asked Pouget to visit Lavaltrie occasionally to ensure that the parish priest "did not do too many silly

Powell

things" before he was removed from the parish the following spring.

Peace had only just been restored to Lavaltrie when a new conflict involving Pouget erupted at Berthier-en-Haut. Since 1789 Louis Labadie* had been teaching school there in a house belonging to the *fabrique*. On 10 May 1792, at the churchwardens' request and for reasons that remain unclear, Pouget expelled Labadie from his school. Labadie responded by suing Pouget in the Montreal Court of Common Pleas. This quarrel was brought to public notice in July, when Labadie published an article in the *Quebec Gazette* stigmatizing the supposedly tyrannical conduct of the parish priest of Sainte-Geneviève-de-Berthier. A few weeks later the same paper carried a denunciation of Labadie's ungrateful and haughty attitude by about 50 residents of Berthier-en-Haut and also a testimony to his good conduct by 30 others. It may have been weariness that in the autumn led Pouget to consider for a moment leaving the parish and becoming a member of the community of the Collège Saint-Raphaël. In any event, Labadie does not seem to have won his case before the courts, and on 24 June 1793 he expressed his regrets to the bishop of Quebec "for having said all that he had, even though it was the truth"; at the same time, having been refused the sacraments from the beginning of the lawsuit, he asked Hubert to allow a priest to give him absolution. He continued to run his own school at Berthier-en-Haut for a year, and then in May 1794 left to establish himself in Verchères.

Pouget was undoubtedly expert at settling differences, for in October 1794 Bishop Hubert put him in charge of another investigation into complaints against the new priest of Saint-Antoine, at Lavaltrie. In November 1795 the bishop again thought of him for the task of putting an end to dissension among the Recollets of Montreal; in the end he changed his mind and entrusted the problem to his coadjutor.

Pouget did not, however, distinguish himself solely through the role he played in various disputes. He was gifted with a talent for oratory that was uncommon for the period, and people did not hesitate to call on his services for great occasions. Hubert and Denaut often took him with them on their pastoral visits, and in addition he was asked to take part in the consecration of Bishop Plessis*. But from 1801 Pouget limited himself exclusively to his parish ministry. The task must have been sufficient to take up all his time, because by 1807 Sainte-Geneviève-de-Berthier had become the most densely populated parish on the north shore of the St Lawrence between Quebec and Montreal, with several hundred more communicants than even the parish of Immaculée-Conception in Trois-Rivières. This development probably explains why Pouget was in a position at the end of his life to bequeath 4,000 *livres* apiece to the Hôtel-Dieu of Montreal, the Congregation of Notre-Dame, the Hôpital Général of Montreal, and the Ursulines of Trois-Rivières, as well as 1,000 *livres* to the poor of Berthier-en-Haut.

Historians have often emphasized the small numbers of Catholic clergy in the years following the conquest, as well as the weak position of the ecclesiastical authority in its dealings with the new rulers. Pouget's career as a priest further illustrates the precarious situation of the Catholic Church in this period, showing how much less influence the clergy had on the people than one might think and dispelling some of the mystery surrounding the difficulties that the bishop of Quebec encountered as he endeavoured to maintain discipline among his clergy.

PIERRE DUFOUR

ANQ-Q, P-1694. ASQ, C 35: 180, 193, 211, 214, 216, 230, 234, 239; Polygraphie, XXV: 179; XLVI: 15d, 15e, 15f; Séminaire, 14/7, nos.57, 69. AUM, P 58, U, Pouget à Haldimand, 25 juin 1780; Pouget à Margane de Lavaltrie, 21 févr. 1800; Pouget à O'Sullivan, 17 juill. 1812, 21 mars 1814, 15 déc. 1815. PAC, MG 24, K3. Hugh Gray, *Letters from Canada, written during a residence there in the years 1806, 1807, and 1808* . . . (London, 1809; repr. Toronto, 1971). George Heriot, *Travels through the Canadas, containing a description of the picturesque scenery on some of the rivers and lakes* . . . (London, 1807). *Invasion du Canada* (Verreau). *Quebec Gazette*, 7 Jan., 27 May, 28 Oct. 1790; 12 July, 2 Aug. 1792; 3 June 1806; 25 May 1818. Caron, "Inv. de la corr. de Mgr Briand," ANQ *Rapport*, 1929–30: 47–136; "Inv. de la corr. de Mgr Denaut," 1931–32: 129–242; "Inv. de la corr. de Mgr Hubert et de Mgr Bailly de Messein," 1930–31: 199–351; "Inv. de la corr. de Mgr Panet," 1933–34: 235–421; "Inv. de la corr. de Mgr Plessis," 1932–33: 3–244. Desrosiers, "Corr. de cinq vicaires généraux," ANQ *Rapport*, 1947–48: 73–133. Jean-Paul de Lagrave, *Les origines de la presse au Québec (1760–1791)* (Montréal, 1975). Lanctot, *Le Canada et la Révolution américaine*. S.-A. Moreau, *Précis de l'histoire de la seigneurie, de la paroisse et du comté de Berthier, P.Q. (Canada)* (Berthierville, Qué., 1889). Trudel, *L'Église canadienne*. Ivanhoë Caron, "Joseph-Octave Plessis," *Le Canada français* (Québec), 2e sér., 27 (1939–40): 193–214, 309–20, 826–41; 28 (1940–41): 71–96, 180–95, 274–92, 784–96, 1029–36. A.[-E.] Gosselin, "Louis Labadie ou le maître d'école patriotique, 1765–1824," RSC *Trans.*, 3rd ser., 7 (1913), sect.i: 97–123. S.-A. Moreau, "L'honorable Jacques Cuthbert, fils, seigneur de Berthier," *BRH*, 8 (1902): 60–63; "L'honorable James Cuthbert, père, seigneur de Berthier," 7 (1901): 341–48. P.-G. Roy, "Les évêques consacrés à Québec," *BRH*, 29 (1923): 97–106; "Saint-Cuthbert," 2 (1896): 177.

POWELL, CHARLES STUART, actor, theatre manager, educator, and office holder; b. *c.* 1749 in England, son of S. Powell; m. Mary Ann —, and they had two daughters, Cordelia and Fidelia; d. 27 April 1811 in Halifax, N.S.

Charles Stewart Powell came from a theatrical family. His father was an actor and manager, and Charles and his younger brother Snelling pursued similar careers. Snelling eventually earned a reputation as "the first successful manager of a theatre in Boston." Charles probably gained his early experience in the west of England, Ireland, and Wales, where his brother was born. In 1781 he joined the company at the Theatre Royal, Bath, then in its heyday and "a splendid training ground for the young actor." He first appeared on the London stage at the Theatre Royal, Covent Garden, on 26 April 1788. From that time until 1792 he was a member of the Covent Garden company, and during the summers of those years he performed with the Theatre Royal in the Haymarket.

In the summer of 1792 Powell emigrated to Boston, Mass. His first appearance there was at Concert Hall on 13 August, when he staged a solo performance of John Collins's "Evening Brush for Rubbing off the Sleeve of Care." Later in the year Powell joined Joseph Harper's Old American Company and played at the New Exhibition Room in productions of *Hamlet* and *Richard III*. The opening of this theatre had flouted an enactment of 1750 that prohibited stage performances, and by the end of the year Harper had been arrested and the theatre itself forced to close. However, with public pressure against the 1750 act mounting, in 1793 the authorities agreed not to launch further prosecutions. That same year Powell was named manager of the new Federal Street Theatre in Boston, and he returned to England to recruit a company that included his wife and brother.

The Federal Street Theatre opened on 3 Feb. 1794 to an enthusiastic reception from Bostonians, though later that month the theatre's musicians published a notice in the local newspapers asking the public to refrain from pelting them with apples, stones, and other assorted objects. Unfortunately, the theatre's financial position was precarious and, to make matters worse, Powell was accused of "improper conduct" towards one of the company's actresses, a charge he publicly denied. After the 1795–96 season, which resulted in his bankruptcy, Powell was replaced as manager. Although he announced his intention of returning to England and publishing an attack on his opponents in the Federal Street Theatre, on 26 Dec. 1796 he emerged as manager of the new Haymarket Theatre in Boston, designed to rival the Federal Street. Here, too, he found himself in pecuniary difficulties, and at the close of the first season he again lost his position as manager. Despite this blow, he and his wife remained members of the Haymarket company.

At about this time Powell was seen by Prince EDWARD AUGUSTUS. Knowing of the problems and quarrels that had thwarted Powell's attempts at theatrical management in Boston, Prince Edward invited him to Halifax to assist in "elevating the public and private morals of the community." In 1789 Canada's first regular theatre had been built on Argyle Street in Halifax by the gentlemen amateurs of the town and garrison. Originally named the New Grand Theatre, it was also called the New Theatre and the Halifax Theatre, but by the time of Powell's arrival in 1797 it was known as the Theatre Royal, no doubt in deference to his patron. The amateurs had attempted, with occasional success, to recruit professionals to perform at the theatre, but scattered comments in the local newspapers indicate that standards were low.

Powell arrived in Halifax in the late summer of 1797, together with his wife and daughters, and an actor who had worked with him in Boston, J. S. Baker. On 15 Sept. 1797, under the auspices of Prince Edward and Lieutenant Governor Sir John WENTWORTH, Powell and Baker presented "Collins Evening Brush." An announcement in the *Royal Gazette and the Nova Scotia Advertiser* introduced them to the Halifax public: "From the efforts of Messrs. Powell and Baker, the lover of Thespian amusement may expect a pleasing entertainment. The former of these gentlemen has frequently shared conspicuousness on English boards, and at different times, two of the first theatres in America have been directed by his management." By early 1798 Powell was able to present regular drama as well as the variety evenings of which his "Brush" is typical. An advertisement in the *Royal Gazette* for Richard Cumberland's *The brothers*, performed on 21 March 1798, shows Powell taking his managerial responsibilities seriously: "The later alterations and additions to the Stage, permitting full scope for working the necessary Machinery, it is intended in the opening Scene of the Play, to represent the Novel sight of a Ship in Distress, etc., stranded on the Coast."

Powell was able to sustain the theatre in Halifax until some time in 1802. He gave more than 40 performances, including Shakespeare's *The tempest* and *Richard III*, George Lillo's *The London merchant; or, the history of George Barnwell*, Sheridan's *The duenna*, and Colley Cibber's and Sir John Vanbrugh's *The provok'd husband*. No doubt the departure of Prince Edward from Halifax in the summer of 1800 had an effect on Powell's prospects; there is a drastic reduction in the number and scale of productions after this date, and he apparently gave up the management in the summer of 1802.

Besides the theatre, Powell operated a dancing academy in Halifax, as well as similar schools in Windsor and Cornwallis. On 9 June 1801, at the opening of a new session of the legislature, he was appointed serjeant-at-arms to the House of Assembly, a position he held until his death. In 1802 he established another school "for the purpose of reading

Prescott

the Classics." He proposed "not only to point out the most distinguished beauties of each author, but to explain to the young reader the moral contained in the several respective passages . . . so as to form the judgment and give them a taste for cultivating the minds with polite literature." In 1806–7 Powell returned to Boston for a season, but he was soon back in Halifax. There, in July 1807, he launched the *Telegraph*, a newspaper that failed to survive. Three years later he visited Saint John, N.B., where he performed and operated a dancing academy for more than three months.

Powell's later years were marked by sickness and by poverty, which was not apparently alleviated by an occasional benefit at the theatre. He died on 27 April 1811, at his home on Prince Street in Halifax, and was buried in an unmarked grave in St Paul's cemetery. His wife and daughters returned to England in the hope of finding employment on the stage, but within six months they were destitute. Hearing of their plight, Prince Edward organized a benefit performance which raised £100, and soon afterwards he obtained a passage for them on a ship sailing to Halifax. There Cordelia Powell re-established her father's dancing academy, giving instruction to such pupils as Joseph Howe* and Beamish Murdoch*.

As an actor, Powell seems to have been somewhat limited, but he was liked and respected by the Halifax audiences of the day. A professional colleague in his Bath days, John Bernard, described him as "a thoroughly artistic, though rather hard, actor." Joseph Howe said that Powell was "a man of some talent, but very narrow and eccentric," and another who had seen him act called him "an educated, facetious and gentlemanly man."

ALAN R. ANDREWS

Nova Scotia Royal Gazette, 1 May 1811. *Royal Gazette and the Nova Scotia Advertiser*, 12 Sept. 1797, 20 March 1798. T. A. Brown, *History of the American stage; containing biographical sketches of nearly every member of the profession that has appeared on the American stage, from 1733 to 1870* (New York, [1870]). *DAB* (biog. of Snelling Powell). *The London stage, 1660–1800* . . . , ed. William Van Lennep et al. (5 parts in 11v., Carbondale, Ill., 1960–68), pt.5. W. W. Clapp, *A record of the Boston stage* (Boston and Cambridge, Mass., 1853; repr. New York and London, [1968]). Barnard Hewitt, *Theatre U.S.A., 1665 to 1957* (New York and Toronto, 1959). Arthur Hornblow, *A history of the theatre in America, from its beginnings to the present time* (2v., Philadelphia and London, 1919; repr. [New York, 1965]). Murdoch, *Hist. of N.S.* S. M. Oland, "Materials for a history of the theatre in early Halifax" (MA thesis, Dalhousie Univ., Halifax, 1966). Cecil Price, *The English theatre in Wales in the eighteenth and early nineteenth centuries* (Cardiff, 1948). G. O. Seilhamer, *History of the American theatre* (3v., Philadelphia, 1888–91; repr. New York and London, 1968). M. E. Smith, *Too soon the curtain fell: a history of theatre in Saint John,*

1789–1900 ([Fredericton, 1981]). R. E. Toscan, "The organization and operation of the Federal Street Theatre from 1793 to 1806" (PHD thesis, Univ. of Ill., Urbana-Champaign, 1970). *Acadian Recorder*, 27 Nov. 1824; 15 Aug. 1896; 6, 13 Nov. 1897. Y. S. Baines, "The New Grand Theatre, Halifax, 1789–1814," *N.S. Hist. Quarterly* (Halifax), 10 (1980): 1–21. P. R. Blakeley, "A royal patron of the theatre," *Atlantic Advocate* (Fredericton), 58 (1967–68), no.5: 42. A. R. Jewitt, "Early Halifax theatres," *Dalhousie Rev.*, 5 (1925–26): 444–59. *Morning Sun* (Halifax), 24 May, 2 June 1858. *Novascotian* (Halifax), 14 June 1838: 189; 24 March 1851.

PRESCOTT, ROBERT, army officer and colonial administrator; b. *c.* 1726 in Lancashire, England, son of Richard Prescott, cavalry officer; m. with at least two daughters; d. 21 Dec. 1815 in Rose Green (West Sussex), England.

Robert Prescott began his career in the British army on 22 June 1745, when he was appointed an ensign in the 15th Foot. He was promoted lieutenant three years later and captain on 22 Jan. 1755. After the outbreak of the Seven Years' War, he participated in 1757 in an expedition against Rochefort, France. The following year he took part in the capture of Louisbourg, Île Royale (Cape Breton Island), under Major-General Jeffery Amherst*, who was also colonel of Prescott's regiment. On 5 May 1759 Prescott received the prestigious appointment of aide-de-camp to Amherst. Early in August he was sent to England with the dispatches announcing the fall of Fort Niagara (near Youngstown, N.Y.). In 1760 he accompanied Amherst in the advance to Montreal, and in late August he was again entrusted with dispatches to England, this time announcing the fall of Fort Lévis (east of Prescott, Ont.). On 22 March 1761 he became major in the 95th Foot. His regiment was sent to Martinique in 1762, arriving shortly after the capture of the island in February, and proceeded to Cuba in May. Prescott exchanged into the 27th Foot in July, and on 10 November he was promoted lieutenant-colonel in the 72nd Foot in succession to Guy CARLETON. He spent the decade after the war unattached to a regiment and probably in Britain.

With the outbreak of the American revolution, Prescott was gazetted lieutenant-colonel of the 28th Foot on 8 Sept. 1775. That year he participated in actions around New York City, including the battle of Long Island, engagements in Westchester County, and the storming of Fort Washington (New York) in November. In August 1777 he was promoted brevet colonel; attached to the expedition against Philadelphia, Pa, he fought at the battle of Brandywine on 11 September. He was with the army of occupation in Philadelphia during the winter of 1777–78 and retreated with it, participating in June 1778 in the battle of Monmouth. The following November he was commander of the 1st Brigade in the British expeditionary force that left New York City to attack St Lucia, and from August 1779 to early 1780 he was in command of the British troops in the Leeward Islands. On 13 Oct. 1780 he was promoted colonel of the 94th Foot; he attained the rank of major-general one year later. After the signing of the peace in 1783 and the disbandment of the 94th Foot that year, he probably returned to England and was placed on half pay; on 6 July 1789 he became colonel of the 28th Foot.

This uneventful interlude ended when war broke out between Britain and revolutionary France; in October 1793 he was promoted lieutenant-general and ordered to Barbados to take command. The following February the British attacked Martinique; Prescott, who was attached to the expedition at the request of the army commander, Lieutenant-General Sir Charles Grey, led the 1st Brigade, landing 2,484 men near Sainte-Luce on the 6th. After the capture of the island, he moved on with Grey's force to Guadeloupe, which was also taken, and he was in command there in December 1794 when the British were obliged to fall back on Martinique. He was appointed civil governor of Martinique, and his firm but conciliatory administration gave great satisfaction to the French planters until ill health forced him to return to England in 1795.

This time Prescott's sojourn at home was short-lived. He was appointed lieutenant governor of Lower Canada on 21 Jan. 1796 in succession to Lord Dorchester [Guy Carleton]; a revised commission of 15 December created him governor-in-chief of the Canadas, New Brunswick, and Nova Scotia, as well as commander of the British forces in North America. On his arrival at Quebec in June 1796 he was deeply concerned about the colony's security. To guard against external invasion and internal subversion he had at his disposal only a small garrison of British troops supplemented by an unreliable militia. He found fortifications inadequate or dilapidated and new barracks urgently required in order to avoid the objectionable practice of quartering soldiers on disgruntled inhabitants, but wartime financial constraints hampered his more ambitious schemes of military works and buildings.

Although Anglo-American relations had improved with the conclusion of Jay's Treaty in 1794 and Britain's final evacuation in 1796 of the frontier posts ceded to the United States, rumours of impending French invasions via the Mississippi valley [*see* Wabakinine*] and the St Lawrence River [*see* Sir Howard Douglas*] caused excitement in the colony throughout 1796 and 1797; the province also seemed to be swarming with elusive French spies and American agitators. What gave Prescott most alarm in these circumstances was the apparent disaffection of the Canadians, whom he suspected of desiring a return to French rule: during the elections of 1796 for the House of Assembly the seigneurs, who generally supported the government, were eliminated as a political force; the same year disturbances occurred in various parts of Lower Canada, but especially at Montreal, where the introduction of a new road act occasioned a serious outbreak of violence in October. Leading members of the British élite, including Chief Justice William Osgoode*, Attorney General Jonathan Sewell*, and the deputies John Richardson* and John YOUNG, believed the riots to have been orchestrated by the French minister to the United States, and were convinced that had they succeeded the British population would have been marked out for massacre. Prescott spent an uneasy winter fearing that the prevalence of secret meetings and inflammatory proclamations presaged a seditious conspiracy. But with a few summary arrests and the exemplary execution the following July of an active American intriguer, David McLane*, as well as the receding prospect of a French invasion, the atmosphere of crisis abated.

Prescott's distrust of the Canadians in a time of tension constrained him to exercise a strict surveillance of the Roman Catholic Church. He stopped the immigration of refugee priests from France, which Dorchester had permitted Bishop Hubert* to undertake, lest they foster among the habitants a fond remembrance of the French régime. Prescott feared that an influx of foreign clerics might also heighten dissatisfaction among the colonists by depriving Canadians of opportunities for ecclesiastical preferment. He was particularly mistrustful of the Sulpicians because they insisted on remaining a French community; he therefore opposed in 1798 the election of the Frenchman Jean-Henri-Auguste Roux* as their superior, and the following year he suggested that the government take over the Sulpician estates.

But Prescott was not hostile to the Roman Catholic Church, whose influence with the population he wished to harness in support of government. Thus, in 1797 when Hubert, who wished to retire, proposed Joseph-Octave Plessis* as coadjutor to Pierre DE-NAUT, Hubert's designated successor, Prescott, once assured of Plessis's moral suitability and loyalty, accepted him. He then firmly defended his decision in the face of protests by Prince EDWARD AUGUSTUS, who had wanted the post to go to a personal favourite, Pierre-Simon Renaud, parish priest at Beauport. In return for his acceptance of Plessis, Prescott demanded from Denaut an annual return of vacant posts and of transfers within the clergy. In making this exaction Prescott was more likely concerned to protect himself from an angered prince by demonstrating a desire "to assert the King's Supremacy," than he was to exercise a royal control of ecclesiastical patronage; in fact he subsequently interfered rarely with clerical placements. For reasons of security, in order to avoid

Prescott

provoking the Canadians, he was determined not to trench upon rights hitherto enjoyed by the Roman Catholic Church. This resolve brought him into conflict with the Church of England bishop of Quebec, Jacob Mountain*, whose single-minded purpose was to place his church on a more secure foundation by extending its privileges and reducing the power and independence of its Roman Catholic rival. The querulous Mountain alienated Prescott's sympathies, but in any case the governor would have recognized the necessity, given the unsettled political state of Lower Canada, to regulate (though with the utmost circumspection) the ecclesiastical authority of the Protestant bishop. The most Prescott would do to help the Church of England was protect the lands reserved for the Protestant clergy from encroachment by individuals – if this could be done without disproportionate trouble or expense.

On his arrival in the colony Prescott had found land affairs in utter chaos. In 1792 the government had solicited applications for township grants from groups of associates, but it was dilatory in making the necessary administrative arrangements to process the resulting flood of claims. Although warrants of survey, supposedly to be completed within six months, were liberally issued for 150 townships involving some 7,000,000 acres, no surveying could begin until the government had appointed commissioners to administer oaths of loyalty and had designated lands reserved to the crown and to the Protestant clergy, preliminaries not completed until 1794. As 1,200 or more applications languished without decision in the Land Granting Department, many settlers returned to the United States disgruntled or financially ruined, while others, in optimism or desperation, began cultivating and spending money on lands to which they had not secured legal title. Then in 1794 the long-suffering petitioners learned that the Executive Council had decided to renege on past pledges and throw open to new applicants all lands for which the original claimants had failed to fulfil the stipulated terms. Since only one township had thus far been legally conveyed, this action represented a wholesale forfeiture of claims and created both a shoal of new petitions and a public outcry from the former applicants against official delays and broken promises.

When Prescott assumed the unenviable responsibility for sorting out this confusion, he devised a scheme that distinguished between bona fide settlers and mere speculators by proportioning the size of township grants to the expenses for development incurred by the applicants. Although his plan was acceptable to the majority of claimants, it failed to satisfy the land speculators, who included members of the Executive Council. From the outset of his investigations Prescott had suspected that, with the connivance of Osgoode,

certain councillors – most prominently Hugh FINLAY, chairman of the land committee, and John Young – had been exploiting their official position to acquire large tracts of land for themselves. The council's ill-judged action in 1794, Prescott believed, had been a deliberate plot by rapacious monopolists to grasp townships actually settled and rendered valuable by the labour and expenditure of the original applicants. When the council condemned his proposed settlement of claims in 1798, Prescott reacted sharply. Irritated by trickery and unaccustomed to opposition, which he considered insubordination, he openly accused his councillors of jobbery, land speculation, and malpractices in office. Thereafter, relations between governor and council rapidly deteriorated as the exchange of charges and recriminations became increasingly acrimonious.

The authorities in London soon grew weary, and then alarmed, at this unseemly slanging match. After an appeal for cordiality had obviously fallen on deaf ears, the British government concluded that imperial interests in Lower Canada were being seriously jeopardized at a critical time, and in April 1799 Prescott was recalled to England for consultations. Robert Shore Milnes* was sent out as lieutenant governor to calm the troubled waters, which he did by allowing the councillors to secure the substantial land grants they coveted.

While he was still in Lower Canada Prescott had been promoted general on 1 Jan. 1798. About that time he had met the British officer George Thomas Landmann*, who later recalled that "the general was a little man, not exceeding five feet four or five inches high, very slender and certainly not much under eighty years of age; he was nevertheless active, a good officer, but exceedingly peppery." It was perhaps Prescott's irascibility that ultimately brought about his recall. As governor he had proved to be a man of integrity and independent judgement, willing to make unpalatable decisions when necessary. However, an old soldier, he was also frank to a fault, impatient of opposition, stubborn, and unskilled in the finer points of colonial politics. Back in England, he agonized bitterly over the censure that his recall implied and for a time tried unsuccessfully to obtain an inquiry into his conduct in order to exonerate himself from the malicious misrepresentations of a self-interested cabal. Although he retained the governorship and its emoluments until 1807, he never returned to Lower Canada, and his death at the age of about 89 in December 1815 went virtually unnoticed in the colony.

PETER BURROUGHS

According to an entry in the catalogue of the BL, Robert Prescott may be the author of *Letter from a veteran to the officers of the army encamped at Boston* (n.p., 1774).

PAC, MG 23, D3; GII, 17; MG 24, B3, 3; MG 30, D1, 25: 409–25; RG 7, G14, 1. PRO, CO 5/34–35; CO 42/105–13; CO 43/17–18. QDA, 73 (C-2). [Jeffery Amherst], *The journal of Jeffery Amherst, recording the military career of General Amherst in America from 1758–1763*, ed. J. C. Webster (Toronto and Chicago, [1931]), 109–10, 140, 156, 158, 210, 212, 214–15, 219, 239–40. *Docs. relating to constitutional hist., 1791–1818* (Doughty and McArthur; 1914). *Gentleman's Magazine*, 1761: 238; 1783: 271; 1797: 979; January–June 1816: 88. Knox, *Hist. journal* (Doughty), 1: 459; 3: 46. Landmann, *Adventures and recollections*, 1: 240. *Quebec Gazette*, 26 Jan., 2 Feb., 4 May, 31 Aug. 1797; 4 April, 18, 25, 29 July, 21 Nov. 1799. *Appleton's cyclopædia of American biography*, ed. J. G. Wilson and John Fiske (7v., New York, 1887–1900), 5: 109. *DNB*. G.B., WO, *Army list*, 1754–1816. H. J. Morgan, *Sketches of celebrated Canadians and persons connected with Canada, from the earliest period in the history of the province down to the present time* (Quebec and London, 1862; repr. Montreal, 1865), 129–30. Wallace, *Macmillan dict*. A. L. Burt, *The United States, Great Britain and British North America from the revolution to the establishment of peace after the War of 1812* (Toronto and New Haven, Conn., 1940), 174–77. Caron, *La colonisation de la prov. de Québec*, 2: 77–140. Christie, *Hist. of L.C.*, 1: 173–203; 6: 23–38. S. D. Clark, *Movements of political protest in Canada, 1640–1840* (Toronto, 1959). F. M. Greenwood, "The development of a garrison mentality among the English in Lower Canada, 1793–1811" (PHD thesis, Univ. of B.C., Vancouver, 1970). R. J. Jones, *A history of the 15th (East Yorkshire) Regiment (the Duke of York's Own), 1685 to 1914* ([Beverley, Eng., 1958]), 127. Lambert, "Joseph-Octave Plessis," 262–65, 288–89, 332–33. Norman Macdonald, *Canada, 1763–1841: immigration and settlement; the administration of the imperial land regulations* (Toronto and London, 1939), 80–84. Millman, *Jacob Mountain*, 268–69.

PREVOST, Sir GEORGE, army officer and colonial administrator; b. 19 May 1767 in New Jersey, the eldest son of Augustin Prévost and Nanette (Ann) Grand; m. 19 May 1789 Catherine Anne Phipps, and they had five children, one of whom died in infancy; d. 5 Jan. 1816 in London, England, and was buried in East Barnet (London).

George Prevost's father was a French-speaking Swiss Protestant who had joined the British army; he was wounded at the siege of Quebec in 1759. At the time of George's birth he was a lieutenant-colonel in the 60th Foot. George's maternal grandfather was a wealthy Amsterdam banker, and his money no doubt later accelerated his grandson's advancement in the British army. After education at schools in England and on the Continent, George was commissioned an ensign in his father's regiment on 3 May 1779. He transferred to the 47th Foot as lieutenant in 1782 and to the 25th Foot as captain in 1784, and then rejoined the 60th on 18 Nov. 1790 with the rank of major. During the opening years of the war with revolutionary France, he saw service in the West Indies,

commanding on St Vincent in 1794 and 1795; on 6 Aug. 1794 he was promoted lieutenant-colonel in the 60th Foot. Wounded twice on 20 Jan. 1796, he returned to England and received an appointment as an inspecting field officer. He was raised to the rank of colonel on 1 Jan. 1798, then brigadier-general on 8 March. In May he became lieutenant governor of St Lucia, where his fluency in French and conciliatory administration won him the respect of the French planters. In 1802 ill health compelled him to return to Britain, but on 27 September, after the resumption of war with France, he was chosen governor of Dominica. In 1803 he fought against the French to retain possession of that island and to recapture St Lucia. Promoted major-general on 1 Jan. 1805, he obtained leave to visit England, where he was placed in command of the Portsmouth district and created a baronet. The following year he became a colonel commandant in his regiment.

On 15 Jan. 1808 Prevost was appointed lieutenant governor of Nova Scotia and given the local rank of lieutenant-general. His appointment, like that of Governor CRAIG for Lower Canada the previous year, was made in accordance with a British decision to replace civil by military colonial administrators at a time of increasing tension in Anglo-American relations. Arriving at Halifax on 7 April, Prevost immediately set about his primary task of strengthening the military security of the Atlantic colonies. By the end of the month he had already taken steps to foment dissension in New England, where much opposition existed to the belligerent attitude of the American government towards Britain. Until hostilities began he sought to encourage New England's violation of President Thomas Jefferson's embargo on trade with Britain by having designated in Nova Scotia and New Brunswick a number of "free ports," where American goods would be exempt from customs duties. The measure gave a substantial boost to Nova Scotia's trade, not only with New England but also with the West Indies. Internally, Prevost could do little about the dilapidated state of fortifications in Nova Scotia, but he did secure from the legislature an amended militia law, which would permit mobilization of a small but efficient force to supplement the regular garrison in an emergency.

This law represented something of an achievement because relations between the executive and the House of Assembly in Nova Scotia had deteriorated under Prevost's predecessor, Sir John WENTWORTH, who had tried to extend the executive's prerogative at the expense of the assembly's powers. When Prevost arrived, the assembly, led by William Cottnam Tonge*, was struggling particularly to assert control over government expenditures. Prevost shrewdly decided to conciliate Tonge, whom he appointed assistant commissary for an expedition that he was organizing as second in command against Martinique. He departed from Halifax on 6 Dec. 1808, taking Tonge with him. In the absence of the lieutenant governor the administration of the colony fell to Alexander Croke*, the senior councillor and a man as stubborn as he was reactionary. Instead of profiting from Tonge's absence to maintain peaceful relations with the assembly, he fought with it over a supply bill, which he finally rejected on the ground that it encroached on royal prerogatives, and then quarrelled with the Legislative Council over the means of breaking the impasse.

Following his return to Halifax on 15 April, after the capture of Martinique, Prevost renounced Croke's actions, restored "good understanding" with his council, and then placated the assembly (still deprived of Tonge, who had found a position in the West Indies) by refusing to quibble over constitutional niceties. On 10 June it not only passed a new supply bill, but also voted 200 guineas for the purchase of a sword for Prevost to mark its approbation of his conduct in the Martinique campaign. In the end, Prevost believed, he had successfully maintained the crown's prerogative. Later in 1809 Prevost took advantage of his good relations with the assembly to secure a tax on distilled liquors in order to meet the cost of arms and accoutrements for the provincial militia. For the rest of his term as lieutenant governor he would ensure that no arbitrary act of the executive united an assembly often torn by each member's scramble to obtain the maximum allocation for road construction in his constituency.

Beginning in 1810 Prevost undertook to buttress the tenuous establishment of the Church of England, thereby risking his hard-won popularity since that church's claims on government alienated other denominations in the colony. He persuaded the British government to permit the use of surplus revenue in the arms fund for completion or repair of Anglican churches and the enlargement of King's College at Windsor. Moreover, he appointed Anglican clergy as civil magistrates, took steps to protect school and glebe lands from encroachment or alienation, and placed Bishop Charles INGLIS on the council. He also obtained an increase in Inglis's salary, provided the bishop, who preferred to rusticate at Aylesford, resided in Halifax. In 1811 Prevost sought to improve clerical salaries by offering to suspend the unpopular collection of quitrents on land grants if the assembly made annual financial provision for Anglican ministers; the proposal was ultimately rejected. Perhaps to reduce criticism from the Presbyterian and Roman Catholic churches, in 1810 Prevost had also appointed a number of their clergy to be magistrates, and the following year he acknowledged the respectability of the Church of Scotland, if not a semi-official status for it, by authorizing a grant from the arms fund to one of its churches.

By May 1811 Prevost was prepared to risk his good relations with the assembly over its annual appropriation to compensate members for their expenses, feeling that it was irregular, liable to abuse, and "an evil highly dangerous to the prerogative of the Crown." Before he came to blows with the assembly over payment of expenses, however, Prevost left Nova Scotia for Lower Canada with instructions to replace Governor Craig. Though Prevost was politically conservative, he had nevertheless remained pragmatic during his administration in Nova Scotia. He considered the contests of factions an unavoidable characteristic of colonial politics, which governors should accept philosophically and seek to temper by diplomacy and conciliation. Prevost also foresaw the drift towards greater local self-government. "My observation leads me to believe," he wrote to the Colonial Office, "that as Nova Scotia becomes sensible of her adolescence, her dislike to control will become more evident, and her attempts to shake off the restraints of the Mother Country more frequent. – In short her ties in my estimation are those of necessity and convenience, more than of gratitude and affection."

On 21 Oct. 1811 Prevost was commissioned governor-in-chief of British North America; having been promoted lieutenant-general on 4 July 1811, he was also made commander of British forces in North America. In this latter capacity he took over the presidency and administration of Lower Canada from Thomas DUNN on 14 September, the day after his arrival at Quebec, and he continued to govern as president until 15 July 1812. As commander-in-chief he was preoccupied with military preparedness. Because of the British army's commitments in Europe, no significant reinforcement could be expected of existing forces in the Canadas, then numbering some 5,600 regular troops and fencibles, of which about 1,200 were stationed in Upper Canada in small, widely scattered garrisons. The Lower Canadian militia could boast 60,000 men on paper but was "ill armed and without discipline." That of the upper province totalled 11,000, of which Prevost thought "it might not be prudent to arm more than 4000," because many inhabitants, recent immigrants from the United States, were of doubtful loyalty.

Worried as well about the disposition of the Canadians if war broke out, Prevost sought to conciliate Canadian political leaders, who had been estranged by the partisan alliance that Craig had formed with the British oligarchy. Prevost soon concluded that the Canadian politicians were men "seeking an opportunity to distinguish themselves as the champions of the Public for the purpose of gaining popularity and . . . are endeavouring to make themselves of consequence in the eyes of government in the hope of obtaining employment from it." He did not disappoint them. Over the course of his administration, through lavish, but judicious, use of patronage, he exploited rivalry in the Canadian party, where the leadership of Pierre-Stanislas Bédard* was contested by several aspirants. In 1812 the dangerously disaffected Bédard was given a judgeship at Trois-Rivières, away from the centre of political affairs; Prevost treated the moderate Louis-Joseph Papineau* as leader. Of the 11 persons nominated by Prevost to the Legislative Council between 1811 and 1815, five were Canadians, who had been virtually excluded from such appointments since 1798; two, Jean-Antoine PANET and Pierre-Dominique Debartzch*, had been prominent critics of Craig. Prevost's strategy, he informed the Colonial Office, was to compose a council "possessed of the consideration of the country, from a majority of its members being independent of the government" in order to transfer to it "the political altercations which have been hitherto carried on by the governor in person."

During a rapid tour of the Montreal region in September 1811, Prevost had "found the country in the hands of the priests," and he determined "to seek the support and influence of the Catholic Clergy." Specifically, he wanted the church's support for a new militia bill, but more generally he saw the clergy as a counterweight to the nationalist and democratically inclined Canadian party. He was no doubt aided by a confidential report from Vicar General Edmund BURKE (1753–1820) of Nova Scotia, who described him to Bishop Plessis* as "a quiet man, good, without prejudices," adding that "never has a governor done more good in such a short time and so little bad." With no control over the clergy and "only persuasion to employ," Prevost offered Plessis an increase in the salary he received from government, civil recognition as bishop of Quebec, and support for a petition to obtain French priests who had emigrated to Britain during the French revolution. Initially sceptical of Prevost, Plessis was ultimately won over by his "obliging disposition." In 1813 a less restrained Alexander McDonell*, Plessis's vicar general in Upper Canada, would be completely conquered by Prevost's personality. "In *patience*, equanimity and abstemiousness, he surpasses all the Bishops, *priests* & even friars I have ever been acquainted with," he exulted to the bishop. "I might even add recluses and recolets."

By early 1812 Prevost had already won over important elements of the Canadian élite, and in April he was able to secure from the House of Assembly a new militia act and funds for defence. Once fighting began, the latter were supplemented by the issue of army bills, an ingenious scheme devised by the merchant John YOUNG. Prevost also obtained a generally faithful participation in the militia on the part of the habitants, in contrast to their virtual boycott of it during the American invasion of 1775–76 [see Benedict ARNOLD; Richard Montgomery*]. The

enthusiasm of virtually all classes of Canadians resulted in part from a changed perception of the Americans: the élite feared the protestantism, anglicization, republican democracy, and commercial capitalism that the Americans represented, whereas the habitants feared the loss to potential American immigrants of an ever diminishing acreage of unused land; all were ready to follow a governor able to acquire their confidence.

In Upper Canada the newly appointed administrator, Isaac BROCK, had less success raising a militia because of the strong American element in the province. Prevost recognized, however, that, since troops could only be moved and supplied speedily by water, any numerical deficiency in land forces would initially be offset by the superiority of the British Provincial Marine over the Americans on the Great Lakes. His strategy, in line with instructions from London, was defensive, the key being to safeguard Quebec, the only permanent fortress in the Canadas. If the Americans launched a substantial, well-organized invasion, Prevost would have no choice but to fall back on Quebec and try to hold it until reinforcements arrived from overseas. Predatory, ill-concerted incursions by the enemy might be repulsed, provided limited resources were not squandered, but Prevost ruled out major offensive operations as imprudent. Initially, too, he wanted to avoid any provocative action, which might unite a divided American public behind the war. Once hostilities started in June 1812, Brock, although momentarily restraining a natural impulse to go to the offence, found this defensive stance irksome. That summer the initiatives taken by Captain Charles ROBERTS in capturing Fort Michilimackinac (Mackinac Island, Mich.) and by Brock in taking Detroit, gave an unexpected fillip to the morale of Upper Canadians and revealed American unpreparedness.

The conditional repeal by Britain of the controversial orders in council relating to the search of neutral ships led Prevost to arrange a local ceasefire early in August. This was rejected by President James Madison, and hostilities resumed in September. After an American invasion of the Niagara peninsula was repulsed at Queenston Heights, where Brock lost his life, and Major-General Henry Dearborn's planned advance on Montreal petered out because his militia refused to cross into Lower Canada, the first season of campaigning closed with no American troops on Canadian soil. Despite pressure from John Strachan* and others that he now adopt Brock's boldly offensive strategy, Prevost held firm to a defensive posture, and was supported in his decision by the Duke of Wellington.

By 1813 the naval contest on the Great Lakes was coming into prominence. Prevost's emphasis on preserving control of the lakes induced the British government to place the Admiralty in charge of

Prevost

marine operations, and Sir James Lucas YEO arrived at Quebec in May to take command. Although directly responsible to the Admiralty in London, Yeo was instructed to cooperate with Prevost in strategic planning and the conduct of operations. Before these measures could take effect, however, British supremacy on the lakes had already been successfully challenged; on Lake Ontario a squadron assembled by Commodore Isaac Chauncey at the important naval base of Sackets Harbor, N.Y., had been able to cross the lake and ravage York (Toronto) in late April 1813. To relieve the mounting pressure on the Niagara peninsula, where land forces under Brigadier-General John Vincent* had been seriously weakened through large-scale desertion from the militia, Prevost created a diversion in May by leading an amphibious expedition against Sackets Harbor while Chauncey's fleet was still absent. Although a landing was effected, Prevost calculated that the forts could not be captured and accordingly withdrew. Thereafter naval operations on Lake Ontario failed to establish the supremacy of either side, and the opposing commanders avoided direct confrontation while they devoted their energies to shipbuilding; ultimately, completion in October 1814 of the 112-gun *St Lawrence* gave control of the lake to Yeo. On Lake Erie in September 1813 the destruction of the small British squadron under Robert Heriot Barclay* gave the Americans a considerable advantage in the struggle for the Niagara peninsula. Fortunately for Prevost, an attempt to sever the province's lifeline in the east by an assault on Montreal failed through the incompetence of the American generals, who were defeated in engagements at Châteauguay, Lower Canada, and Crysler's Farm, Upper Canada, by British forces of far inferior numbers under lieutenant-colonels Charles-Michel d'Irumberry* de Salaberry and Joseph Wanton Morrison* respectively.

In the spring and summer of 1814 the military situation in Upper Canada became grave once again, but in late summer Prevost's prospects brightened considerably with the abdication of Napoleon and the consequent arrival in Canada of an additional 15,000 troops, led by four of Wellington's most able brigade commanders. The British government now expected Prevost to undertake offensive operations, before the campaigning season ended, with two objectives in view: first, to destroy American naval establishments at Sackets Harbor and on lakes Erie and Champlain; and second, to occupy American territory in Michigan so that the British peace commissioners at Ghent (Belgium) could exact a more favourable boundary. Deciding that Sackets Harbor could not be attacked successfully until naval superiority on Lake Ontario had been regained, Prevost planned a combined land and naval operation against Plattsburgh, N.Y., on Lake Champlain. Early in September 1814 he set out

with a powerful army, reinforced by seasoned Peninsular veterans, to which the Americans could oppose only a much smaller force. On reaching Plattsburgh, however, he delayed the assault until the belated arrival of the British fleet, led by Captain George Downie in the hastily completed *Confiance*, whose 36 guns, it was hoped, would wrest control of Lake Champlain from the Americans. Impatiently and precipitately, Prevost had goaded the junior and inexperienced Downie into joining a supposedly combined operation, but then unaccountably failed to provide the promised military backing when the British ships engaged in combat in Plattsburgh Bay. Downie was killed and his force defeated; perhaps prematurely, Prevost abandoned the whole enterprise and retired with a disgruntled army to Lower Canada. Glossing over his share of responsibility for the abortive venture, Prevost justified withdrawal on the ground that, even if Plattsburgh had been captured, it would have been extremely hazardous for the British army to have remained on enemy territory after the loss of naval supremacy on Lake Champlain. Consequently he had withdrawn his army, "which was yet uncrippled for the security of these Provinces." This seemingly craven decision mortified the Peninsular veterans, who had grown accustomed to glorious victories under Wellington. They felt that their newly minted reputation had been tarnished by the pusillanimity of a commander who had gained his laurels in minor Caribbean skirmishes, and who combined incompetence on the field of battle with a niggling insistence on such petty matters as regulation dress, which had never troubled the Iron Duke.

On their return to Quebec and Montreal, officers consorted with leading members of the English-speaking community, many of whom had become Prevost's political enemies. William Smith* commented that the officers were "heartily tired of this Country, as every military man must be, who has any reputation to lose, under such a Goose as our little nincompoop." Smith and others of the English party felt that Prevost's appeasement of the Canadians had been disastrous for their own survival in, and Britain's control of, Lower Canada. The Anglican bishop of Quebec, Jacob Mountain*, whom Prevost described as having "far more disposition for Politics than Theology," considered that he and his church had been abandoned, and that the Roman Catholic Church had been virtually established. One of the most caustic critics of the governor's political strategy was Herman Witsius Ryland*, clerk of the Executive Council and formerly Craig's civil secretary and intimate adviser, who wrote of Prevost: "There he sits, like an Idiot in a Skiff, admiring the Rapidity of the Current which is about to plunge him into the Abyss!!!" In the spring of 1814 Ryland, Mountain, Pierre-Amable DE BONNE, and John Young, enraged by Prevost's unwillingness

696

to block the assembly's impeachment proceedings against chief justices Jonathan Sewell* and James Monk* for alleged misdemeanours during Craig's repressive regime, had organized a cabal in the Executive Council to agitate for the governor's recall. During Prevost's absence from Quebec on military business, the conspirators illegally dispatched an address to the Prince Regent, denouncing the pretensions of the assembly and the governor's servility to it and to the Catholic Church.

Extending their campaign to England, Prevost's critics furnished their London correspondents, such as Sewell, there to fight his impeachment, with malicious gossip based on the complaints of Prevost's officers after Plattsburgh. Prevost and his assistant civil secretary, Andrew William Cochran*, tried to counteract the poisonous reports through Adam Gordon, a personal friend of Prevost in the Colonial Office, but complaints from the colony did not fall entirely on unreceptive ears. British ministers rejected the strident political protests of the Executive Council but were sorely disappointed at being deprived of decisive military victories. Wellington admitted that the war in North America had been successfully conducted until Plattsburgh, and he acknowledged that it was the lack of naval supremacy on the Great Lakes which had prevented Britain from capitalizing on its military superiority in 1814. He advised the ministers, however, that Prevost would have to be recalled for failing to accomplish what had been expected of him militarily, if only to placate public opinion at home.

On 1 March 1815 Prevost heard with relief that the peace treaty signed at Ghent between Britain and the United States had been ratified in Washington. The next day, to his utter amazement and mortification, he learned that he had been superseded as governor and summoned to London to defend his conduct of the Plattsburgh campaign against charges made by Yeo; since they had quarrelled violently after Prevost's return to Quebec from Plattsburgh, there had been no love lost between the two men. Already Prevost's health and spirits had been adversely affected by the persistent, spiteful sniping of his military and political critics; in November 1814 Cochran had remarked to his father that the governor had "a more careworn appearance and more thoughtful manner. He has lost much of that cheerfulness that he had when you first knew him, tho' his good nature remains unchanged." Relentlessly, the English party in the province kept up its attacks. Samuel Gale* and "Veritas" each printed a malevolent series of letters in the *Montreal Herald* and subsequently published them as pamphlets. A diligent investigation ensued to unmask "Veritas." John Richardson*, a Montreal merchant and executive councillor, has been suspected, but the author was Solicitor General Stephen Sewell*, Jonathan's brother,

whom Prevost suspended for his involvement in the campaign against him. On an equally sour note, a vote by the assembly of £5,000 for plate as a testimonial to the departing governor was vetoed by the British majority in the Legislative Council. Early in April 1815 Prevost left Quebec, applauded in numerous addresses by Canadians, reviled by the British.

In England, Prevost at first retired to his estate of Belmont in Hampshire; he soon moved to London, however, as adverse effects on his health from the journey home became alarming. The government accepted his explanations of his military conduct, but in August 1815 a naval court martial of the surviving officers of the Plattsburgh Bay engagement decided, in line with Yeo's evidence, that defeat had been caused principally by Prevost's urging the squadron into premature action and then failing to afford the promised support from the land forces. Prevost requested a military court martial so that he might vindicate his conduct, and this was fixed for 12 Jan. 1816 to allow time for witnesses to travel from Lower Canada. Prevost, however, according to the *Quebec Gazette*, was suffering from "the combined effects of hereditary disease and the peculiar cruelty of his situation during the last few months," and his health necessitated a postponement of the hearing until 5 February; he died of dropsy at the age of 48 exactly one month before the court martial was to convene. Although nothing could then be done legally to clear Prevost's name, the Prince Regent responded to a petition from his widow for some mark of official favour by granting the family additional armorial bearings.

Unfortunately for Prevost's posthumous reputation, this gesture could not repair the damage done by partisan vilification and contemporary strictures on his military conduct. The accusations broadcast by Gale and "Veritas" formed the basis of a censorious article in the *Quarterly Review* of London in 1822. On behalf of Prevost's family and friends, his former civil secretary, Colonel Edward Barbizon Brenton*, replied anonymously, and far from convincingly, the following year in *Some account of the public life of the late Lieutenant-General Sir George Prevost. . . .* By that time the former governor was generally portrayed on both sides of the Atlantic as an affable but weak-willed individual, cautious to a fault, who had been found wanting in a crisis. This deprecatory estimate was made the standard judgement of writers and historians into the 20th century in part because of the myth, assiduously cultivated by John Strachan and the spiritual heirs of the loyalists, that Upper Canada had been saved from American conquest by the bravery of the local militia under Brock. Contrary to the traditional view, however, Prevost's preparations for defending the Canadas with the limited means at

Prevost

his disposal had been energetic, well conceived, and comprehensive, and in the most taxing, hazardous circumstances he had achieved the primary objective of preventing an American conquest. Perhaps his character, abilities, and experience did not so well equip him to be a successful commander of field operations, but his military reputation would have stood higher had his exploits been compared not to those of Wellington, but to those of the opposing American generals.

At the same time, "this tiny, light, gossamer man," as Chief Justice Sampson Salter Blowers* of Nova Scotia described Prevost, had been a most successful colonial administrator. Although like Craig and Wentworth instinctively conservative, Prevost distinguished himself from them by his realism and pragmatism. He was able to analyse the relative force of the social groups in a colony, understand the demands of the most influential, and formulate policies of appeasement that rendered British colonial rule palatable. Unperturbed by the dissensions that characterized relations between the houses of a colonial legislature and blessed with an obliging disposition and winning ways – "smooth & flattering; in manner like a Frenchman," a later governor, Lord Dalhousie [Ramsay*], disparagingly remarked – Prevost's varied employment in the West Indies and North America proved him uncommonly adept at dealing with sensitive colonial politicians, French- as well as English-speaking. In Lower Canada he was in part the undeserving victim of virulent political contests, endemic to a colony with representative institutions and ethnic antagonisms; in the early 1810s political polarization was too intense to be attenuated by personal conciliatory efforts. Nevertheless, the British government highly approved of Prevost's strategy and instructed his successor, Sir John Coape Sherbrooke*, to continue the policy of conciliation that Prevost had resolutely, but vainly, pursued.

PETER BURROUGHS

PAC, MG 23, GII, 10, vol.5; MG 24, A1; A9; A41; B3, 2–4; B16; J48; RG 8, I (C ser.), 366; 676–95B; 1215–27. PANS, MG 100, 152: no.1; RG 1, 58–59, 111, 287–88. PRO, CO 42/143–62; CO 43/22–23; CO 217/82–88; CO 218/19; WO 17/1516–20; WO 71/242; WO 81/52. SRO, GD45/3/542; GD45/3/552. "Campaigns in the Canadas," *Quarterly Rev.* (London), 27 (1822): 405–49. Robert Christie, *Memoirs of the administration of the colonial government of Lower-Canada, by Sir James Henry Craig, and Sir George Prevost; from the year 1807 until the year 1815* ... (Quebec, 1818). *Doc. hist. of campaign upon Niagara frontier* (Cruikshank). *Docs. relating to constitutional hist., 1791–1818* (Doughty and McArthur; 1914). *The life and correspondence of Major-General Sir Isaac Brock* ..., ed. F. B. Tupper (London, 1845). N.S., House of Assembly, *Journal and proc.*, 1808–11. *Official letters of the military and naval officers of the United States, during the war with Great Britain in the years 1812, 13, 14, & 15* ..., comp. John Brannan (Washington, 1823). [John Richardson?], *The letters of Veritas, re-published from the Montreal Herald; containing a succinct narrative of the military administration of Sir George Prevost, during his command in the Canadas* ... (Montreal, 1815). *Select British docs. of War of 1812* (Wood). [John Strachan], *The John Strachan letter book, 1812–1834*, ed. G. W. Spragge (Toronto, 1946). *Montreal Herald*, 1814–15. *Quebec Gazette*, 31 March, 14 April, 26 May, 2 June, 11 Aug., 1 Sept. 1808; 5 Jan., 15 June, 13 July, 28 Sept. 1809; 18 Jan., 15 Feb. 1810; 4 April, 29 Aug., 5, 19, 26 Sept., 3 Oct., 21 Nov. 1811; 7, 16 Jan., 21 Feb., 5 March, 9 April, 7 May, 2, 16 July, 10, 17, 24 Sept., 22 Oct., 26 Nov., 10, 29 Dec. 1812; 18, 25 Feb., 11, 18 March, 1 April, 13 May, 24 June, 7, 21 Oct., 29 Nov., 23 Dec. 1813; 12 Jan., 2 Feb., 16, 23, 30 March, 6, 13 April, 18 May, 10 Aug., 5 Oct. 1815; 29 Feb., 21 March, 21 Nov., 19 Dec. 1816; 8 Dec. 1823. *Appleton's cyclopædia of American biography*, ed. J. G. Wilson and John Fiske (7v., New York, 1887–1900), 5: 116. *DNB*. G.B., WO, *Army list*, 1779–1816. H. J. Morgan, *Sketches of celebrated Canadians and persons connected with Canada, from the earliest period in the history of the province down to the present time* (Quebec and London, 1862; repr. Montreal, 1865). Wallace, *Macmillan dict.*

Henry Adams, *History of the United States* (9v., New York, 1890–91). *After Tippecanoe: some aspects of the War of 1812*, ed. P. P. Mason (East Lansing, Mich., and Toronto, 1963). J. M. Beck, *The government of Nova Scotia* (Toronto, 1957). [E. B. Brenton], *Some account of the public life of the late Lieutenant-General Sir George Prevost, Bart., particularly of his services in the Canadas* ... (London, 1823). A. L. Burt, *The United States, Great Britain and British North America from the revolution to the establishment of peace after the War of 1812* (Toronto and New Haven, Conn., 1940). Christie, *Hist. of L.C.*, vols. 2, 6. Craig, *Upper Canada*. Fingard, *Anglican design in loyalist N.S.* G. S. Graham, *Sea power and British North America, 1783–1820: a study in colonial policy* (Cambridge, Mass., 1941). Hitsman, *Incredible War of 1812; Safeguarding Canada, 1763–1871* (Toronto, 1968). Reginald Horsman, *The causes of the War of 1812* (New York, 1972). Lambert, "Joseph-Octave Plessis." Lemieux, *L'établissement de la première prov. eccl.* C. P. Lucas, *The Canadian War of 1812* (Oxford, 1906). W. S. MacNutt, *The Atlantic provinces: the emergence of colonial society, 1712–1857* (Toronto, 1965). A. T. Mahan, *Sea power in its relations to the War of 1812* (2v., London, 1905). Manning, *Revolt of French Canada*. Murdoch, *Hist. of N.S.*, vol.3. Ouellet, *Bas-Canada; Hist. économique*. Bradford Perkins, *Castlereagh and Adams: England and the United States, 1812–1823* (Berkeley and Los Angeles, Calif., 1964); *Prologue to war: England and the United States, 1805–1812* (Berkeley and Los Angeles, 1961; repr. 1963). J. W. Pratt, *Expansionists of 1812* (New York, 1925). "The late Lieut.-Gen. Sir George Prevost, Bart.," *Naval and Military Magazine* (London), 3 (March 1828): 71–74. "Military services and character of the late Lieut.-Gen. Sir George Prevost, Bart.," *Naval and Military Magazine*, 2 (September 1827): 101–10. J. M. Hitsman, "Sir George Prevost's conduct of the Canadian War of 1812," CHA *Report*, 1962: 34–43.

PRICE, CHARLES. *See* ISHAM, CHARLES THOMAS

PURSS, JOHN, businessman, militia officer, and office holder; b. 12 Dec. 1732 in Elgin, Scotland, son of Alexander Purse, a tailor, and Isabel Blenshel; d. unmarried 8 April 1803 at Quebec, Lower Canada.

John Purss came to Quebec at the time of the conquest. In July 1762 he went into partnership as a merchant with another Scot, James Johnston*. In the late 1760s their firm was buying and selling furs, seal oil, and the products of the Saint-Maurice ironworks. They had been in partnership since 1765 with Jean-Baptiste BOUCHETTE to exploit a trading post and a fishery, probably in the Gulf of St Lawrence, and they had bought a share in the lease of the ironworks in 1767. In 1770 Purss and his partner obtained a 30-year lease on the King's Wharf for 5 shillings annually. This wharf was proving too expensive for the government to maintain but was indispensable for merchants at Quebec; consequently Governor Guy CARLETON had suggested in 1768 that it be rented out, with the lessee assuming responsibility for keeping it in good condition.

During the 1780s the firm of Johnston and Purss ran a distillery with Henry Taylor, who was Johnston's brother-in-law and a distiller. The business, which occupied a two-storey house on Rue Champlain, was a fairly large undertaking, with four stills, four big copper boilers, and eight evaporation tubs. Here an "essence of spruce for making beer" that had been discovered by Taylor and that was exported to New York and the West Indies was prepared. However, like similar establishments in the colony, the enterprise mainly produced regular beer; other alcoholic beverages manufactured were of a poor quality because of a lack of ingredients and experience alike. The two partners also each held 2 of the 48 shares in the Dorchester Bridge, which had been built at Quebec in 1789 [*see* David LYND].

At the end of the 1780s and in the following decade Johnston and Purss leased out some houses they owned on Rue Champlain, Rue du Palais, Rue Sous-le-Fort, and Rue de la Montagne for between £30 and £150 a year, and rented out space on the King's Wharf as well. In April 1789 they sold a lot and stone house on Rue des Pauvres (Côte du Palais) to the merchant Mathew Macnider, Johnston's brother-in-law, for £450. In April 1792 Johnston and Purss let their holdings in the Dorchester Bridge go to William GRANT (1744–1805) for £20 per share. In the course of the 1790s they borrowed about £1,400 from Peter Stuart and Jacques DÉNÉCHAUD, the executor of Barthélemy Cotton*. In 1798 they had to sell the distillery at the demand of the widow of Taylor.

Johnston's death on 8 April 1800 brought about the dissolution of the firm of Johnston and Purss. This solid business partnership had also been a close friendship, and the real estate was therefore divided equally between Purss on one hand and Johnston's widow, the former Margaret Macnider, and children on the other, neither of the joint heirs having the right, however, to sell any property without the other's consent. Moreover, because of the many years the company had been in existence, the confidence the widow had in him, and the great esteem he had for his partner, Purss cancelled the debt of £2,311 1s. 1½d. that Johnston owed him. Before Johnston died, he and Purss had sought renewal of their lease on the King's Wharf, which was due to expire in 1800. They appear to have obtained at least part of the wharf, since Purss complained the following year of encroachments on the King's Wharf; another part had been rented by the government to Alexander MUNN. In the period 1800–2 Purss let a number of properties go. In 1800, in conjunction with Margaret Johnston, he sold the house and lot on Rue de la Montagne for £350. The following year, to honour his debt to the Cotton estate he sold some land with a house on Rue Sous-le-Fort for £800. A few days later he sold a waterfront lot and a wharf in Lower Town and also a lot with a house for a total of £1,700. Lastly, in March 1802 he advertised in the *Quebec Gazette* the auction of a house that had belonged to the firm of Johnston and Purss at Beauport, near Quebec. On the other hand, in January 1803 he received 200 acres in Granby Township and as much again in Milton Township.

At various points in his career Purss joined other merchants of the colony in political and business demands. In 1764 he was one of a group seeking Governor Murray*'s recall, and two years later he signed the address of welcome to his replacement, Lieutenant Governor Carleton. In 1784 he put his name to a petition for repeal of the Quebec Act and the granting of an assembly, habeas corpus, and trial by jury in civil cases. Ten years later, against the background of war between Great Britain and revolutionary France [*see* Robert PRESCOTT], he joined an association founded in June 1794 to support the British government in Lower Canada, and signed the declaration of loyalty to the 1791 constitution. He had subscribed to an agreement on the value of gold currency in 1772. In 1790 he endorsed proposals for the creation of a non-sectarian university in the province, and in 1791 supported demands for the elimination of the seigneurial right of *lods et ventes*; that year as well he signed a petition concerning a bill dealing with guardians and trustees.

Like his partner Purss took part in the town's public life. With John JONES, among others, he played an important part in the beginnings of the Quebec Fire Society, of which he was the treasurer in at least 1786 and 1790. This society, which was founded in 1765, offered its members fire insurance of a kind, organized popular subscriptions to help victims, collaborated with the justices of the peace and army officers in preventing fires, and went into action when conflagrations broke out. In 1790 the Fire Society owned five of the twelve fire pumps at Quebec, the army had four, and Johnston and Purss had at least one. Purss was commissioned lieutenant in the Quebec Battalion of British Militia in 1787, and probably in 1799 was promoted captain. In addition he served as assessor for the town and suburbs of Quebec in 1797.

Purss died on 8 April 1803. In his handwritten will, which was drawn up on 4 Dec. 1802, he had named his friend the Presbyterian minister Alexander SPARK, his cousin James Tullok, and merchant John Munro, all of the town, as his executors. Except for the furniture and household effects, which were bequeathed to Margaret Johnston, Purss gave all his assets to relatives, most of whom lived in Great Britain. On 30 April 1803 Mrs Johnston bought virtually all of his estate for £3,500 sterling, a sum that was paid to his heirs.

ANDRÉ BÉRUBÉ

AC, Québec, Testament olographe de John Purss, 14 April 1803 (*see* P.-G. Roy, *Inv. testaments*, 3: 119). ANQ-Q, CE1-66, 12 April 1803; CN1-83, 17 nov. 1786, 23 avril 1791, 7 avril 1792; CN1-92, 9 sept. 1795, 27 juill. 1797, 29 août 1798; CN1-200, 9 sept. 1782; CN1-202, 26 oct. 1763, 30 août 1765; CN1-205, 14 mars 1778; 22 avril, 18 oct. 1784; CN1-224, 19 juin 1789, 17 juin 1791; CN1-230, 12 juin 1795, 19 mai 1797, 13 févr. 1799, 3 août 1802; CN1-248, 7 janv. 1763; CN1-256, 3 Feb., 12 March, 14 July 1787; 23 April, 18 Dec. 1789; 20 April 1790; 23 April 1795; 27 Feb. 1796; 10 Oct. 1797; 4 June 1798; 2 Sept. 1799; CN1-284, 8, 10 juin, 19 août 1800; 9 mars, 14 avril 1801; 14, 30 avril 1803; CN1-285, 3, 9 déc. 1801. Orkney Arch., Orkney Library (Kirkwall, Scot.), D15/1/3. PAC, MG 11, [CO 42] Q, 69: 326–31. PRO, CO 42/15: f.13 (mfm. at PAC). *Docs. relating to constitutional hist., 1759–91* (Shortt and Doughty; 1918), 1: 212–16, 232–35. *Quebec Gazette*, 29 Sept. 1766; 18 June 1772; 14 June, 26 July 1787; 21 Jan., 4 Nov. 1790; 28 April, 16 June 1791; 3, 10 July 1794; 5 Jan. 1797; 22 March 1798; 4 March 1802; 14 April 1803. "Habitants de la ville de Québec, 1770–1771," F.-J. Audet, compil., *BRH*, 27 (1921): 218. E. H. Dahl *et al.*, *La ville de Québec, 1800–1850: un inventaire de cartes et plans* (Ottawa, 1975), 63, 67. Langelier, *Liste des terrains concédés*, 1757. "Papiers d'État," PAC, *Rapport*, 1890: 208. "Papiers d'État – Bas-Canada," PAC *Rapport*, 1891: 114; 1892: 157, 163, 178, 196; 1893: 53. *Quebec almanac*, 1787: 47; 1799: 99; 1800: 103; 1801: 102. F.-X. Chouinard et Antonio Drolet, *La ville de Québec, histoire municipale* (3v., Québec, 1963–67), 2: 57. Mildred Morgan, "The office of receiver general and its tenure by deputy in the province of Quebec, 1763–1791" ([MA thesis, McGill Univ., Montreal], 1937), 79–80. Ruddel, "Quebec City, 1765–1831," 309–11, 313–14, 542, 603. D. C. Cargill, "John Purse, merchant in Quebec in 1794," *Scottish Genealogist* (December 1966): 33–34. Philéas Gagnon, "Le premier pont sur la rivière Saint-Charles," *BRH*, 4 (1898): 55.

Q

QUENEBENAW (Quinipeno). *See* KINEUBENAE

QUESNEL, JOSEPH, businessman, composer, militia officer, playwright, and poet; b. 15 Nov. 1746 in Saint-Malo, France, third child of Isaac Quesnel de La Rivaudais and Pélagie-Jeanne-Marguerite Duguen; d. 3 July 1809 in Montreal, Lower Canada.

Joseph Quesnel, the son of a prosperous merchant, attended the Collège Saint-Louis in Saint-Malo. When he had finished his studies, he took ship for Pondicherry (India) and visited Madagascar. In 1772 he travelled to French Guiana, the West Indies, and Brazil. After that he took up residence in Bordeaux, France, where he went into partnership with his uncle, Louis-Auguste Quesnel.

In the autumn of 1779 Quesnel embarked on the French privateer *Espoir* for North America. According to tradition he was in command of this vessel, which was carrying war supplies and munitions to help the American colonies in their revolt against Britain. Whatever the case, the ship was captured off Newfoundland by the Royal Navy and taken to Halifax, N.S. Quesnel avoided imprisonment but had to remain in British North America until the end of hostilities. He arrived in Montreal bearing a safe conduct issued by Governor HALDIMAND. There, on 10 April 1780, he married Marie-Josephte Deslandes, who also came from Saint-Malo but whose mother, Marie-Josephe Le Pellé Lahaye, had come to Montreal after her husband's death and had married the merchant Maurice-Régis BLONDEAU.

Quesnel was active in commercial life as Blondeau's partner. He signed a number of petitions from merchants to the government, including one in 1784 calling for a new constitution and one in 1790 asking for settlement of the problems that Montreal merchants were experiencing because of the lack of a customs office there. Quesnel was also interested in the cultural and social life of his adopted town. In 1780 and 1783 he played in amateur theatrical companies. He is supposed to have composed a piece of music that was performed in public at a Christmas party; he lamented, however, that "they call my music sprightly [and] say it is made for the theatre." In 1788 he was an ensign, and from 1791 to 1793 second captain, in the local Canadian militia; at the same time he was serving as a churchwarden in the parish of Notre-Dame.

In October 1788 Quesnel had sailed for England; he then spent the winter in Bordeaux. The purpose of his trip was to establish commercial relations with his family in France, particularly with his brother Pierre, who was in business at Bordeaux. Quesnel also took advantage of the voyage to attend theatrical performances. If he had intended to examine the prospects of returning to France for good, the events of the revolution would have put an end to any such hopes. In November 1789, after his return to Montreal, Quesnel founded a theatrical company, the Théâtre de Société, with his friends Louis Dulongpré*, Pierre-Amable DE BONNE, Jean-Guillaume DE LISLE, Jacques-Clément Herse, Joseph-François Perrault*, and François Rolland. On 11 November Dulongpré undertook to transform his spacious house into a temporary theatre and to supply three stage settings painted on canvas, the lighting, music, wigs, tickets, playbills, caretaker, and ushers. On Sunday 22 November the parish priest of Montreal, François-Xavier Latour-Dézery, preached a vehement sermon denouncing theatrical performances and declared that the church would refuse absolution to those who attended them. At the conclusion of the high mass Quesnel and some of his partners, including De Lisle, protested against this zeal which they termed misdirected. Vicar general Gabriel-Jean Brassier*, who was caught off guard by the firmness of these theatre supporters, all prominent people, wrote to Bishop Hubert* for advice. Hubert censured the conduct of Father Latour-Dézery, by implication acknowledging that his critics were right. The incident was closed in December but a controversy developed in the *Montreal Gazette* over the morality of the theatre: Quesnel joined in the fray with a long letter published on 7 Jan. 1790 defending both the utility and morality of the theatre. Between 29 Dec. 1789 and 9 Feb. 1790 the company gave four evening performances, producing six plays in all, among them *Colas et Colinette, ou le Bailli dupé*, a comic opera by Quesnel. The public and the critics acclaimed this comedy in three acts intermixed with 14 songs. In its second season the Théâtre de Société decided to limit the audience "to a very small number of persons of high birth or noble blood"; but an anonymous correspondent questioned the validity of this decision, given the members' desire to participate in the colony's cultural development. The new policy may have been dictated by the hostile reaction of the clergy. Whatever the case, the company shut down temporarily.

In 1791 and 1792 Quesnel made several trips to the *pays d'en haut*. At that period the sale of furs in London was suffering a serious decline and business was becoming difficult. Furthermore, the trading company he had organized in 1790 with five partners,

including Blondeau and Pierre Bouthillier, was in trouble. Set up to import Bordeaux wines through his brother Pierre's firm, the Compagnie Baignoux-Quesnel, it was facing insurmountable difficulties because of stoppages occasioned by the disruptions of the French revolution.

In 1793 Quesnel partially retired from business and went to live in Boucherville, where he had already bought some land. At the turn of the 19th century Boucherville enjoyed a certain reputation as a centre of Canadian social life in the Montreal region. Lord Selkirk [DOUGLAS] noted in 1804 that "the gentry of the place & neighbourhood hold Assemblies of their own at Boucherville . . . where no English intrude."

Beginning in 1799 Quesnel devoted himself to poetry. His three long poems, written between 1799 and 1805, "L'épître à M. Labadie," "Le rimeur dépité," and "La nouvelle Académie," reveal his wish to make his works known to his friends. He complained bitterly, however, of the lack of attention given them. Quesnel did not publish a collection, but some texts appeared during his lifetime in periodicals; they were either anonymous or else signed with the *nom de plume* "F" (François). His poetic works consist principally of occasional verse. The charming song "À Boucherville," composed about 1798, evokes the quiet joys of life long ago. The poetry of this 18th-century man at times took on a philosophical tone. In his first poem, "À M. Panet," written about 1783 or 1784, he laughs at his friend Pierre-Louis PANET for his faith in Rousseau and Voltaire; he returned to this theme in "Stances marotiques à mon esprit," composed in 1806. And in "Épître à ma femme," written the following year, he claims:

Alas! what use is it to regret
The moments of this brief passage!
Death need not sadden us,
'Tis but the journey's end.

In 1804 he had written his moving "Épître à . . . ," a farewell to health, pleasures, gaiety, and above all to France which he would see no more.

Quesnel's concern about his compatriots' lack of interest in the arts comes out in "L'épître à M. Labadie," written between 1799 and 1801, in which he repeats Boileau's plaint: "The saddest occupation is the poet's trade." In his long autobiographical poem "Le dépit ridicule, ou le sonnet perdu," the poet complains to his wife: "What is the good of the trouble I take for rhyming / If no one ever has time to listen to my verse?" His wife, a more practical person, replies: "I see you every day writing or dreaming, / Whilst I must bring up your children." The poet then announces his great project to her: to invite his friends to a supper, and after carefully double-locking the doors "to read all the lines of my last work." His

Quesnel

concern for interesting his compatriots was still lively when Quesnel dreamed in 1805 of creating an academy of *belles-lettres*. But it was only a dream, at the end of which woke up "Good old François, / Always musing, absent-minded, full of misanthropy, / And, especially to fools, unsociable."

Despite these bitter reflections Quesnel was not ignored by his contemporaries. In January and February 1805 the Théâtre de Société of Quebec performed *Colas et Colinette* at the Théâtre Patagon. A grateful Quesnel, who was in Quebec at the time, presented the amateur actors with a treatise on dramatic art in verse which had appeared in the *Quebec Gazette* under the title "Adresse aux jeunes acteurs" and in which his advice, still topical, shows his knowledge and good taste. On this occasion, moreover, Ignace-Michel-Louis-Antoine d'Irumberry* de Salaberry suggested to the Quebec printer John Neilson* that he publish Quesnel's dramatic works. In 1807, when *Colas et Colinette* was again performed, Neilson decided to publish it. However, because of the difficulties he encountered, it appeared without the music and was not put on sale until 1812.

Quesnel was not indifferent to the great problems of his period. As a result of the upheavals of the French revolution which had directly touched his family in France, a cousin having been guillotined and the property of his brother in Bordeaux confiscated, Quesnel openly displayed pro-British sentiments. In 1799 he wrote the poem "Songe agréable" in which he praised the merits of "George the formidable king" who, "Conquering the unconquerable Frenchman, / Will restore peace to the universe." In 1800 or 1801 Quesnel is believed to have composed a satirical play, *Les républicains français, ou la soirée du cabaret*, which ridiculed the morals of the heads of local sections in Robespierre's time. But Quesnel also reacted to the growing influence of the British who had settled in Lower Canada and to their hostile attitude towards the French and the Canadians. In 1803 he responded to the attacks published in an anonymous poem entitled *L'anti-français*. The preceding year he had composed a satirical play, *L'anglomanie, ou le dîner à l'angloise*, in which he ridiculed the infatuation of part of the seigneurial gentry with English fashions. His thinking developed to the point that in December 1806 he published his poem "Les moissonneurs" in *Le Canadien*, organ of the Canadian party; in it he opposed the pretensions of the British oligarchy in the colony.

Quesnel's final years were passed serenely in a measure of luxury. In 1808 he was preparing another comic opera, *Lucas et Cécile*, but he died before it was finished. In the spring he had leapt into the St Lawrence to save a drowning child, and he succumbed to an attack of pleurisy on 3 July 1809 in the Hôtel-Dieu at Montreal. His widow died the following year. The couple had had 13 children, 6 of whom reached adulthood. Their eldest son, Frédéric-Auguste*, who was called to the bar in 1807, used to hold gatherings for the élite in his Montreal home at which his father enjoyed literary conversation. Jules-Maurice* became a fur trader, thus carrying on a family tradition. Joseph-Timoléon practised medicine, and Mélanie married the lawyer and businessman Côme-Séraphin Cherrier*.

A few days after Quesnel's death Jacques Viger* observed: "It is an irreparable loss for literature and society in this country." In 1830 Michel Bibaud* paid a stirring tribute to the poet who had been dead for more than 20 years: "There is no Canadian with any sort of education who has not read at least some of the late Mr Joseph Quesnel's works." Benjamin Sulte* defined Quesnel's role very lucidly: "The literary awakening perceptible in our country since 1788 owes most to him."

Although his writing is at times a pastiche of Boileau, Ronsard, or Molière, Joseph Quesnel remains a writer of the 18th century. His work is interesting primarily for what it reveals of his time, and his special gift was to be able to convey its artistic and literary atmosphere. He proved the most significant French Canadian writer of the period.

JOHN E. HARE

[Works attributed to Joseph Quesnel appeared during his lifetime in various newspapers, including the *Quebec Gazette*, 7 Feb. 1805; *Le Canadien*, 29 nov., 13 déc. 1806; 10, 17, 24 janv., 14 févr., 3 oct. 1807; the *Montreal Gazette*, the *British American Register* (Quebec), and *Le Courier de Québec*. Some were reprinted in Louis Plamondon, *Almanach des dames, pour l'année 1807* (Québec, 1807). *Colas et Colinette, ou le Bailli dupé* (Québec, 1808) was published by John Neilson; this comic opera was reprinted in the first volume of the *Répertoire national, recueil de littérature canadienne*, comp. James Huston (4v., Montréal, 1848–50), which contains six other pieces by Quesnel. *Colas et Colinette* was also recorded in 1968, the music having been reconstructed by the Toronto composer Godfrey Ridout in 1963. Quesnel's plays, *L'anglomanie, ou le dîner à l'angloise* and *Les républicains français, ou la soirée du cabaret*, were republished in *La Barre du jour* (Montréal), nos.3–5 (1965): 117–41 and no.25 (été 1970): 64–88, respectively.

The Lande collection (PAC, MG 53, 177) contains 24 manuscript poems by Quesnel, some of which were published in *Joseph Quesnel, 1749–1809: selected poems and songs after the manuscripts in the Lande collection*, ed. Michael Gnarowski (Montreal, 1970). Jacques Viger's Saberdache (ASQ, Fonds Viger-Verreau, Sér.O, 095–125) contains the edition he prepared of Quesnel's texts in 1847. The ASQ also holds the vocal score of *Lucas et Cécile* (Fonds Viger-Verreau, Carton 45, no.3). Helmut Kallmann and John E. Hare are preparing a critical edition of Quesnel's works from his recently discovered workbook; this publication should include 30 poems, as well as a few titles attributed to him. J.E.H.]

AD, Ille-et-Vilaine (Rennes), État civil, Saint-Malo, 15 nov. 1746. ANQ-M, CE1-51, 10 avril 1780, 4 juill. 1809. *Quebec Gazette*, 28 Oct. 1790, 25 July 1799, 7 Feb. 1805, 13 July 1809, 19 April 1810. Michel Bibaud, *Épîtres, satires, chansons, épigrammes et autres pièces de vers* (Montréal, 1830), 46. Baudouin Burger, *L'activité théâtrale au Québec (1765–1825)* (Montréal, 1974), 199–215. J. [E.] Hare, *Anthologie de la poésie québécoise du XIXᵉ siècle (1790–1890)* (Montréal, 1979), 21–35. D. M. Hayne, "Le théâtre de Joseph Quesnel," *Le théâtre canadien-français: évolution, témoignages, bibliographie* (Montréal, 1976). Helmut Kallmann, *A history of music in Canada, 1534–1914* (Toronto, 1960), 62–67, 121–22. Camille Roy, *Nos origines littéraires* (Québec, 1909), 125–57. Benjamin Sulte, *Mélanges d'histoire et de littérature* (4v., Ottawa, 1876), 3: 295. Michel Bibaud, "Littérature," *La Bibliothèque canadienne* (Montréal), 2 (1825), no.1: 16–17. Yves Chartier, "La reconstitution musicale de *Colas et Colinette* de Joseph Quesnel," Centre de recherche en civilisation canadienne-française, *Bull.* (Ottawa), 2 (1971–72), no.2: 11–14. J. E. Hare, "Joseph Quesnel et l'anglomanie de la classe seigneuriale au tournant du XIXᵉ siècle," *Co-Incidences* (Ottawa), 6 (1976): 23–31; "Le Théâtre de société à Montréal, 1789–1791," Centre de recherche en civilisation canadienne-française, *Bull.*, 16 (1977–78), no.2: 22–26. É.-Z. Massicotte, "La famille du poète Quesnel," *BRH*, 23 (1917): 339–42.

R

RAIZENNE, MARIE, named **Saint-Ignace**, sister of the Congregation of Notre-Dame and superior (superior general); b. 14 July 1735 at the mission of Lac-des-Deux-Montagnes (Oka, Que.), daughter of Josiah Rising (Shoentakwanni, Ignace Raizenne) and Abigail Nims (Towatogowash, rebaptized Élisabeth); d. 20 April 1811 in Montreal, Lower Canada.

Marie Raizenne's parents had both been born in Deerfield, Mass. Captured by Indians during the War of the Spanish Succession [*see* Jean-Baptiste Hertel* de Rouville] and taken to Sault-au-Récollet (Montreal North) in 1704, they were baptized in the Catholic faith. The two captives, who were "raised in the Indian fashion," attended the mission schools run by the sisters of the Congregation of Notre-Dame and the Sulpicians. At the end of the war they decided not to return to their native land and on 29 July 1715 they were married. Three of their children to dedicate their lives to God. Indeed, when Marie entered the noviciate of the Congregation of Notre-Dame in Montreal in 1752, she was taking the step that her elder sister, Marie-Madeleine, named Saint-Herman, had taken 21 years earlier; her brother, Amable-Simon, had been ordained priest in 1744. Having made her profession in 1754 under the name of Sister Saint-Ignace, she lived through the events of the Seven Years' War in Montreal [*see* Marie-Angélique Lefebvre* Angers]; then in 1761 she helped restore the Sainte-Famille mission on Île d'Orléans. She was serving as mistress of novices in Montreal when the mother house was destroyed by fire in 1768 [*see* Marie-Josèphe Maugue-Garreau*]. However, the following year she was sent to Quebec to take charge of the newly re-established mission in Lower Town, which had had to suspend operations when the town was captured by the British in 1759. Rebuilding the convent had required a loan of 11,000 *livres* from merchant Jean-Baptiste Amiot*. Even though she

could not count on the aid of the townspeople, who were themselves victims of the war, Sister Saint-Ignace was successful in repaying much of this debt within six years, thus demonstrating her administrative abilities. In 1775 she was recalled to Montreal and became assistant to the superior, Véronique BRUNET, *dit* L'Estang, named Sainte-Rose, whom she succeeded in 1778.

During Sister Saint-Ignace's first superiorship the community experienced its share of the woes brought on the country by the War of American Independence. Resources were so scarce that the council of the community refused to repair any of its houses unless "it is raining a great deal [in them]"; in 1780 the sisters were able to buy their supply of wheat (300 bushels) only after receiving a legacy of 3,000 "shillings" from one of their regular benefactors, Étienne Augé*. In 1781 the superior of the Sulpician seminary in Montreal, Étienne Montgolfier*, released the community from the obligation of paying a sum of 1,600 *livres*, which represented the *lods et ventes* owed to the seminary as a result of the sisters' purchase of the Parc à Baron, a property between the St Lawrence River and the road to Lachine. That year, at her request, Governor HALDIMAND freed Sister Saint-Ignace from the requirement of amortizing, by annual payments, the seigneurial dues on the community's fief of Île-Saint-Paul (Île des Sœurs), near Montreal.

Given the financial difficulties facing the community, the sisters in charge of the missions were strongly tempted to take into their schools all the boarders who applied. However, to assure the quality of the services offered and to safeguard the missionaries' health, a regulation was passed in 1780 limiting the number of boarders to 40 and giving priority to pupils who were getting ready for their first communion.

Moreover, the community's dire poverty prompted Sister Saint-Ignace to be extremely prudent when she

Ramage

was called upon in 1782 to examine a proposal for the founding of a mission at Detroit (Mich.). A petition to that end had already been presented in 1755 by the inhabitants of the "lower region of the colony," but to no avail. This time Jean-François Hubert*, who was then parish priest of Notre-Dame-de-l'Assomption, near Detroit, addressed the request to Bishop Briand* of Quebec, and was so confident of receiving a favourable reply that he sent 2,400 *livres* for the missionaries' voyage, promising to provide them with a suitable house. The founding of such a mission, however, posed problems for the Congregation of Notre-Dame. For one thing, it represented a new financial burden for the community, which could barely maintain missions that were already established and were close at hand; moreover, a mission at Detroit would not only be precarious, but might well be short-lived. The superior also thought that she could not compel any sister to move to Detroit, since going so far away had not up to this time been part of the obligations implied in taking vows. In the series of material and spiritual conditions that she considered appropriate to submit to the bishop before agreeing to the proposed mission, the superior revealed not only reservations but also her good sense and respect for her sisters' liberty. Afterwards, having weighed the advantages and disadvantages, she rejected the project. On the other hand, in 1783 the congregation set up a mission at Saint-Denis on the Richelieu, taking possession of a convent built for the sisters by the parish priest, François CHERRIER. The running of the mission was entrusted to Marie-Louise COMPAIN, named Saint-Augustin.

In 1784, when her six-year term of office came to an end, Sister Saint-Ignace became mistress of novices, and four years later second mistress; then in 1790 she was re-elected superior. During her second superiorship she felt some quite legitimate anxieties about the congregation's affairs in France. It was the period of the revolution, and the community's procurator, Jean-Louis Maury, had not been heard from since 25 Feb. 1789. Consequently the community was deprived of the annuity payments which constituted its main income. On learning of the spoliation of the properties belonging to the clergy and the religious communities in France, Sister Saint-Ignace was rightly concerned about the fate of the congregation's possessions there. However, she did not give up hope of seeing Canadian-owned property treated like that of other foreign countries, since the colony had not been under French rule for many years. In a letter dated 11 March 1791 – the last he would send to the community until 1802 – the procurator explained that he could no longer pay the bills of exchange as before, since he was no longer certain he would be reimbursed for the money he advanced. Nor did he give much reassurance as to the future of the property in France belonging to Canadian communities.

By the time her second superiorship ended in 1796, Sister Saint-Ignace still had received no revenues from France and did not know what fate had befallen the congregation's possessions there. It will be readily understood that such a period marked a decided hiatus in the community's development. No new missions were founded. The sisters merely did the essential repairs and raised the monthly board in all the missions to seven *livres* and a bushel of wheat, and the half board to four *livres* and half a bushel of wheat. On 14 May 1793 they sold the Parc à Baron and a property in the *faubourg* Québec, in the east end of Montreal, that had come from a sister's dowry.

During this six-year term of office, the financial foundations and indeed the very future of the congregation Sister Saint-Ignace directed were seriously endangered. Becoming mistress of novices again when the term was over was a welcome rest for her. She carried out this duty until 1802, and then lived in retirement for the last nine years of her life.

ANDRÉE DÉSILETS

Arch. de la Congrégation de Notre-Dame (Montréal), Fichier général; Personnel, V; Reg. général. Louise Dechêne, "Inventaire des documents relatifs à l'histoire du Canada conservés dans les archives de la compagnie de Saint-Sulpice à Paris," ANQ *Rapport*, 1969: 273. [Sœur Saint-Jean l'Évangéliste] [Guillelmine Raizenne], *Notes généalogiques sur la famille Raizenne* ([Ottawa, 1917]). J.-B.-A. Allaire, *Histoire de la paroisse de Saint-Denis-sur-Richelieu (Canada)* (Saint-Hyacinthe, Qué., 1905), 176. C. A. Baker, *True stories of New England captives carried to Canada during the old French and Indian wars* (Cambridge, Mass., 1897), 235–49. C.-P. Beaubien, *Le Sault-au-Récollet, ses rapports avec les premiers temps de la colonie; mission-paroisse* (Montréal, 1898), 182–84, 192–95, 201, 212–18. [Prosper Cloutier], *Histoire de la paroisse de Champlain* (2v., Trois-Rivières, Qué., 1915–17), 2: 144–45. [É.-M. Faillon], *Mémoires particuliers pour servir à l'histoire de l'Église de l'Amérique du Nord* (2v., Paris, 1852–53). Lemire-Marsolais et Lambert, *Hist. de la CND de Montréal*, 4: 237–39, 380–81; vols.5–6. Sulte, *Hist. des Canadiens-français*, vol.6. Trudel, *L'Église canadienne*, 2: 338, 347.

RAMAGE, JOHN, miniaturist and goldsmith; b. *c.* 1748 in Dublin (Republic of Ireland); d. 24 Oct. 1802 in Montreal, Lower Canada.

John Ramage entered the school of the Dublin Society of Artists in 1763. By 1772 he was in Halifax, N.S., where he was sued for small debts that year and in 1774. At Boston, Mass., in 1775, he was painting miniatures on ivory, a popular portrait form of the time. That December, some six months after Bunker Hill, he was a member of the Loyal Irish Volunteers, which was charged with patrolling the streets at night; he joined the British evacuation to Halifax on 17 March 1776.

Nine days prior to his departure from Boston, Ramage had married Victoria Ball. According to the Reverend Mather BYLES of Halifax, he left Victoria in Boston and by March 1777 had married a Mrs Taylor, whose identity remains a mystery. It has been stated by Walter George Strickland, in a work published in 1913, that Ramage contracted a marriage with a woman whose maiden name was Elizabeth Liddel. It may be that this woman was Mrs Taylor. But the date of the marriage to Elizabeth is uncertain. Strickland affirmed that it occurred before Ramage left Dublin and that Elizabeth died in 1784. If Strickland is right, Ramage was guilty of double bigamy in marrying Mrs Taylor in Halifax. Be that as it may, Victoria, who followed Ramage to Halifax, obtained a divorce and returned to Boston.

Ramage left Halifax before mid June 1777 "to avoid the further Pursuits of the Law," according to Byles, and went to New York. In 1780 he was a second lieutenant in the City Militia. A contemporary historian of art, William Dunlap, described him at about this time as "a handsome man of the middle size, with an intelligent countenance and lively eye." He dressed like a beau in scarlet coat, embroidered silk waistcoat, black satin breeches, silver-buckled shoes, and a cocked hat atop his powdered hair. In 1787, however, Dunlap noted that he was "evidently declining through fast living." On 29 January of that year Ramage was married yet again, to Catharine Collins; at the time he had two children by his marriage with Elizabeth Liddel, and he and Catharine were to have three more. Ramage apparently enjoyed success as a miniaturist at New York; according to Dunlap, he painted "all the military heroes or beaux of the garrison, and all the belles of the place." The leading families sat for him, as did the president of the new republic, George Washington, in October 1789. Ramage also made occasional life-size portraits in crayon or pastel.

The British evacuation of New York in 1783 may, however, have affected Ramage's business. Six years later he was suing for bad debts; by 1794 he was in dire straits, and in April a sheriff's sale of his property was announced. Fearful of imprisonment for debt, Ramage fled to Montreal. En route he narrowly escaped drowning but contracted a fever. When he reached Montreal, probably in May, he was in a state of "galloping consumption."

Ramage arrived during a period of acute political tension in Lower Canada. American secret emissaries, favourable to the French revolution, had rendered British officials suspicious of anyone coming from the United States [see David McLane*; Robert PRESCOTT]. After five weeks in bed recuperating from his journey, Ramage found himself in jail, having been denounced as an American sympathizer. "I should have staid where I was," he lamented to his wife, who had remained in New York, "as I think the Accomoda-tion in the gaol in New York is much better, which is all they Could do with me there." Denouncing to her "this Modern Inquisition" at Montreal, he claimed that the accusation against him had resulted from a malicious misconstruction of opinions he had expressed during a stopover at Albany, N.Y., "for there is no sutch thing as a person speaking on Government matters here without Danger." After a month in prison, he was discharged by a grand jury, thanks to the support of several leading Montrealers acquainted with his loyalism during the American revolution, and two letters of recommendation obtained from Colonel Alured Clarke* in 1783. Ramage's anger at his treatment did not push him so far as to demand redress, however. "I am Desired by the Chief Judge [Sir James Monk*] to drop the matter," he wrote to his wife, "as the times are so very Precarious and great aprehensions [exist] of the Canadians Rising into an open insurrection." As late as 1795 he was still complaining of "this Despottick government," adding that its subjects were "the most narrow contracted People I ever came among."

Prior to his imprisonment Ramage had planned to proceed to Quebec, of which town he had "the greatest Expectation." There he hoped to find encouragement from Lieutenant-Colonel George Beckwith and an old Boston acquaintance, Thomas Aston COFFIN, civil secretary and controller of public accounts of Lower Canada. Whether he went or not, his financial situation apparently continued to prevent him from sending money to his wife. In 1795 he claimed that, although he had painted several pictures since his arrival (among the best he had ever executed, he added), he had been paid for only two. In February 1796 he wrote of having done "Some very Extraordinary pictures Lately Sutch as was never Seen in Montreal before." However, as their long separation continued, and as she still received little money, Catharine began to entertain suspicions of Ramage's sincerity. In November 1797 he protested "Some things in your Letters that racks my very soul." "Want of money has been the only thing that has Prevented me from flying to your Arms," he assured her, "as I have never been three weeks at a time in health Since I came to this Place, by my fretting and anxiety of mind for you and my Poor dear Children." In January 1802 he willed his entire estate to his wife and children. They seem never to have rejoined him.

Towards the end of his life Ramage may have obtained some patronage from the family circle of the Montreal merchant James McGILL. A miniature of McGill has been attributed to him. Moreover, the artist's death in October 1802 occurred in the home of one Desrivières, perhaps a son or relative by marriage of McGill's wife, Charlotte Trottier Desrivières, née Guillimin. However, Ramage's exile among a population he disdained apparently remained friendless to the end: his burial record was signed only by the

Ramsay

rector, clerk, and sexton of Christ Church. Typical of Ramage's fortunes was the fate of a land petition he had submitted in February 1802: he was allowed 700 acres of land in Kilkenny Township, but the grant came a few days after his death; moreover, the township was not erected until 30 years later, by which time the allocation had been forgotten.

If the miniature of McGill is indeed Ramage's work it is the sole trace of his artistic production in either Halifax or Montreal. It and miniatures of American sitters, often in chased gold frames of Ramage's own execution and more beautiful than any used by other miniaturists of his time, are reasonably accomplished, precise in drawing, and competent in the handling of colour. However, in the true late 18th-century fashion, established by such leading painters of the period as George Romney, Thomas Lawrence, and Gilbert Stuart, they generally concentrate on prettiness of face, costume, and coiffure. None the less, their excellence bears out Dunlap's affirmation that Ramage was "the best artist in his branch in America."

R. H. HUBBARD

[The miniature of James McGill ascribed to John Ramage is in the McCord Museum. Ramage's portrait of George Washington survives in several versions, one of them being in the Metropolitan Museum (New York). Isabel Stevenson Monro and Kate M. Monro, *Index to reproductions of American paintings; a guide to pictures occurring in more than eight hundred books* (New York, 1948), 520–21, lists about 40 works in public and private collections in the United States. The fullest account of Ramage is John Hill Morgan's monograph, *A sketch of the life of John Ramage, miniature painter* (New York, 1930). It is based on the one contemporary account, William Dunlap, *A history of the rise and progress of the arts of design in the United States*, ed. Rita Weiss, intro. J. T. Flexner (2v. in 3, New York, 1969), 1: 226–27, and on documents gathered from Halifax, Boston, New York, and Montreal, as well as on letters supplied by the Ramage family. R.H.H.]

PAC, RG 1, L3ᴸ: 1668, 1772, 5232–63, 58084–91, 79408–15. W. G. Strickland, *A dictionary of Irish artists . . .* (2v., Dublin and London, 1913), 2: 272–73. R. M. Rosenfeld, "Miniatures and silhouettes in Montreal, 1760–1860" (MA thesis, Concordia Univ., Montreal, 1981). H. B. Wehle and Theodore Bolton, *American miniatures, 1730–1850 . . . & a biographical dictionary of the artists* (Garden City, N.Y., 1927; repr. New York, 1970).

RAMSAY, DAVID, sailor and fur trader; b. probably *c.* 1740 in Leven (Fife), Scotland; d. in or after 1810, probably in Upper Canada.

David Ramsay enlisted as a ship's boy in the Royal Navy and served in the sieges of Louisbourg, Île Royale (Cape Breton Island), in 1758 and Quebec in 1759. Having been posted in 1763 to a British patrol vessel on Lake Ontario, he elected to remain in North America upon his discharge in 1765. At first he worked for an unnamed Montreal fur trader, journeying as far as the upper Great Lakes. In 1768 he was arrested by the commandant at Fort Niagara (near Youngstown, N.Y.) for causing some kind of trouble and was sent to Montreal, where he was held in the guardhouse for several days.

In the fall of 1771 Ramsay undertook a trading expedition with his 17-year-old brother, George. They travelled from Schenectady, N.Y., to the mouth of Kettle Creek, on the north shore of Lake Erie, and from there went some miles upstream to winter with a group of Indians, mainly Mississauga Ojibwas. Exactly what happened during the winter is not clear, but Ramsay obviously did not get along with his clients. He later claimed that the Indians had repeatedly threatened to kill him if he did not give them rum. The Indians said that he had been "drunk and mad" all winter. In March Ramsay killed and scalped a warrior named Wandagan and two women while the rest of the band was absent. The brothers then fled as far as Long Point, on Lake Erie, where some Mississaugas caught up with them. The Indians tied them up but then began drinking. Getting loose, Ramsay killed and scalped five of the party, including a woman and a child. He and his brother proceeded to Fort Erie (Ont.), where Ramsay was arrested and sent to Fort Niagara and then to Montreal.

Ramsay claimed that he had acted in self-defence but the British authorities responsible for the west were incensed. Sir William Johnson*, superintendent of northern Indians, bitterly observed, "Killing a Woman and Child, and then Scalping them afterwards is inexcusable, and the Circumstance of his being able to do all this, is an evident proof that he was not in the danger he represents, and that the Inds. were too much in Liquor, to execute any bad purpose." Johnson was well aware, however, of the ways of white juries in cases of crimes committed against Indians. "I don't think he will Suffer, had he killed a Hundred," he wrote and Ramsay did not. Despite the efforts of the British commander-in-chief, Thomas Gage*, who informed Johnson "I am trying all I can to get Evidence, for if what is related concerning his Cruelty is true no wretch ever more deserved the Gallows," a Montreal jury acquitted him for want of evidence. "I am to presume that nothing was left undone that could be effected to bring Moʳ Ramsay to that Punishment his atrocious Crime deserved," wrote the secretary of state for the American Colonies to Lieutenant Governor Hector Theophilus Cramahé*.

During the American revolution Ramsay served again in the Royal Navy, but once that conflict was over he returned to live among the relatives of the Indians he had killed. The Mississaugas resented his presence, but fearing British retaliation if he were harmed, they simply insisted that he pay the relatives of his victims a certain amount in goods and rum.

When the Indians were drunk, however, they still threatened revenge. In 1793 at the rapids of the Miamis River (Maumee, Ohio), a son of one of his victims intended to kill him, and he was put on a boat for Detroit (Mich.) by Indian agent Alexander McKee*. Ramsay's relationship with the Mississaugas was indeed a complex one. Although he remarked to Patrick Campbell*, a Scottish traveller for whom he was a guide in 1792, that "there was no dependence to be placed in an Indian," he wrote out a petition on behalf of the Mississaugas in the winter of 1793. As late as 1795 he was reported to be living among them – presumably on the sizeable tract of land between present-day Hamilton and Oakville that he had persuaded them to give him in 1789. Moreover, following the murder of Mississauga chief Wabakinine* by a soldier in 1796, Ramsay wrote a letter in support of his sons' petition for compensation in land. According to Lieutenant Governor SIMCOE, he was an adopted Indian.

In the white community Ramsay enjoyed a measure of respect. When Campbell met him he was earning his living carrying dispatches and money for people in the Niagara area. In July 1791 the Executive Council had approved his application for a grant of 600 acres and in 1801 he acquired lands in Kent County. When in 1810 he made out his will, he owned a brig, the *Thames of New York*.

Even in Ramsay's own lifetime the story of the killings had entered local folklore, and the form it took tells much about the attitudes towards native people held by early English-speaking settlers. In his *Voyages and travels of an Indian interpreter and trader* . . . (London, 1791), John Long* recounted the story as he had heard it at Michilimackinac (Mackinaw City, Mich.): some Potawatomis near Fort St Joseph (Niles, Mich.) had tied Ramsay to a stump while they prepared to roast him, but Ramsay's brother got them drunk and the traders escaped after killing the Indians. According to a more traditional account that lived on in the Long Point area until the 1890s at least, a party of nine Indians made an unprovoked attack on Ramsay one night at Long Point in 1760. Becoming drunk on his liquor, they decided to wait until morning before burning him, and while they slept Ramsay got free and killed them all. Although whites remembered "brave" Ramsay's heroic self-defence, Indians thought differently. Joseph Brant [THAYENDANEGEA], the distinguished Iroquois chief, termed him a "mischievous fellow" and an "unworthy rascal."

DONALD B. SMITH

AO, RG 53, ser.1, A, doc.A7 [bound between p.14 and f.1]. PAC, RG 1, L3, 423: R2/7; RG 8, I (C ser.), 251: 116. PRO, CO 42/32: f.27. P. Campbell, *Travels in North America* (Langton and Ganong), 191–206. *Corr. of Lieut. Governor Simcoe* (Cruikshank), 4: 114. *The documentary history of the state of New-York* . . . , ed. E. B. O'Callaghan (4v., Albany, N.Y., 1849–51), 2: 994. *Johnson papers* (Sullivan et al.), 8: 130, 483–84, 497, 512; 12: 967. "Petitions for grants of land" (Cruikshank), *OH*, 26: 359. [Kahkewaquonaby], *Life and journals of Kah-ke-wa-quo-na-by (Rev. Peter Jones), Wesleyan missionary* (Toronto, 1860), 185. John Long, *Voyages and travels of an Indian interpreter and trader* . . . (London, 1791), 147. E. A. Owen, *Pioneer sketches of Long Point settlement* . . . (Toronto, 1898; repr. Belleville, Ont., 1972), 39. J. H. Coyne, "David Ramsay and Long Point in legend and history," *RSC Trans.*, 3rd ser., 13 (1919), sect.II: 111–26. F. C. Hamil, "David Ramsay and the Lees of Kent County," *Western Ontario Hist. Notes* ([London, Ont.]), 2 (1944): 13–15. Donald Smith, "The Mississauga and David Ramsay," *Beaver*, outfit 305 (spring 1975): 4–8.

RANVOYZÉ (Ranvoizé), FRANÇOIS, gold- and silversmith; b. 25 Dec. 1739 at Quebec, son of Étienne Ranvoizé, a button maker, and Jeanne Poitras; m. there 25 Nov. 1771 Marie-Vénérande Pelerin, and they had ten children; d. there 8 Oct. 1819.

François Ranvoyzé had some contact with metal working from his earliest days, since his father made buttons out of brass or copper. He was only ten, however, when his father died. There are a number of indications that Ranvoyzé was apprenticed to the silversmith Ignace-François Delezenne*, although no date can be specified; the usual age for beginning apprenticeship was between 12 and 16. Delezenne's shop was on Rue de la Montagne, a few steps from the Ranvoyzés' house. From 1756 to 1759 Delezenne used the services of many silversmiths and apprentices, sometimes taking them on by written contract, to make phenomenal quantities of the jewellery bartered for furs; Ranvoyzé may have been one of their number. In addition, some of Ranvoyzé's decorative idiom bears a certain similarity to the spirit of the primitive and repetitive motifs found in trade silver.

Ranvoyzé likely completed his apprenticeship by the age of 21, as was customary; the date would have been around 1760 or 1761. Then he probably worked with Delezenne as either journeyman or partner. That there were close links between the two silversmiths was evident on several occasions. In 1771, when the contract for his marriage with Marie-Vénérande Pelerin was signed, Ranvoyzé called Delezenne "his friend who is a father to him." Again, the numerous resemblances in shape and decoration between their articles of silverware can only be understood as the result of close collaboration. This hypothesis might partially explain the fact that Delezenne changed his mark from IF,D to DZ, a mark which suggests two letters from his own name and also the Z in Ranvoyzé, a letter not to be found in the name of any other silversmith of the period. From 1771 until 1775 they

Ranvoyzé

lived within a few steps of each other; in 1772 Ranvoyzé chose Delezenne as godfather for his first-born son; in 1778 during the course of her incredible matrimonial adventures, Marie-Catherine Delezenne*, the silversmith's daughter, was locked up in the Ranvoyzés' house [see Pierre de SALES Laterrière].

When he married, however, Ranvoyzé already owned a "silversmithing shop," with all the necessary tools, and also had savings of 1,500 "shillings in legal currency . . . resulting from his work and industry." The first known professional account that he rendered was for a payment dated 1771 for repairs to two objects belonging to the fabrique of Notre-Dame-des-Victoires at Quebec. Ranvoyzé was living on Rue Saint-Jean at the time; from 1780 he lived, at first as a tenant, in a house that he subsequently bought from the estate of Pascal Soulard. Apparently he remained there until he died. The long and complicated transaction to acquire the dwelling, which involved several heirs, shows Ranvoyzé's persistence, tact, and patience.

There were few events of note in Ranvoyzé's family and social life. Seven of the ten children born of his marriage are mentioned in a will dated 1 April 1817, which was drawn up a year after his wife's death. In addition to his property on Rue Saint-Jean, Ranvoyzé left two others, on Rue des Remparts and Rue des Ursulines, as well as sums amounting to £2,000. At that time two of his four daughters were married, his sons Louis and Étienne* were in practice as notaries, and François-Ignace* was a priest. The division of the property amongst them was done on a very personal basis. Ranvoyzé's public life was limited to his role as a churchwarden of Notre-Dame in Quebec in 1798–99, his affiliation with the Quebec Fire Society, and his financial contribution to the Loyal and Patriotic Society of the Province of Lower Canada in 1813. In 1802 he received two lots in Simpson Township as a reward for service in the militia during the American invasion [see Benedict ARNOLD; Richard Montgomery*]. He soon sold these properties to the merchant Josias Wurtele* for £7 and "other favourable considerations." In 1795 Ranvoyzé joined with six other silversmiths to challenge a law regulating the use of forges [see Michel FORTON]. Following his death in 1819, notices published in several newspapers called him "an old and respectable citizen"; he was buried in the Cimetière des Pauvres.

All the Ranvoyzé children enjoyed a degree of financial and social security that had certainly been attained at the cost of constant efforts to educate and bring them up. The portraits of the parents, which have been attributed to François Baillairgé*, depict Ranvoyzé as a worthy bourgeois, smiling, energetic, honest, hard-working, and well established. It seems clear that he was not involved in contentious lawsuits,

sizeable business deals, or repeated speculation in real estate. In short, he was a quiet man who devoted his life to his family and laboured assiduously turning out a silversmith's wares.

By contrast, Ranvoyzé's work is fascinating in its volume, diversity, quality, and complexity. It is estimated to include several hundred items, perhaps a thousand or more. Their wide dispersal today, reflecting the fact that frequently they are no longer in use for their original purposes, explains why no one has yet managed to compile a descriptive catalogue or make a serious study of them. Fortunately the account-books of the fabriques make some comment possible. There are approximately 200 entries concerning the silversmith, his works, or the repairs he undertook. The statements of account occur at regular intervals from 1771 to 1818. He therefore was engaged in professional activity steadily for at least 48 years, exclusive of any apprenticeship.

Ranvoyzé had such a hold on the market for religious silver that from 1774 until 1794 he worked for a dozen parishes in the Montreal region. It is true that at this period the silversmiths in the town, Michael ARNOLDI, Robert CRUICKSHANK, Charles Duval*, and Pierre HUGUET, dit Latour, were channelling their energies into the production of trade silver. In the 1790s Laurent Amiot* also received a number of orders from the fabriques, and so gradually reduced Ranvoyzé's clientele in the Montreal region. From 1803 this market passed into the hands of Pierre Huguet, who even received orders from as far away as the lower St Lawrence. Ranvoyzé never lacked work, however; in the course of his career several new parishes came into being, and the old ones frequently called upon his services to refurbish or augment what they already possessed.

The requirements of his clientele, which were set down when an order was received, partially explain the variety in form and style of Ranvoyzé's work. Indeed, he knew better than any other silversmith how to adapt his wares to his clients' wishes. His versatility, linked to a creative imagination, enabled him to satisfy every taste. Throughout his career Ranvoyzé copied objects of different styles, often at a client's specific request. His work, therefore, was poles apart from the uniform and repetitive style imposed by Amiot, and that is what makes it so interesting. Ranvoyzé always surprises us with a unique or different shape or decorative motif.

In attending to damaged or old objects, Ranvoyzé made repairs or added further decoration. This was certainly the most economical solution for a fabrique. On the other hand, by putting his mark over earlier ones Ranvoyzé has baffled a number of art historians with the seemingly inconsistent and conflicting decorative styles on the same object.

Sometimes Ranvoyzé entered the prices of the

Ranvoyzé

material and of the workmanship separately on his invoices. Only wealthy clients could afford a richly decorated object that required much of the silversmith's time. Others had to be satisfied with models turned out in several copies, as were certain chalices, processional crosses, and boxes for holy oil. But cost was only one of the relevant factors; in the choice of a silversmith or of the style to be given to a liturgical object, the taste of the parish priest was the preponderant one.

It is very difficult to give a clear picture of the chronological evolution of Ranvoyzé's work. Only about a hundred religious pieces can be dated with precision. Moreover, given the doubtful accuracy of entries in account-books and the hazards of disappearance and destruction, it is uncertain whether this restricted sample is representative. For certain types of object Ranvoyzé reproduced the same models throughout his career: the processional cross in the Séminaire de Québec (1774) is identical to the one at Sainte-Anne-de-Beaupré (1814), and the Ursulines' chalice (1779) to the one at L'Islet (1810) (both being copied from pieces in Louis XIV style). Examination of the ewers, boxes for holy oil, candlesticks, and piscinae yields little information that would enable us to characterize periods in the evolution of Ranvoyzé's style. Only with the following objects can appropriate divisions be established: aspersoria, chalices, ciboria, censers, incense boxes, sanctuary lamps, and salvers.

In the period 1771–81 Ranvoyzé copied forms and decorative motifs from French pieces imported during the French régime and also from the works of Paul Lambert*, *dit* Saint-Paul, and Ignace-François Delezenne. During these early years one motif he seems to have used particularly was a series of small circles irregularly spaced within two lines forming a semicircle. Primitive and naïve, this motif calls to mind the sort of decoration found on trade jewellery. It sometimes crowns a serrated, stylized, and symmetrical leaf that he also used a great deal.

The ciborium of Saint-Roch-des-Aulnets (Saint-Roch-des-Aulnaies), which was made in 1782, is the first object with the distinctive style that made Ranvoyzé's reputation: a decoration of foliage and large exotic fruit running all over the surface freely and in charming fashion. In the 1790s the fruit seems to be used less often and the plant motifs are organized more into the shape of an elongated frieze. In 1798 Ranvoyzé first used a geometrical decoration consisting of garlands of laurel leaves and large bosses inspired by the Louis XVI style brought back from Paris by Laurent Amiot in 1787; this style was, however, to be more characteristic of his work from 1803. The last object decorated with plant motifs that has been found, the aspersorium at Charlesbourg, dates, indeed, from that year; significantly, these motifs are crushed in the vice of two geometrical ones.

As for the numerous chalices copied from the one by Guillaume Loir that is kept at the church of Notre-Dame in Montreal, they were all made in the 1780s.

It is surprising that Ranvoyzé was able to produce such a large collection without the help of apprentices or partners. Some authors have claimed that Joseph-Christophe Delezenne was his apprentice; in fact it seems that Delezenne worked with his father. On the other hand, numerous historical studies, on the basis of a single oral source, report that Laurent Amiot may have done his apprenticeship with Ranvoyzé. But these accounts are so contradictory that it is risky to credit them. According to other hypotheses Ranvoyzé's sons, Étienne and François-Ignace, worked with him. One could even add to the list the name of his brother, Louis Ranvoyzé, for as a gunsmith and locksmith he was already working in metals. There is, however, no documentary evidence to support these theories, which have been advanced to explain the wide variety of marks used by the silversmith, and in particular the marks ER, FIR, and IFR. But the gold monstrance at L'Islet, whose fabrication is abundantly documented, was entirely Ranvoyzé's work, and it bears three of the versions of his marks, including the well-known ER. Moreover, a variation with letters in italics was sometimes badly stamped, thus giving the impression that the vertical line of the R is split, forming an I. As for the styles of all the works bearing variants, they are quite comparable to the pieces definitively attributed to Ranvoyzé. It is possible, therefore, that Ranvoyzé was able to turn out this vast quantity of work by himself, for throughout a very long career all his energies were devoted to his profession. The variety of marks that he used would be but one more expression of his personality, corresponding to the diversity of forms and ornamentation in his creations.

Although François Ranvoyzé's religious work predominates, he did turn out some important pieces of hollow-ware and a good deal of flatware. These items are, however, of little help in establishing the various periods in the evolution of his style or in dating or understanding its development. Nor does he display his greatest originality in this part of his work. As for trade silver, a single object has been attributed to him. Ranvoyzé was the only one of the Quebec silversmiths to leave three items of solid gold – the chalice, ciborium, and monstrance at L'Islet – and he remains unquestionably the most creative and the most imaginative of them. Any anthology of great Quebec artists would have to include his name.

ROBERT DEROME and JOSÉ MÉNARD

[Some of François Ranvoyzé's work is in the Henry Birks Collection of Silver at the National Gallery of Canada

Réaume

(Ottawa) and at the Musée du Québec (Québec). The Fonds Morisset, held at MAC-CD, contains files on Ranvoyzé (2, R213.5/F825) and on Ignace-François Delezenne (2, D348.3/I24.3), both of which provided a great deal of information for this article.

There is still no full biographical study of François Ranvoyzé and no descriptive catalogue of his works and marks. For an account of his early career, clientele, and style, and a résumé of his work, consult *François Ranvoyzé, orfèvre, 1739–1819* (Québec, 1968), a catalogue of an exhibition held at the Musée du Québec. His apprenticeship and service as a journeyman is examined by Robert Derome in "Delezenne, le maître de Ranvoyzé," *Vie des Arts* (Montréal), 21 (1976), no.83: 56–58. Also valuable is the same author's "Delezenne, les orfèvres, l'orfèvrerie, 1740–1790" (MA thesis, univ. de Montréal, 1974), 52, 68–76, 106–7, 172–74. Gérard Morisset*'s *François Ranvoyzé* (Québec, 1942), remains the standard treatment of his activities and the principal stylistic analysis of his output.   R.D. and J.M.]

ANQ-Q, CE1-1, 26 déc. 1739, 4 sept. 1749, 27 oct. 1750, 25 sept. 1758, 7 sept. 1772, 16 nov. 1773, 26 nov. 1774, 10 mars 1776, 25 août 1777, 9 mai 1779, 19 mars 1782, 1er déc. 1785, 3 mai 1787, 17 avril 1789, 2 juill. 1804, 7 janv. 1805; CN1-23, 5 févr. 1813, 5 nov. 1814, 1er avril 1817; CN1-25, 3 févr. 1778; CN1-79, 23 juill. 1756; CN1-83, 14 mars 1787; CN1-178, 15 mai 1799, 10 avril 1801; CN1-189, 9 févr. 1767; CN1-205, 30 nov. 1778, 7 juin 1779; CN1-207, 27 nov. 1752, 25 avril 1771, 13 mai 1772, 21 août 1773; CN1-212, 21 déc. 1816; CN1-230, 13 nov. 1795; CN1-248, 24 nov. 1771; CN1-262, 11 juin 1803; CN1-285, 20 févr. 1801, 26 juill. 1802. AP, Notre-Dame de Québec, Cahiers des délibérations de la fabrique, 1768; Notre-Dame-des-Victoires (Québec), Livres de comptes, 1771. ASQ, Lettres, P, 22, 29, 35. *Le Courrier du Bas-Canada* (Montréal), 16 oct. 1819. *Quebec Gazette*, 3 Jan. 1820. *Quebec Mercury*, 5 March 1816, 12 Oct. 1819. Michel Cauchon, *Jean-Baptiste Roy-Audy, 1778–c.1848* (Québec, 1971). Langdon, *Canadian silversmiths*, 65. Gérard Morisset, *Évolution d'une pièce d'argenterie* (Québec, 1943), 6–7. Traquair, *Old silver of Quebec*. Marius Barbeau, "Anciens orfèvres de Québec," *La Presse* (Montréal), 1er juin 1935: 73. E. A. Jones, "Old church silver in Canada," *RSC Trans.*, 3rd ser., 12 (1918), sect.II: 148–49. Gérard Morisset, "L'œuvre capricieuse de François Ranvoyzé," *L'Action catholique* (Québec), 18 mars 1942: 4; "Les vases d'or de l'église de l'Islet," *La Patrie* (Montréal), 12 mars 1950: 18, 42. "Ranvoyzé, très illustre orfèvre canadien-français," *L'Événement* (Québec), 12 mars 1942: 3, 10. P.-G. Roy, "La famille de Jean Amyot," *BRH*, 25 (1919): 232.

RÉAUME (Rheaume), CHARLES, interpreter and farmer; b. 4 Feb. 1743 in Detroit (Mich.), son of Hyacinthe Réaume, a shoemaker, and Agathe de Lacelle; m. Angélique Beauchamp; d. 20 Dec. 1813 in Kingston, Upper Canada.

By the mid 1760s Charles Réaume had begun his career as an interpreter for the British Indian Department at Detroit. Nor was his activity confined to that vicinity: in 1778 Major Arent Schuyler DePeyster* at Michilimackinac (Mackinaw City, Mich.) entrusted him with correspondence for Governor Frederick HALDIMAND at Montreal, to be taken via the French River (Ont.). His domicile continued to be the region of Detroit, however; he was listed the same year as one of three captains in the Indian Department under Jehu Hay*, the deputy superintendent there.

Réaume also became the proprietor of lots on both sides of the Detroit River, some of which were acquired from the Indians with whom he dealt. In 1776, "in consideration of the sincere friendship and affection that we have for Charles Réaume," Egushwa* and two other principal chiefs of the Ottawa village on the south (Canadian) shore granted him a tract near by. The Detroit census of 1782 shows him to be a well-to-do farmer, whose holdings included a female slave (another slave had died earlier the same year). In 1786 the Potawatomis granted him property on the River Raisin (Mich.).

Réaume not only obtained lands himself; he also played a role in the acquisition of lands by others. In 1780 he acted as an interpreter when the Wyandots conveyed lands on the south shore to Father Pierre-Philippe Potier*, and in 1800 he witnessed the formal conveyance to the crown of the greater part of the Huron Church Reserve, on which the new town of Sandwich (Windsor), Upper Canada, had been begun in 1797.

Réaume achieved some status in the Detroit community, serving from 1781 to 1795 as a warden of Notre-Dame-de-l'Assomption, the south-shore parish. However, an incident that took place in 1797, a year of particularly bad relations between the Indian Department and the local commanding officer, suggests the limitations of Réaume's social standing as well, perhaps, as the haughty character of Captain Hector McLean. Servant-maids at the newly built Fort Malden (Amherstburg), Upper Canada, were reported to have prevented Réaume from seeing McLean by pushing him downstairs, he not being a gentleman and therefore not fit company for an officer. In 1799 McLean approved a list certified by Réaume of 270 Ottawas and Chippewas who had been settled at the Chenal Écarté (on the eastern boundary of the Walpole Island Indian Reserve).

The British naval defeat of 10 Sept. 1813 on Lake Erie [see Robert Heriot Barclay*] resulted in the abandonment of the western frontier and an overland retreat to the northeast [see Henry Procter*]. The hardships had a disastrous effect on the ageing Réaume's health. Somewhere on the Thames River he and his family separated from the British forces, and by early December they had arrived in Kingston. There, on 20 December, he died "of fatigue." During the half century he had served in the Indian Department, Charles Réaume appears to have discharged his responsibilities with such fidelity that he enjoyed the good opinion of both the British and the multitude of native people he encountered.

R. ALAN DOUGLAS

Archdiocese of Detroit, Chancery Office, Reg. des baptêmes, mariages, et sépultures de Sainte-Anne (Detroit), 2 Feb. 1704–30 Dec. 1848, I: 229 (transcript at DPL, Burton Hist. Coll.). *John Askin papers* (Quaife), 1: 170, 249–50, 325–26, 331–33. *Mich. Pioneer Coll.*, 9 (1886): 371–73, 485; 10 (1886): 602; 15 (1889): 585; 20 (1892): 544–45, 641–42. *Windsor border region* (Lajeunesse).

RENAUD D'AVÈNE DES MÉLOIZES, NICOLAS, army officer and seigneur; b. 22 Nov. 1729 at Quebec, son of Nicolas-Marie Renaud* d'Avène Des Méloizes, officer in the colonial regular troops, and Angélique Chartier de Lotbinière; m. 5 Jan. 1767 Agathe-Louise de Fresnoy, and they had three children; d. 30 Aug. 1803 in Blois, France.

Like many an officer's son Nicolas Renaud d'Avène Des Méloizes began serving in the colonial regular troops at an early age, becoming a cadet on 1 Jan. 1741. He participated in the Acadian campaign of 1746–47 [*see* Jean-Baptiste-Nicolas-Roch de Ramezay*] and was commissioned second ensign on 15 Feb. 1748, then ensign on 1 April 1753. From 1753 to 1755 he served in the operations in the Ohio valley [*see* Ange Duquesne* de Menneville] and distinguished himself sufficiently to reach the rank of lieutenant on 1 May 1757.

In February and March 1758 Des Méloizes, acting as attorney for his brother-in-law Michel-Jean-Hugues Péan*, attended to hiring a dozen voyageurs for the *poste du Nord* in the *pays d'en haut*. That same year he took part in the battle at Carillon (near Ticonderoga, N.Y.), and on 1 Jan. 1759 he was promoted captain and adjutant of the garrison at Quebec. Governor Vaudreuil [Pierre de Rigaud*] had recommended him warmly, and the king's order declared: "This officer is a master of all the details connected with the adjutant's duties. He has carried them out with all possible intelligence and dispatch in all the recent campaigns, and he is capable of assisting the adjutant general."

Des Méloizes distinguished himself again in the battle of Sainte-Foy on 28 April 1760 [*see* François de Lévis*], performing "prodigious acts of valour," according to Vaudreuil; his brother Louis-François was killed close by him. Seriously wounded in the thigh by a shell fragment on 13 May, he remained in the Hôpital Général of Quebec, since the surgeon refused to evacuate him. On the strength of the agreement for the exchange of prisoners James Murray* promised that he would be allowed to rejoin the French army as soon as he had recovered, but changed his mind and decided to send him on parole to France. Des Méloizes arrived in La Rochelle early in December 1760 and received the cross of Saint-Louis on 24 March 1761. For a short time he was suspected of complicity in Intendant Bigot*'s malfeasance, but no evidence could be brought against him. On 8 May 1764, therefore, he received a warrant for a pension of 800 *livres*. Although Des Méloizes had, it seems, always been considered "an outstanding officer because of his courage and talents," he then quit the service for good.

In November of that year Des Méloizes was at Quebec. He saw to the managing of the seigneury of Neuville, which he had inherited from his father. He made land grants and bought and sold farms. In September 1765 he turned over his seigneury to Joseph Brassard* Deschenaux for 40,000 *livres*. Then he returned to France. In 1787 he represented the nobility of the bailliage of Senlis at the provincial assembly of Île-de-France.

ÉTIENNE TAILLEMITE

AD, Loir-et-Cher (Blois), État civil, Blois, 30 août 1803. AN, Col., C^{11A}, 104, 105; D^{2C}, 48: f.349; E, 126 (dossier Renaud d'Avène Des Méloizes). ANQ-Q, CE1-1, 22 nov. 1729; CN1-250, 11, 15, 21, 23, 24 févr., 1er, 8, 9, 14 mars 1758; 28 nov., 2, 8, 20 déc. 1764; 23–25 janv., 4, 26, 30 juill., 1er août 1765. Bibliothèque nationale (Paris), MSS, Fr., Chérin 170. Nicolas Renaud d'Avène Des Méloizes, "Journal militaire tenu par Nicolas Renaud d'Avène Des Méloizes, ch^{er}, seigneur de Neuville, au Canada du 19 juillet 1756 au 30 octobre de la même année," ANQ *Rapport*, 1928–29: 4–86. P.-G. Roy, *Inv. concessions*, 2: 27; "La famille Renaud d'Avène Des Méloizes," *BRH*, 13 (1907): 161–81, 193–209.

RICHARDS, WILLIAM, fur trader and watercolour artist; b. *c.* 1785 in the Fort Albany (Ont.) district of Hudson Bay, possibly at Gloucester House (on Washi Lake, Ont.), son of HBC labourer and interpreter John Richards, and grandson of HBC surgeon William Richards of Neath, Wales; d. 9 July 1811 at Moose Factory (Ont.).

The short and rather humble career of William Richards as a Hudson's Bay Company canoeman and cooper in James Bay offers little clue as to how he gained proficiency in a European artistic technique. He apparently never travelled to Europe, and whatever education or training he received clearly resulted from the assistance of senior colleagues rather than of British relatives. On only one occasion would he have met his grandfather: in 1794–95 when the latter was serving at Moose. The elder William had been at Albany and at Henley House (near the junction of the Albany and Kenogami rivers) between 1757 and 1769, when he returned home as a result of disputes with chief factor Humphrey Marten*; suspected of smuggling furs, he was then refused re-employment until 1794.

Young William's contacts with his mixed-blood father, John, were also marked by discontinuity after his first decade of life. Shortly before William's birth, John Richards and his brother Thomas had been hired as labourers at Albany at £6 annually. The London committee's terms suggest that they were not intended

Richmond and Lennox

to advance much higher: Edward Jarvis*, chief at Albany, was told that "in thus employing them as Englishmen, We do not however intend that they should ever be brought to England: We expect that their Abilities be applied to the best Purposes for our Interest." When their father returned to the bay, however, he managed to secure permission for John to travel back to Britain with him in 1795. John spent the next winter in Wales and rejoined the company in 1796. Within a year his "turbulent" nature, and perhaps his slim chance for advancement (despite his apparent literacy), led him to desert to the North West Company. There is no evidence that he saw his son William thereafter.

William is first mentioned in HBC records on 17 Nov. 1800, the day on which he was apprenticed by John Hodgson*, chief factor at Albany, to cooper James Inkster. In August 1802 he was serving aboard the Albany shallop. By late the next summer he and his uncle Thomas Richards, "a Boat steerer &c," had left for Moose; Thomas had requested permission for the trip, "to see his old Mother before she dies." Once at Moose, both men asked chief factor John Thomas* for contracts to serve there, evidently not realizing that such transfers required consent from London. Given "the present situation of affairs" at his post, which like other HBC establishments was employing native-born servants in increasing numbers to make up for a shortage of British labour, Thomas allowed them to stay, meanwhile forwarding their requests to London. The end result was that both uncle and nephew spent the rest of their careers mainly in the Moose area.

In 1804–5 William, a "Canoeman &c" at £8 per annum, served at New Brunswick House (on Brunswick Lake). In 1805–6 he was at Moose except for some inland trips to transport furs and trade goods and later to serve at Fort Kenogamissi (on Kenogamissi Lake). John Thomas characterized him in September 1806 as a good cooper and canoeman, "very zealous & active for the Trade." Thomas's support doubtless encouraged London to rehire Richards for another three years at the terms he asked, £20 annually, from the summer of 1807. After a few months at Fort Abitibi (near La Sarre, Que.) and a summer at Moose, Richards was sent aboard the Eastmain schooner in October 1807 as an extra hand. The onset of winter detained him at Eastmain (Que.) until January 1808, when he returned overland to Moose. During his visit unknown circumstances led Eastmain chief factor George Gladman to charge him with "mutinous refractory Conduct" and urge that he be fined as an example to others, but no fine is on record.

From January 1808 to March of the following year Richards continued as canoeman and cooper at Moose. But on 13 March 1809 John Thomas reported Richards ill and unable to work. In May he was "consumptive" and in September "in a rapid decline" although the doctors thought a trip to England might be helpful "next year *if he survives*." The next summer brought no improvement, and Thomas noted that Richards's "allowance of Wages &c must depend on what the charitable Board may please to grant him." Richards received his wages until he died on 9 July 1811 leaving his widow, Eleanor, and two sons. On that occasion Thomas (then Richards's father-in-law of some years' standing) mourned the death of "a useful Servant and remarkable for his genius in drawing."

Richards had been interested in art since at least 1805, when he is known to have ordered drawing paper and a box of paints from London. It is likely that Thomas encouraged Richards to paint so as to provide portrayals of company posts for the directors in London. Other HBC men, including Humphrey Marten, had used models or plans to describe the posts to their employers, but Richards was not merely a draughtsman: there is human interest as well in his illustration of ice-fishing, wood-cutting, and other local activities. One painting, for instance, is entitled *A man & his wife returning with a load of partridges from their tent*. All of the surviving paintings show fine detail, and in them Richards attains considerable realism despite some difficulties with perspective and scale. The attention paid to shading and to cloud effects above the flat James Bay landscape suggests that, aside from his own talent, Richards developed his skills with the aid of some colleague familiar with the techniques of his chosen medium.

JENNIFER S. H. BROWN

The PAM, HBCA, holds three water-colours by William Richards, entitled *A man & his wife returning with a load of partridges from their tent*, *A south-east view of Albany Factory*, and *A view of Eastmain Factory*; a fourth, untitled and unsigned, has been identified as being by Richards from its similarity to his *East view of Moose Factory*, in the collection of the Glenbow-Alberta Institute (Calgary).

Anglican Church of Canada, Diocese of Moosonee Arch. (Schumacher, Ont.), Diocese of Moosonee papers, ser.III, "Register of births, christenings, deaths and other occurrences at Moose Factory and its inland dependencies belonging to the Honble. Hudson's Bay Company" (mfm. at AO). PAM, HBCA, A.1/40, 43–44, 47; A.6/13; A.16/6, 16–17; A.30/4, 10; B.3/a/104–5; B.59/a/1–122; B.135/a/91–97; B.135/b/27; B.135/f/1–8; B.155/a/12; C.1/740–41. A. M. Johnson, "James Bay artist William Richards," *Beaver*, outfit 298 (summer 1967): 4–10.

RICHMOND and LENNOX, CHARLES LENNOX, 4th Duke of. *See* LENNOX

RIEDESEL, Freifrau zu EISENBACH, FRIEDE-RIKE CHARLOTTE LOUISE VON. *See* MASSOW

RIEUTORD, JEAN-BAPTISTE, doctor; b. *c*. 1733 in Gramont, France, son of Jacques Rieutord and Françoise Deray; m. first 11 Nov. 1760 Pélagie-

712

Roberts

Victoire Perron in Baie-Saint-Paul (Que.); m. secondly 7 July 1788 Marie-Josette Audette, *dit* Lapointe, widow of Samuel Jacobs*, in Trois-Rivières, Que.; d. there 27 March 1818.

Jean-Baptiste Rieutord left Bordeaux on the *Charmante Nancy* and came to New France in 1758, apparently as a military surgeon. Some authors have claimed, without citing sources, that his ship had been captured by the British. By January 1760 Rieutord was practising as a surgeon at Baie-Saint-Paul. In 1762 or early in 1763 he moved to Sainte-Anne-de-Beaupré, but a few months later he decided to settle in Château-Richer. Over 20 years he succeeded in securing a financial status comparing favourably with that of most of his colleagues who lived in the countryside. His landed property was worth 8,750 *livres* and he owed, at least by notarized obligation, only 600 *livres*.

In the spring of 1783, with his experience and success in the rural area behind him, Rieutord moved to the town of Trois-Rivières. He lived comfortably and could indulge in subscribing to the *Quebec Gazette* and owning a black female slave, amenities not within everyone's means. At the professional level his competence was officially recognized on 15 Dec. 1788, when he received a surgeon's licence. In 1790 he exposed the deplorable state of the Trois-Rivières jail, which he had visited at the request of the merchant Malcolm Fraser, whose son was imprisoned there. By 1792 the Ursulines considered it appropriate to make him their official doctor.

Rieutord spent considerable sums of money on some of his children. On 19 Sept. 1781 Thompson and Shaw, Quebec merchants, undertook to furnish his son Jean-Baptiste, who was just 17, with goods so that he could enter into trade at Quebec. Rieutord stood surety for him. The business soon met with disaster. On 5 Oct. 1782 the boy was sentenced to pay 3,360 *livres* to the merchant John JONES. On 24 Feb. 1784 Simon Fraser Sr and John YOUNG, assignees of the body of creditors of Thompson and Shaw, obtained an award of 7,728 *livres* against the Rieutords, father and son, in settlement of goods sold. Of this sum the father put up at least 5,374 *livres*. Subsequently the son decided to move to Saint-Ours and practise as a surgeon. Another son, Louis, who settled at Contrecœur at the end of the 18th century, also practised medicine, but it was François who took over from his father. François is believed to have gone to Europe in 1790, and he then went to study at Queen's College in New Brunswick, N.J., probably before 1793. He chose to practise in Trois-Rivières, where in 1797 he went into partnership with his father as a doctor, surgeon, and apothecary.

On 21 Oct. 1799, feeling the weight of his years and wishing "to free himself of temporal matters in order to attend solely to those concerning his salvation," Jean-Baptiste Rieutord renounced all claims regarding the surgical practice in favour of François, who undertook to support him until he died. His success surpassed his father's. In 1815 his personal estate was worth 12,270 *livres*, including 4,800 *livres* for his surgical instruments and medicines. He owned three farms, four houses in Trois-Rivières, and half of another building lot. His debtors owed him 40,456 *livres*. His liabilities amounted to only 816 *livres*, exclusive of 2,400 *livres* in fees owing to a notary. François Rieutord died less than a year after his father, on 1 Feb. 1819.

MARCEL CADOTTE and RENALD LESSARD

AAQ, 940 CD, II: 99. ANQ-MBF, CE1-48, 7 juill. 1788, 22 févr. 1802, 30 mars 1818, 3 févr. 1819; CN1-4, 21 oct. 1799; CN1-5, 12 juin, 17, 21 juill., 23 sept. 1783; 21 avril 1784; 15 oct. 1790; 16 déc. 1793; CN1-6, 22 févr. 1802, 9 avril 1818; CN1-32, 11 déc. 1816, 8 févr. 1819; CN1-79, 21 juin 1815. ANQ-Q, CE1-6, 24 août 1768; CE4-1, 11 nov. 1760; CN1-76, 28 avril 1762; 10 avril, 11 juin 1763; 26, 29 mars 1764; 31 mars, 25 août 1766; 20 oct. 1769; 27 déc. 1779; 14 janv., 11 févr. 1780; CN1-77, 9 avril, 7, 11, 13, 16 août 1783; CN1-148, 22 mars 1764; CN1-205, 24 août 1781, 14 juill. 1784; CN1-224, 26 avril 1780; CN1-245, 19 sept. 1781; CN1-284, 25 sept. 1788, 13 juill. 1793; CN4-14, 8 nov. 1760; T13-1, mai 1776–mai 1785. PAC, MG 19, A2, ser.3, 5; MG 24, B1, 46; RG 4, B28, 47: 69. *Le Journal des Trois-Rivières* (Trois-Rivières, Qué.), 29 juill. 1886. *Quebec Gazette*, 7 Feb. 1771, 7 Oct. 1790, 17 July 1794, 24 Nov. 1803. M.-J. et G. Ahern, *Notes pour l'hist. de la médecine*, 451–53. "Les docteurs Rieutord père et fils," *BRH*, 18 (1912): 3–7.

ROBERTS, CHARLES, army officer; b. *c.* 1772 in England; d. 4 May 1816 in London, England.

Little is known about Charles Roberts apart from his career in North America. He was commissioned as an ensign in the British army in 1795 and was immediately afterwards sent to the West Indies, where he saw some ten years of service, chiefly in Trinidad, with the 57th and the 37th Foot. He succeeded to a captaincy by purchase in 1801 but suffered repeated attacks of fever, and by 1806, being no longer capable of regular service, he was forced at the age of 34 to "seek for ease in a Veteran Battalion." Roberts joined the 10th Royal Veteran Battalion, which was then being formed in England for garrison duty in the Canadas, and arrived at Quebec in the fall of 1807. Expecting rather easier duties in the veteran battalions, he was somewhat surprised to find himself soon on detached service at Fort St Johns (Saint-Jean-sur-Richelieu), Lower Canada, a state of affairs caused by a shortage of regular troops to meet the threat of war then posed by the United States [*see* Sir George Cranfield BERKELEY]. Moreover, in 1811 Roberts was specifically selected for a more rigorous command, that of Fort St Joseph (St Joseph Island, Ont.), a remote post on Lake Huron established after the

Robertson

abandonment of Michilimackinac (Mackinac Island, Mich.) in 1796 and important to both the fur trade and the maintenance of good relations with the Indians.

On 8 July 1812 Roberts learned that war had been declared by the United States on 18 June, and he determined to take immediate action against the American garrison at Michilimackinac. Operating largely on his own initiative and moving with energy and decision despite a much impaired constitution, he assembled a force consisting of his small garrison of 46 veterans, some 180 Canadian voyageurs and fur traders, and 400 Indians under Robert Dickson* and John Askin Jr and led them against the American post. Michilimackinac's garrison of 61 men was unaware of the commencement of hostilities and surrendered on 17 July soon after the British force appeared.

The implications of this bloodless conquest went far beyond Michilimackinac's immediate value. Roberts's action threw previously doubtful Indian support over to the British, not only ensuring control of the area west of Lake Michigan but also bringing decided pressure on American brigadier-general William Hull at Detroit (Mich.). Hull himself cited the loss of Michilimackinac and the subsequent arousal of the Indian tribes of the northwest as a prime factor in his decision to surrender his forces to BROCK on 16 Aug. 1812. Hull's capitulation was instrumental in securing the British position in western Upper Canada for another year and enabled British resources to be concentrated on the Niagara River to meet the next expected American thrust. Roberts's success was publicly praised, and his superiors, including PRE-VOST, wrote highly of his efforts.

But the strain in capturing Michilimackinac and subsequently in handling the problems of its defence soon broke Roberts's already poor health. In addition, his garrison of veterans was reported as "debilitated and worn down by unconquerable drunkenness," while the Indians' constant demands for food and presents sorely aggravated the problems of isolation at the end of lengthy lines of communication. Working solely on his own initiative, Roberts embodied a company of Canadians (the Michigan Fencibles) in 1813 to bolster his garrison. By May of the same year, however, he was forced to request leave and, suffering from a "great debility of the Stomach and Bowels," he was finally replaced in September. After an exhausting journey he went to Montreal and there reported on conditions at Michilimackinac. But his protracted illness was now "too deeply rooted for him even to indulge the hope of being entirely restored," and he requested retirement on full pay. This request and further solicitations for promotion and various appointments failed and Roberts returned to England in 1815, ostensibly on six months' leave. His health ruined, he was finally retired on full pay, but he died a year after his return. However slight Roberts's

rewards for faithful service had been, his "spirited" behaviour had at least won the respect and approval of both the Indians and his superiors, and the capture of Michilimackinac must stand as a decisive stroke in the successful defence of Upper Canada in the War of 1812.

GLENN A. STEPPLER

PAC, MG 24, A9: 203, 221–25, 233–34 (typescripts); RG 8, I (C ser.), 2; 231: 123; 232: 75–78; 256: 187–88; 676: 183–86, 201–2, 232–33, 236–38; 677–79; 681; 688a–c; 689: 87; 789: 79, 97–99, 109, 123–28; 790: 18–20, 22–23; 1168; 1171: 279–82, 304; 1203½K: 174; 1218: 439–40; 1221; 1227. *John Askin papers* (Quaife). G.B., WO, *Army list*, 1794–1818. C. T. Atkinson and D. S. Daniell, *Regimental history: the Royal Hampshire Regiment . . .* (3v., Glasgow, 1950–55), 1: 151–56, 226. A. R. Gilpin, *The War of 1812 in the old northwest* (Toronto and East Lansing, Mich., 1958), 89–91, 106–7, 128, 241. Walter Havighurst, *Three flags at the straits: the forts of Mackinac* (Englewood Cliffs, N.J., 1966), 113–23. Hitsman, *Incredible War of 1812*, 67–69. Reginald Horsman, "The role of the Indian in the war," *After Tippecanoe: some aspects of the War of 1812*, ed. P. P. Mason (East Lansing and Toronto, 1963), 60–77. C. L. Kingsford, *The story of the Duke of Cambridge's Own (Middlesex Regiment)* (London and New York, 1916), 57–60. G. F. G. Stanley, "The Indians in the War of 1812," *CHR*, 31 (1950): 145–65.

ROBERTSON, DANIEL, army and militia officer, landowner and improver, and office holder; b. *c.* 1733 in Dunkeld, Scotland; d. 5 April 1810 in Montreal, Lower Canada.

Daniel Robertson must have secured some medical training in Scotland before he was appointed to the 42nd Foot as a surgeon's mate in April 1754. His regiment was transferred to North America in June 1756 and stationed at Albany, N.Y.; Robertson was given an ensigncy in July. In 1760 he participated in the capture of Montreal. That, or the following, year he married Marie-Louise Réaume, the 19-year-old widow of Joseph Fournerie de Vézon; through his marriage Robertson gained entry into one of the substantial Canadian families of the colony. The fortunes of war soon took Robertson away from his bride. His regiment participated in the capture of Martinique, where on 29 April 1762 he purchased a lieutenancy. Following the capture of Havana, Cuba, the 42nd was sent back to North America, and in 1763 Robertson participated in Colonel Henry Bouquet's efforts in western Pennsylvania to quell Pontiac*'s uprising. With the reduction of the British army after the Treaty of Paris, Robertson returned to Montreal.

Between 1763 and 1773 the Robertsons had six children, two of whom died in infancy; on 17 Oct. 1773 Marie-Louise herself died. Meanwhile, by 1767 Robertson, in association with Benjamin Price*, seems to have acquired land around Lake Champlain.

He was a member of the grand jury at Montreal in 1768, and was honoured in April with a public notice of thanks by the other members for "your just and spirited Behaviour as a Magistrate and your indefatigable Care to bring Offenders to Justice." In 1773 and 1774 he signed petitions in favour of a house of assembly. At the beginning of the American revolution Robertson was appointed a major in the Montreal militia, and on 14 June 1775 captain-lieutenant of the 1st battalion of the Royal Highland Emigrants. He enlisted about a company of his fellow Scots and was ordered to Fort St Johns (Saint-Jean-sur-Richelieu) to help defend it against the invading Americans [see Richard Montgomery*]. With the besieged fort's surrender on 3 November, Robertson was taken to Connecticut, a dejected prisoner. He was exchanged, and he returned to his regiment early in 1777.

In September 1779 Robertson was appointed commandant of the small post at Oswegatchie (Ogdensburg, N.Y.). There he supervised Indian raids on Americans along the Mohawk frontier; in June 1782 he personally led an attack that destroyed two mills and five houses in a settlement on the Mohawk River. As a result of this success he obtained a commission for his son as an ensign under his command. Moreover, General HALDIMAND secretly appointed Robertson to take over the troubled post at Michilimackinac (Mackinac Island, Mich.), where a fellow Scot, Lieutenant Governor Patrick SINCLAIR, was having serious financial problems. Robertson left for Michilimackinac on 13 August, accompanied by his son and a three-man investigating committee; he assumed command on 18 September.

Although Robertson was permitted by his orders to continue construction of the partially completed fort, he had detailed instructions to curtail expenses in the Indian Department; however, he found it nearly as difficult as had Sinclair to restrain expenditures. Throughout his stay at Michilimackinac, Indian affairs would have a high priority. In late April 1783 he sent George MCBEATH and Charles Mouet de Langlade to inform the Indians around Prairie du Chien (Wis.) that peace with the American colonies was at hand and to encourage the Indians to cease inter-tribal hostilities. A month later word of the peace arrived. Robertson was in a difficult position: he had to stop Britain's Indian allies from fighting among themselves and discourage them from coming to Michilimackinac, where he would have to feed and supply them. In September he was obliged to send Jean-Baptiste CADOT and MADJECKEWISS to Chequamegon Bay (Wis.) to arrange a cessation of hostilities between the Ojibwas and the Foxes and Sioux; the emissaries were unsuccessful.

The dispatch that brought word of peace also revealed that Mackinac Island was to be included within the United States. Concerned that he might have to evacuate the fort, in 1784 Robertson, accompanied by McBeath, carefully inspected the north shore of Lake Superior and selected as a possible location for a new post a site at what is now Thessalon, Ont. After setting forth to Haldimand the advantages of this site, Robertson asked the governor to engage Daniel Sutherland*, Robertson's son-in-law and a merchant at Montreal, to supply certain construction needs. Robertson evidently intended to use Sutherland's business connections and his own position of authority to bolster his precarious financial situation. Even though he had sold his Montreal house on Rue Notre-Dame in December 1782, he had been obliged in September 1783 to borrow £1,000 from David Mitchell*, physician at Michilimackinac, offering a mortgage on an estate called Balmaguard in Scotland. His request for an appointment as Indian agent at Michilimackinac was apparently rejected, as was another, in association with Sutherland, James Grant*, Joseph FROBISHER, and Simon MCTAVISH, for a grant of all the land between Lake Ontario and Lake Huron, through which Robertson felt an all-British route to the west would have to pass.

The British government decided not to abandon Mackinac Island, and Robertson settled in. Between 1785 and 1787 he used his authority as commandant to make a number of land grants to his young daughters, Charlotte and Elizabeth; one of the grants also included among the beneficiaries Grant, McTavish, and Margaret McBeath. Local legend affirms that Robertson built a small summer-house on a rock outcrop at the southeast corner of the island. A variety of lurid tales have become attached to the site, which is still known as Robinson's Folly, a corruption of Robertson's name. In the summer of 1787 Robertson was relieved of his post. Before he left he freed his black slaves, Jean and Marie-Jeanne Bonga; they became prominent tavern keepers on the island, and their sons important fur traders. The merchants at Michilimackinac regretted Robertson's departure and, in October 1787, 42 of them commended him in the *Quebec Gazette*.

Robertson returned to Montreal. He had been placed on half pay in 1784, and on 18 Nov. 1790 he received the rank of major in the army. Late in February 1793 he secured an appointment as captain in the 60th Foot, and on 1 March 1794 he advanced to lieutenant-colonel in the army. Finally, on 1 Jan. 1798 he became a colonel in the army.

Between 1787 and 1806 Robertson amassed over 5,000 acres in a tract of land in Chatham Township on the east bank of the Ottawa River, securing grants for himself and his four children as well as purchasing the grants of some disbanded soldiers of the 84th Foot. He worked to attract settlers and to develop his properties. In 1797 he surveyed 285 lots, and by 1804 he had settled on his lands 43 families comprising 170

Robertson

people. To promote the establishment of a church in the area, in 1806 he gave 96 acres of land to the Anglican missionary Richard BRADFORD.

In the mean time Robertson had achieved a comfortable position in Montreal society. He maintained his ties with the fur-trade merchants through the prestigious Beaver Club, of which he had been elected an honorary member in 1793. He was appointed a justice of the peace in 1799 and a school commissioner in 1805. By 1808 he was colonel of the Argenteuil battalion of militia. He saw to it that his children married well: Margaret had married Daniel Sutherland in 1781; Charlotte married Dr John Farries in 1792; the following year John married Catherine, daughter of the landowner Major-General Gabriel Christie*; and in 1794 Elizabeth married Louis-Hippolyte, son of Joseph-Hippolyte Hertel* de Saint-François, a former army officer and interpreter. This last was an unhappy union, and after Hertel disappeared Elizabeth incurred her father's ire by "living in adultery"; some time before February 1806 she married Theodore Davis, a surveyor at Saint-André-d'Argenteuil.

Robertson's financial situation, however, was once again precarious. Sheriff Edward William GRAY began a series of seizures of property: in January 1802 a wood house, barn, stables, and 3,500 acres of land belonging to Robertson in Chatham Township; in October 1804 a farm on the Rivière Serpentine at Coteau-Saint-Pierre; and in July 1806 5,000 acres in Chatham with several houses and buildings on them. Evidently not all these properties went to auction in the event, for in 1810 Bradford purchased at least 3,000 acres in Chatham from Robertson's estate.

By December 1809 Robertson's health obliged him to live with Margaret and Sutherland. On 8 December he made a will leaving most of his fortune to two granddaughters, Louisa and Maria Sutherland; to Elizabeth he left "one Spanish mill'd Dollar only, on account of her undutiful behaviour and imprudent conduct." He died on 5 April 1810, and was buried three days later with military honours from the Scotch Presbyterian Church, later known as St Gabriel Street Church, at Montreal.

DAVID A. ARMOUR

ANQ-M, CN1-185, 18 Dec. 1809. BL, Add. MSS 21758: 244–56; 21762: 245; 21780 (mfm. at PAC). Mackinac County Courthouse (St Ignace, Mich.), Reg. of the post of Michilimackinac, 1, 11–12, 31–32, 42, 52–67. McCord Museum, Beaver Club minute-book, 1809–11. PAC, RG 1, L3ᴸ: 64480–82, 64486, 64488, 81258–59. PCA, St Gabriel Street Church (Montreal), Reg. of baptisms, marriages, and burials, 8 April 1810 (mfm. at ANQ-M). C. H. Gabriel and Garrett Newkirk, Songs of Mackinac Island: 1, My Mackinac; 2, Robertson's folly (Chicago, 1896). Mich. Pioneer Coll., 10 (1886): 465, 552–53, 638–40, 645, 671–72; 11 (1887): 332–35, 341–42, 350, 356–62, 368–70, 373–80, 383–85, 387–96, 405–7, 413–16, 419–21, 433–35, 442, 449–50, 452–54, 510–11, 568; 12 (1887): 309; 13 (1888): 73–74; 20 (1892): 13, 81, 84, 110, 121, 143, 150–51, 156, 190, 212–13, 217–19, 227, 232–33, 240, 243–45, 253, 264, 268–69, 274–75, 289. H. R. Schoolcraft, Personal memoirs of a residence of thirty years with the Indian tribes on the American frontiers, with brief notices of passing events, facts and opinions, A.D. 1812 to A.D. 1842 (Philadelphia, 1851), 478–79. Statistical account of Upper Canada, compiled with a view to a grand system of emigration, comp. R. [F.] Gourlay (2v., London, 1822; repr. East Ardsley, Eng., and New York, 1966), 1: 604. Wis., State Hist. Soc., Coll., 11 (1888): 164–66, 171–74; 12 (1892): 61–70, 94–96; 17 (1906): 436–38; 19 (1910): 83. Montreal Gazette, 9 April 1810. Quebec Gazette, 27 April 1769; 13 Sept. 1781; 9 Jan. 1783; 11 Oct. 1787; 16 July 1789; 4 Feb. 1802; 8 Nov. 1804; 31 July, 21 Aug. 1806; 15 Nov. 1810. Quebec almanac, 1809: 58. D. A. Armour and K. R. Widder, At the crossroads: Michilimackinac during the American revolution (Mackinac Island, Mich., 1978), 182, 185, 188–91. John Disturnell, Island of Mackinac, giving a description of all the objects of interest and places of resort in the straits of Mackinac and its vicinity . . . also, an account of the early settlement of the country . . . (Philadelphia, 1875), 16–17. B. L. Dunnigan, King's men at Mackinac: the British garrisons, 1780–1796 (Lansing, Mich., 1973). Stanley, Canada invaded, 31, 35, 61, 155. J. A. Van Fleet, Old and new Mackinac; with copious extracts from Marquette, Hennepin, La Houtan, Cadillac, Alexander Henry, and others . . . (Ann Arbor, Mich., 1870), 137. M. C. Williams, Early Mackinac; an historical and descriptive sketch (4th ed., St Louis, Mo., 1903), 146–50. E. O. Wood, Historic Mackinac; the historical, picturesque and legendary features of the Mackinac country . . . (2v., New York, 1918), 1: 584–85; 2: 87–108, 602. J.-J. Lefebvre, "Louise Réaume-Fournerie-Robertson (1742–1773) et son petit-fils le colonel Daniel de Hertel (1797–1866)," RHAF, 12 (1958–59): 323–34.

ROBERTSON, JAMES, printer, publisher, and office holder; b. 1747 in Stonehaven, Scotland; d. 24 April 1816 in Edinburgh, Scotland.

According to his own testimony, James Robertson immigrated to North America in 1766 and was joined there by his brother Alexander two years later. For some time after his arrival James worked as a journeyman with the printing firm of Mein and Fleming in Boston, Mass., but by 1768 he was in New York City, where on 8 May 1769 he and Alexander began publication of the New-York Chronicle. They had apparently learned the printing trade from their father. A rival printer, James Parker, referring to them as "two Scots Paper Spoilers," roundly condemned their workmanship but admitted that "from a large Portion of Impudence, and the National Biass of all Scotch Men in their Favour," they had quickly gained a number of subscribers. The paper was nevertheless dropped the following year.

The Robertsons then removed to Albany, N.Y., where, with the patronage of Sir William Johnson*, they initiated the short-lived Albany Gazette, the first issue appearing on 25 Nov. 1771. Two years later, while maintaining their Albany printing office, they formed a partnership with John Trumbull to publish the *Norwich Packet* in Norwich, Conn. Although this endeavour yielded "a very handsome Profit," they were obliged to give it up in 1776 because "they could no longer carry it on without making it subservient to the Cause of Rebellion." Concentrating on their Albany enterprise, the brothers were active in publishing loyalist pieces. James later claimed that they had been the only printers in America openly to support the crown in an area where there had been no British troops to offer protection. Their activities made them "Obnoxious to the Americans," and in 1776 James was forced to flee to New York City. Alexander, a cripple, was thrown into prison, along with their journeyman, William Lewis*, and was not exchanged until December 1777.

In New York James began a new paper, the *Royal American Gazette*, which he gave over to Alexander on his release, believing that the business could not support them both. James subsequently published the *Royal Pennsylvania Gazette* (Philadelphia) for a few months in 1778 and the *Royal South-Carolina Gazette* (Charleston) from 1780 to 1782. Reunited in New York at the end of the British occupation of Charleston, the brothers continued the *Royal American Gazette* until 1783. They then joined the exodus to Nova Scotia, settling in Shelburne, where they re-established their newspaper. At least from March to July 1784 James was in England, petitioning the loyalist claims commission for compensation for the losses he and his brother had suffered during the war. They estimated their total property losses to have been £650; the annual value of their business in Albany and Norwich was assessed at £350. Eventually they were awarded a settlement of £350.

After his brother's death in 1784 James Robertson carried on the *Royal American Gazette* in Shelburne for at least two years. In 1787, however, at the invitation of Edmund FANNING, lieutenant governor of St John's (Prince Edward) Island, he moved his press to Charlottetown. There, on 15 September, he published the initial issue of the *Royal American Gazette, and Weekly Intelligencer of the Island of Saint John*, the colony's earliest newspaper. Before Robertson's arrival there had been no printing office on the Island, and neither the records of the House of Assembly nor the acts of the legislature had ever been published. In 1788 he not only brought out the assembly's *Journal* for that year but began printing the collected statutes of the colony, revised by Attorney General Phillips Callbeck* and Solicitor General Joseph APLIN. In addition to his printing, Robertson served as deputy postmaster and also as sheriff for a time; he had taken part in local affairs at Shelburne as well, having been a justice of the peace there.

In 1788 the assembly and Council of the Island, supported by Fanning, petitioned Lord Dorchester [Guy CARLETON], stressing the need for a printing office in the colony and emphasizing Robertson's inability to subsist "from the bare Emoluments and Profits of it." "Without some governmental Assistance," they concluded, "the attempt must be dropped, our public Fund being too scanty and inconsiderable, to admit of any provincial Salary or reward." Although the British government was willing to grant Robertson a commission as king's printer, it was reluctant to set a precedent by annexing a salary to the appointment. Apparently unable to support himself, Robertson went to Quebec in 1789, leaving his journeyman, William Alexander Rind, to carry on the printing shop and complete the publication of the statutes. By March 1790, however, Robertson was in England, outlining for the loyalist claims commission the inadequacy of its earlier award to him, a sum that had apparently gone to discharge his and his brother's debts. Noting that no salary had been offered for the position of king's printer on St John's Island, he maintained that "it could answer no purpose for your Memorialist to accept of the Appointment, as the Circumstances of that infant Colony cannot support a Press." Instead, he requested the annual allowance as a loyalist that he claimed other refugee printers in British North America had obtained. Whether his petition had any result is not known. Within a few years Robertson had set up as a printer and bookseller in Edinburgh, where he died in 1816.

Little evidence remains of his personal life. His first wife, Amy, had died in Norwich on 29 May 1776; his second wife was named Mary. No children are mentioned in his petitions to the loyalist claims commission; in 1790 he asked only for compensation "suitable to the support of Himself, and two children of his deceased Brother left in his Charge."

F. L. PIGOT

PRO, AO 12/19; AO 13, bundles 116, 137; CO 226/12: 190–91; 226/13: 222–23; 226/15: 13–16. *The papers of Benjamin Franklin*, ed. L. W. Labaree et al. (21v. to date, New Haven, Conn., [1960]–), 16: 140; 17: 56. C. S. Brigham, *History and bibliography of American newspapers, 1690–1820* (2v., Worcester, Mass., 1947). *DAB*. Tremaine, *Biblio. of Canadian imprints*. W. L. Cotton, "The press in Prince Edward Island," *Past and present of Prince Edward Island* . . . , ed. D. A. MacKinnon and A. B. Warburton (Charlottetown, [1906]), 112–21. D. C. McMurtrie, *The royalist printers at Shelburne, Nova Scotia* (Chicago, 1933). Isaiah Thomas, *The history of printing in America, with a biography of printers, and an account of newspapers* . . . (2nd ed., 2v., Albany, N.Y., 1874; repr. New York, 1972). E. G. Carroll, "History of printing," *Canadian Antiques Collector* (Toronto), 8 (1973), no.[2]: 43–45. Marion Robertson, "The loyalist printers: James and Alexander Robertson," *Nova Scotia Hist. Rev.* (Halifax), 3, no.1 (1983): 83–93.

Robertson

ROBERTSON (Robinson), WILLIAM, merchant, judge, office holder, politician, and militia officer; b. *c.* 1760 in Scotland; m. first 26 Jan. 1798 Cornelia Eleanor Brooks in New York City, and they had one daughter; m. secondly 18 March 1803 Jane Ogilvy, *née* Dunlop, mother of John OGILVY; d. 13 Dec. 1806 in London, England.

William Robertson settled at Detroit (Mich.) in 1782. His brother Samuel, who died that same year, had been a ship's captain there since 1774. William served as clerk to Samuel's father-in-law, John ASKIN, and became his partner on 1 July 1784. Robertson was paid £600 yearly for "conducting the business" until it dissolved on 22 Aug. 1787. He rose rapidly in the southwest fur trade, for which, in 1788, he estimated the value of pelts to be £150,000 to £200,000 annually. Articulate and thoughtful, Robertson was, with Askin and Alexander GRANT, one of the leading merchants in the area and by 1788 he had emerged as the principal spokesman of that group.

In July 1788 Lord Dorchester [Guy CARLETON] established four new administrative districts in western Quebec. Robertson's local prominence was reflected in his appointment to both the Court of Common Pleas and the land board of the District of Hesse. He approved of the former as vital to a commercial society "to protect their Property and redress their wrongs" but opposed the choice of judges, including himself. Because the "Professions of Judge and Merchant combined in the same person are wholly incompatible" and since the main business of the court would be the settlement of debt, he argued the need for a judge "professionally acquainted with the Law." Robertson therefore resigned and carried to Quebec a memorial signed by himself and 33 other merchants. There, on 24 October, he testified before a committee of the Legislative Council. As a result of its favourable report on the petition, William Dummer Powell* became the sole judge of the district. Robertson apparently saw no conflict of interest in his nomination to the land board in 1789 and attended every meeting to the end of August 1790. Despite subsequent non-attendance, he was reappointed in May 1791 and the following year he was named to the board's successor, the land board of the counties of Essex and Kent.

His stature was such that in March 1790 Robertson was recommended by Sir John Johnson* for seats on the executive and legislative councils of the proposed new province of Upper Canada. He was appointed to the former on 9 July 1792 and the latter three days later. Although Lieutenant Governor SIMCOE thought him "a person of very good manners & good sense," he worried about Robertson's ability to devote the time necessary to his new duties. For whatever reason, by 4 November Robertson had resigned both offices.

Robertson's pre-eminence was based on his success as a merchant but little is known of this aspect of his life, especially his major concern – the fur trade out of Detroit. Kinship played a significant role in establishing his business connections. From the outset he was linked to the Askin network through his brother Samuel's widow, Catherine Askin. In 1785 she married Robert HAMILTON, the leading merchant in the Niagara area; Robertson acted as his financier, supplier, patron, and customer. A younger brother, David, had joined Robertson in Detroit by 1790, and in July that year they entered into a partnership, which also included James MacDonell, Robertson's clerk since 1785. MacDonell withdrew in September and David exercised control during William's absence in London, England, between 1791 and 1795. In 1793 the British Treasury awarded Alexander Davison* the contract to supply the troops in the Canadas. He in turn nominated the Montreal merchant John Gray* and the Quebec partnership of Monro and Bell as his Lower Canadian agents. Richard CARTWRIGHT, Hamilton, Askin, and David Robertson then received an exclusive sub-contract to victual the Upper Canadian garrisons between 1793 and 1795 after furious lobbying in London by Robertson and Isaac TODD. Prior to his return in 1795 Robertson entered a new partnership with Askin. That same year he dissolved the partnership with his brother and concluded two new ones with Askin and others for speculation in land. He was given power of attorney in the second indenture, known as the Cuyahoga Purchase, but did not act long in this capacity. In the fall of 1795 he travelled to Philadelphia, Pa, and on his return settled at Montreal. There he acted on Askin's behalf with local merchants and continued to maintain his own business. In 1797, for instance, he supplied the garrison at Amherstburg, Upper Canada, with over 2,000 bushels of Indian corn. Also in this period he and Askin owned a salt spring. In May 1801 he was back at Detroit, presumably to recover the "great amount of my outstanding debts in this quarter."

The death of his wife in 1800 had left Robertson "inconsolable" and the following year he moved to London. Shunning friends, he became an alcoholic; reports filtered back to the Canadas of a life spent in "continual debauch." But a nephew dismissed the rumours as exaggerated and hoped for the reform of his drinking habits through the good influence of his second wife. The marriage did not last long; the couple separated in August 1803, Robertson citing as cause "her insupportable extravagance." Hearsay continued unabated. Hamilton thought him "Lost to every sence of Shame, his Conduct would disgrace the lowest Member of the lowest class of Society." Todd was even harsher, labelling him "a Sot & blackguard . . . infamous as a Liar & Rogue." Only Askin retained any charitable impulses towards "an honest worthy friendly good man" overtaken by fever or drink.

Prior to leaving Detroit in 1791 Robertson had supported the local Church of England clergyman and served as a militia officer. Described by Peter RUSSELL as a "genteel Sensible Scotsman," he possessed a keen mind often at variance with the prevailing opinions of his class. Unlike most merchants he supported the division of the old province of Quebec. While in England in the early 1790s he took a fervent interest in the war against revolutionary France, lamenting "that for the *good* of one another mankind are to cut one anothers throats . . . to a mind possessed by humanity the prospect of carnage is truely afflicting!" He was dispirited by the spectacle of "Europe deluged with human blood, torn to its foundation, & every kingdom in it on the point of political dissolution, from the *unthinking* conduct of kings, priests, ministers & people." Friends reacted to his views with a mixture of shock, rebuke, and even threats.

In the last years of his life Robertson spoke little of his Canadian career. His affairs here were superintended by his nephews. On occasion, perhaps spurred by the pressure of creditors, he wrote a letter complaining of outstanding debts and from 1804 to 1806 he dunned Hamilton. A wealthy man at his death, he left £500 apiece to his two nephews and placed the remainder of his estate in trust for his daughter. In 1820 the value of his land alone was reckoned in excess of £54,000.

There is a pathos to Robertson's life. His natural business acumen and intellect marked him for success. His graciousness of manner and soundness of judgement made him a good friend and worthy counsel. If Robertson was unusual, it was for the delicacy of his sensibilities: the death of a loved one revealed his tragic vulnerability and plunged him into a despair from which he never recovered.

DANIEL J. BROCK

AO, MS 75, Russell to Elizabeth Russell, 9 Feb. 1792; MS 536, Archange Meredith to Mrs Askin, 5 July, 1 Aug. 1803; David Meredith to John Askin, 29 April 1804; Archange Meredith to Askin, 13 April 1805. DPL, Burton Hist. Coll., MS index, file no.95, David, Samuel, and William Robertson, biog. notes, comp. M. M. Quaife; William Robertson papers. PAC, RG 1, L3, 422: R1/19; RG 8, I (C ser.), 115B: 259, 352. UWO, William Robertson papers, docs.42, 45, 50–51, 55, 61, 67, 83, 87, 101n. *Corr. of Lieut. Governor Simcoe* (Cruikshank), 1: 10–11, 47, 121, 253, 300n.; 4: 99n., 211n.; 5: 163, 173–74. *John Askin papers* (Quaife), 1: 208n.; 2: 64n., 297, 392. *Mich. Pioneer Coll.*, 11 (1887): 627–50, 655–56. Armstrong, *Handbook of Upper Canadian chronology*, 13, 33. Burt, *Old prov. of Quebec* (1968), 2: 110. W. R. Riddell, *Michigan under British rule: law and law courts, 1760–1796* (Lansing, Mich., 1926), 52–57.

ROBICHAUX (Robichaud, Robicheau), JEAN-BAPTISTE, fisherman; b. *c.* 1751 in Village des Cadet (Great Village), N.S., son of Joseph Robi-

chaux, *dit* Cadet, and Claire Le Blanc; d. 4 March 1808 in Grand Chipagan (Shippegan), N.B.

Jean-Baptiste Robichaux's father came from Port-Royal (Annapolis Royal, N.S.) but settled in the region of Cobequid (near Truro) at Village des Cadet after his marriage in 1726. Eleven children were born there; Jean-Baptiste was the tenth. Although many of their neighbours responded in the early 1750s to the efforts made by the French government and its agents to persuade Acadians living under British rule to remove to French territory [*see* Jean-Louis Le Loutre*], the Robichaux family remained in Nova Scotia; their distance from Annapolis Royal and the presence of French troops at Louisbourg, Île Royale (Cape Breton Island), and Fort Beauséjour (near Sackville, N.B.) perhaps gave them a sense of security on their lands. Nevertheless, they had eventually to take the weary road to exile. About the time of the deportation in 1755 [*see* Charles Lawrence*] – whether before or after is unclear – Joseph Robichaux took his family by the "emigrants' road" to Tatamagouche, and then by ship to Pointe Prime (Point Prim) on Île Saint-Jean (P.E.I.). It was there that many Acadians from Cobequid, as well as the former parish priest, Jacques Girard*, had settled.

The surrender of Louisbourg to British forces under Jeffery Amherst* and Edward Boscawen* in July 1758 brought with it the capitulation of Île Saint-Jean. In spite of an appeal by Pierre CASSIET and Jean Biscaret, two of the missionaries to the Acadians on the island, it was decided that Colonel Lord Rollo* should proceed with plans to deport the inhabitants. Sent to France, the Robichaux family arrived at Saint-Servan in Brittany at the onset of winter, after a crossing that proved fatal for their father. They settled in the tiny village of Pleudihen on the outskirts of Saint-Servan and, like other Acadian families, were supported for some years by the French government. But they had difficulty adapting to their new life and dreamed of returning home.

On 4 Feb. 1773, at Saint-Servan, Jean-Baptiste married a fellow exile, Félicité Cyr (Sire); they were to have 15 children. At that time the Jersey merchants of the firm Robin, Pipon et·Cie were eager to sign on the Acadian families living on the coasts of France in order to obtain a stable work-force for their settlements in Gaspé and on Cape Breton Island, since the young people from Jersey did not seem to want to take up permanent residence there. Early in the spring of 1774 Jean-Baptiste and his brothers went to Jersey, and in April the Acadian contingent left Saint Helier on two ships, the *Hope* and the *Bee*, bound for Charles Robin*'s establishment at Paspébiac in Gaspé, which they reached the following month. Jean-Baptiste and his wife settled at Bonaventure with their eldest child, Jean-Baptiste, who had been born on 16 Nov. 1773 at Saint-Servan. There they lived in straitened circumstances on his ten-acre plot, com-

Robinson

pletely dependent on the company, Charles Robin having encouraged the Acadians to concentrate on fishing rather than farming. Unable to gain secure possession even of this small property, Robichaux contemplated joining the Acadian families south of the Baie des Chaleurs. About 1790 he crossed the bay with his family to settle at Grand Chipagan, taking up residence on Pointe Brûlé to the west of the harbour. He was the first settler from Grand Chipagan to petition the government for title to his land, in 1798. His rights were recognized, but he was not long to enjoy peaceful possession of his property. He died on 4 March 1808, and was buried the next day in the old cemetery at Caraquet. His widow went to live at Caraquet in the home of one of her daughters, where she died some years later.

Jean-Baptiste Robichaux's story clearly recalls the numerous moves that Acadian families had to endure at the time of the deportation. He was one of the first Acadians to settle at Grand Chipagan and a pioneer of that locality. His brothers all established themselves in New Brunswick, Isidore being an early settler at Pokemouche (Inkerman), and Joseph, Pierre, Michel, and Charles the founders of Saint-Charles (Kent County).

DONAT ROBICHAUD

AAQ, 311 CN, I–VI. AD, Ille-et-Vilaine (Rennes), État civil, Saint-Servan, 1762; 4 févr. 1773. AP, Saint-Bonaventure (Bonaventure), Reg. des baptêmes, mariages et sépultures; Saint-Joseph (Carleton), Reg. des baptêmes, mariages et sépultures. Arch. paroissiales, Caraquet, N.-B., Reg. des baptêmes, mariages et sépultures de l'Acadie, 1768–99. BL, Add. MSS 21862: 17b (transcript at PAC). Northumberland County Registry Office (Newcastle, N.B.), 8: 23–25, testament de J.-B. Robichaux. Placide Gaudet, "Généalogie des Acadiens, avec documents," PAC Rapport, 1905, II, IIIᵉ partie: 333. Patrice Gallant, Les registres de la Gaspésie (1752–1850) (6v., [Sayabec, Québec, 1968]), 5: 454–56. Donat Robichaud, Les Robichaud: histoire et généalogie (Bathurst, N.-B., [1967]), 86–90.

ROBINSON, JOSEPH, judge, politician, militia officer, author, and lawyer; b. c. 1742 in Virginia; m. Lelia —, and they had at least two children, both daughters; d. 24 Aug. 1807 in Charlottetown, P.E.I.

A resident of South Carolina at the outbreak of the American rebellion, Joseph Robinson was major of the militia for Camden District. Ordered by Governor Lord William Campbell* to march against the rebels in Ninety-Six District, he advanced with a party of men and fought the insurgents to a stand-off at the battle of Ninety-Six Court-House in November 1775. In the mean time, however, Campbell had been forced to abandon the province, and Robinson and his men found themselves stranded in the west without money or stores. A price having been put on his head, he

made his way through Cherokee and Creek country to East Florida, where he arrived in 1777; he was joined there by his wife and daughters, who had been driven by the rebels from the family plantation. Robinson was commissioned lieutenant-colonel of the South Carolina Royalists and fought with his regiment in a number of small actions in the south during the remainder of the conflict. Placed on the half-pay list of the British army in 1783, he went with his family to Jamaica the following year, but, finding the climate unsuitable, they moved on to New Brunswick in 1785. Finally, in 1789, Robinson settled on St John's (Prince Edward) Island at the invitation of Lieutenant Governor Edmund FANNING, who particularly enjoyed the company of fellow loyalist officers. There both Robinson's daughters would make good marriages, Rebecca to Robert HODGSON and Matilda to merchant Ralph Brecken.

In 1790 Robinson was appointed an assistant judge, without pay, of Chief Justice Peter STEWART's Supreme Court and was elected to the House of Assembly (which chose him speaker). Well respected by most leading inhabitants, in 1793 he was one of three arbitrators mutually agreed upon to sort out the complex business dispute between the lord chief baron of Scotland, James William Montgomery, and his Island representative, David LAWSON. That same year he was appointed an agent for the loyalists on the Island and colonel of the Prince County militia. The militia's refusal to assemble for him on several occasions was largely a protest against his not being resident in the county rather than an expression of personal animosity. Although he lived in Charlottetown, Robinson leased from Montgomery a farm on Lot 34 in Queens County, where he conducted agricultural experiments and made many improvements. In 1794 he resigned from the assembly to take up an appointment to the Council.

Robinson made his principal mark upon Island politics in 1796, with his pamphlet *To the farmers in the Island of St. John, in the Gulf of St. Lawrence*, which was widely distributed by Hodgson. An extremely brief production – only four pages in length – the pamphlet mainly dealt with the difficulties of soil and climate facing the farmer on the Island. Robinson was also conscious of the problem of land tenure, however, and particularly so since he was himself involved in a dispute with a proprietor (in his case, Montgomery) over land he had hoped to purchase but was obliged to rent. He believed that the existing system of leasehold under large proprietors was producing a population in a "state of low spirits, in much want, misery and distress: devoid of animation," who could well turn into a "grotesque picture of the Highland Clans."

Robinson concluded with a call for a petition from the House of Assembly asking the king to inquire into the grants and to create a court of escheat under which the lands of delinquent proprietors would be taken over and tenants left to pay quitrents to the crown. "Harmony, happiness and tranquillity, must then flourish and succeed, to contention, misery, and distress!" Islanders would no longer migrate to provinces "where lands are given to them and to their heirs forever – where they may cultivate their lands in quietude, and enjoy the fruits of their labours: – where men only look up to God and their King!" Known to most historians only through hostile commentary by Robinson's enemies, *To the farmers* was hardly an inflammatory production. Contemporary critics claimed that Robinson was merely acting as spokesman for the Fanning–Stewart faction in raising and popularizing the escheat issue, and their interpretation may have been valid; however, he did not advocate – as often charged – a popular division of proprietorial lands on a freehold basis.

In 1797 Robinson resigned his judgeship in order to become the Island's only practising attorney besides Peter Magowan. His action permitted the resumption of Supreme Court business, which had virtually ceased in the absence of lawyers for opposing parties. According to John Hill* and John MacDonald of Glenaladale, however, Robinson refused to plead in the Trinity term of 1800 because, given control of the court by the Stewarts, he felt he could not obtain justice for his clients.

Robinson apparently enjoyed a wide intellectual curiosity. In a submission to the loyalist claims commission he mentioned "A Valuable Library of Books consisting of Latin, Greek, Hebrew, Mathematics, Divinity, a Considerable number of the Laws of England," the last in 60 volumes. His grandson Robert Hodgson*, who perused his papers, described him to Egerton Ryerson* in 1861 as "a man of a refined mind, an excellent classical scholar, with a great taste for astronomy, and possessing no ordinary talent in that science, which seems to have amused and occupied his mind in his latter years." His interest in farming evidently continued throughout his life, for in 1803 he was one of those instrumental in organizing an agricultural society on the Island. He died in 1807, after suffering ill health for some years.

J. M. Bumsted

The PAPEI holds a copy of *To the farmers in the Island of St. John, in the Gulf of St. Lawrence* (n.p., n.d.) (Acc. 2702, Smith–Alley coll.); it is likely the only one extant. Robinson's authorship of it is established in SRO, GD293/2/19/6 (James Douglas to James William Montgomery, 26 April 1798).

PAC, MG 11, [CO 226] Prince Edward Island A, 17: 430–31. PAPEI, Acc. 2702, Smith–Alley coll., "Proposal to have meeting of persons interested in forming on the Island an association like the Board of Agriculture in England";

RG 6, Supreme Court records. PRO, AO 12/49: 332–39; AO 13/92: 317–22. SRO, GD293/2/19/6, 9; 293/2/78/12; 293/2/81/2. *Documentary history of the American revolution: consisting of letters and papers relating to the contest for liberty, chiefly in South Carolina . . .* , ed. R. W. Gibbes (2v., New York, 1855–57), 1: 214–19. *Loyalists in East Florida, 1774–1785 . . .* , ed. W. H. Siebert (2v., Deland, Fla., 1929). *Royal Gazette and Miscellany of the Island of Saint John* (Charlottetown), 30 Jan. 1793. Egerton Ryerson, *The loyalists of America and their times: from 1620 to 1816* (2nd ed., 2v., Toronto, 1880), 2: 213–16.

ROE (Row), WALTER, lawyer and office holder; b. *c.* 1760 in London, England; m. 1 March 1790 Ann Laughton of Detroit, Mich., and they had four children; d. 7 Aug. 1801 in Upper Canada.

Walter Roe was one of the first lawyers to practise in Upper Canada. Apparently an only child, he left home after the death of his father, "a man of some means," and the subsequent remarriage of his mother. Joining the Royal Navy in 1779, he served for the duration of the American Revolutionary War and attained the rank of warrant officer before taking up residence in Montreal in the mid 1780s. Evidently well educated, he had greatly impressed his commanding officer during the war, and upon leaving the navy he had been persuaded by the same officer to begin the study of law. After receiving his early legal training in Montreal, he was admitted to the practice of law in the province of Quebec on 13 April 1789.

During his stay in Montreal, Roe undoubtedly came into contact with William Dummer Powell*, then one of the most prominent lawyers in the city, and Powell's patronage and influence may have been useful in launching Roe's legal career. Certainly, it was not long before the careers of the two men became intertwined. In 1788 Governor Lord Dorchester [Guy Carleton] had appointed Alexander McKee*, Jacques Baby*, *dit* Dupéront, and William Robertson judges of the Court of Common Pleas in the newly formed District of Hesse, the most westerly section of what was soon to become the colony of Upper Canada. Baby and Robertson resigned almost immediately, however, claiming that their business activities would prevent them from exercising judicial impartiality. At this point all three appointments were revoked and Powell was made the sole judge of the district. The position of court clerk went to the young Roe.

Roe's arrival on the western frontier coincided with the establishment of civil authority in the region. Following the British conquest, the 1,500 inhabitants residing along both sides of the Detroit River had been under military rule. This situation seemed about to change with the passage of the Quebec Act of 1774, but the American revolution postponed the creation of the civil and legal institutions planned for the interior.

Roe

Only in 1788 was the territory west of the Ottawa River organized into four governmental districts, with the Detroit frontier included in the District of Hesse. Under the proclamation of 1788, the boundaries of Hesse were purposefully left vague so as to encompass the area south of the Great Lakes, an area officially ceded to the United States in 1783 but still occupied by British troops. Given its tenuous claim to the American side of the boundary, Britain was reluctant to include it too formally within an administrative district. Even so, colonial officials were aware that since Detroit was the centre of the fur trade south of the lakes, some institutional authority was required. As a result, although the Court of Common Pleas created in 1788 held its sessions on the Canadian shore, it also had jurisdiction at both Detroit and Michilimackinac (Mackinac Island, Mich.).

As for Roe, he may have been in the west earlier, perhaps while still in military service, for his name appears on a list of loyalists and disbanded troops granted land on the north shore of Lake Erie in 1787. However, he never occupied his Lake Erie grant, residing instead at Detroit, the most important settlement in the region. Within a short time after his arrival there in 1789, Roe found his legal services in constant demand. Besides his official duties as court clerk, he built up a thriving legal practice, including among his clients such prominent people as William Hands*, Sarah Ainse*, John ASKIN, and Angus Mackintosh*. A large part of his business involved collecting debts, certifying land transfers, and attending to the estates of deceased or absentee merchants. During the early 1790s the Montreal merchants Isaac TODD and James McGILL gave Roe the job of watching over their land and other interests in western Upper Canada, and also recommended him to William Robertson, then absent in England, as the best person to handle his substantial property holdings. Unfortunately, there soon developed considerable criticism of Roe's lack of diligence in meeting his responsibilities, and it is clear that by the mid 1790s his career had begun to decline.

Roe's professional difficulties, however, were not entirely the result of personal failings; they were also due partly to the fact that he was no longer the only lawyer in the area, and partly to changes in the administration of justice. Having been trained in French law, Roe was at a distinct disadvantage after the passage of the Constitutional Act of 1791, which provided for the introduction of English law and the creation of a new court system. Always interested in real estate, he now renewed his efforts to accumulate land, no doubt to compensate for his dwindling professional income. Claiming 2,000 acres from the government, he was eventually allotted more than 1,400 acres near York (Toronto), but several years elapsed before the titles were secured and he never cultivated the land.

In 1794 Roe was made a clerk of the peace for the Western District, having been recommended by Attorney General John White* and James Baby*, a member of the Executive and Legislative councils. He was given the rather dubious distinction of surrendering the keys to the fort at Detroit when in 1796 the British evacuated the posts held south of the Great Lakes, and afterwards he and his family joined a number of British subjects who moved across the river to the recently established town of Sandwich (Windsor). In 1797 he was selected as one of the original six benchers, or governors, of the Law Society of Upper Canada, but there is no evidence that he attended any of the meetings. As deputy registrar of the Western District, a post to which he was appointed by Lieutenant Governor SIMCOE in 1796, Roe was required to travel quite regularly the 17 miles from his home in Sandwich to Amherstburg, Britain's new military entrepôt for the Detroit frontier. These trips were both irksome and difficult, and in 1800 Roe, acting in his capacity as clerk of the peace, forwarded to the Executive Council a petition from the grand jury of Sandwich stressing the need for better transportation facilities along the route. Roe was to drown on one of these same trips to Amherstburg. According to John Askin, on 7 August "poor Mr. Rowe was found suffocated where there was very little water." There was some suggestion that Roe had become an alcoholic and had fallen off his horse while intoxicated.

D. R. FARRELL

AO, MU 2438–41. DPL, Burton Hist. Coll., Walter Roe papers (photocopies). PAC, RG 1, L3, 422A: R1/9, 25; 424: R3/76. *Corr. of Hon. Peter Russell* (Cruikshank and Hunter), vols.1–2. *Corr. of Lieut. Governor Simcoe* (Cruikshank). "Grants of crown lands in U.C.," AO *Report*, 1929: 135, 170. *John Askin papers* (Quaife), vol.2. "U.C. land book B," AO *Report*, 1930: 5, 80–81. "U.C. land book C," AO *Report*, 1930: 145. "Upper Canada, District of Hesse; record of the Court of Common Pleas, L'Assomption, 1789," AO *Report*, 1917: 23–177. *Windsor border region* (Lajeunesse). H. P. Beers, *The French & British in the old northwest: a bibliographical guide to archive and manuscript sources* (Detroit, 1964). *The city of Detroit, Michigan, 1701–1922*, ed. C. M. Burton et al. (5v., Detroit and Chicago, 1922). C. M. Burton, *History of Detroit, 1780 to 1850, financial and commercial* . . . (Detroit, 1917). W. R. Riddell, *Legal profession in U.C.*; *Life of William Dummer Powell*; *Old province tales, Upper Canada* (Toronto, 1920). N. V. Russell, *The British régime in Michigan and the old northwest, 1760–1796* (Northfield, Minn., 1939). W. R. Riddell, "Criminal courts and law in early (Upper) Canada," *OH*, 22 (1925): 210–21; "Practice of Court of Common Pleas of the District of Hesse," RSC *Trans.*, 3rd ser., 7 (1913), sect.II: 43–56.

ROLLO, JAMES, cabinet-maker, upholsterer, and furniture importer; b. *c.* 1788, probably in Scotland; m. Frances McCaulay; d. 30 June 1820 in Montreal, Lower Canada.

James Rollo was established as a cabinet-maker in Montreal by 1816. His premises, at that time situated at 1 Rue Saint-Vincent, were removed two years later to Rue Notre-Dame, near Saint-Laurent, a more prestigious location. Like some of the other leading Montreal cabinet-makers of the period, Rollo imported furniture from England. In 1816 he was selling "elegant" English-made mahogany bedsteads, tables, chairs, sofas, and music-stools. Imported furniture provided colonial cabinet-makers with highly saleable stock, as well as fashionable models to be copied in their work-rooms. In 1819, for example, Rollo advertised his usual English goods, "agreeable to the newest fashions," and in the same announcement offered to make, "on the shortest notice," any articles of furniture required "in the newest pattern." Among items he did produce were card- and Pembroke tables in pillar-and-claw style, mahogany bureaux, chests of drawers, wardrobes, dining-tables and chairs, and ladies' work- and toilet-tables, all "manufactured under his immediate superintendance." Handsome mahogany bedsteads, with and without draperies, and sofa-tables in rosewood were also found in his show-rooms. He made use as well of native woods, such as cherry, maple, birch, and ash.

Following the practice of the times, Rollo sold woods to smaller cabinet-makers. He kept ample stocks of both Honduras and what was then called Spanish mahogany, the latter being either Cuban or San Domingo mahogany. Most cabinet-makers of this Regency period also sold articles not necessarily connected with the cabinet trade, and Rollo was no exception. He stocked fowling pieces and paper-hangings, as well as the expected variety of upholstery and curtain materials (haircloth, chintz, moreen) and brass hardware.

That Rollo's customers included John and Thomas* McCord indicates that he managed, within the short time he was in business, to gain the patronage of leading Montrealers. John McCord paid him £5 in 1818 for two "Elbow Chairs," and in March 1820 Thomas purchased for £14 a mahogany couch upholstered in haircloth. For Thomas, Rollo also fitted up a pew in Christ Church, laying a new carpet and restuffing the cushions.

In addition to being prominent in the Montreal cabinet trade, Rollo took an active part in the affairs of the Scotch Presbyterian Church, later known as St Gabriel Street Church, where he was appointed precentor in 1817 and ordained an elder two years later. In 1818 a son and in 1820 a daughter were baptized there.

In the early summer of 1820 Rollo went into partnership with another cabinet-maker, George Gray, who may have been his brother-in-law. The new firm, with Rollo as the senior partner, made a bold start, advertising that it could make up "in the most modern style," and in well-seasoned mahogany, such fashionable articles as Grecian couches and loo- and tea-tables. Within a month, however, Rollo was dead at about age 32. The subsequent sale of his own furniture and other household goods also offered horses, a calèche, a cart, and carrioles, an indication that he had achieved a considerable degree of success.

One of Rollo's former employees, Charles Forrest, opened an upholstery business of his own in 1817, mentioning his experience with Rollo in his advertising. Gray, who acquired the patronage of at least one member of the Molson family, carried on alone, continuing business until well into the Victorian period.

ELIZABETH COLLARD

McCord Museum, McCord papers, bill paid by John McCord, 10 Oct. 1818; bill partially paid by Thomas McCord, 30 March 1820. PCA, St Gabriel Street Church (Montreal), Reg. of baptisms, marriages, and burials, 26 Feb. 1818; 17 April, 20 May, 2 July 1820 (mfm. at ANQ-M). *Montreal Gazette*, 5 July 1820. *Montreal Herald*, 22 June, 2 Nov. 1816; 5, 31 May 1817; 9 May 1818; 24 July 1819; 17, 24 June, 1, 15 July 1820. *An alphabetical list of the merchants, traders, and housekeepers, residing in Montreal; to which is prefixed a descriptive sketch of the town*, comp. Thomas Doige (Montreal, 1819), 162, 192. R. Campbell, *Hist. of Scotch Presbyterian Church*, 320. Elizabeth Collard, "Montreal cabinetmakers and chairmakers, 1800–1850: a check list," *Antiques* (New York), 105 (January–June 1974): 1145.

ROUNDHEAD. *See* STAYEGHTHA

ROUSSEAUX ST JOHN, JOHN BAPTIST (baptized **Jean-Baptiste Rousseau**, *dit* **Saint-Jean**), fur trader, interpreter, businessman, militia officer, and office holder; b. 4 July 1758 in the parish of La Visitation du Sault-au-Récollet (Montreal, Que.), son of Jean-Bonaventure Rousseau, *dit* Saint-Jean, and Marie-Reine Brunet; d. 16 Nov. 1812 in Niagara (Niagara-on-the-Lake), Upper Canada.

Some 20 years before the formation of Upper Canada the Rousseau family of Montreal launched its commercial activities in the Toronto area. In the fall of 1770 Jean-Bonaventure, an interpreter with the Indian Department, was licensed to trade at the Toronto (Humber) River with the local Indians. He transmitted his linguistic skills to his son Jean-Baptiste, who later put them to good use when he in turn joined the department in 1775, on the eve of the American revolution. During the subsequent campaigning he

Rousseaux

may have served with Luc de La Corne* and probably met Joseph Brant [THAYENDANEGEA], the influential Mohawk chief.

On 14 July 1780 Rousseaux married Marie Martineau (Martineaut) at Montreal. In 1783 they reportedly moved to Cataraqui (Kingston, Ont.), where for a few years Rousseaux spent the winter months after lengthy stints of trading at the mouth of the Toronto River, his father's old stamping-ground, and interpreting for the Indian Department. Presumably this erratic life contributed to the breakup of his marriage, which ended in the summer of 1786 after his wife "in her blindness" became involved with another man. Within a year he took a second wife, Margaret Clyne (Cline, Klein), "formerly a prisoner among the Mohock Indians," who had been adopted by Brant. Brant placed a high value on Rousseaux's judgement and ability, and this union strengthened their relationship. On two subsequent occasions the couple renewed their vows before the Church of England clergyman Robert Addison*: first at Brant's home on the Grand River on 15 Oct. 1795 and secondly at Niagara on 30 June 1807. Although Rousseaux's first marriage had been childless, the second produced six children including a son named Joseph Brant.

In the late 1780s Rousseaux was still trading at the Bay of Quinte and "the regions thereabout," the latter doubtless including the Toronto area. When the first surveying party passed along the north shore of Lake Ontario in 1791 it was greeted at Toronto by "Mr. St. John," as he had come to be known locally. That same year he began trading with the Six Nations and built a corn mill near the present site of Brantford. Apparently a year later, after he had been joined by his wife and family, he took up year-round residence on a 500-acre tract on the east bank of the Humber.

By 1792 Rousseaux was established as a shop-keeper, probably the first in what shortly became the town of York (Toronto). As a fur trader and general merchant, he entered partnership with Thomas Barry in 1794, and they soon became regular customers of Richard CARTWRIGHT, the prominent Kingston merchant who supplied most western traders. Rousseaux also continued as an interpreter. On 24 July 1793 Lieutenant Governor SIMCOE urged that he be appointed his personal interpreter. Rousseaux had, Simcoe wrote to Alured Clarke*, the lieutenant governor of Lower Canada, "all the requisites necessary for that office, and is equally agreeable to . . . [Brant] and the Mohawks as to the Missassagas . . . the only person, who possesses any great degree of influence with either of those Nations." Yet once that year Rousseaux had refused to assist Simcoe "on account of the impracticability of quitting his mercantile business for so long a season." However, he did serve during a council called at the Humber for 26 Aug. 1793.

In 1795, in part because he had been refused additional land on the Humber, Rousseaux decamped with his family to the Head of the Lake (the vicinity of present-day Hamilton Harbour) and settled in Ancaster Township. He had prepared the way on 5 Oct. 1794 by purchasing from James Wilson his half share of a grist-mill and sawmill owned by Wilson and Richard Beasley*. In 1797 Rousseaux bought out Beasley's share. Building on his York experience, he opened a general store and entered into a brisk trade with Brant's Mohawks and other Six Nations customers from the Grand River. He opened an inn and a blacksmith shop and over the years amassed considerable landed property. In 1796, in collaboration with Wilson and Beasley, he purchased block 2 of the Six Nations' lands, comprising some 94,000 acres. This sale and others were ratified by the government on 5 Feb. 1798. Shortly thereafter Beasley bought out his partners' interests. Rousseaux's business activities in this period may have been partly financed by a £1,000 bond dated 20 June 1798 from Brant acting on behalf of the Six Nations. On 4 May 1809 Rousseaux sold his mills to the Union Mill Company, whose shareholders, including Abraham Markle*, may have been operating them as early as 1806.

Rousseaux had become a man of parts and he was appointed the township's tax collector. Moreover, this son of old Quebec, who had once affirmed that he was a faithful member of the "Apostolic and Roman Church," became a freemason on 31 Jan. 1796 in the newly formed Barton Lodge. He continued as an interpreter and adviser on Indian affairs, not always, it would appear, to the satisfaction of his superiors. Although Administrator Peter RUSSELL often appreciated his services, he sometimes thought that Rousseaux was interfering with the government's Indian policy. On one occasion in 1798 Russell accused him of trying to block a scheme to curb Brant's power for fear it might threaten the miller's own commercial interests. In spite of these squalls, however, Rousseaux was retained by the Indian Department, and he came to play an active role in the colony's militia establishment as well. On 24 June 1797 Robert HAMILTON, lieutenant of the county of Lincoln, appointed him an ensign in the militia. He was commissioned captain on 15 July 1799 in the West Riding Militia of York and on 16 May 1811 he was promoted lieutenant-colonel in the 2nd York Militia. The following year he was appointed captain in the Indian Department. On the eve of hostilities with the United States, in early June 1812, he reported to William Claus*, deputy superintendent general of Indian affairs, on activities at Grand River of Senecas from New York. They had been sent by the famous chief Red Jacket [Sagoyewatha*] to urge the neutrality of the Six Nations.

Rousseaux was present at the battle of Queenston

Heights on 13 Oct. 1812. He died of pleurisy on 16 November while visiting Fort George (Niagara-on-the-Lake) and was buried with full military honours in St Mark's churchyard at Niagara. He left his estate to his wife, to William Crooks, brother of James*, and to Markle. Aside from his Ancaster properties Rousseaux's estate included 500 acres in Barton Township, 400 acres in Oxford (East and West Oxford) Township, and 200 acres in Beverley Township. He had 69 outstanding accounts totalling in excess of £1,170 and owed £1,151 12s. 1d. His principal creditors were the Crooks brothers, merchants at Niagara, to whom he was in debt for £312 5s., and the Montreal firm of Auldjo and Maitland, which was owed £555 17s. 10d.

Rousseaux made a significant contribution to Indian affairs and to the development of early York and Ancaster. He was also a visible bridge between two régimes, the one French and geared to the ancient fur trade, the other British and responsive to the needs of more varied commercial enterprises and, above all, to the demands of a colony of settlement.

CHARLES M. JOHNSTON

AO, MU 2554–55; RG 22, ser.155, will of J.-B. Rousseaux. MTL, D. W. Smith papers, B7: 227–37; Alexander Wood papers, business letterbooks, I: 7–8 (Wood to R. and S. Hatt, 15 May 1801). PAC, MG 19, F1, 10: 87ff.; RG 1, E3, 7: 9a–c; 68: 206–18; L3, 204: G5/65; 422A: R1/20, 27; RG 5, A1: 15999–6000; RG 10, A2, 27: 511ff.; RG 19, 3741, claim 73. PRO, CO 42/321: 35–36. *Canada, Indian treaties and surrenders* ... [1680–1906] (3v., Ottawa, 1891–1912; repr. Toronto, 1971), 1: 27. *Corr. of Hon. Peter Russell* (Cruikshank and Hunter), 2: 53, 187, 272, 310–11. *Corr. of Lieut. Governor Simcoe* (Cruikshank), 1: 396; 5: 70, 79, 111, 226. [E. P. Gwillim (Simcoe)], *Mrs. Simcoe's diary*, ed. M. Q. Innis (Toronto and New York, 1965), 101, 106. "Surveyors' letters, etc.," AO *Report*, 1905: 472. *Town of York, 1793–1815* (Firth), 1v, lvii, 7–8, 109–12, 212, 215. "U.C. land book C," AO *Report*, 1931: 32. *Valley of Six Nations*, 97, 129–30, 139, 142, 154–55, 160–61.

Illustrated historical atlas of the county of Wentworth, Ont. (Toronto, 1875; repr. Dundas, Ont., 1971), iv, viii, 38–39. W. H. Smith, *Canada: past, present and future* ... (2v., Toronto, [1852]; repr. Belleville, Ont., 1973–74), 1: 170, 229. *Ancaster's heritage: a history of Ancaster Township* (Ancaster, Ont., 1973), 25, 27–28. *Historical sketch of the Barton Lodge No.6, G.R.C., A.F. and A.M.* (Hamilton, Ont., 1895), 183. C. M. Johnston, *Brant County: a history, 1784–1945* (Toronto, 1967). K. M. Lizars, *The valley of the Humber, 1615–1913* (Toronto, 1913), 36–48. Norman Macdonald, *The Barton Lodge, A.F. and A.M., No.6, G.R.C., 1795–1945* (Toronto, [1945]), 39–40. P. J. Robinson, *Toronto during the French régime* ... (2nd ed., Toronto, 1965), 209–20.

ROUTH, RICHARD, office holder and judge; b. in Bristol, England; m. 3 July 1771 Abigail Eppes, daughter of William Eppes of Salem, Mass., and they had seven children, including Randolph Isham*; d. 1801 at sea.

Richard Routh would have been instantly identified by Charles Dickens as being of that classical genus, the inveterate place seeker. He knew little of the revenue service, but moved from the obscurity of his civilian life to the senior customs position in Newfoundland; he knew even less about law, but became chief justice of the island.

Routh emigrated from Bristol to Salem at the age of 17 and became a storekeeper there. For seven years he also acted as deputy collector of customs at Salem and Marblehead. A loyalist, he took part in the evacuation of Boston in March 1776 and at New York that summer he joined the Associated Loyalists of Massachusetts for the defence of the city. In October 1778 he left for England with his family.

Although Routh was without employment he was not without influence. Probably through his father-in-law, he was placed in touch with Benjamin LESTER of Poole, the wealthiest merchant in the Newfoundland trade. Routh's name began to appear in Lester's diary in 1779 and soon after he went to Poole, where he acted as a senior clerk or manager for some of Lester's business affairs. However, by 1782 Lester's son-in-law George Garland had joined the firm, and this event ended Routh's prospects for advancement. He then apparently purchased a vessel and prepared to go into business on his own account. Events in Newfoundland rendered this step unnecessary when the position of collector of customs was declared vacant. It had been untenanted since 1777, but the American war had preoccupied government and no one in Newfoundland was anxious to remind it that there was no longer a custom-house on the island. Lester had substantial political interest, and as a result between 1782 and 1785 he managed to obtain the post of collector of customs for Routh and that of controller of customs for D'Ewes Coke, a surgeon at Lester's main fishery in Trinity Bay.

Routh sailed to Newfoundland in 1782, and returned to Poole on the very day that the merchants met and decided to support those of Dartmouth in a campaign to have the custom-house in Newfoundland abolished. This campaign had nothing to do with him personally and had been going on since 1764, the year in which the commissioners of the customs had first decided that Newfoundland, like the mainland possessions, ought to have a custom-house. Routh reacted quickly to the news that the merchants had voted to abolish his job and spent the end of December 1782 currying favour with as many of them as he could find. At the same time Lester exerted his own much more powerful influence and very soon another meeting of the merchants was held where the resolution "was dropp'd and [it was] agreed that Mr. Routh would [do] everything in his power to lessen the

Routh

grievances they complain'd of and put the fees on a more equitable plan." This reversal placed a wedge between the merchants of Poole and those of Dartmouth and Bristol, who continued to press for the abolition of the custom-house. The division was, however, explicable in wider terms than the influence of Lester or the modest and placatory demeanour of Routh. The Devon merchants had their major interests in St John's and were thus under the direct eye of the customs officials. Only one of the Poole firms was established there, the rest trading to the outports, where the customs officials were all either agents, doctors, or clergymen under the influence of the merchants.

In 1786 the government confirmed the necessity of the custom-house. Routh, although now secure, would meet with hostility from St John's traders almost to the end of his life, but it was muted and generally passive, owing in part to his own discretion in exercising power. The position of collector of customs in Newfoundland carried no fixed salary, and Routh depended upon a share of the fees levied on shipping and cargoes. The job had one supreme attraction, however: the collector, unlike his deputy the controller, was not obliged to reside permanently on the island. Newfoundland's shipping season was confined to the period April–December, and for most of that time the controller could handle all the duties – it was necessary for Routh to be present only at the end of the fishing season. Routh exploited this situation to the full. He never left England until June, sometimes delayed sailing until August, and could be sure of returning to Britain by the end of December. His family was settled in Poole, and his winters were agreeably taken up by dinners, and in trips from Poole into the country, to Bath for "the waters," and up to London, while the rigours of life in Newfoundland were softened by the employment of a maid and the importation of what appears to have been the first coach. His life of pleasant and dignified routine was enlivened only by the dangers of the sea and by a temporary revival of mercantile antagonism to the custom-house between 1790 and 1793. He continued to win the support of previously hostile merchants, obtained the confidence of the government and a succession of naval governors, and retained the warm regard of Benjamin Lester.

In 1798 an unexpected event propelled Routh to the apex of his career when D'Ewes Coke, now chief justice of Newfoundland, was forced to resign. After the departure of John Reeves* in 1793 it had proved impossible to persuade anyone with the slightest legal training to replace him as chief justice, and in the absence of any qualified candidates Coke obtained the job. Although he was not originally required to reside permanently in Newfoundland, in 1798 Governor William Waldegrave prevailed upon the government to order this condition. Coke pleaded ill health and resigned, and strenuous lobbying by the Poole merchants resulted in Routh's appointment; through some oversight he continued to act as the collector of customs as well. The last three years of his life were, however, increasingly unpleasant. He was no more willing than Coke to spend any winters in Newfoundland, and to everyone's consternation he appeared back in England at the end of the year, explaining he had come for his family. An angry government ordered him to return by the first warship which sailed in March; Routh replied with a doctor's certificate to the effect that a serious attack of gout made a journey to Newfoundland most inadvisable.

Routh finally sailed, without his family, in July 1799, and again determined to return home at the end of the year. He waited until Waldegrave had sailed for England and thus had to take passage on a Dartmouth fishing brig. This vessel was taken in January 1800 by a French privateer and for two months Routh underwent an expensive and exhausting captivity. He disconsolately returned to Newfoundland the same year, spent two or three months on the island, and sailed for England in December on the frigate *Camilla*. A heavy gale threw her on her beam ends, and according to Routh forced him under water for five minutes, greatly aggravating his gout and doing nothing to improve his now bitter relationship with his superiors. By this time Routh must have regretted his decision to commute between England and New-foundland, but the needs of his family drove him on. In August 1801 he missed the convoy and had to take passage out on an unknown merchant vessel. By December he had not returned to England and his friends became alarmed. Six months later the government received a letter from Jonathan Ogden, chief surrogate judge in St John's, which with careful sympathy reminded the government that Routh must now be presumed dead, outlined the need for a new chief justice, and recommended himself for the post.

Thus ended the life of Richard Routh. What had he done to affect the world? One is forced to conclude that he had affected it very little. However, he had managed to maintain his wife and to rear his children to maturity. His connection with Lester outlasted both their lives, for most of his sons became merchants, some almost certainly through the influence of Lester's heirs.

K. MATTHEWS

Dorset Record Office, D365/F2–F10; P227/RE3–RE10 (Reg. of marriages, 1770–86). Hunt, Roope & Co. (London), Robert Newman & Co., letterbooks, 1800. PANL, GN 2/1, 1783–1801. PRO, BT 1/2; BT 5/5, 5/9; CO 194/21–43; CO 325/5. G.B., House of Commons, *Reports from committees of the House of Commons which have been printed by order of the house and are not inserted in the Journals*, [1715–1801] (16v., London, [1803–20]),

Roy

10: 391–503, "Reports from the committee on the state of the trade to Newfoundland, severally reported in March, April, & June, 1793." Jones, *Loyalists of Mass.* Stark, *Loyalists of Mass.* (1910).

ROUVILLE, JEAN-BAPTISTE-MELCHIOR HERTEL DE. *See* HERTEL

ROW. *See* ROE

ROY, NARSISE (Narcis, Narcisse, Narsis, Narsisse), silversmith and merchant; b. 27 Nov. 1765 in Montreal, Que., son of Jacques Roy and Marie-Françoise Prud'homme; d. there 23 March 1814.

Narsise Roy must have done his apprenticeship as a silversmith in the period between 1777 and 1786. Robert CRUICKSHANK may have given him his training, since their marks bear striking similarities, particularly in the way the initials RC and NR are formed. However, Roy could have had as master one of the many other silversmiths who were active in Montreal at that time: Louis-Nicolas Gaudin, *dit* La Poterie, Charles-François Delique, Jacques Varin*, *dit* La Pistole, Joseph Schindler*, Louis-Alexandre and Pierre HUGUET, *dit* Latour, Bernard Decousse, Dominique Rousseau*, François Larsonneur, Caspar Frederic Grunewalt, Pierre Foureur, *dit* Champagne, Simon Beaugrand, John Wood, or Michael ARNOLDI.

On 25 June 1787, Roy, "a merchant silversmith," married Marie-Joseph Jérôme, *dit* Latour, in Montreal. The bride brought a dowry of 1,100 *livres*; in addition she received an inheritance from her mother in 1788 and one from her father in 1789, which brought in 1,800 *livres*, 30½ cords of hardwood, and a year's wheat crop. The couple moved into the house belonging to Pierre Roy, Narsise's brother, on Rue Saint-Laurent. Twelve children were born of the marriage.

Roy remained in close touch with his family. From 1794 he kept his mother in his own home and looked after her; hence he gained certain benefits under her will and some minimal financial aid from one of his brothers because "his large family does not permit him to keep his said mother without some compensation." Bonds of family and friendship linked the Roys with a number of silversmiths, in particular Nathan Starns, at whose marriage they were present on 20 Feb. 1794. Roy was also godfather to Narcisse Auclair, who would become an apprentice of Cruickshank in 1805 and then of Starns in 1807. Another of Cruickshank's apprentices, Michel Roy, was a nephew of Narsise. Furthermore Roy appraised the tools of Pierre Huguet, *dit* Latour, and the contents of his silversmith's shop for the inventories made after the deaths of his two wives, the first being done in 1788 with the assistance of Foureur, *dit* Champagne, and the second in 1802 with the help of Starns.

Roy regularly engaged in land and real estate transactions. In 1789 and 1790 he purchased in succession two properties in the *faubourg* Saint-Laurent, one of them from the merchant Louis Cavilhe. It is interesting that the sum of 6,500 shillings required for this purchase was paid entirely in trade silver. The first instalment, made in February 1791, was valued at 1,000 shillings; it consisted of "two thousand ear pendants for the Indians, of thoroughly cleaned and polished silver, half of them small and half large." The final remittance was delivered in 1794. That year Roy bought a third property, again in the *faubourg* Saint-Laurent, from the merchant Joseph Howard*, for 3,000 *livres*, of which 2,400 would be paid "in silverware for the Indians." This debt eventually had to be paid to the merchant Jean-Baptiste-Toussaint Pothier* since Howard's heirs transferred it to him in 1805. In 1796 Roy bought another piece of land in the *faubourg* Saint-Laurent, and in 1798 a lot on Rue Saint-Jacques on which he immediately erected a two-storey stone house. He had another house built in 1808–9. These numerous investments give evidence of real prosperity and business acumen.

The hiring of five apprentices in succession reflected intense activity. Jean-Baptiste Lapointe was taken on in 1793 for six years, and Roy remained in touch with him and acted as a witness at his marriage in 1802; Charles-Olivier Lepage was engaged in 1796, Antoine Delisle in 1797, Louis Tribaut, *dit* Laffriquain, in 1801, and François Leclair in 1802. From 1801 until 1804 Roy filled orders for the North West Company amounting to an impressive total of some 45,000 articles of trade silver: brooches, ear-rings, charms in the shape of crosses, bracelets, and "couettes"; the £1,500 of income they generated was a very large sum at the time. Roy also sold the company other goods, such as bolts of cloth and shoes.

At the end of the 18th century there was a heavy demand for trade silver. Like a number of Montreal silversmiths Roy directed the greater part of his professional activity to that market, having abandoned production of religious silverware. As the articles for the fur trade were not always marked, and as they were dispersed over an immense territory, only a few utensils and pieces of jewellery bearing his mark have been identified. The commercial importance of trade silver, in terms of the number of silversmiths involved and the phenomenal quantities of items produced, has not yet been adequately assessed in the context of an economy in which the fur trade occupied a privileged position.

During the 27 years of his business Narsise Roy hired five apprentices. Over a period of 34 years Cruickshank took on the same number, whereas Huguet in his 35 years of practice relied on two master

Ruckle

silversmiths and eight apprentices. Cruickshank and Huguet, however, made a great deal of religious and domestic silverware as well. Thus Roy may be ranked as one of the largest producers of trade silver, along with the Huguets, Cruickshanks, Arnoldis, Rousseaus, and Schindlers.

ROBERT DEROME and JOSÉ MÉNARD

[John E. Langdon is the only author to mention Narsise Roy's apprenticeship with Robert Cruickshank, but he does not cite the source of this statement. R.D. and J.M.]
ANQ-M, CE1-51, 28 nov. 1765, 25 juin 1787, 4 nov. 1790, 26 mars 1814; CE1-63, 1802; CN1-68, 23 avril 1813; CN1-74, 17 janv. 1788; 30 janv., 27–28 sept. 1802; 12, 26 déc. 1808; 27 avril 1809; CN1-121, 23 nov. 1790, 14 mai 1794; CN1-128, 21 juin 1787; 1ᵉʳ oct. 1788; 30 mars, 30 mai, 21 août 1789; 11 févr. 1793; 20 févr., 29 juill., 25 sept. 1794; 19, 20 août, 25 oct., 23 nov. 1796; 22 sept. 1797; 30 août, 10 sept. 1798; 24 août, 13 sept. 1799; 13 juin 1801; 29 mai 1805; CN1-185, 15 June, 13 Dec. 1802; 4 Nov. 1805; 16 Oct. 1807; CN1-243, 29 mai 1805; CN1-313, 23 mai 1809; 17 févr., 27 mars 1810. MAC-CD, Fonds Morisset, 2, R888/M623/2; R888/N222.5. Langdon, *Canadian silversmiths*. Traquair, *Old silver of Quebec*. Gérard Morisset, "Bibelots et futilités," *La Patrie* (Montréal), 15 janv. 1905: 14–15.

RUCKLE, BARBARA (Heck), b. 1734 in Ballingrane (Republic of Ireland), daughter of Bastian (Sebastian) Ruckle and Margaret Embury; m. 1760 Paul Heck in Ireland, and they had seven children, of whom four survived infancy; d. 17 Aug. 1804 in Augusta Township, Upper Canada.

Normally, the subject of a biography has been a major participant in significant events or has enunciated distinctive ideas or proposals, which have been recorded in documentary form. Barbara Heck, however, left no letters or statements; indeed the evidence for such matters as the date of her marriage is secondary. There are no surviving primary sources from which one can reconstruct her motives and her actions throughout most of her life. Nevertheless she has become an heroic figure in the early history of Methodism in North America. In this instance, the biographer's task is to define and account for the myth and, if possible, to describe the real person enshrined in it.

The Methodist historian Abel Stevens wrote in 1866: "The progress of Methodism in the United States has now indisputably placed the humble name of Barbara Heck first on the list of women in the ecclesiastical history of the New World. . . . The magnitude of her record must chiefly consist of the 'setting' of her precious name, made from the history of the great cause with which her memory is forever identified, more than from the history of her own life." Barbara Heck was involved fortuitously in the inception of Methodism in the United States and Canada, and her fame rests on the natural tendency of a highly successful movement or institution to glorify its beginnings in order to strengthen its sense of tradition and continuity with its past.

Barbara Ruckle was a member of a distinctive community of German refugees, commonly known as the Palatines, who were settled in Ireland by the British government in 1709. In the wake of John Wesley's second visit to Ireland in 1748, which would lead to the establishment of the Irish Conference, many in this group of about 100 families became Methodists. Among the converts who were brought together in Methodist societies were Barbara Ruckle and her future husband, Paul Heck. In 1760, the year of their marriage, the Hecks, along with several other families of their faith, emigrated to New York intending to found a linen factory in New York City. This objective was not achieved and the new settlers took various other forms of employment.

At this time Methodism had not penetrated formally to the British North American colonies and without leadership the little group of German-Irish Methodists became religiously indifferent. The tradition, which is doubtless largely authentic, is that Barbara Heck's concern about their worldliness came to a head in 1766 when she came upon a group of her friends playing cards in her kitchen. Angrily she "lifted a corner of her apron, swept the cards from the table into it with her hand, went to the fire and cast them from her apron into the flames. . . . She put on her bonnet and went to Philip Embury and said to him, 'Philip you must preach to us or we shall all go to hell together, and God will require our blood at your hands!'" Embury, formerly a local preacher in Ireland, hesitantly took up her challenge and held the first service in his home. It was attended by five persons including the Hecks and their African slave. The congregation grew rapidly and in 1768 the Wesley Chapel (John Street Church), the first Methodist church in New York, was opened.

By the mid 1760s continuous emigration from Britain had brought many former Methodists to the North American colonies. The group gathered by Mrs Heck's example was one of several which emerged in Maryland, Pennsylvania, and New York. Wesley's awareness of this development led him to send two missionaries to New York in 1769. They and their successors, notably Francis Asbury, would lay the foundations of the Methodist Episcopal Church in the United States between 1784 and 1800. Meanwhile, through their own movements, the Hecks and other Palatine families participated unwittingly in the diffusion of Methodism.

In 1770, evidently dissatisfied with life in New York, a group including the Emburys and the Hecks settled in Camden Township near modern Bennington, Vt. Again Embury formed a society, at Ash-

728

grove, N.Y., which subsequently became a major centre of Methodism in the New York Conference. The growth of the Camden community was interrupted, however, by the onset of the American Revolutionary War. Paul Heck enlisted in a loyalist regiment and inevitably, in 1778, his farm was confiscated by the rebels. The Hecks, offspring of refugees, now became refugees themselves, members of the motley collection of people who were caught between the bitter proponents of the imperial government and of colonial independence. As such, they sought refuge in Montreal, Que., and as loyalists were resettled in 1785 in Township No.7 (Augusta).

Paul and Barbara Heck and their surviving children established a new home on the third concession of Augusta. They and other former Palatine families who came to this area and to the Bay of Quinte townships apparently sought to keep alive the rudiments of Methodist fellowship and discipline. These two groups were the nuclei of the first circuits in what would become the Canada Conference of the Methodist Episcopal Church. Paul Heck died in 1795; Barbara died suddenly on 17 Aug. 1804 in her son Samuel*'s home. She was buried in the cemetery of the Blue Church (Anglican), near modern Prescott.

In 1909 the Methodist churchman Albert Carman* commented that Barbara Heck "led a humble, holy, blameless life, and died among her kindred with her Bible . . . on her knees." It is characteristic of the legendary quality of that life that the Bible she held was not in German, as tradition has it, but in the Netherlands language; and that the recently demolished Heck house which was claimed to be her home was not the one in which she spent her last years. There is no reason, however, to doubt Dr Carman's assessment. Her determination surely had something to do with the growth of Methodism in New York City; similarly her faith must have influenced her family and her friends to remain loyal to Methodism in adversity and migration. Samuel Heck's career as a prominent local preacher in the St Lawrence settlements was at least in part a testimony to his mother's strong convictions. It is wrong, however, to assert as older Methodist writers have that Barbara Heck and the Palatine families played a decisive part in the foundation of Methodism in the British North American colonies. They were a minute group in an evangelical movement in the North Atlantic world which was fostered by a multitude of persons galvanized by the preaching of John Wesley, George Whitefield, Jonathan Edwards, and many lesser figures.

In retrospect, it is evident that the glorification of Barbara Heck reflected the pride of Canadian and American Methodists in the rapid growth of their denomination in the 19th century and their firm belief that history is the record of the work of Providence in time. Viewed from a longer and different perspective, the study of her life illuminates the ease with which history can become hagiography, and the persistent search in our society for meaningful personal links with the past.

G. S. FRENCH

[The accounts of Barbara Heck in the older secondary sources are essentially hagiographical. They do incorporate, however, letters and reminiscences by persons who knew her children, grandchildren, and other relatives. The information contained in these is consistent with the available documentary evidence, most of which concerns Mrs Heck's relatives and friends. Paul Heck's "German Bible," actually a Dutch New Testament and Psalter, is at the United Church Arch., Central Arch. of the United Church of Canada, Toronto.

In *From Wesley to Asbury*, *infra.*, Professor Baker has clarified the outlines of the first phase of Methodist history in the Thirteen Colonies. G.S.F.]

United Church Arch., Central Arch. of the United Church of Canada, "A collection of documents relating to the Hecks, Emburys, and other clans" (copies). Frank Baker, *From Wesley to Asbury: studies in early American Methodism* (Durham, N.C., 1976). J. [S.] Carroll, *Case and his cotemporaries* . . . (5v., Toronto, 1867–77). William Crook, *Ireland and the centenary of American Methodism* . . . (London, 1866). E. C. Lapp, *To their heirs forever* (Picton, Ont., 1970). Abel Stevens, *The women of Methodism* . . . (New York, 1866). W. H. Withrow, *Barbara Heck: a tale of early Methodism* (Toronto, 1895). J. W. Hamilton, "Address at the unveiling of the monument to Barbara Heck," *Christian Guardian* (Toronto), 4 Aug. 1909: 23–26.

RUSSELL, PETER, office holder, politician, and judge; b. 11 June 1733 in Cork (Republic of Ireland), only son of Richard Russell and his first wife, Elizabeth Warnar; d. 30 Sept. 1808 in York (Toronto), Upper Canada.

Peter Russell was the son of an improvident Irish army officer who claimed without much evidence to be related to the Duke of Bedford. His formal education consisted of boarding for four years with the Reverend Barton Parkinson, first at Cork and then at Kinsale, where he shared studies and a bed with his first cousin William WILLCOCKS and where he became "a very pretty Schollar" according to Parkinson. For six months in 1751 he attended St John's College, Cambridge, but his university career ended abruptly because of his extravagance. He considered entering the army, navy, or trade; he chose the army because he thought he was too weak for the navy and too old for his first choice, trade. Unfortunately there was neither enough money to buy his commission nor enough influence to get one without purchase; Russell had to wait for the Seven Years' War to enter the army.

In 1754 Major-General Edward Braddock, commanding officer of Russell's father's regiment, the 14th Foot, and newly appointed commander-in-chief

Russell

in North America, advised Russell to go there as a volunteer because chances of a commission were good. Russell arrived in South Carolina on 21 May 1755, but delayed joining Braddock's army because of sickness, difficulties in communication, and high living. In July he heard of Braddock's defeat and death, and of his own appointment as an ensign in the 14th, still at Gibraltar. Russell stayed in North America until November, finally arriving in Gibraltar the following May. From July to October 1756 he took part in the second abortive attempt to relieve the garrison on Minorca [see John Byng*]. After becoming a lieutenant on 8 May 1758, Russell returned to England, became dissatisfied, and "quitted his commission in a pet." Realizing, however, that he was too old to begin a new career he accepted Lieutenant-Colonel John Vaughan's offer of a lieutenancy in a new regiment, the 94th Foot, raised for service in North America. Commissioned on 12 Jan. 1760, Russell sailed for North America on 26 August, serving as adjutant and paymaster mostly in the West Indies until the reduction of the regiment on 24 Oct. 1763.

In August 1763 Russell arrived in New York owing more than £1,000 after a disastrous final week of gambling in Martinique. Successful gambling in New York enabled him to settle his army accounts; even greater success in Virginia brought him a 462-acre tobacco plantation 42 miles west of Williamsburg. Here Russell lived on half pay for almost eight years, hiding from his creditors and longing for capital to enter the lucrative slave trade. To raise funds he once more tried gambling, but again he lost; to pay his Virginia debts he had to sell his estate and return to England. Arriving home on 14 Oct. 1771, he was beset with demands for payment of his Martinique debts, and in November 1773 he was forced to fly to the Netherlands where he stayed for ten months before returning. After a humiliating residence within the bounds of Fleet prison he was discharged on 7 Oct. 1774 under the Insolvent Debtors Relief Act.

War in America once more gave him an occupation. On 15 Aug. 1775 Russell was commissioned lieutenant in an additional company of the 64th Foot raised for the war. For several years he recruited in Ireland; finally on 25 Feb. 1778 he sailed for America because promotions were given only to officers there. He succeeded to the captain-lieutenancy of the 64th on 18 August and in October became an assistant secretary to the commander-in-chief, Sir Henry Clinton. After taking part in the capture of Charleston, Russell was appointed judge of the Vice-Admiralty Court of South Carolina on 19 May 1780 by Clinton, but this appointment was disallowed and given to a lawyer with prior claim. On 19 December Russell finally received his captaincy in the 64th. He sold it nine months later at an inflationary price of £2,000 just

before leaving with Clinton on his unsuccessful attempt to relieve Lieutenant-General Charles Cornwallis at Yorktown, Va. On 1 Jan. 1782 Clinton appointed him superintendent of the port of Charleston and on 15 April captain in the Royal Garrison Battalion, but Clinton's career in America was over, and on 13 May 1782 he and Russell sailed for England.

Because of the sale of his commission Russell for the first time in his life had money, which he showered on his father, his half-sister Elizabeth*, and even the mendicant Willcocks family. By 1786, when his father died leaving him only debt and the responsibility for Elizabeth, Russell was once more a poor man begging unsuccessfully for insignificant posts. Since his return to England he had helped Clinton in his controversy with Cornwallis and had written a monumental history of the American campaigns attacking Cornwallis. To protect Russell it was decided to publish it under Clinton's name, although as Clinton wrote, "You have already uttered too many galling truths to be forgiven." Russell's book was too controversial to be published, and it finally appeared under Clinton's name in 1954.

In 1790, then, when Upper Canada was about to come into existence, Russell was struggling to support himself and Elizabeth on a captain's half pay, his patron having lost all influence through his quarrel with Cornwallis. Clinton and other fellow officers, including SIMCOE whom Russell had met in America, still tried to help, and in the summer of 1790, when Simcoe was promised the lieutenant governorship of Upper Canada, it seemed as if Russell too was to be fortunate. In October he accepted the position of secretary to Andrew Elliott, who was going as British minister to the United States, but Elliott eventually declined the posting, destroying Russell's prospects. Simcoe then recommended Russell to Home Secretary Henry Dundas on 12 Aug. 1791 for appointment as Upper Canadian receiver and auditor general with seats on the Executive and Legislative councils. The appointments were approved in September, although Russell's commission was not issued until 31 Dec. 1791 and not received until a year later. He still hoped for something better since he would have to give up his half pay in return for only £300 a year, but when nothing materialized he left England in the spring with his half sister, Chief Justice William Osgoode*, and Attorney General John White*, arriving at Quebec on 2 June 1792.

When Russell arrived in Upper Canada he was 59, much older than most of his colleagues. His closest friends were probably the ablest members of Simcoe's government – Osgoode, White, and Surveyor General David William Smith* – but he disagreed with White and Smith in their criticism of Simcoe's autocratic methods. With Simcoe himself he was on good if not cordial terms. He was a faithful member of the councils and did his share in establishing the working machinery of government. Because all senior government officers were ill-paid, bickering over their relative portion of fees began early and continued for many years; in this squabbling Russell also did his share.

In the beginning there were only four executive councillors, with Russell's name the last on the list. In 1794, however, after Chief Justice Osgoode was transferred to Lower Canada and only one judge was left on the Court of King's Bench in Upper Canada, it was Russell whom Simcoe appointed a temporary puisne judge, with a salary of £500 a year. On 6 July 1795 Russell took over Osgoode's former position as speaker of the Legislative Council. On 1 Dec. 1795 Simcoe requested leave of absence, and recommended that Russell, "the senior Executive Counsellor, (not a Roman Catholick) and . . . in all respects the proper person" be chosen to administer the government. Russell was appointed administrator on 20 July 1796, and on the following day Simcoe left York. At 63, Russell was in a position of authority for the first time in his life.

Russell's administration began auspiciously with the peaceful transfer of six border posts from the British to the Americans under the terms of Jay's Treaty. Even the American occupation of Fort Niagara (near Youngstown), N.Y., within firing range of Fort George (Niagara-on-the-Lake), went off smoothly without the repercussions that were feared. It was a good beginning but Russell's early days in office were marred by the discovery that Simcoe had left him only 12 official documents, taking with him all his other papers including his correspondence with London and Quebec. Throughout his administration, the unfortunate Russell was ignorant of the intentions of both Simcoe and the British authorities on every aspect of government.

At this period the granting of land was the most important responsibility of government. By 1796 the machinery for handling it was grinding slowly and capriciously, not keeping up with the demand for crown grants or for the transfer of property. There was justifiable fear that speculators were acquiring too much land. Russell had always been interested in the problem: 25 years earlier, on his return from Virginia, he had tried to interest the government in his program of reform for land-granting abuses there. In Upper Canada he tightened up the system, closing loopholes and making it more efficient. The loyalist lists were revised; claims for privilege through family relationships were restricted; the surveyor general's office was to keep a list of undesirables; every petitioner was to state clearly what land he had already been granted and this declaration was to be checked; every petition was to be approved by the lieutenant governor or the

administrator; no land was to be transferred until the deed had been issued; the system for the collection of fees was revised.

Because of previous irregular land transfers an act was passed in June 1797 to secure land titles, establishing a land commission to settle individual cases. The Heir and Devisee Commission reported the following month on the grants of townships to proprietors who had agreed to settle and improve them. Simcoe had already rescinded township grants to several proprietors including Russell's cousin, William Willcocks, who had accomplished nothing. Russell went even further and rescinded all township grants, giving compensation for actual settlement only. The most famous instance involved William BERCZY, who lost Markham Township. His vehement protest was in vain for "all the Branches of this Government," according to Russell, "have but one opinion" and thus settlement by township proprietors ended. During Russell's administration there was one other attempt at mass settlement, wished on him by the British government. In the autumn of 1798, 40 French *émigrés* led by Joseph-Geneviève Puisaye*, Comte de Puisaye, arrived and were settled up Yonge Street. Russell obediently followed instructions to assist this scheme, but it was doomed to failure from the outset.

Another vexing problem concerning land was the anomalous status of the large tract on the Grand River belonging to the Six Nations Indians. Joseph Brant [THAYENDANEGEA], the Indian leader, asserted the Indians' right to sell their land; however, Simcoe and Russell maintained that it had been given in perpetuity and could not be alienated. After Simcoe's departure Brant became more insistent; Russell temporized, writing desperately to London for instructions when Brant sold 381,480 acres and demanded that deeds be issued to the purchasers. During the winter of 1796–97 there were rumours of unrest among the Indians on the Mississippi River, so that the continued loyalty of the Upper Canadian Indians was vital. On 29 June 1797 the Executive Council recommended that Russell come to an immediate decision without waiting any longer for instructions from London. Accordingly Russell agreed to issue the deeds. On 15 July, before the details had been settled with Brant, the dispatch from London finally arrived instructing Russell not to accede to Brant's request; the British government would give the Indians an annuity in lieu of permission to sell their land. Brant refused this offer, forcing Russell to disobey his instructions and to issue the deeds on condition that no more land be alienated. In the midst of this controversy Russell learned that responsibility for Indian affairs in Upper Canada had been transferred to him from Quebec on 15 Dec. 1796.

Until the arrival of the new chief justice, John ELMSLEY, on 20 Nov. 1796 Russell's Executive

Ryerse

Council was weak. Unfortunately Elmsley, although strong, opposed Russell almost continually. Their first major battle was over the seat of government. Before Simcoe left he had moved his capital from Newark (Niagara-on-the-Lake) to York, despite the lack of enthusiasm of most government officials, including Russell. Elmsley objected vigorously, but Russell doggedly followed Simcoe's directions, and met his first parliament in York in June 1797. He spent much effort in improving the capital: the New Town was surveyed and opened west of Simcoe's original site; a primitive zoning plan was established; work on public buildings was accelerated; plans were made for adequate defence; some local self-government was granted; police-force regulations were proposed (but blocked by Elmsley); better transportation links with other parts of the province were provided by extending Simcoe's Dundas and Yonge streets into the town and by building the Danforth Road east to Kingston.

Russell's reappointment of himself to the Court of King's Bench was also sharply criticized by Elmsley. Though the reason for his holding the judgeship was no longer valid, Russell kept reissuing his own commission, the last time being on 17 March 1798. He probably did it for the salary; as administrator he received no additional remuneration. With no legal training Russell was vulnerable to ridicule on the bench while at the same time he was breaching the principle of separation of executive and judicial powers. Finally he was ordered to give up the judgeship in return for half Simcoe's salary and fees.

Until the spring of 1798 Russell had expected Simcoe's return to Upper Canada. Thereafter he hoped, without much expectation, to become governor, but in June 1799 he heard of Peter HUNTER's appointment and that August Hunter arrived in Upper Canada. The new lieutenant governor was much impressed by Elmsley, so that Russell's influence as well as his position was greatly diminished. He remained receiver general and was a member of the small committee that governed the province during Hunter's absences, but he had little power. Simcoe had asked that some provision be made for him because he was very old, but nothing was done. After Hunter's death in 1805 Alexander GRANT was appointed administrator because his name preceded Russell's on the official list; Russell protested in vain. Although he owned thousands of acres of land in Upper Canada (as an executive councillor he was given 6,000 acres) he could not find purchasers and could not therefore afford to return to England. He remained in York, tired, sick, and old, still interested in scientific experiments which he had begun long ago in Virginia, still conscientiously doing his duty as receiver general. At his death his estate, which was rapidly increasing in value, passed to Elizabeth, who left it to William Willcocks's daughters in 1822.

Russell has never been considered one of the great men of Ontario. Although later criticism has rather unjustly charged him with greed for land, his contemporaries objected to his greed for fees and offices. As administrator he was cautious, practical, capable, and painstaking. Unlike Simcoe he had little imagination, sometimes had difficulty making decisions, and was willing to devote much thought and effort to detail. Russell, however, was administrator, not lieutenant governor, and he had neither the authority nor the security of governorship. Yet the record of legislation during his administration is impressive, not for great statutes but for those which corrected abuses, improved conditions, or made the machinery of government work more smoothly. Russell was not a great man and his abilities may have been pedestrian, but his accomplishments were very real.

EDITH G. FIRTH

Some of Peter Russell's early correspondence has been published in "The early life and letters of the Honourable Peter Russell," ed. E. A. Cruikshank, *OH*, 29 (1933): 121–40, while a comprehensive collection of his official correspondence as administrator of Upper Canada is available in *Corr. of Hon. Peter Russell* (Cruikshank and Hunter). The journal he kept during the Charleston campaign appears as "The siege of Charleston; journal of Captain Peter Russell, December 25, 1779, to May 2, 1780," ed. James Bain, *American Hist. Rev.* (New York and London), 4 (1898–99): 478–501.

AO, MS 75; MS 517. MTL, Robert Baldwin papers, sect.II; John McGill papers; Elizabeth Russell papers; Peter Russell papers; D. W. Smith papers. PAC, MG 23, HII, 7 (photocopies); RG 1, E1, 46–48; E3, 19. PRO, CO 42/316–48. QUA, Richard Cartwright papers. [Henry Clinton], *The American rebellion: Sir Henry Clinton's narrative of his campaigns, 1775–1782 . . .*, ed. W. B. Willcox (New Haven, Conn., 1954). *Corr. of Lieut. Governor Simcoe* (Cruikshank). Armstrong, *Handbook of Upper Canadian chronology*. G.B., WO, *Army list*, 1756–1808. D. B. Read, *The lieutenant-governors of Upper Canada and Ontario, 1792–1899* (Toronto, 1900), 33–40. *Life and letters of Hon. Richard Cartwright* (Cartwright). E. G. Firth, "The administration of Peter Russell, 1796–1799," *OH*, 48 (1956): 163–81. G. C. Patterson, "Land settlement in Upper Canada, 1783–1840," AO *Report*, 1920. D. R. Plaunt, "The Honourable Peter Russell: administrator of Upper Canada, 1796–1799," *CHR*, 20 (1939): 258–74.

RYERSE (Ryerson), SAMUEL, army officer, miller, office holder, judge, and militia officer; b. 1752 in Saddle River Township, N.J., son of Luke (Luyckes) Ryerse (Ryerson) and Johanna Van der Hoff; m. first Elizabeth Colwell, and they had four children, of whom a son and a daughter survived infancy; m. secondly 22 Jan. 1784 Sarah Davenport, *née* Underhill, and they had ten children, of whom two sons and

Ryerse

one daughter survived infancy; d. 12 June 1812 in Port Ryerse, Upper Canada.

Samuel Ryerse's forebears emigrated from Holland to America in the mid 17th century. They later moved to what became Bergen County, N.J., where young Samuel was raised and presumably educated. According to one family historian, on the outbreak of the American revolution Ryerse was imprisoned for his loyalty. He later escaped and joined the loyalist forces along with his younger brother Joseph*. Samuel became a captain in the New Jersey Volunteers on 25 March 1777. During the next two years he played a conspicuous role in raids into his native province from New York City. On one occasion a rebel newspaper lauded his efforts to prevent plundering by his men and judged him to be "actuated by principles of honour and humanity." Early in 1779 his lands were confiscated and sold.

In the autumn of that year Ryerse was recruited by Major Patrick Ferguson to join an élite force for service in a campaign the following spring against Charleston, S.C. Later Ferguson's force was badly beaten, on 7 Oct. 1780, at the battle of Kings Mountain. Ryerse was wounded in the left hand and wrist and ultimately lost "the ring finger and in great measure the use of my hand." He was taken prisoner and paroled the following February. Of his treatment by the rebels, he wrote to an unknown correspondent: "You would hardly believe it possible that any of the human species could be possessed of so much barbarity. If you will call to mind the most horrid cruelties that have ever been affected by savages you will then in some measure be able to judge what we have seen and suffered." Following his release, he returned to New York City where he rejoined his old unit.

At the conclusion of the war, Ryerse went on half pay. Up to this point he had almost consistently spelt his name Ryerson (on occasion he used Ryerse). Now he began to sign Ryerse. The change has often been ascribed to a clerical error on the army rolls that necessitated his adopting the variant in order to obtain his pay. The most recent study indicates that this interpretation cannot be sustained and suggests that Ryerse probably used the variant to distinguish himself from the rebel branch of his family. His brother Joseph, however, continued to use Ryerson.

The New Jersey Volunteers left New York City in September 1783, arriving in what is now the province of New Brunswick the following month. Ryerse and others in his battalion refused to settle on their designated block of land, the most remote spot then surveyed on the Saint John River. Instead he apparently squatted in the vicinity of St Anne's Point (Fredericton) until June 1784. In 1784 he repeatedly petitioned Governor Thomas CARLETON for land in Sunbury County. Finally, in December 1786, he

received 600 acres on the south bank of the Little River where he farmed and pressed, unsuccessfully, for compensation for his wartime losses. His brother Joseph, who had come with him to New Brunswick, received 400 acres at the same site.

Ryerse was not happy in New Brunswick, "being disappointed both in [its] soil and climate, finding it to be sterile and uncongenial." His wife, too, was unhappy away from her native city of New York. Thus he sold his land and by early 1793 had taken up residence in Brooklyn, N.Y. He then had four children by his second marriage; within eight weeks of his arrival, all had died. In April he returned to New Jersey and purchased land in Morris County, but animosity lingering from the revolution prompted him to seek land in Upper Canada. In the summer of 1794 he travelled to Newark (Niagara-on-the-Lake), where he met with Lieutenant Governor SIMCOE. Ryerse decided to move yet again and returned to the province with his family in the summer of 1795.

Simcoe was struck by Ryerse's "private character and fidelity to the King." Certain that the foundations of loyalty and adherence to the British constitution could be instilled in the population by force of example, Simcoe sought permission from the authorities in Great Britain to extend the boundaries of the settlement at Long Point, Norfolk County, to include Ryerse and others. Moreover, the lieutenant governor went out of his way to enhance Ryerse's status with land and offices. On 1 July 1796 he was named a justice of the peace; he was reappointed continuously until his death. On 15 July the Executive Council granted him the 3,000 acres his military rank entitled him to, and he located them in Norfolk County. He settled at the mouth of Young Creek in Woodhouse Township; there he built a sawmill and a grist-mill which formed the nucleus of the village of Port Ryerse. Unlike the former, the latter mill proved unprofitable; it was burned on 14 May 1814 by a party of American marauders including Abraham Markle*. Before his departure from Upper Canada, Simcoe had directed that Ryerse "may be placed at the head" of the militia with the rank of major at least. In the event, on 17 July 1797, Ryerse received the most important local office, that of county lieutenant [see Hazelton SPENCER], and was commissioned colonel of the 1st Norfolk Militia.

Ryerse was the pre-eminent office holder in the area and played a leading role in the administrative and military affairs of the increasingly populous eastern portion of the Western District. With the formation of the London District on 1 Jan. 1800, he was appointed the first district court judge and, presumably, the first surrogate court judge as well. The following month he became, with Thomas WELCH and Thomas Hornor*, a commissioner of the Court of King's Bench. In August he was included as one of three commissioners

733

Ryerse

responsible for administering the oath of allegiance to individuals claiming land in the district. He performed his duties assiduously. Until June 1803, for instance, he attended and chaired all but one meeting of the Court of Quarter Sessions. Other lesser offices followed: road commissioner in March 1805, trustee of the district school in 1807, and judge of the Court of Requests in 1807, and again in 1809.

Samuel Ryerse was thus part of a regional élite based on office-holding and dominated by the local assemblyman, Surveyor General David William Smith*. Smith had close ties with the powerful merchants of the Niagara peninsula such as Robert HAMILTON. But that interest did not prevent Ryerse in 1800 from heading a petition from 105 inhabitants of Norfolk County protesting "as monopolous and oppressive" the proposed bill to allow Hamilton and his partners to make improvements to the Niagara portage and pay for them by increased freight charges. Late in 1803 Smith decided not to stand for re-election in the riding of Norfolk, Oxford and Middlesex. The resulting power vacuum led to a bitter contest between rival factions.

Ryerse decided to stand, and his candidacy was opposed by Benajah Mallory*. In late May 1804 Lord Selkirk [DOUGLAS] observed that the electioneering "seems here to go on with no small sharpness." In spite of the support of fellow office holders such as Welch, Ryerse was defeated 166 votes to 77. Buoyed by this success his rivals called for the removal of Ryerse and others from office. Tension between the two groups heightened and in January 1805 several shots were fired at Mallory's home. He charged that the attempted assassination was the work of either Ryerse or John Backhouse. Ryerse, in turn, claimed the accusation was part of a conspiracy against him. Several months later the conflict was taken up in the Court of Quarter Sessions and resulted in a welter of charges and counter-charges. Office holders such as Ryerse and Welch characterized their opponents as a Methodist faction motivated by sedition. Indeed, in February 1806, Ryerse petitioned the House of Assembly to declare Mallory ineligible to sit in parliament, "having . . . been a preacher and teacher of the Religious Society or Sect called Methodists." Ryerse's counsel subpoenaed several witnesses who refused to appear; thus one year later the petition was dismissed, on the motion of Solicitor General D'Arcy Boulton*, for lack of evidence.

In 1809 the deputy paymaster general suspended Ryerse's half pay because he held government appointments. Ryerse notified Lieutenant Governor Francis Gore*'s office that he would have to obtain a certificate indicating he had received no remuneration from those offices or ask to "be removed from [them] . . . immediately . . . as they have never paid me for the loss of my time and the Stationary that I have used

on Public Business." Apparently the matter was not resolved in Ryerse's favour; in a letter dated 24 Feb. 1810 he wrote, "Some Embarrassments that I have Unluckily got into with respect to my half Pay have obliged me to resign my Several Provincial Appointments. . . ."

Even after his retirement Ryerse retained a concern for public affairs. He had, as he told Chief Justice Thomas Scott* in 1810, "the good of the Country and the Prosperity of the Province equally at heart in a private Capacity." Ryerse was disturbed about the qualifications of certain men recommended for local office. Few were fit for the situations and some were "Unfriendly" to the Gore administration. He dismissed Duncan McCall* as a trader who occasionally resided in the United States. Moreover, he had been seen in a tavern "deeply Engaged in a game of Chance (throwing Dice and pitching Dollars) which would Seem to indicate a partiality for low Company." He considered Abraham A. Rapelje a better candidate for office but noted, "He has no landed Property nor any fixed residence, and during Judge [Robert Thorpe*'s] residence in this Country was a Strong Advocate of his politiks. . . ."

More than two years after his retirement Samuel Ryerse died of tuberculosis. He had been many things in his life: a soldier, a freemason, a farmer, and a miller. But his enduring reputation was based on his prominence as an office holder. Simcoe had hoped that the principles Ryerse personified – staunch loyalism, toryism, and adherence to the Church of England – would be emulated. As the election of 1804 proved, however, these qualities could not win him the support of the majority of settlers in Norfolk, who were overwhelmingly Methodist and non-loyalist American.

DANIEL J. BROCK

AO, MS 75, Thomas Welch to Peter Russell, 31 Jan. 1805. Donly Museum, Norfolk Hist. Soc. coll., Thomas Welch papers, 892–94, 1517–18. Eldon House (London, Ont.), Commission of Samuel Ryerse as London District Court judge, 1 Jan. 1800. PAC, RG 5, A1: 846–48, 1299, 2121, 4413, 4658–59; RG 9, I, B1, 1: 145–47, 227; RG 68, General index, 1651–1841: ff.288, 290, 293, 403, 406, 408–9, 414–15, 421, 536, 645–46. UWO, John Harris papers, [Amelia Ryerse] Harris, "Mrs John Harris's account of Capt. Samuel Ryerson at Long Point"; London District, U.C., Surrogate Court, estate files, X360; Thomas Walsh papers, Ryerse to Thomas Welch, 20 Nov. 1798. *Corr. of Lieut. Governor Simcoe* (Cruikshank), 4: 46, 191, 314–15, 342–43. *Documents relating to the colonial, revolutionary and post-revolutionary history of the state of New Jersey*, ed. W. A. Whitehead et al. (42v., Newark, N.J., 1880–1949), 22: 328, 499; 23: 350–51. *Documents relating to the revolutionary history of the state of New Jersey*, ed. W. S. Stryker et al. (5v., Trenton, N.J., 1901–17), 3: 65, 77, 92, 265, 350, 593; 4: 269–70; 5: 397. Douglas, *Lord Selkirk's diary* (White), 305. "Journals of Legislative Assembly of

Sales

U.C.," AO *Report*, 1909: 135–36; 1911: 83–84, 126–27, 221–24. "Minutes of the Court of General Quarter Sessions of the Peace for the London District . . . ," AO *Report*, 1933: 1–96, 99, 120. "Political state of U.C.," PAC *Report*, 1892: 53. *Select British docs. of War of 1812* (Wood), 3: 88–91.

Armstrong, *Handbook of Upper Canadian chronology*, 141, 143, 173. *Captain Samuel Ryerse, Bergen County, New Jersey*, [comp. Phyllis Ryerse] ([Port Dover, Ont., 1975]). E. A. Jones, "The loyalists of New Jersey in the revolution," N.J. Hist. Soc., *Proc.* (Newark), new ser., 11 (1926): 484–86. *The Ryerse-Ryerson family history*, comp. Mrs J. E. [S.] [Phyllis] Ryerse (Streetsboro, Ohio, 1964), 4, 16, 22, 45, 47–48, 60, 71n. "State papers – Upper Canada," PAC *Report*, 1892: 375–76. *Wills of the London District, 1800–1839 . . .* , ed. W. R. Yeager (Simcoe, Ont., 1979),

10. J. A. Bannister, *Early educational history of Norfolk County* (Toronto, 1926), 62–64, 68. Brian Dawe, *"Old Oxford is wide awake!" : pioneer settlers and politicians in Oxford County, 1793–1853* (n.p., 1980), 16–21. A. C. Leiby, *The Revolutionary War in the Hackensack valley: the Jersey Dutch and the neutral ground, 1775–1783* (New Brunswick, N.J., 1980), 78–79, 251–52, 302, 313. G. H. Patterson, "Studies in elections and public opinion in Upper Canada" (PHD thesis, Univ. of Toronto, 1969), 10–16. E. A. Cruikshank, "The early history of the London District," *OH*, 24 (1927): 149–50, 164–65, 170. R. M. Keesey, "Loyalism in Bergen County, New Jersey," *William and Mary Quarterly* (Williamsburg, Va.), 3rd ser., 18 (1961): 558–76. G. J. Ryerse, "Port Ryerse; its harbour and former trade," *OH*, 20 (1923): 145–48.

S

SAINT-AUGUSTIN, MARIE-LOUISE COMPAIN, named. *See* COMPAIN

SAINTE-ROSE, VÉRONIQUE BRUNET, *dit* **L'ESTANG (L'Étang),** named. *See* BRUNET

SAINT-IGNACE, MARIE RAIZENNE, named. *See* RAIZENNE

SAINT-JEAN, JEAN-BAPTISTE ROUSSEAU, *dit. See* ROUSSEAUX ST JOHN, JOHN BAPTIST

ST JOHN, JOHN BAPTIST ROUSSEAUX. *See* ROUSSEAUX

SAINT-MARTIN, TOUSSAINT-ANTOINE ADHÉMAR, *dit. See* ADHÉMAR

SALABERRY, ÉDOUARD-ALPHONSE D'IRUMBERRY DE. *See* IRUMBERRY

SALES LATERRIÈRE, PIERRE DE (he did not use his patronymic Fabre in Canada, taking the name of Jean Laterrière on his arrival, Jean-Baptiste in the early 1770s, Jean-Pierre most frequently between 1778 and 1788, and Jean-Pierre or Pierre de Sales Laterrière from 1789), doctor, commissary and inspector of the Saint-Maurice ironworks, seigneur, and author; b. in the 1740s in the Languedoc-Roussillon region of France; m. 10 Oct. 1799 Marie-Catherine Delezenne*, widow of Christophe Pélissier*, at Quebec, and they had three children; d. there 14 June 1815.

Pierre de Sales Laterrière is an enigmatic figure. Called by turns a strange fellow and a pathological liar, this adventurer from the south of France left memoirs, published in 1873, which historians have treated as "the account of the impostures and subterfuges" of a Gascon desperately anxious to carve a place for himself in Canadian society. In the present state of research it is difficult to separate truth from falsehood since the errors, contradictions, improbabilities, and abridgements in his account, whether deliberate or not, help to confuse issues and even tend to cast doubt on his identity.

Pierre de Sales Laterrière purported to be the son of a count from Languedoc, Jean-Pierre de Sales, a descendant of the famous house of de Sales which had given France a great many officers and the church a saint. He based his assertions on a baptismal record dated 23 Sept. 1747 which, although carefully presented as authentic, is impossible to trace. The historian Ægidius Fauteux* has established that he was the son of a man named Fabre from the diocese of Albi and that he reportedly adopted the surname of de Sales in the 1780s. Fauteux casts further doubt on the credibility of Laterrière. Relating in his memoirs his adventures from the time he left the family home until he arrived in the province of Quebec, Laterrière mentions studying naval mathematics in La Rochelle and medicine in Paris. In fact, he is believed simply to have left his birthplace in October 1765 at the instigation of his uncle Pascal Rustan, whose real name was Henri-Marie-Paschal Fabre, *dit* Laperrière. Rustan had been released at the end of April that year from the Châtelet, where he had been imprisoned in connection with the *affaire du Canada*. Laterrière, accompanied by his uncle, is believed to have gone to Paris via La Rochelle, then to England, and finally to Canada. He arrived at Quebec on 5 Sept. 1766.

Laterrière was about 19. By his own description he was naïve and frank, exuberant, and amazed by everything he had seen while sailing up the river. He

Sales

was welcomed by Alexandre Dumas and entertained by a large number of friends to whom Rustan had recommended him. He spent the winter in Montreal, working as a clerk in one of Dumas's stores. He frequently visited his aunt, Catherine Aubuchon, *dit* Lespérance, who lived at Longue-Pointe (Montreal) and who opened the doors of polite society to him: "During the winter, which lasts 8 months, the nights are spent in feasting, suppers, dinners, and balls. The ladies there play cards a great deal before and after the dances. All games are played, but the favourite is an English game called wisk [whist]. Billiards are very fashionable, and many are ruined by them." In the spring Laterrière was back at Quebec; he remained in Dumas's employ until the latter went bankrupt in 1769. Short of resources but not of imagination, Laterrière went off to the parish of Saint-Thomas (at Montmagny) to practise medicine with Jean-Bernard Dubergès. It would appear that, with little or no medical knowledge, he set out to learn the rudiments from Dubergès.

The association did not prove profitable. Laterrière was quite happy to accept the office of agent at Quebec for the shareholders of the Saint-Maurice ironworks in 1771. At the company store, located in Dumas's house near the Lower Town market, Laterrière busied himself with selling, wholesale or retail, the products of the ironworks and sending the pig-iron to England. He restricted his medical concerns to treating "young men suffering from syphilis."

"Of pleasing appearance, well-mannered, and with a passionate fondness for dancing," according to his own assessment, Laterrière did not lack "amusements." He had several love affairs, and only lack of money kept him from marrying Marie-Catherine Delezenne, daughter of the silversmith Ignace-François Delezenne*, whom he considered "very good-looking and witty."

Satisfied with Laterrière's services as commissary and as agent in various matters, Christophe Pélissier, the director of the Saint-Maurice ironworks, invited him to move to Trois-Rivières as works inspector: he would receive a salary of £125 a year, plus one-ninth of the profits. Laterrière left Quebec on 25 Feb. 1775. On 8 March Pélissier married Marie-Catherine Delezenne, who was in love with Laterrière but may have agreed to marry the 46-year-old widower at her father's insistence. In the autumn Pélissier began to supply the American army, which was advancing towards Quebec, with guns, cannon-balls, shells, and various other items. Laterrière later claimed that he had not been aware of Pélissier's dealings with the enemy until the end of March 1776, but this seems improbable. Bearing a note from Pélissier for the officer in command of the American troops besieging Quebec, he went there early in May to get merchandise. He was arrested by the British, imprisoned for

several weeks, and then let go. He was back in Trois-Rivières at the beginning of June. The American army retreated. Worried about his own fate, on 7 June Pélissier fled for New York by way of the Richelieu. The following day the Americans were defeated at Trois-Rivières. Laterrière took over the running of the ironworks, possibly at Governor Guy Carleton's express request. He began to live with Marie-Catherine, who gave birth to a daughter, Dorothée, on 4 Jan. 1778. Having failed in their attempt to separate the lovers, Marie-Catherine's parents disinherited her on 4 Nov. 1780.

At that period the Saint-Maurice ironworks were a substantial enterprise. The region, flat and sandy, was "full of swamps and burnt lands, where the ore is located in veins . . . [and] yields 33 per cent pure and excellent iron." The furnaces and forges were run on charcoal. Between 400 and 800 people worked "in the shop or in the woods, quarries, mines, and on the carts." The company had "a store with goods and provisions," and a "spacious house"; the workers stayed in "about 130 very clean, very liveable houses." Year in year out the operation would bring in "10 to 15 thousand *louis* per seven-month season; expenses took two-thirds of it." Laterrière was happy in the midst of the "little clan" at the ironworks. "The people [were] kind," there were plenty of holidays, and the establishment had numerous visitors. On 6 Oct. 1777, on payment of £900, Laterrière became a shareholder in the enterprise. The following year Pélissier made the lease over to Dumas. Laterrière bought the Île de Bécancour, while continuing to run operations at the ironworks until October 1778. In July he had gone with Marie-Catherine to meet Pélissier, who was passing through Quebec to settle the company's accounts. Pélissier had Marie-Catherine shut up illegally, but she managed to slip away and hide on the Île de Bécancour.

In the autumn Dumas offered Laterrière, who had become the "manager and director" of the ironworks, the opportunity to enter into partnership to run them on a fifty-fifty basis, and in January 1779 they came to an agreement. To make this deal Laterrière had to let Alexis Bigot, *dit* Dorval, a habitant from the seigneury of Cap-de-la-Madeleine, have the Île de Bécancour on 10 February, in exchange for a house and lot at Trois-Rivières and 6,500 *livres*. That month, however, Laterrière was arrested. He was suspected of having incited Michel Delezenne, Marie-Catherine's brother, and an employee, John Oakes*, to go to meet the Americans and pass on information to them. In the preliminary investigation conducted by Conrad Gugy*, François Baby, and Louis-Joseph Godefroy* de Tonnancour, Oakes exonerated Laterrière, but Delezenne heaped accusations upon him. It was a confused affair. Laterrière saw in it a plot hatched by Pélissier before he had left

Sales

permanently for France; he thought that its success had been assured through HALDIMAND's connivance and the complicity of some unscrupulous and ambitious people in Trois-Rivières: the vicar general Pierre Garreau*, *dit* Saint-Onge, Godefroy de Tonnancour, the judge René-Ovide Hertel* de Rouville, and Marie-Catherine's father. A reading of all the documents related to the affair makes the hypothesis of a conspiracy seem flimsy but the accused man's innocence plausible. From the beginning his cohabitation alienated the investigators' sympathy. His version tallied on certain important points with the depositions made by Oakes on 24 February and his own farm labourer on 4 March. Later Michel Delezenne wrote to his father "that what he said at the time of his interrogation concerning Laterrière was said because he was afraid." Moreover, in January 1780 a deposition by Louis Guillon, another of Laterrière's employees, confirmed that of Michel Delezenne, adding details. An embarrassed Haldimand, confident none the less that the investigators "will have done justice to the accused as to the accusers," ordered that the prisoner be taken to Quebec. In March 1779 Laterrière was locked up in the prison, where Valentin Jautard*, Fleury Mesplet*, and Charles Hay* soon joined him. While philosophizing and quarrelling with his companions Laterrière was able to transact business through agents. The request he sent Haldimand from prison for the lease to the Saint-Maurice ironworks reveals that he was thoroughly familiar with foundry techniques. In 1780 he bought a house at Quebec and had his furniture moved there; two years later he sold his house in Trois-Rivières. Nathaniel Day worked in his name at settling accounts with Dumas.

Early in November 1782 Laterrière regained his freedom, but he had to leave Canada "until peace came." The sailing season was nearly over. He would have liked to take ship for Europe, but the only one he found in port was a brig bound for Newfoundland. He spent the winter at Harbour Grace with his daughter. In the spring of 1783 he hired a brig together with William Hardy, a merchant who had a cargo but did not know where to sell it, and they sailed for Quebec, taking time along the way to do some trading in the gulf. Once at Quebec, Laterrière decided on his friends' advice to terminate his association with Hardy and rejoin Marie-Catherine and his friends in Bécancour. He set her up "at the head of a little store" at Saint-Pierre-les-Becquets (Les Becquets), settling down himself at Bécancour, where he practised medicine, did a little trading, and contracted to have "timber for masts and firewood" cut on a woodlot that he had bought in Gentilly (Bécancour). Business was slow.

In the autumn of 1783 Laterrière's inventive mind led him to carry out a plan that on the surface was quite hare-brained. He built a house on a sleigh drawn by two horses. It was a pedlar's sleigh, "covered and quite solid; up front was a well-stocked store; in the middle and crosswise, a cupboard to hold a dispensary and surgical instruments; at the rear, a small room with a stove and chests containing a bed, dishes, and supplies." During the winter he went from parish to parish as far as Saint-Hyacinthe to offer medicaments, merchandise, and his services as a doctor. The experiment aroused people's curiosity but did not turn out to be profitable. In the spring of 1784 Laterrière settled at Gentilly with his family on a farm that he had bought for 600 *livres* the previous autumn. He lived in a house 24 feet square which he called "the château-villa of Belle-Vue." He had some success farming, but met with none speculating in wood for masts and firewood. He survived thanks to his income from practising medicine and his investment in bonds. Late in 1787 he settled at Baie-du-Febvre (Baieville), on the farm of Delezenne, who had been reconciled with his daughter. His reputation as a doctor kept on growing and he made "a lot of money."

The future was promising, until Laterrière learned that a new law required doctors to produce their diplomas and appear before the Medical Board. Since he had no diploma (or had lost it), the examiners made Laterrière return to his books, which led him to register at Harvard College in Boston in the autumn of 1788. There he studied medicine with Benjamin Waterhouse, and anatomy and surgery with John Warren. On 1 May 1789 he took his examination in medicine, and a few weeks later he presented a thesis on puerperal fever. He left Boston on 15 June, and at Quebec on 19 August he successfully took a new examination. After his return to Baie-du-Febvre the number of his patients grew rapidly. He travelled around in the neighbouring parishes, and eventually extended his practice as far as Trois-Rivières and the parishes "north of Lac Saint-Pierre." He lived comfortably and speculated in real estate. On 16 Sept. 1790 he bought three lots in Trois-Rivières; he also purchased a house there belonging to Louis-René-Labadie Godefroy de Tonnancour in which he set up practice, probably in the spring of 1791. He was appointed the prison doctor, and in October in the presence of his colleagues he did a dissection on the body of a woman who had just been hanged. This session in anatomy alienated the local population, and in the spring of 1792 he returned to his house at Baie-du-Febvre, where his son Marc-Pascal* was born on 25 March.

Eager to assure his children of a sound education, in May 1799 Laterrière went with Dorothée and his elder son, Pierre-Jean*, to live in Quebec on Rue de la Montagne. He practised medicine, surgery, and pharmacy, and kept "a dispensary for the gentlemen of the art and other private individuals." Marie-

Sarrebource

Catherine joined him in the autumn, and on 10 Oct. 1799 he married her in the cathedral of Notre-Dame at Quebec, in the presence of the coadjutor designate Joseph-Octave Plessis*. Laterrière was well received by his colleagues. He was one of the rare individuals to be a qualified doctor licensed to practise surgery, pharmacy, and obstetrics as well.

On 24 Feb. 1800 Dorothée married François-Xavier Lehouillier, who according to Laterrière was homosexual. The marriage turned sour, to the great chagrin of Laterrière; deeply affected by his daughter's misfortunes, he returned to live in Trois-Rivières around 1804. But the dangers facing his daughter, who was being ill treated by her husband, brought him back to Quebec in 1805. The matter ended in a separation.

During his short stay in Trois-Rivières Laterrière had renewed contact with the Saint-Maurice ironworks. In May 1806, with Nicholas MONTOUR and ten other partners, he formed Pierre de Sales Laterrière et Compagnie for the purpose of acquiring the lease to the ironworks. He kept 6 of the 32 shares for himself. A disagreement among the partners led to the formation of another company with a capital of £10,000, of which he became the director and ironmaster. The government, however, granted the lease to Mathew Bell*, and the new company was dissolved.

On 26 July 1807 Pierre de Sales Laterrière sailed for Europe to settle a matter of inheritance. War prevented him from going to France. He stayed in Portugal and England, whence he returned in June 1808 with merchandise which he valued at £3,000 and which Dorothée sold in the store she kept in Quebec. This deal brought Laterrière such substantial profits that he was able to send his elder son to study medicine in England and the younger one to Philadelphia; it also enabled him to purchase the seigneury of Les Éboulements on 31 Jan. 1810. "Old and infirm," Laterrière was conscious that "his role was finished." Around 1812 he left his apothecary's shop and his medical practice to his son Pierre-Jean, who later went into partnership with his younger brother, and then he retired to Les Éboulements. On 14 June 1815 he died at Quebec, in his son Marc-Pascal's home: he was buried two days later in the crypt of Notre-Dame.

PIERRE DUFOUR and JEAN HAMELIN

[Pierre de Sales Laterrière is the author of *A dissertation on the puerperal fever* . . . (Boston, 1789) and *Mémoires de Pierre de Sales Laterrière et de ses traverses*, [Alfred Garneau, édit.] (Québec, 1873; réimpr., Ottawa, 1980). Extracts from the latter work were published in *Écrits du Canada français* (Montréal), 8 (janv. 1961): 259–337; 9 (avril 1961): 261–348. P.D. and J.H.]

Arch. de l'univ. Laval (Québec), 298/17. PAC, MG 8, F131. *Quebec Gazette*, 1 Dec. 1808. Charland, "Notre-Dame de Québec: le nécrologe de la crypte," *BRH*, 20: 279.

"Collection Haldimand," PAC *Rapport*, 1888: 169, 809, 818, 984–89. J. [E.] Hare, *Les Canadiens français aux quatre coins du monde: une bibliographie commentée des récits de voyage, 1670–1914* (Québec, 1964). M.-J. et G. Ahern, *Notes pour l'hist. de la médecine*. H.-R. Casgrain, *Œuvres complètes* (3v., Québec, 1873–75), 1: 64–71. Sulte, *Mélanges hist.* (Malchelosse), 6: 123–68; 7: 84, 94–95, 98, 104. J.-P. Tremblay, *La Baie-Saint-Paul et ses pionniers* ([Chicoutimi, Qué.], 1948). Ægidius Fauteux, "La thèse de Laterrière," *BRH*, 37 (1931): 174–75. Gérard Malchelosse, "Mémoires romancés," *Cahiers des Dix*, 25 (1960): 103–44. Benjamin Sulte, "Le docteur Laterrière," *Le Pays laurentien* (Montréal), 1 (1916): 35–38. Albert Tessier, "Les Anglais prennent les forges au sérieux," *Cahiers des Dix*, 14 (1949): 165–85.

SARREBOURCE DE PONTLEROY, NICOLAS, army officer and military engineer; b. 12 June 1717 in Marseilles, France, son of Jacques Sarrebource Pontleroy de Beaulieu and Madeleine Coustan; m. 17 April 1761 Élisabeth Arbalestre de Melun in Sedan, France; d. 6 Aug. 1802 in Château-Thierry, France.

A nobleman, Nicolas Sarrebource de Pontleroy stemmed from a family of the French provinces of Berry and Orléanais. He was admitted to the engineer corps in 1736 and took part in the War of the Austrian Succession from 1744 to 1748, particularly on the Italian front, where he was commended for his ability and courage. Promoted captain in 1745, he was awarded the cross of Saint-Louis eight years later for his services during the war. He was stationed at Perpignan, France, in 1749 and on the Île de Ré five years later.

After 19 years' experience in Europe, Pontleroy was sent to Louisbourg, Île Royale (Cape Breton Island), in 1755 to serve under Louis Franquet*, who had asked for seasoned engineer officers to assist him with the reconstruction of the fortifications. Following a year of observing Pontleroy's surveying, mapping, and construction, Franquet recommended him enthusiastically for the post of chief engineer in New France, which had been made vacant by the death in March 1756 of Gaspard-Joseph Chaussegros* de Léry. In 1757 the court at Versailles appointed Pontleroy over Michel Chartier* de Lotbinière, the choice of Governor Pierre de Rigaud* de Vaudreuil de Cavagnial; Pontleroy's longer service, his membership in the prestigious engineer corps, and Franquet's recommendation were credentials that impressed French officials more than Canadian experience.

Pontleroy left Louisbourg in late September 1757 and arrived at Quebec on 15 October. He soon established himself with Louis-Joseph de Montcalm* and Montcalm's aide-de-camp, Captain Louis-Antoine de BOUGAINVILLE, but he immediately encountered the opposition of Vaudreuil and Lotbinière. Pontleroy complained to the minister of Marine, Massiac, of obstructionism by Vaudreuil, adding: "In this country I am marked with the original sin, that is,

738

of being French." Lotbinière shared the attitude, refusing to accept that France felt it "necessary to send from Europe an engineer to put our [fortified] places in order." When instructed in December 1757 to build at Pointe-Lévy (Lauzon, Lévis, Que.) a hospital for the treatment of communicable diseases, Pontleroy, according to Montcalm, "believed he ought to follow the rules observed in France" by requesting tenders from all the major entrepreneurs of the town. None would bid, however, "from a spirit of faction which had been encouraged in them." A conspiracy on the part of the Vaudreuil faction may not have been necessary, however. The stringent regulations laid down for contractors by the engineer corps, regulations that Chaussegros apparently had never applied, were possibly sufficient in themselves to discourage any of the 30 potential bidders at Quebec. A particular deterrent for Canadians may have been the rule forbidding a contractor to become indebted to the crown during the course of a project. On Île Royale strict application of engineer corps regulations had meant that general contracts were awarded exclusively to French builders brought out for the purpose.

In late June 1758 Pontleroy accompanied Montcalm to Fort Carillon (near Ticonderoga, N.Y.) to reconnoitre its surroundings and make it defensible. There he ostentatiously refused to profit personally from the hauling of building materials, and damned by faint praise the practices of Lotbinière, his predecessor at the post. In his campaign diary, Bougainville characterized Pontleroy as a man who "has an honest and upright heart; he is frank in his remarks and true in his conduct. He has a good theory of his profession, and enough of that routine and that experience of war which make a good campaign engineer." On the recommendations of Montcalm and his senior subordinates, Pontleroy was praised by the French royal court for his performance in strengthening the defences around the fort before the battle of 8 July; the speed at which trenches and abatis were built proved to be an important factor in Montcalm's victory. Pontleroy was promoted lieutenant-colonel on 20 Oct. 1758.

In spite of Montcalm's fear that, in the long run, the expected British offensive against Canada in 1759 would succeed, the chief engineer was instructed to make the colony's fortifications ready for it. Pontleroy directed further construction and repair at Carillon, and then, leaving Jean-Nicolas Desandrouins* to finish the job, moved on to the location of Fort Frontenac (Kingston, Ont.). Vaudreuil wanted the fort, which had been destroyed by John Bradstreet* in August 1758, rebuilt as a supply post, but Pontleroy declared the site indefensible. At Quebec, he found the weakest fortification to be that of the Upper Town, "which, in the state it is in today, is not capable of useful defence in case of siege, having neither ditches, nor counterscarps nor covered way, and being

dominated by heights behind which there is cover facilitating the approaches." On 13 Sept. 1759, when Major-General James Wolfe*'s army stood before those walls, this assessment must have influenced Montcalm's decision not to wait for a siege.

In the last struggle for New France, Pontleroy commanded the engineering detachment, whose strength had been augmented by three officers sent from France. Montcalm noted that during the long bombardment of Quebec in the summer of 1759 "M. de Pontleroy, sensitive to the lot of the unfortunate, opened all the posterns in the fortifications to women and children, but our regret, his and mine, was not to have bread to give to so many destitute." Between 12 July and 18 September Pontleroy was frequently under fire, and during the battle of the Plains of Abraham he served at Montcalm's side. He was at the war council held by Vaudreuil following the battle and voted with the majority for a retreat rather than a counter-attack as favoured by the governor; he thus apparently shared the defeatist attitude of the army.

Pontleroy left for Montreal, stopping at Trois-Rivières to strengthen its defences. In January 1760, asked by François de Lévis* whether an attack should be made on the British advanced posts, he replied in the negative, particularly if Canadians were to be used. "One would be morally certain of being defeated," he asserted. "The Canadian is known to be brave; but he cannot, lacking any discipline, attack in open country; he is not even armed for that, and certainly he will not stand a shock and hold his ground." Pontleroy planned the siege works for the French attack on Quebec in 1760 and on 28 April took part in the battle of Sainte-Foy. The British having retreated within the walls of Quebec, Lévis charged Pontleroy with the management of the siege of the city. It failed, however, and Vaudreuil did not lose the opportunity to criticize Pontleroy: on 17 May he wrote to Lévis, who had retreated to Montreal, that "numerous letters from the army infinitely blame M. de Pontleroy. They attribute to him much caprice and stubbornness."

Pontleroy returned to France with Lévis in 1760. He served in the engineer corps for another 25 years, all of them in France except for a brief stint in Malta in 1761 under the command of François-Charles de Bourlamaque*. He was promoted colonel in 1763, and brigadier five years later. Named director of fortifications for Soissonnais and Picardy in 1770 and for Dauphiné and Provence seven years later, Pontleroy was promoted major-general (*maréchal de camp*) in 1780, five years before his retirement. He died on 18 Thermidor, Year 10 of the revolutionary calendar (6 Aug. 1802).

F. J. THORPE

AD, Aisne (Laon), État civil, Château-Thierry, 6 août 1802. AN, Col., B, 105; C[11A], 103–5; C[11B], 35–37; D[2C], 4,

Sawtelle

58–59; E, 338bis (dossier Pontleroy). Arch. du ministère des Armées (Paris), Inspection du Génie, Arch., article 3, article 8, article 14; Service hist. de l'Armée, A[1], 3392, 3457, 3498–99, 3540, 3574; Y[b], 685; Y[3d]. Arch. municipales, Marseille, France, État civil, Saint-Martin, 13 juin 1717. PAC, MG 18, K3, 2: 461–62. [L.-A.] de Bougainville, "Le journal de M. de Bougainville," A.[-E.] Gosselin, édit., ANQ Rapport, 1923–24: 256, 312–13, 327, 330–31, 333, 353, 363, 365. Coll. des manuscrits de Lévis (Casgrain), vols.1–2, 4, 6–8, 10. [André] Doreil, "Lettres de Doreil," Antoine Roy, édit., ANQ Rapport, 1944–45: 137. "Journal du siège de Québec du 10 mai au 18 septembre 1759," Ægidius Fauteux, édit., ANQ Rapport, 1920–21: 145, 148, 208–11, 214. NYCD (O'Callaghan and Fernow), vol.10. Ægidius Fauteux, Les chevaliers de Saint-Louis en Canada (Montréal, 1940), 154–55. L.-P. d'Hozier et al., Armorial général de la France . . . (7v. in 13, Paris, [1865–1908]; réimpr., [1970]), 2. A.-M. Augoyat, Aperçu historique sur les fortifications, les ingénieurs et sur le corps du génie en France . . . (3v., Paris, 1860–64), 2: 595. Guy Frégault, La guerre de la Conquête (Montréal et Paris, [1955]; réimpr., [1966]). [C.-N.] Gabriel, Le maréchal de camp Desandrouins, 1729–1792; guerre du Canada, 1756–1760; guerre de l'Indépendance américaine, 1780–1782 (Verdun, France, 1887). Alison Hoppen, The fortification of Malta by the Order of St John, 1530–1798 (Edinburgh, 1979), 15, 69–70, 88, 90, 94, 97, 104, 112, 122, 125. [Marquis de Magny], De Sarrebourse, Berry, Orléanais . . . (s.l., s.d.). S. de Morthomier [André Sarrebourse d'Audeville], "De Sarrebourse d'Audeville," Armorial français (Paris), 1 (1889): 361–62; 2 (1890): 4–5. P.-G. Roy, "Le conseil de guerre du 13 sept. 1759," BRH, 29 (1923): 115–17. R.-L. Séguin, "La persévérance d'un Canadien en quête d'une croix de Saint-Louis," RHAF, 9 (1955–56): 365, 368–69, 371–73. Marcel Trudel, "Le gouvernement des Trois-Rivières sous le Régime militaire, 1760–1764," RHAF, 5 (1951–52): 70.

SAWTELLE, JEMIMA (Phipps; Howe; Tute), captive; b. c. 1723, daughter of Josiah Sawtelle and Lydia Parker; d. 7 March 1805 in Vernon, Vt.

Jemima Sawtelle was a young woman in her early twenties when on 5 July 1745 her first husband, William Phipps, was killed at Great Meadow (Putney, Vt) in a skirmish with Indian allies of the French, then at war with the British. Two years later the Indians carried off her younger brother Jonathan to Montreal (Que.). Jemima's family misfortunes had only begun, however. The British and French were engaged in unofficial war in 1755 when, a little before sunset on 27 June, 12 Indians descended on her second husband Caleb Howe, two young sons, and two companions, returning from the fields around Bridgman's Fort (near Hinsdale, N.H.). Howe, the son of a former Indian captive, was mortally wounded, and his sons were captured. The Indians then sprang upon the unmanned fort, where the three wives and the remaining children were easily taken.

After plundering the fort, the Indians started their captives towards Canada. Jemima, accompanied by her seven children aged eleven years to six months, was the most burdened. During the nine-day trek to Fort Saint-Frédéric (near Crown Point, N.Y.), she was surprised – as were many American prisoners – by the kind treatment accorded by the Indians. From Fort Saint-Frédéric some of the captives, including Submit Phipps, Jemima's younger daughter, were taken to Montreal "with a view of selling them to the French," but the market was dull; consequently Submit was given to Governor Pierre de Rigaud* de Vaudreuil de Cavagnial.

All the captives except Submit were then moved via Fort Saint-Jean (Saint-Jean-sur-Richelieu) to the Abenaki village of Saint-François-de-Sales (Odanak), where Jemima and her remaining children were each adopted by separate families; she was allowed, she related later, to keep the baby "for the sake of saving them the trouble of looking after it, and of maintaining it with my milk." When winter set in, Jemima, fearing she could not survive it, persuaded her Indian "mother" to take her to Montreal and sell her and her baby there. No buyers were found, and one lady exclaimed: "Damn it, I will not buy a woman that has a child to look after." The group returned to Saint-François-de-Sales, but the Indian mother had contracted smallpox, from which she soon died. Her daughter and son-in-law became Jemima's family.

With this couple Jemima suffered considerable physical hardship, to which was added mental anguish over the fate of her scattered children. In the winter of 1755–56 she and some of her children were taken separately by their families to hunt around Missisquoi Bay at the northern end of Lake Champlain. Her infant died there, but by chance Jemima was reunited briefly with her two youngest sons, Caleb and Squire. At Fort Saint-Jean in the spring, she was suddenly sold by her Indian master "in a drunken frolic" to a French gentleman, Joachim de Sacépée (Saccapee). Her new situation, although "perfect freedom, of what it had been among the barbarous Indians," was a mixed blessing. She was now able to assist English prisoners who passed through Fort Saint-Jean, but she needed "a large stock of prudence" in dealing with "the good old man" and "a warm and resolute son" both of whom, "at the same time, and under the same roof, became . . . excessively fond of my company." Fortunately, Vaudreuil heard of her predicament, immediately ordered the son, then an officer in the French army, "from the field of Venus to the field of Mars," and warned the father to mind his manners. From this ameliorated situation Jemima and three of her sons were redeemed in November 1758 for 2,600 livres (and 170 livres sundry expenses) by Colonel Peter Schuyler*, and they probably returned to New Hampshire. Her other three children, Moses Howe and Submit and Mary Phipps, remained in Canada. The girls were placed by Vaudreuil's wife, Jeanne-

Charlotte de Fleury Deschambault, with the Ursulines at Quebec; there they met another former captive, Esther Wheelwright*, named de l'Enfant-Jésus, and were converted to Catholicism. Some time after June 1759 Mme de Vaudreuil took the girls with her to Montreal, where she placed them in the convent of the Congregation of Notre-Dame.

After the conquest of Montreal in 1760, Jemima returned to Canada to reclaim her three remaining children. Mary had already been taken to France by Vaudreuil, but Jemima located Moses and Submit. The latter, who was about to depart for France, was persuaded only by an order from the governor of Montreal, Thomas Gage*, to leave the Congregation of Notre-Dame and return with her mother to New England.

The indomitable Jemima Sawtelle, having outlived her third husband, Amos Tute, and both children of their marriage, died on 7 March 1805 at the age of 82, and was buried at Vernon in a cemetery looking over the Connecticut River to Hinsdale, near where she had been taken prisoner 50 years before.

JAMES AXTELL

[Jemima Sawtelle told her story to the Reverend Bunker Gay of Hinsdale, N.H., who recounted it to Jeremy Belknap in a letter. Belknap included Gay's letter in his work *The history of New-Hampshire* (3v., Philadelphia and Boston, 1784–92), 3: 370–88. Subsequently Gay himself published the letter under the title *A genuine and correct account of the captivity, sufferings & deliverance of Mrs. Jemina Howe, of Hinsdale, in New-Hampshire . . .* (Boston, 1792). It was reprinted in a number of other works, but appeared in most accurate form in *Indian captivities: being a collection of the most remarkable narratives of persons taken captive by the North American Indians . . .* , ed. Samuel G. Drake (Boston, 1839), 156–65. The romanticized version of Jemima Sawtelle's adventures presented by David Humphreys in *An essay on the life of the Honorable Major-General Israel Putnam . . .* (Hartford, Conn., 1788; repr. New York and London, 1977), 74, is largely fictional. Emma Lewis Coleman, *New England captives carried to Canada between 1677 and 1760 during the French and Indian wars* (2v., Portland, Maine, 1925), 2: 180, 198, 314–21, contains the known biographical facts concerning Jemima Sawtelle.

Her life was the inspiration for Marguerite Allis's *Not without peril, a novel . . . founded on the life and adventures of Jemima Sartwell, one of the first settlers in Vermont* (New York, 1941), and for the narrative poem written by Angela Marco [A. L. Mearkle], *Fair captive, a colonial story* (Battleboro, Vt., 1937). J.A.]

Arch. du monastère des ursulines (Québec), Livre des entrées et sorties des pensionnaires, 1756–57. PRO, ADM 1/3818: f.10. Benjamin Doolittle, *A short narrative of mischief done by the French and Indian enemy, on the western frontiers of the province of Massachusetts-Bay . . .* (Boston, 1750; repr. New York, 1909), 5–6. *Boston Weekly News-letter*, 4 July 1755. *The affecting history of Mrs. Howe . . .* (London, [1815]; repr. New York and London, 1977).

SAYER, JOHN (also written **Sayers** and **Sayre**, but he signed Sayer), fur trader; b. *c.* 1750; d. 2 Oct. 1818 in Sainte-Anne-de-Bellevue, Lower Canada.

John Sayer first appeared in the fur trade in the late 1770s when he became active in the Fond du Lac district south and west of Lake Superior. He was apparently one of the earliest traders working out of Michilimackinac (Mackinaw City, Mich.) to winter at Lac de la Sangsue (Leech Lake, Minn.). In 1780 Sayer was the Michilimackinac agent for Montreal merchant Joseph Howard* and was granted a licence to send up one canoe to Michilimackinac. That year, upon returning to Lac de la Sangsue for the winter, he found that most of the Ojibwas with whom he had formerly traded had died of smallpox. During the same year he joined with other Michilimackinac merchants in protesting the interference of government officials in the fur trade.

By 1784, following the American revolution, the number of traders around Michilimackinac had grown so alarmingly that Sayer and other merchants formed a committee to regulate the market. The next year, perhaps in response to the recent emergence of the North West Company, Sayer entered an agreement organizing the General Company of Lake Superior and the South (also known as the General Society) [*see* Étienne-Charles Campion*]. Because of his previous experience he was appointed to direct the company's operations in the region south and west of Lake Superior. The pressure of competition and an unpredictable market in the late 1780s, probably combined with the failure of the General Company by 1788, induced Sayer to engage in successive one-year trading alliances with Jean-Baptiste Perrault*, Jean-Baptiste CADOT, and others. In 1789 and 1790 Sayer wintered on the Fond du Lac River (St Louis River, Minn.) under these agreements.

About 1791, apparently having dissolved his long affiliation with Howard, Sayer formed John Sayer and Company and became an agent of the NWC at Sault Ste Marie (Mich.). Two years later he engaged Perrault to build Fort St Louis (Superior, Wis.), the NWC's Fond du Lac district headquarters, and on 12 Sept. 1793 arrived there with his native family to take charge. From then until the summer of 1805 he travelled widely in the region under his command, wintering at Lac de la Sangsue, White Oak Point (near Deer River, Minn.), Upper Red Cedar Lake (Cass Lake, Minn.), Pembina (N.Dak.), and on two tributaries of the St Croix River, the Yellow (Wis.) and Snake (Minn.) rivers. In late April 1798 David Thompson* described him as "poor in flesh" from his winter's subsistence on wild rice and maple sugar at Upper Red Cedar Lake. Sayer's summers were customarily divided between the annual rendezvous, held until 1802 at Grand Portage (near Grand Portage, Minn.) and subsequently at Kaministiquia (Thunder

Schurman

Bay, Ont.), and business at his district headquarters. His chief competitors were the Hudson's Bay Company, which had a post at Pembina, and the New North West Company (sometimes called the XY Company).

John Sayer and Company seems to have been dissolved about 1797, and the following year Sayer was listed as a partner in the NWC. On 5 July 1802 he signed an agreement which extended the coalition of partners and gave him two shares. Following the merger of the New North West Company with the NWC in 1805, Sayer signed a document expanding the NWC from 92 to 100 shares, and apparently that year he took his allotted "rotation," or furlough, to Lower Canada, where he traded for the NWC at the Lac des Chats post (near Quyon) on the Ottawa River. In 1807, having been charged by Duncan McGILLIVRAY with "former irregularities," he was forced to retire from active partnership. The following year Sayer acquired a farm of some 1,000 acres in Onslow Township on Lac des Chats in exchange for one of his company shares. In 1809 he sold this estate to Duncan Cameron* and became a resident of Sainte-Anne-de-Bellevue, selling his second NWC share in 1810 to McTavish, McGillivrays and Company. Though subsequently elected to the Beaver Club, Sayer appears not to have attended any meetings.

With his native wife Obemau-unqua (possibly known as Nancy) Sayer had at least three sons, Pierre-Guillaume*, John Charles, and Henry. The members of his immediate family whom he listed in his will, however, were his wife Elizabeth McPherson and his natural children Margaret, Henry (who may have been Obemau-unqua's son), and James.

DOUGLAS A. BIRK

ANQ-M, CM1, John Sayer, 15 June 1819; CN1-185, 27 June 1810. Minn. Hist. Soc. (St Paul), D. A. Birk, "John Sayer and Fond du Lac fur trade: the history, ecology and archeology of an 1804–1805 North West Company wintering post site (21-PN-11) and its relation to the fur trade in the western Lake Superior region" (1974); Morrison (Allan) papers, Allan Morrison, "History of the fur trade." PAC, MG 19, C1, 12; 17. [This item consists of a journal and some accounts, now identified as Sayer's by the PAC, although the journal has been erroneously attributed to Thomas Connor in *Five fur traders of the northwest . . .*, ed. C. M. Gates ([Minneapolis, Minn.], 1933; [2nd ed.], St Paul, 1965). D.A.B.] *Les bourgeois de la Compagnie du Nord-Ouest* (Masson), 1: 395. *Docs. relating to NWC* (Wallace), 109–10, 207, 247–48, 497. Mackenzie, *Journals and letters* (Lamb), 480, 484. *Mich. Pioneer Coll.*, 10 (1886): 421; 37 (1909–10): 426, 536–37, 537n., 555–57, 568–69, 575. *New light on early hist. of greater north-west* (Coues), 1: 225n.; 2: 1011. [David Thompson], *David Thompson's narrative, 1784–1812*, ed. R. [G.] Glover (new ed., Toronto, 1962), 203–5. Wis., State Hist. Soc., *Coll.*, 19 (1910): 173–74, 181, 238. W. E. Stevens, "The northwest fur trade, 1763–1800," *Univ. of Ill. Studies in the Social Sciences* (Urbana), 14 (1926), no.3: 135–37.

SCHURMAN (Schureman), WILLIAM, businessman, politician, and office holder; b. *c.* 1743 in New Rochelle, N.Y., third child of Jacob Schureman and Jane Parcot; d. 15 Sept. 1819 in Wilmot Valley, P.E.I.

On his father's side William Schurman was descended from Dutch settlers in New Amsterdam (New York City) who witnessed the English capture of New Netherland in 1664 and some 30 years later moved to New Rochelle. His mother's family were French Protestants who had fled France after the revoking of the Edict of Nantes in 1685, sojourned briefly in England, and then come to New York with other Huguenot refugees and established the settlement of New Rochelle. Schurman grew up in a comfortable middle-class home, related by blood or marriage to most of the prominent families in the town. Events leading to the revolution and the revolution itself polarized families in New Rochelle as they did elsewhere; while Schurman's two brothers-in-law adhered to the patriot cause, his own brother was imprisoned for two years after signing a protest against sending local representatives to the 1775 Continental Congress. William, too, cast in his lot with the loyalists. Taking what property he could salvage, and in his own ship, with wife, five sons, and two slaves, he sailed first to Port Roseway (Shelburne), N.S., and then on to Tryon, St John's (Prince Edward) Island.

He arrived at Tryon in 1783 and the following year established himself in the nearby loyalist settlement of Bedeque, on the site of what is now Central Bedeque. He early became the community's most influential resident. Like the other refugees he built a log house and prepared his land for farming, selling in Charlottetown the timber he cleared. Not content with these occupations, he found an outlet for his energies in other ways: he started a shingle-mill (and possibly a grist-mill); he became the agent for a group of settlers whom he brought in 1784 from Shelburne to Bedeque in his own ship; he kept the vessel busy in coastal trade, bringing merchandise to Bedeque and setting up shop in a part of his house to sell it; and he was elected Bedeque's first representative to the colonial legislature in 1785 and later held appointments as justice of the peace and overseer of roads for the district.

In 1792 Schurman's house and store burned to the ground. He rebuilt, restocked the store, and in 1793 invested in a new ship. Six years later the vessel was lost at sea with all aboard, including his 19-year-old son. With characteristic resilience he turned his attention to a new sphere of activity, shipbuilding, and

742

between 1801 and 1803 launched at least three vessels he had built on the shore of his property with the aid of sons and hired men, using lumber from his woods and supplies from his store. The profit from the sale of these ships in St John's, Nfld, and Halifax, N.S., led him to a more ambitious undertaking: in 1808 he bought for £800 a huge tract of land, ten miles long, in the richly wooded valley of the Wilmot River. He soon had the river dammed, a sawmill erected and operating, and shiploads of lumber leaving his wharf for ports on the Island and in nearby provinces. About 1809 he built a new house near his mill, gave the homestead at Bedeque to his eldest son, and moved the short distance to Wilmot Valley, where he spent the last decade of his life, carrying out the duties of local magistrate as occasion arose, and supervising his mill, farm, and store, surrounded by sons and daughters whom he had settled on good properties.

William Schurman was a man of ability and intelligence, with the courage and versatility required for success in his time. He was conspicuously practical as well, apparently able to turn his hand to almost anything, from shipbuilding to coopering and blacksmithing, and able to ride out the forced move from New Rochelle and later losses to arrive at a comfortable old age, a man of substance, entrusted with dispensing justice to those of his neighbours who appeared before him in court. "His public duty as a Member of the Assembly and as a Magistrate," states his death notice in the *Prince Edward Island Gazette*, "were ever of a piece with his other conduct, marked with strong discernment and vigorous activity of mind, which were always evinced by his purity of intention and sound judgment."

Schurman was twice married: in 1768 to Jane Bonnet and in 1778 to Elizabeth Hyatt; four children were born of the first marriage and seven of the second. His family in New Rochelle pronounced the name Skureman and generally spelled it Schureman; William retained the Dutch pronunciation but signed himself Schurman after settling in Bedeque. Although almost all his descendants have followed his spelling, most of those who have left the Maritimes have adopted the pronunciations Shureman or Sherman. The former became widespread because of its use by William's best-known descendant, his great-grandson Jacob Gould Schurman*, author, educator, adviser to American presidents for many years, and minister of the United States to Greece, Montenegro, and China and ambassador to Germany.

ROSS GRAVES

This sketch is based on a more detailed account given in Ross Graves, *William Schurman, loyalist of Bedeque, Prince Edward Island, and his descendants* (2v., Summerside, P.E.I., 1973). The principal sources used are listed below.

North Bedeque Cemetery (North Bedeque, P.E.I.), William Schurman, gravestone. PAPEI, RG 9, Customs, shipping reg., 1 (1787–1824); RG 16, Land registry records, 1792–1833. Private arch., A. Reeves (Bedeque), William Schurman, account book, 1784–1819. Supreme Court of P.E.I. (Charlottetown), Estates Division, liber 1: f.130 (will of William Schurman); Inventories and accounts, William Schurman, inventory of estate. P.E.I., House of Assembly, *Journal. Records of the town of New Rochelle, 1699–1828*, ed. and trans. J. A. Forbes (New Rochelle, N.Y., 1916). *Prince Edward Island Gazette* (Charlottetown), 23 Sept. 1819. *Schuremans of New York*, comp. Richard Wynkoop (New York, 1903). L. U. Fowler, "Bedeque and its people . . . ," *Prince Edward Island Magazine* (Charlottetown), 2 (1900–1): 117–24, 165–68, 259–62. D. S. McHugh, "William Schurman, loyalist," Westchester County Hist. Soc., *Quarterly Bull.* (White Plains, N.Y.), 8 (1932): 121–30.

SCOTHOUSE (Scotus), ALEXANDER MacDONELL OF. *See* MACDONELL

SCOTT, JONATHAN, lay preacher, Congregational minister, and author; b. 12 Oct. 1744 in Lunenburg, Mass., seventh child of John Scott and Lydia Thwing; d. 15 Oct. 1819 in Minot (Maine).

Jonathan Scott's parents, dedicated members of the Congregational Church, taught him to read at an early age and made sure he received a strict religious upbringing based on family prayer and daily readings from the Bible. In spite of this early parental guidance, Scott did not lead a particularly pious life during his adolescent years, largely because from the age of 14 onwards he lived away from home. In 1758, two years after his father's death, Scott was apprenticed to William Goddard, a shoemaker, in Roxbury (Boston), Mass. For the next six years he was confused and unhappy "by reason of being poor, fatherless, and despised, under Servitude, and being from my Mother 50 miles distance." The transition was particularly disturbing because Goddard, according to Scott, "was a man of no religion; he did not so much as pray in his house nor ask a blessing at his table; nor did he bridle his tongue from profaneness." Scott himself later confessed that while living in Roxbury he "learned to provoke God, and corrupt and dishonour man by profane and unclean language."

In April 1764, his apprenticeship completed, Scott took passage from Boston to Yarmouth, N.S., where an elder brother, Moses, had settled in the previous year. This first visit to Yarmouth was disappointing for Scott, since most of his time and hard-earned savings were spent looking after the affairs of his sick brother. Returning to Roxbury in the autumn of the same year, he went to work in the shoemaking business of his old master, Goddard. Because of personal differences, however, he soon left Goddard's

Scott

employ and tried to establish his own trade. Unsuccessful in this venture, he returned to Yarmouth in April 1765. There he was able to earn a small amount of money as a fisherman, and with his savings he began putting down roots in the community. He built a log house in December 1765, and on 14 March 1768 he married Lucy Ring, the daughter of a local trader and fisherman, in a ceremony conducted by the Reverend Ebenezer Moulton*, an itinerant Baptist preacher. Later in the year the couple moved into a frame-house which Scott had built.

The year 1768 was significant in other ways for Scott. Since his childhood days he had retained a deep interest in religious matters, and in the autumn of 1768 he "began to lead in Public Worship at the desire of the people." When in 1770 he was invited to become minister he refused because of divisions within the church based on pro- and anti-evangelical positions. But after a visit by two Congregational ministers from Massachusetts, Solomon Reed and Sylvanus Conant of Middleboro, enough unity was established to encourage Scott to accept the call when it was renewed in January 1772. In March, Scott and a committee from the church travelled to Middleboro, where a council of Congregational ministers organized by Reed and Conant was to examine Scott's qualifications and suitability for the ministry. After a rigorous examination stretching over a two-week period, during which he had to preach and answer doctrinal questions put to him by other ministers, Scott was formally ordained on 28 April 1772. This was a dramatic moment in Scott's life, for here was he, a struggling farmer from a remote settlement, being approved for the ministry by a committee of well-known New England pastors, all holding degrees from Harvard or Yale. Scott was proud of this distinction and from this time on he took seriously the duty of defending the Congregational establishment against evangelical attacks. He returned to Yarmouth in May as the community's first regularly ordained Congregational minister and remained at that post until 1795, when he left to become the minister at Bakerstown (Minot, Maine).

The most interesting aspect of Scott's life during the period from 1772 to 1795 was his role in the great religious revival which swept through Nova Scotia in the 1770s, 1780s, and 1790s but which was particularly intense during the last years of the American Revolutionary War. At the height of the revival in the early 1780s Scott became the leading spokesman for those opposed to the work of Henry Alline*, the itinerant evangelical preacher. Besides visiting and corresponding with other communities throughout the colony in an effort to stem the tide of revivalism, Scott found time to write lengthy and cogent theological tracts designed to refute Alline's often peculiar religious ideas. His major work, *A brief view of the religious tenets and sentiments, lately published and spread in the province of Nova-Scotia*, was a careful and detailed critique of Alline based on the writings of Jonathan Edwards, the famous Massachusetts minister and theologian, whose "new divinity" reconciled the evangelical position with a respect for the existing Congregational establishment. Yet in spite of such efforts, impressive for a man with no formal theological training, Scott was not successful in solidifying the anti-revivalist cause. His weighty theological critiques made scant impression on the farmers and fishermen who responded more easily to the simplistic and emotional preaching of Alline. Even in Yarmouth itself Scott lost most of his people to the revival and became in the early 1780s an embittered and isolated figure. Although he remained as the Congregational minister, his sense of failure in these years contributed to his decision to leave Yarmouth for Bakerstown in 1794.

Jonathan Scott did have his share of human frailties: he had a tendency to be short-tempered in a crisis, and the forthright manner in which he demanded increases in his salary did little to enhance his popularity during the years of the revival. On the whole, however, his failure to obtain support had less to do with his own shortcomings than with conditions in the colony and the effectiveness of Alline's preaching. Scott was much better informed theologically than Alline, particularly in his knowledge of Jonathan Edwards's writings. He was more temperate than Alline, more reasonable, more tolerant, and more cautious in making pronouncements on complicated moral and doctrinal issues. He was also more humane in the sense that he accepted man's limitations when it came to comprehending the mysteries of God's universe. Unsure at times of his own religious condition, he was modest enough to believe that he had not found final solutions to contemporary problems. For this reason, he became somewhat out of place in the 1770s and 1780s, when simplistic preaching, emotional uplift, and a sense of certainty were the order of the day.

GORDON STEWART

Jonathan Scott's writings include *A brief view of the religious tenets and sentiments, lately published and spread in the province of Nova-Scotia* . . . (Halifax, 1784); *The conquest of the last enemy; or, complete victory over death; a discourse, delivered March 9, 1807, at the funeral of the Rev. Samuel Foxcroft, A.M., late pastor of the Congregational Church in New Gloucester* (Charlestown, Mass., 1808); *The life of Jonathan Scott*, ed. C. B. Fergusson (Halifax, 1960); and *A sermon delivered at Hallowell before the Maine Missionary Society, at their first anniversary, June 15, 1808* (Hallowell, Maine, 1808).

PANS, MG 4, 12; RG 1, 222, no.23. Henry Alline, *The life and journal of the Rev. Mr. Henry Alline* (Boston, 1806). *Annals of Yarmouth and Barrington (Nova Scotia) in the revolutionary war, compiled from original manuscripts, etc.*, contained in the *office of the secretary of the Commonwealth, State House, Boston, Mass.*, comp. E. D.

Poole (Yarmouth, N.S., 1899). "Early census rolls of Nova Scotia," PANS, Board of Trustees, *Report* (Halifax), 1934: 52–55. *Plymouth church records, 1620–1859* (2v., [Boston, 1920–23]), 1, pt.I: xxv–xxxvi, xxxix. M. W. Armstrong, *The Great Awakening in Nova Scotia, 1776–1809* (Hartford, Conn., 1948). J. M. Bumsted, *Henry Alline, 1748–1784* (Toronto, 1971). J. R. Campbell, *A history of the county of Yarmouth, in Nova Scotia* (Saint John, N.B., 1876; repr. Belleville, Ont., 1972). C. C. Goen, *Revivalism and separatism in New England, 1740–1800; Strict Congregationalists and Separate Baptists in the Great Awakening* (New Haven, Conn., 1962). G. [T.] Stewart and G. [A.] Rawlyk, *A people highly favoured of God: the Nova Scotia Yankees and the American revolution* (Toronto, 1972). M. W. Armstrong, "Jonathan Scott's 'Brief view,'" *Harvard Theological Rev.* (Cambridge, Mass.), 40 (1947): 121–36. G. [T.] Stewart, "Charisma and integration: an eighteenth-century North American case," *Comparative Studies in Soc. and Hist.* (Cambridge, Eng.), 16 (1974): 138–49; "Socio-economic factors in the Great Awakening: the case of Yarmouth, Nova Scotia," *Acadiensis* (Fredericton), 3 (1973–74), no.1: 18–34.

SCOTT, THOMAS, merchant, office holder, militia officer, and landowner; b. *c.* 1741, probably in England; d. 24 April 1810 near Quebec, Lower Canada.

Thomas Scott had established himself as a merchant at Quebec by August 1762. A Quaker and a pacifist, he found himself embroiled the following July in a vigorous disagreement with a Scottish sergeant that led to the soldier's armed assault upon him. The outburst was probably occasioned in part by the strained relations between the military and the small community of merchants in post-conquest Quebec, and possibly by a degree of antagonism between Scots and English. Scott complained to Governor Murray*, himself a Scot, only to be castigated for his "'*damned English Arrogance.*'"

The nature of Scott's business operations is uncertain. In 1767 he was an attorney, along with two prominent merchants, Thomas DUNN and Richard DOBIE, for another merchant, Edward Harrison*. Scott evidently left business two years later, and on 1 Sept. 1769 he began service in the salaried position of controller of customs, with responsibility for auditing the accounts of the collector, Thomas AINSLIE, and, in his own view, "to be a Compleat checque on the Collector in every part of his conduct." Scott and Thomas Mellish, the deputy collector, immediately became caught up in the lengthy dispute between Ainslie and Governor Guy CARLETON over the collector's jurisdiction and fee schedules, Ainslie maintaining that, as an imperial officer, he was not obliged to submit to audit by provincial authorities. The practical consequences of Scott's refusal to support Ainslie in this dispute are not clear. Although Scott had earned Carleton's praise as a "diligent officer," Ainslie accused him in June 1770 of not performing "official business"; however, the two men

subsequently shelved their differences for a time, aided perhaps by common experiences and mutual friends. Scott entered the British militia at Quebec on 13 Sept. 1775, and as a lieutenant in Ainslie's company he served during the American invasion and occupation of the colony in 1775–76 [*see* Benedict ARNOLD; Richard Montgomery*]. On 14 Aug. 1776 he received a commission, subsequently renewed several times, as justice of the peace at Quebec. Some time after 1769 he had married Jane Phillips, a sister of Mary, wife of postmaster Hugh FINLAY. They had at least two sons baptized in the Anglican church in the 1770s, and their selection of godparents reveals cordial relations with the legislative councillors John Drummond and Adam Mabane* and Ainslie's wife, Elizabeth. Scott's social and financial position are reflected in his residence by 1779 in a two-storey stone house on Rue des Pauvres (Côte du Palais), which had become a street of the wealthy.

The 1780s witnessed the revival of the conflict between Scott and Ainslie. Scott complained to the British Treasury in 1783 and 1787 of Ainslie's steadfast resistance to provincial control and its effect upon his own office. In 1788, during an inquiry into the accounts of Deputy Receiver General William GRANT (1744–1805), Scott pointedly charged Ainslie with having blocked, since 1770, his legitimate access as controller to the records of duties collected and to the collector's official instructions from London. In numerous statements on customs policies, however, Scott and Ainslie stood together in upholding imperial interests; in 1790, for example, they opposed a petition by the merchants of the colony that would have effectively reduced revenues.

Scott's activities as controller were largely confined to the short but feverish navigation season at Quebec, and thus he had ample time to pursue personal business and social interests. He was named curator in 1789 of the estate of Lieutenant-Colonel Christopher Carleton, the governor's nephew and brother-in-law, a further reflection on Scott's good standing in the British community. In 1792, as a leader under the system of township leaders and associates [*see* James CALDWELL], he received a large grant of land in Durham Township on the Rivière Saint-François; he eventually secured personally more than 21,000 acres in Durham. That same year he bought from John Drummond a farm near Quebec on the Rivière Saint-Charles; the purchase included an "elegant villa," later called Sans Souci. He subsequently acquired long-term leases on adjoining properties from Bishop Joseph-Octave Plessis* and Henry CALDWELL. The Scotts apparently spent the spring, summer, and fall on the farm but probably wintered on Rue des Pauvres.

Scott was active publicly as well. In 1787 he was appointed a member of a commission, under the direction of Kenelm CHANDLER, to report on the

Scott

Jesuit estates. He was a founding subscriber two years later of the Quebec branch of the Agriculture Society and one of its directors in 1791 and 1793. On 31 Dec. 1798 he was a steward at an anniversary dinner at which veterans of the Quebec garrison celebrated their stand during the American siege of the city in 1775–76.

In February 1800 he succeeded Ainslie as collector of customs. Scott's service was apparently unmarked by controversy, and any burden caused by customs problems in the distant, new province of Upper Canada was removed when a separate customs establishment was set up there in 1801. In addition to his salary and fees Scott drew income in the 1800s from property rentals and interest on loans, including one of £800 to Thomas Dunn and another to the amount of £2,500 to the firm of Lester and Morrogh [*see* Robert LESTER]. As a result of his relationship with Hugh Finlay, who died in 1801, Scott was responsible along with Robert Morrogh, a merchant and Jane Scott's nephew, for the sale in 1803 of Finlay's farm, Woodside. Scott, whose own sons evidently had died young, was also entrusted with the guardianship of Finlay's three minor sons, Hamilton, Charles, and George, and later with the trusteeship of Morrogh's boy, Robert Lester, a close favourite of the Scotts. Socially, Scott had remained active in the Quebec militia, rising to the rank of lieutenant-colonel in the 3rd battalion in 1809.

Following Jane's death in March 1807, Scott continued to live at his farm and on Rue des Pauvres. In May John YOUNG, looking to succeed him as collector, noted dryly that he was "far advanced in years & requires Assistance." Scott died at about age 69 on 24 April 1810, attended by his nephew William Phillips, who "used to sit up with him night after night during his illness." He was succeeded temporarily as collector by William Somerville and then permanently by Michael Henry Percival*.

At the time of his death Scott was keeping four servants and owned a sizeable estate, which included a modest library, much mahogany furniture, and a quantity of wines and spirits. His real property was extensive: Sans Souci, four other houses, several suburban lots, woodlands (bought from the estate of William Grant), and holdings in Durham, Barnston, and Granby townships. In addition to possessing Bank of England stock worth £11,800 sterling, he was owed more than £1,793 by the failed firm of Lester and Morrogh and £1,140 sterling by Inglis, Ellice and Company of London. The sale of Scott's livestock and his properties in the Quebec area was carried out by his executors, William Burns*, Mathew Lymburner, and Robert Morrogh, and the proceeds were distributed in England among two brothers, two nieces, and a nephew; none of them, however, claimed his remaining estate. In 1833 William Phillips, then a merchant,

became its curator but the claims of settlers in Durham against the legality of Scott's original titles and a series of lawsuits resulted in several decades of contention over the ownership of the lands.

DAVID ROBERTS and JAMES H. LAMBERT

ANQ-Q, CE1-61, 9 July 1775, 6 May 1777, 17 April 1779, 7 July 1787, 8 Aug. 1789, 20 March 1807, 27 April 1810; CN1-83, 12 oct. 1792, 6 déc. 1793; CN1-92, 4 janv. 1802; CN1-230, 24 sept. 1802; 3 mai, 14 oct. 1803; 21 juin, 17 août, 1er déc. 1804; 24 août 1805; 3 oct. 1806; 14 nov. 1808; 27 sept. 1809; 4, 15 mai 1810; 9 févr. 1811; 19 mai, 17 sept., 6 déc. 1813; 19 mai 1815; CN1-250, 19 août 1762; CN1-256, 10 Oct. 1793; CN1-285, 3 mai 1803. PAC, MG 23, D104; I13, 2: 171–73; RG 1, E1, 112: 126–34, 142–43, 150–61; L3ᴸ: 47–48, 793, 1390, 1408, 2442, 4122, 85339–433; RG 4, A1: 22213, 22219, 35473–76; B58, 4–6; 15; RG 68, General index, 1651–1841: ff.181, 185, 309, 324, 338. PRO, CO 42/12, 42/30, 42/69, 42/114, 42/122, 42/124–25, 42/132–33, 42/135. "Les dénombrements de Québec" (Plessis), ANQ *Rapport*, 1948–49: 104, 154, 213. "Les Grant de Longueuil," J.-J. Lefebvre, édit., ANQ *Rapport*, 1953–55: 133. [James Jeffry], "Journal kept in Quebec in 1775 by James Jeffry," ed. William Smith, Essex Institute, *Hist. Coll.* (Salem, Mass.), 50 (1914): 100, 102–3, 115, 117, 119, 135, 138. *Quebec Gazette*, 18 Aug. 1766; 8 Oct. 1767; 18 Jan. 1770; 10 July 1777; 13 May 1779; 17 March, 12 May, 23 June, 3 Nov. 1785; 29 June 1786; 3 May, 5, 12, 26 July 1787; 23 April, 3 Dec. 1789; 28 Jan. 1790; 18, 19 Aug. 1791; 2 Aug. 1792; 11 April, 28 Nov. 1793; 13 Feb., 3 July 1794; 27 Dec. 1798; 1er Aug. 1799; 13 May 1803; 23 May 1805; 23 Jan. 1806; 17 Aug., 7 Dec. 1809; 25 Jan., 26 April, 10 May, 5 July 1810; 18 March 1813. *Quebec almanac*, 1792: 159; 1805: 40; 1809: 47; 1810: 43; 1811: 43; 1812: 43. Kelley, "Church and state papers," ANQ *Rapport*, 1948–49: 309. Gordon Blake, *Customs administration in Canada: an essay in tariff technology* (Toronto, 1957). Neatby, *Quebec*, 35–38.

SCOTT, THOMAS CHARLES HESLOP, self-proclaimed Church of England clergyman; b. *c*. 1753, probably in England; d. 21 March 1813 at Quebec, Lower Canada.

Little is certain about the life of Thomas Charles Heslop Scott. He maintained that his godfather was the Reverend Frederick Keppel, bishop of Exeter from 1762 to 1777, and that Keppel had ordained him in St James Church, London, on 30 Jan. 1774. Scott claimed to have then obtained the post of deputy chaplain of the 34th Foot. Under the command of Lieutenant-Colonel Barrimore Matthew St Leger*, the regiment sailed from Ireland to Quebec, arriving in May 1776, but Scott did not join it until later because, he asserted, his ship was captured by an American privateer; he said he had lost all his belongings, including his certificate of ordination. He turned up in Halifax, N.S., assisted the Reverend John Breynton* at St Paul's Church, and eventually joined the regiment at Sorel, Que.

Scott was carrying out ministerial duties among both soldiers and civilians when early in 1779 he incurred St Leger's strong disapproval, perhaps for misconduct and insubordination. Finally, late in 1781, St Leger dismissed Scott from the chaplaincy, and Governor HALDIMAND forbad him to exercise the office of a minister. Scott protested vigorously, maintaining wryly in 1782 that he had as many good qualities as Haldimand was misinformed he had bad ones. In his own defence he threatened to publish his correspondence with St Leger and appears to have circulated a number of copies of a handbill presumably containing this correspondence in the summer of 1782. Two years later he offered to sell to St Leger the copyright of the correspondence for £210 sterling. No copy of the handbill has been preserved and nothing further is known of the episode.

The Church of England minister, the Reverend Lewis Guerry, a Swiss appointed to Sorel in 1774 to minister in French, had found little opportunity to do so there or elsewhere and, having left in 1776, remained in England on leave of absence. In the eight years after Guerry's departure Scott was the only person to serve as Church of England cleric for the 100 or 150 Protestants, whom he described as "most of them able Artificers, useful Mechanicks, or Shop-Keepers." He found a few supporters in and around Sorel who in 1781 signed a subscription list for his salary. Acting under the orders of Major-General Friedrich Adolph Riedesel, at Sorel in command of Britain's German mercenaries, Captain John BARNES of the Royal Artillery endeavoured to discourage among the subscribers any whose economic dependence on the government made them susceptible to such pressure. Scott had to cease his ministrations for a time and was brought into great penury. In 1783 he sued Barnes for intimidation of subscribers, but in the following year he offered to withdraw the suit if given compensation. How the matter was settled is not known. Meanwhile a search of the London ordination register, conducted for the bishop of London, Robert Lowth, at the request of the military authorities, had produced no evidence of Scott's ordination either by or on orders from Lowth's predecessor Richard Terrick, who would have been authorized to ordain Scott for the ministry in the colonies. In June 1784 Lowth ordered Scott to obey Haldimand's orders.

Despite the bishop's order and despite the discouragement of his subscribers, "the irreverend Mr. Scott," as Captain Barnes called him, continued to conduct religious services at Sorel for a few loyal laymen. These were described as Scott's "besotted followers" by John Doty*, who arrived in Sorel in the summer of 1784 as missionary of the Society for the Propagation of the Gospel and was embarrassed in his work by Scott's presence. Scott claimed to have permission from Bishop Terrick to marry without a

licence from the governor, an authorization which Terrick would have had no power to give. A court of inquiry, established in Sorel in 1787, appears to have concluded that Scott was indeed an impostor.

Scott finally quitted Sorel in 1788, and is reported to have taught school in Quebec. There in November 1789 an indictment for perjury laid against him a year earlier was abandoned by order of Attorney General Alexander Gray, and in 1795 he was acquitted of a charge of libel. In 1797 he signed a four-year lease, at a rent of £15 per annum, for a farm in Sainte-Foy. He died on 21 March 1813 in apparent poverty, after protesting to the last the treatment he had received in the 1780s and demanding compensation. Despite his conflict with the Church of England, he was buried two days later by Salter Jehosaphat Mountain, minister at Quebec. Notwithstanding his lament in 1781 that he was the victim of "the greatest wrongs and injuries that ever innocent man suffered or that the annals of History can possibly produce," and making allowance for the unsettled times in which he was at Sorel, the evaluation of him as an impostor is substantiated by the total lack of evidence supporting his claims. His correspondence, filled with assertions of his importance, as well as threats of character assassination and reprisals, has none of the forbearance and humility that would be expected of a man of the cloth.

THOMAS R. MILLMAN

ANQ-Q, CE1-61, 23 March 1813; CN1-284, 10 avril 1797. BL, Add. MSS 21721: 80; 21732: 7, 75; 21734: 184, 248, 373; 21735/1: 128; 21735/2: 194; 21797: 1; 21799: 97 (copies at PAC). PAC, MG 11, [CO 42] Q, 28: 161–64. USPG, C/CAN/Mont., 1, 31, 34 (mfm. at PAC). *Quebec Gazette*, 15 July 1779, 25 March 1813. Azarie Couillard-Després, *Histoire de Sorel de ses origines à nos jours* (Montréal, 1926), 158–61. *Historical record of the Thirty-Fourth, or the Cumberland Regiment of Foot . . .* (London, 1844). H. C. Stuart, *The Church of England in Canada, 1759–1793; from the conquest to the establishment of the see of Quebec* (Montreal, 1893), 39–40.

SEELY (Seeley, Seelye), JOSEPH, militiaman; b. 1786, probably in western Quebec, son of Augustus Seelye (Sealey); m. with children; last known to be living in 1814.

Details concerning the Seely family are scarce. Seelys from Connecticut were common in New Brunswick and in the Johnstown District of Upper Canada [see Caleb Seely*; Peet Selee*], and it is likely that the various families were related. According to Joseph Seely, his father had served under Jeffery Amherst* during the Seven Years' War and in a corps commanded by Captain James Campbell during the American revolution. The elder Seelye was on the United Empire Loyalist list for Lancaster

Seely

Township, Upper Canada, but the family probably never resided there. By 1801 they were in Elizabethtown (Brockville), where Joseph took the oath of allegiance the same year. Six years later he petitioned for 200 acres of land as the son of a loyalist and received a patent for a lot on Lake Gananoque in Leeds and Lansdowne Township on 24 March 1812.

Here Seely might have spent a life toiling in happy obscurity but for the intervention of the War of 1812. "As became a good subject," he volunteered for duty and served nine months with Captain Charles Jones*'s dragoons. He then enlisted in the 1st Leeds Militia, enticed by Captain Adiel Sherwood*'s "promise of a Sergeants situation and rations for my small family." The higher pay must have seemed a boon to a prospective young farmer and the supply of provisions essential to a family dependent upon the male to clear, sow, and harvest the land. In April 1813 the newly enlisted men were ordered to Prescott, where they were divided into companies the following month.

Seely's hopes were quickly scotched. Since Sherwood had failed to recruit the required quota for his unit, Seely was assigned to Captain Archibald McLean*'s company as a private. The promotion to sergeant was not forthcoming and the rations for his family were never issued. After serving briefly under McLean, Seely was transferred to the "Engineer Employ." Aggrieved, dispirited, and no doubt anxious about his family, the young soldier deserted in late August. About 20 November he was captured "in the Enemy's Camp" on the American shore by a party of Leeds and Grenville militia led by Captain Herman Landen.

It had been a critical year for the civil and military administration of the province. The problems that had confronted Isaac Brock worsened under his successors Roger Hale Sheaffe* and Francis Rottenburg*: disaffection was widespread and desertion endemic among the militia; the House of Assembly was reluctant to allow the administration to use arbitrary powers to meet the civil problem; and initial military successes at Ogdensburg, N.Y., and at Frenchtown (near Monroe, Mich.) had been offset by the capture of York (Toronto) in April, the defeat of Robert Heriot Barclay* on Lake Erie, and the rout of Tecumseh and Henry Procter* at the battle of Moraviantown on 5 October. The outbreak of disorder during the occupation of York had been particularly unsettling [see Elijah Bentley]. In an atmosphere charged with fear and suspicion even judges such as William Dummer Powell* urged dispensing with the due process of civil law to overawe the disaffected. In July Governor Prevost, possibly acting upon information supplied by Powell, empowered Rottenburg to convene courts martial to make examples. The pervasive belief that such action would quell the disloyal culminated in the execution of eight men at the Ancaster "Bloody Assize" in 1814 [see Jacob Overholser].

Charged with desertion to the enemy and with aiding "in piloting one of the Enemy's boat's," Seely was tried before a court martial at Kingston on 9 and 10 Dec. 1813. The court was composed of 13 of the leading militia officers of the Johnstown, Midland, and Eastern districts. The prosecution was handled by the acting judge advocate general, Edward Walker. Seely was left to conduct his own defence – a daunting task for a mere private; he pleaded not guilty. Walker called four witnesses: Landen, Archibald McLean, and two privates from Landen's party. Walker's aim was simple: to establish that Seely had served with the militia until late August and that at his capture he was in an enemy camp within the United States. An unabashed Seely handled his defence with marked aplomb. He did not deny the charges but rather emphasized a family and personal history of loyalty, a laudable record of military service, and a reasonable motive for desertion – the breaking of the promise that had occasioned his enlistment.

Seely's previous military record was not disputed. In testifying to his loyalty, Landen, who had known the prisoner for 16 or 18 years, stated, "No one would I have ventured my life with sooner. . . ." He also mentioned that Seely had fought with "some Americans . . . on account of their celebrating the Independence." After his capture Seely's behaviour was extraordinary. Landen related how he "cried very much and said although you were a prisoner, you were going to a Country you loved, and that you had not been contented since you left it."

Seely's speech in his own defence did not attempt to prove his innocence but rather addressed the circumstances of the case. His loyalty was instinctive, inspired by the attachments of family and by traditions learned from a loyalist father: "I reluctantly left the Country In which I have been brought up from my childhood and to which I was attached by all the ties of Loyalty, Friends and Kindred not with smallest or most distant ideas of *aiding* or *assisting* in the service of an Enemy that I have always been taught to detest. . . . With such a parent to instil the Principles of Loyalty into his Family, it is almost impossible for any member of it, to have any attachment to any other Government than that to which he belongs. . . ." His motivation was simply a sense of injustice – "I considered my promise to serve as void." All the conditions of his enlistment had been broken. Although he had been an acting sergeant for a few days, Seely's application for permanent rank was rejected when McLean called attention to his lack of education. The extra rations, which Landen stated were "the reason that many men with large families engaged," were not delivered. Although Seely was on the ration list, his family was not "in consequence of their being such a number."

The court found Seely guilty of desertion but acquitted him of the second charge. He was sentenced to be transported for seven years but in spite of Rottenburg's approval of the court's judgement he did not meet his fate. Rottenburg had intended to pardon Seely on condition that he enlist in the New Brunswick Fencibles. On 29 Jan. 1814 Rottenburg wrote to his successor, George Gordon Drummond*, on this and other related matters. Drummond acted accordingly and on 18 April 1814 issued a "full, and unlimited Pardon" with the suggested proviso attached. It does not seem that Seely complied with the terms. Neither did he return to his land on Lake Gananoque; it was sold in two instalments many years later.

Seely might have fared worse. Another militia private tried for desertion at the same court martial was promptly shot. What distinguished the two cases was Seely's adroit defence. His ability to combine a sense of just cause and personal loyalty no doubt resulted in the milder sentence and later the pardon. It is commonplace, and perhaps sensible, to see in instances of disaffection and treason the American political sympathies of an Elijah Bentley or an Abraham Markle*. It is also prudent to bear in mind the frustrated self-interest of an Ebenezer ALLAN and an Andrew Westbrook*. And as a reminder that personal lives sometimes do not fit any mode of interpretation, it is instructive to remember the case of Joseph Seely.

ROBERT LOCHIEL FRASER III

AO, MS 4, J. B. Robinson letterbook, 1812–15: 31; MS 519; RG 1, A-IV, 16; C-IV, Lansdowne Township, concession 10, lot 21; concession 11, lot 22; RG 21, sect.A, Elizabethtown, Leeds and Lansdowne townships, census and assessment records. Glengarry Land Registry Office (Alexandria, Ont.), Abstract index to deeds, Lancaster Township: 97–98, 102 (mfm. at AO, GS 4043). Leeds Land Registry Office (Brockville, Ont.), Abstract index to deeds, Lansdowne Township: ff.195, 253 (mfm. at AO, GS 4563). PAC, RG 1, L3, 456: S10/68; RG 5, A1: 6532–35, 6684–709, 7820–21; RG 8, I (C ser.), 166: 54; 679: 148–49; 688C, Allan to Rottenburg, 14 Aug. 1813; RG 9, I, B7: 296–99, 301, 331, 394–97. *Doc. hist. of campaign upon Niagara frontier* (Cruikshank), 5: 94–95. "Grants of crown lands in U.C.," AO *Report*, 1928: 74–76. Reid, *Loyalists in Ont.*, 279. W. M. Weekes, "The War of 1812: civil authority and martial law in Upper Canada," *The defended border: Upper Canada and the War of 1812 . . .* , ed. Morris Zaslow and W. B. Turner (Toronto, 1964), 191–204.

SELBY, PRIDEAUX, army officer, Indian Department official, office holder, and politician; baptized 21 Dec. 1747 in Alnwick, England, son of George Selby and Mary Selby; m. Elizabeth —, and they had at least three children; d. 9 May 1813 in York (Toronto), Upper Canada.

On 21 Dec. 1781 Prideaux Selby was made an ensign in the 5th Foot, then garrisoned in Ireland, and he was promoted lieutenant on 28 Feb. 1785. The first reference to his being in North America appears in

1790, when he was stationed at Detroit (Mich.). He had probably come over with his regiment, which arrived at Quebec on 26 July 1787, and in 1790 accompanied it to Detroit, where he is listed as a housekeeper in a report of 1 Aug. 1791.

In April 1792 Major John Smith, British commander at Detroit and father of David William*, soon to become surveyor general of Upper Canada, recommended Selby to Lieutenant Governor SIMCOE as "a confidential person and competent to give Your Excellency information." During the election contest of that summer Selby actively supported the candidacy of David William Smith for the House of Assembly, and at about the same time Simcoe appointed him assistant secretary of Indian affairs. Little information is available on the functioning of the Indian Department at this time. However, if Selby's experience is any example of the rigours of the schedule, the work must have been gruelling and hectic. There appears to have been a great deal of travel involved; his letters for the next few years were often sent to and from a variety of locations. Moreover, there is some indication that he was entrusted with greater responsibilities than one might have expected to find in an assistant secretary. He was apparently quite close to Simcoe and to Alexander McKee*, the deputy superintendent general of Indian affairs after 1794, and periodically was given general supervision of the department during McKee's not infrequent illnesses, a practice that continued under McKee's successor, William Claus*.

Selby himself had bouts of sickness: in a letter of December 1798 McKee expressed the hope that he would "soon be reestablished in perfect Health, by geting the better of the Cough and Spitting." Soon afterwards Selby asked for permission to take a leave of absence in Europe because of his health. Peter RUSSELL, the administrator of the province and a man who admired Selby's "Ability and principle," forwarded this request to Governor Robert PRESCOTT. As it turned out, with rumours circulating that French and Spanish forces, apparently with Indian assistance, were about to invade British territory by way of the Mississippi valley [*see* Wabakinine*], Prescott decided that it would be "impolitic" to allow Selby to leave his post.

Perhaps because of his ill health, in 1801 Selby received permission from Lieutenant Governor Peter HUNTER to conduct his Indian Department business from his home in Amherstburg. The following May he was appointed a justice of the peace in the Western District. Among his concerns at this time was the proper care of his lands, which led to an interest in the cultivation of hemp. Although there is evidence that his magisterial duties and other preoccupations kept him from some of his departmental work, he continued to play an important role in the Indian Department and his opinion was generally sought and

Selkirk

respected. Amherstburg at this time seems to have been an efficient post with a good record in Indian affairs, and it might not be unreasonable to assume that Selby was at least partly responsible.

Despite his record, or perhaps because of it, Selby was ordered in October 1807 to "remove himself and his office" to York, where he lived the remainder of his life. The culmination of his career came on 8 Oct. 1808 when he was sworn in as a member of the Executive Council. On the same date he was made receiver general and on 1 Jan. 1809, as was usually the practice, he also became auditor general, holding both positions until his death. On appointment to the council Selby took the opportunity to apply to Lieutenant Governor Francis Gore* for the grant of a lot in the town of York, which he received a week later, and in his new capacity as auditor general he signed his own receipt for the patent and surveying fees.

Conscientious as always, Selby rarely missed a meeting of the Executive Council, and by late 1809 John Askin, a prominent figure in the Western District, could claim that the lieutenant governor "pays great attention to what Mr Selby recommends." Nor were his contributions to Upper Canadian life confined to his work in the council. One of the leading members of the Loyal and Patriotic Society of Upper Canada, a benevolent organization established during the War of 1812, he appears to have been the person responsible for proposing the creation of that body: in 1814 John Strachan*, noting that Selby's "sentiments on most subjects, particularly on public affairs were in unison with mine," stated that the Loyal and Patriotic Society was "first suggested by Mr Selby, who gave the credit of it to his excellent daughter." Unfortunately, after reaching the pinnacle of success in Upper Canada and acquiring the land and influence that went with it, Selby became gravely ill in the spring of 1813, ceasing to perform any official duties in April. Close to death during the American occupation of York in late April and early May, he was spared the humiliation of watching the enemy plunder the provincial treasury. On the night before the invasion of 27 April, when Selby was "in a State of insensibility," Chief Justice Thomas Scott* and William Dummer Powell* paid a hurried visit to his house, where the public money was stored. Acting on instructions from the administrator of the province, Sir Roger Hale Sheaffe*, they told Selby's daughter Elizabeth to move this money – more than £3,000 – to a safe hiding-place, a task she carried out that very night. A few days later, however, Major William King of the 15th U.S. Infantry demanded the surrender of the funds in the provincial treasury, and this demand was acceded to after a consultation among Scott, Powell, William Allan*, Duncan Cameron*, and John Strachan.

Selby died on 9 May 1813 and was survived by his daughter Elizabeth, who, along with Matthew Elliott and Alexander Duff, an inhabitant of Sandwich (Windsor), was a joint devisee in trust of her father's real estate holdings, which exceeded 2,000 acres. His death undoubtedly deprived Upper Canada of one of its most respected and influential citizens, whose career demonstrated the opportunities offered in the colony to an enterprising young officer.

Carl Christie

AO, MS 35, letterbook, 1812–34: 96; MS 75 (mfm. at PAC); MU 2100, 1800, no.5; RG 22, ser.155, will of Prideaux Selby. PAC, MG 11, [CO 42] Q, 299, 316–17; MG 19, F1, 5–10; F16; MG 23, HI, 1; 2; RG 1, L1, 22: 481, 523; 25: 141; 26: 88, 98, 151, 401, 412; L3, 447: S misc., 1793–1812/98–100; 448: S1/80, 107, 134; 450: S3/13, 20; 450A: S3/235; 452: S5/115; 454: S9/71; 455: S9/149; RG 5; RG 8, I (C ser.); RG 10, A1, 1–4, 486; A2, 8–12. PRO, CO 42/349: 202; T 28/3: 229–32 (transcripts at PAC). *Corr. of Hon. Peter Russell* (Cruikshank and Hunter), vols.2–3. *Corr. of Lieut. Governor Simcoe* (Cruikshank). "Grants of crown lands in U.C.," AO *Report*, 1929: 99, 138. *John Askin papers* (Quaife). "U.C. land book C," AO *Report*, 1931: 4, 23, 37, 39, 43. *Windsor border region* (Lajeunesse). Armstrong, *Handbook of Upper Canadian chronology*. [J.] B. Burke, *A genealogical and heraldic history of the landed gentry of Great Britain* (12th ed., London, 1914). G.B., WO, *Army list*, 1782, 1786. *The service of British regiments in Canada and North America . . .*, comp. C. H. Stewart ([2nd ed.], Ottawa, 1964).

R. S. Allen, *A history of the British Indian Department in North America, 1755–1830* (Can., National Hist. Parks and Sites Branch, *Manuscript report, no.109*, Ottawa, 1971). Horsman, *Matthew Elliott*. C. W. Humphries, "The capture of York," *The defended border: Upper Canada and the War of 1812 . . .*, ed. Morris Zaslow and W. B. Turner (Toronto, 1964), 251–70; "Upper Canada in 1813" (MA thesis, Univ. of Toronto, 1959). C. C. James, *Early history of the town of Amherstburg . . .* (2nd ed., Amherstburg, Ont., 1909). J. E. Middleton, *The municipality of Toronto: a history* (3v., Toronto, 1923), 1. J. J. Talman, "William Claus: forgotten loyalist" (paper presented to the annual meeting of the CHA, London, Ont., 1978). H. M. Walker, *A history of the Northumberland Fusiliers, 1674–1902* (London, 1919). Alison Ewart and Julia Jarvis, "The personnel of the family compact, 1791–1841," *CHR*, 7 (1926): 209–21.

SELKIRK, THOMAS DOUGLAS, Baron DAER and SHORTCLEUCH, 5th Earl of. *See* DOUGLAS

SEMPLE, ROBERT, HBC territorial governor; b. 26 Feb. 1777 in Boston, Mass., son of Robert Semple and Anne Greenlaw; d. 19 June 1816 at the Red River settlement (Winnipeg, Man.).

Robert Semple's parents espoused the loyalist cause and during or after the American revolution the family returned to England. Robert became a merchant and travelled extensively in Europe, Africa, the Near East, and South America. At the time of the Napoleonic Wars his American birth gave him access to European countries from which British subjects were excluded. Out of these journeys came a number of travel books published between 1803 and 1814. It was probably through his mercantile connections that he came to the attention of Lord Selkirk [DOUGLAS], but it has never been clear what qualifications led the earl to arrange his appointment as governor of the Hudson's Bay Company's territories. Semple was named to the post on 12 April 1815 at a salary of £1,500 per annum.

At this point the Red River settlement had already been established for several years. The first of Selkirk's Scottish settlers, led by Miles Macdonell*, had reached the site in the summer of 1812, and other groups had followed. Semple arrived at York Factory (Man.) in August 1815 with a further party of settlers, mostly from Sutherland. There he learned that the colony had been destroyed by the North West Company [see Duncan Cameron* (d. 1848)], which believed itself seriously endangered by the presence of an HBC settlement on its supply lines. By the time Semple arrived at Red River in November, Colin Robertson*, an HBC man on his way from Montreal to the Athabasca country, had begun re-establishment of the community. In mid December Semple went to Fort Daer (Pembina, N.Dak.), where the settlers had been sent for the winter because of the food shortage, and early in 1816 he set out on a tour of company posts on the upper Assiniboine and Qu'Appelle rivers. He returned to Red River at the end of March. Earlier that month Robertson had seized the Nor'Westers' Fort Gibraltar at the forks of the Red and Assiniboine. Semple approved of the seizure. It was a measure, he said, on which he had "fully determined" and which he believed was justified and necessary.

The relationship between Semple and Robertson was an abrasive one. According to Alexander McDonell*, Semple's successor, they were never on "terms of intimacy," and the differences between them mounted in the face of Métis and NWC hostility. Historians have characterized Semple as a vain, indecisive man, who failed to appreciate the lengths to which Nor'Westers would go to destroy the Red River settlement. Robertson judged him "a proud Englishman, rather too conscious of his own abilities." At first Semple respected Robertson's superior knowledge of the country, but he eventually decided to assert his own leadership. Both men hoped to win over the Métis from the Nor'Westers, and Robertson blamed the failure of this policy on Semple's contempt for the Métis. Robertson hoped to blockade the rivers and prevent the Métis from supplying pemmican to the NWC brigades travelling west. Semple was more concerned with provisions for the settlement than with the blockade. He was aware of intended attacks by the

Métis, whom the NWC had encouraged to think of themselves as a nation with rights to the land, but he vacillated between taking aggressive steps and attempting a reconciliation with them. Disgusted, Robertson left the settlement on 11 June 1816. He was prepared to return, but Semple said there was no need for him.

On 19 June 1816 a party of some 60 or 70 Métis under Cuthbert Grant*, bringing pemmican from the plains for the NWC brigade, reached the settlement. Although Semple knew of their approach and might have expected an attack, he made no defensive plans. With some 25 settlers and HBC men, but apparently without any aggressive intent, he met the Métis along the Red River at an area known as Seven Oaks (Winnipeg). Too late he realized the danger and sent back to the settlement for cannon. A verbal altercation between Semple and one of the Métis led to a skirmish in which the governor and about 20 of his party were killed. Fort Douglas, the settlement headquarters, surrendered the next day and the settlers again dispersed. Selkirk later found evidence that some of those participating in the massacre had been rewarded by the NWC. Two of Grant's party were tried in York (Toronto) for murder and six Nor'Westers for being accessories. All were acquitted. In the battle at Seven Oaks the violence that had marked the contest for the fur trade of the northwest reached a climax and became a determining factor in the amalgamation of the two fur companies in 1821.

HARTWELL BOWSFIELD

Robert Semple is the author of several travel books, including Walks and sketches at the Cape of Good Hope; to which is subjoined a journey from Cape Town to Blettenberg's Bay (London, 1803); Observations on a journey through Spain and Italy to Naples; and thence to Smyrna and Constantinople: comprising a description of the principal places in that route, and remarks on the present natural and political state of those countries (2v., London, 1807); A second journey in Spain, in the spring of 1809; from Lisbon, through the western skirts of the Sierra Morena, to Sevilla, Cordoba, Granada, Malaga, and Gibraltar; and thence to Tetuan and Tangiers (London, 1809); Sketch of the present state of Caracas; including a journey from Caracas through La Victoria and Valencia to Puerto Cabello (London, 1812); and Observations made on a tour from Hamburg, through Berlin, Gorlitz, and Breslau, to Silberberg; and thence to Gottenburg (London, 1814). He also wrote Charles Ellis, or the friends; a novel (2v., London, 1806).

PAC, MG 19, E1, ser.1, 4: 1442–52, 1652–53; 5: 1711–22; 6: 2180, 2403–4; 7: 2711–17, 2735–52 (transcripts). Edinburgh Rev. (Edinburgh and London), 11 (1807–8): 88–100; 15 (1809–10): 384–96. Report of trials in the courts of Canada, relative to the destruction of the Earl of Selkirk's settlement on the Red River; with observations, ed. Andrew Amos (London, 1820), viii. DNB. Encyclopedia Canadiana. J. M. Gray, Lord Selkirk of Red River (Toronto, 1963), 131, 138–48. M. A. MacLeod and W. L. Morton,

Séré

Cuthbert Grant of Grantown, warden of the plains of Red River (Toronto, 1963), 33–52. C. [B.] Martin, *Lord Selkirk's work in Canada* (Toronto, 1916), 96–98, 107–13. Morton, *Hist. of Canadian west* (1973), 573–77.

SÉRÉ (Serré). *See* Cerré

SERRES, ALEXANDRE, surgeon; b. *c.* 1732 in Saramon, France, son of Jean-Baptiste Serres, a notary, and Gabrielle Marleau; m. first Marie Galliay; m. secondly 26 May 1783 Madeleine Lefebvre in Montreal, Que.; m. thirdly 23 Jan. 1804 Thérèse Migneron in Saint-Laurent, near Montreal; d. 18 Aug. 1812 in Montreal.

Little is known of the career of Alexandre Serres before his arrival in the province of Quebec. By his own statement he had received his master's letters from the Académie Royale de Chirurgie in Paris. He is also believed to have served in the French army, since a document dating from 1783 states that he was a former "surgeon-major of Monseigneur le Duc de Guines."

Dr Serres decided to try his luck in the colony, in company with his wife Marie and a child born in London in November 1778. He arrived in August 1779 and on 3 May 1780 sought a post in the army from Governor HALDIMAND, but without success. Two months later he set up practice in Trois-Rivières, where he bought a house and two lots. He purchased a piece of land at Saint-Sulpice in 1781, but in the end decided to move in the winter of 1781–82 and to live in Montreal. On 23 Feb. 1782 he sold his properties at Trois-Rivières to the merchant Louis de La Grave.

At this period Serres was practising in Montreal as a surgeon and obstetrician. He was not always successful. For example, on 6 Oct. 1786 he and Dr George Selby* delivered Marie-Anne Mackay, wife of Charles-Roch Quinson de Saint-Ours, of a child. Serres then prescribed treatment for the mother and is supposed to have added that she should be given only what he ordered. Two days later, on entering the house of his patient, he noticed a syringe that had just been used for an enema. According to a later statement he then expressed surprise to several people and considered his presence was no longer required. He had cause to regret his actions since mother and child died of complications ensuing from the delivery. On 11 October a meeting of surgeons criticized his conduct. Eight days later Serres replied to his detractors through a notice in the *Montreal Gazette* declaring that it "would be better to stick to acting legally and with evidence rather than by any other illicit means." On 13 November a warrant was issued for his arrest on a charge of having caused the deaths of Marie-Anne Mackay and her child by ignorance and negligence. Some days later he begged Lord Dorchester [Guy CARLETON] to defer giving effect to the judgement against him.

Whatever the outcome, this unexpected accident did not prevent Serres from continuing his career. On 27 Sept. 1787 he announced in the *Montreal Gazette* that he was prepared to give "a course on midwifery" for surgeons and midwives from both town and country. Paradoxically it is largely through his observations on the phenomenon of the "great darkness" that he has attracted the attention of historians. On three occasions in October 1785 the sky at Quebec and Montreal grew dark in broad daylight. Serres then noticed that the rain accompanying this event contained sulphur, and he concluded that "the only cause of this phenomenon was the inflammation of some neighbouring mines." Geologists much later attributed the phenomenon to minor volcanic eruptions.

In the light of these details it would seem that Serres had had a scientific education. However, it was not until 1802 that, to comply with the ordinance of 1788 regulating the practice of medicine, he sought a licence as surgeon and obstetrician; it was probably refused him. Around 1804 Serres settled in Saint-Laurent, near Montreal. A few years later he returned to Montreal, where he died in 1812.

Alexandre Serres was quick-tempered and difficult. The newspapers of the period record some of his disputes with the people around him. It seems clear that his professional misfortunes should be imputed more to his personality than to any real incompetence.

RENALD LESSARD

ANQ-M, CE1-44, 23 janv. 1804; CE1-51, 27 sept. 1782, 26 mai 1783, 7 déc. 1791, 19 août 1812; CN1-167, 9, 14 mai 1792; CN1-269, 12 Feb. 1807; CN1-313, 4 mai 1783. ANQ-MBF, CN1-5, 8 juill., 29 sept. 1780. BL, Add. mss 21878: 242; 21879: 39 (copies at PAC). PAC, RG 4, A1: 9970–71; A3, 6, no.120. *Montreal Gazette*, 20 Oct. 1785; 19 Oct. 1786; 27 Sept. 1787; 19 Aug. 1790; 29 March, 5, 19, 26 April 1792. *Quebec Gazette*, 27 Oct. 1785. M.-J. et G. Ahern, *Notes pour l'hist. de la médecine*, 513–14. É.-Z. Massicotte, "Un chirurgien gascon," *BRH*, 42 (1936): 719–21.

SHAW, ÆNEAS, army officer, politician, office holder, and militia officer; b. at Tordarroch House, Scotland, second son of Angus Shaw, chief of Clan Ay, and Anne Dallas of Cantray; m. first Ann Gosline, and they had ten children; m. secondly Margaret Hickman; d. 6 Feb. 1814 in York (Toronto), Upper Canada.

Æneas Shaw emigrated to Staten Island, N.Y., about 1770. Soon after the outbreak of the American revolution he joined the Queen's Rangers as an ensign, and ended the war as a captain, his promotions beginning in November 1777 when a new commander, John Graves SIMCOE, formed a Highland company. Judged adept in the training of light infantry and sharpshooters, he saw much detached service in

Shaw

the Pennsylvania and Virginia campaigns. After surrendering at Yorktown, Va, in 1781, he was evacuated to New York City, and he subsequently joined the loyalist migration to Nova Scotia. He settled on the Nashwaak River (N.B.), where by the fall of 1791 he was an established farmer.

Nevertheless Shaw accepted a commission as a captain-lieutenant in the Queen's Rangers when they were raised as a provincial corps for Upper Canada. Of the five old Rangers who composed half of the new regiment's officers, Shaw was the one who most clearly left a secure position in civilian life. He travelled overland with a dozen recruits to meet Lieutenant Governor Simcoe at Quebec in March 1792 and led the first contingent of Rangers up to Kingston. A year later, when Simcoe had already recommended his appointment to the Executive Council, he brought his family to Niagara (Niagara-on-the-Lake). In Simcoe's words, he was a man of "Education, Ability, & Loyalty . . . one of those Gentlemen who is most likely to effect a permanent Landed Establishment in this Country."

Shaw commanded the Ranger detachment that cleared the site of York in 1793 and he was among the first officials to move his family there. He would have commanded a garrison at Long Point as a nucleus for loyal settlement, if the project had been approved by the imperial government. Delays by the same authority prevented him from being sworn in as an executive councillor until June 1794. In the same month he also took a seat on the Legislative Council, in time to support the administration's bill for a court of king's bench. From then on, although his only other civil appointment was as lieutenant of the county of York (26 Aug. 1796 to 2 Dec. 1798), he was more an official than an officer. He and Receiver General Peter RUSSELL were the only regular attendants at the Executive Council under Simcoe. He was a reliable supporter not only of his patron but also of Russell when the latter became administrator of the province in 1796. Concerned that Shaw's regiment might be withdrawn from Upper Canada, Russell asked permission to have him remain at York because of his indispensability as a councillor. On 31 Aug. 1799 Lieutenant Governor Peter HUNTER, when forming a committee of the council to conduct affairs during his frequent absences, included Shaw; but seniority and his residence at York were probably sufficient reasons. Shaw had neither raised trouble nor made a mark in either council, but his association with Russell was no longer an advantage. His influence on the Executive Council was being eclipsed by the rise of later appointees, notably John McGill*. When the Queen's Rangers were disbanded in 1802, he retired on half pay as a lieutenant-colonel. In the next year his membership in the council became honorary and lasted as such until 1807.

Shaw's public career was not over. Fear of war with

the United States, arising from the *Chesapeake* affair [*see* Sir George Cranfield BERKELEY], revealed that the Upper Canadian militia was almost without arms or training and that its adjutant general, Hugh McDonell* (Aberchalder), was gravely ill. An energetic officer, Sir James Henry CRAIG, came out in late 1807 to fill the vacant post of commander-in-chief at Quebec. In addition, the Upper Canadian militia was provided with 4,000 muskets, a new militia act of 16 March 1808 made it liable for service in defence of the lower as well as the upper province, and Shaw was gazetted on 2 Dec. 1807 with the local rank of colonel to succeed McDonell. Promoted major-general in 1811, Shaw was responsible for training the militia. It was the largest military force in the province, with about a tenth of the total white population enrolled, but it was not subject to training in units larger than local companies nor to fixed periods of service in case of war. Flank companies of volunteers were provided for by a militia act of 6 March 1812, and 2,000 men were subsequently registered in them. Even they could be obliged to train for no more than three days a month. Since the legislature specifically refused to strengthen the law, Shaw can hardly be blamed for the deficiencies of militia units when war came in June 1812. He led them in action once, at the unsuccessful defence of York on 27 April 1813. Nearing his final illness and 32 years away from combat, he moved them too slowly to be of use and unnecessarily withdrew a critically placed company of regulars to their support.

The status that Shaw found in Upper Canada came from office, not wealth. The scale of land grants attached to his rank allowed him 6,000 acres for himself and 1,200 more for each of his children. Nearly all of this land remained unproductive during his lifetime. He began selling it in 1803 at prices that suggest he needed money: his 1,900 acres in Pickering and West Flamborough townships, sold mostly to William Allan*, brought him only £642. About half his grant, in North Dorchester Township, became part of Thomas Talbot*'s settlement. When in 1817 his widow petitioned for the support of his children, however, she was far from poor. Shaw had kept the most valuable of his 500 acres in York Township, and some of it remained in the family until 1862.

S. R. MEALING

[The Shaw family papers, in private hands, are chiefly genealogical. Contemporary references to Shaw are in P. Campbell, *Travels in North America* (Langton and Ganong); *Corr. of Hon. Peter Russell* (Cruikshank and Hunter); *Corr. of Lieut. Governor Simcoe* (Cruikshank); *Select British docs. of War of 1812* (Wood); [J. G.] Simcoe, *A journal of the operations of the Queen's Rangers, from the end of the year 1777, to the conclusion of the late American war* (Exeter, Eng., [1787]); and Gwillim, *Diary of Mrs. Simcoe* (Robertson; 1911; 1934). There are copies of primary documents relating to Shaw in Ont., Ministry of Citizenship and Culture, Heritage Administration Branch (Toronto), Hist. sect. research files, Toronto RF.31, Aeneas Shaw. See also Chadwick, *Ontarian families* and W. J. Rattray, *The Scot in British North America* (4v., Toronto, 1880–84). s.r.m.]

SHEAWAQUANEP. *See* ZHEEWEGONAB

SHENDORETH. *See* DEMASDUWIT

SHEWAQUONAP. *See* ZHEEWEGONAB

SIMCOE, JOHN GRAVES, army officer and colonial administrator: b. 25 Feb. 1752 in Cotterstock, England, son of Captain John Simcoe, a naval officer, and Katherine Stamford; m. 30 Dec. 1782 Elizabeth Posthuma Gwillim*, and they had 11 children; d. 26 Oct. 1806 in Exeter, England.

John Graves Simcoe was the third of four sons, and the only one to live past childhood. His father died, most probably of pneumonia, on the Quebec expedition of 1759, and the family moved to his mother's home, Exeter. Educated at Exeter Grammar School and Eton College, he did not show his father's aptitude for mathematics, but he seems to have been a serious student of modern history (although it was not on the curriculum of either of his schools), and of English and Latin poetry. He continued to write verse occasionally for most of his life. After a year at Merton College, Oxford, he was admitted to Lincoln's Inn, but then decided to follow the military career for which his father had intended him. That officer had drawn up a set of maxims for his sons' education, to which Simcoe often referred. They emphasized industry, devotion to duty, conventional morality, the necessity of formal education in addition to military studies, and the appropriateness of an officer's training for civil as well as military appointments. After a year under a military tutor at Exeter, Simcoe obtained a commission in 1770 as ensign in the 35th Foot, through the influence of his mother's family.

The regiment was sent to Boston, Mass., in 1775, Simcoe arriving two days after the battle of Bunker Hill. During the siege of the town he purchased a captaincy in the 40th Foot, the regiment with which he was to serve in the Long Island campaign, the capture of New York City, and the New Jersey campaigns of 1776–77. He received the first and most serious of his three wounds at the battle of Brandywine, in Pennsylvania; the uncertain health from which he suffered for the rest of his life had, however, begun earlier. Convinced that the British army had no appreciation of light infantry and that no European army had properly organized light cavalry, he wanted to form a combined light corps which would be especially suited for service in America but would also

introduce a more general reform of British military practice. After being refused permission to raise a corps from among the free blacks of Boston, he obtained command on 15 Oct. 1777 of the Queen's Rangers with the provincial rank of major.

The Rangers, a loyalist corps raised a year earlier, had suffered heavy losses. Simcoe brought them up to strength, mainly by recruiting loyalist refugees and American deserters. Organized in 11 companies of about 30 men each – one hussars, one grenadiers, and the rest light infantry – they served continuously for the duration of the war as reconnaissance and outpost troops: in the Pennsylvania campaign of 1778 and the subsequent retreat to New York, in Benedict ARNOLD's raid on Richmond, Va, and in the Yorktown campaign. Their training gave little attention to formal drill, but insisted on physical fitness, rapid movement, bayonet fighting, and, most particularly, discipline in the field. Simcoe made the exaggerated claim that the corps never gave a false alarm, never destroyed civilian property, never had a sentry surprised, and only once lost a patrol. He was himself captured in an ambush in 1779 and spent six months as a prisoner. He was invalided home just before the surrender of Yorktown in 1781. The war had been for him a great personal success: he had risen in army rank from lieutenant to lieutenant-colonel; in action he had been one of the two or three most consistently successful of British regimental commanders; and he had acquired a reputation as a tactical theorist, which was soon enhanced by the publication at Exeter in 1787 of his *Journal of the operations of the Queen's Rangers*.

He convalesced at the Devon home of Admiral Samuel Graves, his godfather, whose ward he married. Elizabeth Posthuma Gwillim was a considerable heiress. She bought a 5,000-acre estate at Honiton in Devon, and built Wolford Lodge, which was to be the family seat until 1923. Simcoe's own financial resources seem to have been trivial in comparison. Unwilling to retire into private life, he was elected to the House of Commons in the government interest for the Cornish borough of St Mawes in 1790. In a brief and obscure parliamentary career, his only reported speeches were on the new constitution for Quebec and on the resumed impeachment of Warren Hastings, although he perhaps also spoke on a motion to abolish the slave trade. His main interest in politics was to secure a military or a colonial appointment. His proposals to raise a corps on the lines of the disbanded Queen's Rangers and (when there seemed danger of a war with Spain) to lead an expedition against Cadiz were unsuccessful, but by the summer of 1790 he was promised the lieutenant governorship of what was to be the new loyalist province of Upper Canada. His hopes that he would not be subordinate to Lord Dorchester [Guy CARLETON] at Quebec, Lower Canada, were disappointed when their commissions, both issued on 12 Sept. 1791, gave the latter authority over both provinces as governor-in-chief.

The Upper Canadian appointment was not Simcoe's first choice – he hoped to exchange it for the post of British minister to the United States – but he brought to it all of his characteristic zeal. By the time he entered Upper Canada on 24 June 1792 he had spent 18 months in preparing to inaugurate its government. Encouraged by his neighbour Sir George Yonge, secretary at War, who was a fellow enthusiast for overseas settlement, Simcoe had offered a series of ambitious and unrealistically expensive plans for the rapid economic, constitutional, religious, and educational development of his new province. Except for his first speech to the legislature at Newark (Niagara-on-the-Lake) on 17 Sept. 1792, his most celebrated utterances on making Upper Canada a model of England overseas date from that period, before he had seen the province.

The political faith that his appointment gave him occasion to express was thoroughly tory, but his toryism was by no means entirely insular. He had retained from the American war a special enthusiasm for North America and for continued British rule in it. His father had been struck by the prospect of mercantilist expansion, based on the St Lawrence and extending into the interior as far as the isthmus of Panama. For Simcoe, who romanticized his father's role in the Seven Years' War, the task of vindicating British imperialism by making it work in Upper Canada was both a filial and a patriotic duty. He had also a genuine sympathy towards loyalist exiles, with some of whom he had maintained a connection. In 1792 he still shared the belief, common among his brother officers, that the Americans were becoming disillusioned with independence, and that the western settlements would not join the union even if it lasted. But he also had a far from grudging admiration for American, especially New England, practicality. Although he once described his opinion of Americans as a mixture of "military contempt" and "civil dessecration," he thought that they had no equals as agricultural settlers or as entrepreneurs of pioneer commerce. The revolution had been, in his view, the result of democratic excess, but he did not think that excessive democracy was the normally dominant characteristic of American society. If his constitutional models for Upper Canada were avowedly British, his models of economic progress were basically American. When he wrote of defeating "the spirit of democratic subversion, in the very Country which gave it existence and growth," he was relying not merely on the transplanting of British institutions but on the underlying strength of conservatism in North America.

He therefore saw no contradiction in depending on American immigration to populate a British colony, although he did once suggest that it might be leavened by transferring the settlers of Newfoundland to Upper Canada. The picture of him as deceived by professions of "late loyalism," first drawn in La Rochefoucauld-Liancourt*'s *Travels*, is false. "The Preference of the British form of Government is alledged by some for quitting the States," he wrote after a year and a half in the province, "but the Oppression of the Land Jobbers, and the uncertainty of the Titles is the more general Reason." He expected that new settlers would be "attached to the British Government or hostile to it by the result of their own comparison and investigation," and that their main concern would be "the undisturbed possession of present benefits and the prospect of future advantages for their families." The loyalty of immigrants would be commanded by a good land-granting system and by the efficient administration of what was basically a familiar constitution.

Clear about the objects of granting land, Simcoe never got a secure grip on its actual administration. He was quick to take an interest in the details of its planning, such as the distribution of crown and clergy reserves throughout townships or the elaborate zoning regulations for town lots in York (Toronto). He was slower to deal with gaps between plans and practice. He began with great faith in granting whole townships to individual applicants, who were to act as organizers of settlement and in turn to be accepted as a sort of local gentry. Twenty-six such grants were made in his first year. Ineffective though the system proved to be, he did not abandon it. The number and size of large grants in fact grew annually, in some part as he and other officials took advantage of their generous land allowances. More than two-thirds of his grants in the new Home District were of over 500 acres, and the best locations generally went to officers of government. He himself seems to have taken only the 5,000 acres due to his military rank, although he was careful to locate more than 1,000 acres in each of the areas – York Township and the Western District – where his government did most to encourage settlement. His family held the lands until 1832, and then sold them all over the next 21 years, mostly to or through William Allan*.

Impatient with the district land boards, set up in 1788 to ensure orderly and loyal settlement, Simcoe often ordered large grants himself. Some of his grants, meant to attract settlement and direct it to particular locations, were of lands to which the title was not clear. His grant to William BERCZY is the notorious but by no means the only case. After he secured the abolition of the land boards in 1794, there was really no machinery left to screen applicants for land. It was fortunate that the most consistently able of his subordinate officials, David William Smith*, was deputy surveyor general. In the short run, the regulations designed to check speculation did not work; in the long run they contributed to confusion

Simcoe

and delay in issuing legal titles. Yet the land system did meet Simcoe's immediate object of making Upper Canada a place where settlers found land easy to get.

In practice, his policy amounted to little more than the acceptance of settlement as it came. The plan he had laid in England was more ambitious, to control not only the location but also the nature of new settlements. The instrument intended for that purpose was his provincial corps, the second Queen's Rangers, and the model of their proposed operation was the Roman military colony. The winter quarters of Ranger detachments were to mark the sites of new towns, settlers being attracted by the clearing and road building that the troops would do, as well as by the markets and protection they would afford. Disbanded Rangers would form the nuclei of settlements; around them immigrants would "coalesce into the general principles of British Subjects." This plan was the most cherished of Simcoe's projects for Upper Canada. He saw it as the antidote to the insidious growth of frontier democracy and as exemplifying the "wise Principle . . . of blending civil & military Advantages." It exemplified, too, his tendency to attach exalted expectations to measures perfectly sensible in themselves and to request financing on the scale of his expectations. The Rangers' function as prophets of social cohesion never received a fair test of its impracticality, because neither the imperial government nor the commander-in-chief at Quebec could be induced to think of them as anything but ordinary troops. The twelve companies that Simcoe proposed, including a cavalry detachment and artificers, were reduced to two infantry companies. His claim to be able to assign them without the commander-in-chief's approval was also denied: Lord Dorchester finally asserted his authority over their employment in June 1796. Until they were disbanded in 1802, the Rangers continued to be important to Upper Canada chiefly as road builders.

More generally, Simcoe was unable to persuade the imperial administration that his province should be treated like a special foundation, not a normal colony. His recommendation that the Indian Department be transferred from the commander-in-chief to the civil government of Upper Canada was later accepted; otherwise, his failure to escape from Dorchester's military authority was complete. His attempt to maintain a separate commissariat in the upper province was disallowed, after his nominee, John McGill*, had served for two years without pay. His practice of requisitioning military supplies for civil works, and even for rations to settlers in the hard winter of 1795–96, was stopped. The Treasury relented in its slow pursuit of his improperly authorized expenditures only after his death. The proposals he endorsed for imperial assistance to capture for Upper Canada the trade of the American west were rejected or ignored. He had to discontinue

appointing lieutenants of counties. He was not allowed to introduce municipal corporations, although he argued for them both as instruments of economic progress and as anti-democratic institutions. Neither the imperial government nor the provincial legislature shared his sense of urgency for the public support of education. His plan for a provincial university, with preparatory schools at Kingston and Newark, was vetoed in Whitehall as premature, besides costing £1,000 a year. The legislature, although it repeated his request for imperial assistance in the year after his departure, did not undertake to assist grammar schools until 1807. His strongest personal disappointment – strongest, at least, after the curbing of his plans for the Queen's Rangers – came from the refusal of full endowment to the Church of England in Upper Canada. His arguments stressed the church's importance in reinforcing social and political conservatism, but he was also deeply if conventionally devout. His hopes, raised a second time by the appointment of Jacob Mountain* as Anglican bishop for the diocese of Quebec in 1793, were dashed by the news that the church would have to wait for the day, which he knew could not be soon, when the clergy reserves were productive. What Simcoe called "due support" for his province could not be fitted into an annual establishment for Upper Canada of £20,000. After four years of almost unrelieved disappointments, his original sense of mission became very like a sense of grievance. He remained convinced that his plans had been eroded by ministerial indifference and warned that his successor must be treated more generously: "a Want of System and [of] a Continuity of Measures in colonial Governments is an evil of serious magnitude."

It was no accident that Simcoe's quarrels were nearly all with his distant superiors. Within the province, his most fundamental task was to provide a framework of civil government, the details of which were not often of special interest to pioneer settlers. He was disappointed in the social status and education of the members of the legislative assembly when he first met them, but in five sessions their objects seldom conflicted with his. Most of the legislation put before them, especially in their first session, was altogether uncontroversial: the adoption of English civil law and of jury trials, of standard English weights and measures and of tavern licensing, and the provision of jails and courthouses in each of the four administrative districts. During his whole term of office, the assembly rejected only two measures that he was anxious for – a land tax and an education bill. In May 1793 it obliged him to settle for the gradual rather than the immediate abolition of slavery in the province. In the next year it accepted a court of king's bench with obvious reluctance. The assembly also faced him with two unwelcome initiatives of its own. He had to concede the legalization of marriages performed by magistrates. He insisted on a qualification: if there were five Anglican clergymen in the district, one of them within eighteen miles, the bill did not apply. He effectively defeated attempts to introduce elective town meetings on the New England model. A bill of 1793 put the election of township officers under the control of justices of the peace, who were appointed by the lieutenant governor and remained the real power of local government. On the whole, he had reason for his annual expressions of satisfaction with the assembly.

He had rather more difficulty with the Legislative Council. His general distrust of merchants and speculators applied with uncomfortable directness to some of its members. There were fewer than ten councillors, never all assembled; and in so small a body his pompously defensive reaction to criticism was a disadvantage. There, also, the developing rivalry of sectional interests found clearer expression. His original idea of the council gave some weight to the independent judgement of its members, but in practice he expected it to act as an adjunct to his administration. Still, he managed after three sessions to find common ground with both of his occasionally outspoken critics on the council: with Robert HAMILTON of the Niagara area on the encouragement of western commerce and with Richard CARTWRIGHT of Kingston on the need for municipal councils.

In the microcosm of Upper Canadian politics, Simcoe's accessibility, candour, and evident desire to please were very serviceable qualities. They made up for his inexperience in civil administration and for his failure to acquire the skills of political manœuvre and compromise. Watchful though he was of his status and perquisites, he was a warm and sympathetic man, with an intense loyalty to his subordinates. Even Chief Justice William Osgoode*, who had a lawyer's contempt for military intellects, conceded him affection. It cannot be said that the provincial administration met his expressed ideal that there should "neither be a *sine cure* mind nor a *sine cure* Body thro' the whole Province," but under him it was at least purposeful and not yet seriously distracted by internal disharmony. Always ambitious, while he was in Upper Canada he identified its progress with his own. Moreover, his zeal for the province, even if it did not prove infectious in Whitehall, was obvious to everyone. He was as suspicious of Montreal merchants as of the loyalty of French Canadians, as insistent on the superior prospects and reliability of Upper Canada as on the folly of imperial parsimony. He had been preferred to Dorchester's nominee, Sir John Johnson*, on the grounds that he was not a resident of the province; but no colonist was a more faithful or partisan advocate.

In truth, however, Simcoe did not take all Upper Canada to be his province. To the main string of loyalist settlements from Kingston eastwards he was relatively indifferent. He saw little of them and made them the objects of no special plans. His interest, like his assiduous travelling, was concentrated on the western part of the province, especially where agricultural settlement was a prospect rather than a fact. Even York, his own choice, was in his design a temporary capital, soon to give way to London. He was not allowed to make that move, which an unnamed official disgruntled at the prospect called "this wild scheme of settling in the bush," but he remained convinced of its inevitability. It was the southwestern peninsula that could become populous by American migration and prosperous by controlling the commerce of the American west. The economic future of the province lay there; and the future importance of Upper Canada, in the continent and in the empire, aroused in him a more enduring enthusiasm than its loyalist origins.

His enthusiasm was not as naïve as it sometimes appeared. He did not expect, as that disappointed loyalist Richard Cartwright thought, "in two or three years [to] put the country into a situation that it is impossible it can arrive at in a century." In civil if not in military matters, he was excited by long-range plans and not by current problems. He thought, too, that planning was the most important part of his function in Upper Canada, whether the results could be rapid or not.

That emphasis showed itself most clearly in his road-building program. He was not interested in roads for the convenience of established settlers; those he left, in the usual and ineffective way, to local authorities. His roads were strategic, both as military communications and as directions for the course of future settlement. It was only with the subsequent projection of the Danforth Road in 1799 that his system came to centre on York. His first priority, on which the Queen's Rangers began work in May 1793, was Dundas Street. It ran from Burlington Bay (Hamilton Harbour) to the valley of the river that he renamed the Thames: "from nowhere to nowhere," so far as existing settlement went, but in Simcoe's design from the head of navigation to the future centre of the province. After the purchase of Indian lands two years later, the road was extended eastward to York. The future that he had in mind for that town, when he began to lay it out in August 1793, was the role which in fact came to be played by Kingston – a garrison, arsenal, and naval base. Yonge Street, finally pushed north to the Holland River by the Rangers in February 1796 after Berczy had built its southern half, was to provide strategic access to the upper Great Lakes. Settlement along it was promoted as much for the security of the road as for its own sake. East of York, Simcoe's plan for strategic communications relied on the control of Lake Ontario. It led to projects for the reform of the Provincial Marine, not to more roads.

Simcoe

Even if the proper use of Americans was to assure Upper Canada's future, there were immediate dangers from them that had to be met. Simcoe had been slow to accept the established facts of American unity and independence, and continued to think that they represented a political rather than a military threat to Upper Canada. His militia bill of May 1793, making local companies liable for service outside their districts, was prompted by the news of war with France. By that fall, however, he was seriously worried about defence against the neighbouring states.

When he arrived, the border posts on American soil were still held by British garrisons, and British diplomacy was briefly pursuing the chimerical prospect of an Indian buffer state. Simcoe exerted himself, as an agent of that diplomacy and subsequently, to maintain British influence with the Ohio valley Indians, both to keep their claims as a counter in Anglo-American negotiations and to avoid their resentment if abandoned. He put as many difficulties as he could in the way of American commissioners seeking an Indian treaty and counted their failure his success. With Alexander McKee*, deputy superintendent general of Indian affairs, he gave the Ohio tribes expectations of British support that exceeded his instructions and bore no relation to the changing objects of imperial policy. His concern for the Indians within Upper Canada, particularly the Six Nations, was limited to the same military context. He had some success in dealing with them: during his administration, one purchase of Indian lands was renegotiated and four others were arranged with more clarity than had been usual. He did not know what to make of Indians who did not conform to his expectations of their present support and ultimate removal; hence the mutual distrust that developed between him and Joseph Brant [THAYENDANEGEA]. While he sought direction, American troops imposed their own solution on the Ohio Indians, in August 1794, at the battle of Fallen Timbers (near Waterville, Ohio).

The American campaign looked from Upper Canada like an intended invasion, the more so because American border garrisons had been strengthened and Simcoe had been ordered to reoccupy an old border fort. In reality, negotiations had already begun for Jay's Treaty which in November 1794 gave up the border posts and removed the danger; but the dispatch giving notice of it took 11 months to reach Upper Canada. The crisis led Simcoe to write some bellicose dispatches on how he would have met the invasion, dispatches which he later regretted but which have given him an exaggerated reputation for anti-Americanism. It also confirmed his growing emphasis on the need to reorganize Upper Canada's defence. He did not regret the loss of the border posts on military grounds, since he found them indefensible in condi-

tion and design. The real necessities were for a naval force on Lake Ontario and for a garrison in Upper Canada large enough to ensure the defence of both provinces. He was urging these with something like his old zeal when, in July 1796, neuralgia and gout took him from the province. Given leave of absence to recover his health in England, he never returned to Upper Canada and resigned early in 1798.

The ten years of service that remained to Simcoe were all military. Still convalescent, he accepted the governorship of St Domingo (Haiti), a difficult post already declined by healthier and more prudent officers, but one that raised his local rank from major-general (3 Oct. 1794) to lieutenant-general (10 Nov. 1796). As part of Henry Dundas's much criticized strategy of colonial warfare against France, the British had intervened in that island at the invitation of royalist French planters. They had found a complex racial war in which the planters were being overwhelmed by free mulattos and by rebel slaves, some of whom accepted French republican authority and some of whom had Spanish support. The British force had no prospect of winning; but in nine months Simcoe was able to bring order to the civil administration, to check corruption in the system of military supply, to reorganize a medical service inadequate to cope with yellow fever, and to restore the collapsing defence of the royalists' plantations. The breakdown of his health after only five months' actual service on the island obliged him to leave in July 1797. The government was displeased, partly because the whole enterprise was not the easy success that had been originally hoped for, and partly because he greatly exceeded the strict budget set for him. The budget was inadequate, but in any case Simcoe was temperamentally unsuited to the stricter ministerial control of the West Indies. Refusing to attempt more than a military stalemate without fresh troops, he persisted in outlining plans of conquest if given the reinforcements that were so clearly not available. Without them, failure was only a matter of time. The sensible course, as his successor realized, would have been to use the authorization that the government had already given him to withdraw.

So long as William Pitt was prime minister, and Dundas secretary of state for War, Simcoe did not receive another active command. After failing to revive his old project of a light corps, he settled for command of the Western District, taking up headquarters at Exeter in December 1797. During the brief ministry of his fellow Devon magnate, Henry Addington, he had hopes of re-entering the House of Commons, of succeeding Robert PRESCOTT as governor of Lower Canada, and even of obtaining a peerage. These came to nothing, but in the end the patronage of the Addingtons brought him the recognition that service alone could not. In July 1806 the

Sinclair

ministry that followed Pitt's death appointed Simcoe commander-in-chief in India. Diverted, in joint command with the Earl of St Vincent of an expedition for the relief of Portugal, he fell ill and was brought back to die at Exeter.

Simcoe's stay in Upper Canada was brief, there is little to suggest that his serious interest in it long survived his departure, and he was unable to alter imperial policy. Yet it is unlikely that any governor before Lord Durham [Lambton*], except Carleton in his first term at Quebec, had so much impact on a Canadian province. His settlement policy determined the course of Upper Canadian development for the next generation. He gave both expression and impetus to the blend of conservatism, loyalty, and emphasis on economic progress that was to dominate the province after the War of 1812. The most persistently energetic governor sent to British North America after the American revolution, he had not only the most articulate faith in its imperial destiny but also the most sympathetic appreciation of the interests and aspirations of its inhabitants.

S. R. MEALING

[Collections of Simcoe's papers are in AO, MS 517, and Devon Record Office, 1038, with copies in PAC, MG 23, H1, 1; ANQ-Q, ZC22-1; the Clements Library; and AD, Vienne (Poitiers), Papiers Dundas. Ernest Alexander Cruikshank* published a selection of careful transcripts in *Corr. of Lieut. Governor Simcoe*, which includes all his numbered dispatches from Upper Canada as well as the bulk of his military correspondence. In addition to *A journal of the operations of the Queen's Rangers, from the end of the year 1777, to the conclusion of the late American war* (Exeter, Eng., [1787]), Simcoe published *Remarks on the travels of the Marquis de Chastellux, in North America* (London, 1787) and *Lieut.-General Simcoe, understanding that the translation of the Duke de Liancourt's "Travels" had been much circulated, thinks it not improper to print an extract from a letter of his to the printer, Mr. Phillips . . .* (Exeter, [1800?]). Mrs Simcoe's diary has been edited by John Ross Robertson* (Toronto, 1911); a revised edition was published in 1934, and a reprint of the original edition appeared in 1973. The diary has also been edited by Mary Quayle Innis (Toronto and New York, 1965). The fullest of his biographies is W. R. Riddell, *The life of John Graves Simcoe, first lieutenant-governor of the province of Upper Canada, 1792–96* (Toronto, [1926]). S.R.M.]

S. R. Mealing, "John Graves Simcoe," *Our living tradition, fourth series*, ed. R. L. McDougall (Toronto, 1962), 57–76. Malcolm MacLeod, "Fortress Ontario or forlorn hope? Simcoe and the defence of Upper Canada," *CHR*, 53 (1972): 149–78. S. R. Mealing, "The enthusiasms of John Graves Simcoe," CHA *Report*, 1958: 50–62. S. F. Wise, "The Indian diplomacy of John Graves Simcoe," CHA *Report*, 1953: 36–44.

SINCLAIR, PATRICK, army officer and colonial administrator; b. 1736 in Lybster, Scotland, son of

Alexander Sinclair and Aemilia Sinclair; m. *c.* 1785 Catherine M. S. Stewart of Inverness, Scotland, and they had at least four sons; d. 31 Jan. 1820 in Lybster.

Like many other Scots, Patrick Sinclair sought adventure and advancement through the British army. He enlisted about 1754, and on 21 July 1758 he became an ensign in the 2nd battalion of the 42nd Foot. Late that year his battalion took part in the successful attack on Guadeloupe. In July 1760 it arrived at Oswego (N.Y.), the rendezvous with other forces that Major-General Amherst* had gathered to move against Montreal (Que.) from the west. While at Oswego, on 27 July 1760, Sinclair was promoted lieutenant. During the descent of the St Lawrence a French brig was captured near Fort Lévis (east of Prescott, Ont.); it was renamed the *Williamson* and Sinclair was given command. He was transferred to the snow *Mohawk* after the fall of the fort and he remained in the vicinity for the rest of Amherst's campaign.

These appointments opened up a new career for the ambitious Scot. In November he gave up his command to join his regiment, but the Great Lakes had fascinated him and on 24 Oct. 1761 he exchanged his commission in the 42nd for one in the 15th Foot in order to join the marine forces on the lakes. For the next year or so he commanded ships on Lake Ontario, but during the Indian uprising of 1763 [*see* Pontiac*] he was transferred to the Upper Lakes. In 1764 he became the first person since René-Robert Cavelier* de La Salle in 1679 to take a sailing vessel up the Huron (St Clair) River to Lake Huron. After his return to Detroit (Mich.) from Michilimackinac (Mackinaw City, Mich.) in the fall, Sinclair was ordered by Colonel John Bradstreet* to construct a small fortification on the Huron River and was allowed to name it Fort Sinclair (Port Huron, Mich.). He sailed lakes Erie, St Clair, Huron, and Michigan during the next three years and travelled to Lake Superior. In 1767 the marine forces were reduced and on 23 September, when Sinclair handed over his vessel, the merchants at Detroit presented him with a silver punch bowl as "a Publick Testimony of their gratitude." He settled at Fort Sinclair, carving out a small estate and securing it by a deed from local Ojibwa chieftains.

Sinclair returned to England in 1769 and, while recruiting there during the next two years, he petitioned for return to the marine forces on the Great Lakes. Though promoted captain on 13 April 1772, he went on half pay and retired to his family estate at Lybster. His attempts to return to North America bore fruit on 7 April 1775 when he was appointed lieutenant governor and superintendent of Michilimackinac, in the recently enlarged province of Quebec. He took ship almost immediately, but two attempts to reach his post via the Thirteen Colonies failed because of the revolutionary turmoil there.

759

Sinclair

Eventually, in 1778, he arrived at Halifax, N.S. A year passed before he was able to proceed overland to Quebec where he presented his credentials to Governor HALDIMAND. On 4 Oct. 1779, more than four years after his commission, he reached Michilimackinac.

Familiar with the post from his sailing days, Sinclair had given considerable thought to the defenceless position of the stockaded fort located almost at the water's edge of a sandy beach. He also knew from experience that sailing vessels had to anchor several hundred yards off the shallow shore. Searching for a better location, he crossed to the rocky heights of Mackinac Island where he explored the fine harbour and a fortifiable bluff. He decided almost immediately that the fort and town should be moved. Even before he secured permission he cleared brush and skidded a few buildings over the ice. During 1780 and 1781 the formidable task of relocating the fort and the village of nearly a hundred houses on the island consumed much of his energy. On 12 May 1781 he formally purchased the island from the local Ojibwas for £5,000 New York currency.

A military man, Sinclair had been disappointed to learn that his position as lieutenant governor would be limited to civil and Indian affairs. Though he would have responsibilities for a vast region he would not have authority over the soldiers at the post. The commander of the garrison, Major Arent Schuyler DePeyster*, noted his pleasure at the appointment of Sinclair because he was liked by both traders and Indians. Soon after the lieutenant governor's arrival DePeyster departed to take command at Detroit. The garrison was left under the nominal authority of Lieutenant George Clowes, but Sinclair exercised the real control. In order to have secure command of the garrison Sinclair purchased a captaincy on 1 April 1780. Brooking no challenges to any aspect of his authority, he had serious clashes with various people including John ASKIN and Joseph-Louis AINSSE. Haldimand supported Sinclair but was distressed by his quarrelsomeness.

Shortly after his arrival at Michilimackinac Sinclair had received a circular letter issued by the secretary of state for the American Colonies which ordered attacks on Spanish possessions. The energetic Scot immediately organized an expedition against St Louis (Mo.). In the spring of 1780 a few traders, including Joseph Calvé and Jean-Marie DUCHARME, and nearly a thousand warriors led by MADJECKEWISS and WAHPASHA, advanced through what is now Wisconsin. Charles-Michel Mouet* de Langlade directed another wave of Indians through the Illinois country. St Louis and Cahokia (Ill.) withstood the assault, however. Sinclair blamed the Canadians, especially Calvé and Ducharme, and the Sauks and Foxes for its failure.

A considerable amount of Sinclair's official funds went to keep the Indians of the Upper Lakes loyal to Britain, and so large were his expenditures that in January 1782 the military cashier at Quebec refused to pay his drafts. Though he was promoted major in the army on 12 June, a board of inquiry consisting of Colonel Henry Hope* and two high officials in the Indian Department, Sir John Johnson* and James Stanley Goddard, came to Michilimackinac to investigate his expenses. Three days after their arrival on 15 September, Sinclair left for Quebec to settle matters. For two years he lived on the Île d'Orléans attempting vainly to untangle his financial affairs. Placed on half pay when his regiment, the 84th (Royal Highland Emigrants), was reduced, Sinclair finally secured permission to return to Lybster. Since his bills had still not been paid, he travelled to London to see Haldimand. On his arrival in late February 1785, his creditors had him thrown into Newgate prison for debt. After obtaining sufficient funds to secure his release Sinclair sued Haldimand for £50,000. The following year the government paid the protested bills, but Sinclair had been impoverished by stiff legal fees and in 1788 he sold his property on the Huron River.

Sinclair's latter years were spent at Lybster, where he experimented with planting wheat and expanding his tenants' fishing fleet. Declared bankrupt in 1804, he was briefly jailed for debt. He died nearly destitute in 1820 and was buried on his estate. Though on half pay he had continued to be promoted: in 1793 he became lieutenant-colonel; in 1797, colonel; in 1803, major-general; in 1810, lieutenant-general. Until the end of his life he drew the salary of lieutenant governor of Michilimackinac, which must have reminded him of that brief moment of power when for three years he was the most important man on the upper Great Lakes.

DAVID A. ARMOUR

Clements Library, Thomas Gage papers, American ser., 25: Campbell to Gage, 3 Oct. 1764; 26: Campbell to Gage, 10 Nov. 1764; 28: Campbell to Bradstreet in Bradstreet to Gage, 7 Dec. 1764; 40: Lieut. Sinclair's report on lakes Michigan and Huron in Campbell to Gage, 2 Aug. 1765; 74: Inventory of schooner *Gladwin* in Sinclair to Gage, 20 Feb. 1768; 79: Turnbull to Gage, 11 July 1768. Thomas Mante, *The history of the late war in North-America and the islands of the West Indies, including the campaigns of MDCCLXIII and MDCCLXIV against his majesty's Indian enemies* (London, 1772), 516. *Mich. Pioneer Coll.*, 6 (1883): 405; 8 (1885): 472–75; 9 (1886): 364–65, 394, 398, 516–632, 655–57; 10 (1886): 355, 357, 378, 382–90, 397–401, 405–8, 413, 415–17, 421–23, 430, 434–43, 452–53, 457–61, 467–71, 477–81, 486–90, 495, 498–500, 502–5, 514–15, 519–22, 529, 534, 548–49, 552–65, 572–73, 579–81, 585, 592–600, 645, 661, 672; 13 (1888): 56–63, 71–72; 19 (1891): 499–501, 529–30, 631–34, 638–40, 671; 20 (1892): 8, 15, 31, 36, 47, 51–54, 56, 65–66, 210–12, 276; 24 (1894): 3–4;

25 (1894): 140, 161. D. A. Armour and K. R. Widder, *At the crossroads: Michilimackinac during the American revolution* (Mackinac Island, Mich., 1978). B. L. Dunnigan, *King's men at Mackinac: the British garrisons, 1780–1796* (Lansing, Mich., 1973). H. B. Eaton, *Patrick Sinclair, builder of Mackinac and founder of Lybster: an account of his life and times* (n.p., 1979). W. L. Jenks, *Patrick Sinclair* (Lansing, 1914). H. B. Eaton, "Lieutenant-General Patrick Sinclair, an account of his military career," Soc. for Army Hist. Research, *Journal* (London), 56 (1978): 128–42, 215–32; 57 (1979): 45–55.

SKERRETT, JOHN, army officer; b. *c.* 1743 in England; d. 18 Aug. 1813 in Heavitree, England.

John Skerrett entered the army on 19 Oct. 1761 as an ensign in the 19th Foot, and he served for 30 years with that regiment in Ireland, North America, and the West Indies. In 1791 he exchanged as a major to the 48th Foot, and in 1794 was promoted lieutenant-colonel in command of a newly raised West India regiment. On its disbandment he returned to England, where on 1 Jan. 1798 he became colonel of the Loyal Durham Fencible Infantry. His success during the Irish rebellion when in command of the fencibles at the battle of Arklow on 9 June 1798 brought him the appointment of brigadier-general to the forces in Ireland.

In 1799 Skerrett arrived in Newfoundland to take over the military command of the island from Lieutenant-Colonel Thomas SKINNER, who remained as his second in command. At that time the St John's garrison of some 560 troops consisted mainly of the Royal Newfoundland Fencible Regiment, raised by Skinner soon after the outbreak of the French revolutionary wars. A high proportion of the men of the regiment were of Irish extraction; 80 of them, Skerrett learned, had taken the oath of the Society of United Irishmen. Strict disciplinary measures introduced by the brigadier resulted in many desertions and a plot to mutiny and assassinate Skinner and his officers. The uprising, planned for 20 April 1800, was averted because Skerrett kept the regiment at exercise all that day following a particularly unsoldierly performance at church parade in the morning. An attempt four days later failed. Skerrett had the ringleaders tried by court martial: eight were hanged and eight others sentenced to life imprisonment.

With the signing of the Treaty of Amiens in 1802 Skinner's regiment was disbanded, and a British regiment sent to St John's after the mutiny was recalled to England. Hostilities between Britain and France were soon renewed, however, and in June 1803 Skerrett was ordered to raise "a Corps of Fencible Infantry in North America." Despite strong competition from the fishery and a ban on recruiting in any year before the close of the fishing season on 25 October, by the summer of 1805 Skerrett had enrolled two-thirds of his establishment of 1,000 men. When in

mid June this new Royal Newfoundland Regiment was transferred to Halifax, N.S., in an exchange with the Nova Scotia Fencibles, Skerrett, who had been promoted major-general on 1 Jan. 1805, remained in St John's as commander of the Newfoundland garrison.

In September 1807, on receiving reports that the United States was preparing for war against Great Britain, Skerrett, who while still in St John's had assumed the acting command of the forces in Nova Scotia, moved to Halifax. Shortly afterwards his eight-year stay in British North America ended with his appointment to the staff in Jamaica, where he briefly held the command of the forces. He subsequently saw service in Sicily and was promoted lieutenant-general on 4 June 1811. When he died two years later he was survived by his widow and an only child, John Byrne, who served with distinction under Wellington in the Peninsular War.

Although Skerrett claimed that he had only a "slender fortune," his memorials seeking some substantial mark of royal favour in recognition of his services resulted in nothing more tangible than cordial thanks for all he had done. It would appear, however, either that his fortune was less slender than he professed or that a belated recognition did indeed materialize. He is reported to have left his son the not inconsiderable inheritance of £7,000 a year.

At a critical time in its history Newfoundland was fortunate in having so experienced a soldier as John Skerrett in command of its garrison. He never hesitated to express to the Colonial Office his concern for the security of Newfoundland and the need for more troops to defend it against both foreign attack and internal uprising. He accused the home government of neglect "in every instance," and declared that "legislating for this island in Portman Square will never do. It will never be preserved by that means." Not confining his efforts merely to matters of defence, Skerrett urged reforms to better the living conditions of the Newfoundlanders. On his departure the leading men of the island expressed their "highest esteem for the zeal you have uniformly manifested to promote the welfare of this island," and successive governors were to pay tribute to the general's efforts for the public good.

G. W. L. NICHOLSON

PANL, GN 2/1, 15, 17–19. PRO, CO 194/42–45, 194/49 (mfm. at PAC); WO 25/40, bundle 18; 25/748. *Gentleman's Magazine*, July–December 1813: 401. *Royal Gazette and Newfoundland Advertiser* (St John's), 1807. G.B., WO, *Army list*, 1763, 1793, 1796–97, 1799, 1812. Richard Cannon, *Historical record of the Nineteenth, or the First Yorkshire North Riding Regiment of Foot* ... (London, 1848). J. W. Fortescue, *A history of the British army* (13v. in 14, London, 1899–1930), 8–10. Russell Gurney, *History of*

Skinner

the *Northamptonshire Regiment, 1742–1934* (Aldershot, Eng., 1935), 85–88. G. W. L. Nicholson, *The fighting Newfoundlander; a history of the Royal Newfoundland Regiment* (St John's, [1964?]). J. J. O'Connell, *The Irish wars; a military history of Ireland from the Norse invasions to 1798* (Dublin, [1920]). Prowse, *Hist. of Nfld.* (1895). H. [G. W.] Smith, *The autobiography of Lieutenant-General Sir Harry Smith, baronet of Aliwal on the Sutlej*, ed. G. C. M. Smith (2v., London, 1901), 1. D. A. Webber, *Skinner's Fencibles: the Royal Newfoundland Regiment, 1795–1802* (St John's, 1964).

SKINNER, ROBERT PRINGLE, army officer; b. 1786 in Gibraltar, third son of Thomas SKINNER and a Miss Power; m. 6 Jan. 1810 Harriet McDonald at Quebec, Lower Canada, and they had at least one child; d. 3 May 1816 in St John's, Nfld.

Robert Pringle Skinner came from a family that had close ties with the British armed forces. His paternal great-grandfather William Skinner had been chief engineer of Great Britain, and his paternal grandfather an infantry captain. His father was an engineer under Robert Pringle*, the commanding engineer at Gibraltar when Skinner was born and after whom he was named. Of his four brothers, three entered the army and one the navy. In 1790 the family came to Newfoundland, where Thomas Skinner had been appointed chief engineer. Five years later Thomas raised the Royal Newfoundland Fencible Regiment, which was disbanded in 1802. However, a successor unit, sometimes called the Royal Newfoundland Regiment of Fencible Infantry but more usually the Royal Newfoundland Regiment, was raised by Colonel John SKERRETT the following year. Although Robert had been too young to serve in his father's regiment, the family connection secured him a lieutenancy, dated 5 Nov. 1803, in the Royal Newfoundland Regiment. The unit transferred to Nova Scotia in 1805, and then in 1807 to Quebec, where it spent five years in garrison. Little is known of Skinner's life at this period save that he was in some minor trouble in 1806 and 1807 for his absence after a period of leave had expired. In November 1809 he was promoted captain.

After the outbreak of the War of 1812 the Royal Newfoundland Regiment was divided into detachments for service on sea and land, and its officers and men were present on several fronts. Skinner himself spent most of the war on the upper St Lawrence around Prescott, Upper Canada. In June 1812 he was ordered to take command of a detachment of gunboats sailing from Quebec to Montreal and he apparently continued upriver, since in October he and 40 Royal Newfoundlanders took part in the abortive assault on Ogdensburg, N.Y. His presence in that region was officially ordered on 23 March 1813, when he was appointed an acting deputy quartermaster general (a common occupation for officers of the regiment) at Prescott,

with command of the gunboats and marines stationed there. During the campaign of 1813 the upper St Lawrence was a lively place, and although assigned to a non-combatant department Skinner managed to see some action. In October he and five men of his regiment captured an American Durham boat in a brief affair near Prescott, and the next month he was present at the battle of Crysler's Farm. Despite the favourable notices given him by lieutenant-colonels Joseph Wanton Morrison* and George Richard John Macdonell*, Skinner received no reward for his services, and indeed the following year was criticized. A certain private in his company claimed that he had received "Extremely ill treatment" when he was arrested on a minor charge, and also that Skinner had withheld the company's pay for six months. The latter charge may have been true – officers of the regiment had already been warned that their pay accounts were inadequate and late – but, since the complaints were about events as much as two years old, they do not appear to have been heeded by higher authority.

Skinner was more or less permanently stationed at Prescott during 1814, although by October he had ceased to be attached to the quartermaster general's department. Most of his regiment had been ordered back to Newfoundland to recruit, but Skinner remained in Canada until after the conclusion of peace. Indeed, he was on his way to reinforce the garrison of Michilimackinac (Mackinac Island, Mich.) with a party of 50 Royal Newfoundlanders when news came that the war was over. By the fall of 1815 he had returned to the regiment, which was now at St John's, but the stresses of the war had damaged his health. On 3 May 1816, just three weeks before his regiment was ordered to Halifax, N.S., to disband, he died, worn out with fatigue. His widow and family returned to Montreal, where they were able to obtain a pension.

STUART R. J. SUTHERLAND

ANQ-Q, CE1-61, 6 Jan. 1810. PAC, RG 8, I (C ser.), 187: 96; 224: 74–75; 231: 220; 506: 121–22; 678: 100–3; 679: 444; 695: 1–4; 721: 2–23, 72–75; 1219: 137–38; 1220: 355. PRO, WO 17/1516–18; 17/2356; 17/2361–63; WO 28/304: f.56; 28/307: f.18. *DNB* (biog. of William Skinner). G.B., WO, *Army list.* G. W. L. Nicholson, *The fighting Newfoundlander; a history of the Royal Newfoundland Regiment* (St John's, [1964?]). Thomas Skinner, *Fifty years in Ceylon: an autobiography*, ed. Annie Skinner (London and Calcutta, 1891), 320.

SKINNER, THOMAS, military engineer; b. 1759 in England, son of William Skinner and Hester Lawder of Berwick-upon-Tweed; m. a Miss Power, and they had five sons and three daughters; d. 6 Feb. 1818 at Le Havre, France.

A grandson of William Skinner, chief engineer of Great Britain in the mid 18th century, Thomas Skinner joined the engineers as an ensign on 27 May 1774. He was stationed for many years at Gibraltar, where the eldest of his children were born. In the late summer of 1790, now a captain, he arrived in Newfoundland as chief engineer. For the next 13 years, serving successively under six governors, he was responsible for maintaining Newfoundland's fortifications and other military works so far as funds pried from the Treasury would permit.

Following the outbreak of war with France in 1793, the departure of an expedition to occupy Saint-Pierre and Miquelon seriously depleted the garrison at St John's [*see* James OGILVIE]. Skinner then raised at his own expense four companies numbering some 150 officers and men and named the Royal Newfoundland Volunteers. In the summer of 1796 the appearance of a French squadron off the coast put St John's in a state of alarm, and the Volunteers acquitted themselves with credit when called out to strengthen the regular garrison. A year later they seized the opportunity presented by a mutiny aboard the *Latona* in St John's harbour to proclaim their readiness "to sacrifice their lives and property in defence of King and Country and their present glorious constitution."

But no such demand was to be made of them, and some time after 1796 the Volunteers quietly disbanded. In the mean time, in April 1795 Skinner had been promoted lieutenant-colonel and authorized to raise immediately a regiment of fencible infantry for service in North America only, similar to those already raised in Nova Scotia by Sir John WENTWORTH and in New Brunswick by Lieutenant Governor Thomas CARLETON. His vigorous recruiting quickly brought the Royal Newfoundland Fencible Regiment to its full strength of 650 men. In 1796 the warlike preparations put in hand by Skinner and Governor Sir James Wallace persuaded the French admiral to abandon any idea of an attack.

Soon afterwards, however, the fortunes of Skinner's regiment went into a decline. In its ranks were many who had taken the oath of the Society of United Irishmen, which pledged to achieve Irish independence, and there is evidence that the mutineers on the *Latona* commanded considerable sympathy from the troops on shore. The strict disciplinary measures taken by Brigadier-General John SKERRETT, who was placed in command of the garrison in 1799 over the head of Skinner, brought increasing disaffection, many desertions, and a plot to mutiny and assassinate Skinner and his officers. The uprising, planned for 20 April 1800, failed, and the ringleaders were tried by court martial, eight of them being hanged. All of the regiment except two picked companies was transferred to Halifax, and a regular British regiment was sent to garrison St John's for the remainder of the war. With peace in 1802 the Royal Newfoundland Fencible Regiment was disbanded. Skinner, who while in

command of the Volunteers and the fencible regiment had continued to serve as chief engineer, relinquished that appointment on being recalled to England in 1803. He retired with full pay on 1 July 1807.

As chief engineer of Newfoundland Thomas Skinner brought the defences of St John's to a high level of efficiency. As a regimental commander his task was not an easy one, and his tendency to act independently of Governor William Waldegrave during the 1790s more than once brought him a sharp reprimand. The governor of Newfoundland was also, by virtue of his commission, commander-in-chief of the troops on the island, and successive governors had upheld this position against the claims of the senior army officers in North America. In 1799 Waldegrave's refusal to recognize the authority of Prince EDWARD AUGUSTUS, commander-in-chief of the army in North America, over the troops in Newfoundland, placed Skinner in the unenviable position of trying to serve two masters. While Waldegrave censured him for withholding information he had received from the prince, Skinner was threatened with a general court martial by the commander-in-chief for not following his orders. "All the officers of my own Regiment, nay, the officers of the Navy themselves," he mournfully informed the prince, "have witnessed my chagrin in not being allowed to follow your Highness's commands."

Thomas Skinner's departure from Newfoundland did not end the military contribution made by his family to the island. His eldest son served there as senior officer of the Royal Artillery from 1821 to 1827, and his third son, ROBERT PRINGLE, was a captain with the Royal Newfoundland Regiment that fought in the War of 1812. A daughter, Harriet, was married to an officer of the 7th Foot, and on hearing of her husband's death in the battle of Salamanca dressed herself in male attire and sought his body on the field. The incident formed the subject for a tragedy performed on the London stage, *The heroine of Salamanca*.

G. W. L. NICHOLSON

PANL, GN 2/1, 12–15, 17. PRO, CO 194/43 (mfm. at PAC); WO 40, bundle 6. *Gentleman's Magazine*, July–December 1812: 297. *DNB* (biog. of William Skinner). G.B., WO, *Army list*, 1775. *Roll of officers of the Corps of Royal Engineers from 1660 to 1898* . . . , ed. R. F. Edwards (Chatham, Eng., 1898). G. W. L. Nicholson, *The fighting Newfoundlander; a history of the Royal Newfoundland Regiment* (St John's, [1964?]). Thomas Skinner, *Fifty years in Ceylon: an autobiography*, ed. Annie Skinner (London and Calcutta, 1891). [This biography of a grandson of Skinner has brief details about the latter's family. G.W.L.N.] D. A. Webber, *Skinner's Fencibles: the Royal Newfoundland Regiment, 1795–1802* (St John's, 1964). [This work reproduces much of the correspondence dealing with the affairs of Skinner's regiment. G.W.L.N.]

Slade

SLADE, THOMAS, ship's captain, agent, and businessman; b. in Poole or Wareham, England, son of Robert Slade and Elizabeth —; d. 1816 in Poole.

Thomas Slade's early life is enveloped in obscurity, and some of the few details we possess come from the will of his uncle John Slade*, a prominent Poole–Newfoundland merchant. After the death of his only son in 1773, John Slade focussed his attention on four of his nephews to provide family continuity within the business: each of the nephews assumed specific areas of responsibility within the firm of John Slade and Company. Over the next several years Thomas was employed in various capacities in his uncle's expansive trade, including that of ship's captain and agent. In 1780 he commanded the 180-ton brig *Fame* from Fogo to Poole, and he continued as a master under his brother John into the 1790s.

The partnership of John Slade and Company spawned a new complex of Poole merchant firms that dominated the trade of outport Newfoundland throughout most of the 19th century. When John Slade Sr died in 1792 the firm possessed major mercantile establishments and sub-establishments along the northeast coast of Newfoundland and in Labrador, owned six brigs, and conducted an extensive supply trade with the growing population on the northeast coast. The estate devolved upon the nephews and their cousin, George Nickleson Allen, who continued the success of the firm, though forced by wartime conditions to reduce their volume of trade during the 1790s. In the next decade the Slades increased their business and were able to take advantage of the lucrative prices for cod, salmon, sealskins, and oil, especially between 1809 and 1812. Moreover, they expanded from the traditional Slade stronghold in the Fogo–Twillingate area southwards into Bonavista, Trinity, and Conception bays, as well as into St Mary's Bay and the Burin region on the south coast.

Despite the increased prosperity, not all the partners wished to continue working within the firm. The first of the Slade heirs to break away was Robert, who in 1804 moved to Trinity and leased the premises previously operated by John Jeffrey of Poole. His business grew steadily and by 1817 his tax rate in Poole was assessed on a trade of more value than that of John Slade and Company. One of the reasons for the apparent decline in the trade of the old firm between 1813 and 1817 was Thomas Slade's departure to form yet another company. By 1817 his firm, Thomas Slade and Company, was rated in Poole on £700 worth of imports and exports, the equivalent in value of John Slade and Company. The principals of the new company were Thomas Slade and his nephew William Cox. It is not clear whether Slade withdrew his capital from the parent firm and struck out on his own, or whether, because of expansion, a decision was taken to manage a branch of the business under a separate name. It appears that John Slade and

Company continued its connections with Twillingate and Fogo, whereas Thomas Slade and Company traded mainly in Bonavista Bay. Thomas Slade's name was attached to the new firm for only a few years. He apparently fell ill in 1816; his will was made on 17 September and probated on 11 November.

Thomas Slade, who evidently did not marry, left a considerable fortune in stocks, money, property, and trade assets, to be divided in a complex manner among his kinfolk. He distributed £53,100 to his immediate relatives, the largest sums going to his brother John and nephew Robert. He also bequeathed a total of £11,000 to some other members of the family and smaller amounts to sundry relations. His lands in the parishes of East and West Morden in Dorset, England, he left to his brother David, and a storehouse in Poole to David's son Thomas. Half of his "Newfoundland trade and all my plantations, rooms, storehouses, flakes, land and estates . . . and also my ships, brigs, sloops, schooners, boats, craft, fishing implements and other effects belonging to the said trade" went to his nephew and partner William Cox. The other half was placed in trust with his cousin Robert for his son Thomas and for the son of his brother David, also named Thomas. It was further enjoined that at the age of 24 the two Thomases were to become partners in Thomas Slade's company, which would take the name of Thomas Slade and Thomas Slade.

Shortly after Thomas Slade's death his company's name was changed to Slade and Cox. By 1824 this company had six ships totalling 904 tons in the Newfoundland trade. The firm traded under this style until 1828, when the Thomas Slades became 24 and the company adopted the name stipulated in Slade's will. By 1836 the house went under the label of Thomas Slade Sr and Company, and was one of six Slade family firms operating in Newfoundland. Thomas Slade therefore represented one of many, but nevertheless important, links in the succession of Slade merchant firms that were involved in Newfoundland from about 1750 to 1868.

Thomas Slade evidently concentrated his energy entirely on commerce and paid little attention to political affairs. He does not appear either to have held or to have sought any political office or appointment in Poole or Newfoundland. In Newfoundland the Slades were one of the last merchant families to conduct trade directly from Poole. They were also notable as one of the last English mercantile families to resist the 19th-century trends towards the centralization of commerce at St John's and a domestically controlled economy on the island.

W. GORDON HANDCOCK

Dorset Record office, P227/CW3–CW5 (Churchwardens, rates and accounts, 1783–1824); P227/OV5–OV6 (Overseers of the poor, rates and accounts, 1827–36). Nfld., Dept. of Culture, Recreation and Youth, Hist. Resources Division

(St John's), W. G. Handcock, "The merchant families and entrepreneurs of Trinity in the nineteenth century" (typescript, St John's, 1981), 90–124. PANL, GN 5/1/B/9; P7/A/6. PRO, ADM 1/47; PROB 11/1239/618; 11/1586/597. *DCB*, vol.4 (biog. of John Slade). Derek Beamish *et al.*, *The pride of Poole, 1688–1851* (Poole, Eng., 1974), 277–78. C. G. Head, *Eighteenth century Newfoundland: a geographer's perspective* (Toronto, 1976), 218–21. Prowse, *Hist. of Nfld.* (1895), 664. *Newfoundlander* (St John's), 14 Oct. 1861: 3. *Public Ledger* (St John's), 3 June 1862: 3.

SMITH, MICHAEL, educator and author; b. 1776 in Chester County, Pa, ten miles from Philadelphia; m. "1806, in one of the southern states" and had at least two children; d. in or after 1816.

Compiler or author of a valuable description of Upper Canada in the years just before the War of 1812, Michael Smith is otherwise a rather shadowy figure, the only biographical material for his life coming from the prefaces he wrote to his various publications and one letter to Lieutenant Governor Francis Gore*'s secretary, William Halton. After he had travelled extensively for nearly ten years through the United States he decided "to go where land could be obtained on easy terms"; he was unwilling "to live in the south, where slavery abounded" and was unable "to get land in Pennsylvania." In January 1810 he moved to the province of Upper Canada which was attracting "the attention of many persons in Pennsylvania and New Jersey" and where "200 acres of land could be got by anyone upon the terms of taking an oath of allegiance to George III and paying $37 50 cents for surveying it." But since he did not wish to go into a new settlement, he bought land, 200 "excellent" acres, near the shore of Lake Erie.

In June 1811 Smith was teaching school three miles from Niagara (Niagara-on-the-Lake). That month he applied for Gore's permission to print "a Geographical and Pollitical view of the province of Upper Canada." This request was granted, and he "travelled extensively for that purpose, for about one year." In the autumn of 1812, after the outbreak of war, he and his family, he states, were constantly harassed and threatened "as a Yankee" by the Indians in the Niagara region, where he was then staying. On 9 Nov. 1812 the administrator, Roger Hale Sheaffe*, ordered "all those who had previously refused to take the oath of allegiance to make application for passports to the United States." Sheaffe's action had been prompted by reports from militia officers such as Richard HATT that some persons had refused to take the oath required by the militia act "for reason their being American Citizens." In his proclamation Sheaffe specified that those failing to report to alien boards set up at Niagara, York (Toronto), and Kingston by 1 Jan. 1813 "shall be taken to be an alien enemy . . . liable to be treated as a Prisoner of War, or as a Spy, as circumstances may dictate." Although Smith stated that he had taken the oath, he and his family, "desirous of returning to the States," travelled to Kingston, where on 26 December he appeared before a board composed of Richard CARTWRIGHT, Allan MacLean*, and Lieutenant-Colonel John Vincent* and received passports. Smith's manuscript was confiscated. The family went on to Prescott and crossed into the United States at Ogdensburg, N.Y. He earned his keep by occasional preaching in Baptist churches as he travelled southward toward New York City and then to Richmond, Va.

On the way, after receiving an offer of financial support for the printing of a "Geographical View of Upper Canada," he hurriedly put together an account based on his memory, "what loose papers [he had] retained," and other papers he had left in Buffalo, N.Y. A first edition of 3,000 copies was published in Hartford, Conn., in 1813, and a second printing, of 10,000, soon appeared in the same city. Later there were further printings in New York City, Philadelphia, and Trenton, N.J. A much enlarged edition was published in Baltimore, Md, in 1814 and another in Richmond in 1815. In that year Smith decided to move to Kentucky, arriving in Lexington in March 1816, where yet another edition of his work came out in several printings within the next year or so. In Lexington he became a school teacher, continued to serve as a Baptist minister, and then dropped from sight.

The success of the various editions suggests the intense American interest in Upper Canada during the years when the United States was trying to conquer that province; Joseph Sabin states that "in one of his prefaces [Smith] made the statement that upwards of thirty thousand volumes of his books had been published altogether." Yet the work would not have made very comfortable reading for American patriots. Smith stresses that at the outbreak of war the people of Upper Canada, predominantly American in background, were generally neutral *vis-à-vis* both the British and Americans, but as the war went on they came to see the Americans as cruel invaders: "They think it their duty to kill all [the Americans] they can while they are coming over, that they may discourage any more from invading the province." Later he described the war as "being carried into Canada, among people of our own nation, who were entirely inoffensive." Apart from the discussion of attitudes toward the war, the work also contains the fullest contemporary account of the geography, population, and customs of the people of Upper Canada in the era of the War of 1812.

G. M. CRAIG

Three of the main editions of Smith's work are: *A geographical view, of the province of Upper Canada, and promiscuous remarks upon the government . . .* (Hartford, Conn., 1813), *A geographical view of the British posses-*

Smith

sions in North America . . . (Baltimore, Md., 1814), and *A narrative of the sufferings in Upper Canada, with his family in the late war, and journey to Virginia and Kentucky, of M. Smith . . .* (3rd ed., Lexington, Ky., 1817). The fullest listing of, and commentary on, the various editions is in *Dictionary of books relating to America, from its discovery to the present time*, comp. Joseph Sabin (29v., New York, 1868–1936; repr. 29v. in 15, Amsterdam, 1961–62), 20: 433–38. Smith also published *On the vanity of human actions; a little sermon, by a big sinner* (Hartford, 1813), *Human sorrow and divine comfort, or a short narrative of the sufferings, travel, present feelings and situation of M. Smith . . .* (Richmond, Va., 1814), and *Beauties of divine poetry; or, appropriate hymns, and spiritual songs, selected, altered and original* (Lexington, 1817).

PAC, RG 5, A1: 5504–5; RG 8, I (C ser.), 688B: 74–76, 87, 105, 127–28, 187. "Proclamations by governors and lieutenant-governors of Quebec and Upper Canada," AO *Report*, 1906: 261–62. E. A. Cruikshank, "The county of Norfolk in the War of 1812," *OH*, 20 (1923): 9–40.

SMITH, WILLIAM, surgeon, army officer, politician, judge, and author; b. in England; m. Sarah MacLean; fl. 1784–1803.

Very little is known of William Smith before his appointment as garrison surgeon of the new colony of Cape Breton on 28 Aug. 1784. He arrived there in November with other English immigrants on the *Blenheim* and was appointed by Lieutenant Governor Joseph Frederick Wallet DesBarres* to the Executive Council of the colony. DesBarres also named him judge of the Court of Exchequer, a largely titular position.

During the autumn of 1785 a dispute developed between DesBarres and the garrison commander, Lieutenant-Colonel John Yorke of the 33rd Foot, over responsibility for the distribution of supplies to the settlers. Smith and the other military men on the council tended to favour Yorke. As a result, in the spring of 1786 DesBarres demanded of this group that they give up either their council seats or their military posts. Smith resigned from the council, and then allied himself with Attorney General David Mathews* and Secretary Abraham Cornelius CUYLER to forward a petition to the British government calling for DesBarres's dismissal. He was restored to the council after DesBarres's recall in November 1786.

Smith enjoyed amicable relations with DesBarres's successor, William MACARMICK, and when Macarmick suspended Chief Justice Richard Gibbons* in March 1788 he named Smith the senior of the three assistant judges appointed to take Gibbons's place. Smith's income, however, was evidently inadequate to allow him to live in Cape Breton, and in the autumn of 1791 he returned to England, although he maintained an interest in the colony. In January 1796 he was superseded as garrison surgeon for neglect of duty and seems to have gone through a difficult period. But thanks to his friendship with Lieutenant Governor Sir John WENTWORTH of Nova Scotia and Lieutenant-General James OGILVIE, then stationed at Halifax, N.S., he was able in March 1798 to obtain the position of joint chief justice of Cape Breton with Ingram BALL. He was sworn in that August, and was later reappointed to the council.

Smith and Ball were soon at odds, since Ball supported a political faction controlled by Mathews, while Smith aligned himself with the opposing group, headed by the Reverend Ranna COSSIT. Both groups contended for dominance in the council and supported various rulers of the colony in an attempt to achieve their ends. Cossit and Smith favoured the policies of Ogilvie, who had become administrator of the colony in June 1798, and those of Ogilvie's successor, Brigadier-General John Murray*. Murray dismissed Ball as joint chief justice in December 1799, leaving Smith alone in the post. Smith's power was then at its peak; he sided with Murray in destroying the power of Mathews and his faction.

In June 1800 Major-General John Despard* arrived in Sydney to become administrator, but Murray refused to surrender the civil command. Since Smith's influence had increased during Murray's administration, he naturally took Murray's part and refused to acknowledge the legality of Despard's appointment. When in the autumn it became obvious that Murray's efforts to retain power were futile, Smith left Cape Breton to present Murray's case to the British government. He was not only unsuccessful in having Murray reinstated but was himself superseded as chief justice, despite his requests to retain the position.

Though Smith never returned to Cape Breton, in 1803 he wrote a 158-page pamphlet entitled *A caveat against emigration to America; with the state of the island of Cape Breton*. The first part of the work is descriptive of the problems encountered by British settlers in North America, and the remainder is an extensive account of the geography and political life of Cape Breton. Smith extolled the attractions of the island: "Intersected by navigable rivers, with numerous deep and commodious bays . . . surrounded by numerous fishing banks, stored with fish . . . with a rich soil [and a] healthy climate, it affords the settler great and tempting advantages." At the same time, the Cape Breton section is highly critical of Smith's political enemies, and biased and pessimistic in its account of events. Nevertheless, its description of the colony and its delineation of life in a newly settled region make it valuable to the student of the period. The pamphlet elicited a reply from DesBarres entitled *Letters to Lord ***** on "A caveat against emigration to America"* in which he attacked Smith for the stands he had taken in Cape Breton. Nothing is known of Smith's career after 1803.

Like others in Cape Breton, William Smith had high hopes of success in the colony, but his experiences there left him disappointed and bitter. He is, however, unique in having left a printed record which gives an insight into events there between 1784 and 1803. It is ironic to reflect that the *Caveat* was published in 1803, at the very time when the colony, now rid of personalities such as Mathews, Gibbons, and Smith, was finally beginning to achieve a measure of self-sufficiency.

R. J. MORGAN

William Smith is the author of *A caveat against emigration to America; with the state of the island of Cape Breton, from the year 1784 to the present year; and suggestions for the benefit of the British settlements in North America* (London, 1803).

PAC, MG 11, [CO 217] Cape Breton A, 3. [J. F. W. DesBarres], *Letters to Lord ***** on "A caveat against emigration to America . . ."* (London, 1804). Morgan, "Orphan outpost."

SMYTHE (Smyth), Sir HERVEY, army officer and topographical painter; b. 30 May 1734 in Ampton, England, son of Sir Robert Smythe and Lady Louisa Carolina Isabelle Hervey, daughter of John Hervey, 1st Earl of Bristol; d. unmarried 25 Sept. 1811 in Elmswell, Suffolk, England, and was buried at West Ham (London).

Hervey Smythe was a page of honour to George II before entering the Royal Horse Guards as a cornet at age 19. On 8 Nov. 1756, at the beginning of the Seven Years' War, he became a captain in the 15th Foot and in 1758 he participated in the expedition against Louisbourg, Île Royale (Cape Breton Island), where he was slightly wounded. He won the admiration of Brigadier-General James Wolfe*, who wrote to Lieutenant-General Lord George Sackville on 30 July that "Little Smith . . . is a most indefatigable, active, and spirited man and has a just claim to your favour and friendship."

On 4 May 1759 Wolfe appointed Smythe one of his aides-de-camp for the campaign against Quebec. The British force arrived at Île d'Orléans on 27 June and the siege of Quebec began. On 22 July Wolfe sent Smythe to Quebec under a flag of truce to escort a large number of women captured the previous day by Lieutenant-Colonel Guy CARLETON during an attack on Pointe-aux-Trembles (Neuville). Wolfe, in a gesture of gallantry, had entertained at table on the evening of the 21st some of the group who were from distinguished families; he was angered, therefore, when his aide-de-camp was rudely received by Quebec's besieged inhabitants and protested this treatment of Smythe to Lieutenant-General Louis-Joseph de Montcalm*. Nine days later Smythe participated in the disastrous attack at Montmorency Falls; on 13 September he was severely wounded in the battle of the Plains of Abraham, where Wolfe himself was killed. In his will Wolfe had left Smythe and several other officers 100 guineas each "to buy swords & rings in remembrance of their Friend."

Smythe, probably because of his wound, returned immediately to England. With him he took a number of sketches he had made of places in the Gulf of St Lawrence and of battles during the siege of Quebec; along with Richard Short* and Thomas DAVIES he was one of the first military artists to record Canada visually. Smythe's sketch of the attack on Quebec, engraved and published at London about 1760, became a popular print at the time. He had supposedly made a profile drawing of Wolfe shortly after the general's death, and in London he painted profiles of Wolfe, which were reproduced in small mezzotints by the well-known engraver Charles Spooner. Smythe is chiefly remembered, however, for *Six elegant views of the most remarkable places in the river and gulph of St Lawrence*, engraved by various hands and published in London by Thomas Jefferys in 1760 with a dedication to William Pitt, secretary of state for the Southern Department. Oil paintings were subsequently executed of several of the same subjects, possibly by the English marine artist, Francis Swaine, Smythe's contemporary.

Smythe became a captain in the 2nd Dragoon Guards on 13 Jan. 1760 and brevet lieutenant-colonel on 26 Nov. 1762. The following year he became a captain in the 3rd Foot Guards. His wound during the battle of the Plains had, however, impaired his health, and he retired on 12 May 1769. In 1783 he succeeded his father as baronet and, having passed the latter part of his life in continual suffering, he died in September 1811 at his farm at Elmswell.

R. H. HUBBARD

[Hervey Smythe's *Six elegant views of the most remarkable places in the river and gulph of St Lawrence* was reproduced in *Scenographia Americana, or a collection of views in North America and the West Indies . . .* (London, 1768). A profile of Wolfe, drawn soon after the general's death, was attributed to Smythe, but John F. Kerslake, in "The likeness of Wolfe," *Wolfe: portraiture & genealogy* (Westerham, Eng., 1959), 42, emphasizes that the identity of the artist has not been established beyond doubt. A tracing of this sketch is held by the National Portrait Gallery, London. Francis Swaine is credited with some canvasses painted from sketches by Smythe of scenes along the St Lawrence River and in the gulf area. Two of these canvasses are in the Royal Ontario Museum, Toronto, and two others are at the National Gallery of Canada in Ottawa. The latter two, *A view of Gaspé Bay* and *A view of Miramichi*, are unsigned and their attribution to Swaine is based only on the word of Smythe himself.

Charles Perry Stacey in "Quebec, 1759: some new documents," *CHR*, 47 (1966): 345, advances the view that either Smythe or Thomas Bell was the author of a "pungent and literate" account of the Quebec campaign. The original is in the Dobbs papers at the Public Record Office of

Spark

Northern Ireland (Belfast), D 162/77, and on microfilm at the PAC.

The claim has been made that Hervey Smythe was the young officer portrayed at the centre of Benjamin West's painting *The death of Wolfe* (1771). A drawing from West's studio, comprising portraits of figures depicted in this well-known canvas, contains one of Smythe that is reproduced in Annie Elizabeth Wolfe-Aylward, *The pictorial life of Wolfe* (Plymouth, Eng., n.d.), 79. Reproductions of another portrait of him are at the PAC and in Knox, *Hist. journal* (Doughty), 1: 331–32, 440. R.H.H.]

Suffolk Record Office (Bury St Edmunds, Eng.), Ampton, Reg. of baptisms, marriages, and burials, 1734. *Bury and Norwich Post* (Bury St Edmunds), 2 Oct. 1811. *Examiner* (London), 20 Oct. 1811. *Allgemeines Lexikon der bildenden Künstler von der Antike bis zur Gegenwart . . .*, ed. Hans Vollmer (37v., Leipzig, German Democratic Republic, 1907–50), 31: 185. *A catalogue of the Sigmund Samuel collection*, comp. C. W. Jeffreys (Toronto, 1948), 10, 17–24, 118, 144, 149. *Complete baronetage*, ed. G. E. Cokayne (5v., Exeter, Eng., 1906), 5: 24. *The National Gallery of Canada, catalogue of paintings and sculpture*, ed. R. H. Hubbard (3v., Ottawa and Toronto, 1957–60), 3: 285. A. G. Doughty and G. W. Parmelee, *The siege of Quebec and the battle of the Plains of Abraham* (6v., Quebec, 1901), 2: 10, 115, 153, 311–12; 3: 221. J. R. Harper, *Painting in Canada, a history* (Toronto and Quebec, 1966), 41, 429. D. A. Ponsonby, *Call a dog Hervey* (London, 1949), 182–84. Robin Reilly, *The rest to fortune; the life of Major-General James Wolfe* (London, 1960), 191. F. St G. Spendlove, *The face of early Canada: pictures of Canada which have helped to make history* (Toronto, 1958), 7–8, 10, 82; plates 16–21. J. C. Webster, *Wolfe and the artists; a study of his portraiture* (Toronto, 1930), 34, 42–43. Beckles Willson, *The life and letters of James Wolfe . . .* (London, 1909), 388, 431, 453. C. P. Stacey, "Benjamin West and *The death of Wolfe*," National Gallery of Canada, *Bull.* (Ottawa), (1966): 1.

SPARK, ALEXANDER, teacher, Church of Scotland clergyman, journalist, and author; b. probably 7 Jan. 1762 in the parish of Marykirk, Scotland, son of John Spark and Mary Low; m. 13 July 1805 Mary Ross at Quebec, Lower Canada; they had no children; d. there 7 March 1819.

Alexander Spark received his primary education at the grammar school in Montrose, Scotland; he later entered King's College (University of Aberdeen). After his graduation with an MA in 1776, he worked as a tutor until 1780 when he accepted an invitation to Quebec by a Mr Reid, director of an academy there, to act as his assistant. Although Spark enjoyed teaching, he turned down the offer of a partnership with Reid and accepted a proposal ultimately to replace the ageing Presbyterian minister at Quebec, George Henry. Spark moved to the country for a time to learn French, and then in 1783 he returned to Scotland to study for the ministry and receive ordination. He came back to Quebec, probably the following year, and became Henry's assistant, but he earned his living as tutor to Henry CALDWELL's son, John*. By 1789 Spark had taken over all ministerial duties from Henry, and when the latter died in 1795 his replacement formally succeeded him.

A number of evangelical members of the Scotch Church, as Spark's congregation was called, were dissatisfied with his theology, and in 1795 they left to form their own congregation. This action was a local manifestation of a dispute among Scottish Presbyterians between moderates, whose views Spark espoused, and populars, or evangelicals. The moderates, of whom two of the most prominent, Alexander Gerard and George Campbell, had been Spark's philosophy and theology professors at King's College, constituted the church's intellectual élite and were the dominant force into the latter half of the 18th century. Strongly influenced by the Enlightenment, moderates were broad-minded and humanistic, latitudinarian in doctrine, and erastian in their conception of the relations between church and state. They were more concerned with moral behaviour than with covenant theology. Spark summarized his "moderate" theology in 1799 when he wrote: "Religion corrects the irregular propensities of the heart, gives strength and stability to virtuous purposes, and cherishes those dispositions, and that temper of mind, which are most friendly to peace, order and good Government."

To the populars, offspring of the 18th-century evangelical revival, the moderates lacked fire in the soul. In 1799 the dissidents who had left Spark's congregation petitioned the Missionary Society in London for a clergyman. It sent Clark BENTOM, who arrived at Quebec on 1 June 1800. He questioned Spark's trinitarian orthodoxy and noted that his communion was "open to any person who chooses to partake without the least previous notice or regard to their character." Having heard Spark preach once, Bentom remarked that "he did not attempt to stimulate his audience to obedience by such frightful Sounds as Hell and Damnation for . . . I am sure there was scarcely anything in his sermon to give them the remotest idea of the Devil, Hell or Wrath." He acknowledged, however, that Spark's moral conduct seemed unimpeachable.

One member of Spark's congregation who appreciated the minister's sermons for their erudition and literary quality was the printer Samuel Neilson*. In 1792 he had named Spark editor of the *Quebec Magazine/Le Magasin de Québec*. Moreover, on Neilson's death in January 1793, Spark, whom Neilson had appointed guardian of his young heir, John Neilson*, took over as managing editor of the *Quebec Gazette/La Gazette de Québec*. Spark's main concern being to ensure the *Gazette*'s financial strength, he abandoned Samuel's late efforts to render the newspaper independent of government and accepted official inspection in return for government advertising. This policy was consistent with Spark's support of British rule in the colony at a time of considerable political turmoil [*see* David McLane*; Robert PRESCOTT]. John Neilson was a bit of a radical, however, and in late 1794 he was obliged to flee to the United States for political reasons. According to Spark, "the enemies of the house, taking advantage of so favourable a crisis to throw the business into disorder," nearly succeeded, and only the greatest personal effort by Spark saved the newspaper for Neilson. Spark continued to manage the *Quebec Gazette* until August 1796.

Meanwhile, despite the withdrawal of its evangelical members, the Scotch Church had been growing steadily in numbers and prosperity under Spark. The minister's income from subscriptions and fees for the performance of baptisms, marriages, and burials increased correspondingly. It was supplemented by fees for his services as estate executor for several of his parishioners and for tutoring; as well, beginning about 1802, he received a salary of £50 from government. By October 1794 he was in a position to lend £300 to Henry Caldwell, and two years later he lent £250 to Neilson. In 1797 he paid £450 for a house on Rue des Pauvres (Côte du Palais), which he rented out and which he would sell along with two lots for £1,200 eight years later. He acquired vacant land in the city in 1801 and 1806. In the latter year he was granted more than 1,200 acres of land in Aston Township. He maintained the social rank expected of a minister of the Kirk, replacing Henry as grand chaplain of Quebec freemasons and attending governors' levees. He was a member of the Quebec Benevolent Society, an exclusive mutual aid society formed by a portion of Quebec's upper class. In 1804 he received a DD from Aberdeen.

By 1800 the Scotch Church was an established institution in Quebec's religious life and its minister a respected member of the minor élite; however, neither had much influence on government. In 1803, when Bentom was arrested on the instigation of Anglican bishop Jacob Mountain* for holding parish registers without legal authorization, the question arose as to whether Spark was authorized to hold them. He argued that, since the Kirk was the established church in Scotland, he had the same rights as the clergy of the Church of England. Attorney General Jonathan Sewell*, who prosecuted Bentom, but whose wife, Harriet Smith, appears to have been a member of the Scotch Church, tried to protect Spark. The judges of the Court of King's Bench asserted, however, that only the Anglican and Roman Catholic clergy could legally hold registers. Thereafter, Mountain himself guided through the legislature a bill validating all past marriages performed by Church of Scotland and dissenting ministers, but a bill to authorize the holding of registers by Church of Scotland clergy was lost.

Nevertheless, Spark continued to perform marriages. "If he has herein acted right," Bentom wrote to the Missionary Society, "it follows all dissenters have the same privilege." In February 1805 a petition by the Scotch Church for equal rights with the Church of England was rejected; not until 1827 were all doubts finally removed about the right of its ministers to hold registers.

The Scotch Church's influence on government was increasing, however. It counted among its members such prominent merchants as John BLACKWOOD, Adam Lymburner*, and John Mure*. By 1805 it also boasted several politicians: Mure, Blackwood, and George Pyke* were members of the House of Assembly and Lymburner an executive councillor; James Irvine* became an executive councillor in 1808. In 1796, shortly after Spark had become titular minister, the congregation had petitioned for a grant of land, but without result. Six years later it petitioned for the site of the former Jesuit chapel on which it proposed to build a church, but again unsuccessfully. In 1807 the congregation was still occupying part of the Jesuit college, where it had been worshipping in a room for more than 40 years, when it received a peremptory order from the commander of the troops in the Canadas, Colonel Isaac BROCK, to move out; most of the college had long since been converted to barracks, but Brock needed more space. Angered by the colonel's arrogance, Spark suggested stiffly that Brock "suffer the matter to terminate, which will be gratifying to me, and may prevent a great deal of trouble." The matter was settled later that year by Governor CRAIG, who accorded Brock the Presbyterians' room and promised Spark land on which to build a church; meanwhile, the congregation worshipped in the court-house. On 30 Nov. 1808 a lot was granted on Rue Sainte-Anne and two years later, on St Andrew's Day, Spark dedicated the church to the patron saint of Scotland.

The congregation became increasingly numerous and prosperous after 1810. In 1803 it had shared with the Church of England congregation one-third of the proceeds of a city-wide collection of funds to provide firewood for the poor. Thereafter, the money in its own poor relief fund increased steadily, and by 1816 Spark could write that none of the congregation's poor was in "immediate extreme want"; he suggested that the money from another city-wide collection that year could best be used among the Roman Catholics. Although long-term charity from the poor relief fund was limited to members of the congregation, Spark often distributed alms to non-members, such as "Gautier – a poor woman," "sick strangers," and "a poor object, name unknown." In 1818 five shillings were dispensed "to redeem slaves." That year Spark, George Jehoshaphat Mountain* of the Church of England, and Joseph Signay*, of the Roman Catholic

Spark

Church, formed a Committee for the Relief of Sick and Destitute Strangers. Spark personally benefited from his congregation's prosperity since in 1810 he began to receive a stable salary of £200 per annum.

As well as establishing the Presbyterian church at Quebec, Spark participated prominently in early efforts to organize Presbyterianism in Lower Canada. In 1793 he joined with John BETHUNE of Upper Canada and John Young* of Montreal to form the Presbytery of Montreal, but it was short-lived. Ten years later he united with Bethune and an elder of the Scotch Presbyterian Church of Montreal, Duncan FISHER, in another ephemeral Presbytery of Montreal, mainly to ordain James Somerville*. Although Somerville was a licentiate of the Relief Presbytery of Glasgow, Spark had taken him under his wing and directed him to the Scotch Presbyterian Church, later known as St Gabriel Street Church. Spark played no part, however, in founding the first durable presbytery in the colony. Either from poor health or fear of jeopardizing his ties with the Church of Scotland, and hence his salary from government, he did not join four secessionist ministers in founding the Presbytery of the Canadas in 1818.

According to his close friend Daniel Wilkie*, Spark was "in stature . . . considerably below the middle size, of a ruddy complexion, and had a fresh, healthful appearance to the last. He pronounced his sermons in a clear and natural, but not a forcible voice. His hair, which he wore powdered, according to the fashion of his earlier days, had a very graceful appearance, and his aspect in the pulpit was venerable in the extreme." Although unambitious, Spark was extremely conscientious; from 1795 until his death he left his post only twice for short visits to Montreal to attend to church business, and in the 15 years that Wilkie knew him he never absented himself from the pulpit at the hour of divine service. He disdained social visits, preferring the privacy of his study or discussions with a small circle of close friends, who were chosen independently of their religion.

Spark was a man of order – "The law of Order is the invariable rule of Divine Government," he asserted – and his concern for order made him a conservative in theology and politics. He was a staunch defender of British colonial government, subscribing to the Association, formed in 1794 to support British rule in Lower Canada, and contributing to a voluntary subscription for the same purpose in 1799. In 1813 he was a director of the Quebec branch of the Loyal and Patriotic Society of the Province of Lower Canada, established to aid needy militiamen and their families. As well, on appropriate occasions he preached sermons stressing the importance of loyalty.

Spark's love of order may also explain his passion for science. From December 1798 at least he daily recorded barometric pressure, wind direction, cloud conditions, and precipitation, if any, at 8:00 a.m and 2:00 or 3:00 p.m.; over a period of 20 years he did not record findings for only 20 days. In addition he was an amateur astronomer and botanist, and he performed electrical experiments with home-made apparatus. These experiments reflected his interest in medicine, for, according to Wilkie, "when electric shocks were supposed to convey relief to those who laboured under various distempers, his door was ever open to the sick, and especially to the indigent, who sought relief from that means." Spark's pastoral concern with emotional problems was characterized by a tendency to view depression as an illness; the ultimate cure was sound Christian faith, but treatment of specific cases of depression should be determined through observation and experimentation.

A well-rounded scholar, Spark was also devoted to the humanities. His library held more than 850 volumes in English, French, Latin, Greek, and Hebrew. He made notations in his journals on philosophy, music, education, and literature, particularly poetry. The *Quebec Gazette* affirmed in 1819 that "he was not meanly skilled in letters"; he had a surprising interest in love poetry, which he wrote in a studied, formal style, when not in a light-hearted vein, such as in "To a Lady returning a lock of her hair":

> Take, dearest maid, your present back,
> For e'er since I possessed it,
> My heart has been upon the rack,
> With cares and fears molested,
> If one small lock culled from your hair,
> Occasions such a pother,
> God help the man, enchanting Fair,
> Who gets you altogether.

Intellectually curious, Spark was at the same time a dedicated educator. After giving up teaching as a career, he tutored students in the classics and mathematics. His land grant in Aston Township had been made on the basis of his "well-known merit as a Public Teacher, & the tendency of his assiduous labours as a Public Instructor of Youth inculcating sound moral and loyal principles." About 1814 the London-based Committee for Promoting the Education of the Poor in Upper and Lower Canada, an initiative of the Reverend Thaddeus Osgood*, asked Spark, Roman Catholic bishop Plessis*, Bishop Mountain, and other prominent Lower Canadians to help it establish schools for the poor. Of the clergymen only Spark accepted the committee's principle of non-sectarian education and helped organize a colonial branch. The following year Spark was proposed as a trustee of the Royal Institution for the Advancement of Learning, which administered Lower Canada's public schools. He died, however, before the nomination could be formally made. On 7 March 1819 –

Spencer

a cold, fine day, he had noted at 8:00 a.m. – he was going to his church in the early afternoon when "he was seized by an apoplectic fit, and expired without a groan." The weather readings for 3:00 p.m. were never recorded.

Few men have been as well suited to their situation as was Alexander Spark to the Scotch Church. Having immigrated to Quebec while still young, and before becoming a clergyman, he was able to adapt to urban colonial society and ideas. As a minister of the Kirk he naturally maintained good relations with the civil authorities, and he was able gradually to raise his congregation from a social position of marginal importance to one of consideration in the eyes of government. In so doing he laid the foundation upon which his successors would build their claims for a part of the clergy reserves. His "moderate" theology equipped him to minister to his young and ambitious middle-class congregation, which was more concerned with matters of practical morality than with theological arguments or spirituality and more attentive to the quiet voice of reasonable persuasion than to hell-and-damnation preaching. Finally, Spark's views on toleration enabled him to work easily in an environment dominated politically by the Church of England and socially by the Roman Catholic Church. There seems little reason to doubt the *Quebec Gazette*'s description of him as "a gentleman beloved and respected by every one in this society."

James H. Lambert

[Most of the documents concerning Alexander Spark are in the archives of St Andrew's Church at Quebec. His sermons (indexed by Spark himself) are of particular interest. His meteorological records for 1798 to 1819 are at McGill Univ. Arch.; there may have been one or more volumes covering the period prior to 1798. The registers often served as a diary, wherein Spark recorded scientific observations, poems, and comments on daily events.

Spark is the author of the following works published at Quebec: *An oration delivered at the dedication of Freemason's Hall in the city of Quebec* (1787); *A sermon preached in the Presbyterian chapel at Quebec on Thursday, the 10th January 1799, being the day appointed for a general thanksgiving* (1799); *A sermon preached in the Scotch Presbyterian Church at Quebec on Wednesday the 1st February 1804, being the day appointed by proclamation for a general fast* (1804); *The connexion between the civil and religious state of society, a sermon preached at the opening of the new Scotch Church, called St Andrew's Church, in the city of Quebec, on Friday the 30th day of November 1810* (1811); *A sermon preached in the Scotch Church in the city of Quebec on Thursday the 21st April 1814, being the day appointed for a general thanksgiving* (1814); and *A sermon delivered in St Andrew's Church, Quebec, by the late Rev. Alex. Spark, D.D., on the 7th March 1819, the day of his death; also a funeral sermon preached on that occasion, the 14th March 1819* (1819). j.h.l.]

AAQ, 210 A, IX: 29; 60 CN, I: 22. ANQ-Q, CE1-61, 13 July 1805, 11 March 1819; CN1-16, 4 avril 1809; 28 sept.

1811; 30 juin, 4 juill. 1812; 28 juin 1815; 9 juill. 1817; 7 juin 1819; 20 mai 1820; CN1-92, 11 janv. 1793; CN1-230, 17 nov. 1803; 23 mai, 3 juin 1806; 12 sept. 1815; CN1-256, 31 Aug., 3 Dec. 1796; CN1-262, 30 mai 1801, 20 mai 1802, 29 juill. 1805, 4 févr. 1808; CN1-284, 24 avril 1797, 26 mars 1800, 28 avril 1801, 14 avril 1803; P-81, 1: 38; P-192; P-193. AP, St Andrew's (Quebec), Corr., Ryland to Lynd, 15 July 1795, Ryland to Spark, 4 Oct. 1796, Ryland to Lymburner, 9 Nov. 1802, Stuart to the Scotch Church, 20 May 1803, Ryland to Spark, 23 Nov. 1804, Spark to Brock, 6 Oct. 1807, Ryland to Spark, 31 Oct., 3 Nov. 1807, Craig to Spark, 14 June 1808, Blackwood to Ryland, 13 Jan. 1809, Spark to Somerville, 13 March 1809, Esson to Spark, 22 Jan. 1818, Ramsay to Spark, 23 July 1818; Kirk session minute-book, 1802–23; Lists of subscriptions for ministers, 1793–1810; Plate collections, 1803–20; Poor relief accounts book, 1803–37; Reg. of baptisms, marriages, and burials, 1786–1819. PAC, MG 24, B1, 20: 75–85; 28: 34, 265; 38: 1006, 1009, 1013; RG 1, L3^L: 508, 1308, 1664, 2134, 17744–48, 17751–59, 17781, 88982–86; RG 4, A1: 3548–49, 4 Dec. 1816. PRO, CO 42/120: ff.6v, 9–10v, 12v–13v; CO 42/125: f.4 (mfm. at PAC). School of Oriental and African Studies, Univ. of London (London), Council for World Mission Arch., Methodist Missionary Soc., Clark Bentom, "Journal and observations on my passage to Quebec arrival &c"; Corr., folder 7, no.1–3, 6–8, 22, 24, 33, 46 (mfm. at ANQ-Q). Quebec Benevolent Soc., *Rules of the Quebec Benevolent Society ...* (Quebec, 1812). [John Strachan], "The death of Dr Spark," *Christian Recorder* (York [Toronto]), 1 (1819–20): 65–73. *Quebec Gazette*, 6 Dec. 1787; 18 Aug. 1791; 28 Nov. 1793; 13 Feb., 10 July 1794; 7 Feb., 18 July, 17 Oct. 1799; 21 April 1803; 14 June 1804; 4 July 1805; 1 Dec. 1808; 17 Jan., 2 March, 10 Aug. 1809; 27 Aug., 7 Dec. 1818; 8, 11 March, 25 Oct. 1819; 25 May 1820. *Quebec Magazine*, 1792–94. Hew Scott et al., *Fasti ecclesiæ scoticanæ: the succession of ministers in the Church of Scotland from the Reformation* (new ed., 9v. to date, Edinburgh, 1915–), 7: 652. William Gregg, *History of the Presbyterian Church in the dominion of Canada ...* (Toronto, 1885), 42, 148, 150–51, 160–61, 206–7. G. D. Henderson, *The burning bush; studies in Scottish church history ...* (Edinburgh, 1957), 74, 130, 139, 164–79. E. A. [K.] McDougall, "The Presbyterian Church in western Lower Canada, 1815–1842" (phd thesis, McGill Univ., Montreal, 1969), 10, 56–57, 83–84. J. S. Moir, *Enduring witness; a history of the Presbyterian Church in Canada* ([Hamilton, Ont.,] 1974?]), 19, 47, 51, 68, 74. W. S. Reid, *The Church of Scotland in Lower Canada* (Toronto, 1936), 25, 41–44, 68, 100–1, 119. *St Andrew's Church, Quebec* (Quebec, 1908), 4. Robert Stewart, *St Andrew's Church (Presbyterian) Quebec: an historical sketch of the church and its ministers* ([Quebec, 1928]), 8. W. C. Clark, "The early Presbyterianism of Quebec under Dr Spark," Literary and Hist. Soc. of Quebec, *Trans.* (Quebec), new ser., 27 (1906–7): 28–31. Daniel Wilkie, "Memoir of the life of the Reverend Alexander Spark, D.D., minister of the Scotch Church, Quebec," *Canadian Christian Examiner and Presbyterian Rev.* (Toronto), 1 (1837): 209–25. S. F. Wise, "Sermon literature and Canadian intellectual history," United Church of Canada, Committee on Arch., *Bull.* (Toronto), 18 (1965): 3–18.

SPENCER, HAZELTON, army officer, office holder, politician, judge, and militia officer; b. 29

771

Spencer

Aug. 1757 in East Greenwich, R.I., son of Benjamin Spencer and Mercy Potter; m. about 1787 Margaret Richards, daughter of John Richards, loyalist, and they had six sons and three daughters; d. 6 Feb. 1813 in Fredericksburgh (North and South Fredericksburgh) Township, Upper Canada.

About 1767 Benjamin Spencer moved his family from Rhode Island to what is now Vermont; in 1775 they were living in Durham Township. A member of the provisional assembly of Vermont in 1777, Benjamin fled from the rebels with his son Hazelton in that year, leaving the rest of his family behind. They joined the British forces commanded by John Burgoyne* in July and that November, en route to Canada, Benjamin died. The following year the family's 300 acres of land in Vermont, later valued at £3,000, was confiscated. Hazelton Spencer served as a volunteer in Sir John Johnson*'s King's Royal Regiment of New York until 1781; he was then commissioned a lieutenant in the 2nd battalion. On 1 March 1781 he was on a list of loyalists quartered at St Johns (Saint-Jean-sur-Richelieu), Que., and described as "a Hatter." In 1783 he was stationed at Cataraqui (Kingston, Ont.) where on 25 June 1784 he went on half pay and thereafter took up land in Fredericksburgh Township.

Like most other loyalist officers, Spencer acquired a good deal of land. In 1792 he and his brother, Abel, were among a group of prominent Upper Canadians who received grants of entire townships from Lieutenant Governor John Graves SIMCOE. Though this grant was later rescinded, Spencer's total landholdings either by grant or by purchase were at least 5,000 acres, located in the counties of Lennox, Addington, Prince Edward, Northumberland, and Durham, and in the town of Kingston.

In January 1795 Spencer was commissioned captain in the second battalion of the newly formed Royal Canadian Volunteer Regiment. He was promoted major in 1797 and served as commandant of the garrison at Kingston from 1797 to 1800. He was then stationed as commandant at Fort George (Niagara-on-the-Lake) from 1800 until 1802, when the regiment was disbanded. On 1 June 1806 Lieutenant Governor Francis Gore* appointed Spencer, Thomas Dorland*, and Archibald McDonell (MacDonell) commissioners for the Midland District to administer the oath to officers on half pay and military allowances. From 1794 until his death in 1813 Spencer was colonel of the 1st Lennox Militia.

Spencer was a member of the Church of England, serving for many years as churchwarden at St Paul's in Fredericksburgh. He was also a member of Masonic Lodge No.7. Like many loyalists Spencer was a slaveholder [see Jack York*].

Although little is known of his early life or education Spencer was regarded as a man of ability and stature in early Upper Canada. He had been appointed justice of the peace for the Mecklenburg District on 16 Oct. 1790. On 1 Jan. 1800 he received his first commission of the peace for the Midland District; the last was dated 16 March 1808. The magistracy of the Midland District met in both an administrative and a legal capacity in the Court of Quarter Sessions, which alternated its location between Adolphustown and Kingston. His military duties took him out of the district between 1800 and 1802, but Spencer attended 6 of 15 sessions of the court between 1800 and 1804. Between 1807 and 1813 he was present at 13 of 25 sessions, a much better record than that of fellow magistrates such as Thomas Dorland, Ebenezer Washburn*, and Joshua BOOTH. On 16 July 1792 his responsibilities had increased with his appointment to the land board of Lennox and Addington, Hastings and Prince Edward, with Booth, Alexander Fisher*, Archibald McDonell, and Peter Van Alstine. The county boards were abolished on 6 Nov. 1794. Meanwhile, on 2 Sept. 1793 Spencer had been named a district judge of the surrogate court which granted probates of wills and letters of administration. He resigned this commission some time after 7 Nov. 1795 at Simcoe's insistence because his new military commission would preclude regular attendance. Alexander Fraser succeeded him on 6 July 1796. On 2 Sept. 1797 Spencer was appointed to the first Heir and Devisee Commission for the Midland District, and was reappointed on 21 July 1800. Of four meetings between 16 Sept. 1802 and 3 Sept. 1803, he attended only one.

In 1792 Spencer had been elected to the House of Assembly for the riding of Lennox, Hastings and Northumberland. His election to the first parliament was not without incident. On 2 Sept. 1792 Ebenezer Washburn swore before a magistrate that Spencer "did obtain the said Election through the Partiality of the Returning Officer." Spencer commented derogatorily upon the character of Washburn, who had falsely accused him of usurping his property in 1786. Spencer's remarks led to an action on 15 Jan. 1793 in the Court of Common Pleas which culminated on 30 March with Washburn's withdrawing because of his inability to produce out-of-district witnesses. Little is known of Spencer's efforts as an assemblyman but in 1794 Simcoe described him as "one of the most respectable Members." In July 1796 Simcoe designated Spencer, Hugh McDonell* (Aberchalder), and Hector McLean as alternates for Richard CARTWRIGHT, John McDONELL (Aberchalder), and John Munro*, the commissioners appointed in 1794 and reappointed two years later to negotiate with Lower Canada agreements to share the customs revenue of the port of Quebec.

The position which best reflects Spencer's local prominence and the esteem in which he was held by

Simcoe was his appointment to the lieutenancy of the county of Lennox on 23 June 1794. This office, modelled on the lord lieutenancies of counties in England, Simcoe conceived as "making a due provision of Power for that legal Aristocracy, which the Experience of Ages has proved necessary to the Ballance & Permanency of her inestimable form of Government." In accordance with British practice the office was conferred upon those "who seem most respectable . . . for their property, Loyalty, Abilities, . . . and who from a Combination of such Possessions and Qualities acquire that weight, respect, and public confidence which renders them the natural support of constitutional authority." The first Upper Canadian appointments had been made in 1792; appointments in other counties came later when their population had grown sufficiently. Usually the lieutenants were chosen from among the legislative councillors or the local senior militia officers. Their duties were to superintend the magistracy and the militia and to appoint or to recommend the magistrates and nominate the officers of militia, subject only to the lieutenant governor's approval. The experiment was a failure. The appointments were for life but no new ones were made after 1807 and by 1812 changes in the militia laws rendered the post largely honorary.

J. K. JOHNSON

AO, MU 3054, "Returns of loyalists quartered at St. Johns, Canada, March 1st, 1781 . . ."; RG 1, A-II-1, 1: 217; A-II-5, 2, 16 Sept. 1802; 2 May, 1, 3 Sept. 1803; RG 22, ser.04, 6: 15, 30 Jan. 1793; ser.54, 1–2; RG 53, ser.2-2, 2: f.245. Lennox and Addington County Museum (Napanee, Ont.), Lennox and Addington Hist. Soc. Coll., T. W. Casey papers: 11411–16 (mfm. at PAC). MTL, William Dummer Powell papers, B85: 66–67; B87: 21. PAC, MG 11, [CO 42] Q, 306: 150; MG 24, D49; RG 1, L3, 447a: S misc. 10; 448: S1/158; 450; 451; 452; 453; 494: S misc., 1788–95/140; RG 5, A1: 2178–79; RG 68, General index, 1651–1841: ff.248, 250, 292, 329, 406, 411, 419–20, 538, 542. *Corr. of Lieut. Governor Simcoe* (Cruikshank), 1: 245; 2: 297–98; 3: 47, 234–35, 259; 4: 131, 327; 5: 234, 327. *Kingston before War of 1812* (Preston), 210. "Notes on land tenure in Canada to A.D. 1800," AO *Report*, 1905: cviii. "Rev. John Langhorn's records, 1787–1813: burials," *OH*, 1 (1899): 63. "United Empire Loyalists: enquiry into losses and services," AO *Report*, 1904: 421, 460. "U.C. land book C," AO *Report*, 1931: 35, 91. Armstrong, *Handbook of Upper Canadian chronology*, 58. Reid, *Loyalists in Ont.*, 305. J. R. Robertson, *The history of freemasonry in Canada from its introduction in 1749 . . .* (2v., Toronto, 1900), 1: 402. T. W. Casey, "Our first representatives in parliament," Lennox and Addington Hist. Soc., *Papers and Records* (Napanee), 4 (1912): 29–33.

SPROULE (Sprowle), GEORGE, army officer, surveyor, office holder, and politician; b. *c.* 1743 in Athlone (Republic of Ireland), eldest son of Adam Sproule and Prudence Lloyd; d. 30 Nov. 1817 in Fredericton, N.B.

George Sproule was born into a military family. After receiving his early education in Athlone and nearby Dublin, he joined the British army in 1762 as an ensign in the 121st Foot and trained as a surveyor and engineer. He eventually attained the rank of captain and was referred to by that title until his death. Of the five children known to have been born to Sproule and his wife Alicia, two sons followed their father into the army and two of his three daughters married military officers.

Sproule's major achievements were in the field of surveying. In 1766, while stationed at Louisbourg, N.S., with the 59th Foot (to which he had transferred the previous year), he was added to the staff of the noted surveyor Captain Samuel Johannes HOLLAND, who described him as "very fit in Knowledge and Constitution for this Business." At that time Joseph Frederick Wallet DesBarres*, James Cook*, and Holland were all busy conducting extensive surveys of the Atlantic coastal region for the British government. In 1766 and 1767 Sproule worked with Holland on Cape Breton Island, and then joined with Thomas WRIGHT and others in mapping the shores of the lower St Lawrence. Anticosti Island and a stretch of the Labrador coast were also surveyed.

In 1770 Sproule was in the party that surveyed the eastern New England coast in conjunction with work being done by DesBarres. His surveying and mapping efforts were eventually incorporated into DesBarres's famous compilation *The Atlantic Neptune . . .* (2v., London, 1777-[81]). Engaged from 1772 in the first thorough survey of New Hampshire's boundaries, Sproule was two years later appointed surveyor general of that colony, a post he held until the American Revolutionary War broke out. Although he had obtained permission to retire from the army in order to establish his family permanently in New Hampshire, at the commencement of hostilities he returned to active service as a lieutenant in the 16th Foot. Having joined the British army in Boston, Mass., he was immediately named an assistant field engineer. On 9 June 1781 he purchased a captaincy in the 16th, "observing but little probability of being restored to his appointment and property in New Hampshire." The following year his lands there were confiscated by the state. At the end of the war Sproule found himself in a difficult situation: not only had he lost both position and property, but he faced the prospect of reduction on half pay. "Justice to his Family" prompted him to sell his company, though he could get only half the price for it that he might have obtained during the war. In memorials to the loyalist claims commission he estimated that his total losses as a result of the revolution exceeded £2,300. In compensation, and as a reward for his military service

Stayeghtha

and his surveying work, he was appointed on 2 Sept. 1784 surveyor general of the recently established colony of New Brunswick at a salary of £150 per annum.

In the spring of 1785 Sproule energetically took up his new post, which he would hold until his death. He was a significant figure in the province's administrative history because he established the Surveyor General's Office, created and maintained essential land records, and in so doing offered a high degree of stability for new settlers during a particularly turbulent time. On his arrival he found matters "in a very perplexed state": earlier surveys had to be corrected and descriptions of grants regularized. He had also to organize his staff, establish guidelines for their activities, and develop procedures for the maintenance of adequate records. A large number of deputy surveyors were appointed, among them Israel PERLEY and Abraham IREDELL, and under Sproule's supervision they undertook the immense task of surveying land for some 12,000 loyalist refugees. Sproule, who insisted on high standards and did much to improve surveying techniques, was also responsible for laying out roads and reserves and for establishing parish and county boundary lines. Provincial boundaries were a matter of concern as well. In 1787 Lieutenant Governor Thomas CARLETON asked Sproule to meet with Hugh FINLAY of Quebec to discuss the conflicting claims of the two colonies to the Madawaska region, a dispute that was eventually settled in New Brunswick's favour. That same year Sproule laid out lots for the Acadians who had settled in this region [see Louis MERCURE]. In 1795 he acted as a surveyor and map-maker in the efforts to determine the Maine–New Brunswick boundary, and three years later he combined the results of surveys done by Dugald CAMPBELL, Thomas Wright, and others into one general map for the use of the commissioners.

Sproule – "that correct, faithful & devoted officer," as Edward WINSLOW described him – was one of New Brunswick's most influential and active government officials during the first decades after the creation of the new province. Not only did he carry out his surveying assignments in an efficient manner, but he further assisted the government by interesting himself in public works. He was frequently involved in the construction of roads and bridges, and he helped erect the new House of Assembly building and the Surveyor General's Office. In 1805 he took on the added responsibility of acting as the province's receiver general and in September 1808 he was appointed a member of the Council. He was also regularly involved with the military establishment in Fredericton, where he served as keeper of the military stores. A member of the Church of England, he acted as a churchwarden and vestryman.

George Sproule's long, distinguished career as a surveyor, soldier, and administrator deserves recognition. To New Brunswick he brought valuable experience and a capacity for leadership that greatly helped the young province during its early stages of development. He served as surveyor general for 33 years; the office was to change hands nine times in the three decades after his death in 1817.

ROBERT FELLOWS

Anglican Church of Canada, Diocese of Fredericton Arch., Christ Church (Fredericton), minutes, 1793–1818 (mfm. at PANB). Old Burying Ground (Fredericton), George and Alicia Sproule, tombstone. PANB, RG 2, RS6, 1: 283; 2: 13; RG 7, RS75, George Sproule, 1817. PRO, AO 12/100: 300; AO 13, bundles 52–53, 79; CO 188/4: 46; 188/15: 74; 188/23: 30–31. Royal Irish Academy (Dublin), Upton papers, no.7, "The Sproules since 1669" (typescript). [S. J. Holland], *Holland's description of Cape Breton Island and other documents*, comp. D. C. Harvey (Halifax, 1935). *Royal commission on American loyalists* (Coke and Egerton). *Winslow papers* (Raymond), 461, 514. G.B., WO, *Army list*, 1762–81. MacNutt, *New Brunswick*, 80–81, 119–20. Murdoch, *Hist. of N.S.*, 2: 128. E. S. Stackpole, *History of New Hampshire* (4v., New York, [1916]), 2: 64–65. D. W. Thomson, *Men and meridians: the history of surveying and mapping in Canada* (3v., Ottawa, 1966–69), 1: 105, 112, 141. Robert Fellows, "The loyalists and land settlement in New Brunswick, 1783–1790: a study in colonial administration," *Canadian Archivist* ([Calgary]), 2 (1970–74), no.2: 5–15.

STAYEGHTHA (Stiahta, Tey-yagh-taw, Ustaiechta, Roundhead), Wyandot war chief; b. mid 18th century; d. 1813 in the Detroit River region.

There was a Wyandot village called Roundhead's Town (Roundhead, Ohio) on the upper Scioto River at the beginning of the 19th century, but at the time Roundhead appears most prominently in the historical record he lived in the Detroit River region. It is likely that he fought in the wars of the early 1790s against the Americans, for he participated in the Treaty of Greenville in 1795, arriving at the council from the vicinity of Detroit with a party of Wyandots, Shawnees, Six Nations, and Delawares. Although he came at the end of July, when proceedings were almost over, he signed the agreement, by which the defeated Indians gave up most of present-day Ohio and part of Indiana. In September 1800 he put his name to a treaty relinquishing to the crown some 2,500 acres on the Canadian side of the Detroit River.

From an early date Roundhead was closely linked with the Prophet [Tenskwatawa*] and TECUMSEH in the movement they organized to defend Indian culture and lands from further white encroachment. In 1807 he was one of the commissioners, along with Tecumseh, Blue Jacket [WEYAPIERSENWAH], and the Panther, sent by an Indian council at Greenville to assure the governor of Ohio that the Prophet intended

Stewart

only peace. Two years later Roundhead was apparently involved, probably under the Prophet's direction, in the execution of the Wyandot chief Leatherlips on a charge of witchcraft.

On the eve of the War of 1812 Roundhead was chief of a group of some 60 Wyandots living on the Canard River (near Windsor), Upper Canada. He became one of the most active of the Indian leaders in the fighting in the Detroit frontier region, no doubt believing as did Tecumseh that alliance with the British offered the only chance of preserving Indian lands from the tide of American settlement. In August 1812 he helped lead the Indians in the engagement at Maguaga (Wyandotte, Mich.) and was prominent in the capture of Detroit. An anecdote first published in 1818 relates that on the latter occasion Tecumseh presented Roundhead with the crimson sash given to him by Brock, commenting that the honour should go to an older and abler warrior.

In September 1812 Roundhead participated in Major Adam C. Muir's unsuccessful expedition against Fort Wayne (Ind.). In January, while Tecumseh was absent, Roundhead and Myeerah led a force of some 500 or 600 Indians in the British-Indian victory over the Americans at Frenchtown (Monroe, Mich.). Roundhead continued to be active throughout the spring of 1813. With Tecumseh he commanded about 1,200 Indians at the siege of Fort Meigs (near Perrysburg, Ohio) in April and May, and his brother Jean-Baptiste was killed during the fighting. At the time American general William Henry Harrison was preparing to invade Upper Canada in September he commented that Roundhead was "entirely in the British interest." Late in the following month, without giving any details, Major-General Henry Procter* stated that "the Indian Cause and ours experienced a serious Loss in the Death of Roundhead."

REGINALD HORSMAN

PRO, CO 42/152: 66–69. *Canada, Indian treaties and surrenders* . . . [1680–1906] (3v., Ottawa, 1891–1912; repr. Toronto, 1971), 1: 1–3, 30–31. *Indian affairs: laws and treaties*, comp. C. J. Kappler ([2nd ed.], 2v., Washington, 1904), 2: 44. *Messages and letters of William Henry Harrison*, ed. Logan Esarey (2v., Indianapolis, Ind., 1922), 2: 537. *Mich. Pioneer Coll.*, 15 (1889): 151–54; 25 (1894): 431. Norton, *Journal* (Klinck and Talman), 300–1, 314–15. "Policy and practice of the United States and Great Britain in their treatment of Indians," *North American Rev.* (Boston), 24 (January–April 1827): 422, 424. [John Richardson], *Richardson's War of 1812; with notes and a life of the author*, ed. A. C. Casselman (Toronto, 1902; repr. 1974), 134–35, 296, 299. *Select British docs. of War of 1812* (Wood), 2: 8, 323, 423. U.S., Congress, *American state papers* (Lowrie et al.), class II, [1]: 578.

Handbook of American Indians (Hodge), 2: 397. Benjamin Drake, *Life of Tecumseh, and of his brother, the Prophet* . . . (Cincinnati, Ohio, 1850), 94–97, 118. B. J.

Lossing, *The pictorial field-book of the War of 1812* . . . (New York, 1868), 291. Erminie Wheeler-Voegelin, *An ethnohistorical report on the Wyandot, Potawatomi, Ottawa, and Chippewa of northwest Ohio* (New York, 1974), 248. Ludwig Kosche, "Relics of Brock: an investigation," *Archivaria* (Ottawa), no.9 (winter 1979–80): 33–103.

STEWART, CHARLES, office holder, lawyer, politician, army officer, and land agent; b. *c.* 1759 in Campbeltown, Scotland, second son of Peter Stewart and Helen MacKinnon; d. 6 Jan. 1813 in Charlottetown, P.E.I.

In 1775 Charles Stewart accompanied his family to St John's (Prince Edward) Island, where his father had been appointed chief justice. A collector of offices – frequently as a deputy doing the work of others – he received his first appointments in 1784, as deputy surveyor of pines for the Island and deputy mustermaster of the disbanded troops and loyalists both on the Island and in Nova Scotia. That same year he assisted his father and his elder brother, John*, in their successful opposition to Lieutenant Governor Walter Patterson* in the House of Assembly elections, and was admitted an attorney before his father's Supreme Court. About this time as well he married Mary, daughter of Thomas Desbrisay, thus cementing an alliance (initiated by his sister Margaret and Theophilus DesBrisay*) between the Island's two most extensive families; the couple were to have 13 children.

Charles's career received a considerable boost during the administration of Lieutenant Governor Edmund Fanning, a 17-year period in the course of which the Stewart clan became closely associated with the executive. First elected to the assembly in 1790 from Prince County, he served in 1797 on the committee which reported on Island settlement and recommended that the proprietors either be compelled to fulfil the terms of their grants or have their lots escheated and regranted to residents. This stand assured him easy re-election in 1803 and 1806.

Although in 1800 Attorney General John Wentworth dismissed Stewart as deputy clerk of the Supreme Court for neglect of duty, he was still a principal office holder, having obtained posts as acting clerk of the Council (where he deputized for his father-in-law), coroner of the crown, clerk of the errors, registrar in Chancery, receiver of inland duties, overseer of working parties for the engineering department, assistant acting engineer, and lieutenant (later captain) in one of the Island's fencible companies. According to one hostile observer, John Hill*, Stewart "had a share" in "all the disputes in the island," generally as "the Governor's Agent and Messenger, when any particular plan was to be set on foot, in which the Governor did not care to appear himself." The loss of his Supreme Court appointment

Stewart

proved a blessing in disguise: by 1802 Stewart was again practising before the courts as an attorney, and he ultimately made a reputation as one of the most able lawyers on the Island.

When in 1804 John Stewart left to become paymaster general to the forces in Newfoundland, Charles became his brother's deputy as receiver of quitrents. Moreover, absentee landowners increasingly turned to him as their local agent, since by this time the Stewarts had made peace with the proprietors in Britain and had become the backbone of their opposition to the administration of Lieutenant Governor Joseph Frederick Wallet DesBarres*. The Stewart faction and the proprietors feared that DesBarres would reopen the land question on the Island, which had been solved to their satisfaction in 1803 with a compromise on the issue of quitrents in arrears. In 1807 Charles was appointed solicitor general, and the success of his career was assured that same year when the Island's principal absentee landholder, the Earl of Selkirk [DOUGLAS], began to put his business into Stewart's hands. On his visits to the Island in 1803 and 1804 Selkirk had been impressed with Stewart's efficiency and knowledge, and by 1810 he was prepared to turn management of his extensive estates over to the Charlottetown attorney. Added to Stewart's other agencies – which included work for the Dundas, Ellice, and Montgomery family interests – the Selkirk connection made him, as he was described in 1810, the "first employed man of business on the Island."

When Attorney General Peter MAGOWAN died in 1810, Stewart was an obvious candidate to replace him. DesBarres opposed Stewart on the grounds that he had only a local education, which afforded "but little knowledge in theory and still less in practice." But the British proprietors were frightened by James Bardin Palmer*, the lieutenant governor's candidate, and, led by Selkirk, succeeded in gaining Stewart the appointment and forcing an investigation of the Loyal Electors, a society that Palmer had helped to organize. This group had entered the political fray in the elections of 1806 in opposition to the official clique, known by its enemies as the "cabal," which had long dominated Island politics and of which Stewart was now the acknowledged leader. Soon after Stewart became attorney general, a packet containing protested bills of exchange drawn by Palmer was placed on the doorstep of his house with the message "Now have at him, Amen – Peter M'Auslane Esq." M'Auslane denied vehemently any involvement in the incident, which nevertheless contributed to a rapidly escalating political crisis. In a hotly contested election in 1812 Stewart was defeated as a candidate for the House of Assembly. Though the Loyal Electors managed to increase their representation, they could not counteract the influence of the proprietors in Britain:

DesBarres was recalled in August 1812 and Palmer was stripped of all his public offices. While these events were taking place Stewart was ordered to attend the September session of the House of Assembly to answer questions about his conduct. He refused, according to one witness replying he would be "damned if he would attend the House." In ill health, he died soon afterwards.

Charles Stewart and his brother John had been an effective partnership for many years in furthering the family's economic and political interests. Unlike John, whose personal notoriety and hot temper had brought him the sobriquet "Hellfire Jack," Charles was a man who preferred to work quietly behind the scenes rather than in the public eye. His epitaph was pronounced by his close friend Caesar Colclough*, who described him as a man "intimately acquainted with the Private Thoughts of any individual on the Island as well as his circumstances." In contrast to most Island politicians, Stewart was a political manager and did not profit personally from his activities; he died in penury, leaving a large family who lived in poverty for many years.

J. M. BUMSTED

National Library of Ireland (Dublin), Dept. of MSS, MS 20287 (5) (O'Hara papers), Caesar Colclough to Charles O'Hara, 13 Jan. 1813. PAC, MG 11, [CO 226] Prince Edward Island A, 17: 437; MG 19, E1, ser.1, 39: 14929–31, 14977–15005 (transcripts); MG 23, D1, ser.1, 25–27 (transcripts at PANS). PAPEI, RG 3, House of Assembly, Journals, 1812–13. PRO, 226/25: 13, 80. SRO, GD51/6/1734; GD293/2/78/63–64. Stewart, *Account of P.E.I.* *Weekly Recorder of Prince Edward Island* (Charlottetown), 26 Dec. 1811. D. C. Harvey, "The Loyal Electors," RSC *Trans.*, 3rd ser., 24 (1930), sect.II: 101–10. MacNutt, "Fanning's regime on P.E.I.," *Acadiensis* (Fredericton), 1, no.1: 37–53.

STEWART, PETER, judge and politician; b. 1725 in Campbeltown, Scotland; d. 10 Oct. 1805 in Charlottetown, P.E.I.

Peter Stewart was a younger son of the Reverend Charles Stuart and Annabella Campbell, daughter of John Campbell of Kildalloig, chamberlain of Kintyre. His father was the Church of Scotland minister at Campbeltown from 1709 to 1765. Peter was apprenticed to an Edinburgh lawyer, served for some years as a law clerk in that city, and subsequently engaged in an unsuccessful fishing business in his native village. In 1758 he married Helen MacKinnon, and they had several children, including John* and CHARLES of Island fame. Left a widower about 1770, Stewart married Sarah Hamilton, daughter of a Captain Hamilton of Drummond and first cousin to Ralph Abercromby, later a distinguished British general. The precise number of Stewart's children is not known.

Family interest in St John's (Prince Edward) Island began in 1770, when Peter's brother Robert undertook a settlement of Highlanders on Lot 18. The venture was not very successful, but the attempt gave Robert some influence with other proprietors and the British government, which he used – with the assistance of Scotland's lord advocate, James William Montgomery – to secure the chief justiceship for his struggling brother in 1775. Paying a salary of only £200 per annum out of the uncollected quitrents of the Island, the appointment was hardly a plum and had gone begging for some time after the death in penury of John Duport in 1774. But Peter lacked proper qualifications for any judicial appointment and could not afford to be selective; moreover, what legal training he had was in Scottish law rather than the English common law that Whitehall always expected to serve as the basis for a colonial judicial system. Since he was already the father of nine children, his principal recommendation for the position was financial need.

Taking up his new opportunity with alacrity, Stewart offered to arrange the transportation of emigrants for Montgomery, and negotiated with Montgomery's partner David Higgins* to lease a large farm on Lot 34. Full of enthusiasm in June 1775, the new chief justice expected no problem in acquiring tenants, "from the passion the Lower Sort of People here have for emigrating." But the accounts of the beginning of the American rebellion – and of hard times on the Island – slowly trickled into Scotland and alarmed prospective emigrants. Stewart himself had second thoughts about a hasty departure into the unknown, claiming he required more time to organize his party. Montgomery, however, refused to encourage delay, believing that, having been made chief justice, Stewart should take up the appointment. Thus Stewart's little group (his wife, two sons, three daughters, and four servants) caught passage at Cork aboard the vessel *Elizabeth*, which set sail for the Island on 10 Sept. 1775.

The autumn voyage was a rough one, but otherwise uneventful. The vessel avoided Yankee privateers, and the only violence experienced was a fight between another gentleman's servant and Jack Stewart in which the youngster was badly cut. His father was extremely upset, and, reported fellow-passenger Thomas Curtis, "If we had got in safe that night as expected I cant gues the consequence as the Judge seem^d a Pasionate man." Instead, the vessel hove to off the north coast of the Island for several days, eventually becoming grounded and breaking up on an uninhabited sand-bar. All passengers were saved but, despite the efforts of George HARDY and others, most of the baggage and freight was lost. The chief justice thus spent his first 16 nights on the Island in a hastily erected wigwam, and was now without almost all his

personal effects including books, clothes, furniture, and provisions. It was not an auspicious beginning for a career in the colonies.

When Stewart finally made his way to Charlottetown in early December 1775, he found little to encourage him. The town had just been pillaged by privateers and the leading government officials, Phillips Callbeck* and Thomas WRIGHT, carried off to Massachusetts. Stewart would later complain that his supposedly improved farm on Lot 34 contained nothing but "a small Hovel not in any respect habitable," and that this solitary building, more than seven miles from Charlottetown, was accessible only by water. Application to London for relief from his losses and for a dwelling-house in the town at public expense was to take some years to produce results. Because of wartime isolation Stewart did not receive his commission as chief justice until July 1776, and, like other officers of the government, he collected no salary until the Island's establishment was put on parliamentary grant in 1777. Nevertheless, like his colleagues, he had to maintain a certain standard of living. Despite his reservations about Lot 34 he attempted to settle it with tenants, and he engaged in some private trading. Throughout the war Stewart lived off credit and the hope that his official position might be turned to advantage in more ways than obtaining numerous public appointments for his sons.

The first real opportunity for the chief justice came in 1779–80, when acting governor Thomas DESBRISAY employed the absence of Governor Walter Patterson* to distribute wholesale to himself and his associates the crown lots in Charlottetown that had not yet been granted to settlers. Many lots were awarded to garrison soldiers, who sold them for a pittance, while others were given directly to councillors on the strength of their large families. Stewart, whose daughter had married young Theophilus DesBrisay*, ended up in possession of 41 town lots and 41 pasture lots, a total exceeded only by the acquisitions of the acting governor himself. Upon his return in the summer of 1780, an enraged Patterson demanded that the lots be handed back. Along with his associates, Stewart refused to comply unless directly ordered to by the home authorities, and Desbrisay wrote to London attempting to explain away the whole sorry business. It was to be three years before the issue was resolved, and then in Patterson's favour, but the governor's attitude would ultimately back-fire upon him.

Meanwhile, the land question came to the fore in an even more serious fashion. On 26 Nov. 1780 a Council meeting, attended by Stewart, agreed unanimously to implement a Treasury minute of 7 Aug. 1776 ordering the Island's receiver general to enforce the payment of quitrents on many of the township lots into which the island had been divided in 1767. The lots of those in arrears were not to be sold until the end

Stewart

of June 1781, and in the mean time advertisements were to be placed three times in the *London Gazette* warning proprietors in Britain that the consequences of non-payment would be distraint or sale of the lots. It is not clear how the Council – given the communications of the time – expected to follow such a timetable, which allowed only seven months for a complicated series of warnings to be received and acted upon. Nor is Stewart's relationship to subsequent government actions easily understood.

When the Privy Council in 1789 conducted an inquiry into the land sales, Stewart submitted a memorial in which he attempted to dissociate himself from the events that had led to Patterson's dismissal. He denied that he had supported the Council's action of 26 Nov. 1780, or its decision of 19 Feb. 1781 to eliminate a critical clause of the Quit Rent Act of 1774 by dispensing with the necessity of distraint; he insisted that on the latter occasion he had advised the governor to have the clause repealed by the House of Assembly instead of in Council. The chief justice argued that, once Patterson had ordered the receiver general of quitrents to institute proceedings against the delinquent lots in the Supreme Court, he had acted to pass judgement against them only in the absence of any defence on the part of the proprietors, and that he could not have interfered in the judicial proceedings. (In 1783, however, he had acknowledged to Montgomery that he viewed the foundations of those proceedings as legally dubious.) He maintained that, when the lots were eventually put up for sale in November 1781, he had bid, successfully, on half of Lot 18 only because, holding the other half of the township, he sought to prevent the part up for sale from getting into the hands of others. (Nevertheless, testimony from Callbeck in 1784 indicated that he had also bid heavily for Lot 35 and was unsuccessful in acquiring it only because he would not pay the price.) Stewart further claimed that, after landowners in Britain had persuaded the imperial authorities of the impropriety of the sales, he was one of four members out of ten at the Council meeting of 20 March 1784 who voted to obey the royal order to place legislation rescinding the sales before the assembly, but that his dissent from the majority had not been entered on the record.

Despite his later denials, Stewart had undoubtedly tacitly supported Patterson and his friends in the initial proceedings against the proprietors in 1780 and 1781. But by 1784 he had plainly broken with Patterson and was entitled to plead innocence in the governor's subsequent defiance of Whitehall. Two provocations by Patterson account for Stewart's shift. One dated back to the Charlottetown lot business. In early 1783 Patterson had read to the Council a letter from the lords of Trade (dated 20 June 1781) opining that the Charlottetown lot transactions were most improper,

and sufficient to justify dismissal for Desbrisay and censure for the others involved, including Stewart. Patterson thereupon proceeded in a self-righteous manner to force return of the lots – although he himself was then holding eight and a half 20,000-acre lots, some of which had been purchased through dummies at the 1781 auction. The inconsistency of Patterson and the embarrassment of having abjectly to restore the lots might be enough for any "passionate man," but about the same time Patterson had "compromised" Stewart's wife, Sarah. Exactly what the governor and Mrs Stewart had done was never made clear, but the chief justice banished her from his house and Patterson removed her to Quebec at his expense.

In any event, by early 1784 the "Stewart party" (led by Jack Stewart but including the Desbrisays and the Townshends) was in the field actively opposing Patterson. In the assembly elections of that spring the chief justice appeared publicly to corroborate his eldest son's insistence that vast new taxes were contemplated by the government, a spectre which led to an easy victory for the Stewart "list" of candidates. This assembly at its first meeting produced a laudatory resolution requesting a substantial salary increase for the chief justice, but Patterson soon dissolved it and planned another election for 1785. Not surprisingly, Stewart wrote to the Home secretary in June 1784, "I have every reason to believe an attempt is now to be made of depriving me of my place of Chief Justice, which I have held since 1775, and of turning me and my numerous family of eleven children out of our only subsistance." Indeed, soon after the 1785 election had destroyed the popular power of the Stewart party, Patterson suspended the chief justice for his political opposition to the government, and particularly "for divulging a secret of Council at the hustings during the time of polling, by saying the Governor intended laying a heavy tax upon the country." According to Solicitor General Joseph APLIN in 1788, the suspension was *pro hac vice*, not intended permanently to affect either Stewart's "Bread" or his dignity. Aplin observed at this time that Stewart was "A Gentleman well stocked with legal Information, and, I believe, possesses the Principles of a Man of . . . Honour."

As might have been expected, the Stewarts actively supported the new lieutenant governor, Edmund FANNING, in his year-long struggle to wrest control of the Island government from Patterson, and in 1789 Jack Stewart personally argued his father's case for restoration to office before the Privy Council. The subsequent decision in London to reinstate Stewart merely confirmed an action which Fanning had taken on his own initiative in June 1789. Soon afterwards, in a last gasp of the old factional warfare of the 1780s, a pro-Patterson group of merchant proprietors (led by John Cambridge*, William Bowley, and John Hill*), insisting that they were being persecuted by the vengeful Stewart clan, brought a series of complaints against Fanning and his leading officers before the Privy Council in 1791. The charges against Stewart – of using his office for political purposes by perverting law in his judgements, of disregarding and refusing evidence, of condoning the malpractice of Aplin (now attorney general), of misdirecting and influencing juries – were not always well documented. But the complainants had a far better case against Stewart than against the other officers, and they might have had more success with the chief justice had they not alleged a conspiracy they could not prove. Thus, only three years after his reinstatement, Stewart was saved by the excesses of his opponents. With Fanning, Aplin, and son-in-law William TOWNSHEND, the chief justice was exonerated by the Privy Council in 1792. He had once again managed to survive.

Despite his exoneration and an increasingly close political alliance with Fanning in the 1790s, Stewart continued to come under considerable criticism for judicial partiality. The fact that one son (Charles) was clerk of the Supreme Court, and another (Jack) its most frequent customer either as plaintiff or defendant, clearly made the chief justice vulnerable. What eventually brought his resignation, however, was a lengthy legal struggle with James William Montgomery. The issue was Stewart's lease of 1,000 acres on Lot 34, for which he had never paid any rental. James DOUGLAS, Montgomery's agent, took Stewart to court in 1797, but complained he could get no justice. Although Montgomery was prepared to compromise, he was enraged when Stewart sued him in the Court of Chancery in 1798 on the basis of uncorroborated statements and half-truths about the initial agreement and subsequent negotiations with Montgomery. The Montgomery–Stewart dispute got entangled with larger political issues on the Island, including the escheat movement (which the Stewarts, with an eye to personal gain, were supporting), the dismissal of Attorney General Aplin, the attacks on Captain John MacDONALD of Glenaladale, and the shuffling of Aplin's replacement John WENTWORTH out of his post after only a few months in office. Montgomery, who for some years had been Scotland's chief legal officer, was not to be out-manœuvered by a colonial judge. In 1801 he wrote Fanning that the chief justice "most likely thinks his power and Influence will prevent any Decree being recovered against him, and that he will tire me out, and make me drop my Action." Insisting "this is not a good Idea in a Chief Justice," Montgomery threatened to bring the proceedings to England, where "they will exhibit a Picture, if the same System is continued, that never before Appeared in any English Judicature." But Stewart had been induced the previous year to step down as chief justice before his activities led to yet

another Whitehall investigation of the Fanning administration. He remained a member of the Council until his death in Charlottetown in 1805. He was survived by a large family of sons and sons-in-law who continued to dominate Island politics for a generation. Whatever his achievements as a judge, Stewart had founded a political dynasty.

J. M. BUMSTED

PAC, MG 11, [CO 226] Prince Edward Island A, 17: 427; MG 23, E12 (transcripts; photocopies at PAPEI). PANS, MG 1, 793, Joseph Aplin to Jonathan Stearns, 14 May 1788. PAPEI, Acc. 2541, Natural Hist. Soc. for P.E.I., item 79; Acc. 2702, Smith–Alley coll., "Minutes of the proceedings of the proprietors of St. John's Island, June 17, 1790–January 27, 1791." PRO, BT 6/102 (copy at PAPEI); CO 226/1: 180–83, 185; 226/7: 75–78, 219–23; 226/8: 71–83, 161–77; 226/9: 71–73; CO 229/1: 180–83, 185. SRO, GD293/2/17/12; 293/2/78/32–34, 45–46, 48, 52a, 59–60, 65–66; 293/2/79/46.

Thomas Curtis, "Voyage of Thos. Curtis," *Journeys to the Island of St. John or Prince Edward Island, 1775–1832*, ed. D. C. Harvey (Toronto, 1955). G.B., Privy Council, *Report of the right honourable the lords of the committee of his majesty's most honourable Privy Council, of certain complaints against Lieutenant Governor Fanning, and other officers of his majesty's government in the Island of St. John* ([London, 1792]); Hist. MSS Commission, *The manuscripts of the Earl of Dartmouth* (3v., London, 1887–96), 2: 605–6. Hew Scott et al., *Fasti ecclesiæ scoticanæ: the succession of ministers in the Church of Scotland from the Reformation* (new ed., 9v. to date, Edinburgh, 1915–), 4: 52. A. B. Warburton, *A history of Prince Edward Island from its discovery in 1534 until the departure of Lieutenant-Governor Ready in A.D. 1831* (Saint John, N.B., 1923), 419, 421. Bumsted, "Sir James Montgomery and P.E.I.," *Acadiensis* (Fredericton), 7, no.2: 76–102.

STIAHTA. *See* STAYEGHTHA

STOUT, RICHARD, merchant, politician, judge, and office holder; b. *c.* 1756; m. 4 Dec. 1797 Martha Wingate Weeks in Guysborough, N.S., and they had five daughters and a son; d. 26 Oct. 1820 in Sydney, N.S.

Richard Stout appears to have come from a New York loyalist family, and there is some possibility that the wife of Jonathan Tremaine*, a loyalist who became a merchant in Halifax, N.S., was his sister. Stout came to Cape Breton some time before December 1788, probably from Halifax, as the local agent and partner of Tremaine. Little is known about the activities of their firm, but Stout appears to have imported mainly general merchandise. Since capital and supplies were scarce in the young colony, he immediately assumed a position of importance, and on 25 April 1791 he was elected to the prestigious position of vestryman of St George's Church in Sydney.

Stout

In May of the following year Lieutenant Governor William MACARMICK transferred the lease for the Sydney coal mines to Stout and Tremaine, which he described as "the principle and indeed the only respectable [mercantile firm] in this place." The mines had been well known for some time, but the British government had persisted in refusing to lease them. Prior to 1784 only the army, a few small operators, and some smugglers had worked the deposits, and in a haphazard fashion, sinking pits and then abandoning them. In 1784, however, Lieutenant Governor Joseph Frederick Wallet DesBarres* had opened regular works at present-day Sydney Mines. His successor, Macarmick, complained that the mines were a source of great expense to the government and strongly recommended that they be leased privately. In January 1788 they were leased to one Thomas Moxley on condition that a government duty be paid on each chaldron mined. The mines developed slowly owing to a lack of capital investment by Moxley, but a report in 1790 of John WENTWORTH, surveyor general of the king's woods in North America, encouraged Macarmick by stating that coal could now compete favourably with wood on the Nova Scotian market. Upon Moxley's death in 1792 Macarmick therefore leased the mines to Stout and Tremaine, who he believed were capable of running them in a more businesslike manner and thus increasing coal exports. The lease was to run for seven years, Stout and Tremaine then becoming tenants at will. Each chaldron mined would be subject to a government duty of five shillings. In order to facilitate the shipping of coal and supplies, Stout began building ships at nearby Big Bras d'Or, and a seagoing vessel was constructed there in 1797.

Miners were hired by Stout from among the Irishmen who had worked in the Newfoundland fishery, and they were paid in supplies shipped by Tremaine. James Miller, who was sent out by the British government in 1792 to supervise the operation of the mines, described this system, in a 1794 report, as making the labourers "bound to his Employer's Shop, Here also they are obliged to take up Articles . . . which they have no occasion to exchange . . . for such as they require." Because the supplies had a high cost, the miners were in constant debt to Stout, who indeed acknowledged that he made most of his profits from this trade and not from the sale of coal.

Since the colliers employed at the mines were not experienced, wasteful and inefficient production methods drove up costs. Miller in his report stated that Stout was "totally unintelligent in Coal Works," and that the mines' full potential was not being exploited. Rather than improve efficiency, Stout brought pressure to bear on Macarmick, claiming that he could not make the mines profitable, and in 1794 the lieutenant governor reduced the duty by one shilling per chaldron. This action lowered prices without threatening Stout's profits.

Not only the miners were in debt to Stout; officials such as David Mathews*, who lived on fixed salaries, were in especially straitened circumstances and thus dependent on Stout's credit. Mathews, who became administrator of the colony on Macarmick's departure in May 1795, appointed Stout to the Executive Council in 1797 to replace William McKINNON. Though he generally avoided the political squabbles that plagued the colony, preferring to watch his own interests, Stout came into conflict with Brigadier-General John Murray*, the colony's fifth ruler. After he took office in 1799 Murray came to believe that Stout was allowing the mines to run down and was not producing coal quickly enough. When Murray demanded that new pits be opened, Stout claimed that the old level which was being worked would last for two more years and that new pits would not be required until the following spring. Murray did not agree and, making use of the terms of the lease, took over the mines himself in the spring of 1800. He also ended Stout's practice of paying in kind, introducing regular wages for the miners.

These actions antagonized Stout, who consequently opposed Murray in his bid to retain office against the challenge of John Despard*. However, when Despard finally assumed the post of administrator in the autumn of 1800 and decided to lease the mines privately, Stout did not return to mining. Moreover, when in 1810 Tremaine made an offer to take over the lease, Stout did not join him, and concentrated instead on the importing business. Although removed from the Executive Council after Mathews was replaced as administrator, he was reappointed by Despard and remained a councillor until 1812, when he resigned for unknown reasons. Administrator Hugh Swayne* reappointed him, as senior councillor, the following spring, but he was dismissed in 1817 by Lieutenant Governor George Robert Ainslie*. His death coincided with the reannexation of Cape Breton to Nova Scotia. In addition to his council seat Stout held numerous small but significant positions such as general surrogate judge of probate and wills, commissioner of escheats, and acting auditor.

The influence of Richard Stout in Cape Breton affairs is difficult to assess. As the most important merchant and the main creditor in the colony as well as an executive councillor, he undoubtedly had considerable personal power. But since few contemporaries commented on his position (although William SMITH did describe him as a "rich storekeeper and haughty despot"), it must be that any influence Stout possessed was wielded covertly. Stout evidently prospered in Cape Breton, for his will left a total of £4,500 to his daughters and his Sydney residence and nearby farm to his wife. The family enjoyed an eminent position in the colonial society: of his daughters one married Hibbert Binney, rector of St George's Church, another married James Crowdy*, clerk of the council, and a third married David Stewart, the last administrator of Cape Breton.

R. J. Morgan

PAC, MG 11, [CO 217] Cape Breton A, 10, 12. PRO, CO 217/113, 217/117–18. Morgan, "Orphan outpost."

STRAHAN, GREGORY. *See* Trahan, Grégoire

STREET, SAMUEL, businessman, politician, office holder, judge, and militia officer; b. 1753 in Wilton, Conn., son of Samuel Street and Elizabeth Smith; m. Phoebe Van Camp, and they had one daughter; d. 3 Feb. 1815 in Thorold, Upper Canada.

During the early years of the American revolution Samuel Street traded with the Indians on the Susquehanna River. In 1778, animated (according to his daughter) by "attachment to the British cause," he left his family in New York and moved to Fort Niagara (near Youngstown, N.Y.). Throughout the war he operated there as a merchant, provisioning the British military and their Indian allies. On 10 July 1780 he formed a partnership with James Burnet and Francis Goring; Burnet subsequently left the company. In the late summer of the following year Goring also left and Street assumed the company's assets of £7,315 and its debts of £5,256. Unlike Robert Hamilton and Richard Cartwright, Street never developed close ties with the British army and, after the war, the lucrative supply of the garrisons was closed to him. Consequently he fell back on the Indian trade and sales to the Indian Department.

To facilitate the latter he attached himself to the interests of John Butler*, an Indian Department official at Niagara. In August 1785 Street formed a partnership, which would last until 4 Jan. 1797, with Butler's son Andrew. The partners maintained a shop at Fort Niagara and in their first two years of business imported goods worth about £15,000 sterling. The Indian trade, however, was rapidly declining, and they now faced competition from American traders. In 1789 the partners built a sawmill on Fifteen Mile Creek which by 1792 had been sold to John Butler. Their company had acquired the reputation of being corrupt. In 1790 Governor Lord Dorchester [Guy Carleton] ordered an investigation of their activities, which included, it was alleged, selling goods stolen from the Indian Department at their shop. Sir John Johnson* deemed their actions "very extraordinary and unaccountable," but assurances by the partners and John Butler laid the matter to rest.

It is clear that Street was in financial trouble as early as 1788. Indeed the need to discharge his debts forced

him to suspend his operations. That year, hopeful of realizing quick profits, he became involved in the land speculation of Oliver Phelps and Nathaniel Gorham in New York. Street acted as agent for his own firm and several individuals in the Niagara area, including John Butler. Known as the Niagara Company, this group purchased 15 shares in the Phelps–Gorham speculation. When Dorchester got wind of the group's purchase, he expressed in the strongest terms his disapproval of this scheme, which would have dispossessed the Six Nations of more of their New York lands by holding out the attraction of migration to their Grand River settlement in Upper Canada. Street was one of the few unwilling to give up his claim. Although he had difficulty making payment on his share, he did not sell it until much later.

More ambitious was his connection with the land settlement scheme of William Berczy and the German Company. Street acted as their agent and in 1794 agreed to purchase one-quarter of Berczy's share in the company. Street also formed a partnership with Elijah Phelps to supply the venture. At its dissolution in 1796 the company owed both Street and the partnership large sums but only relatively small amounts were recovered.

Street's failure as a land speculator probably severely curtailed his mercantile operations. In 1797 Hamilton wrote that he "is at present free from the incumbrances of Business." Street was not, however, wholly inactive as a merchant after this period. In April 1799, for instance, he supplied the Holland Land Company of New York with more than $500 worth of goods. But it seems likely that thenceforth Street relied on the revenue from his Grove Farm in Willoughby Township and the sale of his Upper Canadian lands. By 1796 he had been granted 1,200 acres, of which he claimed the following year to have improved "upwards of 300 acres." In 1798 he sought from the Executive Council confirmation of title on 8,700 acres, probably acquired by purchase or as payment for debt. Of this land, 3,600 acres were in Willoughby. Most of his holdings must eventually have been sold, for at his death he owned only the 500 acres of Grove Farm, 300 acres immediately adjacent to it, and 200 acres of "good Land in the District of Niagara."

In spite of his meagre success in business, Street's early presence in the peninsula and his membership in the mercantile community gave him a public stature that recommended him for office. In 1787 John Butler suggested him for civil position, and the following year he was named a justice of the peace in the newly established administrative district of Nassau. He did not receive his next commission until 1796 and then it was at the instigation of Lieutenant Governor Simcoe; thereafter he was reappointed continuously until his death. In 1797 Hamilton urged Street's appointment

Street

to the commission that would renegotiate the customs-sharing agreement with Lower Canada, praising him as a man whose "knowledge in the Mercantile Interests of the Province I think equal at least, to that of most of the members of our Community." Administrator Peter RUSSELL agreed, apparently, but was unable to reach Street, who was then in the United States. By 1801 Street had achieved an even greater measure of local prominence as Hamilton's deputy for the county lieutenancy of Lincoln. On 7 Jan. 1807 he was appointed judge of the Niagara District court.

Although not a major merchant himself, Street was part of the district's mercantile community and, as such, sensible of its interests. In 1792 he sought election to Upper Canada's first parliament but was soundly defeated by a former officer of Butler's Rangers, Benjamin PAWLING. The merchants, however, were ascendant in the peninsula during the election of 1796 and Street was returned for 2nd Lincoln. There is little that is particularly noteworthy about his participation in the second parliament, but he did vote with the majority supporting Christopher Robinson*'s bill to extend slavery within the province. On 5 June 1800 he was elected speaker, replacing Surveyor General David William Smith*, in spite of the unanimous opposition of Eastern District members, such as John McDONELL (Aberchalder). The speakership was an important position with a tidy yearly allowance of £200 Halifax currency.

In the election of 1800 the merchant candidates, Street and William Dickson*, were defeated by Ralfe Clench* and Isaac Swayze* as a result of the furore over the proposal by Hamilton and others to make extensive improvements to the Niagara portage. According to the poll clerk, Robert Nichol*, Street lost by 22 votes "though every Exertion was made by his friends." Nichol regretted the unfortunate turn of events because Street's "long Acquaintance with the publick business & active talents would have been of great service to the Country & added respectability to the Legislature." According to some sources Street tried for election again in 1804.

The rise of a parliamentary opposition associated with William WEEKES and Robert Thorpe* ended the old division in the peninsula between the merchants and the coalition of office holders and loyalist officers that had opposed them. Street was returned for the riding of 3rd Lincoln in the election of 1808 and, once again, became speaker. On 12 Feb. 1810 the opposition, led by Joseph WILLCOCKS, caused an even division on the School Bill, forcing Street to cast the deciding ballot in its favour. The best-known incident of his speakership was the imbroglio that resulted from the house's contempt proceedings against Nichol. The latter's subsequent arrest on a speaker's warrant led to a ruling by Chief Justice Thomas Scott* that the warrant was invalid since it "appeared in all respects as the personal Act of Mr. Street under his seal, supposing Authority vested in him personally by the House of Assembly." Nichol was released and immediately brought suit against Street. The assembly was outraged by what seemed judicial interference with their privilege. The administrator of the province, Isaac BROCK, supported Nichol against the "inordinate power assumed by [the house]" and regarded its action as a "palpable injustice." The stage was set for a major confrontation that was averted only by the outbreak of the War of 1812.

Street had been a captain in the 3rd Lincoln Militia since 1809, and on 9 Oct. 1812 he was appointed paymaster of the flank companies of the 1st Oxford and 2nd, 3rd, and 5th Lincoln militia. On 22 Oct. 1813 he applied for, and later received, the position of acting deputy paymaster of the militia, and he served in that capacity until 24 May 1814. During the war he held several commissions: on 24 July 1813 he was one of several prominent local figures appointed to take charge of abandoned farms and their produce, and on 24 March 1814 he became a district commissioner to execute the provisions of the recent bill to secure and detain traitors. The Niagara area suffered heavy property damage during the war and Street's holdings were no exception. He claimed £1,878 2s. 6d. provincial currency for his losses, of which £750 resulted from the actions of British troops and their Indian allies; his estate was later awarded £1,333 in compensation.

Unlike his nephew Samuel Street* (usually known as Samuel Street Jr), who lived with him for many years, Street never achieved great commercial success. He was unable to develop an effective post-war economic strategy in the manner of Robert Hamilton. On balance, he was probably more important as a political spokesman of the Niagara merchants. Of the private man, little is known. His will hints at a personal repose based on family, faith, and farm. Such documents often make a perfunctory allusion to religion; Street, however, resigned his soul to the "Great God who made it in hopes through my blessed Saviour Jesus Christ to have a joyful resurrection to life Eternal." He left his beloved farm to his daughter, Mary, "to be quietly and peaceably possessed and enjoyed by her during her natural life." Finally, the man who had dispensed the funds of the Loyal and Patriotic Society to the poor during the war also made provision for them in the event he had no heirs.

In collaboration with BRUCE A. PARKER

AO, MS 500, Cancellation of articles of agreement between Andrew Butler and Street, 4 Jan. 1797; MU 492, "The Goring family" (typescript). BL, Add. MSS 21763: ff.218–19, 224, 227; 21764: f.382. PAC, MG 23, HII, 6, vol.1: 51, 365–75, 444; MG 24, D4: 69–74, 77–82, 90–91, 99–105, 110–11, 128–36; RG 1, E3, 100: 115–23; L3, 446A: S misc., 1793–1812/35; 448A: S2/70, 83, 121; 449: S2/202; RG 5, A1: 108–10, 3712, 3746–47, 4674–75, 6172–74, 7625, 8398, 8421, 8446; RG 19, 3751, claim 1106; RG 68, General index, 1651–1841: ff.326, 402–3, 408, 410, 416, 418, 425, 536. PRO, CO 42/69: ff.222–23, 228–29, 231–32, 235, 255, 261, 277, 280. Wilton Library Assoc., Wilton Hist. Coll. (Wilton, Conn.), G. E. Hubbard, "Supplement to Wilton families," II. "Accounts of receiver-general of U.C.," AO *Report*, 1914: 753. *Corr. of Hon. Peter Russell* (Cruikshank and Hunter), 1: 127–28, 167–68; 2: 44, 145–46, 191–92, 214, 295. *Corr. of Lieut. Governor Simcoe* (Cruikshank), 2: 117, 247; 3: 154, 299; 4: 342–43. "District of Nassau; letter book no.2," AO *Report*, 1905: 334. *Doc. hist. of campaign upon Niagara frontier* (Cruikshank), 3: 56–58; 4: 12–13; 5: 43; 6: 269; 9: 253–55, 259. [Francis Goring], "An early diary of Francis Goring," Niagara Hist. Soc., [*Pub.*], 36 (1924): 63. *Holland Land Company's papers: reports of Joseph Ellicott . . .* , ed. R. W. Bingham (2v., Buffalo, N.Y., 1937–41), 1: 120. "Journals of Legislative Assembly of U.C.," AO *Report*, 1909: 60, 71, 128; 1911: 304; 1912: 70–79. "Names only, but much more," comp. Janet Carnochan, Niagara Hist. Soc., [*Pub.*], 27 (n.d.): 3–4, 8. [Robert Nichol], "Some letters of Robert Nichol," ed. E. A. Cruikshank, *OH*, 20 (1923): 49–51. "The probated wills of persons prominent in the public affairs of early Upper Canada: second edition," ed. A. F. Hunter, *OH*, 24 (1927): 400–2. "Records of Niagara . . . ," ed. E. A. Cruikshank, Niagara Hist. Soc., [*Pub.*], 38 (1927): 60–61, 69; 39 (n.d.): 118–19; 40 (n.d.): 55–56; 41 (1930): 14–15, 28–29, 33–34, 63, 87–88. *The Talbot papers*, ed. J. H. Coyne (2v., Ottawa, 1908–9), 2: 136–38. "United Empire Loyalists: enquiry into losses and services," AO *Report*, 1904: 1105, 1112. "U.C. land book B," AO *Report*, 1930: 66, 72, 90, 117, 119. "U.C. land book D," AO *Report*, 1931: 172, 184–85, 192–93. *Niagara Herald* (Niagara [Niagara-on-the-Lake]), 23 May 1801.

Armstrong, *Handbook of Upper Canadian chronology*, 59, 62, 103. Andre, *William Berczy*, 33. R. W. Bingham, *The cradle of the Queen City: a history of Buffalo to the incorporation of the city* (Buffalo, 1931), 67, 72–73. Janet Carnochan, *History of Niagara . . .* (Toronto, 1914; repr. Belleville, Ont., 1973), 9, 38, 81. Reid, *Loyalists in Ont.*, 323. Wilson, "Enterprises of Robert Hamilton," 49–52, 55, 57, 117, 126, 190, 211, 284, 287, 295, 351–57. E. A. Cruikshank, "A sketch of the public life and services of Robert Nichol, a member of the Legislative Assembly and quartermaster general of the militia of Upper Canada," *OH*, 19 (1922): 10–18. C. L. Perry, "Reminiscences of Francis Goring," Niagara Hist. Soc., [*Pub.*], 28 (n.d.): 19, 24. W. R. Riddell, "The legislature of Upper Canada and contempt: drastic methods of early parliament with critics," *OH*, 22 (1925): 195–97; "Thomas Scott, the second attorney-general of Upper Canada," *OH*, 20 (1923): 134–37.

STREET, THOMAS, ship's captain, shipowner, merchant, and office holder; baptized 1724 in Poole, England, son of John and Mary Street; d. 1805 in Charlton Marshall, England.

Throughout most of the 18th century the Street family of Poole had a strong association with the Newfoundland fishery. Both Thomas Street and his elder brother Peter commanded ships and served as Newfoundland agents for Poole's opulent Quaker family, the Whites, which had its headquarters at Trinity. Thomas Street first appears in 1764 as captain of Joseph White's *Mermaid*, and from 1766 to 1771 he had charge of White's brig *Speedwell*. When Joseph White, the head of the firm, died in 1771, he divided an estate valued at £150,000 among his kinsfolk and Newfoundland agents. The Newfoundland component of his estate, consisting of his "plantations, houses, stages, and other buildings . . . with all . . . ships and vessels . . . boats and fishing craft, goods, effects and stores," was left to his nephew John Jeffrey and his five "Newfoundland servants or agents," Peter and Thomas Street, James and Joseph Randall, and William Munday.

White's will stipulated further that his chief executor and heir, Samuel White, was to provide a partnership consisting of Jeffrey and the Newfoundland agents with £10,000 capital over 14 years so that they could carry on the trade "for their own benefit and advantages" in "equal dividends or proportions," and perhaps establish an independent firm of their own. Under this arrangement a new firm styled Jeffrey, Randall, and Street was formed. Thomas Street had little capital when the company was set up, but accumulated enough so that within a few years he and Jeffrey had bought out the other partners and by 1775 were operating under the name of Jeffrey and Street. This partnership continued until 1789, when it was dissolved and the independent firms of John Jeffrey and Company and Thomas Street and Sons were formed. According to one observer, when Jeffrey and Street separated they divided £40,000 capital, after having repaid Samuel White £33,000, a sum which represented repayment of the £10,000 loan, three per cent of the profits of the trade up to that time, and probably also the purchase price of mercantile properties and ships.

Jeffrey and Street had proved to be formidable competition for other Poole firms. Jeffrey possessed considerable assets apart from his inheritance from White, and was energetic and ambitious for both wealth and power. He managed the Poole end of the trade and actively pursued a political career there. The more practical and sea-experienced Street became manager of the Newfoundland end and resided mainly in Trinity. Jeffrey and Street owned and operated several mercantile establishments in Trinity harbour, and had branches at Bay de Verde, Heart's Content, Old Perlican, Scilly Cove (Winterton), Catalina, Bonavista, Barrow Harbour, and Greenspond. Northward of Cape Freels, the firm was involved from its beginning in the salmon fishery on the Gander River and in 1783 took over the premises and trade formerly belonging to Jeremiah Coghlan* at Fogo. At the height of their trade, about 1786, Jeffrey and Street were exporting annually about 50,000 quintals of salt

Street

codfish, an amount only slightly less than ten per cent of the total exported from the whole of Newfoundland that year, and exceeded only by the 60,000 quintals marketed by the firm of Benjamin LESTER. They were heavily involved in the supply trade with Newfoundland planters, the offshore or bank fishery, the seal fishery, and shipbuilding. Between 1773 and 1787 the firm built 26 vessels at Trinity and Heart's Content, but normally operated between 10 and 15 ships at a given time.

At the outbreak of the American revolution Jeffrey and Street had a fleet of ten vessels ranging from 30 to 250 tons, eight of which had been built in Newfoundland. In 1778 their brig *Dispatch* was captured by privateers while going into San Sebastián, Spain, with a cargo of fish. In 1779 the brig *Triton* was taken while fishing on the Grand Banks, and the next year an American privateer captured their 200-ton *Adventure*, bound from Poole to Greenspond. Despite these losses, the firm actually increased its shipping, and in 1783 had 12 vessels totalling 1,800 tons. In 1788, just before the partnership was dissolved, it owned 15 vessels, one of which was the *Hudson*, commanded by Jeffrey's nephew Joseph W. Jeffrey, and another the *Swift*, captained by Street's son Peter.

The success of the firm of Jeffrey and Street in Trinity between 1775 and 1789 may be attributed to the fact that the firm was well capitalized from the beginning, and to the aggressive and effective management by the two chief partners on both sides of the Atlantic. In the late 1780s, however, when the Newfoundland trade began to decline, Jeffrey became impatient with it and anxious to withdraw his capital. The partners may have had personal differences as well, and in 1789 they decided to terminate their association. Relationships evidently soured considerably after the separation.

In Newfoundland history the name Jeffrey and Street has been mainly associated with that of John August, a Beothuk Indian and one of the few members of that ill-fated tribe to have had a friendly intercourse with the English. According to tradition, John was captured as a child by some fishermen, who chanced upon him and his mother near Red Indian Lake in August 1768 and killed the woman. When George CARTWRIGHT visited Catalina in 1785 he found John in the employ of a Mr Child, an agent of Jeffrey and Street, and recounted that he had been captured when about four years old. John apparently became the master of a fishing vessel, and one writer states that each fall he went up Trinity Bay and travelled into the interior of the island to visit his people. According to John Cartwright, George's brother, John was taken as a child to England, probably by Street, and "exposed as a curiousity to the rabble at Pool for two pence apiece." Trinity burial records show that John August was interred in the churchyard there on 29 Oct. 1788,

and a notation in the burial entry reads "a native Indian of this island, a servant to Jeffrey and Street."

Thomas Street resided with his family in Trinity until 1789, but frequently crossed to Poole on business. According to local parish records, "Capt. Thomas and Christian Street" presented two sons for baptism at Trinity in 1768, another at Heart's Content in 1772, and a daughter at Trinity in 1781. Street's wife was evidently Christian Rowe, daughter of Edward Rowe, a planter who in 1753 was residing at Trinity and who became a justice of the peace. Street's brother-in-law James Rowe became a shipbuilder for his firm and in 1801 was living at Heart's Content on a fishing room owned by Street. As one of the chief inhabitants of Trinity, in 1774 Street became a member of a committee which undertook to build a jail and which established a tax of a quintal per boat and a half quintal per fishing skiff to pay the cost. In 1775 he was appointed a justice of the peace.

Following his separation from Jeffrey, Thomas Street's Newfoundland trade generally declined, and in the period between 1791 and 1801 the number of his ships was reduced from nine to four. Nevertheless, in the winter of 1801 he was employing some 100 servants at his Trinity premises, compared with 150 employed by Benjamin Lester, 22 by Jeffrey, and 16 by Thomas Stone, the other chief merchants in Trinity. He still owned considerable property in Newfoundland, and his main premises at Trinity had four dwelling-houses occupied by his agent and clerks.

To prepare for his retirement, Street bought a country estate at Charlton Marshall, ten miles northwest of Poole, and purchased other properties in Poole itself, among them the High Street mansion and five Hill Street tenements of Thomas Hyde, a Newfoundland trader and oil dealer who had gone bankrupt. In directing this trade, managed in Newfoundland after 1789 by his sons, Street spent most of the winter at Poole and the summers at Charlton Marshall. He became active in local politics, being elected coroner in 1792, sheriff in 1793, and mayor in 1796. Politically, Street aligned himself with the Lester and Garland families, with whom he seems to have had good personal relationships, and actively campaigned for the election of Benjamin Lester as member of parliament for Poole in 1790 and similarly for George Garland in 1800. In many respects Street and Lester had similar traits: both were Anglicans, both had become Newfoundland merchants, both had resided in Trinity during the 1760s, and both had married Trinity-born women. The chief opposition to Lester's party in Poole was one led by Street's former partner, John Jeffrey.

In 1793 Street was called before the House of Commons committee on the Newfoundland trade to address issues raised by some of the other Newfoundland merchants, such as William Newman and Peter OUGIER of Dartmouth and Jeffrey and John WALDRON of Poole. He argued that the establishment of the custom-house in Newfoundland [see Richard ROUTH] was of "great advantage to the fair and lawful trader" and that customs fees "were of little consequence to the trade in general." Street also defended the integrity of John CLINCH, the Anglican missionary and collector of customs at Trinity, against accusations levelled by Jeffrey that Clinch was incompetent in performing his duties.

When Street had retired to England, leaving the trade in the hands of his three sons, it had looked as if the family was secure in the Newfoundland trade for at least another generation. In 1801, however, Peter Street, who had married and resided in Trinity, died suddenly at the age of 34. By Thomas's will, dated 25 Aug. 1805, the year of his death, John inherited the Newfoundland trade, as well as two dwellings in Poole High Street and four "new erected messuages" in Hill Street. Thomas's widow received title to the country estate at Charlton Marshall, and his son Mark acquired the "Storehouses, oil cellars, salt cellars, and coal yards" in Poole. Three years after his father Mark Street also died, leaving John as the only surviving son. The latter left St John's for Poole in January 1809 to administer the affairs of his intestate brother but somewhere in the Atlantic the ship foundered and all hands were lost. The family trade thus came to an abrupt end, the various premises falling into the hands of other families. One of the Trinity properties was acquired by the firm of Bulley, Job, and Cross of St John's, and several others were taken over by Robert Slade of Poole, nephew of John Slade*. The demise of the Street male heirs did not, however, entirely sever the family ties with Newfoundland. John Street had married into the Bulley family of St John's, and one of his brothers-in-law was a principal of Bulley, Job, and Cross. In addition, Thomas Street's daughter Mary married Joseph Bird Jr, a cloth merchant of Sturminster Newton in Dorset. When this business failed Bird struck out into the Newfoundland trade about 1808 and established trading premises at Bonne Bay and on the Strait of Belle Isle. At his death in 1824 his two sons Thomas Street Bird and Joseph Bird continued this trade until the 1840s.

Along with other prominent Newfoundland merchants such as Benjamin Lester, John Slade, and John Waldron, Thomas Street can be classified as a frontier entrepreneur. He moved up through the ranks as seaman, captain, company agent, and finally merchant, and amassed a considerable fortune in the process. Spending much of his active working life at sea and in Newfoundland, he earned a reputation as an outstanding seafarer and master mariner, and bore the title of "Captain" into his old age, long after he became a merchant. In character he was far less aggressive than Lester, Slade, or Waldron, and was certainly much less controversial than his business partner, the petulant John Jeffrey.

W. GORDON HANDCOCK

Anglican Church of Canada, Diocese of Nfld. Arch. (St John's), St Paul's Church (Trinity, Nfld.), Reg. of baptisms, marriages, and burials, I (mfm. at PAC). Dorset Record Office, D365/F2–F10; P70/OV12 (Overseers of the poor, settlement examinations, 1703–1813), John Wheller, 1 Jan. 1807; P227/CW (Churchwardens' records). Maritime Hist. Group Arch., Jeffrey, John, and Street, Thomas, name files. National Maritime Museum, POL (mfm. at PANL). PANL, GN 5/1/B/1, Trinity records, 1805–21; GN 5/1/B/9, Trinity records, 1753–1801. PRO, ADM 1/1225; BT 6/87: 84; C 108/69–71; CO 194/33; PROB 6/184; 11/970/362; 11/1435/863; 11/1523/305. G.B., House of Commons, Reports from committees of the House of Commons which have been printed by order of the house and are not inserted in the Journals, [1715–1801] (16v., London, [1803–20]), 10: 391–503, "Reports from the committee on the state of the trade to Newfoundland, severally reported in March, April, & June, 1793." Lloyd's List, 1753–55, 1764–71. Reg. of shipping, 1783, 1788. Derek Beamish et al., Mansions and merchants of Poole and Dorset (Poole, Eng., 1976), 16, 114, 119. C. G. Head, Eighteenth century Newfoundland: a geographer's perspective (Toronto, 1976), 171–72. F. W. Rowe, Extinction: the Beothuks of Newfoundland (Toronto, 1977), 42–47.

STUART, JOHN, Church of England clergyman; b. 24 Feb. 1740/41 in Paxton Township (near Harrisburg), Pa, son of Andrew Stuart and Mary Dinwiddie; m. 12 Oct. 1775 Jane Okill of Philadelphia, Pa, and they had eight children; d. 15 Aug. 1811 in Kingston, Upper Canada.

John Stuart received his BA from the College of Philadelphia (University of Pennsylvania) in 1763 and his MA in 1770. Between these years he was a schoolmaster in Lancaster County, Pa. Although reared as a strict Presbyterian he became an Anglican, influenced in all probability by the provost of the college, William Smith, a native of Aberdeen who had taken orders in the Episcopal Church of Scotland. His intellectual and social qualifications and even his height, well over six feet, earned him the admiration of his contemporaries. In 1771, following his appointment as a minister of the Society for the Propagation of the Gospel at Fort Hunter, N.Y., Stuart was dubbed "the little Gentleman" by Charles INGLIS, later the first Anglican bishop in British North America.

After the departure of John Ogilvie* in 1760, the Fort Hunter mission had been less closely tended than in the previous decade. Two SPG missionaries, Thomas Browne and Harry Munro, had paid regular visits to the mission, but both whites and Mohawks required greater care. Accordingly Sir William

Stuart

Johnson*, superintendent of northern Indians and a member of the SPG since 1766, was much encouraged when he received strong recommendations in favour of Stuart, who was willing to undertake the task. In a letter dated April 1770 to Samuel Auchmuty, the rector of Trinity Church in New York City, Johnson commented, "I sincerely wish he may turn out to be a Man of Zeal and Attention proportionable to his Size, as you observe."

This indeed proved to be the case. Stuart left New York for England on 27 May 1770, and was ordained deacon on 19 August and priest on 24 August, both by the bishop of London. He then returned to New York without delay and by December had entered on his work at Fort Hunter. He began immediately to hold services for both Indians and whites in the chapel at the fort and to minister to Indians at Canajoharie (near Little Falls). At the latter place he first met Joseph Brant [THAYENDANEGEA], who after becoming a widower in 1771 lived for a short time with Stuart in the Mohawk parsonage near Fort Hunter. The two men later collaborated in the translation of St Mark's Gospel into Mohawk, a work which by 1774 was nearly ready for the press but was not finally printed until 1787. Stuart also supervised a school for Indian children and conducted monthly services at nearby Johnstown. One of his first sad duties there was to officiate at the burial of his friend and protector Sir William Johnson in July 1774.

Stuart's close connection with the Johnson family, avowedly loyal to Great Britain, and his own undisguised political opinions soon made him an object of suspicion to commissioners of the Indian Department who had been appointed by the second Continental Congress to maintain the neutrality of the various tribes. In August 1775, at a commissioner's meeting held in Albany, Teiorhénhsere?*, a Mohawk chief, asked that Stuart not be molested. The request was apparently received favourably since the missionary remained at Fort Hunter in 1776. In 1777 and early in 1778, however, he came under renewed suspicion, his property was plundered, and his church was looted. Soon afterwards, in June 1778, local rebels confined him to Schenectady on parole. Feeling threatened, he went to Albany for brief periods in 1779 and again in the spring of 1780, but on both occasions he was soon ordered to return to Schenectady. In the latter year he was permitted to make a short visit to Philadelphia. Finally, however, in early 1781, his situation became so unpleasant that he applied for permission to leave for the province of Quebec. He eventually obtained an exchange with an army officer held prisoner by the British, quitted Schenectady on 19 Sept. 1781, and arrived at St Johns (Saint-Jean-sur-Richelieu), Que., on 19 October after a fatiguing journey. He was accompanied by his wife and three small children and was permitted to bring personal property, including black slaves.

The choice of loyalism did not come easily to John and Jane Stuart. Both left relatives and friends as well as property behind them when they made their difficult journey. They did not, however, indulge in the bitterness felt by some loyalists. In the year of his departure Stuart wrote to William White, later bishop of Pennsylvania, that he left behind "no personal, altho' many political enemies." Correspondence between Stuart and White continued for nearly 30 years. In 1783 Stuart wrote, "I have taken the Liberty of directing a letter to your care for one of my Rebel Brethren, for whom, notwithstanding, I feel the remains of tenderness." When his young son John had returned to Cataraqui (Kingston, Ont.) after receiving kindness at White's home in Philadelphia in 1785, Stuart acknowledged the courtesy in characteristic bantering fashion: "I just received him home. Time enough to save his political Principles. Six months more would have reconciled him to Republicanism."

Stuart spent four active years, agreeably peaceful after his unpleasant time in New York, in Montreal. He was given a chaplaincy in the 2nd battalion of the King's Royal Regiment of New York by Sir John Johnson*. He operated a school that was open to all denominations, for a short time assisted the clergyman at Montreal, David Chabrand* Delisle, as evening lecturer in the Recollet chapel then used by the Anglicans, preached occasionally at St Johns, and gave oversight to the Fort Hunter Mohawks who were making a temporary home at Lachine [see John DESERONTYON]. In the summer of 1784 he travelled as far as Niagara (Niagara-on-the-Lake, Ont.), where he was welcomed by members of his former Indian flock who had congregated near by and had built a church on what is now the American side of the river. Both going and coming he ministered to loyalist settlers and, as prospects of obtaining a parish in Quebec were poor, he decided to move to Cataraqui, where he hoped to become rector and to obtain the chaplaincy of the garrison. In August 1785 Stuart and his family arrived at Cataraqui, his permanent home until his death in 1811.

In that quarter century Stuart saw the community grow from the day on which the land adjacent to the fort was laid out in lots. His contribution to the religious development of the Kingston area cannot be overestimated, for, until age began to take its toll in the last decade of his life, he showed himself to be a missionary of almost boundless energy. Shortly after his arrival he started the first school west of the Ottawa River, initially in his home, then in a government building. Still later, in 1795, a grammar school was opened in which his son George Okill* was the first teacher. At the beginning, church services were held in the barracks and then in a new church, known as St George's, built in 1792 and twice enlarged. Joseph Brant's sister, Mary [Koñwatsi?tsiaiéñni*], was a member of this church. Stuart kept a watchful eye on the Indians at the Bay of Quinte, and in 1788 he visited the larger Six Nations settlement on the Grand River, taking with him most of the Queen Anne silver formerly used in the Fort Hunter chapel (three pieces stayed with the Bay of Quinte Mohawks). In 1792 a missionary trip in the countryside around Kingston covered roughly 200 miles, and on one occasion he made a 140-mile tour of the "lower settlements" in the Cornwall area. In 1792, after being appointed chaplain of the Legislative Council by Lieutenant Governor John Graves Simcoe, Stuart visited Niagara, and then York (Toronto), as required. He had attended the visitation of his former acquaintance Charles Inglis, now bishop of Nova Scotia, at Quebec in 1789, and was appointed by Inglis commissary for the "western settlements," an office that was again given to him by the first bishop of Quebec, Jacob Mountain*. The post of commissary, the title of which was later changed to "official," entailed considerable visiting of pioneer settlements and the oversight of a few clergy as new missions were opened. In 1799, at his own request and with the support of Bishop White, he was given an honorary DD by his old college in Philadelphia.

In addition to performing his official duties, Stuart devoted himself to the interests of a large family of eight children and allotted such a proportion of his resources to their welfare that even at his death he had accumulated little wealth beyond a few thousand acres of land. When, for example, Sir John Johnson gave him 500 acres on Amherst Island in 1803, he resolved to use it as a portion for one of his daughters. He himself gave basic instruction to several of his children, he sent his boys to school and to college in Schenectady and then to Bishop Inglis's new institution of learning in Windsor, N.S., and he supported his eldest son, George, for a year at Harvard; two girls attended private school in Montreal. At his death George, incumbent of York for a decade, succeeded him as rector of St George's; the third son, James*, had been solicitor general of Lower Canada; the fifth, Andrew*, was well on the way to a brilliant career in law and politics in Quebec. Two other sons were local sheriffs; his daughter Mary had married Charles Jones* of Elizabethtown (Brockville), a prominent businessman who later was to sit both in the House of Assembly and in the Legislative Council.

Throughout his long years at Kingston Stuart received no stipend from his parishioners, but his income from his position as bishop's official and from government sources, as well as a small sum from the SPG as "Missionary to the Mohawks," enabled him to live in comfort. His Kingston farm provided basic security and gave him deep satisfaction. Even before settling at Kingston he wrote, "I am fond of farming and promise myself much Pleasure in the Improvements I intend to make in that new world."

Stuart's judgement of men was generally sound and invariably objective and independent. Of Bishop Mountain he wrote, after due reflection, "He is a man of fine Talents and a good Heart." Of John Strachan* he commented in 1802, "He is a *very good young man* but I doubt he will not be a good *public speaker*." He was dubious about the propriety of the ordination of Richard Pollard*, SPG missionary at Sandwich, and his patience was perpetually exercised by the oddities and religious bigotry of John LANGHORN, his clerical neighbour at Ernestown (Bath). Langhorn's type of old-fashioned high churchmanship led him to confront "schismatics," whether Methodist or Presbyterian, in uncompromising fashion. He apparently read his sermons and, as Stuart wrote to Bishop Inglis in 1788, in his "attention to Church Rituals . . . he is scrupulous to the smallest Punctilio." Stuart, on the other hand, was no less faithful to his principles than Langhorn, yet as a colonial American he was more at home in pioneer society, adapted to it more easily, and met with more success in his ministry than the crusty Welshman. He told the SPG in 1792 that he found it expedient in his late journeys to deliver his discourses without reading. On occasion he even made an extempore prayer before the sermon.

John Beverley Robinson*, who lived with Stuart while attending Strachan's Kingston school, remembered him many years later as "about six feet two inches in height – not corpulent, and not thin, – but with fine masculine features, expanded chest, erect figure; straight, well-formed limbs, and a free, manly carriage, improved by a fondness in his youth for athletic exercises, particularly fencing." Jacob Henry Brooke Mountain, son of Jacob and brother of George Jehoshaphat*, third bishop of the diocese of Quebec, wrote that Stuart was "a very fine elderly man, of lofty stature, and powerful frame; very kind to me, and to every body, though rather caustic and dry in manner. . . . He was diligent and charitable, and sought health and recreation in cultivating his farm and garden . . . and in fine summer evenings he loved to sit on the shore and play upon his flute. . . ." According to Strachan, Stuart was "the Father of the Episcopal Church in this Province." This assessment of his legacy to Ontario Anglicanism is justified, but his total contribution was wider still. In his own person, as well as through his descendants and those whose lives he touched, he exerted an influence on Canadian life in the 19th century that few other loyalists could match.

T. R. MILLMAN

Anglican Church of Canada, Diocese of Ont. Arch. (Kingston), Group 11, John Stuart papers; St George's Cathedral (Kingston), church records. AO, MU 2923, ser.A. BL, Add. MSS 21661–892 (transcripts at PAC). Private arch., Campbell Stuart (Braeside, Ont.), Biog. of John Stuart by A. H. Young (copy in Trinity College Arch., Toronto). USPG, C/CAN/folder 440; Journal of SPG. *The documentary history of the state of New-York . . .*, ed. E. B.

Suárez

O'Callaghan (4v., Albany, 1849–51), 4. Ernest Hawkins, *Annals of the diocese of Toronto* (London, 1848). "History and present state of religion in Upper-Canada," *Christian Recorder* (York [Toronto]), 1 (1819–20): 3–16. *Johnson papers* (Sullivan *et al.*), vols.7–8. *Kingston before War of 1812* (Preston). *Parish reg. of Kingston* (Young). SPG, [*Annual report*] (London), 1782–1811. John Strachan, *A sermon, on the death of the Rev. John Stuart, D.D., preached at Kingston, 25th August, 1811* (Kingston, 1811). A. H. Young, *The Revd. John Stuart, D.D., U.E.L., of Kingston, U.C., and his family: a genealogical study* (Kingston, [1920]). J. W. Lydekker, *The faithful Mohawks* (Cambridge, Eng., 1938). Millman, *Jacob Mountain.* C. W. Robinson, *Life of Sir John Beverley Robinson, bart., C.B., D.C.L., chief-justice of Upper Canada* (Toronto, 1904). J. W. Lydekker, "The Rev. John Stuart, D.D., (1740–1811): missionary to the Mohawks," *Hist. Magazine of the Protestant Episcopal Church* (New Brunswick, N.J.), 11 (1942): 18–64. P. L. Northcott, "The financial problems of the Reverend John Stuart," Canadian Church Hist. Soc., *Journal* (London, Ont.), 6 (1964): 14–27. G. F. G. Stanley, "John Stuart, father of the Anglican Church in Upper Canada," Canadian Church Hist. Soc., *Journal* (Toronto), 3 (1956–59), no.6.

SUÁREZ DE FIGUEROA, JOSÉ MARIANO MOZIÑO LOSADA. *See* MoziÑo

SUZOR (Suzor de Bièvre), FRANÇOIS-MICHEL, doctor; b. 26 May 1756 in Romorantin-Lanthenay, France, son of François Suzor, a merchant, and Marie-Anne Grougnard; d. 15 Dec. 1810 in Saint-Vallier, Lower Canada.

Unlike his father and two of his brothers, François-Michel Suzor was more interested in surgery than in trade and finance. He came to the American colonies with the forces under the Marquis de La Fayette and on 26 Aug. 1778 enlisted as a surgeon's mate in the 7th Massachusetts Regiment. On 11 November some Iroquois from a detachment commanded by an officer of the British forces, Walter Butler*, captured him during the attack on Cherry Valley, N.Y., and took him to Fort Niagara (near Youngstown, N.Y.). Apparently he was accused of trying to bribe the Canadian sailors at this post, and he was subsequently transferred to Montreal and then to Quebec.

At that period a form of syphilis known as the Baie-Saint-Paul malady [*see* Philippe-Louis-François BADELARD; James Bowman*] was raging in several parishes with devastating effects. Thinking that Suzor's skills could be useful, the colonial authorities decided to send him to Baie-Saint-Paul to serve as assistant surgeon under Dr Badelard. Consequently he took ship on 6 May 1780 for Baie-Saint-Paul; he remained there for two and a half years. Some time after his arrival he left the temporary hospital that had been set up and decided to practise medicine in the region on his own.

Electing to remain in the colony, late in 1782 Suzor

chose to set up practice at Pointe-aux-Trembles (Neuville), which had been without a surgeon since Bernard Planté's death that year. He bought some of the books and all the surgical instruments and medicaments in Planté's estate. His marriage to Marie-Anne Larue on 3 March 1783 and the grant of a building site in the village of Pointe-aux-Trembles six months later further helped him to become established. Early in 1784, however, he moved to Saint-Antoine-sur-Richelieu. On 12 June the leading citizens of the region asked Governor HALDIMAND to grant a notary's commission to Suzor, "who through the zeal, charity, and humanity that he possesses" seemed to them to be worthy of occupying such a function. In all probability it was refused him. Some time after his wife's death on 3 July 1785 Suzor returned to the Quebec region and established himself at Cap-Santé; on 28 Aug. 1787 he took as his second wife Louise Laflèche. He lived there until at least 1794, spent some time at Quebec before moving to Île d'Orléans, and finally returned to Cap-Santé around 1801. At his death in 1810 his family was still living there.

It is not known what kind of training Suzor had received, but his handwriting and style give proof of a good education. That prominent people suggested him as a notary lends support to this view. His competence was recognized officially on 30 Dec. 1788 when he received a licence to practise as a surgeon and pharmacist. His experience at Baie-Saint-Paul, where he is supposed to have cured dozens of people, had made a strong impression on him; on several occasions he announced that he "very successfully cures all sorts of venereal diseases, and other illnesses of every kind, [having] a particular secret for curing the infectious malady, so harmful to the health of His British Majesty's subjects, known as the Les Éboulements and Baie-Saint-Paul malady." He also said that he was a very good dentist.

At Suzor's death his second wife was left with seven children, five of whom were still minors. None of the four sons carried on their father's profession.

RENALD LESSARD

AD, Loir-et-Cher (Blois), État civil, Romorantin-Lanthenay, 26 mai 1756. ANQ-M, CE1-13, 3 juill. 1785. ANQ-Q, CC1, 8 oct. 1813; CE1-1, 28 août 1787; CE1-8, 22 avril 1793, 11 févr. 1801; CE1-10, 25 mai 1797; CE1-11, 19 juin 1798; CE1-15, 3 mars 1783, 25 mai 1797; CE2-8, 17 déc. 1810; CN1-21, 1er juill. 1828, 20 juin 1829, 18 mai 1830; CN1-25, 17 sept. 1783; CN1-83, 8 janv., 21 févr. 1783; 25 août 1787; CN1-230, 14 sept. 1802. BL, Add. mss 21732: f.411; 21843: f.54; 21845/2: f.309; 21879: ff.194–95 (copies at PAC). PAC, MG 11, [CO 42] Q, 39: 80; RG 4, A1: 16496–504, 16942–54, 17151; B28, 47: 74–76. *Quebec Gazette*, 3 Oct. 1782, 8 Sept. 1796. F. B. Heitman, *Historical register of officers of the Continental Army during the war of the revolution . . .* (Washington, 1893). *Inventaire des registres paroissiaux de l'île de France (île Maurice), Compagnie des Indes, 1722–1767,* R.-O. Béchet, édit. (Port-Louis, Île Maurice, 1951), 392. Albert Lasnier, "Suzor," *L'Hebdo de Portneuf* (Saint-Raymond, Qué.), 4 déc. 1978: 8. "Nécrologie," *Le Courrier du Canada* (Québec), 23 mai 1877: 2.

T

TANSWELL, JAMES, schoolmaster, journalist, and office holder; b. probably 10 March 1744/45, in Blandford, England; d. 25 April 1819 at Quebec, Lower Canada.

Although he may have studied at a Jesuit college in Europe, James Tanswell himself records only that he spent "the Twenty first Years" of his life "in acquiring a universal Education, & . . . assisting in some of the first Schools in England," until in 1765 he opened his own academy at London. There on 3 June 1768 he married Ann Blacklock; they were to have at least five sons. In 1772, at the request of several people in Nova Scotia, Brook WATSON and Robert Rashleigh persuaded Tanswell to go there "to plant the liberal Arts & Sciences"; shortly after his arrival, he was licensed by government to open a school at Halifax, which he conducted for five years.

In 1778 Tanswell received letters from some residents of Quebec inviting him to move there and intimating that Governor Sir Guy CARLETON had promised him "Protection & Commission." Although Tanswell apparently thought he was coming primarily to tutor Carleton's children, the invitation was likely prompted by a lack of Protestant schools in the city [*see* John FRASER]. When Tanswell arrived in mid September Carleton had departed for England, but on 3 November Governor HALDIMAND granted Tanswell's request for a licence to keep a public school, and on the 23rd he opened an "Academy" and boarding-school on Rue du Parloir. The following year it was moved to the bishop's palace, which the government rented from the Roman Catholic bishop.

In the *Quebec Gazette* of 19 Nov. 1778 Tanswell advertised public and private lessons in reading, writing, arithmetic, the Italian method of bookkeeping, English, French, Latin, Greek, geography, and various branches of mathematics; he also promised that "the exterior Deportment and Behaviour of the Children will be particularly attended to, as well as the Improvement of the Mind." He subsequently widened the range of courses to include ballroom dancing, history ("the most useful study in Life"), German, Spanish, Italian, and the Copernican and Newtonian systems. In 1801 he offered four classes, taught in English and French: reading, writing, and mercantile arithmetic at three guineas per student per annum; French and English grammar and bookkeeping at four guineas; geography, trigonometry, and mensuration at five guineas; and Latin and Greek, geography, the study of globes, the construction of maps and charts, astronomy, navigation, surveying, gauging, architecture, and fortifications at six guineas.

Tanswell taught both boys and girls, but in "separate apartments." Girls, for whom he opened a boarding-school in 1800, were offered "all the necessary, useful and ornamental Branches of Literature, Languages, &c," as well as sciences, and had at their disposal the same materials as the boys, including by 1803 "a *Planetarium, Lunarium, Tellurium* &c. such as have never been seen in this Quarter of the Globe." Boys probably took substantially the same courses in literature and science, but in addition were "expeditiously fitted, for the Army, Navy, University, Accompting House, Mechanicks, &c &c." One subject Tanswell stressed for both sexes was language; he was as keen to help the British attain "a thorough knowledge . . . of that beautiful and necessary Language the *French*" as he was to teach English to the Canadians.

Tanswell made a remarkable effort to facilitate the education of his clientele. He offered courses to both young people and adults mornings, afternoons, and evenings, at first five and then six days a week, in all seasons, and private tutoring in the hours between scheduled classes. In 1789, "from the Hardness of the Times," he educated three British and three Canadian lads free, and he doubled the number the following year. In October 1793, "under the Patronage and Directions" of Prince EDWARD AUGUSTUS, Tanswell opened the Sunday Free School, where instruction was given in both languages in reading, writing, and arithmetic, but where particular attention was accorded the teaching of English to Canadians. At the other end of the social spectrum, in 1815 he proposed "to finish the Education of a small but *very* select number of YOUNG LADIES" and a limited number of young gentlemen. About 1814 he had begun teaching English grammar at the Séminaire de Québec, to whose students he had for a number of years been offering prizes for excellence.

To handle such a wide range of course offerings, times, and types of schools Tanswell required help. His son Thomas assisted from about 1790 until 1803, even though he had opened his own evening-school in

Tanswell

1798, and in 1804 Tanswell had three assistants. Teaching became virtually a family business; in 1817 a grandson, Stephen Joseph, opened a school in the city.

In 1801 Tanswell removed his academy to the Upper Town market; thereafter it was kept successively in various houses in Upper Town. Between 1778 and 1790 the number of Protestant schools at Quebec had increased to six and then stabilized, apparently under conditions of strong competition, for the next 30 years. Unlike most of those who opened schools after him, Tanswell received from the time of his arrival a salary of £100 per annum from government, as well as the usual fees from students; none the less, he found his "arduous, painful & confining Profession of instructing Youth" not very profitable, probably in part because of the competition and his own idealism. He imposed not only a lower, but also an upper limit on the size of his classes; as well, in 1790 half of his 25 students were "free scholars."

Although this proportion of non-paying students was probably unusual even for Tanswell, and although he nearly doubled the number of his students in 1791, he remained constantly in financial difficulty and continually sought new ways to apply his own education to increasing his income while dispelling "the dark Clouds of Ignorance" at Quebec. In 1780 he petitioned Haldimand for three years' salary in advance to help pay the purchase price and cost of repairs on a large house acquired for a boarding-school in which he maintained, often on credit, "many young Gentlemen from the Country." In 1781 he imported "a large and general Assortment of Stationary and Books," which he offered wholesale or retail. In a letter to Haldimand the following year he wrote that, not finding enough work at Quebec, he was ready to abandon teaching for a government job, but that if he must continue teaching, he would need at least a part-time government position. At the same time he solicited from Carleton, commander-in-chief at New York City, permission to set up an academy there. All these requests were apparently refused, as was another in July 1783 for authorization to call his school His Majesty's Royal Quebec Academy. The following year, adducing "a Torrent of unexpected Opposition, a sudden Rise of every specie of Provisions, Infidelity of Servants, and many bad Debts," he requested another room in the bishop's palace. In June 1788 he advertised his services as a copyist of letters, memorials, and petitions, a translator, and a bookkeeper. He had been hired by William Moore* in January of that year to edit Le Courier de Québec ou Héraut françois, the first newspaper in the colony published exclusively in French; only the prospectus and three numbers appeared, however. On 15 Dec. 1788, after the Courier had been discontinued, "there not being subscribers sufficient to pay for the paper,"

Moore advertised a "French Gazette" to be edited by Tanswell, but no issue was ever printed. In 1791 Tanswell was prepared to publish for Canadian students an English grammar with exercises explained in French as well as a French treatise on arithmetic; neither appeared, probably because no way was found to defray the expenses. In 1796 he was appointed interpreter in the courts of King's Bench and Quarter Sessions at £40 per annum, and two years later was made keeper of the Special Gaol for the District of Quebec. He also rented part of his house. In spite of all his efforts to increase his income, however, Tanswell continued intermittently until 1815 to petition the government for aid.

In the early years of his career Tanswell had complained of "the many illiberal & unmerited Aspersions" cast upon his character since 1778, and these unidentified disparagements had perhaps contributed to his financial difficulties. In 1783 his membership in the Thespian Society, a theatre company formed that year, had given rise to the criticism that he had been attending more assiduously to it than to his academy. Opposition to Tanswell may have stemmed most, however, from suspicions about the religious affiliation of the "Protestant schoolmaster." Apparently an Anglican before his arrival at Quebec, and provincial grand secretary of the Society of Free and Accepted Masons in Canada from 1780 to 1784, he none the less had close connections with the Roman Catholic Church, and probably converted to Catholicism at some point. His son Charles was baptized in Notre-Dame Cathedral in 1778 and Ann Tanswell was buried from there in 1797. On 25 June 1799 Tanswell married Marie-Joseph Coutant in Notre-Dame-de-Foy church at Sainte-Foy, and on 27 April 1819 he was buried in the Catholic Cimetière des Picotés. Certainly one notable characteristic of this English schoolmaster's career at Quebec, spanning 41 years, was the ease with which he had moved in the French-speaking and Roman Catholic Canadian society. After Tanswell's death his academy was taken over by the Reverend Daniel Wilkie*, a Presbyterian minister.

MARY JANE EDWARDS

ANQ-Q, CE1-1, 27 avril 1819; CE1-20, 25 juin 1799; CN1-26, 25 avril 1812, 23 févr. 1813; CN1-63, 4 déc. 1811; CN1-178, 14 avril 1812; CN1-262, 14 août 1797; 10 avril 1801; 26 févr., 8 mars 1803. BL, Add. mss 21733: f.161; 21755: ff.37–38; 21877: ff.229–30, 267–69, 336–38 (mfm. at PAC). PAC, RG 1, L3ᴸ: 591; RG 4, A1: 21369, 38199–201, 28 Dec. 1815; RG 68, 90: 114. PRO, CO 42/71: ff.284–86; PRO 30/55, no.10011 (mfm. at PAC). Bas-Canada, chambre d'Assemblée, Journaux, 1801: 276; 1807: 250; 1814, app.A. Le Courier de Québec ou Héraut françois (Québec), 1ᵉʳ janv., 24 nov., 1ᵉʳ déc. 1788. Nova-Scotia Gazette and the Weekly Chronicle, 15 Aug. 1775. Quebec Herald, Miscellany and Advertiser, 1788–92. Quebec

Gazette, 1778–1819. *Quebec almanac*, 1780: 60. *The register book of marriages belonging to the parish of St George, Hanover Square, in the county of Middlesex*, ed. J. H. Chapman and G. J. Armytage (4v., London, 1886–97), 2: 176. P.[-J.] Aubert de Gaspé, *Mémoires* (nouv. éd., Montréal, 1971), 124–25. L.-P. Audet, *Le système scolaire*, 2: 136, 139, 310, 321, 343–44, 346–47; 3: 55, 140; 4: 181, 188–89; 5: 40, 44–45. J. H. Graham, *Outlines of the history of freemasonry in the province of Quebec* (Montreal, 1892), 50–51, 58, 70–71. "L'Académie royale de James Tanswell," *BRH*, 42 (1936): 359. F.-J. Audet, "James Tanswell," *BRH*, 3 (1897): 141.

TARIEU DE LANAUDIÈRE, CHARLES-LOUIS, army and militia officer, seigneur, office holder, politician, and author; b. 14 Oct. 1743 at Quebec, son of Charles-François Tarieu* de La Naudière and Louise-Geneviève Deschamps de Boishébert; d. there 2 Oct. 1811.

Charles-Louis Tarieu de Lanaudière, a godson of Charles de Beauharnois* de La Boische, governor general of New France, came from the seigneurial and military aristocracy. After studying at the Séminaire de Québec from 1752 to 1756, Lanaudière, like many young men of his station, chose a military career, joining the Régiment de La Sarre in 1756. On 28 April 1760 he took part in the battle of Sainte-Foy [*see* François de Lévis*]; wounded in the leg, he spent some months convalescing at the Hôtel-Dieu in Quebec. In September 1760, after the conquest, he left Canada for France with his regiment and his father accompanied him.

In France Lanaudière rejoined other members of his family and continued his military career as an adjutant. In 1767 he travelled with the ambassador of France, the Comte de Châtelet-Lomont, to the court of King George III in London. Obtaining a passport, he returned to his native land in the spring of 1768 to settle some family matters and take up the legacy bequeathed him by his mother, who had died in 1762. Probably influenced by his father, who had come back to Canada in 1763, Lanaudière took up permanent residence in the colony. He sealed his reintegration into Canadian life by marrying Geneviève-Élisabeth de La Corne, daughter of Luc de La Corne* and Marie-Anne Hervieux, in Montreal on 10 April 1769. They had three children but only one daughter reached adulthood.

Having, with his father's help, established himself on intimate terms with the British colonial authorities, Lanaudière was appointed aide-de-camp to Governor Guy CARLETON, who wanted to use the support of the nobility and the clergy to ensure the submission of the Canadians. In 1770 Lanaudière accompanied his superior to London as a representative of the colony's inhabitants. In 1771, probably to reinforce his attachment to their side, the British authorities named him surveyor general of woods and waters and offered to make him a baronet. He refused the baronetcy, however, since the oath that he would be required to take was contrary to his religion.

The American invasion in 1775 [*see* Benedict ARNOLD; Richard Montgomery*] gave Lanaudière the chance of a military role. Travelling through the countryside around Trois-Rivières, he tried to recruit militia for the defence of Montreal in October. But he met with little success. On reaching Berthier-en-Haut (Berthierville) with an unarmed militia detachment, Lanaudière was attacked by the habitants, taken prisoner, and then released. In November that year he accompanied Carleton when the governor evacuated Montreal and embarked with his troops for Quebec. Contrary winds forced the fleet to stop at Sorel, but, with the help of the ship's captain Jean-Baptiste BOUCHETTE, Carleton and Lanaudière escaped. In 1777 Lanaudière, along with his father-in-law, took part in the initial phases of Major-General John Burgoyne*'s expedition into New York. Having returned to Quebec in August, he was not present when the Americans defeated the British troops in the autumn.

Lanaudière was a faithful servant of Carleton and in 1778 again accompanied him to Europe. In 1785 he visited Prussia and met King Frederick II, who permitted him to attend his army's manœuvres in various places. Lanaudière's attachment to the British authorities was rewarded in 1786, when Carleton (now Lord Dorchester) appointed him to the Legislative Council and made him overseer of highways. These appointments were renewed in 1791; in addition he received the title of superintendent of the postal services.

Lanaudière owned vast tracts, inherited from his mother, in the seigneury of Lac-Maskinongé (also called Lanaudière) and similar holdings, given to him by his father in 1772, in the seigneury of Sainte-Anne-de-la-Pérade. As seigneur he rendered fealty and homage for his properties in 1781 and prepared the recognition of suzerainty and census for them the following year. His seigneuries were still sparsely settled and his revenues from them were therefore slim. In 1783 he placed an advertisement in the *Quebec Gazette* inviting loyalists to settle his lands on advantageous terms such as a ten-year exemption from rent. In 1788 he presented a memorial to the government requesting that seigneurial tenure be suppressed on his properties in favour of free and common socage. For Lanaudière a change of this sort would have made his seigneuries much more profitable. But the proposed plan displeased the Canadian seigneurs and *censitaires*, and the request was shelved [*see* Thomas-Laurent Bédard*; William Smith*]. Despite this rebuff Lanaudière retained an interest in agriculture; in 1789 he subscribed to the Agriculture Society in the District of Quebec, which had been

Tarieu

founded that year. He also grew hemp on his lands at Sainte-Anne-de-la-Pérade. However, because he was kept in Quebec by his numerous obligations, Lanaudière did not live on his seigneuries; he entrusted their operation to managers such as Louis Gouin.

Lanaudière was a figure much in the public eye and so he signed addresses of welcome and farewell to British officials, to whom he was completely loyal. In 1792 he was vice-president of the Constitutional Club. Founded that January and composed mainly of British merchants, the club sought to make the constitution better known and to foster economic progress. The government once more recognized Lanaudière's services by appointing him quartermaster general of the militia in 1799. This new post, together with a number of other offices which were largely honorary but also highly lucrative, provided him with an enviable style of life. He had his home on Rue des Pauvres (Côte du Palais), which despite its name was actually one of the most fashionable streets in Quebec at the end of the 18th century. His household included some servants and slaves.

In the last years of his life Lanaudière continued to carry out the duties of the various offices entrusted to him. He died at Quebec on 2 Oct. 1811 and was buried three days later in the crypt of Notre-Dame. He had adapted well to the change in government. Like many other seigneurs he had in self-interest become intimate with the British, who during that period were trying to enhance the social and economic status of the nobility. In the course of a visit to Lower Canada at the beginning of the 19th century, John LAMBERT noted that Lanaudière "is one of the most respectable gentlemen in the colony. . . . He is sincerely attached to the English government, and in his conduct, manners, [and] principles, he seems to be an Englishman."

YVES BEAUREGARD

Charles-Louis Tarieu de Lanaudière is the author of *Chanson* (Québec, 1792); *Le discours suivant, destiné par l'honorable Charles de Lanaudière, pour être prononcé à la dernière assemblée du club constitutionnel; n'a pu l'être parce que plusieurs rapports du comité permanent ont paru devant le club pour avoir sa décision* (Québec, 1792); *A hand-bill against M. Deschenaux* (Quebec, 1792); and *Speech to habitants of Ste. Anne* (Quebec, 1792).

ANQ-Q, CE1-1, 15 oct. 1743, 7 oct. 1777, 27 mars 1779, 5 oct. 1811, 1er avril 1817; P-244. AP, Notre-Dame de Montréal, Reg. des baptêmes, mariages et sépultures, 10 avril 1769, 28 févr. 1770, 17 sept. 1771. PAC, MG 11, [CO 42] Q, 26-2: 515–16, 518; 35: 416–28; 38: 25–33; 48-1: 5; 51-2: 46–47; 89: 117–23; 90: 346–62; 93: 196–97. "Les dénombrements de Québec" (Plessis), ANQ *Rapport*, 1948–49: 15, 65, 115, 166. *Doc. relatifs à l'hist. constitutionnelle, 1759–1791* (Shortt et Doughty; 1921). *Invasion du Canada* (Verreau). [L.-A.-A. Prévôt de Montaubert de Merleval], "La campagne du régiment de La Sarre au Canada (1756–1760)," Pierre Héliot, édit., *RHAF*, 3 (1949–50): 518–36. *Quebec Gazette*, 2 Aug. 1770, 22 Sept. 1774, 23 June 1785, 6 April 1789, 19 Aug. 1791, 31 May 1792, 13 Feb. 1794, 11 Dec. 1800, 22 July 1802, 15 Jan. 1807. Le Jeune, *Dictionnaire*, 2: 58. P.-G. Roy, *Inv. concessions*, vols.2–3. Raymond Douville, *Hommes politiques de Sainte-Anne-de-la-Pérade* ([Trois-Rivières, Qué.], 1973). Tanguay, *Dictionnaire*, 7: 262. Turcotte, *Le conseil législatif.* P.[-J.] Aubert de Gaspé, *Mémoires* (Ottawa, 1866). Caron, *La colonisation de la prov. de Québec*, 2. L.-S. Rhéault, *Autrefois et aujourd'hui à Sainte-Anne de la Pérade* (Trois-Rivières, 1895). P.-G. Roy, *La famille Tarieu de Lanaudière* (Lévis, Qué., 1922). Sulte, *Hist. des Canadiens-français*, 7–8. Trudel, *L'esclavage au Canada français.* Maurice Séguin, "Le régime seigneurial au pays de Québec, 1760–1854," *RHAF*, 1 (1947–48): 382–402. Benjamin Sulte, "L'exploit du capitaine Bouchette," *BRH*, 5 (1899): 318.

TARIEU DE LANAUDIÈRE, XAVIER-ROCH (also called **François-Xavier-Roch**), office holder, lawyer, and militia officer; b. 19 April 1771 at Quebec, son of Charles-François Tarieu* de La Naudière and Marie-Catherine Le Moyne de Longueuil; d. there, unmarried, 5 Feb. 1813.

Xavier-Roch Tarieu de Lanaudière, who was the 13th in a family of 17 children, came from the colony's seigneurial and military aristocracy. From 1782 to 1787 he studied at the Séminaire de Québec. He began his clerkship in the office of notary Pierre-Louis DESCHENAUX in 1793. The following year he obtained the position of secretary and translator to the governor and Executive Council, which he shared with Jacques-François Cugnet until the latter's death in 1797 and then took on alone. In January 1795, following Deschenaux's departure for Trois-Rivières, Lanaudière continued his training with lawyers Pierre-Stanislas Bédard* and Alexis Caron*. In 1801, two years after he had finished, Lieutenant Governor Sir Robert Shore Milnes* granted him the titles of advocate, barrister, attorney, and solicitor. He does not, however, appear to have practised full time, although he kept his titles all his life and on a few occasions acted as attorney or exercised a power of attorney.

As a member of the best society in Quebec, Lanaudière signed the addresses of welcome and farewell to colonial administrators from 1785. In 1790 he signed the petition for a non-sectarian university at Quebec [*see* Jean-François Hubert*]. In 1793 and 1804 he contributed to a fund for disaster victims, and from 1799 he was a member of the Quebec Fire Society. Lanaudière also displayed unwavering attachment to the British crown. In 1797 he gave generously to the war fund to support Great Britain against France. Ten years later he visited the United Kingdom. In 1809, he acted as master of ceremonies at a ball and banquet celebrating a royal birth.

Having lived on Rue Saint-Famille and then Rue Saint-Georges (Côte d'Abraham), Lanaudière in 1802 bought a house at 39 Rue Saint-Louis for £200. He must have lived quite comfortably, since there were some servants in the household. Lanaudière drew mainly on the income from his position as secretary and translator, which brought in £200 a year, and from the rent for a house in the *faubourg* Saint-Roch. In addition he received certain sums as the owner of an eighth of the seigneury of Saint-Vallier which he had inherited from his parents in 1797 and in which he showed a keen interest. In 1810, for example, he took legal action against some of his *censitaires* who had cut hay on his domain without authorization.

Concurrent with his career as an official Lanaudière had a second one as a militia officer. He was serving as a captain in 1798, major in 1805, and lieutenant-colonel in 1810. On 10 Oct. 1811 he was appointed deputy adjutant general of the Lower Canadian militia. Because of the imminence of a clash with the United States, a complete reorganization of the available forces, and particularly of the militia units, was necessary. Lanaudière therefore temporarily handed over his office as secretary and translator to his nephew, Philippe-Joseph Aubert* de Gaspé, to devote himself to running the militia at Quebec. As deputy to adjutant general François Vassal* de Montviel, Lanaudière went to Montreal and Chambly at the end of 1812. Early in 1813 he came back to Quebec to testify before a committee of the House of Assembly. Shortly after his return Lanaudière had problems with his health; he died on 5 Feb. 1813, at the age of 41. The burial took place three days later at Quebec in Notre-Dame church before a large number of civilian and military figures.

His place within his family being what it was, Lanaudière did not have the advantages given the first son. But with the help of his circle of friends he managed to obtain rewarding posts. His career, however, was neither as renowned nor as brilliant as that of his father or of his half-brother CHARLES-LOUIS. He remained a minor official devoted to the British authorities. After his death the *Quebec Gazette* commented: "Mr. F.X. De Lanaudière was one of those rare men whose every moment is devoted to the most scrupulous and exact performance of their duties . . . no one surpassed him in zeal for his Prince."

YVES BEAUREGARD

ANQ-Q, CE1-1, 20 avril 1771, 8 févr. 1813; CN1-83, 23 mars 1793; CN1-178, 29 mars 1798, 18 juin 1803; CN1-230, 14 janv. 1794; 7 janv. 1795; 7 mars 1797; 7 mai 1798; 7 oct., 21 déc. 1802; 1er avril 1809; 16 nov. 1810; CN1-262, 3 mars, 1er, 13 avril 1797; 19 avril 1802; 4 nov. 1803; 10 juill., 8 nov. 1804; 15 mai 1807. "Les dénombrements de Québec" (Plessis), ANQ *Rapport*, 1948–49: 109, 173. *Quebec Gazette*, 24 Nov. 1785; 13 Nov., 11 Dec. 1788; 15 Jan. 1789; 4 Nov. 1790; 18 Aug. 1791; 28 Nov. 1793; 13 Feb., 10 July 1794; 3 Dec. 1795; 27 April 1797; 21 March, 15 Aug. 1799; 10 April 1800; 14 May, 12 Nov. 1801; 26 May 1803; 14 June 1804; 27 June 1805; 9 July 1807; 12 Jan., 14 Sept. 1809; 10 Oct., 17 Dec. 1811; 19 March, 30 April, 23 July, 6 Aug. 1812; 11 Feb. 1813. Charland, "Notre-Dame de Québec: le nécrologe de la crypte," *BRH*, 20: 276. Le Jeune, *Dictionnaire*, 2: 58. Tanguay, *Dictionnaire*, 7: 262. Caron, *La colonisation de la prov. de Québec*, 2. [François Daniel], *Histoire des grandes familles françaises du Canada, ou aperçu sur le chevalier Benoist, et quelques familles contemporaines* (Montréal, 1867). P.-G. Roy, *La famille Tarieu de Lanaudière* (Lévis, Qué., 1922). Benjamin Sulte, *Histoire de la milice canadienne-française, 1760–1897* (Montréal, 1897). P.-B. Casgrain, "Une autre maison Montcalm à Québec," *BRH*, 8 (1902): 329–40.

TASCHEREAU, GABRIEL-ELZÉAR, seigneur, militia officer, office holder, judge, and politician; b. 27 March 1745 at Quebec, son of Thomas-Jacques Taschereau* and Marie-Claire de Fleury de La Gorgendière; m. there first 26 Jan. 1773 Marie-Louise-Élizabeth Bazin; m. secondly 3 Nov. 1789 Louise-Françoise Juchereau Duchesnay, daughter of Antoine JUCHEREAU Duchesnay, in Beauport, Que.; d. 18 Sept. 1809 in Sainte-Marie-de-la-Nouvelle-Beauce (Sainte-Marie), Lower Canada.

At the age of four Gabriel-Elzéar Taschereau lost his father, and he grew up at Quebec with his mother. In 1759 he assisted in the defence of the town against the British; in the course of the siege the family house was burned. There is almost no trace of his activities until 1771, when as owner of a part both of Anticosti Island and of the seigneury of Mingan he granted trading leases to Thomas DUNN and William GRANT (1744–1805). The following year Taschereau, himself heir to a portion of the seigneury of Sainte-Marie-de-la-Nouvelle-Beauce, bought his brothers' and sisters' rights of succession. Early in 1773 he completed his acquisitions by purchasing from his mother for 12,000 shillings half of both the seigneurial rights and the domain of Sainte-Marie-de-la-Nouvelle-Beauce, which comprised her share of the inheritance as widow of the recognized seigneur. Taschereau retained his dwelling at the corner of Rue Buade and Rue de la Montagne in Quebec but took up residence in Sainte-Marie-de-la-Nouvelle-Beauce. He established his mother and sister Marie there, each of them paying 2,000 shillings for a room in the seigneurial manor-house, heat, light, board, and care.

In 1775 the rebel American colonies were preparing to invade the province of Quebec [*see* Benedict ARNOLD]. Consequently, on 14 August Taschereau received a commission as adjutant holding the rank of captain. In September he reviewed the Canadian militia of Quebec, and then on 31 December he took part in the defeat of the Americans in the Lower Town [*see* Richard Montgomery*]. His loyalty to the British

Taschereau

crown drew reprisals from some of his *censitaires* at Sainte-Marie-de-la-Nouvelle-Beauce who had dealings with the American troops. Moreover, early in 1776 the American rebels pillaged his domain and communal mill and sold the effects at auction. After the Americans had withdrawn, Taschereau, François BABY, and Jenkin WILLIAMS were appointed by Governor Guy CARLETON to investigate the nature and extent of collaboration with the enemy in the Quebec region. In September and October Taschereau served on two commissions, one investigating all strangers who arrived in the province, the other the certificates of good conduct required of sellers of spirits. He was also appointed a justice of the peace that year.

In March 1777 Taschereau became a judge of the Court of Common Pleas for the District of Montreal. But he gave up this office soon after because all his interests were at Quebec and in the Beauce. In the course of that year he had bought part of the seigneury of Jolliet. In 1780 and 1781 he gained possession of almost the whole seigneury through the purchase of Joseph Fleury* Deschambault's rights of succession and William Grant's share. In 1778 he had handed over to Grant about £166, the sum he had had invested in a partnership with Nicolas-Joseph de Lafontaine de Belcour, François-Joseph Cugnet*, and François Baby to exploit the post of Saint-Augustin (Que.) on the Labrador coast.

In the next two decades, Taschereau continued his career at Quebec as a minor official. In 1787 Lord Dorchester, as Carleton was now known, appointed him to the commission to examine the Jesuit estates [*see* Kenelm CHANDLER]. Taschereau did his best to protect the church's interests by opposing Sir Jeffery Amherst*'s claims to the property. On 13 Oct. 1788, in his capacity as a seigneur, he signed a petition against the constitution that was being put forward. Three years later he became a commissioner for the building and repair of churches. On 17 July 1792 he was elected to the House of Assembly for Dorchester riding, which he represented with Ignace-Michel-Louis-Antoine d'Irumberry* de Salaberry; he held his seat until 31 May 1796. During his term he was chairman of the committee for establishing courts of justice, and in March 1794 he replaced Jean Renaud* as overseer of highways for the district of Quebec. In this capacity he prepared the first legislation on highways and bridges in the province and secured its adoption in 1796. The act, however, did not meet with favour from the population, who were burdened with additional work and responsibilities.

Taschereau's loyalty to the crown was probably responsible for his appointment to the Legislative Council in 1798, replacing Gaspard-Joseph Chaussegros* de Léry, who had died a short time before. In 1799 he became one of the commissioners to superintend the House of Corrections of Quebec. Two years later he held the appointment of commissioner for building a bridge over the Rivière Jacques-Cartier, as did Jonathan Sewell* and John CRAIGIE. Again in 1801 Sir Robert Shore Milnes* named him a member of the commission appointed to apply a law providing relief to people who owed the state arrears on *lods et ventes* that were often overwhelming. The commission was chaired by Thomas Dunn and its membership included Baby, Robert LESTER, and Jean-Olivier Perrault*. On 17 Feb. 1802 Taschereau replaced Hugh FINLAY as superintendent of post houses in the colony.

According to his obituary in the *Quebec Gazette*, Taschereau "carried out his various charges with remarkable order and discernment." He was a religious, charitable, generous, and well-meaning man. He paid scrupulous attention to the management of his property, and when he took a hand in something, he had at all costs to be master of it. He was uncompromising on the honours due his rank; having a lofty idea of his station, he was determined that those around him should be mindful of it.

When he died in 1809, Gabriel-Elzéar Taschereau left a large estate to his widow and his seven surviving children: Gabriel-Elzéar, Thomas-Pierre-Joseph*, Jean-Thomas*, and Marie-Louise, who had been born of his first marriage, and Antoine-Charles, George-Louis, and Julie-Louise, born of the second. In addition to the goods and chattels, which brought £1,009 at public sale, Taschereau left his heirs the seigneuries of Sainte-Marie-de-la-Nouvelle-Beauce, Saint-Joseph-de-la-Nouvelle-Beauce, and Jolliet, and part of the seigneury of Linière, as well as six properties at Sainte-Marie-de-la-Nouvelle-Beauce and the 700 acres in Nelson Township that he had bought in 1804.

HONORIUS PROVOST

ANQ-Q, CE1-1, 27 mars 1745; CN1-25, 1ᵉʳ févr. 1781; CN1-83, 18 mai 1790; CN1-200, 28 mars 1774; CN1-205, 3 juin 1778; CN1-207, 24 janv., 16 févr. 1773; CN1-230, 3 mai 1804; 6 avril 1808; 24, 29, 30 nov., 1ᵉʳ déc. 1810. PAC, MG 18, H17. "Journal par Baby, Taschereau et Williams" (Fauteux), ANQ *Rapport*, 1927–28: 435–99; 1929–30: 138–40. "La milice canadienne-française à Québec en 1775," *BRH*, 11 (1905): 226–27. *Quebec Gazette*, 20 Feb., 27 March 1794; 25 Feb. 1802; 21 Sept. 1809. "Papiers d'État," PAC *Rapport*, 1890: 183, 186, 305–6, 332. "Papiers d'État – Bas-Canada," PAC *Rapport*, 1891: 170, 175; 1892: 186–87, 189–90, 198–99. *Quebec almanac*, 1780–1805. P.-G. Roy, *Inv. concessions*, 3: 195, 205, 212–13; 4: 142–43; 5: 2, 3, 10–11. Honorius Provost, *Sainte-Marie de la Nouvelle-Beauce; histoire civile* (Québec, 1970); *Sainte-Marie de la Nouvelle-Beauce; histoire religieuse* (Québec, 1967). J.-E. Roy, *Hist. de Lauzon*, 3: 248–54. P.-G. Roy, *La famille Taschereau* (Lévis, Qué., 1901). F.-J. Audet et Édouard Fabre Surveyer,

"Gabriel-Elzéar Taschereau," *La Presse* (Montréal), 12 nov. 1927: 21. Hare, "L'Assemblée législative du Bas-Canada," *RHAF*, 27: 361–95. J.-E. Roy, "La charge de grand voyer," *BRH*, 2 (1896): 139–40. P.-G. Roy, "L'honorable Gabriel-Elzéar Taschereau," *BRH*, 8 (1902): 3–8.

TAYLOR, ALEXANDER, businessman, office holder, and politician; b. *c.* 1736 in Scotland, son of — Taylor and Helen Gordon; twice married, first to Ann Urquhart; father of ten sons and two daughters; d. September 1811 in Newcastle, N.B.

Alexander Taylor claimed his ancestors "for seven Centurys back, were of Consanguinity to His Grace the Duke of Gordon (N. Britain) and his Ancestors." After the sale of his parents' estate he went through "a very generous allowance" in Scotland and within seven years "scarce could command One Shilling." It was at this time that he decided to join his sister and her husband who had come to the Miramichi region (N.B.) in 1777. Travelling with his wife and six children, Taylor went first to Halifax, N.S., where he obtained a grant of 700 acres at Miramichi. When he arrived at his new home in March 1784, he found only a few settlers in the area. Four years later he was appointed a justice of the peace for Northumberland County and he attended the first sessions of the Court of General Sessions in 1789. One of the most interesting of the early Northumberland County magistrates, he showed more concern for the establishment of schools and the welfare of the Indians than any of his colleagues. In 1802 he supported the Micmacs in disputes with white squatters over lands; at that time he claimed "the very road to justice seems to be entangled against these poor creatures." In 1807 he also served as overseer of the poor and commissioner of roads.

Taylor worked hard to develop the Miramichi settlement, where he supported himself by lumbering and fishing. In 1802 he collected information on the area for Edward WINSLOW. In his report of the following year he complained that "we have no Towns in this County which is the ruin of the place," and he suggested that the home government should assist in bringing over more settlers and in establishing towns. He himself claimed to have brought out to New Brunswick more than 150 of his relatives as well as other settlers, and at the time of his death there were two major towns in the area, Chatham and Newcastle, and several flourishing villages. Taylor allied himself with members of the loyalist hierarchy in Fredericton such as Winslow, and he acquired considerable political support within his large family and amongst other Scottish settlers in Northumberland County. In the by-election of 1791, caused by the death of William Davidson*, he helped elect Harris William Hailes, an outsider supported by government, over James Fraser*, a popular local merchant. In 1802

Taylor ran for a seat in the House of Assembly and defeated Samuel LEE, a loyalist. Re-elected to the fifth legislature in 1809, he held his seat until his death two years later.

Taylor was not popular with some of the county magistrates and on occasion caused them considerable embarrassment through incidents in which he was accused of drunkenness and assault and through violations of the fishery regulations. He once attacked a man at the Court of General Sessions and this and other offences led to accusations in 1799 that he had "rendered himself Odious, and a pest to the Community"; as the inspectors of the fishery at Miramichi complained, "The laws have been openly violated, justice buried in oblivion and forsed to seek an assylum in the abyss of obcurity, while licentiousness have marched in triumph Yea! and by a person in authority." "After proper expostulation" with Taylor, who promised "to guard against any further cause of complaint," the other magistrates were able to persuade the complainants to withdraw their charges. However, in 1806 Taylor was again in trouble and was charged with assault and battery. By 1808 he was also in financial difficulty. That year he wrote to Edward Winslow asking him to use his influence to help him retain his positions in the county. Nothing was done, it seems, for Taylor's name does not appear in county records after 1807. Though he had considered returning to Scotland, he apparently straightened out his affairs and decided to stay.

Although frequently involved in disputes with other county officials, Taylor seems to have done more than anyone else to advance the growth of the settlement at Miramichi after the death of William Davidson. He brought out many settlers to the river and he worked for the establishment of schools and towns at a time when the government showed little concern for such matters.

W. A. SPRAY

N.B. Museum, Davidson papers, Alexander Taylor, land grants at Miramichi. PANB, "New Brunswick political biography," comp. J. C. and H. B. Graves (11v., typescript), XI: 84; RG 2, RS8, Appointments and commissions, 2/1: 8, 32, 44; Unarranged Executive Council docs., 1804; RG 10, Northumberland County, petition no.434 (1799); RS108, Petition of John Henderson, 1785; Petitions of Alexander Taylor, 1785, 1810; RG 18, RS153. UNBL, MG H2, A. Taylor to E. Winslow, 15 Oct. 1791; 20 Jan., 25 Oct. 1802; April 1808. "Historical-geographical documents relating to New Brunswick," ed. W. F. Ganong, N.B. Hist. Soc., *Coll.*, 3 (1907–14), no.9: 342. *Winslow papers* (Raymond). W. O. Raymond, "The north shore; incidents in the early history of eastern and northern New Brunswick," N.B. Hist. Soc., *Coll.*, 2 (1899–1905), no.4: 94, 122, 124.

TECUMSEH (Tech-kum-thai), Shawnee chief; his name has been said to mean shooting star or panther

Tecumseh

crouching in wait; b. *c*. 1768, probably near present-day Springfield, Ohio; his father, who may have been named Puckeshinwa, was a Shawnee chief, and his mother may have had some Creek blood; d. 5 Oct. 1813 at what is now Thamesville, Ont., in the battle of Moraviantown.

During the closing decades of the 18th century, Indian lands west of the Appalachian Mountains were increasingly threatened by white colonization. The boundary that Great Britain had tried to erect by the Quebec Act of 1774 was shattered by the American revolution, and in the following years the Americans demonstrated their determination to extend their settlements at Indian expense. Efforts by Little Turtle [Michikinakoua] and others to unify the Six Nations and the various western tribes into a confederacy met with only limited success; the Americans dealt with individual tribes or parts of tribes and absorbed more and more land. Indian resistance to American expansion resulted in three major battles over the Ohio country during the 1790s. Many authorities claim that Tecumseh participated in all of them, but it appears that he was absent from the first. In the second, the defeat in 1791 of an American force near the Miamis Towns (Fort Wayne, Ind.), Tecumseh served as a scout with the warriors of the confederacy. In the third, the battle of Fallen Timbers (near Waterville, Ohio) in August 1794, he headed a small party of Shawnees and distinguished himself when other warriors were retreating by charging a group of Americans who had a field piece, cutting loose the horses, and riding off. Although Indian and American casualties were about the same in this battle, the Indians lost their hope of assistance from the British who, after apparent promises of aid, even refused them shelter in Fort Miamis (Maumee) following the battle. At the Treaty of Greenville in August 1795 the Indians gave up most of present-day Ohio and made other smaller cessions as well. They became caught in a vicious spiral. Scarcity of game and fur-bearing animals meant that to survive they were forced to sell more land to the whites and in so doing they grew even more dependent on them. Between 1803 and 1805 at least 30 million acres were relinquished. Moreover the American insistence on peace both with and among the various tribes weakened the foundations of the Indians' warrior society.

For a few years after Fallen Timbers Tecumseh lived as a band chief at several locations near present-day Piqua, Ohio. He and his band then moved to the west fork of the White River (Ind.). In 1799 he took part in a council near what is now Urbana, Ohio, to smooth out differences between the races, presenting a speech of such "force and eloquence" that the interpreter had trouble translating it. At Chillicothe, Ohio, in 1803 he repeated assurances of peace after the murder of a settler. Two years later, Tecumseh and

his band located at Greenville on the urgings of his brother the Prophet [Tenskwatawa*], who had been instructed by the Great Spirit to set up his headquarters there.

The millenarian religion preached by the Prophet was not unique. Throughout the world such movements have promised supernatural aid to native peoples faced with the realization that their way of life cannot be retained by physical strength alone. Like the leaders of the Delaware nativist revival in the 1750s and 1760s and the prophet of the ghost-dance religion on the prairies in the late 19th century, he predicted that divine intervention would save the Indians from their white oppressors. He taught that their present suffering was a chastisement. If they would purge themselves of white influence, stop practising witchcraft, and return to a purified Indian religion, the Great Spirit would see them live happily as before. There was also a thinly veiled hint that they would be delivered from the Americans, who "grew from the Scum of the great Water when it was troubled by the Evil Spirit." "They are unjust," the Great Spirit had told him, "they have taken away your Lands which were not made for them." Stories of the Prophet's revelations and commandments were soon in circulation all over the country south of the Great Lakes, along with accounts of his miracles. Some Delawares went so far in their fervour that they executed opponents of the movement. Whites at posts as distant as Michilimackinac (Mackinac Island, Mich.) complained of his influence.

There is no evidence that Tecumseh was involved in the evolution of this religion, but as Pontiac* had harnessed the energies of the Delaware revival, so Tecumseh transformed the Prophet's religion into a movement dedicated to retaining Indian land. By the spring of 1807 he revealed a new firmness towards the Americans. When agent William Wells asked him to come to Fort Wayne for talks, Tecumseh replied: "The Great Spirit above has appointed this place for us, on which to light our fires, and here we will remain. As to boundaries, the Great Spirit above knows no boundaries, nor will his red people acknowledge any."

Americans thought they detected the hand of Great Britain in the Indians' activities. Governor William Henry Harrison of Ohio called the Prophet a "fool, who speaks not the words of the Great Spirit but those of the devil, and of the British agents." He was unhappy that the Indians were still in the habit of calling on British posts to trade and to receive gifts from the king. He was also justly suspicious of the activities of Canadian-based traders who came gathering intelligence as well as furs. Indeed the governor-in-chief, Sir James Henry Craig, and lieutenant governor of Upper Canada, Francis Gore*, had set about revitalizing the Indian Department and recruiting Indian allies in the period of tension following the

Chesapeake affair of 1807 [*see* Sir George Cranfield BERKELEY]. In Craig's view, "if we do not employ them, there cannot exist a moment's doubt that they will be employed against us. . . ." Authorities sought out a few Indians who they thought could be trusted with the confidential information that war with the United States might not be far off. In return for support in such an event they were promised aid during the fighting and the eventual return of at least some of their lands. Apparently unaware of Tecumseh's existence, the British were intrigued by stories of the Prophet. Craig suggested that his influence be purchased "at what might be a high price upon any other occasion."

Attempts in 1808 to bring the Prophet to Fort Malden (Amherstburg), Upper Canada, failed because of enmity between him and the Shawnee chiefs visiting there and because he had been instructed by the Great Spirit to move to Tippecanoe (near Lafayette, Ind.). In June the unknown Tecumseh appeared in his place. Gore, who visited the fort in July, met Tecumseh and in a report to Craig called him "a very shrewd intelligent man." The Shawnee chief had told Indian Department officials William Claus* and Matthew ELLIOTT that he and the Prophet were attempting to gather all the tribes into one settlement to defend their lands. They had no intention at the moment of taking part in a war between Britain and the United States, although he added that "if their father the King should be in earnest and appear in sufficient force they would hold fast by him." But though Tecumseh had made an impression, he was to be referred to for some time in British correspondence as the "Brother of the Prophet."

In the spring of 1809 Tecumseh began a journey to the Senecas and Wyandots in the neighbourhood of Sandusky (Ohio) and to the Six Nations Indians in New York State to spread the message of unification against encroachment and to argue the case for common ownership of all Indian land. At Sandusky opposition from Tarhe (Crane), a Wyandot signatory to the Treaty of Greenville, prevented any move by Indians there. On his trip to the Six Nations, Tecumseh had with him as translator Caleb Atwater. According to Atwater, Tecumseh said he "had visited the Florida Indians, and even the Indians so far to the north that snow covered the ground in midsummer." It is not clear if the statements were intended literally. This visit also brought no immediate results. Support for the confederacy continued to come from the tribes south of the Great Lakes and north of the Ohio River. It was strongest among the Potawatomis, Ojibwas, Shawnees, Ottawas, Winnebagos, and Kickapoos, but it could also be found among the Delawares, Wyandots, Menominees, Miamis, Piankeshaws, and others. It tended to come from young warriors, whereas older chiefs were more likely to be opposed,

not the least of their reasons being the fact that the confederacy undermined their authority within their respective tribes. Blue Jacket [WEYAPIERSENWAH] was one of the few older chiefs who remained consistently hostile to the Americans. All sorts of circumstances caused favour for the movement to ebb and flow. The degree of support among a tribe was probably linked to the level of frustration its people felt in their efforts to fend off the American advance and maintain an Indian way of life. On the other hand, some of the most militant adherents were drawn from tribes that had never considered themselves really defeated in previous clashes with the whites, whether French, British, or American. The effect of British agitation must also have been a factor in determining the amount of sympathy with which a group regarded the movement.

The confederacy was threatened with a loss of support later in 1809 when Governor Harrison, judging the organization weak enough to be ignored, purchased another large tract from individual tribes. Tecumseh and the Prophet had promised to stop such transactions, and if they did nothing the movement would appear impotent. Direct action, however, would mean heavy loss of Indian life and withdrawal of British favour. Tecumseh responded therefore by preventing survey of the cession and by threatening death to those chiefs who had signed the treaty if the land were not returned. Tensions ran high, and in August 1810 Tecumseh went to Vincennes to meet with Harrison. He repeated the aims of the confederacy: the unification of the tribes and the establishment of the principle of common ownership of the land so that none of it could be sold without the consent of all Indians. He added that the village chiefs would be stripped of their powers and authority put into the hands of the warriors. The meeting solved nothing, and as fall approached war remained a distinct possibility.

In November Tecumseh was at Fort Malden where he suggested, to Elliott's astonishment, that he was ready to go to war with the Americans. Elliott replied that he would lay the matter before the king; in fact, he wrote to Claus urgently requesting direction. His letter passed up the ladder to Craig, whose main concern was not setting a new policy but avoiding American retribution for his previous belligerent one. He instructed the British chargé d'affaires in Washington to warn the Americans that the Indians might attack. In February 1811, long after the Indians had gone to their hunting and sugaring grounds, he wrote to Gore ordering him to keep them peaceful by whatever means were available, including denial of arms and ammunition to those who appeared bellicose.

Tension between the Indians and the Americans continued to grow. Late in July Tecumseh, accompanied by some 300 Indians, arrived at Vincennes for

Tecumseh

talks with Harrison. Again nothing was solved, and on leaving Tecumseh told Harrison he was going to the south to spread the message of common ownership and unification to the Indians there. In anticipation of his absence Harrison began to plan a march on Tippecanoe in hopes of goading the Prophet to some rash, hostile act that would justify extermination or removal of his followers. When fighting did take place, on the morning of 7 November, casualties on both sides were about the same. The Indians ran out of ammunition and fled, their faith in the Prophet shaken, and the Americans looted and burned their village. Harrison mistakenly equated their disillusionment with the death of the movement. However, the relative strength of their resistance had shown the Indians that they did not have to rely on the supernatural alone to oppose the Americans. The sense of invincibility was perhaps gone, but a new determination to fight had been born.

When Tecumseh returned to Tippecanoe, he found "great destruction and havoc – the fruits of our labour destroyed," the bodies of his friends lying in the dust, and his village in ashes. He began to rebuild his following and prepare for the eventual fight. By June 1812 it was clear that the confederacy was at least as strong as before Tippecanoe. Unaware that war between Britain and the United States had already been declared, Tecumseh boldly announced at Fort Wayne on 18 June that he was on his way to Fort Malden for lead and powder. Though he was warned by the Americans that his trip would be considered "an act of enmity," no other attempt was made to stop him.

The extent of Tecumseh's authority over the Indians who would fight alongside the British in the war is not easily defined. John Mackay Hitsman contends that he was "merely the most forceful of several tribal chiefs," and certainly there were other prominent leaders present on the Detroit frontier, Roundhead [STAYEGHTHA], MYEERAH, Thomas Splitlog [To-oo-troon-to-ra*], and Billy Caldwell* among them. The evidence suggests, however, that the only person who rivalled Tecumseh in his ability to marshal Indian support for the war effort was Robert Dickson*, a Scottish trader from the upper Mississippi valley. Matthew Elliott reported: "Tech-kum-thai has kept . . . [the Indians] faithful – he has shewn himself to be a determined character and a great friend to our Government." It should not be thought, however, that Tecumseh had any sort of absolute control over the Indians who had followed him into Upper Canada. What authority he had had before the war was badly damaged by their loss of faith in the Prophet's teachings. But no Indian leader had ever been able to dictate to the warriors. White officers had that kind of authority because white societies were able to carry on despite huge losses in battle. The Indians could not sustain such losses; the continued existence of a tribe

depended on its having enough young men to hunt and fight, and it was left to the individual warrior to make the decision about his own survival in war. White officers found the practice made Indians unreliable, in their terms, and they strongly disapproved. Nor did they ever come to understand the Indian habit of deciding to fight or not to fight on the basis of omens and visions and dreams. The fact that some Indians were not above using visions to extort special favours from their allies made relations worse. Tecumseh was different. There is no record of his having used such tactics with the British, and they liked working with him because he seemed to understand military operations as if he were a trained soldier.

The first official word of Tecumseh's presence in Upper Canada after the outbreak of the war came on 8 July: he was reported to have played "a conspicuous part" in a council at Sandwich (Windsor) the day before. On 13 July the American forces under Brigadier-General William Hull, governor of the Michigan Territory, seized that village. Then, encouraged by desertions among the Upper Canadian militia and the apparent neutrality of Indians he had expected to support the British, Hull began to send detachments farther into the province. He was fearful, however, that Indians might cut his lines of supply, which ran south by land to Ohio, and indeed on 5 August one of his provision trains was ambushed in the neighbourhood of Brownstown (near Trenton, Mich.) by Tecumseh and some others. This action, combined with the news that the British had captured Fort Michilimackinac [see Charles ROBERTS] and were advancing from the Niagara frontier, prompted Hull's withdrawal of most of his forces from Canadian territory on 8 August. The next day Tecumseh and Roundhead led the Indians who joined some regulars and militia in a bloody skirmish south of Detroit at Maguaga (Wyandotte) with an American force sent out to protect another supply train. Isaac BROCK, the British commander in Upper Canada, reached Fort Malden with reinforcements on 13 August and immediately formulated a bold plan for an attack on Detroit. Tecumseh was delighted, since the Indians, about 600 in number, had been fretting at British caution. On 16 August Brock advanced on the fort, having threatened Hull that "the numerous body of Indians who have attached themselves to my troops, will be beyond controul the moment the contest commences." The American commander surrendered without a fight. Legend has it that Tecumseh rode beside Brock when he entered Detroit and that Brock gave him his sash as a mark of respect. Whatever the case may be, there is no doubt of Brock's esteem for him. "A more sagacious or a more gallant Warrior does not I believe exist," the commander wrote. Moreover, Brock became convinced that an Indian state south of the Great Lakes should be created.

In the early weeks of the war many Indians stood aside from the fighting, remembering broken promises of British aid and feeling the odds against the confederacy too great. The successes of the British at Detroit and Michilimackinac, however, created the impression that they were willing and able to take American territory in this war, and the Potawatomi capture of the garrison from Fort Dearborn (Chicago) on 15 August gave the Indians a new self-confidence. Hundreds of them abandoned their neutrality. By the autumn of 1812 Tecumseh had about a thousand warriors with him.

Tecumseh's whereabouts during the winter of 1812–13 are not clear. Some authorities claim he travelled south again, but the sole notice in primary sources says simply that he was ill for part of the season. When spring came, the British began an offensive out of Fort Malden into the country south of Lake Erie. In April Tecumseh and Roundhead led about 1,200 Indians who joined with some 900 regulars and militia under Major-General Henry Procter* in the siege of Fort Meigs (near Perrysburg, Ohio). The American garrison, which numbered about a thousand, resisted successfully but a relief force was attacked and 500 prisoners were taken. The Indians, carried away with their triumph, began to kill them, and Procter made no effort to stop the slaughter, which ceased only with the arrival of Tecumseh. Indeed, Tecumseh's humanity on this occasion was long remembered and it contributed to his reputation among whites. The Indians were eager to have this fort taken, and after the first siege failed Tecumseh and the others put such pressure on Procter that a second was undertaken in July. The British committed only a few regulars to the attack, depending on the Indians, whose numbers had been augmented from a force of some 1,400 that Robert Dickson brought to Fort Malden from the upper country. Tecumseh and Matthew Elliott began by leading a scouting party eastward to check for approaching reinforcements. The British did not have proper siege equipment with them, and the Indians were apparently relying on a sham battle to draw the garrison out of the fort; so when the trick failed, the operation was abandoned. Procter then chose Fort Stephenson (Fremont, Ohio) as a more vulnerable target, but it too resisted fiercely when besieged at the end of July. Morale among the British and the Indians flagged as a result of the heavy casualties suffered there.

The situation on the Detroit frontier worsened with the defeat of the British fleet under Captain Robert Heriot Barclay* at the battle of Put-in Bay (Ohio) on 10 September. Procter, with about 1,000 regulars and nearly 3,000 warriors and their dependents, had no way now to obtain sufficient provisions, and he knew that the Americans under William Henry Harrison were preparing an invasion. Without consulting the Indians he began dismantling Fort Malden and preparing to retreat towards the head of Lake Ontario. Tecumseh had long suspected that Procter would flee without a fight and he begged him to provide the Indians with arms so that they could carry on their struggle alone. Their goal of retaining their homeland could hardly be achieved from the Niagara frontier. Procter promised to make a stand at the forks of the Thames (Chatham), and some of the Indians, including Tecumseh, agreed to make the retreat. Tecumseh repeatedly urged Procter to stop and face the enemy, but even when the promised location for a fight was reached Procter continued on ahead of the main force, looking for a more defensible site. A number of Indians, believing no stand would be taken, left in disgust. Tecumseh was apparently infuriated by the general's behaviour but was unable to find him.

Finally, on 5 October, Procter met the Americans, in the battle of Moraviantown, not far from the village that missionary David ZEISBERGER had founded in 1792 for converts fleeing the disorder on the American frontier. The British formed their lines with the Indians stationed in swampy ground on the right. The troops were so demoralized that at the first American attack they broke and ran. Their flight left about 500 Indians to face some 3,000 Americans. During this futile resistance Tecumseh was fatally wounded. To this day neither the identity of his slayer nor what his comrades did with his remains is known. With his death, effective Indian resistance south of the lakes practically ceased. Little more than a week later some of the tribes represented at the battle signed a truce with the Americans. Various efforts by the British to re-enlist them failed. By July 1814, months before the end of the war, Harrison met with more than 3,000 Indians to outline his conditions for peace. Neither those talks nor the Treaty of Spring Wells (1815) demanded new land cessions. By 1817, however, the Americans had returned to their old policy. In that year, except for a few left on small reserves, the Indians were removed from Ohio. By 1821 the native inhabitants of Indiana, Illinois, and Michigan had met the same fate. A small number of the displaced came to Upper Canada but most were gradually pushed westward. Of Tecumseh's confederacy nothing remained. Ottawa chief Naywash (Neywash) pronounced its epitaph in 1814 when he said, "Since our Great Chief Tecumtha has been killed we do not listen to one another, we do not rise together. We hurt ourselves by it. . . ." Tecumseh's enemy, Harrison, had described him in 1811 as "one of those uncommon geniuses which spring up occasionally to produce revolutions." The revolution had been crushed.

Tecumseh's struggle and death have haunted the imagination of poets in Canada until the present day. To George Longmore, in his "Tecumthé; a poetical tale, in three cantos" (1824), he was a tragic hero,

Tecumseh

whose flaw was that he was swayed by "nature not reason." John Frederick Richardson* in his poem *Tecumseh, or the warrior of the west* (1828) depicted Tecumseh in a similar manner, the personification of goodness and humanity transformed into a savage fiend by the Americans' murder of his (imaginary) son. In 1886 Charles Mair* published a long verse-drama, *Tecumseh*, in which the Shawnee chief is again the tragic and romantic hero, and in his alliance with the British and his opposition to American expansionists is a symbol of the dual aims of the Canada First movement. An analogy is made in Bliss Carman*'s "Tecumseh and the eagles" (1918) with the struggle of nations for freedom in World War I. In Don Gutteridge's *Tecumseh* (1976) the hero is a potential mediating figure between Indian and white cultures, whose vision, like the poet's, is to "weave a new history from our twin beginnings."

Over the course of the 19th century, historians writing in Upper Canada about the War of 1812 made him into one of its heroes, until he had a place in the mythology alongside Brock, Laura Secord [Ingersoll*], and the Canadian militia. To historian David Thompson he was simply "that great aboriginal hero." To Richardson and Gilbert Auchinleck he was the noble savage, "ever merciful and magnanimous," of a "gallant and impetuous spirit," eloquent, high-minded, and dignified. The fact that he died fighting while a British general retreated before the invading Americans enhanced his appeal to the loyalist mind. The worshipful approach that these tastes inspired had two serious consequences. It encouraged the uncritical embellishment of Tecumseh's image with pieces of hearsay and invention, and it discouraged consideration of his motives. Late in the century Ernest Alexander Cruikshank* broke with the tradition and for the first time Tecumseh's war service was subjected to a scholarly analysis of the records. Historical writers of a lesser stature have, however, perpetuated and extended the old interpretation. In 1910 Katherine B. Coutts wrote, "Of his great gifts he gave all in the Canadian cause." It was and is impossible to cast Tecumseh as a Canadian patriot first and an Indian second. His loyalty was never to Canada or even to the British in Canada. It was to a dream of a pan-Indian movement that would secure for his people the land necessary for them to continue their way of life. The few months he spent fighting with the British forces were in service of that vision. In his failure and death the cynical British and Canadians were only slightly less his enemies than the Americans.

HERBERT C. W. GOLTZ

[Until recently it was thought that Levi Adams had written "Tecumthé; a poetical tale, in three cantos," which appeared in the *Canadian Rev. and Literary and Hist. Journal* (Montreal), 2 (1824): 391–432. Mary Lu MacDonald's introduction to *The charivari, or Canadian poetics* (Ottawa, 1977), 3–10, however, established George Longmore as its author.

The portrait of Tecumseh most likely to be an accurate representation of him is the one drawn in 1808 by trader Pierre Le Dru. The evidence for its authenticity is circumstantial: Le Dru also did a sketch of the Prophet at this time, and his drawing bears a strong resemblance to a later painting of the Prophet done from life by George Catlin. If Catlin's Prophet and Le Dru's Prophet are the same man, then there is a good chance that Le Dru's Tecumseh is also a good likeness. The sketch of Tecumseh that appears in B. J. Lossing, *The pictorial field-book of the War of 1812 . . .* (New York, 1869), and is reproduced in James Mooney, "The ghost-dance religion and the Sioux outbreak of 1890," Smithsonian Institution, Bureau of American Ethnology, *Annual report* (Washington), 1892–93, pt.2, 1896, is a composite, the head being taken from the Le Dru work and the shoulders from a probably unauthentic drawing by an unknown artist. H.C.W.G.]

Fort Malden National Hist. Park Arch. (Amherstburg, Ont.), Information files, Tecumseh. National Arch. (Washington), RG 75, M15. PAC, MG 11, [CO 42] Q, 114: 74–82; MG 19, A3; F1; F2; RG 8, I (C ser.), 257: 211, 217; 678: 267; 682: 101; RG 9, I, B1; B3; RG 10, A1; A2; A6. PRO, CO 42/89, 42/146–52, 42/160, 42/165; FO 5/48, 5/61–62, 5/77, 5/84, 5/87, 5/92, 5/112. Wis., State Hist. Soc., Draper MSS, ser.YY. *Anthony Wayne . . . the Wayne–Knox–Pickering–McHenry correspondence*, ed. R. C. Knopf (Pittsburgh, Pa., 1960; repr. Westport, Conn., 1975). *Corr. of Hon. Peter Russell* (Cruikshank and Hunter). *Corr. of Lieut. Governor Simcoe* (Cruikshank). *Diplomatic correspondence of the United States: Canadian relations, 1784–1860*, comp. W. R. Manning with M. A. Gillis (4v., Washington, 1940–45), 1. *Documents relating to the invasion of Canada and the surrender of Detroit, 1812*, ed. E. A. Cruikshank (Ottawa, 1912). *Fort Wayne, gateway of the west, 1802–1813: garrison orderly books, Indian agency account book*, ed. and intro. B. J. Griswold (Indianapolis, Ind., 1927; repr. New York, 1973). *George Rogers Clark papers . . .* [1771–84], ed. J. A. James (2v., Springfield, Ill., 1912–26). J. [E. G.] Heckewelder, *Narrative of the mission of the United Brethren among the Delaware and Mohegan Indians, from its commencement, in the year 1740, to the close of the year 1808 . . .* (Philadelphia, 1820; repr. [New York], 1971). William Hull, *Memoirs of the campaign of the north western army of the United States, A.D. 1812, in a series of letters addressed to the citizens of the United States . . .* (Boston, 1824). J. D. Hunter, *Manners and customs of several Indian tribes located west of the Mississippi . . .* (Philadelphia, 1823; repr. Minneapolis, Minn., 1957).

Indian affairs: laws and treaties, comp. C. J. Kappler ([2nd ed.], 2v., Washington, 1904). John Johnston, "Recollections of sixty years," ed. C. R. Conover, in L. U. Hill, *John Johnston and the Indians in the land of the Three Miamis . . .* (Piqua, Ohio, 1957), 147–92. *Letter book of the Indian agency at Fort Wayne, 1809–1815*, ed. Gayle Thornbrough (Indianapolis, 1961). *The life and correspondence of Major-General Sir Isaac Brock, K.B.*, ed. F. B. Tupper (2nd ed., London, 1847). Richard M'Nemar, *The Kentucky revival; or, a short history of . . . Shakerism . . .*

(New York, 1846; repr. 1974). [Ma-ka-tai-me-she-kia-kiak], *Black Hawk, an autobiography*, ed. Donald Jackson (Urbana, Ill., 1964). Humphrey Marshall, *The history of Kentucky . . .* (2nd ed., 2v., Frankfort, Ky., 1824). *Memoirs and correspondence of Viscount Castlereagh, second Marquess of Londonderry*, ed. C. [W. Stewart] Vane (12v. in 3 ser., London, 1848–53). *Messages and letters of William Henry Harrison*, ed. Logan Esarey (2v., Indianapolis, 1922). *Mich. Pioneer Coll. The new American state papers [1789–1860], Indian affairs*, ed. T. C. Cochran (13v., Wilmington, Del., 1972). *Outpost on the Wabash, 1787–1791; letters of Brigadier-General Josiah Harmar and Major John Francis Hamtramck . . .*, ed. Gayle Thornbrough (Indianapolis, 1957). [John Richardson], *Richardson's War of 1812; with notes and a life of the author*, ed. A. C. Casselman (Toronto, 1902; repr. 1974); *War of 1812 . . .* ([Brockville, Ont.], 1842). *The St. Clair papers . . .*, ed. W. H. Smith (2v., Cincinnati, Ohio, 1882). *Select British docs. of War of 1812* (Wood). *Tecumseh: fact and fiction in early records*, ed. C. F. Klinck (Englewood Cliffs, N.J., 1961). *The territorial papers of the United States*, comp. C. E. Carter and J. P. Bloom (28v. to date, Washington, 1934– ; repr. vols.1–26 in 25v., New York, 1973). U.S., Congress, *American state papers* (Lowrie *et al.*), class II, vols.[1–2].

Kentucky Gazette (Lexington, Ky.), 1807–12. *National Intelligencer* (Washington), 1807–12. *Quebec Gazette*, 1807–12. *Western Sun* (Vincennes, [Ind.]), 1807–12. Caleb Atwater, *A history of the state of Ohio, natural and civil* (Cincinnati, 1838); *The writings of Caleb Atwater* (Columbus, Ohio, 1833). Gilbert Auchinleck, *A history of the war between Great Britain and the United States of America, during the years 1812, 1813, and 1814* (Toronto, 1855). Pierre Berton, *Flames across the border, 1813–1814* (Toronto, 1981); *The invasion of Canada, 1812–1813* (Toronto, 1980). [These two works perpetuate the romantic and spectacular view of Tecumseh. H.C.W.G.] H. M. Brackenridge, *History of the late war, between the United States and Great Britain; containing a minute account of the various military and naval operations* (4th ed., Baltimore, Md., 1818). C. W. Butterfield, *History of the Girtys . . .* (Cincinnati, 1890). G. C. Chalou, "The red pawns go to war: British-American Indian relations, 1810–1815" (PHD thesis, Indiana Univ., Bloomington, 1971). Moses Dawson, *A historical narrative of the civil and military services of Major-General William H. Harrison . . .* (Cincinnati, 1824). J. B. Dillon, *A history of Indiana from its earliest exploration by Europeans to the close of the territorial government, in 1856 . . .* (Indianapolis, 1859; repr. [New York], 1971). R. C. Downes, *Council fires on the upper Ohio: a narrative of Indian affairs in the upper Ohio valley until 1795* (Pittsburgh, 1940). Benjamin Drake, *Life of Tecumseh, and of his brother, the Prophet . . .* (Cincinnati, 1841). [Still the most reliable secondary source. H.C.W.G.] Dennis Duffy, *Gardens, covenants, exiles: loyalism in the literature of Upper Canada/Ontario* (Toronto, 1982). N. W. Edwards, *History of Illinois, from 1778 to 1833; and life and times of Ninian Edwards* (Springfield, Ill., 1870; repr. New York, 1975). Edward Eggleston and Lillie Eggleston Seelye, *Tecumseh and the Shawnee Prophet . . .* (New York, 1878). E. S. Ellis, *The life of Tecumseh, the Shawnee chief . . .* (New York, 1861).

Timothy Flint, *Indian wars of the west . . .* (Cincinnati, 1833; repr. [New York], 1971). W. A. Galloway, *Old Chillicothe: Shawnee and pioneer history; conflicts and romances in the Northwest territory* (Xenia, Ohio, 1934). H. C. W. Goltz, "Tecumseh, the Prophet, and the rise of the Northwest Indian Confederation" (PHD thesis, Univ. of Western Ont., London, 1973). N. St C. Gurd, *The story of Tecumseh* (Toronto, 1912). H. S. Halbert and T. S. Ball, *The Creek war of 1813 and 1814* (Chicago, 1895). W. H. Harrison, *A discourse on the aborigines of the Ohio valley . . .* (Chicago, 1883). *History of Greene County, together with historic notes on the northwest, and the state of Ohio . . .*, comp. R. S. Dills (Dayton, Ohio, 1881). Hitsman, *Incredible War of 1812*. Reginald Horsman, *Expansion and American Indian policy, 1783–1812* ([East Lansing, Mich.], 1967); *Matthew Elliott*. T. L. M'Kenney and James Hall, *History of the Indian tribes of North America, with biographical sketches and anecdotes of principal chiefs . . .* (3v., Philadelphia, 1838–44). Leslie Monkman, *A native heritage: images of the Indian in English-Canadian literature* (Toronto, 1981). J. M. Oskison, *Tecumseh and his times: the story of a great Indian* (New York, 1938). Bradford Perkins, *Prologue to war: England and the United States, 1805–1812* (Berkeley and Los Angeles, Calif., 1961; repr. 1963). E. T. Raymond, *Tecumseh: a chronicle of the last great leader of his people* (Toronto, 1915). David Thompson, *History of the late war, between Great Britain and the United States . . .* (Niagara [Niagara-on-the-Lake, Ont.], 1832; repr. [New York], 1966). Glenn Tucker, *Tecumseh: vision of glory* (Indianapolis and New York, 1956). [Contains much apocryphal material. H.C.W.G.] K. B. Coutts, "Thamesville and the battle of the Thames," *OH*, 9 (1910): 20–25. E. A. Cruikshank, "The 'Chesapeake' crisis as it affected Upper Canada," *OH*, 24 (1927): 281–322; "The employment of Indians in the War of 1812," American Hist. Assoc., *Annual report* (Washington), 1895: 319–35. Reginald Horsman, "American Indian policy in the old northwest, 1783–1812," *William and Mary Quarterly* (Williamsburg, Va.), 3rd ser., 18 (1961): 35–53.

TESTARD LOUVIGNY DE MONTIGNY, JEAN-BAPTISTE-PIERRE, fur trader, office holder, Indian Department official, and militia officer; b. 1 Nov. 1750 in Montreal (Que.), son of Jean-Baptiste-Philippe Testard* de Montigny and Marie-Charlotte Trottier Desrivières; d. 24 Feb. 1813 and was buried three days later in Montreal.

Jean-Baptiste-Pierre Testard Louvigny de Montigny was a descendant of a family several members of which had had military careers in New France. His father, an officer in the colonial regular troops, had been taken prisoner in 1759 when the British besieged Fort Niagara (near Youngstown, N.Y.). After being released he eventually went with his family to live at Blois, France, in 1764. Unlike most of his brothers and sisters, Jean-Baptiste-Pierre Testard Louvigny de Montigny decided to return to the province of Quebec around 1770. On 12 Aug. 1771, after obtaining a dispensation granted because the degree of their consanguinity was that of second cousins, he married Charlotte Trottier Desrivières, a girl of 16, in

Testard

Montreal. The contract, dated 10 August, gave her a dower of 6,000 *livres* and a preference legacy of 3,000 *livres*. The marriage unfortunately came to an end with her death on 17 Nov. 1779.

Early in the 1770s Louvigny de Montigny went into the fur trade, through which he was to realize substantial profits. During the American invasion in 1775–76 he joined François-Marie Picoté* de Belestre in going to defend Fort St Johns (Saint-Jean-sur-Richelieu); it had already been raided by Benedict ARNOLD's troops on 18 May 1775 and was now once again threatened. Picoté de Belestre's contingent was placed under the orders of the commander of the fort, Major Charles Preston of the 26th Foot, who entrusted Louvigny de Montigny with an important letter for Guy CARLETON in Montreal. Carleton detained the messenger from 9 Sept. 1775 and hence Louvigny de Montigny was not taken prisoner on 2 Nov. 1775 when the garrison of Fort St Johns surrendered to Richard Montgomery*. On 30 October he had joined a raiding party under Carleton which attempted to cross the St Lawrence at Longueuil. They were repulsed by the Americans and had to withdraw.

Louvigny de Montigny took part in the battle at Les Cèdres from 19 to 26 May 1776, although he had only a minor role. It was his brother Jean-Baptiste-Jérémie who particularly distinguished himself by formulating a strategy against the invaders and capturing Major Henry Sherburne. It seems that Louvigny de Montigny subsequently used the brilliant actions of his brother, who died in 1784, to obtain favours from the government. Thus on 1 Jan. 1793 he sent a letter to Lieutenant Governor SIMCOE of Upper Canada requesting a grant of land "opposite Fort Detroit"; he laid emphasis on his military service and credited himself with having been "one of those who devised the plan for the affair at Les Cèdres" in the spring of 1776. He repeated the same theme in 1807, this time declaring that he himself had "put into execution the plan that he had drawn up against Les Cèdres."

Once the American troops had been neutralized, Louvigny de Montigny returned to his trading activities. He was one of the signatories to the address which the Montreal merchants presented to Lieutenant Governor Henry Hamilton* on 16 June 1785 to express their appreciation for his attention to the development of trade in the west. In November 1788 and January 1789 Louvigny de Montigny's name was on two petitions drawn up by some Canadians to protest against the constitutional change then being contemplated [*see* Pierre-Amable DE BONNE].

Towards the end of 1789 Lord Dorchester [Carleton] entrusted a position at Detroit to Louvigny de Montigny. It was here that on 1 March 1790 he took as his second wife Agathe Hay, daughter of Jehu Hay*, the former lieutenant governor of the town. Little is known about his administrative duties, except that he was a member of the land board of the District of Hesse in 1791 and 1792, and then of that of Essex and Kent counties from 1792 to 1794. In any event, he remained in the Detroit area until the beginning of the 19th century.

In 1794, on learning that the American major-general Anthony Wayne was marching against Fort Miamis (Maumee, Ohio), Louvigny de Montigny decided that the 24th Foot, the unit responsible for defending the fort, was in a bad situation, and he raised a corps of 200 Canadians to reinforce the garrison. For this action he received expressions of thanks from Simcoe and from Richard G. ENGLAND, commandant of the post of Detroit, who made a report to Lord Dorchester praising him. The following year Dorchester granted him a captain's commission in the Royal Canadian Volunteer Regiment, which had been created to replace the British troops whose services were required elsewhere. In this capacity Louvigny de Montigny raised a company to garrison Detroit. However, since Dorchester had neglected to give Lieutenant-Colonel England the necessary authority to issue supplies to the new recruits, Louvigny de Montigny had to travel to Montreal and Quebec to obtain approval for the enlistment of 45 men, to whom he had advanced pay at his own risk. After Detroit had been ceded to the Americans in 1796, it may be assumed that, like most of the British nationals, he settled at Amherstburg in Upper Canada; he remained in command of his company until he was discharged in 1802.

Some time between 1802 and 1805 Louvigny de Montigny returned to Lower Canada. As he was without employment, he applied to the Duke of York, offering him his services; despite an encouraging reply, in 1807 he was still not assigned to a specific post. On 6 April 1808 he received a commission as justice of the peace for the District of Montreal which was renewed on 10 July 1810. In the latter year he served as an agent for the Indian Department of Lower Canada. When war broke out with the United States in 1812, he was stationed at the Iroquois reserve of St Regis and was on the staff of the Lower Canadian militia.

Following an enemy raid at St Regis, Louvigny de Montigny was captured on 23 Oct. 1812 and taken the next day to Plattsburgh, N.Y. He returned to Lower Canada on 8 December, having been exchanged for an American colonel. On 24 Feb. 1813, at 62 years of age, he died of his wounds, leaving his wife and several children, one of whom, Pierre-Benjamin Testard de Montigny, would later be a lawyer in Montreal. Louvigny de Montigny's widow received from then on a life pension of £30. This sum did not allow her to live decently, judging by the petition she submitted to the government of Lower Canada in 1815.

FRANÇOIS BÉLAND

ANQ-M, CE1-51, 2 nov. 1750, 12 août 1771, 18 nov. 1779, 27 févr. 1813; CN1-308, 10 août 1771. PAC, MG 11 [CO 42] Q, 112: 306; RG 4, A1; RG 8, I (C ser.), 17: 139. *Corr. of Lieut. Governor Simcoe* (Cruikshank), 2: 400; 4: 106, 275. *John Askin papers* (Quaife), 1: 379–80; 2: 683. *Quebec Gazette*, 16 June 1785; 6, 14 April 1808; 12 July 1810; 1 Oct. 1812. Le Jeune, *Dictionnaire. Quebec almanac*, 1797–1805. Stanley, *L'invasion du Canada* (MacDonald), 181. F.-J. Audet, "Pierre-Jean-Baptiste Testard de Montigny," *BRH*, 33 (1927): 295–300. Louvigny de Montigny, "Le Lorimier et le Montigny des Cèdres," *BRH*, 47 (1941): 33–47. "Le 'Royal Canadien' ou 'Royal Canadian Volunteers,'" *BRH*, 7 (1901): 372. Jacques Viger, "La prise de Saint-Régis," J. M. LeMoine, édit., *BRH*, 5 (1899): 141–44.

TEY-YAGH-TAW. *See* STAYEGHTHA

THAYENDANEGEA (he also signed **Thayendanegen, Thayeadanegea, Joseph Thayendanegea,** and **Joseph Brant**), Mohawk interpreter, translator, war chief, and statesman; Indian Department officer; member of the wolf clan; his Mohawk name means he sets or places together two bets; probably b. *c.* March 1742/43 in Cayahoga (near Akron, Ohio), son of Tehowaghwengaraghkwin; d. 24 Nov. 1807 in what is now Burlington, Ont.

According to testimony Joseph Brant gave to John Norton*, he was "descended from Wyandot prisoners adopted by the Mohawks on both the father and mother's side"; his grandmother had been captured when the Wyandots were living in the vicinity of the Bay of Quinte (Ont.). The tradition that the Mohawk chief Hendrick [Theyanoguin*] was an ancestor of Brant has been affirmed by historian Lyman Copeland Draper. In 1879 an elderly Mohawk woman named Katy Moses, who was a distant relative of Brant's third wife, told Draper that Brant's mother was descended from Hendrick. Charlotte Smith, *née* Brant, a granddaughter of Joseph, said that Brant's mother was Hendrick's granddaughter. When Brant visited England in 1775–76, he was interviewed at length by James Boswell, who wrote an account for the *London Magazine* of July 1776. In it Brant is called the grandson of the chief who visited England in the time of Queen Anne. But Mohawks use the term grandfather to refer also to great- and great-great-grandfathers and to great-uncles, and a chief named Brant (Sa Ga Yeath Qua Pieth Tow) who was also in the 1710 delegation may have been related to Joseph in some way.

Joseph was probably born in March 1742 of the Julian calendar. Estimates of his year of birth made by subtracting his age at death as given by his biographer William Leete Stone produce a date of 1743, but this purely arithmetical calculation ignores the change from Julian to Gregorian calendar which took place in his lifetime. Joseph's father, Tehowaghwengaraghkwin, who was reputed to have been a prominent warrior, died while his son was an infant. A few years before the outbreak of the Seven Years' War, Joseph's mother took him and his sister Mary [Koñwatsiʔtsiaiéñni*] to the Mohawk valley, settling at Canajoharie (near Little Falls, N.Y.), which had been her home before the family's emigration to the Ohio country. She married again, her new husband being a man named Carrihogo, or News Carrier, who was known to the whites as Barnet or Bernard, and by contraction, Brant. Young Joseph was called Brant's Joseph and finally Joseph Brant. Author William Allen, who knew Joseph Brant's son Joseph and possibly obtained the information from him, says that the stepfather, a chief, "was denominated an Onondaga Indian." Stone, who interviewed various descendants, says that the stepfather was a Mohawk.

Brant's first military service with the British came when he was about 15, during the Seven Years' War. He took part in James Abercromby*'s campaign to invade Canada by way of Lake George (Lac Saint-Sacrement) in 1758 and he was with the warriors who accompanied Sir William Johnson*, superintendent of northern Indians, in the 1759 expedition against Fort Niagara (near Youngstown, N.Y.). The next year he was a member of the force led by Jeffery Amherst* that descended the St Lawrence to besiege Montreal.

Brant's stepfather died about 1760. Testimony that Draper received from Brant's godson, John "Smoke" Johnson*, indicates that a warrior known as Old Crooked Neck "took charge" of young Brant and brought him to Sir William Johnson. Impressed by his abilities, Johnson decided to send him to school. In the summer of 1761 Joseph was dispatched along with two other Mohawk boys to the Reverend Eleazar Wheelock in Lebanon (Columbia), Conn., to be enrolled in Moor's Indian Charity School. Wheelock referred to him as "being of a Family of Distinction . . . , was considerably cloathed, *Indian*-fashion, and could speak a few Words of English." His mental capacities and demeanour commended him highly to Wheelock. Brant was soon employed in teaching the Mohawk language to a fellow scholar, Samuel Kirkland, who planned to be a missionary to the Iroquois. On 4 Nov. 1761 Brant and Kirkland went to Iroquois country to secure six more boys for the school. They returned a few weeks later with two Mohawk boys and a promise from Johnson that he would send more when families had returned from the fall hunt.

Thayendanegea

So promising a student was Brant that Wheelock had planned to let him accompany Kirkland when he went on to the College of New Jersey (Princeton University); there Brant could continue tutoring the aspiring missionary in the Mohawk language while he himself studied in the local grammar school, perfecting his English and "pursuing other parts of Useful Learning perhaps fitting for College." The plan did not materialize and in 1762 Kirkland went to the college alone.

Wheelock described Brant in February 1763 as being "of a Sprightly Genius, a manly and genteel Deportment, and of a Modest and benevolent Temper, I have Reason to think began truly to love our Lord Jesus Christ Several Months ago; and his religious Affections Seem Still agreeably increasing." At this time Brant's tutor, Charles Jeffry Smith, was making arrangements to take him with him to Mohawk country, where the two could continue to teach each other their respective languages and where Smith could serve as a missionary to the Mohawks. In May 1763, however, a letter came for Joseph from his sister Mary calling him home, since the Indians were displeased with his being at the school, "don't like the People &c." Wheelock begged Johnson's indulgence for a few more months until Smith could be ready for his mission tour, and until Wheelock had had an opportunity to take Brant on a trip to Boston and Portsmouth, N.H., on school business.

Brant and Smith left for Mohawk country in the summer of 1763, and though both Smith and Wheelock looked forward to Brant's return to the school, it was not to be. Johnson in fact was contemplating sending him to New York City where he could be prepared for entrance into King's College (Columbia University). However, upon advice that prejudice against Indians was running high in the city as a result of Pontiac*'s uprising, Johnson sent him and three other Mohawk youths to missionary Cornelius Bennet in the Mohawk valley to further their education.

Along with other Iroquois allies of the British, Brant participated in the 1764 campaign against the Delaware Indian settlements on the Susquehanna River, and he was one of the volunteers on John Bradstreet*'s expedition against the western Indians that same year. His activities gave rise to the false rumour in New England that he had put himself at the head of a large party of Indians to attack the British. Though Wheelock's confidence in Brant remained unshaken, the tale hurt his school financially. Wheelock later wrote that Brant had been "useful in the War; in which he behaved so much like the Christian and the Soldier, that he gained great Esteem."

On 25 July 1765 Brant married an Oneida woman, Neggen Aoghyatonghsera, whose English name was Margaret, daughter of Isaac of Onoquaga. The ceremony was conducted at Canajoharie by missionary Theophilus Chamberlain*, who described the bride as "a handsome, sober, discreet & a religious young woman." The Brants had two children, Isaac and Christiana, and lived in a comfortable house at Canajoharie where missionaries labouring among the Iroquois were always welcomed. Neggen contracted consumption and died, probably in mid March 1771. Brant then went to live with John STUART, Anglican missionary at Fort Hunter, N.Y. He soon applied to Stuart to marry him to Neggen's half-sister, Susanna. Stuart declined since the Church of England forbad such close kinship marriages, and Brant thereupon approached a German minister, who performed the ceremony. Susanna died after a brief time, leaving no issue. About 1779 Brant married Catharine [Ohtow-aʔkéhson*], reputedly the daughter of former Indian agent George Croghan. She was from a prominent family and later became clan matron of the Mohawk turtle clan; her brother Henry [Tekarihó:ken*] was the tribe's leading sachem. Seven children were born of this marriage: Joseph, Jacob, Margaret, Catharine, Mary, John [Ahyouwaeghs*], and Elizabeth. Brant sent Joseph and Jacob to the Wheelock family at Hanover, N.H., in 1800. Both Dartmouth College and Moor's Indian Charity School were located there by this date, and the boys were entered in the school. It was John, however, who became prominent in Mohawk tribal affairs and in Upper Canadian politics.

During the time Brant spent with John Stuart, he had assisted the missionary in translating the Gospel of St Mark, a concise history of the Bible, and an exposition of the catechism into the Mohawk language. In Stuart's estimation Brant was "perhaps . . . the only Person in America equal to such an undertaking." Brant's services and talents were also valued by Johnson, who used him as an interpreter and a translator of speeches into the languages of the Six Nations. Brant spoke at least three of these languages fluently. Norton states in his *Journal* that shortly before dying in 1774 Johnson used his influence with the Mohawks to have Brant chosen a chief, presumably a war chief, but that Brant accepted the honour with some hesitation. Brant also served Sir William's successor, Guy Johnson*. In 1775 he received the appointment of "Interpreter for the Six Nations Language" at an annual salary of £85 3s. 4d., American army currency.

After the outbreak of hostilities in the Thirteen Colonies in 1775, Brant remained loyal to the king. He went to Montreal with Guy Johnson in the summer and in November embarked for England with Johnson, Christian Daniel Claus*, and a few associates to present their position on Indian affairs to the British government. Brant was generally lionized, introduced to some of the leading men in the arts, letters, and government, inducted into the Falcon Lodge of freemasons, and had his portrait painted. According to Boswell, he "was struck with the appearance of England in general; but he said he chiefly admired the ladies and the horses." He did not, however, neglect the serious side of his mission. He and his Mohawk companion, Oteroughyanento (Ohrante), presented Iroquois grievances about encroachments on their lands to Lord George Germain, secretary of state for the American Colonies. "It is very hard when we have let the Kings subjects have so much of our lands for so little value, they should want to cheat us . . . of the small spots we have left for our women and children to live on," Brant said. Germain fully agreed that the Indians had been wronged by the Americans but stated that the government could not attend to redressing these grievances until the dispute with the king's rebellious subjects had been settled. He hoped that the Six Nations would remain loyal and could, as a consequence, be assured "of every Support England could render Them." The promise satisfied Brant and he later repeated it in a speech to the Six Nations. Indeed, as a result of discussions with numerous English leaders of varying political persuasions, he became more firmly convinced than ever that the welfare of the Indian nations lay in a continuing alliance with the king.

Brant and his companions returned to North America in time to participate in the battle of Long Island in the summer of 1776. Then he and his loyalist friend Gilbert Tice went in disguise through the American-held countryside to Iroquois territory, where Brant urged the Indians to abandon their treaty of neutrality with the Continental Congress and actively support British arms. After persistent effort he eventually raised a force of about 300 Indian warriors and 100 white loyalists. For nearly a year he remained in the Susquehanna River region. Operating out of Onoquaga (near Binghamton, N.Y.), he made several excursions with his Indian-loyalist band to encourage white resistance, rouse the Indians, and confiscate food. In July 1777 he arrived at Oswego, followed by about 300 warriors, to join Barrimore Matthew St Leger*'s campaign. He participated in both the siege of Fort Stanwix (Rome) and the nearby battle of Oriskany that summer.

In January 1778 Brant left Fort Niagara with a party of warriors to reconnoitre in Indian country and be on the look-out for any American invasion attempt. In May and June his forces attacked Cobleskill and Durlach (Sharon). Again quartered at Onoquaga, he continued to send out foraging and scouting parties. Accompanied by a ranger detachment under Captain William Caldwell*, Brant and his warriors attacked and destroyed German Flats (near the mouth of West Canada Creek) in September. During October he and his men continued their raiding operations, mostly in Ulster County. He then joined forces with Captain Walter Butler*'s rangers and some Senecas for an attack on Cherry Valley early in November. During the course of events the Senecas detached themselves from Butler's command and killed indiscriminately, friend and foe alike, throughout the settlement. Brant and his followers tried desperately, and with some success, to save numbers of white non-combatants from the fury of the Seneca warriors. According to every report, wrote Mason Bolton, commandant at Niagara, Brant "behaved with great humanity to all those who fell into his hands at Cherry Valley."

During July 1779 Brant and his Indian-loyalist band attacked the settlement of Minisink (Port Jervis) and cut to pieces the militia sent in pursuit of them. On 29 August at the battle of Newtown (near Elmira), which was the major engagement of the Sullivan–Clinton expedition into Iroquois country, the Indians were less fortunate. A force of Indians, rangers, and a few regulars, commanded by Major John Butler*, Brant, Kaieñʔkwaahtoñ*, and Kaiũtwahʔkũ (Cornplanter), was defeated and obliged to retreat under the onslaught of the American army. The sheer number of the Americans and their superiority in weapons and supplies prevented any further full-scale confrontation for the remainder of the expedition, and the American invaders totally devastated the Indian country as far as the Genesee River before turning back. The Indian refugees were forced *en masse* into the area around Fort Niagara, straining British resources to the utmost.

Far from crushing the Six Nations, the invasion only increased their determination for revenge. Numerous raiding parties spread terror through the American frontier settlements during 1780. In the spring Brant and his band were raiding near Harpersfield, N.Y. In July they laid waste the villages of pro-American Oneidas and Tuscaroras. Brant was also with the Indians and loyalists who devastated the Mohawk valley settlements and the Schoharie region later that year.

Brant had been serving as a captain in the Indian Department at least since early 1779, although he did not have a commission. On 16 April 1779 Germain sent Governor HALDIMAND a commission signed by George III for Joseph Brant as colonel of Indians in appreciation of his "astonishing activity and success" in the king's service. Haldimand suppressed the document, courteously explaining to Germain that Brant, despite his meritorious activity, was relatively young compared to the other Indian war leaders, "has been very lately known in the War Path," and although distinguishing himself was as yet far from being recognized by the senior war chiefs as having an equal footing with the most experienced warriors of the confederacy. Such a mark of distinction, if it were presented to Brant, Haldimand warned, would there-

Thayendanegea

fore "be productive of very dangerous consequences" in stirring up jealousy and animosity towards him among the leading Iroquois warriors. Consequently Brant did not receive an official commission until 13 July 1780 when, on the recommendation of Guy Johnson, Haldimand made him a captain "of the Northern Confederate Indians."

Despite his captaincy, Brant preferred to fight as a war chief. He later explained to Sir John Johnson* that that rank gave him command of more men in battle than was customary with a captain. The British officers who served with Brant and the commanding officers who received reports of his military behaviour always had the highest praise for him. He emerges in the official dispatches as the perfect soldier, possessed of remarkable physical stamina, courage under fire, and dedication to the cause, as an able and inspiring leader, and as a complete gentleman. White volunteers are known to have requested transfer from the rangers so that they could join Brant, "a person they had confidence in & had volunteerly served under with much satisfaction."

In early 1781 Brant and John DESERONTYON were planning to attack the Oneidas once more. Because of a rumoured invasion of the Ohio country by George Rogers Clark, however, Guy Johnson diverted Brant's activities to that quarter. Brant and 17 warriors left Fort Niagara on 8 April 1781 for the Ohio Indian villages, where they remained several months encouraging the inhabitants. On 26 August Brant, with a hundred whites and Indians, utterly defeated an equal number of men from Clark's army, killing or capturing all of them.

Brant's final military service during the revolution came in 1782, when he and his warriors assisted Major John Ross*'s men in repairing Fort Oswego. Then, in July, he set out with a large party of warriors and a company of light infantry from the fort to harry the American settlements; he was summoned back, however, by Haldimand's announcement of peace negotiations and the consequent recall of all war parties. Hostilities were drawing to a close, but Brant's great career as a statesman was just beginning.

In the peace negotiations between Great Britain and the United States, Britain completely ignored its Indian allies and transferred sovereignty over all British-claimed land as far west as the Mississippi River to the Americans, even though almost the entire territory was occupied by Indians, who believed they had never relinquished it to the whites. When Brant learned of the treaty's terms he angrily exclaimed that England had "sold the Indians to Congress." The indignation of the Six Nations at their betrayal led the British administrators in Quebec to attempt to mollify them by various means. Sir John Johnson, superintendent general of Indian affairs, told them that "the

right of Soil belongs to and is in yourselves as sole proprietors" beyond the boundary established by the 1768 Treaty of Fort Stanwix – a line running southwest from that fort to the Ohio River and thence to the Mississippi. Such statements about land title were bound to mislead Indians by obscuring the distinction between ownership of land and sovereignty over it. The British also maintained control of forts Oswegatchie (Ogdensburg, N.Y.), Oswego, Niagara, Detroit, and Michilimackinac (Mackinac Island, Mich.), all in ceded territory, and urged the formation of a confederation by the Iroquois and the Indians to the west. In addition, colonial officials appealed to the home government to secure a land grant within the province for the faithful Iroquois. Haldimand made arrangements for a tract on the Bay of Quinte to be provided for the Mohawks, who had lost all their land as a result of the war, and for other Six Nations Indians and their allies who cared to immigrate. The Senecas, however, objected to the location. They were the westernmost Iroquois tribe and their lands were not immediately threatened by the Americans. Most of them planned to stay where they were, and in their view a settlement on the Bay of Quinte would endanger the Six Nations by dispersing them over too great a distance. They offered the refugees instead a gift of land in the Genesee valley. Though the Mohawks refused the offer, Brant was persuaded that the Seneca reasoning had merit. Through him the Mohawks therefore requested of Haldimand a new grant closer to the traditional Six Nations homeland. In the autumn of 1784 they received a huge tract along the Grand River (Ont.), which the Mississauga Ojibwas had relinquished in May, and, with the exception of the Fort Hunter Mohawks under John Deserontyon who preferred to settle at the Bay of Quinte, they established themselves on this land. A census made in 1785 shows more than 400 Mohawks, several hundred Cayugas and Onondagas, and smaller groups of Senecas, Tuscaroras, Delawares, Nanticokes, Tutelos, Creeks, and Cherokees to a total of 1,843.

Brant played a major role in attempts to forge the Six Nations and the western Indians into a confederacy to oppose American expansion. In August and September 1783 he was present at unity meetings in the Detroit area and on 7 September at Lower Sandusky (Ohio) was a principal speaker at an Indian council attended by Wyandots, Delawares, Shawnees, Cherokees, Ojibwas, Ottawas, and Mingos. There he feelingly presented his grand vision: "We the Chief Warriors of the Six Nations with this Belt bind your Hearts and Minds with ours, that there may be never hereafter a Separation between us, let there be Peace or War, it shall never disunite us, for our Interests are alike, nor should anything ever be done but by the united Voice of us all, as we make but one with you." The confederacy forged at these meetings would continue to be a principal concern of Brant's for a number of years.

From 31 Aug. to 10 Sept. 1784 Brant was at Fort Stanwix for peace negotiations between the Six Nations and New York State officials, but he did not attend the treaty held at the same place with the commissioners of the Continental Congress in October. He did, however, express extreme indignation on learning that the commissioners had detained as hostages several prominent Six Nations leaders, including his friend Kanonraron (Aaron Hill). Brant delayed an intended trip to England attempting to secure their release.

In late 1785 Brant set sail to present Mohawk claims for war losses to the government, to petition for a half-pay pension, to request publication of religious literature in the Mohawk language, and to receive assurance that Indian land had not been given to the United States. Most important, he wished to ascertain whether the faithful Indian allies of the king might expect support from the British government should war break out between the Americans and the confederated Indians over American encroachment on Indian lands. He made the trip over the strong opposition of Sir John Johnson, who urged him to stay at home and attend to the affairs of the confederacy.

In England Brant succeeded in securing his pension and a compensation of about £15,000 for the Mohawks. As for his query whether the Indians would "be considered as His Majesty's faithful allies, and have that support and countenance such as old and true friends expect" should "serious consequences" develop over American encroachments on Indian land, Brant received an assurance from Home Secretary Lord Sydney of the king's continual concern for Indian welfare and a recommendation from the king that the Indians conduct their affairs "with temper and moderation" and a "peaceable demeanor," all of which would "most likely . . . secure to themselves the possession of those rights and privileges which their ancestors have heretofore enjoyed." It was obviously a polite refusal to become militarily involved in the Indians' problems.

The Indian confederacy was not functioning as Brant had planned. The Americans had ignored it and had insisted on making treaties with smaller groups of Indians. The resulting treaties of Fort Stanwix (1784), Fort McIntosh (1785), and Fort Finney (1786), with their extortion of huge land grants, caused deep resentment, growing factionalism, and a disintegration of the unity Brant had sought to establish. He made trips to the Ohio–Detroit region in 1786, 1787, and 1788 to strengthen the confederacy and urge peace with the United States. He also tried hard to secure the

Muskingum River (Ohio) as the boundary between the Indian nations and the United States, but such a settlement was not then acceptable to the American government.

The achievement of unanimity among the diverse Indian nations was one of the most difficult tasks undertaken by Brant and was never fully accomplished. His attempts to halt the treaties held by Major-General Arthur St Clair with the Indians at Fort Harmar (Marietta, Ohio) in 1789 were not successful; the American general conducted one with the Iroquois, exclusive of the Mohawks, and another with the Potawatomis, Sauks, Ottawas, Ojibwas, Wyandots, and Delawares. Predictably – St Clair's policy was to divide and conquer – there was not a full representation even of the nations who were present. The policy led to Indian resentment and reprisals against white settlers and resulted in three full-scale American retaliatory invasions.

Brigadier-General Josiah Harmar's punitive expedition against the Shawnee and Miami villages along the Miamis (Maumee) River in October 1790 was defeated and turned back. Both Governor General Lord Dorchester [Guy CARLETON] and Sir John Johnson told Brant that they wished to effect a peace between the western Indians and the United States, but both men also persisted in deliberately deceiving him concerning the boundaries established by Great Britain and the United States in 1783. They assured him once again that the king had not really given away the Indian lands in the west to the Americans and that the boundary set at the Treaty of Fort Stanwix in 1768 was still in effect. The deception helped provide the British in Canada with an Indian buffer on their frontier and laid the blame for white expansion into the west solely on the Americans.

Brant went into the Indian country south of the Great Lakes in the spring of 1791 to continue his consultation with the western nations. In a council held at Detroit and attended by deputy Indian agent Alexander McKee* and representatives of the confederacy, the Indians agreed that the Muskingum River should be their eastern boundary and sent Brant and 12 other deputies to Quebec to inform the government of their decision. Brant wanted to learn if the British would back the Indians in obtaining recognition of their boundary. Dorchester assured the deputies that the king had not transferred their country to the Americans but he also emphasized that the government could not involve itself in any hostilities. The reluctance of Dorchester to commit the government militarily was a disappointment to Brant. The Americans in 1791 had held a treaty with that portion of the Six Nations living south of the Great Lakes and successfully neutralized them. A treaty with the powerful Cherokees farther to the south had also been

Thayendanegea

concluded. These American diplomatic successes further undercut the strength of the western confederacy.

In November 1791, however, St Clair's army was defeated by western Indian forces under Little Turtle [MICHIKINAKOUA] near the Miamis Towns (Fort Wayne, Ind.). Because of Brant's prestige and great influence with the Indian nations, President George Washington and Secretary of War Henry Knox invited him to the seat of government at Philadelphia in 1792 to seek his good offices in effecting peace in the west. It was the first of several trips Brant would make to confer with American government officials on Indian business. Though he was firm during the visit in protecting the Indian interests and though he rejected the American offer to him of a large land grant and a pension, which he considered a bribe, he believed that a compromise could be worked out on the boundary question and he prepared to travel to the western confederacy in search of a peaceful solution. Because of a sudden sickness he arrived too late for the confederacy council held at the Glaize (Defiance, Ohio) from 30 September until early in October 1792, but he did have several unsuccessful consultations with the various Indian nations, who he now found had hardened their demands and were insisting on the Ohio River as a boundary. At a council between American commissioners and the confederacy Indians at Lower Sandusky in the summer of 1793, Brant had no more success in securing a compromise. Although the American commissioners were authorized to make some concessions so long as their existing settlements in the region could be maintained, the western Indians were adamant that the Ohio River should be the border and that all white settlements should be withdrawn. The failure of the negotiations made war inevitable and led in 1794 to the battle of Fallen Timbers (near Waterville, Ohio), where the western Indians were resoundingly defeated by Major-General Anthony Wayne's army [see WEYAPIERSENWAH].

After Wayne's victory Brant and Lieutenant Governor John Graves SIMCOE both went west in order to encourage the Indians to remain united. Brant promised them warriors from the Six Nations. These attempts to bolster the confederacy proved futile. The Treaty of Greenville conducted by Wayne in 1795 effectively spelled the end of the grand plan of Indian unity. Moreover, the onset of the French revolutionary wars in Europe had made Britain anxious for peace at any cost in North America. By Jay's Treaty of 1794 she had agreed to surrender the border forts to the United States, and in 1796 these symbols of British support for the Indian cause were turned over to the Americans.

With the change in British policy, Brant's persistence in encouraging Indian unity and in maintaining contacts with the other Indian nations became a source of annoyance and suspicion to the British government and to administrators such as Dorchester in the Canadas, who tried to keep the Indians divided, dependent, and subservient. Whereas they had once fostered an Indian confederacy and had encouraged Brant's leadership, they now tried to discourage his diplomacy, undercut his influence, and redirect his activities to his own settlement. Brant was not one to be easily deterred, and the resulting controversy caused tension for many years.

At the Grand River Brant was the main spokesman. Though only a war chief, he served in the capacity of a sachem. He always worked closely with Tekari-hó:ken, the leading Mohawk sachem, but it was to Brant that the chiefs entrusted their diplomacy and land negotiations because of his education, his fluency in English, his many contacts with government officials in England and Canada, and "his knowledge of the laws and customs of the white people." His long association with the Johnson family and his familiarity with the upper classes in Great Britain and North America led him to adopt their manners. He lived in a genteel English style, had about 20 white and black servants, kept a well-stocked table, was waited on by black servants in full livery, and entertained graciously. In 1795 he secured a large tract of land from the Mississauga Indians in the vicinity of Burlington Bay (Hamilton Harbour), which purchase the government confirmed, and he subsequently moved into a fine house he built there. Whites who knew him socially expressed admiration for his intellect, his civility and amiable temperament, his dignity, and his ready wit. Physically impressive, he was 5 feet 11 inches tall, erect, powerful, and well formed, though tending to stoutness in his later years.

Brant had a continuing concern for the intellectual and spiritual advancement of his people. During the Revolutionary War he had obtained a schoolmaster for the Mohawk settlement near Fort Niagara and had a little log chapel built near present-day Lewiston, N.Y. After the immigration to the Grand River he helped secure a school, a schoolmaster, and a church, and by 1789 he had also translated a primer and the liturgy of the Church of England into the Mohawk language. He was planning to write a history for the Six Nations, but evidently, from the press of business, never began the project. He also attempted for a number of years to obtain a resident Anglican clergyman for the settlement and in 1797 turned his attention to Davenport Phelps, a son-in-law of Eleazar Wheelock, who was living in Upper Canada and practising law. He urged Phelps to apply for ordination so that he could serve the Grand River community. Both Peter RUSSELL, administrator of Upper Canada, and Bishop Jacob Mountain* objected to Phelps because of his American military service and his alleged political views and activities. Brant carried on a lengthy correspondence with British officials on his behalf, but to no avail. Finally, through Brant's urging, Phelps obtained his ordination in New York. He preached for a while near Burlington Bay but did not settle at the Grand River and soon returned to the United States. Brant's considerable efforts to secure a resident minister for his people thus came to naught.

A tragic incident occurred in Brant's family in 1795 during the annual distribution of government presents at Burlington Bay. Isaac Brant, who had a violent temper, attacked his father with a knife, wounding him in the hand as his father warded off the blow. Brant drew his dirk in self-defence and in the struggle inflicted a scalp wound on his son. Isaac refused medical attention, and in a few days the wound became badly infected and proved fatal. Brant turned himself in to the authorities but was exonerated. His role in his son's death was a sorrow he bore for the remainder of his days.

A dispute that was to last for several years developed between the Mohawks of the Grand River and the Caughnawaga and St Regis Mohawks during the late 1790s. The latter, by the treaty of 31 May 1796 with the state of New York, abandoned their claim to an extensive area of land in the northern part of the state, the St Regis Indians agreeing to confine themselves to the boundaries of their present reservation along the St Lawrence River. The chiefs, including ATIATOHARONGWEN, who negotiated the treaty later blamed Brant for the sale of their lands. The charge was completely unfounded and unjust. It arose out of a misunderstanding, a desire to shift the blame to another, or deliberate misrepresentation to the Caughnawaga and St Regis Indians on the part of Egbert Benson, the chief New York negotiator. It took Brant four years to secure the complete details of the negotiation from the Caughnawaga and St Regis Indians and from Albany officials, all of whom were reluctant to release information. Through painstaking search and interviews with most of the principals except Benson, who refused to cooperate, Brant was able to clear himself and the Grand River Mohawks.

Scarcely any problem was more enduring or more vexing to Brant than the controversy over the nature of the Six Nations' title to the Grand River lands and the extent of the grant. According to the original Haldimand grant, a tract of approximately two million acres, from the source to the mouth of the river and six miles deep on each side, had been given to the loyalist Six Nations Indians. Later the government claimed that a mistake had been made in the original grant in that the northern portion had never been bought from the Mississaugas and the king accordingly could not grant what he had not bought. Despite repeated urgings by Brant and the other chiefs, the government never made the additional purchase. Brant also believed that the area along the Grand River was too large for the Indian population to farm and too small for hunting. With whites moving into the region in increasing numbers and more land being cleared, game was becoming scarce. He therefore wanted the community to realize a continuing income from the land by sales and leases to whites. Brant also strongly believed that whites living among them and inter-marrying with them would bring and transmit skills needed by the Indians in a changing environment. Though Brant was firmly convinced that the land was, or should have been, granted to the Indians on the same basis as to the white loyalists, in fee simple, to do with as they wished, both Lord Dorchester and Lieutenant Governor Simcoe advanced the curious argument that the king's allies could not have the king's subjects as tenants. The Royal Proclamation of 1763, which had prohibited individual whites from purchasing Indians' land in order to guard the Indians against fraud, was cited. Simcoe further emphasized that the Grand River grant was meant solely for Indians and was never to be alienated. Brant refused a title deed from Simcoe that forbad alienation. By 1796 Dorchester and Simcoe had finally relented to the extent of agreeing that Grand River lands might be leased, although the government would have the right of pre-emption; Brant continued to oppose any restriction of Indian sovereignty.

Brant's leadership did not go unquestioned. Fort Hunter Mohawk Aaron Hill and his brother Isaac (Anoghsoktea) had complained to Lord Dorchester in 1788 about Brant's policy of bringing whites among them. They also resented his growing political influence. Moreover, the land sales resulted in tangled finances because several of the purchasers were unable to keep up with their payments. Some Indians began to blame Brant for the financial mess and the lack of income from the sales. A few even believed he was pocketing the money. Indeed the tensions at the Grand River may have prompted Brant's decision to move to Burlington Bay.

In order to secure for the Six Nations the right of complete control over their Grand River lands, Brant contemplated another trip to England to lay their grievances before the government. Lacking the funds for such an enterprise, he went instead in early 1797 to Philadelphia to relay his complaints to the British minister, Robert Liston. Brant's strategy there was to talk openly about concluding an alliance with the French if his people were not better treated and to let the rumours drift back to Liston. In conference with Liston, he then rehearsed the whole history of the Six Nations' troubles with the government and accused the authorities in the Canadas of refusing to sanction land sales by the Indians because they had personal designs on those same lands.

Brant deliberately associated with the pro-French party in the American capital and studiously avoided mixing with anyone from the administration, even ignoring the repeated invitations of Secretary of War James McHenry to call upon him. McHenry had arranged an appointment for him with Washington, but Brant departed Philadelphia without meeting the president and left behind many complaints that he had not been treated well by the American government officials. Liston's description of Brant as "so determined, so able, and so artful" was apt.

Brant's behaviour was alarming to both Liston and the British authorities in Canada. Rumours were rife of a Franco-Spanish attack on British possessions by way of the Mississippi, and it was feared that discontent among the Indians might lead them to join such an invasion [see Wabakinine*]. Thus in 1797, Brant, through extreme pressure on Peter Russell, received approval for the land dispositions already made. This was only a temporary respite, for the government continued in subsequent years to hold a totally negative attitude toward any Indian right to sell or lease lands to individuals.

Also in 1797 the Mohawks were successful in negotiating a settlement with New York State for the woodlands surrounding their former villages at Fort Hunter and Canajoharie. Brant and John Deserontyon held a treaty at Albany with New York State on 29 March 1797 by which the state awarded the Mohawks a modest compensation of $1,000 and $600 for expenses.

Brant was still determined to secure full Indian sovereignty over the Grand River lands, and he sent his associate John Norton to England in 1804 to present the Indian case and to get the original Haldimand grant confirmed. William Claus*, deputy superintendent general of Indian affairs in Upper Canada, reacted by attempting to manipulate Brant's ouster as chief. Claus sent an Indian emissary, a Cayuga chief named Tsinonwanhonte, to the Grand River to undermine Brant and also wrote to officials in England in an effort to sabotage Norton's mission. Not being able to persuade the great majority of Grand River Indians that Brant and Norton were corrupt and working against their interests, Claus sowed distrust among the Six Nations on the American side of the border. They called a Six Nations council at Buffalo Creek, despite the fact that the grand council fire of the Six Nations Confederacy had been moved several years before to the Onondaga village at the Grand River. This rump council, composed mostly of Senecas, disavowed Norton's mission and deposed Brant as chief. Only a few people from the Grand River attended the meeting. A delegation from the Buffalo Creek council then went to Fort George (Niagara-on-the-Lake), Upper Canada, and held a similar council with Claus, who sent a copy of the proceedings to England and thereby effectively destroyed Norton's mission. Brant later complained that Claus had dictated this document and that a number of the common folk had signed as chiefs to give the pronouncement more weight.

Brant fought back vigorously, berating in council those from the Grand River whom he charged with being Claus's dupes. Then he went to Fort George and held a council on 28 July 1806 to accuse Claus of duplicity, reminding him that the Indians who chose to remain with the Americans had no equity in the Grand River lands and no say in their governance. The Grand River chiefs backed Brant fully and continued him in his chiefly office. He also received support from an anti-government faction that included William Weekes, judge Robert Thorpe*, and missionary Robert Addison*. He was planning another trip to England to plead the Indians' cause and repair the damage Claus had done, but death claimed him.

Joseph Brant had been impressed by much in white culture. He admired the technology of the whites, their style of living, and their industry. He saw that in the changing circumstances in which Indians then lived, the traditional social structure of women farmers and men hunters would not suffice, for game was growing scarce and hunting accordingly declining. As a consequence, there soon would be more likelihood of hunger and only a reduced role in life for the Indian men. For Indians to survive, they would have to adopt white methods of agriculture, raising domestic animals and encouraging the men to become farmers. He invited white families to come and live by his people at Grand River "for the purposes of making roads, raising provisions and teaching us the benefits of agriculture." Brant was furthermore convinced that one of the best means of helping his people through the transition was intermarriage with the whites. There were other features of white culture that Brant valued highly. He was a conscientious Anglican, translating portions of the Bible and helping to found churches for his people. He also saw the necessity of Indians becoming literate in their own language as well as in English and he diligently promoted education.

But there were aspects of white culture that Brant shunned, comparing them unfavourably with the less competitive, more egalitarian ways of the Iroquois. He was repelled by the deep-seated class divisions in white society, the harshness of its laws, the inequitable dispensing of justice, the suppression of the weak by the strong, the horror of the prisons, and the particularly shocking practice of imprisonment for debt. "The palaces and prisons among you form a most dreadful contrast," he reminded a white correspondent. "Go to the former places, and you will see perhaps a *deformed piece of earth* assuming airs that become none but the Great Spirit above. Go to one of your prisons; here description utterly fails!" He was well aware that among whites the laws could often be manipulated or bypassed by the powerful and that

810

"estates of widows and orphans" could be "devoured by enterprising sharpers" – a thing that never happened among Indians. These aspects of white culture Brant considered totally inconsistent with the teachings of Christianity. "Cease, then, to call yourselves Christians, lest you publish to the world your hypocrisy," he admonished the same correspondent. And then he turned back upon the whites a favourite epithet of theirs that had always incensed the Indians: "Cease, too, to call other nations savage, when you are tenfold more the children of cruelty than they."

The moral deficiencies in white society were not only an offence to Brant's idealism. He saw them as practical obstacles that hindered his people from adopting the features of white civilization necessary for their survival. Writing to Samuel Kirkland in 1791 he explained: "A chain of corroborating circumstances, and events, seems to evince to them that the white people, under whatever pretence, aim at their destruction – possess'd with such Idea's their prejudices naturally encrease and seeing the sword in one hand, supported by injustice and corruption, is it any wonder that they suspect the sincerity of any proposals made on the other hand for so great a change as civilization must make. . . ."

Brant was a noble figure who dedicated his whole life to the advancement of his people and who struggled to maintain their freedom and sovereignty. His major failure was his inability to understand the nature of British imperialism and to comprehend the fact that the British would not permit two sovereignties to exist in Upper Canada. The Indians were manipulated and exploited by the British government to serve the purposes of the empire; they were encouraged to cede their land in time of peace, pressured to become military allies in time of war, ignored in the treaty of peace, urged to form an enlarged confederacy as a barrier between the British and the Americans, and coerced to abandon the confederacy when the British had composed their differences with their enemy and growing Indian power threatened to rival their own. British colonial agents were then urged to foster jealousies and divisions among the Indian nations in order to keep them in a state of continual dependency upon the British government. Nor did Brant really understand how dependent the Indians had become in their new environment close to their white neighbours. Even land sales by the Six Nations, which Brant supported for immediately practical reasons, would eventually attach them irreparably to the surrounding white economy as Indian land holdings diminished. Only Brant's larger vision of Indian unity, had it been achieved, would have succeeded in maintaining Indian sovereignty for a longer period and slowing white expansion. In this plan he was defeated by jealousies and divisiveness among the confederated Indian nations, and by American and then British successes in undermining the general confederacy. When TECUMSEH revived the concept of a confederacy in the next generation, it was already too late.

BARBARA GRAYMONT

[There are several portraits of Brant. At least two were made of him during his first visit to England in 1776. Of these, the well-known one by George Romney is in the National Gallery of Canada, Ottawa. Another was the work of an unknown artist commissioned by James Boswell and was reproduced in the *London Magazine* for July 1776. The Benjamin West study of Guy Johnson, painted in England in 1776, shows in the background an Indian often thought to be Brant. From the features, this supposition would seem unlikely. He may be either an idealized Indian or Oteroughyanento. During Brant's second trip to England, in 1786, his portrait was painted twice by Gilbert Stuart. One work was commissioned by the Duke of Northumberland, an acquaintance from the American Revolutionary War, and is still in the private possession of the family at their home in Guildford. The second Stuart portrait, which has become as famous as the earlier Romney one, was commissioned by Francis Rawdon, another war-time acquaintance, and is now at the New York State Historical Association, Cooperstown. A copy is in the British Library. A miniature of this portrait was in the possession of the Brant family in the 19th century. Also during his 1786 visit, a portrait of him wearing the uniform of an officer of the Indian Department and Indian head-dress was painted by John Francis Rigaud. After Brant's return to North America, the portrait was sent to him through the courtesy of Haldimand, who was living in England. The original seems to have disappeared, but a copy is in the New York State Education Department at Albany. There are four studies of Brant by William BERCZY. The earliest, a water-colour bust portrait, was painted some time after 1794 and is in the Musée du Séminaire de Québec. Berczy made what seem to be two copies in oil of this water-colour, but slightly modified, being head to waist portraits, with the right hand resting on a tomahawk. Both are in private collections, in Montreal and Baltimore. Another Berczy, *circa* 1800, is a full-length portrait depicting Brant at the Grand River, and is in the National Gallery of Canada. While on a trip to Philadelphia in 1797, Brant sat for Charles Willson Peale. This painting is now in Independence Hall, Philadelphia. What was probably the last portrait of Brant was painted in Albany in 1805 or 1806 by Ezra Ames. A copy of it was made by George Catlin, and an engraving from the latter by A. Dick was printed as the frontispiece for the second volume of William Leete Stone's biography of Brant. The Catlin copy, which hung in the New York State Library in Albany, was destroyed by fire in 1911. The original Ames portrait is now in Fenimore House, New York State Historical Association.

Brant's house in Burlington was demolished in 1932. Construction of the present Joseph Brant Museum was begun in 1937 on land once owned by Brant. It contains the staircase and some other pieces of the original building.

In the 19th century, Brant's papers were in the possession of his youngest daughter, Elizabeth Brant Kerr, and subsequently of her descendants. These papers were

Thiathoharongouan

borrowed and many of them copied by Stone and Lyman Copeland Draper. Almost all the known Brant manuscripts, either published or unpublished, have been cited by M. J. Smith, "Joseph Brant, Mohawk statesman" (PHD thesis, Univ. of Wis., Madison, 1946). A large amount of Brant correspondence is in BL, Add. MSS 21661–892; PAC, MG 11, [CO 42] Q; MG 19, F1 and F6; and RG 10. The most extensive Brant collection in the United States is Draper MSS, ser.F, held by the State Hist. Soc. of Wis. A number of Brant letters and speeches, some of them in Mohawk, are in the Burke Library, Hamilton and Kirkland Colleges (Clinton, N.Y.), Kirkland MSS; NYPL, Philip Schuyler papers; N.Y. Hist. Soc. (New York), Henry O'Reilly coll. of docs. relating to the Five Nations and other Indians; and the Hist. Soc. of Pa. (Philadelphia), Indian records coll. B.G.]

Additional sources used in the preparation of this article include: Dartmouth College Library (Hanover, N.H.), MS 001329, Account of Wheelock scholars, 1743–61, comp. Frederick Chase; MS 765429.1, Theophilus Chamberlain to Eleazar Wheelock, 29 July 1765. N.Y. Hist. Soc., Jelles Fonda papers, "Journal kept on the expedition of Sir William Johnson and Gen. Jeffrey Amherst against Montreal, June–October 1760." USPG, B, 2 (mfm. at PAC). *Anthony Wayne . . . the Wayne–Knox–Pickering–McHenry correspondence*, ed. R. C. Knopf (Pittsburgh, Pa., 1960; repr. Westport, Conn., 1975). [James Boswell], "An account of the chief of the 'Mohock Indians' who lately visited 'England' (with an exact likeness)," *London Magazine: or, Gentleman's Monthly Intelligencer* (London), 45 (1776): 339. *A brief narrative of the Indian charity-school, in Lebanon in Connecticut, New England; founded and carried on by that faithful servant of God, the Rev. Mr. Eleazar Wheelock*, [ed. Nathaniel Whitaker] (London, 1766; repr. [Rochester, N.Y., 1909?]). P. Campbell, *Travels in North America* (Langton and Ganong). "Census of Niagara, 1783," *Ontario Reg.* ([Madison, N.J.]), 1 (1968): 197–214. *Corr. of Hon. Peter Russell* (Cruikshank and Hunter). *Corr. of Lieut. Governor Simcoe* (Cruikshank). *The documentary history of the state of New-York . . .* , ed. E. B. O'Callaghan (4v., Albany, 1849–51), 4. [Frederick Haldimand], "Private diary of Gen. Haldimand," PAC *Report*, 1889: 127, 129, 131, 135, 139, 145, 151, 157–59, 161, 167, 273. *Johnson papers* (Sullivan et al.). *The letters of Eleazar Wheelock's Indians*, ed. J. D. McCallum (Hanover, 1932). *Loyalist narratives from Upper Canada*, ed. J. J. Talman (Toronto, 1946). *Mich. Pioneer Coll.*, 12 (1887); 20 (1892). Norton, *Journal* (Klinck and Talman). NYCD (O'Callaghan and Fernow), vol.8. "Petitions for grants of land" (Cruikshank), *OH*, 24: 30. *The private papers of James Boswell from Malahide Castle; in the collection of Lt.-Colonel Ralph Heyward Isham*, ed. Geoffrey Scott and F. A. Pottle (18v., [Mount Vernon, N.Y., 1928–34]), 11. "The probated wills of men prominent in the public affairs of early Upper Canada," ed. A. F. Hunter, *OH*, 23 (1926): 341–44. U.S., Congress, *American state papers* (Lowrie et al.), class II, vol.[1]. *Valley of Six Nations* (Johnston). Eleazar Wheelock, *A plain and faithful narrative of the original design, rise, progress, and present state of the Indian charity-school at Lebanon, in Connecticut* (Boston, 1763).

William Allen, *The American biographical dictionary . . .* (3rd ed., Boston, 1857). "Calendar of state papers," PAC *Report*, 1933: 87–88, 100. *Handbook of American Indians* (Hodge), 2: 741–42. Barbara Graymont, *The Iroquois in the American revolution* (Syracuse, N.Y., 1972). R. H. Kohn, *Eagle and sword: the federalists and the creation of the military establishment in America, 1783–1802* (New York and London, 1975). W. H. Mohr, *Federal Indian relations, 1774–1788* (Philadelphia, 1933). W. L. Stone, *Life of Joseph Brant – Thayendanegea . . .* (2v., New York, 1838). M. W. Hamilton, "Joseph Brant painted by Rigaud," *New York Hist.* (Cooperstown, N.Y.), 40 (1959): 247–54; "Joseph Brant: 'the most painted Indian,'" *New York Hist.*, 39 (1958): 119–32. F. W. Hodge, "Some portraits of Thayendanegea," *Indian Notes* (New York), 5 (1928): 207–17. C. M. Johnston, "Joseph Brant, the Grand River lands and the northwest crisis," *OH*, 55 (1963): 267–82. E. H. Phillips, "Timothy Pickering at his best: Indian commissioner, 1790–1794," Essex Institute, *Hist. Coll.* (Salem, Mass.), 102 (1966): 163–202. L. B. Richardson, "The Dartmouth Indians, 1800–1893," *Dartmouth Alumni Magazine* (Hanover), 22 (1929–30): 524–27. G. J. Smith, "Capt. Joseph Brant's status as a chief, and some of his descendants," *OH*, 12 (1914): 89–101.

THIATHOHARONGOUAN. *See* ATIATOHARONGWEN

THIBODEAU (Thibaudeau), SIMON, potter; b. *c.* 1739 in Pisiquid (Windsor, N.S.), son of Alexis Thibodeau and Marie-Anne Blanchard; d. 24 Oct. 1819 in Saint-Denis, on the Richelieu, Lower Canada.

The Thibodeaus, like many Acadian families, were deported in 1755 [*see* Charles Lawrence*] and ended up in Philadelphia, Pa. They went to live in Boston, Mass., around 1763, and then in 1770 settled at Quebec. Simon Thibodeau probably accompanied his family in all its moves and did his apprenticeship in the Thirteen Colonies with Pierre Vincent, a relative who was also in exile.

In 1774 Thibodeau, who was a master potter by then, was living in the *faubourg* Saint-Roch; there he bought a frame-house that was "falling into ruins," likely with the intent of setting up shop. On 12 June 1775, at Quebec, he married Marie-Anne Drolet, daughter of a master blacksmith. In the autumn of that year he enlisted in the Canadian militia of Quebec, and in December he joined his fellow citizens in repulsing the attack by the American forces under Richard Montgomery*.

In 1776 Thibodeau displayed his business sense when he decided to leave Quebec, where there were already several potters, and to buy a lot at Saint-Denis for a workshop. He was in this way recognizing the possibilities of the region for a potter: it was a prosperous rural area within easy reach of the Montreal market via the St Lawrence and of the United States via the Richelieu; it also had abundant greyish-blue clay along the banks of the river as well as in the open fields just a foot below the surface.

At Saint-Denis Thibodeau, who was well informed about both domestic demand and the requirements of the American market, put his capabilities as a businessman and a meticulous craftsman to use in his enterprise. In 1785 he sold his first site at Saint-Denis to Louis Robichaud, who was also a master potter, and moved to the riverside, where the clay was of better quality and easier to extract.

The potter's craft included the tasks of extracting the clay, fashioning the pieces, drying, glazing, and firing. Although shaping the articles and preparing the solution for glazing remained the prerogatives of the master, the other tasks could be carried out by apprentices. With this in mind Thibodeau in 1779 took on Joseph Leprince for 6 years, and then in 1788 engaged Nicolas Prévot for 12 years. Thibodeau's workshop made terrines, bowls, pitchers, and jars for household use, to meet the needs of the habitants, who used earthenware for preparing, cooking, and preserving food.

Thibodeau's business was highly prosperous, and he invested his money in real estate. In 1783 he obtained a site in the *faubourg* Saint-Roch at Quebec from the Jesuits and the following year had it surveyed with a view to putting up a house. In 1788 he rented this house, to which he added a stable, to his brother-in-law François Coupeaux, and in 1815 sold it for £240. Thibodeau also rented his other house in the *faubourg* Saint-Roch to a master cooper. In addition he purchased a farm, a woodlot to supply his kilns with fuel, and pieces of land in the Saint-Denis region.

In his private as in his professional life Thibodeau associated mainly with members of his family and other craftsmen. In particular he continued to maintain relations with Pierre Vincent, who became to some degree his agent at Quebec, assuming responsibility for collecting his rentals. At Saint-Denis he struck up a friendship with Louis Bourdages*, a notary and member of the assembly, who was the son of Acadians; in 1810 Bourdages wrote and promoted the sale of a "seditious" pamphlet entitled *Le sincère ami*, to which Thibodeau subscribed.

Thibodeau's wife, Marie-Anne, died on 6 June 1816. She had borne six children, four of whom died in infancy. Thibodeau then had an inventory drawn up of his assets. He possessed more than 15,000 *livres* in Spanish *piastres*. In addition he held several loans and four pieces of land in the Richelieu valley. His house was very large, comparable in size to the homes of the prominent villagers; his furniture was well made, and his possessions gave proof of his wealth and easy circumstances. A year after his wife's death Thibodeau, who had given up his workshop, made a gift of everything he owned to his son Joseph, a merchant in Saint-Denis. In return he asked Joseph to provide him with board and lodging and to supply him with a horse every year. He also enjoined his son to take care of him and to secure for him the comforts of religion.

Simon Thibodeau died on 24 Oct. 1819 and was buried the next day at Saint-Denis. No one in his family had taken over the workshop to carry on his line of production; but Saint-Denis had, under Thibodeau, become a place favoured by potters and it would continue to be so long after his death.

JACQUELINE ROY

[The author is grateful to Simon Courcy and Daniel Villeneuve for kindly lending documentation relating to their work "Simon Thibaudeau, marchand-potier à Saint-Denis-sur-Richelieu (1776–1819)," a dissertation on ethnography presented at Université Laval in 1973. J.R.]

ANQ-M, CN1-88, 2 mars 1779; CN2-11, 20 févr. 1808; 18 oct. 1811; 26 juin 1813; 25 juin, 2 sept. 1816; 6 avril, 10 mai 1817; CN2-27, 28 mars 1798; 7 janv., 29 nov. 1800; 25 août, 7 sept. 1801; 17 sept. 1802; 7 nov. 1809; 19 mai 1817; CN2-41, 17 août 1776, 19 janv. 1782, 22 nov. 1785, 15 mars 1786; CN2-56, 11 juin 1788. ANQ-Q, CE1-1, 12 juin 1775; CN1-25, 23 août 1783; CN1-26, 28 juin 1815; CN1-205, 8 mars 1774, 6 juin 1775; CN1-284, 29 juill. 1788, 11 août 1802, 20 févr. 1808. AP, Saint-Denis (Saint-Denis, sur le Richelieu), Reg. des baptêmes, mariages et sépultures, 25 oct. 1819. "La milice canadienne-française à Québec en 1775," *BRH*, 11 (1905): 237. Michel Gaumond et P.-L. Martin, *Les maîtres-potiers du bourg Saint-Denis, 1785–1888* ([Québec], 1978). H. H. Lambart, *Two centuries of ceramics in the Richelieu valley: a documentary history*, ed. Jennifer Arcand (Ottawa, 1970).

THORN, JONATHAN, merchant captain; b. 8 Jan. 1779 in Schenectady, N.Y., eldest of the 15 children of Samuel Thorn and Helena Van Slyck; d. *c.* 15 June 1811 in Clayoquot Sound (B.C.).

Jonathan Thorn was a sixth-generation descendant of William Thorne, who arrived in Massachusetts from England in 1638. Jonathan entered the United States Navy on 28 April 1800 as a midshipman and was promoted acting lieutenant on 7 Nov. 1803. He served with distinction in the Barbary Wars, in February 1804 participating in Stephen Decatur's celebrated raid into the harbour of Tripoli (Libya) to destroy the grounded American frigate *Philadelphia*.

On 6 June 1805, at the early age of 26, Thorn was appointed commandant of the New York navy yard and on 16 Feb. 1807 received his lieutenancy. On 18 May 1810, at the request of John Jacob Astor*, he was granted a two-year furlough. Astor had organized the Pacific Fur Company and had chosen him to command the ship that was to carry men and supplies to build Fort Astoria (Astoria, Oreg.) at the mouth of the Columbia River. The vessel selected was the *Tonquin*, 269 tons, which Astor purchased in August. She sailed from New York on 6 Sept. 1810.

Thorn was fitted neither by temperament nor by experience to command such an expedition. He was a strict disciplinarian and clearly despised the Scottish fur traders and Canadian voyageurs who were his passengers. The fact that several of the traders were

Tiffany

partners in the company that owned the ship seems to have weighed with him not at all. Washington Irving, who remembered Thorn "in early life, as a companion in pleasant scenes and joyous hours," characterized him in *Astoria* as "an honest, straightforward, but somewhat dry and dictatorial commander, who, having been nurtured in the system and discipline of a ship of war . . . was disposed to be absolute lord and master on board of his ship." Further, he regarded his passengers "as a set of landlubbers and braggadocios, and was disposed to treat them accordingly." There was evidently a callous streak in his nature. At the Falkland Islands he set sail while eight of his passengers were still ashore and they overtook the ship only after a desperate row of several hours. In the dangerous waters at the mouth of the Columbia he insisted upon attempts to take soundings from small boats, a measure that resulted in the loss of eight lives.

The *Tonquin* entered that river late in March 1811 and, having disembarked men and supplies for the construction of Fort Astoria, on 5 June sailed on a trading cruise up the northwest coast. About 15 June, evidently at anchor in Clayoquot Sound, she was seized by the local Nootka Indians and most on board, including the trader Alexander MacKay, were immediately slain. The only survivor of the entire incident was the interpreter, George Ramsay (called Jack Ramsay by Ross Cox*), son of an English sailor and an Indian mother, who was persuaded to come to Astoria and tell his story, which was recorded by Gabriel Franchère* in his journal. According to Ramsay, Captain Thorn, trading for the first time with Indians, lost patience and ended an attempt to bargain with an important chief by "rubbing his face with the skins that the latter had brought to trade, thus insulting him mightily and causing him to swear vengeance." After lulling their intended victims by peaceful behaviour, Indians carrying concealed weapons contrived to board the vessel and the seizure followed. The next day, when natives swarmed on board seeking plunder, the ship blew up, killing or maiming a large number. It is said in some accounts that a wounded crew member who had managed to remain hidden revenged his comrades in this way.

The United States Navy Department has a portrait of Thorn, and his distinguished naval career has not been forgotten: the destroyer *Jonathan Thorn* was commissioned at the New York navy yard on 1 April 1943.

W. Kaye Lamb

Gabriel Franchère, *Journal of a voyage on the north west coast of North America during the years 1811, 1812, 1813 and 1814*, trans. W. T. Lamb, ed. and intro. W. K. Lamb (Toronto, 1969). [For Ramsay's account of the loss of the *Tonquin* and references to other versions of the story, *see* pp.123–28.] Washington Irving, *Astoria, or anecdotes of an*

enterprise beyond the Rocky Mountains, ed. E. W. Todd (new ed., Norman, Okla., 1964). C. E. Thorn, *Heroic life and tragic death of Lieutenant Jonathan Thorn, United States Navy* (New York, 1944) [a tribute by a great-grand-nephew].

TIFFANY, SILVESTER (Sylvester), officer holder, printer, journalist, and publisher; b. 9 Aug. 1759 in Norton, Mass., eldest son of Gideon Tiffany and Sarah Farrar, *née* Dean; m. first Frances Hopkins, *née* Davis, and they had three children; m. secondly Elizabeth Ralston, and they had five children; d. 24 March 1811 in Canandaigua, N.Y.

Silvester Tiffany entered Dartmouth College, Hanover, N.H., in 1775 and left two years later without graduating, apparently to become a printer and journalist. In the New York census of 1790 he was listed in Albany with his family and a slave, and the following year he appeared in Lansingburgh (Troy), N.Y., where he published the *American Spy* in partnership with William Wands. This journal ceased publication in 1792, and in 1793 Tiffany founded *Tiffany's Recorder*, which folded in 1794. For at least a year he had maintained a printing establishment in Lansingburgh. Tiffany's younger brothers Oliver and Gideon* emigrated to Upper Canada in 1794, settling at Newark (Niagara-on-the-Lake). At the insistence of Lieutenant Governor Simcoe Gideon succeeded Louis Roy* as king's printer. Late in 1795 or shortly thereafter Silvester, accompanied by his family, joined his brothers. On 7 Jan. 1797 he petitioned for lands, his "views being to agriculture," and for a town lot in Newark. On 11 March the Executive Council granted him, as "an assistant to the Kings Printer," 400 acres.

The duties of the king's printer were to print proclamations, speeches, copies of laws, and commissions, but the principal responsibility was the government paper, the *Upper Canada Gazette*. As early as 1795 Simcoe had encouraged Gideon Tiffany to "print all news" and to found the character of the *Gazette* upon truth. The lieutenant governor added that he preferred Tiffany to print, "if it appears to be true, [that] which is most favorable to the British Government." The following year he prohibited Tiffany's practice of obtaining paper from Albany rather than Montreal and directed him to refer to Executive Councillor Peter Russell, the Niagara merchant Robert Hamilton, and Surveyor General David William Smith* for assistance "with subjects" for the paper. Simcoe had decided to remove the capital to York (Toronto) and warned Tiffany that "remaining at Niagara is precarious." Gideon Tiffany ceased to be government printer on 5 July 1797 and by 20 September had been replaced by Titus Geer Simons. Silvester continued as Simons's assistant until 1 May 1798. The paper was moved to York the following September.

Official concern with the political content of Gideon Tiffany's *Gazette* had been hinted at in Simcoe's letter of 1795. By February 1798 Silvester had transformed concern to outright hostility. Chief Justice John ELMSLEY was critical of "unprincipled & unattached republicans" in the province and demanded Simons's dismissal as king's printer because "the Tiffany's are the real managers." Elmsley accused them of having ignored in their columns such important items as the king's address to parliament, "while every trifle relating to the damned States is printed in large character." The following month Elmsley reported to Smith the Tiffanys' "intention of getting up a paper, for the purposes of *disseminating political knowledge*." On 30 April Silvester Tiffany wrote to Russell about "a prosecution . . . to be instituted against me." Apparently the chief justice had broached the subject of treasonable or seditious conduct and Tiffany urged an inquiry. He, in fact, welcomed the notoriety: "Popularity is my object, and interest. . . . I cannot wish it entirely to subside." The self-styled "people's printer," Tiffany believed their interests "inseparable" from the king's. But he alerted Russell that it was beyond his power in his present position to reconcile "the minds of many to present measures, and nothing short of my proposed undertaking can ever effect it."

Silvester and Gideon Tiffany published the first issue of the *Canada Constellation* (later the *Canadian Constellation*) at Newark on 20 July 1799. They addressed it to the "unpredjudiced only . . . of these are our Patrons, lovers and promoters of useful knowledge . . . who wish to see man not debased below, but on a level with man, his capabilities enlarged, and his abilities to serve his God, his King and country strengthened. It is a truth long acknowledged that no men hold situations more influential of the minds and conduct of men, than do printers. . . ." Niagara merchants were not as hostile to the Tiffanys' alleged American political sympathies as were York administrators. On 4 August Hamilton, "anxious to encourage an undertaking which . . . may be usefull," informed John ASKIN that he had put his name down as a subscriber and encouraged Askin to enlist the support of neighbours. But the Tiffanys' supposed political inclinations and general demeanour continued to irritate the government. Earlier that year Gideon had been imprudent enough to add lines to the royal anthem at a social gathering: "God save america and keep us from dispotic Powers." In April Attorney General John White* had informed Russell that Silvester had made allegations about the Executive Council and claimed that the administrator "had charged the public with the expence of advertizing for

a Negro Wench." White insisted that Tiffany and his brothers "cannot be too soon got rid off." Government support was important to early printers and Silvester Tiffany had few friends left in official circles. He drew upon his masonic affiliation with Provincial Secretary William JARVIS, urging him to "assist us." On 11 Jan. 1800 Silvester left the paper, which folded the following July. At some time during that year he became postmaster.

Silvester Tiffany printed the first issue of his new paper, the *Niagara Herald*, on 17 Jan. 1801. He attributed the failure of the *Constellation* to departing from the principle of payment in advance and promised his readers that he had learned a lesson. But he had not learned all his lessons. Not adept politically, he managed in his first issue to raise again the controversy about his alleged American sympathies. Simons had recently printed in the *Gazette* "An ode for Her Majesty's birthday," which Tiffany suggested in the *Herald* had been written by Simons's dog, Sancho. No doubt aware of Elmsley's desire for a printer "of unquestionable attachment to the British Constitution," Simons seized the opportunity. In the *Gazette* he depicted the province as "an asylum to *exiles* and *aliens*, to *atheists* and *prawling democrats*" and challenged Tiffany with having been taught "in the school of embryo republicanism, where you received the rudiments of your faith, your politics and education." Simons could not resist an added gibe at Tiffany's physical appearance, labelling him "mr. Cripple critic." Tiffany replied in kind that although "certainly a cripple . . . [he] is extremely thankful that he is what he is, and anything but Sancho and his poetry." He added that he was neither exile, nor alien, nor atheist. The issue of the political beliefs of American settlers continued to appear in the *Herald*'s columns over the names of various correspondents until 23 May when Tiffany announced he would no longer risk libel by printing anonymous pieces. As late as December "A True Briton" attacked Tiffany in the *Herald* for anti-ministerialist remarks about the peace negotiations between Great Britain and France.

In January 1802 Tiffany began accepting produce in lieu of cash from his subscribers because of the shortage of circulating currency and the following month he increased the cost of subscriptions. That same year he published *Tiffany's Upper Canada almanac*. Plagued by financial problems, the *Herald* continued at least until 28 August. By the end of the year he was settling his affairs, including selling his slave, "to remove from this country early in the spring." He was still grand secretary of the masons as late as 24 April 1803 and thereafter resigned. Tiffany was bitter about his departure to New York State: "Necessity is the choice I make: I unwillingly return. . . . My old, or present [allegiance], I shall consider

Tod

wholly done away." He took up residence on a small lot in Canandaigua and there published the *Ontario Freeman* until his death. In a letter to Jarvis on 12 Feb. 1804 he urged him, "Never let Yankee spirits flag."

DOUGLAS G. LOCHHEAD

AO, MS 517, 22: 58, 61, 77; MU 1730, J. Elmsley to Hunter, 27 March 1800; RG 1, A-I-6: 2921–22; C-I-3, 13: 100; 14: 304. MTL, William Jarvis papers, B50: 351–52; B55: 22–32; Peter Russell papers, J. White to Russell, 23 April 1798; S. Tiffany to Russell, 30 April, 13, 21 May 1798; Henry Weishburn to Russell, 13 March 1799; D. W. Smith papers, B8: 29–32; B11: 190. PAC, MG 24, A6, letterbooks, 1799–1805: 74–75 (transcripts); RG 1, L3, 495: T2/70; 511: T misc., 1791–1819/4, 14; RG 5, A1: 2–3, 19–20. "Accounts of receiver-general of U.C.," AO *Report*, 1914: 753. *Corr. of Hon. Peter Russell* (Cruikshank and Hunter), 2: 103–4. *Corr. of Lieut. Governor Simcoe* (Cruikshank), 3: 346; 4: 196–97, 259. *Doc. hist. of campaign upon Niagara frontier* (Cruikshank), 5: 21–26; 6: 189. *John Askin papers* (Quaife), 2: 239. "Journals of Legislative Assembly of U.C.," AO *Report*, 1909: 58, 91, 118, 121, 163. "Petitions for grants of land" (Cruikshank), *OH*, 24: 140. *Canadian Constellation* (Niagara [Niagara-on-the-Lake, Ont.]), 18 Jan. 1800. *Niagara Herald* (Niagara), 24 Jan., 21 Feb., 6 March, 23 May, 26 Dec. 1801; 16 Jan., 13 Feb. 1802. *Bibliography of Canadiana* (Staton and Tremaine). N. O. Tiffany, *The Tiffanys of America: history and genealogy* ([Buffalo, N.Y., 1901]). Tremaine, *Biblio. of Canadian imprints*, 649–53, 669. Wilson, "Enterprises of Robert Hamilton," 292–93, 311. W. S. Wallace, "The first journalists in Upper Canada," *CHR*, 26 (1945): 372–81; "The periodical literature of Upper Canada," *CHR*, 12 (1931): 4–12.

TOD, JAMES, merchant, politician, militia officer, and seigneur; b. *c.* 1742, probably in Scotland; d. 16 Oct. 1816 at Quebec, Lower Canada.

Details of James Tod's early life and commercial background remain obscure. Although he was at Quebec as early as 1767, when he consigned a book for auction by Samuel Morin, he did not settle there until about 1774. Initially his business, the sale of imported goods, was small; in the fall of 1776, prior to leaving for Britain, he had a "choice" lot of books auctioned at Simpson's Coffee House, where many mercantile transactions and gatherings took place. After his return to the city, in November 1777 he bought from Nicolas-Gaspard BOISSEAU for £750 a house and stores in Lower Town at a location "well situated for trade," between Rue Saint-Pierre and the St Lawrence River. The following year Tod unsuccessfully petitioned the Legislative Council for the grant of an adjacent water-lot and for permission to build a wharf in order to stabilize the deteriorating rear wall of his riverside house. Possibly for domestic service, he bought a black slave, Tom, for £30 in 1779.

In 1782, discouraged perhaps by repeated failures to obtain the water-lot, or finding his location cramped, Tod tried to dispose of his property. Meanwhile, he had begun diversifying his business activities. As early as 1781 he had been active with Simon Fraser of Quebec (possibly Simon Fraser Sr) in exporting furs; two purchases of fur by Tod alone in 1785–86 exceeded £49,000. As well, by 1785 Tod, William GRANT (1744–1805), Peter Stuart, and Mathew and Adam* Lymburner were among the principal Quebec merchants involved in the Gulf of St Lawrence fisheries, then rife with American interlopers. Throughout the late 1780s Tod continued to import, and to sell at his sombre stone establishment, assorted commodities including West Indian and European spirits, sugar, coffee, tobacco, Irish butter, soap, and vinegar, some of which he sold wholesale to other merchants. Obliged on occasion to extend credit to customers, Tod, like most merchants of his time, suffered losses as a result of bankruptcies. His first serious loss occurred as early as 1777, but it was not until the late 1780s, during the depression brought on by the end of the American Revolutionary War, that his extension of credit appears to have become a problem for him. Particularly disquieting for him was a debt of £2,000 sterling which was owed in October 1785 by Alexander Campbell and Company of Quebec, and which it appeared he would have difficulty collecting. By November 1788 Tod was himself in debt to Peter Stuart for £636. Probably to meet with suppliers and creditors, he wintered four times in Britain between 1783 and 1789, and made several return trips in later years, a situation that enabled him to represent in Britain the interest of other Quebec merchants. In 1786, for example, he was trustee in the payment of John JONES's debts in London. Bankruptcies were numerous in Quebec at this time, and Tod acted as a trustee, a role often filled by a creditor, on more than one occasion.

As a member of the closely knit commercial community along Rue Saint-Pierre, where his neighbours included Jones, Robert LESTER, John BLACKWOOD, and John YOUNG, Tod followed, but did not become publicly engaged in, the political debates that engaged such vociferous merchants as George ALLSOPP and William Grant. In the winter of 1785–86 Tod met privately in London with Grant and William Smith* to discuss trade regulations and the mercantile lobby for securing the appointment of Sir Guy CARLETON as governor of Quebec. In the election of 1792 Tod supported Lester's candidacy in Lower Town, and he was himself elected for the lower St Lawrence constituency of Devon, along with the merchant François Dambourgès. During his four years in the province's first assembly, Tod voted against the British minority led by Young and John Richardson* only once, in December 1792, to support the maintenance of a register for the translation into

French of matters introduced in English. He also participated modestly in the sort of social institutions of which the British merchants were often founders. He subscribed to the Agriculture Society, founded in 1789, and was a director of the Quebec Fire Society in 1790 and 1793 and its treasurer in 1792. A lieutenant in the Quebec Battalion of British Militia by 1790, he rose to the rank of captain in 1804.

Although the financial situation of many Quebec merchants in the late 1780s was bleak, Tod appears to have experienced modest success in spite of his difficulties. Assisted by his recently arrived clerk, John Mure*, he was even able to expand his land holdings, particularly in the city. In 1788 he proceeded with the construction of the long-proposed wharf, although he still had not received the grant of the water-lot. Two years later he petitioned for an adjacent water-lot on which he intended to erect a larger wharf "with a Bason in the centre of it for the convenience of loading and unloading" vessels. Both grants were finally made in 1792. Over the next five years he acquired additional property in Quebec and its suburbs, including a Lower Town warehouse owned by Robert Grant, a prominent London merchant.

Outside the city, in 1792 Tod was one of Hugh FINLAY's associates in a petition for 1,200 acres each on the Rivière Saint-François. The same year he purchased for £18 from Simon Fraser Sr the Gaspé seigneury of Rivière-de-la-Madeleine, a prime fishing location; Tod leased the salmon-fishing rights there in 1795 to Joseph Freeman* of Liverpool, N.S. In March 1796, with Mure, Jacob Danford, and Thomas Wilson, Tod acquired the fief of Grosse-Île, in the lower St Lawrence, from the estate of Edward Harrison*. That November the same partners purchased for £50 the nearby fief of Grandville, comprising Île au Canot and Île Patience, which were valued for their hay, timber, and proximity to fishing grounds. In 1799 Tod took the oaths of fealty and homage for Grosse-Île and Grandville, then considered seigneuries. From about the late 1780s, Tod also managed the seigneury of Saint-Gilles in the district of Quebec for Arthur DAVIDSON, a Montreal lawyer.

In 1794, probably during a visit to England, Tod secured the agency to victual the British navy at Quebec, a prized supplement to his normal round of importing, wholesaling, and retailing. Among the goods that he sold were salt, molasses, bricks, "bale goods," and spirits, including "Old London Particular." He was also involved in the grain trade; in July 1796, after bad harvests the year before had resulted in an embargo on agricultural exports, Tod and several other merchants sought permission to supply flour and biscuit to Newfoundland. He owned at least one schooner, the *Charlotte*, and, like most Lower Town merchants, served as agent for numerous vessels

during the short and hectic navigation season at Quebec. The large number of occupants of his house during those months probably included several clerks and servants. By 1799 he had begun constructing a new wharf, possibly the one projected in 1790.

As Tod's business expanded in the 1790s, the list of retail merchants indebted to him grew. Particularly problematic for Tod was the incidence of bankruptcy among those merchants; in 1794 for example, Barthélemy FARIBAULT's son, Barthélemy, failed owing him £868. Between 1795 and 1797 Tod was obliged to borrow £1,150 from the surgeon James Fisher*. His extension of credit, with the corresponding risk of failure, continued in the 1800s. In January 1803 the Quebec shopkeeper Pierre Dumas, who owed Tod £505, failed, and the death in insolvency of another merchant the following year left Tod able to recover only £67 from a debt of nearly £250. By December 1807, 192 debtors from Niagara (Niagara-on-the-Lake), Upper Canada, to Percé in the Gaspé (with the greatest concentration between Chambly and Kamouraska in Lower Canada) owed Tod nearly £24,000; almost one-half of this sum was considered unrecoverable or virtually so. Even among the debts considered good was one of £6,351 owed by Pierre BRUNEAU, who in February had acknowledged his incapacity to pay in full and to whom Tod had not only granted an extension but had promised a discount of more than £1,800 if he paid the rest on time.

By the early 1800s Tod himself was in serious difficulty. He owed £1,654 to Kenelm CHANDLER in 1803. He borrowed nearly £500 the following year, and soon entered a period of spiralling personal indebtedness. His obligations at Quebec were minor compared to his debts in Britain, where he owed more than £28,000. In May 1807, at the suit of Gray, Freeman and Company, a London firm of linen-drapers and Tod's leading creditor, much of his property was seized for sale in partial payment of his British obligations. By November, however, this debt had been reduced only minimally, and it was necessary to assign to it the large sum owed Tod in Canada. The following month Tod failed, a fate, in the knowledgeable opinion of the traveller Hugh Gray, experienced by more than 95 per cent of the British merchants at Quebec since about 1767. He still owed in excess of £28,000, almost all to British suppliers, who included Gray, Freeman and Company and John Gillespie in London, John Lean and Company of Bristol, as well as Meeke, Lowndes and Company, Jones and Smedley, and William Harper at Liverpool. Although the reasons for Tod's collapse are not known, an economic crisis in Great Britain between 1802 and 1805 may have forced his creditors to sue him. The settlement, which was entrusted to Mure, dragged on until at least 1817, a beleaguering circumstance for Tod.

Todd

After his bankruptcy Tod continued in business, much reduced, as a naval supply agent. He was compelled, however, to find new living quarters. In May 1808 he moved from Rue Saint-Pierre to the second floor of a house on Rue de la Montagne. Two years later he was renting the entire house for £100 per annum, but in 1813, after a short residence on Rue Sainte-Famille, he moved into a flat on the corner of Saint-Georges (Hébert) and Laval, where he paid only £50 per annum. He died there on 16 Oct. 1816, aged about 74 years, and was buried three days later from St Andrew's (Presbyterian) Church. It is not known whether Tod ever married, but in 1801 he had transferred to a daughter of full legal age, Charlotte, the 1,200 acres he had bought in Tewkesbury Township. In 1808 he bequeathed to her his furniture and what little remained of his former fortune.

DAVID ROBERTS

AC, Québec, Testament olographe de James Tod, 22 oct. 1816 (*see* P.-G. Roy, *Inv. testaments*, 3: 144). ANQ-Q, CE1-66, 19 Oct. 1816; CN1-16, 6 févr. 1807, 8 mars 1808, 30 nov. 1809, 26 févr. 1810, 6 août 1817; CN1-26, 4, 7 mai, 2 oct. 1804; 20 mai 1807; 2 mai 1810; CN1-27, 9 mai 1811, 18 févr. 1813, 19 févr. 1814; CN1-92, 25 oct., 7, 27 nov. 1788; 13 juill., 13 oct. 1789; 3 août 1791; 9, 11 juill., 14 oct., 9 nov. 1793; 18 août 1794; 22 janv., 6 févr., 21 mars 1796; 12 avril, 10 mai, 28 août 1797; 23 oct., 17 déc. 1798; 10 sept. 1801; CN1-145, 21 juill. 1801, 7 avril 1808, 23 janv. 1810; CN1-147, 2 mars 1807; CN1-178, 27 janv., 23 avril 1795; 15 avril 1797; 5 sept., 5 oct. 1804; 5 avril 1806; CN1-205, 11 oct., 11 nov. 1777; 13 mars 1779; 21 janv., 18 oct. 1780; 7 juill. 1785; CN1-230, 12 sept., 10 oct. 1789; 17 mai 1790; 18 mai 1793; 19 avril 1796; 12 mai 1798; 14 juill. 1803; 15 nov. 1804; 21 juin 1806; 11 déc. 1807; 4 avril 1809; CN1-256, 19 Oct. 1785; 2 June, 7 Aug. 1786; 24 Aug. 1792; 7 Nov. 1793; 16 Jan. 1794; 16 July 1795; CN1-262, 13 juin 1803; 16 oct. 1806; 6 févr., 21 juill. 1807; CN1-284, 3 juin 1791; 27 avril 1793; 9, 11, 13, 27 févr., 21 mars, 2 avril 1795; 7 juin, 11 nov. 1796; 1ᵉʳ mai, 10 juin, 23 sept. 1797; 11 nov. 1799; 4, 31 mars 1800; 23 avril 1801; CN1-285, 28 oct. 1801, 29 janv. 1803. ASQ, C 36: 135; C 37: 177; Polygraphie, XXV: 19H; S, carton 7, no.19: carton 9, nos.2, 2A. BL, Add. MSS 21727: 21 (copy at PAC). McCord Museum, J.-B. Blondeau, account-book, 1779–87: ff.123, 136; Samuel Morin, account-book, 25 août 1767. PAC, MG 8, A7, 5: 306–25; 6: 75–78; MG 23, GII, 26: 7–12; MG 24, B1, 190: 4972–78; L3: 8930–38; MG 30, D1, 29: 181, 183; RG 1, L3ᴸ: 33, 172, 2765–66, 3002, 3019, 41629–36, 92039–76, 92081–85; RG 4, A1: 20499–501, 21707–11; RG 8, I (C ser.), 372: 172A, 179–80A; 599: 22–22A; 1218: 15; RG 42, ser.1, 183: 47. PRO, CO 42/34: 78–82; 42/48: ff.147–50; 42/122: 221 (mfm. at PAC). Bas-Canada, chambre d'Assemblée, *Journaux*, 1792–96. "Les dénombrements de Québec" (Plessis), ANQ *Rapport*, 1948–49: 36, 86, 135, 185. Hugh Gray, *Letters from Canada, written during a residence there in the years 1806, 1807, and 1808* ... (London, 1809; repr. Toronto, 1971), 226–30. Smith, *Diary and selected papers* (Upton), 2: 45–46. *Quebec Gazette*, 13 Oct. 1774; 26 Sept., 3 Oct.

1776; 6 Nov. 1777; 29 Oct. 1778; 24 June 1779; 16 Nov. 1780; 13 Sept. 1781; 14 March, 19 Sept. 1782; 13 Nov. 1783; 17 June 1784; 1, 8 June, 13 July, 16 Nov. 1786; 24 May 1787; 27 March 1788; 28 May, 3, 17 Dec. 1789; 25 March, 1, 22 April, 4 Nov. 1790; 28 April, 5 May 1791; 5 April, 17 May, 20 Dec. 1792; 11 April, 8 Aug., 28 Nov. 1793; 3 July 1794; 7 July 1795; 23, 30 March 1797; 11 Jan. 1798; 9 May, 18 July, 8 Aug. 1799; 23 Jan. 1800; 14 May, 20 Aug. 1801; 20 May, 10 June, 23 Sept. 1802; 8 Sept. 1803; 10 May, 26 July 1804; 25 July 1805; 20 March 1806; 9 April, 14 May, 17 Dec. 1807; 29 Jan., 27 Oct. 1808; 26 Jan. 1809; 22 Feb., 12 April 1810; 19 March 1812; 2 April, 2 Sept., 30 Dec. 1813; 17 Oct. 1816. *Quebec Mercury*, 18 Oct. 1816. Doris Drolet Dubé et Marthe Lacombe, *Inventaire des marchés de construction des Archives nationales à Québec, XVIIᵉ et XVIIIᵉ siècles* (Ottawa, 1977), nos.1615–16. Langelier, *Liste des terrains concédés*, 887. *London directory*, 1806: 87; 1807: 95. *Quebec almanac*, 1791: 44, 85; 1794: 125; 1805: 40. P.-G. Roy, *Inv. concessions*, 1: 222–23; 3: 209. H. A. Innis, *The cod fisheries; the history of an international economy* (rev. ed., Toronto, 1954), 169, 236. Ouellet, *Hist. économique*, 153, 173.

TODD, ISAAC, businessman, office holder, militia officer, and landowner; b. *c.* 1742 in Ireland; d. 22 May 1819 in Bath, England.

Isaac Todd had been a merchant in Ireland before he came to Canada shortly after the conquest. By February 1765 he was established in business at Montreal, and, following a disastrous fire in the city on 18 May, he submitted a claim for £150 in lost merchandise. On 23 May he received a commission as justice of the peace for the District of Montreal. He was quickly attracted to the fur trade, and his early years in it were characterized by numerous partnerships and considerable misfortune. In 1767 he posted bonds totalling nearly £1,500 as security for three traders going to various points in the interior. The following year he suffered a severe financial loss when two of his hired traders were killed by Indians. By 1769, when he invested about £900, he was in association with James McGILL; that year they joined with Benjamin* and JOSEPH Frobisher. Along with his partners Todd again experienced a reverse when the group's canoes were plundered by Indians at Rainy Lake (Ont.). The next year, however, the same partners succeeded in getting their canoes through to the northwest. A subsequent partnership with Richard McNeall was terminated in October 1772. That year Todd was associated with George McBEATH at Michilimackinac (Mackinaw City, Mich.); they received trade goods from Thomas Walker* through Maurice-Régis BLONDEAU at Montreal, and in turn supplied the traders Thomas Corry and John ASKIN. In early 1773 Todd lost two more men killed or starved around Grand Portage (near Grand Portage, Minn.). That spring he and McGill went together to Michilimackinac, taking with them the independent trader Peter POND and some of his goods. By 1774 Todd was acting as the business agent at Montreal for Phyn, Ellice and Company of Schenectady, N.Y. [*see* Alexander ELLICE].

Todd was an early leader in the political activities of British merchants in Canada. In 1765 and 1766 he was among those who petitioned Governor Murray* to reduce restrictions on the fur trade. In March 1769 he was a member of the grand jury for the District of Montreal. Considered by the British merchants as the only representative body in the colony, the grand jury was frequently used by them as a forum for criticizing the policies of the governors and recommending political, social, and economic initiatives. In 1770 Todd signed a petition in favour of an elective assembly, and in the fall of 1774 he had, in the words of Simon McTAVISH, "his hands full of the publick business," having been appointed, along with McGill and others, to a committee charged both with drawing up a petition to the king and British parliament opposing the Quebec Act and with finding means to redress the merchants' grievances. From his position on the committee, Todd was able to advise Phyn, Ellice and Company as to the best method of opposing the Quebec Revenue Act, which threatened that company's profitable supply trade to Montreal merchants by imposing a tax on rum and spirits entering the province from the American colonies; in return Phyn, Ellice gave Todd valuable business information on the state of the fur trade from New York and on the imminent arrival at Quebec of large quantities of rum, which American traders had had shipped there by sea in order to evade the Quebec Revenue Act. Todd's committee corresponded with similar committees in the American colonies but, when the revolution broke out in 1775, Todd remained loyal to Britain and served as a lieutenant in the British militia.

In 1775 Todd and McGill joined Blondeau and the Frobishers to send 12 canoes to Grand Portage in an association that marked the beginning of an extensive trade and presaged the formation of the North West Company. Todd and McGill formalized their association in May or June 1776 when they founded a firm called Todd and McGill; the precedence of Todd's name probably denotes his seniority in the business. Their partnership was cemented by personal friendship. On 2 Dec. 1776 Todd was a witness at McGill's marriage to Charlotte Trottier Desrivières, *née* Guillimin. The following year Todd and McGill loaded six canoes with merchandise valued at £2,700, and in 1778 Todd alone invested about £6,000. In 1779, when the NWC, a co-partnership of 16 shares, was formed by nine firms trading to Michilimackinac, Todd and McGill obtained the maximum allowable two shares. Two shares in the enterprise were held by each of two partnerships with which Todd and McGill were closely associated, Benjamin and Joseph Frobisher and McGill and Paterson, McGill's brother John

being a partner in the latter. In May 1781 Todd and McGill joined the Frobishers and McGill and Paterson in sending to Grand Portage for the northwest trade 12 canoes and 100 men with goods valued at £5,000. That year Todd and McGill became Montreal agents for the Niagara merchants Robert HAMILTON and Richard CARTWRIGHT.

At the end of 1782, when the nature of the preliminary articles of peace between Britain and her rebellious American colonies became known in Montreal, the city's fur-trade community was alarmed at the prospect of losing to the Americans the fur-trade centres of Detroit and Michilimackinac (Mackinac Island, Mich.). Todd, who was in London in February 1783, was a member of a small committee promoting the interests of the Montreal merchants among government officials, and he signed memorials protesting the proposed cession of such key posts and forecasting a loss of business for the Montreal merchants if it occurred. Despite Todd's public prognostications Todd and McGill had sufficient faith in the future of the trade on American territory to withdraw from the northwest about 1783 or 1784 and to concentrate their attention on the trade to the Mississippi and Upper Lakes regions.

Todd and McGill, although they equipped expeditions themselves, acted principally as middlemen, importing from various London firms a wide variety of trade goods. These goods arrived at Quebec and were trans-shipped to Montreal, where they were packed for clients at Detroit, Michilimackinac, and other posts. McGill, who possessed a shrewd judgement but was temperamentally more reserved than Todd, managed affairs at Montreal and conducted most of the correspondence of the partnership. Todd, sociable and cheerful, travelled when business required it, maintaining personal contact with those upon whom depended the success of the company, or of the fur trade in general. He made return voyages to London at least four times between 1778 and 1785; in the latter year, when Lieutenant Governor Henry Hamilton* sent a petition from the fur traders in the *pays d'en haut* to the Home secretary, Lord Sydney, he referred Sydney to Todd for an account of the state of the trade.

In the period immediately following the American revolution Todd and McGill, like other companies trading to Detroit, suffered losses as a result of unstable trade conditions created by conflict between the Indians and the American army. By April 1786 the partnership was so indebted to its English suppliers, McGill informed its Detroit agent, Askin, "that Todd [who was again in London] writes me he was under the necessity of relinquishing every Scheme of business except the shipping of a few dry Goods & some Rum, being afraid to run further in debt & perhaps even meet with a refusal of further credit." When the Detroit traders were driven that year to form a co-partnership

Todd

called the Miamis Company, Todd and McGill, probably through Askin's influence, was named its Montreal agent.

Todd remained active in Montreal's public life. In March 1787 he was a member of the grand jury and a captain in the British militia, but his political activities, unless directly related to commerce, declined as those of McGill intensified. In the 1790s his and McGill's principal commercial pursuits, conducted from warehouses on Rue Saint-Paul, continued to be related to the fur trade. They imported manufactured goods from Britain and tobacco and spirits from the West Indies to sell to other merchants and for their own business. In 1790 they filled 15 canoes and 10 bateaux with goods valued at £11,500. Their activities were still concentrated on the regions south of the Great Lakes. Between 1790 and 1796 they hired at least 518 *engagés*; of these 57 per cent agreed to go wherever they might be sent, a situation that allowed Todd, McGill and Company (as it was called by 1790) to adjust to fluctuations in an unstable field of enterprise. Of those *engagés* whose destination was specified in their contract 24 per cent were sent to Michilimackinac, 19 per cent to the Mississippi region, 17 per cent to Detroit, and the rest to a large number of posts. The year 1797 marked a radical departure from former practice, however; of 70 *engagés* known to have been hired at Montreal, only 14 per cent had no specified destination, while 73 per cent were sent to Michilimackinac.

By the 1790s Todd, McGill and Company had established a contact at St Louis (Mo.) in Auguste Chouteau, who bought their trade goods and shipped to them, via Michilimackinac, peltries gathered along the Missouri and Osage rivers. In 1794, when the Spanish government of Louisiana granted Todd's nephew, Andrew Todd, a monopoly of the upper Mississippi trade, Todd, McGill and Company found itself in a position to monopolize the supply of the entire Mississippi valley. However, the declaration of war between Spain and Britain in October 1796, and Andrew's death later that year, soon dashed grandiose expectations.

The concentration of the trading activities of Todd, McGill and Company on American territory was a source of apprehension to Todd, more so than it was to McGill. In May 1790 Todd, who was in London, and the London merchant John Inglis lobbied Home Secretary William Wyndham Grenville to prevent, or at least delay, the transfer to the United States of western military posts on American territory still garrisoned by British troops. The following year Todd, McGill and Company, along with McTavish, Frobisher and Company [see Simon McTavish] and Forsyth, Richardson and Company, urged Lieutenant Governor SIMCOE to impress upon the British government the need to establish an independent Indian territory in the west, open to both British and American traders; in 1792 Todd lobbied for the idea in London. That April Todd, McGill and other firms complained to Simcoe of American interference with communications between Montreal and the American interior, which, if tolerated by the British government, "would be much the same as a total relinquishment of the Trade." A pessimistic Todd wrote to Askin in August, "I have strongly recommended to the House to curtale & Lessen our connections in that Trade, for when I consider the [uncertainty] of our retaining the Posts the Warr between the Indians and Americans, and the evident fall on furrs I am convinced it is an unsafe and unprofitable business, and will continue so for two or 3 years." In 1794 Todd and Simon McTavish submitted a memorandum to the British government stipulating the conditions that should be demanded of the Americans before the western posts could be turned over to them; of first importance was freedom of trade for the British merchants.

At the same time as Todd struggled to ensure free access for his company to the southwest trade, he sought, in case of failure, to open a door on the northwest, largely controlled since 1787 by the NWC. In 1791 John GREGORY, a partner in the NWC, informed McTavish that Todd, John Richardson*, and Alexander Henry* were determined to get into the northwest trade if McGill would manage the Montreal business of a new company. McGill was not enthused by the idea of opposing the NWC, and he persuaded the others to let him negotiate entry into it with his friend Joseph Frobisher. Frobisher was soon convinced that if Todd, McGill and Forsyth, Richardson were not allowed a share in the northwest trade through the NWC, they would in combination, and with the financial support of Phyn, Ellices, and Inglis of London, constitute a ruinous opposition. On 14 Sept. 1792 Todd, McGill was accorded two shares in a new 46-share arrangement. Three years later, however, perhaps dissatisfied with proposed new conditions of partnership, Todd and McGill did not sign a revised NWC agreement. Instead they agreed with Forsyth, Richardson and two independent traders to operate for three years in the Nipigon country, but they later withdrew from the agreement under pressure from the NWC.

In the 1780s Todd and McGill had begun diversifying their activities, in part as insurance against the vagaries of the fur trade. In addition to conducting their own banking operations, in March 1792 they joined Phyn, Ellices, and Inglis and Forsyth, Richardson in signing a preliminary agreement for a bank in Lower Canada, but the project was stillborn. In 1789 they had associated with the firms of Forsyth, Richardson, Lester and Morrogh [see Robert LESTER], and the merchants Thomas McCord*, George

King, and Jean-Baptiste-Amable Durocher in purchasing for £3,050 the Montreal Distillery Company, of which Jacob Jordan* was formerly the principal backer in Canada. This company seems not to have yielded the expected returns; it was dissolved in 1794 and the property sold to Nicholas MONTOUR for £1,166 that October. Todd also began to envision the supply of grain to the government as an eventual replacement for the fur trade, where all would be lost in a few years, he wrote to Askin in April 1793, "unless there is a change in the mode of Trade and expense that I scarcely think will happen." That year Todd and William ROBERTSON lobbied successfully in London to secure for Todd and McGill's Upper Canadian associate Cartwright and others an exclusive sub-contract to victual the military posts on the Great Lakes. As did many other merchants, Todd and McGill moved into land speculation; through Askin in 1796 they acquired several shares in the Cuyahoga Purchase, a large tract of land along the south shore of Lake Erie. They were occasionally obliged to accept land as payment for debt. One of their largest debtors was Askin, who in 1792 owed them £20,217; he acquitted part of the sum by transferring to them land in and around Detroit. In 1798 Todd also acquired by succession all the property of his nephew, Andrew.

Todd's growing disagreement with McGill about the future of the fur trade on American territory was probably a major contributing factor to the dissolution of his partnership with McGill by early April 1797. Five years earlier James's brother Andrew McGill had been brought into Todd, McGill as a partner, and he had probably been groomed as Todd's eventual successor. Todd's ties with the trade were not immediately severed, however, since it took several years for an outfit to turn a profit or loss; in March 1798 he wrote to Askin of the capture by the French of "the richest of our Furr Ships in which we had to the Amo¹ of £12000." Only after August of that year did he begin to withdraw from active participation. He retired with the reputation of an authority on the trade and a father figure in the fur-trade community. In 1795 he had been admitted to the prestigious Beaver Club. The following year Simcoe wrote to one of his correspondents that the information on communications that the latter had requested was "to be gathered from Carver and Hennepin's Voyages or rather from the conversation of such a man as Mr. Todd." In 1804 Todd exerted his considerable influence in the fur-trade fraternity to promote the union of the NWC and the New North West Company (sometimes called the XY Company) [see Sir Alexander MACKENZIE], seemingly having been, the Earl of Selkirk [DOUGLAS] noted, "almost the only man who has maintained a constant friendly intercourse with both parties."

From 1800 to about 1807 Todd joined with the Quebec firm of Lester and Morrogh to supply provisions to the British army in Lower Canada. He continued his activities in land speculation, alone and with McGill. In October 1801 they acquired 32,400 acres in Stanbridge Township, Lower Canada, from Hugh FINLAY for £3,750. The following August Todd acquired 11,760 acres in Leeds Township through the system of township leaders and associates [see James CALDWELL]. As well, by 1805, in conjunction with McGill and Askin, he had acquired other lands in and around Detroit. After the transfer of that post to the United States in 1796, the refusal of the American government to recognize all of Todd's and McGill's land titles, as well as the failure of the American courts to sustain their prosecutions for debt, had embittered Todd, who in 1808 declared himself to Askin "out of patience with your Rascally Country."

Despite deteriorating health Todd led an active social life. In January 1799 Alexander Henry had written to Askin that Todd "is like myself growing old always complaining"; a year later he specified that Todd "is always complaining when his intestines are empty, but after Dinner recovers wonderfully." The British officer George Thomas Landmann* described him about the same time as an old man who entertained "exceedingly" with numerous anecdotes of his experiences at Michilimackinac; Todd was, Landmann added, affectionately known as "By Jove," for his favourite expression. He was sorely tried by the deaths in July 1804 of McTavish, a close friend, and of a housekeeper. "She was only 31 Years Old," he lamented to Askin, "Lived with me near 10 Years & was Mother to a Little Girl that Calls me and truly her father." He placed this girl in school at Quebec and established a trust fund of £1,000 for each of his housekeeper's other two daughters. "I know of no use Money is but to do good, and to enable me to assist others," he told Askin. "I with pleasure deprive Self of comforts I could enjoy."

In March 1805 Todd presided at a dinner given by the Montreal merchants for local deputies in the House of Assembly. The *Montreal Gazette* reported the tenor of some of the sardonic toasts, including those made by Todd, denouncing a proposal in the assembly to introduce a tax on merchandise for the purpose of funding a new city jail; in February 1806, when the assembly met, those members who supported the tax had the serjeant-at-arms sent from Quebec to arrest Todd, as chairman of the dinner, and Edward EDWARDS of the *Gazette* on a charge of libel. By the time the serjeant-at-arms had arrived at Montreal, however, Todd was nowhere to be found.

Between 1806 and 1813 Todd travelled continuously – to Niagara (Niagara-on-the-Lake), Upper Canada, to New York, and to England – on business and in search of relief from his numerous ailments; however, he always returned to Montreal, craving the

Townshend

company of old friends. A member of the Scotch Presbyterian Church, later known as St Gabriel Street Church, he was elected to its temporal committee in 1809 and later became its president. A trip to New York sparked Henry to observe in February 1810 that Todd's society was missed at Montreal, "he being the only friend, except Mr Frobisher, who has not changed their dispositions, some from geting rich, other from having obtain'd places, &^{ca} [which] has raised them in their own imagination above their old acquaintance." In London the same year the ever gregarious Todd became a founder of the Canada Club, along with Alexander Mackenzie, Edward Ellice*, Simon McGillivray*, and others. By 1812, however, having survived all his friends there, he had returned to Montreal, principally to be with Henry and McGill. "Todd says he is only 68," Henry joked to Askin in February 1811. "Todd was once much older than me but he has grown much younger at present." On 21 Dec. 1813 Todd signed McGill's death certificate; the demise of his friend and former partner prompted him to retire. In May 1815 he was back in England at Bath, taking mineral waters. There he undoubtedly learned of the activities of a NWC ship named in his honour, for in 1813 and 1814 the *Isaac Todd* had participated in a successful operation by the Royal Navy to clear the Pacific Ocean of American naval presence and to capture Fort Astoria, base of the NWC's major competitor on the Pacific coast, John Jacob Astor*. Todd seems never to have returned to Canada, and on 22 May 1819, at the reported age of 77, he died at Bath. The *Montreal Herald* noted that his death was "very sincerely regretted by a numerous and most respectable circle of friends and acquaintances."

In retrospect, given the gradual American exclusion of Montreal traders from the southwest fur trade after 1800, Todd appears to have been the more prescient of the senior partners in Todd, McGill and Company regarding its main economic activity. He may already have had misgivings about leaving the northwest in 1783 or 1784, but clearly by the early 1790s he had realized that the future of the trade lay there. However, by 1792 when, under his pressure, Todd, McGill and Company did join the NWC, Joseph Frobisher and Simon McTavish had already established their preponderance in the co-partnership. Had Todd and McGill remained in the NWC from the beginning they might have proved serious rivals for the dominance of the fur trade from Montreal.

MYRON MOMRYK

ANQ-Q, CN1-16, 27 janv., 17 févr. 1809; CN1-26, 18 déc. 1801; CN1-256, 29 May 1792; CN1-262, 2 oct. 1801. NYPL, William Edgar papers (copies at PAC). PAC, MG 11, [CO 42] Q, 74: 234–35; MG 19, A3, 24; 69; MG 30, D1, 20; RG 4, B1, 12: 4586–91; B28, 115. PRO, CO 42/5: 30–31 (copies at PAC). "The British regime in Wisconsin, 1760–1800," ed. R. G. Thwaites, Wis., State Hist. Soc., *Coll.*, 18 (1908): 313, 326. *Corr. of Lieut. Governor Simcoe* (Cruikshank), 4: 255. *Doc. relatifs à l'hist. constitutionnelle, 1759–1791* (Shortt et Doughty; 1921), 1: 397–98, 886–87. *Docs. relating to NWC* (Wallace). Douglas, *Lord Selkirk's diary* (White). *John Askin papers* (Quaife). Landmann, *Adventures and recollections*, 2: 172. *Montreal Herald*, 19 June 1819. *Quebec Gazette*, 1766–1806. Langelier, *Liste des terrains concédés*, 9. Massicotte, "Répertoire des engagements pour l'Ouest," ANQ *Rapport*, 1942–43. *Quebec almanac*, 1788: 52. M. W. Campbell, *NWC* (1973). R. Campbell, *Hist. of Scotch Presbyterian Church*. B. M. Gough, *The Royal Navy and the northwest coast of North America, 1810–1914: a study of British maritime ascendancy* (Vancouver, 1971), 12–24. Innis, *Fur trade in Canada* (1970). L. P. Kellogg, *The British régime in Wisconsin and the northwest* (Madison, Wis., 1935). Lanctot, *Canada and American revolution* (Cameron). M. S. MacSporran, "James McGill: a critical biographical study" (MA thesis, McGill Univ., Montreal, [1930]). Miquelon, "Baby family," 182, 189. P. C. Phillips, *The fur trade* (2v., Norman, Okla., 1961), 2. Rich, *Hist. of HBC* (1960), vol.2. Rumilly, *La compagnie du Nord-Ouest*. Ivanhoë Caron, "The colonization of Canada under the British dominion, 1800–1815," Quebec, Bureau of Statistics, *Statistical year-book* (Quebec), 7 (1920). R. H. Fleming, "Phyn, Ellice and Company of Schenectady," *Contributions to Canadian Economics* (Toronto), 4 (1932): 30–32. Charles Lart, "Fur trade returns, 1767," *CHR*, 3 (1922): 351–58. E. A. Mitchell, "The North West Company agreement of 1795," *CHR*, 36 (1955): 128–30. Ouellet, "Dualité économique et changement technologique," *SH*, 9: 286. W. E. Stevens, "The northwest fur trade, 1763–1800," *Univ. of Ill. Studies in the Social Sciences* (Urbana), 14 (1926), no.3: 167, 171, 175, 183–84.

TOWNSHEND, GEORGE, 4th Viscount and 1st Marquess TOWNSHEND, army officer and artist; b. 28 Feb. 1723/24; d. 14 Sept. 1807 at Raynham Hall, Norfolk, England.

George Townshend was the eldest son of Charles, 3rd Viscount Townshend, and his wife Audrey Harrison. The Townshends owned extensive estates in Norfolk and elsewhere. George was educated at St John's College, Cambridge, leaving there in 1742. He then went as a volunteer to the British army in Germany, being attached to the staff of Lord Dunmore, one of the general officers. He was present at the battle of Dettingen (16 June 1743) and also apparently at that of Fontenoy (30 April 1745), though a letter of Horace Walpole's says that he was too late for the latter action. In May 1745 he was appointed a captain in Bligh's Regiment (later the 20th Foot). On the outbreak of the Jacobite rebellion in that year he returned to Britain, joined his regiment, and fought with it at the battle of Culloden (16 April 1746). Thereafter he went back to the Continent, having been appointed an aide-de-camp to the Duke of Cumberland. In this capacity he was present at the battle of

Laffeldt (21 June 1747) and carried Cumberland's dispatch back to England. At this time he was elected to the House of Commons for the county of Norfolk, which he continued to represent until he succeeded his father as viscount in 1764. As of 25 Feb. 1747/48 he was appointed to a captaincy in the 1st Foot Guards, which carried with it the rank of lieutenant-colonel in the army. When the War of the Austrian Succession ended in 1748 he returned to England. He fell out with Cumberland, attacked him in parliament, and made him a victim of his notable powers as a caricaturist. At the end of 1750 he resigned from the army. He identified himself with the cause of militia reform and largely as a result of his efforts an effective new militia act was passed in 1757.

In the same year Cumberland ceased to be commander-in-chief, being succeeded by Sir John Ligonier. Townshend now returned to the service, being commissioned as colonel (of no specific regiment) as of 6 May 1758. In August he wrote to William Pitt asking for active employment against the French. In December he was summoned to London and appointed to command a brigade in the expedition under James Wolfe* which was being organized to attack Quebec by way of the St Lawrence. The appointment undoubtedly displeased Wolfe. He had asked Ligonier to let him choose his own subordinates, and he had not asked for Townshend. The "Proposals for the expedition to Quebec" in Pitt's papers suggest as the three brigadiers Robert Monckton*, James Murray*, and Ralph Burton*. Burton, a friend of Wolfe's, was now squeezed out to make room for a man with more influence. Wolfe wrote Townshend a welcoming letter in which he said, "Your name was mentioned to me by the Mareschal [Ligonier] and my answer was, that such an example in a person of your rank and character could not but have the best effects upon the troops in America; and I took the freedom to add that what might be wanting in experience was amply made up, in an extent of capacity and activity of mind, that would find nothing difficult in our business." This reflects the feelings of a hard-working middle-class career officer confronted with the heir to a viscountcy who has always had things made easy for him. It would be strange if Townshend did not resent the reference to inexperience, especially as he had seen a good deal of active service. Here perhaps is the origin of later trouble.

Townshend, junior to Monckton but senior to Murray, was third in command of the expedition. He crossed the Atlantic with Wolfe in Vice-Admiral Charles Saunders*'s flagship *Neptune*. It may have been during the voyage that he made the water-colour drawing of Wolfe which the general's biographer Robert Wright called "the most *convincing* portrait of Wolfe I have ever seen"; it is certainly the best portrait extant. In the last week of June 1759 the British fleet

and army arrived before Quebec, and Wolfe began his long struggle with the problem of bringing the Marquis de Montcalm* to battle. On 9–10 July Townshend's and Murray's brigades landed on the north shore of the St Lawrence below Montmorency Falls and entrenched themselves there. By this time Wolfe's relations with his brigadiers, and particularly Townshend, had deteriorated. On 7 July Wolfe had written in his journal, "Some difference of opinion upon a point termd *slight & insignificant* & the Commander in Chief is threatened wth Parliamentary Inquiry into his Conduct for not consulting an inferior Officer & seeming to disregard his Sentiments!" The "inferior Officer" was presumably George Townshend, MP. Things got worse after the unsuccessful Montmorency attack on 31 July, an operation which the brigadiers had disliked. On 6 September Townshend wrote the rather famous letter to his wife in which he said, "Genl Wolf's Health is but very bad. His Generalship in my poor opinion – is not a bit better; this only between us." Townshend's wickedly clever caricatures of Wolfe which have survived tell a great deal about their relationship.

On or about 27 August Wolfe, then recovering from a severe illness, consulted the brigadiers formally for the first time. He sent them a memorandum begging them to consult together as to the best method of attacking the enemy. He himself suggested three possible lines of attack, all variants of the Montmorency operation which had already failed. After discussion with Admiral Saunders, the brigadiers (it is impossible to distinguish between the three as to their contributions at this point) politely rejected the commander-in-chief's suggestions and recommended a quite different line of operation, bringing the troops away from Montmorency and landing above Quebec: "When we establish ourselves on the North Shore, the French General must fight us on our own Terms; We shall be betwixt him and his provisions, and betwixt him and their Army opposing General [Jeffery Amherst*] [on Lake Champlain]." For the first time, the essential strategic weakness of the French position was pointed out and exploited: Quebec, and the French army outside Quebec, were dependent on provisions brought down the river, and if this supply line were cut Montcalm would have no choice but to fight to open it. Wolfe accepted the brigadiers' recommendation, and thereby made possible the victory on the Plains of Abraham; though the decision to take the risk of landing at the Anse au Foulon, close to the town, was Wolfe's own. The brigadiers had favoured landing farther up the river.

In the battle of the Plains Townshend commanded the British left wing. Wolfe was mortally wounded and Monckton disabled, and Townshend unexpectedly found himself commanding the army. In these circumstances it is not surprising that his direction of

Townshend

the last phase of the action and its aftermath was not particularly effective. His first task was to deal with Colonel Louis-Antoine de BOUGAINVILLE's belated intervention from up the river; this was easily done. But the beaten French field army made good its escape across the Rivière Saint-Charles to its camp; and that night it marched around the British and got away to the west. Townshend prepared to besiege and bombard Quebec, bringing large numbers of guns up the cliff to the Plains of Abraham. But the city surrendered to him on 18 September. He had offered relatively lenient terms in order to get possession of it as soon as possible.

Murray was left in command at Quebec and Townshend returned to England before the winter. He was rewarded with the colonelcy of the 28th Foot and the thanks of parliament. During 1760 his conduct at Quebec was attacked and defended in anonymous pamphlets, which throw little real light on the happenings there. Effective 6 March 1761 he was made a major-general, and took command of a brigade in the British contingent of the allied army in Germany. His brigade was heavily engaged in the battle of Vellinghausen (15–16 July 1761). In 1762 he was sent to Portugal with the local rank of lieutenant-general, and took command of a division of the Anglo-Portuguese army which was protecting Portugal against the forces of France and Spain. No important operations took place here before the conclusion of peace.

In 1767 Townshend was appointed lord lieutenant of Ireland, and held this post until 1772. Traditionally, Townshend in Ireland has been remembered chiefly as a person who was adept at manipulating the Irish parliament by corrupt means and was considerably disliked. Recent research, however, reveals him as an effective and resolute administrator whose financial measures broke the power of the local oligarchy and transferred it to a party in parliament controlled by the government in Dublin Castle. From 1772 to 1782, and again for some months in 1783, he was master general of the Board of Ordnance. He was promoted general in 1782 and field marshal in 1796. He was appointed lord lieutenant of Norfolk in 1792, and also held the office of governor of Jersey. In 1787 he was made a marquess. In 1751 he had married Charlotte Compton, who was Baroness Ferrers of Chartley in her own right. By her, according to some authorities, he had four sons and four daughters. She died in 1770, and in 1773 he married Anne, daughter of Sir James William Montgomery and sister of William*; this marriage is said to have produced six children.

Although Townshend had been so bitter against Wolfe in 1759, time softened his feelings, and in 1774 he discouraged Murray from making an attack on the memory of the dauntless hero. Townshend and his fellow brigadiers have been much abused by Wolfe's admirers; but there is not the slightest doubt that they gave him sound advice at a moment when he was floundering badly, and that it was they, with the support of Saunders, who set Wolfe's feet on the path to victory. Townshend had important artistic abilities; he has been called "the first great English caricaturist." An obituary in the *Times* said, "In his private character he was lively, unaffected, and convivial." His portrait was painted by Sir Joshua Reynolds and by Thomas Hudson.

Townshend was one of the favoured people who in July 1767 received 20,000-acre grants in St John's (Prince Edward) Island, being awarded Lot 56 in the east end of the Island. In 1770, embarrassed by his Irish expenses, he was trying unsuccessfully to sell this land. Like so many of the absentee proprietors, he seems to have done nothing to settle or develop his grant. In 1784, however, he gave up one-quarter of it to "American Loyalists and disbanded troops," and some settlement then took place.

C. P. STACEY

[The biography by Lieutenant-Colonel Charles Vere Ferrers (later Major-General Sir Charles) Townshend, *The military life of Field-Marshal George, first Marquess Townshend, 1724–1807* . . . (London, 1901), is not good but contains important documents. It reprints, on pp.253–60 and 261–74 respectively, the two anonymous pamphlets published in London in 1760: *A letter to an honourable brigadier-general, commander-in-chief of his majesty's forces in Canada*, subsequently ascribed to "Junius," and *A refutation of the letter to an hon^{ble}. brigadier-general, commander of his majesty's forces in Canada*, attributed only to "An officer"; it also reproduces the Reynolds and Hudson portraits.

Townshend's papers for the 1759 campaign are in the Northcliffe collection at PAC (MG 18, M, ser.2); see the printed calendar, *The Northcliffe collection* . . . (Ottawa, 1926). His portrait and caricatures of Wolfe are at the McCord Museum (M245, M905, M1443, M1791–94, M19856–57). The portrait has often been reproduced; it appears in colour in Robin Reilly, *The rest to fortune; the life of Major-General James Wolfe* (London, 1960). Six of the caricatures are reproduced in Christopher Hibbert, *Wolfe at Quebec* (London and Toronto, 1959).

A letter, dated 16 June 1770, from Townshend to Lady Townshend (his mother?) is in the Clements Library, George Townshend papers, letterbooks, 5. Among the printed primary and secondary sources, the following are valuable: John Stewart, *An account of Prince Edward Island, in the Gulph of St. Lawrence, North America* . . . (London, 1806); repr. [East Ardsley, Eng., and New York], 1967); Horace Walpole, *Memoirs of the reign of King George the Second*, ed. [H. R. V. Fox, 3rd Baron] Holland (2nd ed., 3v., London, 1846); *The letters of Horace Walpole, fourth Earl of Oxford* . . . , ed. [Helen] and Paget Toynbee (16v. and 3v. suppl., Oxford, 1903–25); *Times* (London), 19 Sept. 1807; *Burke's peerage* (1963); *DNB*; G.B., WO, *Army list*, 1763, 1806; R. [R.] Sedgwick, *The House of Commons, 1715–1754* (2v., London, 1970), 2; *Canada's smallest prov.*

(Bolger); J. W. Fortescue, *A history of the British army* (13v. in 14, London, 1899–1930), 2; C. P. Stacey, *Quebec, 1759: the siege and the battle* (Toronto, 1959); Thomas Bartlett, "The Townshend viceroyalty, 1767–72," *Penal era and golden age: essays in Irish history, 1690–1800*, ed. Thomas Bartlett and D. W. Hayton (Belfast, 1979), 88–112; "Viscount Townshend and the Irish Revenue Board, 1767–73," Royal Irish Academy, *Proc.* (Dublin), 79 (1979), sect.C: 153–75.   C.P.S.]

TOWNSHEND, WILLIAM, office holder and politician; b. *c.* 1745, probably in Wales, son of Richard Townshend of Wrexham; m. *c.* 1790 Flora Stewart, daughter of Chief Justice Peter STEWART and Helen MacKinnon, and they had six sons and two daughters; d. 5 Dec. 1816 in Plymouth, England.

Little is known of William Townshend's life before he became collector of customs and naval officer for St John's (Prince Edward) Island. He may have obtained the appointments because of a family connection with George, Viscount TOWNSHEND. His enemies later asserted that he had powerful friends in England, although Sir Cecil Wray, an absentee proprietor for whom he acted as agent, is the only one noted as a patron. The office of collector had been given to William Allanby in 1765, but it appears that he had little interest in the colony for Governor Walter Patterson* noted in 1783 that Allanby had been absent for nine years and was not likely to return. During his absence no shipping or customs records had been kept.

Townshend came to the Island in 1784 and that December he was appointed to the Council, Patterson noting that, as he had been "so unexceptionable since his arrival," he could not be refused a seat. The appointment placed him firmly within the colony's little establishment and he was quickly involved in Patterson's lengthy efforts to seize land from absentee proprietors. A member of Council in April 1786 when legislation relating to the seizure was passed, Townshend was named in the charges later made against officers of the government. He had, however, objected to the measures because of irregularities in their passage and resigned as a result of their adoption. The complainants noted in their summary of evidence in 1789 that Townshend, who had resumed his seat in April 1787, had temporarily "admitted the advances of his brother officers." When the Privy Council brought down its report in 1789 it concluded that he had innocently been drawn into the affair, and he was one of the few officers in the colony who was able to avoid dismissal and disgrace.

On the arrival of Lieutenant Governor Edmund FANNING in November 1786 Townshend had promptly aligned himself with the anti-Patterson faction. Fanning responded by writing in November 1787 to the Home secretary praising Townshend as a "zealous advocate in support of the measures of His Majesty's Government." No doubt some of Fanning's enthusiasm stemmed from the part Townshend had taken in the elections of July and August 1787 by which Fanning hoped to end the hold Patterson's group had on the House of Assembly. Charges were made to Council on 20 August that Townshend had campaigned vigorously in the election and although he denied the accusation it is clear he was an active Fanning supporter.

Townshend's zeal extended beyond political action. From the time of his arrival on the Island he was energetic in administering customs legislation, and after the ease of the Allanby period his enforcement soon created difficulty in the colony. He crossed Patterson in 1786 by seizing the property of merchants who had imported goods from the United States with Patterson's consent. Townshend's action was precipitated by a complaint made that year by another merchant, John Cambridge*, but Townshend delayed acting until he had checked at Halifax, N.S., to obtain "more qualified and discriminating ideas of the Powers of a Governor & Council." This delay, and allegations from Cambridge that Townshend had been allowing smuggling from the Îles de la Madeleine, led to an investigation by the commissioners of customs. When the case was settled early in 1788 Townshend was cleared and the report concluded that Patterson and Attorney General Phillips Callbeck* had "very improperly interfered in the Business of the Customs."

In June 1788 Townshend tried to seize goods that had been brought ashore at Patterson's farm. He landed there with a party of soldiers but was repelled by 25 men, most of whom were Patterson's servants. He was later successful: the goods and the schooner from which they had been landed were seized and sold by order of the Vice-Admiralty Court sitting in Charlottetown. Over the next two years he made several seizures, including vessels belonging to John Cambridge and his fellow merchants William Bowley and John Hill*. Whether these were legitimate seizures is difficult to determine because Townshend was over strict in his application of the customs laws, making no allowance for the conditions existing in the colony. By challenging the leading merchants he involved himself in protracted litigation.

The result was that in 1791 Townshend was named by Cambridge, Bowley, Hill, and several leading absentee proprietors as one of those forming an illegal combination to rule the Island. Besides reviving charges of exorbitant and illegal fees which had been made against Townshend to the commissioners of customs, Cambridge and the others accused him of such offences as connivance in the smuggling of tobacco, disposing of blank registration forms, and oppressive seizures. Several of the accusations grew

Trahan

out of an incident in which Townshend had charged Hill with illegal acts in relation to the registration of a new vessel; in fact, these were merely technical irregularities which could have been overlooked. The general tenor of the 1791 action was that Townshend, in league with Chief Justice Stewart, Lieutenant Governor Fanning, and Attorney General Joseph APLIN, had planned to oppress Hill and Cambridge. Townshend, the deponents alleged, had told Hill that the government officials were preparing to "carry things with an high hand against those who had opposed them." When the accusations were heard in London that year Townshend presented a detailed defence but it does not appear to have impressed the investigating committee. However, the following year the committee concluded that the claims could not be considered proved because they were "as fully and positively denied, as they are charged."

Whether it was Townshend or the merchants who had been chastened by their experience the number of smuggling cases heard before the Island courts dropped considerably. The only one to attract attention after 1792 was that brought against James DOUGLAS, agent to James William Montgomery, in 1797. Douglas complained that it had been initiated in retaliation for his having brought a suit against Chief Justice Stewart. Three years were to pass before Douglas was acquitted.

Although Townshend was reported to be seeking a post in a more eligible spot at this time, whatever efforts he made were not successful. His health declined after 1800 but in spite of continuing illness it was Townshend rather than senior councillor Thomas DESBRISAY who was named "Temporary Commander in Chief" of the Island in October 1812 following the removal of Lieutenant Governor Joseph Frederick Wallet DesBarres*. As administrator, Townshend seems to have done little more than follow the instructions of the Colonial Office during his tenure of less than a year. His most significant act was the removal of James Bardin Palmer* from the posts he had held under DesBarres, but the move had been requested by officials in London. This did not prevent Townshend from boasting that rather than a "turbulent divided and . . . Anarchial Colony" the new lieutenant governor, Charles Douglass Smith*, would find a "peaceable regular and . . . a well satisfied People."

The remainder of Townshend's life appears to have been uneventful. His health continued to decline and he died on a visit to England in 1816. Although linked to the Island establishment by marriage and by virtue of his post, he seems to have been able to avoid becoming embroiled in the politics of the colony. The increase in trade and shipbuilding in the latter years of his service was easily handled without incident by the office he supervised. Despite a stormy beginning he

had become by the end of his career what Patterson had first suggested in 1784 – an unexceptionable man.

H. T. HOLMAN

PAC, MG 9, C3; MG 23, E5; E7, 2; RG 7, G8D, 44: 88, 249. PAPEI, Acc. 2810, Ira Brown papers, no.138; Acc. 2849, Palmer family papers, no.8; RG 1, Commission book, 1812; RG 5, Minutes, 1784–1817; RG 6, Supreme Court, case papers, 1784–1800; minutes, 1784–1800; RG 9, Customs, shipping reg., 1 (1787–1824). PRO, CO 226/8: 63, 163; 226/9: 172; 226/11: 193; 226/12: 3, 22, 24, 26, 240, 247; 226/13: 282; 226/14: 73, 90, 400; 226/16: 186; 226/18: 118, 131, 166, 214; 226/19: 221; 226/22: 229; 226/23: 57; 226/24: 74; 226/26: 13, 15; 226/27: 31; 226/28: 24; 226/30: 7; 226/31: 5, 12; 226/32: 251, 304, 308, 311; 226/43: 257. SRO, GD 293/2/19–20. Supreme Court of P.E.I. (Charlottetown), Estates Division, liber 1: f.116 (will of William Townshend). [John MacDonald?], *Remarks on the conduct of the governor and Council of the Island of St. John's, in passing an act of assembly in April of 1786 to confirm the sales of the lands in 1781 . . .* (n.p., [1789]), 64–65. [J.] B. Burke, *A genealogical and heraldic history of the colonial gentry* (2v., London, 1891–95; repr. 2v. in 1, Baltimore, Md., 1970), 2: 684.

TRAHAN, GRÉGOIRE, known as **Gregory Strahan**; soldier; b. *c.* 1752, son of Charles Trahan of Grand Pré, N.S., and Marie-Anne Landry; d. 21 Sept. 1811 in Philadelphia, Pa.

When still quite young Grégoire Trahan was caught up in the deportation of the Acadians [*see* Charles Lawrence*]. With his parents and elder sister Madeleine he was exiled to Concord, Mass., probably at the time of the main expulsion in the summer and autumn of 1755. About 12 years later the family, which had grown with the birth of five children in exile, immigrated to the province of Quebec. The Trahans settled at Yamachiche, where other Acadian exiles had begun moving in some three years before; they joined in opening up two concessions of unequal length, called La Grande-Acadie and La Petite-Acadie, making their own home on the former.

When the American invasion began in 1775 [*see* Benedict ARNOLD; Richard Montgomery*], Grégoire Trahan enlisted for six months as a soldier in the rebel army. Having been posted to a company in James Livingston*'s regiment, in December he took part in the siege of Quebec, during which commissary John M. Taylor entrusted him with the keys to the army storehouse because he spoke "a little English." When his period of enlistment ended in the spring of 1776 Trahan was discharged at Sorel. Colonel Livingston sent him to Albany, N.Y., and from there to Philadelphia with General Philip John Schuyler's dispatches. Because of his service in the American army Trahan could not return to Quebec without some risk; consequently he lived in Philadelphia, where on

18 Sept. 1780 he married Marguerite Bourque. In 1783 he came back to Quebec, but he was treated as a rebel and was dispossessed of the 80 acres of land he owned on the concession of La Grande-Acadie. He had to return with his family to Philadelphia, and there he followed the occupations of innkeeper and carter.

In 1810 Trahan petitioned the American government for the reward promised to those Canadians who had enlisted in the American army in 1775. His claims were not satisfied until 1826, 15 years after his death, following a new petition by his son Joseph. His widow and his children Joseph, Paul, Charles, and Mary are believed to have received a thousand acres near Lake Erie. Today most of Grégoire Trahan's descendants in the United States bear the name Strahan.

MAURICE FLEURENT

ANQ-MBF, CE1-52, 27 févr. 1764; 2 sept., 7, 25 oct. 1767. Arsenault, *Hist. et généal. des Acadiens* (1978), 1: 198; 3: 1310–13. Raphaël Bellemare, *Les bases de l'histoire d'Yamachiche, 1703–1903* . . . (Montréal, [1903]). Napoléon Caron, *Histoire de la paroisse d'Yamachiche (précis historique)* (Trois-Rivières, Qué., 1892).

TRESTLER (Tröstler), JEAN-JOSEPH, soldier, businessman, landowner, and politician; b. *c.* 1757 in Mannheim (Federal Republic of Germany), son of Henry Tröstler and Magdeleine Feitten; d. 7 Dec. 1813 in Vaudreuil, Lower Canada.

Jean-Joseph Trestler came to Quebec in 1776 with the Hesse-Hanau Chasseurs, a German mercenary unit. He may also have performed the duties of a military surgeon, as his continuing interest in medicine suggests. For example, in 1804, in exchange for the "secret of curing cankers" he made over a piece of land with buildings to Antoine Hamel, a surgeon in the village of Rigaud. Over the years he built up an impressive medical library of some 130 volumes, most of them in German. One of his sons, Jean-Baptiste, became a surgeon and a professor at the Montreal School of Medicine and Surgery.

Having been discharged from the army by 1783 at the latest, Trestler became a pedlar in Montreal. Here in November 1785 he married Marguerite Noël, a girl of 16. On 8 Aug. 1786 he purchased a house 30 feet square in the seigneury of Vaudreuil, with a hen-house, pigsty, and bake-oven; he paid 1,300 *livres*, including a down payment of 400 *livres* cash, and opened a general store in it. In 1791 he went into the production of potash and built a factory with ash, furnace, and potash sheds. His wife died in October 1793, leaving him with four little girls, and in February 1794 he married 23-year-old Marie-Anne-Joseph Curtius, whose father, a merchant of German origins, had moved from the Richelieu valley and

become a schoolteacher in Vaudreuil. At that time Trestler had a personal estate valued at 42,210 *livres* and also owned two houses, several buildings, 120 acres of land, and a building lot; his debts amounted to 19,935 *livres*.

Trestler's strategic location on the banks of the Ottawa River enabled him to participate in the lucrative fur trade. Although at that time competition and high operating costs were causing the merchants in the fur trade to amalgamate, he did not enter into partnership with another merchant or fur company. From 1803 he shared the running of a general store at Les Cèdres with merchant Jacques-Hubert Lacroix. He apparently also engaged in alongshore trading with the four boats, two ferries, and lighter that he owned.

Trestler's profits from trade and industry enabled him to make loans and in particular to invest in real estate. He bought an impressive number of farms, buildings, and properties, not only at Vaudreuil but also in the surrounding areas of Les Cèdres and Rigaud, as well as in the towns of Montreal and Quebec. He even owned islands in the Ottawa River and in the seigneury of Villechauve, commonly called Beauharnois. In addition he acquired a veritable domain for himself. After buying a number of lots and buildings next to his property at Vaudreuil, he erected on a site now in Dorion a stone dwelling as large as a manor-house with a façade of 139 feet and a depth of 40 feet. The central portion was put up in 1798; the section on the west end, which housed the general store and the fur warehouse, was built in 1805 and the east-end one in 1806. He also had an ashery, barn, byres, stables, and sheds on his estate. The enterprise became one of the busiest places west of Montreal Island.

Having become a prosperous businessman, Trestler could not resist the attractions of a political career. He represented the riding of York in the fifth parliament of Lower Canada from 18 June 1808 until 2 Oct. 1809. In the course of the only session, held in the spring of 1809, he took an interest in the laws regulating commerce, particularly trade with the United States, at a time when the embargo which the American Congress had decreed in December 1807 was proving advantageous to the colony's merchants. He sat on a committee appointed to study the consequences of developing a new market in the port of Montreal, which threatened the continued existence of the old one.

This session gave rise to virulent confrontations between Canadian and British members of the assembly. Whereas the other member for York, John Mure*, and Ignace-Michel-Louis-Antoine d'Irumberry* de Salaberry, from the neighbouring riding of Huntingdon, sided with the English party, Trestler unconditionally and unwaveringly supported the

Trottier

Canadians led by Pierre-Stanislas Bédard*, particularly on the choice of Jean-Antoine PANET as speaker and the bills to expel judge Pierre-Amable DE BONNE and Ezekiel Hart*. Trestler attended the assembly for the last time on 26 April 1809. The merchant from Vaudreuil was not to participate in the new parliament convoked by Governor CRAIG the following year, perhaps because of the tense nature of the debates, or through fear of neglecting his business for a career that was certainly fascinating but scarcely remunerative.

Although Trestler encountered nothing but success in business, his family life was marked by unhappy and trying episodes. In the year following his first wife's death he lost two daughters who were still quite young, Marie-Marguerite and Marie-Josephte. In 1806 Michel-Joseph, who at nine was the eldest of the four sons born of his second marriage, was drowned near the family home. In 1809 and 1810 Trestler objected to the marriages of his daughters Catherine and Marie-Madeleine with his clerks Joseph Eleazar Hays and Patrice Adhémar, and he cut their inheritance to five shillings each. He was taken to court by Catherine, who sought the share of the joint estate that was to come to her upon her mother's death; in 1812 he had to pay her 4,000 *livres* to redeem the succession rights on the landed property. In September of the following year Trestler lost his third son, Henry-Daniel, who was eight. Three months later, following a brief "but very violent" illness, Trestler himself died at the age of 56; he was buried on 9 December in the crypt of the church of Saint-Michel at Vaudreuil. His second wife lived for another 38 years; his second son, Jean-Baptiste, was the only one of his children to carry on the family line. Iphigénie, Jean-Baptiste's youngest child, married Antoine-Aimé Dorion*.

Jean-Joseph Trestler, who was no Croesus when he arrived in Canada, nevertheless succeeded through trade and industry in rapidly building up a large fortune, even though he did not belong to the British plutocracy in the colony. When he died, his assets, aside from his numerous pieces of real estate, were worth about 90,000 *livres*. He owed an estimated 22,717 *livres* to 15 creditors, including James DUNLOP, but some 400 people, almost all from the region and more than three-quarters with debts of less than 300 *livres*, owed him a total of 108,390 *livres*. His clients and most of the parties with whom he had dealings were Canadian. On the political scene he made common cause with the first nationalist leaders of French Canada. Having become fully integrated into the French-speaking and Catholic community in Lower Canada, he had earned the respect of the habitants of Vaudreuil and the surrounding regions, who were present in large numbers at his funeral.

PIERRE ANGRIGNON

[Copies of a number of documents used to prepare this biography are held at the Maison Trestler in Dorion, Que. After Jean-Baptiste Trestler's death in 1871 this house was used by his son-in-law Antoine-Aimé Dorion as a summer residence and remained in family hands until 1927. The spacious building was designated an architectural monument of national importance by the Canadian government in 1969 and a historic monument by the Quebec government in 1976. In the latter year Judith and Louis Dubuc bought the house with the intention of restoring it and living there while at the same time assuring that it would play a cultural role. Open for guided tours, it now serves as a centre for multicultural and interdisciplinary gatherings. The Fondation Trestler looks after the house's preservation and program and possesses material relating to the Trestler family, including lists, photocopies of birth, marriage, and death certificates, and notarized contracts. P.A.]

AC, Terrebonne (Saint-Jérôme), Minutiers, Augustin Dumouchelle, 27 oct. 1812. ANQ-M, CE1-50, 26 mai 1787; 4 juill. 1788; 27 sept. 1789; 21 mai 1792; 25 oct. 1793; 26 févr., 5 mars 1794; 25 mars 1797; 28 juill. 1798; 7 avril 1805; 8 août 1806; 19 mars 1809; 1er oct. 1810; 28 févr. 1811; 9 sept., 9 déc. 1813; 15 avril 1851; CE1-51, 21 nov. 1785, 24 févr. 1794; CN1-74, 18 mars, 14 sept. 1809; CN1-117, 2 juill. 1804, 29 janv. 1810; CN1-313, 10 oct. 1810, 3 janv. 1814. Private arch., Fondation Trestler (Dorion), Louis Dubuc, "La maison Trestler, 1798" (s.l., [1979]); "Liste de tous ceux qui ont été congédiés du Corps des Chasseurs de Hesse-Hanau depuis l'année 1777 jusqu'à présent" (s.l., s.d.). Bas-Canada, chambre d'Assemblée, *Journaux*, 10 avril–15 mai 1809. "Michel-Eustache-Gaspard-Alain Chartier de Lotbinière (1748–1822)," J.-J. Lefebvre, édit., ANQ *Rapport*, 1951–53: 385, 389. *Montreal Gazette*, 14 Dec. 1813, 21 July 1814. *Quebec Gazette*, 6 March 1800; 20 April 1809; 28 March, 12 Sept. 1811; 3 June 1813; 14, 21 Nov. 1816. Desjardins, *Guide parl.*, 144. Marc Fréchette et al., "Rapport et relevé de la maison Trestler" (3v., travail présenté à l'école d'architecture, univ. de Montréal, 1978) (copy at MAC-CD). [P.-G. Roy], *Vieux manoirs, vieilles maisons* (3 sér., Québec, 1927), 1: 155. F. J. Audet, "Les députés de la vallée de l'Ottawa," CHA *Report*, 1935: 12. Gilles Paquet et J.-P. Wallot, "Les inventaires après décès à Montréal au tournant du xixe siècle: préliminaires à une analyse," *RHAF*, 30 (1976–77): 213, 217. R.-L. Séguin, "L'apport germanique dans le peuplement de Vaudreuil et Soulanges," *BRH*, 63 (1957): 43, 56–58; "'L'apprentissage' de la chirurgie en Nouvelle-France," *RHAF*, 20 (1966–67): 598–99; "Des familles de Vaudreuil-Soulanges sont d'ascendance germanique," *La Patrie* (Montréal), 31 mai 1959: 44.

TROTTIER DESRIVIÈRES BEAUBIEN, EUSTACHE-IGNACE, businessman, seigneur, militia officer, and office holder; b. 10 Feb. 1761 in Montreal (Que.), son of Eustache Trottier Desrivières Beaubien, a merchant, and Marguerite Malhiot; d. 3 Oct. 1816 in Varennes, Lower Canada.

Eustache-Ignace Trottier Desrivières Beaubien came from a family that had been in business and the fur trade since the 17th century. During the 1780s his father, who was a merchant in Montreal and then at the Lac-des-Deux-Montagnes mission (Oka), engaged in fur trading, particularly on lakes Abitibi and Timis-kaming, but stiff competition from British merchants had forced him to abandon this activity and to concentrate almost exclusively on his retail business at Lac-des-Deux-Montagnes. It seems then that Desrivières Beaubien did his apprenticeship in the business world alongside his father.

On 7 Oct. 1783, at Varennes, Desrivières Beaubien married Marie-Appolline Bailly de Messein, who came from one of the leading merchant families of the locality. As dowry she brought her share in the estate of her father, François-Augustin Bailly de Messein; for his part Desrivières Beaubien benefited from a 9,000-*livre* advance on his inheritance. The young couple took up residence in Varennes, where Desrivières Beaubien opened a general store. His wife died on 29 Oct. 1793, a year after their sixth child was born. In 1794, in addition to his store, which was inventoried at 14,415 *livres* 18 *sous*, Desrivières Beaubien owned at Varennes two houses, two lots, and a meadow, as well as the animals that he leased to habitants living on the seigneury. Since the debts owed to him exceeded his liabilities, his net worth was 16,706 *livres*.

On 7 Aug. 1796, having been a widower for several years, Desrivières Beaubien married Charlotte Boucher de La Bruère, daughter of René Boucher de La Bruère, at Boucherville. The bride, who had a large dowry, added to his fortune by bringing into the community of property two farms and a lot in the seigneury of Boucherville, a third of the seigneury of Montarville, and 8,000 *livres*.

During the next two decades Desrivières Beaubien invested in real estate. He bought farms in the seigneuries of Varennes, Belœil, Boucherville, and Montarville, as well as in the barony of Longueuil. In 1816 he owned 26 farms or sections of land in these various places, which he leased with a view to selling the crops in his store at Varennes, or in Montreal. In addition he operated a potashery and a bakery and owned half of a carding-mill.

Like many of his compatriots Desrivières Beaubien suffered under Governor CRAIG's administration. In May 1810, with no explanation, the governor withdrew his commissions as justice of the peace for the District of Montreal, an office he had filled since 1791, and as major in the Boucherville militia, a post he had held for two years. Desrivières Beaubien protested, claiming that the authorities had listened to false information and slanderous complaints. In July 1812 he sent a petition to the new governor, Sir George PREVOST, asking him to investigate the grounds for his dismissal. A military court presided over by Louis Guy* was set up that month.

Desrivières Beaubien must have won his case, for in the autumn of 1813 he took part in an action at the head of a militia battalion at Châteauguay. He was also reinstated as a justice of the peace.

It seems that his war service was too hard on his health. After a long and painful illness, Desrivières Beaubien died on 3 Oct. 1816. As lieutenant-colonel in the Verchères militia he was buried with full military honours. In addition to his farms and lots he left an estate valued at 22,568 *livres* to his surviving children, Henri* and Édouard Desrivières-Beaubien, who were both minors.

RAYMOND DUMAIS

ANQ-M, CE1-10, 7 oct. 1783, 29 oct. 1793, 11 mai 1810; CE1-22, 7 août 1796, 5 oct. 1816; CE1-51, 11 févr. 1761; CN1-117, 21 oct. 1806; CN1-121, 14 juill. 1794, 15 août 1795; CN1-150, 6 oct. 1783; CN1-167, 7 août 1796; 15 sept., 30 oct., 4 nov. 1816; CN1-269, 31 Jan. 1798; CN1-313, 7 mai 1795, 14 févr. 1800, 9–12 févr. 1801, 24 sept. 1807, 26 sept. 1809; P-10, octobre 1806, cause no.267. Arch. du séminaire de Trois-Rivières (Trois-Rivières, Qué.), Coll. Montarville Boucher de La Bruère. ASQ, Fonds Viger-Verreau, Carton 18, no.67. AUM, P 58, P2/191, 195, 198; U, Desrivières-Beaubien à Jordan, 16 août 1802. *Montreal Gazette*, 14 Oct. 1816. *Quebec Gazette*, 11 Aug. 1791; 3, 17 May 1810. Tanguay, *Dictionnaire*, 7: 359. "La loyauté des Canadiens en 1775," *BRH*, 31 (1925): 370–75. "Le 'Royal Canadien' ou 'Royal Canadian Volunteers,'" *BRH*, 7 (1901): 372.

TURNER, WILLIAM, Moravian missionary; b. 3 July 1743 in Halifax, England; d. 1804 in Fulneck (near Pudsey), England.

William Turner, a wool carder by trade, came of an Anglican family, but in June 1762 he joined the Moravian Brethren; the following year he was accepted as a member of their congregation at Fulneck. There in the late 1760s he undoubtedly met Jens Haven* and Christian Larsen Drachart* who were attempting to organize a Moravian mission to the Labrador Inuit. In 1771 Turner became one of three English bachelors in a party of 14 persons, most of whom were German or Danish, sent to establish such a mission. A junior member of the group, he rose slowly in status, having to learn both German and Inupik. He was apparently competent in the latter by late 1775, and three years later he was allowed to preach his first sermon in that language.

The objective of the mission, which centred on Nain on the Labrador coast, was to create settled coastal communities of Christian Inuit. One impediment to this goal was the reliance of the natives on the caribou for meat, skins, and sinew, which necessitated their making lengthy expeditions inland in summer and sometimes in winter. Mission authorities were concerned that the hunt, which took the Inuit beyond the Moravians' direct influence, should be as brief as possible and that all the meat and skins should be brought out to the coast. Mission superiors also considered the feasibility of sending a missionary to accompany the hunters on a regular basis, not only to urge speed but also to ensure that converts did not relapse into their old ways. In 1780 Turner was sent on two journeys inland from Nain, his task being to provide the information upon which mission policy could be based.

Alone with local Inuit, Turner travelled for most of February, and again from 8 August to 25 September, suffering in mind and body on both occasions and deriving no enjoyment from his adventures. He was the only Moravian in Labrador ever to accompany the Inuit on a hunt, and possibly the first white man to do so in Canada. His journals provide a unique and valuably detailed account of the caribou hunt and of the Inuit way of life on the Labrador plateau before the introduction of firearms. More immediately, his experiences evidently persuaded the mission authorities that it was not possible to control the caribou hunt, since the Inuit travelled long distances over difficult terrain, broke up into small, constantly shifting bands, and endured considerable hardships.

In 1782 Turner left Nain to join the staff of a new station called Hoffenthal in German or Hopedale in English, and built that year under Haven's direction. Now recognized as a competent and experienced missionary, he was ordained deacon on 12 May 1784 and given permission to marry. As was frequently the case, Turner's marriage, on 25 August to Sybilla Maria Willin, probably from the Moravian settlement at Barby, Saxony (German Democratic Republic), occurred shortly after his ordination. Wives were often provided to missionaries by the European settlements, and it is probable that the couple had never met before Maria's arrival at Hopedale four days earlier.

In 1789 Turner made a short trip to England, returning to Hopedale in July 1790 as one of its senior missionaries. The early 1790s were a difficult time for the mission in general and for Hopedale in particular, since the Inuit, whether or not they had been baptized, were being strongly attracted south by traders at Baie des Esquimaux (Hamilton Inlet), Sandwich Bay, and other places; this attraction compromised the missionaries' goals of converting and settling the natives, a task rendered difficult in any case by their religious leaders or *angakut* [see Tuglavina*]. Between 1790 and 1792 Moravian authorities seriously considered abandoning Hopedale. Not until later in the 1790s were significant gains of converts made.

Possibly the tensions of a difficult period, but certainly ethnic prejudice, led to bad relations between Turner and the German first helper or leader of the Labrador missions, Brother Christian Ludwig Rose. In January 1791 Rose and the Turners had a violent disagreement from which Mrs Turner, who was pregnant with their second child (they already had a son), was obliged to retreat to bed. Their daughter was born in April but survived only 11 days, and Mrs Turner never fully recovered from the difficult birth, which Turner blamed on their tense relations with Rose. In September Turner wrote the Brethren in England that Rose "is such an enimy to the English Brethren as I have never met with in the Cong^n. he can scarce bear to hear anyone speak of England." That month Turner was transferred to the Okak station to take charge of trade; he remained there until his retirement to England in 1793, possibly as a result of continuing friction with his German superiors.

J. K. HILLER

Manuscripts relating to the establishment of the Moravian missions in Labrador are held at the Moravian Arch. in Bethlehem, Pa., and in the Moravian Church in Great Britain and Ireland Arch., London. Both the PAC (MG 17, D1) and Memorial Univ. of Nfld. (St John's) possess microfilm copies of documentary material. Personal information concerning William Turner was found in the Okak church book, now in the Moravian Mission Arch. in Nain, Nfld. Turner is the author of a journal housed in the Moravian archives in London; edited by J. Garth Taylor, it was published as "William Turner's journeys to the caribou country with the Labrador Eskimos in 1780," in *Ethnohistory* (Tucson, Ariz.), 16 (1969): 141–64.

J. K. Hiller, "The foundation and the early years of the Moravian mission in Labrador, 1752–1805" (MA thesis, Memorial Univ. of Nfld., [1968]).

TUTE, JEMIMA. *See* SAWTELLE

U

UPHAM, JOSHUA, judge and politician; b. 3 Nov. 1741 in Brookfield, Mass., second son of Dr Jabez Upham and Katharine Nichols; d. 1 Nov. 1808 in London, England.

Joshua Upham was both the most typical and the least typical of the band of loyalist brethren who formed the first governing class of New Brunswick. In terms of birth, education, wealth, profession, and marriage, he was a classic example of the Massachusetts tory élite which supported the British cause during the American revolution. At the same time he displayed a genuine sympathy for the grievances of the American colonists, and in his subsequent career he manifested a sensitivity to popular needs and a willingness to question government policy which stamp him as unusual among his loyalist colleagues.

After graduating from Harvard College in 1763, Upham began his legal career in Brookfield. On 27 Oct. 1768 he married Elizabeth Murray, daughter of the prosperous John Murray of Rutland, and he later took her brother Daniel into partnership with him. Upham's position in the debate preceding the American revolution was ambivalent. Trying desperately to placate both sides in order to retain his pleasant mode of life, on the one hand he supported the non-importation and non-consumption measures urged by the aggrieved patriots, while on the other he signed public addresses of homage to Governor Thomas Hutchinson and Lieutenant-General Thomas Gage*. Called before the Brookfield committee of public correspondence in 1775 to explain his political principles, he stated his willingness to submit to the resolution of the majority of his compatriots even though personally he opposed American independence. Yet he did not become a declared loyalist until 1777, when a Massachusetts law required all lawyers to take the oath of allegiance to the new state. Unwilling to comply, Upham sold his property and made his way to New York City to join the British military effort.

Once committed, Upham became an exemplary loyalist and soldier, serving as an officer on several raids in New England. In January 1779 he was appointed by the commander-in-chief, Sir Henry Clinton, inspector of refugee claims on Long Island, and the following year he was authorized to raise a regiment of Associated Loyalists there and with them was placed in command of Fort Franklin at Lloyd Neck. He ended the war as a major in the King's American Dragoons and an aide-de-camp to Sir Guy CARLETON. Since the war had sapped his financial resources, in late 1783 he decided to join his patron Carleton in London in hopes of getting a government post in Nova Scotia. Yet he made clear to his American friends that he left his homeland out of necessity, not malice.

Upham was a vigorous supporter of the movement to partition Nova Scotia and establish a separate loyalist province north of the Bay of Fundy. When the province of New Brunswick was in fact established in 1784, he received an appointment as a judge of the Supreme Court, with a salary of £300 per annum, and a seat on the Council. He arrived in his new home that November. Upham's initial years in New Brunswick were marred by personal hardship. His wife had died in 1782, leaving him with five children, and he himself was afflicted with rheumatism which gave him constant pain. None the less, he performed his duties on the Supreme Court and Council faithfully, and he developed his 1,000-acre farm near French Village, not far from Fredericton. In 1792 he remarried, his wife being Mary Chandler, sister-in-law of Amos BOTSFORD, speaker of the House of Assembly.

Upham was involved in three notable issues during his New Brunswick years. The first was the dispute between the assembly and the Council over whether assembly members should be paid for attendance. Despite the disapproval of the lieutenant governor, Thomas CARLETON, Upham in company with Daniel Bliss strenuously opposed the Council's stand against payment and defended the constitutional right of the assembly to control appropriations. In 1800 he became involved in another controversial question when the legality of slavery in New Brunswick was tested in the Supreme Court. Upham voted to uphold it, a natural action since he was himself a slave-owner, but the court was divided on the matter and no decision was rendered [see Caleb JONES]. Perhaps Upham's most distinguished service to the province occurred in 1807, when he was deputized by the Council and the assembly to go to England to protest the fact that public officials in New Brunswick were not being treated as well as their counterparts in Upper and Lower Canada. Specifically, he asked the British government to put the salaries of the Supreme Court judges on a par with those of the other provinces, to make their appointments run during good behaviour, to give New Brunswick separate legislative and executive councils, and finally, and most interestingly, to appoint a governor general for the four colonies of Nova Scotia, New Brunswick, Prince Edward Island, and Cape Breton. Upham's petitions containing these requests graphically describe the rigours endured by public servants in backwoods New Brunswick, the province's resentment at its inferior treatment by the imperial government, and the loyalists' continuing sense of pride in their record of service to the empire.

Although Upham was successful in getting the judges' salaries raised, he did not live to enjoy the victory. He died in London as he was preparing to return home, survived by his wife and seven children. One of his daughters married John Murray Bliss*, who became solicitor general of New Brunswick and a judge of the Supreme Court; another married John Wesley Weldon, also a well-known lawyer and politician; his son Charles Wentworth became a prominent Unitarian clergyman, congressman, and historian in Massachusetts. In recognition of Upham's services the New Brunswick House of Assembly granted £200 to his widow and £100 to an unmarried daughter of his first marriage.

The few personal papers that remain reveal Upham to have been a man of unusual sublety, grace, and conviction. To date, he has been a footnote in New Brunswick's recorded history, but his personal qualities and record of service clearly mark him out for larger print.

ANN GORMAN CONDON

Mass. Hist. Soc., Henry Knox papers, Joshua Upham to Knox, 1 Dec. 1783; Timothy Pickering papers, Joshua Upham to Pickering, 18 Nov. 1783. PAC, MG 23, D1, ser.1, 4: 1318–21. PRO, CO 188/13; PRO 30/55 (copies at PAC). UNBL, MG H2, Joshua Upham to Edward Winslow, 27 Aug. 1783. *American arch.* (Clarke and Force), 4th ser., 2: 852. N.B., Legislative Council, *Journal*, [1786–1830], 1: 204–6, 3 Feb. 1797. *Royal commission on American loyalists* (Coke and Egerton). Jones, *Loyalists of Mass.* Shipton, *Sibley's Harvard graduates*, 15: 495–96, 499–500. F. K. Upham, *The descendants of John Upham, of Massachusetts, who came from England in 1635, and lived in Weymouth and Malden; embracing over five hundred heads of families, extending into the tenth generation* (Albany, N.Y., 1892). Condon, "Envy of American states." J. W. Lawrence, *The judges of New Brunswick and their times*, ed. A. A. Stockton [and W. O. Raymond] ([Saint John, N.B., 1907]).

USTAIECHTA. *See* STAYEGHTHA

V

VIETS, ROGER, Church of England clergyman and poet; b. 9 March 1738 in Simsbury, Conn., second of four children of John Viets and Lois Phelps; m. first 19 Nov. 1772 Hester Botsford, and they had eight children; m. secondly 18 July 1802 Mary Pickett of Kingston, N.B., widow of Benjamin Isaacs; d. 15 Aug. 1811 in Digby, N.S.

Roger Viets went to school at Salmon Brook (near Granby), Conn., and subsequently attended Yale College. Although born into a Presbyterian family, he prepared himself at Yale for Church of England orders, and upon graduation in 1758 he became lay reader at St Andrew's Church, Simsbury. On 17 April 1763 he was ordained priest in London, England, and afterwards was appointed missionary at Simsbury, a post he retained until 1785.

During the American revolution Viets sympathized with the loyalists, and in late 1776 he was jailed at Hartford, Conn., on suspicion of having aided fugitive British officers. However, his leaving Simsbury after the war may have been motivated as much by economics as by politics: when the Society for the Propagation of the Gospel withdrew financial support from its American missions and instead offered salaries to clergymen willing to move to British North America, Viets applied for a post in Nova Scotia. On 1 Dec. 1785 he was assigned to Digby, and in May of the following year he set out to inspect his new mission. Arriving in July after an unusually harrowing 64-day voyage, he immediately began his pastoral duties and visited many of the outlying areas of his mission. In October he returned to Connecticut for his wife and children; on 12 June 1787, accompanied by his family, he was back in Digby.

Throughout his career at Digby, Viets travelled extensively to serve all the people in his mission, which stretched from Clementsport to Yarmouth and down Digby Neck. In Digby itself he and his parishioners built Trinity Church in 1791. He was a popular preacher and was always conscientious in fulfilling his religious responsibilities. Yet his dabbling in commerce – in 1789, for example, he visited Connecticut and returned with a boatload of goods – drew criticism; one of his detractors, the Reverend William Clark, noted that Viets "is a mere Tool to any Body & anything, by which he can get money; I never knew his equal for a mercenary Disposition." Viets's friends, however, argued that he merely provided items badly needed by the settlers. Whatever his motives, Viets never became wealthy through commerce.

In diocesan affairs Viets initially supported Samuel Andrew Peters for the bishopric of Nova Scotia; however, he became an enthusiastic supporter of Charles INGLIS when Inglis was appointed bishop in 1787. In 1788 he preached the sermon at Inglis's first ecclesiastical visitation. Some years later, in 1800, he became involved in an important test case involving the province's marriage laws. In that year he informed Inglis that Enoch Towner, the Baptist preacher at Sissiboo (Weymouth), had illegally performed a marriage. Inglis, eager to reassert the Church of England's exclusive right to solemnize marriages, promptly lodged a complaint with the registrar of the Court of Marriage and Divorce, and shortly afterwards a trial was held in Halifax, with Richard John Uniacke* prosecuting on behalf of the crown and Simon Bradstreet Robie* representing the defendant.

At length the court decided in Towner's favour and, what was even more important, it categorically denied that the Church of England had been made the established church by an act of the Nova Scotia legislature. This decision was a significant landmark in the weakening of Church of England authority in Nova Scotia.

Viets, described by Joseph Peters* as "a Strange Mortal: Whimsical, Quiddling, Stingy, Close-Shin'd, Strait-laced, Iron bound," had strong views on the importance of observing the sabbath: on one occasion, according to Peters, Viets became so impassioned after seeing pleasure-boats on a Sunday that John WISWALL, a fellow Anglican clergyman, had to intervene to hold him in check. He was a writer of some merit, publishing seven sermons and a topographical poem, *Annapolis-Royal*. The latter work, which describes the Annapolis area and the simple pleasures of life there, was the first poem to be published as a separate imprint in British North America.

Viets's death on 15 Aug. 1811 was caused by "Quick Consumption" (probably pneumonia). He had been preaching on the Granville side of Digby Gut and had returned by open boat in a chilling fog. At his request, he was buried in an unmarked grave outside the east window of Trinity Church. He was succeeded at Trinity by his son Roger Moore Viets.

THOMAS B. VINCENT

[Roger Viets is the author of *Annapolis-Royal* (Halifax, 1788; repr. with intro. by T. B. Vincent, Kingston, Ont., [1979]); *A serious address and farewell charge to the members of the Church of England in Simsbury and the adjacent parts* (Hartford, Conn., 1787); *A sermon, on the duty of attending the public worship of God; preached at Digby in Nova-Scotia, April 19th, 1789* (Hartford, 1789); *A sermon preached at Hartford, on Lord's-day, December 30th, 1764* (Hartford, 1765); *A sermon, preached at Sissaboo, now called Weymouth, in Nova-Scotia, on the 15th October, 1797* (Saint John, N.B., 1799); *A sermon, preached before the lodge of Free and Accepted Masons, at Granby . . . called St. Mark's Lodge; on the 9th July, 1800* (Hartford, 1800); *A sermon, preached in St. Andrew's Church, Simsbury, in New-England, on April 9th, 1784; being the anniversary of the crucifixion of Christ, commonly called Good-Friday* (Hartford, 1787); *A sermon, preached in St. Peter's Church, in Granby, formerly Simsbury, in Connecticut, New-England, on the 29th day of June 1800* (Hartford, 1800); and *A sermon preached to the ancient and worshipful society of Free and Accepted Masons, at their anniversary festival of the blessed evangelist St. John, 1792, in Trinity Church, Digby, Nova-Scotia* (Halifax, 1793). His church records have also been published under the title *Records of Rev. Roger Viets, rector of St. Andrews, Simsbury, Conn., and missionary from the Society for the Propagation of the Gospel in Foreign Parts, 1763–1800*, ed. A. C. Bates (Hartford, 1893). Manuscript sermons by Viets are found in PAC, MG 23, D1, ser.1, 14, and in the Univ. of King's College Library (Halifax).   T.B.V.]

F. H. Viets, *A genealogy of the Viets family with biographical sketches; Dr. John Viets of Simsbury, Connecticut, 1710, and his descendants* ([Hartford], 1902). I. W. Wilson, *A geography and history of the county of Digby, Nova Scotia* (Halifax, 1900; repr. Belleville, Ont., 1975). "Epitaphs, Church of England graveyard, Kingston, Kings County, N.B.," comp. W. O. Raymond, *Acadiensis* (Saint John), 8 (1908): 136.

VIGER, DENIS, carpenter, wood-carver, merchant, and politician; b. 6 June 1741 in Montreal (Que.), son of Jacques Viger, a shoemaker, and Marie-Louise Ridé (Riday-Beauceron); d. there 16 June 1805.

Almost nothing is known of Denis Viger's formative years, but presumably he served his apprenticeship in Montreal, where he first began doing pieces of carpentry. On 30 June 1772 he married Périne-Charles, daughter of the notary François-Pierre Cherrier*, in a big wedding at Saint-Denis on the Richelieu. The couple went to live in Montreal, in a stone house Viger owned on the northeast corner of Rue Saint-Paul and Rue Saint-Vincent. At the time of his marriage Viger already possessed two lots in Montreal, probably by inheritance from his father.

In 1774 Viger and Jean-Louis Foureur*, *dit* Champagne, received 904 *livres* for carving various wooden pieces in the church of Saint-Denis, where Viger's brother-in-law François CHERRIER was parish priest. These included the tabernacles, candlesticks ornamented with carved crosses and crucifixes for the side-chapels, the high altar, the decoration on the churchwardens' and acolytes' pews, a prie-dieu chair with turned columns for the celebrant, and two other chairs for the two chief cantors.

From then until 1783, Viger worked mainly for the Hôtel-Dieu in Montreal, where he did several pieces of work in wood and iron. His accounts, however, reveal a diversity of activities, such as repairing carrioles and making coffins and packing-cases. In addition, during the 1790s he engaged in the potash business; he would buy the product, have it inspected, and ship it to England.

While he was pursuing these occupations, Viger became interested in politics. In 1792 he openly supported the candidatures of his wife's brother-in-law Joseph Papineau*, Pierre FORETIER, and others in Montreal ridings. Four years later he decided to run with Papineau in Montreal East. The two men sent a letter to the voters, which was published in the *Montreal Gazette* on 27 June 1796; in it they observed: "The only return we can offer is an ardent desire of rendering service to our Country." Viger was elected on 29 July 1796 but took part in just two sessions, in which he supported the Canadian bloc wholeheartedly; however, he remained in office until 4 June

Villemonde

1800. He died five years later; his wife lived another two decades, dying in Montreal on 3 Feb. 1825.

Over the years Denis Viger had seen his social status improve. His marriage linked him with the great Papineau, Cherrier, and Lartigue families. He was able to give his son, Denis-Benjamin*, who became a lawyer and influential politician, an education with the Sulpicians, rather than keeping him with himself, as craftsmen usually did. Denis Viger was the uncle of Jacques Viger*, the first mayor of Montreal, and Louis-Michel Viger*, a lawyer, member of the assembly, and president of the Banque du Peuple.

LOUISE DÉSY

ANQ-M, P-24; CE1-51, 6 juin 1741, 25 avril 1776, 18 juin 1805; CE2-12, 30 juin 1772. AP, Saint-Denis (Saint-Denis sur le Richelieu), Livres de comptes, I (1755–1821), 1774: f.20v. Arch. des Religieuses hospitalières de Saint-Joseph (Montréal), Affaires temporelles de la communauté, Comptabilité, 1744–83. MAC-CD, Fonds Morisset, 2, V674/D395. F.-J. Audet, *Les députés de Montréal*, 45–46. Tanguay, *Dictionnaire*, 7: 465–66. É.-Z. Massicotte, "Les demeures de Denis-Benjamin Viger," *BRH*, 47 (1941): 269–70.

VILLEMONDE, LOUIS LIÉNARD DE BEAUJEU DE. *See* LIÉNARD

VONDENVELDEN, WILLIAM, army officer, translator, surveyor, office holder, printer, and politician; b. *c.* 1753 in Hesse-Kassel (Federal Republic of Germany), son of Isaac Vondenvelden and Marie Young; m. 24 Oct. 1801 Marie-Suzanne Voyer at Quebec, and they had one child; d. there 20 June 1809.

William Vondenvelden came to Quebec in June 1776 with the Hesse-Hanau Chasseurs, a unit in which he held the rank of lieutenant and adjutant. Some time between 1777 and 1782 he left the army and went to live at Quebec, where in the latter year he became a translator for the *Quebec Gazette*, owned by William Brown*. In September 1783 he obtained a commission as a surveyor and opened an office in his house on Rue Champlain; here he also gave courses in surveying, mathematics, and French. In January 1785 he launched a subscription to support publication of a work he had written entitled "The Canadian surveyor, or a treatise on surveying of lands," which had received the approval of the surveyor general of the province, Samuel Johannes HOLLAND. Despite advertising, particularly in the *Quebec Gazette*, Vondenvelden was not able to attract enough subscribers.

In 1786 Vondenvelden received a commission as justice of the peace for the District of Gaspé and moved to New Carlisle. The following year he became clerk of the Court of Common Pleas and clerk of the peace for the same district. At this time he was practising as a surveyor and in 1789 he drew up the survey of Île Bonaventure. In 1793 he was hired by the provincial government, which wanted to open up land south of the St Lawrence and so called upon experienced surveyors.

Vondenvelden settled permanently at Quebec in 1793 and in the same year, with the backing of the Quebec merchant John JONES, ordered the equipment to set up a printing shop, which he installed at 21 Rue de la Montagne. The death of Samuel Neilson*, owner of the *Quebec Gazette*, and the disappearance of William Moore*'s *Quebec Herald, Miscellany and Advertiser*, both of which occurred early in the year, spurred Vondenvelden and Jones to launch a new weekly. The first issue of the *Times/Cours du tems* appeared on 4 Aug. 1794. Despite Vondenvelden's good intentions the *Times* did not turn out to be a vehicle for intellectual discussion. He was extremely prudent and exercised firm control over the articles. He assured the British authorities of his support, while at the same time demonstrating his independence of political parties. Advertisements, official communications, and extracts from foreign newspapers filled the eight pages of every issue. On 13 May 1795 Jones terminated the partnership, selling his interests to Vondenvelden for £342. On 27 July Vondenvelden announced that his weekly would cease publication because of the limited number of subscribers.

Vondenvelden's printing activity had not, however, come to an end. On 27 Aug. 1795 Governor Lord Dorchester [Guy CARLETON] appointed him official printer for the statutes. The year before, he had printed the acts passed in the second session of the first parliament. After Vondenvelden's appointment, 600 copies of the statutes adopted during the sessions of each parliament were printed as a fascicle with a title page. Vondenvelden set up his printing shop on Rue des Pauvres (Côte du Palais) in 1796 and worked principally for the government, which paid him £472 for printing costs and paper that year. By the time his shop was sold to Pierre-Édouard Desbarats* and Roger Lelièvre on 23 May 1798, he had also published some 30 books and pamphlets.

Vondenvelden, who had been appointed assistant surveyor general in 1795, continued to practise as a surveyor. On 16 July 1798 he joined with Louis CHARLAND for the purpose of bringing out a topographical map of Lower Canada, accompanied by a book. Their map, largely inspired by one made by Samuel Gale* and Jean-Baptiste Duberger* in 1794–95, was published in London in 1803 under the title of *A new topographical map of the province of Lower Canada*. This was the first map of Lower Canada to be printed and it took into account the best principles of topography. Their book, which came out the same year at Quebec and was entitled *Extraits des titres des* *anciennes concessions de terre en fief et seineurie*, gave a brief description of the location of the seigneuries as well as the date on which they were granted. The success of the undertaking inspired Joseph Bouchette* to bring out in 1815 his edition of maps and his work *A topographical description of the province of Lower Canada*. . . .

On 20 June 1799 Vondenvelden was appointed surveyor of the highways, streets, and lanes in the town and parish of Quebec, and as such became responsible for road-works. In the autumn of 1800 he stood as a candidate in the riding of Gaspé and defeated John Mure*, a leader of the British mercantile bourgeoisie, by 113 votes. He supported the Canadian party in the House of Assembly. This created difficulties for him and he had to resign from his official post as surveyor on 21 May 1801. During the winter of 1802–3 he visited London to supervise the printing of his map of Lower Canada. At the time of the 1804 elections he thought it prudent to withdraw from politics.

From 1804 William Vondenvelden gave his attention to his practice, maintaining a surveying office across from the garden of the Château Haldimand in Upper Town. He died on 20 June 1809, following a carriage accident. The estate he left his widow and son William consisted mainly of accounts receivable and numerous landed properties that had for the most part been acquired according to the system of township leader and associates [*see* James CALDWELL]. He owned in all 56,400 acres located in the townships of Thetford, Compton, Kildare, Marston, Kingsey, Clinton, Wentworth, and Buckland.

JOHN E. HARE

William Vondenvelden published, in collaboration with the surveyor Louis Charland, *A new topographical map of the province of Lower Canada compiled from all the former as well as the latest surveys* . . . (London, 1803). This topographical map was accompanied by a book entitled *Extraits des titres des anciennes concessions de terre en fief et seineurie, faites avant et depuis la Conquête de la Nouvelle France par les armées britanniques dans la partie actuellement appellée le Bas-Canada* . . . , compiled by the same two authors and published at Quebec in 1803.

ANQ-Q, CE1-61, 24 oct. 1801, 22 juin 1809; CN1-92, 24 oct. 1801; CN1-99, 29, 30 août 1809; CN1-230, 16 juill. 1798; CN1-256, 13 May 1795; CN1-262, 23 mai 1798. *Quebec Gazette*, 10 July 1794; 25 June, 3 Sept., 24 Dec. 1795; 23 Aug. 1798; 20 June 1799; 1 Sept. 1808; 22 June 1809. Beaulieu et Hamelin, *La presse québécoise*, 1: 11–12. *Quebec almanac*, 1788–1810. Benjamin Sulte, "Trois noms," *BRH*, 1 (1895): 40–42.

W

WACHICOUESS. *See* MADJECKEWISS

WAHPASHA (Wabasha, Wapasha, Ouabachas, La Feuille, La Oja; the name means red leaf), a civil chief of the Mdewakanton band of the Santee Sioux; probably b. *c.* 1720; probably d. before 1805. He had at least one son, Wahpasha, and one daughter, Mar-pi-ya-ro-to-win (Grey Cloud), who became the wife of James AIRD.

In March 1740 Wahpasha and Ninsotin met Paul Marin* de La Malgue at the Rock River (Ill./Wis.) "to deliver up our bodies" in apology for the recent killing of two Ottawas, allies of France, by a party of Sioux. The attack, which had taken place at the Wisconsin portage (near Portage, Wis.), had been provoked by rumours that two Sioux envoys sent to Montreal about 1738 had died at the hands of the French. Leaders of the tribe, however, recognized the need for good relations with France; since the 1730s the Sioux had been warring with the Ojibwas, who were pressing down from the north, and European goods, particularly guns and powder, were vital to the struggle. After Marin had accepted the apology, Wahpasha and Sintez, another young Sioux, accompanied him to Montreal. There Wahpasha pleaded for the improvement of trade relations. The next July, however, he was accused of killing a son of Sieur Gatineau near Fort Saint-Joseph (Niles, Mich.). He was probably at the battle of Kathio, later in the 1740s, which saw traditionally armed Sioux defeated by the French guns of the Ojibwas and driven from their villages around Mille Lacs Lake (Minn.), and he is reputed to have led a migration which finally settled at Kioxsa (Winona, Minn.).

As long as the French controlled the Great Lakes and the western fur trade the Sioux had to maintain contact with them. With the fall of Canada in 1760 came the need for a new alliance. In 1763 James Gorrell*, the British commandant at La Baye (Green Bay, Wis.), met with 12 Sioux who, offering him command of their warriors, told him of their hatred of the Ojibwas, expressed a desire for British trade goods, and said they hoped to return the next year with their "king." This king was probably Wahpasha. In the following years Wahpasha must have cemented his ties with the new imperial power, for by the outbreak of the American revolution the British considered him an important ally.

Wahpasha

Ordered to recruit the Indians of the upper Mississippi for the British, trader Charles Gautier de Verville contacted Wahpasha late in the winter of 1777–78. In March the chief reached Gautier's camp at the mouth of the St Croix River (Wis.) with 20 men and together they went up the Mississippi to gather others. By June the party, consisting of more than 200 warriors of various nations and their families, had arrived at La Baye, and shortly afterwards it continued on to Montreal. Whether or not Wahpasha accompanied it east is unknown.

In the late winter or early spring of 1779 Wahpasha set out to join Henry Hamilton* at Vincennes (Ind.) but stopped at Prairie du Chien (Wis.) when he heard of Hamilton's surrender. He sent his son to Fort Michilimackinac (Mackinaw City, Mich.) to ask for instructions and suggested an attack on the Sauks and Foxes, who had treated with the Americans. Commandant Arent Schuyler DePeyster*, fearing the effect an intertribal war would have on the British effort in the west, sent Wahpasha gifts and probably counselled him against attacks on the offending tribes. Governor HALDIMAND called the chief's proposal a "very uncommon one from an Indian" and added that "the zeal he has manifested merits our attention."

Spain's entry into the conflict opened a new front, and early in 1780 the British urged Wahpasha to attack Spanish territory. That April at Prairie du Chien the chief received a commission as a "general" and was reported "well contented" with it. In May he and Emmanuel Hesse set out with some traders and a number of Indians as one part of a large expedition against Spanish St Louis (Mo.) [see Patrick SINCLAIR]. This campaign marked a high point in Sioux–Ojibwa relations, with Wahpasha and MADJECKEWISS, an Ojibwa chief, both promoting unity. By June Wahpasha had evidently returned to Michilimackinac since in that month he left the post with trader John Long* for Prairie du Chien, where furs had been held for safekeeping. Before the year was out he again visited Michilimackinac, receiving gifts for his people.

The alliance among the western Indians that the British had encouraged was tenuous at best. In February 1783 a trader was killed in the cross-fire between one of Wahpasha's war parties and some Ojibwas. Trade to the upper Mississippi was suspended and a council was held at Prairie du Chien on 24 May. The Foxes hastened to blame Wahpasha. He in turn assured the British that the "bad men who have killed the Whites" would be sent for justice and he asked that trade be re-established. By 1786, however, warfare was general among the western Indians. Wahpasha probably played a leading role, and in July 1787 he attended the conference arranged by the British and held at Fort Michilimackinac (by then on Mackinac Island, Mich.) [see Joseph-Louis AINSSE].

After making peace with one another, the Indians signed a treaty with the whites. They promised not to molest the traders and agreed to pay their debts, render up the killers of whites, and report those who would disturb their loyalty to the king. Wahpasha was one of the signatories.

Tradition has it that Wahpasha was expelled from his tribe because of internal jealousies and spent his last days on the Hoka River (Root River, Minn.). American explorer Zebulon Montgomery Pike conferred on the Mississippi in 1805 with his son Wahpasha, and the fact that the young chief had taken his father's name suggests that the old chief had died by that date.

It has been claimed that Wahpasha was the first hereditary civil chief of the Sioux. According to this story Wahpasha travelled to Quebec some time after the conquest to plead for resumption of the commerce that had been withdrawn when a Sioux killed a trader near Mendota (Minn.). The British, impressed by the chief's earnestness, gave him a medal which became a symbol of his authority and served to establish the position of civil chief, which became hereditary. The tale no doubt results from the compressive effect of oral tradition. There is no documentary evidence that Wahpasha visited Quebec during the British régime and, although the existence of hereditary positions in Sioux society before white contact is difficult to establish, they were certainly present by the 1760s. It is true, however, that Wahpasha owed much of his prestige, which he passed on to his son, to his ties with the French and British. His authority was based not only on his fighting skills but on his ability to command the presents so vital to his people's livelihood. In turn this authority enhanced his importance in the eyes of the whites. Sinclair called him a chief "of very singular & uncommon abilities" and declared the Sioux "a People undebauched addicted to War" and "accustomed to all the attention and obedience required by discipline." The ability to raise 200 such warriors with ease gave Wahpasha a strong bargaining position in his dealings with the whites. For a brief period the Sioux were able to exploit to their own advantage the conflicting imperial designs of the French, British, and Americans. Subsequent history has not been so kind.

GUS RICHARDSON

BL, Add. MSS 21758: ff.214–15, 220–21 (transcript at PAC). PAC, MG 19, A13, 2: 381 (transcript). Jonathan Carver, Travels through the interior parts of North-America, in the years 1766, 1767, and 1768 (London, 1778; repr. Toronto, 1974), 257. [A. S. DePeyster], Miscellanies, by an officer (Dumfries, Scot., 1813). John Long, Voyages and travels of an Indian interpreter and trader . . . (London, 1791; repr. New York, 1968, and Toronto, 1971), 185–90. Mich. Pioneer Coll., 9 (1886): 382, 384, 544, 548, 568; 11

(1887): 483–93; 23 (1893): 606–8. *New light on early hist. of greater northwest* (Coues), 1: 273. J.-B. Perrault, "Narrative of the travels and adventures of a merchant voyageur in the savage territories of northern America . . . ," ed. J. S. Fox, *Mich. Pioneer Coll.*, 37 (1909–10): 538. [Z. M. Pike], *The journals of Zebulon Montgomery Pike, with letters and related documents*, ed. Donald Jackson (2v., Norman, Okla., 1966), 1: 93, 126; 2: 25, 211; "Pike's explorations in Minnesota," Minn. Hist. Soc., *Coll.* (St Paul), 1 (1872): 370n. Wis., State Hist. Soc., *Coll.*, 1 (1855): 36–41; 6 (1872): 250–51; 11 (1888): 111–64; 12 (1892): 49; 17 (1906): 323, 362, 397.

DAB. "Haldimand collection, calendar: continuation," PAC *Report*, 1886: 685, 688, 697, 703, 706, 715. *Handbook of American Indians* (Hodge), vol.2. *The aborigines of Minnesota: a report . . .* , comp. N. H. Winchell (St Paul, 1911), 532, 540–43. T. C. Blegen, *Minnesota: a history of the state* (Minneapolis, Minn., 1963), 21–22. Harold Hickerson, *Mdewakanton band of Sioux Indians* (New York and London, 1974). Thomas Hughes, *Indian chiefs of southern Minnesota; containing sketches of the prominent chieftains of the Dakota and Winnebago tribes from 1825 to 1865* ([2nd ed.], Minneapolis, 1969), 21–24. W. R. Hurt, *Dakota Sioux Indians* (New York and London, 1974). Gontran Laviolette, *The Sioux Indians in Canada* (Regina, 1944), 23. R. W. Meyer, *History of the Santee Sioux: United States Indian policy on trial* (Lincoln, Nebr., 1967). E. D. Neill, *The history of Minnesota: from the earliest French explorations to the present time* (Philadelphia, 1858), 225–31. Doane Robinson, *A history of the Dakota or Sioux Indians . . .* (Aberdeen, S.Dak., 1904; repr. Minneapolis, 1967), 57, 64, 119–20. H. R. Schoolcraft, *Historical and statistical information, respecting the history, condition and prospects of the Indian tribes of the United States . . .* (6v., Philadelphia, 1851–57; repr. New York, 1969), 2: 169n., 182; 3: 613.

J. H. Case, "Historical notes of Grey Cloud Island and its vicinity," Minn. Hist. Soc., *Coll.* (St Paul), 15 (1915): 371. L. F. Jackson, "Sioux land treaties," N.Dak. Hist. Soc., *Coll.* (Bismarck), 3 (1910): 498–528. E. D. Neill, "Dakota land and Dakota life," Minn. Hist. Soc., *Coll.* (St Paul), 1 (1872): 262, 290–91. C. C. Willson, "The successive chiefs named Wabasha," Minn. Hist. Soc., *Coll.* (St Paul), 12 (1908): 503–12.

WALDRON, JOHN, surgeon, ship's captain, shipowner, merchant, and office holder; b. 12 Nov. 1744 in Burton Bradstock, England, son of Joseph and Martha Waldron; m. 14 Jan. 1775 Mary Young in Poole, England, and they had two sons and one daughter; d. in or after 1818, probably in Poole.

Though most of John Waldron's career in the Newfoundland trade is well documented, the early phase of his life is somewhat obscure. At the time of his marriage to the daughter of one of his employers he was a parishioner of Burton Bradstock. Thereafter he resided mainly in Poole, living there permanently from his retirement in 1802. During his active working life Waldron spent most of his summers at sea and in Newfoundland. He occasionally wintered on the island in Harbour Breton, where for about 38 years he was an agent and later a partner in a Poole–Newfoundland firm.

Waldron was certainly not the first of his name involved in the Newfoundland fishery, and possibly not the first of his own family: records show that several Waldrons captained ships to Newfoundland from ports in south Devon during the early 1700s. His associates, the Clarke and Young families, also had a lengthy term in the Newfoundland fishery: the Clarkes, for example, had initiated a merchant business around 1700. Before the preliminary Anglo-French treaty of 1762 the firm of Samuel Clarke and Robert Young had established its headquarters in Saint-Pierre; Waldron had come out from England about 1760 as a surgeon for this firm. When Saint-Pierre was ceded by the treaty to the French, the English traders and settlers were ordered to remove. Samuel Clarke and Waldron, who had become a ship's captain and agent in the employ of Clarke and Young, elected to relocate in nearby Fortune Bay and built their main premises on Harbour Breton. James Cook*, exploring and charting Fortune Bay a few years later, commented that Clarke and Young's establishment was the "best situated for carrying on a fishery . . . of any place on the No. side of Fortune Bay."

The year 1775 proved to be a significant one in Waldron's career. He married into the Young family and after the death of his father-in-law, Robert Young, that same year had his name attached to the firm. The three major partners were now Samuel Clarke, Waldron, and Samuel Young, possibly a relative of Robert. From Clarke's death in 1785 to 1794 the firm styled itself Waldron and Young, but after two of the Clarke heirs became involved it reverted to Clarke, Waldron and Young. This arrangement lasted only until 1797 when the partnership was dissolved; it was reorganized to become Clarke and Waldron. After Waldron retired the firm continued as Samuel and John Clarke until it went bankrupt in 1819.

As the resident agent of one of the more important trading companies in Fortune Bay, Waldron not only managed a shore and bank fishery but also developed a supply trade with the pioneering inhabitants in Fortune Bay and districts to the westward. Similarly, in their respective districts of Newfoundland most of the leading Poole merchant firms were able to establish a strong control over the fishery and supply trade with settlers. In 1785 Waldron and Young, together with Thomas Tremlett* of Dartmouth and some Jerseymen, were identified as the major entrepreneurs "who carry on the Fishery and supply the Planters in [Fortune Bay]." Most important, the merchants controlled and directed the patterns of migration and settlement. Thus it is not surprising that a large proportion of the population settling around Fortune Bay were formerly servants and passengers

Waldron

who had been transported from Poole and Dorset by Waldron's firm and were also, on becoming planters in the fishery, provisioned from his Harbour Breton stores.

Waldron's shipping suffered greatly during the American and French revolutionary wars; in the first conflict American privateers using Saint-Pierre as a base captured four of the firm's vessels in two months, and in 1796–97 several other ships were taken. Though these losses were severe, the trade survived, and in 1800 Clarke and Waldron were rated in Poole on exports and imports valued at £700 per year and the ownership of five vessels – *Navigation* (112 tons), *Fanny* (40 tons), *Calerus* (66 tons), *Commerce* (78 tons), and *Jane* (102 tons). The firm's export and import rates that year were small compared to those of other Poole–Newfoundland merchants (£3,000 for Benjamin LESTER and £1,800 each for the firms of Thomas Saunders, George Kemp, and William Spurrier) but still larger than those of some of the smaller merchants, such as George Neave and Joseph Garland. Similarly, Clarke and Waldron's ship tonnage of 398 tons was far less than Lester's 1,743, Kemp's 1,166, Spurrier's 1,035, and Saunders's 706, but still greater than that of smaller firms. These indices placed Waldron's firm within the middle rank of Poole companies.

From 1782 until his retirement Waldron held the offices of justice of the peace and naval officer for Fortune Bay, but in fact his jurisdiction covered the whole of the south coast of Newfoundland between Point May and Cape Ray. Part of his responsibility involved the collection of statistics on the fishery and population, which he handed to the governor's surrogate on his annual visit to Fortune Bay. His long experience in the Saint-Pierre–Fortune Bay area qualified him as one of the leading English experts on the French fishery in southern Newfoundland waters, and it was for this reason that he was summoned to give testimony before the committee of the House of Commons which in 1793 was appointed to inquire into the state of the trade to Newfoundland. According to his testimony, he sent an employee to Saint-Pierre with some regularity "privately to examine that Fishery, and to observe the general state of the island." In August 1792, for example, he found that the French had "40 sail of brigs and ships, of the average of about 150 tons each" and "between 110 and 120 of fishing shallops, each carrying three men; about 100 bankers, upon an average carrying eight men."

When Britain and France were engaged in peace negotiations in 1802 Waldron submitted a written brief through his member of parliament, George Garland, on the disposition of the French fishery in Saint-Pierre and Miquelon. He claimed that after 1783, when the French government gave financial incentives, "the fishery was prosecuted with the utmost avidity – The Number of Adventurers were greatly increased, the Coast of these Islands swarmed with their Bateaux and our fishery as might be expected from the vicinity of the Islands to Fortune Bay, was very materially injured." He also stated that the islands were used by the French as a "Mart for all their European Manufacturers for the United States" and that French fishers had "in the space of two months . . . destroyed more Trees [in the Fortune Bay region] than the English had done in Twenty years previous." His allusions to relations between the French and Micmacs in Newfoundland constitute one of the few documentary sources on this topic. Waldron claimed that the French from "Motives of Policy" supplied the Indians with ammunition, and that the Indians visited Saint-Pierre regularly to receive "absolution . . . Gratís" from the Catholic priests resident there. One consequence of this intercourse, he contended, was "that the Indians were attached to them and hostile to us." On the subject of the future development of Newfoundland, Waldron made a most unusual proposal, one that astounded even Garland: he suggested that Newfoundland be made into a "receptacle for Convicts," arguing that they could be employed in cultivation and that their settlement in the colony would be vastly cheaper than their transportation to Australia, and went on to make proposals for crops and livestock. Garland forwarded Waldron's letter to the government, commending Waldron's eminent qualifications to make observations on the French fishery but disassociating himself from the proposal for a convict colony. Much of Waldron's testimony before the commons committee in 1793 and many of his comments in his letter to Garland do appear to be valid, but there is little doubt that he was prone to exaggerate on some issues and lacked credibility on others. His optimistic remarks on the agricultural potential of Newfoundland, particularly in his own region, constitute but one example where his judgement might be questioned. A more flagrant example of his unreliability occurred in 1793 when he testified on the role of the custom-office in Fortune Bay.

The establishment of custom-houses in Newfoundland in 1764 had been bitterly opposed by the West Country and Poole merchants [*see* Richard ROUTH]. Merchants appearing before the committee of 1793, including William Newman and Peter OUGIER of Dartmouth and John Jeffrey of Poole, were still contending that the activities of customs officers and the high customs fees were a hindrance to the Newfoundland trade. When Waldron appeared, he declared that his own trade had suffered from the establishment of the custom-house because the process delayed his vessels. Questioned about Charles Cramer, customs officer and justice of the peace in

Walker

Fortune Bay, Waldron claimed that he had been dismissed as a justice for neglect of duty and bad conduct. Richard Routh, however, offered testimony about conflicts and retaliation between the two ending in Cramer's delaying a ship and Waldron's agent then clapping him in irons for three months.

John Waldron was clearly an energetic, physically robust, and somewhat ruthless and hard-driving individual, who was fairly well-educated, literate, and intelligent. Compared to his contemporaries he had an exceptionally long and arduous career in the Newfoundland trade: few other merchants lasted longer than a decade before they handed over the management to younger relatives and agents. Waldron's pioneering was also exceptional in that he played a major role in establishing the frontier of English exploitation and settlement southward and westward in Newfoundland. He spent so much of his working life in Newfoundland that he had little time to make himself a political figure in Poole, but he did participate in several committees of Poole merchants formed to represent their interests in Newfoundland affairs and in 1800 he supported George Garland's candidacy for parliament. As far as can be determined, neither of his two sons established himself in the Newfoundland trade, but a John Waldron who captained ships between Poole and Trinity and Greenspond in the 1820s for the firm of Sleat and Read may have been either a son or grandson.

W. GORDON HANDCOCK

Dorset Record Office, D203/A4–A5; D365; P227/CW3 (Churchwardens, rates and accounts, 1783–1802); OV1 (Overseers of the poor, rates and accounts, 1764–73); RE7 (Reg. of marriages, 1770–86). Hunt, Roope & Co. (London), Robert Newman & Co., company records (mfm. at PANL). Maritime Hist. Group Arch., Waldron, John, name file. Nfld. Hist. Soc. (St John's), Keith Matthews, "The West Country merchants in Newfoundland" (paper read to the Nfld. Hist. Soc., 1968). Nfld. Public Library Services, Provincial Reference Dept. (St John's), Phillip Saunders and Pierce Sweetman, "Letter book of Saunders and Sweetman," 1788–1804. PANL, GN 2/1, 2/2. PRO, ADM 7/373; BT 6/84, 6/87; CO 194/30, 194/43, 324/7; PROB 11/1609/481; RG 4/464. G.B., House of Commons, *Reports from committees of the House of Commons which have been printed by order of the house and are not inserted in the Journals*, [1715–1801] (16v., London, [1803–20]), 10: 391–503, "Reports from the committee on the state of the trade to Newfoundland, severally reported in March, April, & June, 1793." Derek Beamish et al., *Mansions and merchants of Poole and Dorset* (Poole, Eng., 1976). C. G. Head, *Eighteenth century Newfoundland: a geographer's perspective* (Toronto, 1976).

WALKER, THOMAS, advocate and politician; b. c. 1759; m. first 6 Nov. 1782 Jane Finlay in Montreal, Que.; m. secondly 30 Oct. 1797 in Berthier-en-Haut (Berthierville), Lower Canada, Anna Louisa Vial de Sainbel, widow of Charles Vial de Sainbel, and they had at least one child, Louisa Nash; d. January 1812 in William Henry (Sorel), Lower Canada.

The first record of Thomas Walker places him in Montreal in June 1778. After serving as clerk of the Court of Common Pleas for that district during the next year, he was admitted to the bar on 9 Oct. 1780. He subsequently moved to Quebec, where in June 1783 he was employed by the trustees of Thompson and Shaw, merchants. This partnership had gone into bankruptcy, its assets being assigned to the firm of Fraser and Young [see John YOUNG], and Walker acted in the several suits brought before the Court of Common Pleas for the recovery of sums and merchandise. His experience with that court lends some authority, and perhaps a hint of personal vexation, to his testimony on 2 Aug. 1787 before Chief Justice William Smith*'s inquiry into the administration of justice in Quebec [see Arthur DAVIDSON].

Walker's chief complaint was that the laws and practices followed by the Court of Common Pleas were too uncertain. He was not so concerned about its inclination to disregard the English legal system; on the contrary, he actually advocated a fuller recognition of French mercantile laws and more reliance on the French civil code in the determination of costs. The root of the trouble lay, rather, in the judges. They seldom explained the legal grounds of their decisions; their failure to ensure that the records of the court were kept in order added to the incertitude; their habitual procrastination made denials of justice "very frequent and very prejudicial"; their flagrant use of "grace and favour" raised doubts about their impartiality; and all this, together with what was either a "want of professional knowledge" or "gross neglect and inattention," produced "a State of disorder, confusion and uncertainty in points of rules of Law and practice, out of which it was highly necessary we should be extricated." With regard to the judges themselves, the irregular behaviour of John Fraser had clearly distorted the decision of the court in at least two cases; Adam Mabane*'s "great intimacy with and favor for others at the Bar, was very injurious to the rest, and particularly to me"; Pierre PANET was "allways ready to join in the measures and desires of Mr. Mabane on the Bench"; and as for René-Ovide Hertel* de Rouville, "I never considered an Englishman and Canadian had an equal chance before him."

Soon after giving this testimony, Walker returned to Montreal, where he established a private practice. His career as a lawyer thereafter does not seem to have been particularly distinguished, and only two records of legal business have been found: in February 1794 he offered his services to Johannes Ruyter, known as

Walk-in-the-Water

John Ruiter, who was Thomas DUNN's business agent for the seigneury of Saint-Armand, and in June of the same year he acted as attorney for the London administrator who was managing the estate of the fur trader Germain Maugenest* and his heir. Still, Walker evidently enjoyed the social life of Montreal, joining both the Protestant Congregation, an Anglican body, and the local branch of the Agriculture Society. Indeed, according to the British officer George Thomas Landmann*, while undoubtedly "a very clever lawyer," he was "more attached to the pleasures of good dinners and to merry companions than to the dry occupations of his profession" – which might account for his recurrent indebtedness.

Walker also seems to have rather petered out as a politician. Elected in July 1800 as member of the House of Assembly for Montreal County, a constituency that his brother James had represented from 1792 to 1796, he retained his seat till 1804. However, he was absent for most of the second and third sessions, as well as all of the fourth, and his name figures in the *Journals* for this period in connection with only three measures, all of which he supported: the expulsion of Charles-Jean-Baptiste Bouc*, who had been convicted of a crime; the continuation of the statute providing for returning officers; and the reduction of the quorum required for assembly meetings.

In contrast, Walker was positively diligent during his initial session, when he helped to frame legislation dealing with the civil courts, trials by jury in commercial actions, witnesses in civil suits, wills and testaments, copartnerships, deserting seamen, the salaries of translators in the assembly, customs duties between Lower and Upper Canada, the Montreal water supply, and the removal of the walls and fortifications surrounding that city. He also played a part in three developments that entailed fundamental questions of principle concerning the appropriation of taxation, parliamentary privilege, and educational policy.

It is not clear, however, whether Walker appreciated the significance of those developments – and extremely doubtful whether he would have supported some of the principles that might be read into them. Thus although the tax he initiated on billiard tables licensed for hire did enable the assembly to appropriate the proceeds, there is no indication that he was anxious to increase the influence of the legislature, let alone that he was anticipating the struggle for responsible government. Similarly, there is nothing to suggest that his attitude in the Bouc affair, which had got under way in March of 1800, was dictated by a wish to bolster the constitutional position of the assembly by invoking the privileges of the House of Commons at Westminster. Indeed, Walker might well have been primarily intent in both these instances on providing support for the government.

This suspicion as to his motives, and underlying affiliation, is strengthened if not confirmed by his behaviour over the Education Act of 1801. Essentially an anglicizing measure, as evidenced by its promotion of English-language teaching and creation of a preponderantly Protestant school board, this statute nevertheless enabled the creation of an educational system more in keeping with Roman Catholic, and Canadian, interests by permitting the existence of separate schools. In his endeavours to get this permission revoked, Walker seem to have shown his true colours. Whatever the reasons for his having endorsed the application of some French laws in 1787, by 1801 he had apparently become a partisan of that English party which was working hand in glove with government to promote the anglicization of Lower Canada.

G. P. BROWNE

PAC, MG 11, [CO 42] Q, 29: 542–79; MG 23, GIII, 3, vol.1: 61–65; MG 24, B1, 190: 5033; MG 30, D1, 30: 560–63, 566; RG 4, A1: 24878–81; B17, 18, 9 May 1800; 23, 10 March, 9 May 1804; 25, 5 April 1805. Bas-Canada, chambre d'Assemblée, *Journaux*, 1801–4. *Docs. relating to constitutional hist., 1791–1818* (Doughty and McArthur; 1914). Landmann, *Adventures and recollections*, 2: 62–64. *Quebec Gazette*, 16 July 1778; 5 June, 9 Oct. 1783; 21 Oct. 1784; 16 July 1789; 10 July 1794; 24 July 1800; 9 Jan. 1812. F.-J. Audet, *Les députés de Montréal*, 356. L.-P. Audet, "Attempts to develop a school system for Lower Canada, 1760–1840," *Canadian education; a history*, ed. J. D. Wilson *et al.* (Scarborough, Ont., 1970), 145–66; *Le système scolaire*, vol.3. T.-P. Bédard, *Histoire de cinquante ans (1791–1841), annales parlementaires et politiques du Bas-Canada, depuis la Constitution jusqu'à l'Union* (Québec, 1869). Christie, *Hist. of L.C.* Duncan McArthur, "Constitutional history, 1763–1840," *Canada and its prov.* (Shortt and Doughty), 4: 439–503. Manning, *Revolt of French Canada*. Robert Rumilly, *Histoire de Montréal* (5v., Montréal, 1970–74), 2. F.-J. Audet et Édouard Fabre Surveyer, "James Walker," *La Presse* (Montréal), 19 nov. 1927: 67.

WALK-IN-THE-WATER. *See* MYEERAH

WALSH. *See* WELCH

WAPASHA. *See* WAHPASHA

WARREN, JOHN, soldier, merchant, office holder, and militia officer; m. Mary —, and they had at least three sons and one daughter; d. May 1813 at Fort Erie, Upper Canada.

Little is known about John Warren's early life. On 13 Oct. 1778 Robert MATHEWS, adjutant of the 8th Foot, recommended Warren, then a drum major in the regiment, for the post of commissary at Fort Erie. Mathews noted Warren's "extraordinary good behaviour during a service of near 23 years, his having numerous family to support, and his possessing a Character and abilities that will do credit to any recommendation in his favour." Warren himself corroborated this statement about his military career. In a letter of 1797 to the surveyor general of Upper Canada, David William Smith*, Warren stated that his father had served the government for 18 years, and he himself had "served ever since the year Fifty five."

The first evidence of Warren's activity after his appointment as commissary is a letter dated 9 Dec. 1779 to Francis Goring, a clerk at Fort Niagara (near Youngstown, N.Y.), complaining of the difficulties he had encountered: the severe winter and the shortage of winter clothing and ammunition. By March 1780 conditions had improved and he was able to joke to Goring that "tho you should proceed from your garrett even to the top of the big house, we Fort Erie folks are much higher than any of you Niagara people." The commissary was responsible for garrison supply, military contracts, and the trans-shipment of goods at the western end of the Niagara portage. He had to be aware of impending shortages of staples and kept a close watch on trade fluctuations, informing his military superiors when shortages in flour and wheat seemed imminent. His principal contacts were with two of the major army suppliers, Robert HAMILTON at Queenston and John ASKIN at Detroit (Mich.). Warren's position at an important military and commercial crossroads assured him a measure of success when he took advantage of his post and moved into private trade. In 1796 he received permission to occupy a lot on the military reserve and constructed a frame dwelling.

By the late 1780s Warren had become a figure of some local prominence in public affairs. On 27 Dec. 1787 he was on the list of men recommended by Sir John Johnson* for "civil trusts" in the proposed new administrative districts, which were established the following July by Lord Dorchester [Guy CARLETON]. He was appointed a justice of the peace for the Nassau District on 24 July 1788 and reappointed in 1800 and 1806, receiving his last commission on 8 Oct. 1807. In the spring of 1790 he was named a road commissioner of the district. His most important appointment was to the district land board. On 1 May 1791 he and Robert Kerr* joined the original appointees: John Butler*, Hamilton, Benjamin PAWLING, and Nathaniel PETTIT. He was reappointed to the board's successor, the land board of Lincoln County, on 20 Oct. 1792; of 14 meetings after his original appointment he attended 3. The board was abolished by order in council in November 1794.

On 19 Oct. 1797 Warren was named to the first Heir and Devisee Commission for the Home District with such men as Pawling, Pettit, and Hamilton and was reappointed on 21 July 1800 for Lincoln County. The evidence for his attendance is fragmentary but it is known that he attended only one of the seven sessions between 1 Oct. 1800 and 15 Sept. 1803. The legislation establishing the commission, the work of Chief Justice John ELMSLEY, was intended to secure titles to land based on certificates acquired "by inheritance, by legitimate purchase, or by exchange." A problem had arisen with the wording of the certificates, which made no provision for conveyances to anyone other than the heirs or devisees of the original holder. The settlement of title was of crucial importance to major merchants such as Hamilton and Richard CARTWRIGHT who had acquired certificates through the settlement of outstanding debts. Warren's sympathies lay with the merchants; writing to Surveyor General Smith about a meeting of the commission on 1 March 1798, Elmsley mentioned a firm refusal he had had to give to a request by Hamilton that certain warrants of council he had received be admitted for consideration: "Warren of Fort Erie argued in his [Hamilton's] favour: & so did Dr. [Robert] Kerr, but I was inexorable; The Country Gentlemen such as Pawling, Tenbrook [Peter Ten Broeck] & [John] MacNabb said nothing, but I construed their silence into approbation of what I did."

Warren seems, however, to have had little inclination for landholding on the grand scale of local speculators such as Hamilton, William Dickson*, Robert Addison*, or Samuel STREET. He had successfully petitioned for 1,540 acres of land and by 1796 had patented all but 100 acres, these holdings being located in Bertie Township. On 17 June 1800, Warren and his wife sold 500 acres for $632.90 and on 4 Dec. 1805 he sold another 500 acres. His only purchase was a complementary lot of 226 acres on 23 Aug. 1804.

In 1801 the Upper Canadian legislature had passed an act which regulated trade with the United States, providing for customs duties and designating 11 ports of entry. Fort Erie was one of them and on 6 August Warren was appointed collector of customs there, a position he held until his death. The same year Ebenezer Washburn* and Richard Beasley* had introduced a bill authorizing the appointment of inspectors of flour, pot and pearl ashes. Warren had been made an inspector on 1 August and served until 7 April 1809 when he tendered his resignation to William Halton, Lieutenant Governor Francis Gore*'s private secretary, because "advanced Age renders me incompetent to the Duty."

Throughout his life Warren had a community of interest with the Niagara merchants. The election of 1800 provides a demonstration. The year before, Hamilton and his associates, Thomas Clark* and George Forsyth, had attempted to secure from the assembly improvements by road and canal to the Niagara portage, anticipated costs to be covered by increased tolls, and subsequently David McGregor

Watson

Rogers* introduced a bill to this effect. The bill was put over till the next session. In the mean time the election was called and it provided a focus for the opposition in the Niagara region to the merchant interest. In Lincoln the merchants' candidates, Samuel Street and William Dickson, were opposed by Ralfe Clench* and Isaac Swayze*. A number of merchants, including Warren, Hamilton, and James Crooks*, attempted to get the powerful Surveyor General Smith elected in the riding of Norfolk, Oxford and Middlesex; Warren, indeed, conveyed letters from them to the politically active Norfolk merchant Thomas WELCH, personally urging "that you will exert your interest in his favour." Smith prevailed but the merchant candidates in Lincoln were defeated. A massive campaign by petition against the portage bill as "monopolous and oppressive" ensured that it was not revived.

The clash between interests had not abated when in 1806 Warren became involved in justice Robert Thorpe*'s opposition to the administration of Lieutenant Governor Francis Gore. On 3 October Thorpe presided over a civil case at the Niagara assizes brought against Magistrate Warren by a Mr Hawn. Hawn had been jailed by Warren for plundering part of the cargo of a ship wrecked on Lake Ontario, and had been subsequently released by justice William Dummer Powell* because of the "Irregularity" of the commitment. In the trial at the assizes, Hawn called as witnesses Clench and Swayze, the old antagonists of the merchants, and his counsel, William WEEKES, was allowed by Thorpe to berate Warren as "a man of turpitude without and turbulence within the Court." Warren's conduct was held up by Weekes as an example of the necessity "to curb the power of these petty Tyrants [the magistrates]." Hawn was awarded £100 damages by the jury.

This treatment of Warren led an outraged magistracy including Hamilton, Street, Thomas Dickson*, and William Claus* to petition Gore, requesting that "in future [the magistrates] be protected from such unwarranted abuse." In a separate letter to Halton, Hamilton described Warren's situation as "one of the hardest that has ever occurred among us." Hamilton feared "that if the Bonds of respect from the People to the Magistrates are once broken there is an end to all order and to all well doing." The execution of the judgement in the Hawn case was pending for some years. It was the subject of charges of misconduct by John Mills Jackson* in 1808 and was raised by Gore himself in 1810 on behalf of Warren when he wrote to the secretary of state for War and the Colonies, Lord Liverpool, asking for authorization "to pay the Damages and Expenses incurred by Mr. Warren." It is not known whether any action was taken upon Gore's request.

For many years Warren had served as lieutenant-colonel of the 3rd Lincoln Militia. The War of 1812 increased his duties as commissary and militia officer. The strain proved too much; on 7 April 1813 he offered his resignation to Adjutant General Æneas SHAW because of the "rapid decline of my health from the two months last past." He died "two or three days before the actions at Fort George [(Niagara-on-the-Lake), 27 May 1813]." His sons Henry and John succeeded to most of his official positions.

In collaboration with BRUCE A. PARKER

AO, MS 75, John Warren to Peter Russell, 12 Oct. 1801; MS 537, T. Ridout to S. S. Ridout, 24 Jan. 1799; RG 1, A-I-1, 1: 99; A-I-6: 1054–55; A-II-5, 1: Niagara District reports, 1800–3; C-I-9, 1; C-IV, Bertie Township, concession 1, lot 4; concession 2, lot 4; concession 3, lot 5; concession 4, lots 9–13; concession 11, lots 10–12; RG 4, A-I, 1; RG 22, ser.134, 2: 92–93; ser.6-2, Lincoln County, will of John Warren. BL, Add. MSS 21851: 14–17 (copies at PAC). Donly Museum, Norfolk Hist. Soc. coll., Thomas Welch papers, 1044–45, 1476–77, 1525–26, 1624–26, 1744–45 (mfm. at PAC). MTL, U.C., Court of Common Pleas, Nassau District, minutes. Niagara South Land Registry Office (Welland, Ont.), Abstract index to deeds, Bertie Township, 28, 63, 98, 133, 143, 153, 164, 274–78, 291–95 (mfm. at AO, GS 2794). PAC, RG 1, L3, 523: W3/73; 524: W6/23 (mfm. at AO); RG 5, A1: 3995–96, 3862–63, 3966–67, 4859–60; RG 9, I, B1, 1: 294–95, 297; RG 16, A1, 84; RG 19, 3751, claim 1139; RG 68, General index, 1651–1841: ff.182, 249–50, 289–90, 292, 326, 408, 410, 416, 418, 525. PRO, CO 42/350: ff.12, 76–79, 175. UWO, Thomas Walsh papers, John Warren to Thomas Welch, 21 July 1800.

Corr. of Hon. Peter Russell (Cruikshank and Hunter), 2: 109. *Corr. of Lieut. Governor Simcoe* (Cruikshank), 4: 140–41. "District of Nassau: minutes and correspondence of the land board," AO *Report*, 1905: 295–306. [J. M. Jackson], *A view of the political situation of the province of Upper Canada, in North America . . .* (London, 1809), 11–12. *John Askin papers* (Quaife), 1: 583–84, 587; 2: 42, 289–90, 360, 756. "Journals of Legislative Assembly of U.C.," AO *Report*, 1909: 104, 106–7, 110–11, 114, 135–36, 139. Loyal and Patriotic Soc. of U.C., *Report, with an appendix, and a list of subscribers and benefactors* (Montreal, 1817), 382. "Notes on land tenure in Canada to A.D. 1800," AO *Report*, 1905: xcii, cviii. "Records of Niagara . . . ," ed. E. A. Cruikshank, Niagara Hist. Soc., [*Pub.*], 39 (n.d.): 119; 40 (n.d.): 62; 41 (1930): 113; 42 (1931): 50; 44 (1939): 30. U.C., House of Assembly, [*A bill intituled an act to amend and improve the communication by land and water between the lakes of Ontario and Erie*] (Niagara [Niagara-on-the-Lake], 1799). Janet Carnochan, "United Empire loyalists," Niagara Hist. Soc., [*Pub.*], 37 (1925): 13. E. A. Cruikshank, "The old fort at Fort Erie," Welland County Hist. Soc., *Papers and Records* (Welland), 5 (1938): 96–97. "The settlement of the township of Fort Erie, now known as the township of Bertie: an attempt at a Domesday Book," comp. E. A. Cruikshank, Welland County Hist. Soc., *Papers and Records*, 5 (1938): 30–32, 35, 80–81.

WATSON, Sir BROOK, political merchant; b. 7 Feb. 1735/36 in Plymouth, England, son of John

Watson and Sarah Schofield; d. 2 Oct. 1807 in East Sheen (London), England.

Orphaned at the age of six, Brook Watson was sent to a distant relative in Boston, Mass., and in 1750 was employed by Andrew Huston trading with the French and Indians in Nova Scotia. In 1752 Watson became secretary to Lieutenant-Colonel Robert Monckton* at Fort Lawrence (near Amherst, N.S.) and assisted Huston and Chief Commissary Joshua WINSLOW. Three years later he was sent to supervise the expulsion of the Acadians from the Baie Verte area. In 1758 he formed a business partnership with Joseph Slayter of Halifax, acting as agent for the Cumberland region. He moved to London the following year and in 1762 formed an association with John Lymburner, brother of Adam*, to enter the Quebec trade. From then on, Watson's fortunes were were founded on a series of partnerships. One of the most important was with Gregory Olive, the most durable with Robert Rashleigh; at one time all three men were in partnership. Their commercial interests concentrated on Nova Scotia and Quebec.

Watson's involvement in both colonies became the greater as a result of his association with Joshua Mauger*. Mauger had established the basis of his wealth in Nova Scotia in the 1750s and maintained his interests there through a network of business associates that included Michael Francklin* and John Butler*. In developing his own interests in the colony Watson worked closely with the Mauger–Franklin group and lobbied in London on its behalf. Watson travelled to Quebec in 1766 and 1767 and made a good impression on Lieutenant Governor Guy CARLETON; it was likely on one of these visits that he engaged George ALLSOPP as his principal business agent there. Around 1768 Mauger, who some years earlier had joined with a group of London merchants in a company to furnish supplies to the Quebec trade, brought Watson into the group and transferred his business to him. Watson's commercial interests included trading fish from Labrador and Nova Scotia waters to Spain, and furs from Quebec to Britain; he engaged in the timber trade and the whale fishery and with Christophe Pélissier* and others he had a share of the Saint-Maurice ironworks. By the early 1770s he was the dominant figure in Nova Scotia's commerce and he had also acquired considerable land holdings there. In 1775 he sent £32,000 worth of furs and £8,000 worth of other products from Quebec to his London warehouse; it was estimated that, but for the American invasion of Quebec that year [see Benedict ARNOLD; Richard Montgomery*], he could have shipped an extra £10,000 worth of goods.

Business interests of this magnitude naturally held political implications. In the 1770s Watson lobbied in London for the continuation of the timber bounty and in 1775 presented Lord Dartmouth with William Smith*'s plan for reorganizing the North American empire. In May that year he went to New York, where he talked in conciliatory tones to a number of future rebels while privately condemning the British government for its lack of firmness in the face of colonial resistance. With a *laissez-passer* from the Continental Congress he travelled to Crown Point (N.Y.) and on 10 July arrived in Quebec overland. After visiting Montreal, he sailed from Quebec on 11 November at the start of the siege, travelling on the *Adamant* together with Joseph Brant [THAYENDANEGEA] and Indian Department officials Christian Daniel Claus* and Guy Johnson*. Within a year reports were circulating that Carleton was ordering defective goods for the Indian Department from Watson. The growing connection between the two men was demonstrated in 1778 when Carleton spoke to Chief Justice Peter Livius* in favour of Watson's claim in a legal action involving Jean-Louis Besnard*, *dit* Carignant: Livius found against Watson's side and was immediately dismissed from office.

When Sir Guy Carleton went to New York City as commander-in-chief in 1782, Watson accompanied him as commissary general. His principal responsibility was to oversee the evacuation of the loyalists to Nova Scotia, almost 30 years after he had helped expel the Acadians from the colony. Watson himself appreciated the irony of the situation. Despite the unpleasantness of the task he stood well with the loyalists. On his return to London he acted for many individuals claiming compensation for their losses and organized charitable subscriptions for the indigent. The new colony of New Brunswick appointed him agent in 1786, a post he held until 1794. Nova Scotia offered him the post of second agent, but he apparently declined; Lieutenant Governor Henry Hamilton* wrote from Quebec that he should be the agent for that province as well.

By the early 1780s Watson's business house was carrying about one-quarter of Quebec's trade. He was hard hit by the immediate post-war depression, when several of his correspondents failed. Merchants cast much of the blame on the "absurd Mixture of French & English Law," which was the "Handle for Oppressive Partialities," and on Governor Frederick HALDIMAND for countenancing them. Watson told the House of Commons – he had been elected for the City of London in 1784 – that the Quebec Act of 1774 had set up "a weak and inadequate system of government" and he wished to see English law, especially in commercial matters, introduced. He had strong ties with the English party in Quebec through such men as Lieutenant Governor Hamilton, Attorney General James Monk*, and councillors William GRANT (1744–1805) and Thomas DUNN. He was convinced that his upright friend Sir Guy Carleton should return to Quebec as governor.

Between 1784 and 1786 Watson acted as Carleton's chief advocate with the British government. He was

Waugh-we-ya-pe-yis-sin-ious

able to use his position as an MP and as a distant relative by marriage of William Pitt to compensate for Carleton's own lack of family connections and diffidence about pushing himself forward. Whenever Carleton came to London he visited Watson, and the visits increased as the negotiations intensified. Both men received parliamentary pensions in their wives' names on the same day in June 1786. When Carleton, who had obtained a peerage from a reluctant administration, returned to Quebec, he took two of Watson's men with him: Thomas Aston COFFIN as civil secretary and William Smith as chief justice. Smith repaid Watson's confidence in him by his first decision from the bench: the Quebec Act, he ruled, had not taken English law away from Englishmen.

From 1793 to 1796 Watson acted as commissary general to the army in Flanders and from 1798 to 1806 as commissary general of Great Britain. In the later years of his life he also served as chairman of Lloyd's of London and deputy governor of the Bank of England. One of his principal claims to fame among his contemporaries was that he became, in 1796, the first one-legged lord mayor of London. At the age of 14 he had lost a leg to a shark in Havana harbour. In 1778 he commissioned John Singleton Copley to depict the scene in a painting that quickly became a popular mezzotint. When he received his baronetcy on 5 Dec. 1803, Watson's new coat of arms featured "a human Leg crest and erased below the Knee" as well as Neptune "repelling a Shark in the Act of securing its Prey."

Watson had married, in 1760, Helen, daughter of Colin Campbell, goldsmith of Edinburgh, Scotland. There were no surviving children. A great-nephew inherited the baronetcy.

L. F. S. UPTON

[Sir Brook Watson bequeathed the painting by John Singleton Copley, *Watson and the shark* (1778), to Christ's Hospital, then situated in London, since it "holds out a useful lesson" for youth. The painting is now in the National Gallery of Art (Washington). A second version by Copley (1778) is in the Boston Museum of Fine Arts, and the Beaverbrook Art Gallery (Fredericton) has a miniature. An engraving of the original painting, by Valentine Green (1779), is in N.B. Museum, Webster coll. of Canadiana, no.1792, as is a cruder, undated French engraving, which prints the scene in reverse.

In 1788 James Bretherton made an etching of Watson addressing the House of Commons, and Robert Dighton published a coloured caricature of him in 1803; copies of both are in N.B. Museum, Webster coll. of Canadiana, nos.1794, 1795. The same collection has an undated portrait by Copley of Watson in robes that have been erroneously described as those of lord mayor but are perhaps those of sheriff (no.1791); another version is in the Indianapolis Museum of Art. The Webster collection also has an oil painting by a Mr Callender (1805), *Brook Watson and cattle incident at Chignecto in April, 1755* (no.1797). The Church

of St Mary the Virgin in Mortlake (London), where Watson lies buried, also has an engraving of him.

No family or business papers have survived. Watson's papers as commissary general in America are in PRO, WO 60/12–15; in Flanders, WO 1/166–73; and of Great Britain, WO 58/1–57. L.F.S.U.]

ASQ, Fonds Viger–Verreau, Carton 37, no.238. BL, Add. MSS 19071: ff.249–50. NYPL, Philip Schuyler papers, no.1522, Gen. Richard Montgomery to Schuyler, 13 Nov. 1775. PANS, A. J. H. Richardson, "Sir Brook Watson" (mfm.); MG 1, 936B (transcript). PRO, PROB 11/1470/ 930. G.B., Hist. MSS Commission, *The manuscripts of the Earl of Dartmouth* (3v., London, 1887–96), 2: 82–83, 262. N.S., House of Assembly, *Journal and proc.*, 1784: 96. *The parliamentary history of England from the earliest period to the year 1803*, comp. William Cobbett and John Wright (36v., London, 1806–20), 27: 524. *Proceedings in the case of Peter Livius* ([London, 1790]), 37. Smith, *Diary and selected papers* (Upton), 1: 217–18; 2: 56, 94. *Quebec Gazette*, 13 July, 16 Nov. 1775. *DNB*. "State papers," PAC *Report*, 1890: 79. C. A. M. Edwards, *Brook Watson of Beauséjour* (Toronto, 1957). J. C. Webster, "Sir Brook Watson: friend of the loyalists, first agent of New Brunswick in London," *Argosy* (Sackville, N.B.), 3 (1924–25): 3–25.

WAUGH-WE-YA-PE-YIS-SIN-IOUS. *See* WEYA-PIERSENWAH

WAUNATHOAKE. *See* DEMASDUWIT

WAWAPESSENWA. *See* WEYAPIERSENWAH

WEEKES, WILLIAM, lawyer and politician; b. in Ireland; d. 11 Oct. 1806, probably in Niagara (Niagara-on-the-Lake), Upper Canada.

In 1798 William Weekes settled at York (Toronto), Upper Canada, where, having been admitted to the bar, he soon became embroiled in factional politics. Because he was Irish, because he had lived for a time in the United States, and because he became a fierce critic of the provincial government, it has sometimes been suggested that he sympathized with the cause of Irish independence, admired the republican and democratic institutions of the United States, and was predisposed to the pursuit of radical politics in Upper Canada. This was not the case. The "blessings" of the United States, he wrote privately in 1801, were "evinced in the broil of faction, the spirit of enmity, and the practices of fraud"; its independence was "a savage licentiousness, uncontrolled by authority and undignified by Sovereignty." Were the "inflammatory Innovators in Ireland" but to travel in that country, he declared, they would lose "all rage for democracy, all furor for reform."

For a time Weekes supported the administration of Lieutenant Governor Peter HUNTER, whom he initially discovered to be "rigorous in his mandates, and deliberate and judicious in his measures," and from whom he had hopes of advancement. It is possible that

844

he hoped to win official favour when he attempted to secure the election of judge Henry ALLCOCK to the House of Assembly in 1800. As the agent of Allcock, but apparently upon his own initiative, Weekes contrived to have the poll closed, by reason of riot, when his candidate was in the lead. This election was voided, however, upon appeal to the assembly [*see* Samuel HERON].

In 1804 Weekes himself stood for election at Durham, Simcoe, and the East Riding of York. Defeated by the incumbent, Angus MACDONELL (Collachie), Weekes blamed government influence. The following year, having campaigned against the Sedition Act passed during the previous session, and against the removal of moneys from the treasury by the executive without approval of the assembly, he was returned in a by-election for the same riding. Immediately upon taking his seat he gave notice of motion to consider "the disquietude which prevails in this province by reason of the administration of public affairs." The money issue was settled when the administration restored the amount to the treasury; Weekes's motion was defeated by a vote of ten to four.

In 1806, when arguing at the Niagara assizes before judge Robert Thorpe*, Weekes referred to the late Lieutenant Governor Hunter as a "Gothic Barbarian whom the providence of God . . . removed from this world for his tyranny and Iniquity." His fellow counsel, William Dickson*, took issue with the propriety of the remark. Two days later Weekes challenged him to a duel that was fought on 10 October in the vicinity of Fort Niagara (near Youngstown), N.Y. Weekes was mortally wounded and died the following day. The funeral was held at the home of the Niagara merchant John MacKay; Ralfe Clench*, Robert Nelles*, and Isaac Swayze* were among the special mourners, most probably because they were fellow assemblymen.

Weekes's career was distinguished by the extravagance of his rhetoric, which perhaps truly reflected an unbalanced political judgement. He is chiefly important by reason of his influence upon Thorpe, a fellow Irishman who, having arrived in the province only in 1806, knew little of local politics and came to entertain the views of his friend Weekes. He was apparently stunned by Weekes's death, writing that "this sudden and shocking catastrophe has shaken me much . . . my heart is wrung." He moved into Weekes's house and succeeded him as the focus for opposition in the assembly to the administration now headed by Lieutenant Governor Francis Gore*. At the opening of the poll that resulted in his election to the assembly, Thorpe invoked the image of Weekes "looking down from Heaven with pleasure on . . . [the electors'] exertions in the cause of liberty."

G. H. PATTERSON

MTL, William Weekes, letter to George Alps, 16 Jan. 1801 (transcript). York County Surrogate Court (Toronto), will of William Weekes, 10 Oct. 1806 (photocopy at MTL). "Political state of U.C.," PAC *Report*, 1892: 32–135. *Town of York, 1793–1815* (Firth). *Upper Canada Gazette*, 2 March 1805. S. D. Clark, *Movements of political protest in Canada, 1640–1840* (Toronto, 1959). J. E. Middleton and Fred Landon, *The province of Ontario: a history, 1615–1927* (5v., Toronto, [1927–28]). H. H. Guest, "Upper Canada's first political party," *OH*, 54 (1962): 275–96. G. [H.] Patterson, "Whiggery, nationality, and the Upper Canadian reform tradition," *CHR*, 56 (1975): 25–44.

WEH-YAH-PIH-EHR-SEHN-WAW. *See* WEYA-PIERSENWAH

WELCH (Walsh, Welsh), THOMAS, surveyor, office holder, militia officer, and judge; b. 5 Nov. 1742 in Maryland, son of Francis Welch and Elizabeth Pierce; m. first in 1769 a Miss Johnson; m. secondly 11 May 1788 Mary (Polly) Mitchell in Harford County, Md, and they had two children; d. 2 July 1816 in Charlotteville Township, Upper Canada.

Francis Welch emigrated from Dungannon (Northern Ireland) about 1740 and settled in Philadelphia, Pa, where he engaged in maritime activities. Later, after his father had been captured and imprisoned by the French, young Thomas Welch was taken to live with one of his mother's wealthy Quaker uncles near Philadelphia. Welch was sent to school and received a sound education. He served with the British provincial forces during the Seven Years' War. At the conclusion of the war, he completed mathematical studies and was later appointed surveyor and under-sheriff in Berks County, Pa. In 1769 he removed to Frederick County, Md, where he was employed as a deputy surveyor, conveyancer, and coroner.

In February 1775 Welch refused reappointment as deputy surveyor and coroner and later declined a commission in the revolutionary forces. Fearing for his safety on the outbreak of hostilities, he conveyed his farm to a friend and made his way to the British lines. In October 1778 he was commissioned quartermaster of the Maryland Loyalists. The unit was stationed at Pensacola (Fla) for three years, during which time he also served as assistant engineer. The Spanish captured Pensacola in May 1781; the British prisoners were exchanged in July and then sent to New York City, where Welch learned of his wife's death.

At New York Welch was appointed captain of a company of loyalist refugees which he accompanied to what is now New Brunswick. He was soon named a deputy surveyor and may also have been engaged as a conveyancer. He received a grant of 550 acres of land, only 25 of which he considered cultivable. After residing in New Brunswick and Quebec for nearly five years, he decided to return to Maryland to look after his affairs there. En route he was shipwrecked and lost

Welch

all his possessions, including the deed to 1,000 acres in Florida which he had purchased while stationed there. With the aid of friends he eventually made his way back to Frederick County where he resumed his former professions; soon after, he moved to Havre de Grace, remarried, and became manager of the Legh Furnace, an ironworks owned by an old business associate, Legh Master. Unable to recover his pre-revolution properties or debts, Welch appealed to the British consulate at Philadelphia for aid, but to no avail. He was, however, advised that generous grants of land were being made to loyalists who settled in Upper Canada.

In mid September 1793 Welch left Maryland with his family and several members of his wife's family, arriving at Queenston, Upper Canada, in November. He was appointed a deputy surveyor in Lincoln County and became a captain in the local militia. In June 1794 he was granted 2,500 acres in Lincoln; he moved to the vicinity of the Sugar Loaf in Humberstone Township and subsequently to Thorold Township. Welch surveyed several townships in Lincoln and Norfolk counties. As early as January 1794 he had expressed a desire to settle at Long Point in Norfolk. When on 3 Dec. 1796 he was designated Norfolk's first land registrar, he took the opportunity to move there. He had already achieved a measure of local prominence when Robert HAMILTON recommended him as justice of the peace in June 1796; he was commissioned the following month.

Welch brought his family to Charlotteville Township in January 1797 and settled on a farm which in time became moderately prosperous. In 1808 he owned two houses (both made of round logs) and 500 acres, of which 88 had been cultivated; three years later he still had two homes but now one was two storeys and made of square timber. His total acreage had increased to 560 acres but the amount of land under cultivation was down to 26 acres. Besides farming, he operated a mill for a time and, in addition to his official duties, he became a captain in the 1st Norfolk Militia. Provision had been made in 1798 for the establishment of the London District; Welch requested that he be appointed its deputy surveyor. He was readily recognized by government officials as a man of proven ability, with all the proper credentials for higher office. He had informed Thomas Ridout* of the Surveyor General's Office of his wish for a position in the new local government. The information was passed to Chief Justice John ELMSLEY who offered Welch either the shrievalty or the clerkship of the peace. As a result of a misunderstanding, he requested the latter. On 1 Jan. 1800 he was appointed clerk of the peace, clerk of the district court, and registrar of the surrogate court. Other responsibilities soon followed which he executed to the satisfaction of his superiors and colleagues. In February, for instance, he was

appointed one of the district commissioners of the Court of King's Bench, and he was named deputy secretary of the district on 7 May 1802. Nevertheless Welch was having financial difficulties and, in the spring of 1803, asked to be relieved of his offices to enable him to return to Lincoln County and manage his affairs there. By the autumn, however, he decided to retain his posts because his eldest son, Francis Legh (Leigh) Walsh, was too young to be appointed in his stead. In June 1806 he resigned the offices of clerk of the peace and clerk of the district court because his "Age . . . as well as infirmities commonly attending that age" and the increase in public business made it impossible for him to perform his duties "in the manner I could wish."

Welch was, with Samuel RYERSE, one of the most prominent members of a local élite that was based on office holding. In the election of 1800 this élite acquired a powerful patron in Surveyor General David William Smith*, who became the local assemblyman. Welch had been appointed returning officer for the riding and, at the urging of Smith's supporters such as Robert Hamilton, John WARREN, and James Crooks*, he handled the local campaign. Smith's unsuccessful opponent, Richard Cockrell*, later contested the election on the grounds that Welch had acted improperly.

Welch's plurality of offices made him a perfect symbol of the élite. Moreover, the performance of his duties, particularly those of a legal nature, often brought him into direct contact with disgruntled individuals such as Ebenezer ALLAN or political opponents such as Benajah Mallory*. The election of 1804 was contested by Ryerse and Mallory after Smith decided not to stand again. Political rivalry was acute; it was intensified by Mallory's victory which led to a direct challenge of the office holders themselves. In 1805 Welch characterized the group calling for the removal of Ryerse and his brother, Sheriff Joseph Ryerson*, as a Methodist faction combined with "the most Seditious and abandoned Characters." Welch was deeply suspicious of what he considered its self-interested motives, its Methodism, and its non-loyalist American background.

In spite of the agitated nature of public affairs within the district, he continued to accept the offices which were thrust upon him. In 1807 he was appointed a trustee of the district school, in October of the same year he was empowered to carry out the provisions of the Sedition Act, and in January 1808 he became deputy lieutenant of the county. He also served for a time as one of the district's road commissioners. On 2 April 1810 he was commissioned judge of the district and surrogate courts and recommissioned justice of the peace. Two days later he was succeeded as land registrar by his son Francis Legh, who the following month succeeded him as surrogate court registrar as

Wentworth

well. On 14 April Francis appointed his father deputy land registrar and in February 1813 he also appointed him deputy registrar of the surrogate court.

Beginning in 1810 Welch began to withdraw from some of the offices he had amassed. That April he relinquished his militia commission because of his "advanced Age." In November he handed over his judgeships because of his "extreme indisposition." He was also, like Ryerse, concerned about the imminent loss of his half pay if he did not rid himself of his offices. In February 1812 he was named a commissioner under the Sedition Act but resigned immediately, pleading that his illness over the past year and a half had left him physically and mentally incapable of performing the duties.

Thomas Welch was a member of the Church of England and a freemason. He died in 1816 and was survived by his widow and their two sons. Both the hamlet and railway point of Walsh were named after the family he had founded in Norfolk County during the early years of its settlement.

DANIEL J. BROCK

AO, MS 75, Thomas Welch to Peter Russell, 31 Jan. 1805; RG 1, A-I-1, 42: 5, 52, 71–74, 114, 123, 126. Donly Museum, Norfolk Hist. Soc. coll., Family Bible transcripts, vol.B; Supplementary papers, II: 3–4; F. L. Walsh papers, 2084–87, 2965; Thomas Welch papers, 87, 89, 96–99, 864–65, 886–89, 893–94, 901–6, 963–64, 1030–33, 1053–55, 1072–73, 1139–42, 1208–9, 1235, 1310–11, 1342–43, 1356, 1358, 1398, 1409–26, 1462–63, 1666–69, 1684–85, 1722–27, 1755, 1757. MTL, Thomas Walsh papers. PAC, RG 1, L3, 522: W1/21; 523A: W4/69; RG 5, A1: 926–27, 1872–73, 2111, 2514–27, 4761, 4918, 5243, 5936, 5970–71, 6056; RG 9, I, B1, 1: 227, 401. Private arch., F. H. Armstrong (London, Ont.), Magisterial files. UWO, London District, U.C., Surrogate Court, estate files, X361; Thomas Walsh papers, corr., William Caldwell Jr to Thomas Welch, 6 Nov. 1789; Thomas Dickson to Welch, 19 July 1800; John Elmsley to Welch, 12 Nov. 1799; Andrew Havner to Welch, 23 July 1790; William Jarvis to Welch, 12 Feb. 1800; Patrick Kennedy to Welch, 7 June 1783; William and Thomas Pagan to Welch, 15 May 1787; Thomas Ridout to Welch, 20 Sept., 14, 20, 30 Nov. 1799; David Secord Jr to Welch, 17 May 1799; Jon Sellman to Welch, 16 June 1790; D. W. Smith to Welch, 11 Nov. 1800; letter of leave to Welch, 4 July 1783; unsigned letter to Welch, 14 Aug. 1784; magisterial and military notations, 4 Aug. 1796–24 Jan. 1799. Charlotteville Township assessments for the years 1808–1811, ed. W. [R.] Yeager (Simcoe, Ont., 1976), 11–12, 21–22. Corr. of Hon. Peter Russell (Cruikshank and Hunter), 1: 187; 2: 296. Corr. of Lieut. Governor Simcoe (Cruikshank), 4: 299. "Petitions for grants of land" (Cruikshank), OH, 26: 366–67. Pioneers of Charlotteville Township, Norfolk County, 1798–1816, ed. W. [R.] Yeager (Simcoe, 1977), 6–7. "U.C. land book B," AO Report, 1930: 67. Armstrong, Handbook of Upper Canadian chronology, 172–73. Illustrated historical atlas of the counties of Haldimand and Norfolk (n.p., [1972]), 61. Wills of the London District, 1800–1839 . . . , ed. W. R. Yeager (Simcoe, 1979), 12. J. A. Bannister, Early educational history of Norfolk County (Toronto, 1926), 52–54. Brian Dawe, "Old Oxford is wide awake!": pioneer settlers and politicians in Oxford County, 1793–1853 (n.p., 1980). E. A. Owen, Pioneer sketches of Long Point settlement . . . (Toronto, 1898; repr. Belleville, Ont., 1972), 37–41, 311–12, 316–17. G. H. Patterson, "Studies in elections and public opinion in Upper Canada" (PHD thesis, Univ. of Toronto, 1969), 6–20. E. A. Cruikshank, "The early history of the London District," OH, 24 (1927): 166, 170, 226. "Thomas Welch," Assoc. of Ont. Land Surveyors, Annual report (Toronto), 1919: 77–78.

WENTWORTH, JOHN, lawyer, office holder, and politician; b. c. 1768 in Portsmouth, N.H., son of Thomas Wentworth and Anne Tasker; d. c. 1820, probably in Paris, France.

John Wentworth was born into the premier family of New Hampshire, one that had provided a number of the colony's leading administrators. His father died about the time of his birth, and his mother in 1770 was remarried to Captain Henry Bellew; the family moved to England at the outset of the American revolution. John was educated at the Inner Temple in London, and between 1797 and 1799 published a ten-volume legal compilation always known as "Wentworth on Pleading." Popular at the time, the work was not of lasting value; its author, in spite of his claims to originality, had cannibalized a small number of similar collections, and one later critic pronounced it of "no authority at all," and "extremely incorrect." Nevertheless, the tomes attracted the attention of someone within the Home Department, and in 1799 Wentworth found himself appointed attorney general of Prince Edward Island in the place of Joseph APLIN. Wentworth's distant relationship to the lieutenant governor of Nova Scotia, Sir John WENTWORTH, may also have influenced his appointment.

Given the many complaints about legal practice on the Island, a man of Wentworth's competence must have seemed particularly attractive to the home authorities. His appointment having been made after the sailing of the ships for Halifax in 1799, Wentworth was forced to travel via New York, and he did not arrive in Charlottetown until May 1800. Lieutenant Governor Edmund FANNING used the delay to press for the appointment of his own preferred candidate, the acting attorney general, Peter MAGOWAN.

The political and legal situation into which Wentworth stepped was a tangled and complex one. For years a number of legal cases had lain dormant, largely because of the difficulty of obtaining justice in the Supreme Court; many of the suits involved the family of Peter STEWART, himself chief justice, and his son CHARLES, the clerk of the court. Inevitably, in his private practice Wentworth found himself acting for the political opponents of the administration, as

Wentworth

well as for the many proprietors and ordinary settlers who were attempting to take legal action against members of the tightly organized Fanning government. He took on briefs for proprietors James William Montgomery, Edward Ellice*, and Captain John MacDonald of Glenaladale, as well as for a large number of Acadians opposing eviction from their lands by John Stewart*. According to John Hill*, Wentworth was almost immediately retained in more than 200 causes, at least 50 of them involving the chief justice and his relatives. He applied for the chief justiceship in succession to Peter Stewart, and he managed to dismiss Charles Stewart as clerk of the Supreme Court, greatly frightening government officials. To their relief, Fanning received authorization in September 1800 to appoint Magowan attorney general, the Home Department having assumed that Wentworth's delay in reaching the Island meant that he would not take up his post. Although the slowness of communications gave Wentworth good grounds for retaining his position, Fanning, in a political manœuvre typical of the Island, made no attempt to present his case and in fact dismissed him from the Council. Wentworth's own protests against his treatment were ignored in London, perhaps because the lieutenant governor had convinced the home authorities that the former attorney general had excited "a litigious spirit hitherto unknown." After losing the attorney generalship Wentworth remained to see his cases through; however, he soon found himself charged with malpractice by John Cambridge*. His supporters claimed that he could prove his innocence in any impartial court, but was being hounded off the Island as others had been before him. James Douglas wrote to William Montgomery* that Wentworth would return to England "with such an Account of the Misconduct here that would quite surprize you."

Instead of returning to England to protest his treatment, Wentworth made his way back to the United States and was soon practising law in Portsmouth. On 7 Jan. 1802 he married Martha Wentworth, granddaughter of the former governor, Benning Wentworth, and by 1804 he was sufficiently settled in New Hampshire to deliver a Fourth of July oration and compose a patriotic ode for the national celebration. The oration supported the Republican party of Thomas Jefferson and strongly attacked the British "system of tyranny and corruption," a subject about which Wentworth understandably had strong feelings. But he did not in the long run prosper in Portsmouth, and returned to London in 1816. Wentworth took up residence on Charles Street in Westminster, and spent his final years piteously memorializing Whitehall as a suffering loyalist who had unfairly lost his appointment on Prince Edward Island. He died around 1820, probably in Paris where his last petitions were written.

J. M. Bumsted

John Wentworth is the author of *A complete system of pleading: comprehending the most approved precedents and forms of practice; chiefly consisting of such as have never before been printed* . . . (10v., London, 1797–99); *An oration, delivered at Portsmouth, New-Hampshire, on the fourth July, 1804* (Portsmouth, 1804); and "Patriotic odes; composed for the national jubilee, July 4th, 1804" (broadside, n.p., [1804]) (copy at American Antiquarian Soc., Worcester, Mass.).

PAC, MG 11, [CO 226] Prince Edward Island A, 17: 272–77. PAPEI, RG 6, Supreme Court, docket book, 1788–1843. PRO, CO 226/1: 31, 36. SRO, GD293/2/19/1, 10. C. H. Bell, *The bench and bar of New Hampshire, including biographical notices of deceased judges of the highest court, and lawyers of the province and state, and a list of those now living* (Boston and New York, 1895), 726. John Wentworth, *The Wentworth genealogy: English and American* (3v., Boston, 1878), 554.

WENTWORTH, Sir JOHN, office holder and colonial administrator; b. 9 Aug. 1737 in Portsmouth, N.H., the elder surviving son of Mark Hunking Wentworth and Elizabeth Rindge; m. 11 Nov. 1769 in Portsmouth his cousin Frances Deering Wentworth, widow of their mutual cousin, Theodore Atkinson; d. 8 April 1820 in Halifax, N.S., leaving one legitimate and one illegitimate son.

After an uneventful career at Harvard College, where he graduated ba in 1755 and ma in 1758, John Wentworth returned to Portsmouth and entered his father's merchant house, on whose behalf he travelled to England in the early 1760s. There he successfully sought the patronage of Charles Watson-Wentworth, Marquess of Rockingham, for himself and his family. During his sojourn in London he also represented the colony of New Hampshire, in which his family had been prominent for three generations, as an official spokesman against the Stamp Act in 1765. He was on hand for the exposure of the misdoings of Benning Wentworth, governor of New Hampshire and surveyor general of the king's woods in North America. The incident proved to be a fortunate turn of events since John was chosen to succeed to his uncle's offices in 1766.

It was not in the younger Wentworth's nature to take lightly the responsibility of these virtually hereditary positions. On his return to America he applied himself with great assiduity and judiciousness to the enforcement of the reservation to the Royal Navy of all trees suitable for ships' masts, displaying a taste for pioneer travel and an adaptability to frontier conditions which stood in sharp contrast to the ostentatious display that accompanied his governorship. With the help of his English supporters, Wentworth managed to defend himself in 1773 against the most serious challenge to his administration, a charge of corruption made by one of his former councillors, Peter Livius*. At the same time the governor retained his popularity at home, being endowed with a genuine common touch that strengthened his social relations with the colonists, and with sufficient influence and power to enable him to treat successfully with the critics of his family's oligarchic control. Eventually, however, the dissatisfaction with Wentworth's administration ripened into, and was joined by, opposition to British policies. By 1775 the governor's relations with the House of Assembly, which had embraced the revolutionary cause, and with the town of Portsmouth, which chafed under British naval surveillance, finally and irrevocably broke down. He fled to Boston, Mass., next to Halifax, and then to New York City where he organized a company of loyalist volunteers in 1776. His active military support of the British earned him the proscription of the Continental Congress. Shortly after he sailed for England in 1778, the New Hampshire legislature passed a bill of attainder against him.

In England for the next five years the erstwhile governor and absentee surveyor resumed his relations with the Wentworth nobility, enjoyed a pension in recognition of his loyalty to the crown, and served on the board of loyalist agents. The office of surveyor general for North America was briefly abolished in 1782, but the return of Charles James Fox and Lord North to political power saw Wentworth reappointed and dispatched to Nova Scotia in 1783. Further advancement, particularly the coveted governorship of Nova Scotia, eluded him, but he became a familiar and well-respected figure in that province and the surrounding colonies as he regularly traversed the forests to oversee the protection of white pine and to reserve what he considered to be fine quality timberland for the use of the Royal Navy. He claimed that he did his utmost, as he had been instructed, to avoid interfering with the settlement of loyalist refugees, many of whom were completely destitute. Indeed, he considered mast policy and settlement policy perfectly compatible in circumstances where "the best timber, especially pines, seldom grow on the best land." Between his expeditions into the wilds he flourished on the fringes of Halifax society, avoiding the quarrels and intrigues of the hectic 1780s. He made his residence in a rural situation on Bedford Basin known as Friar Lawrence's Cell. None the less, he naturally remained ambitious for a more eminent situation. Frances, too, despaired of her fate as wife of the surveyor general, a position that not only lacked lustre but also took her conscientious husband away from home for months at a time. The liaison that developed between Mrs Wentworth and the young Prince William Henry during the 1780s when he visited Halifax with the North Atlantic squadron was an attempt to escape the loneliness and the tedium of a society that was beneath her contempt. It illustrates the liberalized relationship she and John maintained, which included extramarital affairs for both in a style typical of the most civilized as well as the most debauched of Georgian aristocracy in England.

"Governor" Wentworth, as he continued to be styled, happened to be in London in 1792 attending to his normally chaotic financial affairs when the news of the death of Lieutenant Governor John Parr* late in 1791 provided him with the opportunity to press his case for the appointment. The subsequent choice of Wentworth as lieutenant governor was universally welcomed because of his amiable personality and proven loyalist principles; above all, his background and experience provided Nova Scotia with an administrator of tried ability. The 1790s proved to be a rewarding decade as Sir John (created a baronet in 1795) joined the efforts of the executive with those of the assembly and successfully pulled Nova Scotia out of stagnation, expunging the public debt by 1797, yet, in the absence of surplus revenue, avoiding the inevitable quarrel over appropriations until the turn of the century. Wartime trade and privateering occasioned a general return to prosperity. The capital, and especially the Wentworth household, glittered with the social events attending the frequent visits of Prince EDWARD AUGUSTUS, commander-in-chief in Nova Scotia, who schemed with Sir John for the division between them of the civil and military administrations of British North America and used his friend's suburban retreat as one of his abodes with his French mistress, Thérèse-Bernardine Mongenet*, known as Mme de Saint-Laurent, during the years of his Nova Scotian and British North American commands, 1794–1800.

The 1790s, however, also provided challenges and disquietude for the lieutenant governor. Amongst the former, the unexpected addition to the population of the maroons, expelled *en masse* from Jamaica as punishment for their persistent guerrilla warfare against authority, preoccupied his public attention for much of the period from 1796 to 1801. He tried unsuccessfully to settle the blacks as Christianized farmers and labourers. In a pig-headed fashion, spurred on by what one historian has infelicitously described as a "search for life's merit badges," Wentworth pursued his plans for permanent, segregated settlement in Nova Scotia in opposition to the preferences of the Jamaican commissioners, the settled populace, and ultimately the maroons themselves. To realize his misguided object, Wentworth

Wentworth

lavished public funds on feeding, placating, and charming the maroons. In these circumstances the Duke of Portland, the Home secretary, seized with enthusiasm the offer of the Sierra Leone Company to provide a tropical home for the maroons, as it had for the black loyalists of Nova Scotia before them [*see* David GEORGE; Thomas Peters*]. Wentworth had no choice but to see that all the maroons were packed off to Africa and to sit by while his official salaries were debited to cover such expenses as cocked hats, scarlet cloth, and gold lace for the uniforms of the maroon regiment of militia formed for service in Nova Scotia, as well as brandy and tobacco for the comfort of the hapless exiles on their voyage.

Meanwhile, for a man of Wentworth's temperament and recent experience in the American colonies, the outbreak of the French revolution and subsequent Anglo-French wars took on more than a mere strategic significance. Admittedly, the initial fear of French attack elicited a conventional response from the lieutenant governor. With little concern for the high cost of his actions, he called out the militia, raised a new regiment – the Royal Nova Scotia – and placated the poverty-stricken, roving Indians, who were always regarded in wartime both as a terrorist threat and as potential French allies. But far more unsettling was his apprehension of the enemy within – disloyal elements with overtly democratic aspirations. Steadfast supporters of church and state such as Wentworth made little distinction between disloyalty and dissent: the heretical notions of dissenters on church and state were thought to pose a threat to social and political order. Wentworth's rhetoric, like that of Bishop Charles INGLIS, did not fail to single out religious dissenters as potential subversives, but it was more particularly directed at political dissentients, especially William Cottnam Tonge*, who challenged executive supremacy in government and drove the governor to the kind of autocratic excesses that served only to hasten his official demise.

The struggle between Wentworth and Tonge, a pre-loyalist from Newport, broadened into a constitutional struggle between the governor-in-council and the House of Assembly and marred much of the last decade of the Wentworth administration. It occurred against the background of a more fundamental socio-economic conflict. Wentworth, not surprisingly, surrounded himself with loyalists who had had to wait until his advent to power for their fair share of place and influence. He made no attempt to conceal his favouritism, which also included the usual Wentworthian nepotism: the calling of his brother-in-law Benning Wentworth and his own son Charles Mary Wentworth to his Council and their appointment as successive provincial secretaries. More neglected by Wentworth than the non-loyalist elements, how-

ever, were the country interests, whose preferences invariably ran counter to the mercantile preoccupations of the capital and to the control it exercised. Although Wentworth's varied experiences and intimate acquaintance with the province as surveyor general should have made him sympathetic to other sectors of the community, the "merchantocracy" had the ear of a man who had been trained in his father's counting-house and for whom the encouragement of large-scale commercial ventures was a source of challenge. Contemporaries such as Lord Dalhousie [George Ramsay*] believed that Wentworth was the innocent dupe of certain merchants more astute and cunning than himself. Certainly he relied on the friendship of such ambitious loyalist entrepreneurs as Lawrence Hartshorne* and Michael Wallace*, whom he promoted from the assembly to the Council and subsequently remembered affectionately in his will.

Whatever the wider causes, the rivalry with Tonge for political leadership appears to have been fired by personal animosity. For some inexplicable reason Wentworth seems to have taken a decided aversion to Tonge. Their relationship got off to a bad start as early as 1792 when Wentworth's personal nominee for the position of naval officer in Halifax lost to this upstart son and deputy of the former incumbent, Winckworth Tonge*. Since the reformist element in the assembly was to collapse after Tonge's departure from Nova Scotia in 1808, Wentworth made no mistake in recognizing this man as the leading inspiration of the anti-government faction. In particular, Wentworth was distressed by Tonge's resort to the kind of political clubs favoured by contemporary English radicals during election campaigns, and by his clever electoral tactics, especially when he ran and won in Halifax County in 1799 despite his failure to satisfy the property qualification. Above all, Wentworth firmly believed that, as a public servant, Naval Officer Tonge had no right to oppose government policies, the only alternative to active support being discreet neutrality. Far from taking either course, Tonge led the assembly to pass consolidated appropriation bills and challenge the governor's right to interfere in financial matters, particularly the assembly's appropriations for roads and bridges. Wentworth responded with stunning ineptitude and lack of constitutional acumen: in 1804 he claimed the sole right to appropriate colonial revenues; in 1806 he rejected the assembly's nomination of Tonge as speaker and claimed the authority to decide the outcome of contested elections; in 1807 he dismissed Tonge from the naval office.

His increasing extremism and the prospect that an Anglo-American conflict would require a military governor were responsible for Wentworth's peremptory removal from office in 1808 and his replacement by PREVOST. This blow was a final one in a series of misfortunes and disappointments since the optimistic days of the early 1790s. The scandal surrounding his excessive expenditure on the maroons, defence, and a new government house had led Wentworth to fear in 1801–2 that he would be demoted to a West Indian post. Appointment as governor general of British North America did not materialize despite continued English patronage in the person of Rockingham's nephew, Earl Fitzwilliam, and the steadfast support of the Duke of Kent [Edward Augustus], who pressed Wentworth's case on the Prince Regent. Wentworth's personal financial affairs had also been a disaster. Many years before he had been disinherited by his governor uncle in favour of a young wife; the dispossession occasioned by the revolution had been followed by a more shattering disinheritance, that by his own parents. Parliamentary compensation for his losses as a loyalist was swallowed up by debts to his English agent and kinsman Paul Wentworth. While he was lieutenant governor, his loss of salary as a result of over-expenditure not only caused him financial embarrassment but carried with it the suspicion that he had misappropriated public funds. Both the British government and the Nova Scotia assembly, however, granted him annuities for life which enabled him in 1810 to take the ailing Frances to England where she died in 1813. Meanwhile Wentworth was forced to leave England in 1812 in order to escape his creditors, who were clamouring for the payment of his debts. Out of necessity he returned to Nova Scotia where he could continue to draw the much needed surveyor general's salary. A stroke in 1816 largely incapacitated him. He sank under his distress, as popular sentiment would have it, at the news of the deaths of the Duke of Kent and George III in the spring of 1820, and was buried beneath St Paul's Church in Halifax.

The record of Wentworth's career in Nova Scotia might have been more flattering if he had served a normal length of term as colonial administrator. Sixteen years gave him enough rope with which to hang himself. His many years of prominence in the province exposed his weaknesses to friends and advisers and they did not scruple to use his good services for their own ends. Over the years he remade the Council in his own image and by 1800 revealed his determination to pay scant attention to the assembly in affairs of government. Such a reactionary constitutional stand was bound to excite critics even without the additional element of the governor's feud with Tonge. Arguably, Wentworth's inflated notion of the governor's prerogative, his worst fault, could have been derived as much from a reading of supposed British intentions for British North America as from any inherent extremism in his nature. Equally important for a loyalist, however, was the fear that

forces unleashed by the American revolution and carried forth by the French would, in the absence of vigilance and suppression, undermine the *status quo*. Margaret Ells summed up Wentworth's weaknesses and over-reactions when she accused him of losing "all sense of proportion." Yet despite the stormy final years of his administration, Wentworth was by all accounts a well-beloved governor, a kind, charming, earthy little man, devoted to the service of his monarch and hospitable to citizen and stranger alike.

JUDITH FINGARD

Halifax County Court of Probate (Halifax), Book 4: 54–55 (will of John Wentworth) (mfm. at PANS). Leeds City Libraries (Leeds, Eng.), Rockingham papers, corr. 1776–1812, Sir John and Lady Frances Wentworth to Lady Rockingham and others (copy at PANS). Northamptonshire Record Office (Northampton, Eng.), Fitzwilliam (Milton) papers. PANS, MG 1, 939–40; RG 1, 49–54; 139: 55; 214: 367; 227: doc.132; 328: doc.16. PRO, AO 12/12: ff.1–11, 16–19; 12/62: f.1; 12/104: f.71; 12/109: 320–21; AO 13, bundle 40: ff.244–483; bundle 53: nos.479, 499; CO 217/63–90. Portsmouth Athenaeum (Portsmouth, N.H.), Peirce papers, corr., 1763–1803 (copy at PANS). Sheffield City Libraries (Sheffield, Eng.), Wentworth Woodhouse muniments, Sir John and Sir Charles Wentworth, corr.; Fitzwilliam papers (courtesy of the trustees of the Fitzwilliam Wentworth Estates and the director of the Sheffield City Libraries). SRO, GD45/3/541, 6 June 1818; GD45/3/543, 9 April 1820. *The correspondence of George, Prince of Wales, 1770–1812*, ed. [Arthur] Aspinall (8v., London, 1963–71), 3: 21–23. [William Dyott], *Dyott's diary, 1781–1845: a selection from the journal of William Dyott, sometime general in the British army and aide-de-camp to His Majesty King George III*, ed. R. W. Jeffery (2v., London, 1907), 1. *DAB*. *DNB*. Shipton, *Sibley's Harvard graduates*, vol.13. John Wentworth, *The Wentworth genealogy: English and American* (3v., Boston, 1878).

R. G. Albion, *Forests and sea power: the timber problem of the Royal Navy, 1652–1862* (Cambridge, Mass., 1926). J. R. Daniell, *Experiment in republicanism: New Hampshire politics and the American revolution, 1741–1794* (Cambridge, 1970). Fingard, *Anglican design in loyalist N.S.* Mollie Gillen, *The prince and his lady: the love story of the Duke of Kent and Madame de St Laurent* (London, 1970). L. S. Mayo, *John Wentworth, governor of New Hampshire, 1767–1775* (Cambridge, 1921). M. B. Norton, *The British-Americans: the loyalist exiles in England, 1774–1789* (Boston and Toronto, 1972). K. E. Stokes, "Sir John Wentworth and his times, 1767–1808" (PHD thesis, Univ. of London, 1938). J. [E.] Tulloch, "Conservative opinion in Nova Scotia during an age of revolution, 1789–1815" (MA thesis, Dalhousie Univ., Halifax, 1972). Susan Whiteside, "Colonial adolescence: a study of the maritime colonies of British North America, 1790–1814" (MA thesis, Univ. of B.C., Vancouver, 1965). R. W. Winks, *The blacks in Canada: a history* (London and New Haven, Conn., 1971). Philip Ziegler, *King William IV* (London, 1971). [A. G.] Archibald, "Life of Sir John Wentworth, governor of Nova Scotia, 1792–1808," N.S. Hist. Soc., *Coll.*, 20 (1921):

Weyapiersenwah

43–109. Margaret Ells, "Governor Wentworth's patronage," N.S. Hist. Soc., *Coll.*, 25 (1942): 49–73.

WEYAPIERSENWAH (Weh-yah-pih-ehr-sehn-waw, Wey-a-pic-e-sen-waw, Waugh-we-ya-pe-yissin-ious, Wawapessenwa, Blue Jacket), Shawnee war chief; b. mid 18th century; d. *c.* 1810, probably in the Detroit River region.

One of the earliest mentions of Blue Jacket in white records dates from January 1773 when missionary David Jones visited "Blue Jackets Town" near the Scioto River (Ohio). In the following year Blue Jacket was one of the Indian leaders at the battle of Point Pleasant (W.Va) in Lord Dunmore's War, and during the American revolution he was an ally of the British. By 1778 his town on the Scioto was deserted, and he had a new one on the site of present Bellefontaine, Ohio. This town was burnt in the expedition of Kentucky frontiersman Benjamin Logan in 1786. Blue Jacket negotiated with the Kentuckians at Limestone (Maysville, Ky) in 1787 but was raiding into Kentucky the following year.

By the late 1780s Blue Jacket had settled in the region of the Miamis (Maumee) River in what is now northwestern Ohio and northeastern Indiana. In 1788 he had "a fine plantation well stocked with cattle" in the vicinity of the present Fort Wayne, Ind. Along with the Miami chief Little Turtle [MICHIKINAKOUA] he was one of the main Indian leaders in the successful engagements with the American armies of Josiah Harmar and Arthur St Clair in 1790 and 1791.

By 1792 Blue Jacket had a village on the Miamis River shortly below the Auglaize. A young American captive who was there at that time described him as "the most noble in appearance of any Indian I ever saw." The following year an American Quaker called him "a brave, masculine figure of a man." Less complimentary was Richard G. ENGLAND, British commandant at Detroit, who commented, "I have not the highest Opinion of either his Zeal, or Abilities."

Blue Jacket was active along the Miamis throughout 1793 and 1794, and he travelled farther afield recruiting Indians to resist the Americans. He wanted to go to Montreal to confer with Sir John Johnson*, superintendent general of Indian affairs, but was prevented from doing so by the British authorities at Detroit. After the unsuccessful Indian attack on Fort Recovery (Ohio) in June 1794 Blue Jacket took over general command of the Indian forces from Little Turtle, who counselled caution, and he led the Indians in their defeat at the battle of Fallen Timbers (near Waterville, Ohio) in August 1794. Early in 1795 Blue Jacket decided to make peace with American general Anthony Wayne. He signed preliminary articles on 11 February and was active in persuading the Indians to attend the conference at Greenville (Ohio) to be held that summer. Alexander McKee*, deputy superintendent general of Indian affairs for Upper Canada, reproached him, reportedly saying, "You have deranged, by your imprudent conduct, all our plans for protecting the Indians. . . . You must now be viewed as the enemy of your people. . . ." Nevertheless, Blue Jacket took part in the Greenville council, signing on 3 August the treaty by which the Indians ceded much of what is now Ohio to the Americans. At the council he said, "You see me now present myself as a war chief, to lay down that commission, and place myself in the rear of my village chiefs, who, for the future, will command me. . . . We must think of war no more."

After Greenville Blue Jacket lived for a time near Fort Wayne, later moved to the Auglaize River near the present Wapakoneta, Ohio, and by 1801 had a home on the Detroit River. No doubt he visited Fort Malden (Amherstburg), Upper Canada, from time to time, since it was from that post after 1796 that the British distributed presents to the Indians south of the border. He signed the Treaty of Fort Industry in July 1805, by which part of northern Ohio was ceded to the United States. Early in their movement he became associated with the Prophet [Tenskwatawa*] and TECUMSEH; for a time he apparently lived with them at Greenville, and he visited Chillicothe in 1807 as one of the Indian emissaries to the Ohio government.

Blue Jacket was probably married at least twice – once to an American prisoner named Moore, and once to a half-Indian daughter of Jacques Baby*, *dit* Dupéront. His children included Nancy; Mary, who married Jacques Lacelle; George Blue Jacket, who was an interpreter for the British during the War of 1812; and Jim Blue Jacket, who was associated with Tecumseh and also took part in the war.

REGINALD HORSMAN

PAC, MG 19, F1, 5: 233–35. Wis., State Hist. Soc., Draper MSS, 11YY33. *Anthony Wayne . . . the Wayne–Knox–Pickering–McHenry correspondence*, ed. R. C. Knopf (Pittsburgh, Pa., 1960; repr. Westport, Conn., 1975), 296, 384, 390. *Documentary history of Dunmore's War, 1774 . . .*, ed. R. G. Thwaites and L. P. Kellogg (Madison, Wis., 1905), 374n. [L. C. Draper], "Biographical field notes of Dr. Lyman C. Draper: Toledo and vicinity, 1863–66," Hist. Soc. of Northwestern Ohio, *Quarterly Bull.* (Toledo), 5 (1933), no.4: items 175–76, 181–82. *Indian affairs: laws and treaties*, comp. C. J. Kappler ([2nd ed.], 2v., Washington, 1904), 2: 39–45, 77–78. *John Askin papers* (Quaife), 2: 34n., 743. David Jones, *A journal of two visits made to some nations of Indians on the west side of the river Ohio, in the years 1772 and 1773* (Burlington, Vt., 1774; repr. New York, 1971), 51–52. *Mich. Pioneer Coll.*, 17 (1890); 20 (1892); 24 (1894); 40 (1929). Norton, *Journal* (Klinck and Talman), 187. *The revolution on the upper Ohio, 1775–1777 . . .*, ed. R. G. Thwaites and L. P. Kellogg (Madison, 1908; repr. Port Washington, N.Y., and London, 1970), 44n. [Thomas Ridout], "Narrative of the captivity among the Shawanese Indians, in 1788, of Thomas Ridout, afterwards surveyor-general of Upper Canada, from the original manuscript in possession of the family," *Ten years of Upper Canada in peace and war, 1805–1815; being the Ridout letters*, ed. Matilda Edgar (Toronto, 1890), 366. H. R. Schoolcraft, *Travels in the central portions of the Mississippi valley . . .* (New York, 1825; repr. Millwood, N.Y., 1975), 49. O. M. Spencer, *Indian captivity: a true narrative of the capture of Rev. O. M. Spencer by the Indians, in the neighbourhood of Cincinnati* (New York, 1835; repr. Ann Arbor, Mich., 1966), 86–87. U.S., Congress, *American state papers* (Lowrie *et al.*), class II, [1]: 564, 568, 571, 579.

Handbook of American Indians (Hodge), 1: 155. Henry Howe, *Historical collections of Ohio . . . an encyclopedia of the state . . .* (3v. in 2, Columbus, Ohio, 1889–91), 1: 300. J. [E.] Bakeless, *Daniel Boone* (New York, 1939; repr. Harrisburg, Pa., 1965), 322–23. John Bennett, *Blue Jacket, war chief of the Shawnees, and his part in Ohio's history* (Chillicothe, Ohio, 1943). [This is a standard work on Blue Jacket but contains material about his youth that is unproven and likely incorrect. R.H.] C. W. Butterfield, *History of the Girtys . . .* (Cincinnati, Ohio, 1890), 410. Benjamin Drake, *Life of Tecumseh, and of his brother, the Prophet . . .* (Cincinnati, 1858), 37, 94–97, 191. Henry Harvey, *History of the Shawnee Indians, from the year 1681 to 1854, inclusive* (Cincinnati, 1855; repr. New York, 1971), 112–14. L. U. Hill, *John Johnston and the Indians in the land of the Three Miamis . . .* (Piqua, Ohio, 1957), 8. C. E. Slocum, *History of the Maumee River basin from the earliest account to its organization into counties* (Defiance, Ohio, 1905), 243, 437. C. G. Talbert, *Benjamin Logan, Kentucky frontiersman* (Lexington, Ky., 1962), 210–11. Erminie Wheeler-Voegelin, "Ethnohistory of Indian use and occupancy in Ohio and Indiana prior to 1795," *Indians of Ohio prior to 1795* (2v., New York and London, 1974), 2: 532, 571; *Indians of northwest Ohio; an ethnohistorical report on the Wyandot, Potawatomi, Ottawa and Chippewa of northwest Ohio* (New York and London, 1974), 158, 243. B. R. Long, "Joseph Badger, the first missionary to the Western Reserve," *Ohio Archæological and Hist. Pubs.* (Columbus), 26 (1917): 17–18.

WILKIE, WILLIAM, pamphleteer and reformer; fl. 1820.

Dislocation caused by the transition from war to peace after 1815 prompted an eruption of agitation across British North America. Robert Gourlay* of Upper Canada is the best-known radical of this era, but Nova Scotia had a parallel to Gourlay in the person of William Wilkie.

Little is known about Wilkie, either prior to or after his attaining political notoriety. He was the son of Walter Coltheart Wilkie, a Halifax sea captain, who was descended from the pioneer settlers of 1749. By the beginning of the 19th century the Wilkie family had acquired modest status in Halifax society. Walter gained a seat on the grand jury in 1817 and, in 1825, one of his sons, James Charles William, became clerk to the Halifax Banking Company. Although no confirmation can be obtained from Anglican church records, it appears that William Wilkie was born in the mid to late 1790s. He received what was, for the

times, an above-average education and probably went to work as clerk in a merchant counting-house. His name appears in no public or private document until April 1820, when the crown charged him with criminal libel for having issued, anonymously, a pamphlet entitled *A letter to the people of Halifax, containing strictures on the conduct of the magistrates. . . .*

Wilkie's venture into print took place against a background of business failures, unemployment, crime, poor crops, and large-scale emigration to the United States. The sudden disappearance of wartime prosperity left Nova Scotians confused and ready to listen to self-proclaimed experts professing to know what had gone wrong. John Young*, Thomas McCulloch*, and others ventured into the weekly press with remedies for hard times. Most critics offered comment that was either neutral or conservative in political tone. Occasionally, however, a radical note crept in. This was particularly true of the pamphlet written by William Wilkie.

His 21-page epistle, apparently printed by Anthony Henry Holland*, proprietor of the *Acadian Recorder*, focused on the alleged deficiencies of Halifax's appointed civic authorities. Their prime failing, in Wilkie's eyes, lay in allowing municipal taxes to rise by 85 per cent between 1817 and 1819. This large increase, caused mainly by escalating welfare costs, was attributed by Wilkie to extravagance and corruption. Civic officials, he maintained, received excessive incomes, charged exorbitant fees, allowed the sheriff to extort money from imprisoned debtors, exploited inmates of the workhouse for private benefit, exempted friends from taxes, and refused to render proper accounts for public expenditures. The indictment, at least some of which appears justified, climaxed with the impassioned observation: "We are governed by a set of drivellers, from whom we can expect no remedy, but in *poison*, no relief but in *death*."

After dealing with the magistrates, Wilkie proceeded to denounce virtually every other component of constituted authority. The courts received criticism because their high fees denied justice to small businessmen seeking to collect debts. As well, the laws against theft were enforced in so lax a manner as to undermine the security of property. The Council, a body dominated by Halifax's wealthy élite, was condemned for having vetoed a bank bill, thereby perpetuating a scarcity of credit in the province. The assembly also was attacked for its failure to carry out a redistribution of seats, as well as for the members' decision to raise their sessional indemnity. The nature of these grievances, with their emphasis on the plight of those with small property, suggests that Wilkie belonged to and identified with the shopkeeper stratum of Halifax society.

Willcocks

Wilkie's pamphlet might have been overlooked had his language been less hysterical or his social status more elevated. As it was, he aroused both the ire and the paranoia of leading members of the establishment. They struck back with criminal prosecution, bringing Wilkie to trial in the Supreme Court in April 1820. He sought and was granted the right to conduct his own defence; the prosecuting attorney was Samuel George William Archibald*, king's counsel and member of the House of Assembly. Far from being evasive or deferential, Wilkie "acknowledged himself the author of the libel, and undertook to repeat and comment upon it, in terms so much more offensive than the language of the libel itself, as to remove from any candid mind the smallest doubt of his guilt." After a mere five minutes' deliberation the jury returned a guilty verdict. The court then sentenced Wilkie to two years at hard labour in the local workhouse. As a gesture of leniency, Chief Justice Sampson Salter Blowers* ruled that the duration of the sentence would be halved if Wilkie maintained good behaviour.

The case had attracted wide public interest, and a contemporary later observed that "the sympathy in his [Wilkie's] favour was very general throughout the town." Anonymous threatening letters were sent to the press, but no one dared come to his defence openly. The Halifax press, including Holland's *Acadian Recorder*, denounced Wilkie as a "misguided and foolish young man" who deserved what he got. No one, it appeared, had a desire to be publicly associated with expressions of "licentious spirit."

As far as is known, Wilkie served a term in the workhouse and then disappeared, probably migrating to the United States. He appears to have been forgotten by Halifax society. Reformers of the 1830s, such as Joseph Howe*, never brought up his name when building their critique of Nova Scotia's oligarchy. Nevertheless, Wilkie's abortive political career heralded much of what would follow in the campaign for responsible government; it also suggested that protest, when it arose on a large scale, would be concentrated not among the very poor but rather within the petite bourgeoisie of urban society.

D. A. SUTHERLAND

William Wilkie is the author of *A letter to the people of Halifax, containing strictures on the conduct of the magistrates with regard to the police office, Court of Quarter Session, work house, poor house, jail, &c; also, strictures on the court of commissioners, Supreme Court, &c.; also, strictures on his majesty's Council and House of Assembly, bank bill, militia, issuing tickets for [seats], Digby election, raising the pay, &c. &c*, by a Nova Scotian ([Halifax], 1820).

PANS, RG 34-312, P, 8–9. [George Ramsay, Earl of Dalhousie], *The Dalhousie journals*, ed. Marjorie Whitelaw ([Toronto], 1978). *Acadian Recorder*, 2 March 1816; 18 Sept., 30 Oct., 6 Nov. 1819; 22 April 1820. *Free Press* (Halifax), 21 Sept., 14 Dec. 1819. *Nova Scotia Royal Gazette*, 19 April 1820. *Weekly Chronicle* (Halifax), 21 April 1820. Akins, *Hist. of Halifax City*. W. M. Brown, "Recollections of old Halifax," N.S. Hist. Soc., *Coll.*, 13 (1908): 79. G. V. V. Nicholls, "A forerunner of Joseph Howe," *CHR*, 8 (1927): 224–32.

WILLCOCKS (Wilcox), JOSEPH, diarist, office holder, printer, publisher, journalist, politician, and army officer; b. 1773 in Palmerston (Republic of Ireland), second son of Robert Willcocks and Jane Powell; d. unmarried 4 Sept. 1814 at Fort Erie, Upper Canada.

A man of some education and modest contacts, Joseph Willcocks left Ireland on 1 Dec. 1799 and arrived at York (Toronto), Upper Canada, on 20 March 1800. He stayed first with his kinsman William WILLCOCKS. On 1 May he became private clerk to a distant cousin, Receiver General Peter RUSSELL. Later, as a result of Russell's influence, he became receiver and payer of fees in the Surveyor General's Office. Willcocks petitioned successfully for a town lot in York on 15 July; on 12 August another petition for 1,200 acres was also granted, and he later located this land in Hope Township. On 7 August he moved into the Russell household, remaining there until 23 Aug. 1802 when he was dismissed for courting Russell's half-sister Elizabeth*. The same day Willcocks visited Chief Justice Henry ALLCOCK, who remonstrated with Russell, to no avail, on Willcocks's behalf. On 13 October Willcocks moved into the home of Allcock, who proved a worthy patron. He soon received a position engraving deeds for the provincial secretary, William JARVIS. He was appointed registrar of the probate court and marshal of assize on 9 May 1803 and sheriff of the Home District on 4 Sept. 1804.

To this point, there was little indication that Willcocks's career would be controversial. His diary and letters covering his first three years in the province reveal a man interested mainly in social life and good connections who claimed that "mediocrity . . . is the summit of my ambition." He noted that "there are not more than 100 Persons of Consequence in the Whole Province," and he counted many of them among his intimates. Willcocks was not, however, without an interest in politics and was a close observer of events in Ireland. Of Upper Canada, he declared that "politics never ran higher in Ireland than they do here," and that he was careful to assure the government of his loyalty. Consequently, he had "no intercourse with the Republican party." Willcocks was in the gallery of the House of Assembly on 30 May 1801 when Allcock denounced the claim of Angus MACDONELL (Collachie) to continue as that body's clerk. The following month Willcocks and his friend William WEEKES were among Allcock's first visitors after his election to the assembly had been voided by the house. In the subsequent by-election Willcocks voted for the administration's candidate, John Small*, who, however, lost to Macdonell. Relations between Allcock and Weekes became strained after the by-election, and Weekes soon accused Willcocks of being "under the Pay of Government as their informer."

Allcock's influence grew after 1802 as Lieutenant Governor Peter HUNTER came to rely more and more upon his judgement. Willcocks basked in the security of his appointment to the shrievalty: "No Governor or King can dismiss me without [my] having committed some high offence." Although the "officers of Government disagree very much," he noted, "I have the good fortune to be always at the strongest side." In the fall of 1804 Allcock left for England and the following year he was appointed chief justice of Lower Canada. Willcocks was no longer on the strongest side.

Willcocks had been contented with his lot in Upper Canada and had expressed no regrets about leaving his native land. However, the equipoise of his life in the colony seems to have been undermined by the loss of Allcock as a patron and by a gradual rethinking (since 1803) of recent events in Ireland. He had not supported the rebellion by the Society of United Irishmen in 1798. He had had doubts about the wisdom of the legislative union of Ireland with Great Britain in 1800 but had accepted it as a matter of loyalty. The immediate post-union period had, however, occasioned even graver doubts. When in 1803 his brother warned authorities in Dublin of imminent uprisings, Willcocks wondered if he were right in doing so. Willcocks became increasingly certain that true loyalty was to withstand arbitrary rule.

Willcocks's views began to crystallize around his understanding of 18th-century whiggism. According to that tradition, the revolution of 1688 represented successful resistance to authoritarian rule. Even though the British parliament was dominated by whigs throughout the 18th century, the concern over arbitrary power remained a dominant thread of their thought. Given the mixed or balanced constitution, in their view any increase in power by the executive or the crown meant a loss of liberty elsewhere. Consequently, the loyal subject needed to be ever vigilant. Willcocks's outlook on these points was influenced by justice Robert Thorpe* and Charles Burton Wyatt*, the surveyor general.

A successor to Allcock as mentor and friend, Thorpe arrived in Upper Canada in late September or early October 1805. He was Willcocks's neighbour in York, and by coincidence they had cousins who were neighbours in Palmerston. Willcocks was attracted to Thorpe's extraordinary self-confidence, his Irishness,

and his clear criticism of the arbitrariness of the administrations of Hunter and his successor, Alexander GRANT. In May 1806 Willcocks considered Thorpe "my most particular friend." A principle championed by Thorpe and later espoused by Willcocks was that colonial legislatures were independent. Basing his assertion on the authority of Sir William Blackstone's *Commentaries on the laws of England*, Thorpe argued that the legislature of a colony such as Upper Canada, was, as Blackstone put it, "subject . . . to the control of Parliament though (like Ireland, Man, and the rest) not bound by any acts of Parliament, unless particularly named." Thorpe, following Weekes, was struck by how far removed colonial government seemed to be from that ideal. Indeed, the possibility of misrule seemed to increase with distance from the seat of power. Men such as Willcocks and Thorpe were therefore even more sensitive to supposed abuses of power, and even more certain that the only solution to the problem of misrule was to recognize the legitimate legislative independence of the colony and to ensure that executive councillors considered themselves responsible to the legislature rather than to the governor. Many officials in Upper Canada were surprised by these views, not only because the colonial government seemed to them to be comparatively independent but, more important, because such attitudes seemed to show that critics were abusing the positions of trust they held.

What in practice sparked the rise of a political opposition in Upper Canada was the widespread reaction against government changes in land policy, implemented between 1802 and 1804, which increased the fees on land grants and tightened the rules concerning the eligibility of loyalists for free land grants. That opposition was given a parliamentary focus by Weekes's election to the assembly in 1804. In October 1806 he was killed in a duel, and when Thorpe ran, successfully, in the subsequent by-election Willcocks was active in his campaign. Between 1806 and 1808 an opposition group in the assembly formed around whig ideas and around the leadership of Thorpe and then Willcocks. This group seems to have derived its support from those with Irish roots and the small farmers and loyalists who had borne the brunt of the so-called reforms in land policy.

Thorpe and Willcocks had a good perspective on the land issue. Willcocks, for instance, had worked at the land office; moreover, as sheriff, he had seen many people forced to sell their land at auction to pay off debts to merchants. Both had been involved in the foundation and proceedings of the Upper Canada Agricultural and Commercial Society, of which Thorpe was chairman, formed to encourage the cultivation of hemp and to report on improvements made in agriculture and on the need for government assistance to farmers. Since the Executive Council

Willcocks

had responsibility for land grants, after 1802 it became the focus of criticism and the symbol of arbitrary power. The concern with the council combined with the Irishness of Thorpe and Willcocks to add an overtone of nationality to an issue which was, at heart, one of constitutional proprieties and interpretations of law. Condemning the influence of merchants such as Robert HAMILTON, Thorpe characterized the administrations of Hunter, Grant, and Francis Gore* as being "surrounded with the same scotch Pedlars." To this group could be added such key office holders as John McGill* and Thomas Scott*, both from Scotland. John Mills Jackson*, the author of a pamphlet highly critical of the Gore administration, was reported to have reviled "that damned Scotch faction, with the Governor at the head." Willcocks himself denounced the policies originating from the executive since 1802 as nothing less than the "tyrannical" actions of a Scotch clique.

In the face of this challenge to the structure of authority in the colony, Gore moved swiftly to assert the power of his office. Much to the amazement of Willcocks and his friends, who were confident of the security of their appointments and the importance of their connections in Britain, in a short space of time the British government withdrew the appointments of Thorpe and Wyatt and on 23 April 1807 Gore removed Willcocks from the shrievalty, ostensibly for "general and notorious bad conduct." These actions confirmed the group's concern about the dangers of arbitrary authority in the hands of a colonial governor.

Shortly after his dismissal from office, Willcocks moved to Niagara (Niagara-on-the-Lake) where he established the *Upper Canada Guardian; or, Freeman's Journal*. A small four-page sheet, the paper was published from 24 July 1807 to 9 June 1812, "avowedly calculated," as he wrote in the last issue, "to disseminate the principles of political truth, check the progress of inordinate power, and keep alive the sacred flame of a just and rational liberty." Willcocks's criticism of government was well within the limits of these touchstones of whig canon. Yet such was the world of Upper Canadian politics that many in official circles believed that his paper was financed by the United Irishmen, aided by American editors, and controlled by Thorpe. There were reports that Willcocks intended "to revolutionize the province," and that he personally believed the government would censor him within six months of the paper's founding. His friends worried because he was prone to trouble, unaccustomed to business practices, and unlikely to heed advice.

The few issues of the paper that have survived indicate Willcocks's continuing concern with liberty, oppressive land laws, and arbitrary power. Letters in early numbers from "A Loyalist," reputedly Thorpe, argued that civic duty did not involve support for bad rulers: "Surely it would not be loyalty to assist a monarch in rendering himself absolute, who would overturn the constitution, and subvert the law?" The paper received widespread notice. Judge William Dummer Powell* complained in 1809 that it was in almost every house, and Gore lamented the "vulgar attacks" by the "Seditious Printer" which were "relished too much, by the good people of Upper Canada." In fact, however, the paper contained remarkably little editorial matter, and it was premature for Willcocks's enemies to label him and his followers "Rebels, and supporters of unprincipled demagogues." In addition to the newspaper, Willcocks carried on a conveyancing business at Niagara. As he explained in the *Guardian* of 14 April 1810, this undertaking was in part an effort to obviate the exorbitant charges of "the learned and conscientious gentlemen of the Long Robe." He had problems with the paper and does not seem to have published between July 1810 and July 1811. In June 1812 he sold the press, which he said was "growing old and crazy," to Richard HATT for $1,600. He was certain that he could purchase "a new and complete set of Types and Press" for a quarter of the price.

Willcocks won the by-election called in 1807 to replace Solomon Hill in the riding of West York, 1st Lincoln, and Haldimand and took his seat on 26 Jan. 1808. The fact of his election was significant. In the Niagara peninsula Thorpe's opposition and particularly his stinging attack in 1806 upon local magistrates such as John WARREN had, it seemed, unified a number of disparate, but pro-government, political groupings. Certainly the merchants led by Robert Hamilton had closed ranks with their old opponents, loyalist officers such as Ralfe Clench* and small office holders such as Isaac Swayze*. Despite this change Willcocks was re-elected in 1808 and 1812.

Willcocks participated briefly in the fourth session of the fourth parliament before being jailed for contempt of the house. In the election held after parliament was dissolved on 21 May 1808, he was re-elected, without opposition, for the constituency of 1st Lincoln and Haldimand. Although the legislative record of the first session of the fifth parliament (February–March 1809) has not survived, it is clear from the observations of contemporaries that Willcocks assumed the leadership of the parliamentary opposition. He may not have been as clever as Thorpe, who once remarked that Willcocks "did not possess a sufficiency of brains to bait a mouse trap"; none the less, Weekes was dead and Thorpe and Wyatt were no longer on the scene. As the editor of the only newspaper critical of government, Willcocks was in a position to coordinate and sustain the grievances of various groups against the administration. Moreover, as a man who had been dismissed by the governor and jailed by the assembly, he evoked the sympathy of other victims of supposed arbitrariness – small farmers on the one hand and petty loyalists anxious to retain their privileges with respect to land grants on the other. The opposition group for which Willcocks provided a focus throughout his legislative career grew steadily within the assembly; at the peak of its power in 1812 it controlled half the votes in the house. How Willcocks felt about his new political role is not clear. However, this active leadership contrasted sharply with his early years in the colony when as a diarist and a journalist his function was mainly to observe.

Considerable controversy has surrounded the group, and Willcocks in particular, as successive generations of historians have sought to explain the basis of its political opposition. Most often, Willcocks and his associates have been understood simply as "intriguing spirits" frustrated in their search for political appointment. More probably, the opposition group was held together by pragmatic, but not entirely selfish, responses to legitimate grievances related to land-granting, executive power, and social inequities.

The cohesiveness of the parliamentary opposition and its ability to affect the legislative process have also been the subject of a good deal of historiographical debate. Often that debate has concerned the extent to which it is accurate to label the group a "party." It was not a party in the modern political sense. There was no formal structure although, for a time, Thorpe may have used the Upper Canada Agricultural and Commercial Society to provide some cohesion for the group's efforts. Moreover, the parliamentary composition of the group fluctuated over time and, when disagreements occurred, there was not sufficient cohesion to enforce discipline and prevent members from voting independently. But it did mark a departure from the usual pattern of assemblymen working as individuals. The group's composition and behaviour may be examined through a study of the division lists, that is, the recorded votes on individual motions, especially as the number of them increased during Willcocks's career as an MLA. An analysis of the divisions of the second session of the fifth parliament in 1810 indicates that Willcocks had a high percentage of voting agreement with six other members. Among them, David McGregor Rogers*, who had given only lukewarm support to Thorpe in 1807, worked closely with Willcocks and sided with him on 18 of the 21 divisions in which he participated. Benajah Mallory* supported him on 16 of 21 divisions, Peter Howard* on 18 of 23, and John Roblin on 18 of 20. His greatest backing came from John Willson*, who voted with him on 25 of 26 divisions. This group made a number of demands which the administration and its supporters in the assembly opposed: a civil list controlled by the legislature, lower salaries for public officials, easier regulations with respect to loyalist and

military claims for land, and tighter controls over jury practices and electoral procedures. Particularly noteworthy was the group's resistance to several motions to unseat members on the grounds that they were Methodist ministers, and the motions citing John Mills Jackson for libel.

During the third session in 1811, Willcocks, Howard, Mallory, and Willson were in almost complete accord in 18 recorded divisions. Moreover, there was considerable support from Rogers and from the recently elected Willet Casey, Abraham Marsh, David Secord*, and Philip Sovereign. This group continued the fights of the previous session as well as seeking to exclude crown appointees from sitting in the assembly, to broaden the availability of schooling, and to reconsider the rates of assessment.

The high point of the group's opposition came in the last session of the fifth parliament in February and March 1812, under the threat of war with the United States. The colony's administrator, Isaac BROCK, was determined to push through the assembly measures calculated to put the province on a war footing. But he was not to have his way. The nine assemblymen of the previous session who had coalesced under Willcocks's leadership were joined by Thomas Dorland* and John Stinson. Thus, in a house that contained 23 members Willcocks's group now had a near majority. It received timely support from Thomas Barnes Gough, and the speaker, Samuel STREET, who could vote only in instances of a tie, never did. Moreover, the group had considerable legislative experience which Willcocks and Rogers marshalled well. In the face of this strong opposition Brock dissolved parliament on 5 May and called an election, determined to get a loyal (and more pliant) assembly on the eve of war.

Many members were not returned, but Willcocks was among the half-dozen re-elected. He won a resounding victory in 1st Lincoln and Haldimand, defeating Abraham Nelles by 154 votes to 40. Brock had high hopes for the new parliament with its many new members, including his highly regarded attorney general, John MACDONELL (Greenfield). He called an emergency session, which was to run from 27 July to 5 August. Yet even during a time of war, the assembly under the influence of Willcocks and the Ancaster miller Abraham Markle* refused to grant Brock such controversial legislation as the partial suspension of habeas corpus. Unable to secure the house's cooperation, a disgusted Brock lost no time in proroguing it.

Some historians have judged Willcocks's performance in the assembly as if it were nothing more than a prelude to his treason in 1813. In fact, the invasion of Upper Canada by American forces in the summer of 1812 affected neither his opposition nor his loyalty. It needs to be reiterated that he saw no contradiction between the two. In the last issue of the *Guardian* on 9

Willcocks

June 1812 he maintained that he was an enemy "of the measures of the Kings Servants in this colony," asserting at the same time that he was a "constant adherent to the interests of the Country." Indeed, Brock appealed to this loyalty in August 1812 when he sought Willcocks's cooperation in securing an alliance with the Six Nations Indians, whose reserve was in his constituency. Brock's concern was that the Niagara peninsula would be flanked on both sides, should the Indians' support go to the Americans. In spite of ill health, Willcocks took up the task willingly. Early in September he reported to John Macdonell (Greenfield), one of Brock's aides-de-camp, that the mission had been completed successfully and that he was prepared to serve again if called upon. He then returned to Niagara, and he was subsequently mentioned in British army dispatches as one of several gentleman volunteers who served at the battle of Queenston Heights.

Nor was Willcocks's loyalty called into question during the first few months of 1813. The second session of the sixth parliament, held from 25 February to 13 March 1813, passed without incident. The Niagara merchant William Hamilton Merritt* wrote that Willcocks had become a "zealous loyalist": "He has behaved very well on all occasions and so have all his party, altho' they are trusted with no office whatever." Furthermore, early in April William Warren Baldwin*, one of Willcocks's earliest acquaintances in York, noted that his friend was then actively recruiting for the Incorporated Militia. One must either take a cynical approach to Willcocks's actions in the months following the outbreak of the war, or seek another explanation for his treason in the summer of 1813. It is the timing that suggests there was more to his career than a pattern of disloyalty.

His loyalty was shaken when the climate of civil opinion within the province was altered shortly following the capture of York in April 1813 and the invasion of the Niagara peninsula in May. With the stabilization of the military situation after the battle of Stoney Creek on 5 June 1813, local élites, in both the Niagara and the Home districts, were able to demand the imposition of harsh military measures to curb the disaffected [see Elijah BENTLEY]. Willcocks, who had accepted with Thorpe the argument that colonial legislatures had, *de jure*, independent powers, had become convinced during his years in the assembly, and particularly during the important legislative sessions of 1812, that the maintenance of those powers required constant vigilance against executive despotism and arbitrary rule; if the legislature were to retain the right to act independently, it must prove itself worthy of the trust. The collapse of virtually all resistance to the erosion of the constitution by the executive dashed his hopes for the province. When during the *Chesapeake* affair of 1807 [see Sir George

Cranfield BERKELEY] the British forcibly asserted their right to search American ships for deserters, Willcocks wrote to an American correspondent: "The honest part of us say that if the States pocket the indignity they can no longer style themselves a nation." The events of 1813 showed Willcocks that Upper Canadians were willing to pocket the indignity of arbitrary and, what was worse, military rule. No longer were they concerned to defend their liberties. Willcocks was not pro-American. He probably had never overcome his early conviction that the Americans were "not an honest people." But he was certain they would never challenge or subvert the supremacy of the local legislature. Some time in July 1813 Willcocks crossed the Niagara River and offered his services to the American forces.

By the end of August 1813 he had raised and was commanding a unit of expatriate Upper Canadians known as the Company of Canadian Volunteers. Among his fellow officers were such prominent figures from the parliamentary opposition in Upper Canada as Mallory and Markle. Indeed most of the unit's 120 or so recruits were from the constituencies that these three men had represented in the assembly. The Americans valued Willcocks for his "zeal, activity and local knowledge." In November and December 1813 he led scouting and foraging parties to Stoney Creek and the Forty (Grimsby), aided in the burning of Niagara, and participated in the subsequent retreat to Buffalo, N.Y. "Surpassed by none in enterprise and bravery," Willcocks commanded his volunteers at Fort George (Niagara-on-the-Lake) and Fort Erie until on 4 Sept. 1814 he "received a mortal wound by a shot through the right breast" during an action before the latter.

Willcocks was important as an observer of Upper Canadian politics, as the leader of its first sustained opposition group, and as a traitor. Trying to find a consistent thread in his career, some historians have come to the conclusion that his early professions of loyalty must have been lies. In other words, a traitor must be understood in the light of his treason. But this interpretation fails to take account of the developments in Willcocks's maturing political opinions. During the course of his Upper Canadian career he became convinced that resistance to bad government was a duty demanded of loyal subjects. Individuals, colonies, and even nations had to prove that they deserved their independence through the vigilant defence of their rights. He came to see similarities among the situations in Upper Canada, Ireland, and the United States. Having concluded that the union of Ireland and Great Britain was a mistake, he was persuaded by 1806 that the United Irishmen had been right in their active opposition to misrule and that he himself had let Ireland down when she needed him most. Similarly, in their resistance to the British in the critical tests of 1807 and 1812 the Americans proved themselves worthy of nationhood in Willcocks's eyes. When in the summer of 1813 Upper Canadians failed to defend their constitutional liberties and the maintenance of civil law, they forfeited not only Willcocks's sympathy but also his allegiance. To find a consistent and rational thread in Willcocks's political career it is not necessary to discount his words and emphasize his treason; rather, it may be found by paying closer attention to what he said, when he said it, what he did, and when he did it. Firmly in the opposition whig tradition, Willcocks opposed arbitrary and distant power, valued loyalty to his country rather than to his rulers, and believed in the independence of colonial legislatures. At great inconvenience to his own position, he pursued a public course consistent with those whig principles.

ELWOOD H. JONES

[Joseph Willcocks's letterbook and diary are preserved at the PAC in MG 24, C1; the latter has been published under the title "The diary of Joseph Willcocks from Dec. 1, 1799, to Feb. 1, 1803," as an appendix in J. E. Middleton and Fred Landon, *The province of Ontario, infra.*, 2: 1250–322. Scattered issues of the *Upper Canada Guardian; or, Freeman's Journal* (Niagara [Niagara-on-the-Lake, Ont.]), the newspaper he edited from 1807–12, are still extant: the major run is in PRO, CO 42/347 and 42/350; two issues (22 Jan. 1808 and 14 April 1810) have been microfilmed by the Canadian Library Assoc. The other major source of information on Willcocks is PRO, CO 42 (mfm. at PAC); much of the relevant material here has been published as "Political state of U.C.," PAC *Report*, 1892: 32–135. E.H.J.]

AO, MS 503, D-2 (voters' lists, 1812). William Blackstone, *Commentaries on the laws of England* (4v., Oxford, 1765–69; repr. Chicago and London, 1979), 1: 104–5. [Richard Cartwright], *Letters, from an American loyalist in Upper Canada, to his friend in England; on a pamphlet published by John Mills Jackson, esquire: entitled, A view of the province of Upper Canada* (Halifax, [1810]). *Doc. hist. of campaign upon Niagara frontier* (Cruikshank). [J. M. Jackson], *A view of the political situation of the province of Upper Canada, in North America* ... (London, 1809). "Journals of Legislative Assembly of U.C.," AO *Report*, 1911. *Town of York, 1793–1815* (Firth), 157–91, 232–37. H. J. Morgan, *Bibliotheca Canadensis: or, a manual of Canadian literature* (Ottawa, 1867; repr. Detroit, 1968), 393–94. Bernard Bailyn, *The origins of American politics* (New York, 1967). R. M. and Joyce Baldwin, *The Baldwins and the great experiment* (Don Mills, Ont., 1969). C. E. Beardsley, *The victims of tyranny: a tale* (2v., Buffalo, N.Y., 1847). Gates, *Land policies of U.C.* William Kingsford, *The history of Canada* (10v., Toronto and London, 1887–98), 8. J. E. Middleton and Fred Landon, *The province of Ontario: a history, 1615–1927* (5v., Toronto, [1927–28]). H. H. Guest, "Upper Canada's first political party," *OH*, 54 (1962): 275–96. G. [H.] Patterson, "Whiggery, nationality, and the Upper Canadian reform tradition," *CHR*, 56 (1975): 25–44. W. R. Riddell, "Joseph Willcocks: sheriff, member of parliament and traitor," *OH*, 24 (1927): 475–99.

WILLCOCKS, WILLIAM, colonizer, merchant, judge, and office holder; b. January 1735/36, probably in Cork (Republic of Ireland), son of Charles Willcocks and Margaret Russell; m. *c.* 1760 Phoebe Jackson of Birr (County Offaly), and they had eight children; d. 7 Jan. 1813 in York (Toronto), Upper Canada.

William Willcocks spent his childhood with his first cousin, Peter RUSSELL, on one occasion infecting him with lice at their school in Cork. After a seven-year apprenticeship with a Cork wine merchant and two years in Dublin engaged in successful litigation concerning an inheritance, he married about 1760 and began business as a commission merchant in Cork. Although at first he did well he was forced to stop payment in 1778 and thereafter he was in financial difficulties. In 1782 the loss of his two ships reduced him to bankruptcy from which he was finally discharged three years later. His election as sheriff of Cork in 1765 made him eligible for election as mayor, but this prize eluded him. By 1792 Willcocks was an unsuccessful merchant with unfulfilled municipal ambitions; thus he was easily persuaded to leave his family and follow Russell to Upper Canada.

Even before Willcocks's arrival in Niagara (Niagara-on-the-Lake) on 24 Nov. 1792, Russell had procured for him and his son Charles a prestigious front lot in Toronto and 200 acres each in its neighbourhood. On 31 Dec. 1792 Willcocks and some associates were granted Norwich (Whitby and East Whitby) Township; Willcocks received 1,000 acres and each immigrant he settled there would get 200 acres. In January he left for Ireland and Wales to recruit settlers. His return was delayed by the outbreak of war with France, and by his election as mayor of Cork. After serving his year as mayor, in November 1794 he advertised land in Norwich, now Whitby, at prices from one to five guineas per 100 acres plus an annual rent. He sailed from Cork with 33 settlers on 10 May 1795, arriving in New York City on 15 July. Here everything went wrong – all his settlers deserted him, and he finally reached Kingston that October in an open boat, having abandoned at Oswego, N.Y., the goods for his proposed shop in York. While in Albany he again advertised land in Whitby "on moderate terms."

Townships had been granted to accelerate settlement and to permit like-minded people to settle together; all grants were to be free except for government fees. Willcocks's advertisements were "in manifest violation of the principles and conditions," and on 25 May 1796 Whitby was taken from him by Lieutenant Governor SIMCOE. Meanwhile Willcocks's second group of Irish settlers had been

Williams

captured at sea by the French. After Simcoe's departure in July 1796 Russell, now administrator of Upper Canada, persuaded the Executive Council on 4 October to reserve Whitby to Willcocks for two more years, since he had been unaware he could not sell the land and had tried to bring settlers. Willcocks's claims in Whitby were finally rescinded on 28 June 1797 because the French war made it unlikely that he could fulfil the conditions of the grant. The war also postponed the arrival of his family; it was not until 1801 that his wife, three daughters, and his son and daughter-in-law were all in Canada.

By the turn of the century Willcocks was established in York as a shopkeeper, magistrate, and first postmaster, resigning the last position in 1801. In January 1800 he had been appointed a judge of the Home District court – the only judge not a barrister – and judge of the Home District Surrogate Court. He had bought 15,000 acres in Norwich (North and South Norwich) Township, Oxford County, in 1799, but his land speculation proved disastrous; by 1803, when his second daughter, Phoebe, married William Warren Baldwin*, everything Willcocks had was under execution. Although not as radical as Joseph WILLCOCKS, his second cousin once removed, he supported judge Robert Thorpe*'s political activities in 1806–7. In his old age he lived with the Baldwins, but spent much time at his property at Millbrook (Markham) involved in "useless schemes at Mill building," according to his son-in-law. His debts were paid by selling land, and his property, like Peter Russell's, eventually passed to the Baldwin family.

Willcocks's Upper Canadian career owed more to Peter Russell's influence than to his own ability; it demonstrates the power and limitation of 18th-century nepotism.

EDITH G. FIRTH

AO, MS 75. MTL, Robert Baldwin papers, sect.II; W. W. Baldwin papers, sect.[I]–II; Elizabeth Russell papers; Peter Russell papers. PAC, MG 23, HII, 7 (photocopies); RG 1, E1, 46–48; E3, 19. PRO, CO 42/316–22. *Corr. of Hon. Peter Russell* (Cruikshank and Hunter). *Corr. of Lieut. Governor Simcoe* (Cruikshank). C. B. Gibson, *The history of the county and city of Cork* (2v., London, 1861), 2. E. A. Cruikshank, "An experiment in colonization in Upper Canada," *OH*, 25 (1929): 32–77. G. C. Patterson, "Land settlement in Upper Canada, 1783–1840," AO *Report*, 1920.

WILLIAMS, JAMES, land agent and office holder; b. in Kirkcudbrightshire, Scotland; m. secondly Elizabeth Stewart on Prince Edward Island, and they had two sons and two daughters; fl. 1803–15.

Although a detailed biographical background for James Williams survives on Prince Edward Island, little of it can be substantiated. According to this tradition – no doubt originally an oral one – Williams was a native of Kirkcudbright, apprenticed to a tailor, who ran away to serve with a Highland regiment, first in Ireland and then in Canada. According to Thomas DOUGLAS, 5th Earl of Selkirk, however, Williams was a Kirkcudbrightshire man who had worked for his family for many years. Whatever the case, Williams had somehow acquired a knowledge of Gaelic and sufficient business experience to prompt Selkirk to employ him in 1802 as an agent for his projected settlements in North America. When early in 1803 Selkirk acquired lands on Prince Edward Island upon which to place 800 Highland emigrants, Williams was placed in charge of the operation. He was not initially expected to depart for North America with the settlers, his first wife being seriously ill with consumption, but he was nevertheless on board the *Oughton*, which reached the Island on 27 Aug. 1803 with a group of Roman Catholic passengers from North and South Uist. The *Polly* and Selkirk's ship, the *Dykes*, bringing Presbyterian settlers from the Isle of Skye, had arrived some weeks earlier.

Selkirk remained on the Island only long enough to see that his settlers were disembarked and that the process of land allocation had begun on his properties in the Orwell Bay–Pinette River region. Departing then for Upper Canada, he left detailed instructions for Williams to implement over the autumn and winter. Even before his departure, however, hostility between Williams and Dr Angus McAulay*, who with his son had recruited most of the emigrants, was evident, and several confrontations were to occur during Selkirk's absence. McAulay accused Williams of not working hard enough to build houses before winter or to obtain provisions. He also complained of unfairness in the allocation of land, and objected to the easy familiarity between Williams and the official class of the colony. Williams, he maintained, spent most of the winter in Charlottetown and left supervision of the settlement at Belfast to another Kirkcudbright man, who "behaved with insolence." Selkirk was forced to forbid Williams to involve himself in local politics by running for the House of Assembly, although after his return to the Island in September 1804 he was prepared to countenance an appointment to the Council (which, however, was never made). In October, having again left detailed instructions with his agent, Selkirk sailed for home. He would not return to his settlement.

As was typically the case with his North American agents, Selkirk expected far too much from Williams. Accustomed to loyal and dependable Scottish estate managers who knew their place and remained in it, Selkirk was never able to adjust his thinking to conditions in North America, where – especially in his prolonged absence an ocean away – his agents were regarded as important men in their own right and came to behave accordingly. Almost inevitably they acquired their own interests and pretensions, and began to ignore the interests of the employer upon whom their position ultimately depended. The political ambitions of Williams were symptomatic of the problem, which Selkirk was unable to resolve at any of his settlements.

In the first years of his Island agency, Williams apparently was active on Selkirk's behalf. He sought a market for the settlement's anticipated produce in Newfoundland, even buying a schooner for the trade, and successfully established additional emigrants sent by his employer. He also began to build a sawmill at Pinette, intended to cut 600,000 board feet of timber per year. But despite continual drawing of cash upon Selkirk's account, he failed to report to his employer, who by July 1806 was understandably worried about the progress of his settlement. Writing that month to James Stewart, whom he had met in Halifax, N.S., in 1804, Selkirk was not certain Williams had turned "rogue," but he felt there was enough evidence to fit with numerous instances of the "malignant effect of the American climate on . . . honesty." At the same time he advised Williams to allow Stewart to examine the books in Halifax, to report to Stewart monthly, and to clear all bills of exchange with him. In the event, however, Williams managed to defer the ordered visit to Nova Scotia.

Selkirk was soon to be further alarmed by the report of a Nova Scotia attorney, John Fraser, whom Stewart sent to the Island to investigate in late October 1806. That Williams had supposedly received a good deal of money in cash and produce, and that the mill had plainly "turned out to good advantage," cast considerable suspicion on his continued failure to communicate with an employer who had thus far received no return from his lands. Selkirk was now convinced of the need to send a confidential agent to the Island, and the news that his sister Helen's young son Basil Hall had been stationed at Halifax under Sir George Cranfield BERKELEY provided him with his man. Hall visited the Island late in 1807, his mother subsequently complaining to a friend that he was not suited to the business: "You see he has mismanaged matters in the first outset, for by blabbing his intentions all over Halifax, openly before he set out, he infallibly spread the report of himself. . . ." If young Hall's lack of circumspection helped prevent him from getting to the bottom of the affair, his visit nevertheless led Williams to send Selkirk a letter "written under . . . much emotion." Vigorously defending himself against the suspicion of fraud, Williams insisted that he had worked hard on Selkirk's behalf, and denied that the sawmill had been profitable, although much effort and money had been expended upon it. "Your Lordship must not expect every twenty shillings your Agent receives will produce the same to you." Williams here referred to the fact that payment was

often in kind, and the produce hard to market, but his employer could have been pardoned for thinking in other terms.

Nevertheless, James Stewart was well pleased with the effect of Hall's visit and, as a result of his recommendation and a further letter from Williams, Selkirk accepted his agent's explanations. Williams was to return to Britain to justify his conduct in person – as he himself had insisted must be done – but not until he had accommodated another party of Highlanders coming to the Island in 1808. It soon became clear, however, that Williams was unwilling to return to Britain or to keep in touch. By the end of 1809 Selkirk was again in despair.

With Napoleon's blockade of the Baltic ports in 1807 the opening of the colonial timber trade had begun in earnest. Prince Edward Island was one of the first areas to be exploited, and the increased prices of lumber brought many adventurers to the colony. In January 1809 Williams informed Selkirk that he had leased the sawmill and the timber rights on lots 10, 58, 60, and 62 to a William Spraggon, whose references seemed adequate. James Stewart was not impressed with the lessee's line of credit, however, and when Selkirk checked with Spraggon's London bankers they refused to honour any bills of exchange. Moreover, the earl's lawyer informed him that, because of the manner of framing the contract, Spraggon fulfilled its terms by paying bills drawn in London, honoured or not. Whether Williams had been duped or was a party to the business was not at all clear.

Late in 1809 Selkirk wrote a lengthy letter to Captain John MACDONALD of Glenaladale, rehearsing his dealings with Williams and requesting the old Highlander's assistance. There were large arrears of advances to settlers, as well as returns from sales of land, to be accounted for; although Selkirk was not certain that Williams was cheating him, he could no longer leave a man in charge who so neglected making reports and had disobeyed a positive order to present his accounts. By this point Selkirk had given up on the Island and was not prepared to replace Williams, preferring if possible to sell his holdings. A separate letter to Williams informed him that he was under MacDonald's supervision.

In the spring of 1810 Captain John wrote reassuringly to Selkirk of Williams's performance, but his assessment was likely based more on old acquaintance and approval of Williams's politics than on any investigation of the situation, for he was permanently confined to his house. By this time Williams had been absorbed into the "old party": he had married into the family of the former chief justice, Peter STEWART, had become friendly with Chief Justice Caesar Colclough*, and in 1810 was elected sheriff to the complaints of the Loyal Electors, among them Angus

Williams

McAulay. MacDonald had long been an enemy of the Stewart clique, but his dislike of the Loyal Electors had apparently buried old antagonisms. Political overtones were endemic in all Island dealings and help explain why active proprietors such as Selkirk were seldom well served.

In June 1810 Williams indicated his intention of returning to Britain in six weeks (although "the extreme perturbation of mind I labour under rather retards my movements"); two months later he explained that a serious illness made it impossible for him to consider the trip. That illness did not, however, prevent him from becoming embroiled, early the following year, in a heated dispute with Angus McAulay over the building of a road through the Selkirk lands. While Williams and McAulay were publicly jousting, Selkirk was attempting to sort out the affairs of the Island, on both a public and a private level. The two, of course, were inextricably intertwined. In 1810 Selkirk had led the successful efforts of the Island's proprietors to have Charles STEWART appointed attorney general instead of James Bardin Palmer*, leader of the Loyal Electors, and he had temporarily turned his Island affairs over to Stewart until a permanent arrangement could be made. The immediate issues were recovering assets from Spraggon and getting an accounting from Williams. In August 1811 Stewart reported that he was taking legal action against Spraggon; but he complained that he could not hope to succeed against the timber merchant, who had initiated a counter suit in the Court of Chancery, as long as Joseph Frederick Wallet DesBarres*, who was closely allied with Palmer, remained lieutenant governor.

As for Williams, he had attempted in the summer of 1811 to sell nearly 500 tons of pine timber from Selkirk's lots, perhaps in anticipation of his return home. Yet his enemies charged that he was "notoriously known to be in embarrassed circumstances," and even Charles Stewart, who was a friend, had later to admit that Williams was anxious neither to leave the Island nor to turn over papers relating to the Selkirk estates. His failure to provide documentation made it difficult for Stewart to defend Selkirk in the Chancery suit, where Spraggon and his lawyer, William Roubel*, tried to sequester Selkirk's lands for failure to answer the plaintiff's charges. The legal issue, Palmer later insisted, was whether Williams could speak for Selkirk. The court decided that Selkirk must appear personally, a principle that penalized absentee proprietors, whose agents could dispose of their assets but not recover them.

Stewart's death in 1813 forced Selkirk to employ the new attorney general, William Johnston*, as his legal counsel in the maze of Island litigation. The sketchiness of the court records and the loss of many Selkirk papers make it impossible to follow all the litigation through to its conclusion. But late in 1813 Johnston was representing Selkirk before the Court of Chancery in an action to recover the estate papers from Williams (who was appointed inspector of emigrants that same year). This case dragged on through 1814 and 1815. Ultimately, on 22 May 1815, the court ordered an attachment on Williams. It was never served, probably because Williams had left the Island – according to local tradition for Louisiana.

Not only was Selkirk unable to recover his papers from Williams, but his agent had decamped owing him considerable money. It is not clear exactly when Williams had turned "rogue," but in the end he fulfilled his employer's worst suspicions and left the Selkirk property on the Island in complete disarray. Neither Selkirk nor his executors succeeded in sorting out the confusion.

J. M. BUMSTED

PAC, MG 19, E1, ser.1, 37: 14190–92; 39; 50: 19123–44 (transcripts). PAPEI, Acc. 2849, Palmer family papers, nos.14, 129; RG 6, Supreme Court, case papers, 1812, King v. Williams; RS2, Chancery Court, Minutes, 1813–19; James Williams, advertisement, Pinette sawmill, 9 Feb. 1811. Private arch., J. D. Bates (Anton's Hill, Berkshire, Eng.), Hall of Dunglass family letters, Lady Hall to Jean, Lady Hunter, 3 Jan. 1808 (photocopies at National Library of Scotland, Edinburgh). PRO, CO 226/28: 7–23. Douglas, *Lord Selkirk's diary* (White); *Observations on the present state of the Highlands of Scotland, with a view of the causes and probable consequences of emigration* (London, 1805; repr. New York, 1969), 177–98. *Weekly Recorder of Prince Edward Island* (Charlottetown), 18 June 1811, 25 Nov. 1813. Andrew Macphail, "The history of Prince Edward Island," *Canada and its prov.* (Shortt and Doughty), 13: 355–56. M. A. Macqueen, *Skye pioneers and 'the Island'* ([Winnipeg, 1929]), 12. J. M. Bumsted, "Settlement by chance: Lord Selkirk and Prince Edward Island," *CHR*, 59 (1978): 170–88. G. F. Owen, "The voyage of the Polly," reprinted in Archibald Irwin, "Lord Selkirk's settlers in Prince Edward Island," *Prince Edward Island Magazine* (Charlottetown), 4 (1902–3): 421–25; 5 (1904–5): 29–33, 137–40.

WILLIAMS, JENKIN, lawyer, office holder, seigneur, judge, and politician; b. *c.* 1734 in Wales; m. Anne Jones, and they had at least three children; d. 30 Oct. 1819 at Quebec, Lower Canada.

Jenkin Williams left Wales in 1767 in order to avoid a lawsuit against him for forgery. He emigrated to New York to continue practising as a lawyer without harassment. There he met William Smith*, who advised him to settle at Quebec instead. Williams reached that town in September 1767 and on 16 October secured a commission as a lawyer. He quickly succeeded in making a favourable impression on people. Only a few months after he arrived Attorney General Francis Maseres* judged him to be "a very worthy well-behaved man, very sober and assiduous, and of sufficient abilities to make a good attorney"; already he foresaw a profitable career for Williams in the colony.

In 1768 Williams was appointed register of the Court of Chancery. In the autumn of 1773 he was made a commissioner, along with Adam Mabane* and Thomas Dunn, to act during the absence in England of the province's chief justice, William Hey*. In May 1776 Governor Guy Carleton selected him to serve, together with François Baby and Gabriel-Elzéar Taschereau, as a commissioner to visit the parishes between Trois-Rivières and Kamouraska in order to conduct an inquiry about people who might have helped the rebels during the American invasion [see Benedict Arnold; Richard Montgomery*]. Less than a decade after his arrival in the colony Williams was regarded by Maseres as one of the two foremost British lawyers there, the other being Henry Kneller*. The Canadians held him in high esteem and often called on his services, according to the attorney general; even François-Joseph Cugnet*, whom Maseres termed a severe critic, was said to have expressed the opinion that Williams was worthy of being elevated to the bench.

Williams also soon succeeded in ensuring for himself a comfortable financial situation if not prosperity; he was able to have his children educated in England and to purchase several properties by the 1770s. In November 1770 he paid 10,000 livres, the equivalent of £450 or £500, for a large property on Rue Saint-Jean, where he took up residence. Two years later he purchased by tender another lot next to his home, with a house and outbuildings. In addition, from 1772 to 1776 he bought several lots on the Rivière Saint-Charles, where he made his country home. In July 1777 Williams sold his residence to Chief Justice Peter Livius* for £1,250 but continued living in Upper Town with his family, which included at least one son. On 4 September he and his wife purchased the fief of Montplaisant, a property detached from the fief of Villeray and located outside the Saint-Louis gate; Williams took the oath of fealty and homage for it in May 1781.

By 1777, as his career developed, Williams had become justice of the peace, clerk of the Legislative Council, and clerk of the Court of Appeal. He kept the first clerkship until 1791 but had to give up the second to become solicitor general, a position to which he was named on 14 Dec. 1782 and which he held until Jonathan Sewell* replaced him in October 1793. In appointing Williams to the solicitor generalship, to which was attached the office of inspector general of the royal domain, Governor Haldimand was filling a post that had long been vacant. The decision was in fact directed against Attorney General James Monk*, who had alienated the governor's trust through his conduct and who was thus deprived of some of the lucrative functions he had exercised till then. As a result Monk developed a hostility to his colleague. When Haldimand decided in 1783 to retain the services of Williams in his action against John Cochrane [see James Dunlop] because he thought Monk too deeply compromised with the merchant group, his choice did nothing to heal the breach between the two men.

In 1784 Williams returned to England, where he saw Smith and Carleton. During his meetings with Lord Sydney, the Home secretary, he apparently asked for the chief justiceship of Quebec, which was vacant. In fact, since Livius's removal from office in 1778, Williams had been serving as one of the three commissioners appointed to act in his place. Lord Sydney gave him to understand, however, that the old charge of forgery still standing against him impeded his accession to such a high office, especially since the unhappy matter was not unknown in the province of Quebec. Because he was sympathetic towards Williams, Sydney told him to take steps to have the criminal proceedings lifted, and Williams eventually succeeded in doing so. Otherwise his services were giving complete satisfaction to his superiors; his presence in the colony was considered indispensable and he was soon asked to return to his post. He received instructions from Carleton and sailed on 2 Nov. 1785 for Quebec.

When Monk was dismissed in the spring of 1789, Williams anticipated that the choice of attorney general would fall on him; then, with the resignation of Edward Southouse, he hoped to succeed to the post of judge of the Court of Common Pleas. But in vain. This double disappointment left him with the impression that his long record of service was rather badly rewarded. After being chosen as clerk of the new Executive Council which had been created by the Constitutional Act of 1791, he finally was elevated to the bench on 12 Jan. 1792, succeeding Mabane, who had died a few days earlier, on the Court of Common Pleas in the District of Quebec. When the judiciary was reorganized in December 1794, he moved to the Court of King's Bench.

During the 25 years in which he had practised as a lawyer Williams had never disappointed the expectations held of him. His legal opinions reveal that he was a competent jurist, able to make fine distinctions and be completely impartial, even on the politically divisive questions of the day. Of a temperate, even conservative bent, he generally remained aloof from partisan struggles. Although he did play an active role in the committee set up in the autumn of 1773 to demand an assembly, a year later he avoided joining his compatriots who sought repeal of the Quebec Act. On the question of the law in force in the province, his opinions, without showing bias, were nevertheless

Williams

rather of a kind that the Canadians found gratifying. For example, he deplored the attitude of the British who were demanding that English law be reinstituted, particularly in commercial matters; he considered that their position was based on ignorance fostered "by some misinformed English Practitioners." But he correctly judged that under the Quebec Act English law had to govern in all transactions concerning land held in free and common socage, particularly in matters of descent and dower. Again, on the question of replacing the seigneurial system he submitted to the Legislative Council at the time of the 1790 inquiry [see Thomas-Laurent Bédard*] a report which, far from echoing the prejudices of the British, was confined to a descriptive analysis of the consequences of instituting land tenure in free and common socage; it was apparent that in his opinion the great majority of censitaires, who were of small means, would suffer seriously from the change in land tenure and that this disadvantage would in the end be more important than the advantages which the crown and the seigneurs might draw from it. His views were of a sort to please Carleton, as well as Haldimand. Neither of them had, for that matter, failed to show him their esteem, since they had called upon him over the years to discharge increasingly important duties.

Although he was in his 60s, Williams nevertheless continued to be active. From the 1790s he also exercised the functions of commissioner to receive the oath from assemblymen and legislative councillors as well as from office holders. He was a member of the commission responsible for administering the Jesuit estates. As attorney for Haldimand's sole legatee, Williams sold the fief of Grand-Pabos to Felix O'HARA in 1796; in 1801 he was appointed attorney for the executors of former governor Murray* to conduct the sale of the seigneuries of Rivière-du-Loup and Madawaska to Henry CALDWELL. He continued to engage in land transactions on his own account. Having repurchased in 1801 the two properties that he had previously owned on Rue Saint-Jean, he lived on one and then resold it for £1,500 in February 1806. Two months later he bought the house on Rue Saint-Louis owned by John ELMSLEY, who had died the previous year; he let it go in March 1811 for £1,200, having purchased from John Richardson* the previous month two properties, one with a large stone house and outbuildings on Rue des Pauvres (Côte du Palais), for £1,800, paying £450 in cash. Williams had also received 400 acres in Milton Township in 1803 and 26,810 acres in Stanfold Township in 1807.

After 20 years on the bench Williams retired on 22 May 1812 because of his advanced age. He then received an annual pension of £500 as a "reward for his long and meritorius services." He retained until death the office as honorary member of the Executive Council to which he had been appointed on 7 Jan.

1801, and as well remained a member of the Legislative Council, to which he had acceded two years later. On 13 July 1819 he bequeathed almost all his property to his wife, as well as some lands to his grandchildren Anne Margaret and John Jenkin McLean. Williams died at Quebec on 30 Oct. 1819. He had had a long career during which he commanded respect and won well-deserved honours through his loyalty and competence. His funeral was held in the Cathedral of the Holy Trinity on 3 Nov. 1819.

ANDRÉ MOREL

AC, Québec, Testament olographe de Jenkin Williams, 20 Nov. 1819 (see P.-G. Roy, Inv. testaments, 3: 154). ANQ-Q, CE1-61, 3 Nov. 1819, 17 Sept. 1824; CN1-16, 4 févr. 1806, 5 mai 1810, 25 févr. 1811, 29 janv. 1812, 26 juill. 1815; CN1-25, 4 sept. 1777; CN1-205, 24 mars 1775; 12 août 1776; 2 janv., 26 mai, 19 juill. 1777; 23 oct., 9 nov. 1778; 30 sept. 1780; 5 juill. 1781; CN1-207, 28 août 1769, 3 nov. 1770; CN1-230, 10 sept. 1793; 26 janv. 1796; 24 juin, 22 oct. 1799; 17 août 1801; 29 janv. 1802; 18 janv., 5 févr. 1803; 21 août 1806; 16 juin 1807; 16 janv., 9 mars 1811; CN1-248, 19 janv. 1773; CN1-262, 20 avril 1805, 26 avril 1806. BL, Add. mss 21736 (copy at PAC). PAC, MG 11, [CO 42] Q, 92: 166; MG 23, GI, 5; MG 24, I153. Bas-Canada, chambre d'Assemblée, Journaux, 1798: 117; 1799–1800: 82; 1801: 264; 1802: 179: 1812–13, app.E, no.17; 1814, app.A; Statuts, 1793–94, c.6. "Les dénombrements de Québec" (Plessis), ANQ Rapport, 1948–49: 67, 104, 117, 154, 213. Docs. relating to constitutional hist., 1759–91 (Shortt and Doughty; 1918), 1: 487–501; 2: 589–91, 711–22; 1791–1818 (Doughty and McArthur; 1914), 68, 348–49. Extract of the proceedings of a committee of the whole Council under the following order of reference relative to a conversion of the present tenures in the province of Quebec into that of free and common soccage (Quebec, 1790). "Journal par Baby, Taschereau et Williams" (Fauteux), ANQ Rapport, 1927–28: 435–99; 1929–30: 138–40. Kelley, "Jacob Mountain," ANQ Rapport, 1942–43: 231. [Francis Maseres], Additional papers concerning the province of Quebeck: being an appendix to the book entitled, "An account of the proceedings of the British and other Protestant inhabitants of the province of Quebeck in North America, [in] order to obtain a house of assembly in that province" (London, 1776), 9; Maseres letters (Wallace), 69–70, 76. Smith, Diary and selected papers (Upton), 1: 153, 159, 184, 189–90, 193–94, 284; 2: 5, 10, 173, 175, 311. The trial of David McLane for high treason, at the city of Quebec, in the province of Lower-Canada; on Friday, the seventh day of July, A.D. 1797: taken in short-hand, at the trial (Quebec, 1797), 3. Quebec Gazette, 2 Nov. 1769; 18 June 1772; 12 Dec. 1776; 2 May, 12 June 1777; 29 June 1786; 1 March, 1 Aug. 1787; 31 July 1788; 25 March 1790; 21 July, 1, 19 Aug. 1791; 19 Jan., 23 Aug. 1792; 11 April, 10 Oct. 1793; 13 Feb., 3 July 1794; 29 Jan., 25 June 1795; 27 June 1805; 28 May 1812; 15 April 1813; 19 Oct. 1815; 24 June, 1 Nov. 1819. Quebec Mercury, 2 Nov. 1819. F.-J. Audet, "Solliciteurs généraux et inspecteurs généraux du domaine du Roy," BRH, 39 (1933): 277. Bouchette, Topographical description of L.C., 371. Caron, "Inv. de la corr. de Mgr Briand," ANQ Rapport, 1929–30:

128; "Inv. de la corr. de Mgr Hubert et de Mgr Bailly de Messein," 1930–31: 204, 226. Desjardins, *Guide parl.*, 29, 57. *The encyclopedia of Canada*, ed. W. S. Wallace, (6v., Toronto, [1948]), 6. Langelier, *Liste des terrains concédés*, 10, 979. J.-J. Lefebvre, "Tableau alphabétique des avocats de la province de Québec, 1765–1849," *La rev. du Barreau de la prov. de Québec* (Montréal), 17 (1957): 285–92. Lucien Lemieux, "Juges de la province du Bas-Canada de 1791 à 1840," *BRH*, 23 (1917): 87–90. "Papiers d'État," PAC *Rapport*, 1890: 150, 207, 278, 304. "Papiers d'État – Bas-Canada," PAC *Rapport*, 1891: 8, 11, 26, 28, 35–36, 59, 143; 1892: 159, 170, 174, 182, 185–86, 198, 208, 265, 268–69, 271, 273, 280, 291; 1893: 40, 66, 73, 85, 109. *Quebec almanac*, 1780: 33–34; 1791: 40, 83; 1792: 98–99, 104, 152; 1794: 68, 72, 74; 1796: 67; 1800: 87–88; 1805: 14, 17, 21; 1815: 40, 43, 46–48. P.-G. Roy, *Inv. concessions*, 1: 25; 2: 96, 98; 3: 115, 286; 4: 129; *Les juges de la prov. de Québec*, 509, 577. Turcotte, *Le Conseil législatif*, 18, 63–64, 303–4. Burt, *Old prov. of Quebec* (1968), 2: 32, 39–40, 117. *Canada and its prov.* (Shortt and Doughty), 15: 148. Caron, *La colonisation de la prov. de Québec*, 1: 141, 214, 256, 263, 304–15. R. C. Dalton, *The Jesuits' estates question, 1760–1888: a study of the background for the agitation of 1889* (Toronto, 1968), 37–38, 44–46. F.-X. Garneau, *Histoire du Canada depuis sa découverte jusqu'à nos jours*, Hector Garneau, édit. (8e éd., 9v., Montréal, 1944–46), 6: 264–65, 275–76, 285. William Kingsford, *The history of Canada* (10v., Toronto and London, 1887–98), 6: 451; 7: 196. Lanctot, *Le Canada et la Révolution américaine*, 173. Neatby, *Administration of justice under Quebec Act*, 58, 63–64, 88–89, 185–87, 192, 245–53, 259–60, 300, 305–6, 324, 340–41, 351–54; *Quebec*, 156–57. Sulte, *Hist. des Canadiens-français*, 8: 78; *Mélanges hist.* (Malchelosse), 3: 41–49. Trudel, *L'esclavage au Canada français*, 142, 344, 364. L. F. S. Upton, *The loyal whig: William Smith of New York & Quebec* (Toronto, 1969), 162, 185. "Panet *vs* Panet," *BRH*, 12 (1906): 120–23. J.-P. Wallot, "Plaintes contre l'administration de la justice (1807)," *RHAF*, 20 (1966–67): 283.

WINSLOW, EDWARD, army officer, politician, judge, office holder, and author; b. 20 Feb. 1746/47 in Plymouth, Mass., son of Edward Winslow and Hannah Dyer; m. Mary Symonds, and they had at least 14 children; d. 13 May 1815 in Fredericton, N.B.

Edward Winslow was the direct descendant of the first Edward Winslow to settle in North America, who arrived on the *Mayflower* in 1620 and became the valued deputy of Governor William Bradford of Plymouth Colony. Members of the family continued to serve Plymouth Colony and later Massachusetts Bay Colony in a variety of posts at the local, provincial, and imperial levels. Our subject, "Ned" Winslow, was imbued with this tradition of public service from his earliest years. He grew up in a great mansion, overlooking Plymouth Rock, which his father had built to entertain the social élite of Massachusetts. After graduating from Harvard College in 1765, Winslow began to follow in his father's footsteps as a local official in Plymouth, and served as naval officer, registrar of wills, and clerk of the Court of General Sessions. He also moved conspicuously in the governing circles of tory Boston. At one time he devised an elaborate system to reorganize the chaotic provincial records which won the approbation of Governor Thomas Hutchinson, and in 1769 he was a prime mover in the establishment of the Old Colony Club, an organization devoted to memorializing the founders of Plymouth Colony. When in 1770, at the age of 23, Winslow was asked to deliver the public address celebrating the 150th anniversary of the landing at Plymouth Rock, he could fairly believe that his career was launched.

Two shadows threatened these bright prospects. One was a heavy load of debt. The family's lavish style of life far exceeded the money available, and these "old debts" would hamper Winslow's ambitions for the rest of his life. Even more ominous was festering public discontent with the Massachusetts colonial government. A tory since birth, Winslow responded to radical criticism with an intense partisanship that was characteristic of his personality. His authorship in 1773 of the "Plymouth Protest," condemning the Sons of Liberty as a "sett of cursed, venal, worthless Raskalls," may have been admirably loyal but it was also reckless. Likewise, by refusing to cooperate with the Plymouth County Convention and by organizing a private tory police company to maintain order in Plymouth, Winslow eventually made himself so "obnoxious" to his countrymen that he was stripped of his public offices, and in October 1774 "the Great Mob ... hunted me from the Country. ..."

When hostilities broke out on 19 April 1775 Winslow rushed to fight with the British regulars at Lexington. Commended for valour by his commander, Lord Hugh Percy, he continued to serve the army in a paramilitary capacity throughout the rebels' eight-month siege of Boston; during this time he was appointed by Lieutenant-General Thomas Gage* collector for the port of Boston and registrar of probate for Suffolk County. In early 1776 Winslow made the painful decision to leave his family and his native land and go with the British troops to Halifax, N.S. There, on 30 July, he was commissioned muster master general of the loyalist forces in North America with the provincial rank of lieutenant-colonel, a post he held until the end of the war. The appointment stirred his love of display: informed that no particular uniform was prescribed, he ordered one "'with a blue coat, scarlet cape, and a scarlet lining with plain white buttons.'" Later in the summer he accompanied the troops under General Sir William Howe to their new base in New York.

The American revolution brought real suffering and deprivation to the Winslow family. Eventually his

Winslow

aged parents, his two maiden sisters, and his own young family had to abandon their beloved Plymouth and huddle as indigent exiles in the garrison town of New York, totally dependent on Edward and the British army for their future. Their distress pained Winslow deeply. Yet the war also brought Winslow's personal talents and sensibilities into brilliant juxtaposition: his gallantry, his organizational flair, and his passionate sympathies all expanded and found new purpose. His periodic visits to the loyalist army units and his work with the muster rolls and pay sheets brought him into frequent contact with the men of the regiments and he established a close bond with all ranks of loyalist soldiers. Like them, he deeply resented British favouritism to rebel deserters, "scoundrels who have just emerged from the very center of rebellion," over the steadfast loyalist corps. Like them, he based his hopes on the outcome of the war. And like them also, he increasingly blamed Great Britain for the frustration of those hopes: "There has been such a damnable series of treating & retreating – pidling, Conciliating – & commissionering that fighting (which is the only remedy for the American disorder) has been totally suspended." The loyalist troops' disdain for British timidity reached its height with General Sir Henry Clinton, who provoked Winslow's most scathing comments: "The Stupor which Seem^d to seize his Excy, & which nothing short of a Supernatural event can rouse him from – effectually prevented any military enterprise."

Except for an exciting and successful series of coastal raids on Rhode Island, directed by Edmund FANNING, during the summer of 1779, Winslow spent most of the war monitoring muster rolls. At the end of hostilities, he had but little choice as to his future. He could not go to Massachusetts where he was legally proscribed. Family debts and responsibilities kept him from taking the preferred course to England where the best jobs lay. He thus reluctantly accepted Sir Guy CARLETON's suggestion that he go to Nova Scotia as an agent for the loyalist regiments and lay out lands for the 6,000 troops and their families who would eventually follow.

After having settled his own family in Granville, N.S., in early 1783, Winslow worked assiduously to get the best possible situation for himself and his loyalist troops. He cultivated the friendship of Governor John Parr* and other Halifax officials; but, while these gentlemen proved willing to share their table with Winslow, they clung tight to their power over land grants. In particular, they resisted Winslow's determination to settle his loyalist regiments and their families on a single block of land because they understood that realization of this plan would in effect establish a separate, potentially competitive political community within Nova Scotia.

The rebuffs of the "Nabobs of Nova Scotia," as he

later called them, simply spurred Winslow on. He abandoned his original plan to settle his troops in peninsular Nova Scotia and, in company with several other loyalist officers, began to explore the possibilities on the north side of the Bay of Fundy. When they reached the Saint John River valley, where many loyalist refugees were already encamped, they knew they were home. The bounteous natural resources of the river valley coupled with its great distance from Halifax immediately appealed to the loyalist officers. And it was there in July 1783 that Winslow made his provocative suggestion that the area north of the Bay of Fundy be partitioned from Nova Scotia to become a separate loyalist province, "& if it does it shall be the most Gentlemanlike one on earth."

Winslow's proposal singles him out as the prophet of the future province of New Brunswick and remains the most distinctive contribution of his long career. The structural elements in his suggestion were not, however, entirely new. The need for a separate loyalist province to serve as a haven for those supporters of the British cause who could not return to their former homes in America had long been recognized by the British government, and an abortive attempt to meet it was made in 1780 when the northern portion of what is now Maine was designated the province of New Ireland [see John CALEFF]. Moreover, the policy of resettling the loyalist troops in British North America along regimental lines, so that they could be easily called up again if the need arose, was first suggested by Sir Guy Carleton. Winslow's key contribution was in combining the idea of a separate loyalist province with Sir Guy's wish to keep the loyalist military organization intact and in affixing these concepts to a particular site – the northern region of Nova Scotia, centring on the Saint John River valley.

Underlying Winslow's proposal were a number of ideological assumptions which he shared with many of his fellow loyalists and which were vitally important to the development of New Brunswick. Two of these were epitomized by his vow that the new province would be "the most Gentlemanlike one on earth." First and foremost, it was to be a loyalist province, governed by the valiant exiles with no concessions to the Acadians, Indians, or "old inhabitants" already living in the area. Secondly, its leaders were to be members of the loyalist élite, the officers and gentlemen whose impeccable backgrounds and long experience in colonial affairs would enable them to establish a model government. Thirdly, the active support of the British government was assumed. By appointing firm loyalists to the chief positions, by supporting such key social institutions as education and the Church of England, and by reserving the West Indian trade for her colonial subjects, Britain was to lay the social and economic foundations of the new province. Finally, Winslow foresaw a competitive relationship with the United States. He dreamed fondly of the day when the very cream of American society, disillusioned by their faltering republic and deprived of their vital West Indian trade, would move north and settle in his projected province. This theme of ultimate revenge provoked Winslow's most famous prophecy (words now engraved in bronze in the Centennial Building at Fredericton):

Yes – by God! we will be the envy of the American states. . . . When the people of the neighboring states shall observe our operations. When they see us in the enjoyment of a regular system of Government – protected by the mother Country – not sad'led with enormous taxes and compare their state with ours, Will they not envy us? Surely they will. Many of their most respectable inhabitants will join us immediately.

To realize his goal of a separate loyalist province, Winslow communicated his proposals and his hopes to numerous colleagues in Nova Scotia and Great Britain. The project won ready assent among refugees frustrated by lack of employment and difficulties in obtaining land grants, and an intricate, year-long political struggle ensued between the advocates of a new province and those wishing to retain the political integrity of Nova Scotia. This campaign is known in Canadian history as the partition movement. Winslow was only one of several protagonists in the struggle, but he was an important one. His most significant conquest was Brigadier-General Henry Edward Fox, the commander-in-chief of British forces at Halifax and brother to the powerful British politician, Charles James Fox. In July 1783, through the agency of his good friends George Duncan LUDLOW and Ward Chipman*, Winslow was appointed Fox's secretary and he met with the general in Halifax that August. Chipman had sternly admonished Winslow to "be a man of business, indulge your *convivial penchant* with caution," and Winslow clearly took the hint. Fox not only became his warm friend but joined his own ambitions to Winslow's plans for the new loyalist settlements, at one point seeking the governorship of the proposed new province for himself. Among other important allies whom Winslow helped organize in favour of partition were the Penobscot Associated Loyalists, the community of Maine timber merchants who had emigrated *en masse* to St Andrews in order to remain within the British navigation system [*see* William GALLOP]; several key leaders of the loyalist refugee groups who were settling along the Saint John River, such as Amos BOTSFORD, Gilfred Studholme*, and George Leonard*; and William HAZEN, the most prominent of the pre-loyalist settlers.

The second key task that Winslow performed during the partition movement was to gather information regarding the economic and political condition of British North America and transmit it to London. This information was used by his loyalist colleagues and their supporters to convince the imperial government not only of the need for a separate loyalist province but also of its viability. The political arguments advanced to support their cause centred on the inability of Halifax to govern the distant settlements across the Bay of Fundy. Wartime promises of a separate loyalist establishment were also emphasized, as was the incompatibility of the refugees with the inhabitants of Nova Scotia, many of whom had supported the American revolution. Unspoken, but surely not unnoticed by London, was the welcome relief a new province would offer in providing jobs for some of the loyalist placemen who had been besieging Whitehall since the onset of the war. The economic arguments supporting partition emphasized the natural resources of the area. Winslow and his colleagues sent to London detailed estimates of the timber, fishing, and agricultural potential of the proposed new colony. These were used to convince the British government that the area had a solid economic base and could look forward to a brisk supply trade with the British West Indies.

The partition movement did not, of course, go unopposed. Governor Parr and the Nova Scotia Council used their influence to belittle the need for a separate province, which would diminish their political jurisdiction and present a formidable rival in London, the loyalists having many highly placed friends there. Halifax officials, moreover, held immense tracts of unoccupied land in the Saint John River valley and the Cumberland area; these would, they knew, fall forfeit if a new government took over the northern region. Resistance came as well from within the proposed new province. Along the Saint John River a majority of the old inhabitants and many dissident loyalist soldiers and refugees clustered around the lawyer Elias Hardy* in order to oppose partition and express their desire to remain part of Nova Scotia. Basically, these men resented the way in which Winslow and the other loyalist agents had favoured themselves and their allies in the distribution of lands, and they did not wish to see this exclusive officer group permanently established in power. Yet despite the strenuous opposition, the campaign organized by Winslow and his colleagues, and backed by powerful English friends, proved decisive. On 18 June 1784 the Privy Council approved the establishment of the province of New Brunswick, expressly to provide an adequate refuge for the "great number of Your Majesty's Loyal Subjects," and in September of the same year the Great Seal was passed, bearing the significant motto *Spem Reduxit* ("Hope Restored").

Unfortunately for Edward Winslow his labours for

Winslow

the new province were not capped by a personal triumph. At the last moment Fox declined the governorship of New Brunswick and Winslow had no other such patron in England. As he saw it, all the lucrative posts went to a "pack of heavy ass'd pensioners living in England," while those actually working out in the new settlements had to settle for high-sounding, low-paying appointments. "The assault on St. James," he noted bitterly, "was more successful than the assault on St. John." Nevertheless, Winslow's actual appointments in New Brunswick were prestigious. A member of the Council and surrogate general of the province since its inception, he became deputy paymaster of contingent expenses for the army in 1785, judge of the Inferior Court of Common Pleas for York County, commissioner of the New England Company in 1791, muster-master of the King's New Brunswick Regiment, secretary to the international boundary commission in 1796 and 1798, and deputy surveyor of the king's woods in 1806. Thus he did have considerable public influence. In his first years in New Brunswick he made imaginative contributions to public policy, among them his suggestions regarding the accoutrements Governor Thomas CARLETON's dignity would require: "He shall have an elegant house – a Church a State house – an assembly room – & a playhouse if he pleases." Such fancies were soon stilled by the economic necessities of pioneer New Brunswick and Winslow's own state of personal indebtedness. "Blast Poverty – 'tis a devil incarnate," he fumed in 1786, and in 1792 he regaled John Graves SIMCOE with the inability of new, sparsely settled colonies to support men of education and refined sensibilities in public life. Winslow's frustrations over the brutal economics of the frontier were shared by many of New Brunswick's loyalist élite, with the result that "our Gentlemen have all become potato farmers – & our Shoemakers are preparing to legislate."

Winslow's deep commitment to public life had therefore to take a back seat while he concentrated his energies on farming in order to support his wife and children, two sisters, and three household slaves. Yet he never lost faith in the province he had helped establish. Two visits to prosperous New England in the 1790s produced much nostalgia but no change of heart. And his most notable publication, the "Tammany" letters published in the *Royal Gazette and New-Brunswick Advertiser* in 1802, was an extended denunciation of his faint-hearted comrades who were deserting New Brunswick for lusher pastures. Winslow characterized those returning south as "a few giddy eccentric and discontented characters [who] . . . meanly skulked into the United States . . . there they have become literally 'hewers of wood and drawers of water' and . . . they are compelled to consider the most meritorious actions of their lives as the most atrocious offences which they ever committed." Those who had left for Upper Canada were "not quite so culpable" but were "influenced by the same extraordinary caprice."

Ironically, relief finally came to Winslow not out of his services to New Brunswick but from a brief wartime contact. In 1804 he was called to England to justify his accounts as deputy paymaster of contingencies, and while he was there his old military commander, Lord Hugh Percy, now Duke of Northumberland, arranged for his appointment to the New Brunswick Supreme Court. When the appointment was made in 1807, the fact that Winslow was not a lawyer upset the local bar and Lieutenant Governor Carleton, but he himself was grateful for the opportunity to put his affairs in order at last. In 1808 Winslow served briefly as president of the province and courageously disobeyed his instructions in order to disband a mutinous militia in time for spring planting. His deep-seated resentment of the United States surfaced anew during the War of 1812, and he prayed that Great Britain would finally give the Americans "the chastisement which they so richly deserve." He died in 1815, pursued to the grave by his twin nemeses, debt and gout. His wife and several children survived him. In 1816 the New Brunswick House of Assembly granted £100 apiece to Winslow's two unmarried daughters in recognition of his "numerous services" to the province.

Winslow's correspondence is the single most important collection of loyalist personal papers in Canada. By turns erudite, passionate, vitriolic, and high humoured, his letters vividly record the drama of the loyalist exodus to British North America as well as the minutiae of daily life in early New Brunswick. Winslow could pierce an opponent with a phrase. Thus Elias Hardy was a "pettifogging notary public," Richard John Uniacke* "a great lubberly insolent irish rebel," and the waspish Jonathan ODELL "a High priest of the order of Melchisedec." Mainly, however, Winslow's rhetoric reflected his enormous zest for life and his profound love of humanity. The climate of New Brunswick had "all the marks of virginity about it. It breaks wind furiously – spits a little – but we continue to manage it." And the disputatious New Brunswick Assembly was simply another "Lilliput," composed of "fellows here who three years agoe did not know that Magna Charta was not a Great Pudding." As for himself, Winslow confided, "If I was to be transformed into an instrument of musick . . . I would chuse to be a fiddle because it would requre some skill and taste to play upon me." Winslow certainly was a finely tuned instrument, not adept at clearing a wilderness, but admirably suited to civilizing and cultivating a community of people.

ANN GORMAN CONDON

868

A large selection from Winslow's correspondence, edited by William Odber Raymond*, has been published as *Winslow papers, A.D. 1776–1826* (Saint John, N.B., 1901). The letters he wrote under the pseudonym Tammany appeared in the *Royal Gazette and New-Brunswick Advertiser* (Saint John) on 21 July and 8 Sept. 1802. Raymond also edited Winslow's "A sketch of the province of Nova Scotia, and chiefly of such parts as are settled," N.B. Hist. Soc., *Coll.*, 2 (1899–1905), no.4: 142–62.

N.B. Museum, H. T. Hazen coll.: Ward Chipman papers. PAC, MG 23, D1, ser.1, 1: 356–60; 4: 1318–49, 1362–67; 6: 7–8; 10: 297–99; D4: 10–10b; GII, 10, vol.2: 1035–42. PANB, RG 2, RS6. PANS, MG 1, 939: 22; 940: 4. PRO, CO 188/1–19, CO 217/56–59; PC 2/129: 192, 412; PRO 30/55 (copies at PAC). UNBL, MG H2, Edward Winslow, affidavit to loyalist claims commission, 28 Oct. 1783; fragment of letter, c.1780; letters, Winslow to Joseph Chew, c.1797; to Ward Chipman, 7 July 1783, 27 April 1784, 25 April 1785; to John Coffin, 4 Oct. 1784; to Robert Hallowell, 2 May 1778; to George Leonard, 5 Oct. 1784; to Daniel Lyman, 12 March 1800; to Benjamin Marston, 16 March 1786; to J. G. Simcoe, 7 April 1792; to Gregory Townsend, 17 Jan. 1793; to Benning Wentworth, 9 July 1778; to Sir John Wentworth, 25 July 1807; to Edward Winslow Jr, 13 June 1811; Ward Chipman to Winslow, 25 June 1783, 14 March 1784; H. E. Fox to Winslow, 14 April 1784; E. G. Lutwyche to Winslow, 5 Jan. 1807. William Bradford, *Of Plymouth Plantation, 1620–1647*, ed. S. E. Morison (New York, 1952), 86n. G.B., Hist. MSS Commission, *Report on American manuscripts in the Royal Institution of Great Britain*, [comp. B. F. Stevens, ed. H. J. Brown] (4v., London, 1904–9), 4: 243. N.B., House of Assembly, *Journal*, 1786–1814; Legislative Council, *Journal*, [1786–1830]. *Royal commission on American loyalists* (Coke and Egerton). *New Brunswick Royal Gazette* (Saint John), 1785–1815. *Saint John Gazette* (Saint John), 1783–1807.

Jones, *Loyalists of Mass.* Sabine, *Biog. sketches of loyalists.* Shipton, *Sibley's Harvard graduates*, vol.16. Condon, "Envy of American states." Margaret Ells, "Loyalist attitudes," *Historical essays on the Atlantic provinces*, ed. G. A. Rawlyk (Toronto, 1967; repr. 1972), 44–60. G. S. Graham, *Sea power and British North America, 1783–1820: a study in colonial policy* (Cambridge, 1941). J. W. Lawrence, *The judges of New Brunswick and their times*, ed. A. A. Stockton [and W. O. Raymond] ([Saint John, 1907]). W. S. MacNutt, *The Atlantic provinces; the emergence of colonial society, 1712–1857* (Toronto, 1965); *New Brunswick.* R. W. Sloan, "New Ireland: loyalists in eastern Maine during the American revolution" (PHD thesis, Mich. State Univ., East Lansing, 1971). Wright, *Loyalists of N.B.* Marion Gilroy, "The partition of Nova Scotia, 1784," *CHR*, 14 (1933): 375–91. C. W. Rife, "Edward Winslow, Junior: loyalist pioneer in the Maritime provinces," CHA *Report*, 1928: 101–12.

WINSLOW, JOSHUA, army and militia officer, diarist, office holder, judge, and politician; b. 23 Jan. 1726/27 in Portsmouth, N.H., youngest of three children of John Winslow and Sarah Peirce (Pierce); d. June 1801 at Quebec, Lower Canada.

In 1745, at the age of 18, Joshua Winslow became a lieutenant in a New Hampshire regiment raised for William Pepperrell*'s expedition against Louisbourg, Île Royale (Cape Breton Island). Continuing his military career after the fall of the fortress, he exchanged his provincial commission for a regular one as ensign in Pepperrell's newly formed 66th Foot. Winslow also received an appointment as commissary general of the British forces in Nova Scotia. It was in this capacity that in 1750 he accompanied the two expeditions commanded by Charles Lawrence* which resulted in the construction of Fort Lawrence on the Chignecto Isthmus the same year. He continued his service as commissary at Fort Lawrence and then at Fort Cumberland (near Sackville, N.B.), the former Fort Beauséjour captured in 1755. At this time he met and had as an assistant Brook WATSON, who later was to be of considerable help when Winslow became a loyalist refugee.

On 3 Jan. 1758 Winslow married his cousin Anna Green; the two sons and two daughters they eventually had were to die relatively young. There is some evidence that Winslow was involved in business in Massachusetts in the early 1760s, but for most of that decade he was in Nova Scotia. In August 1761 he was appointed to "a committee to admit persons into the township of Sackville" and, along with John Huston, one of its earliest settlers, he had an important influence on the township's composition. The committee decided on the layout of settlement areas within the township, formulated guidelines on the allotment of acreage, and distributed tracts of land. In 1765 Winslow was among the leading men of Cumberland County who petitioned for the county's representation in the House of Assembly. When this request was granted Winslow was chosen as the area's representative, although he did not serve as one of Cumberland's officially elected members until 1770–72. In April 1764 he had been appointed a judge of the Inferior Court of Common Pleas for Cumberland County, and he had been a colonel in the militia since June 1762, justice of the peace for Cumberland County, and truckmaster for Indian trade.

Despite his acquisition of land and offices in Nova Scotia, as well as his continuing duties as commissary, Winslow retained his New England connections. In 1770 his ten-year-old daughter Anna was sent to Boston, Mass., "for schooling" and, judging by Anna's diary, in April 1772 her parents were "preparing to quit [their] present habitation" at Cumberland in favour of their residence at Marshfield, Mass. In 1776, some years after Winslow had "sold out and removed," John Eagleson*, one of his critics in Nova Scotia, surmised that he would find in "New England his native country, a Clime better suited both to his Civil and Religious Sentiments." Instead, the increasingly rebellious climate of Massachusetts

Wiswall

proved unacceptable to Winslow and he soon was identified as a tory sympathizer. Arrested, and then released, by one of his nephews, he decided escape to Halifax was necessary.

In August 1780 he was still in Halifax. Recommended that month "by some eminent Merchants of London as a person of great Honour & conversant in Business," he was soon appointed to oversee payment of "the Subsistence & Extraordinaries of the Forces serving at Quebec." For some reason the letter of appointment did not reach Governor Frederick HALDIMAND until the fall of 1782, but a "Variety of difficulties" had retarded Winslow's arrival until the spring of that year. Winslow carried with him a supporting letter from Welbore Ellis, secretary of state for the American colonies, and Haldimand also soon received a strong recommendation concerning Joshua's "Merit" from Brook Watson. Ellis in his letter emphasized to Haldimand Winslow's suitability for a seat on the Legislative Council but felt it would be better "for the King's Service that he should owe it to you, and therefore your Recommendation of him will be waited for before any step is taken for his Appointment." Although Haldimand on several occasions recommended Winslow to fill any vacancy which might occur on the council, Winslow never was appointed.

Winslow nevertheless settled at Quebec and served as deputy paymaster until his death. After the war ended he was reunited with his wife but in the interval, probably in 1779, their last living child, Anna, had died. With the division of Quebec into Upper and Lower Canada in December 1791, additional responsibilities were entrusted to Winslow. That month he became Lower Canada's receiver general and held this office until Henry CALDWELL took over in July 1794. His health must have deteriorated considerably during his last years, for after his death one of his colleagues commented: "If death be ever desirable it surely was so in his case."

Even allowing for the exaggerated comments of his friends and patrons, Winslow appears to have been an individual who was respected and trusted as a man of principle. Despite the acceptance of the revolutionary cause by relatives and friends, and despite the threat to his immediate family, Winslow felt his interests were best protected by supporting the crown. Once his choice was made, his friends in London saw to it that he was reasonably well rewarded. Ironically, after his death his wife wasted no time in returning to New England, where she died in 1816.

W. G. GODFREY

Joshua Winslow's journal has been published as *The journal of Joshua Winslow, recording his participation in the events of the year 1750 memorable in the history of Nova Scotia*, ed. and intro. J. C. Webster (Saint John, N.B., 1936).

BL, Add. MSS 21705: 16; 21707: 101–2; 21710: 214–15; 21715: 172–73; 21716: 74; 21717/2: 487; 21723: 49, 270, 429; 21724: 298, 360; 21727: 76; 21733: 167–68; 21752/2: 426–27, 442, 455, 457, 522; 21753: 65–66 (transcripts at PAC). PAC, MG 11, [CO 42] Q, 67: 16, 21, 229, 313, 362; 69/2: 331; 71: 386–87, 392, 398, 400; MG 23, D4; RG 8, I (C ser.), 76: 1–11; 223: 62; 224: 29–30. PRO, WO 34/61: 57 (mfm. at PAC). [A. G. Winslow], *Diary of Anna Green Winslow, a Boston school girl of 1771*, ed. A. M. Earle (Boston and New York, 1894). [John Winslow], "Journal of Colonel John Winslow of the provincial troops, while engaged in removing the Acadian French inhabitants from Grand Pre . . . ," N.S. Hist. Soc., *Coll.*, 3 (1883): 105, 133–34, 139–40. *Directory of N.S. MLAs*, 371, 383, 385, 389. G.B., WO, *Army list*, 1790: 326. "Louisbourg soldiers," comp. Charles Hudson, *New-England Hist. and Geneal. Reg.* (Boston), 24 (1870): 379. Wallace, *Macmillan dict.*

Merrill Jensen, *The founding of a nation: a history of the American revolution, 1763–1776* (New York and Toronto, 1968), 437. J. D. Snowdon, "Footprints in the marsh mud: politics and land settlement in the township of Sackville, 1760–1800" (MA thesis, Univ. of N.B., Fredericton, 1975), 20–22, 69. Howard Trueman, *The Chignecto Isthmus and its first settlers* (Toronto, 1902; repr. Belleville, Ont., 1975), 29–30, 33. J. C. Webster, *The forts of Chignecto: a study of the eighteenth century conflict between France and Great Britain in Acadia* ([Shediac, N.B.], 1930), 104; "Sir Brook Watson: friend of the loyalists, first agent of New Brunswick in London," *Argosy* (Sackville, N.B.), 3 (1924–25): 3–25.

WISWALL, JOHN, Church of England clergyman; b. 15 April 1731 in Boston, Mass., son of Peleg Wiswall and Elizabeth Rogers; m. first 17 Dec. 1761 Mercy Minot of Brunswick (Maine), and they had four children; m. secondly March 1784 Margaret Hutchinson of New Jersey; d. 2 Dec. 1812 in Wilmot, N.S.

The son of a well-known schoolmaster, John Wiswall graduated from Harvard College in 1749 and taught at various schools in the vicinity of Boston. In 1753 he began studying divinity under Jonathan Mayhew and other Congregational ministers, and for the next couple of years he travelled about Massachusetts as a supply preacher. Eventually, in 1755 or 1756, he was made minister of a Congregational church at Falmouth (Maine), then part of Massachusetts and literally a "frontier post." Life here had its pleasures, for in 1761 Wiswall married Mercy Minot, a "tall and genteel" woman who had captivated him with her "lively blue eyes," "graceful modesty," and "indescribable sweetness." Yet all was not domestic bliss. A week after his marriage Wiswall was "taken distracted," and the following year he was placed in the care of a leading Boston physician, who attempted to cure his patient by confining him in a "dark chamber." Notwithstanding this treatment, in early 1763 Wiswall regained his health and made his way back to Falmouth.

Wiswall became the object of public abuse when in

1764 he announced his conversion to Anglicanism – a decision he defended on the grounds that there was no "essential difference" between the Church of England and the "congregational communion." Newspapers as distant as New York commented on his conversion, and one journal blamed his apostasy on the fact that he was "very much disordered in his upper House." Wiswall, however, ignored his critics, and in late 1764 he travelled to England for ordination, sponsored by Benning Wentworth, the governor of New Hampshire. Ordained priest by the bishop of London in February 1765, Wiswall was back in Falmouth by the following May and ministered faithfully to his new Anglican congregation until the "publick Distractions" of the early 1770s. When he was arrested in 1775 he insisted that "not the severest punishment, not the fear of death" would shake his allegiance to the crown. Released on the understanding that he would remain in Falmouth, Wiswall broke his parole and travelled to Boston, arriving there in early June. He immediately appealed for assistance to commander-in-chief Thomas Gage*, but his petition yielded only an appointment as deputy chaplain to two regiments. To add to his misfortunes, his wife and one of his daughters died that summer. A disconsolate Wiswall wrote that "the sufferings and Persecutions I have Undergone: together with the rebellious spirit of the People has entirely weaned my Affection from my native Country – the further I go from it the better."

Made a navy chaplain in late 1775, Wiswall spent most of the next few years in wartime service. In 1781 he accepted a curacy in Suffolk, England, but within a year he was serving in a parish in Kent, and later still he moved to another parish in Essex. Early in 1783, after obtaining a temporary pension of £60 annually in compensation for his losses during the American revolution, he emigrated to Nova Scotia to succeed Jacob BAILEY as the Anglican clergyman in Cornwallis.

Wiswall arrived in Cornwallis in August and the following February was formally inducted as the clergyman of the parish, the ceremony being performed by Jacob Bailey. In March 1784 Bailey, now stationed in Annapolis Royal, married Wiswall to Margaret Hutchinson, a widow from New Jersey whom Bailey termed "very clever" and "sensible and . . . prudent in the management of family affairs." As before, however, Wiswall was far from happy. Although he lived in a "decent house," received an annual salary of £100 from the Society for the Propagation of the Gospel (to which was added a grant of more that £200 from the loyalist claims commission), and was married to a woman with "the gleanings of a very ample estate," Wiswall felt just as poverty-stricken as the most humble of the settlers among whom he laboured. He also complained bitterly of the state of religion in his district. Besides

facing opposition from his own congregation, some of whom criticized him as a "passionate man" and tried to eject him from the Cornwallis glebe, Wiswall had the difficult task of strengthening the Church of England in an area that was overrun with dissenters. Soon after arriving in Cornwallis he wrote that in his mission, which also included the settlements of Horton and Wilmot, Anglicans were greatly outnumbered by "wild enthusiasts" of every denomination. Whereas Wiswall was the only Anglican clergyman in the district, no fewer than six non-Anglican ministers – the most prominent being the Methodist itinerant William Black* – served Cornwallis and its surrounding settlements. With these rival preachers, moreover, Wiswall was not on the best of terms: he dismissed the Baptist Nicholas Piersons as an "illiterate shoemaker," and he had to resort to the courts before a dispute with the Presbyterian clergyman James Murdoch over the ownership of the Horton glebe was resolved in his favour.

In 1788 a bitter Wiswall wrote: "I regret that ever I came to this Country – I was wretchedly deceived . . . I am banished from my Friends – and doomed to lead a most laborious life, pinched with poverty and oftimes not knowing where to procure the common conveniences not to say necessarys of life." Despairing that "the church should ever flourish in Cornwallis," by the late 1780s Wiswall had begun concentrating his energies on the neighbouring communities of Aylesford and Wilmot. In 1789 he resigned his Cornwallis charge and was given responsibility for these settlements; he moved to Wilmot that fall. Even a change of scene, however, could not improve his spirits. Most of the people in his new mission were Baptists and Methodists, and soon Wiswall was complaining of "strolling, fanatical teachers" and their "deluded hearers." His own flock refused to contribute to his financial support, claiming that a combination of apathy and physical infirmity was preventing him from discharging his duties. This charge seems to have had some basis in fact. Many years earlier the SPG had rebuked Wiswall for his lack of missionary zeal, and Charles INGLIS, the Anglican bishop of Nova Scotia, made the same point in a letter of 1791. "Wiswall is an infirm man," he wrote, "& rather incapable of that exertion which the state of the country requires – like too many of the Clergy here, he does not seem to have such notions of order, conformity to the Rubrics, & subordination as I could wish; nor of the necessity of vigorous exertions in the Clergy. . . ."

Wiswall, for his part, resented Inglis's criticisms and made no effort to change his ways. From the 1790s he seems to have spent more time cultivating his glebe than ministering to his parishioners. In 1796 he asked to be relieved of Aylesford, but on the recommendation of Bishop Inglis the SPG refused this request. Abiding by the society's decision, Wiswall continued to serve his two parishes until 1801, when John Inglis*, the bishop's son, was appointed to Aylesford. That same year Wiswall was seriously injured in a fall from his horse, and for the last decade of his life he was too crippled and frail to minister to his Wilmot flock on a regular basis. He died on 2 Dec. 1812, at the age of 81, and was buried near the Anglican church in Middleton. One of his sons, Peleg, was elected to the House of Assembly and later became a judge of the Nova Scotia Supreme Court.

MAUD M. HUTCHESON

Acadia Univ. Arch. (Wolfville, N.S.), John Wiswall, journal, 1771–1812 (mfm. at PANS). PRO, AO 12/10: f.309; 12/61: f.39; 12/99: f.42; 12/109: f.312; AO 13, bundles 51, 82–83. USPG, Journal of SPG, 24: 134–36, 262–64, 314–17, 337–41, 358–62; 25: 2–5, 37, 69–71, 100, 144, 149–50, 157–59, 184–85, 201–4, 211; 26: 19, 99, 193–94, 415–17; 27: 117–19, 128–30, 204–8, 277–78, 284–86, 377–78; 28: 25, 52, 80–81, 177, 184–86, 359–61, 382–84; 29: 8–9, 95–97, 175–76, 205–7, 335–56; 30: 10–13, 151–52, 284. [Jacob Bailey], "Nova Scotia, 1784: a letter of Jacob Bailey," ed. David Siegenthaler, Canadian Church Hist. Soc., Journal (Sudbury, Ont.), 19 (1977): 131–37. Glimpses of Nova Scotia, 1807–24, as seen through the eyes of two Halifax merchants, a Wilmot clergyman and the clerk of the assembly of Nova Scotia, ed. C. B. Fergusson (Halifax, 1957). Journals of the Rev. Thomas Smith, and the Rev. Samuel Deane, pastors of the first church in Portland . . . , ed. William Willis ([2nd ed.], Portland, Maine, 1849). "United Empire Loyalists: enquiry into losses and services," AO Report, 1904: 172–73, 188. Jones, Loyalists of Mass. Sabine, Biog. sketches of loyalists, vol.2. Calnek, Hist. of Annapolis (Savary). A. W. [H.] Eaton, The Church of England in Nova Scotia and the tory clergy of the revolution (New York, 1891). Fingard, Anglican design in loyalist N.S. Stark, Loyalists of Mass. (1910). E. M. Saunders, "The life and times of the Rev. John Wiswall, M.A., a loyalist clergyman in New England and Nova Scotia, 1731–1821," N.S. Hist. Soc., Coll., 13 (1908): 1–73.

WRIGHT, GEORGE, educator and Church of England clergyman; b. 1752 in Omagh (Northern Ireland), son of William Wright; m. 12 Sept. 1787 Mary Cochran in New York City; d. 1 Aug. 1819 in Halifax, N.S.

George Wright was educated at Trinity College, Dublin (Republic of Ireland), and graduated with a BA in 1782. Shortly thereafter he emigrated to New York where he taught school and officiated for a time at St Mark's Church by the Ferry in Brooklyn. In 1788 he was recommended by the lord primate of Ireland and "several persons of judgement & veracity at New York" for missionary service with the Society for the Propagation of the Gospel. Two years later he moved to Halifax to succeed his brother-in-law, William Cochran*, as headmaster of the grammar school. On 7 April 1799 he was appointed minister of St George's

Church, which had been built in 1758 to serve the "foreign Protestants" of Halifax. Although the congregation was still composed mainly of German Lutherans, Wright reported that only a few members of his flock retained their own language.

Immediately after his appointment to St George's, Wright became involved in the building of a new church. With the help of the Duke of Kent [EDWARD AUGUSTUS], who was then serving as commander of forces in British North America, a grant of £500 was obtained from the British government, and to this sum the province later added £1,000. Plans for a circular structure, a design favoured by the duke, were drawn by William Hughes, master builder in the royal dockyard, with the assistance of John Merrick* and J. Flieger of the surveyor general's department. The result, St George's Round Church, still stands – an architectural landmark of downtown Halifax. Wright officiated at the laying of the cornerstone by Lieutenant Governor Sir John WENTWORTH on 10 April 1800. He also preached the sermon at the first service in the new structure on 19 July 1801.

From 1790 until his death Wright simultaneously pursued three careers: chaplain of the garrison, headmaster of the grammar school, and rector of St George's. Since his church was not legally constituted as a parish until 1827, jurisdictional disputes with St Paul's, the other Anglican church in the city, inevitably arose. The most serious of these, concerning the issuance of marriage licences, developed in 1800 and led to a breach between Wright and the rector of St Paul's, Robert Stanser*. To add to Wright's problems, the grammar school was in constant financial difficulty. During the period from 1808 to 1812 the House of Assembly repeatedly vetoed the annual grant to the headmaster, and each year Wright petitioned for redress. Reasons for the assembly's position are obscure; however, Bishop Charles INGLIS, who sided with Wright, suggested that in the minds of some assemblymen the Halifax grammar school was no more entitled to financial aid than any other school in the province. The grant was restored in 1813 and continued thereafter.

Wright was apparently a spirited individual: he was always ready to leap to the defence of his school, and on one occasion he shouldered a musket and marched to the Grand Parade when an alarm was spread that French transports were preparing to land an invading force. In 1817 he suffered a stroke and was largely inactive for the remainder of his life. There is some reason to believe that he married twice, but only his wife Mary appears in historical sources; it was she who inherited the bulk of his estate upon his death in 1819. His son William Wright was a business partner of Andrew Belcher*, a prominent Halifax merchant.

WILLIAM B. HAMILTON

Halifax County Court of Probate (Halifax), W138 (will and estate papers of George Wright) (mfm. at PANS). PANS, MG 4, St George's Anglican Church, Halifax, Reg. of baptisms, marriages, and burials; MG 9, no.43: 300–27; MG 20, 677, no.14; MG 100, 151, nos.4b–4c; RG 1, 298. PRO, CO 217/130. USPG, Journal of SPG, 25: 92, 414; 26: 391; 27: 10, 54, 313, 317–18, 366, 412–13, 415–20; 28: 53–57, 172, 302–3, 386, 438; 29: 170, 325, 418–19; 30: 8, 33–34, 151; 32: 281. *Acadian Recorder*, 7 Aug. 1819. *Royal Gazette and the Nova Scotia Advertiser* (Halifax), 3 Jan. 1794. *Weekly Chronicle* (Halifax), 13 Aug. 1819. Akins, *Hist. of Halifax City*. Fingard, *Anglican design in loyalist N.S.* R. V. Harris, *The Church of Saint Paul in Halifax, Nova Scotia: 1749–1949* (Toronto, 1949).

WRIGHT, THOMAS, surveyor, astronomer, politician, judge, and author; b. *c.* 1740, possibly in London, England, son of Thomas Wright and Martha Bisse; m. 6 Dec. 1769 Susanna Turner of Cumberland, N.S., and they had ten children; d. 7 Dec. 1812 on Prince Edward Island.

Little is known of the early life of Thomas Wright. According to his own testimony, he studied drawing and mathematics at Christ's Hospital in London and in 1758 went to North America where he furthered his education with practical work under the surveyor general of Georgia. Returning to England in 1763, he came out the following year as deputy to Captain Samuel Johannes HOLLAND, surveyor general of the Northern District of North America. Wright assisted in the survey of St John's (Prince Edward) Island and Cape Breton Island and took charge of the survey of Anticosti. He returned to England in 1767 to deliver plans on which he had been working and two years later came out again to North America to observe the transit of Venus from Quebec. The survey of the Northern District continued, and Wright worked with Holland along the coast of the Bay of Fundy and in New England. During this time he requested a military commission but his application was unsuccessful. As a result, he offered to take the first civil employment in the colonies that would allow him to continue with the survey.

In 1769 St John's Island was made a separate colony from Nova Scotia, and when Governor Walter Patterson* arrived the following year he appointed Wright a member of the Council, even though Wright was absent much of each year on the survey. At Patterson's request Wright was appointed surveyor general of the colony in 1773, but he may have continued to work with Holland. The following year he became a judge of the Supreme Court on the death of Chief Justice John Duport, and he continued as an assistant judge after the arrival of Duport's successor, Peter STEWART. His position as one of the senior members of the administration led to his being taken prisoner in 1775 by American privateers who raided Charlottetown, but he and the administrator, Phillips Callbeck*, were soon released by order of General George Washington.

As a member of the Council Wright almost unavoidably became entangled in the controversy over the land question. The British government had agreed to the establishment of a separate administration for St John's Island on the condition that it be supported through the collection of quitrents. Proprietors were unwilling or unable to pay, however, and the colony soon found itself in financial difficulty. In 1781 Governor Patterson seized several townships for arrears of quitrents and had them sold at auction. Most members of the administration took advantage of the irregular way in which the sale was conducted to acquire property, but there is no indication that Wright benefited from the governor's actions. Nevertheless, because he was later party to efforts to block the adoption of reversing legislation explicitly demanded by the Home Department after complaints by the proprietors, Wright was implicated in the affair. In an attempt to settle the dispute the British government in 1786 ordered Patterson to return to England and dispatched Lieutenant Governor Edmund FANNING to replace him. Patterson refused to give up his post on Fanning's arrival and during the winter of 1786–87 the Island had two governors, both claiming to represent the crown. Along with some other members of the administration Wright continued to support Patterson and refused to cooperate with Fanning. Following the re-opening of communication with Britain in the spring of 1787, Patterson was formally dismissed and Wright suspended from the Council and the post of surveyor general. The suspensions lasted only a few months, but Wright's return to the administration was also of short duration. Led by Captain John MACDONALD of Glenaladale and Robert Clark*, the proprietors brought criminal charges against Patterson and members of his government, and the case was finally heard before the British Privy Council in 1789. At the trial Wright presented his own defence and, according to MacDonald, "never was a human being made so ridiculous a figure." Wright was removed from the Council and it was only by reason of his large family and his poverty that he was permitted to retain his post as surveyor general. The trial appears to have ended his direct participation in the government of the colony, although a Thomas Wright, either he or his eldest son, sat in the House of Assembly from 1797 to 1802.

Wright was more successful in his professional activities. In 1788 he was given a vote of thanks by the assembly for his efforts as a surveyor and for his work, unpaid, as a judge. But Wright soon found that he had only routine tasks to perform as surveyor general, since the colony, because of its land-holding system, had little crown land. Several of his sons took up surveying, and by 1791 Wright was complaining to

Yeo

Lord Grenville, the Home secretary, "I wish but to be useful to the publick as well to my family, here I am of little to either." Throughout his career Wright experienced difficulty in obtaining his salary, which was originally to have come from the quitrents. Once it was understood that the payment of salaries from quitrents was unworkable, adjustments were made, and Wright claimed that his salary was reduced in error. By 1790 he was pleading that he and his family were in desperate circumstances, and he requested a post in the proposed new colony of Upper Canada or elsewhere. No action was taken on the request and his salary was not adjusted until 1806.

A year after the establishment in 1796 of a commission to determine the boundary between New Brunswick and the District of Maine (then part of Massachusetts), Wright was appointed astronomer for the British side; Thomas Barclay* was Britain's representative on the commission, Edward WINSLOW served as its secretary, and Ward Chipman* argued the British case. Wright had surveyed the entire area in 1772, and with Samuel Webber, the American astronomer, he now took highly accurate sightings to establish the exact location of the several rivers claimed to be the border. In the summer of 1797 he and Robert Pagan* excavated a small island in the St Croix or Scoodic River and uncovered the remains of buildings erected by Pierre Du Gua* de Monts and Samuel de Champlain* in 1604. By establishing which of the three rivers referred to as the St Croix was in fact the St Croix of the exploration period, their findings to a great extent ended the boundary dispute.

At the time of his death in 1812 Wright had been active in surveying and mapping the Atlantic shore of North America for almost 50 years; he had covered the entire coast of what are now the Maritime provinces of Canada and had worked as far south as Georgia. Surveyors who achieved more fame, such as Holland and Joseph Frederick Wallet DesBarres*, used his reports to prepare the first accurate maps of the region. However, Wright is now known not for his cartographic contribution but rather for his political activi-

ties. His involvement with the land question almost ruined him, and after the "unfortunate business" Wright promised to "render my future conduct unexceptionable." He succeeded all too well.

After Wright's death the post of surveyor general went in turn to his sons Charles* and George* and to his grandson George*, who held the position until 1854. For an 80-year period, then, the Island's only surveyors general were members of the Wright family. Even in an age of nepotism their hold on the office, like that of Charles Morris* and his family on the same position in Nova Scotia, was remarkable.

H. T. HOLMAN

Thomas Wright is the author of *Description of the island of Anticosti* (London, 1768). Observations he communicated to the astronomer royal, Nevil Maskelyne, formed the basis of Maskelyne's article, "Immersions and emersions of Jupiter's first satellite, observed at Jupiter's Inlet, on the island of Anticosti, North America, by Mr. Thomas Wright, deputy surveyor-general of lands for the Northern District of America . . . ," Royal Soc. of London, *Philosophical Trans.*, 64 (1774): 190–93.

PAC, MG 24, K2, 6: 53, 61, 121, 151, 260, 284 (transcripts). PAPEI, Acc. 2702, Smith–Alley coll., Thomas Wright docs.; RG 3, House of Asembly, Journals, 1788; RG 5, Minutes, 11, 18, 24 April, 23 May, 29 Oct. 1787; 15 Sept. 1790; RG 16, Land registry records, Conveyance reg., liber 1234: ff.2–5, 7–9, 15. Private arch., Mrs J. T. McIntyre (Calgary), Charles Wright papers, pp.1–4 (photocopies at PAC). PRO, CO 5/115: 20–21; 5/154: 202–3 (mfm. at PAC); CO 226/1: 15, 23, 35, 53, 83; 226/10: 176–77, 331–32; 226/13: 337–38; 226/14: 341, 370, 380–81; 226/18: 118, 128, 131–32, 211, 219; 226/21: 145, 149–50, 157; 226/22: 219–20; CO 227/2: 26, 35, 43, 50–51, 61–62; 227/21: 26; CO 323/24: 623. Supreme Court of P.E.I. (Charlottetown), Estates Division, Administrations, file 23, Thomas Wright. [John MacDonald?], *Remarks on the conduct of the governor and Council of the Island of St. John's, in passing an act of assembly in April of 1786 to confirm the sales of the lands in 1781 . . .* (n.p., [1789]). Stewart, *Account of P.E.I.*, 181–203. *Canada's smallest prov.* (Bolger), 45, 52–65. R. D. and J. I. Tallman, "The diplomatic search for the St. Croix River, 1796–1798," *Acadiensis* (Fredericton), 1 (1971–72), no.2: 59–71.

Y

YEO, Sir JAMES LUCAS, naval officer; b. 7 Oct. 1782 in Hampshire, England, elder son of James Yeo, sometime agent victualler to the Royal Navy at Minorca; d. unmarried 21 Aug. 1818 at sea.

After a brief schooling at Bishop's Waltham near Winchester, Hampshire, James Lucas Yeo joined the Royal Navy in March 1793 as a boy volunteer. Promoted lieutenant on 20 Feb. 1797, he was advanced to commander on 21 June 1805 and captain

on 19 Dec. 1807, by which time he had already been recognized as an intrepid practitioner of unconventional sea warfare. Typically, he had captured his own first command, the 22-gun French privateer *Confiance*, during a lightning raid of 4 June 1805 on Muros, a small fortified port on the northwest coast of Spain. At the time of the raid he was first lieutenant on the 46-gun *Loire* and was in charge of a shore party which was to act against a local fort of unknown strength. In the event, he was required to neutralize a potentially dangerous harbour battery before moving against the fort, which by this time was firing on the *Loire*. Although he had only 50 men under his command, he stormed the place, which was garrisoned by 250 men and equipped with 12 cannon; this successful assault led to the capture of the *Confiance* and other substantial prizes. Yeo was promptly appointed to command the *Confiance*, an action which was as promptly endorsed by the Admiralty. Two years later he achieved the coveted rank of post-captain, a promotion undoubtedly influenced by sterling services to Vice-Admiral Sir William Sidney Smith in the negotiations and effort which led to the successful evacuation of the Portuguese royal family to Brazil in the face of a French invasion of Portugal. In the winter of 1808–9 he led an Anglo-Portuguese expedition against Cayenne, French Guiana. With only 400 men and a few heavy guns he compelled the surrender of a garrison of some 1,200, protected by strong fortifications and more than 200 cannon. This extraordinary feat resulted in the expulsion of the French from South America and won Captain Yeo signal honours: on 17 Aug. 1809 a knight commander's cross of the Portuguese order of St Benedict of Avis – he was the first Protestant to be so honoured – and, on 20 June 1810, a knighthood. For some months after his return to England he was on half pay, convalescing from a severe bout of malaria, but early in 1811 he was assigned to the 32-gun *Southampton* and ordered to Jamaica.

On 19 March 1813 Sir James was appointed commodore and commander-in-chief on the lakes of Canada. Prior to this date he had never commanded a capital ship, much less a squadron, but in his new assignment he was strictly enjoined never to undertake operations without "the full concurrence and approbation" of Sir George PREVOST, the captain-general and governor-in-chief of British North America. Moreover, he would speedily discover that in the Canadas his instinct for daring initiatives had to be disciplined in the interests of an imperious necessity: maintenance of control over Lake Ontario, the crucial link between the arsenal and dockyard at Kingston, Upper Canada, and the British force on the Niagara peninsula.

Yeo and his immediate command of 437 officers and other ranks disembarked at Quebec on 5 May. The next day he was en route to Upper Canada, spurred by the news that York (Toronto) had fallen to the Americans on 27 April, and that this disaster had also cost the British the cutter *Duke of Gloucester* and a warship burned on the stocks to prevent its capture. He reached Kingston with Prevost on 15 May and within a fortnight had deployed his men and readied his ships for action. He had at his disposal the newly launched 23-gun *Wolfe*, the 22-gun *Royal George*, the 16-gun *Prince Regent*, the 14-gun brig *Earl of Moira*, two 8-gun schooners, and a number of gunboats. Against

him the Americans could muster only the 24-gun *Madison*, the 16-gun *Oneida*, and some ten schooners bought after the outbreak of war and hastily armed with long guns. For the time being Yeo was unquestionably superior, but his squadron was seriously understrength in men and his prime weapon was the 32-pounder carronade, lethal in close combat but of limited range. The Americans, in contrast, had ample manpower, and were equipped with the long 24-pounder gun, which gave them a distinct advantage at a distance.

Haste in Yeo's preparations was essential since Prevost hoped to take advantage of the presence of the enemy squadron at the other end of the lake to effect a strike against Sackets Harbor, N.Y., the principal American naval base on Lake Ontario. The operation was intended to relieve pressure by sea and land on Brigadier-General John Vincent*'s force on the Niagara peninsula and, if possible, to destroy both the American dockyard and a ship under construction which threatened to outgun any vessel available to the British. It was duly mounted on 28–29 May but because of adverse weather and Prevost's excessive caution proved a failure. The British effected considerable damage but suffered many casualties, and although the American squadron hastened to return on receiving news of the attack, its sailing came too late to benefit Vincent. Yeo, however, held effective control of the lake and rendered valuable assistance to the army until 23 July, when his opponent Commodore Isaac Chauncey sailed from Sackets Harbor with a powerful squadron led by his new ship, the 28-gun *General Pike*. For the next two weeks the two commanders manœuvred inconclusively. Yeo won a modest victory on 10 August but on 28 September, in an engagement known as the "Burlington Races," he felt obliged to break contact and beat for Kingston. In the mean time, his squadron on Lake Erie, commanded by Robert Heriot Barclay*, had been destroyed on 10 September at Put-In-Bay, Ohio, by Oliver Hazard Perry.

The campaign of 1813 had been intensely frustrating to both commanders: Chauncey, superior in long guns, had failed to find or create an opportunity to use them decisively, while Yeo had consistently lacked the favourable winds which would have enabled him to make effective use of his powerful but short-range carronades. Yeo's reaction was to devote the winter of 1813–14 to rearmament and the building of more powerful ships. In both endeavours he was at a decided disadvantage: parallel American efforts were favoured by secure internal communications, but British supplies, equipment, and reinforcements could reach Kingston only via the exposed route of the St Lawrence.

In the event, however, Sir James was able to leave Kingston on 3 May 1814 with a heavily armed squadron, now reinforced by two powerful frigates, the 56-gun *Prince Regent* and the 42-gun *Princess Charlotte*. With this force he was still superior in carronades, and could oppose 87 long guns to Chauncey's reputed 61. Moreover, he had on the stocks a 112-gun ship which, as the *St Lawrence*, would become the strongest warship ever launched in the Canadas. On the 6th he cooperated with Lieutenant-General George Gordon Drummond*, the army commander in Upper Canada, in a highly successful attack on the American base at Oswego, N.Y., and on the 9th he blockaded Sackets Harbor. He raised the blockade on 6 June to return to Kingston but remained in control of the lake until 9 August, when Chauncey appeared off the town with his new frigate *Superior*, mounting 32 long guns and 30 42-pounder carronades. Since he also had a new 42-gun frigate, the *Mohawk*, his effective strength was appreciably greater than Yeo's.

The American squadron withdrew on 1 September, but Sir James remained in port, unwilling to risk his squadron on open water pending completion of the *St Lawrence*. This great ship had become the subject of acute concern in command circles. It had absorbed the total resources of the Kingston dockyard for months, and by the time it was launched early in September Drummond's army on the Niagara peninsula was desperately in need of supplies and reinforcements. A further five weeks were required for outfitting but on 15 October the *St Lawrence* sailed for the Head of the Lake (the vicinity of present-day Hamilton Harbour) accompanied by an armada of support and supply ships. Thereafter Chauncey remained discreetly at Sackets Harbor. He had little choice: no two of his largest ships could have withstood the 112 guns – 68 of which were long 24- and 32-pounders – of Yeo's new flagship.

On 11 September Yeo's deputy at Île aux Noix, Lower Canada, Captain George Downie, had lost both his life and his squadron at the battle of Lake Champlain during Prevost's attempt to invade the United States from Montreal. This disaster was the second suffered by Sir James's command, but in both cases his subordinates had been forced into premature action by army commanders of superior rank: Barclay on Lake Erie by Major-General Henry Procter*, and Downie on Lake Champlain by Prevost himself. The last was especially culpable. He was fully aware that Downie's new ship the *Confiance* was not ready for action, and he withheld promised army support at the critical stage of the battle. Hitherto relations between Yeo and Prevost had been distant but correct. The commodore had been antagonized by his commander-in-chief's caution and vacillation at Sackets Harbor, and since then he had had reason to resent demands that he support the army, requests which he considered unrealistic in terms of the safety and capability of his Lake Ontario squadron. But the war was still

raging, and Yeo limited his formal reaction to the Lake Champlain disaster to a report addressed to the Admiralty on 29 September which clearly implicated Prevost as the author of Downie's tragedy. It is unlikely that this report had any direct effect on Prevost's future. By the time it reached London the secretary of state for War and the Colonies had apparently already decided to recall him.

The inland naval campaign of 1814 ended on 21 November. Once again Yeo devoted the comparative peace of winter to reinforcing his squadron. During his 19 months in the Canadas the shipbuilding war with the Americans had accelerated to an extraordinary degree, and his plans for 1815 were appropriately bold and ambitious. The 56-gun frigate *Psyche* was launched at the end of December, and before the end of January he had two 110-gun ships on the stocks. The *Psyche* never saw service, and the other ships were never completed, since on 1 March 1815 Prevost received notice of the ratification of the Anglo-American peace signed at Ghent (Belgium) on 24 Dec. 1814. On the following day the commander-in-chief was informed that his appointment had been cancelled and that he was to report to London to account for his conduct of the Plattsburgh campaign.

Sir James was also summoned home immediately, but he had no reason for concern, whether for his reputation or for his professional future. His health, however, was precarious: he was suffering from overwork and from the debilitating effects of the marsh fever peculiar to Kingston. He was succeeded by Commodore Sir Edward Campbell Rich Owen on 20 March 1815, and shortly thereafter embarked for England. He arrived in the United Kingdom on 16 May, and on the 30th addressed a lengthy report to the Admiralty on his experiences in the Canadas. In his opinion, British successes in this sector had been conditioned to an unusual degree by the "stupidity" of the enemy, which was particularly demonstrated by the American failure to cut the vulnerable line of the St Lawrence. He did not think that this fundamental error would be repeated or that the British could hold the Upper Lakes in any future conflict, and forcefully recommended that Kingston be transformed into a major fortress linked to Montreal by an inland waterway along the Ottawa and Rideau river systems.

On 5 June 1815 Yeo was appointed commander-in-chief on the west coast of Africa with special responsibility for the anti-slavery patrol, a congenial posting since he was a convinced abolitionist. He was to fly his broad pennant in the *Inconstant*. It is a measure of his standing with the Admiralty that he received this position: by midsummer 1815 the navy was being rapidly demobilized, and scores of post-captains and other senior officers were being placed on half pay. He was not able to leave England for several weeks after his appointment, since he was required to testify at the court martial in mid August of those of his officers who had survived the battle of Lake Champlain. In the event all were honourably acquitted, responsibility for the disaster having been placed with Prevost.

Yeo's African assignment proved to be his last. He died, aged 35, "of general debility" on board the *Semiramis*, to which he had transferred in October 1817 while en route from Jamaica to England. His burial took place with full service honours at the Royal Garrison Chapel in Portsmouth on 8 Sept. 1818. He was survived by his parents, sisters, and his only brother, Lieutenant George Cosby Yeo, who was killed in a shipboard accident in the spring of 1819.

James Lucas Yeo was a brilliant officer whose selfless devotion to duty contributed in large measure to his early death. He deserved well of his country, and he has justly earned an honoured place among the heroes of the War of 1812.

JOHN W. SPURR

PRO, ADM 1/2736–38 (mfm. at PAC). William James, *A full and correct account of the military occurrences of the late war between Great Britain and the United States of America* . . . (2v., London, 1818). "Memoir of the public services of Sir James Lucas Yeo, knt., captain in the Royal Navy," *Naval Chronicle*, 24 (July–December 1810): 265–85 (includes a portrait); *Naval Chronicle*, 40 (July–December 1818): 243–44. *Select British docs. of War of 1812* (Wood), vol.2; vol.3, pt.1. *Kingston Gazette*, 1813–15. Colledge, *Ships of Royal Navy*, vol.1. *DNB*. H. J. Morgan, *Sketches of celebrated Canadians and persons connected with Canada, from the earliest period in the history of the province down to the present time* (Quebec and London, 1862; repr. Montreal, 1865), 221–22. W. L. Clowes, *The Royal Navy: a history from the earliest times to the present* (7v., London, 1897–1903), 5. Hitsman, *Incredible War of 1812*. A. T. Mahan, *Sea power in its relations to the War of 1812* (2v., Boston, 1905). Theodore Roosevelt, *The naval war of 1812, or the history of the United States Navy during the last war with Great Britain, to which is appended an account of the battle of New Orleans* (New York and London, 1882), esp. 251, 355, 367. E. A. Cruikshank, "The contest for the command of Lake Ontario in 1812 and 1813," RSC *Trans.*, 3rd ser., 10 (1916), sect.II: 161–223; "The contest for the command of Lake Ontario in 1814," *OH*, 21 (1924): 99–159. C. P. Stacey, "The ships of the British squadron on Lake Ontario, 1812–14," *CHR*, 34 (1953): 311–23. C. Winton-Clare [R. C. Anderson], "A shipbuilder's war," *Mariner's Mirror* (Cambridge, Eng.), 29 (1943): 139–48; repr. in *The defended border: Upper Canada and the War of 1812*, ed. Morris Zaslow and W. B. Turner (Toronto, 1964), 165–73.

YOUNG, JOHN, merchant, entrepreneur, seigneur, politician, militia officer, office holder, landowner, and judge; b. *c.* 1759, possibly in Scotland; d. 14 Sept. 1819 at Quebec, Lower Canada.

John Young was an energetic champion of Lower Canada's commercial interests. This great merchant and entrepreneur exemplified the strengths and weaknesses of the English-speaking mercantile group. What he did in aid of commerce, his city, and public finance went beyond self-interest. In politics, however, he became a self-righteous and self-serving conservative. His egotism brought about his own financial ruin and disturbed the province.

John Young first appeared at Quebec in about May 1783, having been a merchant in London. He had been engaged by the London firms of Anderson and Parr and Alexander Anderson and Davidson, as well as by the Liverpool firm of John Owen Parr and Company, to collect debts owed by Thompson and Shaw of Quebec, and probably other colonial companies there and in Halifax. In that year he formed the partnership of Fraser and Young with Simon Fraser Sr of Quebec. In 1787 Fraser retired and Young formed a new partnership of the same name with Simon Fraser Jr. The partners engaged in the wholesale and retail trade, supplying traders at Quebec, in communities down river from L'Islet to Rivière-du-Loup, and in Trois-Rivières. By 1789 their firm had acquired three or more small schooners to carry its merchandise, beer appearing to be the principal commodity. Ships were also accepted as surety or as payment from debtors. The company became a creditor to many persons for personal loans and unpaid merchandise. For example, in 1788 Alexander Fraser, a wood merchant at Chambly, owed Fraser and Young more than £4,500 and a Quebec shipowner, Jean-Baptiste BOUCHETTE, acknowledged his debt of £1,359. The partners were also active in land transactions in the Quebec region and beyond. In September 1790 they sold 600 acres of cultivated land in Vermont for £4,000.

Young failed to recover Anderson and Parr's claims against Thompson and Shaw in 1783–84 because of the legal manœuvres of a rival creditor. This bitter experience with French civil law may have spurred Young to become a spokesman for the city's English-speaking merchants who wished to change the colony's laws and constitution [*see* George ALLSOPP; William GRANT (1744–1805)]. He was a member of the mercantile group that met at the British Coffee House, where such matters were undoubtedly discussed. In 1786 the merchants elected him to a committee that pressed the Legislative Council to adopt English commercial law and weights and measures. The following year he and Robert LESTER led the merchants' public opposition to a bill introduced by Paul-Roch Saint-Ours to strengthen the position of French civil law. Young's ascendancy was also evident from his presence on a grand jury that in May 1789 deplored the state of Quebec's streets, the condition of the city's poor, and the lack of rehabilitation for inmates of the prison. In the same year he was a founding member of the Agriculture

Young

Society, whose object was the improvement of farming.

Young's emergence as a social and political leader among the merchants was confirmed in June 1792 during Lower Canada's first elections, when he and Lester were chosen as the representatives of Lower Town in the House of Assembly. Canadian supporters of Jean-Antoine PANET, an unsuccessful candidate, charged Young with preventing others from standing for election by claiming they were aliens and with opening taverns, "where Hams were sliced and strong liquors given to Tradesmen and Labourers, who were also influenced by sundry other unwarrantable Acts of His Servants or Hirelings"; the latter, they said, had promised electors well-paid jobs and had distributed oranges, ribbons, and cockades. Young's personal papers confirm this charge, with the correction that he had actually plied the voters with madeira, Burton ale, and turkey meat. Understandably, he did not contest the accusation; rather, he threatened the complainants with his own petition against the actions of Michel-Amable BERTHELOT Dartigny in Charlesbourg.

In the assembly Young became a leader of the English party and, with Pierre-Amable DE BONNE, acted as its election manager before 1800. In December 1793 Governor Lord Dorchester [Guy CARLETON] recommended that Young be made an honorary, unpaid member of the Executive Council, and this appointment was made by the crown in June 1794. It is ironic that in the mean time Young, who would become a defender of the executive branch of government against encroachments by the assembly, provided the lower house with its first opportunity for self-enhancement. In November 1793 he had been arrested for debt at the suit of an ironmonger. The warrant had been signed by Panet as notary; although defeated in Quebec's Lower Town constituency in 1792, he had been elected for Upper Town and, despite Young's opposition, chosen as speaker of the assembly. With Young's encouragement, the assembly successfully claimed that its members enjoyed the British parliamentary privilege of immunity from civil arrest. Moreover, Panet was censured for having signed the writ and obliged to apologize to the assembly. Young won a personal victory, and in future the Canadian party would invoke the precedents of the House of Commons as a means of extending the colonial legislature's powers. When Young was re-elected for Lower Town in 1796, De Bonne nominated him for speaker. Panet, however, retained that position.

Young was politically active outside the assembly. When the French revolution turned to regicide and mass executions in the winter of 1792–93, he joined others in Lower Canada in subscribing to loyal declarations to defend the existing constitution and the British empire from revolution. He had become an ensign in the Quebec Battalion of British Militia in about 1790, and he was promoted lieutenant in 1794. He supported the institution of compulsory and universal service in a standing militia. The resistance of the country-folk to this service was interpreted by the British of the colony as a prelude to revolution. David McLane*, an agent of the French Directory, approached John BLACK, a Quebec shipwright known to Young, to enlist Black's aid in a scheme to seize the city. The shipbuilder denounced McLane to Young in May 1797. McLane was arrested, brought before a commission of oyer and terminer of which Young was a member, and then tried for treason by 12 jurymen. The convicted agent was then publicly hanged and disembowelled outside the city walls as an object-lesson to those who might sympathize with revolution.

Young had testified to Black's loyalty and services as a government *agent provocateur*. Black was later captured at sea by the French, and for this misfortune, his material losses, and his role in the McLane affair he was given five-sevenths of Dorset Township in 1799. He promptly mortgaged the more than 50,000 acres to Young, who was his creditor for £3,144. Ownership passed to Young, and he employed a Canadian to buy out other landowners in the township. In July 1807 Young sold the entire parcel to Simon McTAVISH of Montreal for £4,000.

Throughout the anti-revolutionary panic and the Anglo-French war, Young provided leadership in the affairs of the city. In 1792 he was elected a director of the Quebec Fire Society, and the following year he was its president. In 1793 he was among the first and most generous subscribers to a fund to aid victims of a fire on Rue du Sault-au-Matelot. He was also one of 13 prominent citizens who in 1799 began a voluntary subscription to help finance Britain's war effort. In the same year he was president of a mutual aid association, the Quebec Benevolent Society. Given the public spirit he showed in civic affairs, Young could be credited with compassion in his treatment of the black slave Rubin, whom he had bought in 1795. Two years later the young black was promised a monthly salary and emancipation in 1804, to encourage his fidelity, "honesty and assiduity."

John Young's business fortunes reached their zenith in the 1790s. By 1792 Fraser and Young had long-term leases on prime locations in Lower Town: St Andrew's Wharf off Rue Saint-Pierre and a building on that street. In October 1791 the partners had joined Thomas Grant, a distiller, to form Thomas Grant and Company and to buy the St Roc Brewery on Rue Saint-Charles; they paid £3,850 for it. Despite the firm's name, Fraser and Young held a two-thirds interest. In May 1792 the associates acquired a large lot in the seigneury of Beauport from a *censitaire*, and the following month they purchased a majority interest in another property, buildings included, from the seigneur of Beauport, Antoine JUCHEREAU Duchesnay. In addition to the total purchase price of £2,250, the firm invested a large sum in the construction of a new brewery and distillery on the seigneury. Grant attended to the brewing and distilling, Young to the business in Quebec, and Fraser to the company's affairs in London.

Young quickly outgrew his partners; for example, of the ships arriving at Quebec in 1793, two were consigned to Fraser and Young and 12 were exclusively in the service of Young as carriers of coal, salt, and West Indian products. That July Thomas Grant and Company was replaced by Young and Company, in which Grant had only one share to his associates' seven; in 1794 he sold out to Young. Meanwhile Young and Fraser Jr had acquired a new partner in Thomas AINSLIE, collector of customs at Quebec. He was sold two shares in the brewing and distilling company for £6,000, to be invested in the business.

Ainslie was to be more than a powerful ally; he became Young's father-in-law. On 2 June 1795 Young married 19-year-old Christian (Christianna) Ainslie at Quebec. Their marriage contract stipulated "that no 'Communauté des Biens' shall at any time . . . exist or be . . . notwithstanding the Coutume de Paris and all and every other Law, Usage and Custom of the said Province of Lower Canada." In this stipulation there may have been some dislike of French civil law, but it was also a prudent safeguard for Christian, who had a sharp business sense and a dowry of £2,000 from her father. The pride of the Ainslies was evident in her signature, "Christian Ainslie Young," and in the fact that all her children received Ainslie as a second name. From 1796 to 1800 four children were born to the couple: Catherine, Thomas*, Elizabeth, and Gilbert. The boys' names were drawn from Christian's family. Such a distinguished wife deserved better than Young's old quarters next door to Fraser on Rue Saint-Pierre. In May 1796 Young bought a two-storey stone house on Rue Sainte-Anne, in the shadow of the governor's palace and far from the lubricious haunts of sailors.

The same month Christian's brother Gilbert replaced their father in Young and Company. Young bought out Fraser for ten shillings and resold Fraser's portion to Gilbert and the distiller David Harrower for £4,000. Harrower sold his one-seventh interest back to the company in 1800. On behalf of the firm and his own interests, Young petitioned the government for more dock space, a reduction in the duties on the molasses he imported from Martinique, and permission to export oats. His wheat exports helped to pay for the wines and liquors he obtained through Alexander Young of London.

The St Roc Brewery and the Beauport distillery and brewery were, as the Earl of Selkirk [DOUGLAS]

testified, large even by European standards. The building stone had come from the company's own quarry at Pointe-Lévy (Lauzon and Lévis). For these enterprises Young made bulk purchases of barley and wheat. The barley was secured by long-term contracts with farmers and merchants in Lower Canada. Brewers and maltsters were recruited from Britain, and over time hundreds of local labourers were hired. Until 1801 the St Roc Brewery was operated by a brewer-associate, James Mason Godard (Goddard). The company's fleet of schooners grew in order to carry grain and to deliver beer, malt liquor, and Burton ale throughout the colony. In 1798 Young also participated in a speculative venture with Black and Henry CALDWELL to refit and sell a ship in Europe.

Young had always speculated in land. Since 1787 he had held the seigneury of Vitré, and he trafficked in real estate in Upper and Lower Canada. In addition to the returns from Dorset Township and sundry town and farm lots that he sold, Young realized £3,750 in 1801 by selling two-thirds of St Andrew's Wharf to the merchant James McCallum*. While on the Executive Council's land committee, Young sought crown grants for himself and his friends. These activities brought him into conflict with Governor PRESCOTT, who was trying to curb land speculation. The influence of Young and some fellow councillors was sufficient to obtain Prescott's removal in 1799. Young received crown grants in 1801, 1812, and 1817; a concession made in 1802, however, was nullified to avert a scandal. The 1812 grant was delayed for two years to allow London to signify its consent or disapproval. Young's influence on the land board was acknowledged in April 1804 when Surveyor General Joseph Bouchette* wrote to a co-petitioner, "I spoke to Mister Young, who I believe will do much in our business."

At the turn of the century the gap between Young's debts and credits widened alarmingly. Between 1791 and 1801 he was owed at least £5,000. On 15 occasions in the period 1793–1802, he had sheriffs seize the property of delinquent debtors. Young's own debts were on a characteristically grand scale: in 1798 he owed nearly £5,000 sterling to two London firms, and a year later he acknowledged a debt of £1,000 sterling to a Liverpool merchant. Two creditors at Quebec were owed a total of £1,000. To these personal obligations were added the debts of Young and Company, known by 1802 as Young and Ainslie. In the counting-house at the St Roc Brewery, Young and Gilbert Ainslie watched their liabilities mount: in 1801 alone they contracted debts of £1,368 to Peter Stuart of Quebec and £4,383 sterling to Samuel Baker of King's Lynn, in England. The partners responded to their crisis with expansion rather than retrenchment. In 1803, while acknowledging a debt of £6,000 to two grain suppliers, Young and Ainslie ordered

Young

another 30,000 bushels of barley on credit. In the same month they bought land behind their brewery along the Rivière Saint-Charles for 4,800 *livres*. The company borrowed some £2,200 in addition to making purchases on credit in 1803–4. Even Young's father-in-law felt obliged to sue it for £668. Gilbert Ainslie had also had enough, and on 1 Sept. 1804 he sold his one-third interest to Young for ten shillings.

Young alone faced the financial consequences of the firm's reckless over-expansion, and he showed considerable ingenuity. A barley supplier who sued him was paid with 100 hogsheads of beer. An obligation to one man's estate was reduced by transferring an account receivable to the widow. In 1805 Young resorted to land sales to satisfy his creditors. The following year, however, he withdrew from the struggle: the company's Beauport grist-mill was leased out in August, and in December the distillery and both breweries were rented to William Meiklejohn. Joseph Bouchette's verdict that Young and Ainslie's enterprises had been "undertaken upon too great a scale for the consumption of the province at that period" tells only part of the story. Young invested more than he could afford in a brewing and distilling business that faced stiff competition. There were other breweries in the colony; imported rum was cheap; and domestic spirits were considered to be inferior to Scotch whisky.

The collapse of Young and Ainslie did not destroy the entrepreneur's reputation. Young's partners in the formation of the Union Company of Quebec in 1805 twice elected him a director, and, on their behalf, Young bought a large house on Rue Notre-Dame in Lower Town, which, fitted up as the Union Hotel with coffee and assembly rooms, became a political and social gathering place.

As ever, Young was the champion of commerce. In 1799 Lieutenant Governor Robert Shore Milnes* appointed him chairman of a commission for the regulation of pilots, the improvement of harbours, and the establishment of safe navigation on the St Lawrence River. This experience led Young in 1805 to introduce a bill in the assembly for the foundation of Trinity House of Quebec, which, like its counterpart on the Thames, would regulate pilotage and navigation and erect aids to shipping [*see* François BOUCHER]. The bill passed, and in May Young was appointed the first master of the new institution. He resigned from this unpaid office in 1812.

Young's financial troubles may have stimulated the malign spirit that began to mark his attitude toward Canadians in the legislative assembly. He was not a bigot; he used French in his private and business affairs and maintained good social relations with Canadians of similar rank and political outlook. After the French revolution the English speakers became very uneasy about the loyalty of the Canadian lower classes, and projects for cultural assimilation of the Canadians were discussed. Young's enthusiasm for public schools evolved in this direction. In 1793 he supported William Grant's education bill; he proposed one of his own in 1797. Two years later, as an executive councillor, he approved Anglican bishop Jacob Mountain*'s assimilationist plan for a centralized education system. In the assembly Young seconded a motion to appropriate the Jesuit estates to finance the establishment of public schools. Despite the opposition of Young and others, a bill in 1801 to place all primary and secondary education under the direction of a public body, to be called the Royal Institution for the Advancement of Learning, was amended to permit the existence of separate and independent schools. Joseph-François Perrault* still objected to the amended proposal, but his attempt to substitute an entirely new bill was defeated by an opposing group led by Young.

As a merchant, a political conservative, and a would-be anglicizer, Young was on a collision course with the Canadian party. Led by lawyers, notaries, and tradesmen, this party drew electoral support from the farming population. Young sat in the assembly for 14 sessions, with two absences on trips to Britain. In that time he became disillusioned with the legislature. To his mind, it had become a forum for ungrateful demagogues bent on usurping the prerogatives of the crown, their protector. Young's attitude was inconsistent: he lamented that the Canadian members were ignorant of British law and custom yet derided their efforts to read and translate books on British government. He moved in 1806 "that the British Constitution should only be studied in the language of the Empire." In 1819, when he looked back on his experiences in the assembly, he wrote, "The little Education & Knowledge that was in it lay with the English members, & without them the Canadians could not go on; it is now changed, the English members are reduced one half in number, & much more in quality, for scarcely any gentleman will go into the House; the Canadian members prove the observation that a little learning is a dangerous thing; they think they are now sufficiently instructed to walk alone. . . ."

To combat the apparent decline in the quality of members in the assembly, Young worked for the election of "loyal" candidates and opposed the payment of salaries to members. He also proposed a literacy test in order to exclude uneducated persons, since a few deputies could not sign their names. He believed that membership in the legislature ought to be limited to literate gentlemen of independent means. When his efforts to alter the composition of the house failed, he tried to persuade his correspondents, including Prince EDWARD AUGUSTUS, to have the Constitutional Act of 1791 amended to curb the assembly's powers. In 1805 Young prepared a memorandum for Milnes, the departing lieutenant governor, recommending the union of the legislatures of Upper and Lower Canada to overcome "the present difficulties." As a merchant he had been offended that year by the assembly's decision to finance the building of prisons through increased duties on commerce and not by land taxes, which would have affected farmers.

Young's conflict with the Canadian party went on outside the assembly. In 1807 he was sued for debt by Juchereau Duchesnay's widow, Catherine Le Comte Dupré, whose lawyers were Panet and Pierre-Stanislas Bédard*, leaders of the Canadian party. On Young's behalf, Attorney General Jonathan Sewell* argued that the will upon which the widow's claim was based had not been proved in accordance with English common law. The will had only been deposited with a notary, as was customary under French law. The newspaper *Le Canadien* reported the case in detail and treated it as an attack on Canadian traditions. The judges, De Bonne, Jenkin WILLIAMS, and Chief Justice Henry ALLCOCK, found in favour of Young.

In the assembly Young's political enemies had the upper hand, his attempts to prevent their ascendancy having miscarried. He knew that, as a member of the minority, he was no longer of service to his friends in commerce and the administration. Therefore, in 1808, he decided not to run for re-election. However, he was induced by a petition, allegedly signed by 81 electors, to stand for Upper Town in the election of October 1809. He polled only 33 votes before withdrawing from the contest.

Young remained mired in debt. In 1807 he admitted owing 22 creditors more than £4,600. Increasingly, he turned to the government for his financial salvation. In May he went to Britain, presumably to seek a salary as master of Trinity House and appointment as assistant collector of customs at Quebec. These rewards were not forthcoming, although Young was given a salary as a regular member of the Executive Council. In 1808 Governor CRAIG endorsed a petition by Young for a land grant, while opposing another request for a salary as master. According to Craig, Young's treatment of his creditors was a scandal at Quebec.

Christian intervened to save the family's remaining assets. The St Roc Brewery had been leased to the merchant Jacob Pozer in October 1808. In December this establishment, along with the Beauport facilities and the Youngs' own home, was seized by the sheriff at the suit of two English creditors, Baker and John Walter. To make matters worse, the St Roc Brewery was damaged by fire in January 1809. At the public auction of Young's assets in May, Christian bought all the properties. She had managed Young's concerns during his absences; now she was manager and owner, with her husband's agreement. In April 1810 the

Beauport properties were again seized while Christian endeavoured to revive the St Roc Brewery, where she had undertaken major repairs. In 1811 she contracted for the building of a new wharf. She also arranged for a large purchase of barley on credit from one of the brewery's old suppliers, James McCallum. In April 1812 Christian leased a two-storey stone house outside the Saint-Louis gate for £160 a year. The substantial rent indicates that, whatever their situation, the Youngs were not willing to live with frugality.

Christian also set about to eliminate her husband's debts. In 1811 she paid the widow of Peter Stuart £200 against a debt of £1,300. In June 1813 she used Pozer as an intermediary to recover a £704 debt acknowledgement to the estate of Robert Wood by giving Wood's widow £228. The St Roc Brewery must have disappointed her, for in the same month she sold it to her creditor McCallum for £16,000. McCallum also bought Young's long-awaited land grant in Sherrington Township soon after Young received it in 1812. When Pozer had 50,000 acres owned by Young in Tingwick Township seized, Christian was obliged to buy the land back in 1817.

Even as Christian manœuvered to avoid insolvency, Young remained active in the public affairs of Lower Canada. As a justice of the peace, he co-signed the warrant for the arrest of Bédard in January 1810. Bédard was an editor of the newspaper *Le Canadien*, which Governor Craig regarded as a treasonous publication. Young's expertise in law placed him in the Court of Appeals as a judge for four years, and his knowledge of finance earned him a seat on the committees of the Executive Council that dealt with lands and public accounts. At the outbreak of the War of 1812 he was placed in charge of a committee to devise a circulating medium to supplement the moneys available for the civil administration and defence of the Canadas. In July 1812 the committee recommended the creation of interest-bearing "army bills" with values of from $1 to $400. The issue of this currency between 1812 and 1815 created an emergency fund of £250,000. Measures taken by Young assured the acceptance of the bills in Lower Canada, where the population was mistrustful of paper money, and even in the state of New York. He was prevented from overseeing the circulation of the bills, however, when critics suggested that he would profit from their issue and redemption. After 1811, when Craig's successor, Sir George PREVOST, deferred to majority opinion in the assembly and would not submit to his council, Young joined others of the English party in successfully conniving at his removal. This action, along with its role in the earlier downfall of Prescott, makes it clear that the English party was only loyal to the governor as long as he shared its viewpoint, as had Craig.

Young

In April 1812 Young had written to the Colonial Office asking to be appointed either collector or controller of customs; this was his third such petition. Feeling that a representation in person would be more effective, he sailed with his family for London in July 1814. Lord Bathurst, secretary of state for War and the Colonies, and Henry Goulburn, under-secretary, would not grant Young an interview, nor did they accept his offer to act as an adviser during the negotiations leading to the Treaty of Ghent. Young suspected that his enemies had turned these officials against him, and he begged to answer any charges. Meanwhile, because of his prolonged absence from Quebec, his yearly salary of £100 as an executive councillor was being challenged. In 1816 he gave the British government yet another account of his services and declared that "his Slender funds are exhausted by the Expences of his family & the education of his Children since his arrival in England, & he has not the means of replacing them." In apparent defeat, he and his family returned to Quebec in the summer of 1817.

Having resumed his place on the Executive Council, Young gave advice on taxation, duties, and other fiscal matters to governors Sir John Coape Sherbrooke* and Charles LENNOX, 4th Duke of Richmond and Lennox. In Richmond he found a most pliant governor. The duke placed the preparation of accounts and budgets completely in the hands of Young, who in 1819 led him into a confrontation with the assembly over government finances. Through Richmond, Young was able to influence Bathurst, the duke's brother-in-law. The historian Helen Taft Manning described Young as Richmond's "finance minister" and "one of the arch-intriguers and trouble-makers of the English party."

Currency, commerce, and banking still occupied Young's mind as he lay dying in the summer of 1819. He drew up a proposal for a "Royal Bank of British North America" for all the colonies. He had renewed his requests for some extraordinary reward for his past services to government and for originating the army bills, but apart from two lots in Tingwick, granted in 1817, all he received was a commission to administer oaths to half-pay officers.

The estate inventory made after Young's death reveals how low his fortunes had sunk. Except for a piano, a chequers table, and 36 bottles of white wine, his effects were undistinguished; no books or paintings were enumerated. His furnishings and clothes were valued at £215, and he had only £12 on hand. His debts surpassed £7,000, of which £2,800 were owed to John Richardson* of Montreal and £1,000 to Christian. She had paid off more than a score of his debts, and she was now left to raise three young children with the aid of her eldest son, Thomas Ainslie. Young left her nearly £470 in personal effects and money, the Tingwick grants, and the tiny

seigneury of Vitré, as well as 1,800 acres of land in Upper Canada. Of about £1,300 owed to Young, £900 were considered "doubtful" or beyond recovery.

Young had one posthumous victory. A few months after his death, Thomas Ainslie Young received the post of controller of customs at Quebec, which his father had persistently sought. Thomas was destined for a prominent place in government and, as inspector of police after 1837, would zealously pursue the rebel Patriotes, who were the spiritual heirs of the Canadian party that had outraged his father. It was, however, the self-righteous and intransigent conservatism of such men as John Young that had driven many liberal reformers in Lower Canada to rebellion.

PETER N. MOOGK

ANQ-Q, CN1-16, 4 avril, 24, 26 déc. 1806; 8, 10, 19, 31 janv., 6 févr. 1807; 22, 25 oct., 14 déc. 1808; 23 juin, 12 oct. 1809; 13 juin, 1er, 21 sept., 24 oct. 1810; 13 mars, 7 juin, 20, 25, 27 sept., 31 déc. 1811; 10 avril, 30 mai, 24 oct., 12 nov. 1812; 8, 30 juin, 9 juill. 1813; 27 mai, 8, 20 juin, 11, 14–16, 18 juill. 1814; 4, 11 oct. 1817; CN1-26, 8 août 1800, 16 sept. 1802, 12 oct. 1805, 29 janv. 1806, 3 juin 1807; CN1-63, 5 mars 1812; CN1-83, 9 nov. 1785; 2, 25 sept. 1786; 9 mars, 23 mai, 11 juill. 1787; 18, 24 sept. 1788; 17 juin 1789; 17, 21, 22 mars, 14 mai 1792; CN1-92, 12 juill. 1788; 16, 17, 28 sept., 13 oct., 12 déc. 1789; 30 mars 1792; 18 août, 17 oct. 1794; CN1-178, 11 avril 1796; 20, 23, 28 févr., 2 mars 1797; 22 déc. 1803; 21 juin 1805; 14 janv., 6 mai 1807; CN1-230, 10 oct. 1789; 19 nov. 1798; 30 juin 1803; 31 juill., 10 août 1804; 1er avril, 26 juin, 9, 24 juill. 1806; 17, 27 mai 1809; 25 nov. 1819; 22 févr. 1821; CN1-256, 7 Aug. 1784; 31 May, 20 June 1787; 26 Aug., 22, 26 Sept. 1788; 11 May, 29 July 1789; 21 Nov., 6 Dec. 1789; 29 April, 14 May, 9, 16 June, 22 July, 14 Sept. 1791; 25, 29 June, 8 Sept., 17 Nov. 1791; 17 Feb. 1792; 13, 16, 22 Nov. 1793; 18, 21 Feb., 28 June, 25 Sept. 1794; 28 Feb., 4, 24 March, 1, 5 June, 3, 15 Aug., 28 Nov. 1795; 18 May 1796; 20 Jan., 8, 9 June 1797; 10 Feb., 6, 8, 26 March, 28 April, 11 May, 4, 6 June, 10, 15, 23 Aug. 1798; 27 April, 13, 29 Aug., 20 Feb. 1800; 20 April 1802; CN1-262, 11, 23, 25, 27 mai, 2 juin, 8 août 1796; 15 avril, 18 mai, 26 juin, 1er juill. 1797; 27 févr., 15 oct. 1799; 30 avril, 30 juin, 17 oct. 1800; 21 janv., 1er avril, 23 mai, 21 août 1801; 2 août, 18 nov. 1802; 11 juin, 29 sept., 1er, 15 oct. 1803; 24 août 1804; CN1-284, 12 oct., 27 déc. 1791; 11 août 1792; 21 nov. 1793; 4 oct. 1800; 16 juill. 1801; CN1-285, 13 mai, 20, 29 juill., 12 août, 5, 18 sept. 1800; 9 juin, 18 juill., 10 sept. 1801; 20 avril, 9 août, 26 oct. 1802; 3, 10 févr., 23 mai, 17 juin, 7 oct. 1803; 14, 15 août, 12, 18 sept., 4 déc. 1804; 11 janv., 1er, 29 avril 1805; 4 août 1806. PAC, MG 11, [CO 42] Q, 29: 468–82, 890–98; 59: 564; 69: 330, 355–56; 72-73: 111; 75: 205, 220; 77: 71; 77A: 151, 195; 81: 577, 615; 85: 166; 101: 274, 276, 355; 102: 55, 64; 106: 379; 107: 332; 108: 114–15; 117: 230–36; 127: 98–102; 135-2: 65; 140: 562–71, 586–87, 595, 597; 153: 470, 480, 489; MG 24, B4, 1–5; 7; 10; RG 1, L3L; RG 8, I (C ser.), 99: 26, 29; 372: 176; 373: 177; 603: 4–20, 123; 688E: 376, 398–417, 437, 474; 704: 262; 718: 78; 1707: 16; RG 68, General index, 1651–1841: ff.59, 83, 345. Private arch., P. N. Moogk (Vancouver), letter from Samuel Phillips to Jonathan Sewell, 16 Jan. 1794.

"Les dénombrements de Québec" (Plessis), ANQ *Rapport*, 1948–49: 86, 119, 189. *Docs. relating to constitutional hist., 1759–91* (Shortt and Doughty; 1907), 614–19; *1791–1818* (Doughty and McArthur; 1914), 162–65, 170. [Joseph Hadfield], *An Englishman in America, 1785, being the diary of Joseph Hadfield*, ed. D. S. Robertson (Toronto, 1933), 125–26. [Robert Hunter], *Quebec to Carolina in 1785–1786; being the travel diary and observations of Robert Hunter, Jr., a young merchant of London*, ed. L. B. Wright and Marion Tinling (San Marino, Calif., 1943), 20. "La vente des esclaves par actes notariés sous les Régimes français et anglais," ANQ *Rapport*, 1921–22: 122–23. *Quebec Gazette*, 5 June 1783; 7, 10 Oct. 1784; 26 May, 9 June 1785; 26 March, 24 May, 11 June, 3 Dec. 1789; 17, 31 May, 14 June, 20 Dec. 1792; 17 Jan., 7 March 1793; 9 Jan., 26 June, 10 July, 23 Oct. 1794; 17 Dec. 1795; 26 Jan. 1797; 17 Oct. 1799; 5 June, 3 July 1800; 12 April, 10 May, 12 July, 27 Dec. 1804; 10 Jan., 11 April, 16 May 1805; 25 Aug., 22 Dec. 1808; 12 Jan., 5 Oct. 1809; 12 April 1810; 19 May 1811; 8 July 1813; 16 Feb. 1815; 21 July 1817; 17 Sept. 1819. *Quebec Mercury*, 22 July 1817, 17 Sept. 1819. Kelley, "Jacob Mountain," ANQ *Rapport*, 1942–43: 245, 247, 258. Langelier, *Liste des terrains concédés*, 1919. *Quebec almanac*, 1790: 44; 1796: 82. L.-P. Audet, *Le système scolaire*, 2: 115, 235; 3: 15, 17, 23, 38, 40, 47, 59–63, 83. Christie, *Hist. of L.C.*, 1: 127, 178, 200, 213, 230–31, 352; 2: 14–15, 252. F. M. Greenwood, "The development of a garrison mentality among the English in Lower Canada, 1793–1811" (PHD thesis, Univ. of B.C., Vancouver, 1970). J.-J. Jolois, *Joseph-François Perrault (1753–1844) et les origines de l'enseignement laïque au Bas-Canada* (Montréal, 1969), 92–93. Manning, *Revolt of French Canada*. Paquet et Wallot, *Patronage et pouvoir dans le Bas-Canada*, 23, 42, 59. P.-G. Roy, *La famille Juchereau Duchesnay* (Lévis, Qué., 1903). Ruddel, "Quebec City, 1765–1831," 250, 306–14. Trudel, *L'esclavage au Canada français*. F.-J. Audet et Édouard Fabre Surveyer, "L'honorable John Young," *La Presse* (Montréal), 3 déc. 1927: 53. P.-G. Roy, "John Black," *BRH*, 27 (1921): 4–5; "La Trinity-House ou Maison de la Trinité à Québec," 24 (1918): 105–10. J.-P. Wallot, "La querelle des prisons (Bas-Canada, 1805–1807)," *RHAF*, 14 (1960–61): 69–70, 262–68; "Une émeute à Lachine contre la conscription (1812)," 18 (1964–65): 211–12.

Z

ZEISBERGER, DAVID, Moravian clergyman and author; b. 11 April 1721 in Zauchtenthal, Moravia (near Ostrava, Czechoslovakia), son of David Zeisberger and his wife Rosina (Anna); m. 4 June 1781 Susanna Lekron (Susan Lecron) in Lititz, Pa; d. 17 Nov. 1808 in Goshen (near Gnadenhutten, Ohio).

In 1726 or 1727 the Zeisberger family moved to Herrnhut, Saxony (German Democratic Republic), where some fellow members of the Moravian Church had settled. When in 1736 his parents emigrated to a Moravian colony in Georgia, David Zeisberger remained behind in school, joining them two years later and moving with them to eastern Pennsylvania in 1740. Although it was decided by the elders of the church that he should return to Europe, early in 1743 Bishop David Nitschmann, noticing the young man's sadness at departing, advised him to stay. Zeisberger spent the next two years learning the Delaware and Mohawk languages in preparation for missionary work; he would eventually become conversant in the Onondaga, Cayuga, Mahican, and Ojibwa tongues and another Delaware dialect. During the later 1740s he ministered to the Delawares at Shamokin (Sunbury, Pa) and on 27 Feb. 1750 was ordained. Towards the end of that year he visited Herrnhut, where he reported on the success of the missions. As a result of the high regard that Count von Zinzendorf, leader of the Moravian Church, had for him, Zeisberger was appointed "perpetual" missionary to the Indians at this time. For the next decade he carried on his ministry at various locations in the Thirteen Colonies, occasionally acting as an interpreter as well.

Pacifism was part of the Moravian creed but extremely difficult for Indians to practise during the conflicts of the Seven Years' War and Pontiac*'s uprising. Many converts drifted away from the missions or were killed. By the spring of 1765 peace had been restored in the west and Zeisberger led the surviving Moravian Indians, mostly Delawares and Mahicans, up the east branch of the Susquehanna to establish the settlement of Friedenshütten (near Wyalusing, Pa). For the next few years he worked mainly among various Indian bands in the northern Pennsylvania wilderness.

The pressure exerted by white settlers in the Susquehanna valley began to make life difficult for the Moravian Indians there, and an invitation from Netawatwees (King Newcomer), chief of the Unami Delawares, led to the removal of the Indians from Friedenshütten and a nearby colony to the Muskingum (Tuscarawas) valley. There, at Schœnbrunn (near Gnadenhutten, Ohio) in 1772, Zeisberger founded a new settlement, and several other communities subsequently were established. During the American revolution he attempted to have the Moravian Indians and their Delaware neighbours maintain a passive stance, but he and his converts came under the suspicion of all the belligerents and many lost their lives [*see* Glikhikan*]. In 1781 the Schœnbrunn colony was forcibly removed by a large war party

Zeisberger

accompanied by British Indian agent Matthew ELLIOTT, and over the next year or so the converts were dispersed along the shores of Lake Erie. Zeisberger was taken to Detroit, questioned by British commandant Arent Schuyler DePeyster*, and released. He gathered a number of his scattered converts and, with the commandant's assistance, set up a temporary settlement north of Detroit at New Gnadenhütten (Mount Clemens, Mich.). In 1786, prompted by news that the Americans had set aside land in the Muskingum valley for the Moravian Indians, he led the community back in that direction. Local Delawares, however, warned against settling on the reserved lands, and Zeisberger took the colonists closer to Lake Erie, where they founded New Salem (near Milan, Ohio).

In 1788 the community contained 164 people, about one-third of the number who had lived in the Muskingum villages before the revolution, and war was still a threat. A confederacy of Indian tribes in the region south of the Great Lakes had been formed to block the advance of American settlement [see MICHIKINAKOUA], and the resulting clashes between Indians and whites led in 1791 to the evacuation of New Salem by its residents. Seeking refuge in British territory, they crossed the Detroit River and formed a temporary village near present-day Amherstburg, Ont. For Zeisberger it was essential that his converts live apart from the threats and temptations of white society, and early in 1792 he secured permission to found a settlement along the La Tranche (Thames) River. There, not far from modern Thamesville, they ceased their wanderings. Under his guidance the new colony of Schœnfeldt, or Fairfield as it was known in English, began to flourish. Thirty-eight lots were laid out for a village, and a meeting-house, schools, and barns were built. Corn, wheat, and vegetables were grown, cattle raised, bees kept, maple sugar produced, and salt and oil obtained from springs nearby. Lieutenant Governor SIMCOE and his suite were entertained at Fairfield in February 1793, and although Simcoe reproved the missionaries for having too close ties with Moravian headquarters in Bethlehem, Pa, in July more than 50,000 acres were granted to the colony. By 1798, some 2,000 bushels of corn were being sold annually to the North West Company and 5,000 pounds of maple sugar were being produced.

Zeisberger's life at Fairfield was not without difficulties, however. Whites who came to settle in the vicinity coveted the land and, he wrote, "if they could drive us away from here . . . would do so gladly." Passing war parties urged converts to join in the fight to save Indian lands south of Lake Erie. Traders and neighbours, white, Indian, and black, tempted them with liquor. They found it hard, moreover, to give up ancestral beliefs and customs and were frequently perplexed by their adopted religion. Often individuals had to be sent away from the community, the ultimate disciplinary measure. In many cases they returned and made further attempts to adapt to the required standards, but unconverted family and friends continued urging them to come back to the old ways. Zeisberger's diary contains frequent references to "backslidings and transgressions" among "the brethren" and to the "dark heathenism" of their Ojibwa neighbours, who came begging for food but resisted conversion. By the end of 1793 there were 159 Indians in the community; four years later the number had risen only to 172.

Meanwhile, in 1797 the Muskingum lands had been surveyed, and the Fairfield Indians were encouraged by both the American government and the Moravian bishop at Bethlehem, John Ettwein, to return to them. Allowing his sense of duty to hold his better judgement in check, Zeisberger made the agonizing decision to go, although it was agreed that two missionaries and most of the Indians would remain behind. In August 1798 he left Fairfield and with his departure went the moving figure and inspiration behind the mission. Zeisberger was utterly dedicated to his ministry and possessed of great abilities as a leader. A missionary who had served with him wrote later: "Amid distressing and perilous circumstances, not only his fellow missionaries, but the Indian converts, invariably looked to him; and his courage, his undaunted readiness to act, his comforting words cheered them all."

A new colony, Goshen, was begun not far from the former settlements on the Muskingum, and there Zeisberger spent the final decade of his life, haunted by a sense of failure. In fact, although he had not made vast numbers of converts he left a valuable legacy. Over the years he had produced extensive writings on the Delaware and Onondaga languages, which remain basic to their study, and his personal and official journals are an important source for the history of the tribes among whom he spent more than 60 years of his life. Fairfield was razed by the Americans during the War of 1812 but was rebuilt across the Thames as New Fairfield, and the Moravian mission continued there until 1903. Descendants of Zeisberger's converts still live on the remainder of the lands, now known as the Moravian Indian Reserve.

DANIEL J. BROCK

[During his very active life Zeisberger managed to publish several works in the Delaware tongue. These include his translation of hymns from the German and English hymn-books of the Moravian Church, which appeared as *A collection of hymns, for the use of the Christian Indians, of the missions of the United Brethren, in North America* (Philadelphia, 1803); *Essay of a Delaware-Indian and English spelling-book, for the use of the schools of the*

Christian Indians on Muskingum River (Philadelphia, 1776), a second edition of which, omitting the appendix, was published under the title *Delaware Indian and English spelling book, for the schools of the mission of the United Brethren; with some short historical accounts from the Old and New Testaments* (Philadelphia, 1806); and a collection of *Sermons to children*, issued with his translation of A. G. Spangenberg's treatise, *Something of bodily care for children* (Philadelphia, 1803).

He also left numerous unpublished manuscripts, most of them concerning the Delaware and Onondaga languages. The Indian mission records of the Moravian Church, housed at the Moravian Arch. (Bethlehem, Pa.), include extensive Zeisberger papers, among them the manuscripts of his major work, the "Deutsch und Onondagoische wörter-buch," a seven-volume German-Onondaga lexicon, and a complete Onondaga grammar, the "Onondagoisch grammatica." An English translation of the latter was prepared by Peter Stephen Du Ponceau under the added title, "A grammar of the Onondago language," and this likewise remains in manuscript at the Moravian Arch. Harvard College Library, Harvard Univ. (Cambridge, Mass.), possesses a collection of 20 Delaware-language manuscripts by Zeisberger and others (MS Am 767), and the library of the American Philosophical Soc. in Philadelphia holds several items, including his "Onondago & German vocabulary."

Three of Zeisberger's manuscript works were published after his death. A Delaware grammar now at Harvard (MS Am 767, 6) was edited and translated by Du Ponceau and appeared under the title *Grammar of the language of the Lenni Lenape or Delaware Indians* (Philadelphia, 1827). A dictionary of Indian languages, also at Harvard (MS Am 767, 1), was edited by Eben Norton Horsford and published under the title *Zeisberger's Indian dictionary, English, German, Iroquois: the Onondaga, and Algonquin: the Delaware* (Cambridge, 1887). Zeisberger's translation into Delaware of a life of Christ compiled by Samuel Lieberkühn was published in New York in 1821 under the title *The history of Our Lord and Saviour Jesus Christ: comprehending all that the four evangelists have recorded concerning him; all their relations being brought together in one narration . . . in the very words of Scripture*. Zeisberger's personal copy of this manuscript can be found at Harvard (MS Am 767, 2).

Two diaries kept by Zeisberger have also been published. His personal journals for the years 1781–98 have appeared as *Diary of David Zeisberger, a Moravian missionary among the Indians of Ohio*, ed. and trans. E. F. Bliss (2v., Cincinnati, Ohio, 1885). The official journals Zeisberger sent to the Moravian Church in Bethlehem can be found in "David Zeisberger's official diary, Fairfield, 1791–1795," trans. and ed. P. E. Mueller. Mueller's translation, originally prepared as a PHD thesis (Columbia Univ., New York, 1956), was printed with a few added introductory remarks in Moravian Hist. Soc., *Trans.* (Nazareth, Pa.), 19 (1963): 3–229. According to Mueller, Zeisberger "used his personal diary as a basis, sometimes copying verbatim, sometimes rewording the same content, often omitting, frequently adding information" to the official journals. This volume supplements Bliss's work, and the 33-page introduction supplements E. [A.] De Schweinitz's biography, *The life and times of David Zeisberger, the western pioneer and apostle of the Indians* (Philadelphia, 1870).

Useful studies of Zeisberger's life appear in *DAB* and in E. E. and L. R. Gray, *Wilderness Christians, the Moravian mission to the Delaware Indians* (Toronto and Ithaca, N.Y., 1956). D.J.B.]

ZHEEWEGONAB (Shewaquonap, Sheawaquanep, meaning duck feather), band leader among the Northern Ojibwas, probably a member of the sturgeon clan; fl. 1780–1805.

Zheewegonab's father, Nonosecash (known as Assakis prior to the early 1760s), traded regularly at the Hudson's Bay Company's Fort Albany (Ont.) between 1761 and 1771. In 1766 his large band numbered 12 canoes, or some 30 persons. He appears to have been murdered in 1772 or 1773, and his brother Shuwescome was killed in 1774. Probably Zheewegonab became leader of the band about this time.

He is first mentioned by John Kipling, chief trader at Gloucester House (Washi Lake, Ont.), who reported in 1780 that Zheewegonab was on his way to Albany with three canoes. Kipling's later remark that the Indian was pleased with the treatment he received there may indicate that Zheewegonab had been dealing with Montreal-based traders during the 1770s. In 1781 he traded at Gloucester House, but did not appear there again until 1783, when he reported that the smallpox epidemic of 1781–82 had killed a number of his band members, as well as many Indians southwest of Lake St Joseph.

During the summer of 1784 James Sutherland* of the HBC, exploring west of Gloucester House, met captains Zheewegonab and Cannematchie (possibly Zheewegonab's brother) and their bands, totalling 15 men plus women and children, camped at Pashkokogan Lake just southeast of Lake St Joseph. Zheewegonab told Sutherland that late in the summer of 1783, upon finding Gloucester deserted, he had thrown his furs away. That winter he apparently traded his catch to the men from Montreal. Sutherland made a speech to the Indians to attract them back to Gloucester, and then smoked the sacred calumet with them, aware that "none but he who is or intends to be your real friend will smoak the great Pipe." The Indians held a dance and a feast involving the eating of a dog. Sutherland's guide and Zheewegonab then exchanged guns, gift exchanges being important in establishing alliances.

Zheewegonab's band appears to have hunted in the vicinity of Lake St Joseph, especially near its northwest end. Sutherland's encounter with them in 1786 occurred near the Crownest River (probably present-day Cat River). After Osnaburgh House was established close to the east end of Lake St Joseph in the summer of 1786, and the Cat Lake outpost two years later, Zheewegonab traded at these two settlements, especially the former. Nevertheless, he dealt with men of the North West Company whenever they offered better bargains. Because of his great influence

Zheewegonab

over the Indians around Lake St Joseph, his business was eagerly sought; he called it his lake, suggesting that his influence determined where the Indians of the area traded. In 1790 he requested the establishment of an HBC outpost some 90 miles west of Osnaburgh House to overcome the attractions offered by the Nor'Westers there. The request was ignored, and the following year Robert Goodwin, chief trader at Osnaburgh, acknowledged that "plainly they will not come to us when they can get better with the Canadians."

Throughout the 1790s Zheewegonab's band played off the HBC against the NWC. In 1800 John MCKAY of Osnaburgh commented that he "as well as his whole Blackguard family are such expensive Indians that I am sure they never brought a skin to this house, since first settled, that ever cleared itself in England."

Nevertheless, Zheewegonab arrived annually at Osnaburgh House with from 6 to 14 canoes and was considered to be "the chief Captain at Osnaburgh" as late as 1805.

Zheewegonab does not appear in the Osnaburgh House records after 1805 and it may be assumed that he either died or was replaced as leader about that time. The band appears to have numbered about 30 to 35 members during the period of his leadership. Some of Zheewegonab's descendants now belong to the Osnaburgh House treaty band.

CHARLES A. BISHOP

PAM, HBCA, B.3/a/50–67; B.30/a/1–6; B.78/a/1–14; B.86/a/1–18; B.155/a/1–36; B.155/e/1–6. C. A. Bishop, *The Northern Ojibwa and the fur trade: an historical and ecological study* (Toronto and Montreal, 1974).

886

Appendix

HALDIMAND, Sir FREDERICK (baptized **François-Louis-Frédéric**), army officer and colonial administrator; b. 11 Aug. 1718 in Yverdon, Switzerland, second of four sons of François-Louis Haldimand, receiver for the town, and Marie-Madeleine de Treytorrens; d. there unmarried 5 June 1791.

Frederick Haldimand came from a German family of comparatively humble origins which apparently settled at Thun in Switzerland during the 16th century. In 1671, however, Gaspard Haldimand, Frederick's grandfather and a wet cooper by trade, became an inhabitant of the commune of Yverdon. Frederick's position as the son of a minor functionary may have been responsible for his receiving only a limited education. He evidently possessed a strong interest in military life from an early age, but the various cantonal and city forces of Switzerland offered limited possibilities for advancement. Haldimand later commented that his native land was no place for someone with ambition, and this belief may have persuaded him to look for a career with a foreign army, a course of action very popular in his homeland.

Various accounts have been given of Haldimand's early military service, but it now appears that in 1740 he joined the Markgraf Heinrich infantry regiment of the Prussian army, evidently with commissioned rank. During the War of the Austrian Succession the regiment was in the thick of the action. In addition to being present at the battle of Mollwitz (Małujowice, Poland) in 1741 Haldimand probably also participated in the fighting at Hohenfriedberg (Dąbromierz, Poland) and Kesseldorf (German Democratic Republic) in 1745. This experience may have been responsible for his being offered a position in the regiment of Swiss Guards in the Dutch army. In 1748 he became a first lieutenant, and on 1 July 1750 he was promoted captain commandant, with the army rank of lieutenant-colonel. While in the Guards he formed a close friendship with Henry Bouquet, a fellow Swiss who would also serve with distinction in North America.

In November 1755, as Britain and France were edging closer to full-scale war in North America, Jacques Prévost, a former Swiss officer of the French army, proposed to the British government that a regiment be raised among the numerous deserters from various armies who had taken refuge in Germany. He soon modified his plan to suggest that the regiment also recruit from among the Swiss and German settlers of Pennsylvania. Prévost's scheme appeared to satisfy the government's need to augment its forces in North America and its desire to have the Pennsylvania settlers defend themselves, and he received provisional royal authorization to approach suitable Protestant Swiss and German officers in other armies. By March 1756 some 90 officers and non-commissioned officers, among them Haldimand, Bouquet, Samuel Johannes HOLLAND, and Prévost's brother Augustin, had agreed to transfer to the British army, where they were to be joined by such persons as Conrad Gugy* and Joseph Frederick Wallet Des-Barres*. In the mean time, the British government had introduced bills into the House of Commons to permit the raising of the regiment and to allow the foreign officers to hold British commissions, which an act of 1701 forbad them to do. The bills were duly passed, but "certain Restrictions and Qualifications" were laid upon the foreigners. There were to be only 50 of them – or about one-third of the officers – and they could hold active commands only in North America. It also appears that they could not serve outside the new regiment. The unit, named the Royal Americans (62nd, later 60th, Foot), was officially approved in March 1756, at a strength of four battalions. To ensure that seniority would be retained, the officers' commissions were backdated to late 1755 and early 1756. Haldimand received the rank of lieutenant-colonel of the 2nd battalion with effect from 4 Jan. 1756.

In June of that year some 40 foreign officers, including Haldimand, arrived at New York. The remainder of 1756 and most of 1757 were taken up with the physical creation and training of the new regiment, and during these formative months clashes occurred between the British and foreign officers. The influx of foreigners into an army almost totally national in composition, combined with the widespread tendency of Britons to dislike foreigners, resulted in British officers slighting and harassing their new comrades in arms. Haldimand's unhappy experiences undoubtedly helped form his conviction that the British service would never completely accept foreigners, as did the failure of the British government to honour its promise to appoint Bouquet and himself

Haldimand

colonels commandant. But in order to deal immediately with the antipathy of British officers, he and Bouquet agreed to serve "with application and activity" during the war and to avoid involvement in army politics. After the conflict, if hostility towards them persisted, they could retire honourably. As it happened, both men had little to fear personally, since their intelligent professionalism soon made them respected and admired by many British officers. Indeed, as early as March 1757 Lord Loudoun, the commander-in-chief in North America, commented, "These two Lieu^t Colonels will do extremely well, and are very good officers."

At the beginning of 1758 Haldimand was at Annapolis, Md, but he was soon called to Philadelphia, Pa, to supervise preparations for the embarkation of troops, including his battalion, for the expedition against Louisbourg, Île Royale (Cape Breton Island). But Major-General James Abercromby*, Loudoun's successor, valued his services so highly that he persuaded Haldimand to exchange temporarily into the 4th battalion of the Royal Americans, which was to accompany him on his expedition against Fort Carillon (near Ticonderoga, N.Y.). During the disastrous British attack of 8 July on that post Haldimand was slightly wounded while occupying the prestigious post of commander of the massed British grenadiers. He spent the winter of 1758–59 at Fort Edward (also called Fort Lydius; now Fort Edward, N.Y.), occasionally sending Robert Rogers* and his rangers on patrols.

For the 1759 campaign Haldimand and the 4th battalion were assigned to Brigadier-General John Prideaux's expedition against Fort Niagara (near Youngstown, N.Y.), and he was appointed second in command. But on Amherst*'s orders Haldimand and his battalion were left behind at Oswego to guard Prideaux's communications and to build a fort to replace the ones that Louis-Joseph de Montcalm* had destroyed three years previously. The latter task was not even begun when on 5 July a force under Louis de La Corne* swooped down on the British positions. Haldimand disposed his men in hastily dug trenches and exchanged a desultory fire with the enemy. The next morning, when La Corne attempted to mount an attack, the cannon that Haldimand had concealed and the musketry "played w^t such fury" that the French retreated, and soon afterwards made off. Both sides suffered only minor casualties, and La Corne probably did not press his attack because the British force was larger and more aggressive than he had believed. At all events, Oswego was not attacked again during the war.

Late in July Haldimand heard of Prideaux's death before Niagara and he immediately set out for that post. However, on his arrival, he found that Sir William Johnson* had not only taken the fort but was also unwilling to part with the command he had assumed. Rather than start a dispute with the Indian affairs agent, a chagrined Haldimand returned to Oswego to await Amherst's instructions. His superior praised Haldimand's tact, but at the same time sent Brigadier-General Thomas Gage* to assume command in the region. Haldimand remained at Oswego over the winter, continued to work on the fort, and kept watch for French activity. Since Oswego was the assembly point of Amherst's army for the 1760 campaign, Haldimand worked during the spring on preparing transports and storing supplies. His services during the ensuing campaign won him the honour of taking possession of Montreal after its surrender on 8 September. Moreover, his non-British background and command of French were probably responsible for his being named liaison officer with Governor Vaudreuil [Pierre de Rigaud*] and François de Lévis* to arrange the embarkation of the French troops and civil officials.

Haldimand then became second in command to Gage, the military governor of the District of Montreal. Although the war had brought him distinction and advancement (to colonel in America on 8 Jan. 1758), he believed that his foreign birth still militated against his chances of rising in the British service. Just after the capture of Montreal he therefore fulfilled his pact with Bouquet and asked Amherst for leave to resign. He was, however, dissuaded from this course. Peace-time left comparatively little of military importance to do in Montreal, although its social life was some compensation for the periods of isolation Haldimand had spent in frontier posts. On 28 Feb. 1762 he was promoted full colonel.

That May Haldimand got his first opportunity to direct a civil administration when he became acting military governor of Trois-Rivières with the departure of Ralph Burton* on campaign. He occupied the post until March 1763, when Burton returned. The same year he again went from Montreal to Trois-Rivières, Burton having transferred to Montreal on Gage's appointment as commander-in-chief. This time he held the governorship from October 1763 to the establishment of civil government in September 1764. In accordance with the policy of the other two military governors, Burton had retained the majority of the French laws and regulations governing commerce, agriculture, currency, and other matters. These Haldimand also retained, but he made one significant change in the administration of justice. Influenced by the system Gage had used in Montreal, in June 1762 he established four courts of militia captains in the district to hear cases on a regular basis, and he also set up four councils of military officers to hear appeals from those courts. The arrangement was an improvement over Burton's system of using the militia captains as arbiters in their own parishes, and if the captains and the officers were somewhat ignorant of French civil law, this disadvantage was offset by the conferral of greater responsibility on local officials.

Haldimand also took an interest in the operation of the Saint-Maurice ironworks, which had been mismanaged and neglected in the latter part of the French régime [see François-Étienne Cugnet*; René-Ovide Hertel* de Rouville]. The works had been reopened by Burton in 1760 and soon made a profit on the iron produced. Under Haldimand's active supervision they became, in addition to a source of new iron, the depot for the rendering down of surplus iron from old cannon and other objects. In the military régime production went from 30,000 pounds in 1760 to more than 150,000 pounds in 1763, and the profits made were sufficient to pay the costs of the military government of Trois-Rivières. The works were enlarged, much iron was sold to the local merchants François Lévesque* and Jacques Terroux*, and badly needed hard currency was disbursed in the district in the form of workers' salaries, pay for casual labourers, and money paid to habitants for providing firewood and making access roads. Haldimand cannot be given sole credit for this improvement, but his keen interest ensured that Burton's initial work would be continued.

Little of real importance occurred at Trois-Rivières during the military régime. In the spring of 1764, however, Haldimand was unwillingly drawn into the controversy that surrounded James Murray*'s appointment as civil governor of Quebec. Murray had been officially appointed in November 1763, but Gage had directed Burton and Haldimand to continue as independent military governors until Murray's commission arrived. This order led to friction since Murray claimed, as governor-designate, to have overall military command from the beginning of 1764, and he also tried to take sole responsibility for the raising of the Canadian volunteers who were to assist in the suppression of Pontiac*'s uprising. This dispute had unpleasant consequences for Haldimand. Since he was without extensive private means – a state of affairs not as unusual for British officers as has been represented – his lavish spending to uphold the dignity of the governor's office had caused him financial problems. He believed, however, that a partial compensation could be provided by one of the two salaried positions of lieutenant governor established for the civil government. But the assistance he expected from Murray in attaining this position was not forthcoming, since the governor was piqued by Haldimand's earlier refusal to cede any of his powers prematurely. Thus, once Haldimand handed over the civil administration of Trois-Rivières to Hector Theophilus Cramahé* on 28 Sept. 1764, he was reduced to commander of the troops. Refused leave to

go to Europe, he spent a cheerless winter, a season worsened by his failure to obtain the sinecure of lieutenant governor of the garrison of Quebec, even though this time he had Murray's support. Despite his failure and his belief that foreigners were badly treated in the British service, he remained philosophical and confided to Gage that he had decided to forget his disappointments, promising, "I will shut myself up . . . in my trade."

In May 1765 Haldimand learned of Burton's appointment as brigadier of the Northern Department and the cessation of his own independent command, and he immediately and successfully applied for leave. He apparently left Quebec in September for Europe, but when he arrived at New York his plans changed once again: Bouquet had died in September at Pensacola (Fla), where he had gone to take up his appointment as brigadier of the Southern Department. The death of his closest friend ironically was beneficial to Haldimand, since as senior colonel in North America he was now promoted brigadier-general in Bouquet's place. Moreover, Burton had been recalled from Quebec, and Gage intended to appoint Haldimand brigadier of the Northern Department in his room. But when the British government appointed Guy CARLETON lieutenant governor of Quebec in April 1766 to act in Murray's absence, it also decided to make him brigadier of the Northern Department in order to avoid renewal of the sorts of quarrels that had developed between Murray and Burton and had hampered the operation of government. Consequently, despite Haldimand's eagerness for the Northern Department appointment, Gage was obliged to send him to the remote and much less desirable Southern Department.

In March 1767 Haldimand arrived at his headquarters of Pensacola, where he was to remain, with the exception of one year at St Augustine (Fla) between April 1769 and April 1770, until the spring of 1773. As brigadier, he was responsible, under Gage's supervision, for military affairs in the provinces of West and East Florida. Problems of communication between the two, however, confined his command to whichever colony he was stationed in. Fortunately, his relations with the governors of both provinces were, apart from minor disputes, good, and he was able to avoid the rather spectacular confrontations, paralleling incidents in Quebec [see George ALLSOPP], that had previously occurred between the military and civil authorities. Nor was there much danger externally. The powerful Indian tribes on the northern border of West Florida were by and large friendly and, apart from a short period in 1770 when Britain and Spain were on the verge of war, relations with the Spaniards in Louisiana were amicable.

Haldimand's years in the Floridas were nevertheless frustrating. The poor condition of the forts in

Haldimand

his command gave him constant concern, and a parsimonious government refused to advance much money for their repair and improvement. Their dilapidated state would have made little difference to Haldimand if his recommendations to withdraw most of the garrisons to Charleston, S.C., and leave the defence of the Floridas to the navy had been accepted. A promising start was made in 1769 when much of the West Florida garrison was transferred to St Augustine, but complaints from the inhabitants of West Florida forced the British government to return the troops and Haldimand in 1770. On a day-to-day level, Haldimand had ongoing disputes with the provincial board of ordnance about the employment of engineers and the responsibility for military stores, and with the barracks officials about the regulation of their department. These imbroglios were accompanied by the constant problems of poor communications, extremes of climate, the high cost of living, and the rough-and-ready style of frontier life. It is hardly surprising, therefore, that he should have bombarded Gage with bitter complaints about the "frightful labyrinth" of his command or that he should have described his service as "the most disagreeable . . . of my life." Haldimand was also troubled by his failure to advance in the army, which he rightly attributed to his distance from the seats of power in London and New York. His principal object was the colonelcy of a battalion, since the considerable income of that rank would help him deal with the debts contracted in the Floridas. But despite his efforts to persuade his superiors of his merits, it was not until 25 May 1772 that he was appointed a colonel commandant in the 60th Foot. Exactly five months later he was promoted major-general by the normal process of seniority.

In the spring of 1773 Haldimand was pleasantly surprised when he was summoned by Gage to New York, where he became acting commander-in-chief on the latter's departure on leave to England in June. His period in office, from June 1773 to May 1774, was relatively uneventful, despite the worsening political climate. On two occasions, however, he was called upon to make decisions of some importance. In the autumn of 1773 he successfully resisted the demand of Governor William Tryon of New York for troops to intervene in the ongoing dispute with New Hampshire over the "Hampshire grants" (now Vermont). Then, early in 1774, in the wake of the Boston Tea Party, when it was feared that New York would oppose the landing of East India Company tea, Haldimand decided not to provide military protection for the tea unless formally requested and authorized to do so by the civilian authorities. He was determined not to weaken the military's position by involving it in situations that could lead to violence with the population. Both decisions were fully supported by the home government, and his "Temper and Prudence" were applauded.

When Gage arrived at Boston in June 1774, Haldimand became second in command but remained at New York. The dangerous situation in Massachusetts soon forced Gage to concentrate his forces in Boston, and in September he ordered Haldimand and the New York garrison there. Gage's position as governor of Massachusetts left him little time for military duties, and in November he appointed Haldimand commander of the army at Boston. Haldimand remained in the background, however, because of Gage's policy of deliberately avoiding confrontations with the inhabitants. It is also of interest that Gage did not inform him of the expedition to Concord in April 1775.

In the mean time, the British government's increasing concern at Gage's gloomy reports prompted it in February 1775 to assign major-generals William Howe, John Burgoyne*, and Henry Clinton to be advisers to Gage. This step naturally entailed the supersession of Haldimand, and in April he was advised that his foreign birth made him unsuitable for command in what was then seen as a civil war. He was also informed that he had been granted leave and was urged to take advantage of the permission. The government's reasoning must have seemed familiar to Haldimand, whose appointment as commander-in-chief had been delayed while the legality of giving a foreigner such a position had been debated. It was, however, tactless for his replacements to arrive on the same boat as the government's letter, and for them to be junior officers with little collective experience of North American conditions. From a purely military standpoint, Haldimand's removal was ill advised, and it was a pity for the British cause that he was not given an active command. Not only was he probably the best British general on the continent, but apart from Gage he had the most experience of North American conditions in both peace and war. He was also, in contrast to his superior, widely respected in the army.

Haldimand left Boston the day before the battle of Bunker Hill, and after a stop in New York arrived in London on 9 Aug. 1775. Partly because of his knowledge of the colonists and partly because of government embarrassment over his recall, he was well received. Private interviews with the king and with Lord North, the leader of the government, were followed in September by his appointment to the sinecure of inspector general of the forces in the West Indies. Moreover, in July 1776 he was granted £3,000 as indemnification for expenses incurred while commander-in-chief. But while these events were gratifying, they did not conceal the fact that there was no chance of his receiving a military command against the rebels. Thus late in 1776 Haldimand could undertake his long-postponed journey to his home town. There he purchased the property of Champettit, on whose improvement he was to spend lavishly.

In the spring of 1777 Guy Carleton, now governor

of Quebec, learned that Burgoyne was to command the army which would invade the rebel colonies from that province during the summer, and in a fit of pique he promptly submitted his resignation. It was just as promptly accepted, primarily because of the poor relations he had had with Lord George Germain, secretary of state for the American Colonies. Germain had evidently been considering Haldimand as a potential successor to Carleton for some time, since soon after the latter's resignation was received the minister informed Haldimand that he had been successfully recommended to the king as the new governor of Quebec.

Although he had often proved his devotion to the crown since agreeing to serve under the British flag, Haldimand owed his selection for this new responsibility to his long experience in the North American colonies. His various posts and duties had allowed him to acquire a good geographical knowledge of this vast domain and adapt himself to the social and cultural diversity of its inhabitants. He had been able to familiarize himself with the numerous problems – particularly those of territorial organization, colonial administration, and defence – arising from the expansion of the British empire in North America.

Since Haldimand had left that continent in 1775, the imperial government had been engaged in a military operation of considerable magnitude to quell the revolt of the Thirteen Colonies, an operation undertaken in the hope – as tenacious as it was illusory – of averting an unhappy conclusion to the grave crisis. When Haldimand informed Germain that he accepted with gratitude the governorship at Quebec, the course of large-scale military operations [see John Burgoyne] was so preoccupying the secretary of state's attention that he apologized for being unable to give Haldimand any details or clear indications of what was expected of him. But even under these conditions Germain did not fail to stress to Haldimand the importance of the office being entrusted to him by the king. His insistent reminders that he owed this office to the king clearly indicated that in the eyes of the British authorities he was still a Swiss mercenary. It was probably because there were no other candidates of the same calibre seeking the post that the military command and the government of one of the crown's colonies were both entrusted to this foreigner. In addition to his commission as "Captain General and Governor in Chief in and over our Province of Quebec in America" Haldimand was entrusted with the same powers of commander-in-chief that had been granted Carleton.

Nine months were to elapse before the new governor could occupy his headquarters, because continuing bad weather in early October 1777 prevented him from leaving Portsmouth. His departure was put off until spring, and then was delayed again. When he finally landed at Quebec on 26 June 1778, the situation in North America had changed greatly. The disaster at Saratoga (Schuylerville, N.Y.) in October 1777 had wrecked Germain's original plan for suppressing the rebels, and the official entry of France into the conflict on 6 Feb. 1778 had forced the British government to disperse its resources in men and material more widely. Fortunately Haldimand's situation as commander-in-chief of Quebec enabled him to escape, at least in part, the constraints that the strategy of dispersal of forces imposed upon his colleague Sir Henry Clinton, commander-in-chief for the rest of North America. Although that policy created problems for Haldimand, in particular serious ones concerning troop reinforcements and supply procurement, he did not have to suffer such disastrous consequences as Clinton did in regard to strategic organization. Haldimand was not faced with instructions from the home authorities obliging him to give up sensitive places, withdraw to defensive positions, and part with a portion of his forces.

Because of the turn of events it had become of paramount importance, from London's point of view, to hold on to the province of Quebec, maintain its territorial integrity, repel any external attack, and repress any internal agitation. These were the main objectives assigned Haldimand, on which he was to focus in performing his dual function as commander-in-chief and governor. When reminded of them by the home authorities before his departure, he is said to have replied, "I shall do my Duty as a Soldier."

Haldimand could not have described better his line of conduct. He was governed by a sense of duty, as much by temperament as by military training and the professional commitment of a mercenary, and he tended to govern the province with the general's baton. How can he be blamed? To praise his conduct as commander-in-chief but stigmatize his behaviour as governor is to risk making an unsound judgement. All factors conspired to favour his combining the civil and military roles in the discharge of his duties: the mission he was to carry out, the situation itself, which allowed no choice in means and methods, and the system of government that had been established under the Quebec Act and that Carleton had brought under his authority, thus preparing the way for his successor.

The circumstances did not lend themselves to the setting up of a constitutional régime devised to protect the rights and liberties of British subjects. In fact, not only did the Quebec Act seem to have as much *raison d'être* as when it had been passed by the imperial parliament in 1774, but Haldimand's mission was similar to the one entrusted to Gage under the Massachusetts Government Act. Haldimand, who had been Gage's assistant in Boston for more than six months and had witnessed the difficulties he experienced at the head of a rebellious province, knew very well where he himself stood. His stay in Boston had

Haldimand

made him deeply distrust the operations of the Sons of Liberty, and certainly the American invasion could not have reassured him about their designs. For example there is a note in the personal memorandum that he wrote with his return to Canadian soil in mind "to tell [the Catholic clergy] that their religion and rights will suffer if the rebels, and especially the Bostonnais, gained the upper hand . . . [and that] the latter are most interested in reducing Canada in order to settle it with their own people so as to assure their independence."

Haldimand must have been somewhat relieved to receive the welcoming addresses from the English-speaking citizens of Quebec and Montreal, who seemed to be aware of the dangers in prospect and were counting on obtaining both military and civil protection to promote their economic interests and their political rights as British subjects. The French-speaking citizens of the town of Quebec also paid their respects, expressing their wish to continue under the protection of the crown's representative to enjoy the benefits of the Quebec Act, which guaranteed "the ownership and peaceful enjoyment of our property and our rights as citizens." These addresses showed respectively what the spokesmen of the two opposing communities were anticipating. They conveyed publicly the expectations that the legislative councillors entertained of the new governor and gave a foretaste of their different viewpoints.

Divergence of opinion was a normal state of affairs among legislative councillors since, in the absence of representative institutions, the council constituted the only centre of power where the political forces of the colony came face to face. When Haldimand arrived, there was already a well-defined split between two parties: the French party rallied the defenders of the authoritarian system put in place by Carleton; the English party grouped the forces opposed to that system and in favour of innovation. Whereas the latter party drew recruits exclusively from the Protestant minority and basically represented the views of the British bourgeoisie, the French party not only had in its ranks representatives of both peoples but contained elements from different social and professional groups. As reconstituted under Haldimand's administration the French party would include, in addition to the seigneurs and French Canadian militia officers, the commander of the British militia (subsequently the receiver general), Henry CALDWELL, judges John Fraser and Adam Mabane*, and surveyors John Collins* and Samuel Johannes Holland.

Haldimand quite naturally found within the French party his strongest support for maintaining the system of government that had been set up since the Quebec Act; but if by doing so he was able to exercise his authority as he thought best, it was less from a desire to consolidate his personal power, as Carleton had

done, than from the wish to serve the interests of the crown as best he could. Haldimand's civil administration was characterized by resistance to change. It was as much through the force of circumstance as through personal choice that he resolutely set out along the path traced by his predecessor. He soon perceived that the established system would make it easier to maintain political control of the situation at a time when he had to concentrate on assuring the province's security and defence.

Despite the vigilance that his heavy responsibilities required, Haldimand displayed some flexibility from the earliest days of his administration. Having learned of the presence in Montreal of printer Fleury Mesplet*, who had been in the service of the Philadelphia-based Continental Congress, he at first ordered him expelled from the province but changed his mind following the intervention of "respectable" Montrealers on their fellow citizen's behalf. The weekly newspaper that Mesplet and his partner, Valentin Jautard*, had founded a month before the new governor's arrival continued to appear for nearly a year. The two journalists were, however, kept under close surveillance by Lieutenant Governor Cramahé and were required to avoid involvement in politics. They did not escape ecclesiastical censure from the vicar general and Sulpician superior, Étienne Montgolfier*; he had little liking for their literary efforts, which were inspired by the Enlightenment. Montgolfier hastened to put Haldimand on his guard against these members of the Académie de Montréal. The governor preferred to play for time, replying that "the matter . . . merited careful reflection" and that he had "very explicitly had attacks on religion or the clergy forbidden."

Time had its limits, of course. In April 1779 Mesplet was summoned before the Court of Common Pleas for daring to reflect in public on the administration of justice. Jautard, who as a lawyer could enter the "sanctuary of justice," had revealed to the public the judicial irregularities being committed there, and Pierre Du Calvet* entered the fray in his turn to denounce the judges' abuses of powers and to call René-Ovide Hertel de Rouville to account. Losing patience with the "misconduct of these insolent people," the latter urged Haldimand to deal severely with them. The decision was not long in coming: it was directed against not only the newspaper, but also Mesplet and Jautard, who were put behind bars on 3 June 1779. Even though they were detained for political reasons, Haldimand justified his action by alleging reasons of security such as stifling "the licentious spirit" which had been infecting the atmosphere of the town of Montreal from the time of the American invasion.

The bad reputation Montreal had acquired as a centre for plots and a hotbed of agitation for seditious and turbulent minds lent some weight to the presumption, if not to the demonstration, of the two prisoners' guilt, but above all it was the fact that they were natives of France which made them suspect in Haldimand's eyes. Previously, in the spring of 1779, another French immigrant, Pierre de SALES Laterrière, had been imprisoned on suspicion of collaboration and conspiracy [see Christophe Pélissier*]. The governor waited until the spring of 1780 before proceeding with other arrests as warnings: these included the apprehension of Charles Hay*, a Scottish merchant at Quebec, and François CAZEAU, a Montreal merchant of French origin. In September 1780 Brigadier-General Allan Maclean* had Du Calvet and the master surgeon Boyer Pillon, both of Montreal, detained.

In his well-known indictment, which he published in London in 1784 under the title *Appel à la justice de l'État*, Du Calvet claimed that the arrests of citizens under Haldimand's "despotic and tyrannical" administration could be counted "by the hundreds." Less than a month after his arrival Haldimand had published in the *Quebec Gazette* an act of the British parliament which from the spring of 1777 had authorized in the North American colonies the arrest and detention, without right to bail, of any person suspected or accused of high treason. This legislation justified in the governor's eyes the prolonged imprisonment without legal recourse of persons considered undesirable or dangerous. The situation warranted such security measures, he informed Germain when explaining his actions. Consequently he waited until peace returned before releasing, in the spring of 1783, the people he considered mainly responsible for an espionage network. A year later he finally complied with article 13 of his instructions and issued an ordinance establishing habeas corpus.

Haldimand's mission appeared the more difficult and sensitive since he was taking charge of a former French colony populated largely by erstwhile subjects of the king of France who could not remain indifferent to the alliance between France and the American colonies. After a French squadron had reached Delaware Bay in July 1778, schemes for conquering Canada began to give rise to rumours of invasion. However, an attempt to reconquer Canada did not enter into the plans of France because, as the French foreign minister, the Comte de Vergennes, observed, it was in that country's interest to leave her former colony in the hands of the British to be "a useful source of unease and vigilance on the part of the Americans, because it will make them even more conscious of their need for the king's friendship and alliance." The minister plenipotentiary to the American Congress, Conrad-Alexandre Gérard, was none the less supposed "always to lend himself readily to anything that may suit the United States and to co-operate willingly

in the execution of their plan for conquest as far as circumstances permit . . . but without making any formal commitment to do so."

France's secret designs were kept well hidden by the proposals for conquering the province of Quebec that the Marquis de La Fayette advanced. Early in the autumn of 1778 Congress studied and approved an invasion plan to be carried out with the assistance of France in the spring and summer of 1779. This plan envisaged the occupation of the province through a vast deployment of forces and a series of military operations both in the west, where capture of Detroit and Niagara and control of Lake Ontario were to be secured, and in the St Lawrence valley, which was to be penetrated through a double thrust via the Rivière Saint-François and the St Lawrence. While the soldiers of the revolutionary army setting off from the mouth of the Saint-François would invade the south shore, a French expeditionary corps would sail from Brest across the Atlantic to take the town of Quebec by surprise, incorporate as many Canadian volunteers as possible into its regiments, and then join the American troops to seize Montreal. But this invasion strategy, which was modelled on British operations during the Seven Years' War, was considered impracticable by General George Washington; for him, freeing American soil of the British presence was the prime necessity. In the end Congress decided to put aside the proposed plan, without however abandoning any measures that might favour "the liberty and independence of Canada and its union with the United States."

The French vice-admiral Jean-Baptiste-Charles d'Estaing joined in Vergennes's diplomatic game, pretending to give his support to the plan. Late in October 1778 d'Estaing had a declaration printed on board the *Languedoc* addressed "to all former French people in North America." Essentially it was rhetoric intended to revive the conquered people's memory of the former mother country: "You were born French, you cannot have ceased to be so." The manifesto began circulating and appearing on a few church doors in the spring of 1779. The allusion to the possibility that French flags might appear in the valley of the St Lawrence caught the imagination of those who, through real attachment, self-interest, or other reasons, hoped for France's return.

It was as much the skilful dissimulation involved in spreading the proclamation as the actual infecting of people's minds that worried Haldimand in the extreme. "I see myself surrounded by enemies," he confided to his friend Jacques de Budé, "since France has allied herself with the rebels." What he feared, he admitted to Clinton, was less an outright attack by an invading army than infiltration into the heart of the country by detachments that would take advantage of collaborators in all classes of the population. He explained that he had every reason to believe the

Haldimand

distribution of the proclamation was linked to a network for corresponding with the rebels, even though he had not yet succeeded in obtaining proof. At this moment Mesplet and Jautard were arrested.

It was nevertheless time that Haldimand moderated his obsession with the subversive influence of the Franco-American alliance on the inhabitants of the St Lawrence valley and turned his attention elsewhere. News from the west heralded much more real dangers of subversion among the Indian tribes, both the Six Nations and those of the Illinois country.

The geographical immensity of Quebec presented enormous problems for its defence. A month after his arrival, however, Haldimand was in a position to outline his strategy. The building of a citadel at Quebec did not seem to him a matter of great urgency: its completion would take several years and commencing works of fortification in the present circumstances "might only serve to intimidate the people, and no ways answer immediate exigencies." What was particularly urgent was to ensure control of the main access routes – the Richelieu and Lake Champlain on one hand, the upper St Lawrence and the Great Lakes on the other – by strengthening Fort St Johns, occupying Cataraqui (Kingston, Ont.), reinforcing Niagara and Detroit, and reoccupying Oswego and if possible Fort Presque Isle (Erie, Pa). Communications with the western posts had to be maintained at all costs, because they were indispensable not only to the colony's economy but also for the protection of the settled region in the St Lawrence valley. It might well be because of the sheer size of Quebec that Great Britain could hope to maintain her hold on North America.

The preservation of such a huge territory would require a mobilization of human resources that was to constitute one of Haldimand's major preoccupations until the end of the war. Before leaving England he had been told by Germain that a force of nearly 1,200 men was being dispatched. These reinforcements, together with some 5,500 soldiers already stationed in Quebec, were considered by Germain quite sufficient to defend the province. He left to Haldimand's discretion the creation of a corps of Canadians, of not more than a thousand men recruited from the local militia on an alternating basis and for a limited period, to conduct diversionary operations along the frontiers and back up larger-scale undertakings.

Once in the colony, Haldimand thought Germain's confidence unfounded. There were fewer than 6,000 soldiers fit for duty and of these about 900 were in fact beyond his control in the western posts. In addition these military forces were a motley collection: on the one hand a few thousand British regulars and nearly as many German auxiliaries, and on the other units of provincial troops, including Brigadier-General Maclean's Royal Highland Emigrants and the American loyalists recruited by Sir John Johnson* who formed the one-battalion-strong King's Royal Regiment of New York. In addition there were the ranger companies under Major Commandant John Butler*, who was stationed at Fort Niagara.

Within less than a month Haldimand began to clamour for more reinforcements. In the face of invaders familiar with the terrain, trained to withstand the climate and used to finding shelter in the woods, his "stolid German troops," who could be employed only on garrison duty, would be of no use. As for the British soldiers, they had not been in the country long enough to hold their own against the rebels' tactics. It thus seemed absolutely essential for Britain to send a large body of troops whose presence could readily inspire enthusiasm among the conquered population and thus make possible the recruitment of a corps of provincials entirely commanded by Canadian officers.

The fear, which indeed amounted to an obsession, of a second American invasion so preoccupied Haldimand that he saved his resources in men and supplies to protect the St Lawrence valley region. The early months of his administration were devoted to organizing his defensive system, and in particular to fortifying the Richelieu axis. He made Sorel his main operational base and accordingly fitted it up to quarter the largest part of his troops and store munitions and supplies. These facilities were to attain such a scale that two years later the seigneury of Sorel became crown property through Haldimand's agency. After the war he turned it into a temporary reception area for thousands of loyalist refugees.

As he was completely absorbed in reinforcing the defences of the St Lawrence valley, Haldimand paid too little attention to the more real danger of attacks that were being planned by the Americans in the west. The situation even had to deteriorate gravely before he resolved to consider the consequences seriously and try belatedly to make up for his lack of vigilance. Haldimand really became conscious of the gravity of the situation and began to concern himself seriously with the problems of security and defence west of the upper St Lawrence in the spring of 1779. In April he sent an aide-de-camp, Captain Dietrich Brehm, to inspect the line of communication between Montreal and Detroit. Brehm was to examine fortifications, recommend essential repairs, and above all investigate means of improving the supply system. Supplying the troops was indeed of such fundamental concern to Haldimand that he was to make it the foundation of his defensive strategy for the west.

Haldimand had not given up his plan for reestablishing a post at Oswego that would offer "the most effectual means to secure the fidelity of the Indians," whom the rebels were contriving to entice away by exploiting the Franco-American alliance for propaganda purposes. While awaiting reinforcements he had been busy since early spring dispatching provisions to re-supply the posts in the west, which had been sadly depleted following Lieutenant Governor Henry Hamilton*'s "unfortunate Expedition" of 1778–79. The tempting promises that Hamilton had made to the Indian warriors who accompanied him had encouraged a great many Indian families to take refuge near the posts. Supply requirements had virtually doubled, and Haldimand did not see how they could be met because of the inadequacy of stores.

Having to contend with this double and crucial problem of shortages in personnel and supplies, Haldimand opted for a strategy aimed at retaining the most important western posts. And just as he had tried to consolidate his defensive positions in the St Lawrence valley, henceforth he would do his utmost to extend his control along the Montreal–Detroit axis by concentrating on the improvement of communications. His objective was to facilitate supplying the posts and to ensure their defence. He turned his efforts, therefore, to building canals around the rapids between Lac Saint-Louis and Lake St Francis. His biggest achievement was the construction of a canal about a thousand feet long at Coteau-du-Lac, which was completed in less than two years.

Meanwhile Washington was preparing to strike a blow at the heart of the Six Nations. His plan called for a large-scale and devastating march through the lands of the Senecas and Cayugas, who were known as the most "pro-British" of the Iroquois nations; it was entrusted to Major-General John Sullivan, who was joined by Brigadier-General James Clinton [see John Butler; Kaieñʔkwaahtoñ*; THAYENDANEGEA].

The success of this expedition was in part due to Haldimand's inaction. Indeed, Washington, who had striven to conceal his objectives, could congratulate himself on having been so successful in his feint that Haldimand, in a council of Iroquois convoked at Quebec by Guy Johnson*, held as groundless the deep fears voiced by the warriors in face of the danger threatening them [see Teyohaqueande*]. The expedition was at its assembly point at Tioga (near Athens, Pa) before Haldimand finally took seriously the risk that the Six Nations Confederacy might disintegrate. On 1 Sept. 1779 he pressed Sir John Johnson to assume command of a relief expedition comprising loyalist provincials from the KRRNY, a detachment of light infantry, a company of German light infantry, and a few hundred Iroquois and Canadian Indians recruited by the Indian agents Christian Daniel Claus* and John Campbell*. This force totalled 700 men, who were hastily assembled at Lachine, and the expedition had to be organized en route, as correspondence between Johnson and Haldimand indicates.

In late September, the Continental Army's punitive expedition was complete. Under the shock of the invasion the Iroquois tribes that had been hard hit at first displayed resentment towards their British allies, who had not responded to either their expectations of protection or their requests for help. Forced to seek refuge at Niagara and to depend upon their suppliers for survival, they had, however, no choice but to remain pro-British. Early in the autumn of 1779 more than 5,000 Indians flocked into the area around the post, seeking help from Lieutenant-Colonel Mason Bolton's garrison. Bolton had to cope with this new situation, which was going to turn Niagara into a centre for food and shelter and consequently to increase substantially the cost of supplying the west. Johnson had by then reached the relay point on Carleton Island at the entrance to Lake Ontario, and was imagining himself fully engaged in action. He was busily thinking up scenarios for counter-attacks and calculating his chances of surprising the enemy. Meanwhile Haldimand was worrying about having to feed this influx of people into the west over the coming winter. Having anticipated that Sullivan's troops would march on Niagara and then on Detroit, it was with a certain relief that he learned of their withdrawal.

In the event Johnson was not even able to give a severe lesson to the Oneidas, who had taken the rebels' side. Reaching Oswego in mid October, he had to be satisfied with the capture of three Iroquois spies and to go back down the St Lawrence with part of his expeditionary force. Although at the beginning of October Haldimand had approved the idea of a winter camp on Carleton Island in anticipation of military operations in the west, a month later he thought better of it, fearing that the supplies intended for shipment to Niagara the following spring would be consumed. It was his duty to take increased precautions, following the bad crops that year, which had already obliged him to issue a proclamation forbidding the export of wheat from the province in order to forestall a real shortage. Then in January 1780 he endeavoured to fix the price of wheat by ordinance. He was defeated by the single vote of Cramahé, who sided with the English party, and had to be satisfied with renewing the embargo on exporting wheat by an ordinance on 9 March 1780. On 15 Jan. 1781, despite continuing strong opposition from Cramahé, he issued a decree making it obligatory to thresh wheat. Offended, the lieutenant governor resigned and left the country for good.

The recall of Johnson from the west was also linked with Haldimand's constant dread of losing control of the situation in the lower part of the St Lawrence valley. By his own admission Johnson's expedition included "the best and most experienced woodsmen" in the colony. Men of that sort seemed to him even more indispensable for defending "Canada" – a term Haldimand significantly reserved for the region of the St Lawrence valley – because, being unable to count

Haldimand

on his German auxiliary troops or on the Canadians' loyalty, he was still waiting for further reinforcements. Until 1780 Haldimand complained constantly and bitterly about the first German contingents in the colony, but when more carefully chosen auxiliaries were sent, and particularly when Major-General Friedrich Adolph Riedesel, who had been taken prisoner at Saratoga, came back, Haldimand would tone down and then cease his criticism.

The extension of the conflict into the west had placed Haldimand in a serious dilemma: should he lose the settled part of the province or the *pays d'en haut*? But from the beginning of his administration he had made his choice. Now, having failed to win the Six Nations' loyalty by providing military protection – for example by re-occupying the abandoned post at Oswego – Haldimand endeavoured to retain their attachment by helping them with supplies and by distributing presents.

In the spring of 1780 at Niagara, Colonel Guy Johnson as superintendent of the Six Nations was supporting the efforts of the Iroquois war chiefs to mobilize their people and assisting them in organizing raids, which were carried out jointly with loyalist light infantry. At Quebec Haldimand was authorizing an initial and daring incursion to free the loyalists settled in the Mohawk valley around Johnstown, N.Y., from the rebels' grasp. The operation, which was carried out by Sir John Johnson, ended in less than complete success: fewer than a hundred loyalists joined the ranks of the "liberators" who had come to spread terror in the settlements of the region.

The following autumn, probably emboldened by the intensified guerrilla war being waged by the more loyal of the Iroquois chiefs – among them Joseph Brant (as Thayendanegea was known), Kaiũtwah⁷kũ (Cornplanter), and Kaień⁷kwaahtoñ – Haldimand wanted to strike harder. This time a large-scale operation was involved. Its main objective was to wipe out grain production in the Mohawk valley, one of the rebels' wheat-growing regions. Again Haldimand relied on Sir John Johnson to conduct the undertaking, which used much of the light infantry in the province and included the loyalists of the KRRNY and the rangers, as well as several hundred Iroquois warriors who assembled at Oswego early in October 1780. Two weeks later the expedition reached the fertile Schoharie valley and systematically devastated the farming settlements. Johnson reported to Haldimand that within a 50-mile radius between Fort Plain and Fort Hunter he had burned a thousand houses and as many barns in which were stored more than half a million bushels of grain – the equivalent of about a fifth of the grain produced in the St Lawrence valley. Faced with the loss of this supply essential to his troops, Washington expressed his concern to the president of Congress.

To cover this daring stroke Haldimand had turned to the diversionary strategy favoured by Germain. He had instructed Major Christopher Carleton, the commander of the garrison at Île aux Noix, in the Richelieu, to lead a punitive expedition against the rebel forts south of Lake Champlain. Assembling forces as numerous as those at Johnson's disposal, Major Carleton succeeded in taking Fort Ann, N.Y., and Fort George (also called Fort William Henry; now Lake George) after surprising their garrisons, and took more than a hundred men prisoner. He burned the two forts and several dwellings and other buildings in the vicinity.

These striking successes so alarmed the governor of New York, George Clinton, that to prevent a repetition in 1781 he made a moving appeal to the president of Congress for help from the other American states. While expressing satisfaction with the results, Haldimand for his part voiced some anxiety to his colleague Sir Henry Clinton: these successes, he suggested, might be "an Additional Motive for the Enemy to Attempt the Reduction of this Province for the Security of their Frontiers." Haldimand was indicating in his own way that he did not intend to multiply his bold initiatives at the risk of imperilling the province's safety.

During the time they had held their respective posts, the two commanders-in-chief had often in their mutual correspondence expressed a desire to coordinate military operations. But the immense size of the theatre of war and the degree to which their troops were dispersed forced them to act independently most of the time. Haldimand never undertook important operations, however, without advising his colleague in the hope that Clinton could take advantage of them and perhaps even attempt an offensive of his own. This hope became even more uncertain when the conflict was extended into the colonies to the south and Clinton became engrossed in planning for large-scale British operations at Charleston and Yorktown in the period from the spring of 1780 to the autumn of 1781. In a final attempt at collaboration Clinton proposed a plan for joint action: to ensure the success of an expedition being planned by the southern army at the head of Chesapeake Bay and as far as possible along the Potomac and Susquehanna rivers, Clinton suggested to Haldimand a major offensive from the north. For strategic and logistical reasons Haldimand refused his cooperation.

These reasons were reinforced by the fact that Haldimand already had a well-filled agenda as the autumn of 1781 began. He had, in fact, to risk everything in the most crucial phase of his negotiations with the representatives from "the republic of Vermont." This tactical plan he had already revealed to Clinton. In a repetition of his bold diversionary venture of the preceding autumn he was going to send

896

a "strong detachment" south of Lake Champlain, while an expeditionary corps and some Iroquois war parties would carry out raids in the Mohawk valley and on the frontiers of Pennsylvania. This time, however, the objective in occupying Crown Point, N.Y., was to lead not to a destroying operation but rather to an attempt to entice the Vermonters into allegiance to Britain. For nearly four years, from 1779 to 1783, Haldimand was to make his negotiations with Vermont a major concern. Unfortunately they achieved no concrete results. Each of the interested parties, however, got something out of them: Vermont admitted having seen them as "a necessary political manœuver" to shield its frontiers from an invasion or a foray by the British and as a "necessary step" for maintaining its independence. Indeed, during these four years Vermonters enjoyed a complete cessation of hostilities against them. For his part, as long as the truce with Vermont lasted, Haldimand did not have to fear an invasion by the rebels via Lake Champlain, "for without her Assistance, or assent, nothing can be carried on against this Province by that Route."

Early in 1782 Lord Shelburne had assumed responsibility for colonial affairs when he became Home secretary, and the first dispatch he sent Haldimand would have tried the most seasoned military officer, with its avalanche of news and directives from a minister obviously too busy to spare the pride of a mere mercenary. Without preamble he announced that France was preparing to send a sizeable armed force of perhaps 6,000 soldiers from the port of Brest. In the face of a possible attack on the colony, Carleton had been asked to move to Quebec from New York with some of his troops if he considered it necessary. Furthermore, in the event that the colony became "the Seat of the War," the very reasons that had necessitated Haldimand's recall at the beginning of the revolutionary war would prevail. In anticipation of Carleton's return Shelburne had obtained the king's permission for Haldimand to take a leave without losing his pay or his commission as civil head and military commander. This dispatch nearly put an end to Haldimand's long years of service; had it not been for his strong professional sense of duty, he would have given up the governorship. His decision to postpone returning to London earned him a knighthood in the Order of the Bath in September 1785 – an honour which he owed entirely to the personal merit shown in 30 years of faithful and loyal service to the crown, for he could not gain entry to this distinguished order of chivalry through any connection with the aristocratic world in Britain.

Though he had been cut to the quick, Haldimand nevertheless gave himself time to reflect before sending a reply to Shelburne on 17 July 1782 that reveals the proud and dignified bearing of this mercenary, who chose not to sacrifice his professional honour and commitment to his wounded pride. He began his letter by noting the security measures he had taken to meet any prospective French attack; then he again expressed his humble submission and devotion to the king's wishes, adding that he could not entertain for a moment the idea of embarrassing the British government or through his military rank hindering any measure judged propitious for the defence of the empire. He declared however that it would be impossible for him to agree to serve under Carleton's orders, suggesting that pride, dignity, and health all prompted him to avail himself of his leave and return to Europe. Despite everything, he said that he was ready to put off his departure until the spring of 1783 unless, of course, Carleton arrived in the province before then.

On 29 July 1782 Haldimand advised Carleton of his resolve to leave Quebec by autumn "if Circumstances should oblige you to come to this Province." Far from taking offence at Haldimand's frankness, Carleton informed him not only that he did not envisage going to Quebec the following autumn but that it was most unlikely he would come "at any Time"; he declared peremptorily that he had not relinquished the government of the province with the intention of returning to it one day, however things might turn out. He was even less willing to take over from Haldimand in a large-scale military campaign there since in agreeing to come to New York he had been eager to play a great role as mediator in the peace negotiations.

However mortified he was, Haldimand did not neglect the responsibilities of his office. In a letter dated 26 Oct. 1782 he advised Thomas Townshend, who had succeeded Lord Shelburne, that he was duty-bound to extend his stay because hostilities had not yet been brought to a close in the *pays d'en haut* despite negotiations for peace. The Americans' determination to seize the western posts forced him to remain on the spot to defend the interests of His Majesty and the empire. But if he thus consented to put off his departure, he did not intend to reconsider his irrevocable decision to return to Europe once this "critical period" was over. In the autumn of 1782 Haldimand was thoroughly preoccupied with the relentless determination of Pennsylvania and Virginia frontiersmen and Kentucky pioneers to continue their punitive attacks on the Indian tribes – in particular the Shawnees, whose villages were in the territory that was to become Ohio. Ever since the great march of devastation by the Sullivan–Clinton expedition, Haldimand had taken very seriously the danger to which the native peoples were exposed, and in consequence the growing threat to British positions in the west.

In his defensive strategy Haldimand had constantly counted upon the support of the Indian tribes, and principally of the Six Nations, and he had repeatedly

Haldimand

insisted on the "indispensable need" of maintaining the alliance with the Indians in order to safeguard the *pays d'en haut* and the western posts, and thus ensure the security of the province. Having long since learned that the best and surest means of maintaining good relations with the native peoples entailed exchanges of goods and services, Haldimand did his utmost to convince the authorities in Britain that they had to pay the price. And he in fact argued the case so well that the estimated value of the goods distributed as gifts through the Indian Department increased sixfold in a four-year administrative period, rising from about £10,000 in 1778 to £63,861 in 1782.

If Haldimand had been successful in obtaining backing for his policy of extending bounty to the Indian allies up until 1782, the change of ministries and the peace negotiations forced him to take another approach to upholding the cause of the Indians. His position was the more delicate and difficult since Shelburne would completely ignore the Indians' case during the six months of negotiations that ended on 30 Nov. 1782 with the signing of the preliminary articles of peace between the British government and Congress. Not only did these accords fail to provide any protective measures for the Indians, they did not recognize any property rights for them or even a right to live on any part of the vast domain that had been assigned to them 20 years earlier by virtue of the Royal Proclamation of October 1763.

Concerned that relations with the native peoples might deteriorate, Haldimand did his best through skilful diplomacy to prevent any rupture. He could count on the help of the devoted post-commandants, and he was able to draw upon the long experience of the men responsible for Indian matters. Thus, when Sir John Johnson arrived back in the province as the new superintendent general of Indian affairs Haldimand entrusted him with the important diplomatic mission of reassuring the native peoples that the king's protection would continue in peace-time as in war. The recommendations given Johnson before he left for the west in September 1782 show the vigilant attention that the governor intended to give this crucial problem. Haldimand remained conscious of the stakes at the negotiating table, where people were about to dispose of the whole of the old northwest and thus to decide the fate of the Indians. Apprehending the serious consequences of this peace-making and hoping to forestall them, he undertook to make the new minister aware of the seriousness of the situation.

The dispatch that Haldimand sent Townshend at the end of October 1782 established the framework of a long argument that the governor would develop and return to until it bore fruit to the extent of influencing the home authorities not to hand over the western posts, despite the provision for evacuation laid out in the seventh article of the preliminary treaty.

Late in April 1783 Haldimand received the official proclamation of the end of hostilities and the text of the preliminary articles of the treaties signed separately with the United States on one hand and with France and Spain on the other. These accords had been the subject of lengthy debate in the British parliament, and the harsh criticism of the opposition had brought about Shelburne's resignation and the formation of a coalition headed by Lord North and Charles James Fox, who divided the two posts of secretary of state between them. Although the generous territorial concessions to the Americans were widely criticized, there was only one member of the House of Lords who denounced "the cruelty and perfidy" of the peace agreements with regard to the Indian allies, who were being dispossessed of their ancestral lands in a "shameful and impardonable" manner. This cavalier indifference was reflected in the final letter that Townshend, as Home secretary, sent to Haldimand, instructing him to see to the security of the superintendents and agents of the Indian Department, as well as to the protection of the traders and their property. Only the situation of the white colonists, it seemed, merited the attention and solicitude of the empire's rulers.

London's obvious lack of interest hardly made the task easier for Haldimand, who in the absence of instructions was left to his own devices. Displaying remarkable tenacity, he persisted in his praiseworthy endeavour to make people in Britain aware of the situation. Far from giving up, he redoubled his diplomatic efforts among those who would lose the most under the peace agreements and tried to find a solution that would be acceptable to at least the main allies, the Iroquois. This solution came to him in the willingness expressed by the influential Mohawk chief Joseph Brant to abandon the ancestral lands of his nation in the Mohawk valley, which following the treaty of Fort Stanwix in 1768 had been invaded by New York frontiersmen. The long guerrilla war that the Mohawks had carried on against these invaders during the American revolution made a return to their former villages virtually impossible. Conscious of this fact, Brant had unburdened himself to Sir John Johnson, giving him to understand that his people could agree to settle west of Lake Ontario. When Johnson passed along this information, Haldimand took advantage of the Mohawk chief's visit to Quebec late in May 1783 to explore the possibilities.

Brant, who had come from Niagara as the delegate of the Six Nations and their allies, appeared before Haldimand to enquire "in behalf of all the King's Indian Allies" if there were grounds for crediting the alarming news that they had been completely overlooked in the peace agreements. Haldimand, on his own admission "much embarrassed" by the question, endeavoured to reassure the chief of the king's continued protection by suggesting that the area around Cataraqui and westwards along the north shore of Lake Ontario be examined by Surveyor General Samuel Johannes Holland. Then, since he very much wanted to have his proposal endorsed by London, Haldimand hastened to refer it to Lord North, the new Home secretary, in the first letter he sent him, on 2 June 1783. Clearly more at ease corresponding with a minister well versed in the problems under discussion, Haldimand told him directly of Brant's initiative and his own response, justifying it in the following terms: "Actions, not words, can make impression upon the Indians." This more assured tone also came from an element of personal satisfaction, since Lord North had informed him of the king's gratitude and request that he remain at his post until "the necessary Arrangements are made consequent to a Peace Establishment."

Events themselves left Haldimand no choice: his presence on the scene had become even more indispensable. There was indeed "much to be done . . . to arrange everything," particularly with peace agreements which, far from appeasing the Indians, risked provoking them to an uprising. The comments of the principal Iroquois chiefs, which the post commandant at Niagara, Brigadier-General Allan Maclean, had picked up, justified the governor's vigilance. Maclean reported to Haldimand in May 1783 that the Indians regarded the conduct of the British towards them as "cruel and perfidious." Considering themselves "a free People Subject to no Power upon Earth," they stated that they had been "faithful Allies of the King of England, but not his Subjects," and that he could not dispose of "their Rights or properties without a manifest breach of all justice and Equity, and they would not Submit to it"; what is more, "they would defend their own just Rights or perish in the attempt to the last Man . . . which they thought preferable to Misery & distress if deprived of their hunting grounds." They would, however, wait for Haldimand to inform them of London's real intentions before acting, because, they said, "you at all times treated them Well, and had been a true friend to them, and had always kept your Word with them and therefore they had great Confidence in Your Excellency." Fearing an unconditional surrender of the western posts that would put them "at the Mercy of their Enemies," the Iroquois chiefs insisted upon obtaining guarantees of protection.

Haldimand urged Sir John Johnson to visit Niagara again and try to calm the Indians' apprehensions by giving them at least some reason to hope that the king's protection would be continued. It took a great deal of insistence on the governor's part to persuade the superintendent to carry out a diplomatic mission that he found repugnant after ratification of the "infamous" peace agreement. Johnson gave in to

Haldimand's entreaties, and he managed to attain the twofold goal which the governor had sought: soothing the Indians' anxieties and hearing what they had to say in order to explain their expectations to the home authorities. In the reports on the meetings held at Niagara in the superintendent's presence Haldimand found ample material for pleading the native peoples' cause.

Early in August 1783 Washington's envoy, Baron Friedrich Wilhelm von Steuben, who had come to the province to lay the groundwork for the transfer of the western posts, gave Haldimand another opportunity to take the matter up again with Lord North. Courteously but firmly the governor had refused to listen to von Steuben, giving him to understand that there could be no discussion of terms for evacuating the posts before the peace treaty had been definitively concluded. In his account of the interview Haldimand explained to Lord North that it was incumbent upon him to avoid any gesture that might provoke the Indians, who were "in general extremely exasperated at the Americans." "The longer the Evacuation is delayed, the more time is given to our traders to remove their Merchandize, or to convert it into Furs, and the Greater Opportunity is given to the Officers under my Command to reconcile the Indians to a Measure, for which they Entertain the greatest abhorence."

In the middle of November, more than five months after proposing to Brant that the Mohawk nation be resettled in the colony, Haldimand received royal assent to proceed as he saw fit. Furthermore, Lord North stated specifically that this authorization also applied to any other allied Indian nation and to any tract of land the governor might choose within the bounds of the province. Finally Haldimand's efforts to heighten awareness were bearing fruit, and for the first time since peace talks had begun someone in authority in Britain deigned to concern himself with the fate of the Indians. Encouraged by this partial victory, Haldimand made a final attempt to prevent the western posts from being handed over and asked Lord North to abide by the terms of the treaty of Fort Stanwix.

By the time Haldimand's letter reached London in March 1784, Townshend, who had become Lord Sydney, had again been made Home secretary. In his first dispatch to Haldimand, dated 8 April, he reviewed the various questions raised by the governor that had remained unanswered since the previous autumn. On the matter of the western posts Haldimand had the satisfaction of seeing that the home government was finally giving in to his arguments. Sydney pointed out that by virtue of the seventh article of the definitive peace treaty no date had been set for commencing the evacuation of the posts, and as the Americans had not yet complied with a single one of the articles in the treaty, the British could, under the circumstances, delay at least until such time as they

Haldimand

could ensure the security of the property of the traders in the *pays d'en haut*.

Although he was authorized to grant the allied Indian nations any territory that he considered suitable for them, Haldimand had to wait for those most directly affected to make their choice before proceeding with the resettlement. Brant, who had at first been in favour of the Bay of Quinte region, finally in the winter of 1783–84 chose a stretch of land along the Grand River extending from its source to Lake Erie, a location not so far from Niagara and the ancestral lands of the other Iroquois nations. In March 1784 he sent the governor a formal request for the grant of the territory and sought the government's assistance, requesting an advance of funds from the indemnity claimed by the Mohawks for their losses in the war, which were evaluated at nearly £16,000 New York currency. Haldimand was delighted to reach an agreement and undertook to acquire the territory in question; he also promised he would recommend to the king that they be compensated for their losses. Then, despite the fact it was not up to him to grant an indemnity, he declared that he was prepared to advance the Mohawks £1,500 to provide relief in their difficulties, and as well to supply the whole of the Six Nations with clothing. He would arrange to give them food for a reasonable length of time, taking into account the available resources and the needs of the loyalists.

To acquire the territory an arrangement had to be made with the Mississaugas, and Haldimand put Lieutenant-Colonel John Butler in charge of settling this matter. It took nearly two months to conclude an agreement, which was ratified at Niagara on 22 May 1784. For £1,180 7s. 4d. the Mississaugas agreed to give up about half of their hunting-grounds between lakes Ontario, Erie, and Huron, for the benefit of the British crown and for the use of the loyalist settlers and their "Six-Nations brothers." But Haldimand thought it best to wait until the autumn of 1784 to proclaim that this territory was placed under the king's protection; he wanted to be sure that the region chosen would be suitable for regrouping the largest possible number of native people. Since he was, in fact, convinced that their survival depended upon this union, he took advantage of his final months at the head of the government of the province to make further recommendations in favour of bringing together the Six Nations. On his return to London, in a long report that he presented to Lord Sydney on public matters in the province of Quebec, Haldimand did not neglect to deal first of all with the "Means suggested as the most probable to retain the Six Nations and Western Indians in the King's Interest." Referring to the settlement on the Grand River, which was so close to his heart, Haldimand called upon the British government to welcome it warmly and give it every encouragement,

"not only in consideration of their past Services, but in proportion as it shall be thought necessary to preserve the Friendship & Alliance of the Indians." In all likelihood, it was, as he stressed, the best trump card that the mother country held for safeguarding the *pays d'en haut* and the fur trade.

From the beginning to the end of his term as commander-in-chief of the Northern Department Haldimand remained faithful to his mission of seeing to the defence and security of the province. Having made alliance with the native peoples the cornerstone of his defensive strategy for the immense territory of the *pays d'en haut*, he was drawn further into upholding the Indians' cause than the British government had anticipated. Although the efforts that he had to put forth for this purpose may appear out of proportion with the results obtained, they were none the less praiseworthy. Unfortunately Haldimand's commitments to the Iroquois nations were either unknown to most of Haldimand's contemporaries and their descendants or ignored by them.

The other group of refugees for whom Haldimand had to provide were, of course, the loyalists. Since 1776 they had been arriving from the adjacent American frontier regions, many taking service in the provincial regiments under the governor's command. By the end of hostilities there were small bodies of such troops, together with some civilians, in the Niagara region, at Detroit, and near Cataraqui, in addition to the main concentration at Montreal. More civilians were being subsisted at Montreal and Sorel, and in the summer of 1783 another group arrived from New York City. While never as numerous as their brethren in the Maritime provinces, by the peace the loyalists in the colony numbered some 6,000.

As long as a British victory had seemed possible Haldimand had given little thought to the placing of these refugees, though by 1783 it was imperative that something be done. The governor favoured a military settlement in the Detroit region, but this plan was abandoned following news of the cession of the area to the Americans. Haldimand had also considered the area around the Baie des Chaleurs, although he never actively supported the idea. The British government itself had advised that the loyalists be allowed to settle in what are now the Eastern Townships, but the governor persuaded it to change its mind: not only would the refugees be too close for comfort to their late foes, but he wished to reserve the area for the expanding Canadian population.

There remained the upper part of the province, and here Haldimand had initially been opposed to allowing white settlement because he did not wish to antagonize the Indians. But during the early part of 1783 he began to come to the conclusion that the lands along the St Lawrence west of Montreal could be used, and to consider the possibility of making

Cataraqui a focus for settlement. The preliminary surveys were favourable, the land could be readily acquired from the local Mississaugas, and the Mohawks who were to settle around the Bay of Quinte were pleased at the prospect of the loyalists' coming. Moreover, the leading loyalists wished to establish themselves there, and as Haldimand always believed that the refugees were "entitled to every Consideration and assistance" because of their loyalty he at length acquiesced. Accordingly, during the summer of 1783 he ordered more extensive surveys, and a start was made on essential buildings at Cataraqui. The enthusiastic reports from loyalists investigating the lands led Haldimand to solidify his opinions, and by the autumn he could justify selection of the region to the British government. Preparations went on through the rest of 1783 and into 1784, and by the late spring of the latter year the majority of those loyalists who wished to settle the new regions were ready to move. Eight townships were established along the upper St Lawrence from the westernmost seigneury to the vicinity of present-day Brockville, Ont., and five more around Cataraqui. By the fall of 1784 some 4,000 persons were established there. Of the remaining loyalists, some 300 chose to form communities on lands offered on the Baie des Chaleurs, and several hundred more decided on Sorel. Lastly, a small loyalist settlement across from Fort Niagara had already been formed by troops disbanded there.

But if the refugees had a place to settle, they lacked many of the necessary items that would enable them to create homes in the wilderness. All required seeds, tools, clothing, and other supplies, which were often insufficient or simply unavailable. Moreover, the loyalists' demands often took no account of scarcities. Fortunately, the government stores could still dispense provisions, which Haldimand had decided to continue for a year after the official disbanding of the provincial regiments, although these rations too were sometimes in short supply. The governor had to employ agents to purchase seed and provisions surreptitiously in the United States, but this source was erratic. Haldimand was also hampered because he had no clear idea of the limits of his responsibilities, since the British government had given only general instructions about the distribution of supplies. However, it is to his credit that he was determined to give the loyalists all the materials that could be spared, and that he was ready to exceed his powers from the genuine concern he felt for their plight. When in the summer of 1784 he received orders from London to reduce the rations to two-thirds allowance, and then to one-third the following year, the united protests of the loyalists that the step would cause great difficulty persuaded him to continue full rations on his own cognizance.

Despite the governor's good intentions, he was continually plagued by disputes and complaints. Disgruntled loyalists circulated petitions asking for freehold tenure instead of the seigneurial system which had been put in place, and others tried to circumvent Haldimand's plan for distributing the township lots impartially. The confusion and delays attendant on the moving meant that many refugees reached their lands too late to plant crops, and there were more or less continual disputes about the grants themselves. These and other problems were still persisting when Haldimand left, but at least some of the loyalists were well on their way to establishing themselves. Any examination of the founding of what was to become Ontario must therefore conclude that without the generous and unwavering support of Haldimand the original settlers would have faced much greater hardships.

In November 1784 Haldimand sailed from Quebec for London on leave. While he was in Britain, the government consulted him on provincial matters. In 1786, however, he was replaced as governor by Carleton, now Lord Dorchester. Despite the termination of his governorship, Haldimand was kept informed of events in Quebec by Adam Mabane, Robert MATHEWS, Henry Hope*, and other friends, and his sense of indignation was kept fuelled by their reports of the activities of Dorchester's chief justice, William Smith*, whom Haldimand disliked, and by their accounts of the agitation for a house of assembly and more English laws. Such unpleasant tales would have been less disturbing had Haldimand been employed elsewhere, but there was little chance of that. His foreign birth made him ineligible to hold "any Office or Place of Trust, either Civil or Military" in Britain, and he was too senior to assign to a minor overseas station. There were also less important irritations: other generals had made their service during the revolution personally profitable, Dorchester refused to re-purchase some of the items generously bought from him in 1778, and a country house he had built at Montmorency Falls was proving to be a white elephant.

Still, there were compensations. Besides his income from the 60th Foot, Haldimand received the pay of a lieutenant-general, drew rents from various lands, and held some stocks. When these assets were combined with his natural parsimony and the financial expertise of his nephew Anthony Francis Haldimand, a London banker, he was able to live in some comfort at his home in the fashionable Mayfair district of London and to maintain and improve his property at Yverdon. High social status assured him access to the court and to upper-class drawing-rooms, and the many dinners, card parties, levees, and excursions in the park were all carefully recorded in his diary. At the same time he made extended visits to his home town, and it was on one such visit that he died. He had never

Haldimand

married – his correspondence reveals nothing about any romantic involvement – and in his will he left his nephew Anthony Francis all his property. Its exact size is unknown, but it must have been considerable, for no less than £13,000 was ordered to be set aside in legacies to various persons and institutions. The bulk went to sundry relations, but £625 passed to Mabane, and £100 each to Mathews and Jenkin WILLIAMS.

Outside of his official duties, a good deal of Haldimand's time was occupied with his relations and his lands. His position made him vulnerable to requests from his family to provide for young relatives, in particular the brothers of Anthony Francis. Beginning in 1756 with Peter Frederick*, three nephews came to North America, where Haldimand dutifully obtained them commissions in the army. Unfortunately, all three proved less than perfect, falling heavily into debt, displaying a lack of talent in the tasks he set them, and embarrassing the friends who volunteered to look after them in his absence. In 1786 Haldimand's grand-nephew Frederick Devos was sent out as an ensign, and promptly showed the same unendearing characteristics. By early 1791, after repeated complaints, Haldimand was grumbling that he would send Devos "back to his dear mother's to guard her sheep" if he did not improve. But he always took pains to recommend all four for advancement, and in his will he left Devos £2,500. At the same time he continued to mutter that the family never seemed to appreciate his efforts.

Haldimand's cumulative experiences with land were not much happier. During the early period of his North American service he collected a considerable amount of property, but like many officers failed to make much of it. His two principal holdings were the seigneury of Grand-Pabos in the Gaspé and one-fifth of the township of Hopewell on the Petitcodiac River (N.B.). He purchased Grand-Pabos from François Lefebvre* de Bellefeuille in 1765, intending it for his nephew Peter Frederick. The latter's death the same year destroyed this plan, and for the remainder of his life Haldimand never seems to have been quite sure about what to do with the seigneury. Although he invested a certain amount of money and from time to time took an interest in it, he also constantly toyed with the idea of selling it. The net result was that Grand-Pabos remained largely unsettled and undeveloped but still in his hands. It was not until 1796 that Anthony Francis Haldimand disposed of it to Felix O'HARA, who had cared for it during the American revolution.

In contrast to his lackadaisical attitude towards Grand-Pabos, Haldimand maintained a lively interest in his share of Hopewell Township, which was granted to himself, Bouquet, and some New York merchants in 1765. The partners invested a fair amount, attracted some settlers, and seemed to be making reasonable progress until about 1772, when a series of complicated, lengthy, and expensive legal battles with their agent Thomas Calhoun, his executors, and various others resulted in part of the township being sold. The disruption of the American revolution depressed the settlement, and in 1783 the Nova Scotia government started proceedings for escheat for non-fulfillment of the conditions of settlement. Despite intensive efforts, Haldimand and the remaining proprietors were unsuccessful in staving off the escheat, which put him personally out of pocket for a considerable sum. None of the other lands he possessed ever attracted his attention as much as Hopewell or Grand-Pabos. Some property on the Saint John River (N.B.) was disposed of almost as soon as it was granted, and a farm in Maryland which came to him as a legacy from Bouquet was sold in 1772. Haldimand also received grants in Pennsylvania and the Floridas, and the former were in his possession as late as 1788 and at that time were still producing rents.

STUART R. J. SUTHERLAND, PIERRE TOUSIGNANT, and MADELEINE DIONNE-TOUSIGNANT

Algemeen Rijksarchief (The Hague), Raad van State, no.1542: f.49. Arch. cantonales vaudoises (Lausanne, Switzerland), État civil, Yverdon, 11 août 1718, 9 juin 1791. Bibliothèque publique, Yverdon (Switzerland), J.-G. Pillichody, "Remarques curieuses et intéressantes . . . manuscrit commencé le 5 septembre 1742," 57. BL, Add. MSS 21644: ff.328–32; 21661–892. N.S., Dept. of Lands and Forests (Halifax), Crown land grants, book 5: 400–2; book 6: 420, 423, 454; book 7: 43, 47, 51, 90. PAC, MG 11, [CO 42] Q, 14: 5; 19: 56, 257–63; 25: 295 et seq.; MG 23, GII, 1; MG 40, B1; RG 4, B9, 9: 33–43. PANB, RG 10, RS107/1/6: 13; RS107/5/1: 89; RG 10, RS108, Petition of John Wentworth, 1786. PRO, WO 1/7: ff.40–61, 71–72v, 119, 241–41v; 1/9: ff.285–340, 353–53v; WO 17/1489–95; WO 34/9.

[Jeffery Amherst], *The journal of Jeffery Amherst, recording the military career of General Amherst in America from 1758 to 1763*, ed. J. C. Webster (Toronto and Chicago, [1931]), 139–40, 147. [John Barker], "The diary of Lieutenant John Barker, Fourth (or the King's Own) Regiment of Foot, from November, 1774, to May, 1776," Soc. for Army Hist. Research, *Journal* (London), 7 (1928): 81–109, 145–74. [Henry Clinton], *The American rebellion: Sir Henry Clinton's narrative of his campaigns, 1775–1782* . . . , ed. W. B. Willcox (New Haven, Conn., 1954), 397–99. *The correspondence of General Thomas Gage with the secretaries of state, 1763–1775*, ed. C. E. Carter (2v., New Haven and London, 1931–33; repr. [Hamden, Conn.], 1969). *The correspondence of King George the Third from 1760 to December 1783* . . . , ed. J. [W.] Fortescue (6v., London, 1927–28; repr. 1967), 3: 196, 363. *Correspondence of William Pitt, when secretary of state, with colonial governors and military and naval commissioners in America*, ed. G. S. Kimball (2v., New York and London, 1906). *Despatches and instructions of Conrad-Alexandre Gérard, 1778–1780* . . . , ed. J. J. Meng (Baltimore, Md., 1939),

Haldimand

129. *Docs. relating to constitutional hist.*, *1759–91* (Shortt
and Doughty; 1907), 2: 676, 694–96, 721. Jeremiah Fogg,
*Journals of the military expedition of Major General John
Sullivan against the Six Nations*, ed. Frederick Cook
(Auburn, N.Y., 1887), 101. G.B., Hist. MSS Commission,
The manuscripts of the Earl of Dartmouth (3v., London,
1887–96), 2: 134–35; House of Commons, *Journals*
([London]), 27: 423–24, 440, 463, 466, 480. [Frederick
Haldimand], "Private diary of Gen. Haldimand," PAC
Report, 1889. [William Hervey], *Journals of the Hon.
William Hervey, in North America and Europe, from 1755 to
1814; with order books at Montreal, 1760–1763* (Bury St
Edmunds, Eng., 1906). *Invasion du Canada* (Verreau), 1:
49–50. *Johnson papers* (Sullivan et al.), 3: 116. *Journals of
the Continental Congress, 1774–1789*, ed. W. C. Ford et al.
(34v., Washington, 1904–37), 12: 1042–48; 13: 11–14.
[Stephen Kemble], *The Kemble papers* (2v., New York,
1884–85), 1: 41. *Kingston before War of 1812* (Preston).
Knox, *Hist. journal* (Doughty), 3: 93. *Military affairs in
North America, 1748–1765* . . . , ed. S. [McC.] Pargellis
(New York and London, [1936]; repr. [Hamden], 1969),
323, 326–30, 420. "Ordonnances édictées pour la province
de Québec par le gouverneur et le conseil de celle-ci, de 1768
à 1791 . . . ," PAC *Rapport*, 1914–15: 142–50. "Proclamations issued by the governor-in-chief . . . ," PAC *Report*,
1918: 88–194. *The settlement of the United Empire Loyalists
on the upper St Lawrence and Bay of Quinte in 1784; a
documentary record*, ed. E. A. Cruikshank (Toronto, 1934;
repr. 1966). Smith, *Diary and selected papers* (Upton), 1:
62. [John Sullivan], *The letters and papers of Major General
John Sullivan*, ed. O. G. Hammond (3v., Concord, N.H.,
1930–39), 3: 132–36. "United Empire Loyalists: enquiry
into losses and services," AO *Report*, 1904. *Valley of
Six Nations* (Johnston), 44–48. Vt. Hist. Soc., *Coll.*,
(Montpelier), 2 (1871). [George Washington], *The writings
of George Washington, from the original manuscript
sources, 1745–1799*, ed. J. C. Fitzpatrick (39v., Washington, 1931–44), 13: 223–44, 254–57; 17: 150.

La Gazette littéraire pour la ville et le district de Montréal,
25 nov., 30 déc. 1778; 21 avril 1779. *Quebec Gazette*, 23
July 1778. *DNB*. G.B., WO, *Army list*, 1756–95. P.-G.
Roy, *Inv. concessions*, 4: 128–30. Tremaine, *Biblio. of
Canadian imprints*, no.291. J. R. Alden, *General Gage in
America: being principally a history of his role in the
American revolution* (Baton Rouge, La., 1948); *John Stuart
and the southern colonial frontier* . . . (Ann Arbor, Mich.,
1944). Rodney Atwood, *The Hessians, mercenaries from
Hessen-Kassel in the American revolution* (Cambridge,
Eng., 1980), 254, 257. Norman Baker, *Government and
contractors: the British Treasury and war supplies, 1775–
1783* (London, 1971), 200–1. J. F. Bannon, *The Spanish
borderlands frontier, 1513–1821* (New York, 1970),
190–205. E.-H. Bovay, *Le Canada et les Suisses, 1604–
1974* (Fribourg, Switzerland, 1976), 15, 17. G. S. Brown,
*The American secretary: the colonial policy of Lord George
Germain, 1775–1778* (Ann Arbor, 1963), c.4. A. L. Burt,
Old prov. of Quebec (1968), 1: 27; *The United States, Great
Britain and British North America from the revolution to the
establishment of peace after the War of 1812* (Toronto and
New Haven, 1940). L. W. G. Butler and S. W. Hare, *The
annals of the King's Royal Rifle Corps* . . . (5v., London,
1913–32), 1. Evan Charteris, *William Augustus, Duke of
Cumberland, and the Seven Years War* . . . (London,

[1925]), 192–93. Alexandre Crottet, *Histoire et annales de
la ville d'Yverdon* . . . (Geneva, Switzerland, 1859), 391,
511–12, 515–16, 621–25. E. B. De Fonblanque, *Political
and military episodes* . . . *derived from the life and
correspondence of the Right Hon. John Burgoyne* . . .
(London, 1876), 120, 128. J. O. Dendy, "Frederick
Haldimand and the defence of Canada, 1778–1884" (PHD
thesis, Duke Univ., Durham, N.C., 1972). Henri Doniol,
*Histoire de la participation de la France à l'établissement
des États-Unis d'Amérique, correspondance diplomatique et
documents* (6v., Paris, 1886–99), 3: 237–38, 464–66.
G. N. D. Evans, *Uncommon obdurate: the several public
careers of J. F. W. DesBarres* (Toronto and Salem, Mass.,
1969), 7. Allen French, *The first year of the American
revolution* (Cambridge, Mass., 1934), 208. M. B. Fryer,
King's men: the soldier founders of Ontario (Toronto and
Charlottetown, 1980). J. F. C. Fuller, *British light infantry
in the eighteenth century* . . . (London, [1925]), 97. Gunter
Gieraths, *Die Kampfhandlungen der brandenburgisch-
preussischen Armee, 1626–1807: ein Quellenbuch* (West
Berlin, 1964), 43–47. L. H. Gipson, *The British empire
before the American revolution* (15v., New York and
Caldwell, Idaho, 1936–70), 9: 176–99, 200–31; 13:
88–109. Barbara Graymont, *The Iroquois and the American
revolution* (Syracuse, N.Y., 1972), 198–99, 220, 240, 256.
D. [R.] Higginbotham, *The war of American independence;
military attitudes, policies, and practice, 1763–1789* (New
York, 1971), c.6. W. A. Hunter, *Forts on the Pennsylvania
frontier, 1753–1758* (Harrisburg, Pa., 1960), 208.

C. A. Jellison, *Ethan Allen, frontier rebel* (Syracuse,
1969), 18–181, 225, 243–44, 254, 257, 260–64, 277,
282–85, 287, 290–91. Cecil Johnson, *British West Florida,
1763–1783* (New Haven, 1943). Lanctot, *Le Canada et la
Révolution américaine*, 94–95, 209. J. N. McIlwraith, *Sir
Frederick Haldimand* (Toronto, 1906). H. C. Mathews,
*Frontier spies; the British secret service, Northern Depart-
ment, during the Revolutionary War* (Fort Myers, Fla.,
1971), 122–23. C. L. Mowat, *East Florida as a British
province, 1763–1784* (Berkeley, Calif., and Los Angeles,
1943; repr. Gainsville, Fla., 1964), 27. S. McC. Pargellis,
Lord Loudoun in North America (New Haven and London,
1933; repr. [Hamden], 1968), 62–64, 316–18. *The parliamentary history of England from the earliest period to the
year 1803*, comp. William Cobbett and John Wright (36v.,
London, 1806–20), 23: 384–85, 410. Prussia, Great
General Staff, Military History Section, *Der Kriege Fried-
richs des Grossen* (21v., Berlin, 1890–1914), 1–2. H. L.
Shaw, *British administration of the southern Indians,
1756–1783* (Lancaster, Pa., 1931). John Shy, *A people
numerous and armed: reflections on the military struggle
for American independence* (New York, 1976), 73–107;
*Toward Lexington: the role of the British army in the coming
of the American revolution* (Princeton, N.J., 1965). Marcel
Trudel, *Louis XVI, le Congrès américain et le Canada,
1774–1789* (Québec, 1949); *Le Régime militaire dans
le gouvernement des Trois-Rivières, 1760–1764* (Trois-
Rivières, Qué., 1952), 59, 61–97, 101–24. P.-E. de
Vallière, *Honneur et fidélité: histoire des Suisses au service
étranger* (Lausanne, 1940). N. W. Wallace, *A regimental
chronicle and list of officers of the 60th, or King's Royal Rifle
Corps, formerly the 62nd, or the Royal American Regiment
of Foot* (London, 1879), app., 31–33, 35–37. Horace
Walpole, *Memoirs of the reign of King George the Second*,

Haldimand

ed. [H. R. V. Fox, 3rd Baron] Holland (2nd ed., 3v., London, 1846), 2: 160. W. B. Willcox, *Portrait of a general: Sir Henry Clinton in the War of Independence* (New York, 1964), 37. B. [G.] Wilson, *As she began: an illustrated introduction to loyalist Ontario* (Toronto and Charlottetown, 1981). E. C. Wright, *The Petitcodiac: a study of the New Brunswick river and of the people who settled along it* (Sackville, N.B., 1945). J. L. Wright, *Anglo-Spanish rivalry in North America* (Athens, Ga., 1971), 111–20.

E. D. Branch, "Henry Bouquet: his relict possessions," *Western Pa. Hist. Magazine* (Pittsburgh), 22 (1938): 201–8. A. L. Burt, "The quarrel between Germain and Carleton: an inverted story," *CHR*, 11 (1930): 202–22. Willis Chipman, "The life and times of Major Samuel Holland, surveyor-general, 1764–1801," *OH*, 21 (1924): 11–90. Allen French, "General Haldimand in Boston, 1774–1775," Mass. Hist. Soc., *Proc.* (Boston), 66 (1942): 90–95. R. W. McLachlan, "Fleury Mesplet, the first printer at Montreal," RSC *Trans.*, 2nd ser., 12 (1906), sect.II: 242–43. C. L. Mowat, "The southern brigade: a sidelight on the British military establishment in America, 1763–1775," *Journal of Southern Hist.* (Baton Rouge), 10 (1944): 59–77. S. M. Scott, "Civil and military authority in Canada, 1764–1766," *CHR*, 9 (1928): 117–36. P. H. Smith, "Sir Guy Carleton, peace negotiations, and the evacuation of New York," *CHR*, 50 (1969): 245–64.

GENERAL BIBLIOGRAPHY AND
LIST OF ABBREVIATIONS

List of Abbreviations

AAQ	Archives de l'archidiocèse de Québec	MAC-CD	Ministère des Affaires culturelles, Centre de documentation
AC	Archives civiles		
AD	Archives départementales	MTL	Metropolitan Toronto Library
ADB	*Australian dictionary of biography*	NWC	North West Company
AN	Archives nationales	*NYCD*	*Documents relative to the colonial history of the state of New-York*
ANQ	Archives nationales du Québec		
ANQ-M	Archives nationales du Québec, Centre régional de Montréal	NYPL	New York Public Library
		OH	*Ontario History*
ANQ-MBF	Archives nationales du Québec, Centre régional de la Mauricie–Bois-Francs	PAC	Public Archives of Canada
		PAM	Provincial Archives of Manitoba
		PANB	Provincial Archives of New Brunswick
ANQ-Q	Archives nationales du Québec, Centre d'archives de la Capitale	PANL	Provincial Archives of Newfoundland and Labrador
AO	Archives of Ontario	PANS	Public Archives of Nova Scotia
AP	Archives paroissiales	PAPEI	Public Archives of Prince Edward Island
ASQ	Archives du séminaire de Québec		
ASSM	Archives du séminaire de Saint-Sulpice, Montréal	PCA	Presbyterian Church in Canada Archives
AUM	Archives de l'université de Montréal	PRO	Public Record Office
BL	British Library	QDA	Quebec Diocesan Archives
BRH	*Le Bulletin des recherches historiques*	QUA	Queen's University Archives
CCHA	Canadian Catholic Historical Association	*RHAF*	*Revue d'histoire de l'Amérique française*
CÉA	Centre d'études acadiennes	RSC	Royal Society of Canada
CHA	Canadian Historical Association	SCHÉC	Société canadienne d'histoire de l'Église catholique
CHR	*Canadian Historical Review*		
CND	Congregation of Notre-Dame	SGCF	Société généalogique canadienne-française
DAB	*Dictionary of American biography*		
DBF	*Dictionnaire de biographie française*	*SH*	*Social History, a Canadian Review*
DCB	*Dictionary of Canadian biography*	SPG	Society for the Propagation of the Gospel
DNB	*Dictionary of national biography*		
DOLQ	*Dictionnaire des œuvres littéraires du Québec*	SRO	Scottish Record Office
		UNBL	University of New Brunswick Library
DPL	Detroit Public Library	USPG	United Society for the Propagation of the Gospel
DSB	*Dictionary of scientific biography*		
GRO	General Register Office for Scotland	UTL-TF	University of Toronto Library, Thomas Fisher Rare Book Library
HBC	Hudson's Bay Company		
HBCA	Hudson's Bay Company Archives	UWO	University of Western Ontario
HBRS	Hudson's Bay Record Society		

General Bibliography

The General Bibliography is based on the sources most frequently cited in the individual bibliographies of volume V. It should not be regarded as providing a complete list of background materials for the history of Canada in the 18th and early 19th centuries.

Section I describes the principal archival sources and is arranged by country. Section II is divided into two parts: part A contains printed primary sources including documents published by the various colonial governments; part B provides a listing of the contemporary newspapers most frequently cited by contributors to the volume. Section III includes dictionaries, indexes, inventories, almanacs, and directories. Section IV contains secondary works of the 19th and 20th centuries, including a number of general histories and theses. Section V describes the principal journals and the publications of various societies consulted.

I. ARCHIVAL SOURCES

CANADA

ARCHIVES CIVILES. *See* Québec, ministère de la Justice

ARCHIVES DE L'ARCHIDIOCÈSE DE QUÉBEC. A guide to the collection is available in SCHÉC *Rapport*, 2 (1934–35): 65–73.

Series cited in volume V:

A: Évêques et archevêques de Québec
    12 A: Registres des insinuations ecclésiastiques
    20 A: Lettres manuscrites des évêques de Québec
    210 A: Registres des lettres expédiées. Inventories of the correspondence of a number of the bishops of Quebec, compiled by Ivanhoë Caron, are available in ANQ *Rapport* [*see* section III].
    22 A: Copies de lettres expédiées
C: Secrétairerie et chancellerie
    CB: Structures de direction
    1 CB: Vicaires généraux
    CD: Discipline diocésaine
    303 CD: Titres cléricaux
    42 CD: Abjurations
    516 CD: Séminaire de Québec
    61 CD: Paroisses
    69 CD: Visites pastorales
    71-31 CD: Sulpiciens
    940 CD: Procès-verbaux de liberté au mariage

Diocèse de Québec (in process of reclassification)
    CM: Église universelle
    10 CM: Correspondance de Rome
    7 CM: États-Unis
    9 CM: Europe
    90 CM: Angleterre
    CN: Église canadienne
    30 CN: Terre-Neuve
    301 CN: Îles de la Madeleine
    310 CN: Île-du-Prince-Édouard
    311 CN: Nouveau-Brunswick
    312 CN: Nouvelle-Écosse
    320 CN: Haut-Canada
    60 CN: Gouvernement du Canada

ARCHIVES DE L'UNIVERSITÉ DE MONTRÉAL. The Service des archives of the Université de Montréal has prepared an important series of publications relating to the archive groups and collections in its custody; a list of these can be found in *Bibliographie des publications du Service des archives* (3ᵉ éd., Montréal, 1980), compiled by Jacques Ducharme and Denis Plante.

The following collection is cited in volume V:
P 58: Collection Baby. The researcher may usefully consult the *Catalogue de la collection François-Louis-Georges Baby*, compiled by Camille Bertrand, with preface by Paul Baby and introduction by Lucien Campeau (2v., Montréal, 1971). Transcripts of the bulk of the

Collection Baby, which is being classified at present, are located at the PAC.

A: Documents d'ordre familial
 A1: Actes d'état civil
 A2: Notes généalogiques et biographiques
 A3: Contrats de mariage
 A4: Testaments et donations
 A5: Successions et tutelles
C: Colonisation
 C2: Ventes et échanges
 C3: Accords, arbitrages, arpentages
G: Commerce et finance
 G1: Grandes compagnies de fourrures
 G2: Commerce, finance, affaires
H: Affaires religieuses et communautés
 H2: Jésuites
 H3: Paroisse Notre-Dame de Montréal
J: Archives judiciaires
 J2: Documents judiciaires
L: Affaires politiques et parlementaires
P: Documents militaires
 P1: Commissions militaires
 P2: Papiers militaires
S: Papiers de William Berczy
U: Correspondance générale

ARCHIVES DU SÉMINAIRE DE QUÉBEC. Analytical and chronological card indexes as well as numerous inventories are available in the archives.

The following series were cited in volume V:
C: Livres de comptes du séminaire
 C 11: 1749–77
 C 35: 1753–80
 C 36: 1771–1801
 C 37: 1781–1809
Évêques
Fichier des anciens
Fonds Viger–Verreau
 Cartons: Papiers de H.-A.-J.-B. Verreau; Jacques Viger
 Série O: Cahiers manuscrits
  019: Registre des baptêmes, mariages et sépultures, Saint-Joseph des Illinois (Mich.)
  095–125; 0139–52: Jacques Viger, "Ma Saberdache." See Fernand Ouellet, "Inventaire de la Saberdache de Jacques Viger," ANQ Rapport, 1955–57: 31–176.
  0165–71: Journal personnel de Jacques Viger
Lettres
 M: 1685–1789
 P: 1685–1887
 R: 1686–1946
 S: 1663–1871
 T: 1731–1875

MSS: Cahiers manuscrits divers
 11: Élèves du petit séminaire
 12: Grand livre du séminaire
 13: Plumitif du conseil du séminaire commencé en 1678
 342: A.-E. Gosselin, Notes biographiques des prêtres du séminaire
 431–32: A.-E. Gosselin, Liste d'élèves, d'ordinations du grand séminaire
 433: A.-E. Gosselin, Officiers et professeurs du séminaire de Québec
 436–37: A.-E. Gosselin, Prêtres du séminaire
MSS-M: Cahiers de cours manuscrits
 134: P.-J. Bossu, Cours de géométrie par l'abbé Antoine Robert
 208: Joseph Signay, Cours de théologie par l'abbé P.-J. Bossu
 427: N.-C. Fortier, Cours de catéchisme par l'abbé H.-F. Gravé
 978: F.-C. Gagnon, Cours d'histoire ancienne par l'abbé Joseph Signay
Paroisse de Québec
Polygraphie: Affaires surtout extérieures
S: Seigneuries du séminaire
 S-11: Terrier, Île Jésus, Saint-François, Saint-Elzéar, Saint-Antoine, Sainte-Rose
 S-168: Terrier censier, Petite-Rivière, Baie-Saint-Paul, Saint-Urbain, Île aux Coudres
 S-169: Terrier censier, Ange-Gardien, Château-Richer, Sainte-Anne, Saint-Joachim
Séminaire: Affaires diverses

ARCHIVES DU SÉMINAIRE DE SAINT-SULPICE, Montréal.

The following sections were used in the preparation of volume V:
Section 8: Seigneuries, fiefs, arrière-fiefs et domaines
 A: Seigneurie du Lac-des-Deux-Montagnes
Section 11: Enseignement
 47–49: Enseignement secondaire
Section 14: Successions
 Dossier 9: Rente viagère
 Dossier 18: Huet de La Valinière, Pierre
Section 15: Testaments
Section 19: Statistiques
Section 21: Correspondance générale
Section 24: Histoire et géographie, biographies, divers
 Dossier 2: Biographies
 Dossier 5: Catalogue des prêtres de Saint-Sulpice
 Dossier 6: Cahiers Faillon
Section 25: Séminaire de Saint-Sulpice
 Dossier 1: Règlements, visites, comptes rendus des assemblées
Section 33: Sépultures, certificats

Section 36: Missions
Section 49: Prédication

ARCHIVES NATIONALES DU QUÉBEC. In 1980 the archives undertook to establish a new uniform classification system for its regional centres. Inventories, catalogues, guides, conversion tables, and finding aids are available on microfiche in all the regional repositories of the ANQ.

CENTRE D'ARCHIVES DE LA CAPITALE, Québec
    The following sources were used in volume V:
C: Pouvoir judiciaire, archives civiles
  CA: Arpenteurs
    1: Québec
      3: Bédard, J.-B.
  CC: Tutelles et curatelles
    1: Québec
  CE: État civil
    1: Québec
      1: Notre-Dame de Québec
      5: Notre-Dame de Miséricorde (Beauport)
      6: La Visitation de Notre-Dame (Château-Richer)
      7: Saint-Charles-Borromée (Charlesbourg)
      8: Sainte-Famille (Cap-Santé)
      10: Saint-Laurent (île d'Orléans)
      11: Sainte-Famille (île d'Orléans)
      12: Saint-Pierre (île d'Orléans)
      15: Saint-François-de-Sales (Neuville)
      19: Saint-Joseph-de-la-Pointe-Lévy (Lauzon)
      20: Notre-Dame-de-Foy (Sainte-Foy)
      28: Saint-Ambroise (Loretteville)
      61: Cathedral of the Holy Trinity (Quebec)
      66: St Andrew's (Quebec)
    2: Montmagny
      2: Notre-Dame de l'Assomption (Berthier-en-Bas)
      7: Saint-Thomas (Montmagny)
      8: Saint-Vallier (Bellechasse)
    3: Kamouraska
      1: Notre-Dame-de-Liesse (Rivière-Ouelle)
      3: Saint-Louis (Kamouraska)
      12: Sainte-Anne-de-la-Pocatière (La Pocatière)
    4: Saguenay
      1: Saints-Pierre-et-Paul (Baie-Saint-Paul)
  CN: Notaires
    1: Québec
      11: Barolet, Claude
      16: Bélanger, Jean
      21: Bernard, Joseph
      25: Berthelot Dartigny, M.-A.
      26: Berthelot, Michel
      27: Besserer, L.-T.
      49: Campbell, Archibald

      60: Chavigny de La Chevrotière, Ambroise
      63: Chevalier, F.-X.
      76: Crespin, Antoine (père)
      77: Crespin, Antoine (fils)
      79: Decharnay, J.-B.
      83: Deschenaux, P.-L.
      91: Du Laurent, C.-H.
      92: Dumas, Alexandre
      99: Faribault, Barthélemy
      103: Fortier, Joseph
      107: Gagnon, Pierre
      115: Genest, André
      122: Gouget, Jacques
      145: Jones, John
      147: Laforce, Pierre
      148: Lemaître Lamorille, François
      151: Lanoullier Des Granges, P.-A.-F.
      157: Larue, F.-X.
      168: Lebrun de Duplessis, J.-B.
      171: Lee, Thomas
      178: Lelièvre, Roger
      189: Louet, Claude
      193: Martineau, J.-M.
      197: McPherson, L. T.
      200: Miray, Louis
      202: Moreau, F.-E.
      205: Panet, J.-A.
      206: Panet, J.-B.
      207: Panet, J.-C.
      209: Panet, P.-L.
      212: Parent, A.-A.
      224: Pinguet, J.-N.
      230: Planté, J.-B.
      245: Rousseau, F.-D.
      248: Saillant, J.-A.
      250: Sanguinet, Simon
      253: Scott, W. F.
      256: Stewart, Charles
      262: Têtu, Félix
      284: Voyer, Charles
      285: Voyer, Jacques
    2: Montmagny
      7: Boisseau, N.-G.
    3: Kamouraska
      11: Cazes, Louis
      18: Dionne, Joseph
    4: Saguenay
      14: Lavoye, Michel
      16: Néron, Jean
E: Pouvoir exécutif
  1: Intendants
  4: Secrétaire provincial
  17: Justice
  18: Registraire
  21: Terres et forêts
P: Fonds et collections privées
  20: Henry Caldwell

81: Famille Fraser
92: J.-J. Girouard
128: Papiers Laforce
192: Famille Neilson
193: Imprimerie Neilson
200: J.-A. Panet
238: J.-T. Taschereau
239: P.-G. Roy
240: Seigneuries
244: Famille Tarieu de Lanaudière
289: Famille Salaberry
297: Famille Fraser
313: George Allsopp
319: Jonathan Sewell
398: François Baillairgé
417: Famille Papineau
1694: J.-B.-N. Pouget
P1000: Petits fonds
11-185: M.-A. Berthelot Dartigny
18-334: Jacques Cartier
19-347: Famille Céloron de Blainville
27-502: Davidson and John Lees
32-592: Joseph Drapeau
54-1047: Famille Juchereau
55-1053: Duc de Kent
80-1666: J.-R. Piuze
93-1905: Édouard-Alphonse Salaberry
95-1936: François Signay
R: Représentation du pouvoir royal
G: Gouverneurs
T: Pouvoir judiciaire
6-1: Cours de justice, Régime anglais
11-1: Cour supérieure
13-1: Cour provinciale
Z: Copies de documents conservés au-dehors des ANQ-Q
C: Canada (en dehors du Québec)
22: Simcoe, John Graves
Q: Québec (en dehors des ANQ)
60: État civil, Catholiques, Sainte-Anne (Restigouche)
75: Mal de la Baie-Saint-Paul

CENTRE RÉGIONAL DE LA MAURICIE–BOIS-FRANCS, Trois-Rivières
The following sources were used in volume V:
C: Pouvoir judiciaire, archives civiles
CE: État civil
1: Trois-Rivières
13: Saint-Jean-Baptiste (Nicolet)
15: Saint-Antoine-de-Padoue (Louiseville)
48: Immaculée-Conception (Trois-Rivières)
50: St James (Trois-Rivières)
52: Sainte-Anne (Yamachiche)
CN: Notaires
1: Trois-Rivières
4: Badeaux, A.-I.

5: Badeaux, J.-B.
6: Badeaux, Joseph
29: Dielle, Paul
32: Dumoulin, J.-E.
76: Poulain, Pierre
79: Ranvoyzé, Étienne
80: Rigaud, É.-F.
91: Trudel, Augustin

CENTRE RÉGIONAL DE MONTRÉAL
Sources cited in volume V include:
C: Pouvoir judiciaire, archives civiles
CA: Arpenteurs
1: Montréal
16: Charland, Louis
CC: Tutelles et curatelles
CE: État civil
1: Montréal
3: La Nativité (Laprairie)
4: La Visitation-de-la-Bienheureuse-Vierge-Marie (Sault-au-Récollet)
10: Sainte-Anne (Varennes)
12: Saint-Antoine (Longueuil)
13: Saint-Antoine-de-Padoue (Saint-Antoine-sur-Richelieu)
22: Sainte-Famille (Boucherville)
23: Saint-François d'Assise (Montréal)
26: Saint-François-Xavier (Verchères)
37: Saint-Joachim (Pointe-Claire)
39: Saint-Joseph (Chambly)
44: Saint-Laurent (Montréal)
46: Saint-Marc-de-Cournoyer (Saint-Marc)
50: Saint-Michel (Vaudreuil)
51: Notre-Dame de Montréal
63: Christ Church (Montreal)
79: St Stephen (Chambly)
141: Hôtel-Dieu de Montréal
2: Saint-Hyacinthe
12: Saint-Denis (Saint-Denis, sur le Richelieu)
CL: Licitations, adjudications, ventes par les shérifs
CM: Testaments olographes
1: Montréal
CN: Notaires
1: Montréal
16: Barron, Thomas
29: Beek, J. G.
43: Boileau, René
68: Cadieux, J.-M.
74: Chaboillez, Louis
88: Cherrier, F.-P.
100: Courville, Louis de
108: Danré de Blanzy, L.-C.
117: Deguire, J.-B.
120: De Lisle, Jean
121: De Lisle, J.-G.

126: Desautels, Joseph
128: Desève, J.-B.
134: Doucet, N.-B.
150: Duvernay, P.-C.
158: Foucher, Antoine
167: Gauthier, J.-P.
184: Gray, E. W.
185: Gray, J. A.
187: Griffin, Henry
189: Grisé, Antoine
194: Guy, Louis
200: Henry, Edme
217: Jorand, J.-J.
243: Latour, L.-H.
254: Leguay, François (père)
255: Leguay, François (fils)
259: Lepallieur, François
269: Lukin, Peter
290: Mézière, Pierre
295: Mondelet, J.-M.
308: Panet, Pierre
309: Panet, P.-L.
313: Papineau, Joseph
339: Raimbault, J.-C.
363: Sanguinet, Simon
364: Saupin, J.-J.
372: Simonnet, François
375: Soupras, L.-J.
383: Thibaudault, Louis
2: Saint-Hyacinthe
11: Bourdages, Louis
27: Dutalmé, P.-P.
41: Jehanne, Marin
56: Michaud, Christophe
3: Verchères
31: Glandon-Desdevens. M.-L. de
P: Fonds et collections privées
10: Documents judiciaires, Cour du banc du roi
24: Viger, famille
P1000: Petits fonds
14-633: Lettres diverses
48-1020: Documents judiciaires, Cour des plaidoyers communs
S: Seigneuries
1: Montréal
1-11: L'Assomption

ARCHIVES OF ONTARIO, Toronto. Unpublished inventories, calendars, catalogue entries, guides, and other finding aids are available in the archives, which is also making available finding aids on microfiche.
Materials used in volume V include:
MS: Microfilm Series
4: Robinson (John Beverley) papers
35: Strachan (John) papers
43: Richard Cartwright, letterbook, 1793–96
74: Merritt (William Hamilton) papers

75: Russell family papers
78: Macaulay papers
87: Eli Playter, diary
88: Baldwin (William Warren and Robert) papers
392: Hiram Walker Historical Museum collection
444: Macdonald (Father Ewen) collection
496: Tupper (Ferdinand Brock) papers
497: Gilkison (William and Jasper T.) papers
500: Street (Samuel) papers
503: Nelles (Robert) papers
517: Simcoe (John Graves) papers, Canadian section
519: Stone (Joel) papers
520: Jones (Solomon) papers
521: Jessup (Edward) papers
522: Rogers papers
525: Galt (Alexander T.) papers
526: Berczy (William) papers
536: Askin (John) papers
537: Ridout papers
MU: Manuscript Units
490–92: Canniff (William) papers
500–15: Cartwright family papers
1106–9: French (Frederick John) papers
1368: High treason register
1532–37: Jarvis–Powell papers
1730: Peter Hunter, letterbook
1750: McCall (Daniel Abial) papers
1776–78: Macdonell (Alexander) papers
2095–143: Miscellaneous collection
2438–41: Roe family papers
2554–55: Rousseau collection
2828–31: Smith (F. P.) papers
2923: Stuart family papers
3054: United Empire Loyalists collection
RG 1: Records of the Ministry of Natural Resources
A: Offices of surveyor general and commissioner of crown lands
I: Correspondence
1: Letters received, surveyor general
2: Surveyor general's letterbooks (available on microfilm as MS 627)
6: Letters received, surveyor general and commissioner (available on microfilm as MS 563)
II: Reports and statements
1: Surveyor general's reports
5: Heir and Devisee Commission reports
IV: Schedules and land rolls
C: Lands Branch
I: Land grants
3: Fiats and warrants
4: Locations
9: Miscellaneous
IV: Township papers
CB-1: Survey diaries, field notes and reports

911

RG 4: Records of the attorney general
  A: Attorney general
    I: Pre-confederation records
RG 21: Municipal records
  sect.A: Records of municipalities
RG 22: Court records
    ser.04: Court of Common Pleas (pre-1794)
    ser.6-2: Records of the Surrogate Court of Ontario
    ser.54: Midland District, Court of General Quarter Sessions of the Peace, minutes
    ser.131: King's Bench, judgement docket-book
    ser.134: King's Bench, assize minute-books, criminal
    ser.155: Probate Court estate files
RG 53: Records of the department of the provincial secretary, recording office
    ser.1: Land patents
    ser.2-2: Index to patents by name

ARCHIVES PAROISSIALES. The more noteworthy of the holdings of Quebec parish archives are the registers of baptisms, marriages, and burials; copies are deposited with the Archives civiles of the judicial district in which the parish is located. Parish archives usually contain many other documents, including parish account-books, records of the *fabriques*, and registers of parish confraternities.

CENTRE D'ÉTUDES ACADIENNES, Université de Moncton, N.-B. For further information about the collections *see* CÉA, *Inventaire général des sources documentaires sur les Acadiens* (3v., Moncton, N.-B., 1975–77), 1.
  Materials used in volume V include:
A: Fonds personnels
  Gaudet, Placide

EVA BROOK DONLY MUSEUM, Simcoe, Ont. For information on the Norfolk Historical Society collection housed in the museum see *Collections of the Norfolk Historical Society, preliminary inventory* (Ottawa, 1957), published by the PAC in cooperation with the society.
  The following materials were used in the preparation of volume V:
Norfolk Historical Society collection
  Thomas Welch papers
  Miscellaneous papers

HUDSON'S BAY COMPANY ARCHIVES. *See* Provincial Archives of Manitoba

McCORD MUSEUM, Montreal.
  The following material was used in the preparation of volume V:
Beaver Club minute-book
J.-B. Blondeau, account-book

Arthur Davidson papers
William Grant papers
McCord papers
Samuel Morin, account-book
Riedesel papers

MARITIME HISTORY GROUP ARCHIVES, Memorial University of Newfoundland, St John's. For information on the collections held at the archives see: *Preliminary inventory of records held at the Maritime History Group*, comp. Roberta Thomas under the direction of Keith Matthews ([St John's, 1978]); *Check list of research studies pertaining to the history of Newfoundland in the archives of the Maritime History Group* (4th ed., [St John's], 1981), a listing of research studies prepared by Memorial University students which is housed in the archives; and *An index to the name files . . .* , comp. Gert Crosbie under the direction of Keith Matthews ([St John's], 1981). Various other indexes to individual collections at the archives are also available.
  Materials cited in volume V include:
Name file collection. This collection consists of some 20,000 files, arranged by surname, concerning anyone connected in any way with the Newfoundland trade or fisheries, 1640–1850. The files are compiled from a wide range of sources, and each entry includes a reference to the original source.

METROPOLITAN TORONTO LIBRARY. For information on the library's manuscript holdings, see *Guide to the manuscript collection in the Toronto Public Libraries* (Toronto, 1954).
  Manuscripts consulted for volume V include:
William Allan papers
Robert Baldwin papers, sect.II
William Jarvis papers
William Dummer Powell papers
Elizabeth Russell papers
Peter Russell papers
D. W. Smith papers
U.C., Court of Common Pleas, Nassau District, minutes
Alexander Wood papers
York, U.C., minutes of town meetings and lists of inhabitants

MINISTÈRE DES AFFAIRES CULTURELLES, CENTRE DE DOCUMENTATION. *See* Québec, ministère des Affaires culturelles

NEW BRUNSWICK MUSEUM, Saint John, N.B. For a description of its holdings *see* New Brunswick Museum, Archives Division, *Inventory of manuscripts, 1967* ([Saint John, 1967]).
  Materials used in volume V include:

F41: Scrapbook, newspaper clippings – New Brunswick
F49: Land petitions, typescript abstracts
F50: Muster rolls
F53: Typescripts relating to Kingston, King's County, N.B.
F71: Miscellaneous records, 1786–1860
Hazen family papers
H. T. Hazen collection
  Ward Chipman papers
Odell family papers
Petitions, Northumberland County (abstracts)
SB 39: Scrapbook, newspaper clippings – "Historic homes of Fredericton"
Simonds, Hazen, and White papers

PRESBYTERIAN CHURCH IN CANADA ARCHIVES, Toronto.
  The following material was used in the preparation of volume V:
St Gabriel Street Church (Montreal), Register of baptisms, marriages, and burials

PROVINCIAL ARCHIVES OF MANITOBA, Winnipeg.
  The following series was consulted in the preparation of volume V:
Hudson's Bay Company Archives. The PRO and the PAC hold microfilm copies of the records for the years 1670 to 1870. For more information concerning copies held at the PAC and the finding aids that are available see *General inventory, manuscripts, 3*. The articles by R. H. G. Leveson-Gower, "The archives of the Hudson's Bay Company," *Beaver*, outfit 264 (December 1933): 40–42, 64, and by Joan Craig, "Three hundred years of records," *Beaver*, outfit 301 (autumn 1970): 65–70, provide useful information to researchers. For series of HBCA documents published by the HBRS, *see* section II.
Section A: London office records
  A.1/: London minute-books
  A.5/: London correspondence books outwards – general
  A.6/: London correspondence books outwards – official
  A.11/: London inward correspondence from HBC posts
  A.16/: Officers' and servants' ledgers and account-books
  A.30/: Lists of servants
  A.32/: Servants' contracts
  A.36/: Officers' and servants' wills
Section B: North American trading post records
  B.3/a: Albany journals
  B.3/b: Albany correspondence books
  B.10/e: Lake Attawapiskat, report on districts
  B.22/a: Brandon House journals

B.30/a: Cat Lake journals
B.42/a: Fort Churchill journals
B.59/a: Eastmain journals
B.59/z: Eastmain miscellaneous items
B.78/a: Gloucester House journals
B.86/a: Henley House journals
B.105/a: Lac La Pluie journals
B.123/a: Martin Fall journals
B.135/a: Moose journals
B.135/b: Moose correspondence books
B.135/f: Moose lists of servants
B.149/a: Nipigon House journals
B.155/a: Osnaburgh House journals
B.155/e: Osnaburgh House reports on districts
B.166/a: Portage de l'Île journals
B.198/a: Severn journals
B.203/a: Somerset House (Swan River) journals
B.220/a: Trout Lake journals
B.239/a: York Factory journals
B.239/b: York Factory correspondence books
B.239/f: York Factory lists of servants
Section C: Records of ships owned or chartered by the HBC
  C.1: Ships' logs
Section D: Governors' papers
  D.13: Commissioners' outward letterbooks to London
Section E: Miscellaneous records
  E.2: "Observations on Hudson's Bay." Pieces 1–3 are by James Isham, 4–13 by Andrew Graham.
  E.3: Peter Fidler, journals
Section F: Records of allied and subsidiary companies
  F.3: North West Company correspondence

PROVINCIAL ARCHIVES OF NEW BRUNSWICK, Fredericton. The archives is in the process of reorganizing and reclassifying some material. As a result, individual references to PANB collections in volume V will not always correspond to those currently in use at the archives, although the old references are still usable for the purposes of location and retrieval. The following description is an attempt to indicate the latest changes as the volume goes to press. For information on the manuscript holdings, *A guide to the manuscript collections in the Provincial Archives of New Brunswick*, comp. A. C. Rigby (Fredericton, 1977), remains useful, although the classification system used when it was published is now obsolete.
  Materials used in the preparation of volume V include:
MC 58: "Bishop Inglis letters, 1787–1842." Compiled by W. O. Raymond.
"New Brunswick political biography." Compiled by J. C. and H. B. Graves. 11 vols., typescript.

RG 1: Records of the lieutenant-governor
RS330: Thomas Carleton
A1–A8: Letterbooks
RG 2: Records of the central executive
RS6: Minutes and orders-in-council of the Executive Council
RS7: Executive Council records, Ottawa series (being reorganized)
RS8: Executive Council records, New Brunswick series (being reorganized)
Appointments and commissions
Indians
Unarranged Executive Council documents
RG 4: Records of the New Brunswick Legislative Assembly
RS24: Legislative Assembly sessional papers
RG 5: Records of the superior courts
RS55: Court of Equity records, original jurisdiction
RG 7: Records of the probate courts
RS63: Charlotte County Probate Court records
RS72A: Sunbury County Probate Court records
RS75: York County Probate Court records
RG 10: Records of the Department of Natural Resources
RS107: Crown Lands and Lands Branch records
RS108: Land petitions
RG 18: Records of the Department of Municipal Affairs
RS153: Northumberland County records
Minutes of the courts of quarter sessions

PROVINCIAL ARCHIVES OF NEWFOUNDLAND AND LABRADOR, St John's. For information on the collections see *Preliminary inventory of the holdings . . .* and *Supplement . . .* (2 nos., St John's, 1970–74).

The following materials were cited in volume V:
GN: Government records – Newfoundland
GN 1: Governor's office
13: Census records
4: St John's, 1794–95
GN 2: Department of the Colonial secretary
1: Letterbooks, outgoing correspondence
2: Incoming correspondence
GN 5: Court records
1: Surrogate Court
A: Central District
1: Minutes
B: Northern District
1: Minutes
9: Estate records
C: Southern District
1: Minutes
2: Supreme Court
A: Central District
1: Minutes
4: Sessions Court

A: Central District
P: Private records
P 1: Governors' private papers
5: Duckworth papers
P 5: Miscellaneous groups
11: Job Brothers, papers
P 7: Businesses
A: Fishing related
6: Slade & Sons, Fogo, ledgers
53: Munn & Co., Ltd., Harbour Grace, records

PUBLIC ARCHIVES OF CANADA, Ottawa. The PAC has published a *Guide to the manuscript groups and record groups of the Manuscript Division*, compiled by Grace Maurice Hyam (1978), and *Federal Archives Division*, a guide compiled by Terry Cook and G. T. Wright (1983). Collections at the PAC are listed in the *Union list of MSS*, which it also publishes [*see* section III]. Addenda to published inventories, unpublished inventories of manuscript and record groups, and finding aids to individual collections are available at the PAC, which also makes available a large number of finding aids on microfiche.

The following inventories to materials in the Manuscript and the Federal Archives divisions which were used in the preparation of volume V have been published:
General inventory, manuscripts, volume 1, MG 1–MG 10 (1971)
General inventory, manuscripts, volume 2, MG 11–MG 16 (1976)
General inventory, manuscripts, volume 3, MG 17–MG 21 (1974)
General inventory, manuscripts, volume 4, MG 22–MG 25 (1972)
General inventory, manuscripts, volume 7, MG 29 (1975)
General inventory, manuscripts, volume 8, MG 30 (1977)
General inventory series, no.1: records relating to Indian affairs (RG 10) (1975)
An older series of inventories has been largely superseded by unpublished inventories available at the PAC, but the following are still of some limited use:
Record group 1, Executive Council, Canada, 1764–1867 (1953)
Record group 4, civil and provincial secretaries' offices, Canada East, 1760–1867; Record group 5, civil and provincial secretaries' offices, Canada West, 1788–1867 (1953)
Record group 7, governor general's office (1953)
Record group 8, British military and naval records (1954)
Record group 9, Department of Militia and Defence, 1776–1922 ([1957])

Record groups, no.14: records of parliament, 1775–1915; no.15: Department of the Interior; no.16: Department of National Revenue (1957) Material from the following collections was cited in volume V:

MG 5: Ministère des Affaires étrangères, Paris
    B: Mémoires et documents
        2: Angleterre

MG 8: Documents relatifs à la Nouvelle-France et au Québec (XVIIᵉ–XXᵉ siècle)
    A: Documents généraux
        7: Actes de foi et hommage
    F: Documents relatifs aux seigneuries et autres lieux
        25: Gaspé
        57: Montréal
        131: Les Éboulements
        138: île Bizard
    G: Archives paroissiales
        65: Montreal, Christ Church (Anglican)

MG 9: Provincial, local and territorial records
    A: New Brunswick
        12: Local records
            11: Westmorland County
    B: Nova Scotia
        9: Local records
            14: Shelburne
    C: Prince Edward Island
        3: Collector of customs
    D: Ontario
        7: Church records
            2: Boston, Baptist Church
        8: Local records
            8: Eastern District
            21: Lunenburg District

MG 11: Public Record Office, London, Colonial Office papers
    [CO 42]. Q series. The Q transcripts were prepared by the PAC before the PRO reorganization of 1908–10 and include most of what is now in CO 42, material now found in CO 43, and items from other series. Documents for the period covered by volume V are calendared in PAC *Report*, 1890–93, 1896.
    [CO 188]. New Brunswick A. Pre-1784 documents relating to the area now known as New Brunswick are found in the Nova Scotia classes of the CO records. For the period 1784–1801 the New Brunswick A series is a composite collection of transcripts from a number of British sources which were not included in CO 188 as established by the PRO reorganization of 1908–10. From 1802 on the transcripts and CO 188 are virtually identical. A calendar for vols. 1–14 (1784–1801) is available in the PAC *Report*, 1895.

[CO 217]. Nova Scotia A; Cape Breton A. Up to 1801 these series are composites of transcripts from various sources in Great Britain, especially the PRO. By the time the work of transcription had reached 1802 the PRO had established the CO 217 series. From 1802 the transcripts are from CO 217 only. Documents of Nova Scotia A for the period covered by volume V have been calendared in PAC *Report*, 1894 and 1946, and of Cape Breton A in *Report*, 1895.

[CO 220]. Cape Breton B (minutes of the Executive Council, 1785–1807). A composite series taken principally from sources now part of PRO, CO 220.

[CO 226]. Prince Edward Island A. For the period prior to 1820 this is a composite series of transcripts derived primarily from sources now in PRO, CO 226, but also including material copied from the Dartmouth papers (PAC, MG 23, A1). Post-1820 documents are from CO 226 only. A calendar for vols.1–16 (1763–1801) appears in PAC *Report*, 1895.

MG 17: Ecclesiastical archives
    A: Roman Catholic Church
        7-2: Séminaire de Saint-Sulpice, Montréal
    D: Moravian Brethren
        1: Moravian Brethren

MG 18: Pre-conquest papers
    H: New France
        17: Taschereau, famille
    K: French officers
        3: Chartier de Lotbinière, Michel-Eustache-Gaspard, marquis de
    L: British officers
        4: Amherst family
    M: Northcliffe collection
        ser.2: George Townshend papers
    N: Military and naval documents
        13: Beaujeu, Louis Liénard de
        20: Laforce, le sieur

MG 19: Fur trade and Indians
    A: Fur trade, general
        1: Edgar, William
        2: Ermatinger estate
        3: Askin family
        5: McTavish, Frobisher & Co.
        7: Mackenzie, Sir Alexander
        13: Henry, Alexander, the younger
        35: McGillivray, Simon
    B: Fur trade, companies and associations
        1: North West Company
        3: Beaver Club
    C: Fur trade, collections
        1: Masson collection

E: Red River settlement
    1: Selkirk, Thomas Douglas, 5th Earl of
    2: Red River settlement
    4: Macdonell, Miles
F: Indians
    1: Claus family
    2: Johnson family
    6: Brant family
    16: McKee, Alexander and Thomas
MG 22: Autographs
  A: Canadian autographs
    9: Sandham, Alfred, collection
MG 23: Late eighteenth-century papers
  A: British statesmen
    1: Dartmouth, William Legge,
      2nd Earl of
    3: Sydney, Thomas Townshend,
      1st Viscount
    4: Shelburne, William Fitzmaurice
      Petty, 2nd Earl of, 1st Marquis of
      Lansdowne
    6: Germain, George Sackville,
      1st Viscount Sackville
    8: Richmond and Lennox, Charles
      Lennox, 3rd Duke of
  B: American revolution
    1: British headquarters papers
    7: Quebec: journal of events of the
      siege, 1775–76
    14: Purdy, Gilbert
    19: Cazeau, François
  C: Nova Scotia
    6: Inglis family
    8: Grant, John
    9: Committee for loyalists
  D: New Brunswick
    1: Chipman, Ward, Sr and Jr
    3: Carleton, Thomas
    4: Botsford, Amos
    6: Byles family
    104: Price, Evan John
  E: Prince Edward Island
    5: Fanning, Edmund
    7: Townshend, William
    12: DesBrisay, Thomas de la Cour
  F: Cape Breton
    1: DesBarres, Joseph Frederick Wallet
  GI: Quebec and Lower Canada: government
    5: Quebec: administration of justice
    6: Montréal: petition des citoyens et
      habitants catholiques
  GII: Quebec and Lower Canada: political
    figures
    1: Murray, James
    3: Gray, Edward William
    6: Dorchester, Sir Guy Carleton,
      1st Baron

    9: Finlay, Hugh
    10: Sewell, Jonathan, and family
    14: Smith, William
    15: Gray, Alexander
    17: Prescott, Robert
    19: Monk family
    20: Coffin, Thomas Aston
    22: Haldimand, Sir Frederick
    23: Mabane, Adam
    26: Ainslie, Thomas
  GIII: Quebec and Lower Canada: merchants
    and settlers
    1: Allsopp family
    3: Ruiter (Ruyter) family
    8: Birnie, Samuel
    23: Nairne, John and Thomas
    32: Fisher, Duncan
  GV: Quebec and Lower Canada: miscellaneous
    1: Boisseau, Nicolas-Gaspard
    7: Verreau, Hospice-Anthelme-Jean-
      Baptiste
    8: Badelard, Philippe-Louis-François
  HI: Upper Canada: political figures
    1: Simcoe, John Graves
    2: Russell family
    3: Jarvis family
    4: Powell, William Dummer, and
      family
    5: White, John
    7: Cartwright, Richard
  HII: Upper Canada: merchants and settlers
    1: McDonald–Stone family
    6: Berczy, William von Moll
    7: Farmer, Hugh Hovell
    11: Gray, Robert Isaac Dey
    18: Pettit, Nathaniel
  I: Colonies general
    13: Sharpe, Joshua
  J: Exploration and travel
    9: Mathews, Robert
  K: Military documents
    1: Fraser family
    12: Jessup, Edward
MG 24: Nineteenth-century pre-confederation papers
  A: British officials and political figures
    1: Brock, Sir Isaac
    6: Hunter, Peter
    9: Prevost, Sir George
    14: Richmond and Lennox, Charles
      Lennox, 4th Duke of
    41: Drummond, Sir Gordon
    45: Duckworth, Sir John Thomas
  B: North American political figures and events
    1: Neilson collection
    2: Papineau, famille
    3: Ryland, Herman Witsius, and family
    4: Young, John, and family

7: Jones, Charles
10: Dunn, Thomas
16: Cochran, Andrew Wilson
118: Caldwell, Henry
130: Clark(e), Thomas, and family
C: Correspondents of political figures
1: Willcocks, Joseph
D: Industry, commerce, and finance
4: Goring, Francis
15: Brehaut, Peter
49: Spencer papers
99: Birnie, George and Alexander
F: Military and naval figures
4: Bisshopp, Cecil
I: Immigration, land, and settlement
8: Macdonell of Collachie family
9: Hill collection
20: Bridge, Samuel Southby
26: Hamilton, Alexander
153: Williams, Jenkin
179: Foretier, Pierre
J: Religious figures
48: Whittaker, John William
K: Education and cultural development
2: Coventry, George
3: Painchaud, Abbé Charles-François
L: Miscellaneous
3: Collection Baby
MG 25: Genealogy
59: Jessup family
MG 29: Nineteenth-century post-confederation
manuscripts
A: Economic
5: Strathcona and Mount Royal, Sir
Donald Alexander Smith, 1st Baron
D: Cultural
72: LeMoyne, James MacPherson
MG 30: Manuscripts of the first half of the
twentieth century
C: Social
5: Mercure, Prudent-L.
D: Cultural
1: Audet, Francis-Joseph
56: Leymarie, A.-Léo
136: Brunet, Pierre
MG 40: Records and manuscripts from British
repositories
B: Letters patent, commissions, instructions
1: Letters patent, 1610–1869
L: Great Britain: General Post Office
MG 53: Lande collection
55: Early records of business transactions
in Canada
177: The manuscript poems of Joseph
Quesnel
MG 55: Miscellaneous documents
RG   1: Executive Council: Quebec, Lower Canada,

Upper Canada, Canada, 1764–1867
E: State records
1: Minute-books (state matters)
3: Upper Canada: submisssions to the
Executive Council, state matters
14: Executive Council office: correspondence and records of the clerk
15: Public accounts: Board of Audit
17: Quebec and Lower Canada:
committee on highways, roads, and
bridges
L: Land records
1: Minute-books (land matters)
3: Upper Canada and Canada: petitions
for land grants and leases
3L: Quebec and Lower Canada: land
petitions and related records
4: Upper Canada, land board: minutes
and records
7: Miscellaneous records
RG   4: Civil and provincial secretaries' offices:
Quebec, Lower Canada, and Canada East
A: Secretaries' correspondence
1: S series
3: Reference books, registers, day
books, and miscellaneous correspondence
B: Office records
1: Addresses
3: Proclamations
6: Ordinances
8: Notaries and advocates: applications to act as
9: Commissions
16: Court records
17: Suits
28: Bonds, licences, and certificates
33: Civil service records
43: Records of the committee of the
Executive Council investigating the
claims of Dr James Bowman and his
work combatting the St Paul's Bay
disease
58: Customs records
RG   5: Civil and provincial secretaries' offices:
Upper Canada and Canada West
A: Secretaries' correspondence
1: Upper Canada sundries
B: Miscellaneous records
2: Records of the Robert Isaac Dey Gray
estate
11: Records relating to education
RG   7: Canada: governor general's office
G1: Despatches from the Colonial Office
G2: Despatches to the Colonial Office
G5: Letterbooks of despatches from the Colonial
Office

G8D: Records from the lieutenant-governors' offices, Prince Edward Island
G14: Miscellaneous records
G15C: Letterbooks, Quebec and Lower Canada: civil secretary's letterbooks
G16C: Letterbooks, Upper Canada: civil secretary's letterbooks
G18: Miscellaneous records
RG   8: British military and naval records
   I: C series (British military records)
RG   9: Department of Militia and Defence
   I: Pre-confederation records
   A: Adjutant general's office, Lower Canada
     1: Correspondence
     7: Nominal rolls and paylists, 1812–15
   B: Adjutant general's office, Upper Canada
     1: Correspondence
     3: Militia: general orders
     4: Pensions and land grants
     7: Nominal rolls and paylists, 1812–15
RG 10: Indian affairs
   A: Administrative records of the imperial government
     1: Records of the governor general and the lieutenant governors
       1–7: Upper Canada, civil control
       486–87: Lower Canada, civil control
     2: Records of the superintendent's office
       8–21: Superintendent general's office
       26–46: Deputy superintendent general's office, correspondence
     6: General office files
       659: General administration records, Quebec and Lower Canada
   B: Ministerial administration records
     8: General headquarters administration records
       766–68A: G. M. Mathieson, notes and indices
RG 14: Records of parliament, 1791–1867
   A: Lower Canada
     1: Legislative Council, minutes, addresses, and petitions
     3: Legislative Assembly, journals
RG 16: Department of National Revenue
   A: Customs, excise and inland revenue
     1: Correspondence and returns
RG 19: Department of Finance
RG 42: Department of Marine
   I: Shipping registers
RG 68: Registrar general of Canada

PUBLIC ARCHIVES OF NOVA SCOTIA, Halifax. For a description of the collections see *Inventory of manuscripts in the Public Archives of Nova Scotia* (Halifax, 1976).

Materials used in the preparation of volume V include:

MG   1: Papers of families and individuals
     12–14: William Bruce Almon, accounts
     91–104: Jacob Bailey documents
     161: Burbidge family papers
     163–64A: Byles family documents
     219: John Clarkson documents
     258: Isaac Deschamps documents
     277–311: Arthur W. H. Eaton documents
     313B: Fawson family documents
     328: Gillmore family genealogy, "The Gillmore saga"
     332D: Francis Green, "Genealogical and biographical anecdotes of the Green family" (1806)
     472–74A: Edward How, documents
     479–80: Charles Inglis documents
     481–82: John Inglis documents
     544: T. H. Lodge collection, genealogies
     583–695: Miller family documents
     731A–B: O'Brien family documents
     742–44: George Patterson documents
     748A: Simeon Perkins documents
     749–52: Simeon Perkins diary (copy)
     793: Simon B. Robie documents
     817–63: Thomas B. Smith, genealogy
     936B: Sir Brook Watson, "Autobiographical sketch"
     939–41: Sir John Wentworth, documents
     947–62: White family documents
     979–80: Peleg Wiswall documents
MG   3: Business papers
     150–51: William Forsyth, Halifax, sales and letterbook
MG   4: Churches and communities
     12: Chebogue church records
     18: Cornwallis Township church records
     77–79: Liverpool church records
     91: Lunenburg, Anglican church records
     92: Lunenburg County documents
     94–105: Lunenburg County genealogies, comp. E. A. Harris
     140–41, 143: Shelburne County church and community records
MG   9: Scrapbooks
     no.43: H. W. Cunningham, "St George's parish notes"
     no.109: F. S. Crowell, "New Englanders in Nova Scotia"
     no.170: Miscellaneous
MG 12: Great Britain, Army
MG 13: Great Britain, Navy

MG 20: Societies and special collections
    61–70: Charitable Irish Society, Halifax, collection
    211–25: Nova Scotia Historical Society
    215, no.10: Log of the privateer Charles Mary Wentworth
    670–707: Nova Scotia Historical Society, unpublished papers
    677, no.14: D. A. Story, "Old St George's Church, Halifax, N.S."

MG 24: Shubenacadie Canal papers

MG 100: Documents, newspaper clippings and miscellaneous items

RG 1: Bound volumes of Nova Scotia records for the period 1624–1867
    29–185: Documents relating to the governing of Nova Scotia: dispatches, letterbooks, and commission books
    186–214½H: Council, minutes
    219–85: Miscellaneous documents
    286–300: Legislative Council, selections from the files
    301–14: Legislative Assembly, selections from the files
    326–30: Miscellaneous papers relating to Cape Breton
    341–96c: Special subjects
    409: Papers relating to settlement on the River Saint John
    419–22: Negro and maroon settlement
    423: Extracts from the Dorchester papers concerning negroes
    424–26½: Government establishment on Sable Island
    443–54: Census and poll tax
    458–65½: Mines and minerals
    499–501: Letters of agency of the Vice-Admiralty Court of Nova Scotia

RG 5: Records of the Legislative Assembly of Nova Scotia
    A: Assembly papers
    E: Election writs
    GP: Governor's petitions
    S: Statutes

RG 8: Records of the Central Board of Agriculture of Nova Scotia

RG 20: Lands and Forests
    A: Land grants and petitions

RG 34: Court of General Sessions of the Peace
    312: Halifax County
    318: Pictou County
    321: Shelburne County

RG 36: Chancery Court

RG 39: Supreme Court
    C: Civil and criminal cases
    J: Judgement books

RG 46: Commissions, oaths, and bonds
    folder 3: Commissions as justices of the peace

PUBLIC ARCHIVES OF PRINCE EDWARD ISLAND, Charlottetown.
    Materials used in the preparation of volume V include:

Acc. 2333: Unnamed. Contains architectural plans by John Plaw.
    2541: Natural History Society for Prince Edward Island
    2702: Smith–Alley collection
    2810: Ira Brown papers
    2849: Palmer family papers
    2987: Unnamed. Concerns visit of Bishop Plessis, 1812.

RG 1: Lieutenant governor, Commission books

RG 3: House of Assembly

RG 5: Executive Council, Minutes

RG 6: Courts, Supreme Court records
    RS2: Chancery Court records

RG 9: Customs, shipping registers

RG 16: Registry Office, Land Registry records Conveyance registers

RG 20: City of Charlottetown records

QUÉBEC, MINISTÈRE DE LA JUSTICE. The Archives civiles and the Archives judiciaires of Quebec, which are under the joint jurisdiction of the courts and the Ministère de la Justice, are now separate repositories as a result of the reclassification of the former Archives judiciaires. They are deposited at the court-houses in the administrative centres of the 34 judicial districts of Quebec.

ARCHIVES CIVILES. At the time of the reorganization, these archives were supposed to retain documents for the last 100 years, including registers of births, marriages, and deaths, notaries' *minutiers* (minute-books), and records of surveyors active in the district; all earlier documents were to be moved to the ANQ. This transfer, however, was not completed until December 1982. Since the early documents had not been accessioned or classified by the ANQ when volume V went to press, they are cited as Archives civiles.

QUÉBEC, MINISTÈRE DES AFFAIRES CULTURELLES, CENTRE DE DOCUMENTATION, Québec. The Ministère des Affaires culturelles has consolidated into one documentation centre the collections of all its previously existing centres, including that of the Inventaire des biens culturels.
    The following materials were used in the preparation of volume V:
Fonds Morisset

2: Artistes et artisans
  A762/J65.3.2: Arnoldi, Johann Peter
  A762/M621.1: Arnoldi, Michael
  B157/J43: Baillairgé, Jean
  B157/P622.7: Baillairgé, Pierre-Florent
  C226/E25.5/1: Cannon, Edward
  C747.3/P622: Conefroy, Pierre
  C958.8/R639: Cruickshank, Robert
  D348.3/I24.3: Delezenne, Ignace-François
  E54.5/P622: Émond, Pierre
  F744/M623: Forton, Michel
  G933.5/F825: Guernon, dit Belleville,
      François
  H243/J27.5/2: Hanna, James
  H459/L888.4: Heer, Louis-Chrétien de
  H894.5/L888.9: Huguet, dit Latour, Louis
  H894.5/P622/1: Huguet, dit Latour, Pierre,
      père
  L716.4/P551: Liébert, Philippe
  N282/J43: Natte, dit Marseille, Jean
  R213.5/F825: Ranvoyzé, François
  R888/M623/2: Roy, Michel
  R888/N222.5: Roy, Narsise
  S336/J83: Schindler, Joseph
  V674/D395: Viger, Denis

QUEBEC DIOCESAN ARCHIVES, Quebec. For a description of this archives *see*: A. R. Kelley, "The Quebec Diocesan Archives; a description of the collection of historical records of the Church of England in the Diocese of Quebec," ANQ *Rapport*, 1946–47: 181–298; [A.] M. Awcock, "Catalogue of the Quebec Diocesan Archives" (typescript, Shawinigan, Que., 1973; copy available at the archives).
  The following sections were cited in volume V:
Section B: Parish reports, correspondence and other material relating to the parishes
  58 (B-12): Letters testimonial concerning clergy and church in the District of Montreal, prior to the formation of the Diocese of Montreal
  60 (B-14): Quebec cathedral
Section C: Correspondence of the Right Reverend Jacob Mountain
  72 (C-1)–80 (C-9): 1792–1821
Section D: Copies of letters and papers referring to the Diocese of Quebec
  83 (D-2): 1781–88
  84 (D-3): 1789–93

QUEEN'S UNIVERSITY ARCHIVES, Kingston, Ont. For information on the collection see *A guide to the holdings of Queen's University Archives* (Kingston, 1978).
  Materials used in volume V include:
Richard Cartwright papers

UNIVERSITY OF NEW BRUNSWICK LIBRARY, Archives and Special Collections Department, Fredericton.
  Materials used in volume V include:
MG H: Historical
  H 2: Winslow family papers

UNIVERSITY OF TORONTO LIBRARY, Thomas Fisher Rare Book Library. For a description of holdings see *The Thomas Fisher Rare Book Library: a brief guide to the collections* (Toronto, 1982).
  Materials consulted in the preparation of volume V include:
MS coll. 30: J. N. Wallace, "Encyclopedia of the fur trade, biographical & geographical"
MS coll. 31: W. S. Wallace collection

UNIVERSITY OF WESTERN ONTARIO, D. B. Weldon Library, London, Ont. A description of the municipal record and personal manuscript collections is available on microfiche in *Regional collection: the D. B. Weldon Library catalogue*, ed. S. L. Sykes (4 fiches, London, 1977).
  The following material proved useful in the preparation of volume V:
London District, U.C., Surrogate Court, estate files
William Robertson papers
Thomas Walsh papers

FRANCE

ARCHIVES DÉPARTEMENTALES. For a list of analytical inventories *see*: France, Direction des archives, *État des inventaires des archives nationales, départementales, communales et hospitalières au 1er janvier 1937* (Paris, 1938); *Supplément, 1937–1954* [by R.-H. Bautier] (Paris, 1955); *Catalogue des inventaires, répertoires, guides de recherche et autres instruments de travail des archives départementales, communales et hospitalières . . . à la date du 31 décembre 1961* (Paris, 1962). For copies of documents held by the PAC see *General inventory, manuscripts, 1*: 87–99. There is a uniform system of classification for all departmental archives. A list of the various series may be found in *DCB*, 2: 683–84.
  The following series was cited in volume V:
E: Titres de famille, états civils, notaires [The registers of births, marriages, and deaths (*états civils*) are often more complete in the municipal archives.]

ARCHIVES NATIONALES, Paris. The basic inventories of the Archives nationales are: France, Direction des archives, *Inventaire sommaire et tableau méthodique des fonds conservés aux Archives nationales, 1re partie, régime antérieur à 1789* (Paris, 1871); *État sommaire par séries des documents conservés aux Archives nationales* (Paris, 1891); and *Catalogue des manuscrits conservés aux Archives nationales* (Paris, 1892). More recent finding aids include: *État des inventaires des archives nationales, départementales, communales et hospitalières au 1er janvier 1937* (Paris, 1938), and its *Supplément, 1937–1954* [by R.-H. Bautier] (Paris, 1955), published by the Direction des archives; Gilles Héon, "Fonds intéressant le Canada conservés en France: quelques instruments de recherche," *Archives* (Québec), 5 (1973), no.1: 40–50. J.-E. Roy, *Rapport sur les archives de France relatives à l'histoire du Canada* (Ottawa, 1911), and H. P. Beers, *The French in North America: a bibliographical guide to French archives, reproductions, and research missions* (Baton Rouge, La., 1957), give sketches of the history and organization of the archives. For information on copies of AN documents available at the PAC, see *General inventory, manuscripts, 1*: 5–48.

Series cited in volume V:

Fonds des Colonies. For a description of the series and sub-series, *see* Étienne Taillemite, "Les archives des colonies françaises aux Archives nationales," *Gazette des Archives* (Paris), 46 (1964): 93–116.

B: Correspondance envoyée. For the 17th and 18th centuries, *see* Étienne Taillemite, *Inventaire analytique de la correspondance générale avec les colonies, départ, série B (déposée aux Archives nationales), I, registres 1 à 37 (1654–1715)* (Paris, 1959), and Édouard Richard, "Report of Mr. Édouard Richard," PAC *Report*, 1899, supp., 245–548, and his "Summary of documents in Paris . . . ," PAC *Report*, 1904, app.K: 1–312; 1905, 1, pt.vi: 3–446.

C: Correspondance générale, lettres reçues

  C^{11}: Canada et colonies d'Amérique du Nord

    C^{11A}: Canada. A calendar is available in PAC *Report*, 1885: xxix–lxxix; 1886: xxxix–cl; 1887: cxl–ccxxxix. *See also* D. W. Parker, *A guide to the documents in the manuscript room at the Public Archives of Canada* (Ottawa, 1914), 227–29. There is an unpublished index to this series at the PAC.

    C^{11B}: Île Royale. Volumes 1 to 38 are calendared in Parker, *Guide*, 241–45, and PAC *Report*, 1887: cclxxxii–cccxciv.

    C^{11E}: Canada, divers. Letters, etc., dealing with boundary disputes. Calendared in Parker, *Guide*, 240–41, and PAC *Report*, 1887: cclxiii–cclxxxii.

  C^{12}: Saint-Pierre et Miquelon

D: Matricules des troupes

  D^{2C}: Troupes des colonies. Selected volumes are calendared in PAC *Report*, 1905, 1, pt.vi: 508–18.

  D^{2D}: Personnel militaire et civil

E: Personnel individuel

F: Documents divers

  F^1: Commerce aux colonies

    F^{1A}: Fonds des colonies. Financial documents.

  F^3: Collection Moreau de Saint-Méry. Papers relating to Canada, Louisiana, Île Royale, Saint-Pierre, and Miquelon have been copied and microfilmed by the PAC. Calendared in PAC *Report*, 1899, supp., 39–191; 1905, 1, pt.vi: 447–505; Parker, *Guide*, 249–53.

Fonds de la Marine. For descriptions of the archives, *see* Didier Neuville, *État sommaire des archives de la Marine antérieures à la Révolution* (Paris, 1898); Roy, *Rapport sur les archives de France*, 157–243; and Étienne Taillemite, *Les archives anciennes de la Marine* (Paris, [1961]).

B: Service général. Calendared in Didier Neuville *et al.*, *Inventaire des archives de la Marine, série B: service général* (8v., Paris, 1885–1963).

  B^2: Correspondance, lettres envoyées

  B^3: Correspondance, lettres reçues. For a name and subject index to this and the preceding sub-series, *see* Étienne Taillemite *et al.*, *Table de noms de lieux, de personnes, de matières et de navires (sous-séries B^1, B^2 et B^3)* (Paris, 1969).

  B^4: Campagnes

C: Personnel

  C^1: Officiers militaires de la Marine

  C^2: Officiers civils de la Marine

  C^6: Rôles d'équipages

  C^7: Personnel individuel

Service central hydrographique

  3^{JJ}: Journaux, mémoires, correspondance

Section Outre-mer.

Dépôt des fortifications des colonies. A manuscript inventory of the various series in this section is available at the AN. *See also* PAC *Report*, 1905, 1, pt.iii: 1–44, and Roy, *Rapport sur les archives de France*, 535–59.

G: Dépôt des papiers publics des colonies

  G^1: Registres d'état civil, recensements et documents divers

GREAT BRITAIN

BRITISH LIBRARY, London. For a brief guide to catalogues and indexes of the manuscript collections, *see* T. C. Skeat, "The catalogues of the British Museum, 2: manuscripts," *Journal of Documentation* (London), 7 (1951): 18–60, which has been revised as *British Museum: the catalogues of the manuscript collections* (London, 1962), and M. A. E. Nickson,

The British Library: guide to the catalogues and indexes of the Department of Manuscripts ([London], 1982). Information on some collections of Canadian interest is available in *A guide to manuscripts relating to America in Great Britain and Ireland*, ed. J. W. Raimo (Westport, Conn., 1979). For copies of documents from the British Library in the PAC see *General inventory, manuscripts, 3*.

Used in the preparation of volume V were the King's Maps and King's, Stowe, and Additional manuscripts:

Add. MSS 7972–8090: Puisaye (Joseph de), Count, correspondence and papers relating to the affairs of the French royalists

Add. MSS 11038: A collection of philological papers

Add. MSS 15332: Ten large maps and plans of Asia and America

Add. MSS 19069–70: Letters and papers of Jean-Paul Mascarene, commander-in-chief of Nova Scotia

Add. MSS 19071–73, 19075–76: Papers relating to Nova Scotia collected by Dr Andrew Brown

Add. MSS 21631–60: Henry Bouquet papers

Add. MSS 21661–892: Official correspondence and papers of Lieutenant Governor Sir Frederick Haldimand

Add. MSS 24322: Miscellaneous letters and papers relating to American affairs

Add. MSS 35349–6278: Hardwicke papers

Add. MSS 37216–22: Correspondence of the Rev. Philip Morant, historian of Essex

Add. MSS 37842–935: Windham papers

Add. MSS 38190–489: Liverpool papers

Add. MSS 41262–67: Clarkson papers

Add. MSS 58855–9494: Dropmore papers

King's MSS 208–9: Robert Morse, "A general description of the province of Nova Scotia, and a report of the present state of its defences . . ."

King's Maps CXIX, 107b: "Plan of Trinity's Harbour, Newfoundland, 1748"

Stowe MSS 793: [Sir Alexander Mackenzie], "Journal of a Voyage performed by order of the N.W. Company, in a bark canoe, in search of a passage by water through the N.W. Continent of America from Athabasca to the Pacific Ocean, in summer 1789"

DEVON RECORD OFFICE, Exeter, Eng. Descriptions of some materials appear in *Devon Record Office: brief guide, part 1: official and ecclesiastical* (1v. to date, [Exeter, 1969–   ]); *A guide to manuscripts relating to America in Great Britain and Ireland*, ed. J. W. Raimo (Westport, Conn., 1979); and *Britain and the Dominions: a guide to business and related records in the United Kingdom concerning Australia, Canada, New Zealand, and South Africa*, comp. C. A. Jones (Boston, 1978). Many of the parish registers held by the office are listed in *Original parish registers in record offices and libraries* ([Cambridge, Eng.], 1974) and its *First supplement* (1976).

The following materials were used in the preparation of volume V:

53/6, box 34: Kingskerswell, documents relating to land, 1657–1811

73A: Coffinswell

PO: Settlement examinations

1038: Simcoe papers

2537A: St Petrox, Dartmouth, parish records

2659A: Broadhempston, parish records

2954A: Abbotskerswell, parish records

2992A: St Saviour, Dartmouth, parish records

2993A: St Clement, Townstall (Dartmouth), parish records

3119A: Kingskerswell, parish records

3289S: Exeter, shipping registers

3419A: Combeinteignhead, parish records

3420A: Stokeinteignhead, parish records

DD60501–8053: Dartmouth Corporation records

Exeter City Archives

Town customs accounts

DORSET RECORD OFFICE, Dorchester, Eng. Descriptions of some materials concerning Canada appear in *A guide to manuscripts relating to America in Great Britain and Ireland*, ed. J. W. Raimo (Westport, Conn., 1979), and in *Britain and the Dominions: a guide to business records in the United Kingdom concerning Australia, Canada, New Zealand, and South Africa*, comp. C. A. Jones (Boston, 1978).

The following were used in the preparation of volume V:

D: Deposited documents

    D203: Bridport–Gundry records

        A1–A54: Joseph Gundry & Co. records

    D365: Records of the Lester and Garland families

        F2–F10: Benjamin and Isaac Lester, diaries

P: Parish records

    P70: Blandford Forum

        OV: Overseers' records

    P227: St James Church, Poole

        CW: Churchwardens' records

        OV: Overseers' records

        RE: Registers of baptisms, marriages, and burials

GENERAL REGISTER OFFICE FOR SCOTLAND, Edinburgh. Information concerning the parish registers held by the GRO is available in the *Detailed list of Old Parochial Registers of Scotland* (Edinburgh, 1872). Registers of baptisms, marriages, and burials for several Scottish parishes were used in the preparation of volume V.

NATIONAL MARITIME MUSEUM, London. For information on the manuscript collections see *Guide to the*

manuscripts in the National Maritime Museum, ed.
R. J. B. Knight (2v., London, 1977–80).

The following materials have been used in the preparation of volume V:

Artificial collections
    AGC: Letters
    JOD: Journals and diaries
    LBK: Letterbooks
Personal collections
    DUC: Duckworth papers
    GRV: Graves papers
    KEA: Keats papers
    POL: Pole papers
    YOR: Yorke papers
Public records
    HAL: Halifax Dockyard records
        F: Commissioners' letterbooks

PUBLIC RECORD OFFICE, London. For an introduction to the holdings and arrangement of this archives see *Guide to the contents of the Public Record Office* (3v., London, 1963–68). For copies of PRO documents available at the PAC see *General inventory, manuscripts, 2*.

The following series were used in the preparation of volume V:

Admiralty
    Accounting departments
        ADM 36: Ships' musters, series I
        ADM 42: Yard pay books
    Admiralty and Secretariat
        ADM 1: Papers
        ADM 2: Out-letters
        ADM 6: Various
        ADM 7: Miscellanea
        ADM 9: Returns of officers' services
        ADM 50: Admirals' journals
        ADM 51: Captains' logs
        ADM 52: Masters' logs
        ADM 55: Log books, supplementary, series II:
            explorations
    Greenwich Hospital
        ADM 68: Accounts and ledgers, various
        ADM 80: Miscellanea, various
    Navy Board
        ADM 106: Navy Board records
        ADM 107: Passing certificates
Board of Customs and Excise
    CUST 65: Outport records, Dartmouth,
        England
Board of Inland Revenue
    IR 26: Estate duty office: death duty
        registers
Board of Trade
    General
        BT 1: In-letters and files, general
        BT 5: Minutes

BT 6: Miscellanea
Registrar general of shipping and seamen
    BT 98: Agreements and crew lists, series I
Chancery
    Judicial proceedings (equity side)
        C108: Masters' exhibits
Colonial Office. [*See* R. B. Pugh, *The records of the Colonial and Dominions offices* (London, 1964).]
        CO 1: Colonial papers, general series
    America and West Indies
        CO 5: Original correspondence
    Barbados
        CO 33: Miscellanea
    Bermuda
        CO 41: Miscellanea
    Canada
        CO 42: Original correspondence
        CO 43: Entry books
    New Brunswick
        CO 188: Original correspondence
        CO 189: Entry books
        CO 190: Acts
        CO 191: Sessional papers
        CO 193: Miscellanea
    Newfoundland
        CO 194: Original correspondence
        CO 195: Entry books
        CO 199: Miscellanea
    Nova Scotia and Cape Breton
        CO 217: Original correspondence
        CO 218: Entry books
    Prince Edward Island
        CO 226: Original correspondence
        CO 227: Entry books
        CO 229: Sessional papers
    Sierra Leone
        CO 267: Original correspondence
        CO 270: Sessional papers
    Colonies general
        CO 324: Entry books, series I
        CO 325: Miscellanea
    Maps and plans
        CO 700: Maps
Exchequer and Audit Department
        AO 1: Declared accounts (in rolls)
        AO 3: Accounts, various
        AO 12: Claims, American loyalists, series I
        AO 13: Claims, American loyalists, series II
Exchequer, King's Remembrancer
        E 190: Port books
Foreign Office. [See *Records of the Foreign Office, 1782–1939* (London, 1969).]
    General correspondence
        FO 5: America, United States of, series II
High Court of Admiralty
        HCA 26: Letters of marque

Indexes (available for various classes)
    IND 16663: Chancery proceedings, modern series,
        index to pleadings
Paymaster General's Office
    PMG 4: Half pay
Prerogative Court of Canterbury (formerly held at
    Somerset House)
        PROB 6: Act book: administrations
        PROB 11: Registered copy wills
Privy Council Office
        PC 2: Registers
Public Record Office
    Documents acquired by gift, deposit, or purchase
        PRO 30/8: Chatham papers
        PRO 30/55: Carleton papers
Registrar General
    RG 4/464: Authenticated register, Presbyterian
        Old Meeting, Poole
Treasury
    In-letters and files
        T 1: Treasury Board papers
    Out-letters
        T 28: Various
    Miscellanea
        T 50: Documents relating to refugees
        T 64: Various
War Office
    Correspondence
        WO 1: In-letters
        WO 40: Selected unnumbered papers
    Returns
        WO 17: Monthly returns
        WO 25: Registers, various
    Miscellanea
        WO 28: Headquarters records
    Private collections
        WO 34: Amherst papers
        WO 36: American rebellion: entry books
    Judge Advocate General's Office
        WO 71: Courts martial, proceedings
        WO 81: Letterbooks
    Commissariat department
        WO 57: In-letters
        WO 58: Out-letters
        WO 60: Accounts

SCOTTISH RECORD OFFICE, Edinburgh. A comprehensive listing of materials relating to Canada is provided by the SRO's "List of Canadian documents" (typescript, 1977, with updates to 1981). An appendix records Canadian documents in private archives as surveyed by the National Reg. of Arch. (Scotland). This guide is based on an earlier compilation, *A source list of manuscripts relating to the U.S.A. and Canada in private archives preserved in the Scottish Record Office* (Edinburgh, 1970), and is available at the PAC, all provincial archives, and other selected Canadian

institutions. Some items are also described in *A guide to manuscripts relating to America in Great Britain and Ireland*, ed. J. W. Raimo (Westport, Conn., 1979), and *Britain and the Dominions: a guide to business and related records in the United Kingdom concerning Australia, Canada, New Zealand, and South Africa*, comp. C. A. Jones (Boston, 1978).

The following were cited in volume V:
Church of Scotland records
    CH2: Presbytery records
Gifts and deposits
    GD1: Miscellaneous gifts and deposits
        151: James Dunlop, letterbook
    GD45: Dalhousie muniments
    GD51: Melville Castle muniments
    GD293: Montgomery estate papers in the muniments of Messrs. Blackwood and Smith, W.S., Peebles, estate papers

UNITED SOCIETY FOR THE PROPAGATION OF THE GOSPEL, London. The archives is in the process of reorganizing and reclassifying some material. Thus classifications used by Canadian archives holding USPG microfilm do not always correspond to those of the archives itself. Indexes are available at USPG, however, and most dated references are easily transferred. For copies of USPG documents available at the PAC, see *General inventory, manuscripts, 3.*

The following were consulted in the preparation of volume V:
B: Original letters received from the American colonies, the West Indies, Newfoundland, Nova Scotia
C/Am: Unbound letters from the American colonies
C/CAN: Unbound letters from Canada. Letters from Montreal, New Brunswick, Newfoundland, Nova Scotia, Quebec, and Pre-Diocesan groupings were used. A nominal card index is available at USPG.
X: Miscellaneous volumes and papers, 18th–20th centuries
Dr Bray's Associates, minute-books and unbound papers
Journal of proceedings of the Society for the Propagation of the Gospel. Comprises bound and indexed volumes of the proceedings of the general meetings held in London from 1701, and four appendices, A, B, C, D (1701–1860).

UNITED STATES

DETROIT PUBLIC LIBRARY, Burton Historical Collection, Detroit, Mich. The Collection's holdings are listed in *The national union catalog of manuscript collections* . . . (18v. plus 7 index vols. to date, Ann Arbor and Washington, 1962–   ).

Materials used in volume V include:
John Askin papers
J.-B. Barthe papers
Thomas Williams papers

MASSACHUSETTS HISTORICAL SOCIETY, Boston. For information about the collections *see:* S. T. Riley, *The Massachusetts Historical Society, 1791–1959* (Boston, 1959); "The manuscript collections of the Massachusetts Historical Society: a brief listing," *M.H.S. Miscellany* (Boston), 5 (December 1958); *Catalog of manuscripts of the Massachusetts Historical Society* (9v. to date, Boston, 1969–).

The following items were used most frequently in the preparation of volume V:
Robert Haswell, "A voyage round the world onboard the ship Columbia-Rediviva and sloop Washington," [1787–89]
——— "A voyage on discoveries in the ship Columbia Rediviva," [1791–93]

NEW YORK PUBLIC LIBRARY, Rare Books and Manuscripts Division. For information on the manuscript collections see *Dictionary catalog of the Manuscript Division* (2v., Boston, 1967) and *Guide to the research collections of the New York Public Library*, comp. S. P. Williams (Chicago, 1975), 41–47.

Manuscripts cited in volume V include:
William Edgar papers
Phillip Schuyler papers

STATE HISTORICAL SOCIETY OF WISCONSIN, Madison. For information on the manuscript collection see *Guide to the manuscripts of the Wisconsin Historical Society*, ed. A. M. Smith (Madison, 1944), *Supplement number one*, ed. J. L. Harper and S. C. Smith (1957), and *Supplement number two*, ed. J. L. Harper (1966). The Draper MSS are not included in any of these volumes, but are discussed at length in the *Guide to the Draper manuscripts*, ed. J. L. Harper (Madison, 1983).

Materials used in the preparation of volume V include:
Consolidated returns of trade licences
Draper MSS

WILLIAM L. CLEMENTS LIBRARY, University of Michigan, Ann Arbor. Brief descriptions of the manuscript collections of the Clements Library appear in *The national union catalog of manuscript collections . . .* (18v. plus 7 index vols. to date, Ann Arbor and Washington, 1962–), and *Guide to the manuscript collections in the William L. Clements Library*, comp. A. P. Shy assisted by B. A. Mitchell (3rd ed., Boston, 1978).

Materials used in the preparation of volume V include:
Thomas Gage papers
  American series
  Supplementary accounts

II. PRINTED PRIMARY SOURCES

A. OFFICIAL PUBLICATIONS AND CONTEMPORARY WORKS

"Accounts of the receiver-general of Upper Canada . . . [1801–2]." AO *Report*, 1914: 729–81.
[AINSLIE, THOMAS.] *Canada preserved; the journal of Captain Thomas Ainslie.* Edited by Sheldon S. Cohen. [Toronto, 1968.]
American archives: consisting of a collection of authentick records, state papers, debates, and letters and other notices of publick affairs, the whole forming a documentary history of the origin and progress of the North American colonies. . . . Compiled by Matthew St Clair Clarke and Peter Force. 2 ser. in 9 vols. Washington, 1837–53; reprinted [New York, 1972]. Six series covering the years up to 1787 were projected but only the 4th and part of the 5th series appeared, covering the years 1774–76.
ARCHIVES NATIONALES DU QUÉBEC, Québec
  PUBLICATIONS [*see also* section III]

Rapport. 54 vols. 1920/21–77. There is an index to the contents of the first 42 volumes: *Table des matières des rapports des Archives du Québec, tomes 1 à 42 (1920–1964)* ([Québec], 1965).
ARCHIVES OF ONTARIO, Toronto
  PUBLICATIONS
  Report. 22 vols. 1903–33.
BAS-CANADA. *See* LOWER CANADA
"Board of land office for the District of Hesse, 1789–1794; minutes of meetings, etc." AO *Report*, 1905: 1–268.
Les bourgeois de la compagnie du Nord-Ouest: récits de voyages, lettres et rapports inédits relatifs au Nord-Ouest canadien. Louis-[François-]Rodrigue Masson, éditeur. 2 vols. Québec, 1889–90; réimprimé New York, 1960.
CAMPBELL, PATRICK. *Travels in the interior inhabited parts of North America in the years 1791 and 1792. . . .* Edinburgh, 1793. [New edition.] Edited by Hugh Hornby Langton and William Francis

Ganong. (Champlain Society publications, 23.) Toronto, 1937.

CHAMPLAIN SOCIETY, Toronto

PUBLICATIONS

52 vols. to date, exclusive of the Hudson's Bay Company series [*see* HBRS], the Ontario series, and the unnumbered series.

8–10: Knox, *Hist. journal* (Doughty).

13–15, 17: *Select British docs. of War of 1812* (Wood).

21: *Journals of Hearne and Turnor* (Tyrrell).

22: *Docs. relating to NWC* (Wallace).

23: P. Campbell, *Travels in North America* (Langton and Ganong).

29: Perkins, *Diary, 1766–80* (Innis).

35: Douglas, *Lord Selkirk's diary* (White).

36: Perkins, *Diary, 1780–89* (Harvey and Fergusson).

39: Perkins, *Diary, 1790–96* (Fergusson).

41–42: Smith, *Diary and selected papers* (Upton).

43: Perkins, *Diary, 1797–1803* (Fergusson).

46: Norton, *Journal* (Klinck and Talman).

50: Perkins, *Diary, 1804–12* (Fergusson).

ONTARIO SERIES

11 vols. to date.

3: *Kingston before War of 1812* (Preston).

4: *Windsor border region* (Lajeunesse).

5: *Town of York, 1793–1815* (Firth).

7: *Valley of Six Nations* (Johnston).

Collection des manuscrits du maréchal de Lévis. Henri-Raymond Casgrain, éditeur. 12 vols. Montréal et Québec, 1889–95.

The correspondence of Lieut. Governor John Graves Simcoe, with allied documents relating to his administration of the government of Upper Canada. Edited by Ernest Alexander Cruikshank. (Ontario Historical Society publication.) 5 vols. Toronto, 1923–31.

The correspondence of the Honourable Peter Russell, with allied documents relating to his administration of the government of Upper Canada during the official term of Lieut.-Governor J. G. Simcoe, while on leave of absence. Edited by Ernest Alexander Cruikshank and Andrew Frederick Hunter. (Ontario Historical Society publication.) 3 vols. Toronto, 1932–36.

"Les dénombrements de Québec faits en 1792, 1795, 1798 et 1805." Joseph-Octave Plessis, compilateur. ANQ *Rapport*, 1948–49: 1–250.

The documentary history of the campaign upon the Niagara frontier. . . . Edited by Ernest [Alexander] Cruikshank. (Lundy's Lane Historical Society publication.) 9 vols. Welland, Ont., [1896]–1908.

Documents relatifs à l'histoire constitutionnelle du Canada. . . . Adam Shortt *et al.*, éditeurs. (PAC publication.) 3 vols. Ottawa, 1911–35.

[1]: *1759–1791.* Adam Shortt et Arthur George Doughty, éditeurs. 2ᵉ édition. (PAC, Board of Historical Publications.) 2 parties. 1921.

[2]: *1791–1818.* Arthur George Doughty et Duncan A. McArthur, éditeurs.

[3]: *1819–1828.* Arthur George Doughty et Norah Story, éditeurs.

Documents relating to the constitutional history of Canada. . . . Edited by Adam Shortt *et al.* (PAC publication.) 3 vols. Ottawa, 1907–35.

[1]: *1759–1791.* Edited by Adam Shortt and Arthur George Doughty. 2nd edition. (PAC, Board of Historical Publications.) 2 parts. 1918.

[2]: *1791–1818.* Edited by Arthur George Doughty and Duncan A. McArthur.

[3]: *1819–1828.* Edited by Arthur George Doughty and Norah Story.

Documents relating to the North West Company. Edited by William Stewart Wallace. (Champlain Society publications, 22.) Toronto, 1934.

Documents relative to the colonial history of the state of New-York. . . . Edited by Edmund Bailey O'Callaghan and Berthold Fernow. 15 vols. Albany, N.Y., 1853–87.

[DOUGLAS, THOMAS.] *Lord Selkirk's diary, 1803–1804; a journal of his travels in British North America and the northeastern United States.* Edited by Patrick Cecil Telfer White (Champlain Society publications, 35.) Toronto, 1958; reprinted New York, 1969.

"Early records of St. Mark's and St. Andrew's churches, Niagara." Compiled by Janet Carnochan. *OH*, 3 (1901): 7–85.

"État général des billets d'ordonnances dont j'ay fait la vérification sur les bordereaux que m'en ont remis les porteurs et propriétaires d'ycelles du gouvernement de Montréal, au désir du règlement fait le vingt-deux may dernier approuvé de son excellence monsieur le gouverneur. . . ." Pierre Panet, compilateur. ANQ *Rapport*, 1924–25: 231–342.

Gentleman's Magazine. London, 1731–1907. Monthly.

"Grants of crown lands in Upper Canada . . . [1792–98]." AO *Report*, 1928: 7–228; 1929: 9–177; 1930; 1931.

[GWILLIM, ELIZABETH POSTHUMA.] *The diary of Mrs. John Graves Simcoe, wife of the first lieutenant-governor of the province of Upper Canada, 1792–6.* Edited by John Ross Robertson. Toronto, 1911; reprinted [1973]. [Revised edition.] 1934.

HENRY, ALEXANDER. *Travels and adventures in Canada and the Indian territories, between the years 1760 and 1776.* New York, 1809. New edition. Edited by James Bain. Toronto, 1901; Boston, 1901; reprinted Edmonton, [1969], New

York, [1969], Rutland, Vt., [1969], and St Clair Shores, Mich., 1972. Part I of the original has also been published as *Attack at Michilimackinac . . .* , ed. D. A. Armour (Mackinac Island, Mich., 1971).

HUDSON'S BAY RECORD SOCIETY, Winnipeg
PUBLICATIONS
32 vols. to date. General editor for vols.1–22, Edwin Ernest Rich; vols.23–25, Kenneth Gordon Davies; vols.26–30, Glyndwr Williams; vols.31– , Hartwell Bowsfield. Vols.1–12 were issued in association with the Champlain Society [*q.v.*] and reprinted in 1968 in Nendeln, Liechtenstein.
21–22: Rich, *Hist. of HBC* [*see* section IV].
27: [Graham, Andrew.] *Andrew Graham's observations on Hudson's Bay, 1767–91*. Edited by Glyndwr Williams, introduction by Richard [Gilchrist] Glover. London, 1969.

Invasion du Canada. [Hospice-Anthelme-Jean-Baptiste] Verreau, éditeur. Montréal, 1873. A collection of five pamphlets originally issued separately between 1870 and 1872. Further volumes were projected but only one additional pamphlet appeared. See *Biblio. of Canadiana* (Staton and Tremaine) [section III].

The John Askin papers. Edited by Milo Milton Quaife. (DPL, Burton historical records, 1–2.) 2 vols. Detroit, 1928–31.

Johnson papers (Sullivan *et al.*). See *The papers of Sir William Johnson*

"Journal par Messrs Franˢ Baby, Gab. Taschereau et Jenkin Williams dans la tournée qu'ils ont fait dans le district de Québec par ordre du général Carleton tant pour l'établissement des milices dans chaque paroisse que pour l'examen des personnes qui ont assisté ou aider les rebels dont nous avons pris notes." Ægidius Fauteux, éditeur. ANQ *Rapport*, 1927–28: 435–99; 1929–30: 138–40.

Journals of Samuel Hearne and Philip Turnor. Edited by Joseph Burr Tyrrell. (Champlain Society publications, 21.) Toronto, 1934; reprinted New York, 1968.

"The journals of the Legislative Assembly of Upper Canada . . . [1792–1821]." AO *Report*, 1909, 1911–13. The journals for part of 1794 and for 1795–97, 1809, 1813, and 1815 are missing.

Kingston before the War of 1812: a collection of documents. Edited by Richard Arthur Preston. (Champlain Society publications, Ontario series, 3.) Toronto, 1959.

KNOX, JOHN. *An historical journal of the campaigns in North-America, for the years 1757, 1758, 1759, and 1760. . . .* 2 vols. London, 1769. [New edition.] Edited by Arthur George Doughty. (Champlain Society publications, 8–10.) 3 vols. Toronto, 1914–16; reprinted New York, 1968.

LANDMANN, [GEORGE THOMAS]. *Adventures and recollections of Colonel Landmann, late of the Corps of Royal Engineers*. 2 vols. London, 1852.

LOWER CANADA/BAS-CANADA
HOUSE OF ASSEMBLY/CHAMBRE D'ASSEMBLÉE
Journals/Journaux. Quebec, 1792/93–1820.
LEGISLATIVE COUNCIL/CONSEIL LÉGISLATIF
Journals/Journaux. Quebec, 1792/94–1820.
Provincial statutes/Les statuts provinciaux. Quebec, 1792/96–1820.
For further information *see* Thériault, *Les pub. parl.* [section III].

[MACKENZIE, ALEXANDER.] *The journals and letters of Sir Alexander Mackenzie*. Edited by William Kaye Lamb. (Hakluyt Society, [Works], extra series, 41.) Cambridge, Eng., 1970; Toronto, 1970.

[MASERES, FRANCIS.] *The Maseres letters, 1766–1768*. Edited by William Stewart Wallace. (University of Toronto studies, History and economics series, vol.3, no.2.) Toronto, 1919.

Michigan Pioneer Collections. Lansing. 40 vols. 1874/76–1929. To avoid confusion the Michigan Historical Commission, Department of State, Lansing, has standardized the citation for the volumes, which were originally published by various historical agencies and under various titles. Volumes are traditionally cited by their spine dates.

Military operations in eastern Maine and Nova Scotia during the revolution, chiefly compiled from the journals and letters of Colonel John Allan, with notes and a memoir of Col. John Allan. Edited by Frederic Kidder. Albany, N.Y., 1867; reprinted New York, 1971.

"Minutes of the Court of General Quarter Sessions of the Peace for the Home District, 13th March, 1800, to 28th December, 1811." AO *Report*, 1932.

The Naval Chronicle . . . containing a general and biographical history of the Royal Navy of the United Kingdom; with a variety of original papers on nautical subjects. London. 1 (January–June 1799)–40 (July–December 1818).

NEW BRUNSWICK
HOUSE OF ASSEMBLY
Journal. Fredericton, 1786–1842. Title varies; *see* Bishop, *Pubs. of governments of N.S., P.E.I., N.B.* [section III].
LEGISLATIVE COUNCIL
Journal of the Legislative Council of the province of New Brunswick . . . [1786–1830]. 2 vols. Fredericton, 1831.

NEW BRUNSWICK HISTORICAL SOCIETY, Saint John
PUBLICATIONS
Collections. 12 nos. in 4 vols. and 21 additional nos. to date. 1894/97– . Used primarily for the documents reproduced.

New light on the early history of the greater northwest: the manuscript journals of Alexander

Henry, fur trader of the Northwest Company, and of David Thompson, official geographer and explorer of the same company, 1799–1814. . . . Edited by Elliott Coues. 3 vols., New York, 1897; reprinted 3 vols. in 2, Minneapolis, Minn., [1965].

[NORTON, JOHN.] *The journal of Major John Norton, 1816.* Edited by Carl Frederick Klinck and James John Talman. (Champlain Society publications, 46.) Toronto, 1970.

NOVA SCOTIA
HOUSE OF ASSEMBLY
  Journal and proceedings. Halifax, 1761–1820. Title varies; *see* Bishop, *Pubs. of governments of N.S., P.E.I., N.B.* [section III].

ONTARIO HISTORICAL SOCIETY, Toronto
PUBLICATIONS
  Corr. of Hon. Peter Russell (Cruikshank and Hunter).
  Corr. of Lieut. Governor Simcoe (Cruikshank).

[OSGOODE, WILLIAM.] "Letters from the Honourable Chief Justice William Osgoode: a selection from his Canadian correspondence, 1791–1801." Edited by William Colgate. *OH*, 46 (1954): 77–95, 149–68.

The papers of Sir William Johnson. Edited by James Sullivan *et al.* 14 vols. Albany, N.Y., 1921–65.

The parish register of Kingston, Upper Canada, 1785–1811. Edited by Archibald Hope Young. (Kingston Historical Society publication.) Kingston, Ont., 1921.

[PERKINS, SIMEON.] *The diary of Simeon Perkins. . . .* Edited by Harold Adams Innis *et al.* (Champlain Society publications, 29, 36, 39, 43, 50.) 5 vols. Toronto, 1948–78.
  [1]: *1766–1780.* Edited by Harold Adams Innis.
  [2]: *1780–1789.* Edited by Daniel Cobb Harvey with notes by Charles Bruce Fergusson.
  [3]: *1790–1796;* [4]: *1797–1803;* [5]: *1804–1812.* Edited by Charles Bruce Fergusson.

"Petitions for grants of land . . . [1792–99]." Edited by Ernest Alexander Cruikshank. *OH*, 24 (1927): 17–144; 26 (1930): 97–379.

"Political state of Upper Canada in 1806–7." PAC *Report*, 1892: 32–135.

PRINCE EDWARD ISLAND
HOUSE OF ASSEMBLY
  Journal. Charlottetown, 1788–1820. Title varies; *see* Bishop, *Pubs. of governments of N.S., P.E.I., N.B.* [section III].

PUBLIC ARCHIVES OF CANADA, Ottawa
BOARD OF HISTORICAL PUBLICATIONS
  Doc. relatifs à l'hist. constitutionnelle, 1759–91 (Shortt et Doughty; 1921).
  Docs. relating to constitutional hist., 1759–91 (Shortt and Doughty; 1918).
  NUMBERED PUBLICATIONS [*see* section III]
  OTHER PUBLICATIONS [*see also* section III]
  Doc. relatifs à l'hist. constitutionnelle, 1759–91 (Shortt et Doughty; 1911).

Doc. relatifs à l'hist. constitutionnelle, 1791–1818 (Doughty et McArthur; 1915).
Doc. relatifs à l'hist. constitutionnelle, 1819–28 (Doughty et Story; 1935).
Docs. relating to constitutional hist., 1759–91 (Shortt and Doughty; 1907).
Docs. relating to constitutional hist., 1791–1818 (Doughty and McArthur; 1914).
Docs. relating to constitutional hist., 1819–28 (Doughty and Story; 1935).
Report/Rapport. 1881– . Annually, with some omissions, until 1952; irregularly thereafter. For indexes, *see* section III.

QUEBEC
CONSEIL LÉGISLATIF/LEGISLATIVE COUNCIL
  Ordonnances. Québec, 1777–92.
For further information *see* Thériault, *Les pub. parl.* [section III].

The royal commission on the losses and services of American loyalists, 1783 to 1785, being the notes of Mr. Daniel Parker Coke, M.P., one of the commissioners during that period. Edited by Hugh Edward Egerton. Oxford, Eng., 1915.

Royal Society of London. *Philosophical Transactions.* . . . 1 (1665–66)–177 (1886). Carried on from 178 (1887) in two separate series: A, *Mathematical and physical sciences*; B, *Biological sciences*. Title and volume numbering vary.

Select British documents of the Canadian War of 1812. Edited by William [Charles Henry] Wood. (Champlain Society publications, 13–15, 17.) 3 vols. in 4. Toronto, 1920–28; reprinted New York, 1968.

Le séminaire de Québec: documents et biographies. Honorius Provost, éditeur. (ASQ publication, 2.) Québec, 1964.

SMITH, WILLIAM. *The diary and selected papers of Chief Justice William Smith, 1784–1793.* Edited by Leslie Francis Stokes Upton. (Champlain Society publications, 41–42.) 2 vols. Toronto, 1963–65.

STEWART, JOHN. *An account of Prince Edward Island, in the Gulph of St. Lawrence, North America. . . .* London, 1806; reprinted [East Ardsley, Eng., and New York], 1967.

"Surveyors' letters; notes, instructions, etc., from 1788 to 1791." AO *Report*, 1905: 405–99.

The town of York, 1793–1815: a collection of documents of early Toronto. Edited by Edith Grace Firth. (Champlain Society publications, Ontario series, 5.) Toronto, 1962.

"United Empire Loyalists: enquiry into the losses and services in consequence of their loyalty; evidence in the Canadian claims." AO *Report*, 1904.

UNITED STATES, CONGRESS. *American state papers: documents, legislative and executive, of the Congress of the United States. . . .* Edited by Walter Lowrie *et al.* 38 vols. in 10 classes. Washington, 1832–61.

"Upper Canada land book B, 19th August, 1796, to 7th April, 1797." AO *Report*, 1930: xi–126.

"Upper Canada land book C, 29th June, 1796, to 4th July, 1796; 1st July, 1797, to 20th December, 1797." AO *Report*, 1931: ix–98.

"Upper Canada land book C, 11th April, 1797, to 30th June, 1797." AO *Report*, 1930: 127–75.

"Upper Canada land book D, 22nd December, 1797, to 13th July, 1798." AO *Report*, 1931: 99–194.

The valley of the Six Nations; a collection of documents on the Indian lands of the Grand River. Edited by Charles Murray Johnston. (Champlain Society publications, Ontario series, 7.) Toronto, 1964.

The Windsor border region, Canada's southernmost frontier; a collection of documents. Edited by Ernest Joseph Lajeunesse. (Champlain Society publications, Ontario series, 4.) Toronto, 1960.

Winslow papers, A.D. 1776–1826. Edited by William Odber Raymond. Saint John, N.B., 1901.

WISCONSIN, STATE HISTORICAL SOCIETY, Madison
PUBLICATIONS
Collections. 31 vols. 1854–1931.

B. NEWSPAPERS

The following newspapers were particularly useful in the preparation of volume V. Numerous sources have been used to determine their various titles and their dates of publication. The printed sources include, for all areas of the country: Canadian Library Assoc., *Canadian newspapers on microfilm, catalogue* (2 pts. in 3, Ottawa, 1959–69), *Union list of Canadian newspapers held by Canadian libraries/Liste collective des journaux canadiens disponibles dans les bibliothèques canadiennes* (Ottawa, 1977), and for pre-1800 newspapers, Tremaine, *Biblio. of Canadian imprints* [see section III]; for Newfoundland: "Chronological list of Newfoundland newspapers in the public collections at the Gosling Memorial Library and Provincial Archives," comp. Ian MacDonald (copy deposited in the Reference Library, Arts and Culture Centre, St John's); for Nova Scotia: G. E. N. Tratt, *A survey and listing of Nova Scotia newspapers, 1752–1957, with particular reference to the period before 1867* (Halifax, 1979), and *An historical directory of Nova Scotia newspapers and journals before confederation*, comp. T. B. Vincent (Kingston, Ont., 1977); for Ontario: *Catalogue of Canadian newspapers in the Douglas Library, Queen's University*, [comp. L. C. Ellison *et al.*] (Kingston, 1969), *Early Toronto newspapers, 1793–1867* . . . , ed. E. G. Firth, intro. H. C. Campbell (Toronto, 1961), and W. S. Wallace, "The periodical literature of Upper Canada," *CHR*, 12 (1931): 4–22; and for Quebec: Beaulieu et Hamelin, *La presse québécoise*, vol.1 [see section III].

Acadian Recorder. Halifax. Began publication on 16 Jan. 1813 as a weekly. A tri-weekly began on 5 Sept. 1864, and was joined by a daily on 1 Dec. 1868. Both editions ceased publication in May 1930.

Le Canadien. Québec; Montréal. A prospectus appeared on 13 Nov. 1806; the paper was published in Quebec as a weekly from 22 Nov. 1806 to 2 March 1825. It resumed publication on 7 May 1831 as a semi-weekly, becoming a tri-weekly on 9 May 1832 and a daily on 8 May 1857. Published in both tri-weekly and daily editions from 1874 to 1890. The paper moved to Montreal in 1891 and ceased publication in 1893, reappearing between 22 Dec. 1906 and December 1909.

Le Courier de Québec. Prospectus issued on 29 Oct. 1806. A semi-weekly, it was published from 3 Jan. 1807 to 31 Dec. 1808.

Herald, Miscellany & Advertiser. Quebec. Began publication on 24 Nov. 1788 as a weekly. The title of this first issue was *Quebec Herald and Universal Miscellany*, but for the rest of the paper's run from 1 Dec. 1788 to 16 Nov. 1789 the title was shortened to *Herald and Universal Miscellany*. The paper continued as the *Herald, Miscellany & Advertiser*, and became a semi-weekly from 23 Nov. 1789 until 19 May 1791, when it reverted to its original weekly format. It appears to have ceased publication on 11 Feb. 1793, although the last issue extant is that of 23 July 1792. The paper was numbered in volumes of 52 issues apiece (the two semi-weekly editions had separate volume, issue, and page numbering), for which indexes and separate title pages were published annually. The title page for the first volume retained the original title *Quebec Herald and Universal Miscellany*; those of subsequent volumes were entitled *Quebec Herald, Miscellany and Advertiser*, a title under which the paper is commonly known.

Kingston Gazette. Kingston, [Ont.]. A weekly, the paper was published under this title from 25 Sept. 1810 to 29 Dec. 1818. It continued as the *Kingston Chronicle* from 1 Jan. 1819 to 22 June 1833, and then appeared as the *Chronicle & Gazette* (which became semi-weekly in 1835) from 29 June 1833 until 1847.

Lloyd's List. London. Began publication as a weekly in 1733/34 and seems to have become semi-weekly at the beginning of 1736/37; the earliest surviving issue is that of 2 Jan. 1740/41. It became a daily on 1 July 1837, and has continued, with several changes in title, to the present.

Montreal Gazette/La Gazette de Montréal. A bilingual continuation of *La Gazette littéraire pour la ville et district de Montréal* (1778–79), the paper was published as a weekly from 3 Aug. 1785 to 31 Jan. 1824. From August 1822 to the present time the paper has appeared only in English with several changes in title and frequency.

Montreal Herald. Published under various titles from 19 Oct. 1811 to 18 Oct. 1957. Frequency varied until the 1830s when it became a daily; a weekly edition also appeared under differing titles beginning in 1834.

Nova Scotia Royal Gazette. Halifax. Published under this title from 3 Jan. 1801 to 9 Feb. 1843. A weekly, it began publication as the *Halifax Gazette* on 23 March 1752. It was continued under various titles, including the *Nova-Scotia Gazette and the Weekly Chronicle* (4 Sept. 1770–31 March 1789) and the *Royal Gazette and the Nova-Scotia Advertiser* (7 April 1789–30 Dec. 1800). On 16 Feb. 1843 the paper became the *Royal Gazette*, which continues to the present.

Quebec Gazette/La Gazette de Québec. Published weekly from 21 June 1764 to 25 Dec. 1817, and semi-weekly from 19 Jan. 1818 to 30 April 1832. The paper appeared tri-weekly from 2 May 1832 until its last issue on 30 Oct. 1874, except for a brief period between 1848 and 1850 during which it alternated between daily and tri-weekly publication. It remained bilingual from 2 May 1832 until 30 April 1842 but the French and English editions were published separately; from 29 Oct. 1842 to 30 Oct. 1874 only the English edition appeared.

Quebec Herald, Miscellany and Advertiser. See *Herald, Miscellany & Advertiser*

Quebec Mercury. Began publication on 5 Jan. 1805 as a weekly, becoming a semi-weekly on 14 May 1816. The paper was issued tri-weekly from 17 May 1831 to 29 April 1848 and from 31 Oct. 1848 to 8 Jan. 1863. It appeared daily between 1 May and 30 Oct. 1848, and resumed daily publication from 12 Jan. 1863 until its last issue of 17 Oct. 1903.

Royal Gazette and Newfoundland Advertiser. St John's. Published from 27 Aug. 1807 as a weekly. In October 1924 the paper became the *Newfoundland Gazette*, the official government gazette which continues to the present.

Royal Gazette and the Nova-Scotia Advertiser. See *Nova Scotia Royal Gazette*

Upper Canada Gazette. Published at Newark, later Niagara [Niagara-on-the-Lake, Ont.], from its inception on 18 April 1793 to 25 Aug. 1798, and then at York [Toronto]. Irregular until 1800, when it became a weekly. Its full title to 28 March 1807 was the *Upper Canada Gazette; or, American Oracle*; from 15 April 1807 to the end of 1816 it appeared under the title *York Gazette*, switching back to *Upper Canada Gazette* in 1817. From 1821 to 1828 it was issued in two parts, with official government announcements appearing as *Upper Canada Gazette* and the newspaper portion under a variety of other titles. It is believed to have ceased publication in 1849, though no copies later than March 1848 seem to have survived.

York Gazette. See *Upper Canada Gazette*

III. REFERENCE WORKS

ALLAIRE, JEAN-BAPTISTE-ARTHUR. *Dictionnaire biographique du clergé canadien-français*. 6 vols. Montréal et Saint-Hyacinthe, Qué., 1908–34.
[1]: *Les anciens*. Montréal, 1910.
[2]: *Les contemporains*. Saint-Hyacinthe, 1908.
[3]: [*Suppléments*.] 6 parts in 1 vol. Montréal, 1910–19.
[4]: *Le clergé canadien-français: revue mensuelle* ([Montréal]), 1 (1919–20). Only one volume of this journal was published.
[5]: *Compléments*. 6 parts in 1 vol. Montréal, 1928–32.
[6]: Untitled. Saint-Hyacinthe, 1934.

Almanach de Québec. See *Quebec Almanac*

ARCHIVES NATIONALES DU QUÉBEC, Québec
PUBLICATIONS [*see also* section II]
P.-G. Roy, *Inv. concessions*.
—— *Inv. testaments*.
—— *Les juges de la prov. de Québec*.

ARMSTRONG, FREDERICK HENRY. *Handbook of Upper Canadian chronology and territorial legislation*. (University of Western Ontario, Lawson Memorial Library publication.) London, 1967.

AUDET, FRANCIS-JOSEPH. *Les députés de Montréal (ville et comtés), 1792–1867*. . . . Montréal, 1943.
—— "Les législateurs du Bas-Canada de 1760 à 1867." Manuscript held by the Morisset Library, University of Ottawa, 3 vols., 1940.
—— ET ÉDOUARD FABRE SURVEYER. *Les députés au premier Parlement du Bas-Canada [1792–1796]*. . . . Montréal, 1946.

Australian dictionary of biography. Edited by Douglas Pike *et al*. 8 vols. to date. Melbourne, [1966]– . Vols. 1–2 cover the years 1788–1850; vols. 3–6, the years 1851–90; and vols. 7–8, "A to Gib" for the years 1891–1939.

BEAULIEU, ANDRÉ, ET JEAN HAMELIN. *La presse québécoise des origines à nos jours*. [2e édition.] 5 vols. to date [1764–1919]. Québec, 1973– .

A bibliography of Canadiana, being items in the Public Library of Toronto, Canada, relating to the early history and development of Canada. Edited by Frances Maria Staton and Marie Tremaine. Toronto, 1934; reprinted 1965.

A bibliography of Canadiana: first supplement. . . . Edited by Gertrude Mabel Boyle with Marjorie Colbeck. Toronto, 1959; reprinted 1969.

Biographie universelle, ancienne et moderne. . . . [Joseph-François et Louis-Gabriel Michaud, éditeurs.] 85 vols. [vols.1–52, "A" to "Z"; vols.53–55, *Partie mythologique*, "A" to "Z"; vols.56–85, *Supplément*, "A" to "Vil"]. Paris, 1811–62. Nouvelle édition. [Louis-Gabriel Michaud et Eugène-Ernest Desplaces, éditeurs.] 45 vols. [1854–65]; réimprimé Graz, Austria, 1966–70.

BISHOP, OLGA BERNICE. *Publications of the governments of Nova Scotia, Prince Edward Island, New Brunswick, 1758–1952.* (National Library of Canada publication.) Ottawa, 1957.

BOATNER, MARK MAYO. *Encyclopedia of the American revolution.* New York, [1966]. [Revised edition.] 1974.

BOUCHETTE, JOSEPH. *A topographical description of the province of Lower Canada, with remarks upon Upper Canada, and on the relative connexion of both provinces with the United States of America.* London, 1815; reprinted [Saint-Lambert, Que., 1973]. Published in French as *Description topographique de la province du Bas Canada, avec des remarques sur le Haut Canada, et sur les relations des deux provinces avec les États Unis de l'Amérique* (Londres, 1815; réimprimé, John Ellis Hare, éditeur, [Montréal, 1978]).

BURKE, JOHN. *A general and heraldic dictionary of the peerage and baronetage of the United Kingdom.* London, 1826. 105th edition. Edited by Peter Townend. 1970.

"Calendar of state papers, addressed by the secretaries of state for the colonies to the lieutenant governors or officers administering the province of Upper Canada, 1796–1820." PAC *Report*, 1933: 83–171.

CANADIAN PERMANENT COMMITTEE ON GEOGRAPHICAL NAMES

TOPONYMY STUDIES

1: Rayburn, *Geographical names of P.E.I.*
2: —— *Geographical names of N.B.*

CARON, IVANHOË. "Inventaire de la correspondance de Mᵍʳ Bernard-Claude Panet, archevêque de Québec." ANQ *Rapport*, 1933–34: 235–421.

—— "Inventaire de la correspondance de Mᵍʳ Jean-François Hubert, évêque de Québec et de Mᵍʳ Charles-François Bailly de Messein, son coadjuteur." ANQ *Rapport*, 1930–31: 199–351.

—— "Inventaire de la correspondance de Mᵍʳ Jean-Olivier Briand, évêque de Québec." ANQ *Rapport*, 1929–30: 47–136.

—— "Inventaire de la correspondance de Mᵍʳ Joseph-Octave Plessis, archevêque de Québec,

1797–1825." ANQ *Rapport*, 1927–28: 215–316; 1928–29: 89–208; 1932–33: 3–244.

—— "Inventaire de la correspondance de Mᵍʳ Louis-Philippe Mariaucheau D'Esgly, évêque de Québec." ANQ *Rapport*, 1930–31: 185–98.

—— "Inventaire de la correspondance de Mᵍʳ Pierre Denaut, évêque de Québec." ANQ *Rapport*, 1931–32: 129–242.

CHADWICK, EDWARD MARION. *Ontarian families: genealogies of United-Empire-Loyalist and other pioneer families of Upper Canada.* 2 vols. Toronto, 1894–98; reprinted 2 vols. in 1, Lambertville, N.J., [1970]. Vol.1 reprinted with an introduction by William Felix Edmund Morley, Belleville, Ont., 1972.

CHARLAND, PAUL-VICTOR. "Notre-Dame de Québec: le nécrologe de la crypte ou les inhumations dans cette église depuis 1652." *BRH*, 20 (1914): 137–51, 169–81, 205–17, 237–51, 269–80, 301–13, 333–47.

COLLEDGE, JAMES JOSEPH. *Ships of the Royal Navy: an historical index.* 2 vols. Newton Abbot, Eng., [1969–70].

DESJARDINS, JOSEPH. *Guide parlementaire historique de la province de Québec, 1792 à 1902.* Québec, 1902.

DESROSIERS, LOUIS-ADÉLARD. "Correspondance de cinq vicaires généraux avec les évêques de Québec, 1761–1816." ANQ *Rapport*, 1947–48: 73–133.

Dictionary of American biography. Edited by Allen Johnson *et al.* 20 vols., index, and 2 supplements [to 1940]. New York, 1928–[58]; reprinted, 22 vols. in 11 and index, [1946?–58]. 4 additional supplements to date [to 1960]. Edited by Edward Topping James *et al.* [1973]– . *Concise DAB.* [1964.] 2nd edition. [1977.] 3rd edition. [1980.]

Dictionary of national biography. Edited by Leslie Stephen and Sidney Lee. 63 vols., 3 supplements, and index and epitome [to 1900]. London, 1885–1903; reissued without index, 22 vols., 1908–9. 7 additional supplements to date [to 1970]. Edited by Sidney Lee *et al.* 1912– . *Concise DNB.* 2 vols. [1953]–61. *Corrections and additions to the Dictionary of national biography.* Boston, 1966.

Dictionary of scientific biography. Edited by Charles Coulston Gillispie *et al.* 15 vols. New York, [1970–78].

Dictionnaire de biographie française. Jules Balteau *et al.*, éditeurs. 15 vols. to date ["A" to "Gilbert"]. Paris, 1933– .

Dictionnaire des œuvres littéraires du Québec. Maurice Lemire *et al.*, éditeurs. 3 vols. to date [to 1959]. Montréal, [1978]– .

A directory of the members of the Legislative Assembly of Nova Scotia, 1758–1958. Introduction by Charles Bruce Fergusson. (PANS publications, Nova Scotia series, 2.) Halifax, 1958.

Encyclopædia Britannica. [14th edition.] Edited by Warren E. Preece *et al.* 23 vols. and index. Chicago and Toronto, [1966]. 15th edition. 30 vols. [1977.]

Encyclopedia Canadiana. Edited by John Everett Robbins *et al.* 10 vols. Ottawa, [1957–58]. [Revised edition.] Edited by Kenneth H. Pearson *et al.* Toronto, [1975].

Encyclopedia of music in Canada. Edited by Helmut Kallmann *et al.* Toronto and Buffalo, N.Y., [1981].

GAUTHIER, HENRI. *Sulpitiana*. n.p., 1912. [2ᵉ édition.] Montréal, 1926.

Grand Larousse encyclopédique. 10 vols. Paris, [1960]–64. Nouvelle édition. 1973. 2 supplements to date. 1969– .

GREAT BRITAIN, ADMIRALTY. *The commissioned sea officers of the Royal Navy, 1660–1815*. [Editing begun by David Bonner Smith; project continued by the Royal Naval College in cooperation with the National Maritime Museum.] 3 vols. n.p., [1954?].

—— WAR OFFICE. *A list of the general and field officers as they rank in the army*. . . . [London, 1754–1868.] The first known official army list was published in 1740 and has been reprinted as *The army list of 1740 . . . with a complete index of names and of regiments* (Soc. for Army Hist. Research, Special no., 3, Sheffield, Eng., 1931).

Guide to the reports of the Public Archives of Canada, 1872–1972. Compiled by Françoise Caron-Houle. (PAC publication.) Ottawa, 1975.

Handbook of American Indians north of Mexico. Edited by Frederick Webb Hodge. 2 parts. (Smithsonian Institution, Bureau of American Ethnology, Bulletin, 30.) Washington, 1907–10; reprinted New York, 1971. The Canadian material in this work has been revised and republished as an appendix to the tenth report of the Geographic Board of Canada, entitled *Handbook of Indians of Canada* (Ottawa, 1913; repr. New York, 1969).

Handbook of North American Indians. Edited by William C. Sturtevant *et al.* (Smithsonian Institution publication.) 4 vols. to date [6, 8–9, 15]. Washington, 1978– .

HARE, JOHN [ELLIS], ET JEAN-PIERRE WALLOT. *Les imprimés dans le Bas-Canada, 1801–1840: bibliographie analytique*. Montréal, 1967. Only one volume, *1801–1810*, was published.

Index to reports of Canadian archives from 1872 to 1908. (PAC publications, 1.) Ottawa, 1909.

JONES, EDWARD ALFRED. *The loyalists of Massachusetts: their memorials, petitions and claims*. London, 1930; reprinted Baltimore, Md., 1969.

KELLEY, ARTHUR READING. "Church and state papers . . . being a compendium of documents relating to the establishment of certain churches in the province of Quebec [1759–91]." ANQ *Rapport*, 1948–49: 297–340; 1953–55: 75–120.

—— "Jacob Mountain, first lord bishop of Quebec: a summary of his correspondence and of papers related thereto for the years 1793 to 1799. . . ." ANQ *Rapport*, 1942–43: 177–260.

[LANGELIER, JEAN-CHRYSOSTÔME.] *List of lands granted by the crown in the province of Quebec from 1763 to 31st December 1890*. Quebec, 1891. Published in French as *Liste des terrains concédés par la couronne dans la province de Québec de 1763 au 31 décembre 1890* (1891).

LEBŒUF, JOSEPH-[AIMÉ-]ARTHUR. *Complément au dictionnaire généalogique Tanguay*. (Société généalogique canadienne-française publications, 2, 4, 6.) 3 séries. Montréal, 1957–64. *See also* Tanguay, *Dictionnaire*.

LEFEBVRE, JEAN-JACQUES. "Engagements pour l'Ouest, 1778–1788." ANQ *Rapport*, 1946–47: 303–69. *See also* Massicotte, "Répertoire des engagements pour l'Ouest."

LE JEUNE, LOUIS[-MARIE]. *Dictionnaire général de biographie, histoire, littérature, agriculture, commerce, industrie et des arts, sciences, mœurs, coutumes, institutions politiques et religieuses du Canada*. 2 vols. Ottawa, [1931].

MARION, MARCEL. *Dictionnaire des institutions de la France aux XVIIᵉ et XVIIIᵉ siècles*. Paris, 1923; réimprimé 1968, 1969.

MASSICOTTE, ÉDOUARD-ZOTIQUE. "Répertoire des engagements pour l'Ouest conservés dans les Archives judiciaires de Montréal . . . [1670–1821]." ANQ *Rapport*, 1929–30: 195–466; 1930–31: 353–453; 1931–32: 243–365; 1932–33: 245–304; 1942–43: 261–397; 1943–44: 335–444; 1944–45: 309–401; 1945–46: 227–340. *See also* Lefebvre, "Engagements pour l'Ouest."

MIKA, NICK AND HELEN. *Places in Ontario: their name origins and history*. 2 parts to date. Belleville, Ont., 1977– .

Officers of the British forces in Canada during the War of 1812–15. Compiled by L. Homfray Irving. (Canadian Military Institute publication.) [Welland, Ont., 1908.]

"Papiers d'État [1761–99]." PAC *Rapport*, 1890: 1–340. *See also* "State papers."

"Papiers d'État – Bas-Canada [1791–1830]." PAC *Rapport*, 1891: 1–206; 1892: 155–293; 1930, app. A: 1–199. *See also* "State papers."

Place-names and places of Nova Scotia. Introduction by Charles Bruce Fergusson. (PANS publications, Nova Scotia series, 3.) Halifax, 1967; reprinted Belleville, Ont., 1976.

PUBLIC ARCHIVES OF CANADA, Ottawa
  NUMBERED PUBLICATIONS
  1: *Index to reports of PAC*.
  OTHER PUBLICATIONS [*see also* section II]

Guide to reports of PAC (Caron-Houle).

Inventories of holdings in the Manuscript Division [*see* section I].

Union list of MSS (Gordon *et al.*; Maurice).

Union list of MSS, supp. (Maurice and Chabot).

PUBLIC ARCHIVES OF NOVA SCOTIA, Halifax
NOVA SCOTIA SERIES
2: *Directory of N.S. MLAs.*
3: *Place-names of N.S.*

Quebec almanac . . . /Almanach de Québec. . . . Quebec, 1780–1841 (except in 1781, 1790, and 1793). Publishers: William Brown, 1780–89; Samuel Neilson, 1791–92; John Neilson, 1794–1823; Neilson and Cowan, 1824–36; S. Neilson, 1837; W. Neilson, 1838–41. Title varies as to spelling, and also as to language.

Quebec directory. Used in volume V were: *The directory for the city and suburbs of Quebec . . .* , comp. Hugh MacKay ([Quebec], 1790); *Number II of the directory for the city and suburbs of Quebec . . .* , comp. Hugh MacKay (Quebec, 1791).

RAYBURN, ALAN. *Geographical names of New Brunswick.* (Canadian Permanent Committee on Geographical Names, Toponymy study, 2.) Ottawa, 1975.

——— *Geographical names of Prince Edward Island.* (Canadian Permanent Committee on Geographical Names, Toponymy study, 1.) Ottawa, 1973.

The register of shipping. . . . London, [1760?]– . Title varies: *Lloyd's register of British and foreign shipping*, 1834–1913/14; *Lloyd's register of shipping*, 1914/15– .

A register of the regiments and corps of the British army: the ancestry of the regiments and corps of the regular establishment. Edited by Arthur Swinson. London, [1972].

REID, WILLIAM DANIEL. *The loyalists in Ontario: the sons and daughters of the American loyalists of Upper Canada.* Lambertville, N.J., [1973].

ROY, PIERRE-GEORGES. *Inventaire des concessions en fief et seigneurie, fois et hommages et aveux et dénombrements, conservés aux Archives de la province de Québec.* (ANQ publication.) 6 vols. Beauceville, Qué., 1927–29.

——— *Inventaire des testaments, donations et inventaires du Régime français conservés aux Archives judiciaires de Québec.* (ANQ publication.) 3 vols. Québec, 1941.

——— *Les juges de la province de Québec.* (ANQ publication.) Québec, 1933.

SABINE, LORENZO. *Biographical sketches of loyalists of the American revolution, with an historical essay.* [2nd edition.] 2 vols. Boston, 1864; reprinted Port Washington, N.Y., [1966]. First published as *The American loyalists, or biographical sketches of adherents to the British crown in the war of the revolution . . .* (Boston, 1847).

The service of British regiments in Canada and North America: a resume with a chronological list of uniforms portrayed in sources consulted. Compiled by Charles Herbert Stewart. (Canada, Department of National Defence Library publications, 1.) Ottawa, 1962. [2nd edition.] 1964.

SHIPTON, CLIFFORD KENYON. *Sibley's Harvard graduates. . . .* (Massachusetts Historical Society publication.) 17 vols. to date [1690–1771]. Cambridge and Boston, Mass., 1933– . A continuation of J. L. Sibley, *Biographical sketches of graduates of Harvard University, in Cambridge, Massachusetts* [1642–89] (3v., Cambridge, 1873–85), the volumes are numbered consecutively from it.

SMITHSONIAN INSTITUTION, Washington
PUBLICATIONS
Handbook of American Indians (Hodge).
Handbook of North American Indians (Sturtevant *et al.*).

"State papers [1761–99]." PAC *Report*, 1890: 1–325.

"State papers – Lower Canada [1791–1830]." PAC *Report*, 1891: 1–200; 1892: 153–285; 1930, app.A: 1–187.

TANGUAY, CYPRIEN. *Dictionnaire généalogique des familles canadiennes depuis la fondation de la colonie jusqu'à nos jours.* 7 vols. [Montréal], 1871–90; réimprimé [New York, 1969]. *See also* Lebœuf, *Complément.*

——— *Répertoire général du clergé canadien par ordre chronologique depuis la fondation de la colonie jusqu'à nos jours.* Québec, 1868. [2e édition.] Montréal, 1893.

THÉRIAULT, YVON. *Les publications parlementaires d'hier et d'aujourd'hui.* (Vie parlementaire, 2.) Québec, 1978. 2e édition. 1982.

TREMAINE, MARIE. *A bibliography of Canadian imprints, 1751–1800.* Toronto, 1952.

TURCOTTE, GUSTAVE. *Le Conseil législatif de Québec, 1774–1933.* Beauceville, Qué., 1933.

Union list of manuscripts in Canadian repositories/ Catalogue collectif des manuscrits des archives canadiennes. Edited by Robert Stanyslaw Gordon *et al.* (PAC publication.) Ottawa, 1968. Revised edition. Edited by E. Grace Maurice. 2 vols. 1975. *Supplement/Supplément.* Edited by E. Grace Maurice *et al.* 3 vols. to date. 1976– .

WALBRAN, JOHN THOMAS. *British Columbia coast names, 1592–1906, to which are added a few names in adjacent United States territory: their origin and history. . . .* (Geographic Board of Canada publication.) Ottawa, 1909; reprinted with an introduction by G. P. V. Akrigg, Vancouver, 1971; reprinted Seattle, Wash., and London, 1972.

WALLACE, WILLIAM STEWART. *The Macmillan dictionary of Canadian biography.* Edited by William

Angus McKay. 4th edition. Toronto, [1978]. First published as *The dictionary of Canadian biography* (1926).

WATTERS, REGINALD EYRE. *A check list of Canadian literature and background materials, 1628–1950. . . .* (Humanities Research Council of Canada publication.) Toronto, [1959]. 2nd edition [. . . *1628–1960*]. Toronto [and Buffalo, N.Y., 1972].

IV. STUDIES (BOOKS AND THESES)

ABBOTT, MAUDE ELIZABETH [SEYMOUR]. *History of medicine in the province of Quebec.* Toronto, 1931; Montreal, 1931.

AHERN, MICHAEL-JOSEPH ET GEORGE. *Notes pour servir à l'histoire de la médecine dans le Bas-Canada depuis la fondation de Québec jusqu'au commencement du XIXe siècle.* Québec, 1923.

AKINS, THOMAS BEAMISH. *History of Halifax City.* Belleville, Ont., 1973. First published as N.S. Hist. Soc., *Coll.*, 8 (1895) [*see* section V].

ANDRE, JOHN. *William Berczy, co-founder of Toronto; a sketch.* [Toronto, 1967.]

ARSENAULT, BONA. *Histoire et généalogie des Acadiens.* 2 vols. Québec, [1965]. [2e édition.] 6 vols. [1978.] Vol.1 of first edition translated and revised in collaboration with Brian M. Upton and John G. McLaughlin as *History of the Acadians* (Quebec, [1966]).

AUDET, LOUIS-PHILIPPE. *Le système scolaire de la province de Québec* [1635–1840]. 6 vols. Québec, 1950–56.

BELL, WINTHROP PICKARD. *The "foreign Protestants" and the settlement of Nova Scotia: the history of a piece of arrested British colonial policy in the eighteenth century.* Toronto, [1961].

BREBNER, JOHN BARTLET. *The neutral Yankees of Nova Scotia, a marginal colony during the revolutionary years.* New York, 1937; republished, introduction by William Stewart MacNutt, Toronto and Montreal, [1969]; reprint of 1937 edition, New York, [1970].

BURNS, ROBERT JOSEPH. "The first elite of Toronto: an examination of the genesis, consolidation and duration of power in an emerging colonial society." PHD thesis, University of Western Ontario, London, 1974.

BURT, ALFRED LEROY. *The old province of Quebec.* Toronto and Minneapolis, Minn., 1933; republished, introduction by Hilda [Marion] Neatby, 2 vols., [Toronto, 1968]; reprint of 1933 edition, New York, [1970].

CALNEK, WILLIAM ARTHUR. *History of the county of Annapolis, including old Port Royal and Acadia, with memoirs of its representatives in the provincial parliament, and biographical and genealogical sketches of its early English settlers and their families.* Edited and completed by Alfred William Savary. Toronto, 1897; reprinted Belleville, Ont., 1972. *See also* Savary, *Supplement to hist. of Annapolis.*

CAMPBELL, MARJORIE [ELLIOTT] WILKINS. *The North West Company.* Toronto, 1957. [Revised edition.] [1973.]

CAMPBELL, ROBERT. *A history of the Scotch Presbyterian Church, St. Gabriel Street, Montreal.* Montreal, 1887.

Canada and its provinces: a history of the Canadian people and their institutions. Edited by Adam Shortt and Arthur George Doughty. 23 vols. Toronto, 1913–17.

Canada's smallest province: a history of P.E.I. Edited by Francis William Pius Bolger. [Charlottetown, 1973.]

CARON, IVANHOË. *La colonisation de la province de Québec.* 2 vols. Québec, 1923–27. [1]: *Débuts du Régime anglais, 1760–1791.* [2]: *Les cantons de l'Est, 1791–1815.*

CHAPAIS, [JOSEPH-AMABLE-]THOMAS. *Cours d'histoire du Canada* [1760–1867]. 8 vols. Québec, 1919–34. Another edition. 8 vols. Montréal, [1944–45]. Réimprimé. [Trois-Rivières, 1972.]

CHRISTIE, ROBERT. *A history of the late province of Lower Canada, parliamentary and political, from the commencement to the close of its existence as a separate province. . . .* 6 vols. Quebec and Montreal, 1848–55. [2nd edition.] Montreal, 1866.

CONDON, ANN GORMAN. "'The envy of the American states': the settlement of the loyalists in New Brunswick: goals and achievements." PHD thesis, Harvard University, Cambridge, Mass., 1975.

COOK, WARREN LAWRENCE. *Flood tide of empire: Spain and the Pacific northwest, 1543–1819.* New Haven, Conn., and London, 1973.

CRAIG, GERALD MARQUIS. *Upper Canada: the formative years, 1784–1841.* (Canadian centenary series, 7.) [Toronto], 1963.

CREIGHTON, DONALD GRANT. *The commercial empire of the St Lawrence.* Toronto, 1937; reprinted under the title *The empire of the St. Lawrence,* [1956] and [1970].

DAVIDSON, GORDON CHARLES. *The North West Company.* Berkeley, Calif., 1918; reprinted New York, [1967].

IV. STUDIES

[Dooner, Alfred James, named] Brother Alfred. *Catholic pioneers in Upper Canada.* Toronto, 1947.

Fingard, Judith. *The Anglican design in loyalist Nova Scotia, 1783–1816.* London, 1972.

Galarneau, Claude. *La France devant l'opinion canadienne (1760–1815).* (Université Laval, Institut d'histoire, Cahiers, 16.) Québec et Paris, 1970.

Gates, Lillian Frances [Cowdell]. *Land policies of Upper Canada.* (Canadian studies in history and government, 9.) Toronto, [1968].

Gosselin, Auguste[-Honoré]. *L'Église du Canada après la Conquête* [1760–89]. 2 parties. Québec, 1916–17.

Hannay, James. *History of New Brunswick.* 2 vols. Saint John, N.B., 1909.

Hitsman, John Mackay. *The incredible War of 1812: a military history.* Toronto, [1965].

Horsman, Reginald. *Matthew Elliott, British Indian agent.* Detroit, 1964.

Innis, Harold Adams. *The fur trade in Canada: an introduction to Canadian economic history.* New Haven, Conn., and London, 1930. Revised edition. [Edited by Mary Quayle Innis, Samuel Delbert Clark, and William Thomas Easterbrook.] Toronto, 1956. [Abridged edition (based on the revised edition, foreword by Robin William Winks).] [1962.] Revised edition (reprint of 1956 edition with revised foreword from the 1962 edition). [1970.]

Johnston, Angus Anthony. *A history of the Catholic Church in eastern Nova Scotia.* 2 vols. Antigonish, N.S., 1960–71.
1: *1611–1827.*
2: *1827–1880; with a brief appendix surveying the years 1880–1969.*

Lambert, James Harold. "Monseigneur, the Catholic bishop: Joseph-Octave Plessis; church, state, and society in Lower Canada: historiography and analysis." D. ès L. thesis, Université Laval, Québec, [1981].

Lanctot, Gustave. *Le Canada et la Révolution américaine.* Montréal, 1965. Translated by Margaret M. Cameron as *Canada & the American revolution, 1774–1783* (Toronto and Vancouver, 1967).

Langdon, John Emerson. *Canadian silversmiths, 1700–1900.* Toronto, 1966.

Lemieux, Lucien. *L'établissement de la première province ecclésiastique au Canada, 1783–1844.* (Histoire religieuse du Canada, 1.) Montréal et Paris, [1968].

[Lemire-Marsolais, Darie-Aurélie, named Sainte-Henriette, et] Thérèse Lambert, named Sainte-Marie-Médiatrice. *Histoire de la Congrégation de Notre-Dame de Montréal.* 11 vols. in 13 and an index to date. Montréal, 1941– . Before her death in 1917 Sister Sainte-Henriette had completed nine volumes of her history as well as an index; only two volumes were published, in 1910. In 1941 her complete work was published and the first two volumes reissued. The index for the first nine volumes, prepared by Sister Sainte-Henriette, was published in 1969.

Life and letters of the late Hon. Richard Cartwright, member of Legislative Council in the first parliament of Upper Canada. Edited by Conway Edward Cartwright. Toronto and Sydney, Australia, 1876.

MacDonald. "Hon. Richard Cartwright." See *Three hist. theses*

McLintock, Alexander Hare. *The establishment of constitutional government in Newfoundland, 1783–1832: a study of retarded colonisation.* (Imperial studies, 17.) London and Toronto, 1941.

Macmillan, David Stirling. "The 'new men' in action: Scottish mercantile and shipping operations in the North American colonies, 1760–1825." In *Canadian business history; selected studies, 1497–1971,* edited by David Stirling Macmillan, 44–103. [Toronto, 1972.]

MacNutt, William Stewart. *New Brunswick, a history: 1784–1867.* Toronto, 1963.

Manning, Helen Taft. *The revolt of French Canada, 1800–1835; a chapter in the history of the British Commonwealth.* Toronto, 1962.

Maurault, Olivier. *Le collège de Montréal, 1767–1967.* 2ᵉ édition. Antonio Dansereau, éditeur. Montréal, 1967. The first edition was published in Montreal in 1918 under the title *Le petit séminaire de Montréal.*

Millman, Thomas Reagh. *Jacob Mountain, first lord bishop of Quebec; a study in church and state, 1793–1825.* (University of Toronto studies, History and economics series, 10.) Toronto, 1947.

Miquelon, Dale Bernard. "The Baby family in the trade of Canada, 1750–1820." MA thesis, Carleton University, Ottawa, [1966].

Morgan, Robert J. "Orphan outpost: Cape Breton colony, 1784–1820." PHD thesis, University of Ottawa, 1972.

Morisset, Gérard. *Coup d'œil sur les arts en Nouvelle-France.* Québec, 1941; réimprimé, 1942.

Morton, Arthur Silver. *A history of the Canadian west to 1870–71, being a history of Rupert's Land (the Hudson's Bay Company's territory) and of the North-West Territory (including the Pacific slope).* London and Toronto, [1939]. 2nd edition. Edited by Lewis Gwynne Thomas. Toronto [and Buffalo, N.Y., 1973].

MURDOCH, BEAMISH. *A history of Nova-Scotia, or Acadie.* 3 vols. Halifax, 1865–67.

NEATBY, HILDA MARION. *The administration of justice under the Quebec Act.* London and Minneapolis, Minn., [1937].

—— *Quebec: the revolutionary age, 1760–1791.* (Canadian centenary series, 6.) [Toronto, 1966.]

OUELLET, FERNAND. *Le Bas-Canada, 1791–1840: changements structuraux et crise.* (Université d'Ottawa, Cahiers d'histoire, 6.) Ottawa, 1976. Translated and adapted by Patricia Claxton as *Lower Canada, 1791–1840: social change and nationalism* (Canadian centenary series, 15, [Toronto, 1980]).

—— *Histoire économique et sociale du Québec, 1760–1850: structures et conjoncture.* (Histoire économique et sociale du Canada français.) Montréal et Paris, [1966]. Translated as *Economic and social history of Quebec, 1760–1850: structures and conjonctures* (n.p., [1980]).

PAQUET, GILLES, ET JEAN-PIERRE WALLOT. *Patronage et pouvoir dans le Bas-Canada (1794–1812); un essai d'économie historique.* Montréal, 1973.

PROWSE, DANIEL WOODLEY. *A history of Newfoundland from the English, colonial, and foreign records.* London and New York, 1895. 2nd edition. London, 1896. 3rd edition. Edited by James Raymond Thoms and Frank Burnham Gill. St John's, 1971. Reprint of 1895 edition. Belleville, Ont., 1972.

RAYMOND, WILLIAM ODBER. *The River St. John: its physical features, legends and history from 1604 to 1784.* Saint John, N.B., 1910. [2nd edition.] Edited by John Clarence Webster. Sackville, N.B., 1943; reprinted, 1950.

RICH, EDWARD ERNEST. *The history of the Hudson's Bay Company, 1670–1870.* (HBRS publications, 21–22.) 2 vols. London, 1958–59. [Trade edition.] 3 vols. Toronto, 1960. A copy of this work available at PAC contains notes and bibliographical material omitted from the printed version.

RIDDELL, WILLIAM RENWICK. *The legal profession in Upper Canada in its early periods.* Toronto, 1916.

—— *The life of William Dummer Powell, first judge at Detroit and fifth chief justice of Upper Canada.* Lansing, Mich., 1924.

Robertson's landmarks of Toronto; a collection of historical sketches of the old town of York from 1792 until 1833, and of Toronto from 1834 to [1914]. Edited by John Ross Robertson. 6 series. Toronto, 1894–1914; vols. 1 and 3 reprinted Belleville, Ont., 1976, 1974.

ROY, JOSEPH-EDMOND. *Histoire de la seigneurie de Lauzon* [1608–1840]. 5 vols. Lévis, Qué., 1897–1904.

—— *Histoire du notariat au Canada depuis la fondation de la colonie jusqu'à nos jours.* 4 vols. Lévis, Qué., 1899–1902.

RUDDEL, DAVID THIERRY. "Quebec City, 1765–1831: the evolution of a colonial town." D. ès L. thesis, Université Laval, Quebec, 1981.

RUMILLY, ROBERT. *La compagnie du Nord-Ouest: une épopée montréalaise.* 2 vols. [Montréal, 1980.]

SAVARY, ALFRED WILLIAM. *Supplement to the history of the county of Annapolis.* . . . Toronto, 1913; reprinted Belleville, Ont., 1973. See also Calnek, *Hist. of Annapolis* (Savary).

STANLEY, GEORGE FRANCIS GILMAN. *Canada invaded, 1775–1776.* (Canadian War Museum, Historical publications, 8.) Toronto, 1973. Translated by Marguerite MacDonald as *L'invasion du Canada, 1775–1776* (Soc. hist. de Québec, Cahiers d'hist., 28, Québec, 1975).

STARK, JAMES HENRY. *The loyalists of Massachusetts and the other side of the American revolution.* Boston, [1907]. Another edition. 1910.

SULTE, BENJAMIN. *Histoire des Canadiens-français, 1608–1800.* . . . 8 vols. Montréal, 1882–84.

—— *Mélanges historiques.* . . . Gérard Malchelosse, éditeur. 21 vols. Montréal, 1918–34. This series is a mixture of volumes of articles and monographs.

Three history theses. (Ontario, Department of Public Records and Archives publication.) [Toronto, 1961.] Particularly useful was Donald C. MacDonald, "Honourable Richard Cartwright, 1759–1815."

TOUSIGNANT, PIERRE. "La genèse et l'avènement de la constitution de 1791." Thèse de PHD, université de Montréal, 1971.

TRAQUAIR, RAMSAY. *The old silver of Quebec.* (Art Association of Montreal publication.) Toronto, 1940.

TRUDEL, MARCEL. *L'Église canadienne sous le Régime militaire, 1759–1764.* 2 vols. [Montréal et] Québec, 1956–57.

—— *L'esclavage au Canada français: histoire et conditions de l'esclavage.* Québec, 1960.

WALLOT, JEAN-PIERRE. *Un Québec qui bougeait: trame socio-politique du Québec au tournant du XIXe siècle.* [Québec, 1973.]

WILSON, BRUCE GORDON. "The enterprises of Robert Hamilton: a study of wealth and influence in early Upper Canada: 1776–1812." PHD thesis, University of Toronto, 1978.

WRIGHT, ESTHER CLARK. *The loyalists of New Brunswick.* Fredericton, [1955]; reprinted Moncton, N.B., [1972].

V. JOURNALS AND STUDIES (ARTICLES)

Acadiensis: a Quarterly devoted to the Interests of the Maritime Provinces of Canada. Saint John, N.B. 1 (1901)–8 (1908).

Acadiensis: Journal of the History of the Atlantic Region/Revue de l'histoire de la région atlantique. Fredericton. Published by the Department of History of the University of New Brunswick. 1 (1971–72)– .

Beaver: Magazine of the North. Winnipeg. Published by the HBC. 1 (1920–21)– . *Index:* 1 (1920–21)– outfit 284 (June 1953–March 1954). Title varies.

Le Bulletin des recherches historiques. Published usually in Lévis, Qué. Originally the organ of the Société des études historiques, it became in March 1923 the journal of the Archives de la province de Québec (now the ANQ). 1 (1895)–70 (1968). *Index:* 1 (1895)–31 (1925) (4v., Beauceville, Qué., 1925–26). For subsequent years there is an index on microfiche at the ANQ-Q.

BUMSTED, JOHN MICHAEL. "Sir James Montgomery and Prince Edward Island, 1767–1803." *Acadiensis* (Fredericton), 7 (1977–78), no.2: 76–102.

Les Cahiers des Dix. Montréal et Québec. Published by "Les Dix." 1 (1936)– .

CANADIAN CATHOLIC HISTORICAL ASSOCIATION/ SOCIÉTÉ CANADIENNE D'HISTOIRE DE L'ÉGLISE CATHOLIQUE, Ottawa. Publishes simultaneously a *Report* in English and a *Rapport* in French, of which the contents are entirely different. 1 (1933–34)– . *Index:* 1 (1933–34)–25 (1958). Title varies: *Study sessions/Sessions d'étude* from 1966.

CANADIAN HISTORICAL ASSOCIATION/SOCIÉTÉ HIS- TORIQUE DU CANADA, Ottawa. *Annual report.* 1922– . *Index:* 1922–51; 1952–68. Title varies: *Historical papers/Communications historiques* from 1966.

Canadian Historical Review. Toronto. 1 (1920)– . *Index:* 1 (1920)–10 (1929); 11 (1930)–20 (1939); 21 (1940)–30 (1949); 31 (1950)–51 (1970). Université Laval has also published an index: *Canadian Historical Review, 1950–1964: index des articles et des comptes rendus de volumes,* René Hardy, compil. (Québec, 1969). A continuation of the *Review of Historical Publications relating to Canada:* 1 (1895–96)–22 (1917–18); *Index:* 1 (1895–96)–10 (1905); 11 (1906)–20 (1915).

Canadian Historic Sites: Occasional Papers in Archaeology and History/Lieux historiques cana- diens: cahiers d'archéologie et d'histoire. Ottawa. Published by Canada, National Historic Parks and Sites Branch. No.1 (1970)– .

Dalhousie Review. Halifax. Published by Dalhousie University. 1 (1921–22)– .

HARE, JOHN [ELLIS]. "L'Assemblée législative du Bas-Canada, 1792–1814: députation et polarisa- tion politique." *RHAF,* 27 (1973–74): 361–95.

Island Magazine. Charlottetown. Published by the Prince Edward Island Heritage Foundation. No.1 (fall–winter 1976)– .

MACNUTT, WILLIAM STEWART. "Fanning's regime on Prince Edward Island." *Acadiensis* (Frederic- ton), 1 (1971–72), no.1: 37–53.

MASSICOTTE, ÉDOUARD-ZOTIQUE. "Les Chaboillez: une famille de traitants au 18e et au 19e siècle." *BRH,* 28 (1922): 184–88, 207–9, 241–42, 274– 76, 311–13, 325–32, 355–59.

NIAGARA HISTORICAL SOCIETY, Niagara-on-the- Lake, Ont. [*Publication.*] 1 (1896)–44 (1939). The first number is called *Transactions;* nos.2 (1897)– 44 list titles of articles included but have no main title; nos.38 (1927)–44 are all called "Records of Niagara."

NOVA SCOTIA HISTORICAL SOCIETY, Halifax. *Collec- tions.* 1 (1878)– ; vols.1–8 reprinted, 2v., Belle- ville, Ont., 1976–77. Index: 1 (1878)–32 (1959) in 33 (1961).

Ontario History. Toronto. Published by the Ontario Historical Society. 1 (1899)– ; vols.1–49 (1957) reprinted Millwood, N.Y., 1975. An index to volumes 1 (1899) to 64 (1972) appears in *Index to the publications of the Ontario Historical Society, 1899–1972* (1974). Title varies: *Papers and Records* to 1946.

OUELLET, FERNAND. "Dualité économique et changement technologique au Québec (1760– 1790)." *SH,* 9 (1976): 256–96.

Revue canadienne. Montréal. 1 (1864)–53 (1907); nouvelle série, 1 (1908)–27 (1922). Vols.17 (1881)–23 (1887) are also numbered nouvelle série, 1–7; vols.24 (1888)–28 (1892) are also called 3ᵉ série, 1–[5]. *Tables générales:* 1 (1864)– 53 (1907).

Revue d'histoire de l'Amérique française. Montréal. Published by the Institut d'histoire de l'Amérique française. 1 (1947–48)– . Index: 1 (1947–48)– 10 (1956–57); 11 (1957–58)–20 (1966–67); 21 (1967–68)–30 (1976–77).

ROYAL SOCIETY OF CANADA/SOCIÉTÉ ROYALE DU CANADA, Ottawa. *Proceedings and Transactions/ Mémoires et comptes rendus.* 1st ser., 1 (1882– 83)–12 (1894); 2nd ser., 1 (1895)–12 (1906); 3rd ser., 1 (1907)–56 (1962); 4th ser., 1 (1963)– . *General index:* 1st ser.–2nd ser.; *Author index:* 3rd ser., 1 (1907)–35 (1941). The Canadian Library Association has published *A subject index to the Royal Society of Canada Proceedings and Trans- actions: third series, vols. I–XXXI, 1907–1937,* comp. M. A. Martin (Reference publications, 1, Ottawa, 1947).

Social History, a Canadian Review/Histoire sociale, revue canadienne. Ottawa. Published under the direction of an interdisciplinary committee from various Canadian universities. No.1 (April 1968)– .

Société généalogique canadienne-française, Montréal. *Mémoires*. 1 (1944–45)– . The society's numbered publications include 2, 4, 6: Lebœuf, *Complément* [*see* section III].

CONTRIBUTORS

Contributors

ALLAIRE, GRATIEN. Professeur adjoint d'histoire, University of Alberta, Edmonton, Alberta.
Charles Chaboillez. Charles-Jean-Baptiste Chaboillez.

ALLEN, ROBERT S. Deputy chief, Treaties and historical research, Department of Indian Affairs and Northern Development, Ottawa, Ontario.
Cecil Bisshopp.

ANDREW, SHEILA MURIEL. Graduate student in history, University of New Brunswick, Fredericton, New Brunswick.
Louis Mercure.

ANDREWS, ALAN. Professor of theatre, Dalhousie University, Halifax, Nova Scotia.
Charles Stuart Powell.

ANGRIGNON, PIERRE. Professeur d'histoire, Collège d'enseignement général et professionnel de Valleyfield, Québec.
Jean-Joseph Trestler.

ANGUS, MARGARET SHARP. Writer, Kingston, Ontario.
William Fairfield.

ARCHER, CHRISTON I. Professor of history, University of Calgary, Alberta.
Pedro de Alberni. Dionisio Alcalá-Galiano.

ARMOUR, DAVID A. Assistant superintendent, Mackinac Island State Park Commission, Michigan, U.S.A.
Joseph-Louis Ainsse. Jean-Baptiste Cadot. John Dease. Joseph-Marie Ducharme. Madjeckewiss. Daniel Robertson. Patrick Sinclair.

ARMSTRONG, FREDERICK H. Professor of history, University of Western Ontario, London, Ontario.
Henry Allcock. Duncan Fisher.

ARSENAULT, GEORGES. Professeur invité en études acadiennes, University of Prince Edward Island, Charlottetown, Prince Edward Island.
Xavier Gallant, known as Pinquin.

AXTELL, JAMES. Professor of history, College of William and Mary, Williamsburg, Virginia, U.S.A.
Jemima Sawtelle (Phipps; Howe; Tute).

BAILEY, ALFRED G. Professor emeritus of history, University of New Brunswick, Fredericton, New Brunswick.
Jonathan Odell.

BEAMISH, DEREK F. Principal lecturer in history, Dorset Institute of Higher Education, Bournemouth, England.
Benjamin Lester.

BEAUREGARD, YVES. Étudiant au doctorat en histoire, Université Laval, Québec, Québec.
Charles-Louis Tarieu de Lanaudière. Xavier-Roch Tarieu de Lanaudière.

BECK, J. MURRAY. Formerly professor of political science, Dalhousie University, Halifax, Nova Scotia.
John Creighton. Dettlieb Christopher Jessen.

BÉLAND, FRANÇOIS. Étudiant à la maîtrise en histoire, Université Laval, Québec, Québec.
Maurice-Régis Blondeau. François Malhiot [in collaboration with H. Paré]. *Nicholas Montour. Jean-Baptiste-Pierre Testard Louvigny de Montigny.*

BERGERON, ADRIEN, S.S.S. Montréal, Québec.
Cécile Boudreau (Pitre; Pellerin).

BERNIER, JACQUES. Professeur d'histoire, Université Laval, Québec, Québec.
Philippe-Louis-François Badelard.

BÉRUBÉ, ANDRÉ. Chef adjoint, Sites industriels, Parcs Canada, Québec, Québec.
John Purss.

BEST, HENRY B. M. President, Laurentian University, Sudbury, Ontario.
Jacques Cartier.

BIRK, DOUGLAS A. Chairman, Institute for Minnesota Archaeology, Minneapolis, Minnesota, U.S.A.
John Sayer.

BISHOP, CHARLES A. Professor of anthropology, State University of New York, Oswego, New York, U.S.A.
Chejauk. Zheewegonab.

BLAKELEY, PHYLLIS R. Provincial archivist, Public Archives of Nova Scotia, Halifax, Nova Scotia.
Francis Green. Sir Richard Hughes. Alexander McNutt.

BOWLER, REGINALD ARTHUR. Associate professor of history, State University of New York, Buffalo, New York, U.S.A.
Edward Jessup.

BOWSFIELD, HARTWELL. Associate professor of history, York University, Downsview, Ontario.
Owen Keveny. Robert Semple.

BRISSON, RÉAL. Étudiant au doctorat en histoire, Université Laval, Québec, Québec.
Antoine Juchereau Duchesnay.

BROCK, DANIEL JAMES. Teacher, London and Middlesex County Roman Catholic Separate School Board, London, Ontario.
Ebenezer Allan. Abraham Iredell. William Robertson. Samuel Ryerse. Thomas Welch. David Zeisberger.

BROWN, JENNIFER S. H. Associate professor of history, University of Winnipeg, Manitoba.
Charles Thomas Isham. Duncan McDougall. Duncan McGillivray [in collaboration with S. M. Van Kirk]. *William Richards.*

BROWN, WALLACE. Professor of history, University of New Brunswick, Fredericton, New Brunswick.
Mather Byles.

†BROWNE, G. P. Professor of history, Carleton University, Ottawa, Ontario.
Guy Carleton, 1st Baron Dorchester. Arthur Davidson. Thomas Walker.

BUGGEY, SUSAN. Chief, Historical research, Parks Canada, Winnipeg, Manitoba.
Edward Mortimer.

BUMSTED, J. M. Professor of history, University of Manitoba, Winnipeg, Manitoba.
Joseph Aplin. Jonathan Binney. William Burn. James Curtis. Edmund Fanning. Robert Hodgson. David Lawson. Helen MacDonald of Glenaladale (MacDonald). Peter Magowan. Seth Noble. Joseph Robinson. Charles Stewart. Peter Stewart. John Wentworth. James Williams.

BURGESS, JOANNE. Professeur d'histoire, Université du Québec à Montréal, Québec.
Richard Dobie. Pierre Foretier. William Grant (1743–1810).

BURNS, ROBERT J. Historian, Parks Canada, Ottawa, Ontario.
Robert Isaac Dey Gray. William Jarvis.

BURROUGHS, PETER. Professor of history, Dalhousie University, Halifax, Nova Scotia.
Robert Prescott. Sir George Prevost.

BURTON HISTORICAL COLLECTION STAFF. Detroit Public Library, Michigan, U.S.A.
Philippe Dejean.

CADOTTE, MARCEL. Professeur agrégé de pathologie, Université de Montréal, Québec.
Jean-Baptiste Rieutord [in collaboration with R. Lessard].

CAMPBELL, LYALL. Free-lance writer and editor, Vancouver, British Columbia.
James Rainstorpe Morris [in collaboration].

CAMPBELL, MARJORIE WILKINS. Writer, Toronto, Ontario.
François Decoigne [in collaboration]. *John Gregory. John Ogilvy.*

CAMPBELL, ROD. Director of professional development, New Brunswick Teachers' Association, Fredericton, New Brunswick.
William Hazen.

CASTONGUAY, JACQUES. Doyen des études collégiales, Collège militaire royal de Saint-Jean, Saint-Jean-sur-Richelieu, Québec.
James Bell.

CAUCHON, MICHEL. Directeur, Études et Inventaires, Ministère des Affaires culturelles, Québec, Québec.
Antoine Jacson. Philippe Liébert.

CAYA, MARCEL. University archivist, McGill University, Montreal, Quebec.
Henry Caldwell. Thomas Aston Coffin.

CHAPUT, DONALD. Curator of history, Natural History Museum, Los Angeles, California, U.S.A.
Jean-Gabriel Cerré.

CHARD, DONALD F. Historic park planner, Parks Canada, Halifax, Nova Scotia.
Charles Morris.

CHARD, ELIZABETH A. Registrar, Saint Mary's University, Halifax, Nova Scotia.
George Gillmore [in collaboration].

CHAUSSÉ, GILLES, S.J. Professeur d'histoire, Collège Jean-de-Brébeuf, Montréal, Québec.
François Cherrier.

CHIASSON, ANSELME, O.F.M. CAP. Ex-directeur, Centre d'études acadiennes, Université de Moncton, Nouveau-Brunswick.
Gabriel Champion.

CHRISTIE, CARL A. Historian, Directorate of History, National Defence Headquarters, Ottawa, Ontario.
Joseph Bunbury. Prideaux Selby.

CLARKE, JOHN. Associate professor of geography, Carleton University, Ottawa, Ontario.
François Baby. Thomas McKee.

COLLARD, ELIZABETH. Writer and museum consultant, Ottawa, Ontario.
James Rollo.

COLTHART, JAMES M. Marketing manager, Sinclair Radio Laboratories Ltd, Concord, Ontario.
Alexander Ellice.

CONDON, ANN GORMAN. Assistant professor of history, University of New Brunswick, Saint John, New Brunswick.
John Caleff. Joshua Upham. Edward Winslow.

COOK, CYRIL STEWART. Minister, McLeod-Stewarton United Church, Ottawa, Ontario.
Clark Bentom.

COOPER, JOHN IRWIN. Professor emeritus of history, McGill University; Tillsonburg, Ontario.
James McGill.

CRAIG, G. M. Professor of history, University of Toronto, Ontario.
Michael Smith.

CUTHBERTSON, BRIAN C. U. Public records archivist, Public Archives of Nova Scotia, Halifax, Nova Scotia.
Moses Delesdernier.

CUTTER, DONALD C. Professor of history, St Mary's University, San Antonio, Texas, U.S.A.
Manuel José Antonio Cardero. Tadeo Haenke. Alejandro Malaspina.

CYR, CÉLINE. Rédactrice-historienne, *Dictionnaire biographique du Canada/Dictionary of Canadian biography*, Les Presses de l'université Laval, Québec, Québec.
René-Amable Boucher de Boucherville. Louis Chaboillez. Joseph Drapeau [in collaboration with P. Dufour]. *Jean-Baptiste-Melchior Hertel de Rouville. Jean-Baptiste Le Comte Dupré. Jérôme Martineau.*

DAY, RÉGINALD. Agent des relations internationales, Ministère de l'Énergie, des Mines et des Ressources, Ottawa, Ontario.
Felix O'Hara.

DEROME, ROBERT. Professeur d'histoire de l'art, Université du Québec à Montréal, Québec.
Michael Arnoldi. Robert Cruickshank. Michel Forton. Pierre Huguet, dit Latour [in collaboration with N. Morgan]. *François Ranvoyzé. Narsise Roy.* [Biographies written in collaboration with J. Ménard.]

DÉSILETS, ANDRÉE. Professeur d'histoire, Université de Sherbrooke, Québec.
Véronique Brunet, dit L'Estang, named Sainte-Rose. Marie-Louise Compain, named Saint-Augustin. Marie Raizenne, named Saint-Ignace.

DESJARDINS, ÉDOUARD, M.D. Rédacteur émérite, *L'Union médicale du Canada*, Montréal, Québec.
Jacques Dénéchaud.

DESJARDINS, MARC. Chercheur, Institut québécois de recherche sur la culture, Québec, Québec.
Jean-Baptiste Allain.

DESLOGES, YVON. Agent de recherche en histoire, Parcs

Canada, Québec, Québec.
Malcolm Fraser. René-Hippolyte Laforce.

DÉSY, LOUISE. Recherchiste; étudiante à la maîtrise en histoire de l'art, Université du Québec à Montréal, Québec.
Denis Viger.

DEVEAU, J. ALPHONSE. Directeur, Centre acadien, Université Sainte-Anne, Church Point, Nouvelle-Écosse.
Amable Pichard.

DIONNE-TOUSIGNANT, MADELEINE. Recherchiste, Montréal, Québec.
Sir Frederick Haldimand [in collaboration with S. R. J. Sutherland and P. Tousignant].

†DONNELLY, JOSEPH P., s.J. Professor emeritus of English, College of the Holy Cross, Worcester, Massachusetts, U.S.A.
Pierre Gibault.

DOUGLAS, R. ALAN. Curator, Hiram Walker Historical Museum, Windsor, Ontario.
Charles Réaume.

DOUGLAS, W. A. B. Director, Directorate of History, National Defence Headquarters, Ottawa, Ontario.
Jean-Baptiste Bouchette.

DOUVILLE, RAYMOND. Ex-sous-secrétaire et ex-archiviste du gouvernement du Québec, Québec.
Joseph-Laurent Bertrand. Pierre-Louis Deschenaux.

DUCHARME, JACQUES. Conservateur adjoint, Archives nationales du Québec, Montréal, Québec.
Marie-Catherine-Françoise Céloron.

DUFOUR, PIERRE. Historien, Parcs Canada, Québec, Québec.
Joseph Boucher de Niverville. Joseph Drapeau [in collaboration with C. Cyr]. *Clément Gosselin. Pierre-Paul Margane de Lavaltrie.* [Biographies written in collaboration with G. Goyer.] *Jean-Baptiste-Noël Pouget. Pierre de Sales Laterrière* [in collaboration with J. Hamelin].

DUMAIS, RAYMOND. Chef, Division des services, Archives nationales du Québec, Montréal, Québec.
Pierre Panet. Eustache-Ignace Trottier Desrivières Beaubien.

DUNLOP, ALLAN C. Assistant provincial archivist, Public Archives of Nova Scotia, Halifax, Nova Scotia.
James Brenton. John Burbidge.

EDWARDS, MARY JANE. Professor of English, Carleton University, Ottawa, Ontario.
James Tanswell.

EDWARDS, RON. Toronto, Ontario.
Patrick McNiff.

ELLIOTT, SHIRLEY B. Formerly legislative librarian, Nova Scotia Legislative Library, Halifax, Nova Scotia.
Benjamin Belcher.

ENGSTRAND, IRIS H. WILSON. Professor of history, University of San Diego, California, U.S.A.
José Mariano Moziño Losada Suárez de Figueroa.

ERICKSON, VINCENT O. Professor of anthropology, University of New Brunswick, Fredericton, New Brunswick.
Noël Bernard.

EVANS, CALVIN D. Assistant librarian, University of Alberta, Edmonton, Alberta.
Aaron Graham.

EVEREST, ALLAN S. Professor of history, State University College of Arts and Science, Plattsburgh, New York, U.S.A.
Moses Hazen.

FAHEY, CURTIS. Manuscript editor, *Dictionary of Canadian biography/Dictionnaire biographique du Canada*, University of Toronto Press, Ontario.
Benedict Arnold.

FARIBAULT-BEAUREGARD, MARTHE. Bibliothécaire-archiviste, Société généalogique canadienne-française, Montréal, Québec.
Barthélemy Faribault [in collaboration with C. Lessard].

FARRELL, DAVID R. Associate professor of history, University of Guelph, Ontario.
Toussaint-Antoine Adhémar, dit *Saint-Martin. John Askin. Walter Roe.*

FELLOWS, JO-ANN CARR. Director, Economic research, Department of Fisheries, Fredericton, New Brunswick.
Jacob S. Mott.

FELLOWS, ROBERT. Archivist, Provincial Archives of New Brunswick, Fredericton, New Brunswick.
George Sproule.

†FERGUSSON, CHARLES BRUCE. Archivist emeritus, Public Archives of Nova Scotia, Halifax, Nova Scotia; associate professor of history, Dalhousie University, Halifax, Nova Scotia.
Simeon Perkins.

FINGARD, JUDITH. Professor of history, Dalhousie University, Halifax, Nova Scotia.
Charles Inglis. Sir John Wentworth.

FIRTH, EDITH G. Formerly head, Canadian History Department, Metropolitan Toronto Library, Ontario.
Jabez Collver. John Elmsley. Peter Russell. William Willcocks.

FISHER, ROBIN. Associate professor of history, Simon Fraser University, Burnaby, British Columbia.
Muquinna.

FLEURENT, MAURICE. Chargé de cours, Université du Québec à Trois-Rivières, Québec.
Louis Demers. Grégoire Trahan, known as *Gregory Strahan.*

FRASER, ROBERT LOCHIEL, III. Hamilton, Ontario.
Elijah Bentley. John Macdonell (Greenfield) [in collaboration with C. M. Whitfield]. *Edward McSwiney. Mary Osborn (London). Jacob Overholser. Angelique Pilotte. Joseph Seely.*

FRENCH, G. S. President, Victoria University, Toronto, Ontario.
James Man. Barbara Ruckle (Heck).

FRENETTE, YVES. Étudiant au doctorat en histoire, Université Laval, Québec, Québec.
John Lees.

GALARNEAU, CLAUDE. Professeur titulaire d'histoire, Université Laval, Québec, Québec.
Jean-Baptiste Lahaille. Henry-Antoine Mézière.

GAUTHIER, RAYMONDE. Professeur d'histoire de l'art, Université du Québec à Montréal, Québec.
Pierre-Florent Baillairgé. Edward Cannon. Pierre Émond.

GERVAIS, JEAN-FRANCIS. Directeur de sociétés, Limalonges, France.
François Cazeau.

943

GILMAN, RHODA R. Assistant director for education, Minnesota Historical Society, St Paul, Minnesota, U.S.A.
James Aird.

GODFREY, WILLIAM GERALD. Associate professor and head, History Department, Mount Allison University, Sackville, New Brunswick.
Thomas Carleton. James Glenie. Joshua Winslow.

GOLTZ, HERBERT C. W., JR. Associate professor of history, St Thomas University, Fredericton, New Brunswick.
Michikinakoua. Tecumseh.

GOUGH, BARRY MORTON. Professor of history, Wilfrid Laurier University, Waterloo, Ontario.
Joseph Billings. James Colnett. Robert Haswell. Alexander Henry. John Meares. Peter Pond. Nathaniel Portlock.

GOYER, GÉRARD. Archiviste, Division des archives, Université Laval, Québec, Québec.
Clément Gosselin. Pierre-Paul Margane de Lavaltrie. [Biographies written in collaboration with P. Dufour.]

GRAVES, ROSS. Senior English teacher and school librarian, South Colchester High School, Brookfield, Nova Scotia.
William Schurman.

†GRAY, JOHN MORGAN. Director, The Macmillan Company of Canada, Toronto, Ontario.
Thomas Douglas, Baron Daer and Shortcleuch, 5th Earl of Selkirk.

GRAYMONT, BARBARA. Professor of history, Nyack College, New York, U.S.A.
Atiatoharongwen. Thayendanegea.

GREENHILL, BASIL. Director, National Maritime Museum, London, England.
George Hardy.

GREENWOOD, F. MURRAY. Associate professor of history, University of British Columbia, Vancouver, British Columbia.
John Black.

GWYN, JULIAN. Professor of history, University of Ottawa, Ontario.
Sir George Cranfield Berkeley.

HAMELIN, JEAN. Directeur général adjoint, *Dictionnaire biographique du Canada/Dictionary of Canadian biography*, Les Presses de l'université Laval; professeur d'histoire, Université Laval, Québec, Québec.
Pierre Denaut [in collaboration with M. Paquin]. *Pierre de Sales Laterrière* [in collaboration with P. Dufour].

HAMILTON, WILLIAM B. Director, Atlantic Institute of Education, Halifax, Nova Scotia.
George Wright.

HANDCOCK, GORDON. Associate professor of geography, Memorial University of Newfoundland, St John's, Newfoundland.
Charles Garland. Thomas Slade. Thomas Street. John Waldron.

HARE, JOHN E. Professeur agrégé d'histoire, Université d'Ottawa, Ontario.
Edward Edwards. Alexandre Menut. Joseph Quesnel. William Vondenvelden.

HAREL, BRUNO, P.S.S. Archiviste, Séminaire de Saint-Sulpice, Montréal, Québec.
Jean-Baptiste-Jacques Chicoisneau. Charles Ecuier. Michel Leclerc. Claude Poncin.

HEAD, C. GRANT. Associate professor of geography, Wilfrid Laurier University, Waterloo, Ontario.
Sir Erasmus Gower.

HERON, CRAIG. Assistant professor of history, York University, Downsview, Ontario.
Samuel Heron. Abner Miles.

HILLER, JAMES K. Associate professor of history, Memorial University of Newfoundland, St John's, Newfoundland.
William Turner.

HOENIGER, JUDITH F. M. Associate professor of microbiology, University of Toronto, Ontario.
André Michaux.

HOLMAN, H. T. Law student, Ottawa, Ontario.
Peter Byers, known as *Black Peter. William Townshend. Thomas Wright.*

HORSMAN, REGINALD. Distinguished professor of history, University of Wisconsin–Milwaukee, Wisconsin, U.S.A.
Matthew Elliott. Myeerah. Stayeghtha. Weyapiersenwah.

HUBBARD, R. H. Honorary historian to the governor general, Ottawa, Ontario.
Thomas Davies. John Ramage. Sir Hervey Smythe.

HUTCHESON, MAUD M. Toronto, Ontario.
John Wiswall.

JANSON, GILLES. Archiviste, Université du Québec à Montréal, Québec.
Charles Blake. Pierre-Joseph Compain. Dominique Mondelet.

JANZEN, CAROL ANNE. Businesswoman, Kentville, Nova Scotia.
Thomas Millidge.

JARRELL, RICHARD A. Associate professor of natural science, York University, Downsview, Ontario.
Francis Masson.

JOANETTE, GINETTE. Étudiante à la maîtrise en histoire, Université de Montréal, Québec.
Pierre Guy [in collaboration with C. Joron].

JOBLING, J. KEITH. Programme director, History and comparative education, Department of Administration and Policy Studies, McGill University, Montreal, Quebec.
Finlay Fisher.

JOHNSON, J. K. Professor of history, Carleton University, Ottawa, Ontario.
Joshua Booth. Richard Duncan. Benjamin Pawling. Hazelton Spencer.

JOHNSTON, CHARLES M. Professor of history, McMaster University, Hamilton, Ontario.
John Deserontyon. John Baptist Rousseaux St John.

JONES, ELWOOD H. Professor of history, Trent University, Peterborough, Ontario.
Joseph Willcocks.

JONES, FREDERICK. Senior lecturer in business and professional studies, Dorset Institute of Higher Education, Bournemouth, England.
James Balfour. John Clinch. John Harries.

JORON, CLAIRE. Recherchiste, Pierrefonds, Québec.
Pierre Guy [in collaboration with G. Joanette].

KAREL, DAVID. Professeur agrégé d'histoire, Université Laval, Québec, Québec.
Jean-Sébastien Natte, dit *Marseille.*

KERNAGHAN, LOIS KATHLEEN. Historical researcher, Bou-

tilier's Point, Nova Scotia.
William James Almon. Duncan Clark. Deborah How (Cottnam). Alexander Howe. John Philipps.

KNIGHT, R. J. B. Deputy head, Department of Printed Books and Manuscripts, National Maritime Museum, London, England.
Henry Duncan.

LaBRÈQUE, MARIE-PAULE R. Directrice, Bibliothèque municipale, Acton-Vale, Québec.
James Caldwell. John Coffin.

LACASSE-GALES, SUZANNE. Consultante, Ottawa, Ontario.
Louis-Chrétien de Heer [in collaboration with P. N. Moogk].

LACELLE, CLAUDETTE. Historienne, Parcs Canada, Ottawa, Ontario.
Pierre Conefroy.

LACHANCE, ANDRÉ. Professeur titulaire d'histoire, Université de Sherbrooke, Québec.
Nicolas-Gaspard Boisseau.

LAHEY, RAYMOND J. Vicar-general, Archdiocese of St John's, Newfoundland.
Edmund Burke (fl. 1785–1801). *Patrick Lambert.*

LAMB, W. KAYE. Formerly dominion archivist and national librarian; Vancouver, British Columbia.
Robert Gray. Sir Alexander Mackenzie. Jonathan Thorn.

LAMBERT, JAMES H. Rédacteur-historien, *Dictionnaire biographique du Canada/Dictionary of Canadian biography*, Les Presses de l'université Laval, Québec, Québec.
David-François de Montmollin. Thomas Scott [in collaboration with D. Roberts]. *Alexander Spark.*

LANGELIER, GILLES. Archiviste, Collection nationale de cartes et plans, Archives publiques du Canada, Ottawa, Ontario.
Jean-Baptiste Bédard. Louis Charland. Étienne Guy.

LaPLANTE, CORINNE. Bathurst, Nouveau-Brunswick.
Michel Bastarache, dit Basque.

LAPOINTE, GABRIELLE, O.S.U. Québec, Québec.
Marguerite Davanne, named de Saint-Louis de Gonzague.

LAUZIER, ROCH. Travailleur autonome, Québec, Québec.
François Boucher. James Frost. John Painter.

LEE, DAVID. Historian, National Historic Parks and Sites Branch, Department of the Environment, Ottawa, Ontario.
Francis Le Maistre.

LEIGHTON, DOUGLAS. Associate professor of history, University of Western Ontario, London, Ontario.
Simon Girty.

LEMIEUX, LUCIEN. Vicaire épiscopal, Longueuil, Québec.
Pierre Huet de La Valinière.

LESSARD, CLAUDE. Professeur d'histoire, Université du Québec à Trois-Rivières, Québec.
Barthélemy Faribault [in collaboration with M. Faribault-Beauregard].

LESSARD, RENALD. Étudiant à la maîtrise en histoire, Université Laval, Québec, Québec.
Jean-Baptiste Rieutord [in collaboration with M. Cadotte]. *Alexandre Serres. François-Michel Suzor.*

L'HEUREUX, JACQUES. Professeur titulaire de droit, Université Laval, Québec, Québec.
Jean-Baptiste Lebrun de Duplessis. Maurice Morgann.

LOCHHEAD, DOUGLAS G. Director, Centre for Canadian

Studies, Mount Allison University, Sackville, New Brunswick.
Silvester Tiffany.

LORTIE, LÉON. Professeur à la retraite, Montréal, Québec.
Jean De Lisle. Jean-Guillaume De Lisle.

†LYSAGHT, AVERIL M. London, England.
Sir Joseph Banks.

McCLOY, T. R. Librarian emeritus, Glenbow-Alberta Institute, Calgary, Alberta.
John McKay.

MacDONALD, ALLAN J. Archivist, Archives of Ontario, Toronto, Ontario.
John McDonell (Aberchalder). Angus Macdonell (Collachie).

MacDONELL, MARGARET. Professor of Celtic studies, St Francis Xavier University, Antigonish, Nova Scotia.
Calum Bàn MacMhannain.

McDOUGALL, ELIZABETH ANN KERR. Historian, Montreal, Quebec.
John Bethune. John Dun.

McGAUGHEY, ELVA RICHARDS. Kingston, Ontario.
Ephraim Jones.

†MACKAY, DONALD C. Principal, Nova Scotia College of Art, Halifax, Nova Scotia.
Charles Oliver Bruff.

MacKENZIE, A. ANTHONY. Associate professor of history, St Francis Xavier University, Antigonish, Nova Scotia.
James Jones. Ranald McKinnon. Robert Patterson.

MacKINNON, NEIL J. Associate professor of history, St Francis Xavier University, Antigonish, Nova Scotia.
George Panton.

MacLEAN, R. A. Professor of history, St Francis Xavier University, Antigonish, Nova Scotia.
Edmund Burke (1753–1820). John Harris.

MacMILLAN, DAVID S. Professor of history, Trent University, Peterborough, Ontario.
James Douglas. James Dunlop [in collaboration with A. J. H. Richardson]. *Joseph Forsyth. William Pagan* [in collaboration with R. Nason].

McMULLEN, LORRAINE. Professor of English, University of Ottawa, Ontario.
Friederike Charlotte Louise von Massow (Riedesel, Freifrau zu Eisenbach).

†MacNUTT, WILLIAM STEWART. Professor emeritus of history, University of New Brunswick, Fredericton, New Brunswick.
Edward Augustus, Duke of Kent and Strathearn [in collaboration].

MANNION, JOHN. Associate professor of geography, Memorial University of Newfoundland, St John's, Newfoundland.
Archibald Nevins.

MARTIN, ALBERTUS. Évêque de Nicolet, Québec.
Pierre-Michel Cressé. Benjamin-Nicolas Maillou.

MATTEAU, PIERRE. Conseiller pédagogique aux professeurs, Collège d'enseignement général et professionnel de La Pocatière, Québec.
Jean Digé. Jacques-Nicolas Perrault.

MATTHEWS, KEITH. Professor of history; chairman, Maritime History Group, Memorial University of Newfoundland, St John's, Newfoundland.
Samuel Bulley. Richard Hutchings. Robert Newman.

945

Peter Ougier. Andrew Pinson. Richard Routh.

MEALING, STANLEY R. Professor of history, Carleton University, Ottawa, Ontario.
Æneas Shaw. John Graves Simcoe.

MÉNARD, JOSÉ. Étudiante à la maîtrise en histoire de l'art, Université du Québec à Montréal; recherchiste, Musée des beaux-arts, Montréal, Québec.
François Ranvoyzé. Narsise Roy. [Biographies written in collaboration with R. Derome.]

MILLMAN, THOMAS R. Formerly archivist, Anglican Church of Canada, Toronto, Ontario.
Richard Bradford. Jehosaphat Mountain. Thomas Charles Heslop Scott. John Stuart.

MIMEAULT, MARIO. Professeur d'histoire, Polyvalente C.-E.-Pouliot, Gaspé, Québec.
Claude Guitet.

MOMRYK, MYRON. Archivist, Manuscript Division, Public Archives of Canada, Ottawa, Ontario.
Edward William Gray. Isaac Todd.

MOODY, BARRY M. Associate professor of history, Acadia University, Wolfville, Nova Scotia.
James DeLancey.

MOOGK, PETER N. Associate professor of history, University of British Columbia, Vancouver, British Columbia.
Louis-Chrétien de Heer [in collaboration with S. Lacasse-Gales]. *Colin McNabb. John Young.*

MOREL, ANDRÉ. Professeur titulaire de droit, Université de Montréal, Québec.
David Lynd. Pierre-Louis Panet. Jenkin Williams.

MORGAN, NORMA. Graduate student in art history, Concordia University, Montreal, Quebec.
Pierre Huguet, dit Latour [in collaboration with R. Derome].

MORGAN, ROBERT J. Director, Beaton Institute, University College of Cape Breton, Sydney, Nova Scotia.
Ingram Ball. Ranna Cossit. Abraham Cornelius Cuyler. William Macarmick. William McKinnon. James Ogilvie. William Smith. Richard Stout.

MORIN, JACQUES. Rimouski, Québec.
Liveright Piuze.

MORRISON, JEAN. Historical research officer, Old Fort William, Thunder Bay, Ontario.
Alexander MacKay. Kenneth MacKenzie. Donald McTavish.

NASON, ROGER. Bicentennial coordinator, City of Fredericton, New Brunswick.
William Gallop. William Pagan [in collaboration with D. S. Macmillan].

†NICHOLSON, G. W. L. Military historian, Ottawa, Ontario.
John Skerrett. Thomas Skinner.

NOPPEN, LUC. Professeur titulaire d'histoire de l'art, Université Laval, Québec, Québec.
Jean Baillairgé.

NORMAND, SYLVIO. Étudiant à l'école du Barreau du Québec, Québec, Québec.
James G. Hanna.

O'GALLAGHER, MARIANNA, S.C.H. High school teacher, Quebec, Quebec.
John Fraser. John Jones [in collaboration]. *Robert Lester* [in collaboration].

OUELLET, FERNAND. Professeur d'histoire, Université d'Ottawa, Ontario.

Joseph Frobisher. George McBeath. Simon McTavish. Joseph Périnault.

PAIKOWSKY, SANDRA. Associate professor of art history; curator, Sir George Williams Art Galleries, Concordia University, Montreal, Quebec.
Robert Field.

PAQUETTE, NORMAND. Professeur d'histoire, Collège d'enseignement général et professionnel de Trois-Rivières, Québec.
John Antrobus.

PAQUIN, MICHEL. Codirecteur de la rédaction, *Dictionnaire biographique du Canada/Dictionary of Canadian biography,* Les Presses de l'université Laval, Québec, Québec.
Pierre Denaut [in collaboration with J. Hamelin].

PARÉ, HÉLÈNE. Recherchiste, Montréal, Québec.
François Malhiot [in collaboration with F. Béland].

PARKER, BRUCE A. Teacher, Port Hope High School, Ontario.
Richard Hatt. Nathaniel Pettit. Samuel Street. John Warren [in collaboration].

PATTERSON, GRAEME H. Associate professor of history, University of Toronto, Ontario.
William Weekes.

PATTERSON, STEPHEN E. Professor of history, University of New Brunswick, Fredericton, New Brunswick.
Israel Perley.

PELLETIER, GÉRALD. Diplômé de 2ᵉ cycle en histoire, Université d'Ottawa, Ontario.
Joseph-Dominique-Emmanuel Le Moyne de Longueuil.

PIGOT, F. L. Librarian, Robertson Library, University of Prince Edward Island, Charlottetown, Prince Edward Island.
Thomas Desbrisay. John MacDonald of Glenaladale. James Robertson.

PINCOMBE, C. A. Researcher and writer, Moncton, New Brunswick.
John Beardsley.

PLAMONDON, LILIANNE. Québec, Québec.
Marie-Catherine Payen de Noyan, named *de Saint-Alexis.*

PORTER, JOHN R. Professeur d'histoire de l'art, Université Laval, Québec, Québec.
François Guernon, dit Belleville.

POTTER, JANICE. Research associate in history, University of Saskatchewan, Saskatoon, Saskatchewan.
Richard Cartwright [in collaboration with G. A. Rawlyk].

POZZO-LAURENT, JEANNINE. Recherchiste, Parcs Canada, Québec, Québec.
Jean-Guillaume Plantavit de Lapause de Margon.

PRESTON, RICHARD A. W. K. Boyd professor of history emeritus, Duke University, Durham, North Carolina, U.S.A.
James Clark [in collaboration].

PRITCHARD, JAMES. Associate professor of history, Queen's University, Kingston, Ontario.
Joseph-Bernard de Chabert de Cogolin, Marquis de Chabert.

PROVOST, HONORIUS, PTRE. Archiviste retraité, Séminaire de Québec, Québec.
Pierre-Jacques Bossu, dit Lyonnais, named *Brother Félix. Charles-Ange Collet. Henri-François Gravé de La Rive. Gabriel-Elzéar Taschereau.*

RAWLYK, GEORGE A. Professor of history, Queen's

University, Kingston, Ontario.

Richard Cartwright [in collaboration with J. Potter].

†RICH, EDWIN ERNEST. Emeritus Vere Harmsworth professor of imperial and naval history, University of Cambridge, England.

Robert Longmoor.

RICHARDSON, A. J. H. Formerly assistant chief of research, National Historic Parks and Sites Branch, Department of Indian and Northern Affairs, Ottawa, Ontario.

James Dunlop [in collaboration with D. S. Macmillan].

RICHARDSON, GUS. Toronto, Ontario.

Wahpasha.

RIOUX, CHRISTIAN. Historien, Parcs Canada, Québec, Québec.

John Barnes. John Craigie.

ROBERTS, DAVID. Manuscript editor, *Dictionary of Canadian biography/Dictionnaire biographique du Canada*, University of Toronto Press, Toronto, Ontario.

Thomas Ainslie. George Allsopp. Alexandre Dumas. William Grant (1744–1805). Ralph Gray. James McNabb. Thomas Scott [in collaboration with J. H. Lambert]. *James Tod.*

ROBICHAUD, MGR DONAT. Curé, Saint-Nom-de-Jésus, Beresford, Nouveau-Brunswick.

Jean-Baptiste Robichaux.

RODGER, ANDREW C. Archivist, National Photography Collection, Public Archives of Canada, Ottawa, Ontario.

Nicolas Gautier.

ROGERS, IRENE L. Historian, Prince Edward Island Heritage Foundation, Charlottetown, Prince Edward Island.

John Plaw.

ROME, DAVID. Associate professor of history, Concordia University, Montreal, Quebec.

Jacob Raphael Cohen.

ROMPKEY, RONALD. Lecturer in English, University of Lethbridge, Alberta.

Bruin Romkes Comingo.

ROSS, JULIE MARTHA. Graduate student in history, University of New Brunswick, Fredericton, New Brunswick.

Jacob Bailey [in collaboration with T. B. Vincent].

ROUSSEAU, FRANÇOIS. Historien, Monastère de l'Hôtel-Dieu de Québec, Québec.

Marie-Vénérande Melançon, named *de Sainte-Claire*. *Marie-Geneviève Parent*, named *de Saint-François d'Assise.*

ROUSSEAU, LOUIS. Professeur de sciences religieuses, Université du Québec à Montréal, Québec.

Joseph Borneuf.

ROY, JACQUELINE. Rédactrice-historienne, *Dictionnaire biographique du Canada/Dictionary of Canadian biography*, Les Presses de l'université Laval, Québec, Québec.

Pierre-Joseph Carrefour de La Pelouze. John Lambert. John Nairne. Simon Thibodeau.

RUDDY, DAVID DANIEL. Associate professor of history and political science, Collège militaire royal de Saint-Jean, Saint-Jean-sur-Richelieu, Québec.

Louis Liénard de Beaujeu de Villemonde.

RYDER, DOROTHY E. Formerly reference collection development specialist, National Library of Canada, Ottawa, Ontario.

John Bentley.

RYERSON, STANLEY BRÉHAUT. Professeur invité d'histoire, Université du Québec à Montréal, Québec.

Pierre Brehaut. Louis Dunière.

SÉGUIN, GEORGETTE, S.G.M. Secrétaire, Centre Marguerite-d'Youville, Montréal, Québec.

Marie-Angélique Dussaus.

SMITH, DONALD B. Associate professor of history, University of Calgary, Alberta.

Kineubenae. David Ramsay.

SMITH, SHIRLEE ANNE. Keeper, Hudson's Bay Company Archives, Provincial Archives of Manitoba, Winnipeg, Manitoba.

Joseph Colen.

SNOWDON, JAMES D. Sessional lecturer in history, Acadia University, Wolfville, Nova Scotia.

Amos Botsford. Charles Dixon.

SPRAY, WILLIAM A. Vice-president (academic), St Thomas University, Fredericton, New Brunswick.

Caleb Jones. Samuel Lee. Alexander Taylor.

†SPURR, JOHN W. Chief librarian emeritus, Royal Military College of Canada, Kingston, Ontario.

Ralph Henry Bruyeres. George Glasgow. Sir Robert Hall.

STACEY, C. P. University professor emeritus, University of Toronto, Ontario.

Sir Isaac Brock. George Townshend, 4th Viscount and 1st Marquess Townshend. Sir James Lucas Yeo.

STAGG, RONALD J. Professor of history, Ryerson Polytechnical Institute, Toronto, Ontario.

William Berczy.

STANLEY, DELLA M. M. Lecturer in history, Mount Saint Vincent University, Halifax, Nova Scotia.

Pierre Cassiet.

STANLEY, GEORGE F. G. Professor emeritus, Royal Military College of Canada, Kingston, Ontario, and Mount Allison University, Sackville, New Brunswick.

Charles Lennox, 4th Duke of Richmond and Lennox.

STEELE, IAN K. Professor of history, University of Western Ontario, London, Ontario.

Hugh Finlay.

STEPPLER, GLENN A. Graduate student in history, University of Oxford, England.

Kenelm Chandler. Charles Roberts.

STEWART, ALICE R. Professor of history, University of Maine at Orono, Maine, U.S.A.

John Allan.

STEWART, GORDON T. Associate professor of history, Michigan State University, East Lansing, Michigan, U.S.A.

Jonathan Scott.

STORY, G. M. Professor of English, Memorial University of Newfoundland, St John's, Newfoundland.

George Cartwright. Demasduwit.

SUTHERLAND, DAVID A. Associate professor of history, Dalhousie University, Halifax, Nova Scotia.

William Forsyth. Samuel Hart. Philip Marchinton. William Wilkie.

SUTHERLAND, MAXWELL. Chief, Historical Research Division, Parks Canada, Ottawa, Ontario.

Robert Morse.

SUTHERLAND, STUART R. J. Military historian, Toronto, Ontario.

Robert Mathews. James Moody. Robert Pringle Skinner. Sir Frederick Haldimand [in collaboration with P. Tousignant and M. Dionne-Tousignant].

TAILLEMITE, ÉTIENNE. Inspecteur général des Archives de France, Paris, France.
Jacques Bedout. Louis-Antoine de Bougainville, Comte de Bougainville. Nicolas Renaud d'Avène Des Méloizes.

THÉORÊT, MARC. Notaire, Laval, Québec.
Jean d'Olabaratz.

THOMPSON, FREDERIC FRASER. Professor emeritus, Royal Military College of Canada, Kingston, Ontario.
Mark Milbanke. Francis Pickmore.

THORPE, F. J. Chief, History Division, National Museum of Man, National Museums of Canada, Ottawa, Ontario.
Samuel Johannes Holland. Nicolas Sarrebource de Pontleroy.

TOUSIGNANT, PIERRE. Professeur agrégé d'histoire, Université de Montréal, Québec.
Pierre-Amable De Bonne. Thomas Dunn. Jean-Antoine Panet. [Biographies written in collaboration with J.-P. Wallot.] *Sir Frederick Haldimand* [in collaboration with S. R. J. Sutherland and M. Dionne-Tousignant].

TRATT, GERTRUDE E. N. Teacher, Halifax, Nova Scotia.
James Humphreys.

†TRATT, GRACE M. Special collections librarian, Dalhousie University, Halifax, Nova Scotia.
Isaac Deschamps.

TUNIS, BARBARA R. Research historian, Ottawa, Ontario.
George Longmore.

TURNER, H. E. Associate professor of history, McMaster University, Hamilton, Ontario.
John Langhorn.

TURNER, LARRY P. Graduate student in history, Queen's University, Kingston, Ontario.
Michael Grass.

†UPTON, L. F. S. Professor of history, University of British Columbia, Vancouver, British Columbia.
John Julien. Sir Brook Watson.

VACHON, CLAUDE. Chef de division, Gestion des documents, Régie des rentes du Québec, Québec.
Michel-Amable Berthelot Dartigny.

VAN KIRK, SYLVIA M. Associate professor of history, University of Toronto, Ontario.
Isabel Gunn. Duncan McGillivray [in collaboration with J. S. H. Brown].

VINCENT, THOMAS B. Associate professor of English, Royal Military College of Canada, Kingston, Ontario.
Jacob Bailey [in collaboration with J. M. Ross]. *Roger Viets.*

WALKER, JAMES W. ST G. Associate professor and chairman, Department of History, University of Waterloo, Ontario.
David George. Boston King.

WALLACE, CARL MURRAY. Associate professor of history, Laurentian University, Sudbury, Ontario.
Gabriel George Ludlow. George Duncan Ludlow.

WALLOT, JEAN-PIERRE. Vice-recteur aux études; professeur titulaire d'histoire, Université de Montréal, Québec.
John Blackwood. James Campbell. Sir James Henry Craig. Pierre-Amable De Bonne [in collaboration with P. Tousignant]. *Thomas Dunn* [in collaboration with P. Tousignant]. *Édouard-Alphonse d'Irumberry de Salaberry. Jean-Antoine Panet* [in collaboration with P. Tousignant].

WHITE, STEPHEN A. Généalogiste, Centre d'études acadiennes, Université de Moncton, Nouveau-Brunswick.
Pierre Cormier. Amable Doucet.

WHITELEY, W. H. Professor of history, Memorial University of Newfoundland, St John's, Newfoundland.
Sir Roger Curtis. Sir John Thomas Duckworth. Thomas Graves, 1st Baron Graves. Pierre Marcoux.

WHITESIDE, M. SUSAN. Librarian, Nova Scotia Museum, Halifax, Nova Scotia.
Isaac Hildrith.

WHITFIELD, CAROL M. Chief of research, Halifax Defence Complex, Parks Canada, Halifax, Nova Scotia.
Alexander Grant [in collaboration]. *John Macdonell (Greenfield)* [in collaboration with R. L. Fraser].

WICKWIRE, FRANKLIN B. Professor of history, University of Massachusetts, Amherst, Massachusetts, U.S.A.
Richard G. England.

WILLIAMS, GLYNDWR. Professor of history, University of London, England.
Andrew Graham.

WILLIAMSON, JOHN L. Deputy minister, Energy Secretariat, Fredericton, New Brunswick.
Samuel Andrews.

WILSON, BRUCE GORDON. Chief, London Office, Public Archives of Canada, London, England.
Robert Hamilton.

YOUNG, D. MURRAY. Professor of history, University of New Brunswick, Fredericton, New Brunswick.
Dugald Campbell.

INDEX OF IDENTIFICATIONS

CATEGORIES

Agriculture	Engineers	Miscellaneous
Architects	Explorers	Native peoples
Armed forces	Fur traders	Notaries
Artisans	Indian affairs	Office holders
Arts	Journalists	Politicians
Authors	Law	Religious
Blacks	Mariners	Scientists
Business	Medicine	Surveyors
Education		Women

Index of Identifications

Like the network of cross-references within biographies, this index is designed to assist readers in following their interests through the volume. Most of the groupings are by occupations carried on within Canada, but some have been established to help readers who approach the past from other perspectives. Women appear in one grouping, as do blacks, a reflection of the interest in their history, but they may also be found under the occupations in which they engaged. Native peoples are given by tribe. Readers interested in immigration or in the history of ethnic groups in Canada should consult the Geographical Index, where subjects are listed by their place of birth.

Some of the occupational categories require explanation so that users will be better able to find biographies of particular interest. Under "agriculture" is to be found a variety of people known to have been engaged in the development of land. "Seigneurs" form a readily identifiable sub-group; "improvers" include land agents, gentlemen farmers, and colonizers; listed as "settlers" are habitants, tenants, and small landowners for whom farming was the prime occupation. Those who speculated in seigneuries or others lands are to be found under "business." "Arts" includes both fine and performing arts. A distinction between fine arts and "artisans" was difficult to make in some instances; silversmiths, for example, appear under "arts" and potters under "artisans."

Although the engineers in this volume are military officers and so appear under "armed forces," it was decided also to list them separately as "engineers." Related occupations, those of surveyor, hydrographer, and cartographer, are found under "surveyors." Readers wishing to pursue the history of education and medicine should consult, as well as "education" and "medicine," the category "religious." Fur traders, although they might have appeared under "business," are given a separate listing for the benefit of readers interested in this aspect of the economy. "Mariners" includes civilian captains, pilots, and navigators; naval officers appear as a sub-group of "armed forces." Within "office holders," the sub-division "administrators" includes high-ranking officials: governors, lieutenant governors, and administrators.

The DCB/DBC attempts by its assignments to encourage research in new areas as well as familiar ones, but its selection of individuals to receive biographies reflects the survival of documentation and the areas historians have chosen to investigate. The index should not, therefore, be used for quantitative judgements; it is merely a guide to what is contained in volume V.

AGRICULTURE

"Improvers"

Askin, John
Berczy, William
Burbidge, John
Burn, William
Campbell, James
Chandler, Kenelm
Curtis, James
Delesdernier, Moses
Dixon, Charles
Douglas, James
Douglas, Thomas, Baron Daer and
   Shortcleuch, 5th Earl of Selkirk
Dunière, Louis
Fanning, Edmund

Guy, Pierre
Harris, John
Holland, Samuel Johannes
Lawson, David
MacDonald of Glenaladale, Helen
   (MacDonald)
MacDonald of Glenaladale, John
McNutt, Alexander
Ogilvy, John
Robertson, Daniel
Robinson, Joseph
Stewart, Charles
Stewart, Peter
Willcocks, William
Williams, James

Seigneurs

Allsopp, George
Baby, François
Blackwood, John
Boucher de Boucherville,
   René-Amable
Boucher de Niverville, Joseph
Caldwell, Henry
Cressé, Pierre-Michel
De Bonne, Pierre-Amable
Drapeau, Joseph
Dunn, Thomas
Ellice, Alexander
Finlay, Hugh
Foretier, Pierre

INDEX OF IDENTIFICATIONS

Fraser, Malcolm
Gray, Ralph
Hazen, Moses
Hertel de Rouville, Jean-Baptiste-
  Melchior
Juchereau Duchesnay, Antoine
Le Comte Dupré, Jean-Baptiste
Le Moyne de Longueuil, Joseph-
  Dominique-Emmanuel
Liénard de Beaujeu de Villemonde,
  Louis
Lynd, David
McTavish, Simon
Margane de Lavaltrie, Pierre-Paul
Montour, Nicholas
Nairne, John

Panet, Jean-Antoine
Panet, Pierre-Louis
Périnault, Joseph
Perrault, Jacques-Nicolas
Renaud d'Avène Des Méloizes,
  Nicolas
Sales Laterrière, Pierre de
Tarieu de Lanaudière, Charles-Louis
Taschereau, Gabriel-Elzéar
Tod, James
Trottier Desrivières Beaubien,
  Eustache-Ignace
Williams, Jenkin
Young, John

Settlers

Bastarache, *dit* Basque, Michel
Bentley, Elijah
Collver, Jabez
Cormier, Pierre
Gallant, Xavier, known as Pinquin
Guitet, Claude
Hibbard, Jedediah
Lawson, David
MacMhannain, Calum Bàn
Mercure, Louis
Overholser, Jacob
Pawling, Benjamin
Réaume, Charles
Ruckle, Barbara (Heck)

ARCHITECTS

Baillairgé, Jean
Baillairgé, Pierre-Florent
Berczy, William

Charland, Louis
Conefroy, Pierre

Demers, Louis
Plaw, John

ARMED FORCES

American

Army: officers

Arnold, Benedict
Gosselin, Clément
Hazen, Moses
Willcocks, Joseph

Army: soldiers

Trahan, Grégoire, known as Gregory
  Strahan

British

Army: officers

Badelard, Philippe-Louis-François
Barnes, John
Bisshopp, Cecil
Blake, Charles
Boucher de Boucherville, René-
  Amable
Brock, Sir Isaac
Bruyeres, Ralph Henry
Bunbury, Joseph
Burbidge, John
Caldwell, Henry
Campbell, Dugald

Carleton, Guy, 1st Baron Dorchester
Carleton, Thomas
Coffin, John
Craig, Sir James Henry
Davies, Thomas
Duncan, Richard
Eddy, Jonathan
Edward Augustus, Duke of Kent and
  Strathearn
England, Richard G.
Fanning, Edmund
Fraser, Malcolm
Glasgow, George
Glenie, James
Grant, Alexander
Green, Francis
Haldimand, Sir Frederick (Appendix)
Hazen, Moses
Heer, Louis-Chrétien de
Hertel de Rouville, Jean-Baptiste-
  Melchior
Hodgson, Robert
Holland, Samuel Johannes
Howe, Alexander
Hunter, Peter
Jessup, Edward
Juchereau Duchesnay, Antoine
Le Maistre, Francis
Le Moyne de Longueuil, Joseph-
  Dominique-Emmanuel

Longmore, George
MacDonald of Glenaladale, John
McDonell (Aberchalder), John
McKee, Thomas
McKinnon, Ranald
McNabb, Colin
McNutt, Alexander
Marcoux, Pierre
Margane de Lavaltrie, Pierre-Paul
Mathews, Robert
Mercure, Louis
Moody, James
Morse, Robert
Nairne, John
Ogilvie, James
Pawling, Benjamin
Philipps, John
Pond, Peter
Prescott, Robert
Prevost, Sir George
Roberts, Charles
Robertson, Daniel
Ryerse, Samuel
Selby, Prideaux
Shaw, Æneas
Simcoe, John Graves
Sinclair, Patrick
Skerrett, John
Skinner, Robert Pringle
Smythe, Sir Hervey

952

INDEX OF IDENTIFICATIONS

Spencer, Hazelton
Sproule, George
Stewart, Charles
Townshend, George
Vondenvelden, William
Winslow, Edward
Winslow, Joshua

Army: soldiers

Booth, Joshua
Burbidge, John
Fraser, John
Gray, Ralph
Jones, Ephraim
Macdonell (Greenfield), John
Trestler, Jean-Joseph
Warren, John

Militia: officers

Ainslie, Thomas
Askin, John
Baby, François
Badelard, Philippe-Louis-François
Baillairgé, Pierre-Florent
Belcher, Benjamin
Blackwood, John
Blondeau, Maurice-Régis
Boisseau, Nicolas-Gaspard
Booth, Joshua
Boucher de Boucherville, René-
  Amable
Boucher de Niverville, Joseph
Bouchette, Jean-Baptiste
Brenton, James
Bruneau, Pierre
Burbidge, John
Caldwell, Henry
Caldwell, James
Cartier, Jacques
Cartwright, Richard
Chaboillez, Charles-Jean-Baptiste
Chaboillez, Louis
Charland, Louis
Coffin, John
Creighton, John
Cressé, Pierre-Michel
Cruickshank, Robert
De Bonne, Pierre-Amable
De Lisle, Jean-Guillaume
Dobie, Richard
Dumas, Alexandre
Dunière, Louis
Dunlop, James
Edwards, Edward
Elliott, Matthew
Foretier, Pierre
Fraser, Malcolm
Frobisher, Joseph
Gray, Edward William
Guy, Étienne
Guy, Pierre

Hatt, Richard
Heron, Samuel
Hertel de Rouville, Jean-Baptiste-
  Melchior
Jarvis, William
Jessen, Dettlieb Christopher
Jessup, Edward
Jones, John
Juchereau Duchesnay, Antoine
Laforce, René-Hippolyte
Le Comte Dupré, Jean-Baptiste
Lees, John
Le Maistre, Francis
Le Moyne de Longueuil, Joseph-
  Dominique-Emmanuel
Lester, Robert
Liénard de Beaujeu de Villemonde,
  Louis
Lynd, David
McBeath, George
McDonell (Aberchalder), John
Macdonell (Greenfield), John
McGill, James
McKee, Thomas
McKinnon, Ranald
McNabb, Colin
McTavish, Simon
Magowan, Peter
Malhiot, François
Marcoux, Pierre
Margane de Lavaltrie, Pierre-Paul
Millidge, Thomas
Moody, James
Mortimer, Edward
Nairne, John
Ogilvy, John
Painter, John
Panet, Jean-Antoine
Patterson, Robert
Pawling, Benjamin
Perkins, Simeon
Perrault, Jacques-Nicolas
Purss, John
Quesnel, Joseph
Robertson, Daniel
Robertson, William
Robinson, Joseph
Rousseaux St John, John Baptist
Ryerse, Samuel
Scott, Thomas
Shaw, Æneas
Spencer, Hazelton
Street, Samuel
Tarieu de Lanaudière, Charles-Louis
Tarieu de Lanaudière, Xavier-Roch
Taschereau, Gabriel-Elzéar
Testard Louvigny de Montigny, Jean-
  Baptiste-Pierre
Tod, James
Todd, Isaac
Trottier Desrivières Beaubien,
  Eustache-Ignace
Warren, John
Welch, Thomas

Winslow, Joshua
Young, John

Militiamen

McSwiney, Edward
Seely, Joseph
Thibodeau, Simon

Navy: officers

Berkeley, Sir George Cranfield
Bouchette, Jean-Baptiste
Curtis, Sir Roger
Duckworth, Sir John Thomas
Duncan, Henry
Frost, James
Gower, Sir Erasmus
Graves, Thomas, 1st Baron Graves
Hall, Sir Robert
Hughes, Sir Richard
Laforce, René-Hippolyte
Milbanke, Mark
Pickmore, Francis
Portlock, Nathaniel
Yeo, Sir James Lucas

Navy: sailors

Billings, Joseph
Ramsay, David

French

Army: officers

Badelard, Philippe-Louis-François
Boucher de Boucherville, René-
  Amable
Boucher de Niverville, Joseph
Bougainville, Louis-Antoine de,
  Comte de Bougainville
Carrefour de La Pelouze, Pierre-Joseph
Hertel de Rouville, Jean-Baptiste-
  Melchior
Juchereau Duchesnay, Antoine
Le Moyne de Longueuil, Joseph-
  Dominique-Emmanuel
Liénard de Beaujeu de Villemonde,
  Louis
Margane de Lavaltrie, Pierre-Paul
Plantavit de Lapause de Margon, Jean-
  Guillaume
Renaud d'Avène Des Méloizes,
  Nicolas
Sarrebource de Pontleroy, Nicolas
Tarieu de Lanaudière, Charles-Louis

Army: soldiers

Guernon, *dit* Belleville, François
Jacson, Antoine
Mondelet, Dominique
Natte, *dit* Marseille, Jean-Sébastien

953

INDEX OF IDENTIFICATIONS

Navy: officers

Bedout, Jacques
Chabert de Cogolin, Joseph-Bernard
   de, Marquis de Chabert
Olabaratz, Jean d'

Militia: officers

Gautier, Nicolas
Le Comte Dupré, Jean-Baptiste

Spanish

Army: officers

Alberni, Pedro de

Navy: officers

Alcalá-Galiano, Dionisio
Malaspina, Alejandro

Navy: sailors

Cardero, Manuel José Antonio

ARTISANS

Baillairgé, Jean
Baillairgé, Pierre-Florent
Bédard, Jean-Baptiste
Bell, James
Brehaut, Pierre
Cannon, Edward
Edwards, Edward
Émond, Pierre
Fisher, Duncan

Gosselin, Clément
Gray, Ralph
Hanna, James G.
Hodgson, Robert
Huguet, *dit* Latour, Pierre
Humphreys, James
Mézière, Henry-Antoine
Mott, Jacob S.
Pawling, Benjamin

Périnault, Joseph
Robertson, James
Rollo, James
Thibodeau, Simon
Tiffany, Silvester
Viger, Denis
Vondenvelden, William
Willcocks, Joseph

ARTS

Gold and silver work

Arnoldi, Michael
Bruff, Charles Oliver
Cruickshank, Robert
Forton, Michel
Hanna, James G.
Huguet, *dit* Latour, Pierre
Ramage, John
Roy, Narsise

Music

Bentley, John
Ecuier, Charles
MacMhannain, Calum Bàn
Quesnel, Joseph

Painting

Berczy, William
Cardero, Manuel José Antonio
Davies, Thomas
Field, Robert
Heer, Louis-Chrétien de
Lambert, John
Liébert, Philippe
Natte, *dit* Marseille, Jean-Sébastien
Ramage, John
Ranvoyzé, François
Richards, William
Smythe, Sir Hervey
Townshend, George, 4th Viscount
   and 1st Marquis Townshend

Sculpture

Baillairgé, Jean
Baillairgé, Pierre-Florent
Émond, Pierre
Guernon, *dit* Belleville, François
Jacson, Antoine
Liébert, Philippe
Viger, Denis

Theatre

Natte, *dit* Marseille, Jean-Sébastien
Powell, Charles Stuart

AUTHORS

Diaries and memoirs

Askin, John
Douglas, Thomas, Baron Daer and
   Shortcleuch, 5th Earl of Selkirk
King, Boston

Massow, Friederike Charlotte Louise
   von (Riedesel, Freifrau zu
   Eisenbach)
Mézière, Henry-Antoine
Perkins, Simeon

Plantavit de Lapause de Margon, Jean-
   Guillaume
Sales Laterrière, Pierre de
Willcocks, Joseph
Zeisberger, David

Pamphlets, essays, polemics, and sermons

Badelard, Philippe-Louis-François
Bentom, Clark
Berthelot Dartigny, Michel-Amable
Bethune, John
Burke, Edmund (1753–1820)
Cartwright, Richard
De Bonne, Pierre-Amable
Gillmore, George
Huet de La Valinière, Pierre
Inglis, Charles
Lebrun de Duplessis, Jean-Baptiste
Mountain, Jehosaphat
Robinson, Joseph
Sales Laterrière, Pierre de
Smith, William
Spark, Alexander
Tarieu de Lanaudière, Charles-Louis
Wilkie, William
Winslow, Edward

Poetry, prose, and drama

Bailey, Jacob
Berczy, William
Byles, Mather
Cartwright, George
Delesdernier, Moses
Odell, Jonathan
Quesnel, Joseph
Scott, Jonathan
Viets, Roger

Travel accounts, journals, narratives, and scientific works

Ainslie, Thomas
Banks, Sir Joseph
Bentom, Clark
Bougainville, Louis-Antoine de, Comte de Bougainville
Caldwell, Henry
Caleff, John
Carrefour de La Pelouze, Pierre-Joseph
Cartwright, George
Cartwright, Richard
Chabert de Cogolin, Joseph-Bernard de, Marquis de Chabert

Colnett, James
Curtis, Sir Roger
De Lisle, Jean
Douglas, Thomas, Baron Daer and Shortcleuch, 5th Earl of Selkirk
Finlay, Hugh (?)
Graham, Aaron
Haswell, Robert
Henry, Alexander
Holland, Samuel Johannes
Laforce, René-Hippolyte
Lambert, John
McGillivray, Duncan
Mackenzie, Sir Alexander
Meares, John
Michaux, André
Moody, James
Morse, Robert
Moziño Losada Suárez de Figueroa, José Mariano
Pond, Peter
Portlock, Nathaniel
Smith, Michael
Winslow, Joshua
Wright, Thomas

BLACKS

Byers, Peter, known as Black Peter

George, David

King, Boston

BUSINESS

Ainslie, Thomas
Allan, Ebenezer
Allsopp, George
Antrobus, John
Arnold, Benedict
Askin, John
Baby, François
Belcher, Benjamin
Bell, James
Binney, Jonathan
Black, John
Blackwood, John
Blake, Charles
Booth, Joshua
Botsford, Amos
Boucher, François
Bouchette, Jean-Baptiste
Brehaut, Pierre
Bruneau, Pierre
Bulley, Samuel
Caldwell, Henry

Caldwell, James
Cannon, Edward
Cartier, Jacques
Cartwright, George
Cartwright, Richard
Cazeau, François
Cerré, Jean-Gabriel
Chaboillez, Charles-Jean-Baptiste
Clark, James
Coffin, John
Craigie, John
Cruickshank, Robert
Curtis, James
Dejean, Philippe
De Lisle, Jean
Deschamps, Isaac
Dixon, Charles
Dobie, Richard
Drapeau, Joseph
Dumas, Alexandre
Dun, John

Duncan, Richard
Dunière, Louis
Dunlop, James
Dunn, Thomas
Edwards, Edward
Ellice, Alexander
Elliott, Matthew
Fairfield, William
Finlay, Hugh
Foretier, Pierre
Forsyth, Joseph
Forsyth, William
Forton, Michel
Frobisher, Joseph
Gallop, William
Garland, Charles
Glenie, James
Grant, Alexander
Grant, William (1744–1805)
Grant, William (1743–1810)
Gray, Edward William

INDEX OF IDENTIFICATIONS

Gray, Ralph
Gregory, John
Guy, Pierre
Hamilton, Robert
Hanna, James G.
Hardy, George
Harris, John
Hart, Samuel
Hatt, Richard
Hazen, Moses
Hazen, William
Heron, Samuel
Hildrith, Isaac
Hodgson, Robert
Holland, Samuel Johannes
Huguet, *dit* Latour, Pierre
Humphreys, James
Hutchings, Richard
Jessup, Edward
Jones, Ephraim
Jones, John
Laforce, René-Hippolyte
Lebrun de Duplessis, Jean-Baptiste
Le Comte Dupré, Jean-Baptiste
Lee, Samuel
Lees, John
Lester, Benjamin
Lester, Robert
Longmore, George
Lynd, David

McGill, James
McNabb, James
McTavish, Simon
Malhiot, François
Marchinton, Philip
Marcoux, Pierre
Martineau, Jérôme
Menut, Alexandre
Mézière, Henry-Antoine
Miles, Abner
Mondelet, Dominique
Montmollin, David-François de
Mortimer, Edward
Mott, Jacob S.
Munn, Alexander
Nevins, Archibald
Newman, Robert
Ogilvy, John
O'Hara, Felix
Ougier, Peter
Pagan, William
Painter, John
Patterson, Robert
Pawling, Benjamin
Périnault, Joseph
Perkins, Simeon
Perley, Israel
Perrault, Jacques-Nicolas
Philipps, John
Pinson, Andrew

Purss, John
Quesnel, Joseph
Robertson, James
Robertson, William
Rollo, James
Rousseaux St John, John Baptist
Roy, Narsise
Ryerse, Samuel
Sales Laterrière, Pierre de
Schurman, William
Scott, Thomas
Slade, Thomas
Stout, Richard
Street, Samuel
Street, Thomas
Taylor, Alexander
Tiffany, Silvester
Tod, James
Todd, Isaac
Trestler, Jean-Joseph
Trottier Desrivières Beaubien,
  Eustache-Ignace
Viger, Denis
Waldron, John
Warren, John
Watson, Sir Brook
Willcocks, Joseph
Willcocks, William
Young, John

EDUCATION

Bossu, *dit* Lyonnais, Pierre-Jacques,
  named Brother Félix
Burke, Edmund (1753–1820)
Champion, Gabriel
Chicoisneau, Jean-Baptiste-Jacques

Fisher, Finlay
Fraser, John
How, Deborah (Cottnam)
Man, James
Powell, Charles Stuart

Smith, Michael
Spark, Alexander
Tanswell, James
Wright, George

ENGINEERS

Bruyeres, Ralph Henry
Glenie, James

Holland, Samuel Johannes
Morse, Robert

Sarrebource de Pontleroy, Nicolas
Skinner, Thomas

EXPLORERS

Alcalá-Galiano, Dionisio
Billings, Joseph
Gray, Robert

Haenke, Tadeo
Henry, Alexander
MacKay, Alexander

Mackenzie, Sir Alexander
Malaspina, Alejandro
Pond, Peter

FUR TRADERS

Adhémar, *dit* Saint-Martin, Toussaint-
    Antoine
Ainsse, Joseph-Louis
Aird, James
Askin, John
Blondeau, Maurice-Régis
Cadot, Jean-Baptiste
Chaboillez, Charles
Chaboillez, Charles-Jean-Baptiste
Colen, Joseph
Colnett, James
Decoigne, François
Dobie, Richard
Ducharme, Jean-Marie
Frobisher, Joseph
Graham, Andrew

Grant, William (1743–1810)
Gray, Robert
Gregory, John
Gunn, Isabel
Haswell, Robert
Henry, Alexander
Isham, Charles Thomas
Keveny, Owen
Longmoor, Robert
McBeath, George
McDougall, Duncan
McGillivray, Duncan
MacKay, Alexander
McKay, John
Mackenzie, Sir Alexander

MacKenzie, Kenneth
McTavish, Donald
McTavish, Simon
Meares, John
Montour, Nicholas
Pangman, Peter
Périnault, Joseph
Pond, Peter
Portlock, Nathaniel
Ramsay, David
Richards, William
Rousseaux St John, John Baptist
Sayer, John
Testard Louvigny de Montigny, Jean-
    Baptiste-Pierre

INDIAN AFFAIRS

Ainsse, Joseph-Louis
Boucher de Niverville, Joseph
Bunbury, Joseph
Cadot, Jean-Baptiste
Dease, John

Elliott, Matthew
Girty, Simon
McKee, Thomas
Réaume, Charles
Rousseaux St John, John Baptist

Selby, Prideaux
Testard Louvigny de Montigny, Jean-
    Baptiste-Pierre
Thayendanegea (Joseph Brant)

JOURNALISTS

Edwards, Edward
Mézière, Henry-Antoine
Pawling, Benjamin

Spark, Alexander
Tanswell, James
Tiffany, Silvester

Vondenvelden, William
Willcocks, Joseph

LAW

Judges

Allcock, Henry
Ball, Ingram
Berthelot Dartigny, Michel-Amable
Binney, Jonathan
Botsford, Amos
Brenton, James
Burbidge, John
Campbell, Dugald
Cartwright, Richard

Clinch, John
Creighton, John
Curtis, James
Davidson, Arthur
De Bonne, Pierre-Amable
Dejean, Philippe
Deschamps, Isaac
Deschenaux, Pierre-Louis
Dixon, Charles
Duncan, Richard
Dunn, Thomas

Elmsley, John
Garland, Charles
Graham, Aaron
Gray, Robert Isaac Dey
Green, Francis
Hamilton, Robert
Harris, John
Hatt, Richard
Howe, Alexander
Jessen, Dettlieb Christopher
Jessup, Edward

Jones, Ephraim
Lee, Samuel
Lees, John
Ludlow, Gabriel George
Ludlow, George Duncan
McDonell (Aberchalder), John
Millidge, Thomas
Morris, Charles
Mortimer, Edward
O'Hara, Felix
Panet, Jean-Antoine
Panet, Pierre
Panet, Pierre-Louis
Pawling, Benjamin
Perkins, Simeon
Pettit, Nathaniel
Robertson, William
Robinson, Joseph
Routh, Richard
Russell, Peter
Ryerse, Samuel
Smith, William
Spencer, Hazelton
Stewart, Peter
Stout, Richard
Street, Samuel
Taschereau, Gabriel-Elzéar
Upham, Joshua
Welch, Thomas
Willcocks, William
Williams, Jenkin
Winslow, Edward
Winslow, Joshua
Wright, Thomas
Young, John

Justices of the peace

Adhémar, *dit* Saint-Martin, Toussaint-
  Antoine
Ainslie, Thomas
Allan, John
Allsopp, George
Antrobus, John
Askin, John
Baby, François
Binney, Jonathan
Blackwood, John
Blake, Charles
Blondeau, Maurice-Régis
Boisseau, Nicolas-Gaspard
Booth, Joshua
Boucher de Niverville, Joseph
Burbidge, John
Caldwell, James
Cartwright, Richard
Chaboillez, Louis
Clinch, John
Coffin, John
Coffin, Thomas Aston
Creighton, John
Cruickshank, Robert
De Bonne, Pierre-Amable

Dejean, Philippe
Delesdernier, Moses
Deschamps, Isaac
Deschenaux, Pierre-Louis
Dixon, Charles
Doucet, Amable
Duncan, Richard
Dunn, Thomas
Elliott, Matthew
Fairfield, William
Finlay, Hugh
Foretier, Pierre
Forsyth, Joseph
Forsyth, William
Fraser, Malcolm
Frobisher, Joseph
Gallop, William
Garland, Charles
Graham, Aaron
Grant, Alexander
Grant, William (1743–1810)
Grass, Michael
Green, Francis
Hamilton, Robert
Harries, John
Harris, John
Hatt, Richard
Hazen, Moses
Hertel de Rouville, Jean-Baptiste-
  Melchior
Hodgson, Robert
Holland, Samuel Johannes
Howe, Alexander
Humphreys, James
Iredell, Abraham
Jessen, Dettlieb Christopher
Jessup, Edward
Jones, Caleb
Jones, Ephraim
Le Comte Dupré, Jean-Baptiste
Lee, Samuel
Lees, John
Lester, Benjamin
Longmore, George
Ludlow, Gabriel George
McBeath, George
McDonell (Aberchalder), John
McGill, James
McKinnon, Ranald
McNabb, James
McTavish, Simon
Malhiot, François
Marchinton, Philip
Margane de Lavaltrie, Pierre-Paul
Millidge, Thomas
Montour, Nicholas
Moody, James
Morris, Charles
Morris, James Rainstorpe
O'Hara, Felix
Painter, John
Panet, Pierre

Patterson, Robert
Pawling, Benjamin
Périnault, Joseph
Perkins, Simeon
Perley, Israel
Perrault, Jacques-Nicolas
Pettit, Nathaniel
Philipps, John
Robertson, Daniel
Robertson, James
Ryerse, Samuel
Schurman, William
Selby, Prideaux
Spencer, Hazelton
Street, Samuel
Street, Thomas
Taschereau, Gabriel-Elzéar
Taylor, Alexander
Testard Louvigny de Montigny, Jean-
  Baptiste-Pierre
Todd, Isaac
Trottier Desrivières Beaubien,
  Eustache-Ignace
Vondenvelden, William
Waldron, John
Warren, John
Welch, Thomas
Willcocks, William
Williams, Jenkin
Winslow, Joshua
Young, John

Lawyers

Aplin, Joseph
Berthelot Dartigny, Michel-Amable
Botsford, Amos
Brenton, James
Chaboillez, Louis
Clark, James
Davidson, Arthur
De Bonne, Pierre-Amable
Deschenaux, Pierre-Louis
Dumas, Alexandre
Gray, Edward William
Gray, Robert Isaac Dey
Hodgson, Robert
Lebrun de Duplessis, Jean-Baptiste
Macdonell (Collachie), Angus
Macdonell (Greenfield), John
Magowan, Peter
Panet, Jean-Antoine
Panet, Pierre
Panet, Pierre-Louis
Robinson, Joseph
Roe, Walter
Stewart, Charles
Tarieu de Lanaudière, Xavier-Roch
Walker, Thomas
Weekes, William
Wentworth, John
Williams, Jenkin

MARINERS

Boucher, François
Bouchette, Jean-Baptiste
Bulley, Samuel
Colnett, James
Digé, Jean
Frost, James
Gautier, Nicolas

Gray, Robert
Hardy, George
Hutchings, Richard
Laforce, René-Hippolyte
Newman, Robert
Ougier, Peter

Pinson, Andrew
Portlock, Nathaniel
Slade, Thomas
Street, Thomas
Thorn, Jonathan
Waldron, John

MEDICINE

Almon, William James
Badelard, Philippe-Louis-François
Bentom, Clark
Blake, Charles
Caleff, John
Clark, Duncan
Clinch, John

Compain, Pierre-Joseph
Dénéchaud, Jacques
Longmore, George
Mondelet, Dominique
Philipps, John
Piuze, Liveright

Rieutord, Jean-Baptiste
Sales Laterrière, Pierre de
Serres, Alexandre
Smith, William
Suzor, François-Michel
Waldron, John

MISCELLANEOUS

Byers, Peter, known as Black Peter

Pilotte, Angelique

Robichaux, Jean-Baptiste

NATIVE PEOPLES

Abenakis

Atiatoharongwen

Beothuks

Demasduwit

Malecites

Bernard, Noël

Miamis

Michikinakoua

Micmacs

Julien, John

Mohawks

Atiatoharongwen
Deserontyon, John
Thayendanegea (Joseph Brant)

Nootkas

Muquinna

Northern Ojibwas

Zheewegonab

Ojibwas

Chejauk (?)
Kineubenae
Madjeckewiss

Ottawas

Chejauk (?)

Shawnees

Tecumseh
Weyapiersenwah

Sioux

Wahpasha

Wyandots

Myeerah
Stayeghtha

NOTARIES

Berthelot Dartigny, Michel-Amable
Chaboillez, Louis
Dejean, Philippe
De Lisle, Jean
De Lisle, Jean-Guillaume

Deschenaux, Pierre-Louis
Dumas, Alexandre
Faribault, Barthélemy
Gray, Edward William
Lebrun de Duplessis, Jean-Baptiste

Mondelet, Dominique
Panet, Jean-Antoine
Panet, Pierre
Panet, Pierre-Louis

OFFICE HOLDERS

Administrators

Brock, Sir Isaac
Carleton, Guy, 1st Baron Dorchester
Carleton, Thomas
Craig, Sir James Henry
Desbrisay, Thomas
Duckworth, Sir John Thomas
Dunn, Thomas
Fanning, Edmund
Glasgow, George
Gower, Sir Erasmus
Grant, Alexander
Graves, Thomas, 1st Baron Graves
Haldimand, Sir Frederick (Appendix)
Hughes, Sir Richard
Hunter, Peter
Le Maistre, Francis
Lennox, Charles, 4th Duke of
   Richmond and Lennox
Ludlow, Gabriel George
Macarmick, William
Milbanke, Mark
Ogilvie, James
Pickmore, Francis
Prescott, Robert
Prevost, Sir George
Russell, Peter
Semple, Robert
Simcoe, John Graves
Sinclair, Patrick
Townshend, William
Wentworth, Sir John
Winslow, Edward

Officials

Adhémar, *dit* Saint-Martin, Toussaint-
   Antoine
Ainslie, Thomas
Allan, John
Allsopp, George
Antrobus, John
Aplin, Joseph
Askin, John
Baby, François

Baillairgé, Pierre-Florent
Bentley, Elijah
Bentley, John
Binney, Jonathan
Blackwood, John
Blake, Charles
Blondeau, Maurice-Régis
Boisseau, Nicolas-Gaspard
Booth, Joshua
Botsford, Amos
Boucher, François
Boucher de Boucherville, René-
   Amable
Brenton, James
Burbidge, John
Caldwell, Henry
Caldwell, James
Campbell, Dugald
Cartwright, Richard
Chaboillez, Louis
Chandler, Kenelm
Charland, Louis
Clark, James
Clinch, John
Coffin, John
Coffin, Thomas Aston
Craigie, John
Creighton, John
Curtis, James
Cuyler, Abraham Cornelius
De Bonne, Pierre-Amable
Dejean, Philippe
Delesdernier, Moses
Desbrisay, Thomas
Deschamps, Isaac
Deschenaux, Pierre-Louis
Digé, Jean
Dixon, Charles
Doucet, Amable
Douglas, James
Dun, John
Duncan, Henry
Duncan, Richard
Dunn, Thomas
Eddy, Jonathan
Edwards, Edward

England, Richard G.
Fairfield, William
Faribault, Barthélemy
Finlay, Hugh
Foretier, Pierre
Forsyth, Joseph
Forsyth, William
Fraser, Malcolm
Frobisher, Joseph
Frost, James
Gallop, William
Garland, Charles
Gautier, Nicolas
Glenie, James
Graham, Aaron
Grant, Alexander
Grant, William (1744–1805)
Gray, Edward William
Gray, Robert Isaac Dey
Green, Francis
Hamilton, Robert
Hardy, George
Harris, John
Hatt, Richard
Hazen, Moses
Hazen, William
Heron, Samuel
Hertel de Rouville, Jean-Baptiste-
   Melchior
Hodgson, Robert
Holland, Samuel Johannes
Howe, Alexander
Hughes, Sir Richard
Humphreys, James
Iredell, Abraham
Jarvis, William
Jessen, Dettlieb Christopher
Jessup, Edward
Jones, Ephraim
Lebrun de Duplessis, Jean-Baptiste
Le Comte Dupré, Jean-Baptiste
Lees, John
Longmore, George
Ludlow, Gabriel George
Lynd, David
McBeath, George

INDEX OF IDENTIFICATIONS

McDonell (Aberchalder), John
Macdonell (Collachie), Angus
Macdonell (Greenfield), John
McGill, James
McKinnon, Ranald
McKinnon, William
McNabb, Colin
Magowan, Peter
Marcoux, Pierre
Miles, Abner
Millidge, Thomas
Moody, James
Morgann, Maurice
Morris, Charles
Morris, James Rainstorpe
Mott, Jacob S.
Odell, Jonathan
O'Hara, Felix
Painter, John
Panet, Pierre
Panet, Pierre-Louis
Pawling, Benjamin
Périnault, Joseph
Perkins, Simeon

Perley, Israel
Perrault, Jacques-Nicolas
Pettit, Nathaniel
Philipps, John
Powell, Charles Stuart
Purss, John
Robertson, Daniel
Robertson, James
Robertson, William
Roe, Walter
Rousseaux St John, John Baptist
Routh, Richard
Russell, Peter
Ryerse, Samuel
Schurman, William
Scott, Thomas
Selby, Prideaux
Shaw, Æneas
Spencer, Hazelton
Sproule, George
Stewart, Charles
Stout, Richard
Street, Samuel

Tanswell, James
Tarieu de Lanaudière, Charles-Louis
Tarieu de Lanaudière, Xavier-Roch
Taschereau, Gabriel-Elzéar
Taylor, Alexander
Testard Louvigny de Montigny, Jean-Baptiste-Pierre
Tiffany, Silvester
Todd, Isaac
Townshend, William
Vondenvelden, William
Waldron, John
Warren, John
Welch, Thomas
Wentworth, John
Wentworth, Sir John
Willcocks, Joseph
Willcocks, William
Williams, James
Williams, Jenkin
Winslow, Edward
Winslow, Joshua
Young, John

POLITICIANS

Appointed

Allcock, Henry
Allsopp, George
Aplin, Joseph
Baby, François
Ball, Ingram
Binney, Jonathan
Blackwood, John
Boucher de Boucherville, René-Amable
Brenton, James
Caldwell, Henry
Cartwright, Richard
Cossit, Ranna
Craigie, John
Creighton, John
Cuyler, Abraham Cornelius
De Bonne, Pierre-Amable
DeLancey, James
Desbrisay, Thomas
Deschamps, Isaac
Duncan, Henry
Dunn, Thomas
Elmsley, John
Finlay, Hugh
Forsyth, William
Grant, Alexander
Hamilton, Robert
Hazen, William
Hertel de Rouville, Jean-Baptiste-Melchior

Holland, Samuel Johannes
Howe, Alexander
Juchereau Duchesnay, Antoine
Le Comte Dupré, Jean-Baptiste
Lees, John
Le Moyne de Longueuil, Joseph-Dominique-Emmanuel
Ludlow, Gabriel George
Ludlow, George Duncan
McGill, James
McKinnon, William
Morris, Charles
Pagan, William
Panet, Jean-Antoine
Panet, Pierre-Louis
Perrault, Jacques-Nicolas
Robertson, William
Robinson, Joseph
Russell, Peter
Selby, Prideaux
Shaw, Æneas
Smith, William
Sproule, George
Stewart, Peter
Stout, Richard
Tarieu de Lanaudière, Charles-Louis
Taschereau, Gabriel-Elzéar
Townshend, William
Upham, Joshua
Wentworth, John
Williams, Jenkin
Winslow, Edward

Wright, Thomas
Young, John

Elected

Allan, John
Allcock, Henry
Aplin, Joseph
Barnes, John
Belcher, Benjamin
Berthelot Dartigny, Michel-Amable
Binney, Jonathan
Black, John
Blackwood, John
Booth, Joshua
Botsford, Amos
Brehaut, Pierre
Brenton, James
Bruneau, Pierre
Burbidge, John
Cartier, Jacques
Chaboillez, Louis
Craigie, John
Creighton, John
Curtis, James
De Bonne, Pierre-Amable
DeLancey, James
Deschamps, Isaac
Digé, Jean
Dixon, Charles
Drapeau, Joseph
Ducharme, Jean-Marie

INDEX OF IDENTIFICATIONS

Dumas, Alexandre
Dunière, Louis
Elliott, Matthew
Fairfield, William
Frobisher, Joseph
Glenie, James
Grant, William (1744–1805)
Gray, Ralph
Gray, Robert Isaac Dey
Guy, Étienne
Harris, John
Hart, Samuel
Hatt, Richard
Hertel de Rouville, Jean-Baptiste-
 Melchior
Hodgson, Robert
Howe, Alexander
Humphreys, James
Jessen, Dettlieb Christopher
Jones, Ephraim
Jones, John
Juchereau Duchesnay, Antoine
Lawson, David
Lee, Samuel

Lees, John
Lester, Robert
Lynd, David
McBeath, George
McDonell (Aberchalder), John
Macdonell (Collachie), Angus
Macdonell (Greenfield), John
McGill, James
McKee, Thomas
McNabb, James
Magowan, Peter
Malhiot, François
Marchinton, Philip
Margane de Lavaltrie, Pierre-Paul
Martineau, Jérôme
Menut, Alexandre
Millidge, Thomas
Montour, Nicholas
Moody, James
Morris, Charles
Mortimer, Edward
Pagan, William
Panet, Jean-Antoine
Panet, Pierre

Panet, Pierre-Louis
Pawling, Benjamin
Périnault, Joseph
Perkins, Simeon
Perrault, Jacques-Nicolas
Pettit, Nathaniel
Philipps, John
Robinson, Joseph
Schurman, William
Spencer, Hazelton
Stewart, Charles
Street, Samuel
Taschereau, Gabriel-Elzéar
Taylor, Alexander
Tod, James
Trestler, Jean-Joseph
Viger, Denis
Vondenvelden, William
Walker, Thomas
Weekes, William
Willcocks, Joseph
Winslow, Joshua
Wright, Thomas
Young, John

RELIGIOUS

Baptists

Bentley, Elijah
George, David
Hibbard, Jedediah

Church of England

Andrews, Samuel
Bailey, Jacob
Balfour, James
Beardsley, John
Bradford, Richard
Byles, Mather
Clinch, John
Cossit, Ranna
Harries, John
Inglis, Charles
Langhorn, John
Montmollin, David-François de
Mountain, Jehosaphat
Odell, Jonathan
Panton, George
Scott, Thomas Charles Heslop
Stuart, John
Viets, Roger
Wiswall, John
Wright, George

Congregationalists

Noble, Seth
Scott, Jonathan

German Reformed

Comingo, Bruin Romkes

Jews

Cohen, Jacob Raphael

Methodists

King, Boston
Man, James
Marchinton, Philip

Moravians

Turner, William
Zeisberger, David

Presbyterians

Bentom, Clark (?)
Bethune, John
Collver, Jabez
Dun, John
Gillmore, George
Spark, Alexander

Roman Catholics

Capuchins

Jones, James

Congregation of Notre-Dame

Brunet, *dit* L'Estang, Véronique,
 named Sainte-Rose
Compain, Marie-Louise, named Saint-
 Augustin
Raizenne, Marie, named Saint-Ignace

Dominicans

Burke, Edmund (fl. 1785–1801)

Franciscans

Lambert, Patrick
O'Donel, James Louis

*Hospital nuns of the Hôpital Général
(Quebec)*

Payen de Noyan, Marie-Catherine,
 named de Saint-Alexis
Melançon, Marie-Vénérande, named
 de Sainte-Claire
Parent, Marie-Geneviève, named de
 Saint-François d'Assise

Recollets

Bossu, *dit* Lyonnais, Pierre-Jacques,
 named Brother Félix
Demers, Louis

INDEX OF IDENTIFICATIONS

Religious Hospitallers of St Joseph

Céloron, Marie-Catherine-Françoise

Seculars

Allain, Jean-Baptiste
Bertrand, Joseph-Laurent
Bossu, *dit* Lyonnais, Pierre-Jacques,
    named Brother Félix
Burke, Edmund (1753–1820)
Cassiet, Pierre
Champion, Gabriel
Cherrier, François
Collet, Charles-Ange

Compain, Pierre-Joseph
Conefroy, Pierre
Denaut, Pierre
Gibault, Pierre
Gravé de La Rive, Henri-François
Lahaille, Jean-Baptiste
MacDonell of Scothouse, Alexander
Maillou, Benjamin-Nicolas
Pichard, Amable
Pouget, Jean-Baptiste-Noël

*Sisters of Charity of the Hôpital
Général (Montreal)*

Dussaus, Marie-Angélique

Sulpicians

Borneuf, Joseph
Chicoisneau, Jean-Baptiste-Jacques
Ecuier, Charles
Huet de La Valinière, Pierre
Leclerc, Michel
Poncin, Claude

Ursulines

Davanne, Marguerite, named de Saint-
    Louis de Gonzague

SCIENTISTS

Banks, Sir Joseph
Graham, Andrew
Haenke, Tadeo

Masson, Francis
Michaux, André

Moziño Losada Suárez de Figueroa,
    José Mariano
Wright, Thomas

SURVEYORS

Bédard, Jean-Baptiste
Campbell, Dugald
Chabert de Cogolin, Joseph-Bernard
    de, Marquis de Chabert
Charland, Louis
Guy, Étienne
Hibbard, Jedediah

Hildrith, Isaac
Holland, Samuel Johannes
Iredell, Abraham
McNiff, Patrick
Millidge, Thomas
Morris, Charles
Patterson, Robert

Perley, Israel
Plaw, John
Pond, Peter
Sproule, George
Vondenvelden, William
Welch, Thomas
Wright, Thomas

WOMEN

Boudreau, Cécile (Pitre; Pellerin)
Brunet, *dit* L'Estang, Véronique,
    named Sainte-Rose
Céloron, Marie-Catherine-Françoise
Compain, Marie-Louise, named Saint-
    Augustin
Davanne, Marguerite, named de Saint-
    Louis de Gonzague
Demasduwit
Dussaus, Marie-Angélique

Gunn, Isabel
How, Deborah (Cottnam)
MacDonald of Glenaladale, Helen
    (MacDonald)
Massow, Friederike Charlotte Louise
    von (Riedesel, Freifrau zu
    Eisenbach)
Melançon, Marie-Vénérande, named
    de Sainte-Claire

Osborn, Mary (London)
Parent, Marie-Geneviève, named de
    Saint-François d'Assise
Payen de Noyan, Marie-Catherine,
    named de Saint-Alexis
Pilotte, Angelique
Raizenne, Marie, named Saint-Ignace
Ruckle, Barbara (Heck)
Sawtelle, Jemima (Phipps; Howe; Tute)

GEOGRAPHICAL INDEX

CANADA

Alberta

British Columbia
Mainland
Vancouver Island

Manitoba

New Brunswick

Newfoundland and Labrador
Labrador
Newfoundland

Northwest Territories

Nova Scotia
Cape Breton Island
Mainland

Ontario
Centre
East
Niagara
North
Southwest

Prince Edward Island

Quebec
Bas-Saint-Laurent–Gaspésie/
   Côte-Nord
Montréal/Outaouais
Nord-Ouest/Saguenay–Lac-Saint-Jean/
   Nouveau-Québec
Québec
Trois-Rivières/Cantons-de-l'Est

Saskatchewan

OTHER COUNTRIES

PLACE OF BIRTH

Channel Islands
Czechoslovakia
Federal Republic of Germany
France
German Democratic Republic
Gibraltar
Ireland
Italy
Mexico
Netherlands
Poland

Republic of Ireland
Spain
Switzerland
United Kingdom
United States of America

CAREER

Corsica
France
Saint-Pierre and Miquelon
Spain
United States of America

ONTARIO

V North

I East
II Centre
III Niagara
IV Southwest
V North

QUEBEC

I

V

II

III

IV

I Bas-Saint-Laurent–Gaspésie/Côte-Nord
II Québec
III Trois-Rivières/Cantons-de-l'Est
IV Montréal/Outaouais
V Nord-Ouest/Saguenay–Lac-Saint-Jean/
   Nouveau-Québec

Geographical Index

The Geographical Index, in two parts, provides a regional breakdown of subjects of biographies according to place of birth and according to career. Each part has two sub-sections: Canada and Other Countries.

For the purposes of this index, Canada is represented by the present provinces and territories, listed alphabetically. (The Yukon Territory does not appear here, however, since no one in volume V lived in or visited the region.) Five provinces are further subdivided. British Columbia, Newfoundland and Labrador, and Nova Scotia each have two subdivisions. Ontario and Quebec appear in five subdivisions as shown on the maps; those for Quebec are based on the administrative regions defined by the Direction général du domaine territorial. The section Other Countries is based for the most part on modern political divisions, but overseas territories of European countries are listed separately. Only the United Kingdom is subdivided.

Place of Birth. This part of the index lists subjects of biographies by their birthplace, whether in Canada or elsewhere. Where only a strong probability of birth in a particular region exists, the name of the subject is followed by a question mark. It should be noted that the use of modern political divisions produces some anachronisms; a person born in Moravia, for example, appears under "Czechoslovakia." To accommodate those individuals known only to have been born in Ireland, a separate listing under "Ireland" has been provided; readers interested in Irish personalities or in immigration from Ireland should consult also "Republic of Ireland" and "United Kingdom: Northern Ireland."

Career. Subjects appear here on the basis of their activity as adults. Places of education, retirement, and death have not been considered. Persons whose functions gave them jurisdiction over several regions, such as a bishop or governor, are listed according to their seat of office, but their activities as described in the biographies have also been taken into consideration. Merchants appear only in the area of the primary location of their business, unless the biographies indicate active personal involvement in other regions. Explorers are found in the areas they discovered or visited. Only individuals who were born in the territory of present-day Canada and whose lives took them elsewhere are listed in the section Other Countries; they are listed under the country or countries in which they had a career or were active.

PLACE OF BIRTH

Canada

MANITOBA

Isham, Charles Thomas (?)

NEWFOUNDLAND AND LABRADOR

Newfoundland

Garland, Charles   Hutchings, Richard (?)

NOVA SCOTIA

Mainland

Bastarache, *dit* Basque, Michel
Boudreau, Cécile (Pitre; Pellerin)
Cormier, Pierre
Doucet, Amable

Gautier, Nicolas
How, Deborah (Cottnam)
Howe, Alexander

Melançon, Marie-Vénérande, named
de Sainte-Claire
Robichaux, Jean-Baptiste
Thibodeau, Simon

ONTARIO

East

Boucher de Boucherville, René-
Amable
Seely, Joseph

North

Richards, William

PRINCE EDWARD ISLAND

Byers, Peter, known as Black Peter

Mercure, Louis

QUEBEC

Bas-Saint-Laurent–Gaspésie/Côte-Nord

Gallant, Xavier, known as Pinquin

Montréal/Outaouais

Adhémar, *dit* Saint-Martin, Toussaint-
Antoine
Arnoldi, Michael
Baby, François
Bertrand, Joseph-Laurent
Blondeau, Maurice-Régis
Boucher de Niverville, Joseph
Brunet, *dit* L'Estang, Véronique,
named Sainte-Rose
Bruyeres, Ralph Henry
Céloron, Marie-Catherine-Françoise
Cerré, Jean-Gabriel
Chaboillez, Charles
Chaboillez, Louis
Cherrier, François
Compain, Marie-Louise, named Saint-
Augustin

Compain, Pierre-Joseph
De Bonne, Pierre-Amable
Decoigne, François
Denaut, Pierre
Ducharme, Jean-Marie
Ecuier, Charles
Foretier, Pierre
Gibault, Pierre
Guy, Étienne
Guy, Pierre
Laforce, René-Hippolyte
Leclerc, Michel
Le Comte Dupré, Jean-Baptiste
Le Moyne de Longueuil, Joseph-
Dominique-Emmanuel
Liénard de Beaujeu de Villemonde,
Louis
Malhiot, François
Margane de Lavaltrie, Pierre-Paul
Mézière, Henry-Antoine
Panet, Pierre-Louis
Périnault, Joseph
Pouget, Jean-Baptiste-Noël
Raizenne, Marie, named Saint-Ignace

Rousseaux St John, John Baptist
Roy, Narsise
Testard Louvigny de Montigny, Jean-
Baptiste-Pierre
Trottier Desrivières Beaubien,
Eustache-Ignace
Viger, Denis

Québec

Baillairgé, Pierre-Florent
Bédard, Jean-Baptiste
Bedout, Jacques
Berthelot Dartigny, Michel-Amable
Boisseau, Nicolas-Gaspard
Borneuf, Joseph
Bossu, *dit* Lyonnais, Pierre-Jacques,
named Brother Félix
Boucher, François
Bouchette, Jean-Baptiste
Bruneau, Pierre
Cartier, Jacques
Charland, Louis
Conefroy, Pierre

Cressé, Pierre-Michel
Davanne, Marguerite, named de Saint-Louis de Gonzague
Demers, Louis
Deschenaux, Pierre-Louis
Drapeau, Joseph
Dunière, Louis
Dussaus, Marie-Angélique
Émond, Pierre
Forton, Michel
Gosselin, Clément
Huguet, *dit* Latour, Pierre

Irumberry de Salaberry, Edouard-Alphonse d'
Juchereau Duchesnay, Antoine
Maillou, Benjamin-Nicolas
Marcoux, Pierre
Martineau, Jérôme
Panet, Jean-Antoine
Parent, Marie-Geneviève, named de Saint-François d'Assise
Payen de Noyan, Marie-Catherine, named de Saint-Alexis
Perrault, Jacques-Nicolas
Ranvoyzé, François

Renaud d'Avène Des Méloizes, Nicolas
Tarieu de Lanaudière, Charles-Louis
Tarieu de Lanaudière, Xavier-Roch
Taschereau, Gabriel-Elzéar

Trois-Rivières/Cantons-de-l'Est

Cadot, Jean-Baptiste
Clark, James (?)
Hertel de Rouville, Jean-Baptiste-Melchior

Other Countries

CHANNEL ISLANDS

Brehaut, Pierre

Brock, Sir Isaac

Le Maistre, Francis

CZECHOSLOVAKIA

Haenke, Tadeo

Zeisberger, David

FEDERAL REPUBLIC OF GERMANY

Berczy, William
Jessen, Dettlieb Christopher

Trestler, Jean-Joseph

Vondenvelden, William

FRANCE

Allain, Jean-Baptiste
Badelard, Philippe-Louis-François
Baillairgé, Jean
Bougainville, Louis-Antoine de, Comte de Bougainville
Carrefour de La Pelouze, Pierre-Joseph
Cassiet, Pierre
Cazeau, François
Chabert de Cogolin, Joseph-Bernard de, Marquis de Chabert
Champion, Gabriel

Chicoisneau, Jean-Baptiste-Jacques
Dejean, Philippe
De Lisle, Jean
Dénéchaud, Jacques
Digé, Jean
Dumas, Alexandre
Faribault, Barthélemy
Grass, Michael
Gravé de La Rive, Henri-François
Guernon, *dit* Belleville, François
Guitet, Claude

Heer, Louis-Chrétien de
Huet de La Valinière, Pierre
Jacson, Antoine
Lahaille, Jean-Baptiste
Lebrun de Duplessis, Jean-Baptiste
Liébert, Philippe
Menut, Alexandre
Michaux, André
Mondelet, Dominique
Natte, *dit* Marseille, Jean-Sébastien
Olabaratz, Jean d'

971

GEOGRAPHICAL INDEX

Panet, Pierre
Pichard, Amable
Plantavit de Lapause de Margon, Jean-
  Guillaume

Poncin, Claude
Quesnel, Joseph
Rieutord, Jean-Baptiste
Sales Laterrière, Pierre de

Sarrebource de Pontleroy, Nicolas
Serres, Alexandre
Suzor, François-Michel

GERMAN DEMOCRATIC REPUBLIC

Massow, Friederike Charlotte Louise
  von (Riedesel, Freifrau zu
  Eisenbach)

GIBRALTAR

Belcher, Benjamin

Craig, Sir James Henry

Skinner, Robert Pringle

IRELAND

Caldwell, Henry
Cannon, Edward
Carleton, Thomas

Hanna, James G.
McNiff, Patrick
Magowan, Peter (?)

O'Hara, Felix
Todd, Isaac
Weekes, William

ITALY

Malaspina, Alejandro

MEXICO

Moziño Losada Suárez de Figueroa,
  José Mariano

NETHERLANDS

Comingo, Bruin Romkes

Holland, Samuel Johannes

POLAND

Piuze, Liveright

REPUBLIC OF IRELAND

Burke, Edmund (fl. 1785–1801)
Burke, Edmund (1753–1820)
Dease, John
Desbrisay, Thomas
Elliott, Matthew
England, Richard G.
Hall, Sir Robert

Inglis, Charles
Jones, James
Keveny, Owen
Lambert, Patrick
Lester, Robert
Nevins, Archibald
O'Donel, James Louis

Ramage, John
Ruckle, Barbara (Heck)
Russell, Peter
Sproule, George
Willcocks, Joseph
Willcocks, William

SPAIN

Alberni, Pedro de

Alcalá-Galiano, Dionisio

Cardero, Manuel José Antonio

SWITZERLAND

Delesdernier, Moses

Haldimand, Sir Frederick (Appendix)

Montmollin, David-François de

UNITED KINGDOM

Barnes, John (?)

England

Allcock, Henry
Allsopp, George
Antrobus, John (?)
Ball, Ingram
Banks, Sir Joseph
Bell, James (?)
Bentley, John
Bentom, Clark
Billings, Joseph (?)
Blackwood, John (?)
Blake, Charles
Bradford, Richard
Bulley, Samuel

Burbidge, John
Burn, William
Cartwright, George
Chandler, Kenelm
Clinch, John
Colen, Joseph
Colnett, James
Creighton, John
Curtis, Sir Roger
Davies, Thomas
Dixon, Charles
Duckworth, Sir John Thomas
Duncan, Henry
Duncan, Richard
Dunn, Thomas
Edward Augustus, Duke of Kent and
    Strathearn

Elmsley, John
Field, Robert
Frobisher, Joseph
Frost, James (?)
Graves, Thomas, 1st Baron Graves
Gray, Edward William
Gregory, John
Hardy, George
Hart, Samuel (?)
Hatt, Richard
Hildrith, Isaac
Hodgson, Robert
Hughes, Sir Richard
Lambert, John
Lennox, Charles, 4th Duke of Rich-
    mond and Lennox
Lester, Benjamin

Macarmick, William
Marchinton, Philip
Mathews, Robert
Milbanke, Mark
Morgann, Maurice
Morse, Robert
Mountain, Jehosaphat
Newman, Robert
Painter, John
Pickmore, Francis (?)
Pinson, Andrew
Plaw, John
Portlock, Nathaniel
Powell, Charles Stuart
Prescott, Robert
Roe, Walter
Routh, Richard
Scott, Thomas
Scott, Thomas Charles Heslop
Selby, Prideaux
Simcoe, John Graves
Skerrett, John
Skinner, Thomas
Slade, Thomas
Smith, William
Smythe, Sir Hervey
Street, Thomas
Tanswell, James
Turner, William
Waldron, John
Watson, Sir Brook
Wright, Thomas (?)
Yeo, Sir James Lucas

Northern Ireland

Askin, John
Carleton, Guy, 1st Baron Dorchester
Gillmore, George
McNutt, Alexander (?)
Wright, George

Scotland

Ainslie, Thomas
Aird, James

Allan, John
Balfour, James
Bethune, John
Black, John
Campbell, Dugald
Clark, Duncan
Craigie, John
Cruickshank, Robert (?)
Davidson, Arthur
Dobie, Richard
Douglas, James
Douglas, Thomas, Baron Daer and
    Shortcleuch, 5th Earl of Selkirk
Dun, John
Dunlop, James
Ellice, Alexander
Finlay, Hugh
Fisher, Duncan
Fisher, Finlay
Forsyth, Joseph
Forsyth, William
Fraser, John
Fraser, Malcolm
Glenie, James
Graham, Andrew
Grant, Alexander
Grant, William (1744–1805)
Grant, William (1743–1810)
Gray, Ralph (?)
Gunn, Isabel
Hamilton, Robert
Heron, Samuel
Hunter, Peter
Lawson, David
Lees, John
Longmoor, Robert
Longmore, George
Lynd, David (?)
McBeath, George
MacDonald of Glenaladale, Helen
    (MacDonald)
MacDonald of Glenaladale, John
McDonell (Aberchalder), John
Macdonell (Collachie), Angus
Macdonell (Greenfield), John

MacDonell of Scothouse, Alexander
McDougall, Duncan
McGill, James
McGillivray, Duncan
McKay, John (?)
Mackenzie, Sir Alexander
MacKenzie, Kenneth
McKinnon, Ranald
McKinnon, William
MacMhannain, Calum Bàn
McTavish, Donald
McTavish, Simon
Masson, Francis
Mortimer, Edward
Munn, Alexander
Nairne, John
Ogilvie, James (?)
Ogilvy, John
Pagan, William
Panton, George
Patterson, Robert
Purss, John
Ramsay, David
Robertson, Daniel
Robertson, James
Robertson, William
Rollo, James (?)
Shaw, Æneas
Sinclair, Patrick
Spark, Alexander
Stewart, Charles
Stewart, Peter
Taylor, Alexander
Tod, James (?)
Williams, James
Young, John (?)

Wales

Gower, Sir Erasmus
Harries, John
Langhorn, John
Philipps, John
Townshend, William (?)
Williams, Jenkin

UNITED STATES OF AMERICA

Ainsse, Joseph-Louis
Allan, Ebenezer
Almon, William James
Andrews, Samuel
Aplin, Joseph
Arnold, Benedict
Atiatoharongwen
Bailey, Jacob

Beardsley, John
Bentley, Elijah
Binney, Jonathan
Bisshopp, Cecil
Booth, Joshua
Botsford, Amos
Brenton, James
Bruff, Charles Oliver

Byles, Mather
Caleff, John
Cartwright, Richard
Chaboillez, Charles-Jean-Baptiste
Coffin, John
Coffin, Thomas Aston
Collet, Charles-Ange
Collver, Jabez

Cossit, Ranna
Cuyler, Abraham Cornelius
DeLancey, James
De Lisle, Jean-Guillaume
Deserontyon, John
Eddy, Jonathan
Fairfield, William
Fanning, Edmund
George, David
Girty, Simon
Graham, Aaron
Gray, Robert
Gray, Robert Isaac Dey
Green, Francis
Harris, John
Haswell, Robert
Hazen, Moses
Hazen, William
Hibbard, Jedediah
Humphreys, James
Iredell, Abraham
Jarvis, William
Jessup, Edward
Jones, Caleb
Jones, Ephraim

King, Boston
Lee, Samuel
Ludlow, Gabriel George
Ludlow, George Duncan
MacKay, Alexander
McKee, Thomas
McNabb, Colin
McNabb, James
Man, James
Miles, Abner
Millidge, Thomas
Montour, Nicholas
Moody, James
Morris, Charles
Morris, James Rainstorpe
Mott, Jacob S.
Noble, Seth
Odell, Jonathan
Osborn, Mary (London)
Overholser, Jacob
Pangman, Peter
Pawling, Benjamin
Perkins, Simeon
Perley, Israel
Pettit, Nathaniel

Pond, Peter
Prevost, Sir George
Réaume, Charles
Robinson, Joseph
Ryerse, Samuel
Schurman, William
Scott, Jonathan
Semple, Robert
Smith, Michael
Spencer, Hazelton
Street, Samuel
Stuart, John
Tecumseh (?)
Thayendanegea (Joseph Brant)
Thorn, Jonathan
Tiffany, Silvester
Upham, Joshua
Viets, Roger
Welch, Thomas
Wentworth, John
Wentworth, Sir John
Winslow, Edward
Winslow, Joshua
Wiswall, John

CAREER

Canada

ALBERTA

Decoigne, François
Henry, Alexander
Isham, Charles Thomas
Longmoor, Robert

McGillivray, Duncan
MacKay, Alexander
Mackenzie, Sir Alexander

McTavish, Donald
Pangman, Peter
Pond, Peter

BRITISH COLUMBIA

Mainland

Mackenzie, Sir Alexander

Vancouver Island

Alberni, Pedro de
Alcalá-Galiano, Dionisio

Billings, Joseph
Cardero, Manuel José Antonio
Colnett, James
Gray, Robert
Haenke, Tadeo
Haswell, Robert
MacKay, Alexander

Malaspina, Alejandro
Meares, John
Moziño Losada Suárez de Figueroa,
  José Mariano
Muquinna
Portlock, Nathaniel
Thorn, Jonathan

MANITOBA

Blondeau, Maurice-Régis
Boucher de Niverville, Joseph
Chaboillez, Charles
Colen, Joseph
Decoigne, François
Douglas, Thomas, Baron Daer and
  Shortcleuch, 5th Earl of Selkirk

Graham, Andrew
Henry, Alexander
Isham, Charles Thomas
Keveny, Owen
Longmoor, Robert
McDougall, Duncan

MacKay, Alexander
McKay, John
Montour, Nicholas
Pond, Peter
Semple, Robert

NEW BRUNSWICK

Allan, John
Andrews, Samuel
Arnold, Benedict
Barnes, John
Bastarache, *dit* Basque, Michel
Beardsley, John
Bernard, Noël
Botsford, Amos
Boudreau, Cécile (Pitre; Pellerin)
Byles, Mather
Caleff, John
Campbell, Dugald
Carleton, Thomas
Cormier, Pierre
Davies, Thomas
Delesdernier, Moses
Dixon, Charles
Eddy, Jonathan

Gallop, William
George, David
Glenie, James
Hazen, Moses
Hazen, William
Holland, Samuel Johannes
How, Deborah (Cottnam)
Iredell, Abraham
Jones, Caleb
Julien, John
Lee, Samuel
Liénard de Beaujeu de Villemonde,
  Louis
Ludlow, Gabriel George
Ludlow, George Duncan
McNutt, Alexander
Man, James
Mercure, Louis

Morse, Robert
Mott, Jacob S.
Noble, Seth
Odell, Jonathan
Pagan, William
Perley, Israel
Powell, Charles Stuart
Robichaux, Jean-Baptiste
Robinson, Joseph
Ryerse, Samuel
Shaw, Æneas
Sproule, George
Taylor, Alexander
Upham, Joshua
Welch, Thomas
Winslow, Edward
Winslow, Joshua
Wright, Thomas

NEWFOUNDLAND AND LABRADOR

Labrador

Banks, Sir Joseph
Cartwright, George
Curtis, Sir Roger
Duckworth, Sir John Thomas
Marcoux, Pierre
Pinson, Andrew
Turner, William

Newfoundland

Balfour, James
Banks, Sir Joseph
Berkeley, Sir George Cranfield
Bulley, Samuel

Burke, Edmund (fl. 1785–1801)
Cannon, Edward
Cartwright, George
Chabert de Cogolin, Joseph-Bernard
  de, Marquis de Chabert
Clinch, John
Demasduwit
Duckworth, Sir John Thomas
Garland, Charles
Gower, Sir Erasmus
Graham, Aaron
Graves, Thomas, 1st Baron Graves
Harries, John
Howe, Alexander
Hutchings, Richard
Lambert, Patrick

Lester, Benjamin
Milbanke, Mark
Nevins, Archibald
Newman, Robert
O'Donel, James Louis
Ougier, Peter
Pickmore, Francis
Pinson, Andrew
Routh, Richard
Skerrett, John
Skinner, Robert Pringle
Skinner, Thomas
Slade, Thomas
Street, Thomas
Waldron, John

NORTHWEST TERRITORIES

McDougall, Duncan

Mackenzie, Sir Alexander

NOVA SCOTIA

Cape Breton Island

Allain, Jean-Baptiste
Badelard, Philippe-Louis-François
Ball, Ingram
Burbidge, John
Caldwell, Henry
Caleff, John
Carrefour de La Pelouze, Pierre-Joseph
Chabert de Cogolin, Joseph-Bernard
  de, Marquis de Chabert
Champion, Gabriel
Cossit, Ranna
Cuyler, Abraham Cornelius
Davies, Thomas
Fraser, Malcolm
Gautier, Nicolas
Gray, Ralph
Green, Francis
Hazen, Moses
Holland, Samuel Johannes
Inglis, Charles
Macarmick, William
McKinnon, William
Nairne, John
Ogilvie, James
Olabaratz, Jean d'
Prescott, Robert
Ramsay, David
Sarrebource de Pontleroy, Nicolas
Smith, William
Smythe, Sir Hervey
Sproule, George
Stout, Richard
Winslow, Joshua
Wright, Thomas

Mainland

Ainslie, Thomas
Allan, John
Almon, William James
Aplin, Joseph
Bailey, Jacob
Belcher, Benjamin
Berkeley, Sir George Cranfield
Bethune, John
Binney, Jonathan

Botsford, Amos
Brenton, James
Bruff, Charles Oliver
Burbidge, John
Burke, Edmund (fl. 1785–1801)
Burke, Edmund (1753–1820)
Byles, Mather
Caleff, John
Chabert de Cogolin, Joseph-Bernard
  de, Marquis de Chabert
Clark, Duncan
Coffin, Thomas Aston
Comingo, Bruin Romkes
Cossit, Ranna
Creighton, John
Davies, Thomas
DeLancey, James
Delesdernier, Moses
Deschamps, Isaac
Dixon, Charles
Doucet, Amable
Duncan, Henry
Eddy, Jonathan
Edward Augustus, Duke of Kent and
  Strathearn
Fanning, Edmund
Field, Robert
Forsyth, William
George, David
Gillmore, George
Green, Francis
Harris, John
Hart, Samuel
Hildrith, Isaac
Holland, Samuel Johannes
How, Deborah (Cottnam)
Howe, Alexander
Hughes, Sir Richard
Humphreys, James
Inglis, Charles
Jessen, Dettlieb Christopher
Jones, James
King, Boston
Liénard de Beaujeu de Villemonde,
  Louis
McKinnon, Ranald
McNabb, Colin
McNutt, Alexander

Man, James
Marchinton, Philip
Mercure, Louis
Millidge, Thomas
Moody, James
Morris, Charles
Morris, James Rainstorpe
Morse, Robert
Mortimer, Edward
Ogilvie, James
Panton, George
Patterson, Robert
Perkins, Simeon
Philipps, John
Pichard, Amable
Plaw, John
Powell, Charles Stuart
Prevost, Sir George
Robertson, James
Scott, Jonathan
Skerrett, John
Tanswell, James
Viets, Roger
Watson, Sir Brook
Wentworth, Sir John
Wilkie, William
Winslow, Edward
Winslow, Joshua
Wiswall, John
Wright, George
Wright, Thomas

ONTARIO

Centre

Allcock, Henry
Bentley, Elijah
Berczy, William
Brock, Sir Isaac
Bruyeres, Ralph Henry
Clark, James
Deserontyon, John
Douglas, Thomas, Baron Daer and
    Shortcleuch, 5th Earl of Selkirk
Elmsley, John
Grant, Alexander
Gray, Robert Isaac Dey
Heron, Samuel
Hunter, Peter
Iredell, Abraham
Jarvis, William
Kineubenae
Lennox, Charles, 4th Duke of Rich-
    mond and Lennox
Macdonell (Collachie), Angus
Macdonell (Greenfield), John
McNabb, James
Miles, Abner
Rousseaux St John, John Baptist
Russell, Peter
Selby, Prideaux
Shaw, Æneas
Simcoe, John Graves
Thayendanegea (Joseph Brant)
Weekes, William
Willcocks, Joseph
Willcocks, William
Yeo, Sir James Lucas

East

Atiatoharongwen
Barnes, John
Bethune, John
Booth, Joshua
Bouchette, Jean-Baptiste
Bruyeres, Ralph Henry
Bunbury, Joseph
Cartwright, Richard
Clark, James
Fairfield, William
Forsyth, Joseph
Glenie, James
Grass, Michael
Gray, Robert Isaac Dey
Hall, Sir Robert
Holland, Samuel Johannes
Jessup, Edward
Jones, Ephraim
Laforce, René-Hippolyte

Langhorn, John
McDonell (Aberchalder), John
MacDonell of Scothouse, Alexander
McNabb, James
McNiff, Patrick
McSwiney, Edward
Masson, Francis
Rousseaux St John, John Baptist
Ruckle, Barbara (Heck)
Seely, Joseph
Sinclair, Patrick
Skinner, Robert Pringle
Spencer, Hazelton
Stuart, John
Yeo, Sir James Lucas

Niagara

Bentley, Elijah
Bisshopp, Cecil
Brock, Sir Isaac
Bruyeres, Ralph Henry
Bunbury, Joseph
Burke, Edmund (1753–1820)
Burn, William
Cartwright, Richard
Clark, James
Dease, John
Dun, John
Duncan, Richard
Elliott, Matthew
Hamilton, Robert
Hatt, Richard
Heron, Samuel
Iredell, Abraham
Jarvis, William
Kineubenae
Lennox, Charles, 4th Duke of Rich-
    mond and Lennox
Macdonell (Collachie), Angus
Macdonell (Greenfield), John
McNabb, Colin
Masson, Francis
Osborn, Mary (London)
Overholser, Jacob
Pawling, Benjamin
Pettit, Nathaniel
Pilotte, Angelique
Ramsay, David
Rousseaux St John, John Baptist
Russell, Peter
Simcoe, John Graves
Smith, Michael
Spencer, Hazelton
Street, Samuel
Tiffany, Silvester
Warren, John

Welch, Thomas
Willcocks, Joseph
Willcocks, William
Yeo, Sir James Lucas

North

Cadot, Jean-Baptiste
Chaboillez, Charles-Jean-Baptiste
Chejauk
Dease, John
Decoigne, François
Douglas, Thomas, Baron Daer and
    Shortcleuch, 5th Earl of Selkirk
Graham, Andrew
Gunn, Isabel
Isham, Charles Thomas
Keveny, Owen
Liénard de Beaujeu de Villemonde,
    Louis
McDougall, Duncan
McGillivray, Duncan
MacKay, Alexander
McKay, John
MacKenzie, Kenneth
McTavish, Donald
Madjeckewiss
Masson, Francis
Richards, William
Sayer, John
Sinclair, Patrick
Todd, Isaac
Zheewegonab

Southwest

Adhémar, *dit* Saint-Martin, Toussaint-
    Antoine
Allan, Ebenezer
Askin, John
Brock, Sir Isaac
Burn, William
Collver, Jabez
Douglas, Thomas, Baron Daer and
    Shortcleuch, 5th Earl of Selkirk
Elliott, Matthew
Elmsley, John
England, Richard G.
Girty, Simon
Grant, Alexander
Iredell, Abraham
McKee, Thomas
McNiff, Patrick
Myeerah
Ramsay, David
Réaume, Charles
Roberts, Charles

GEOGRAPHICAL INDEX

Roe, Walter
Rousseaux St John, John Baptist
Ryerse, Samuel
Selby, Prideaux

Stayeghtha
Tecumseh
Testard Louvigny de Montigny, Jean-
  Baptiste-Pierre

Thayendanegea (Joseph Brant)
Welch, Thomas
Zeisberger, David

PRINCE EDWARD ISLAND

Aplin, Joseph
Boucher de Niverville, Joseph
Byers, Peter, known as Black Peter
Cassiet, Pierre
Champion, Gabriel
Curtis, James
Desbrisay, Thomas
Deschamps, Isaac
Douglas, James
Douglas, Thomas, Baron Daer and
  Shortcleuch, 5th Earl of Selkirk
Fanning, Edmund

Gallant, Xavier, known as Pinquin
Gautier, Nicolas
Hardy, George
Hodgson, Robert
Holland, Samuel Johannes
Howe, Alexander
Lawson, David
MacDonald of Glenaladale, Helen
  (MacDonald)
MacDonald of Glenaladale, John
MacMhannain, Calum Bàn
Magowan, Peter

Pichard, Amable
Plaw, John
Robertson, James
Robinson, Joseph
Schurman, William
Stewart, Charles
Stewart, Peter
Townshend, William
Wentworth, John
Williams, James
Wright, Thomas

QUEBEC

Bas-Saint-Laurent–Gaspésie/Côte-Nord

Allain, Jean-Baptiste
Champion, Gabriel
Cormier, Pierre
Gallant, Xavier, known as Pinquin
Gautier, Nicolas
Guitet, Claude
Holland, Samuel Johannes
Jacson, Antoine
Le Maistre, Francis
Longmore, George
Michaux, André
O'Hara, Felix
Perrault, Jacques-Nicolas
Piuze, Liveright
Robichaux, Jean-Baptiste
Sproule, George
Vondenvelden, William
Wright, Thomas

Montréal/Outaouais

Ainsse, Joseph-Louis
Arnold, Benedict
Arnoldi, Michael
Atiatoharongwen
Baby, François
Baillairgé, Pierre-Florent
Barnes, John

Bell, James
Bentley, John
Berczy, William
Bethune, John
Blake, Charles
Blondeau, Maurice-Régis
Borneuf, Joseph
Boucher de Boucherville, René-
  Amable
Boucher de Niverville, Joseph
Bouchette, Jean-Baptiste
Bougainville, Louis-Antoine de,
  Comte de Bougainville
Bradford, Richard
Bruneau, Pierre
Brunet, dit L'Estang, Véronique,
  named Sainte-Rose
Caldwell, James
Carleton, Guy, 1st Baron Dorchester
Carrefour de La Pelouze, Pierre-Joseph
Cartier, Jacques
Cazeau, François
Céloron, Marie-Catherine-Françoise
Cerré, Jean-Gabriel
Chaboillez, Charles
Chaboillez, Charles-Jean-Baptiste
Chaboillez, Louis
Chandler, Kenelm
Charland, Louis
Cherrier, François
Chicoisneau, Jean-Baptiste-Jacques

Clark, James
Cohen, Jacob Raphael
Collet, Charles-Ange
Compain, Marie-Louise, named Saint-
  Augustin
Compain, Pierre-Joseph
Conefroy, Pierre
Cruickshank, Robert
Cuyler, Abraham Cornelius
Davidson, Arthur
Davies, Thomas
De Bonne, Pierre-Amable
De Lisle, Jean
De Lisle, Jean-Guillaume
Demers, Louis
Denaut, Pierre
Deserontyon, John
Dobie, Richard
Ducharme, Jean-Marie
Dunlop, James
Dussaus, Marie-Angélique
Ecuier, Charles
Edwards, Edward
Ellice, Alexander
England, Richard G.
Faribault, Barthélemy
Fisher, Duncan
Fisher, Finlay
Foretier, Pierre
Fraser, Malcolm
Frobisher, Joseph

979

Frost, James
Gillmore, George
Glenie, James
Gosselin, Clément
Grant, William (1744–1805)
Grant, William (1743–1810)
Gravé de La Rive, Henri-François
Gray, Edward William
Gregory, John
Guernon, François, *dit* Belleville
Guy, Étienne
Guy, Pierre
Haldimand, Sir Frederick (Appendix)
Hazen, Moses
Heer, Louis-Chrétien de
Hertel de Rouville, Jean-Baptiste-
  Melchior
Hibbard, Jedediah
Huet de La Valinière, Pierre
Huguet, *dit* Latour, Pierre
Jacson, Antoine
Jessup, Edward
Jones, Ephraim
Juchereau Duchesnay, Antoine
Lambert, John
Lebrun de Duplessis, Jean-Baptiste
Leclerc, Michel
Le Comte Dupré, Jean-Baptiste
Lees, John
Le Moyne de Longueuil, Joseph-
  Dominique-Emmanuel
Lennox, Charles, 4th Duke of Rich-
  mond and Lennox
Liébert, Philippe
Liénard de Beaujeu de Villemonde,
  Louis
McBeath, George
McDonell (Aberchalder), John
Macdonell (Collachie), Angus
MacDonell of Scothouse, Alexander
McGill, James
McGillivray, Duncan
Mackenzie, Sir Alexander
MacKenzie, Kenneth
McTavish, Simon
Maillou, Benjamin-Nicolas
Malhiot, François
Margane de Lavaltrie, Pierre-Paul
Masson, Francis
Massow, Friederike Charlotte Louise
  von (Riedesel, Freifrau zu
  Eisenbach)
Mézière, Henry-Antoine
Michaux, André
Mondelet, Dominique
Montour, Nicholas
Mountain, Jehosaphat
Nairne, John
Ogilvy, John
Panet, Jean-Antoine
Panet, Pierre
Panet, Pierre-Louis

Pangman, Peter
Périnault, Joseph
Plantavit de Lapause de Margon,
  Jean-Guillaume
Pond, Peter
Pouget, Jean-Baptiste-Noël
Quesnel, Joseph
Raizenne, Marie, named Saint-Ignace
Ramage, John
Roberts, Charles
Robertson, Daniel
Robertson, William
Roe, Walter
Rollo, James
Roy, Narsise
Sales Laterrière, Pierre de
Sawtelle, Jemima (Phipps; Howe; Tute)
Sayer, John
Scott, Thomas Charles Heslop
Serres, Alexandre
Spencer, Hazelton
Stuart, John
Suzor, François-Michel
Testard Louvigny de Montigny, Jean-
  Baptiste-Pierre
Thibodeau, Simon
Todd, Isaac
Trestler, Jean-Joseph
Trottier Desrivières Beaubien,
  Eustache-Ignace
Viger, Denis
Walker, Thomas

**Nord-Ouest/Saguenay–Lac-
Saint-Jean/Nouveau-Québec**

Gunn, Isabel
McDougall, Duncan
Michaux, André

Québec

Ainslie, Thomas
Ainsse, Joseph-Louis
Allcock, Henry
Allsopp, George
Antrobus, John
Arnold, Benedict
Atiatoharongwen
Baby, François
Badelard, Philippe-Louis-François
Baillairgé, Jean
Baillairgé, Pierre-Florent
Barnes, John
Bédard, Jean-Baptiste
Bentley, John
Bentom, Clark
Berczy, William
Berthelot Dartigny, Michel-Amable
Bertrand, Joseph-Laurent
Black, John
Blackwood, John

Blake, Charles
Boisseau, Nicolas-Gaspard
Borneuf, Joseph
Bossu, *dit* Lyonnais, Pierre-Jacques,
  named Brother Félix
Boucher, François
Boucher de Boucherville, René-
  Amable
Boucher de Niverville, Joseph
Bouchette, Jean-Baptiste
Bougainville, Louis-Antoine de,
  Comte de Bougainville
Brehaut, Pierre
Brock, Sir Isaac
Bruneau, Pierre
Brunet, *dit* L'Estang, Véronique,
  named Sainte-Rose
Bruyeres, Ralph Henry
Burke, Edmund (1753–1820)
Caldwell, Henry
Campbell, Dugald
Cannon, Edward
Carleton, Guy, 1st Baron Dorchester
Carleton, Thomas
Carrefour de La Pelouze, Pierre-Joseph
Cartier, Jacques
Chandler, Kenelm
Charland, Louis
Cherrier, François
Coffin, John
Coffin, Thomas Aston
Collet, Charles-Ange
Compain, Marie-Louise, named Saint-
  Augustin
Compain, Pierre-Joseph
Conefroy, Pierre
Cormier, Pierre
Craig, Sir James Henry
Craigie, John
Cuyler, Abraham Cornelius
Davanne, Marguerite, named de Saint-
  Louis de Gonzague
Davidson, Arthur
Davies, Thomas
Dease, John
De Bonne, Pierre-Amable
Demers, Louis
Denaut, Pierre
Dénéchaud, Jacques
Deschenaux, Pierre-Louis
Deserontyon, John
Digé, Jean
Drapeau, Joseph
Dumas, Alexandre
Dunière, Louis
Dunlop, James
Dunn, Thomas
Ecuier, Charles
Edward Augustus, Duke of Kent and
  Strathearn
Elmsley, John
Émond, Pierre

England, Richard G.
Faribault, Barthélemy
Finlay, Hugh
Forton, Michel
Fraser, John
Fraser, Malcolm
Frost, James
Gibault, Pierre
Gillmore, George
Glasgow, George
Gosselin, Clément
Grant, William (1744–1805)
Gravé de La Rive, Henri-François
Gray, Ralph
Green, Francis
Guitet, Claude
Haldimand, Sir Frederick (Appendix)
Hanna, James G.
Hazen, Moses
Heer, Louis-Chrétien de
Holland, Samuel Johannes
Huet de La Valinière, Pierre
Hunter, Peter
Jacson, Antoine
Jones, John
Juchereau Duchesnay, Antoine
Laforce, René-Hippolyte
Lahaille, Jean-Baptiste
Lambert, John
Lebrun de Duplessis, Jean-Baptiste
Leclerc, Michel
Le Comte Dupré, Jean-Baptiste
Lees, John
Le Maistre, Francis
Le Moyne de Longueuil, Joseph-
 Dominique-Emmanuel
Lennox, Charles, 4th Duke of Rich-
 mond and Lennox
Lester, Robert
Liénard de Beaujeu de Villemonde,
 Louis
Longmore, George
Lynd, David
Macdonell (Collachie), Angus
MacDonell of Scothouse, Alexander
Marcoux, Pierre
Margane de Lavaltrie, Pierre-Paul
Martineau, Jérôme
Massow, Friederike Charlotte Louise

von (Riedesel, Freifrau zu
 Eisenbach)
Mathews, Robert
Melançon, Marie-Vénérande, named
 de Sainte-Claire
Menut, Alexandre
Mercure, Louis
Michaux, André
Mondelet, Dominique
Montmollin, David-François de
Morgann, Maurice
Mountain, Jehosaphat
Munn, Alexander
Nairne, John
Natte, *dit* Marseille, Jean-Sébastien
Painter, John
Panet, Jean-Antoine
Panet, Pierre
Panet, Pierre-Louis
Parent, Marie-Geneviève, named de
 Saint-François d'Assise
Payen de Noyan, Marie-Catherine,
 named de Saint-Alexis
Perrault, Jacques-Nicolas
Pichard, Amable
Piuze, Liveright
Plantavit de Lapause de Margon, Jean-
 Guillaume
Pouget, Jean-Baptiste-Noël
Prescott, Robert
Prevost, Sir George
Purss, John
Raizenne, Marie, named Saint-Ignace
Ramsay, David
Ranvoyzé, François
Renaud d'Avène Des Méloizes,
 Nicolas
Rieutord, Jean-Baptiste
Sales Laterrière, Pierre de
Sarrebource de Pontleroy, Nicolas
Scott, Thomas
Sinclair, Patrick
Skinner, Robert Pringle
Smythe, Sir Hervey
Spark, Alexander
Suzor, François-Michel
Tanswell, James
Tarieu de Lanaudière, Charles-Louis

Tarieu de Lanaudière, Xavier-Roch
Taschereau, Gabriel-Elzéar
Thibodeau, Simon
Tod, James
Townshend, George, 4th Viscount and
 1st Marquess Townshend
Trahan, Grégoire, known as Gregory
 Strahan
Vondenvelden, William
Walker, Thomas
Watson, Sir Brook
Williams, Jenkin
Winslow, Joshua
Wright, Thomas
Young, John

Trois-Rivières/Cantons-de-l'Est

Antrobus, John
Baby, François
Bertrand, Joseph-Laurent
Boucher de Niverville, Joseph
Boudreau, Cécile (Pitre; Pellerin)
Campbell, James
Carleton, Guy, 1st Baron Dorchester
Cohen, Jacob Raphael
Cressé, Pierre-Michel
De Bonne, Pierre-Amable
Demers, Louis
Deschenaux, Pierre-Louis
Dumas, Alexandre
Ecuier, Charles
Faribault, Barthélemy
Grant, William (1743–1810)
Haldimand, Sir Frederick (Appendix)
Lambert, John
Longmore, George
Maillou, Benjamin-Nicolas
Massow, Friederike Charlotte Louise
 von (Riedesel, Freifrau zu
 Eisenbach)
Montour, Nicholas
Mountain, Jehosaphat
Pouget, Jean-Baptiste-Noël
Rieutord, Jean-Baptiste
Sales Laterrière, Pierre de
Sawtelle, Jemima (Phipps; Howe; Tute)
Serres, Alexandre

SASKATCHEWAN

Cadot, Jean-Baptiste
Chaboillez, Charles
Decoigne, François
Gregory, John

Isham, Charles Thomas
Longmoor, Robert
MacKay, Alexander
Mackenzie, Sir Alexander

McTavish, Donald
Montour, Nicholas
Pangman, Peter
Pond, Peter

Other Countries

CORSICA

Hertel de Rouville, Jean-Baptiste-
  Melchior

FRANCE

Baby, François
Bedout, Jacques
Hertel de Rouville, Jean-Baptiste-
  Melchior
Le Moyne de Longueuil, Joseph-
  Dominique-Emmanuel
Margane de Lavaltrie, Pierre-Paul
Mézière, Henry-Antoine
Renaud d'Avène Des Méloizes, Nicolas
Tarieu de Lanaudière, Charles-Louis

SAINT-PIERRE AND MIQUELON

Gautier, Nicolas

SPAIN

Irumberry de Salaberry, Édouard-
  Alphonse d'

UNITED STATES OF AMERICA

Adhémar, *dit* Saint-Martin, Toussaint-
  Antoine
Bedout, Jacques
Boucher de Boucherville, René-
  Amable
Boucher de Niverville, Joseph
Cadot, Jean-Baptiste
Cerré, Jean-Gabriel
Ducharme, Jean-Marie
Foretier, Pierre
Gibault, Pierre
Gosselin, Clément
Juchereau Duchesnay, Antoine
Laforce, René-Hippolyte
Le Moyne de Longueuil, Joseph-
  Dominique-Emmanuel
Liénard de Beaujeu de Villemonde,
  Louis
Mézière, Henry-Antoine
Périnault, Joseph
Renaud d'Avène Des Méloizes, Nicolas
Tarieu de Lanaudière, Charles-Louis
Testard Louvigny de Montigny, Jean-
  Baptiste-Pierre
Trahan, Grégoire, known as Gregory
  Strahan

NOMINAL INDEX

VOLUME I	1000–1700
VOLUME II	1701–1740
VOLUME III	1741–1770
VOLUME IV	1771–1800
VOLUME V	1801–1820
VOLUME VI	1821–1835
VOLUME VII	1836–1850
VOLUME VIII	1851–1860
VOLUME IX	1861–1870
VOLUME X	1871–1880
VOLUME XI	1881–1890
VOLUME XII	1891–1900

As of 1983 the following volumes have been published, volumes I–V, IX–XI, and an *Index, volumes I to IV*.

Nominal Index

Included in this index are the names of persons mentioned in volume V. They are listed by their family names, with titles and first names following. Wives are entered under their maiden names with their married names in parenthesis. Persons who appear in incomplete citations in the text are fully identified when possible. An asterisk indicates that the person has received a biography in a volume already published, or will probably receive one in a subsequent volume. A death date or last floruit date refers the reader to the volume in which the biography will be found. Numerals in bold face indicate the pages on which a biography appears. Titles, nicknames, variant spellings, married and religious names are fully cross-referenced.

AARON. *See* Kanonraron
Abbot, Jonas, 422
Abbott, Edward, 147
Abbott, Harriet. *See* Bradford
Abbott*, Joseph (d. 1862), 107
Aberchalder. *See* MacDonell; McDonell
Abercromby*, James (1706–81), 40, 163, 295, 681, 803, 888
Abercromby, Sir Ralph, 110, 776
Ackmobish. *See* Akomápis
Adam, James, 424
Adam, Robert, 424
Adams, John, 15
Adams, Levi, 800
Addington, Henry, 1st Viscount Sidmouth, 674, 758
Addison*, Robert (d. 1829), 279, 519, 640, 724, 810, 841
Adhémar, Catherine. *See* Moreau
Adhémar, Geneviève. *See* Blondeau
Adhémar*, Jean-Baptiste (d. 1754), 3
Adhémar*, Jean-Baptiste-Amable (1736–1800), 3, 90, 241, 380
Adhémar, Marie-Madeleine. *See* Trestler
Adhémar, Patrice, 828
Adhémar, *dit* Saint-Martin, Toussaint-Antoine (Martin), 3–4
Adhémar* de Lantagnac, Gaspard (1681–1756), 97
Adonwentishon. *See* Ohtowa'kéhson
Agashawa. *See* Egushwa
Agmabesh. *See* Akomápis
Agnew*, Stair (d. 1821), 94, 160, 456
Ahdohwahgeseon. *See* Ohtowa'kéhson
Ah je juk. *See* Chejauk
Ahyouwaeghs* (1794–1832), 804
Ailleboust d'Argenteuil, Louise-Charlotte d' (Margane de Lavaltrie), 578
Ailleboust de La Madeleine, Catherine d', named de la Visitation, 186
Ailleboust de Manthet, Louise-Catherine d' (Charly Saint-Ange; Payen de Noyan et de Chavoy), 661
Ainse. *See also* Ainsse
Ainse*, Sarah (Montour; Maxwell; Willson) (d. *c.* 1823), 602, 722
Ainslie, Christian. *See* Rutherford

Ainslie, Christian (Christianna) (Young), 6, 879, 881, 882
Ainslie, Elizabeth. *See* Williamson
Ainslie, Elizabeth. *See* Martin
Ainslie*, George Robert (1776–1839), 780
Ainslie, Gilbert (grandfather), 4
Ainslie, Gilbert, 6, 879
Ainslie, John, 4
Ainslie, Mary. *See* Potts
Ainslie, Thomas, 5–7, 191, 745, 746, 879
Ainsse, Constante. *See* Chevalier
Ainsse, Joseph (grandfather), 7
Ainsse, Joseph, 9
Ainsse, Joseph-Louis, 7–9, 229, 760
Ainsse, Marie-Thérèse. *See* Bondy
Aird, George, 10
Aird, James, 8, 9–10, 835
Aird, Margaret (Anderson), 10
Aiton, William, 56, 580
Akomápis*, Nicholas (fl. 1778–80), 435
Akwirente, Joseph. *See* Onasakenrat, Joseph
Alary, Pierre, 51
Albarade, Jean d', 591
Albemarle, Earl of. *See* Keppel
Alberni, Pedro de, 10–11, 12, 399, 411, 571, 615
Alcalá-Galiano, Antonia (Alcalá-Galiano), 11
Alcalá-Galiano, Dionisio, 11–12, 140, 141, 571, 615
Alcalá-Galiano Pareja y Valera de la Serna, Antonio, 11
Alder, Thomas, 526
Alembert. *See* Le Rond
Allain, Jean-Baptiste, 12–13, 181, 458
Allain, Jeanne. *See* De Lille
Allain, Marie (Gautier, *dit* Bellair), 338
Allain, Pierre, 12
Allaire, Marie, 331
Allamand*, Jeanne-Charlotte (Berczy) (fl. 1760–1833), 70
Allan, Aaron, 14
Allan, Ebenezer, 13–15, 749, 846
Allan, Isaac, 35, 158, 349, 456
Allan, Isabella. *See* Maxwell
Allan, John, 15–17, 257, 295, 296, 416, 465, 627
Allan, Lucy. *See* Chapman
Allan, Mary. *See* Gregory

Allan, Mary. *See* Patton
Allan, Sally. *See* Kyen-da-nent
Allan, William, 15
Allan*, William (1770–1853), 65, 285, 366, 549, 643, 750, 753, 755
Allanby, William, 825
Allchechaque. *See* Chejauk
Allcock, Hannah (wife of HENRY), 17
Allcock, Henry, 17
Allcock, Henry, **17–19**, 292, 304, 420, 440, 441, 453, 519, 639, 845, 854, 855, 881
Allcock, Mary. *See* Askin
Allen. *See also* Allan
Allen, Ann (Gillmore), 343
Allen, Edward, 66
Allen, Elizabeth. *See* Saul
Allen, Ethan, 29, 167
Allen, George Nickleson, 764
Allen, Mary (Jones), 456
Allen, William, 803
Alliés, Geneviève (Amyot de Vincelotte; Marcoux), 577
Allin. *See* Allan
Alline*, Henry (1748–84), 665, 744
Allmon. *See* Almon
Allsopp, Anna Marie. *See* Bondfield
Allsopp, Carleton, 22
Allsopp, George, **19–23**, 44, 142, 164, 215, 289, 290, 317, 368, 369, 370, 371, 372, 426, 427, 602, 816, 843
Allsopp*, George Waters (1768–1837), 22, 23
Allsopp, James, 22
Allsopp, John, 22
Allsopp, Robert, 22
Allsopp, William, 22
Almon, James, 23
Almon, Rebecca. *See* Byles
Almon, Ruth. *See* Hollywood
Almon*, William Bruce (1787–1840), 23
Almon, William James, **23–24**, 128, 187, 297
Alvord, Clarence Walworth, 175
Ambroise. *See* Saint-Aubin
Ames, Ezra, 811
Amherst*, Jeffery, 1st Baron Amherst (d. 1797), 104, 134, 163, 172, 182, 227, 253, 339, 348, 363, 384, 415, 454, 478, 479, 528, 545, 650, 681, 690, 719, 747, 759, 794, 803, 823, 888
Amherst, William, 338, 381, 430
Amiot, Jean-Baptiste, 26
Amiot*, Jean-Baptiste (1717–69), 667, 703
Amiot, Jean-Nicolas, 329
Amiot*, Laurent (1764–1839), 218, 329, 437, 708, 709
Amiot, Marie-Anne (Perrault), 667
Amyot de Vincelotte, Geneviève. *See* Alliés
Ance, 9
Anderson, Andrew, 23
Anderson, Elizabeth Ann. *See* Hamilton
Anderson, Joseph, 549
Anderson, Margaret. *See* Aird
Anderson*, Thomas Gummersall (1779–1875), 10
André, John, 34, 629
André* de Leigne, Louise-Catherine (Hertel de Rouville) (1709–66), 421
Andrews, Abigail. *See* Tyler
Andrews, Hannah Ann. *See* Shelton

Andrews, Samuel, 24
Andrews, Samuel, **24–26**, 59, 135
Andriani, Paolo, Count Andriani, 563
Angeac*, François-Gabriel d' (1708–82), 339
Angers. *See also* Lefebvre
Angers, Geneviève (Blondeau), 89
Anglebert. *See* Poitevin
Angulo. *See* Flórez
Anne, Queen of Great Britain and Ireland, 803
Anoghsoktea (Isaac Hill), 255, 256, 809
Anspach*, Lewis Amadeus (1770–1823), 275
Antill, Edward, 414
Antill, Harriet (Blake; Panet), 88
Antrobus, Catherine Betsey Isabella. *See* Cuthbert
Antrobus*, Edmund William Romer (d. 1852), 27
Antrobus, John, **26–27**, 283, 576
Anville, Duc d'. *See* La Rochefoucauld
Aoghyatonghsera, Neggen (Margaret) (Brant), 804
Aplin, John, 27
Aplin, Joseph, **27–28**, 239, 263, 309, 310, 311, 425, 516, 568, 569, 717, 778, 779, 826, 847
Apsley, Baron. *See* Bathurst
Apthorp, Charles Ward, 374
Aque-Noch-Quah, 593
Arbalestre de Melun, Élisabeth (Sarrebource de Pontleroy), 738
Arboulin, Marie-Françoise d' (Bougainville), 102
Arbuthnot*, Mariot (1711–94), 382, 434
Arce. *See* Lom
Archibald*, Samuel George William (1777–1846), 854
Argenson, Comte d'. *See* Voyer
Argenteuil. *See* Ailleboust
Armitinger. *See* Ermatinger
Arnaud, Olive (Huet de La Valinière), 431
Arnold, Benedict, 28
Arnold, Benedict, 16, **28–36**, 64, 118, 130, 147, 167, 277, 413, 414, 481, 492, 588, 604, 629, 754
Arnold, Hannah. *See* Waterman
Arnold, Hannah, 35
Arnold, Henry, 35
Arnold, Margaret. *See* Mansfield
Arnold, Margaret. *See* Shippen
Arnold, Richard, 35
Arnoldi, Charles, 37, 218
Arnoldi, Michael, **36–37**, 218, 708, 727
Arnoldi, Peter (father), 36
Arnoldi, Peter, 37, 218
Arnoldi*, Phebe (rebaptized Apolline), named de Sainte-Angèle (Diehl) (1767–1825), 36
Arnoldi, Philipina Maria. *See* Horn
Arouet, François-Marie (Voltaire), 165, 232, 248, 372, 486, 668, 701
Arrowsmith, Aaron, 198
Arsac* de Ternay, Charles-Henri-Louis d' (1723–80), 381, 491
Arseneau, Geneviève (Compain), 201
Artigny. *See* Berthelot; Rouer
Asbury, Francis, 728
Ashbridge, Mrs Sarah, 419
Ashbridge, Sarah (Heron), 419
Ashburton, Baron. *See* Dunning
Askin, Alice. *See* Rea
Askin, Catherine (Robertson; Hamilton), 39, 402, 405, 718

Askin, Charles, 39
Askin, James, 37
Askin, John, 3, 14, 15, 17, **37–39**, 129, 168, 178, 179, 306, 364, 365, 366, 367, 402, 403, 404, 495, 527, 528, 529, 536, 552, 553, 565, 718, 722, 750, 760, 815, 818, 819, 820, 821, 822, 841
Askin, John, 38, 39, 178, 548, 553, 714
Askin, Madelaine (Richardson), 39
Askin, Marie-Archange. *See* Barthe
Askin, Mary (Allcock), 17
Askin, Thérèse (McKee), 39, 536
Assakis. *See* Nonosecash
Assheton, Susanna (Humphreys), 438
Assomption. *See* Maugue-Garreau
Astor*, John Jacob (1763–1848), 318, 418, 526, 528, 529, 533, 544, 559, 562, 635, 813, 822
Atiatoharongwen (Louis Atayataghronghta), **39–41**, 809
Atkins, Martha (Gray), 388
Atkinson, Frances Deering. *See* Wentworth
Atkinson*, George (d. 1792), 451
Atkinson, George (Sneppy), 526
Atkinson, Theodore, 848
Atwater, Caleb, 797
Aubert* de Gaspé, Philippe-Joseph (1786–1871), 498, 622, 793
Aubert* de Gaspé, Pierre-Ignace (1758–1823), 44
Aubert* de La Chesnaye, Charles (1632–1702), 108
Aubert* de La Chesnaye, François (d. 1725), 288
Aubert de La Chesnaye, Ignace-François, 288
Aubrey, Thomas, 348
Aubuchon, *dit* Lespérance, Catherine (Fabre, *dit* Laperrière), 736
Aubussargues. *See* Vergese
Aubut, Marie-Anne (Piuze), 676
Auchechaque. *See* Chejauk
Auchinleck, Gilbert, 800
Auchmuty, Samuel, 59, 445, 786
Auclair, Narcisse, 218, 727
Audet*, Francis-Joseph (1867–1943), 183, 395, 429, 530, 572, 577
Audette, *dit* Lapointe, Marie-Josette (Jacobs; Rieutord), 713
Audin. *See* Daudin
Augé*, Étienne (d. 1780), 394, 703
Augé, Jeanne (Digé), 256
Augé, Marie-Louise (Dejean), 237
Augooshaway. *See* Egushwa
August, John. *See* John August
Auldjo*, Alexander (1758–1821), 133, 259, 320, 461
Aulte, Catherine, 198
Aupetit, Anne (Cazeau), 173
Aureil. *See* Doreil
Avène. *See* Renaud
Aylwin*, Thomas (d. 1791), 283
Ayotte, Pierre, 358

Baby, Antoine, 41, 42
Baby*, Charles-François-Xavier (1794–1864), 217
Baby, François, **41–46**, 149, 164, 165, 289, 290, 396, 398, 484, 492, 577, 736, 794, 863
Baby, François (son of François), 45
Baby*, François (1768–1852), 366, 449
Baby*, James (1763–1833), 44, 365, 536, 722
Baby, Louis, 41

Baby, Marie-Anne. *See* Tarieu de Lanaudière
Baby, Raymond, 41
Baby, Thérèse. *See* Le Comte Dupré
Baby*, *dit* Dupéront, Jacques (d. 1789), 41, 42, 44, 396, 721, 852
Baby-Chenneville, Angélique (Chaboillez), 180
Backhouse, John, 734
Backus, Abigail (Perkins), 664
Bacon, Miss, 126
Bad Bird. *See* Madjeckewiss
Badeaux, Antoine-Isidore, 603
Badeaux, Geneviève. *See* Berthelot
Badeaux*, Joseph (1777–1834), 76
Badel, Antoine, 417
Badel, Marie-Angélique (Heer), 417
Badelard, Bernard, 649
Badelard, Esther. *See* Bruyer
Badelard, Louise-Philippe (Panet), 46, 648
Badelard, Louise-Suzanne, 46
Badelard, Marie-Charlotte. *See* Guillimin
Badelard, Philippe-Louis-François, **46–47**, 329, 330, 501, 648, 788
Badelard, Philippe-Martin, 46
Badgley*, Francis (1767–1841), 259, 260, 283, 376, 566
Bailey, David, 47
Bailey, Jacob, **47–48**, 430, 871
Bailey, Mary. *See* Hodgkins
Bailey, Sally. *See* Weeks
Baillairgé*, Charles (1826–1906), 50
Baillairgé*, François (1759–1830), 49, 50, 51, 61, 139, 140, 193, 305, 329, 452, 708
Baillairgé, Georges-Frédéric, 48
Baillairgé, Jean, 48
Baillairgé, Jean, **48–51**, 305, 452
Baillairgé, Jeanne. *See* Bourdois
Baillairgé, Marie-Louise. *See* Cureux, *dit* Saint-Germain
Baillairgé, Marie-Louise. *See* Parent
Baillairgé, Pierre, 48
Baillairgé, Pierre-Florent, 49, 50, **51–52**, 61, 305
Baillairgé*, Thomas (1791–1859), 50, 51, 305
Bailly, Catherine Margaret (Comingo), 199
Bailly* de Messein, Charles-François (1740–94), 58, 150, 179, 186, 246, 449, 459, 667
Bailly de Messein, François-Augustin, 829
Bailly de Messein, Marie-Appolline (Trottier Desrivières Beaubien), 829
Baker, Abigail (Fairfield), 307
Baker, Mrs Dorinda (Dorine), 389
Baker (Littlehales), Sir Edward Baker, 519
Baker, J. S., 689
Baker, John, 389
Baker*, Samuel, 879, 881
Baker, Simon, 389
Baldwin, David, 681
Baldwin, Phoebe. *See* Willcocks
Baldwin*, William Warren (1775–1844), 521, 858, 860
Balfour, Ann. *See* Emray
Balfour, James, **52–53**, 492
Ball, Sir Alexander John, 53
Ball, Anna. *See* Coutts
Ball, Mrs Betsy, 678
Ball, Catherine (Carleton; Skelton), 141, 155
Ball, Ingram, **53–54**, 204, 634, 766

Ball, John, 341
Ball, Joseph, 678
Ball, Margaret. *See* Childs
Ball, Mary. *See* Dickerson
Ball, Robert, 53
Ball, Victoria (Ramage), 705
Ballard, Michael, 491
Banks, Dorothea, Lady Banks. *See* Weston-Hugessen
Banks, Sir Joseph, **54–56**, 71, 166, 167, 502, 581
Banks, Sarah. *See* Bate
Banks, William, 54
Bannerman, James, 560, 561
Barbeau, François, 622
Barbeau, Joseph, 622
Barbeau, Marie-Louise. *See* Fluette
Barbée. *See* Barbet
Barbel*, Marie-Anne (Fornel) (1704–93), 277, 576
Barbet (Barbée), Marie-Charlotte (Michaux), 592
Barclay*, Robert Heriot (1785–1837), 696, 748, 799, 875, 876
Barclay*, Thomas (1753–1830), 106, 574, 874
Barham, Baron. *See* Middleton
Barker. *See also* Berker
Barker, Hannah (Noble), 627
Barker, Joseph, 627
Barnes, Isabella. *See* Johnson
Barnes, Jane, 560
Barnes, John, **56–57**, 747
Barnet. *See* Carrihogo
Barnsfare, Adam, 191
Barolet, Françoise (Bedout), 61
Barolet, Marie-Louise (Panet), 648
Barolette. *See* Papin
Baron, Catherine. *See* Hubert
Baron, Thomas, 322
Barré, Isaac, 145
Barrell, Joseph, 387, 410, 411
Barrin* de La Galissonière, Roland-Michel, Marquis de La Galissonière (1693–1756), 176
Barrington, Daines, 221
Barrington, Samuel, 220, 221
Barron, Thomas, 322
Barry, Thomas, 724
Barsalou, Jean-François, 322
Barthe, Jean-Baptiste, 129
Barthe, Marie-Archange (Askin), 39
Barthe, Thérèse (Grant), 363, 366, 367
Bartholomy, Néron, 385
Bartolozzi, Francesco, 382
Barton, Joseph, 669
Basque. *See* Bastarache
Bastarache, Jean-Baptiste, 57
Bastarache, Pierre, 57, 58
Bastarache, *dit* Basque, Marguerite. *See* Gaudet
Bastarache, *dit* Basque, Michel, **57–58**
Bastarache, *dit* Le Basque, Marguerite. *See* Forest
Bastarache, *dit* Le Basque, Pierre, 57
Bate, Sarah (Banks), 54
Bathurst, Henry, 1st Baron Apsley and 2nd Earl Bathurst, 479
Bathurst, Henry, 3rd Earl Bathurst, 268, 489, 490, 672, 673, 674, 882
Batt*, Isaac (d. 1791), 450, 500

Batt, Thomas, 296
Baudin, Nicolas, 105, 593
Baüyn, Bonaventure, 680
Bayer, Justina Sophia (Clark), 187
Bayne, William, 277
Bazan. *See* Valdés
Bazin, Marie-Angélique (Berthelot Dartigny), 74
Bazin, Marie-Louise-Élizabeth (Taschereau), 793
Bazin, Pierre, 74
Bear. *See* Saint-Aubin
Beardsley, Anna (wife of JOHN), 59
Beardsley*, Bartholomew Crannell (1775–1855), 60, 643, 673
Beardsley, Catharine. *See* Brooks
Beardsley, Gertrude. *See* Crannell
Beardsley, Hannah (Dibblee), 60
Beardsley, John, 58
Beardsley, John, 24, **58–60**
Beardsley, John Davis, 60
Beardsley, Keziah. *See* Wheeler
Beardsley, Sylvia. *See* Punderson
Beasley, Joanne (Cartwright), 167
Beasley*, Richard (1761–1842), 440, 669, 724, 841
Beaton, David, 101
Beatson, John, 617
Beatson*, Patrick (1758–1800), 283
Beatson, William, 617
Beaubien. *See* Desrivières-Beaubien; Trottier
Beauceron. *See* Riday-Beauceron
Beauchamp, Angélique (Réaume), 710
Beaucour; Beaucourt. *See* Malepart
Beaugrand, Simon, 436, 727
Beauharnois* de La Boische, Charles de, Marquis de Beauharnois (d. 1749), 791
Beaujeu. *See* Liénard; Saveuse
Beaulieu. *See* Sarrebource
Beaumarchais. *See* Caron
Beauséjour. *See* Godin
Beauvais. *See* Legardeur
Beck. *See* Beke
Beckwith, George, 705
Beckwith, Nehemiah, 35
Bédard, Jean-Baptiste, **60–61**
Bédard*, Jean-Charles (1766–1825), 212
Bédard, Madeleine. *See* Daigle
Bédard, Marie-Angélique. *See* Fiset
Bédard, Marie-Anne. *See* Toupin
Bédard*, Pierre-Stanislas (1762–1829), 207, 208, 210, 211, 212, 233, 234, 460, 580, 651, 695, 792, 828, 881
Bédard, Thomas, 60
Bédard*, Thomas-Laurent (1747–95), 60
Bedford, Duke of. *See* Russell
Bedout, Françoise. *See* Barolet
Bedout, Jacques, **61–63**
Bedout, Jean-Antoine, 61
Bedout, Jeanne. *See* Lafont
Bedout, Marie-Jeanne. *See* Daigre
Beechey, Sir William, 587
Beek. *See* Beke
Bégin, Charles, 278
Behzer, Traugott Leberecht. *See* Piuze, Liveright
Beikie, John, 521
Beke (Beck, Beek), Margaret S. (Jones), 457

Bélair. *See also* Dalpech; Plessis
Bélair, Ann. *See* Fraser
Bélair, Louis, 269, 270, 271
Bélanger, Ann. *See* Fraser
Bélanger, Louise (Marcoux), 231
Belcher*, Andrew (1763–1842), 423, 872
Belcher, Benjamin, **63**, 122
Belcher, Benjamin, 63
Belcher*, Clement Horton (1801–69), 63
Belcher, Jonathan, 127
Belcher*, Jonathan (1710–76), 63, 81, 554, 555
Belcher, Sarah. *See* Post
Belcour. *See* Lafontaine
Belestre. *See* Picoté
Belknap, Jeremy, 741
Bell, Alexander, 64
Bell, Ann (Forsyth), 325
Bell, James, **63–65**, 414
Bell, Jane (Montmollin), 600
Bell, Margaret. *See* Christie
Bell, Margaret, 64
Bell*, Mathew (1769–1849), 182, 214, 484, 566, 738
Bell, Thomas, 767
Bell, William, 64
Bellair. *See* Gautier
Bellecour (Bellecourt). *See* Lafontaine
Bellefeuille. *See* Lefebvre
Bellefontaine. *See* Godin
Bellenoy, Thérèse (Brehaut; Sheppard), 107
Belleville. *See* Guernon
Bellew, Anne. *See* Tasker
Bellew, Henry, 847
Benar. *See also* Bernard
Benar, Sunum, 74
Benard, Marie-Josephe, 293
Bender, François-Xavier, 294
Benedict, Elizabeth. *See* Smith
Bennet, Cornelius, 804
Bennett, Bertha (Botsford), 94
Benson, Egbert, 809
Bentinck. *See* Cavendish
Bentley, Benjamin, 66
Bentley, Catherine (wife of JOHN), 66, 67
Bentley, Deborah. *See* McKay
Bentley, Elijah, **64–66**, 749
Bentley, Ira, 65, 66
Bentley, John, **66–68**
Bentley, Margaret (Hutton; wife of JOHN), 68
Bentley, Mary Colley. *See* Gill
Bentley, Reuben, 65
Bently, Samuel, 64, 65, 66
Bentom, Clark, **68–70**, 768, 769
Berczy, Albert-Guillaume. *See* Berczy, William
Berczy*, Charles Albert (1794–1858), 70
Berczy, Jeanne-Charlotte. *See* Allamand
Berczy, William, **70–72**, 114, 417, 419, 420, 428, 440, 448, 496, 596, 597, 614, 731, 755, 757, 781, 811
Berczy*, William Bent (1791–1873), 70, 72
Berey Des Essarts, Félix (Charles), 570
Bergeaux, Anne-Marie. *See* Gautier, *dit* Bellair
Berkeley, Augustus, 4th Earl of Berkeley, 72
Berkeley, Elizabeth, Countess Berkeley. *See* Drax
Berkeley, Emilia Charlotte, Lady Berkeley. *See* Lennox

Berkeley, Sir George Cranfield, **72–73**, 861
Berkeley, Sir George Henry Frederick, 73
Berker (Barker), Mercy (Millidge), 598
Bernard. *See also* Carrihogo
Bernard, Antoinette (wife of NOËL), 74
Bernard, Jean-Baptiste, 74
Bernard, John, 690
Bernard, Louis, 73, 74
Bernard, Madeleine de (Chabert), 176
Bernard, Marie, 74
Bernard, Marie-Madeleine, 74
Bernard, Noël (Neville), **73–74**
Bernard, Zacharie, 74
Bernera. *See* MacLeod
Bernstorff, America von, Countess von Bernstorff. *See* Riedesel
Berryer, Nicolas-René, Comte de La Ferrière, 103, 104
Berthelet, Joachim, 242
Berthelet, Radegonde (De Lisle), 242
Berthelette, Catherine. *See* Vallée
Berthelot*, Amable (1777–1847), 75, 649
Berthelot, Charles, 74
Berthelot, Charlotte-Archange. *See* Mézière
Berthelot, Émilie (Girouard), 51
Berthelot, Geneviève (Badeaux), 76
Berthelot, Michel, 76
Berthelot, Thérèse. *See* Roussel
Berthelot Dartigny, Marie-Angélique. *See* Bazin
Berthelot Dartigny, Michel-Amable, **74–76**, 234, 508, 649, 650, 878
Bertin, Louise, 192
Bertrand, Jacques, 76
Bertrand, Joseph-Laurent, **76–77**
Bertrand, Marie-Louise. *See* Dumouchel
Bertrand, Marie-Thérèse. *See* Dulignon
Besnard*, *dit* Carignant, Jean-Louis (1734–91), 4, 272, 843
Besné. *See* Du Chaffault
Best, William, 63
Bethune*, Alexander Neil (1800–79), 79
Bethune, Angus, 77
Bethune*, Angus (1783–1858), 79, 526
Bethune, Cecilia (Kirby), 79
Bethune, Christian. *See* Campbell
Bethune*, Donald (1802–69), 79
Bethune*, James Gray (1793–1841), 79
Bethune, John, **77–79**, 280, 320, 520, 770
Bethune*, John (1791–1872), 79
Bethune*, Norman (1899–1939), 79
Bethune, Véronique. *See* Waddens
Bétourné, Marguerite (Leclerc), 480
Bezeau, Michel-Charles, 77
Bibaud*, Michel (1782–1857), 243, 702
Bidwell*, Barnabas (1763–1833), 308
Bienville. *See* Le Moyne
Bièvre. *See* Suzor
Bigot*, François (d. 1778), 88, 104, 164, 276, 638, 652, 711
Bigot, *dit* Dorval, Alexis, 736
Billinger, William, 127
Billings, Ekaterina. *See* Pestel
Billings, Elizabeth (Fairfield), 307
Billings, Joseph, **79–81**
Billopp*, Christopher (1737–1827), 349
Binney, Hannah Adams. *See* Newton

Binney, Hibbert,781
Binney, Hibbert Newton, 82, 216
Binney, Jonathan, **81–82**
Binney, Lucy. *See* Creighton
Binney, Margaret. *See* Miller
Binney, Martha. *See* Hall
Binney, Stephen Hall, 82
Binney, Thomas, 81
Birch. *See also* Burch
Birch, Samuel, 468
Bird, Henry, 301, 345, 346
Bird*, James (d. 1856), 531
Bird, Joseph (father), 785
Bird, Joseph, 785
Bird, Mary. *See* Street
Bird, Thomas Street, 785
Birnie, Eleanor (Davidson), 224
Birnie, Samuel, 684
Biscaret, Jean, 172, 719
Bishop, Charles, 618
Bisse, Martha (Wright), 872
Bisshopp, Cecil, **82–83**
Bisshopp, Cecil, 12th Baron Zouche, 83
Bisshopp, Charlotte Barbara. *See* Townshend
Bisshopp, Harriet Anne, Baronne Zouche. *See* Southwell
Blache, François, 436
Blache, René, 218
Blachford, Christabella (Curtis), 220
Black, Henry, 85
Black, Jane. *See* McMun
Black, Jane. *See* Rawson
Black, John, **83–85**, 878, 879
Black*, John (d. 1823), 328, 646, 647
Black, William, 83
Black*, William (1760–1834), 468, 469, 573, 664, 665, 871
Black*, William (1771–1866), 646, 647
Blackburn, Augustin, 621
Blackburn, Hugh, 331
Blackburn, John, 364
Blackburn, Mary. *See* Nairne
Black Jack. *See* Byers, John
Blacklock, Ann (Tanswell), 789, 790
Black Peter. *See* Byers, Peter
Blackstone, Sir William, 165, 372, 486, 855
Blackwood, Jane. *See* Holmes
Blackwood, John, 27, **85–88**, 95, 182, 211, 270, 493, 494, 769, 816
Blackwood, John, 87
Blackwood*, Thomas (1773–1842), 528
Blaine, Alexander, 301
Blainville. *See* Céloron
Blair, Andrew, 349, 351
Blais, Jean-Baptiste, 165
Blais*, Michel (d. 1783), 499
Blaise Des Bergères de Rigauville, Jean-Baptiste-Marie, 143
Blake, Charles, 46, **88–89**, 318, 584
Blake, Harriet. *See* Antill
Blake, John, 88
Blake, Mary. *See* Sunderland
Blanchard, Marie-Anne (Thibodeau), 812, 813
Blanchet, Catherine-Henriette. *See* Juchereau Duchesnay
Blanchet*, François (1776–1830), 211, 212

Blanzy. *See* Danré
Blaskowitz, Charles, 611
Blay. *See* Blais
Blenshel, Isabel (Purse), 699
Bligh, William, 55, 686
Bliss, Daniel, 350, 831
Bliss*, John Murray (1771–1834), 456, 831
Bliss*, Jonathan (1742–1822), 35, 94, 157, 350, 416, 456, 630
Blodget, Samuel, 415
Blondeau, François, 89
Blondeau, Geneviève. *See* Angers
Blondeau, Geneviève (Adhémar), 3
Blondeau, Jean-Baptiste, 89
Blondeau, Joseph, 89
Blondeau, Joseph-Barthélemy, 602
Blondeau, Marie-Josephe. *See* Le Pellé Lahaye
Blondeau, Maurice, 89
Blondeau, Maurice-Régis, **89–90**, 241, 242, 511, 528, 662, 663, 700, 701, 818, 819
Blondeau, Thomas, 89
Blowers*, Sampson Salter (1743–1842), 35, 94, 446, 630, 698, 854
Blue Jacket. *See also* Weyapiersenwah
Blue Jacket, George, 852
Blue Jacket, Jim, 852
Blue Jacket, Mary (Lacelle), 852
Blue Jacket, Nancy (Stewart), 852
Bodega* y Quadra, Juan Francisco de la (d. 1794), 11, 387, 411, 615
Bodoin, Louis, 269
Bodquin. *See* Flórez
Bohle, Charles-David, 218
Bohle, Peter, 218
Boileau, *dit* Boileau-Despréaux, Nicolas, 486, 701, 702
Boiret*, Urbain (1731–74), 379
Boisdale. *See* MacDonald
Boishébert. *See* Deschamps
Boisseau, Claire. *See* Jolliette
Boisseau, Marie-Anne. *See* Pagé, *dit* Carcy
Boisseau*, Nicolas (1700–71), 90
Boisseau, Nicolas-Gaspard, **90–91**, 492, 507, 654, 816
Boisseau*, Nicolas-Gaspard (1765–1842), 91, 580
Boisseau, Thérèse. *See* Couillard
Boit, John, 387, 388
Bolingbroke, Viscount. *See* Saint-John
Bolton, Mason, 676, 805, 895
Bolvin*, Gilles (d. 1766), 497
Bonaparte, Elizabeth. *See* Patterson
Bonaparte, Jérôme (Jérôme, King of Westphalia), 660
Bonaparte, Joseph (Joseph, King of Naples; Joseph, King of Spain), 616
Bonaparte, Napoleon. *See* Napoleon 1st
Bonaventure. *See* Denys
Bondfield, Acklam, 21
Bondfield, Anna Marie (Allsopp), 20
Bondfield, John, 21, 385
Bondfield, John Taylor, 20
Bondy, Marie-Thérèse (Ainsse; Godefroy), 7
Bonga, Jean, 715
Bonga, Marie-Jeanne (wife of Jean), 715
Bonnaventure. *See* Denys
Bonne* de Missègle, Louis de (d. 1760), 128, 230, 487

Bonne de Missègle, Louise. *See* Prud'homme
Bonner, Eleanor. *See* Pritchard
Bonnet, Jane (Schurman), 742
Bonnet, Joseph, 95
Bontein, Helen McKellar (Howe), 430
Boone, Henry, 283, 322
Booth, Benjamin, 91
Booth, Joshua, **91–92**, 170, 550, 772
Booth, Margaret. *See* Fraser
Borgia. *See* Levasseur-Borgia
Borneuf, Joseph, **92–93**, 480
Borneuf, Marie-Madeleine. *See* Degrès
Borneuf, Pierre, 92
Borrel, Joseph, 436
Boscawen*, Edward (1711–61), 172, 273, 274, 339, 393, 510, 719
Boscawen, George Evelyn, 3rd Viscount Falmouth, 510
Bossu, Catherine. *See* Jean
Bossu, Jean-Michel-Jacques, 93
Bossu, *dit* Lyonnais, Pierre-Jacques, named Brother Félix, **93–94**
Bossuet, Jacques-Bénigne, 165
Bostwick, Henry, 8, 129
Boswell, James, 166, 803, 805, 811
Botsford, Amos, **94–95**, 160, 258, 353, 354, 416, 607, 831, 867
Botsford, Bertha. *See* Bennett
Botsford, Gideon, 94
Botsford, Hester (Viets), 832
Botsford, Sarah. *See* Chandler
Botsford*, William (1773–1864), 94, 416, 456
Bouc*, Charles-Jean-Baptiste (1767–1832), 234, 395, 840
Boucher, François, 95
Boucher, François, **95–96**, 334, 482
Boucher, François-Claude, 164
Boucher, Jonathan, 628
Boucher, Joseph, 588
Boucher, Louis-Michel, 95
Boucher, Marie-Anne. *See* Martel
Boucher, Marie-Joseph. *See* Tremblay
Boucher, Pierre, 95
Boucher de Boucherville, Charles-Marie, 96
Boucher de Boucherville, Charlotte (Perrault), 667
Boucher de Boucherville, Madeleine. *See* Raimbault de Saint-Blaint
Boucher de Boucherville, Madeleine-Charlotte (Chaussegros de Léry), 96
Boucher de Boucherville, Marguerite. *See* Raimbault
Boucher* de Boucherville, Pierre (1689–1767), 96, 667
Boucher de Boucherville, Pierre-Amable, 96
Boucher de Boucherville, René-Amable, **96–97**
Boucher* de Boucherville, Thomas-René-Verchères (1784–1857), 96
Boucher de La Bruère, Charlotte (Trottier Desrivières Beaubien), 829
Boucher de La Bruère, René, 248, 829
Boucher de La Bruère de Montarville, Joseph, 165
Boucher de Niverville, Jean-Baptiste, 98
Boucher* de Niverville, Jean-Baptiste (1673–1748), 97
Boucher de Niverville, Joseph, 26, **97–100**, 216, 217, 225
Boucher de Niverville, Marguerite-Thérèse. *See* Hertel de La Fresnière
Boucher de Niverville, Marie-Josephte. *See* Châtelin

Boucher de Niverville (Nebourvele) Grandpré, François, 97, 98
Boucher de Niverville Montizambert, Pierre-Louis, 98
Boucherville. *See* Boucher
Bouchette, Adélaïde. *See* Chaboillez
Bouchette, Jean-Baptiste, 99, **100–1**, 699, 791, 877
Bouchette*, Joseph (1774–1841), 61, 72, 101, 179, 183, 228, 235, 428, 460, 835, 879, 880
Bouchette, Luce (Rolette), 101
Bouchette (Bouchet), Marc, 100
Bouchette, Marie-Angélique. *See* Duhamel
Bouchette, Marie-Thérèse. *See* Grenet
Boudreau, Cécile (Pitre; Pellerin), **102**
Boudrot, Charles, 102
Boudrot, Marie-Josephe. *See* Landry
Bougainville, Louis-Antoine de, Comte de Bougainville, **102–5**, 462, 738, 739, 824
Bougainville, Marie-Françoise de. *See* Arboulin
Bougainville, Marie-Joséphine de. *See* Longchamps-Montendre
Bougainville, Pierre-Yves de, 102
Boulton*, D'Arcy (1759–1834), 521, 559, 734
Boulton, Eliza. *See* Jones
Boulton*, Henry John (1790–1870), 458, 673
Boulton, Matthew, 55
Bouquet, Henry, 301, 714, 887, 888, 889, 902
Bourdages*, Louis (1764–1835), 165, 269, 813
Bourdois, Jeanne (Baillairgé), 48
Bourdon* de Dombourg, Jean-François (b. 1720, d. in or after 1789), 339
Bourdon de Dombourg, Marguerite. *See* Gautier, *dit* Bellair
Bourg*, Joseph-Mathurin (1744–97), 458, 587, 687
Bourk (Bourke). *See* Burke
Bourlamaque*, François-Charles de (1716–64), 164, 638, 677, 739
Bourneuf*, François-Lambert (1787–1871), 261
Bouron, Henri, 652
Bourque, Marguerite (Trahan), 827
Bourret, François-Emmanuel, 207, 495
Bouthillier, Pierre, 701
Bowdoin, James, 238
Bowie, Barbara (Graham), 363
Bowker, John, 672
Bowley, William, 27, 219, 310, 568, 778, 825
Bowman*, James (d. 1787), 88, 788
Bowyer, Henry, 442
Boyd, Sir Robert, 206
Boyer, Charles, 534, 656
Boyer, Françoise (Denaut), 245
Braddock, Edward, 40, 729, 730
Bradford, Harriet (Abbott), 107
Bradford, Richard, 106
Bradford, Richard, **106–7**, 716
Bradford, Sarah. *See* Jefferey
Bradford, Susanna. *See* Cole
Bradford, William (Pilgrim father), 865
Bradford, William (printer), 438
Bradley, Arthur Granville, 152
Bradstreet*, John (1714–74), 253, 739, 759, 804
Brady, Jane Sarah (Curtis, Lady Curtis), 220
Brady, Matthew, 220
Braidwood, Thomas, 390
Branssat (Bransac). *See* Migeon

Brant. *See also* Carrihogo; Sa Ga Yeath Qua Pieth Tow

Brant, Catharine. *See* Ohtowa?kéhson

Brant, Catharine (John), 804

Brant, Charlotte (Smith), 803

Brant, Christiana (Hill), 804

Brant, Elizabeth (Kerr), 804, 811

Brant, Isaac, 804, 809

Brant, Jacob, 804

Brant, John. *See* Ahyouwaeghs

Brant, Joseph. *See* Thayendanegea

Brant, Joseph, 803, 804

Brant, Margaret (Powless), 804

Brant, Mary. *See* Koñwatsi?tsiaiéñni

Brant, Mary (Hill), 804

Brant, Neggen. *See* Aoghyatonghsera

Brant, Susanna (wife of THAYENDANEGEA), 804

Brant's Joseph. *See* Thayendanegea

Brassard*, Louis-Marie (1726–1800), 216, 217, 253

Brassard, Pierre, 217

Brassard Deschenaux. *See also* Deschenaux

Brassard* Deschenaux, Charles-Joseph (1752–1832), 47

Brassard* Deschenaux, Joseph (1722–93), 252, 576, 711

Brassard Deschenaux, Madeleine. *See* Vallée

Brassier*, Gabriel-Jean (1729–98), 92, 294, 432, 480, 524, 680, 701

Braun, Antoine-Théodore, 480

Brebner*, John Bartlet (1895–1957), 109, 554

Brecken, John, 424

Brecken, Matilda. *See* Robinson

Brecken, Ralph, 720

Brehaut, Marie. *See* Todevin

Brehaut, Pierre, 107

Brehaut, Pierre, 84, **107–8**, 283, 637

Brehaut, Thérèse. *See* Bellenoy

Brehm, Dietrich, 894

Brenton*, Edward Barbizon (d. 1845), 108, 697

Brenton, Elizabeth. *See* Russell

Brenton, Frances. *See* Cranston

Brenton, Jahleel, 108

Brenton, James, 63, **108–9**, 251, 431, 574

Brenton, Rebecca. *See* Scott

Bretherton, James, 844

Breynton*, John (d. 1799), 128, 430, 746

Briand*, Jean-Olivier (1715–94), 46, 49, 76, 92, 118, 143, 146, 185, 196, 201, 202, 224, 241, 245, 246, 294, 305, 342, 343, 379, 380, 432, 433, 452, 471, 481, 569, 570, 658, 667, 687, 704

Brien, *dit* Dérocher (Desrochers). *See* Desrochers

Brigham, Moses, 14

Brisay. *See* La Cour

Bristol, Earl of. *See* Hervey

Brock, Elizabeth. *See* De Lisle

Brock, Irving, 111

Brock, Sir Isaac, 14, 72, 83, **109–15**, 191, 518, 521, 522, 643, 695, 697, 714, 748, 769, 775, 782, 798, 800, 857, 858

Brock, John (father), 109

Brock, John, 109, 110

Brock, William, 111

Brooke, Frances. *See* Moore

Brooke*, John (d. 1789), 600, 601, 620

Brooks, Catharine (Beardsley), 59

Brooks, Cornelia Eleanor (Robertson), 718

Brooks, Thankful (Cossit), 204

Brouague. *See* Martel

Broughton, William Robert, 12

Brown, Mr. *See* Comingo, Bruin Romkes

Brown, Alexander, 126

Brown*, Andrew (d. 1833 or 1834), 58, 240

Brown, Charles, 298

Brown*, James (1776–1845), 87, 211, 298

Brown, John, 34, 64

Brown, Mather, 128

Brown, Robert, 55

Brown*, William (d. 1789), 224, 298, 834

Browne*, George (1811–85), 678

Browne, Thomas, 785

Bruce, Jessy (Chaboillez), 177

Bruce, William (fur trader), 602

Bruce, William (physician), 23

Bruff, Charles Oliver, **115–16**

Bruff, James Earle (father), 115

Bruff, James Earle, 115

Bruff, Mary. *See* Letellier

Bruff, Peter Schuyler, 116

Bruix, Eustache, 62

Bruneau, Julie (Papineau), 116

Bruneau, Marie-Anne. *See* Robitaille

Bruneau, Marie-Élizabeth. *See* Morin, *dit* Chêneverd

Bruneau, Pierre, 108, **116–17**, 817

Bruneau, Pierre-Guillaume, 116

Bruneau, René-Olivier, 116

Bruneau, Théophile, 117

Brunet, Marie-Reine (Rousseau, *dit* Saint-Jean), 723

Brunet, *dit* L'Estang, Jean, 117

Brunet, *dit* L'Estang, Marguerite. *See* Dubois

Brunet, *dit* L'Estang, Véronique, named Sainte-Rose, **117–18**, 703

Brunswick, Duke of. *See* Ferdinand; Karl Wilhelm Ferdinand

Brutelles. *See* L'Héritier

Bruyer, Esther (Badelard), 46

Bruyères, Catherine-Élisabeth. *See* Pommereau

Bruyeres, Janet. *See* Dunbar

Bruyères*, John (d. before 1787), 118

Bruyeres, Ralph Henry, **118–19**

Brymer, Alexander, 281

Brymner*, Douglas (1823–1902), 610, 611

Buchan*, David (b. 1780, d. in or after 1838), 243, 244, 275, 672

Buchanan, Flora. *See* MacLeod

Buchanan, Malcolm Bàn. *See* MacMhannain, Calum Bàn

Buck. *See* Burch

Buckingham, Marquess of. *See* Grenville

Buckinghamshire, Earl of. *See* Hobart

Budden, Mrs. *See* Fisher

Budé, Jacques de, 893

Budgell, Elizabeth (Graves), 380

Buffalo, 419

Buffon, Comte de. *See* Leclerc

Bulkeley, Peter, 628

Bulkeley*, Richard (1717–1800), 108, 121, 251

Bull, Captain, 15

Buller, Catherine (Macarmick), 510

Buller, Susannah Catherine (Duckworth, Lady Duckworth), 273

Buller, William, 273
Bulley, Joanna. *See* Wood
Bulley, John, 119
Bulley, Samuel, **119–20**
Bulley, Samuel, 120
Bulley, Thomas, 120
Bulley, William Wilking, 120
Bullock, Mary Elizabeth. *See* Clinch
Bullock*, William (1797–1874), 190
Bunbury, Joseph, **120–21**
Bunbury, Thomas, 348
Burbidge, Elizabeth (wife of JOHN), 121
Burbidge, John, 63, **121–22**
Burbidge, Rebecca. *See* Dudley
Burch*, John (1741–97), 402
Burghley, Baron. *See* Cecil
Burgoyne*, John (1722–92), 32, 33, 34, 40, 64, 88, 96,
    146, 147, 148, 181, 206, 222, 231, 254, 282, 306, 307,
    319, 321, 343, 347, 422, 454, 457, 548, 567, 575, 582,
    583, 772, 791, 890, 891
Burke, Edmund, 145
Burke, Edmund (fl. 1785–1801), **122–23**, 124, 408, 459,
    632
Burke, Edmund (1753–1820), **123–25**, 181, 306, 494, 524,
    695
Burn, William, **125–27**
Burnet, James, 781
Burney, James, 80
Burns, David, 389, 520
Burns*, John (1774–1822), 279
Burns, Phoebe Maria (Fanning), 309
Burns*, William (d. 1829), 566, 746
Burr, Aaron, 72
Burritt, Stephen, 457
Burt*, Alfred Leroy (1888–1970), 147, 152, 585
Burton, Clarence Monroe, 237
Burton*, Sir Francis Nathaniel (1766–1832), 96
Burton*, Ralph (d. 1768), 142, 181, 272, 823, 888, 889
Bushnell, Charles Ira, 605
Bute, Earl of. *See* Stuart
Butler, Andrew, 781
Butler, John, 407
Butler*, John (d. 1791), 82, 257, 607, 843
Butler*, John (d. 1796), 14, 15, 121, 147, 168, 229, 254,
    439, 454, 517, 660, 661, 669, 781, 805, 841, 894, 900
Butler, Samuel, 48
Butler*, Walter (1752–81), 517, 788, 805
By*, John (1779–1836), 106
Byers, Amelia (mother of PETER), 127
Byers, John, known as Black Jack, 127
Byers, Peter, known as Black Peter, **127**
Byers, Sancho, 127
Byles, Anna. *See* Noyes
Byles, Katherine, 128
Byles, Mary, 128
Byles, Mather, 127
Byles, Mather, 23, **127–28**, 250, 430, 705
Byles, Rebecca. *See* Walter
Byles, Rebecca (Almon), 23, 24, 430
Byles, Sarah. *See* Lyde
Byles, Susanna. *See* Lawlor
Byng*, John (d. 1757), 730
Byrne, Michael, 229

Byrne, Rebecca (Hart), 409, 410
Byron*, John (1723–86), 52, 359, 369, 382
Byssot* de La Rivière, François (d. 1673), 288

CADET. *See also* Robichaux
Cadet*, Joseph-Michel (1719–81), 90, 131, 368
Cadot, Athanasie (wife of JEAN-BAPTISTE), 129, 130
Cadot, Jean-Baptiste, 90, **128–30**, 242, 568, 682, 715, 741
Cadot, Jean-Baptiste, 129, 130, 177, 178
Cadot, Jean-François, 128
Cadot, Joseph-Marie, 130
Cadot, Marie. *See* Mouet
Cadot, Marie-Josephe. *See* Proteau
Cadot, Michel, 129, 130
Cairns, Catherine (Cuthbert), 26
Caldwell, Alexander, 133
Caldwell, Amelia (Mary), 133
Caldwell, Ann. *See* Hamilton
Caldwell, Ann, 132
Caldwell, Anne, Lady Caldwell. *See* French
Caldwell*, Billy (d. 1841), 798
Caldwell, Henry, 30, 31, 44, 57, 84, **130–33**, 149, 191, 215,
    331, 371, 428, 460, 486, 502, 566, 600, 602, 621, 745,
    768, 769, 864, 870, 879, 892
Caldwell, Sir Henry John, 132
Caldwell, James, 177, 285
Caldwell, James, **133–34**
Caldwell, Sir John, 130
Caldwell*, Sir John (1775–1842), 132, 768
Caldwell, Louisa. *See* Melvin
Caldwell, Louisa, 133
Caldwell*, William (d. 1822), 302, 517, 805
Calef, Margaret. *See* Staniford
Calef, Robert, 134
Caleff, Dorothy. *See* Jewett
Caleff, John, **134–35**, 336
Caleff, Margaret. *See* Rogers
Calhoun, Thomas, 902
Callbeck, Ann. *See* Coffin
Callbeck*, Phillips (d. 1790), 27, 219, 220, 250, 309, 515,
    568, 717, 777, 778, 825, 873
Callender, Mr (painter), 844
Callicum, 411
Calonne, Charles-Alexandre de, 671
Calonne*, Jacques-Ladislas-Joseph de (1743–1822), 181,
    671
Calvé, Joseph, 273, 760
Cambridge*, John (1748–1831), 27, 219, 310, 568, 679,
    778, 825, 826, 848
Camden, Earl and Marquess of. *See* Pratt
Cameron*, Duncan (d. 1838), 65, 113, 453, 521, 522, 750
Cameron*, Duncan (d. 1848), 544, 742
Cameron, Hector Charles, 56
Campbell, Alexander, 135
Campbell, Annabella (Stuart), 776
Campbell, Christian (Bethune), 77
Campbell, Colin, 337, 844
Campbell, Coll, 221
Campbell, Donald, 101
Campbell, Dugald, **135–38**, 159, 161, 355, 456, 774
Campbell, George, 768
Campbell, Helen (Watson, Lady Watson), 844
Campbell, Jacobina. *See* Drummond

Campbell, James, 747
Campbell, James, **138–39**, 373, 472
Campbell, John (general), 136, 157, 158
Campbell, John (governor), 122, 361, 595, 632
Campbell*, John (d. 1795), 895
Campbell, John, 4th Earl of Loudoun, 134, 425, 888
Campbell*, Patrick (fl. 1759–1824), 135, 136, 137, 506, 549, 646, 707
Campbell, William, 121
Campbell*, Lord William (d. 1778), 199, 215, 720
Campbell*, William (d. 1823), 504, 647
Campbell*, Sir William (1758–1834), 557, 558, 559, 643, 672, 673, 674
Campbell of Kildalloig, John, 776
Campeau, Michel-Archange (Mézière), 590
Campion*, Étienne-Charles (d. 1795), 9, 178, 259, 260, 377
Candolle, Augustin-Pyramus de, 616
Caner, Henry, 128
Cannematchie, 885
Canniff*, William (1830–1910), 307
Canning, George, 286
Cannon, Ambrose, 139
Cannon, Edward, 51, **139–40**
Cannon, Helena. *See* Murphy
Cannon*, John (1783–1833), 139, 140
Cannon, Laurence, 139
Cannon, Martin, 61
Cannon*, Mary (d. 1827), 204
Cantray. *See* Dallas
Captain Bull. *See* Bull
Captain John. *See* Deserontyon, John
Captain Pipe. *See* Konieschguanokee
Captain Tinnewabano. *See* Tinnewabano
Carbouere. *See* Rocques
Carcy. *See* Pagé
Cardero, Antonia Romero de. *See* Romero
Cardero, Gregoria Rosalia de la Vega de. *See* Vega
Cardero, Manuel José Antonio, 12, **140–41**, 571
Cardero, Salvador Dieguez, 140
Carignant. *See* Besnard
Carleton. *See also* Pigott-Carleton
Carleton, Anne, 161
Carleton, Catherine. *See* Ball
Carleton, Christopher (grandfather), 141, 155
Carleton, Christopher, 584, 745, 896
Carleton, Emma, 161
Carleton, Guy, 1st Baron Dorchester, 5, 6, 19, 20, 21, 22, 26, 30, 31, 32, 33, 42, 43, 44, 46, 87, 88, 94, 98, 99, 100, 101, 121, 124, 130, 132, 133, 136, **140–55**, 157, 158, 161, 162, 180, 182, 185, 186, 191, 192, 224, 225, 229, 230, 232, 237, 238, 241, 242, 246, 254, 260, 271, 282, 289, 290, 300, 316, 317, 318, 324, 331, 334, 351, 364, 369, 371, 378, 383, 393, 398, 413, 414, 427, 432, 439, 442, 445, 454, 455, 457, 468, 470, 471, 478, 479, 482, 485, 486, 487, 493, 494, 499, 507, 509, 518, 528, 552, 553, 576, 577, 578, 585, 588, 594, 600, 601, 606, 607, 621, 630, 637, 650, 652, 653, 663, 669, 684, 690, 691, 699, 717, 718, 721, 736, 745, 752, 754, 756, 757, 759, 767, 781, 789, 790, 791, 794, 802, 807, 808, 809, 816, 831, 834, 841, 843, 844, 863, 864, 866, 878, 889, 890, 891, 892, 897, 901
Carleton, Hannah. *See* Van Horn
Carleton, Henrietta Anne (Pigott-Carleton; Leir), 152
Carleton, Maria, Baroness Dorchester. *See* Howard

Carleton, Thomas, 25, 56, 60, 136, **155–63**, 347, 348, 349, 350, 351, 352, 353, 354, 355, 356, 357, 504, 505, 506, 507, 589, 590, 630, 631, 646, 733, 763, 774, 831, 868
Carleton, William, 161
Carman*, Albert (1833–1917), 729
Carman*, Bliss (1861–1929), 800
Carmichael-Smyth, Harriet, Lady Carmichael-Smyth. *See* Morse
Carmichael-Smyth*, Sir James (1779–1838), 609
Caron*, Alexis (1764–1827), 792
Caron, Marie-Anne (Paré; Hotesse; Foretier), 321
Caron de Beaumarchais, Pierre-Augustin, 233
Carpentier, Claude, 432
Carrefour de La Pelouze, Abraham, 163
Carrefour de La Pelouze, Gabrielle-Marie. *See* Vernas
Carrefour de La Pelouze, Pierre-Joseph, **163–64**
Carreño, Alberto M., 616
Carrihogo (News Carrier, Barnet, Bernard, Brant), 803
Carroll, Charles, 31
Carroll, John, 186, 343, 434
Carson*, William (1770–1843), 274, 275
Carter, Christopher (fl. 1818), 27
Carter, Christopher (inventor), 519
Carteret (Thynne), Henry Frederick, 1st Baron Carteret, 315, 316, 317
Cartier, Cécile. *See* Gervaise
Cartier, Cécile (Hubert), 164
Cartier*, Sir George-Étienne (1814–73), 164
Cartier, Jacques, **164–65**
Cartier, Jacques, 164, 165
Cartier, Joseph (brother of JACQUES), 164
Cartier, Joseph (nephew of JACQUES), 165
Cartier, *dit* L'Angevin, Jacques, 164
Cartier, *dit* L'Angevin, Marguerite. *See* Mongeon
Cartwright, Anne (Cartwright), 165
Cartwright, Edmund, 166
Cartwright, Edward, 333
Cartwright, Elizabeth (Robison), 168
Cartwright, George, 166
Cartwright, George, 55, **165–67**, 221, 576, 577, 641, 675, 784
Cartwright, Hannah, 171
Cartwright, James, 171
Cartwright, Joanne. *See* Beasley
Cartwright, John, 55, 166, 167, 243, 784
Cartwright*, John Solomon (1804–45), 172
Cartwright, Magdalen. *See* Secord
Cartwright, Mary Magdalen (Dobbs), 172
Cartwright, Richard (father of RICHARD), 167, 168
Cartwright, Richard, 17, 38, 92, **167–72**, 189, 304, 326, 402, 404, 442, 443, 492, 494, 519, 550, 718, 724, 757, 765, 772, 781, 819, 821, 841
Cartwright, Richard (son of RICHARD), 171
Cartwright*, Sir Richard John (1835–1912), 172
Cartwright, Robert David, 172
Cartwright, Stephen, 171
Cartwright, Thomas Robison, 172
Cartwright, William, 165
Carver, Jonathan, 682, 684, 821
Cary*, Thomas (1751–1823), 225
Casey, Willet, 857
Casgrain*, Pierre (1771–1828), 668
Casot*, Jean-Joseph (1728–1800), 90, 247
Cassiet, Jeanne. *See* Dangoumau

Cassiet, Pierre, 172
Cassiet, Pierre, **172–73**, 719
Castanet*, Jean-Baptiste-Marie (1766–98), 493
Castlereagh, Viscount. *See* Stewart
Catherine II, Empress of Russia, 80
Catlin, George, 800, 811
Cavagnial. *See* Rigaud
Cavelier, Monsieur (doctor), 248
Cavelier* de La Salle, René-Robert (1643–87), 759
Cavendish, Lord John, 145
Cavendish Bentinck, William Henry, 3rd Duke of Portland,
   28, 35, 121, 149, 152, 160, 161, 186, 279, 303, 354, 388,
   440, 510, 634, 655, 850
Cavilhe, Louis, 242, 727
Cazeau, Anne. *See* Aupetit
Cazeau, François, **173–74**, 893
Cazeau, Léonard, 173
Cazeau, Marguerite. *See* Vallée
Cecil, William, 1st Baron Burghley, 54
Céloron, Marie-Catherine-Françoise, **174**
Céloron, Marie-Madeleine, 174
Céloron de Blainville, Catherine. *See* Eury de La Pérelle
Céloron* de Blainville, Pierre-Joseph (1693–1759), 98, 174
Cerré, Catherine. *See* Giard
Cerré, Jean-Gabriel, **174–75**, 654, 663
Cerré, Marie-Anne (Panet), 653, 654
Cerré, Marie-Thérèse (Chouteau), 175
Cerré, Paschal, 175
Chabert, Joseph-François de, 176
Chabert, Madeleine de. *See* Bernard
Chabert de Cogolin, Hélène-Marguerite-Barbe de, Marquise
   de Chabert. *See* Tascher
Chabert de Cogolin, Joseph-Bernard de, Marquis de
   Chabert, **175–77**
Chabert* de Joncaire, Philippe-Thomas (fl. 1707–66), 98
Chabert* de Joncaire de Clausonne, Daniel-Marie (d. 1771),
   143
Chaboillez, Adélaïde (Bouchette), 179
Chaboillez, Angélique. *See* Baby-Chenneville
Chaboillez, Charles, 178
Chaboillez, Charles, **177–78**, 179, 535
Chaboillez, Charles-Jean-Baptiste, 177, **178–79**, 180, 333,
   527, 564, 566
Chaboillez, Jessy. *See* Bruce
Chaboillez, Louis, **180**, 636
Chaboillez, Louis-Joseph, 180
Chaboillez, Marguerite. *See* Conefroy
Chaboillez, Marguerite. *See* Larchevêque
Chaboillez, Marie-Anne. *See* Chevalier
Chaboillez, Marie-Anne (Parent), 436
Chaboillez, Marie-Charlotte-Domitille (Doëy), 178
Chaboillez, Marie-Marguerite (McTavish), 179, 566
Chaboillez, Pierre-Louis, 178
Chaboillez, Rachel (Marie-Louise) (McKenzie), 179
Chabrand* Delisle, David (1730–94), 78, 321, 333, 369,
   527, 600, 602, 663, 786
Chalmers, George, 149
Chamard, Louise (Forton), 329
Chamberlain*, Theophilus (1737–1824), 423, 431, 804
Chamberland, Marie-Marguerite (Jacson), 451
Chamblain. *See* Volant
Champagne. *See* Foureur
Champigny, Marie de (Lebrun de Duplessis), 478
Champion, Anne. *See* Cordon

Champion, Gabriel, 13, **180–81**, 458
Champion, Gilles, 180
Champlain*, Samuel de (d. 1635), 874
Chandler, Charlotte. *See* Dunière
Chandler, Kenelm, **181–83**, 284, 745, 817
Chandler, Kenelm Conor, 182, 217
Chandler, Mary (Upham), 831
Chandler, Nathaniel, 181
Chandler, Sarah (Botsford), 94
Chandler, Thomas, 181
Chandler, Thomas Bradbury, 657
Chapel, Mr (slave owner), 340
Chapman, George, 406
Chapman, Lucy (Allan), 15
Chaptes de La Corne. *See* La Corne, Luc de
Charest*, Étienne (1718–83), 368, 481
Charest, Joseph, 481
Charland, Alexis, 183
Charland, Louis, **183–84**, 834
Charland, Marie. *See* Poulin
Charland, Marie-Joseph. *See* Fearson
Charland, Sarah. *See* Jones
Charles, the Young Pretender, 514
Charlotte Sophia of Mecklenburg-Strelitz, Queen of Great
   Britain and Ireland, 297
Charly* Saint-Ange, Louis (b. 1703, d. 1767 or 1768), 368,
   369
Charly Saint-Ange, Louise-Catherine. *See* Ailleboust de
   Manthet
Chartier de Lotbinière, Angélique (Renaud d'Avène Des
   Méloizes), 711
Chartier* de Lotbinière, Eustache (François-Louis) (b.
   1716, d. after 1785), 432
Chartier de Lotbinière, Louise (De Bonne), 231
Chartier de Lotbinière, Louise-Madeleine, Marquise de
   Lotbinière. *See* Chaussegros de Léry
Chartier de Lotbinière, Marie-Françoise (Juchereau Duches-
   nay), 462
Chartier* de Lotbinière, Michel, Marquis de Lotbinière
   (1723–98), 42, 231, 300, 462, 652, 738, 739
Chartier* de Lotbinière, Michel-Eustache-Gaspard-Alain
   (1748–1822), 96, 99, 207, 231, 232, 233, 650
Chase, Samuel, 31, 629
Chassebœuf, Constantin-François, Comte de Volney, 594
Châtelet, Florent-Louis-Marie du, Comte et Duc du
   Châtelet-Lomont, 791
Châtelin, Marie-Josephte (Boucher de Niverville), 97
Chatellereaux, Marie-Anne (Parent), 658
Chatham, Earl of. *See* Pitt
Chatillonnet. *See* Sauvage
Chaudrue, Jean, 276
Chauncey, Isaac, 696, 875, 876
Chaussat, Armand-Joseph, 49
Chaussegros de Léry, Alexandre-André-Victor, 270
Chaussegros* de Léry, Charles-Étienne (1774–1842), 75
Chaussegros* de Léry, Gaspard-Joseph (1682–1756), 49,
   738, 739
Chaussegros* de Léry, Gaspard-Joseph (1721–97), 60, 75,
   143, 481, 794
Chaussegros de Léry, Louise-Madeleine (Chartier de
   Lotbinière, Marquise de Lotbinière), 231
Chaussegros* de Léry, Louis-René (1762–1832), 97, 270
Chaussegros de Léry, Madeleine-Charlotte. *See* Boucher de
   Boucherville

Chauveaux, Charles, 242
Chavoy. *See* Payen
Chejauk, **184–85**
Chenard de La Giraudais, François, 105
Chêneverd. *See* Morin
Chenneville. *See* Baby-Chenneville
Cherrier, Benjamin-Hyacinthe-Martin, 186
Cherrier*, Côme-Séraphin (1798–1885), 186, 702
Cherrier, François, **185–86**, 200, 704, 833
Cherrier*, François-Pierre (d. 1793), 185, 833
Cherrier, Marie. *See* Dubuc
Cherrier, Mélanie. *See* Quesnel
Cherrier, Périne-Charles (Viger), 833
Cherrier, Séraphin, 186
Chesterfield, Earl of. *See* Stanhope
Chevalier, Angélique (De Lisle), 241
Chevalier, Constante (Ainsse), 7
Chevalier, Jacques, 249
Chevalier*, Jean-Baptiste (d. 1746 or 1747), 7, 179
Chevalier, Marie-Anne (Chaboillez), 178
Chevallier, Louis-Thérèse, 7, 8
Chevert, François de, 103
Chevrières. *See* La Croix
Chew, John, 121
Chew*, Joseph (d. 1798), 147
Chewett*, William (1753–1849), 519
Chiasson, Agnès (Gaudet), 203
Chiasson, Anne (Gallant), 335
Chicoisneau, Guillaume, 186
Chicoisneau, Hélène. *See* Gaulthier
Chicoisneau, Jean-Baptiste-Jacques, **186–87**, 680
Chicou, *dit* Duvert, Pierre, 248
Chief Joseph. *See* Onasakenrat, Joseph
Child, Mr (commercial agent), 784
Child, Isabella (Coffin), 190
Childs, Margaret (Ball), 53
Chinic*, Martin (1770–1836), 84, 270
Chinn, Edward, 20, 142
Chinn, John, 129
Chipman*, Ward (1754–1824), 35, 156, 157, 161, 390, 416, 456, 504, 505, 506, 630, 867, 874
Choiseul, Étienne-François, Duc de Choiseul, 104, 105
Chouinard, Jean-Marie, 359
Chouteau, Auguste, 175, 820
Chouteau, Marie-Thérèse. *See* Cerré
Christie, Mr (teacher), 321
Christie, Catherine (Robertson), 716
Christie*, Gabriel (1722–99), 63, 164, 331, 413, 414, 716
Christie, Margaret (Bell), 63
Christie, William, 63
Christopher, John, 626
Chubb*, Henry (1787–1855), 613
Churchill, Charles, 629
Churchill, John, 1st Duke of Marlborough, 166, 486
Cibber, Colley, 689
Cimère, Marie-Josephte (Ecuier), 294
Cirier*, Antoine (1718–98), 392, 393, 497
Clairaut, Alexis, 102
Claire. *See* Petit-Claire
Clameron, Marie (Poncin), 680
Clapp, Lucy (Creighton), 215
Clark, Benjamin, 642, 643, 644
Clark, Duncan, 24, **187–88**

Clark, Elizabeth. *See* Hare
Clark, George Rogers, 3, 8, 175, 238, 342, 567, 806
Clark, James, 188
Clark, James, **188–89**
Clark, Jemima. *See* Mason
Clark, John (merchant), 611
Clark, John (politician), 188
Clark, Justina Sophia. *See* Bayer
Clark, Mary Margaret. *See* Kerr
Clark, Peter, 188
Clark*, Robert (d. 1794), 407, 873
Clark*, Robert (1744–1823), 169, 188
Clark*, Thomas (1770–1835), 403, 405, 549, 672, 673, 674, 841
Clark, William (clergyman), 832
Clark, William (explorer), 9, 418, 419
Clarke*, Sir Alured (d. 1832), 151, 206, 318, 372, 433, 479, 552, 705, 724
Clarke*, Isaac Winslow (d. 1822), 138
Clarke, Richard Samuel, 25
Clarke, Samuel, 837
Clarkson, John, 341, 469
Claus*, Christian Daniel (1727–87), 147, 229, 254, 256, 260, 272, 600, 804, 843, 895
Claus*, William (1765–1826), 256, 365, 467, 536, 673, 724, 749, 797, 810, 842
Clausonne. *See* Chabert
Claye, Cécile (Michaux), 592
Clement XIII, 173
Clench*, Ralfe (1762–1828), 279, 405, 520, 549, 782, 842, 845, 856
Cleveland, 258
Clinch, Hannah. *See* Hart
Clinch, John, 190
Clinch, John, **189–90**, 785
Clinch, Joseph Hart, 190
Clinch, Mary Elizabeth (Bullock), 190
Clinch, Thomas, 189
Cline. *See* Clyne
Clinton, George, 896
Clinton, Sir Henry, 34, 148, 222, 604, 629, 730, 831, 866, 890, 891, 893, 896
Clinton, James, 895
Clive, Robert, 1st Baron Clive, 166
Clober. *See* Dunlop; McGregor
Cloud, Daniel, 557, 558
Clowes, George, 760
Clyne (Cline, Klein), Margaret (Rousseau St John), 724
Coates, Susanna (Dixon), 257
Cobb, Elizabeth (Eddy), 295
Cochin. *See* Cocking
Cochran*, Andrew William (1792–1849), 697
Cochran, James, 494
Cochran, Mary (Wright), 872
Cochran, Thomas, 389, 494
Cochran, William, 494
Cochran*, William (d. 1833), 124, 872
Cochrane, Sir Alexander Forrester Inglis, 314
Cochrane, John, 284, 863
Cochrane, Thomas, 220
Cock, Daniel, 344
Cockan. *See* Cocking
Cockburn*, Sir Francis (1780–1868), 72

Cockburn*, James Pattison (1778–1847), 228
Cocking*, Matthew (1743–99), 129, 363, 450, 682
Cockrell*, Richard (1769–1829), 846
Codner, Daniel, 119
Coffin, Ann (mother of JOHN), 190
Coffin, Ann (Callbeck), 220, 515
Coffin*, Sir Isaac (1759–1839), 13, 281
Coffin, Isabella. See Child
Coffin, James, 191
Coffin, John, 31, 182, **190–91**, 192, 214, 370, 509
Coffin, John (son of JOHN), 191
Coffin*, John (1756–1838), 137, 354, 504, 505
Coffin, Louisa, 192
Coffin, Margaret (Sheaffe), 191
Coffin, Marie-Louise, 192
Coffin, Mary (mother of THOMAS ASTON), 192
Coffin*, Nathaniel (1776–1846), 191
Coffin, Sarah, 192
Coffin, Susannah (Grant; Craigie), 191, 214
Coffin*, Thomas (1762–1841), 191, 214, 291, 372, 603
Coffin, Thomas Aston, **192–93**, 486, 508, 705, 844
Coffin, William (grandfather), 190
Coffin, William (uncle), 192
Coffin, William, 191
Coffin*, William Foster (1808–78), 191
Coghlan*, Jeremiah (fl. 1756–88), 166, 491, 783
Cogolin (Cogollin). See Chabert
Cohen, Abraham Haim, 194
Cohen, Jacob Raphael, **193–94**
Cohen, Rebecca. See Luria
Coke, D'Ewes, 492, 725, 726
Coke, Thomas, 573
Colclough*, Caesar (1764–1822), 220, 335, 474, 678, 776, 861
Colden, Cadwallader, 506, 646
Colden, Elizabeth (De Lancey), 239
Cole*, John (d. 1779), 363, 656, 682
Cole, Susanna (Bradford), 106
Coleman, Seth, 608
Coleman, Thomas, 551
Colen, Joseph, **194–95**, 451
Coleridge, Samuel Taylor, 167
Collachie. See Macdonell; McDonell
Collas, Marguerite-Angélique (Olabaratz), 638
Collégien. See Saillant
Collet, Charles-Ange, **195–96**
Collet, Claude, 195
Collet, Marguerite. See Fauché
Collier*, Sir George (1738–95), 16, 296
Collins, Catharine (Ramage), 705
Collins, Charles W., 590
Collins, John, 689
Collins*, John (d. 1795), 146, 149, 426, 428, 519, 552, 892
Collnett, James (father), 197
Collnett, James, 197, 387
Collnett, Sarah (wife of James, father), 197
Collver. See also Culver
Collver, Anna (wife of JABEZ), 196
Collver, Freelove. See Lamb
Collver, Jabez, **196–97**
Collver, John, 196
Collyer, Joanne (Hughes, Lady Hughes), 434
Colnett, Elizabeth Caroline, 198

Colnett, James, **197–99**, 387, 571, 586
Colonel Louis. See Atiatoharongwen
Colquhoun, Patrick, 219
Coltman*, William Bacheler (d. 1826), 268
Colvile (Wedderburn), Andrew, 266
Colvill*, Alexander, 7th Baron Colvill (1717/18–70), 381
Colwell, Elizabeth (Ryerse), 732
Combe, William, 541, 542
Comcomly, 419, 526
Comingo, Bruin Romkes, **199–200**
Comingo, Catherine Margaret. See Bailly
Comingo, Ebjen (Eljen, Fruche) (wife of BRUIN ROMKES), 199
Comingo, Renée. See Des Camps
Compain, Geneviève. See Arseneau
Compain, Marie-Louise, named Saint-Augustin, 186, **200–1**, 704
Compain, Pierre-Joseph, 200, **201–2**, 501, 502
Compain, dit L'Espérance, Françoise. See Vacher
Compain, dit L'Espérance, Pierre, 200, 201
Compton, Charlotte, Baroness Ferrers (Townshend, Viscountess Townshend), 824
Conant, Sylvanus, 744
Conefroy, Marguerite (Chaboillez), 180
Conefroy, Marie-Josette. See Métivier
Conefroy, Pierre, 97, **202–3**, 247, 248
Conefroy, Robert, 202
Connor, Thomas, 742
Conor, Elizabeth, 183
Conott (Connott), Sarah (Heron), 420
Contrecœur. See Pécaudy
Conway, Henry Seymour, 142, 148, 149
Cook*, James (1728–79), 55, 80, 107, 197, 274, 381, 387, 425, 538, 539, 570, 580, 684, 686, 773, 837
Cook, Louis. See Atiatoharongwen
Cook*, William Hemmings (d. 1846), 194
Cooley, Mary (Hatt), 411
Cooper, Myles, 630, 657
Cooper*, William (d. 1840), 597
Copley, John Singleton, 844
Corbin, Madeleine (Laforce), 470
Cordis, Mary (Haswell), 410
Cordon, Anne (Champion), 180
Cormack*, William Eppes (1796–1868), 244
Cormier, Anne. See Gaudet
Cormier, Cécile. See Thibodeau
Cormier, François, 203
Cormier, Jacques, 203
Cormier, Pierre, 203
Cormier, Pierre, **203–4**
Cornplanter. See Kaiũtwahʔkũ
Cornwallis, Charles, 2nd Earl and 1st Marquess Cornwallis, 53, 134, 227, 657, 730
Cornwallis*, Edward (1712/13–76), 215, 239, 250
Cornwallis, Sir William, 359
Corps, Mary (Dixon), 257
Corrigal, Jacob, 185
Corry (Curray, Currie), Thomas, 818
Cort, John, 465
Cossit, Ranna, 53, **204–5**, 446, 546, 634, 766
Cossit, Thankful. See Brooks
Cossitt, Phoebe. See Hillyer
Cossitt, Rene, 204

Costin, Thomas, 590
Cotté*, Gabriel (d. 1795), 90, 376, 663
Cottnam, Deborah. *See* How
Cottnam, Grizelda Elizabeth, 430
Cottnam, Martha Grace (Tonge), 430
Cottnam, Samuel, 430
Cotton*, Barthélemy (d. 1780), 249, 699
Cotton*, Charles Caleb (1775–1848), 106
Couagne*, René de (d. 1767), 662
Couc*, Elizabeth (La Chenette, Techenet; Montour) (b. 1667, d. *c.* 1750), 602
Couc, *dit* Lafleur, Pierre, 602
Coughlan*, Laurence (d. 1784 or 1785), 52
Couillard, Louis, 91
Couillard, Thérèse (Boisseau), 91
Couillard Des Islets, Louis, 654
Coulon, Marie (Guernon), 392
Coulon* de Villiers, Louis (1710–57), 96, 486
Coulon* de Villiers de Jumonville, Joseph (1718–54), 96, 470, 486
Coupeaux, François, 813
Coursol. *See also* Coursolles
Coursol, Mélanie. *See* Quesnel
Coursolle, Jean-Marie, 572
Coursolles (Coursol), Charlotte (Jones), 456
Courthiau, Pierre-Noël, 312
Courval. *See* Poulin
Coustan, Madeleine (Sarrebource Pontleroy de Beaulieu), 738
Coutant, Marie-Joseph (Tanswell), 790
Coutlée*, Thérèse-Geneviève (1742–1821), 293
Couton. *See* Cotton
Coutts, Anna (Ball), 53
Coutts, Katherine B., 800
Couturier, Jean, 432
Coventry*, George (1793–1870), 419
Cox, Christiana (Christina) Lætitia (Longmore), 501
Cox*, Nicholas (d. 1794), 485, 501, 502, 503, 637
Cox*, Ross (1793–1853), 419, 526, 560, 814
Cox, William, 764
Craig, Hew, 205
Craig, Sir James Henry, 13, 18, 51, 85, 86, 87, 111, 119, 138, 161, 165, **205–14**, 215, 225, 235, 236, 286, 291, 292, 386, 461, 489, 651, 693, 694, 695, 696, 697, 753, 769, 796, 797, 828, 829, 881
Craigie, John, 214
Craigie, John, 61, 191, 192, **214–15**, 291, 326, 442, 485, 495, 496, 794
Craigie, Susannah. *See* Coffin
Cramahé*, Hector Theophilus (1720–88), 44, 132, 142, 144, 146, 289, 481, 508, 706, 889, 892, 895
Cramer, Charles, 838, 839
Crandall*, Reuben (1767–1853), 65
Crane. *See also* Chehauk; Tarhe
Crane, Jonathan, 63
Crannell, Gertrude (Beardsley), 59
Cranston, Frances (Brenton), 108
Cranston, Samuel, 108
Crausee, Miss von (Massow), 582
Crawford, William, 302, 345, 346
Creighten, Christian (Christen) (Fisher), 319
Creighton*, Donald Grant (1902–79), 153, 288
Creighton, John, **215–16**

Creighton, John, 216
Creighton, Joseph, 216
Creighton, Lucy. *See* Clapp
Creighton, Lucy (Binney), 216
Creighton, Maria (wife of JOHN), 215
Creighton, Sarah (Wilkins), 216
Crénier, Louis-Alexandre, 680
Crépeaux, Geneviève (Gosselin), 358
Cressé. *See also* Poulin
Cressé, Marie-Victoire. *See* Fafard Laframboise
Cressé, Michel, 216
Cressé, Pierre-Michel, **216–17**, 377
Croghan, George, 804
Croisille (Croizille). *See* Legardeur
Croke*, Sir Alexander (1758–1842), 108, 109, 446, 694
Crooke, Margaret (Inglis), 444
Crooks*, James (1778–1860), 189, 405, 639, 643, 673, 725, 842, 846
Crooks*, Ramsay (1787–1859), 526
Crooks, William, 189, 725
Crosby, Ann (O'Donel), 631
Crouckeshanks, Alexander, 217
Crowdy*, James (1794–1867), 781
Cruickshank, Ann (Kay; wife of ROBERT), 218
Cruickshank, Elizabeth (Webster), 218
Cruickshank, Robert, 36, 37, **217–19**, 437, 595, 614, 708, 727, 728
Cruikshank*, Ernest Alexander (1853–1939), 759, 800
Cuadra. *See* Bodega
Cugnet*, François-Étienne (1688–1751), 252, 498
Cugnet*, François-Joseph (1720–89), 43, 144, 252, 253, 606, 794, 863
Cugnet, Gilles-Louis, 196
Cugnet, Jacques-François, 482, 792
Cugnet, Louise-Charlotte (Liénard de Beaujeu de Villemonde), 462, 498
Cugnet, Louise-Madeleine. *See* Dusautoy
Cugnet, Marie-Angélique. *See* Le Comte Dupré
Cugnet, Thomas-Marie, 368
Cullen, William, 260
Culver. *See also* Collver
Culver (Collver), Nathan, 197
Cumberland, Duke of. *See* William Augustus
Cumberland, Richard, 689
Cummings, Samuel, 94
Cunningham, Archibald, 402
Cuoq*, Jean-André (1821–98), 480
Curatteau*, Jean-Baptiste (1729–90), 51, 143, 164, 241, 242, 294
Cureux, Marguerite (Dumas), 276
Cureux, *dit* Saint-Germain, Marie-Louise (Baillairgé), 51
Curray (Currie). *See* Corry
Currey, William Samuel, 443
Curtis, Mr, 244
Curtis, Christabella. *See* Blachford
Curtis, Elizabeth. *See* Lawson
Curtis, James, **219–20**, 263, 335, 477
Curtis, Jane Sarah, Lady Curtis. *See* Brady
Curtis, Sir Lucius, 221
Curtis, Roger (grandfather), 220
Curtis, Roger, 221
Curtis, Sir Roger, **220–22**
Curtis, Thomas, 407, 777

Curtius, Charles, 315
Curtius, Marie-Anne-Joseph (Trestler), 827
Cusson, Marie-Joseph (Périnau), 662
Cuthbert, Alexander, 312, 687
Cuthbert, Catherine. *See* Cairns
Cuthbert, Catherine Betsey Isabella (Antrobus), 26
Cuthbert*, James (d. 1798), 21, 26, 142, 312, 313, 432, 579, 636, 687
Cuthbert*, James (1769–1849), 636
Cuthbert*, Ross (1776–1861), 209, 210
Cuttan (Cutten), Josiah, 639
Cuyler, Abraham Cornelius, 204, **222–23**, 510, 545, 552, 766
Cuyler, Catalyntje. *See* Schuyler
Cuyler, Cornelius, 222
Cuyler, Jane Elizabeth. *See* Glen
Cygne, Le. *See* Onasakenrat, Joseph
Cyr (Sire), Félicité (Robichaux), 719
Cyrier. *See* Cirier

DAER and Shortcleuch, Baron. *See* Douglas
Daer and Shortcleuch, Baroness. *See* Wedderburn
Daigle, Madeleine (Bédard), 60
Daigre, Marie-Jeanne (Bedout), 61
Dalciat, Marie-Louise (Petit-Claire; Huguet, *dit* Latour), 437
Dale, David, 69
Dalhousie, Earl of. *See* Ramsay
Dallas of Cantray, Anne (Shaw), 752
Dalpech, *dit* Bélair, Marie (Guernon, *dit* Belleville), 392
Dalrymple, Alexander, 541, 684
Dambourgès, François, 654, 816
Dame, George, 584
Dandin. *See* Daudin
Dandridge, Martha (Washington), 313
Danford, Jacob, 817
Dangeac (Danjaique). *See* Angeac
Dangoumau (Dengomau), Jeanne (Cassiet), 172
Danré* de Blanzy, Louis-Claude (b. 1710, d. in or after 1770), 652
Darby*, Nicholas (d. 1785), 166, 675
Darce. *See* Lom
Darris, Marie-Charlotte. *See* Sajos
Darris, Pierre, 257
Dartigny. *See* Berthelot
Dartmouth, Earl of. *See* Legge
Dashwood, Francis, 15th Baron Le Despencer, 315
Daudin*, Henri (d. 1756), 172
Davanne, Louis, 223
Davanne, Marguerite. *See* Germain
Davanne, Marguerite, named de Saint-Louis de Gonzague, **223–24**
Davenport, Sarah. *See* Underhill
David*, David (1764–1824), 193
David, Phoebe. *See* Samuel
Davidson. *See also* Davison
Davidson, Arthur, 99, **224–26**, 492, 817
Davidson, Eleanor. *See* Birnie
Davidson, Elizabeth, 224
Davidson, Jane. *See* Fraser
Davidson, Jane (Ross), 224
Davidson, Walter, 224
Davidson*, Walter (1790–1825), 224, 225

Davidson*, William (d. 1790), 328, 350, 416, 465, 795
Davies, David, 226
Davies, Mary (wife of THOMAS), 226
Davies, Thomas, **226–28**, 767
Davis, Elizabeth. *See* Robertson
Davis, Frances (Hopkins; Tiffany), 814
Davis, Theodore, 716
Davison*, Alexander (1750–1829), 22, 43, 71, 181, 182, 277, 289, 483, 484, 718
Davison*, George (d. 1799), 43, 132, 289, 371, 484
Dawes, William, 341
Dawson*, John William (1820–99), 529, 530
Day, Nathaniel (fl. 1782), 737
Day, Nathaniel (office holder), 214, 584
Dean, Sarah (Farrar; Tiffany), 814
Dearborn, Henry, 66, 113, 695
Dease, Anne. *See* Johnson
Dease, Jane. *See* French
Dease, John, 8, 9, **228–30**
Dease*, Peter Warren (1788–1863), 228
Dease, Richard, 228
Debartzch*, Pierre-Dominique (1782–1846), 695
De Bonne, François, Duc de Lesdiguières, 230
De Bonne, Louise. *See* Chartier de Lotbinière
De Bonne, Louise-Élizabeth. *See* Marcoux
De Bonne, Pierre-Amable, 87, 96, 207, 208, 210, 211, 226, **230–36**, 243, 385, 386, 464, 487, 650, 651, 654, 696, 701, 828, 878, 881
DeBurgo. *See* Burke
Decatur, Stephen, 813
D'echambault (Déchambault). *See* Fleury
Dechinique*, Martin (d. 1825), 95
Decoigne, François, **236–37**
De Cou, Anne (Odell), 628
Decousse, Bernard, 727
Decrès, Denis, Duc Decrès, 62
Dees, Robert, 139
Degeay*, Jacques (1717–74), 432
Degrès, Marie-Madeleine (Borneuf), 92
De Guerne. *See* Le Guerne
Deguire*, *dit* Desrosiers, Joseph (1704–89), 143
Deiaquande. *See* Teyohaqueande
Dejean, Jeanne. *See* Rocques de Carbouere
Dejean, Josette. *See* Larchevêque
Dejean, Marie-Louise. *See* Augé
Dejean, Philippe, 237
Dejean, Philippe, **237–38**
Dejean, Théotiste. *See* Saint-Cosme
Delafontaine. *See* Lafontaine
De Lancey, Elizabeth. *See* Colden
DeLancey, James, **238–39**
DeLancey, Martha. *See* Tippett
De Lancey, Oliver, 604
De Lancey, Peter, 238
DeLancey, Stephen, 239, 552
Deland, Marie (Menut), 588
Delaunay, Louis, 77
Delavall, Ann (Milbanke, Lady Milbanke), 595
Delavall, Edward, 595
Delesdernier, Eleanor. *See* Pritchard
Delesdernier, Gideon, 239, 240
Delesdernier, Judith. *See* Martin
Delesdernier, Lewis Frederick, 240

Delesdernier, Moses, **239–41**

Delezenne*, Ignace-François (d. 1790), 218, 707, 708, 709, 710, 736, 737

Delezenne, Joseph-Christophe, 709

Delezenne*, Marie-Catherine (Pélissier; Sales Laterrière) (1755–1831), 708, 735, 736, 737, 738

Delezenne, Michel, 736, 737

De Lille, Jeanne (Allain), 12

Delique, Charles-François, 727

Delisle. *See also* Chabrand

De Lisle, Angélique. *See* Chevalier

De Lisle, Ann. *See* Denton

Delisle, Antoine, 727

De Lisle*, Augustin (1802–65), 241

De Lisle, Elizabeth (Brock), 109

Delisle, Frédéric, 218

De Lisle, Jean, **241–42**, 380, 398, 663

De Lisle, Jean-Guillaume, 241

De Lisle, Jean-Guillaume, 180, 211, 233, 241, **242–43**, 701

De Lisle, Marie-Louise. *See* Heer

De Lisle, Pierre-Guillaume, 417

De Lisle, Radegonde. *See* Berthelet

De Lisle, Suzanne. *See* Lacroix-Mézière

Delor. *See* Levasseur

Delorme, Monsieur (fur trader), 533

Demasduwit, **243–44**

Demers, Alexis, 245

Demers*, Jérôme (1774–1853), 245

Demers, Louis, 244

Demers, Louis (baptized Jean), **244–45**

Demers, Thérèse. *See* Gagnon

Demers, *dit* Dumé, Françoise (Ducharme), 272

Denaut, André, 245

Denaut, Françoise. *See* Boyer

Denaut, Marguerite-Amable, 217, 248

Denaut, Pierre, 77, 93, 123, 186, 203, 217, 224, **245–48**, 292, 294, 374, 380, 471, 494, 516, 524, 525, 659, 671, 680, 687, 688, 691

Dénéchaud, Angélique. *See* Gastonguay

Dénéchaud, Antoinette. *See* Lubet

Dénéchaud, Charles-Denis, 249

Dénéchaud*, Claude (1768–1836), 249, 651

Dénéchaud, Jacques, **248–49**, 699

Dénéchaud, Pierre (grandfather), 248

Dénéchaud, Pierre, 249

Dengomau. *See* Dangoumau

Denis. *See* Denys

Denis* de Saint-Simon, Antoine-Charles (1734–85), 104

Denison, John, 326

Denniston, John, 287

Denton, Ann (De Lisle), 241, 242

Denys. *See* Denis

Denys* de Bonnaventure, Claude-Élisabeth (1701–60), 339

Denys de Vitré, Marie-Anne-Noële, 323

Denys de Vitré, Mathieu-Théodore, 323

DePeyster*, Arent Schuyler (1736–1822), 8, 9, 38, 39, 567, 568, 682, 710, 760, 836, 884

Deray, Françoise (Rieutord), 712

Derenzy, Elizabeth. *See* Selby

Dérocher. *See* Desrochers

Derosiers. *See* Deguire

Desandrouins*, Jean-Nicolas (1729–92), 739

Desauniers. *See* Trottier

Desbarats*, Pierre-Édouard (1764–1828), 139, 834

DesBarres*, Joseph Frederick Wallet (1721–1824), 204, 222, 223, 335, 427, 430, 510, 516, 569, 607, 766, 773, 776, 780, 826, 862, 874, 887

Des Bergères. *See* Blaise

Desbrisay, Ellen. *See* Landers

DesBrisay, Magdalen. *See* Vergese d'Aubussargues

DesBrisay, Margaret. *See* Stewart

Desbrisay, Mary (Stewart), 775

DesBrisay, Theophilus (Samuel-Théophile de La Cour de Brisay) (father of THOMAS), 249

DesBrisay, Theophilus (grandson of THOMAS), 250

DesBrisay, Theophilus (great-grandson of THOMAS), 250

DesBrisay*, Theophilus (1754–1823), 250, 263, 775, 777

Desbrisay, Thomas, 128, 219, **249–50**, 263, 569, 775, 777, 778, 826

Des Camps, Renée (Comingo), 199

Deschaillons. *See* Saint-Ours

Deschambault. *See* Fleury

Deschamps, George, 251

Deschamps, Isaac, 63, 109, **250–52**, 431, 574

Deschamps, Sarah. *See* Ellis

Deschamps* de Boishébert, Henri-Louis (1679–1736), 668

Deschamps de Boishébert, Louise-Geneviève (Tarieu de La Naudière), 791

Deschamps* de Boishébert et de Raffetot, Charles (1727–97), 102, 451, 668

Deschamps* de La Bouteillerie, Jean-Baptiste-François (d. 1703), 668

Deschenaux. *See also* Brassard

Deschenaux, Geneviève. *See* Dumon

Deschenaux, Marie-Joseph. *See* Perrault

Deschenaux (Brassard Deschenaux), Pierre-Louis, 84, **252–53**, 289, 290, 792

Desdevens* de Glandons, Maurice (1742–99), 146

Deserontyon, John, **253–56**, 806, 810

Deserontyon, Peter John, 255

Des Essarts. *See* Berey

Desève, Charlotte (Leheup, *dit* Latulippe; Huguet, *dit* Latour), 435

Desève, Jean-Baptiste, 437

Desfonds, Bazile, 322

Desglis (Desgly). *See* Mariauchau

Désilets. *See* Huard

Des Islets. *See* Couillard

Desjardins*, Philippe-Jean-Louis (1753–1833), 380, 494, 659

Desjardins*, *dit* Desplantes, Louis-Joseph (1766–1848), 659

Deslandes, Marie-Josephe. *See* Le Pellé Lahaye

Deslandes, Marie-Josephte (Quesnel), 700

Deslandes, Pierre-Louis, 89

Des Méloizes. *See* Renaud

Despard*, John (1745–1829), 53, 205, 546, 766, 780

Despiaube, Catherine (Olabaratz), 638

Desplantes. *See* Desjardins

Des Porques, Anne (Liébert), 497

Desprez. *See* Guyon

Desrivières. *See also* Trottier

Desrivières, Monsieur (of Montreal), 705

Desrivières, François, 133

Desrivières-Beaubien, Édouard, 829

Desrivières-Beaubien*, Henri (1799–1834), 829

Desrochers*, Urbain (1780–1860), 497
Desrochers, Vital, 570
Desrosiers. *See* Deguire
Devos, Frederick, 902
Deyohninhohhakarawenh. *See* Theyanoguin
Dézery. *See* Latour-Dézery
Diaquande. *See* Teyohaqueande
Dibble, Abigail (Jessup), 454
Dibblee*, Frederick (d. 1826), 73, 74
Dibblee, Hannah. *See* Beardsley
Dick, A., 811
Dickens, Charles, 725
Dickerson, Mary (Ball), 53
Dickinson, Temperance (Odell), 628
Dickson, Jean (Hunter, Lady Hunter), 630, 631
Dickson*, Robert (1768–1823), 9, 10, 403, 714, 799
Dickson, Thomas, 258, 355
Dickson*, Thomas (1775–1825), 403, 549, 642, 643, 842
Dickson*, William (1769–1846), 403, 520, 549, 639, 782, 841, 842, 845
Diderot, Denis, 202
Diehl, John Justus, 36, 484
Diehl, Peter, 37, 88
Diehl, Phebe. *See* Arnoldi
Dieskau*, Jean-Armand, Baron de Dieskau (1701–67), 98, 393, 677
Digby, Robert, 148
Digby, William, 152
Digé, Geneviève (Pelletier), 257
Digé, Jacques, 256
Digé, Jean, **256–57**, 654
Digé, Jean, 256
Digé, Jeanne. *See* Augé
Digé, Marie-Charlotte. *See* Sajos
Digé, Véronique. *See* Lévêque
Dighton, Robert, 844
Dijean. *See* Dejean
Dinwiddie, Mary (Stuart), 785
Dionne, Germain, 358
Dionne, Marie (Gosselin), 358
Disney, Daniel, 98
Dixon, Charles, 257
Dixon, Charles, 94, **257–58**
Dixon*, George (fl. 1776–91), 586, 686
Dixon, Mary. *See* Corps
Dixon, Susanna. *See* Coates
Dixon, Thomas, 355
Dobbs, Alexander Thomas, 172
Dobbs, Mary Magdalen. *See* Cartwright
Dobie, Richard, **258–61**, 320, 376, 391, 745
Dodd, Ann (Pinson), 674
Dodd*, Archibald Charles (d. 1831), 53, 205, 546
Dodd, Jane. *See* Lynd
Dodd, Robert, 687
Dodd, Thomas, 509
Dodsley, Robert, 298
Doëy, Marie-Charlotte-Domitille. *See* Chaboillez
Dolabarats. *See* Olabaratz
Dombourg. *See* Bourdon
Donaldson, William, 349
Don Jacque. *See* Angeac
Donkley, John, 359
Donovan, Sarah (Elliott), 303

Dorchester, Baron. *See* Carleton
Dorchester, Baroness. *See* Howard
Doreil*, André (Jean-Baptiste) (fl. 1749–59), 677
Dorion*, Sir Antoine-Aimé (1818–91), 828
Dorion, Iphigénie. *See* Trestler
Dorland*, Thomas (1759–1832), 550, 772, 857
Dorrill*, Richard (d. 1762), 337, 632
Dorval. *See* Bigot
Dosquet*, Pierre-Herman (1691–1777), 4
Doty*, John (1745–1841), 27, 139, 600, 747
Doucet, Amable, **261–62**
Doucet, François, 261
Doucet, Madeleine (Magdalene) (Gallant), 335
Doucet, Marguerite. *See* Petitot, *dit* Saint-Sceine
Doucet, Marie (Doucet), 261
Doucet, Marie-Gertrude. *See* Gaudet
Doucet, Marie-Josèphe. *See* Robichaud
Doucet, Pierre, 261
Doucet*, Pierre (b. 1750, d. in or after 1799), 261
Douglas. *See also* Hamilton
Douglas*, Sir Charles (d. 1789), 31, 33, 36, 100, 281, 381, 686
Douglas, Helen (Hall, Lady Hall), 861
Douglas*, Sir Howard (1776–1861), 691
Douglas, James, 28, 220, **262–64**, 311, 424, 478, 516, 569, 779, 826, 848
Douglas, Jean, Baroness Daer and Shortcleuch, Countess of Selkirk. *See* Wedderburn
Douglas, John (father), 262
Douglas, John, 262
Douglas, Lady Katherine (Halkett), 266, 269
Douglas, Thomas, Baron Daer and Shortcleuch, 5th Earl of Selkirk, 125, 126, 195, 237, **264–69**, 309, 440, 465, 466, 516, 518, 529, 531, 533, 542, 544, 547, 591, 636, 657, 701, 734, 751, 776, 821, 860, 861, 862, 879
Douglas, Waitsill. *See* Haszard
Douglas, William, 586
Downie, George, 696, 876
Downman, John, 615
Dowset. *See* Doucet
Drachart*, Christian Larsen (1711–78), 54, 829
Drake*, Francis William (d. 1788 or 1789), 596
Drapeau, Charles, 271
Drapeau, Joseph, 165, **269–72**, 278, 301, 580
Drapeau, Marie-Geneviève. *See* Noël
Drapeau, Marie-Joseph. *See* Huard
Drapeau, Pierre, 269
Draper, Lyman Copeland, 803, 812
Drax, Elizabeth (Berkeley, Countess Berkeley), 72
Drolet, Marie-Anne (Thibodeau), 812
Drummond, Colin, 289
Drummond, Donald, 135
Drummond*, Sir George Gordon (1772–1854), 66, 107, 114, 117, 267, 550, 558, 559, 643, 644, 749, 876
Drummond, Henrietta Martha (Hamilton, Lady Hamilton), 244
Drummond, Jacobina (Campbell), 135
Drummond, John, 214, 745
Drummond, Peter, 282
Drummond, Susan (McLean), 135
Dryden, John, 629
Drysdale, John, 617
Duberger*, Jean-Baptiste (1767–1821), 834

Dubergès, Jean-Bernard, 736
Dubois, Marguerite (Brunet, *dit* L'Estang), 117
Dubreil* de Pontbriand, Henri-Marie (d. 1760), 48, 195, 276, 379, 432
Dubuc, Marie (Cherrier), 185
Du Calvet*, Pierre (1735–86), 21, 58, 75, 144, 398, 484, 649, 892, 893
Du Chaffault, Louis-Charles, Comte Du Chaffault de Besné, 62
Duchambon. *See* Du Pont
Ducharme*, Dominique (François) (1765–1853), 273
Ducharme, Françoise. *See* Demers, *dit* Dumé
Ducharme, Jean-Marie, **272–73**, 394, 567, 760
Ducharme, Joseph, 272
Ducharme*, Laurent (fl. 1723–87), 273
Ducharme, Marie-Angélique. *See* Roy, *dit* Portelance
Ducharme, Paul, 273
Ducharme, Thérèse. *See* Trottier
Ducheneau, *dit* Sanregret, Marguerite (Natte, *dit* Marseille), 622
Duchesnay. *See* Juchereau
Duchouquet. *See also* Lefebvre-Duchouquet
Duchouquet, Charlotte (Dumoulin), 329
Duckworth, Anne. *See* Wallis
Duckworth, Henry, 273
Duckworth, Sir John Thomas, **273–76**
Duckworth, Sarah. *See* Johnson
Duckworth, Susannah Catherine, Lady Duckworth. *See* Buller
Ducondu, Jean, 479
Ducros, *dit* Laterreur, Marguerite, 331
Dudevant*, Arnauld-Germain (b. 1751, d. *c.* 1798), 146, 471
Dudley, Rebecca (Gerrish; Burbidge), 121
DuFaradon. *See* Normant
Duff, Alexander, 750
Dufresne*, Nicolas (1789–1863), 480
Dufrost, Charles. *See* Youville, Charles-Marie-Madeleine d'
Dufrost* de Lajemmerais, Marie-Marguerite (Youville) (1701–71), 241, 293, 498, 680
Dufy. *See* Trottier
Dugré, Alexandre, 603
Du Gua* de Monts, Pierre (d. 1628), 874
Duguen, Pélagie-Jeanne-Marguerite (Quesnel), 700
Duhamel, Julien, 100
Duhamel, Marie-Angélique (Bouchette), 100
Du Jaunay*, Pierre (d. 1780), 8, 129
Dulignon, Marie-Thérèse (Bertrand), 76
Dulongpré*, Louis (1759–1843), 51, 71, 243, 417, 437, 529, 701
Dumas, Alexandre, 74, 271, **276–79**, 289, 315, 470, 484, 736, 737
Dumas, Antoine-Libéral, 276
Dumas, Catherine. *See* Lee
Dumas, Jean, 276
Dumas*, Jean-Daniel (1721–94), 276, 487
Dumas, Marguerite. *See* Cureux
Dumas, Marie. *See* Favar
Dumas, Marie-Françoise. *See* Fornel
Dumas, Marie-Joseph. *See* La Roche
Dumas, Pierre, 817
Dumas* Saint-Martin, Jean (1725–94), 241, 276, 277, 289
Dumé. *See* Demers

Dumon, Geneviève (Deschenaux), 252
Dumont. *See* Lambert
Dumontier, Baptiste, 576
Dumouchel, Marie-Louise (Bertrand), 76
Dumoulin, Charlotte. *See* Duchouquet
Dumoulin, Louise-Charlotte. *See* Poulin de Courval Cressé
Dun, James, 279
Dun, John, **279–80**, 639
Dunbar, Janet (Bruyeres), 118
Dunbar, William, 118
Duncan, Adam, 1st Viscount Duncan, 280
Duncan, Arthur, 281
Duncan*, Charles (fl. 1786–92), 197, 500, 586
Duncan, Frances (Ludlow) (wife of Gabriel Jr), 503, 505
Duncan, Frances (Ludlow) (wife of GEORGE DUNCAN), 505
Duncan, Henry, 187, **280–81**, 435
Duncan, Henry, 281
Duncan, Isabella (Twisden), 281
Duncan, John, 281, 282, 299
Duncan, Maria. *See* March
Duncan, Mary. *See* French
Duncan, Mary. *See* Wright
Duncan, Richard, 279, **281–83**, 285, 518
Dundas, Henry, 1st Viscount Melville, 131, 149, 152, 159, 160, 262, 318, 351, 452, 730, 758
Dunière, Charlotte (Chandler), 182
Dunière, Élisabeth. *See* Trefflé, *dit* Rottot
Dunière, Geneviève (Wills), 603
Dunière, Louis, 283
Dunière, Louis, 67, 107, 182, 233, **283–84**, 470, 566, 575, 576, 577, 650, 653
Dunière*, Louis-François (1754–1828), 283
Dunière, Marguerite. *See* Durand
Dunière, Marie-Anne (Marcoux), 576
Dunlap, William, 705, 706
Dunlop, Alexander, 284, 286
Dunlop, David, 284
Dunlop, James, **284–87**, 646, 828
Dunlop, James, 287
Dunlop, Jane (Ogilvy; Robertson), 635, 718
Dunlop, Robert, 284, 286
Dunlop of Clober, Alexander, 284, 287
Dunlop of Garnkirk, James, 286
Dunmore, Earl of. *See* Murray
Dunn. *See also* Dun
Dunn, Henriette. *See* Guichaud
Dunn, Robert, 290
Dunn, Thomas (paymaster), 289
Dunn, Thomas, 18, 43, 44, 69, 100, 108, 111, 138, 142, 146, 150, 191, 214, 215, 224, 226, 234, 277, **287–93**, 332, 368, 369, 370, 371, 373, 374, 422, 460, 492, 493, 494, 496, 576, 637, 694, 745, 746, 793, 794, 840, 843, 863
Dunn, Thomas (son of THOMAS), 290
Dunn, William, 290
Dunning, John, 1st Baron Ashburton, 145
Dupasquier, Abram, 239
Dupéré, Jean-Baptiste, 436
Dupéré, Magdeleine. *See* Huguet
Dupéront (Dupéron, Duperron). *See* Baby
Duplessis. *See* Lebrun
Duplessis-Sirois, Pascal, 588
Du Ponceau, Peter Stephen, 885

Du Pont* Duchambon de Vergor, Louis (b. 1713, d. after 1775), 104
Duport, John, 777, 873
Dupré. *See* Le Comte; Le Conte
Dupré, *dit* Le Conte. *See* Le Conte Dupré
Duquesne* de Menneville, Ange, Marquis Duquesne (d. 1778), 272, 276, 312
Durand, Marguerite (Dunière), 283
Durand, Servant, 276
Durham, Earl of. *See* Lambton
Durkee, Martha (Hebbard), 422
Durocher, Jean-Baptiste-Amable, 285, 370, 663, 821
Dusautoy (Dusaultoir), Louise-Madeleine (Cugnet), 252, 253
Dusourdy. *See* Landriaux
Dussau, Joseph, 249
Dussaus, Jean, 293
Dussaus, Marie-Angélique. *See* Huard
Dussaus, Marie-Angélique, **293**
Duval*, Charles (fl. 1767–1828), 436, 708
Duval, Joseph, 577
Duverger. *See* Forget
Duvert. *See* Chicou
Dyer, Hannah (Winslow), 865
Dysan. *See* Dejean

EAGLESON*, John (fl. 1765–90), 446, 869
Eaststaff*, Thomas George William (d. 1854), 274
Ecuier, Charles, **294–95**
Ecuier, Jean, 294
Ecuier, Marie-Josephte. *See* Cimère
Eddy, Eleazar, 295
Eddy, Elizabeth. *See* Cobb
Eddy, Jonathan, 15, 16, 240, 257, 258, 416, 627, 666
Eddy, Mary. *See* Ware
Edgar, William, 511, 560, 561
Edward Augustus, Duke of Kent and Strathearn, 24, 45, 84, 85, 87, 93, 101, 108, 119, 122, 136, 159, 160, 161, 187, 188, 192, 205, **296–98**, 318, 354, 356, 366, 372, 405, 425, 431, 439, 449, 504, 508, 541, 605, 608, 622, 634, 635, 649, 689, 690, 691, 763, 789, 849, 851, 872, 880
Edward, Catherine (Munn), 616
Edwards, Edward, **298–99**, 383, 821
Edwards, Jonathan, 729, 744
Edwards, Mary Ann, 401
Edwards*, Richard (d. 1795), 52, 361
Effingham. *See* Howard
Egan, William, 632
Egmont, Earl of. *See* Perceval
Egremont, Earl of. *See* Wyndham
Egushwa* (d. *c.* 1800), 710
Eisenbach, Freifrau zu. *See* Massow
Eisenbach, Freiherr zu. *See* Riedesel
Eldon, Earl of. *See* Scott
Eliza* y Reventa, Francisco de (1759–1825), 10, 11, 12, 198, 411, 615
Ellice, Alexander, 270, 282, **299–301**, 326, 333, 494, 511
Ellice, Ann. *See* Russell
Ellice*, Edward (1783–1863), 86, 300, 301, 531, 822, 848
Ellice, James, 299
Ellice, Mary. *See* Simpson of Gartly
Ellice*, Robert (1747–90), 299, 300, 512
Ellice of Knockleith, William, 299

Elligood, Anne (Elmsly), 303
Elliot, John, 123, 359, 361, 632
Elliott, Alexander, 302, 303
Elliott, Andrew, 730
Elliott, Francis Gore, 303
Elliott, Matthew, **301–3**, 306, 345, 449, 535, 536, 750, 797, 798, 799, 884
Elliott, Matthew, 303
Elliott, Robert Herriot Barclay, 303
Elliott, Sarah. *See* Donovan
Ellis, Henry, 20, 555
Ellis, John, 228
Ellis, Sarah (Deschamps), 250, 252
Ellis, Welbore, 1st Baron Mendip, 870
Ells, Margaret, 851
Elmsley, John, 17, 18, 188, 226, **303–4**, 389, 440, 453, 731, 732, 815, 841, 846, 864
Elmsley*, John (1801–63), 303
Elmsley, Mary. *See* Hallowell
Elmsly (Elmslie), Alexander, 303
Elmsly, Anne. *See* Elligood
Elmsly (Elmslie), Peter, 303
Elphinston, James, 628
Elphinstone, George Keith, 1st Viscount Keith, 206
Embury, Catherine (Fisher), 320
Embury, Margaret (Ruckle), 728
Embury, Philip, 320, 728
Emery, Christiana (Nairne), 620
Emery, Ruhama. *See* Rich
Emich Charles, Prince of Leiningen, 298
Emmanuel, Father. *See* Veyssière, Leger-Jean-Baptiste-Noël
Émond, Françoise. *See* Navarre
Émond, Pierre, 304
Émond, Pierre, 51, **304–5**, 452, 659
Emray, Ann (Balfour), 52
England, Anne. *See* O'Brien
England, Poole, 307
England, Sir Richard, 307
England, Richard G., **306–7**, 365, 552, 802, 852
English, Thomas, 678
English Chief* (fl. 1789–1821), 538
Entremont*, Bénoni d' (d. 1841), 545
Eppes, Abigail (Routh), 725
Eppes, William, 725
Ermatinger*, Frederick William (d. 1827), 285, 383, 384, 614
Ermatinger*, Lawrence (d. 1789), 258, 382, 383
Erskine. *See also* Askin
Erskine, John, 23rd Earl of Mar, 37
Esdaile, Robert, 320
Esgly (Esglis). *See* Mariauchau
Espinosa y Tello, José, 140
Estaing, Jean-Baptiste-Charles (Charles-Henri) d', Comte d'Estaing, 105, 173, 176, 893
Estimauville*, Jean-Baptiste-Philippe d' (1783–1823), 61
Etches, Richard Cadman, 686
Etherington, George, 7, 567
Ettwein, John, 884
Eury de La Pérelle, Catherine (Céloron de Blainville), 174
Evans*, Thomas (1777–1863), 113
Ewer*, Thomas Anthony (d. 1833), 632
Exmouth, Viscount. *See* Pellew

FABRE. *See also* Sales Laterrière
Fabre, Monsieur (probably father of Pierre de SALES Laterrière), 735
Fabre, *dit* Laperrière, Catherine. *See* Aubuchon, *dit* Lespérance
Fabre, *dit* Laperrière, Henri-Marie-Paschal (Pascal Rustan), 277, 735, 736
Fabre Surveyer, Édouard, 37, 530, 577
Fafard, *dit* Laframboise, Marguerite (Grant), 376
Fafard Laframboise, Marie-Victoire (Cressé), 216
Fainante, Monsieur (NWC employee), 564
Fairfield, Abigail. *See* Baker
Fairfield, Benjamin, 307, 308
Fairfield, Clarissa. *See* Fulton
Fairfield, Elizabeth. *See* Billings
Fairfield, Stephen, 307, 308
Fairfield, William, 307
Fairfield, William, **307–8**
Falcon, Pierre, 535
Falmouth, Viscount. *See* Boscawen
Fanning, Edmund, 27, 28, 219, 250, 262, 263, **308–12**, 424, 425, 431, 478, 515, 516, 568, 569, 717, 720, 775, 778, 779, 825, 826, 847, 848, 866
Fanning, Hannah. *See* Smith
Fanning, James, 308
Fanning, Phoebe Maria. *See* Burns
Fargues, Henriette. *See* Guichaud
Fargues, Jean, 290
Fargues, Pierre, 287, 290, 492, 601
Fargues*, Thomas (1780–1847), 290, 291
Faribault, Barthélemy, 271, **312–13**, 817
Faribault, Barthélemy, 817
Faribault, Bernard, 312
Faribault, Catherine-Antoine. *See* Véronneau
Faribault*, Georges-Barthélemi (1789–1866), 330, 649
Faribault*, Joseph-Édouard (1773–1859), 313
Faribault, Madelaine. *See* Hamon
Farquerson. *See* Ferguson
Farrar, Sarah. *See* Dean
Farries, Charlotte. *See* Robertson
Farries, John, 716
Fauché, Marguerite (Collet), 195
Fauteux*, Ægidius (1876–1941), 735
Favar, Marie (Dumas), 276
Favell, Mrs John. *See* Titameg
Favell, John, 534
Favell, Mary (McKay), 534
Fearson, Marie-Joseph (Charland), 183
Feitten, Magdeleine (Tröstler), 827
Féligonde. *See* Pélissier
Félix, Brother. *See* Bossu, *dit* Lyonnais
Feltz*, Charles-Elemy-Joseph-Alexandre-Ferdinand (d. 1776), 201
Ferdinand, Duke of Brunswick, 166, 584
Ferdinand I, King of the Two Sicilies (Ferdinand IV of Naples), 400
Ferguson*, Bartemas (d. 1832), 661
Ferguson, Henry, 556
Ferguson, Isabella (Gregory), 391
Ferguson*, John (d. 1830), 256
Ferguson, Patrick, 733
Fernández. *See* Martínez
Ferrer* Maldonado, Lorenzo (d. 1625), 571

Ferrers, Baroness. *See* Compton
Ferris, John Horatio, 88
Feuille, La. *See* Wahpasha
fforbes. *See* Forbes
ffraser. *See* Fraser
Fidalgo, Salvador, 12, 80
Fidler*, Peter (1769–1822), 236, 684
Fiedmont. *See* Jacau
Field, Robert, 24, **313–14**, 612
Figueroa. *See* Moziño
Filmer, Sir Robert, 628
Finlay, Charles, 746
Finlay, Elizabeth. *See* Grant
Finlay, George, 746
Finlay, Hamilton, 746
Finlay, Hugh, 21, 44, 146, 150, 165, 278, **314–19**, 427, 484, 503, 552, 692, 745, 746, 774, 794, 817, 821
Finlay, James, 260, 390, 537, 682
Finlay, Jane (Walker), 839
Finlay, John, 543
Finlay, Mary. *See* Phillips
Finlay, Robert, 314
Finlay, Susanna. *See* Parkins
Finucane, Andrew, 158
Finucane, Bryan, 109, 251
Firth*, William (1768–1838), 521
Fiset, Marie-Angélique (Bédard), 60
Fisher, Mrs (Budden; King; wife of Duncan, son of DUNCAN), 320
Fisher, Alexander (brother of DUNCAN), 319, 321
Fisher, Alexander (brother of FINLAY), 319, 321
Fisher*, Alexander (1755–1830), 92, 772
Fisher, Catherine. *See* Embury
Fisher, Christian. *See* Creighten
Fisher, Duncan (father of DUNCAN), 319
Fisher, Duncan (son of DUNCAN), 320
Fisher, Duncan, **319–21**, 770
Fisher, Elizabeth (Torrance), 320
Fisher, Finlay, 319, **321**
Fisher, James, 319, 321
Fisher*, James (d. 1822), 6, 318, 331, 493, 494, 495, 496, 501, 502, 817
Fisher, Jannet (Hick), 320
Fisher, John, 319, 320, 321
Fisher, Margaret (Hutchison; Lunn), 320
Fisher, Nancy (Mackenzie), 320
Fitzroy, Augustus Henry, 3rd Duke of Grafton, 142
Fitzwilliam, William, 4th Earl Fitzwilliam, 851
Fleming, Mrs (wife of Sampson), 39
Fleming, Sampson, 39
Fletcher, Alexander, 219, 309
Fletcher, Sir Richard, 450
Fleurimont. *See* Noyelles
Fleury, Madeleine (Jacson), 451
Fleury de La Gorgendière, Marie-Claire de (Taschereau), 793
Fleury Deschambault, Jeanne-Charlotte de (Le Verrier de Rousson; Rigaud de Vaudreuil de Cavagnial, Marquise de Vaudreuil), 741
Fleury* Deschambault, Joseph (1709–84), 143, 413, 794
Fleury* Deschambault, Louis-Joseph de (1756–1824), 374
Fleury Deschambault, Marie-Anne-Catherine (Le Moyne de Longueuil, Baronne de Longueuil; Grant), 288, 369

Flieger, J., 872
Flinders, Matthew, 55
Floquet*, Pierre-René (1716–82), 369, 414, 432
Florence, Pierre, 668
Florence, Thérèse-Esther. *See* Hausman, *dit* Ménager
Flórez Maldonado Martínez de Angulo y Bodquin, Manuel Antonio, 197, 198
Fluette, Marie-Louise (Barbeau; Natte, *dit* Marseille), 622
Fonblanche. *See* Quesnel
Forbes, Alexander, 486
Forbes, Geneviève (Grant), 376
Forbes*, John (1707–59), 545
Ford, Polly (wife of MICHIKINAKOUA), 593
Forest, Marguerite (Bastarache, *dit* Le Basque), 57
Foretier, Catherine. *See* Hubert
Foretier, Étienne, 322
Foretier, Jacques, 321, 322
Foretier, Marie-Anne. *See* Caron
Foretier, Pierre, 241, 259, **321–25**, 662, 663, 833
Foretier, Thérèse. *See* Legrand
Forget* Duverger, Jacques-François (fl. 1753–64), 342
Fork. *See* Nissowaquet
Fornel*, Louis (d. 1745), 277, 576
Fornel, Marie-Anne. *See* Barbel
Fornel, Marie-Françoise (Meignot; Dumas), 277
Forrest, Charles, 723
Forrest, Robert, 320
Forster, George, 32
Forster, Johann Reinhold, 362
Forsyth, Alexander, 299
Forsyth, Alice. *See* Robins
Forsyth, Ann. *See* Bell
Forsyth, George, 189, 262, 402, 405, 841
Forsyth*, James Bell (1802–69), 325, 617
Forsyth, Jane Prescott (Gregory), 391
Forsyth, Jean. *See* Phyn
Forsyth*, John (1762–1837), 101, 287, 300, 325, 326, 391
Forsyth, Joseph, 92, 168, 170, **325–27**, 402
Forsyth, Thomas (brother of JOSEPH), 259, 325, 512
Forsyth, Thomas (son of WILLIAM), 328
Forsyth, William, 325
Forsyth, William, 299, **327–29**, 350, 410, 608, 646
Fortier, François, 676
Fortier, Julie-Louise. *See* Taschereau
Fortin, Jean-Marie, 651
Forton, Jean (father), 329
Forton, Jean, 329
Forton, Louise. *See* Chamard
Forton, Michel, **329**
Foster, Augustus John, 113
Foucault*, François (1690–1766), 315
Foucher, Antoine, 602
Foucher*, Louis-Charles (1760–1829), 207, 322, 434, 591
Foucher, Marie-Madeleine-Françoise (Panet), 652
Fourche, La. *See* Nissowaquet
Foureur*, *dit* Champagne, Jean-Louis (1745–1822), 392, 833
Foureur, *dit* Champagne, Pierre, 436, 727
Fournel. *See* Fornel
Fournerie de Vézon, Joseph, 714
Fournerie de Vézon, Marie-Louise. *See* Réaume
Fournier, Joseph, 329
Fox, Charles James, 145, 849, 867, 898

Fox, Henry Edward, 156, 630, 867, 868
Fox, Theophilus, 502
Foxcroft, John, 315
Foy, Edward, 584
Foy, Hannah. *See* Van Horn
Foy, Nathaniel, 161
Fraisses de Long, Antoine, 276
Franchère*, Gabriel (1786–1863), 236, 237, 419, 533, 534, 814
Francis. *See* Leblanc, *dit* Latour, François
Francklin*, Michael (1733–82), 16, 81, 240, 251, 257, 409, 416, 435, 465, 556, 607, 608, 843
François*, Luc (baptized Claude) (1614–85), 497
Franklin, Benjamin, 31, 315, 316
Franklin, Thomas, 647
Franklin, William, 438, 628, 629, 657
Franks, Jacob, 9
Franquet*, Louis (d. 1768), 738
Fraser, Agnes. *See* Maxwell
Fraser, Alexander (apprentice), 437
Fraser, Alexander (judge), 772
Fraser, Alexander (merchant), 877
Fraser, Alexander (officer), 132, 317, 318, 374, 427
Fraser, Alexander (of Grenada), 349
Fraser*, Alexander (d. 1799), 224, 225
Fraser, Ann. *See* Hudson
Fraser, Ann (Bélanger; Bélair), 331
Fraser, Donald, 330
Fraser*, James (1759–1822), 58, 795
Fraser, Jane. *See* McCord
Fraser, Jane (Davidson), 224
Fraser, Janet. *See* McIntosh
Fraser, John (businessman), 283, 333, 562, 563, 564, 565
Fraser, John (judge), 142, 146, 149, 150, 216, 225, 232, 599, 839, 892
Fraser, John (lawyer), 861
Fraser, John, 46, **329–30**
Fraser*, John Malcolm (d. 1860), 331
Fraser, Joseph, 331
Fraser, Malcolm (father), 713
Fraser, Malcolm (son), 99
Fraser, Malcolm, 131, **330–31**, 620
Fraser, Margaret (Booth), 91
Fraser, Mary Ann (McNabb), 550
Fraser, Simon (merchant), 816
Fraser, Simon (father), 64, 713, 816, 817, 877
Fraser, Simon (son), 270, 877, 879
Fraser, Simon (son of MALCOLM), 331
Fraser*, Simon (1776–1862), 531, 541
Fraser*, Thomas (1749–1821), 282
Fraser, William, 331
Fréchette*, Louis-Honoré (1839–1908), 130
Frederick II, King of Prussia, 166, 582, 791
Frederick Augustus, Duke of York, 110, 206, 346, 356, 488, 802
Freeman, Anne (Grant), 260
Freeman*, Joseph (1765–1837), 817
French, Anne (Caldwell, Lady Caldwell), 130
French, Arthur, 640
French, Jane (Dease), 228
French, Mary (Duncan), 280
Fresnoy, Agathe-Louise de (Renaud d'Avène Des Méloizes), 711

Frichet, Jean-Baptiste, 185
Friedel, Ignace, 248
Frobisher*, Benjamin (d. 1787), 90, 178, 179, 258, 331, 332, 512, 528, 561, 562, 563, 564, 602, 818
Frobisher*, Benjamin Joseph (1782–1821), 291, 333
Frobisher, Charlotte. See Jobert
Frobisher, Joseph, 331
Frobisher, Joseph, 8, 90, 129, 134, 177, 178, 214, 215, 218, 258, 291, 301, **331–34**, 391, 495, 500, 512, 528, 561, 562, 564, 565, 566, 592, 602, 614, 636, 682, 715, 818, 820, 822
Frobisher, Rachel. See Hargrave
Frobisher, Thomas, 129, 331, 332, 500, 682, 683, 685
Fromenteau, Louis, 225
Frost, James, 95, **334–35**, 386
Frost, Jeremiah, 545
Frost, John, 545
Frost, Phoebe. See Wallen
Fubbister, John; Fubbister, Mary. See Gunn, Isabel
Fuller, Andrew, 557, 558
Fulton, Clarissa (Fairfield), 307
Fulton*, James (1740–1826), 612
Fulton, Joseph, 656

Gage*, Thomas (d. 1787), 146, 147, 282, 312, 389, 413, 457, 478, 479, 706, 741, 831, 865, 871, 888, 889, 890, 891
Gagnon, Thérèse (Demers), 244
Gaiachoton. See Kayahsota?
Galaup*, Jean-François de, Comte de Lapérouse (1741–88), 80, 103, 105, 194, 363, 500
Gale, Anna. See Noyes
Gale*, Samuel (1747–1826), 184, 834
Gale*, Samuel (1783–1865), 268, 697
Galiano. See Alcalá-Galiano
Gallant, Anne. See Chiasson
Gallant, Fidèle, 335
Gallant, Jean-Baptiste, 335
Gallant, L'Ange, 335
Gallant, Louis, 335
Gallant, Madeleine. See Doucet
Gallant, Victor, 335
Gallant, Xavier, known as Pinquin, **335–36**
Galliay, Marie (Serres), 752
Gallop, William, **336–37**, 646
Galloway, Agnes (Munn), 616, 617
Galloway, Joseph, 438
Galphin (Gaulfin, Gaulphin), George, 340
Gambier*, James, 1st Baron Gambier (1756–1833), 360
Gamelin, Charlotte (Malhiot), 571
Gamelin, Élisabeth (Malhiot), 572
Gamelin*, Ignace (1663–1739), 571
Gamelin*, Ignace (1698–1771), 572
Ganong*, William Francis (1864–1941), 136, 137
Garaut. See Garreau
Gardiner, Sylvester, 5
Gardner, William, 127
Garennes, Louis, 269
Garland, Charles, **337–38**
Garland, George (father of CHARLES), 337
Garland, George (politician), 492, 624, 725, 784, 838, 839
Garland*, George (1793–1833), 492
Garland, John, 337

Garland, John Bingley, 492
Garland, Joseph, 838
Garneau, Jean, 463
Garnkirk. See Dunlop
Garnom, Marie-Anne (Poitevin d'Anglebert), 294
Garreau. See Maugue-Garreau
Garreau*, dit Saint-Onge, Pierre (1722–95), 570, 582, 737
Garrettson, Freeborn, 468, 573
Garth. See McDonald
Garthbeg. See McTavish
Gartly. See Simpson
Gaspé. See Aubert
Gassin, Françoise (Natte), 622
Gaston, Jean, 497
Gastonguay, Angélique (Dénéchaud), 248
Gastonguay, Jean-Baptiste, 248
Gates, Horatio, 33
Gatineau, Monsieur (fur trader), 835
Gaudet, Agnès. See Chiasson
Gaudet, Anne (Cormier), 203, 204
Gaudet, Augustin, 203
Gaudet, Gertrude. See Le Blanc
Gaudet, Joseph, 261
Gaudet, Marguerite (Bastarache, dit Basque), 57
Gaudet, Marie-Gertrude (Doucet), 261
Gaudet*, Placide (1850–1930), 58, 203
Gaudin, dit La Poterie, Louis-Nicolas, 727
Gaudot, Salomé (Montmollin), 600
Gaulfin (Gaulphin). See Galphin
Gaulthier, Hélène (Chicoisneau), 186
Gaultier* de Varennes et de La Vérendrye, Pierre (1685–1749), 498, 563
Gautier, Madame (pauper), 769
Gautier, Anne. See Leblanc, dit Le Maigre
Gautier, Jean-Baptiste, 339
Gautier, Joseph, 339
Gautier, Nicolas, **338–40**
Gautier (Gauthier), Pierre, 339
Gautier, dit Bellair, Anne-Marie (Bergeaux; Mercure), 589
Gautier*, dit Bellair, Joseph-Nicolas (1689–1752), 338, 339, 589
Gautier, dit Bellair, Marguerite (Bourdon de Dombourg), 339
Gautier, dit Bellair, Marie. See Allain
Gautier de Verville, Charles, 8, 230, 836
Gay, Bunker, 741
Gayahgwaahdoh. See Kaieñʔkwaahtoñ
Genêt, Edmond-Charles, 152, 591, 592
George II, King of Great Britain and Ireland, 141, 767
George III, King of Great Britain and Ireland, 55, 142, 212, 241, 297, 313, 397, 408, 432, 434, 465, 488, 583, 630, 765, 791, 805, 851
George IV, King of Great Britain and Ireland, 114, 213, 268, 336, 400, 449, 536, 559, 674, 697, 851
George, David, **340–42**, 469
George, Phillis (wife of DAVID), 340
Gerard, Alexander, 768
Gérard, Conrad-Alexandre, 893
Germain (Sackville), George, 1st Viscount Sackville, 142, 146, 147, 148, 225, 238, 433, 482, 767, 805, 891, 893, 894, 896
Germain, Marguerite (Davanne), 223
Gerrard, Ann. See Grant

Gerrard*, Samuel (1767–1857), 260, 377, 635
Gerrish*, Benjamin (1717–72), 121
Gerrish*, Joseph (1709–74), 109, 240
Gerrish, Rebecca. *See* Dudley
Gervaise, Cécile (Cartier), 164
Gervaise, Michel, 164, 165, 185
Geyesutha. *See* Kayahsota⁇
Ghernish. *See* MacDonald
Giard*, Antoine (b. 1682, d. 1746 or 1747), 174
Giard, Catherine (Cerré), 174
Gibault, Marie-Joseph. *See* Saint-Jean
Gibault, Pierre, 342
Gibault, Pierre, **342–43**, 433
Gibbon, Edward, 182
Gibbons*, Richard (d. 1794), 108, 510, 766, 767
Gibson, James, 127
Gibson, Margaret (McGill), 527
Giengwahtoh. *See* Kaieñ⁇kwaahtoñ
Giffard* de Moncel, Robert (1587–1668), 288
Gigon, Faustin, 436
Gilbert, Joseph, 274
Gill, Mary Colley (Bentley), 67
Gill, William, 67
Gillespie*, George (1772–1842), 635, 636
Gillespie, John, 817
Gillmore, Ann. *See* Allen
Gillmore, George, **343–45**
Gilmore*, Thomas (d. 1773), 224
Girard. *See also* Giard
Girard*, Jacques (d. 1782), 719
Girouard, Émilie. *See* Berthelot
Girouard*, Jean-Joseph (1795–1855), 49, 50
Girty, Catharine. *See* Malott
Girty, George, 345
Girty, James, 345
Girty, Mary. *See* Newton
Girty, Simon, 345
Girty, Simon, 301, **345–46**
Givins*, James (d. 1846), 120
Gladman, George, 526, 712
Glandons. *See* Desdevens
Glapion*, Augustin-Louis de (1719–90), 146
Glasgow, George, **346–47**
Glasgow, Margaret. *See* Green
Glasier*, Beamsley Perkins (d. 1784), 413, 415
Glegg, John Bachevoye, 522
Glen, Jane Elizabeth (Jannetie) (Cuyler), 222
Glenaladale. *See* MacDonald; M'Donald
Glenie, James, 94, 136, 158, 159, 160, 162, 258, **347–58**, 506, 646
Glenie, Mary Anne. *See* Locke
Glenie, Melville, 356
Glennie, Professor, 357
Glikhikan* (Glickhican) (d. 1782), 301, 345, 882
Glynn, John, 145
Godard (Goddard), James Mason, 495, 879
Goddard, James Stanley, 322, 368, 760
Goddard, William, 743
Godefroy, Marie-Thérèse. *See* Bondy
Godefroy* de Tonnancour, Charles-Antoine (1755–98), 216, 217
Godefroy* de Tonnancour, Louis-Joseph (d. 1784), 143, 570, 687, 736, 737

Godefroy de Tonnancour, Louis-René-Labadie, 737
Godin, Sophia (Morse), 609
Godin*, *dit* Bellefontaine, *dit* Beauséjour, Joseph (b. 1697, d. after 1774), 412
Godsman, John. *See* Davidson, William
Goff*, Fade (1780–1836), 336
Goguet*, Denis (1704–78), 395, 396
Goldfrap, James, 142
Gonwatsijayenni. *See* Koñwatsi⁇tsiaiéñni
Goodwin, Robert, 886
Goold (Gould), Arthur, 666
Goold, Nathan, 135
Gordon, Mr (justice of the peace), 432
Gordon, Adam, 697
Gordon, Lord Adam, 214
Gordon, Alexander, 4th Duke of Gordon, 488, 795
Gordon, Lady Charlotte (Lennox, Duchess of Richmond and Lennox), 488, 489
Gordon, Helen (Taylor), 795
Gordon, James, 349
Gordon, Margaret. *See* MacDonell of Scothouse
Gordon, William (office holder), 507
Gordon, William (of Fredericton), 349, 350
Gordon of Wardhouse, Isabella (MacDonald of Glenaladale), 515
Gore*, Francis (1769–1852), 65, 111, 171, 189, 366, 441, 521, 550, 551, 734, 750, 765, 772, 796, 797, 841, 842, 845, 856
Goreham*, Joseph (1725–90), 58, 63, 204, 240, 258, 295, 296
Gorham, Nathaniel, 781
Goring, Francis, 781, 841
Gorrell*, James (fl. 1757–69), 835
Gosline, Ann (Shaw), 752
Gosling*, William Gilbert (1863–1930), 221
Gosselin, Catherine. *See* Monty
Gosselin, Charlotte. *See* Ouimet
Gosselin, Clément, 146, **358–59**
Gosselin, Gabriel, 358
Gosselin, Geneviève. *See* Crépeaux
Gosselin, Louis, 359
Gosselin, Marie. *See* Dionne
Goudie*, John (d. 1828), 67
Gough, Thomas Barnes, 857
Gouin, Louis, 792
Goulburn, Henry, 882
Gould. *See also* Goold
Gould, John, 501
Gourlay*, Robert Fleming (1778–1863), 551, 661, 674, 853
Gower, Abel, 359
Gower, Sir Erasmus, **359–61**, 633
Gower, Letitia. *See* Lewes
Grabot, Barthelemie (Lahaille), 471
Grace*, Thomas, known as Father James (1755–1827), 458
Grafton, Duke of. *See* Fitzroy
Graham, Aaron, **361**, 596, 641
Graham, Andrew, **362–63**, 450
Graham, Barbara. *See* Bowie
Graham, Felix, 681, 682
Graham*, Hugh (1758–1829), 344
Graham, Jane (McBeath), 512
Graham, Patricia. *See* Sherer
Granby, Marquess of. *See* Manners

Grand, Nanette (Ann) (Prévost), 693
Grandpré. *See* Boucher
Grand Sauteux, Le. *See* Minweweh
Granger, Eli, 597
Grant, Alexander, 17, 39, 189, **363–67**, 441, 443, 536, 718, 732, 855, 856
Grant, Ann. *See* Lynd
Grant, Ann (Gerrard), 260
Grant, Anne. *See* Freeman
Grant, Catherine (Jordan), 260
Grant, Charles, 85, 86, 144, 364
Grant*, Charles William, Baron de Longueuil (1782–1848), 373, 375
Grant*, Cuthbert (d. 1854), 268, 751
Grant, David (brother of WILLIAM, 1744–1805), 370
Grant, David (fur trader), 531
Grant, David Alexander, 64, 246, 370, 371, 372, 373, 374, 603
Grant, Elizabeth (Finlay), 260
Grant, Geneviève. *See* Forbes
Grant, Isobel (Grant), 363
Grant, James, 214
Grant*, James (fl. 1777–99), 259, 512, 715
Grant, Jane. *See* Holmes
Grant, Jane Elizabeth (Maitland), 372
Grant, Jean. *See* Tyrie
Grant, John (father of WILLIAM, 1743–1810), 376
Grant, John (fur trader), 90, 259, 260, 376
Grant, John (son of ALEXANDER), 367
Grant, John (supply contractor), 368, 373
Grant, Marguerite. *See* Fafard, *dit* Laframboise
Grant, Marguerite, 509
Grant, Marie-Anne-Catherine. *See* Fleury Deschambault
Grant, Patrick, 363
Grant, Peter, 531
Grant*, Peter (1764–1848), 534
Grant, Richard, 260
Grant, Robert (fur trader), 561, 603, 656
Grant, Robert (merchant), 368, 369, 817
Grant, Susannah. *See* Coffin
Grant, Thérèse. *See* Barthe
Grant, Thomas (distiller), 878, 879
Grant, Thomas (son-in-law of David LYND), 460, 509
Grant, William (father of WILLIAM, 1744–1805), 367
Grant, William (1744–1805), 21, 22, 43, 44, 45, 67, 87, 91, 108, 132, 142, 191, 233, 277, 288, 289, 290, 291, 317, 318, **367–76**, 385, 427, 460, 483, 493, 509, 527, 576, 603, 699, 745, 746, 793, 794, 816, 843, 880
Grant, William (1743–1810), 259, 260, **376–77**, 563
Grant*, Sir William (1752–1832), 87, 142, 148, 149
Grass, Margaret. *See* Swartz
Grass, Mary Ann (wife of MICHAEL), 377
Grass, Michael, **377–79**
Grasse, François-Joseph-Paul de, Comte de Grasse, 62, 105, 176
Gravé de La Rive, Charles-Yves, 379
Gravé de La Rive, Henri-François, **379–80**, 459, 492, 523, 524, 580
Gravé de La Rive, Louise-Jeanne-Marguerite. *See* Mercier
Graves, Algernon, 679
Graves, Booty, 512, 602, 656, 683
Graves, Elizabeth. *See* Budgell
Graves, Elizabeth, Baronne Graves. *See* Williams

Graves, Samuel, 754
Graves, Thomas, 380
Graves, Thomas, 1st Baron Graves, 62, 176, **380–82**, 491
Gravier, Charles, Comte de Vergennes, 433, 893
Gray, Alexander, 8, 150, 747
Gray, Andrew, 366
Gray, Edward William, 218, 298, 373, **382–84**, 391, 614, 652, 716
Gray, Elizabeth. *See* Low
Gray, Elizabeth (mother of ROBERT), 387
Gray, Frost Ralph, 386
Gray, George, 723
Gray, Hugh, 210, 495, 817
Gray, James, 388
Gray, John (father), 382, 383
Gray, John (merchant), 142, 288
Gray*, John (d. 1829), 71, 384, 420, 581, 718
Gray, Jonathan Abraham, 218, 383, 384, 614
Gray, Margaret. *See* Oakes
Gray, Martha. *See* Atkins
Gray, Mary Ann. *See* Scott
Gray, Phoebe. *See* Wallen
Gray, Ralph, 83, 369, **384–86**, 509
Gray, Robert, **387–88**, 410, 411
Gray*, Robert (d. 1828), 220, 309, 310, 311, 335
Gray, Robert Don Quadra, 388
Gray, Robert Isaac Dey, 17, 326, **388–89**, 518, 520
Gray, William, 387
Grece*, Charles Frederick (fl. 1805–21), 138, 373
Green, Anna (Winslow), 486, 869
Green, Benjamin, 390
Green*, Benjamin (1713–72), 389, 430
Green, Charles, 390
Green, Francis, **389–90**
Green, Harriet. *See* Mathews
Green*, James (1751–1835), 440
Green, Margaret. *See* Pierce
Green, Margaret (Glasgow), 347
Green, Margaret Ann (Howe), 430
Green, Susanna (Green), 389
Green, Timothy, 72
Green, Valentine, 844
Greenfield. *See* Macdonell
Greenhow, Robert, 388
Greenlaw, Anne (Semple), 750
Gregory, George, 391
Gregory, Isabella. *See* Ferguson
Gregory, Jane Prescott. *See* Forsyth
Gregory, John, 332, 333, **390–92**, 512, 537, 561, 562, 564, 565, 566, 603, 656, 820
Gregory, Maria (Mitchell), 391
Gregory, Mary (Milly) (Allan), 15
Gregory, William, 605
Grenet, Marie-Thérèse (Bouchette; Rollet), 100
Grenville, George Nugent Temple, 1st Marquess of Buckingham, 542
Grenville, Richard, 2nd Earl Temple, 54
Grenville, William Wyndham, 1st Baron Grenville, 22, 149, 151, 152, 586, 820, 874
Grey. *See also* Gray
Grey, Charles, 1st Earl Grey, 35, 691
Grey, William de, 1st Baron Walsingham, 605
Grey Cloud. *See* Mar-pi-ya-ro-to-win

Griffin, Robert, 259, 260
Grothé, Christian, 36, 436
Grougnard, Marie-Anne (Suzor), 788
Grunewalt, Caspar Frederic, 727
Gubbins, Joseph, 356
Güemes Pacheco Horcasitas Padilla, Juan Vicente de, 2nd Count of Revilla Gigedo, 10, 11, 198, 615
Guerne. *See* Le Guerne
Guernish. *See* MacDonald
Guernon, François, 392
Guernon, Marie. *See* Coulon
Guernon, *dit* Belleville, François, **392–93**
Guernon, *dit* Belleville, Jean-Baptiste, 392
Guernon, *dit* Belleville, Marie. *See* Dalpech, *dit* Bélair
Guernon, *dit* Belleville, Marie (Martin; wife of FRANÇOIS), 392
Guerry, Lewis, 747
Gugy*, Conrad (d. 1786), 214, 277, 484, 736, 887
Guichard, Simon, 680
Guichart* (Guichart de Kersident), Vincent-Fleuri (1729–93), 480
Guichaud, Henriette (Fargues; Dunn), 287, 290, 492
Guichaud, Jacques, 290
Guilford, Earl of. *See* North
Guillaume, 241
Guillimin, Charlotte (Trottier Desrivières; McGill), 526, 529, 705, 819
Guillimin*, Guillaume (1713–71), 478
Guillimin, Marie-Charlotte (Badelard), 46, 47, 648
Guillon, Louis, 737
Guillot*, *dit* Larose, François (b. 1727, d. before 1785), 99
Guillouet, Louis, Comte d'Orvilliers, 62
Guinaud, Henry, 42
Guines, Duc de, 752
Guío, José, 140
Guitet, Claude, **393–94**
Guitet, Élisabeth. *See* Peyrot
Guitet, Joseph, 393
Guitet, Modeste. *See* Landry
Guitet, René, 393
Guiyahgwaahdoh. *See* Kaieñ?kwaahtoñ
Gunn, Isabel, **394**
Guy, Catherine. *See* Vallée
Guy, Étienne, **394–95**, 398, 399
Guy, Jeanne. *See* Truillier, *dit* Lacombe
Guy, Joseph, 398, 399
Guy*, Louis (1768–1850), 398, 399, 829
Guy, Marie-Josephte. *See* Hervieux
Guy*, Pierre (1701–48), 97, 395
Guy, Pierre, 42, 43, 44, 241, 243, 278, 394, **395–99**, 663
Guyasuta. *See* Kayahsota?
Guyon Desprez, Élisabeth (Périnault), 662
Gwillim*, Elizabeth Posthuma (Simcoe) (1766–1850), 405, 428, 754, 759
Gyart. *See* Giard
Gyrard. *See* Girard

HACKETT, William, 83
Hadfield, Joseph, 318
Haenke, Tadeo, **399–400**, 571
Hailes, Harris William, 795
Hains. *See also* Ainsse
Hains, Joseph, 599

Hains, Marie-Françoise (Mondelet), 599
Haldimand, Anthony Francis, 901, 902
Haldimand, François-Louis, 887
Haldimand, Sir Frederick, 3, 8, 9, 14, 21, 43, 44, 57, 64, 91, 95, 96, 131, 132, 147, 148, 150, 156, 158, 173, 182, 204, 214, 224, 229, 231, 238, 240, 241, 252, 254, 255, 256, 259, 262, 273, 277, 284, 290, 298, 313, 316, 317, 332, 334, 343, 347, 348, 359, 364, 370, 371, 378, 384, 398, 425, 427, 433, 434, 454, 455, 470, 482, 492, 517, 537, 552, 576, 583, 584, 585, 589, 599, 602, 621, 637, 649, 654, 687, 700, 703, 710, 715, 737, 747, 752, 760, 788, 789, 790, 805, 806, 811, 836, 843, 863, 864, 870, **887–904**
Haldimand, Gaspard, 887
Haldimand, Marie-Madeleine. *See* Treytorrens
Haldimand*, Peter Frederick (d. 1765), 426, 902
Hale*, John (1765–1838), 193
Hale, William, 557
Halkett* (Wedderburn), John (1768–1852), 266
Halkett, Katherine. *See* Douglas
Hall, Basil, 861
Hall*, George Benson (d. 1821), 366
Hall, Helen, Lady Hall. *See* Douglas
Hall, Martha (Binney), 81
Hall, Mary (Roche; mother of ROBERT), 400, 401
Hall, Robert, 401
Hall, Sir Robert, **400–1**
Hall, Stephen, 81
Hallam, Lewis, 66
Halliburton*, Sir Brenton (1775–1860), 109
Halliburton, John, 24, 109, 187, 297
Hallowell, Benjamin, 303
Hallowell, James, 333, 562, 565, 566
Hallowell, Maria. *See* Sutherland
Hallowell, Mary (Elmsley), 303
Hallowell, William, 565
Halton, William, 765, 841
Hamel, Antoine, 827
Hamel*, Théophile (François-Xavier) (1817–70), 72
Hamilton, Captain, 776
Hamilton, Alexander, 553
Hamilton*, Alexander (1790–1839), 406, 453
Hamilton, Ann (Caldwell), 130
Hamilton, Catherine. *See* Askin
Hamilton*, Sir Charles (1767–1849), 243, 672
Hamilton, Elizabeth Ann (Anderson), 672, 673, 674
Hamilton*, George (d. 1836), 406, 453
Hamilton, Helen (Hamilton Douglas, Countess of Selkirk), 264
Hamilton, Henrietta Martha, Lady Hamilton. *See* Drummond
Hamilton*, Henry (d. 1796), 3, 8, 21, 26, 43, 44, 74, 100, 132, 148, 150, 238, 242, 253, 271, 273, 283, 289, 290, 298, 301, 317, 343, 344, 371, 427, 433, 637, 647, 649, 684, 802, 819, 836, 843, 895
Hamilton, Hugh, 130
Hamilton, Jean. *See* Wight
Hamilton, John, 402
Hamilton*, John (1802–82), 406
Hamilton, Mary. *See* Herkimer
Hamilton, Robert, 38, 39, 168, 280, **402–6**, 439, 442, 453, 492, 548, 549, 639, 660, 661, 669, 718, 719, 724, 734, 757, 781, 782, 814, 815, 819, 841, 842, 846, 856
Hamilton, Sarah (Stewart), 776, 778

Hamilton Douglas, Dunbar, 4th Earl of Selkirk, 264
Hamilton Douglas, Helen, Countess of Selkirk. *See* Hamilton
Hamon, Madelaine (Faribault), 312
Hamond, Sir Andrew Snape, 94, 148, 434
Hamtramck, John Francis, 553
Hancock, Thomas, 554
Hands. *See also* Ainse
Hands*, William (1755–1836), 722
Hänke, Elias Georg Thomas, 399
Hänke, Rosalia (mother of Tadeo HAENKE), 399
Hankey, Robert (merchant), 42
Hanna, Elizabeth. *See* Saul
Hanna, James G., 329, **406–7**
Hanna*, James Godfrey (d. 1851), 407, 461
Hanna, Jane (Orkney), 406
Hanna, Mary (Macnider), 406
Hannah (niece of Richard CARTWRIGHT), 168
Hannay*, James (1842–1910), 162, 353, 646
Hardy*, Sir Charles (d. 1780), 382
Hardy*, Elias (d. 1798), 35, 157, 352, 353, 504, 867, 868
Hardy, George, **407–8**, 777
Hardy, William, 737
Hare, Elizabeth (Clark), 188
Harel, Marie-Élizabeth (Périnault), 662
Harffy, William, 449
Hargrave, Rachel (Frobisher), 331
Harkness, John, 287
Harmar, Josiah, 3, 594, 807, 852
Harmon*, Daniel Williams (1778–1845), 543
Harper, Joseph, 689
Harper, William (merchant), 817
Harper, William (schoolmaster), 394
Harries, John, 123, **408**, 473, 633
Harries, Phoebe (wife of JOHN), 408
Harris, Elizabeth. *See* Scott
Harris, John, **408–9**, 660
Harris, Mary. *See* McKinney
Harris, Matthew, 409
Harris, Robert, 409
Harris, Thomas, 408, 409
Harrison, Audrey (Townshend, Viscountess Townshend), 822
Harrison*, Edward (d. 1794), 164, 460, 745, 817
Harrison, Margaret (Jones), 460, 461
Harrison, William Henry, 594, 619, 775, 796, 797, 798, 799
Harrower, David, 879
Hart*, Aaron (d. 1800), 194, 484, 494
Hart, Asher Alexander, 194
Hart*, Benjamin (d. 1855), 194
Hart*, Ezekiel (d. 1843), 27, 194, 207, 208, 210, 235, 828
Hart, Hannah (Clinch), 189
Hart, Joseph, 190
Hart, Moses, 410
Hart*, Moses (1768–1852), 64
Hart, Rebecca. *See* Byrne
Hart, Samuel, **409–10**
Hartshorne*, Lawrence (1755–1822), 850
Harvey, Augustus, 464
Harvey*, Daniel Cobb (1886–1966), 429
Harvey*, Sir John (1778–1852), 82
Hassard. *See* Haszard
Hasse, Gertrude (Holland), 425, 426
Hastings, Marquess of. *See* Rawdon-Hastings

Hastings, Selina, Countess of Huntingdon. *See* Shirley
Hastings, Warren, 754
Haswell, Mary. *See* Cordis
Haswell, Robert, 388, **410–11**, 586
Haswell, William, 410
Haszard (Hassard), Waitsill (Douglas), 262
Hatsell, John, 292
Hatt, Mary. *See* Cooley
Hatt, Mary (mother of RICHARD), 411
Hatt, Richard, 411
Hatt, Richard, 280, 405, **411–12**, 643, 765, 856
Hatt*, Samuel (d. 1842), 280, 411, 412, 643
Hauser, Frederick, 94
Hausman, *dit* Ménager, Thérèse-Esther (Florence; Perrault), 668
Haven*, Jens (1724–96), 54, 829, 830
Haviland*, William (1718–84), 104
Havy*, François (1709–66), 41, 276
Hawkins*, Ernest (1802–68), 475, 476
Hawn, Mr (of Upper Canada), 842
Hay, Agathe (Testard Louvigny de Montigny), 802
Hay*, Charles (fl. 1770–83), 737, 893
Hay, George, 523
Hay*, Jehu (d. 1785), 710, 802
Hay, John, 284
Hay, Thomas, 9th Earl of Kinnoull, 347
Hay, William, 284
Hays, Catherine. *See* Trestler
Hays, Joseph Eleazar, 828
Hayt, Monson, 35
Hazen, Charlotte. *See* La Saussaye
Hazen, Moses, 31, 34, 146, 358, 359, **412–15**, 415, 416
Hazen*, Robert Leonard (1808–74), 416
Hazen, Sarah. *See* Le Baron
Hazen, William, 16, 94, 413, **415–17**, 504, 506, 630, 867
Hazeur*, Joseph-Thierry (1680–1757), 196
Hazzen, Abigail. *See* White
Hazzen, Moses, 412, 415
Headley, Elizabeth. *See* Young
Headley, John, 664
Hearne*, Samuel (1745–92), 363, 450, 500, 656, 683
Heath, Elizabeth (Pettit), 669
Hebbard. *See also* Hibbard
Hebbard, John, 422
Hebbard, Martha. *See* Durkee
Heck, Barbara. *See* Ruckle
Heck, Paul, 728, 729
Heck*, Samuel (1774–1844), 729
Hedden (Heddon), Isaac, 136, 355
Heer, Frédérique-Louise. *See* Ouvrier
Heer, Jean-Tobie, 417
Heer, Louis-Chrétien de, **417**
Heer, Marie-Angélique de. *See* Badel
Heer, Marie-Louise de (De Lisle), 417
Hefele, Johanna Josepha Walpurga (Moll), 70
Heister, Leopold Philipp von, 427
Henday*, Anthony (fl. 1750–62), 363
Henderson, John, 424
Henderson, William, 530
Hendrick (Hendrick Peters). *See* Theyanoguin
Heney*, Hugues (1789–1844), 323
Hennepin*, Louis (baptized Antoine) (b. 1626, d.c. 1705), 821
Henniker, John, 413

Henry. *See also* Tekarihó:ken
Henry, Alexander, 177, 236, 237, 394, **418–19**, 501, 526, 560, 656
Henry*, Alexander (1739–1824), 38, 39, 129, 260, 377, 418,495,496,500,529,536,553,562,592,682,684,820, 821, 822
Henry, George, 509, 600, 768, 769
Henry, Jane (Lynd), 509
Henry*, John (d. 1853), 209, 532
Henry, Robert, 418
Henry*, Robert (1785–1859), 418
Henry, William, 418
Herchmer, Lawrence, 169
Heriot*, Frederick George (1786–1843), 228
Heriot*, George (1759–1839), 228, 319
Herkimer, Mary (McLean; Hamilton), 402
Heron, Andrew, 279, 419
Heron, Lucy (wife of SAMUEL), 420
Heron*, Patrick (fl. 1709–52), 430
Heron, Samuel, 17, 65, 71, **419–21**, 453, 519, 597
Heron, Sarah. *See* Ashbridge
Heron, Sarah. *See* Conott
Herrington, M. Eleanor, 256
Herriot. *See* Heriot
Herron*, William (1784–1838), 473
Herse, Jacques-Clément, 243, 701
Hertel de La Fresnière, Marguerite-Thérèse (Boucher de Niverville), 97
Hertel* de Rouville, Jean-Baptiste (1668–1722), 703
Hertel de Rouville, Jean-Baptiste-Melchior, 236, **421–22**
Hertel* de Rouville, Jean-Baptiste-René (1789–1859), 421
Hertel de Rouville, Louise-Catherine. *See* André de Leigne
Hertel de Rouville, Marie-Anne. *See* Hervieux
Hertel de Rouville, Marie-Anne-Julie (Irumberry de Salaberry), 421
Hertel* de Rouville, René-Ovide (1720–92), 96, 146, 216, 225, 232, 383, 421, 599, 652, 737, 839, 892
Hertel de Saint-François, Elizabeth. *See* Robertson
Hertel de Saint-François, Françoise-Catherine (Irumberry de Salaberry), 449
Hertel* de Saint-François, Joseph-Hippolyte (1738–81), 716
Hertel de Saint-François, Louis-Hippolyte, 716
Hervé, Zacharie, 201
Hervey, John, 1st Earl of Bristol, 767
Hervey, Lady Louisa Carolina Isabelle (Smythe, Lady Smythe), 767
Hervieux, Jean-Baptiste, 421
Hervieux, Louise. *See* Quesnel Fonblanche
Hervieux*, Louis-François (1711–48), 395
Hervieux, Marie-Anne (Hertel de Rouville), 236, 421
Hervieux, Marie-Anne (La Corne), 791
Hervieux, Marie-Anne (Le Comte Dupré), 320, 481
Hervieux, Marie-Josephte (Guy), 394, 395
Hesse, Emmanuel, 836
Hester, James, 526
Hester, John, 526
Hesther, Nancy, 526
Hey*, William (d. 1797), 20, 142, 144, 145, 146, 606, 863
Hibbard, Jedediah, **422–23**
Hibbard, Martha. *See* Porter
Hiché*, Henry (d. 1758), 368
Hiché, Marie-Josephte-Madeleine (Perthuis), 368
Hick, Jannet. *See* Fisher

Hick, John, 320
Hickman, Margaret (Shaw), 752
Hicks*, John (1715–90), 554
Higginbottom, Thomas, 107
Higgins, Cornelius, 477
Higgins*, David (d. 1783), 219, 263, 477, 478, 777
Hildrith, Ann. *See* Wood
Hildrith, Isaac, **423–24**, 658
Hill, Aaron. *See* Kanonraron
Hill, Christiana. *See* Brant
Hill, Isaac. *See* Anoghsoktea
Hill*, John (d. 1841), 27, 219, 310, 516, 568, 721, 775, 778, 825, 826, 848
Hill, Margaret (Morris), 629
Hill, Mary. *See* Brant
Hill, Solomon, 856
Hill, Wills, 1st Earl of Hillsborough, 142, 143, 145, 606
Hillier*, George (d. 1841), 661
Hillyer, Phoebe (Cossitt), 204
Hine, John, 675
Hinman, Benjamin, 29
Hins. *See* Ainsse
Hinton, Ann (Mott), 613
Hipps, George, 385
Hitsman, John Mackay, 798
Hiyoua. *See* Wikinanish
Hobart, Robert, 4th Baron Hobart and 4th Earl of Buckinghamshire, 319, 542
Hobbes, Thomas, 486
Hocquart*, Gilles (1694–1783), 90
Hodgkins, Mary (Bailey), 47
Hodgson*, John (d. 1833), 394, 712
Hodgson, Rebecca. *See* Robinson
Hodgson, Robert, 28, **424–25**, 516, 720
Hodgson*, Sir Robert (1798–1880), 425, 721
Hodgson, Thomas, 679
Hogan, Hugh, 139
Holburne, Francis, 280
Holdsworth, Ann (Newman), 625
Holdsworth, Mary (Newman), 625
Holland*, Anthony Henry (1785–1830), 612, 853, 854
Holland, Gertrude. *See* Hasse
Holland, Henry, 426
Holland*, John Frederick (d. 1845), 335, 426, 428, 541
Holland, Marie-Joseph. *See* Rollet
Holland, Samuel Johannes, 101, 149, 183, 222, 255, 378, **425–29**, 457, 499, 552, 589, 773, 834, 873, 874, 887, 892, 899
Holland, Samuel Lester, 428
Holloway*, John (1747–1826), 360
Hollywood, Ruth (Almon; Nash), 23
Holmes, Jane (Grant; Blackwood), 85, 86
Holmes*, John (rebaptized Jean) (1799–1852), 295
Holmes*, William (d. 1792), 451, 561, 603, 656
Holmes*, William (d. 1834), 502
Holroyd, John Baker, 1st Earl of Sheffield, 21, 149, 491
Hooker, Philip, 678
Hope*, Henry (d. 1789), 56, 96, 148, 149, 156, 214, 283, 343, 523, 576, 760, 901
Hopkins, Frances. *See* Davis
Hopkins, Samuel, 519
Horcasitas. *See* Güemes
Horn, Philipina Maria (Phébé) (Arnoldi), 36
Hornor*, Thomas (1767–1834), 733

Horsford, Eben Norton, 885
Hoskins, John Box, 388, 411, 586
Hotesse, Marie-Anne. *See* Caron
Hough, Franklin Benjamin, 40, 41
Hounsom, John, 373
How, Deborah (Cottnam), **429–30**
How*, Edward (d. 1750), 429, 430
How, Marie-Madeleine. *See* Winniett
Howard, John, 684
Howard*, Joseph (d. 1797), 20, 21, 142, 727, 741
Howard, Lady Maria (Carleton, Baroness Dorchester), 141
Howard*, Peter (d. 1843), 857
Howard, Thomas, 2nd Earl of Effingham, 140, 145
Howard, William, 129
Howe, Alexander, **430–31**
Howe, Caleb (father), 740
Howe, Caleb, 740
Howe, Helen McKellar. *See* Bontein
Howe, Jemima. *See* Sawtelle
Howe*, Joseph (1804–73), 692, 854
Howe, Margaret Ann. *See* Green
Howe, Moses, 740, 741
Howe, Richard, 4th Viscount Howe, 221, 274, 280, 281, 382, 435, 595
Howe, Squire, 740
Howe, William, 5th Viscount Howe, 23, 115, 147, 222, 227, 505, 629, 657, 865, 890
Huard, Marie-Angélique (Dussaus), 293
Huard, *dit* Désilets, Marie-Joseph (Drapeau), 269
Hubbard, Mary (Pond), 681
Hubbard, William, 353
Hubert, Catherine (Baron; Foretier), 322
Hubert, Cécile. *See* Cartier
Hubert*, Jean-François (1739–97), 12, 13, 77, 92, 124, 125, 150, 179, 180, 186, 202, 245, 246, 247, 294, 343, 380, 434, 480, 493, 509, 523, 524, 570, 587, 633, 663, 667, 687, 688, 691, 701, 704
Hudson, Ann (Naper; Fraser), 330
Hudson, Thomas, 824
Huet de La Valinière, Charles, 431
Huet de La Valinière, Olive. *See* Arnaud
Huet de La Valinière, Pierre, **431–34**
Hugessen. *See* Weston-Hugessen
Hughes, James, 531
Hughes, Jane, Lady Hughes. *See* Sloane
Hughes, Joanne, Lady Hughes. *See* Collyer
Hughes, Sir Richard, 434
Hughes, Sir Richard, **434–35**
Hughes, William, 872
Huguet, Charlotte. *See* LaMotte
Huguet, Claude, 435
Huguet*, Joseph (1725–83), 432
Huguet, Magdeleine (Dupéré), 436
Huguet, *dit* Latour, Agathe-Henriette (McDonell), 436, 437
Huguet, *dit* Latour, Charlotte. *See* Desève
Huguet, *dit* Latour, Claire. *See* Trudeau
Huguet, *dit* Latour, Josette. *See* Valois
Huguet, *dit* Latour, Louis, 435, 436, 437
Huguet, *dit* Latour, Louis-Alexandre, 435, 436, 437, 727
Huguet, *dit* Latour, Louis-Maximilien-Théodore, 436
Huguet, *dit* Latour, Marie-Louise. *See* Dalciat
Huguet, *dit* Latour, Pierre, 218, 219, **435–38**, 708, 727, 728
Huguet, *dit* Latour, Pierre, 435, 436, 437

Huguet, *dit* Latour, Scholastique, 436
Huiquinanichi. *See* Wikinanish
Hull, William, 14, 112, 522, 543, 643, 714, 798
Hullett, William, 495
Humbert, François-Joseph-Michel, 481
Humboldt, Friedrich Wilhelm Karl Heinrich Alexander von, 400
Hume, David, 182, 486
Humphreys, David, 741
Humphreys, James, 438
Humphreys, James, **438–39**
Humphreys, Mary. *See* Yorke
Humphreys, Susanna. *See* Assheton
Hunt, Henry, 675
Hunt, Henry Holdsworth, 626
Hunter, Charles D., 344
Hunter, Euphemia. *See* Jack
Hunter, James, 327
Hunter, Jean, Lady Hunter. *See* Dickson
Hunter, John, 189
Hunter, Peter, 17, 18, 101, 265, 280, 303, 304, 365, 366, 405, 420, **439–43**, 453, 470, 495, 502, 548, 549, 732, 749, 753, 844, 845, 855, 856
Hunter, Robert, 617
Hunter of Knap, John, 439
Huntingdon, Countess of. *See* Shirley
Huntingdon, Jabez, 664
Huot*, François (1756–1822), 580
Hurtin, William, 613
Husbands, Hermon, 309
Huston, Andrew, 843
Huston*, James (1820–54), 702
Huston, John, 869
Hutchings, Charles, 444
Hutchings, Hannah. *See* Sparke
Hutchings, Henry, 444
Hutchings, Richard, **443–44**, 596
Hutchings, Robert, 443
Hutchins*, Thomas (d. 1790), 362
Hutchinson, Margaret (Wiswall), 870, 871
Hutchinson, Thomas, 831, 865
Hutchison, Margaret. *See* Fisher
Hutchison, William, 320
Hutton, James, 68
Hutton, Margaret. *See* Bentley
Hyatt, Elizabeth (Schurman), 743
Hyde, Thomas, 784

INGERSOLL, Jared, 94
Ingersoll*, Laura (Secord) (1775–1868), 83, 168, 800
Inglis, Archibald, 444
Inglis, Charles, 25, 59, 60, 109, 124, 128, 135, 204, 205, 219, 314, 318, 344, **444–48**, 475, 476, 573, 601, 602, 605, 637, 657, 694, 785, 787, 832, 850, 871, 872
Inglis, John, 86, 820
Inglis*, John (1777–1850), 446, 872
Inglis, John Bellingham, 86
Inglis, Margaret. *See* Crooke
Inglis, Mary. *See* Vining
Ingraham, Joseph, 387
Inkster, James, 712
Innis*, Harold Adams (1894–1952), 528, 683, 685
Innis, Mary Emma. *See* Quayle

Iredell, Abraham, **448–49**, 553, 774
Iredell, Hannah. *See* Luckens
Iredell, Hester. *See* Marsh
Iredell, Robert, 448
Irelande, Bazile, 564
Irish, Charles, 218
Irumberry* de Salaberry, Charles-Michel d' (1778–1829), 297, 421, 449, 450, 696
Irumberry de Salaberry, Édouard-Alphonse d', 297, **449–50**
Irumberry de Salaberry, Françoise-Catherine d'. *See* Hertel de Saint-François
Irumberry de Salaberry, François-Louis d', 449, 450
Irumberry* de Salaberry, Ignace-Michel-Louis-Antoine d' (1752–1828), 75, 174, 297, 449, 461, 508, 702, 794, 827
Irumberry de Salaberry, Marie-Anne-Julie d'. *See* Hertel de Rouville
Irumberry de Salaberry, Maurice-Roch d', 449, 450
Irvine*, James (d. 1829), 461, 769
Irving*, Paulus Æmilius (1714–96), 142
Irving, Washington, 472, 814
Isaac. *See* Anoghsoktea
Isaac. *See* Glikhikan
Isaac of Onoquaga, 804
Isaacs, Benjamin, 832
Isaacs, Mary. *See* Pickett
Isham, Charles Thomas, 194, **450–51**, 500
Isham, James, 451
Isham*, James (d. 1761), 362, 450
Isham, Jane, 451
Isham, Mary, 451
Isham, Price, 451
Isham, Thomas (great-uncle), 450
Isham, Thomas, 451

Jacau* de Fiedmont, Louis-Thomas (d. 1788), 104
Jack, 239
Jack, Euphemia (Hunter), 439
Jackson, Francis James, 533
Jackson, James, 330
Jackson*, John (1765–1839), 496
Jackson*, John Mills (1764–1836), 170, 171, 842, 856, 857
Jackson, Phoebe (Willcocks), 859
Jacob. *See* Jacau
Jacobs*, Ferdinand (d. 1783), 450, 656
Jacobs, Marie-Josette. *See* Audette, *dit* Lapointe
Jacobs*, Samuel (d. 1786), 20, 164, 368, 369, 385, 713
Jacquerault (Jacquero). *See* Jacrau
Jacquin, Nikolaus Josef, 399
Jacrau*, Joseph-André-Mathurin (d. 1772), 144, 379
Jacson, Antoine, 49, **451–52**
Jacson, Antoine-Joseph, 451
Jacson, Louis (grandfather), 451
Jacson, Louis, 452
Jacson, Madeleine. *See* Fleury
Jacson, Marie-Marguerite. *See* Chamberland
James, Father. *See* Grace, Thomas
James, Abigail (Jessup), 454
Jamet*, John (d. 1763), 129
Jamieson, Neil, 646
Jarvis, Abraham, 25
Jarvis*, Edward (d. *c.* 1800), 712
Jarvis*, George Stephen Benjamin (1797–1878), 113
Jarvis, Hannah Owen. *See* Peters

Jarvis, Leonard, 413, 415, 416
Jarvis, Martha. *See* Seymour
Jarvis, Mary Boyles. *See* Powell
Jarvis*, Munson (1742–1825), 647
Jarvis, Samuel (father of WILLIAM), 452
Jarvis, Samuel (political candidate), 94
Jarvis*, Samuel Peters (1792–1857), 453
Jarvis, William, 65, 420, 441, 449, **452–53**, 597, 815, 816, 854
Jauge, Simon, 42
Jautard*, Valentin (d. 1787), 621, 737, 892, 894
Jay, John, 629
Jean, Catherine (Bossu), 93
Jean-Baptiste, 775
Jefferey, John, 106
Jefferey, Sarah (Bradford), 106
Jefferson, Thomas, 313, 583, 693, 848
Jefferys, Thomas, 767
Jeffrey. *See also* Jefferey
Jeffrey, John, 491, 641, 764, 783, 784, 785, 838
Jeffrey, Joseph W., 784
Jemison, Mary, 14
Jenison, Jean, 599
Jenkins, George, 614
Jenkinson, Robert Banks, 2nd Earl of Liverpool, 213, 521, 522, 655, 842
Jenner, Edward, 189, 190
Jenner, George Charles, 190
Jérôme, 261
Jérôme, King of Westphalia. *See* Bonaparte, Jérôme
Jérôme, *dit* Latour, Marie-Joseph (Roy), 727
Jervis, John, 1st Earl of St Vincent, 759
Jessen, Dettlieb Christopher, **453–54**
Jessen, Francisca Barbara. *See* Rudolf
Jessup, Abigail. *See* Dibble
Jessup, Abigail. *See* James
Jessup, Ebenezer, 454
Jessup, Edward, 307, **454–55**, 457
Jessup, Edward, 455
Jessup, Joseph, 454
Jewett, Dorothy (Caleff), 134
Jewett, Jedediah, 47
Jewitt*, John Rodgers (1783–1821), 618, 619
Job, John, 119, 120
Jobert, Charlotte. *See* Larchevêque
Jobert, Charlotte (Frobisher), 332, 333
Jobert, Jean-Baptiste, 333
John (father of David GEORGE), 340
John, Captain. *See* Deserontyon, John
John, Catharine. *See* Brant
John August, 784
Johnson, Miss (Welch), 845
Johnson, Anne (Dease), 228
Johnson*, Guy (d. 1788), 147, 229, 254, 262, 804, 806, 811, 843, 895, 896
Johnson, Isabella (Barnes), 57
Johnson*, Sir John (1742–1830), 149, 179, 229, 230, 254, 255, 282, 291, 302, 320, 365, 388, 405, 454, 517, 518, 519, 537, 552, 660, 669, 718, 757, 760, 772, 781, 786, 787, 806, 807, 841, 852, 894, 895, 896, 898, 899
Johnson*, John (1792–1886), 803
Johnson, Samuel (college president), 58
Johnson, Samuel (lexicographer), 56, 166

Johnson, Sarah (Duckworth), 273
Johnson, Smoke. *See* Johnson, John
Johnson*, Sir William (d. 1774), 129, 228, 229, 253, 299, 454, 517, 519, 523, 567, 681, 706, 716, 786, 803, 804, 888
Johnston*, Alexander (d. 1778), 507
Johnston*, Hugh (1755–1828), 647
Johnston*, James (d. 1800), 19, 142, 289, 509, 699
Johnston, Margaret. *See* Macnider
Johnston, Sarah, 192
Johnston*, William (d. 1828), 862
Johnstone, George, 136
Johnstone, John, 681
Johnstone, William, 482
Jolliet*, Louis (d. 1700), 288
Jolliette, Claire (Volant de Chamblain; Boisseau), 91
Jolliffe, Peter, 491
Joly, Angélique. *See* Marchand
Joncaire. *See* Chabert
Jones, Mr (surveyor), 183
Jones, Alpheus, 458
Jones, Anne (Williams), 862
Jones, Caleb, 137, **456**, 506
Jones*, Charles (1781–1840), 458, 748, 787
Jones, Charlotte. *See* Coursolles
Jones, Charlotte (Sherwood), 457
Jones, David, 852
Jones, Elisha (father), 456
Jones, Elisha, 457
Jones, Eliza (Boulton), 457
Jones, Elizabeth (wife of CALEB), 456
Jones, Elizabeth Vaughan (Ross), 461
Jones, Ephraim, 455, **456–58**
Jones, Inigo, 678
Jones, James, 647
Jones, James, 12, 123, 125, **458–59**, 524, 671
Jones, John (grand jury member), 462
Jones, John (nephew of JOHN), 462
Jones, John (notary), 462
Jones, John (politician), 462
Jones, John (schoolmaster), 462
Jones*, John (1737–1800), 408, 633
Jones, John, 67, 373, **459–62**, 494, 699, 713, 816, 834
Jones, John Paul, 264
Jones*, Jonas (1791–1848), 457, 458, 558
Jones, Jonathan, 222
Jones, Joseph, 462
Jones, Josiah, 457
Jones, Margaret. *See* Harrison
Jones, Margaret S. *See* Beke
Jones, Mary. *See* Allen
Jones, Mary. *See* Stuart
Jones, Peter. *See* Kahkewaquonaby
Jones, Richard W., 139
Jones, Robert, 502
Jones, Sarah (Charland), 183
Jones, Simeon, 457
Jones*, Solomon (1756–1822), 455
Jones, Stephen, 457
Jones, William, 458
Jordan, Catherine. *See* Grant
Jordan*, Jacob (1741–96), 164, 191, 656, 684, 821
Jordan*, Jacob (1770–1829), 260, 566

Joseph, King of Naples; Joseph, King of Spain. *See* Bonaparte, Joseph
Joseph*, Henry (1775–1832), 194
Joseph, Naphtali, 193
Joseph, Rachel. *See* Solomons
Jourdain, Michel-Augustin, 305
Jourdain*, *dit* Labrosse, Charles (b. 1734, d. in or after 1824), 140, 495
Jourdain*, *dit* Labrosse, Paul-Raymond (d. 1769), 497
Jouy, Comte de. *See* Rouillé
Joybert de Soulanges, Marie-Geneviève (Le Moyne de Longueuil), 486
Joyeuse. *See* Villaret
Juchereau* de Saint-Denis, Nicolas (d. 1692), 463
Juchereau de Saint-Denys, Thérèse-Denise. *See* Migeon de Branssat
Juchereau Duchesnay, Antoine, 462
Juchereau Duchesnay, Antoine, 231, **462–64**, 470, 482, 793, 879, 881
Juchereau* Duchesnay, Antoine-Louis (1767–1825), 464
Juchereau Duchesnay, Catherine. *See* Le Comte Dupré
Juchereau Duchesnay, Catherine-Henriette (Blanchet), 464
Juchereau* Duchesnay, Jean-Baptiste (1779–1833), 464
Juchereau Duchesnay, Julie-Louise. *See* Liénard de Beaujeu de Villemonde
Juchereau Duchesnay, Julie-Marguerite, named de Saint-Antoine, 464
Juchereau Duchesnay, Louise-Françoise (Taschereau), 464, 793
Juchereau Duchesnay, Marie-Catherine, named de Saint-Ignace, 462
Juchereau Duchesnay, Marie-Eustache, 462
Juchereau Duchesnay, Marie-Françoise. *See* Chartier de Lotbinière
Juchereau* Duchesnay, Michel-Louis (1785–1838), 464
Judah, Abraham, 193
Judith (mother of David GEORGE), 340
Julie-Marguerite de Saint-Antoine. *See* Juchereau Duchesnay
Julien, Francis, 465
Julien, John, **464–65**
Jumonville. *See* Coulon
Jussieu, Bernard de, 592

KAHKEWAQUONABY* (1802–56), 467
Kaieñ?kwaahtoñ* (d. 1786), 254, 805, 896
Kaigwiaidosa. *See* Madjeckewiss
Kain*, William (1809–30), 640
Kaiũtwah?kũ (Cornplanter), 805, 896
Kalm*, Pehr (1716–79), 228
Kanonraron (Aaron Hill), 255, 807, 809
Karl Wilhelm Ferdinand, Duke of Brunswick, 582
Katem, Michael, 337
Kay, Ann. *See* Cruickshank
Kay, John, 512
Kay, William, 512
Kayahsota?* (Kayashoton) (fl. 1755–93), 253
Kayenquaraghton. *See* Kaieñ?kwaahtoñ
Kaygill, Thomas, 678
Kaylus. *See* Thubières
Keats*, Sir Richard Goodwin (1757–1834), 473, 474, 671
Keith, Viscount. *See* Elphinstone
Kelly*, Jean-Baptiste (1783–1854), 186

Kelly, Joseph, 413
Kélus. *See* Thubières
Kemp, George, 838
Kendrick*, John (d. 1794), 387, 410, 411
Kennedy, Elspeth (Elspy) (McKay), 532
Kennedy, Hugh Alexander, 676
Kent and Strathearn, Duchess of. *See* Victoria Mary Louisa
Kent and Strathearn, Duke of. *See* Edward Augustus
Kenwick (Kenwrick). *See* Kendrick
Keppel, Frederick, 746
Keppel, George, 3rd Earl of Albemarle, 141
Kerr, Elizabeth. *See* Brant
Kerr*, James (1765–1846), 234
Kerr, Lady Louisa (Lennox), 488
Kerr, Mary Margaret (Clark), 673
Kerr*, Robert (d. 1824), 279, 639, 841
Kerr, William Henry, 4th Marquess of Lothian, 488
Kerr*, William Johnson (1787–1845), 673
Kersident. *See* Guichart
Keveny, Owen, 267, **465–66**
Kiashuta. *See* Kayahsota[?]
Kildalloig. *See* Campbell
Kimber, Joseph, 406
Kineubenae, **466–67**
King, Mrs. *See* Fisher
King, Boston, 341, **468–69**
King*, Edwin Henry (1828–96), 320
King, George (Montreal merchant), 821
King, George (Quebec merchant), 406
King, Hannah. *See* Waterman
King*, James (1750–84), 55
King, Violet (wife of Boston), 468, 469
King, William (shipbuilder), 83
King, William (soldier), 750
King Hendrick. *See* Theyanoguin
King Newcomer. *See* Netawatwees
King of Kanadesaga. *See* Kaieñ?kwaahtoñ
Kinnoull, Earl of. *See* Hay
Kipling, John, 885
Kirby, Cecilia. *See* Bethune
Kirby*, John (1772–1846), 79, 168, 327
Kirkland, Samuel, 803, 804, 811
Kirouac*, Conrad, named Brother Marie-Victorin (1885–1944), 593
Kiyasuta. *See* Kayahsota[?]
Klein. *See* Cline
Kluck, William, 507
Knap. *See* Hunter
Kneller*, Henry (d. 1776), 224, 863
Knockleith. *See* Ellice
Knox, Henry, 40, 415, 808
Knox, Thomas (customs collector), 4
Knox, Thomas (muster master), 630
Knox, William, 149, 351, 353
Konieschguanokee (Captain Pipe), 345
Koñwatsi?tsiaiéñni* (d. 1796), 786, 803, 804
Kruzenshtern, Ivan Fedorovich, 80
Kyen-da-nent (Sally) (wife of Ebenezer Allan), 15

Labadie*, Louis (1765–1824), 688
La Balme. *See* Mottin
Labbé, Charles, 116
La Boische. *See* Beauharnois

La Bouteillerie. *See* Deschamps
La Brède, Baron de. *See* Secondat
Labrie*, Jacques (1784–1831), 211
Labrosse. *See* Jourdain
La Brosse*, Jean-Baptiste de (1724–82), 201
La Bruère. *See* Boucher
La Cailleterie. *See* De Lisle
Lacasta. *See* Sessé
Lacelle, Agathe de (Réaume), 710
Lacelle, Jacques, 852
Lacelle, Mary. *See* Blue Jacket
La Chenette, Mme. *See* Couc, Elizabeth
La Chesnaye. *See* Aubert
Laclède Liguest, Pierre de, 272
Lacombe. *See* Truillier
La Corne, Élisabeth de. *See* Ramezay
La Corne, Geneviève-Élisabeth de (Tarieu de Lanaudière), 791
La Corne*, Louis de, known as Chevalier de La Corne (1703–61), 98, 888
La Corne, Louis de, known as La Corne l'aîné, 578
La Corne*, Luc de, known as Chaptes de La Corne or La Corne Saint-Luc (d. 1784), 96, 143, 724, 791
La Corne, Marie-Angélique de (Margane de Lavaltrie), 578
La Corne, Marie-Anne. *See* Hervieux
La Cour de Brisay, Samuel-Théophile de. *See* DesBrisay, Theophilus
Lacroix, Hubert, 233
Lacroix, Jacques-Hubert, 827
La Croix* de Chevrières de Saint-Vallier, Jean-Baptiste de (1653–1727), 245
Lacroix-Mézière, Suzanne (De Lisle), 241, 591
La Fayette, Marquis de. *See* Motier
La Ferrière, Comte de. *See* Berryer
La Feuille. *See* Wahpasha
Laffont, Jean-Baptiste, 342
Laffriquain. *See* Tribaut
Laflèche, Louise (Suzor), 788
Lafleur. *See* Couc
Lafont, Jeanne (Pécholier; Bedout), 62
Lafontaine. *See* Marion
Lafontaine* de Belcour, Jacques de (1704–65), 426
Lafontaine de Belcour, Nicolas-Joseph de, 43, 794
Laforce. *See also* Pépin
Laforce, Madeleine. *See* Corbin
Laforce, René-Hippolyte, 462, **470–71**
Laforge, Monsieur (manufacturer), 259
La Fourche. *See* Nissowaquet
Laframboise. *See also* Fafard
Laframboise, Claude, 377
Lafrance, Jean-Baptiste, 418
La Fresnière. *See* Hertel
La Galissonière, Marquis de. *See* Barrin
Lagimonière*, Jean-Baptiste (1778–1855), 267
La Giraudais. *See* Chenard
La Gorgendière. *See* Fleury
Lagrave, Augustin, 436
La Grave, Louis de, 752
Lahaille, Barthelemie. *See* Grabot
Lahaille, Jean-Baptiste, 146, **471–72**
Lahaille, Joseph, 471
Lahaye. *See* Le Pellé
Lahontan, Baron de. *See* Lom

Lajemmerais. *See* Dufrost
Lajimonière. *See* Lagimonière
La Jonquière, Marquis de. *See* Taffanel
Lalancette. *See* Landriaux; Lebreton
La Madeleine. *See* Ailleboust
La Malgue; La Marque. *See* Marin
La Marche, Jean-François de, 180, 671
La Marre. *See* Varin
Lamb, Freelove (Collver), 196
Lambert, John, 138, **472–73**, 792
Lambert, Patrick, **473–74**, 633
Lambert*, *dit* Saint-Paul, Paul (1691–1749), 709
Lambert Dumont, Charlotte-Louise (Poulin de Courval Cressé), 216
Lambert Dumont, Eustache, 481
Lambly, John, 96
Lambton*, John George, 1st Earl of Durham (1792–1840), 759
Lamorille. *See* Lemaître
LaMotte, Charlotte (Huguet), 435
Lampen, William, 52, 53
Lanaudière; La Naudière. *See* Tarieu
Lanctot*, Gustave (1883–1975), 359
Landen. *See also* Landers
Landen, Herman, 748
Landergan. *See* Lonergan
Landers (Landen), Ellen (Desbrisay), 249
Landmann*, George Thomas (1779–1854), 366, 391, 486, 502, 692, 821, 840
Landriaux*, Louis-Nicolas (d. 1788), 201
Landrican, Michael, 338
Landry, Claude, 393
Landry, Jean, 393
Landry, Marie-Anne (Trahan), 826
Landry, Marie-Josephe (Boudrot), 102
Landry, Modeste (Guitet), 393
Lane, Michael, 274
Langdon, John E., 728
L'Angevin. *See* Cartier
Langhorn, John, **474–77**, 787
Langlade. *See* Mouet
Langlois, Michel, 418
Langlois, Pierre, 87
Languedoc*, François (1791–1840), 117
Lantagnac. *See* Adhémar
La Oja. *See* Wahpasha
Laparre, Élie, 248
Lapause. *See* Plantavit
La Pelouze. *See* Carrefour
La Pérelle. *See* Eury
Lapérière. *See* Desjardins
Lapérouse, Comte de. *See* Galaup
Laperrière. *See* Fabre
Lapierre. *See* Lebourdais
La Pistole. *See* Varin
Lapointe. *See also* Audette
Lapointe, Jean-Baptiste, 727
La Poterie. *See* Gaudin
Larchevêque, Charlotte (Jobert), 333
Larchevêque, Josette (Marie-Joseph) (Dejean), 237
Larchevêque, Marguerite (Chaboillez), 177, 178
Larchevêque, *dit* La Promenade, Jacques, 178
La Rivaudais. *See* Quesnel

La Rive. *See* Gravé
La Rivière. *See* Byssot
La Roche, Marie-Joseph (Requiem; Dumas), 276
La Rochefoucauld* de Roye, Jean-Baptiste-Louis-Frédéric de, Marquis de Roucy, Duc d'Anville (1709–46), 97, 498
La Rochefoucauld-Liancourt*, François-Alexandre-Frédéric de, Duc de La Rochefoucauld-Liancourt (1747–1827), 101, 639, 755
Larocque, François-Antoine, 512
Larocque*, François-Antoine (1784–1869), 177
Larose. *See* Guillot
Larsonneur, François, 436, 727
Lartigue*, Jean-Jacques (1777–1840), 93, 186
Larue, Marie-Anne (Suzor), 788
La Rue, Pierre de, Abbé de L'Isle-Dieu, 172, 471
La Salle. *See* Cavelier
La Saussaye, Charlotte de (Hazen), 412
Lassare, Ignace, 676
Laterreur. *See* Ducros
Laterrière. *See also* Sales
Laterrière, Jean (Jean-Baptiste, Jean-Pierre). *See* Sales Laterrière, Pierre de
Latham, John, 227, 362
Latour. *See* Huguet; Jérôme; Leblanc
Latour-Dézery, François-Xavier, 233, 243, 701
Latulippe. *See* Leheup
Laubara (Laubaras). *See* Olabaratz
Lauderdale, Earl of. *See* Maitland
Laughton, Ann (Roe), 721
Laurens, Henry, 630
Lauriot, François, 51
La Valinière. *See* Huet
Lavaltrie. *See* Margane
La Vérendrye. *See* Gaultier
Lavergne, Pierre, 77
Lavimaudier (Lavimaudière). *See* Lagimonière
Lavine, 389
Lavoisier, Antoine-Laurent de, 187
Lawder, Hester (Skinner), 762
Lawe, George, 621
Lawlor, Susanna (Reid; Byles), 128
Lawrason, Lawrence, 670
Lawrence*, Charles (d. 1760), 240, 554, 869
Lawrence, Sir Thomas, 543, 706
Lawson, David, 219, 262, 263, 310, **477–78**, 720
Lawson, Elizabeth (Curtis), 219
Lawson, Ellen (wife of DAVID), 477
Leach, Mary (Mountain), 613
Leatherlips, 775
Le Baron, Sarah (Hazen), 415
Le Basque. *See* Bastarache
Lebert, Michelle (Pépin, *dit* Laforce), 470
Le Blanc, Claire (Robichaux, *dit* Cadet), 719
Leblanc*, Étienne (d. 1831), 27
Le Blanc, Gertrude (Gaudet), 261
Le Blanc*, Pierre (d. 1799), 261
Leblanc, *dit* Latour, François, 656
Leblanc, *dit* Le Maigre, Anne (Gautier), 339
Leblanc*, *dit* Le Maigre, Joseph (1697–1772), 339
Lebourdais, *dit* Lapierre, Jacques, 77
Lebreton, *dit* Lalancette, Pierre-Henri, 248
Lebrun de Duplessis, Jean-Baptiste, 478
Lebrun de Duplessis, Jean-Baptiste, **478–80**

Lebrun de Duplessis, Marie. *See* Champigny
Lebrun de Duplessis, Marie-Catherine. *See* Mettot
Leclair, François, 727
Leclerc, Georges-Louis, Comte de Buffon, 182
Leclerc, Ignace, 242
Leclerc, Marguerite. *See* Bétourné
Leclerc, Michel, 480
Leclerc, Michel, 92, **480–81**
Lecompte. *See* Le Conte Dupré
Le Comte Dupré, Catherine. *See* Martel de Brouague
Le Comte Dupré, Catherine (Juchereau Duchesnay), 231, 463, 464, 482, 881
Le Comte Dupré, Françoise (Le Moine), 482
Le Comte* Dupré, Georges-Hippolyte, known as Saint-Georges Dupré (1738–97), 43, 383, 481, 482, 652
Le Comte* Dupré, Jean-Baptiste (d. 1765), 320, 481
Le Comte Dupré, Jean-Baptiste, 95, 231, 463, **481–82**
Le Comte Dupré, Jean-Baptiste (son of JEAN-BAPTISTE), 482
Le Comte Dupré, Louise-Charlotte, 482
Le Comte Dupré, Marie-Angélique (Cugnet), 482
Le Comte Dupré, Marie-Anne. *See* Hervieux
Le Comte Dupré, Thérèse (Baby), 41
Le Conte* Dupré, Louis (1654–1715), 481
Lecron. *See* Lekron
Le Cygne. *See* Onasakenrat, Joseph
Le Derniers. *See* Delesdernier
Le Despencer, Baron. *See* Dashwood
Ledru*, Jean-Antoine (b. 1752, d. after 1794), 124, 306
Le Dru, Pierre, 800
Ledyard, John, 80
Lee, Catherine (Dumas), 278
Lee, Charles, 147
Lee, Joseph, 482
Lee, Lucy (mother of SAMUEL), 482
Lee, Samuel, **482–83**, 795
Lee, Sarah (wife of SAMUEL), 482
Lee, Thomas, 278
Lee*, Thomas (1783–1832), 84
Leeds, John, 614
Leek. *See* Macdonell
Lees, Jane, 485
Lees, John, 483
Lees, John, 181, 182, 277, 283, **483–85**
Lees, Nancy, 485
Lees, Sarah, 485
Lefebvre*, Jean (1714–60), 41, 276
Lefebvre, Madeleine (Serres), 752
Lefebvre* Angers, Marie-Angélique, named Saint-Simon (1710–66), 703
Lefebvre de Bellefeuille, Antoine, 217
Lefebvre* de Bellefeuille, François (1708–80), 902
Lefebvre-Duchouquet, Charles-Joseph, 164
Lefrançois, Alexis, 13
Lefrançois*, Charles (1773–1829), 211
Legardeur de Beauvais, Madeleine. *See* Marchand
Legardeur* de Croisille et de Montesson, Joseph-Michel (d. *c.* 1776), 97
Legardeur* de Repentigny, Louis (1721–86), 128, 129, 231
Legardeur* de Saint-Pierre, Jacques (1701–55), 98
Légaré*, Joseph (1795–1855), 72
Legge*, Francis (d. 1783), 81, 82, 216, 545, 548, 607, 608, 660, 670

Legge, William, 2nd Earl of Dartmouth, 142, 143, 145, 146, 147, 220, 843
Leggett, Elizabeth Bond (Morris), 607
Legrand, Jean-Baptiste, 322, 323, 324
Legrand, Thérèse (Foretier), 322, 323, 324, 325
Le Grand Sauteux. *See* Minweweh
Legris, Marie-Angélique (Martineau), 579
Le Guerne*, François (1725–89), 102
Leheup, *dit* Latulippe, Charlotte. *See* Desève
Leheup, *dit* Latulippe, Jean, 435
Leheup, *dit* Latulippe, Marguerite, 436
Lehouillier, Dorothée. *See* Sales Laterrière
Lehouillier, François-Xavier, 738
Leigh*, John (d. 1823), 244
Leigne. *See* André
Leiningen, Prince of. *See* Emich Charles
Leiningen, Princess of. *See* Victoria Mary Louisa
Leir, Henrietta Anne. *See* Carleton
Leith*, James (1777–1838), 635
Lejamtel*, François (1758–1835), 12, 13, 181, 458, 671
Lekron (Lecron), Susanna (Susan) (Zeisberger), 883
Lelièvre, Roger, 834
Le Loutre*, Jean-Louis (1709–72), 172, 203
Le Maigre. *See* Leblanc
Lemaire, *dit* Saint-Germain, Venance, 259
Lemaire de Saint-Germain, Charles-François, 432
Le Maistre, Élizabeth. *See* Théodore
Le Maistre, Francis, 132, **485–86**, 553, 584
Le Maistre, François-Guillaume, 485
Le Maistre, Margaret. *See* Stuart
Lemaître Lamorille, François, 478
Le Mercier*, François-Marc-Antoine (b. 1722, d. *c.* 1798), 677
Lemesurier, Peter, 107
Lemire Marsolet, Isidore (baptized Charles-Antoine), 569
Le Moine, Françoise. *See* Le Comte Dupré
Le Moine, John Francis, 482
Lemonier, François, 592, 622
Le Monnier, Louis-Guillaume, 592
Le Moyne* de Bienville, Jean-Baptiste (d. 1767), 487
Le Moyne* de Longueuil, Charles, Baron de Longueuil (1687–1755), 97
Le Moyne de Longueuil, Charles-Jacques, Baron de Longueuil, 369
Le Moyne de Longueuil, Geneviève (Liénard de Beaujeu de Villemonde), 49
Le Moyne de Longueuil, Joseph-Dominique-Emmanuel, 96, 231, 232, 233, **486–88**, 499
Le Moyne de Longueuil, Louise. *See* Prud'homme
Le Moyne de Longueuil, Marie-Anne-Catherine, Baronne de Longueuil. *See* Fleury Deschambault
Le Moyne de Longueuil, Marie-Catherine (Tarieu de La Naudière), 792
Le Moyne de Longueuil, Marie-Geneviève. *See* Joybert de Soulanges
Le Moyne* de Longueuil, Paul-Joseph, known as the Chevalier de Longueuil (1701–78), 231, 486, 498
Lennox, Charles, 3rd Duke of Richmond and Lennox, 141, 142, 149, 348, 349, 350, 357, 425, 488
Lennox, Charles, 4th Duke of Richmond and Lennox, 72, **488–90**, 882
Lennox, Charlotte, Duchess of Richmond and Lennox. *See* Gordon

Lennox, Emilia Charlotte (Berkeley, Lady Berkeley), 72
Lennox, Lord George Henry, 488
Lennox, Lady Louisa. *See* Kerr
Lenoir, Françoise (Liébert), 497
Lenoir, Vincent, 497
Leonard*, George (1742–1826), 389, 867
Leonard, Jemima (Perkins), 665
Lepage, Charles-Olivier, 727
Lepage, Geneviève (Marcoux), 575
Lepage, René, 270
Le Pellé Lahaye, Marie-Josephe (Deslandes; Blondeau), 89, 700
Leprince, Joseph, 813
Leprohon*, Jean-Philippe (1765–1831), 243
Lerche, Jean-Henry, 218, 436
Lernoult, Richard Berrenger, 147
Le Rond d'Alembert, Jean, 102
Le Roux*, Thomas-François (1730–94), 458
Léry. *See* Chaussegros
Lesage, Joseph, 77
Le Saulnier*, Candide-Michel (1756–1830), 92
Les Derniers. *See* Delesdernier
Lesdiguières, Duc de. *See* De Bonne
Lespérance. *See* Aubuchon
L'Espérance. *See also* Compain
L'Espérance*, Charles-Gabriel-Sébastien de, Baron de L'Espérance (1725–91), 339
L'Estang. *See* Brunet
Lester, Benjamin, 166, 189, **490–92**, 725, 726, 784, 785, 838
Lester, Francis, 490
Lester, Isaac, 491
Lester, Sir John, 492
Lester, Rachel. *See* Taverner
Lester, Robert, 332, 460, **492–97**, 566, 794, 816, 877, 878
Lester, Susannah. *See* Taverner
L'Étang. *See* Brunet
Letellier, Mary (Bruff), 115
Létourneau, Michel, 436
Lett*, Benjamin (1813–58), 114
Levasseur*, François-Noël (d. 1794), 49, 304
Levasseur, Pierre, 638
Levasseur*, René-Nicolas (d. 1784), 638
Levasseur*, *dit* Delor, Jean-Baptiste-Antoine (d. 1775), 304
Levasseur-Borgia*, Joseph (1773–1839), 208
Léveillé, Monsieur (merchant), 185
Lévêque, François, 256
Lévêque, Véronique (Digé), 256
Le Verrier de Rousson, Jeanne-Charlotte. *See* Fleury Deschambault
Lévesque, Catherine. *See* Trottier Desauniers Beaubien
Lévesque, François, 635
Lévesque*, François (1732–87), 494, 601, 889
Lévis*, François de, Duc de Lévis (1719–87), 40, 41, 96, 104, 164, 498, 638, 677, 739, 888
Lévis-Mirepoix, Gaston-Charles-Pierre de, Duc de Lévis-Mirepoix, 103
Levy. *See* Thubières
Lewes, Letitia (Gower), 359
Lewis, Andrew, 554
Lewis, Meriwether, 9, 418, 419
Lewis*, William (fl. 1777–87), 506, 717
L'Héritier de Brutelles, Charles-Louis, 593

Liancourt. *See* La Rochefoucauld-Liancourt
Liard, 419
Liddel, Elizabeth (Ramage), 705
Liddell, Andrew, 611
Liddell, John, 611
Liddell, William, 611
Lieberkühn, Samuel, 885
Liébert, Anne. *See* Des Porques
Liébert, Françoise. *See* Lenoir
Liébert, Philippe (father), 497
Liébert, Philippe, 392, 393, **497–98**
Liébert, Philippe (rebel), 146
Liele, George, 340
Liénard* de Beaujeu, Daniel-Hyacinthe-Marie (1711–55), 41, 498
Liénard* de Beaujeu, Louis (1683–1750), 498
Liénard de Beaujeu, Thérèse-Denise. *See* Migeon de Branssat
Liénard de Beaujeu de Villemonde, Charles-François, 499
Liénard de Beaujeu de Villemonde, Geneviève. *See* Le Moyne de Longueuil
Liénard de Beaujeu de Villemonde, Julie-Louise (Juchereau Duchesnay), 462, 498
Liénard de Beaujeu de Villemonde, Louis, 6, 358, 462, **498–99**
Liénard de Beaujeu de Villemonde, Louise-Charlotte. *See* Cugnet
Ligonier, John (Jean-Louis), 1st Earl Ligonier, 141, 823
Liguest. *See* Laclède
Lillo, George, 689
Linch, Thomas, 396
Lindsay*, William (d. 1834), 287, 509
Lindsey*, Charles (1820–1908), 685
Linnaeus (Linné, von Linné), Carl (Carolus), 581
L'Isle-Dieu, Abbé de. *See* La Rue
Liston, Sir Robert, 809, 810
Little Abraham. *See* Teiorhéñhsere?
Littlehales. *See* Baker
Little Turtle. *See* Michikinakoua
Liverpool, Earl of. *See* Jenkinson
Livingston*, James (1747–1832), 146, 413, 414, 826
Livius*, Peter (1739–95), 21, 142, 146, 148, 260, 843, 849, 863
Lloyd, Nathaniel, 373
Lloyd, Philip, 373
Lloyd, Prudence (Sproule), 773
Locke, John, 372
Locke, Mary Anne (Glenie), 347, 349, 356
Loedel*, Henry Nicholas Christopher (d. 1830), 88, 89
Logan, Benjamin, 852
Logan, Hart, 286
Loir, Guillaume, 709
Lom* d'Arce, Louis-Armand de, Baron de Lahontan (b. 1666, d. before 1716), 684
London, Bartholomew, 639, 640
London, Catherine (Rictenburgh), 640
London, Mary. *See* Osborn
Londonderry, Marquess of. *See* Stewart
Lonergan (Landergan), Patrick, 122, 632
Long. *See also* Fraisses
Long*, John (fl. 1768–91), 567, 707, 836
Longchamps-Montendre, Marie-Joséphine de (Bougainville), 102

Longmoor. *See also* Longmore
Longmoor, Robert, 450, **500–1**, 682
Longmoor, Robert, 501
Longmoor, William, 500
Longmore, Alexander, 501
Longmore, Christiana Lætitia. *See* Cox
Longmore, George, 201, 202, **501–2**
Longmore, George, 799, 800
Longueuil. *See* Le Moyne
Longueuil, Baron de. *See* Grant; Le Moyne
Longueuil, Baronne de. *See* Fleury Deschambault
Loring*, Joshua (1716–81), 363
Losada. *See also* Moziño
Losada, Manuela (Mosiño), 615
Lotbinière. *See* Chartier
Lotbinière, Marquis de. *See* Chartier
Lotbinière, Marquise de. *See* Chaussegros de Léry
Lothian, Marquess of. *See* Kerr
Loubert, Pierre, 393
Loudoun, Earl of. *See* Campbell
Louis, Colonel. *See* Atiatoharongwen
Louis XVI, King of France, 671
Louvigny. *See* Testard
Low, Elizabeth (Gray), 388
Low, Mary (Spark), 768
Lowth, Robert, 747
Lubet, Antoinette (Dénéchaud), 248
Lucas*, Francis (d. 1770), 166
Lucas, Joseph, 329, 436
Luckens, Hannah (Iredell), 448
Luckman, Lieutenant, 674
Ludlow, Ann. *See* Ver Planck
Ludlow, Daniel, 505
Ludlow, Frances (wife of Gabriel Jr). *See* Duncan
Ludlow, Frances (wife of GEORGE DUNCAN). *See* Duncan
Ludlow, Gabriel (father), 505
Ludlow, Gabriel, 503, 505
Ludlow, Gabriel George, 156, 157, 161, **503–5**, 506
Ludlow, Gabriel Ver Planck, 504
Ludlow, George Duncan, 349, 456, 503, **505–7**, 630, 867
Lugrin*, George Kilman (1791–1835), 613
Lukens, John, 448
Lumsden, John, 218
Lunn, Margaret. *See* Fisher
Lunn*, William (1796–1886), 320
Luria, Rebecca (Cohen), 193
Lutwyche, Edward Goldstone, 94, 161, 162
Lyde, Sarah (Byles), 128
Lyman, Daniel, 350, 353
Lymburner*, Adam (d. 1836), 150, 151, 232, 270, 283, 370, 373, 493, 566, 576, 647, 650, 769, 816, 843
Lymburner, John, 843
Lymburner, Mathew, 370, 746, 816
Lynd, Ann (Grant), 509
Lynd, David, 75, 91, 192, 385, **507–10**
Lynd, Hutchinson, 509
Lynd, Jane. *See* Henry
Lynd, Jane (Dodd), 509
Lynd, John, 508
Lynson, Jane. *See* Robinson
Lyon, James, 626
Lyon*, James (1735–94), 199
Lyonnais. *See* Bossu

Lyons, Barnett, 194
Lyons, Charles, 478
Lyons, Jacques Judah, 194
Lyons, John, 419
Lysaght, Averil M., 221

MABANE*, Adam (d. 1792), 44, 91, 142, 145, 146, 149, 150, 181, 215, 277, 278, 284, 317, 371, 583, 745, 839, 863, 892, 901, 902
Mabane, Isabell, 215
McAlpin, Daniel, 585
Macarmick, Catherine. *See* Buller
Macarmick, James, 510
Macarmick, Philippa (mother of WILLIAM), 510
Macarmick, William, 53, 204, 223, **510–11**, 546, 634, 766, 780
McArthur, Duncan, 232
Macartney, George, 1st Earl Macartney, 359
McAulay*, Angus (1759–1827), 547, 860, 862
Macaulay*, James (1759–1822), 502
Macaulay*, Robert (1744–1800), 326, 492
Macaulay, Zachary, 68
MacAulay*, Zachary (1739–1821), 146
M'Auslane, Peter, 776
McBeath, Erie. *See* Smyth
McBeath, George, 299, 300, 333, **511–13**, 561, 603, 682, 683, 715, 818
McBeath, Jane. *See* Graham
McBeath, Margaret, 715
McCall*, Duncan (1769–1832), 734
McCallum*, James (d. 1829), 648, 879, 881
McCarthy*, Jeremiah (d. 1828), 217, 278
McCaulay, Frances (Rollo), 723
McCauley. *See* Macaulay
McClellan (McLellan), Robert, 526
McClement, Patrick, 330
McColl*, Duncan (1754–1830), 25, 573
McCord, Jane (Fraser), 224
McCord, John (brother of Thomas*), 723
McCord, John (merchant), 142, 331, 406, 508, 637
McCord*, Thomas (1748–1824), 723, 820
MacCormick. *See* Macarmick
McCormick, Charles, 602, 656
McCormick, Martha (O'Hara), 637
McCrae, David, 512
McCrae, Erie. *See* Smyth
McCulloch*, Thomas (1776–1843), 124, 612
McCurdy, John (doctor), 190
McCurdy, John (officer), 412
McDavitt, Catherine (McNiff), 551
MacDhòmhnaill, Eilidh. *See* MacDonald of Glenaladale, Helen
MacDhòmhnaill, Iain. *See* MacDonald of Glenaladale, John
MacDhòmhnaill, Seumas. *See* MacDonald, James
MacDhòmhnuill, Alasdair. *See* MacDonell of Scothouse, Alexander
MacDonald; McDonald. *See also* MacDonell; Macdonell
Macdonald, Alexander, 523
McDonald*, Archibald (1790–1853), 466
MacDonald, Augustine (Austin), 516
MacDonald, Donald, 513, 514, 515
McDonald*, Donald (1795–1854), 516
MacDonald, Flora Anna Maria (Macdonell), 516

McDonald, Harriet (Skinner; Macdonell (Greenfield)), 762
MacDonald, Helen. *See* MacDonald of Glenaladale
MacDonald*, James (1736–85), 514, 524
McDonald, John, 635
McDonald*, John (d. 1874), 516
MacDonald, Roderick C., 516
MacDonald, Ronald, 514
MacDonald, William, 516
MacDonald*, Sir William Christopher (1831–1917), 516
MacDonald of Boisdale, Colin, 514
McDonald* of Garth, John (d. 1866), 236, 266, 559, 560
MacDonald of Ghernish (Guernish), Margaret (MacDonald of Glenaladale), 514, 515, 516
M'Donald of Glenaladale, Alexander, 513, 514
MacDonald of Glenaladale, Helen (MacDonald), **513–14**, 515
MacDonald of Glenaladale, Isabella. *See* Gordon of Wardhouse
MacDonald of Glenaladale, John, 28, 219, 220, 263, 311, 424, 425, 513, **514–17**, 569, 721, 779, 848, 861, 862, 873
MacDonald of Glenaladale, Margaret. *See* MacDonald of Ghernish
M'Donald of Glenaladale, Margaret. *See* MacDonell of Scothouse
MacDonald of Glenaladale, Margaret, 513
McDonell, Agathe-Henriette. *See* Huguet, *dit* Latour
McDonell*, Alexander (fl. 1815–24), 751
McDonell*, Alexander (1762–1840), 78, 440, 518, 521, 525, 695
Macdonell*, Alexander Greenfield (d. 1835), 268, 520, 544
Macdonell, Ann, 523
McDonell (MacDonell), Archibald, 772
McDonell*, Archibald (d. 1830), 92
MacDonell, Catherine. *See* MacLeod of Bernera
McDonell, Donald, 550
McDonell, Duncan Cameron, 437
Macdonell, Flora Anna Maria. *See* MacDonald
Macdonell*, George Richard John (d. 1870), 79, 762
McDonell, Helen. *See* MacNab
McDonell, Helen. *See* Yates
MacDonell, James, 718
MacDonell*, John (1768–1850), 656
Macdonell*, Miles (1769–1828), 266, 267, 268, 451, 466, 523, 525, 751
MacDonell, Roderic, 40, 524
McDonell* (Aberchalder), Hugh (d. 1833), 518, 753, 772
Macdonell (Aberchalder), Janet (Macdonell of Greenfield), 520
McDonell (Aberchalder), John, 282, **517–18**, 519, 520, 772, 782
McDonell* (Collachie), Alexander (1762–1842), 126, 265, 266, 519, 520, 521, 522
Macdonell (Collachie), Angus, 188, 189, 388, 389, 420, **518–20**, 845, 854, 855
Macdonell (Collachie), James, 523
McDonell (Collachie), James, 519
Macdonell* (Greenfield), Donald (1778–1861), 522, 523
Macdonell (Greenfield), Harriet. *See* McDonald
Macdonell (Greenfield), John, 83, 113, 114, **520–23**, 857, 858
McDonell of Aberchalder, Alexander, 517
McDonell of Collachie, Allan, 517, 518, 519
Macdonell of Greenfield, Alexander, 520

Macdonell of Greenfield, Janet. *See* Macdonell (Aberchalder)
Macdonell of Leek, John, 517
MacDonell of Scothouse, Alexander, **523–25**
MacDonell of Scothouse, Angus (Æneas), 523
MacDonell of Scothouse (Scotus), Margaret (M'Donald of Glenaladale; Gordon), 513, 514
McDonnell, Elizabeth (McNiff), 551
McDougall, Mrs. *See* Shaw
McDougall*, Alexander (d. 1821), 525, 526
McDougall, Anne, 526
McDougall, Duncan, 525
McDougall, Duncan, **525–27**, 533
McDougall, George, 526, 527
McDowall*, Robert (1768–1841), 308, 476
MacEachern*, Angus Bernard (d. 1835), 125, 458, 516, 671
McFarland, Margaret (Pettit), 669
McGill, Andrew, 179, 286, 436, 529, 655, 821
McGill, Ann. *See* Wood
McGill, Charlotte. *See* Guillimin
McGill, Isobel, 529
McGill, James, 527
McGill, James, 8, 38, 90, 134, 168, 179, 180, 183, 211, 218, 233, 285, 286, 287, 299, 300, 319, 320, 332, 333, 372, 384, 402, 436, 460, 484, 485, 489, 496, **527–30**, 561, 564, 566, 572, 581, 614, 663, 681, 705, 706, 722, 818, 819, 820, 821, 822
McGill, John, 527, 529, 819
McGill*, John (1752–1834), 326, 365, 440, 441, 442, 548, 549, 753, 756, 856
McGill, Margaret. *See* Gibson
McGillivray, Anne. *See* McTavish
McGillivray, Donald, 530
McGillivray, Duncan, **530–32**, 561, 565, 742
McGillivray, Magdalene, 532
McGillivray*, Simon (1783–1840), 544, 822
McGillivray, William, 532
McGillivray*, William (1764–1825), 134, 265, 266, 267, 333, 391, 530, 532, 542, 544, 559, 561, 564, 565, 566, 684
McGowan. *See* Magowan
McGregor, Coll, 285
McGregor*, James (1759–1830), 660
McGregor of Clober, James, 284
McHenry, James, 810
Machiquawish. *See* Madjeckewiss
Macho, B., 321
McIntosh, Donald, 534
McIntosh, Janet (Fraser), 330
Maciver, Isabella (Mackenzie), 537
McKay, Alexander, 385
MacKay, Alexander, 526, **532–34**, 540, 814
McKay, Alexander Ross, 532
MacKay, Donald, 534
McKay, Donald (father), 532
McKay, Donald, 534
McKay, Elspeth. *See* Kennedy
Mackay, Francis, 315
McKay, Hugh, 67
MacKay, John, 280, 411, 845
McKay, John, **534–36**, 886
McKay*, John Richards (d. 1877), 535
MacKay, Marguerite. *See* Waddens

Mackay, Marie-Anne (Quinson de Saint-Ours), 752
McKay, Mary. *See* Favell
McKay, Samuel, 231, 315, 413
McKay, Thomas, 532, 533, 534
MacKay, William, 535
McKay*, William (1772–1832), 532
McKee*, Alexander (d. 1799), 39, 229, 301, 302, 306, 345, 365, 535, 536, 552, 707, 721, 749, 758, 807, 852
McKee, Thérèse. *See* Askin
McKee, Thomas, 39, 302, 365, **535–36**
Mackellar*, Patrick (1717–78), 425
McKenzie, Mr (fur trader), 538
Mackenzie, Alexander, 277
Mackenzie, Sir Alexander, 266, 391, 512, 532, 533, **537–43**, 562, 563, 564, 565, 581, 603, 635, 636, 656, 683, 684, 685, 822
McKenzie*, Alexander (d. 1830), 533, 544
McKenzie*, Charles (d. 1855), 177
MacKenzie, Colin, 543
McKenzie*, Daniel (d. 1832), 267, 544
McKenzie*, Donald (1783–1851), 526, 533
Mackenzie, Geddes (Mackenzie, Lady Mackenzie), 537, 542
Mackenzie, George, 542
Mackenzie, Holt, 101
Mackenzie, Isabella. *See* Maciver
Mackenzie, James, 377
Mackenzie, John (businessman), 320
Mackenzie, John (uncle of Sir Alexander), 537
Mackenzie, Kenneth, 537
MacKenzie, Kenneth, **543–44**
MacKenzie, Louisa (wife of KENNETH), 544
MacKenzie, Margaret (daughter of KENNETH), 544
MacKenzie, Margaret (mother of KENNETH), 543
Mackenzie, Murdoch, 543
Mackenzie, Nancy. *See* Fisher
McKenzie, Rachel. *See* Chaboillez
MacKenzie, Roderick, 339
McKenzie*, Roderick (d. 1844), 177, 179, 391, 537, 538, 539, 541, 542, 544, 565, 684
McKinney, Mary (Harris), 408
McKinnon, Mrs (wife of WILLIAM), 546
MacKinnon, Helen (Stewart), 775, 776, 825
McKinnon, John, 544
McKinnon, Letitia. *See* Piggott
McKinnon, Ranald, **544–45**
McKinnon, William, 204, **545–46**, 634, 780
McKinnon*, William Charles (1828–62), 545
Mackintosh*, Angus (1755–1835), 722
Mackintosh, Duncan, 543
McLane*, David (d. 1797), 84, 87, 462, 486, 691, 878
MacLaomuinn, Eoghan, 547
McLean. *See also* McLane
Maclean*, Allan (1725–98), 30, 78, 131, 191, 282, 515, 517, 584, 893, 894, 899
MacLean*, Allan (1752–1847), 169, 765
McLean, Anne Margaret (Wilson), 864
McLean, Archibald, 135
McLean*, Archibald (1791–1865), 521, 522, 558, 748
McLean*, Francis (d. 1781), 16, 134, 336, 434, 557
McLean, Hector, 536, 710, 772
McLean, John Jenkin, 864
McLean, Mary. *See* Herkimer

McLean*, Neil (d. 1795), 402
MacLean, Sarah (Smith), 766
McLean, Susan. *See* Drummond
McLellan. *See also* McClellan
McLellan, Archibald, 466
McLeod*, Archibald Norman (fl. 1781–1839), 268, 466, 559
MacLeod, Flora (Buchanan), 546
MacLeod*, Normand (d. 1796), 390, 391, 537, 562, 603, 656
MacLeod of Bernera, Catherine (MacDonell), 523
McLoughlin*, John (1784–1857), 534, 544
McLoughlin, Marguerite. *See* Waddens
McMartin*, Alexander (1788–1853), 522
McMaster, James, 646
MacMhannain, Calum Bàn, **546–48**
McMullen, Élisabeth, 293
McMun, Jane (Black), 83
MacNab, Helen (McDonell), 519
McNabb, Alexander, 549, 550
McNabb, Colin, **548–50**
McNabb, Colin A., 549
McNabb, Elizabeth (wife of COLIN), 548
McNabb, James, 548, 550
McNabb, James, 548, 549, **550–51**
MacNabb, John, 841
McNabb, Mary Ann. *See* Fraser
McNabb, Simon, 549, 550
McNair, Andrew, 287
McNeall, Richard, 818
McNicol, Magdalen. *See* Nairne
McNicol, Peter, 621
Macnider*, Adam Lymburner (1778–1840), 287
Macnider*, John (1760–1829), 372, 406
Macnider, Margaret (Johnston), 699, 700
Macnider, Mary. *See* Hanna
Macnider, Mathew, 372, 699
McNiff, Catherine. *See* McDavitt
McNiff, Elizabeth. *See* McDonnell
McNiff, Patrick, 38, 306, 448, **551–53**
McNutt, Alexander, 553
McNutt, Alexander, 409, **553–57**
McNutt, Benjamin, 556, 557
McNutt, Jane (wife of Alexander), 553
MacNutt*, William Stewart (1908–76), 157, 356, 605
Macomb, Alexander, 299, 512
Macomb, William, 3, 299, 511, 512
Macormick. *See* Macarmick
Macpherson, Daniel, 499
McPherson, Elizabeth (Sayer), 742
McQueen, Mary, 673
McSwiney, Edward, **557–59**
McTavish, Alexander, 559
McTavish, Anne (McGillivray), 530
McTavish, Donald, 419, **559–60**
McTavish*, John George (d. 1847), 526
McTavish, Marie-Marguerite. *See* Chaboillez
McTavish, Simon, 177, 179, 260, 284, 287, 299, 300, 332, 333, 377, 384, 391, 511, 512, 525, 530, 531, 532, 541, 542, 559, **560–67**, 603, 682, 683, 715, 819, 820, 821, 822, 878
McTavish of Garthbeg, John, 560
MacTier, Grace (Pangman), 656
Macuina. *See* Muquinna

Madison, James, 113, 695
Madjeckewiss, 129, 130, **567–68**, 715, 760, 836
Madjeckewiss, 568
Maera. *See* Myeerah
Magon* de Terlaye, François-Auguste (1724–77), 118, 392
Magowan, Peter, **568–69**, 721, 776, 847, 848
Mailhiot. *See* Malhiot
Maillard*, Pierre (d. 1762), 172, 379, 393
Maillou, Angélique. *See* Marchand
Maillou, Antoine, 245
Maillou, Benjamin, 569
Maillou, Benjamin-Nicolas, **569–70**
Mainville, Monsieur (NWC employee), 466
Mair*, Charles (1838–1927), 800
Maitland, Sir Alexander, 515
Maitland, James, 8th Earl of Lauderdale, 35
Maitland, Jane Elizabeth. *See* Grant
Maitland*, Sir Peregrine (1771–1854), 489
Maitland, William, 259, 372
Maitwaywayninnee. *See* Matayawenenne
Malard, Anthelme, 480
Malartic. *See* Maurès
Malaspina, Marchioness of. *See* Melilupi
Malaspina, Marquis of. *See* Morello
Malaspina, Alejandro, 11, 140, 399, 400, **570–71**
Malchelosse, Gérard, 530
Maldonado. *See* Ferrer; Flórez
Malepart* de Beaucourt, François (1740–94), 417, 497
Malhiot*, Charles-Christophe (1808–74), 603
Malhiot, Charlotte. *See* Gamelin
Malhiot, Élisabeth. *See* Gamelin
Malhiot, François, **571–73**
Malhiot, François-Victor, 572
Malhiot*, François-Xavier (1781–1854), 572
Malhiot, Jean, 571
Malhiot*, Jean-François (1692–1756), 571
Malhiot, Julie-Éliza. *See* Montour
Malhiot, Madeleine. *See* Marchand
Malhiot, Marguerite (Trottier Desrivières Beaubien), 828
Malhiot, Pierre-Ignace, 572
Mallory*, Benajah (d. 1853), 734, 846, 857, 858
Malott, Catharine (Girty), 345
Man, James, **573–74**
Man (Mann), John, 573
Manette (Monette), 39
Mann*, Gother (1747–1830), 118, 441, 442
Mann, Isaac, 637
Manners, Charles, 4th Duke of Rutland, 120
Manners, John, Marquess of Granby, 166, 610
Manseau*, Antoine (1787–1866), 181, 671
Mansfield, Earl of. *See* Murray
Mansfield, Margaret (Arnold), 28
Manthet. *See* Ailleboust
Manuel, Dolly, 99
Maquilla (Maquinna). *See* Muquinna
Mar, Earl of. *See* Erskine
Marakle. *See* Markle
March, Maria (Duncan), 281
March, Mary. *See* Demasduwit
Marchand, Angélique (Joly; Maillou), 569
Marchand*, Étienne (1707–74), 185, 245
Marchand, Geneviève (Marcoux), 575
Marchand*, Jean-Baptiste (1760–1825), 92, 186, 242

Marchand, Louis, 576
Marchand, Louis (Louis-Martin), 575, 576, 577
Marchand, Madeleine (Malhiot; Legardeur de Beauvais), 571
Marchand, Marguerite, named de Sainte-Ursule, 224
Marchand, Marie-Geneviève. *See* Marcoux
Marchinton, Elizabeth (wife of PHILIP), 575
Marchinton, Joseph, 575
Marchinton, Mary (Welsford), 575
Marchinton, Philip, **574–75**
Marcle. *See* Markle
Marcoux, André, 231
Marcoux, François-Xavier, 77
Marcoux, Geneviève. *See* Alliés
Marcoux, Geneviève. *See* Lepage
Marcoux, Geneviève. *See* Marchand
Marcoux, Germain, 575
Marcoux, Jean-Baptiste, 576, 577
Marcoux, Louise. *See* Bélanger
Marcoux, Louise-Élizabeth (De Bonne), 231
Marcoux, Marie-Anne. *See* Dunière
Marcoux, Marie-Geneviève (Marchand), 576
Marcoux, Pierre, 231, 575, 576, 577
Marcoux, Pierre, 283, **575–78**
Margane de Lavaltrie, Louise-Charlotte. *See* Ailleboust d'Argenteuil
Margane de Lavaltrie, Marie-Angélique. *See* La Corne
Margane de Lavaltrie, Pierre-Paul, 578
Margane de Lavaltrie, Pierre-Paul, **578–79**, 687
Margane de Lavaltrie, Séraphin, 578
Margane de Lavaltrie, Suzanne-Antoinette (Tarieu de Lanaudière), 579
Margon. *See* Plantavit
Marguerite de Sainte-Ursule. *See* Marchand
Marguerite de Saint-Louis de Gonzague. *See* Davanne
Mariauchau d'Esgly, Louise (Martel de Brouague), 481
Mariauchau* d'Esgly, Louis-Philippe (1710–88), 76, 143, 150, 202, 380, 433, 434, 458, 480, 481, 524
Marie* (d. 1759 or 1760), 98
Marie-Angélique de Saint-Martin. *See* Viger
Marie-Anne de la Nativité. *See* Migeon de Branssat
Marie-Anne-Archange de Saint-Bernard. *See* Panet
Marie-Catherine de Saint-Alexis. *See* Payen de Noyan
Marie-Catherine de Saint-Ignace. *See* Juchereau Duchesnay
Marie-Charlotte (wife of ATIATOHARONGWEN), 40
Marie-Françoise de Saint-Jacques. *See* Panet
Marie-Geneviève de Saint-François d'Assise. *See* Parent
Marie-Joseph de l'Enfant-Jésus. *See* Wheelwright
Marie-Vénérande de Sainte-Claire. *See* Melançon
Marie-Victorin, Brother. *See* Kirouac
Marin* de La Malgue, Paul (d. 1753), 40, 835
Marion*, Salomon (1782–1830), 436, 437
Markland*, Thomas (1757–1840), 326, 492
Markle*, Abraham (1770–1826), 643, 724, 725, 733, 749, 857, 858
Marlborough, Duke of. *See* Churchill
Marleau, Gabrielle (Serres), 752
Marler, George Carlyle, 602
Marmontel, Jean-François, 233
Mar-pi-ya-ro-to-win (Grey Cloud), 10, 835
Marrant*, John (1755–91), 469
Marriott, Sir James, 145
Marseille. *See* Natte

Marsh, Mr (settler), 335
Marsh, Abraham, 857
Marsh, Hester (Hetty) (Iredell), 448
Marsh, Thomas, 335
Marsh, William, 422
Marsolet. *See* Lemire
Marston*, Benjamin (1730–92), 162, 465, 468, 506
Marteilhe, John (Jean), 146, 369
Martel, Marie-Anne (Boucher), 95
Martel de Brouague, Catherine (Le Comte Dupré), 481
Martel* de Brouague, François (b. 1692, d. *c.* 1761), 481
Martel de Brouague, Louise. *See* Mariauchau d'Esgly
Marten*, Humphrey (fl. 1750–86), 194, 450, 500, 711, 712
Martin. *See also* Marten
Martin, Elizabeth (Ainslie), 4, 745
Martin (Martine), Judith (Delesdernier), 239
Martin, Marie. *See* Guernon, *dit* Belleville
Martineau, Augustin, 579
Martineau, Françoise. *See* Mercier
Martineau, Jérôme, 271, **579–80**
Martineau (Martineaut), Marie (Rousseaux St John), 724
Martineau, Marie-Angélique. *See* Legris
Martínez. *See also* Flórez
Martínez* Fernández y Martínez de la Sierra, Esteban José (1742–98), 10, 197, 387, 571, 586
Mary (daughter of ATIATOHARONGWEN), 41
Maseres*, Francis (1731–1824), 42, 49, 142, 144, 145, 151, 224, 317, 348, 357, 369, 479, 600, 605, 606, 862
Mash-i-pi-nash-i-wish. *See* Madjeckewiss
Maskelyne, Nevil, 874
Mason, Jemima (Clark), 188
Massiac, Claude-Louis de, known as Marquis de Massiac, 738
Massiot, Gamaliel, 226
Masson, Francis, **580–81**
Massow, Mrs. *See* Crausee
Massow, Friederike Charlotte Louise von (Riedesel, Freifrau zu Eisenbach), **582–84**
Massow, Hans Jürgen Detloff von, 582
Master, Legh, 846
Masters, John, 491
Matayawenenne (Maitwaywayninnee), 185
Matchekewis. *See* Madjeckewiss
Mather, Increase, 127
Mathews*, David (d. 1800), 53, 204, 205, 222, 223, 389, 510, 511, 546, 634, 766, 767, 780
Mathews, Harriet (Green), 389
Mathews, Mary. *See* Simpson
Mathews, Robert, 14, 378, **584–85**, 840, 901, 902
Mathieson*, Alexander (1795–1870), 320
Matonabbee* (d. 1782), 683
Maude, John, 636
Maudon, Grâce (Plantavit de Lapause de Margon), 678
Maugenest*, Germain (d. 1792), 840
Mauger*, Joshua (d. 1788), 81, 250, 556, 607, 666, 843
Maugue-Garreau*, Marie-Josèphe, named de l'Assomption (d. 1785), 117, 143
Maurès* de Malartic, Anne-Joseph-Hippolyte de, Comte de Malartic (1730–1800), 104, 677
Maury, Alexandre, 200
Maury, Jean-Louis, 200, 704
Maxwell, Agnes (Fraser), 330
Maxwell, Isabella (Allan), 15

Maxwell, Margaret (Pagan), 645
Maxwell, Sarah. *See* Ainse
Mayar. *See* Myeerah
Mayar (Mayard). *See* Maillard
Mayer, Johann Michael, 37
Mayhew, Jonathan, 870
Mazel, Mr (engraver), 687
Mea ire. *See* Myeerah
Meares, John, 197, 198, 387, 541, **585–87**, 686
Medley, Henry, 380
Meignot, Marie-Françoise. *See* Fornel
Meiklejohn, William, 880
Melançon, Jean-Baptiste, 587
Melançon, Marie-Anne. *See* Robichaud
Melançon, Marie-Vénérande, named de Sainte-Claire, **587–88**, 659
Melilupi, Catalina (Morello, Marchioness of Malaspina), 570
Mellish, Thomas, 745
Melo. *See* Rivera
Melun. *See* Arbalestre
Melville, Viscount. *See* Dundas
Melvin, Louisa (Caldwell), 133
Ménager. *See* Hausman
Mendip, Baron. *See* Ellis
Menehwehna. *See* Minweweh
Méneveau, Anne (Mondelet), 599
Menneville. *See* Duquesne
Menut, Alexandre, 75, **588–89**
Menut, Marie. *See* Deland
Menzies, Dr, 46
Menzies*, Archibald (1754–1842), 56, 540
Mercier. *See also* Le Mercier
Mercier, Françoise (Martineau), 579
Mercier, Louise-Jeanne-Marguerite (Gravé de La Rive), 379
Mercier, Louis-Sébastien, 233
Mercure, Anne-Marie. *See* Gautier, *dit* Bellair
Mercure, François, 589
Mercure, Joseph, 589
Mercure, Louis, **589–90**
Mercure, Louis-Michel, 589
Mercure, Madeleine. *See* Thibodeau
Mercure, Michel, 589
Merle*, Jacques, named Father Vincent de Paul (1768–1853), 125
Merlet, Monsieur (rebel), 687
Merrick*, John (d. 1829), 872
Merritt*, William Hamilton (1793–1862), 522, 673, 858
Merry, Anthony, 20
Meshecunnaqua (Me-She-Kin-No-Quah). *See* Michikinakoua
Mesplet*, Fleury (1734–94), 173, 298, 383, 590, 591, 621, 737, 892, 894
Messein. *See* Bailly
Métivier, Marie-Josette (Conefroy), 202
Mettot, Marie-Catherine (Lebrun de Duplessis), 478, 479
Meurin, Sébastien-Louis, 342
Meyers*, John Walden (1745–1821), 550
Meynardie, Mr (businessman), 395
Mézière. *See also* Lacroix-Mézière
Mézière, Charlotte-Archange (Berthelot), 591
Mézière, Henry-Antoine, 241, **590–91**
Mézière, Marie-Eugénie. *See* Passy

Mézière, Michel-Archange. *See* Campeau
Mézière, Pierre, 590
Mézière, Pierre-François, 590, 652
Mézière, Simon-André, 590
Michaux, André, 592
Michaux, André, 581, **592–93**
Michaux, Cécile. *See* Claye
Michaux, François-André, 592, 593
Michaux, Marie-Charlotte. *See* Barbet
Michiconiss (Michiguiss). *See* Madjeckewiss
Michikinakoua (Michikiniqua), 3, **593–95**, 796, 808, 852
Mickle, Sara, 114
Middleton, Charles, 1st Baron Barham, 281
Mieray. *See* Myeerah
Migeon* de Branssat, Marie-Anne, named de la Nativité (d. 1771), 224
Migeon de Branssat, Thérèse-Denise (Juchereau de Saint-Denys; Liénard de Beaujeu), 498
Mighells. *See* Miles
Mignault*, Pierre-Marie (1784–1868), 186
Migneron, Thérèse (Serres), 752
Milan, William, 465
Milbanke, Ann, Lady Milbanke. *See* Delavall
Milbanke, Mark, 361, 408, **595–96**, 632
Milbanke, Mary. *See* Webber
Milbanke, Sir Ralph, 595
Miles, Abner, 419, 420, **596–98**
Miles*, Elijah (1753–1831), 355
Miles, James, 597
Miles, Mercy (wife of ABNER), 596
Miles*, Stephen (1789–1870), 169
Millage (Milledge). *See* Millidge
Milledge*, John (d. 1830), 598
Miller, Andrew, 608
Miller, George, 373
Miller, James, 204, 546, 634, 780
Miller, Margaret (Binney), 81
Miller, Maria Frances Ann. *See* Morris
Miller, William, 608
Millidge, John, 598
Millidge, Mercy. *See* Berker
Millidge, Thomas, 94, **598–99**
Millidge*, Thomas (d. 1838), 598, 647
Mills*, Joseph Langley (1788–1832), 489
Mills*, Sir Thomas (d. 1793), 142, 191, 289, 370
Milmine, Alexander, 259
Milnes*, Sir Robert Shore (1746–1837), 18, 45, 95, 106, 121, 206, 209, 212, 213, 214, 215, 218, 226, 234, 246, 247, 291, 292, 319, 374, 384, 398, 439, 449, 470, 486, 494, 577, 579, 648, 649, 651, 655, 659, 692, 792, 794, 880, 881
Milton, John, 630
Minavavana. *See* Minweweh
Minot, Mercy (Wiswall), 870
Minweweh* (d. 1770), 129, 567
Miray, Louis, 463
Mirepoix. *See* Lévis-Mirepoix
Missègle (Misèle). *See* Bonne
Mitchell, David, 391
Mitchell*, David (d. 1832), 715
Mitchell, John, 68
Mitchell, Maria. *See* Gregory
Mitchell, Mary (Polly) (Welch), 845
Mitchell, William, 327

Mitchikiweese. *See* Madjeckewiss
Mit'tee'na'pew. *See* Matonabbee
Mociño. *See* Moziño
Moffatt*, George (1787–1865), 544, 636
Molière. *See* Poquelin, Jean-Baptiste
Moll. *See also* Berczy
Moll, Albrecht Theodor, 70
Moll, Johanna Josepha Walpurga. *See* Hefele
Moll, Johann Albrecht Ulrich (Wilhelm Albert Ulrich von). *See* Berczy, William
Moncel. *See* Giffard
Monckton*, Robert (1726–82), 58, 203, 227, 412, 823, 843
Mondelet, Anne. *See* Méneveau
Mondelet*, Charles-Elzéar (1801–76), 600
Mondelet, Didier, 599
Mondelet, Dominique, **599–600**
Mondelet*, Dominique (1799–1863), 600
Mondelet*, Jean-Marie (d. 1843), 183, 591, 600
Mondelet, Marie-Françoise. *See* Hains
Monette. *See* Manette
Mongan, Charles, 600
Mongenet*, Thérèse-Bernardine, known as Mme de Saint Laurent (1760–1830), 297, 298, 449, 849
Mongeon, Marguerite (Cartier, *dit* L'Angevin), 164
Monk*, Sir James (1745–1826), 77, 81, 84, 149, 150, 151, 152, 192, 226, 370, 373, 492, 508, 697, 705, 843, 863
Monro*, David (1765–1834), 182, 484, 566
Montaño. *See* Rivera
Montarville. *See* Boucher
Montbrun, Pierre, 258
Montcalm*, Louis-Joseph de, Marquis de Montcalm (1712–59), 47, 103, 104, 163, 164, 191, 196, 369, 487, 677, 738, 739, 767, 823, 888
Montendre. *See* Longchamps-Montendre
Montesquieu, Baron de. *See* Secondat
Montesson. *See* Legardeur
Montgolfier*, Étienne (1712–91), 92, 146, 241, 245, 294, 396, 432, 480, 498, 680, 687, 703, 892
Montgomery, Anne (Townshend, Viscountess and Marchioness Townshend), 824
Montgomery, Sir James, 268
Montgomery, Sir James William, 219, 220, 262, 263, 310, 311, 477, 478, 514, 720, 777, 778, 779, 824, 826, 848
Montgomery, Mary. *See* Ross
Montgomery*, Richard (1736–75), 5, 30, 31, 36, 40, 64, 98, 131, 147, 164, 191, 254, 272, 331, 358, 383, 396, 414, 492, 572, 575, 652, 802, 812
Montgomery*, William (1765–1800), 262, 477, 824, 848
Monthelet. *See* Mondelet
Montigny. *See* Testard
Montizambert. *See* Boucher
Montmollin, David-François de, 146, **600–2**, 613
Montmollin, Élyse de, 602
Montmollin, Francis Godot de, 601
Montmollin, Jane de. *See* Bell
Montmollin, John Frederick de, 601
Montmollin, John Samuel de, 601
Montmollin, Louis de, 600
Montmollin, Salomé de. *See* Gaudot
Montour, Mme. *See* Couc, Elizabeth
Montour, Andrew (Henry), 602
Montour, Geneviève. *See* Wills
Montour, Henry Isaac Horatio, 603

Montour, Nicholas, 373, 494, 561, 562, **602–4**, 738, 821
Montour, Nicholas, 604
Montour, Sarah. *See* Ainse
Montresor*, John (1736–99), 657
Monts. *See* Du Gua
Montviel. *See* Vassal
Monty, Catherine (Gosselin), 358
Moody, James, **604–5**
Moody, Jane. *See* Robinson
Moody, John, 604
Mooers (Moores), Elizabeth (Perley), 665
Mooney, Sophia M. (Pond), 685
Moore, Miss or Mrs (wife of WEYAPIERSENWAH), 852
Moore*, Frances (Brooke) (d. 1789), 130, 228, 582
Moore, John, 69
Moore, Sir John, 110
Moore, Stephen, 314, 315
Moore, Thomas, 642, 643
Moore*, William (fl. 1779–98), 66, 460, 790, 834
Moores. *See* Mooers
Morand*, Paul (Hypolithe) (d. 1854), 436, 437
Moreau, Catherine (Adhémar), 3
Moreau*, Jean-Baptiste (d. 1770), 199
Morello, Carlo, Marquis of Malaspina, 570
Morello, Catalina Melilupi de, Marchioness of Malaspina. *See* Melilupi
Morgan, Daniel, 31
Morgan*, Henry James (1842–1913), 18
Morgann, Maurice, 144, 148, **605–7**
Morice, William, 204, 476
Morin, Samuel, 816
Morin, William, 117
Morin, *dit* Chêneverd, Marie-Élizabeth (Bruneau), 116
Morisset*, Gérard (1898–1970), 49, 710
Morrin*, Joseph (1794–1861), 249
Morris*, Charles (1711–81), 108, 426, 607, 608, 874
Morris, Charles, 94, 407, 598, **607–8**
Morris*, Charles (1759–1831), 109, 607, 612
Morris, Elizabeth Bond. *See* Leggett
Morris, Gouverneur, 630
Morris, James Rainstorpe, **608–9**
Morris, Margaret. *See* Hill
Morris*, Maria Frances Ann (Miller) (1813–75), 608
Morris, Mary. *See* Read
Morris, Robert, 629
Morris, Susannah (wife of JAMES RAINSTORPE), 608
Morrison, Alexander, 313
Morrison*, Joseph Wanton (d. 1826), 696, 762
Morrogh, Francis, 493
Morrogh, Robert, 332, 492, 493, 494, 495, 566, 746
Morrogh, Robert Lester, 746
Morse, Harriet (Carmichael-Smyth, Lady Carmichael-Smyth), 609
Morse, Robert, **609–11**
Morse, Sophia. *See* Godin
Morse, Thomas, 609
Mortimer, Alexander, 611
Mortimer, Edward, **611–12**, 660
Mortimer, Mary. *See* Smith
Mortimer, Sarah. *See* Patterson
Morton*, Arthur Silver (1870–1945), 531, 532, 683
Moschell*, Johann Adam (1795–1849), 199
Moses, Katy, 803

Mosiño. *See also* Moziño
Mosiño, Juan Antonio, 615
Mosiño, Manuela Losada de. *See* Losada
Mosley. *See* Mozely
Motier, Marie-Joseph-Paul-Yves-Roch-Gilbert, Marquis de La Fayette, 238, 414, 583, 788, 893
Mott, Mrs (mother of JACOB S.), 613
Mott, Amelia (Ryan), 612
Mott, Ann. *See* Hinton
Mott, Gabriel F., 613
Mott, Jacob S., **612–13**
Mott, John, 612
Mott, William Hinton, 613
Mottin de La Balme, Augustin, 3, 594
Mouet, Marie (Cadot), 130
Mouet de Langlade, Charles, 715
Mouet* de Langlade, Charles-Michel (d. *c.* 1800), 8, 499, 567, 568, 760
Moulton*, Ebenezer (1709–83), 744
Mounier*, François (d. 1769), 142, 276, 369
Mounier*, Jean-Mathieu (fl. 1715–74), 276
Mountain, Ann. *See* Postle
Mountain*, George Jehoshaphat (1789–1863), 602, 769, 787
Mountain, Jacob, 613
Mountain*, Jacob (1749–1825), 18, 68, 69, 106, 212, 246, 292, 330, 334, 445, 476, 489, 494, 579, 601, 613, 614, 692, 696, 756, 769, 770, 787, 808, 880
Mountain, Jacob Henry Brooke, 787
Mountain, Jehosaphat, 106, 134, 601, **613–15**
Mountain, Mary. *See* Leach
Mountain, Salter Jehoshaphat, 614, 747
Mower*, Nahum (1779–1830), 298
Moxley, Thomas, 511, 780
Mozely (Mosley), Nancy, 506
Moziño, María Rita Rivera de. *See* Rivera y Melo Montaño
Moziño Losada Suárez de Figueroa, José Mariano, 11, 198, **615–16**
Mudjeckewiss. *See* Madjeckewiss
Muir, Adam C., 302, 775
Mulgrave, Baron. *See* Phipps
Munday, William, 783
Munn, Agnes. *See* Galloway
Munn, Alexander, **616–18**, 699
Munn, Catherine. *See* Edward
Munn, David, 617
Munn, James (brother of ALEXANDER), 617
Munn, James (shipbuilder), 617
Munn, John (father of ALEXANDER), 616
Munn, John (father of JOHN*), 617
Munn*, John (d. 1859), 617
Munro. *See also* Monro
Munro, Duncan, 385
Munro, Harry, 785
Munro, Henry, 543
Munro, John, 285, 460, 461, 700
Munro*, John (1728–1800), 282, 518, 519, 772
Muquinna* (fl. 1778–95), 11, 12, 411, 571, 586, 615, 618
Muquinna, **618–19**
Murdoch*, Beamish (1800–76), 690
Murdoch, James, 199, 344, 871
Mure*, John (d. 1823), 84, 319, 461, 635, 636, 769, 817, 827, 835

Murphy, Helena (Eleanor) (Cannon), 139
Murray*, Anne (Powell) (1758–1849), 189, 521, 522
Murray, Daniel, 354, 831
Murray, Elizabeth (Upham), 831
Murray*, James (1721/22–94), 4, 19, 20, 91, 98, 130, 131,
132, 141, 142, 143, 144, 153, 181, 224, 225, 272, 277, 288,
289, 315, 330, 331, 368, 369, 379, 384, 389, 412, 413, 425,
426, 427, 462, 478, 479, 494, 507, 511, 578, 588, 620, 658,
699, 711, 745, 819, 823, 824, 864, 889
Murray, John, 831
Murray*, John (d. 1824 or 1825), 53, 205, 546, 634, 766,
780
Murray, John, 2nd Earl of Dunmore, 822
Murray, John, 4th Earl of Dunmore, 301, 340, 423, 852
Murray*, Walter (d. 1772), 142
Murray, William, 1st Earl of Mansfield, 145
Musgrave, Sir Thomas, 156
Myeerah (Myecruh), **619–20**, 775, 798
Myers, Hyam, 193

NADEAU, Louis, 277
Nagot, François-Charles, 186
Nairne, Christiana. See Emery
Nairne, Christine, 621
Nairne, John, 31, 330, 585, **620–22**
Nairne, John, 621
Nairne, Magdalen (McNicol), 621
Nairne, Mary (Blackburn), 621
Nairne, Thomas, 621
Nancy (Ann), 456
Naper, Ann. See Hudson
Napier, Peter, 95, 334
Napoleon I, Emperor of the French, 68, 69, 131, 242, 347,
489, 655, 660, 696, 861
Nash, Ruth. See Hollywood
Natte, Françoise. See Gassin
Natte, Jean-Noël, 622
Natte, dit Marseille, Jean-Sébastien, **622–23**
Natte, dit Marseille, Marguerite. See Ducheneau, dit
Sanregret
Natte, dit Marseille, Marie-Louise. See Fluette
Navarre, Françoise (Émond), 304
Naywash (Neywash), 799
Neave, George, 838
Nebourvele. See Boucher
Necker, Jacques, 486
Neé, Luis, 399
Negushwa. See Egushwa
Neilson*, John (1776–1848), 67, 84, 298, 702, 768, 769
Neilson*, Samuel (1771–93), 768, 834
Nelles, Abraham, 857
Nelles*, Robert (1761–1842), 520, 639, 643, 673, 845
Nelson, Horatio, 1st Viscount Nelson, 110, 435, 585, 631,
636
Nelson, John, 636
Nemiers (Nemire), George, 639, 640
Nepean, Sir Evan, 21, 317, 350, 351, 371, 427
Néron, Jean, 271
Nesbitt*, William (d. 1784), 108, 556
Netawatwees (King Newcomer), 883
Nevers, Phineas, 556
Nevins, Archibald, 623
Nevins, Archibald, **623–25**

Nevins, Grace. See Penrose
Nevins, Jane (wife of ARCHIBALD), 623
Nevins, Penrose, 623
Nevins, Pim, 623
Nevins, Robert, 624
Nevins, Thomas, 623, 624
Newcomer, King. See Netawatwees
Newell, Susanna (Pond), 681
Newman, Ann. See Holdsworth
Newman, Holdsworth, 625
Newman, John (brother of ROBERT), 625, 626
Newman, John (merchant), 625
Newman, Lydston, 625, 626
Newman, Mary. See Holdsworth
Newman, Richard (uncle), 625
Newman, Richard, 625, 626
Newman, Robert, 625
Newman, Robert, **625–27**, 641
Newman, Sir Robert William, 626
Newman, Thomas (father), 625, 626
Newman, Thomas, 626
Newman, William, 641, 785, 838
News Carrier. See Carrihogo
Newsom, George, 623
Newton, Hannah Adams (Binney), 81
Newton, Henry, 81
Newton, John, 81
Newton, Mary (Girty; Turner), 345
Neywash. See Naywash
Nichol*, Robert (d. 1824), 403, 522, 643, 782
Nichols, Katharine (Upham), 830
Nims, Abigail (Towatogowash, rebaptized Élisabeth)
(Raizenne), 703
Ninãkon. See Minweweh
Ninsotin, 835
Nissowaquet* (d. 1797), 8, 229
Nitachinon. See Chabert de Joncaire, Philippe-Thomas
Nitschmann, David, 883
Nivard Saint-Dizier, Étienne, 286
Niverville. See Boucher
Noble*, Arthur (d. 1746/47), 498
Noble, Hannah. See Barker
Noble, John, 675
Noble, John Hatt, 675
Noble, Mary (Margaret) (Riddle; wife of SETH), 627
Noble, Ruhama. See Rich
Noble, Seth, 296, **627–28**, 666
Noble, Thomas, 627
Noel, Bernard. See Bernard, Noël
Noël, Jean-Baptiste, 165, 269
Noël, Marguerite (Trestler), 827
Noël*, Marie-Geneviève (Drapeau) (1766–1829), 269
Noiseux*, François-Xavier (1748–1834), 77, 253, 295
Nonosbawsut, 243, 244
Nonosecash (Assakis), 885
Nooth*, John Mervin (d. 1828), 202, 471, 501, 502, 503,
592, 684
Normandeau, Joseph, 436
Normant* Du Faradon, Louis (1681–1759), 498
North, Frederick, 2nd Earl of Guilford, 134, 148, 152, 241,
479, 849, 890, 898, 899
Northcote, James, 382
Northumberland, Duke of. See Percy

Norton*, John (fl. 1784–1826), 114, 255, 412, 803, 804, 810
Norton*, Moses (d. 1773), 451
Nosawaguet. *See* Nissowaquet
Noyan. *See* Payen
Noyelles* de Fleurimont, Nicolas-Joseph de (1695–1761), 97
Noyes, Anna (Gale; Byles), 127
Nutter, Valentine, 438

OAKES*, Forrest (d. 1783), 368, 382, 656, 683
Oakes*, John (d. 1832), 36, 37, 436, 736, 737
Oakes, Margaret (Gray), 382
Oakley, George, 495
O Bask. *See* Bastarache
Obemau-unoqua (Nancy?), 742
Oberholser. *See* Overholser
O'Brien, Anne (England), 306
O'Brien, James, 306
Obwandiyag. *See* Pontiac
Odell, Anne. *See* De Cou
Odell, John, 628
Odell, Jonathan, 34, 155, 156, 157, 162, 355, 589, **628–31**, 868
Odell, Temperance. *See* Dickinson
Odell, William, 628
Odell*, William Franklin (1774–1844), 465, 630
Odeserundiye. *See* Deserontyon, John
O'Donel, Ann. *See* Crosby
O'Donel, James Louis, 122, 123, 360, 408, 473, 494, 595, **631–34**
O'Donel, Michael (father), 631
O'Donel, Michael, 631
Ogden*, Isaac (1739–1824), 211, 226, 388, 538, 614, 684
Ogden, Jonathan, 726
Ogilvie, James, 53, 205, 339, 546, **634–35**, 766
Ogilvie, John, 636
Ogilvie*, John (1724–74), 785
Ogilvie, Penelope (wife of JAMES), 634
Ogilvy, Jane. *See* Dunlop
Ogilvy, John, 286, 564, **635–37**, 718
O'Hara*, Edward (1767–1833), 637
O'Hara, Felix, **637–38**, 864, 902
O'Hara, Henry, 637
O'Hara, Hugh, 637
O'Hara, Martha. *See* McCormick
O'Hara, Oliver, 637
Ohrante. *See* Oteroughyanento
Ohtowaʔkéhson* (1759–1837), 804
Oja, La. *See* Wahpasha
Okill, Jane (Stuart), 785, 786
Olabaratz, Catherine d'. *See* Despiaube
Olabaratz, Jean d', 363, **638–39**
Olabaratz*, Joannis-Galand d' (d. 1778), 638
Olabaratz, Marguerite-Angélique d'. *See* Collas
Old Crooked Neck, 803
Olding, Nicholas Purdue, 660
Old King; Old Smoke. *See* Kaieñʔkwaahtoñ
Oliva*, Frédéric-Guillaume (d. 1796), 501
Olive, Gregory, 843
Olivier, Captain, 313
Olry, Joseph-Antoine, 478
Onasakenrat* (Onesakenarat), Joseph (1845–81), 480

Onoquaga. *See* Isaac
Oreil. *See* Doreil
Orford, Earl of. *See* Walpole
Orillat*, Jean (1733–79), 178, 185, 277, 322, 654, 662
Orillat, Thérèse-Amable. *See* Viger
Orkney*, James (1760–1832), 329, 406
Orkney, Jane. *See* Hanna
Orléans, Philippe, Duc d', Regent of France, 449
Orvilliers, Comte d'. *See* Guillouet
Osborn*, Henry (d. 1771), 596
Osborn, Mary (London), **639–40**
Osgood*, Thaddeus (1775–1852), 770
Osgoode*, William (1754–1824), 18, 71, 84, 152, 234, 285, 291, 304, 602, 691, 692, 730, 731, 757
Oteroughyanento (Ohrante), 805, 811
Ouabachas. *See* Wahpasha
Ouasson. *See* Wasson
Ougier, Benedict, 641
Ougier, Peter, **640–42**, 785, 838
Ougier, Peter, 641
Ouimet, Charlotte (Gosselin), 358
Ousson. *See* Wasson
Ouvrier, Frédérique-Louise (Heer), 417
Overholser, Barbara (wife of JACOB), 642
Overholser, Jacob, **640–45**
Owasser. *See* Wasson
Owen, Sir Edward Campbell Rich, 401, 876
Owen, Robert, 297
Owen, William, 146
Oxford, James, 465

PACHECO; Padilla. *See* Güemes
Pagan, David, 645
Pagan, George, 645
Pagan, John (uncle), 645
Pagan, John, 284, 645, 646
Pagan, Margaret. *See* Maxwell
Pagan*, Robert (1750–1821), 134, 161, 336, 337, 351, 355, 645, 646, 874
Pagan, Thomas (uncle), 645
Pagan, Thomas, 645, 646
Pagan, William, 645
Pagan, William, 94, 337, **645–47**
Pagé, *dit* Carcy, Marie-Anne (Boisseau), 90
Paillet, Mr (businessman), 395
Painchaud*, Joseph (1787–1871), 202
Painter, Elizabeth, 648
Painter, John, 284, **647–48**
Painter, Margaret. *See* Stuart
Palliser*, Sir Hugh (1722/23–96), 54, 55, 73, 166, 220, 274, 338, 369, 381, 641, 675
Palmer, Mr (Baptist preacher), 340
Palmer*, James Bardin (d. 1833), 127, 220, 335, 569, 776, 826, 862
Palmer, Wait, 340
Panet, Bernard-Antoine, 648, 649
Panet*, Bernard-Claude (1753–1833), 77, 292, 649, 668, 676
Panet*, Bonaventure (1765–1846), 653
Panet, Charles, 648
Panet, Harriet. *See* Antill
Panet*, Jacques (1754–1834), 648
Panet, Jean-Antoine, 45, 46, 87, 182, 208, 226, 233, 235,

257, 283, 292, 372, 373, 421, 484, 493, 578, 588, 603, **648–52**, 653, 654, 695, 828, 878, 881
Panet*, Jean-Claude (d. 1778), 91, 146, 149, 150, 648, 652, 653
Panet, Jean-Nicolas, 652
Panet, Léon, 654
Panet, Louis, 648
Panet, Louise-Amélie, 654
Panet, Louise-Philippe. *See* Badelard
Panet, Marie (Taschereau), 648, 649
Panet, Marie-Anne. *See* Cerré
Panet, Marie-Anne. *See* Trefflé, *dit* Rottot
Panet, Marie-Anne-Archange, *dite* de Saint-Bernard, 649
Panet, Marie-Françoise, *dite* de Saint-Jacques, 649
Panet, Marie-Louise. *See* Barolet
Panet, Marie-Madeleine-Françoise. *See* Foucher
Panet*, Philippe (1791–1855), 648, 649
Panet, Pierre, 277, 288, **652–53**, 654, 839
Panet, Pierre-Louis, 106, 175, 234, 257, 290, 373, 508, 650, **653–55**, 663, 701
Pangman, Bastonnais (Joseph?), 656
Pangman, Grace. *See* MacTier
Pangman, John, 656
Pangman, Peter, 391, 537, 562, 566, 602, 603, **656–57**, 682, 684
Panther, 774
Panton, George, **657–58**
Paoli, Pascal, 421
Papin, *dit* Barolette, Catherine, 293
Papineau, Antoine, 165
Papineau*, Joseph (1752–1841), 233, 241, 373, 572, 833
Papineau, Julie. *See* Bruneau
Papineau*, Louis-Joseph (1786–1871), 117, 186, 208, 489, 651, 695
Paradis, Augustin, 139
Parcot, Jane (Schureman), 742
Paré, Jacques, 322
Paré, Marie-Anne. *See* Caron
Pareja. *See* Alcalá-Galiano
Parent, Joseph, 658
Parent, Marie-Anne. *See* Chaboillez
Parent, Marie-Anne. *See* Chatellereaux
Parent, Marie-Geneviève, named de Saint-François d'Assise, 587, **658–59**
Parent, Marie-Louise (Baillairgé), 49, 51
Parent, Pierre, 436
Park, Mungo, 55
Parker, Sir Hyde, 110
Parker, James, 716
Parker, Lydia (Sawtelle), 740
Parker, William, 635
Parkins, Susanna (Finlay), 314
Parkinson, Barton, 729
Parkman, Francis, 412
Parkyns, John, 664
Parr*, John (1725–91), 25, 94, 109, 128, 136, 148, 156, 158, 222, 251, 281, 309, 310, 344, 431, 435, 445, 465, 589, 605, 610, 634, 657, 658, 866, 867
Parry*, Sir William Edward (1790–1855), 56
Pascaud, Jean, 395
Pascoe, Charles Frederick, 107
Passy, Marie-Eugénie de (Mézière), 591
Pasteur, Charles-Bernard, 591
Paterson, Charles, 8, 9, 39, 229, 561, 656, 682

Patterson, Elizabeth (Bonaparte), 660
Patterson, George, 660
Patterson, John (brother of Walter*), 309, 310
Patterson, John (deacon), 660
Patterson, Robert, 409, 611, **659–60**
Patterson, Sarah (Mortimer), 611, 660
Patterson*, Walter (d. 1798), 27, 219, 249, 250, 309, 310, 477, 513, 515, 775, 777, 778, 825, 826, 873
Patton, Mary (Allan), 15
Pawling, Benjamin, **660–61**, 669, 782, 841
Pawling, Jesse, 660
Pawling, Peter Ten Broeck, 661
Pawling, Susan (wife of BENJAMIN), 660
Payen de Noyan, Marie-Catherine, named de Saint-Alexis, **661–62**
Payen de Noyan et de Chavoy, Louise-Catherine. *See* Ailleboust de Manthet
Payen* de Noyan et de Chavoy, Pierre-Jacques (1695–1771), 661
Payet, Marie-Joseph (Pouget), 687
Payne, Hiram, 204
Peachey*, James (d. 1797), 228, 428
Peale, Charles Willson, 313, 811
Péan*, Michel-Jean-Hugues (d. 1782), 104, 164, 191, 711
Pearley. *See* Perley
Peaslie, Robert, 415
Pécaudy* de Contrecœur, Claude-Pierre (1705–75), 98, 143, 185, 272
Péché (Peshe), Monsieur (*engagé*), 684
Pécholier, Jeanne. *See* Lafont
Pecholier, Thomas, 42
Peirce (Pierce), Sarah (Winslow), 869
Pelegrin. *See* Pellegrin
Pelerin, Marie-Vénérande (Ranvoyzé), 707
Pélissier*, Christophe (b. 1728, d. before 1800), 21, 277, 289, 735, 736, 843
Pélissier, Marie-Catherine. *See* Delezenne
Pélissier de Féligonde, Jean-François, 680
Pellegrin*, Gabriel (1713–88), 103
Pellerin, Cécile. *See* Boudreau
Pellerin, Pierre, 102
Pelletier, Geneviève. *See* Digé
Pelletier, Joseph, 257
Pelletier, Pierre, 599
Pellew, Edward, 1st Viscount Exmouth, 444
Pellisier. *See* Pélissier
Pemberton, Jeremy, 251
Penman, George, 407
Pennant, Thomas, 54, 167, 221, 362
Penrose, Grace (Nevins), 623
Penrose, Richard, 623
Penrose, Thomas, 623
Penrose, William, 623
Pépin*, Joseph (1770–1842), 497
Pépin, *dit* Laforce, Michelle. *See* Lebert
Pépin, *dit* Laforce, Pierre, 470
Pepperrell*, Sir William (1696–1759), 134, 869
Perceval, John, 2nd Earl of Egmont, 315
Percival*, Michael Henry (d. 1829), 746
Percy, Hugh, 2nd Duke of Northumberland, 811, 865, 868
Périnau, Jacques, 662
Périnau, Marie-Joseph. *See* Cusson
Périnau, Toussaint, 662
Périnault, Élisabeth. *See* Guyon Desprez

Périnault, Joseph, 241, 322, 323, **662–63**
Périnault, Marie-Élisabeth. *See* Harel
Périnault, Pierre-Joseph, 663
Perkins, Abigail. *See* Backus
Perkins, Elizabeth. *See* Young
Perkins, Jacob, 663
Perkins, Jemima. *See* Leonard
Perkins, Simeon, 63, 116, 410, 573, 608, **663–65**
Perkins, Thomas, 166
Perkins, Zebulon, 116
Perley, Elizabeth. *See* Mooers
Perley, Eunice. *See* Putnam
Perley, Israel, 555, 627, **665–67**, 774
Perley, Thomas, 665
Perrault, Charles-François, 570
Perrault, Charlotte. *See* Boucher de Boucherville
Perrault*, François (d. 1745), 283
Perrault, Guillaume-Michel, 667
Perrault, Jacques, 667
Perrault*, Jacques, known as Perrault *l'aîné* (1718–75), 6, 368, 481, 499, 667
Perrault, Jacques-Nicolas, 283, 576, **667–69**
Perrault*, Jean-Baptiste (1761–1844), 533, 635, 741
Perrault*, Jean-Olivier (1773–1827), 234, 668, 794
Perrault*, Joseph-François (1753–1844), 225, 233, 241, 243, 386, 508, 651, 701, 880
Perrault, Marie-Anne. *See* Amiot
Perrault, Marie-Joseph (Deschenaux), 252
Perrault, Marie-Louise. *See* Taschereau
Perrault, Michel, 668
Perrault, Pierre, 668
Perrault, Thérèse-Esther. *See* Hausman, *dit* Ménager
Perrault *l'aîné*. *See* Perrault, Jacques; Perrault, Jacques-Nicolas
Perrinault. *See* Périnault
Perron, Pélagie-Victoire (Rieutord), 713
Perry, Oliver Hazard, 875
Perthuis, Marie-Josephte-Madeleine. *See* Hiché
Peshe. *See* Péché
Pestel, Ekaterina von (Billings), 79
Peter (schoolmaster), 255
Peters*, Charles Jeffery (d. 1848), 456
Peters, Hannah Owen (Jarvis), 452, 453
Peters, Hendrick. *See* Theyanoguin
Peters*, Joseph (1729–1800), 318, 833
Peters, Samuel Andrew, 344, 832
Peters*, Thomas (d. 1792), 341, 469
Petit. *See* Pettit
Petit-Claire, Claude-Joseph, 437
Petit-Claire, Marie-Louise. *See* Dalciat
Petitot, *dit* Saint-Sceine (Sincennes), Marguerite (Doucet), 261
Petrequin. *See* Pettrequin
Petters. *See* Peters
Pettit, Elizabeth. *See* Heath
Pettit, Margaret. *See* McFarland
Pettit, Nathaniel, 669
Pettit, Nathaniel, 639, 660, 661, **669–70**, 841
Pettrequin*, Jean (d. 1764), 250
Petty, William, 2nd Earl of Shelburne, 142, 143, 144, 148, 149, 155, 156, 158, 162, 606, 607, 610, 897, 898
Peyrot, Élisabeth (Guitet), 393
Peyton*, John (1749–1829), 243
Peyton, John, 243, 244

Phebe de Sainte-Angèle. *See* Arnoldi
Phelan, Patrick, 122, 632
Phelan, William, 458, 459
Phelps, Benajah, 199
Phelps, Davenport, 808, 809
Phelps, David, 412
Phelps, Elijah, 781
Phelps, Lois (Viets), 832
Phelps, Oliver, 781
Philipps, John, 670
Philipps, John, **670**
Philipps, Judith. *See* Wood
Phillipps, John, 670
Phillips, Charles, 377
Phillips, Jane (Scott), 745, 746
Phillips, Mary (Finlay), 314, 318, 745
Phillips, Samuel, 333
Phillips, William, 746
Phipps, Catherine Anne (Prevost), 693
Phipps, Constantine John, 2nd Baron Mulgrave, 54, 55
Phipps, Jemima. *See* Sawtelle
Phipps, Mary, 740, 741
Phipps, Submit (Willard), 740, 741
Phipps, William, 740
Phyn, James, 282, 299, 646
Phyn, Jean (Forsyth), 325
Picard*, Louis-Alexandre (d. 1799), 37, 329, 436
Picard, Marie-Madeleine (Serré), 174
Pichard, Amable, 458, **670–71**
Pickett, Mary (Isaacs; Viets), 832
Pickmore, Francis, **671–72**
Picoté* de Belestre, François-Marie (1716–93), 96, 98, 143, 232, 487, 802
Pier. *See* Saint-Aubin
Pierce. *See also* Peirce
Pierce, Elizabeth (Welch), 845
Pierce, Margaret (Green), 389
Piers, Harry, 635
Piersons, Nicholas, 871
Piggott, Letitia (McKinnon), 544
Pigott-Carleton, Henrietta Anne. *See* Carleton
Pike, Zebulon Montgomery, 9, 836
Pillon, Boyer, 893
Pilotte, Angelique, **673–74**
Pineda, Antonio, 399
Pinet, Alexis, 51
Pinquin (Pinquaing). *See* Gallant, Xavier
Pinson, Andrew (father of ANDREW), 675
Pinson, Andrew (grandson of ANDREW), 675
Pinson, Andrew, 576, **674–76**
Pinson, Ann. *See* Dodd
Pinson, William, 675
Pipe, Captain. *See* Konieschguanokee
Pitchy. *See* Peachey
Pitre, Cécile. *See* Boudreau
Pitre, François, 102
Pitre, Jean, 102
Pitre, Jean-Baptiste, 102
Pitt, John, 2nd Earl of Chatham, 155, 356
Pitt, William, 21, 148, 149, 156, 488, 492, 566, 758, 759, 844
Pitt, William, 1st Earl of Chatham, 130, 141, 145, 155, 767, 823
Pius V1, 242, 246, 632

Piuze, Édouard-Ferdinand, 676
Piuze, J.-R., 676
Piuze, Liveright, **676**
Piuze, Marie-Anne. *See* Aubut
Piuze, Rémi, 676
Piza, David, 194
Place, Thomas, 193
Plamondon*, Antoine (1804–95), 72
Plamondon*, Louis (1785–1828), 702
Plantavit de Lapause de Margon, Grâce. *See* Maudon
Plantavit de Lapause de Margon, Henri, 678
Plantavit de Lapause de Margon, Jean-Guillaume, **676–78**
Planté, Bernard, 788
Plante, George, 576
Planté*, Joseph-Bernard (1768–1826), 580
Platt, John, 614
Plaw, John, 678
Plaw, John, **678–80**
Plaw, Mary (mother of JOHN), 678
Plaw, Mary (wife of JOHN), 678
Playter, Ely, 597
Playter, James, 597
Plessis*, Joseph-Octave (1763–1825), 13, 45, 123, 125, 181, 186, 200, 203, 207, 209, 211, 213, 217, 236, 246, 247, 248, 271, 290, 292, 374, 380, 459, 471, 473, 489, 493, 494, 495, 588, 633, 651, 659, 662, 671, 678, 688, 691, 695, 738, 745, 770
Plessis-Bélair, François, 77
Poitevin d'Anglebért, Joseph, 294
Poitevin d'Anglebért, Marie-Anne. *See* Garnom
Poitras, Jeanne (Ranvoizé), 707
Pole, Sir Charles Morice, 190, 360
Pollard*, Richard (1752–1824), 787
Pollock, William, 507
Pommereau, Catherine-Élisabeth (Bruyères), 118
Poncin, Claude, 187, **680–81**
Poncin, Jean, 680
Poncin, Marie. *See* Clameron
Pond, Charles Hobby, 685
Pond, Mary. *See* Hubbard
Pond, Nathan Gillette, 685
Pond, Peter, 681
Pond, Peter, 129, 300, 391, 512, 537, 538, 539, 561, 592, 602, 603, 656, **681–86**, 818
Pond, Sophia M. *See* Mooney
Pond, Susanna. *See* Newell
Pondiac (Pondiak, Pondiag). *See* Pontiac
Pontbriand. *See* Dubreil
Pontiac* (d. 1769), 38, 89, 129, 253, 300, 462, 511, 567, 714, 796, 804, 883, 889
Pontleroy. *See* Sarrebource
Pope, Alexander, 629
Poquelin, Jean-Baptiste (Molière), 233, 248, 702
Portelance. *See* Roy
Porteous, Andrew, 284, 286
Porteous, John (fur trader), 282, 284, 286 , 299, 326
Porteous, John (merchant), 566
Porteous*, Thomas (d. 1830), 566
Porteous, William, 566
Porter, Asa, 509
Porter, Martha (Hibbard), 422
Porter, Nathaniel, 422
Portland, Duke of. *See* Cavendish

Portlock, Joseph Ellison, 686
Portlock, Nathaniel, 587, **686–87**
Post, Sarah (Belcher), 63
Postle, Ann (Mountain), 613
Pote, Jeremiah, 337
Pothier. *See also* Potier
Pothier*, Jean-Baptiste-Toussaint (1771–1845), 324, 727
Potier*, Pierre-Philippe (d. 1781), 710
Potter, Mercy (Spencer), 772
Potter, William W., 238
Pottié (Pottier). *See* Potier
Potts, James, 4
Potts, Mary (Ainslie), 4
Pouget, Jean-Baptiste-Noël, 313, **687–88**
Pouget, Marie-Joseph. *See* Payet
Pouget, Paul, 687
Poulin, Louis, 331
Poulin, Marie (Charland), 183
Poulin de Courval Cressé, Charlotte-Louise. *See* Lambert Dumont
Poulin de Courval Cressé, Claude, 216
Poulin de Courval Cressé, Louise-Charlotte (Dumoulin), 216
Poulin* de Courval Cressé, Louis-Pierre (1728–64), 216
Powell, Anne. *See* Murray
Powell, Charles Stuart, **688–90**
Powell, Cordelia, 688, 690
Powell, Fidelia, 688
Powell, Jane (Willcocks), 854
Powell, John, 189
Powell, Mary Ann (wife of CHARLES STUART), 688
Powell, Mary Boyles (Jarvis), 522
Powell, S. (father of CHARLES STUART), 688
Powell, Snelling, 689
Powell, William, 523
Powell*, William Dummer (1755–1834), 17, 18, 65, 172, 268, 366, 440, 521, 522, 523, 643, 644, 718, 721, 748, 750, 842, 856
Power, Miss (Skinner), 762
Power*, John (d. 1823), 474
Power, Patrick, 632
Powless, Margaret. *See* Brant
Pownall*, Sir George (1755–1834), 21, 224, 225, 318
Pownall, John, 407
Powys, Thomas, 21
Pozer, Jacob, 881
Pratt, John Jeffreys, 2nd Earl and 1st Marquis of Camden, 366
Prenties, Miles, 508
Prescott, Harriet. *See* Skinner
Prescott, Richard, 690
Prescott, Robert, 71, 84, 87, 140, 152, 236, 246, 253, 319, 439, 455, 536, 649, **690–93**, 749, 758, 879, 881
Pressart*, Colomban-Sébastien (1723–77), 144, 379
Preston, Charles, 413, 802
Preston*, Richard (d. 1861), 342
Prévost, Augustin, 693, 887
Prevost, Catherine Anne. *See* Phipps
Prevost, Sir George, 45, 87, 112, 113, 119, 138, 140, 213, 292, 314, 346, 401, 424, 489, 529, 558, 643, 651, 668, **693–98**, 714, 748, 829, 851, 875, 876, 881
Prévost, Jacques, 887
Prévost, Nanette. *See* Grand

Prévot, Nicolas, 813
Price, Mr (merchant), 322
Price*, Benjamin (d. 1768), 289, 413, 714
Price, Charles. *See* Isham, Charles Thomas
Price, Walter, 633
Prideaux, John, 681, 888
Priestley, Joseph, 182
Prince Regent. *See* George IV
Pringle*, Robert (d. 1793), 762
Pritchard, Edward W., 347
Pritchard, Eleanor (Bonner; Delesdernier), 240
Pritchard*, John (1777–1856), 535
Procter*, Henry (1769–1822), 302, 346, 748, 775, 799, 876
Prophet. *See* Tenskwatawa
Proteau, Marie-Josephe (Cadot), 128
Proulx, Basile, 497
Prowse*, Daniel Woodley (1834–1914), 382
Prud'homme, Louise (Bonne de Missègle; Le Moyne de Longueuil), 230, 487
Prud'homme, Marie-Françoise (Roy), 727
Puckeshinwa, 796
Puisaye*, Joseph-Geneviève, Comte de Puisaye (1755–1827), 86, 440, 519, 731
Pullman (Pulman), John, 321
Punderson, Ebenezer, 59
Punderson, Sylvia (Beardsley), 59, 60
Purcell, Thomas, 108
Purse, Alexander, 699
Purse, Isabel. *See* Blenshel
Purss, John, 493, 509, **699–700**
Putnam, Eunice (Perley), 665
Putnam, Israel, 666
Pyke*, George (1775–1851), 27, 90, 769

QUADRA. *See* Bodega
Quaife, Milo Milton, 553
Quain, Mrs Mary, 59, 60
Quayle, Mary Emma (Innis), 759
Quélus. *See* Thubières
Quenebenaw. *See* Kineubenae
Querno, Camillo. *See* Odell, Jonathan
Quesnel*, Frédéric-Auguste (1785–1866), 702
Quesnel, Joseph, 233, 243, **700–3**
Quesnel, Joseph-Timoléon, 702
Quesnel*, Jules-Maurice (1786–1842), 702
Quesnel, Louis-Auguste, 700
Quesnel, Marie-Josephte. *See* Deslandes
Quesnel, Mélanie (Coursol; Cherrier), 702
Quesnel, Pélagie-Jeanne-Marguerite. *See* Duguen
Quesnel, Pierre, 701
Quesnel de La Rivaudais, Isaac, 700
Quesnel Fonblanche, Louise (Hervieux), 395
Queylus. *See* Thubières
Quiasutha. *See* Kayahsota?
Quinipeno. *See* Kineubenae
Quinson de Saint-Ours, Charles-Roch, 231, 752
Quinson de Saint-Ours, Marie-Anne. *See* Mackay
Quiquinanis. *See* Wikinanish
Quitawape. *See* Atiatoharongwen

RABY*, Augustin (d. 1782), 95
Raby*, Augustin-Jérôme (1745–1822), 373, 493
Racine, Jean, 248

Racy, John, 291
Raddish (Reddish), Thomas, 303
Radstock, Baron. *See* Waldegrave
Rae. *See* Rea
Raeburn, Henry, 314
Raffetot. *See* Deschamps
Raikes, Robert, 189
Raimbault, Marguerite (Boucher de Boucherville), 96
Raimbault de Saint-Blaint, Madeleine (Boucher de Boucherville), 96
Raizenne, Amable-Simon, 703
Raizenne, Élisabeth. *See* Nims, Abigail
Raizenne, Ignace. *See* Rising, Josiah
Raizenne, Marie, named Saint-Ignace, 118, **703–4**
Raizenne, Marie-Madeleine, named Saint-Herman, 703
Ralfe, James, 276
Ralston, Elizabeth (Tiffany), 814
Ramage, Mrs (Taylor; wife of JOHN), 705
Ramage, Catharine. *See* Collins
Ramage, Elizabeth. *See* Liddel
Ramage, John, **704–6**
Ramage, Victoria. *See* Ball
Ramezay, Élisabeth de (La Corne), 578
Ramezay*, Jean-Baptiste-Nicolas-Roch de (1708–77), 97, 108, 128, 498
Ramsay, David, **706–7**
Ramsay, Donald, 407
Ramsay, George, 706
Ramsay, George (Jack), 814
Ramsay*, George, 9th Earl of Dalhousie (1770–1838), 698, 850
Randall, James, 783
Randall, Joseph, 783
Ranvoizé, Étienne, 707
Ranvoizé, Jeanne. *See* Poitras
Ranvoyzé*, Étienne (1776–1826), 708, 709
Ranvoyzé, François, 51, 218, 329, 437, **707–10**
Ranvoyzé*, François-Ignace (1772–1843), 709
Ranvoyzé, Louis (uncle), 709
Ranvoyzé, Louis, 708
Ranvoyzé, Marie-Vénérande. *See* Pelerin
Rapelje, Abraham A., 734
Rashleigh, Robert, 173, 396, 416, 494, 789, 843
Rastel de Rocheblave, Philippe-François, 175, 243
Rastel* de Rocheblave, Pierre (d. 1840), 544
Raux, Joseph-Alexandre, 271
Ravel, Jean-Baptiste, 680
Rawdon-Hastings, Francis, 1st Marquess of Hastings, 811
Rawson, Jane (Black), 84
Rawson, Sentlow, 84
Raymond*, William Odber (1853–1923), 60, 155, 590, 869
Raynal, Guillaume, 165, 202, 233, 248, 486
Rea (Rae), Alice (Askin), 37
Read, Mary (Morris), 607, 608
Réaume, Agathe. *See* Lacelle
Réaume, Angélique. *See* Beauchamp
Réaume, Charles, **710–11**
Réaume, Hyacinthe, 710
Réaume, Marie-Louise (Fournerie de Vézon; Robertson), 714
Rêche. *See* Resche
Récher*, Jean-Félix (1724–68), 379
Reddish. *See* Raddish

Reddy, Thomas, 139
Red Jacket. *See* Sagoyewatha
Redouté, Pierre-Joseph, 592
Reed, Solomon, 744
Reeves*, John (d. 1829), 53, 361, 444, 596, 632, 726
Regnard, Jean-François, 233
Reiche. *See* Resche
Reid, Mr (schoolmaster), 768
Reid, James, 655
Reid, Susanna. *See* Lawlor
Reinhard, Charles, de, 466
Reische. *See* Resche
Renaud*, Jean (d. 1794), 601, 794
Renaud, Pierre-Simon, 691
Renaud d'Avène Des Méloizes, Agathe-Louise. *See* Fresnoy
Renaud d'Avène Des Méloizes, Angélique. *See* Chartier de
    Lotbinière
Renaud d'Avène Des Méloizes, Louis-François, 711
Renaud d'Avène Des Méloizes, Nicolas, **711**
Renaud* d'Avène Des Méloizes, Nicolas-Marie (1696–
    1743), 711
Rendell, Elias, 119, 120
Repentigny. *See* Legardeur
Requiem, Marie-Joseph. *See* La Roche
Resche*, Pierre-Joseph (1695–1770), 196
Reventa. *See* Eliza
Revilla Gigedo, Count of. *See* Güemes
Révol, Marie-Charlotte. *See* Roy
Révol*, Pierre (d. 1759), 276
Reynolds, Sir Joshua, 824
Riall*, Sir Phineas (1775–1850), 642
Rich, Edwin Ernest, 683, 685
Rich, Ruhama (Emery; Noble), 627
Richard, Louis-Claude, 593
Richards, Eleanor. *See* Thomas
Richards, John (father of WILLIAM), 711, 712
Richards, John (loyalist), 772
Richards, Margaret (Spencer), 772
Richards, Thomas, 711, 712
Richards, William, 711
Richards, William, **711–12**
Richardson*, John (d. 1831), 183, 212, 233, 300, 320, 326,
    327, 333, 372, 374, 384, 485, 512, 566, 572, 636, 691, 697,
    816, 820, 864, 882
Richardson*, John Frederick (1796–1852), 800
Richardson, Madelaine. *See* Askin
Richery, Joseph de, 675
Richmond and Lennox, Duchess of. *See* Gordon
Richmond and Lennox, Duke of. *See* Lennox
Rictenburgh, Catherine. *See* London
Riday-Beauceron. *See* Ridé
Riddle, Mary. *See* Noble
Ridé (Riday-Beauceron), Marie-Louise (Viger), 833
Ridout*, George (1791–1871), 522
Ridout*, Thomas (1754–1829), 65, 66, 846
Riedesel, America (Bernstorff, Countess von Bernstorff),
    583
Riedesel, Friederike Charlotte Louise, Freifrau zu Eisen-
    bach. *See* Massow
Riedesel, Friedrich Adolph, Freiherr zu Eisenbach, 457,
    582, 583, 747, 896
Riedesel, Georg Karl, Freiherr zu Eisenbach, 583
Riedesel, Louisa Augusta Elizabeth Canada, 583

Rieutord, François, 713
Rieutord, Françoise. *See* Deray
Rieutord, Jacques, 712
Rieutord, Jean-Baptiste, 315, **712–13**
Rieutord, Jean-Baptiste, 713
Rieutord, Louis, 713
Rieutord, Marie-Josette. *See* Audette, *dit* Lapointe
Rieutord, Pélagie-Victoire. *See* Perron
Rigaud, John Francis, 811
Rigaud* de Vaudreuil, François-Pierre de (1703–79), 487
Rigaud de Vaudreuil de Cavagnial, Jeanne-Charlotte de,
    Marquise de Vaudreuil. *See* Fleury Deschambault
Rigaud* de Vaudreuil de Cavagnial, Pierre de, Marquis de
    Vaudreuil (1698–1778), 41, 58, 103, 104, 164, 368, 470,
    498, 499, 677, 711, 738, 739, 740, 741, 888
Rigauville. *See* Blaise
Rind, William Alexander, 717
Rindge, Elizabeth (Wentworth), 848
Ring, Lucy (Scott), 744
Rising, Josiah (Shoentakwanni, Ignace Raizenne), 703
Ritchie, Ann (Zouch), 385, 386
Ritchie, Benjamin, 385
Ritchie, Hugh, 385
Rivera y Melo Montaño, María Rita (Moziño), 615
Riverin*, Joseph (1699–1756), 46
Robe, William, 61
Robert*, Antoine-Bernardin (1757–1826), 93, 659
Robert, Jean-de-Dieu-François, 432
Roberts*, Benjamin (fl. 1758–75), 8
Roberts, Charles, 112, 695, **713–14**
Robertson, Alexander, 716, 717
Robertson, Amy (wife of JAMES), 717
Robertson, Catherine. *See* Askin
Robertson, Catherine. *See* Christie
Robertson, Charlotte (Farries), 715, 716
Robertson*, Colin (1783–1842), 237, 266, 267, 751
Robertson, Cornelia Eleanor. *See* Brooks
Robertson, Daniel, 106, 129, 413, 512, 568, **714–16**
Robertson, David, 168, 404, 718
Robertson, Elizabeth (Hertel de Saint-François; Davis), 715,
    716
Robertson, George, 327
Robertson, James, 505
Robertson, James, 27, 438, **716–17**
Robertson, Jane. *See* Dunlop
Robertson, John, 716
Robertson*, John Ross (1841–1918), 375, 759
Robertson, Margaret (Sutherland), 716
Robertson, Marie-Louise. *See* Réaume
Robertson, Mary (wife of JAMES), 717
Robertson, Samuel, 402, 718
Robertson, William, 38, 168, 365, 403, 404, 449, **718–19**,
    722, 723, 821
Robeshaw. *See* Robichaux
Robespierre, Maximilien de, 105, 702
Robichaud, Louis, 813
Robichaud, Marie-Anne (Melançon), 587
Robichaud, Marie-Josèphe (Doucet), 261
Robichaux, Charles, 720
Robichaux, Félicité. *See* Cyr
Robichaux, Isidore, 720
Robichaux, Jean-Baptiste, **719–20**
Robichaux, Jean-Baptiste, 719

Robichaux, Joseph, 720
Robichaux*, Louis (1704–80), 393
Robichaux, Michel, 720
Robichaux, Pierre, 720
Robichaux, Prudent, 261
Robichaux, *dit* Cadet, Claire. *See* Le Blanc
Robichaux, *dit* Cadet, Joseph, 719
Robie*, Simon Bradstreet (1770–1858), 832
Robin*, Charles (1743–1824), 637, 719, 720
Robins, Alice (Forsyth), 325
Robins, James, 326
Robinson. *See also* Robertson
Robinson, Beverley, 59, 349, 646
Robinson*, Christopher (1763–98), 307, 388, 518, 782
Robinson, Jane (Lynson; Moody), 604
Robinson*, John (1762–1828), 646
Robinson*, Sir John Beverley (1791–1863), 65, 66, 113, 114, 457, 520, 521, 522, 558, 559, 643, 644, 787
Robinson, Joseph, 28, 127, 263, 309, 310, 311, 424, 425, 478, 515, **720–21**
Robinson, Lelia (wife of JOSEPH), 720
Robinson, Matilda (Brecken), 720
Robinson*, Peter (1785–1838), 65
Robinson, Rebecca (Hodgson), 424, 720
Robinson*, William Benjamin (1797–1873), 453
Robison, Elizabeth. *See* Cartwright
Robitaille, François, 285
Robitaille, Marie-Anne (Bruneau), 116
Robitaille, Romain, 285
Roblin, John, 857
Roche, Mary. *See* Hall
Rocheblave. *See* Rastel
Rockingham, Marquess of. *See* Watson-Wentworth
Rocques de Carbouere, Jeanne de (Dejean), 237
Rodgers. *See also* Rogers
Rodgers, David, 301, 345
Rodney, George Brydges, 1st Baron Rodney, 274
Roe, Ann. *See* Laughton
Roe, Walter, 449, **721–22**
Rogers*, David McGregor (1772–1824), 388, 520, 549, 842, 857
Rogers, Elizabeth (Wiswall), 870
Rogers, Margaret (Caleff), 134
Rogers*, Robert (1731–95), 7, 8, 38, 129, 412, 585, 589, 888
Rogers, Samuel, 556
Rolette*, Charles-Frédéric (1783–1831), 101
Rolette, Luce. *See* Bouchette
Rolland, François, 243, 701
Rollet, Marie-Joseph (Holland), 426, 428
Rollet, Marie-Thérèse. *See* Grenet
Rollin, Charles, 486
Rollo*, Andrew, 5th Baron Rollo (1703–65), 172, 719
Rollo, Frances. *See* McCaulay
Rollo, James, **723**
Romero, Antonia (Cardero), 140
Romney, George, 706, 811
Ronsard, Pierre de, 702
Roque*, Jacques-Guillaume (1761–1840), 187
Roquefeuil, Camille de, 618
Rose, Christian Ludwig, 830
Ross*, Alexander (1783–1856), 419, 533, 534
Ross, David, 614

Ross, Elizabeth Vaughan. *See* Jones
Ross, James, 461
Ross, Jane. *See* Davidson
Ross, John, 391, 537, 538, 562, 656, 683, 684
Ross*, John (fl. 1762–89), 40, 378, 806
Ross*, Malchom (d. 1799), 451, 500
Ross, Mary (Spark; Montgomery), 768
Rosslyn, Earl of. *See* Wedderburn
Rottenburg*, Francis, Baron de Rottenburg (1757–1832), 65, 66, 558, 643, 748, 749
Rottot. *See* Trefflé
Roubaud*, Pierre-Joseph-Antoine (b. 1724, d. after 1789), 143
Roubel*, William (fl. 1801–34), 220, 862
Roucy, Marquis de. *See* La Rochefoucauld
Rouer* d'Artigny, Louis (1667–1744), 76
Rouffio*, Joseph (b. 1730, d. in or after 1764), 276
Rouillé, Antoine-Louis, Comte de Jouy, 172, 638
Roundhead. *See* Stayeghtha
Roupe*, Jean-Baptiste (1782–1854), 481
Rousseau*, Dominique (1755–1825), 36, 436, 727
Rousseau, Jean-Jacques, 233, 248, 701
Rousseau, *dit* Saint-Jean, Jean-Bonaventure, 723
Rousseau, *dit* Saint-Jean, Marie-Reine. *See* Brunet
Rousseaux, Joseph Brant, 724
Rousseaux St John, John Baptist, **723–25**
Rousseaux St John, Margaret. *See* Clyne
Rousseaux St John, Marie. *See* Martineau
Roussel, Thérèse (Berthelot), 74
Roussel*, Timothée (d. 1700), 74
Rousson. *See* Le Verrier
Routh, Abigail. *See* Eppes
Routh*, Sir Randolph Isham (1782–1858), 725
Routh, Richard, 190, 492, **725–27**, 839
Rouville. *See* Hertel
Roux*, Jean-Henri-Auguste (1760–1831), 93, 187, 200, 247, 295, 494, 680, 691
Row. *See* Roe
Rowe, Christian (Street), 784
Rowe, Edward, 784
Rowe, James, 784
Rowland, John Hamilton, 658
Roy, Jacques, 727
Roy, Joseph-Marie, 298
Roy*, Louis (1771–99), 298, 814
Roy, Marie-Charlotte (Révol), 276
Roy, Marie-Françoise. *See* Prud'homme
Roy, Marie-Joseph. *See* Jérôme, *dit* Latour
Roy, Michel, 218, 436, 727
Roy, Narsise, 436, **727–28**
Roy, Pierre, 727
Roy, William, 55, 348
Roy, *dit* Portelance, Marie-Angélique (Ducharme), 272
Roye. *See* La Rochefoucauld
Rubin, 878
Ruckle, Barbara (Heck), **728–29**
Ruckle, Bastian (Sebastian), 728
Ruckle, Margaret. *See* Embury
Rudd, James Sutherland, 27, 68, 106
Rudolf, Francisca Barbara (Jessen), 453
Ruiter, John. *See* Ruyter, Johannes
Rumsey, Benjamin, 181
Russell, Ann (Anne) (Ellice), 299

Russell, Elizabeth. *See* Warnar
Russell, Elizabeth (Brenton), 108
Russell*, Elizabeth (1754–1822), 189, 730, 732, 854
Russell, John, 4th Duke of Bedford, 729
Russell, Margaret (Willcocks), 859
Russell, Peter, 35, 71, 189, 303, 304, 307, 326, 365, 440, 453, 519, 536, 548, 719, 724, **729–32**, 749, 753, 782, 808, 810, 814, 815, 854, 859, 860
Russell, Richard, 729
Rustan, Pascal. *See* Fabre, *dit* Laperrière, Henri-Marie-Paschal
Rutherford, Christian (Ainslie), 4
Ruthven, John, 381
Rutland, Duke of. *See* Manners
Ruyter, Johannes, known as John Ruiter, 839
Ryan, Amelia. *See* Mott
Ryan*, John (d. 1847), 506, 612, 613
Ryerse, Elizabeth. *See* Colwell
Ryerse, Johanna. *See* Van der Hoff
Ryerse (Ryerson), Luke (Luyckes), 732
Ryerse, Samuel, 59, 196, **732–35**, 846, 847
Ryerse, Sarah. *See* Underhill
Ryerson*, Egerton (1803–82), 721
Ryerson*, Joseph (1761–1854), 733, 846
Ryland*, Herman Witsius (1760–1838), 18, 45, 84, 207, 208, 212, 213, 246, 292, 651, 655, 696

SABIN, Joseph, 765
Sacépée (Saccapee), Joachim de, 740
Sackville, Viscount. *See* Germain
Sagaunash. *See* Caldwell, Billy
Sa Ga Yeath Qua Pieth Tow (Brant), 803
Sage, John, 35
Sageot. *See* Sajos
Sagoyewatha* (d. 1830), 121, 724
Saillant*, Jean-Antoine (1720–76), 74, 288, 289, 478
Sainbel. *See* Vial
Saint-Ange. *See* Charly
Saint-Aubin*, Ambroise (d. 1780), 16, 295
Saint-Augustin. *See* Compain
Saint-Auron. *See* Maugenest
Saint-Blaint. *See* Raimbault
St Cir, Monsieur (North West Company employee), 564
St Clair, Arthur, 3, 553, 594, 807, 808, 852
Saint-Cosme, Théotiste (Dejean), 237, 238
Saint-Denis; Saint Denys. *See* Juchereau
Saint-Dizier. *See* Nivard
Sainte-Rose. *See* Brunet, *dit* L'Estang
Saint-François. *See* Hertel
Saint-Georges Dupré. *See* Le Comte Dupré, Georges-Hippolyte
Saint-Germain. *See* Cureux; Lemaire
Saint-Herman. *See* Raizenne
Saint-Horan. *See* Maugenest
Saint-Ignace. *See* Raizenne
Saint-Jean. *See also* Rousseau
Saint-Jean, Marie-Joseph (Gibault), 342
St John. *See* Rousseaux
Saint-John, Henry, 1st Viscount Bolingbroke, 486
Saint-Jorand. *See* Maugenest
Saint-Laurent, Mme de. *See* Mongenet, Thérèse-Bernardine
St Leger*, Barrimore Matthew (d. 1789), 33, 57, 88, 254, 347, 584, 746, 747, 805

Saint-Luc. *See* La Corne
Saint-Martin. *See* Adhémar; Dumas
Saint-Onge. *See* Garreau
Saint-Ours. *See also* Quinson
Saint-Ours, Paul-Roch, 149, 150, 208, 877
Saint-Ours Deschaillons, Pierre-Roch de, 98
Saint-Paul. *See* Lambert
Saint-Pierre. *See also* Legardeur
Saint-Pierre, Paul de, 433
Saint-Sceine. *See* Petitot
Saint-Simon. *See* Denis; Lefebvre Angers
Saint-Terone. *See* Maugenest
Saint-Vallier. *See* La Croix
St Vincent, Earl of. *See* Jervis
Sajos (Sageot), Marie-Charlotte (Darris; Digé), 257
Sakayengwaraton. *See* Johnson, John
Salaberry. *See* Irumberry
Sales, Jean-Pierre de, 735
Sales Laterrière, Dorothée de (Lehouillier), 736, 737, 738
Sales* Laterrière, Marc-Pascal de (1792–1872), 737, 738
Sales Laterrière, Marie-Catherine de. *See* Delezenne
Sales Laterrière, Pierre de, 100, 277, **735–38**, 893
Sales* Laterrière, Pierre-Jean de (1789–1834), 737, 738
Sally. *See* Kyen-da-nent
Salter, John, 618
Samuel, Phoebe (David), 193
Sandby, Paul, 227
Sandys, Francis, 678
Sanguinet, Joseph, 322
Sanguinet*, Simon (1733–90), 242, 289
Sanregret. *See* Ducheneau
Sargeant, Winthrop, 574
Sargent, Charles Sprague, 593
Sargent, Winthrop (grandfather), 4
Sargent, Winthrop, 629
Sarrebource de Pontleroy, Élisabeth. *See* Arbalestre de Melun
Sarrebource de Pontleroy, Nicolas, **738–40**
Sarrebource Pontleroy de Beaulieu, Jacques, 738
Sarrebource Pontleroy de Beaulieu, Madeleine. *See* Coustan
Sarychev, Gavriil Andreevich, 80
Sasseville*, François (1797–1864), 218
Saswee. *See* Leblanc, *dit* Latour, François
Sauer. *See also* Sower
Sauer, Martin, 80
Saul, Elizabeth (Hanna; Allen), 406
Saulnier, Joseph, 58
Saunders*, Sir Charles (d. 1775), 141, 142, 145, 823, 824
Saunders*, John (1754–1834), 456
Saunders, Thomas, 838
Saur. *See* Sower
Sauvage de Chatillonnet, Jean-Louis-Melchior, 480
Saveuse* de Beaujeu, Jacques-Philippe (1770–1832), 488
Sawtelle, Jemima (Phipps; Howe; Tute), **740–41**
Sawtelle, Jonathan, 740
Sawtelle, Josiah, 740
Sawtelle, Lydia. *See* Parker
Sayenqueraghta. *See* Kaieñ?kwaahtoñ
Sayer, Mrs (wife of JOHN). *See* Obemau-unoqua
Sayer, Elizabeth. *See* McPherson
Sayer, Henry (son of JOHN and Obemau-unoqua), 742
Sayer, Henry (son of JOHN and possibly Obemau-unoqua), 742

Sayer, James, 742
Sayer, John, 533, **741–42**
Sayer, John Charles, 742
Sayer, Margaret, 742
Sayer*, Pierre-Guillaume (fl. 1796–1849), 742
Sayre, James, 59
Sayre, John, 59
Scallan*, Thomas (d. 1830), 474
Scarth, John, 394
Schank*, John (1740–1823), 364
Schindler*, Joseph (d. 1792), 329, 436, 727
Schleiger, Marie-Magdelaine, 509
Schofield, Sarah (Watson), 843
Schureman, Jacob, 742
Schureman, Jane. *See* Parcot
Schurman, Elizabeth. *See* Hyatt
Schurman*, Jacob Gould (1854–1942), 743
Schurman, Jane. *See* Bonnet
Schurman, William, **742–43**
Schuyler, Catalyntje (Cuyler), 222
Schuyler, Hon Yost, 33
Schuyler*, Peter (1710–62), 740
Schuyler, Philip John, 29, 30, 33, 40, 413, 519, 826
Scoresby, William, 55
Scothouse. *See* MacDonell
Scott, Elizabeth (Harris), 408
Scott, Jane. *See* Phillips
Scott, John (father of JONATHAN), 743
Scott, John (seaman), 166
Scott, John, 1st Earl of Eldon, 18
Scott, Jonathan, **743–45**
Scott, Lucy. *See* Ring
Scott, Lydia. *See* Thwing
Scott, Mary Ann (Gray), 384
Scott, Moses, 743
Scott, Rebecca (Brenton), 108
Scott, Robert, 166
Scott, Thomas, 8, 229
Scott, Thomas, 6, 182, 332, 495, **745–46**
Scott*, Thomas (1746–1824), 17, 66, 304, 365, 389, 440, 443, 521, 549, 639, 643, 644, 734, 750, 782, 856
Scott, Thomas Charles Heslop, 56, **746–47**
Scott, Sir Walter, 264
Scotus. *See* MacDonell
Scovil, James, 25
Seabury, David, 431
Seabury, Samuel, 94
Sealey. *See* Seelye
Seccombe*, John (1708–92), 199
Seccombe, Thomas, 258
Secondat, Charles de, Baron de La Brède et de Montesquieu, 372
Secord*, David (1759–1844), 857
Secord, Laura. *See* Ingersoll
Secord, Magdalen (Cartwright), 167, 168
Seely*, Caleb (1787–1869), 747
Seely, Joseph, **747–49**
Seelye (Sealey), Augustus, 747
Seixas, Gershom Mendas, 194
Selby, Elizabeth (wife of PRIDEAUX), 749
Selby, Elizabeth (Derenzy), 750
Selby, George, 749
Selby*, George (1759–1835), 566, 752

Selby, Mary (Selby), 749
Selby, Prideaux, 120, 121, 449, 536, **749–50**
Selee*, Peet (1766–1844), 747
Selkirk, Countess of. *See* Hamilton
Selkirk, Countess of. *See* Wedderburn
Selkirk, Earl of. *See* Douglas
Selkirk, Earl of. *See* Hamilton Douglas
Semple, Anne. *See* Greenlaw
Semple, Robert, 750
Semple, Robert, 267, 466, 544, **750–52**
Seneca King. *See* Kaieñˀkwaahtoñ
Senilh, Joseph, 276
Sentner, Caleb, 335
Séré (Serré). *See* Cerré
Serna. *See* Alcalá-Galiano
Serré, Joseph, 174
Serré, Marie-Madeleine. *See* Picard
Serres, Alexandre, **752**
Serres, Gabrielle. *See* Marleau
Serres, Jean-Baptiste, 752
Serres, Madeleine. *See* Lefebvre
Serres, Marie. *See* Galliay
Serres, Thérèse. *See* Migneron
Sessé y Lacasta, Martín de, 615, 616
Sewell, Harriet. *See* Smith
Sewell*, Jonathan (d. 1839), 18, 45, 60, 69, 77, 84, 193, 208, 212, 225, 231, 234, 246, 247, 292, 373, 374, 494, 691, 697, 769, 794, 863, 881
Sewell*, Stephen (d. 1832), 133, 218, 614, 697
Seymour, Martha (Jarvis), 452
Shakespeare, William, 607, 689
Shakoyenˀkwaráhton. *See* Johnson, John
Shanks. *See* Schank
Sharples, James, 114, 543
Shash. *See* Leblanc, *dit* Latour, François
Shaw, Dr, 126
Shaw, Miss (McDougall), 525
Shaw, Æneas, 303, 365, 440, **752–54**, 842
Shaw, Alexander, 376, 534
Shaw, Angus (father of ÆNEAS), 752
Shaw, Angus (fur trader), 534
Shaw*, Angus (d. 1832), 525, 530, 531, 559
Shaw, Ann. *See* Gosline
Shaw, Anne. *See* Dallas of Cantray
Shaw, Isaiah, 598
Shaw, Margaret. *See* Hickman
Shaw, Phineas, 350
Shaw*, William (fl. 1759–89), 390
Shawnandithit* (d. 1829), 240
Sheaffe, Margaret. *See* Coffin
Sheaffe*, Sir Roger Hale (1763–1851), 82, 110, 111, 114, 191, 215, 522, 748, 750, 765
Sheawaquanep. *See* Zheewegonab
Shedden, Robert, 646
Shedden, William, 646
Shee, Sir George, 18
Sheffield, Earl of. *See* Holroyd
Shelburne, Earl of. *See* Petty
Shelton, Hannah Ann (Andrews), 24
Shendoreth. *See* Demasduwit
Sheppard, Peter, 107
Sheppard, Thérèse. *See* Bellenoy
Sheppard, William Grant, 107, 108

Sherbrooke*, Sir John Coape (1764–1830), 267, 268, 314, 489, 698, 882
Sherburne, Henry, 802
Sherer, Patricia (Graham), 363
Sheridan, Richard Brinsley Butler, 438, 689
Sherwood*, Adiel (1779–1874), 748
Sherwood, Charlotte. *See* Jones
Sherwood, Justus, 637
Sherwood*, Levius Peters (1777–1850), 457
Sherwood, Reuben, 557
Shewaquonap (Shewequenap). *See* Zheewegonab
Shippen, Margaret (Peggy) (Arnold), 28, 34, 35, 36
Shirley, Selina (Hastings, Countess of Huntingdon), 135
Shoentakwanni. *See* Rising, Josiah
Shoolbred, John, 483
Short*, Richard (fl. 1754–66), 50, 228, 767
Shreve, Thomas, 446
Shuldham*, Molyneux, 1st Baron Shuldham (d. 1798), 220, 221, 369, 595
Shuwescome, 885
Sidmouth, Viscount. *See* Addington
Sierra. *See* Martínez
Signay*, Joseph (1778–1850), 769
Sigogne*, Jean-Mandé (1763–1844), 458
Sills, Jonathan, 99
Sills, Joseph, 99
Silvia (servant), 216
Simcoe, Elizabeth Posthuma. *See* Gwillim
Simcoe, John, 754
Simcoe, John Graves, 15, 35, 71, 78, 93, 101, 120, 121, 124, 151, 152, 170, 188, 196, 255, 279, 282, 297, 303, 306, 326, 365, 388, 404, 405, 428, 439, 448, 452, 453, 455, 518, 519, 541, 552, 553, 594, 596, 597, 661, 669, 707, 718, 722, 724, 730, 731, 732, 733, 734, 749, 752, 753, **754–59**, 772, 773, 781, 787, 802, 808, 809, 814, 815, 820, 821, 859, 860, 868, 884
Simcoe, Katherine. *See* Stamford
Simonds*, James (1735–1831), 16, 415, 416, 608
Simonds, Richard, 415
Simonnet*, François (1701–78), 436
Simons, Titus Geer, 814, 815
Simpson*, Sir George (d. 1860), 532
Simpson, Mary (Mathews), 584
Simpson of Gartly, Mary (Ellice), 299
Sincennes. *See* Petitot
Sinclair, Aemilia (Sinclair), 759
Sinclair, Alexander, 759
Sinclair*, Alexander Maclean (1840–1924), 547
Sinclair, Catherine M. S. *See* Stewart
Sinclair, Patrick, 8, 38, 129, 260, 273, 567, 715, **759–61**, 836
Sinnott, James, 473
Sintez, 835
Siongorochti. *See* Kaieñ?kwaahtoñ
Sire. *See* Cyr
Sirier. *See* Cirier
Sirois. *See* Duplessis-Sirois
Sivert. *See* L'Espérance
Skelton, Catherine. *See* Ball
Skelton, Thomas, 141
Skerrett, John, 633, **761–62**, 763
Skerrett, John Byrne, 761

Skinner, Mrs. *See* Power
Skinner, Harriet. *See* McDonald
Skinner, Harriet (Prescott), 763
Skinner, Hester. *See* Lawder
Skinner, Robert Pringle, **762**, 763
Skinner, Thomas, 633, 761, **762–63**
Skinner, William (father), 762
Skinner, William, 762
Slade, David, 764
Slade, Elizabeth (mother of THOMAS), 764
Slade, John, 764
Slade*, John (1719–92), 491, 675, 764, 785
Slade, Robert (grandfather), 764
Slade, Robert (uncle), 764, 785
Slade, Robert (cousin), 764
Slade, Robert, 764
Slade, Thomas (cousin of THOMAS), 764
Slade, Thomas (nephew of THOMAS), 764
Slade, Thomas, **764–65**
Slayter, Joseph, 843
Sloane, Jane (Hughes, Lady Hughes), 434
Small, John, 515
Small*, John (1746–1831), 17, 420, 441, 453, 519, 855
Small, Patrick, 561, 562, 603
Smith*, Charles Douglass (d. 1855), 250, 336, 679, 826
Smith, Charles Jeffry, 804
Smith, Charlotte. *See* Brant
Smith, David, 344
Smith*, Sir David William (1764–1837), 120, 279, 282, 302, 326, 388, 405, 448, 518, 519, 552, 597, 730, 734, 749, 755, 782, 814, 815, 841, 842, 846
Smith, Edward, 56
Smith, Elizabeth (Street; Benedict), 781
Smith, Fraser, 559, 560
Smith, George (merchant), 611, 612
Smith, George (minister), 190
Smith, Hannah (Fanning), 308
Smith, Harriet (Sewell), 769
Smith, Henry, 679
Smith, Isaac, 679
Smith, John, 749
Smith, Mary (Mortimer), 611
Smith, Michael, 65, **765–66**
Smith*, Peter (d. 1826), 168, 169
Smith*, Samuel (1756–1826), 673, 674
Smith, Sarah. *See* MacLean
Smith, Thomas, 595
Smith, William (educator), 785
Smith, William (geologist), 55
Smith, William (merchant), 328
Smith*, William (1728–93), 21, 45, 90, 132, 148, 149, 150, 153, 192, 232, 242, 300, 317, 371, 372, 373, 427, 479, 505, 816, 839, 843, 844, 862, 863, 901
Smith, William, 53, **766–67**, 780
Smith*, William (1769–1847), 696
Smith, Sir William Sidney, 875
Smollett, Tobias George, 486
Smyth. *See also* Carmichael-Smyth; Smith; Smythe
Smyth, Erie (McCrae; McBeath), 512
Smyth*, George Stracey (d. 1823), 162
Smythe, Sir Hervey, 228, **767–68**
Smythe, Lady Louisa Carolina Isabelle. *See* Hervey
Smythe, Sir Robert, 767

Sneppy. *See* Atkinson, George
Snow, Stephen, 573
Solander, Daniel Carl, 55, 167
Solomons, Ezekiel, 376
Solomons*, Lucius Levy (1730–92), 194
Solomons, Rachel (Joseph), 194
Somerville*, James (1775–1837), 320, 770
Somerville, William, 746
Sonneck, Oscar George Theodore, 68
Sorbier* de Villars, François (1720–88), 380
Sosawaket. *See* Nissowaquet
Sosé. *See* Onasakenrat, Joseph
Soulanges. *See* Joybert
Soulard, Pascal, 708
Southey, Robert, 166
Southouse, Edward, 216, 225, 232, 863
Southwell, Harriet Anne (Bisshopp, Baroness Zouche), 82
Sovereign, Philip, 857
Sower*, Christopher (1754–99), 318, 613
Spark, Alexander, 69, 320, 330, 700, **768–71**
Spark, John, 768
Spark, Mary. *See* Low
Spark, Mary. *See* Ross
Sparke, Hannah (Hutchings), 443
Sparke, Henry, 443, 444
Spence, James, 194
Spencer, Abel, 772
Spencer, Benjamin, 772
Spencer, Hazelton, 92, 170, **771–73**
Spencer, Margaret. *See* Richards
Spencer, Mercy. *See* Potter
Spiesmacher, Frederick Christopher, 7, 8
Spittal, John, 127
Splitlog, Thomas. *See* To-oo-troon-to-ra
Spooner, Charles, 767
Spraggon, William, 861, 862
Springer, Daniel, 14
Sproule, Adam, 773
Sproule, Alicia (wife of GEORGE), 773
Sproule, George, 356, 448, 589, 590, 667, **773–74**
Sproule, Prudence. *See* Lloyd
Spurrier, William, 838
Stairs, John, 390
Stamford, Katherine (Simcoe), 754
Stanhope, Philip Dormer, 4th Earl of Chesterfield, 182, 486
Staniford, Margaret (Calef), 134
Stansbury, Joseph, 34, 629, 631
Stanser*, Robert (1760–1828), 124, 872
Starns, Nathan, 218, 436, 727
Stayeghta, 619, **774–75**, 798, 799
Stealing, John, 123
Steedman, William, 684
Steel*, John (fl. 1776–1822), 101
Sterling*, James (fl. 1759–83), 282, 364
Sterne, Laurence, 438
Sterns, Jonathan, 109, 251
Steuben, Friedrich Wilhelm von, 899
Stevens, Abel, 728
Stevens*, Abel (d. 1825 or 1826), 65
Stewart (Stuart), Alexander, 418, 532
Stewart, Bonaventure, 473
Stewart, Catherine M. S. (Sinclair), 759
Stewart, Charles (customs officer), 4

Stewart, Charles (notary), 252, 289, 385, 509
Stewart, Charles, 250, 309, 311, 335, 425, 569, **775–76**, 779, 847, 848, 862
Stewart*, Charles James (1775–1837), 422
Stewart, David, 781
Stewart, Elizabeth (Williams), 860
Stewart, Flora (Townshend), 825
Stewart, Helen. *See* MacKinnon
Stewart, James, 861
Stewart*, John (d. 1834), 309, 516, 775, 776, 777, 778, 779, 848
Stewart, Margaret (DesBrisay), 775
Stewart, Mary. *See* Desbrisay
Stewart, Nancy. *See* Blue Jacket
Stewart, Peter, 27, 28, 219, 220, 250, 263, 309, 310, 311, 424, 516, 568, 720, 775, **776–79**, 825, 826, 847, 848, 861, 873
Stewart, Robert, 777
Stewart, Robert, 1st Viscount Castlereagh and 2nd Marquess of Londonderry, 18, 85, 94, 161, 210, 292, 365, 504, 542
Stewart, Sarah. *See* Hamilton
Stewart, Sir William, 110
Stiahta. *See* Stayeghtha
Stieglitz, Christian Ludwig, 678
Stiles, Ezra, 684
Stinson, John, 857
Stirling. *See* Sterling
Stobo*, Robert (1726–70), 470
Stocking, Abner, 29
Stone*, Joel (1749–1833), 552
Stone, Thomas, 784
Stone, William Leete, 256, 584, 803, 811, 812
Stout, Martha Wingate. *See* Weeks
Stout, Richard, 511, **779–81**
Stoyell, Thomas, 597
Strachan, Ann. *See* Wood
Strachan*, John (1778–1867), 65, 68, 79, 83, 170, 457, 520, 529, 557, 695, 697, 750, 787
Strahan, Gregory. *See* Trahan, Grégoire
Strange*, James Charles Stuart (1753–1840), 618
Street, Christian. *See* Rowe
Street, Elizabeth. *See* Smith
Street, John (grandfather), 783
Street, John, 785
Street, Mark, 785
Street, Mary (mother of THOMAS), 783
Street, Mary (Bird), 785
Street, Mary (Ussher), 673, 782
Street, Peter (uncle), 783
Street, Peter, 784, 785
Street, Phoebe. *See* Van Camp
Street, Samuel, 781
Street, Samuel, 70, 71, 388, 518, 661, **781–83**, 841, 842, 857
Street*, Samuel (1775–1844), 548, 549, 643, 672, 782
Street*, Samuel Denny (1752–1830), 136, 137, 161, 353, 355, 356, 456
Street, Thomas, 491, 641, **783–85**
Strickland, Walter George, 705
Stuart. *See also* Stewart
Stuart, Andrew, 785
Stuart*, Andrew (1785–1840), 329, 787
Stuart, Annabella. *See* Campbell

Stuart, Charles, 776
Stuart, David, 533
Stuart*, George Okill (1776–1862), 17, 401, 786, 787
Stuart, Gilbert, 314, 594, 706, 811
Stuart*, Sir James (1780–1853), 787
Stuart, Jane. *See* Okill
Stuart, John, 17, 255, 321, 445, 475, 476, 524, **785–88**, 804
Stuart, John, 786
Stuart, John, 3rd Earl of Bute, 315
Stuart, Margaret (Le Maistre), 486, 647
Stuart, Margaret (Painter), 647
Stuart, Mary. *See* Dinwiddie
Stuart, Mary (Jones), 787
Stuart, Peter, 43, 289, 368, 369, 372, 373, 374, 494, 509, 699, 816, 879, 881
Stuart, Robert, 533
Studholme*, Gilfred (1740–92), 16, 296, 416, 589, 867
Suárez. *See* Moziño
Suckling*, George (fl. 1752–80), 426, 605
Sullivan, James, 329
Sullivan, John, 32, 147, 414, 895
Sulte*, Benjamin (1841–1923), 702
Sunderland, Mary (Blake), 88
Suria*, Tomás de (1761–1835), 140
Surveyor. *See* Fabre
Sutherland*, Daniel (d. 1832), 106, 284, 564, 715, 716
Sutherland*, George (fl. 1774–99), 531
Sutherland*, James (d. 1797), 535, 885
Sutherland, Louisa, 716
Sutherland, Margaret. *See* Robertson
Sutherland, Maria (Hallowell), 716
Suzor, François, 788
Suzor, François-Michel, **788–89**
Suzor, Louise. *See* Laflèche
Suzor, Marie-Anne. *See* Grougnard
Suzor, Marie-Anne. *See* Larue
Swain, James, 185
Swaine, Francis, 767
Swanton*, Robert (d. 1765), 203
Swartz, Margaret (Grass), 377
Swayne*, Hugh (d. 1836), 780
Swayze*, Isaac (1751–1828), 405, 661, 782, 842, 845, 856
Swediaur, François-Xavier, 46
Swift, Jonathan, 486
Sydney, Viscount. *See* Townshend
Symes, George, 374
Symonds, Mary (Winslow), 865
Syrier. *See* Cirier

TABEAU, Antoine, 177
Tabeau, Jean-Baptiste, 259
Taché*, Jean (1698–1768), 277
Taché*, Pascal-Jacques (1757–1830), 75
Taffanel* de La Jonquière, Jacques-Pierre de, Marquis de La Jonquière (1685–1752), 98, 176
Talbot, James, 632
Talbot*, Thomas (1771–1853), 14, 112, 440, 753
Tanswell, Ann. *See* Blacklock
Tanswell, Charles, 790
Tanswell, James, 330, 373, **789–91**
Tanswell, Marie-Joseph. *See* Coutant
Tanswell, Stephen Joseph, 790
Tanswell, Thomas, 789
Tarhe (Crane), 797

Tarieu* de La Naudière, Charles-François (1710–76), 43, 143, 791, 792
Tarieu de Lanaudière, Charles-Gaspard, 578
Tarieu de Lanaudière, Charles-Louis, 44, 99, 100, 372, 380, 687, **791–92**, 793
Tarieu de Lanaudière, Geneviève-Élisabeth. *See* La Corne
Tarieu de La Naudière, Louise-Geneviève. *See* Deschamps de Boishébert
Tarieu de Lanaudière, Marie-Anne (Baby), 43, 45
Tarieu de La Naudière, Marie-Catherine. *See* Le Moyne de Longueuil
Tarieu de Lanaudière, Suzanne-Antoinette. *See* Margane de Lavaltrie
Tarieu de Lanaudière, Xavier-Roch, **792–93**
Tascher, Hélène-Marguerite-Barbe (Chabert de Cogolin, Marquise de Chabert), 176
Taschereau, Antoine-Charles, 794
Taschereau, Gabriel-Elzéar, 43, 45, 61, 146, 182, 370, 577, 650, **793–95**, 863
Taschereau, Gabriel-Elzéar, 794
Taschereau, George-Louis, 794
Taschereau*, Jean-Thomas (1778–1832), 87, 208, 211, 212, 235, 649, 794
Taschereau, Julie-Louise (Fortier), 794
Taschereau, Louise-Françoise. *See* Juchereau Duchesnay
Taschereau, Marie. *See* Panet
Taschereau, Marie, 793
Taschereau, Marie-Claire. *See* Fleury de La Gorgendière
Taschereau, Marie-Louise (Perrault), 794
Taschereau, Marie-Louise-Élizabeth. *See* Bazin
Taschereau*, Thomas-Jacques (1680–1749), 793
Taschereau*, Thomas-Pierre-Joseph (1775–1826), 794
Tasker, Anne (Wentworth; Bellew), 847
Taverner, Jacob, 491
Taverner, Rachel (Lester), 491
Taverner, Susannah (Lester), 491
Taverner*, William (d. 1768), 491
Taylor, Colonel, 605
Taylor, Mr (father of ALEXANDER), 795
Taylor, Mrs. *See* Ramage
Taylor, Alexander, 483, **795**
Taylor, Ann. *See* Urquhart
Taylor, Helen. *See* Gordon
Taylor, Henry, 699
Taylor, John M., 826
Taylor, Nathaniel, 509
Taylor, William (lawyer), 109, 251
Taylor, William (merchant), 262
Tayorheasere. *See* Teiorhéñhsere?
Techenet, Mme. *See* Couc, Elizabeth
Tecumseh (Tech-kum-thai), 113, 114, 302, 594, 619, 748, 774, 775, **795–801**, 811, 852
Tee Yee Neen Ho Ga Row. *See* Theyanoguin
Tehoragwanegen* (d. 1849), 40
Tehowaghwengaraghkwin, 803
Teiorhéñhsere?* (d. 1780), 786
Teiyoquande. *See* Teyohaqueande
Tekarihó:ken. *See also* Ahyouwaeghs
Tekarihó:ken* (d. 1830), 804, 808
Tello. *See* Espinosa
Tempest, Sir Henry, 361
Temple, Earl. *See* Grenville
Templer, Dudley, 652
Ten Broeck, John, 643

Ten Broeck, Peter, 669, 841
Tenskwatawa* (d. 1836), 302, 594, 774, 775, 796, 797, 798, 800, 852
Teoniahigarawe. *See* Theyanoguin
Terlaye. *See* Magon
Ternay. *See* Arsac
Terrick, Richard, 600, 747
Terroux*, Jacques (fl. 1725–77), 889
Testard de Montigny, Jean-Baptiste-Jérémie, 32, 802
Testard* de Montigny, Jean-Baptiste-Philippe (1724–86), 801
Testard de Montigny, Marie-Charlotte. *See* Trottier Desrivières
Testard de Montigny, Pierre-Benjamin, 802
Testard Louvigny de Montigny, Agathe. *See* Hay
Testard Louvigny de Montigny, Charlotte. *See* Trottier Desrivières
Testard Louvigny de Montigny, Jean-Baptiste-Pierre, 306, 552, **801–3**
Têtu, Félix, 231, 253
Têtu, Henri, 248
Tewennihata. *See* Thewanihattha
Teyarhasere. *See* Teiorhéñhsere ͻ
Teyohaqueande* (fl. 1756–83), 895
Teyoninhokarawen. *See* Norton, John
Tey-yagh-taw. *See* Stayeghtha
Thain*, Thomas (d. 1832), 635
Thayendanegea (Thayendanegen, Thayeadanegea), 40, 72, 121, 229, 254, 255, 256, 440, 517, 549, 707, 724, 731, 758, 786, **803–12**, 843, 896, 898, 899, 900
Théodore, Élisabeth (Le Maistre), 485
Thesiger, George, 390
Thewanihattha (Tewennihata), Marguerite (Monique) (wife of Atiatoharongwen), 40
Theyanoguin* (d. 1755), 803
Thiathoharongouan. *See* Atiatoharongwen
Thibodeau, Alexis, 812
Thibodeau (Thibaudeau), Cécile (Cormier), 203
Thibodeau, Joseph, 813
Thibodeau, Madeleine (Mercure), 589
Thibodeau, Marie-Anne. *See* Blanchard
Thibodeau, Marie-Anne. *See* Drolet
Thibodeau, Simon, **812–13**
Thomas, Eleanor (Richards), 712
Thomas, George, 281
Thomas, John, 31
Thomas*, John (d. 1822), 712
Thomas, William, 185
Thomey, John, 338
Thompson, David, 800
Thompson*, David (1770–1857), 177, 236, 418, 500, 526, 531, 541, 559, 563, 656, 685, 741
Thompson, John, 618, 619
Thompson*, Mary (fl. 1823–24), 673
Thompson, William, 99, 147
Thorn, Helena. *See* Van Slyck
Thorn, Jonathan, 526, 533, 534, **813–14**
Thorn, Samuel, 813
Thorne, William, 813
Thorpe*, Robert (d. 1836), 18, 65, 171, 365, 366, 405, 441, 442, 443, 453, 643, 734, 782, 810, 842, 845, 855, 856, 857, 858, 860
Thubières* de Levy de Queylus, Gabriel (1612–77), 658
Thurlow, Edward, 1st Baron Thurlow, 145

Thwing, Lydia (Scott), 743
Thynne. *See* Carteret
Tiahoqwando. *See* Teyohaqueande
Tice, Gilbert, 805
Tiffany, Elizabeth. *See* Ralston
Tiffany, Frances. *See* Davis
Tiffany, Gideon, 814
Tiffany*, Gideon (1774–1854), 14, 814, 815
Tiffany, Oliver, 639, 814
Tiffany, Sarah. *See* Dean
Tiffany, Silvester, 639, 640, **814–16**
Tigoransera. *See* Teiorhéñhsere ͻ
Tinnewabano (Tinpot), 184, 185
Tippett (Tippetts), Martha (DeLancey), 239
Tipping, William, 586
Titameg (wife of John Favell), 534
Tiyanoga. *See* Theyanoguin
Tiyerhasere. *See* Teiorhéñhsere ͻ
Tobacco's Son, 343
Tod, Charlotte, 818
Tod, James, 116, 117, 182, 270, 278, 329, 459, 493, 667, **816–18**
Todd, Andrew, 820
Todd, Isaac, 14, 38, 90, 168, 180, 287, 298, 299, 319, 332, 333, 371, 402, 404, 440, 492, 494, 495, 496, 511, 527, 528, 529, 561, 564, 580, 603, 681, 718, 722, **818–22**
Todevin, Marie (Brehaut), 107
Tolfrey, Frederic, 490
Tom, 816
Tomah*, Pierre (fl. 1775–80), 17
Tomison*, William (1739–1829), 194, 195, 450, 451, 500, 531, 566, 656
Tonge, Martha Grace. *See* Cottnam
Tonge, Richard Peter, 334
Tonge*, William Cottnam (b. 1764, d. in or after 1825), 410, 612, 693, 694, 850, 851
Tonge*, Winckworth (1727/28–92), 430, 850
Tonnancour. *See* Godefroy
To-oo-troon-to-ra* (d. 1838), 798
Toosey*, Philip (d. 1797), 57, 182, 601, 613, 614
Torrance, Elizabeth. *See* Fisher
Torrance*, John (1786–1870), 320
Toupin, Marie-Anne (Bédard), 60
Tournois*, Jean-Baptiste (b. 1710, d. in or after 1761), 40
Towatogowash. *See* Nims, Abigail
Towne, Benjamin, 438
Towner, Enoch, 832, 833
Townshend, Anne, Viscountess and Marchioness Townshend. *See* Montgomery
Townshend, Audrey, Viscountess Townshend. *See* Harrison
Townshend, Charles, 3rd Viscount Townshend, 822
Townshend, Sir Charles Vere Ferrers, 824
Townshend, Charlotte, Viscountess Townshend. *See* Compton
Townshend, Lady Charlotte Barbara (Bisshopp), 82
Townshend, Flora. *See* Stewart
Townshend, George, 4th Viscount and 1st Marquess Townshend, 82, 141, 310, 311, 347, 348, 477, **822–25**
Townshend, Richard, 825
Townshend, Thomas, 1st Viscount Sydney, 145, 148, 149, 150, 151, 156, 157, 158, 241, 309, 585, 807, 819, 863, 897, 898, 899, 900
Townshend, William, 27, 250, 262, 263, 310, 425, 516, 779, **825–26**

Trahan, Charles (grandfather), 826
Trahan, Charles, 827
Trahan, Grégoire, known as Gregory Strahan, **826–27**
Trahan, Joseph, 827
Trahan, Madeleine, 826
Trahan, Marguerite. *See* Bourque
Trahan, Marie-Anne. *See* Landry
Trahan, Mary, 827
Trahan, Paul, 827
Trefflé, *dit* Rottot, Élisabeth (Dunière), 283
Trefflé, *dit* Rottot, Marie-Anne (Panet), 652, 654
Tremaine*, Jonathan (d. 1823), 511, 779, 780
Tremblay, Marie-Joseph (Boucher), 95
Tremlett*, Thomas (d. 1829), 127, 837
Trestler, Catherine (Hays), 828
Trestler, Henry-Daniel, 828
Trestler, Iphigénie (Dorion), 828
Trestler, Jean-Baptiste, 827, 828
Trestler, Jean-Joseph, **827–28**
Trestler, Marguerite. *See* Noël
Trestler, Marie-Anne-Joseph. *See* Curtius
Trestler, Marie-Josephte, 828
Trestler, Marie-Madeleine (Adhémar), 828
Trestler, Marie-Marguerite, 828
Trestler, Michel-Joseph, 828
Treytorrens, Marie-Madeleine de (Haldimand), 887
Tribaut, *dit* Laffriquain, Louis, 727
Tröstler, Henry, 827
Tröstler, Magdeleine. *See* Feitten
Trottier, Thérèse (Ducharme), 272
Trottier Desauniers Beaubien, Catherine (Lévesque), 494
Trottier Desrivières, Charlotte. *See* Guillimin
Trottier Desrivières, Charlotte (Testard Louvigny de Montigny), 801
Trottier* Desrivières, François-Amable (1764–1830), 527, 528, 529
Trottier Desrivières, James McGill, 527, 529
Trottier Desrivières, Marie-Charlotte (Testard de Montigny), 801
Trottier Desrivières, Thomas-Hippolyte, 527
Trottier Desrivières Beaubien, Charlotte. *See* Boucher de La Bruère
Trottier Desrivières Beaubien, Eustache, 480, 828
Trottier Desrivières Beaubien, Eustache-Ignace, **828–29**
Trottier Desrivières Beaubien, Marguerite. *See* Malhiot
Trottier Desrivières Beaubien, Marie-Appolline. *See* Bailly de Messein
Trottier* Dufy Desauniers, Thomas-Ignace (d. 1777), 143, 383
Troy, John Thomas, 473
Trudeau, Claire (Huguet, *dit* Latour), 436
Trudel, Augustin, 271
Truillier, *dit* Lacombe, Jeanne (Guy), 395
Trumbull, John (painter), 41
Trumbull, John (printer), 717
Truteau, Toussaint, 165
Tryon, William, 94, 239, 308, 657, 890
Tsinonwanhonte, 810
Tucker, Joseph, 8
Tucker, Lewis, 27
Tucker, Robert, 431
Tuglavina* (Tuglawina, Tukelavinia) (d. 1798), 830
Tullok, James, 700

Tunstall*, James Marmaduke (1760–1840), 298, 614
Tupper, Edith, 114
Tupper, Ferdinand Brock, 114
Turgeon, Joseph, 580
Turnbull, George, 8, 129, 237
Turner, Mary. *See* Newton
Turner, Nicholas, 382, 383
Turner, Samuel, 68
Turner, Susanna (Wright), 873
Turner, Sybilla Maria. *See* Willin
Turner, William, **829–30**
Turnor*, Philip (d. 1799 or 1800), 450, 500, 539
Tute, Amos, 741
Tute, Jemima. *See* Sawtelle
Tüyaguande. *See* Teyohaqueande
Twining, William, 446
Twisden, Isabella. *See* Duncan
Twisden, Thomas, 281
Twiss*, William (d. 1827), 347, 348
Tyler, Abigail (Andrews), 24
Tyler, Moses Coit, 629, 631
Tyorhansera. *See* Teiorhéñhsere?
Tyrie, Jean (Grant), 367
Tyrrell*, Joseph Burr (1858–1957), 539

UMFREVILLE*, Edward (fl. 1771–89), 362, 450
Underhill, Sarah (Davenport; Ryerse), 732
Uniacke*, Richard John (1753–1830), 124, 239, 240, 832, 868
Upham, Charles Wentworth, 831
Upham, Elizabeth. *See* Murray
Upham, Jabez, 830
Upham, Joshua, 35, 456, 506, **830–32**
Upham, Katharine. *See* Nichols
Upham, Mary. *See* Chandler
Urquhart, Ann (Taylor), 795
Usakechack, 184
Ussher (Usher), John, 672, 673
Ussher, Mary. *See* Street
Ustaiechta. *See* Stayeghtha

VACHER, Françoise (Compain, *dit* L'Espérance), 200, 201
Valdés y Flores Bazán, Cayetano, 11, 140, 571
Valera. *See* Alcalá-Galiano
Valin, Marie, 479
Vallée, Catherine (Berthelette; Guy), 394
Vallée, Madeleine (Brassard Deschenaux), 252
Vallée, Marguerite (Cazeau), 173
Valois, Josette (Huguet, *dit* Latour), 436
Van Alstine, Peter, 92, 378, 552, 772
Vanbrugh, Sir John, 689
Van Camp, Phoebe (Street), 781
Vancouver*, George (1757–98), 12, 80, 387, 540, 541, 615
Van der Hoff, Johanna (Ryerse), 732
Van Dyke, Sir Anthony, 496
Vanfelson*, George (1784–1856), 649
Van Horn, Hannah (Foy; Carleton), 155
Van Slyck, Helena (Thorn), 813
Var. *See* Saint-Aubin
Varennes. *See* Gaultier
Varin*, *dit* La Pistole, Jacques (d. 1791), 218, 727
Varin* de La Marre, Jean-Victor (b. 1699, d. in or after 1780), 652

Vassal* de Montviel, François (1759–1843), 45, 270, 793
Vasseur. *See* Levasseur
Vaudreuil. *See* Rigaud
Vaughan, Sir John, 730
Vauquelin*, Jean (1728–72), 203
Vavasour*, Henry William (d. 1851), 673
Vega, Gregoria Rosalia de la (Cardero), 140
Vergennes, Comte de. *See* Gravier
Vergese d'Aubussargues, Magdalen de (DesBrisay), 249
Vergor. *See* Du Pont
Vernas, Gabrielle-Marie (Carrefour de La Pelouze), 163
Véronneau, Catherine-Antoine (Faribault), 312
Ver Planck, Ann (Ludlow), 503, 504
Verville. *See* Gautier
Veyssière*, Leger-Jean-Baptiste-Noël, known as Father
  Emmanuel (1728–1800), 146, 600, 602, 614
Vézina, Pierre, 226
Vézon. *See* Fournerie
Vialar, Anthony, 492
Vialars, Antoine, 396
Vialars, Daniel, 395, 396
Vial de Sainbel, Anna Louisa. *See* Walker
Vial de Sainbel, Charles, 839
Victoria, Queen of Great Britain and Ireland, 298
Victoria Mary Louisa, Princess of Leiningen, Duchess of
  Kent and Strathearn, 298
Vienne*, François-Joseph de (d. *c.* 1775), 369
Vienne, Jean, 396
Viets, Hester. *See* Botsford
Viets, John, 832
Viets, Lois. *See* Phelps
Viets, Mary. *See* Pickett
Viets, Roger, **832–33**
Viets, Roger Moore, 833
Viger, Denis, **833–34**
Viger*, Denis-Benjamin (1774–1861), 186, 208, 209, 235,
  322, 324, 649, 651, 834
Viger, Jacques (father of DENIS), 833
Viger, Jacques (father of Jacques*), 75
Viger*, Jacques (1787–1858), 184, 702, 834
Viger*, Louis-Michel (1785–1855), 834
Viger, Marie-Angélique, named de Saint-Martin, 659
Viger, Marie-Louise. *See* Ridé
Viger, Périne-Charles. *See* Cherrier
Viger, Thérèse-Amable (Orillat), 654
Villaret de Joyeuse, Louis-Thomas, Comte de Villaret de
  Joyeuse, 62
Villars. *See* Sorbier
Villemonde. *See* Liénard
Villiers. *See* Coulon
Vincelotte. *See* Amyot
Vincent, Mr (teacher), 255
Vincent*, John (1765–1848), 82, 643, 696, 765, 875
Vincent, Pierre, 812, 813
Vincent de Paul, Father. *See* Merle, Jacques
Vining, Mary (Inglis), 444
Visitation. *See* Ailleboust de La Madeleine
Vitré. *See* Denys
Volant de Chamblain, Claire. *See* Jolliette
Volant de Chamblain, François, 91
Volney, Comte de. *See* Chassebœuf
Voltaire. *See* Arouet, François-Marie
Vondenvelden, Isaac, 834

Vondenvelden, Marie. *See* Young
Vondenvelden, Marie-Suzanne. *See* Voyer
Vondenvelden, William, 67, 139, 183, 184, 428, 460,
  834–35
Vondenvelden, William, 835
Voyer*, Jacques (1771–1843), 165, 270
Voyer, Marie-Pierre de, Comte d'Argenson, 102
Voyer, Marie-Suzanne (Vondenvelden), 834
Vuadens. *See* Waddens

WABACUMAGA. *See* Wabbicommicot
Wabakinine* (Wabacoming) (d. 1796), 707
Wabasha. *See* Wahpasha
Wabbicommicot* (d. 1768), 467
Wabicanine. *See* Wabakinine
Wachicouess. *See* Madjeckewiss
Waddens*, Jean-Étienne (d. 1782), 77, 259, 532, 538, 683,
  684
Waddens, Marguerite (MacKay; McLoughlin), 532, 534
Waddens, Véronique (Bethune), 77, 78
Wadins. *See* Waddens
Wahpasha, 10, 760, **835–37**
Wahpasha, 835, 836
Waipykanine. *See* Wabakinine
Waldegrave, William, 1st Baron Radstock, 360, 408, 726,
  763
Waldron, John, 641, 785, **837–39**
Waldron, John, 839
Waldron, Joseph, 837
Waldron, Martha (mother of JOHN), 837
Waldron, Mary. *See* Young
Wales, Prince of. *See* George IV
Walker*, Alexander (1764–1831), 618
Walker, Anna Louisa (Vial de Sainbel; wife of THOMAS),
  839
Walker, Edward, 748
Walker, James, 572, 840
Walker, Jane. *See* Finlay
Walker, Louisa Nash, 839
Walker*, Thomas (d. 1788), 20, 64, 98, 142, 146, 382, 413,
  432, 517, 527, 818
Walker, Thomas, **839–40**
Walker*, William (d. 1792), 451, 683
Wallace, Sir James, 763
Wallace*, Michael (d. 1831), 608, 612, 850
Wallace, William, 287
Wallace*, William Stewart (1884–1970), 331
Wallen, Phoebe (Phebe) (Frost; Gray), 334, 386
Wallis, Anne (Duckworth), 273
Wallis, John, 273
Walpole, Horatio (Horace), 4th Earl of Orford, 822
Walsh. *See also* Welch
Walsh, Francis Legh (Leigh), 846, 847
Walsingham, Baron. *See* Grey
Walter, John, 881
Walter, Rebecca (Byles), 128
Walter, William, 657, 658
Wandagan, 706
Wands, William, 814
Wapackcamigat (Wapaumagen). *See* Wabbicommicot
Wapasha. *See* Wahpasha
Ward, William, 190
Wardhouse. *See* Gordon

Ware, Mary (Eddy), 295
Waring, Richard, 468
Warnar, Elizabeth (Russell), 729
Warren, Henry, 842
Warren, John (doctor), 737
Warren, John, 405, 548, 642, 643, 644, 660, 661, 669, **840–42**, 846, 856
Warren, John (son of JOHN), 642, 644, 842
Warren, Sir John Borlase, 69, 82
Warren, Mary (wife of JOHN), 840
Warren*, Sir Peter (d. 1752), 134
Warsong. *See* Wasson
Washburn*, Ebenezer (d. 1826), 521, 550, 772, 841
Washburn*, Simon Ebenezer (d. 1837), 521
Washington, George, 16, 24, 28, 29, 30, 33, 34, 36, 40, 96, 148, 227, 239, 295, 313, 343, 414, 604, 627, 629, 705, 706, 808, 810, 873, 893, 895, 896, 899
Washington, Martha. *See* Dandridge
Wasson* (Wassong) (fl. 1763–76), 567
Waterhouse, Benjamin, 737
Waterman, Hannah (King; Arnold), 28
Waterman, Richard, 491
Watson, Sir Brook, 20, 22, 23, 173, 192, 277, 289, 371, 396, 416, 494, 789, **842–44**, 869, 870
Watson, Helen, Lady Watson. *See* Campbell
Watson, John, 843
Watson, Sarah. *See* Schofield
Watson, Simon Zelotes, 14
Watson-Wentworth, Charles, 2nd Marquess of Rockingham, 149, 848, 851
Waugh-we-ya-pe-yis-sin-ious (Wawapessenwa). *See* Weyapiersenwah
Waunathoake. *See* Demasduwit
Wawatam* (fl. 1762–64), 129
Wayne, Anthony, 121, 535, 553, 556, 594, 802, 808, 852
Webb*, James (d. 1761), 381
Webber, Mary (Milbanke), 595
Webber, Samuel, 874
Webster, Arthur, 218
Webster, Elizabeth. *See* Cruickshank
Wedderburn. *See also* Colvile; Halkett
Wedderburn, Alexander, 1st Earl of Rosslyn, 145
Wedderburn, Jean (Douglas, Baroness Daer and Shortcleuch, Countess of Selkirk), 264, 265, 266, 269
Weekes, William, 17, 171, 366, 405, 420, 441, 443, 519, 643, 782, 810, 842, **844–45**, 854, 855, 856
Weeks, Joshua Wingate, 48, 128
Weeks, Martha Wingate (Stout), 779
Weeks, Sally (Bailey), 47
Weh-yah-pih-ehr-sehn-waw. *See* Weyapiersenwah
Weis, George, 248
Welch, Mrs. *See* Johnson
Welch, Elizabeth. *See* Pierce
Welch, Francis, 845
Welch, Mary. *See* Mitchell
Welch, Thomas, 405, 733, 734, 842, **845–47**
Weld*, Isaac (1774–1856), 228, 302, 472
Weldon, John Wesley, 831
Well, Bernard, 432
Welles, John, 20, 21
Wellesley, Arthur, 1st Duke of Wellington, 489, 695, 696, 697, 698, 761
Wells, William, 796
Welsford*, Augustus Frederick (1817–55), 575

Welsford, John, 575
Welsford, Mary. *See* Marchinton
Welsh. *See* Welch
Wenman*, Richard (d. 1781), 670
Wentworth. *See also* Watson-Wentworth
Wentworth, Anne. *See* Tasker
Wentworth, Benning (uncle), 848, 871
Wentworth, Benning, 850
Wentworth, Sir Charles Mary, 850
Wentworth, Elizabeth. *See* Rindge
Wentworth, Frances Deering (Atkinson; Wentworth, Lady Wentworth), 848, 849, 851
Wentworth, John, 311, 569, 775, 779, 780, **847–48**
Wentworth, Sir John, 48, 124, 188, 240, 281, 297, 310, 314, 316, 328, 349, 350, 351, 354, 355, 356, 410, 423, 424, 431, 445, 608, 609, 634, 635, 646, 689, 693, 698, 763, 766, 847, **848–52**, 872
Wentworth, Mark Hunking, 848
Wentworth, Martha (Wentworth), 848
Wentworth, Paul, 851
Wentworth, Thomas, 847
Wesley, John, 258, 468, 573, 574, 575, 728, 729
West, Benjamin, 768, 811
Westbrook*, Andrew (1771–1835), 14, 749
Weston-Hugessen, Dorothea (Banks, Lady Banks), 54
Wetherall*, Sir Frederick Augustus (1754–1842), 449
Wetmore*, Thomas (1767–1828), 456, 647
Weyapiersenwah (Wey-a-pic-e-sen-waw), 594, 774, 797, **852–53**
Wheeler, Keziah (Beardsley), 58
Wheelock, Eleazar, 803, 804, 808
Wheelwright*, Esther (rebaptized Marie-Joseph), named de l'Enfant-Jésus (1696–1780), 224, 741
White, Aaron, 423, 658
White, Abigail (Hazzen), 412, 415
White, Alexander, 57
White, Henry, 364
White, James, 16, 415, 416
White*, John (d. 1800), 17, 307, 389, 453, 639, 722, 730, 815
White, Joseph, 491, 783
White, Samuel, 491, 783
White, William, 786, 787
Whitefield, George, 135, 729
White Head. *See* Theyanoguin
Whitlaw, Mrs Elizabeth, 287
Wight, Jean (Hamilton), 402
Wikinanish* (Wickananish) (fl. 1788–93), 387, 618, 619
Wilberforce, William, 68, 531, 575
Wilcox. *See* Willcocks
Wilds, George, 47
Wilkes, John, 82
Wilkie*, Daniel (1777–1851), 330, 770, 790
Wilkie, James Charles William, 853
Wilkie, Walter Coltheart, 853
Wilkie, William, **853–54**
Wilkins*, Lewis Morris (1768–1848), 216
Wilkins, Sarah. *See* Creighton
Wilkinson, James, 9, 32, 171
Wilkinson, Moses, 468
Willard, Submit. *See* Phipps
Willcocks, Charles (grandfather), 859
Willcocks, Charles, 859
Willcocks, Jane. *See* Powell

Willcocks, Joseph, 66, 171, 405, 412, 443, 643, 782, **854–59**, 860
Willcocks, Margaret. *See* Russell
Willcocks, Phoebe. *See* Jackson
Willcocks, Phoebe (Baldwin), 860
Willcocks, Robert, 854
Willcocks, William, 65, 71, 420, 597, 729, 731, 732, 854, **859–60**
Willet, Marinus, 40
William. *See* Tuglavina
William IV, King of Great Britain and Ireland, 122, 123, 128, 408, 632, 849
William Augustus, Duke of Cumberland, 141, 822, 823
William Henry, Prince. *See* William IV
Williams, Anne. *See* Jones
Williams, Elizabeth. *See* Stewart
Williams, Elizabeth (Graves, Baroness Graves), 380
Williams, James, **860–62**
Williams, Jenkin, 8, 18, 43, 45, 224, 226, 234, 493, 794, **862–65**, 881, 902
Williams, Thomas. *See* Tehoragwanegen
Williams, Thomas, 511, 682
Williams*, Sir William Fenwick (1800–83), 298
Williams, William Peere, 380
Williamson, Charles, 70, 71
Williamson, David, 345
Williamson, Elizabeth (Ainslie), 4
Willin, Sybilla Maria (Turner), 830
Wills, Geneviève. *See* Dunière
Wills, Geneviève (Montour), 603
Wills, Meredith, 283, 603
Willson*, John (1776–1860), 857
Willson, Sarah. *See* Ainse
Wilmot, Allen C., 9
Wilmot*, Montagu (d. 1766), 261, 409, 415, 555, 556
Wilmot, Samuel Street, 550
Wilson, Alexander, 499
Wilson, Anne Margaret. *See* McLean
Wilson, James, 724
Wilson, Thomas, 817
Winman. *See* Wenman
Winn, Joseph, 65
Winniett, Marie-Madeleine (How), 430
Winslow, Anna. *See* Green
Winslow, Anna, 869, 870
Winslow, Edward (great-great-grandfather of EDWARD), 865
Winslow, Edward (father of EDWARD), 865
Winslow, Edward, 35, 155, 156, 157, 161, 162, 354, 356, 390, 504, 505, 590, 613, 630, 774, 795, **865–69**, 874
Winslow, Hannah. *See* Dyer
Winslow, John, 869
Winslow*, John (1703–74), 295
Winslow, Joshua, 6, 132, 485, 486, 843, **869–70**
Winslow, Mary. *See* Symonds
Winslow, Penelope, 390
Winslow, Sarah. *See* Peirce
Wiswall, Elizabeth. *See* Rogers
Wiswall, John, 48, 122, 833, **870–72**
Wiswall, Margaret. *See* Hutchinson
Wiswall, Mercy. *See* Minot
Wiswall, Peleg (grandfather), 870
Wiswall, Peleg, 872
Witherspoon, John, 646

Wolfe*, James (1726/27–59), 104, 130, 141, 164, 412, 425, 428, 739, 767, 823, 824
Wood*, Alexander (d. 1844), 65, 285, 326
Wood, Ann (Hildrith), 423
Wood, Ann (McGill; Strachan), 529
Wood, Henry, 477
Wood, Joanna (Bulley), 119
Wood, John, 727
Wood, Judith (Philipps), 670
Wood, Robert, 881
Wood*, Thomas (1711–78), 670
Wood, William Charles Henry, 152
Woodin, William, 239
Wool, John Ellis, 113
Woolrich, James, 294
Woolsey*, John William (1767–1853), 566
Wooster, David, 31, 32, 64, 383, 414, 652
Wray, Sir Cecil, 825
Wright, Mr (fur trader), 512
Wright*, Charles (1782–1828), 874
Wright, George, **872–73**
Wright*, George (d. 1842), 874
Wright*, George (1810–87), 874
Wright, Martha. *See* Bisse
Wright, Mary. *See* Cochran
Wright, Mary (Duncan), 281
Wright, Robert, 823
Wright, Susanna. *See* Turner
Wright, Thomas (father of THOMAS), 873
Wright, Thomas (MHA), 873
Wright, Thomas, 426, 678, 773, 774, 777, **873–74**
Wright, William (grandfather), 872
Wright, William, 872
Wulff, George, 182
Wurtele*, Josias (d. 1831), 6, 708
Wyatt*, Charles Burton (d. in or after 1822), 855, 856
Wyer*, Thomas (d. 1824), 336, 337
Wyndham, Charles, 2nd Earl of Egremont, 4

YATES, Helen (McDonell), 517
Yeo, George Cosby, 8, 877
Yeo, James, 874
Yeo, Sir James Lucas, 83, 400, 401, 696, 697, **874–77**
Yeoward, Thomas, 635
Yockney, Samuel, 679
Yonge, Sir George, 755
Yore. *See* Ewer
York, Duke of. *See* Frederick Augustus
York*, Jack (fl. 1800), 639
Yorke, Charles, 605
Yorke, John, 223, 766
Yorke, Mary (Humphreys), 438
Young, Alexander, 460, 879
Young, Archibald Hope, 476
Young, Catherine Ainslie, 879
Young, Christian. *See* Ainslie
Young, Elizabeth (Headley; Perkins), 664
Young, Elizabeth Ainslie, 879
Young, George Edme, 179, 564
Young, Gilbert Ainslie, 879
Young, John, 6, 83, 84, 100, 101, 133, 212, 234, 270, 278, 317, 373, 464, 484, 489, 493, 494, 495, 603, 648, 650, 691, 692, 695, 696, 713, 746, 816, **877–83**
Young*, John (d. 1825), 78, 279, 320, 321, 770

Young*, John (1773–1837), 612, 853
Young, Marie (Vondenvelden), 834
Young, Mary (Waldron), 837
Young, Robert, 837
Young, Samuel, 837
Young*, Thomas Ainslie (d. 1860), 879, 882
Youville*, Charles-Marie-Madeleine d' (1729–90), 202, 293
Youville, Marie-Marguerite d'. *See* Dufrost de Lajemmerais
Youville Dufrost, Charles. *See* Youville, Charles-Marie-Madeleine d'

ZEISBERGER, David, 883
Zeisberger, David, 346, 799, **883–85**
Zeisberger, Rosina (Anna) (mother of DAVID), 883
Zeisberger, Susanna. *See* Lekron
Zheewegonab, **885–86**
Zinzendorf, Nikolaus Ludwig, Count von Zinzendorf, 883
Zouberbuhler*, Sebastian (d. 1773), 250
Zouch, Ann. *See* Ritchie
Zouch, John Thomas, 386
Zouche, Baron. *See* Bisshopp
Zouche, Baroness. *See* Southwell